CHILDREN'S NEEDS II:

Development, Problems and Alternatives

EDITED BY

George G. Bear
University of Delaware

Kathleen M. Minke
University of Delaware

Alex Thomas
Miami University

National Association of School Psychologists

Bethesda, Maryland

First Printing, 1997

Published by the National Association of School Psychologists
Bethesda, MD

Library of Congress Cataloging-in-Publication Data

Children's needs II : development, problems, and alternatives / edited
   by George G. Bear, Kathleen M. Minke, Alex Thomas.
     p. cm.
    Includes bibliographical references and index.
    ISBN 0-932955-96-7
     1. School psychology—United States. 2. Child development—United
States. 3. Child psychology—United States. I. Bear, George G.
II. Minke, Kathleen M. III. Thomas, Alex. IV. National Association
of School Psychologists.
LB1027.55.C46 1997
370.15—dc21   97-3781
                                                    CIP

Printed in the United States of America

Contents

93019

III. Children's Academic Needs: Development, Problems, and Alternatives

A. Motivation and Learning

B. Classroom Practices

C. Other Related Issues

IV. Children's Family-Related Needs: Development, Problems, and Alternatives

A. Family Organization and Practices

B. Family-Based Problems

C. Family and Culture

Acknowledgments

This project has been an enormous undertaking and has benefitted from the care and attention of many individuals. We wish to particularly thank the many reviewers who took the time to read chapters and provide careful, detailed, and thoughtful feedback to the authors. Our reviewers included:

Ruth Adams	Charles Deupree	Steve Landau	Kathy Pluymert
Carolyn Allen	Betty Dizney	James Larson	Thomas Power
Laura Bailet	Patricia Ellis	Jeff Laurent	Fred Provenzano
Thomas Barry	Allan Ensor	Philip Lazarus	Mary Ann Rafoth
Lisa Bischoff	Tom Fagan	Kathy Lemanek	M.K. Randolph
JoKay Boyle	Ervi Farkas	David Lemire	James Raths
Bruce Bracken	Craig Frisby	Bridget Lillis	Chuck Rechsteiner
Jeffrey Braden	Lane Geddie	Gloria Miller	Ronald Reeve
Steve Breckheimer	Shelly Greggs	R.V. Moran	Ron Russell
Michael Brown	Shaunna Griffin	Stacy Morrone	Gail Rys
Sue Burkholder	Debra Grilly	Steve Morse	Marcia Sachs
Mei Mei Burr	Leslie Hale	Judy Oehler-Stinnett	Geraldine Scholl
Carolyn Callahan	Pamela Hawkins	Tom Ollendick	Robbie Sharp
Kathryn Carroll	Robyn Hess	Randy Olley	Anne Teeter
Servio Carroll	Jan Hughes	Leslie Paige	Paul Trivette
Al Cavalier	Deborah Johnson	Steven Pfeiffer	Kathryn Michele Turner
Arlene Crandall	Gloria Johnson	William Pfohl	Ena Vasquez-Nuttal
Peg Dawson	Nadine Kaslow	Le Adelle Phelps	Richard Veit
Ebenezer de Oliveira	Carol Kelly	Jack Pikulski	T. Steuart Watson

Many of our graduate students have had the opportunity to experience the "glory" of the publication process by assisting us with management of chapters, correspondence with authors and reviewers, and proof reading galleys. Our thanks go to: Jon Cooper, Ebenezer de Oliveira, Sandy Deemer, Michael Fernandes, Susan Davies, Jami Van Ryswyk, Vicky Gunn, Christy Howard, Karl Kurt, Megan Farrell, Connie Bowling, and Megan Kakela.

Particular gratitude is extended to Shaunna Griffin, doctoral student extraordinaire at the University of Delaware, whose organizational skills were essential in tracking all of the bits of paper involved and whose good humor never flagged despite the constant demand for more of her time! Likewise, special thanks goes to James Raths, department chair extraordinaire, who provided the necessary resources for the project, constant encouragement, and much appreciated guidance when needed. Departmental office staff, especially Doris Davidson, Kathy Murphy, and Nancy Pysher, deserve recognition for secretarial and budgeting assistance.

We thank Servio Carroll and the NASP Publications Board for their support and guidance. Also, our thanks to Paul Mendez, NASP Director of Publications, for his attention to details and marketing expertise. Thanks, also, to Susan Gorin, NASP Executive Director, for her ability to consistently provide the calming voice of reason.

Mary Fitzsimmons provided timely and accurate copy editing under rushed and harried circumstances. Mary Boss, who oversaw the myriad details of typesetting and corrections, was wonderfully unflappable. Our sincere appreciation to you both.

We'd also like to acknowledge the few among our supportive family, friends, and colleagues who never spoke a word but remained steadfastly glad to see us no matter how late or grumpy we were when we got home: Hiro, Hobbs, Shadow, and Teddy. Let's go for a walk!

From George Bear: To my wife, best friend, and the greatest teacher, Patti, and the two soccer bears, Brian (RMC #22) and Adam (MHS #33). Thanks for your understanding, especially when the book's tasks seemed overwhelming (700+ days), and for reminding me of my cherished priorities.

From Kathleen Minke: My deepest gratitude to my friend and spouse, Bob Sekinger, who takes away all my blues. Thanks to Honey Vickers, Patrice Hall, and Janet Minke for listening! I'd also like to thank my parents, Don and Bette Minke, who are celebrating 50 years of marriage this year, for providing an incredible model of devotion, humor, and perseverance in the face of adversity.

From Alex Thomas: Thanks to Bonnie, the "boys," and the thousands of school psychologists who are able to provide excellent services and maintain professional fervor in often difficult circumstances.

Finally, we thank each of the 100+ authors who contributed to yet another important NASP publication. It is our hope that this volume will be of service to the thousands of dedicated school psychologists and educators who choose to face the challenge of meeting children's needs in today's society.

George Bear, Kathleen Minke, Alex Thomas

Introduction: Children's Needs and School Psychology's Response

Kathleen M. Minke and George G. Bear

University of Delaware

Today's children face enormous challenges. Recent figures from the National Center for Education Statistic's *Youth Indicators* (Snyder & Shafer, 1996) highlight some of the stressors that impinge on children's daily lives. For example, family work patterns have changed dramatically in the last 45 years. In 1950, 11.9% of married women with children under six were employed or seeking employment. In 1993, this figure was 59.6%. Concurrent with this change in work patterns, changes in family composition have occurred. In 1994, 59% of Black children, 29% of Hispanic children, and 19% of White children lived in single-parent homes. These families are particularly vulnerable socioeconomically; 53% of children in female-headed households lived in poverty in 1994. Clearly, large numbers of children are experiencing the effects of poverty and family stress, just two of the multiple and interrelated factors associated with the ever-expanding needs of children in our society.

Children need help. They need help not just from families but also from schools and communities. Their needs demand effective prevention and treatment programs addressing the multiplicity of physical, social, emotional, and academic problems they present. These needs range from brain injury due to motor vehicle accidents, homicide, suicide, and HIV/AIDS (four of the six leading causes of death among youth ages 10–24 [see Health promotion, this volume]) to more common, but nevertheless serious, problems, such as reading difficulties, low achievement motivation, aggression and bullying, fears, peer rejection, social skills deficits, and loneliness (see related chapters, this volume).

Given the expanding range of children's needs, it should come as no surprise that approximately 20% of all children need mental health services. For example, McDermott and Weiss (1995) classified 5.2% of their national sample as "seriously maladjusted" and an additional 16.2% as "at-risk" for serious maladjustment. After reviewing 12 recent epidemiological studies, Doll (1996) concluded that, in a typical school of 1,000 students, between 180 and 220 students would be expected to have diagnosable psychiatric disorders.

Studies of children's physical health-related problems are equally disturbing. For example, survival rates among preterm infants are improving, but as many as 30% of infants requiring neonatal care will have a disability identified in the preschool years (A. R. Fuchs, F. Fuchs, & Stubblefield, 1993; see also Prematurity, this volume). Further, by age 18, around 10% to 15% of children experience at least one chronic medical condition; these illnesses and injuries may significantly challenge the coping skills of the individuals involved (Tarnowski & Brown, 1995). HIV infection is affecting increasing numbers of children and adolescents, both directly (e.g., through prenatal exposure) and indirectly (e.g., through infection and death of family members [see HIV/AIDS, this volume]). Other health-related difficulties, while not always life-threatening, often compromise children's developmental outcomes. For example, children with chronic seizures (approximately 1% of all children) frequently experience academic and social problems (see Epilepsy, this volume). Children who are obese (as many as 1 of 4 school-age children) are at increased risk for low self-esteem, loneliness, and mood disorders (see Obesity, this volume). Common allergies, affecting as many as 20% of children, can result in frequent school absences, decreased attention and concentration, and anxiety related to breathing problems (see Allergies and Asthma, this volume).

Children's healthy development is further compromised by the severely limited availability of services to youth (see Doll, 1996). Bowe (1995) estimated that states are serving no more than 70% of infants and toddlers with disabilities, and only around 5% of youth access mental health services (Inouye, 1988, cited in McDermott & Weiss, 1995). As described by Doll (1996), even under the recommended psychologist/student ratio of 1:1000, the school psychologist would have to work with a different student each day of the school year to even meet every student with a psychiatric disorder!

Schools, therefore, are called to serve a population with a tremendous multiplicity of needs and limited access to scarce resources. They are asked to serve students in an atmosphere of public dissatisfaction with general education, which has increased in the years since the publication of *A Nation at Risk: The Imperative for Educational Reform* (National Commission on Excellence in Education, 1983). The press for reform resulted in the adoption of the highly ambitious National Education Goals (Goals 2000, 1994). For example, the goals call for 90% of students to graduate from high school and for United States students to be first in the world in science and math achievement by the year 2000.

At the same time that regular education is attempting to dramatically improve student outcomes, special education has come under increased scrutiny. Some have essentially called for eliminating the cascade of services and serving all children in regular education (see D. Fuchs & L. S. Fuchs, 1991, 1994, for discussion of inclusion issues). As a result of these reform movements in general and special education, teachers are expected to promote both academic excellence and equity of opportunity to all children, a daunting task. As stated by Kauffman (1989), "teachers must choose between (a) allocating more time to the production of expected mean outcomes for the group, which sacrifices gains of the least capable learners, or (b) allocating more time to the least capable learners to narrow the variance among students, which inevitably sacrifices achievement of the students who learn most easily" (p. 266). Unquestionably, schools as systems are under tremendous and competing pressures.

School Psychology's Response

Recently, both the National Association of School Psychologists (NASP) and the American Psychological Association (APA) have lodged national campaigns to convince legislators and school administrators outside of the profession, as well as school psychology trainers and practitioners within, of the importance of expanded and integrated psychological services in the schools and the role school psychologists can play in producing better student outcomes. As reflected in *Best Practices III* (Thomas & Grimes, 1995), school psychologists are considered problem solvers—individuals with expertise in both psychology and education who can apply this knowledge to issues of child development and systems change. Advocating for an expanded role to include consultation and intervention for school psychologists is not new; such roles were recommended in the 1954 Thayer Conference (Cutts, 1955) and subsequent documents and proceedings of the NASP and the APA (e.g., *Specialty Guidelines for the Delivery of Services,* APA, 1981). NASP examples include

- Spring Hill conference (Ysseldyke & Weinberg, 1982)
- Olympia conference (Brown, Cardon, Coulter, & Meters, 1982).

- *Standards for the Provision of School Psychological Services* (NASP, 1984a, 1994a).
- *Standards for Training and Field Placement Programs in School Psychology* (NASP, 1984b, 1994b).

What is new, however, is an increased recognition of the expanding academic, social, emotional, and physical needs of children and an emphasis on consultation and intervention applied in the context of reform initiatives in special education and school health services.

Central to both of these reform initiatives is the decreased emphasis on diagnostic *testing* and data collection for the purpose of classifying and placing children into special education. *Assessment* would continue to play a critical role but primarily in the service of interventions. From this perspective, every issue, whether preventive or remedial in nature, is understood through a problem-solving approach to assessment. Once an issue is identified, defined, and analyzed, interventions are developed, implemented, and evaluated. Thus, problem-solving assessment is linked to interventions, preferably interventions that are broad based and that integrate special education, general education, home, and community services. Coordination and collaboration with others are critical to the assessment and intervention process. Moreover, while not neglecting the value of crisis intervention and treatment, preventive interventions are preferred, especially those that promote the healthy social, emotional, physical, and academic development of *all* children. This shift in emphasis from current practices is reflected in several recent NASP and APA documents and publications, including *Assessment and Eligibility in Special Education* (NASP/NASDSE/OSEP, 1994), *Standards for Training and Field Placement Programs in School Psychology* (NASP, 1994b), *Home-School Collaboration* (Christenson & Conoley, 1992), *Comprehensive and Coordinated Psychological Services for Children* (APA, 1994), and *Reforming America's Schools: Psychology's Role* (APA, 1995). Likewise, it is seen throughout most chapters in this book.

Translating Research Into Practice

It is much easier to write about best practices and preferred roles and functions than to implement them, particularly in light of the strong resistance to change which characterizes most schools (Sarason, 1995). Major system-related obstacles to an expanded role for school psychologists abound, including high psychologist-to-student ratios (averaging 1:2,100) as well as system preferences and incentives for school psychologists to function primarily within the role of "sorter" instead of "repairer" (Fagan & Wise, 1994).

It is important to recognize, however, that obstacles

and barriers to change do not lie solely outside our profession, nor are they beyond our influence. The knowledge base of the profession, and actual competencies of school psychologists, profoundly influence which services are delivered and how effective they are. To overcome system barriers, school psychologists must not only advocate actively for a broader role but be prepared to deliver a broad range of services and demonstrate the effectiveness of those services. Even within the context of a restricted role, the majority of practicing school psychologists can take steps to offer additional services and to increase the demand for them (see Family Systems and the Family-School Connection, this volume).

A major strength of our profession is its theoretical and empirical bases in the disciplines of psychology and education. This broad base is evident throughout this book, with multiple chapters emphasizing the importance of integrating research and theory from differing theoretical perspectives, including developmental psychology, cognitive-behavioral psychology, educational psychology, family systems theory, applied behavior analysis, psychopathology, and multicultural psychology. Such breadth of knowledge provides the foundation for effective assessment, prevention, and intervention practices responsive to the complex interaction of individual and environmental factors that influence children's needs.

As is evident in many chapters (e.g., Anger, Lying, Physical and Emotional Abuse, Suicidal Ideation and Behavior), complex behaviors often call for complex and broad-based interventions. For example, diagnosing a child as having a conduct disorder and prescribing narrow techniques to be implemented in the confines of the classroom or in a social skills training group is hardly sufficient for producing lasting and significant change. In recent years it has become increasingly apparent that prevention and treatment programs must also address the faulty cognitive and emotional processes that underlie conduct disorders as well as the social, cultural, and situational factors that reinforce and maintain aggressive and coercive behaviors (Dodge & Price, 1994; Guerra & Slaby, 1990; Huesmann, 1994; Hughes & Cavell, 1995; Kazdin, 1995).

Promotion of Healthy Development for All Children

To serve the needs of all children, many school psychologists may find it necessary to refresh their knowledge, or acquire new knowledge, about individual and environmental factors that contribute to healthy development. The understanding and promotion of wellness among children has tended to take a back seat to the diagnosis and treatment of problem behaviors (see chapters on Life Satisfaction and Happiness and Health Promotion, this volume). If recent reforms envisioned by leaders in school psychology are to be realized, school psychologists will need to radically shift the time spent in psychoeducational assessment and systems/organizational consultation (currently about 55% and 5%, respectively; Reschly & Wilson, 1995). Moreover, within the general consultation role, a shift from the current emphasis on problem-centered behavioral consultation (Bergan & Kratochwill, 1990) will be necessary. Such changes would require greater application of what Bergan and Kratochwill refer to as "developmental consultation," a more preventive model. These changes would also require incorporating perspectives other than operant behavioral ones and giving greater emphasis to problem analysis. As is evident in multiple chapters of this book (see, for example, chapters on Prosocial Behavior, Giftedness, Self-Concept, Sociomoral Reasoning and Behavior, Substance Use and Abuse, Adolescent Pregnancy and Parenting), cognitive and social-developmental factors must be analyzed and addressed in the promotion of healthy development. Likewise, critical knowledge of cultural and student diversity and the ways it relates to healthy development are necessary (e.g., see Sexual Minority Youth, Religion, Ethnic and Racial Diversity, Family Systems and the Family-School Connection). What defines and explains "healthy" or "normal" behavior is not necessarily the same at all ages nor across diverse cultural groups. Where appropriate, these points are emphasized throughout this volume, especially within the context of the problem-analysis step in the problem-solving process.

Collaboration with Others

Regardless of whether the focus is on problem-centered or developmental consultation, it is apparent in recent reform initiatives that school psychologists will need to collaborate more with parents and with school-based health service providers (e.g., school counselors, nurses, and teachers). The need for collaboration reflects a shift in emphasis from viewing children primarily as "academic students" to viewing them as individuals with a variety of academic, social, emotional, and physical needs that cannot be adequately addressed by schools alone. Therefore, it will be necessary for school psychologists to also collaborate more with health service providers who have traditionally operated outside of the school (e.g., physicians, social workers, clinical psychologists). The increasing use of psychotropic medications to modify children's behavior and learning provides one example of the urgent need for greater collaboration. These medications are often prescribed independently of school-based interventions, the quality of outcomes would likely be improved by communication and collaboration among professionals (see Pediatric Psychopharmacology, this volume).

Importantly, if school health initiatives take hold, many health professionals will be working in "full-service" school settings, with the potential of improving possibilities for collaboration. However, simple propinquity of professionals will not guarantee improved services for children. Although the extent of children's needs clearly indicates room for many helping professionals within schools, differences in theoretical orientations, preferred intervention techniques, and professional/agency "cultures" make it likely that conflicts will arise as individuals attempt to work collaboratively (Romualdi & Sandoval, 1995). School psychologists at both the specialist and doctoral levels of training (see Brown & Minke, 1986; Minke & Brown, 1996; Reschly & Wilson, in press) have the advantage of understanding both psychological science and schools as systems—training not shared by other psychologists or mental health professionals outside of schools. This training should make them ideal candidates for leadership roles in developing integrated school-based service models. In addition to the roles of consultant and direct service provider, potential roles include those of "resource broker" and program evaluator (Romualdi & Sandoval, 1995).

If school psychologists are to fulfill their potential as leaders for coordinated services, it is essential that internal struggles do not deflect us from that goal. The APA and the NASP historically have had periods of both cooperation and conflict between the organizations. The most recent, substantive debate has centered around the need for each of the existing specialty areas within the APA, one of which is school psychology, to reapply for recognition as a specialty prior to the year 2002. It has been suggested that perhaps doctoral school psychology should join forces with child clinical psychology and develop a new specialty of professional child psychology (see, e.g., Curley, 1996; Kamphaus & Conoley, 1996). Such proposals, in our view, tend to overemphasize the differences between the two levels of training and downplay the similarities. The primary differences lie in preparation to practice *outside* of schools, not within them (Reschly & Wilson, in press). Only school psychologists are prepared both to understand schools as systems and to apply knowledge of psychological principles to those systems. Any reconceptualization of the specialty at either level of training must not neglect this linking function. Furthermore, should doctoral school psychology undergo radical change, this change would not lessen the need for doctoral and specialist-level practitioners to collaborate, cooperate, and respect one another's professional expertise.

Consumer Satisfaction

Schools, and many school psychologists, must become more sensitive to the needs of consumers, acknowledging what parents, teachers, students, and others perceive to be desired, needed, and acceptable services. Although consumer preferences cannot take precedence over activities that yield meaningful and positive outcomes for students, school psychologists should not promote solutions that are insensitive to consumers (Cummings, 1996; Gresham & Lopez, 1996). According to Gresham and Lopez, school psychologists providing consultation services should ask three fundamental questions directly linked to the social validity concepts of social significance, social acceptability, and social importance: "What should we change? How should we change it? How will we know it was effective?" (p. 205). With respect to social significance, curriculum-based measurement, standardized testing, social skills training, and classroom management training may be dear to many school psychologists and special educators, but not to the masses of general educators now trained in the popular whole language approach to literacy and in authentic assessment nor to those who understand that frequent use of extrinsic rewards can be detrimental to self-regulation (Lepper, Keavney, & Drake, 1996). Many chapters in this volume incorporate different theoretical perspectives (e.g., see Reading, Socially Responsible Behavior), recognizing that research and theory rarely support only one approach to all problems. "One size fits all" is a dangerous practice: Those who limit their practice to a single method of intervention or assessment are likely to be replaced by more flexible (and effective) interventionists.

Evident in the different theoretical perspectives reflected in the chapters of this volume is a more tempered position toward assessment and intervention than that proposed in recent years by advocates of "outcome-based" education (e.g., Reschly & Ysseldyke, 1995). As noted by Fagan (1995), "a long-standing paradigm of assessing skills through underlying supportive characteristics (e.g., intelligence) has shifted to a paradigm of direct assessment of skills and direct remedial instruction irrespective of underlying abilities and traits" (p. 65). Consistent with the paradigm shift, behaviors (i.e., observable skills) are directly assessed and remediated, with limited attention to motivation, attributions, emotions, and other internal processes. With some exceptions (particularly those chapters focusing on specific problem behaviors of young children, such as Temper Tantrums), the positions of the authors of this volume tend to be more consistent with the balanced (i.e., "traditional") assessment paradigm advocated by Fagan and Wise (1994), Hyman and Kaplinski (1994), Harrison (1996), and Trachtman (1981)—a paradigm in which problem analysis (linked to intervention) is not limited to a functional analysis of operant behaviors but includes the roles of motivation, emotions, attributions, learning strategies, and other processes supported by theory and research.

Furthermore, nearly all of the chapters in this volume highlight that every problem is not an intrachild problem (see, for example, chapters in the sections on Family Organization and Practices and Family and Culture). As noted by Brinker (1990), "if we continue to conceptualize the child only as a learner, dissociated from the many other ecologies that define the child, we will probably continue to fail in our attempts to meet individual educational needs" (p. 182). Thus, assessment and problem analysis include attention to the reciprocal influences among intrachild, family, school, and other contextual variables. From this perspective, "problems" are broadly defined, and solutions may encompass activities that have been traditionally defined as prevention as well as remediation.

Overview of the Volume

Children's Needs II: Development, Problems, and Alternatives presents a broad array of issues important in helping children attain healthy developmental outcomes. The volume is designed to serve as a research-based resource to school psychologists (in practice and in training), as well as other health service providers to children and adolescents both in and outside of school settings. Because children's developmental issues are discussed in the context of how they affect school learning, helping professionals working with children in clinic, community, and school settings should find the book helpful in designing interventions that are considered socially valid by school personnel. Consistent with the diversity of topics presented, authors were encouraged not to limit themselves to a single theory or orientation. Rather, the chapters represent integration of research across a variety of relevant perspectives, as appropriate to the subject. To promote the accuracy and usefulness of the volume, each chapter underwent an anonymous peer review process prior to publication; suggestions for revision were made by at least one authority on the topic, a school psychology practitioner, and one of the editors.

The book is organized into five broad sections (Social, Emotional, Academic, Family, and Health and Wellness Needs). Within most sections, subheads are provided to facilitate access to related chapters. We have attempted to include topics that address both healthy development and specific developmental challenges.

With a few exceptions, each chapter in the volume follows the same basic headings. First, current research on a specific topic, including relevant developmental factors, is presented (Background and Development), fol-lowed by implications of the topic for children's developmental outcomes (Problems and Implications). The information presented in these sections is essential for a detailed problem analysis; it will alert readers to important developmental aspects of the topic and the outcomes that might be expected with or without intervention. Each chapter also provides suggested avenues for intervention (Alternative Actions). Although it is expected that interventions will vary depending on the elements identified as critical for an individual child or situation based on the problem analysis, the information presented in this section should provide a starting point for intervention design, grounded in the most current research. Finally, suggestions for further reading are provided along with resources for parents and children, where appropriate (Recommended Resources). In sum, this volume is intended as a resource to support the problem-solving role. School psychologists and other helping professionals can use the information presented to (a) increase their knowledge of the most recent research in a topic area; (b) develop detailed problem analyses; and (c) translate the research into effective interventions for children, educators, families, and communities.

Authors' Notes

We gratefully acknowledge the helpful comments made by Steven Landau and Thomas K. Fagan on an earlier draft of this introduction. The material in the chapter, of course, reflects our own views, not necessarily those of the reviewers or the National Association of School Psychologists.

The authors played an equal role in the writing of this chapter. Order of authorship was determined by a coin toss.

References

American Psychological Association. (1981). Specialty guidelines for the delivery of services by school psychologists. In American Psychological Association (Ed.), *Specialty guidelines for the delivery of services* (pp. 33–44). Washington, DC: Author. See also *American Psychologist, 36,* 640–681.

American Psychological Association. (1994). *Comprehensive and coordinated psychological services for children: A call for service integration.* Washington, DC: Author.

American Psychological Association. (1995). *Reforming America's schools: Psychology's role.* Washington, DC: Author.

Bergan, J. R., & Kratochwill, T. R. (1990). *Behavioral consultation and therapy.* New York; Plenum Press.

Bowe, F. G. (1995). Population estimates: Birth-to-5, children with disabilities. *The Journal of Special Education, 28,* 461–471.

Brinker, R. P. (1990). In search of the foundation of special education: Who are the individuals and what are the differences? *Journal of Special Education, 24,* 174–184.

Brown, D. T., Cardon, B. W., Coulter, W. A., & Meyers, J. (Eds.). (1982). The Olympia proceedings [Special issue]. *School Psychology Review, 11.*

Brown, D. T., & Minke, K. M. (1986). School psychology graduate training: A comprehensive analysis. *American Psychologist, 41,* 1328–1338.

Christenson, S. L., & Conoley, J. C. 1992). *Home-school collaboration: Enhancing children's academic and social competence.* Washington, DC: National Association of School Psychologists.

Cummings, J. A. (1996). Responding to school needs: The role of the psychologist. In R. C. Talley, T. Kubiszyn, M. Brassard, & R. J. Short (Eds.). *Making psychologists in schools indispensable: Critical questions & emerging perspectives* (pp. 77–81). Washington, DC: American Psychological Association.

Curley, J. F. (1996). Professional child psychology revisited. *The School Psychologist, 50, 97,* 102.

Cutts, N. E. (Ed.). (1955). *School psychologists at mid-century.* Washington, DC: American Psychological Association.

Dodge, K. A., & Price, J. M. (1994). On the relation between social information processing and socially competent behavior in early school-aged children. *Child Development, 65,* 1385–1397.

Doll, B. (1996). Prevalence of psychiatric disorders in children and youth: An agenda for advocacy by school psychology. *School Psychology Quarterly, 11,* 20–46.

Fagan, T. K. (1995). Trends in the history of school psychology in the United States. In A. Thomas & J. Grimes (Eds.), *Best practices in school psychology III* (pp. 59–67). Washington, DC: National Association of School Psychologists.

Fagan, T. K., & Wise, P. S. (1994). *School psychology: Past, present, and future.* New York: Longman.

Fuchs, A. R., Fuchs, F., & Stubblefield, P. G. (Eds.). (1993). *Preterm birth: Causes, prevention, and management* (2nd ed.). New York; McGraw-Hill.

Fuchs, D., & Fuchs, L. S. (1991). Framing the REI debate: Abolitionists versus conservationists. In J. W. Lloyd, N. N. Singh, & A. C. Repp (Eds.), *The regular education initiative: Alternative perspectives on concepts, issues, & models* (pp. 241–255).

Fuchs, D., & Fuchs, L. S. (1994). Inclusive schools movement and the radicalization of special education reform. *Exceptional Children, 60,* 294–309.

Goals 2000: Educate America Act, Pub. L. No. 103-227. 103rd Congress, 2nd. session (1994).

Gresham, F., & Lopez, M. F. (1996). Social validation: A unifying concept for school-based consultation research and practice. *School Psychology Quarterly, 11,* 204–227.

Guerra, N. G., & Slaby, R. R. (1990). Cognitive mediators of aggression in adolescent offenders: II. Intervention. *Developmental Psychology, 26,* 269–277.

Harrison, P. L. (1996). Enduring expertise of school psychologists and the changing demands of schools in the United States. In R. C. Talley, T. Kubiszyn, M. Brassard, & R. J. Short (Eds.), *Making psychologists in schools indispensable: Critical questions & emerging perspectives* (pp. 62–70). Washington, DC: American Psychological Association.

Huesmann, I. R. (Ed.). (1994). *Aggressive behavior: Current perspectives.* New York: Plenum Press.

Hughes, J. N., & Cavell, T. A. (1995). Cognitive-affective approaches: Enhancing competence in aggressive children. In G. Cartledge & J. F. Miburn (Eds.), *Teaching social skills to children and youth: Innovative approaches* (3rd ed., pp. 199–236). Boston: Allyn and Bacon.

Hyman, I. A., & Kaplinski, K. (1994). Will the real school psychologist please stand up: Is the past a prologue for the future of school psychology—role and function. *School Psychology Review, 23,* 564–583.

Hynd, G. W. (1996). More than a change is needed. *The School Psychologist, 50,* 97, 103, 119.

Inouye, D. K. (1988). Children's mental health issues. *American Psychologist, 43,* 813–816.

Kamphaus, R. W., & Conoley, J. C. (1996). Nurturing doctoral school psychology: Vision, home, and message. *The School Psychologist, 50,* 65, 68–71.

Kauffman, J. M. (1989). The Regular Education Initiative as Reagan-Bush policy. A trickle-down theory of education of the hard-to-teach. *Journal of Special Education, 3,* 256–278.

Kazdin, A. E. (1995). *Conduct disorders in childhood and adolescence* (2nd ed.). Thousand Oaks, CA: Sage.

Lepper, M. R., Keavney, M., & Drake, M. (1996). Intrinsic motivation and extrinsic rewards: A commentary on Cameron and Pierce's meta-analysis. *Review of Educational Research, 66,* 5–32.

McDermott, P. A., & Weiss, R. V. (1995). A normative typology of healthy, subclinical, and clinical behavior styles among American children and adolescents. *Psychological Assessment, 7,* 162–170.

Minke, K. M., & Brown, D. T. (1996). Preparing psychologists to work with children: A comparison of curricula in child-clinical and school psychology programs. *Professional Psychology: Research and Practice, 27,* 631–634.

NASP/NASDSE/OSEP. (1994). *Assessment and eligibility in special education: An examination of policy and practice with proposals for change.* Alexandria, VA: National Association of State Directors of Special Education.

National Association of School Psychologists. (1984a). *Standards for the provision of school psychological services.* Washington, DC: Author.

National Association of School Psychologists. (1984b). *Standards for training and field placement programs in school psychology.* Washington, DC: Author.

National Association of School Psychologists. (1994a). *Standards for the provision of school psychological services* (rev. ed.). Washington, DC: Author.

National Association of School Psychologists. (1994b). *Standards for training and field placement programs in school psychology* (rev. ed.). Washington, DC: Author.

National Commission on Excellence in Education. (1983). *A nation at risk: The imperative for educational reform.* Washington, DC: U.S. Government Printing Office.

Reschly, D. J., & Wilson, M. S. (1995). School psychology practitioners and faculty: 1986 to 1991–1992 trends in demographics, roles, satisfaction, and system reform. *School Psychology Review, 24,* 62–80.

Reschly, D. J., & Wilson, M. S. (in press). Characteristics of school psychology graduate education: Implications for the entry level discussion and doctoral level specialty definition. *School Psychology Review.*

Reschly, D. J., & Ysseldyke, J. (1995). School psychology paradigm shift. In A. Thomas & J. Grimes (Eds.), *Best practices in school psychology III* (pp. 17–31). Washington, DC: National Association of School Psychologists.

Romualdi, V., & Sandoval, J. (1995). Comprehensive school-linked services. Implications for school psychologists. *Psychology in the Schools, 32,* 306–317.

Sarason, S. B. (1995). *School change: The personal development of a point of view.* New York: Teachers College Press.

Snyder, T., & Shafer, L. (1996). *Youth indicators: 1996.* Washington, DC: U.S. Department of Education, National Center for Education Statistics.

Tarnowski, K. J., & Brown, R. R. (1995). Psychological aspects of pediatric disorders. In M. Hersen & R. T. Ammerman (Eds.), *Advanced abnormal child psychology* (pp. 393–410). Hillsdale, NJ: Lawrence Erlbaum.

Thomas A., & Grimes, J. (Eds.). (1995). *Best practices in school psychology III.* Washington, DC: National Association of School Psychologists.

Trachtman, G. M. (1981). On such a full sea. *The School Psychology Review, 10,* 138–181.

Ysseldyke, J. E., & Weinberg, R. A. (Eds.). (1982). The future of psychology in the schools: Proceedings of the Spring Hill Symposium [Special issue]. *School Psychology Review, 10* (2).

1

Prosocial Behavior

Nancy Eisenberg
Jerry D. Harris
Arizona State University

When preschooler Sally deftly grabs a puzzle from Eric's hand, Eric immediately breaks into tears. Classmate Randy, observing this exchange, pats Eric on the back and offers to share a toy helicopter with which he has been playing.

The focus of this chapter is not on Sally or Eric but rather on Randy—or more correctly, on his prosocial response to a classmate. This interest in Randy's behavior is different from the focus in much of this volume. The target behavior is not problematic; that is, it does not occur too often nor under the wrong circumstances. And, strictly speaking, the absence of prosociality is not normally considered a deficit deserving the same attention as many other social and academic deficits that come to the attention of the school psychologist. For example, concern for a child who is exceptionally socially reticent or who has failed to master basic reading skills is typically greater than for a child who bypasses opportunities to be helpful to others.

Nonetheless, there is reason to assert the value both to the individual and to society of fostering caring, sharing, and helping. For example, children who are prosocial may be somewhat less likely to develop difficulties in peer relationships. Prosocial, sympathetic children tend to be popular, to have friends, and to be socially competent (Eisenberg et al., in press, Farver & Branstetter, 1994; see Eisenberg & Fabes, in press). Moreover, children who use low levels of prosocial moral reasoning exhibit relatively poor social behavior which, in turn, is associated with low sociometric status (Bear & Rys, 1994). If prosocial children have higher quality peer relationships, they are likely to have fewer socioemotional problems (Parker & Asher, 1987). Consequently, fostering the development of prosocial behavior and reasoning among children seems a worthwhile goal for parents and educators.

Background

In the psychological literature, *prosocial behavior* often is defined as voluntary behavior intended to benefit another and includes helping, donating, sharing, and comforting. Prosocial behavior that is intrinsically motivated is said to be altruistic. Thus, *altruism* refers to assisting others when one's acts are internally motivated by concern for others or by internalized values, goals, and self-rewards (Eisenberg & Fabes, in press). Altruistic acts generally are viewed as reflecting moral rather than egoistic motivation. However, behaviors helpful to others may also reflect mere compliance with the demands of the situation or fear of punishment, the desire for reward, or some other nonmoral factor.

It usually is impossible for an observer to differentiate between altruistically motivated actions and those motivated by less noble concerns. However, altruistic motives and behaviors may evolve from nonaltruistic prosocial actions as children develop. Thus, an understanding of factors influencing the broader domain of prosocial behavior is of value.

Prosocial behavior, including altruism, frequently may be motivated by empathy-related emotional reactions. *Empathy* is commonly defined in developmental psychology as an affective response that stems from the apprehension of another's emotional state or condition, and which is identical or very similar to what the other person is feeling or would be expected to feel. Thus, if Randy is saddened by Eric's crying, or from what he infers from the crying about Eric's emotional state, he is experiencing empathy (Eisenberg & Fabes, in press). If Eric recovers and cheerfully plays with the new toy and Randy feels happy as a consequence of Eric's shift in emotion, this would also be an empathic response.

It is important to differentiate empathy from related emotional responses, especially sympathy and personal distress. *Sympathy,* an affective response that frequently stems from empathy, consists of feelings of concern for a distressed or needy other. Thus, if Randy feels concern regarding Eric's well-being, he is experiencing sympathy. However, personal distress may also result when one vicariously experiences another's emotional state or condition. *Personal distress* involves a self-focused, aversive emotional reaction such as discomfort, anxiety, or self-oriented distress (see Batson, 1991). Accordingly, if Randy's affective response to Eric's crying is a feeling of negative emotional arousal or discomfort, a reaction that might also motivate action, Randy is feeling personal distress.

Empathy-related emotional reactions have been strongly implicated in prosocial development and action (see Batson, 1991; Eisenberg & Miller, 1987; Hoffman, 1982). However, sympathy and personal distress are believed to be associated with different motivations and to relate differently to prosocial behavior. Specifically, sympathy is viewed as associated with other-oriented motives and, consequently, with other-oriented, altruistic helping behavior. In contrast, personal distress is believed to evoke the egoistic motivation of alleviating one's own distress. For example, if he responds to Eric's crying with personal distress, Randy would be expected to engage in prosocial behavior only if that is the easiest way to stop the crying. If personal distress motivates his action and if Randy can easily escape contact with Eric's crying, he would be expected to leave the situation rather than help.

In general, the empirical research is consistent with the notion that sympathy is more likely to be associated with helping than is personal distress when it is easy for one to escape contact with the person needing assistance. In a series of studies, Eisenberg, Fabes, and their colleagues examined the relations of self-report, facial, and physiological (e.g., heart rate and skin conductance) markers of sympathy and personal distress to prosocial behavior in situations in which escape was relatively easy. When children were shown a variety of empathy-inducing videotapes, those who exhibited facial or physiological markers of sympathy tended to be relatively prosocial if given an opportunity to assist someone in the film or a group of people similar to those in the film (e.g., hospitalized children). In contrast, children (especially boys) who exhibited evidence of personal distress tended to be less prosocial (see Eisenberg & Fabes, in press). Due to the conceptual and empirical links between empathy-related reactions and prosocial behavior, an understanding of factors that promote sympathy provides information relevant to fostering prosocial behavior.

Development of Prosocial Responding

For a long time most philosophers, psychologists, and others believed infants, toddlers, and young children to be quite self-interested and amoral. This view was exemplified by Sigmund Freud's theory in which infants were born possessing only the id, the structure of personality concerned with innate, instinctual, irrational impulses and self-gratification. In most of Freud's writings the superego or con-

science was said to develop only after children were 4 to 6 years of age. Jean Piaget also promulgated the belief that young children are concerned only with their own needs. He asserted that children do not have the ability to understand others' perspectives until they are 6 or 7 years of age. If children are unaware of another's perspective, they are unlikely to assist. It is now clear from empirical work, however, that children develop a rudimentary understanding of others' perspectives in the first few years of life. Furthermore, children engage in other-oriented, prosocial behavior at an early age, although the nature of prosocial responding does seem to change somewhat during the first few years of life.

Reactions to Others' Distress

Much of the research on the early development of prosocial behavior concerns infants' and toddlers' reactions to others' distress. Six-month-olds infrequently respond with distress to that of a peer, although they often display interest in peers' discomfort (Hay, Nash, & Pedersen, 1981). Hoffman (1982) argued that infants in the first year of life do not clearly differentiate between self and other and, therefore, are unsure who is experiencing any distress they witness. By 10 to 14 months of age, infants often become agitated and disturbed when they view others in distress (Radke-Yarrow & Zahn-Waxler, 1984). It is not entirely clear in these situations whether children are genuinely concerned about the other person or whether the other person's distress merely upsets the infant. However, children of this age often seek comfort for themselves as a reaction to viewing another's distress, which supports the later explanation. Becoming distressed as a response to the distress of others decreases in relative frequency during the second year of life.

Between 12 and 18 months, children sometimes try to interact in a positive manner with others in distress such as by patting someone who is upset. Randy's sharing of a toy in response to Eric's whimpering is typical of comforting behaviors that emerge and become more common during this period (Radke-Yarrow & Zahn-Waxler, 1984). Hoffman (1982) argued that although the 1- to 2-year-old appears to experience empathy and sometimes is prosocial, the child experiences "egocentric empathy." That is, although some children have become fully aware of the difference between the self and another as physical entities and recognize who is experiencing distress, they do not yet fully distinguish between the other person's inner states and their own. Thus, a young child is prone to assist in ways appropriate for oneself but perhaps not for the other person. For example, a girl may give a distressed adult her own beloved doll or bring her own mother to comfort a crying peer, even if the other child's mother is present. Although increasing in frequency during the second year of life, prosocial behavior, including attempts to help others in distress, is far from commonplace during this period. In fact, 2-year-olds are more likely than younger children to aggress against those whom they have hurt (Radke-Yarrow & Zahn-Waxler, 1984). Children aged 18 to 36 months often ignore or watch their siblings' distress and frequently exacerbate the situation when they have upset their siblings (Dunn, 1988). Similarly, young children more often ignore peers' distress than respond in a positive manner. In one study of 16- to 33-months-olds, a peer responded to another's distress within a play episode only 22% of the time, and children were three times as likely to respond to the distress of a friend than to that of a peer who was not a friend (Howes & Farver, 1987).

These findings notwithstanding, children's prosocial interventions do increase in frequency in the first few years of life (Dunn, 1988). Moreover, it appears that 3-year-olds can respond to others' distresses more appropriately and competently than can 18-month-olds. These changes are due, perhaps, to increases with age in children's ability to take another's perspective or to understand how other people think and feel. Because preschool children are better able to understand the perspective of others than are younger children, they are more motivated and better able to pinpoint the source of another's distress and to help in ways sensitive to the other's need (Hoffman, 1982). Nonetheless, comforting of distressed others, particularly peers, is still a relatively infrequent act, especially in the preschool classroom (see Eisenberg, Cameron, Tryon, & Dodez, 1981).

Children of school age typically spend more time with their peers than do younger children and begin to develop intimate friendships. Moreover, with increasing age children are more likely to view emotional support as an important component of friendship and provide more support (see Hartup, 1983; Youniss, 1980). In addition, older children are more likely than younger children to take the perspective of the distressed person when attempting to help or comfort them. Hence, the quality of their assistance often is superior to that of younger children (see Bar-Tal, 1982; Krebs & Van Hesteren, 1994).

It also is likely that preadolescents and adolescents sympathize with and comfort a broader range of individuals than do younger children. Hoffman (1982) hypothesized that the ability to sympathize with the distress of abstract others (i.e., those who are not in the immediate situation) and with the chronic distress of others develops in late childhood or early adolescence. Hoffman suggested that this age-related change is based upon the child's newfound ability to view others as having personal identities and life experiences beyond the immediate situation. If Hoffman is correct, adolescents, in comparison to younger children, would be expected to be more sympathetic (and therefore more prosocial) toward members of disadvantaged groups and other individuals whose distress is chronic or not immediately observable.

Sharing, Donating, and Helping

Not only do young children sometimes intervene when another is distressed, they also share with and help others in a variety of ways. One- to 2-year-olds often share objects in social interactions that do not involve distress, and such sharing increases during the first year of life (see Eisenberg & Fabes, in press; Radke-Yarrow, Zahn-Waxler, & Chapman, 1983). Sharing of objects may not be motivated primarily by concern for others; rather, exchange of objects appears to be an effective way for young children to sustain positive interactions with other people.

In addition, even 18-month-olds frequently participate in everyday housekeeping tasks without being directed to do so. They spontaneously assist their mothers, fathers, and unfamiliar adults with such tasks, and their behavior often is goal oriented and not limited to imitation of adults' behaviors. Although it is not clear that children assist with chores primarily to assist another, their behavior has positive consequences for others (Rheingold, 1982).

Sharing and helping behaviors, although more frequent in the preschool classroom than comforting behaviors, are still relatively infrequent. Estimates of sharing behaviors per child in the classroom range from less than 1 to 4 times per hour (Eisenberg et al., 1981; Eisenberg & Fabes, in press).

It is not clear whether naturally occurring sharing behaviors increase with age during the preschool years (Radke-Yarrow et al., 1983). However, older school-aged children are more likely than younger children to share objects or money with unknown others (Radke-Yarrow et al., 1983). Moreover, older children may be slightly more likely than younger children to assist in emergency situations in which someone else is hurt. There is some evidence that helping increases in the midelementary school years, declines later in elementary school or early high school, and then increases again in the high school years. Interview data indicate that young children often are inhibited from helping because they feel unable to assist. In contrast, young adolescents and older preadolescents frequently are inhibited by fear of social disapproval for helping (e.g., if their help is not wanted) or fear of embarrassing the potential recipient of help (Midlarsky & Hannah, 1985). Older children may also help more in some situations than younger children because they have relatively greater experience, resulting in more task-relevant skills and knowledge. In addition, older children may help more, in part, because they may be better able to discern others' needs (Pearl, 1985).

Age Changes in Motives and Reasoning About Prosocial Behavior

Older and younger children also seem to differ somewhat in their motivations for engaging in prosocial behaviors.

For example, older children are more likely to help or donate in situations in which they are not promised a reward or pressured to help (see Bar-Tal, 1982; Eisenberg, 1986). Moreover, there are developmental trends in the reasons children give for their prosocial actions. Even preschoolers occasionally give simple, other-oriented, and pragmatic reasons for their peer-directed prosocial actions, but in general, self-oriented, hedonistic reasons for prosocial behavior appear to decrease with age. With increasing age, children are more inclined to cite reasons that reflect perspective taking and empathy/sympathy (Bar-Tal, 1982; Eisenberg, 1986). Moreover, there is evidence, albeit mixed, that children who express more mature motives for their prosocial actions engage in more prosocial behavior (see Eisenberg, 1986).

Similar age-related trends have been noted in studies of children's moral reasoning, most of which involved interviews of children regarding hypothetical moral dilemmas (Eisenberg, 1986). Respondents were asked what the story protagonist, faced with the dilemma, should do and why. The responses of young children tended to emphasize hedonistic reasoning or needs-oriented (primitive empathic) prosocial reasoning. Needs-oriented reasoning involves mere recognition of the other person's needs or condition. For example, Randy might explain that he helped "because Eric was crying" with no further elaboration. In elementary school, children's moral reasoning begins to reflect concern with approval and enhancing interpersonal relationships, as well as the desire to behave in stereotypically "good" ways. However, such reasoning appears to decrease in use somewhat in high school. Beginning in late elementary school or thereafter, children begin to express reasoning reflecting abstract principles, internalized affective reactions (e.g., guilt or positive affect about the consequences of one's behavior for others or living up to internalized principles), and self-reflective sympathy and perspective taking. However, individuals of all ages sometimes verbalize immature modes of reasoning, and developmental trends do not always involve linear progressions. For example, hedonistic reasoning drops off sharply in use from age 4 to age 11 or 12, but appears to reemerge somewhat in adolescence and early adulthood (see Eisenberg, 1986; Eisenberg, Carlo, Murphy, & Van Court, 1995). For a more detailed discussion of moral reasoning, see "Moral Reasoning and Behavior" in this volume.

Eisenberg (1986) has argued that, when considering prosocial options, prosocial moral reasoning provides a window into the hierarchy of children's goals, needs, and values. Findings from research involving hypothetical moral dilemmas and studies concerning motives for real-life prosocial behavior suggest essentially the same developmental course. With either methodology, children become more other-oriented and concerned with abstract value-related reasons for prosocial behavior with age. Customarily, they become less self-oriented in the preschool and elementary school years. Thus, even if the quantity of some types of prosocial behaviors does not change with age, the quality of children's prosocial actions generally becomes more altruistic with age. Furthermore, with increasing age children appear more capable of understanding value- and other-oriented rationales for enacting prosocial behaviors.

Sex Differences in Prosocial Development

There appear to be modest sex differences with girls reporting or evidencing somewhat more prosocial behavior than boys. These differences are larger for measures of kindness/considerateness than for instrumental helping (Eisenberg & Fabes, in press). Moreover, girls tend to report more sympathy and empathy than boys, although sex differences in facial or physiological measures of empathy-related responding are small (see Eisenberg & Lennon, 1983; Eisenberg & Fabes, in press). It is likely that people, including children, believe that females should be and are more prosocial; thus, children may come to view themselves as helpful and empathic and, consequently, sometimes may act in ways consistent with these perceptions.

The Socialization of Prosocial Behavior

Although biological factors may play a role in the development of empathy and prosocial behavior (see Eisenberg, Fabes, & Miller, 1990; Zahn-Waxler, Robinson, & Emde, 1992), clearly children's prosocial behavior is also related to some types of socialization experiences. Some of the relevant data on socialization is correlational, but other research involves experimental designs from which inferences about causality can be made with some confidence. Moreover, patterns of findings from laboratory and naturalistic studies generally converge, which increases professional confidence in this body of knowledge concerning parental practices. Relations that have received particular scrutiny by researchers are between prosocial behavior and empathy-related responses, on the one hand, and, on the other, disciplinary practices, parental warmth, modeling, parental nondisciplinary verbalizations, reinforcement, assignment of the child to prosocial activities, parental emotion-related practices, parental emphasis on prosocial values, and expressions of emotion and conflict in the home.

Disciplinary Practices

Parental discipline that involves induction (i.e., reasoning) rather than power assertion appears to be associated with prosocial behavior, particularly for middle-class children in Western cultures. Inductions that are victim- or peer-oriented, for example those that point out the consequences of the child's behavior on others, have been linked with children's prosocial behavior. However, inductions seem to be most effective for children who have a history of exposure to inductive discipline. Inductions also appear to be most effective when combined with a democratic parenting style including support and demands for mature behavior (see Eisenberg & Fabes, in press; Hoffman, 1983; Janssens & Gerris, 1992).

Hoffman (1983) reasoned that inductions are likely to promote moral development for a number of reasons, including the following:

- They induce an optimal level of arousal for learning—that is, they elicit the child's attention but are unlikely to produce high levels that are disruptive to learning.
- Inductions are unlikely to be viewed by the child as arbitrary and therefore are not apt to induce resistance.
- Inductions focus children's attention on consequences of their behavior for others, thereby capitalizing on children's capacity to empathize and experience guilt.

Hoffman further argued that over time, inductive messages are experienced as internalized (i.e., deriving from within the child) because the child plays an active role in processing the information embedded in the induction. This information is encoded and integrated with information contained in other inductions and becomes disassociated from the particular disciplinary event. Furthermore, the focus when socializers use inductions is on the child's action and its consequences rather than on the parent as the disciplinary agent. Consequently, over time children are likely to remember the causal link between their actions and consequences for others rather than the external pressure or the specific disciplinary context.

In contrast to inductive discipline, power-assertive discipline is defined as involving physical punishment, deprivation of privileges, or the threat of these punishments. In general, power assertion has been found to be either unrelated or negatively related to children's prosocial behavior (Eisenberg & Fabes, in press). Moreover, physical abuse of children appears to be associated with low levels of children's empathy and prosocial behavior, as well as with inappropriate behavior (Main & George, 1985; see Miller & Eisenberg, 1988). As asserted by Hoffman (1983), children often attribute prosocial behavior induced by power-assertive techniques to external motives such as fear of detection or punishment (Dix & Grusec, 1983). Further, power assertion may focus children's attention on punishment rather than on the consequences of their behavior for others and likely induces a level of arousal inimicable to learning (Hoffman, 1983).

Nonetheless, there is a difference between the occasional use of power-assertive techniques in the context of a positive parent-child relationship and the use of punishment as the preferred, predominant mode of discipline. When power-assertive techniques are used in a measured and rational manner by parents who generally are supportive and use nonpower-assertive disciplinary techniques, there may be no negative effects on children's social behavior.

Of course, punishment can induce immediate compliance with socializers' demands for prosocial behavior if the socializer monitors the child's behavior. However, there is little evidence that physical punishment, particularly when used as a primary mode of discipline, fosters the development of internalized prosocial behavior.

Parental Warmth

The relation between children's prosocial behavior and the variables of parental warmth and support is a complex one. Parental warmth by itself is not consistently related to prosocial behavior (e.g., Iannotti, Cummings, Pierrehumbert, Milano, & Zahn-Waxler, 1992; see Eisenberg & Fabes, in press; Radke-Yarrow et al., 1983), although sympathetic parents tend to have same-sex children who are prone to sympathy rather than to personal distress (Eisenberg et al., 1992). Moreover, there is evidence, albeit limited, that children with secure attachments at a young age are more sympathetic and prosocial as preschoolers (e.g., Kestenbaum, Farber, & Sroufe, 1989; Iannotti et al., 1992).

It is likely that parental warmth and support provide a context within which other positive parental practices are optimally effective. For example, in a study with Dutch children, Dekovic and Janssens (1992) examined relations between prosocial behaviors, as reported by teachers and peers, and measures of parenting practices. They found that prosocial behavior was associated with democratic parenting, involving both parental warmth and support, combined with inductions; demandingness; and the provision of suggestions, information, and positive comments. In contrast, parental warmth combined with a highly permissive parenting style may result in low levels of prosocial behavior.

Modeling

One of the most consistent findings in the prosocial literature is that children emulate prosocial and selfish behavior that they observe, be it enacted by unknown adults or parents (see Eisenberg & Fabes, in press; Radke-Yarrow et al., 1983). This finding has occurred regularly in laboratory studies in which exposure to models was manipulated as well as in correlational studies of families. Nurturant models who have ongoing relationships with children may be particularly effective models. For example, preschoolers who viewed lifelike prosocial behaviors enacted by adults with whom they had nurturant interactions over a period of time in the classroom were likely to exhibit prosocial behavior at a later time (Yarrow, Scott, & Waxler, 1973). Although powerful and competent models are imitated more than other models, children may also imitate prosocial actions of their peers (Owens & Ascione, 1991; see Eisenberg & Fabes, in press).

Nondisciplinary Verbalizations

In general, children are more likely to share or donate with others if they hear an adult say that he or she is going to help. In addition, children tend to engage in more prosocial behavior if exposed to pronouncements from adults (usually called *preachings* in the literature) that are other oriented in content (e.g., point out the effects of assisting another) and that focus on the positive effects of prosocial action on others' emotional states (e.g., "They would be so happy and excited if they could buy food and toys . . ."). Typically, preachings normative in content, that is, indicating it is good or right to give, are less effective than preachings emphasizing the effects of prosocial behavior on others (e.g., Smith, Leinbach, Stewart, & Blackwell, 1983; see Eisenberg & Fabes, in press). Preachings also may be most effective when children feel that they have a choice about whether to provide assistance. For example, McGrath, Wilson, and Frassetto (in press) found that adults' appeals increased donating by children if the peer-beneficiary was referred to in the appeal *and* if the children did not feel forced to give. In addition, children were more generous if exposed to a message stating that the intended beneficiary of the appeal (adult or child) would be happy about the donation rather than sad if the donation did not occur.

Positive Reinforcement

Concrete rewards and social reinforcement (e.g., praise) often increase the rate or frequency of children's prosocial behavior in the immediate context. However, concrete rewards do not seem to enhance prosocial tendencies outside of the rewarded context. The effects of praise seem to vary with the type of praise and age of the recipient. Praise that attributes a child's positive behavior to dispositional kindness seems to be more effective than praise that simply labels the act as positive (e.g., Grusec & Redler, 1980). In this context, *dispositional kindness* refers to motives that stem from the child's stable traits or dispositions (e.g., "I guess you're the kind of person who likes to help others whenever you can—yes, you are a very nice and helpful person").

Social reinforcement for prosocial actions, with or without a dispositional attribution, appears to be positively related to the occurrence of prosocial behavior in the immediate context among elementary school children.

However, praise without a dispositional attribution was not associated with the generalization of prosocial behavior to a new situation for 5- or 8-year-olds. In contrast, 10-year-olds exposed to either dispositional praise or nondispositional praise evidenced generalization to a different prosocial behavior (one that had not been reinforced). Grusec and Redler (1980) hypothesized that older children may interpret reinforcement for a specific action (i.e., nondispositional praise) as having implications for a variety of situations whereas younger children do not view praise for a given act as having broader relevance.

Assignment of Prosocial Activities

Children who are induced to engage in prosocial behavior without feeling forced to do so seem to be relatively more prosocial in other contexts (see Staub, 1979). In addition, the assignment of chores that have positive consequences for others has been linked to prosocial proclivities in children. Thus, practice in assisting others or learning by doing seems to foster prosocial tendencies, at least in some circumstances (Eisenberg & Fabes, in press). It is possible that children who behave prosocially come to think of themselves as helpful people, although evidence for this explanation is mixed (Eisenberg, Cialdini, McCreath, & Shell, 1987; Eisenberg & Fabes, in press).

Emotion-Related Practices

Parental practices that help children to cope with their own negative emotion appear to foster sympathy and prosocial behavior rather than egoistic personal distress. This may occur because children who fail to adequately cope with their emotions tend to become overly aroused and, consequently, experience a self-focused aversive response (i.e., personal distress) rather than sympathy when confronted with another's distress. For example, investigators have found that parental emphasis on controlling one's own self-related negative emotion (e.g., sadness, anxiety) is related to levels of personal distress among boys who are confronted with an empathy-inducing stimulus. Parental focus on instrumentally dealing with the cause of the negative emotion, on the other hand, was associated with boys' sympathy (Eisenberg, Fabes, Schaller, Carlo, & Miller, 1991). Parents' willingness to discuss emotion with their children is related to children's empathy and prosocial behavior; however, such discussions likely foster sympathy and prosocial behavior primarily when the parents explain emotions and do not allow their children to become overaroused emotionally (Eisenberg et al., 1993).

Parental Emphasis on Prosocial Values

As might be expected, parents who hold and try to teach prosocial values to their children tend to have children who are relatively kind and helpful (Eisenberg & Fabes, in press). One of the more dramatic pieces of evidence for this assertion comes from a study of people who have exhibited unusual tendencies toward altruism such as rescuers in Nazi Europe. These individuals assisted potential holocaust victims, often at the risk of losing their own lives. Many rescuers recalled learning values of caring from parents or from another person influential in their development. Rescuers also reported that their parents felt that ethical values were universal, that is, were to be extended to all human beings. Interestingly, rescuers did not differ from nonrescuers in reported exposure to nonprosocial values such as honesty or equity, only in prosocial-relevant values (Oliner & Oliner, 1988).

Expression of Emotion and Conflict in the Home

Frequency and valence of emotion expressed in the family seems to play a role in children's prosocial behavior, albeit in a complex manner. In regard to positive emotion, relations, when obtained, generally are positive (e.g., Garner, Jones, & Miner, 1994; Eisenberg & Fabes, in press).

Findings regarding conflict in the home are more complex. Conflict seems to be positively correlated with young children's prosocial behavior toward family members, such as parents and siblings, particularly if conflict is frequent and physical in nature (Cummings, Zahn-Waxler, & Radke-Yarrow, 1984). However, conflict also is associated with problem behaviors and emotional dysregulation in children (Davies & Cummings, 1994). Moreover, in general, reports and displays of maternal anger and externalizing emotion have been associated with low levels of peer-directed prosocial behavior, low sympathy, and high levels of personal distress (e.g., Eisenberg et al., 1992). Eisenberg and Fabes (in press) noted that this apparently discrepant pattern of findings can be interpreted in a meaningful way: Children exposed to high intensity or ongoing anger may tend to become overaroused when exposed to others' negative emotions and experience self-focused personal distress as a consequence. Exposure to adult conflict would tend to undermine children's emotional security, inducing distress and evoking coping responses from the child calculated to minimize the stress in the child's social environment (see Davies & Cummings, 1994). If this were true, children would be expected to try to escape from dealing with others' distress if possible. Often children cannot readily escape from conflict in the home; thus, they may attempt to alleviate their own distress by intervening and comforting family members.

In brief, it appears that exposure to high levels of anger and conflict may elicit attempts by children to minimize self-related negative emotional and physical consequences of conflict but undermines a more general propensity for sympathy or other-oriented prosocial behavior.

Although prosocial development likely is due, in part, to factors other than socialization, it appears that adults can foster prosocial tendencies by using a variety of socialization practices. These practices are listed in Table 1. Of course, it is important to realize that many people and factors play a role in the development of prosocial actions, motives, and reasoning. Nonetheless, it appears that schools, teachers, and parents can play a role in enhancing prosocial development.

Prosocial Behavior in the Schools

Although some consider schools to be primarily a resource for academic development, children receive indirect (and in some cases direct) classroom instruction regarding aspects of morality such as the valuing of prosocial behavior. Prosocial behavior is regarded by most in our society as desirable, at least in the abstract, and such norms and values are embedded in instructional materials and practices. Promotion of prosocial behavior and reasoning would also be expected to have a positive effect on the quality of classroom interaction. Thus, many teachers may wish to promote prosocial behavior as a way of optimizing the learning environment.

Descriptive Research

Given the potential impact of educational institutions, it is surprising that the knowledge base regarding the ef-

Table 1 *Summary of Recommended Practices and Related Factors Associated with Prosocial Development*

Use of authoritative parenting, including inductive discipline and low levels of power assertion
Prosocial modeling
Use of preachings and other verbalizations that encourage the child to emphatize
Use of dispositional praise for prosocial behavior
Provision of practice in prosocial behavior
Encouragement of constructive regulation of negative emotion
Adults' encouragement and valuing of prosocial values
Expression at home of positive emotion rather than conflict
Participation in cooperative activities
Development of supportive relationships in classrooms including teacher expression of affection and approval
Encouragement of emotional role taking through discussion of naturally occurring events at school
Student participation in classroom governance and rule setting
Creation of a caring, cohesive school community

Note. Listed practices and related factors are discussed in text.

fects of the school experience on children's prosocial behavior is not extensive. Furthermore, little of the existing research concerning the schools and prosocial development addresses the effects of socialization in typical school settings under routine conditions. One finding from this limited body of research literature is that a relation exists between quality of out-of-home care in the early years (e.g., preschool or day care) and children's prosocial development (Phillips, McCartney, & Scarr, 1987; see Eisenberg & Fabes, in press). For example, Howes, Matheson, and Hamilton (1994) found that children classified as securely attached to their current and first preschool teachers were rated as more considerate and emphatic with unfamiliar peers than were children classified as having an insecure relationship (especially ambivalent) with their teachers. Thus, a supportive relationship between young children and their teachers may be important for prosocial development. Another finding from descriptive studies is that naturally occurring prosocial behaviors are not very frequent in the classroom and that teachers, although presumed to value them, usually do not actively reward instances of prosocial behavior (Eisenberg et al., 1981).

Intervention Research

The bulk of research concerning prosocial behavior and reasoning in schools consists of intervention studies. Unfortunately, most formal attempts to facilitate prosociality in schools have involved relatively weak, short-duration interventions. Moreover, evaluation of programs has been difficult in some cases because control groups have been exposed to some aspects of the intervention (e.g., Ascione, 1992). Treatment integrity has suffered in some instances when teachers have improvised rather than adhering to the planned curriculum.

Among the best known and conducted intervention studies is the Child Development Project (see Battistich, Watson, Solomon, Schaps, & Solomon, 1991; Solomon, Watson, Delucchi, Schaps, & Battistich, 1988). This longitudinal program included some school-wide elements and parent involvement, but the primary component of the intervention focused on teacher education. Teachers were trained in procedures for creating classrooms conducive to the development of prosocial behavior and reasoning, then were assisted in implementing these procedures; treatment integrity was monitored on an ongoing basis. The procedures with which teachers were familiarized included techniques for expressing affection and approval, for interacting informally with children through games and other activities, and for discussing personal opinions and experiences. Moreover, teachers were trained to use a child-centered, developmental approach to classroom management that emphasized inductive discipline. For example, when Sally took the toy from Eric, the teacher might have directed Sally's attention to Eric's affective response and to how Sally might have felt if the situation had been reversed. Great emphasis was placed on student participation in rule setting and self-control and on student commitment to agreed-upon rules and shared values. Another important program element was participation in cooperative activities—interdependent, joint activities in which children have common goals and must work together, negotiate, state their positions, and compromise. Other aspects of the program that played a less prominent role included promoting social understanding, highlighting prosocial values, and providing helping activities (Battistich et al., 1991). Considerable importance was attached to discussion of naturally occurring events. A generous act or classroom conflict often became a springboard for discussion focusing, for example, on perspective taking and others' needs and feelings.

Across five consecutive years of implementation (kindergarten through fourth grade), students in the program classrooms in three schools, compared to comparable control classes, obtained higher ratings for spontaneous prosocial behavior across all five grades (although the difference was marginally significant during first grade and nonsignificant during fourth grade). These patterns held when both teachers' general competence and students' participation in cooperative activities were controlled, suggesting that program effects on children's prosocial behavior were not simply due to differences in teacher-initiated cooperative interactions nor to more efficiently organized and managed classrooms. This pattern of findings was replicated in a second cohort consisting of kindergarten and first grade classrooms. Moreover, there was evidence that supportive and friendly behavior at school increased, particularly in the first cohort (Solomon et al., 1988). Participation in the program did not affect children's academic performance or their observed negative interpersonal behavior.

The aforementioned findings are particularly impressive because teachers in the first cohort had only one year of experience in implementing program components. With additional time to refine their technique and fully integrate the program into the routine of the classroom, the program might be expected to have even stronger effects. It should be noted, however, that the program was implemented in schools that consisted of mostly white, middle-to-upper-class students who were, for the most part, academically and socially competent. The extent to which the program would be effective with more diverse samples of children is still unknown.

Solomon, Battistich, and Watson (1993) also examined the program's effects on children's prosocial moral reasoning and conflict resolution. All students in one group received the intervention from kindergarten until at least Grade 4 and some as long as through Grade 6; monitoring of effects continued through eighth grade. Comparison students earned higher prosocial reasoning scores than program children in kindergarten, but the program group subsequently obtained higher scores. Program students also received higher scores on conflict resolution (indicating consideration of others' needs and a reliance on the use of compromise and sharing) than did comparison students at each grade level and scored significantly higher at fourth- and eighth-grade levels. These results provide some evidence that the program can have prolonged effects. It should be noted that the outcomes of the program were greater when data were aggregated across years; findings were not consistently significant within years. Moreover, due to the relatively small sample size in the later grades and the high attrition rate, any conclusions must be viewed cautiously.

More recently, the concept of the school as community has become central to these researchers' understanding of the efficacy of their intervention (Battistich, Solomon, Watson, & Schaps, 1994). Most relevant to this discussion is the finding that prosocial behavior and reasoning appear to be fostered in schools and classrooms in which a sense of a caring community exits. The caring school community is one in which members support and care about one another; participate in and influence group decisions; share values, goals, and norms; and feel a sense of belonging.

It appears that many approaches within the cooperative education movement may also serve to facilitate outcomes that are prosocial in nature. However, in the cooperative education literature, behavior and reasoning are not often identified by investigators as prosocial, and to date, no systematic integration of the two bodies of literature has appeared.

Some school-based attempts to promote prosocial tendencies have extended the scope of the intervention to include—or have specifically emphasized—animals as beneficiaries. For example, Ascione (1992) examined the effects of a humane education program (NAHEE's "People and Animals") involving about 40 hours of intervention across the school year, with first through fifth graders. Younger children evidenced relatively little immediate effect, but an effect on humane attitudes was noted a year later (Ascione & Weber, 1993). On an immediate posttest, humane attitudes were enhanced for fourth graders; on a posttest one year later, humane attitudes were enhanced among fourth and fifth graders. Most notable, perhaps, was that humane-directed empathy also increased for both fourth and fifth graders on both the initial test and the one-year posttest.

opment. Parents are most likely to rear prosocial children if the parents are supportive; use inductive discipline; provide opportunities for prosocial activity; model, value, and preach other-oriented behavior; uphold high standards for their children; and encourage the development of sympathy and perspective taking. Moreover, practices that help children to manage their own negative emotion seem to be related to the development of prosocial and sympathetic responding, as does parental provision of an emotionally positive home environment. It is likely that characteristics of the child such as temperament, compliance, and other aspects of personality interact with parental characteristics and beliefs in determining the quality of the parent-child relationship and parental socialization efforts. To date, however, researchers studying correlates of prosocial responding have given relatively little consideration to the role of the child's characteristics in the socialization process. Furthermore, most of the research has involved middle-class children and mothers so the generalizability of the work to other populations and to socializers besides mothers is not known. Fortunately, however, the results of research conducted in schools generally are consistent with findings from studies of socialization effects in the family.

Prosocial behavior and reasoning are doubtlessly valued by most educators although not frequently reinforced in typical classrooms. Quality early schooling and supportive relationships between children and their teachers have been associated with the development of prosocial behavior. Moreover, school-based programs designed to enhance prosocial values, behaviors, and attitudes in children can be effective in enhancing children's prosocial proclivities with respect to both humans and animals. Prosociality can be enhanced in classrooms in which teachers communicate well and share governance with students, use inductive discipline, focus on feelings, and structure cooperative learning activities. These conditions are associated with the perception of the school as a caring community.

Recommended Resources

Battistich, V., Watson, M., Solomon, D., Schaps, E., & Solomon, J. (1991). The Child Development Project: A comprehensive program for the development of prosocial character. In W. M. Kurtines & J. L. Gerwirtz (Eds.), *Handbook of moral behavior and development: Vol. 3. Application* (pp. 1–34). New York: Erlbaum.

or

Solomon, D., Watson, M. S., Delucchi, K. L., Schaps, E., & Battistich, V. (1988). Enhancing children's prosocial behavior in the classroom. *American Educational Research Journal, 25,* 527–554.

Summary

A constellation of socializers' practices, beliefs, and characteristics, as well as the emotional atmosphere of the home, seems to be related to children's prosocial devel-

In both of these references, the Child Development Project is described and results presented following several years of implementation. Program methodology is explained and effects on classroom behavior are presented for two cohorts of students.

Eisenberg, N. (1989). *Empathy and related emotional responses.* In W. Damon (Series Ed.), *New Directions for Child Development, 44.*
This edited monograph in the New Directions for Child Development *series is written for professionals with some knowledge of the emotion or prosocial literatures. Articles focus on the development of empathy and related emotions from infancy on and on relations between empathy and prosocial behavior.*

Eisenberg, N. (1992). *The caring child.* Cambridge, MA: Harvard University Press.
Written for a general audience, this book is part of the Harvard University Press series on the developing child. It provides an account of the motives underlying prosocial behavior and the evolution of these motives. Biological bases, cultural influences, and socialization are discussed as is the role played by situational factors.

Eisenberg, N., & Fabes, R. A. (in press). Prosocial development. In W. Damon (Series Ed.) & N. Eisenberg (Vol. Ed.), *Handbook of child psychology: Vol. 3. Social and personality development* (5th ed.). New York: Wiley.
This chapter presents, perhaps, the most extensive and up-to-date summary of major research findings and theory regarding prosocial behavior and reasoning. The reference list includes all major studies in this area published in English in the past 15 years.

References

Ascione, F. R. (1992). Enhancing children's attitudes about the humane treatment of animals: Generalization to human-directed empathy. *Antrozoos, 5,* 176–191.

Ascione, F. R., & Weber, C. V. (1993, March). *Children's attitudes about the humane treatment of animals and empathy: One-year follow up of a school-based intervention.* Paper presented at the biennial meeting of the Society for Research in Child Development, New Orleans, LA.

Bar-Tal, D. (1982). Sequential development of helping behavior: A cognitive-learning approach. *Developmental Review, 2,* 101–124.

Batson, C. D. (1991). *The altruism question: Toward a social-psychological answer.* Hillsdale, NJ: Erlbaum.

Battistich, V., Solomon, D., Watson, M., & Schaps, (1994, April). *Students and teachers in caring classrooms and school communities.* Paper presented at the meeting of American Educational Research Association, New Orleans, LA.

Battistich, V., Watson, M., Solomon, D., Schaps, E., & Solomon, J. (1991). The Child Development Project: A comprehensive program for the development of prosocial character. In W. M. Kurtines & J. L. Gerwirtz (Eds.), *Handbook of moral behavior and development: Vol. 3. Application* (pp. 1–34). New York: Erlbaum.

Bear, G. G., & Rys, G. S. (1994). Moral reasoning, classroom behavior, and sociometric status among elementary school children. *Developmental Psychology, 30,* 633–638.

Cummings, E. M., Zahn-Waxler, C., & Radke-Yarrow, M. (1984). Developmental changes in children's reactions to anger in the home. *Journal of Child Psychology and Psychiatry, 25,* 63–74.

Davies, P. T., & Cummings, E. M. (1994). Marital conflict and child adjustment: An emotional security hypothesis. *Psychological Bulletin, 116,* 387–411.

Dekovic, M., & Janssens, J. M. (1992). Parents' child-rearing style and children's sociometric status. *Developmental Psychology, 28,* 925–932.

Dix, T., & Grusec, J. E. (1983). Parental influence techniques: An attributional analysis. *Child Development, 54,* 645–652.

Dunn, J. (1988). *The beginnings of social understanding.* Cambridge, MA: Harvard University Press.

Eisenberg, N. (1986). *Altruistic emotion, cognition, and behavior.* Hillsdale, NJ: Erlbaum.

Eisenberg, N., Cameron, E., Tryon, K., & Dodez, R. (1981). Socialization of prosocial behavior in the preschool classroom. *Developmental Psychology, 17,* 773–782.

Eisenberg, N., Carlo, G., Murphy, B., & Van Court, P. (1995). Prosocial development in late adolescence: A longitudinal study. *Child Development.*

Eisenberg, N., Cialdini, R., McCreath, H., & Shell, R. (1987). Consistency-based compliance: When and why do children become vulnerable? *Journal of Personality and Social Psychology, 52,* 1174–1181.

Eisenberg, N., & Fabes, R. A. (in press). Prosocial development. In W. Damon (Series Ed.) & N. Eisenberg (Vol. Ed.), *Handbook of child psychology: Vol. 3. Social, emotional, and personality development* (5th ed). New York: Wiley.

Eisenberg, N., Fabes, R. A., Carlo, G., Speer, A. L., Switzer, G., Karbon, M., & Troyer, D. (1993). The relations of empathy-related emotions and maternal practices to children's comforting behavior. *Journal of Experimental Child Psychology, 55,* 131–150.

Eisenberg, N., Fabes, R. A., Carlo, G., Troyer, D., Speer, A. L., Karbon, M., & Switzer, G. (1992). The relations of maternal practices and characteristics to children's vicarious emotional responsiveness. *Child Development, 63,* 583–602.

Eisenberg, N., Fabes, R. A., Karbon, M., Murphy, B. C., Wosinski, M., Polazzi, L., Carlo, G., & Juhnke, C. (in press). The relations of children's dispositional prosocial behavior to emotionality, regulation, and social functioning. *Child Development.*

Eisenberg, N., Fabes, R. A., & Miller, P. A. (1990). The evolutionary and neurological roots of prosocial behavior. In L. Ellis & H. Hoffman (Eds.), *Crime in biological, social, and moral contexts* (pp. 247–260). New York: Praeger.

Eisenberg, N., Fabes, R. A., Schaller, M., Carlo, G., & Miller, P. A. (1991). The relations of parental characteristics and practices to children's vicarious emotional responding. *Child Development, 62,* 1393–1408.

Eisenberg, N., & Lennon, R. (1983). Gender differences in empathy and related capacities. *Psychological Bulletin, 94,* 100–131.

Eisenberg, N., & Miller, P. (1987). The relation of empathy to prosocial and related behaviors. *Psychological Bulletin, 101,* 91–119.

Farver, J. A. M., & Branstetter, W. H. (1994). Preschoolers' prosocial responses to their peers' distress. *Developmental Psychology, 30,* 334–341.

Garner, P. W., Jones, D. C., & Miner, J. L. (1994). Social competence among low-income preschoolers: Emotion socialization practices and social cognitive correlates. *Child Development, 65,* 622–637.

Grusec, J. E., & Redler, E. (1980). Attribution, reinforcement, and altruism: A developmental analysis. *Developmental Psychology, 16,* 525–534.

Hartup, W. W. (1983). Peer relations. In P. H. Mussen (Series Ed.) and E. M. Hetherington (Vol. Ed.), *Handbook of child psychology: Vol. 4. Socialization, personality, and social development* (pp. 103–196). New York: Wiley.

Hay, D. F., Nash, A., & Pedersen, J. (1981). Responses of six-month-olds to the distress of their peers. *Child Development, 52,* 1071–1075.

Hoffman, M. L. (1982). Development of prosocial motivation: Empathy and guilt. In N. Eisenberg (Ed.), *The development of prosocial behavior* (pp. 281–313). New York: Academic Press.

Hoffman, M. L. (1983). Affective and cognitive processes in moral internalization. In E. T. Higgins, D. N. Ruble, & W. W. Hartup (Eds.), *Social cognition and social development: A sociocultural perspective* (pp. 236–274). Cambridge, MA: Cambridge University Press.

Howes, C., & Farver, J. (1987). Toddlers' responses to the distress of their peers. *Journal of Applied Developmental Psychology, 8,* 441–452.

Howes, C. Matheson, C. C., & Hamilton, C. E. (1994). Maternal, teacher, and child care history correlates of children's relationships with peers. *Child Development, 65,* 264–273.

Iannotti, R. J., Cummings, E. M., Pierrehumbert, B., Milano, M. J., & Zahn-Waxler, C. (1992). Parental influences on prosocial behavior and empathy in early childhood. In J. M. A. M. Janssens & J. R. M. Gerris (Eds.), *Child rearing: Influence on prosocial and moral development* (pp. 77–100). Amsterdam: Swets & Zeitlinger.

Janssens, J. M. A. M., & Gerris, J. R. M. (1992). Child rearing, empathy and prosocial development. In J. M. A. M. Janssens & J. R. M. Gerris (Eds.), *Child rearing: Influence on prosocial and moral development* (pp. 57–75). Amsterdam: Swets & Zeitlinger.

Kestenbaum, R., Farber, E. A., & Sroufe, L. A. (1989). Individual differences in empathy among preschoolers: Relation to attachment history. In N. Eisenberg (Ed.), *New directions for child development: Vol. 44. Empathy and related emotional responses* (pp. 51–64). San Francisco: Jossey-Bass.

Krebs, D. L., & Van Hesteren, F. (1994). The development of altruism: Toward an integrative model. *Developmental Review, 14,* 103–158.

Main, M., & George, C. (1985). Responses of abused and disadvantaged toddlers to distress in agemates: A study in the day care setting. *Developmental Psychology, 21,* 407–412.

McGrath, M. P., Wilson, S. R., & Frassetto, S. J. (in press). Why some forms of inductive reasoning are better than others: Effects of cognitive focus, choice, and affect on children's prosocial behavior. *Merrill-Palmer Quarterly.*

Midlarsky, E., & Hannah, M. E. (1985). Competence, reticence, and helping by children and adolescents. *Developmental Psychology, 21,* 534–541.

Miller, P., & Eisenberg, N. (1988). The relation of empathy to aggression and externalizing/antisocial behavior. *Psychological Bulletin, 103,* 324–344.

Oliner, S. P. & Oliner, P. M. (1988). *The altruistic personality: Rescuers of Jews in Nazi Europe.* New York: Free Press.

Owens, C. R., & Ascione, F. R. (1991). Effects of the model's age, perceived similarity, and familiarity on children's donating. *Journal of Genetic Psychology, 152,* 341–357.

Parker, J. G., & Asher, S. R. (1987). Peer relations and later personal adjustment: Are low accepted children "at risk"? *Psychological Bulletin, 102,* 357–389.

Pearl, R. (1985). Children's understanding of others' need for help: Effects of problem explicitness and type. *Child Development, 56,* 735–745.

Phillips, D., McCartney, K., & Scarr, S. (1987). Childcare quality and children's social development, *Developmental Psychology, 23,* 537–543.

Radke-Yarrow, M., & Zahn-Waxler, C. (1984). Roots, motives, and patterns in children's prosocial behavior. In E. Staub, D. Bar-Tal, J. Karylowski, & J. Reykowski (Eds.), *Development and maintenance of prosocial behavior: International perspectives on positive behavior* (pp. 81–99). New York: Plenum.

Radke-Yarrow, M., Zahn-Waxler, C., & Chapman, M. (1983). Prosocial dispositions and behavior. In P. Mussen (Series Ed.) & E. M. Hetherington (Vol. Ed.), *Manual of child psychology: Vol. 4: Socialization, personality, and social development* (4th ed., pp. 469–545). New York: John Wiley & Sons.

Rheingold, H. L. (1982). Little children's participation in the work of adults, a nascent prosocial behavior. *Child Development, 53,* 114–125.

Smith, C. L., Leinbach, M. D., Stewart, B. J., & Blackwell, J. M. (1983). Affective perspective-taking, exhortations, and children's prosocial behavior. In D. L. Bridgeman (Ed.), *The nature of prosocial development* (pp. 113–137). New York: Academic Press.

Solomon, D., Battistich, & Watson, M. (1993, March). *A longitudinal investigation of the effects of a school intervention program on children's social development.* Paper presented at the biennial meeting of the Society for Research in Child Development, New Orleans, LA.

Solomon, D., Watson, M. S., Delucchi, K. L., Schaps, E., & Battistich, V. (1988). Enhancing children's prosocial behavior in the classroom. *American Educational Research Journal, 25,* 527–554.

Staub, E. (1979). *Positive social behavior and morality: Vol 2: Socialization and development.* NY: Academic Press.

Yarrow, M. R., Scott, P. M., & Waxler, C. Z. (1973). Learning concerning for others. *Developmental Psychology, 8,* 240–260.

Youniss, J. (1980). *Parents and peers in social development: A Sullivan-Piaget perspective.* Chicago: University of Chicago Press.

Zahn-Waxler, C., Robinson, J., & Emde, R. N. (1992). The development of empathy in twins. *Developmental Psychology, 28,* 1038–1047.

2

Sociomoral Reasoning and Behavior

George G. Bear

University of Delaware

Herbert C. Richards

University of Virginia

John C. Gibbs

Ohio State University

Perhaps no other phase of human society is causing greater concern in the present generation than the moral trend of young people. There is universal recognition among the civilized nations of the urgent need for the salvaging of civilization. The adult generation is convinced that the moral situation is bad and frantically insists that matters be set right. . . . The neglect of character training has been due in a large measure to three causes: First, . . . lack of agreement as to what constitutes morality. . . . Second, . . . insufficient agreement as to the proper procedure in salvaging the morals of our present civilization. Third, . . . an undue amount of evading responsibility and attempting to place responsibility with other social agencies (Troth, 1930, p. 3).

Many educators, parents, and the public at large have become alarmed about what appears to be widespread moral deterioration—a decay aggravated by fragmentation of traditional families, declining trust in public institutions, increases in ethically questionable business practices, and frequent exposure to violence through mass media (ASCD Panel . . . , 1988). According to the most recent Phi Delta Kappa/Gallup poll, lack of discipline, fighting/violence/gangs, and drug abuse are perceived by the public as the respectively first, third, and fourth most serious problems facing public schools today (Elam & Rose, 1995).

Alarmed by what they see as a wholesale moral decline in public schools, parents, educators, and other professionals argue for a return to a golden era when children respected their parents and students their teachers—a time of orderly classrooms and firm discipline—a time when juvenile crime was rare and substance abuse nonexistent. Recent publications, such as *Reclaiming our Schools: A Handbook on Teaching Character, Academics, and Discipline* (Wynne & Ryan, 1993) and the *Book of Virtues* (Bennett, 1994), have become

popular, contributing to the renewed interest in moral instruction in public schools. For these authors, character education entails teaching morality and social responsibility as directly and efficiently as possible. This is in accord with what Wynne and Ryan (1993) call "the great tradition," wherein morality is thought to be a special kind of knowledge imposed on children by *cultural transmission* (Pressley & McCormick, 1995).

Important as promoting the character education practices of the past may be, it is sobering to remember that every generation has had its concerns about the morality of its youth (exemplified in our introductory quotation from 1930) and its own moral limitations. For example, it is difficult to believe that today's young people are collectively less morally responsible than their forebearers who accepted institutionally sanctioned racism or embraced Hitler's vision. Nor do we believe that past generations were right to publicly endorse such "moral" educational practices as the rote repetition of scripture which children could not understand or the use of severe corporal punishment to correct minor transgressions. In fact, after reading about the prevalent moral ideas of past generations, we question if there ever was a "golden era" when nearly all children respected their elders and grew into adults who behaved morally. For this reason, we caution educators against naively embracing "traditional" practices.

But we must agree with Bennett (1994), Wynne and Ryan (1993), and other advocates of character education when they document the urgent need for change. There is overwhelming evidence that many kinds of moral problems, especially violent crime, drug abuse, gang membership, and teenage pregnancy, have risen in the past several decades. Moreover, today's school personnel seldom act proactively by implementing systematic programs to promote moral responsibility, choosing instead to focus on ways to deal with behavior problems once they have occurred.

We also agree with advocates of character education that the direct teaching of moral knowledge and the systematic application of behavioral principles are important, and often necessary, for promoting moral development. However, as reflected throughout this chapter, we also believe that such strategies are not sufficient for fostering prosocial conduct and curtailing antisocial behaviors. As argued eloquently by Lickona (1991), and perhaps best exemplified in practice in the Child Development Project (Battistich, Watson, Solomon, Schaps, & Solomon, 1991), educators should also adopt the applications of the constructivist approach to moral education, with its emphasis on promoting reflective moral thought.

Background and Development

In this chapter, acting morally means choosing to do whatever is necessary to ensure benevolent and fair social interaction—understanding and doing what one *ought* to do. To act in a moral way, a person must first understand how his or her actions affect the welfare of others, judge whether such actions are right or wrong, intend to act in accord with this judgment, and follow through with this intention (Rest, 1983). Because moral development necessarily entails social interaction and because the term *moral* often connotes misleading impressions, we tend to use the term *sociomoral* throughout this chapter, especially when referring to reasoning.

Acting in a morally mature manner also requires one to be self-governing. Piaget (1932/1965) and Kohlberg (1981, 1984) referred to this quality as *moral autonomy*— the "ability to think for oneself and to decide between right and wrong in the moral realm and between truth and untruth in the intellectual realm by taking all relevant factors into account, independently of rewards or punishments" (Kamii, Clark, & Dominick, 1994). Acting in a moral way when there is no other choice does not exemplify moral maturity. Even criminals who perform the most hideous acts behave appropriately provided the environment is coercive enough.

When people act in a morally autonomous way, they are referencing their behavior to moral values. Such values, grounded in sociomoral reasoning, entail an obligation to act in a certain way, even when an individual would rather do something else (Lickona, 1991). Take "honesty," for example. If you tell the truth, when it would be to your advantage to lie, you are behaving in accord with this moral value. Although moral values vary from culture to culture (Schweder, Mahapatra & Miller, 1987), nearly all contemporary authorities (Damon, 1990; Lickona, 1991; Power, Higgins, & Kohlberg, 1989; Wynne & Ryan, 1993, to name a few) agree that at least a few universal

ones exist. For example, few would disagree with the following six moral values or characterological ideals: (a) trustworthiness; (b) respect; (c) responsibility; (d) justice and fairness; (e) caring; and (f) civic virtue and citizenship. These "Six Pillars of Character" emerged from the 1992 Aspen Summit Conference on Character Education, a conference in which a diverse group of educators and youth leaders were asked to identify values that "transcend cultural, religious, and socioeconomic differences" ("Six pillars of character," 1992, p. 64).

More than six decades ago, a team of researchers (Hartshorne, May, & Shuttleworth, 1930) thought they had empirically demonstrated what was argued centuries earlier by Aristotle: Learning about moral values does not necessarily translate into morally responsible behavior. In an impressive series of studies under controlled conditions, these investigators found that when children were tempted to lie, steal, or cheat, those who had been taught the Scout's code and rarely missed Sunday School were as apt to be dishonest as peers who had less moral training. Relying on the analytic methods then available to interpret their data, these investigators concluded that behaving morally depended more on context than background. There seemed to be little evidence for the existence of honesty as a character trait.

In more recent years, Burton (1976) revisited the Hartshorne et al. (1930) studies. Using sophisticated multivariate statistics, Burton uncovered subtle evidence that the earlier investigators were too extreme in their conclusions. The reanalysis not only revealed a single, general factor for "honesty" but demonstrated that the link between moral knowledge and behavior was stronger than previously thought. By aggregating the measures in both domains, Burton found a correlation of .46 between moral knowledge and actual behaviors—much larger than any of the pairwise correlations reported by Hartshorne et al. Like Burton, most investigators today believe "a small but consistently manifested honesty factor distinguishes individuals" (p. 176) and that such a factor is associated with moral knowledge. Nevertheless, there is also consensus that situational context profoundly influences behavior.

Development of Sociomoral Reasoning

Since Hartshorne et al.'s (1930) pioneering research efforts, many theories about the origins, development, and promotion of moral autonomy have been proposed. More than any other approach to moral development, the cognitive-developmental stage theories of Piaget (1932/ 1965) and Kohlberg (1981, 1984; Power et al., 1989) have stimulated research and inspired innovative educational practice. Piaget and Kohlberg offered an alternative to the behaviorist approach in which conformity to external norms received emphasis. Kohlberg (1981, 1984; Colby & Kohlberg, 1987a) refined and extended the earlier work of Piaget and demonstrated that children and adolescents construct increasingly adequate concepts of morality—at least under appropriate social conditions. Such concepts develop in unison with cognitive development and with the maturity of social perspective taking.

According to cognitive-developmental theory, sociomoral reasoning, rather than moral knowledge or content per se, underlies children's moral development. That is, although important, knowing what behaviors are right or wrong is much less important than understanding and appreciating why the behaviors should (or should not) be exhibited. Kohlberg (1981, 1984) envisioned stages of sociomoral reasoning grouped according to three levels: *preconventional* (Stages 1 and 2), *conventional* (Stages 3 and 4), and *postconventional* (Stages 5 and 6). Postconventional thinking seldom appears before adulthood and then only rarely (Colby & Kohlberg, 1987a). In the practical realm of the school psychologist, therefore—and possibly in the theoretical realm as well (see Gibbs, 1991b)—only the first four stages are relevant; only these will be described here. In the tradition of Piaget (1932/1965), Kohlberg coined technical names for his six stages. In order of appearance, they are

1. Heteronomous morality.
2. Individualism, instrumental purpose, and exchange.
3. Mutual interpersonal expectations, relationships, and interpersonal conformity.
4. Social system and conscience.
5. Social contract or utility and individual rights.
6. Universal ethical principles. (Colby & Kohlberg, 1987, pp. 18–19).

Descriptions of Kohlberg's first four stages are given in Table 1. Note that as a memory aid, we use the more descriptive labels recently introduced by Gibbs, Potter, and Goldstein (1995). In accordance with Gibbs's revision (1991b; Gibbs, Basinger, & Fuller, 1992), the "preconventional" level is labeled Immature and the "conventional" level is labeled Mature.

According to cognitive-developmental theory, all children advance through the stages of sociomoral judgment in the same order but not at the same rate. Nor do all attain the same sociomoral stage at the end of childhood, adolescence, or adulthood. Whereas it is considered "normal" to exhibit Stages 1 and 2 during the lower elementary grades, Stages 2 and 3 during the upper elementary and intermediate grades, and Stage 3 and some Stage 4 during high school, there is a great deal of variation. Such differences are due to variations in both cognitive maturity and cumulative social experience. Children who are mentally retarded, emotionally disturbed, or learning disabled tend to develop less mature sociomoral reasoning strategies than nonhandicapped peers, whereas more advanced reasoning is typically found among intellectually gifted children (Bear, 1987). In general, mature sociomoral reasoning is positively correlated (typically in the .30's) with socioeconomic status, level of formal education, performance on IQ tests, and perspective-taking ability (Colby & Kohlberg, 1987a).

Most researchers in the cognitive tradition now agree that learning about right and wrong—that is, acquiring content—may be necessary, but not sufficient, to promote moral development. Kohlberg (1981, 1984) argued that advancement depends on cognitive conflict in a social context. Over time sociomoral growth occurs as an individual attempts to apply his or her current sociomoral thinking to novel situations, finds it to be inadequate, and, as a result, experiences internal conflict. The resulting "disequilibration" stimulates cognitive reorganization and the construction of more advanced reasoning in order to coordinate the conflicting perspectives of self and others (inter-individual conflict), or conflicting cognitions held by the individual (intra-individual conflict), or both. Advancement requires appropriate social contexts—ones in which there are opportunities to experience cognitive conflict.

A number of empirical investigations have supported many of Kohlberg's broader claims: The sequence of the first four stages appears universal; stage structures tend to be hierarchical; regressions from higher to lower stages and stage skipping rarely occur; and stages are correlated with age (see Colby & Kohlberg, 1987a, and Snarey, 1985, for reviews). Moreover, contrary to the popular claims of Gilligan and others (Gilligan, 1982), there is little empirical evidence of a structural bias in favor of males (Garmon, Basinger, Gregg, & Gibbs, 1996; Walker, 1991).

In recent years, however, the role of cognitive conflict in the promotion of moral development has been a topic of much debate. Some researchers (e.g., Bandura, 1986; Gilly, 1991) have pointed out that no one has fully explained how cognitive changes are actually internalized. Moreover, they argue, such changes frequently occur in the absence of any observable cognitive conflict. As such, a variety of other mechanisms, such as scaffolding and modeling, may also promote changes in sociomoral reasoning.

Walker and Taylor (1991) found evidence to support the notion that simply inducing cognitive conflict is not the only, or best, means of promoting sociomoral growth. In a longitudinal study, data on the sociomoral reasoning of children and their parents were collected together with information about how parents discussed important matters with their children. These researchers found that a parent's level of sociomoral reasoning, particularly if it were about one stage above the child's, in conjunction with a particular style of discussion, facilitated the long-term growth in their child's sociomoral reasoning. Interestingly, neither a challenging, "conflictual" style nor an information-giving, "lecturing" style proved to be the best way to promote growth. Rather, the most effective style—the one that best pro-

Table 1 *Stages of Moral Reasoning of School-Age Children*

Immature Level

Stage 1. Power: Might makes right

Reasoning is characterized by three core beliefs: The moral significance of an action resides in its inherent goodness or badness; authority figures dictate what is right or wrong; and punishment is an inevitable consequence of wrongdoing. Once children learn that lying, stealing, or hurting someone is wrong, no further justification is needed to establish the moral status of such actions. Moreover, authority figures, not cooperating individuals, determine standards of right or wrong—at least those not already self-evident. This means that right action is construed as deference to a superior power. Morally good means doing what one is told by a powerful authority—someone older, bigger, stronger, or more prominent. Stage 1 core beliefs also translate into the idea that you can get what you want if you are powerful enough.

Stage 2. Deals: You scratch my back, I'll scratch yours.

Individuals reasoning at Stage 2 no longer believe punishment to be an inevitable consequence of transgression. Given their improved perspective taking, they recognize that punishment is dependent on situational variables. Judgments continue to be concrete, pragmatic, and individualistic, but right and wrong are construed in a situational context. *If* you get caught, and who catches you, determines whether the behavior is right or wrong. The fundamental operating philosophy is now naive, instrumental hedonism—the belief that every individual has the right to pursue his or her own best interests. Making a deal is important in that it allows two individuals to advance their respective self-interests simultaneously. Moreover, one person should help another because the favor will be returned. The same notions of instrumental exchange apply to aggressive actions: If one is hit, one should hit back.

Mature Level

Stage 3. Mutuality: Treat others as you would like to be treated.

Conventional moral reasoning begins with Stage 3, a major advancement from the two preconventional stages. In the Gibbs, Basinger, and Fuller's (1992) revision of Kohlberg's work, Stages 1 and 2 are labelled "immature" and 3 and 4 "mature." Most young people discover that moral decisions based on individual self-interest are flawed. For one thing, there is no reliable way to resolve disagreements when one-on-one negotiations break down. For another, increasing social awareness promotes a more comprehensive view of the moral domain. Stage 3 reasoning coordinates colliding individual perspectives and, as a consequence, constructs reference points outside the two-party framework. Moral decisions are now based on shared values and norms. One manifestation of such thinking is that one should abide by the Golden Rule by putting oneself into another person's shoes. Another is that good intentions as well as actions must be considered when judging the moral transgressions of others.

Stage 4. Systems: Are you contributing to society?

Stage 4 reasoning widens the reference group still further. Just as individual needs were subordinated to the values of limited reference groups during the transition to Stage 3, these values, in turn, are subordinated to or integrated into the laws and ideals of society as a whole. Individuals reasoning at Stage 4 act out of the conviction that without laws and authorities to enforce them, competing self-interests (Stage 2) and limited group loyalties (Stage 3) would erode the social fabric and society would break down. It is in the best interest of everyone, then, to be law abiding. The Stage 4 perspective is "generally that of a societal, legal, or religious system that has been codified into institutionalized laws and practices" (Colby & Kohlberg, 1987, p. 28). For some individuals, however, Stage 4 reasoning may be grounded in religious law rather than secular. Gibbs, Basinger, and Fuller (1992) describe "ideal" versions of Stages 3 and 4 evidenced by some adolescents and adults.

moted advances in sociomoral reasoning—was Socratic. Gains were greatest for children of parents who frequently elicited their child's opinion, asked questions that clarified an issue, paraphrased what their child said, and checked for understanding. These findings are, for the most part, consistent with the tenets of cognitive-developmental theory. But they do suggest that Kohlberg and Piaget seriously underestimated the influence of parents on a child's moral development. Moreover, they suggest that "heavy-handed" cognitive challenges that so effectively promote

sociomoral growth during peer discussions "may be counterproductive in a family context involving a discussion among individuals of differing status and power" (Walker & Taylor, 1991, p. 281).

Misunderstandings of Kohlberg's Theory

Although Kohlberg's theory continues to inform educational practice today, it has attracted a number of criticisms from educators (e.g., Leming, 1993; Wynne &

Ryan 1993), psychologists (e.g., Bandura, 1991), and philosophers (e.g., Phillips, 1987). Unfortunately, several criticisms come from misunderstandings of Kohlberg's work. Two are central to the educational focus of this chapter:

First, perhaps because of the emphasis Kohlberg placed on stage descriptions, some practitioners assume that children can be homogeneously classified according to stage. But, as noted by Rest (1983, p. 586), a cognitive-developmentalist, the "acquisition of cognitive structures is gradual rather than abrupt; acquisition is not an all-or-nothing matter but rather is better depicted as a gradual increase in the probability of occurrence." Like Rest, Kohlberg recognized that stage mixtures and fluctuations are common, and level of reasoning often varies according to the social context. For example, as shown by Krebs, Vermeulen, Carpendale, and Denton (1991), individuals continue to apply their old stages of reasoning after acquiring new ones and are likely to reason one stage lower when confronted with real-life dilemmas compared to hypothetical dilemmas (which are typically used to measure sociomoral reasoning). Moreover, making matters more complex in respect to stage mixture and classification of reasoning, later in his career Kohlberg included substages or "stage types" within each stage: Heteronomous or Type A, and Autonomous or Type B (Candee & Kohlberg, 1987; Colby & Kohlberg, 1987a).

It follows that a school psychologist generally should not expend valuable resources on the formal assessment and labeling of a child's general "stage" of sociomoral reasoning but instead should focus on understanding the sociomoral reasoning that might underlie a child's behavior in a given situation. There is one exception, however. Whenever a pervasive developmental delay is suspected (Gregg, Gibbs, & Basinger, 1994), such assessments might be useful. (If interested in assessing moral reasoning, we suggest use of the Sociomoral Reflection Measure-Short Form [Gibbs et al., 1992], an 11-item open-ended questionnaire that correlates .69 with Kohlberg's substantially more complex interview and scoring manual [Colby & Kohlberg, 1987b].)

The second misunderstanding of Kohlberg's approach is that it is preoccupied with the *structure* of sociomoral judgment to the exclusion of *content* and *behavior*. (By content we mean moral knowledge, e.g., "stealing, lying, and cheating are wrong.") In fact, Bandura (1991) maintains there is little point in considering the stage of sociomoral reasoning at all. He writes:

The way in which moral principles are applied in coping with diverse moral dilemmas varies, depending on situational imperatives, activity domains and constellations of social influence. It is not uncommon for sophisticated moral justifications to subserve inhumane endeavors. (p. 46)

In essence, Bandura argues that almost any course of action can be justified at each stage of sociomoral rea-

soning. For example, it would be difficult to convince a teacher that a violent act grounded in Stage 3 reasoning ("If I didn't kick the punk's ass, my friends wouldn't trust me any more. You've got to be loyal to your friends") is somehow more mature morally than a nonviolent act grounded in Stage 1 ("I didn't hit him because my parents would have killed me"). An educator who focuses exclusively on promoting stage growth may find problematic the absence of a direct and immediate linkage between reasoning and behavior.

Unlike Bandura (1991), however, cognitive developmentalists recognize the critical importance of content and behavior while also arguing that how children (or anyone) construe matters of right and wrong (i.e., how they structure sociomoral thought) is important in its own right. They also believe educators should allocate at least some of their resources to promoting stage growth. For one thing, as reported later, stage advances do positively influence the probability of morally responsible behavior—at least beyond Stage 2. For another, it is important for children to make mature sociomoral decisions autonomously, in the absence of authority and in a variety of social contexts. Nevertheless, as argued by Bandura, decisional choice and actual behavior are no less important than sociomoral reasoning per se. Later in his career, Kohlberg came to realize this point himself, as reflected in his inclusion of a decision function (deontic choice—deciding which action is right) and a follow-through function (judgment of responsibility or obligation to act) into a model of the relation of moral reasoning and action (Candee & Kohlberg, 1987).

Kohlberg also came to recognize, when he started working in the public schools, that there is much more to moral behavior than moral reasoning. In the 1970s Kohlberg's moral education approach was centered on the use of classroom moral discussion in which the primary role of the teacher was to create cognitive conflict via Socratic-style discussions of moral dilemmas. Later in his life, he advocated a multifaceted "Just Community" approach to moral education—one that focused on the school's overall moral climate and governance, with an emphasis on active student involvement. He also encouraged teachers to become advocates for morally responsible behavior, not just moral discussion moderators (Power et al., 1989). Similarly, recent "neo-Kohlbergian" moral education programs cast educators in the role of "coaches" who directly address content, reasoning, and social skills (Gibbs et al., 1995).

It is intriguing that as cognitive-developmental investigators came to recognize that observable behavior was a critically important aspect of morality, their social learning counterparts began to recognize that principles of reinforcement and observational learning were not sufficient in explaining sociomoral behavior—that the critical role of social cognitions needed to be explored. Bandura (1986, 1991), for example, offered a social cognitive theory of morality in which behavior, cognition, and environmental influences "all operate as interacting determinants of each other" (1991, p. 70). Bandura's work is especially helpful in understanding why individuals who hold high internal standards of morality sometimes behave inhumanely. Thus, perhaps largely in response to respective criticisms of the two predominant approaches to moral development and education (social learning/character training and cognitive-developmental), contemporary moral education projects and models address multiple components of sociomoral maturity. Examples are the Child Development Project (Battistich et al., 1991), Lickona's (1991) Educating for Character model, the Just Community Approach (Power et al., 1989), and most recently, the EQUIP program (Gibbs et al., 1995).

Components of Sociomoral Maturity

Achieving sociomoral maturity is not a simple matter. Indeed, a multitude of research findings support a more general proposition: Acting in a morally responsible or mature way is influenced by multiple factors, both internal and external to the individual. Many of these factors are covered in other chapters of this volume, including Aggressive Behavior, Anger, Prosocial Behavior, Social Responsibility, Social Problem Solving, and Social Skills. No single process is sufficient to explain all or even most of what is commonly meant by moral maturity. As a consequence, efforts have been made to partition the moral domain. For example, some have divided the area into affective, cognitive, and behavioral aspects. However, we prefer a functional framework like the one offered by James Rest (1983). According to Rest, the moral domain is composed of four interacting components. To function as a morally mature individual, all four components must be actively engaged.

Component 1

A person must interpret a given situation as one in which someone's welfare may be affected. To act morally, one must first be alerted to the possibility that a moral response (either exhibition or inhibition of a behavior) is needed. That is, there must be *arousal,* or at least *awareness,* regarding the anticipated consequences of one's decision to act, or failure to act. Individuals vary dramatically in sensitivity to potentially moral situations, and a variety of personal qualities such as background experience, history of making moral choices, attentiveness to situational cues, feelings of empathy and guilt, and awareness of the feelings, thoughts, and needs of others will all profoundly influence the moral salience of an event and degree of arousal stimulated (Hoffman, 1982, 1991). Situational factors, such as clarity of circumstance, length of exposure to the problem, perceived moral seriousness, emotional ties with others who are involved, and physical

distance from those affected by the moral choice, also affect the likelihood of moral thought or action (Piliavin, Dovidio, Gaertner, & Clark, 1981).

In emergencies, moral arousal may lead directly to altruistic actions. For example, a teenager who dove into an icy river to save a young child later told reporters that he acted "automatically"; there was no time to think. Emotions, particularly empathy, prevailed. Of course, emotional arousal, especially anger and rage, often results in transgressions against others (see Anger Control, this volume). In such cases the actor may not be consciously aware of how his or her actions affect the welfare of others. In other situations, however, emotions and behavior are not directly linked. Instead, arousal or awareness triggers the second component, that of moral reflection.

Component 2

A person must determine an optimal course of moral action. Once alerted to the possibility that alternative courses of action might have differential consequences for the welfare of others, sociomoral reasoning is activated. As will become apparent later, the quality of such thinking is heavily dependent on the individual's developmental level (Kohlberg, 1981, 1984). Through stage-related reasoning, moral values are weighed and compared. In this fashion, an individual reasoner determines what *ought* to be done—the moral ideal. Component 2 has generated a great deal of research, most of it suggesting that the stage of sociomoral reasoning influences, but does not completely determine, what people intend to do in situations of moral conflict.

For example, there is ample evidence that delinquent youth who engage in antisocial or illegal activities reason at lower levels than nondelinquent peers (Blasi, 1980; Chandler & Moran, 1990; Gregg, et al., 1994; Trevethan & Walker, 1989). Positive relationships have also been found between sociomoral judgment and resistance to cheating (Harris, Mussen, & Rutherford, 1976), prosocial behaviors (Bear & Rys, 1994; Eisenberg, 1982), and absence of classroom conduct problems (Bear, 1989; Bear & Richards, 1981; Richards, Bear, Stewart, & Norman, 1992). We will return to the relation between moral reasoning and behavior in later sections.

Component 3

A person must choose among valued outcomes and decide the intended course of action. Moral considerations are not the only ones influencing behavior, and a variety of other, nonmoral values compete with those of the moral domain in formulating a goal or intention to act (Rest, 1983). For this reason, deciding what is right does not necessarily determine how someone chooses to act. For example, in a classic study, Damon (1977) found that children, interviewed about how they ought to distribute candy bars as a reward for making bracelets, described a variety of schemes by which the confections could be fairly divided. But when given the goodies, these same children gave themselves a disproportionate share.

Sociomoral reasoning (Component 2) and goal selection (Component 3) are interrelated and tend to occur at the same time. As such, nonmoral alternatives often compete with moral ones as the individual weighs moral considerations against personal costs or benefits. Unfortunately, self-serving biases often prevail (Nisan, 1991).

Component 4

A person must act on what was intended. As noted in 1913 by moral educator Arthur Holmes: "Almost everybody thinks it is easy enough to know what is right: but to *do* what is right—there comes the rub" (Holmes, 1913/ 1930, p. 19). Intentions, linked to reasoning and goals, incline a person to act in a morally responsible way, but all too often behaviors are inconsistent with such intentions. That is, the child knows what is right, intends to act morally, and has the necessary social skills to do so— but just does not do the right thing. In recent years, researchers have focused on three interrelated factors that help to explain why people, especially children, fail to act in accord with their own convictions:

1. Emotions such as empathy or guilt have not been cultivated and linked to prosocial cognitions in order to motivate appropriate behavior (Hoffman, 1991). The child knows what is right but just does not care enough to act.
2. Other cognitions compete with moral reasoning in determining behavior. Included would be immature, self-serving personal considerations that override the more deliberative reasoning of Components 2 and 3. For example, a child's (or anyone's) good intentions can be easily undermined by the contingencies of the moment—the presence or absence of rewards and punishments and nonmoral personal goals (Eisenberg, 1986; Gibbs, 1994). Additional cognitions that might override a moral decision based on reasoning would be judgments of self-efficacy (Eisenberg, 1986) and judgments of responsibility to act (Candee & Kohlberg, 1987). Far too often individuals decide that they *should* help others but do not do so because they feel that they are not able to help or that helping is the responsibility of others (e.g., helping children in poverty).
3. Other cognitions might disengage self-regulatory mechanisms and allow a person to deny responsibility for his or her own irresponsible behavior (Bandura, 1991; Gibbs, 1994). Bandura argued that in most circumstances, children and adults are inclined to act humanely—especially when internal standards are well matched to the social environment. However, it is not uncommon for someone to act reprehensibly when co-

erced by social expectations (e.g., peer pressure to conform) that run counter to internalized values. To better understand how "good" people sometimes act irresponsibly, Bandura identified several cognitive mechanisms that disengage moral controls in specified social contexts. For example, one way to avoid responsibility for aggressive behavior is to divert blame—either to the victim or the circumstance. As any school principal knows, aggressive children routinely externalize blame by claiming that their antagonist "had it coming" or they were "just getting even." In children and adults, self-exoneration can also be achieved by blaming circumstances. In either case, "not only are one's own actions excusable but one can even feel self-righteous in the process" (Bandura, 1991, p. 92). These and other cognitive mechanisms identified by Bandura (1991) are presented elsewhere in this volume (see Social Responsibility).

Problems and Implications

Explanations for social failures are not hard to come by— the breakup of the traditional family (see Family Functioning, this volume), lack of parental discipline (see Parenting and Aggressive Behavior, this volume), violent programming on television (Comstock & Paik, 1991), failure to teach moral values in school (Wynne & Ryan, 1993), and the availability of weapons (see School Violence, this volume), to name several. Our own research, however, has focused more on sociomoral reasoning (Component 2) and self-centered cognitions that preempt moral considerations (Components 3 and 4). We are especially interested in the sociomoral reasoning associated with antisocial conduct and the precursors of such reasoning. In general, we have found that delinquents and children who exhibit classroom conduct problems typically verbalize more Stage 2 sociomoral justifications than any other kind (Bear & Rys, 1994; Gibbs et al., 1995). In fact, in a study of elementary and middle school children, those who reasoned at Stage 1, the least advanced of Kohlberg's hierarchy, were as well behaved in the classroom as their more mature peers at the conventional level (Stages 3 and 4; Richards et al., 1992). The "might makes right" orientation proved to be as effective as the more mature "mutuality" perspective in buffering conduct problems, perhaps, however, only as long as authority figures were around.

It appears, then, that Stage 2 sociomoral judgment is the kind most associated with antisocial behavior. However, as one study recently demonstrated (Bear & Rys, 1994), not every aspect of Stage 2 reasoning predisposes young people to act out their aggressions or act in socially incompetent ways. Rather, only those elements that encourage the reasoner to be self-centered, hedonistic, lacking in empathy and interpersonal sensitivity, and disrespectful of rules are linked to unacceptable conduct. Boys with a hedonistic perspective, for example, not only exhibited more behavior problems but were viewed less favorably by peers than classmates who reasoned in more empathetic or interpersonal ways. Even when measures of social competence and acting-out were controlled, the type of sociomoral judgment continued to predict social preference. These findings suggest that sociomoral judgment affects popularity (sociometric status) not only indirectly by curtailing aggressive behavior but directly as well. A child who fights for the "right" reason (to defend himself or another) is likely to be viewed more favorably by peers than one who fights for the "wrong" reason (to get even or achieve a personal reward).

For most children, self-centered, hedonistic reasoning declines as they benefit from the many social-perspective-taking opportunities afforded by the elementary school years. But not all children progress in this way. For those with conduct disorders, perspective-taking opportunities all too often turn into coercive exchanges which actually reinforce egocentric thinking. Indeed, aggressive children typically come from homes where coercive exchanges are common and caretakers seldom employ inductive disciplinary techniques (see Aggressive Behavior, this volume). As a consequence, the self-centered thinking of early childhood persists. As children grow into adolescents, such thinking becomes consolidated and eventually manifests itself as a cognitive distortion—an inaccurate or rationalizing attitude, thought, or belief about the social behaviors of oneself or others (Gibbs, 1987, 1991a). Similar to the mechanisms of cognitive disengagement discussed by Bandura (1991), cognitive distortions protect the individual from painful self-evaluations. Gibbs (1991a) identifies four types of cognitive distortions, as follows:

1. *Self-centered.* One ignores or dismisses the perspectives and needs of others as well as one's own long-term best interest. Instead, behavior is regulated by an egocentric and hedonistic perspective in which immediate feelings and desires prevail.
2. *Minimizing/Mislabeling.* Antisocial behavior is viewed as causing no real harm or as being acceptable or even admirable. Others are referred to with belittling or dehumanizing labels.
3. *Assuming the Worst.* One attributes hostile intentions to others, assumes a worst-case (and inevitable) scenario for a social situation, or believes that improvement is impossible in one's own or others' behavior.
4. *Blaming Others.* Others, or external factors, are incorrectly blamed for one's harmful actions. Blame may also be misattributed to a momentary aberration (one was drunk, high, in a bad mood, etc.).

Alternative Actions

Whether working with children or adolescents in regular classrooms or intervening with those who exhibit conduct disorders, school psychologists and educators should devise and implement multiple strategies for promoting sociomoral development. In this section we offer some general recommendations for promoting moral development in schools and more specific recommendations for helping antisocial children advance their sociomoral reasoning and improve their conduct.

General Recommendations for Promoting Sociomoral Reasoning

An excellent guide for anyone interested in practical techniques for promoting sociomoral growth in school settings is Thomas Lickona's (1991) book, *Educating for Character: How Our Schools Can Teach Respect and Responsibility.* This highly readable compendium is well informed by both recent research and actual school practice. Many of the following alternative actions are clearly explained and illustrated in Lickona's book:

1. Do whatever is necessary to ensure that schools are safe communities for all who learn and work there. Violence and intimidation have no place at any school and, if present, must be eradicated (see School Violence, this volume, for related alternative actions).
2. Promote a caring school environment and community. Noddings (1995) recommends reorganizing the curriculum around themes of care: "caring for self, for intimate others, for strangers and global others, for the natural world and its nonhuman creatures, for the human-made world, and for ideas" (p. 675). For specific ideas about how to develop a caring school environment, we recommend Noddings (1992) book on the topic, *The Challenge to Care in Schools,* as well as Carducci and Carducci's *The Caring Classroom* (1982). (The chapter Prosocial Behavior, this volume, also provides ideas for promoting prosocial behaviors, including the Child Development Project.)
3. Do whatever possible to influence television viewing. Young people must be encouraged to view programs that feature prosocial themes rather than violent ones. Teachers can influence such viewing through specific assignments and parent conferences (Pressley, 1995); school psychologists by exhorting parents and other adults to exercise some control over children's viewing habits. These recommended practices also apply to children's playing of violent video games and listening to music that advocates violence.
4. Highlight the importance of adults modeling exemplary sociomoral behavior and reasoning. It is also a good idea to expose students to prominent individu-

als who lead exemplary lives. There is overwhelming evidence that both prosocial behavior and sociomoral reasoning are profoundly influenced by observational learning (Bandura, 1986). The more positive the models, the better.

5. Teach morality by telling as well as modeling. Direct teaching works best when students are given understandable explanations for why they should behave as instructed (see Prosocial Behavior and Social Responsibility, this volume.)

6. Promote cooperative learning practices. If the object is to foster caring and justice, cooperative educational environments work better than competitive ones.

7. Use story-telling, literature, and other aspects of the curriculum to strengthen appreciation for moral values. In virtually every subject, there are opportunities to link course content with moral responsibility.

8. Provide frequent and multiple opportunities for children to assume, and challenge, differing moral perspectives. Arrange for moral discussions that incorporate Socratic dialogue, debate, and role-playing. Discussions should entail moral dilemmas involving real-life problems, hypothetical situations, as well as content-specific issues appearing in history or literature. One review of the moral discussion literature concluded that teachers, peers, and parents require little training to be effective discussion leaders; that the most effective discussions include a mixture of discussants who express different stages of sociomoral reasoning; and stage change should not be expected over a short period of time—when such change does occur it is unlikely to be lasting (Bear, 1987).

9. Teach social problem-solving skills (see Social Problem Skills, this volume) while incorporating a moral discussion or social decision-making component (see next section).

10. Promote active student involvement in real-life decisions pertaining to school climate, governance, discipline, conflict resolution, and peer relations. For example, encourage students to help resolve conflicts among classmates, to determine "fair" rules and consequences, and to develop and participate in school and community projects that demonstrate moral and social responsibility.

Recommendations for Promoting Moral Development in Classroom Social Decision-Making Discussions

In addition to the 10 actions just listed, a critical part of any program for promoting moral development in the classroom should be *social decision-making sessions,* a derivative of Kohlbergian moral discussions included as part of the EQUIP curriculum recently developed by Gibbs et al. (1995). Although EQUIP was designed specifically for motivating and equipping antisocial youth to help one another achieve responsible behavior, its strategies also are appropriate for *preventing* antisocial behavior. Most of our recommendations for how to use group decision making to promote moral development are drawn from EQUIP. Another good source of recommendations (and topics for moral discussions) in dealing with aggressive youth can be found in *The Prepare Curriculum: Teaching Prosocial Competencies* (Goldstein, 1988).

Although social decision-making sessions essentially constitute moral education, we prefer the term "social decision making" because "moral education" may have certain misleading connotations. After all, the activity of promoting moral development means the facilitation of moral-cognitive development so that young people will make more mature decisions in social situations.

In social decision-making meetings, the group strives to develop the capacity to make mature decisions concerning specified problem situations. Unlike moral dilemmas, the problem situations generally *do* have right or responsible answers—for example, deciding to try to persuade a friend against taking a ride in a stolen car. The "problem" is that the right answer may not be immediately apparent (for example, the group may decide to take the ride if it is misrepresented with the Minimizing/Mislabelling cognitive distortion of "doing fun things with a friend"). Similarly, problem situations in which the right answer is to tell on a friend (for example, if the friend is dealing in drugs) may at first be experienced as dilemmas because the peer norm against "ratting" or "narking" is so strong.

The problem situations are designed to create opportunities for participants to take the perspectives of others; on a controversial question, this opportunity can involve active challenges from peers (or, if necessary, from the school psychologist or teacher serving as group leader). Even among antisocial adolescents, group majority positions and reasoning on the problem-situation questions tend to be positive, responsible, and mature. A student who makes a negative decision and justifies it with Stage 1 or 2 reasoning may lose to a more mature challenge and experience the conflict or disequilibration of having to acquiesce to the majority. Disequilibration may be crucial if a student using predominantly immature stages of sociomoral judgment is to achieve more mature moral development. Preferably, to allow adequate preparation, the problem situations in the EQUIP book should be given to the students before the problem-situation sessions begin. However, social decision-making sessions can also be based on students' answering the problem-situation questions at the beginning of the class. At the start of the session, the teacher should display some simple rules:

- Listen to what others have to say.
- If you criticize another group member, give that person a chance to answer.
- Never put down or threaten anyone.
- Stay on the subject when you disagree.
- Never talk to anyone outside the group about what is said in the group.

The teacher next promotes sociomoral development in four phases: (a) introducing the problem situation, (b) cultivating mature morality, (c) remediating moral developmental delay, and (d) consolidating mature morality. At the close of each session, the group leader should conduct a self-evaluation using a checklist (see Table 2) that corresponds to the four phases.

Phase 1:
Introducing the Problem Situation

To have an effective social decision-making session, all students must understand clearly what the problem sit-

uation is and how it relates to their lives. The teacher should ask what the problem is, why it is a problem, whether problems like this actually happen, and so forth.

Phase 2: Cultivating Mature Morality

The purpose of this phase is to cultivate a group atmosphere of mature morality characterized by both positive decisions and mature sociomoral reasoning. The makings of a mature moral climate are typically available from the students themselves (at least from the majority). The teacher's job is to cultivate the resources available in the class in order to render mature morality prominent and to set the tone for the remainder of the meetings. The teacher highlights mature morality by asking group members who indicated positive decisions about the reasons for those decisions and then writing those reasons on the flip pad or chalkboard for the group to consider. (The leader should write down reasons offered for a negative decision separately—after the reasons for the positive choice have been listed.)

Table 2   *Checklist for Teacher Review/Self-Evaluation*

Date: _____   Class: _____   Session discussed _____

In the various phases, did you ask questions to:

Phase 1. Introducing the problem situation

_____ 1. Remind the class or group of the ground rules for discussion?

_____ 2. Make sure the group understood the problem situation (e.g., "Who can tell the group just what Jerry's problem is? Why is that a problem?")?

_____ 3. Relate the problem situation to students' everyday lives (e.g., "Do problems like this happen? Who has been in a situation like this? Tell the class about it.")?

Phase 2: Cultivating mature morality

_____ 4. Establish mature morality as the tone for the rest of the session (e.g., eliciting, reconstructing, and listing on flip-pad or chalkboard mature reasons for each positive majority decision)?

Phase 3: Remediating moral developmental delay

_____ 5. Use more mature group members and the list of reasons (Phase 2) to challenge the hedonistic or pragmatic arguments of some students?

_____ 6. Create role-taking opportunities in other ways as well (e.g., "What would the world be like if everybody did that?" "How would you feel if you were Bob?")?

Phase 4: Consolidating mature morality

_____ 7. Make positive decisions and mature reasons unanimous for the group (e.g., "Any strong objections if I circle that decision as the group decision/underline that reason as the group's number one reason?")?

_____ 8. Praise the group for their positive decisions and mature reasons (e.g., "I'm really pleased that the group was able to make so many good, strong decisions and back them up with good, strong reasons." "Would the group like to tape this sheet onto the wall?")?

In General

_____ 9. Were all the group members interested and involved?

_____ 10. Was some constructive value found in every serious group member comment?

_____ 11. Was the "should" supported and relabeled as strong (e.g., "Yes, it does take guts to do the right thing . . .")?

Note. From *The EQUIP Program: Teaching Youth to Think and Act Responsibly through a Peer-Helping Approach* by J. C. Gibbs, G. B. Potter, and A. P. Goldstein, 1995, Champaign, IL: Research Press. Copyright 1995 by Research Press, Inc. Adapted with permission.

Phase 3: Remediating Moral Developmental Delay

If a mature moral atmosphere has been cultivated in the class, the teacher has accomplished crucial preparation for the next phase, which addresses the reality that—despite majority tendencies toward mature reasoning—many of today's adolescents are at least moderately developmentally delayed, particularly with regard to reasons for the importance of not stealing (see Gregg et al., 1994). These students can seriously undermine the group "culture" and will do so if allowed. The mature moral atmosphere established at the outset is a crucial defense against the onslaught of these students as they are brought into the discussion and challenged.

In theoretical terms, remediating moral developmental delay means creating social-perspective-taking opportunities or challenging individuals to consider other—especially other more mature—viewpoints. Such opportunities can reduce self-centered cognitive distortion by engendering disequilibration and stimulating more mature sociomoral judgment. Exposure to mature sociomoral reasons for positive decisions will already have provided delayed group members with an opportunity or a challenge to grow. But mere exposure is not sufficient. The teacher should (a) invite the negative group members to explain their views, (b) publicly record on a flip pad or chalkboard their explanations or reasons for their decision, and (c) invite members of the majority to respond.

Particular types of probe questions are especially helpful in creating perspective-taking opportunities. Self-centered reasoners should be challenged to generalize ("What would the world be like if everybody did that?") or to consider the point of view or feelings of another party in the problem situation. Students with puzzling or contradictory response patterns should be asked to clarify. Quiet students should be brought out, and members with "cannot decide" responses should be probed for both sides of their thinking.

Phase 4: Consolidating Mature Morality

Once mature morality has been cultivated and challenged, it needs to be consolidated. The group's mature morality is consolidated—and the group's culture becomes more positive and cohesive—as the teacher seeks consensus for positive decisions and mature reasons. In the process, students with initially immature sociomoral judgment reasons continue to feel pressure to defer to and even embrace mature morality. In the discussion of the problem situation, the goal is to convert as many of the positive majority positions as possible into unanimous group decisions. In any event, the group should be praised or encouraged at the conclusion of the social decision-making session.

Conclusion

As school psychologists become more involved in implementing interventions designed to promote prosocial behavior and decrease antisocial behavior, it is likely that the limitations of many popular programs for social skills training and social problem solving will become readily apparent. This is particularly true if the school psychologist's goal is to develop self-discipline, or morally responsible behavior in the absence of external control. Too few programs target sociomoral reasoning and decision making—the internal process by which children determine what is "right" or "wrong" and come to adopt moral values. Although not sufficient for developing morally and socially responsible behavior, the development of reasoning should be a critical component of school-based interventions for developing responsible behavior.

Recommended Resources

Print Resources

Gibbs, J. C., Potter, G. B., & Goldstein, A. P. (1995). *The EQUIP program: Teaching youth to think and act responsibly through a peer-helping approach.* Champaign, IL: Research Press.
Unlike the other recommended resources in this section, this book focuses on antisocial youths. The authors argue that three primary problems typify antisocial youths: social skill deficiencies, delays in sociomoral reasoning, and social cognitive distortions. A program provided to remediate these problems includes curriculum activities that primarily focus on developing mature sociomoral reasoning, teaching specific social skills, managing anger, and correcting thinking errors.

Kurtines, W. M., & Gewirtz, J. L. (1991). *Handbook of moral behavior and development.* Hillsdale, NJ: Erlbaum.
Written more for scholars and researchers than for educators, this three-volume set provides the most complete and authoritative source of information on research, theory, and practice in moral development. Chapters are contributed by the most highly respected authorities in the field (e.g., Bandura, Eisenberg, Enright, Hoffman, Power, Rest, Staub, Turiel).

Lickona, T. (1991). *Educating for character: How our schools can teach respect and responsibility.* New York: Bantam.
Written for educators, this book provides an excellent example of applying research and theory to practice. Lickona addresses the basic controversies in moral education (Whose values should be taught? Sex education, etc.) and offers practical guidelines and specific strategies for promoting moral reasoning and behavior.

Wynne, E. A., & Ryan, K. (1993). *Reclaiming our schools: A handbook on teaching character, academics, and discipline.* New York: Macmillan.
Similar to Lickona's book, this book is written for educators and addresses important areas of controversy in moral edu-

cation. Although important reading, guidelines tend to be more general and opinionated. The authors make a compelling argument for a return to traditional methods of teaching character.

Informational Networks for Character Education

Character Education Partnership, Association for Supervision and Curriculum Development, 1250 N. Pitt St., Alexandria, VA 22314-1453 (703-549-9110, Ext. 305).

Character Education Network, Center for the Advancement of Ethics and Character, Boston University, School of Education, 605 Commonwealth Ave., Rm. 356, Boston, MA 02215 (617-353-3262).

Jefferson Center for Character Education, 2700 E. Foothill Blvd., Suite 302, Pasadena, CA 91107.

Josephson Institute of Ethics, 4640 Admiralty Way, Suite 1001, Marina del Rey, CA 90292 (310-306-1868).

References

ASCD Panel on Moral Education. (1988). *Moral education in the life of the school.* Alexandria, VA: Association for Supervision and Curriculum Development.

Bandura, A. (1986). *Social foundations of thought and action: A social cognitive theory.* Englewood Cliffs, NJ: Prentice-Hall.

Bandura, A. (1991). Social cognitive theory of moral thought and action. In W. M. Kurtines & J. L. Gewirtz (Eds.), *Handbook of moral behavior and development: Vol. 1. Theory* (pp. 45–103). Hillsdale, NJ: Erlbaum.

Battistich, V., Watson, M., Solomon, D., Schaps, E., & Solomon, J. (1991). The Child Development Project: A comprehensive program for the development of prosocial character. In W. M. Kurtines & J. L. Gewirtz (Eds.), *Handbook of moral behavior and development: Vol. 3. Application* (pp. 1–34). New York: Erlbaum.

Bear, G. G. (1987). Moral responsibility. In A. Thomas & J. Grimes (Eds.), *Children's needs: Psychological perspectives* (pp. 365–371). Bethesda, MD: National Association of School Psychologists.

Bear, G. G. (1989). Sociomoral reasoning and antisocial behaviors among normal sixth graders. *Merrill-Palmer Quarterly, 35,* 183–196.

Bear, G. G., & Richards, H. C. (1981). Moral reasoning and conduct problems in the classroom. *Journal of Educational Psychology, 73,* 644–670.

Bear, G. G., & Rys, G. S. (1994). Moral reasoning, classroom behavior, and sociometric status among elementary school children. *Developmental Psychology, 30,* 633–638.

Bennett, W. J. (1994). *The book of virtues: A treasury of great moral stories.* New York: Simon & Schuster.

Blasi, A. (1980). Bridging moral cognition and moral action: A critical review of the literature. *Psychological Bulletin, 88,* 1–45.

Burton, R. V. (1976). Honesty and dishonesty. In T. Lickona (Ed.), *Moral development and behavior: Theory, research, and social issues* (pp. 173–197). New York: Holt, Rinehart and Winston.

Candee, D., & Kohlberg, L. (1987). Moral judgment and moral action: A reanalysis of Haan, Smith, and Block's (1968) Free Speech Movement data. *Journal of Personality and Social Psychology, 52,* 554–564.

Carducci, D. J., & Carducci, J. B. (1984). The caring classroom: A guide for teachers troubled by the difficult student and classroom disruption. New York: Bull.

Chandler, M., & Moran, T. (1990). Psychopathy and moral development: A comparative study of delinquent and nondelinquent youth. *Development and Psychopathology, 2,* 227–246.

Colby, A., & Kohlberg, L. (1987a). *The measurement of moral judgment: Vol. 1. Theoretical foundations and research validation.* New York: Cambridge University Press.

Colby, A., & Kohlberg, L. (1987b). *The measurement of moral judgment: Vol. 2. Standard issue scoring manual.* New York: Cambridge University Press.

Comstock, G. A., & Paik, H. (1991). Psychopathy and moral development: A comparative study of delinquent and nondelinquent youth. *Development and Psychopathology, 2,* 227–246.

Damon, W. (1977). *The social world of the child.* San Francisco: Jossey Bass.

Damon, W. (1990). *The moral child.* New York: The Free Press.

Eisenberg, N. (1982). The development of reasoning regarding prosocial behavior. In N. Eisenberg (Ed.), *The development of prosocial behavior* (pp. 219–249). New York: Academic Press.

Eisenberg, N. (1986). *Altruistic emotion, cognition, and behavior.* Hillsdale, NJ: Erlbaum.

Eisenberg, N., Shea, C. L., Carlo, G., & Knight, G. P. (1991). Empathy-related responding and cognition: A "children and the egg" dilemma. In W. M. Kurtines & J. L. Gewirtz (Eds.), *Handbook of moral behavior and development: Vol. 2. Research* (pp. 63–88). Hillsdale, NJ: Erlbaum.

Elam, S. M., & Rose, L. C. (1995). The 27th Annual Phi Delta Kappa/Gallup Poll of the public's attitudes towards the public schools. *Phi Delta Kappan, 77,* 41–56.

Garmon, L. C., Basinger, K. S., Gregg, V. R., & Gibbs, J. C. (1996). Gender differences in stage and expression of moral judgment. *Merrill-Palmer Quarterly, 42,* 418–437.

Gibbs, J. C. (1987). Social processes in delinquency: The need to facilitate empathy as well as sociomoral reasoning. In W. M. Kurtines & J. L. Gewirtz (Eds.), *Moral development through social interaction* (pp. 301–321). New York: Wiley-Interscience.

Gibbs, J. C. (1991a). Sociomoral developmental delay and cognitive distortion: Implications for the treatment of antisocial youth. In W. M. Kurtines & J. L. Gewirtz (Eds.), *Handbook of moral behavior and development: Vol. 3. Application* (pp. 95–110). Hillsdale, NJ: Erlbaum.

Gibbs, J. C. (1991b). Toward an integration of Kohlberg's and Hoffman's theories of morality. In W. M. Kurtines & J. L. Gewirtz (Eds.), *Handbook of moral behavior and development: Vol. 1. Theory* (pp. 183–222). Hillsdale, NJ: Erlbaum.

Gibbs, J. C. (1994). Fairness and empathy as the foundation for universal moral education. *Comenius, 14,* 12–23.

Gibbs, J. C., Basinger, K. S., & Fuller, D. (1992). *Moral maturity: Measuring the development of sociomoral reflection.* Hillsdale, NJ: Erlbaum.

Gibbs, J. C., Potter, G. B., & Goldstein, A. P. (1995). *The EQUIP program: Teaching youth to think and act responsibly through a peer-helping approach.* Champaign, IL: Research Press.

Gilligan, C. (1982). In a different voice: Women's conception of the self and of morality. *Harvard Educational Review, 47,* 481–517.

Gilly, M. (1991). Social psychology of cognitive constructions: European perspectives. In M. Carretero, M. L. Pope, P. Simons, & J. J. Pozo (Eds.), *Learning and instruction: European research in an international context: Vol. 3* Oxford, England: Pergamon.

Goldstein, A. (1988). *The Prepare Curriculum: Teaching prosocial competencies.* Champaign, IL: Research Press.

Gregg, V. R., Gibbs, J. C., & Basinger, K. S. (1994). Patterns of developmental delay in moral judgment by male and female delinquents. *Merrill-Palmer Quarterly, 40,* 538–553.

Harris, S., Mussen, P. H., & Rutherford, E. (1976). Some cognitive, behavioral, and personality correlates of maturity of moral judgement. *Journal of Genetic Psychology, 128,* 123–135.

Hartshorne, H., May, M. A., & Shuttleworth, F. K. (1930). *Studies in the nature of character: Vol. III. Studies in the organization of character.* New York: Macmillan.

Hoffman, M. L. (1982). Development of prosocial motivation: Empathy and guilt. In N. Eisenberg (Ed.), *The development of prosocial behavior* (pp. 281–313). New York: Academic Press.

Hoffman, M. L. (1991). Empathy, social cognition, and action. In W. M. Kurtines & J. L. Gewirtz (Eds.), *Handbook of moral behavior and development: Vol. 1. Theory* (pp. 275–301). Hillsdale, NJ: Erlbaum.

Holmes, A. (1930). Good character. In D. C. Troth (Ed.), *Selected readings in character education* (pp. 8–12). Boston: Beacon Press. (Reprinted from *Principles of character making,* pp. 264–284, 1913. Philadelphia: J. B. Lippincott)

Kamii, C., Clark, F. B., & Dominick, F. B. (1994). The six national goals: A road to disappointment. *Phi Delta Kappan, 75,* 672–677.

Kohlberg, L. (1981). *Essays on moral development: Vol. 1. The philosophy of moral development.* New York: Harper & Row.

Kohlberg, L. (1984). *Essays on moral development: Vol. 2. The psychology of moral development.* New York: Harper & Row.

Krebs, D. L., Vermeulen, S. C. A., Carpendale, J. I., & Denton, K. (1991). Structural and situational influences on moral judgment: The interaction between stage and dilemma. In W. M. Kurtines & J. L. Gewirtz (Eds.), *Handbook of moral behavior and development: Vol. 2. Theory* (pp. 139–169). Hillsdale, NJ: Erlbaum.

Leming, J. S. (1993). In search of effective character education. *Educational Leadership, 51,* 63–71.

Lickona, T. (1991). *Educating for character: How our schools can teach respect and responsibility.* New York: Bantam.

Nisan, M. (1991). The moral balance model: Theory and research extending our understanding of moral choice and deviation. In W. M. Kurtines & J. L. Gewirtz (Eds.), *Handbook of moral behavior and development: Vol. 3. Application* (pp. 213–249). Hillsdale, NJ: Lawrence Erlbaum.

Noddings, N. (1992). *The challenge to care in schools.* New York: Teachers College Press.

Noddings, N. (1995). Teaching themes of care. *Phi Delta Kappan, 76,* 675–679.

Phillips, D. C. (1987). *Philosophy, science, and social inquiry.* New York: Pergamon Press.

Piaget, J. (1926). *Judgment and reasoning in the child.* New York: Harcourt.

Piaget, J. (1965). *The moral judgment of the child.* Glenco, IL: Free Press. (Original work published 1932)

Piliavin, J. A., Dovidio, J. F., Gaertner, S. L., & Clark, R. (1981). *Emergency intervention.* New York: Academic Press.

Power, F. C., Higgins, A., & Kohlberg, L. (1989). *Lawrence Kohlberg's approach to moral education.* New York: Columbia University Press.

Pressley, M., & McCormick, C. B. (1995). *Advanced educational psychology: For educators, researchers, and policy makers.* New York: Harper Collins.

Rest, J. R. (1983). Morality. In J. H. Flavell & E. M. Markman (Eds.), *Handbook of child psychology* (4th ed., Vol. 3, pp. 556–629). New York: Wiley.

Richards, H. D., Bear, G. G., Stewart, A. L., & Norman, A. D. (1992). Moral reasoning and classroom conduct: Evidence of a curvilinear relationship. *Merrill-Palmer Quarterly, 38,* 176–190.

Shweder, R. A., Mahapatra, M., & Miller, J. G. (1987). Culture and moral development. In J. Kagan & S. Lamb (Eds.), *The emergence of morality in young children* (pp. 1–82). Chicago: University of Chicago Press.

Six pillars of character: Developing moral values in youth. (1992). (Special issue). *Ethics: Easier Said Than Done, 19 & 20,* 34–88.

Snarey, J. R. (1985). Cross-cultural universality of social-moral development: A critical review of Kohlbergian research. *Psychological Bulletin, 97,* 202–232.

Trevethan, S. D., & Walker, L. J. (1989). Hypothetical versus real-life moral reasoning among psychopathic and delinquent youth. *Development and Psychopathology, 1,* 91–103.

Troth, D. C. (1930). *Selected readings in character education.* Boston: Beacon Press.

Walker, L. J. (1991). Sex differences in moral reasoning. In W. M. Kurtines & J. L. Gewirtz (Eds.), *Handbook of moral behavior and development: Vol. 2. Research* (pp. 333–364). New York: Erlbaum.

Walker, L. J., & Taylor, J. H. (1991). Family interactions and the development of moral reasoning. *Child Development, 62,* 264–283.

Wynne, E. A., & Ryan, K. (1993). *Reclaiming our schools: A handbook on teaching character, academics, and discipline.* New York: Merrill and imprint of Macmillan Publishing Co.

3

Social Problem Solving Skills

Maurice J. Elias

Rutgers University

Background

Hamburg (1990) has written eloquently that the social foundation necessary to provide guidance to children in their attempts to develop social and academic competence and to carve out an interdependent identity can no longer be presumed to exist in the normal course of childhood experiences. Relationships of adults and children have changed as relationships of adults to the workplace, their communities, and to each other have changed. The skills needed to cope effectively with life's everyday challenges must be taught and explicitly nurtured to avoid having too many students become social casualties.

Daniel Goleman's (1995) book, *Emotional Intelligence,* has provided a public, popular platform from which to pursue the promulgation of the competencies needed for sound social functioning. Goleman shows that data from a wide range of disciplines and various parts of the life span converge to suggest that one's social and affective skills are at least as important to one's future life success as what are traditionally seen as "intellectual" skills.

Thus, in pursuit of academic excellence, education professionals must not lose the child as a person. As students move through the elementary school years, they are being watched less and less vigilantly by the adults around them. Schools must be equipped with handholds throughout, and lifelines around the ship, extending far into the sea for those who do fall overboard. Among the most important handholds and lifelines are social decision-making and problem-solving skills.

The focus on social decision making and problem solving reflects a growing belief that decisions are central to social interactions and to what is defined as "success" for students, workers, family members, citizens, and, indeed, all people (Wales, Nardi, & Stager, 1986). On an everyday, common-sense basis, it is obvious that many problem conditions from which children suffer can be traced to how they handle concrete decision-making situations. A child can find himself or herself at a personal

and interpersonal crossroads by such everyday situations as these: "Who are you going to hang out with on the school yard?" "C'mon, let's spray paint the school." "I can't believe you're worried about school work. Forget it and forget class. Come with us!" "You gotta smoke—everyone else is." "Are you going to listen to what they tell you about health in those assemblies?"

Do students have the social competence skills needed to handle such temptations? A child's pathway on the road to higher risk or greater competence will be influenced strongly by the *decisions* made when confronting these and related situations. Strategies and skills that help them gather the appropriate information from their environments, make decisions, and follow through in these and related situations truly are *life skills* that can serve to guide children as they face everyday challenges.

Social decision-making and problem-solving approaches are future oriented. They look ahead to the period of time when children become adolescents and then move on to take adult roles as citizens in a democracy, with all of the many challenges and responsibilities that follow. Children's capacity to respond to situations they find themselves in with peers, teachers, and parents and their ability to think clearly and make decisions under stress affect their ability to handle the problematic areas—both small and large—that they inevitably will face. Their ability to handle these problems—not in isolation, but in partnership with classmates and the adults in their lives—exercises considerable influence on their identity as capable, confident people.

Indeed, as children move from direct and intensive adult supervision toward greater independence, their capacity for sound social judgment and appropriate personal decision making becomes as important as their basic academic abilities. Kolbe (1985) astutely pointed out that one's "independent" health decisions are in fact mediated through one's social relationships and therefore can in no real sense be viewed as "autonomous." If a teenager smokes, it affects others. If a middle school student drinks beer in the park alone or with a few friends, there are clear ramifications for parent-child and other familial relationships. Children's eating habits may lead to distractible or lethargic, inattentive behaviors which may impact upon peer and teacher relationships in school. The ability to make interpersonal and health decisions and choose and enact constructive, interdependent social behaviors illustrates that social decision making and problem solving should be a focal construct in conceptualizing children's needs. Hence, Goleman echoes others when he says that success in the adult world is no less dependent on academic ability than it is on interpersonal, intrapersonal, or practical intelligence (Blythe & Gardner, 1990; Sternberg & Wagner, 1986) or on social decision-making and problem-solving skills (Elias & Clabby, 1992).

Development

Competence in social decision making and problem solving requires the ability to adapt and integrate behaviors (actions), cognition (thinking) and emotions (feelings) to achieve specific goals. Therefore, these skills and their coordination must be developed. Critical skills necessary in these areas are (Consortium on the School-Based Promotion of Social Competence, 1991, 1994; Hawkins, Catalano, & Associates, 1992):

- *Self-Control Skills.* These are skills necessary for accurate processing of social information, for delay of behavior long enough to engage in thoughtful accessing of one's social decision-making abilities, and for being able to approach others in a way which avoids provoking their anger or annoyance. They include the ability to listen carefully and accurately, follow directions, calm oneself down when under stress, and talk to others in a socially appropriate manner.
- *Social-Awareness and Group-Participation Skills.* These skills underlie the exercise of social responsibility and positive interactions in groups. They include learning how to recognize and elicit trust, help, and praise from others; how to recognize others' perspectives; how to choose friends wisely; how to share, wait, and participate in groups; how to give and receive help and criticism; and how to understand others' perspectives.
- *Social Decision-Making Skills.* This is a set of skills that combine to form a strategy to guide one in thoughtful decision making when facing choices or problematic situations, particularly when one is under stress. Steps for social decision making should be taught to children from elementary school through high school age, as well as to the parents and educators who work with them. These steps include understanding signs of one's own and others' feelings and accurately labeling and expressing feelings; deciding on one's goals; thinking of alternate ways to solve a problem, especially when planning a solution and making a final check for

possible obstacles; and thinking in terms of long- and short-term consequences and consequences both for oneself and others. Teaching these steps serves to create a common language and shared perspective on competence which reinforces and solidifies learning over time.

Table 1 presents a comprehensive list of skills of social decision making and problem solving in an assessment framework that focuses on the expression of these skills in different situations in which school-aged children need to be able to show social and affective mastery. For children to develop their social decision-making and problem-solving skills, there is a pattern of growth that must be fostered. While the description of skills and the assessment outline presented can be helpful in monitoring children's progress and arranging for necessary intervention, much has been learned about the context of skill development that needs to be added to the existing knowledge base. Specifically, the development of social decision-making and problem-solving skills requires an understanding of the simultaneous development of other cognitive and affective skills and the interpersonal contexts in which the skills are mobilized for use.

An overarching developmental framework is provided by Erikson (1954) in his notion of adaptational tasks. His discussion of development can be thought of as a set of roughly sequential hurdles that are confronted and mastered over the course of succeeding age periods. These provide guidelines for school psychologists and others who work with children to provide the proper match of developmental task, skill area, and application context. The tasks are separated into *personal, family, school, community,* and *event triggered* (referring to stressful life events and transitions that, while unplanned, tend to occur in particular developmental periods). Each of these tasks are arenas in which to understand and nurture the development of social decision-making and problem-solving skills. Table 2 presents an outline of key tasks by developmental period, grouped into the domains of personal, family, peer, school related, community related, and event triggered. The latter refers to stressors that impact on the lives of children, at times without warning and at times gradually, with some "official" markers (as in the case of divorce). To facilitate service planning, this category is included as a guide to those event-triggered situations most likely to occur at given age periods. The developmental outline and Table 2 are based on information in Elias and Associates (1992) and Elias and Clabby (1992).

What follows next is a brief overview of the Eriksonian context within which the tasks in each domain must be resolved within each developmental period. Such a perspective allows skill development to be framed by the emerging identity of the child.

Table 1   *A Checklist of Students' Social Decision Making and Problem Solving Strengths Across Situations*

Skills Demonstrated	Situations*
A. Self-Control Skills	
1. Listens carefully and accurately.	_____
2. Remembers and follows directions.	_____
3. Concentrates and follows through on tasks.	_____
4. Calms him or herself down.	_____
5. Carries on a conversation without upsetting or provoking others.	_____
B. Social Awareness and Group Participation Skills	_____
6. Accepts praise or approval.	_____
7. Chooses praiseworthy and caring friends.	_____
8. Knows when help is needed.	_____
9. Asks for help when needed.	_____
10. Works as part of a problem-solving team.	_____
C. Social Decision Making Skills	
11. Recognizes signs of feelings in self.	_____
12. Recognizes signs of feelings in others.	_____
13. Describes accurately a range of feelings.	_____
14. Puts problems into words clearly.	_____
15. States realistic interpersonal goals.	_____
16. Thinks of several ways to solve a problem or reach a goal.	_____
17. Thinks of different types of solutions.	_____
18. Does items 16 and 17 for different types of problems.	_____
19. Differentiates short- *and* long-term consequences.	_____
20. Looks at effects of choices on self and others.	_____
21. Keeps positive *and* negative possibilities in mind.	_____
22. Selects solutions that can reach goals.	_____
23. Makes choices that do not harm self or others.	_____
24. Considers details before carrying out a solution (who, when, where, with whom, etc.).	_____
25. Anticipates obstacles to plans.	_____
26. Responds appropriately when plans are thwarted.	_____
27. Tries out his or her ideas.	_____
28. Learns from experiences or from seeking out input from adults, friends.	_____
29. Uses previous experience to help "next time."	_____

*Situations can be recorded by entering the numbers of those situations in which particular skills appear to be demonstrated, using the following codes:

1 = with peers in classroom
2 = with peers in other situations in school
3 = with teachers
4 = with other adults in school
5 = with parents
6 = with siblings or other relatives
7 = with peers outside of school
8 = when under academic stress or pressure
9 = when under social or peer-related stress or pressure
10 = when under family related stress or pressure
11 = other: _____

The Early Childhood Period: PreKindergarten to Grade 2, Ages 3–7

Erikson's *stages of trust and autonomy* cover the years from birth to the age of two (approximately; the sequence is more reliable than the specific age boundaries). Successful social adaptation is linked to children receiving physical and emotional security, as they begin to recognize their capacity to explore and interact with their environments. Rudiments of social decision-making abilities develop during the first 2 years. Even infants exhibit precausal, "if-then," motor association as they learn what they must do to have their needs met. They learn how to get people to hold them, feed them, and change their diapers long before they can ask for such things directly. Nevertheless, their early verbal behavior is part of their current and future adaptational success. From these early experiences, children begin to develop a nonverbal sense of expectancy concerning their ability to exercise an in-

Table 2 *Social Problem-Solving Tasks for Each Age Level Grouped by Domain*

Early Childhood	Middle Childhood	Early Adolescence	Adolescence
Personal Domain			
Learning self-management. Learning social norms about appearance, such as washing face, washing hair, brushing teeth. Recognizing medication and household product warning labels.	Understanding safety for latchkey kids. Interviewing people at the door. Saying "no" to strangers in person or on the phone. Exercising. Managing time. Being aware of sexual factors. Recognizing and accepting body changes. Recognizing and resisting inappropriate sexual behaviors.	Recognizing the importance of alcohol and other drug abuse prevention. Establishing norms for health. Developing request and refusal skills. Acknowledging the importance of self-statements and self-rewards. Understanding sexual factors such as body changes. Recognizing inappropriate sexual behaviors.	Taking care of self. Recognizing consequences of risky behaviors (e.g. delinquency, sexual activity, smoking, drug use). Protecting self from negative outcomes. Earning and budgeting money. Planning a career. Preparing for adult roles. Living with others. Living alone. Making a home.
Family Domain			
Being in a family. Making a contribution at home (e.g. chores, responsibilities). Relating positively with siblings.	Understanding families and different family forms and structures. Understanding closeness, touch, and its boundaries.	Recognizing conflict between parents' and peers' values (e.g. clothes and style, media, importance of achievement). Learning about stages in parents' (adults') lives.	Becoming independent. Talking with parents about daily activities and family plans. Learning self-disclosure skills.
Peers Domain			
Initiating conversations. Being a member of a group. Sharing. Taking turns. Cooperating.	Expanding peer groups. Learning to include and exclude others. Learning to set boundaries, deal with secrets. Learning to cope with peer pressure to conform (e.g. clothes), to be assertive, self-calming, cooperative.	Choosing friends. Developing peer leadership skills. Dealing with conflict among friends. Recognizing and accepting alternatives to aggression.	Initiating and maintaining cross-gender friends and romantic relationships. Practicing request and refusal skills. Preparing for parenting and family responsibilities.

(Continued)

fluence on having their needs met and concerning the nature of the outcomes to situations in which they are involved. Later, a sense of self-efficacy emerges from this early, generalized sense of trust.

The *stage of initiative,* which is linked to the early childhood period, brings with it new requirements for social adaptation as children encounter day-care, preschool, and school environments. Children must improve their motor and verbal control and begin to show awareness of and accommodation to social rules (in addition to parental rules). In early childhood, growing language and cognitive capacities fuel advances in social decision making. Children can be expected to identify basic feelings, pick up on a central theme in situations, decenter both in communication and in their sense of space, consider alternative ways to reach a goal, and recognize alternative consequences to their actions. Language and conceptual skills that are prerequisite to mature social decision mak-

ing evolve at this time. Children acquire terms to help them with integration and differentiation (is-is not; and-or; same-different; all-some), divergent production (other; else), causal inferences (if-then; why-because); and qualification or specification (where; with whom; when; now-later; before-after). Expectancies become more closely linked to perception of ongoing experiences, and children begin to develop an early sense of what Rotter (1982) calls an "expectancy" for the usefulness of being a good problem solver.

The Middle Childhood Period: Grades 3–5, Ages 8–10

Children enter the *stage of industry* during what is usually called middle childhood. In school and in extracurricular activities, successful adaptation requires more focus and continuity than in prior stages. Self-awareness of goals

Table 2   *Continued*

Early Childhood	Middle Childhood	Early Adolescence	Adolescence
School-Related Domain			
Following school rules. Understanding similarities and differences such as skin color or physical disabilities. Accepting responsibility in the classroom. Respecting authority.	Setting academic goals. Planning study time. Completing assignments. Learning to work in teams. Accepting similarities and differences (e.g. appearance, ability levels).	Learning skills for participating in setting policy. Learning planning and management skills to complete school requirements. Preventing truancy. Learning refusal skills. Setting personal standards.	Making a realistic academic plan. Recognizing personal strengths. Persisting to achieve goals in spite of setbacks. Participating in school and community service. Being a role model for younger students. Getting involved in out-of-school, year-abroad, apprenticeship, or work-study programs.
Community Domain			
Recognizing a pluralistic society. Awareness of holidays, different cultural groups, and customs. Accepting responsibility for the environment. Taking care of the classroom.	Joining groups outside of school. Accepting cultural differences. Helping people in need.	Developing involvement in community projects. Identifying and resisting negative group influences. Accepting group differences.	Contributing to community service projects. Accepting responsibility for the environment. Participating in community service or environmental projects. Getting involved in local government, youth, or issue advocacy.
Event-Triggered Domain			
Coping with divorce. Dealing with a death in the family. Becoming a big brother or big sister to a sibling. Dealing with family moves.	Same as Early Childhood tasks.	Same as Early Childhood tasks. Dealing with a classmate's drug use or delinquent behavior.	Same as Early Childhood tasks. Dealing with a classmate's drug use, delinquent behavior, injury or death due to violence, pregnancy, suicide, HIV/AIDS, or the like.

and goal attainment is needed if children are to be able to carry out projects and participate in teams and performances. These attributes are also behind their penchant for collecting things and reading book series during the latter part of this age period. Their growing ability to focus also prepares them for the period of identity, which extends from preadolescence into the teen years. Students build on prior experiences to attempt to answer the questions "Who am I?" and "What can I become?" These questions take on an emotional charge and a sense of reality as children move into formal, operational cognitive capacities.

In middle childhood, key abilities in social-decision making include a broadening vocabulary to label a range of feelings in self and others; an improved ability to link sequences of events; a more accurate sense of perspective; an expanded ability to consider alternative solutions and consequences and to formulate elaborated plans for means-ends linkage; and the beginning of an ability to anticipate obstacles to one's plans.

Early Adolescence: Grades 6–9, Ages 11–14

Early adolescence—the middle school years—is most obviously a time of intense physical changes. This includes a growth spurt, a reduction in "baby fat," and the appearance of secondary sex characteristics related to the onset of puberty. What is perhaps most significant is the varying rates at which all of these changes occur, both for a given child and across children. This means that the middle school child can look like an elementary school child, a high school child, or anywhere in between. As children see their schoolmates reach various milestones at different times, they inevitably make comparisons, and all too often see themselves as deficient.

Nevertheless, the belief that adolescence should be defined as a period of stress, turmoil, and rebellion has been declared by many to be a myth. And the evidence certainly bears them out. Rather, it is helpful to examine developmental tasks that early adolescents must work through on their path toward adulthood, and these certainly can be sources of both exhilaration and consternation. These tasks will be addressed next (Carnegie Council on Adolescent Development, 1989; Dorman & Lipsitz, 1984).

Early adolescence is a time of cognitive awakening when individuals make a transition from the *stage of industry* to the *stage of identity*. Children awaken to the world of possibility and potential, of abstract thinking and going from the specific to the general. They retain a certain egocentrism, which leads them to believe they are unique, special, even invulnerable to harm. At the same time, there is a concern with the great anonymous "they" and what "they" think. To help deal with this vast cognitive awakening, early adolescents often see things in black-and-white or "good-or-bad" terms. This leads to the possibilities of catastrophizing, denial, and overgeneralization. At the same time, increased social concern emerges, fueled by the beginnings of their realization about the importance of what they do in the present influencing what they will be able to do in the future, and by the innocent exuberance they bring to so many of life's issues and challenges.

Erikson (1954) noted that a sense of "industriousness" characteristic of early adolescence can be seen both in a strong orientation to certain tasks and in a faddish commitment to certain things for relatively short periods of time. This partly explains why middle-school-aged children can be such avid collectors. It is important during the middle-school years for children to achieve some sense of mastery in one or more activities in which they are displaying their industriousness. Unfortunately, this does not necessarily translate into motivation relating to school achievement. Having the best baseball card or audiotape collections may be more than sufficient for some children.

There is no doubt that peer relationships begin to increase in their importance and influence during the early adolescent years. Yet, teachers, as well as parents and other adults, must not be lulled into thinking that their influence as role models and sources of advice is in any way diminished. Rather, children are less likely to admit or acknowledge this influence during the middle-school years than they might have in prior years. Thus, being a source of support at this time in a child's life is often a thankless and even at times frustrating role. However, that support can be a lifeline for youth who otherwise would derive most of their views from their peers. What adults can do is to stimulate these children's social decision-making and problem-solving abilities, to provide them with much needed reflective exercise.

Adolescence: Grades 10–12, Ages 15–17

Adolescence requires both more mature expectancies and better integrated social-decision-making skills. With

regard to expectancies, successful adaptation is aided by an appropriate internal locus of control; a realistic sense of which situations will have positive outcomes; and a general tendency to consider multiple alternatives, consequences, and plans before acting. With regard to decision making, advances in reciprocal perspective taking fuel improvements in the identification of emotions and causal inference; in the ability to consider multiple alternatives, consequences, and plans; in the formation of contingency plans; and in the ability to supply a flexible response to obstacles. Finally, by the time of adolescence, children should have the capabilities to exhibit all of the self-control and social-awareness and group-participation skills listed in Table 1. To the extent that these are impaired, there will be limits placed on the effectiveness of an adolescent's use of constructive social-problem-solving strategies.

Summary

In general, the psychosocial stages are the engines of development, fueled by the emergence of new language and social-decision-making capabilities at each level. It must be remembered, however, that it is the forces of social adaptation—other people, norms, rules, and structures—that forge a greater integration of skills, mobilization of expectancies before action, precise use of language, and the capacity for flexibility and synergistic use of skills. Here, one must be cognizant of the living environment of the child and the opportunities, challenges, and resources provided in support of mastery of the adaptational tasks just outlined, as well as many other related ones that were not described here due to space limitations.

Problems and Implications

The presentation of the skills of social decision making and problem solving, both overall and in a developmental context, is designed to make clear that these are essential skills for everyday functioning. To the extent to which children experience deficits in these skills, their functioning will be compromised. School practitioners will find that many traditional problems can be redefined in terms of a predominant set of deficiencies in social decision making. Social problem solving draws on a variety of conceptual contributions, many of which have been made in the context of studying specific problem groups or age groups. Because the schools are places in which all children of varying age groups converge, adherents of a comprehensive social-problem-solving perspective are able to draw parallels among various literatures, noting the commonalities of concepts that might be hidden by differences in terminology. The assessment framework provided in Table 1 can serve as a guide to identifying these similarities.

Problem-Solving Models

While it is beyond the scope of this chapter to review all of the relevant theoretical points (cf. Elias & Clabby, 1992), two examples that can serve as useful illustrations are the work of Selman in interpersonal understanding and Dodge in social information processing. Selman's model grew from early work on the importance of perspective taking in successful interpersonal interaction. When children grow into middle childhood and adolescence and lack the ability to coordinate the perspective of multiple individuals—peers, family members, school staff—with whom they must interact, as well an integrate these perspectives with their own sense of self, their interpersonal relationships are likely to be impaired. Children's deficiencies in this area have been linked to aggressive behavior, impaired friendships, social rejection, and delinquent behavior. Selman's intervention approaches focus a great deal on role-play interactions with much feedback, to help children learn how to "read" others and develop insights into alternative ways others might be thinking and feeling in situations (Selman et al., 1992; Yates & Selman, 1988).

An important related conceptual contribution with strong intervention implications is the social information processing model of Dodge and colleagues (Crick & Dodge, 1994). From this point of view, interpersonal interactions can be understood as progressive encounters with information, leading to decisions about appropriate actions. Cues from others must be encoded and interpreted; responses must be generated and selected in the context of one's goals in a particular interaction, and then the appropriate behavior is enacted (cf. Dodge, 1986; also see Aggressive Behavior, this volume).

Dodge's model is compatible with Selman's view and fits well within the larger rubric of social problem solving. It is especially useful in providing school psychologists with conceptual tools to understand how deficiencies in social information processing and other elements of the social-problem-solving process can lead to aggressive behavior. How children process the initial cues in social interactions—such as facial expressions and their ability to interpret those social cues by taking another's perspective, reading another's intentions, and empathizing—will influence their social problem solving and subsequent behavior. The hostile attribution bias is an example of how aggressive children tend to encode neutral social cues as threatening, thus leading to misunderstanding and/or strong affect, particularly anger, fear, threat, or rage (Dodge, Price, Bachorowski, & Newman, 1990). Under such conditions, aggressive behavior in the form of a preemptive strike would not be unexpected, nor would flight or other avoidant behaviors that might look

to an observer to be without apparent stimulus. Dodge, Bates, and Pettit (1990) further illustrate how accrued harm due to a history of receiving aggression, rejection, and verbal abuse shapes children's information processing, with resulting processing deficits affecting behavior in ways that increase the likelihood for further harm.

Much as Dodge has focused on externalizing problems, Seligman (1995) and colleagues have looked at the implications of social-problem-solving deficiencies for internalizing disorders. For example, depression can be linked to an inability to consider alternative ways to reach a goal, an underemphasis on positive consequences of possible actions, or the failure to articulate a clear and reachable goal. Negative social interactions often stem from an inability to label and manage one's strong feelings; to recognize the signs of different feelings in others; to understand the "politics" of successful interaction, involving thinking through when, where, and how to act, and what to say and how to say it; and to learn from experiences of social rejection. Anxiety is an outgrowth of trying to pursue too many goals simultaneously, of pursuing goals unrealistically set by oneself or perhaps by others, or of not having clear goals to pursue. Following peer pressure can be reframed as following others' goals for oneself. School-based, short-term (9 to 12 sessions) group interventions designed by Seligman based on these frameworks have shown initial success in field trials (Goleman, 1995).

What should be clear from these examples is that deficiencies in social decision making and problem solving are associated with a wide range of problem behaviors. Approaches at assessment, prevention and remediation that do not incorporate substantial attention to social decision making and problem-solving skills will be reduced in their potential effectiveness.

Multicultural Considerations

One aspect of social decision making and problem solving that requires special consideration is its multicultural application. This is an area that has been neglected in theoretical writing and especially in research. Nevertheless, it is clear that possession of self-control, social awareness, and group participation skills and the skills and strategies needed for making thoughtful social decisions, particularly when one is under stress, can be seen by virtually all groups as valuable in their everyday social and academic tasks. Generalization to multicultural situations will be improved as the latter are built into social-decision-making instruction as examples and then brought in more systematically as a set of application-phase activities.

Because this area has been so neglected, and because current knowledge of the developmental task framework has been so ill-informed by systematic study of various population groups, two brief examples are presented to show how the skills in Table 1 should be reconsidered for application to different cultural and ethnic groups.

Skill: Listening

Multicultural link to social decision making and problem solving

To function in a multicultural context, one must be able to *recognize and understand the perspectives of others*. The first step in seeing and understanding multiple perspectives must be to listen for them. Instruction in social decision making builds children's skills in active listening and questioning for clarification. One result can be a deeper understanding of others. Students will tend to rely less on prejudiced views when they listen actively and "fill in missing information," not with stereotypes, but by seeking more information. When a student learns to listen attentively and to question, he or she is not blindly accepting views but is learning to identify, grapple with, and understand multicultural perspectives.

Another quality derived from listening skills is related to the capacity to be *"media literate"*—the ability to use, and not be used by, the media. Social-decision-making and problem-solving skills help students learn to transfer listening skills developed in the classroom to the "intentional and unintentional multicultural teachings" of the news and entertainment media (Banks, Cortes, Gay, Garcia, & Ochos, 1976; Cortes, 1990). Children who listen actively and critically will learn to fill in the gaps in what is presented in the media—often in oversimplified form—through intelligent questioning and by not passively "soaking in" what is offered.

Skill-building approach

A prompt such as "Listening Position" reminds students that it is time to pay attention; not to talk out of turn; and when the speaker is finished, to ask questions if they want more information about the who, what, where, or when of what was said.

Skill: Group Participation

Multicultural link to social decision making and problem solving

Social-decision-making activities enhance children's understanding of the significance of groups and highlights for them what group membership feels like on a personal level (as a member of a class, sharing circle group, or smaller activity groups). The idea in social decision making is to augment group cohesiveness, not by making students feel as if they are all the same, but by emphasizing both similarities and differences among classmates. In meeting new people and learning what may be different about them, ethnically or otherwise, the students become closer as a group and more aware of the

diversity within it. As students realize that they and the students about whom they learn more "interesting" things are members of many groups (classroom, lunch time, or ethnic groups, to mention only a few), their definition of groupness may become less rigid. Group generalizations will then be less likely to harden into inflexible distortions or group stereotyping (Banks et al., 1976; Cortes, 1990).

Skill-building approach

Group cohesiveness and trust is presented to students using a practical rationale: "In many classes," a teacher might say, "we get to know our classmates only in a limited way. There are many other things that we can learn about our classmates that are interesting to know. We can act better as a team when our classmates see us as more than just people who can write well or add and subtract." Specific skills-building activities include learning and practicing ways of approaching new people and starting a conversation and keeping it going.

Alternative Actions

A number of systematic, well researched interventions exists in the area of social decision making and problem solving. In addition to the programs mentioned earlier, other application examples currently in use in the context of school-based practice are presented next as a source of ideas, with follow-up information available in the Recommended Resources section at the end of this chapter.

Classroom-Level Applications

Curricula exist that will allow a classroom teacher—often in consultation or collaboration with a school psychologist, guidance counselor, social worker, or health educator—to carry out a program related to social decision making that extends from the preschool through high school grades. Skill emphases vary in accordance with the developmental considerations presented earlier. Two examples of well-researched classroom-based curricular programs follow.

Interpersonal Cognitive Problem-Solving (or I Can Problem Solve; ICPS) by Shure (1994) has been evaluated over a period of 25 years and more recently in a 5-year longitudinal study. This curriculum is geared toward the promotion of mental health in students from Kindergarten through Grade 6. It includes a pre-problem-solving phase (e.g., identifying feelings and perspective taking) followed by problem-solving training, both of which use games, stories, puppets, and role-playing. Results show gains in interpersonal as well as academic behavior, including a reduction in impulsive behavior; how ever, it is also clear that effects disappear in the absence of "booster" or follow-up sessions.

Like ICPS, Skillstreaming (Goldstein, Sprafkin, Gershaw, & Klein, 1980) is a method of promoting social skills that emphasizes interpersonal and problem-solving skills. The Skillstreaming Curriculum aims to improve interpersonal communication in prosocial skills such as classroom survival, making friends, dealing with feelings, and alternatives to aggression. Skillstreaming uses modeling, role-playing, performance feedback, and transfer of training to promote prosocial skills. A study by Miller, Midgett, and Wicks (1992) found that Skillstreaming used for 6 weeks with a group of middle school students with emotional disturbances yielded improvements in beginning social skills, advanced social skills, dealing with feelings, alternatives to aggression, dealing with stress, and planning skills.

Grade-Level Applications

Because of the curriculum-based nature of many of the intervention programs, the school psychologist or other pupil services provider can coordinate intervention programs across classrooms at a given grade level. Further, because these interventions are structured, it is possible to create sequences of intervention that continue from grade level to grade level. The developmental sequence of adaptational tasks as presented in Table 2 provide both a rationale and guide for school practitioners paying special attention to the continuity of programs from year to year, an intervention feature that is seen far too infrequently (Consortium on the School-Based Promotion of Social Competence, 1994).

School-Wide Applications

While the programs just described and similar programs have shown some success, it has become clear that results tend to be stronger, more generalizable, and more enduring if programs are ongoing and long term (Weissberg & Elias, 1993). Thus, a "second generation" of social problem solving programs has emerged with a dual emphasis on the integration of the program into the classroom structure and on continuity and reinforcement of skills.

Weissberg, Jackson, and Shriver (1993) assert that infusing a decision making model into the health curriculum can be especially valuable, as it provides a common framework and language to address diverse content and problem areas. Their social-problem-solving (SPS) program integrates the affective, cognitive, and behavioral aspects of problem solving in both content and instruction. Students are taught steps to use when responding to health and life-skills-related challenges and problems. These steps are

1. Stop, calm down and think before you act.
2. Say the problem and how you feel.
3. Set a positive goal.
4. Think of lots of solutions.
5. Think ahead to the consequences.
6. Go ahead and try the best plan.

In a longitudinal study of the program, students who received SPS training were compared to students who did not receive the training. Results indicated that students receiving SPS training showed significant gains in their ability to generate more cooperative solutions to hypothetical problems and endorse assertive and cooperative strategies to resolve interpersonal conflict (Elias & Weissberg, 1990).

This chapter's author and my colleague (Elias & Clabby, 1989) developed a social problem solving program that has been studied since 1979. The program has been delivered to students with and without disabilities in mainstream settings, as well as in school-based and residential special education contexts. The scope of the program is multiyear, and those trained in the program learn how to integrate it into all aspects of the school day in an ongoing manner. Major documented effects of the program are that, compared to control groups, children involved in the programs were more sensitive to others' feelings; were seen by their teachers as displaying more positive prosocial behavior; were sought out by their peers more for help with problems; displayed lower than expected levels of antisocial, self-destructive, and socially disordered behavior, even when followed up in high school; and felt that they learned more about their classmates. Also important is that this program has been subjected to external evaluation and has been designated as a program of educational excellence by the Program Effectiveness Panel of the U.S. Department of Education's National Diffusion Network (Elias & Clabby, 1992).

Another important SPS application has been to address school-wide matters such as the discipline system. Using a computer software program that incorporates the social decision making steps, an "SPS Lab" has been set up so that children who are in trouble, such as detention, can go there and work with the computer to review how their thinking got them into trouble and then develop a computer-generated action plan that the students, school staff, and parents can follow up on. The Lab also is used as a place where students who are having an academic, peer, health, or family problem can go to try to work it through, again developing an action plan (Elias & Tobias, 1996).

The Child Development Program (Battistich, Elias, & Branden-Muller, 1992) is another example of an effective SPS approach that seeks to impact on the entire school environment. The program was designed to create a caring and participatory school community in which children are given opportunities to learn about others' needs and perspectives, to collaborate with one another, and to engage in a variety of prosocial actions, all in balance with their own needs. Group activities include working in small cooperative groups toward common goals in academic and nonacademic tasks. Goals of fairness and consideration are reached through direct training in group interaction skills. Group discussions and meetings are also geared toward increased helping of other students and sensitivity to and understanding of others' feelings, needs, and perspectives. The program operates at all grade levels, and staff must agree to the principles and procedures of the program before Child Development Project staff will support implementation.

Results from a longitudinal study of three suburban, middle-class elementary schools (and three control schools) using the Child Development Program (Battistich et al., 1992) indicate that improvement relative to the control group was shown on spontaneous prosocial behavior (helpfulness, support, cooperation), student ratings of the extent to which the classroom was a "caring community," greater ability to take the perspectives of others as well as consider one's own needs, and peer acceptance. Also found was a decrease in loneliness and social anxiety. Based on these and other data, the Child Development Project has also been approved by the Program Effectiveness Panel of the U.S. Department of Education's National Diffusion Network.

District-Wide Applications

As the work of Goleman (1995) and others in the area of emotional intelligence and social and emotional learning gains popular appeal, more and more districts will consider social decision making and problem solving as a district-wide goal. Because there are individual programs and related programs that exist across grade levels, and because many proponents of the approach favor staff development models involving not only teachers but support staff and administrators, social decision making approaches are ideal for coordinated, district-wide use. It allows for maximal instructional and content continuity, something of particular importance for self-contained and included special education populations. (See Elias & Weissberg, 1990, & Weissberg & Elias, 1993, for a discussion of the implementation of such a program in the New Haven, Connecticut Public Schools.)

Social-decision-making and problem-solving skills are enhanced best when linked to appropriate levels of related cognitive and affective skills and in areas of highest salience to children. Therefore, the developmental guidelines presented earlier should be valuable for district-wide intervention planning. Note that for children with special education classifications, extra challenges are afforded by the fact that there often are mismatches between their level of skills and of skill integration and the adaptational tasks they are facing. Generally, they will need more instructional time, more direct practice, more review time, and more focused attention to generalization if lasting gains are to be expected, compared to their same-age nonclassified peers. When these program features have taken place, classified and at-risk children have been successful recipients of programs (Elias & Clabby, 1992; Elias & Tobias, 1996).

If public pressures to build children's social and emotional learning escalate, school psychologists and other practitioners will find that demands will outstrip the current knowledge base. While groups such as the Consortium on the School-Based Promotion of Social Competence (1994) and the Collaborative for the Advancement of Social and Emotional Learning (in preparation) work to elaborate guidelines for interventions based increasingly on research and practice that are replicated and sensitive to learner and implementer diversity, practitioners will have to act when the opportunity arises. This may require "brushing up" on such approaches as action research, program planning, implementation, evaluation, and consultation. However, if these are the tools required to meet the needs of children in comprehensive ways, it is necessary to rise to meet the challenge.

Individual and Small-Group Applications

Many school practitioners will find that their circumstances will not allow them to begin with the kinds of systematic and extensive applications represented by the programs just presented. However, all of these programs contain materials and procedures that allow for adaptations at the individual and small-group levels, in both preventive and remediative contexts. The skills in Table 1 can be used for individual assessment and intervention planning, drawing from the materials available. In addition, through a technique known as dialoguing or facilitative questioning, students' skills can be developed in a counseling context. Interventions of this kind have been elaborated elsewhere (see Elias & Tobias, 1996).

Students who are at risk for academic failure and drop out benefit from problem-solving groups to assist them in self-organization, self-management, goal setting, and study skills. Problem solving also is valuable for small groups formed around event-triggered situations such as divorce or bereavement.

Summary

The skills needed to cope effectively with life's everyday challenges must be taught and explicitly nurtured if schools are to prevent too many students from turning into social casualties. As they move from direct and intensive adult supervision toward greater independence, children's capacity for sound social judgment and appropriate personal decision making becomes as important as their basic academic abilities. This chapter presented an overview of these social-decision-making and problem-solving skills, an assessment framework for use by school practitioners, and an overview of the development of these skills in the context of adaptational challenges of childhood and adolescence in the personal, family, peer, school, and community domains, as well as situations triggered by the occurrence of stressful life events. Linkages of skill deficits to dysfunction, considerations for applications in multicultural settings and with children who have special education classifications, and examples of the many well-researched and well-articulated interventions at the individual, small-group, classroom, grade-level, school-wide, and district-wide levels were provided.

Recommended Resources

Collaborative for the Advancement of Social and Emotional Learning (CASEL).
Located at the Yale Child Study Center, CASEL is serving as a central resource for information about social and emotional learning in children and adolescents. It is a clearinghouse for program information and a source of networking for professionals, educators, administrators, community members, parents, legislators, and policy makers. (CASEL, Dept. of Psychology (M/C 285), University of Illinois at Chicago, 1007 W. Harrison Street, Chicago, IL 60607-7137; 312-413-1008, 312-413-4122 (fax).

Elias, M. J. (Ed.). (1993). *Social decision making and life skills development: Guidelines for middle school educators.* Gaithersburg, MD: Aspen.
Practitioners and action researchers who have been implementing social problem solving programs in the field for years have written up their most creative and successful work for inclusion in this volume. Included are applications for self-contained and other special education classes, community service and environments science, urban youth, and how to provide SPS-based workshops and newsletters for parents. One chapter is devoted entirely to multicultural applications. Among the authors are Weissberg, Snow, Grady, Clabby, Friedlander, Welland, Bruene, and Chung.

Elias, M. J., & Clabby, J. F. (1992). *Building social problem solving skills: Guidelines from a school-based program.* San Francisco: Jossey-Bass.
This volume provides a guide for those intending to do comprehensive school-based SPS programs. It includes a step-by-step action research plan, principles of curriculum design, counseling applications, ways to engage parents, examples of how standard programs can be adapted to local circumstances, and curriculum modules of vocationally based SPS at the high school level.

Elias, M. J., & Tobias, S. E. (1996). *Social problem solving: Interventions in the schools.* New York: Guilford.
Designed for school psychologists in particular, this book contains practical activities to build the social decision making

skills of students at all grade levels, but with particular emphasis on the elementary and middle school periods. Included are the latest multimedia applications such as the Video Critique Club and the Student Conflict Manager/Personal Problem Solving Guide Computer Software.

Goleman, D. (1995). *Emotional intelligence.* New York: Bantam.
Goleman, a science writer for the New York Times, *provides a clear, literate, multidisciplinary overview of the underpinnings of social and emotional learning and why these skills are essential for everyday life success in terms that are useful for presentation to parents, teachers, and school board members. He also identifies examples of model programs from around the country.*

Shure, M. B. (1994). *I Can Problem Solve! (ICPS).* Champaign, IL: Research Press.
This work, as well as others by Myrna Shure and her collaborator, George Spivack, represents pioneering work in the field of social problem solving. ICPS actually consists of a series of curriculum modules that provide specific skills-building exercises from the preschool years through Grade 6.

References

Banks, J. A., Cortes, C., Gay, G., Garcia, R., & Ochos, A. (1976). *Curriculum guidelines for multicultural education.* Washington, DC: National Council for the Social Studies.

Battistich, V. A., Elias, M. J., & Branden-Muller, L. R. (1992). Two school-based approaches to promoting children's social competence. In G. W. Albee, L. A. Bond, & T. V. Cook-Monsey (Eds.), *Improving children's lives: Global perspectives on prevention* (pp. 217–234). Newbury Park, CA: Sage.

Blythe, T., & Gardner, H. (1990). A school for all intelligences. *Educational Leadership, 47*(7), 33–37.

Carnegie Council on Adolescent Development. (1989). *Turning points: Preparing American youth for the 21st century.* Washington, DC: Carnegie Corporation of New York.

Collaborative for the Advancement of Social and Emotional Learning. (in preparation). *The missing piece: Guidelines and examples for promoting academic and interpersonal success through social and emotional skill development.* Alexandria, VA: Association for Supervision and Curriculum Development.

Consortium on the School-Based Promotion of Social Competence. (1991). Preparing students for the twenty-first century: Contributions of the prevention and social competence promotion fields. *Teachers College Record, 93,* 297–305.

Consortium on the School-Based Promotion of Social Competence. (1994). The school-based promotion of social competence: Theory, research, practice, and policy. In R. Haggerty, L. Sherrod, N. Garmezy, & M. Rutter (Eds.), *Stress, risk, and resilience, in children and adolescents* (pp. 268–316). New York: Cambridge University Press.

Cortes, C. (1990, March). A curricular basis for multicultural education. *Doubts and Uncertainties, 4,* 1–5.

Crick, N., & Dodge, K. A. (1994). A review and reformulation of social information-processing mechanisms in children's social adjustment. *Psychological Bulletin, 115,* 74–101.

Dodge, K. A. (1986). A social information processing model of social competence in children. In M. Perlmutter (Ed.), *Cognitive perspectives on children's social and behavioral development* (pp. 77–125). Hillsdale, NJ: Erlbaum.

Dodge, K. A., Bates, J. E., & Pettit, G. (1990). Mechanisms in the cycle of violence. *Science, 250,* 1678–1683.

Dodge, K. A., Price, J. M., Bachorowski, J., & Newman, J. P. (1990). Hostile attribution biases in severely aggressive adolescents. *Journal of Abnormal Psychology, 99,* 385–392.

Dorman, G., & Lipsitz, J. (1984). Early adolescent development. In G. Dorman (Ed.), *Middle grades assessment program* (pp. 3–8). Carrboro, NC: Center for Early Adolescence.

Elias, M. J., & Associates. (1992). Drug and alcohol prevention curriculum. In J. D. Hawkins, R. F. Catalano, & Associates (Eds.), *Communities that care: Action for drug abuse prevention* (pp. 129–148). San Francisco: Jossey-Bass.

Elias, M. J., & Clabby, J. F. (1989) *Social decision making skills: A curriculum guide for the elementary grades.* Gaithersburg, MD: Aspen.

Elias, M. J., & Clabby, J. F. (1992). *Building social problem solving skills: Guidelines from a school-based program.* San Francisco: Jossey-Bass.

Elias, M. J., & Tobias, S. E. (1996). *Social problem solving: Interventions in the schools.* New York: Guilford.

Elias, M. J., & Weissberg, R. P. (1990). School-based social competence promotion as a primary prevention strategy: A tale of two projects. In R. Lorion (Ed.), *Protecting the children: Strategies for optimizing human development* (pp. 177–200). New York: Haworth.

Erikson, E. H. (1954). *Childhood and society.* New York: Norton.

Goldstein, A., Sprafkin, Gershaw, & Klein, (1980). *Skillstreaming the adolescent.* Champaign, IL: Research Press.

Goleman, D. (1995). *Emotional intelligence.* New York: Bantam.

Hamburg, B. (1990). *Life skills training: Preventive interventions for young adolescents.* New York: Carnegie Council on Adolescent Development.

Hawkins, J. D., Catalano, R. F., & Associates (Eds.). (1992). *Communities that care: Action for drug abuse prevention.* San Francisco: Jossey-Bass.

Kolbe, L. (1985). Why school health education? An empirical point of view. *Health Education, 16,* 116–120.

Miller, M. G., Midgett, J., & Wicks, M. L. (1992). Student and teacher perceptions related to behavior change after Skillstreaming training. *Behavioral Disorders, 17,* 291–295.

Rotter, J. B. (1982). *The development and application of social learning theory.* New York: Praeger.

Seligman, M. E. P. (1995) *The optimistic child.* New York: HarperPerennial.

Selman, R., Schultz, L, Nakkula, M., Barr, D., Watts, C., & Richmond, J. (1992). Friendship and fighting: A developmental approach to the study of risk and prevention of violence. *Development and Psychopathology, 4,* 529–558.

Shure, M. B. (1994). *I Can Problem Solve! (ICPS).* Champaign, IL: Research Press.

Sternberg, R., & Wagner, R. (Eds.). (1986). *Practical intelligence: Nature and origins of competence in the everyday world.* New York: Cambridge University Press.

Wales, C., Nardi, A., & Stager, R. (1986). Decision making: A new paradigm for education. *Educational Leadership, 43,* 37–42.

Weissberg, R. P., & Elias, M. J. (1993). Enhancing young people's social competence and health behavior: An important challenge for educators, scientists, policymakers, and funders. *Applied & Preventive Psychology, 2,* 179–190.

Weissberg, R. P., Jackson, A. S., & Shriver, T. P. (1993). Promoting positive social development and health practices in young urban adolescents. In M. J. Elias (Ed.), *Social decision making and life skills development: Guidelines for middle school educators* (pp. 45–78). Gaithersburg, MD: Aspen.

Yates, K., & Selman, R. (1988). Social competence in the schools: Toward an integrative developmental model for intervention. *Developmental Review, 9,* 64–100.

4

Social Skills

Frank M. Gresham
University of California-Riverside

The ability to interact successfully with peers and significant adults is one of the most important aspects of a child's development. The extent to which children, adolescents, and adults are able to establish and maintain satisfactory interpersonal relationships and terminate pernicious interpersonal relationships in many ways defines social competence and predicts successful psychological adjustment (Kupersmidt, Coie, & Dodge, 1990; Parker & Asher, 1987). Social competence is important because it has become clear that the development of oppositional, antisocial behavior problems begins early in life and these problems are stable over time (Kazdin, 1987; Oleweus, 1979). Oleweus for example, found that aggressive, antisocial behavior in boys was as stable as measures of intelligence over one-year ($r = .76$) and five-year ($r = .69$) intervals.

Patterson, DeBaryshe, and Ramsey (1989) presented a developmental model showing that antisocial behavior begins early in life (ages 2–3 years) and continues throughout the school years. School entry represents a particularly critical period for children having early onset difficulties in social behavior. Reid and Patterson (1991) indicated that many children exhibiting antisocial behavior patterns before school will continue coercive and aggressive behavior patterns with peers and teachers upon school entry. In the absence of intervention, this behavior pattern will be maintained throughout their school careers and beyond (see Kazdin, 1987; Patterson et al., 1989; Reid & Patterson, 1991). When children come to school with an oppositional, antisocial style of interacting, they fail to acquire and/or perform appropriate social skills in the school settings. Consequently, these children are at early risk for school maladjustment, as well as for referrals to special education services (Gresham & Reschly, 1988; Walker & McConnell, 1995; Walker & Severson, 1992).

Social competence deficits and antisocial behavior patterns are particularly salient in school settings. Several reviews have suggested that the primary reason some children have academic problems is because they are disruptive in classrooms and have low compliance rates with school rules (Eme, 1979; Hinshaw, 1992). This relationship between academic underachievement and social competence deficits appears to be more common in boys than in girls. However, longitudinal research by Robins (1986) showed that girls who experience social competence problems and antisocial behavior are at risk for developing later psychological disorders (i.e., internalizing and externalizing disorders) in adolescence and on into adulthood and this risk is equal for boys and girls.

Schools, by virtue of their accessibility to all children, their parents, and teachers, represent an ideal locale for teaching and refining children's social behavior. As a microcosm of society, the school is a place where children and adults work, play, eat, and live together for 6 hours per day, 5 days per week, and at least 180 days per year. By Grade 5 children will spend a minimum of 5,400 hours in school. During this time, these children will be exposed to literally tens of thousands of social interactions with both peers and adults. Not surprisingly, schools represent a major socializing institution in society.

A variety of terms have been used to describe one's success in establishing and maintaining satisfactory interpersonal relationships including social competence, social skills, assertion skills, prosocial behavior, social-cognitive skills, interpersonal skills, and social problem-solving skills. Unfortunately, there is less than unanimity of agreement on the meaning of these terms. The purpose of this chapter is to define and describe the concept of social skills; highlight its importance to children's development and adjustment, particularly in school settings; identify negative outcomes associated with difficulties in social competence; and outline specific intervention procedures having empirical support in remediating social competence deficits.

Background and Development

Definitional Issues

Various approaches to measuring and defining social competence have been proposed in the literature. Some individuals may define a person as socially skilled if that person is well-accepted by peers. Others may define social skills as behaviors that result in reciprocal positive social exchanges among two or more persons. On a general level, social skills might be defined as socially acceptable behaviors that enable a person to interact effectively with others and to avoid socially unacceptable or aversive responses from others.

Social competence can be conceptualized as a multidimensional construct that includes adaptive behavior, social skills, and peer relationship variables (e.g., peer acceptance, peer rejection, and friendship; Gresham & Reschly, 1988). McFall (1982) offered a useful conceptualization of social competence by articulating a distinction between *social skills* and *social competence.* In McFall's view, social skills are the specific behaviors that a person exhibits to perform competently on a social task. Social competence, on the other hand, is an evaluative term based on judgments that a person has performed a social task adequately. These judgments may be based on opinions of significant others (e.g., teachers, parents, or peers), comparisons to explicit criteria (e.g., number of social tasks correctly performed), or comparisons to a normative sample. In short, this view of social competence considers social skills to be *specific behaviors* that result in *judgment(s)* about those behaviors.

Building on McFall's (1982) conceptualization, I offered a *social validity* perspective on social skills (Gresham, 1983). According to this view, social skills are specific behaviors or behavior patterns that predict important social outcomes within certain situations. In school settings, important social outcomes include but are not limited to (a) peer acceptance, (b) significant others' judgments of social competence (teachers, peers, and parents), (c) academic achievement, (d) adequate self-concept, and (e) absence of maladaptive problem behaviors. The advantage of this definition is that it identifies behaviors in which a child may be deficient and can relate these deficiencies to socially important criteria or outcomes. It should be noted that social validity represents an important type of validity in interventions with children and has been a useful standard against which the success of interventions has been judged (Gresham & Noell, 1993; Noell & Gresham, 1993; Schwartz & Baer, 1991).

Social competence has been a basic notion associated with the definition and classification criteria for individuals with disabilities. For example, the modern classification criteria in mental retardation have consistently emphasized and equally weighted the importance of cognitive and social competence (i.e., adaptive behavior; MacMillan, Gresham, & Siperstein, 1993). In fact, *social skills* represent one of the 10 adaptive skills areas specified in the 1992 definition of mental retardation proposed by the American Association on Mental Retardation (AAMR). According to AAMR, social skills are:

related to social exchanges with other individuals, including initiating, interacting, and terminating interaction with others; receiving and responding to pertinent social cues; recognizing feelings; providing positive and negative feedback; . . . sharing . . . being aware of peers and peer acceptance. (p. 40)

The definition and classification criteria of children as seriously emotionally disturbed (SED) use social competence deficits to identify, classify, and place students into this disability category (Forness & Knitzer, 1992). For example, two crucial criteria specified in the Individuals With Disabilities Education Act (IDEA) for classification of students as SED are (a) an inability to build or maintain satisfactory interpersonal relationships with peers and teachers and (b) inappropriate types of behaviors or feelings under normal circumstances. Although social skills are not included in the identification criteria for children with learning disabilities, these children experience substantial difficulties in social skills and peer acceptance (Gresham, 1992; Kavale & Forness, in press; LaGreca & Stone, 1990; Swanson & Malone, 1992).

Domains of Social Competence

Upon entering school, children have to negotiate two important social-behavioral adjustments: teacher-related and peer-related (Walker, McConnell, & Clark, 1985). Teacher-related adjustment reflects the extent to which children meet the demands of teachers and accomplish tasks in classroom settings. Most teachers would consider a behavioral repertoire to be indicative of successful adjustment if it (a) facilitates academic performance and (b) is marked by the absence of disruptive or unusual behaviors that challenge the teacher's authority and disturb the classroom ecology (Gresham & Reschly, 1988; Hersh & Walker, 1983). This pattern of social behavior has been described by Hersh and Walker as the *model behavior profile* expected by most teachers.

Walker and colleagues (see Walker, Irvin, Noell, & Singer, 1992) have presented an extremely useful model of interpersonal social-behavioral competence for school settings. Based on a multiple-measure, multiple-indicator assessment approach, Walker et al. provide a construct score approach to the assessment of social competence and its outcomes. Their model presented in Figure 1 describes both adaptive and maladaptive teacher and peer social-behavioral domains and outcomes. Note that the adaptive teacher-related adjustment behaviors operationalize the model behavior profile described earlier and result in teacher acceptance and school success. The maladaptive domain is characteristic of behaviors that disrupt the classroom ecology and result in teacher rejection, school failure, and referral to special education.

The social behaviors in the adaptive peer-related adjustment domain are substantially different from those in

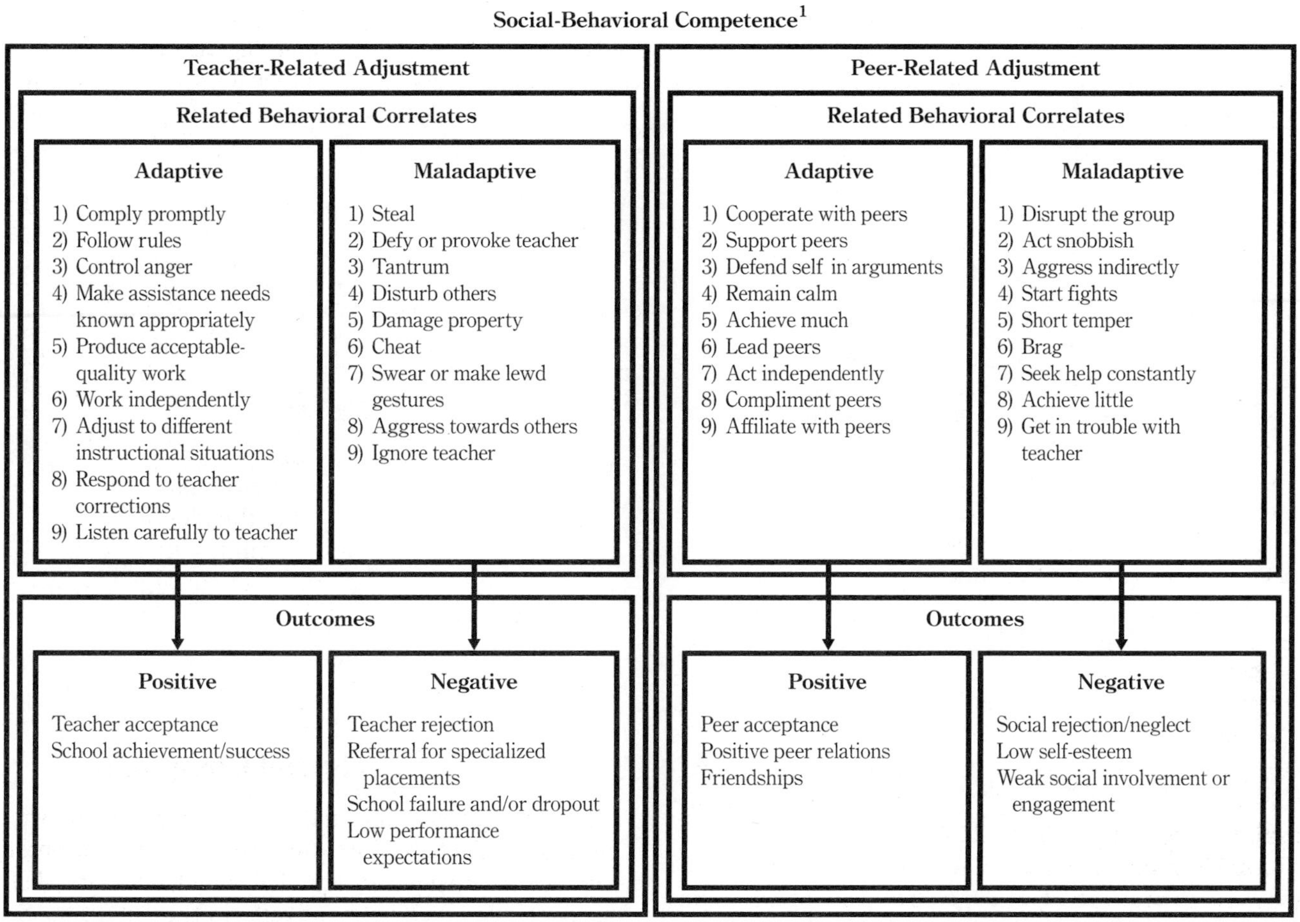

Social-Behavioral Competence[1]

Teacher-Related Adjustment	Peer-Related Adjustment
Related Behavioral Correlates	**Related Behavioral Correlates**

Adaptive	Maladaptive	Adaptive	Maladaptive
1) Comply promptly	1) Steal	1) Cooperate with peers	1) Disrupt the group
2) Follow rules	2) Defy or provoke teacher	2) Support peers	2) Act snobbish
3) Control anger	3) Tantrum	3) Defend self in arguments	3) Aggress indirectly
4) Make assistance needs known appropriately	4) Disturb others	4) Remain calm	4) Start fights
5) Produce acceptable-quality work	5) Damage property	5) Achieve much	5) Short temper
6) Work independently	6) Cheat	6) Lead peers	6) Brag
7) Adjust to different instructional situations	7) Swear or make lewd gestures	7) Act independently	7) Seek help constantly
8) Respond to teacher corrections	8) Aggress towards others	8) Compliment peers	8) Achieve little
9) Listen carefully to teacher	9) Ignore teacher	9) Affiliate with peers	9) Get in trouble with teacher

Outcomes (Teacher-Related) / **Outcomes** (Peer-Related)

Positive	Negative	Positive	Negative
Teacher acceptance	Teacher rejection	Peer acceptance	Social rejection/neglect
School achievement/success	Referral for specialized placements	Positive peer relations	Low self-esteem
	School failure and/or dropout	Friendships	Weak social involvement or engagement
	Low performance expectations		

[1]From "A Construct Score Approach to the Assessment of Social Competence: Rationale, Technological Considerations, and Anticipated Outcomes" by H. Walker, L. Irvin, J. Noell, & G. Singer, 1992, *Behavior Modification, 16,* 448–474. *Reprinted with permission of the authors.*

Figure 1. *Model of Interpersonal Social-Behavioral Competence within School Settings[1]*

the teacher-related adjustment domain. These behaviors are essential for the formation of friendships and peer acceptance but have little to do with classroom success and teacher acceptance (Gresham & Elliott, 1990; Walker et al., 1992). The maladaptive behaviors in this domain are likely to result in peer rejection or neglect but share many similarities with the maladaptive behaviors in the teacher-related adjustment domain.

Classification of Social Skills Deficits

A useful distinction to make when considering children's social-behavioral difficulties is the differentiation between *acquisition* and *performance* deficits (Gresham, 1981). This distinction is important because it suggests different intervention approaches in remediating social competence deficits and may suggest different venues for carrying out these interventions (classroom-based versus pullout groups). Social skills acquisition deficits refer to

the absence of knowledge for executing particular social skills even under optimal conditions. Social performance deficits represent the presence of social skills in a behavioral repertoire but the failure to perform these skills at acceptable levels in given situations. In short, acquisition deficits describe "Can't do" deficits and performance deficits reflect "Won't do" deficits.

This two-way classification has been extended into a four-category classification scheme particularly relevant in the assessment of and intervention with social skills deficits Gresham & Elliott, 1990). This extended classification scheme incorporates two dimensions of behavior: social skills and interfering problem behaviors (see Figure 2). Children may have social skill acquisition or performance deficits with or without interfering problem behaviors. Interfering problem behaviors include internalizing or overcontrolled (e.g., anxiety, depression) and externalizing (e.g., aggression, impulsivity) or undercontrolled behavior patterns that prevent either the acquisition or performance of socially skilled behaviors.

Problem Behavior Dimension	Acquisition Deficit	Performance Deficit
Problem Behavior Present	Acquisition deficit with interfering problem behavior(s)	Performance deficit with interfering problem behavior(s)
Problem Behavior Absent	Acquisition deficit without interfering problem behavior(s)	Performance deficit without interfering problem behavior(s)

Figure 2. *Social Skills Deficit Classification Model*

Problems and Implications

Behavioral Correlates of Students with Mild Disabilities

A substantial body of literature suggests that children within all mild disability groups exhibit deficient social skills and excesses of interfering problem behaviors (Gresham, 1992; Kavale & Forness, in press; Landau & Moore, 1991; Merrell, Johnson, Merz, & Ring, 1992; Swanson & Malone, 1992). This holds true for children with learning disabilities, mild mental retardation, emotional and behavioral disorders, and attention deficit/hyperactivity disorders as well as for children who are low in academic achievement but not classified as mildly disabled.

Several studies have shown that students with mild disabilities exhibit deficient social skills and excesses in interfering problem behaviors relative to nondisabled students. Almost all of these studies, however, have shown no differences among mild disability groups. One study (Gresham, Elliott, & Black, 1987) contrasted three groups (Grades 1–8) defined as learning disabled, mildly mentally retarded, and behavior disordered with nondisabled controls using teacher ratings of social skills. These ratings tapped the social skills dimensions of cooperation, self-control, and social initiation. No differences were found among the mild disability groups, but large differences were found between these groups and the nondisabled group. On average, the mild disability groups scored approximately one standard deviation below the nondisabled group. A discriminant function analysis correctly classified 71% of the mild disability group and 78% of the nondisabled group using the total social skills score. Studies contrasting students with learning disabilities and nondisabled students have reported similar effect sizes (Gresham & Reschly, 1988; Kistner & Gatlin, 1989).

A comprehensive investigation by Merrell et al. (1992) contrasted four groups (Grades K-6) classified as learning disabled, mildly mentally retarded, behavior dis-

ordered, and low achieving with nondisabled controls using teacher-rated social skills as the dependent measure. Consistent with Gresham et al.'s (1987) findings, no differences were found between learning disabled or mildly mentally retarded groups nor were there any differences between these groups and the low-achieving group. There were, however, substantial differences between the behavior disordered group and the other mild disability groups. Merrell et al. concluded that social skills is a weak discriminating variable in differentiating among learning disabled, mildly mentally retarded, and low-achieving groups but is a strong predictor of membership in the behavior disorder group.

Two meta-analytic investigations have been conducted recently regarding the social-behavioral correlates of students classified as learning disabled (Kavale & Forness, in press; Swanson & Malone, 1992). Swanson and Malone reviewed 39 studies and found that students with learning disabilities had poorer social problem-solving skills than 79% of nondisabled groups, were on task less than 80% of nondisabled groups, and had more interfering problem behaviors (internalizing and externalizing) than 78% of nondisabled students. In a more comprehensive meta-analytic investigation, Kavale and Forness reviewed 152 studies involving 6,353 students classified as either learning disabled or non-learning-disabled. The results of this meta-analysis yielded effect sizes similar to the Swanson and Malone investigation. Overall, students with learning disabilities had poorer social skills than 75% of their nondisabled peers.

An investigation by McConaughy and colleagues (McConaughy, Mattison, & Peterson, 1994) used both teacher and parent ratings of externalizing and internalizing problem behaviors gathered from three states with groups of children classified as behavior disordered or learning disabled and normal controls. Results indicated that 73% of the students with behavior disorders and almost 79% of those with learning disabilities could be accurately classified.

In summary, students with mild disabilities have poorer social skills than 75% to 90% of their nondisabled peers, with students having behavior disorders being the most deficient. It is safe to conclude that social skills deficits and interfering problem behavior excesses of students with behavior disorders represent part of the diagnostic criteria for defining this group. Social skills deficits appear to characterize all mild disability groups; however, it is unclear whether this represents a cause, an effect, or a concomitant of a mild disability.

Behavior Correlates Based on Sociometric Status

A great deal of research has focused on the behavioral correlates of different sociometric status groups. One of the most comprehensive narrative reviews of this literature was conducted by Coie, Dodge, and Kupersmidt (1990). These authors found that the best behavioral predictors or correlates of *rejected* sociometric status are behaviors fitting an externalizing behaviors pattern (e.g., aggressive, disruptive, and noncompliant behaviors) whereas children classified as *neglected* tended to engage in more solitary play and to engage in less aggressive social interactions. Children classified as *controversial* share many of the behaviors of rejected children (i.e., externalizing behaviors) but are liked by about half of their peers.

The most comprehensive meta-analytic review of the behavioral correlates in the two-dimensional sociometric status literature was conducted by Newcomb, Bukowski, and Pattee (1993). These authors reviewed 41 studies conducted with children between 5 and 12 years of age and contrasted popular, rejected, neglected, and/or controversial sociometric-status groups with average sociometric-status comparison groups. This review categorized the behavioral correlates of sociometric status into three areas: (a) *sociability* (e.g., initiating, communicating, problem solving, positive social behavior), (b) *aggression* (e.g., disruptive, negative affect/emotion, fighting), and (c) *withdrawal* (e.g., loneliness, depression, anxiety).

The behavioral profile of children classified as rejected indicated higher levels of aggression and withdrawal coupled with lower levels of positive social behavior and cognitive skills (Newcomb et al., 1993). In contrast, controversial children displayed a similar pattern of aggression; however, they exhibited much higher levels of positive social behavior than rejected children. In fact, controversial children are equal to popular children in social interactions, positive social actions, positive traits, and friendship skills. Newcomb et al. suggested that the aggressive behavior pattern of controversial children is balanced by their relatively high levels of prosocial and cognitive skills. This review also showed that controversial children inhibit their aggressive behaviors with adults (teachers and parents) but not with peers. This same pattern of aggressive behavior is not true of rejected children. Newcomb et al. indicated that neglected children show the fewest differences from average children. In fact, these authors argue that children classified as neglected lack a clear behavioral profile and are simply choosing to interact at a lower level than other sociometric groups.

Alternative Actions

The foregoing review suggests that many children who are poorly accepted or rejected by peers as well as those with mild disabilities may require some form of social skills interventions that will enhance the quality of their social interactions and improve their peer relationships. As mentioned earlier, the school is an ideal setting for teaching social skills based on its accessibility by children, teachers, and parents. Fundamentally, social skills intervention takes place in schools both informally and formally using either *universal* or *selected* intervention procedures. *Informal* social skills intervention is based on the notion of incidental learning which takes advantage of naturally occurring behavioral incidents or events to teach appropriate social behavior. Most social skills instruction in home, school, and community settings can be characterized as informal or incidental. Thousands of behavioral incidents occur in home, school, and community settings creating an opportunity for making each of these behavioral incidents a successful learning experience.

Formal social skills instruction can take place in a classroom setting in which the entire class is exposed to a social skills "curriculum" or in a small-group setting removed from the classroom. Walker, Colvin, and Ramsey (1995) refer to these teaching formats as *universal* and *selected* interventions, respectively. Universal interventions are not unlike vaccinations, school-wide discipline plans, or school rules in that they are designed to affect all children under the same conditions. Universal interventions are designed to prevent more serious problems from developing later in a student's school career and beyond (i.e., primary prevention). Selected interventions are typically conducted with children who have been identified as being at risk for behavior problems and are based on an individual assessment of a student's social skills deficits and problem behavior excesses. These interventions are undertaken to prevent existing behavior problems from developing into more serious behavior problems (i.e., secondary or tertiary prevention).

Universal social skills interventions focus on impacting all students using the same procedures in the same setting (Walker et al., 1995). For example, a class-wide social skills intervention program designed to teach conflict resolution and social problem solving is an example of a universal social skill intervention. Other examples of universal social skills intervention programs include *The Prepare Curriculum,* (Goldstein, 1988), *The ACCEPTS PROGRAM* (Walker et al., 1983), and *Social Skills Intervention Guide* (Elliott & Gresham, 1992). These universal interventions are likely to be used as a means of primary prevention rather than secondary or tertiary prevention. *Selected* social skills interventions, on the other hand, are designed for a select or target group of students using individually tailored intervention procedures based on the specific social skills deficits of these targeted students. Examples of selected intervention procedures are use of differential reinforcement and response cost with a target student, using positive practice to teach appropriate verbal interactions with other students, or teaching self-control skills to a selected group of impulsive and aggressive youngsters. Selected social skills interventions are more likely to be used at the levels of secondary and tertiary prevention.

Efficacy of Social Skills Training

Obviously, an important question is whether social skills training (SST) is effective in promoting the acquisition, performance, and generalization of prosocial behaviors and in facilitating peer acceptance. Several qualitative and quantitative (meta-analyses) reviews have summarized and integrated the outcomes of controlled SST investigations.

I conducted a qualitative review of the literature on SST with children having behavioral and intellectual disabilities (Gresham, 1981). Based on this review of 70 studies, I concluded that SST procedures using manipulation of antecedents, manipulation of consequences, modeling, and coaching were effective in teaching social skills to children. The evidence for generalization and maintenance of trained social skills was considerable weaker.

I also reviewed 33 studies that used cognitive-behavioral techniques to teach social skills (Gresham, 1985). The cognitive-behavioral techniques included modeling, coaching, treatment packages (treatments in combination), and social problem solving. These techniques were evaluated across seven criteria: (a) subject characteristics, (b) treatment specification, (c) type of outcome measure, (d) statistical analysis, (e) experimental design, (f) generalization, and (g) cost effectiveness. I concluded that some cognitively based techniques, particularly modeling and coaching, were effective in teaching social skills to children. The effects of self-instruction and social problem solving on the social relationships of children was not adequately demonstrated. Two major gaps were found in this literature: (a) lack of data on generalization and maintenance and (b) the tendency of cognitive-behavioral studies to use outcome measures lacking social validity (e.g., social problem-solving tasks, behavioral role-play measures, measures of social cognition). There was little evidence in the 33 reviewed studies that cognitive-behavioral techniques lead to greater generalization and maintenance than the applied behavior analysis studies reviewed earlier (Gresham, 1981).

McIntosh, Vaughn, and Zaragoza (1991) reviewed 22 SST studies conducted with 572 children having learning disabilities (ages 5–19 years). SST strategies primarily included combinations of modeling, coaching, behavioral rehearsal, role-playing, and feedback. This review indicated that 14 out of 22 studies (63.6%) showed positive effects. There was a significant positive relationship between the amount of SST and intervention effects. Specifically, studies showing positive effects of intervention provided over three times as much SST as studies not showing intervention effects. McIntosh et al. also re-

ported that studies matching social skills deficits with intervention strategies were more likely to show positive results. Zaragoza, Vaughn, and McIntosh (1991) reported similar effects of SST in their review of 27 studies conducted with children having behavior disorders.

In a meta-analysis, Schneider (1992) reviewed 79 SST controlled-outcome studies published between 1942 and 1987. Effect size estimates indicated that SST was most effective with withdrawn children and least effective with children described as aggressive and unpopular. In terms of outcome variables, SST produced the largest effect on social interaction and lower effect sizes for aggression and peer acceptance. SST procedures based on operant strategies produced the largest effect sizes. Schneider concluded that between 60% and 65% of the children receiving SST improved their social behavior compared to 30% to 35% of children not receiving such training. Hanson (1989) reported similar effect sizes in a review of SST studies with children in grades K-12.

A more recent meta-analysis of the SST literature was conducted by Beelmann, Pfingsten, and Losel (1994) in which 49 studies between 1981 and 1990 were reviewed. These authors reported somewhat smaller effect sizes than Schneider (1992) and demonstrated that the effects of SST varied according to the type of outcome variable content (social-cognitive skills, social interaction skills, social adjustment, and self-related cognitions/affect). As expected, social problem-solving interventions produced the largest effect sizes on social-cognitive skills but had virtually no effect on more socially valid outcomes of social-interaction skills, social adjustment, or self-related cognitions/affect. This finding is consistent with my 1985 review of cognitive-behavioral social skills interventions. Multimodal, behavioral SST interventions had moderate effects on social cognitive skills and social interaction skills but virtually no effect on social adjustment or self-related cognitions/affect. Similar to previous reviews, Beelman et al. concluded that evidence for generalization and maintenance of SST effects was weak.

In summary, both qualitative and quantitative reviews of the SST literature suggest that it can be an effective intervention for changing social behavior. However, there is far less support for the generalization of these changes across settings, situations, persons, and time. A similar weakness was uncovered by DuPaul and Eckert (1994) in their review of generalization effects of studies using commercially available SST programs. The reasons for SST not producing more generalized effects, in part, can be attributed to three things: (a) failure of researchers and practitioners to "match" social skills instructional strategies with specific types of social skills deficits, (b) failure to adequately program for generalization, and (c) using "weak" treatments in restricted settings to change social behavior. These issues will be addressed later in this chapter.

Paramount Principles and Objectives of Social Skills Training

Social skills instruction should emphasize the acquisition, performance, and generalization of prosocial behaviors and the reduction and/or elimination of competing interfering problem behaviors. A large number of intervention procedures have been identified for teaching social skills to children. These procedures are based on the 10 paramount principles of social skills training presented in Table 1. These principles were derived from a comprehensive review of the SST literature and the work of Walker et al. (1994).

SST has four primary objectives: (a) promoting skill acquisition, (b) enhancing skill performance, (c) reducing or removing interfering problem behaviors, and (d) facilitating the generalization and maintenance of social skills. It should be noted that children will likely have some combination of acquisition and performance deficits, some of which may be accompanied by interfering problem behaviors and others which will not. Thus, any given child may require some combination of acquisition, performance, and behavior reduction strategies. All children will require procedures to facilitate the generalization and maintenance of social skills. Based on space constraints in this chapter, only a brief description is given of the first three objectives of SST. Specific procedures for all four objectives are listed in Table 2. A more comprehensive discussion of SST can be found in two chapters in *Best Practices in School Psychology-III* (Elliott, Racine, & Bruce, 1995; Gresham, 1995). A more complete discussion of facilitating generalization of trained social

skills is provided because this is the most consistent weakness of SST programs.

Social skills intervention procedures based on acquisition deficits assume that the child either does not have the skill in his or her repertoire or is missing a particular step in performing a social skill sequence. As such, it is extremely important that an adequate social skills assessment be conducted prior to SST. Table 2 lists the primary SST procedures for promoting skill acquisition.

Procedures for enhancing the performance of social skills are based on the arrangement of antecedents and consequences for social behavior. This suggests that most social skills interventions for most children will take place in naturalistic environments (e.g., classrooms, playgrounds) rather than in small, pullout SST groups. As such, most social skills interventions can be facilitated by using a consultative framework for interventions implemented in classrooms or other naturalistic settings. Specific strategies for accomplishing this objective are listed in Table 2.

Although the focus in SST is clearly upon the development and refinement of prosocial behaviors, many children fail to acquire or perform these prosocial behaviors because of the presence of interfering problem behaviors. In the case of acquisition deficits, the interfering problem behavior(s) may block social skill acquisition. For instance, self-stimulatory behaviors of an autistic child may prevent the development of eye contact and conversation skills. In performance deficits, aggressive behavior might be performed instead of prosocial behavior because aggressive behavior is more effective in producing desired outcomes. For example, a preschooler may learn that grabbing a toy from a peer is more effective than asking for the toy. Table 2 lists procedures of removing or reducing interfering problem behaviors.

Table 1 *Paramount Principles of Social Skills Training*

1. Social skills are learned behaviors.
2. Social skills can be either acquisition deficits or performance deficits.
3. Social skills are highly contextualistic and relativistic.
4. Social skills are best taught in naturalistic settings and situations.
5. Social skills are governed by the Principle of Social Reciprocity.
6. Social skills should be taught by the same procedures used to teach academic skills.
7. There is a direct, positive relationship between the amount and quality (integrity) of social skills training and the amount of change in social behavior.
8. Social skills training strategies must be accompanied by reductive techniques for the reduction or elimination of interfering problem behaviors.
9. Social skills training must be supplemented by behavioral rehearsal opportunities,performance feedback, and contingency systems in naturalistic settings to promote theiroccurrence, fluency, and mastery.
10. For social skills to be integrated into a behavioral repertoire, they must be as or more efficient and reliable in producing desired outcomes as competing behaviors.

Facilitating Generalization: Form and Function

At its most basic level, only two processes are essential to all behavioral interventions: *discrimination* and *generalization.* Discrimination and generalization represent polar opposites on the continuum of behavior change. Discrimination represents the control of behavior by some stimuli but not others, and it is highly adaptive and essential for survival. For example, people do not put gasoline on kitchen fires but do put it in cars. One's ability to generalize across various aspects of the environment gives some stability, consistency, and efficiency to behavior (Edelstein, 1989). Because the environment is constantly changing, it is improbable that an individual will always contact stimuli in identical forms. Thus, you cannot count on learning how to use all variations of telephones in order to use unfamiliar telephones; you must be able to generalize.

Table 2 *Social Skills Training Objectives and Strategies*

I. PROMOTING SKILL ACQUISITION
- A. Modeling
- B. Coaching
- C. Behavioral Rehearsal

II. ENHANCING SKILL PERFORMANCE
- A. Manipulation of Antecedents
  1. Peer initiation strategies
  2. Sociodramatic play activities
  3. Proactive classroom management practices
  4. Peer tutoring
  5. Incidental teaching
- B. Manipulation of Consequences
  1. Contingency contracting
  2. Group-oriented contingency systems
  3. School/home notes

III. REMOVING INTERFERING PROBLEM BEHAVIORS
- A. Differential Reinforcement
  1. Differential reinforcement of other behavior (DRO)
  2. Differential reinforcement of low rates of behavior (DRL)
  3. Differential reinforcement of incompatible behavior (DRI)
- B. Overcorrection
  1. Restitution
  2. Positive practice
- C. Response Cost
- D. Time-out
  1. Nonexclusion (contingent observation)
  2. Exclusion
- E. Systematic Desensitization
- F. Flooding/Exposure

IV. FACILITATING GENERALIZATION
- A. Topographical Generalization
  1. Training diversely
     a. Use sufficient stimulus exemplars
     b. Teach sufficient response exemplars
     c. Make antecedents less discriminable (train "loosely")
     d. Make consequences less discriminable ("thin" reinforcement schedule)
  2. Exploit functional contingencies
     a. Teach relevant behaviors
     b. Modify environments supporting interfering problem behaviors
     c. Recruit natural communities of reinforcement
     d. Reinforce occurrences of generalization
  3. Incorporate functional mediators
     a. Incorporate common salient social stimuli
     b. Incorporate common salient physical stimuli
     c. Incorporate salient self-mediated physical stimuli
     d. Incorporate salient self-mediated verbal or covert stimuli
- B. Functional Generalization
  1. Identify strong competing stimuli
  2. Identify strong competing interfering problem behaviors
  3. Identify functionally equivalent socially skilled behaviors
  4. Increase reliability and efficiency of socially skilled behaviors (build fluency)
  5. Decrease reliability and efficiency of interfering problem behaviors

A major problem confronting social skills trainers is that they have been relatively successful in getting some behaviors to occur in one place for a limited period of time. In other words, SST has been highly effective in teaching *discriminations.* On the other hand, getting social behavior to occur in more than one place for an extended period of time has been more difficult to achieve. That is, generalizations of SST across participants, settings, behaviors, and time have been largely unsuccessful mainly because, the way social skills are taught works in almost direct opposition to generalization. That is, social skills are taught under conditions of discrimination (e.g., do this here but not there, or do this but not that) rather than under conditions leading to ultimate generalization (e.g., here are 10 situations where you can do this or here are 10 things you can do in this situation).

Generalization is typically regarded from two perspectives. One emphasizes behavioral *form* or *topography* and the other emphasizes behavioral *function* (Edelstein, 1989; Stokes & Osnes, 1989). The topographical description of generalization refers to the occurrence of relevant behaviors under different, nontraining conditions (Stokes & Osnes). The so-called "relevant" behaviors (e.g., social skills) can occur across settings/situations (setting generalization), behaviors (response generalization), and/or time (maintenance). The topographical approach to generalization suggests that relevant behaviors occurred in other settings or were maintained over time but does not indicate *why* this occurred. Topographical generalization merely describes an observed outcome or correlate of a given SST intervention program.

The *functional* approach to generalization consists of two types: (a) stimulus generalization which is the occurrence of the same behavior under variations of the original stimulus (the greater the difference between the training stimulus and subsequent stimuli, the less generalization) and (b) response generalization which is the control of multiple behaviors by the same stimulus (a functional response class).

Stokes and Osnes (1989) suggest that topographical and functional generalization answers two fundamental questions: (a) Did the social skill occur in generalized circumstances (i.e., across settings, situations, persons, and time)? and (b) What are the functional variables that explain that generalization? Current knowledge sheds much more light on the former than on the latter. Why is it that the literature consistently shows that SST interventions show behavior change in some situations for a limited period of time but do not show generalized behavior changes? One feasible explanation is that the training environment is unlike the generalization environment (i.e., the generalization environment is too far out on the generalization gradient). Errors in response generalization can be explained by the fact that social skills being taught are not part of a desired functional response class.

Part IV of Table 2 presents 12 specific topographical generalization strategies listed under three broad categories: (a) training diversely, (b) exploiting functional contingencies, and (c) incorporating functional mediators. These strategies can be used to increase the odds that SST will produce generalized responding (see Stokes & Osnes, 1989). However, these strategies are not based on the functional control of behavior. In spite of these suggestions and strategies, the bottom line in topographical generalization is that it is correlational rather than functional. If behavior does generalize, it is not usually known exactly why and if behavior does not generalize, it is not known exactly why not. This is certainly better than the "Train and Hope" approach to generalization (train the behavior and hope it generalizes), but it may not inform future efforts in programming for generalization.

One way of understanding generalization errors, *functionally,* is within the context of competing behaviors. Horner, Dunlap, and Koegel (1988) offer the following scenario: A child has acquired a new, adaptive social skill and demonstrates excellent generalization across new situations. A new situation is presented that contains a strong, competing stimulus. This competing stimulus is likely to elicit old, undesirable behavior. The practical effect is the new adaptive social skill does not generalize to situations containing the strong competing stimulus.

This situation would create no problems if the child did not have to encounter environments with the strong competing stimulus. However, this is not always possible such as when the strong competing stimulus is a classmate or a teacher. The notion of strong competing stimuli may be why so many problem drinkers "fall off the wagon" (bars and alcohol represent strong competing stimuli for undesirable drinking behavior).

Generalization errors result from inadequate stimulus control over social skills relative to interfering problem behaviors. One reason, among many, that socially skilled behaviors may fail to generalize is because the newly taught behavior is masked or overpowered by older and stronger competing behaviors. This is an important concept for understanding why some behaviors generalize to new situations but not others and why a behavior that has been maintained well for a long time may suddenly deteriorate.

Competing behaviors are performed instead of socially skilled behaviors often because the competing behavior is more *efficient* than the socially skilled behavior in obtaining desired outcomes. For instance, whining and grabbing for food by young children is more efficient in obtaining food than politely asking and waiting for food. Horner et al. (1988) have termed this the *functional equivalence of behavior.* That is, two or more behaviors can be equal in their ability to produce reinforcement. Thus, with many preschoolers, grabbing toys is more efficient than asking for toys, and pushing peers out of the way is more efficient than asking them to move.

In summary, current research would suggest that all things being equal, preexisting behaviors are likely to compete successfully with newly trained social skills if the preexisting behaviors lead to more powerful or immediate reinforcers or more efficiently produce the same reinforcement as the social skill alternative (i.e., they are more cost-beneficial). Horner et al. (1988) suggest that the following questions be answered when attempting to program for functional generalization:

(a) *Does the child engage in undesirable behaviors that achieve the same result as the socially skilled target behavior? In other words, are the undesirable behaviors equally or perhaps more functional in obtaining reinforcement? For example, does pushing a peer out of line achieve the same result as asking him or her to move?*

(b) *If undesirable behaviors are equally or more functional, are they more efficient and reliable in achieving that function? That is, do the undesirable behaviors achieve the same reinforcer more quickly and more consistently that the socially skilled alternative behavior? For instance, grabbing a toy may be more efficient and reliable in obtaining the toy than requesting it.*

(c) *Are competing behaviors correlated with the presence of a specific stimulus (e.g., a person, place, or thing) or are they associated with the presence of many stimuli and situations? For example, does the child only hit others during free play, but not other times?*

Answers to these questions imply two classes of intervention strategies: (a) Decrease the efficiency and reliability of competing, inappropriate behaviors and (b) Increase the efficiency and reliability of socially skilled alternative behaviors. The former can be accomplished by many of the procedures listed in Table 2 under Removing Interfering Problem Behaviors. The latter can be achieved by spending more time and effort in building the *fluency* of trained social skills using combinations of modeling, coaching, and, most importantly, behavioral rehearsal.

Generalization should never be considered an afterthought with respect to SST. The most important and functional question is how to get social skills to generalize across settings, situations, persons, and time. Social skills that do not generalize are not functional for individuals. Topographical approaches based on training diversely, exploiting functional contingencies, and incorporating functional mediators may be effective. However, the functional approach based on competing behaviors and functional equivalents has more promise for facilitating generalization of trained social skills.

Summary

Social skills are socially acceptable behaviors that enable a person to interact effectively with others and to avoid socially unacceptable or aversive responses from others. Social skills are specific behaviors that allow individuals to perform competently on a social task. Social competence, on the other hand, is an evaluative term based on judgments by significant others (e.g., peers, teachers, parents) that a given behavioral performance was socially skilled.

Children have to negotiate two important social-behavioral adjustments upon school entry: teacher-related and peer-related. Teacher-related adjustment reflects the extent to which children meet demands of teachers and accomplish tasks in classroom settings whereas peer-related adjustment are behaviors essential to the formation of friendships, peer acceptance, and the resolution of conflicts. These two adjustment domains require different behaviors and have differential outcomes for children. Some children cannot successfully negotiate these adjustments because of either acquisition deficits (Can't do) or performance deficits (Won't do).

Social skills training (SST) strategies designed to remediate children's social skills deficits can be classified under four broad categories reflecting specific training objectives: (a) promoting skill acquisition, (b) enhancing skill performance, (c) removing interfering problem behaviors, and (d) facilitating generalization. The largest gap in the SST literature is the failure to adequately demonstrate the generalization and maintenance of trained social skills. Procedures based on a functional approach to generalization are recommended to accomplish the goal of producing generalized changes in children's social behavior.

Author's Note

The present work was supported, in part, by Grants No. H023C20002 and H023C30103 from the Office of Special Education Research, U.S. Department of Education. Opinions expressed herein are those of the author's alone and should not be interpreted as having agency endorsement.

Recommended Resources

Alberg, J., Petry, C., & Eller, S. (1994). *A social skills planning guide.* Longmont, CO; Sopris West.
This practical and clearly written guide to planning social skills assessment and intervention programs is invaluable to the practitioner. This guide is divided into three chapters and an appendix. Chapter 1 entitled "The Need for Social Skills Instruction" defines social skills, discusses reasons students may lack social skills, gives a rationale why schools should be in the business of teaching social skills, describes cultural issues in social skills instruction, and the benefits of teaching social skills. Chapter 2 entitled "Social Skills Instruction" describes types of social skills deficits, discusses how one determines which social skills to teach, reviews methods of social skills instruction, indicates how social skills instruction can be integrated within an existing curriculum, and identifies resources to assist in teaching social skills. Chapter 3 entitled "Selecting a Social Skills Program" discusses the identification and prioritization of social skills needs of students, choosing social skills programs, implementation issues, and social skills program-evaluation strategies. The appendix provides summaries of eight social skills programs for preschool, elementary, middle/junior high, and senior high/postsecondary programs.

Asher, S., & Coie, J. (Eds.). (1990). *Peer rejection in childhood.* New York: Cambridge University Press.
This book is one of the most comprehensive and scholarly treatments of peer rejection, its causes and correlates, and strategies for remediation. Written from a developmental perspective, this book contains 13 chapters written by many world authorities in the area of children's social competence. The book is divided into five parts: Part I reviews the behavioral characteristics of peer-rejected children in three chapters, and Part II discusses social-cognitive processes. Part III describes parent-child relations and peer rejection. Part IV indicates the consequences of peer rejection, and Part V reviews issues in social competence intervention research. The book concludes with a chapter by John Coie offering a theory of peer rejection. This book is a "must read" for serious students of social competence and peer rejection in children and adolescents.

Walker, H., Colvin, G., & Ramsey, E. (1995). *Antisocial behavior in school: Strategies and best practices.* Pacific Grove, CA: Brooks/Cole.
Probably the best book ever written on the understanding, identification, assessment, and intervention with children displaying antisocial behavior patterns. This book is one of the most clearly written, practical, and scholarly treatises on this subject available. The book contains 13 chapters and three appendices. It is full of tables, figures, examples, and case studies that make the understanding of this complex behavior pattern clear. Chapters 1–4 deal with descriptions of antisocial behavior characteristics, issues in effective school-based interventions for these problems, and the acting-out behavior cycle and its management. Chapters 5–8 discuss establishing a school-wide discipline plan, managing the classroom environment, using instructional approaches to teaching adaptive behavior patterns, and managing antisocial behavior on the playground. Chapters 9 and 10 review social skills assessment, intervention, and generalization strategies. Chapter 11 deals with parent in-

volvement, Chapter 12 presents case studies, and Chapter 13 describes school violence, gangs, and school safety. Every school psychologist, school counselor, school principal, and teacher who deals with antisocial children should read this book.

References

Beelman, A., Pfingsten, U., & Losel, F. (1994). Effects of training social competence in children: A meta-analysis of recent evaluation studies. *Journal of Clinical Child Psychology, 23,* 260–271.

Coie, J., Dodge, K., & Kupersmidt, J. (1990). Peer group behavior and social status. In S. Asher & J. Coie (Eds.), *Peer rejection in childhood* (pp. 17–59). New York: Cambridge University Press.

DuPaul, G., & Eckert, T. (1994). The effects of social skills curricula: Now you see them, now you don't. *School Psychology Quarterly, 9,* 113–132.

Edelstein, B. (1989). Generalization: Terminological, methodological, and conceptual issues. *Behavior Therapy, 20,* 311–324.

Elliott, S. N., & Gresham, F. M. (1992). *Social skills intervention guide.* Circle Pines, MN: American Guidance Service.

Elliott, S. N., Racine, C., & Bruce, R. (1995). Preschool social skills training. In A. Thomas & J. Grimes (Eds.), *Best practices in school psychology-III* (pp. 1009–1020). Washington, DC: National Association of School Psychologists.

Eme, R. (1979). Sex differences in childhood psychopathology: A review. *Psychological Bulletin, 86,* 574–595.

Forness, S., & Knitzer, J. (1992). A new proposed definition and terminology to replace "serious emotional disturbance" in Individuals With Disabilities Education Act. *School Psychology Review, 21,* 12–20.

Goldstein, A. (1988). *The Prepare Curriculum.* Champaign, IL: Research Press.

Gresham, F. M. (1981). Social skills training with handicapped children: A review. *Review of Educational Research, 51,* 139–176.

Gresham, F. M. (1983). Social validity in the assessment of children's social skills: Establishing standards for social competency. *Journal of Psychoeducational Assessment, 1,* 299–307.

Gresham, F. M. (1985). Utility of cognitive-behavioral procedures for social skills training with children. *Journal of Abnormal Child Psychology, 13,* 411–423.

Gresham, F. M. (1992). Social skills and learning disabilities: Causal, concomitant, or correlational? *School Psychology Review, 21,* 348–360.

Gresham, F. M. (1995). Social skills training. In A. Thomas & J. Grimes (Eds.), *Best practices in school psychology-III* (pp. 1021–1029). Washington, DC: National Association of School Psychologists.

Gresham, F. M., & Elliott, S. N. (1990). *Social Skills Rating System.* Circle Pines, MN: American Guidance Service.

Gresham, F. M., Elliott, S. N., & Black F. L. (1987). Teacher-rated social skills of mainstreamed mildly handicapped and nonhandicapped children. *School Psychology Review, 16,* 78–88.

Gresham, F. M., & Noell, G. H. (1993). Documenting the effectiveness of consultation outcomes. In J. Zins, T. Kratochwill, & S. Elliott (Eds.), *Handbook of consultation services for children: Applications in educational and clinical settings* (pp. 249–273). San Francisco: Jossey-Bass.

Gresham, F. M., & Reschly, D. J. (1988). Issues in the conceptualization and assessment of social skills in the mildly handicapped. In T. Kratochwill (Ed.), *Advances in school psychology* (vol. 6, pp. 203–247). Hillsdale, NJ: Lawrence Erlbaum.

Hanson, R. (1989). Social skill training: A critical meta-analytic review (Doctoral dissertation, Texas Women's University, 1988). *Dissertation Abstracts International, 50,* 903A.

Hersh, R., & Walker, H. M. (1983). Great expectations: Making schools effective for all students. *Policy Studies Review, 2,* 147–188.

Hinshaw, S. (1992). Externalizing behavior problems and academic underachievement in childhood and adolescence: Causal relationships and underlying mechanisms. *Psychological Bulletin, 111,* 125–155.

Horner, R., Dunlap, G., & Koegel, R. (Eds.). (1988). *Generalization and maintenance: Lifestyle changes in applied settings.* Baltimore: Paul H. Brookes.

Kavale, K., & Forness, S. (in press). Social skill deficits and learning disabilities: A meta-analysis. *Journal of Learning Disabilities.*

Kazdin, A. (1987). Treatment of antisocial behavior in children: Current status and future directions. *Psychological Bulletin, 102,* 187–203.

Kistner, J., & Gatlin, D. (1989). Sociometric differences between learning disabled and nonhandicapped students: Effects of sex and race. *Journal of Educational Psychology, 81,* 118–120.

Kupersmidt, J., Coie, J., & Dodge, K. (1990). The role of peer relationships in the development of disorder. In S. Asher & J. Coie (Eds.), *Peer rejection in childhood* (pp. 274–308). New York: Cambridge University Press.

LaGreca, A. M., & Stone, W. (1990). Children with learning disabilities: The role of achievement in their social, personal, and behavioral functioning. In H. L. Swanson & B. Keogh (Eds.), *Learning disabilities: Theoretical and research issues* (pp. 333–352). Hillsdale, NJ: Lawrence Erlbaum.

MacMillan, D. L., Gresham, F. M., & Siperstein, G. (1993). Conceptual and psychometric concerns about the 1992 AAMR definition of mental retardation. *American Journal on Mental Retardation, 98,* 325–335.

McConaughy, S., Mattison, R., & Peterson, R. (1994). Behavioral/emotional problems of children with serious emotional disturbances and learning disabilities. *School Psychology Review, 23,* 81–98.

McFall, R. (1982). A review and reformulation of the concept of social skills. *Behavioral Assessment, 4,* 1–35.

McIntosh, R., Vaughn, S., & Zaragoza, N. (1991). A review of social interventions for students with learning disabilities. *Journal of Learning Disabilities, 24,* 451–458.

Merrell, K., Johnson, E., Merz, J., & Ring, E. (1992). Social competence of students with mild handicaps and low achievement: A comparative study. *School Psychology Review, 21,* 125–137.

Newcomb, A., Bukowski, W., & Pattee, L. (1993). Children's peer relations: A meta-analytic review of popular, rejected, neglected, controversial, and average sociometric status. *Psychological Bulletin, 113,* 99–128.

Noell, G. H., & Gresham, F. M. (1993). Functional outcome analysis: Do the benefits of consultation and prereferral intervention justify the costs? *School Psychology Quarterly, 8,* 200–226.

Oleweus, D. (1979). Stability of aggressive reaction patterns in males: A review. *Psychological Bulletin, 86,* 852–875.

Parker, J., & Asher, S. (1987). Peer relations and later personal adjustment: Are low-accepted children at risk? *Psychological Bulletin, 102,* 357–389.

Patterson, G., DeBaryshe, B., & Ramsey, E. (1989). A developmental perspective on antisocial behavior. *American Psychologist, 44,* 329–335.

Reid, J., & Patterson, G. (1991). Early prevention and intervention with conduct problems: A social interactional model for the integration of research and practice. In G. Stoner, M. Shinn, & H. Walker (Eds.), *Interventions for achievement and behavior problems* (pp. 715–740). Washington, DC: National Association of School Psychologists.

Robins, L. (1986). The consequences of conduct disorder in girls. In D. Oleweus, J. Block, & M. Radke-Yarrow (Eds.), *Development of antisocial and prosocial behavior: Research, theories, and issues* (pp. 385–414). San Diego: Academic Press.

Schneider, B. (1992). Didactic methods for enhancing children's peer relations: A quantitative review. *Clinical Psychology Review, 12,* 363–382.

Schwartz, I., & Baer, D. (1991). Social validity assessment: Is current practice state of the art? *Journal of Applied Behavior Analysis, 24,* 189–204.

Stokes, T., & Osnes, P. (1989). An operant pursuit of generalization. *Behavior Therapy, 25,* 429–432.

Swanson, H. L., & Malone, S. (1992). Social skills and learning disabilities: A meta-analysis of the literature. *School Psychology Review, 21,* 427–443.

Walker, H. M., Colvin, G., & Ramsey, E. (1995). *Antisocial behavior in school: Strategies and best practices.* Pacific Grove, CA: Brooks/Cole.

Walker, H. M., & McConnell, S. (1995). *Walker-McConnell Scale of Social Competence and School Adjustment, Elementary Version: User's Manual.* San Diego: Singular Publishing Group.

Walker, H. M., McConnell, S., & Clark, J. (1985). Social skills training in school settings: A model for the social integration of handicapped children into less restrictive settings. In R. McMahon & R. Peters (Eds.), *Childhood disorders: Behavioral developmental approaches* (pp. 140–168). New York: Brunner-Mazel.

Walker, H. M., McConnell, S., Holmes, D., Todis, B., Walker, J., & Golden, N. (1983). *The Walker Social Skills Curriculum: The ACCEPTS Program (A curriculum for children's effective peer and teacher skills).* Austin, TX: PRO-ED.

Walker, H. M., Irwin, L., Noell, J., & Singer, G. (1992). A construct score approach to the assessment of social competence: Rationale, technological considerations, and anticipated outcomes. *Behavior Modification, 16,* 448–474.

Walker, H. M., Schwarz, I., Nippold, M., Irwin, L., & Noell, J. (1994). Social skills in school-age children and youth: Issues and best practices in assessment and intervention. *Topics in Language Disorders: Pragmatic and Social Skills in School-Age Children and Adolescents, 14,* 70–82.

Walker, H. M., & Severson, H. (1992). *Systematic screening for behavior disorders.* Longmont, CO: Sopris West.

Zaragoza, N., Vaughn, S., & McIntosh, R. (1991). Social skills interventions and children with behavior problems: A review. *Behavioral Disorders, 16,* 260–275.

5

Socially Responsible Behavior

George G. Bear

University of Delaware

Cathy F. Telzrow

Cuyahoga Special Education Service Center

Ebenezer A. deOliveira

University of Delaware

Background

During a biweekly social skills training session, both Tim and Rick demonstrate the appropriate social skills of listening to the speaker and staying in one's seat. After receiving praise and a token, they return to their class, only to be sent to the principal's office an hour later for clowning around while the teacher was talking. For Tim, this was the first time he has ever been sent to the office, although not the first time he disobeyed class rules. For Rick, the office is a familiar setting. Although Tim and Rick's discrete actions are similar, the two boys exhibit remarkably different behavioral patterns. Tim generally complies with school rules but often questions, and sometimes disobeys, rules he views as being "ridiculous and unfair." Unlike Tim, Rick is almost always unprepared for class, rarely completes his homework, and frequently gets into trouble for more serious infractions of classroom rules, including fighting and stealing. Rick was referred to the social skills group as a means of treating behaviors associated with his conduct disorder. In contrast, Tim was nominated to participate as a prosocial model for the group. Despite their differences in behavioral patterns, this week both boys were described by their teacher as being "socially irresponsible."

This chapter is more about Tim than it is about Rick. Behaviors associated with Rick's conduct disorder are not the center of focus here because they are covered elsewhere in this volume (see Aggressive Behavior, Anger Control, Bullying, Conduct Disorders, Lying, Stealing). Likewise, prosocial behavior, another important dimension of socially responsible behavior, is not discussed extensively because this topic is addressed in the chapter "Prosocial Behavior." Instead, in this chapter we focus on children who possess exemplary social skills but who nevertheless exhibit common behaviors deemed "irresponsible" by teachers and parents.

Children who are socially responsible tend to follow school rules and conform to social role expectations (Ford, 1985). They also act prosocially: They share with others, help others, and cooperate with others (Wentzel, 1992). These behaviors are included typically under the rubric of social skills. In this chapter, however, we prefer the term *socially responsible behavior*. Unlike social skills, which refers to a wide range of observable and situation-specific social behaviors learned and maintained "through the processes of observational, instrumental (operant), and respondent (classical) learning" (Gresham, 1995, p. 1022), the term socially responsible behavior highlights the importance of *internalization*. Internalization refers to "taking over the values and attitudes of society as one's own so that socially acceptable behavior is motivated not by anticipation of external consequences but by intrinsic or internal factors" (Grusec & Goodnow, 1994, p. 4). Central among these internal factors are self-constructed, or self-chosen, *values, goals,* and *standards* (Bandura, 1989; Eisenberg, 1986; Grusec & Lytton, 1988).

For purposes of this chapter, *values* are preferences about ways of behaving, which tend to generalize across situations (Rokeach, 1973). Children who value, or fail to value, socially responsible behaviors hold certain beliefs and understandings about the desirability of such behaviors. For example, many aggressive children hold the belief that aggression is not wrong but an acceptable way of responding to a variety of situations (Guerra & Slaby, 1990), and they view the negative consequences of aggression to be of little importance (Boldizar, Perry, & Perry, 1989). *Goals* are closely related to values. As defined by Staub (1984, p. 243), goals are "cognitive orientations that are associated with the desirability of certain outcomes." Goals are largely directed by what one values. Common goals among aggressive children are dominance and revenge rather than the valued goal of affiliation, which characterizes nonaggressive children (Lochman, Wayland, & White, 1993).

Values and goals are important because they motivate children to pursue desired outcomes and to act in self-satisfying ways (Bandura, 1986, 1989). In this manner, values and goals also imply affect. For example, although their values and goals differ, it is likely that both Tim and Rick anticipate and experience self-satisfaction or pride when goals based on their values are achieved and self-dissatisfaction or guilt when their goals are not achieved.

To determine if Tim or Rick believe that they have achieved their personal goals, one must also examine their *standards*. Standards are the criteria individuals use to judge whether their behavior is consistent with their values and goals. Just as a child's values and goals might differ from those of the school, so too might the child's standards. Thus, Tim, and possibly Rick, might value good behavior and actually achieve their personal goals of "having a good day in school." However, because of differing personal standards, Rick's goal might be achieved simply by not being sent to the principal's office. For Tim, who generally holds higher self-standards, the same goal would be achieved if he simply were not reprimanded by the teacher. As such, in the realm of social behavior, self-regulation in achieving one's goals is not based solely on objective criteria but also on subjective standards of what constitutes "good," "bad," "right," and "wrong."

Values, goals, and standards provide both the foundation and motivation for self-regulatory behavior. They are transmitted primarily by the family but also by social and institutional systems (including schools, peers, mass media, religion, etc.). Socialization explains why children, in general, share similar values, goals, and standards. Social systems generally model and reward normative behaviors and discourage deviant ones. However, because values, goals, and standards, as well as behaviors, vary across and within systems, they are rarely uniform (Bandura, 1986).

Values, goals, and standards also differ among children because children play an active role in their adoption and construction. The predominant theories of social and moral development (i.e., social cognitive theory [Bandura, 1986]), social information processing theory (Dodge, 1986; Dodge & Crick, 1990), and cognitive developmental theory (Damon, 1977; Kohlberg, 1984; Turiel, 1983) differ in their explanations of the cognitive and emotional processes that account for responsible behavior. However, each agrees that children do not passively absorb what is modeled, taught, and rewarded in society. Instead, children interpret and add meaning to environmental events, constructing their own values, goals, and standards. Moreover, as they develop, children increasingly monitor their own behaviors, inhibiting socially inappropriate behaviors and exhibiting prosocial behaviors

that are intentional and consistent with their own values, goals, and standards. When such consistency occurs in the absence of external monitors, sanctions, and rewards, socially responsible behavior, or self-regulation, is in place (Bandura, 1991; Kopp, 1987).

The teaching of socially responsible values and behavior has long been an important function of America's educational system. For example, Wentzel (1991a) documented a 150-year commitment to the promotion of social-responsibility goals by America's schools and argued that "the development of social responsibility in the form of citizenship skills and moral character is often considered to be a primary function of schooling" (p. 1). Despite recent objections to the teaching of values in schools (Manno, 1995) and debates over how values should be taught (Leming, 1993), both the government and the general public still expect that social responsibility will be taught in the public schools. This was reflected recently in a Gallup Poll (Elam & Rose, 1995) and in the U. S. Department of Education encouraging schools (via grants) to develop programs that teach six social and moral values: responsibility, respect, justice and fairness, trustworthiness, caring, and civic virtue and citizenship (*Federal Register,* March 13, 1995).

In addition to being important to cultivate in its own right, there is ample evidence that socially responsible behavior correlates positively with academic achievement (Wentzel, 1991a; 1991b, 1993). Wentzel (1991a) offers two explanations for this relationship: socially responsible behavior (a) helps create safe, orderly, and positive school environments that facilitate learning and interpersonal relationships, and (b) motivates students to become more engaged in learning activities. For example, striving to be cooperative and compliant facilitates the expression of achievement-oriented behaviors. Indeed, Wentzel (1993) reported that school interventions intended to increase socially responsible behavior result in higher achievement levels, although the reverse is not true (i.e., academic enrichment does not increase social responsibility). Research also indicates that successful students pursue both academic and social goals simultaneously (Wentzel, 1993). Those who pursue only social goals (e.g., to be compliant and responsible) do less well in school (Wentzel, 1991b, 1992).

Socially responsible behavior also is important for developing and maintaining positive peer relations. Numerous studies have linked peer acceptance and friendships to various social behaviors, especially the presence of prosocial behavior and the absence of chronic antisocial behaviors (see Peer Relations, this volume). Note that it is chronic antisocial behavior, and not occasional aggression or questioning and disobeying of classroom rules, that predicts social rejection. For example, in Wentzel's (1994) study of sixth and seventh graders, the pursuit of academic prosocial goals (e.g., helping classmates) correlated positively with peer acceptance, but a strict pursuit of rule-following goals correlated negatively (but positively to teacher acceptance).

Studies also have linked peer acceptance and rejection to peer perceptions of responsibility for one's behavior. Graham and Hoehn (1995) showed that a primary reason why aggressive children are rejected by peers is that, as early as first grade, peers perceived aggressive children as being responsible for their behavior problems and thus deserving of anger (but not sympathy). Withdrawn children, who were more socially accepted than their aggressive counterparts, were not perceived as responsible for their behavior and thus were judged to be deserving of sympathy, not anger. Juvonen (1991) found similar results in a sample of sixth graders. More anger, less sympathy, and less acceptance and anticipated social support were shown toward deviant peers perceived to be responsible for their behavior problems (e.g., aggression, bragging) than toward deviant peers judged not to be responsible for either shyness or a physical disability.

In short, social responsibility should be a topic of interest to school psychologists and other school personnel because (a) it is at the crux of citizenship development, a traditional goal of American schools, and (b) it facilitates both academic learning and positive peer relations.

Development

Influence of Social-Cognitive Abilities and Habits

Over the course of development, emphasis in socialization tends to shift from the direct teaching of social skills necessary for self-regulation to inculcating the desire to self-regulate (Grusec & Goodnow, 1994). As such, internal values, goals, and standards become increasingly important. This shift in emphasis coincides with increased complexity and sophistication in social cognitive abilities, especially during the early elementary grades (ages 6–8; Yeates & Selman, 1989). Central among social cognitive abilities that continue to develop from the early elementary school years through adolescence are perspective taking, sociomoral reasoning, and social conventional reasoning as shown in the developmental theories and research of, among others, Damon (1977), Eisenberg (1986), Kohlberg (1984), and Turiel (1983). These researchers have found that the development of social cognitive abilities largely accounts for the following:

- Increased understanding of the intentions and perspectives of others.
- Decreased unilateral respect for authority and rules.
- Decreased belief that rules are to be followed because punishment is inevitable.

- Increased mutual respect for rules and obligations and the understanding that rules are alterable.
- Increased understanding that "just" rules are fair to everyone: A rule is not fair simply because it is dictated by an authority.
- Increased use of social comparisons in evaluating one's behavior and a related desire to conform to social expectations of others (which may be those of the peer group or those of respected adults).
- Increased understanding that rules foster cooperation and are needed to coordinate and maintain social order.
- A shift from a preconventional hedonistic "seek rewards, avoid punishment" perspective to conventional sociomoral reasoning that reflects a concern about others and the social order.

With age, children also become more competent in their use of specific, social information-processing skills, which increase in sophistication. For example, Dodge and Price (1994) found increased skills in encoding of hostile and nonhostile cues, interpreting hostile intent, generating more behavioral responses, endorsing aggressive responses less, and enacting a skill.

Although the relationships among the social cognitive variables just enumerated are often complex, as are the relations to behavior, each has been theoretically and empirically linked to socially responsible behavior either in the classroom or at home. Correlations between such measures of social-cognitive abilities and socially responsible classroom behavior tend to fall only in the .30's (e.g., Bear, 1989; Eisenberg, 1986; Geiger & Turiel, 1983) but are higher when specific, social information-processing skills are matched with specific problem situations (Dodge & Price, 1994). Stronger relations should not be expected given the complexity of relations between thought and action and given that the variance in behavior is explained by a multitude of situational and individual factors (Baumeister, Heatherton, & Tice, 1994; Eisenberg, 1988). As Eisenberg notes (1988, p. 483), these additional factors include "(a) situational factors (e.g., cost of assisting, likelihood of disapproval for aggression); (b) other personal factors (e.g., self-identity with regard to helpfulness or aggressiveness, level of self-esteem and self-focus); (c) cognitive-evaluative processes (e.g., evaluation of the expected utility of a behavior, attributions regarding the cause of another's aggression or need for assistance, beliefs about expectations of one's reference group); and (d) relevant personal competencies (e.g., knowledge of skills or strategies for carrying out a given behavior, sense of self-efficacy)."

Increased complexity and sophistication in social cognitive abilities also coincides with increased stability and consistency in behavior (Huesmann, Guerra, Miller,

& Zilli, 1992). Note, however, that the correlation does not imply causation: Most developmental theorists agree that the thought-action relation is reciprocal. For example, the direct teaching and modeling of habits of socially appropriate behavior is critical to internalization, especially during the early years of childhood when social-cognitive abilities are limited and externally oriented methods of discipline often are necessary. As argued by Perry and Perry (1983), these habits continue to serve as the foundation for good behavior as the child becomes older. However, with age, children come to recognize that their behavior is rarely under the constant surveillance of parents and teachers: No longer can they attribute their habits of good behavior to external causes. Thus, internal attributions are made, fostering the internalization of values, goals, and standards which may have actually followed rather than preceded good behavior.

Influence of Emotions

Over the past decade, the relation of emotions to social cognitive abilities and the motivational role of emotions in responsible behavior have gained increased attention among many prominent researchers (e.g., Bandura, 1989; Eisenberg, 1986; Hoffman, 1982; Weiner, 1986). The public popularity of such recent books as *Emotional Intelligence* (Goleman, 1995) and *Shame: The Exposed Self* (Lewis, 1995) reflects such attention. Hoffman's (1982, 1988) developmental theory of moral development and empathy is perhaps the most widely known and researched theory of the relation between emotions, thought, and responsible behavior. According to Hoffman, the emotions of empathy and guilt develop in parallel and function as motives for morally and socially responsible behaviors. Closely linked to cognitive and moral development, these two emotions often prompt a child to help a peer in need, to control the impulse to harm a peer, or to adhere to valued rules. Drawing from a large body of research, including his own studies on parental disciplinary practices, Hoffman (1982, 1988) argues that parental use of *inductions* fosters the internalization of values by linking them to the emotions of empathy and guilt. Inductions are disciplinary techniques that emphasize the effects of one's behavior on others (see Prosocial Behavior, this volume, for a discussion of inductions). These may include simple statements ("Don't take things from your sister, she'll miss them and cry") or more complex explanations and discussions used with older children. Inductions are used more often by parents with an authoritative, rather than authoritarian or permissive, parenting style. Authoritative parents combine inductions with firm controls, clear expectations of socially responsible behavior, flexibility in disciplinary practices based on mitigating circumstances, and consid-

eration of the child's perspective. Likewise, a modest degree of power assertion might be used, when necessary, to gain the child's attention.

Consistent with Hoffman's theory and research, others have independently shown that parents and teachers who use induction in a nurturant, caring way tend to receive self-regulated, compliant responses from children (e.g., Crockenberg & Litman, 1990). Through such an interactional style, parents and teachers train children in self-assertion and power sharing, which are indispensable skills as children responsibly seek to achieve their own goals without disrespecting the goals of others. By contrast, parents and teachers tend to foster social conformity dependent upon adult surveillance and behavioral consequences when they are preoccupied with mechanical procedures, give excessive negative feedback, and offer no explanations about why norms should be followed (cf. Blumenfeld, Pintrich, & Hamilton, 1987).

Several researchers have shown a link, which becomes stronger as children mature, between emotions and perception of responsibility, controllability, and intentionality (Ferguson, Stegge, & Damhuis, 1991; Graham & Weiner, 1986; Hoffman, 1988). For example, Ford, Wentzel, Wood, Stevens, and Siesfeld (1989) reported additional evidence for the linkage between emotions and responsibility, with implications for socialization. They found that adolescents' predictions of behavioral choices (i.e., whether they would behave in a socially responsible or socially irresponsible manner) are associated with emotions theoretically linked to social responsibility. Anticipated guilt and pride are the two emotions found to be most consistently linked to responsible choices, regardless of whether social sanctions are present. Their findings suggest that parents and teachers may be more successful in stimulating self-regulation and social responsibility in children by appealing to children's pride (e.g., desire to be treated as grownups) and guilt (e.g., sorrow about wrongdoing, which leads to interpersonal reconciliation and future resistance to temptation) than to their fear or shame. The findings also support the arguments of emotion theorists and developmental researchers (e.g., Baumeister, Stillwell, & Heatherton, 1994; Crockenberg & Litman, 1990; Izard, 1991) that conformity elicited by fear or shame differs from conformity elicited by guilt or pride. Whereas the former requires external monitoring and regulation, the latter develops through self-regulatory processes which reflect autonomy.

In sum, research and theory in developmental psychology highlight the important roles of social cognitive abilities and emotions in the shift in behavioral control from that of the adult to the developing child. Educators desiring to promote socially responsible behavior (i.e., internalization) should combine strategies, such as induction, with the judicious use of externally oriented behavioral techniques commonly used in the schools.

Problems and Implications

The cognitive, emotional, and interactional processes described in the previous section are helpful to construe the development of socially responsible values and behavior, but they guarantee no reliable prediction. As educators are well aware, children (and adults) often affirm that they value rule-abiding behaviors and strive to conform to social standards, and yet, in a given situation, their behavior does not adhere to their own standards, much less the rules of the classroom. As noted previously, any one or combination of multiple cognitive, emotional, behavioral, and situational factors are likely to explain why someone, such as Tim, occasionally disobeys classroom rules. Although important, and certainly worthy of analysis in problem-solving consultation or assessment, an examination of each of these factors is far beyond the scope of this chapter. For conducting a thorough problem-solving analysis of rule-violating related behaviors, we refer the reader to other chapters in this volume, as noted in parentheses, for purposes of addressing the following necessary questions:

- Is the behavior serious enough to indicate the need for formal diagnosis and/or systematic treatment? (see Conduct Disorders, Cheating, Lying, Stealing)
- Has the child failed to acquire appropriate social skills? (see Social Skills)
- Does the behavior reflect problems controlling one's emotions, especially anger? (see Anger Control)
- Does the behavior reflect interfering behavior problems such as aggression, a poor sense of self-efficacy, impulsivity, anxiety, depression, or the like? (see Aggressive Behavior, Social Skills, Attention Deficit/Hyperactivity Disorder, Anxiety, Depression, and Temperament)
- Does the behavior reflect deficiencies in empathy-related emotions across situations? (see Prosocial Behavior)
- Does the behavior reflect deficient or biased styles of social problem solving or information processing? (see Social Problem Solving Skills and Anger Control)
- Does the behavior reflect a developmental delay in sociomoral reasoning? (see Sociomoral Reasoning and Behavior)

A negative response to the just listed questions would suggest that the child's rule-related disobedience, while still a problem to the classroom teacher, may well reflect normal social development. An important remaining question, however, is Why does a child who has no significant social-cognitive, emotional, or behavioral deficiencies act in a socially irresponsible manner? Social cognitive theorists offer several explanations:

1. It Is Normal, and Healthy, to Question and Disobey Rules and Other Social Conventions

Research on children's differentiation of the moral and social conventional domains offers valuable insights into the thinking children use when they naturally question, and disobey, common classroom rules. According to Turiel and colleagues (e.g., Nucci, 1982; Smetana, 1995; Turiel, 1983), children understand that some rules are grounded in moral values, some in social conventions, and others concern prudential issues. Transgressions against moral-based rules entail actions that have nonarbitrary, negative implications concerning justice or the welfare and rights of others (e.g., "Don't hurt others," "don't steal or damage others' property"). In contrast, violations of social conventions are actions that conflict with arbitrary, commonly agreed-upon behavioral practices and rules of the social system (e.g., "Walk quietly in the halls," "complete homework on time," "raise your hand"). Violations of social conventional rules generally are not perceived as harming others or as being unjust. It is not inherently wrong to disobey such rules: Remove the rule (or the fear of external consequences) and there is little reason to engage in the rule-governed behavior. Rules concerning prudential issues pertain to behaviors that affect the health, safety, or comfort of oneself (e.g., "Brush your teeth," "don't chew on your pencil").

Children view moral, social-conventional, and prudential behaviors as legitimately subject to parent and teacher authority, but this especially holds true with moral transgressions because they are viewed as being inherently wrong (i.e., regardless of whether there are governing rules; Smetana & Bitz, 1996). In the eyes of many children, unprovoked fighting is wrong, but there is little wrong with running in the halls and chewing gum in class, especially when an adult is absent. Moreover, in the eyes of some, but especially adolescents, certain rule violations, such as use of alcohol and cigarettes, shift from the moral and social conventional domains to either the prudential or personal domains (Smetana, 1988, 1995). The personal domain encompasses actions generally seen to be issues of personal choice or perspective (e.g., style of clothing and hair, dating preferences)— behaviors perceived by the child to have little, if any, impact on others. Such distinctions are not always clear and often are dependent on the social situation and the child's developmental perspective, as well as individual differences. For example, research by Smetana (1988) shows that adolescents are much more likely than younger children to reject social conventions and to view them as crossing over into the personal domain, contributing to common conflicts that parents and teachers have with adolescents over social conventions such as homework and cleaning their rooms. Likewise, research also shows that compared to nondelinquent youth, delinquent youth are more likely to classify moral transgressions as matters of personal choice (Guerra, Nucci, & Huesmann, 1994).

Turiel and his collaborators (e.g., Turiel, 1983) have empirically identified seven levels in the development of social conventions. In progressing from one level to the next, children shift between affirming and negating the validity of social conventions, such as many classroom rules. That is, a period (or level) of understanding and appreciating rules is followed by a period in which children recognize the inadequacy of their previously held thinking about rules. For example, at level 1 (approximately 6 to 7 years of age) children follow rules simply because they are dictated by persons in authority. At level 2 (approximately 8 to 9 years) children recognize that there are exceptions to rules and that others fail to follow them, thus concluding that other than for pragmatic reasons there is no reason to adhere to the rules. This is followed by level 3 (approximately 10 to 11 years), a period of affirmation in which conventions are complied with because they are perceived as necessary elements of rule systems and because important people in positions of authority expect conventions to be followed. Negation returns at level 4 (approximately 12 to 13 years), when children tend to view many classroom and school-wide rules as unnecessary and unjust constraints; consequently, they often act in unconventional ways, especially when the peer group reinforces such behaviors. By 15 to 16 years of age, however, most adolescents have a greater appreciation of the role of social structure and institutions. Consequently, they view adherence to conventions and rules as important for participation in a social system (Turiel's level 5). Failure to move from level 4 to level 5 leads to persistence in rule violations.

Significant problems arise when a child fixates at a lower level (especially a level of negation) or frequently fails to differentiate the moral, social, prudential, and personal domains (e.g., the child views most, if not all, behaviors as matters of personal choice). Although research does not support a direct association between stage of social conventional reasoning and behavior, it does show maturity of social conventional reasoning to be correlated with socially responsible behavior in the classroom (Geiger & Turiel, 1983). But perhaps the greatest contribution of research on social conventional reasoning is the finding that the negation of social rules is critical to reorganization of thought and, thus, to healthy social development.

Whereas Turiel's research highlights the internal structure of social-conventional thinking, it is widely recognized that environmental factors exert a powerful influence on children's questioning of rules. For example, as noted by Eccles et al. (1993), the increased desire for autonomy and the questioning of authority that characterizes adolescence coincides not only with increased cognitive maturity but also with wider exposure to different viewpoints and belief systems. This includes increased opportunities for unsupervised interactions with peers in which the relationship is no longer asymmetrical with respect to power and authority. Such opportunities foster the questioning of rules, particularly those rules set by teachers and parents without input from the child or consideration thereof.

2. Not All Social Behavior Requires Reflection

Many socially responsible and irresponsible acts occur automatically, without social-cognitive reasoning or problem-solving skills ever becoming engaged (Langer, Blank, & Chanowitz, 1978). That is, the first step in most social problem-solving models—stop and think—never occurs. For example, Tim observes others roughhousing on the playground and readily joins the fray without thinking of rules, possible outcomes, or the impact of the behavior on others.

A popular social-cognitive explanation of automatic, seemingly impulsive or mindless behavior is that children's standards of appropriate behavior become more linked to scripts, or cognitive representations of the sequence of behavioral steps that occur in common situations (Huesmann, 1988). These scripts serve to guide behavior, especially reoccurring or habitual behaviors (e.g., behaviors ranging from saying "please" and "thank you" to reacting nonaggressively toward those who bother you). Different scripts are retrieved from memory and activated, affecting both emotions and behavior, and accounting for many behaviors performed "without thinking" such as Tim, but not Rick, refraining from aggressing toward a peer who teases or shoves him.

3. Self-Interest and a Self-Serving Bias Tend to Influence Behavior

In their research on the development of children's reasoning about distributive justice (e.g., How should five candy bars be distributed among four children?), Gerson and Damon (1978) concluded that, although level of reasoning was related to decisional choice, "there was a strong tendency for all children to prefer themselves to some extent" (p. 44). Likewise, research in attributional theory shows that individuals tend to have a self-serving bias in attributions of causality, assuming greater responsibility for successful outcomes (especially controllable outcomes) than for negative outcomes, perhaps as a means of protecting or bolstering self-esteem (Weiner, 1992). Together, such research studies strongly suggest that, irrespective of other factors (e.g., level of moral reasoning, environmental factors), children's actions and thoughts, including those of both Tim and Rick (and most adults), tend to be self-serving.

4. The Relation Between Social-Cognitive Abilities and Socially Responsible Behavior Often Is Mediated by Situational Context

Multiple aspects of the situational context are likely to influence both the extent to which social-cognitive abilities are engaged and the choice of one's personal goals. Common classroom factors that interact with social cognitions and behavior would include the clarity and fairness of rules; the stated, and actual, consequences of rule violations and the consistency in their enforcement; the degree of monitoring by the teacher; physical arrangements of the class; and teacher, parent, and peer expectations.

Eisenberg (1986) has shown that behavior's relation to social-cognitive abilities and emotions is often mediated by the perceived costliness of the act. Less cognitive reflection (e.g., social and moral reasoning) occurs when the negative consequences of rule violations are perceived to be minor, such as Tim being verbally reprimanded for running in the halls. Likewise, less cognitive reflection occurs when the cost of helping others is low (e.g., sharing a pencil versus donating one's allowance to the needy). Social cognition is most likely to be related to behavior in situations that require decision-making processes, especially those processes that entail conflicting values or goals associated with perceived costliness of the act.

Unfortunately, values and goals that reflect social responsibility do not always prevail in situations of conflicting choices. This is perhaps most evident in the powerful influence of peers on situational behaviors, as well as on more enduring values, attitudes, and behavior. Drawing from extensive research on adolescent peer relations and attitudes, Steinberg (1996), in his recent book *Beyond the Classroom: Why School Reform Has Failed and What Parents Need to Do,* makes a compelling case that an adolescent's friendship group is equally, or more, influential than parents and teachers in determining many socially responsible behaviors, particularly those perceived to be in the prudential or personal domains such as drug and alcohol use and school achievement. Steinberg argues that school reform efforts are destined to fail if they do not address adolescent peer influences on behavior. It should be noted, however, that friendship groups can support, as well as undermine, values taught in home and in the classroom. Thus, one key factor differentiating Tim and Rick may well be the values held by their chosen peer groups.

5. Processes of Cognitive and Emotional Disengagement Are Linked to Social and Moral Actions

Processes of disengagement, or cognitive distortions, allow individuals to construe their violations of social conventions, as well as more serious moral transgressions, as nonproblematic, not their fault, or not deserving punishment. Disengagement protects oneself from self-disteeming feelings of failure to achieve one's goals or failure to act in a manner consistent with one's values and standards. Mechanisms of disengagement identified by Bandura (1989) and relevant to violations of classroom rules include moral or social justification, euphemistic labeling, advantageous comparison, displacement of responsibility, dehumanization, and blame-shifting.

Moral or social justification: "But I meant well"
Moral reasoning can be used to justify not only one's responsible behavior, but also one's socially reprehensible conduct. Self-condemnation for a rule-violating action can be avoided by justifying to oneself (and hopefully to others) that "it was the 'right' thing to do." For example, Tim might justify his running in the halls by arguing that, if he had not run, he would have been late for class.

Euphemistic labeling: "I was just kidding"
As stated by Bandura (1989), "through convoluted and sanitizing verbiage, detrimental conduct is made benign, and those who engage in it are relieved of a sense of personal agency" (p. 67). Thus, Tim may blind himself to the irresponsible nature of a given rule-governed behavior by applying a more acceptable label to it: Behavior that destroys school property is labeled as "just clowning around," cruel teasing becomes "just joking," and fighting is referred to as "just horseplay."

Advantageous comparison: "But others are worse"
In the eyes of a teenage offender, a violation of rules is insignificant, perhaps even praiseworthy, and certainly not worthy of punishment, when compared against the greater violations of others. Thus, Tim might alleviate his incipient guilt about not turning in a homework assignment by comparing himself with Rick, who has failed to turn in *all* the assignments during the last marking period.

Displacement of responsibility: "But he forced me to do it"
By placing the responsibility on another, one minimizes not only internal self-prohibiting reactions but also personal concern about the consequences of his or her irresponsible behavior on others (Bandura, 1989). At a recent New York Giants football game, for example, the throwing of snowballs led to the injury of dozens of fans and the arrest of many more. When the news reporters questioned the culprits about their actions, many expressed the view that the stadium authorities "made them do it" by selling too much beer and not clearing the snow. Likewise, Tim might seek to convince himself (and maybe others) that the teacher "forced" him to return a

book late to the library when she postponed the due date of the last reading assignment.

Victim-Blaming: "He deserved it"

Extreme, self-serving cognitive distortions can take the form of victim-blaming. Gibbs, Potter, and Goldstein (1995) report a personal discussion that one of the authors once had with juvenile felons concerning shoplifting. During the discussion, Gibbs asked rather rhetorically, "Who's to blame in this situation?" He was astonished to hear several boys in the group assert quite seriously that the store owner was at fault. "Their reasoning was that if the store owner wasn't alert enough to spot and catch a shoplifter, he *deserved* to be robbed" (p. 99). On a much less serious level, Tim is likely to excuse his teasing of a classmate by stating that the classmate started it or excuse his failure to complete homework by stating that the teacher assigned too much homework.

The foregoing examples show how children may resort to self-serving cognitive distortions as a defense against self-punitive affect and thinking and, thus, lowered self-esteem. Such distortions are more likely to be employed when irresponsible behavior has obvious negative consequences to oneself or to others. Self-serving cognitive distortions may either be kept internal or be verbalized as excuse-giving, depending on whether the situation involves a potential need to escape punishment. Research reviewed by Bandura (1989) indicates that a combination of several self-protective strategies yields multiplicative, rather than additive, effects. This finding constitutes a great challenge to school psychologists involved in correction of ongoing socially irresponsible behavior and points in the direction of preventive intervention.

Alternative Actions: Teacher-Student Interactions That Promote Internalization

Due to space limitations (and recognition that multiple resources on the topic exist elsewhere), we do not cover common classroom-management practices and behavior techniques for teaching socially responsible behavior, nor do we devote adequate attention to district- and building-level policies related to socially responsible behavior and internalization. Although dyadic interactions are highlighted in this section, we strongly recommend that schools not limit their focus to the teacher-student level but also closely examine more general policies and comprehensive, broad-based programs, procedures, and practices for promoting social responsibility. Questions in Table 1 should be helpful for this purpose.

Table 1 *Some General Questions That Schools Should Address When Examining Whether Current Policies and Practices Promote Internalization*

- To what extent is the goal of social responsibility translated into existing school policies and practices?

- Have the community's values, goals, and standards been identified and highlighted in policies and curricula? (For example, has a committee of parents, citizens, and educators developed or adopted a list of common values? Does the school emphasize these values in social studies, language arts, and other areas? Does it encourage or recognize community service by students?).

- Do teachers and support staff model exemplary values, goals, and high standards related to socially responsible behavior? (For example, are teachers held to a lower standard in respect to foul language, tardiness, smoking? Do outstanding role models mentor students in student government and community service projects?)

- Is democratic governance taught, practiced, and encouraged among the student body? (For example, do students participate in important district-, building-, and classroom-level decisions, such as issues of fairness in disciplinary policies?) At the classroom level, do students of all ages participate in the discussion of classroom problems and solutions pertaining to issues of social responsibility? (For example, are class meetings held, such as those described by Glasser (1976)? To what extent does the teacher reflect an authoritarian versus authoritative style during class meetings?)

- Are socially responsible individuals and their actions spotlighted in the school? In the community? In the curriculum? (For example, are moral and social issues highlighted in English literature, social studies, science? Are "good deeds" recognized?)

- Are prevention-oriented programs being implemented to promote social development and curtail irresponsible behavior? (For example, does the school implement conflict-resolution, peer-mediation, or social problem-solving programs? Do such programs include a home-school component?)

- Do existing programs emphasize social responsibility, or reliance on external rewards and consequences? Do they balance the adolescent's desire for autonomy and self-determination with the teacher's responsibility to manage and monitor social behavior?

- Where appropriate, do classroom-management practices include students in the decision-making process, especially decisions pertaining to social behavior? Are school and classroom rules clear, fair, developmentally appropriate?

- Is a systematic inservice program provided that focuses on both the development and promotion of socially responsible behavior and the prevention and management of undesirable behavior?

- To what extent are parents, the community, and students included in existing programs? Are rules and disciplinary practices, and their rationale, communicated clearly to parents and students?

- Are existing practices evaluated? (For example, how are they perceived by teachers, parents, and students? Are they effective in promoting positive behavior and self-discipline? Are both behaviors and cognitions evaluated?)

Importance of the Disciplinary Message

Although multiple aspects of the teaching process, the school environment, and peer relations clearly impact on the internalization process, everyday disciplinary encounters between children and their parents and teachers focus most directly on the teaching of socially responsible behavior. Grusec and Goodnow (1994) recently integrated research on the social-cognitive and emotional bases of behavior into a provocative formulation of how children come to internalize society's values. Note that although their model focuses specifically on parent-child interactions, we generalize the model to teacher-student interactions. In so doing, we recognize that our recommended actions are somewhat speculative. However, in the absence of research on teacher-student interactions that promote internalization per se, and given that parent-student and teacher-student relations are very similar, we argue that the practical applications of Grusec and Goodnow's research- and theory-based model should be considered by school psychologists and educators.

According to Grusec and Goodnow (1994), messages conveyed during disciplinary actions are central to the internalization process. They emphasize, however, that disciplinary practices often fail to promote internalization because the child (a) does not accurately perceive the message the parent is attempting to communicate, (b) decides not to accept the message, or (c) both.

Message features that promote the child's accurate perception of the message

Drawing from a wealth of research and theory in developmental psychology, Grusec and Goodnow (1994) argue that messages are likely to be accurately perceived if they

- Are clear, consistent, and repeated often.
- Are understandable, relevant, and fit the developmental level of the child's schemas.
- Capture the child's attention (the message might include, for example, the use of mild power assertion).
- Signal that the message is important to the adult.
- Convey positive attention.
- Emphasize the reasoning behind the rule (especially empathy- or other-oriented reasoning.)

Message features that promote the child's acceptance of the message

In identifying features of messages that determine the child's acceptance or rejection of the message, Grusec and Goodnow (1994) divided features into three categories: (a) features that influence the child's evaluation of the adult's behavior as being appropriate, (b) features that influence the child's motivation to accept the message, and (c) features that influence the child's perception of the message's value or standard as originating internally, rather than externally. These features, with the addition of features drawn from the school psychology literature on student acceptability of interventions, are reviewed next within the context of teacher-student interactions.

Perceptions of Appropriateness and Fairness

Students are more likely to comply with disciplinary interventions if they perceive these interventions to be acceptable or appropriate (see Elliott, 1988, and Reimers, Wacker, & Koeppl, 1987, for literature reviews of research on intervention acceptability). The one dimension of appropriateness that has been of foremost interest among researchers is that of fairness, especially the extent to which an intervention is perceived by the student to fit a rule violation. As one might predict, children judge harsh interventions (e.g., being suspended or sent to the principal) as fair for severe problems such as moral transgressions (e.g., fighting, cheating) but unfair for problems of less severity such as violations of social conventional rules (e.g., disturbing the classroom; Bear & Fink, 1991; Bear & Stewart, 1990). In addition to being related to the severity of the problem, perceptions of fairness were related to the transgressor's history of misbehavior (i.e., reputation, Bear and Fink). Reputation, in turn, was related to the predicted effectiveness of the intervention. Students, particularly eighth graders more so than fifth graders, judged that, although a harsh intervention would be fair for someone with a history of misbehaving, it would be of questionable effectiveness.

Studies of student acceptability also indicate that

- Boys, compared to girls, are more likely to view classroom behavior problems as less wrong and to reject corresponding interventions (Bear & Fink, 1991; Bear & Stewart, 1990; Elliott, Witt, Galvin, & Moe, 1986).
- Boys are particularly more likely to reject verbal-mediated interventions such as counseling, social problem solving, and moral discussions (Bear & Stewart, 1990).
- Familiar interventions (e.g., being sent to the principal, detention, loss of recess) are preferred by most students over less familiar interventions (Bear & Stewart, 1990; Elliott et al., 1986).
- Students prefer private teacher-student interventions, group reinforcement, negative sanction, and home-based interventions over public reprimands and negative group-contingencies (used when only one child misbehaves) (Elliott et al., 1986; Turco & Elliott, 1986).
- Whereas students agree that it is fair to punish a child for a moral transgression, it is unfair to punish someone for failing to be prosocial (Grusec & Pedersen, 1989).

In addition to the intervention fitting the misdeed, Grusec and Goodnow (1994) add that children are more likely to accept an intervention if

- The adult's actions are viewed as consistent with the authority associated with the adult's given position. For example, a recent study by Laupa and Turiel (1993) showed that children rejected the authority of a school principal to punish children for their behavior outside of the school setting.
- The adult follows due process procedures. Acceptance is facilitated if the child's perspective, including any extenuating circumstances, is heard and respected. Bringing up problem behaviors that occurred in the past, especially those for which the child was already punished, would be viewed as unfair.
- The adult's procedures are consistent with what the child has come to expect from the adult. Grusec and Goodnow cite cultural differences in respect to children's expectations and parental disciplinary style and their relation to acceptance. Although power assertion is most effective when accompanied by warmth and nurturance, children who are recipients of frequent power assertion are more likely to expect, and accept, its use than those for whom power assertion is used less frequently.
- The adult's actions are viewed by the child as being well intentioned.
- The intervention matches the child's temperament, mood, and developmental status.
- The child agrees with the evidence the adult uses to support the use of the intervention (e.g., the facts are not disputed; cognitive distortions, as referred to previously, are not prevalent).

Motivational Aspects of Messages

Other features likely to determine acceptance or rejection relate to the motivational value of the message. Drawing once again from theory and research in developmental psychology, Grusec and Goodnow (1994) conclude that the following features enhance the prospects that the child will be motivated to accept the message:

- The message arouses empathy. As argued by Hoffman (1994), empathy-based inductions foster internalization by attaching emotions to the reasoning underlying the message.
- The message arouses insecurity. Negative forms of power assertion such as screaming, humiliation, and public reprimands are likely to frighten a child (and are clearly discouraged). Nevertheless, they may actually promote compliance and in some cases internalization. However, compliance will remain externally oriented unless the child comes to attribute the compliance to intrinsic reasons and not to parental pressure.

- The message emphasizes that the behavior and supporting value(s) are important to the adult.
- Warmth and reciprocity characterize the adult-child relationship, promoting identification with the adult. The child not only appreciates the adult's immediate warmth and loving support but also recalls previous instances during which the adult provided the same.
- The message minimizes threats to the child's autonomy. The use of humor, indirect messages, and low levels of power assertion lessens the threat to one's autonomy (especially during adolescence), thus decreasing the likelihood of rejection. There is some evidence that the same messages, or interventions, are less threatening when delivered by peers than by adults.

Self-Generational Aspects

The features just listed determine the accuracy of the student's perceptions of a message, the fairness of the message as perceived by the student, and the child's motivation to accept the message. Some of the same features also determine the extent to which the child comes to view the value(s) conveyed in the message as being self-generated. Of particular importance to perceived self-generation are (a) the minimal threat to autonomy and (b) the use of implicit messages (i.e., messages requiring the child to reflect upon the message while decoding its important elements). These two features are important because they contribute to attributions of intrinsic motivation. Related to intrinsic attributions for acceptance is the degree to which the child comes to discount external attributions for acceptance. As noted by Grusec and Goodnow (1994), it is not until the second to fourth grades that children come to view internal and external causes of behavior as independent. Prior to this point, instead of discounting the role of external pressure on their behavior, children perceive external and internal motivation as being directly related (greater external pressure increases the self-perceptions that the behavior was self-generated).

Although Grusec and Goodnow's (1994) formulation of the internalization process is not without its critics (see Hoffman, 1994; Kochanska, 1994; Perry, 1994), it serves as a useful heuristic for school psychologists when working with teachers and parents in curtailing discipline problems and promoting prosocial behavior via a preventive approach. An important element of such an approach would be a focus on the *student's* perspective during disciplinary actions, especially features of disciplinary actions that enhance the likelihood that the message conveyed in the action will be accepted by the student. This element should mesh well with social problem-solving and sociomoral decision-making components (see Social Problem Solving and Sociomoral Reasoning and Behavior, this volume) as well as with such classroom management strategies as clear rules and teacher expectations, student goal setting, contracting, and the appropriate use of behavioral principles (for practical recommendations related to these strategies, see Kaplan & Carter, 1995; Sprick, Sprick, & Garrison, 1993)—components that should comprise a comprehensive, prevention-oriented program for developing socially responsible behavior.

Summary

Programs and practices that focus exclusively on external control absolve children of responsibility for their actions. Schools cannot hold children accountable for their actions if their policies and practices do not recognize that behavior is determined by both personal and external factors. In this chapter, we emphasized the personal factors involved in the internalization process, especially cognitions related to the acceptance or rejection of rules and interventions. In so doing, we do not dismiss the value of external-oriented behavioral techniques frequently used in the classroom, especially reinforcement and mild forms of power assertion (e.g., time-out, response cost, verbal reprimands). Such behavioral techniques clearly serve the important purposes of maintaining classroom order (particularly in the presence of the teacher), teaching habits of appropriate behavior, and perhaps focusing the student's attention on the message that the intervention attempts to convey. They are problematic only when not combined with practices that promote internalization and, thus, socially responsible behavior.

Recommended Resources

Devries, R., & Zan, B. (1994). *Moral classrooms, moral children: Creating a constructivist atmosphere in early education.* New York: Teacher's College Press.
Based on principles of constructivist education, the authors provide practical guidelines and strategies for promoting social and moral responsibility in the elementary grades. Chapters, and corresponding teaching strategies, include Conflict and Its Resolution, Rule Making and Decision Making, Voting, Social and Moral Discussions, and Cooperative Alternatives to Discipline. The text should serve as an excellent companion to books that focus on the use of traditional behavioral techniques for children with more serious behavior problems.

Grusec, J. E., & Goodnow, J. J. (1994). Impact of parental discipline methods on the child's internalization of values: A reconceptualization of current points of view. *Developmental Psychology, 30,* 4–19.
This article offers a model of discipline effectiveness based on current research and theory in the areas of social-cognitive and emotional development. The model emphasizes that the child's interpretation and evaluation of disciplinary methods is the most critical factor in determining the effects of discipline, particularly as it relates to internalization of social values. Factors influencing interpretation and evaluation are reviewed, with emphasis on the parent-child relationship and parental goals. Following the articles are commentaries on the model by three recognized authorities on internalization: Hoffman, Kochanska, and Perry.

Decisions, Decisions [Computer software] (varying dates). Watertown, MA: Tom Snyder Productions. *Choices, Choices* [Computer software] (varying dates). Watertown, MA: Tom Snyder Productions.
Unique among the wealth of curriculum materials for developing social responsibility are these two award-winning educational software series which focus on real-life historical and contemporary issues. Learning strategies include role-playing, debate, group social problem solving, and group sociomoral decision making. Among the 17 titles in the **Decisions, Decisions** *series (mostly for grades 5–12) are Lying, Cheating, Stealing; Prejudice; Substance Abuse; AIDS; and Drinking and Driving.* **Choices, Choices** *(grades K or 2, through 4) consists of three programs: Kids and the Environment, On the Playground, and Taking Responsibility.*

References

Bandura, A. (1986). *Social foundations of thought and action: A social cognitive theory.* Englewood Cliffs, NJ: Prentice-Hall.

Bandura, A. (1989). Self-regulation of motivation and action through internal standards and goal systems. In. L. A. Pervin (Ed.), *Goal concepts in personality and social psychology* (pp. 19–85). Hillsdale, NJ: Erlbaum.

Bandura, A. (1991). Social cognitive theory of moral thought and action. In W. M. Kurtines & J. L. Gewirtz (Eds.), *Handbook of moral behavior and development: Vol. 1. Theory* (pp. 45–103). Hillsdale, NJ; Lawrence Erlbaum.

Baumeister, R. F., Heatherton, T. F., & Tice, D. M. (1994). *Losing control: How and why people fail at self-regulation.* San Diego, CA: Academic Press.

Baumeister, R. F., Stillwell, A. M., & Heatherton, T. F. (1994). Guilt: An interpersonal approach. *Psychological Bulletin, 115,* 243–267.

Bear, G. G. (1989). Sociomoral reasoning and antisocial behaviors among normal sixth graders. *Merrill-Palmer Quarterly, 35,* 183–196.

Bear, G. G., & Fink, A. (1991). Judgments of fairness and predicted effectiveness of classroom discipline: Influence of problem severity and reputation. *School Psychology Quarterly, 6,* 83–102.

Bear, G. G., & Stewart, M. (1990). Early adolescents' acceptability of interventions: Influence of problem severity, gender, and moral development. *Journal of Early Adolescence, 10,* 191–208.

Blumenfeld, P. C., Pintrich, P. R., & Hamilton, V. L. (1987). Teacher talk and students' reasoning about morals, conventions, and achievement. *Child Development, 58,* 1389–1401.

Boldizar, J. P., Perry, D. G., & Perry, L. (1989). Outcome values and aggression. *Child Development, 60,* 571–579.

Crockenberg, S., & Litman, C. (1990). Autonomy as competence in 2-year-olds: Maternal correlates of child defiance, compliance, and self-assertion. *Developmental Psychology, 26,* 961–971.

Damon, W. (1977). *The social world of the child.* San Francisco: Jossey-Bass.

Dodge, K. A. (1986). A social information processing model of social competence in children. In M. Perlmutter (Ed.), *Minnesota Symposia on Child Psychology* (Vol. 18, pp. 77–125). Hillsdale, NJ: Lawrence Erlbaum.

Dodge, K. A., & Crick, N. R. (1990). Social information-processing bases of aggressive behavior in children. *Personality and Social Psychology Bulletin, 16,* 8–22.

Dodge, K. A., & Price, J. M. (1994). On the relation between social information processing and socially competent behavior in early school-aged children. *Child Development, 65,* 1385–1397.

Eccles, J. S., Midgley, C., Wigfield, A., Buchanan, C. M., Reuman, D., Flanagan, C., & MacIver, D. (1993). Development during adolescence: The impact of stage-environment fit on young adolescents' experiences in schools and in families. *American Psychologist, 48,* 90–101.

Eisenberg, N. (1986). *Altruistic emotion, cognition, and behavior.* Hillsdale, NJ: Erlbaum.

Eisenberg, N. (1988). The development of prosocial and aggressive behavior. In M. H. Bernstein and M. E. Lamb (Eds.), *Development psychology: An advanced textbook* (2nd ed., pp. 461–495). Hillsdale, NJ: Erlbaum.

Elam, S. M., & Rose, L. C. (1995). The 27th Annual Phi Delta Kappa/Gallup Poll of the public's attitudes towards the public schools. *Phi Delta Kappan, 77,* 41–56.

Elliott, S. N. (1988). Acceptability of behavioral treatments: Review of variables that influence treatment selection. *Professional Psychology: Research and Practice, 19,* 68–90.

Elliott, S. N., Witt, J. C., Galvin, G. A., & Moe, G. L. (1986). Children's involvement in intervention selection: Acceptability of interventions for misbehaving peers. *Professional Psychology: Research and Practice, 17,* 235–241.

Federal Register, March 13, 1995.

Ferguson, T., Stegge, H., & Damhuis, I. (1991). Children's understanding of guilt and shame. *Child Development, 62,* 827–839.

Ford, M. E. (1985). The concept of competence: Themes and variations. In H. A. Marlowe & R. B. Weinberg (Eds.), *Competence development: Theory and practice in special populations* (pp. 3–49). Springfield, IL: Charles C. Thomas.

Ford, M. E., Wentzel, K. R., Wood, D., Stevens, E., & Siesfeld, G. A. (1989). Processes associated with integrative social competence: Emotional contextual influences on adolescent social responsibility. *Journal of Adolescent Research, 4,* 405–425.

Geiger, K., & Turiel, E. (1983). Disruptive school behavior and concepts of social convention in early adolescence. *Journal of Educational Psychology, 75,* 677–685.

Gerson, R., & Damon, W. (1978). Moral understanding and children's conflict. In W. Damon (Ed.), *New directions for child development* (Vol. 1, pp. 41–59). San Francisco: Jossey-Bass.

Gibbs, J. C., Potter, G. G., & Goldstein, A. P. (1995). *The EQUIP program: Teaching youth to think and act responsibly through a peer-helping approach.* Champaign, IL: Research Press.

Glasser, W. (1976). *Reality therapy: A new approach to psychiatry.* New York: Harper-Row.

Goleman, D. (1995). *Emotional intelligence.* New York: Bantam.

Graham, S., & Hoehn, S. (1995). Children's understanding of aggression and withdrawal as social stigmas: An attributional analysis. *Child Development, 66,* 1143–1161.

Graham, S., & Weiner, B. (1986). From an attributional theory of emotion to developmental psychology: A round trip ticket? *Social Cognition, 4,* 152–179.

Gresham, F. M. (1995). Best practices in social skills training. In A. Thomas & J. Grimes (Eds.), *Best practices in school psychology-III* (pp. 1021–1030). Washington, DC: National Association of School Psychologists.

Grusec, J. E., & Goodnow, J. J. (1994). Impact of parental discipline methods on the child's internalization of values: A reconceptualization of current points of view. *Developmental Psychology, 30,* 4–19.

Grusec, J. E., & Lytton, H. (1988). *Social development: History, theory, and research.* New York: Springer-Verlag.

Grusec, J. E., & Pedersen, J. (1989, April). *Children's thinking about prosocial and moral behavior.* Paper presented at the Biennial Meeting of the Society for Research in Child Development, Kansas City, KS.

Guerra, N. G., Nucci, L., & Huesmann, R. (1994). Moral cognition and childhood aggression. In L. R. Huesmann (Ed.), *Aggressive behavior: Current perspectives* (pp. 13–33). New York: Plenum.

Guerra, N. G., & Slaby, R. G. (1990). Cognitive mediators of aggression in adolescent offenders: II. Intervention. *Developmental Psychology, 26,* 269–277.

Hoffman, M. (1994). Discipline and internalization. *Developmental Psychology, 30,* 26–28.

Hoffman, M. L. (1982). Development of prosocial motivation: Empathy and guilt. In N. Eisenberg (Ed.), *The development of prosocial behavior,* (pp. 281–313). San Diego, CA: Academic Press.

Hoffman, M. L. (1988). Moral development. In M. Bornstein & M. Lamb (Eds.), *Developmental psychology: An advanced textbook* (pp. 497–548). Hillsdale, NJ: Erlbaum.

Huesmann, L. R. (1988). An information-processing model for the development of aggression. *Aggressive Behavior, 14,* 13–24.

Huesmann, L. R., Guerra, N. G., Miller, L. S., & Zelli, A. (1992). The role of social norms in the development of aggressive behavior. In A. Fraczek & H. Zumkley (Eds.), *Socialization and aggression* (pp. 139–152). New York/Heidelberg: Springer-Verlaz.

Izard, C. (1991). *The psychology of emotions.* New York: Plenum Press.

Juvonen, J. (1991). Deviance, perceived responsibility, and negative peer reactions. *Developmental Psychology, 27,* 672–681.

Kaplan, J. S., & Carter, J. (1995). *Beyond behavior modification* (3rd ed.). Austin, TX: PRO-ED.

Kochanska, G. (1994). Beyond cognition: Expanding the search for the early roots of internalization and conscience. *Developmental Psychology, 30,* 20–22.

Kohlberg, L. (1984). *Essays on moral development: Vol. 2. The psychology of moral development.* San Francisco: Harper & Row.

Kopp, C. B. (1987). The growth of self-regulation: Caregivers and children. In N. Eisenberg (Ed.), *Contemporary topics in developmental psychology* (pp. 35–52). New York: Wiley.

Langer, E. J., Blank, A., & Chanowitz, B. (1978). The mindlessness of ostensibly thoughtful action. *Journal of Personality and Social Psychology, 36,* 635–642.

Laupa, M., & Turiel, E. (1993). Children's concepts of authority and social contexts. *Journal of Educational Psychology, 85,* 191–197.

Leming, J. S. (1993). In search of effective character education. *Educational Leadership, 51,* 63–71.

Lewis, M. (1995). *Shame: The exposed self.* New York: The Free Press.

Lochman, J. E., Wayland, K. K., & White, K. J. (1993). Social goals: Relationships to adolescent adjustment and to social problem-solving. *Journal of Abnormal Psychology, 21,* 135–151.

Manno, B. V. (1995). The new school wars: Battles over outcome-based education. *Phi Delta Kappan, 76,* 720–726.

Nucci, L. P. (1982). Conceptual development in the moral and conventional domains: Implications for values education. *Review of Educational Research, 52,* 93–122.

Perry, D. G. (1994). Comments on the Grusec and Goodnow (1994) model of the role of discipline in moral internalization. *Developmental Psychology, 30,* 23–25.

Perry, D. G., & Perry, L. C. (1983). Social learning, causal attribution, and moral internalization. In J. Bisanz, G. L. Bisanz, & R. Kail (Eds.), *Learning in children: Progress in cognitive development research* (pp. 105–136). New York: Springer Verlag.

Reimers, T. M., Wacher, D. P., & Koeppl, G. (1987). Acceptability of behavioral interventions: A review of the literature. *School Psychology Review, 16,* 212–227.

Rokeach, M. (1973). *The nature of human values.* New York: Macmillan.

Smetana, J. G. (1988). Adolescents' and parents' conceptions of parental authority. *Child Development, 59,* 321–335.

Smetana, J. G. (1995). Parenting styles and conceptions of parental authority during adolescence. *Child Development, 66,* 299–316.

Smetana, J. G., & Bitz, B. (1996). Adolescents' conceptions of teachers' authority and their relations to rule violations in school. *Child Development, 67,* 1153–1172.

Sprick, R., Sprick, M., & Garrison, M. (1993). *Interventions: Collaborative planning for students at risk.* Longmont, CO: Sopris West.

Staub, E. (1984). Steps toward a comprehensive theory of moral conduct: Goal orientation, social behavior, kindness, and cruelty. In W. M. Kurtines & J. L. Gewirtz (Eds.), *Morality, moral behavior, and moral development* (pp. 241–260). New York: John Wiley.

Steinberg, L. (1996). *Beyond the classroom: Why school reform has failed and what parents need to do.* New York: Simon & Schuster.

Turco, T. L., & Elliott, S. N. (1986). Assessment of students' acceptability of teacher-initiated interventions for classroom misbehaviors. *Journal of School Psychology, 24,* 307–313.

Turiel, F. (1983). *The development of social knowledge: Morality and convention.* Cambridge, England: Cambridge University Press.

Weiner, B. (1986). *An attributional theory of motivation and emotion.* New York: Springer-Verlag.

Weiner, B. (1992). *Human motivation: Metaphors, theories, and research.* Newbury Park, CA: Sage.

Wentzel, K. R. (1991a). Social competence at school: Relation between social responsibility and academic achievement. *Review of Educational Research, 61*(1), 1–24.

Wentzel, K. R. (1991b). Relations between social competence and academic achievement in early adolescence. *Child Development, 62,* 1066–1078.

Wentzel, K. R. (1992). Motivation and achievement in adolescence: A multiple goals perspective. In D. H. Schunk & J. L. Meece (Eds.), *Student perceptions in the classroom* (pp. 287–306). Hillsdale, NJ: Erlbaum.

Wentzel, K. R. (1993). Does being good make the grade? Social behavior and academic competence in middle school. *Journal of Educational Psychology, 85,* 357–364.

Wentzel, K. R. (1994). Family functioning and academic achievement in middle school: A social-emotional perspective. *Journal of Early Adolescence, 14*(2), 268–291.

Yeates, K. O., & Selman, R. L. (1989). Social competence in the schools: Toward an integrative developmental model for intervention. *Developmental Review, 9,* 64–100.

6

Peer Relations

Jaana Juvonen

University of California, Los Angeles

Background and Development

Social adjustment, in particular satisfying peer relations, is an essential component of school success. Children who have friends and feel accepted among their classmates are more likely to engage in school activities than those who feel lonely or left out (cf. Goodenow, 1992). Furthermore, different forms of peer relationships, such as dyadic friendships and group-based affiliations, facilitate school adjustment in unique ways. For example, during the transition from small elementary schools and self-contained classes to large, often anonymous, compartmentalized middle schools, a friendship provides emotional support, whereas affiliation in a clique facilitates belongingness (Brown, 1990). Peer relationships are not only intertwined with school adjustment and achievement behaviors, they are also associated with integral social-emotional adjustment outcomes, such as the development of social skills and psychological well-being.

Three interrelated aspects of school-based peer relations—friendships, sociometric status, and peer reputation—as well as their associations with adjustment outcomes, are examined here. Each of the three forms of peer relations highlights different aspects and functions of affiliation with individuals of equal status. In addition, developmental changes in social needs and peer networks are discussed. This is followed by a consideration of problems associated with poor peer relationships and actions that can be taken to remediate such difficulties.

Friendships

Friendships are defined as close, dyadic, and reciprocal relationships (e.g., Sullivan, 1953). Whether two children are friends is typically assessed by examining the mutuality of their friendship nominations (i.e., whether two children name one another as friends or as people with whom they like to do things). Friendships are most likely to develop between children with similar backgrounds (of the same sex, ethnicity, family socioeconomic status) and with common interests (Hartup, 1983). These common interests and activities are the proximal determinants of a friendship: Children consider others as friends if they are able to share and do things with them (e.g., play games during recess, have lunch, attend extracurricular activities).

The social needs and behavior patterns of children and their friends vary as a function of age. During the first years in elementary school, friendships are formed in the context of a small group or a clique (Berndt, 1988). Hence, children have more than just one friend. Social bonds within such a clique are held together by common activities. By early adolescence, close relationships with peers come to serve new psychological functions (e.g., provide acceptance and intimacy). Common activities can still tie individuals together in a clique, but it is the qualitative aspects of close relationships that determine who is considered a friend. Preadolescents describe friendships in terms of closeness, equality, trustworthiness, and loyalty (e.g., Berndt, 1988). Consequently, friends also replace some of the roles that parents or other significant adults serve in childhood (i.e., that of a companion; Buhrmester & Furman, 1986).

In spite of developmental differences, it is presumed that friendships serve important social developmental functions for all children. Close friends, or "chums," are considered imperative in providing a context in which children develop an understanding of social concepts and skills (e.g., Selman & Shultz, 1990; Sullivan, 1953). For example, children might come to realize what trustworthiness and loyalty mean only when they encounter such issues with friends (e.g., when social engagements are broken or secrets are spread). Furthermore, children are likely to learn to understand or empathize with other people's feelings best when disappointments and positive events are shared with close companions. Also, conflict situations with equals are likely to teach youngsters about multiple perspectives and improve their skills at negotiating and resolving disagreements (Piaget, 1932; see also Shantz & Hartup, 1992). Given such integral social developmental functions of friendships, it is presumed that children without friends do not have the same opportunities to master social concepts and practice interpersonal skills as youngsters with close relationships.

Although friendships are known to serve several positive functions, the influence of friends must be understood in the context of the youngsters' needs to affiliate with certain (e.g., similar) others. A student with academic difficulties is likely to find others who do not value academic accomplishments or aspire to achieve in school. Teachers and parents may not view such friendships as adaptive or developmentally desirable, but these friendships can be supportive in that a child who is in conflict with teachers and parents (because of anti-achievement attitudes) now has a niche in which one's deviation from that of an ideal student is accepted. Similar dynamics characterize peer networks of aggressive youths (Cairns & Cairns, 1994). Therefore, when discussing the supportive functions of school-based friendships, one needs to remember that while some friends might facilitate classroom engagement and healthy habits, others may endorse anti-academic values and illicit activities. Given that conformity to peer norms and values peaks in early adolescence (Clasen & Brown, 1987), it is not surprising that one potential source of conflict between adults and adolescents involves the selection of friends.

Sociometric Status

Peer status, or social standing, most typically refers to children's sociometric position within their peer group (see Hartup, 1983) or the general attitude of a group toward its individual members. Sociometric status can be assessed using rating scales or a combination of positive and negative nominations from questions, such as: "With whom would you like to play/hang out?" or "With whom would you not like to play/hang out?" (see Asher & Hymel, 1981, for further discussion on assessment methods). Although some practitioners have ethical concerns about using negative nominations, such nominations provide an important distinction between two unpopular groups in that children who are actively disliked (rejected) are differentiated from those who are neither liked nor disliked (neglected). In addition, the most commonly used classification schemes utilize the liking and disliking nominations to compute two additional scores that describe the social impact (a sum of positive and negative scores) and the overall preference (a difference between positive and negative scores) of a child (Newcomb & Bukowski, 1984).

Typically, five sociometric status groups—popular, controversial, neglected, rejected, and average—are identified. Children are classified as popular if they obtain exclusively positive nominations from their peers, whereas controversial youngsters are liked by some and disliked by others. Neglected children receive both low positive and low negative endorsements, whereas those who are classified as rejected are predominantly disliked. Although different classification rules and schemes vary,

generally 8% to 12% of children belong to any of the four extreme sociometric groups. The majority of students receive one or two positive and negative endorsements. These children, who compose the largest sociometric group, are labelled as average in social standing.

There is a large body of research on the behavioral correlates of the extreme sociometric status groups in elementary school (see Coie, Dodge, & Kupersmidt, 1990, and Newcomb, Bukowski, & Pattee, 1993, for reviews). Popular children are typically described as cooperative, helpful, and skillful negotiators; controversial peers are socially skillful, yet also aggressive; neglected youngsters are timid and asocial; and rejected peers are aggressive, antisocial, and disruptive. There is little descriptive information about the social status of groups beyond elementary school because the sociometric method lends itself best to the analysis of self-contained groups as found in elementary classrooms.

Although sociometric status is often used as an indicator of social adjustment, empirical evidence shows that social status is not always related to children's own views of peer approval. There are significant developmental changes in the relation between peer-rated likability and self-perceptions of peer acceptance. This association is strongest in preadolescence (Harter, 1990). Thus, youngsters may be most realistic in assessing their social status at the time when peer relations are salient and important aspects of their identity.

The variable and sometimes weak association between sociometric ratings and self-perceptions of peer approval (or loneliness) may also reflect some qualitative, as opposed to quantitative, aspects of peer relationships (Berndt & Keefe, 1995). A child liked by many can still feel lonely because she does not have any close friends. Furthermore, a child who is unpopular (i.e., rejected or neglected) in the class might feel socially quite satisfied because he has one friend with whom he can interact. Thus, sociometric status and friendships can complement but not compensate for each other.

Sociometric status can change during a school year and can certainly vary as the composition of a class changes. Rather than attributing changes in social status to variations in the social adjustment of an individual, the contribution of the peer group must be considered. Peer-group norms or values in part determine who is popular or rejected (Hartup, 1983). Although there is little direct research on how peer group norms and values develop and get enforced, many teachers can certainly cite the specific behaviors or physical characteristics that their students despise or devalue as well as those that are respected or admired.

There is higher consensus regarding disliked than liked classmates (e.g., Hartup, 1983). In general, there also is higher agreement among children of the same age on what is negative than on what is considered desirable (Peevers & Secord, 1973). One factor contributing to such a disparity is that, among the positive components, pre- and especially early adolescents make a distinction between characteristics that elicit respect (e.g., fairness, cooperativeness) and those that are admired (e.g., trendy haircuts or clothing). Whereas respect appears to be related to liking, admiration seems to be associated with popularity. Hence, the determinants of positive peer relations vary depending on the specific aspects under consideration.

Peer Reputation

Whereas friendships and sociometric status describe certain aspects of peer relationships, reputation is a more indirect measure of children's relational or social status. However, peer reputation may be more informative in respect to the reasons underlying peer reactions. For example, a timid classmate who is frequently victimized by others may be labelled a "wimp." Similarly, a student who is academically oriented and hence despised may be called a "teacher's pet." Reputations with such negative connotations can be very stable and detrimental to the social adjustment of a child. First, reputations are difficult to change because they are shared by a collective. In addition, they are likely to affect one's self-definition given that others treat one not according to one's actions but according to one's reputation (cf. Rogosch & Newcomb, 1989). For example, a "bully" gets blamed for being mean (e.g., wanting to hurt others), and his actions bring retaliations from his classmates. In contrast, a "cool" peer might be given the benefit of doubt for the same behavior and hence elicit no negative responses from peers (Hymel, 1986).

A child's reputation can be assessed using peer assessment methods. In elementary school, one such approach is called the "Revised Class Play" (Masten, Morison, & Pellerini, 1985). Instead of classifying children based on their likability, students assign their classmates into roles that reveal some stable behavior characteristics. Such assessments can provide important clinical information. Although teachers and other school personnel may recognize children displaying overt forms of maladaptive behavior, such as aggression, only children themselves may be able to identify those who display covert forms of aggression (e.g., verbal, relational) or those who are victimized.

As students move to larger schools, they tend to label their schoolmates according to their peer affiliations. That is, the reputational characteristics change from behavioral or other concrete descriptions to relational ones. Peer reputation then refers to crowd labels, such as "preppies," "brains," and "burnouts." Adolescents use these names to describe the looks, values, attitudes, and behavior (e.g., family background, taste in dress or music, school orientation, and habits) of their peers. It is presumed that such labels or classifications provide

structure and hence enhance the mastery of a new expanding school environment (Brown, 1990; Eckert, 1989). Furthermore, these reputation-based social formations can also serve as reference groups and thus aid the identity development of early adolescents. However, adolescents labelled as "burnouts" may not identify themselves as such but rather perceive or wish to belong to a more desirable crowd. Thus, self-definition or desired self may not correspond with reality (see Kupersmidt, Buchele, Voeller, & Sedikides, 1996, for a related discussion). Also, given that crowds differ in prestige, it is difficult to change one's reputation, for example, from a "burnout" to a "preppie" (see Brown, 1990). Such problems capture the increasingly complex social worlds of adolescence.

In sum, schools provide children with a context for social life. Many students view school as a place to meet and spend time with friends rather than as an institution for academic learning and achievement. Three interrelated aspects of peer relationships were reviewed:

1. Friendships, which serve integral social developmental functions (e.g., the development of social skills, sources of support).
2. Sociometric standing, which describes students' social success within a peer group and distinguishes five classifications.
3. Peer reputation, which defines a student according to one or more salient characteristics.

These three aspects of school-based peer relationships are meaningful in understanding children's behavior in school as well as for the prediction of social and personal adjustment.

Problems and Implications

Children without friends, children who are not accepted by their peers, and children with negative reputations have developmental disadvantages. As mentioned earlier, youth without a reciprocal relationship with a peer lack opportunities to learn social concepts (e.g., the meaning of equality and loyalty) and skills (e.g., how to negotiate rules, constructively resolve conflicts). Furthermore, a child without a companion is likely to feel lonely, particularly in situations when others affiliate with their friends (e.g., during recess or lunch; Asher, Parkhurst, Hymel, & Williams, 1990; Parkhurst & Asher, 1992).

Lack of friends, unpopularity, and negative peer reputation are associated with a range of social and personal adjustment difficulties. While each aspect of peer-related problems can contribute to maladjustment, they are not independent: A child without friends is likely to be unpopular and have a negative peer reputation. Because distinctions between these various aspects of peer relationships are rarely made in any one study, it is difficult to determine their unique effects. While most of the research discussed next pertains to the correlates of unpopular peer status, similar outcomes might be associated with lack of friends, negative peer reputation, or both.

Concurrent Correlates

A large bulk of studies have examined the concomitant correlates of peer-relationship difficulties. In general, there appear to be at least two distinct categories of unpopular children. One group is submissive or withdrawn: They tend to be socially anxious, report high levels of loneliness, and display low self-perceptions of peer approval (e.g., Rubin, LeMare, & Lollis, 1990). Whereas these submissive youngsters (also, see Loneliness, this volume) are not actively disliked during elementary school, they appear to be more socially ostracized in middle school (Coie et al., 1990). Observational studies suggest that withdrawal is more likely a cause rather than an antecedent of negative peer reactions. It appears that children who become submissive actively seek the company of others, but their social overtures are frequently dismissed by peers (Coie et al., 1990; Rubin et al., 1990). Hence, they may get discouraged and withdraw from peer interactions.

The second group of unpopular peers act aggressively (see Aggressive Behavior, this volume). In spite of active peer rejection in elementary school, they do not display a high degree of loneliness or social anxiety nor have low self-perceptions of peer approval (e.g., Asher et al., 1990). Rather than internalizing their difficulties with peers, aggressive children seem to blame others for unpleasant interpersonal encounters (Dodge, 1980). This bias may in part explain their relatively positive self-perceptions and low levels of loneliness. Also, whereas withdrawn children are social isolates (Rubin et al., 1990), aggressive youngsters tend to affiliate with others who display antisocial tendencies (Cairns & Cairns, 1994; Cairns et al., 1987; Dishion, Andrews, & Crosby, 1995). In addition, peer reactions to aggressive youngsters appear to generally improve rather than worsen by middle school (see Coie et al., 1990). Given that aggression (along with other antisocial behaviors) peaks in early adolescence (Moffitt, 1993), hostile acts may become less salient and thus less negatively viewed by peers.

In addition to the correlational studies on unpopular peer status, there are laboratory investigations of emerging peer status in novel play groups (see Putallaz & Wasserman, 1990, for a review). To examine which behaviors best predict low peer acceptance and rejection and whether peer relationship problems generalize across different peer groups and settings, children's sociometric standing is first assessed in natural social environments (e.g., classrooms). Then the behaviors and strategies of children of extreme status groups (e.g., rejected and neglected children) are compared in an experimental setting as they attempt to join a small group of unacquainted peers engaged in an activity (e.g., playing a board game). The findings of these investigations, typically referred to as peer-group-entry studies, show that different patterns of behavior predict neglect and rejection. Neglected children are timid in approaching the new group and tend to "hover" as they try to initiate contact with the unacquainted peers. They bid for entry but tend to retreat quickly. In contrast, rejected children use coarse tactics and appear to take over the situation as they plunge into the activity. Whereas the neglected children are eventually ignored, the rejected youngsters are rejected by their new peers within the first few sessions.

In addition to the two general types of behavior patterns associated with peer relationship problems (i.e., withdrawal and aggression), students with disabilities also have difficulties getting along with their classmates. A recent review shows that children with learning disabilities (LD) are less accepted and more rejected than their non-LD classmates (e.g., Ochoa & Olivarez, 1995). Similarly, children with mild mental retardation who are included in general education settings tend to be less accepted and more rejected than their nondisabled peers (Madden & Slavin, 1983). Also, children with emotional and behavioral problems (e.g., Sabornie & Kauffman, 1985) and those with attention deficit/hyperactivity disorders (e.g., Erhardt & Hinshaw, 1994) are more likely to experience peer rejection than are their nondisabled classmates. Given that emotional and behavioral problems as well as attention deficit/hyperactivity disorders are in part defined by, or associated with, externalizing behaviors (i.e., aggression, disruptiveness, impulsivity), the peer-related difficulties of students with emotional and behavioral problems and attention deficit/hyperactivity disorders are not surprising.

When discussing the peer-relationship problems of children with mild disabilities, it should be noted that the causes of these difficulties are not fully understood. It may be that children with LD have neurologically based, information-processing deficits that affect their ability to read social cues (cf. Dodge, 1980). Alternatively, social difficulties may be secondary to the disability condition. It may be that academic problems or social behaviors *associated with* learning disabilities are the primary determinants of low peer acceptance and rejection. Thus, a child with LD may not be liked by classmates because he is perceived as "slow" or "dumb" and may be rejected because he acts out.

The effects of classroom environments and instructional practices have not been systematically tested in most studies that examine the social status of children with mild disabilities. When a child with a disability is included in a class in which she is the only one with such a condition, classmates are unlikely to immediately accept her. Similarly, certain instructional practices that set children with disabilities apart from others (e.g., pullout programs) are likely to emphasize the differences rather than similarities between them and the rest of the class, thereby hurting the peer status of children with special needs.

Long-Term Correlates

There is a wealth of research on the long-term correlates of children's negative sociometric status. These studies document that children who are not accepted are more likely than other children to have long-term adjustment problems. Some of the early studies in this area revealed that peer-relationship problems at third grade were more predictive of mental health problems by early adulthood than behavior ratings of teachers, achievement performance, and IQ scores (Cowen, Pederson, Babigian, Izzo & Trost, 1973). Subsequent reviews of the research suggest that children not accepted by their peers are at higher risk for dropping out, having mental health problems, and getting involved in criminal activities (Kupersmidt, Coie & Dodge, 1990; Parker & Asher, 1987).

Because peer-relationship difficulties are associated with other problems (e.g., externalizing or internalizing behaviors), the predictiveness of peer status per se is unclear. For example, in the case of children with psychiatric disorders, there are at least three pathways that explain the long-term social difficulties of these youngsters. It may be that their condition (e.g., affective disorder) directly influences long-term maladjustment, regardless of their social difficulties with peers. Alternatively, it may be that the stress created by peer rejection (elicited by atypical behavior of the child) functions as the primary predictor of subsequent adjustment problems. Finally, the two problems can have cumulative effects on long-term adjustment outcomes. That is, children who have psychiatric disorders *and* are chronically rejected by their peers are most likely to have personal and social adjustment difficulties in adulthood. Hence, peer-relationship problems can be conceptualized as another set of stressors that children with special needs are more likely to experience than other children.

Two mediating factors of peer-relationship problems that in part explain some of their detrimental long-term effects are the *onset* and *stability* of low acceptance (cf. lack of friends, negative peer reputation). There are particular developmental periods or psychologically core events during which lack of acceptance is likely to be especially detrimental (e.g., during difficult family events, school transitions). Also, the long-term effects are likely to be worse the longer a child remains neglected or rejected (cf. without a close friend or with a negative reputation). Eventually, the negative interpretations and presumptions of peers regarding a classmate may become internalized by the youngster: The unpopular child comes to expect that no one will like him (Rabiner & Coie, 1989). These children then become trapped in a vicious cycle of maladaptive behavior, bad reputation, and negative expectations of peers' reactions (Price & Dodge, 1990).

Although various types of relationship problems have cumulative effects and certain conditions can exacerbate the influence of problematic peer relations, such effects can be moderated by one's social needs at any time (e.g., Kupersmidt et al., 1996). Children who desire to be popular or liked by all classmates might be especially sensitive to peer reactions, whereas youngsters whose social aspirations are more modest might be quite adjusted although they do not have close friends or in spite of their neglected status or unfavorable reputation. Also, friendships or satisfying peer relationships in other environments (e.g., in the neighborhood) can buffer the effects of low social status, lack of friends, or negative reputation at school.

In sum, peer-related difficulties can be conceptualized as stressors or risk factors that contribute to concurrent and long-term adjustment problems. Although lack of friends, low social status, and negative peer reputation are not independent of one another, they each have specific antecedents and consequences. Thus, on a conceptual level, predictions can be made about the effects of each type of peer-related problem. In Figure 1, one hypothetical sequence is presented that depicts how the three aspects of peer-relationship problems might be linked with one another.

The figure starts with a lack of a friends because it is presumed that a friendship provides an ideal (and perhaps necessary) context for the development of social skills. Low social skills, in turn, predict unpopular peer status. Unpopularity is related to low self-perceptions of peer approval, on one hand, and negative peer reputation, on the other. Whereas self-perceptions of peer difficulties and feelings of loneliness may directly predict future adjustment problems (e.g., internalizing behaviors), the relation between reputational factors and future adjustment problems (e.g., externalizing behaviors) is likely to be mediated by the stability or chronicity of difficulties in peer relations (e.g., Kupersmidt et al., 1990).

Alternative Actions

When students are identified as having no friends, being unpopular, or having unfavorable peer reputations, intervention strategies should be undertaken to prevent the negative short- and long-term effects of peer-relationship problems. Previous research efforts have focused on interventions, that is, how to fix a problem, whereas prevention tactics have been rarely discussed or proposed. This is somewhat surprising because the type of students most at risk for developing chronic peer-relationship difficulties are known. Given this disparity in emphasis, I

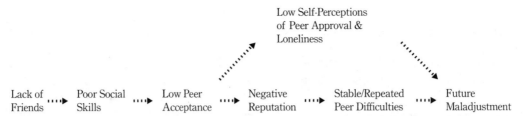

Figure 1. *A hypothetical sequence of peer-related difficulties and future maladjustment.*

will first discuss issues that are most relevant for prevention purposes. Although these issues have not been empirically tested as prevention tactics, they may be helpful for practitioners as different placement options are considered for children and youth with special needs or otherwise at risk for social difficulties with peers. Discussion of possible prevention tactics is followed by a review of intervention programs.

Prevention Efforts

As discussed earlier in the context of the meaning of sociometric status, the social success of any one child is determined not only by her behavior or personality characteristics, but also by peer-group norms. Hence, certain social environments bring out certain idiosyncrasies which, in turn, can negatively impact the social adjustment of the individual. Children who stand out in their class are most likely to have a negative reputation and to be unpopular among their classmates (Juvonen, 1992). Therefore, class environments where "different" students (e.g., children with disabilities, gifted students, ethnic minority children, youth with homosexual orientation) are placed plays a critical role.

According to one common inclusion policy, students with special needs are placed in typical classrooms so that no more than two or three such students are in one classroom. These ratios (i.e., 2:25 or 3:30) are likely to highlight the uniqueness and problems of these individuals rather than facilitate their social integration. In addition, the student who feels different or inferior is likely to engage in social comparisons that are detrimental to his or her self-perceptions. These effects are exacerbated when these students are also pulled out for part of the school day (e.g., for remedial education). Such instructional practices decrease the physical proximity between students with disabilities and the rest of the class and further stigmatize those in need of services. Thus, a student who qualifies for special education may feel inferior or left out when services are provided outside of the typical class.

There is some evidence that alternative environments facilitate the adjustment of children with special needs. For example, in one study (Juvonen & Bear, 1992), children with learning disabilities, especially boys, tended to be socially adjusted in regular classrooms in which approximately one third of the students were children with LD. These classes were cotaught by a special education and a regular education teacher; no children were pulled out for special education. Given that feelings of acceptance and belongingness are known to promote achievement motivation and school success, the classroom social context may indeed be a more crucial factor than the academic curriculum for a child with a disability. Recent reviews of the effects of cooperative learning methods and alternative classrooms appear to add some viable choices for teachers and school personnel (e.g., Slavin, 1990).

Intervention Programs

When a child does not get along with his peers and is excluded from peer activities, the most common assumption is that the child lacks social skills (Asher & Renshaw, 1981). Therefore, the child may be referred to participate in a program that teaches how to make friends, how to communicate appropriately, how to cooperate and share, and so forth (Coie & Koeppl, 1990; see Social Skills, this volume). Although children are rejected by their peers because of *negative* behaviors (see Hartup, 1983), social skills intervention programs have traditionally been assigned to teach *prosocial* behavior. Only recently have there been programs that also focus on the negative behaviors or the cognitive precursors of hostility (e.g., Graham & Hudley, 1992). Regardless of the specific focus of interventions, social skills programs typically involve adult coaching, peer modeling, and role-playing as the primary methods (see Social Skills, this volume). Children develop strategies or evaluate the effectiveness of tactics suggested by others. Such methods can be used not only to teach children effective strategies but also to increase the perception of risks and potential negative outcomes of poor strategies.

Whereas social skills interventions are typically conducted with a small group, another intervention approach involves two children at a time. Pair therapy (Selman & Schultz, 1990) utilizes the (semi-)natural context of a peer dyad to develop children's social understanding and prosocial behaviors. That is, the other child is expected to function as if a friend, while the therapist facilitates the interactions and negotiation strategies between the two.

This structure allows children "to interact directly with each other over issues that are real and meaningful to them" (Selman & Schultz, 1990, p. 134). In addition to the behavioral goals similar to those of group-based social skills interventions (e.g., developing turn taking, improving negotiation skills), this method includes specific cognitive aims (e.g., ability to self-reflect) and affective objectives (e.g., developing trust). Compared to traditional social skills interventions, pair therapy is more labor intensive, but practitioners may find some of the main principles helpful when dealing with children who have long histories of peer-relationship problems.

Social skills interventions have been fairly successful in changing the behavior of target children (e.g., LaGreca & Santogrossi, 1980; Ladd, 1981; see Social Skills, this volume). However, positive changes in behavior have not necessarily resulted in improved social status (see Hymel, 1986). As discussed in the context of peer reputation, the peer group is unlikely to change its view of an individual. Hence, a bully may remain perceived as a bully in the minds of classmates even when no longer causing trouble or retaliating. Furthermore, the expectations of unpopular children do not automatically change as a function of social skills intervention. They may learn new skills yet they expect others to dislike them. Hence, the generalization and maintenance of learned skills is typically poor. Whether pair therapy fares better in this respect than traditional group-based interventions remains to be seen.

One way to address the problem of low maintenance and generalization of learned social skills is to further probe the beliefs of the child in intervention as well as the perceptions of the rejectors. Rabiner and Coie (1989) showed that peer status of rejected children can be improved by simply raising their positive expectations of others' (new playmates') sentiments toward them. If a child makes a better impression on others when she expects these others to like her, then it is important to target the maladaptive thoughts of children with chronic difficulties with peers.

Likewise, it is essential to take into consideration the perceptions of the children who reject a classmate. Judgments of responsibility for deviant characteristics appear to determine, in part, the affective and behavioral reactions toward hypothetical peers (Juvonen, 1992). For example, if children hold a classmate responsible for being obese ("He is so fat because he eats and eats all the time!"), then they are likely to dislike the person and exclude him from activities. In contrast, if they understand that someone might be heavy because of a biological condition (e.g., thyroid malfunction), then they are less likely to reject this person and instead feel sympathy. In sum, it may be necessary to complement traditional social skills interventions by addressing the perceptions of the rejectors as well as the beliefs of the rejected children.

When intervention efforts are not successful, one needs to examine not only the assumptions and the methods of the program but also the motivation of the client. An aggressive child who has been referred to a social skills program may claim not to care whether classmates like him or not (Boldizar, Perry, & Perry, 1989). Likewise, an unpopular child may not feel lonely or in need of treatment as long as she has a friend. In these cases, children see the intervention efforts as unnecessary or irrelevant. It is unlikely that any intervention can be effective unless the target child sees its advantages or is motivated to change his or her social image (Asher et al., 1990). Hence, before a child is referred for a treatment, it is important to assess the subjective perceptions and feelings of the child.

In sum, the consideration of the classmates' perceptions as well as the expectations of students with peer-related difficulties are essential for both prevention and intervention purposes. Prevention efforts include the manipulation of the classroom composition by increasing its diversity (e.g., the number of students with disabilities) and developing unobtrusive methods of providing services for children with special needs. Intervention programs (traditional group-based social skills training or pair therapy) that aim to improve the peer relations of unpopular children should include, in addition to traditional social skills instruction, an evaluation of the targets' and their classmates' perceptions (e.g., expectations, interpretations of intent) and social motivation.

Summary

Schools provide children with a rich social arena. Although peer relationships are associated with achievement behaviors, they are also related to important social-emotional adjustment outcomes. Three interrelated aspects of peer relations were discussed in this chapter:

1. Friendships, which serve integral social developmental functions, such as development of interpersonal skills.
2. Sociometric standing, which describes children's social status within a peer group.
3. Peer reputation, which depicts how a student is viewed and classified by classmates, and hence can provide clinical insights.

Peer-related difficulties, on the other hand, were conceptualized as stressors or risk factors that contribute to concurrent and long-term adjustment problems. Based on concomitant symptoms, two distinct groups of unpopular children were identified. One group consists of submissive or withdrawn children who tend to be socially anxious, report high levels of loneliness, and display low self-perceptions of peer approval. Another group of un-popular peers are those who act aggressively. In spite of active peer rejection, they do not display a high degree of loneliness or social anxiety nor have low self-perceptions of peer approval. The long-term correlates of peer-related difficulties include dropping out, mental health problems, and involvement in criminal activities. Different pathways and links between peer-relationship problems and sub-sequent maladjustment (e.g., direct, indirect, spurious) were delineated.

Discussion on alternative actions was divided into two sections: prevention and intervention. Prevention efforts include the manipulation of the classroom composition by increasing its diversity (e.g., diminishing the salience of one or two students with apparent problems or disabilities) and developing unobtrusive methods for providing services for children with special needs. Two types of intervention programs designed to improve the peer relations of unpopular children were described: pair therapy and group-based social skills interventions. Also, the importance of evaluating the target children's as well as their classmates' perceptions (e.g., expectations, inter-pretations of intent) and motivation to get along with oth-ers were discussed.

Recommended Resources

Asher, S. R., & Coie, J. D. (Eds.). (1990). *Peer rejection in childhood.* Cambridge, England: Cambridge University Press.
The recent advances in the study of children's peer-relationship problems are presented in this book. The volume includes chapters on the personality and behavior characteristics of children with social difficulties, the concurrent as well as longitudinal correlates of peer rejection, and reviews on intervention programs.

Asher, S. R., & Hymel, S (1981). Children's social competence in peer relations: Sociometric and behavioral assessment. In J. D. Wine & M. D. Smye (Eds.), *Social competence* (pp. 125–157). New York: Guilford.
This chapter provides an overview of various assessment methods and instruments that can be used to evaluate children's peer relations. Short reviews of relevant research are also included. The chapter is a practical guide for school psychologists.

Berndt, T. J., & Ladd, G. W. (Eds.). (1989). *Peer relationships in child development.* New York: Wiley.
One of the most comprehensive set of chapters on the developmental functions of peer relations is presented in this book. Intriguing conceptual analyses and empirical findings highlight the centrality of positive peer relations on children's personal, social, and emotional adjustment. Although the book is written for professional audience, the chapters are also appropriate for parents.

Hartup, W. W. (1983). Peer relations. In E. W. Hetherington

(Ed.), *Handbook of child psychology: Vol 4. Socialization, personality, and development* (4th ed., pp. 103–196). New York: Wiley.
This classic handbook chapter covers a wide range of issues related to the developmental changes in children's interaction patterns, adaptive functions of peer relations, peer socialization effects, individual differences in social adaptation, and the comparison between peer and family systems.

Selman, R. L., & Schultz, L. H. (1990). *Making a friend in youth: Developmental theory and pair therapy.* Chicago: Chicago University Press.
A conceptual model for relationships as well as guidelines for intervention are presented in this book. Pair therapy provides an alternative approach to group-based social skills intervention programs. Two children act as if friends, while a therapist functions as a facilitator. Such a contextualized approach may prove to enhance the maintenance and generalizability of newly learned social competencies and skills.

References

Asher, S. R., & Hymel, S. (1981). Children's social competence in peer relations: Sociometric and behavioral assessment. In J. D. Wine, & M. D. Smye (Eds.), *Social competence* (pp. 125–157). New York: Guilford.

Asher, S. R., Parkhurst, J. T., Hymel, S., & Williams, G. A. (1990). Peer rejection and loneliness in school. In S. R. Asher & J. D. Coie (Eds.), *Peer rejection in childhood* (pp. 253–273). Cambridge, England: Cambridge University Press.

Asher, S. R., & Renshaw, P. D. (1981). Children without friends: Social knowledge and social skills. In S. R. Asher, & J. M. Gottman (Eds.), *The development of children's friendships* (pp. 273–296). Cambridge, England: Cambridge University Press.

Berndt, T. J. (1988). The nature and significance of children's friendships. *Annual Child Development, 5,* 155–186.

Berndt, T. J., & Keefe, K. (1995). Friends' influence on adolescents' adjustment to school. *Child Development, 66,* 1312–1329.

Boldizar, J. P., Perry, D. G., & Perry, L. C. (1989). Outcome values and aggression. *Child Development, 60,* 571–579.

Brown, B. B. (1989). The role of peer groups in adolescents' adjustment to secondary school. In T. J. Berndt, & G. W. Ladd (Eds.), *Peer relationships in child development* (pp. 188–215). New York: Wiley.

Brown, B. B. (1990). Peer groups and peer cultures. In S. S. Feldman, & G. R. Elliott (Eds.), *At the threshold: The developing adolescent* (pp. 171–196). Cambridge, MA: Harvard University Press.

Buhrmester, D., & Furman, W. (1986). The changing functions of friends in childhood: A Neo-Sullivanian perspective. In V. J. Derlega & B. A. Winstead (Eds.), *Friendship and social interaction* (pp. 41–62). New York: Springer Verlag.

Cairns, R. B., & Cairns, B. D. (1994). *Lifelines and risks: Pathways of youth in out time.* Cambridge, England: Cambridge University Press.

Clasen, D. R., & Brown, B. B. (1987). The multidimensionality of peer pressure in adolescence. *Journal of Youth and Adolescence, 14,* 451–468.

Coie, J. D., Dodge, K. A., & Kupersmidt, J. B. (1990). Peer group behavior and social status. In S. R. Asher & J. D. Coie (Eds.), *Peer rejection in childhood* (pp. 17–59). Cambridge, England: Cambridge University Press.

Coie, J. D., & Koeppl, G. K. (1990). Adapting intervention to the problems of aggressive and disruptive rejected children. In S. R. Asher & J. D. Coie (Eds.), *Peer rejection in childhood* (pp. 309–337). Cambridge, England: Cambridge University Press.

Cowen, E. L., Pederson, A., Babigian, H., Izzo, L. D., & Trost, M. A. (1973). Long-term follow-up of early detected vulnerable children. *Journal of Consulting and Clinical Psychology, 41,* 438–446.

Dishion, T. J., Andrews, D. W., & Crosby, L. (1995). Antisocial boys and their friends in early adolescence: Relationship characteristics, quality, and interactional process. *Child Development, 66,* 139–151.

Dodge, K. A. (1980). Social cognition and children's aggressive behavior. *Child Development, 51,* 162–170.

Eckert, P. (1989). *Jocks and burnouts: Social categories and identity in high school.* New York: Teachers College Press.

Erhardt, D., & Hinshaw, S. (1994). Initial sociometric impressions of attention-deficit hyperactivity disorder and comparison boys: Predictors from social behaviors and from nonbehavioral variables. *Journal of Consulting and Clinical Psychology, 62,* 833–842.

Goodenow, C. (1992). Strengthening the links between educational psychology and the study of social contexts. *Educational Psychologist, 27,* 177–196.

Graham, S., & Hudley, C. (1982). An attributional approach to aggression in African-American children. In D. H. Schunk, & J. L. Meece (Eds.), *Student perceptions in the classroom.* Hillsdale, NJ: Erlbaum.

Harter, S. (1990). Self and identity development. In S. S. Feldman, & G. R. Elliott (Eds.), *At the threshold: The developing adolescent* (pp. 352–387). Cambridge, MA: Harvard University Press.

Hartup, W. W. (1983). Peer relations. In E. W. Hetherington (Ed.), *Handbook of child psychology: Vol 4. Socialization, personality, and development* (4th ed., pp. 103–196). New York: Wiley.

Hymel, S. (1986). Interpretations of peer behavior: Affective bias in childhood and early adolescence. *Child Development, 57,* 431–445.

Juvonen, J. (1992). Negative peer reactions from the perspective of the reactor. *Journal of Educational Psychology, 84,* 314–321.

Juvonen, J., & Bear, G. (1992). Social adjustment of children with and without learning disabilities in integrated classrooms. *Journal of Educational Psychology, 84,* 322–330.

Kupersmidt, J. B., Buchele, K. S., Voeller, M. E., & Sedikides, C. (1996). Social self-discrepancy: A theory relating peer relationship problems and school maladjustment. In J. Juvonen, & K. R. Wentzel (Eds.), *Social motivation: Understanding children's school adjustment.* Cambridge, England: Cambridge University Press.

Kupersmidt, J. B., Coie, J. D., & Dodge, K. A. (1990).

The role of poor peer relationships on the development of disorder. In S. R. Asher & J. D. Coie (Eds.), *Peer rejection in childhood* (pp. 274–305). Cambridge, England: Cambridge University Press.

LaCreca, A. M., & Santogrossi, D. A. (1980). Social skills training with elementary school students: A behavioral group approach. *Journal of Consulting and Clinical Psychology, 48,* 220–227.

Ladd, G. W. (1981). Effectiveness of a social learning method for enhancing children's social interaction and peer acceptance. *Child Development, 52,* 171–178.

Madden, N., & Slavin, R. (1983). Mainstreaming students with mild handicaps: Academic and social outcomes. *Review of Educational Research, 58,* 519–569.

Masten, A., Morison, P., & Pellerini, D. (1985). A Revised Class Play method of assessment. *Developmental Psychology, 3,* 523–533.

Moffitt, T. E. (1993). Adolescence-limited and life-course persistent antisocial behavior: A developmental taxonomy. *Psychological Review, 4,* 674–701.

Newcomb, A. F., & Bukowski, W. M. (1984). A longitudinal study of the utility of social preference and social impact sociometric classification schemes. *Child Development, 55,* 1434–1447.

Newcomb, A. F., Bukowski, W. M., & Pattee, L. (1993). Children's peer relations: A meta-analytic review of popular, rejected, neglected, controversial, and average sociometric status. *Psychological Bulletin, 113,* 99–128.

Ochoa, S., & Olivarez, A. (1995). A meta-analysis of peer rating sociometric studies of pupils with learning disabilities. *The Journal of Special Education, 29,* 1–19.

Parker, J. G., & Asher, S. R. (1987). Peer relations and later personal adjustment: Are low accepted children at risk? *Psychological Bulletin, 102,* 357–389.

Peevers, B., H., & Secord, P. F. (1973). Developmental changes in attribution of descriptive concepts to persons. *Journal of Personality and Social Psychology, 27,* 120–128.

Piaget, J. (1932). *The moral judgment of the child.* London: Routledge & Keagan.

Price, J. J., & Dodge, K. A. (1989). Peers' contribution to children's maladjustment. In T. J. Berndt, & G. W. Ladd (Eds.), *Peer relationships in child development* (pp. 341–370). New York: Wiley.

Putallaz, M., & Wasserman, A. (1990). Children's entry behavior. Peer rejection and loneliness in school. In S. R. Asher & J. D. Coie (Eds.), *Peer rejection in childhood* (pp. 60–89). Cambridge, England: Cambridge University Press.

Rabiner, D. L., & Coie, J. D. (1989). Effects of expectancy inductions on rejected children's acceptance by unfamiliar peers. *Developmental Psychology, 25,* 450–457.

Rogosch, F. A., & Newcomb, A. F. (1989). Children's perceptions of peer reputations and their social reputations among peers. *Child Development, 60,* 597–610.

Rubin, K. H., LeMare, L. J., & Lollis, S. (1990). Social withdrawal in childhood: Developmental pathways to peer rejection. In S. R. Asher & J. D. Coie (Eds.), *Peer rejection in childhood* (pp. 253–273). Cambridge, England: Cambridge University Press.

Sabornie, E., & Kauffman, J. (1985). Regular classroom sociometric status of behaviorally disordered adolescents. *Behavioral Disorders, 10,* 268–274.

Selman, R. L., & Shultz, L. H. (1990). *Making a friend in youth: Developmental theory and pair therapy.* Chicago: University of Chicago Press.

Shantz, C. U., & Hartup, W. W. (Eds.), *Conflict in child and adolescent development.* Cambridge, England: Cambridge University Press.

Slavin, R. E. (1990). *Cooperative learning: Theory, research, and practice.* Engelwood Cliffs, NJ: Prentice Hall.

7

Play

Roslyn P. Ross

Queens College and the Graduate School of the City University of New York

Background and Development

On one level, it has been important to study play simply because young children play. They do so exuberantly, spontaneously, voluntarily, creatively, and with pleasure. In seeking to explain why children play, early theorists variously cited surplus energy, energy deficits necessitating relaxation and recreation, the practice of instinctively based skills necessary for adult activities, and humanity's cathartic need for recapitulation of the different epochs in human development to rid itself of primitive features of behavior. (An excellent description of these, as well as 20th century theories, can be found in Rubin, Fein, & Vandenberg, 1983.)

On another level, it has been important to study play because it is inextricably entwined with so many aspects of human development and functioning. The three theorists (Freud, Piaget, Vygotsky) who dominated play theory in the first half of the 20th century were actually addressing more general aspects of psychological functioning. In doing so they stumbled across children's play and extended their work to include it. Freud, for example, was interested in how drives are satisfied, how conflicts are resolved, and how thought originates. It was in this context, during the first decade of the 20th century, that he saw how play functions as wish fulfillment and catharsis. Later, as Freud began to focus more on ego functioning, he also saw play as an opportunity for mastery—an attempt by repetition to work over and assimilate anxiety-provoking situations. Play functions as a spontaneous way of liquidating anxiety. In play, unlike the original frightening situation which had to be endured passively, children are able to exercise control. Children may stop and start play at will, allowing in things in manageable bits. They also may play the role of the doer, the powerful one, instead of the one done to. Play's perceived coping potential paved the way for its use as therapy. The window it provides into the child's conscious and not-so-conscious concerns led to its use in assessment.

Ego psychologists studying play, most notably Erik Erikson (1950), expanded on its mastery aspects; they came to regard play and fantasy as autonomous ego functions which did not inevitably derive from conflict or anxiety. Erikson regards play as a cognitive skill used in the service of adjustment; it is an infantile way of thinking over difficult experiences and restoring a sense of mastery.

Piaget (1945/1962) was primarily interested in cognitive processes and cognitive development and linked symbolic play with general intellectual growth. He saw in play an example of assimilative activity; play is the child's way of gradually integrating new information into a limited experiential background. The form that play takes reflects the child's level of cognitive development or intelligence. Thus, *practice play, symbolic play,* and *games-with-rules* are play counterparts of sensorimotor, preoperational, and concrete operational intelligence, respectively. The view of play as a useful cognitive skill suggested the value of enhancing a child's ability to engage in pretense play to achieve cognitive gains, something Piaget called the "American question."

Vygotsky (1967, 1978), a Soviet psychologist whose writings first became available in English in the 1960s, was also concerned with the development and functioning of higher mental processes. He differed from Piaget in two respects. Firstly, he introduced notions about the sociocultural formation of the mind and emphasized the essentially social character of play. Vygotsky's view of play as a social symbolic activity influenced researchers who traced the effects of the social world by focusing on interactions between caretakers and infants and interactions among siblings or groups of children. Secondly, Vygotsky also saw play as a more active causal agent in development compared to Piaget. Vygotsky proposed that play actually sets the stage for subsequent development and leads to the development of imaginative processes, language acquisition, and problem solving. Play does not just reflect thought; play creates it. A child's play with someone else actually creates a condition for jumping above the level of his or her normal behavior (a zone of proximal development).

As shall be seen later, the issue of whether play reflects (is a simple correlate of) other psychological functions or is a causal agent for subsequent development remains controversial. There is no doubt, however, that play experiences are associated with a plethora of developmental virtues in cognitive-linguistic and affective-social domains (Fisher, 1992). Its study reveals a great deal about children's social, emotional, and cognitive functioning. Its study also allows inferences about the effects of different experiences on children. Currently, play behavior is used to study such diverse things as symbolic development in atypical populations and security of infant attachment to their caretakers as it affects subsequent development. The need for school psychologists to understand play behavior also increases as more and more young children are cared for in institutionalized settings (e.g., daycare facilities) and as psychologists are increasingly asked to make decisions about preschool services for youngsters who may be developmentally delayed.

Defining Play

An agreed-upon definition of *play* does not exist because play has been studied from different, and sometimes incompatible, theoretical perspectives. The approach to definition that has generated the greatest consensus attempts to characterize play in terms of a small number of dispositional characteristics (Fisher, 1992; Garvey, 1977; Rubin et al., 1983). Play is considered to be different from other behaviors in that it is

1. Intrinsically motivated.
2. Focused on means rather than ends or on activities rather than goals.
3. Pleasurable.
4. Voluntary.
5. Organism dominated rather than stimulus dominated (asks what the child can do with the object rather than what the object can do).
6. Nonliteral, that is, involving pretense and an "as if" stance.
7. Free from external rules.
8. Actively engaged in as an activity.

The latter four features are accepted variously by some theoreticians and not by others. Each excludes an activity that others might consider play. Exploration, for example, is excluded and contrasted with play by considering play to be organism dominated rather than stimulus dominated (#5). Sensorimotor activities, like going down a slide in different ways, are excluded by disposition (#6); games with rules are excluded by disposition (#7); daydreaming is excluded by disposition (#8).

A second approach to defining play consists of describing distinctive types of play, often within a developmental framework (Rubin et al., 1983). These classifications also tend to reflect theoretical judgments. Piaget's (1962) taxonomy of play, for example, is based on his theory of cognitive development; the three types of play

he describes are related to periods of sensorimotor, preoperational, and concrete operational functioning, respectively:

1. *Practice play* (also known as functional or sensorimotor play) appears after a sensorimotor skill has been acquired. It involves repetitive muscle movements and the introduction of a deliberate complication into the way of doing something. Examples include running, gathering, dumping, and manipulating objects.
2. *Symbolic play* (also known as pretense or pretend play) is behavior that is nonliteral, acting as if something is the case when it is not in reality. Examples include using a plastic medicine dropper as if it were a telephone (make-believe transformation) and pretending to cook like a parent (role-playing). A distinction is sometimes made by others between *sociodramatic play* in which children adopt familiar roles (e.g., parent, teacher, doctor) and *thematic fantasy play* in which children adopt fantastic or fictitional roles removed from everyday (Superman, Wonderwoman, the Little Mermaid).
3. *Games* involve rules which have been agreed upon beforehand and competition in the pursuit of goals. Examples include checkers, hide and seek, and baseball.

A fourth type of play described by Piaget and others, *Constructive play,* does not appear to fit into this classification system. Constructive play is the manipulation of objects to construct or create something. It is the most common form of activity in most preschool and kindergarten classes (Rubin et al., 1983). Piaget suggested that "constructive games" occupy a position halfway between play and work.

Parten's (1932) influential classification scheme involves social levels of play and distinguishes four types:

1. *Solitary play* is solitary or independent play in which there is no reference to others.
2. *Parallel play* involves children pursuing similar activities near or among others but without seeking social contact; they play beside, but not with, each other.
3. *Associative play* involves children playing with others; there is social contact and conversation about common activity, but individual interests are not subordinated to those of the group.
4. *Cooperative play* involves organized activity, differentiation of roles, and complementing actions.

Other social play classification systems are summarized by Johnson, Christie, and Yawkey (1987, p. 50). Additional classification systems describe different types of adult-child play, object play, and pretend play. (For reviews, see Beeghley, 1993; Johnson et al., 1987; Rubin et al., 1983.) Still others describe play from anthropological, sociological, comparative, and cultural perspectives.

Development of Play

The properties of play change with and reflect development. Because each perspective on play brings with it a different set of classifications and milestones, it is exceedingly difficult to paint a satisfactory developmental portrait in a brief article such as this one. It is also difficult to credit the many individual researchers whose discoveries went into building the portraits. For a more extensive picture, see Johnson et al. (1987), Rubin et al. (1983), and Westby (1991), whose reviews of the development of play provide the basis for the account of selected milestones that follows.

It is hard to say at which point behavior should be called play. During the first months of life, infants certainly have playful interactions with adults which have important repercussions for emotional development. They explore the objects of the outside world between 4 and 8 months by looking, reaching, and mouthing. By 8 months of age, they begin to use objects when they play with people. They can attend to objects that others are interested in; they can share that interest and intentionally communicate. Children also begin to differentiate the functions of objects and do not indiscriminately mouth or bang things. The 8-to-12-month-old child is developing object permanence; children of this age search for missing toys as well as adults. They tend to attend to only one toy at a time. The child over one year of age is much more likely to use more than one object in play. In addition, the physical characteristics of playthings are more likely to direct the play. This means that objects are used with some predictability and understanding of how they are used in daily life.

For the first year and a half or so of life, children's play remains sensorimotor (also called practice or functional) or presymbolic, although the first pretense gestures appear at 12 or 13 months of age. These are harbingers of true pretense activities that develop gradually. Symbolic or pretense play appears with the onset of representation and language. It is behavior that is simulative or nonliteral, acting as if something is the case when in reality it is not. It indicates that the child can understand that one thing (sound patterns, images) can signify something else, even when the something is not present. Piaget's notion that early markers of symbolic representation, such as the onset of pretend play and language comprehension, are related has been born out by research (Rubin et al., 1983). Research has concentrated on the gradual development of symbolism in play, concentrating on four developmental trends:

■ *Decontextualization*—moving away from using realistic objects in pretense.

■ *Decentration*—moving away from self-as-agent to other-as-agent in pretense.

■ *Substitution*—substituting one object for another and eventually dispensing altogether with a material base.

■ *Integration*—coordinating pretend acts into sequences.

Infants as young as 12 months have been observed engaging in the simplest type of pretend play involving self-as-agent. They may pretend to eat or to talk on the phone using realistic props. During the second year of life, children become increasingly engaged in pretend play and can use substitute objects (e.g., a long plastic medicine dropper or block for a telephone). At about 18 months, children are capable of transforming the objects and agents of pretend play in a way that Piaget considers genuine symbolic play. Thus the toddler, who previously pretended to talk on the realistic toy phone, may now make a mother or doll pretend to do so. Eventually, substitute objects may not even be necessary; the presence of a phone may be imagined. Pretend play becomes more elaborate and organized and contains more sequences as children mature.

The content or theme of symbolic play also shows developmental changes. At first, children represent only highly familiar events in which they have personally participated. Within some months (at about 19 to 22 months), their pretend representations also include adopting the role of another person with whom they are familiar. At about 3 to 3 1/2 years, children start to include play in which they enact roles that are removed from the familiar and domestic. They adopt stereotypic occupational roles and fictional or fantastic roles from the media. Earliest forms of group pretense also involve familial, relational roles (sociodramatic play) and gradually change to include fictional roles (thematic fantasy play).

Pretense play can be either solitary or social. In general, researchers agree that there is an increase in interactive play, corresponding with social skill development, as children grow older. Pretense play becomes an increasingly social activity between 2 and 5 years of age. Even during infancy there is a great deal of interactive play with adults and older siblings in cultures where infant play is initiated. From mutual engagement comes imitation of facial expressions and sounds and turn taking. During the second half of the first year, infants enjoy such games as peek-a-book, clap hands, give-and-take, and being chased. At first, infants have a passive role though they are very attentive and amused when adults initiate play. At approximately 8 months, infants begin to assume an active role and by 12 months begin to initiate their own games with adults and willing pets. By the time children reach about two, the caregiver's role tends to shift from that of a direct participant to that of an attentive spectator or coach who encourages play and may teach some play skills.

It is at about this time (2 years) that direct participation with peers begins to be important in children's play. Parten's (1932) classic studies showed a progression from solitary (2 to 2 1/2 years) to parallel (2 1/2 to

3 1/2 years) to associative (3 1/2 to 4 1/2 years) to co-operative (4 1/2 years) play. While many children show this progression, it is no longer believed that these are invariant stages of increasing developmental complexity. Some children, for example, do not follow this trend. More recent research suggests that toddlers are capable of some playful interactive exchanges. Older children appear to alternate between solitary and interactive play as they outgrow a tendency to engage in simple side-by-side or parallel play. While the frequency of solitary pretense play decreases with age during the preschool years, it increases again during the late-kindergarten and early-first-grade years. Solitary play follows an upright U-shaped developmental function. It may reflect personality and play orientation as well as developmental level.

The third type of play which Piaget describes is games-with-rules. This type of play rarely occurs before the period of 4 to 7 years and belongs preeminently to the period from 7 to 11 years. Rules, agreed upon in advance and often handed down from a previous generation, determine the game. The object of a game is to compete, to win. Piaget postulated that rule-governed behavior was more complex than symbolic play and would replace it as children became increasingly competent cognitively. While it is true that games-with-rules increase dramatically during the school years, imaginative play persists well beyond the 7-year-old child's leap into concrete operational thinking. Indeed, solitary pretense play, which was in decline relative to social pretense play from the ages of 3 to 5, shows an increase starting at age 6. Singer and Singer (1990) describe how symbolic play goes underground during middle childhood and adulthood. It becomes internalized in the form of private thought, fantasy, daydreaming and imagination. It may even show up in such adult play as Dungeons & Dragons, costume balls, and Mardi Gras festivals.

Problems and Implications

The Nature of Play Disturbances

Because play reflects developmental processes, it also reflects difficulties children may face in their cognitive and socioemotional development. Play disturbances can indicate something about the developmental progress a child is making or failing to make as well as something about environmental stressors. Disturbances in play refer to such things as the delay shown by a two-year-old who is still engaged in exploring objects by mouthing, shaking, and dropping them rather than using them in pretend play. It refers also to absence or paucity of play that may reflect either refusal or inability to play. It refers to

inhibitions in play in response to certain circumstances or around certain play themes, to play that is disorganized or perseverative, to pretend play with unhappy endings and unresolved conflicts, or to pretend play that remains solitary in the company of others. Readers interested in anecdotal descriptions of pretend play difficulties should look at the work of Erikson (1950), Gould (1972), and Gordon (1993).

Some difficulties in play are characteristic of normally developing children. It is not unusual, for example, for one-year-old children to temporarily cease playing when they are subject to maternal departure in an unfamiliar setting (Kagan, 1984). Infants and young children generally need the proximity of their caretaker to feel secure enough to engage in exploration and play. Kagan and other researchers studying early attachment behavior see play inhibition as a particularly reliable indicator of temporary distress in response to unexpected or threatening events in the first 3 years of life.

It is also not unusual to see preschoolers suddenly stop their play when fearful themes are introduced (Dilalla & Watson, 1988). Their difficulty in maintaining pretense at such times has been linked to their difficulty in maintaining a boundary between fantasy and reality. Older children, too, may find themselves too frightened by a play theme to continue playing. In describing how anxiety could disrupt play, Erikson (1950) wrote:

The *microsphere*—i.e., the small world of manageable toys—is a harbor which the child establishes, to return to when he needs to overhaul his ego. . . . Often the microsphere seduces the child into an unguarded expression of dangerous themes and attitudes which arouse anxiety and lead to sudden play disruption. This is the counterpart in waking life of the anxiety dream; it can keep children from trying to play just as the fear of night terror can keep them from going to sleep. (p. 194)

Dangerous play themes are certainly generated by every child as he or she encounters the progression of developmental tasks that growing up involves. Some anxiety, disrupted play episodes, and periods of regression (play and otherwise) are to be expected. When do they become matters of concern? There are no hard and fast guidelines; this question must be answered in terms of how pervasive, intense, and long lasting the disruptions are. Concern is warranted when regression ceases to be a temporary time of self-protective withdrawal from encounters that produce anxiety and when regrouping fails to take place.

Another sort of play difficulty is shown when a child is able to portray powerful negative feelings or strong conflict in play but is unable to find some kind of pretend resolution. In other words, the negative feelings do not inhibit play, but the child cannot come up with a benign solution to a play conflict. Unhappy endings are unlikely to reduce anxiety or to leave a child feeling he or she has mastered some problem. According to Gordon (1993), play that is an expression of intense negative emotion must include cognitive reorganization to promote emotional adaptation. She cites the literature on trauma and cognitive-behavioral theory, both of which stress the importance of cognitive reappraisal with respect to change, in support of this position. Catharsis without affect modulation or conflict resolution is not adaptive. Indeed, dozens of experimental studies have discredited the catharsis theory (Biblow, 1973) despite its continued defense by purveyors of televised violence.

Gordon (1993) maintains that emotional adaptation is also compromised in play which is perseverative (the same action is compulsively repeated with little creative variation) or disorganized. Disorganized or fragmented play comes across as cognitively impaired to the onlooker. Organic cognitive limitations may well be at the root of some disorganized play, but anxiety may also go a long way in explaining impaired cognitive functioning. Fragmented play behaviors have occasionally been likened to self-protective dissociative symptoms found in some traumatized children (Gil, 1991). It is as if the child does not piece things together in fragmented play or recall painful events in their entirety.

Play in Children with Disabilities

Play difficulties also have been linked empirically to certain pathological states in young children; these include organic and emotional difficulties as well as physically handicapping conditions. In general, however, research on the play of children with disabilities is relatively scarce compared to what is known of normally developing children (Hellendoorn, 1994). Perhaps this is because there are so many different kinds of disabilities, all with their own specific characteristics. At any rate, for some reason, play has not always been considered an important part of the development of children with severe disabilities. This is reflected in the absence of the topic in many handbooks on the development of children with disabilities.

One contributing reason for this may be that some children with disabilities, particularly those with multiple disabilities, do not appear to play (Hellendoorn, 1994; Rubin et al., 1983). This may not be because of innate deficits which preclude development of play skills, however, but rather because of secondary conditions. Severely restricted mobility, for example, requires that adults make special efforts to put toys within reach and to provide toys in the first place. An adult who thinks a child cannot play is unlikely to make such efforts. Some children with disabilities may feel demoralized because of repeated lack of success in affecting the environment and may show a subsequent lack of initiative. For example, unseen dangers may make a blind child afraid of exploring. The reported delay and failure of blind children to engage in certain forms of play may be a consequence of their dependency and learned helplessness (Singer & Streiner, 1966; Tait, 1972). Language difficulties may not prevent the emergence of symbolic play in deaf children but may become more critical in the development of more complex, imaginative play and social play. Social play may become restricted, for example, because a deaf child is unable to negotiate play with other children (Blum, Fields, Scharfman, & Silber, 1994).

A number of studies indicate that there is a relationship between play maturity and cognitive and language development for children with and without developmental delays. Indeed, if children have play skills more mature than their language skills, it is often a sign that they are second-language learners or lack experience with the concepts and interaction patterns required by standardized testing (Westby, 1991). Mental or developmental age, rather than chronological age, is the predictor of most measures of play maturity, including symbolic play, for children with mental retardation and Down's syndrome. A minimal mental age of about 20 months (and equivalent competency in language comprehension) is required for the emergence of symbolic play in children both with mental retardation and with normal development (Piaget, 1962; Wing, Gould, Yeates, & Brierly, 1977). The symbolic play skills of children who are language delayed but not autistic are comparable to or a bit better than their language skills (Sigman & Sena, 1993). Although there is also a significant association between play and language skills for children with autism, language ability within the 18- to 25-month-old range is still associated with documented deficiencies in symbolic play for these youngsters. Children with autism who achieve language abilities comparable to 5-year-olds are able to use symbols in play (Lewis & Boucher, 1988).

One may expect slower development of play in children with mild to moderate retardation and children with Down's syndrome, but the sequence will be approximately the same as in normally developing children (Cicchetti, Beeghly, & Weiss-Perry, 1994; Sigman & Sena, 1993). If children with retardation reach this minimal mental age of 20 months and do not demonstrate symbolic play or show play that is qualitatively different, it is likely that secondary conditions rather than an innate play disability are responsible. Hellendoorn (1994) describes how motor handicaps may further impede the exploratory urge of a child with mental retardation. Understimulation and lack of encouragement by caregivers who may be demoralized by seeing so little progress also can have an effect as can the tendency of these children to avoid the unknown.

The play behavior of children with autism is more problematic or impaired than that of children with mental retardation and markedly different from that of children of similar developmental abilities (Cicchetti et al., 1994;

Jarrold, Boucher, & Smith, 1993; Rubin et al., 1983; Sigman & Sena, 1993). Indeed, a paucity of symbolic play is considered characteristic of autism. One of the ways to rule out a diagnosis of autism is to observe spontaneous, exhuberant pretend play in the absence of preoccupation with lining up objects or spinning or twirling toy parts in a repetitive way. Currently, many researchers believe that children with autism have unique, specific deficits in symbolic play and language that cannot be accounted for by level of cognitive development or degree of mental retardation alone. Evidence suggests that children with autism also engage in less spontaneous functional play (exploring objects or making use of objects like a brush to comb a doll's hair), the type of play that preceeds symbolic play. When they are actively encouraged to explore objects, object exploration does increase to the levels found in normal children and those with mental retardation of the same developmental level. The one exception to this is doll play. One wonders whether this is part of a basic *social*-cognitive deficit. Whether or not it is, doll play appears to be a specific correlate of language comprehension.

Play Difficulties: Effects, Causes, or Simple Correlates?

Children who have delays or deficits in language, in cognitive functioning, or in socioemotional functioning also are likely to have play difficulties. It is not possible, however, to draw conclusions about what causes play difficulties from these correlations. Neither can conclusions be drawn about the consequences of play difficulties from correlations between play competence and positive developmental outcomes. The effect of the link between play variability and variability in other factors may go in either direction; it is also possible that the links may be mediated by common determinants.

As Bretherton (1989) points out, evidence of a relationship between a fantasy predisposition and cooperation, social competence, and peer acceptance has sometimes been taken to imply that collaborative make-believe is a training ground for social competence. However, children need a good deal of social competence to engage in collaborative make-believe in the first place. They need to be able to communicate clearly with their play partners, manage conflicts, negotiate the course of the play, and take alternative perspectives. It is just as likely that a propensity to engage in collaborative make-believe is the outcome rather than the cause of competent social and emotional functioning. It is also possible that children could use contexts other than collaborative make-believe to exercise or develop social cognitive skills. (e.g., building a model together, working on shared projects).

In 1983, Rubin et al. concluded that "in general, researchers have been unable to provide convincing evidence that pretend play is either a prerequisite for language or cognitive abilities, a concurrent achievement, or a consequence of having acquired such abilities" (p. 758). A decade later, that still appears to be the case. In 1993, Gordon noted "only future, longitudinal research will help to determine whether cognitive and socioemotional phenomena are effects, causes, or simple correlates of play inhibition" (p. 229).

Despite the lack of certainty about what causes play difficulties, much is known about factors that disrupt play processes. Play processes can be disrupted by events that vary from mildly to intensely upsetting. Thus, play has been found to be disrupted by mildly upsetting events like a mother's temporary departure from her infant in an unfamiliar setting (Kagan, 1984), by more upsetting events like hospitalization and divorce (Hetherington, Cox, & Cox, 1979), and by traumas like abuse and kidnapping (Gil, 1991; Terr, 1991). Anxiety which disrupts play may be stirred by internal conflicts (the threatened emergence of unacceptable or ambivalent feelings) and intensified needs, as well as traumatic events (Erikson, 1940).

Play processes can also be disrupted (or enhanced) by a multitude of environmental events like verbal stimulation, parental involvement, and crowding as well as biological factors like nutrition and organic conditions. (See reviews by Rubin et al., 1983; Wachs, 1993.) Individual differences have also been implicated. Gordon (1993) and Bretherton (1989) cite evidence that children who are less securely attached to their mothers (as judged in the Ainsworth Strange Situation), less ego resilient, or less well-adjusted are more likely to show play disruption and poorer quality play. Both comment on the irony that the very children who are most in need of the opportunity for emotional mastery offered by play may be the ones who are least able to avail themselves of it. "Aside from therapeutic situations, exploration and mastery of the internal world through make-believe play is primarily available to those children who can form supportive relationships with parents and peers" (Bretherton, 1989, p. 399).

Whether one is trying to understand what can disrupt or enhance play behavior, a multidimensional approach is recommended (Wachs, 1993). Play behavior is best understood when interactions between individual characteristics and environmental stimuli are taken into account. In support of an interactionist approach, Wachs cites findings that infants who are characterized as highly active show higher levels of mastery play and exploratory play competence when their parents are less stimulating or less involved; the reverse is true for low active infants. Findings reviewed in Chapter 10 by Singer and Singer (1990) on the impact of television violence also demonstrate that factors have to be studied in interaction; the effect of television violence on behavior, including play and fantasy, differs remarkably as a function of developmental level, propensity for fantasy, and impulse control.

Alternative Actions

Assessment

Using play for assessment

The study of play provides an excellent alternative assessment strategy for children who are difficult to test with standardized instruments (Beeghley, 1993; Cicchetti & Wagner, 1990). Thus, it is particularly appropriate for very young children and children who are or are at risk of being developmentally delayed, that is, children who may be difficult to test because of attentional deficits, motivational problems, or behavioral problems. Fortunately, play assessment can be repeated endlessly without children becoming bored or showing practice effects. It is also appropriate for children with language problems (caused by delays or deficits or learning a second language) for whom standardized tests relying on language tell little about cognitive development. In some instances, play provides the only alternative for assessing skills or behaviors; there is a lack of useful standardized tests to tap the interactional, affective, motivational, and self-regulatory behaviors that young children exhibit regularly in play. Even when appropriate standardized instruments are available to assess behaviors of interest and even when children respond well to such tests, it is still a good idea to include alternative assessment strategies. It is a general principle that sound assessment is multifaceted assessment, and play behaviors indicate a great deal about children's functioning.

At least five different approaches to using play for assessment may be discerned. Because structural forms of play are so closely related to cognitive development, structural forms are assessed to indicate children's exploratory competence and symbolic skills. In this approach, a cognitive skill (e.g., ability to symbolize) is inferred from a play skill (e.g., pretense play). In a second approach, play is used as the context or setting for assessing other domains of interest; play skills per se are not the main interest. Rather, play is used to assess such things as parent-child interaction, peer interaction, social skills, motor skills, infant temperament, infant attention, and the like. Thirdly, play themes may be assessed to indicate children's concerns and interests as well as the balance they achieve between coping and defensive strategies. A fourth approach to assessment involves using play and drawing techniques as tools for interviewing traumatized children. A well-known example of this approach is the use of anatomically detailed dolls to interview young children about possible sexual abuse. Finally, a fifth approach involves assessing children's play behavior itself and using the information to facilitate play skills.

How play is assessed

There are many different formats for play assessment. Examples can be found in the book on play diagnosis and assessment by Schaefer, Gitlin, and Sandgrund, (1991). Generally the format involves direct observation of play, although some procedures rely on reports by others familiar with the child's play. Play may be observed in naturalistic or structured play settings. Naturalistic observations take place in the child's natural and, therefore, familiar setting and usually involve observing the child in free play or interchange with others. Naturalistic observations most clearly illuminate environmental influences and have the potential for leading to hypotheses about a child's functioning. The disadvantage of this technique is that it is difficult to establish the reliability of naturalistic observations. Its usefulness also depends greatly on the thoroughness in recording, knowledge base, and clinical astuteness of the observer. A naturalistic observation is often a good way to start—to get a feeling for the lay of the land. It can be followed by a targeted observation or another naturalistic observation in which selected play data are appraised through the use of rating scales. Rating scales have the advantage of providing practitioners with an informed sense of what to observe (e.g., Linder, 1993; Westby, 1991). Many of the play scales were originally developed as research instruments and are not commercially available. They are obtained through journal articles or by contacting authors. Efforts to develop reliable scales that have sound psychometric properties have been called "promising" in reviews for the last two decades.

Direct observation of play may also be done in structured settings—in clinic or laboratory playrooms—or in structured format. Such observations are usually structured so that there is a period of spontaneous play and one of facilitated play in which the play partner (examiner or parent) tries to elicit a best performance or demonstration of advanced skills. In contrast to a naturalistic observation, a structured play observation limits the nature of the data available but increases the possibility of developing norms and more reliable observations and interpretations.

Interactional play paradigms are a particular type of structured play observation. They were originally devised to gain basic knowledge about development, and some have been shown to be remarkably productive in this regard. A few familiar play paradigms may illustrate this point (see Cicchetti & Wagner, 1990, for descriptions). Much has been learned about security of attachment from the Ainsworth Strange Situation paradigm, about the reciprocity of emotional communication between parent and infant from Tronick's face-to-face mother-infant interaction procedure, and about object permanence from Piaget's disappearing-object paradigm. Each of these research-derived play paradigms provides substantial assessment information as well. Unfortunately, it is often difficult to use these paradigms in clinical and school settings. They require information and resources (equipment, space, and personnel) that may not be readily available. Cicchetti and Wagner argue that the information available from research-derived play paradigms is so rich that efforts need to be made to help professionals involved in the assessment of infants and toddlers profit from them; the authors describe steps that may be taken in this direction.

The same principles that apply to sound assessment in general apply to using play for assessment. A few examples follow. It is important to observe play in several contexts because play is significantly influenced by setting variables (Beeghley, 1993; Rubin et al., 1983). Play behavior should constitute one of several sources of information, not the only source. Just as it is difficult to know what to make of projective data without knowing what behavior is actually like in various settings, play content cannot be reliably interpreted without additional sources of information. Play content may reflect a characteristic response style or a wished-for response style, or it may be imitative of observed behavior. It may be an expression of impulses usually inhibited or reflect an enactment of doing onto others what has been done onto oneself as one way of reasserting a sense of control. Additionally, there is a need for normative data using standardized settings equipped with specified sets of objects to make sense of most play data. The use of reliable and valid scales also facilitates meaningful interpretation as does following best practices in designing targeted observations. Finally, assessment needs to be linked to intervention (Bagnato, Neisworth, & Munson, 1989).

Intervention

Play is often used to influence development because it has so many important developmental consequences and because it is so easily influenced. It is highly susceptible to change from direct feedback, the presence of others, modeling by adults or peers, and ecological influences like space and equipment (Rubin et al., 1983). As knowledge of children's play has grown over the last decades, so has the use of play for all kinds of interventions. An international symposium on play held in the Netherlands in 1991 (Hellendoorn, van der Kooij, & Sutton-Smith, 1994) was devoted to play interventions. The interventions considered were

1. Play therapy emphasizing emotional aspects.
2. Play programs for children with special needs which emphasize developmental possibilities.
3. Play as general education curriculum emphasizing cognitive effects.

Additional interventions which are variants on or extensions of number 3 include

■ Programs training parents to play with their infants which emphasize parenting skills.

■ Training studies of pretense play which emphasize emotional growth or the development of social skills.
■ School play interventions which emphasize the development of attitudes about gender, aggression, cooperation, and other social behaviors.

What follows is a selected review that focuses on the bases for considering play the powerful means for change that it has been considered to be.

Play therapy

This is probably the best known of the play interventions. What distinguishes play therapy as a treatment modality is its use of play as a medium for communication. Play is the child's language; a play therapist needs to be able to understand this language and know how to skillfully communicate therapeutic messages through play. Older children, those about 8 to 11 or 12 years, may use games, rather than toys, to converse. Although play therapy was first developed in the 1920s by psychoanalysts, it is no longer linked with any one theoretical position. Play therapy may be used by practitioners with vastly different theoretical positions and methods (O'Conner & Schaefer, 1994).

Play therapy is widely used in clinical practice (Tuma & Pratt, 1982) and has been called this century's "major growth industry in the play field" (Hellendoorn et al., 1994, p. 217). Its foundation has been theoretical rather than empirical. Child psychotherapy research, in general, has been relatively neglected in comparison to adult psychotherapy research (Kazdin, 1993). It is only in the last several decades that significant progress has been made in conducting outcome studies. Various meta-analyses of child psychotherapy, which include play therapy, have shown average effect sizes ranging from .71 to .79 depending upon the review (Kazdin, 1993). This means that the difference between children and adolescents receiving treatment and those, similarly troubled, receiving none is about three-quarters of a standard deviation on relevant outcome measures. If Cohen's (1977) guidelines for interpretation are used, an effect size of .50 is a moderate effect, corresponding to group differences people would normally notice, and an effect size of .80 is a large effect, corresponding to very readily perceived group differences. This means that the effect of psychotherapy on children and adolescents on average is relatively large and has positive practical, as well as statistical, significance. These findings are comparable to findings for psychotherapy with adults.

Unfortunately, meta-analytic studies have not provided firm guidelines for which form of treatment (e.g., play therapy) is better than others or for which problem. This is because there are too few studies of certain strategies or populations to make meaningful comparisons. Only about 5% of the outcome research, for example, has addressed play therapy (Kazdin, 1993) despite the fact that it is a commonly used treatment for young children (Tuma & Pratt, 1982). Very little outcome research has specifically addressed the treatment of children below the age of 7 years or preschoolers in particular (Eyberg, 1992).

There are some tentative conclusions that can be drawn (and easily debated) from large-scale reviews. Behavioral-modification procedures and parent-management training tend to be more effective than short-term play therapy or other nonbehavioral techniques for aggressive and noncompliant youngsters, and treatments tend to be more effective for children than adolescents (e.g., Eisenstadt, Eyberg, McNeil, Newcomb, & Funderburk, 1993; Kazdin, 1993; Patterson, DeBarsyshe, & Ramsey, 1989). At this point it is necessary to turn to exemplary studies with specific techniques and populations for promising leads about which techniques are appropriate for which problems. The review article by Kazdin cites several good leads. In addition, Kratochwill and Morris (1991) examine the treatment research separately by clinical problem area.

The term play therapy is often misused for all kinds of supposedly helpful play activities. A potential for such misuse exists when Individual Educational Plans for preschoolers who are or are at risk of becoming developmentally delayed include play therapy indiscriminately. Too often, the goals for the intervention are left vague or are ones that would seem to be better served by educational programs. Blurring the distinction between play programs and play therapy leads to an unacceptable watering down of the different goals of intervention and of the different professional competencies involved. Hellendoorn et al., (1994, p. 221) suggest that it is useful to distinguish between play therapy, which aims at diminishing emotional problems and disturbances by means of play, and play programs, which aim at developing normal play skills.

Play programs for children with special needs

Interventions for children with special needs consist of helping them discover stages of play that they might not do on their own because of their handicaps. Generally this involves training the child's caregiver to observe the child's specific possibilities in order to help him or her acquire play skills. Hellendoorn et al. (1994) describe programs for children with special needs as being in the pioneering stage.

Play as curriculum and other play training interventions

There is considerable evidence that play training benefits children in their cognitive, linguistic, social, and emotional development. (Articles by Fein and Rivkin, 1986; Fisher, 1992; Hellendoorn et al., 1994; MacDonald, 1993; and Singer and Singer, 1990, chapter 6 provide excellent reviews of the evidence.) This is so for parent-child play

starting in infancy and for teacher-child play or training. Though there is agreement that training children to engage in socio-dramatic play can enhance their functioning in a number of ways (e.g., literacy, mathematical readiness, waiting behavior and self-control, group cooperation, concentration, originality), there is still no agreement about the reason. It has even been suggested that being able to play may just make children feel good in school and thus more accessible to whatever school wants them to learn. There is also controversy over whether play training is better than instruction that focuses only on the specific ability in question. Play as academic strategy is also constrained by the reasonable assumption that there are different routes to competence. For some children, it may be play; for others, it may be other routes.

A note of caution

Although play interventions have often been welcomed enthusiastically, their acceptance has not been unqualified. Sutton-Smith (1993, 1994), a prominent play theorist and researcher, for example, provocatively argues that many professionals are overcontrolling and oversupervising children's play in the service of adult interests. These interests have included inculculating manliness in the last century, controlling sexist play and abolishing play fighting and war toys in this century, emphasizing academic outcomes, and socializing lower classes according to middle-class standards by advocating parent-child play. Sutton-Smith is concerned that the genuine playfulness and autonomy of children's play, may be compromised.

Summary

The properties of play change with and reflect development. Piaget (1945/62), for example, maintained that the form play takes reflects the child's level of cognitive development or intelligence. Thus, practice play, symbolic or pretend play, and games-with-rules are play counterparts of sensorimotor, preoperational, and concrete operational intelligence, respectively. While it is true that games-with-rules increase dramatically during the school years, imaginative play persists well beyond the preschool years. It becomes internalized in the form of private thought, fantasy, daydreaming, imagination, and adult play (e.g., Dungeons & Dragons, costume balls, Mardi Gras festivals).

In general, researchers agree that there is an increase in interactive or social play, corresponding with social skill development as children grow older. Pretense play, for example, becomes an increasingly social activity between 2 and 5 years of age. However, the progression from solitary to socially collaborative play is not an invariant process. Some children continue to engage in solitary pretense play at the same time that they are involved in social pretense play.

Children who have delays or deficits in language, in cognitive functioning, or in socioemotional functioning are also likely to have play difficulties. It is not possible, however, to come to any conclusions about what causes play difficulties from these correlations. Neither is it possible to come to any conclusions about the consequences of play difficulties from correlations between play competence and positive developmental outcomes. The effect of the link between play variability and variability in other factors may go in either direction; it is also possible that the links may be mediated by common determinants. Nevertheless, these links make play behaviors of particular interest to psychologists interested in diagnosis and assessment of young children needing help. Play difficulties, for example, have been linked empirically to certain pathological states. As knowledge of children's play has grown over the last decades, so has the use of play for all kinds of interventions.

Recommended Resources: Professionals

Gould, R. (1972). *Child studies through fantasy: Cognitive-affective patterns in development.* New York: Quadrangle Books.
Nursery school children's fantasy materials form the foundation blocks for developmental considerations on aggression, identification and individuation, and ego and superego development. Gould's theoretical premises are grounded in vivid records of children at play.

Hellendoorn, J., van der Kooij, R., & Sutton-Smith, B. (Eds.). (1994). *Play and intervention.* Albany, NY: State University of New York Press.
A description of play interventions used for (a) therapy, (b) children with special needs, and (c) regular classrooms and elementary school curriculum.

Rubin, K. H., Fein, G. G., & Vandenberg, B. (1983). Play. In P. H. Mussen (Series Ed.) & E. M. Hetherington (Vol. Ed.), *Handbook of child psychology: Vol. 4, Socialization, personality, and social development* (4th ed., pp. 693–774). New York: Wiley.
Although the review of research benefits from updated reading, this chapter provides such a solid foundation for understanding children's play and the issues that are still being considered that it is an important reference.

O'Connor, K. J., & Schaefer, C. E. (Eds.). (1994). *Handbook of play therapy: Vol. 2. Advances and innovations.* New York: Wiley.
This book serves as a single source to get an idea of different approaches to play therapy, especially recent applications.

Schaefer, C. E., Gitlin, K., & Sandgrund, A. (Eds.). (1991). *Play diagnosis and assessment.* New York: John Wiley & Sons.

This volume presents a collection of recent contributions to play assessment which will be of interest to researchers and clinicians. The book is divided into six parts: "Developmental Play Scales," "Diagnostic Play Scales," "Parent-Child Interaction Scales," "Peer Interaction Scales," "Projective Play Assessment," and "Play Therapy Scales." The annotated bibliographies at the end of each section are useful.

Slade, A., & Wolf, D. P. (Eds.). (1994). *Children at play: Clinical and developmental approaches to meaning and representation.* New York: Oxford University Press.
This volume includes articles by child clinicians and researchers. Examples of children's symbolic play abound and will be instantly recognizable to those who have had any experience child-watching. This book will be useful to readers interested in the role played by affect and relationships in symbolic play in both normal and abnormal development.

Recommended Resource: Parents

Singer, D. G., & Singer, J. L. (1990). *The house of make-believe: Children's play and the developing imagination.* Cambridge: Harvard University Press.
This book could as easily be listed under the bibliography for professionals as under the one for parents. These authors manage to cover available research at the same time that they unfold a wonderful tale—"the special mystery of how we develop our human capacity for mental travel through time and space."

References

Bagnato, S. J., Neisworth, J. T., & Munson, S. M. (1989). *Linking developmental assessment and early intervention: Curriculum-based prescriptions.* Rockville, MD: Aspen.

Beeghley, M. (1993). Parent-infant play as a window on infant competence: An organizational approach to assessment. In K. MacDonald, (Ed.), *Parent-child play* (pp. 71–112). Albany, NY: State University of New York Press.

Biblow, E. (1973). Imaginative play and the control of aggressive behavior. In J. L. Singer (Ed.), *The child's world of make-believe: Experimental studies of imaginative play* (pp. 104–128). New York: Academic Press.

Blum, E. J., Fields, B. C., Scharfman, H., & Silber, D. (1994). Development of symbolic play in deaf children aged 1 to 3. In A. Slade & D. P. Wolf (Eds.), *Children at play: Clinical and developmental approaches to meaning and representation* (pp. 238–260). New York: Oxford University Press.

Bretherton, I. (1989). Pretense: The form and function of make-believe play. *Developmental Review, 9,* 383–401.

Cicchetti, D., Beeghly, M., & Weiss-Perry, B. (1994). Symbolic development in children with Down syndrome and in children with autism: An organizational, developmental psychopathology perspective. In A. Slade, & D. P. Wolf (Eds.), *Children at play: Clinical and developmental approaches to meaning and representation* (pp. 206–237). New York: Oxford University Press.

Cicchetti, D., & Wagner, S. (1990). Alternative assessment strategies for the evaluation of infants and toddlers: An organizational perspective. In S. J. Meisels & J. P. Shonkoff (Eds.), *Handbook of early childhood intervention* (pp. 246–277). New York: Cambridge University Press.

Cohen, J. (1977). *Statistical power analysis for the behavioral sciences* (Rev. ed.). San Diego, CA: Academic Press.

Dilalla, L. F., & Watson, M. W. (1988). Differentiation of fantasy and reality: Preschoolers' reactions to interruptions in their play. *Developmental Psychology, 24,* 286–291.

Eisenstadt, T. H., Eyberg, S., McNeil, C. B., Newcomb, K., & Funderburk, B. (1993). Parent-child interaction therapy with behavior problem children: Relative effectiveness of two stages and overall treatment outcome. *Journal of Clinical Child Psychology, 22,* 42–51.

Erikson, E. H. (1940). Studies in the interpretation of play: Clinical observation of play disruption in young children. *Genetic Psychology Monographs, 22,* 557–671.

Erikson, E. H. (1950). *Childhood and society,* New York: Norton.

Eyberg, S. M. (1992). Assessing therapy outcome with preschool children: Progress and problems. *Journal of Clinical Child Psychology, 21,* 306–311.

Fein, G., & Rivkin, M. (Eds.). (1986). *The young child at play: Reviews of research* (Vol. 4). Washington, DC: National Association for the Education of Young Children.

Fisher, E. P. (1992). The impact of play on development: A meta-analysis. *Play & Culture, 5,* 159–181.

Garvey, C. (1977). *Play.* Cambridge, MA: Harvard University Press.

Gil, E. (1991). *The healing power of play: Working with abused children.* New York: Guilford Press.

Gordon, D. E. (1993). The inhibition of pretend play and its implications for development. *Human Development, 36,* 215–234.

Gould, R. (1972). *Child studies through fantasy: Cognitive-affective patterns in development.* New York: Quadrangle Books.

Hellendoorn, J. (1994). Imaginative play training for severely retarded children. In J. Hellendoorn, R. van der Kooij, & B. Sutton-Smith (Eds.), *Play and intervention* (pp. 113–122). Albany, NY: State University of New York Press.

Hellendoorn, J., van der Kooij, R., & Sutton-Smith, B. (Eds.). (1994). *Play and Intervention.* Albany, NY: State University of New York Press.

Hetherington, E. M., Cox, M., & Cox, R. (1979). Play and social interaction in children following divorce. *Journal of Social Issues, 35,* 26–49.

Jarrold, C., Boucher, J., & Smith, P. (1993). Symbolic play in autism: A review. *Journal of Autism and Developmental Disorders, 23,* 281–307.

Johnson, J. E., Christie, J. F., & Yawkey, T. D. (1987). *Play and early childhood development.* Glenview, IL: Scott, Foresman and Company.

Kagan, J. (1984). The idea of emotion in human development. In C. Izard, J. Kagan, & R. Zajonc (Eds.), *Emotions, cognition, and behavior* (pp. 38–72). New York: Cambridge University Press.

Kazdin, A. E. (1993). Psychotherapy for children and adolescents: Current progress and future research directions. *American Psychologist, 48,* 644–657.

Kratochwill, T. R., & Morris, R. J. (Eds.). (1991). *The practice of child therapy* (2nd ed.). Elmsford, NY: Pergamon Press.

Lewis, V., & Boucher, J. (1988). Spontaneous, instructed, and elicited play in relatively able autistic children. *British Journal of Developmental Psychology, 6,* 325–339.

Linder, T. W. (1993). *Transdisciplinary play-based assessment: A functional approach to working with young children* (Rev. ed.). Baltimore: Paul H. Brookes Publishing Co.

MacDonald, K. (Ed.). (1993). *Parent-child play.* Albany, NY: State University of New York Press.

O'Connor, K. J., & Schaefer, C. E. (Eds.). (1994). *Handbook of play therapy: Vol. 2, Advances and innovations.* New York: Wiley.

Parten, M. B. (1932). Social participation among preschool children. *Journal of Abnormal and Social Psychology, 27,* 243–269.

Patterson, G. R., DeBarsyshe B. D., & Ramsey, E. (1989). A developmental perspective on anti-social behavior. *American Psychologist, 44,* 329–335.

Piaget, J. (1945/1962). *Play, dreams, and imitation in childhood.* New York: Norton.

Rubin, K. H., Fein, G. G., & Vandenberg, B. (1983). Play. In P. H. Mussen (Series Ed.) & E. M. Hetherington (Vol. Ed.), *Handbook of child psychology: Vol. 4, Socialization, personality, and social development* (4th ed., pp. 693–774). New York: Wiley.

Schaefer, C. E., Gitlin, K., & Sandgrund, A. (Eds.). (1991). *Play diagnosis and assessment.* New York: John Wiley & Sons.

Sigman, M., & Sena, R. (1993). Pretend play in high-risk and developmentally delayed children. In M. H. Bornstein & A. W. O'Reilly (Eds.), *The role of play in the development of thought* (pp. 29–42). San Francisco: Jossey-Bass.

Singer, D. G., & Singer, J. L. (1990). *The house of make-believe: Children's play and the developing imagination.* Cambridge, MA: Harvard University Press.

Singer, J. L., & Streiner, B. F. (1966). Imaginative content in the dreams and fantasy play of blind and sighted children. *Perceptual and Motor Skills, 22,* 475–482.

Sutton-Smith, B. (1993). Dilemmas in adult play with children. In K. MacDonald (Ed.), *Parent-child play* (pp. 15–40). Albany, NY: State University of New York Press.

Sutton-Smith, B. (1994). Paradigms of intervention. In J. Hellendoorn, R. van der Kooij, & B. Sutton-Smith (Eds.), *Play and intervention* (pp. 3–21). Albany, NY: State University of New York Press.

Tait, P. (1972). The implications of play as it relates to the emotional development of the blind child. *Education of the Visually Handicapped, 10,* 52–54.

Terr, L. C., (1991). Childhood traumas: An outline and overview. *American Journal of Psychiatry, 148,* 10–20.

Tuma, J. M., & Pratt, J. M. (1982). Clinical child psychology practice and training: A survey. *Journal of Clinical Child Psychology, 11,* 27–34.

Vygotsky, L. S. (1967). Play and its role in the mental development of the child. *Soviet Psychology, 12,* 62–76.

Vygotsky, L. S. (1978). *Mind in society: The development of higher mental processes.* Cambridge, MA: Harvard University Press.

Wachs, T. D. (1993). Multidimensional correlatives of

individual variability in play and exploration. In M. H. Bornstein & A. W. O'Reilly (Eds.), *The role of play in the development of thought* (pp. 43–53). San Francisco: Jossey-Bass Publishers.

Westby, C. E. (1991). A scale for assessing children's pretend play. In C. E. Schaefer, K. Gitlin, & A Sandgrund, (Eds.), *Play diagnosis and assessment* (pp. 131–161). New York: John Wiley & Sons.

Wing, L., Gould, J., Yeates, S. R., & Brierly, L. M. (1977). Symbolic play in severely mentally retarded and in autistic children. *Journal of Child Psychology and Psychiatry, 18,* 167–178.

8

Sports

Ronald E. Reeve

University of Virginia

Strong support for the value of sport participation is prominent in American society. Discussing athletic competition, for example, sociologist David Riesman wrote, "The road to the board room leads through the locker room" (cited in Tutko & Burns, 1976, pp. 41–42). James Michener (1976) in his landmark book *Sports in America* stated, "I believe that children, like little animals, require play and competition in order to develop. . . . I believe that competition . . . is essential to the full maturing of the individual" (Margenau, p. 2). To a greater or lesser extent, most Americans agree that participation in youth sports is healthy, physically and psychologically, for children.

Background and Development

Other than school, involvement in age-group athletics likely is the out-of-home activity in which school-aged children engage most frequently. An estimated 30 million children participate annually in youth sports activities (Lapchick, 1986), including nonschool- and school-sponsored activities. Thus about two-thirds of all youth ages 6 to 18 are involved in some type of athletics. Add to that approximately 5 million coaches, officials, and administrators and perhaps another 100 million parents and other relatives who provide transportation, watch practices and games, and the like and it is clear that youth sport is a major American enterprise, involving more than half the total population in some manner. With this level of participation, one would assume that a consensus exists that competitive athletics are good for children.

However, enormous variability exists within youth sports, such that the experience for one child may be markedly dissimilar from that of another child, with very different physical and emotional outcomes of participation resulting. Among the variables which may differ are the following: what the age (chronologically and cognitively), size, and skill level of the participants are; whether the sport is an individual or team sport; what the gender of participants is; whether the sport involves rep-

resenting a school or other group; and whether the coaches are trained or are merely volunteers.

Age Differences

Perhaps the most important psychological dimension involved in whether a given activity is "healthy" for children and youth is the impact of participating in that activity on the individual's self-concept and related motivational patterns. The theoretical and research model most often applied to youth sports was developed in the last two decades, primarily by Susan Harter (1983, 1986). Harter began with White's (1959) notion of "competence," the innate need of individuals to master their environment. The energy which drives this need is referred to by White as "effectance," and the emotional satisfaction attained is called "feelings of efficacy." When an individual is successful at mastering important developmental tasks, what develops is a general sense of themselves as efficacious, or competent, in the world. That feeling, in turn, promotes favorable feelings about oneself and increases the likelihood that the person involved will attempt and be successful at subsequent developmental tasks.

Harter (1983, 1986) expanded White's notions by relating them to cognitive-developmental stages and by noting that the reactions of significant others help shape children's evolving beliefs about themselves and their abilities. While competence is a more or less unitary construct for young children, a developmental shift occurs around age 8 or 9. Prior to that time, children see themselves as competent or incompetent, for example, "dumb" or "smart," globally. If a child succeeds at a task, the view of self is adjusted in a positive direction; if failure occurs on a particular task, the whole of self-esteem may move downward. During development, especially after 8 or so and continuing through 11 or 12, children become increasingly able to differentiate among activities and to see themselves, for example, as lousy at math but good at music or competent at sports but not at drawing. These multifaceted domains of self then get assigned varied levels of importance by the child/adolescent, eventually combining to form a global self-worth that is reliable over time. (See Self-Concept, this volume.)

As global self-esteem develops, perceived competence, affect, and motivation are interwoven. Children engage in mastery attempts throughout development. These are perceived as successful based initially on the feedback received from significant others. Early on, up to age 11 or so according to Harter (1983, 1986), Weiss (1995), and others who work in this area, children rely heavily on feedback from adults—parents, teachers, and coaches (in the case of sports). After age 11 or so, peer feedback and self-evaluation take on relatively greater importance. When mastery attempts are perceived as successful in the child's eyes (based on whatever feedback is received), feelings of competence are reinforced, and internal locus of control, positive affect, and subsequent competence motivation increase. (See Achievement Motivation, this volume.)

In sports (as in other developmental tasks), an internal locus of control, or "intrinsic motivation," is enhanced when children are reinforced for independent mastery attempts, encouraged to improve specific and concretely observable skills, and focused on enjoyment of an activity. In contrast, when children learn to view success at a task primarily in relation to others' performance (i.e., whether the child won or lost a contest), the outcomes are based less on variables which they can control. Perceived competence decreases, and an extrinsic motivational orientation is more likely to develop (Weiss, McAuley, Ebbeck, & Wiese, 1990). A sense of physical, athletic competence can contribute to the evolution of a positive global self-esteem and an intrinsic motivational style which potentially carries over into all parts of one's life.

Gender Differences

Differences between males and females in motor skills are present beginning in preschool years, though these differences remain small up through middle childhood. Girls usually are better at fine motor tasks, including handwriting and drawing, and in those gross motor skills that depend on precise movements (e.g., dancing, hopping, skipping). Boys typically outperform girls to a small extent in other gross motor areas throughout childhood, with the greatest male advantage occurring in throwing and kicking (Cratty, 1986; Thomas & French, 1985). Some difference in muscle mass in favor of boys exists. However, that genetic advantage is not sufficient to explain boys' superiority in so many gross motor skills. Environment likely plays a considerable role (Berk, 1993). Parents' expectations appear to be part of the reason for gender differences in children's skills. In a study of 800 parents of elementary students, for example, Eccles and Harold (1991) reported finding markedly higher expectations for sons to perform athletically than for daughters.

Not surprisingly, their children appeared to have absorbed these messages: Kindergarten through third grade boys *and girls* viewed sports as much more important for boys.

During adolescence, dramatic differences between genders in development of motor skills occur. Females make gradual skill gains, usually leveling off at around 14 years of age. Males, on the other hand, show marked increases in speed, strength, and endurance at puberty and continue to gain in these areas throughout their teen years (Beunen et al., 1988). By mid-adolescence, little overlap exists in motor skills between genders; that is, few girls are able to outperform the average boy in gross motor tasks by the age of 16. Thus, by early adolescence, most sports competition, and most physical education in schools, is sex segregated.

Females' sport participation clearly has increased since the 1970s. However, it still is not equal to males' (Coakley, 1990). Title IX of the federal Education Amendments of 1972 required schools receiving public funds to provide equal access for males and females in all programs, including sports. Despite the great impact of Title IX, Berk (1992) reported that, in high school sports, about 64% of all males participate while only 41% of females are involved.

Problems and Implications

Proponents of sports for children and youth point to potential outcomes such as improved fitness levels (and subsequent healthier adult lifestyles), enhanced social/emotional adjustment, better academic performance, and character development. Unfortunately, sports participation also has numerous possible drawbacks. For every positive outcome attributed to age-group athletic competition there exists a downside. A national panel of children's sports experts identified a series of issues which frame the debate over children's sports participation (Cahill & Pearl, 1993). These issues are summarized here briefly, with some reorganization.

Competitive stress, if too great, leads to anxiety and loss of fun. Over time, burnout and dropout often result. If competitive stress is kept at low to moderate levels, however, children can learn to cope with competition such as they are likely to face in their adult lives. Sports competition might serve to inoculate participants against debilitating stress reactions in competitive situations later in life.

Each year approximately one third of participants in any given youth sport drop out (Gould, 1987b). Sometimes that occurs simply because other activities are even more appealing. However, dropping out may be the result of remediable problems with the way in which sports are organized and run for children. Martens (1980) discussed the six most common reasons children gave for dropping out of sports. These included *not getting to play* (90% said they would rather play for a losing team than ride the bench for a winning team); *constant criticism of mistakes; mismatching* (e.g., the child who never experiences winning or where size is markedly different—"I had to tackle a monster"); *psychological stress,* as manifested in the feeling that the child dreads the approach of game time; *failure* (e.g., the child is cut or sits on the bench always); and *overorganization,* including too lengthy practices, military-style calisthenics, and too little fun in practices and games.

Some parents and critics of youth sport worry that the stress of competition in athletics is always too great. A landmark study by Simon and Martens (1979) should help alleviate some of the concern. They evaluated stress levels of children competing in seven sports as well as of those engaging in other evaluative activities including tests in school, participation in band, and performing in solo music competitions. The most anxiety-producing activity of all was the band solos. Additionally, the only sport which elicited more anxiety than tests in school was wrestling. Overall, team sports were less stressful than individual sports. Thus, unless a child is to be protected from all evaluative situations, there is little to suggest that sports participation places such stress on children and youth that athletics are to be avoided.

Moral development may be retarded when children are exposed to unsportsperson-like behaviors in other children and adults. It is all too common to observe coaches and athletes at all levels cheating, behaving violently, and using intimidation to achieve goals. In contrast, sports potentially provide unparalleled opportunities to test and learn to obey rules, as well as to see why rules exist and to learn to value fairness. This occurs when children observe positive role models and when they experience reinforcement for appropriate behavior in a competitive context.

Research data do not support the contention that sports participation necessarily builds character or otherwise enhances moral development (Rees, Howell, & Miracle, 1990). Rather, as with other activities in which children engage, how the experience is structured is the key to its effects.

Attitudes toward health can be impaired if participants experience constant criticism and repeated failure and when physical activity is used as punishment. Children may then come to associate exercise with these negative emotional experiences. The likelihood of future involvement in physical activity is decreased in such situations. A positive experience in sports increases the chances of lifelong participation in physical activity.

Development of a sense of responsibility for one's own actions may be diminished if the sport experience of a child is a negative one. An external locus of control may develop which predisposes the individual to blame others

for failures and not to take credit for successes. However, if adults allow children to share in decision making and provide opportunities for them to see the relation of specific individual actions to their own skill improvement, children can become increasingly responsible and independent—that is, internally controlled.

Social development can be negatively impacted if children expend so much time and effort on athletic activities that they fail to develop well-rounded personalities. Academic, social, and artistic development may well be impeded in those cases. Athletes who over-focus on sport often become quite self-centered and narrow. This appears to occur more commonly in individual sports such as ice skating, gymnastics, and swimming, where long hours of individual training are the norm. On the positive side, sport can provide great opportunities to interact with a variety of different children and adults, many of whom would not otherwise be a part of the child's social group, and to practice social and leadership skills as they work within a team to pursue mutual goals.

Athletes have been found to be the most popular group of children among 9- to 12-year-olds (Buchanan, Blankenbaker, & Cotten, 1976), indicating that being an athlete often is a social asset, especially for boys. A more recent follow-up study of nearly 500 fourth, fifth, and sixth graders (Chase & Dummer, 1992) examined which criteria were most important for popularity. For boys, sports success was considered the number one determinant for males to be popular, while physical appearance was considered most important for females and academic achievement somewhat less important. Girls considered physical appearance to be the most important determinant of personal popularity for both males and females.

Competitiveness, at its worst, can produce a "win at all costs" mentality. At the extreme negative end of the competitiveness continuum, sports has been viewed by some as a sort of organized child abuse. This is particularly true in girls gymnastics and, to a slightly lesser extent, in elite youth tennis and figure skating. In these sports the emphasis in the last several decades has been on identifying potentially gifted athletes at younger and younger ages; putting them in isolated training facilities where they practice for many hours each week and where their caloric intake can be monitored and their outside involvements controlled; and getting them into intense, win-lose competitions at ever earlier ages.

Since the 1970s, when Olga Korbut and then Nadia Comaneci captured Olympic gold medals in their early teens competing with bodies of young girls, thousands of little girls have been pushed to emulate their success. The ideal body for a gymnast in international competition is seen as being that of a prepubescent girl, with small buttocks, no breast tissue, and abnormally low body fat. Maintaining that "ideal" physique into teenage years requires that competitors' diets be restricted and that exercise volume and intensity be extreme in order to retard puberty. According to a recent report on "60 Minutes" (October 8, 1995), the 1976 U.S. National Gymnastics Team averaged 17 years of age, 5 feet 3 inches in height, and 110 pounds. The 1994 U.S. team averaged 15 years old, 4 feet 11 inches, and less than 90 pounds. Perhaps the elite gymnasts on the national team could make a case that the payoff was worth their sacrifices. Some of those individuals do get substantial economic benefits, and all at least have experienced considerable competitive success and have seen the world as part of their experience in gymnastics. However, there are only about 20 spots on the national team. There are approximately 20,000 girls in serious training in the U.S. (Margenau, 1990).

Children and youth who must make weight limits in sports or whose caloric intake is otherwise drastically restricted are at considerable risk for developing serious eating disorders. Weight-limit sports include wrestling and junior football for boys. However, concerns communicated by coaches to young competitors about weight are quite common in swimming, distance running, and especially gymnastics. It appears that females generally are more susceptible to continuing problems in this area than are males: Anorexia and bulimia are reported in approximately 4% of female athletes in "lean" sports such as women's gymnastics, while rates for girls in other sports are close to zero (Azar, 1996).

Fortunately, the extreme exemplified by girls' gymnastics at the elite level and to some extent by figure skating, tennis, and perhaps some swimming programs is not the mean for youth sports. The other end of the continuum might be "house league" soccer or T-ball, where everybody plays and where the young participants often have to ask who won on the way home, *if* the question ever occurs to them. Unquestionably, at least for young children, the T-ball end of the spectrum is much closer to ideal.

One problem with athletics for children is traceable to adults. Because adults usually must organize the activities, their values (emphasis on winning, etc.) sometimes get in the way of healthier motives for athletic activity. Unfortunately, some adults appear to live out their sports fantasies vicariously through their own children. Parents may threaten to (or may actually) withhold love and affection to motivate their children to meet parent goals for their children's performance.

Youth coaches also may be a part of the problem. (Of course, many youth coaches are also parents of participants.) Coaches, in the absence of having training in how to coach children and youth, too often model their own behavior on the most viable models available. The most visible are college and pro coaches whose jobs are on the line with every call (and whose players are at elite skill levels and are much older). Or they coach as they themselves were coached. The bottom line is that there is a significant lack of knowledge among youth coaches

about the emotional, social, cognitive, and physical characteristics and needs of children.

Based on their own perceptions and desires, adults make questionable decisions such as organizing preteen leagues so that there will be playoffs, all-star games, publicized batting averages and won-lost records, and the like. Children's needs frequently are sacrificed as children are encouraged to act like big leaguers or pros, instead of acting their age.

Elitism also is a problem. The most gifted often get the bulk of playing time, and they pitch or play quarterback. Certainly the game is not much fun for *either* team if a great pitcher strikes out everyone on the opposition. Children get stereotyped at a very early age: Heavy and slow children play on the line in football or play catcher in softball, never getting a chance to develop skills for other positions. Yet those who know about physical development of children are quite aware that body types change drastically for many children over the course of their childhood, with especially dramatic changes occurring during early adolescence. That chubby, slow 10-year-old may have a halfback or shortstop body at 14, but if no opportunity is provided to try different positions and to develop skills necessary for being a halfback or shortstop, odds are good that the child will have given up on football or softball some time before. Coaches make a serious error by trying to get maximum payoff *now* (e.g., winning) by playing children only in their current best positions, no matter what the child wants and with no eye to the child's future as an athlete.

Alternative Actions

Implications of Harter's developmental perspective for youth sports are several. Perhaps most importantly, it is not good practice to place too much emphasis on one activity (sports or anything else) in childhood. If a child experiences failure at the one central activity in his or her life, that child's self-esteem may be permanently impaired. Thus it would be better to place less emphasis on externally judged win-lose activities and more on participating in a variety of activities, with skill development and fun as the primary goals.

What can be done to improve the sports experience for children? Vogler and Schwartz (1993) make a number of suggestions which represent a consensus among those who study this field. *First* (and foremost), in order to allow as many children and youth as possible to receive the benefits of participation in sports, *de-emphasize winning*. This is especially critical at young ages, when children's self-concepts are initially forming. The adults' role in sports should be to teach the necessary skills, rules, and strategies for the games in a safe and appropriate environment. Most leagues for young children (those below 11 or 12) should be recreational in philosophy and orientation. For these young children, such things as league standings, play-offs, and all-star games should be downplayed or eliminated.

Too much emphasis on winning too early leads to unnecessary stress and frequently to burnout (Gould, 1987b). Mini-bikers have national championships beginning at age 6; 3-year-olds compete in a baton twirling olympics, and a national pee-wee golf tournament includes 4-year-olds. When pressures such as these occur too early, many participants often end up ready to burn their equipment by the time they reach adolescence.

For young children, the goals of skill development and fun must be paramount. The most direct route to letting children have fun is by eliminating the emphasis on winning. For team sports at the recreational level, the teams could be realigned as necessary to equalize competition, even after the season begins. Equal playing time should be assured for all children, and all children should have the opportunity to play all positions. Coaches could be rotated among teams from season to season, so that players would get the benefit of teaching from a variety of coaches.

A *second* strong suggestion is to *educate the coaches.* Clinics should be available in all local leagues for all coaches. The content of the clinics should include prevention of and care for injuries; techniques for teaching skills and strategies of the game; and, most importantly, the psychological needs of children who are in the age group involved. Canada, Australia, and New Zealand all require youth coaches to be formally certified by examination (Micheli, 1990).

Obviously, requiring that all coaches go through a training program will require time and energy for those providing the training as well as for potential coaches. Most sports for preadolescent children rely on volunteer coaches, and those typically are drawn from the ranks of parents. Fortunately, good models exist which have been successful and which can be adapted to fit local needs. Among the excellent coaching courses available are the American Coaching Effectiveness Program (ACEP) of the National Youth Sports Coaches' Association (2611 Old Okeechobee Road, West Palm Beach, FL, 33409) and the Program for Athletic Coaches' Education (PACE), 213 I. M. Sports Circle, Michigan State University, East Lansing, MI, 48824. Information about youth sports certification programs is available from the National Youth Sports Foundation, 10 Meredith Circle, Needham, MA, 02192.

Third, evaluate coaching behavior. While it is important to be as selective as possible in choosing coaches initially, it is at least as important to check in later to see how coaches are doing. Among the behaviors which should be prohibited are arguing with officials and berating players. Instances of these should be dealt with vigorously. Of course, other behaviors also should be evaluated. These include such things as dependability in organizing and getting to practices and games; providing specific and constructive feedback to players about their skills and structuring appropriate activities for skill improvement; keeping up with playing time so all players get their share; and (perhaps most importantly) making the experience fun.

Unfortunately, parents and other spectators also can be part of the problem with youth sports. Parents may yell inappropriately at their own and at other children, and they too often vocally dispute referees' calls. They also may interfere with the coaches' ability to coach during games. For these reasons, a *fourth* suggestion is to *keep adult spectators at a distance.* Some leagues have successfully required adults other than coaches to stay behind fences and/or in the stands, rather than allowing stray adults to roam the sidelines. If such rules were implemented and made clear early on, most adults would understand and comply, and the experience for children would be improved substantially.

Fifth, and very importantly, youth sports could be dramatically improved if organizers would *adapt special rules to increase action and the likelihood of success.* "Boring" sports such as Little League baseball, which have lost participants steadily, might experience a rebirth if hitters and fielders spent more time hitting and fielding than standing around and watching. At T-ball levels, the batting tee allows every batter to put the ball in play, and there is a defensive opportunity for every batter. Continuing this general notion, coaches or other players on the team could pitch to their own hitters. Other adaptations would be the use of a pitching machine or a different player to pitch each inning instead of having the one or two most precocious 12-year-olds do all the pitching. The increased chances for fielders to get involved would bring much more excitement and participation than now exist in the sport.

Similar rule alterations could improve the likelihood of success in other sports as well. In basketball, lowering the goal to 8 feet or 9 feet (depending on participants' ages) can increase scoring while also helping children to develop better shooting mechanics. Forbidding teams from using a full-court press likewise helps children who might not yet have developed the advanced skill necessary to evade several defenders while simultaneously maintaining a dribble. Further, using smaller basketballs for young participants recognizes the developmental fact that younger participants have smaller hands than do fully developed high school and college players. In basketball and other sports (e.g., soccer and football), changing the court or field size and limiting the number of players on the field or court at any one time also are likely to aid skill development.

Finally, take every reasonable safety precaution. Fortunately, the injury rate in organized sports is not high. In fact, more children are injured falling off swings, bicycles, and skateboards each year than by participating in youth sports (Taft, 1991). However, there is risk, and preventable injuries are unacceptable. The injury rate in Little League baseball, for example, is higher than necessary. Requiring batters to wear helmets has reduced injuries, but further injury reduction could occur. For example, a low-impact, softer covered, and safer baseball has been available for a number of years but has been rejected by Little League because of "tradition." It is the same size as a regulation ball, it bounces similarly to the "hardball," and it "carries" about as far when hit. While baseball may be the most obvious violator, other sports also must consider physical safety issues. Helmets and other protective gear should be mandatory in sports where danger is present. Fields and gyms must be checked regularly for potential safety hazards, and these problems should be dealt with expeditiously. Given the level of risk for serious injury, boxing and contact karate simply have no place as sports for children.

Should all sports competition be so controlled? Certainly the foregoing perspective makes good sense from a developmental perspective for most sports for children under the age of 12 or so. However, consistent with the implications of Harter's model as well as with what is known about the typical physiological development patterns of youth, older children are much better prepared to deal with the psychological and physical demands of more highly competitive sports. Thus, most experts recommend that an advanced level of sports competition be available as an avenue for the relatively more skilled athletes beginning at 12 or 13. At that point, programs catering to two or more ability levels are best. Thus, those who choose to compete at a higher level, with more emphasis on skilled performance, have opportunities to do so. However, those who wish to continue to play primarily for the joy of the activity also will have venues in which to participate.

Should Jane/John participate in sports? Parents face this question every day. School psychologists can help parents answer this important question by reviewing with them which issues must be considered. In general, given the potential benefits of sports, all children *should* be given the opportunity to participate. Some cautions, however, are important. The sport under consideration should be investigated, with an "intelligent consumer's" mindset, including consideration of a number of questions:

- Is the sport, as offered in this specific locale, safe? Check out the condition of the facilities, ask questions about equipment, and so forth. Is first-aid equipment, including ice, available at all practices and games? Is there an emergency plan in the event of injury to a child?
- Who are the coaches; how are they selected, trained, and evaluated; and what rules or principles guide their behavior? Is the emphasis of the sport on skill building

and fun or on winning? Do all players get to play? How are players selected and assigned? Do the coaches have training in first aid and CPR?
- Does the child *want* to play, or is she or he being asked to play to meet other needs such as to help parents to relive lost (or never found) sports glory through the child or to be able to keep pace with neighbors' or friends' children?

Answering these questions can maximize the likelihood that the sports activities chosen will be beneficial physically and emotionally.

Summary

Youth sports are part of the experience of most children in our society. When that experience is positive, the results can include enhanced health, self-esteem, and character development. On the other hand, participating in athletics sometimes leads to unnecessary injuries and negative attitudes toward exercise; it may lower self-concept (and thus weaken motivation to attempt new challenges); and sport may produce "characters" rather than enhancing character development. Much depends on how the adults involved structure the experience.

Recognizing that the physical and psychological needs of children vary across the developmental spectrum, best practice for at least a substantial majority of young children (through ages 11 or 12) includes de-emphasizing winning and focusing primarily on evaluating and improving the individual skills of participants and on making the experience fun for children. Beginning in early adolescence, two (or more) levels of competition should be provided so that more able athletes can have the opportunity to develop advanced athletic skills while those who choose to do so can still participate in primarily recreational youth sports.

Other changes which would substantially improve the sports experience for children and youth include

- Educating coaches.
- Controlling the behavior of adult spectators.
- Adapting rules to increase the likelihood of success (e.g., lowering the goal for basketball) and to provide more action and more opportunities for practicing the skills involved.
- Taking every possible precaution to ensure the safety of participants.

Psychologists should encourage parents to actively check out how a sport is conducted and make informed decisions about what is in the best interests of their children. Those concerned about the welfare of children should be advocates for making the youth sport experience a positive one for all children and youth.

Recommended Resources for Parents and Professionals

Cahill, B. R., & Pearl, A. J. (Eds.). (1993). *Intensive participation in youth sports.* Champaign, IL: Human Kinetics Publishers.

This book, published by the American Orthopaedic Society for Sports Medicine, includes a great deal of technical information about physiology of children's sports participation (e.g., resistance training and injuries in children). However, it also has excellent sections on competitive stress and burnout and on self-esteem and motivation. Also included are well-written, research-based chapters on social development of children involved in intensive, highly competitive sports-training programs.

Danish, S. J., Petitpas, A. J., & Hale, B. D. (1990). Sport as a context for developing competence. In T. P. Gullotta, G. R. Adams, & R. Montemayor (Eds.), *Developing social competency in adolescence.* Newbury Park: Sage.

This excellent chapter provides an insightful discussion linking sports with the developmental theories of Erickson, White ("effectance motivation"), and Harter. Research on the degree to which sports participation can enhance a sense of competence in children and youth is critically reviewed, and suggestions for designing sport activities to aid in healthy development are made.

Margenau, E. (1990). *Sports without pressure.* New York: Gardner Press.

Written in an informal, nonscientific, conversational style by a sports psychologist, this book would be very useful for parents and coaches. It provides a common-sense discussion of the developmental needs of children at various ages and offers good advice for parents and coaches about restructuring competition to make it more developmentally appropriate.

Micheli, L. J. (with Jenkins, M. D.). (1990). *Sportswise: An essential guide for young athletes, parents, and coaches.* Boston: Houghton Mifflin.

Micheli is a physician who specializes in youth sports injuries. He provides excellent suggestions for preventing and treating common sports injuries, and his presentation of appropriate training methods for children is useful. In addition, he shows pariticular insight into the psychological needs of children in his discussions of stress and "psychological injuries."

Seefeldt, V. D. (Ed.). (1987). *Handbook for youth sports coaches.* Reston, VA: American Alliance for Health, Physical Education, Recreation, and Dance.

This book includes chapters by many of the leading researchers and writers in the field of children's athletic competition. The chapters are unusually well integrated for an edited book and easy to read. All are addressed to the youth coach, and each offers practical suggestions on topics such as "Preventing Common Injuries," "Teaching Sportsmanship and Values," "How to Conduct Effective Practices," "Conducting a Sport Orientation Meeting for Parents," "What About Co-ed Competition?" and "Principles for Effective Coach-Athlete Interactions."

References

Azer, B. (1996). Public scrutiny sparks some eating disorders. *APA Monitor, 27,* 33.

Berk, L. E. (1992). The extracurriculum. In P. W. Jackson (Ed.), *Handbook of research on curriculum* (pp. 1002–1043). New York: Macmillan.

Berk, L. E. (1993). *Infants, children, and adolescents.* Boston: Allyn and Bacon.

Beunen, G. P., Malina, R. M., Van't Hof, M. A., Simons, J., Ostyn, M., Renson, R., & Van Gerven, D. (1988). *Adolescent growth and motor performance.* Champaign, IL: Human Kinetics.

Buchanan, H. T., Blankenbaker, J., & Cotten, D. (1976). Academic and athletic ability as popularity factors in elementary school children. *Research Quarterly, 47,* 320–325.

Cahill, B. R., & Pearl, A. J. (Eds.). (1993). *Intensive participation in children's sports.* Champaign, IL: Human Kinetics Publishers.

Chase, M. A., & Dummer, G. M. (1992). The role of sports as a social status determinant for children. *Research Quarterly for Exercise and Sport, 63,* 418–424.

Coakley, J. (1990). *Sport and society: Issues and controversies* (4th ed.). St. Louis, MO: Mosby.

Cratty, B. J. (1986). *Perceptual and motor development in infants and children* (3rd ed.). Englewood Cliffs, NJ: Prentice-Hall.

Eccles, J. S., & Harold, R. D. (1991). Gender differences in sport involvement: Applying the Eccles' expectancy-value model. *Journal of Applied Sport Psychology, 3,* 7–35.

Gould, D. (1987a). Promoting positive sport experiences for children. In J. R. May, & M. J. Asken (Eds.), *Sport psychology: The psychological health of the athlete.* Elmsford, NY: Pergamon.

Gould, D. (1987b). Understanding attrition in children's sport. In D. Gould & M. R. Weiss (Eds.), *Advances in pediatric sport sciences, Vol 2: Behavioral issues* (pp. 61–85). Champaign, IL: Human Kinetics.

Harter, S. (1983). The development of the self-system. In M. Hetherington (Ed.), *Handbook of child psychology: Social and personality development* (Vol. 4, pp. 275–385). New York: Wiley & Sons.

Harter, S. (1986). Processes underlying the construction, maintenance, and enhancement of the self-concept in children. In J. Suls, & A. Greenwald (Eds.), *Psychological perspectives on the self* (vol. 3, pp. 137–181). Hillsdale, NJ: Erlbaum.

Lapchick, R. E. (1986). *Fractured focus.* Lexington, MA: D. C. Heath.

Margenau, E. (1990). *Sports without pressure.* New York: Gardner Press.

Martens, R. (1980). The uniqueness of the young athlete: Psychological considerations. *American Journal of Sportsmedicine, 8,* 382–385.

Micheli, L. J. (1990). *Sportswise: An essential guide for young athletes, parents, and coaches.* Boston: Houghton Mifflin.

Michener, J. A. (1976). *Sports in America.* NY: Random House.

Rees, C. R., Howell, F. M., & Miracle, A. W. (1990). Do high school sports build character? A quasi-experiment on a national sample. *The Social Science Journal, 27,* 303–315.

Simon, J. A., & Martens, R. (1979). Children's anxiety in sport and nonsport evaluative activities. *Journal of Sport Psychology, 1,* 160–169.

Taft, T. N. (1991). Sports injuries in children. *The Elementary School Journal, 91,* 429–435.

Thomas, J. R., & French, K. E. (1985). Gender differences across age in motor performance: A meta-analysis. *Psychological Bulletin, 98,* 260–282.

Tutko, T., & Burns, W. (1976). *Winning is everything and other American myths.* New York: Macmillan.

Vogler, C. C., & Schwartz, S. E. (1993). *The sociology of sport: An introduction.* Englewood Cliffs, NJ: Prentice Hall.

Weiss, M. R. (1995). Children in sports: An educational model. In S. M. Murphy (Ed.), *Sport psychology interventions* (pp. 39–69). Champaign, IL: Human Kinetics.

Weiss, M. R., McAuley, E., Ebbeck, V., & Wiese, D. M. (1990). Self-esteem and causal attributions for children's physical and social competence in sport. *Journal of Sport and Exercise Psychology, 12,* 21–36.

White, R. W. (1959). Motivation reconsidered: The concept of competence. *Psychological Review, 66,* 297–333.

9

Sexual Interest and Expression

Deborah J. Tharinger
Jon Lasser

University of Texas at Austin

Background

An understanding of the development and meaning of children's sexual interest and expression, as well as the sexuality socialization of children, is of utmost importance to all child health and mental health professionals. For those professionals who practice in the schools, additional expertise is required to navigate, competently and sensitively, the complexities inherent in dealing with the interface of the topics of children, sexuality, gender, values and morals, parental and familial views, and cultural and political impact. Schools are an educational and social context where (a) children explore and express aspects of their sexuality individually and interpersonally; (b) opportunities and challenges exist for the provision of sexuality education; and (c) local cultural and political climates influence how personnel in schools are inclined or even allowed to respond to children's sexual interest and expression.

Most attention to sexuality today by parents, educators, health officials, and policy makers concerns the developmental period of adolescence. Dominant are concerns about adolescents being sexually active and the resulting consequences, such as contracting sexually transmitted diseases and becoming pregnant. Concerns in the adolescent period also center on the sexual interest and expression of sexual minority youth (see Sexual Minority Youth, this volume). Little attention, however, is paid to the development and meaning of sexuality in the period of childhood. From a scholarly perspective, barriers to research have been many (Goldman, 1994; Gordon, Schroeder, & Abrams, 1990), and in the popular literature there continues to be a denial of childhood sexual interest and expression and an uncomfortableness about addressing it. Although Freud's rich insights into infant and child sexuality were first published in 1905, and there has been a marked liberalization in adult attitudes toward sexuality over the past 40 years (Yates, 1982), little change has occurred in cultural attitudes toward childhood sexuality. As Strong and Devault note, "the silence

that surrounds sexuality in most families and in most communities carries its own important messages. It communicates that some of the most important dimensions of life are secretive, off limits, bad to talk or think about" (1988, p. 235).

Unfortunately, due to the prevalence of adult denial, many children are left to construct their own knowledge base about sexuality, often by going underground and getting information from peers, siblings, and older children that is often inaccurate, distorted, frightening, or at a level they cannot understand. Media, including television, movies, and advertisements in print and in visual form continue to market products, from cereal to perfume to jeans to cars with sexual images that bombard children. Sexualized images also are pronounced in children's popular media. Recent examples include Roger Rabbit's girlfriend in the movie of that name and the Pocahontas character in the 1995 movie marketed primarily to young girls. Even more recently concern has been voiced about children's access to sexually explicit information on the Internet (Cyberporn . . . , 1995). Children are left to struggle with how to make sense of the somewhat overwhelming and often contradictory images, unfortunately often without adult awareness, assistance, or supervision.

Although sexuality development is one of many domains of development, such as social, cognitive, emotional, physical, and moral (in fact, it transcends all of these), it is not well represented in courses on child development, in teacher education courses, or in professional psychology training programs, including school psychology programs. Psychology and education courses and textbooks do an adequate job presenting theory and research findings on sex differences and sex roles but have not integrated and disseminated the knowledge base that exists on sexuality development and socialization. Thus, psychologists and educators need knowledge to guide them in navigating the controversies inherent in offering information, assessment, and interventions in regard to children's developing sexuality. As in other domains of development, the psychologist needs to be able to differentiate and address, in context, what is relatively normal (or acceptable) from that which is abnormal (or unacceptable). The child experiencing the latter may be in need of a continuum of interventions targeted at a child, caretaker, or system. Psychologists also need to be aware of and sensitive to shifting notions of normalcy.

However, what may seem fairly straightforward in assessing and intervening in other domains of development can become unduly complex in the area of sexual development, which, as discussed earlier, falls in the midst of heated diversity of political, religious, family, educational, and community beliefs and values. Thus, it is not surprising that the area of children's sexuality development continues to be extremely controversial, with right- and left-wing groups opposing each other on the national, state, and local levels on the interface of public schools and sexuality education, AIDS awareness and education, education about sexual abuse, and educational curricula addressing diversity of sexual decision making and lifestyles. As an example, at hearings in December of 1995 before a congressional committee, both the American Psychological Association and the National Association of School Psychologists provided testimony. Congress held the hearings in response to parents' concern that the federal government condones the teaching of questionable values by allowing unrestricted sexuality education about issues such as HIV/AIDS, birth control, and condom use. Congress was asked to specify what can be taught in classes about sex and to use federal funding to school districts as a means of exerting control in the matter. The testimony of the psychologists stressed that sexuality education in schools ought to be comprehensive and unrestricted by the federal government—decisions should be left up to local school districts, with strong input from parents (APA Testifies . . . , 1996; NASP Responds . . . , 1996).

Despite political controversies, limited societal interest in finding out about the nature of child sexuality, and the lack of funds for research on children's developing sexuality, there has been a slow increment in knowledge about children's sexuality (Martinson, 1990). The appearance of the 1995 book, *Handbook of Child and Adolescent Sexual Problems,* edited by Rekers, is a welcome source of information for professionals who work with children. It covers early identification and prevention of sexual problems, problems of psychosexual adjustment to physical development, problems associated with sexual victimization, problems of gender development and sexual orientation, and problems of sexual behavior. Recent clinical and empirical research examining the consequences of child sexual abuse, especially the impact of abuse on sexuality development, has also been useful (Tharinger, 1990).

To help address the knowledge gap and promote attitude change, this chapter focuses on children's sexuality development, exclusive of the adolescent period. Depending on the definition of the beginning of adolescence, some of the concerns noted for adolescents are apparent for older children—that is, 11- and 12-year-olds—in terms of the consequences of being sexually active or sexually victimized, which include pregnancy, sexually transmitted diseases, and the need to be knowledgeable about contraception. However there are unique aspects of the development of children's sexuality that set the stage for the challenges most adolescents face in the area of sexuality, developments that are vital for professionals who work with children to understand. Thus, to better equip the school psychologist to respond to the questions and needs of children, parents, and educators in the area of children's sexuality, this chapter focuses on the development of children's sexual interest and expression, including expressions of sexuality in the elementary school setting.

Sexual interest is defined broadly as curiosity and concern about the physical, biological, cognitive, emotional, social, moral, and behavioral aspects of sexuality. *Sexual expression* is defined as the behavioral manifestation of sexual interest. In this chapter, the natural course of children's sexual development is traced and discussed, from infancy through middle childhood, along with central aspects of the sexual socialization process within the home and within the school. Four levels of concerns that children, parents, and educators have about children's sexuality are then presented. Then guidelines for assessment, intervention, and prevention activities for school psychologists are addressed, following the framework of the four levels of concern. Throughout, the need for school psychologists to be capable and comfortable in supporting the healthy development of children is emphasized. An approach to childhood sexuality is recommended that is open and honest, acknowledges the complex nature of sexuality, and is respectful. The task for parents and educators is to be knowledgeable, comfortable, approachable, communicative, and age appropriately responsive and yet protective of children. The task for children seems even more difficult—how to negotiate this complex and often perplexing area of development. The role for school psychologists is to assist children and their parents and educators to more successfully navigate these waters.

The Role and Preparation of School Psychologists

School psychologists, by the nature of their psychological knowledge and professional role in the schools, can be in a key position to reinforce parental and societal understanding and acceptance of children as sexual persons. They can

- Educate parents and teachers about what is normal and abnormal.
- Usually serve to defuse parents' and educators' fears that sexual expression in children leads to irresponsible or pathological sexual conduct in adult life.
- Facilitate communication between adults and children about sexuality.
- Participate in the selection, administration, and evaluation of sexuality education programs.
- Attend to the sexual interest and expression of special population children, such as those who are mentally retarded, physically disabled, or emotionally disturbed.
- Provide interventions to address child sexual victimization.
- Provide guidance to school-based responses to childhood sexual aggression.

However, school psychologists typically have little education, training, or experience in this area, perhaps because of the long-held attitude that sexual matters are not part of the school curriculum, because of the lack of graduate training programs to provide the knowledge and experiential base, and because sexuality has traditionally been medicalized. Although school psychologists interview and consult with parents and teachers about children's physical, intellectual, educational, social, and emotional development, they typically do not inquire about children's sexual development. In addition, school psychologists are rarely asked questions about children's sexuality, although almost all parents, teachers, and children have questions or concerns in this area. To begin communication, children's sexuality should be considered a domain of human life that can be discussed with both adults and children—not a difficult and embarrassing topic to be avoided (Jensen, 1979). Thus, the school psychologist must endorse sexuality as a legitimate topic of discussion and intervention. Sexual attitudes and behaviors can be explored as a preventive measure as well as a treatment of existing concerns (Haroian, 1992).

However, to be appropriately responsive, school psychologists must be approachable and knowledgeable. They must be open and comfortable with the topic, which requires obtaining knowledge and examining and clarifying personal attitudes about sexuality (Juhasz, 1983). In addition, they constantly must examine the effects of changing sexual mores on the broader social context. Once permission is given and comfortableness is modeled, questions will be raised by children, parents, and educators. Most of adults' questions will pertain to behavior within the normal range, that is, questions about children who are manifesting basically normal behavior that adults regard as wrong, abnormal, deviant, or inappropriate for a given setting. For most of these situations,

parents and educators can be helped by education, reassurance, and possibly brief counseling—interventions that help them respond to children in a manner that does not create a problem or exacerbate a minor problem. Most of children's questions will also fall along the continuum of what is abnormal and what is normal, in terms of thoughts, feelings, and behaviors, and can be addressed by similar psychoeducational and counseling interventions. However, other questions asked may suggest a serious problem, as exemplified by the presence of abnormal sexual behaviors, including sexual behavior that is inappropriate, precocious, or coercive and aggressive. Often, but not always, these behaviors are related to having been sexually abused. These concerns require thorough assessment and intervention for the child and family and typically involve collaborative referral to outside or school-linked health or mental health agencies. To be well grounded on the continuum of children's sexual behavior, school psychologists need to be familiar with the developmental nature of children's sexuality.

Sexual Development and Socialization

Children are developing sexual beings; they are developing physically, biologically, cognitively, emotionally, socially, morally, and behaviorally in relation to their sexuality. Sexual development is a natural, necessary, and complex process that begins at conception and continues throughout the life cycle (Petty, 1995). During the prenatal period, sexual development is controlled mainly by biological factors. But from the moment of birth, a child's sexual development is profoundly influenced by psychosocial factors, primarily parents and extended family, schooling, peers, and media, all interacting with the child's biological heritage. This process of being acculturated about sexuality is called *sexual socialization* (Calderone, 1983) and it cannot be prevented—it happens in one way or another. However, it can be weighted toward the healthy or the unhealthy. The goal is sexual adjustment; that is, individuals who, at every stage of their life cycles, are confident, competent, and responsible in their sexuality. Viewing sexual interest and expression, as well as its socialization, as developmental is useful in understanding the range of behavior included in the concept of normalcy rather than perceiving all childhood sexual interest and behavior as abnormal. In addition, knowing what is normal is essential to determining what is abnormal. A description of the normal developmental progressions of children's sexual interest can be organized into the stages of infancy, early childhood, and middle-to-late childhood.

Sexuality in Infancy

Sonograms show that the sexual response system begins functioning in utero, as shown by periodic erections of the penis and the findings that the vagina of the infant girl lubricates cyclically from birth on, by the same mechanism that operates later on in sexual responsiveness (Langfeldt, 1980). Also, orgasm-like behavior clearly is apparent in very young infants (Martinson, 1991). Furthermore, the discovery of various parts of the body inevitably leads a baby of around 6 months to discover its genital pleasure area, the penis in the boy and the clitoris and vulva in the girl. Baby boys and girls rub their genitals as soon as they develop the necessary motor coordination. There appears to be a genuine sense of pleasure leading to repetition of self-stimulation in infancy. The potential to respond to sexual stimuli in infancy suggests that the foremost "principle" in childhood sexuality is that "genital stimulation feels good" (Abramson, 1980).

The development of sexuality is thought to be greatly influenced by the infant's interactions with primary caregivers, consisting of sensuous closeness through holding, clinging, and cuddling (Biehr, 1989). This parent-child bonding begins at birth and extends to include nursing, bathing, dressing, and other physical interactions between parents and their newborn child. These interactions correspond to Bowlby's (1969) concept of attachment and to Erikson's (1968) first psychosocial stage of development, trust versus mistrust, and they are viewed as the beginnings of sexual education (Bettelheim, 1981). Children who are deprived of warm, close bonding during infancy can experience later difficulties in forming intimate relationships and perhaps in being comfortable with their sexuality (Trause, Kennell, & Klaus, 1977).

As infants develop social attachment and seek to secure and maintain closeness and trust, they begin to regulate self-stimulation to conform to external reactions. Thus, early parental reactions to an infant's genital exploration influence the regulatory character of his or her principles for acceptable sexual conduct (Petty, 1995). As the infant grows, sensorimotor intelligence also unfolds and matures, and genital stimulation becomes a predetermined rather than a random response, making the connection between genital play and positive feelings more assured. However, as this sequence becomes more practiced, parental awareness of this behavior also is more likely.

Thus, although self-stimulation begins early in infancy, many parents even today continue to regard genital play as wrong and unhealthy and are fearful of imagined consequences (Leung & Robson, 1993). Conscious self-pleasuring of the genitals can upset a parent who has not been prepared for acceptance of its occurrence as normal; it can lead to constant interference by well-meaning but uninformed adults who, because of their fear, do not permit children to explore their bodies. As a result of parental interference many children stop the behavior, but the experience may leave a lasting negative outlook on their own sexuality (Petty, 1995).

It is important for parents and educators to understand and accept that genital play and self-stimulation are a normal part of growing up and are viewed as an important step in the development of the erotic response (Martinson, 1991). The instances in which parents and educators need to give children special guidance are those in which the child engages in genital play or masturbates in situations felt to be inappropriate such as, in public, in the presence of persons outside the family, or even in the view of parents or family members who are upset by it. A parent or educator can be advised to direct the child simply to confine masturbating to a private place. This brings out a major principle in the sexual socialization of children, applicable from infancy on: Socialize for privacy. That is, the child's sexual interest, curiosity, or behavior should not be labeled "bad" but simply not appropriate for the time, place, or person (Calderone, 1983). Children as young as age two can begin to distinguish between appropriate contexts.

Instances do occur in infancy and later stages of development when self-pleasuring or masturbation is not an aspect of healthy development and necessitates more than guidance for privacy. This is when masturbation is excessive, compulsive, or both and not under the rational control of the child. When this is the case, the behavior can be viewed as a means of warding off anxiety or other distressing feelings and can be interpreted as defensive behavior (Jensen, 1979) or as emotional disturbance, especially when coupled with withdrawn behavior (Chilman, 1983). However, there are no norms for masturbation frequencies, and so-called "excessive masturbation" is a matter of judgment. Excessive masturbation is a subjective quantification interpreted as preoccupation with masturbatory activity to the exclusion of other age-appropriate activities or resulting in stigma and censure from others that may create secondary adjustment problems for the child (Haroian, 1992). In these instances, assessment and intervention may be needed.

Sexuality in Early Childhood

The onset of language signals a critical new stage in the development of sexual interest (Gadpaille, 1978). Children seek and are provided with labels for sexual feelings, functions, and organs that can serve to initiate a unified sense of sexuality (Abramson, 1980). It is important for adults to provide appropriate, accurate labels, and professionals can be helpful by enabling parents and early childhood educators to have a suitable vocabulary easily understood by the child.

During early childhood, most children begin asking questions about how babies are made and how birth occurs (Martinson, 1980). When parents are open, honest, and emotionally positive, the child senses that future question asking is welcomed. Parents also can anticipate questions and be prepared. The use of picture books to provide information and elicit questions is helpful. Some parents respond to their children's questions with matter-of-fact and developmentally appropriate answers, but others are obviously uncomfortable and reluctant to discuss sexual information at any length. Research has suggested that U.S. children are lagging in their knowledge of the facts and language of sexuality. In a cross-culture study, U.S. children were shown to be significantly delayed in the area of sexual thinking, that is, in their understanding of concepts about basic sexual development and behavior, compared with Australian, British, and Swedish children but to be equal on tests of general cognitive reasoning (Goldman & Goldman, 1982). In a study of U.S. children ages 2 to 7 years, Gordon et al. (1990) report a surprising lack of knowledge in several areas of sexuality studied.

At the same time that parents need to provide their children with accurate information, they need to remain cautious about how much information they give a youngster when a question is asked and to remember the child's age and developmental level. It is helpful to determine what the child really wants to know, which may be very different from the answer the adult is inclined to give (Bettelheim, 1981). The young child is ready for only a little information at a time. A now classic study on the thinking of children aged 3 to 12 about how people get babies continues to be an excellent source for understanding what children know and can understand at various stages of development (Bernstein & Cowan, 1975).

By age 5, most children are fascinated with learning slang words about sexual body parts. Jokes about sex and genital function begin to make their rounds, often heard first from an older child or adult and then repeated. Obscene words, especially "fuck," are used. The fascination and use continue into the school years, although these words are not used in a sexual way. Rather, they are used as part of growing up and being like one's peers or to convey status, anger, or frustration. Unfortunately, because even young children quickly learn the difference between a "clean" and a "dirty" word or joke, the idea that sex is dirty is reinforced. Parents may respond to children's experimentation with these new words by simply ignoring this benign behavior or by explaining to the child that some words are inappropriate in various settings.

During this stage, children continue to be curious about body parts, and unless harshly reprimanded for the behavior in infancy, they engage in genital stimulation, first as a solitary activity and later in social games like "show me yours and I'll show you mine" and "doctor." This behavior is usually related more to curiosity than sexuality (Petty, 1995). Children also continue to be aware of parental attitudes of disapproval of genital play

and can be confused by parental encouragement to be aware of their bodies but to exclude the genitals from such awareness. This confusion is compounded by many children's assumption, based on messages received during toilet training, that their genitals are "dirty." Parents need to be advised not to refer to aspects of the toileting process as negative or dirty but rather to convey a sense of pride in their child being able to successfully use the potty. Child-oriented books and videos on the topic can be useful to children *and* parents beginning the toilet training process.

Genital exhibitionism, a concern of some parents, is common and normal among 3- and 4-year-olds when it is occasional (Jensen, 1979). It generally indicates pride in one's body—a wholesome trait. Boys and girls up to 3 or 4 years enjoy being nude either at nursery school or in public. After that age, however, the public frowns on it, and they get the message and cover up. Normal genital exhibitionism is best accepted by parents for what it is— a healthy behavior. Parents simply need the education and reassurance to ignore the behavior or to act appropriately, and to avoid overreacting and creating a problem for the child.

Children also form ideas about sexuality based on their observation of physical interactions between their parents. Parents are both conscious and unconscious role models to their impressionable youngsters. Seeing one's parents hugging and kissing, and obviously enjoying it, is a good advertisement for the pleasure of physical and emotional intimacy. On the other hand, seeing parents constantly fighting and not being mutually responsive can have just the opposite effect.

In summary, it is normal for young children to want information about sexuality, to become fascinated by dirty words, to continue to self-stimulate and engage in social games involving sexual exploration, to feel proud of their bodies and want to exhibit them, and to be influenced greatly by their parents' affectionate behavior toward each other and toward them. What is not normal is excessive or compulsive self-stimulation or exhibitionism; coercive and aggressive sexual behavior toward others; and detailed and age-inappropriate understanding of adult sexual behavior. It is likely that children manifesting these types of behavior have been overly sexually stimulated for their age. They may be victims of sexual abuse (see Sexual Abuse, this volume), or they may have witnessed on television or in person sexual activity that they cannot comprehend or integrate, and they are preoccupied or disturbed by it. These behaviors require evaluation and possibly intervention.

Sexuality in Middle-to-Late Childhood

During the middle-to-late-childhood stage of development, many children undergo significant physical changes that impact their sexual and reproductive capacities. The biological sexual changes in physical appearance and functioning—the development of pubic hair, development of breasts, the appearance of wet dreams—can be troublesome to the child, who is often not sure how to react to such phenomena. Biological puberty, defined by the beginning of menarche in girls and by the capacity for ejaculation in boys, begins between the ages of 8 and 15 (Martinson, 1991). The average range for the onset of menstruation is 12 to 13 (Petty, 1995). Girls who present with early or precocious puberty have significant developmental struggles, while boys with early puberty are often heralded as leaders and capable athletes. The psychological impact of precocious puberty can be a significant childhood trauma for girls. It separates the child from her peers, undermines the security of sameness, and may produce tension within her family (Haroian, 1992). For example, a pubescent female third grader must prematurely attend to the rituals of menstruation and breast development and may be the target of ostracism from peers and undesired attention from older boys, taking her off the normal developmental track of age-appropriate sexual and gender play.

A natural and continuing aspect of sexual development during this stage is sexual play and gender play between same-sex and opposite-sex peers. Clinicians have described normal child sexual exploration or play as an "information gathering process of limited duration where children of similar ages explore each other's bodies, visually and tactually" (Johnson, 1990, p. 64). Children involved in normal sex play are near the same size and age and participate voluntarily. This type of normal sexual behavior generally occurs only a few times in discrete periods of a child's life and does not leave children with feelings of anger, shame, fear, or anxiety, although there may be some embarrassment and silly or giggly affect. Normal sexual behaviors among children may include kissing, hugging, peeking, touching, and exposing of genitals that tend to diminish and then stop if children are discovered and asked to stop (Johnson, 1991).

Sexual play is usually secretive, conducted out of the sight of adults. Boys initiate sex play more often than girls (Kinsey, Pomeroy, & Martin, 1948; Kinsey, Pomeroy, Martin, & Gebhard, 1953). In a survey, parents noted that 76% of their daughters and 83% of their sons had participated in some sex play (Kolodny, 1980). By age 8 or 9, children have awareness of the erotic element of self-stimulation and sexual play (Masters, Johnson, & Kolodny, 1982). Engaging in these experiences can help children learn how to relate to others, with important consequences for their adult psychosexual adjustment (Martinson, 1976). Thus, ordinary sex play is not psychologically harmful; it is simply a stage of development. It generally occurs between playmates of like age, is cooperative, and is limited to a few episodes (Kinsey et al., 1953). It may consist of mutual touching or imitating intercourse. However, if sexual exploration involves an older child, (e.g., an adolescent with a school-age or younger child), coercion, or aggression, it is not a case of sexual play. It is sexual abuse and needs to be addressed accordingly.

The harm arising from ordinary sexual play among children generally comes from any ensuing crisis that might arise—the punishment and guilt induced by the parents' and other adults' reactions. The child who has been expressing normal sexual curiosity can come to feel bad and shameful. The episode can be traumatic; it can shape attitudes that interfere with healthy adult sexuality. Parental reactions to the discovery of sex play in children frequently operate on a double standard. Girls often are cautioned strongly against sexual play, especially with boys. Boys, on the other hand, tend to get mixed messages from their parents; they may be warned or even punished for such activity, but there is a hint of resignation or even pride in the attitude that "boys will be boys." In general, there is far more parental and societal acceptance of sexual interest in talk and behavior in boys than in girls. Little girls are expected to demonstrate awareness and interest in the reproductive aspects of sex rather than the pleasure or recreational aspects.

The unspoken permission for boys to follow their sexual curiosity applies except in homosexual situations, where parents consistently react in a negative way. However, many parents are unaware that homosexual play among children is a normal part of growing up. Homosexual experiences have been reported by more than half the boys and more than a third of the girls in a study of children of ages 4 to 14 (Elias & Gebhard, 1969). These homosexual activities are a common part of sexual development in this culture, and such experiences are usually unrelated to sexual orientation in adulthood (Bell, Weinberg, & Hammersmith, 1981).

Gender play was the focus of a recent study that involved extensive observations in elementary schools (Thorne, 1993; Thorne & Luria, 1986). The authors noted that what appears to be sexual to an adult observer may have little or no sexual content for children: "In elementary school life the overtly sexual is mostly a matter of words, labels, and charged rituals of play. In identifying this behavior as 'sexual,' we (the authors) are cautious about imposing adult perspectives. When children say words like 'fag' or 'fuck,' they rarely share adult meanings, as was apparent in their use of 'fag' essentially as a synonym for 'nerd' and as an epithet occasionally applied to girls as well as boys" (Thorne & Luria, p. 185). The authors further explain that "from an early age children draw on sexual meanings to maintain gender segregation, that is, to make cross-gender interaction risky and to mark and ritualize boundaries between "the boys" and "the girls." In their separate gender groups, girls and boys learn somewhat different patterns of bonding—boys sharing the arousal of group rule-breaking; girls emphasizing the construction of intimacy and themes of romance. Coming to adolescent sexual intimacy from different and asymmetric gender subcultures, girls and boys bring somewhat different needs, capacities, and types of knowledge" (Thorne & Luria, 1986, p. 188).

This discussion of sexuality development in middle to late childhood calls into question Freud's concept of a period of sexual latency—a time when sexual interests and impulses are diverted into nonsexual behaviors and interests. Although after age 8 separation of the sexes in play activities is common and the term *homosocial* has been used to explain this phase of sexual development—a time when males play and associate with other males and females play and associate with other females—the existence of a period of sexual latency is not widely accepted (Petty, 1995). During late childhood, children play primarily with members of their own sex, but research indicates that they discuss sex-related topics frequently, show keen interest in the opposite sex, desire to be in the presence of the opposite sex, and under certain circumstances desire to engage in sexual activities with members of the opposite sex. Children in this age period begin to form attachments or crushes on others their age, in what becomes for many children the beginning of a series of close relationships with peers of the opposite sex. During this time, many older children learn how to kiss, how to dance, how to talk to peers of the opposite sex, and how to fondle and caress. The process of navigating this stage of development and learning these skills is often exciting and dramatic but can also be painful and embarrassing, requiring adult input and guidance if offered or welcomed (Martinson, 1991).

Problems and Implications

Having reviewed the development of children's sexual interest and behavior, the reader may now find it useful to examine and contrast the questions that children, parents, and educators have about children's developing sexuality. Concerns or problems that arise regarding children's sexual development are discussed in the following paragraphs using a four-level framework. Again, concerns or problems are examined from the perspective of children, parents, and educators.

Questions About Sexual Interest and Expression

Children's questions

When most adults think about children's interest in sexuality, the question of where do babies come from and the names of body parts often come to mind. These are classic concerns and usually refer to questions asked by 2- and 3-year-old children. It is important to examine the range of questions that children are asking or thinking

about and not asking. These exemplar questions reflect a need that children have for information and understanding—preferably from adults. These may include:

- Why are there so many mixed messages about sex?
- How come adults act so differently when anything about sex comes up?
- What is sex anyway?
- What is all the fuss about?
- Why are these called "dirty" words and why are they dirty?
- Is my curiosity OK?
- What is normal?
- Where can I get accurate information?
- What are the rules and when do they apply?
- How come the rules seem to apply differently for boys and girls?
- Where do I fit in?
- Are my thoughts, feelings, and behavior normal?
- Why am I being teased?
- Why would an adult want or try to be sexual with a child?

Parents' questions

Parents' questions are somewhat different from children's but reflect the same need for information and communication. Their questions may include:

- How do I respond to my children's sexual questions, interest, and behavior?
- Do I wait for questions, or do I proactively give information, and if so, when and how?
- How do I balance my child's sexual curiosity and expression with protecting him or her from knowing and expressing too much?
- Am I promoting feelings of shame, guilt, embarrassment, and fear in my child about his or her sexual development?
- How do my own attitudes about sexuality impact my child's?
- Is my child's sexual behavior pattern normal or abnormal?
- Is my child's sexual behavior just normal curiosity or a sign of a developmental deviation?
- Will educating my child about sexuality encourage permissive attitudes, resulting in active sexual involvement or sexual behaviors that deviate from a pattern normally accepted by society?
- Does my child need treatment for a potential sexual problem?
- What are the chances that my child will or won't have a normal adult sex life?

Educators' questions

Educators' and school administrators' questions are somewhat different from those of children and parents in that they are more systemic and involve setting school policy. Their questions are likely to include:

- What is the responsibility of the local school in terms of educating children about sexuality?
- What is the responsibility of the school for responding to children's sexual expression, including masturbation, sexual language, touching, teasing, harassment, and sexual aggression?
- What is the responsibility of the school for ensuring that children are safe from sexual harassment, teasing, name calling, and the like?
- How do schools effectively address children's use of sexual terms, slang, and labels and sexually charged rituals of play?
- How do children use sexual meanings to maintain gender segregation and when is it appropriate and inappropriate?
- How do school personnel recognize when adults are adultmorphizing the meaning of children's sexual interest and expression and overreacting to it?
- How does one recognize signs that children have been sexually abused?
- How can school professionals work with groups of local parents to develop effective policies for our school?

Thus, it is apparent that children, parents, and educators have many questions about developing sexuality, some very similar and some distinct based on their unique responsibilities. These questions can be examined for their common basis and underlying concerns.

Analysis of Concerns

From an examination of the common anxieties of children, parents, and educators described earlier as well as the questions just presented, four levels of concern are proposed by this chapter's authors as a framework from which to conceptualize perceived sexual concerns about children's sexual interest and expression. Each progressive level represents a more serious problem and the need for more extensive assessment and intervention. These levels are depicted in the following discussion and then revisited with an eye toward intervention.

Level 1: Lack of knowledge about children's sexual development

Many concerns that children, parents, and educators voice are due to their lack of knowledge about the normal development of child sexuality. Because of this lack of knowledge, the concern is that the interests and behaviors are abnormal when, in relation to most standards, they fall in the normal range.

Level 2: Lack of effective communication among children, adults, and systems

Other concerns are due to poor communication about sexuality. Parents and educators are confused about how to respond to children's behavior and questions: They are unsure about how to sexually socialize children—how to educate and yet protect them. These adults are uncomfortable with childhood sexuality and perhaps affected by their own sexual issues. Children do not know how or where to get information or how to initiate a discussion with adults.

Level 3: Fear of social rejection resulting from sexual expression

Concerns at this level are related to the emotional and social consequences adults fear for children and, in the case of parents, sometimes for themselves. Parents and educators want to protect children from engaging in behavior that the children cannot handle cognitively and emotionally, for example intercourse, and of course almost all adults want to protect children from any sort of sexual abuse. Parents also may want to protect children from engaging in thoughts, behaviors, and interests that would render them victims of social prejudice and harassment, for example, homosexuality and pervasive cross-gender behavior, particularly for boys. Interestingly, although children themselves may share the same fears as adults in terms of being shamed or rejected because of their sexual expression, some children may fear peer rejection for not participating in what adults may view to be premature or precocious sexual behaviors.

Level 4: Presence of abnormal sexual behavior: Inappropriate, precocious, or aggressive/coercive

The concerns at Level 4 involve a child's abnormal sexual expression. The child's sexual expression, self-directed or directed at others at home, at school, or in the neighborhood may be related to past or present sexual abuse or sexual overstimulation, to severe stress or neglect, or to the inability to regulate sexual behavior as a result of being traumatized, retarded, autistic, or psychotic. A model delineating three levels of abnormal sexual behavior has been suggested by Berliner and Rawlings (1991). These levels include inappropriate sexual behavior, developmentally precocious sexual behavior, and coercive/aggressive sexual behavior.

Alternative Actions

Assessment

The goal of an evaluation is to recommend and provide or refer for appropriate intervention. The higher the level of concern and the poorer the fit among the child, parents, and educational system, the more extensive the intervention will need to be. Many factors must be considered when evaluating a child's sexual interest or expression as being possibly inappropriate and in need of intervention. Although a discussion of assessment in this area is beyond the scope of this chapter, the following factors are suggested as important components of the evaluation.

- Aspects of the Sexual Interest and Behavior
  □ Type, frequency, intensity, duration, and context (e.g., individual, dyadic, group) of expression of sexual behavior the child is displaying.
- Aspects of the Child
  □ Age, sex, and physical, cognitive, social, and emotional level of the child.
  □ Degree of distress experienced by the child as a result of his or her sexual expression.
  □ Child's level of understanding of his or her sexuality development.
  □ Current stressors present in the child's life.
  □ Presence and nature of current or previous sexual abuse.
  □ Presence and nature of intrusive medical procedures regarding genitalia.
  □ Motivation of the child to participate in the intervention.
- Aspects of the Family
  □ Family composition.
  □ Degree of distress experienced by family members as a result of the child's sexual expression.
  □ Degree of accurate parental knowledge of childhood sexuality.
  □ Parents' ability to communicate effectively about sexuality with their child.
  □ Parental attitudes and values regarding sexuality, including cultural and religious attitudes.
  □ Presence of recent or current family stressors.
  □ Presence and nature of previous or current domestic violence.
  □ Motivation of the parents to participate in an intervention.
- Aspects of the School Environment
  □ Teachers' and administrators' knowledge of sexuality, ability to communicate with children and parents, and attitudes and values.
  □ Cultural, religious, and political influences on the school environment.
  □ Degree of distress experienced by school personnel as a result of the child's sexual behavior.
  □ Quality of the relationship between the family and the school.
  □ Motivation of educators to participate in the intervention.
- *Aspects of the Peer Group:* Characteristics, behavior, sexual experiences, and strength of influence of the child's peer group.

- *Aspects of the Culture:* Norms of subcultural group to which the child and family belong

Interventions

Available interventions are not unique to the topic of children's sexual interest and expression and are familiar to many school psychologists. They include psychoeducational methods; mental health or behavioral consultation; crisis intervention and related problem-solving techniques; school-based individual, group, and family counseling and therapy; and referral to other mental health and health professional for similar and additional services. School psychologists need to be informed and comfortable about applying these interventions to sexual concerns with children, parents, families, and educators. To be effective, school psychologists must examine their own personal attitudes about sexuality, must gain knowledge about child sexuality and sexual socialization, must consider the consequences of entering an area where cultural denial and prohibition continue to be strong, and must seek out school district and parental support. Interventions are described that are appropriate at each of the four levels of concern just described, followed by suggestions for prevention activities.

Interventions for level 1: Lack of knowledge
If an evaluation reveals that the perceived sexual concern or problem results from lack of knowledge on the part of the children, parents, or educators regarding what is developmentally appropriate, information needs to be provided, either directly by the school psychologist through a one-to-one format or by referring the parents and educators to readings, courses, or in-service training workshops focused on childhood sexuality. Suggested goals for parental sexuality education programs that also can be applied with teachers are offered by Klein and Gordon (1992) and Walters and Walters (1983). Children can be referred to sexuality education courses, possibly offered through the school or through church or community organizations. Children and adults are well served by accurate information, endorsement of the normalcy of children's sexual feelings and desires and of their right to be sexual, and an opportunity to learn culturally acceptable sociosexual skills and sexual socialization skills.

Interventions for level 2: Lack of effective communication
If an evaluation reveals that a perceived sexual concern or problem stems from poor or negative communication between parents and child or educator and child, it is appropriate for the school psychologist to intervene by directly working with the parents or educator to aid them in feeling knowledgeable, confident, comfortable, and secure in talking to children about sexuality. In the early 1950s, Kinsey suggested that if parents wanted to be the

ones to tell their child about the "facts of life," they should do it before the child reaches the age of nine. With today's proliferation of sexual images, information, and misinformation in the media, that age should probably be revised downward to about age five. Referral to a parent group or communication group within the school or to a local mental health facility also can be effective. If the parent or educator appears to be seriously distressed by the idea of communicating about sexuality, a referral for individual or couple counseling may be timely. If parents accept and endorse the child's interest in sex and encourage the acquisition of sex information, trial and error learning will become less necessary and children will look to parents for information, discussion, and support. The acknowledgment of the child's interest in sex, supervision of play with other children, distraction from sexually stimulating situations, and specified acceptable times and ways to experience sexual gratification or satisfy sexual interest will in time bring sex talk and behavior into an acceptable range (Haroian, 1992).

It also can be beneficial for school psychologists to work directly with children, individually or in groups, to provide them with age-appropriate information about sexuality and the means to feel comfortable in communicating about their sexuality. As discussed earlier, children have many questions about the area of sexuality and their development. Intense and continued or intermittent sexual interest in children should be accommodated as any other interest would be. Age-appropriate books and conversations with parents endorse the child's curiosity about this important aspect of life and encourage an open and unashamed quest for sexual knowledge (see Recommended Resources). In contrast, a child who shows little interest or curiosity about sex should not be overwhelmed with sex information by overzealous parents or educators.

Interventions for level 3: Fear of social rejection resulting from sexual expression

If an evaluation reveals that a child's perceived sexual problem is a result of the child's engaging in behavior that parents, teachers, or both believe he or she cannot cognitively and emotionally handle, such as being sexually active, and the problem cannot be resolved by providing knowledge and communication skills to the adults and child involved, crisis intervention and therapy are recommended. Family therapy may be the treatment of choice because the whole family's functioning, and how it may be supporting or even encouraging the child's behavior, can be reviewed and targeted for change.

In the case of children for whom evaluation reveals that the perceived sexual problem is a result of their engaging in interests and behaviors that can render them and perhaps their family victims of social prejudice, such as homosexual or excessive cross-gender behavior, multiple interventions may be required. In the case of homosexuality, for example, the children need the psycho-

logical protection of a counseling or therapy relationship from which to explore these interests and determine their meaning (see Sexual Minority Youth, this volume). Education about the normality of homosexual fantasies and behavior in childhood can relieve fears and distress and eliminate the concern. Children who determine that their sexual orientation is exclusively or primarily toward members of the same sex need continued support to integrate this information into their identity and relationships in the world. In this case, some parents may also need support through outside counseling, community support groups, and possibly family therapy to cope with what they may perceive as a loss and rejection and to reach the stage of acceptance. Other parents may not perceive their child's homosexuality as a loss but rather as an important part of their child to embrace and support. In addition, school psychologists can aid teachers by providing consultation to allow them to work on their own emotional reactions to homosexuality and to assist them with other students' reactions.

Intervention for level 4: Presence of abnormal sexual behavior

If an evaluation reveals that a child's perceived sexual problem falls on the continuum of abnormal sexual behavior, that is, inappropriate sexual behavior, developmentally precocious sexual behavior, or coercive/aggressive sexual behavior, child, group, and family therapy may be warranted, teacher consultation is recommended, and in case of coercive and aggressive sexual behavior, a residential treatment setting may be needed. Children exhibiting these behaviors typically have been sexually abused or sexually overstimulated. Sexual abuse has serious initial and ongoing emotional and behavioral consequences for the child that continue if untreated and also can endanger others (Berliner & Elliot, 1996).

The level of intervention depends on where they fall on the continuum of exhibiting abnormal sexual behavior. Inappropriate sexual behavior may include persistent, public, or painful masturbation; touching others' or asking others to touch their breasts or genitals; expressing excessive interest in sexual matters, materials, or sexual behavior of others; sexualization of nonsexual situations, sexually stylized behavior imitative of adult sexual relationships; sexualized content to play, art, or conversation; and repeatedly publicly showing genitals (Berliner, Manaois, & Monastersky, 1986). Based on clinical reports, it is believed that children demonstrating inappropriate sexual behaviors have almost always been sexually abused or sexually overstimulated (Johnson, 1990). Developmentally precocious sexual behaviors include engaging in extensive sexual behaviors with other children, including oral copulation and vaginal and anal intercourse (Berliner & Rawlings, 1991). These behaviors are typically the result of having been sexually abused and then abusing others—typically similarly aged peers, such as siblings or other children in foster care (Johnson,

1990). Sexual behaviors at the coercive/aggressive end of this continuum are the most serious and may be associated with other forms of antisocial behavior. Aggressive sexual behavior may involve physical force to obtain submission and to prevent reporting. Coercive sexual behavior does not use force; however, serious threats to gain compliance are utilized. Behaviors at this extreme end of the continuum are by far the most serious, may be associated with other forms of antisocial behavior, and are in need of extensive intervention.

Prevention Activities

In addition to providing intervention services, school psychologists can be involved actively in school-based prevention programs by conducting parent education groups on childhood sexuality and communication skills and by providing workshops for educators on sexual development and on ways that school personnel can respond more appropriately and effectively to children's sexual interest and behavior. School psychologists also can meet a prevention need by supporting and being involved in sexuality education programs for children in the schools (Klein & Gordon, 1992). Parents and teachers may also involve themselves in prevention efforts by controlling the subtle messages about sexuality that adults communicate to children. Negative reactions to nudity, dirty words, and sexual behaviors can have a deleterious impact on children's development. An awareness of this impact, combined with a solid knowledge base of children's sexual development, can help parents and educators respond to children's sexuality in a positive, nurturing manner.

School psychologists work extensively with children who have disabilities of one kind or another. These children require sex education, and many have the same needs, desires, rights, and responsibilities as the nondisabled child. To teach sex education to children with disabilities, professionals need a positive attitude toward the children and to know the particular medical and psychosocial implications of the disability. Suggestions for providing sex education for children with emotional disturbance, behavior disorders, mental retardation, sensory impairments, and orthopedic impairments are provided by Harioan (1992), Warzak, Kuhn, and Nolten (1995), and Tharinger, Burrows-Horton, and Millea (1990).

Summary

School psychologists have the opportunity to be involved in the identification and prevention of ignorance and silence about childhood sexuality. Although most people associate sexuality solely with adolescence and adulthood, infants and children are developing sexual beings and they express natural interest and curiosity about their sexuality. Most adults, including parents and educators, find it difficult to accept and to allow expression of childhood sexuality, to communicate with children about sexuality, and to provide a positive sexual socialization experience for children. As a result, many children may associate the negative feelings of shame, guilt, embarrassment, fear, and helplessness with sexuality. Ironically and unfortunately, as parents, these children may pass on to their offspring similar attitudes and feelings.

To aid school psychologists, this chapter discussed the controversies that ensue in this area and presented the normal developmental progressions of children's sexual interest from infancy through middle-to-late childhood. Questions that children, parents, and educators ask about children's sexuality were reviewed and concerns that they express about children's sexual interest, using four progressive levels of seriousness, were delineated. Following, guidelines for conducting comprehensive assessments were provided, suggestions for appropriate interventions under each of the four levels of concern were offered, and the need for school psychologists to be involved in prevention activities was argued.

School psychologists can be in a key position to reinforce parental and societal acceptance of children as sexual persons; to educate adults and children about sexual development; and to promote honest, accurate, and open communication about sexuality among adults, children, and systems. School psychologists can evaluate adults' concerns about children's sexual interest and recommend and provide appropriate interventions. The goal for school psychologists is to support and promote practices that allow children to feel confident, competent, accepting, and responsible about their sexuality. To be effective, school psychologists must be knowledgeable, comfortable, approachable, and willing to enter a controversial area.

Recommended Resources

For Children*

Ages 0–5

Baby Brendon's Busy Day: A Sexuality Primer. Donna A. Jennings. 1993, 30 pp., $15.95 plus postage and handling. Goose Pond Publishing, PO Box 14602, Tallahassee, FL 32317; 904-385-6659.
Using rhyming text and color illustrations, this book labels parts of the body, including the genitals; identifies stages of infant development; depicts family affection; and presents mothers and fathers as equal caregivers for children. It includes a foreword and introduction to help guide parents in their role

---

*Recommended Resources for Children and for Parents were selected from SIECUS Annotated Bibliographies with permission from SIECUS, 130 West 42nd Street, Suite 350, New York, NY 10036.

as the primary sexuality educators of their children. A companion book, Baby Brenda's Busy Day, *is in production.*

Bellybuttons Are Navels. Mark Schoen. 1990, 44 pp., $14.95. Prometheus Books, 700 East Amherst Street, Buffalo, NY 14215; 800-853-7545.
Intended to help parents create a relaxed environment for the comfortable discussion of sexuality, this colorful book will help adults to initiate and guide matter-of-fact, accurate discussions about anatomy.

Ages 5–8

A Kid's First Book About Sex. Joani Blank. 1983, 48 pp., $6.00. Yes Press, 938 Howard Street, #101, San Francisco, CA 94103; 415-974-8985.
With an emphasis on self-esteem and body image, this illustrated book covers "the other parts of sex besides making babies." It discusses body parts; sexual feelings and behaviors and orientation; and the pleasures of sexual and personal relationships with other people.

Let's Talk About Sex and Loving. Gail Jones Sanchez. 1994, 69 pp., $9.95. Empty Nest Press, PO Box 361842, Milpitas, CA 95035; 408-946-5757.
This book, designed to be read to children, provides information about gender differences, puberty, intercourse, reproduction, masturbation, slang words, sexual abuse, adoption, and love. Asterisks in the text highlight opportunities for discussion. The book includes a foreword to parents, glossary, bibliography, and list of helpful organizations.

How Babies and Families are Made. Patricia Schaffer. 1988, 52 pp., $6.95. Tabor Sarah Books, 3345 Stockton Place, Palo Alto, CA 94303; 415-494-7846.
In a clear manner, this illustrated book covers reproduction and discusses the variety of ways in which babies can be conceived and families can be formed. In addition, it discusses the changing composition of families in today's world.

Ages 9–12

Asking About Sex and Growing Up. Joanna Cole. 1988, 90 pp., $4.95. Morrow Junior Books, 1359 Avenue of the Americas, New York, NY 10019. 800-237-0657.
Using a question-and-answer format, this book offers scientific facts and practical guidance about puberty, masturbation, intercourse, pregnancy, sexual abuse, and sexually transmitted diseases.

Period. JoAnn Gardner-Loulan, Bonnie Lopez, and Marcia Quackenbush. 1991, 98 pp., $9.95. Volcano Press, PO Box 270, Volcano, CA 95689; 202-296-3445.
Written for females approaching puberty, this book discusses physical changes and gynecological care, placing special emphasis on the physical and emotional significance of menstruation. The chapter, "Pads, Pins, or Tampons?" discusses the pros and cons of different products on the market. Illustrations and personal stories bring humor to the discussion. The book includes a removable parents' guide. Also available in Spanish.

Sex Stuff for Kids 7–17. Carol Marsh. 1994, 94 pp., $14.95. Gallopade Publishing Group, 359 Milledge Avenue, #100, Atlanta, GA 30312; 404-370-0420.
In a straightforward and, where appropriate, humorous man-

ner, the author provides factual information about puberty, feelings, dating, contraception, sexually transmitted diseases, pregnancy, peer relationships, and sexual violence.

For Parents*

Sexual Development of Young Children. Virginia Lively and Edwin Lively. 1991, 198 pp. Delmar Publishers, 2 Computer Drive, West, Box 15015, Albany, NY 12212; 518-459-1150.
This resource helps to clarify issues in the sexual development of children. An appropriate book for both parents and teachers, the book is especially helpful for answering questions, focusing discussions, and providing information.

When Sex is the Subject: Attitudes and Answers for Young Children. Pamela M. Wilson. 1991, 101 pp. Network Publications, P.O. Box 1830, Santa Cruz, CA 95061-1830; 408-438-4081.
For teachers and parents, this book concerns itself with addressing the questions of children age 10 and younger. The psychosocial development and learning process of children is discussed. Guidelines to help parents respond accurately and comfortably are offered.

A Parent's Guide to Teenage Sexuality. Jay Gale. 1989, 242 pp. Henry Holt & Co., 115 West 18th Street, New York, NY 10011; 212-886-9200.
This guide discusses the role of parents and family in an adolescent's sexual education program and provides guidelines about how to talk to teenagers. The topics covered include the biology of maturation and the special situations and needs that adolescents must confront.

Sex is More Than a Plumbing Lesson: A Parent's Guide to Sexuality: Education for Infants Through the Teen Years. Patty Stark. 1990, 203 pp. Preston Hollow Enterprises, Inc., P.O. Box 670935, Dallas, TX 75367-0935; 214-368-7201.
This book stresses the complex nature of human sexuality and the parent's role as a sexuality educator. Written clearly and directly, it encourages parents to communicate with their children about sexuality.

For School Psychologists

Sex Education: Theory and Practice. Clint E. Bruess and Jerrold S. Greenberg. 1981, 319 pp. Wadsworth Publishing Company, Belmont, CA.
School psychologists involved in the development and evaluation of sexuality education programs will find this book to be both comprehensive and practical. The authors provide the theoretical foundations of sexuality education followed by strategies for the implementation of programs in schools. School psychologists will also benefit from the sections on sex education research and evaluation. Although the book was published over a decade ago, it remains relevant and useful.

Adolescent Sexuality and Sex Education: A Handbook for Parents and Educators. John Gasiorowski. 1988, 152 pp. Wm. C. Brown Company Publishers, Dubuque, Iowa.
Although the title suggests that this book is for parents and educators, it is also useful for those school psychologists who are engaged in the development and support of sexuality education.

The author provides data regarding adolescent sexual behavior and development so that parents, teachers, and school administrators can design education programs that best meet the needs of students. Particularly helpful are the chapters on the evaluation and effectiveness of sexuality education.

Sexuality Education Across Cultures: Working With Differences. Janice M. Irvine. 1995, 183 pp. Jossey-Bass Publishers, 350 Sansome St., San Francisco, CA 94194.
Recognizing the need to address cultural differences within classrooms, the author provides useful information backed by research findings for developing sexuality education programs in schools. The book provides a theoretical perspective on sexuality and sexuality education, followed by useful chapters on the constructions of race and gender and their interactions with sexuality.

Sexuality and the Curriculum: The Politics and Practices of Sexuality Education. James T. Sears. 1992, 366 pp. Teachers College Press, New York, NY 10027.
This edited volume provides new theoretical insights in the area of sexuality education. Integrating curriculum theory into sexuality education practice, the authors challenge current practice and recommend nontraditional ways of thinking about sexuality education in the schools.

Guidelines for Comprehensive Sexuality Education: Kindergarten–12th Grade. SIECUS National Guidelines Task Force. 1993, 52 pp. SIECUS, 130 W 42nd St, New York, NY 10036.
Based on the belief that the content of sexuality education should be developmentally appropriate, this set of guidelines was designed to provide a blueprint for the development of new sexuality education programs.

References

Abramson, P. R. (1980). Cognitive development and sexual expression in childhood. In J. M. Samson (Ed.), *Childhood and sexuality: Proceedings of the international symposium on childhood and sexuality* (pp. 137–142) Montreal, Canada: Editions Etudes Vivantes.

APA testifies against tighter controls on sex education. (February, 1996). *APA Monitor,* p. 17.

Bell, A. R., Weinberg, M. S., & Hammersmith, S. K. (1981). *Sexual preference: Its development in men and women.* Bloomington, IN: Indiana University Press.

Berliner, L., & Elliot, D. (1996). Sexual abuse of children. In J. Briere, L. Berliner, L. Bulkley, C. Jenny, & T. Reid (Eds.), *The APSAC handbook on child maltreatment* (pp. 51–71). Newbury Park, CA: Sage.

Berliner, L., Manaois, O., & Monastersky, C. (1986). *Child sexual behavior disturbance: An assessment and treatment model.* Unpublished manuscript.

Berliner, L., & Rawlings, L. (1991). *A treatment manual: Children with sexual behavior problems.* Unpublished manuscript.

Bernstein, A. C., & Cowan, P. A. (1975). Children's concepts of how people get babies. *Child Development, 46,* 77–91.

Bettelheim, B. (1981, July). Our children are treated like idiots. *Psychology Today,* pp. 28–43.

Biehr, B. (1989). Problem sexual behavior in school-aged children and youth. *Theory into Practice, 28,* 221–226.

Bowlby, J. (1969). *Attachment.* New York: Basic Books.

Calderone, M. S. (1983). Childhood sexuality: Approaching the prevention of sexuality disease. In G. W. Albee, S. Gordon, & H. Leitenberg (Eds.), *Promoting sexual responsibility and preventing sexual problems* (pp. 333–344). Hanover and London: University Press of New England.

Chilman, C. S. (1983). The development of adolescent sexuality. *Journal of Research and Development in Education, 16,* 16–26.

Culley & Flanagan.

Cyberporn: Exclusive: A new study shows how pervasive and wild it really is. Can we protect our Kids—and free speech? (1995, July 3). *Newsweek,* pp. 38–45.

Elias, J., & Gebhard, P. (1969). Sexuality and sexual learning in childhood. *Phi Delta Kappan, 3,* 401–405.

Erikson, E. H. (1968). Childhood and society (rev. ed.). New York: Norton.

Gadpaille, W. J. (1978). Psychosexual developmental tasks imposed by pathologically delayed childhood: A cultural dilemma. In S. Feinstein & P. Giovacchini (Eds.), *Adolescent psychiatry* (Vol. 6). Chicago: University of Chicago Press.

Goldman, J. D. G. (1994). Some methodological problems in planning, executing and validating a cross-national study of children's sexual cognition. *International Journal of Intercultural Relations, 18,* 1–27.

Goldman, R., & Goldman, J. (1982). *Children's sexual thinking: A comparative study of children aged 5 to 15 years in Australia, North America, Britain and Sweden.* London: Routledge & Kegan Paul.

Gordon, B. N., Schroeder, C. S., & Abrams, J. M. (1990). Age and social-class differences in children's knowledge of sexuality. *Journal of Clinical Child Psychology, 19,* 33–43.

Haroian, L. M. (1992). Sexual problems of children. In C. E. Walker & M. C. Roberts (Eds.), *Handbook of clinical child psychology* (pp. 431–450). New York: Wiley.

Jensen, G. D. (1979). Childhood sexuality. In R. G. Green (Ed.), *Human sexuality: A health practitioner's text (2nd ed.)* Baltimore: Williams & Wilkins.

Johnson, T. C. (1990). Children who act out sexually. In J. McNamara & B. H. McNamara (Eds.), *Adoption and the sexually abused child.* City: Human Services Development Institute, University of Southern Maine.

Johnson, T. C. (1991). Understanding the sexual behaviors of young children. *SIEUCS Report, 5,* 8–15.

Juhasz, A. M. (1983). Variation in sexual behavior. *Journal of Research and Development in Education, 16,* 53–59.

Kinsey, A. C., Pomeroy, W. B., & Martin, C. E. (1948). *Sexual behavior in the human male.* Philadelphia: Saunders.

Kinsey, A. C., Pomeroy, W. B., Martin, C. E., & Gebhard, P. H. (1953). *Sexual behavior in the human female.* Philadelphia: Saunders.

Klein, M., & Gordon, S. (1992). Sex education. In C. E. Walker & M. C. Roberts (Eds), *Handbook of clinical child psychology* (pp. 933–949). New York: Wiley.

Kolodny, R. C. (1980). *Adolescent sexuality.* Paper presented at the Michigan Personnel and Guidance Association Annual Convention, Detroit, MI.

Leung, K. C. L., & Robson, W. L. M. (1993). Childhood masturbation. *Clinical Pediatrics, 238*–241.

Martinson, F. M. (1976). Eroticism in infancy and childhood. *Journal of Sex Research, 12,* 251–262.

Martinson, F. M. (1980). Child sexuality: Trends and consequences. In J. M. Samson (Ed.), *Childhood and sexuality: Proceedings of the international symposium on childhood and sexuality.* Montreal, Canada: Editions Etudes Vivantes.

Martinson, F. M. (1990). Current legal status of the erotic and sexual rights of children. In M. E. Perry (Ed.), *Handbook of sexology: Vol. 7. Childhood and adolescent sexuality* (pp. 113–124).

Martinson, F. M. (1991). Normal sexual development in infancy and childhood. In G. D. Ryan & S. L. Lane (Eds.), *Juvenile sexual offending: Causes, consequences, and correction* (pp. 57–82) Lexington, KY: Lexington Books.

Masters, W. H., Johnson, V. E., & Kolodny, R. C. (1982). *Human sexuality.* Boston: Little, Brown.

NASP responds to 'social values' hearing. (1996). *NASP Communiqué, 24* (5), p. 1.

Petty, D. L. (1995). Sex education toward the prevention of sexual problems. In G. A. Rekers (Ed.), *Handbook of child and adolescent sexual problems* (pp. 1–54). Lexington, KY: Lexington Books.

Rekers, G. A. (1995). *Handbook of child and adolescent sexual problems.* Lexington, KY: Lexington Books.

Strong, B., & Devault, C. (1988). *Understanding our sexuality* (2nd ed.). St. Paul, MN: West Publishing Company.

Tharinger, D. (1990). The impact of child sexual abuse on developing sexuality. *Professional Psychologist: Research and Practice, 21,* 331–337.

Tharinger, D., Burrows-Horton, C., & Millea, S. (1990). Sexual abuse and exploitation of children and adults with mental retardation and other handicaps. *Child Abuse and Neglect: The International Journal, 14,* 301–312.

Thorne, B. (1993). *Gender play: Girls and boys in school.* New Brunswick, Canada.

Thorne, B., & Luria, Z. (1986). Sexuality and gender in children's daily worlds. *Social Problems, 33,* 176–190.

Trause, M. A., Kennell, J., & Klaus, M. (1977). Parental attachment behavior. In J. Money & H. Musaph (Eds.), *Handbook of sexology* (pp. 789–799). New York: Elsevier/North-Holland.

Walters, J., & Walters, L. H. (1983). The role of the family in sex education. *Journal of Research and Development in Education, 16,* 8–15.

Warzak, W. J., Kuhn, B. R., & Nolten, P. W. (1995). Obstacles to the sexual adjustment of children and adolescents with disabilities. In G. A. Rekers (Ed.), *Handbook of child and adolescent sexual problems* (pp. 81–100). Lexington, KY: Lexington Books.

Yates, A. (1982). Childhood sexuality in the psychiatric textbook. *The Journal of Psychiatric Education, 6,* 217–226.

10

Attention-Deficit/Hyperactivity Disorder[1]

Kathy L. Bradley
George J. DuPaul

Lehigh University

Background and Development

Children and adolescents diagnosed with Attention-Deficit/Hyperactivity Disorder (ADHD) exhibit developmentally inappropriate levels of inattention, impulsivity, and overactivity (American Psychiatric Association, 1994). Between 3% and 5% of school-aged children in the United States have this disorder (Barkley, 1990). Despite the fact that the term ADHD was first coined in the last decade, the disorder is not new. In fact, an historical review of the literature indicates that children displaying symptoms of what is now called ADHD have been identified since the early part of the 20th century (see Barkley, 1990, for a review of the history of this disorder). For example, labels such as brain-injured children, minimal brain dysfunction, and hyperkinetic impulse disorder have been used to diagnose children displaying problems with attention and behavior control. Thus, educators have been faced with the challenge of accommodating the needs of students with ADHD for decades.

Diagnostic Criteria

The current definition of ADHD is set forth in the *Diagnostic and Statistical Manual of Mental Disorders* (*DSM-IV;* American Psychiatric Association, 1994). ADHD, therefore, represents a category for psychiatric diagnosis, even though it is technically not an educational disability entity. Because they are frequently called upon to assist in the diagnosis of ADHD as well as to develop appropriate interventions and/or recommend options for educational placement, school psychologists need to be

cognizant of the diagnostic criteria. This knowledge is also important given the need for communication with medical and mental health communities.

The symptoms of ADHD are divided into two main categories: inattention (e.g., distractibility, difficulties completing tasks) and hyperactivity-impulsivity (e.g., difficulty staying seated, frequently interrupting other's activities). At least six of nine symptoms in each category must be present on a frequent basis over a minimum of 6 months to be considered clinically significant. Further, some of the disabling symptoms must have been present prior to the age of 7 years. ADHD-related behaviors should be associated with impairment in two or more settings across one or more areas of functioning (e.g., social, academic, and occupational). The fact that ADHD symptoms must be cross-situational increases the importance of school personnel being involved in the diagnostic evaluation. That is, it is not enough that a parent reports ADHD symptoms. These symptoms must be present in more than the home setting for the diagnosis to be made. Finally, alternative hypotheses (e.g., presence of other emotional or behavior disorders) must be considered prior to a diagnostic decision. The main features of the *DSM-IV* criteria for ADHD are displayed in Table 1.

There are three subtypes of ADHD: Predominantly Inattentive, Predominantly Hyperactive-Impulsive, and Combined (American Psychiatric Association, 1994). Children in the Combined Type display significant symptoms of both inattention and hyperactivity-impulsivity. These "classic" cases of ADHD are the most common subtype; as such, the bulk of the research literature has included these children as subjects. The Predominantly Inattentive type describes children who exhibit significant inattention symptoms but do not display most of the hyperactive-impulsive symptoms. This latter subtype was previously labelled Attention Deficit Disorder without Hyperactivity and described children who are likely to have problems with concentration and work completion but not with impulse control, aggression, or defiance

---

[1]Many people distinguish between two designations when referring to attention disorders, that is, whether the hyperactive impulsive symptom cluster is or is not present. For consistency, ADHD is used throughout this chapter to refer to children who present a symptom picture consistent with the diagnostic criteria in *DSM-IV,* which may or may not include the hyperactive and impulsive components.

Table 1 *Main Features of the Diagnostic Criteria for ADHD*

1. Child must display at least six of nine symptoms of Inattention.
2. Child must display at least six of nine symptoms of Hyperactivity-Impulsivity.
3. Some of the symptoms must have been present by the age of 7 years.
4. Duration of symptoms must be at least 6 months.
5. Symptoms must be present in two or more settings.
6. Symptoms cause impairment in academic, social, and/or occupational functioning.
7. Symptoms are not due to another disorder (e.g., Autistic Disorder).
8. There are three subtypes: Combined, Predominantly Inattentive, Predominantly Hyperactive-Impulsive.

Note. Criteria from *Diagnostic and Statistical Manual of Mental Disorders* (Fourth Edition) by American Psychiatric Association, 1994, Washington, DC: Author. Copyright 1994 by American Psychiatric Association.

(Barkley, DuPaul, & McMurray, 1990). Little is known about the newest subtype of this disorder: the Predominantly Hyperactive-Impulsive type. Children with this subtype of ADHD exhibit significant symptoms of hyperactivity and impulsivity but are not particularly inattentive. The field trials conducted to establish *DSM-IV* criteria (McBurnett, Lahey, & Pfiffner, 1993) indicated that a large percentage of children with this subtype are of preschool age (i.e., 3 to 5 years old). Given the lack of research on the Hyperactive-Impulsive subtype, we will primarily focus our discussion on the Combined and Predominantly Inattentive subtypes.

Developmental Aspects

One of the popular myths about this disorder is that children outgrow their ADHD symptoms as they reach adolescence and, thus, the disorder is unique to the elementary school years. Unfortunately, it is clear that ADHD is, in most cases, a lifelong disorder beginning in early childhood and extending into adulthood (Barkley, 1990; Weiss & Hechtman, 1993). ADHD has an early onset and the typical child with this disorder exhibits significant behavior-control difficulties as early as infancy. More commonly, once children with ADHD enter preschool and/or daycare settings, teachers and other adult supervisors complain of high activity level, poor attention to group activities (e.g., circle time), impulsive behavior (e.g., interrupting conversations, butting into games), and physical aggression. Additional difficulties associated with ADHD in the preschool years include delayed speech development, accident proneness, disrupted family relationships, and poor peer relations, particularly when interacting with children in structured settings

(Ross & Ross, 1982). Longitudinal investigations have indicated that approximately 50% of young children diagnosed with ADHD as preschoolers will receive the same diagnosis in later childhood or early adolescence (Campbell, 1990). Alternatively, about half of preschool students exhibiting significant inattention, impulsivity, and overactivity can be expected to improve within a year. However, the group of children displaying chronic ADHD-related difficulties represents a significant proportion of the population. Palfrey, Levine, Walker, and Sullivan (1985) found that up to 40% of 4-year-old children were reported by parents and teachers to display frequent symptoms of ADHD. Although the behavior-control problems of most of these children improved by the time they reached second grade, approximately 5% of the total sample evidenced disruptive behavior and academic performance difficulties that, in some cases, warranted the provision of special education services.

As mentioned previously, approximately 3% to 5% of the elementary school population can be considered to have ADHD. These students have difficulties succeeding in many activities such as the completion of independent seatwork, getting along with classmates, following teacher directives, attaining grades commensurate with their abilities, and participating appropriately in class discussions or group activities (DuPaul & Stoner, 1994). It is in elementary school that most children with ADHD are first referred for psychological or educational evaluations or both. Because of their ADHD symptoms and associated behavior difficulties (i.e., noncompliance and physical aggression), these children are at high risk for academic underachievement, grade retention, placement in special education, and peer rejection relative to their normal counterparts (Barkley, DuPaul et al., 1990).

As children with ADHD progress into their teenage years, the absolute frequency and intensity of their symptoms decline (Hart, Lahey, Loeber, Applegate, & Frick, 1995). That is, they improve with respect to inattention, impulsivity, and especially overactivity as compared to their own behavior during preschool and elementary school years. Of course, their peers are exhibiting similar improvements in behavior control, which contributes to an ongoing discrepancy between adolescents with ADHD and their classmates. In fact, 70% to 80% of children with ADHD will continue to display prominent ADHD-related behavior relative to their agemates during adolescence (Barkley, Fischer, Edelbrock, & Smallish, 1990).

There are at least four key areas of adolescent development that may be compromised by the presence of ADHD. These include physical maturation, the rising influence of the peer group, the transition into secondary school, and a drive for independence. First, changes in physical appearance may, in combination with the difficulties associated with ADHD, significantly impact the adolescent's self-esteem and may also exacerbate the coordination deficits sometimes associated with this disorder.

Second, teenagers with ADHD may be more prone than their agemates to associate with a deviant peer group given their tendencies towards aggression and rejection from mainstream peer activities (Barkley, 1990). In fact, more than 40% of teens with ADHD display significant antisocial behaviors such as physical fighting, stealing, and vandalism (Barkley, Fischer et al., 1990; Gittelman, Mannuzza, Shenker, & Bonagura, 1985). Third, the transition to secondary school can heighten the organizational difficulties of the student with ADHD given the presence of multiple teachers, increased demands for independent work, greater emphasis on note-taking and study skills, and the variant levels of tolerance and understanding among faculty members. Therefore, it is no surprise that teenagers with ADHD are at higher than normal risk for grade retention, suspensions, and school dropout (Barkley, 1990; Weiss & Hechtman, 1993). Finally, the typical drive for adolescent independence is associated with a rejection of authority figures such as parents and teachers. Over 60% of adolescents with this disorder have been found to exhibit frequent defiance and noncompliance with rules and directives relative to 11% of normal-control teenagers (Barkley, Fischer et al., 1990).

Several prospective longitudinal investigations have followed children with ADHD into young adulthood (i.e., 18 to 25 years old). In general, these studies have found that over 50% of children with ADHD will continue to evidence symptoms of the disorder into adulthood, especially with respect to inattention and impulsivity (Barkley, Fischer et al., 1990; Gittelman et al., 1985; Weiss & Hechtman, 1993). Problems for adolescents with ADHD in the domains of academic achievement and antisocial behavior continue to be the greatest risks for this group in adulthood. Almost a third of these adults will have dropped out of high school, with only 5% completing a university degree program (Barkley, Fischer et al., 1990). Approximately 25% or more of these individuals will develop chronic patterns of antisocial behavior that persist into adulthood and are associated with adjustment problems such as substance abuse, occupational instability, and interpersonal difficulties (Barkley, Fischer et al., 1990). On a more positive note, about one-third of individuals followed into adulthood are found to be symptom free and are relatively well adjusted (Barkley, 1990). Yet, it is no longer prudent to view ADHD as a benign disorder restricted to childhood. Clearly a large percentage of this population experiences chronic and debilitating difficulties.

Factors Contributing to Outcome

Given the variant outcomes associated with ADHD, researchers have sought to identify variables that can reliably predict which individuals are at highest risk for poor adolescent and adult adjustment. Few specific predictors

have been identified beyond those factors predictive of adjustment for the general population. Students with higher than average cognitive abilities who come from affluent family backgrounds and whose parents are not experiencing significant mental health difficulties have the best outcomes (Weiss & Hechtman, 1993). Beyond the general predictors of IQ, socioeconomic status, and family background, there are at least two additional variables that play a prominent role in the adjustment of individuals with ADHD. First, an early onset (i.e., before 10 years old) of antisocial behaviors, especially lying, stealing, and fighting, is predictive of later antisocial outcome and perhaps continued ADHD (Barkley, 1990). Second, being rejected by one's peers in childhood is predictive of continued interpersonal adjustment problems in adolescence and adulthood (Barkley, 1990; Parker & Asher, 1987). Therefore, to identify the students with the greatest need for intervention, practitioners should consider as the optimal predictive scheme the combination of the child's cognitive ability, the child's level of aggressiveness and peer rejection, parental psychopathology, socioeconomic status, and family child-rearing practices (Barkley, 1990; Weiss & Hechtman, 1993).

Problems and Implications

Problems

The difficulties associated with ADHD appear to be exacerbated under a variety of circumstances. In particular, certain aspects of the educational setting are problematic for most students with ADHD. Specific factors associated with the severity of the symptoms displayed by these individuals include frequency of feedback, immediacy of consequences, and saliency of consequences (Barkley, 1990). The type of rich schedule of feedback and reinforcement that benefits individuals with ADHD is often difficult to provide in many classrooms. Students with ADHD tend to perform better in one-to-one situations versus groups and may display less severe symptoms in highly structured environments. These environmental characteristics are not necessarily typical of most general education settings.

Other factors contributing to the problems faced by these individuals may be related to family and parent-child relationships. Investigations of parent and family characteristics of children with ADHD have indicated an increased risk of separation and divorce, higher levels of maternal depression, and more issues of conflict and anger during communication (Barkley, Anastopoulos, Guevremont, & Fletcher, 1992). Studies investigating the relationship of children with ADHD and their parents have shown that these children tend to be less compliant with maternal directives and more negative than most children. Mothers of children with ADHD have been shown to be more negative, issue more commands to their children, and pay less attention to their children during positive interactions (Barkley, 1990).

Significant levels of stress have been reported by parents of children with ADHD, particularly in relation to the defiant behavior displayed by these children (e.g., Cunningham, Benness, & Siegel, 1988). Parental psychopathology, which is reportedly higher in families of children with ADHD than for other families, also contributes to the multiple problems often encountered by these children (Biederman et al, 1986). Barkley and colleagues (1992) reported that there were more reports of conflict and greater negative interactions during a neutral discussion between teens with ADHD and their parents when compared to a control group of adolescents.

The severity of ADHD also is compounded in many individuals through the development of cormorbid disorders. ADHD is frequently associated with academic underachievement. It has been estimated that up to 80% of children with ADHD may have an associated learning disability or achievement problem (Semrud-Clikeman et al., 1992). Cantwell and Baker (1991) also suggested a relationship between children with early speech/language impairments and the increased prevalence of both learning disabilities and ADHD.

In addition to these academically related problems, a significant number of children with ADHD develop conduct problems such as lying, stealing, and fighting. According to Barkley (1990), up to 40% of children and 65% of adolescents may meet criteria for the diagnosis of oppositional defiant disorder. A subset of these individuals may be diagnosed with more serious problems indicative of a conduct disorder. Research also suggests that children with ADHD are more likely to exhibit greater symptoms of depression and anxiety than other children (Barkley, 1995).

Another factor contributing to the problems of individuals with ADHD is their problematic social relationships. It is estimated that over 50% of children with ADHD have significant difficulties developing interpersonal relationships and experience peer rejection (Landau & Moore, 1991). Children with ADHD may be viewed by their peers as more disruptive, off-task, and domineering than other children (Madam-Swain & Zentall, 1990). It only takes a few encounters with a child with ADHD for a peer to witness these behaviors and withdraw from contact with the child (Barkley, 1990). Studies suggest that children with ADHD do not necessarily have a deficit in social skills that causes their difficulties. Instead, it appears that their problems are related to an inability to perform appropriate skills when confronted with specific social situations (Landau & Moore, 1991).

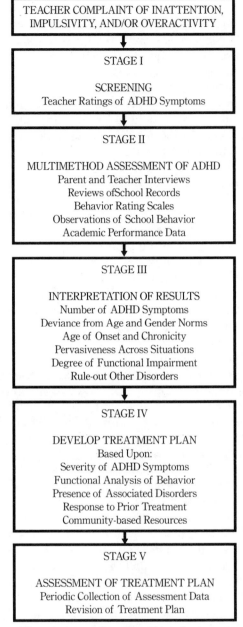

Figure 1. *Five stages of the school-based assessment of ADHD.*

Note: *From "How to Assess Attention-Deficit/Hyperactivity Disorder Within School Settings" by G. J. DuPaul, 1992,* **School Psychology Quarterly, 7,** *p. 60–74. Copyright 1992 by National Association of School Psychologists. Reprinted with permission.*

Assessment

Because of the complexity of this disorder, a multimethod assessment approach is recommended. A model of such an assessment process was presented by this chapter's co-author (DuPaul, 1992) and includes five stages of evaluation (see Figure 1). Following the initial referral, Stage 1 of the model involves screening through the completion of teacher-rating scales. Stage 2 focuses on a more thorough assessment including both teacher and parent interviews and rating scales, a review of the student's educational history, observations of the student in the school setting, and a review of the student's permanent classroom products.

Despite the apparent promise of clinic-based tests of attention and impulse control for the diagnosis of ADHD, measures such as the Matching Familiar Figures Test (Kagan, 1966) and the Vigilance Tasks (Gordon, 1983) have not been found to provide clinically meaningful information beyond the previously mentioned measures. Given the limited ecological validity of clinic tests (Barkley, 1991), it is premature to recommend their inclusion in the school-based assessment battery.

During Stage 3 of the process, the assessment data are evaluated and interpreted with respect to the criteria for diagnosis presented in the *DSM-IV* (American Psychiatric Association, 1994). A treatment plan is then developed during Stage 4 of the model followed by an assessment of treatment outcome during Stage 5 (DuPaul & Stoner, 1994). Based upon the results of this multimethod stage assessment, a variety of intervention strategies may be used to develop a comprehensive treatment package.

Medication Issues

Stimulant medication is the most common intervention for ADHD (Milich, Licht, Murphy, & Pelham, 1989). It is estimated that between 1% and 2% of the school-age population receive stimulant mediation as a treatment for ADHD (Safer & Krager, 1988). Stimulant medications are so called because of their ability to increase the arousal or alertness of the central nervous system. In addition to stimulant medications, other less frequently used pharmacological interventions include tricyclic antidepressants, clonidine, and monoamine oxidase inhibitors (see Werry & Aman, 1993). The use of medication for this disorder has expanded to include students across all age and grade levels (DuPaul & Stoner, 1994). For example, the number of adolescents receiving medication for ADHD has increased over the last several years (Safer & Krager, 1988). Nevertheless, concerns regarding the reliance on medication as the sole treatment for this disorder focus on its limited long-term effectiveness and its failure to "normalize" the individual's behavior and academic performance in comparison to their same-age and grade-level peers (Evans & Pelham, 1991; Hoza, Pelham, Sams, & Carlson, 1992).

Numerous investigators have consistently demonstrated short-term enhancement of behavioral, academic, and social functioning of the majority of children being treated with stimulant medication (see Pelham, 1993, for a review). Alternatively, long-term follow-up investigations have not revealed advantages for stimulant medication, in isolation, on social, vocational, or educational outcomes (Hechtman, Weiss, & Perlman, 1984). However, many studies contain flaws in such areas as the definition of ADHD used to identify subjects, experimental procedures, dependent measures, and data analysis (Pelham, 1983).

It is estimated that 70% to 80% of children with ADHD exhibit a positive response to stimulant medication (Barkley, 1977). The primary responses to this medication include increases in attention span and decreases in impulsive, disruptive, and inappropriate behaviors. With respect to the enhancement of academic performance, some studies have shown that students receiving stimulant medication have made improvements in academic productivity (Douglas, Barr, O'Neill, & Britton, 1988; DuPaul & Rapport, 1993; Evans & Pelham, 1991). However, the effects of stimulant medication on academic productivity do not necessarily generalize to acquisition of skills or to accuracy of responses.

The potential limitations of pharmacotherapy have led to the adoption of multimodal treatment approaches for ADHD. Stimulants appear to exert greater behavior-changing effects when combined with other effective treatment approaches, such as behavior modification (DuPaul & Stoner, 1994). There is agreement in the literature that if medication is warranted, it should not be used in isolation. The use of stimulant medication should be in conjunction with other psychoeducational and behavioral strategies (DuPaul, Barkley, & McMurray, 1991; Pelham & Milich, 1991).

Alternative Actions

One approach to providing behavioral interventions for students with ADHD is to modify the environmental and/or task characteristics associated with their difficulties. Focusing on the antecedents of behaviors, these strategies might include moving the child's desk closer to the teacher and away from the possible distractions of other students, providing the student with a separate desk to increase the opportunity to maintain attention to tasks, and varying the presentation format of new material to enhance attention. An additional strategy would include ensuring a correct match between the difficulty level of the curriculum and the student's abilities (Pfiffner & Barkley, 1990).

Another approach to intervention with this population of students is to apply consequences contingent upon the student's performance of particular target behaviors. These strategies may include the provision of praise and/or rewards for the display of appropriate behaviors or withdrawing attention when inappropriate behaviors are exhibited. Token reinforcement procedures, involving the accumulation of tokens or points contingent upon positive behaviors and, in some cases, the loss of tokens or points for negative behaviors, have been shown to be effective with individuals with ADHD (Abramowitz & O'Leary, 1991; Pfiffner & Barkley, 1990). The use of time-out from positive reinforcement may also prove to be an effective strategy for the behavior of some students but not for those whose main function of their behavior is to escape from situations or to avoid particular tasks (Pfiffner & Barkley, 1990).

Home-school contingencies are sometimes recommended for students with ADHD as a means of combining school and parent efforts to improve students' classroom behavior. Typically such a program proceeds by having school personnel complete a daily checklist that reports on the child's behavior throughout the school day. The child then takes the checklist home to the parent(s) who provides appropriate consequences based upon the number of points earned on the checklist (DuPaul & Stoner, 1994). One advantage of this type of intervention is that it tends to require less teacher time and effort than a classroom-based program. For this reason, some teachers are more accepting of the home-school program (Barkley, 1990).

There are limitations with these strategies as well. The application of contingency-based interventions must be viewed in terms of the relevancy of these strategies to the particular age or grade level of the student. Contingency-based strategies may be more practical at the elementary than at the secondary level. Considering the fact that adolescents with ADHD may encounter at least seven different teachers during the course of a typical day, it may be difficult to ensure that a behavioral intervention is implemented across all settings with the same degree of integrity (Abramowitz & O'Leary, 1991). It also may be difficult to engage a large team of teachers in following a prescribed and structured behavior-management plan. In addition, it may not be feasible for teachers to implement a contingency-based strategy given the number of students they encounter during the school day. Finally, difficulties may be encountered as educators become more concerned with the public reaction regarding reinforcement of a student for behavior that is "expected" of other students at the adolescent level.

One class of interventions that may be successful with individuals with ADHD involves self-management strategies. These interventions focus on the development of skills that allow students to become more independent and to act as their own change agents (Hinshaw, Henker, & Whalen, 1984). Self-management strategies can be conceptualized into two types of procedures: those with a focus on cognitive control and those based on contingency management (see Shapiro & Cole, 1994, for a review). The main difference between these two types of procedures is that cognitive-based strategies focus on antecedents of behavior while contingency-based procedures focus more on the consequences of behaviors.

Although the rationale behind the use of self-management procedures appears to make intuitive sense, there have been those who question the efficacy of such strategies with students diagnosed with ADHD. In a critical review of the literature, Abikoff (1985) listed a number of concerns related to studies investigating the use of strategies emphasizing cognitive training with individuals with ADHD. These criticisms focus on the types of instruments used to assess change in student performance, the variety of training procedures that fall under the rubric of cognitive-behavior strategies, and the lack of long-term evidence that these strategies are effective for this population of students. Alternatively, the use of contingency-based self-management strategies may have more potential in the treatment of ADHD. These strategies involve teaching individuals skills to assist them in evaluating their own behavior. Individuals subsequently learn to apply the appropriate consequence after their response has occurred. More empirical work is necessary to demonstrate the effectiveness of contingency-based self-management strategies (DuPaul & Stoner, 1994).

Based upon the research to date, no one intervention strategy appears to be of optimal use for students with ADHD. Instead, research shows the need for multi-method interventions applied across a variety of settings. For example, a study of multimodal treatment for ADHD is currently underway at several sites across the United States and Canada that will help to determine the optimal combination of treatment strategies for children with this disorder (Richters et al., 1995). Interventions also need to be monitored over time and adapted accordingly as the developmental needs and the environmental demands upon the student change. Whalen and Henker (1991) argue that pitting different treatments (pharmacologic vs. psychosocial) against each other to identify the single superior (or optimal) approach is an "untenable and untestable" quest (p. 126). Instead, the individual needs of the student with ADHD should be taken into consideration as well as the needs of others in the student's environment. With these variables in mind, the most appropriate methods for intervention can be applied in an effort to enhance the success of the student in the educational environment.

Finally, school practitioners should be aware that students diagnosed with ADHD are protected under two federal laws: the Individuals with Disabilities Act (IDEA, 1990) and Section 504 under the Rehabilitation Act of 1973. Children with ADHD can be classified under IDEA as "Other Health Impaired" if it is demonstrated that their handicap significantly interferes with their learning. Section 504 is not an aspect of special education but is a responsibility of the comprehensive general public education system. According to Section 504, if a child with ADHD is classified as "handicapped" but is not eligible for special education services under IDEA, a school must implement a plan of action to prevent discrimination if the child's handicap results in a substantial limitation in learning.

Summary

The symptoms of ADHD impact a significant number of students across all age and grade levels in the educational environment. Once thought to be a disorder of childhood, it is now understood that ADHD is a chronic disorder that persists into adulthood for most individuals with the diagnosis. Along with the primary symptoms associated with this disorder (inappropriate levels of inattention, impulsivity, and hyperactivity), students with ADHD may develop additional difficulties such as poor academic performance, conduct problems, stressful parent-child relationships, and inadequate social relationships.

Assessment of ADHD involves a complex, multistep process that includes gathering information across a variety of sources and environments. Once the assessment process is complete, the most appropriate interventions are selected, and methods for monitoring the effectiveness of the interventions are established.

Although stimulant medication is the most commonly chosen intervention for students with ADHD, there are limitations to the use of medication as the sole intervention strategy. Behavior-modification techniques which focus on antecedents, consequences, or both have also been shown to be effective with individuals with ADHD. However, these traditional behavior-modification strategies also have drawbacks with respect to the practicality of their use with the adolescent population in a typical classroom setting. Self-management strategies, particularly those focused on contingency-based procedures, may provide a viable alternative for use with adolescents with ADHD. Researchers are in agreement that the most effective treatment for ADHD involves multimethod interventions applied across a number of different settings over a long time period.

Practitioners in the field of psychology must become aware of the significant problems that students with ADHD encounter as they mature and move through the educational system. Professionals must also be cognizant of the research regarding the variety of interventions available for students with ADHD and should be familiar with the federal laws protecting the rights of these individuals. Research in the area of ADHD continues to grow and the challenge for practitioners is to remain knowledgeable and contribute to the ongoing investigations related to diagnosis, assessment, and treatment of students with ADHD.

Recommended Resources

Practitioners

Barkley, R. A. (1990). *Attention-deficit hyperactivity disorder: A handbook for diagnosis and treatment.* New York: Guilford Press.
Considered to be one of the single best sources of information about ADHD, this book provides a comprehensive review of research in all areas related to this disorder. This volume covers such topics as nature and diagnosis, assessment, and treatment of ADHD.

DuPaul, G. J., & Stoner, G. (1994). *ADHD in the schools: Assessment and intervention strategies.* New York: Guilford Press.
A valuable resource for school psychologists and educators, this book covers a variety of school-related problems associated with ADHD. Discussions of academic-related problems, school-based assessment procedures, problematic peer relationships, and effective strategies are included in this resource.

Shapiro, E. S., & Cole, C. L. (1994). *Behavior change in the classroom: Self-management interventions.* New York: Guilford Press.
An excellent resource for school-based practitioners who wish to address the needs of all school-aged children and adolescents. This text reviews the research on self-management strategies and translates this research into practical procedures for use in the educational setting.

Teachers

Fowler, M. (1992). *CH.A.D.D. Educators manual.* Plantation, FL: CH.A.D.D.
This book, written by several leaders in the field, explains to teachers, school administrators, and others in education Attention Deficit Disorders (ADD) and the best ways to educate students with ADD. Sections include: "ADD Goes to School," "Parents and Schools Working Together," and "ADD: A Brief Legal Summary."

Parker, H. (1992). *The ADD hyperactivity handbook for schools.* Florida: Specialty Press.
This comprehensive text explains current education policies and their effects on children with ADD. Also included are methods of evaluation and helping to teach children with ADD as well as sample Individualized Education Plans (IEPs).

Reif, S. F. (1994). *How to reach and teach ADHD children.* New York: Prentice Hall.
This book focuses on practical techniques, strategies, and interventions for helping children with attention problems and hyperactivity.

Parents

CH.A.D.D.ER. [semi-annual publication]. Plantation, FL.: CH.A.D.D.
A magazine published by CH.A.D.D., a national support organization for parents of children and adults with attention deficit disorder. The publication includes articles regarding assessment, treatment and legal/placement issues.

Greenberg, G. S., & Horn, W. F. (1991). *Attention deficit hyperactivity disorder: Questions and answers for parents.* New York: Research Press.
This book answers questions frequently asked by parents about ADHD. Also included are behavior-management and cognitive-therapy techniques.

Ingersoll, B. (1988). *Your hyperactive child: A parent's guide to coping with ADD.* Garden City, NY: Doubleday.
Included in this book are a general overview of ADHD, diagnosis, causes, treatment, daily life, special problems, school, and behavior modification.

References

Abikoff, H. (1985). Efficacy of cognitive training interventions in hyperactive children: A critical review. *Clinical Psychology Review, 5,* 479–512.

Abramowitz, A. J., & O'Leary, S. G. (1991). Behavioral interventions for the classroom: Implications for students with ADHD. *School Psychology Review, 20,* 220–234.

American Psychiatric Association. (1994). *Diagnostic and statistical manual of mental disorders* (4th ed.). Washington, DC: Author.

Barkley, R. A. (1977). A review of stimulant drug research with hyperactive children. *Journal of Child Psychology and Psychiatry, 18,* 137–165.

Barkley, R. A. (Ed.). (1990). *Attention deficit hyperactivity disorder: A handbook for diagnosis and treatment.* New York: Guilford Press.

Barkley, R. A. (1991). The ecological validity of laboratory and analogue assessment methods of ADHD symptoms. *Journal of Abnormal Child Psychology, 19,* 149–178.

Barkley, R. A. (1995). *Taking charge of ADHD: The complete, authoritative guide for parents.* New York: Guilford Press.

Barkley, R. A., Anastopoulos, A. D., Guevremont, D. C., & Fletcher, K. E. (1992). Attention-deficit hyperactivity disorder in adolescents: Mother-adolescent interactions, family beliefs and conflicts, and maternal psychopathology. *Journal of Abnormal Child Psychology, 20,* 263–288.

Barkley, R. A., DuPaul, G. J., & McMurray, M. B. (1990). A comprehensive evaluation of attention deficit disorder with and without hyperactivity as defined by research criteria. *Journal of Consulting and Clinical Psychology, 58,* 775–789.

Barkley, R. A., Fischer, J., Edelbrock, C., & Smallish, M. (1990). The adolescent outcome of hyperactive children diagnosed by research criteria: An eight year follow-up study. *Journal of the American Academy of Child & Adolescent Psychiatry, 29,* 546–557.

Biederman, J., Munir, K., Knee, D., Habelow, W., Armentano, M., Autor, S., Hoge S. K., & Waternaux, C. (1986). A family study of patients with attention deficit disorder and normal controls. *Journal of Psychiatric Research, 20,* 263–274.

Campbell, S. B. (1990). *Behavior problems in preschool children: Clinical and developmental issues.* New York: Guilford Press.

Cantwell, D. P., & Baker, L. (1991). Association between attention deficit-hyperactivity disorder and learning disorders. *Journal of Learning Disabilities, 24,* 88–91.

Cunningham, C. E., Benness, B. B., & Siegel, L. S. (1988). Family functioning, time allocation, and parental depression in the families of normal and ADDH children. *Journal of Clinical Child Psychology, 17,* 169–177.

Douglas, V. I., Barr, R. G., O'Neill, M. E., & Britton, B. G. (1988). Dosage effects and individual responsivity to methylphenidate in attention deficit disorder. *Journal of Child Psychology and Psychiatry, 29,* 453–475.

DuPaul, G. J. (1992). How to assess attention-deficit hyperactivity disorder within school settings. *School Psychology Quarterly, 7,* 60–74.

DuPaul, G. J., Barkley, R. A., & McMurray, M. B. (1991). Therapeutic effects of medication on ADHD: Implications for school psychologists. *School Psychology Review, 20,* 203–219.

DuPaul, G. J., & Rapport, M. D. (1993). Does methylphenidate normalize the classroom performance of children with attention deficit disorder? *Journal of the American Academy of Child and Adolescent Psychiatry, 32,* 190–198.

DuPaul, G. J., & Stoner, G. (1994). *ADHD in the schools: Assessment and intervention strategies.* New York: Guilford Press.

Evans, S. W., & Pelham, W. E. (1991). Psychostimulant effects on academic and behavioral measures for ADHD junior high school students in a lecture format classroom. *Journal of Abnormal Child Psychology, 19,* 537–552.

Gittelman, R., Mannuzza, S., Shenker, R., & Bonagura, N. (1985). Hyperactive boys almost grown up. *Archives of General Psychiatry, 42,* 937–947.

Gordon, M. (1983). *The Gordon Diagnostic System.* DeWitt, NY: Gordon Systems.

Hart, E. L., Lahey, B. B., Loeber, R., Applegate, B., & Frick, P. J. (1995). Developmental change in attention-deficit hyperactivity disorder in boys: A four-year longitudinal study. *Journal of Abnormal Child Psychology, 23,* 729–750.

Hechtman, L., Weiss, G., & Perlman, T. (1984). Young adult outcome of hyperactive children who received long-term stimulant treatment. *Journal of the American Academy of Child Psychiatry, 23,* 261–269.

Hinshaw, S. P., Henker, B., & Whalen, C. K. (1984). Self-control in hyperactive boys in anger-inducing situations: Effects of cognitive-behavioral training and of methylphenidate. *Journal of Abnormal Child Psychology, 12,* 55–77.

Hoza, B., Pelham, W. E., Sams, S. E., & Carlson, C. (1992). An examination of the "dosage" effects of both behavior therapy and methylphenidate on the classroom performance of two ADHD children. *Behavior Modification, 16,* 164–192.

Kagan, J. (1966). Reflection-impulsivity: The generality and dynamics of conceptual tempo. *Journal of Abnormal Psychology, 71,* 17–24.

Landau, S., & Moore, L. A. (1991). Social skill deficits in children with attention-deficit hyperactivity disorder. *School Psychology Review, 20,* 235–251.

Madam-Swain, A., & Zentall, S. S. (1990). Behavioral comparisons of liked and disliked hyperactive children in play contexts and the behavioral accommodations by their classmates. *Journal of Consulting and Clinical Psychology, 58,* 197–209.

McBurnett, K., Lahey, B. B., & Pfiffner, L. J. (1993). Diagnosis of attention deficit disorders in *DSM-IV*: Scientific basis and implications for education. *Exceptional Children, 60,* 108–117.

Milich, R., Licht, B. G., Murphy, D. A., & Pelham, W. E. (1989). Attention-deficit hyperactivity disordered boys' evaluations of and attributions for task performance on medication versus placebo. *Journal of Abnormal Psychology, 98,* 280–284.

Palfrey, J. S., Levine, M. D., Walker, D. K., & Sullivan, M. (1985). The emergence of attention deficits in early childhood: A prospective study. *Developmental and Behavioral Pediatrics, 6,* 339–348.

Parker, J. G., & Asher, S. R. (1987). Peer relations and later personal adjustment: Are low-accepted children at risk? *Psychological Bulletin, 102,* 357–389.

Pelham, W. E. (1983). The effects of psychostimulants on academic achievement in hyperactive and learning disabled children. *Thalamus, 3,* 1–47.

Pelham, W. E. (1993). Pharmacotherapy for children with attention-deficit hyperactivity disorder. *School Psychology Review, 22,* 199–227.

Pelham, W. E., & Milich, R. (1991). Individual differences in response to Ritalin in classwork and social behavior. In L. L. Greenhill & B. B. Osman (Eds.), *Ritalin: Theory and patient management* (pp. 203–221). New York: Mary Ann Liebert, Inc.

Pfiffner, L. J., & Barkley, R. A. (1990). Educational placement and classroom management. In R. A. Barkley (Ed.), *Attention-deficit hyperactivity disorder: A handbook for diagnosis and treatment* (pp. 498–539). New York: Guilford Press.

Richters, J. E., Arnold, L. E. Jensen, P. S., Abikoff, H., Conners, C. K., Greenhill, L. L., Hechtman, L., Hinshaw, S. P., Pelham, W. E., & Swanson, J. M. (1995). NIMH collaborative multisite multimodal treatment study of children with ADHD: I. Background and rationale. *Journal of the American Academy of Child and Adolescent Psychiatry, 34,* 987–1000.

Ross, D. M., & Ross, S. A. (1982). *Hyperactivity: Current issues, research and theory* (2nd ed.). New York: Wiley.

Safer, D. J., & Krager, J. M. (1988). A survey of medication treatment for hyperactive/inattentive students. *Journal of the American Medical Association, 260,* 2256–2258.

Semrud-Clikeman, M., Biederman, J., Sprich-Buckminster, S., Lehman, B. K., Faraone, S. V., & Norman, D. (1992). Comorbidity between ADHD and learning disability: A review and report in a clinically referred sample. *Journal of the American Academy of Child and Adolescent Psychiatry, 31,* 439–448.

Shapiro, E. S., & Cole, C. L. (1994). *Behavior change in the classroom: Self-management interventions.* New York: Guilford Press.

Weiss, G., & Hechtman, L. R. (1993). *Hyperactive children grown up* (2nd ed.). New York: Guilford Press.

Werry, J. S. & Aman, M. G. (Eds.), (1993). *Practitioners guide to psychoactive drugs for children and adolescents.* New York: Plenum Press.

Whalen, C. K., & Henker, B (1991). Therapies for hyperactive children: Comparisons, combinations, and compromises. *Journal of Consulting and Clinical Psychology, 59,* 126–137.

11

Conduct Disorders

Russell J. Skiba

Indiana University

The problem of disruptive conduct has been, and continues to be, among the most pressing problems facing educators (Gottfredson, Gottfredson, & Hybl, 1993). Recently, increased attention on the integration of students with disabilities, as well as the rising tide of school violence (see School Violence, this volume), has lent an urgency to consideration of issues posed by children who exhibit conduct disorders.

The origins of conduct and behavior problems are complex, as are the way in which they are expressed. Students who exhibit disruptive and delinquent behavior often are exposed to a variety of stress factors including community violence (Garbarino, Kostelny, & Dubrow, 1991), family discord (Emery, 1988), inconsistent and inadequate discipline and monitoring (Patterson, 1992), and parents who themselves face a wide range of adjustment difficulties (Wahler, 1990). As a result, these children and youth exhibit a broad range of coexisting emotional and behavioral difficulties (McConaughy & Skiba, 1993).

Outcomes for children with severe behavioral difficulties are not encouraging. Students with conduct problems are most likely to be served in special education as seriously emotionally disturbed (Pullis, 1992) and as such tend to be significantly overrepresented in the most restrictive continuum placements, particularly residential care (Kauffman & Lloyd, 1992). Longitudinal studies continue to indicate a distressingly high rate of stability for the disorder (Esser, Schmidt, & Woerner, 1990) predicting high rates of school dropout (Cairns, Cairns, & Neckerman, 1989a) and of delinquency and incarceration (Patterson, Crosby, & Vuchinich, 1992).

Yet despite such frustrations, knowledge concerning antisocial behavior and conduct disorder has expanded greatly in the past 20 years. A sufficient database has been developed from which to generate and test specific hypotheses regarding the genesis and maintenance of conduct disorders (Patterson, 1992). Longitudinal investigations have begun to provide an important understanding of the developmental nature of antisocial behavior (Loeber, 1990). A new appreciation of the complexity and interrelationship among etiological factors has led to

awareness of the need for multicomponent assessment and intervention (Kazdin, 1987b). All of these developments have important implications for the manner in which to approach assessment and intervention for children with conduct disorders. The purpose of this chapter is to focus on developments in current knowledge about conduct disorders and to explore the implications of those advances for school psychological practice.

Background

Definition

The fourth edition of the *Diagnostic and Statistical Manual of Mental Disorders (DSM IV);* American Psychiatric Association [APA], 1994) continues, as in earlier editions, to define the essential feature of conduct disorder as a "repetitive and persistent pattern of behavior in which the basic rights of others or major age-appropriate societal norms or rules are violated" (p. 85). Criterion behaviors used in diagnosing the disorder fall into four main groupings: (a) aggression to people and animals, (b) nonaggressive destruction of property, (c) deceitfulness or theft, and (d) serious violations of rules. Subtypes in the current *DSM* are childhood-onset type (prior to age 10) and adolescent-onset type, that is, an absence of any of the criteria prior to age 10. Although both antisocial behavior and delinquent behavior are terms used extensively in this chapter because of their considerable overlap, the terms can be distinguished to a certain extent. The term *antisocial behavior* is typically used to refer to the broader class of externalizing behavior, regardless of the severity of the behavior (Kazdin, 1987b); the term *conduct disorder* may refer to more severe examples of the behavior that violate the rights of others. *Delinquency,* while clearly an outcome for which students with conduct disorder are at risk, represents severely disordered behavior that is law violating or has come under the purview of the law (Kazdin, 1987a).

The occurrence of any specific disruptive or antisocial act is extremely common, necessitating other criteria for differentiating the more severe disorders. It has been estimated that 50% or more of all children and youth exhibit, or report having engaged in, at least one disruptive or delinquent behavior (Kazdin, 1987a). The presence or absence of conduct disorder is thus indexed not merely by the presence of certain behaviors, but by the pattern of their occurrence over time and situations. Severe conduct problem behavior appears more likely to show cross-situational consistency across *multiple settings,* increased *frequency* of disruptive behavior, a greater *variety* of problem behaviors, and an earlier *onset* of the problem behavior (Loeber, 1990).

Prevalence and Comorbidity

Epidemiological studies have estimated the prevalence of conduct disorders to range between 3% and 10% of the general population (Fergusson, Horwood, & Lynskey, 1993; Kazdin, 1987a; Quay, 1986). Conduct disorders are the most frequently diagnosed disorder of childhood, accounting for one-third to one-half of all specific disorders (Quay, 1986) and a similar proportion of child clinic referrals (Kazdin, 1987b). Boys are typically diagnosed more frequently than girls (APA, 1994), although there have been reported exceptions to this pattern (Fergusson et al., 1993).

Prevalence estimates of conduct disorder are complicated by the relatively high rates of co-occurrence, or comorbidity, with other disorders. There appears to be a high degree of overlap between the most common externalizing disorders: conduct disorder, oppositional defiant disorder, and attention deficit/hyperactivity disorder. Extremely high rates of co-occurrence between conduct disorder and oppositional defiant disorder rate has led to some speculation that oppositional defiant disorder may be simply a developmental precursor to conduct disorder (Rey et al., 1988). Similarly, data showing co-occurrence of conduct disorder and attention deficit/hyperactivity disorder ranging up to half or more of all cases (Biederman, Newcorn, & Sprich, 1991) have raised questions concerning the extent to which attention deficit/hyperactivity disorder and conduct disorder represent separate syndromes (Hinshaw, 1987). Fergusson, Horwood, and Lloyd (1991) caution that while it may be possible to distinguish between conduct and attentional disorders in theory, "the practical and clinical utility of this distinction may be limited, given that these variables are so highly correlated" (p. 270).

Prevalence studies have also identified a fairly substantial comorbidity of conduct disorder and a number of internalizing disorders. Cross-sectional studies of clinic populations identified using the *DSM* typically report comorbidity rates between conduct disorders and affective/anxiety disorder between 32% and 37% (Kovacs, Paulaskas, Gatsonis, & Richards, 1988). Studies using broad-band quantitative rating scales completed by teachers or parents have reported rates of comorbidity between internalizing and externalizing syndromes as high as 52% (McConaughy & Skiba, 1993). Such findings suggest that programs designed to treat only externalizing problems run the risk of neglecting co-occurring internalizing problems (Cole & Carpentieri, 1990).

Complexity of disorder appears to be the norm rather than the exception for children displaying behaviors associated with conduct disorder. In reviewing comorbidity studies, Forness, Kavale, King, and Kasani (1994) concluded that at least 60% of all children with conduct disorder are likely to display one or more other disorders as well. Such figures suggest that both assessment and intervention must be multifaceted and multicomponent in order to address the complex needs of children with conduct problems and their families.

Is Conduct Disorder a Disability?

In recent years, a number of authors (e.g., Slenkovich, 1983) have argued that students with conduct and behavioral problems are properly classified as *socially maladjusted* and hence excluded from service under the definition of serious emotional disturbance (SED) in the Individuals with Disabilities Education Act (IDEA). The arguments have been debated extensively elsewhere (Cline, 1990; Nelson, 1992; Skiba & Grizzle, 1991; Slenkovich, 1992), but several are worth reviewing here.

In general, there appears to be little data supporting this exclusionary interpretation and a great deal of evidence contradicting it. Historical and legal analyses (Bower, 1982; Cline, 1990) suggest that students with conduct and behavior problems have always been considered part of the mandate of special education, while investigations of current programs suggest that conduct disorders are the most typical behavior pattern exhibited in SED classrooms (Pullis, 1991). Further, both a lack of appropriate assessment methodology (Skiba & Grizzle, 1991) and the high rate of comorbidity between internalizing and externalizing syndromes (McConaughy & Skiba, 1993) suggest that it is simply not possible to make such distinctions in a way that guarantees the rights of children to a technically valid and unbiased assessment.

Thus, the policy of excluding children with conduct disorders from service under the IDEA is remarkably unsupported by empirical data, current service patterns, historical precedent, or best practice in assessment. Some authors have suggested that pressure to exclude children with conduct problems is related to fiscal concerns because these children are among the most expensive and challenging to serve (Nelson, 1992). Yet, left untreated, children who exhibit antisocial behavior and conduct disorder are at high risk for school dropout, delinquency, and criminality. It becomes highly questionable, then, whether the short-term savings engendered by refusing to treat children with conduct disorders will be worth the long-term costs to society in terms of decreased productivity and increased crime Skiba and Grizzle (1992).

Development and Implications

The complexity of the lives and behaviors of children exhibiting conduct problems has made definition, diagnosis, and exact prevalence estimates difficult. Yet research in the past 20 years has made great strides in identifying some of the correlates of conduct disorder and antisocial behavior in children and youth. It is important, however, in reviewing this literature to be clear that these are factors *associated with* conduct disorder. Most of the literature to date is correlational in nature, and it is more often than not difficult to glean the direction of causality. Thus, rather than speculating on direction of causality, it may be best to regard conduct disorders and antisocial behavior as a complex developmental process involving personal characteristics, parent factors, academic or cognitive deficits, and social interactional factors.

Personal Characteristics

Behavioral characteristics
Almost by definition, it is the externalizing behaviors associated with conduct disorder and their effect in violating the rights of others that are its most salient feature. *DSM-IV* lists 13 behavioral criteria, organized into four categories: aggression to people and animals, destruction of property, deceitfulness or theft, and serious violation of rules. Of these, aggression appears to be the most widely studied and perhaps most stable feature of conduct disorder (see Aggressive Behavior, this volume). Aggression appears to be strongly predictive of a variety of negative outcomes from early childhood (Lochman & the Conduct Problems Prevention Research Group, 1995) and, it has been argued, may be as stable over time as IQ (Olweus, 1979). Others have argued that overactivity is also a distinguishing characteristic of conduct disorder, especially in its early stages (Loeber, 1990). As noted later, specific aggressive and disruptive behaviors appear to be developmental and probably age-specific. Behaviors associated with the disorder appear over time to become more serious and endangering (Cairns, Cairns, Neckerman, Ferguson, & Gariepy, 1989b) as well as more diverse and covert (Loeber, 1990).

Temperament
Individual child temperament has been posited as a risk factor for the development of aggression and antisocial behavior, in that a cluster of temperamental attributes, often labeled "fussy" or "difficult" may be more difficult for caregivers to manage (Thomas & Chess, 1977; see also Temperament, this volume). Landy and Peters (1992) note that aggression and affect regulation are developmental processes beginning in early infancy and suggest that temperamental differences in these processes may play a role in the development of aggression. There does appear to be an association between early temperament factors and later aggression (Bates, 1990). Yet the variance explained by temperament is typically small relative to other factors, causing some to question whether that contribution is clinically useful for predicting or treating conduct disorders (Quay, 1986).

Biological or genetic factors
In reviewing research on psychobiological correlates of conduct disorders, Shapiro and Hynd (1993) concluded that research seeking neuroanatomical correlates of conduct disorder have provided only inconsistent or preliminary evidence of such a link. Somewhat stronger evidence has been found for a link between some neurotramsmitters (i.e., seratonin) or neurohormones, such as cortisol or testosterone, and increased levels of juvenile delinquency and conduct disorder. Some psychophysiological correlates, such as increased heart rate or lowered skin conductance, have also been reported (Quay, 1986). Thus, studies seeking a physiological basis for conduct disorder have yielded some suggestive evidence of neurophysiological correlates. Yet measurement difficulties and the tentative nature of the findings means that possible organic links with conduct disorder must at present be interpreted cautiously (Shapiro & Hynd).

Implications
The stability, early onset, and implications of the overt and covert behaviors associated with conduct disorder would argue that the personal characteristics of children are an important associated feature of that disorder. Yet there is a great deal of room for caution in interpreting the contribution of individual-difference factors to conduct disorder. There appears to be insufficient evidence to justify the inference of a lack of conscience or heightened intentionality from externalizing behavior. While there is more evidence of temperament or biological contributions to risk of conduct disorder, measurement concerns (Quay, 1986) and inconsistent or weak relationships (Kazdin, 1987a) argue that such associations would best be viewed as preliminary. Thus, rather than focus on inferred individual differences, the most productive perspective for treatment would appear to involve treating specific behaviors (e.g., early aggression) associated with later poor outcomes and focusing on features that appear to be more reliably associated with the disorder, as outlined later in the chapter.

Parental Factors

Correlates of conduct disorder

Family factors have been implicated as playing a central role in the development and maintenance of conduct disorders (Patterson, 1992), yet untangling the relative importance of specific familial factors in predicting risk for disordered behavior is a complex process. Parental antisocial behavior appears to be moderately to strongly correlated with child conduct disorder (Frick et al., 1992). Maternal depression has also been identified as moderately to strongly correlated with conduct disorder (Downey & Coyne, 1990), yet depression appears to be a nonspecific risk factor, placing a child at risk for a range of disorders, not simply conduct disorder (Frick, 1993). Divorce has likewise been implicated as a very significant stressor in the lives of children (Amato & Keith, 1991). Yet reviews (e.g., Amato & Keith) also indicate that conduct disorder is less likely to be associated with divorce per se than with marital discord and conflict either before or after marital separation. Finally, while lower socioeconomic status clearly places a child at increased risk for conduct disorder and delinquency (West, 1982), it may not be poverty itself that is the risk factor, so much as the stressors associated with poverty. Multivariate analyses indicate that the effects of poverty may be largely explained by the effects of stressful events and beliefs that may be associated with lower economic status (Guerra, Huesmann, Tolan, Van Acker, & Eron, 1995).

Thus, factors such as parental psychopathology or marital conflict appear to be important correlates of conduct disorder but probably have their effect on child behavior through more proximal mechanisms (Reid & Patterson, 1991). The strongest candidates as direct influences for the development and maintenance of conduct disorders appear to be parental behavior management and monitoring. In their analysis of longitudinal studies of antisocial behavior, Loeber and Dishion (1983) reported that parent-child interactions, especially harsh and inconsistent discipline, inadequate monitoring, and low parental involvement, proved the best early predictors of male delinquency. Two important processes have been consistently identified in the literature: coercive family process (Patterson, 1982) and inconsistent or inadequate parental monitoring (Wahler & Dumas, 1986).

Coercive cycle of management

Based on some 25 years of research, Patterson and his colleagues (see Patterson, 1992) have implicated a specific process of family interaction, coercive family interchanges, as critical in the genesis of antisocial behavior and conduct disorders. The process is a developmental and interactive one. Research has consistently shown that children identified as aggressive and antisocial receive high rates of aversive behavior from other family members (Patterson, 1982) and learn to respond aver-

sively as well. If functional in turning off the attacks of others, then those aversive child responses will be negatively reinforced. While such an interaction may maintain the short-term equilibrium of the family by ending the conflict, in the long term it tends to increase the likelihood of coercive behavior. As the cycle becomes established, accelerations toward more aversive responses by either the parent or the child are extremely likely to be met with a similarly accelerating aversive response, trapping both parent and child in a mutually accelerating coercive pattern of behavior. As the frequency of such coercive interactions increases, so does the likelihood that at least some of these interactions will end in physical abuse (Reid, Patterson, & Loeber, 1982).

This basic training in coercion appears to be predictive of a variety of negative outcomes for children as they approach school age and has been elaborated into a multicomponent model for predicting the development of antisocial behavior and conduct disorders (Patterson, 1992; Reid & Patterson, 1991). Pettit, Bates, and Dodge (1993) reported that children exposed to negative, coercive parenting were rated significantly higher on measures of externalizing behavior at school entry and tended to show continued increases in externalizing behavior over time. This parenting style seems to be predictive of both later poor school adjustment in middle childhood (Ramsey, Walker, Shinn, O'Neill, & Stieber, 1989) and self-reported delinquency in adolescence (Patterson & Stouthamer-Loeber, 1984). Extensive causal models testing hypotheses derived from the basic coercive family interaction process (Patterson; Reid & Patterson) suggest that the basic training in coercion received in the home creates a high risk for peer rejection and academic failure once the child enters school. These factors, combined with inadequate parental supervision, later place that youngster at further risk for association with deviant peers and eventual delinquency.

Inconsistent and inadequate monitoring

Consistency and predictability of parental supervision has long been implicated as an important variable in the development of antisocial behavior. Glueck and Glueck (1950) found that a pattern of inconsistent parental discipline and poor supervision was predictive of delinquency. Parents of children with conduct problems have been shown to be more likely to respond negatively to both positive and negative child behaviors (Hetherington & Martin, 1979). The aversive behavior of these children may be an attempt to escape from the anxiety-provoking unpredictability of inconsistent or indiscriminate parenting (Wahler & Dumas, 1986). Acting-out behavior designed to "test the limits" may thus be reinforced by an escape from unpredictability, regardless of whether the resulting parental attention is positive or negative. Experimental tests among clinic referred mother-child dyads have supported the model, showing that child aversive behavior covaries predictably with inconsistent or indiscriminate maternal attention (Wahler, Williams, & Cerezo, 1990).

Other studies have suggested that inadequate parental supervision or involvement may be in itself sufficient to contribute to delinquency and antisocial behavior, especially in middle childhood and adolescence (Wilson, 1980). As is the case with coercive parenting, parental monitoring and supervision appear to be consistently associated with school adjustment (Ramsey et al., 1989). Patterson et al. (1992) note that while a decrease in parental supervision over time is probably normative in contemporary society, for antisocial youth who may be rejected by peers and experiencing school failure, that lack of monitoring may be especially salient in allowing increased contact with deviant peer culture.

Implications
The central importance of parental discipline and monitoring has obvious implications for school personnel in terms of working closely with the parents of children with conduct disorders to improve management skills and school-home communication. These will be detailed in the Alternative Actions section later in this chapter. In addition, because home discipline and monitoring have a clear and ongoing relationship with school conduct (Pettit et al., 1993), these data also have important implications for school-based intervention. If acting-out behavior is an attempt to define the boundaries of unpredictable and inconsistent home environments (Wahler & Dumas, 1986), then effective classroom management must provide a safe and structured environment characterized by consistent and predictable consequences. Yet at the same time, an overemphasis on control in many programs for students with emotional and behavioral disorders has led to sterile and aversive environments (Knitzer, Steinberg, & Fleisch, 1990). Shores, Gunter, and Jack (1993) suggest that punitive classroom management procedures are likely to produce the same coercive cycle in the school environment. Given the extensive history of coercive training many children with conduct disorders bring with them, discipline policies based primarily on control and coercion are likely to backfire. Rather, sound principles of positive and preventive behavior management (Gettinger, 1988; Sprick & Nolet, 1991) provide a method for increasing academic engagement and preventing acceleration of coercive student behavior.

Academic and Cognitive Deficits

Cognitive or academic deficits are among the most widely reported correlates of conduct disorder. An association between achievement deficits and disruptive or antisocial behavior has been found as early as first grade (Tremblay et al., 1992) to be an important predictor during elementary and middle school (Walker, Stieber, Ramsey, & O'Neill, 1991) and to extend in longitudinal studies as far as age 30 (Huesmann, Eron, & Yarmel, 1987). McGee, Williams, Share, Anderson, and Silva (1986) found that up to 50% of all boys with reading disabilities in a large-scale epidemiological study were at risk for some form of externalizing disorder by age 11, a rate three times that of non-reading-disabled students.

Yet the relationship between cognitive ability, academic skill, and conduct disorder appears to be complex and the direction of causation unclear. Earlier theories of delinquency suggested a progression from academic failure to antisocial behavior (Rutter, Tizard, & Whitmore, 1970); that is, students experiencing academic failure will be at greater risk for lowered self-esteem, decreased teacher attention, and acting-out behavior in order to escape from academic demands. Some more recent investigations, however, have supported the alternative hypothesis, that conduct disorder is more likely to disrupt learning (Huesmann et al., 1987; Tremblay et al., 1992). A third possibility is that both conduct disorder and poor achievement are the product of some third variable, such as socioeconomic status (Offord, Alder, & Boyle, 1986) or the presence of an attentional disorder (Frick et al., 1991). Though there has been support for each of the three hypotheses, there does not appear to be sufficient research to conclusively choose from among the three (Hinshaw, 1992).

Despite lack of a clear understanding of causal connections, research in this area has succeeded in identifying developmental relationships that may prove useful in treatment planning. First, there appears to be differential risk for conduct or behavior problems depending upon whether the academic deficit is general or specific. McGee et al. (1986) found that while children whose reading disabilities were consistent with low cognitive ability showed increases in teacher-reported problem behavior between age 5 and 7, children whose reading disability was specific (that is, discrepant from their IQ) tended to exhibit behavior problems later, from age 7 to 9. Second, the data are strongly suggestive of a developmental course for both conduct disorders and underachievement. Hinshaw (1992) suggests that while underachievement in the early grades is more likely to be associated with attentional problems, academic difficulties in later elementary school and adolescence are more likely to be associated with antisocial behavior and conduct disorder. Thus, underachievement and problem behavior might be conceived of as reciprocal risk factors: Whatever the direction of initial causality, the presence of low academic skill places a child at risk for problem behavior, while those problem behaviors are a continuing risk factor for poor educational attainment.

The importance of the relationship between academic underachievement and antisocial behavior cannot be overestimated. Cairns et al. (1989a) found that a combination of academic underachievement and aggressive behavior in the seventh grade was highly predictive (82%) of early dropout from school. Because the relative importance of disruptive behavior and underachievement in predicting later conduct disorder and delinquency is unclear, it is important that both be assessed. Whenever there are indications of conduct problems, academic performance should be assessed. Whenever academic difficulties surface, especially in the early grades, the implications of these for classroom behavior should be explored.

Social Interaction

A strong and consistent link has been identified between the quality of peer interaction and risk for later negative behavioral outcomes. Ollendick, Weist, Borden, and Greene (1992) found associations between peer rejection and increased criminal offenses, conduct disorder, and substance abuse. Children exhibiting aggressive behaviors toward their peers receive higher rates of negative initiations from peers (Walker, Shinn, O'Neill, & Ramsey, 1987) and higher rates of negative consequences and commands from teachers (Wehby, Symons, & Shores, 1995). Both aggression and peer rejection appear to place children at risk for later disorder. Coie, Lochman, Terry, and Hyman (1992) followed two cohorts of third-grade children from low-income homes into early adolescence. Both aggression and peer rejection in the third grade, measured by peer nomination, predicted parent and teacher ratings of school adjustment and externalizing disorders in middle school.

At least one theoretical formulation suggests that such difficulties in social interaction are related to deficiencies in social cognitive processing. Dodge and his colleagues (Dodge, 1980; Steinberg & Dodge, 1983) have found that aggressive children are more likely to misattribute a hostile intent to nonhostile or neutral social initiations from peers and to respond in an inflexible hostile manner. Aggressive boys have been found to minimize their own aggressiveness and maximize the aggressiveness of their peers (Lochman, 1987). Dodge (1993) has postulated a social-information processing framework for the development of conduct disorders, suggesting that, at each step of cognitive processing, aggressive children are likely to make cognitive errors that will result in an increased probability of inferring hostile intent and reacting in a hostile manner. While associations between any single step in processing and deviant behavior may be relatively small ($r = .30$), multiple correlations of cognitive processing stages and deviant behavior may range as high as $r = .94$, providing impressive evidence of the link between faulty social cognition and aggressive behavior (Dodge, 1993).

The focus on the deviant peer interactions of students with conduct disorders implies a deficit model of skills. That is, the aggressive student may lack sufficient behavioral alternatives to respond to diverse social situations, resulting in an increased likelihood of hostile responding. Thus, social skills training (see Social Skills, this volume) becomes an important component in any intervention program, in order to broaden the child's repertoire of potential responses. The social cognitive model of aggression also implies a cognitive deficit: At every step in the process of encoding and responding to social cues, aggressive and disruptive youngsters make cognitive errors that increase the probability that they will respond with hostility to all incoming social stimuli. Thus, training in appropriate social skills may also need to address the faulty social perceptions of students rejected by their peers for aggressive behavior (Lochman, Dunn, & Klimes-Dougan, 1993).

Developmental Course

One of the more important recent developments in the field of conduct disorders has been an increased understanding of the developmental course of the disorder. While the relatively high stability seems to yield a poor prognosis for conduct disorders (Kazdin, 1987b), it has also led to a focus on specific risk factors and predictors. This developmental understanding may in turn yield important new perspectives on the treatment of conduct disorders.

Stability and prognosis
This high stability of childhood conduct disorders has been extensively noted. Longitudinal studies have shown that aggression and antisocial behavior in childhood is reliably associated with increased criminality, poor academic achievement, and increased substance abuse well into adulthood (Hodgins, 1994; Huesmann et al., 1987). These data provide a generally pessimistic picture regarding prognosis and treatment. Students exhibiting early conduct problems are much more likely to be placed in some form of special services (Walker et al., 1991) and to be at risk for school dropout (Cairns et al., 1989a), juvenile delinquency (Reid & Patterson, 1991), and incarceration (Patterson, et al., 1992).

Yet closer examination of that stability indicates some important details and qualifications concerning the continuity of antisocial behavior over time. First, the association of early disruptive behavior, adolescent delinquency, and adult personality disorder means that conduct disorders do not spring up, full blown, overnight (Loeber, 1990). Adolescents who are incarcerated due to a pattern of conduct disorder are highly likely to have a significant history of disruptive behavior, academic failure, and inadequate parental discipline and supervision. Second, because the correlations between early disruptive behavior and later conduct disorder are not perfect (i.e, 1.00), by definition a large proportion of children exhibiting behavioral difficulty will not become conduct disordered. Only a small propor-

Early Childhood		Middle Childhood		Adolescence	
Coercive Parenting	Cognitive/ Language Deficit	Lack of Parental Engagement	Academic Difficulty	Poor Parental Supervision	School Alienation or Dropout
Early Aggression/ Hyperactivity	Poor Social Skills	Increased Aggression/ Covert Acts	Cognitive Set: Hostile Attributions	Increased Likelihood of Delinquency	Association with Deviant Peers

Figure 1. *A developmental sequence for conduct disorders, tracing the course of the disorder across four factors: parenting, cognitive/academic, personal characteristics, and social interactions.*

tion of those children exhibiting childhood aggression will proceed to juvenile delinquency or adult antisocial personality (Loeber, 1983).

Developmental models of conduct disorder

Examination of the risk and protective factors associated with conduct disorder at various ages has led to a number of formulations concerning the developmental course of that disorder (Dodge, 1993; Loeber, 1990; Patterson, 1992; Reid & Patterson, 1991; Tolan, Guerra, & Kendall, 1995). Figure 1 represents a hypothetical developmental sequencing of the four dimensions presented earlier. Given the relatively recent emergence of the developmental approach to antisocial behavior and delinquency (Patterson, 1992), the sequencing and placement in time of developmental issues must be regarded as speculative, representing examples of the types of issues and problems identified by research to date in each of the four dimensions.

A number of considerations flow out of the developmental approach to conduct disorders. First, risk factors are not independent but interact in significant ways; a single risk factor may have an important influence in a number of domains. Cognitive deficits, for example, have been associated with school alienation (Cairns et al., 1989a; Reid & Patterson, 1991) as well as social interaction difficulties (Dodge, 1993). Second, early risk factors may set the context for patterns of behavior that are themselves risk factors for further disorder. Early conduct problems and aggression appear to increase the risk of academic failure in later grades (Tremblay et al., 1992). Yet that failure is itself a risk factor for further antisocial behavior, as the adolescent with behavior disorders engages in disruptive behavior in order to escape from academic demands (Center, Deitz, & Kaufman, 1982). Loeber (1990) has termed this phenomenon *stacking,* suggesting a cumulative effect of risk factors over time. Third, the actual behaviors constituting conduct disorder will change over time. While young children may engage primarily in inattentive, noncompliant, or mildly disruptive behavior, antisocial behaviors become progressively more diverse (Loeber, 1983) and more dangerous over time, as the physical capacities of youth and adolescents grow (Cairns et al, 1989b). Finally, a developmental per-

spective implies that both child behavior and environmental responses evolve over time. Patterson (1992) notes that the inadequate parental discipline and monitoring predictive of antisocial behavior is itself developing and changing over time. While escalating cycles of coercion appear to be the parenting pattern most predictive of behavioral disturbance in early childhood, inadequate supervision appears to become more predictive of negative outcomes as the youth enters adolescence.

Alternative Actions

The complexity of both the etiology and course of conduct disorder has led to some pessimism regarding the availability of effective treatments. Indeed, in his review of effective treatments, Kazdin (1987b) notes that no single treatment has been shown to be consistently successful in ameliorating the course of conduct disorder. Rather, multifaceted treatments, simultaneously addressing a number of need areas, appear to be warranted (Tolan et al., 1995). A comprehensive program might include multimethod assessment and early identification, family-based intervention, school-based interventions, service coordination, and skills training.

Early Identification and Primary Prevention

Studies of the course of conduct disorders suggest that patterns of behavior associated with conduct disorder become more intransigent and less amenable to successful intervention as the child matures (Loeber, 1990). Thus early identification and intervention are essential in order to maximize the possibilities of diverting the course of the disorder. Multiple-gating approaches (Lochman et al., 1995; Walker & Severson, 1990) offer a promising approach to early identification.

The necessity of early intervention and broad-based prevention approaches has also been widely recognized. Zigler, Taussig, and Black (1992) suggest that the extremely high costs of delinquent and predelinquent behavior in both fiscal and social terms have led to a new focus on a preventive and ecological approach to intervention. The programs they review often start in preschool and include parent training, social instruction, enriched academic environments, and even community contacts with social service agencies. Hawkins and Weis (1985) have presented an integrated model of delinquency prevention that includes components that address family, school, and community issues. While the approach is still nascent, preliminary data appear promising: Graduates of a multisystemic treatment program showed improved family and behavioral outcomes at the completion of the program and fewer significant criminal offenses and arrests up to 4 years later (Borduin et al., 1995).

Family-Based Intervention

Parent management training

Extensive research has implicated behavior management as among the factors, perhaps the most critical factor, in the development and maintenance of child antisocial behavior. Increasing the skills of parents in managing disruptive and aversive behavior thus appears to be an important target for intervention. The direct training of parents in less coercive and more preventive management techniques has been found to be consistently effective in reducing deviant child behavior (Webster-Stratton, 1993) and may be the most consistently effective of currently available interventions (Kazdin, 1987b).

A number of models of parent training in behavior management have demonstrated effectiveness (Forehand & McMahon, 1981; Patterson, 1982; Webster-Stratton, 1993). In general, these programs train parents to systematically attend to specific behaviors of their children; to consistently reinforce positive behaviors; and to use mild but specific, contingent, and consistent punishment for coercive behaviors. In addition to training in reinforcement techniques, procedures such as distraction, selective attention, and ignoring are modeled, role-played and implemented, usually in feedback situations. While time-out is often a component of such programs in dealing with externalizing problems such as hitting, there is also an emphasis on skills that enhance closeness and parental emotional availability.

Although positive results have been consistently demonstrated for parent behavior-management training, the effectiveness of such approaches appears to be limited by the personal challenges that many such families face (Webster-Stratton, 1993). Thus, parent training models have come to include a focus on these interpersonal stressors. In a model termed *synthesis teaching,* Wahler, Carter, Fleischman, and Lambert (1993) investigated the impact of addressing personal stressors in conjunction with behavior management training for 29 clinic-referred mother-child dyads. The mothers in the synthesis teaching group showed both significant gains in appropriate maternal attention and decreases in child aversive behavior at both 6-month and one-year follow-ups, when compared to a group that had received only parent management training. These and other similar results (Griest et al., 1982) suggest that, to ensure generalization, attention to the interpersonal stressors that often characterize the lives of families of children with conduct disorders may be a necessary adjunct to parent management training.

Parent involvement in school

Given the pervasiveness of family problems in the lives of multiproblem children, a primary goal of any intervention program must be to change the nature of the relationship between home and school. Yet attitudes held by both parents and teachers may impede the development of effective working relationships: Parents often attribute their child's poor school performance to teacher factors, while teachers attribute poor academic performance to lack of parental concern or skill (Vernberg & Medway, 1981).

Whatever the obstacles, however, school involvement by parents appears to yield clear benefits for their child. Parent involvement in the schooling of their children can lead to strong increments in academic performance, regardless of family socioeconomic status or parent education level (Keith et al., 1992). Epstein (1992) offers a framework for increasing parent involvement in a number of areas, including communications from the schools, volunteering, learning activities at home, and parental participation in school decision making. By using such approaches (see also Christenson & Conoley, 1992) to make parents partners rather than adversaries in the educational process, school psychologists can increase available school resources for dealing with students with conduct and behavior problems.

School-Based Intervention

Teacher training in behavior management

Successful school intervention for students with conduct disorder may also require a significant commitment to teacher training in behavior management. Classroom management of disruptive behavior is typically viewed as among the most critical skills in dealing with youngsters with behavior problems in either regular or special education classrooms (Myles & Simpson, 1989). Yet teachers often feel that their training is most inadequate in precisely this area (Brophy & McCaslin, 1992). As the trend toward the integration of greater numbers of learners with learning and behavior problems continues, teachers will be called upon to manage a greater diversity and severity of problem behaviors. Thus, additional teacher training in preventative management techniques may be critical for effective school programs. Such procedures appear to be especially effective when implemented as part of a school-wide behavior plan (Gottfredson et al., 1993).

The principles constituting sound behavior management have been documented extensively (Alberto & Troutman, 1995; Gettinger, 1988; Sprick & Nolet, 1991) and need little repetition here. What may be important to address, however, is the typical disciplinary climate in many middle and secondary schools. Field-based investigations have consistently documented classroom environments in which positive reinforcement is all but lacking (Shores et al., 1993). Negative, coercive disciplinary practices appear to be little more effective in school settings than they are in the family; student alienation caused by the perception of harsh and unfair discipline appears to be a significant determinant of the decision to dropout (Wehlage & Rutter, 1986).

A promising alternative in the area of behavior management is the emerging technology of functional analysis (Horner, Albin, & O'Neill, 1991). The primary goals of functional assessment are to use interview and observation to identify setting events and functions of severely disruptive behavior (Foster-Johnson & Dunlap, 1993). These data have been viewed as useful in the field of severe disabilities in specifying the communicative function and context of behavior (Harding, Wacker, Cooper, Millard, & Jenson-Kovolan, 1994) and identifying replacement behaviors that will serve a similar function (Horner et al., 1991). Applications of this approach to emotional and behavioral disorders are relatively recent and exploratory (Dunlap et al., 1993). Yet the goals and technology of functional assessment may hold great promise for increasing understanding of conduct and behavior problems.

Appropriate curricular placement

The link between antisocial or aggressive behavior and underachievement has been extensively documented in longitudinal and correlational studies (Hinshaw, 1992). Experimental studies have supported the hypothesis that a significant proportion of disruptive classroom behavior may be an attempt to escape academic demands that are perceived as too difficult. Center et al. (1982) demonstrated that students in a classroom for students with emotional and behavioral disorders were three times as likely to engage in disruptive behavior when academic demands were mismatched to student ability levels than when students were working in materials appropriately matched to their level of academic skill. Gickling and Thompson (1985) showed that appropriate curricular placement yields increases in both time on-task and work completed. For children with attention deficit/hyperactivity disorder, appropriate curricular placement appears to have an impact on appropriate behavior at least as powerful as psychostimulant medication.

Thus, for children with conduct disorders, appropriate curricular placement appears to be an effective means for reducing disruptive classroom behavior. In particular, the technology of curriculum-based assessment (Howell & Morehead, 1987) can provide important information about the appropriate instructional level. Although the classroom behavior of students with conduct disorder is more likely to capture attention, the data suggest programming that emphasizes successful academic performance is more likely to be productive in the long term. Ayllon and Roberts (1974) showed that, while attention solely to behavior management does not have an impact on the academic performance of disruptive children, improving academic performance can have an effect on both academic performance and classroom behavior.

Service Coordination

The complexity of the problems associated with conduct and behavior disorders makes it apparent that no one educational or social service agency can address all of those problems. In response to concerns about fragmentation and failure to serve children in need of mental health services (Knitzer, 1982), the National Institutes of Mental Health launched the Children and Adolescent Service System Program (CASSP) in 1984. The program emphasizes a child-centered, family-focused, and community-based approach whose goal is to develop a comprehensive system of care for children and youth with severe emotional disturbance and their families (Stroul & Friedman, 1986). In the 10 years since the CASSP initiative was launched, model programs have sprung up around the country. Such interagency ventures have demonstrated impressive outcomes, including increased placement in the community, decreased costs, improvements in behavioral and academic functioning, decreased involvement with juvenile justice and corrections, and increased parent satisfaction with services (Jordan & Hernandez, 1990).

An important development in this model has been the notion of individualized care or wraparound services (Burchard & Clarke, 1990). In this model, rather than expending local and state resources on expensive residential placements, communities use those resources to bring in local services, which are "wrapped around" the child and family in an effort to successfully maintain the child in the local community. Several features have been identified as important in making individualized wraparound services effective (Skiba, Polsgrove, & Nasstrom, 1995), including *interagency collaboration* (Nelson & Pearson, 1991), *case management* (Burns & Friedman, 1990), *flexible funding* (Dollard, Evans, Lubrecht, & Schaeffer, 1994), and *unconditional care* (Burchard & Clarke, 1990).

In a system of services strongly conditioned to provide programming based on categorical labels and specific program components (Burchard & Clarke, 1990), it may seem a daunting task for psychologists to reach across those barriers and begin to coordinate school services with other social service agencies. Yet children and youth exhibiting severe conduct and behavior problems are highly likely to have been involved with several agencies, including the courts, mental health agencies, private hospitals, and welfare (Shamsie, Sykes, & Hamilton, 1994). To the extent that these services fail to communicate, all involved with the individual child run the risk of providing programs that duplicate or conflict with other agencies.

Skills Training

Interpersonal skill deficits may cause children at risk of conduct disorder to choose less adaptive means of engaging peers; hence, skills training approaches teach interpersonal and intrapersonal skills in order to build a repertoire for improved social interaction. Social skills packages may emphasize training in individual skills, such as conversation (Bierman & Furman, 1984) or classroom and peer interaction skills (Walker et al., 1983). Other programs, such as the Anger Coping Program (Lochman et al., 1993), emphasize a social problem-solving model that trains children to generate and attempt behavioral alternatives in problem situations. It is important to note that successful social skills programs are not limited to cognitive or social instruction but are set within a framework of an ongoing behavioral programming to establish reinforcement contingencies that can maintain appropriate social responses as they emerge (Lochman et al., 1993). Further discussion of skills training approaches may be found elsewhere in this volume (see Anger Control, Social Problem Solving, and Social Skills, this volume).

Summary and Conclusions

Disruptive and aggressive students create chaos in the environments with which they interact. Aggression creates discomfort and anger among peers and teachers at the elementary level and may endanger the safety of others as the youngster reaches adolescence (Cairns et al., 1989b). As the disruptive behavior continues, the child is at high risk for peer rejection and negative teacher interaction (Wehby et al., 1995). Over time, a continuing cycle of disruption is created and maintained that eventually yields a strong probability that the adolescent with conduct disorder will become alienated from school, attracted to deviant peer groups outside the school, and engaged in law-violating behavior.

Yet as compelling as these disruptive behaviors are, they are not by any means the whole story of conduct disorder. Conduct disorders are inextricably woven into a fabric of causes and correlated factors. Within this context, the seemingly inexplicable paradoxes of disordered behavior become more comprehensible. Against a family background of coercion and abuse, disruptive behaviors that appear volitional may in fact be the only alternatives available to a youngster whose family history has left a highly limited repertoire of appropriate responses. Nor is it surprising, considering the likelihood that many youngsters with conduct disorder are exposed to high levels of aversive behavior (Reid & Patterson, 1991), that they will come to routinely misinterpret everyday social cues, attributing hostility where none was intended. Even classroom disruptions that threaten classroom order and safety may, for the antisocial youngster, provide the sole means of escape from what seem to be incomprehensible and overwhelming academic demands.

Thus, programs and interventions for children with severe conduct problems tread a fine line. In the face of a range of behaviors that violate the rights of others to a safe environment, limits must be imposed. Consistency and structure probably also serve an educational function for the child who may have learned to engage in disruptive behavior in order to define the limits of a characteristically chaotic family environment (Wahler & Dumas, 1986). Yet without an understanding of the overall context and development of conduct disordered behavior, an overemphasis on control can create sterile and confrontational programs and classrooms (Knitzer et al., 1990). Analyses of classroom environments (Shores et al., 1993) indicate that a pattern of coercion and counter-coercion is no less predictable in the school setting than in the home.

The one firm conclusion that can be reached amid the complex interrelationships of conduct disorder is that no single approach to treatment and intervention will be sufficient. Antisocial behavior is multiply determined; treatment programs that fail to account for that fact do so at their peril. Simply managing classroom behavior becomes an overwhelming task if the home environment continues to provide the conditions that support and maintain disruptive behavior. Instructing a child in appropriate classroom behaviors through social skills training may well be insufficient if a curriculum mismatch creates an urge to escape from academic demands through whatever means necessary. Multiple component interventions, addressing the cognitive, social, academic, and even family needs of multiproblem children, are necessary to address the developmental complexity of conduct disorder (Conduct Disorders Prevention Research Group, 1992).

If the potential risks of ignoring the problems of children with conduct disorder are great, so are the potential benefits of making a commitment to preventive programs. Lochman et al. (1993) noted that multicomponent school-based prevention programs can accrue both short- and long-term benefits to disruptive children, as well as their peers and teachers. In the short term, classroom environments become less jarred by disruptive outbursts, children become less rejected as their own behavior becomes less aggressive, and youngsters with a long history of aggression achieve some measure of security and personal competence over time. In the long term, prevention programs can reduce the risk associated with behaviors highly predictive of future delinquency, underachievement, and criminality (Zigler et al., 1992). Although there is abundant room for pessimism in approaching intervention with conduct disordered behavior, there appears to be little alternative but to continue to develop comprehensive prevention-oriented models that can address the complexity of conduct disordered behavior.

Recommended Resources

Clark, L. (1985). *SOS! Help for Parents.* Bowling Green, KY: Parents Press.
This book is a very practical, yet research-based guide for parents on handling behavior problems of children. The author does a fine job of taking the best available research and presenting it in an accessible format. Illustrations are clear and well-organized and accompanied by abundant examples. This should be a valuable resource in helping avoid some of the parenting problems that often occur in families with a child with conduct disorder.

Forness, S. R., Kavale, K. A., King, B. H., & Kasari, C. (1994). Simple versus complex conduct disorders: Identification and phenomenology. *Behavioral Disorders, 19,* 306–312.
Forness and his colleagues explore phenomena associated with comorbidity of conduct disorders and conclude that complexity of the disorder may well be the rule for children with conduct disorders. They demonstrate how the most common classroom disruptive behaviors, not paying attention and disruptive behavior, may be indications of a number of possible disorders.

Kazdin, A. E. (1987). Treatment of antisocial behavior in children: Current status and future directions. *Psychological Bulletin, 102,* 187–203.
Kazdin's article on treatment of antisocial behavior is a classic in the field, identifying treatments that appear most promising for children with conduct disorder. Presenting several models that might guide intervention, he makes the intriguing suggestion that antisocial behavior be viewed in the context of a "chronic-disease" model, requiring more or less constant treatment and monitoring.

Loeber, R. (1990). Development and risk factors of juvenile antisocial behavior and delinquency. *Clinical Psychology Review, 10,* 1–41.
This paper provides an enlightening summary of research related to the field of antisocial behavior. Focusing on how risk factors influence the development of antisocial behavior at different points in time, Loeber explores how such factors lead to increased risk for, or desistance from, conduct disorders and delinquency.

Patterson, G. R. (1992). Developmental changes in antisocial behavior. In R. D. Peters, R. J. McMahon, & V. L. Quinsey (Eds.), *Aggression and violence throughout the life span* (pp. 52–82). Newbury Park, CA: Sage.
This book chapter provides an insightful analysis of how both antisocial behavior and the parenting problems that often accompany it evolve over time. From the basic unit of coercive interchanges, Patterson builds an elegant model showing how the form, intensity, and setting of antisocial and aggressive behavior shift over time.

References

Alberto, P. A., & Troutman, A. C. (1995). *Applied behavior analysis for teachers* (4th ed.). Englewood Cliffs, NJ: Merrill.

Amato, P. R., & Keith, B. (1991). Parental divorce and the well-being of children: A meta-analysis. *Psychological Bulletin, 110,* 26–46.

American Psychiatric Association. (1994). *Diagnostic and statistical manual of mental disorders* (4th ed.). Washington, DC: Author.

Bates, J. (1990). Conceptual and empirical linkages between temperament and behavior problems: A commentary on the Sanson, Prior, and Kyrios study. *Merrill-Palmer Quarterly, 36*(2), 193–199.

Biederman, J., Newcorn, J., & Sprich, S. (1991). Comorbidity of attention deficit hyperactiveity disorder with conduct, depressive, anxiety, and other disorders. *American Journal of Psychiatry, 148,* 564–577.

Bierman, K. L., & Furman, W. (1984). The effect of social skills training and peer involvement on the social adjustment of preadolescents. *Child Development, 55,* 151–162.

Bloom, R. B., & Hopewell, L. R. (1982). Psychiatric hospitalization of adolescents and successful mainstream reentry. *Exceptional Children, 48,* 352–357.

Borduin, C. M., Mann, B. J., Cone, L. T., Henggeler, S. W., Fucci, B. R., Blaske, D. M., & Williams, R. A. (1995). Multisystemic treatment of serious juvenile offenders: Long-term prevention of criminality and violence. *Journal of Consulting and Clinical Psychology, 63,* 569–578.

Bower, E. M. (1982). Defining emotional disturbance: Public policy and research. *Psychology in the Schools, 19,* 55–60.

Brophy, J., & McCaslin, M. (1992). Teachers' reports of how they perceive and cope with problem students. *The Elementary School Journal, 93,* 3–68.

Burchard, J. D., Burchard, S. N., Sewell, R., & VanDenBerg, J. (1993). *One kid at a time: Evaluative case studies and description of the Alaska Youth Initiative Demonstration Project.* Washington, DC: Georgetown University Child Development Center, CASSP Technical Assistance Center.

Burchard, J. D., & Clarke, R. T. (1990). The role of individualized care in a service delivery system for children and adolescents with severely maladjusted behavior. *Journal of Mental Health Administration, 17(1),* 48–60.

Burns, B. J., & Friedman, R. M. (1990). Examining the research base for child mental health services and policy. *Journal of Mental Health Administration, 17*(1), 87–99.

Cairns, R. B., Cairns, B. D., & Neckerman, H. J. (1989a).

Early school dropouts: Configurations and determinants. *Child Development, 60,* 1437–1452.

Cairns, R. B., Cairns, B. D., Neckerman, H. J., Ferguson, L. L., & Gariepy, J. L. (1989b). Growth and aggression: 1. Childhood to early adolescence. *Developmental Psychology, 25,* 320–330.

Center, D., Deitz, S. M., & Kaufman, M. E. (1982). Student ability, task difficulty, and inappropriate classrom behavior: A study of children with behavior disorders. *Behavior Modification, 6,* 355–374.

Christenson, S. L., & Conoley, J. C. (1992). *Home-school collaboration: Enhancing children's academic and social competence.* Silver Spring, MD: National Association of School Psychologists.

Cline, D. H. (1990). Interpretations of emotional disturbance and social maladjustment as policy problems: A legal analysis of initiatives to exclude handicapped/disruptive students from special education. *Behavioral Disorders, 15,* 159–173.

Coie, J. D., Lochman, J. E., Terry, R., & Hyman, C. (1992). Predicting early adolescent disorder from childhood aggression and peer rejection. *Journal of Consulting and Clinical Psychology, 60,* 783–792.

Cole, D. A., & Carpentieri, S. (1990). Social status and the comorbidity of child depression and conduct disorder. *Journal of Consulting and Clinical Psychology, 58,* 748–757.

Conduct Disorders Prevention Research Group. (1992). A developmental and clinical model for the prevention of conduct disorders: The FAST track program. *Development and Psychopathology, 4,* 509–527.

Deur, J. L. & Parke, R. D. (1970). Effects of inconsistent punishment or aggression in children. *Developmental Psychology, 2,* 403–411.

Dodge, K. A. (1980). Social cognition and children's aggressive behavior. *Child Development, 51,* 162–170.

Dodge, K. A. (1993). Social-cognitive mechanisms in the development of conduct disorder and depression. *American Review of Psychology, 44,* 559–584.

Dollard, N., Evans, M. E., Lubrecht, J., & Schaeffer, D. (1994). The use of flexible service dollars in rural community-based programs for children with serious emotional disturbance and their families. *Journal of Emotional and Behavioral Disorders, 2*(2), 117–125.

Downey, G., & Coyne, J. C. (1990). Children of depressed parents: An integrated review. *Psychological Bulletin, 108,* 50–76.

Dunlap, G., Kern, L., dePerczel, M., Clarke, S., Wilson, D., Childs, K. E., White, R., & Falk, G. D. (1993). Functional analysis of classroom variables for students with emotional and behavioral disorders. *Behavioral Disorders, 18,* 275–291.

Emery, R. E. (1982). Interparental conflict and the children of discord and divorce. *Psychological Bulletin, 92,* 310–330.

Emery, R. E. (1988). *Marriage, divorce, and children's adjustment.* Newbury Park, CA: Sage.

Esser, G., Schmidt, M. H., & Woerner, W. (1990). Epidemiology and course of psychiatric disorders in school-age children: Results of a longitudinal study. *Journal of Child Psychology and Psychiatry, 31,* 243–263.

Faretra, G. (1981). A profile of aggression from adolescence to adulthood: An 18-year follow-up of psychiatrically disturbed and violent adolescents. *American Journal of Orthopsychiatry, 5,* 439–453.

Fendrich, M., Warner, V., & Weissman, M. M. (1990). Family risk factors, parental depression, and psychopathology in offspring. *Developmental Psychology, 26,* 40–50.

Fergusson, D. M., Horwood, L. J., & Lloyd, M. (1991). Confirmatory factor models of attention deficit and conduct disorder. *Journal of Child Psychology and Psychiatry, 32,* 257–274.

Fergusson, D. M., Horwood, J., & Lynskey, M. T. (1993). Prevalence and comorbidity of *DSM-III-R* diagnoses in a birth chort of 15 year olds. *Journal of the American Academy of Child and Adolescent Psychiatry, 32,* 1127–1134.

Forehand, R. L., & McMahon, R. J. (1981). *Helping the noncompliant child: A clinician's guide to parent training.* New York: Guilford Press.

Forness, S. R., Kavale, K. A., King, B. H., & Kasari, C. (1994). Simple versus complex conduct disorders: Identification and phenomenology. *Behavioral Disorders, 19,* 306–312.

Foster-Johnson, L., & Dunlap, G. (1993). Using functional assessment to develop effective, individualized interventions for challenging behaviors. *Teaching Exceptional Children, 25*(3), 44–50.

Frick, P. J. (1993). Childhood conduct problems in a family context. *School Psychology Review, 22,* 376–385.

Frick, P. J., Kamphaus, R. W., Lahey, B. B., Loeber, R., Christ, M. A., Hart, E. L., & Tannenbaum, L. E. (1991). Academic underachievement and the disruptive behavior disorders. *Journal of Consulting and Clinical Psychology, 59,* 289–294.

Frick, P. J., Lahey, B. B., Loeber R., Stouthamer-Loeber, M., Christ, M. A., & Hanson, K. (1992). Familial risk factors to oppositional disorder and conduct disorder: Parental psychopathology and maternal parenting. *Journal of Consulting and Clinical Psychology, 60,* 49–55.

Gettinger, M. (1988). Methods of proactive classroom management. *School Psychology Review, 17,* 227–242.

Glueck, S., & Glueck, E. T. (1950). *Unravelling juvenile delinquency.* New York: Commonwealth Fund.

Goldstein, A. P., Harootunian, B., & Conoley, J. C. (1994). *Student aggression: Prevention, management, and replacement training.* New York: Guilford Press.

Gottfredson, D. C., Gottfredson, G. D., & Hybl, L. G. (1993). Managing adolescent behavior: A multiyear, multischool study. *American Educational Research Journal, 30*(1), 179–215.

Griest, D. L., Forehand, R., Rogers, T., Breiner, J. L., Furey, W., & Williams, C. A. (1982). Effects of Parent Enhancement Therapy on the treatment outcome and generalization of a parent training program. *Behaviour Research and Therapy, 20,* 429–436.

Guerra, N. G., Huesmann, L. R., Tolan, P. H., Van Acker, R., & Eron, L. D. (1995). Stressful events and individual beliefs as correlates of economic disadvantage and aggression among urban children. *Journal of Consulting and Clinical Psychology, 63,* 518–528.

Harding, J., Wacker, D. P., Cooper, L. J., Millard, T., & Jenson-Kovolan, P. (1994). Brief hierarchical assessment of potential treatment components with children in an outpatient clinic. *Journal of Applied Behavior Analysis, 27,* 291–300.

Hawkins, J. D., & Weis, J. G. (1985). The social development model: An integrated approach to delinquency prevention. *Journal of Primary Prevention, 6*(2), 73–97.

Hetherington, E. M. & Martin, B. (1979). Family interaction. In H. C. Quay & J. S. Werry (Eds.), *Psychopathological disorders of childhood.* New York: Wiley and Sons.

Hinshaw, S. P. (1987). On the distinction between attentional deficits/hyperactivity and conduct problems/aggression in child psychopathology. *Psychological Bulletin, 101,* 443–463.

Hinshaw, S. P. (1992). Externalizing behavior problems and academic underachievement in childhood and adolescence: Causal relationships and underlying mechanisms. *Psychological Bulletin, 111,* 127–155.

Hodgins, S. (1994). Status at age 30 of children with conduct disorders. *Studies on Crime and Crime Prevention, 3,* 41–62.

Horner, R. H., Albin, R. W., & O'Neill, R. E. (1991). Supporting students with severe intellectual disabilities and severe challenging behavior. In G. Stoner, M. R. Shinn, & H. M. Walker (Eds.), *Interventions for achievement and behavior problems* (pp. 269–288). Silver Spring, MD: National Association of School Psychologists.

Howell, K. W., & Morehead, M. K. (1987). *Curriculum-based evaluation for special and remedial education.* Columbus, OH: Merrill.

Huesmann, L. R., Eron, L. D., & Yarmel, P. W. (1987). Intellectual functioning and aggression. *Journal of Personality and Social Psychology, 52,* 232–240.

Jordan, D. D., & Hernandez, M. (1990). The Ventura Planning Model: A proposal for mental health reform. *The Journal for Mental Health Administration, 17*(1), 26–47.

Kauffman, J. M., & Lloyd, J. W. (1992). Restrictive educational placement of students with emotional or behavioral disorders: What we know and what we need to know. *Severe Behavior Disorders Monograph, 15,* 35–43.

Kazdin, A. E. (1987a). *Conduct disorders in childhood and adolescence.* Beverly Hills, CA: Sage.

Kazdin, A. E. (1987b). Treatment of antisocial behavior in children: Current status and future directions. *Psychological Bulletin, 102,* 187–203.

Keith, T. Z., Bickley, P. G., Keith, P. B., Trivette, P. S., Singh, K., & Troutman, G. C. (1992). *Does parent involvement raise eighth grade student achievement? Evidence from the National Educational Longitutidinal Study of 1988.* Paper presented at the Annual Meeting of the National Association of School Psychologists, Nashville, TN.

Knitzer, J. (1982). *Unclaimed children: The failure of public responsibility to children and adolescents in need of mental health services.* Washington, DC: Children's Defense Fund.

Knitzer, J., Steinberg, Z., & Fleisch, B. (1990). *At the schoolhouse door: An examination of programs and policies for children with behavioral and emotional disorders.* New York: Bank Street College.

Kovacs, M., Paulaskas, S., Gatsonis, C., & Richards, C. (1988). Depressive disorders in childhood III: A longitudinal study of comorbidity with and risk for conduct disorders. *Journal of Affective Disorders, 15,* 205–217.

Landy, S., & Peters, R. D. (1992). Toward an understanding of a developmental paradigm for aggressive conduct problems during the preschool years. In R. D. Peters, R. J. McMahon, & V. L. Quinsey (Eds.), *Aggression and violence throughout the life span* (pp. 1–30). Newbury Park, CA: Sage.

Lochman, J. E. (1987). Self- and peer perceptions and attributional biases of aggressive and nonaggressive boys in dyadic interactions. *Journal of Consulting and Clinical Psychology, 55,* 404–410.

Lochman, J. E., & The Conduct Problems Prevention Research Group. (1995). Screening of child behavior problems for prevention programs at school entry. *Journal of Consulting and Clinical Psychology, 63,* 549–559.

Lochman, J. E., Dunn, S. E., & Klimes-Dougan, B. (1993). An intervention and consultation model from a social cognitive perspective: A description of the anger coping program. *School Psychology Review, 22,* 458–471.

Loeber, R. (1983). The stability of antisocial and delinquent child behavior: A review. *Child Development, 53,* 1431–1446.

Loeber, R. (1990). Development and risk factors of juvenile antisocial behavior and delinquency. *Clinical Psychology Review, 10,* 1–41.

Loeber, R., & Dishion, T. J. (1983). Early predictors of male delinquency: A review. *Psychological Bulletin, 94,* 68–99.

Loeber, R., & Dishion, T. J. (1984). Boys who fight at home and school: Family conditions influencing cross-setting consistency. *Journal of Consulting and Clinical Psychology, 52,* 759–768.

McConaughy, S. H., & Skiba, R. J. (1993). Comorbidity of externalizing and internalizing problems. *School Psychology Review, 22,* 421–436.

McGee, R., Williams, S., Share, D. L., Anderson, J., & Silva, P. A. (1986). The relationship between specific reading retardation, general reading backwardness and behavioural problems in a large sample of Dunedin boys: A longitudinal study from five to eleven years. *Journal of Child Psychology and Psychiatry, 27,* 597–610.

Myles, B. S., & Simpson, R. L. (1989). Regular education teacher modifications for mainstreaming mildly handicapped students. *The Journal of Special Education, 22,* 479–491.

Nelson, C. M. (1992). Searching for meaning in the behavior of antisocial pupils, public school educators, and lawmakers. *School Psychology Review, 21,* 35–39.

Nelson, C. M., & Pearson, C. A. (1991). *Integrating services for children and youth with emotional/behavioral disorders.* Reston, VA: Council for Exceptional Children.

Offord, D., Alder, R. J., & Boyle, M. H. (1986). Prevalence and sociodemographic correlates of conduct disorder. *American Journal of Social Psychiatry, 6,* 272–278.

Olweus, D. (1979). Stability of aggressive reaction patterns in males: A review. *Psychological Bulletin, 86,* 852–875.

O'Neill, R. E., Horner, R. H., Albin, R. W., Storey, K., & Sprague, J. R. (1990). *Functional analysis: A practical assessment guide.* Eugene, OR: University of Oregon Research and Training Center on Community-Referenced Nonaversive Behavior Management.

Patterson, G. R. (1982). *Coercive family process.* Eugene, OR: Castalia.

Patterson, G. R. (1992). Developmental changes in antisocial behavior. In R. D. Peters, R. J. McMahon, & V. L. Quinsey (Eds.), *Aggression and violence throughout the life span* (pp. 52–82). Newbury Park, CA: Sage.

Patterson, G. R., Crosby, L., & Vuchinich, S. (1992). Predicting risk for early police arrest. *Journal of Quantitative Criminology, 8,* 335–355.

Patterson, G. R., & Stouthamer-Loeber, M. (1984). The correlation of family management practices and delinquency. *Child Development, 55,* 1299–1307.

Peterson, J. L., & Zill, N. (1986). Marital disruption, parent-child relationships, and behavior problems in children. *Journal of Marriage and the Family, 48,* 295–307.

Pettit, G. S., Bates, J. E., & Dodge, K. A. (1993). Family interaction patterns and children's conduct problems at home and school: A longitudinal perspective. *School Psychology Review, 22,* 403–420.

Pullis, M. (1991). Practical considerations of excluding conduct disordered students: An empirical analysis. *Behavioral Disorders, 17,* 9–22.

Ramsey, E., Walker, H. M., Shinn, M., & O'Neill, R. E., (1989). Parent management practices and school adjustment. *School Psychology Review, 18,* 513-525.

Reid, J. B., & Patterson, G. R. (1991). Early prevention and intervention with conduct problems: A social interactional model. In G. Stoner, M. R. Shinn, & H. M. Walker (Eds.), *Interventions for achievement and behavior problems* (pp. 715–740). Silver Spring, MD: National Association of School Psychologists.

Reid, J. B., Patterson, G. R., & Loeber, R. (1982). The abused child: Victim, instigator, or innocent bystander? In M. Bernstein (Ed.), *Response structure and organization.* Lincoln, NE: University of Nebraska Press.

Rey, J. M., Bashir, M. R., Schwarz, M., Richards, I. N., Plapp, J. J., & Stewart, G. W. (1988). Oppositional disorder: Fact or fiction? *Journal of the American Academy of Child and Adolescent Psychiatry, 27,* 157–162.

Robins, L. N. (1979). Problems amenable to investigation through follow-up studies. In H. C. Quay & J. S. Werry (Eds.), *Psychopathological disorders of childhood* (2nd ed.) New York: Wiley.

Rubin, R. A., & Balow, B. (1978). Prevalence of teacher identified behavior problems: A longitudinal study. *Exceptional Children, 45,* 102–111.

Rutter, M., Tizard, J., & Whitmore, K. (1970). *Education, health, and behavior.* London: Longman.

Quay, H. C. (1986). Conduct disorders. In H. C. Quay & J. S. Werry (Eds.), *Psychopathological disorders of childhood* (3rd ed., pp 35–72). New York: Wiley.

Shamsie, J., Sykes, C., & Hamilton, H. (1994). Continuity of care for conduct disordered youth. *Canadian Journal of Psychiatry, 39,* 415–420.

Shapiro, S. K., & Hynd, G. (1993). Psychobiological basis for conduct disorder. *School Psychology Review, 22,* 386–402.

Shores, R. E., Gunter, P. L., & Jack, S. L. (1993). Classroom management strategies: Are they setting events for coercion? *Behavioral Disorders, 18,* 92–102.

Skiba, R., & Grizzle, K. (1991). The social maladjust-

ment exclusion: Issues of definition and assessment. *School Psychology Review, 20,* 577–595.

Skiba, R., & Grizzle, K. (1992). Qualifications v. logic and data: Excluding conduct disorders from the SED definition. *School Psychology Review, 21,* 23–28.

Skiba, R., Polsgrove, L., & Nasstrom, K. (1995). *Developing a system of care: Interagency collaboration for students with emotional/behavioral disorders.* Reston, VA: Council for Children with Behavioral Disorders.

Slenkovich, J. E. (1983). *PL 94-142 as applied to DSM III diagnoses: An analysis of DSM III diagnoses vis-a-vis special education law.* Cupertino, Ca: Kinghorn Press.

Sprick, R. S., & Nolet, V. (1991). Prevention and management of secondary-level behavior problems. In G. Stoner, M. R. Shinn, & H. M. Walker (Eds.), *Interventions for achievement and behavior problems* (pp. 519–538). Silver Spring, MD: National Association of School Psychologists.

Sternberg, M. D., & Dodge, K. A. (1983). Attributional bias in aggressive adolescent boys and girls. *Journal of Social and Clinical Psychology, 1,* 312–321.

Stewart, M. A., Cummings, C., Singer, S., & deBlois, C. S. (1981). The overlap between hyperactive and unsocialized aggressive children. *Journal of Child Psychology and Psychiatry, 22,* 35–45.

Stroul, B. A., & Friedman, R. M. (1986). *A system of care for children and youth with severe emotional disturbances.* (Rev. ed.). Washington, DC: Georgetown University Child Development Center, CASSP Technical Assistance Center.

Tolan, P. H., Guerra, N. G., & Kendall, P. C. (1995). A developmental-ecological perspective on antisocial behavior in children and adolescents: Toward a unified risk and intervention framework. *Journal of Consulting and Clinical Psychology, 63,* 579–584.

Tremblay, R. E., Masse, B., Perron, D., Leblanc, M., Schwartzmann, A. E., & Ledingham, J. E. (1992). Early disruptive behavior, poor school achievement, delinquent behavior and delinquent personality: Longitudinal analyses. *Journal of Consulting and Clinical Psychology, 60,* 64–72.

Uchitelle, S., Bartz, D., & Hillman, L. (1989). Strategies for reducing suspensions. *Urban Education, 24*(2), 163–176.

Vernberg, E. M., & Medway, F. J. (1981). Teacher and parent causal perceptions of school problems. *American Educational Research Journal, 18,* 29–37.

Wahler, R. G., Cartor, P. G., Fleischman, J., & Lambert, W. (1993). The impact of synthesis teaching and parent training with mothers of conduct-disordered children. *Journal of Abnormal Child Psychology, 21,* 425–440.

Wahler, R. G., & Dumas, J. E. (1986). Maintenance factors in coercive mother-child interactions: The compliance and predictability hypotheses. *Journal of Applied Behavior Analysis, 19,* 13–22.

Wahler, R. G., Williams, A. J., & Cerezo, A. (1990). The compliance and predictability hypotheses: Sequential and correlational analyses of coercive mother-child interactions. *Behavioral Assessment, 12,* 391–407.

Walker, H. M., McConnell, S. R., Holmes, D., Todis, B., Walker, J., & Golden, H. (1983). *The Walker social skills curriculum: The ACCEPTS program.* Austin, TX: Pro-Ed.

Walker, H. M., & Severson, H. (1990). *Systematic screening for behavior disorders.* Longmont, CO: Sopris West.

Walker, H. M., Shinn, M. R., O'Neill, R. E., & Ramsey, E. (1987). A longitudinal assessment of the development of antisocial behavior in boys: Rationale, methodology, and first year results. *Remedial and Special Education, 8*(4), 7–16.

Walker, H. M., Stieber, S., Ramsey, E., & O'Neill, R. E. (1991). Longitudinal predication of the school achievement, adjustment, and delinquency of antisocial versus at-risk boys. *Remedial and Special Education, 12*(4), 43–51.

Webster-Stratton, C. (1993). Strategies for helping early school-aged children with oppositional defiant and conduct disorders: The importance of home-school partnerships. *School Psychology Review, 22,* 437–457.

Wehby, J. H., Symons, F. J., & Shores, R. E. (1995). A descriptive analysis of aggressive behavior in classrooms for children with emotional and behavioral disorders. *Behavioral Disorders, 20,* 87–105.

Wehlage, G. G., & Rutter, R. A. (1986). Dropping out: How much do schools contribute to the problem? *Teachers College Record, 87,* 374–392.

West, D. J. (1982). *Delinquency: Its roots, careers, and prospects.* Cambridge, MA: Harvard University Press.

Will, M. (1986). Educating students with learning problems: A shared responsibility. *Exceptional Children, 52,* 411–415.

Wilson, H. (1980). Parental supervision: A neglected aspect of delinquency. *Journal of Criminology, 20,* 203–235.

Wolf, M. M., Braukman, C. J., & Ramp, K. A. (1987). Serious delinquent behavior as part of a significantly handicapping condition: Cures and supportive environments. *Journal of Applied Behavior Analysis, 20,* 347–359.

Zigler, E., Taussig, C., & Black, K. (1992). Early childhood intervention: A promising preventative for juvenile delinquency. *American Psychologist, 47,* 997–1006.

12

Aggressive Behavior

Gregory S. Pettit

Auburn University

Background and Development

Aggression is highly salient and aversive, with pronounced consequences for the aggressor, the victim, and society at large. Numerous articles and book chapters, written for both academic and applied audiences, have discussed its origins, manifestations, and treatment (e.g., Huesmann, 1994; Hughes & Cavell, 1995; Parke & Slaby, 1983). Rather than attempt to provide a highly compressed summary of this voluminous literature, in the present chapter I highlight issues, themes, and recent developments of particular relevance for those working with aggressive children in school settings.

Definitions and Types

Aggression has been defined and operationalized in many different ways over the years, with some writers emphasizing its topography (i.e., its forms and features) and others stressing its underlying mechanisms and motivational determinants (see Berkowitz, 1993; Dodge, 1991; Parke & Slaby, 1983). A general definition, and one with which most writers probably would agree, is that aggression is a behavioral act that results in hurt or harm to another person. Beyond this simple definition, however, there is considerable divergence of opinion on the relative importance that should be placed on the intentions of the aggressor and the conditions serving to instigate—or to reinforce—the aggressive act. Consequently, many commentators have tended to characterize aggressive behavior in terms of contrasting dimensions, such as physical versus verbal aggression, hostile versus instrumental aggression, or overt versus covert aggression (Parke & Slaby, 1983). By attempting to more clearly differentiate among different aspects of aggression, researchers and practitioners hope to better understand the contexts within which aggression is expressed and the inter- and intrapersonal consequences associated with aggression.

An evolving framework that seems especially promising as a way of describing and *explaining* aggressive behavior is one that focuses on the distinction between reactive aggression and proactive aggression (Dodge & Coie, 1987; Price & Dodge, 1989). This framework encompasses other aggression-subtyping models, such as the hostile-versus-instrumental aggressive-behavior distinction (e.g., Berkowitz, 1993) and specifies the antecedents, social correlates, and social information-processing mechanisms that are presumed to be responsible for the development and maintenance of aggressive behavior. Because this framework—and the proactive-reactive distinction more generally—has implications for both the identification and treatment of aggression, it will be discussed at some length.

To illustrate what is meant by proactive aggression and reactive aggression, brief profiles of hypothetical children are presented. These profiles were taken from Dodge (1991, p. 201) and represent an amalgam of characteristics detailed in case records of highly aggressive youth in a comprehensive treatment program.

Billy is 12 years old and has been arrested four times for vandalism, theft, and similar offenses. He is reported to be a major behavior problem in school. He is a bully among peers, in that he regularly coerces other boys into deferring to him. He teases peers, threatens them, dominates them, laughs at them, and starts fights with them. Billy most likely would fit criteria as socially rejected (highly disliked and not at all liked by peers).

Reid is also 12 years old. He has been arrested for assault on his teacher. One day following her ridicule of him for failing an exam, he pulled a knife on her in the school parking lot and cut her in the arm. He is also considered highly aggressive and socially rejected among peers, but he doesn't seem to start fights as much as he escalates conflicts and can't avoid them. He overreacts to minor provocations and is viewed as volatile and short-tempered. Nobody wants to get too close to Reid because he might strike at any time.

These vignettes highlight some of the central features of proactive and reactive aggression. Proactively aggressive children typically use aggression instrumentally as a strategy for achieving particular goals. These may be nonsocial goals, such as acquiring a desired object (e.g., by grabbing a toy away from another child), or they may be social goals in the sense of dominating or bullying others in order to get one's way. Reactively aggressive children, on the other hand, do not "use" aggression as a means of pursuing a desired goal. Rather, reactively aggressive children tend to be easily provoked and irritated. They lash out angrily in confrontational situations which may be real or imagined. As succinctly stated by Dodge (1991), the proactively aggressive child "is troubling *to* others," whereas the reactively aggressive child "is troubled *by* others" (p. 201). The notion of proactive aggression fits with views of aggression as being "pulled" by anticipated rewards and positive outcomes (Bandura, 1983). The concept of reactive aggression is consistent with the view that aggressive behavior is "pushed" by a child's perception of threat, experience of anger, or frustration in having personal goals blocked by others (Berkowitz, 1993).

Research on aggression in children typically has been concerned with one or the other of these two broad aggression types. Thus, for example, some have examined the proactive aggression of the playground bully (see Chapter 15, this volume), whereas others have investigated the reactive aggression of the threatened child. The techniques used to combat aggression also tend to differ according to the type of aggression being targeted, with some treatment procedures being directed toward altering the contingencies (anticipated outcomes) for aggressive behavior (e.g., Patterson, 1982), and others toward alleviating the push to aggression through training in anger control (see Anger Control, this volume).

Empirical support for the distinction between reactive and proactive aggression is accumulating. One of the most comprehensive studies designed to evaluate the construct validities of the two types of aggression was undertaken by Dodge and Coie (1987). A six-item questionnaire was devised, with three items reflecting proactive aggression (sample: "This child uses physical force to dominate other kids") and three items describing reactive aggression (sample: "When this child has been teased or threatened, he or she gets angry easily and strikes back"). The questionnaire was administered to teachers of several hundred elementary-school-aged boys. There was evidence of strong convergent validity but only modest discriminant validity. Composite scores based on the two sets of items correlated .76, which indicates that teachers see a high degree of covariation among the two types of aggression. In related research, Dodge, Lochman, Harnish, Bates, and Pettit (in press) found that a majority of children rated by teachers as high-aggressive fall into what might be called a mixed or pervasively aggressive group, with proportionally smaller numbers of children comprising the reactively and proactively aggressive groups, respectively.

In spite of the empirical overlap of proactive and reactive aggression, the two types of aggression have some distinct social correlates. For example, Dodge and Coie

(1987) found that proactively aggressive boys were more likely than reactively aggressive boys to be nominated by peers as leaders. Price and Dodge (1989) reported that reactive aggression was more strongly related to negative peer evaluations than was proactive aggression. Along these lines, Dodge et al. (in press) found that reactively aggressive children, compared to proactively aggressive children, had lower peer preference scores and were judged by teachers to be more poorly adjusted overall. It appears, therefore, that reactively aggressive children tend to be seen as more socially and behaviorally deviant than proactively aggressive children.

Sex Differences

Most of the research on children's aggression has been conducted only with boys or has contained disproportionate numbers of boys in the aggressive groups. The justification for excluding girls in studies of aggression often hinges on issues of practicality: Because boys consistently have been found to be more aggressive than girls (Parke & Slaby, 1983)—at least in terms of *overt* aggression—boys' aggression as a topic of study has been a priority. In effect, sample sizes can be cut in half by studying boys only. The study of girls' aggressive behavior also is important, however, because there is evidence that the "gender gap" in aggression is narrowing (Loeber, 1990). In fact, although the frequency of aggressive, violent acts committed by minors in the United States has increased steadily over the past 20 years for both sexes, the rate for girls has increased at a faster rate than that for boys (U.S. Department of Justice, 1990).

It has been postulated that the predominant form of girls' aggression and boys' aggression differs and that this difference reflects prevailing gender norms for each sex. Building upon the distinction between direct and indirect aggression (see Bjorkqvist, Osterman, & Kaukiainen, 1992), Crick and Grotpeter (1995) recently proposed a broad reformulation of aggression that distinguishes between its overt features (the basis for most standard definitions of aggression) and its relational features (defined as attempts to harm others through manipulation or control of relationships with others). Although both boys and girls have been found to display each type of aggression, boys more commonly show the former (e.g., physical aggression), whereas girls are more likely to display the latter (e.g., teasing, ruining reputations). Because the Crick and Grotpeter (1995) study is one of the very few efforts to systematically assess relational aggression, and hence *girls'* aggression, it will be described in some detail.

Crick and Grotpeter (1995) developed a peer-nomination scale to assess relational aggression and overt aggression among third-through sixth-grade boys and girls. The use of a peer-nomination scheme was predicated on the successful employment of this method in past research on childhood aggression (see Huesmann, 1994). Moreover, a peer-nomination approach was seen as desirable because it was expected that the relatively indirect and subtle nature of relational aggression might be difficult for those outside the peer group to reliably evaluate. Scales describing overt aggression (sample: "starts fights") and relational aggression (sample: "tries to keep certain people from being in their group during activity or play time") were created and were found to be moderately correlated. Based on extreme scores, children were classified as relationally aggressive, overtly aggressive, both relationally and overtly aggressive, or nonaggressive. Boys and girls were equally likely to be classified as nonaggressive. However, the overtly aggressive group consisted almost exclusively of boys, whereas the relationally aggressive group consisted mainly of girls. The combined group was made up of both boys and girls. The relationally aggressive children were more likely to be disliked by peers and more likely to report social-psychological distress (e.g., loneliness and depression) than nonaggressive children, even after taking into account overt aggression. Rys and Bear (1995) replicated the finding that school-age children high in relational aggression tend to be girls. They also report that girls' peer rejection was associated more strongly with relational aggression than with overt aggression, whereas boys' peer rejection was associated more strongly with overt aggression than with relational aggression.

The relational aggression concept is of interest because it points to the deleterious effects of a kind of behavior more likely to be seen in girls than in boys. However, questions remain about its meaning and measurement. Because a particular act of aggression may be complex in its topography and functions, the distinction between relational aggression and other kinds of aggression can be easily blurred. For instance, a child may engage in an overt and physical act of aggression, such as hitting, in order to pursue the interpersonal (i.e., relational) goal of public humiliation. Moreover, one might argue that the behaviors cast under the rubric "relational aggression" are not, strictly speaking, aggressive behaviors. Clearly, they *are* maladaptive, but whether they fit best conceptually and empirically as markers of aggression (as opposed to, say, antisocial behavior) is a topic for future research.

Developmental Changes

At first glance, it might appear relatively straightforward to document whether children become more or less aggressive with the passage of time. However, this task is made more challenging by the fact that the aggressive acts of a young child are not directly comparable to the aggressive acts of an older child or adolescent. As a result, researchers have studied age-related changes in both the form of aggressive behavior and the situations that tend to elicit aggression.

Much of what is known about the aggressive behavior of preschoolers has come from two studies. The first is a classic study conducted by Goodenough (1931) in an especially fertile period of research on aggression and social process—the late 1920s and early 1930s. Goodenough asked mothers of 2- to 5-year-old children to keep diaries in which they recorded angry outbursts displayed by their children, their apparent cause, and the ensuing consequences. The second was an important observational study conducted by Hartup (1974), who analyzed the causes and consequences of aggressive acts that occurred over a 5-week period in groups of children aged 4 to 6 and 6 to 7 years. Based on the findings reported in these and related studies (summarized in Parke & Slaby, 1983), it may be concluded that physical, instrumental forms of aggression decrease across development, but verbal aggression and hostile aggression show a slight increase.

What might account for the decline in physical forms of aggression during the preschool-to-school transition? One explanation is that parents and teachers may show less tolerance for aggression and punish it (or redirect it) more consistently at later ages than at earlier ages. It also is possible that most children learn through experience that desired outcomes may be achieved in more efficient ways than through a show of force. The finding that hostile aggression increases during the school years has been attributed to the fact that older children are acquiring the social-perspective-taking skills that enable them to infer the intentions of others and to retaliate when they judge that someone is out to hurt them (Hartup, 1974). Indeed, research has shown that preschoolers and kindergartners are less skilled than older elementary-school-aged children in correctly identifying peer's intentions (Dodge & Feldman, 1990). For many young children, a negative outcome in an encounter with a peer, such as having one's block tower knocked over, leads to an inference of hostility ("He did it on purpose!") regarding the harm doer, irrespective of mitigating circumstances and cues. As children get older, they increasingly are capable of taking into consideration the contexts within which a provocation occurs and are able to discriminate between acts clearly hostile from those clearly benign or accidental (Crick & Dodge, 1994).

Age differences in aggression also appear to be tied to the type of eliciting stimulus (Parke & Slaby, 1983). For example, an aggressive act by a young child is most likely to occur in response to goal blocking, whereas for an older child, aggression is more likely to occur in response to frustrations that involve threats to one's self-esteem. Moreover, the link between the form of aggression displayed and the eliciting stimulus appears to change across development (Hartup, 1974). Among older children, derogations such as teasing, tattling, and put-downs are likely to elicit an insult designed to threaten another's self-esteem, but they are relatively unlikely to elicit hitting. This kind of reciprocated derogation occurs much less frequently in preschool-aged children. Hartup (1974) found no age differences in responses to "blocking" (i.e., interfering with one's possessions, activities, or space), which elicited a hostile response about 25% of the time in both the older and younger groups. It would appear that as children get older, insults, put-downs, and other threats to self-esteem become more important as triggers for a reciprocated, hostile aggressive response.

As a whole, the developmental literature suggests that understanding school children's aggression requires appreciation of the social context within which the aggressive act occurs, awareness of differences in children's abilities to read and accurately interpret situational cues, and recognition of children's strong motivation to employ whatever face-saving strategies are necessary to protect their self-esteem.

Problems and Implications

Aggression occurs naturally among children. Roughhousing is common, especially among younger children, and provides opportunities for learning norms for playful and nonplayful aggression. A certain amount of aggression is to be expected in peer interactions from early childhood, as conflicts emerge over favorite toys, activities, and playmates (Ross & Conant, 1992). Moreover, the social norms of the school years often indicate that some level of aggressiveness (or counteraggressiveness) is appropriate for defending oneself against insults and attacks. As noted earlier, the social context—including the physical setting; the age, sex, and ethnic composition of the group; and local norms—figure importantly in children's judgments of the acceptability of an aggressive act. The type of relationship that children enjoy also affects the norms for aggression. Even friends engage in disputes, but these disputes rarely escalate to the point of hostile confrontations (Hartup, 1992). Friends, compared to nonfriends, appear to be better able to recognize the potential destructiveness of aggressive behavior. Friends therefore seek to resolve conflicts amicably, before the conflicts escalate to the point where there is a danger of physical or psychological injury.

Even though aggression is to a certain extent normative in children's development, it nonetheless is the case that some children "cross the line" by engaging in problem aggression. Children who display chronically high rates of aggression quickly find themselves alienated from their parents, peers, and teachers. In this section I consider issues related to the prevalence, stability, and short- and long-term consequences associated with chronic aggressive behavior, as well as the distal and proximal mechanisms presumed to be responsible for the development and maintenance of aggression.

Prevalence and Stability

The prevalence of chronic aggressive behavior is somewhat difficult to estimate because aggression typically is considered a manifestation of antisocial behavior or conduct disorder. Conduct disorders are discussed elsewhere in this volume (see Conduct Disorders). The prevalence of conduct disorders in the United States has been estimated to range from approximately 4% to 10% (Kazdin, 1987). The increasing frequency of aggressive, violent acts committed by minors in the United States over the past two decades is especially alarming given that aggression is among the most intractable of child behavioral problems and among the most stable of personal attributes (approaching that of the intelligence quotient in some studies; see Kazdin, 1987).

Outcomes

Prospective longitudinal studies have demonstrated that childhood aggression predicts a wide array of adolescent and adult adjustment difficulties, including juvenile delinquency and adult criminal acts, academic failure (dropping out of school), adolescent pregnancy, drug use, alcoholism, and mental health problems (see Kupersmidt, Coie, & Dodge, 1990). Aggressive children also tend to be lonely, to have lower self-esteem, and to do more poorly in school. In fact, aggressive, antisocial children seem to lack many of the skills necessary for effective classroom learning, including basic reading skills and an ability to stay seated and pay attention (Hughes & Cavell, 1995).

Because aggression tends to be associated with peer rejection, which is itself a predictor of concurrent and subsequent maladjustment (Parker & Asher, 1987), researchers have wondered whether the joint influence of low peer status and high aggression is responsible for the negative effects. To address this issue, Kupersmidt and Coie (1990) conducted separate assessments of aggression and peer rejection in a large sample of elementary-school-aged children. Analyses were designed to disentangle the effects of peer rejection and aggression on subsequent delinquent behavior and school maladjustment. A high rate of aggression toward peers during the school years was significantly related to both juvenile delinquency and dropping out of school 7 years later, even after controlling for early peer rejection. High rates of aggression in the grade school years thus seem to forecast socially significant negative outcomes for children.

Distal Mechanisms: Families, Peers, and School

The types of factors typically discussed with respect to the onset and maintenance of chronic aggressive behavior may be broadly grouped along a proximal-distal continuum. At the most proximal level are biological factors. Considerable progress has been made in the search for underlying biological substrates of aggression (e.g., hormonal and neurological factors). The interested reader will find extensive treatments of these issues elsewhere (e.g., Dodge, 1991; Huesmann, 1994). At the most distal level are sociocultural factors. Sociocultural explanations for aggression also have been discussed extensively, with particular reference in the past several years to the role of media violence (e.g., the impact of television, movies, and popular music). Detailed discussions of socio-contextual influences on children's aggressive behavior may be found in several recent, edited volumes (e.g., Eron, Gentry, & Schlegel, 1994; Huesmann, 1994). The current presentation will focus on a more limited set of distal factors (family, peer group, and school experiences) and proximal factors (the child's social-cognitive makeup).

Family influences

Several family background characteristics have been linked with childhood aggression, including degree of economic deprivation, ethnicity, family size, and single parent status (Parke & Slaby, 1983). These factors often are highly intercorrelated with one another, making it difficult to disentangle the effects of one factor from the effects of others, or from cumulative effects. Family socioeconomic status (SES) has shown the strongest and most consistent links with aggressive behavior (Loeber, 1990), but the effects of SES are thought to operate primarily through disruption of parenting effectiveness (Patterson, 1982).

A large amount of research on the social antecedents of children's aggressive behavior have been concerned with the quality of family relationships. Parents' attitudes and child-rearing styles have been assumed to play a major role in shaping children's aggressive behavior (Parke & Slaby, 1983). Some of the more reliable findings indicate that aggressive children, compared to nonaggressive children, are more likely to have parents who (a) are cold and rejecting, (b) use power assertive discipline strategies (such as physical punishment) in an erratic fashion, (c) often permit the display of aggression, and (d) poorly monitor their children's whereabouts and acquaintances. Cold and rejecting parents frustrate their children's emotional needs and model a lack of concern for others by their detachment. By ignoring many of their children's aggressive acts, permissive parents tacitly "legitimize" aggressive behavior and fail to provide opportunities for children to control their aggressive urges.

When aggression escalates to the point where permissive parents step in and spank their children, the results may be counterproductive for two major reasons. First, the parents are punishing a class of behavior that previously was allowed to go unpunished. Research clearly has shown (see Parke & Slaby, 1983) that aggressive behavior punished in an erratic, inconsistent fashion becomes extremely difficult to eliminate. The situation is worsened if one parent punishes the aggression while the other parent ignores it or occasionally encourages it. Second, power assertive discipline may have counterproductive results because parents are serving as models for the very behavior (aggression) that they are seeking to curb in the child. It is therefore not surprising that parents who rely on physical punishment to discipline aggression often have children who are highly aggressive outside the home setting. Children who have learned that they will be physically punished when they irritate their parents are likely to direct the same kind of response toward peers who irritate them. An extreme instance of the aggression-transfer notion has been documented in physically maltreated children (Dodge, Bates, & Pettit, 1990). Such children are far more likely to display aggression in peer relations than are nonmaltreated children.

Parents also may indirectly influence their children's aggression via their management and monitoring of their children's social activities. In fact, parental monitoring (i.e., awareness of what the child is doing and with whom) emerges as a key predictor of aggression in middle childhood and early adolescence (Patterson, Reid, & Dishion, 1992). To some degree, poorly monitoring parents have abdicated their parental responsibility by allowing their children free rein; children growing up in such families are more likely to gravitate to deviant peer groups where antisocial behavior is modelled and reinforced (Reid & Patterson, 1991).

It is generally accepted that some degree of parental vigilance is necessary to ensure that children's best interests are safeguarded. However, to determine just how much control and supervision is appropriate one must place parental management strategies in cultural perspective. Whereas in ethic-majority, suburban families high degrees of restrictive control may be associated with heightened levels of aggressiveness, in ethnic-minority, urban families restrictive control may be critical for deterring the development of problem aggression. This may be because differing environmental niches necessitate lesser or greater amounts of behavioral control and monitoring, depending on, among other things, levels of crime, delinquent activity, and neighborhood safety. There also may be ethnic and cultural differences in the appraisal of the "harshness" of certain parenting techniques (Deater-Decker, Dodge, Bates, & Pettit, in press). That is, what some groups of parents might view as punitive or even abusive might be interpreted by other groups of parents as signals to the child of support and concern.

Among the most complete and compelling theories of the connection between parenting behaviors and child aggression is the family coercion model articulated and tested by Patterson (e.g., Patterson, 1982; Reid & Patterson, 1991; Patterson et al., 1992). Patterson and his colleagues have painstakingly documented the operation of coercive processes within the family that reinforce aggression. Compared to families with nonproblem children, the families of aggressive children are more negative and disapproving, with high levels of "nattering" (needling, threatening, irritating behavior) and lower levels of affection and warmth. Patterson describes these negative family settings as coercive environments because a high percentage of interactions center on one family member's attempts to stop another from irritating him or her. Although some modeling and positive reinforcement are involved, the training of aggressive behavior relies heavily on negative reinforcement or escape conditioning. Extended coercive episodes occur regularly in these families and include situations in which the parent makes a demand, the child resists, and the cycle repeats until the parent fails to enforce the directive. They also include situations where the child makes a demand and the parent initially resists but subsequently capitulates in the face of continued child demands. For example, when a mother demands that a child clean up his or her room, the child will learn to whine, yell, scream, or hit because these actions often lead to a termination of the mother's demand (and thus are reinforced). The aggressor who forces other family members to withdraw their aversive behavior first is encouraged by successfully ending the aversive behavior of the other. This would occur when the child succeeds in getting the mother to drop her demand, or the mother succeeds through coercion in getting the child to clean up. Consequently, the aggressor is even more likely to direct such behavior toward these family members in the future. Moreover, children who successfully use coercive behavior to escape their parents' attempts to control them are likely to apply such tactics in nonfamilial settings, such as school, when confronted with a demanding or resistant peer or teacher.

Parents who participate in coercive episodes with their children do not behave in a consistent fashion. In a detailed analysis of the contingency systems operating in problem and nonproblem families, Snyder (1977) reported that, compared to families of nonaggressive children, families of aggressive children were characterized by more aversive and fewer positive consequences for positive behavior. They were also characterized by more positive and fewer aversive consequences for negative behavior. This indicates that in problem families there is a relative absence of contingency in parental response to child behavior. Wahler and Dumas (1986) relied on such findings to develop a model of family dysfunction that stresses the indiscriminate nature of parental responses in families of aggressive children. This model highlights the inherent aversiveness of unpredictability in social relations. Observational data on problem families reveal an

indiscriminate (inconsistent and unpredictable) parenting style *except* during extended coercive (and hence, predictable) episodes (Wahler & Dumas, 1986). This suggests that children may misbehave and act aggressively to reduce maternal indiscriminate attention, presumably because children find unpredictability more aversive than involvement in a coercive bout.

A question currently being asked by researchers is whether different types of aggressive behavior have common family origins or whether there are unique formative experiences that give rise to the different types of aggression (Dodge, 1991). This question was addressed in a recent investigation of the role of maltreatment in the development of reactive aggression versus proactive aggression (Dodge et al., in press). Dodge and his colleagues speculated that the experiential antecedents of reactive aggression would more likely lie in abusive conditions that produced fear and anger and disrupted a sense of security, such as when a child has been the target of maltreatment. Indeed, reactive aggression was found to be associated strongly with an early history of maltreatment. Of those children identified as high-reactive-aggressive on the basis of third grade teachers' ratings, 26% had a prior history of maltreatment. None of the children identified as high-proactive-aggressive had a prior history of maltreatment. Interestingly, the proactively aggressive group did not differ significantly from the nonaggressive group on measures of parenting or family background characteristics such as stress and socioeconomic status.

The antecedents of proactive aggressive behavior remain elusive. Some researchers (e.g., Bandura, 1983; Dodge, 1991) have speculated that chronic proactive aggression is more likely to develop when a child has a history of early positive reinforcement for aggression and has been exposed to models of aggressive behavior in social environments that endorse aggression as an acceptable means for resolving conflicts and disputes. These are intriguing possibilities that await future empirical examination.

Peer influences

Although family experience often is considered to provide the crucible within which an aggressive behavioral style is first acquired, the peer group is presumed to play a pivotal role either in exacerbating this interpersonal orientation or in helping to lessen it as a problem. Peer influences in early and middle childhood may be described in terms of social preferences within the group and in terms of close affiliations (friendships) between individual children (Parker & Asher, 1993). Peer rejection is strongly associated with aggression, with about half of all rejected children also being identified as aggressive (Cillessen, van IJzendoorn, van Lieshout, & Hartup, 1992). The proportion of aggressive children who are rejected is even higher, with studies indicating that only about one-third of all aggressive children avoid peer rejection (Coie, 1990).

In this arena it is difficult to determine the extent to which peer rejection antecedes child aggressive tendencies, occurs concomitantly with those tendencies, or is an outcome of the child's aggressiveness (Coie, 1990). For example, it may be that the aggressive child acquired the behavioral orientation in early childhood, possibly as a result of parental disciplinary ineffectiveness, and then carried this antagonist style of interacting with others into the classroom (Pettit, Clawson, Dodge, & Bates, 1996). Because peers found this child to be an unsatisfactory companion, the child was shunned and acquired a negative reputation. Even if the child adapted to the classroom and became less aggressive, the child's reputation would persist, resulting in continued peer rejection. In contrast, consider a child who shows up the first day of class without a repertoire of social skills but is not unduly aggressive. Perhaps the child also possesses some characteristic or set of characteristics that set him or her apart from the majority peer group (e.g., physical unattractiveness, minority ethnic status, or unkempt appearance). The child could become rejected even in the absence of aggression. In this instance, the peer group's negative reaction to the child may lead to heightened frustration and feelings of incompetence. The child may then behave aggressively as a way of combatting these feelings and as a way of asserting some control over the peer group experience.

Although aggressive children are more likely to be rejected by peers than are nonaggressive children, aggressive children are not isolated from their peers and many do, in fact, establish friendships with other children. However, their friendship networks are likely to be composed of other aggressive children, and their interactions with friends have a more negative quality (Dishion, Andrews, & Crosby, 1995), compared to the friendship interactions of nonaggressive children. Association with aggressive peers appears to heighten the likelihood that an aggressive child will stay on a deviant trajectory and gravitate to delinquent and other antisocial activity (Dishion et al., 1995). Several factors may be responsible for the elevated risk of children whose peer networks are made up of aggressive children. Selection processes (i.e., that aggressive children seek out other aggressive children) appear to account for some of the similarity between aggressive children and their peers. Peer influence also appears to be a factor, in that exposure to deviant peers leads to increases in antisocial behavior beyond initial levels (Patterson et al., 1992). Because most peers avoid them or systematically exclude them, many aggressive children also fail to benefit from interacting with nonaggressive children.

School and academic influences

Aggressive behavior in children has been linked to academic problems in several studies (see Parke & Slaby, 1983), although the underlying reasons for this connection are not yet clear. Several explanations have been put forth (e.g., Hughes & Cavell, 1995), including that aggressive children are more likely to be rejected by peers and therefore come to find the school environment more generally to be aversive, or that some underlying neurodevelopmental deficit may contribute to both the development of aggressive behavior and correlated academic problems. These are not mutually exclusive explanations. The main point here is that aggressive behavior and academic problems often covary in school-age populations.

It also is the case that schools and individual classrooms differ in the level of aggressiveness that is tolerated. Teachers, like parents, vary in their effectiveness in dealing with aggressive behavior problems, and children often take their cues from teachers in deciding how to react to a child's aggressive behavior (Hughes & Cavell, 1995). In some schools aggression may be an adaptive response to a specific cultural pressure (as in not allowing oneself to be "dissed"). Whether school personnel will find it necessary to intervene usually will depend on decisions about whether the aggressive display is judged to have potential for adverse consequences for the child and others.

Finally, one might argue that the school context itself creates a milieu that can be conducive to aggression. Some empirical evidence suggests that relationships among individual teachers, teacher hostility, and lack of rapport among school personnel adversely affect the school environment with respect to aggression (Larson, 1994).

Summary

Family, peer, and school experiences appear to be instrumental in the development of aggression. Although family experience may serve to launch a child on an aggressive trajectory, subsequent experiences with peers and at school serve to maintain (or possibly deflect) this path. The interplay of these multiple social influences underscores the need for broad-based assessment of the conditions giving rise to children's aggressive behaviors.

Proximal Mechanisms of Influence: The Role of Social-Cognitive Processes

In recent years, a social-information-processing model of children's social behavior has emerged providing significant advances in the understanding of childhood aggression (Crick & Dodge, 1994; Dodge, Pettit, McClaskey, & Brown, 1986). This model is comprehensive, drawing on a number of theoretical and empirical perspectives, including social-learning theory, attribution theory, and decision-making theory. Social information processing describes the cognitive processes involved in an individual's response to a specific social situation. Of particular importance is an understanding of how individuals perceive social cues, make attributions and inferences about those cues, generate solutions to social dilemmas or problems, and make behavioral decisions about how to respond to those problems (including decisions whether or not to aggress).

Research based on this model has demonstrated the significance of this approach for understanding child-hood aggression. In contrast to past theories of aggression, including motivational approaches (e.g., frustration-instigated aggression) and general social-cognitive approaches (e.g., perspective taking), social-information-processing theory describes the processes involved in aggressive events in specific terms (Dodge, 1991; Dodge et al., 1986). For example, the steps involved in the processing of information, described later, have been laid out in a very detailed way. These steps are interdependent in the sense that performance at earlier stages affects performance at later stages. An aggressive behavioral response, therefore, is the outcome of the social-information-processing steps that precede it.

Social-information-processing theory also is specific with respect to situational attributes. Situation here refers to the particular context within which children may have social difficulties. For example, some children may find it difficult to gain access to a group of peers already at play. Other children have problems in situations in which they have been bothered or irritated by a peer. These two kinds of situations—termed peer group entry and response to provocation—are especially challenging for rejected-aggressive children (Dodge & Feldman, 1990). Assessments of children's social information processing in peer-group-entry situations have been found to be significantly related to children's actual behavior in analogous situations but not in provocation-type situations. The reverse, processing about provocation situations predicting response to provocation but not peer-group-entry behavior, also has been found (Dodge et al., 1986). These findings suggest that to understand the role of social information processing in aggression one must consider the situational context within which the aggressive act is displayed.

In the social-information-processing model developed by Dodge and colleagues, it is posited that aggressive behavior occurs as a function of several cognitive steps: (a) encoding of social cues, (b) interpretation of those cues, (c) response generation, (d) response decision and evaluation, and (e) behavioral enactment. (Note: Six steps are described in a newly reformulated social-information-processing model. This reflects the inclusion of a goal-clarification and selection component immediately prior to response generation; see Crick & Dodge, 1994.) Encoding describes the perceptual task of scanning the environment and paying attention to relevant cues. Aggressive children have been found to selectively attend to and recall aggressive cues (Dodge & Feldman, 1990). Partly this is because aggressive children and ad-

olescents respond too quickly to social cues, without taking advantage of all the available cues. But aggressive children also are more likely to notice aggressive cues and to fail to notice nonaggressive cues.

The second step is to mentally represent the encoded cues and to interpret them in an accurate and meaningful way. This step requires the application of a set of interpretation rules to the encoded cues to derive meaning. For example, if a child has acquired a rule structure that calls for an interpretation of peer hostility when a scowl is observed on a peer's face, then if a scowl is encoded the child will interpret the situation as one of hostility. Hostile intent attributions have been shown to increase the likelihood that a child will respond aggressively (see Dodge et al., 1986). Because aggressive children more often infer hostility in peers, they are more likely to respond in an aggressive, retaliatory manner. In many instances, these inferences are erroneous in that the peer meant no harm; thus, the peer is likely to view the aggressive child's action as an unwarranted provocation. Repeated exchanges like this eventually will result in the aggressive child acquiring a negative reputation, which may produce even more opportunities for peer provocation, and help to solidify the aggressive child's negative status in the peer group.

In the third step, the child generates one or more potential behavioral responses to the interpreted cues. Even a young child has a repertoire of many possible behavioral responses. Although some have argued that the sheer number of solutions generated may lead to more effective responding (see Dodge & Feldman, 1990), the content of the generated solutions appears to be more strongly linked with aggressive behavior. Generally, a larger proportion of the responses generated by aggressive children are aggressive, inept, or irrelevant to the social problem (Dodge et al., 1986). Having generated possible responses, the child must now decide on a particular response and evaluate its likely outcome (fourth step). Aggressive children are more likely to report that acting in an aggressive way is easy for them, that they expect being aggressive will produce tangible rewards (in the sense that it will lead to desirable instrumental and social outcomes), and that they believe being aggressive will reduce aversive treatment from peers (Crick & Dodge, 1994). In short, aggressive children are more likely than nonaggressive children to believe that aggression is a legitimate solution leading to positive outcomes with minimal negative costs.

The final step in the social-information-processing model is behavioral enactment, whereby the actual behavioral performance is executed and monitored. Aggressive children have been shown in role-playing contexts to be less effective in implementing nonaggressive behavioral responses (see Dodge & Feldman, 1990). This may be because they lack the necessary behavioral skills or because they lack the motivation to perform a competent response. If motivational factors are responsible for the aggressive child's disinclination to perform competently, then social-skills-training approaches would not be expected to lead to demonstrable improvements in behavior (Hughes & Cavell, 1995).

Links Between Family Experience, Social-Information-Processing Patterns, and Child Aggression

Several investigators recently have posited that the effects of family experience on children's aggressive behavior may at least be partially explained by their shared associations with social information processing. In this view, social-cognitive patterns mediate the association between parenting practices and children's aggressive orientations. Evidence suggests that, indeed, social information processing may serve as a connecting link between harsh discipline and children's aggressiveness. For instance, Dodge et al. (1990) found that

- Physically maltreated children, compared to nonmaltreated children, were more aggressive at school (their teacher-rated aggressive scores were, on average, 93% higher than those of nonharmed children).
- Physically harmed children, relative to nonharmed children, developed more deviant processing styles (i.e., they were significantly less attentive to relevant cues, more biased toward attributing hostile intent, and less likely to generate competent solutions to interpersonal problems).
- These information-processing styles were strongly predictive of children's school aggression. Maltreatment status no longer had a statistically significant effect on later child aggression once social-information-processing patterns were controlled.

These findings are consistent with the hypothesis that early physical maltreatment has its effects on a child's development of aggressive behavior largely by altering a child's social-information-processing patterns.

Chronic aggressive behavior in childhood clearly constitutes a risk marker for both current and future maladjustment. The general persistence of aggression and its resistance to change point to the need for early and comprehensive intervention.

Alternative Actions

Because of the large individual, interpersonal, and societal costs of child aggressive behavior, there has been intense interest in developing effective intervention strategies. Only a few years ago Kazdin (1987) concluded that there were as yet no empirically established, effective

treatments for aggressive, antisocial children, although several techniques were judged to be promising. The techniques receiving the most systematic attention are training in cognitive-problem-solving skills and parent management (Hughes & Cavell, 1995; Kazdin, 1987; Larson, 1994). The effectiveness of each of these approaches likely hinges on how carefully the program is tailored to the needs of the individual child and family. For example, some children may be more prone to aggression in certain kinds of situations than in others (Dodge et al., 1986) and may have particular deficiencies in selected social-cognitive skills (e.g., misreading social cues). Along these lines, parents may require special training and remediation in particular problematic areas. Optimally effective interventions—whether focused on the child or the parent—may require the development of individual profiles that emphasize specific problem areas.

Approaches Using Problem-Solving Skills

Many different treatment approaches include elements of social skills training (see Social Skills, this volume) and social problem solving (see Social Problem Solving, this volume). Each of these approaches share a focus on the individual child's lack of interpersonally effective skills. Problem-solving skills-training (PSST) programs use a combination of instruction, coaching, modeling, behavioral rehearsal, and feedback to teach low-accepted children prosocial behaviors such as helping, sharing, and asking questions, as well as more general skills in accurately "reading" social situations and social cues (Hughes & Cavell, 1995). Application of PSST with aggressive children is based on the premise that these children lack the skills necessary for successful peer interaction. Evidence for the effectiveness of PSST is mixed (Kazdin, 1987), partly because many aggressive children do not necessarily lack prosocial skills (Price & Dodge, 1989), and partly because aggression is multiply determined and maintained by the comparatively more distal factors (family and peers) discussed earlier.

A more effective variation on PSST has been developed by Lochman (Lochman & Curry, 1986; see Anger Control, this volume). The Lochman approach combines problem-solving skills training with instruction in the use of anger-control techniques. Children are first taught to "stop and think" in anger-provoking situations and then to apply problem-solving skills, such as defining the problem, identifying a goal, generating alternative responses, evaluating the likely consequences of the response, selecting a response, and monitoring its effectiveness. Application of this approach has been shown to result in both short-term and long-term reductions in aggressive behavior and related behavior problems (Lochman & Curry, 1986). A more complete description of the anger-control training framework and its use by school psychologists involved in violence prevention is provided by Larson (1994).

Parent Management Training

Parent management training (PMT) consists of a set of procedures designed to train parents to interact differently with their child. The guiding premise is that aggressive behavior inadvertently develops and is nurtured in the home by maladaptive parent-child interactions (Kazdin, 1987). As described earlier, research consistently has shown connections between ineffective and hostile parenting behavior and children's aggression. Because coercive styles of interaction seem to play a central role in promoting aggressive behavior, training programs concerned with reducing coercion and increasing positive parenting behavior have been among the most successful intervention strategies.

The predominant parent training model has evolved from the coercive family theory of Patterson and colleagues (Patterson, 1982; Patterson et al., 1992). As a core feature, parents are trained to identify, define, and observe problem behavior in new ways. A careful specification of the problem is a crucial ingredient for learning how to deliver reinforcing or punishing consequences. Specific elements typically involve training parents to track their children's behavior more carefully, to enforce directives more consistently, to resist giving in to child demands, and to apply time-out to systematically shape child behavior. PMT also includes components designed to ensure that parents serve as positive role models by being nonaversive interaction partners and using noncoercive, conflict-resolution styles. Some variations on PMT stress compliance training and parent-child play and coping with parental stressors (see Kazdin, 1987; Larson, 1994).

Following an examination of the empirical evidence, Kazdin (1987) concluded that PMT holds considerable promise for treating antisocial behavior. PMT approaches typically are well grounded in theory and research, the benefits of treatment appear to be general and often extend beyond the target child (e.g., siblings also appear to profit), and the widespread application of PMT make it accessible for many families with aggressive children. At the same time, Kazdin (1987) notes that some families do not respond to PMT, and some of those that do may not see concomitant changes in their children owing to countervailing family and peer influences. Some have argued that the most effective interventions are likely to be those that combine elements of PMT and of individual social skills training for the child (e.g., Kazdin, Siegel, & Bass, 1992).

Comprehensive Interventions

Comparatively greater success has been achieved by interventions that include multiple components. For ex-

ample, Kazdin et al. (1992) contrasted the relative effectiveness of (a) cognitive problem-solving skills training (i.e., cognitive and behavioral techniques designed to teach problem solving in interpersonal situations), (b) parent management training (i.e., use of positive reinforcement, shaping, contracting, and providing time-out), and (c) a combination of the two treatment approaches. The combined treatment program was found to be markedly superior to either approach alone in leading to more pervasive and durable changes in child functioning.

An ambitious and potentially important comprehensive preventive/intervention effort is the FAST Track program (Conduct Problems Prevention Research Group, 1992). The intervention is currently being implemented in four different communities with children identified as extremely high risk on the basis of a multiple-gating procedure. The design incorporates a developmental perspective, with multistage preventive interventions divided into five components: (a) parent training designed to teach parents to be more consistent and less punitive in their disciplining of the child; (b) home visit/case management to assist the often highly disorganized families; (c) social skills training with children to help them acquire anger-control skills and nonaggressive-response repertoires; (d) academic tutoring; and (e) teacher-based classroom interventions intended, in part, to train teachers to more effectively manage disruptive behavior. Although data describing the effectiveness of the program in combatting the development of serious antisocial behavior have not yet been published, the overall effort is impressive and eventually may merit consideration as a model program.

Summary

Aggressive behavior in childhood is a significant problem for the individual and society. This chapter has highlighted the normative developmental course of childhood aggression and has described some key distinctions among the characteristic forms taken by aggression, their implications for understanding the contexts in which aggression is expressed, and sex differences in boys' and girls' aggression. Family, peer, and school factors that contribute to aggressive behavior problems were discussed. Breakdowns in effective parenting, such as capitulating to the child's coercive demands, inconsistently enforcing directives, and failing to monitor the child's activities were identified as important contributors to the development of children's aggressive orientations. Peer rejection, exposure to a deviant peer group, and attending a school where aggression is tolerated were discussed as factors that serve to maintain and exacerbate aggressive inclinations. At a more proximal level, social-information-processing patterns—including difficulty in attending to relevant social cues, a propensity to make hostile attributional biases, an impoverished response repertoire, and a tendency to evaluate aggression favorably—were described as robustly related to the actual display of aggression. Moreover, evidence was summarized suggesting that these social-cognitive processes may serve as the more proximal mediators of the association between early family experiences (such as maltreatment) and subsequent aggressive behavior. Several promising intervention programs were briefly summarized, and it was noted that the most successful programs likely will have multilevel components that address parent management practices, children's problem-solving skills, and community and school conditions that may unintentionally foster aggressive behavior.

Author's Note

Preparation of this chapter was supported in part by grants from the National Institute of Child Health and Human Development (HD30572) and the National Institute of Mental Health (MH49869). Author's address: Department of Family and Child Development, 203 Spidle Hall, Auburn University, AL 36849.

Recommended Resources

Dodge, K. A., Bates, J. E., & Pettit, G. S. (1990). Mechanisms in the cycle of violence. *Science, 250,* 1678–1683.
This is the first major report from the ongoing Multi-site Child Development Project, an intensive study of the early family origins of childhood aggression. This article argues that socially transmitted social-information-processing patterns may help to account for the development of aggression. Children who had been physically maltreated by parents were less attentive to relevant social cues, more biased in interpreting peers' intentions, and less likely to generate competent solutions to social conflicts. These processing patterns were associated with grade-school aggression and mediated the linkage between child maltreatment and aggressive behavior. This investigation suggests that interventions targeting social-cognitive mechanisms may prove useful in breaking the cross-generational cycle of violence.

Hughes, J. N., & Cavell, T. A. (1995). Cognitive-affective approaches: Enhancing competence in aggressive children. In G. Cartledge & J. F. Miburn (Eds.), *Teaching social skills to children and youth: Innovative approaches* (3rd ed., pp. 199–236). Boston: Allyn and Bacon.
This comprehensive but highly readable survey of treatment models and approaches for aggressive children stresses the role of social-cognition and emotional processes in the development and maintenance of childhood aggression. Both authors have contributed importantly to the literature on clinical interven-

tions with behavior-problem children. A special strength of this chapter is that it contains sections devoted to the need to explicitly link assessment of aggression (including biological, family, peer, and academic factors) with intervention planning.

Huesmann, L. R. (Ed.). (1994). *Aggressive behavior: Current perspectives.* New York: Plenum Press.
This volume is dedicated to Leonard Eron, one of the pioneers in the study of aggression, and contains several up-to-date chapters on the origins, functions, and consequences of childhood aggression. Eron himself contributes a chapter on theories of aggression. A partial list of other contributors include Nancy Guerra and colleagues (on moral cognition and aggression), Leonard Berkowitz (on anger and negative affect), Thomas Dishion and colleagues (on the peer relations of aggressive adolescents), Dan Olweus (on bullying at school and what to do about it), Kirsti Lagerspetz and Kaj Bjorkqvist (on differences in boys' and girls' aggression), and Rowell Huesmann and Laurie Miller (on long-term effects of exposure to media violence).

Kazdin, A. E. (1994) Interventions for aggressive and antisocial children. In L. D. Eron, J. H. Gentry, & P. Schlegel (Eds.), *Reason to hope: A psychological perspective on youth and violence* (pp. 341–382). Washington, DC: American Psychological Association.
This important chapter provides a thorough overview of recent advances in the assessment and treatment of childhood aggression. Major family-, school-, and community-based interventions are described and critiqued. Issues, challenges, and future research directions are highlighted, with special reference to the interplay of basic and applied research. A statement of priorities for research and public policy is articulated. The chapter is authored by one of the major contributors to current research, theory, and interventions with aggressive children.

Larson, J. (1994). Violence prevention in the schools: A review of selected programs and procedures. *School Psychology Review, 23,* 151–164.
This informative review examines selected commercially available and research literature approaches for violence-prevention efforts in school settings. The emphasis in on primary prevention (such as broad-based social skills training), secondary prevention (working with at-risk youth using techniques such as anger control), and tertiary prevention (intensive efforts devoted to remediating chronic aggression). Implications for school psychologists are laid out clearly, within the context of an overall model of alternative prevention procedures in a comprehensive school safety plan.

References

Bandura, A. (1983). Psychological mechanisms of aggression. In R. G. Green & E. I. Donnerstein (Eds.), *Aggression: Theoretical and empirical views* (Vol. 1, pp. 101–140). New York: Academic Press.

Berkowitz, L. (1993). *Aggression: Its causes, consequences, and control.* Philadelphia: Temple University Press.

Bjorkqvist, K., Osterman, K., & Kaukiainen, A. (1992). The development of direct and indirect aggressive strategies in males and females. In K. Bjorkqvist & P. Niemela

(Eds.), *Of mice and women: Aspects of female aggression* (pp. 51–64). San Diego, CA: Academic Press.

Cillessen, A. H. N., van I Jzendoorn, H. W., van Lieshout, C. F. M., & Hartup, W. W. (1992). Heterogeneity among peer-rejected boys: subtypes and stabilities. *Child Development, 63,* 893–905.

Coie, J. D. (1990). Toward a theory of peer rejection. In S. R. Asher & J. D. Coie (Eds.), *Peer rejection in childhood.* (pp. 365–401) New York: Cambridge University Press.

Conduct Problems Prevention Research Group. (1992). A developmental and clinical model for the prevention of conduct disorders: The FAST Track program. *Development and Psychopathology, 4,* 509–527.

Crick, N. R., & Dodge, K. A. (1994). A review and reformulation of social-information-processing mechanisms in children's social adjustment. *Psychological Bulletin, 115,* 74–101.

Crick, N. R., & Grotpeter, J. K. (1995). Relational aggression, gender, and social-psychological adjustment. *Child Development, 66,* 710–722.

Deater-Deckard, K., Dodge, K. A., Bates, J. E., & Pettit, G. S. (in press). Physical discipline among African-American and European-American mothers: Links to children's externalizing behaviors. *Developmental Psychology.*

Dishion, T. J., Andrews, D. W., & Crosby, L. (1995). Antisocial boys and their friends in early adolescence: Relationship characteristics, quality, and interactional process. *Child Development, 66,* 139–151.

Dodge, K. A. (1991). The structure and function of reactive and proactive aggression. In D. J. Pepler & K. H. Rubin (Eds.), *The development and treatment of childhood aggression* (pp. 201–218). Hillsdale, NJ: Erlbaum.

Dodge, K. A., Bates, J. E., & Pettit, G. S. (1990). Mechanisms in the cycle of violence. *Science, 250,* 1678–1683.

Dodge, K. A., & Coie, J. D. (1987). Social-information-processing factors in reactive and proactive aggression in children's peer groups. *Journal of Personality and Social Psychology, 53,* 1146–1158.

Dodge, K. A., & Feldman, E. (1990). Issues in social cognition and sociometric status. In S. R. Asher & J. D. Coie (Eds.), *Peer rejection in childhood* (pp. 119–155). New York: Cambridge University Press.

Dodge, K. A., Lochman, J. E., Harnish, J. D., Bates, J. E., & Pettit, G. S. (in press). Reactive and proactive aggression in school children and psychiatrically impaired chronically assaultive youth. *Journal of Abnormal Psychology.*

Dodge, K. A., Pettit, G. S., McClaskey, C. L., & Brown, M. (1986). Social competence in children. *Monographs of the Society for Research in Child Development, 51,* (2, Serial No. 213).

Eron, L. D., Gentry, J. H., & Schlegel, P. (Eds.). (1994). *Reason to hope: A psychological perspective on youth and violence.* Washington, DC: American Psychological Association.

Goodenough, F. L. (1931). *Anger in young children.* Minneapolis: University of Minnesota Press.

Hartup, W. (1974). Aggression in childhood: Developmental perspectives. *American Psychologist, 29,* 336–341.

Hartup, W. W. (1992). Peer relations in early and middle childhood. In V. B. Van Hasselt & M. Hersen (Eds.), *Handbook of social development: A lifespan perspective* (pp. 257–281). New York: Plenum.

Huesmann, L. R. (Ed.). (1994). *Aggressive behavior: Current perspectives.* New York: Plenum Press.

Hughes, J. N., & Cavell, T. A. (1995). Cognitive-affective approaches: Enhancing competence in aggressive children. In G. Cartledge and J. F. Miburn, *Teaching social skills to children and youth: Innovative approaches* (3rd edition, pp. 199–236). Boston: Allyn and Bacon.

Kazdin, A. E. (1987). Treatment of antisocial behavior in children: Current status and future directions. *Psychological Bulletin, 102,* 187–203.

Kazdin, A. E., Siegel, T. C., & Bass, D. (1992). Cognitive problem-solving skills training and parent management training in the treatment of antisocial behavior in children. *Journal of Consulting and Clinical Psychology, 60,* 733–747.

Kupersmidt, J. B., & Coie, J. D. (1990). Preadolescent peer status, aggression, and school adjustment as predictors of externalizing problems in adolescence. *Child Development, 61,* 1350–1362.

Kupersmidt, J. B., Coie, J. D., & Dodge, K. A. (1990). The role of poor peer relationships in the development of disorder. In S. R. Asher & J. D. Coie (Eds.), *Peer rejection in childhood* (pp. 274–305). New York: Cambridge University Press.

Larson, J. (1994). Violence prevention in the schools: A review of selected programs and procedures. *School Psychology Review, 23,* 151–164.

Lochman, J. E., & Curry, J. F. (1986). Effects of social-problem-solving training and self-instructional training with aggressive boys. *Journal of Clinical Child Psychology, 15,* 159–164.

Loeber, R. (1990). Developmental and risk factors of juvenile antisocial behavior and delinquency. *Clinical Psychology Review, 10,* 1–42.

Parke, R. D., & Slaby, R. G. (1983). The development of aggression. In E. M. Hetherington (Ed.), P. H. Mussen (Series. Ed.), *Handbook of child psychology: Vol. 4. Socialization, personality, and social development* (pp. 547–641). New York: Wiley.

Parker, J. G., & Asher, S. R. (1987). Peer relations and later personal adjustment: Are low-accepted children at risk? *Psychological Bulletin, 102,* 357–389.

Parker, J. G., & Asher, S. R. (1993). Friendship and friendship quality in middle childhood: Links with peer group acceptance and feelings of loneliness and social dissatisfaction. *Developmental Psychology, 29,* 611–621.

Patterson, G. R. (1982). *Coercive family process.* Eugene, OR: Castalia.

Patterson, G. R., Reid, J., & Dishion, T. (1992). *Antisocial boys.* Eugene, OR: Castalia.

Pettit, G. S., Clawson, M. A., Dodge, K. A., & Bates, J. E. (1996). Stability and change in peer-rejected status: The role of child behavior, parenting, and family ecology. *Merrill-Palmer Quarterly, 42,* 91–118.

Price, J. M., & Dodge, K. A. (1989). Reactive and proactive aggression in childhood: Relations to peer status and social context dimensions. *Journal of Abnormal Child Psychology, 17,* 455–471.

Reid, J. B., & Patterson, G. R. (1991). Early prevention and intervention with conduct problems: A social interactional model for the integration of research and practice. In

G. Stoner, M. Shinn, & H. M. Walker (Eds.), *Interventions for achievement and behavior problems* (pp. 715–739). Silver Spring, MD: National Association of School Psychologists.

Ross, H. S., & Conant, C. L. (1992). The social structure of early conflict: Interaction, relationships, and alliances. In C. U. Shantz & W. W. Hartup (Eds.), *Conflict in child and adolescent development* (pp. 153–185). New York: Cambridge University Press.

Rys, G. S., & Bear, G. G. (1995). *Relational aggression and peer rejection: Gender and developmental issues.* Manuscript submitted for publication.

Snyder, J. J. (1977). Reinforcement analysis of interaction in problem and nonproblem families. *Journal of Abnormal Psychology, 86,* 528–535.

U.S. Department of Justice, Federal Bureau of Investigation. (1990, April). *Age-specific arrest rates and race-specific arrest rates for selected offenses, 1965–1988.* Washington, DC: Government Printing Office.

Wahler, R. G., & Dumas, J. E. (1986). Maintenance factors in coercive mother-child interactions: The compliance and predictability hypotheses. *Journal of Applied Behavior Analysis, 19,* 13–22.

13

Anger

John E. Lochman
Duke University Medical Center

Susanne E. Dunn
Children's Psychiatric Institute

Elizabeth E. Wagner
Duke University

Background and Development

Anger has typically been defined as a response to a "demeaning offense against me or mine" (Lazarus, 1991, p.) or to a sense of being endangered. The danger may be relatively broad, ranging from physical to symbolic threats to one's self-esteem or dignity. Thus, anger necessarily involves at least some minimal level of cognitive appraisal of a threatening situation, and dysfunctional anger-related behaviors typically are accompanied by stereotypical cognitive distortions and deficiencies.

Anger can have notably positive effects by energizing individuals to action (Goleman, 1995) and by organizing and focusing the individual's cognitive processing around the threatening event and his or her goal in the situation. The arousal associated with anger can have mobilizing and even exhilarating effects in directing the individual to directly grapple with the threatening adversaries. Anger is the emotion that corresponds to the "fight" response in the fight-flight arousal mechanism; this innate action tendency involves an attack on the agent perceived to be blameworthy (Lazarus, 1991). However, anger is the mood that people have most difficulty controlling (Goleman, 1995), and intense uncontrolled anger arousal can be a central component of externalizing behavior problems.

The Emergence of Anger

The expression and experience of anger changes developmentally throughout childhood but has defined roots during infancy. While negative facial expressions are seen in infants of all ages, there are developmental changes in infants' facial expressions themselves. By one month of age, infants can express negative facial affect.

However, their negative expressions are difficult to differentiate (e.g., anger vs. fear vs. sadness) and their negative vocalizations are not consistently associated with the source of provocation. Clear facial expressions of anger emerge prior to the 4th month of life and have been interpreted as reflecting the infant's acquired (though primitive) comprehension of the means-end relationship. Also, the targets of facial expressions of anger change with age. Initially, anger expressions are directed toward the immediate source of frustration (e.g., the source of pain or physical restraint); by 7 months, the expressions are directed toward the mother. This pattern is not surprising as the expression and direction of anger would be expected to develop as the infant's motor and cognitive skills develop (Stenberg & Campos, 1990).

Investigations of developmental changes in the direction of anger expressions following frustration (Izard, Hembree, & Heubner, 1987; Stenberg, Campos, & Emde, 1983) support this analysis. Specifically, one-month-olds' facial expressions, clearly negative yet undifferentiated, were not directionally selective. The infants looked at nonsocial or irrelevant targets. Older infants were directionally selective with their anger reactions. At 4 months, facial expressions were event oriented with infants attending to the source of frustration both at its onset and following its termination. At 7 months, facial expressions were oriented toward humans. The infants attended briefly to the source of frustration and then addressed their facial expressions primarily to humans and overwhelmingly toward the mother—the most likely source of help. Similar patterns have been observed with negative vocalizations. These findings have been interpreted as reflecting a developmental progression from undifferentiated to event-specific to person-directed responding, and finally, to person-specific responding, thus illustrating infants' increasing understanding of the source of frustration as well as their changing expectations about their mothers as a source of potential safety and comfort (Stenberg & Campos, 1990).

The Socialization of Anger

Parents as socializers of anger

Children's expression and experience of anger are facilitated by frustrating or aggressive responses emitted by children's significant others to the children or to each other and are inhibited by parents' socialization practices. Parents respond differentially to their infants' facial expressions of emotion. Observations of parent-infant interactions indicate that parents' socialization goals involve the reinforcement and modeling of positive affect and the discouragement of negative affect. Generally, parents mirror infants' positive facial expressions while responding to infants' negative expressions with a different emotion such as concern or interest. Thus, the infants' emotion expressions are shaped over time, becoming increasingly positive and less labile (Lemerise & Dodge, 1993).

Kochanska (1987) analyzed mothers' responses to their toddlers' (age 2 to 31/2 years) anger displays and found that, as children mature, they are clearly given the message that anger is inappropriate. Specifically, the older the child, the more likely the mother is to tell the child that anger is not appropriate and that he or she should stop expressing it, and the less likely the mother is to respond to anger with affection and support or to inquire regarding the cause of the child's anger. Within these developmental trends, mothers respond differentially to boys' and girls' anger regulation. Boys' anger is rarely ignored; their anger displays are more likely to elicit maternal attention and to result in their getting what they want. Conversely, girls' anger is likely to be ignored and rarely elicits maternal reward or support. Radke-Yarrow and Kochanska (1990) have interpreted these data as consistent with gender stereotypes regarding the expression of anger.

Eisenberg and Fabes (1994) examined and found meaningful the relationship between mothers' self-reported socialization practices with their 4- to 6-year-old preschool children and their children's real-life expressions of anger. Specifically, unsupportive parental practices such as severe or avoidant maternal reactions to child negative behaviors were associated with low levels of nonconstructive anger reactions by their children. While supportive parental practices such as maternal comforting were associated also with low levels of nonconstructive anger reactions, they were related as well to higher levels of constructive reactions by the children when angered. Interestingly, maternal socialization practices were related to children's behavior when angered regardless of child temperament. These findings lend support to the conclusion that mothers' reactions to their children's negative

emotions influence and shape their children's subsequent expression of anger-based behaviors.

As children get older, social relationships play an increasingly important role in the self-regulation of interpersonal anger. For example, Karniol and Heiman (1987) found that elementary-school children, although reporting feeling equally angry at provocations from low-status provokers (peers) and high-status provokers (adults), responded differentially to their provocations. When angered by peers, children employed more active coping responses (e.g., retaliation or yelling); when angered by adults, children employed more passive responses (e.g., ignoring or internalizing). This pattern of responding reflects the children's understanding of, and responsiveness to, variations in social status.

In summary, parental socialization of anger begins with the earliest parent-infant interactions, with parents reinforcing positive affect and discouraging negative affect. As children mature, parents become increasingly less tolerant of their anger displays and respond in various direct and indirect ways. In terms of children's self-regulation of their own interpersonal anger, social relationships and variations in social status play an increasingly important role.

The effects of anger in the environment on young children

When one-year-olds are exposed to events of anger (defined as anger by overt actions of raised volume of voice, intensified tone, hitting, facial expressions, gestures, etc.), they respond with "troubled attention" characterized by mothers as frowns, concerned expressions, whining, or whimpering. Responses to anger at this young age, however, are typically indistinguishable from responses to other displays of emotion (e.g., intense crying or loud laughing). Over the next several months, along with the troubled attention comes a social referencing (the infants look toward their mothers) following confrontation with unfamiliar situations (Klinert, Campos, Soce, Emde, & Svejda, 1983).

Beginning at 16 to 18 months and thereafter, responses of concerned attention are often organized into a "flight or fight" response pattern. Typical responses include demanding that the argument stop, clutching a blanket, hiding, or covering the ears. Children of this age have also been reported to engage in imitative responses (imitate certain aspects of their parents' angry behaviors such as their facial expression, words, intonation, or rhythm), self-referential responses, and verbal comments indicating which aspects of the ambient anger are most salient to the child ("Be quiet, Mommy." "Stop yelling, Daddy.").

By 2 years to 30 months, most children behave as if they are able to organize what appear to be quite divergent events into meaningful patterns that measurably impact their immediate psychological and physiological state and ultimately their own response patterns. Regardless of the particular response employed—the subtlety ("Hi Mommy, hi Daddy. What are you doing?") or directness ("Stop it! You have to stop screaming at each other.") of the child's response to the ambient anger—most children appear to experience the anger as unpleasant and are concerned primarily with fleeing from or stopping the angry exchange (Radke-Yarrow & Kochanska, 1990).

Using various paradigms, Cummings and colleagues (Cummings, Vogel, Cummings, & El-Sheikh, 1989; Cummings, Ballard, & El-Sheikh, 1991) have examined children's reactions (feelings, perceptions, and coping strategies) to angry behavior between adults. In one paradigm, children watched videotaped segments of various forms of angry and friendly interactions between adults (see Cummings et al., 1989, for descriptions of the various interactions) and were then interviewed regarding their reactions. The types of anger expression depicted included nonverbal anger, verbal anger, verbal physical anger (anger involving physical contact), unresolved anger (interactions beginning positively but ending with anger between the adults), and resolved anger (interactions beginning with anger but ending with reconciliation and friendly exchanges). Across all ages, 4 to 19 years, children perceived all forms of anger expression as negative and responded with negative emotion. Children of all ages considered nonverbal anger equally as negative as overt verbal expressions of anger. Anger involving physical aggression (toward either people or objects) was considered by far to be the most negative type of anger expression. Interestingly, unresolved anger was viewed as much more negative than resolved anger and led to higher levels of anger and distress in children. Anger resolution appeared to ameliorate the negative effects of exposure to anger.

In terms of age effects, children from ages 4 to 9 increasingly said they would attempt to intervene and appeared to be increasingly distressed by the conflict. Negative emotional responses declined, however, as the children approached adolescence. So, while the adolescents perceived the adult anger as negative (as the younger children did), they did not report experiencing as intense negative emotions in response to the anger as the younger children reported experiencing. This pattern has been interpreted variously as reflecting a growing ability to modulate negative arousal in adolescence and as a decreased threat from adults' conflicts as adolescents mature and achieve greater social competence and independence.

The studies reviewed converge in demonstrating that exposure to environmental anger impacts childrens' behaviors in meaningful and observable ways. Not surprisingly, there is a positive association among family members' frequency of anger expression (Radke-Yarrow & Kochanski, 1990). Thus, when anger expression by an individual family member is high, it would be less likely that empathic and positive interpersonal behaviors by either the parents or the children in such a home would be present. While it is difficult to determine the direction of influence in these families, it does appear that the child's expression of anger would be primed by the preponderance and synchrony of family members' anger displays.

Problems and Implications

Although anger can also create psychological and social problems when individuals excessively inhibit and constrain their anger, this chapter is focused on the more common and serious problems associated with excessive, uncontrolled discharge of intense anger. Aggressive behavior in children and adults has been conceptualized as being due in part to an inability to regulate emotional responses to anger-producing stimuli (Lochman & Wells, in press). Children's aggressive behavior has been related to intense emotional arousal in general (e.g., Cummings, Iannotti, & Waxler, 1995) and to high levels of anger in particular (Eisenberg, Fabes, Nyman, Bernzweig, & Pinuelas, 1994).

When individuals perceive themselves as endangered or threatened, they have common physiological responses at two levels (Goleman, 1995). First, there is an energy rush, lasting for a period of minutes, as a result of a limbic surge that releases catecholamines. Second, a general background state of action readiness, which can last for hours or days, is created by the action of the amygdala on the adrenocortical branch of the nervous system. The second level of activation can also be stimulated by stress of all kinds, and individuals become more prone to anger arousal if they already are activated at this second level by being provoked or somewhat irritated. When in this state of readiness, even minor triggers can produce highly intense anger responses. Thus, anger builds on anger (Goleman, 1995), because escalating anger is a result of a series of perceived provocations, each of which trigger arousal which dissipates slowly. Anger is capable of developing very rapidly due to the initial limbic surge and can be manifest overtly in increased cardiovascular activity. Highly aggressive boys have been found to have lower resting heart rates than nonaggressive boys, but they display a sharp surge in heart rate following interpersonal provocation in laboratory situations in comparison to nonaggressive boys (Craven, 1996). These sharp changes in arousal may contribute to highly aggressive boys' distorted perceptions of others and to their sense of being unable to control their emotions.

Based on these two levels of physiological response to threat, two types of anger are apparent (Goleman, 1995). When threat is perceived, the thalamus signals the neocortex, which then processes the perceived causes and perceived responses to the threat. The result can be a deliberate, calculated anger response. In addition, the thalamus also signals the amygdala, and separate from the collateral cortical processing, the amygdala can directly trigger a surge in heart rate and blood pressure, producing a rage response. These two types of anger approximate a distinction between reactive and proactive aggression, which will be noted later in this chapter.

Anger Arousal and Social Cognitive Distortions and Deficiencies

Angry, rage-filled aggression can be readily conceptualized within a social information-processing model of anger arousal (Crick & Dodge, 1994; Lochman, White, & Wayland, 1991). The specific distortions and deficiencies in processing for aggressive children are detailed in Aggressive Behavior (this volume). Briefly, aggressive children have been found to have social-cognitive difficulties at all five stages of processing in this model. Aggressive children have cue-encoding difficulties as they excessively recall hostile social cues and their distorted initial attention to, and recall of, cues lead to the hostile attributional bias typical of many aggressive children. Especially in ambiguous social situations, aggressive children overperceive the hostile intentions of others. In live dyadic interactions, aggressive children not only overperceive the aggressiveness of dyadic partners in competitive situations, they also are relatively unaware of how aggressive they appear to others. This linked pattern of distorted perceptions of self and other leads to aggressive children's attributions that they are not responsible for conflict within these interactions (Lochman, 1987).

These encoding and attributional distortions in the appraisal stages of processing contribute to aggressive children's subsequent difficulties in generating competent solutions to social problems. Aggressive children overly rely on action-oriented and aggressive solutions and underrely on verbal strategies such as verbal assertion and compromise solutions. In addition, in contrast to nonaggressive children, many aggressive children believe that aggressive solutions are effective in stopping aversive treatment from others and are not negatively evaluated by peers. Finally, some aggressive children also have notable difficulties in the final enactment phase of processing, indicating basic inadequacies in their understanding of the intricacies of effective social skills.

Emotion and information processing

Notably missing from this description of the cognitive processing problems of aggressive children is the role of emotion, specifically anger. Information-processing models of psychopathology have historically neglected the way in which emotion results from and contributes to individuals' cognitive activity in interpersonal situations.

Anger can have powerful effects on information processing in at least three ways. Anger can be a direct effect of an initial appraisal of threat, anger can arise out of schema activation, and a preexisting anger mood can alter cognitive processing.

First, in an application of Zillman's emotion theory to the arousal-aggression linkage, a perception of provocation produces arousal and the potential for aggression (Zillman, 1983). An example of how cognitive processes can produce excitatory emotional activity is evident in Graham, Hudley, and Williams' (1992) study in which aggressive boys in an ambiguous intent condition were found to have more biased inferences about intent and reported more feelings of anger. Anger mediated the link between attributions of hostile intent and the boys' tendency to act aggressively. In this regard, emotions have been hypothesized to be the glue between both attributions and behavior (Weiner, 1990) and the adaptation system which motivates individuals to solve their problems (Smith & Lazarus, 1990).

Similarly, another model of anger arousal (Lochman, White, & Wayland, 1991) depicts anger as an affective stress reaction. Children's cognitive appraisal and interpretation of an event leads to two kinds of internal activities: generation of cognitive plans and activation of anger-related physiological arousal, which then impacts subsequent moment-to-moment processing.

Second, an individual's schemas stored in memory can also be activated by an initial appraisal of a threatening situation, and these schemas can then have direct and indirect effects on information processing (Lochman & Lenhart, 1995). For example, after an individual initially perceives a peer interacting in a competitive way during a classroom task, the individual's well-entrenched schema about how people never seem to treat him fairly in competitive situations can become activated, contributing to emotional arousal and to potentially biased interpretations of others' intentions. These moderately provocative events are likely to produce some emotional and physiological arousal in most children, but the intense reactive anger and rage of some aggressive individuals can be due to the activation of schemas about the general unfairness and unjustness of others.

Schemas about accountability and responsibility, with their implications for who received blame or credit for events, are clearly linked to the experience of anger. Accountability appraisals generate "hot" emotional reactions when the provocative person is perceived to act intentionally unjustly and in a controllable manner (Smith & Lazarus, 1990). When a child attributes blame for conflict to self, then the child experiences anger. These schema-driven attribution-emotion linkages then produce quite different decisions about behavioral responses, with anger leading more often to aggressive solutions than to apologies, help seeking, nonconfrontation, or compromise solutions.

Third, a preexisting anger mood can disrupt individuals' cognitive processing when they subsequently encounter a potentially provocative stimulus. Being in a bad mood primes cognitive appraisals and plans which have affective tags consistent with that mood. Like other emotions, anger's effect on cognition operates with an inverted U-function. While mild levels of anger can have a positive, energizing effect, high levels of anger impair subsequent information processing, leading to impulsive aggression (Zillman, 1983). Studies of affective arousal and attributions in parents of aggressive children have found that (a) moods bias cognitive processes in parenting, such as determining who was at fault for a misdeed in a parent-child conflict and (b) attributions lead to affect (Dix & Lochman, 1990). These findings suggest that similar emotion-cognitive linkages operate for parents as for children and that intervention should ultimately begin to target parents' as well as children's affect regulation.

Effects of anger

Thus, anger can generally affect information processing after being stimulated by initial appraisals in a situation, after key schemas are activated, or through an individuals' pervasive angry mood which already exists before information can be processed in a situation. Once activated, anger can have a variety of reverberating effects on individuals' appraisal and cognitive problem-solving activities during provocative situations. Anger can sustain and reaffirm a string of increasingly distorted attributions of the intentions of a possible antagonist. Once anger-aroused, the child is likely to scan the ongoing situation for further cues that the possible antagonist is acting to harm the child in an unfair, unjustified manner, and he or she is unlikely to attend to mitigating or neutral cues. The child explicitly or implicitly also appraises and interprets the arousal he or she experiences. Aggressive children defensively minimize their labeling of the emotional states associated with a sense of vulnerability (e.g., fear, sadness), especially as they approach adolescence (Lochman & Dodge, 1994), and they have been found to report fewer negative emotions overall than nonaggressive peers (Lochman & Dodge, 1994; Quiggle, Garber, Panak & Dodge, 1992; Waas, 1988).

Arousal and intense emotional reactions in early stages of interactions can flood the information-processing system of aggressive children by causing children to use a rapid automatic processing style and by activating their beliefs that they are unable to control their emotions. (Brandon-Muller, Elias, Gara & Schneider, 1992). When aggressive children use quick, automatic processing rather than slower, deliberate processing, they retrieve from memory more action-oriented and fewer verbal, competent problem-solving strategies (Rabiner, Lenhart & Lochman, 1990). However, when they slow down and comparatively evaluate solutions, sifting through the strategies in their memory bins, the competence of the

solutions substantially improves. Automatic processing is an adaptive, efficient way to process information in routine situations but can be maladaptive when initiated preemptively by affect-laden schemas and arousal in ambiguous, potentially threatening situations.

Once aroused, anger maintains itself through retrieval of arrays of anger-laden schemas about the usual blameworthiness of others and through the ruminating self-talk that aggressive children can use. Brooding thoughts about a provocative incident do not permit the arousal to decay and instead fuels an ongoing angry state, which the child can come to perceive is well justified.

Angry Aggression and Reactive Aggressive Children

Recent research has found important subtypes of aggressive children, with one particularly useful classification being the distinction between proactive and reactive aggressive children (Dodge, Lochman, Harnish, Pettit, & Pettit, in press; Pettit, this volume). Proactive aggressive children display either instrumental aggression, in which aggressive behavior is used to reach a desired goal or desired object, or bullying aggression, which is meant to meet these children's goals to dominate and intimidate others. Reactive aggression is characterized by the presence of "hot-blooded" anger, defensive aggression in response to perceived threats, and intensive autonomic activation. In contrast, proactive aggression is more highly organized, more cold-blooded, and with little autonomic activation. Reactive aggression is a frustration response with a lack of self-control, while proactive aggression is less emotional. Although substantial overlap exists between these two types of aggressive children, distinct groups can be reliably identified. The reactive-aggressive children, with their display of angry aggression, have the most profound social information-processing deficits, which are particularly evident in the initial social information-processing steps involving encoding of cues and attributions.

The reactive-proactive distinction is similar in certain ways to distinctions between hostile versus instrumental aggression and expressive versus instrumental aggression (Campbell, Munor, & Coyle, 1992). Hostile aggression is regarded as a defensive, provoked act initiated by threatening attacks or insults and is person oriented rather than task oriented. Expressive aggression occurs when internal controls are lost in response to frustration and stress. Thus, angry, reactive aggressive children typically seem to display these forms of poorly controlled hostile, expressive aggression.

The anger-modulation difficulties of reactive aggressive children derive in part from the problematic socialization histories of these children. Reactive aggressive children have been found to experience higher rates of physical abuse in the first 5 years of life, causing an early onset of angry aggression (Dodge et al., in press). In addition, although exposure to parent-to-child physical aggression has been found to predict both reactive and proactive aggression in sons, between-parent aggression has also added to the prediction of reactive aggression (Lochman & Lenhart, 1993). Between-parent aggression, and parents' accompanying emotional dysregulation, influences children's aggression through modeling and interference with parenting skills, in addition, appear directly to influence children's emotional reactions, their inability to regulate emotions, and their display of reactive aggression. These parental contributions to reactive aggression are strikingly similar to research reported about the impact of adult-adult conflict on children's anger and fear (El-Sheikh & Cheskes, 1995). The coexisting anger and attribution problems of reactive aggressive children are paralleled by associations between the negative attributional inferences and negative affect of mothers of aggressive children (Dix & Lochman, 1990; Miller, 1995), suggesting the intergenerational transmission of these social-cognitive and emotional regulation difficulties to angry, reactive aggressive children.

Children's inability to constructively cope with their negative emotions is associated with their peers' dislike of them (Eisenberg et al., 1993), apparently contributing to the high levels of peer social rejection experienced by reactive aggressive children and to the high levels of depression they display (Dodge et al., in press). The developmental course for rejected aggressive children is especially malignant, as they are at high risk for delinquency, school failure, and early substance use (Lochman & Wayland, 1994), indicating the particular need for intervention and prevention with angry, reactive aggressive children.

Alternative Actions

Several intervention or prevention programs have been developed to help reduce anger problems. Most programs teach skills to manage the affective arousal associated with anger. Some also teach skills to improve social problem solving and others target social skills. Further, some programs focus on the social-cognitive deficits discussed earlier (e.g., hostile-attributional bias). The various intervention programs will be reviewed in turn.

The Anger Coping Program

The Anger Coping Program is a school-based, cognitive-behavioral group intervention. As described in a session-by-session format (Lochman, Lampron, Gemmer, & Harris, 1987), the program is most appropriate for fourth through sixth graders but can be adapted for younger or older children. During the school day, children attend 18 weekly group sessions which typically last from 45 minutes to one hour. Groups are usually made up of four to six children who have been identified by school personnel as aggressive or disruptive or as having difficulty managing anger. The group leaders typically consist of one coleader from within the school system (e.g., counselor, psychologist) and one coleader from a local mental health clinic.

The program aims to correct some of the social-cognitive deficits discussed earlier (e.g., hostile-attributional bias). Group topics include teaching perspective-taking skills (so that social interactions and the intentions of others are more accurately perceived), teaching strategies for managing the affective arousal associated with anger, and improving social problem-solving skills. These latter two goals are accomplished by

1. Identifying physiological (e.g., tight muscles, heart beating fast) and other cues of anger (e.g., fists clenched, scowling face).
2. Using self-instruction statements when angry (e.g., "Stop, think, what should I do?").
3. Using a social problem-solving model in which participants are taught *how* to think about problems: (a) What is the problem? (b) What are my feelings? (c) What are my choices? and (d) What will happen?

Use of videotapes, videotaping, and role-playing allows observation and practice of the skills learned. Goal setting in the classroom encourages generalization of the skills within the school setting. Information regarding the acquisition of a videotape developed by Jim Larson for use in the Anger Coping intervention may be obtained from this chapter's first author or from Jim Larson (Department of Psychology, University of Wisconsin-Whitewater, Whitewater, WI 53190).

Outcome research (as reviewed in Lochman, Dunn, and Klimes-Dougan, 1993) indicates program participants display less disruptive-aggressive behavior, more time on task in the classroom, lower levels of parent-rated aggression, higher self-esteem or perceived social competence, and a trend toward a reduction in teacher-rated aggression. These findings have been noted using pre-post assessments as well as comparisons between program participants and control groups. Examination of the longer term preventive effects of the program have shown indicators of maintenance of gains and preventive effects but have also found that some other behavioral gains were not maintained (Lochman, 1992). Compared to untreated controls and nonaggressive boys, program participants had higher levels of self-esteem; lower rates of irrelevant solutions to problems on a problem-solving measure; and lower rates of alcohol, marijuana, and other drug use at a follow-up period 3 years after the intervention. On these follow-up measures, the program participants were functioning in a range comparable to the nonaggressive boys indicating a prevention effect for substance use and a relative normalization of self-esteem and social problem-solving skills.

Positive program effects have also been found in a recent dissemination study in which training was provided to the coleaders (school psychologists, school counselors) of 41 Anger Coping groups provided in elementary schools in an urban school district. The intensive training program included three full-day workshop sessions prior to the start of the groups and follow-up monthly workshops and telephone consultations while groups were being implemented. When pre-post changes were examined, parents reported that the children had fewer externalizing and internalizing problems at posttest, parent and teacher ratings indicated reductions in attentional problems, and children reported improved perceived social competence and improved social problem-solving skills.

An extended version of the Anger Coping program, known as the Coping Power Program, is currently being implemented and evaluated (Lochman & Wells, in press) with boys identified in fourth and fifth grades. The 33-session, child-component program addresses resistance to peer pressure as well as extended coverage of affect awareness and anger-management strategies. This prevention research project will examine the additive or synergistic effects of combining the child-component program with a 16-session, behaviorally oriented parent-training group for some children's families.

The Art of Self-Control

This cognitive and behaviorally oriented, group (and individual), adolescent control program is described in a session-by-session format in Feindler and Ecton (1986). The group program consists of 12 sessions lasting from 45 to 90 minutes once weekly in outpatient settings and twice weekly in residential treatment settings. The groups typically consist of 8 to 12 members, and the leaders may come from a variety of settings, (e.g., child care workers, counselors, nurses, probation officers, psychiatrists, psychologists, social workers, teachers, or even involved parents).

This program provides training in relaxation, self-instructions, the use of coping statements, assertiveness, self-monitoring of anger and conflictual situations, and problem solving. It utilizes Stress Inoculation Training (SIT) based on Meichenbaum and Goodman's (1971) and Novaco's (1975) intervention program. SIT particularly emphasizes the cognitive components of anger, encouraging adolescents to moderate, regulate, and prevent out-of-control anger and to utilize problem-solving skills in response to conflictual situations. In this program, the SIT approach involves an Educational/Cognitive Preparation Phase, a Skill Acquisition Phase (consisting of a

cognitive component and a behavioral component skills training), and a Skill Application Phase. In the first phase, participants are taught to recognize their personal anger patterns (including cognitive, physiological, and behavioral components) and their situational antecedents or "triggers" which lead to their out-of-control anger. Leaders then encourage adolescents to use these cues to "chill out" and to substitute cognitive-behavioral anger-control techniques.

In the Skill Acquisition Phase, participants are taught cognitive-behavioral techniques to utilize in anger-provoking situations. Feindler and Ecton (1986) utilize the mnemonic "*C-A-L-M-D-O-W-N*" to indicate the different cognitive and behavioral skills to be learned:

1. Cue for anger provocation.
2. Alter views of anger provocation.
3. Let adolescents use self-instructions to help with anger control.
4. Moderate physiological anger arousal by providing skills in relaxation.
5. Direct adolescents to communicate anger verbally and nonverbally by providing them with training in assertiveness.
6. Organize the manner in which anger-related problems are solved by teaching problem-solving skills.
7. Work through the proper timing sequences and conditions that will enhance the effectiveness of the skills learned (using modeling and behavioral rehearsal formats).
8. Negotiate a contract to use the skills learned (to promote generalization to other settings).

In the Skill Acquisition Phase, participants are taught how to utilize the skills just enumerated by exposing them to graduated anger-provoking situations through role-plays and real-life situations. Videotapes and written homework are used to assist with this process. The three phases of this program occur simultaneously, rather than successively as they are described here.

As summarized in Feindler and Ecton (1986), outcome research for this program has indicated reductions in aggressive and disruptive behavior and improvements in problem-solving abilities, social skills, cognitive reflectivity, and adult-rated impulsivity and self-control. These improvements were noted from pre-post comparisons as well as when comparisons were made between program participants and a control group. The populations examined consisted of adolescents who had experienced fairly extreme or chronic histories of aggression (e.g., adolescents at an in-school junior high school program for multisuspended and delinquent youth, adolescents at an inpatient psychiatric facility).

This program also has been adapted for use primarily with incarcerated adolescents. This adaptation, called Anger Control Training, is part of a larger program (i.e.,

Aggression Replacement Training) aimed to help reduce adolescent aggression. A detailed description of this program (in a session-by-session format) can be found in Goldstein and Glick (1994).

Positive Adolescent Choices Training (P.A.C.T.)

This cognitive-behavioral violence-prevention program (specifically developed for African-American adolescents) consists of training in anger management as well as training in social skills and violence awareness (see Larson, 1994, for more information about this program). When used with middle school students, P.A.C.T. participants receive 20 one-hour weekly sessions. The anger-management portion of the program relies heavily on a series of videotapes depicting conflicts between African-American youth. The videotapes and their respective topics are "Givin' It" (giving negative feedback, such as expressing criticism or displeasure), "Takin' It" (receiving negative feedback, such as reacting to criticism and anger from others), and "Workin' It Out" (negotiation, such as identifying problems and solutions, and learning to compromise). As reviewed by Larson (1994), the videotapes are now being marketed alone as an anger-management program, entitled "Dealing with Anger: A Violence Prevention Program for African-American Youth" (Hammond, 1991).

Outcome research has indicated that during the 3 years following the intervention, P.A.C.T. participants were less likely to have been referred to juvenile court or to have been charged with violent offenses (Guerra, Tolan, & Hammond, 1994). The potential treatment effects of the anger-management portion of the program (now being marketed alone as an intervention) have yet to be evaluated separately from the effects of the P.A.C.T. program in its entirety (Larson, 1994).

Think First: Anger and Aggression Management for Secondary-Level Students

This intervention program is an expansion of Feindler's program (Feindler & Ecton, 1986) for use exclusively in the school setting, and particularly at the middle and high school levels (Larson, 1992), from whom a detailed treatment manual of the program is available. This 14-session program relies heavily on the use of a prerecorded videotape in which students model anger-control skills in a series of vignettes. The student's role-play the following skills: arousal-management techniques, self-instruction, and consequential thinking. In a final portion of the videotape, students are provided training in cognitive-behavioral problem solving. In outcome research with this program, program participants were helped to use more self-guiding verbalizations and received fewer dis-

ciplinary referrals. More extensive outcome research has yet to be conducted.

Second Step: A Violence Prevention Curriculum

This is a primary prevention program designed to help reduce impulsive and aggressive behavior as well as improve social competence in children (Committee for Children, 1992). Skill areas targeted are anger management, empathy, and impulse control. There are three separate curricula for elementary school children (one for preschool-Kindergarten, one for Grades 1 to 3, and one for Grades 4 to 5) as well as a middle school curriculum. Each curriculum contains approximately 50 to 60 lessons, and recommendations are for sessions to occur no more than twice per week. Exercises which encourage generalization are built into each session.

Preliminary outcome research for the program has indicated increased knowledge and improved skills in anger management, impulse control, empathy, social problem solving, and conflict resolution; no data are available indicating reductions in aggressive behavior (Guerra et al., 1994). A larger scale outcome study is being conducted. A recent study using the middle school curriculum showed program participants to have somewhat increased assertive versus aggressive responses given on the Children's Action Tendency Scale (see Larson, 1994). Additionally, a questionnaire for teachers and administrators of students taught the curriculum indicated that the program was held in very positive regard (see Larson, 1994). No data on the long-term preventive effects of the program are available.

Violence Prevention Curriculum for Adolescents

This is a school-based, primary prevention program designed as a 10-session health education curriculum for high school students (Prothrow-Stith, 1987). The curriculum is aimed at presenting anger as a normal and potentially constructive feeling. In particular, students are encouraged to explore anger as a normal emotion, discover the ways they express anger, and assess the likely outcome of using fighting as a way of expressing anger. The curriculum also provides information about the statistics on adolescent violence and homicide, teaches some problem-solving skills, and aims to create an environment in which nonviolence and violence prevention is valued. Role-playing as well as videotaping role-plays are done to encourage practice of the concepts and skills learned.

Outcome research indicated that, following program participation, high school students showed significant differences on instruments which measured knowledge and attitudes about anger, violence, and homicide and that fewer fights and arrests were reported (as per self-report) (see Guerra et al., 1994; Larson, 1994). No data on the long-term preventive effects of the program are available.

Other Interventions

As summarized in Hinshaw, Buhrmester, and Heller (1989), several studies have examined the effect of stimulant medication on anger control for a specific population of children who often exhibit anger-control problems, namely children suffering from Attention-Deficit/Hyperactivity Disorder (ADHD). The findings have been mixed as to the effectiveness of stimulant medication on anger-control problems of ADHD boys; however, the most recent study did show that stimulant medication improved self-control, decreased physical retaliation, and tended to increase coping strategies when ADHD boys were verbally provoked by peers. The medication appeared to enhance the boys' abilities to utilize anger-control skills they had learned in a cognitive-behavioral program. Thus, the findings indicate that stimulant medication may be an effective adjunct treatment for use with behavioral or cognitive-behavioral interventions to improve social skills or anger control in ADHD children (see Hinshaw et al., 1989, for additional information).

Summary

This chapter has reviewed developmental changes in the expression and experience of anger, especially highlighting the roles of parents and peers as socializers of anger expression. Anger-modulation difficulties are conceptualized within a social information-processing model, and the role of anger in disrupting this processing is discussed. Angry rage responses appear to be characteristic of reactive aggressive children. The prevention or intervention programs reviewed are all aimed at helping reduce anger problems. Numerous variables must be considered in choosing the best intervention. Some programs have been utilized primarily in school settings, while others have been used to treat youth experiencing more serious problems, of which anger may be only one (e.g., youth admitted to a psychiatric facility).

Programs are available for both children and adolescents, although very young children are somewhat underrepresented. One of the two primary prevention programs discussed offers a curriculum for children as young as preschool; however, most of the intervention programs are for mid-elementary to high-school-aged youth. The programs also vary in the amount of treatment outcome research which has been conducted. To be most effective, comprehensive prevention programs for children at high risk of adolescent conduct problems may need to begin at the transition to elementary school and continue at least through the transition to middle school, while focusing broadly on children's emotional and social skills, parents' skills, and home-school involvement (Conduct Problem Prevention Research Group, 1992).

As for the content of the various programs reviewed, similarities and differences exist. Typically, participants are taught ways to manage the affective arousal associated with anger. Many programs also contain a component in which participants are taught social problem-solving skills, and, in others, participants are taught social skills. Some programs then focus on the social-cognitive deficits discussed earlier (e.g., hostile-attributional bias). Lastly, with ADHD children, stimulant medication may be an effective adjunct treatment for use with behavioral or cognitive-behavioral interventions to improve anger control.

Authors' Note

This chapter's authors acknowledge the support of grant DA 08453 from the National Institute of Drug Abuse in the preparation of this chapter. Correspondence can be addressed to John Lochman, Box 2917, Department of Psychiatry, Duke University Medical Center, Durham, NC 27710.

Recommended Resources

Crick, N. R., & Dodge, K. A. (1994). A review and reformulation of social information-processing mechanisms in children's social adjustment. *Psychological Bulletin, 115,* 74–101.
This article reviews research on the relation between social information processing and social adjustment in childhood and provides a reformulated model of human performance and social exchange. The review suggests that overwhelming evidence supports the empirical relation between characteristic processing styles and children's social adjustment. Some aspects of processing (such as hostile attributional biases, inaccurate detection of intervention cues, competence of problem solutions, and evaluation of response outcomes) appear to have causal effects on behavior and social status, but other aspects (such as perceived self-competence) appear to be the result of peer status.

Cummings, E. M., & El-Sheikh, M. (1991). Children's coping with angry environments: A process-oriented approach. In E. M. Cummings, A. L. Green, & K. H. Karraker (Eds.), *Life span developmental psychology* (pp. 131–150). Hillsdale, NJ: Lawrence Erlbaum Associates.
This chapter considers the effects of discordant emotional environments, specifically anger between adults, on the psychological health and development of young children. The authors present accumulating evidence that, regardless of form—verbal, physical, silent treatment—and social context, anger be-

tween adults represents a significant stressor throughout childhood. Issues of developmental continuity and change, individual adaptation and maladaptation, and buffers and resilience factors regarding chronic exposure to angry environments are highlighted.

Larson, J., (1994). Violence prevention in the schools: A review of selected programs and procedures. *School Psychology Review, 23,* 151–164.
This article reviews a number of violence-prevention programs, most of which contain a component targeting anger control or anger management. The programs reviewed are both those available commercially and those published in the research literature. The emphasis is on interventions which can be utilized in the school setting. The article presents primary, secondary, and tertiary interventions summarized in a chart identifying prevention level (e.g., elementary school), concern (e.g., proactive or reactive aggression), and the specific intervention recommended. Implications for school psychologists are particularly addressed.

Lochman, J. E., Dunn, S. E., & Klimes-Dougan, B. (1993). An intervention and consultation model from a social cognitive perspective: A description of the Anger Coping Program. *School Psychology Review, 22,* 456–469.
In this article, a rationale for and a description of the Anger Coping program is presented. The need for such school-based preventive interventions for aggressive children is discussed. In addition, the article reviews the social-cognitive model on which the program is based and reviews relevant outcome-research findings. Universal intervention and teacher consultation is also discussed as ways to augment such programs. In concluding, the article advocates for comprehensive social-cognitive interventions, including ones which provide program for parents.

Lochman, J. E., White, K. J., & Wayland, K. K. (1991). Cognitive-behavioral assessment and treatment with aggressive children. In P. C. Kendall (Ed.), *Child and Adolescent therapy: Cognitive-behavioral procedures* (pp. 25–65). New York: Guilford.
*This chapter reviews the historical roots of cognitive-behavioral therapy and the negative outcomes which accrue in later years to children identified as aggressive in elementary school. A social-cognitive model for aggression is presented which includes social information-processing deficits and distortions (as described in Crick and Dodge, 1994) and which also emphasizes the recursive effects of physiological arousal and affect labeling on information processing. The impact of cognitive processing style (automatic **vs.** deliberate) and of schemas (social goals, beliefs about outcome expectations) on information processing and on aggression is also explored. The chapter also reviews cognitive-behavioral interventions for aggressive children, with a particular focus on the Anger Coping Program.*

Radke-Yarrow, M., & Kochanska, G. (1990). Anger in young children. In N. L. Stein, B. Leventhal, & T. Trabasso (Eds.), *Psychological and biological approaches to emotion,* (pp. 297–310). Hillsdale, NJ: Lawrence Erlbaum Associates.
This chapter considers the development of anger in children from 1 to 8 years of age through four lines of inquiry. The first set of questions addresses the effects of the experience of anger, not in the children themselves but in their social environment.

The second explores normative developmental issues related to anger. Next, the socialization of anger is discussed, with emphasis on maternal response to children's anger expression. Finally, the origins of anger in young children are explored. In considering these issues the authors draw from their own frequently referenced naturalistic and empirical research on children's affective behavior and development.

References

Branden-Muller, L. R., Elias, M. R., Garg, M. J., & Schneider, K. (1992). The development and interrelationship of affective cognitive and social-cognitive skills in children: Theoretical implications: *Journal of Applied Developmental Psychology, 13,* 271–291.

Campbell, A., Muncer, S. & Coyle, E. (1992). Social representations of aggression as an explanation of gender differences: A preliminary study. *Aggressive Behavior, 18,* 95–108.

Committee for Children. (1992). *Second Step: A violence prevention curriculum.* Seattle, WA: Author.

Conduct Problems Prevention Research Group. (1992). A developmental and clinical model for the prevention of conduct disorder: The FAST Track Program. *Developmental and Psychopathology, 4,* 509–527.

Craven, S. (1996). *Examination of the role of physiological and emotional arousal in reactive aggressive boys' hostile attribution biases in peer provocation situations.* Unpublished manuscript, Duke University, Durham, NC.

Crick, N. R., & Dodge, K. A. (1994). A review and reformulation of social-information processing mechanisms in children's social adjustment. *Psychological Bulletin, 115,* 74–101.

Cummings, E. M., Ballard, , & El-Sheikh, M. (1991). Children's coping with angry environments: A process-oriented approach. In E. M. Cummings, A. L. Greene, & K. H. Karraker (Eds.), *Life-span developmental psychology* (pp. 131–150). Hillsdale, NY: Lawrence Erlbaum Associates.

Cummings, E. M., Iannotti, R. V., & Zahn-Waxler, C. (1985). Influence of conflict between adults on the emotions and aggression of young children. *Developmental Psychology, 21,* 495–507.

Cummings, E. M., Vogel, D., Cummings, J. S., & El-Sheikh, M. (1989). Children's responses to different forms of expression of anger between adults. *Child Development, 60,* 1392–1404.

Dix, T., & Lochman, J. E. (1990). Social cognition and negative reactions to children: A comparison of mothers of aggressive and nonaggressive boys. *Journal of Social and Clinical Psychology, 9,* 418–438.

Dodge, K. A., Lochman, J. E., Harnish, J. D., Pettit, J. E., & Pettit, G. S. (in press). Reactive and proactive aggression in school children and psychiatrically impaired chronically assaultive youth. *Journal of Abnormal Psychology.*

Eisenberg, N., & Fabes, R. A. (1994). Mother's reactions to children's temperament and anger behavior. *Merrill-Palmer Quarterly, 41,* 138–156.

Eisenberg, N., Fabes, R. A., Bernzweig, J., Karbon, M., Poulin, R., & Hanish, L. (1993). The relations of emotionality and regulation to preschoolers' social skills and sociometric status. *Child Development, 64,* 1418–1438.

Eisenberg, N., Fabes, R. A., Nyman, M., Bernzweig, J., & Pinuelas, A. (1994). The relations of emotionality and regulation to children's anger-related reactions. *Child Development, 65,* 109–128.

El-Sheikh, M., & Cheskes, J. (1995). Background verbal and physical anger: A comparison of children's responses to adult-adult and adult-child arguments. *Child Development, 66,* 446–458.

Feindler, E. L., & Ecton, R. B. (1986). *Adolescent anger control: Cognitive-behavior techniques.* New York: Pergamon Books.

Goldstein, A. P., & Glick, B. (1994). *The Prosocial Gang: Implementing aggression replacement training.* Thousand Oaks, CA: Sage Publications.

Goleman, D. (1995). *Emotional intelligence.* New York: Bantam Books.

Graham, S., Hudley, C., & Williams E. (1992). Attributional and emotional determinates of aggression among African-American and Latino young adolescents. *Developmental Psychology, 28,* 731–740.

Guerra, N. G., Tolan, P. H., & Hammond, W. R., (1994). Prevention and treatment of adolescent violence. In L. D. Eron, J. H. Gentry, & P. Schlegel (Eds.), *Reason to hope: A psychosocial perspective on violence and youth.* Washington, DC: American Psychological Association.

Hammond, W. R. (1991). *Dealing with anger: A violence prevention program for African-American Youth.* Champaign, II: Research Press.

Hinshaw, S. P., Buhrmester, D., & Heller, T. (1989). Anger control in response to verbal provocation: Effects of stimulant medication for boys with ADHD. *Journal of Abnormal Child Psychology, 17,* 393–407.

Izard, C. E., Hembree, E. A., & Huebner, R. R. (1987). Infants' emotional expressions to acute pain: Developmental change and stability of individual differences. *Developmental Psychology, 23,* 105–113.

Karniol, R., & Heiman, T. (1987). Situational antecedents of children's anger experiences and subsequent responses to adult versus peer provokers. *Aggressive Behavior, 13,* 109–118.

Klinnert, M., Campos, J., Soce, I., Emde, R., & Svejda, M. (1983). Emotions as behavior regulators: Social referencing in infancy. In R. Plutchik & H. Kellerman (Eds.), *Emotions in early development: Vol. 2. The Emotions* (pp. 57–86). New York: Academic Press.

Kochanska, G. (1987 month). *Socialization of young children's anger by well and depressed mothers.* Paper presented at the Biennial Meeting of the Social for Research in Child Development, City.

Larson, J. D. (1992). *Think first: Anger and aggression management for secondary level students* (Treatment Manual). Whitewater, WI: Author

Larson, J. D. (1994). Violence prevention in the schools: A review of selected programs and procedures. *School Psychology Review, 23,* 151–164.

Lazarus, R. S. (1993). From psychological stress to the emotions: A history of changing outlooks. In L. W. Porter, & M. R. Rosenzweig (Eds.), *Annual Review of Psychology, 44,* 1–21.

Lemerise, E. A., & Dodge, K. A. (1993). The development of anger and hostile interactions. In M. Lewis & J. M. Haviland (Eds.), *Handbook of emotions,* (pp. 537–546). New York: Guilford Press.

Lochman, J. E. (1987). Self and peer perceptions and attributional biases of aggressive and nonaggressive boys in dyadic interactions. *Journal of Consulting and Clinical Psychology, 55,* 404–414.

Lochman, J. E. (1992). Cognitive-behavioral intervention with aggressive boys: Three-year follow-up and preventive effects. *Journal of Consulting and Clinical Psychology, 60,* 426–432.

Lochman, J. E. & Dodge, K. A. (1994). Social cognitive processes of severely violent, moderately aggressive, and nonaggressive boys. *Journal of Consulting and Clinical Psychology, 62,* 366–374.

Lochman, J. E., Dunn, S. E., & Klimes-Dougan, B. (1993). An intervention and consultation model from a social-cognitive perspective: A description of the Anger Coping Program. *School Psychology Review, 22,* 456–469.

Lochman, J. E., Lampron, L. B., Gemmer, T. C., & Harris, S. R. (1987). Anger coping intervention with aggressive children: A guide to implementation in school settings. In P. A. Keller & S. R. Heyman (Eds.), *Innovations in clinical practice: A source book* (Vol. 6, pp. 339–356). Sarasota, FL: Professional Resource Exchange.

Lochman, J. E. & Lenhart, L. A. (1993). Anger coping intervention for aggressive children: Conceptual models and outcome effects. *Clinical Psychology Review, 13,* 785–805.

Lochman, J. E., & Lenhart, L. (1995). Cognitive behavioral therapy of aggressive children: Effects of schemas. In H. P. G. van Bilsen, P. C. Kendall, & J. H. Slavenburg (Eds.), *Behavioral approaches for children and adolescents: Challenges for the next century* (pp. 145–166). New York: Plenum.

Lochman, J. E. & Wayland, K. K. (1994). Aggression, social acceptance and race as predictors of negative adolescent outcomes. *Journal of the American Academy of Child and Adolescent Psychiatry, 33,* 1026–1035.

Lochman, J. E., & Wells, K. C. (in press). A social-cognitive intervention with aggressive children: Prevention effects and contextual implementation issues. In R. De V. Peters & R. J. McMahon (Eds.), *Prevention childhood disorders, substance abuse, and delinquency.* Thousand Oaks, CA: Sage Publications.

Lochman, J. E., White, K. J., & Wayland, K. K., (1991). Cognitive-behavioral assessment and treatment with aggressive children. In P. C. Kendall (Eds.), *Child and adolescent therapy: Cognitive-behavioral procedures* (pp. 25–35). New York: Guilford Press.

Meichenbaum, D., & Goodman, J. (1971). Training impulsive children to talk to themselves: A means of developing self-control. *Journal of Abnormal Psychology, 77,* 115–126.

Miller, S. A. (1995). Parents' attribution for their children's behavior. *Child Development, 66,* 1557–1584.

Novaco, R. W. (1975). *Anger control: The development and evaluation of an experimental treatment.* Lexington, MA: D.C. Heath.

Prothrow-Stith, D. (1987). *Violence prevention curriculum for adolescents.* Newton, MA: Education Development Center.

Quiggle, N. L., Garber, J., Panak, W. F., & Dodge, K. A.

(1992). Social information processing in aggressive and depressed children. *Child Development, 63,* 1305–1320.

Rabiner, D. L., Lenhart, L., & Lochman, J. E. (1990). Automatic versus reflective problem solving in relation to children's sociometric status. *Developmental Psychology, 71,* 535–543.

Radke-Yarrow, M., & Kochanska, G. (1990). Anger in young children. In N. L. Stein, B. Leventhal, & T. Trabasso (Eds.), *Psychosocial and biological approaches to emotion* (pp. 297–310). Hillsdale, NJ: Lawrence Erlbaum Associates.

Smith, C. A., & Lazarus, R. W. (1990). Emotion and adaptation. In L. Pervin (Ed.), *Handbook of personality: Theory and research* (pp. 609–637). New York: Guilford Press.

Stenberg, C. R., & Campos, J. J. (1990). The develop-ment of anger expressions in infancy. In N. L. Stein, B. Leventhal, & T. Trabasso (Eds.), *Psychological and biological approaches to emotion* (pp. 247–282). Hillsdale, NJ: Lawrence Erlbaum Associates.

Stenberg, C. R., Campos, J. J., & Emde, R. N. (1983). The facial expression of anger in seven month old infants. *Child Development, 54,* 178–184.

Weas, 1988Weiner, B. (1990). Attribution in personality psychology, In L. Pervin (Ed.), *Handbook of personality: Theory and research* (pp. 609–637). New York: Guilford Press.

Zillman, D. (1983). Arousal and aggression. In R. G. Green & E. I., Donnerstein (Eds.), *Aggression: Theoretical and empirical reviews* (Vol. 1, pp. 75–101). New York: Academic Press.

14

Temper Tantrums

Susan M. Sheridan
Sondra Russman
University of Utah

Background and Development

Temper tantrums are acknowledged by professionals and parents as being developmentally appropriate for children in the toddler years. However, under certain conditions temper tantrums are indicative of more serious problems (Schaefer & Millman, 1981). For example, temper tantrums can be a part of generalized noncompliance in a child. Likewise in the *Diagnostic and Statistical Manual of Mental Disorders-Fourth Edition* (*DSM-IV;* American Psychiatric Association, 1994), behaviors often associated with temper tantrums (e.g., loss of temper) are recognized as one of the criteria for diagnosing Oppositional Defiant Disorder.

Temper tantrums are common and normal in most children between 1 and 4 years of age (Bhatia et al., 1990; Le Couteur, 1993; Needleman, Stevenson, & Zuckerman, 1991). However, actual prevalence rates are difficult to discern given discrepancies across studies. For example, Bhatia et al. (1990) used an outpatient clinic sample and found that 75.3% of children between the ages of 3 and 5 had temper tantrums, with boys exhibiting them three times more frequently than girls. Using a more stringent definition of temper tantrums, including both frequency and duration (3 or more tantrums per day lasting more than 15 minutes), Needleman et al. (1991) indicated that temper tantrums occur at least once a week in 50% to 80% of preschool children. Finally, Douglas (1989) cited that at least 19% of 2-year-olds, 18% of 3-year-olds, and 11% of 41/2-year-olds have tantrums daily. The discrepancies in these studies are likely attributable to the use of different definitions of temper tantrums, combined with the use of different clinic samples.

In summary, from a developmental perspective temper tantrums are considered normal in toddlers, decreasing in frequency as children become older (Schaefer & Millman, 1981). This provides little solace to a frustrated, embarrassed, or helpless parent of a 10-year-old or an adolescent, who is exhibiting tantruming behavior. Though temper tantrums are developmentally appropri-ate for toddlers, they are developmentally inappropriate for older children.

Definitional Issues

Many different visual images are evoked when a parent describes a child as having a "temper tantrum." For example, the child could be on the floor screaming and banging his or her head, throwing things and being verbally abusive, or kicking and hitting others. A temper tantrum could entail any combination of these and other behaviors. Interestingly, there does not seem to be an agreed-upon set of discrete behaviors that describe temper tantrums. In a seminal chapter, Trieschman (1969) acknowledged that temper tantrums are difficult to define because several behaviors co-occur to comprise a "tantrum." There does seem to be consensus among professionals that temper tantrums (a) contain both verbally and physically aggressive behaviors, (b) are extreme and spontaneous reactions not justified by the situation, (c) contain at least one adult and one child, and (d) likely occur in a public setting (Bath, 1994; Douglas, 1989; Schaefer & Millman, 1981). For the purpose of this chapter, temper tantrums are defined as severe behaviors (e.g., biting, kicking, swearing, screaming, shouting, hitting, and throwing things) that are generally exhibited in response to an adult directive and are disproportionate to the situation. They can be conceptualized as learned behaviors that occur as a result of repeated behavioral events (i.e., the use of a class of behaviors that produce a tantrum episode), resulting in the attainment of desirable outcomes for the child.

Stages of Temper Tantrums

Both Trieschman (1969) and Bath (1994) described temper tantrums as occurring in a series of progressive stages. Although their stage-wise conceptualizations of temper tantrums allow for an organized assessment and analysis, it should not be concluded that all tantrums will progress systematically in an identical fashion. Likewise, it does not presume that application of seemingly appropriate interventions will always stop a tantrum from going through its course.

Bath (1994) and Trieschman (1969) discussed complimentary, though slightly different, stages of a temper tantrum. Bath referred to the first phase as the pretantrum arousal stage, better known to most parents as the "rumbling and grumbling" phase described by Trieschman. Here, the child is grouchy, irritable, and unsatisfiable. It is as if the child is seeking a situation in which to make an issue, such as searching for a lost toy, finding something broken, or wanting something such as a candy bar right before dinner. The child becomes aroused, setting the stage for a tantrum to occur. The second stage is known as the "encounter" (Bath) or "help-help" stage (Trieschman). During this phase, the child becomes noisy, breaks rules, violates accepted behavior, and oversteps the boundary of propriety by doing or saying something that will demand attention. This stage can be initiated by someone, usually an adult, asking the child to start or stop doing something. The "outburst" is considered by Bath to be the core of the tantrum. Trieschman identified it as the "either-or" and "no! no!" stage. The child's behavior is at its apex, ranging from undirected screaming and flailing to goal-directed verbal and physical aggression. This phase generally runs its course, bringing the child into the calming phase, better known as the "leave me alone" period. Verbal and physical outbursts are reduced, leaving the child sad and placid. According to Bath, children's needs will vary from withdrawing because of "defeat" in the interaction to needing both reassurance and comfort from the adult. Trieschman identified a posttantrum phase as the "hangover." During this period some children act as if nothing happened, though they may be tired. Others feel guilty or upset with themselves and have a difficult time accepting any responsibility for their behavior.

Development

Temper tantrums are found in children from infancy through adolescence and into the adult years. Depending upon the developmental stage of the child, tantrums are characterized as "normal" behavior or are associated with more severe behavior problems.

Infancy
As indicated previously, temper tantrums are considered to be a part of the normal development of children between the ages of 3 and 5 years. However, infants can also express tantrum-like behaviors. In the course of normal development, infants express their needs via smiling, crying, gurgling, and grabbing at interesting objects. When their basic needs are compromised (e.g., warmth, food, and drink) or when they experience pain, illness, or fatigue, infants are likely to express their rage with screaming and flailing limbs (Bath, 1994). These behaviors typically are attended to immediately and readily by parents and caregivers, both to appease the infant and calm the adult. According to Bath, rage changes developmentally as children move into their toddler years.

Toddler years
Professionals and parents seem to agree that temper tantrums are a "rite of passage" into the toddler years and are rarely considered a serious emotional disturbance during this time (Schaefer & Millman, 1981). Toddlers are actively striving for competence and autonomy. Having acquired mobility and limited communication, they enthusiastically set out to explore their environment. During this stage, parents are primarily concerned about their children achieving developmental milestones such as walking and talking. However, the child's newfound freedom means that household rules and consequences need to be established and enforced to ensure safety and maintain control of the child. Attempts at exploration by the toddler are often met with adult intervention. Lacking the ability to understand why their efforts have been thwarted by the adult, combined with natural physical and verbal inabilities, toddlers may become frustrated and will often respond with a temper tantrum.

As more rules are placed on the toddler, disagreements between the parent and child are inevitable. These disagreements are not always worked out in the child's favor, and therefore the child is likely to exhibit tantrum behaviors. There may, however, be a positive side to this behavior (Lieberman, 1993). For example, screaming, defiance, and physical and verbal aggression toward adults are a necessary component of the need to test and enrich the toddler's individuality.

It is theorized that between the ages of 18 months and 3 years children begin asserting themselves and developing a sense of autonomy (Erikson, 1950). In this developmental stage, children often "test limits" as they expand their boundaries and attempt to exert more control over their environment. Tantrums may occur as children test their ability to control others in their lives (e.g., parents, siblings, caretakers). In this context, tantrums are not considered abnormal behavior. However, they become a sign of abnormality when they are used frequently and over a prolonged period of time (Schaefer, Millman, Sichel, & Zwilling, 1986), especially into the middle childhood years.

Early and middle childhood
A significant reduction in temper tantrums from the toddler into the early childhood years was confirmed by Bhatia et al. (1990). These researchers found that only 21% of children between the ages of 6 and 8 had temper tantrums, a marked reduction from children in their toddler years. A decline in tantrums will first be noted by a longer

time between their occurrence. Though the intensity of the tantrum may still be high, the child begins to consider possible outcomes of the behavior, and the posttantrum pouting time may be shorter. The completion of a tantrum may be followed by expressions of remorse and possible affection for the parents, marking the second possible change. A third change is noted by a decrease in tantrum time. Whereas at one time a tantrum may have lasted 15 minutes, it may now taper to 1 to 2 minutes in duration. Finally, parents and caregivers often find that they can discuss problems with the child and avert the tantrum behaviors altogether.

Problems and Implications

If tantrums continue to persist after the age of 5 years, it may be that they have become a preferred means of problem solving by the child (Douglas, 1989). It is probable that the longer the tantrum behaviors have been practiced and reinforced, the more entrenched they have become. It is important to note that the continuation of tantrums can be associated with more severe problems. For example, Oppositional Defiant Disorder, Attention Deficit/Hyperactivity Disorder, and Antisocial Personality Disorder found in the *DSM-IV* describe tantrum-like behaviors such as physical and verbal aggression, defiant behavior, and loss of temper as part of their diagnostic criteria.

The life histories of children who at the age of 10 were still experiencing severe temper tantrums in reaction to frustration and adult authority were investigated by Caspi, Elder, and Bem (1987). Using archival data from 1928, they argued that having tantrums is not a "personality trait" maintained across time from early childhood to adulthood, but an *interactional style* they labeled "interactional continuity." These researchers suggest that the explosive, undercontrolled interactional style that appears as temper tantrums will manifest itself later in life, especially in times of frustration and negotiation. These tantrum-like behaviors are consistent with a diagnosis of Intermittent Explosive Disorder (*DSM-IV*, 1994) characterized by extreme aggressive outbursts out of proportion to any psychosocial stressors. However, this diagnosis can only be made after other mental disorders are ruled out (e.g., Antisocial Personality Disorder, Conduct Disorder, Attention Deficit/Hyperactivity Disorder).

Comorbidity

Children with communication disorders, mental retardation, or a pervasive developmental disorder, that is, children who experience a delay in or total lack of spoken language may develop a pattern of severe temper tantrums (Durand, 1993; Gross, 1994). Children who are de-

pressed exhibit mood swings and an inability to tolerate frustration. Angry outbursts, aggression, isolation, and withdrawal are often how children with depression respond to minor provocation (Ingersoll & Goldstein, 1995). According to Ingersoll and Goldstein, "depressed preschoolers are often sulky and uncooperative, with frequent crying spells and temper tantrums" (p. 18). Likewise, children with Separation Anxiety Disorder are also at risk for severe temper tantrums, especially if forced to separate from their parents or to leave their homes or other familiar areas (Ingersoll & Goldstein).

Temper tantrums can occur in isolation or be part of a pattern of generalized noncompliance. From a school psychologist's viewpoint, it is important to distinguish between children who present with isolated incidents of temper tantrums and those whose tantrums are accompanied by other severe behaviors. This understanding and knowledge will affect both diagnostic and therapeutic decisions.

Temper tantrums can also be accompanied by a myriad of other behavior problems not necessarily associated with a *DSM-IV* diagnosis (Bath, 1994; Bhatia et al, 1990; Douglas, 1989; Needleman et al., 1991). In a study on prevalence and etiology, Bhatia et al. reported the following problems were exhibited at a higher rate among tantruming children compared to control children: (a) thumb sucking, (b) head banging, (c) sleep disturbances, (d) mutism, (e) school avoidance, (f) underachievement, (g) speech and eating problems, and (h) delinquent behavior.

Psychosocial and Familial Correlates

Needleman et al. (1991) investigated the psychosocial correlates of temper tantrums in a study comprised of 502 mothers from a combined referred and nonreferred clinic population. Temper tantrums were defined as shouting, banging, kicking, or screaming, which occurred three or more times a day and lasted longer than 15 minutes. The researchers found that 6.8% of the mothers identified severe tantrums in their child, with 52% also identifying other behavior problems. Factors associated with temper tantrums included (a) maternal depression and stress, (b) low education, (c) use of corporal punishment, (d) manual social class, (e) child care provided predominately by the mother, and (f) poor child health. Gender, maternal employment, low social support, and single parenthood were not associated with tantrums.

In a retrospective family study, Mattes and Fink (1987) evaluated the heritability of "having temper outbursts" and associated diagnoses. An average of 18.2% of patients with temper outbursts had relatives with temper problems, compared to 4.3% for patients with diverse psychiatric conditions without temper problems. Although their sample was small, results suggested familial transmission of temper problems. The trait of having temper outbursts was more strongly transmitted than were specific diagnoses such as Intermittent Explosive Disorder. However, it cannot be concluded that tantrums are genetically caused. It is also likely that parent modeling contributes to the demonstration of tantrum behavior in their children.

Child and Family Factors Contributing to Temper Tantrums

Temper tantrums do not occur in a vacuum. Rather, they are best conceptualized as occurring as a result of an interaction between the child and his or her environment (Caspi et al., 1987). Many personal and interpersonal factors are likely to contribute to the behavioral outbursts of a tantrum-prone child. Although some of these may not be amenable to change, a careful analysis of tantrums is useful for purposes of intervention. Specifically, analysis of conditions that surround a tantrum and of the functions that a temper tantrum may serve can broaden a school psychologist's interpretation of the behaviors and lead directly to effective interventions.

It has been suggested that young children with developmentally appropriate cognitive and language abilities may demonstrate temper tantrums in response to frustration (Douglas, 1989). In these cases, children's cognitive capacities (i.e., knowing what they want) may supersede their motor or communicative abilities (i.e., the developmental ability to attain what is desired). For example, 2-year-olds may have a strong desire to dress themselves independently. However, such efforts may be met with great frustration if their fine motor skills are not adequately developed to manipulate the buttons or snaps on their clothing. This mismatch between what is desired and what can be accomplished motorically may result in a behavioral outburst (i.e., tantrum).

Tantrums may also serve a communicative function for children with language impairments (Durand, 1993). For example, children with severe disabilities may exhibit temper tantrums as a means to communicate needs, wishes, or messages. Attempts to communicate via aggressive tantrum behaviors are often reinforced by others who respond to the child, even in response to inappropriate communication gestures.

Tantrums can also be understood as a result of interactional factors between the child exhibiting the tantrum and others in the child's environment. Patterson (1976) found high rates of aggression (especially toward the mother) in families with a "difficult" child. These mothers were found to engage in punitive behaviors toward their child, even when the child was behaving appropriately.

Children in "insular" families (Wahler & Dumas, 1984) are also at risk for developing negative or aggressive behaviors such as tantrums. Insular families are those with little (usually negative) social contact outside of the immediate family, such as with friends, relatives, or others. Such families are often from low socioeconomic conditions and tend to reject assistance from outside the home. Research on insular mothers has found that they (a) are unhappy and aggressive in many social interactions, even outside of the family; (b) tend to be angry and irritable toward their children regardless of the children's behaviors; (c) consistently respond aggressively toward their children behaving aggressively; (d) often become detached and uninterested in their children; and (e) use immature behaviors in conflict interactions with their children.

Patterson and his colleagues (1975) have explained dysfunctional interactions between children and their parents in terms of a "coercive cycle" (see Aggressive Behavior, this volume). Specifically, the coercion hypothesis states that unclear boundaries and limits on a child's behavior may lead to a power struggle between a parent and child. Negative interactions are frequent and progressively more aggressive. In some situations, a child's behavior may escalate to violent or severe tantruming until the parent accommodates his or her wishes (i.e., the child's behaviors are reinforced). In other situations, the parent may continue engaging in the negative interaction by yelling or screaming until the child discontinues the inappropriate behaviors (i.e., the parent's behaviors are negatively reinforced). A cycle of anger and aggression often develops with the parent and child becoming increasingly more negative toward each other. This recurrent interactional pattern models aggression for the child and reinforces the behavior when it results in a desirable state of affairs (Patterson, Reid, Jones, & Conger, 1975).

Inconsistency in reactions to a child's tantrums may also result in increased frequency and intensity of the inappropriate behaviors. From a behavioral perspective, intermittent reinforcement of tantrums may encourage a child to use them regularly because they are effective at least some of the time. Such inconsistency also results in behaviors that are very difficult to extinguish because the child has learned that, on some occasions, they will lead to desirable results.

Analysis of Temper Tantrums

Temper tantrums serve various functions, some of which are listed in Table 1. In general, children tend to exhibit tantrums to exert control over their environment, gain attention of others, or communicate. When used to obtain a desired wish or elicit a predictable response, the tantrum serves a *control function;* when used to gain attention from others, they serve an *attention function;* and when they communicate the child's frustration or needs, they serve a *communicative function.*

In general, functional analyses can be considered *descriptive* or *experimental.* In descriptive approaches, var-

Table 1 *Functions of Temper Tantrums and Possible Interventions*

Function	Intervention
Control	
Gain access to or obtain desired wish. Elicit predictable response.	■ Extinction-based procedures (ignoring, time-out from reinforcement). ■ Firm, consistent limit setting. ■ Differential reinforcement of other behaviors.
Attention	
Gain attention from others.	■ Positive reinforcement of appropriate behaviors. ■ "Catch them being good" procedures.
Communication	
Express need. Express frustration.	■ Alternative communication techniques. ■ Training in verbal and social skills.

iables are not manipulated experimentally to examine their controlling influence on behavior. In an experimental approach, hypothesized relationships are tested directly by manipulating those variables presumed to affect target behaviors (e.g., tantrums) and then measuring concomitant changes.

A careful functional analysis can determine the purpose or function of a temper tantrum. Functional analyses identify "important, controllable, causal functional relationships applicable to a specified set of target behaviors for an individual client" (Haynes & O'Brien, 1990, p. 654). Thus, they require attention to the antecedents and consequences of a tantrum as well as situational events or conditions that coincide with their occurrence.

A useful framework for conducting a functional analysis is presented by O'Neill, Horner, Albin, Storey, and Sprague (1990). These authors indicate that a functional analysis must include (a) a description of the undesirable behavior (i.e., "tantrum") in operational terms, (b) a prediction of the times and situations when the tantrum behavior will or will not be performed across various routines (e.g., such as in a classroom), and (c) a definition of functions, such as maintaining reinforcers that the tantrums produce for the child. The Functional Analysis Interview (O'Neill et al.) investigates a range of variables that influence problematic behavior. In addition, these authors recommend an observational format and have developed a Functional Analysis Observation Form which can assist in the direct observation of tantrum behaviors and allow information gathering on behavior, setting events, discriminative stimuli, functions, and actual con-

sequence of behavior. The final phase of their approach involves direct manipulation of variables (such as withholding attention) to examine the responsiveness of the problematic tantrum behaviors. This approach to functional analysis allows one to test hypotheses through observation of actual behavior change.

School psychologists should consider the use of a variety of descriptive procedures (e.g., questionnaires, checklists, and rating scales) to supplement direct observational procedures in a functional analysis. Descriptive data may be helpful in the development of important hypotheses regarding variables that maintain problematic behaviors of the child, teacher, or parent. Two questionnaires useful for this purpose are the Motivational Assessment Scale (MAS; Durand & Crimmins, 1988) and the Problems Behavior Questionnaire (PBQ; Lewis, Scott, & Sugai, 1994). The MAS is a 16-item questionnaire designed to generate information and evaluate hypotheses pertaining to functions of behavior, including tantrums. The PBQ is a 15-item scale that assesses behavior problems in relation to three response classes: (a) behaviors that function to gain peer or teacher attention; (b) behaviors that function to avoid peer or teacher attention; and (c) setting events.

The intervention chosen to address temper tantrums can vary depending on the function of the behaviors. Therefore, attention to functional analysis is important in developing both a thorough understanding of the problem and an appropriate intervention. For this reason, various interventions are presented next in the context of possible functions of tantrum behaviors.

Alternative Actions

Extinction-based Procedures

Extinction procedures (i.e., withholding reinforcers) should be considered when the function of a temper tantrum is to somehow control the child's interaction with a parent, teacher, or other adult. The goal is to break the learned and reinforced link between the inappropriate behavior and the desired outcome (e.g., removal of an aversive stimulus such as a command). Ignoring and time-out from reinforcement are two common extinction procedures used in the treatment of temper tantrums.

Endo, Sloane, Hawkes, McLoughlin, and Jenson (1991) used self-instructional manuals to teach parents procedures by which to reduce the frequency of temper tantrums. In Phase 1 of the program, parents were given specific instructions on ignoring the tantrum. For example, they were instructed to leave the room and not return for 5 minutes or until the child stopped tantruming. If another tantrum occurred, they were to repeat the procedure and respond to any verbalization of the child with "I don't have to listen to that." Whenever Phase 1 was ineffective, parents were taught to use a brief (5-minute) time-out. Phase 2 was identical to Phase 1, except that a time-out room was used. Six of 10 children showed improvements from baseline to treatment. When measuring outcomes based on the last part of treatment, all but one child showed improvements. Further, all parents reported satisfaction with the self-instructional program.

Ralph (1987) used extinction coupled with differential reinforcement in treating tantrums of a 7-year-old boy with Down's syndrome. In this case study, family members were encouraged to withhold reinforcement (i.e., attention) when the boy demonstrated tantrum behaviors. Specifically, when he began to tantrum, family members removed themselves from his presence or placed him in a quiet place away from toys or other pleasurable activities. This time-out from reinforcement was coupled with positive reinforcement of appropriate behaviors (i.e., quiet or nontantrum behaviors) whenever possible. The behavioral objective of 3 consecutive days without tantrums was reached 18 days after the program began and was maintained for an additional 7 days with one minor relapse in a new setting. Unfortunately, although similar problematic behaviors occurred in the school, the intervention was not implemented in that setting nor was generalization assessed.

A "gradual extinction" procedure was described by Rolider and Van Houten (1984b) to decrease bedtime tantrums (i.e., excessive crying) of three toddlers. Parents were instructed to put their children to bed and leave them alone for a minimum prespecified amount of time (e.g., 10 minutes). Every two nights, the criterion was increased by 5 minutes until the crying behavior was extinguished. For each child, results showed that once the criterion time exceeded the tantrum's duration, the duration of the tantrum quickly declined to at or near zero. During three follow-up sessions, none engaged in bedtime tantrum behaviors.

A problem with extinction procedures, especially in school settings, is the difficulty controlling all sources of reinforcement that are contingent upon tantruming. For example, other students may provide attention to tantrum behaviors and reinforce their occurrence. Additionally, it is often difficult to consistently ignore tantrum behaviors. Petty (1976) reported two case studies in which extinction (ignoring) was used in combination with contingent reinforcement and desensitization training for parents (this procedure was employed after ignoring was found to be ineffective when used alone). The mothers underwent relaxation procedures by hypnosis, wherein they were instructed to visualize themselves calm and undisturbed during their child's most recent tantrum. After desensitization, the mothers reported that they were able to ignore the tantrum behaviors and that the tantrums occurred less frequently and were less bothersome. It

should be noted that formal data were not collected in these case studies, nor was a controlled design used to evaluate effects of the procedures.

Reinforcement Procedures

In treating temper tantrums, reinforcement is typically combined with extinction procedures to increase preferred alternative behaviors. Positive reinforcement is useful when the function of a child's tantrums is to gain attention if the treatment agents (e.g., parents, teachers) are careful to deliver reinforcers only for alternative, nontantrum behaviors. This is often termed *differential reinforcement of alternative behaviors* (DRA). In setting up DRA programs, caregivers must be careful to identify appropriate behaviors that are exhibited in place of tantrum behaviors. For example, instead of pleading, crying, or screaming after being denied a candy bar, a child, although disappointed, simply agrees and says "O.K." The parent immediately praises the child's verbal response and accepting behavior.

Repp and Karsh (1994) used positive reinforcement for alternative behaviors, in combination with other treatment components, to treat tantrum behaviors of two students with developmental disabilities. Through a careful functional analysis, they identified the function of tantrums as gaining teacher attention. The intervention included (a) withholding of attention for tantrums; (b) providing frequent reinforcement for task engagement in the form of "high fives," pats on the back, and the like; and (c) increasing the opportunities for social interaction between each student and the teacher and teaching assistant. The intervention resulted in a substantial reduction in the frequency of each child's tantrums, with maintenance of the behavioral improvements at a one-year follow-up.

Slightly different from DRA programs are reinforcement systems that reinforce the absence of inappropriate target behaviors. These programs, coined *differential reinforcement of other behaviors* (DRO), generally do not identify specific alternative behaviors with which to replace tantrum behaviors. Rather, reinforcement is delivered at specific times or in specific intervals if tantrums have not been exhibited. In the treatment of tantrum-like behaviors of a 6-year-old girl at bedtime, Rolider and Van Houten (1984a) examined the effects of DRO plus extinction and DRO plus reprimands. In the DRO-plus-extinction condition, the child was placed on an intermittent schedule of reinforcement wherein she earned a star for refraining from crying and asking to get out of bed. For every three stars, she was allowed to select among several small back-up reinforcers. All instances of crying or asking to get out of bed were ignored by the parents. In the DRO-plus-reprimand condition, the same reinforcement procedures were used, but instances of crying were responded to with a reprimand. Specifically, the parent was instructed to make a firm statement (i.e., "Look at me!"), point a finger, and command the child to stop and go to sleep. Both procedures led to a decrease in bedtime tantrum behaviors. However, the DRO-plus-reprimand condition produced a more marked decline in the average amount of time elapsed from bedtime to the end of the child's last vocalization.

Communication Training

Some children, particularly those with severe language or cognitive disabilities, use temper tantrums to communicate with others. For these children, school psychologists should consider communication training, a method of teaching children to convey their needs, desires, or frustrations, using socially appropriate alternatives to tantrums.

Durand (1993) provided functional communication training to children with severe language and cognitive disabilities who exhibited temper tantrums and other challenging behaviors. The children were taught to appropriately request objects and activities previously obtained by displaying tantrum behaviors. Assistive communication devices were used to augment their communication. Following a functional analysis of their problem behaviors, they were taught to use their devices to request the objects or activities (e.g., social attention, breaks from work) that were maintaining their tantrums. Multiple baseline data collected across students showed decreases in aberrant behavior in all children with the onset of communication training. In addition, the children displayed increases in positive facial expression in relation to training.

Matson, Fee, Coe, and Smith (1991) used communication-based social skills training in the treatment of preschoolers with developmental delays who demonstrated tantrums. The children were taught appropriate verbal behavior (such as greetings and initiating play) that would replace inappropriate social behaviors, including tantrums and aggression. Appropriate verbal behavior was taught with puppets, peer modeling, role playing, instructions, and reinforcement. Following treatment, significant differences were found between children who participated in treatment and those in a control group, with negative social behaviors (including tantrums) decreasing and positive social skills increasing dramatically.

Additional Procedures

Several additional procedures to treat temper tantrums have been described in the intervention literature. Milan, Mitchell, Berger, and Pierson (1982) reported the effectiveness of "Positive Routines," a chaining and fading technique to rapidly eliminate the bedtime tantrums of three children with severe handicaps. Classical conditioning was used by Gross (1994), whereby a nonaversive odor was paired with feelings of contentment to allow a teacher to intervene and decrease aggressive tantrums in a blind, noncommunicative child. Amatea (1994) described the use of brief, systemic family therapy (i.e., emphasizing the use of paradox and reframing) to decrease tantrums in a 5-year-old girl.

Psychopharmacological interventions also have been shown to reduce aggressiveness in patients with temper outbursts. Carbamazepine (CMZ), propranolol (PPL), and lithium have been identified as particularly effective to reduce rage outbursts (Mattes, 1986).

Finally, physical restraint was used by Swerissen and Carruthers (1987) and by Prasad, Sitholey, Dutt, and Srivastava (1992) to address dangerous tantruming behaviors (e.g., head banging, self-injury) of children with severe intellectual disabilities. However, the use of such procedures in a school setting is not recommended due to the potential for misuse and ethical violations.

Summary

Temper tantrums represent a common, albeit challenging class of behaviors for children between approximately one and four years of age. The focus of this chapter has been on the normal and abnormal developmental courses of tantrums. Specific attention was paid to conditions under which tantrums may be considered problematic and atypical. These include the demonstration of tantrum behaviors in relation to dysfunctional adult-child interactions, the consistent and preferred use of tantrums in children over the age of 5 years, and tantrums in children with developmental disabilities.

An important approach to treating temper tantrums is to understand the function they serve for individual children. If environmental variables that maintain temper tantrums can be identified, they can be manipulated to reduce or eliminate the behavior.

Several interventions successful in treating temper tantrums were reviewed briefly. These interventions, presented in the context of the various functions of tantrum behaviors, include:

- Extinction and differential reinforcement procedures when the function of tantrums is to control aspects of the environment (including parents and teachers).
- Operant reinforcement of appropriate behaviors when the function is gaining attention.
- Communication and social skills training when the function is to communicate needs or desires.

A combination of treatment interventions is generally recommended.

Functional analysis is offered as a framework by which to structure a school psychologist's work with students who exhibit temper tantrums. It is particularly beneficial when used in the context of ongoing consultation with teachers and parents. In this way, school psychologists can provide much-needed assistance to those who must deal with the extremely challenging behaviors that constitute tantrums.

Recommended Resources

Cohen, J. J., & Fish, M. C. (Eds.). (1993). *Handbook of school-based interventions: Resolving student problems and promoting healthy educational environments*. San Francisco: Jossey-Bass.
In this book, researchers present a variety of strategies and empirically based interventions to deal with various problem behaviors (e.g., temper tantrums, annoying or bothering others, noncompliance) students may exhibit in the classroom from kindergarten through twelfth grade. Each chapter includes a description of the problem behavior by the author. Next, research-based investigations with potential value for the school setting are described. For example, five studies were presented on managing tantrums in the school setting including (a) a paradoxical intervention to reduce tantrums; (b) delayed mediated punishment to reduce tantruming; and (c) treating temper tantrums on the school bus. Finally, each author provides commentaries to assist in the practical application of the techniques. This book is considered a valuable resource for teachers, psychologists, counselors, and other school professionals who deal with a wide range of behavior problems.

Phelan, T. W. (1984). *1-2-3: Magic!* Plantation, FL: ADD Warehouse.
This easy-to-read booklet provides parents with a straightforward discipline program that enables them to manage their children, ages 2 to 12, without arguing, yelling, hitting, or tantruming. The beginning of the booklet explains normal childhood problems that can be expected. Phelan then provides parents with some basic discipline strategies before addressing specific behavior problems. In the second part of the booklet, Phelan describes to parents effective ways of handling difficult behaviors such as screaming, tantruming, and fighting. Each section also describes how parents can encourage positive behavior such as eating, cleaning rooms, and going to bed.

Repp, A. C., & Karsh, K. G. (1994). Hypothesis-based interventions for tantrum behaviors of persons with developmental disabilities in school settings. *Journal of Applied Behavior Analysis, 27,* 21–31.
This article provides an excellent demonstration of the use of functional analysis in the assessment and treatment of students who exhibit temper tantrums. The tantruming behaviors of two students with developmental disabilities during instruction and other demand conditions were the focus. Informal assessments (e.g., teacher interviews and narrative recording) suggested two competing hypotheses for the behaviors (i.e., positive and negative reinforcement). Through careful functional analytical procedures, including direct observations during ongoing classroom activities, the authors identified gaining attention (i.e., positive reinforcement), as compared to avoiding or escaping demands (i.e., negative reinforcement), as a likely function of the behaviors. Based on this hypothesis, they developed an intervention that included (a) withholding of attention for tantrums; (b) providing differential reinforcement of alternative behaviors; and (c) increasing the opportunities for social interaction between each student and the teacher and teaching assistant. Results of a multiple-baseline-across-subjects design demonstrated a substantial reduction in the percentage and frequency of tantrums for each child, with maintenance of the behavioral improvements at a one-year follow-up.

Sloane, H. N. (1979). *The good kid book: How to solve the 16 most common behavior problems*. Champaign, IL: Research Press.
This book provides parents with self-instructional chapters to decrease a variety of children's problem behaviors (e.g., tantrums, avoiding chores and homework, whining). Each chapter provides a description of the behavior and a rationale for its remediation. A specific but flexible program is presented followed by an easy, step-by-step approach for implementation. For example, Sloane presents specific procedures for helping parents deal with tantrums. Methods for both decreasing the target behavior and increasing socially appropriate behaviors are described. Reproducible sheets are available at the end of each section.

References

Amatea, E. S. (1994). Brief systemic intervention with school behavior problems: A case of temper tantrums. *Psychology in the Schools, 25,* 174–183.

American Psychiatric Association. (1994). *Diagnostic and statistical manual of mental disorders* (4th ed.). Washington, DC: Author.

Bath, H. I. (1994). Temper tantrums in group care. *Child and Youth Care Forum, 23,* 5–27.

Bhatia, M. S., Dhar, N. K., Singhal, P. K., Nigam, V. R., Malik, S. C., & Mullick, D. N. (1990). Temper tantrums: Prevalence and etiology in a non-referral outpatient setting. *Clinical Pediatrics, 29,* 311–315.

Caspi, A., Elder, G. H., & Bem, D. J. (1987). Moving against the world: Life-course patterns of explosive children. *Developmental Psychology, 23,* 308–313.

Douglas, J. (1989). *Behaviour problems in young children: Assessment and management*. New York: Tavistock/Routledge.

Durand, V. M. (1993). Functional communication training using assistive devices: Effects on challenging behavior and affect. *Augmentative and Alternative Communication, 9,* 168–176.

Durand, V. M., & Crimmins, D. (1988). Identifying the variables maintaining self-injurious behavior. *Journal of Autism and Developmental Disorders, 18,* 99–117.

Endo, G. T., Sloane, H. N., Hawkes, T. W., McLoughlin, C., & Jenson, W. R. (1991). Reducing child tantrums through self-instructional parent training materials. *School Psychology International, 12,* 95–109.

Erikson, E. H. (1950). *Childhood and society*. New York: Norton.

Gross, E. R. (1994). Nonaversive olfactory conditioning to control aggressive behaviors of a blind, hearing impaired, and noncommunicating child. *Journal of Developmental and Physical Disabilities, 9,* 77–82.

Haynes, S. N., & O'Brien, W. H. (1990). Functional analysis in behavior therapy. *Clinical Psychology Review, 10,* 649–668.

Ingersoll, B. D., & Goldstein, S. (1995). *Lonely, sad and angry: A parent's guide to depression in children and adolescents.* New York: Doubleday.

Le Couteur, A. (1993). Clinical syndromes in early childhood. In D. Black & D. Cottrell (Eds.), *Seminars in child and adolescent psychiatry* (pp. 95–98). London: Gaskell.

Lieberman, A. (1993). *The emotional life of the toddler.* New York: The Free Press.

Lewis, T. J., Scott, T. M., & Sugai, G. (1994). The Problem Behavior Questionnaire: A teacher based instrument to develop functional hypotheses of problem behavior in general education classrooms. *Diagnostique, 19,* 103–115.

Matson, J. L., Fee, V. E., Coe, D. A., & Smith, D. (1991). A social skills program for developmentally delayed preschoolers. *Journal of Clinical Child Psychology, 20,* 428–433.

Mattes, J. A. (1986). Psychopharmacology of temper outbursts: A review. *The Journal of Nervous and Mental Disease, 174,* 464–470.

Mattes, J. A., & Fink, M. (1987). A family study of patients with temper outbursts. *Journal of Psychiatric Research, 21,* 249–255.

Milan, M. A., Mitchell, Z. P., Berger, M. I. & Pierson, D. F. (1982). Positive routines: A rapid alternative to extinction for elimination of bedtime tantrum behavior. *Child Behavior Therapy, 3,* 13–25.

Needleman, R., Stevenson, J., & Zuckerman, B. (1991). Psychosocial correlates of severe temper tantrums. *Developmental and Behavioral Pediatrics, 12,* 77–83.

O'Neill, R. E., Horner, R. H., Albin, R. W., Storey, K., & Sprague, J. R. (1990). *Functional analysis: A practical assessment guide.* Brooks/Cole.

Patterson, G. R. (1976). The aggressive child: Victim and architect of a coercive system. In L. A. Hamerlynck, L. C., Handy, & E. J. Mash (Eds.), *Behavior modification and families: Vol. I. Theory and research.* New York: Brunner/Mazell.

Patterson, G. R., Reid, J. G., Jones, R. R., & Conger, R. E. (1975). *A social learning approach to family intervention.* Eugene, OR: Castalia Press.

Petty, G. L. (1976). Desensitization of parents to tantrum behavior. *The American Journal of Clinical Hypnosis, 19,* 95–97.

Prasad, M., Sitholey, P., Dutt, K., & Srivastava, R. P. (1992). ADL (Activity of Daily Living) training and treatment of temper-tantrums in a severely retarded aphasic child. *Indian Journal of Clinical Psychology, 19,* 37–39.

Ralph, A. (1987). Utilising family resources to manage tantrum behaviour: A home-based single-subject study. *Behaviour Change, 4*(4), 30–35.

Repp, A. C., & Karsh, K. G. (1994). Hypothesis-based interventions for tantrum behaviors of persons with developmental disabilities in school settings. *Journal of Applied Behavior Analysis, 27,* 21–31.

Rolider, A., & Van Houten, R. (1984a). The effects of DRO alone and DRO plus reprimands on the undesirable behavior of three children in home settings. *Education and Treatment of Children, 7,* 17–31.

Rolider, A., & Van Houten, R. (1984b). Training parents to use extinction to eliminate nighttime crying by gradually increasing the criteria for ignoring crying. *Education and Treatment of Children, 7,* 119–124.

Schaefer, C. E., & Millman, H. L. (1981). *How to help children with common problems.* New York: Van Nostrand Reinhold.

Schaefer, C. E., Millman, H. L., Sichel, S. M., & Zwilling, J. R. (1986). *Advances in therapies for children.* San Francisco: Jossey-Bass.

Swerissen, H., & Carruthers, J. (1987). The use of a physical restraint procedure to reduce a severely intellectually disabled child's tantrums. *Behaviour Change, 4*(1), 34–38.

Trieschman, A. E. (1969). Understanding the stages of a typical temper tantrum. In A. E. Trieschman, J. K. Whittaker, & L. K. Brendtro (Eds.), *The other 23 hours* (pp. 170–197). New York: Aldine.

Wahler, R. G., & Dumas, J. E. (1984). Changing the observational coding styles of insular and noninsular mothers: A step toward maintenance of parent training effects. In R. F. Dangel & R. A. Polster (Eds.), *Parent training: Foundations of research and practice* (pp. 379–416). New York: Guilford Press.

15

Bullying

George M. Batsche
University of South Florida

Background and Development

In 1993, 29% of eighth-grade students reported being threatened without a weapon and 18% reported being threatened with a weapon (National Education Goals Panel, 1994). In addition, 23% of these eighth graders reported being injured without a weapon and 9% reported being injured with a weapon. Finally, 40% of these students reported theft of their property and 31% reported vandalism of their property.

School violence traditionally has been defined as acts of assault, theft, and vandalism. Violence should, however, be defined more broadly to include any conditions or acts that create a climate in which individual students and teachers feel fear or intimidation in addition to being the victims of assault, theft, or vandalism. This latter description would include "bullying" in the definition of violence and greatly expand the discussion of violence and safety in the schools (Furlong & Morrison, 1994).

Bullying is defined as a form of aggression in which one or more students physically and/or psychologically (and more recently, sexually) harass another student repeatedly over a period of time. Typically, the action is unprovoked and the bully is perceived as stronger than the victim (Hazler, Hoover, & Oliver, 1992; Olweus, 1991).

The majority of research on bullying has been conducted in Scandinavian countries (e.g., Olweus, 1978, 1984, 1991a, 1991b), England (e.g., Boulton & Underwood, 1992; Stephenson & Smith, 1989) and Japan (e.g., Murakami, 1985). Although relatively little attention has been given to bullying in the United States, a few studies have addressed the problem (e.g., Hazler et al., 1992; Hoover, Oliver, & Hazler, 1992; Perry, Kusel, & Perry, 1988; Perry, Williard, & Perry, 1990). Olweus (1978, 1991a) reported that about 15% of school students in Norway were involved in bully/victim problems now and then. In two separate studies involving elementary and secondary students in England, Stephenson and Smith (1989) and Lane (1988) reported that approximately 23% of children and adolescents experienced bullying.

Similar results have been obtained in the United States. In a 1984 study by the National Association of Secondary School Principals, it was reported that 25% of students surveyed stated that one of their most serious concerns was fear of bullies. Perry et al. (1988) reported that about 10% of their sample of American students could be characterized as extreme victims of bullying. Plus there are the eighth-grade students cited in the opening paragraph of this chapter who experienced varying degrees of assault, theft, or vandalism. Clearly, there is a great deal of similarity across studies and countries in the percentages of students reporting experiences with bullying. A statement that 15% to 20% of all students will experience some form of bullying during their school years is certainly supported by the literature. Therefore, bullying may be the most prevalent form of violence in the schools and the form that is likely to affect the greatest number of students.

Is student victimization increasing? Olweus (1991b, 1993) suggested that bullying in Norway, occurs more frequently than it did 10 to 15 years ago and has taken on more serious forms. In a special report for the National Education Goals Panel, Johnston, O'Malley, and Bachman (1993) reported an increase, from 19% in 1980 to 25% in 1992, in the percentage of U.S. 12th graders threatened without a weapon. The majority of the increase took place between 1980 and 1985, and the figures remained quite stable during the next 7 years. Whether or not there is an increase in student victimization, the fact that one in five students is at risk for victimization is cause for serious concern and action on the part of school personnel.

Victimization by students is not limited to other students. Johnston et al. (1993) reported that 28% of public school teachers were verbally abused, 15% threatened with injury, and 3% physically attacked by students during the 1991 school year. Although teachers (and parents, for that matter) may not fit the "physically weaker" profile of the typical peer victim, bullies nonetheless will intimidate those who they believe cannot, or will not, retaliate or those whom they have been successful in bullying in the past. Many bullies come from environments where they have been successful in bullying adults for personal gain, where they have established a positive reputation with their peers, or where they have escaped an undesirable situation.

Development of a Bully

There is evidence to suggest that bullying is intergenerational and that a bully at school is often a victim at home (Floyd, 1985; Greenbaum, 1988). Bullies come from homes where parents (a) prefer physical means of discipline (authoritarian); (b) are sometimes hostile and rejecting; (c) are described as both hostile and permissive (inconsistent parenting/little supervision); (d) have poor problem-solving skills; and (e) teach their children to strike back at the least provocation (Floyd, 1985; Greenbaum, 1988; Loeber & Dishion, 1984). Olweus (1991) reported that bullies are often characterized by impulsivity, a strong need to dominate others, and scant empathy with victims. However, he found no indications that bullies are anxious or insecure or lack self-esteem. Perhaps this is the case because bullies report that they "like" being a bully and perceive their actions as justified (Greenbaum, 1988). They are reinforced for their actions through both positive-reinforcement (goal attainment) and negative-reinforcement (removal of threat) paradigms. These studies suggest that bullying may be related to control: When they are in control, bullies feel more secure and less anxious. Unfortunately, that security is at the expense of their victims. In general, bullies can be described as having aggressive behavior profiles combined with physical strength (Olweus, 1991). Aggressive boys are confident of achieving success through their aggression, are unaffected by the possibility of inflicting pain and suffering, and process information about victims in a rigid and automatic fashion (Perry et al., 1988). Bullies believe that they pick on other children because they are provoked by the victim or because they do not like the victim. In one study where bullies were asked how they feel when they bully other children, the most common responses were that they felt good/happy or that they felt mad or angry (Boulton & Underwood, 1992).

Follow-up studies of bullies do not project a positive picture. Olweus (1991) reported that approximately 60% of boys identified as bullies in Grades 6 through 9 had at least one conviction at the age of 24 and that 35% to 40% had three or more convictions. This was true of only 10% of the control group. By comparison, Olweus also noted that former *victims* had an average or below-average level of criminality in early adulthood. Eron, Huesmann, Dubow, Romanoff, and Yarnel (1987), in a sample of U.S. students, reported that bullies identified early in school had a one-in-four chance of having a criminal record by age 30.

Oliver, Hoover, and Hazler (1994) investigated the perceived roles of bullies. Most of the participants in their study (middle and high school students in small midwestern schools) agreed that bullied students were at least partly to blame for their own victimization and agreed that weakness, emotionality, and poor social skills were reasons for bullying. In this study, girls agreed that bullies attained a higher social status than victims. Finally, most participants agreed that bullying served the function of making victims tougher.

Victims

Some students are at greater risk for bullying and physical violence than others. Boys are more likely to be victims, students with lower grades are twice as likely to be victims, and victims are more likely to attend a school that provides a lesser quality of education or a school that has problems with vandalism (Metropolitan Life Insurance Company, 1994). However, students who have been victims of violent incidents are not more likely to attend urban public schools and only somewhat higher proportions are minorities (24% versus 19%).

Olweus (1978) identified two types of victims: the *passive* victim and the *provocative* victim. Passive victims are described as anxious, insecure, appearing to do nothing to provoke attacks, and appearing not to defend themselves. Provocative victims are described as hot-tempered, restless, anxious, and ones who will attempt to retaliate when attacked. Perry et al. (1988) identified victims in a similar manner, using the terms "high-aggressive" and "low-aggressive victims." However, Perry et al. found that the probability of a victim being provocative or passive was approximately equal whereas Olweus (1984) reported fewer than one in five victims as provocative.

Olweus (1978) described passive victims as lonely and abandoned at school, often without friends. They were not aggressive, did not tease, and were likely (if boys) to be physically weaker than same-age peers. Results of parent interviews suggested that these boys were sensitive at a young age and had closer contact and more positive relations with their parents (particularly their mothers) than boys in general. Teachers identified these children as *overprotected* by parents. The majority of victims believed that they were picked on because they were smaller or weaker or for no reason at all. Few believed that they provoked the bully. In addition, the vast majority of victims believed that bullies feel good, happy, brilliant, or clever when they pick on a victim (Boulton & Underwood, 1992).

Perry et al. (1988) investigated the relationship between victimization, aggression, and peer rejection. They found that aggression and victimization were orthogonal dimensions. That is, some of the most extreme victims were also some of the most aggressive children in their sample. Perry et al. (1988) suggested that victims constitute a heterogeneous group and can be categorized in the following manner: victimized/rejected, aggressive/rejected, and victimized/aggressive/rejected. The victimized/rejected child would reflect Olweus's "passive victim" profile while the victimized/aggressive/rejected would reflect the "provocative victim" profile. As Perry et al. suggested, the victimized/aggressive/rejected student might aggress against weaker children but then be victimized by stronger, aggressive peers. This would explain the fact that some of the most extreme victims in their sample were also some of the most aggressive students.

Clearly, it is necessary to understand the type of victim one is working with in order to implement successful interventions. If one views all victims as passive and weak, then strategies such as assertiveness training and presenting a stronger visual profile might be recommended. However, the provocative victims would require strategies designed to reduce aggressive behaviors (e.g., interpreting hostile bias) as well as strategies to use more assertive/less aggressive solutions to threats (Dodge, Coie, Pettit, & Price, 1990). These highly aggressive/victimized students are among the most disliked members of the peer groups and are at risk for later adjustment problems. Perry et al. (1988) cautioned that the form and seriousness of the problems associated with peer rejection may depend on the ability of school personnel to accurately identify the type of rejection that the student is experiencing.

Victimization is generally unrelated to most physical characteristics of children. In two separate studies, Olweus (1978) demonstrated that the only physical characteristic related to victimization was physical strength. No other physical characteristic was associated with victim status. Weaker children were more likely to be victims and bullies were more likely to be physically stronger (than their victims). Students who were fat, red-haired, wore glasses, spoke in an unusual dialect, dressed differently, and so forth were no more likely to be victims than other students without these characteristics.

Merton (1996) and others (Coie, 1990; Evans & Eder, 1993; Kinney, 1993) have conducted an interesting series of research studies investigating the responses to rejection by nonaggressive students. Merton concluded that rejection becomes socially "institutionalized" in junior high school students who are rejected by their peers. The rejected students had tremendous difficulty changing their status and typically required a change in school settings to do so. Hymel, Wagner, and Butler (1990) attributed this to reputational bias. The strength of the bias other students have toward rejected students is strengthened when institutional labels (e.g., nerd) are attached to these students. Coie (1990) believes that these labels not only encourage reputational bias but also satisfy the need of the social group to have students who can serve as negative examples. Merton (1996) demonstrated that re-

jected students who actively engaged in behavioral changes to modify their reputational bias were unsuccessful unless those changes were dramatic. Typically, rejected students *believed* that their status had changed even though interviews with peers did not support this view. Status changes did not occur unless the student became more like the dominant peer group *and* actively negated the labeled (nerd) identity. In order to successfully negate the labeled identity, rejected students had to engage in behavior that exceeded the expectations (conforming behavior) of the dominant peer group and was blatantly inconsistent with previous rejected-status behavior. The implications of Merton's research for the bully/victim problem are profound. First, although rejected students may believe that they have changed their behavior and their image, few peers would recognize those changes and increase levels of peer acceptance. Second, simply adding replacement behaviors (prosocial) through skills training may be insufficient to increase peer acceptance of these rejected students. Third, direct interventions with the peer group to reduce reputational bias are necessary.

Gender Differences

Boys bully and are bullied more than girls. Victims report that about 65% of bullying is perpetrated by boys, 15% by girls, and 19% by boys and girls (Boulton & Underwood, 1992). In a recent study Olweus (1991) found more than 60% of girls bullied in Grades 5 through 7 were bullied by boys only and an additional 15% to 20% were bullied by both boys and girls. More than 80% of victimized boys were bullied by boys.

The *type* of bullying also varies according to gender. Boy bullies are three to four times more likely to inflict physical assaults than girl bullies (Eron et al., 1987), whereas girls use more ridicule and teasing (Hoover et al., 1992). Olweus has labeled open attacks as *direct bullying* and social isolation and exclusion from the group as *indirect bullying*. Boys are more likely to employ direct bullying.

School Variables

Researchers in England and Scandinavian countries investigated the relationship between the rate of bullying and school size, class size, ethnic mix, and socioeconomic levels. The size of the schools ranged from 100 to 1,200 students and the class size from 18 to 31 students. Results indicated no positive relationship between the relative frequency or level of bully/victim problems and the size of the school or the size of the class (Olweus, 1991; Whitney & Smith, 1993). Nor was there a relationship between the proportion of White/non-White students and the frequency of bullying behavior. However, a significant negative correlation was found between socio-economic status of the families that the school served and the frequency of bullying in junior/middle schools (Whitney & Smith, 1993). To date, there are no studies that report similar comparisons for schools in the United States. However, the average school size, class size, and percent of students by ethnic group in the Whitney and Smith study were very similar to that of schools in the United States.

Age/Grade Trends

The percentage of students bullied decreases significantly with age and grade. The rate of decline is less during junior high and high school. Olweus (1991) reported that the average percentage of students bullied was 11.6% in Grades 2 through 6 and 5.4% in Grades 7 through 9. More than 50% of students in the lowest grades are bullied by older students whereas older students are bullied primarily by same-age peers (Boulton & Underwood, 1992; Olweus, 1991). However, it is the youngest students in a particular school setting (regardless of age) who are most at risk for being bullied. This is logical given the fact that the younger students in a building are usually physically weaker and more vulnerable than older, stronger students. There is a general decline in direct, physical bullying as age and grade increase while the relatively higher level of verbal abuse/aggression remains constant (Boulton & Underwood, 1992; Perry et al., 1988). Specifically, Perry et al. (1988) reported nearly equal victimization scores for third-grade males on the physical and verbal (15 verbal, 16 physical) Peer Nomination Inventory (PNI)—a peer rating system designed to rank students on dimensions of inappropriate behavior. However, there was a significant reduction in the physical victimization score for males in Grade 6 (15 verbal, 9 physical) on the PNI.

Problems and Implications

It is logical to assume that victims of bullying would be fearful and anxious in the environment in which the bullying took place. Victims might respond with avoidance/withdrawn/escape behaviors (skipping school, avoiding places at school, running away, suicide), more aggressive behaviors (such as bringing a weapon to school for self-defense or retaliation), and poor academic performance. It is important to remember that Perry et al. (1988) identified different *types* of victims and that the effects of bullying would differ as a function of victim type.

Avoidance and withdrawal behaviors are likely to occur in the victims of bullies. The presence of a bully at school creates a climate of fear and intimidation for the individual victims of that bully, regardless of how pervasive the problem is. Students who are chronic victims of even mild abuse are likely to view school as an unhappy setting (Gilmartin, 1987) and to avoid places within the school setting or the school completely. Data from the 1992 school year (Johnston et al., 1993) indicated that 16% of eighth graders felt unsafe at school some or most of the time and 7% of eighth graders did not go to school during the previous month because they felt unsafe at school. Even greater numbers of students take precautions while at school to ensure their own safety. Thus, 20% stay away from certain places in school, 22% stay away from certain places on school grounds, and 8% stay away from school-related events. Although not completely responsible for creating a school climate that students strive to avoid, bullying contributes to the serious problem of making school a place to be feared for many students. Effective schooling cannot occur under conditions of intimidation and fear.

In the *Violent Schools-Safe Schools* report (National Institute of Education, 1978), 56% of assault victims reported being afraid at school sometimes and 15% of attack victims reported staying home sometimes out of fear of being hurt. In addition, 29% of victims reported that they occasionally brought weapons to school when only 9% of other students did so. Nine percent of 8th graders and 10% of 10th graders reported bringing a weapon (gun, knife, or club) to school at least once in the previous month. In extreme cases, students have committed suicide as a result of bullying or have killed the bully (Greenbaum, 1988). These data support the notion that fear for one's safety in school results in skipping school, avoiding areas of school, or engaging in illegal activities (weapons at school) in significant numbers. Almost one-in-five students reported having either no, one, or two friends at school, indicating that many victims have few peer-level resources for either problem solving or support. When a condition exists in which students fear for their safety (or their lives) and feel that they have little or no peer and/or teacher support, it is not surprising that increases in school avoidance, in the number of weapons, and in both self-directed and interpersonal aggression are seen in the school setting.

Although the impact of bullying on academic performance is less well understood, it would be logical to assume that the effects of skipping school, avoiding school-related activities, and fear for one's safety would be detrimental to academic progress. There is some evidence to support this position. Hazler et al., (1992) reported that 90% of students who were bullied stated that they experienced a drop in school grades. Olweus (1978) found that male victims of bullying had somewhat lower grades than their peers. Perry et al. (1988) found a significant, negative correlation between intelligence and level of victimization for males.

Effects of Bullying on Student Perceptions of School and Schooling

Research conducted by Louis Harris and Associates for the Metropolitan Life Insurance Survey of the American Teacher (1994) found that

1. Students who reported being victims of threats and violence in school reported significantly different perceptions about school, their peers, and their teachers than students who reported not being a victim.
2. Students who experienced violence were more likely to have had other negative experiences in school, including academic failure and a belief that their school provided a lesser quality of education and that their parents had infrequent contact with the school. Of the students who had not been victims, 85% did not hold these beliefs.
3. Of students who had been victims, 34% stated that they were less respectful of other students because of the violence (compared to only 15% of students who had not been victims) and 53% said that they trusted other students.
4. The vast majority of students who had been victims of violence believed that sometimes teachers in their school thought of them as "numbers." Victims reported significantly less attention from teachers than nonvictims, were less likely to talk with teachers about the problem, and felt that teachers could not help.

Response of School Personnel to Bullying

The response of school personnel to bullying is, at best, disappointing. Results of research conducted at different times and in different countries provide a similar picture. More than 60% of the victims reported that school personnel responded poorly, responded only sometimes or never, or tried to put a stop to the bullying only once in a while or almost never (Boulton & Underwood, 1992; Hoover et al., 1992; Olweus, 1991a). It is clear that school personnel do relatively little to intervene in the bullying cycle at school. There may be a number of reasons for this.

First, Stephenson and Smith (1989) report that 25% of teachers feel that it is sometimes helpful to ignore the problem. Because bullying often occurs in the form of verbal intimidation, isolation, and exclusion, teachers may view these behaviors as less serious than physical assaults, where the damage is easily visible. Second, the social skills (skill deficits) of the victims may be such that teachers are less motivated to intervene. Third, the behavior of the victim may play an important role as well. Boulton and Underwood (1992) reported that the effect size for the correlation between reported victimization and intervention by teachers was less than the reported frequency of bullying and intervention by teachers. This suggests that the child who is bullied will get less atten-

tion from adults than the child who bullies. Interviews with victims indicate that children who do not tell do so out of fear of reprisal. If this is the case, then victims might perceive that teachers and other school personnel either will not be sympathetic to their plight or will not be able to protect them.

The majority of the research cited throughout this chapter was consistent in stating that in order for bullying to be reduced significantly, schools must send a strong message to students and staff that bullying is inappropriate. Students are quick to indict school personnel for their failure to act both to protect victims and to deal effectively with bullies (Hazler et al., 1992). Victims of bullies already believe that they are victims of their peers (the bullies). If these students also believe that they are victims of the system through the lack of protection and support by the school staff, then one can understand more clearly why students resort to avoidance and/or retaliation. It is clear that schools must promote the idea that adults will be supportive of victims and that school officials can provide a safe haven for all students while at school.

Alternative Actions

A few studies have evaluated the effects of school-based intervention programs to reduce bullying (Olweus, 1991, 1994), but most have provided only anecdotal reports and limited outcome data. School-based intervention programs must seek to integrate strategies gleaned from research on topics that include organizational change, effective parent involvement, behavioral programs for students with aggressive and/or withdrawn behavior profiles, group counseling for perpetrators and victims, and effective building-based discipline procedures. In May 1987, a "Schoolyard Bully Practicum," sponsored by the National School Safety Center, was held at Harvard University to develop a prevention program for the United States. A wide range of strategies was identified to help educators and others control and prevent bullying. It was clear that the development of a comprehensive, integrated plan that could be implemented by school buildings across the United States was necessary in order to achieve the control and prevention of bullying. Many researchers and practitioners (e.g., Coie, Underwood, & Lochman, 1991; Goldstein, 1988; Olweus, 1994) have suggested a variety of district-, building-, classroom-, and student-level interventions. Drawing largely from these interventions, what follows is a set of recommended strategies and components necessary to construct a comprehensive plan to control and prevent bullying in schools.

1. Promote facts, not myths about bullying: Bullying is a significant and pervasive problem in America's schools. Fear has become a significant factor in the school behavior of many students (15% to 20%). There is evidence that truancy, avoidance of school activities and peers, possible academic difficulties, and in extreme cases, suicide, are linked to bullying. Films and videos are available for use with students and professional staff that can facilitate the promotion of accurate information (e.g., National School Safety Center; Summerhill Productions; see references).

2. Dispel beliefs about aggressive behavior: The prevailing attitude that fighting and other forms of aggressive behavior are a normal part of growing up must be discarded. Schools must promote the belief that this type of behavior is completely unacceptable, must develop policies and programs to deal effectively and quickly with aggression, and must teach students directly about alternatives to aggression. The use of specific skill-based programs involving aggression control/replacement training (e.g., Goldstein & Glick, 1987) are recommended.

3. Conduct a school-wide assessment of bullying: Schools must determine how pervasive the bullying problem is, what the attitudes and beliefs of bullies and victims are, what the perception of students is regarding how well the school handles bullying, and what students believe should be done. Olweus (1978, 1984) developed a direct assessment device for his research and Perry et al. (1988) developed a peer-nomination procedure to assess the nature of bullying within student groups.

4. Develop a student code of conduct: Most schools have an existing code of conduct. However, students should participate in the development of the code that includes provisions to deal with bullying. The code should specify both *appropriate* and inappropriate relationships between students and students and students and faculty. The majority of school codes of conduct specify only inappropriate behaviors and do not include student involvement in their development.

5. Provide individual counseling and group skill-building services for bullies and victims: Counseling services are most effective when there is an emphasis on the development of skills to replace aggressive behaviors with more appropriate ones or to replace avoidance/withdrawn behaviors with more assertive ones. The use of group social-skills training is the intervention of choice (see Goldstein, 1988). The implementation of building-wide social skills training will facilitate the generalization of skills learned in "pull-out" (small group) training focused only on bullies and/or their victims.

6. Involve parents in the intervention process: The school usually involves the parents of the bully when disciplinary action is required, such as suspension or expulsion. Few schools routinely involve the parents of victims or the parents of bullies for purposes other than discipline. Some schools have adopted a "10 Day/10 Minute Suspension" program designed to encourage the parent's involvement in interventions for bullies. In this program, the length of the student's suspension is dependent on whether or not the parents will become involved with school personnel in an intervention program. The earlier the parents become involved, the shorter the suspension. Parents often have the same problems with their children at home that teachers have in school. Therefore, involving parents in parent education, teaching parenting and child-management skills, and linking home and school intervention programs are desirable components of a comprehensive plan.

7. Implement intervention strategies specific to aggressive children: Approaches to intervention with aggressive students and their victims fall into five general categories: behavior management; self-control strategies; social skills training; information processing; and cognitive perspective taking (Coie et al., 1991). Larson (1994) provides a critical review of intervention programs for aggressive students. How intervention programs are implemented is as important as the particular programs selected. Bullying is an interpersonal act conducted within a social setting. For that reason, interventions designed to reduce the bullying behavior and increase prosocial behavior should be implemented in a group setting and in a consistent manner. Intervention programs targeted at bully behavior should be implemented building-wide, with all school staff (instructional, administrative, support, cafeteria, custodial, bus) trained to implement preventative and intervention strategies. This building-wide strategy will facilitate generalization of both the intervention strategies and the effects of those strategies on student behavior. In addition, the building-wide program should be a multifaceted intervention process (Dubow, Huesmann, & Eron, 1987) that addresses the multiple components recommended by Coie et al. (1991).

8. Implement interventions with the peer group to facilitate changes in the peer perceptions of rejected (aggressive and nonaggressive) students who have successfully modified their behavior. Classroom-based and small-group interventions that directly teach students to make objective evaluations of peer behavior are needed. The repeated use of peer-nomination and evaluation inventories can provide both teachers and peers with concrete measures of those changes. The work of Merton (1996) makes it clear that the failure to reduce the reputational bias of peers will result in little opportunity for rejected students to succeed without a complete change in environments.

9. Build in accountability and evaluation: Teachers and students alike should be informed, on a regular basis,

of the effects of the comprehensive school-wide plan. A school-wide tracking system should document the frequency of bully/victim problems (such as behavior referrals to the office, suspensions, expulsions) and these data should be reported to teachers and students monthly. Bullies and victims should be identified and included in intervention programs on a continuing basis. Teachers and students should be encouraged to set specific goals designed to reduce the rate of aggressive behavior while increasing the rate of prosocial behavior. Unless data are routinely provided to teachers and students, the true picture of a bully problem will not emerge. When this happens, the sensitivity of the students and staff to the problem will diminish and the motivation to support intervention programs will decline. Conversely, if the students and staff do receive data on the effectiveness of the intervention programs they are implementing, then the motivation to continue these programs will increase.

members. The intervention programs implemented in the school setting (social skills training, conflict resolution, anger control training) must be coordinated and co-implemented in the home setting. Community agencies must be involved in supporting a prevention-based approach to bullying and harassment and must work with school settings to provide this message to students and their families.

Bullying begins with the attitudes an individual holds toward other people. These attitudes are developed through family values, the context of the school and community culture, and the extent to which individuals take the time to influence the behavior of those who bully and the victims of bullying. The school environment has the resources to initiate a comprehensive solution to this problem. However, if the intervention stops at the school door, then little will be done to influence the attitudes and behavior of the next generation of children and youth.

Summary

The effects of bullying contribute substantially to the development of an unsafe environment in schools and to a decline in the performance (academically and socially) of students involved in bully/victim experiences. The presence of bullying in a school indicates that the level of prosocial behavior is inadequate and respect for one another is lacking. Too many students, teachers, and parents are poorly equipped to respond to bullies. Students believe that the adults in the school environment do little to discourage bullying. In essence, bullies believe that they can use power and intimidation to control their environment where few would want to spend their day. Whether bullying occurs in the form of physical aggression, intimidation in a power struggle, sexual harassment, ridicule, or teasing, the bottom line is that bullies are unable to demonstrate appropriate interpersonal skills and their victims fear the environment they are in. Bullying is always inappropriate. The environment will change and the climate improve only when school systems choose to develop and implement a *comprehensive* plan designed to teach prosocial behavior, to limit aggressive behavior, and to teach skills that promote positive interactions between students. More importantly, however, school personnel must recognize that the problem is pervasive, that it contributes to the decline in academic and social progress of students, and that a comprehensive intervention plan must be implemented by the entire staff, throughout the school setting.

Bullying is a pervasive problem that does not recognize home, community, or school borders. Effective intervention plans for bully/victim problems must include collaboration between school personnel and family

Author Note

This chapter was based, in part, on the article "Bullies and Their Victims: Understanding a Pervasive Problem in the Schools" by G. Batsche and H. Knoff which appeared in *The School Psychology Review*.

Recommended References

Garrity, C., Jens, K., Porter, W., Sager, N., & Short-Camilli, C. (1994). *Bully-proofing your school.* Longmont, CO: Sopris West.
This workbook presents steps for the development of a comprehensive approach to identifying and intervening with bullies. The curriculum includes steps for the adoption of a school-wide program, a staff training curriculum, student instruction, victim support, and parent collaboration.

Goldstein, A. P., Palumbo, J., Striepling, S., & Voutsinas, A. M. (1995). *Break it up.* Champaign, IL: Research Press.
This publication provides step-by-step procedures for safely handling student disruptiveness and aggression as well as student fights. The comprehensive fight management system detailed in this publication is demonstrated in the videotape, also available from Research Press.

Goldstein, A. P. (1988). *The prepare curriculum.* Champaign, IL: Research Press.
The **Prepare Curriculum** *is a series of coordinated psycho-educational courses explicitly designed to teach an array of prosocial competencies to aggressive, antisocial youth as well as to those who are withdrawn and isolated (victims).*

Larson, J. (1994). Violence prevention in the schools: A review of selected programs and procedures. *School Psychology Review, 23,* 151–164.
This article reviews selected commercially published and research literature curricula and procedures available for violence prevention in the school setting. The article focuses on those programs considered to have potential for effective outcomes. Curricula are selected that must be implemented as part of a multidimensional program.

Olweus, D. (1993). *Bullying at school: What we know and what we can do.* Cambridge, MA: Blackwell.
This book is an excellent resource guide for those individuals interested in knowing basic information about bullies and victims. The book contains special sections on intervention programs at the building, class, and individual levels. In addition, a section on practical advice provides intervention ideas for less structured settings (e.g., recess, lunch) and for working with parents.

References

Boulton, J. J., & Underwood, K. (1992). Bully/victim problems among middle school children. *British Journal of Educational Psychology, 62,* 73–87.

Coie, J. D. (1990). Toward a theory of peer rejection. In S. R. Asher & J. D. Coie (Eds.), *Peer rejection in childhood* (pp. 365–401). New York: Cambridge University Press.

Coie, J. D., Underwood, M., & Lochman, J. E. (1991). Programmatic intervention with aggressive children in the school setting. In I. Rubin & D. Pepler (Eds.), *The development and treatment of childhood aggression* (pp. 389–410). Hillsdale, NJ: Erlbaum.

Dodge, K. A., Coie, J. D., Pettit, G. S., & Price, J. M. (1990). Peer status and aggression in boys' groups: Developmental and contextual analyses. *Child Development, 61,* 1289–1309.

Dubow, E. F., Huesmann, L. R., & Eron, L. D. (1987). Mitigating aggression and promoting prosocial behavior in aggressive elementary schoolboys. *Behavior Research and Therapy, 25,* 527–531.

Eron, L. D., Huesmann, R. L., Dubow, E., Romanoff, R., & Yarmel, P. W. (1987). Childhood aggression and its correlates over 22 years. In *Childhood aggression and violence.* New York: Plenum.

Evans, C., & Eder, D. (1993). "No exit": Processes of social isolation in the middle school. *Journal of Contemporary Ethnography, 22,* 139–170.

Floyd, N. M. (1985). "Pick on somebody your own size!" Controlling victimization. *The Pointer, 29,* 9–17.

Furlong, M. J., & Morrison, G. M. (1994). Introduction to miniseries: School violence and safety in perspective. *School Psychology Review, 23,* 139–150.

Gilmartin, B. G. (1987). Peer group antecedents of severe love-shyness in males. *Journal of Personality, 55,* 467–489.

Goldstein, A. P. (1988). *The prepare curriculum.* Champaign, IL: Research Press.

Goldstein, A. P., & Glick, B. (1987). *Aggression replacement training.* Champaign, IL: Research Press.

Goldstein, A. P., Sprafkin, R. P., Gershaw, J. J., & Klein, P. (1980). *Skillstreaming the adolescent.* Champaign, IL: Research Press.

Greenbaum, S. (1987, November). What can we do about schoolyard bullying? *Principal,* 21–24.

Greenbaum, S. (1988). School bully and victimization. (Resource Paper). Malibu, CA: National School Safety Center.

Guetzloe, E. (1992). Violent, aggressive, and antisocial students: What are we going to do with them? *Preventing School Failure, 36,* 4–9.

Hazler, R. J., Hoover, J. H., & Oliver, R. (1992, November). What kids say about bullying. *The Executive Educator,* 20–22.

Hoover, J., & Hazler, R. J. (1991). Bullies and victims. *Elementary School Guidance and Counseling, 25,* 212–219.

Hoover, J. H., Oliver, R., & Hazler, R. J. (1992). Bullying: Perceptions of adolescent victims in the midwestern USA. *School Psychology International, 13,* 5–16.

Johnston, L. D., O'Malley, P. M., & Bachman, J. G. (1993). *Monitoring the future study for goal 6 of the national education goals: A special report for the National Education Goals Panel.* Ann Arbor: University of Michigan's Institute for Social Research.

Kinney, D. A. (1993). From nerds to normals: The recovery of identity among adolescents from middle school to high school. *Sociology of Education, 66,* 21–40.

Lane, D. A. (1989). Bullying in school: The need for a integrated approach. *School Psychology International, 10,* 211–215.

Larson, J. (1994). Violence prevention in the schools: A review of selected programs and procedures. *School Psychology Review, 23,* 151–164.

Loeber, R., & Dishion, T. J. (1984). Boys who fight at home and school: Family conditions influencing cross-setting consistency. *Journal of Consulting and Clinical Psychology, 52,* 759–768.

McGinnis, E., & Goldstein, A. P. (1984). *Skillstreaming the elementary school child.* Champaign, IL: Research Press.

Merton, D. E. (1996). Visibility and vulnerability: Responses to rejection by nonaggressive junior high school boys. *Journal of Early Adolescence, 16,* 5–26.

Metropolitan Life Insurance Company. (1994). *The American teacher 1994.* New York: Author.

Murakami, Y. (1985). Bullies in the classroom. *Japan Quarterly, 32,* 407–409.

National Education Goals Panel. (1993). *The national education goals report: Volume one.* Washington, DC: U.S. Government Printing Office.

National Education Goals Panel. (1994). *National education goals report.* Washington, DC: Author.

National Institute of Education. (1978). *Violent schools-safe schools.* Washington, DC: U.S. Department of Health, Education and Welfare.

Oliver, R., Hoover, J. H., & Hazler, R. (1994). The perceived roles of bullying in small-town midwestern schools. *Journal of Counseling and Development, 72,* 416–420.

Olweus, D. (1978). *Aggression in the schools: Bullies and whipping boys.* New York: Wiley.

Olweus, D. (1984). Aggressors and their victims: Bullying at school. In N. Frude & H. Gault (Eds.), *Disruptive behavior disorders in schools* (pp. 57–76). New York: Wiley.

Olweus, D. (1991a). Bully/victim problems among school children: Basic facts and effects of a school based intervention program. In I. Rubin & D. Pepler (Eds.), *The development and treatment of childhood aggression* (pp. 411–447). Hillsdale, NJ: Erlbaum.

Olweus, D. (1991b). Victimization among school children. In R. Baenninger (Ed.), *Targets of violence and aggression.* Holland: Elsevier Science Publishers.

Olweus, D. (1993). *Bullying at school: What we know and what we can do.* Cambridge, MA: Blackwell Publishers.

Olweus, D. (1994). Annotation: Bullying at school: Basic facts and effects of a school-based intervention program. *Journal of Child Psychology and Psychiatry and Allied Disciplines, 35,* 1171–1190.

Perry, D. G., Kusel, S. J., & Perry, L. C. (1988). Victims of peer aggression. *Developmental Psychology, 24,* 807–814.

Perry, D. G., Williard, J. C., & Perry, L. C. (1990). Peers' perceptions of the consequences that victimized children provide aggressors. *Child Development, 61,* 1310–1325.

Stephenson, P., & Smith, D. (1989). Bullying in the junior school. In D. P. Tattum & D. A. Lane (Eds.), *Bullying in schools* (pp. 45–57). Stoke-on-Trent, England: Trentham Books.

Whitney, I., & Smith, P. K. (1993). A survey of the nature and extent of bullying in junior/middle and secondary schools. *Educational Research, 35,* 3–25.

16

Lying

Jan N. Hughes
Archna Prasad-Gaur

Texas A&M University

Background and Development

In its broadest sense, a lie refers to a nonaccidental false statement. However, not all forms of lying serve the same function or have the same developmental and psychological significance. *Antisocial lying,* the primary focus of this chapter, is defined as a deliberate attempt to deceive another person in order to avoid blame, obtain a reward, avoid an obligation, or inflict harm. Thus, antisocial lying serves hedonistic or malicious motivations. Antisocial lying is often associated with other behaviors that violate societal norms or rules and may be either a precursor to or a manifestation of conduct disorder (Loeber et al., 1993). Examples of antisocial lies include the following:

- A girl accidently breaks a vase; her mother asks how the vase broke, and the girl replies, "I don't know."
- A boy falsely tells his mother that he has finished his homework.
- A girl tells a classmate that another classmate is spreading unkind rumors about her, in hopes of starting a fight between the two classmates; the accusation, however, is false.

A second form of lying, referred to as *defensive lying,* is motivated by the desire to protect oneself from threats to one's sense of felt security and self-worth (Hughes & Baker, 1990). Examples include the following:

- An eight-year-old girl whose neglectful mother abandoned her to the care of an aunt tells classmates that her mother is on a business trip and is going to bring her lots of presents when she returns.
- A 10-year-old boy says that he is one of the most popular children in his class; however, he is actively rejected by his peers.
- A six-year-old girl denies pinching her baby brother, even when confronted with overwhelming evidence that she did, indeed, pinch him. Because the pain and discomfort that acknowledging the behavior would

produce cannot be tolerated, she excludes this information from consciousness.

In each of these examples, the child's lie is motivated by the desire to protect the self from heavily negatively laden information that threatens the child's self-concept and sense of security. In the first two examples, the child is unable to acknowledge his or her rejection by others. In the third example, the child is unable to acknowledge her aggressive impulses. Because denial operates at an unconscious level, there is no conscious attempt to deceive another.

Although the focus of this chapter is on antisocial lying, defensive lying is also discussed. Excluded from consideration in this chapter are *prosocial falsehoods,* or white lies. Prosocial falsehoods are motivated by positive social motives, such as avoiding hurting another's feelings, entertaining another, and helping another. Also excluded from consideration are false statements that reflect a child's inability to distinguish reality from fantasy. For example, a boy says that two girls followed him all day at school, staring at him constantly and whispering about him. The boy believes this assertion, even though no one followed him all day.

Incidence

Lying is a common behavior. In a study on developmental changes in conceptions of lying, Peterson, Peterson, and Seeto (1983) found that adults and all children 11 years of age and older admit to lying at least some of the time (although the type of lie was not ascertained). Because everyone lies at some time, the frequency, nature, and severity of the consequences of lying are important considerations in defining lying as a problem behavior. In her review of seven studies on the prevalence of lying in normal children ages 4 to 16 years, Stouthamer-Loeber (1986) reported a prevalence rate of 19.4% for parent reports and 14.4% for teacher reports, after averaging over all subjects in the different studies, leaving out prevalence rates for frequent or chronic lying. The prevalence rate for frequent or chronic lying was 3%, as reported by parents or teachers, and retrospective self-reports of chronic lying was at a fair higher rate (15%-23%). Because these prevalence data are based on raters' definitions of "often," "sometimes," and "rarely," the criteria or exact frequencies that determine these ratings cannot be ascertained.

Regarding consequences, lying is regarded as a problem behavior when it interferes with the development and maintenance of satisfying interpersonal relationships. This criterion for determining when lying is a problem recognizes that lying is an interpersonal behavior that tends to destroy the trust essential to satisfying relationships with others. A second criterion is whether lying occurs as part of a constellation of antisocial behaviors. As discussed later, when lying is one of several behaviors that warrant a diagnosis of conduct disorder, the child requires a broad-based intervention addressing the multiple causes of disruptive and antisocial behaviors.

There are no reliable data on sex differences in antisocial lying. Although moral reasoning and moral behavior are not the same, researchers investigating sex differences in moral reasoning relative to lying and stealing found no sex differences (Peisach & Hardeman, 1983). Stouthamer-Loeber (1986) reported prevalence rates for lying among girls about one third lower than those among boys. However, she attributed the differences to rating biases. In a study of sixth graders, Bear (1989) found that boys and girls reported similar levels of covert aggressive behaviors (i.e., stealing, lying, and cheating), although boys reported much higher levels of physically and verbally aggressive behaviors (see Conduct Disorders, this volume).

Developmental Considerations

No significant age differences in antisocial lying among children ages 4 to 18 years were reported in a study conducted by Achenbach and Edelbrock (1981). However, the reasons for lying and types of lies probably differ at different ages. For example, first- and second-grade children may lie to avoid punishment, whereas adolescents may lie to protect a friend from detection or to fit in with a peer group. Furthermore, older children and adolescents are probably more likely to justify their lying on the basis of moral principles (Blasi, 1980).

Because honesty is a moral behavior, theories of moral development are relevant to the development of lying. Several researchers have investigated the relationship between stages of moral reasoning and moral behavior (for review see Blasi, 1980). Kohlberg (1969) formulated a series of three broad levels of moral development, subdivided into six stages. At the first level, that of preconventional morality, there is no internalization of moral standards. Moral acts are judged on the basis of their consequences. "You should not lie because

you would be punished" is an example of Level 1 moral reasoning. At Level 2, the conventional level, ethical standards are internalized and judgments of right and wrong are based on the approval or disapproval of others rather than on the physical consequences of the behavior. "You should not lie because other people will not trust you" is an example of Level 2 reasoning. At Level 3, moral judgments are based on a rational and internalized ethical code and are relatively independent of approval or negative sanction from others: "You should not lie because a society in which people trust each other benefits all members of the society." Although the ages at which individuals attain each stage vary, Kohlberg believed that individuals progress through the stages in an invariant order and that a child's cognitive abilities determine the stage of moral development (see Moral Reasoning and Behavior, this volume).

Applying Kohlberg's theory of moral development, researchers consistently find significant differences between antisocial and non-antisocial youth in stages of moral reasoning (Blasi, 1980). Furthermore, children's level of moral reasoning predicts their level of conduct problems in the classroom. Specifically, children who reason at a conventional level (which recognizes that group interests, rules, and expectations are more important than the instrumental desires of the individual) are less disruptive in the classroom and more socially competent and engage in more prosocial behaviors (Bear & Richards, 1981; Bear & Rys, 1994). However, specific associations between stages of moral reasoning and lying have not been established.

Problems and Implications

Role of Antisocial Lying in Other Childhood Problems

Lying is associated with several childhood problems, including poor peer relationships, conduct disorders, and disturbed parent-child relationships. Stouthamer-Loeber (1986) found an average prevalence rate of lying among clinical populations of 49%, or 2 1/2 times greater than that in normal samples. In addition, a lower-than-normal rate for lying was indicated in children with a diagnosis of neurotic problems and a higher-than-normal rate in children with a diagnosis of conduct problems. Thus, viewing lying as part of a constellation of behaviors is more useful than viewing lying as an isolated behavior problem.

Lying and peer relationships

Trust is an essential characteristic of friendship, especially in later childhood and adolescence. Thus, the child who lies will have difficulty being accepted by peers and developing close friendships. In turn, satisfactory peer relationships are very important to a child's behavioral adjustment and learning. It is well established that children who are rejected by their peers achieve less well in school and are more likely to experience a wide range of adjustment difficulties in later adolescence (see Peer Relations, this volume).

The finding that rejected-aggressive children develop internalizing problems in adolescence may be due to the adolescent's greater awareness of his or her social acceptance. Whereas younger aggressive and rejected children overestimate their level of peer acceptance (Patterson, Kupersmidt, & Griesler, 1990), adolescents accurately perceive their low level of acceptance and, consequently, experience higher levels of depression.

Lying and conduct disorders

According to the *Diagnostic and Statistical Manual, Fourth Edition* (American Psychiatric Association, 1994), lying is one of the criteria for a diagnosis of conduct disorder. The conduct-disordered child or adolescent violates societal norms of conduct by persistently engaging in behavior in which the basic rights of others, societal norms, or rules are violated. A diagnosis of conduct disorder requires that the individual manifest at least 3 of 15 criteria in the past 12 months, with at least one criterion present in the past 6 months. These 15 criteria are grouped into four categories of antisocial behavior: aggression to people and animals, destruction of property, deceitfulness or theft, and serious violation of rules. The criterion "often lies to obtain goods or favors or to avoid obligations" is one of three criteria within the "Deceitfulness or theft" grouping.

When lying is included as an item on behavior rating scales, it is invariably included in a delinquent, conduct problem, or antisocial scale, such as the Delinquency scale of the Child Behavior Checklist (Achenbach & Edelbrock, 1991; Reynolds & Kamphaus, 1992). Loeber and Schmaling (1985) subjected data from 28 factor and cluster analytic studies on child psychopathology to a multidimensional scaling analysis in order to empirically determine the dimensions of antisocial behavior. The analysis yielded one dimension with two poles: overt or confrontative behaviors and covert or concealing behaviors. Lying falls on the covert side and is related to behaviors such as theft, truancy, and drug use. This distinction between overt and covert antisocial behavior has been replicated by other researchers (Achenbach, 1993).

Conduct disorders are highly stable from early childhood into adulthood (Loeber et al., 1993; Robins, 1979). Children under the age of 11 who exhibit antisocial behaviors are likely to continue their antisocial behaviors into adulthood. Children who exhibit this early-onset pathway to antisocial behavior progress from oppositional and defiant behaviors in early childhood to early

symptoms of conduct disorder (e.g., lying, fighting, petty stealing) to serious property crimes and interpersonal violence in adolescence and adulthood (Hinshaw, Lahey, & Hart, 1993). Furthermore, youth with early-onset conduct disorder are markedly more aggressive than those whose conduct problems begin in adolescence (Hinshaw, Lahey, & Hart, 1993).

Researchers have identified three pathways to delinquency: (a) an early authority conflict pathway, consisting of early manifestation of stubborn behavior, defiance, and authority avoidance; (b) a covert pathway, consisting of lying and other covert behaviors, property damage, and moderate to serious forms of delinquency; and (c) an overt pathway, consisting of aggression, fighting, and violence (Loeber et al., 1993). In a longitudinal study using both retrospective and prospective methods with a sample of community boys, Loeber and his colleagues reported that the majority of boys displaying behavioral characteristics of one pathway also display behavioral characteristics of other pathways. However, whereas approximately one-third of the boys who fit the covert pathway had not shown an onset of behaviors characteristic of the overt pathway, fewer than 10% of boys who fit the overt pathway had not shown an onset of behaviors characteristic of the covert pathway. Thus, escalations in overt behaviors are more predictive of escalations in covert behaviors than escalations in covert behaviors are predictive of escalations in overt behaviors. Importantly, boys in the triple pathways and in a dual pathway that includes the covert pathway (i.e., covert-overt and covert-authority conflict pathways) were most likely to have a petition filed in the juvenile court for a violent offense. These data underscore the importance of examining lying within the context of developmental pathways to delinquency. When lying is part of a combination of covert aggression and either overt aggression or authority conflict, the child is at greatest risk for delinquency, which itself is associated with adult criminality and substance abuse.

When lying is part of a pattern of antisocial, rule-violating behavior, it requires a broad-based approach to assessment and to intervention. A broad-based approach is required because conduct disorders are the result of multiple and interactive causes and because single-focused interventions have been found to be ineffective in altering the negative developmental trajectory of children exhibiting high levels of physical and covert aggression (Hughes & Cavell, 1995). Among the factors contributing to conduct disorders are home and parenting factors (e.g., harsh and inconsistent parenting, low parental monitoring, low maternal warmth and acceptance, marital discord, parent criminality), school factors (school failure, school norms), community factors (high levels of neighborhood violence, few recreational facilities, poverty, media violence), child factors (temperament and intelligence), and peer group factors (association with antisocial peers) (Hughes & Cavell, 1995; Patterson, Reid, & Dishion, 1992).

Defensive Lying

Children may use denial to cope with potentially threatening information. Defensive exclusion refers to the unconscious denial of negative self-reference information (Bowlby, 1980). The child who has a fragile self-concept, perhaps resulting from an insecure attachment relationship, is unable to tolerate the stress associated with negative information about the self. Thus, the child is unable to admit to imperfections, rigidly adhering to a globally positive but distorted view of self (Cassidy, 1988). This child may falsely state the he or she is good at school work, has many friends, and does not receive much punishment from his or her parents. These statements do not reflect an intent to deceive others so much as an attempt to defend the self against overwhelming negative feelings associated with acknowledgement of one's limitations and vulnerabilities.

Aggressive and rejected children, as well as maltreated children, are especially likely to have difficulty accurately processing negative self-relevant information (Cassidy, 1988; Hughes, Cavell, & Grossman, 1995; Patterson, Cohn, & Kao, 1989). These children's denial of negative self-relevant information is best understood in the context of the attachment theory (Bowlby, 1980). Theoretically, children who receive consistently sensitive and responsive care can tolerate some negative or harsh behavior on the part of the parent without threatening the self-system (or internal working model of attachment; Main, Kaplan, & Cassidy, 1985). Eventually, secure children integrate negative or conflicting information about the parent or self into the self-system. If a child experiences harsh, rejecting parenting or otherwise inadequate parenting on a consistent basis, threats to maintaining the positive aspects of the self-system may be intolerable. At this point the process of defensive exclusion, either ignoring or denying negative self-relevant information, may shore up the weakened self-system, allowing the child to maintain an essentially positive, if inaccurate, model of self and others.

Idealized perceptions of self and others require denial of imperfections in the self and of conflict in relationships. In the attachment literature, idealization of the self is characteristic of avoidant persons (see Main et al., 1985). Insensitive and harsh parenting in early life leads to defenses that entail some sort of cognitive and affective distortion in an attempt to suppress an otherwise overwhelming negative emotion. Main's work with insecure infants suggests that one defense against negative emotions in the attachment relationship is "splitting," in which negative affects are disconnected from their cognitive appraisal in an attempt to ignore the emotional conflict and its associated distress. The infant attempts to manage the conflicted emotional relationships through such avoidance strategies as gaze aversion (Lewis, 1993).

Aggressive and rejected children's denial of negative self-relevant information may be akin to this splitting of affective experience and cognitive appraisals characteristic of avoidant infants. Cassidy (1988) found that 6-year-old children classified as insecure/avoidant on the basis of a reunion episode were unable to admit imperfections and insisted they were perfect in every way on two interview measures of self-esteem. In contrast, secure children evidenced a generally positive self-view but admitted to personal flaws. In general, secure children perceived themselves as being accepted despite flaws. Hughes et al. (1995) found that aggressive children in Grades 2 and 3 were more likely than average children to report higher levels of maternal acceptance. Furthermore, their reports of support from peers were no different from reports of average children, despite the fact that they were much less well-accepted by peers. Of special interest is the finding that, among aggressive children, a tendency to inflate perceptions of competence and support from others was related to higher levels of externalizing problems.

The self-system is an internal model of self and others that encompasses expectations, attitudes, and affects regarding one's self, others, and the interactions between the two (Sroufe, 1990). As children increase in age, their self-systems become more complex and differentiated (Harter, 1986). However, aggressive and rejected children's reliance on distorted processing of negative self-relevant information may interfere with the development of more mature models of self and others. McKeough, Yates, and Marini (1994) found that the cognitive complexity of aggressive children's understanding of social relationships both lagged behind that of average children and was qualitatively different. McKeough et al. proposed that defensive processes, primarily denial and idealization, interfered with aggressive children's integration and organization of social information and contributed both to their slower rate of social reasoning and to qualitative differences in their models of social interaction.

Alternative Actions: Assessment

When a teacher or parent asks for help regarding a child's lying, the psychologist must conduct an assessment of the lying behavior as well as an assessment of the child's overall functioning. The assessment of the lying behavior establishes the parameters of the lying, its frequency, and associated antecedents and consequences. The assessment of the child's overall functioning determines whether the child's lying is best understood as a precursor or manifestation of conduct disorder, peer rejection, a disturbed parent-child relationship, or other problem. Alternatively, lying may reflect the psychological defense of denial.

Assessment of Lying Behavior

What behaviors does the referring adult classify as lying? What is the content and context of the child's lying? How frequently does the child lie? Is lying a recent or a long-standing problem? In an interview with the referring adult(s), the psychologist asks for specific examples of the referred child's lying behavior. By analyzing the context of the child's lies and environmental antecedents and consequences, the psychologist and teacher or parent formulate hypotheses about the child's motivations. Is the child avoiding punishment? Is the child attempting to harm another or to gain some advantage? Such antisocial motives are indicative of antisocial lying. On the other hand, the child's lies may reflect a psychological defense against potentially threatening information or an attempt to gain acceptance from the peer group.

There are very real problems in obtaining an accurate count of lying. Lying is difficult to observe; a child may be a skilled liar and only gets caught on occasion. Nevertheless, an estimate of the frequency of lying helps the psychologist determine the seriousness of the problem and serves as an important baseline against which to evaluate improvement following the intervention. The psychologist asks the referring adult to maintain a written record of the child's lying for a period of 7 to 14 days. The definition of lying arrived at in the interview serves as the operational definition. If possible, both the child's parents and teachers record instances of lying in order to determine the specifics of the behavior. Because the adults will not be able to judge, with complete confidence, whether an assertion made by the child is true or false, they record all assertions they have just reason to believe are false. When possible, the adults should attempt to determine the veracity of the child's suspected lie. For example, a teacher can contact the parent to check out the child's assertion that he was unable to complete his homework due to a family emergency. When lying is part of covering up for stealing, intervention should focus on stealing (see Stealing, this volume).

It may be helpful to conduct a functional analysis of the lying, in order to determine the situations associated with lying and the consequences that follow lying. For each reported or suspected lie, the observer records the following information: the actual content of the lie, antecedent events, and consequent events. Antecedent events refer to all the characteristics of the situation that obtained just before the lie occurred and the person to whom the lie was directed. Consequent events are simply whatever happened just after the lie occurred. Examples of antecedent events include bragging by another child, criticism of the target child, or an unstructured play situation. Examples of consequent events include someone

calls the child a liar; the child avoids punishment; or another child is unjustly blamed. A notepad with three columns marked off facilitates the record keeping. In the center column, the observer writes the child's suspected false assertion, and antecedents and consequences are recorded in the left and right columns, respectively. The results of the functional analysis may be used to identify motivations as well as unintended rewards for lying.

What Other Problems Does the Child Have?

It is important to determine if lying is part of other childhood problems such as peer rejection, conduct problems, or a disturbed parent-child relationship. Several behavioral rating scales and checklists are useful in assessing a child's overall behavioral problems and social competencies. For example, the Behavior Assessment System for Children (Reynolds & Kamphaus, 1992) and the Child Behavior Checklist (Achenbach & Edelbrock, 1991) have good reliability and evidence of validity. By taking a broad view of the child's behavior problems as well as areas of strength, the lying can be put into perspective. When lying is part of a pattern of antisocial behavior, the assessment and the intervention should target the broader class of conduct problems rather than only lying. When the lying is part of peer rejection, an assessment of the child's social competencies through behavioral observations, teacher ratings, or peer ratings is appropriate.

When lying is part of pattern of antisocial behavior, the assessment should include an assessment of the multiple factors associated with the development of conduct problems in children. These factors include biological, family, parenting, peer, academic, school, and community factors (Hughes & Cavell, 1995). For example, children with a diagnosis of Attention Deficit/Hyperactivity Disorder (ADHD) are likely to exhibit conduct problems. A general deficit in self-regulation may contribute to the ADHD child's lying.

Among family factors to assess are the parents' effectiveness as disciplinarians, their reliance on overly punitive forms of discipline, the extent to which they provide emotional acceptance to their child, their level of involvement and monitoring, and the level of family stress. The Parenting Stress Index (Abidin, 1983) is a reliable and valid measure of parents' views of the child as well as sources of family stress. Some families view lying and other antisocial behavior as justified due to perceived mistreatment by society and a sense of alienation from mainstream society. In this case, lying to "outsiders" may constitute part of a deviant lifestyle that may be valued by the child's extended family. Similarly, the level of peer and community support for antisocial behavior and attitudes should be assessed. If the child associates with antisocial peers, it is likely that rule-breaking behavior receives peer support. The level of violence in the school and community should also be considered. Chapters in this volume on stealing and conduct disorders discuss assessment practices relevant to assessment of lying when lying is part of a pattern of antisocial behavior.

Lying may reflect deficiencies in social and moral reasoning. Aggressive and rejected children, compared to nondeviant peers, exhibit poor perspective-taking ability, under-attention to relevant social cues, selective attention to hostile cues, a tendency to infer hostile intent to others in ambiguous situation, a reliance on ineffective and aggressive solutions to interpersonal conflict, belief that aggression results in positive consequences for the aggressor, and a lack of empathy for the victim of aggression (see Crick & Dodge, 1994; Hughes & Cavell, 1995). These social-information processes can be assessed through semistructured interviewing procedures based on vignettes (Guerra & Slaby, 1989; Hughes & Baker, 1990), in which the child is presented with a situation involving some provocation and asked a series of questions that elicit the child's attributions, likely behavioral response, and beliefs about the effectiveness of both antisocial and socially competent responses.

A child's reasoning about lying should also be assessed. The child may believe that lying is justified when one's needs have been thwarted by another or when the person lied to is an "outsider" versus a member of the child's social network. A child may be unaware or unperturbed by the effect of lying on another person or may expect that "everyone lies, so it is okay." A child may be unaware of the long-term consequences of lying in terms of further isolation from peers and loss of potential sources of support from adults (e.g., teachers, friends).

Integrating Assessment Data into a Case Conceptualization: Two Examples

Case 1

Phillip, age 10, was referred to the school psychologist by his classroom teacher for excessive lying. In the initial interview, the teacher recounted several of Phillip's recent lies, including claims of having given a crippled child a ticket to Disneyland that he had won, having a pet tiger when he was younger, having raised $1,000 for the American Red Cross in a marathon jump rope context, and having lived in a mansion in Virginia before a flood washed it away. The teacher agreed to record Phillip's lying behavior, using the three-column technique, for seven school days. The teacher recorded an average of two lies a day. The lies were told to the entire class, usually during social studies, when class discussions were common. The lies often involved material possessions or outstanding accomplishments. Other children argued with Phillip, trying to prove that he was lying, but Phillip stuck to his assertions. His measured intelligence was average, and he earned grades of "B" and "C." On a so-

ciometric questionnaire, Phillip received no best friend nominations, but he chose two of the most popular boys in class as his best friends. The teacher reports that other children ignore Phillip or actively exclude him from their play. Phillip's attempts to enter play groups are awkward and ineffective. He tends to dominate and monopolize the play equipment. Phillip rarely gives compliments, shares, or offers help to classmates. In response to actual or perceived rejection from classmates, he becomes verbally or physically aggressive or complains to the teacher. On a self-report questionnaire, Phillip described himself as lonely and unpopular with his classmates.

Phillip, a single child, lives with his parents in a lower-middle-income neighborhood, similar to that of most children attending Phillip's school. His parents are concerned about his lying, but they blame the lying on other children who pick on Phillip and do not accept him. Phillip's parents are in their mid-50s, and they report being overwhelmed by the demands of an active boy and not engaging in many shared family recreational activities.

On the basis of this assessment, the psychologist believed that Phillip's lying was a problem because it occurred frequently and interfered with his peer acceptance. His lying appeared to be motivated by his desire to be accepted by his classmates. He lacked social skills for relating positively with peers, and he had a poor self-concept. Thus, the intervention for Phillip should include social skills training along the lines of Lochman and Curry's (1986) anger coping program (see Anger Control, this volume). The teacher should attempt to minimize the disruption caused by Phillip's lies by moving the discussion on rather than allowing students to argue with Phillip. Additionally, Phillip might benefit from brief individual counseling that would increase his awareness of the long-term consequences of his lying (i.e., increased peer rejection) and provide him with an additional source of adult support and acceptance so that his need to lie to gain a sense of importance is lessened.

Case 2

Heather, a 12-year-old girl, was referred to the psychologist by her parents for lying. Example lies included saying she did not phone the emergency 911 number after calling it three times, spilling honey and then blaming it on her sister, and telling her parents she made a "B" on a spelling test so that she could stay up late to watch a TV program. The psychologist called a meeting with the parents and the teacher for the purpose of determining whether Heather also lied at school, as well as to assess Heather's overall school functioning. The teacher said that Heather had made up some highly unlikely excuses for not turning in her homework. It was also discovered during the meeting that Heather had told lies that the teacher had not detected. Although her parents did not allow her to wear makeup to school, Heather wore a great deal of it at school, especially eye makeup. When the teacher asked her what her mother thought about her wearing so much makeup, Heather had responded that her mother did not mind. She was putting the makeup on when she got to school and washing it off before going home. Heather also had signed her mother's name to a note excusing her from dressing out for P.E.

Heather's teacher and parents agreed to record instances of Heather's lying for 2 weeks, and they agreed to communicate with each other two or three times a week to verify information that Heather had given one of them. The teacher detected five lies, four involving untrue reasons for not doing homework and one involving reasons for being tardy to class. The parents recorded 10 lies at home, all of which involved avoiding blame or getting out of some obligation. Additionally, Heather had been found with a cassette recorder she said she borrowed from a friend, when she actually had stolen it from the library.

Heather is popular with a small group of girls who tend to be "trouble makers" at school. She is a "C" student, but her aptitude test scores indicate that she is underachieving. On the teacher version of the Child Behavior Checklist (Achenbach & Edelbrock, 1991) her teacher endorsed a large number of items reflecting the externalizing syndrome, particularly within the aggression scale (argues, disobeys at school, lies and cheats, is stubborn).

Heather's parents are critical of her and tend to rely primarily on punitive discipline techniques. Relatively minor behavior infractions result in significant punishment, including spanking and being grounded for several weeks. On the parent version of the Child Behavior Checklist, Heather obtained elevated scores on the Aggression and Delinquency scales. Heather is one of four siblings, and high levels of family conflict characterize the family environment.

Based on this assessment, the psychologist hypothesized that Heather's lying was part of a pattern of child defiance against parental authority and of covert aggression. Thus, Heather exhibits characteristics of both the covert and authority conflict pathways to delinquency. The recommended intervention included parent training that incorporates both control skills and acceptance of the child, such as the Parent and Child Series (Webster-Stratton, 1990) and involvement in peer group activities with prosocial peers. Specifically, Heather's parents agreed to enroll her in soccer, a sport in which she could excel and which would increase her time spent with prosocial peers. Heather was assigned a college student "mentor" who provided an additional source of acceptance and a positive role model.

Alternative Actions: Interventions

In applied behavior analysis, specific target behaviors are identified, and principles of learning are applied to their modification. The concept of target behaviors in behavior therapy has been criticized on the grounds that it encourages a simplistic, static, and monosymptomatic view of client difficulties (Mash & Terdal, 1988). The target behavior metaphor has particular problems when applied to a complaint of lying. Lying is the "deceleration" target behavior (the behavior to be eliminated or decreased), and telling the truth is the incompatible "acceleration" behavior. According to applied behavior analysis, the problem behavior is either ignored or punished, and the incompatible behavior is rewarded. Yet, rewarding telling the truth is problematic. A child could easily obtain rewards by making truthful assertions while continuing unabated lying. But punishing lying behavior poses problems, too. Punishing each lie a child tells may succeed only in making the child a more skillful liar. Also, "getting at the truth" places parents and teachers in the role of grand inquisitor and provides the child with attention that may inadvertently reinforce the lying behavior.

Whereas a strict contingency-management approach to lying may be unproductive, it is important to alter contingencies of reinforcement for lying and telling the truth so that the rewards for lying are lessened, and the rewards for telling the truth are increased. For example, when the child lies to avoid punishment and is detected in the lie, the punishment that would have been administered for the original behavior should stand, and a punishment for lying should be added. When a child admits to a wrongdoing on his or her own, the punishment for the wrongdoing should be less than it would be if the child had not admitted guilt.

When lying is viewed as part of another problem, such as antisocial behavior, peer rejection, or a disturbed parent-child relationship, the intervention should address the constellation of behaviors comprising the disorder as well as factors contributing to the problem.

Lying as Part of Antisocial Behavior

Single-focused interventions for children exhibiting aggression and other disruptive behavior disorders are unlikely to be effective (Hughes & Cavell, 1995). A consensus has been achieved that early intervention in the development of conduct disorders, before a relative "window of opportunity" closes, is most likely to be effective in altering the negative developmental trajectory (Kazdin, 1993). Furthermore, interventions will need to be broad based, addressing at least two of the multiple systems that influence the development and maintenance of antisocial behavior. The most extensively researched interventions for childhood antisocial behaviors are parent-training approaches and skill-training approaches.

Parent training with conduct-problem youth.
The efficacy of parent training (PT) with parents of children with conduct disorders is supported by research

spanning three decades (for review see McMahon & Forehand, 1984, or Kazdin, 1993). Gerald Patterson and his colleagues were pioneers in developing and evaluating parent-training programs (Patterson, Chamberlain, & Reid, 1982; Patterson & Fleischman, 1979). Their approach to parent training was based on social learning principles, especially on altering parent-delivered contingencies for antisocial and prosocial behaviors. Other researchers have made modifications to this approach and contributed to the systematic evaluation of parent-training approaches with parents of conduct-disordered children (e.g., McMahon, Forehand, & Griest, 1981; Webster-Stratton, 1984). These programs of research have greatly increased the knowledge of who responds to parent training, mechanisms responsible for improved child functioning, and the impact of modifications in treatment procedures on client outcomes.

In recent years, training in parent-management skills has been combined with training in positive parent-child interactional skills, especially nondirective play skills (Eyberg, 1988). The emphasis on parental acceptance and positive parenting skills is based on findings that a combination of parental warmth and appropriate behavioral controls result in best child outcomes (Parke & Slaby, 1983) and that parents of conduct-disordered children are overly controlling and provide lower levels of acceptance (Greenberg, Speltz, & DeKlyen, 1993). Thus, current programs represent a merger of behavioral management approaches and relationship enhancement approaches (Eyberg, 1988). More recent approaches also emphasize the establishment of cooperative parent-child interactions through the use of problem solving and communication skills (Webster-Stratton, 1987).

Both individual and group formats of parent training have been found to be effective, and therapist, or leader, manuals are available for both formats (Barkley, 1987; Webster-Stratton, 1987). Although individual-versus-group formats have not been directly compared, a comparison of training utilizing videotaped materials and parent workbooks with and without group discussion found that only parents who received group discussion maintained gains 3 years after treatment (Webster-Stratton, Hollingsworth, & Kolpocoff, 1989). Despite variations, all programs in this genre include instruction, modeling, and rehearsal of targeted parenting skills, homework assignments to promote generalization of skills to home settings, and discussion of homework assignments to identify obstacles and modifications needed in strategies.

A number of studies have documented marked improvements for children and parents in parent training relative to treatment control conditions (see McMahon & Forehand, 1984 and Parenting, this volume). Despite the overall effectiveness of parent training, 30% to 40% of treated parents report that children's problems remain in the clinical range after treatment, and 25% to 50% of teachers report child externalizing problems are within the clinical range (Webster-Stratton, 1990). Parents least likely to respond positively to parent training are those experiencing significant stress. Mothers who are socially isolated, with few sources of social support outside the family; socioeconomically disadvantaged families; children whose problems are more severe; and parents who evince psychopathology are less likely to benefit from parent training (Webster-Stratton, 1985). These same characteristics predict attrition from parent training (Kazdin, 1990). Multiple demands interfere with commitment to learning and practicing skills taught. With such parents, attention to family stress and parents' personal issues and worries may be a necessary adjunct to parent training.

When the scope of parent training is broadened to include family problems characteristic of families of children with conduct disorders, its effects are increased (Dadds et al., 1987). A supportive and positive alliance with parents may also be especially important in working with parents who experience high levels of stress and few sources of support. Families with more severe problems may also require more than the typical 10 to 12 sessions. Kazdin et al. (1989) provided between 50 and 60 hours of parent training with parents of children with severe problems. Combining parent training with other therapies, such as problem-solving-skills training for children, enhances the effects of parent training alone (Kazdin, Siegel, & Bass, 1992).

Parent training is less successful with adolescents (Henggeler & Borduin, 1990). Whereas parenting factors loom as the most significant influence on the development of aggression and conduct problems in the preschool years, other systems become increasingly important after children enter school. By adolescence, the peer group is the preeminent influence on conduct disorders. Adolescents need multisystemic approaches that recognize the influence of additional systems, peers, and school.

Skill-training approaches
Interventions designed to remedy aggressive children's social cognitive deficits and distortions have produced positive but limited effects. For example, Kazdin and his colleagues (Kazdin, Bass, Siegel, & Thomas, 1989) demonstrated that problem-solving-skills training resulted in significant behavioral improvement in highly aggressive children that lasted up to one year after treatment. Despite these gains, a majority of treated children continue to exhibit clinically significant levels of aggressive/disruptive behavior. Tremblay and his colleagues (Tremblay, Pagani-Kurtz, Masse, Vitaro, & Pihl, 1995) report that a combination of problem-solving-skills training for the children and home-based parent training for a 2-year period resulted in the children being less likely to receive special class placements at ages 10 to 13, but not after age 13, and no group-by-time interaction effects were

found for teacher-rated disruptiveness or court reports of offenses in mid-adolescence. More promising results were reported by Lochman (Lochman & Curry, 1986), who documented that children provided self-control and problem-solving skills intervention decreased disruptive/aggressive classroom behavior and improved on parent-completed measures of aggression, and reported increased self-esteem relative to controls. Three years after treatment, treated boys displayed lower levels of substance use, improved self-esteem, and lower levels of behavior deviance but did not differ in level of classroom behavior (Lochman, 1992). The author suggested treatment effects could be strengthened by longer treatments that also focus on children's social cognitive schemata (beliefs) and include parents.

Lying as Part of a Pattern of Deficient Social Skills

When lying is part of low peer acceptance, it is important to determine if the child is also aggressive. Peer rejection is often associated with aggressive behavior, in which case the rejected/aggressive child is likely to benefit from the same social-cognitive interventions just described for antisocial children. When the child who has a problem with lying is nonaggressive but low accepted, a focus on friendship-making skills and skills needed for positive group participation, such as cooperating, supporting others, leading, and assertion, may be most helpful (Bierman & Furman, 1984; Ladd, 1981). The focus in these cases is on prosocial skills rather than on inhibiting aggressive impulses. An important aspect of these programs is the opportunity to practice newly introduced skills in play sessions with a peer, followed by an opportunity to "debrief" the child's use of the skill. Including well-accepted classmates in the training and using cooperative learning tasks also contribute to the effectiveness of social skills training for low-accepted, nonaggressive children (Bierman & Furman, 1984).

Lying as Part of Disturbed Parent-Child Relationship

When lying occurs in context of a parent-child relationship characterized by harsh and inconsistent discipline and low acceptance, the child is likely to exhibit other antisocial behaviors, in which case parent-training strategies similar to those discussed earlier would be appropriate. However, sometimes the lying may occur in the context of a parent-child relationship characterized by high parental expectations and contingent approval. In this case, the child's lying may occur only at home and may result from the child's desire to avoid perceived parental displeasure or rejection. Harter and Monsour (1992) have described a process by which children develop a "false self" which they present to their parents in

order to maintain their parents' approval. Thus, a child might lie to his or her parents as an attempt to maintain their approval. When this dynamic is present, the recommended intervention is one that addresses the quality of the affective bond between the parent and the child. Specifically, the parents need to more clearly communicate acceptance of the child and distinguish between approving of a child's behaviors and approving of the child. By giving the child more security, affection, and positive attention, the need for lying may disappear.

Lying as Denial or Wishful Thinking

Young children who state as fact what is really a wish need help in learning how to express desires. Parents and teachers can rephrase an untrue assertion as a wish, accepting the child's feelings while gently confronting the factual accuracy of the statement. This rephrasing, or reframing technique, shows respect for the child and conveys acceptance of the child's feelings. For example, when the girl whose mother abandoned her states that her mother calls her each night, the adult might respond, "You're thinking about how nice it would be to talk with your mother, and you wish you could visit with her every day." If the child insists on the factual accuracy of the assertion, the adult just moves on to another topic or activity.

When lying is part of defensive exclusion, the child needs help in integrating negative self-relevant information. If one accepts the premise that the child's need to exclude negative information derives from an insecure model of self and others, the intervention should provide the child with an opportunity to develop a more adaptive internal model of self and others. The provision of consistently supportive relationships with one or more adults (e.g., teachers, mentors, parent) provides the opportunity for the child to modify expectations about the self as unworthy of being cared for and of others as unavailable or unwilling to provide support and acceptance. Within a new, accepting, and close relationship, the child receives accurate feedback about himself or herself. The adult does not just provide positive feedback, however. Only providing positive feedback would not assist the child in learning how to integrate negative feedback into a basically secure sense of self. Because negative feedback is embedded in a caring relationship, the child learns how to incorporate negative information into his or her self-concept. Sensitive child psychotherapists provide the conditions for positive changes in the child's internal working models. However, other adults, including teachers and mentors, can also provide new relationship experiences that challenge the child's views of self and others (Cavell, Hughes, Henington, Edens, & Delagarza, 1995; Pianta, 1992).

Summary

Lying is associated with several childhood problems, and an assessment of the child's overall adjustment and relationships with parents, teachers, and peers is necessary in order to focus one's intervention efforts on the constellation of problems of which lying is a part. Lying may signify difficulty in peer relationships, conduct disorder, a disturbed parent-child relationship, or an inability to acknowledge information that is potentially threatening to the child's self-system. Effective interventions address the broader problem rather than focusing exclusively on lying as an isolated, discrete behavior.

Recommended Resources

Bussey, K. (1992). Lying and truthfulness: Children's definitions, standards, and evaluative reactions. *Child Development, 63,* 129–137.
In this cross-sectional study, the authors investigate preschool, second grade, and fifth grade children's definitions of lying and moral reasoning about lying. Developmental changes in children's understanding of lying, evaluative reactions to lying, and moral standards related to lying were found. As children mature, they rely more on internal standards and reactions and less on external aspects of the lying in evaluating lying. Older children report feeling proud when they tell the truth. The authors provide some implications of their findings for encouraging children to be truthful.

Eisenstadt, T.H., Eyberg, S., McNeil, C.B., Newcomb, K., & Funderburk, B. (1993). Parent-child interaction therapy with behavior problem children: Relative effectiveness of two stages and overall outcome. *Journal of Clinical Child Psychology, 22,* 42–51.
This empirical article describes Parent-Child Interaction Therapy (PCIT) and reports evidence of its efficacy. PCIT is especially helpful in reducing child behavioral problems with younger children (ages 3–7). PCIT emphasizes teaching parents child-relationship skills such as play skills as well as strategies for managing behavior problems.

Patterson, G.R., & Forgatch, M.S. (1987). *Parents and adolescents living together. Part 1: The basics.* Eugene, OR: Castalia.
The authors provide parents sage advice about how to establish healthy, mutually respectful relationships with their adolescents. The book stresses the importance of the quality of the relationship with the adolescent as well as strategies for preventing and responding to behavioral problems, including lying.

Robin, A.L., & Foster, S.L. (1984). Problem-solving communication training: A behavioral-family systems approach to parent-adolescent conflicts. In P. Karoly & J.J. Steffen (Eds.), *Adolescent behavior disorders: Foundations and contemporary concerns* (pp. 195–240). Lexington, MA: Lexington Books.

This model "involves multidimensional assessment and treatment techniques, guided by an evolving social learning theory of parent-adolescent conflict that blends cognitive-behavioral and family systems orientations with developmental considerations concerning adolescence" (p. 196). Behavioral assessment techniques are used to assess family communication, problem solving, developmental status, belief systems, family structure, and functional interaction patterns. Training involves restructuring and family systems techniques.

Stouthamer-Loeber, M. (1986). Lying as a problem behavior in children: A review. *Clinical Psychology Review, 6,* 267–289.
This article presents a review of empirical studies on lying by children. Data on prevalence of lying in normal and clinic samples of children and on adults' perceptions of the seriousness of lying are provided. Longitudinal and cross-sectional studies are reviewed that demonstrate an association between lying and conduct problems and delinquency. The article provides a few suggestions for treatment. For example, they suggest increasing parental monitoring and supervision and punishing the lie and the misbehavior that prompted the lie separately.

Webster-Stratton, C. (1988). *Parent and children series.* Eugene, OR: Castalia Press.
This series is a course in parenting skills and consists of a leader's guide, videotapes, and participant workbooks. The program teaches parents of young children (ages 3–9) skills in establishing warm, accepting relationships as well as skills in promoting prosocial skills and decreasing problem behaviors. The program has been extensively tested, and a body of well-respected published literature documents its success in decreasing child problem behaviors.

References

Abidin, R. (1983). *Parenting Stress Index Manual.* Charlottesville, VA Pediatric Psychology Press.

Achenbach, T. M. (1993). Taxonomy and comorbidity of conduct problems: Evidence from empirically based approaches. *Development and Psychopathology, 5,* 51–64.

Achenbach, T. M., & Edelbrock, C. (1981). Behavioral problems and competencies reported by parents of normal and disturbed children, aged 4 through 16. *Monographs of the Society for Research in Child Development, 46,* 1–82.

Achenbach, T. M., & Edelbrock, C. (1991). *Manual for the Child Behavior Checklist and Revised Child Behavior Profile* (2nd ed.). Burlington, VT: University of Vermont, Department of Psychiatry.

American Psychiatric Association. (1994). *Diagnostic and statistical manual of mental disorders* (4th ed.). Washington, DC: Author.

Barkley, R. A. (1987). *Defiant children: A clinician's manual for parent training.* New York: Guilford Press.

Bear, G. G. (1989). Sociomoral reasoning and antisocial behaviors among normal sixth graders. *Merrill-Palmer Quarterly, 35,* 181–196.

Bear, G. G., & Richards, H. C. (1981). Moral reasoning and conduct problems in the classroom. *Journal of Educational Psychology, 73,* 644–670.

Bear, G. G., & Rys, G. S. (1994). Moral reasoning, classroom behavior, and sociometric status among elementary school children. *Developmental Psychology, 30,* 633–638.

Bierman, K. L., & Furman, W. (1984). The effects of social skills training and peer involvement on the social adjustment of preadolescents. *Child Development, 55,* 151–162.

Blasi, A. (1980). Bridging moral cognition and moral action: A critical review of the literature. *Psychological Bulletin, 88,* 1–45.

Bowlby, J. (1980). *Attachment and loss: Vol. 3. Loss.* New York: Basic Books.

Bussey, K. (1992). Lying and truthfulness: Children's definitions, standards, and evaluative reactions. *Child Development, 63,* 129–137.

Cassidy, J. (1988). Child-mother attachment and the self in six-years olds. *Child Development 59,* 121–134.

Cavell, T. A., Hughes, J. N., Henington, C., Edens, J., & Delagarza, S. (March 1995). *Prime time: Corrective attachment experiences as prerequisites to problem solving skills training.* Paper presented at biennial meeting of the Society for Research in Child Development, Indianapolis, IN.

Crick, N. R., & Dodge, K. A. (1994). A review and reformulation of social information-processing mechanisms in children's social adjustment. *Psychological Bulletin, 115,* 74–101.

Dadds, M. R., Sanders, M. R., & Behrens, B. C. (1987). Marital discord and child behavior problems: A description of family interactions during treatment. *Journal of Clinical Child Psychology, 16,* 192–203.

Eyberg, S. (1988). Parent-Child Interaction Therapy: Integration of traditional and behavioral concerns. *Child and Family Behavior Therapy, 10,* 33–45.

Greenberg, M. T., Speltz, M. L., & DeKlyen, M. (1993). The role of attachment in the early development of disruptive behavior problems. *Development and Psychopathology, 5,* 191–214.

Guerra, N. J., & Slaby, R. G. (1989). Evaluative factors in social problem solving by aggressive boys. *Journal of Abnormal Child Psychology, 17,* 277–289.

Harter, S. (1986). Cognitive-developmental precesses in the integration of concepts about emotions and the self. *Social Cognition, 4,* 119–151.

Harter, S., & Monsour, A. (1992). Developmental analysis of conflict caused by opposing attributes in the adolescent self-portrait. *Developmental Psychology, 28,* 251–260.

Henggeler, S. W., & Borduin, C. M. (1990). *Family therapy and beyond: A multisystemic approach to treating the behavior problems of children and adolescents.* Pacific Grove, CA: Brooks/Cole.

Hinshaw, S. P., Lahey, B. B., & Hart, E. L. (1993). Issues of taxonomy and comorbidity in the development of conduct disorder. *Development and Psychopathology, 5,* 31–49.

Hughes, J. N., & Baker D. B. (1990). *The clinical child interview.* New York: Guilford Press.

Hughes, J. N., & Cavell, T. A. (1995). Enhancing competence in aggressive children. In G. Cartledge & J. F. Milburn (Eds.), *Teaching social skills to children: Innovative approaches* (3rd ed., pp. 199–236). New York: Pergamon Press.

Hughes, J. N., Cavell, T. A., & Grossman, P. B. (1995). *A positive view of self and others: Risk or protection for aggressive children?* Manuscript submitted for publication.

Kazdin, A. E. (1990). Premature termination from treatment among children referred for antisocial behavior. *Journal of Child Psychology and Psychiatry, 31,* 415–425.

Kazdin, A. E. (1993). Treatment of conduct disorder: Progress and directions in psychotherapy research. *Development and Psychopathology, 5,* 277–310.

Kazdin, A. E., Bass, D., Siegel, T., & Thomas, C. (1989). Cognitive-behavioral therapy and relationship therapy in the treatment of children referred for antisocial behavior. *Journal of Consulting and Clinical Psychology, 57,* 522–535.

Kazdin, A. E., Siegel T. C., & Bass, D. (1992). Cognitive problem-solving skills training and parent management training in the treatment of antisocial behavior in children. *Journal of Consulting and Clinical Psychology, 60,* 733–747.

Kohlberg, L. (1969). *Stages in the development of moral thought and action.* New York: Holt.

Ladd, G. W. (1981). Effectiveness of a social learning model for enhancing children's social interaction and peer acceptance. *Child Development, 52,* 171–178.

Lewis, M. D. (1993). Emotion-cognition interactions in early infant development. *Cognition and Emotion, 7,* 145–170.

Lochman, J. E. (1992). Cognitive-behavioral intervention with aggressive boys: Three year follow-up and preventive effects. *Journal of Consulting and Clinical Psychology, 60,* 426–432.

Lochman, J. E., & Curry, J. F. (1986). Effects of social problem-solving training and self-instructional training with aggressive boys. *Journal of Clinical Child Psychology, 15,* 159–164.

Loeber, R., & Schmaling, K. B. (1985). Empirical evidence of overt and covert patterns of antisocial conduct problems: A meta-analysis. *Journal of Abnormal Child Psychology, 13,* 337–352.

Loeber, R., Wung, P., Keenan, K., Giroux, B., Stouthamer-Loeber, M., Van Kannen, W. B., & Maughan, B. (1993). Developmental pathways in disruptive child behavior. *Development and Psychopathology, 5,* 103–133.

Main, M., Kaplan, N., & Cassidy, J. (1985). Security in infancy, childhood, and adulthood: A move to the level of representation. Monographs of the Society for Research in Child Development, 50 (1–2, Serial No. 209).

Mash, E.J., & Terdal, L. G. (1988). Behavioral assessment of child and family disturbance. In E.J. Mash & L. G. Terdal (Eds.), *Behavioral assessment of childhood disorders* (2nd ed., pp. 3–65). New York: Guilford Press.

McKeough, A., Yates, T., & Marini, A. (1994). Intentional reasoning: A developmental study of behaviorally aggressive and normal boys. *Development and Psychopathology, 6,* 285–304.

McMahon, R. J., & Forehand, R. (1984). Parent training for the noncompliant child: Treatment outcome, generalization, and adjunctive therapy procedures. In R. F. Dangel & R. A. Polster (Eds), *Parent training: Foundations of research and practice* (pp. 298–328). New York: Guilford Press.

McMahon, R. J., Forehand, R., & Griest, D. L. (1981). Effects of knowledge of social learning principles on enhancing treatment outcome and generalization in a parent training program. *Journal of Consulting and Clinical Psychology, 49,* 562–532.

Parke, R. D., & Slaby, R. G. (1983). The development

of aggression. In E. M. Hetherington (Ed.), *Handbook of child psychology: Vol. 4. Socialization, personality and social development* (pp. 547–641). New York: Wiley.

Patterson, C. J., Cohn, D. A., & Kao, B. T. (1989). Maternal warmth as a protective factor against risks associated with peer rejection among children. *Development and Psychopathology, 1,* 21–38.

Patterson, C. J., Kupersmidt, J. B., & Griesler, P. C. (1990). Children's perceptions of self and relationships with others as a function of sociometric status. *Child Development, 61,* 1335–1349.

Patterson, G. R., Chamberlain, P., & Reid, J. B. (1982). A comparative evaluation of a parent training program. *Behavior Therapy, 13,* 638–650.

Patterson, G. R., & Fleischman, M. J. (1979). Maintenance of treatment effects: Some considerations concerning family systems and follow-up data. *Behavior Therapy, 10,* 168–185.

Patterson, G. R., Reid, J. B., & Dishion, T. J. (1992). *Antisocial boys.* Eugene, OR: Castalia.

Peisach, E., & Hardeman, M. (1983). Moral reasoning in early childhood: Lying and stealing. *The Journal of Genetic Psychology, 142,* 107–120.

Peterson, C. C., Peterson, J. L., & Seeto, D. (1983). Developmental changes in ideas about lying. *Child Development, 54,* 1529–1535.

Pianta, R. (1992). Conceptual and methodological issues in research on relationships between children and non-partental adults. In R. Pianta (Ed.), *Beyond the parent: The role of other adults in children's lives* (pp. 121–129). San Francisco: Jossey-Bass.

Reynolds, C. R., & Kamphaus, R. W. (1992). *Behavior assessment system for children.* Circle Pines, MN: American Guidance Service.

Robins, L. N. (1979). Follow-up studies. In H. C. Quay & J. S. Werry (Eds.), *Psychopathological disorders of childhood* (pp. 483–513). New York: John Wiley & Sons.

Sroufe, L. A. (1990). An organizational perspective on the self. In D. Cicchetti & M. Beeghly (Eds.), *The self in transition: Infancy to childhood* (pp. 281–307). Chicago: University of Chicago Press.

Stouthamer-Loeber, M. (1986). Lying as a problem behavior in children: A review. *Clinical Psychology Review, 6,* 267–289.

Tremblay, R. E., Pagani-Kurtz, L., Masse, L. C., Vitaro, F., & Pihl, R. O. (1995). A bimodal preventive intervention for disruptive kindergarten boys: Its impace through mid-adolescence. *Journal of Consulting and Clinical Psychology,* 63(4), 560–568.

Webster-Stratton, C. (1984). Randomized trial of two parent-training programs for families with conduct disordered children. *Journal of Consulting and Clinical Psychology. 52,* 666–678.

Webster-Stratton, C. (1985). Predictors of treatment outcome in parent training for conduct disordered children. *Behavior Therapy, 16,* 223–242.

Webster-Stratton, C. (1987). *The parents and children series.* Eugene, OR: Castalia.

Webster-Stratton, C. (1990). Long-term follow-up of families with young conduct problem children: From preschool to grade school. *Journal of Consulting and Clinical Psychology, 19,* 144–149.

Webster-Stratton, C., Hollingsworth, T., & Kolpocoff, M. (1989). The long term effectiveness and clinical significance of three cost-effective training programs for families with conduct problem children. *Journal of Consulting and Clinical Psychology, 57,* 550–553.

17

Stealing

Gloria E. Miller

University of Denver

Background and Development

Nonconfrontative stealing can be defined as the unlawful taking of someone's property without the use of force or violence. Such behavior is considered a pervasive juvenile problem and is viewed as one of the most difficult to address by parents and school professionals (Belson, 1975). It is contrasted with other theft behavior that involves face-to-face contact with a victim (i.e., robbery) or illicit entry (i.e., burglary).

The Safe School Study, a national survey on school crime undertaken by the National Institute of Education (1977), cited nonconfrontative theft of personal property as the major crime occurring in elementary and secondary schools. In the schools surveyed, an average of 1 out of 8 teachers and 1 out of 9 students reported incidents of personal theft within any one-month period. Similarly, in a national survey reported by the National School Boards Association (cited in Baker, 1979) the proportion of students who reported they had been victims of nonconfrontative stealing ranged from 43% to 72%. The true level of stealing that occurs in schools, however, is underestimated due to imprecise and nonstandardized record keeping and the fact that countless incidents of less conspicuous, minor stealing offenses are never reported, especially with young offenders (Miller & Moncher, 1988). As of 1994, only five states (SC, NC, VA, FL, CA) required records to be kept on school crime, but the variation in data collection and reporting methods makes it difficult to get a consistent picture of the scope of the problem (Morrison, Furlong, & Morrison, 1994). Underestimates are also due to the pervasive unwillingness of school officials to report theft or other acts of violence due to fears of reprisal or appearances of inadequacy (Goldstein, 1994).

Information about the incidence of youth stealing in normal populations is sparse and outdated. An early longitudinal study of 110 middle- to upper-class children indicated that 10% of parents reported stealing as a problem in their sons at age 8, although this fell to 4% by age 10 (MacFarlane, Allen, & Honzik, 1962). In the Isle of Wight

study conducted in 1970, approximately 6% of parents and 4% of teachers were concerned about stealing in boys ages 10 to 13 (3% were concerned about girls stealing; Rutter, Tizard, & Whitmore, 1970). On the most recent revalidation of the Child Behavior Checklist (Achenbach & Edelbrock, 1991), adult reports of "stealing at home" in referred populations ranged from 15% in the youngest age group (i.e., 4 to 7 years) to 30% in the oldest age groups and reports of "stealing out of the home" ranged from 20% to 30%, respectively. In nonreferred populations, reports of these behaviors did not exceed 5% of the population.

On self-report surveys, a majority of adolescents admit to high levels of petty theft during childhood (Belson, 1975; Weger, 1987). In a recent self-report study of stealing behavior in 167 nondelinquent youths (ages 10 to 15 years), Moncher and Miller (in press) found that 45% reported some form of occasional stealing and 7% reported frequent stealing behavior within the last school year (i.e., defined as taking money or possessions from desks, lockers, machines, school buildings, stores, or homes). These levels are consistent with past studies in which reported involvement in petty stealing ranged from 50% to 80% of the populations surveyed (Klemke, 1982). Also consistent with past findings, self-reported stealing behavior was higher in older (13- to 15-year-olds) than younger respondents (10- to 12-year-olds) and more males than females reported occasional or frequent theft behavior, especially in the older age groups.

Age-related increases in self-reported stealing may simply reflect more occasion to engage in these behaviors. For example, as children get older, they possess larger amounts of money and are allowed to shop independently which may give them more opportunity or perceived need to steal. Alternatively, these findings may reflect the increased influenced of peer-group attitudes that condone such behavior (Berndt, 1979). Only recently have studies included or focused exclusively on the nature and development of female antisocial behavior. Thus, cautions must be raised against generalizing about gender differences in stealing or other antisocial behavior because the variability between females is greater than any observed differences between males and females (Hyde, 1984) and because of the limited research directed at this issue (Kavanagh & Hops, 1994).

At the national level, the most recent Uniform Crime Report index (U.S. Department of Justice, 1995) indicates that while the total number of Larceny/Theft arrests (i.e., not including motor vehicle theft) has decreased 9% from 1990 to 1994 for adults, these figures have increased 10% over the same time period for the under-18-years age group. Moreover, this category of offenses represents the majority of all recorded crimes, and over 33% of these offenses are committed by persons under the age of 18. Theft and burglary offenses also constitute more than half of all criminal arrests in youth aged 18 or under with continued increases in rates of referrals through age 16 (Butts & Poe, 1993). Similarly, nonconfrontative theft comprises the majority of crime that occurs in schools, with increased levels reported from elementary to middle school (U.S. Department of Justice, 1991). Such age-related increases can be due either to the involvement of more individuals or to fewer individuals who engage in increasingly severe and more frequent criminal behavior.

Clearly, the cost of youth stealing impacts both individuals and the community at large. Theft committed by juveniles accounts for billions of dollars of loss to victims each year (Nimick, 1990). Estimates of nonconfrontative crime in the workplace, which includes theft, fraud, and vandalism, have been projected to cost between $30 and $40 billion a year in lost revenue (Hollinger, 1983). Most significantly, personal property offenses negatively affect feelings regarding safety and well-being and can lead to increased avoidance, insecurity, generalized fear, and alienation from authority figures and institutions (Gottfredson & Gottfredson, 1985; Rubel, 1977). High levels of theft and other covert antisocial behaviors in schools also have been strongly associated with lower staff morale and commitment, lower student achievement, and less positive student and staff affiliation (Baker & Rubel, 1980).

Problems stemming from persistent stealing behavior in children are among the most serious complaints made by parents and educators. Yet adults often are at a loss as to how to address nonconfrontative stealing. One reason for this difficulty is the acknowledgment that incidents of "taking another person's possession" are quite common in childhood and are viewed as normal manifestations of social development as children learn about rules of ownership, possession, and sharing (Eisenberg, 1982). Stealing may be a part of an individual's growing social awareness which advances from an impersonal egocentric stance to an insightful interpersonal perspective (Selman, 1980). Moreover, other developmental factors, such as empathy and moral reasoning, can significantly affect expressions of dishonest behavior in children (Bear & Rys, 1994; Kahn, 1992). Nevertheless, concerns about excessive stealing behavior are found

with children as young as age four (Achenbach & Edelbrock, 1991), and examinations of referrals to child and family clinics indicate that 30% to 50% evidence excessive nonconfrontative stealing (Patterson, 1982).

Another reason for the widespread frustration in dealing with stealing is the lack of agreement on what constitutes problematic levels of the behavior. In the latest revision of the *Diagnostic and Statistical Manual of Mental Disorders-IV* (American Psychiatric Association, 1994), "Theft and Deceitfulness" is one of four major diagnostic categories for childhood and adolescent conduct disorder. Three behavioral criteria comprise this category: has broken into a home, building, or car; lies to obtain goods or favors or to avoid obligations; and steals nontrivial items without confrontation. A diagnosis is made if three criteria (i.e., those listed here or any of the other 12 associated criteria) have been present over the past year with at least one criterion exhibited within the last 6 months. Such definitions stress the need to take note of isolated incidents that occur over extended periods of time or occur in conjunction with other conduct problems. Referrals heighten after kindergarten or when repetitive stealing is noted (Reid & Patterson, 1989). But even so, adults often hesitate to target stealing as a major reason for referral in young children because of its association with labels such as thievery, juvenile delinquency, and dishonesty (Miller & Klungness, 1989).

Problems and Implications

A substantial body of literature points to the dire consequences associated with excessive childhood stealing. The findings of both retrospective and prospective studies have shown that antisocial behaviors persist across childhood and into adulthood and are quite resistant to change by junior high (Loeber, 1982; Robins & Rutter, 1990). Nonconfrontative stealing has been hypothesized as an important precursor to other covert and overt antisocial behavior in adolescence (Patterson, 1986). Moreover, convincing relationships have been found between childhood antisocial behavior such as stealing and later social maladjustment, school dropout, delinquency, or criminality (Loeber, 1990; Moore, Chamberlain, & Mukai, 1979). More immediate repercussions of excessive stealing include academic failure and peer rejection (Patterson, DeBaryshe, & Ramsey, 1989). Thus, there is consensus that early and persistent stealing leads to significant individual and social repercussions.

The extant literature on delinquency in general and on youth violence in particular can be used to draw conclusions about individual and contextual factors that place a child at risk either for initial stealing or continued patterns of stealing (Eron, Gentry, & Schlegel, 1994). Patterson and his colleagues have supported the idea that disturbed social relations and child-rearing practices within the family are a critical link in the development of antisocial behaviors across settings and time (Patterson, 1986; Patterson et al., 1989). The dysfunctional interpersonal relations a child exhibits in the family are assumed to spill over into school settings, to impede academic progress, and to disrupt the development of relations with peers and teachers (Reid & Patterson, 1989). Continued school failure and peer rejection are hypothesized to increase a child's association with antisocial peers which then sets the stage for new forms of problem behavior in adolescence (Vuchin, Bank, & Patterson, 1992). Similarly, Loeber (1990) has proposed a developmental progression of antisocial behavior that begins with initial parental accounts of early temperamental difficulties, followed by increased reports of impulsivity and inattention, incidents of hostility and aggression, inappropriate interpersonal relations (i.e., first within the family and then in other settings), academic deficiencies, and finally association with an antisocial peer group that predicates delinquent behavior.

Cognitive theories emphasizing internal mediators and self-regulative processes also have advanced current knowledge of factors that may affect stealing and other antisocial behavior. Attribution theory suggests that people make decisions and are motivated to act based on interpretations made in social situations about why people behave as they do and how behavior relates to outcomes in a situation (Weiner, 1986). Strong evidence has been found between anger and specific perceptions of having been wronged, including biased interpretations of situational cues and faulty attributions or response expectations regarding social situations (Dodge, 1993; Hudley, 1994). Perceptions of personal motivation, justice, fairness, and punishment have been shown to directly influence youth's judgment and decision making about stealing (Bell, Peterson, & Hautaluoma, 1989; Kahn, 1992). Generalized beliefs about social behavior and attitudes towards school and authority can impact levels and perceptions of stealing (Moncher & Miller, in press).

Finally, broad social contexts relate to levels and persistence of antisocial behavior in children. Theorists have long hypothesized that involvement in delinquency is related to a weakening commitment to a conventional set of community values (Gottfredson & Gottfredson, 1985). Organizational variables such as climate, communication, and rule systems have been related to greater levels of self-reported antisocial behavior in schools and communities (Rubel, 1977). Olweus (1993) found that bully and victimization patterns are contingent on the attitudes, routines, and behaviors of peers and adults in school and community settings. Stressful life conditions can alter interpersonal relations and set the stage for increased antisocial behavior in children possibly through the disruption of healthy family interactions, the exacerbation of dysfunctional relationships, or the fostering of a negative social climate that promotes criminal behavior (Tremblay, Masse, Perron, Leblanc, Schwartzman, & Ledingham, 1992; Webster-Stratton, 1990). School and community cohesiveness and commitment to safety and prosocial alternatives are also predictors of juvenile crime (U.S. Department of Justice, 1991).

Assessment Recommendations

Past work on the etiology of nonconfrontative stealing and other antisocial behavior points to the need to conduct broad assessments that address critical factors and relationships within and between all of the child's major life environments (Miller & Moncher, 1988). Such comprehensive assessments involve multiple procedures (i.e., interviews, ratings, observations, self-reports) across a variety of informants and settings (i.e., child, peers, parents, teachers, relatives, neighbors, community members). The following guidelines are offered to conduct an effective problem analysis of stealing.

Establish Adult Expectations

It is important to establish a framework of openness that allows for the expression of personal attributions, perceptions, and beliefs about the problem with all adults who have regular contact with the child. Prior work on parental treatment engagement strongly suggests that attention to such internal expectancies contribute greatly to retention and long-term success by fostering an atmosphere of support, cooperation, and trust and by strengthening a client's perseverance especially in the face of difficulty (Meichenbaum & Turk, 1987; Miller, 1994). This is particularly important with families of children who steal because these families are often difficult to engage and keep in treatment (Patterson, 1982; Seymore & Epston, 1989).

Begin with the recognition that everyone shares a responsibility and a desire to promote the child's well-being and success. The next step is to gain an understanding of adults' beliefs and attributions about the problem, including reasons for, concerns about, and personal reactions to the child's stealing. Such information can often reveal attitudes that inadvertently reinforce or condone the behavior, as when stealing is viewed as an inevitable "right of passage" (e.g., Everyone does it, I did it too), an unalterable genetic trait (e.g., She was born to act out) or an assumed emotional reaction (e.g., He does it to get even with his Dad). Personalized beliefs that lead to externalized blame (e.g., The school is at fault. It is those friends of his), self-blame (e.g., I am a bad parent. My divorce led to this) or feelings of resentment and anger (e.g., How can she do this to me) can reduce adult effectiveness and immobilize them from taking effective actions. Facilitating a discussion can help to reframe the issue and provide alternative explanations that release adults from debilitating self-blame, helplessness, or fatalistic excuses for the behavior (Prinz & Miller, 1994).

Finally, attitudes about seeking help (e.g., a sign of weakness versus a sign of strength) and about prior experiences of receiving help in the community or at the child's school must be addressed. Such discussions may uncover areas of resistance and negative perceptions associated with therapeutic efforts (e.g., Nothing ever worked; I was made to feel like the villain) and helping relationships (e.g., You are going to turn him in. You don't really care, you're just doing your job). This information can then be used to normalize the need for intervention, facilitate joint goal setting, and clarify each person's role in the process. A critical message to convey is that the success of future efforts depends on the ability to work collaboratively as peers.

Build a Consensus Definition and Focus on Competence

The development of an objective definition of stealing is fundamental to diagnosis and intervention (Miller & Klungness, 1986, 1989). Agreeing on what constitutes stealing is especially important because recognition of the behavior is likely to differ significantly across settings due to varying tolerances for and reluctance to label acts of stealing. First, consideration must be given to dominant attitudes and lifestyle patterns that relate to the sharing of personal property. Such information can quickly identify situations where stealing may be a function of differences in rules of possession across the child's major environments.

Next, it is important to determine if there is a tendency for involved adults to identify only extreme property violations (e.g., taking things worth more than $10), to accept alternative "plausible" explanations (e.g., finding, borrowing, receiving a gift), or to ignore "suspected" stealing acts that are not easy to document. Differences of opinion on what constitutes theft behavior can then be debated and reframed to build a consensus that includes all documented and suspected theft behavior. Authorities have recommended that stealing be defined as any time the child possesses something that cannot be accounted for or whenever there is an accusation of stealing by an authority or peer (Reid, 1975). Such an overinclusive definition is essential to take the burden of proof from concerned adults, which can inadvertently reinforce stealing, and to place the onus of responsibility on the child to "prove innocence."

This "guilty until proven innocent" standard should be invoked after the child has been found to have stolen on repeated occasions. The child should understand that this standard is a consequence of past behavior and may result in occasions where he or she will be accused and punished when not guilty. Adults will need to acknowledge that this is regrettable but absolutely necessary to help overcome the problem. This standard will help everyone involved to avoid lengthy interrogation or heated arguments and ultimately will lessen the need to use such an overinclusive standard in the not so distant future.

Finally, diagnostic information should identify instances where the child has demonstrated a strong sense of honesty or resistance to temptation (e.g., turned in a lost item; paid for a broken item). Such efforts are essential to the design of interventions that target improved honesty in addition to reductions in stealing (Seymour & Epston, 1989). This information also helps to refocus on the child's competence and creates a framework of confidence that the child can have influence and control over his or her own problem.

Gather Background and Historical Information

When gathering background information about a covert behavior such as stealing, it is best not to rely on singular third-party reports (Loeber, Green, Lahey, & Stouthamer-Loeber, 1990). Multiple sources of data must be collected including child self-reports. Clarify the occurrence and severity of stealing by asking how often the behavior has been reported *or suspected* because many stealing acts remain unsubstantiated. It also is important to determine the extent to which the behavior takes place across a variety of settings (i.e., home, school, at a relative's, in the community). Historical information should include inquiries about the age of onset as well as evidence of concomitant behavior problems, early temperamental difficulties, or both. It is also important to assess whether adult or sibling family members are knowingly or inadvertently modeling or condoning the child's theft behavior through past or present involvement in theft (or other antisocial behaviors).

Strong empirical evidence indicates that young children who exhibit the early onset of a variety of oppositional, aggressive, and covert antisocial behaviors may be most at risk for serious delinquency as adolescents. Such versatile antisocial patterns before age 10 have been associated with continued or escalating antisocial behavior and a significantly higher chance of police involvement during adolescence (Loeber, Tremblay, Gragnon, & Charlebois, 1989). The early emergence of covert and overt behavioral difficulties clearly indicate the need for more immediate and comprehensive intervention efforts and intensive family efforts. Later onset or singular antisocial involvement may suggest the need for individual and peer interventions (McCord & Tremblay, 1992).

Identify Setting Characteristics

The characteristics of the settings where stealing occurs, including the place, time of day, the people present, and the level of surveillance or adult monitoring in the area can provide information about critical events that can instigate or perpetuate stealing. Additional information can be obtained from questions about the type of item(s) taken and what is typically done with the item. Such information can be used to immediately clarify whether basic or essential needs contribute to the theft behavior and to determine if simple environmental changes such as increased security measures or increased adult monitoring might lead to immediate and significant reductions in stealing (Olweus, 1993; Stevens, 1994). Another important setting factor concerns a child's academic standing and performance. Limited academic success may contribute to feelings of incompetence, frustration, and nonrecognition that can lead to a variety of attention-getting behaviors, including stealing. Such information can quickly identify children who may need alternative academic remediation, support, and reinforcement in addition to interventions that target stealing (Miller & Prinz, 1991).

Evaluate Cognitive Processes and Mediators

Cues about what maintains or provokes stealing can be determined by evaluating the child's attributions, beliefs, and response expectations. Faulty cognitive processes, such as hostile interpretations of the situation (e.g., He harmed me on purpose), faulty outcome expectations (e.g., I will get even), and limited flexibility in generating alternative responses or in evaluating consequences can lead to expressions of anger or revenge and give rise to motivations to steal (Dodge, 1993; Pepler & Slaby, 1994). A child could be asked to describe perceptions and thought processes where a decision was made to steal either in an actual or a hypothetical situation. Determinations of moral reasoning skills and general perceptions of justice, fairness, and punishment also provide insight into judgments and decision making about stealing (Bear & Rys, 1994; Kahn, 1992).

Finally, assessments should focus on perceived external and internal deterrents to theft behavior. For example, a child could be asked to rate the likelihood a person would steal given certain conditions (e.g., a personal need, a need for another person, everyone is doing it, it is easy to get away with) or perceptions (e.g, God would think it was wrong. My parents would lose trust). Such an approach was recently employed by Moncher and Miller (in press), who asked youths to make judgments about what may encourage or inhibit stealing in hypothetical same-aged peers. External situational factors (i.e., financial need, unlikely detection, peer pressure) were viewed as highly likely to promote stealing by a majority of respondents and internal factors (i.e., family or religious values, self or parental disappointment) were not perceived as successful deterrents. Moreover,

higher levels of reported stealing, especially in males older than 13, were related to beliefs that a person would steal when viewed as acceptable by peers or in instances where there was a perceived need for themselves or a loved one. Thus, greater adolescent participation in theft may be likely if stealing is viewed as a means of gaining peer approval or acceptance.

Investigate Peer-Group Factors

Prevalent attitudes in the child's peer group regarding antisocial behavior in general and stealing in particular must be assessed, possibly through routine attitude surveys of the whole student body (Miller & Moncher, 1988). It is especially important to determine the similarity of attitudes between the child and his or her best friend because continued involvement in antisocial behavior is highly related to association with at-risk peers who condone or engage in similar behavior (Kupersmidt, Coie, & Dodge, 1990; Loeber, 1990). Interviews should determine if a child's social network supports delinquent behavior such as theft. A child who frequently observes peers (or adults) enjoying profits from theft without experiencing any negative consequences will be reinforced vicariously for stealing (Reid & Patterson, 1989).

The peer group also plays a major role in the creation and maintenance of a child's reputation and peer status (Hymel, Wagner, & Butler, 1990). Children make reputational decisions based on situational attributions about the cause and intentionality of social behavior (i.e., Was it justified? Was it done intentionally?) which can lead to negative attributions or dispositional inferences about the child (e.g., He is mean). Such reputational biases then create expectancies that contribute to decisions about whether and how to interact with the peer. Sociometric analysis, interviews, and observation will be needed to assess whether negative reputational biases have developed about the child leading to peer rejection. This is especially likely if peers have been personally victimized by the theft behavior (i.e., personal belongings taken) or if the child's behavior is viewed as revengeful or hostile in nature (Waas & Honer, 1990). Reputational biases are especially critical to assess in older children (i.e., aged 10 and above) because they become increasingly entrenched and can lead to continued rejection by prosocial peers even in the face of a child's successful behavioral change.

Appraise School and Community Environments

The social climate within school and community environments must be addressed in comprehensive evaluations of stealing (Baker, 1979). Two major factors consistently discriminate schools with high versus low levels of pupil disruption—the lack of clear rules to forbid moral transgression and inconsistently administered consequences for such offenses (Baker & Rubel, 1980). In fact, Stevens (1994) recommends that a first step in the formation of any school safety program must be a thorough analysis of the systems used to develop, communicate, and implement policies and procedures regarding all forms of personal and property violations.

Other important areas to address are students' attitudes toward and affiliation with authority figures in school and community settings (Hawkins, Catalano, & Associates, 1992). Positive attitudes and alliances with significant prosocial role models have been identified as protective factors against adversity while negative feelings and few alliances have been tied to alienation that promotes continued antisocial behavior (Rolf, Masten, Cicchetti, Neuchterlein, & Weintraub, 1990). Moncher and Miller (in press) found that youths who account for the highest levels of self-reported stealing also gave the most negative school ratings regarding the fairness of policies and teachers' respect and treatment of students. These results clearly suggest that children's impressions of interpersonal relations with adults in school and community environments mediate covert antisocial patterns such as stealing.

Consider Family Characteristics

The level, sophistication, and consistency of control strategies within the family are critical to address. Chaotic, rigid, or harsh discipline and poor communication are common in families of children with behavior disorders (Patterson, 1982). In a large retrospective study of over 1,000 cases at a child clinic, Heath and Kosky (1992) found that the families of children referred for stealing lacked warmth and evidenced less personal contact between family members in comparison to children referred solely for aggression or for a variety of other reasons. Such detachment appears to substantially lower levels of social reinforcement and parental monitoring (Reid & Hendriks, 1973). In fact, Wahler and Dumas (1987) found that children who experience inconsistent or erratic adult monitoring may actually increase their level of misbehavior as a means of decreasing such unpredictability. Parent-child relationships may play an indirect role in children's stealing behavior through their influence on a child's attitudes toward school and peers (Moncher & Miller, in press). These findings strongly point to the need to address parental monitoring and supervision of the child's whereabouts and activities and to assess the family's interpersonal relationships.

The daily hassles and long-term stressors that affect a family's functioning also must be clarified and understood. Assessments of this nature would strive to identify families under great stress due to severe environmental conditions (e.g., unemployment, poverty, high crime neighborhood), marital distress, or personal difficulties

(e.g., depression, alcoholism, health, criminal involvement). Many studies point to the negative effects of stress on personal reactions in general and on parent-child relations and parent treatment in particular (Eyberg, Boggs, & Rodriguez, 1992; Webster-Stratton, 1990). Goodyer, Kolvin, and Gatzanis (1987) found that clinically referred conduct-disordered youths who exhibited high levels of theft had experienced a greater number of stressful events in the 12 months prior to referral than had children exhibiting other clinical symptoms. Indeed, families with conduct-disordered youth who also face significant psychosocial problems may need additional support to increase the success of structured family interventions (Kazdin, 1990; Miller & Prinz, 1990).

Finally, it is important to identify family strengths and capabilities in regards to child management as well as obstacles that may block or hinder the effective use of such competencies (Dunst & Trivette, 1987; Meichenbaum & Turk, 1987). This would include assessments of the extent and availability of parental social support (Wahler, 1980) as well as an understanding of parental competencies and skills and family resources (Blechman, 1984). Such information is especially critical for families of children who steal because these families are at risk for limited treatment receptiveness and engagement (Reid & Hendriks, 1973).

Alternative Actions

Despite widespread agreement that nonconfrontative stealing is a relatively common problem faced by school professionals, there are surprisingly few empirical studies of interventions specific to stealing. Nevertheless, one overwhelming conclusion to be drawn from past work is that early prevention is essential to reduce escalation to other antisocial behavior during adolescence (McCord & Tremblay, 1992). This is especially true for young children who display a variety of conduct disorders in addition to evidence of persistent stealing across settings (Loeber, 1990). Such prevention efforts will require multisystemic approaches conducted across a variety of settings and directed at the individual (e.g., conflict resolution, social skills, academic remediation, vocational development) as well as at peer, family, and school levels (Henggeler & Borduin, 1990).

Prevention efforts optimally occur before fourth grade when social rejection and reputational biases have not yet become fully crystallized, or they may be strategically implemented during critical periods of social transitions (i.e., kindergarten to first grade, elementary to middle school; Coie et al., 1993; McCord & Tremblay, 1992). Other characteristics of successful efforts to prevent youth involvement in antisocial behavior include extensive outreach and coordination to develop partnerships across a child's major life settings (Evans, Okifuji, & Engler, 1993), the incorporation of supportive adult mentors (Hawkins, Catalano Associates, 1992), and a focus on empowering children and families. Finally, academic skills remediation and consultation with teachers and parents to reduce disruptive behavior across classroom and home settings have been a part of most successful school-based prevention efforts.

Secondary prevention with children already exhibiting nonconfrontative stealing have emphasized efforts to change social contingencies and interaction patterns within families. Parents learn effective strategies to reduce oppositional and antisocial behavior, foster prosocial behavior, and enhance effective communication and problem solving. Structured social-learning family interventions have been most successful in this regard, especially when designed to (a) match the needs, daily routines, and unique lifestyle of each family (Meichenbaum & Turk, 1987); (b) capitalize on family competencies, resources, and dominant cultural attitudes (Dunst & Trivette, 1987); (c) utilize already existing social support networks, including relatives, friends, and community or church leaders (Boyd-Franklin, 1989); and (d) provide concomitant services for significant personal and family needs (Miller & Prinz, 1991). Treating parents with respect, involving them as partners in dealing with their child's behavior, and providing many opportunities for a variety of positive parent-child interactions are characteristics of interventions that lead to high levels of parental participation, involvement, and satisfaction (McMahon & Slough, in press).

Individual interventions have been most successful when the child has been involved in establishing his or her own solution for change and when there has been a dual focus on improved honesty and reduced stealing (Seymore & Epston, 1989). Other recommendations for the design of successful child-focused interventions include the administration of simple and consistent consequences for any suspected instances of stealing (e.g., one hour of work around the house, the elimination of one hour of TV or video games) and the requirement that the child compensate for the stolen item (e.g., "trading in" a favorite toy, giving up a favorite activity, completing extra chores; Reid, 1975).

Many child-focused interventions also have been designed to modify faulty, incomplete, or inaccurate cognitive processes that interfere with the development of positive adult and peer relationships. Such efforts seek to increase a child's awareness of internal states associated with arousal and use of specific problem-solving and self-regulation skills that encourage accurate processing of social events (Miller & Prinz, 1991). Outcomes are enhanced through concomitant endeavors to reduce reputational biases (Hymel et al., 1990). Specific guidelines to improve the effectiveness of social cognitive interventions include direct work with the child in naturalistic situations to maximize prosocial involvement with highly regarded peers, and especially, to ensure subsequent positive experiences with victims of the child's theft behavior (Waas & Honer, 1990).

Summary

Nonconfrontative stealing is a common manifestation of social development which makes it difficult to know when to become concerned about such behavior. Acts of theft often are not reported until the child gets older, takes a nontrivial item, or is caught by authorities. Unfortunately, adult hesitancy to identify stealing increases the likelihood that it will become more entrenched which can lead to reputational biases in peers and later maladjustment. Assessments of nonconfrontative stealing must begin with the understanding that concerns should surface as early as possible, especially when other behavioral difficulties are noted.

A variety of diagnostic approaches are necessary to account for the multiple contexts and factors hypothesized to affect the development and continuance of nonconfrontative stealing in children and adolescents. Adult attitudes, expectations, and beliefs concerning the stealing behavior must be addressed before a consensus definition of stealing is built. Complete background information regarding the onset of stealing and other behavior problems is essential to effective diagnosis as is an evaluation of critical characteristics of the settings where stealing typically occurs. Appraisals of social cognitive processes, peer group relations, and school and community environments also are fundamental to a complete problem analysis of stealing.

Attempts to prevent and reduce nonconfrontative stealing and other forms of antisocial behavior must be conducted within a multisystemic framework that would involve individual, classroom, home, peer, and community approaches. Such collaborative home, school, and community partnerships require integrated intervention strategies, interagency cooperation, and long-term follow-up similar to the service delivery model recommended by the Task Force on Psychology in the Schools (American Psychological Association, 1993a).

School psychologists are ideally suited to play a central role in the design and implementation of such comprehensive efforts. The considerable expenditures of time and energy, the poor long-term prognosis, and the detrimental psychological, social, and economic costs associated with nonconfrontative stealing provide strong justification for continued efforts to enhance service delivery models. Indeed, the deterrence of such a serious precursor of later antisocial behavior was a major recommendation of the Commission on Violence and Youth (American Psychological Association, 1993b).

Recommended Resources

Hawkins, J. D., Catalano, R. F., & Associates. (1992). *Communities that care: Action for drug abuse prevention.* San Francisco: Jossey-Bass.

This book is an excellent resource for individuals interested in the development and implementation of a comprehensive community-wide prevention program that is applicable to a wide variety of at-risk behaviors.

Miller, G. E., & Prinz, R. J. (1991). Designing interventions for stealing. In G. Stoner, M. R. Shinn, & H. M. Walker (Eds.), *Interventions for achievement and behavior problems* (pp. 593–617). Silver Spring, MD: National Association of School Psychologists.

This chapter offers a thorough review of the nature, scope, and etiology of juvenile stealing as well as the significant obstacles professionals face when screening and assessing for this behavior. Specific recommendations are forwarded to enhance effectiveness with individuals, schools, and families when designing intervention and prevention procedures.

Moncher, F. J., & Miller, G. E. (in press). Nondelinquent youth's stealing behavior and their perceptions of parents, school, and peers. *Journal of Adolescence.*

This article presents the results of a comprehensive survey study of 167 nondelinquent youths who reported on a variety of covert theft acts common in school and community settings. Youths' perceptions of situations, feelings, and behaviors that encourage or inhibit stealing in peers and personal attitudes toward family, peers, and school were assessed. The results provide insight into factors that can impact upon adolescent involvement in stealing.

Morrison, R., Furlong, F., & Morrison, S. (1994). School violence to school safety: Reframing the issue for school psychologists. *School Psychology Review, 23,* 236–256.

These authors provide an extensive overview of significant issues that must be considered when designing school-based prevention programs that seek to enhance safety and foster positive educational environments as a means of reducing crime and violence.

Seymore, F. W., & Epston, D. (1989). An approach to childhood stealing with evaluation of 45 cases. *Australian and New Zealand Journal of Family Therapy, 10,* 137–143.

This article describes a therapeutic program that emphasizes direct child involvement during a comprehensive family-based intervention. The elements of the program are carefully outlined and evaluated. The intervention succeeded in keeping families engaged and promoted positive immediate and long-term behavior changes in the child as reported by the child and parent.

References

Achenbach, T. J., & Edelbrock, (1991). *Manual for the Child Behavior Checklist and Revised Child Behavior Profile* (2nd Ed.). Burlington, VT: University of Vermont Press.

American Psychiatric Association. (1994). *Diagnostic and statistical manual of mental disorders* (4th ed.). Washington, DC: Author.

American Psychological Association. (1993a). *Delivery of comprehensive school psychological services: An educator's guide.* Task Force on Psychology in the Schools. Washington, DC: Author.

American Psychological Association. (1993b). *Violence and youth: Psychology's response: Volume I. Summary report of the American Psychological Association Commission on Violence and Youth.* Washington, DC: Author.

Baker, K. (1979). Crime and violence in schools: A challenge to educators. In T. Kratochowill (Ed.), *Advances in school psychology* (Vol. 5, pp. 57–85). NJ: Lawrence Erlbaum Associates.

Baker, K., & Rubel, R. J. (Eds.) (1980). *Violence and crime in the schools.* Lexington, MA: Lexington Books.

Bear, G., & Rys, G. S. (1994). Moral reasoning, classroom behavior, and sociometric status among elementary school children. *Developmental Psychology, 30,* 633–638.

Bell, P. A., Peterson, T. R., & Hautaluoma, J. E. (1989). The effect of punishment probability on overconsumption and stealing in a simulated commons. *Journal of Applied Social Psychology, 19,* 1483–1495.

Belson, W. A. (1975). *Juvenile theft: The causal factors.* London: Harper & Row.

Berndt, T. J. (1979). Developmental changes in conformity to peers and parents. *Developmental Psychology, 15,* 608–616.

Blechman, E. A. (1984). Competent parents, competent children: Behavioral objectives of parent training. In R. F. Dangel & R. A. Polster (Eds.), *Parent training* (pp. 34–66). New York: Guilford, Press.

Boyd-Franklin, N. (1989). *Black families in therapy: A multisystems approach.* New York: Guildford Press.

Butts, J., & Poe, E. (1993). *Offenders in juvenile court, 1990* (Juvenile Justice Bulletin). Washington, DC: U.S. Department of Justice.

Coie, J. D., Watt, N. F., West, S. G., Hawkins, J. D., Asarnow, J. R., Markman, H. J., Ramey, S. L., Shure, M. B., & Long, B. (1993). The science of prevention: A conceptual framework and some directions for a national research program. *American Psychologist, 48,* 1013–1022.

Dodge, K. A. (1993). Social-cognitive mechanisms in the development of conduct disorder and depression. *Annual Review of Psychology, 44,* 559–584.

Dunst, C. J., & Trivette, C. M. (1987). Enabling and empowering families: Conceptual and intervention issues. *School Psychology Review, 16,* 443–456.

Eisenberg, N. (1982). *The development of prosocial reasoning.* New York: Academic Press.

Eron, L. D., Gentry, J. H., & Schlegel, P. (1994). *Reasons to hope: A psychosocial perspective on violence & youth.* Washington, DC: American Psychological Association.

Evans, I. M., Okifuji, A., & Engler, L. (1993). Home-school communication in the treatment of childhood behavior problems. *Child and Family Behavior Therapy, 15,* 37–60.

Eyberg, S. M., Boggs, S. R., & Rodriguez, C. M. (1992). Relationships between maternal parenting stress and child disruptive behavior. *Child and Family Behavior Therapy, 14,* 1–10.

Federal Bureau of Investigation. (1992). *Uniform crime report*. Washington, DC: U.S. Government Printing Office.

Goldstein, A. P. (1994). School violence I: Aggression towards persons and property in America's schools. *The School Psychologist, 48*, 6–21.

Goodyer, I., Kolvin, I., & Gatzanis, S. (1987). The impact of recent undesirable life events on psychiatric disorders in childhood and adolescence. *British Journal of Psychiatry, 151*, 179–184.

Gottfredson, G., & Gottfredson, D. (1985). *Victimization in the schools*. New York: Plenum Press.

Hawkins, J. D., Catalano, R. F., & Associates. (1992). *Communities that care: Action for drug abuse prevention*. San Francisco: Jossey-Bass.

Heath, E., & Kosky, R. (1992). Are children who steal different from those who are aggressive? *Child Psychiatry and Human Development, 23*, 9–18.

Henggeler, S. W., & Borduin, C. M. (1990). *Family therapy and beyond: A multisystemic approach to treating behavior problems of children and adolescents*. Pacific Grove, CA: Brooks/Cole.

Hollinger, R. C. (1983). *Theft by employees*. New York: Harcourt Brace Jovanovich.

Hudley, C. A. (1994). Perceptions of intentionality, feelings of anger, and reactive aggression. In M. J. Furlong & D. C. Smith (Eds.), *Anger, hostility and aggression: Assessment, prevention, and intervention strategies for youth* (pp. 83–116). Brandon, VT: Clinical Psychology.

Hyde, J. S. (1984). How large are gender differences in aggression? A developmental meta-analysis. *Developmental Psychology, 20*, 722–736.

Hymel, S., Wagner, E., & Butler, L. J. (1990). Reputational bias: View from the peer group. In S. R. Asher & J. D. Coie (Eds.), *Peer rejection in childhood* (pp. 156–188). Cambridge, England: Cambridge University Press.

Kahn, P. H. (1992). Children's obligatory and discretionary moral judgments. *Child Development, 63*, 416–430.

Kavanagh, K., & Hops, H. (1994). Good girls? Bad boys?: Gender and development as contexts for diagnosis and treatment. In T. H. Ollendick & R. J. Prinz (Eds.), *Advances in Clinical Child Psychology* (Vol. 16, pp. 45–79). New York: Plenum, Press.

Kazdin, A. E. (1990). Premature termination from treatment among children referred for antisocial behavior. *Journal of Child Psychology and Psychiatry, 31*, 415–425.

Klemke, L. W. (1982). Exploring juvenile shoplifting. *Sociology and Social Research, 67*, 59–75.

Kupersmidt, J. B., Coie, J. D., & Dodge, K. A. (1990). The role of poor peer relationships in the development of disorder. In S. R. Asher & J. D. Coie (Eds.), *Peer rejection in childhood* (pp. 247–308). Cambridge, England: Cambridge University Press.

Loeber, R. (1982). The stability of antisocial and delinquent child behavior: A review. *Psychological Bulletin, 94*, 68–99.

Loeber, R. (1990). Development and risk factors of juvenile antisocial behavior and delinquency. *Clinical Psychology Review, 10*, 1–42.

Loeber, R., Green, S. M., Lahey, B. B., & Stouthamer-Loeber, M. (1990). Optimal informants of childhood disrup-tive behaviors. *Development and Psychopathology, 1*, 317–337.

Loeber, R., Tremblay, R. E., Gragnon, C., & Charlebois, P. (1989). Continuity and desistance in disruptive boys' early fighting at school. *Development and Psychopathology, 1*, 39–50.

MacFarlane, J., Allen, L., & Honzik, M. (1962). *A developmental study of behavior problems of normal children between 21 months and 14 years*. Berkeley, CA: University of California Press.

McCord, J., & Tremblay, R. E. (1992). *Preventing antisocial behavior: Interventions from birth through adolescence*. New York: Guilford Press.

McMahon, R. J., & Slough, N. (in press). Family-based intervention in the FAST track program. In R. DeV. Peters & R. J. McMahon (Eds.), *Prevention and early intervention: Childhood disorders, substance abuse, and delinquency*. Newbury Park, CA: Sage.

Meichenbaum, D., & Turk, D. C. (1987). *Facilitating treatment adherence: A practitioners guidebook*. New York: Plenum Press.

Miller, G. E. (1994). Enhancing family-based interventions for managing childhood anger and aggression. In M. J. Furlong & D. C. Smith (Eds.), *Anger, hostility and aggression: Assessment, prevention,and intervention strategies for youth* (pp. 83–116). Brandon, VT: Clinical Psychology.

Miller, G. E., & Klungness, L. (1986). Treatment of non-confrontative stealing in school-aged children. *School Psychology Review, 15*, 24–35.

Miller, G. E., & Klungness, L. (1989). Childhood theft: A comprehensive review of assessment and treatment. *School Psychology Review, 18*, 82–97.

Miller, G. E., & Moncher, F. J. (1988). Critical issues in the assessment of childhood stealing behavior. In R. Prinz (Ed.), *Advances in behavioral assessment of children and families* (Vol. 4, pp. 73–96). Greenwich, CT: JAI Press.

Miller, G. E., & Prinz, R. J. (1990). Enhancement of social learning family interventions for childhood conduct disorder. *Psychological Bulletin, 108*, 291–307.

Miller, G. E., & Prinz, R. J. (1991). Designing interventions for stealing. In G. Stoner, M. R. Shinn, & H. M. Walker (Eds.), *Interventions for achievement and behavior problems* (pp. 593–617). Silver Spring, MD: National Association of School Psychologists.

Moncher, F. J., & Miller, G. E. (in press). Non-delinquent youth's stealing behavior and their perceptions of parents, school, and peers. *Journal of Adolescence*.

Moore, D. R., Chamberlain, P., & Mukai, Z. H. (1979). Children at risk for delinquency: A follow-up comparison of aggressive children and children who steal. *Journal of Abnormal Child Psychology, 7*, 345–355.

Morrison, R., Furlong, F., & Morrison, S. (1994). School violence to school safety: Reframing the issue for school psychologists. *School Psychology Review, 23*, 236–256.

National Institute of Education, U.S. Dept. of Health, Education, and Welfare. (1977). *Violent schools—Safe schools. The safe school study report to the Congress* (Vol. 1). Washington, DC: U.S. Government Printing Office.

Nimick, E. H. (1990). *Juvenile court property cases* (Juvenile Justice Bulletin). Washington, DC: U.S. Department of Justice.

Olweus, D. (1993). *Bullying at school: What we know and what we can do.* Cambridge, MA: Blackwell.

Patterson, G. E. (1982). *Coercive family processes.* Eugene, OR: Castalia.

Patterson, G. E. (1986). Performance models for antisocial boys. *American Psychologist, 41,* 432–444.

Patterson, G. E., DeBaryshe, B. D., & Ramsey E. (1989). A developmental perspective on antisocial behavior. *American Psychologist, 44,* 329–335.

Pepler, D. J., & Slaby, R. G. (1994). Theoretical and developmental perspectives on youth and violence. In L. D. Eron, J. H. Gentry, & P. Schlegel (Eds.), *Reasons to hope: A psychosocial perspective on violence and youth* (pp. 27–58). Washington, DC: American Psychological Association.

Prinz, R. J., & Miller, G. E. (1994). Family-based treatment for childhood antisocial behavior: Experimental influences on dropout and engagement. *Journal of Consulting and Clinical Psychology, 62,* 645–650.

Reid, J. B. (1975). The child who steals. In G. R. Patterson, J. B. Reid, R. Jones, & R. E. Conger (Eds.), *A social learning approach to a family intervention: Vol 1. The socially aggressive child* (pp. 135–138). Eugene, OR: Castalia.

Reid, J. B., & Hendriks, A. (1973). Preliminary analysis of the effectiveness of direct home intervention for the treatment of predelinquent boys who steal. In L. A. Hamerlynck, L. C. Hardy, & L. J. Mash (Eds.), *Behavior therapy: Methodology, concepts, and practice* (pp. 209–220). Champaign, IL: Research Press.

Reid, J. B., & Patterson, G. R. (1989). The development of antisocial behavior patterns in childhood and adolescence. *European Journal of Personality, 3,* 107–120.

Robins, L. N., & Rutter, M. (Eds.). (1990). *Straight and devious pathways to adulthood.* New York: Cambridge University Press.

Rolf, J., Masten, A. S., Cicchetti, D., Neuchterlein, K. H., & Weintraub, S. (1990). *Risk and protective factors in the development of psychopathology.* New York: Cambridge University Press.

Rubel, R. J. (1977). *Unruly schools: Disorders, disruptions, and crimes.* Lexington, MA: D.C. Heath.

Rutter, M., Tizard, J., & Whitmore, R. (1970). *Education, health and behavior.* New York: Wiley.

Selman, R. L. (1980). *The growth of interpersonal understanding.* San Diego, CA: Academic Press.

Seymore, F. W., & Epston, D. (1989). An approach to childhood stealing with evaluation of 45 cases. *Australian and New Zealand Journal of Family Therapy, 10,* 137–143.

Stevens, R. D. (1994). Planning for safer and better schools: School violence prevention and intervention strategies. *School Psychology Review, 23,* 204–215.

Tremblay, R. E., Masse, B., Perron, D., Leblanc, M., Schwartzman, A., & Ledingham, J. (1992). Early disruptive behavior, poor school achievement, delinquent behavior, and delinquent personality: Longitudinal analyses. *Journal of Consulting and Clinical Psychology, 60,* 64–72.

U.S. Department of Justice. (1991). *School crime: A national crime victimization survey report.* Washington, DC: Bureau of Justice Statistics.

U.S. Department of Justice. (1995). *Crime in the United States* (Uniform Crime Reports). Washington, DC: Federal Bureau of Investigation.

Vuchin, S., Bank, L., & Patterson, G. R. (1992). Parenting, peers, and the stability of antisocial behavior in preadolescent boys. *Developmental Psychology, 28,* 510–521.

Waas, G. A., & Honer, S. A. (1990). Situational attributions and dispositional inferences: The development of peer reputation. *Merrill-Palmer Quarterly, 36,* 239–260.

Wahler, R. G. (1980). The insular mother: Her problems in parent-child treatment. *Journal of Applied Behavior Analysis, 13,* 207–219.

Wahler, R. G., & Dumas, J. E. (1987). Stimulus class determinants of mother-child coercive interchanges in multidistressed families: Assessment and intervention. In J. D. Burchard & S. N. Burchard (Eds.), *Prevention of delinquent behavior* (pp. 190–219). Beverly Hills, CA: Sage.

Webster-Stratton, C. (1990). Stress: A potential disrupter of parent perceptions and family interactions. *Journal of Clinical Child Psychology, 19,* 302–312.

Weger, R. M. (1987). Children and stealing. In A. Thomas & J. Grimes (Eds.), *Children's needs and psychological perspectives* (pp. 571–578). Washington, DC: National Association of School Psychologists.

Weiner, B. (1986). *An attributional theory of motivation and emotion.* New York: Springer-Verlag.

18
Cheating

F. Clark Power
Ann Marie R. Power

University of Notre Dame

Background and Development

Cheating in school has always been a significant problem, but it has become decidedly worse in recent years. In 1969, for example, 33.8% of high school students confessed to using a cheat sheet on a test; in 1989, more than double that number (67.8%) confessed to such use (Schab, 1991). Although the high incidence of cheating evokes cries of outrage from adult leaders, few students seem concerned. An overwhelming majority of students (78%) report that they are not at all offended by cheating, and more students approve of cheating than disapprove (Johnston, Bachman, & O'Malley, 1990). Some educators and social scientists believe that the pervasiveness of student cheating signals the moral decay of the nation's youth; others, however, attribute cheating to broader problems in the culture and organization of schools and society. Cheating in school is, after all, not a new problem. Over 60 years ago, Willard Waller (1932) reported widespread use of "cribbing" on examinations: "Certainly, a large percentage of any student body cribs occasionally, and another group cribs habitually" (p. 360). The purpose of this chapter is to understand why students cheat; what the rising incidence of cheating means for those who work in schools; and how school psychologists working with teachers, administrators, and counselors can effectively address this problem.

Cheating and Character

In the popular media, cheating is typically seen as a defect of character or a lack of virtue. This view led Hartshorne and May (1928–1930) to conduct their well known "Studies of Character." Hartshorne and May found very little behavioral consistency across a number a situations in which students were tempted to cheat. These researchers discovered that in spite of what students say about honesty, they will cheat when the rewards are high and the risks are low. The Hartshorne and May studies debunked the notions of character and virtue by showing that situational factors, such as the probability of detection, were far more powerful than internal factors, such as a virtue of honesty, in predicting cheating.

Since the Hartshorne and May studies, social learning theorists have elaborated how situational factors regulate moral behavior. Their research shows that anticipated sanctions, whether in the form of concrete rewards and punishments or social approval and disapproval (cf. Bandura, 1991), influence behavior. Sanctions help to explain why children may espouse the virtue of honesty but not always practice it. Adults want to hear that children esteem the virtues, but they also want children to get good grades. Adults, moreover, do not always practice what they preach. When conflicts occur between preaching and practice, research on modeling shows that practice predominates (Bandura, 1986).

The rise of cheating over the last 30 years may in part be due to a lack of positive role models, leading to a growing cynicism about adult society. In 1969, 49.1% of high school students agreed that people in the U.S. were honest; in 1989, 23.8% agreed (Schab, 1991). The majority of students think that adults in almost all professions (the exceptions are judges and medical doctors) are dishonest sometimes. Whether or not adolescents' perceptions are correct, they no doubt influence how seriously adolescents regard their own and their peers' cheating. If students believe that everyone cheats some of the time, it is easy to excuse cheating as a human foible or even as a necessity. Moreover, it is easy to dismiss moral admonitions about cheating as hypocritical.

The rise of cheating may also be explained as a reaction to ever constricting opportunities for social advancement (Michaels & Miethe, 1989). In this sense, cheating is the by-product of a highly competitive society that values winning at any cost (Kohn, 1992). Examples abound of athletes, business executives, building contractors, and adults from all walks of life who cheat to gain a competitive edge. Competition is fruitful insofar as individuals are willing to abide by the rules that regulate any particular activity. Unfortunately the heat of competition often seems to lead individuals to focus selfishly on their own goals, making it easier to cheat and to disregard others' welfare (Staub, 1978). The negative effects of competition may well be magnified by a meritocratic system that richly compensates the winners and provides little or nothing to the losers. The recognition given to virtue pales in comparison to that given to material success. Unfortunately, children witness the rewards gained by cheating and find little compensation in the practice of virtue.

Although psychologists now recognize that situational factors have a major influence on cheating, psychologists are coming to a renewed appreciation for the role of character in moral behavior. Re-analyses of the Hartshorne and May data indicate greater behavior consistency across situations than had originally been noticed (Burton, 1963). Moreover, Kohlberg's (1984) research bridged the gap between words and deeds by showing that stages of moral reasoning are related to moral action. More recently cognitive developmentalists have begun to identify personality factors that influence moral agency (Arnold, 1993; Higgins, 1995; Nisan, 1985). Adolescents, for example, may be more likely to resist the temptation to cheat if their self-concept or sense of identity is rooted in moral values.

Developmental Perspective

Most studies of cheating, whether focused on the individual or the social context, fail to examine the problem from a developmental perspective. Cheating is all too often regarded as the violation of a socially approved standard for behavior. Yet, clearly, cheating has different meanings for students as they mature. Young children, for example, may violate rules unknowingly. Older children may think of cheating as wrong only if it would hurt the teacher's feelings. The escalating severity of sanctions for cheating from elementary school through college suggests that as children develop, the social significance of their cheating grows as does their moral responsibility for honest behavior.

Social learning theorists view the development of children's standards of moral behavior as becoming more cognitively complex and internalized as children grow older (Bandura, 1991). Initially parents give children simple prohibitions backed by concrete rewards and punishments. Later parents and other authorities teach children more abstract rules and rely on more subtle expressions of social approval and disapproval. Ultimately parents and teachers attempt to help children to regulate their own behavior according to agreed upon standards of conduct.

Cheating is a very general term for all kinds of behavior from plagiarism to taking too much time to complete a test. Cheating also depends upon directly stated and implied rules for collaboration and research. These rules may change abruptly from one grade level to an-

other. For example, in the third grade children may be permitted to copy a research paper from an encyclopedia. In the seventh grade such copying may be seen as plagiarism, yet paraphrasing from an encyclopedia may be permitted. The seriousness of cheating is often difficult to gauge because its negative consequences are difficult to apprehend. For example, suppose 12-year-old Billy was unable to prepare for a test because his parents got into a terrible fight the night before. If Billy does not cheat, he may get an undeserved low grade. If Billy cheats, who will be hurt?

Jean Piaget (1932/1965) offered a penetrating developmental analysis of cheating that is particularly sensitive to the social context. He described cheating as a "defensive reaction" brought on by an unnecessarily individualistic educational system (p. 287). In Piaget's view, children are logically disposed to learn cooperatively and, in particular, to "emulate" successful students. The social structure of schools forces students either to comply with the teacher or to resist. In either case, cheating is likely to result. Compliance encourages weaker students to cheat in order to keep up with their peers, while resistance takes the form of organized cheating or at the very least a strictly enforced code of silence. Given the significant role that authority plays in maintaining the competitive system, Piaget was not surprised to find that children regarded cheating primarily as a violation of the teachers' rules and expectations. Piaget and his colleagues asked children between the ages of 6 and 12 years to respond to the question: "Why must you not copy from your friend's book?" They coded the children's answers into one of the following categories: (a) authority because copying violates an adult prohibition, (b) equality because copying hurts another student, and (c) utility because cheating is useless, you learn nothing. They found that the appeal to authority was made by 100% of children between the ages of 6 and 7 but dropped to 15% at age 12. On the other hand, the appeal to equality was not made by children until age 10 (26%) and rose to 62% by the ages of 11 and 12. The appeal to utility was relatively uncommon; it did not appear until age 10 (5%) and rose to only 25% by age 12.

Piaget's results indicate that children's reasons for not cheating develop with age, beginning with authority and ending with equality. His results less clearly support his view of cheating as the by-product of a competitive and adult-dominated social structure. Although young children align cheating with disobedience rather than dishonesty, the majority of older children see cheating as unfairness or hurting others. Few children, moreover, state that cheating is justifiable "solidarity" in response to a harsh social order, although Piaget suggests that many more may have thought it. Piaget cites the following example from an 11-year-old as an expression of this kind of solidarity: "For those who can't learn they ought to be allowed to have a little look, but for those who can learn it isn't fair. . . . He ought not have copied. But if he was not clever it was more or less all right for him to do it" (p. 289). This answer indicates a genuine moral conflict. On the one hand, cheating is clearly seen as wrong ("one ought not to cheat"); on the other hand, a child's inability to learn entitles that child to extra help. This example suggests that children's understanding of the problem of cheating should not be isolated from their understanding of larger issues of justice in the process of classroom instruction.

Thorkildsen (1989) explored children's thinking about fair instructional practices by asking students from first grade through college to evaluate five different ways of modifying instruction in response to differences in learning pace. Students from all age groups believed that the practice of peer tutoring, of having the faster students assist the slower students, was the most fair followed by the practice of giving the faster students enrichment exercises while the slower students completed the assignment. Students from all age groups also believed that the practice of allowing slower students not to complete their assignments was the least fair. An analysis of the reasoning students used to justify their evaluation yielded a developmental scale with five levels, which describe different goals for doing schoolwork. At the first level, the goal of schoolwork is to gain rewards. The concern for slower students is whether they get the extrinsic reward rather than whether they complete their assignment. At the second level, the goal is that all students finish their work. At the third level, the goal is not that everyone completes their work but that everyone learns equally well. At the fourth level, there is a recognition that the more capable students should have an opportunity to move ahead. There is also the goal that everyone should learn equally well. Students tend to vacillate between these goals. At the fifth level, the notion that the more able should be allowed to move ahead is accepted without vacillation.

Thorkildsen refers to the work of Nichols, Patashnick, and Mettetal (1986) in noting parallels between their levels of children's conceptions of intelligence and her levels. Students at her Level 3 believe that fairness requires an equality of learning. They understand learning to mean the accumulation of information rather than the development of reasoning skills. Students at the fifth level think of learning as the development of reasoning skills, which may explain why they think it is fair that the faster learners have an opportunity to move ahead.

Thorkildsen's research suggests that cheating has different meanings for students at different levels. Students at the first two levels (usually before the age of 10) focus on the completion of work rather than learning. Thus they are unlikely to understand why students who complete their work first should not be able to share their answers with slower students. Students at the next level (usually between the ages of 10 and 18 years) appreciate the distinction between finishing an assignment and learning the material. Because they regard learning as acquiring information, however, they emphasize the product—getting the right answer—over the process—developing an intellectual skill. Therefore, they are unlikely to see much harm in sharing information. Only at the fourth and fifth levels can students really appreciate the fairness of the meritocratic system of instruction and the ways in which cheating subverts this system.

Kohlberg's moral stage theory (see Moral Reasoning and Behavior, this volume) provides the most sensitive approach to the reasoning that informs children and adolescents' notions of honesty and their rationalizations for cheating. Studies conducted on the relationship between Kohlberg's stages of moral judgment and cheating indicate that the higher the individual's stage of moral judgment, the less likely he or she is to cheat (cf. Blasi, 1980; Kohlberg, 1984). Kohlberg (1970) first explained this relationship in terms of the Socratic principle that reasoning leads directly to action. Later, however, Kohlberg (1984) offered a more nuanced interpretation not only of the cheating studies but of other moral judgment—moral action studies. Kohlberg (1984) pointed out that the child's moral stage does not lead to different conclusions about whether cheating is right or wrong; most subjects at all stages acknowledge that cheating is wrong. On the other hand, moral stage does correlate with the likelihood that students will refuse to cheat in a temptation situation (Kohlberg, 1984). This latter fact led Kohlberg to conclude that moral stage may influence students' sense of responsibility to act on the judgment that cheating is wrong by supporting or rejecting "excuses" to cheat.

Kohlberg's earlier and later positions are not mutually exclusive. At higher stages, individuals will be more motivated to act because they have a better understanding of the value of honesty and because their higher reasoning makes it more difficult to rationalize cheating than at the lower stages.

Taken together, the research on moral development and on students' perceptions of the evaluation process indicates that elementary and high school students think of cheating very differently. Cheating in the elementary grades seems largely synonymous with disobedience. Students are likely to see little intrinsic value in making sure that individuals do their own work because they equate learning with completing assignments or acquiring information. Cheating at the junior high school and high school level takes on more significance as students move to a Stage 3 morality based on meeting expectations of good behavior and upholding trust. Students also come to appreciate differences in achievement and the ways these differences are reflected in grading.

Problems and Implications

The research evidence indicates that cheating should be approached as both a social and a characterological problem. Because of the prevalence of cheating at the junior high and high school level, interpretations of the seriousness of particular instances of cheating should be made with caution. Generally, cheating behavior can be attributed to situational factors and most efficiently remedied through interventions at the level of the classroom group. Cheating may, however, be a manifestation of a characterological problem. *The Diagnostic and Statistical Manual of Mental Disorders* (American Psychiatric Association, 1994) does not specifically include cheating as a criterion of a conduct disorder, although the manual does include the related behaviors of deceitfulness and theft. Cheating is, of course, a form of deceit and may in certain instances be seen as a form of theft (e.g., in cases of plagiarism, copying another's exam answers, or fraudulently obtaining a test).

Achenbach and Edelbrock (1981) include cheating with lying as a single item on the Child Behavior Checklist. They find that approximately 50% to 85% of children referred for professional treatment are reported to lie or cheat, whereas only 15% to 20% of children in a normal sample are. In the more recent and comprehensive Achenbach-Conners-Quay Questionnaire (ACQ), cheating and lying are distinguished, and both are found to contribute to a delinquency factor (Kazdin, 1995). A delinquent pattern typically includes not only lying and cheating but also such behaviors as theft, running away, setting fires, and truancy (Achenbach, 1993). Another way of classifying cheating is to see it along with lying and stealing as part of a covert (as opposed to an overt) polarity of antisocial behavior (Loeber, Lahey, & Thomas, 1991).

This volume's chapters on conduct disorders, lying, and stealing provide a good summary of the research and issues relevant to the clusters of behaviors labeled as delinquent or covert. These chapters note that particular attention must be paid to early manifestations of antisocial behavior because the onset of character disorders occurs in early childhood. Conduct disorders may also be accompanied by other disorders such as Attention-Deficit/Hyperactivity Disorder and Oppositional Defiant Disorder (Kazdin, 1995). Cheating may in certain instances be a response to difficulties in paying attention during class and preparing for examinations. Cheating may also be a way of opposing teachers' authority. Clearly to assess the significance of any particular act of cheating or even pattern of cheating, one must ascertain both the context in which cheating occurs and the motivation for the cheating. Several personality factors have been shown to be correlated with cheating, such as low self-esteem, fear of failure, and difficulty with authority figures (Bushway & Nash, 1977; Evans & Craig, 1990; Murphy, 1993). Cheating has also been related to pressures at home, part-time work, and absences from school (Evans & Craig, 1990).

Cheating Within the School Context

Many social psychologists regard cheating as a form of deviance insofar as cheating entails the violation of an agreed-upon expectation for behavior. Michaels and Miethe (1989), for example, maintain that cheating is explicable by an integrated model of deviance drawing from deterrence, rational-choice, social-bond, and social-learning theories. Deterrence theory stipulates that undesirable behavior can be curtailed by a high risk of detection and swift and severe sanctions. The high incidence of cheating may be partly due to a perception that it is easy to get away with cheating and that those who get caught are not severely punished. Teachers and administrators endorse deterrence theory insofar as they typically respond to cheating and other discipline problems with greater surveillance and harsher punishments.

Rational-choice theory unmasks the simplicity of deterrence theory by proposing that anticipated rewards as well as punishments enter into the calculated choice to engage in deviant behavior (Piliavin, Thornton, Gartner, & Matsueda, 1986). Schools mimic the wider society by ignoring the virtuous (except with token citizenship awards) and rewarding top athletes and scholars. Therefore, students may decide to cheat in order to gain the rewards most readily proffered by schools. One serious shortcoming of rational-choice theory, however, is that it focuses on the decision maker without considering the social context in which choices are made. Social-bond theory postulates that deviant behavior occurs as a result of loosened ties to society (Hirschi, 1969). Michaels and Miethe (1989) note, however, that strong social ties may predict cheating if those ties are to peers who cheat.

All of the just mentioned theories may be related to social learning theory. Of particular relevance, however, is differential association-reinforcement theory, which builds on social-bond theory by postulating that deviant behavior is fostered through relationships with those who engage in such behaviors. Thus, students who socialize with others who cheat will find reinforcement in the form of social approval for their cheating and social disapproval when they refuse to cooperate in cheating or in covering it up.

Michaels and Miethe (1989) conclude that all four of these social-psychological theories of deviance predict self-reported cheating (in a sample of college students at a large university with an honor code). In reaching this conclusion, however, they criticize the premise that cheating is a form of deviance. Because the majority of students in their sample perceived cheating as an acceptable way of attaining good grades and the benefits that go with them, they suggest that cheating, from a statistical point of view, is a "normative" behavior (Michaels & Miethe, 1989, p. 882). The term "normative" is a misleading one, however, because although the majority of students may engage in and accept cheating, they also see cheating as wrong. Norms can be defined from a descriptive, behavioral perspective as how most subjects *do* act and from a prescriptive, evaluative perspective as how most subjects believe that they *should* act. As Power, Higgins, and Kohlberg (1989) note, the fact that subjects may tolerate and sometimes encourage the violation of rules against cheating does not mean that students think cheating ought to be practiced as a moral ideal. Most students recognize that cheating is wrong but see it as a way of life.

Power et al. (1989) argue that, in many schools, the honesty norm (considered from a prescriptive, evaluative perspective) has not taken hold or become institutionalized as a group norm. Students have personal objections to cheating but do not see cheating as violating a shared expectation for behavior. Peer pressure to share answers and to cover up cheating constitutes a "counter norm" to honesty insofar as students experience a need to conform in the sense of fitting in with others in the group. Yet this expectation to go along with the crowd does not have the obligatory force of an expectation based on values and on reason. Thus cheating may be a quasi-norm from a descriptive point of view, while also being a form of deviance from a prescriptive point of view.

Surprisingly little attention has been given to understanding how students regard cheating. Most students of all ages think that cheating is wrong, but few stress that cheating is unfair to or harms others. For example, 73.5% of high school students agree with the statement, "Cheating only hurts the cheater" (Schab, 1991). This response suggests that most students think of cheating primarily as a prudential rather than as a moral issue (Tisak & Turiel, 1994). Perhaps the fact that cheating rules are imposed from above leads students to focus primarily on the risks and consequences of getting caught rather than on the intrinsic immorality of cheating. Students may, of course, realize that cheating is unfair in the abstract but in the context of school regard such unfairness as trivial. Nisan (1985) argues that individuals allow themselves and others to deviate to a degree from the moral ideal insofar as those deviations are seen as excusable. These deviations are permitted presumably because they are due to strong temptations or because they are relatively unimportant in the context of competing considerations. In Nisan's view, individuals define a level of "limited acceptable morality" in which they may knowingly violate moral norms without believing that they are immoral persons or that they have done something really wrong. Students may regard cheating as "limited acceptable morality" (or immorality) insofar as students acknowledge that cheating is wrong but excuse cheating as necessary in certain situations (Schab, 1991).

This chapter's authors believe that the acceptance of cheating among most students can best be understood within the context of a school structure that is meritocratic and authoritarian. Students are required to earn status in schools through their performance on daily assignments, periodic tests, and papers. Teachers assign grades by comparing students with each other, although the teachers may not distribute student grades strictly along a bell curve. While children do learn to compete in other contexts (e.g., by playing games with their friends or in more structured athletic programs), classrooms are the main locus of competition in childhood.

The assignment of students to ability-level classes and tracks and the emphasis given to grades and academic awards are predicated on the assumption that students will work independently and achieve according to their abilities and effort. According to Dreeben (1968), students need to internalize the norms of independence and achievement in order to be prepared for adult society. Teachers play a major role in helping students become independent workers by regulating when they can work with one another and when they must work alone. Teachers must sometimes intervene in children's relationships with their parents and friends in order to foster children's independence. This intervention may appear to be artificial because parents and friends are naturally inclined to offer help. It may also seem arbitrary because the teacher decides which tasks are to be done independently for the sake of evaluation and which are to be done cooperatively for the sake of instruction. Yet even when teachers attempt to clarify their expectations, the line between cooperation and collusion remains fuzzy. This fuzziness is due to the fact that helping behavior which is ordinarily thought of as praiseworthy can be construed as cheating in certain teacher-defined situations.

Differing Perceptions of Rules and Situations

To explain why a particular student cheats, it is necessary to ascertain how that student defines the situation in which he or she decides to cheat. Sociologists use the term "definition of the situation" to refer to both a "process" and a "product" (Waller, 1932, p. 292). As a process, an "individual explores the behavior possibilities of a situation, marking out particularly the limitations which the situation imposes upon his [or her] behavior, with the final result that the individual forms an attitude toward the situation, or, more exactly, in the situation" (Waller, p. 292). Waller claims that this process is "intimately subjective" and "must be worked out anew in the mind of every human being" (p. 293). In the case of cheating, students attend not only to a teacher's prohibitions against cheating but also to classroom peers' expectations for help. This leads to a dilemma or to what Waller calls a "conflict of moralities" (1932, p. 361).

Obviously, differences between the ways in which teachers and students define the situation lead to problems. While teachers may see cheating as a matter of character and honesty, students may see it as a matter of peer solidarity or as a game of fooling the teacher. Students and teachers confront very different *received* definitions of the cheating situation (the definition of the situation as product) because of the different cultural contexts in which they reside. Within the students' culture, letting others copy their answers and keeping silent about cheating violations are well established counter norms. Teachers, on the other hand, belong to an adult culture that opposes cheating and encourages vigilance, particularly in the school setting. Teachers generally assume that many of their students will cheat if they have an opportunity to do so. Students recognize that their teachers do not trust them and are trying to catch them cheating. Both teachers and students thus find themselves engaged in a "cat and mouse" dynamic. This dynamic severely limits what teachers believe are possible ways of addressing the cheating problem.

The split between teacher and student cultures is due primarily not to the generational gap but to the authority structure of school. Teachers and administrators have almost absolute responsibility for making and enforcing school rules. This allocation of responsibility may be justifiable insofar as students are ignorant of what is right and wrong and are so immature that they need almost complete external regulation. Yet there is no evidence that students are so ignorant and irresponsible that they can have no meaningful role in the disciplinary process. In fact, this allocation of responsibility alienates students and thus undermines the effectiveness of disciplinary policies. Is it surprising to find that students care little about violations of school rules, like the cheating rule, when they have no investment in such rules? Or is it surprising to find that students ban together to protect themselves from teachers and administrators who do not seek their opinion or seem to care about the effects of school rules on the students? The authoritarian structure of schools drives students and teachers apart fostering mutual ignorance and suspicion. Furthermore, an authoritarian structure aimed at control rather than moral education deprives students of an opportunity to learn responsibility.

Alternatives

Classroom Strategies

Despite the fact that educators regard cheating as a serious problem, only 5.4% of high school students agree that schools are an effective "source of guidance concerning honesty" (Schab, 1991). Why are schools so ineffective? Part of the problem may well be structural;

schools, as noted, are meritocracies. Rewards, such as track placement, access to special classes, recognition in awards ceremonies, scholarships, and admission into selective prep schools and universities depend on getting high grades. Failure to achieve high grades can lead to such negative sanctions as teacher and parent disapproval, disadvantageous track and course placement, and diminished employment opportunities. Students may find that teachers' pleas for honesty ring hollow in a highly competitive environment in which so much emphasis is placed on grades. One way to limit cheating is to strike a better balance in the classroom between competition and cooperation. The academic and social benefits of cooperative learning strategies are well documented and approaches are readily available (Johnson & Johnson, 1989). As Thorkildson (1989) has found, students of all ages believe that they should help other students in the learning process. Unfortunately, she also reports that few teachers take advantage of cooperative-learning and peer-tutoring approaches. The use of cooperative approaches demonstrates that teachers sincerely support students' natural desire to assist their peers. Once cooperation has been legitimized, teachers are in a better position to explain why, in certain cases, individual assignments and tests are necessary.

A second way to limit cheating is to give more attention to the moral and civic ends of education. Students cheat not only to gain a competitive edge but to win approval or avoid disapproval. They correctly perceive that virtue receives little recognition outside of their school's handbook, graduation speeches, and a token citizenship award. Moral and values education programs have long been under attack by conservatives and liberals for indoctrinating values or failing to respect the barrier between church and state. The result can be that values essential to the school and wider society, such as honesty, are not taught in the classroom.

It is far easier to respond to cheating with prevention tactics, such as strict test supervision, alternate test forms, and greater spacing between desks, than it is to deal with cheating as a moral issue. Prevention tactics may well curtail cheating behavior, but they fail to address the mentality that gives rise to cheating in the first place. Moreover, as noted earlier, such tactics are based on the uninvestigated presupposition that students will cheat if they have the opportunity to do so. Many students do, in fact, construe teachers' lack of vigilance as an invitation to cheat because students have become accustomed to their teachers' mistrust. On the other hand, students typically respond favorably to teachers open to a more trusting relationship.

Instead of automatically resorting to prevention tactics, teachers would be well served if they negotiated a contract of trust with their students. In return for a promise of honesty on tests and assignments, teachers could promise to act in ways consistent with trust. For example, if students pledge honesty, teachers could pledge to leave the classroom during tests. This kind of agreement is at the heart of the honor code programs at the service academies and many universities. Honor code programs go on, of course, to stipulate that students who observe cheating must report it to an honor code committee. Reporting is the most difficult part of this honor code because students generally think of reporting as a form of betrayal. Teachers are rightly skeptical that students will agree to report another student. Yet the teachers could negotiate a contract focused on mutual trust. If students or teachers observe cheating, then the contract would be dissolved and teachers would be free to resort to prevention tactics. The teachers should, of course, make every effort to renegotiate the honesty contract because of the onus of teaching in a situation in which mistrust has become publicly acknowledged.

Once they establish an effective honesty contract, teachers can explore with students the desirability of having an honor code for their classroom and perhaps their school. Student concern about reporting another student can be partly alleviated in a situation in which students do not have to hand over a fellow student to an adult authority. Schools that have enjoyed success with honor codes have active student-led honor code committees. These committees may receive adult input as long as students play a major role. Student concern about reporting can also be lessened by granting honor code committees some flexibility in determining the severity of punishment. Students are understandably reluctant to report other students if the penalties are likely to be severe. Severe penalties may also inhibit students from admitting to cheating.

The idea of negotiating a student/teacher contract applies certain features of the just-community approach to moral education described by Power et al. (1989). The just-community approach involves students and teachers in a democratic process of making and enforcing disciplinary rules and policies. The key to this process is having teachers share responsibility with all students, not only those elected to a student council or appointed to an honor board. Teachers' unilateral use of prevention tactics sends students the message that cheating is the teachers' problem. The contractual approach lets students know that the cheating problem belongs to everyone, especially the students. The purpose of negotiating a contract is to break the barrier between the student and teacher cultures in order to build a common norm opposed to cheating.

Negotiating such a contract requires time and effort. In the just-community approach, problems like cheating are discussed in regularly scheduled community meetings. Teachers who wish to employ a contractual approach to cheating need to set aside time for discussing why students should not cheat. Moral-discussion research indicates that teachers are effective only when they facilitate student participation (Colby, Kohlberg, Fenton, Speicher-Dubin, & Lieberman, 1977). This requires that teachers give up their role as authorities and encourage students to think about how cheating affects other students and why cheating is wrong. Teachers must resist the temptation to give students a lecture on honesty or to ask closed questions, such as, "Don't you all see that cheating is wrong?" The moral-discussion approach derives from cognitive developmental research indicating that students actively construct their moral reasoning. A good discussion stimulates cognitive conflict, challenging students to rethink why they hold certain values and behave as they do.

Moral discussion over the course of a semester has been shown to promote significant moral stage development (Higgins, 1980). Although resistance to cheating is positively correlated with stage development, moral discussion interventions alone have not been successful in changing student behavior (Blatt & Kohlberg, 1975). This lack of change is probably due to the fact that moral discussions only produce a modest amount of change and that the hypothetical moral dilemmas used in these discussions do not address cheating directly. Moral discussion can more profitably be used in the context of making a real decision about classroom cheating.

As one of the parties to an honesty contract, teachers can and should insist that students be sincere in promising trust and that students understand why trust is important. Teachers should help students to see that the primary purpose of the honesty policy is to prevent dishonest students from gaining an unfair advantage over honest students. When teachers lose sight of this custodial responsibility and simply assert their authority as teachers, it becomes difficult for students to regard cheating as anything more than disobedience. Teachers should also be cautious about advancing the argument that cheaters only hurt themselves. This argument may easily be interpreted as supporting the student view that cheaters hurt *only* themselves. Teachers need to be clear with students that the moral evil of cheating resides in the act of deception. Of course, teachers should also discourage the copying of routine assignments out of laziness. Care should be taken, however, to distinguish this kind of copying, which students find trivial, with copying on a test or paper.

Teachers who use the contractual approach should be willing to discuss and modify their testing and grading practices. Students report that tests surveying large amounts of material, grading on a curve, and assessments based on very few tests or assignments increase the likelihood of cheating (Bushway & Nash, 1977; Evans & Craig, 1990). Teachers will have an easier time persuading students to be fair to fellow students by not cheating if students perceive that their teachers are making a sincere effort to make their tests fair. Moreover, teachers will have an easier time building a climate of trust if students feel that they can openly raise issues concerning when a test is being given, how much material is to be covered in it, and whether special help may be required.

Individual Assessment

Although cheating can generally be approached at the level of the classroom, individual students may require special attention. Assessment for a cheating problem should proceed according to the framework provided in the chapters on lying and stealing. The psychologist must first determine the forms of cheating that the child has engaged in, their severity, their frequency, and their history. Certain forms of cheating, such as plagiarism, may be due to teachers' failures to explain their expectations effectively or to students' inattention to these explanations. Because cheating is such a widespread phenomenon and because teachers do not always have an accurate view of the cheating situation in the classrooms (Evans & Craig, 1990), the psychologist may need to ask some of the referred child's classmates about the extent of cheating in their classrooms.

In trying to understand a child's cheating, the school psychologist should determine whether a child's cheating tends (a) to be a response to peer pressure, test anxiety, learning or study problems, or low self-esteem; (b) to stem from hostility toward a particular teacher or authority figures in general; or (c) to be an attempt to gain an unfair advantage over others, to meet the unreasonably high expectations of parents and teachers, or to avoid humiliation. Many children cheat because they are doing poorly in school. In such cases, learning or attention problems may be present. Given that children with conduct disorders generally manifest a cluster of behavior problems, ratings scales or checklists may be a helpful way of ascertaining whether cheating is symptomatic of a more pervasive antisocial problem. Finally the psychologist should evaluate the child's moral reasoning about cheating. This can be done by asking the referred child to discuss some of the reasons why students may be tempted to cheat and why cheating is wrong.

Individual Interventions

The therapeutic approaches discussed in the preceding chapters on lying and stealing are all applicable to the cheating problem. Parental training approaches are most relevant when cheating is symptomatic of a character disorder or when cheating is a response to parental pressure to succeed. Skill training approaches are helpful in addressing children's difficulties in coping with their schoolwork and with problems of peer acceptance. Behavioral approaches are difficult to apply to cheating because the rewards for cheating are so great in contrast to the risks of being caught. Teachers may be helped,

however, to find ways of acknowledging prosocial behavior. In cases in which individuals are suspected of cheating, the punishment for cheating should be lessened if individuals admit to it.

Summary

Cheating in school is a growing problem brought about by factors in society and the school as well as in the individual student. Although teachers regard cheating as an antisocial behavior, many children accept cheating as part of coping with the demands of school. Because of its pervasiveness, cheating must be addressed at the classroom level through approaches that elicit the cooperation of the teacher and the students. In individual cases, cheating may be symptomatic of a character disorder, of attentional and learning disabilities, or of difficulties in peer and parental relationships. Interventions at the individual level should take into account the extent to which cheating is part of a broader problem or complex of problems.

Recommended Resources

Evans, E. D., & Craig, D. (1990). Teachers and student perceptions of academic cheating in middle and senior high schools. *Journal of Educational Research, 84*(1), 44–52.
This article contrasts the ways in which teachers and students regard cheating.

Hartshorne, H., & May, M. A. (1928–1930). *Studies in the nature of character: Vol. 1: Studies in deceit.* New York: Macmillan.
This is the classic study of cheating. It undermined the notion of character and strongly supported the belief that cheating was best explained by situational variables.

Kazdin, A. E. (1995). *Conduct disorders in childhood and adolescence* (2nd ed.). Thousand Oaks, CA: Sage.
This book provides a concise but comprehensive discussion of character disorders, their diagnosis and assessment, their origins and trajectories, treatment approaches, prevention, and research issues.

Power, F. C., Higgins, A., & Kohlberg, L. (1989). *Lawrence Kohlberg's approach to moral education.* New York: Columbia University Press.
The authors provide an overview of Kohlberg's theory of moral development and then present the just-community approach to moral education. They discuss how the problem of cheating was resolved through a democratic process of rule making.

Schab, F. (1991). Schooling without learning: Thirty years of cheating in high school. *Adolescence, 26,* 839–847.
The author shows how cheating has grown over thirty years and how adolescents have become more cynical about the behavior of adult "role models."

References

Achenbach, T. M. (1993). Taxonomy and comorbidity of conduct problems: Evidence from empirically based approaches. *Development and Psychopathology, 5,* 51–64.

Achenbach, T. M., & Edelbrock, C. (1981). Behavioral problems and competencies reported by parents of normal and disturbed children aged 4 through 16. *Monographs of the Society for Research in Child Development, 46,* 1–82.

American Psychiatric Association. (1994). *Diagnostic and statistical manual of mental disorders* (4th Ed.). Washington, DC: Author.

Arnold, M. L. (1993). *The place of morality in the adolescent self.* Unpublished Ph.D. dissertation, Harvard University.

Bandura, A. (1986). *Social foundations of thought and action: A social cognitive theory.* Englewood Cliffs, NJ: Prentice Hall.

Bandura, A. (1991). Social cognitive theory of moral thought and action. In. W. M. Kurtines & J. L. Gewirtz (Eds.), *Handbook of moral behavior and development: Volume 1. Theory* (pp. 45–103). Hillsdale, NJ: Lawrence Earlbaum Associates.

Blatt, M., & Kohlberg, L. (1975). The effects of classroom moral discussion upon children's moral judgement. *Journal of Moral Education, 4,* 129–161.

Blasi, A. (1980). Bridging moral cognition and moral action: A critical review of the literature. *Psychological Bulletin, 88,* 1–45.

Burton, R. V. (1963). Generality of honesty reconsidered. *Psychological Review, 70,* 481–499.

Bushway, A., & Nash, W. R. (1977). School cheating behavior. *Review of Educational Research, 47,*(4), 623–632.

Colby, A., Kohlberg, L., Fenton, T., Speicher-Dubin, B., & Lieberman, M. (1977). Secondary school moral discussion programmes led by social studies teachers. *Journal of Moral Education, 6,* 90–111.

Dreeban, R. (1968). *On what is learned in school.* Reading, MA: Addison-Wesley.

Evans, E. D., & Craig, D. (1990). Teachers and student perceptions of academic cheating in middle and senior high schools. *Journal of Educational Research, 84,*(1), 44–52.

Hartshorne, H., & May, M. A. (1928–1930). *Studies in the nature of character: Vol. 1. Studies in deceit.* New York: Macmillan.

Higgins, A. (1995). Understanding the moral self: Research goals for the next five years. *Moral Education Forum,* 20 (2), 30–37.

Higgins, A. (1980). Research and measurement issues in moral education interventions. In R. Mosher (Ed.), *Moral education: A first generation of research and development* (pp. 92–107). New York: Praeger.

Hirschi, T. (1969). *Causes of deliquency.* Berkeley: University of California Press.

Johnson, D., & Johnson, R. (1989). *Cooperation and competition: Theory and research.* Edina, MN: Interaction Books.

Johnston, L., Bachman, J., & O'Malley, P. (1990). *Monitoring the future: A continuing study of the lifestyles and values of youth, 1989 Computer File.* Conducted by University of Michigan, Survey Research Center. ICPSR Ed. Ann Arbor, MI: Inter-University Consortium for Political and Social Research, Producer and Distributor.

Kazdin, A. E. (1995). *Conduct disorders in childhood and adolescence* (2nd. ed.). Thousand Oaks, CA: Sage.

Kohlberg, L. (1970). Education for justice: A modern statement of the Platonic view. In N. Sizer & T. Sizer (Eds.), *Moral education: Five lectures* (pp. 56–83). Cambridge MA: Harvard University Press.

Kohlberg, L. (1976). Moral stages and moralization: The cognitive developmental approach. In T. Lickona (Ed.), *Moral development, and behavior: Theory, research, and social issues* (pp. 31–53). New York: Holt, Rinehart, and Winston.

Kohlberg, L. (1984). *Essays on moral development: Vol. 2. The psychology of moral development.* San Francisco: Harper and Row.

Kohn, A. (1992). *No contest: The case against competition.* Boston: Houghton Mifflin.

Loeber, R., Lahey, B. B., & Thomas, C. (1991). Diagnostic conundrum of oppositional defiant disorder and conduct disorder. *Journal of Abnormal Psychology, 100,* 379–390.

Michaels, J. W., & Miethe, T. D. (1989). Applying theories of deviance to academic cheating. *Social Science Quarterly, 70*(4), 870–885.

Murphy, J. P. (1993). The nature of cheating. In J. J. Cohen & M. C. Fish (Eds.), *The handbook of school-based interventions: Resolving student problems and promoting health educational environments* (pp. 18–20). San Francisco: Jossey-Bass.

Nicholls, J. G., Patashnick, M., & Mettetal, G., (1986). Conceptions of ability and intelligence. *Child Development, 57,* 636–645.

Nisan, M. (1985). Limited morality: A concept and its educational implications. In M. Berkowitz & F. Oser (Eds.), *Moral education: Theory and application* (pp. 403–420). Hillsdale, NJ: Lawrence Erlbaum Associates.

Piaget, J. (1932/1965). *The moral judgement of the child.* Glencoe, IL: Free Press

Piliavin, I., Thornton, G., Gartner, R., & Matsueda, R. L. (1986). Crime, deterrence, and rational choice. *American Sociological Review, 51,* 101–19.

Power, F. C., Higgins, A., & Kohlberg, L. (1989). *Lawrence Kohlberg's approach to moral education.* New York: Columbia University Press.

Schab, F. (1991). Schooling without learning: Thirty years of cheating in high school. *Adolescence, 26,* 839–847.

Staub, E. (1978). *Positive social behavior and morality: Vol. 1. Social and personality differences.* New York: Academic Press.

Thorkildsen, T. (1989). Justice and the classroom: The student's view. *Child Development, 60,* 323–334.

Tisak, M., & Turiel, E. (1984). Children's conceptions of moral and prudential rules. *Child Development, 55,* 1030–1039.

Waller, W. (1932). *The sociology of teaching.* New York: John Wiley & Sons.

19

Fire Setting

Kristal E. Ehrhardt
Kevin J. Armstrong
Western Michigan University

David W. Barnett
Mark Winters
University of Cincinnati

Background and Development

Few things are more frightening to school personnel and parents than children who set fires. Fire setters threaten lives and property. The actual amount of human and property loss related to children's fire-related behaviors each year is difficult to pinpoint. Researchers explain that fire statistics are inexact for a number of reasons (Pokalo, 1993). One reason is that not every fire is countable. Some fires go undetected, are extinguished quickly, or occur in an isolated environment (Kolko & Kazdin, 1994). Other fires are observed but not revealed to authorities. For example, Kolko and Kazdin (1988a) found that up to 35% of children who were interviewed said that they had set fires but that only 9% had been reported to the authorities. It seems likely that even when fire-related behavior is known adults, parents, and school personnel may prefer to handle matters privately. Another shortcoming of the database is that, until recently, researchers had not reported children's descriptions of their fire-related behavior (Kolko & Kazdin, 1994). While it seems reasonable to be skeptical of the validity of self-report data from these children, the issue merits empirical investigation. These kinds of data could be especially helpful in clarifying children's motivations and knowledge/skill base and in understanding fire setting in general.

Prevalence and Impact

Despite the limitations in developing a complete database, several findings have been offered. Fires are one of the leading causes of death in children (Peterson, 1988). In 1985, children in the United States set approximately 57,000 fires and constituted 35% of this country's arson arrests (Cook, Hersch, Gaynor, & Roehl, 1989 as cited by Kolko & Kazdin, 1992). Fires set by children resulted

in over 200 deaths in 1990, and property loss is estimated to be in the billions of dollars per year (Pokalo, 1993). Characteristics of the fire-setting incidents vary according to data taken from retrospective reports. Showers and Pickrell (1987) reported that 71% of fires were set alone, 78% were set at home, 49% involved a motive of curiosity, and 14% of the fires resulted in damages in excess of $20,000.

School psychologists would most likely become involved with fire-setting children based on either parent or teacher request. This request would ordinarily follow an adult's observation of fire-related behaviors in the child. Fortunately for school officials, the great majority of fires set by children are at home. However, some fires occur at schools, and these need to be taken especially seriously. Fires set at school almost necessarily require more planful behavior given that schools are unlikely to have incendiary materials easily available for children. Thus, school-based fire setters must typically bring these materials or gather them in a deliberate fashion. Whether the fire-setting behaviors are observed at home, school, or the community, school psychologists should be familiar with related key terms and concepts developed by researchers in this area.

Definition of Key Terms and Concepts

Consistent with Kolko and Kazdin's (1986) request to separate match players from fire setters, Gaynor and Hatcher (1987) outlined four categories of fire-related behavior: fire interest, fire play, fire setting, and arson. These categories fall on a continuum based on the degree of involvement with fire. Note how both the role of intention and the risk of serious consequences grow considerably along this continuum.

Fire interest

On one end of the continuum is a simple interest in fire. It is common for children to be curious about fire (Jackson, Glass, & Hope, 1987). Typically, this characterizes boys more than girls, begins around age two, and extends up to at least age six. Opportunities for children to express interest in fire occur when adults light matches, birthday candles, log fires, or gas stoves. This interest, often expressed through requests to help or simply by watching the events closely, appears to be a normal behavior. It is presumed that most parents take advantage of moments when their children express curiosity (i.e., naturalistic teaching situations) to instruct them in fire safety behaviors.

Fire play

Fire play incidents are unplanned and occur two or fewer times in a child's life. Resulting fires, if they occur, are described as accidental. The motivations for the behavior seem to be curiosity and experimentation. Most of these children are boys between the ages of five and ten. Fire play should be taken seriously. Estimates are that only 33% of first-time fire play behavior actually cause a fire but that this increases to 80% for second-time fire play incidents. This is an important justification for supporting parents in providing a speedy intervention following first fire-play incidents.

Fire setting

Fire setting is differentiated from fire play in that the child deliberately seeks out the materials necessary to start the fire and, after starting it, neither attempts to extinguish the fire nor notify any one that it has started. Motivations appear complex but most frequently are reported as revenge, anger, pain, and need for excitement. Fire setting usually involves boys older than seven. For example, 89% of reported fire setters in 1987 were male (Uniform Crime Reports, 1987). In a relatively large community sample ($N = 95$), Kolko and Kazdin (1994) found that 79% of the identified fire setters were boys. Importantly, there is general agreement among researchers that children who set fires frequently engage in other antisocial behaviors (Pokalo, 1993). These behaviors are likely to continue unless immediate and appropriate interventions are implemented.

Arson

At the other end of the continuum is deliberate, malicious fire starting where the child is aware of the probability of destruction but shows no apparent concern for these consequences. Arson is a legally defined behavior, and the definition can vary somewhat from state to state. However, before finding a child guilty of arson, the courts must typically determine that a fire-setting child has reached the age of accountability. Thus, not all fire-setting children may be charged with arson. Keep in mind that fires set at school involve material not easily gathered in most school buildings. This increases the chances that fires set at school would be better classified as stemming from fire setting or arson rather than fire play.

Developmental Issues

So, why is it that some children develop appropriate fire safety behaviors while others do not? Why is it that some children act in ways to prevent fires while others start them? It is not completely clear how either normal (i.e., safe) or abnormal (i.e., dangerous) fire-related behaviors develop in children. Fire-setting children appear to differ from non-fire-setting children in at least four areas (Kolko & Kazdin, 1992). First, their risk is higher due to greater exposure to fire or fire models, increased fire curiosity, or advanced knowledge of fire. Kolko and Kazdin (1986) proposed a tentative model of risk factors including references to learning experiences and cues related to fire setting. Specifically, they argue that limited fire-awareness and fire-safety skills (cognitive components) interact with interpersonal ineffectiveness/skills deficits and motivational components to help establish a personal repertoire which supports fire setting. However, they acknowledge that there are no firm data showing a causal link between early experiences with fire setting and later fire setting because early fire *interest* seems almost universal and early fire *play* occurs in a large portion of children (especially boys).

Second, fire-setting children exhibit more psychopathology and antisocial behavior such as general social skills deficits, aggression, and delinquency. Patterson (1976a) reported that children who set fires typically exhibit empirically established, lower order behavior problems such as noncompliance, lying, stealing, and other acts of vandalism. Also, fire setters are more likely to engage in covert antisocial behaviors such as lying and truancy rather than overt antisocial behavior such as arguing, temper tantrums, or fighting (Loeber & Schmaling, 1985). Identifying abnormal motivations in these children is difficult due to the usual methodological limitations associated with relying on the self-report of a low-frequency behavior typically exhibited in private. However, based on interview data, curiosity and anger have been identified as primary motives of children who set fires.

Specifically, Kolko and Kazdin (1991) provide a detailed analysis of parent-reported data showing that both children's curiosity and anger are related to measures of fire-setting risk. However, the high-anger children in their sample were involved in more fire-related activities than were the high-curiosity children. Interestingly, the long-held notion that fire setting is linked to enuresis and cruelty to animals as a unique behavioral triad has not been supported by the majority of group studies describing fire setters (e.g., Showers & Pickrell, 1987). However, one study with psychiatric inpatients found that fire setters engaged in significantly more cruelty to animals, property destruction, lying, stealing and vandalism than non-fire-setters although they did not engage in more aggressive behaviors (Kuhnley, Hendren & Quinlan, 1982).

Third, researchers generally agree that parenting and child factors interact to help maintain problem behaviors. Parents may demonstrate more pathology, and their parenting practices may involve low monitoring, limited discipline, and reliance on negative parenting strategies. For example, mothers of fire setters have reported significantly higher levels of depressive symptomatology than mothers of non-fire-setters (Kazdin & Kolko, 1986). Further, fire setters also characterized their parents' behaviors as involving lax discipline, nonenforcement of rules and consequences, and anxiety induction (Kolko & Kazdin, 1990). As one would expect, it is difficult to determine if the child's behavior occurs as an antecedent or consequent to these parental characteristics.

Fourth, family dysfunction is characterized by low cohesion and high conflict. Kazdin and Kolko (1986) reported greater marital dysfunction in homes of fire setters compared to homes of non-fire-setters. Parents of fire setters also reported less marital satisfaction, cohesion, and expression of affection (Kolko & Kazdin, 1990). Note that data do not support the once-held belief that parental absence differentiates fire setters from non-fire-setters. Instead, it is the quality of the parent-child interaction, the specific parenting practices, and the presence of adult psychopathology which are more strongly implicated. Again, it is unclear whether the children's behavior is a product of and/or a contribution to family dysfunction. However, their coexistence is generally acknowledged by clinical researchers in this area.

Problems and Implications

Immediate and Future Implications of Problems

Self

Recidivism is a substantial problem with firesetters. In one sample, retrospective data indicated that 52% of outpatient and 72% of inpatient fire setters set a second fire within a one-year period (Kolko & Kazdin, 1988b). Other studies have found 50% to 65% recidivism rates for community children aged 6–13 years (Kolko & Kazdin, 1992). School psychologists should be aware that previous fire-setting behavior is an important predictor of future fire setting. Additionally, school psychologists should be aware of the link between firesetting and other, generally covert, antisocial behavior.

Family

As mentioned earlier, the maintenance of child antisocial behavior has been linked to different aspects of family functioning. Implicated factors include ineffective parental monitoring, rule enforcement, use of discipline, and basic safety (Barnett & Carey, 1992). Kazdin and Kolko (1986) report that antisocial behavior has been related to coercive parent-child interactions, marital discord, parent insularity, parent psychopathology, and indiscriminate caretaking. Specifically, parents and fire-setting children engage in more aversive interactions (teasing, arguing, humiliation, negative statements) than parents of normal children. Other family background variables of known fire-setting children include reports of family disruption and chaos, single-parent homes, parental absences and abandonment, and abuse. Parents of these children may be more likely to experience psychosis, depression, or antisocial behavior. In particular, maternal depression has been strongly linked to the development of antisocial behavior in boys (Patterson, 1982). Regardless whether such antisocial behavior develops before or after the parent's psychopathology, school psychologists should be aware that these factors can be reciprocally determined and maintained. Family and individual therapy may be needed to deal with related issues.

School

Although a careful assessment is indicated anytime a child engages in fire-related behaviors, it is imperative that the assessment be completed quickly when the behaviors occur in a place where planning was likely to be involved. In any case, school officials should be informed about any fire-related behavior because, as described later in this chapter, it is likely that schools are a good place for education-based prevention programs and identifying children who may be at risk for developing more severe conduct disorders. Schools can also be a source of information for parents interested in prevention at home. School officials are encouraged to communicate with local fire fighting professionals or national organizations (e.g., the National Firehawk Foundation in San Francisco, CA, or the National Fire Protection Agency in Quincy, MA) in developing a curriculum for prevention. Additional suggestions will be made in a later section of this chapter.

Related Problems

As described earlier, fire-setting children often come from dysfunctional families (Kolko & Kazdin, 1990) and would typically be diagnosed with conduct disorder (American Psychiatric Association, 1994; see Conduct Disorder, this volume). While it is generally agreed that antisocial behavior heightens a child's risk for fire setting (Forehand, Wierson, Frame, Kempton, & Armistead, 1991), Edelbrock, as cited in McMahon and Forehand

(1988), has proposed an empirically based developmental model for conduct disorder which describes a progression through four stages: oppositional, offensive, aggressive, and delinquent behaviors. Fire setting is one of the behaviors in the final and most severe stage. These data support the notion that noncompliance is a keystone behavior which places children at risk for developing more significant antisocial problems such as fire setting. If noncompliance in a student has developed into delinquent behavior (especially the covert types), conservative professionals will conclude that a fire-setting assessment is indicated. It is also important to support families with children in one of these four stages to secure professional assistance as soon as possible to stop the progression of conduct-disorder-related problems. Interventions requiring parental involvement should be implemented only after careful consideration of the family's capabilities and resources. Home-based skills training may have to be postponed or prioritized differently if the parental/familial circumstances are prohibitive. Although some school psychologists may have sufficient training and resources to assist multiproblem families, others may find it more practical to include a family therapist or clinical psychologist in evaluation or treatment of the family.

Alternative Actions

Obviously, fire setting poses immediate physical dangers both to the child who sets the fire and to family members and friends. Further, there is the possibility of severe long-term social, legal, and familial effects. Given the potentially serious consequences, intervention strategies for young fire setters and their care providers (e.g., parents and teachers) are needed. Unfortunately, in the school psychology literature there are virtually no empirical treatment outcome studies on fire setting. In related fields (e.g., clinical psychology and social work), a limited amount of treatment outcome research exists, composed primarily of case studies and single-case experimental designs. Although this body of research has sample and methodological limitations including sampling bias, few reports of treatment integrity, definitional ambiguity, few replications, and minimal attention to generalization and maintenance, several prevention and treatment programs have promising outcomes. In the following section, we discuss available strategies for prevention and intervention with young fire setters and their care providers. These strategies may be provided by a school psychologist or related professional through parent and teacher consultation.

Primary Prevention Strategies

Barnett and Carey (1992) suggest that parents take advantage of natural supervised opportunities (e.g., birthday candles, campfires, barbeques) to educate their children about fire and its uses. It seems likely that this is how most children acquire safe fire-related behaviors. However, given the serious consequences associated with fire setting and given that fire interest and fire play appear most common among young children (Baizerman & Emshoff, 1984; Federal Emergency Management Agency, 1988), early education and prevention programs are needed.

Strategies for selecting a target audience for prevention programs

Peterson (1988) suggests three common tactics for school psychologists to use when implementing prevention programs. They are (a) population-wide programs, described as a "media campaign" that may be directed at a nationwide audience; (b) high-risk group interventions, aimed at potentially high-risk children and families; and (c) milestone prevention, directed at "children as they pass a certain developmental milestone" (p. 595). Prevention programs aimed at high-risk groups and milestone groups (i.e., children aged two through ten) may be particularly appropriate targets for school psychologists. However, schools may choose to participate in population-wide programs such as "The Learn Not to Burn Campaign" by the National Fire Protection Association (1995).

Components of prevention programs

To teach children fire-safety skills and the impact of fire, prevention programs should inform children about:

- The functions and characteristics of fire (e.g., uses of fire such as cooking and ways fires can injure people).
- Ways to distinguish between fire-related objects that they may use under adult supervision (e.g., a sparkler) and those that may be used only by an adult (e.g., a match).
- What action to take if they find a lighter or match (e.g., immediately take it to an adult).
- Self-protective skills to use in the event of a fire (e.g., they should leave a burning house without stopping to get their possessions). (Kolko, Watson, & Faust, 1991).

Additionally, children might be taught to use skills such as "stop, drop, and roll" if their clothing catches fire. An important consideration when developing and implementing a prevention program is that empirical evidence demonstrates that programs employing behavioral rehearsal combined with frequent feedback and small, concrete extrinsic rewards are much more effective than programs relying on more didactic and passive educational models (Peterson, 1988).

An Overview of Strategies for Intervening with Child Fire Setters

Several authors have stressed the need for comprehensive multicomponent approaches to the treatment of young fire setters (e.g., Adler, Nunn, Northam, Lebnan, & Ross, 1994; Cox-Jones, Lubetsky, Fultz, & Kolko, 1990; Koles & Jenson, 1985; Kolko, 1983; McGrath, Marshall, & Prior, 1979). Although these programs vary in content and procedure, the intent of each is to intervene directly on the target variable of fire setting as well as on correlated keystone behaviors of the child (e.g., noncompliance and knowledge of fire safety) and parents (e.g., discipline approaches and request-making skills). A description of various potential intervention components follows.

Establishing risk

When a referral for fire setting is presented to the school psychologist, the first action should be to establish the seriousness of the problem situation. Although the risk of property damage, injury, or death are too grave for the parent or school psychologist to take any fire-setting incident lightly, interventions may vary depending upon the nature of the incident(s) and related risk factors. Kolko and Kazdin (1989a, 1989b) offer two fire-setting-risk interviews, one for children and one for parents, to assess factors related to risk (e.g., high curiosity, limited parental supervision). Both of these interviews, embedded within a problem-solving assessment approach, will assist with problem analysis and help to identify avenues for plan development.

Informing parents of their responsibilities

The Federal Emergency Management Agency (1988) and Barth (1986) recommend that, at an early stage, the school psychologist or other professional inform parents of their civil and legal responsibilities (e.g., financial responsibilities and criminal liability) for damages their child may cause. Additionally, they suggest that parents be informed of possible consequences of noncompliance with intervention procedures. Barnett and Carey (1992) advise collaboratively developing a contingency contract with parents to clarify the responsibilities of the parents, school, child, and community agencies related to fire-setting intervention. While a formal contract may not be necessary, it can serve to prompt appropriate action and to document the professional's recommendations.

Safety proofing the home and establishing a plan for parental monitoring

As mentioned previously, fire safety education is a critical part of any fire prevention plan. Fire proofing the home by removing or limiting child access to possible incen-

diary devices and combustibles is another preventative step (Barnett & Carey, 1992). For example, parents might add safety knobs to stoves or hide lighters and matches. Smoke detectors and fire extinguishers can be added to the house and emergency procedures established (e.g., emergency telephone numbers and evacuation plan). Relatedly, school psychologists may help parents to establish plans for monitoring child behaviors related to fire setting. As one suggestion, Barnett and Carey (1992) recommend the use of "off limit" areas, demarcated by brightly colored tape (e.g., dad might put a strip of orange tape in front of the fireplace). Contingencies could be added for situations in which the child enters the "off limits" area (e.g., the child must immediately go to time-out).

Investigating sources of parental stress and possible sources of support

As mentioned earlier, young firesetters may often live in families experiencing parental stress and dysfunction (Kolko & Kazdin, 1986). Obviously then, it is critical to assess sources of familial stress or parental functioning when developing interventions for child firesetters (Barnett & Carey, 1992). Due to safety concerns for the family, parents must be extremely vigilant when monitoring the behavior of children who set fires. However, parental stress and dysfunction may impede their ability to closely monitor children. With cases involving multiproblem families, the school psychologist may wish to consider utilizing other professionals in the community such as a clinical psychologist or marital/family therapist to address parent or family issues which may interfere with a child's intervention program.

The school psychologist can provide further assistance to the families by brainstorming about sources of support they might enlist to help monitor child behavior. Sources of support might include grandparents, adult friends, or older siblings. Use of an eco-map (Hartman, 1978) is one tool the psychologist might consider to help identify parental supports and stress. As an additional strategy, the school psychologist may provide support for the family by establishing a plan for close contact with parents (Barnett & Carey, 1992; Carstens, 1982). For example, in an unreported case study by the first author, daily contact was established through the use of a school-home note and a quick office visit as the parent dropped the child off at school. On the brief home-school note, the parent indicated whether the child had engaged in any match play and whether the parent was able to adhere to the plan for monitoring.

Suggesting parental participation in a structured-parenting-skills program

As noted previously, children who set fires may engage in other conduct problems, especially covert behaviors such as noncompliance or lying but also overt behaviors such as aggression or temper tantrums (Loeber & Schmaling, 1985; Patterson, 1976a). Therefore, the school psychologist may consider suggesting the parents participate in a structured-parenting-skills program for dealing with noncompliant children. Examples include programs by Barkley (1987), Forehand and McMahon (1981), and Sanders and Dadds (1993). By intervening on a keystone variable such as noncompliance, reductions may be seen in related or correlated behaviors such as aggression and temper tantrums. Minimally, parents can be provided with Patterson's (1976b) classic text on *Living with Children.* This book is an invaluable source for child-management approaches.

Considering a range of behavioral interventions for fire setting

Several behavioral interventions have been effective at reducing fire-setting behaviors and may be practical for school psychologists. Outcome studies using positive practice (Welsh, 1971), satiation (Adler et al., 1994; Holland, 1969; Wolff, 1984), and overcorrection (Koles & Jensen, 1985; McGrath et al., 1979) have appeared frequently in the literature. These procedures provide children with opportunities to be repeatedly exposed to fire-setting experiences coupled with naturalistic consequences and educational components. As an example, during satiation the child is taught the appropriate way to light a match and to extinguish it. Then, the child must light matches repeatedly until the session has ended (as many as 200 matches may be used in one session). Following this procedure, the child is required to clean the area where matches were lit. Obviously, use of these procedures require strict and careful adult supervision.

Response cost and restitution procedures have been employed with young fire setters (Adler et al., 1994; Carstens, 1982; Holland, 1969). These procedures attach loss of privileges or other consequences, (e.g., cleaning the house) to occurrence of fire-setting behaviors. Similarly, positive reinforcement procedures for nonoccurrence of fire-related behaviors have been used successfully with children (Adler et al., 1994; Holland, 1969; Kolko, 1983; Cox-Jones et al., 1990). Finally, some authors recommend the use of social skills training for children who set fires (Koles & Jensen, 1985; McGrath et al., 1979; Kolko & Ammerman, 1988) to develop overall social competence and to increase incompatible, prosocial behaviors.

In conclusion, a range of intervention options are available for use with young fire setters. During problem solving and consultation with parents and teachers, school psychologists will wish to consider specific components of an intervention package for young fire setters and their families, based upon careful consideration of the situation.

Ensuring Successful Interventions for Young Fire Setters

Collaborative relationships between educators and other school professionals, community mental health professionals, and local fire fighters are vital when dealing with juvenile fire setters (Barth, 1986; Cox-Jones et al., 1990; Federal Emergency Management Administration, 1988; Webb, Sakheim, Towns-Miranda, & Wagner, 1990). In fact, Webb et al. (1990) cite "assessment, preventive intervention, and interdisciplinary collaboration between the fire department and mental health services . . . as key factors in the identification and treatment of juvenile firesetters and their families" (p. 305). School psychologists may play a critical role in developing and facilitating relationships between these professionals. Relatedly, they may serve to coordinate services among these agencies and professionals to achieve the most beneficial outcomes for young fire setters and their families.

Summary

Fire setting by children poses serious threats to lives and property. Useful educational and behavioral interventions have been developed for treating child fire setters. School psychologists can serve an important role in developing and/or facilitating both individual interventions for children and marital/family therapy for their families, if needed. Further, school psychologists may assist in implementing fire safety programs in schools, possibly preventing the occurrence of some fire setting by children.

Recommended Resources

Barnett, D. W., & Carey, K. T. (1992). *Designing interventions for preschool learning and behavior problems.* San Francisco: Jossey-Bass.
Chapter 8 provides an overview of interventions for safety-related issues with preschool children, including fire setting. The authors present a comprehensive, multicomponent list of suggestions for addressing fire-setting behaviors with young children. These suggestions range from strategies for safety proofing the house to descriptions of specific behavioral interventions for fire setting.

Federal Emergency Management Agency. (1994). *The National Juvenile Firesetter/Arson Control and Prevention Program.* Washington, DC: U.S. Fire Administration, U.S. Government Printing Office.
This series of manuals is a continuation of a federal prevention program begun in 1987. The focus of this work is to provide the necessary information to develop collaborative prevention programs between fire departments, mental health workers, and juvenile justice workers. This program is well-organized

and contains valuable lists of resources (e.g., school curricula, national fire service programs). Manuals may be obtained by contacting the Office of Planning and Education, United States Fire Administration, Federal Emergency Management Agency, Washington, DC 20472.

Kolko, D. J. (1985). Juvenile firesetting: A review and methodological critique. *Clinical Psychology Review, 5,* 345–376. *This comprehensive review of the early literature describes descriptive characteristics, assessment, and intervention of juvenile firesetters. Even though the article is now somewhat dated, it is still the most extensive review in the literature. It is an excellent resource for professionals who want an overview of issues regarding child fire setting.*

References

Adler, R., Nunn, R., Northam, E., & Lebnan, V., & Ross, R. (1994). Secondary prevention of childhood firesetting. *Journal of the American Academy of Child & Adolescent Psychiatry, 33,* 1194–1202.

American Psychiatric Association. (1994). *Diagnostic and statistical manual of mental disorders* (4th ed.). Washington, DC: Author.

Baizerman, M., & Emshoff, B. (1984). Juvenile firesetting: Building a community based prevention program. *Children Today,* 8–12.

Barkley, R. A. (1987). *Defiant children: A clinician's manual for parent training.* New York: Guilford Press.

Barnett, D. W., & Carey, K. T. (1992). *Designing interventions for preschool learning and behavior problems.* San Francisco: Jossey-Bass.

Barth, R. P. (1986). *Social and cognitive treatment of children and adolescents.* San Francisco: Jossey Bass.

Carstens, C. (1982). Application of a work penalty threat in the treatment of a case of juvenile fire setting. *Journal of Behavior Therapy and Experimental Psychiatry, 13,* 159–161.

Cox-Jones, J. C., Lubetsky, M. J., Fultz, S. A., & Kolko, D. J. (1990). Inpatient psychiatric treatment of a young recidivist firesetter. *Journal of the American Academy of Child and Adolescent Psychiatry, 29,* 936–941.

Federal Emergency Management Agency. (1988). *Pre-adolescent firesetter handbook: Ages 0–7.* Washington, DC: U.S. Fire Administration, U.S. Government Printing Office.

Firehawk Children's Program. (1984, Spring). *Firehawk Dispatch,* 6–7.

Forehand, R., & McMahon, R. (1981). *Helping the noncompliant child: A clinician's guide to parent training.* New York: Guilford Press.

Forehand, R., Wierson, M., Frame, C. L., Kempton, T. & Armistead, . (1991). Juvenile firesetting: A unique syndrome or an advanced level of antisocial behavior? *Behavior Research and Therapy, 29,* 125–128.

Gaynor, J., & Hatcher, C. (1987). *The psychology of child firesetting.* New York: Brunner/Mazel.

Hartman, A. (1978, October). Diagrammatic assessment of family relationships. *Social Casework,* pp. 465–476.

Holland, C. J. (1969). Elimination by the parents of fire-setting behavior in a 7 year old boy. *Behavior Research Therapy, 7,* 135–137.

Jackson, H., Glass, C., & Hope, S. (1987). A functional analysis of recidivistic arson. *British Journal of Clinical Psychology, 26*(3), 175–185.

Kazdin, A. E., & Kolko, D. J. (1986). Parent psychopathology and family functioning among childhood firesetters. *Journal of Abnormal Child Psychology, 14,* 315–329.

Koles, M. R., & Jensen, W. R. (1985). Comprehensive treatment of chronic fire setting in a severely disordered boy. *Journal of Behavior Therapy and Experimental Psychiatry, 16,* 81–85.

Kolko, D. J. (1983). Multi component parental treatment of firesetting in a six year old boy. *Journal of Behavior Therapy and Experimental Psychiatry, 14,* 349–353.

Kolko, D. J. (1985). Juvenile firesetting: A review and methodological critique. *Clinical Psychology Review, 5,* 345–376.

Kolko, D. J., & Ammerman, R. T. (1988). Firesetting. In M. Hersen, & C. G. Last (Eds.), *Child behavior therapy casebook* (pp. 00–00). New York: Plenum Press.

Kolko, D. J., & Kazdin, A. E. (1986). A conceptualization of firesetting in children and adolescents. *Journal of Abnormal Child Psychology, 14,* 49–61.

Kolko, D. J., & Kazdin, A. E. (1988a). Parent-child correspondence of firesetting among child psychiatric patients. *Journal of Child Psychology and Psychiatry and Allied Disciplines, 29,* 175–184.

Kolko, D. J., & Kazdin, A. E. (1988b). Prevalence of firesetting and related behaviors among child psychiatric patients. *Journal of Consulting and Clinical Psychology, 56,* 628–630.

Kolko, D. J., & Kazdin, A. E. (1989a). Assessment of dimensions of childhood firesetting among patients and nonpatients: The firesetting risk interview. *Journal of Abnormal Child Psychology, 17,* 157–176.

Kolko, D. J., & Kazdin, A. E. (1989b). The children's firesetting interview with psychiatrically referred and nonreferred children. *Journal of Abnormal Child Psychology, 17,* 609–624.

Kolko, D. J., & Kazdin, A. E. (1990). Matchplaying and firesetting in children: Relationship to parent, marital, and family dysfunction. *Journal of Clinical Child Psychology, 19,* 229–238.

Kolko, D. J., & Kazdin, A. E. (1991). Aggression and psychopathology in matchplaying and firesetting children: A replication and extension. *Journal of Clinical Child Psychology, 20,* 191–201.

Kolko, D. J., & Kazdin, A. E. (1992). The emergence and recurrence of child firesetting: A one-year prospective study. *Journal of Abnormal Child Psychology, 20,* 17–37.

Kolko, D. J., & Kazdin, A. E. (1994). Children's descriptions of their firesetting incidents: Characteristics and relationship to recidivism. *Journal of the American Academy of Child and Adolescent Psychiatry, 33,* 114–122.

Kolko, D. J., Watson, S., & Faust, J. (1991). Fire safety/prevention skills training to reduce involvement with fire in young psychiatric inpatients: Preliminary findings. *Behavior Therapy, 22,* 269–284.

Kuhnley, E. J., Hendren, R. L., & Quinlan, D. M. (1982). Firesetting by children. *Journal of the American Academy of*

Child Psychiatry, 21, 560–563.

Loeber, R. & Schmaling, K. B. (1985). Empirical evidence for overt and covert patterns of antisocial conduct problems: A meta-analysis. *Journal of Abnormal Child Psychology, 13*(2), 337–353.

McGrath, P., Marshall, P., & Prior, K. (1979). A comprehensive treatment program for a firesetting child. *Journal of Behavior Therapy and Experimental Psychology, 10,* 69–72.

McMahon, R. J. & Forehand, R. (1988). Conduct disorders. In E. J. Mash & L. G. Terdal (Eds.), *Behavioral assessment of childhood disorders* (2nd ed., pp. 185–219). New York: Guilford Press.

National Fire Protection Agency. (1995, August). *New directions for the learn not to burn program: The champion model* [World Wide Web]. Available WWW: http//:www.wpi.edu/depts/academic/fire/nfpa/pubed-newdirections.html

Patterson, G. (1976a). The aggressive child: Victim and architect of a coercive system. In L. Hamerlynck, L. Handy, & E. Marsh (Eds.), *Systematic common sense.* Eugene, OR: Castalia Press.

Patterson, G. (1976b). *Living with children* (rev.). Champaign, IL: Research Press.

Patterson, G. R. (1982). *A social learning approach: Vol. 3. Coercive family process.* Eugene, OR: Castalia Press.

Peterson, L. (1988). Preventing the leading killer of children: The role of the school psychologist in injury prevention. *School Psychology Review, 17,* 593–600.

Pokalo, M. (1993, April). *Childhood firesetting: Identification and treatment.* Presented at the annual meeting of the National Association of School Psychologists, Washington, D.C..

Sanders, M. R., & Dadds, M. R. (1993). *Behavioral family intervention.* Boston: Allyn and Bacon.

Showers, J., & Pickrell, E. (1987). Child firesetters: A study of three populations. *Hospital and Community Psychiatry, 38,* 495–501.

Uniform Crime Reports. (1987). *Crime in the United States.* Washington, DC: U.S. Government Printing Office.

Webb, N. B., Sakheim, G. A., Towns-Miranda, L., & Wagner, C. R. (1990). Collaborative treatment of juvenile firesetters: Assessment and outreach. *American Journal of Orthopsychiatry, 60,* 305–310.

Welsh, R. S. (1971). The use of stimulus satiation in the elimination of juvenile firesetting behavior. In A. Graziani (Ed.), *Behavior therapy with children* (pp. 283–289). Chicago: Atherton Press.

Wolff, R. (1984). Satiation in the treatment of inappropriate fire setting. *Journal of Behavior Therapy and Experimental Psychiatry, 15,* 337–340.

20

Temperament

Hedy Teglasi

University of Maryland

Background

Temperament refers to basic dimensions of personality that are intrinsic to the child and normally distributed within the population. It is commonly identified with (a) components of personality that appear early in life (before the impact of socialization) and that are strongly heritable and biological in origin (Buss & Plomin, 1984; Strelau, 1983); (b) traits that are relatively stable, cross-situationally consistent, and evident throughout the age span and diverse cultures (Rothbart & Derryberry, 1981; Strelau & Eysenck, 1987); and (c) the style (how) rather than the content (what) or purpose (why) of behavior (Strelau, 1983; Thomas & Chess, 1977).

Each of these defining characteristics of temperament has been questioned. For example, researchers have argued that temperament should not be restricted to early appearing traits, even if the genetic basis is kept, because genes come into play at different times over the course of development as features of the nervous system mature (Rothbart, 1989b). Heritability for most characteristics has been said to increase as children grow older (at least up to middle childhood; see Rutter, 1994). Furthermore, constitutional characteristics are not necessarily genetically determined but can be influenced by environmental factors. Neural development, for instance, is subject to experiential input (Blakemore, 1991).

The utility of the temperament concept does not rest on the assumption of genetic origin. Heritability estimates rarely exceed 50%, and although this level is substantial, the rest of the story is told by other influences including the environment (see Plomin, 1994). The other side of the coin is that measures of the "environment" show genetic influence. For example, children's perceptions of parental behavior toward them have a significant genetic component. Plomin concludes that "correlations between environmental measures and developmental outcomes cannot be assumed to be environmental in origin" (p. 184). When more than one child in a family is studied, differences between siblings are striking. These differences are associated with "nonshared" perceptions

of the "same" environment, and it is these nonshared experiences that are most predictive of outcomes (Dunn, Stocker, & Plomin, 1990).

Although there is diversity of opinion on the matter (see Kohnstamm, 1986), the dominant view is that temperament is cross-situationally consistent (Strelau & Eysenck, 1987). This position is reflected in most temperament questionnaires that minimize the impact of situationally specific variables by aggregating items that sample a broad range of situations (e.g., Buss & Plomin, 1984; Carey & McDevitt, 1978; Martin, 1988; Windle & Lerner, 1986). Despite conceptions of temperament that insist on generality across types of responses and situations, there is increasing evidence for behavioral style being dependent on context. Goldsmith and Campos (1990) found negligible correlations between parameters of intensity, duration, and latency across responses to different laboratory situations. Thus, infants could not be generally classified as "intense" or "slow to respond" without reference to the type and context of the response. Goldsmith and Campos concluded that "the view of temperament that our results support is not the outmoded view of temperament as present at birth, rigidly stable across time, and invariant across situations." (p. 1961). Instead, these authors see temperament as comprised of behavioral tendencies that are moderated by situations, occasions, and other dispositions. Temperament represents a style of engagement with a range of environments, and cross-situational consistency does not mean that a trait will be expressed identically in all situations. Indeed, prototypical aspects of situations such as their novelty or the degree of stimulation they afford are built into the definition of some of the temperament dimensions. Adaptability and approach-avoidance are temperament concepts grounded in the style of responding to unfamiliar situations. A child may approach familiar people easily but remain wary in responding to new people.

These situation-specific properties of temperament dimensions permit the drawing of linkages to theories involving arousal regulation or stimulus seeking that may relate to different biological subsystems. Situational specificity is compatible with notions of activation, reactivity, and optimum arousal that play a key role in various theories of temperament and in biologically rooted conceptions of personality (e.g., Buss & Plomin, 1984; Mehrabian, 1980; Strelau, 1983; Zuckerman, 1979). Temperament implies situation-specificity because situations and tasks have different stimulative value and individuals vary in their reactions to various levels and types of stimulation. Preferences reflected in approach or avoidance of new people, tasks, or situations as defined by Thomas and Chess (1977) bear on theories that adhere to arousal regulation. The question is not whether differences exist across situations but how to view these differences. Consistency across situations should be defined in terms of correlations across situations similar in functional relationships to the temperament trait being considered because different demands of situations call into play different temperamental attributes. Eliasz (1990) argues that the "continuity of behavior within well-defined classes of situations enables adequate prediction of behavior despite the existence of cross-situational differences" (p. 290).

The generally accepted definition of temperament emphasizes the formal, stylistic characteristics of individuality (Buss & Plomin, 1984; Thomas & Chess, 1977). This emphasis on behavioral style may be suited to infants and toddlers but is seen as too restrictive for older ages. As the child matures, developments in the cognitive areas interplay with emotions and with behavioral styles (Sroufe, Schork, Motti, Lawroski, & La Freniere, 1984), and these reciprocally influence one another.

Temperament and Personality

Generally, temperament is viewed as a subclass of personality and constitutes its "core" (Hofstee, 1991). Personality serves as a central organizer of behavior that influences the expression of temperamental traits. Difficulty in distinguishing between temperament and the more general concept of personality stems in part from the overlap between behavioral style (process) and the content of awareness and of coping strategies that develop over time. The contrast between temperament and personality is also obscured by the following: (a) a common descriptive vocabulary; (b) overlapping concepts; and (c) failure of empirical data to differentiate between temperament and personality on the basis of biological factors (Prior, 1992). Heritability estimates for temperament and personality dimensions are very similar. Concepts like values, interests, and attitudes may be influenced by biological factors (Eaves, Eysenck, & Martin, 1989). Attempts are being made to identify temperament dimensions singly or in combination that form the cornerstone for the development of more complex dimensions such as the widely-agreed-upon Five Factor Model describing the dimensions of adult personality (e.g., Dig-

man & Inouye, 1986). Some authors do not differentiate between temperament and personality because of their narrow conception of personality (e.g., Eysenck, 1970; Gray, 1982; Zuckerman, 1979).

The concept of self-regulation as both a personality variable and a behavioral style is an example of how identical terms are used differently with respect to personality and temperament. Self-regulation as personality appears to be defined in general terms (Karoly, 1993) as performing a central organizing function (e.g., ego), whereas the temperament view of self-regulation refers to basic processes involved in optimizing stimulation, alertness, and affective arousal. When viewed as temperament, self-regulation is comprised of processes that modulate reactivity (arousability of motor and emotional responses) such as attention, responsiveness to cues signaling reward and punishment, behavioral inhibition to intense or novel stimuli, and effortful inhibitory control (Rothbart & Posner, 1985).

A dichotomized view of temperament and personality polarizes temperament as purely intrinsic to the child as opposed to personality as the product of interactions with others. However, the emphasis should be on discovering how temperamental attributes contribute to the development of the functional whole that is personality.

Specific Traits Included Within the Temperament Rubric

Although there is consensus about the importance of temperament and agreement on some defining characteristics, there is a diversity of opinion on the specific traits that constitute temperament. The term is very broad, encompassing behavioral qualities of emotion, attention, and activity (Bates, 1989). Different approaches to investigating temperament have emphasized different traits.

Much of the work in relation to temperament has focused on basic emotions and individual differences in their expression. Some theorists limit the temperamental domain to emotions (e.g., Goldsmith & Campos, 1986). Many others give a prominent role to the emotions (e.g., Buss & Plomin, 1984; Gray, 1982). Some theorists argue for the necessity of establishing biological correlates and for selecting temperamental traits on the basis of a network of constructs tied to psychobiological theories (see Rothbart, 1989a, for a review of the biological bases of temperament). These researchers apply their knowledge about neuropsychological and biochemical mechanisms to explain individual differences in temperament characteristics. Gray (1982), for instance, postulates three dimensions of personality corresponding to three neurological constructs underlying the emotion system—Behavioral Inhibition System, Behavioral Approach System, and Fight/

Flight System. According to Gray's conceptualization, individuals differ in their responsiveness to cues signalling rewards and punishments. Zuckerman (1979) examines the physiological and biochemical mediators of sensation seeking. Mehrabian (1980) distinguished three basic traits: pleasure-displeasure, arousal-nonarousal, and dominance-submissiveness. Eysenck (1970) proposed three dimensions of extraversion, neuroticism, and psychoticism. Some researchers follow a hypothetical-deductive strategy that combines biological mechanisms and developmental regularities (see Rothbart, 1991). Those with a homeostatic self-regulatory focus define temperament as individual differences in those biological processes that relate to physiological arousal (reactivity) and the automatic or deliberate actions to moderate physiological arousal to optimum levels. Researchers acknowledge the complexity of the linkages between physiological mechanisms and temperamental traits. They, therefore, suggest that studies focus on configurations of various physiological and biochemical correlates of temperament rather than attempt to identify one-to-one correspondences or reduce one system to another.

Temperament dimensions derived from the well-known New York Longitudinal Study (NYLS, Thomas & Chess, 1977) were based on a descriptive approach to temperament. Close observations of infants yielded nine dimensions of temperament that have received much attention from practitioners: Activity, Rhythmicity, Approach/Withdrawal, Adaptability, Intensity, Mood, Persistence/Attention Span, Distractibility, and Sensory Threshold. Many temperament measures currently used are based in whole or in part on these nine dimensions. Factor analyses of the items constituting these nine dimensions have generated five to seven factors based on parent ratings and three factors with teacher ratings (Martin, Wisenbaker, & Huttunen, 1994). Factor analytic studies have shown that the nine NYLS dimensions overlap, and these findings are used to justify the construction of scales with fewer dimensions. However, it should be noted that the use of factor analytic techniques to eliminate potentially clinically useful dimensions is a source of debate within the temperament field (Carey & McDevitt, 1995).

Exactly which traits are temperamental is still an open question. Furthermore, specific temperament traits have separate definitions specific to a particular theoretical position. For example, *approach* has been defined in reference to responsiveness to environmental stimuli associated with primary rewards (Wilson, Barrett, & Gray, 1989) as well as in relation to typical response patterns to new persons, situations, or events (Thomas & Chess, 1977).

Dimensions drawn from various theoretical perspectives and extensively validated are grouped next into seven categories. These dimensions, however, are *not* independent.

Negative emotionality

This dimension constitutes the disposition to show various forms of negative affect such as generalized distress, fear, and anger. Buss and Plomin (1984) include negative emotionality (plus activity and sociability) in their definition of temperament suggesting that general distress differentiates over the first year into anger and fear. The *quality of mood* dimension on the nine-dimensional scheme of Thomas and Chess (1977) puts negative and positive mood quality at opposite ends of the same continuum. They define quality of mood as the amount of smiling, pleasant, joyful, and friendly behavior, as contrasted with unpleasant, moody, complaining, fussy, and unfriendly behavior. Negative emotionality is *not* the same as depression, nor is it pathological, but a manifestation of style. Chess and Thomas also proposed the dimension of *intensity* which relates to the manner of expressing emotions. Similarly, Buss and Plomin (1984) include in their emotionality construct the strength of the response, intensity of the stimulus eliciting the response, and how easily the child is pacified. Rothbart (1981) differentiates negative emotionality into components of fear, distress, and soothability.

The negative mood of a baby is likely to cause parents to feel inadequate and describe their baby as "difficult" (Bates, 1980). As they get older, children can display negative mood in two ways: by being worried, serious, timid, anxious, and whining; or by being aggressive, angry, or argumentative. The angry child tends to have frequent temper tantrums and antagonistic interactions. Timid or anxious children tend to remain excessively dependent on caregivers or may be hard to soothe if their distress is intense. Parental tolerance for timidity and fearfulness tends to wane as a child gets older, despite the child's continued susceptibility to negative mood (Stevenson-Hinde & Simpson, 1982). Negative emotionality such as extreme fear or anger interferes with the development of social skills and positive interactions.

The *"difficult" temperament* concept introduced by Thomas, Chess, and Birch (1968) has a strong negative emotionality component and includes five dimensions: negative mood; withdrawal; poor adaptability to new situations; high intensity; and low regularity of biological rhythms. Others have redefined the construct of the difficult temperament on the basis of factor analysis (e.g., Bates, 1987) as involving frequent and intense expressions of negative affect. Parentally defined difficultness has at its core the variables of negative mood and poor adaptability.

Adaptability

The Thomas and Chess (1977) conceptualization of *adaptability* and *approach-avoidance* are distinct, yet they tend to cluster together empirically. Adaptability is the capacity to get used to new or altered situations after the initial reaction. The initial response (approach-avoidance) reflects how the child handles novelty; adaptability reflects adjustment as the situation becomes more familiar. An adaptable child accepts new foods after initial rejection and takes changes of routine in stride. Adaptability is also related to negative emotionality. Kagan and his colleagues focused on shyness or behavioral inhibition in the face of novelty (Kagan, Reznick, & Snidman, 1989). Shy children are reluctant to approach new people and adapt less well to new social situations.

A poorly adaptable child takes a very long time to get used to unfamiliar situations or to changes in routine. Transitions such as entering school may remain difficult for a long time. The poorly adaptable child's trouble with transitions is due to difficulty in getting used to new ideas or situations and not to problems with leaving an activity, as is true for the child with high persistence. Poorly adaptable children remain overly focused on one idea (or one aspect of a situation) and do not alter their expectations to anticipate or plan for changes. A 12-year-old incessantly fussing about being late as parents change a flat tire is an example of such inflexibility. Parents frequently report difficulty when their child is inflexible in the face of relatively normal deviations from the routine. The causes for a child's poor adaptability may include various emotional and cognitive components. Thus, adaptability is a broad term that needs to be refined relative to age and situational context. In their Dimensions of Temperament Scale Revised (DOTS-R), Windle and Lerner (1986) substituted flexibility/rigidity for the adaptability dimension because the former is more specific than the latter.

Reactivity

Reactivity is best articulated by Strelau (1983) and Rothbart and Derryberry (1981). Reactivity (Strelau, 1983) has two interacting components: how *intense a stimulus* must be to evoke a reaction and the *intensity of the reaction itself.* The *threshold of responsiveness* of Thomas and Chess (1977) touches on *reactivity,* and Buss and Plomin's (1984) *emotionality* includes this as part of their definition.

The dimension of reactivity is theoretically central to a variety of other temperament constructs, including negative emotionality and adaptability. Other traits viewed by some as temperamental, such as introversion-extraversion, sensation seeking, differential sensitivity to rewards and punishment, and behavioral inhibition also involve differential thresholds for responding. An individual's reactive processes have many possible components (somatic, autonomic, cognitive, neuroendocrine) organized into the two broad categories of positive and negative reactivity (Rothbart, 1989a). These processes are influenced by objective and subjective stimulus qualities such as their intensity, their perceived meaning (positive or negative), and expectations about their occurrence. The

manner in which stimuli are interpreted changes with maturation and experience. Furthermore, individuals who vary in responsiveness to specific stimuli also vary in their preference for seeking or avoiding such stimuli (see the self-regulation section). Thomas and Chess (1977) define *threshold of responsiveness* as the intensity of stimulation needed to provoke a response. A child with a low threshold is sensitive to sound, lights, temperature, feel of clothes, and physical discomfort, as well as textures and smells of food. An infant with a low threshold may cry in the bath if it is too hot or cold, may refuse new foods, and may even react to changes such as a haircut in a family member.

A preschooler with a low threshold often says, "I don't like it" or "It bothers me." Sensitivity to taste and texture of food may result in rejection of a familiar food when there is a minor substitution in the recipe or if it is not presented on the plate in the customary way. A child's behavior may provoke constant power struggles particularly if the parents view her or him as manipulative or demanding rather than as sensitive.

According to Thomas and Chess (1977), *intensity of reaction* is the energy level of the response for both positive and negative emotions. A highly intense child expresses protest by screaming with anger; a less intense child may frown, grumble, or sulk. Similarly, an intense child expresses happiness with exuberance and may roar with laughter, whereas a child with low intensity would smile or grin. Intensity as a basic dimension of temperament has been difficult to validate because the intensity levels of behaviors across different domains are not correlated, and intensity items from different domains do not cluster together in factor analyses (McClowry, Hegvik, & Teglasi, 1993).

Self-regulation

This construct is tied to reactivity and constitutes efforts to maintain optimal arousal (by a low-reactive person seeking out stimulating activities or a high-reactive person avoiding stimulation). Strelau (1983) refers to the modulation of *reactivity* as *activity,* whereas Rothbart (1989b) uses the term *self-regulation.*

Approach-withdrawal, defined by Thomas and Chess (1977) as the initial response to unfamiliar situations, persons, or tasks, could be construed as serving self-regulatory functions by regulating the amount of stimulation. An individual could withdraw attention from or avoid contact with aversive stimuli. However, aversive stimuli might be tolerated or deliberately sought to achieve a purpose or goal (see Rothbart, 1989b). These deliberate choices are reminiscent of the conceptualization of personality as regulating and organizing behavior. Excessive avoidance interferes with learning needed skills, and failure to avoid overstimulation results in being overwhelmed. Strelau and Eliasz (1994) suggest that prevention and intervention programs should be directed primarily to parents and teachers by instructing them in how to help youngsters engage in *activity* that moderates the emotional tension and the stimulus overload that can disrupt learning and produce stress.

Infants may show withdrawal responses by tuning out their attention or by initially reacting negatively to new experiences such as foods or a bath. A baby may protest when left with strangers either by clinging or throwing a tantrum. A child may look frightened and hang back in new situations or may hide when unexpected company arrives. In older children, withdrawal responses are shown by initial reactions to a new peer group or new academic subjects. An older child with a moderate tendency to withdraw might be cautious before joining a conversation or game. Depending on the extent of the withdrawal tendency, such caution may be a positive trait, and the opposite extreme of approaching new things with little reflection might be problematic. Low threshold may increase the likelihood of initial withdrawal from physical stimuli such as noises and new foods, places, and activities.

Parents of a child who avoids new experiences are faced with decisions about how much to encourage their child to approach unfamiliar situations. Children who are allowed to avoid new situations may not get a chance to learn needed skills and may miss the opportunity to get accustomed to these situations. The cumulative effect of withdrawal can lower confidence, thus increasing future tendencies to withdraw. If the child is gently introduced to new experiences at a tolerable pace (depending on adaptability), the adverse impact of a tendency to avoidance can be minimized. Conversely, pushing a child into situations or activities prematurely may exacerbate the withdrawal tendency.

Activity

Most temperament frameworks include this dimension which typically refers to frequency and intensity of motor activity (e.g., Buss & Plomin, 1984; Eaton & Enns, 1986). A child's activity level is the extent to which he or she is in motion during routine activities such as eating, dressing, playing, or even sleeping. Highly active children may have "run before they walked." Such children are "restless" during quiet activities when not absorbed. A highly active child virtually never sits still and responds at a high frequency, always touching things, talking, and the like. Physical activity, especially if it is vigorous, plays a possible role in arousal (Rothbart & Derryberry, 1981; Strelau, 1983) by increasing or reducing tension. Problems arise when children do not modulate their level of activity appropriately to avoid friction with others or to engage in the learning process in school. Excessive activity interferes with home and classroom routines and with interpersonal or academic demands. When activity level is low, problems pertain to lack of energy or engagement. A low-activity level is generally not regarded as a problem

during infancy, but an older child may be viewed as lacking initiative and drive.

Active children at 42 and 50 months have been found to have more tantrums, make more refusals, and seek attention more than do less active children (Stevenson-Hinde & Simpson, 1982). Active infants are less "cuddly" and sleep less than average as toddlers; they are described as "getting into everything." When older, they have difficulty sitting in their seats at school and may engage in rough play with other children.

Attention Regulation

Distractibility is defined by Thomas and Chess (1977) as the degree to which extraneous stimuli interfere with ongoing behavior. This dimension has different implications for adjustment at various ages. During infancy, distractibility refers to the extent to which a distressed child will be soothed in response to external stimuli (Rothbart, 1981). A distractible baby stops fussing when given a pacifier or stops crying when picked up. In later years, distractibility can show itself by frequent changes of activity during play, topic changes during discussions, or apparent "absent mindedness" when something intrudes into ongoing activity. Duration of attention to an activity when not distracted is referred to by Thomas and Chess as *attention span/persistence* and by Rothbart as *duration of orienting*. Though distractibility and attention span/persistence are conceptually distinct, they are empirically related.

Attention deployment is seen as a way to regulate affect or arousal. Mehrabian's (1978) concept of *stimulus screening* (the cognitive counterpart of the trait arousability) differentiates individuals on the basis of the degree to which they habitually and selectively process environmental information. Screeners select out less relevant components of everyday stimuli and are better able to moderate arousal in response to a sudden increase in the rate of information (complexity, novelty, variability) than are nonscreeners. A highly distractible child is greatly influenced by the immediacy of the environmental stimulation or even by internal stimulation. Such a child will be "captured" by the strongest stimulus present and has difficulty voluntarily focusing attention. This child can attend for a long time to TV or puzzles because these stimuli may be strong enough to screen out sources of distraction. Lego blocks with notches may rivet attention because, unlike wooden ones, they provide cues (structure) so that each step leads to the next.

As distractible children get older, they have problems at home and school and in social situations. Parents describe such children as lacking in responsibility, dawdling in the morning, not completing chores on schedule, and not listening. Much to the dismay of parents, these children often do not keep promises and have difficulty planning and prioritizing their behavior because their susceptibility to environmental stimulation may override a previous commitment. In school, they may have difficulty concentrating in a "busy" classroom, cannot work independently, do not follow directions, and have problems organizing their work or managing their time. They appear to be "unmotivated," but the problem is that they cannot focus their attention when other stimuli impinge. Peer relationships may be disrupted because of difficulty staying in tune with others. Distractible children may be described as "uncaring," for when caught up in the stimulation of the moment, they may not be aware of others' feelings.

Persistence (attention span) is the continuation of activity in the face of obstacles or requests to stop (Thomas & Chess, 1977). A persistent child will insist on continuing an activity despite requests from parents or teachers to stop and will return to the task after interruption. While persistence is related to distractibility, they are different concepts. A distractible child can be persistent if other stimuli are not strong enough to divert attention from an ongoing activity. In fact, a distractible child can become highly persistent in some activities such as computer games.

Both the high and low extremes of attention span/persistence can be problematic at different ages. High persistence is related to difficulty changing an activity abruptly; a child may throw a tantrum when asked to come to dinner while absorbed in play or may protest when a teacher requests a change of activity. On the other hand, absorption in games or puzzles and the ability to stay with activities for a long time is viewed as positive. Such children tend to do homework carefully, watch others intently to learn skills, and practice an activity until it is mastered. The stubborn form of persistence (i.e., not taking *no* for an answer) needs to be more carefully studied because it may involve poor adaptability (inflexibility) and, depending on the situation, may entail different temperamental processes.

Factor analysis of teacher ratings of the nine NYLS temperament dimensions produce three clusters (Keogh, 1982, 1986): *task orientation* (high persistence, low distractibility, and low activity level); *personal social flexibility* (high adaptability, approach, and positive mood); and *reactivity* (high intensity, low threshold, and negative mood). The *task orientation* factor correlates with grades and standardized tests of achievement (Martin, 1994). This correlation is linear so that children with low task orientation do less well than those with average task-orientation scores. Likewise, children with average task orientation do less well than those rated high on this factor. Low *task orientation* overlaps with the criteria for Attention Deficit Hyperactivity Disorder (ADHD) found in the *Diagnostic and Statistical Manual of Mental Disorders* (American Psychiatric Association, 1994; *DSM-IV*). In their discussion of the relationship between temperament and the clinical disorder of ADHD, Carey and McDevitt (1995) point out the importance of *low adapt-*

ability (or inflexibility) as a characteristic of children diagnosed with ADHD. They suggest that poor adaptability may account for Barkley's (1990) observation that central to ADHD is an inability to regulate behavior according to rules or consequences.

Sociability and positive emotionality

Sociability is the enjoyment of the company of others and seeking out companionship. Buss and Plomin (1984) include sociability in the temperament rubric but exclude positive emotionality due to insufficient evidence regarding heritability. However, *sociability and positive emotionality* overlap empirically and conceptually. Sociability is distinct from shyness because the latter refers to responses to new people or unfamiliar groups (inhibited, anxious, self-conscious), whereas the former is a preference for company which could be expressed through interactions with familiar people. There is a modest correlation between shyness and sociability but it is worthwhile to distinguish between them (Cheek & Buss, 1981). Although sociability and positive emotionality seem to be positive traits, restriction of emotional experiences to the extreme positive range may have its drawbacks. Without some apprehension about future consequences, the youngster may not anticipate problems in time to take constructive action.

Developmental Issues

Development reflects the constantly evolving interactional process between the individual and the environment. Some temperament features drive development without much environmental interaction. Infants with high activity level and vigor will meet earlier locomotion or motor milestones such as walking (Carey & McDevitt, 1995). An extreme tendency to withdraw is likely to interfere with the acquisition of social skills. Distractibility and short attentional span (including low persistence) will influence the focus and thoroughness of information processing apart from any feedback that such a behavioral style might elicit from others. Although the temperament concept highlights the individual's own contribution to his or her development, it brings the impact of the environment to the surface. Individual differences in temperament may "define" the relevant dimensions of the environment (Scarr, 1994). Environmental influences within the family that do not have the same effect on all siblings are most relevant for adjustment (Plomin, 1994).

The "goodness-of-fit" concept synthesizes the environmental and personological perspectives. The individual's contribution to the developmental process is embedded in a matrix of other influences including the family system, physical environment, and cultural expectations in reference to a child's age and gender (Kohnstamm, 1989b). Accordingly, psychological development proceeds through the interplay of temperament with other characteristics of the individual and the environment. When environmental demands are consonant with the predispositions of the child, development proceeds optimally. However, an environment that places demands for adaptation beyond the child's capacity undermines development. Continuous friction and antagonism with parents and teachers result in the development of emotional and behavioral problems such as school refusals, overreaction to feedback, and poor self-image (Carey & McDevitt, 1995; Thomas & Chess, 1977). Some temperamental characteristics such as low task orientation may interfere with finding a congenial niche in the environment, especially in the educational system. Negative emotionality and inflexibility are sources of friction in virtually any environment.

Changes in the goodness-of-fit between the person and the environment can occur due to environmental pressures (e.g., Chess & Thomas, 1984), maturation of the nervous system (Rothbart & Derryberry, 1981), and delayed gene action (e.g., Goldsmith & Campos, 1982). A harmonious fit can be disrupted by new demands that are incompatible with the child's temperament. Conversely, a poor fit may be altered by the emergence of a talent (e.g., unusual musical ability) or gradual mastery of the demands.

Appropriate behavioral manifestations of the underlying temperament are expected to change in accordance with age (Thomas & Chess, 1977). Thomas and Chess indicated that the "behavioral criteria for any temperamental trait must necessarily change over time as the child's psychological functioning develops and evolves. What remains consistent over time is the *definitional identity* of the characteristic" (p. 159). What changes is not the temperament trait but its expression. Rothbart (1991) argues that physiological changes in the process of maturation alter the quality as well as the number of temperament traits. For example, the temperament quality of "effortful control" is evident in preschoolers but not in infants. As children mature, the process of self-regulation (central to Rothbart's conception of temperament) becomes increasingly refined.

Temperament influences the reciprocal interplay between the person and the environment in four ways. The first three are widely accepted. The fourth has received very little attention.

- *Temperament shapes the responses of others.* Children's temperamental qualities influence their reactions to environmental stimuli, and the resultant behaviors influence how others will react (Bell, 1968; Dunn & Kendrick, 1982; Keogh, 1982). For example, a school-aged child who is easily distracted or does not persist on tasks is likely to elicit more control and structure from parents and teachers. Even after extensive professional guidance, middle-class parents seem unable to accept the individuality of children who are temperamentally distractible and nonpersistent (Thomas et al., 1968). Such parents stubbornly continue to make demands on their children (e.g., to sit still and concentrate for long periods of time) that are at odds with the child's capacity. The reactions of others further amplify the individuality of the child's experiences. The prevailing values and expectations of the environment determine the acceptability of various temperamental traits and influence others' reactions.

- *Temperament dictates the selection of activities and environments.* The most striking manifestations of individual differences are in the selection and interpretation of the meanings of situations. Substantial correlations have been reported between preferences for different types of situations and temperament (see Van Heck, 1991). Differences in emotional reactivity are related to preferences for situations differing in degree of stimulation (Strelau, 1983). Highly reactive individuals will avoid high levels of arousal, stress, or risk. People with a high activity level seek environments that are fast paced, and sociable people seek out other people (Buss & Plomin, 1984).

- *Temperament modifies the impact of the environment.* Some temperamental qualities increase vulnerability or foster resilience in the face of adversity. Likewise, the influence of the family environment on the development of siblings who differ on a variety of temperamental attributes is not the same (see Plomin, 1994).

- *Temperament shapes the subjective world.* What becomes internally represented (e.g., schema, expectations) are not measurable "objective" events but the individual's subjective experience of the event as it is filtered through temperament and other traits. The appraisal of a situation is limited by what enters awareness through the attentional process. Emotions control sensitivity and attention to stimuli (Derryberry & Rothbart, 1988; Frijda, 1986) and guide activation of prior memories (Blaney, 1986; Bower, 1981). Thus, the memories that influence the appraisal of a current event are themselves influenced by the prevailing affective states and prior cognitive/affective appraisals. According to the constructivist position, the starting point in understanding one's world is in the "facts" of experience or the individual's moment-to-moment awareness. For instance, feeling anger, boredom, or disconnection is an incontrovertible reality. Next is the interpretation of the "facts" into a "theory" that explains experiences through postulating causal connections, intentions, and so forth. Finally, the dynamic interplay between "fact" and "theory" develops over time and is often the focus of therapy. The temperamental predisposition to experience negative emotionality has been shown to influence the internal representations of children as measured with a storytelling task

(Bassan-Diamond, Teglasi, & Schmitt, 1995). The internal representations of prior experience provide the memories and mind set for understanding subsequent experiences. In this fashion, individual differences are further magnified.

Problems and Implications

Even as currently and incompletely conceptualized, temperament has demonstrated utility to explain behavioral individuality as well as to predict the development of mental health disorders (e.g., Carey & McDevitt, 1995; Maziade, 1994), particularly in combination with other risk factors (e.g., Sanson, Oberklaid, Pedlow, & Prior, 1991). Research, which included temperament, has identified these attributes as placing children at risk for developing mental health disorders or fostering resilience and resourcefulness in the face of adversity (e.g., Grizenko & Fisher, 1992; Rutter, 1987).

At least at the extremes, certain temperamental dispositions constitute risk factors for psychiatric disorder (Bates, 1989; Rutter, 1989). Three possible mechanisms for the development of disorder have been suggested by Rutter (1994):

■ *Extreme of temperament as a subclinical manifestation of the disorder.* This might be seen, for example, in the connection between behavioral inhibition and anxiety disorders (Kagan, 1994) or in the similarity between behaviors characterizing task orientation (temperament dimensions of high distractibility, high activity, and low persistence) and the *DSM-IV* descriptions of ADHD (American Psychiatric Association, 1994).

■ *Temperament as increasing susceptibility to psychosocial stress and adversity.* An example of this view would be the increased vulnerability of behaviorally inhibited children to experiencing stress in new situations. Such children are described as reactive (Kagan, 1994) and prone to high levels of physiological arousal. The converse of being unusually low in physiological reactivity is associated with increased risk for criminality and recidivism (Magnusson, 1988) because such children are less responsive to normal societal controls. It has been argued that the most crucial temperament traits in human functioning are *reactivity* and *self-regulatory activity* (e.g., Rothbart & Derrybery, 1981; Strelau, 1983). *Reactivity* refers to ease of arousability of the central nervous system. *Activity* constitutes behavior to seek situations or engage in actions that foster optimal stimulation. When a highly reactive individual cannot reduce stimulation to tolerable levels, the quality of performance may decrease and/or the individual is subject to stress. On the other hand, individuals with low reactivity may seek increased stimulation to avert

discomfort in routine or less stimulating situations. An extended discrepancy between level of reactivity and level of activity may cause disturbances in behavior. Thus, difficulty regulating *activity* to correspond with *reactivity* constitutes a temperament risk factor.

■ *Temperament as eliciting negative reactions and contributing to poor social interactions.* The direct effect of temperament on interpersonal interactions has been linked to the constellation of traits referred to as "difficult" (Thomas & Chess, 1977; Thomas et al., 1968). This cluster has been popular because of its prediction of psychiatric disorder (Maziade, Caron, Cote, Boutin, & Thivierge, 1990). As the name implies, this pattern tends to elicit negative responses from parents, teachers, and peers and promotes a poor "fit" with the environment. Caution is needed, however, because these reactions depend on the characteristics of the respondent, as well as the familial and cultural context including age-and gender-related expectations.

Given that aspects of behavior, emotion, and cognition converge in cohesive ways, these interrelated components of individuality should be examined in relation to development. An example of how the manifestation of temperament can change as a result of the interplay of various traits and experience is that of a 4½-year-old girl who was described by her mother as becoming suddenly introverted and withdrawn from peers. Previously, she was very gregarious and outgoing. At a recent party with her preschool classmates, the children were asked to dance, and she was the only one who volunteered. After having danced in an uninhibited way, her peers teased her. She subsequently became unhappy and isolated. How she puts this incident into perspective and how she comes to understand and regulate her temperament will influence her affect and behavior in the future.

A contrasting example (cited in Teglasi, 1993) is of a 4½-year-old boy who was cautious and shy in new situations. When he arrived at a bowling alley for a birthday party with his preschool friends, he declared that he would neither put on bowling shoes nor bowl. He decided to watch and keep his friends company. Upon leaving, he told his mother that if he first went bowling with his family, he could do it next time at a party. The boy's insight, initiative, and persistence in mastering uncomfortable feelings, coupled with the responsiveness of his family, resulted in his becoming a well-liked leader among his peers by the fourth grade. Again, the interplay of multiple factors in development is evident.

The list of traits included in the temperament rubric will no doubt be refined in the future. Global and situation-specific aspects of traits will be designated, and attributes that are combinations of two or more discrete dimensions of temperament will be distinguished from unidimensional constructs. For instance, the interplay of aspects of emotionality and sociability may relate to shyness (Buss & Plomin, 1986). With increased conceptual clarity, more appropriate measures can be devised.

Alternative Actions

General Guidelines

The goodness-of-fit concept explicates the interplay of situational factors with the characteristics of the individual. The idea that the influence between the child and others in the environment is bidirectional allows parents, caregivers, teachers, and mental health professionals to collaborate as partners to promote the child's development (through an optimal match) rather than casting blame on one another. It should be noted that children who have some extremely adverse temperamental qualities might be accommodated only by a narrow range of environments. Furthermore, children with developmental delays and other diagnosable impairments also vary on the normal continuum of temperamental traits. These temperamental differences should be addressed by the professional because they shape reactions to stress or other difficulties and influence the outcomes of intervention (see Carey & McDevitt, 1995).

In determining the appropriate intervention to resolve a problem, those concerned with the child's care need to ascertain whether the problem is based on a mismatch between environmental demands and temperament, whether it represents an attempt to manipulate, or whether it is a combination of the two. A behavior that is purely an expression of temperament can become manipulative. For example, a child with negative mood whose parents struggle to make him "happy" could use these "moods" to manipulate parents. The cardinal rule regarding intervention is to support a child with behavior problems due to temperament and to alter contingencies for behaviors that are primarily manipulative. When dealing with a temperamentally difficult child, parents and teachers are more likely to be objective rather than respond with irritation if the following are kept in mind:

- A child who behaves in a way that upsets parents and teachers does not necessarily *intend* to do this.
- Temperament is a relatively durable trait and generally must be managed rather than changed.
- Misbehavior caused by temperament-environment mismatch should not be punished.

When working with parents and teachers, it is important for the professional to convey an understanding of the emotional impact of the child's behavior and to acknowledge that what they are doing might be satisfactory for a child with different temperament traits. Thus,

the *intent* of the teachers' and parents' approach can be separated from its *effect* on the child. In the management of a child with difficult temperament attributes, the goal is not to accept all the youngster's behavior in all situations but to reduce or eliminate the adverse influence of temperament. The aims of the intervention strategies are (a) avoidance of demands or expectations substantially dissonant with the child's temperament and (b) enforcement of schedules and activities that will minimize the undesirable future consequences of the child's temperament.

Interventions depend on the child's age. During the first year or two, the focus is on helping parents or other caregivers accommodate the child's temperament by gearing stimulation, feeding, and other caregiving activities to the requirements of the child. At later ages, parents continue to respond to their child's individuality but also begin to foster the development of self-regulation by helping the child identify feelings, verbalize needs, and understand the impact of his or her behavior on the responses of others. The ultimate goal of management techniques is for the child to learn self-understanding and ways of coping with temperamental difficulties. There is a progression from a great deal of parental and teacher effort, involvement, and guidance to gradually increasing self-direction on the part of the maturing child. A "difficult" child may require a slower shift from external sources of regulation to increasing responsibility for self-regulated behavior. The following general guidelines should be helpful to school psychologists in addressing these goals.

Provide parents and teachers with an understanding of the child's behaviors

A common ground of understanding among parents, teachers, and professionals facilitates communication and promotes a problem-solving atmosphere. The assessment of temperament relies on concrete descriptive material from a variety of functionally similar life situations (Thomas & Chess, 1977). Temperament must be defined in the context within which the behavior occurs; assessment of temperament must be individually tailored to the extent that children differ in their life experiences. Difficulties can arise from one problematic temperament trait or from the joint impact of several attributes. As children get older, their lives become more individualized, and the temperament roots of behavior may be more difficult to assess.

Parents and teachers can be helped to identify temperament characteristics of children by the availability of short questionnaire forms that expedite the delineation of temperament. For specific descriptions and critiques of measures, the reader is referred to several reviews (e.g., Bates, 1989; Carey & McDevitt, 1995; Slabach, Morrow, & Wachs, 1991).

The professional who is familiar with temperament constructs and measures is in a position to synthesize information gathered from various sources such as parents, teachers, systematic observations in the classroom, and the performance of tasks administered during individual assessments. The goal is to develop a cohesive understanding of the child, to distinguish extremes of temperament from disorders, and to use this information to design strategies for intervention that are responsive to present concerns and work toward minimizing (preventing) the adverse impact of temperament extremes on subsequent development.

Devise strategies for managing situations based on a common framework for understanding the child's behaviors

Parents and teachers bristle when they are given simplistic solutions or strategies to address what they know to be complex problems. Smith (1994) suggests that professionals provide general understandings and strategies and collaborate with parents and teachers on the specifics in accordance with their values and circumstances. One of the goals of intervention/prevention strategies is to improve the interactions of the child with others in the environment. Strengthening the relationship between the child and parent is of paramount importance.

Foster optimal development in the child and use strategies to compensate for possible future adverse impact of temperament characteristics

Smith (1994) gives an example of a 5-year-old boy, Andy, whose parents were concerned about his defiant, argumentative behavior at home (e.g., rageful tantrums, constant demands to be played with) which was in dramatic contrast to his model behavior in public. Parents were also concerned about his difficulty with separating from them for any length of time including his refusal to attend preschool and kindergarten and current protest about starting the first grade. After an assessment, Andy's behavioral problems were viewed as stemming directly from his temperament. Andy was very shy and behaved cautiously in any unfamiliar environment. He preferred to be at home with his parents where he felt he could exercise control by insisting on getting his way. The temperament counselor helped Andy's parents to understand that the most important skill Andy needed to develop at this time was the ability to let them influence his behavior. Many learning strategies were developed to promote this skill. Although Andy started first grade with home schooling, halfway through the year his parents were able to begin transitioning him to attend school. As Andy began to accept his parents' influence, they were able to help him learn other skills to cope with his temperament such as modulating the expression of his emotional intensity by practicing his "inside voice" and his "outside voice."

The example of Andy highlights the advantage of separating the temperamental and motivational *origins* of behavior (see Thomas & Chess, 1989). Andy's behavior was motivated by his desire to avoid the anxiety experienced outside the home, but this motivation was shaped by temperament which played a primary role in determining a pattern of behavior that subsequently became motivated by its consequence. Understanding Andy's behaviors as a reaction to distress in new situations circumvented a focus on what the parents had done to create such insecurity in the child or on the manipulativeness of the child. Rather than blaming the parents or pathologizing a "normal" child, the parents, school personnel, and mental health professionals worked together to ensure a successful school entry.

Specific Guidelines

The following discussion provides specific guidelines for managing children with one or more difficult temperamental characteristics. The discussion points are consistent with the literature (Thomas & Chess, 1977; Carey & McDevitt, 1995; Chess & Thomas, 1995; Turecki & Tonner, 1989) and the author's experience.

Structure

Despite detailed explanation of what is expected, some children cannot organize their own behavior nor sustain effort without continued supervision and guidance. One cannot simply tell a distractible child to "clean your room" but may need to start with a request to "put library books on the bottom shelf." After providing feedback, the next task can be given. Elaborate behavior management programs may provide the structure and supervision required.

A school-aged child with low task orientation (high distractibility, low attention span/persistence, and possibly high activity level) needs supervision with homework, redirection to the task, and regular feedback. Teachers may need to stand physically close to a distractible child when giving instructions and to keep gently reminding the child to return to the task. A predictable routine can keep an easily overstimulated or distractible child from becoming "revved up," ease the adjustment problems of the poorly adaptable child, and provide comfort for the fearful child.

Preemptive action

Understanding the child's temperament and anticipating the situations in which difficulties will arise can help parents and teachers avoid confrontations and minimize dissonance between the child and the environment. Changes in routine for a poorly adaptable child can be planned to allow time for adjustment. Parents and teachers need to anticipate how long a distractible child can stay on task without frustration and to provide short breaks.

An active, distractible child may expend so much effort struggling to pay attention in school that parents may wish to ease up on their expectations at home. Parents may decide that maintaining a tidy home with artwork and breakables is not worth the conflict with a very active child. Steps may be taken to prevent the escalating sequence that results in the "wild" behavior often seen in active, distractible children. Preemptive action is necessary before such children are out of control by removing them from the situation, distracting them, or allowing them to "blow off steam."

A sensitive child may benefit from reduced stimulation. A light sensitive child who wakes at dawn needs blackout shades. A child especially sensitive to the taste and texture of foods should be provided with a balanced meal of preferred foods. New foods can be introduced gradually, with familiar alternatives provided as a back-up.

A persistent child who finds it difficult to stop an activity abruptly needs time to disengage. Parents or teachers can preempt a tantrum by giving notice a few minutes before switching an activity or by allowing the child to bring the activity to another setting ("let's bring the puzzle or doll along").

Preparation

When parents and teachers cannot change the environment or their demands to suit a child's needs, they can help prepare the child for upcoming stressful events. Poorly adaptable children and those with a tendency toward initial withdrawal do not like surprises and welcome being able to anticipate changes by being told of upcoming sequences of events. Parents can explain what will happen on a trip, discuss when company will arrive, and role-play an anticipated visit to the doctor's office.

Teaching coping skills and self-understanding

When children are old enough, discussions about their sensitivities or about their reactions to change may be helpful. Parents can label their child's reactions with a nonjudgmental attitude and convey understanding. As children get older, they can label their own reactions and verbalize their needs. A poorly adaptable child might say, "I need more time to get used to it." A persistent child who is pulled away from an absorbing activity may learn to express frustration without tantrums.

Children who are taught to recognize that their problems lie in initial reactions to novelty may be encouraged to persevere long enough to enjoy activities. Nonpersistent children may learn to break up tasks into small components and take breaks during a difficult task. Distractible children can do homework in a quiet place away from interfering stimuli. Children with a high activity level may learn to channel their energies, and those with

intense reactions may learn to understand the impact of their intensity on others.

Acceptance

Parents or teachers may feel that unless they attempt to "change" a child's irritating behaviors, they are guilty of reinforcing them. However, there is not much one can do to change negative mood quality or high activity. In fact, it is damaging to require a child to "cheer up," because such admonitions convey that the child's natural mood state is unacceptable. The key lies in recognizing that negative mood quality is not a manifestation of unhappiness but a reflection of temperament style so that subtle expressions of happy feelings can be appreciated. Similarly, a child's energetic activity, while jarring at times, must simply be channeled constructively. Children whose innate tendencies are constantly challenged may not develop the self-esteem necessary to cope with their adverse temperamental characteristics.

Building relationships

Because parents and teachers are human, there are inevitable frictions and irritations elicited by some temperament characteristics. Yet criticism and hostility should not be allowed to pervade relationships with temperamentally difficult children. Parents can capitalize on pleasant situations, such as car rides or calm times before going to bed. Enjoyable activities in which a child's temperament is an asset should be planned to help solidify the bond between parents and child. Teachers can be alert for situations that bring out the "best" in a child. It takes a great deal of patience and perseverance to promote a solid relationship with a difficult child. However, in the context of a basically positive relationship, inevitable frictions that arise from difficult temperament qualities can be put into perspective.

Summary

Temperament is the basis for individual differences in the style of engaging with the environment. The resultant behaviors, in turn, shape the reactions of others. Although the temperament concept highlights the person's own contribution to development, it also clarifies the impact of the environment because specific factors of the environment come into play according to the given patterns of temperament characteristics. Optimizing the goodness-of-fit between an individual and the environment is important because psychological development proceeds through the interplay of temperament with other characteristics of that individual and the environment.

Recommended Resources

Carey, W. B., & McDevitt, S. C. (Eds.) (1994). *Prevention and early intervention: Individual differences as risk factors for the mental health of children.* New York: Brunner/Mazel.
This edited book honoring the contributions of Thomas and Chess is intended for the professional. A basic premise of this work is that normal variations in temperament may be risk factors in the mental health of children, and that goodness-of-fit between a child and the environment is influenced by the reciprocal interplay between the child's characteristics and the environment. Complexities involved in the definition and influence of temperament are explicated, and several ongoing intervention and prevention programs are described.

Carey, W. B., & McDevitt, S. C. (1995). *Coping with children's temperament.* New York: Basic Books.
This book is geared to a professional audience, but parents may find it useful. The authors apply temperament concepts to the understanding and management of children at various ages (neonates, infants toddlers, preschoolers, and school age to adolescence). They emphasize the nine dimensions of temperament proposed by Thomas and Chess.

Chess, S., & Thomas, A. (1995). *Temperament in clinical practice.* New York: Guilford.
This paperback reissue of the original work, published in 1986, is a useful guide for professionals to apply theory to prevention and intervention programs.

Kohnstamm, G. A., Bates, J. E., & Rothbart, M. K. (Eds.). (1989). *Temperament in childhood.* New York: Wiley.
The variety of well written chapters capture the diversity of methods and viewpoints in the field of temperament. It is recommended for the professional who wants a comprehensive understanding of the complexities involved in temperament conceptualization and research.

Turecki, S., & Tonner, L. (1989). *The difficult child* (Rev. ed.). New York: Bantam Books.
This book is intended primarily for parents of children who are temperamentally difficult to raise. It helps parents identify and understand the temperamental bases of unconstructive interactions with children. Guidelines for assessment of temperament and management techniques are provided.

References

American Psychiatric Association. (1994). Diagnostic and statistical manual of mental disorders (4th ed.). Washington, DC: Author.

Bassan-Diamond, L., Teglasi, H. & Schmitt, P. (1995). Temperament and a storytelling measure of self regulation. *Journal of Research in Personality, 29,* 109–120.

Barcley, R. A. (1990). *Attention-deficit hyperactivity disorder: A framework for diagnosis and treatment.* New York: Guilford.

Bates, J. E. (1980). The concept of difficult temperament. *Merrill-Palmer Quarterly, 26,* 299–319.

Bates, J. E. (1987). Temperament in infancy. In J. D. Osofsky (Ed.), *Handbook of infant development.* New York: Wiley.

Bates, J. E. (1989). Applications of temperament concepts. In G. A. Kohnstamm, J. E. Bates, & M. K. Rothbart (Eds.), *Temperament in childhood* (pp. 321–355). New York: Wiley.

Bell, R. Q. (1968). A reinterpretation of the direction of effects in studies of socialization. *Psychological Review, 75,* 81–95.

Blakemore, C. (1991). Sensitive and vulnerable periods in the development of the visual system. In G. R. Bock & J. Whelan (Eds.), *The childhood environment and adult disease: Ciba Foundation Symposium 156* (pp. 129–147). Chichester, England: John Wiley.

Blaney, P. H. (1986). Affect and memory: A review. *Psychological Bulletin, 99,* 229–246.

Bower, G. H. (1981). Mood and memory. *American Psychologist, 36,* 129–148.

Buss, A. H., & Plomin, R. A. (1984). *Temperament: Early developing personality traits.* Hillsdale, NJ: Erlbaum.

Buss, A. H., & Plomin, R. (1986). The EAS approach to temperament. In R. Plomin & J. Dunn (Eds.), *The study of temperament: Changes, continuities and challenges.* Hillsdale, NJ: Erlbaum.

Carey, W. B., & McDevitt, S. C. (1978). Revision of the infant temperament questionnaire. *Pediatrics, 61,* 735–739.

Carey, W. B., & McDevitt, S. C. (1995). *Coping with children's temperament.* New York: Basic Books.

Cheek, J. M. & Buss, A. H. (1981). Shyness and sociability. *Journal of Personality and Social Psychology, 41,* 330–339.

Chess, S., & Thomas, A. (1984). *Origins and evolution of behavior disorders from infancy to early adult life.* New York: Brunner Mazel.

Chess, S., & Thomas, A. (1995). *Temperament in clinical practice.* New York: Guilford.

Derryberry, D., & Rothbart, M. K. (1988). Arousal, affect, and attention as components of temperament. *Journal of Personality and Social Psychology, 55,* 953–966.

Digman, J. M., & Inouye, J. (1986). Further specification of the five robust factors of personality. *Journal of Personality and Social Psychology, 50,* 116–123.

Dunn, J. & Kendrick, C. (1982). Temperamental differences, family relationships, and young children's response to change within the family. *Temperamental differences in infants and young children* (Ciba Foundation Symposium; 89). London: Pitman Books.

Dunn, J., Stocker, C., & Plomin, R. (1990). Nonshared experience within the family: Correlates of behavioral problems in middle childhood. *Development and Psychopathology, 2,* 113–126.

Eaton, W. O., & Enns, R. (1986). Sex differences in human motor activity level. *Psychological Bulletin, 100,* 19–28.

Eaves, L., Eysenck, H. J., & Martin, N. (1989). *Gene, culture, and personality: An empirical approach.* New York: Academic Press.

Eliasz, A. J. (1990). Broadening the concept of temperament: From disposition to hypothetical construct. *European Journal of Personality, 4,* 287–302.

Eysenck, H. J. (1970). *The structure of human personality* (3rd Ed.). London: Methuen.

Frijda, N. H. (1986). *The emotions.* Cambridge, England: Cambridge University Press.

Goldsmith, H. H., & Campos, J. J. (1982). Toward a theory of infant temperament. In R. N. Emde & R. J. Harmon (Eds.), *The development of attachment and affiliative systems* (pp. 161–193). New York: Plenum.

Goldsmith, H. H., & Campos, J. J. (1986). Fundamental issues in the study of early temperament: The Denver Twin Temperament Study. In M. H. Lamb & A. Brown (Eds.), *Advances in developmental psychology* Hillsdale, NJ: Erlbaum.

Goldsmith, H. H., & Campos, J. J. (1990). The structure of temperamental fear and pleasure in infants: A psychometric perspective. *Child Development, 61,* 1944–1964.

Gray, J. A. (1982). *The neuropsychology of anxiety: An enquiry into the functions of the septo-hippocampal system.* Oxford, England: Oxford University Press.

Grizenko, N., & Fisher, C. (1992). Review of studies of risk and protective factors for psychopathology in children. *Canadian Journal of Psychiatry, 37,* 711–721.

Hofstee, W. K. B. (1991). *The concepts of personality and temperament.* In J. Strelau & A. Angleitner (Eds.), *Explorations in temperament: International perspectives in theory and measurement* (pp. 177–188). New York: Wiley.

Kagan, J. (1994). Inhibited and uninhibited temperaments. In W. B. Carey & S. C. McDevitt (Eds.), *Prevention and early intervention: Individual differences as risk factors for the mental health of children* (pp. 35–41). New York: Brunner/Mazel.

Kagan, J., Reznick, J. S., & Snidman, N. (1989). Issues in the study of temperament. In G. A. Kohnstamm, J. E. Bates, & M. K. Rothbart (Eds.), *Temperament in childhood* (pp. 133–144). Chichester, England: John Wiley.

Karoly, P. (1993). Mechanisms of self-regulation: A systems view. *Annual Review of Psychology, 44,* 23–51.

Keogh, B. K. (1982). Children's temperament and teachers' decisions. In R. Porter & G. M. Collins (Eds.), *Temperamental differences in infants and young children* (pp. 269–279). London: Pitman.

Keogh, B. K. (1986). Temperament and schooling: Meaning of "goodness of fit"? In J. V. Lerner & R. M. Lerner (Eds.), *Temperament and social interaction in infants and children* (pp. 89–108). San Francisco: Jossey Bass.

Kohnstamm, G. A. (1986). *Temperament discussed: Temperament and development in infancy and childhood.* Leiden, Swets-Zeitlinger.

Kohnstamm, G. A. (1989a). Historical and international perspectives. In G. A. Kohnstamm, J. E. Bates, & M. K. Rothbart (Eds.), *Temperament in childhood* (pp. 557–566). New York: Wiley.

Kohnstamm, G. A. (1989b). Temperament in childhood: Cross-cultural and sex differences. In G. A. Kohnstamm, J. E. Bates, & M. K. Rothbart (Eds.), *Temperament in childhood* (pp. 483–508). New York: Wiley.

Magnusson, D. (Ed.). (1988). *Paths through life: A longitudinal research program.* Hillsdale, NJ: Erlbaum.

Martin, R. P. (1988). *The temperament assessment battery for children.* Brandon, VT: Clinical Psychology Publishing.

Martin, R. P. (1994). Special theme section: Impact of temperament on theory, research, and practice in school psychology. *Journal of School Psychology, 32,* 117–166.

Martin, R. P., Wisenbaker, J., Huttunen, M. (1994). Review of factor analytic studies of temperament measures based on the Thomas-Chess Structural Model: Implications for the Big Five. In C. Halverson, Jr., G. Kohnstamm, & R. P. Martin (Eds.). *The developing structure of temperament and personality from infancy to adulthood* (pp. 157–172). Hillsdale, N.J.: Erlbaum.

Maziade, M. (1994). Temperament research and practical implications for clinicians. In W. B. Carey & S. C. McDevitt (Eds.), *Prevention and early intervention: Individual differences as risk factors for the mental health of children* (pp. 69–80). New York: Brunner/Mazel.

Maziade, M., Caron, C., Cote, R., Boutin, P., & Thivierge, J. (1990). Extreme temperament and diagnosis: A study in a psychiatric sample of consecutive children. *Archives of General Psychiatry, 47,* 477–484.

McClowry, S. G., Hegvik, R. L. & Teglasi, H. (1993). An examination of the construct validity of the middle childhood temperament questionnaire. *Merrill-Palmer Quarterly, 39,* 279–293.

Mehrabian, A. (1978). A measure of individual difference in temperament. *Educational and Psychological Measurement, 38,* 1105–1117.

Mehrabian, A. (1980). *Basic dimensions for a general psychological theory.* Cambridge, MA: Oelgeschlager, Gunn & Hain.

Plomin, R. (1994). Interface of nature and nurture in the family. In W. B. Carey & S. C. McDevitt (Eds.), *Prevention and early intervention: Individual differences as risk factors for the mental health of children* (pp. 179–189). New York: Brunner/Mazel.

Prior, M. (1992). Childhood temperament. *Journal of Child Psychology and Psychiatry, 33,* 249–279.

Rothbart, M. K. (1981). Measurement of temperament in infancy. *Child Development, 52,* 569–578.

Rothbart, M. K. (1989a). Biological processes in temperament. In G. Kohnstamm, J. Bates, & M. K. Rothbart (Eds.), *Temperament in childhood* (pp. 77–110). New York: Wiley.

Rothbart, M. K. (1989b). Temperament and development. In G. Kohnstamm, J. Bates & M. K. Rothbart (Eds.), *Temperament in childhood* (pp. 187–247). New York: Wiley.

Rothbart, M. K. (1991). Temperament: A developmental framework. In J. Strelau & A. Angleitner (Eds.), *Explorations in temperament: International perspectives on theory and measurements* (pp. 61–74). New York: Wiley.

Rothbart, M. K., & Derryberry, D. (1981). Development of individual differences in temperament. In M. E. Lamb & A. L. Brown (Eds.), *Advances in developmental psychology* (Vol. 1, pp. 37–86). Hillsdale, NJ: Erlbaum.

Rothbart, M. K., & Posner, M. J. (1985). Temperament and the development of self-regulation. In L. C. Hartlage & C. F. Telzrow (Eds.), *The neuropsychology of individual difference: A developmental perspective* New York: Plenum Press.

Rutter, M. (1987). Psychosocial resilience and protective mechanisms. *American Journal of Orthopsychiatry, 57,* 316–331.

Rutter, M. (1989). Temperament: Conceptual issues and clinical implications. In G. A. Kohnstamm, J. E. Bates, & M. K. Rothbart (Eds.), *Temperament in childhood* (pp. 463–479). New York: Wiley.

Rutter, M. L. (1994). Temperament: Changing concepts and implications. In W. B. Carey & S. C. McDevitt (Eds.), *Prevention and early intervention: Individual differences as risk factors for the mental health of children* (pp. 23–34). New York: Brunner/Mazel.

Sanson, A., Oberklaid, F., Pedlow, R., & Prior, M. (1991). Risk indicators: Assessment of infancy predictors of pre-school behavioral maladjustment. *Journal of Child Psychology and Psychiatry, 32,* 609–626.

Scarr, S. (1994). Genetics and individual differences: How Chess and Thomas shaped developmental thought. In W. B. Carey & S. C. McDevitt (Eds.), *Prevention and early intervention: Individual differences as risk factors for the mental health of children* (pp. 170–178). New York: Brunner/Mazel.

Slabach, E. H., Morrow, J., & Wachs, T. D. (1991). Questionnaire measurement of infant and child temperament. In J. Strelau & A. Angleitner (Eds.), *Explorations in temperament: International perspectives on theory and measurement* (pp. 205–234). New York: Plenum Press.

Smith, B. (1994). The Temperament Program: Community-based prevention of behavior disorders in children. In W. B. Carey & S. C. McDevitt (Eds.), *Prevention and early intervention: Individual differences as risk factors for the mental health of children* (pp. 257–266). New York: Brunner/Mazel.

Sroufe, L. A., Schork, E., Motti, F, Lawroski, N., & LaFreniere, P. (1984). The role of affect in social competence. In C. E. Izard, J. Kagan, & R. B. Zajonc (Eds.), *Emotions, cognition and behavior* (pp. 289–319). Cambridge, England: Cambridge University Press.

Stevenson-Hinde, J., & Simpson, A. E. (1982). Temperament and relationships. In R. Porter & G. M. Collins (Eds.), *Temperamental differences in infants and young children:* Ciba Foundation Symposium 89 (pp. 51–61). London, England: Pittman.

Strelau, J. (1983). *Temperament, personality, activity.* New York: Academic Press.

Strelau, J., & Eliasz, A., (1994). Temperament risk factors for Type A behavior patterns in adolescence. In W. B. Carey & S. C. McDevitt (Eds.). *Prevention and early intervention: Individual differences as risk factors for the mental health of children* (pp. 42–49). New York: Brunner/Mazel.

Strelau, J., & Eysenck, H. J. (Eds.). (1987). *Personality dimensions and arousal.* New York: Plenum.

Teglasi, H. (1993). *Clinical use of story telling: Emphasizing the T.A.T. with children and adolescents.* Boston: Allyn & Bacon.

Thomas, A., & Chess, S. (1977). *Temperament and development.* New York: Brunner/Mazel.

Thomas, A., & Chess, S. (1989). Temperament and personality. In G. A. Kohnstamm, J. E., Bates, & M. K. Rothbart (Eds.), *Temperament in childhood* (pp. 249–261). New York: Wiley.

Thomas, A., Chess, S., & Birch, H. G. (1968). *Temperament and behavior disorders in children.* New York: New York University Press.

Turecki, S., & Tonner, L. (1989). *The difficult child* (Rev. ed.). New York: Bantam Books.

Van Heck, G. L. (1991). Temperament and the Person-Situation Debate. In J. Strelau & A. Angleitner (Eds.), *Explorations in temperament: International perspectives on theory and measurement* (pp. 163–175). New York: Wiley.

Windle, M., & Lerner, R. M. (1986). Reassessing the dimensions of temperamental individuality across the life span: The Revised Dimensions of Temperament Survey (DOTS-R). *Journal of Adolescent Research, 1,* 213–230.

Zuckerman, M. (1979). *Sensation seeking: Beyond the optimal level of arousal.* Hillsdale, NJ: Erlbaum.

21

Corporal Punishment

Irwin A. Hyman
Barbara M. Barrish
Jeffrey Kaplan
Temple University

Background and Development

Ask any American to define discipline and the most likely response will be that it is punishment. Punishment of children in home and school includes withdrawal of privileges; yelling, screaming, and nagging at them; and various versions and perversions of time-out and hitting. The latter, the topic of this chapter, is generally classified as corporal punishment and is one of the most controversial parenting and pedagogical issues with which psychologists must deal.

Corporal punishment cannot be properly understood by isolating the discussion to school issues. Support for this practice in America is pervasive, and it too often rises to the level of legally defined abuse in both homes and schools (National Committee for the Prevention of Child Abuse, 1991). Its use is sustained by tradition (Straus, 1994), individual beliefs and experiences (Barrish, 1996; Kaplan, 1995), religion (Greven, 1991; Wiehe, 1990) and political ideology (Hyman, 1995).

Widespread support for the use of corporal punishment reflects both many individuals' punitive attitudes and public policy toward youth misbehavior, deviance, and nonconformity. This support suggests that the United States may be one of the most punitive of Western democracies (Hyman, 1995). For instance, corporal punishment is forbidden in the schools of Continental Europe, Britain, Japan, Israel, the former Communist nations, Ireland, parts of Australia, Cyprus, Canada, Puerto Rico, Jordan, Ecuador, Iceland, Mauritius, and the Philippines and at the high school level in New Zealand. In the home, Sweden, Norway, Finland, Denmark, and Austria forbid parental spanking (Deley, 1988; Haeuser, 1992; Kinkead, 1994). Germany, Switzerland, Australia, and Canada have been considering similar legislation. By 1960, only New Jersey and Massachusetts forbad corporal punishment in schools. By 1995, 27 states, many suburban upper middle class schools, and most of the largest cities had banned it (Hyman, 1990; Hyman & Wise, 1979).

Perceptions of appropriateness and efficacy of corporal punishment are correlated with the frequency, intensity, duration, and context of how individuals experienced it as children (Barrish, 1996; Hyman, 1990; Kaplan, 1995). Thus, because most Americans have been recipients of corporal punishment in home, school, or both, they consider it appropriate. This poses a unique ethical problem for many school psychologists, a problem which can be especially difficult when working with those whose religious beliefs and/or personal experiences imply that it is an effective way to deter misbehavior.

Should all school psychologists' practice be guided by the fact that both the American Psychological Association and the National Association of School Psychologists have passed resolutions against the use of corporal punishment in schools? While these organizations offer no guidelines regarding parental spanking, most child abuse experts are unfavorable toward it (National Committee for the Prevention of Child Abuse, 1991; Straus, 1994). For psychologists who are also unfavorable toward spanking, practice issues may not be problematic. But what should psychologists do when working with educators and parents in the South, in rural areas, or with specific groups who consider corporal punishment to be part of their culture? And what if a school psychologist believes that paddling and spanking are necessary and effective in certain situations?

This chapter is framed by the authors' admitted bias against the use of corporal punishment in any setting. With that stated, however, we attempt to present material which reflects the current state of research and practice.

Definition

Dictionary (Barnhart, 1963), legal (Black, 1968), educational (Hyman, 1988) and psychological (Hyman, 1996) definitions of corporal punishment indicate that it consists of the infliction of pain on the human body as a penalty for an offense. It may also consist of painful confinement. Inflicters' and inflictees' definitions and perceptions of pain may vary. Therefore, accurate definitions in individual cases are debatable, especially in drawing a line between allowable corporal punishment and abuse. State and local education regulations allowing the use of corporal punishment normally include regulations meant to ensure that its use is not abusive. Users are admonished to use reasonable force, to ensure that they are not striking in anger, and to have a witness present. While written reports are required and parents must normally be notified, data and the personal observations of this chapter's authors indicate that most school districts sustain some amount of unreported, informal corporal punishment (Hyman, 1990). Most corporal punishment in schools is administered with wooden paddles, and some schools specify the shape, size, and thickness of the paddle and the number of blows per offense.

Legal precedents have broadened the definition of corporal punishment when the courts have considered it excessive (Hyman, 1990; Pokalo & Hyman, 1993). It can include painful confinement in a restricted space, forcing a child to assume a fixed posture for a long time, excessive exercise and drills, forced ingestion of noxious substances, and exposure to painful environments (Hyman, Clarke, & Erdlen, 1987).

Prevalence

It is difficult to determine the extent to which schools use corporal punishment because of obvious problems of data collection. Biannual surveys of the Office of Civil Rights and extrapolations have resulted in this chapter's first author estimating about 3 million school incidents per year in the early 1980s to about 1/2 million in the early l990s (Hyman, 1990).

In American homes, corporal punishment, administered by hitting with an open hand, is widely used by most parents. A Harris poll in 1992 revealed that 86% of Americans approved of parental spankings (Hyman, 1990). Straus (1994), in reviewing the literature, found that between 32% and 90% of all parents surveyed were using some form of physical punishment on their children, with the lowest rates reported for parents of adolescents and the highest for those with children aged 3 to 6 years. In fact, studies of toddlers almost always show rates of over 90% receiving physical punishment, with one survey reporting a rate of physical punishment of almost 100% for children around 3 years of age.

National surveys and Gallup polls taken up until 1983 consistently found approximately 50% of all teachers, parents, and administrators favored the use of corporal punishment in the schools (Rust & Kinnard, 1983). Recent surveys of psychologists suggest that at least 30% favor the use of physical punishment as a disciplinary practice in the home (Kaplan, 1995).

Parent-reported rates of hitting, spanking, and slapping have generally been lower than those described retrospectively by young adults who also indicate higher rates occurring in younger childhood (91% to 93.2%) than during adolescence (32% to 50.7%) (Graziano, 1992). A study of 679 college students by Graziano and Namaste (1990) found that over 93% had experienced some physical punishment, primarily by parents (88%) and secondarily by teachers (22%). The research has also shown that adults who physically punish their children were more likely to have themselves been hit as children than parents who do not spank (Weller, Romney & Orr, 1987). In a study by Bryan and Freed (1982), 95% of students surveyed in a community college population reported that they had received some corporal punishment during their lifetimes.

In schools, corporal punishment occurs more frequently in the primary and intermediate levels, and boys are hit much more frequently than girls (Hyman, 1990). Minority and poor White school children receive paddlings four to five times more frequently than middle and upper class White students (Richardson & Evans, 1992). There are mixed data on the extent of use in the home as a function of race and class (Kelly, Power, & Wimbush, 1992).

Most of the corporal punishment in American schools occurs in states in the South and Southwest—Florida, Texas, Arkansas and Alabama have consistently been among the leaders in the frequency of hitting school children (Hyman, 1990). The least frequent use of corporal punishment occurs in schools in the Northeast. The only identified study of personality traits of teachers who frequently paddle indicated that they tend to be authoritarian, dogmatic, relatively inexperienced, impulsive, and neurotic as compared to their peers (Rust & Kinnard, 1983). This study has methodological problems that limit generalization. Yet, anecdotal and observational data collected during litigation in corporal punishment cases do suggest that educators who use it more than the norm are different from their peers (Pokalo & Hyman, 1993). Teachers who do not paddle are most often those who were rarely if ever spanked or paddled as children (Lennox, 1982). This modeling effect has been demonstrated in studies of parents (Straus, 1994) and psychologists (Kaplan, 1995).

Schools with high rates of corporal punishment also have high rates of suspensions and are generally more punitive in all discipline responses than schools with low rates of corporal punishment (Farley, 1983). Also, studies show that corporal punishment, rather than being used as a "last resort," is too often the first punishment for nonviolent and minor misbehaviors (Hyman et al., 1987). In descending order of support for school corporal punishment are school board members, school administrators, teachers, parents, and students (Reardon & Reynolds, 1979).

People who indicate that they are Fundamentalists, Evangelicals, Literalists, and/or Baptists tend to respond more punitively to disciplinary situations than those who identify with other major religions and orientations (Barnhart, 1972; Greven, 1991; Wiehe, 1990). Demographic studies of corporal punishment in schools support these findings (Hyman, 1989, 1990).

Developmental Issues

A comprehensive discussion of developmental issues is beyond the scope of this chapter. Also, much of the research is deeply embedded in theoretical constructs which tend to flavor the methodology and conclusions. However, a few studies are mentioned here that highlight salient developmental issues.

In terms of severe corporal punishment, Jaffe, Wolfe, Wilson, and Zak (1986) studied the effects of family violence, including all levels of corporal punishment, on boys between 6 and 16 years of age, both as victims and as witnesses. Both internalizing and externalizing behaviors were investigated. Aggression was considered externalizing behavior along with disobedience at home or school, lying and cheating, destroying things belonging to self or others, cruelty to others, associating with bad friends, and fighting. Internalizing included clinging to adults, complaining of loneliness, feeling unloved, feeling sadness or jealously, and excessive worrying. Boys who witnessed family violence developed similarities in behavioral and social maladjustment to boys who were abused by their parents, while differing significantly from children of nonviolent families. However, those who merely witnessed the violence were more likely to internalize their symptoms. Weiss, Dodge, Bates and Pettit (1992) found that internalizing problems were more difficult to assess in the kindergarten children they studied. They postulated that one reason may be because early physical discipline can have a delayed effect on internalizing problems so that they do not become apparent until later childhood or adolescence.

The idea of a latency period in the development and demonstration of internalizing problems is also suggested by the findings that adolescents and adults who received any level of corporal punishment as children are more prone to suicide and depression than those who were not physically punished (Deykin, Alpert & McNamara, 1985). As Straus (1994) demonstrated, the more corporal punishment experienced as a child, the higher the probability for that individual of depression and suicidal thoughts in adulthood. He concludes that corporal punishment puts a child at risk of serious injury, both physical and psychological.

Miller (1983), using a psychoanalytic perspective, attributes the latent and long-lasting psychological effects of physical punishment to the facts that (a) the punishment may occur before conscious memory is formed and, therefore, become implanted more powerfully and with ultimately greater impact in the unconscious; and (b) children are expected to love, respect, and even show gratitude to the adults who hit them and, therefore, must bury and deny any feelings of humiliation or anger associated with the pain of being spanked. These buried feelings manifest in deeper feelings of despair or rage as the child reaches adulthood. Miller states, "the conscious use of humiliation (whose function is to satisfy the parents' needs) destroys the child's self-confidence, making him or her insecure or inhibited; nevertheless this approach is considered beneficial" (p. 21).

Two developmentally relevant components of personality that are strongly influenced by the quality of one's early experiences with one's parents are self-concept, or how we perceive ourselves, and self-esteem, the evaluations associated with these judgments (Ponterotto, 1993). In terms of overall parenting styles, Litovsky and Dusek (1985) demonstrated that adolescents who rated their parents as warm and accepting and as allowing psychological autonomy had higher self-esteem scores than those who experienced their parents as rejecting and controlling (i.e., as using guilt, hostility and intrusiveness to force compliance with parental desires). Straus (1994) suggests that physical punishment accompanied by verbal assaults may increase the risk of damage to the child's self-esteem compared to physical punishment administered in the context of a supportive relationship.

One of this chapter's authors (Barrish, 1996) studied college students' memories of the use of corporal punishment to investigate Straus's (1994) assumption that the effects of corporal punishment might be mediated by the type of parenting. The results indicate that even mild or moderate parental physical punishment can have negative psychological consequences for those who experience it as children. That is, ordinary, everyday, legally sanctioned corporal punishment does not appear to be benign or beneficial to its recipients. The most salient point to be made from this study is that other methods of disciplining children are more conducive to the development of a child's psychological well-being (Barrish, 1996).

Power and Chapieski (1986) and Trickett and Kuczynski (1986) found that many punitive interventions do not even result in compliance with the parents' requests or demands but end simply with the administration of punishment. Discipline administered as part of a teaching or modeling process and based on mutual respect, communication, and positive regard may be more likely to promote internal motivations for compliance (Trickett & Kuczynski, 1986) than more punitive methods. In addition to enhancing the child's self-concept, persuasion rather than punishment may help children to develop a higher level of moral judgment. This occurs when behavioral choices are based on rational considerations of the rightness or wrongness of one's actions, rather than on fear of punishment (see Sociomoral Development and Behavior, this volume).

We do not imply that punishment, or at least the threat of it, may not sometimes be necessary in children rearing and education. However, the preponderance of data favors the use in most situations of noncorporal techniques such as time-out, overcorrection, and response cost (Axelrod & Apsche, 1984). Even in the area of aversive procedures with children with severe disturbances, most experts do not favor the use of corporal punishment as described here.

Socioeconomic and Racial Factors

A series of studies of school corporal punishment indicate that lower class minority and White children are hit four to five times more often than middle and upper class White children (Hyman, 1990). Because it is statistically more likely that a child who is African-American or Hispanic will also be poor, it is difficult to determine whether paddlings are racially motivated. Further, while no data are available, observations suggest that minority teachers may be just as likely to use corporal punishment on poor minority children as are White teachers. Our research and clinical experience indicate that educators rarely paddle children of wealthy and/or influential families. All of the cases of severe paddlings with which we are familiar involve children of poor or working class parents.

Early research on social class and corporal punishment was inconclusive, although the consensus appeared to favor the belief that parents of a higher socioeconomic status (SES) were less likely to hit their children. Some contemporary research continues to suggest that parents in higher SES groups are less likely to use or approve hitting children as a means of discipline (Wiley, 1989). However, artifacts including the types of questions asked and who is asking them may bias responses.

Straus (1994) suggests viewing SES as existing on a continuum rather than simply comparing groups, such as working and middle class. He and his colleagues offer data on adolescents which indicate a curvilinear relationship, with middle class adolescents receiving the most corporal punishment.

Although SES is important, educational level may be crucial in how respondents to surveys answer questions about corporal punishment. Perhaps one's availability of financial resources or occupational experiences are not as important as educational attainment. Education can shape attitudes and beliefs and exposes people to thinking that contradicts traditional beliefs or transgenerational values regarding discipline. Further, respondents from higher SES may be more sophisticated about surveys and more likely to respond in terms of the perceived social desirability of their answers.

Techniques Used to Administer Corporal Punishment

A series of epidemiological articles which document and analyze school corporal punishment reported in the national press reveal that instruments used include leather straps, thin rattan switches, baseball bats, plastic bats, the soles of size 13 cowboy boots, and a variety of other handy or favored instruments (Czumbil, Hopkins, Wilson, & Hyman, 1993; Hyman et al., 1987). Students have been confined for long periods in storerooms, boxes, cloakrooms, closets, and school vaults. They have been thrown against lockers, walls, desks, or concrete pillars and forced to run a "gauntlet" or "belt line."

The cases reported are relatively rare; however, they are often considered necessary, acceptable, and legal in the schools and communities where they happen. Yet, the damage caused by the educators often rises to the legal definition of abuse when committed by parents or adults in any other setting (Pokalo & Hyman, 1993).

In homes, cases of excessive corporal punishment which end in death are frequently reported in the media. One study of college students (Barrish, 1996) revealed that parental corporal punishment included spanking (63%), slapping (42%), hair or ear pulling (20%), punching (9%), pinching (14%), whipping (11%), arm twisting (9%), shaking (9%), and kicking (6%).

Practical and scientific issues make it very difficult to draw an exact line between "normal" spanking and abuse. Medical and legal definitions of abuse require evidence such as bruises, broken bones, and other obvious signs of injury. From a social/psychological perspective, many practitioners find that acceptable levels of force, definitions of spanking, and individual children's physical and emotional reactions vary quite widely as a function of factors such as culture, transgenerational patterns of child rearing, and individual thresholds for pain and bruising (Hyman, 1990).

Legal Issues

In 1867 New Jersey became the first state to abolish corporal punishment in the schools; Massachusetts followed in 1971. As of 1995, it was banned by either statute or regulation in 27 states.

The most well-known federal case involving corporal punishment in the schools is *Ingraham v. Wright* (1977). James Ingraham was a junior high school student in Miami who received more than 20 paddlings from the principal. Medical diagnoses indicated hematomas of the buttocks which required hospital visits. In this case the U.S. Supreme Court ruled that corporal punishment does not violate certain constitutional safeguards against cruel and unusual punishment and due process (Hyman & Wise, 1979; Van Dyke, 1984). The legal theory supporting use of corporal punishment is that schools serve "in loco parenti" and therefore can use parental methods of discipline which reflect cultural practices.

On the issue of substantive due process, involving how severely one may corporally punish a school child and on the issue of whether parents may prevent its use on their children, federal district courts have issued contradictory opinions. Whether excessive punishment might violate the substantive due process rights embodied in the Fourteenth Amendment has yet to be established by the Supreme Court. Some states, such as Pennsylvania, allow corporal punishment for regular students but forbid it with children with disabilities. In any state, the Individual Education Plan for a child with a disability can forbid the use of corporal punishment. This is especially relevant, from a legal and clinical perspective, if the student has been a victim of any type of abuse.

Abolition of corporal punishment in homes is highly unlikely in the foreseeable future. However, it is generally forbidden in foster homes and institutions which serve both children and adolescents and in most boarding schools.

Problems and Implications

Physical Injuries

The effects of corporal punishment vary widely. A series of studies document injuries resulting from corporal punishment in schools (Czumbil et al., 1993; Hyman et al., 1987). They include reports of red and blistering welts, hematomas on the legs and buttocks, and injuries to almost every external and many internal body parts. Some injuries have resulted in deaths.

Children with disabilities are particularly vulnerable to maltreatment in school. For instance, a high proportion of children with disabilities who are aggressive, especially those with conduct disorders, have been victims of abuse in the home (McCord, 1988; Miller, 1983; Straus, 1994; Weiss et al., 1992). Their parents frequently justify severe beatings and verbal abuse as being necessary for discipline. They may even encourage teachers to do the same with a claim such as "that is all the kid understands." It simply is not logical to continue to hit children who are aggressive when frequent and severe corporal punishment has been documented as a major cause of their aggression. If necessary, therapeutic physical restraint may be judiciously used in extreme situations, but inflicting more pain is just counterproductive.

Psychological Damage

Studies of stress symptoms resulting from corporal punishment in schools evidence short- and long-term psychological damage. This chapter's first author and col-

leagues developed the *My Worst School Experience* survey to examine the effects of both physical and psychological maltreatment on school children (Hyman, 1990; Hyman, Zelikoff, & Clarke, 1988; Kohr, 1996). Using this instrument both normatively and in clinical evaluations, researchers demonstrated that any level of corporal punishment may result in stress symptoms in over 50% of the recipients and post-traumatic stress disorder in 1% to 2% of the victims.

Children who are physically punished are more likely to grow up approving of it (Graziano, 1992; Kelder, McNamara, Carlson & Lynn; Weller et al., 1987) and using it to settle interpersonal conflicts (Carlson, 1986; Kaufman & Cicchetti, 1989; Larzelere, 1986; McCord, 1988; Weiss et al., 1992). These effects are not limited to victims of severe child abuse. Even children who experienced only socially sanctioned, legal, and "ordinary" physical punishment were almost three times more likely to have seriously assaulted a sibling in the previous year when compared to children who were not physically disciplined (Straus, 1994). Larzelere (1986), despite his support for "moderate" spanking, found a linear, positive association between physical punishment and child aggression. Studies have also shown that men raised by aggressively punitive parents are more likely to commit crimes than those reared by nonviolent methods (McCord, 1988).

Researchers have posited numerous theories to explain the mechanism of the intergenerational transmission of the implicit acceptance of violence as it is expressed in hitting (Levinson, 1989). Models include learning theory and the impact of modeling behaviors (Bandura, 1973; Graziano, 1992) and spillover of cultural norms that support the use of violence in face-to-face situations (Parke, 1982; Straus, 1994). Weiss et al. (1992), using a prospective design, found support for their idea that children subject to early harsh discipline develop maladaptive social-information-processing styles, including inattention to relevant social cues, hostile attributional biases, and a tendency to access aggressive responses as solutions to interpersonal problems. Harsh discipline may include frequent and/or severe spankings. However, parents or legal authorities may not deem that it is physically damaging enough to be legally considered abuse.

Psychologists' Attitudes About Corporal Punishment

A random sample of psychologists from four divisions of the American Psychological Association (APA) indicated that 31% of respondents recommended parental use of corporal punishment (Kaplan, 1995). This finding is similar to that of Ragsdale (1994) whose survey of members of the APA Division of Children, Youth, and Families and Division of Clinical Psychology indicated that 30% would suggest a spank "rarely" or "sometimes." Kaplan's study indicated that over 75% of the respondents opposed or strongly opposed the use of corporal punishment and that 55% believed spanking to be an abusive act while 8% felt it is child abuse. Yet, 48% reported having used corporal punishment on their own children. Ragsdale's study showed that although 70% of psychologists would never recommend that a parent spank a child, 62% reported slapping or spanking their own child more than once.

Kaplan (1995) found that females were more likely to oppose the use of corporal punishment than males. Other predictors of opposition were being raised in higher SES classes than lower ones, Jewish religious orientation as compared to Protestant orientation, and never having received corporal punishment at home as a child. Psychologists who perceived the corporal punishment they received as a child as helpful were more likely to use and recommend the use of corporal punishment than those who perceived it as harmful, regardless of how severe the punishment.

Arguments in Favor of Corporal Punishment and Responses

Because most Americans support the use of corporal punishment, it is important to understand their rationale. Most arguments in favor of corporal punishment are based on personal experiences, interpretations of the Bible, and so-called "common sense" assumptions, such as "I was hit and it didn't do me any harm."

Defenders of corporal punishment in school claim that it works, that its use should be determined at the local level, that it is needed to maintain discipline, and that publicized abuses appear so bizarre and infrequent they should not trigger policy decisions (Hyman, 1990). With few exceptions, the majority of abuses we have investigated were all legally sanctioned and the educators' actions were defended—and all too frequently approved—by local teachers unions, administrators, school boards, and many citizens. Also, teachers are frequently immune to charges of child abuse, even though there are observable physical injuries that would lead to prosecution if done by any other adult, including parents.

Teacher resistance to banning corporal punishment is often based on the argument that its use, or at least the threat that it can be used, is needed to stem student violence. However, all laws and regulations regarding corporal punishment in schools protect teachers' rights to use force to quell disturbances and to protect themselves, others, property, or students from self-injury. A teacher is not liable for the incidental infliction of pain as a result of the legitimate use of any of the aforementioned. In any event, teachers rarely paddle big, strong, potentially violent students, as most hitting occurs in the lower grades (Hyman & Wise, 1979).

While there is no research we know of to support corporal punishment in schools, a small group of researchers support "moderate" parental spanking (Fore-

hand & McMahon, 1981; Larzelere, 1986; Roberts & Powers, l990). Some support for their position is based on a few studies of clinically referred, noncompliant children. In these experimental studies, mothers of oppositional 2- to 6-year-old children were assigned to one of four chair time-out enforcement procedures. To qualify for the study, a child had to refuse at least 30% of 30 pairs of parental "pick up" or "put" requests during an experimental setting. Noncompliant children were randomly assigned to "enforcement" procedures if they would not stay in time-out chairs. Enforcement included either spanking, holding, placing behind a barrier for 60 seconds, or releasing if the child attempted to escape from time-out. All treatment procedures were effective for some children, but from an individual perspective, placing behind barriers and spanking were more effective in some cases in making children stay in time-out chairs. Looking at compliance data before the data were analyzed for individual differences, it is hard to believe that these studies could be used to support any broad policy position.

In these studies and others, supporters of moderate spanking never adequately define "moderate" (Larzelere, 1986; Roberts & Powers, 1990). Further, these studies do not address how the children became noncompliant, why the restraint condition was so brief, or whether it consisted of a non-pain-inflicting basket hold. This hold is accompanied by calming and reassuring words which assure the child that he or she must complete the punishment and that there is no intention to inflict physical pain as part of it. Nor do the studies indicate the extent and sophistication of positive, preventive disciplinary techniques used before hitting or the other punishment procedures. Also, in assigning parental hitting, parents' perceptions of what is mild, moderate, or severe is purely subjective. It is very much dependent on their own childhood accommodations to being spanked by their parents.

Even though some studies may show that moderate spanking appears to do no harm, there is little scientific evidence that it is necessary. The overwhelming evidence is that reward, praise, and interactions with children which promote the development of a positive self-concept are the most powerful motivators for learning. Because almost every popular discipline-training program for educators promotes well-proven positive and preventive techniques (Hyman, et al., 1997) and because the infliction of pain is, a priori, a violent act, the promotion of corporal punishment only adds to the already unacceptable levels of violence in the lives of American children.

Alternative Actions

There is ample evidence that the politics of punitiveness have fertile ground in America. The data support, at least at a hypothetical level, that the slow progress in eliminating corporal punishment, especially when it rises to the level of legally defined abuse, is explainable in terms of American punitiveness in comparison to other Western democracies which have banned it. We recognize that the roots of the problems addressed here are multifaceted. While the reasons for the acceptance of hitting children may be complex, the outcome is simple to understand. When hitting children becomes an unacceptable notion to most Americans, a great deal of child abuse, and the other ills documented here, will be eliminated.

Through experimental studies, survey research, and advocacy research, psychologists must continue to provide social science data on the effects of punitiveness. The increasingly successful battle to eliminate corporal punishment in U.S. schools illustrates how social science data, based on advocacy research, can help advocates to change public policy. The following recommendations flow from over two decades of public policy efforts.

The next generation of parents and teachers must be taught that there is no reason to yell, scream, ridicule, or hit children in the name of discipline. APA and the National Association of School Psychologists (NASP) should pass resolutions against spanking in the home. These actions could have profound, positive effects on other major national organizations, just as their joint 1974 resolution on corporal punishment in schools did.

To effectively minimize the victimization of American children, *every year Congress should consider a bill to ban spanking in the home.* Such a bill was introduced in the Wisconsin legislature in 1992. While such Congressional bills have little chance of passing in the near future, introduction each year will draw attention to abuse problems and raise the public's consciousness about the inherent problems with hitting children and the connection between abuse and violence.

All preservice and in-service psychologists and teachers should take complete courses in discipline which include work in anger control and crisis management so that they do not model punitiveness as a solution to problems. There is ample and overwhelming evidence that, when religion and theme interference from individuals' own experiences of being hit as children are mediated by data, they are open to a multitude of well-documented approaches to discipline that do not require the infliction of pain (Hyman et al., 1996). Further, training must provide strategies to deal with the pro-corporal-punishment attitudes of parents, employers, teachers, and regional cultures. This is especially crucial for school psychologists who work in the conservative areas of the South and Southwest, and in predominantly rural communities.

All public schools should include curricula, such as conflict resolution and peer mediation, on nonviolent solutions to problems. They should promote critical analyses of TV shows which depict simple-minded, violent answers to complex problems.

History courses should teach the reality of violence against children and other minorities in society. Educa-tors need to stop romanticizing violence in history and promote an understanding of the consequences of policies based on punitiveness.

Media involvement is needed in promoting the message of nonviolent solutions to misbehavior. Media public service announcements can demonstrate a variety of proper discipline techniques for common misbehaviors. Parenting courses should be increased, improved, and made mandatory, especially for at-risk populations with a strong likelihood of early parenthood.

Summary

This chapter has presented a brief overview of the literature on corporal punishment. The writers admit to their bias against it but also present the major arguments in support. The movement to forbid the use of corporal punishment in schools, in institutions, and eventually in the home is supported by emerging studies of family violence which suggest a link between spanking and child abuse. Current research indicates correlations between spanking and such demographic factors as social class, religion, geography, and race.

Because of obvious ethical and legal limitations on experimental studies of corporal punishment in which students are assigned hitting, the research base has been varied. Our arguments against corporal punishment in schools have been based on sources such as the Bible (Greven, 1991), literature (Gibson, 1978), medicine (Hyman, 1990), history (Miller, 1983), government studies (Hyman, 1990), newspaper articles (Hyman et al., 1987), special education, cross-cultural studies (Haeuser, 1992; Levinson, 1989), experimental studies (Bandura, 1973), and sociology (McCord, 1988).

Finally, imagine an America in which no adult ever hit a child. In that America, every parent and teacher would use positive, reinforcing, self-esteem-building procedures to shape appropriate behavior in children. Punishments such as time-out and loss of privileges would be used appropriately. Is there a school psychologist who does not believe that such an America would have vastly reduced rates of child abuse and many more well-behaved, happy, achieving children?

Recommended Resources

Greven, P. (1991). *Spare the child: The religious roots of punishment and the psychological impact of physical abuse.* New York: Vintage Books.
The religious and historical roots of belief in corporal punishment is traced to English Protestant influences in American parenting. The material is especially helpful to psychologists working in conservative and rural regions.

Hyman, I. A. (1990). *Reading, writing and the hickory stick: The appalling story of physical and psychological abuse in American Schools.* Lexington, MA: Lexington Books.
Causes, history, demographics, legal issues, and clinical case studies regarding corporal punishment in the schools are presented. This book also offers strategies for eliminating corporal punishment in all settings. Research-based answers for the most common arguments in favor of corporal punishment in home or school are included.

Hyman, I., Dahbany, A., Blum, M., Weiler, E., Brooks-Klein, V. & Pokalo (1997). *School discipline and school violence: The teacher variance approach,* Needham Heights, MA: Allyn & Bacon.
This book offers a comprehensive discussion of the relation of American punitiveness toward children and school misbehavior and violence. Included are teacher tests of punitiveness and their orientation to discipline as well as a theory-driven approach, written for teachers, to five orientations for diagnosis and remediation of student misbehavior.

Straus, M. A. (1994). *Beating the devil out of them: Corporal punishment in American families.* New York: Lexington Books.
Using an extensive research base of surveys on family discipline and violence, Straus offers compelling data about the negative effects of any type or level of parental spanking. Especially cogent is its relation to depression, aggression, and criminal behavior.

References

Axelrod, S., & Apsche, J. (Eds.). (1984). *The effects of punishment on human behavior.* New York: Academic Press.

Bandura, A. (1973). *Aggression: A social learning analysis.* Englewood Cliffs, NJ: Prentice Hall.

Barnhart, C. (1963). *American college dictionary.* New York: Random House.

Barnhart, J. (1972). *The Billy Graham religion.* Philadelphia: The Pilgrim Press.

Barrish, B. (1996). The relationship of remembered parental physical punishment to adolescent self-concept. Unpublished doctoral dissertation, Temple University, Philadelphia.

Black, H. (1968). *Black's law dictionary (4th ed.).* St. Paul, MN: West Publishing.

Carlson, B. E. (1986). Children's beliefs about punishment. *American Journal of Orthopsychiatry, 56*(2), 308–312.

Czumbil, M., Hopkins, K., Wilson, D., & Hyman, I. (1993, April). An analysis of recent corporal punishment cases reported in national newspapers. Paper presented at the 25th Annual Convention of the National Association of School Psychologists, Washington, D.C.

Deley, W. (1988). Physical punishment of children: Sweden and the U.S.A. *Journal of Comparative Family Studies, 19,* 419–431.

Deykin, E. Y., Alpert, J. J., & McNamara, J. J. (1985). A pilot study of the effect of exposure to child abuse or neglect on adolescent suicidal behavior. *American Journal of Psychiatry, 142*(11), 1299–1303.

Farley, A. (1983). National survey of the use and non-use of corporal punishment as a disciplinary technique within the United States public schools. Unpublished doctoral dissertation, Temple University, Philadelphia.

Forehand, R. L., & McMahon, R. J. (1981). *Helping the non-compliant child: A clinician's guide to parent training.* New York: Guilford Press.

Gibson, I. (1978). *The English vice,* London: Duckworth.

Graziano, A. M. (1992). Why we should study sub-abusive violence against children. *The Child, Youth, and Family Services Quarterly, 15*(4), 6–8.

Greven, P. (1991). *Spare the child: The religious roots of punishment and the psychological impact of physical abuse.* New York: Vintage Books.

Haeuser, A. (1992). Swedish parents don't spank. *Mothering, 63,* 42–49.

Hyman, I. (1988). Corporal punishment. In R. Gorton, G. Schneider, & J. Fisher (Eds.), *Encyclopedia of school administration and supervision* (pp. 79–80). New York: Oryx Press.

Hyman, I. (1989, October). *Using advocacy research to change public policy: The case of corporal punishment in the schools.* Paper presented at the Poster Session of the Policy and Research Forum of the Eighth National Conference on Child Abuse and Neglect, Salt Lake City, UT.

Hyman, I. A. (1990). *Reading, writing, and the hickory stick: The appalling story of physical and psychological abuse in American Schools.* Lexington, MA: Lexington Books.

Hyman, I. (1995). Corporal punishment, psychological maltreatment, violence, and punitiveness in America: Research, advocacy, and public policy. *Applied & Preventive Psychology, 4,* 113–130.

Hyman, I. (1996). Corporal punishment. In T. Fagan & P. Wardon (Eds.), *Historical encyclopedia of school psychology* (pp. 92–93). Westport, CT: Greenwood Publishing Group.

Hyman, I., Clarke, J., & Erdlen, R. (1987). An analysis of physical abuse in American schools. *Aggressive Behavior, 13,* 1–7.

Hyman, I., Dahbany, A., Blum, M., Weiler, E., Brooks-Klein, V. & Pokalo, M. (1997). *School discipline and school violence: The teacher variance approach.* Needham Heights, MA: Allyn & Bacon.

Hyman, I. A., & Wise, J. (1979). *Corporal punishment in American education.* Philadelphia: Temple University Press.

Hyman, I., Zelikoff, W., & Clarke, J. (1988). Psychological and physical abuse in schools: A paradigm for understanding post-traumatic stress disorder in children. *Journal of traumatic Stress, 1*(2) 243–267.

Ingraham V. Wright, 97 S.Ct. (1971).

Jaffe, P., Wolfe, D., Wilson, S., & Zak, L. (1986). Similarities in behavioral and social maladjustment among child victims and witnesses to family violence. *American Journal of Orthopsychiatry, 56*(1), 142–146.

Kaplan, J. (1995). Psychologists' attitudes towards corporal punishment. Unpublished doctoral dissertation, Temple University, Philadelphia.

Kaufman, J., & Cicchetti, D. (1989). The effects of maltreatment on school-aged children's socioemotional development: Assessments in a day-camp setting. *Developmental Psychology, 25,* 516–524.

Kelder, L. R., McNamara, J. R., Carlson, B., & Lynn, S. J. (1991). Perceptions of physical punishment: The relation to childhood and adolescent experiences. *Journal of Interpersonal Violence, 6(4),* 432–445.

Kelly, M., Power, T., & Wimbush, D. (1992). Determinants of disciplinary practices in low income black mothers. *Child Development, 63*(3), 573–582.

Kinkead, G. (1994, April 10). Spock, Brazelton and now Penelope Leach. *New York Times Magazine,* 32–35.

Kohr, M. (1996). Validation of the my-worst-experience scale. Unpublished doctoral dissertation, Temple University, Philadelphia.

Larzelere, R. E. (1986). Moderate spanking: Model or deterrent of children's aggression in the family? *Journal of Family Violence, 1*(1), 27–36.

Lennox, N. (1982). Teacher use of corporal punishment as a function of modeling behavior. Unpublished doctoral dissertation, Temple University, Philadelphia.

Levinson, D. (1989). *Family violence in cross-cultural perspective.* Newbury Park, CA: Sage Publications.

Litovsky, V. G., & Dusek, J. B. (1985). Perceptions of child rearing and self-concept development during the early adolescent years. *Journal of Youth and Adolescence, 14*(5), 373–387.

McCord, J. (1988). Parental behavior in the cycle of aggression. *Psychiatry, 51,* 14–23.

Miller, A. (1983). *For your own good.* New York: Farer, Straus & Giraux.

National Committee for the Prevention of Child Abuse. (1991). *Public attitudes and behaviors with respect to child abuse prevention, 1987–1991.* Chicago: Author.

Parke, R. D. (1982). Theoretical models of child abuse: Their implications for prediction, prevention and modification. In R.H. Starr, Jr. (Ed.), *Child abuse prediction: Policy implications* (pp. 31–66). Cambridge, MA. Ballinger Publishing.

Pokalo, M., & Hyman, I. (1993, April). *Case studies in community sanctioned abuse of school children.* Paper presented at the 25th Annual Convention of the National Association of School Psychologists, Washington, D.C.

Ponterotto, J. G. (1993). Review of the multidimensional self-esteem scale. *Mental Measurements Yearbook, 10,* 580–582.

Power, T., & Chapieski, M. (1986). Childrearing and impulse control in toddlers: A naturalistic investigation. *Developmental Psychology, 22*(2), 271–275.

Ragsdale, E. (1994). *Ethical beliefs and professional practices of psychologists regarding parental use of corporal punishment.* Unpublished master's thesis, University of Alabama, Tuscaloosa.

Reardon, F., & Reynolds, R. (1979). A survey of attitudes toward corporal punishment in Pennsylvania schools. In I. Hyman & J. Wise (Eds.), *Corporal punishment in American education* (pp. 301–328). Philadelphia: Temple University Press.

Richardson, R., & Evans, E. (1992, June). *African-American males: Endangered species and the most paddled.* Paper presented at the Annual Conference of the Louisiana Association of Multicultural Education, Southern University, Baton Rouge, LA.

Roberts, M., & Powers, S. (1990). Adjusting chair timeout enforcement procedures for oppositional children. *Behavior Therapy, 21,* 257–271.

Rust, J. O., & Kinnard, K. Q. (1983). Personality characteristics of the users of corporal punishment in the schools. *Journal of School Psychology, 21,* 91–105.

Straus, M. A. (1994). *Beating the devil out of them: Corporal punishment in American families.* New York: Lexington Books.

Tricket, P. K., & Kuczynski, L. (1986). Children's misbehaviors and parental discipline strategies in abusive and nonabusive families. *Developmental Psychology, 22,* 115–123.

Van Dyke, (1984). Corporal punishment in our schools. *Clearing House, 57*(7), 296–300.

Wiehe, E. (1990). Religious influence of parental attitudes toward the use of corporal punishment. *Journal of Family Violence. 5,* 173–186.

Weiss, B., Dodge, K. A., Bates, J. E., & Pettit, G. S. (1992). Some consequences of early harsh discipline: Child aggression and a maladaptive social information processing style. *Child Development, 63,* 1321–1335.

Wiley, E. (1989). Educators call for fairer, more effective means of discipline in schools. *Black Issues in Higher Education, 5*(21), 3–16.

22

School Violence

Michael Furlong
Gale M. Morrison
Annie Chung
Michael Bates
University of California at Santa Barbara

Richard L. Morrison
Ventura (California) Unified School District

Background and Development

According to the 27th annual Phi Delta Kappa-Gallup Poll (Elam & Rose, 1995), for the past several years "lack of discipline" and "fighting/violence/gangs" are among the biggest concerns adults have about America's public schools. As such, it behooves school psychologists and other educators to be aware of what is known about the occurrence of violence in schools and which prevention and intervention strategies have been implemented to reduce its incidence. School violence obviously violates fundamental tenets about providing safe conditions in which teaching and learning take place. However, many publications and other media sensationalize violent incidents occurring on school campuses, contributing to the development of negative attitudes toward schools (Elam & Rose, 1995). Although the popular media may serve to motivate much needed school safety action, there is also a need for thoughtful, informed program development.

The reader is encouraged to consider the topic of school violence as encompassing more than responding to obvious violent, criminal behavior in schools, although such interventions may at times be necessary. This chapter emphasizes the importance of critical analysis of (a) what is known about school violence and its impacts, (b) how school violence prevention fits into the broader educational mission of schools, and (c) the implementation of prevention programs that are thoughtfully embedded within broader support efforts to promote student personal and social development and to enhance the context in which learning occurs.

Definition Confusion

Only two studies have examined school psychologists' own experiences with school violence and the types of violence that occur on school grounds. Furlong, Babinski, Poland, Muñoz, and Boles (1996) found that school psychologists were unlikely to be the victims of even mild forms of violence at school but that a wide range of incidents occurred to students and other individuals at their respective schools. An interesting finding was that school psychologists' perceptions of the size of the "violence" problem was strongly associated with the type of incidents that occurred. Bullying and harassment behaviors (both verbal and milder physical forms of pushing and punching) occurred in almost all schools, even those described as having little or no violence problem. In contrast, school psychologists tended to describe their schools as having a "moderate" school violence problem when property incidents (e.g., stealing and vandalism) occurred and as having a "big or very big" violence problem when serious physical assaults (e.g., hit on the head, cut with a sharp object, or threatened with a gun) occurred. A second study (Dear et al., 1995) found this same pattern of responses from teachers, school counselors, school administrators, and education credential candidates.

Consistent with these findings, Kameoka (1988) found a surprising amount of diversity among which specific school behaviors were considered "violent." He asked a sample of recent high school graduates to rate the level of violence in 71 behaviors that could occur at school. Even for the incident rated as most violent across the sample (sexual assault on campus), about 25% of the respondents rated this behavior as completely nonviolent. This lack of consensus about which behaviors characterize school violence may have its roots in the fact that youth antisocial behavior has strong and traditional ties to law enforcement and juvenile justice disciplines. Educators may be more comfortable addressing the "antisocial" behavior of specific youth as part of a broader developmental perspective rather than addressing "violent" behavior, which can be considered a widespread social problem.

Given the confusion surrounding the term "school violence," questions arise regarding the nature of what school violence is and why it should be investigated. In American society, schools are the primary social setting in which intimate, caring relationships develop. As complex and intimate social settings, perhaps the ones shared most generally by all children, the influence of schools as norm-setting environments can transcend the individuals involved. Because children expect schools to be safe, secure, and nurturing environments, the effects of violence at school can be quite damaging to a child's fundamental sense of security and interpersonal trust. Thus, the term "school violence" encompasses not just the behaviors of individual students, staff, and intruders, but also the broader impact to the social setting in which these behaviors occur (Furlong, Morrison, & Clontz, 1991). The construct of school violence is therefore similar to the construct of family violence, in that the context in which violence occurs is crucial to its understanding.

From an educator's perspective, it is helpful to think about school violence as including a range of behaviors that occur at school and that lead to some form of personal harm (Furlong, Morrison, & Dear, 1994; G. M. Morrison, Furlong, & R. L. Morrison, 1994). Such classes of behavior include bullying, anger-control problems, aggressive behavior, sexual harassment, and even corporal punishment (Hyman, Zelikoff, & Clarke, 1988; see related chapters, this volume). With students' developmental risk factors in mind, school personnel can conceptualize school violence as a continuum of behaviors with harmful effects that progress from accidental to neglectful to finally intentional acts. Consistent with a broad developmental perspective, Dear & CTC Advisory Panel on School Violence (1995) define school violence as

a public health and safety condition that often results from individual, social, economic, political and institutional disregard for basic human needs. [It] includes physical and nonphysical harm which causes damage, pain, injury or fear [and it] disrupts the school environment and results in the debilitation of personal development which may lead to hopelessness and helplessness. (p. 15)

How Often Does School Violence Occur?

Popular conceptions of school violence are derived from increasing media coverage and incidence surveys sponsored by special interest groups. These sources of information are not subjected to the scrutiny of scientific review, use nonuniform methodologies, and do not include standard reliability and validity checks in survey instruments (Furlong, Flam, & Smith, 1996). Of the relatively few school violence studies that employed strict scientific

methodology, the most extensive was *Violent Schools— Safe Schools* (National Institute of Education, 1978), which is now outdated. One of the few studies to provide a longitudinal perspective on school violence was the National Educational Longitudinal Study (NELS; Hafner et al., 1990), which included a school safety item ("I do not feel safe at this school") in its survey. Responses to this item showed that more seventh graders felt unsafe at school in 1980 (12.2%) than in 1990 (8.8%), a finding at odds with popular beliefs about the upward spiraling of school violence.

Given the NELS findings, there is reason to recognize that many students report being safe at school and may be more concerned with matters other than personal safety (e.g., academics, social relationships). Nevertheless, students are victimized on school campuses and an understanding of their plight is needed. The biannual *Youth Risk Behavior Surveillance Survey (YRBSS),* conducted by the Center for Disease Control and Prevention (Kann et al., 1995), is a useful source of information about how frequently school violence occurs. This survey involved a large, nationally representative sample ($N = 16,296$) of high school students (Grades 9 to 12) drawn from surveys conducted in 32 states and U.S. territories. With respect to school violence, specific questions addressed (a) avoiding school because of unsafe feelings, (b) getting into physical fights on campus, (c) being threatened or injured at school, and (d) weapon carrying at school. This database provides the best single source of information about the incidence of school violence, although these few questions limit the scope of the data.

Avoiding School Because of Unsafe Feelings

Because self-reported fear alone does not necessarily reflect objective danger in a setting, asking students how many times they actually stay home because of insecure feelings is a useful place to start examining school violence and safety issues. As shown in Figure 1, 4.4% of all students in this national sample (Kann et al., 1995) indicated that they stayed home at least one day in the previous month because of personal safety concerns. There were no difference in the rates reported by females (4.4%) and males (4.3%). Differences by age were noted with ninth graders (6.1%) twice as likely as twelfth graders (3.0%) to stay home. Strong differences were noted by sociocultural groups with Hispanic students (10.1%) the most likely to stay home. Among all of the regions included in the survey, students in American Samoa (23.1%) were by far the most likely to say they had stayed home. Students in the Virgin Islands (8.6%), Nevada (7.8%), and Louisiana (7.3%) were the next most likely to stay home. The regions with the lowest proportion of students staying home were Montana (2.5%), Nebraska (3.0%), and South Dakota (3.1%).

Felt Too Unsafe To Go To School
In Past 30 Days

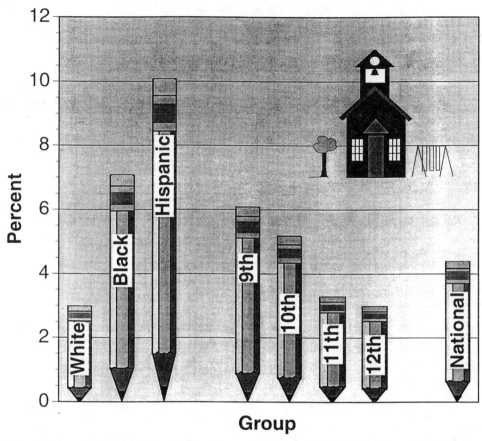

Note. Data from "Youth Risk Behavior Surveillance—United States, 1993," by L. Kann, C. W. Warren, W. A. Harris, J. L. Collins, K. A. Douglas, M. E. Collins, B. I. Williams, J. G. Ross, and L. J. Kolbe, 1995, *Morbidity and Mortality Weekly, 44,* p. 1–55.

Figure 1. *Percentage of high school students reporting they felt too unsafe to go to school at least once in the previous 30 days.*

Getting into Physical Fights on Campus

American folklore sometimes romanticizes scuffles that occur on schoolyards. With concern about more serious incidents of violence has come increasing interest in preventing these less serious forms of aggression on campus in the hope that an escalation of aggressive behavior can be avoided. The *YRBSS* (Kann et al., 1995) asked students if they had been in a physical fight at school in the previous year. Across the national sample, 16.8% of the students indicated they had been in a fight. Again, a strong developmental component emerged, with ninth graders (23.1%) more than twice as likely as twelfth graders (11.4%) to have been in a fight, perhaps reflecting the stress associated with the transition to secondary school and the comparatively lower social status of younger students. Differences by sociocultural group were not strong, but African-American students (22.0%) were the

most likely to say they had been in a fight. As one would expect, males (23.5%) were almost three times as likely as females (8.6%) to have fought. Not too surprisingly, regional differences mirrored those for students staying home because of safety concerns. American Samoan students (39.1%) were nearly twice as likely as the next highest regional group (Nevada students, 20.1%) to indicate they had been in a fight. There was little difference across other regions; all ranged from 12.5% (Nebraska) to 17.9% (Louisiana).

Being Threatened or Injured at School

In the *YRBSS* (Kann et al., 1995), the combination of incidents used to measure threats or injuries at school is narrow in focus. As one might expect when an item refers to physical injury, fewer students (7.3%) reported being "threatened or injured" at school than being in physical fights. The same grade level and sociocultural group patterns found for schoolyard fighting held for threats and injury. Ninth graders (9.4%) and African-Americans (11.2%) were the most likely to have been threatened or injured at school. Students in American Samoa (15.2%) and Nevada (10.3%) were the most likely to say they were threatened or injured, whereas students from South Dakota (6.3%) were the least likely.

Weapon Carrying at School

The specter of students toting weapons is perhaps the strongest image that the public has about the potential for violence on school campuses. There is no central source of information, nor an established procedure to document weapon confiscations on America's school campuses (see Furlong, Flam, & Smith, 1996, for a detailed review of studies examining the incidence of guns on school campuses). Consequently, the best source of information is student self-reports of bringing weapons to school. In the *YRBSS* (Kann et al., 1995), students were asked if they had carried a weapon (e.g., "gun, knife or club") on school property during the previous month (note that it need not have been specifically during regular school hours). Nationally, 11.8% of the students indicated they had brought a weapon onto school property at least once. Differences in weapon carrying by age and sociocultural groups were not pronounced. Similar to the other safety patterns just described, ninth graders (12.6%) and African Americans (15.0%) were the most likely to say they had brought a weapon to school. Males in all groups (17.9%) were much more likely than females (5.1%) to bring weapons to school. By region, Tennessee had the highest (18.2%) reported weapon-carrying rate; Hawaii had the lowest (7.9%) rate.

Perpetrators of School Violence

To date, there are no analyses of students who commit acts of school violence. However, research examining the backgrounds of youth with antisocial behavior suggests that these youth exhibit multiple risk factors. For example, Walker, Colvin, and Ramsey (1995) report that students who repeatedly commit violent acts have identifiable high-risk profiles that include being male, academic difficulties, peer rejection, interpersonal skill deficits, prior history of antisocial and/or aggressive behavior that has progressed with increasing severity, involvement in numerous high-risk behaviors, and low self-esteem. For students with a long history of increasingly severe antisocial behavior, this pattern begins in early childhood and remains stable over the course of adolescence and into adulthood (see Aggressive Behavior, this volume).

The work of Walker et al. (1995) suggests a developmental pattern for those youths most likely to commit school violence. Deficits in interpersonal social skills are manifested early and can often be identified by the age of four. When these youths reach school age, they often have academic and social difficulties yet lack the academic and social skills to cope. As a consequence, they engage in inappropriate and/or antisocial behavior when interacting with peers, are rejected, and then often form their own referent groups with other rejected, antisocial youths. These deviant peer groups often develop attitudes and values that support violent behavior. Social control theory (Felson, Liska, South, & McNulty, 1994) suggests that, even if the student ascribes to nonviolent personal values, the group norms of the deviant peer group override these personal values and elicit violent behavior from the individual. Over time, as the severity of antisocial behaviors increases, the proviolence group values may become internalized.

School Violence Victimization

Much research to date has focused on the rates of negative, criminal acts on school grounds. Only a few studies have sought to better understand the profiles of students who are victims of school violence. Furlong, Chung, Bates, and Morrison (1995) compared students who reported no victimization experiences with those students who reported 12 or more types of victimization in the previous month (less than 5% of the total sample). Compared with nonvictims, victims of multiple forms of violence at school were more likely to be male than female (3:1 ratio) and to be poorly bonded to the school community. Victims of multiple forms of violence were nearly 10 times as likely as nonvictims to feel unsafe at school and 7 times more likely to report low levels of interpersonal trust. The strongest finding was that multiple victims were nearly 22 times more likely than nonvictims to score high on a scale measuring hostile interpersonal attitudes and beliefs. The experience of being a victim of school violence has powerful negative effects that erode a student's connectedness and bonding to the broader school community. In general, experiencing or witnessing any type of violence has a dampening effect on children's development (Pynoos & Nader, 1988). This pattern also holds for violence that occurs at school, with the qualification that as a setting in which one should expect to have positive interpersonal relationships, like in a family, the impact of being a victim of violence is magnified.

Violence victimization at school is a strong developmental risk factor (G. M. Morrison, Furlong, & R. L. Morrison, 1994), but reports of its occurrence contribute to the impression that *many* students are *frequently* victimized. The authors have administered the *California School Climate and Safety Survey* (*CSCSS*, described later in this chapter) to more than 10,000 students in southern California attending schools in rural, suburban, and urban areas (see Furlong, Chung et al., 1995). Students were asked to indicate which of 21 violent incidents they had personally experienced at school in the previous month. The incidents fell on a continuum of experiences involving *bullying, harassment, property intrusion, serious physical intrusion,* and *threats related to deviant behavior.* Differences across rural, suburban, and urban communities were negligible—54.3%, 55.3%, and 54.1% of the students in each region, respectively, reported experiencing three or fewer incidents. For 64% of the students, the worst form of violence they experienced in a given month was being called names by another student. Consistent with this finding, 59.8% of the students reported that getting good grades is their biggest worry, compared with just 12.1% whose biggest worry was school violence. Interestingly from a developmental perspective, younger children were more likely than older pupils to worry about school violence. (See also Furlong & Morrison, 1994; R. L. Morrison, Furlong, & G. M. Morrison, 1994.)

Summary of School Violence Research Findings

The school violence prevalence and incident studies cited here show that schools are places where most students feel safe. Nonetheless, a subgroup of youths commit violent acts at school, are the victims of these violent acts, or both. The information just presented suggests that school violence-prevention or -reduction programs should address the needs of both types of students. Even students who are usually nonvictims must learn how to be effective citizens in communities where violence occurs, just as victims need social support and perpetrators need programs to reduce their aggressive tendencies and involvement in numerous high-risk behaviors.

Alternative Actions: Multicomponent School Violence-Reduction Programs

Efforts to address the multiple facets of school violence clearly call for a multicomponent approach. The needs of staff, student victims, witnesses, and even the perpetrators themselves must be managed within the framework of a comprehensive school safety plan. In addition, it is necessary to examine how the school context itself may contribute to the occurrence of violence. A useful model to guide this process, one that encompasses these diverse perspectives, is the Subculture of Violence theory (DuRant, Pendergast, & Cadenhead, 1994; Felson et al.,

1994). This model proposes that youth are more likely to engage in violent behavior when they have observed models in their home, community, and school settings that demonstrate and/or validate violent behaviors and attitudes. The model suggests that in school settings it is necessary to examine and then address the needs of students who have largely accepted a violent value system (as in gangs subcultures) and to examine how school norms may sanction or tolerate violent acts. Drawing upon this theoretical perspective, we describe a multicomponent strategy that guides the development of a comprehensive school violence-reduction program. Most schools should find useful some weighted combination, reflecting local needs and conditions, of the violence reduction components listed next.

Component I: Reducing School Violence by Intervening with Aggressive Students

As a result of public policy demands to punitively respond to the threat of violence at school through "zero-tolerance" programs, schools have tended to focus disciplinary actions on perpetrators of violence. Similarly, researchers have begun to investigate the root causes of violence and the development of programs designed to prevent future violence. A comprehensive approach to school violence prevention should encompass multiple components, starting with efforts to modify the behavior of students as well as school staff who have engaged in or are at risk of engaging in violent behavior. The work of Batsche (this volume), Lochman (this volume), and Pettit (this volume) provide valuable resources for this component of a general violence-reduction effort. As shown by Walker and Sylwester (1991), three simple measures (teacher ratings of student social skills, observed aggressive behavior on the playground, and the number of disciplinary referrals to the school administration) are highly effective in identifying students with long-term antisocial and aggressive tendencies. These youth are very disproportionately involved in community and school-related antisocial behaviors, and consequently, programs designed to promote prosocial behaviors among them can reduce school violence.

An example of a complex, empirically tested program that has high contextual validity for addressing individual students' aggressive behaviors in the schools is the program developed by Walker et al. (1995). Their program emphasizes the early identification of and intervention with youth with aggressive behaviors. Once these youths are identified, specific interventions focus on study skills development, social skills development, increased awareness of health risks associated with aggressive behaviors, and development of coping strategies to prevent future substance use or abuse. Interventions are implemented on a case-by-case basis by combining social skills training, positive reinforcement, and response cost procedures in order to produce socially desirable behavioral changes. Useful classroom management strategies, instructional techniques, and playground management considerations for modifying students' behaviors are also utilized.

Component II: Implement Victimization Support Programs

Surveys show that the overwhelmingly typical response to antisocial and aggressive behavior at school is disciplinary actions, to the near exclusion of counseling and developmentally appropriate behavior programs (Elam & Rose, 1995; Furlong et al., 1996; Larson, 1993). In the rush to placate public fears about violence by administering swift disciplinary actions, the conditions and needs of student and staff victims may be overlooked. A second level of response to school violence should incorporate needs assessments with the implementation of prevention and intervention programs for victims. As shown earlier in this chapter, most students, fortunately, do not experience a great deal of violence at school. However, a small group does experience multiple forms of violence (Finkelhor & Dziuba-Leatherman, 1994). At school, these individuals develop a negative perception of the interpersonal security and support in the school community, which are hallmarks of individuals who have Post Traumatic Stress Disorder (Pynoos & Nader, 1988; Zins, Travis, Brown, & Knighton, 1994). This fact is particularly important because victims and witnesses of repeated violence are themselves more likely to engage in violence in the future (Richters & Martinez, 1993).

Slaby and colleagues (Slaby, Wilson-Brewer, & Dash, 1994) have developed a violence prevention curriculum that addresses the needs of victims of school violence. This program, *Aggressors, Victims, and Bystanders: Thinking and Acting to Prevent Violence,* focuses on violence among peers and specifically on the roles youth adopt during potentially violent situations. It is targeted at the entire student body. Adolescents examine their roles as aggressors, victims, and bystanders of violence and learn new ways to think about how they respond to conflict. The cognitive-behavioral orientation of this curriculum is apparent in its reliance on a four-step model of conflict resolution: (a) keep cool, (b) size up the situation, (c) think it through, and (d) do the right thing. The unique aspect of this curriculum is its emphasis on the role of the bystander as a critical player in potentially violent situations. One of the primary objectives of the program is to give students the skills to assume a different role in conflict situations—the role of the nonviolent problem solver. Exercises are presented in a variety of ways, including classroom discussions, role-playing activities, brainstorming, small-group work, case studies, self-directed analysis, and homework.

Component III: Implementing School-Wide Violence Prevention Programs

A third level of response involves the implementation of general peacemaking, peer mediation, or conflict resolution programs in school settings. Such programs are natural bridges between components that focus on individual change and those that seek to change the school context in which violent and nurturing behaviors occur. Although there is limited research that has critically examined the impact of these programs on the incidence of school violence (Posner, 1994), several programs have been widely used. These include the *Second Step Violence Prevention Curriculum* (Committee for Children, 1988) and *Violence Prevention Curriculum for Adolescents* (Prothrow-Stith, 1987). A survey review of 51 violence-prevention programs implemented in U.S. schools is provided by Wilson-Brewer, Cohen, O'Donnell, and Goodman (1991). Additionally, peer mediation programs based upon the curricula of the San Francisco Community Board Mediation Program have also been integrated into violence-prevention and -reduction approaches in many schools (see Johnson & Johnson, 1994; Lane & McWhirter, 1992). A brief review of the most widely used, general, school violence-reduction programs follows.

Second Step Violence Prevention Curriculum

This program (Committee for Children, 1988) seeks to develop skills in deficit areas related to social isolation, lack of empathy, impulse-control problems, poor decision-making skills, and anger-control problems. The program targets preschool through middle school students and is divided into elementary and middle school curricula. Both curricula are founded on cognitive-behavioral procedures such as self-instruction, problem solving, modeling, and behavioral rehearsal. A typical lesson involves group discussions centered around stimulus photographs, such as a picture of two boys arguing over a playground ball. The class discussion addresses the consequences of fighting and generates alternative solutions. The middle school curriculum involves a slightly different presentation format and introduces problem-solving skills into the lessons.

Integration of the *Second Step Curriculum* has been a vital aspect of many schools' attempts to prevent and/or reduce violence on their campuses. In the Milwaukee Public Schools, this curriculum has been used since 1991 in 78 elementary schools in conjunction with (a) school staff inservices focusing on violent incident management, (b) peer mediation programs, and (c) parent workshops. Coordinating these services are two school psychologists who work closely with a school team consisting of administrators, counselors, social workers, and teachers. Strategies to incorporate the empathy, impulse-control, and anger-management skills emphasized in the *Second Step Curriculum* into the classroom lessons and into the school environment are designed by the cooperative efforts of the school psychologist, counselor, and classroom teachers so that students are given opportunities not only to learn about positive ways in which to deal with anger but also to practice these new skills.

Violence Prevention Curriculum for Adolescents

Drawing upon a public health model of violence reduction, this program deals almost exclusively with violence between peers (Prothrow-Stith, 1987). It aims to raise the students' threshold to engage in aggressive behaviors by creating an atmosphere of nonviolence in the classroom and by building alternative responses to anger. The curriculum uses didactic presentation, student brainstorming, role-play, and creative homework techniques to explore global, inter-, and intrapersonal aspects of violence. Over the course of 10 sessions, students examine national and local homicide statistics, explore anger as a normal emotion, analyze how they express anger, evaluate the consequences of fighting, and discuss alternatives to fighting.

Peer mediation strategies

Combining elements of the San Francisco Community Board Mediation Program as well as the School Mediators' Alternative Resolution Team, Johnson and Johnson (1994) developed and implemented a peer mediation program in U.S. and European schools. In this four-step program, students are taught specific negotiation and mediation skills that include:

1. De-escalating angry outbursts and facilitating calm behaviors amongst those in conflict.
2. Introducing the mediation process and rules as well as obtaining the disputants agreement to this process.
3. Facilitating honest, respectful communication between disputants by allowing each to present his or her perspective of the problem by remaining neutral and restating each of the disputant's position to the other.
4. Binding the final solution to the problem via a verbal and/or formal contract.

Ultimately, the goal of peer mediation is to enable students to self-regulate their own behavior, particularly when conflicts arise. All students participate and are given opportunities to practice the skills taught in this program. Once an entire class receives training, a typical format for handling student disputes utilizes two mediators (daily selection of mediators by a teacher, for example) who intervene and prompt the use of mediation procedures when signs of potential hostility between two other students develop.

Until recently, the empirical investigation of such peer mediation programs has been limited. However, anecdotal reports and brief survey responses of various school personnel and students indicate that participation in peer mediation programs have decreased the frequency of conflicts 47% to 50% (Lane & McWhirter, 1992).

Component IV: Interventions Designed to Improve School Climate

The fourth component of a comprehensive school violence-reduction program involves efforts to impact the general climate of the school itself. Such programs may not focus directly on specific violent behaviors per se but rather seek to change the conditions on the school campus that may directly or indirectly manifest themselves in violent acts (Dear et al., 1995). Thus, programs to decrease racism, increase appreciation of diversity, and improve levels of interpersonal trust can decrease violence by improving a school's climate and the quality of the interpersonal relationships among and between students and staff.

Research by Felson et al. (1994) shows that when schools are influenced by subgroups ascribing to a culture of violence the general normative standards of the school can still be strong enough to override the influence of personal violence values. Factors shown to protect schools from being dominated by a subculture that supports violence include having (a) a high proportion of academically capable students, (b) an ethos that stresses academic values, and (c) firm but fair disciplinary procedures. At the same time, exclusive focus on excessive security procedures and discipline may alienate students and create a climate that discourages trusting interactions. This balanced perspective has been recognized by almost every school-community group that has gathered to discuss how to create safe and effective schools (Dear et al., 1995; Ontario Ministry of Education, 1994; Safe Schools Project, 1993). These study groups have all concluded that to reduce school violence it is necessary to implement programs in the three components already described, but it is also necessary to create a comprehensive safe school strategic plan, one that involves the school and its community. Procedures to complete school safety planning have been described by Stephens (1994) and the California Department of Education (1989, 1994).

National School Safety Center Model

Stephens (1994), of the National School Safety Center, outlines an approach to school safety planning that addresses interventions at the systemic level. He states that for a school safety plan to be effective it must be comprehensive, continuing, and broad based. The school safety planning process is unique in that it includes whichever prevention or intervention programs meet local school needs. Thus, an essential component of this planning process is conducting an initial needs assessment. Regardless of the specific interventions used, for a safety plan to be successful it must have support from the district as a long-term agenda priority and buy-in from the site administrators as a continuing school priority. Stephens describes a variety of potential safety plan actions which include

- Establishing a parent center that encourages proactive parent participation in the school community.
- Ensuring active student input and participation in the planning process.
- Enhancing extracurricular programs for students.
- Integrating the safety plan into the school curricula.
- Supporting staff development through in-service training.
- Making behavior guidelines for students clear and prominent.
- Establishing a crisis response plan.
- Paying special attention to the needs of the victims of school violence.
- Creating partnerships among youth service professionals to coordinate violence prevention efforts.
- Building a state-of-the-art communication network between campus buildings and to off-site facilities such as law enforcement and fire departments.

California Department of Education Model

A guide for developing comprehensive school safety plans was developed by the California Department of Education (1989). The manual, *Safe Schools: A Planning Guide for Action,* presents a conceptual framework to guide the planning process based on the work of Furlong et al. (1991). Procedures are presented to examine the safety and violence risks in the physical, social, and cultural dimension of a school climate. Forms for writing a school safety plan are included along with a videotape discussing key considerations for establishing a school safety planning team.

Summary and Conclusions

A basic human need for children is to be safe and secure. In order for children to learn and to benefit from the education that American schools provide, school personnel must ensure that school environments are free from violence. Whereas the statistics about school violence reviewed in this chapter are sometimes misleading, there are enough incidents on school campuses to warrant serious attention to their reduction. Violence and threats to safety and security are, at the least, an impediment to children's development.

The statistics about school violence suggest that children and school faculty and staff are affected differentially by school violence. Different, but identifiable, groups of children are likely to be touched by violent acts. The perpetrators are likely to have a long history of antisocial

behavior. We identified programs that utilize proven strategies to modify this behavior; such strategies include social skill training combined with behavioral techniques.

Another, less visible, group involved in school violence are the victims. Although not as much is known about how they become victims in the first place, research has documented certain demographic characteristics such as belonging to the youngest grade group on a school campus and being African-American or American Samoan. Social alienation and attitudes of hostility and mistrust have also been associated with victims of school violence. Support programs for these students as well as potential bystanders and observers of school violence include counseling services and the development of conflict resolution skills.

School-wide prevention programs attempt to include all students in the process of gaining skills in interpersonal problem solving and conflict resolution and reducing negative behaviors such as lack of empathy, impulsiveness, and angry or aggressive responses to conflict situations. These programs include a variety of strategies including classroom instruction, curriculum focus on global or community issues of peace, peer-mediation programs, parent workshops, and staff in-service.

Work with individual students, student groups, and school-wide communities must be enhanced by policies, procedures, and climate development provided by a comprehensive school safety planning process (see Table 1). We have provided references and resources to guide such a process (see Table 2). While we have provided information and perspective on the players and the strategies in reducing school violence, it is important to note that implementing what is known in a consistent and ongoing manner may be the biggest challenge. Educators are inundated by an increasing "goal" list for what must be included in children's education and what must be achieved in terms of student outcomes. Although school psychologists resonate to the need for strategies to reduce school violence in terms of student development and juvenile justice professionals are alert to the criminal or delinquency consequences, mainline educators, of necessity, must have their eye on student outcomes, in particular academic outcomes.

Therefore, as G. M. Morrison, Furlong, and R. L. Morrison (1994) outlined, educators need to embrace school safety as part of their mission. Perhaps the role of the school psychologist in this challenge is to help communicate the connections that school safety has to both the major academic mission of the schools and to major school reform efforts. What is the "umbrella" or conceptual superstructure that will allow safety and education to combine efforts? The answer to this question requires the appreciation of the complexity of the problem as well as its solution. In this chapter we have attempted to outline both. One bottom line for educators and support personnel to recognize is that class lists consist of students who

Table 1 *Essential Actions for Reducing School Violence on a School-Wide Level*

1. *Needs Assessment:* Conduct a needs assessment to determine what needs to be addressed at your school. Ask students, parents, and staff members about their views of what happens on campus and what needs to be done about it.

2. *School Safety Plan:* Develop a comprehensive school safety plan that (a) responds to the identified needs of the school, (b) involves the entire school community, (c) incorporates multiple intervention techniques, and (d) targets students and staff at all three levels of intervention.

3. *View Others With Respect:* View all students as competent, valuable, and trustworthy members of the school community. The goal should be to build rapport between all students and staff, ideally creating a feeling of connectedness to the school through mutual respect and trust.

4. *Commitment and Leadership:* For a school safety plan to be most effective, it must have support from school and community leaders. Strong commitment to the plan must come from the district and from the principal at the school site.

5. *Think Long-Term:* Think of the school safety plan as a long-term investment (i.e., several years or more). Incorporate violence prevention and intervention techniques into the curriculum. Change the thinking to make violence prevention and intervention a normal and permanent part of the school day.

6. *Choose Reinforcement Over Punishment:* Focus intervention on building desired behaviors and strengthening existing protective factors, not just on eliminating unwanted behaviors. Avoid punitive and aversive programs. Violations of rules and misbehaviors should be viewed as opportunities to learn rather than opportunities to punish.

7. *Clarify Rules and Procedures:* Make school rules and policies as clear as possible to students, parents, and staff members. Apply contingencies of rules violations fairly and consistently. Suggestions include posting and rules and policies in highly visible areas around campus, creating and distributing student handbooks, and implementing peer mediation.

8. *Respect Individual Differences:* Accommodate individual differences in the classroom. For those at-risk students having academic difficulties, adjust class lessons to give them more chances to be successful. Successful experiences can create bonding between student and school.

9. *Facilitate Student Bonding With School:* Other ways to facilitate school bonding include developing teacher teams (or houses) that follow the students over several years and sponsoring more after-school or weekend events on campus.

10. *Increase Support for Teachers and Staff:* Provide more support for teachers and staff through recognition programs for meritorious service. Establish in-service training programs for classroom management techniques, crisis response planning, and other safety issues.

11. *Involve Parents and Community:* Involve parents in the school community by creating parent centers, offering parent training, encouraging volunteers, and enhancing parent-classroom communication. Also develop school-community links through neighborhood watch programs and meaningful interagency cooperation.

Table 2 *Useful School Violence Assessment Tools*

Though other sources are available for gathering information regarding violence incidents on school campuses, the following are three resources that provide complementary perspectives and meaningful information about school violence related campus conditions. See Furlong (1994) for a more extensive review of school safety assessment tools.

California School Climate and Safety Survey (CSCSS)

■ Available from Michael J. Furlong, Ph.D., Graduate School of Education, CCSP Program, UCSB, Santa Barbara CA 93106-9490. email: mfurlong@education.ucsb.edu.

■ Available for upper elementary school (Grades 4 and 5, 67 items) and secondary school (Grades 6 to 12). Staff and parent revisions are also available.

■ Addresses four major areas pertaining to student perceptions of (a) general safety conditions on campus; (b) quality of the physical, social, and cultural dimensions of their school's climate; (c) personal victimization experiences; and (d) sociocultural information.

■ Used to collect information about risk and resiliency conditions on school campuses as part of the school safety planning process described in *Safe Schools: A Planning Guide for Action* (California Department of Education, 1989).

■ Data and results have been used in school safety research (e.g., Furlong et al., 1995) and by school-site safety-planning teams as part of their needs assessment and evaluation procedures.

Youth Risk Behavior Surveillance Survey (YRBSS)

■ Available from the Centers for Disease Control and Prevention.

■ Developed by a panel convened by the Centers for Disease Control and Prevention to measure progress toward the Healthy People 2000 national goals (Kann et al., 1995).

■ Assesses numerous dimensions of high school students' risk behaviors (e.g., substance abuse, car driving habits, weapons possession). However, the focus is not exclusively on matters related to violence occurring on school campuses.

■ Includes several school safety/violence questions pertaining to students' self-reported feelings of safety on campus.

■ Provides biannual survey results for readily available regional and national comparison information, periodically published in the Center for Disease Control's *Morbidity and Mortality Research Reports.*

California Safe Schools Assessment (CSSA)

■ Available from the Butte County Office of Education, CA.

■ Recently revised and reinstituted in July 1995 by the Butte County (California) Office of Education.

■ As mandated by California state law, requires the reporting of 20 legally defined crimes divided into four broad categories: (a) Drug and Alcohol Offenses, (b) Crimes Against Persons, (c) Property Crimes, and (d) Other Incidents (e.g., possession of weapon) that might occur on a school campus (Hanson & Kleaver, 1995).

■ May be used as part of a broader school safety assessment that includes positive indicators of school climate to help schools and law enforcement agencies develop and evaluate plans to address more serious forms of violence that occur on school campuses.

are victims, perpetrators, and bystanders. The goal is to teach them skills for getting along with others in learning and living. School organizations and their norms will help or hinder in this goal.

Recommended Resources

Furlong, M. J., & Morrison, G. M. (Eds.). (1994). School violence miniseries [Special issue]. *School Psychology Review, 23* (2).
This special issue addresses the importance of critically examining the notion and prevalence of school violence from an educational perspective. Topics covered include violence-prevention programs to use in the schools, bullying, school violence-intervention strategies, legal issues pertaining to school violence, and cultural issues of school violence. Available from the National Association of School Psychologists, 4340 East West Highway, Suite 402, Bethesda, MD 20814.

Goldstein, A. P., Harootunian, B., & Conoley, J. C. (1994). *Student aggression: Prevention, management, and replacement training.* New York: Guilford.
Outlined in this book are an introduction to the concern of violence and aggression amongst youth and ideas for the prevention of its occurrence, followed by a two-tier focus on interventions that encompass student-specific and system strategies. Using examples from society at large, the authors present crime statistics as well as the prevalence of violence in the mass media to explain school violence in the context of current societal trends. As solutions to this problem, several therapeutic approaches including psychological skills training, behavior modification techniques, psychodynamic and humanistic interventions, and gang-oriented interventions are outlined. In addition, separate chapters address teacher, school, and family roles in the intervention process.

Gorski, J. D., & Pilotto, L. (Eds.). (1995). Violence in educational settings [Special issue]. *Educational Psychology Review, 7* (1).
Compilations of issues regarding violence in the context of various educational settings from risk factors associated with adolescent violence, the prevalence of gangs in schools, implementing school health curricula in order to prevent violence, to college campus violence. Additionally, a resource section with listings and brief descriptions of other relevant publications is provided.

Kadel, S., & Follman, J. (1993). *Hot topics: Reducing school violence.* Tallahassee, FL: SouthEastern Regional Vision for Education (SERVE).
In this publication, research-supported issues relating to crisis management, strategies to prevent school violence, and the causes and effects of youth violence are examined and presented with practical "how to" procedures for implementing various violence reduction techniques in schools. Also provided is an extensive resource section that includes numerous agencies, publications, and specific violence prevention curricula. Available from SERVE, 345 S. Magnolia Dr., Suite D-23, Talla-hassee, FL 32301-2950; (904) 922-2300; 800-352-6001, FAX (904) 922-2286.

Nelson, C. M., & Shores, R. E. (Eds). (1994). Dealing with aggressive and violent students [Special issue]. *Preventing School Failure, 38* (3).
This special issue provides an overview as well as practical applications of prevention and intervention strategies regarding aggressive and violent behaviors of students. The contributing authors address issues concerning violence among youth, the development of aggression in children, assessment of aggressive behavior, school violence, the implementation of classroom programs to reduce negative behaviors, and a framework for the understanding and prevention of youth violence. Available from Heldref Publications, 1319 Eighteenth St., NW, Washington, DC 20036-1902; 1-800-365-9753.

School Safety, National School Safety Center Newsjournal. Thousand Oaks, CA: National School Safety Center.
This quarterly journal published by the National School Safety Center (NSSC) provides a well balanced perspective on school safety issues, such as improving school climate, gangs on school campuses, and descriptions of programs that are making a difference. A wide range of other school safety resources are maintained by the center. Available from the National School Safety Center, 4165 Thousand Oaks Blvd., Suite 290, Thousand Oaks, CA 91362; (805) 373-9977, FAX (805) 373-9277.

Internet Resources. There are several World Wide Web locations with information about school safety and school violence.
http://cgcs.org:80/
The Council of Great City Schools, a national coalition of urban school districts, provides a source list of information about urban education in general, and school violence in particular. It provides links to on-line newsletters with articles about school violence.

gopher://gopher.rbs.org:70/11/goals/goal7
The Department of Education (DOE) maintains this site pertaining to the National Education Goals: Goal 7 "Safe, Disciplined, and Drug-Free Schools." It contains: (a) a statement about Goal 7, (b) a list of U.S. DOE resources, (c) on-line digests and publications about school safety and violence, (d) news and announcements, and (e) other sources of information.

http://ericweb.tc.columbia.edu/administration/safety
The ERIC Clearinghouse on Urban Education provides direct links to articles pertaining to (a) school safety and school violence, including information on conflict resolution and gangs, (b) several relevant bibliographies on crime and gangs, and (c) a short list of other references, including several ERIC and other journal articles.

http://www.bcpl.lib.md.us/~sandyste/school_psych.html
In addition to providing information on many topics of interest for school psychologists, the following page includes easy links to ERIC clearinghouses, and several links to school violence articles. It also includes on-line psychology journals and links to the Partnership Against Violence (PAVNET) site.

gopher://gophercysfernet.mes.umn.edu:4242/11/
YAR/ProgAbstracts
*The Youth at Risk community strengthening programs are
projects for at-risk children and their families involving public
and private agencies in more than 400 communities nationwide. This page enables access to abstracts that provide detailed
information about specific interventions (including those addressing school violence). Search for the keywords "school violence."*

http://www.ncrel.org/ncrel/sdrs/areas/SaDcont.htm
*The Safe and Drug-Free Schools site contains information
about critical issues in safe and drug-free schools, a guide to
supporting materials, and an extensive list of additional resources. Some of the content areas were still under development
at press time.*

References

California Department of Education. (1989, Revised in 1994). *Safe schools: A planning guide for action.* Sacramento, CA: Author (CDE, Sacramento, CA 95814).

Committee for Children. (1988). *Second Step: A Violence Prevention Curriculum.* Seattle, WA: Author. (2203 Airport Way S., Suite 500, Seattle, WA 98134–2027)

Dear, J. D. & CTC Advisory Panel on School Violence (1995). *Creating caring relationships to foster academic excellence: Recommendations for reducing violence in California schools. Final report of the California Commission on Teacher Credentialing Advisory Panel on School Violence.* Sacramento, CA: California Commission on Teacher Credentialing. (1812 9th St., Sacramento, CA 95814–7000).

DuRant, R. H., Pendergast, R. A., & Cadenhead, C. (1994). Exposure to violence and victimization and fighting behavior by urban Black adolescents. *Journal of Adolescent Health, 15,* 311–318.

Elam, S. M., & Rose, L. C. (1995). The 27th annual Phi Delta Kappa/Gallup Poll of the public's attitudes toward the public schools. *Phi Delta Kappan, 77,* 41–56.

Felson, R. B., Liska, A. E., South, S. J., & McNulty, T. L. (1994). The subculture of violence and delinquency: Individual versus school context effects. *Social Forces, 73,* 155–173.

Finkelhor, D., & Dziuba-Leatherman, J. (1994). Victimization of children. *American Psychologist, 49,* 173–183.

Furlong, M. (1994). Evaluating school violence trends. *School Safety,* (Winter), 23–27.

Furlong, M. J., Babinski, L., Poland, S., Muñoz, J., & Boles, S. (1996). Factors associated with school psychologists perceptions of campus violence. *Psychology in the Schools, 33,* 29–38.

Furlong, M. J., Chung, A., Bates, M., & Morrison, R. (1995). Profiles of non-victims and multiple-victims of school violence. *Education and Treatment of Children, 18*(3), 282–298.

Furlong, M. J., Flam, C., & Smith, A. (1996). Guns and schools: Disarming the myths. *California School Psychologist, 1,* 4–13.

Furlong, M. J., & Morrison, G. M. (1994). Introduction to mini-series: School violence and safety in perspective. *School Psychology Review, 23,* 139–150.

Furlong, M. J., Morrison, G. M., & Dear, J. (1994). Addressing school violence as part of the school's educational mission. *Preventing School Failure, 38*(3), 10–17.

Furlong, M. J., & Morrison, R. L. (1994). Status update of research related to National Educational Goal Seven: School violence content area. In *Proceedings of the National Education Goals Panel/National Alliance of Pupil Service Organizations Safe Schools, Safe Students Conference.* (ERIC Document Reproduction Service No. ED 384 829).

Furlong, M. J., Morrison, R. L., & Clontz, D. (1991). Broadening the scope of school safety. *School Safety* (Winter), 23–27.

Hafner, A. et al. (1990). *A profile of the American eighth grader: NELS: 88 Student Descriptive Summary.* Washington, DC: National Center for Educational Statistics.

Hanson, P., & Kleaver, L. (1995). *California safe schools assessment: Understanding and reporting school crime.* Butte County, CA: CA Department of Education and Butte County Office of Education.

Hyman, I. A., Zelikoff, W., & Clarke, J. (1988). Psychological and physical abuse in the schools: A paradigm for understanding Post-Traumatic Stress Disorder in children and youth. *Journal of Traumatic Stress, 1,* 243–267.

Johnson, D. W., & Johnson, R. T. (1994). Constructive conflict in the schools. *Journal of Social Issues, 50*(1), 117–137.

Kameoka, K. Y. (1988). *Perceptions of school violence: A psychometric analysis.* Unpublished master's thesis, Department of Educational Psychology, University of Hawaii, Manoa.

Kann, L., Warren, C. W., Harris, W. A., Collins, J. L., Douglas, K. A., Collins, M. E., Williams, B. I., Ross, J. G., & Kolbe, L. J. (1995). Youth Risk Behavior Surveillance—United States, 1993. *Morbidity and Mortality Weekly Reports, 44* (SS-1), 1–55.

Lane, P. S., & McWhirter, J. J. (1992). A peer mediation model: Conflict resolution for elementary and middle school children. *Elementary School Guidance and Counseling, 27,* 15–23.

Larson, J. (1993). School psychologists' perceptions of physically aggressive student behavior as a referral concern in nonurban districts. *Psychology in the Schools, 30*(4), 345–350.

Morrison, G. M., Furlong, M. J., & Morrison, R. L. (1994). School violence to school safety: Reframing the issue for school psychologists. *School Psychology Review, 23,* 236–256.

Morrison, G. M., Furlong, M. J., & Smith, G. (1994). Factors associated with the experience of school violence among general education, leadership class, opportunity class, and special day class pupils. *Education and Treatment of Children, 17*(3), 356–369.

Morrison, R. L., Furlong, M. J., & Morrison, G. M. (1994). Knocking the wheels off the school violence bandwagon. *Educational Leadership, 24*(2), 6–9.

National Institute of Education. (1978). *Violent schools—Safe schools: The safe school student report to the Congress*

[Executive Summary]. Washington, DC: Author.

Ontario Ministry of Education. (1994). *Violence-free schools policy, 1994*. Toronto, Ontario: Queen's Printer for Ontario.

Posner, M. (1994). Research raises troubling questions about violence prevention programs. *Harvard Education Letter, 10*(3), 1–4.

Prothrow-Stith, D. (1987). *Violence Prevention Curriculum for Adolescents*. Newton, MA: Education Development Center. (55 Chapel Street Newton, MA 02158, (800) 225–4276).

Pynoos, R. S., & Nader, K. (1988). Psychological first aid and treatment approach to children exposed to community violence: Research implications. *Journal of Traumatic Stress, 1*, 445–473.

Richters, J. E., & Martinez, P. (1993). The NIMH community violence project: I. Children as victims of and witnesses to violence. *Psychiatry: Interpersonal and Biological Processes, 56*, 46–54.

Safe Schools Project. (1993). *Safe schools project report: A blueprint for violence reduction in the Pittsburgh Public Schools*. Pittsburgh, PA: Pittsburgh Public Schools.

Slaby, R. G., Wilson-Brewer, R., & Dash, K. (1994). *Aggressors, victims, and bystanders: Thinking and acting to prevent violence*. Newton, MA: Education Development Center. (55 Chapel Street Newton, MA 02158, (800) 225–4276).

Stephens, R. D. (1994). Planning for safer and better schools: School violence prevention and intervention strategies. *School Psychology Review, 23*(2), 204–215.

Walker, H. M., Colvin, G., & Ramsey, E. (1995). *Antisocial behavior in school: Strategies and best practices*. Pacific Grove, CA: Brooks/Cole.

Walker, H. M., & Slywester, R. (1991). Where is school along the path to prison? *Educational Leadership, 49*(1), 14–16.

Wilson-Brewer, R., Cohen, S., O'Donnell, L., & Goodman, I. (1991). *Violence prevention for young adolescence: A survey of the state of the art*. Washington, DC: Carnegie Council on Adolescent Development. (ERIC Document Reproduction Service No. ED 356 442).

Zins, J. E., Travis, L., Brown, M., & Knighton, A. (1994). Schools and the prevention of interpersonal violence: Mobilizing and coordinating community resources. *Special Services in the Schools, 8*, 1–19.

23

Self-Concept

George G. Bear
Kathleen M. Minke
Shaunna M. Griffin
Sandra A. Deemer

University of Delaware

Self-esteem is the likeliest candidate for a *social vaccine,* something that empowers us to live responsibly and that inoculates us against the lures of crime, violence, substance abuse, teen pregnancy, child abuse, chronic welfare dependency, and educational failure. The lack of self-esteem is central to most personal and social ills plaguing our state and nation as we approach the end of the twentieth century (California Task Force to Promote Self-Esteem and Personal and Social Responsibility, 1990, p. 4).

The associations between self-esteem and its expected consequences are mixed, insignificant, or absent. The nonrelationship holds between self-esteem and teenage pregnancy, self-esteem and child abuse, self-esteem and most cases of alcohol and drug abuse. . . . If the association between self-esteem and behavior is so often reported to be weak, even less can be said for the causal relationship between the two. Over the years, other reviewers have offered fairly similar readings of the available research, pointing to results that are unimpressive or characterized by "massive inconsistencies and contradictions" (Smelser, 1990 as cited in Kohn, 1994, p. 274).

The first passage appears in a task force report that precipitated the most recent self-esteem movement in American schools. Ironically, the second passage appears in the introduction to the research monograph developed to accompany, and substantiate, the task force report. As indicated by these two conflicting passages, few popular constructs in education and psychology have received as much research yet remain as misunderstood as the construct of self-esteem. Such misunderstanding is reflected in several *myths* commonly held by educators, as recently identified by Kohn (1994):

1. Aggression, substance abuse, and similar social deviances result from low self-esteem.
2. People with high self-esteem are most likely to help others and to exhibit other prosocial behaviors.

3. Academic achievement and self-esteem are substantially related.
4. Self-esteem programs enhance academic performance.
5. Academic skill programs enhance self-esteem.

We add other myths, more specific to children with learning disabilities (LD) and the practice of school psychology.

6. Children with LD have low self-esteem.
7. Children with LD will have higher self-esteem when placed in regular classrooms than in special education classrooms.
8. Classification labels, such as "LD," result in lowered self-esteem.
9. Self-esteem is best measured by aggregating scores across multiple and various dimensions of self-concept.

Confusion and myths about self-esteem are likely to remain among educators and school psychologists who are unfamiliar with recent advances in theory, research, and measurement about self-esteem and the related construct of self-concept. As recently noted by Marsh, Byrne, and Shavelson (1992), "such advances were slow during the heyday of behaviorism. It is only in the last twenty-five years that there has been a resurgence in self-concept research" (p. 47). In this chapter we present a brief review of self-concept theory and research, with a focus on research related to self-esteem and self-perceptions of children with learning disabilities. Such a focus is intended to help school psychologists and educators design and implement efficacious interventions with children who perceive themselves negatively.

257

Background

Self-Concept as Multidimensional and Hierarchical

Foremost among the changing views toward self-concept is the increased recognition that self-concept is a multidimensional, rather than a unidimensional, construct. Consistent with a multidimensional view, and drawing from the earlier work of Shavelson, Hubner, and Stanton (1976), Marsh (1990a) defines self-concept as "a person's perceptions regarding himself or herself. These perceptions are formed through experience with and interpretations of one's environment. They are influenced especially by evaluations by significant others, by reinforcements, and by attributions of one's own behavior" (p. 32). When viewed multidimensionally, self-concept is best represented not by a single score on a measure of self-concept but by a *profile* of an individual's self-perceptions across specific domains.

Theorists also tend to agree that self-concept is hierarchical, with a general self-concept or self-esteem at the apex, but disagree as to how the hierarchy should be organized. For example, in Marsh's theory (Marsh, Byrne, & Shavelson, 1988) and related measures, global self-esteem is at the top of the hierarchy, similar to Spearman's "g," and specific behaviors are at its base. In the middle are first-order factors, or subdomains, (e.g., Physical Abilities, Peer Relations, Reading) which are subsumed under two or three broader domains (e.g., Nonacademic and Academic, or Nonacademic, Verbal/Academic, and Math/Academic). In contrast, Harter's (1987) model includes domains, similar to Marsh's subdomains, that are placed directly below global self-esteem in the hierarchy. Such differences in theory and measures, together with the failure of research efforts to replicate a clearly defined hierarchical structure across age groups, has continued to generate much debate among researchers about the hierarchical nature of self-concept (see Bracken, 1996; Byrne & Worth Gavin, 1996; Harter, 1986; and especially Marsh, 1989, for different opinions).

Table 1 shows the domains portrayed in the theories and measures of two of the most widely respected modern-day theorists and researchers in self-concept, Susan Harter and Herbert Marsh. It also presents the domains included in the more recently published, and perhaps most psychometrically sound, measure of self-concept: *The Multidimensional Self Concept Scale* (MSCS; Bracken, 1992).

Self-Esteem as One Dimension of Self-Concept

Some researchers use the terms *self-esteem* and *self-concept* interchangeably, noting that studies have failed to demonstrate conceptual and empirical distinctions between the two (e.g., Bracken, Bunch, Keith, & Keith, 1992). Others, however, view self-esteem as a specific component of an individual's self-concept, representing one's global, or overall, feelings of self-worth—feelings of general happiness, satisfaction, or affect about oneself. Although largely determined by one's self-perceptions of competence or adequacy in important specific domains (e.g., academics, social acceptance, and behavioral conduct), self-esteem from this perspective is a conceptually separate dimension of self-concept (Coopersmith, 1967; Harter, 1985a, 1987; Marsh, 1986; Rosenberg, 1979). The scale measuring what is typically referred to as self-esteem is called "Global Self-Worth" by Harter and "General-Self" by Marsh. The items consist predominantly of self-evaluative items tapping general affect (e.g., "I am a happy person"; "I am proud of myself").

Bracken's (1992) model differs from those of Harter and Marsh in that the apex of his model is represented not by a separate measure of general self-esteem but by a Total Scale score consisting of the sum of scores across the diverse domains of self-concept. However, the "Affect" scale on Bracken's MSCS contains items similar to those measuring self-esteem on Harter's and Marsh's scales (e.g., "I am happy with myself just the way I am"). Thus, although it includes an affective dimension separate from overall self-concept, this model represents a different hierarchical structure. As such, practitioners should not assume that scores representing the apex of Bracken's model measure the same construct as measured by the general self-esteem scales of Harter and Marsh.

As a further complication, whereas self-esteem scales focus primarily on general affective self-evaluations, domain-specific scales tend to include both affect-related self-evaluations (e.g., "I am pleased with my reading") and non-affect-related self-descriptions (e.g., "I receive good grades in reading"). Although self-evaluative and self-descriptive items correlate positively, thus loading on the same factor, combining these item types may obscure important differences among children, especially among children who receive special education services. As will become apparent in the Problems and Implications section of this chapter, the dissimilar item content across measures and the failure to clearly distinguish between self-descriptions and self-evaluations have contributed to the confusion, myths, and inconsistent findings in the field of self-concept.

Process Versus Content in Self-Concept

In recent years, researchers have increased their attention to the processes by which children develop and protect their self-concepts. However, relatively little of this research has appeared in school psychology journals. Whereas school psychology researchers have contrib-

Table 1   *Comparison of Domains Assessed in Three Theoretically and Empirically Derived Multidimensional Measures of Self-Concept for School-Age Children*

Self-Perception Profile for Children (Grades 3–8; Harter, 1985b)	Self-Description Questionnaire I (Grades 2–6; Marsh, 1988)	Multidimensional Self Concept Scale (Grades 5–12; Bracken, 1992)
Global Self-Worth	General-Self	Affect*
Scholastic Competence	Reading	Academic
	Mathematics	
	General-School	
Social Acceptance	Peer Relations	Social
Athletic Competence	Physical Abilities	Physical*
Behavioral Conduct		Competence*
Physical Appearance	Physical Appearance	Physical*
	Parent Relations	Family
Self-Perception Profile for Adolescents (Grades 9–12) (Harter, 1988)	**Self-Description Questionnaire II (Grades 7–10) (Marsh, 1990a)**	
Global Self-Worth	General Self	
Scholastic Competence	Verbal	
	Math	
	General School	
Social Acceptance	[Same Sex Relations & Opposite Sex Relations, below]	
Athletic Competence	Physical Abilities	
Behavioral Conduct	Honesty/Trusworthiness	
Physical Appearance		
Physical Appearance		
Job Competence		
Close Friendship	Same-Sex Relations	
Romantic Appeal	Opposite-Sex Relations	
	Emotional Stability	
	Parent Relations	

Note. Scales denoted by an asterisk, in our judgment, do not measure the same construct as similarly named scales on the other measures, although they share similar items and, in some cases, similar labels.

uted psychometrically sound measures of self-concept (e.g., Bracken's [1992] MSCS) and have furthered the professional knowledge base of external factors that correlate with self-concept, there is a dearth of articles in the school psychology literature on the internal processes that explain (a) the complex relations between self-concept and important outcomes, (b) the development of self-concept, and (c) the mechanisms by which one protects self-esteem when faced with external evidence of incompetency or inadequacy. To gain an understanding of these internal processes, discussed in the next section, one must turn to research on self-concept that has been primarily the focus of researchers in developmental and educational psychology. In focusing on such research in this chapter, we do not mean to deemphasize the critical importance of measurement issues in self-concept research and clinical practice, which are the focus of excellent reviews and critiques appearing elsewhere (e.g., see Byrne, 1996b; Huebner, 1995; Keith & Bracken, 1996).

Development

Age Differences

Self-concept becomes increasingly differentiated with age, at least until early adolescence (Harter, 1990; Marsh, 1989). As early as age 5, children perceive differences in their competence across various domains (Eccles, Wigfield, Harold, & Blumenfeld, 1993a; Marsh, Craven, & Debus, 1991), with the number of recognized domains increasing from childhood to adulthood (Harter, 1990; Marsh, 1989). For example, consistent with her developmental model of self-concept, Harter's (1985b) factor-analytic studies of self-concept measures show a change from five domains (in addition to the measure of global self-worth) for children in grades 3 to 8 to eight domains in grades 9 to 12 (as shown in Table 1).

According to Harter (1986), not only do the number of domains increase, but the manner by which children describe themselves also changes. In early childhood, children give concrete, and overly positive, descriptions of their behavior (e.g., "I can run fast"); in middle childhood, they use more trait-like psychological constructs (e.g., "I'm smart," "I'm attractive," "I'm a good athlete"); and upon adolescence they use more abstract psychological constructs (e.g., "I'm an extrovert").

With development, it appears that the overly optimistic self-evaluations of young children come under increased self-scrutiny. Some recent researchers (e.g., Eccles et al., 1993a; Marsh, 1989), but not all (e.g., see Bracken, 1992; Crain, 1996), have reported age-related declines in perceptions of competence in various domains of self-concept during the early school years. For example, Eccles et al. (1993a) found declining self-perceptions of competence in the areas of math, reading, and instrumental music among children in grades 1, 2, and 4. Similarly, Marsh (e.g., 1989) reported a general decline in most areas of self-concept through early adolescence (about grade 8 or 9), with a rising trend occurring around grade 10 and continuing into early adulthood.

Whereas reasons for the increase in self-concept in late adolescence are unclear, research strongly suggests that the declines in self-esteem and domain-specific self-perceptions during the elementary and middle school years largely can be explained by the extremely positive self-perceptions held during the first few years of school. As children progress through the elementary grades, their self-evaluations become more consistent with evaluations by their teachers and with evaluations based on objective criteria (Beneson & Dweck, 1986; Stipek, 1981). Moreover, prior to second or third grade, children engage in few social comparisons (Ruble, Boggiano, Feldman, & Loebl, 1980; Stipek & Tannatt, 1984); that is, they do not judge their own competence by considering the performance of their peers.

In addition to the limited use of social comparisons in judging their competencies, there are several other reasons why young children's self-perceptions are overly-positive:

1. They seldom consider the difficulty level of tasks performed and the relation of difficulty to effort needed to succeed on the task (Nicholls, 1978) and, thus, view success on even easy tasks as evidence of high ability (Stipek & Tannatt, 1984).
2. They evaluate their ability on the basis of amount of effort expended (Nicholls, 1978; Stipek & Tannatt, 1984).
3. They are likely to ignore evidence of low competence (Stipek & Tannatt, 1984).
4. They lack the ability to integrate evaluative information from multiple sources (Harter, 1985a; Surber, 1984).

Although decreasing over the course of the elementary years, a tendency to overestimate one's abilities is still apparent in adolescence. For example, Eccles (1986, as cited in Stipek & Mac Iver, 1989) found that less than 17% of seventh graders ranked themselves below the middle of the class in math ability.

Developmental changes do not act alone in influencing children's self-perceptions but act in concert with contextual factors such as the home and school environments that children experience (Eccles et al., 1993b; Midgley, Anderman, & Hicks, 1995). For example, children's perception of social support from important others (e.g., parents, peers, teachers, close friends) is a key determinant of general self-esteem as well as of more domain-specific self-perceptions. In elementary and middle school, general self-esteem is strongly related to support from parents and classmates and less so to perceived support of close friends or teachers (Harter, 1987). In adolescence, although parental support remains an important determinant of general self-esteem, approval from a generalized peer group becomes the strongest predictor of general self-esteem (Robinson, 1995).

Gender Differences

Boys' and girls' self-perceptions tend to be more similar than different. In fact, in a recent study by Crain and Bracken (1994), gender differences were reported only on the Physical scale, in favor of boys. In general, when gender differences are reported they tend to be consistent with traditional gender-role stereotypes. Among elementary-school children, gender differences favor boys in the areas of math and science (Eccles, et al., 1993a; Marsh, Barnes, Cairns, & Tidman, 1984; Stipek, 1990), athletics, and general self-concept (Bear, Clever, & Proctor, 1991; Marsh et al., 1984). Girls tend to hold higher self-perceptions in the areas of music (Eccles et al., 1993a), behavioral conduct (Harter, 1985b), reading, and general school (Marsh, 1989). Boys also score higher on physical appearance, except in the very early grades when girls score somewhat higher than boys (Marsh et al., 1991).

Among adolescents, girls tend to have higher self perceptions in the areas of verbal/reading, general school, honesty/trustworthiness, religion/spiritual value and same-sex relationships, whereas boys report higher self-perceptions in the areas of math, physical abilities appearance, problem solving, general self, and emotional stability (Marsh, 1989). It is important to note, however that although gender differences have been consistently reported in particular domains of self-concept, they usually account for a very small proportion of the variance in self-concept scores (about 1% or less for all areas, except physical ability and appearance which reach 2% to 3%) and, thus, are of little clinical importance (Crain, 1996 Marsh, 1989).

Problems and Implications

Low self-esteem has been associated with a host of negative academic and social outcomes, including low grades and achievement scores, aggression and delinquency, dropping out of school, and poor peer relations (see related chapters, this volume). There is very little evidence, however, that low self-esteem *causes* these problems. As noted in reviews by Byrne (1996a) and Strein (1993), the causal relation between achievement and dimensions of self-concept is unclear, with some studies suggesting that low self-concept precedes low achievement, others indicating the opposite directionality, and still others indicating no causal relation or a reciprocal one that varies with age. The near absence of longitudinal studies has contributed greatly to confusion about the direction of causality.

Correlations between general self-esteem and academic achievement are quite small, generally falling in the low to mid .20s (Hattie, 1992; Marsh, 1993a). Such low correlations reflect not only problems in the measurement of self-concept, but also the complexity of the phenomenon itself: Academics is only one of many variables influencing self-esteem, and its influence is mediated by multiple cognitive and affective variables. Coefficients are appreciably higher when achievement in specific academic domains is correlated with self-perceptions of competence in the respective academic domain. For example, across samples of preadolescents, Marsh (1993a) reported median correlations of .39 between English achievement and English self-concept and .33 between math achievement and math self-concept. Among adolescents, Marsh (1992) reported similar correlations ranging from .45 to .70.

It should be noted that *high* self-esteem may actually be problematic, especially among children with behavior problems. This is particularly true among children who continue to maintain overly positive self-perceptions that contradict objective indices of related behaviors. Consistent with several prior studies, Hughes, Cavell, and Grossman (in press) recently reported inflated ratings of self-competence and social support among aggressive children. They concluded that, rather than serving as a developmental self-protecting asset, such an unrealistic view of self may be detrimental in that it contributes to the denial of negative affect and behaviors, to external attributions of blame, and to resistance to change. As also noted by Lochman (1992), Hughes et al. indicated that an important implication of their findings is that the effectiveness of treatment programs for aggressive children may be indicated by a *decrease* on measures of self-concept.

In light of the just reviewed findings and the paucity of causal research in the social and emotional areas, there is little theoretical or empirical support for educators, school counselors, and school psychologists to focus on general self-esteem in hopes of preventing or remediating children's academic or interpersonal problems. (There is some support, however, for programs that focus on domain-specific self-perceptions.) Nevertheless, the importance of general self-esteem, especially when accurately linked to external indices of functioning, should not be dismissed: Positive self-esteem, given its direct relation to feelings of happiness (and depression), should be an important educational goal in its own right (see Happiness and Life Satisfaction, this volume). School psychologists should be prepared to address children's low self-esteem, regardless of any causal relationship with other school-related problems.

Problem Analysis

Attempts to understand and improve a child's self-esteem should begin with a problem-solving analysis of the multiple behavioral, cognitive, affective, and environmental factors that influence self-concept. This analysis should include an understanding of the developmental and individual differences presented previously, such as recognition that inflated self-perceptions are normal in early grades and are likely to last longer among children with academic and behavior problems. In conjunction with a normative and ipsative examination of the child's profile of scores on a multidimensional self-concept instrument (see Bracken, 1992, 1996, for related guidelines), a clinical interview should be used to (a) examine self-perceptions in domains or subdomains not tapped by that instrument (e.g., music); (b) assess the importance or value the child attaches to a wide variety of self-concept domains; (c) pursue responses to individual items, especially item responses that reflect specific areas of difficulty or sources of low self-perceptions; (d) differentiate affective self-evaluations from self-descriptions of behavior; (e) determine the types of comparisons and standards (or "frames of reference") used in the process of self-evaluation; and (f) determine perceived support from important others. Each of these steps, and its importance, is briefly reviewed next. Sample interview questions for each step are provided in Table 2.

Identify domains, subdomains, or specific areas of self-perceived importance that are not represented in the child's profile scores

As argued pointedly by Damon and Hart (1986, p. 105), a major limitation of standardized self-report measures of self-concept is that they force subjects to respond as efficiently as possible to items and domains predetermined to be important by the test developer. Consequently, the published measures may overlook categories that the *child* thinks are important. This may be particularly true with measures designed for a wide age range (e.g., measures that do not differentiate same and opposite sex relations in adolescence). Thus, scores on none of the self-

Table 2 *Clinical Interview Sample Questions*

Goal	Sample Questions
Elicit and examine self-perceptions and self-evaluations across a variety of domains.	How would you describe yourself? How do you feel about yourself? How might others describe you? What are you most proud of? What do you do very well? What things are difficult for you? What are some things you would like to do much better?
Assess importance attached to domains, especially areas of concern.	On as scale of 1 to 10, how important to you is it to be good at _____?
Explore individual item responses that are strongly negative or that differ from other items in the domain.	I noticed that you disagreed with the item, "My parents understand me." Tell me more about that.
Examine individual items for inconsistencies in responses to *descriptions* of competence and *feelings* about competence.	You said that you get good grades in reading, but that you're not pleased with your reading. Tell me about that.
Determines frames of reference (social and ipsative comparisons).	When I asked you about you how well you're doing in _____, how did you decide how well (or poorly) you're doing? (Were you thinking about kids who are your own age? Older? In other classes? Were you thinking of how well you do in other areas?) Do you think you *should* compare yourself to _____? How about if you compare how well you're doing in _____ (weak area) with _____ (other group or other area)?
Evaluate perceptions of social support.	When you are having problems, whom can you turn to for help? How about others (e.g., parents, teachers, peers, close friends, relatives, and neighbors)?

concept measures in Table 1 would indicate that a child's negative self-perceptions lie specifically in music, art, or writing. Only Marsh's scales would reflect that a child's low self-perceptions of academics are not pervasive but rather restricted to reading. And none would reveal that an outstanding athlete is experiencing low esteem because of his or her recent poor performances in gymnastic events. Because of these limitations, the school psychologist should ask, and probe, responses to open-ended questions designed to elicit self-perceptions of competency in areas of self-perceived importance.

Interview questions also are often necessary to identify self-perceived difficulties. As noted by Chapman and Tunmer (1995), many children experience difficulties in areas in which their self-perception scores may not be low, and such difficulties may influence their affective state and self-esteem. Thus, children may respond favorably to scale items that tap self-perceptions of academics or reading, while simultaneously recognizing that they have specific, and serious, difficulties in the same area (e.g., the child who reads poorly but excels in math or the child with excellent phonetic skills but poor comprehension). In one recent study (Bear & Minke, 1996), third graders with LD responded that they were just as smart as other children and that they performed well in the classroom; however, they also responded that they had difficulties learning. Indeed, as noted by Renick and Harter (1989), it is not uncommon for teachers and par-

ents to inform children with LD that they are doing well, despite performance that is seriously below grade level, thus explaining inconsistencies between self-perceptions and achievement test scores. Whether children with LD focus on their reading difficulties or the positive feedback they receive greatly influences their satisfaction with reading and, ultimately, their self-esteem (Bear, Minke, Griffin, & Deemer, in press).

Assess the importance or value the child attaches to each domain

According to several theorists (e.g., Harter, 1986; James, 1892/1963), perceived importance mediates the relation between domain-specific self-perceptions and global self-esteem. For example, whereas low self-perceptions of athletic competence are likely to impact the self-esteem of a child who aspires to play varsity or professional sports, similar self-perceptions would have little, if any, impact on the self-esteem of the child who does not value athletics. Self-perceived importance may also mediate the relation between domain-specific self-perceptions and behavior. For example, as found in the classic studies of Bem and Allen (1974), friendly behavior was associated with self-perceptions of friendliness, but only among those who highly valued friendliness—construing it as a central characteristic of their personality.

Attached importance can be assessed by administering Harter's Importance Rating Scale (1985b) or more informally by simply asking the child to rate the importance of each domain on a scale of 1 to 10. Harter (1985b) argues that such information should also be used to determine if a discrepancy exists between self-perceptions and perceived importance ratings in each domain assessed. Although Harter (1986) posits that discrepancy scores are more predictive of general self-esteem than are self-perceptions scores per se, several studies have failed to support this position (Bear et al., 1991; Marsh, 1993b). As recognized by Harter (1996), most children highly value each of the domains included on commonly used self-concept scales; thus, there is little variance in importance scores. For example, despite their problems in academics and behavior, and related self-perceptions of inadequacy in these areas, children with LD value these domains as highly as other children (Bear et al., 1991). Moreover, children are rarely given the option of valuing some domains while discounting the importance of others (Harter, 1996). Nevertheless, among those who perceive a domain to be of little importance, self-perceptions in that domain are likely to have little impact on their self-esteem or behavior.

Where appropriate, probe responses to individual items or sets of items with similar content

While cautioning that this level of interpretation is "the least reliable and most subjective," Bracken (1996) states that an examination of clusters of items with similar content and individual items, "can provide meaningful clues and provide a segue into the exploration of examinees' feelings, beliefs, or concerns about specific events, actions, or aspects of their lives" (p. 484). For example, as noted by Bracken, a strong negative response to the item on the MSCS Academic scale "My parents care about my education" should warrant attention. Such a perception might provide clues as to why a child perceives himself or herself to be academically competent but obtains a low score on the Affect scale of the MSCS.

An examination of item-level responses also is valuable when the examiner suspects that the child defines terms or interprets items differently than other children. For example, in responding to the item "I'm doing well in my classroom," a student who previously earned failing grades but now earns Ds and Cs is likely to define "well" differently than a straight-A student. As such, they would interpret the item differently while giving the same positive response.

Differentiate affective self-evaluations from self-descriptions of behavior

In examining responses to scale items or interview questions, we recommend that school psychologists assess not only self-perceptions of competency or adequacy in important domains but also feelings of satisfaction (or dissatisfaction) attached to the respective self-perceptions. As noted earlier, self-concept scales tend to blend subjective, affectively loaded self-evaluative items (e.g., "I am happy with my reading") with more objective, self-descriptive items ("I get good grades in reading"). Although such items often yield similar responses, we agree with several theorists (Chapman & Tunmer, 1995; Harter, 1985a) that the items represent separate yet related constructs in the self-concept network. Self-evaluations of competence do not necessarily translate into feelings of satisfaction. For example, especially in the early grades, children are very satisfied with their reading despite recognition of their reading difficulties (Chapman & Tunmer). Likewise, based on positive teacher feedback and grades, older children with LD may respond favorably to many items on an academic scale but be unhappy that their reading skills are greatly below those of peers.

As argued by Bandura (1986), Harter (1987), and Weiner (1994), affects such as satisfaction, dissatisfaction, pride, and shame follow from self-evaluations and mediate subsequent motivation and behavior. A recent study (Bear et al., in press) found that feelings of satisfaction toward one's reading decreased from third to sixth grade (for both children with and those without LD) and that satisfaction mediated the relation between self-perceptions of positive teacher feedback and overall feelings of self-worth. That is, the perception that the classroom teacher was pleased with one's reading was related to positive self-esteem but primarily among those who felt satisfied about their reading.

Determine frames of reference

Although emphasis varies across models, all major self-concept theorists recognize that variations in self-concept among children with similar competencies often can be attributed to children using different comparison groups and standards. For example, Marsh (1987, 1990b, 1991) emphasizes the "Big-Fish-Little-Pond Effect" (BFLPE), in which students' self-concepts are affected by the general skill level of the reference group. His studies have demonstrated that secondary-level students are more likely to have lower academic self-concepts when they attend schools where average achievement is quite high than when they attend schools of lower average achievement. In turn, the lower self-concepts were found to lead to other negative academic outcomes, including the selection of less challenging courses, lower educational aspirations and subsequent achievement, and a reduced likelihood of attending college.

Researchers have shown that the social comparison process is a critical factor in the development of self-concept among children with LD, especially beyond elementary school. In Renick and Harter's (1989) study, children with LD who attended resource rooms for only part of the school day tended to compare themselves to higher achieving children in their regular classrooms, resulting in lower self-esteem. Likewise, we (Bear et al., in press) found that among sixth graders (with and without LD), social comparison information was a good predictor of reading satisfaction (although much less so than teacher feedback).

The findings just reviewed have important implications for the self-concepts of children in inclusive classrooms, countering the arguments of some researchers (e.g., Wang & Birch, 1984) that such placements enhance self-concepts of children with disabilities. As later research indicates (e.g., Bear et al., 1991), unless accommodations are made and "protected resources" provided, it is more likely that global self-esteem of children with disabilities suffers in inclusive classes, while self-esteem of children without disabilities is enhanced.

Fortunately (especially for those below the norm in achievement, physical ability, etc.), social comparison is not the only frame of reference children use in making self-evaluations. Children also use an internal comparison process in which they compare their competence in one domain with their competence in other domains. As noted by Marsh (1986) and Marsh and Hattie (1996), this internal, ipsative process can have a compensatory effect (e.g., "I'm not very good in reading, but I do well in math and have friends"). Indeed, Kloomak and Cosden (1994) found that children with LD who maintain high self-esteem in spite of low academics have significantly higher self-perceptions in the nonacademic domains of social competence, behavioral conduct, and physical appearance.

In addition to social comparative and ipsative standards, Bracken (1992, 1996) highlights the importance of two other standards studied by self-concept theorists and researchers: the *absolute* standard (e.g., "Is my performance acceptable to my teacher or parent?" "Did I pass the test?") and the *ideal* standard (e.g., "Did I get an 100 on the test?" "Was I the fastest in the race?"). In Bracken's model of self-concept, each of these four evaluative standards can be viewed from either the *personal* perspective or the *other* perspective, resulting in eight combinations of perspectives and standards. Children commonly use one of these four standards (comparative, ipsative, absolute, and ideal) and two perspectives, or combinations thereof, in the process of evaluating themselves and in developing their self-concepts. Problems can occur when the standards are unrealistic or irrational and lead to experiences of failure. Thus, school psychologists should analyze not just self-concept scores but also the perspectives and standards reflected in item responses.

Assess self-perceptions of social support

Social support from others should also be assessed, given that both theory and research show that it is a major determinant of self-worth (Harter, 1987). Among children with LD, Forman (1988) found perceived social support from classmates to be the best predictor of global self-worth. Results of a study by Kloomak and Cosden (1994)

suggest that perceived social support, especially from parents, may well compensate for low academic self-perceptions. Thus, the analysis of perceived social support from significant others (e.g., parents, teachers, close friends, classmates) should be analyzed both to understand the causes of low self-esteem and to target factors for interventions. Perceptions of social support can be gleaned from interview questions, from responses to individual items on self-concept scales, and from several specific measures of social support such as Harter's (1985c) Social Support Scale for Children and the Survey of Children's Social Support (Dubow & Ullman, 1989).

It may also be beneficial to observe the child interacting with significant adults (i.e., parents and teachers) and/or to interview these adults to assess (a) the extent to which they perceive that they provide support to the child, and (b) the extent to which they share the child's perceptions of the relative importance of the various domains. Consider the following case example.

A 7-year-old boy was referred by his father for an evaluation because of poorly developed physical skills. The father was particularly concerned because the boy could not throw and catch at the level the father felt he should. An evaluation revealed that the child's gross and fine motor skills were roughly age appropriate. Further, the child attained an IQ in the gifted range, was highly interested in science and learning, was quite pleased with his abilities and school successes, and reported little interest in athletic skills. His father's belief in the importance of athletics and his limited appreciation of his son's other well-developed skills, suggested avenues of intervention that would have gone unnoticed without investigating contextual factors.

Alternative Actions

One Size Does Not Fit All

As implied by the foregoing discussion, simple, "one size fits all" prescriptions for improving general self-esteem or even specific domains of self-concept are not likely to be successful due to the complex nature of children's self-perceptions. However, following a detailed problem analysis, the school psychologist should have well-developed hypotheses concerning

1. The specific areas or domains of self-concept in which the child reports both positive and negative self-perceptions and the domains in which the child is unhappy about those self-perceptions.
2. The manner in which the child makes self-evaluations (i.e., the primary frames of reference used).
3. The child's perception of support and other contextual factors that influence the child's self-evaluations.

In turn, these hypotheses should suggest whether intervention would be most efficaciously directed at (a) the child, (b) the classroom and peers, or (c) the family.

Interventions Directed Toward the Child

There are large numbers of activities available that are intended to improve children's overall feelings of self-esteem. Most school psychologists are familiar with popular, affectively oriented programs such as Developing Understanding of Self and Others (Dinkmeyer & Dinkmeyer, 1982) and activity books such as *100 Ways to Enhance Self-Esteem* (Canfield & Wells, 1994). Unfortunately, there is limited empirical support for such affectively oriented programs and activities (see Huebner, 1995, and Strein, 1988, for reviews). When studies have been done, they frequently are methodologically weak, calling into question the limited effects that have been documented. Even more disturbing, fewer significant effects are found in the more rigorous studies; when placebo control groups are used, there is an "almost complete lack of supportive evidence" for affective education programs (Strein, 1988, p. 294).

Given the multidimensional nature of self-concept, it should not be surprising that general self-esteem programs have limited effects. Further, because these programs rarely attend to the school and family environments in which a child's self-esteem grows and changes, limited effects should be expected (Beane, 1991).

If self-esteem enhancement programs are unlikely to be successful, what can be done for the individual child who suffers from low self-esteem? Although there are no clear-cut answers, cognitive-behavioral and problem-solving approaches have faired somewhat better in evaluation studies (Huebner, 1995). For example, Hajzler and Bernard (1991), in a review of Rational-Emotive Education (REE) studies, concluded that REE interventions of at least 12 hours can reduce irrational thoughts and anxiety and improve self-esteem and locus of control in students as young as fourth grade. Still, it is rare to find studies that include placebo control groups and long-term follow-up, so the efficacy of these approaches remains largely unknown.

Attribution-retraining interventions, such as the one described in Craven, Marsh, and Debus (1991), also appear promising. This intervention involved providing internally focused feedback that emphasized children's strengths in a particular academic subject and modeled an internal attribution for success (e.g., "Look at how well you add and subtract. You must feel good about your ability in math"). Improvements in academic self-concept and general self-concept were documented when the intervention was delivered by a researcher but not when delivered by a classroom teacher (see Huebner, 1995, and Strein, 1993, for discussion of the implications of this study).

An additional avenue of intervention for children with learning disabilities is suggested by Heyman (1990).

Children with LD who have less negative perceptions of their disabilities (i.e., those who see LD as limited rather than global, as modifiable rather than permanent, and as less stigmatizing) have more positive academic self-concepts and general self-esteem (Heyman, 1990). Thus, there may be some benefit to helping children understand the nature of learning disabilities as a means of supporting positive self-perceptions (Rothman & Cosden, 1995).

Although cognitive-behavioral interventions show potential for improving children's self-perceptions, it must be remembered that they are most likely to be successful when targeted toward the specific dimensions of self-concept judged as problematic and when based on the child's interpretation of cues in the environment. Shirk and Harter (1996) describe a cognitive, case-formulation approach to treating low self-esteem, similar to the process advocated in this chapter. Their case studies provide excellent examples of the ways in which a detailed problem analysis leads to different treatment choices.

Interventions Directed Toward the Classroom

Because children's self-perceptions are affected by environmental factors, teacher and classroom practices are potential targets for intervention. It is likely that classroom practices associated with effective teaching and positive behavior management will also be associated with positive self-perceptions in children (Blumenfeld, Pintrich, Meece, & Wessels, 1982; see Evertson & Harris, 1993, and Good & Brophy, 1991, for a review of these areas). Further, practices associated with the development of "mastery goals" in students may also promote positive self-perceptions through the attribution process (see chapter on Achievement Motivation, this volume). To a large extent, however, recommendations for classroom practices to foster positive self-perceptions remain speculative and await the outcome of further research. Still, a number of suggestions can be made on the basis of current theory.

Earlier in the chapter, research related to the social comparison process was reviewed. As children get older, they more often compare themselves to peers in drawing conclusions about their own skills and abilities. Children who judge their own attributes negatively relative to their peers are at risk for developing negative self-perceptions. Although it is unlikely that the social comparison process could (or even should) be eliminated, there are steps teachers can take to reduce the salience of social comparison cues in the classroom (see Table 3). By making social comparison cues less available, teachers may encourage students to rely on other standards for self-evaluation such as personal improvement and effort.

Table 3 *Methods to Reduce the Availability of Social Comparison Cues and Limit Negative Social Comparison Effects*

Area of Practice	Method to Reduce Social Comparisons
Grading and evaluation	Make grades private not public (do not post grades or "best work").
	Allow students to improve grades by redoing work.
	Avoid grading such that only a few students can achieve high grades (e.g., use of normal curve).
Grouping	Avoid use of ability groups for instruction.
	Make group membership flexible; allow for movement from one group to another.
Tasks	Provide individualized tasks at which all children can be succesful.
	Reduce emphasis on competition against other students.
	Utilize cooperative learning strategies that allow all children to participate successfully.

Note. Adapted from "Classroom Factors Affecting Students Self-Evaluations: An Interactional Model" by H. M. Marshall and R. S. Weinstein, 1984, *Review of Educational Research, 54,* 301–325, and from "Achievement Goals and the Classroom Motivational Climate" by C. Ames, 1992, in *Student Perceptions in the Classroom*, D. H. Schunk and J. L. Meece, Eds., pp. 327–348, Hillsdale, NJ: Lawrence Erlbaum.

Teachers should also be aware of the power of positive feedback in maintaining children's positive self-perceptions. For example, one study (Bear et al., in press) demonstrated that sixth graders' feelings of satisfaction with their reading skills were enhanced by positive teacher feedback. Similarly, Blumenfeld et al. (1982) showed that higher self-perceptions of ability were associated with the amount of positive feedback provided by the teacher. However, the effects of positive feedback are complex and are embedded in the child's interpretation of factors such as task difficulty (e.g., praise for success on an easy task may be perceived negatively [Barker & Graham, 1987]) and the overall quality of the relationship with the teacher (Marshall & Weinstein, 1984).

Finally, both teachers and parents influence opportunities for children to develop peer relationships. Such opportunities (e.g., cooperative learning activities, participation in sports) can foster quality friendships that may protect children's feelings of general self-worth. For example, children with LD, who are often rejected by their classmates, may be buffered from the impact of such rejection because they have at least one good friend (Bear, Juvonen, & McInerney, 1993; Juvonen & Bear, 1992).

Interventions Directed Toward Parents

It has long been established that children's self-perceptions are affected by their parents' perceptions (e.g.,

Helper, 1958). As stated by Hamachek (1971), "it's not difficult to see how a parent can negatively influence a youngster's feelings about his ability to do schoolwork by telling him he's stupid or by inferring that he inherited bad genes which make it impossible to do well" (p. 191). Although it must be remembered that such negative messages do not directly cause negative self-perceptions (because the child's internalization and acceptance of the messages are also critical), parents do have powerful effects on children's developing self-esteem.

According to Bednar and Peterson (1995), parents should be encouraged to examine three areas in supporting the development of self-esteem: acceptance, expectations, and autonomy. These elements involve expression of warmth, a commitment to parenting, consistent and reasonable demands for age-appropriate behavior, and developmentally appropriate autonomy. These parenting qualities are also those associated with an authoritative parenting style (see chapter on Parenting Styles, this volume). Recent work has suggested that permissive and authoritarian parenting may be associated with lower child self-esteem (Philips, 1993). Thus, interventions directed toward the development of effective, authoritative parenting skills is recommended.

Summary

Over the course of the elementary school years, children develop increasingly differentiated self-concepts, encompassing self-descriptions and self-evaluations across a variety of domains and subdomains. These self-perceptions are linked with important developmental outcomes, although most likely not in a directly causal fashion. To understand the complexity of self-perceptions and the ways they influence individual children, school psychologists should conduct a detailed problem analysis that assesses self-evaluations across multiple domains, the value attached to these domains by the child, the standards of reference the child typically employs, and the social supports available to the child. Interventions should be individualized; however, efforts to promote effective teaching and positive parenting practices are likely to be influential in helping children develop healthy self-concepts.

Recommended Resources

Bracken, B. A. (Ed.). (1996). *Handbook of self-concept: Developmental, social, and clinical considerations.* New York: John Wiley.
This book provides one of the most comprehensive discussions of theoretical and applied issues in self-concept. Written by leaders in the field (e.g., Bracken, Marsh, Harter, Byrne), chapters

address a range of topics, including instrumentation, global and domain-specific aspects of self-concept, and factors influencing self-perceptions. The book contains a useful appendix listing psychoeducational instruments that tap various self-concept domains.

Harter, S. (1987). The determinants and mediational role of global self-worth in children. In N. Eisenberg (Ed.), *Contemporary topics in developmental psychology* (pp. 00–00). City, State: John Wiley.
In this chapter, Harter provides a thorough, concise description of her model of self-concept. The historical basis of the theory is discussed, as well as the complex relationship among social support, perceived competence and importance, affect, motivation, and self-concept. The robustness of this model across ages is also examined.

Kohn, A. (1994). The truth about self-esteem. *Phi Delta Kappan, 76,* 272–283.
This article presents a nontechnical discussion of common misconceptions regarding self-esteem. Conceptual and methodological problems are discussed in light of available research. The value of affective education programs is examined, considering the positions of both proponents and critics of these programs.

Marsh, H. W., Byrne, B. M., & Shavelson, R. J. (1992). A multidimensional, hierarchical self-concept. In T. M. Brinthaupt & R. P. Lipka (Eds.), *The self: Definitional and methodological issues* (pp. 44–95). Albany, NY: State University of New York Press.
This chapter provides an overview of Marsh's hierarchical model of self-concept, highlighting the empirical basis for the model and the uniqueness of the model in comparison to other models of self-concept. The relation between various dimensions of self-concept and academic achievement indicators is discussed. In addition, Marsh and his colleagues provide a developmental account of the changing self-concept.

References

Ames, C. (1992). Achievement goals and the classroom motivational climate. In D. H. Schunk & J. L. Meece (Eds.), *Student perceptions in the classroom* (pp. 327–348). Hillsdale, NJ: Lawrence Erlbaum.

Bandura, A. (1986). The social learning perspective: Mechanisms of aggression. In H. Tock (Ed.), *Psychology of crime and criminal justice* (pp. 198–236). Prospect Heights, IL: Waveland Press.

Barker, G. P., & Graham, S. (1987). Developmental study of praise and blame as attributional cues. *Journal of Educational Psychology, 79,* 62–66.

Beane, J. A. (1991). Sorting out the self-esteem controversy. *Educational Leadership, 49,* 25–30.

Bear, G. G., Clever A., & Proctor, W. A. (1991). Self-perceptions of nonhandicapped children and children with learning disabilities in integrated classes. *The Journal of Special Education, 24,* 409–426.

Bear, G. G., Juvonen, J., & McInerney, F. (1993). Self-perceptions and peer relations of boys with and boys without learning disabilities in an integrated setting: A longitudinal study. *Learning Disability Quarterly, 16,* 127–136.

Bear, G. G., & Minke, K. M. (1996). Positive bias in the maintenance of self-worth among children with LD. *Learning Disability Quarterly, 19,* 23–31.

Bear, G. G., Minke, K. M., Griffin, S. M., & Deemer, S. A. (in press). Achievement-related perceptions of children with learning disabilities and normal achievement: Group and developmental differences. *Journal of Learning Disabilities.*

Bednar, R. L., & Peterson, S. R. (1995). *Self-Esteem: Paradoxes and innovations in clinical theory and practice* (2nd ed.). Washington, DC: American Psychological Association.

Bem, D. J. & Allen, A. (1974). On predicting some of the people some of the time: The search for cross-situational consistencies in behavior. *Psychological Review, 81,* 506–520.

Beneson, J. F., & Dweck, C. S. (1986). The development of trait explanations and self-evaluations in the academic and social domains. *Child Development, 57,* 1179–1187.

Blumenfeld, P. C., Pintrich, P. R., Meece, J., & Wessels, K. (1982). The formation and role of self-perceptions of ability in elementary classrooms. *Elementary School Journal, 82,* 401–420.

Bracken, B. A. (1992). *Examiner's manual for the Multidimensional Self-Concept Scale.* Austin, TX: Pro-Ed.

Bracken, B. A. (1996). Clinical applications of a context-dependent, multidimensional model of self-concept. In B. A. Bracken (Ed.), *Handbook of self-concept: Developmental, social, and clinical considerations* (pp. 463–504). New York: John Wiley.

Bracken, B. A. Bunch, S., Keith, T. Z., & Keith, P. B. (1992, August). *Multidimensional self-concept: A five instrument factor analysis.* Paper presented at the American Psychological Association's annual conference, Washington, DC.

Byrne, B. M. (1996a). Academic self-concept: Its structure, measurement, and relation to academic achievement. In B. A. Bracken (Ed.), *Handbook of self-concept: Developmental, social, and clinical considerations* (pp. 287–316). New York: John Wiley.

Byrne, B. M. (1996b). *Measuring self-concept across the lifespan: Issues and instrumentation.* Washington, DC: American Psychological Association.

Byrne, B. M., & Worth Gavin, D. A. (1996). The Shavelson model revisited: Testing for the structure of academic self-concept across pre-, early, and late adolescents. *Journal of Educational Psychology, 88,* 215–228.

California Task Force to Promote Self-Esteem and Personal and Social Responsibility. (1990). *Toward a state of esteem: The final report of the California Task Force to Promote Self-Esteem and Personal and Social Responsibility.* Sacramento, CA: Author.

Canfield, J., & Wells, H. C. (1994). *100 ways to enhance self-concept in the classroom* (2nd ed.). Boston: Allyn and Bacon.

Chapman, J. W., & Tunmer, W. E. (1995). Development of young children's reading self-concepts: An examination of emerging subcomponents and their relationships with reading achievement. *Journal of Educational Psychology, 87,* 154–167.

Coopersmith, S. (1967). *The antecedents of self-esteem.* Palo Alto, CA: Consulting Psychologists Press.

Crain, R. M. (1996). The influence of age, race, and gender on child and adolescent multidimensional self-concept. In B. A. Bracken (Ed.), *Handbook of self-concept: Developmental, social, and clinical considerations* (pp. 395–420). New York: John Wiley.

Crain, R. M., & Bracken, B. A. (1994). Age, race, and gender differences in child and adolescent self-concept: Evidence from a behavioral-acquisition, context-dependent model. *School Psychology Review, 23,* 496–511.

Craven, R. G., Marsh, H. W., & Debus, R. L. (1991). Effects of internally focused feedback and attributional feedback on the enhancement of academic self-concept. *Journal of Educational Psychology, 83,* 17–26.

Damon, W., & Hart, D. (1986). Stability and change in children's self-understanding. *Social Cognition, 4,* 102–118.

Dinkmeyer, D., & Dinkmeyer, D., Jr. (1982). *Developing understanding of self and others, DUSO-2* (rev.). Circle Pines, MN: American Guidance Service.

Dubow, E. F., & Ullman, D. G. (1989). Assessing social support in elementary school children: The survey of children's social support. *Journal of Clinical Child Psychology, 18,* 52–64.

Eccles, J., Wigfield, A., Harold, R. D., & Blumenfeld, P. (1993a). Age and gender differences in children's self-and task-perceptions during elementary school. *Child Development, 64,* 830–847.

Eccles, J. S., Wigfield, A., Midgley, C., Reuman, D., Mac Iver, D., & Feldlaufer, H. (1993b). Negative effects of traditional middle schools on students' motivation. *Elementary School Journal, 93,* 553–574.

Evertson, C. M., & Harris, A. H. (1993). What we know about managing classrooms. *Educational Leadership, 49,* 74–78.

Forman, S. (1988). The effects of social support and school placement on the self-concepts of LD students. *Learning Disability Quarterly, 11,* 115–124.

Good, T. L., & Brophy, J. E. (1991). *Looking in classrooms* (5th ed.). New York: Harper and Row.

Hajzler, D. J., & Bernard, M. E. (1991). A review of rational-emotive education outcome studies. *School Psychology Quarterly, 6,* 27–49.

Hamachek, D. E. (1971). *Encounters with the self.* New York: Holt, Rinehart, and Winston.

Harter, S. (1985a). Competence as a dimension of self-evaluation. Toward a comprehensive model of self-worth. In R. L. Leahy (Ed.), *The development of the self* (pp. 55–121). San Diego, CA: Academic Press.

Harter, S. (1985b). *The Self-Perception Profile for Children: Revision of the Perceived Competence Scale for Children, Manual.* Denver, CO: University of Denver Press.

Harter, S. (1985c). *The Social Support Scale for Children, Manual.* Denver, CO: University of Denver.

Harter, S. (1986). Processes underlying the construction, maintenance, and enhancement of the self-concept in children. In J. Suls & A. G. Greenwald (Eds.), *Psychological perspectives on the self* (Vol. 3, pp. 137–181). Hillsdale, NJ: Erlbaum.

Harter, S. (1987). The determinants and mediational role of global self-worth in children. In N. Eisenberg (Ed.),

Contemporary topics in developmental psychology (pp. 219–242). New York: John Wiley.

Harter, S. (1988). *The Self-Perception Profile for Adolescents, Manual.* Denver, CO: University of Denver Press.

Harter, S. (1990). Issues in the assessment of self-concept of children and adolescents. In A. La Greca (Ed.), *Childhood assessment: Through the eyes of a child* (pp. 292–325). Needham Heights, MA: Allyn and Bacon.

Harter, S. (1996). Historical roots of contemporary issues involving self-concept. In B. A. Bracken (Ed.), *Handbook of self-concept: Developmental, social, and clinical considerations* (pp. 1–37). New York: John Wiley.

Hattie, J. (1992). *Self-Concept.* Hillsdale, NJ: Lawrence Erlbaum.

Helper, M. M. (1958). Parental evaluations of children and children's self-evaluations. *Journal of Abnormal and Social Psychology, 56,* 190–194.

Heyman, W. B. (1990). The self-perception of a learning disability and its relationship to academic self-concept and self-esteem. *Journal of Learning Disabilities, 23,* 472–475.

Huebner, E. S. (1995). Assessment and intervention with children with low self-esteem. In A. Thomas & J. Grimes (Eds.), *Best practices in school psychology—III* (pp. 831–840). Washington, DC: National Association of School Psychologists.

Hughes, J. N., Cavell, T. A., & Grossman, P. B. (in press). A positive view of self: Risk of protection for aggressive children. *Development and Psychopathology.*

James, W. (1963). *Psychology.* New York: Fawcett. (Original work published in 1892).

Juvonen, J., & Bear, G. G. (1992). Social adjustment of children with and without learning disabilities in integrated classrooms. *Journal of Educational Psychology, 84,* 322–330.

Keith, L. K., & Bracken, B. A. (1996). Self-concept instrumentation: A historical and evaluative review. In B. A. Bracken (Ed.), *Handbook of self-concept: Developmental, social, and clinical considerations* (pp. 91–170). New York: John Wiley.

Kloomak, S., & Cosden, M. (1994). Self-concept in children with learning disabilities: The relationship between global self-concept, academic "discounting," nonacademic self-concept, and perceived social support. *Learning Disability Quarterly, 17,* 140–153.

Kohn, A. (1994). The truth about self-esteem. *Phi Delta Kappan, 76,* 272–283.

Lochman, J. E. (1992). Cognitive-behavioral intervention with aggressive boys: Three year follow-up and preventive effects. *Journal of Consulting and Clinical Psychology, 60,* 426–432.

Marsh, H. W. (1986). Verbal and math self-concepts: An internal/external frame of reference model. *American Educational Research Journal, 23,* 129–149.

Marsh, H. W. (1987). The big-fish-little-pond effect on academic self-concept. *Journal of Educational Psychology, 79,* 280–295.

Marsh, H. W. (1988). *Self-Description Questionnaire, I.* San Antonio. TX: The Psychological Corporation.

Marsh, H. W. (1989). Age and sex effects in multiple dimensions of self-concept: Preadolescence to early adulthood. *Journal of Educational Psychology, 81,* 417–430.

Marsh, H. W. (1990a). *Self-Description Questionnaire, II.* San Antonio. TX: The Psychological Corporation.

Marsh, H. W. (1990b). Influences of internal and external frames of reference on the formation of math and English self-concepts: A multiwave, longitudinal, panel analysis. *Journal of Educational Psychology, 82,* 107–116.

Marsh, H. W. (1991). The failure of high ability high schools to deliver academic benefits: The importance of academic self-concept and educational aspirations. *American Educational Research Journal, 28,* 445–480.

Marsh, H. W. (1992). Content specificity of relations between academic achievement and academic self-concept. *Journal of Educational Psychology, 84,* 35–42.

Marsh, H. W. (1993a). Academic self-concept: Theory, measurement, and research. In J. Suls (Ed.), *Psychological perspectives on the self* (Vol. 4, pp. 59–98). Hillsdale, NJ: Erlbaum.

Marsh, H. W. (1993b). Relations between global and specific domains of self: The importance of individual importance, certainty, and ideals. *Journal of Personality and Social Psychology, 65,* 975–992.

Marsh, H. W., Barnes, J., Cairns, L., & Tidman, M. (1984). The Self-Description Questionnaire (SDQ): Age effects in the structure and level of self-concept for preadolescent children. *Journal of Educational Psychology, 75,* 940–956.

Marsh, H. W., Byrne, B. M., & Shavelson, R. J. (1988). A multifaceted academic self-concept: Its hierarchical structure and its relation to academic achievement. *Journal of Educational Psychology, 80,* 366–380.

Marsh, H. W., Byrne, B. M., & Shavelson, R. J. (1992). A multidimensional, hierarchical self-concept. In T. M. Brinthaupt & R. P. Lipka (Eds.), *The self: Definitional and methodological issues* (pp. 44–95). Albany, NY: State University of New York Press.

Marsh, H. W., Craven, R. G., & Debus, R. (1991). Self-concepts of young children 5 to 8 years of age: Measurement and multidimensional structure. *Journal of Educational Psychology, 83,* 377–392.

Marsh H. W., & Hattie, J. (1996). Theoretical perspectives on the structure of self-concept. In B. A. Bracken (Ed.), *Handbook of self-concept: Developmental, social, and clinical considerations* (pp. 38–90). New York: John Wiley.

Marshall, H. M., & Weinstein, R. S. (1984). Classroom factors affecting students self-evaluations: An interactional model. *Review of Educational Research, 54,* 301–325.

Midgley, C., Anderman, E., & Hicks, L. (1995). Differences between elementary and middle school teachers and students: A goal theory approach. *Journal of Early Adolescence, 15,* 90–113.

Nicholls, J. G. (1978). The development of the concept of effort and ability, perceptions of academic attainment, and the understanding that difficult tasks require more ability. *Child Development, 49,* 800–814.

Philips, E. L. (1993). *Permissiveness in child rearing and education: A failed doctrine?* Lanham, MD: University Press of America.

Renick, M. J., & Harter, S. (1989). Impact of social comparisons on the developing self-perceptions of learning disabled students. *Journal of Educational Psychology, 81,* 631–638.

Robinson, N. S. (1995). Evaluating the nature of perceived support and its relation to perceived self-worth in adolescents. *Journal of Research on Adolescents, 5,* 253–280.

Rosenberg, M. (1979) *Conceiving the self.* New York: Basic Books.

Rothman, H. R., & Cosden, M. (1995). The relationship between self-perception of a learning disability and achievement, self-concept, and social support. *Learning Disability Quarterly, 18,* 203–212.

Ruble, D. N., Boggiano, A. K., Feldman, N. S., & Loebl, J. H. (1980). Developmental analysis of the role of social comparison in self-evaluation. *Developmental Psychology, 16,* 105–115.

Shavelson, R. J., Hubner, J. J., & Stanton, G. C. (1976). Self-concept: Validation of construct interpretations. *Review of Educational Research, 46,* 407–441.

Shirk, S., & Harter, S. (1996). Treating low self-esteem. In M. Reinecke, F. Dattilio, & A. Freeman (Eds.), *Cognitive therapy with children and adolescents.* New York: Guilford.

Stipek, D. J. (1981). Children's perceptions of their own and their classmates' ability. *Journal of Educational Psychology, 73,* 404–410.

Stipek, D. J. (1990). Self-concept development during the toddler years. *Developmental Psychology, 26,* 972–977.

Stipek, D., & Mac Iver, D. (1989). Developmental changes in children's assessment of intellectual competence. *Child Development, 60,* 521–538.

Stipek, D., & Tannatt, L. (1984). Children's judgements of their own and their peers' academic competence. *Journal of Educational Psychology, 76,* 75–84.

Strein, W. (1988). Effectiveness of classroom-based elementary school affective education programs: A critical review. *Psychology in the Schools, 25,* 288–296.

Strein, W. (1993). Advances in research on academic self-concept: Implications for school psychology. *School Psychology Review, 22,* 273–284.

Surber, C. E. (1984). Influences of ability and effort: Evidence for two different processes. *Journal of Personality and Social Psychology, 46,* 249–268.

Wang, M. C., & Birch, J. W. (1984). Effective special education in regular classes. *Exceptional Children, 50,* 391–398.

Weiner, B. (1994). Integrating social and personal theories of achievement striving. *Review of Educational Research, 64,* 557–573.

24

Life Satisfaction and Happiness

E. Scott Huebner

University of South Carolina

Background

A primary concern of parents is enhancing their children's well-being. For most parents, this concern includes their children's happiness, which is considered the central element in many conceptualizations of the good life (Kamman, Farry, & Herbison, 1983). The happiness of Americans was considered so crucial to the authors of the Declaration of Independence that it was defined as an inalienable right of all citizens.

Despite the importance of happiness and related constructs (e.g., life satisfaction), researchers have only recently begun to investigate the nature and correlates of these positive well-being constructs. This neglect may be related to the fact that models of children's adaptation have typically defined psychological well-being as the absence of psychopathological symptoms. Unfortunately, such models fail to capture the full range of one's sense of well-being. A child reporting few psychopathological symptoms may still experience a sense of well-being ranging from "low" to "OK" to "great."

As proposed by the World Health Organization (1964), mental health is a state of complete physical, mental, and social well-being—not merely the absence of disease. Cowen (1991) shares this view, arguing that psychological wellness should be considered on the basis of positive indicators, including "a basic satisfaction with oneself and one's existence . . . or life satisfaction" (p. 404).

Life satisfaction has been defined in various ways, but definitions converge on the notion that global life satisfaction reflects a cognitive judgment of one's satisfaction with life as a whole (Diener, 1994). According to Diener (1994), life satisfaction is one of three related, yet partially distinct, dimensions of psychological well-being. The other two dimensions are positive affect (happy, proud) and negative affect (anxious, bored). In this model, psychological well-being is thus defined by the relative presence of positive emotions, absence of negative emotions, and satisfaction with life as a whole.

More comprehensive, multidimensional models of well-being have been proposed. For example, Ryff (1989)

argued that well-being models should include multidimensional criteria. In addition to traditional indicators of happiness and life satisfaction, criteria would include self-acceptance, autonomy, positive interpersonal relations, environmental mastery, and others. Unfortunately, Ryff's model was developed for adults in the context of successful aging, not for children. In Huebner's (1994) model, which applies to children, judgments of life satisfaction are made with respect to various specific domains or contexts in an individual's life, including satisfaction with family, friends, self, school experiences, and living environment as well as satisfaction with life in general (Huebner, 1994). Similar to Ryff's model, this model incorporates additional positive indicators, like global self-satisfaction or self-esteem and satisfaction with friends (see Figure 1). The specific domains together constitute the general judgment of life satisfaction. Such multidimensional models should serve to enhance the study of children's well-being as they require a more focused, differentiated consideration of children's adaptation.

Life Satisfaction and Related Constructs

Many early studies of global and domain-specific life satisfaction were conducted within the quality-of-life tradition in sociology and gerontology. Researchers in these traditions differentiated objective and subjective indicators of the quality of life. *Objective* indicators are quantifiable features of places (e.g., availability of recreational services) or persons (e.g., income). *Subjective* indicators, like life satisfaction reports, measure people's judgments of the conditions of their lives and their satisfaction with the conditions. The degree of congruence between people's satisfaction reports and objective environmental circumstances was a frequent concern of researchers. Specifically, particular objective demographic variables (e.g., socioeconomic status, quality of living environment) were expected to contribute to life satisfaction. However, mostly weak relationships have been reported between various objective indicators and subjective life satisfaction reports of adults and children (see Development and Correlates section).

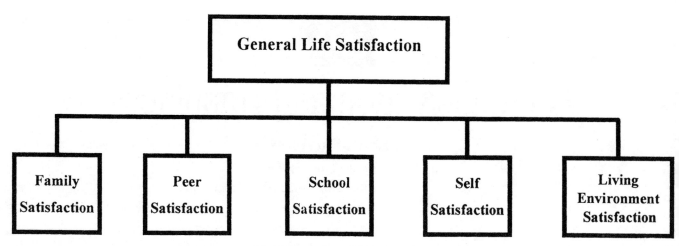

Figure 1. *Multidimensional Life Satisfaction Model.*

More recently, psychological well-being research has been conducted within the realm of psychology. Researchers have begun to explore the relationships between life satisfaction and traditional psychological constructs. For example, life satisfaction and self-esteem have been differentiated. Global self-esteem generally refers to a summary evaluation of one's self-worth or satisfaction with one's behavior and personal characteristics (see Self-concept, this volume). In contrast, life satisfaction is construed to be a more comprehensive construct, which may include but is not limited to judgments of satisfaction with the self. Using Chamberlain's (1988) model, life satisfaction evaluations reflect both inner-directed (e.g., self) and outer-directed evaluations (e.g., satisfaction with peer relationships, school experiences, etc.).

General or global life satisfaction thus may be considered superordinate constructs that encompass various contexts, including the subordinate context of self-satisfaction or self-esteem. Hence, items in global self-esteem scales, such as the Self-Perception Profile for Children (Harter, 1988) focus exclusively on aspects of the self (e.g., "Some kids are often unhappy with themselves," "Some kids like the kind of person they are") whereas items in global life satisfaction scales, such as the Students' Life Satisfaction Scale (Huebner, 1991c) are context-free ("My life is going well," "I would like to change many things in my life"). With respect to specific domain-based evaluations, life satisfaction and self-concept domains can be distinguished on the basis of the target of the evaluation. For example, family satisfaction judgments require respondents to report how positively they evaluate their family life (e.g., I think well of my parents) whereas self-esteem scales typically include items that require respondents to consider how family members (e.g., parents) evaluate *them* (e.g., My parents think well of me).

Empirical support for the separability of life satisfaction and self-esteem has been provided by factor analytic studies (e.g., Huebner, 1995, Terry & Huebner, 1995).

Students may thus report both high self-esteem and low life satisfaction. Further support has been provided by findings of differential correlations between the two constructs as a function of cultural differences. For example, in a study of 31 countries, E. Diener and M. Diener (1995) found strong relationships between life satisfaction and self-esteem in individualistic countries, but much weaker relationships in collectivist countries.

Life satisfaction among children and adolescents has been shown to be related, but separable from various indexes of psychopathology. Huebner and Alderman (1993) found that life satisfaction correlated moderately negatively with self-reported anxiety, loneliness, and depression as well as with teacher-reported internalizing and externalizing behavior problems in the classroom. Likewise, they found life satisfaction discriminated children with emotional difficulties from children without emotional difficulties.

The value of differentiating life satisfaction from depression was illustrated in a large longitudinal study of adults (Lewinsohn, Redner, & Seeley, 1991). In this study, life satisfaction demonstrated a prodromal relationship with depression. That is, low life satisfaction *preceded* the onset of clinical depression. This relationship is particularly important because it suggests that global life satisfaction reports may serve as a predictor of depression.

The separability of measures of life satisfaction and psychopathology (e.g., depression, anxiety) provides support for the notion that traditional conceptualizations that focus on measuring (the absence of) negative reactions alone may provide an incomplete assessment of a person's well-being. To obtain the most comprehensive assessments of well-being, psychologists need to include positive indicators to complement the traditional symptom-focused negative ones (Diener, 1994).

The reconceptualization of psychological well-being has significant implications for psychological interventions in children's lives. Cowen (1991) has argued forcefully that psychologists need to focus research and program-development efforts toward the enhancement of psychological well-being rather than continuing to focus on the repair of established psychopathology. Prevention and competence building should thus become the focus of concern—targetting all children, not just children who are at risk for or already demonstrating serious dysfunction. Likewise, research programs would be aimed at identifying conditions relating to positive manifestations of well-being as well as those relating to negative manifestations (e.g., anxiety, depression).

This chapter will focus on the development of children's positive well-being, with an emphasis on children's life satisfaction and positive affect. Although research with adults has been described as "extensive, broad-ranging, and conceptually diffuse . . . and growing rapidly" (Andrews & Robinson, 1991), there is a dearth of research with children. Nevertheless, many of the findings are consistent with those from adult studies, offering important implications for the design of environments and experiences to maximize children's sense of well-being and adaptational competence.

Development and Correlates

Studies of life satisfaction and self-reported positive affect have been limited to children of approximately age 8 years and above. This is because of (a) researchers' reliance on self-report measures and (b) the cognitive limitations of young children, especially difficulties formulating appraisals of global life satisfaction. It has been assumed that younger children's responses would reflect attention to only one domain of life satisfaction instead of an integrative summary across various domains.

Contemporary cognitive psychology suggests that children use information from both their inner (self) and outer (e.g., environmental) worlds to construct judgments of satisfaction with their life as a whole and with specific domains. Similar to the development of global self-esteem (e.g., see Harter, 1989), the manner in which such integration occurs, as well as the number of relevant domains included, likely changes as a function of the child's development and environmental circumstances (e.g., relocating, death of a parent, school transition, starting a job). Children, as well as adults, formulate such cognitive appraisals, which predispose them to particular emotional reactions, positive or negative. Children who report high life satisfaction are those who most frequently assess their lives in a positive manner and thus increase the probability of frequent ongoing positive emotions (Diener, 1994).

As noted previously, an individual's positive subjective well-being has typically been investigated through the use of self-report questionnaires. Unfortunately, although numerous measures exist that are appropriate for adults (see Andrews & Robinson, 1991), few measures appropriate for children and adolescents have been developed. With respect to general or global life satisfaction, the Perceived Life Satisfaction Scale (Adelman, Taylor, & Nelson, 1989) has been developed for adolescents and the Students' Life Satisfaction Scale (Dew & Huebner, 1994; Huebner, 1991c) has been developed for students in Grades 3 to 12. With respect to positive and negative affect, there are a number of measures, although the Affect scale of the Multidimensional Self Concept Scale (Bracken, 1992) and the Positive and Negative Affect Scale (Watson, Clark, & Tellegen, 1988) are perhaps the most promising at present.

Because of the psychometric limitations often associated with self-report scales, many well-being researchers recommend the use of multiple measures (e.g., parent reports, teacher reports) to supplement self-reports. Nevertheless, advantages of life satisfaction scales, in particular, include (a) relatively strong correlations with the reports of significant others, such as parents (e.g., Dew & Huebner, 1994); (b) sensitivity to changing life circumstances (Diener, 1994); and (c) low correlations with social desirability measures (Diener, 1994; Huebner, 1991c). Thus, although additional work needs to be done in developing appropriate instrumentation, the research to date supports the usefulness of current approaches to the assessment of life satisfaction.

Demographic Variables

Summative judgments of global life satisfaction do not appear to be related to age (Dew & Huebner, 1994; Huebner, 1991a, 1991c). However, some studies have demonstrated small age effects for frequencies of reported positive and negative affect. For example, Greene (1990) found higher frequencies of positive affect among elementary school students compared to junior and senior high students. Greater affective variability has also been observed in senior high students compared to middle school students (Larson, Csikszentmihalyi, & Graef, 1980). That is, adolescents report a wider range of emotions, with more intense positive and negative emotional experiences. Despite the greater intensity of their emotions, the "highs" and "lows" tend to be short-lived compared to adults, however.

Domain-based predictors of global life satisfaction may also remain consistent across age levels. Studies of elementary, middle, and senior high students have demonstrated satisfaction with family life to be judged more important than satisfaction with peers and/or satisfaction with school experiences and physical attributes (Dew & Huebner, 1994; Huebner, 1991a; Man, 1991; Terry & Huebner, 1995). The value of strong family ties apparently continues even into late adolescence, when female and male students have begun to spend disproportionately greater amounts of time with peers than their parents. The relative importance of satisfying family and peer relationships, compared to other domains, underscores the importance of these close interpersonal relationships to the maintenance of children's well-being.

Nevertheless, the *structure* of life satisfaction may change as children mature. For example, Dew (1995) has found that adolescents differentiate more life-satisfaction domains than younger students. Specifically, adolescent reports of satisfaction with peers split into two domains, that is, satisfaction with same-sex peers and satisfaction with opposite-sex peers.

Life satisfaction does not appear to be related to gender (Dew & Huebner, 1994; Huebner, 1991a). Boys and girls appear equally satisfied with their lives as a whole.

The geographic location of a child's residence has been found to be modestly but significantly related to a child's level of satisfaction. Homel and Burns (1989) found that the location of children's residences predicted their life satisfaction scores above and beyond the contribution of social status variables. Specifically, children living in commercial streets, particularly in inner city areas, reported greater unhappiness and dissatisfaction with their lives.

It is unclear, however, if socioeconomic status (SES) is related to life satisfaction. The results of studies investigating the relationship between SES and life satisfaction have been equivocal, with some studies indicating modest relationships (e.g., Dew & Huebner, 1994) and others indicating negligible relationships (e.g., Huebner, 1991a). Based upon studies with adults, it is possible that once children's basic needs (e.g., food, clothing, and shelter) have been met, economic resources have little impact upon well-being. Despite the increasing economic affluence of Americans over the past several decades, *objective* indicators have suggested a decline in the well-being of American youth.

Overall, the contributions of demographic variables in explaining children's life satisfaction are modest at best. The findings are consistent with those reported for adults, suggesting weak linkages between such objective indicators and well-being perceptions across the life span.

Personal Factors

Life satisfaction does not appear to be related to intelligence or school achievement (Huebner & Alderman, 1993; Huebner, 1991a) but does appear to be associated with several personality factors. Research has shown life satisfaction to be related to both locus of control and self-esteem (Huebner, 1991a, 1991c). Children with an internal locus of control tend to be more satisfied with their lives than those who believe that the events of their lives are caused by luck, chance, or powerful others. Life satisfaction is also strongly associated with high self-esteem

among American students (Huebner, 1991a, 1991c). However, as noted previously, some children report considerable dissatisfaction with their overall life circumstances while maintaining high levels of self-worth.

A moderate relationship has also been reported between life satisfaction and extraversion, with extraverts reporting higher life satisfaction (Heaven, 1989; Huebner, 1991a). Given the aforementioned importance of satisfying interpersonal relationships, it may be that extraverts participate in more social activities, leading to an increased likelihood of encountering many satisfying experiences (Diener, 1994).

Motivational factors have also been found to be involved in the development and maintenance of happiness in children and adolescents. A particularly intriguing study by Wong and Csikszentmihalyi (1991) investigated two kinds of motivation among adolescents. One focused on long-term goals and the other, on ongoing experiences. Only intrinsic motivation was associated with positive affect and satisfaction, which in turn was associated with the difficulty level of courses in which students enrolled during their high school years. Enjoyment appeared to determine students' willingness to undertake longer term challenging tasks; hence, positive affect connected with specific tasks may not influence shorter term achievement outcomes, such as grades, but may influence longer term outcomes. Wong and Czsikzentmihalyi speculated that the ongoing pursuit of more difficult tasks likely facilitates the development of increasing skills, leading to enduring high levels of subjective well-being.

Csikszentmihalyi and colleagues have also conducted numerous studies showing that happiness and life satisfaction are related to the nature and frequency of the various activities of adolescents. For example, the difficulty level of the activity and the level of the person's skills interact to influence the affect associated with the activity (Csikszentmihalyi & Wong, 1991). When the difficulty level of the task exceeds an individual's skills, anxiety is produced. In contrast, when the individual's skills exceed the difficulty level of the task, boredom results. According to Csikszentmihalyi and Wong, between anxiety and boredom lies the experience of flow, in which the person's skills correspond to the level of challenge demanded by the activity. The highest levels of well-being are associated with frequent flow conditions. Happiness is thus a by-product of frequent engagement in particular activities.

Different types of activity relate differentially to well-being. Studies of the immediate experiences of adolescents (e.g., Csikszentmihalyi & Wong, 1991) have indicated that the highest levels of satisfaction have been reported for structured recreational activities, socializing with friends, eating, and arts and hobbies. The lowest levels of satisfaction have been reported for resting, studying, thinking, watching television, and being alone. In short, a sense of well-being has been associated with active engagement in challenging activities, not with mindless leisure activities. In a study of at-risk inner-city adolescents, Maton (1990) also reported a positive correlation between participation in meaningful activities and life satisfaction.

The degree to which the decision to engage in an activity has been perceived as voluntary also impacts upon the person's experience of well-being. Activities imposed by external authority (e.g., studying) are more likely to be associated with unpleasant experiences than self-selected activities, such as hobbies.

Stressful Life Events

The experience of major stressful life events (e.g., death of a parent, significant illness) has been correlated moderately with negative affect in a variety of studies. The moderate level of the relationships suggests the importance of other mediators (e.g., cognitive interpretations, coping skills, social support) in long-term adaptation. Overall, additional research with children is badly needed, particularly investigations that consider the interactions among various stressful events, positive events, coping, and developmental levels.

A related, emerging area of stress-related research is the study of resilient children. Resilient children are those who grow up healthy despite highly stressful environmental circumstances. One particularly robust finding from this body of literature is that resilient children identify at least one adult who provides significant emotional support for them (see Phillips, 1993 for a review). Teachers represent the most frequently identified "significant adult" for such children, suggesting the important role that school personnel can play in contributing to children's well-being, especially for children from troubled families.

Summary of Development and Correlates

Much additional research is needed in this area, particularly in understanding the processes by which children and adolescents make satisfaction judgments (e.g., social comparison, level of aspirations). Nevertheless, to date, findings converge nicely with those from adult studies. For example, overall high levels of life satisfaction have been found for children and adolescents, as has been the case for adults. Also, the relatively greater importance of person, social, and task variables in relation to demographic variables is consistent with adult research. Together, these studies suggest that a *variety* of variables influence the experience of high levels of psychological well-being, many of which should be amenable to prevention and intervention efforts. School psychologists should carefully note, however, that the preponderance of well-being studies are correlational in nature. Thus, the direction of causality is unclear. For example, positive

interpersonal relationships may be an *effect* of positive affect or life satisfaction rather than an antecedent. Bidirectional effects are also possible. Thus, much additional research is needed to tease out the causal connections related to children's happiness and life satisfaction.

Alternative Actions

Little has been written about the classroom implications of psychological well-being. In a major review of school reform movements in the 1980s and 1990s, Phillips (1993) concluded that "in our zealous pursuit of higher school achievement, we have somehow lost track of the emotions of children and adolescents and the affective aspects of school learning and behavior" (p. 10). Phillips further states that "allocation of energies and resources in our schools must go increasingly to building wellness and lifetime competence rather than just struggling to contain the school failures of children and adolescents. . . . The challenge is to identify factors or conditions that advance optimal development" (p. 14).

As noted previously, research in life satisfaction and happiness is in its infancy. Nevertheless, several generic implications for educators may be offered that should form the foundation for efforts to develop programs and policies to enhance the positive mental health of children and youth. These central implications are (a) the promotion of supportive interpersonal relationships and (b) the encouragement of participation in meaningful activities.

Promoting Supportive Interpersonal Relationships

The relationships between psychological well-being and inappropriate classroom behavior suggest the need for educators to pay greater attention to the interrelationships among learning, motivation, emotion, and socialization. The well-being studies reviewed herein underscore the importance of facilitating supportive interpersonal relationships, particularly positive family and peer relationships, throughout childhood. School psychologists should thus direct attention in their assessments to the inclusion of measures of children's perceptions of the quality of their interpersonal relations, such as those with family and friends. Comprehensive assessments should incorporate a variety of methods, including teacher ratings, peer ratings, and self-reports. Given the frequent finding of a lack of congruence between objective indicators (e.g., single parent families, presence of siblings with disabilities in a family) and subjective indicators, school psychologists should directly investigate an individual student's interpretations and evaluations of particular objective events and circumstances in his or her interpersonal life.

Considering the importance of high-level social skills to both academic and social competence, it seems imperative that formal, developmentally appropriate, social-competence programs should be incorporated into the mainstream academic curriculum. Cowen (1994) has reviewed numerous social-competence programs for children and adolescents with documented efficacy. Further, Elias (see Social Problem Solving, this volume) has described efforts to design a comprehensive, district-wide social-competence program appropriate for students across Grades K to 12.

The apparent importance of positive family relations in providing a solid foundation for a child's overall well-being also provides further support for those who advocate the provision of enhanced support to parents. Support may be increased through many possible home-school activities, including parent education programs, support groups (e.g., parents of children with special needs), and frequent parent conferences.

Although family members and peers provide significant sources of well-being for the majority of children, other relationships become particularly crucial for some children. The studies of resilient children who overcome difficult economic and family circumstances indicate that in times of stress these children often turn to teachers and other school personnel for support. Such findings suggest the central role that educators can serve in the mediation of children's positive adaptations to stress-laden environments.

One systemic recommendation offered to accomplish this role is the creation of smaller, more personalized school environments in which "every student is well known by at least one adult" (Carnegie Council on Adolescent Development, 1989). The implementation of this difficult but powerful challenge might go a long way toward increasing the impact of schools on children's well-being.

Encouraging Involvement in Meaningful Activities

The findings of Csikszentmihalyi and his colleagues regarding motivation, affect, and educational outcomes imply the need for schools to provide opportunities to explore a variety of potentially meaningful activities (e.g., mentoring, structured sports, art, specific academic enrichment programs) in addition to the traditional "reading, writing, and arithmetic" to discern which ones constitute flow activities for them. Once various flow activities have been identified, school experiences might be geared toward providing the opportunity for students to select such activities frequently, possibly through increased individualization of classroom activities and methods, as well as the provision of a wide variety of course options and extracurricular activities. The challenge for educational programs may be to integrate the key elements of peer interactions and challenging activities to enhance motivational and educational adaptation. As Csikszentimihalyi and Wong (1991) speculate, "if the environment of the school were to utilize the enjoyment of friendship for the purpose of learning, the educational process might become much more happy and intrinsically motivating" (p. 210).

Some work experiences for older high school students may also provide flow experiences. However, studies have also indicated that students who work long hours, particularly on jobs that are repetitive, unchallenging, and devoid of opportunities for adult contact and reinforcement, experience negative outcomes. These negative outcomes include decreased participation in extracurricular activities and thus perhaps decreased exploration of other, possibly meaningful experiences. When jobs do not consume too much time, they may be beneficial to the extent that they are challenging and provide opportunities to learn new skills and earn positive adult feedback (Chinman & Linney, 1996; Greenberger & Steinberg, 1986). The availability of comprehensive vocational counseling services is thus crucial in helping students plan and evaluate their participation in various in-school and extra-school occupational experiences.

Numerous studies have documented the benefits of student participation in community service activities. Chinman and Linney (1996) have reviewed a variety of service-oriented programs that have been shown to enhance well-being from an "adolescent empowerment" perspective. For example, they described the benefits of mentoring programs for both the mentor and the mentee. Similarly, class-wide peer tutoring programs have been implemented in schools with positive educational and affective benefits.

Because the vast majority of research on intervention-program outcomes has involved at-risk populations, greater research attention is needed on the usefulness of well-being programs that target *all* children. Given the limited influence of demographic variables (except in cases of extreme economic deprivation), it is apparent that all children have the potential to experience satisfying lives, regardless of social status, gender, race, and so forth. Focusing on enhancing the psychological well-being and related interpersonal competencies of all children, rather than simply "treating" students who exhibit symptoms of psychopathology, should yield the most cost-effective approach to educational intervention.

Summary

This chapter has summarized the extant research on children's positive well-being in the forms of life satisfaction and positive affect. Several multidimensional models of children's well-being were noted, and it was argued that such multidimensional models are necessary to achieve a comprehensive understanding of children's psychological well-being and adaptation. Studies of the correlates of life satisfaction and positive affect were reviewed. To date, these positive indicators of well-being have not been found to relate consistently or strongly to demographic variables (e.g., age, gender). Stronger relationships have been demonstrated with personality (e.g., internal locus of control), social (e.g., quality of family relationships), and task (e.g., voluntariness, meaningfulness, level of challenge) variables.

Although children's positive well-being research is just beginning, it provides clues to general guidelines for school personnel to consider in developing comprehensive programs to optimize children's overall well-being. The general guidelines included (a) the promotion of supportive interpersonal relationships and (b) the opportunity to participate in meaningful competence-building activities. It was concluded that greater attention should be paid to the interrelationships among affect, motivation, and learning of all children and youth in an effort to enhance their intellectual and affective competence.

Resources

Bender, T. A. (in press). Assessment of personal well-being during childhood and adolescence. In G. D. Phye (Ed.), *Handbook of classroom assessment: Learning, achievement, and adjustment.* San Diego, CA: Academic Press.
This chapter provides a good synthesis of the research literature on the assessment of children's subjective well-being, focusing on life satisfaction in particular. Developmental and methodological issues are highlighted.

Diener, E. (1994). Assessing subjective well-being: Progress and opportunities. *Social Indicators Research, 31,* 103–157.
This article presents an outstanding summary of issues in the assessment of subjective well-being by one of the world's foremost researchers in the area. The author integrates well-being research with recent basic psychological research in cognition, personality, and emotion.

Lorion, R. P. (1990). *Protecting the children: Strategies for optimizing emotional and behavioral development.* New York: Haworth.
This edited book includes chapters describing 10 prevention-based programs covering early-childhood, middle-childhood, and adolescent age groups.

Phillips, B. N. (1993). *Educational and psychological perspectives on stress in students, teachers, and parents.* Brandon, VT: Clinical Psychology Publishing Company.
This book provides an excellent overview of stress and coping research with students, educators, and parents. It includes an excellent discussion of the need for including a focus on facilitating **optimal** *social-emotional development in school reform efforts.*

Veenhoven, R. (1993). *Bibliography of happiness: 2472 contemporary studies of subjective appreciation of life.* Rotterdam, Netherlands: RISBO.

This source book (also available as a computer diskette) includes 2,472 references on subjective well-being. It is the most complete bibliography of the field that is currently available. Included is a subject index to help the reader locate references on specific aspects of this rapidly growing area of inquiry. For detailed information and ordering information, see Veenhoven, R. (1995). World database of happiness. Social Indicators Research, 34, *299–313.*

References

Adelman, H., Taylor, L., & Nelson, P. (1989). Minors' dissatisfaction with their life circumstances. *Child Psychiatry and Human Development, 20,* 135–147.

Andrews, F. M., & Robinson, J. P. (1991). Measures of subjective well-being. In J. P. Robinson, P. R. Shaver, & L. S. Wrightsman (Eds.), *Social psychological attitudes: Vol. 1. Measures of personality and social psychological attitudes* (pp. 61–114). San Diego, CA: Academic Press.

Bracken, B. (1992). *Multidimensional Self Concept Scale.* Austin, TX: PRO-ED.

Carnegie Council on Adolescent Development. (1989). *Turning points: Preparing America's youth for the 21st century.* New York: Carnegie Corporation of New York.

Chamberlain, K. (1988). On the structure of well-being. *Social Indicators Research, 20,* 581–604.

Chinman, M., & Linney, J. A. (1996). *Toward a model of adolescent empowerment: Theoretical and empirical evidence.* Manuscript submitted for publication.

Cowen, E. (1991). In pursuit of wellness. *American Psychologist, 46,* 404–408.

Cowen, E. (1994). The enhancement of psychological wellness: Challenges and opportunities. *American Journal of Community Psychology, 22,* 149–179.

Csikszentmihalyi, M., & Wong, M. (1991). The situational and personal correlates of happiness: A cross-national comparison. In F. Strack, M. Argyle, & N. Schwarz (Eds.), *Subjective well-being: An interdisciplinary perspective* (pp. 193–212). New York: Pergamon.

Dew, T. (1995). *The development and validation of a life satisfaction scale for adolescents.* Unpublished doctoral dissertation, University of South Carolina, Columbia.

Dew, T., & Huebner, E. S. (1994). Adolescents' perceived quality of life: An exploratory investigation. *Journal of School Psychology, 32,* 185–199.

Diener, E. (1994). Assessing subjective well-being: Progress and opportunities. *Social Indicators Research, 31,* 103–157.

Diener, E., & Diener, M. (1995). Cross-cultural correlates of life satisfaction and self-esteem. *Journal of Personality and Social Psychology, 68,* 653–663.

Greenberger, E., & Steinberg, L. D. (1986). *When teenagers work: The psychological and social costs of adolescent employment.* New York: Basic Books.

Greene, A. L. (1990). Patterns of affectivity in the transition to adolescence. *Journal of Experimental Child Psychology, 50,* 340–356.

Harter, S. (1988). *Manual for the Self-Perception Profile*

for Children. Unpublished manuscript, University of Denver.

Harter, S. (1989). Causes, correlates, and functional role of global self-worth: A life span perspective. In J. Kolligan & R. Sternberg (Eds.), *Perceptions of competence and incompetence across the life span* (pp. 67–100). New Haven, CT: Yale University Press.

Heaven, P. C. (1989). Extraversion, neuroticism, and satisfaction with life among adolescents. *Personality and Individual Differences, 10,* 489–492.

Homel, R., & Burns, A. (1989). Environmental quality and the well being of children. *Social Indicators Research, 21,* 133–158.

Huebner, E. S. (1991a). Correlates of life satisfaction in children. *School Psychology Quarterly, 6,* 103–111.

Huebner, E. S. (1991b). Further validation of the Students' Life Satisfaction Scale: The independence of satisfaction and affect ratings. *Journal of Psychoeducational Assessment, 9,* 363–368.

Huebner, E. S. (1991c). Initial development of the Students' Life Satisfaction Scale. *School Psychology International, 12,* 231–240.

Huebner, E. S. (1994). Preliminary development and validation of a multidimensional life satisfaction scale for children. *Psychological Assessment, 6,* 149–158.

Huebner, E. S., & Alderman, G. L. (1993). Convergent and discriminant validation of a children's life satisfaction scale: Its relationship to self- and teacher-reported psychological problems and school functioning. *Social Indicators Research, 30,* 71–82.

Kamman, R., Farry, M., & Herbison, P. (1983). The analysis and measurement of happiness as a sense of well-being. *Social Indicators Research, 15,* 91–115.

Larson, R., Csikszentmihalyi, M., & Graef, R. (1980). Mood variability and the psychosocial adjustment of adolescents. *Journal of Youth and Adolescence, 9,* 469–490.

Lewinsohn, P. M., Redner, J. E., & Seeley, J. R. (1991). The relationship between life satisfaction and psychosocial variables: New perspectives. In F. Strack, M. Argyle, & N. Schwarz (Eds.), *Subjective well-being: An interdisciplinary perspective* (pp. 193–212). New York: Pergamon.

Man, P. (1991). The influence of peers and parents on youth life satisfaction in Hong Kong. *Social Indicators Research, 24,* 347–365.

Maton, K. I. (1990). Meaningful involvement in instrumental activity and well-being: Studies of older adolescents and at risk urban teenagers. *American Journal of Community Psychology, 18,* 297–320.

Phillips, B. N. (1993). *Educational and psychological perspectives on stress in students, teachers, and parents.* Brandon, VT: Clinical Psychology Publishing Company.

Ryff, C. (1989). Beyond Ponce de Leon and life satisfaction: New directions in quest of successful aging. *International Journal of Behavioral Development, 12,* 35–55.

Terry, T., & Huebner, E. S. (1995). The relationship between self-concept and life satisfaction in children. *Social Indicators Research, 35,* 39–52.

Watson, D., Clark, L., & Tellegen, A. (1988). Development and validation of brief measures of positive and negative affect: The PANAS scales. *Journal of Personality and Social Psychology, 54,* 1063–1070.

Wong, M., & Csikszentmihalyi, M. (1991). Motivation and academic achievement: The effects of personal traits and the quality of experience. *Journal of Personality, 59,* 537–574.

World Health Organization. (1964). *Basic documents* (15th ed.). Geneva, Switzerland: Author.

25

Loneliness in Childhood

Steven R. Asher
Andrea Hopmeyer
University of Illinois at Urbana-Champaign

It is fitting that a chapter on loneliness appears in a book on *Children's Needs* because feelings of loneliness are a direct consequence of children having certain relationship needs that go unfulfilled. These needs include the desire to be accepted by others, to be integrated into a group, and to participate in a close and intimate relationship. Within the context of a close relationship, a child has the possibility of someone to confide in and rely upon and someone who is validating and emotionally supportive. Loneliness would not exist if children did not need emotional connections to the significant people in their lives. It is this need for connectedness that makes children vulnerable to experiencing loneliness.

Even the most socially competent person will sometimes experience loneliness. Indeed, it could be argued that participating in relationships makes people more vulnerable to loneliness because of the separations or disappointments that can inevitably occur: A planned get-together with family or friends is canceled, a hoped-for invitation is not forthcoming, a friend moves, a parent dies. In these circumstances, loneliness is an inevitable by-product of a life that involves attachments and connections to others. Thus, there is little cause for concern about short-term or situational loneliness.

There is reason to be concerned, however, about people who are chronically lonely. The distinction between situational loneliness and chronic loneliness is widely made in the adult loneliness literature (see Beck & Young, 1978). Persons who suffer from short-term loneliness recover when they form new social bonds (for a review, see Rook, 1988). For example, Cutrona (1982), in a study of student transition to college, found that 80% of the students reporting loneliness in their first term of school did not report loneliness in the second term. Chronic loneliness, by contrast, refers to loneliness which is persistent and enduring (Rook, 1988). The term is typically used to describe persons who have been dissatisfied with their relationships for a period of two or more consecutive years (Young, 1982). An example would be students who are lonely during their entire col-

lege career because they are unable to take advantage of the opportunities on campus to meet others and form friendships. Chronically lonely people are living with a disproportionate share of emotional pain and there is evidence that chronic loneliness is associated with depression and other adjustment difficulties (e.g., Horowitz, French, & Anderson, 1982).

Given the universality of the experience of loneliness, it is remarkable that psychologists have only recently begun to systematically study this significant human emotion. The first research-based, edited volume on loneliness in adults appeared in 1982 (Peplau & Perlman, 1982), and the first research-based, edited volume on loneliness in childhood is only now in preparation (Rotenberg & Hymel, in press). Those who study loneliness in children actually have certain advantages compared to those who study loneliness in adults. Although children may be less verbal and less reflective than adults about their relationships, they may also be less defensive and more willing to report emotions, such as loneliness, that are viewed by adults as socially undesirable (Rotenberg & Kmill, 1992). Furthermore, with children it is far easier to reliably measure the "objective" features of their social relationships. Because children spend most of their waking hours with peers in school and because schools are fairly accessible for research, it is possible to measure indexes such as the degree to which children are accepted by peers, their participation in close friendships, and the quality of their friendships. With the exception of studies of college students in dormitories (e.g., Cutrona, 1982), most studies of these relationship factors in adults have relied on self-reports from adults, due to the difficulties of gaining independent access to those they interact with in the diverse settings of their lives (e.g., workplace, family, neighborhood, clubs and organizations).

This chapter will focus on what is known about loneliness in children. In the section on Background and Development, we will provide a brief history of this newly emerging topic of inquiry. Because this is a recent focus of study, attention will be given to how loneliness is defined, how children conceptualize loneliness, and how loneliness can be formally assessed. In the next section, Problems and Implications, we will describe how loneliness might affect a child's overall adjustment to school and what has been learned about several different sources of loneliness. As will be seen, most of the research on the sources of loneliness has focused on the effects of children's peer relationships on loneliness. However, some evidence exists on the influence of parents and on the role of internal psychological processes, such as children's expectations, standards, and attributional styles.

In the third major section, Alternative Actions, several strategies will be suggested for helping children experiencing high levels of loneliness. We will focus particularly on intervention efforts that could be conducted in a school context. To date, little intervention research has been done with lonely children. Accordingly, the section on Alternative Actions will be necessarily speculative. However, useful leads exist because intervention research has been done on related topics such as how to teach social skills to children who are poorly accepted by their peers. Our proposals for future interventions will be informed by various types of intervention efforts but will need to be directly tested using loneliness as an explicit outcome criterion.

Background and Development

Children's Understanding and Experience of Loneliness

Do children have an understanding of what loneliness means and do children experience loneliness? These are essential questions for there would be little point in administering formal measures of loneliness if the concept of loneliness had no meaning to children. Research on loneliness in children has lagged behind research on loneliness in adults partly because certain prominent relationship theorists such as Robert Weiss (1973) and Harry Stack Sullivan (1953) speculated that loneliness is not experienced in childhood but instead awaits certain developmental attainments that occur in early adolescence. For example, according to Sullivan the need for intimacy in preadolescence manifests itself in the youth's desire for a "compeer" or close friendship, someone with whom the young adolescent can share intimate information. Feelings of loneliness are said to develop when the young adolescent is unable to form a close friendship.

However, there is now evidence that even young children understand and experience loneliness well before adolescence. In several recent studies, children have been asked about their ideas concerning loneliness. In

one study (Williams & Asher, 1992), the vast majority of 8- through 11-year-old children with mental retardation conceptualized loneliness in terms of being alone (without a companion) and feeling sad. Similar results were obtained from interviews with 5- and 6-year-old children in regular education classrooms (Cassidy & Asher, 1992). Even children at this age level can sometimes use apt metaphors in their descriptions of the loneliness experience. For example, one child told the interviewer, "Like if you're a Martian, and you don't eh, eh, uh, and you only live on one planet and . . . nobody's, um, with ya, on that planet."

In a third, more extensive study, Hayden, Tarulli, and Hymel (1988) interviewed third- through eighth-grade regular education students. These children described loneliness in terms of being psychologically as well as physically distant from others. For example, children described loneliness as resulting from conflicts or broken loyalties. Hayden et al.'s results suggest that as children get older they come to understand that a person can feel lonely even in the presence of others when significant relational ties are disrupted or damaged.

These interview studies encourage the formal assessment of loneliness in children because they suggest that children have a basic understanding of the meaning of loneliness. School psychologists and other professionals can therefore employ formal loneliness measures with confidence that school-age children appreciate that loneliness involves some form of depressed affect and that there is a difference between loneliness and solitude.

Definition and Measurement of Loneliness

Formal measures of loneliness are based, either implicitly or explicitly, on how loneliness is defined by the test developer. Table 1 lists a series of definitions that Hopmeyer (1995) recently culled from the literature. Although variability in definitions exists, certain elements reoccur. Most definitions emphasize the affective side of loneliness; researchers recognize that loneliness involves an "unpleasant experience," "the painful awareness of feeling apart," or "a feeling of emptiness." Many definitions also include a cognitive element, namely the person's realization that one's relationships are deficient in some manner. Most researchers join affective and cognitive elements into their definition. For example, Peplau and Perlman (1982) define loneliness as "the unpleasant experience that occurs when a person's network of social relationships is deficient in some way, either quantitatively or qualitatively" (p. 31). Other definitions are somewhat similar. For example, "loneliness is a painful feeling of isolation, that is, of being alone, cut-off, or distanced. This is accompanied by a felt deprivation of, or longing for, association, contact, or closeness" (Parkhurst & Hopmeyer, in press). These definitions offer a kind of "mini-theory" of loneliness because they include a description

Table 1 *Selective Summary of Definitions of Loneliness*

Author(s)	Definition
Perlman & Peplau (1981)	"... the unpleasant experience that occurs when a person's network of social relationships is deficient in some way, either quantitatively or qualitatively" (p. 31).
Ponzetti & Cate (1988)	"... a perceived interpersonal problem in which a person's network of relationships is either smaller or less satisfying than desired" (p. 292).
Rook (1984)	"... an enduring condition of emotional distress that arises when a person feels estranged from, misunderstood, or rejected by others and/or lacks appropriate social partners for desired activities, particularly activities that provide a sense of social integration and opportunities for emotional intimacy" (p. 1391).
Sullivan (1953)	"... the exceedingly unpleasant and driving experience connected with an inadequate discharge of the need for human intimacy, for interpersonal intimacy" (p. 290).
Williams (1983)	"... the painful awareness of feeling apart from desired or wanted close relationships with others" (p. 52).
Young (1982)	"... the absence or perceived absence of satisfying social relationships, accompanied by symptons of psychological distress that are related to the actual or perceived absence" (p. 380).
Zilboorg (1938)	"... a feeling of emptiness ..." (p. 47).

of the cause, namely that loneliness results when people become aware of a deficiency in their relationships or of certain needs going unmet.

Definitions such as these have led researchers to generate measures of loneliness which, in addition to assessing feelings of loneliness, also assess children's perceptions of their relationship strengths and inadequacies. Table 2 presents the items on the most widely used measure with adults and adolescents, the revised UCLA Loneliness Measure (Russell, Peplau, & Cutrona, 1980). Table 3 lists the items from the most widely used measure for children, the Illinois Loneliness and Social Dissatisfaction Questionnaire (Asher & Wheeler, 1985, originally developed by Asher, Hymel, & Renshaw, 1984). Most of the items on both the measure for adults and the one for children ask respondents to reflect on the nature of their social relationships and to identify deficiencies. Although people's perceptions of their relationships or appraisals of deficiencies in their relationships are generally correlated with feelings of loneliness, perceptions of deficiencies do not inevitably lead people to feel lonely (Shute & Howitt, 1990). Furthermore, interpretation problems can result when a measure designed to assess loneliness is correlated with other measures of a person's social network. For example, if someone wants to study the connection between loneliness and variables such as whether people have friends or have their relationship needs met, it would be important to use a loneliness measure which does not include content overlapping with these variables (see Nicholls, Licht, & Pearl, 1982, for a broader discussion of this issue). The implication is that, for certain purposes, measures are needed which directly assess children's feelings of loneliness without assessing related cognitions about their relationships. Several investigators have begun to create measures that meet this need (e.g., Asher, Gabriel, & Hopmeyer, 1993; Ladd, Kochenderfer, & Coleman, in press; Parker & Asher, 1993b).

Table 2 *The Revised UCLA Loneliness Scale*

*1. I feel in tune with people around me
2. I lack companionship
3. There is no one I can turn to
*4. I do not feel alone
*5. I feel part of a group of friends
*6. I have a lot in common with the people around me
7. I am no longer close to anyone
8. My interests and ideas are not shared by those around me
*9. I am an outgoing person
*10. There are people I feel close to
11. I feel left out
12. My social relationships are superficial
13. No one really knows me
14. I feel isolated from others
*15. I can find companionship when I want it
*16. There are people who really understand me
17. I am unhappy being so withdrawn
18. People are around me but not with me
*19. There are people I can talk to
*20. There are people I can turn to.

Note. The total score on the scale is the sum of all 20 items. Items with asterisks should be reversed (i.e., 1 = 4, 2 = 3, 3 = 2, 4 = 1) before scoring. The four item survey version of the UCLA Loneliness Scale consists of items 1, 13, 15 and 18. Reprinted from "The Revised UCLA Loneliness Scale: Concurrent and Discriminant Validity Evidence" by D. Russell, L. A. Peplau, and C. E. Cutrona, 1980, *Journal of Personality and Social Psychology, 39,* p. 475. Copyright 1980 by the American Psychological Association. Reprinted with permission.

Existing loneliness measures for children all rely on children's self-reports due to the inherently subjective nature of loneliness and the assumption that direct observational measures or teacher and peer assessments of children's loneliness would have less validity. Nonetheless, the existing self-report measures take several different forms. Some focus exclusively on the context of peer

Table 3 *Illinois Loneliness and Social Dissatisfaction Questionaire*

1. It's easy for me to make new friends at school
2. I like to read
3. I have nobody to talk to in class
4. I'm good at working with other children in my class
5. I watch TV a lot
*6. It's hard for me to make friends at school
7. I like school
8. I have lots of friends in my class
*9. I feel alone at school
10. I can find a friend in my class when I need one
11. I play sports a lot
*12. It's hard to get kids in school to like me
13. I like science
*14. I don't have anyone to play with at school
15. I like music
16. I get along with my classmates
*17. I feel left out of things at school
*18. There's no other kids I can go to when I need help in school
19. I like to paint and draw
*20. I don't get along with other children in school
*21. I'm lonely at school
22. I'm well liked by the kids in my class
23. I like playing board games a lot
*24. I don't have any friends in class

Note. The total score on the scale is the sum of the 16 primary items. Items with asterisks should be reversed in scoring. Items 2, 5, 7, 11, 13, 15, 19, and 23 are classified as hobby or interest items. Items 9, 17, and 21 are "pure" loneliness items and have the highest loadings in factor analyses of the measure. From "Children's Loneliness: A Comparison of Rejected and Neglected Peer Status" by S. R. Asher and V. A. Wheeler, 1985, *Journal of Counseling and Clinical Psychology, 53,* p. 502. Copyright 1985 by the American Psychological Association. Adapted with permission.

relations, whereas others include items that assess the family context as well as the peer context. Some measures treat loneliness as a unitary construct, whereas other measures are designed to distinguish so-called "social loneliness" (feelings of not being integrated into a group) from "emotional loneliness" (lacking sufficient intimacy and emotional support). Finally, as just noted, measures vary in terms of the number of items that focus explicitly on feelings of loneliness. Some measures include no items that specifically assess loneliness, other measures include only items that directly concern loneliness, and still other measures include a mixture of loneliness items and items that assess related cognitions. Because this is a newly emerging area of research, we will provide an overview of existing measures for children.

Heinlein and Spinner's (1985) measure contains 11 items designed to assess emotional loneliness in children. The items assess two related constructs: (a) children's feelings of loneliness (e.g., "When I am with my family I feel lonely") and (b) children's perceptions about the degree to which important emotional provisions are

being met by their family (e.g., "My family really cares about me"). Third- through ninth-grade children were asked to respond to the items using a 4-point Likert scale ranging from "always" to "never." A principal-components factor analysis with varimax rotation indicated one factor. The measure was found to demonstrate good internal reliability; the coefficient alpha for the measure was .88.

Marcoen and Brumagne (1985) developed a 28-item questionnaire, with half of the items assessing relations with peers (e.g., "I feel excluded by my classmates"; "I wish I had more friends") and the other half assessing relations with parents (e.g., "Mother and Father do not listen to me when I say something"; "I feel left out at home"). The results of a factor analysis with fifth- through eighth-grade children indicated two factors: (a) peer-related loneliness and (b) parent-related loneliness. The coefficient alpha was .88 for peer-related loneliness and .68 for parent-related loneliness.

Another measure focusing on peers and family contexts is the Relational Provisions Loneliness (RPLQ) questionnaire constructed by Hayden-Thomson (1989). The measure was designed to assess four constructs: (a) a child's sense of group integration in the family (e.g., "In my family, I feel part of a group of people who do things together"), (b) a sense of group integration in the peer group (e.g., "I am part of a group of friends that does things together"), (c) a sense of personal intimacy in the family (e.g., "There is someone in my family who I can turn to"), and (d) a sense of personal intimacy in the peer group (e.g., "There is someone my age I could go to if I were feeling down"). Children are asked to respond to the items using a 5-point Likert scale ranging from "always true" to "not at all true." The results of a factor analysis with third- through eighth-grade children indicated the four hypothesized factors. The coefficient alpha for each factor was: group integration in peer context = .82; personal intimacy in peer context = .86; group integration in family context = .89; personal intimacy in family context = .90.

Note that none of the items on the Hayden-Thomson questionnaire directly ask about feelings of loneliness. Accordingly, Hayden-Thomson assessed the construct validity of the measure by correlating each subscale with children's responses to separate items that explicitly focused on loneliness. These correlations were: group-integration in peer context = .48; personal-intimacy in peer context = .40; group-integration in family context = .55; personal-intimacy in family context = .60. Although these correlations are statistically significant, they are not high and suggest that caution be used in interpreting measures where loneliness is not directly assessed.

In the Illinois Loneliness and Social Dissatisfaction Questionnaire (Asher et al., 1984), all of the items focus on the peer context. The questionnaire consists of 16 primary items and 8 filler items that ask about hobbies, interests, and school subject preferences. The primary items assess four related constructs: (a) children's feelings of loneliness (e.g., "I'm lonely"); (b) children's perceptions of the degree to which certain important relationship provisions are being met (e.g., "There's nobody I can go to when I need help"); (c) children's perceptions of their social competence (e.g., "I'm good at working with other children"); and (d) children's appraisals of their current peer relationships (e.g., "I have lots of friends"). Children are asked to respond to the items using a 5-point Likert scale ranging from "that's always true about me" to "that's never true about me." The measure was modified slightly (Asher & Wheeler, 1985) by providing an explicit school focus to each of the sixteen primary items (e.g., "I'm lonely at school"; "I can find a friend in my class when I need one"). This adaptation (see Table 3) makes the questionnaire particularly useful for school psychologists who are interested in children's feelings of loneliness in school.

The original versions of the Illinois Loneliness and Social Dissatisfaction Questionnaire were used with third- through sixth-grade children. Recently, variations also have been developed for use with middle-school children (Parkhurst & Asher, 1992), kindergarten and first-grade children (Barth & Parke, 1993; Cassidy & Asher, 1992), and mid-elementary-school students with mild retardation (Williams & Asher, 1992). The modifications of the measure for young children and older children with mild retardation involve using a 3-point scale rather than a 5-point scale and wording items in question format. For example, children are asked "Are you lonely at school?" and they respond by selecting one of three options: "yes," "sometimes," or "no."

There is considerable evidence that the original measure and its variations are psychometrically sound (e.g., Asher et al., 1984; Asher & Wheeler, 1985; Barth & Parke, 1993; Cassidy & Asher, 1992; Parkhurst & Asher, 1992; Williams & Asher, 1992). In several elementary and middle school samples, children's responses have been factor analyzed, using a quartimax solution. The results of these analyses generally indicate a single factor composed of the 16 primary items. Furthermore, the "pure" loneliness items (i.e., items 9, 17, and 21) tend to be the highest loading items. The internal reliability of the 16-item loneliness scale (measured using coefficient alpha) is consistently about .90 with both middle school students and regular education students in mid-elementary school. The reliability is lower (e.g., .79) but still acceptable with younger children and with older elementary school children with mild retardation. Additionally, there is evidence for both short-term and long-term stability in children's reports of loneliness. For example, Renshaw and Brown (1993) found that initial loneliness scores correlated .66 with loneliness scores assessed 10 weeks later, and .56 with loneliness scores assessed one year later.

Hymel et al. (1983) reported similar stability over a one-year period.

A recently developed Loneliness in School Contexts Questionnaire is designed to focus all items explicitly and exclusively on children's feelings of loneliness (Asher et al., 1993). There are only a few different ways in which one can ask children whether they feel lonely and still have each item unequivocally focused on feelings of loneliness. Therefore, the questionnaire presents three questions that directly focus on loneliness but asks each question about four different school contexts: the classroom, physical education, the lunchroom, and the playground. Thus, for example, children are asked to respond to the following three items about the playground: "The playground is a lonely place for me"; "I feel sad and alone on the playground"; "I feel lonely on the playground." By asking three questions about each of four contexts it was possible to create twelve "pure" loneliness items. Fifteen filler items were also used, and items about a particular context were separated from one another. Students were asked to respond to the items using a 5-point Likert scale ranging from "always" to "never." The measure was tested in a study with fourth- and fifth-grade children. A principal-components analysis with varimax rotation of the questionnaire yielded four factors corresponding to the four contexts. The coefficient alphas for each context were: (a) playground = .86; (b) physical education = .86; (c) lunchroom = .85; and (d) classroom = .82. The internal reliability for the entire 12-item measure was .94 (Asher et al., 1993).

In sum, several reliable measures exist for assessing children's feelings of loneliness. In the next section we will examine what has been learned about loneliness in childhood from using these measures.

Problems and Implications

Assessments of loneliness in children reveal that about 10% of children report extreme feelings of loneliness and social dissatisfaction. For example, 11.8% of kindergarten children responded affirmatively to the question "Are you lonely at school"? (Cassidy & Asher, 1992). Likewise, on the item "I'm lonely," 5.8% of third- through sixth-grade children indicated "that's always true about me," and another 5.6% said "that's true about me most of the time" (Asher et al., 1984).

Longitudinal research is needed to compare the nature and rate of loneliness among different age groups, including children. A number of researchers have speculated that adolescents are particularly vulnerable to loneliness and experience greater loneliness than individuals at other ages (e.g., Brennan, 1982; Ostrov & Ofer, 1978). Estimates vary across studies but as a generalization 10% to 20% of adolescents report chronic feelings of loneliness (Davis, 1990). To date, however, it appears that only one study (Shultz & Moore, 1988) has directly compared the incidence of loneliness of adolescents to individuals of different ages, and this study was with high school students, college students, and older adults. Results indicated that high school students experienced the greatest degree of loneliness.

One reason for being concerned about loneliness is that it may be a potential risk factor for school withdrawal. It has long been known that children who are poorly accepted by peers are at greater risk for dropping out of school (see Kupersmidt, Coie, & Dodge, 1990, and Parker & Asher, 1987, for reviews), and there is some evidence that loneliness may interfere with successful school performance among adolescents. Dodson, Campbell, and Dobson (1987) administered the revised UCLA loneliness scale and the Quality of School Life Scale (QLS) to a sample of 163 high school juniors. The QLS is designed to assess students' satisfaction with school, commitment to classwork, and reactions to teachers. Lonely students reported less satisfaction with school, less commitment to classwork, and more negative reactions to teachers. In addition, lonely students had lower grade point averages. Dodson et al. speculated that the painful experience of loneliness may be "all consuming" and distract the students from their academic endeavors.

Given the possible consequences of loneliness for school adjustment, it is important to identify the major sources of loneliness in children and adolescents. Most of the research on this topic has focused on the effects of "objective" relationship deficits on children's loneliness. From this work it is becoming clear that problems in social relationships can affect children's feelings of well-being. Children's more "subjective" perceptions of their interpersonal relationships can also play a powerful role. Research on both types of influences is discussed next.

Relationship Influences on Loneliness

A widely held view is that individuals are lonely because their relational ties are deficient either qualitatively or quantitatively. According to this perspective, causes of loneliness are located in the individual's current and past relationship history. Advocates of this approach (e.g., Sullivan, 1953; Weiss, 1973, 1974) suggest that individuals' relationships must adequately satisfy a set of interpersonal needs (such as the needs for social integration and intimacy) or they will experience loneliness. Because these approaches focus on the individual's social needs, they are often termed "social needs" theories (e.g., Hymel & Woody, 1991; Maragoni & Ickes, 1989).

One possible explanation for why children experience chronic loneliness is that the parent-child relationship is deficient in some way. Theorists writing from psychodynamic and attachment perspectives stress the importance of the infant's relationship with his or her primary caregiver on emotional development. Within this literature, three potential mechanisms have been proposed to mediate the relationship between a dysfunctional early relationship with the parents and the development of loneliness. Sullivan (1953) stressed that deficits in the early parent-child relationship prevent the child from acquiring the necessary social skills for establishing and maintaining healthy relationships with others in later years. Fromm-Reichmann (1959) and Zilboorg (1938) proposed that deficits in this early relationship affect the child's beliefs and expectations about others. Bowlby (1969) and other attachment theorists (e.g., Bretherton, 1985; Main, Kaplan & Cassidy, 1985; Sroufe & Waters, 1977) also proposed that the nature and quality of the parent-child bond establishes an orientation towards others. They suggested that, in the context of the infant's early interactions with the caregiver (generally, the mother), the child constructs a general representation of what social relationships are like. This representation, referred to as a "working model," includes both a conception of what others are like in relationships (e.g., whether others can be trusted) and a concept of the self (e.g., whether the self is worthy of love and respect). The nature of this representation is said to affect how the individual responds in later relationships. A third explanation is suggested by Winnicott (1958). He proposed that a lack of intimacy in infancy arrests the development of the child's ability to be comfortable when alone.

Despite the fact that numerous scholars have speculated that loneliness originates in the early parent-infant relationship, only one longitudinal study appears to have been conducted on the linkage between parent-child relations and loneliness. Berlin, Cassidy, and Belsky (1995) examined whether 12-month-old infants classified as insecure-ambivalent using Ainsworth's Strange Situation would report greater loneliness at both ages 5 and 7, compared to other children. The results showed that the insecure-ambivalent attachment style predicted greater loneliness in children at both 5 and 7 years of age.

The preponderance of research on how relationship problems influence children's loneliness has been done by researchers interested in children's peer relationships at school. There are several sources of motivation for this research. First, there is observational evidence that children disliked by peers (as measured sociometrically) receive more negative treatment from peers (e.g., Dodge, Schlundt, Schocken, & Delugach, 1983). Second, as noted earlier, research indicates that peer rejection in childhood is associated with an elevated risk for dropping out of school. There is also emerging evidence that children's success versus failure in peer relations plays a role even in children's adaptation to the earliest years in school (Ladd, 1990). It seems plausible, therefore, that loneliness could help explain the connection between peer relationship problems and early school adjustment and later withdrawal from school.

Another factor motivating loneliness research has been prior research on intervention with poorly accepted children. Beginning two decades ago, researchers used sociometric measures to identify children who were poorly accepted by peers and then taught social relationship skills to children (e.g., Gottman, Gonso, & Schuler, 1976; Oden & Asher, 1977). Such efforts were often successful (see Coie & Koeppl, 1990, and Asher, Parker, & Walker, 1996, for recent reviews), but this work was done without evidence that poorly accepted children were lonely or wanted help with peer relationship problems.

Various investigators have recently addressed this knowledge gap. In the process, ideas about the nature of children's peer adjustment have become increasingly differentiated, and there is now evidence that at least four different indicators of peer adjustment are related to children's loneliness at school. These four indexes are acceptance by peers, participation in best friendships, the quality or supportiveness of one's closest friendships, and the extent to which one is victimized by peers.

Peer acceptance refers to the extent to which children are liked or disliked by the peer group as a whole. Peer acceptance can be assessed using rating-scale sociometric measures (e.g., Oden & Asher, 1977) or a combination of positive and negative sociometric nomination measures (e.g., Coie, Dodge, & Coppotelli, 1982). There is a consistent body of evidence that children who are poorly accepted by peers report higher levels of loneliness at school. This pattern emerges in studies of middle school students (Parkhurst & Asher, 1992), mid-elementary-school students (e.g., Asher & Wheeler, 1985; Crick & Ladd, 1993), and even in the kindergarten and first-grade school years (Cassidy & Asher, 1992). Furthermore, this pattern exists in various school contexts. Low-accepted children reported being more lonely in the classroom, physical education, the lunchroom, and the playground (Asher et al., 1983). No school context seems to provide a safe haven for children who are poorly accepted by their peers.

Children's participation in best friendships is a second somewhat independent indicator of peer adjustment. Recent research has underscored the need to distinguish friendship from overall peer acceptance (Bukowski & Hoza, 1989; Parker & Asher, 1993a). Whereas peer acceptance refers to the liking for a child by the group as a whole, friendship refers to a close dyadic relationship, one characterized by mutual affection and a shared history. Friendship can be assessed sociometrically by asking children to indicate the names of their best friends (i.e., circling names on a class roster) and then identifying children who reciprocally nominate one another. The fact that some highly accepted children lack friends and some poorly accepted children actually have friends (Parker & Asher, 1993b) suggests the potential value of differentiating friendship participation from peer acceptance.

Recent research with third- through fifth-grade students suggests that children's participation in friendship makes a contribution to their well-being independent of peer acceptance (Parker & Asher, 1993b; Renshaw & Brown, 1993). Children at all levels of peer acceptance have been found to benefit from having a best friend and to suffer greater loneliness from not having one. It seems plausible that friendships meet certain needs such as the need for a reliable companion, intimacy, or emotional closeness—needs that are somewhat distinct from those met by being accepted or included by the group as a whole. A recent study by Parker and Seal (in press), done at a summer camp, indicated that the most lonely group were children who never made a friend throughout the time at camp. Interestingly, the next most lonely group were children whose pattern was to make and lose friends.

The particular features or qualities of children's peer relationships is another indicator of peer adjustment. Friendship quality refers to the specific features of a friendship, such as the extent to which it provides companionship and recreation, help and guidance, emotional support, and shared intimacy. Friendship qualities also include how much conflict exists in the friendship and how easily conflict gets resolved. Several efforts have been made recently to assess the quality of children's best friendships (see, for example, Berndt & Perry, 1986; Bukowski, Hoza, & Boivin, 1994; Furman & Buhrmester, 1985; Parker & Asher, 1993b). In one study (Parker & Asher, 1993b), children were presented with an individually customized questionnaire in which the name of their very best friend was inserted into each item. A total of 40 items were used to assess six different friendship features:

- Companionship and Recreation (e.g., "Jamie and I always play together at recess").
- Help and Guidance (e.g., "Jamie and I help each other with school work a lot").
- Validation and Caring (e.g., "Jamie cares about my feelings").
- Intimate Exchange (e.g., "Jamie and I talk about the things that make us sad").
- Conflict and Betrayal (e.g., "Jamie and I get mad at each other a lot").
- Conflict Resolution (e.g., "Jamie and I always make up easily when we have a fight").

All six features were measured reliably (coefficient alpha's ranged from .73 to .90), and each feature was found to make an independent contribution to children's feelings of loneliness, even after statistically controlling for children's level of peer acceptance. Of the six different features, conflict resolution, validation and caring, and companionship and recreation seem to have had the strongest associations with loneliness.

One final dimension of peer adjustment, being overtly victimized by peers, may prove to be a particularly important influence on loneliness. It seems plausible that children who are poorly accepted by peers, who lack friends, or whose friends are not supportive and reliable allies would be more likely to be victimized by peers. There is evidence that poor acceptance by the peer group is associated with being victimized by classmates (Perry, Kussel, & Perry, 1988). There is also emerging evidence suggesting a link between victimization and loneliness. For example, low-accepted children who were also described by peers as easy to push around were lonelier than low-accepted children who were described as starting fights (Parkhurst & Asher, 1992). Parkhurst, Roedel, Bendixen, and Pontenza (1991) found in two samples of seventh- and eighth-grade students that students' concerns about victimization predicted their feelings of loneliness at school. Kochenderfer and Ladd (in press) found that being verbally or physically victimized by peers is associated with higher levels of loneliness even among kindergarten children.

In addition to various objective indicators of a child's peer adjustment, it is clear that children's own subjective evaluations of their peer relations are important in explaining feelings of loneliness. For example, children's satisfaction with various aspects of their friendships adds significantly to the prediction of loneliness over and above children's level of peer group acceptance or number of reciprocated friendships (Cohn, Lohrmann, & Patterson, 1985; Parker & Asher, 1993b; Renshaw & Brown, 1993). Furthermore, Williams (1996) found that children's perceptions that they are victimized by peers were more important in predicting feelings of loneliness than peer reports of whether children were victimized. Taken together, these findings suggest that children's subjective appraisals of their relationships contribute to feelings of loneliness independently of "objective" relationship indexes. This "subjectiveness" is discussed next.

Influence of Cognitive Appraisal on Loneliness

A cognitive-appraisal approach to the study of loneliness does not assume that a direct causal relationship exists between the objective features of people's social relationships and their feelings of loneliness. Instead, primary emphasis is placed on individuals' subjective perceptions and standards. It is proposed that these subjective evaluations mediate the relationship between the "objective" factors of people's social network and their feelings of loneliness. According to this perspective, individuals' perceptions that their social needs are going unmet underlie the experience of loneliness. Although two people may have "objectively" similar patterns of social relationships, one person may feel lonely and the other person may feel content because they evaluate their relationships differently. Along these lines, W. H. Jones (1982) speculated that lonely individuals may have unrealistically high standards for their friends, their lover, or their spouse. Consistent with this view, Shaver, Furman, and Buhrmester (1985) found that chronically lonely individuals hold exceedingly high expectations for interpersonal relationships compared to both situationally lonely and nonlonely individuals.

Advocates of this approach (e.g., Delegara & Margulis, 1982; Peplau, Russell & Heim, 1979; Perlman & Peplau, 1981) explain that loneliness occurs when individuals perceive that their network of social relationships is smaller or less satisfying than they desire. Following from this, they propose that loneliness feelings can be heightened or reduced by changing a person's subjective standards for relationships. Because these scholars emphasize the discrepancy between desired and achieved social relationships, their ideas are often subsumed under the heading of "cognitive discrepancy models."

Empirical support for the important mediating role that cognitions play in the experience of loneliness comes from a variety of sources (see Peplau, Miceli, & Morasch, 1982, for a review of this literature). Most studies have indeed found that individuals' subjective evaluations of their relationships are more important in predicting loneliness than the objective features of their lives (e.g., Cuffell & Akamatsu, 1989; D. C. Jones, 1992; W. H. Jones, 1982; Stokes, 1985; Williams & Solano, 1983). For instance, Cuffell and Akamatsu (1989) examined differences in the qualitative and quantitative features of lonely and nonlonely college students' social relationships. They found that the quantitative aspects of the students' social relationships, such as their number of friends and their frequency of contact with friends, were not highly related to their scores on the UCLA Loneliness Scale. By contrast, the students' reported satisfaction with their social relationships was strongly associated with these scores.

Individuals' attributions or explanations regarding the causes of their social difficulties may also play a critical role in modulating their loneliness experience. Consistent with this view, research with adults indicates that individuals who suffer from chronic loneliness can be distinguished from other individuals in terms of their cognitive style (see Peplau, Miceli, & Morasch, 1982, for a review of this literature). They are significantly more likely to provide dysfunctional explanations for social events compared to both situationally lonely and nonlonely individuals. In particular, they tend to explain social failures in terms of stable and internal characteristics (i.e., traits, abilities). Evidence that lonely children exhibit dysfunctional cognitive schemata is provided by Bukowski and Ferber (1985) in a study with fifth- and sixth-grade children. Low-accepted children who tended to explain social failures in terms of stable and internal characteristics were lonelier than other children. In addition, their loneliness was stable over a 6-month period. Similar findings are reported by Renshaw and Brown (1993). They found that children's attributional style was an important factor in predicting their current and later experiences (i.e., at 10 weeks and 1 year after the initial assessment) of loneliness in school.

Alternative Actions

Perhaps because of the recency of research on children's loneliness, virtually no intervention research has yet been conducted with lonely children. Accordingly, our recommendations for alternative actions are necessarily brief and somewhat speculative. Still, there are some promising leads that could be pursued. Our emphasis here will be on interventions that could be employed in schools. In particular, we will highlight interventions designed to improve children's relationships and social experiences at school. It is clear from existing research that children's relationships at school play a significant role in their feelings of loneliness. So this domain is a plausible one for intervention efforts. It is also clear that many children would like help improving their social relationships. Recently, this chapter's co-author and his colleagues (Asher, 1993; Asher, Zelis, Parker, & Breune, 1991) asked children if they would like help learning more about how to make friends and get along with other children. Here is the wording of the question (children could answer by indicating "yes," "maybe," or "no"):

Some kids are kind of worried about how they are getting along with other kids. These children are having some problems making friends or keeping friends. Imagine that there was a person in the school whose job was to help children learn how to make friends and get along better with other kids. This person's job would be to help children change how well they get along with other kids. Now imagine that all the kids in the school had a chance to get help from this person. Would you like to get help if this person really worked at the school?

In response to this question, a substantial percentage of children indicated an interest in getting help. Furthermore, children who were poorly accepted by peers, lacked friends, or were lonely at school were significantly more likely to express an interest in help. For example, in one sample, about 47% of low-accepted children said "yes," 38% said "maybe," and only 15% said "no." Similar patterns were found when children were asked if they would like to talk to the school social worker (rather than a hypothetical expert). These findings suggest that school professionals have a window of opportunity to assist children because a desire for help is generally predictive of beneficial outcomes from intervention. Our suggestions, then, focus on different ways to improve children's peer relationships.

Research reviewed earlier on the connection between peer relationships and loneliness indicates that feelings of loneliness are influenced by peer acceptance, victimization, participation in friendship, and the quality of children's friendships. Accordingly, efforts aimed at improving each of these dimensions of children's peer adjustment should help prevent future loneliness or help children who are currently lonely. With regard to these distinct dimensions, the majority of intervention research has focused on promoting peer acceptance and has attempted to help children by teaching them social-relationship skills. In these studies, children have been taught skills found in previous research to correlate with being accepted by peers (e.g., cooperativeness, responsiveness, helpfulness). Furthermore, the assumption made in many of these studies is that children lack basic knowledge about how to respond to key social tasks and that children's problems go beyond performance difficulties brought about by factors such as self-consciousness or anxiety.

Certainly there is reason to believe that lonely individuals could benefit from direct instruction in social-relationship skills. Research with adults (e.g., W. H. Jones, 1982) and with children (e.g., Cassidy & Asher, 1992) suggests that lonely individuals are less prosocial in their interactions with others and are more likely to be negative or withdrawn and nonresponsive. There is an ironic quality to the findings concerning behavioral style and loneliness. One would think that a lonely person, being particularly in need of contact with others, might be on especially "good behavior" when meeting with or interacting with other people. Unfortunately, this does not appear to be the case. Research with adults by W. H. Jones (1982) indicates that lonely individuals are actually less friendly and more nonresponsive when meeting someone for the first time.

This kind of pattern suggests that lonely people might be helped by receiving direct instruction in social-relationship skills. Research with poorly accepted children indicates that teaching children relationship skills often leads to significant improvements in peer acceptance (for a recent review, see Asher et al., 1996). In particular, the game-playing or activity context seems like a useful one for teaching relationship concepts such as sustaining participation, cooperating, being a responsive communicator, and being supportive or validating of others (for examples, see social-skills-coaching studies by Bierman & Furman, 1984; Gresham & Nagle, 1980; Ladd, 1981; Lochman, Coie, Underwood, & Terry, 1993; Oden & Asher, 1977).

The relevance of game contexts to children's social interactions with peers suggests that another alternative action would be to help children by promoting their competence at games and sports. Suggestive research has been done on the links between children's athletic ability and their feelings of loneliness at school (Page, Frey, Talbert, & Falk, 1992). Children in first through sixth grade completed a loneliness rating scale and several fitness tests. Results indicated that lonely children were both less physically fit and less physically active than non-lonely children. The authors speculated that, because sports activities are important social arenas for children in the elementary school years, children who lack the skills necessary to participate in these activities may come to feel isolated and lonely. Further evidence for the link between participation in athletics and children's experiences of loneliness was reported by a study using the Illinois Loneliness Questionnaire (Asher & Wheeler, 1985). Recall that this questionnaire includes eight filler items focusing on children's hobbies, interests, and activity preferences. Of these eight items, only one item was found to relate to feelings of loneliness: Children who strongly endorsed the item "I play sports a lot" were less lonely. Perhaps lonely children could be helped not only by acquiring new social relationship skills but also by learning game-playing competencies so that they can be more comfortable and involved in this important peer context.

Research on the effects of being victimized by peers suggests that another approach to reducing loneliness at school would be to reduce the level of bullying that occurs in school (see Bullying, this volume). Because poorly accepted children are at greater risk for being victimized, reducing bullying in school should be especially helpful for children who are poorly accepted and therefore most vulnerable. Olweus (1991) has recently described a large-scale intervention effort undertaken in Norway. The focus of this effort was to change policies and practices in schools so that bullying would not be tolerated. Major components included increasing school professionals' knowledge about the problem and its causes; promoting an attitude of active involvement on the part of teachers and parents; communicating clear rules against bullying enforced by nonhostile, nonphysical sanctions; and providing closer surveillance and supervision of recess. Olweus reported substantial reductions in bullying activity as a result of these efforts.

Another approach to intervention would be to modify the ecology of classroom life to promote cohesiveness among children. A considerable amount of work has been done in recent years on creating more cooperative and more caring school environments. Unfortunately, virtually no research exists on the effects of these efforts on children's loneliness at school. Research is badly needed, for example, on the types of teacher-student interactions that promote a sense of well-being and community for children. There is large variation in how the teacher-student relationship unfolds, with some relationships characterized by high levels of attachment, warmth, and support, others characterized by considerable child dependency on the teacher, and still others characterized by high levels of interpersonal conflict (e.g., Birch &

Ladd, 1996; Howes & Hamilton, 1992; Pianta & Steinberg, 1992). Certainly a child's relationship to the teacher must affect a child's level of loneliness at school, yet little is known about this important feature of school life. What is known is that children who are disliked by peers also tend to be disliked by teachers (Taylor & Trickett, 1989). Indeed it is possible that at least young children are taking their cues from teachers. Many years ago Flanders and Havumaki (1963) reported that it was possible to increase a child's sociometric status by having teachers increase the rate with which they praise a student in front of the rest of the class.

There is also a need for research on the effects of school organizational patterns. As discussed earlier, there is some evidence that loneliness may be relatively high during adolescence. To what extent is this the result of how secondary schools are organized with classes and peer composition changing every hour. Would adolescents be less lonely if they functioned in self-contained classrooms or at least teams as in the widely adopted middle school model?

Another organizational variable is multi-age versus same-age grouping. Katz and McClellan (in press) speculate that multi-age classrooms would reduce competition and aggression and that this context would also provide older, less mature students with an opportunity to interact with younger children (for related research, see Ladd, 1983; Furman, Rahe, & Hartup, 1979). Still another organizational variable discussed by Katz and McClellan that needs research is "looping," namely the practice of having teachers stay for several years with children as together they move from one grade level to the next. This practice is common in one-room schools and in schools that use multi-age classrooms, but it could be adopted in any type of school. Hopefully, future efforts at intervention will include attention to important organizational factors and school policies as well as to improving children's competencies.

Summary

Approximately 10% of elementary school children report extremely high levels of loneliness, and there is reason to believe that loneliness is associated with making a poor adjustment to school and withdrawing from school in the later years. This chapter reviewed the emerging research literature on loneliness in children. Because research on children's loneliness is at beginning stages, attention was given in the first major section (Background and Development) to how loneliness is defined, how children at various ages conceptualize loneliness, and how loneliness has been formally assessed in school-age populations. Evidence here indicates that even young children have a basic understanding of the concept of loneliness.

Furthermore, it is clear that loneliness in school can be reliably measured from age five or six onward.

The second major section, Problems and Implications, described what has been learned about the factors that influence loneliness at school. Most of the research on this topic has focused on how children's peer relationships influence their feelings of loneliness. Findings indicate that loneliness is affected by the degree to which children are accepted by peers, whether children participate in best friendships, the quality of children's friendships, and whether children are victimized by peers. Children's subjective appraisals of their relationships also play an important role.

The third major section, Alternative Actions, considered possible interventions to reduce loneliness. Given the recency of research on children's loneliness, relatively little work has been done of the effects of intervention. Accordingly, this section proposed several approaches to intervention that draw on related research on how to promote more positive relationships at school. These include social-relationship skills training, interventions to reduce victimization, and efforts to promote a more caring and participatory school environment.

More research is needed not only on this pervasive childhood problem but also on intervention strategies so that school psychologists and others working with children who are lonely can offer effective help and guidance.

Recommended Resources

Asher, S. R., Parker, J. G., & Walker, D. L. (1996). Distinguishing friendship from acceptance: Implications for intervention and assessment. In W. M. Bukowski, A. F. Newcomb, & W. W. Hartup (Eds.), *The company they keep: Friendship in childhood and adolescence* (pp. 366–405). New York: Cambridge University Press.
This chapter reviews evidence that social-relationship skills training has beneficial effects on children's peer acceptance. It seems plausible that many of the interventions discussed could be helpful with lonely children. The chapter also makes a strong distinction between peer acceptance and friendship and proposes that promoting friendship may require teaching skills relevant to the "social tasks of friendship."

Asher, S. R., Parkhurst, J. T., Hymel, S., & Williams, G. A. (1990). Peer rejection and loneliness in childhood. In S. R. Asher & J. D. Coie (Eds.), *Peer rejection in childhood* (pp. 253–272). New York: Cambridge University Press.
This chapter provides a review of the first wave of research on loneliness in childhood. Particular attention is given to the experience of loneliness in childhood, issues in the assessment of loneliness, and the connection between peer acceptance and children's reports of loneliness.

Parker, J. G., Rubin, K. H., Price, J. M., & DeRosier, M. E. (1995). Peer relationships, child development, and adjustment: A developmental psychopathology perspective. In D.

Cicchetti & D. Cohen (Eds.), *Developmental psychopathology: Vol. 2. Risk, disorder, and adaptation* (pp. 96–161). New York: Wiley.
This chapter reviews theory and evidence that children's adjustment in their peer relations has "broad developmental and clinical significance for children." The chapter provides an excellent treatment of the complex connections between peer relations and children's social competence and well-being.

Peplau, L. A., & Perlman, D. (1982). *Loneliness: A sourcebook of current theory, research and therapy.* New York: Wiley & Sons.
This book provides an excellent treatment of the topic of loneliness. Attention is given to definitional and measurement issues, to various theoretical approaches, to factors associated with loneliness, and to treatment perspectives. Chapters are authored by researchers who pioneered in the study of loneliness, and most focus on loneliness in adulthood.

Rotenberg, K. J., & Hymel, S. (Eds.). (in press). *Childhood loneliness.* New York: Cambridge University Press.
This volume is now in preparation with an expected publication date of late 1997. It will be the first research-based, edited volume on loneliness in children. A strong feature of the book will be its attention to developmental issues and to a sociocultural perspective. Many of the chapters will focus on assessment issues and on the links between loneliness and the nature of children's social relationships.

References

Asher, S. R. (1993, March). Inviting children to self-refer. In Celia Fisher (Chair), *Ethical issues in the reporting and referring of research participants.* Symposium conducted at the biennial meeting of the Society for Research in Child Development, New Orleans.

Asher, S. R., Gabriel, S. W., & Hopmeyer, A. (1993, April). *Children's loneliness in different school contexts.* Paper presented at the biennial meeting of the Society for Research in Child Development, New Orleans.

Asher, S. R., Hymel, S., & Renshaw, P. D. (1984). Loneliness in children. *Child Development, 55,* 1456–1464.

Asher, S. R., Parker, J. G., & Walker, D. L. (1996). Distinguishing friendship from acceptance: Implications for intervention and assessment. In W. M. Bukowski, A. F. Newcomb, & W. W. Hartup (Eds.), *The company they keep: Friendship in childhood and adolescence* (pp. 366–405). New York: Cambridge University Press.

Asher, S. R., & Wheeler, V. A. (1985). Children's loneliness: A comparison of rejected and neglected peer status. *Journal of Consulting and Clinical Psychology, 53,* 500–505.

Asher, S. R., Zelis, K. M., Parker, J. G., & Breune, C. M. (1991). Self-referral for peer relationship problems among aggressive and withdrawn low-accepted children. In J. T. Parkhurst, & D. L. Rabiner (Co-Chairs), *The behavioral characteristics and the subjective experiences of aggressive and withdrawn rejected children.* Symposium conducted at the biennial meeting of the Society for Research in Child Development, Seattle.

Barth, J. M., & Parke, R. D. (1993). Parent-child relationship influences on children's transition to school. *Merrill-Palmer Quarterly, 39,* 173–195.

Beck, A. T., & Young, J. E. (1978, September). College blues. *Psychology Today.*

Berlin, L. J., Cassidy, J., & Belsky, J. (1995). Loneliness in young children and infant-mother attachment: A longitudinal study. *Merrill-Palmer Quarterly, 41,* 91–103.

Berndt, T. J., & Perry, T. B. (1986). Children's perceptions of friendships as supportive relationships. *Developmental Psychology, 22,* 640–648.

Bierman, K. L., & Furman, W. (1984). The effects of social skills training and peer involvement on the social adjustment of preadolescents. *Child Development, 55,* 151–162.

Birch, S. H., & Ladd, G. W. (1996, April). Continuity and change in the quality of teacher-child relationships: Links with children's early school adjustment. In S. Birch (Chair), *Children's relationships with teacher: Assessment, continuity, and linkages with school adjustment.* Symposium conducted at the annual meeting of the American Educational Research Association, New York.

Bowlby, J. (1969). *Attachment and loss: Vol. 1. Attachment.* New York: Basic Books.

Brennan, T. (1982). Loneliness at adolescence. In L. A. Peplau & D. Perlman (Eds.), *Loneliness: A sourcebook of current theory, research and therapy* (pp. 166–179). New York: Wiley.

Bretherton, I. (1985). Attachment theory: Retrospect and prospect. In I. Bretherton & E. Waters (Eds.), Growing points of attachment theory and research. *Monographs of the Society for Research in Child Development, 50,* (1–2, Serial No. 209), 3–35.

Bukowski, W. M., & Ferber, J. S. (1985). *A study of peer relations, attribution style, and loneliness during early adolescence.* Unpublished manuscript, University of Maine.

Bukowski, W. M., & Hoza, B. (1989). Popularity and friendship: Issues in theory, measurement, and outcome. In T. J. Berndt & G. W. Ladd (Eds.), *Peer relationships in child development* (pp. 15–45). New York: Wiley.

Bukowski, W. M., Hoza, B., & Boivin, M. (1994). Measuring friendship quality during pre- and early adolescence: The development and psychometric properties of the Friendship Qualities Scale. *Journal of Social and Personal Relationships, 11,* 471–484.

Cassidy, J., & Asher, S. R. (1992). Loneliness and peer relations in young children. *Child Development, 63,* 350–365.

Cohn, D. A., Lohrmann, B. C., & Patterson, C. (1985, April). *Social networks and loneliness in children.* Paper presented at the biennial meeting of the Society for Research in Child Development, Toronto, Ontario.

Coie, J. D., Dodge, K. A., & Coppotelli, H. (1982). Dimensions and types of social status: A cross-age perspective. *Developmental Psychology, 18,* 557–570.

Coie, J. D., & Koeppl, G. (1990). Adapting intervention to the problems of aggressive and disruptive rejected children. In S. R. Asher & J. D. Coie (Eds.), *Peer rejection in childhood* (pp. 309–337). New York: Cambridge University Press.

Crick, N. R., & Ladd, G. W. (1993). Children's perceptions of their peer experiences: Attributions, loneliness, social anxiety, and social avoidance. *Developmental Psychology, 29,* 244–254.

Cuffell, B. J., & Akamatsu, T. J. (1989). The structure of loneliness: A factor-analytic investigation. *Cognitive Therapy and Research, 13,* 459–474.

Cutrona, C. E. (1982). Transition to college: Loneliness and the process of social adjustment. In L. A. Peplau & D. Perlman (Eds.), *Loneliness: Current theory research and therapy* (pp. 291–309). New York: Wiley.

Davis, B. D. (1990). Loneliness in children and adolescents. *Issues in Comprehensive Pediatric Nursing, 13,* 59–69.

Delegara, V. J., & Margulis, S. T. (1982). Why loneliness occurs: The interrelationship of social-psychological and privacy concepts. In L. A. Peplau & D. Perlman (Eds.), *Loneliness: Current theory, research and therapy* (pp. 152–165). New York: Wiley.

Dobson, J. E., Campbell, N. J., & Dobson, R. (1982). Relationships among loneliness, perceptions of school, and grade point averages of high school juniors. *The School Counselor, 35,* 143148.

Dodge, K. A., Schlundt, D. G., Schocken, I., & Delugach, J. D. (1983). Social competence and children's social status: The role of peer group entry strategies. *Merrill-Palmer Quarterly, 29,* 309–336.

Flanders, T. Z., & Havumaki, S. (1963). The effects of teacher-pupil contacts involving praise on the sociometric choices of students. In J. M. Seidman (Ed.), *Education for mental health.* New York: Crowell.

Fromm-Reichmann, F. (1959). Loneliness. *Psychiatry, 22,* 1–15.

Furman, W., & Buhrmester, D. (1985). Children's perceptions of the personal relationships in their social networks. *Developmental Psychology, 6,* 1016–1024.

Furman, W., Rahe, D. F., & Hartup, W. W. (1979). Rehabilitation of socially withdrawn preschool children through mixed-age and same-age socialization. *Child Development, 50,* 915–922.

Gottman, J. M., Gonso, J., & Schuler, P. (1976). Teaching social skills to isolated children. *Journal of Abnormal Child Psychology, 4,* 179–197.

Gresham, F. M., & Nagle, R. J. (1980). Social skills training with children: Responsiveness to modeling and coaching as a function of peer orientation. *Journal of Consulting and Clinical Psychology, 48,* 718–729.

Hayden, L., Tarulli, D., & Hymel, S. (1988, May). *Children talk about loneliness.* Paper presented at the biennial University of Waterloo Conference on Child Development, Waterloo, Ontario.

Hayden-Thomson, L. (1989). *The development of the Relational Provision Loneliness Questionnaire for children.* Unpublished doctoral dissertation, University of Waterloo, Waterloo, Ontario.

Heinlein, L., & Spinner, B. (1985, April). *Measuring emotional loneliness in children.* Paper presented at the biennial meeting of the Society for Research in Child Development, Toronto.

Hopmeyer, A. (1995). *Loneliness: An integrative review.* Unpublished manuscript, University of Illinois at Urbana-Champaign.

Horowitz, L. M., French, R., & Anderson, C. A. (1982). The prototype of a lonely person. In L. A. Peplau & D. Perlman (Eds.), *Loneliness: A sourcebook of current theory, research, and therapy* (pp. 183–205). New York: Wiley.

Howes, C., & Hamilton, C. E. (1992). Children's relationships with teachers: Stability and concordance with parental attachments. *Child Development, 63,* 859–866.

Hymel, S., Freigang, R., Franke, S., Both, L., Bream, L., & Borys, S. (1983, June). *Children's attributions for social situations: Variations as a function of social status and self-perception variables.* Paper presented at the annual meeting of the Canadian Psychological Association, Winnipeg, Manitoba.

Hymel, S., & Woody, E. (1991). Popular and unpopular children: Strategies for maintaining self-concept. In F. D. Alsaker & S. R. Asher (Co-Chairs), *Self-perceptions among children with poor peer relationships.* Symposium presented at the biennial meeting of the International Society for the Study of Behavioral Development, Minneapolis, Minnesota.

Jones, D. C. (1992). Parental divorce, family conflict and friendship networks. *Journal of Social and Personal Relationships, 2,* 219–235.

Jones, W. H. (1982). Loneliness and social behavior. In L. A. Peplau & D. Perlman (Eds.), *Loneliness: A sourcebook of current theory, research, and therapy* (pp. 238–252). New York: Wiley & Sons.

Kochenderfer, B. J., & Ladd, G. W. (in press). Peer victimization: Manifestations and relations to school adjustment. *Journal of School Psychology.*

Kupersmidt, J. B., Coie, J. D., & Dodge, K. A. (1990). The role of poor peer relationships in the development of disorder. In S. R. Asher & J. D. Coie (Eds.), *Peer rejection in childhood* (pp. 274–305). New York: Cambridge University Press.

Ladd, G. W. (1981). Effectiveness of a social learning method for enhancing children's social interaction and peer acceptance. *Child Development, 57,* 171–178.

Ladd, G. W. (1990). Having friends, keeping friends, making friends, and being liked by peers in the classroom: Predictors of children's early school adjustment? *Child Development, 61,* 1081–1100.

Ladd, G. W., Kochenderfer, B. J., & Coleman, C. C. (in press). Friendship quality as a predictor of young children's early school adjustment. *Child Development.*

Lochman, J. E., Coie, J. D., Underwood, M. K., & Terry, R. (1993). Effectiveness of a social relations intervention program for aggressive and nonaggressive, rejected children. *Journal of Consulting and Clinical Psychology, 61,* 1053–1058.

Main, M., Kaplan, I., & Cassidy, J. (1985). Security in infancy, childhood, and adulthood: A move to the level of representation. In I. Bretherton & E. Waters (Eds.), Growing points of attachment theory and research. *Monographs of the Society for Research in Child Development, 50,* (1–2, Serial No. 209), 66–104.

Maragoni, C., & Ickes, W. (1989). Loneliness: A theoretical review with implications for measurement. *Journal of Social and Personal Relationships, 6,* 93–128.

Marcoen, A., & Brumagne, M. (1985). Loneliness among children and young adolescents, *Developmental Psychology, 3,* 1025–1031.

Nicholls, J. G., Licht, G. B., & Pearl, R. A. (1982). Some dangers of using personality questionnaires to study personality. *Psychological Bulletin, 92,* 572–580.

Oden S., & Asher S. R. (1977). Coaching children in social skills for friendship making. *Child Development, 48,* 495–506.

Olweus, D. (1991). Bully/victim problems among school children: Basic facts and effects of a school based intervention program. In D. J. Pepler & K. H. Rubin (Eds.), *The development and treatment of childhood aggression* (pp. 411–448). Hillsdale, NJ: Erlbaum.

Ostrov, E., & Offer, D. (1978). Loneliness and the adolescent. *Adolescent Psychiatry, 6,* 34–50.

Page, R. M., Frey, J., Talbert, R., & Falk, C. (1992). Children's feelings of loneliness and social dissatisfaction: Relationship to measures of physical fitness and activity. *Journal of Teaching in Physical Education, 11,* 211–219.

Parker, J. G., & Asher, S. R. (1987). Peer relations and later personal adjustment: Are low-accepted children at risk? *Psychological Bulletin, 102,* 357–389.

Parker, J. G., & Asher, S. R. (1993a). Beyond group acceptance: Friendship adjustment and friendship quality as distinct dimensions of children's peer adjustment. In D. Perlman & W. H. Jones (Eds.), *Advances in personal relationships* (Vol. 4, pp. 261–294). London: Kingsley.

Parker, J. G., & Asher, S. R. (1993b). Friendship and friendship quality in middle childhood: Links with peer group acceptance and feelings of loneliness and social dissatisfaction. *Developmental Psychology, 29,* 611–621.

Parker, J. G., & Seal, J. (in press). Forming, losing, renewing, and replacing friendships: Applying temporal parameters to the assessment of children's friendship experiences. *Child Development.*

Parkhurst, J. T., & Asher, S. R. (1992). Peer rejection in middle school: Subgroup differences in behavior, loneliness and interpersonal concerns. *Developmental Psychology, 28,* 231–241.

Parkhurst, J. T., & Hopmeyer, A. (in press). Developmental change in the sources of loneliness among children and adolescents: Constructing a theoretical model. In K. J. Rotenberg & S. Hymel (Eds.), *Childhood loneliness.* New York: Cambridge University Press.

Parkhurst, J. T., Roedel, T. D., Bendixen, L. D., & Pontenza, M. T. (1991, April). Subgroups of rejected middle school students: Their behavioral characteristics, friendships, and social concerns. In J. T. Parkhurst & D. L. Rabiner (Co-Chairs), *The behavioral characteristics and the subjective experience of aggressive and withdrawn/submissive rejected children.* Symposium presented at the biennial meeting of the Society for Research in Child Development, Seattle.

Peplau, L. A., Miceli, M., & Morasch, B. (1982). Loneliness and self-evaluation. In L. A. Peplau & D. Perlman (Eds.), *Loneliness: Current theory research and therapy* (pp. 135–151). New York: Wiley & Sons.

Peplau, L. A., & Perlman, D. (1982). *Loneliness: A sourcebook of current theory, research and therapy.* New York: Wiley & Sons.

Peplau, L. A., Russell, D., & Heim, M. (1979). The experience of loneliness. In I. H. Freize, D. Bar-Tal, & J. S. Carroll (Eds.), *New approaches to social problems: Applications of attribution theory.* San Francisco: Jossey-Bass.

Perlman, D., & Peplau, L. A. (1981). Toward a social psychology of loneliness. In R. Gilmour & S. Duck (Eds.), *Personal relationships: Vol. 3. Personal relationships in disorder* (pp. 31–44). London: Academic Press.

Perry, D. G., Kussel, S. J., & Perry, L. C. (1988). Victims of peer aggression. *Developmental Psychology, 24,* 807–814.

Pianta, R. C., & Steinberg, M. (1992). Teacher-child relationships and the process of adjusting to school. *New Directions for Child Development, 57,* 61–80.

Renshaw, P. D., & Brown, P. J. (1993). Loneliness in middle childhood: Concurrent and longitudinal predictors. *Child Development, 64,* 1271–1284.

Rook, K. S. (1988). Toward a more differentiated view of loneliness. In S. W. Duck (Ed.), *Handbook of personal relationships* (pp. 571–589). New York: John Wiley & Sons.

Rotenberg, K. J., & Hymel, S. (in press). *Childhood loneliness.* New York: Cambridge University Press.

Rotenberg, K. J., & Kmill, J. (1992). Perception of lonely and non-lonely persons as a function of individual differences in loneliness. *Journal of Social and Personal Relationships, 9,* 325–330.

Russell, D., Peplau, L. A., & Cutrona, C. E. (1980). The revised UCLA loneliness scale: Concurrent and discriminant validity evidence. *Journal of Personality and Social Psychology, 39,* 472–480.

Shaver, P., Furman, W., & Buhrmester, D. (1985). Transition to college: Network chances, social skills and loneliness. In S. Duck & D. Perlman (Eds.), *Understanding personal relationships: An interdisciplinary approach* (pp. 193–219). London: Sage Publications.

Shultz, N. R., & Moore, D. (1988). Loneliness: Differences across three age levels. *Journal of Social and Personal Relationships, 5,* 275–284.

Shute, R., & Howitt, D. (1990). Unravelling the paradoxes of loneliness: Research and elements of a social theory of loneliness. *Social Behaviour,* 169–184.

Sroufe, L. A., & Waters, E. (1977). Attachment as an organizational construct. *Child Development, 48,* 1184–1199.

Stokes, J. P. (1985). The relation of social network and individual difference variables to loneliness. *Journal of Personality and Social Psychology, 48,* 981–990.

Sullivan, H. S. (1953). *The interpersonal theory of psychiatry.* New York: Norton.

Taylor, A. R., & Trickett, P. K. (1989). Teacher preference and children's social status in the classroom. *Merrill Palmer Quarterly, 35,* 343–361.

Weiss, R. S. (1973). *Loneliness: The experience of emotional and social isolation.* Cambridge, MA: MIT Press.

Weiss, R. S. (1974). The provisions of social relationships. In Z. Rubin (Ed.), *Doing unto others: Joining, molding conforming, helping, loving* (pp. 17–26). Englewood Cliffs, NJ: Prentice-Hall.

Williams, G. A. (1996). *Peer relationship processes and children's loneliness at school.* Unpublished doctoral dissertation, University of Illinois, Urbana-Champaign.

Williams, G. A., & Asher, S. R. (1992). Assessment of loneliness at school among children with mental retardation. *American Journal of Mental Retardation, 96,* 373–385.

Williams, J. G., & Solano, C. H. (1983). The social reality of feeling lonely: Friendship and reciprocation. *Personality and Social Psychology Bulletin, 9,* 237–242.

Winnicott, D. W. (1958). The capacity to be alone. *International Journal of Psychoanalysis, 39,* 416–420.

Young, J. E. (1982). Loneliness, depression and cognitive therapy: Theory and application. In L. A. Peplau & D. Perlman (Eds.), *Loneliness: A sourcebook of current theory, research, and therapy* (pp. 379–406). New York: Wiley & Sons.

Zilboorg, G. (1938, January). Loneliness. *Atlantic Monthly,* 45–54.

26

Stress

Robyn S. Hess

University of Nebraska at Kearney

Ellis P. Copeland

University of Northern Colorado

The transition to adulthood for today's youth is a difficult journey filled with risk, rapid change, and seemingly boundless choices. Both children and adolescents face the specter of AIDS and other sexually transmitted diseases; the disintegration of the family through divorce and teen pregnancy; increased levels of poverty and violence; and constant, oftentimes negative media images of drug and alcohol use, sexual stimuli and themes, and violent conflict resolution. They observe technological advances that become obsolete daily and are forced to question their role in an economy in which the younger generation is unlikely to match the financial security enjoyed by their parents (Rice, 1996). This constant bombardment of stressful stimuli calls into question the ability of youth to adapt. Phillips (1993) concluded that the number of teenage suicides, homicides, and pregnancies support the notion that American children and adolescents need assistance to more effectively cope with the stress in their lives.

The serious and wide-ranging effects of long-term exposure to stress are well documented (e.g., Compas, 1987). Psychosocial stress has been correlated with lower school functioning and academic achievement (Grannis, 1992); behavior disorders, short-term adjustment reactions, and depression (Compas, 1987); and a wide variety of somatic symptoms (Barr, Boyce, & Zeltzer, 1994). Helping children and adolescents to understand and prevent the negative consequences of stress is an integral part of the role of school psychologists and other concerned school professionals.

Background and Development

Stress is an ubiquitous part of human existence. One cannot escape the natural challenges of life, whether they be death of a parent, transition to a new school, or the hassles of everyday living. As a part of its omnipresence, the term *stress* is used on television, radio, newspapers, and in daily conversations. Yet, to make matters more complex, few people define stress the same way (Selye, 1993). Selye (1956) first defined stress as the body's nonspecific response to any environmental demand. Within the context of a biological and stimulus-response phenomenon, chemical changes occur in the body as a response to an environmental stressor/stimuli.

Selye's tenet initiated a host of subsequent studies into the stress-illness relationship. Although it is not precisely known how the psychological and physiological variables interact, stress has been found to assault physical functioning and the immune system in a variety of ways. Trait theory has implicated personality traits such as temperament or hardiness, whereas process theory talks of a direct link between stress and the immune system. Others speculate that individuals under stress engage in behaviors that make them more likely to fall ill. Independent of theory, the link between stress and illness has been clearly established (e.g., Dohrenwend & Dohrenwend, 1978).

The "illness-linked" stressors that have received the most attention include both major life events and the study of daily hassles. Drawing on the work of Holmes and Rahe (1967), Coddington (1972) was among the first to study the overall stress level of the "normal" adolescent. He first developed an adolescent major-life-events scale that included items such as parent divorce or death of a relative. It was hypothesized that the degree of stress an individual experienced could be measured in terms of the number of life changes he or she had undergone. Later efforts in stress research examined daily hassles which have been defined by Lazarus and his associates (Lazarus & Cohen, 1977; Lazarus & Delongis, 1983) as the irritating, frustrating, distressing demands that characterize everyday transactions with the environment. It is generally agreed that life-change events and daily hassles are experiences that extract demands on an individual's psychological resources and are typically experienced as stressful. Life-change events are stressful as they require immediate and often major adjustments, whereas daily hassles are more often cumulative in their demands on the individual.

Lazarus and his associates view stress from a process or cognitive phenomenological perspective. Within this context, daily hassles are perceived as proximal measure of stress, whereas major life events are seen as distal (as such, more difficult to study). The proximal-distal dimension refers to the ordering of various environments, according to their conceptual proximity to experience, to perceive, and to interpret or psychologically respond. For each event, Lazarus uses the term *cognitive appraisal* to describe how the individual perceives a stressful situation. Appraisals are placed into three categories: harm or loss, threat, or challenge. So, each proximal or recent event can be observed as an immediate indicator of a child's or adolescent's appraisal and the personal distress and disruption connected with the "stressor" event. In contrast, interpreting the effects of a major life event is more removed and complex. As such, Lazarus hypothesized that daily hassles would have a stronger relationship to adaptational outcomes than major life events. Indeed, research using a measure of daily hassles and a measure of major life events has recently found daily hassles to be the superior predictor of psychological and physiological adaptation (e.g., Ham & Larson, 1990). Still, more empirical studies with children and adolescents are needed.

Due to the promising predictive status of hassles on adaptation outcome, efforts have been made to establish the types of daily hassles that children and adolescents identify as most stressful. Compas, Davis, Forsythe, and Wagner (1987) classified daily hassles into five areas or events: network, intimacy, family, peer, and academic. Similarly, other studies have found school, family, and difficulties with friends as the areas that most concern adolescents (e.g., Armacost, 1989; Stern & Zevon, 1990).

Although the relationship between hassles and adaptation, and life events and adaptation has been shown, stress research has recently taken a new direction to include an examination of the variables that moderate stress in an individual. It is now believed that coping variables or protective factors in the stress-illness relationship promote a better understanding of how to effectively intervene and prevent deleterious responses to stress. The most frequent protective factors mentioned and studied are those related to "hardiness" or "resilience" (Blocker & Copeland, 1994). The mediating variables most often studied in the stress-illness relationship are the repertoire of coping behaviors employed by the individual to ward off stress. Albee (1982) proposed that the etiology of mental illness or adaptation can be attributed to the interaction of stress and organic vulnerability moderated by positive coping strategies such as social competence, self-esteem, and social support. With chil-

dren and adolescents, a number of different perspectives on the moderating effects of coping behaviors have emerged. Again, studies are limited, yet positive coping strategies such as problem-focused abilities, interpersonal skills, and reframing of emotionally sensitive information or interactions demonstrate considerable promise (Blocker & Copeland, 1994; Patterson & McCubbin, 1987).

It is only recently that researchers have started to explore stress in children and adolescents. Initially, it was believed that children did not experience stress or were isolated from the stress of the adult world. Subsequently, the study of stress focused on the application of adult models of stress to children and adolescents. It is now evident that child and adolescent stress is a complex topic best viewed from several different perspectives including biological, developmental, cultural, and social-cognitive standpoints. Taken together, these differing views provide a comprehensive understanding of the impact of stress on children and adolescents.

Biological Perspective

Stress research has long recognized the fundamental connection between biological functions and stress (e.g., Selye, 1956). One important consideration in understanding the impact of stress is the biological disposition or temperament of the individual. There are wide variations in children with regard to their emotional responses and behavior. Garmezy (1987) has noted that personality dispositions are associated with how certain individuals cope with stressful situations. Many of these personality traits or dispositions undoubtedly have their foundation in the individual's physiological makeup. For example, infants who display consistent negative reactions in response to mild stress and novelty, behaviors which might be associated with a difficult temperament, have greater activity of the right frontal lobe (Fox, 1992). Conversely, the data indicated that children demonstrating greater left frontal activation, associated with attention and verbal strategies, are less likely to cry when separated from their mothers and less likely to withdraw from novel situations. Fox (1992) suggested that children demonstrating this pattern of brain activity may be better able to regulate their emotions than children showing greater activity in the opposite or right frontal lobe. Furthermore, it was proposed that a link may exist between emotion regulation and the types of strategies that infants and children use to modulate arousal. Similarly, Wertlieb, Weigel, Springer, and Feldstein (1987) have found that certain temperament orientations such as high activity level, low adaptability, withdrawal from new stimuli, and distractibility are associated with a greater number of behavioral symptoms and that temperament is related to socioemotional functioning and the ability to cope with stressful situations. These predispositions may interact with a child's environment and result in either a vulnerability or a resiliency to the effects of stress.

A biological perspective is instrumental in understanding an individual's predisposition to stress as well as the long-term impact of stressful events. It has been consistently documented that stressful situations are correlated with changes in physiological immunity in humans (Zakowski, Hall, & Baum, 1992). In children, the association between stress and health status has been demonstrated across a variety of problems including infections, accidents, and psychiatric disorders (Barr et al., 1994). Stressful life events such as the death of a loved one, marital discord, and even more minor stressors such as taking examinations have been associated with reductions in some aspect of immune function which, in turn, could seriously affect health. Indeed, the emerging field of psychoneuroimmunology (PNI), the study of the interactions between behavior, the brain, and the immune system, is providing new insights into how stress alters immunity (Maier, Watkins, & Fleshner, 1994). It has also helped to point out the complexity of the relationship between stress and the immune system. Different stressors will elicit differing responses and are influenced by various moderating variables such as personality and coping responses. In effect, there is a bidirectional relationship between the brain and the immune system with psychological processes influencing this network and being regulated by it (Maier et al., 1994).

Developmental Perspective

In examining stress, it is necessary to consider the child's and adolescent's developmental level and the representative tasks for each level (Phillips, 1993). The source of stress, an individual's vulnerability, and the individual's ability to deal with stressors vary with the developmental stage. Human beings are exposed to stresses from conception onward. In infancy and early childhood, individuals experience stress in response to meeting various developmental milestones such as walking and toilet training, addressing separation issues, and dealing with their families. Stress at this stage is commonly viewed as a reciprocal activity between an infant and his or her environment with stress occurring because of deficits in the infant, the environment, or their interactions (Goodyer, 1988). The bonds formed between parent and child during the child's early years have a profound impact on subsequent personal and social development. When these bonds are not well formed, children are more vulnerable to subsequent stress in their lives (Chandler & Shermis, 1990). Infant and preschool children tend to respond to stress through defensive responses (e.g., crying) or seeking comfort from caretakers (Goodyer, 1988).

In middle childhood, as the child begins to interact with society, the major sources of stress expand to include school, peers, and neighborhood. Cognitive abilities are more advanced and marked by a greater sense of inquiry and exploration of the world. This curiosity and risk taking brings about the desire for mastery of tasks and also the accompanying chance of failure which can become a source of stress to children. Parents continue to play an important role as they help children to understand the world so that the child can gain a sense of control over stressful situations (Chandler & Shermis, 1990). Peer relationships grow in importance and conflicts with peers are viewed as particularly stressful (Phillips, 1993). At this developmental level as with all subsequent ones, gender differences must be considered for a better understanding of the impact of stress on children. In several studies of younger children, boys have been found to be more vulnerable than girls with respect to stress caused by hospital admission, birth of a sibling, parental discord or divorce, and day care (Rutter, 1983). After puberty, this trend reverses itself and females appear to become more vulnerable to the effects of stress (Brooks-Gunn, 1991). In middle childhood, individuals tend to respond to stress through affective expression (e.g., sadness, anger) and behavioral expression (e.g., disruptiveness, school refusal; Goodyer, 1988).

A frequently ignored transition in the individual life cycle is the move from late childhood into early adolescence. The individual typically moves to a new school and, during early adolescence, begins to experience major body and hormonal changes. These social transitions combined with physical changes have been shown to adversely impact psychological variables such as self-esteem and self-efficacy, and these adverse effects appear more evident with females (Blyth, Simmons, & Bush, 1978). This period represents a particularly vulnerable time as longitudinal research clearly demonstrates that youngsters who encounter multiple simultaneous life changes in early adolescence are more likely to experience emotional and behavioral disturbances (e.g., Compas, Howell, Phares, Williams, & Giunta, 1989; Simmons, Burgeson, Carlton-Ford, & Blyth, 1987). Students undergoing school change, puberty, and onset of dating at the same time are more likely to show declines in self-esteem, reduced school performance, and diminished participation in extracurricular activities. Females, in particular, may be vulnerable to the effects of stress as they are required to cope with puberty and its associated social and emotional roller coaster of events at an earlier age than boys. Thus, it is not surprising that females experience self-competency problems and are more likely to report a negative mood as they enter adolescence (Brooks-Gunn, 1991; Miller & Kirsch, 1987).

Although the traditional perspective of "storm and stress" during adolescence is not as readily accepted as it once was, this earlier emphasis did highlight the simultaneous stressors experienced by adolescents (Hauser & Bowlds, 1990). Indeed, children tend to experience a greater number of life-change units with increasing age, peaking at about age 16 (Forman, 1993). Furthermore, Larson and Ham (1993) found that the higher rates of distress associated with adolescence are likely related to the greater number of negative life events experienced by these youth. Preadolescents tend to experience significantly fewer negative stressors than early adolescents. Thus, adolescents are facing not only more stressors but also more negative life events. It is a time of extreme change—physiologically, socially, emotionally, and cognitively—presenting a period of rapid transitions.

As adolescents progress toward adulthood, their dependence on the family continues to decrease and the influence of peers is paramount. For older adolescents, the biological changes that impact early adolescents have largely subsided, and cognitive growth is nearly complete. Concurrently, ego development and identity take place as the adolescent grows toward adult status. As adolescents progress through subsequent developmental stages, they begin to internalize the rules of social interaction, become increasingly aware of their own cognitive complexity, develop an ability to tolerate ambiguity, and develop more objective reasoning (Hauser & Bowlds, 1990). These changes allow adolescents to exert greater control over their perceptions of stress and to regulate their resulting actions. Older adolescents generally possess a broader range of coping strategies, especially problem-solving ones, and their chosen coping strategies are generally closer to those of adults than those of children (Hauser & Bowlds, 1990).

Cultural Perspective

Like gender, cultural background affects an individual's perception of, and reaction to, stressful life events (Newcomb, Huba, & Bentler, 1986; Phinney, Lochner, & Murphy, 1990). In a study of the impact of life change events with adolescents, Newcomb et al. (1986) reported ethnic differences between Hispanic and Black adolescents in their perceptions of stressfulness. Although tentative, these results suggest that youth from diverse cultural backgrounds may differ in their perceptions of stress. Not only can minority youth face chronic stressors such as cultural conflicts, negative stereotypes, and disadvantaged status, but they also can experience additional stress due to developmental changes and their ethnic status (Phinney et al., 1990).

For culturally diverse youth, ethnicity comprises a central component of the quest for identity, and it presents difficult, sometimes overwhelming challenges (Phinney, 1989). As minority youth shift their identification from family to peer group during late childhood and adolescence, ethnic identity becomes especially salient as peers begin to have more impact on self-evaluation than does the family. Among individuals from culturally diverse backgrounds, some adolescents face complex psy-

chological issues in relation to their ethnicity because of their developmental level and broader range of experiences in school and the community (Phinney et al., 1990). For example, adolescents are becoming more sensitive to feedback, both positive and negative, from the social environment at a time when they are also trying to develop a healthy sense of identity as an individual and as a member of a particular ethnic or cultural group. Ethnic identity (defined as a sense of belonging and positive attitudes toward one's membership in an ethnic group) has been shown to be related to positive self-concept, a greater sense of mastery over the environment, and more positive family and peer relationships (Phinney, 1989; Phinney, Chavira, & Williamson, 1992).

Social-Cognitive Perspective

One of the most important tasks of adolescence is the development of one's own identity. According to Erikson's (1968) theory, a stable sense of ego identity creates a foundation for effectively adapting to the unpredictable changes of life. In their work, Hauser and Bowlds (1990) have outlined four developmental paths or profiles of adolescent ego development which is defined as "differing psychosocial stages through which an adolescent progresses" (p. 399). Each profile type identifies the base level of ego development for individuals in early adolescence and characterizes their progression, or stability, in development throughout high school. These developmental paths represent the profile of stages that the adolescent demonstrates over a period of several years.

The earliest stage of ego development as conceptualized by Hauser and Bowlds (1990) is the preconformist stage. It is characterized by those young teens who are still highly dependent on parents, are basically unaware of differences between self and others, engage in either/or thinking, and have relationships with peers and adults marked by manipulation or exploitation. Many of the stressors at this stage result from the adolescent's relatively poor adaptive skills and family conflicts. Generally, this stage is not considered problematic unless the adolescent continues to display this form of development for 2 years or more, at which point the individual's development is considered to be *severely arrested*. Another path, the conformist stage of ego development, is characterized by an intense concern with peer acceptance and conformity. This emphasis can create major stress in the life of an adolescent because of the accompanying pressure to experiment with risky behaviors such as drug and alcohol use, sex, and reckless driving. If the adolescent does not advance to a higher stage, they are referred to as following the *steady conformist* path.

The more advanced stages of ego development are also referred to as the postconformist stages. The third path is referred to as *accelerated* ego development and is characterized by increasing autonomy of thought and action, an emphasis on inner standards, and an interest in forming mutual relationships with others. Finally, those adolescents who demonstrate *progressive* ego development transition from earlier preconformist or conformist stages to the more advanced postconformist stages of ego development. For example, an adolescent who began at the earliest stage of ego development but then advanced to conformist and then a postconformist level would be considered to have progressive ego development.

As adolescents advance through these psychological ego stages, they develop greater cognitive abilities to understand and tolerate diversity, complexity, and incongruities of life. Successful progression through these stages seems to be related to a broader range of coping skills to life's stressors (Hauser & Bowlds, 1990). These characteristics are likely related to the individual's development of a sense of self-efficacy, a perception that one can handle life's stressors. Bandura's (1977) self-efficacy theory postulates that high self-efficacy is associated with greater motivation and effort, while low self-efficacy is related to decreased initiative or output of energy.

The relationship between positive self-view and self-efficacy is an important concept to teach children and adolescents in dealing with stress. This connection is especially a concern with females who tend to develop a negative self-view soon after entering middle school (Brooks-Gunn, 1991; Miller & Kirsch, 1987). This negative self-view is limiting and potentially inhibits individuals from believing they have the ability and self-reliance necessary for successful stress management. Left unattended, these negative biases may perpetuate problem behaviors and depression as the adolescent grows older. Some research indicates that females tend to amplify negative moods and generalize failure more than males. For example, Dweck, Goetz, and Strauss (1980) found that girls tended to base their expectations of future performance more on past or current failures rather than past or current successes whereas boys' expectations of future performance did not seem to be negatively affected by present or past failures. Furthermore, in a series of experiments with children, girls tended to attribute failure to internal, stable factors such as lack of ability, while boys tended to attribute failure to external factors such as the teacher or to unstable factors such as effort (e.g., Dweck & Goetz, 1978). Similar studies have not been able to replicate these gender effects (e.g., Diener & Dweck, 1980; Licht & Dweck, 1984); thus, these results must be considered with caution. However, these negative expectations may contribute to a skewed self-esteem and lead to lowered persistence and avoidance of previously failed tasks. This cognitive pattern could be especially harmful in relation to managing stressful experiences.

A related concept, locus of control—or an individual's perception of control over a certain event or situation—is also important to consider in relation to stress. Internal control credits agency to oneself, which is a critical aspect of coping, whereas external control gives agency to others or fate, which is thought to contribute to a sense of helplessness. Werner and Smith (1982) identified both internal locus of control and positive self-concept as two protective factors important in ameliorating the risk associated with stress. The relationship between these two factors and more positive outcomes was most apparent in those individuals experiencing the greatest amount of stress. In a group of adolescents who had not experienced a great deal of stress, these factors did not discriminate resilient individuals from those with poor outcomes.

The most recent social-cognitive perspective to be advanced has been broadly labeled by Goleman (1995) as *emotional intelligence*. Drawing from neuroscience and cognitive-behavioral research, Goleman defined emotional intelligence as self-knowledge, impulse control, persistence, zeal and optimism, empathy, and social competence. Repeatedly he demonstrates that those with lower emotional intelligence are not well equipped to handle stress in their lives, whereas those with high emotional intelligence possess the qualities of people who excel in the real world. The downside of Goleman's emotional intelligence is its breadth; it is a "construct" with a great deal of face validity but it offers few of the specific application ideas one can derive from the efficacy literature cited earlier. However, the optimistic aspect of Goleman's message is that emotional intelligence can be taught, nurtured, and strengthened.

Problems and Implications

Stress can take many forms and have an infinite number of sources in the life of an individual. Most of the studies described have addressed normative stresses, those considered to be a part of life for almost any child or adolescent. Daily stressors or hassles in life are considered to be a source of normative stress as are some major life events such as graduating from high school because these major yet normal events can cause stress in the life of a young person. Additional consideration must be given to those nonnormative stressors, or risk factors, which increase the likelihood of maladaptive outcomes. These risk factors might include divorce, marital discord, loss or separation from either parent, child abuse, foster care, a paternal record of criminality, or complications of chronic illness.

From a broader social perspective, nonnormative environmental stressors within which the family system is embedded, including socioeconomic status and diverse ethnic background, exert complex challenges and strains on the family and child. Today it is estimated that 22% of American children live in poverty (Sherman, 1994); these conditions contribute heavily to the adverse life experiences of many minority children and adolescents. Among specific populations, poverty runs as high as 54% among children in single-parent homes, 40% among Hispanic children, and 47% among Black children (Sherman). The constant stress or strain that accompanies poverty can gradually weaken a family system by diminishing the ability of parents to provide warmth, guidance, and consistent discipline for their children (Sherman). Children who live in impoverished households experience stress both directly and indirectly. They face their parents' frustration and tension caused by daily hassles such as paying bills, threatened loss of welfare or unemployment payments, child-care dilemmas, and transportation needs. So too, the more direct stressors related to violence, insufficient medical care, and inadequate housing and nutrition negatively impact children. The impact of poverty is so pervasive that Sherman concluded, "in sum, poverty forces children to fight a many-front war simultaneously, often without the armors of stable families, adequate health care and schooling, or safe and nurturing communities" (p. xvii).

Of particular concern is the wave of violence impacting today's youth. Indeed, violence has become an undeniable part of the lives of many children and adolescents (Singer, Menden Anglin, Song, & Lunghofer, 1995). A recent survey of 3,735 adolescents from two large cities, a smaller midwestern city, and a midwestern suburb indicated that anywhere from 0.5% to 33.4%, depending on their geographic location, reported having been shot at or shot. These figures nearly doubled when students were asked whether they had witnessed such an event, 4.7% to 62.2%, respectively (Singer et al., 1995). The rate of violent victimization among 12- to 19-year-olds is twice that of adults over the age of 25 years (Bureau of Justice Statistics, 1992). As a result, many of our youth live the daily stress of fear. About 24% of Black students in central cities and 18% of the White students feared being attacked going to and from school (Bureau of Justice Statistics, 1991).

Violence is not isolated to the neighborhood or school but is often found in the homes of children and adolescents. In fact, the Singer et al. (1995) study indicated that female adolescents were more likely to be exposed to violence, including sexual abuse/assault, in their homes than in the community. For example, in the suburban area investigated in this study, 34.2% females reported being slapped, hit, or punched at home; only 13.7% reported being a victim of this type of abuse at school and 2.6% in the neighborhood.

These grim statistics are of special concern because research has demonstrated that exposure to violent events can result in lasting symptoms of stress (e.g., Singer et al., 1995; Wallen, 1993). When enough of these symptoms (e.g., recurrent distressing dreams and/or recollections of the event, irritability or outbursts of anger, feelings of detachment from others, restricted range of affect) occur in combination and persist for at least a month, an individual may be diagnosed as suffering from post-traumatic stress disorder (PTSD). Certain variables such as actual physical proximity to the violence, knowing the victim, and previous exposure to violence are factors that increase the likelihood that a child will experience PTSD symptoms (Pynoos et al., 1987). Age or developmental level is also an important factor to consider. Children under the age of 11 seem to be more vulnerable to PTSD than older children and adolescents (Davidson & Smith, 1990). School psychologists, because of their ability to impact large numbers of individuals, hold a key position in helping schools, families, and youth to successfully manage the stress of sometimes overwhelming normative events (e.g., puberty, school transition) and to provide support and intervention in response to the nonnormative stressors (e.g., violence, poverty) that are so prevalent in today's society.

Alternative Actions

Over the last 25 years, researchers have begun to recognize the value in studying factors that enable youth to be resistant to stressors. Alternative actions directed toward helping youth with problems related to stress might focus on creating conditions which help all children and adolescents to be more resilient. Forman (1993) noted that because of their access to virtually the entire child population at an early age, schools have the potential to effect major positive changes in children and adolescents by providing preventive interventions as part of the curriculum. The school environment teaches, prepares, and promotes a "safe" environment in which adolescents may experience trials and errors in preparation for adulthood. Furthermore, school personnel can provide social support in the form of emotional support, informational guidance, and tangible assistance. In particular, the school psychologist can consult with other school professionals to help design school-wide stress-prevention and management programs. These efforts should focus on helping all children successfully meet the challenge of stressful life events. In addition to prevention, schools must also offer intervention programs that include training in coping skills and in social interactions for those students experiencing short-term or intermittent stressors and, for those students who are most vulnerable, strategies which develop the resiliency of these youth through multifaceted resource development.

Preventative Actions

Emphasis on affective training with children and the development of their emotional intelligence seems imperative. Goleman (1995) noted, from the Head Start literature, the following emotional and social measures as predictors of early school success: "being self-assured and interested; knowing what kind of behavior is expected and how to rein in the impulse to misbehave; being able to wait, to follow directions, and to turn to teachers for help; and expressing needs while getting along with other children" (p. 193). Learning emotional expression may allow students to examine the importance of understanding and releasing intense feelings in appropriate ways. Allowing students opportunities to learn real-life problem solving will allow them an opportunity to resolve conflict situations and develop a repertoire of skills to use in similar situations. Not only knowledge of the "feeling" words but also an emphasis on knowing themselves, knowing others, and effective interaction skills must be a part of any training program.

Students need to feel included in the microcosm of their reality—school. Cooperative learning arrangements allow students to participate as partners in classroom experiences and help them develop leadership and teamwork skills. In the classroom, a majority of studies of cooperative learning techniques such as Jigsaw II, Teams-Games-Tournaments (TGT), and Student Team Achievement Divisions (STAD) have found positive effects on some aspect of self-esteem (see Slavin, 1995, for a more detailed description of these programs). In addition, there is some evidence to suggest that cooperative learning methods make students feel that they have a chance to succeed and that their efforts will lead to success. Slavin (1995) supports the idea that students' believing they are valuable and important individuals is of critical importance in their ability to be resilient to stress, to be effective problem solvers, and to be happy and productive members of society. As adolescents' cognitive abilities develop, they begin to observe and evaluate themselves relative to their peers. If this introspection brings disappointing results, a student's self-esteem may suffer, resulting in a belief system that may be inaccurate and lead to more stress. In order to evaluate themselves as worthwhile, children and adolescents must be given the opportunity for success. Another possibility is to provide additional opportunities for mastery in extracurricular activities and equal opportunities for students to secure positions of responsibility in school clubs, by tutoring other students, or the like.

Coping-Skills Training

Some researchers believe that the thoughts and behaviors associated with coping can be modified educationally and/or therapeutically. Teaching coping skills beginning with young children and continuing through early and late adolescence presents a potentially significant method of preventing and/or modifying dysfunctional or maladaptive behaviors. In the life of a child or adolescent, many events occur that are perceived as uncertain, novel, perhaps threatening, and most certainly important. Each of these events can lead to a perception or feeling of stress. In response to these stressful feelings, individuals are forced to develop coping skills. Ineffective coping skills can lead to a life of disorganization and distress.

According to Lazarus and Folkman (1984), there are two basic types of coping: emotion-focused and problem-focused. Some individuals try to cope with stressful events by managing the tension. This approach is considered emotion-focused coping and often includes attempts to alleviate stress by ventilating feelings, denial, distraction, and avoiding the situation(s) that caused it. Emotion-focused coping is often seen as less effective because it treats the symptom rather than the cause (Hauser & Bowlds, 1990; Patterson & McCubbin, 1987). Problem-focused coping involves taking some direct action to either reduce the demands of a stressor that poses a threat or to increase one's inner resources. An example might be creating a plan or strategy for completing a difficult project. A third type of coping identified by Patterson and McCubbin (1987) is called appraisal-oriented coping where an individual copes with stressful events by redefining the stress into manageable demands. Examples might include attempts to make light of a situation by being humorous or re-evaluating the perceived severity of a situation. The latter two methods of coping are considered more effective because they generate solutions or alter one's perception of the stressor. In general, avoidance is associated with high symptomatology, whereas active efforts such as positive cognitive restructuring and problem-focused coping are related to lower symptoms (Kliewer, Sandler, & Wolchik, 1994). For example, Goodman, Gravitt, and Kaslow (1995) found that among children who experienced high levels of stress, those with less effective social problem-solving skills reported higher levels of depression than a similar group of children who had more effective social problem-solving skills.

In reality, however, most adolescents use an overlapping array of coping skills with a primary focus on one method over the others (Patterson & McCubbin, 1987). In support of this idea, Hauser and Bowlds (1990) stated that both emotion-regulating and problem-solving coping strategies are used in nearly all stressful situations. Furthermore, developmental, gender, and ethnic differences may also impact coping choices. Younger children tend to use more problem-focused strategies than older children; thus, it is not until children are older that they begin to use emotion-focused strategies (Wertlieb, Weigel, & Feldstein, 1987). In general, research indicates that female adolescents use social support as a strategy more often than male adolescents; males use humor or engaging in physical activity as a coping strategy more often than do females (Copeland & Hess, 1995; Patterson & McCubbin, 1987). An individual's ethnic background can impact the use of coping strategies as well. For example, among an early adolescent population, Hispanics reported using social support strategies and spiritual support more often than did Whites (Copeland & Hess, 1995).

In developing coping-skills training programs, professionals need to consider not only the variables that impact coping-strategy choices but also the developmental tasks facing the child or adolescent. For example, it would be especially important to train students in effective coping strategies prior to entry into middle school or junior high as these school transitions are stressful for students. Furthermore, training in coping skills is not an inoculation; that is, once a student is trained he or she is not prepared for life. Coping-skills training must take place over several different developmental stages with increasing information and opportunities for practice occurring over the course of a student's educational career. For the most effective results, coping-skills training should be offered in conjunction with social-skills training and affective education to help the student develop a variety of effective responses to stressful events. So too, students must be provided ample opportunities and support for the application of these newfound skills.

Developing Resiliency in Vulnerable Youth

Some youth come to school with a number of risk factors impacting their lives. However, it is believed that certain constitutional and environmental factors can help these children be more resistant or resilient to the effects of the negative stressors. Specific traits related to individual personality, social environment, and family have been linked to resilience in children and adolescents. The characteristics that relate to resiliency may not remain static across different developmental levels. For example, Werner and Smith (1982) reported that constitutional factors such as health and temperament were most influential during infancy and early childhood; problem-solving and communication skills and alternative care-takers played a major role in middle childhood; and intrapersonal factors were most important in adolescence. Although some aspects of resiliency may be traits that cannot be changed with intervention, other basic characteristics of resiliency (e.g., social skills, social support, problem-solving skills) may be used as an organizing framework for various intervention strategies to help vulnerable young people to effectively meet the demands of their stressful environments.

Social-cognitive factors

A positive sense of self, or a sense of personal power to exercise a degree of control over the environment, is one of the personality variables associated with resiliency. According to Forman (1993), programs focusing on the development of social-cognitive problem solving are among the most frequently used and best developed programs for social enhancement and emotional competence. Affective curricula can be introduced to teach students how negative thoughts can actually contribute to their own perceptions of stress. Positive self-talk and methods for cognitive restructuring can also be taught to help students develop an effective buffer against stress. To cope with the physiological aspects of stress, children and adolescents can be taught relaxation techniques. These exercises can be used at home or school to release pent-up stress and muscle tension.

Teaching children and adolescents how to reduce stressful thought patterns focuses on changing the appraisal of the stressor. Accurate perception is an important element in responding appropriately. Decreasing irrational beliefs may have a positive effect on the perception of, and the response to, a perceived stress. Teaching students a rational-emotive approach to problem solving gives them additional tools to use in their repertoire of coping skills (Forman, 1993). Similarly, stress-inoculation training is a structured approach to helping individuals learn to deal with stressful situations through cognitive-behavioral procedures (Forman, 1993). Although the results of recent research are mixed, evidence exists to suggest that many of the strategies associated with stress-inoculation training such as progressive muscle relaxation, anxiety management, cognitive restructuring, and assertiveness training are helpful in reducing state and trait anxiety and stress-related symptoms in adolescents (e.g., Hains, 1992; Kiselica, Baker, Thomas, & Reedy, 1994). Finally, attribution retraining can be used to teach students to see and internalize the direct relationship between effort and success and to reduce their sense of hopelessness or learned helplessness in the face of stressful situations (Forman, 1993).

An example of a program that includes many of these components is the Improving Social Awareness-Social Problem Solving Project (ISA) described by Elias and Clabby (1992). This program consists of a curriculum that provides training in social problem-solving readiness and critical thinking skills at the elementary-school level. Preventative efforts are directed at the secondary level at specific problem areas, such as substance abuse and suicide. Teachers are taught to incorporate ISA approaches into the academic curriculum, extracurricular activities, study skills, and discipline. Parents are also involved as skill elicitors and home trainers. Because the program provides a multicomponent, multilevel approach to helping children to deal with stress, the chances for success are increased. Evidence is presented by Elias and Clabby (1992) which supports the use of this program in different applications (e.g. elementary school, middle school transition) with positive longitudinal results in various areas of social decision making (e.g., problem-solving concepts, prosocial behavior, coping skills).

Social factors

It appears that social support can reduce the negative impact of stress on health and social functioning for children (e.g., Wertlieb, Weigel, & Feldstein, 1987) and adolescents. Other researchers have endorsed the importance of social support in the development of effective coping skills and resiliency to life events and believe that social support interventions hold great promise in working with adolescents (e.g., Gottlieb, 1991). However, Grannis (1992) cautioned that social support can only temporarily reduce stress unless it is accompanied by an increased sense of control over the stressful event. Thus, to deal effectively and constructively with other people, children and adolescents must learn problem-solving techniques that facilitate productive social interaction and allow them to generate an active solution to their problems. Schools also must provide a positive environment which allows numerous opportunities for children and adolescents to be involved constructively with others.

Family factors
During childhood and early adolescence, the parent is still considered the primary social support of a child and should be recruited as a key player in a stress-management program. Families can impact stress and coping efforts in a number of fundamental ways by meeting basic psychological needs, influencing self-esteem, shaping values, controlling exposure to stressful events, and providing support. Adaptive responses to stress are enhanced by the provision of a warm, supportive, predictable, cohesive, and communicative family environment (Kliewer et al., 1994). School psychologists can provide parents with educational and support groups that may affect the efficacy of their coping strategies and help them to model effective behaviors, attitudes, and stress-management techniques to their children. Coaching, in which parents directly instruct children on how to appraise stressful events, suggest specific actions, and reinforce subsequent coping behavior can also influence how children perceive stressful situations (Kliewer et al., 1994).

An adequate identification figure does not necessarily have to originate within the family. Resilient adolescents have been found to have extensive contacts outside the immediate family with concerned and caring ministers, teachers, older friends, and peers (Hauser, Vieyra, Jacobson, & Westlieb, 1985; Werner & Smith, 1982). This information highlights the role that caring educational personnel can serve in the life of a child.

Summary

Helping today's youth develop necessary and effective strategies for dealing with the unavoidable stresses encountered in life will ultimately create adults who have the skills and necessary psychological resources to cope with life. It is unrealistic to think children and adolescents can be sheltered from stressors. Rather it is more positive

to view stressful experiences as helping the individual to develop effective coping strategies, increase personal resources, and lead to a sense of mastery and competence in social development. Those individuals who have been taught emotional awareness as well as a variety of effective coping strategies stand a much greater chance of success in the world of business, family and personal relationships, and social interactions. The more skills an individual has, the greater the possibility of successful maneuvering through life with a minimum of distress and heartache. The necessity of enhancing coping skills has considerable potential for educators, researchers, childcare advocates, parents, and others concerned about the health and future status of our world.

Recommended Resources

Professionals

Elias, M. J., & Clabby, J. F. (1992). *Building social problem-solving skills: Guidelines from a school-based program.* San Francisco: Jossey-Bass.
The authors have created a comprehensive, practical guide for the development of a social decision-making and problem-solving skills program that can be implemented in the schools. Their approach emphasizes a complete understanding of the child, his or her school environment, and the collaboration needed between different areas.

Forman, S. G. (1993). *Coping skills interventions for children and adolescents.* San Francisco: Jossey-Bass.
Forman's work describes specific intervention strategies geared toward helping children and adolescents cope with stress. Any one of these approaches could be used as part of a more comprehensive plan or several of them used together to create a customized program for particular grade levels or schools.

Phillips, B. N. (1993). *Educational and psychological perspectives on stress in students, teachers, and parents.* Brandon, VT: Clinical Psychology.
After extensive review of the field of stress in children and adolescence, Phillips has created a useful, comprehensive book addressing stress as it applies to the educational system. He includes chapters on stress in teachers and parents as well which is consistent with the ecological perspective of this book.

Parents

Mendler, A. N. (1990). *Smiling at yourself: Educating young children about stress and self-esteem.* Santa Cruz, CA: Network Publications.
This easy-to-read paperback, designed for children under the age of 10, is filled with suggestions and activities for teachers and parents in helping them to educate children on feelings and reactions to stressful events.

References

Albee, G. (1982). Preventing psychopathology and promoting human potential. *American Psychologist, 37,* 1043–1050.

Armacost, R. L. (1989). Perceptions of stressors by high school students. *Journal of Adolescent Research, 4,* 443–461.

Bandura, A. (1977). *Social learning theory.* Englewood Cliffs, NJ: Prentice-Hall.

Barr, R. G., Boyce, W. T., & Zeltzer, L. K. (1994). The stress-illness association in children: A perspective from the biobehavioral interface. In R. J. Haggerty, L. R. Sherrod, N. Garmezy, & M. Rutter (Eds.), *Stress, risk, and resilience in children and adolescents: Processes, mechanisms, and interventions* (pp. 182–224). New York: Cambridge University Press.

Blocker, L. S., & Copeland, E. P. (1994). Determinants of resilience in high-stressed youth. *The High School Journal, 77,* 286–293.

Blyth, D. A., & Simmons, R. G., & Bush, D. (1978). The transition into early adolescence: A longitudinal compression of youth in two educational contexts. *Sociology of Education, 51,* 149–162.

Brooks-Gunn, J. (1991). How stressful is the transition to adolescence for girls? In M. E. Colten & S. Gore (Eds.), *Adolescent stress: Causes and consequences* (pp. 131–149). New York: Aldine de Gruyter.

Bureau of Justice Statistics. (1991). *School crime, 1991.* Washington, DC: U.S. Department of Justice. (Publication NCJ-131645)

Bureau of Justice Statistics. (1992). *Criminal victimization in the United States, 1992.* Washington, DC: U.S. Department of Justice. (Publication NCJ-144776)

Chandler, L. A., & Shermis, M. D. (1990). A paradigm for the study of childhood stress. In J. H. Humphrey (Ed.), *Human stress: Current selected research,* (Vol. 4, pp. 111–124). New York: AMS Press.

Coddington, R. D. (1972). The significance of life events as etiologic factors in the diseases of children: Vol. 2. A study of a normal population. *Journal of Psychosomatic Research, 16,* 205–213.

Compas, B. E. (1987). Stress and life events during childhood and adolescence. *Clinical Psychology Review, 7,* 275–302.

Compas, B. E., Davis, G. E., Forsythe, C. J., & Wagner, B. M. (1987). Assessment of major and daily stressful events during adolescence: The Adolescent Perceived Events Scale. *Journal of Consulting and Clinical Psychology, 55,* 534–541.

Compas, B. E., Howell, D. C., Phares, V., Williams, R. A., & Giunta, C. T. (1989). Risk factors for emotional/behavioral problems in young adolescents: A prospective analysis of adolescent and parental stress and symptoms. *Journal of Consulting and Clinical Psychology, 57,* 732–740.

Copeland, E. P., & Hess, R. S. (1995). Differences in young adolescents' coping strategies based on gender and ethnicity. *Journal of Early Adolescence, 15,* 203–219.

Davidson, J., & Smith, R. (1990). Traumatic experiences in psychiatric outpatients. *Journal of Traumatic Stress Studies, 3,* 459–475.

Diener, C. I., & Dweck, C. S. (1980). An analysis of learned helplessness: Vol. 2. The processing of success. *Journal of Personality and Social Psychology, 39,* 940–952.

Dohrenwend, B. S., & Dohrenwend, B. P. (1978). Some issues in research on stressful life events. *Journal of Nervous and Mental Disease, 166,* 7–15.

Dweck, C. S., & Goetz, T. E. (1978). Attributions and learned helplessness. In J. H. Harvey, W. Ickes, & R. F. Kidd (Eds.), *New directions in attribution research,* (Vol. 2, pp. 157–179). Hillsdale, NJ: Lawrence Erlbaum.

Dweck, C. S., Goetz, T. E., & Strauss, N. L. (1980). Sex differences in learned helplessness: Vol. 4. An experimental and naturalistic study of failure generalization and its mediators. *Journal of Personality and Social Psychology, 38,* 441–452.

Elias, M. J., & Clabby, J. F. (1992). *Building social problem-solving skills: Guidelines from a school-based program.* San Francisco: Jossey-Bass.

Erikson, E. H. (1968). *Identity, youth, and crisis.* New York: Norton.

Forman, S. G. (1993). Coping skills interventions for children and adolescents. San Francisco: Jossey-Bass.

Fox, N. A. (1992). Frontal brain symmetry and vulnerability to stress: Individual differences in infant temperament. In T. M. Fields, P. M. McCabe, & N. Schneiderman (Eds.), *Stress and coping in infancy and childhood* (pp. 83–100). Hillsdale, NJ: Lawrence Erlbaum.

Garmezy, N. (1987). Stress, competence, and development: Continuities in the study of schizophrenic adults, children vulnerable to psychopathology, and the search for stress-resistant children. *American Journal of Orthopsychiatry, 57,* 159–174.

Goleman, D. (1995). *Emotional intelligence.* New York: Bantam.

Goodman, S. H., Gravitt, G. W., & Kaslow, N. J. (1995). Social problem solving: A moderator of the relations between negative life stress and depression symptoms in children. *Journal of Abnormal Child Psychology, 23,* 473–485.

Goodyer, I. M. (1988). Stress in childhood and adolescence. In S. Fisher & J. Reason (Eds.), *Handbook of life stress, cognition and health* (pp. 23–40). New York: John Wiley & Sons.

Gottlieb, B. H. (1991). Social support in adolescence. In M. E. Colten & S. Gore (Eds.), *Adolescent stress: Causes and consequences* (pp. 281–306). New York: Aldine de Gruyter.

Grannis, J. C. (1992). Students' stress, distress, and achievement in an urban intermediate school. *Journal of Early Adolescence, 12,* 4–27.

Hains, A. A. (1992). A stress inoculation training program for adolescents in a high school setting: A multiple baseline approach. *Journal of Adolescence, 15,* 163–175.

Ham, M., & Larson, R. (1990). The cognitive moderation of daily stress in early adolescence. *American Journal of Community Psychology, 18,* 567–585.

Hauser, S. T., & Bowlds, M. K. (1990). Stress, coping, and adaptation. In S. S. Feldman & G. R. Elliot (Eds.), *At the threshold: The developing adolescent* (pp. 388–413). Cambridge, MA: Harvard University Press.

Hauser, S. T., Vieyra, M. A. B., Jacobson, A. M., & Wertlieb, D. (1985). Vulnerability and resilience in adolescence:

Views from the family. *Journal of Early Adolescence, 5,* 81–100.

Holmes, T. H., & Rahe, R. H. (1967). The Social Readjustment Rating Scale. *Journal of Psychosomatic Research, 11,* 213–218.

Kiselica, M. S., Baker, S. B., Thomas, R. N., & Reedy, S. (1994). Effects of stress inoculation training on anxiety, stress, and academic performance among adolescents. *Journal of Counseling Psychology, 41,* 335–342.

Kliewer, W., Sandler, I., & Wolchik, S. (1994). Family socialization of threat appraisal and coping: Coaching, modeling, and family context. In F. Nestmann & K. Hurrelman (Eds.), *Social networks and social support in childhood and adolescence* (pp. 271–292). New York: Walter de Gruyter.

Larson, R., & Ham, M. (1993). Stress and "Storm and Stress" in early adolescence: The relationship of negative events with dysphoric affect. *Developmental Psychology, 29,* 130–140.

Lazarus, R. S., & Cohen, J. B. (1977). Environmental stress. In I. Altman & J. F. Wohlwill (Eds.), *Human behavior and the environment,* (Vol. 2, pp. 89–127). New York: Plenum.

Lazarus, R. S., & Delongis, A. (1983). Psychological stress and coping in aging. *American Psychologist, 38,* 245–254.

Lazarus, R. S., & Folkman, S. (1984). *Stress, appraisal, and coping.* New York: Springer.

Licht, B. G., & Dweck, C. S. (1984). Determinants of academic achievement: The interaction of children's achievement orientations with skill area. *Developmental Psychology, 20,* 628–636.

Maier, S. F., Watkins, L. R., & Fleshner, M. (1994). Psychoneuroimmunology: The interface between behavior, brain, and immunity. *American Psychologist, 49,* 1004–1017.

Miller, S. M., & Kirsch, N. (1987). Sex differences in cognitive coping with stress. In R. C. Barnett, L. Biener, & G. K. Baruch (Eds.), *Gender and stress* (pp. 278–307). New York: The Free Press.

Newcomb, M. D., Huba, G. J., & Bentler, P. M. (1986). Desirability of various life change events among adolescents: Effects of exposure, sex, age, and ethnicity. *Journal of Research in Personality, 20,* 207–227.

Patterson, J. M., & McCubbin, H. I. (1987). Adolescent coping style and behaviors: Conceptualization and measurement. *Journal of Adolescence, 10,* 163–186.

Phillips, B. N. (1993). *Educational and psychological perspectives on stress in students, teachers, and parents.* Brandon, VT: Clinical Psychology.

Phinney, J. S. (1989). Stages of ethnic identity development in minority group adolescents. *Journal of Early Adolescence, 9,* 34–49.

Phinney, J. S., Chavira, V., & Williamson, L. (1992). Acculturation attitudes and self-esteem among high school and college students. *Youth and Society, 23,* 299–312.

Phinney, J. S., Lochner, B. T., & Murphy, R. (1990). Ethnic identity development and psychological adjustment in adolescence. In A. R. Stiffman & L. E. Davis (Eds.), *Ethnic issues in adolescent mental health* (pp. 53–72). Newbury Park, CA: Sage.

Pynoos, R. S., Frederick, C., Nader, K., Arroyo, W., Steinberg, A., Eth, S., Nunez, F., & Fairbanks, L. (1987). Life threat and posttraumatic stress in school-aged children. *Archives of General Psychiatry, 44,* 1057–1063.

Rice, F. P. (1996). *The adolescent: Development, relationships, and culture* (8th ed.). Boston: Allyn & Bacon.

Rutter, M. (1983). Stress, coping, and development: Some issues and some questions. In N. Garmezy & M. Rutter (Eds.), *Stress, coping, and development in children* (pp. 1–41). New York: McGraw-Hill.

Selye, H. (1956). *The stress of life.* New York: McGraw-Hill.

Selye, H. (1993). History of the stress concept. In L. Goldberger & S. Breznitz (Eds.), *Handbook of stress: Theoretical and clinical aspects* (pp. 7–17). New York: The Free Press.

Sherman, A. (1994). *Wasting America's future: The Children's Defense Fund report on the costs of child poverty.* Boston: Beacon Press.

Simmons, R. G., Burgeson, R., Carlton-Ford, S., & Blyth, D. A. (1987). The impact of cumulative change in early adolescence. *Child Development, 58,* 1220–1234.

Singer, M. I., Menden Anglin, T., Song, L., & Lunghofer, L. (1995). Adolescents' exposure to violence and associated symptoms of psychological trauma, *JAMA, 273*(6), 477–482.

Slavin, R. E. (1995). *Cooperative learning* (2nd ed.). Boston: Allyn & Bacon.

Stern, M., & Zevon, M. A. (1990). Stress, coping, and family environment: The adolescent's response to naturally occurring stressors. *Journal of Adolescent Research, 5,* 290–305.

Wallen, J. (1993). Protecting the mental health of children in dangerous neighborhoods. *Children Today, 22*(3), 24(5).

Werner, E., & Smith, R. S. (1982). *Vulnerable but invincible: A study of resilient children.* New York: McGraw-Hill.

Wertlieb, D., Weigel, C., & Feldstein, M. (1987). Stress, social support, and behavior symptoms in middle childhood. *Journal of Clinical Child Psychology, 16,* 204–211.

Wertlieb, D., Weigel, C., & Springer, T., & Feldstein, M. (1987). Temperament as a moderator of children's stressful experiences. *American Journal or Orthopsychiatry, 57,* 234–245.

Zakowski, S., Hall, M. H., & Baum, A. (1992). Stress, stress management, and the immune system. *Applied & Preventative Psychology, 1,* 1–13.

27
Anxiety

Thomas J. Huberty
Indiana University

Background and Development

Although anxiety is a term frequently used in psychology and common parlance, it is a rather unique emotional condition because it can be viewed both positively and negatively. In a positive mode, it occurs normally in children and adults and can be used as an indicator that development is progressing at an expected rate. Anxiety also can be adaptive as it may alert a person to impending danger or threat or be a motivator to take action or perform at optimal levels. From a negative perspective, anxiety at extremely high levels may suggest the presence of emotional or behavioral difficulties that require intervention. Anxiety can exist alone or with other disorders and becomes a psychological disorder when it is at a level that personal and social functioning are impaired.

Defining Anxiety

Although anxiety is a common term and a key concept in various psychological theories (e.g., psychoanalytic perspectives), it has not received much attention in childhood research until the last several years (Kendall et al., 1992). It has been defined as "apprehension without apparent cause" (Johnson & Melamed, 1979) and also as "apprehension, tension, or uneasiness related to the expectation of danger, whether internal or external. Anxiety may be focused on an object situation or activity that is avoided, as in phobia, or it may be unfocused" (Morris & Kratochwill, 1985, p. 84). More specifically, anxiety has cognitive, behavioral, and physiological components. For the purposes of this discussion, *anxiety* is defined as apprehension, distress, or tension about real or anticipated internal or external threats that may be shown in cognitive, behavioral, or physiological patterns.

Attempts have been made to distinguish anxiety from fear by describing anxiety as apprehension about subjective phenomena or threats that do not exist (e.g., irrational concerns about contracting an incurable disease). In contrast, fear has been seen as apprehension about a known event or object (e.g., a large barking dog near a toddler). Phobias are considered to be more like fears, because the child can identify the object which promotes the fear, although the reaction may appear irrational to an adult. Upon further investigation, however, what appears to be fear of an object may only be a symptom of a more pervasive problem, which may include anxiety (e.g., separation anxiety, which will be discussed later). There is considerable overlap of behavioral symptomatology in anxiety and fear, making it difficult to differentiate the two patterns. Nevertheless, there is research evidence to suggest that anxiety disorders are reasonably definable diagnostic entities and are included in the *Diagnostic and Statistical Manual of Mental Disorders-Fourth Edition* (*DSM-IV;* American Psychiatric Association, 1994). The reader is referred to Kratochwill (this volume) who provides an excellent discussion of fears and phobias in childhood.

The Components of Anxiety

Anxiety has three components which may be shown in varying degrees by an individual child: cognitive, behavioral, and physiological. The *cognitive* component includes difficulties with worry, concentration, memory, attention, oversensitivity, and problem solving. *Behavioral* patterns consistent with high levels of anxiety may be motor restlessness, "fidgety" behaviors, avoidance of an anxiety-producing situation, verbal statements about being "uptight," and erratic or irrational behavior. In extreme cases, actual physical flight or escape may be seen. *Physiological* manifestations may be recurrent, localized pain (e.g., stomach aches); enuresis; tics; heart palpitations; flushing of the skin; rapid heart rate; perspiration; headache; feeling "jittery"; nausea; vomiting; and muscle tension (Huberty, 1987; Huberty & Eaken, 1994; Kendall et al., 1992). The pattern and intensity of specific symptoms will vary from child to child as a function of age, experience, and coping skills. Further, different situations may create a variety of response patterns.

The cognitive components of anxiety have importance for the description, diagnosis, and intervention for anxiety problems. Extensive research has indicated that anxiety disorders involve cognitive dysfunctions in two broad categories: *cognitive distortions* and *cognitive deficiencies.* Cognitive distortions refer to the tendency to misconstrue or misperceive social and environmental events. Information processing is occurring, but it may be illogical, irrational, or otherwise distorted from the real or probable circumstances. For example, the anxious youngster may be worried that a parent going on a business trip will be in an airplane crash. Although possible, such an event is highly unlikely. The child is convinced to an irrational extent that the crash will occur, thereby distorting (overestimating) the probability of the event occurring.

Cognitive deficiencies represent the *absence* of information processing; that is, the child lacks the cognitive skills necessary to resolve a problem and cope with real or perceived threat. For example, a child may be anxious about giving a speech in class, which would be common for many children. However, the student becomes so anxious that he or she becomes almost immobilized and does not engage in problem-solving or coping strategies. The intervention implications are to help the child engage in effective cognitive processing to develop effective methods to resolve anxiety. It should be noted that a child could show both types of cognitive dysfunction, which may become the focus for differential diagnosis and intervention (Kendall et al., 1992).

A related topic in cognitive dysfunction refers to the *attributional style* of anxious children, that is, how they perceive and describe the causal nature of events. This concept is familiar to most psychologists and will not be reviewed in detail here. However, locus of control, stability, and globalness are central concepts to the nature of attributional style, with a fourth aspect being controllability, or the perceived ability to change or control perceived causes of events (Bell-Dolan & Wessler, 1994). Most of the research with regard to internalizing problems and attributional style has focused on depression; however, there tends to be considerable overlap in children between anxiety and depression. Thus, there may be similarities with regard to attributional style and anxiety. For example, a child who views failure as internal and stable could become apprehensive and seek to avoid perceived threatening situations. If anxious and depressed children do have similar attributional styles, there could be implications for better understanding of internalizing problems and interventions (Bell-Dolan & Wessler, 1994).

Anxiety as a Normal Developmental Pattern

Although anxiety may be viewed as a negative emotional condition, it is part of a normal pattern of development for all children. *Stranger anxiety* emerges at about 7 to 8 months of age, when children show increased behavioral and physiological signs of distress in the presence of strangers, such as crying, clinging to familiar adults, and withdrawal from the new person. When the stranger leaves, the child returns to normal. This pattern usually dissipates by about one year of age. Later in the second year of life, *separation anxiety* begins to emerge, as children show distress about being left by their parents or primary caretaker. As with stranger anxiety, the child often shows crying, clinging, and anger. This pattern normally has subsided by the end of the second year of life. If these patterns are shown at the expected ages, then they may be used as indicators that the child's cognitive abilities are developing as expected.

Children's normal fears and anxiety have been the focus of several studies over the last few decades. Jersild and Holmes (1935) found that preschool children showed an average of 4.6 fears, as reported by the mother. The fears shown by preschoolers are of specific objects and events (e.g., large dogs, separation from parents). Developmentally, however, specific fears and anxiety change over time, but the actual number of reported fears remains fairly stable, as old fears are replaced by new ones consistent with the child's developmental level. The normal development of fear and anxiety appears to progress from global, undifferentiated, and externalized patterns to increased differentiation, abstractness, and internalization (Kendall & Ronan, 1990). The sequence of these developmental patterns seems to be fairly constant up to adolescence, when anxiety about moral, religious, and sexual issues becomes more prominent (Miller, 1983).

A significant developmental concomitant of anxiety and its most prominent characteristic is *worry.* Worry has been defined as "an anticipatory cognitive process involving repetitive thoughts related to possible threatening outcomes and their potential consequences" (Vasey, Crnic, & Carter, 1994, p. 530). As a central component to anxiety, worry also demonstrates a predictable developmental sequence. Being able to worry requires that a child be able to anticipate a future event. At preschool and early childhood levels, children have difficulty anticipating the future and likely cannot think about more than one possibility simultaneously. At middle childhood, the ability to appreciate and consider multiple possibilities and potential negative outcomes increases the likelihood for anxiety to occur. At adolescence and beyond, the normal development of increasing abstraction, hypothetico-deductive reasoning, and metacognition contributes to the appreciation of multiple solutions to problems. The necessary condition for a child to experience worry and associated anxiety is unknown, but it is presumed that the ability to anticipate even one threatening situation could lead to anxiety (Vasey et al., 1994).

Anxiety as a Disorder

Although anxiety is a common developmental pattern and is experienced by everyone at some time, it can become problematic when it persists at high levels and contributes to problems with personal and social functioning. For the school-aged child or youth, anxiety may contribute to learning and performance problems or be present as disorders that are pervasive across a variety of settings.

In the *DSM-IV* (American Psychiatric Association, 1994) section on "Disorders First Identified in Childhood and Adolescence," only *separation anxiety disorder* (SAD) is specifically identified as emerging during childhood or adolescence. The primary characteristic of SAD is that the child has significant difficulty in separating from a primary caretaker, usually a parent and most often the mother. Separation anxiety is considered to be one of the bases for school refusal behaviors (see the chapter by Paige, this volume). Under *DSM-IV* criteria, other anxiety-related diagnoses can be given to children that also apply to adults, such as post-traumatic stress disorder (PTSD), social phobia, obsessive-compulsive disorder (OCD), and generalized anxiety disorder. (See Curry & Murphy, 1995.)

The anxiety disorders specific to children and adolescents in *DSM-IV* are very different from those presented in the *Diagnostic and Statistical Manual of Mental Disorders-Third Edition-Revised* (*DSM-III-R;* American Psychiatric Association, 1987). In *DSM-III-R, overanxious anxiety disorder* (OAD) and *avoidant anxiety disorder* (AAD) of childhood and adolescence were unique diagnostic categories. The primary characteristics of OAD were excessive worry and fearful behavior unrelated to a specific situation but tending to be pervasive. AAD was shown by marked avoidance of new situations, persons, or events and a preference for familiar surroundings. Although SAD was retained in *DSM-IV* as being unique to childhood and adolescence, OAD was subsumed under generalized anxiety disorder. Avoidant disorder was removed from the *DSM-IV* completely, in part because of the difficulty distinguishing AAD from social phobia (Kendall et al., 1992).

Incidence figures

Anxiety disorders are among the most common psychological disorders, and estimates suggest that approximately 15% of the population will experience an anxiety disorder at some point in their lives. Approximately 7.5% to 10% of children have anxiety disorders (Bernstein & Borchardt, 1991; Kashani & Orvaschel, 1990). However, that estimate may not be accurate because evidence exists that children who receive an anxiety diagnosis may receive an additional diagnosis, including disruptive behavior disorders (Last, Strauss, & Francis, 1987). In their classic Isle of Wight study, Rutter, Tizard, and Whitmore (1970) found anxiety states to be the most common in middle childhood, accounting for two-thirds of all emotional disorders. Their estimates of the frequency of anxiety disorders ranged from 2.5% to 5%. Anxiety disorders are equally represented across social class and ethnicity, although the specific symptoms and causes for the anxiety may differ.

Gender differences

Girls tend to show higher levels of anxiety on self-report measures, but the differences may be more due to boys' reluctance to admit to anxiety. A sociocultural factor may be operating, because girls' reports of anxiety are more acceptable to adults than are similar reports from boys (Harris & Ferrari, 1983; Ollendick, Matson, & Helsel, 1985). Marks (1987) notes that gender differences are of little importance for ages 10 to 11. At that time, boys' fears tend to dissipate faster than do those of girls, leaving girls to show more fear and anxiety at early adolescence. However, boys and girls may be anxious about different things. For example, Dweck and Bush (1976) reported that while girls may be more prone to anxiety about social approval from adults, boys appear more concerned about how their peers perceive or evaluate them. It may be that when social expectations are considered, "true" gender differences may be nonsignificant or minor differences may be over-emphasized.

Problems and Implications

Relationship of Anxiety to Performance, Cognitive Functioning, and Social Development

Performance and test anxiety

Although there are many reasons for poor performance in the classroom, anxiety often is not recognized as a primary factor in some children's difficulties. Anxiety about school performance to the point of being problematic is far more common than many professionals realize and has been estimated to affect as many as 10 million students in the United States (Hill, 1984). Therefore, the problem is not insignificant but may not be well recognized or properly addressed. It should be within the realm and expertise of school psychologists and other professionals to be aware of the possibility of performance or test anxiety, recognize its characteristics within the school population, and develop procedures to prevent or reduce it at the classroom and school level. For many years, psychologists and educators have been interested in the relationship of anxiety to learning and school performance. Areas that have been investigated include academic performance, task performance, cognitions during performance, and task-relevant behavior.

One of the seminal studies on test anxiety was conducted by Sarason, Lighthall, Davidson, Waite, and Ruebush (1960). They gave high-anxiety and low-anxiety students two tasks that required analytic problem-solving skills under timed (pressured) and untimed (unpressured) conditions. The high-anxiety students made fewer errors in the untimed condition. Conversely, the low-anxiety students performed better than their high-anxiety counterparts in the timed condition. Therefore, although high-anxiety students may have difficulty in pressure situations, they may perform at a higher level in unpressured situations. If that is true, then the high-anxious child may be more motivated to perform and do better if there is little pressure.

Other studies have investigated various aspects of the relationship of anxiety to performance and learning. Leibert and Morris (1967) identified two aspects of anxiety: worry (the cognitive component) and emotionality (the physiological/affective component). They found that worry is most related to cognitive and attention cues, whereas emotionality, an involuntary conditioned response, is most associated with evaluation. Worry and emotionality are hypothesized to be distinct but correlated factors in test anxiety. Worry is believed to be more strongly and negatively associated with test anxiety than is emotionality. Other studies have found similar results, with the consensus being that worry is most related to concerns about performance and one's ability to do particular tasks and accounts for the majority of the variance.

Other investigators have focused on the cognitive components of anxiety, particularly with regard to off-task thoughts. For example, Wine (1971, 1980) proposed that high- and low-anxious individuals differ in their ability to maintain their attention to tasks. While low-anxious children are attending to the task and sustaining effort, high-anxious children divide attention between the task and thoughts about how they are doing, leading to lowered performance. Many of the off-task thoughts of high-anxious children are irrelevant, self-evaluative in a negative way, and self-deprecatory (Wigfield & Eccles, 1990). Children with high levels of test anxiety tend to show debilitating off-task and self-evaluative thoughts and difficulties with task completion (Zatz & Chassin, 1985), increased attentional problems as reported by teachers (Strauss, Frame, & Forehand, 1987), and higher frequency of anxiety and phobic disorders (Beidel & Turner, 1988). This last finding suggests that if a child is identified as having test anxiety, there is a high probability of an accompanying anxiety disorder that explains the original symptoms. Therefore, the practitioner who encounters a child with test anxiety may be advised to investigate whether an anxiety disorder is present.

Test anxiety during school years

Table 1 presents some of the correlates of test or performance anxiety in children and adolescents. In general, test anxiety begins to show during the early elementary years and gradually increases during the school years to a peak during adolescence. The reasons for this anxiety are not fully understood, but high teacher and parent expectations or reactions likely play a role. As children progress through school and become exposed to evaluative situations, they learn how to evaluate feedback from parents, teachers, and peers and can form attitudes and perceptions about their ability. Consequently, it may become difficult to determine if performance problems cause anxiety or if anxiety causes performance problems. There is evidence that both causal directions exist, particularly as children continue through school and evaluation becomes more intense, grading standards change, standardized assessment increases, and more emphasis is put on test performance and grade point averages for admission to college (Wigfield & Eccles, 1990).

Impact on social development

In addition to cognitive and learning problems, children and adolescents with high levels of anxiety are more likely to develop social problems. These problems also appear to be of a reciprocal nature; that is, anxiety tends to create social development problems, which may cause

Table 1 *Some Characteristics and Correlates of Performance or Test Anxiety*

- Independent of cognitive ability
- Onset as early as age six
- Intensity declines until about age 11, then returns with increased intensity
- Often is chronic
- Associated with high levels of worry and emotionality
- Concerns about poor performance
- Physiological responses (e.g., increased heart rate)
- Attention problems, many off-task thoughts, and distractions
- Problems with information processing
- Negative self-deprecatory and self-evaluation thoughts
- Frequent use of coping cognitions (attempts to control anxiety and attention)
- Somatic concerns
- Misinterpretation of information
- Poor social relationships and fewer friends
- Low self-esteem
- More non-school-related fears
- Higher generalized anxiety
- Generally more negative mood states

Note. Adapted from "Cognitions in Test-Anxious Children: The Role of On-Task and Coping Cognition Reconsidered," by P. J. M. Prins, M. J. M. Groot, and G. J. F. P. Hanewald, 1994, *Journal of Consulting and Clinical Psychology, 62,* 409–414, and "Test Anxiety in African American School Children," by B. G. Turner, D. C. Beidel, S. Hughes, and M. W. Turner, 1993, *School Psychology Quarterly, 8,* 140–152.

further anxiety. Costanzo, Miller-Johnson, and Wencel (1995) provide an excellent discussion of the relationship of anxiety to social development. They propose that anxiety is a socialized state or trait highly influenced by how children cognitively interpret and construct the social environment. Social factors can have significant effects on a child's development. All children develop general expectancies and interpretations about the world, but the anxious child's cognitions are characterized by fear and apprehension about the meaning of the world and his or her relationship with it. As the child continues to develop and experience changes in cognitive development, these cognitions, expectations, and social constructions will change. Included in these changes are social comparison processes, peer group development, social attributions, and attachments to others.

Issues in the Diagnosis of Anxiety Disorders

Normal versus abnormal anxiety

Because anxiety has a normal developmental course and is manifested in some form at every age of childhood, it may be difficult to determine when anxiety is at the syndrome or disorder level and intervention is needed. There is little research or theory to help the practitioner determine when normal anxiety crosses a threshold to a level of abnormality. Such a lack of data is reasonable, however, given that anxiety varies across persons, age, and situations. *DSM-IV* does not provide guidance about what are "normal" and "abnormal" levels of anxiety. Therefore, the determination of when anxiety is not normal and a disorder is present is left to the practitioner, who must have a thorough knowledge of the typical developmental course and decide whether an individual child's anxiety is within those expected parameters. Two considerations may be helpful to the professional when trying to make this decision: First, the symptoms of anxiety may be normal for the child's age or developmental stage but are at such an extreme level that they are dysfunctional. Or secondly, the symptoms may be mild but are not expected at the child's current developmental status. As an example, consider separation anxiety disorder. Although it is quite normal for a young child to experience apprehension at separating from a primary caretaker, severe reactions are not normal and can indicate a problem. For the adolescent, however, separation anxiety can occur to a mild degree but be problematic if it is causing difficulties, because it is not expected at that age. In both instances, interventions may be indicated, despite the fact that the level of anxiety shown varies across persons of different ages.

Comorbidity

One of the most challenging problems in diagnosis is the degree of overlap or comorbidity with other anxiety disorders or non-anxiety disorders, such as depression. Comorbidity is not assumed in *DSM-IV;* that is, each category is presumed to be diagnostically distinct from all others, and multiple diagnoses represent multiple disorders. Comorbidity of anxiety disorders is a rather recent area of research, which Brown and Barlow (1992) attribute to the hierarchical exclusionary criteria of *DSM-III-R.* Because anxiety was given a lower priority in the hierarchical system, "many diagnoses were excluded if their defining symptoms occurred only during the course of a coexisting disorder that occupied a higher position in the hierarchy. Most broad categories of disorders ranked above anxiety disorders" (p. 835).

Anxiety disorders may be comorbid with non-anxiety disorders as well and create a more complex picture of an individual child. Last et al. (1987) examined comorbidity in adolescents referred to an anxiety disorders clinic for OAD, SAD, or depression. When more than one diagnosis was given, an anxiety disorder was present in 50% to 75% of the cases, indicating a high rate of comorbidity. Kovacs, Feinberg, Crouse-Novak, Paulauskas, and Finklestein (1984) found co-occurrence of anxiety with depression, dysthymia, conduct disorder, and attention deficit disorder. Of particular interest in this latter study was the authors' conclusion that anxiety disorders appeared to precede depressive disorders in most cases that were comorbid, and conduct disorders tended to develop before depression when they were comorbid. Although early research indicated that children with internalizing, anxiety-related problems did not carry these problems into adulthood, more recent research is mixed and supports both the absence and continuation of problems (Wenar, 1994).

Anxiety and depression

The relationship between anxiety and depression and their co-occurrence has received much research and clinical attention in recent years. Although it has been assumed that anxiety and depression are separate entities, there have been several studies to contradict those assumptions. High, significant correlations between self reports of anxiety and depression have been shown. Several clinical studies have shown that a child who is given a diagnosis of either depression or anxiety often shows symptoms of the other disorder (see Ollendick & King, 1994). Thus, the search for "pure" diagnoses of anxiety and depression can be difficult in clinical research studies. Despite the overlap of the disorders, there does appear to be evidence of cognitive, behavioral, social, and family differences between anxiety and depression, which may be useful for assessment and intervention. Stark, Humphrey, Laurent, Livingston, and Christopher (1993) found that these variables helped to differentiate a group of children who were screened for anxiety and depression and met cut-off criteria on self-report measures. Depressed children had more negative cognitions about themselves, the world, and the future; showed more anger and impulsiveness; were more likely to live in a dysfunctional family; and were more impulsive and recalcitrant than the children with an anxiety disorder. Thus, although symptoms of anxiety and depression may overlap to a great degree, there are differences between the constructs at the syndrome or disorder level.

Negative affectivity (NA) is a mood-based construct proposed by Watson and Clark (1984) to explain the frequent finding of significant overlap of anxiety and depression. NA can be present in adults or children and is described as a general negative affective state characterized by tension and distress (Lonigan, Carey, & Finch, 1994). When considering the overlap of anxiety and depression, *positive affectivity* (PA) also must be considered. PA is the obverse of NA and refers to a positive mood where the child does not show significant levels of tension and distress. High NA appears to be unique to depression, while both high NA and PA are associated with anxiety. Objective assessment of PA is not usually done, however, because most self-report instruments of depression and anxiety tend to have items that predominantly are negatively loaded.

Alternative Actions

Assessment of Anxiety Problems and Disorders

The assessment of anxiety disorders is a complex task involving many considerations, and it is beyond the scope of this chapter to address all the issues or to review assessment measures. However, the practitioner should consider the following points when attempting to assess anxiety and its effects.

Developmental nature of anxiety
There may be a tendency among professionals to conclude that if anxiety is present, a psychological intervention is a matter of course. Several developmental factors (indicated in Table 2) should be considered when assessing anxiety.

Multimethod, multisetting, multitrait assessment
Because anxiety is a complex pattern involving normal developmental considerations along with the possibility of psychopathology, a multifaceted approach is necessary. *Multimethod* approaches should involve objective assessment and include (a) observation; (b) behavioral interviews with the child, parents, teachers, or significant others; (c) behavior-rating scales completed by parents and teachers; (d) self-report measures of anxiety; and (e) multidimensional personality scales. It is important to

Table 2 *Developmental Considerations for Assessment of Anxiety*

- What is the child's current developmental level?
- Are the signs of anxiety a normal aspect of development?
- If so, are these signs expected, considering the child's developmental level?
- Are the signs of anxiety excessive for the child's developmental level?
- Are the signs of anxiety of a long-standing nature or have they emerged as a temporary increase in severity for the child?
- If the anxiety is a normal developmental phenomenon (e.g., social anxiety at adolescence), is it nevertheless sufficiently intense to interfere with the individual's social or academic functioning?

conduct *multisetting* assessment, because anxiety can be shown differently across settings. If setting variations exist, there are implications for differential interventions that may be linked to the events, precipitating factors, or persons in each setting. The reader is referred to Lann (1991), March (1995), and Ollendick, King, and Yule (1994) for more information on assessment issues.

As discussed earlier, anxiety can be correlated with other behavior patterns or syndromes, be comorbid with other disorders, or represent a disorder itself. Therefore, *multitrait* assessment is essential to an accurate description or diagnosis of anxiety and should include areas such as internalizing behaviors, particularly depressive symptoms. Because there often is a correlation between internalizing and externalizing patterns, assessment of the latter should be completed as well. Other related areas that should be assessed include self-esteem, coping skills, family functioning, peer relationships, and the child's thoughts, beliefs, and attributions about anxiety and academic performance.

The practitioner should remember that, although the multimethod, multisetting, and multitrait approach is necessary to describe anxiety, problems in assessment often occur. One of the most disconcerting outcomes of assessment is the observation that much of the data are conflicting. For example, it is common for teachers and parents to report differences in the child's behavior at school and at home. These discrepancies may be due to setting differences, variations in instruments used, the informant's ability to report anxiety-related symptoms, or other possibilities. It is a common finding that parents and teachers do not agree on specific behaviors, and, in general, adults are not very accurate when asked to report a child's internal mood state. Even when such information is obtained from the child, it may offer little clarity, depending on the child's age, ability to communicate about feelings and moods, or willingness to reveal information. When assessment information is discrepant, the practitioner should try to determine the overall pattern and base conclusions on those data. Highly discrepant information should not be ignored, because it may be useful later, but it should be given secondary consideration if it is inconsistent with most other data.

Interventions for Anxiety Problems and Disorders

Performance or test anxiety

The research on reducing performance or test anxiety has been primarily focused on adults but may have some applications for children and adolescents. It should be noted, however, that reduction of test anxiety may not necessarily improve performance. Nevertheless, attempts to reduce the anxiety are necessary. Two approaches to reducing this type of anxiety are (a) working directly with the child and (b) changing performance or testing conditions. Research has suggested that systematic desensitization, cognitive restructuring, relaxation, and observing models completing tasks successfully can be effective in reducing pre-performance or pre-evaluation experiences. Some authorities suggest focusing more on the worry about performance and emphasizing attention to the task rather than to off-task thoughts that may occur (Wigfield & Eccles, 1990). "Practice runs" in which the student rehearses and repeats the required actions may help reduce the anxiety. The second approach of changing testing conditions may be effective, such as removing time limits, breaking up testing sessions into smaller time periods, altering the instructions, and trying other techniques designed to reduce the stress on the child (Huberty & Eaken, 1994).

Anxiety disorders

There are many approaches to addressing anxiety disorders in children and adolescents, including traditional psychotherapy and counseling, with a focus on helping the client to develop insight into the problem. The most effective methods of intervention, however, have been behavior therapy and related approaches. The majority of promising interventions are of the cognitive-behavioral type and include techniques such as self-monitoring, self-reinforcement, constructive self-talk, and relaxation. In cognitive-behavioral approaches, the therapist must act as a diagnostician, educator, and consultant, who focuses on the client's thoughts, feelings, attitudes, and other cognitive material to understand and treat the problem (Kendall et al., 1992). The emphasis is on helping the child to become a more effective problem solver and to process information more efficiently. Kendall et al. (1992) discuss several approaches to cognitive-behavioral interventions, which focus on reducing the cognitive distortions that cause or maintain anxiety. Space prohibits detailed discussion of these techniques, some of which are summarized below.

Reducing negative self-talk may be accomplished by helping the child to focus on the maladaptive thoughts or beliefs and trying to create other cognitions that are more rational and realistic. The following example shows how a therapist might address the anxiety a child has about giving a speech in class.

Child: I have to give this speech in class next week and I'm terrified about it.

Therapist: What terrifies you about giving this speech?

Child: I just know that I'll get up there and stutter and make a fool of myself and everyone will laugh at me. The other kids will tease me later and be talking for weeks about how bad I did.

Therapist: It is normal for people to feel anxious when they have to perform before their friends like that. Even people who do that a lot sometimes get nervous in front of a group.

Child: Yeah, but they've done it before and they know how to handle it. I am such a total klutz in front of people.

Therapist: So, you're convinced that this will go badly because you're a klutz and there's not much you can do about it. Do you think you're a total klutz or is it just this speech that worries you?

Child: Well, I guess I'm not a total klutz, 'cause I'm a pretty good student. I just haven't done much speaking before.

Therapist: So, you're not a klutz, but you're worried about this speech. Do you know the material well?

Child: Oh, yeah. I know this stuff frontwards and backwards and I actually enjoyed learning about it, but I still am worried about giving the speech.

Therapist: You just said you are "worried" about this speech, while a few minutes ago, you said you were "terrified." What has changed here?

Child: Well, I guess I know the material well, and if I practice it a lot, I should feel better about it. I guess I'll still be nervous, but I'll figure a way to get through it. After all, I do pretty well otherwise.

Therapist: So, now you're not terrified, but worried. That seems normal. You think that you're just worried about this one thing, and that you know the material well. If you practice and rehearse, do you think it should go pretty well?

Child: Yeah, I guess so. I know I'll be a little nervous, but I know my stuff, so I think it will go O.K.

In this example, the therapist is successful in helping to change the child's distorted cognitions about being a "total klutz," a self-attribution that is irrational but is increasing the level of fear. By helping the child to develop alternative cognitions and coping strategies, the anxiety is reduced to a normal level. It would be unrealistic for the child to expect to be anxiety free when giving the speech, but the goal should be to keep it at a manageable level.

Self-monitoring is a technique to help children increase their ability to recognize when thoughts and feelings become too frequent or intense. These thoughts might be recorded on a tally sheet or in a daily journal, and the child has a record of the frequency of these occurrences. Becoming more aware of how often these thoughts occur may lead to a spontaneous reduction in frequency, as well as give the therapist baseline and treatment-efficacy information upon which to base further intervention.

Self-reinforcement occurs when students give themselves rewards for decreasing negative thoughts or self-talk. This technique requires a highly motivated client who is willing and able to record negative thoughts. For example, a goal might be set to reduce the number of negative thoughts to a specific level over a period of several days. If the goal is met, then the child would be able to reward herself or himself for being successful.

Relaxation techniques are useful for children and adults to reduce anxiety and include progressive relaxation, deep breathing exercises, and imagery techniques. The essential feature of these techniques is to put the child into a relaxed state which is incompatible with anxiety. After the child learns these techniques with the help of a therapist, they can be used independently.

In addition to cognitive behavioral techniques, some anxious children may receive benefit from *social skills training*, particularly those who tend to have social phobic or avoidant behaviors. It is possible that some of these children have *skill deficits* rather than *performance deficits*. When one encounters an anxious child, it may be hypothesized that the child has the necessary social skills, but the anxiety interferes with the ability to perform appropriately (i.e., a performance deficit). An alternative possibility is that the child may not have the skill or knowledge to perform adequately in a social situation (i.e., a skill deficit). Further, the lack of ability to interact in a socially appropriate way may make the child more anxious. The practitioner should determine if social skills problems exist, whether they are skill or performance deficits, and whether social skills training is needed.

Family interventions might also be helpful. Although practitioners may focus on the child with an anxiety disorder, they should not neglect the role that the family may play in the development and maintenance of the problem. Although the research suggests that children with anxiety disorders tend to have families with better functioning than depressed children (Stark et al., 1993), it is possible that the individual case may have family factors as contributors to the problem that must be addressed. For example, if a child's parents are having severe marital problems, the child may experience anxiety about what the future holds for the family. Table 3 presents a set of questions or guideposts that may be useful to the practitioner when considering family variables.

Table 3 *Family Considerations in Childhood Anxiety Disorders*

- Are there difficulties within the family that create uncertainty about the future?
- Is the child a major focus of the family problems?
- Is there evidence of related problems that contribute to the anxiety (e.g., abuse or neglect)?
- What expectations do the parents have for the child?
- Are expectations of the child realistic, based upon the child's developmental level?
- Are discipline practices appropriate for the child's age or level?
- Are discipline practices consistent across siblings and situations?

Summary

Anxiety problems and disorders represent significant sources of difficulty for as many as 15% of children and youth yet may go unrecognized or be given insufficient intervention attention. Anxiety is characteristic of all children at some time but becomes problematic when it is out of proportion to the situation or inconsistent with normal developmental expectations. If anxiety is left untreated, significant impairments in personal, social, and academic problems can result.

Assessment requires a multimethod approach, including cognitive, affective, and social aspects. Of particular importance to assess are cognitions, attributions, beliefs, and self-deprecating thoughts that form the basis for the anxiety. Intervention for anxiety problems and disorders can be varied and may often include working with the family. The most effective interventions are of a cognitive-behavioral nature, with the goal to alter cognitive distortions and deficiencies that form the basis for anxiety problems. The practitioner must be aware of both the normal developmental aspects of anxiety and the clinical syndromes that may exist independently or that represent specific disorders.

Recommended Resources

Kendall, P. C., Chansky, T. E., Kane, M. T., Kim, R. S., Kortlander, E., Ronan, K. R., Sessa, F. M., & Siqueland, L. (1992). *Anxiety disorders in youth.* Boston: Allyn & Bacon.
This book provides an excellent overview of issues, characteristics, and diagnoses of anxiety disorders in children and youth. It emphasizes a cognitive-behavioral approach to interventions and gives the reader practical examples and specific suggestions for techniques to address anxiety problems.

Kendall, P. C., Kane, M., Howard, B., & Siqueland, L. (1990). *Cognitive-behavioral treatment of anxious children: Treatment manual.* [Available from Philip C. Kendall, Department of Psychology, Temple University, Philadelphia, PA 19122.]

This manual contains materials, specific suggestions, and treatment plans for anxiety problems. Based upon available research, it is a practical tool that can be used in an applied context with children. The practitioner should find it a useful adjunct to a repertoire of intervention skills.

March, J. S. (Ed.). (1995). *Anxiety disorders in children and adolescents.* New York: Guilford Press.
This book is divided into three sections covering foundations of anxiety problems, specific disorders, and treatment. Topics include the neuropsychology of anxiety, assessment, comorbidity, and major treatment approaches (cognitive-behavioral, pharmacotherapy, psychodynamic, and family therapy). It concludes with a chapter about how to organize an anxiety-disorders clinic.

Ollendick, T. H., & King, N. J. (1994). Diagnosis, assessment, and treatment of internalizing problems in children: The role of longitudinal data. *Journal of Consulting and Clinical Psychology, 62,* 918–927.
This excellent article discusses a number of issues regarding internalizing problems. Treatment of anxiety issues includes comorbidity, developmental course, longitudinal findings, and a review of selected treatment outcome studies. The article has an extensive reference list, which will provide the reader with a valuable index for some of the major articles and research available.

Ollendick, T. H., King, N. J., & Yule, W. (Eds.). (1994). *International handbook of phobic and anxiety disorders in children and adolescents.* New York: Plenum Press.
This volume provides a synthesis of current thinking and research on anxiety disorders in childhood. It is divided into four sections addressing current issues in anxiety, specific phobic and anxiety disorders, assessment procedures, and specific treatment and prevention strategies.

References

American Psychiatric Association. (1987). *Diagnostic and statistical manual of mental disorders* (3rd ed., rev.). Washington, DC: Author.

American Psychiatric Association. (1994). *Diagnostic and statistical manual of mental disorders* (4th ed.). Washington, DC: Author.

Beidel, D. C., & Turner, S. M. (1988). Comorbidity of test anxiety and other anxiety disorders in children. *Journal of Abnormal Child Psychology, 16,* 275–287.

Bell-Dolan, D., & Wessler, A. E. (1994). Attributional style of anxious children: Extensions from cognitive theory and research on adult anxiety. *Journal of Anxiety Disorders, 8,* 79–96.

Bernstein, G. A., & Borchardt, C. M. (1991). Anxiety disorders in childhood and adolescence: A critical review. *Journal of the American Academy of Child and Adolescent Psychiatry, 30,* 519–533.

Brown, T. A., & Barlow, D. H. (1992). Comorbidity among anxiety disorders: Implications for treatment and DSM-IV. *Journal of Consulting and Clinical Psychology, 60,* 835–844.

Costanzo, P., Miller-Johnson, S., & Wencel, H. (1995). Social development. In J. S. March (Ed.), *Anxiety disorders in children and adolescents* (pp. 82–108). New York: Guilford Press.

Curry, J. F., & Murphy, L. B. (1995). Comorbidity of anxiety disorders. In J. S. March (Ed.), *Anxiety disorders in children and adolescents* (pp. 301–317). New York: Guilford Press.

Dweck, C. S., & Bush, E. S. (1976). Sex differences in learned helplessness: I. Differential debilitation with peer and adult evaluators. *Developmental Psychology, 12,* 147–156.

Harris, S. L., & Ferrari, M. (1983). Developmental factors in child behavior therapy. *Behavior Therapy, 14,* 54–72.

Hill, K. T. (1984). Debilitation motivations and testing: A major educational problem, possible solutions, and policy applications. In R. E. Ames & C. Ames (Eds.), *Research on motivation in education* (Vol. 1, pp. 245–274). New York: Academic Press.

Huberty, T. J. (1987). Children and anxiety. In A. Thomas & J. Grimes (Eds.), *Children's needs: Psychological perspectives* (pp. 46–51). Washington, DC: National Association of School Psychologists.

Huberty, T. J., & Eaken, G. J. (1994). Interventions for children's anxiety disorders. *Special Services in the Schools, 9,* 97–117.

Jersild, A. T., & Holmes, F. B. (1935). *Children's fears* (Child Development Monograph No. 20).

Johnson, S. B., & Melamed, B. G. (1979). The assessment and treatment of children's fears. In B. B. Lahey & A. E. Kazdin (Eds.), *Advances in clinical child psychology* (Vol 2, pp. 107–139). New York: Plenum Press.

Kashani, J. H., & Orvaschel, H. (1990). A community study of anxiety in children and adolescents. *American Journal of Psychiatry, 147,* 313–318.

Kendall, P. C., Chansky, T. E., Kane, M. T., Kim, R. S., Kortlander, E., Ronan, K. R., Sessa, F. M., & Siqueland, L. (1992). *Anxiety disorders in youth.* Boston: Allyn & Bacon.

Kendall, P. C., & Ronan, K. R. (1990). Assessment of children's anxieties, fears, and phobias: Cognitive-behavioral models and methods. In C. R. Reynolds & R. W. Kamphaus (Eds.), *Handbook of psychological and educational assessment of children* (pp. 223–244). New York: Guilford Press.

Kovacs, M., Feinberg, T. L., Crouse-Novak, M., Paulauskas, S. L., & Finkelstein, R. (1984). Depressive disorders in childhood: I. A longitudinal prospective study of characteristics and recovery. *Archives of General Psychiatry, 41,* 229–237.

Lann, I. S. (Ed.). (1991). Assessment of childhood anxiety disorders. *Journal of Anxiety Disorders* (Special Issue), *5,* 101–103.

Last, C. L., Strauss, C. C., & Francis, G. (1987). Comorbidity among childhood anxiety disorders. *The Journal of Nervous and Mental Disease, 175,* 726–730.

Leibert, R. M., & Morris, L. W. (1967). Cognitive and emotional components of test anxiety: A distinction and some initial data. *Psychological Reports, 20,* 975–978.

Lonigan, C. J., Carey, M. P., & Finch, A. J. (1994). Anxiety and depression in children and adolescents: Negative affectivity and the utility of self-reports. *Journal of Consulting and Clinical Psychology, 62,* 1000–1008.

March, J. S. (Ed.). (1995). *Anxiety disorders in children and adolescents.* New York: Guilford Press.

Marks, I. (1987). The development of normal fear: A review. *Journal of Child Psychology and Psychiatry, 28,* 680–697.

Miller, L. C. (1983). Fears and anxieties in children. In C. E. Walker & M. C. Roberts (Eds.), *Handbook of clinical child psychology* (pp. 337–380). New York: Wiley.

Morris, R. J., & Kratochwill, T. R. (1985). Behavior treatment of children's fears and phobias: A review. *School Psychology Review, 14,* 84–93.

Ollendick, T. H., & King, N. J. (1994). Diagnosis, assessment, and treatment of internalizing problems in children: The role of longitudinal data. *Journal of Clinical and Consulting Psychology, 62,* 918–927.

Ollendick, T. H., King, N. J., & Yule, W. (Eds.). (1994). *International handbook of phobic and anxiety disorders in children and adolescents.* New York: Plenum Press.

Ollendick, T. H., Matson, J. L., & Helsel, W. J. (1985). Fears in children and adolescents: Normative data. *Behavior Research and Therapy, 23,* 465–467.

Prins, P. J. M., Groot, M. J. M., & Hanewald, G. J. F. P. (1994). Cognitions in test-anxious children: The role of on-task and coping cognition reconsidered. *Journal of Consulting and Clinical Psychology, 62,* 409–414.

Rutter, M., Tizard, J., & Whitmore, K. (1970). *Education, health, and behavior.* New York: Wiley.

Sarason, S. B., Lighthall, F. F., Davidson, K. S., Waite, R. R., & Ruebush, B. K. (1960). *Anxiety in elementary school children.* New York: Wiley.

Stark, K. D., Humphrey, L. L., Laurent, J., Livingston, R., & Christopher, J. (1993). Cognitive, behavioral, and family factors in the differentiation of depressive and anxiety disorders during childhood. *Journal of Consulting and Clinical Psychology, 61,* 878–886.

Strauss, C. C., Frame, C. L., & Forehand, R. (1987). Psychosocial impairment associated with anxiety in children. *Journal of Clinical Child Psychology, 16,* 235–239.

Turner, B. G., Beidel, D. C., Hughes, S., & Turner M. W. (1993). Test anxiety in African American school children. *School Psychology Quarterly, 8,* 140–152.

Vasey, M. W., Crnic, K. A., & Carter, W. G. (1994). Worry in childhood: A developmental perspective. *Cognitive Therapy and Research, 18,* 529–549.

Watson, D., & Clark, L. A. (1984). Negative affectivity: The disposition to experience aversive emotional states. *Psychological Bulletin, 96,* 455–490.

Wenar, C. (1994). *Developmental psychopathology* (3rd ed.). New York: McGraw-Hill.

Wigfield, A., & Eccles, J. S. (1990). Test anxiety in the school setting. In M. Lewis & S. M. Miller (Eds.), *Handbook of developmental psychopathology* (pp. 237–250). New York: Plenum Press.

Wine, J. D. (1971). Test anxiety and direction of attention. *Psychological Bulletin, 76,* 92–104.

Wine, J. D. (1980). Cognitive-attentional theory of test anxiety. In I. G. Sarason (Ed.), *Test anxiety: Theory, research, and applications* (pp. 349–385). Hillsdale, NJ: Lawrence Erlbaum.

Zatz, S., & Chassin, L. (1985). Cognitions of test-anxious children under naturalistic test-taking conditions. *Journal of Consulting and Clinical Psychology, 53,* 393–401.

28

Fears and Phobias

Sylvia Z. Ramirez
University of Texas at Austin

Thomas R. Kratochwill
University of Wisconsin-Madison

Richard J. Morris
University of Arizona

Background and Development

Literature on children's and adolescents' fears and phobias has grown extensively in the last 25 years. In particular, there has been increased attention given to understanding how fears develop in children and how normal fears are related to the development of more severe fears, called "clinical fears" or "phobias," and anxiety (e.g., Craig & Dobson, 1995; King, Hamilton, & Ollendick, 1988; Reynolds, 1992). This chapter provides an overview of some definitional issues in children's fears and phobias, reviews some of the fears and phobias that children and adolescents are likely to experience, discusses some theories related to the development of more severe phobias or debilitating fears, and reviews some common psychological intervention strategies often used by mental health professionals to treat children's fears and phobic disorders.

Definitional Issues

Fear Versus Phobia

The definitional issues are complex and require differentiation between fears, phobias, and related emotional states. In the professional literature, there is a great deal of confusion regarding definitions and criteria for these terms (Morris & Kratochwill, 1983, 1985). What one finds is an interchanging and mixing of terms such as *fear, phobia, anxiety, stress,* and *worry.* Graziano, DeGiovanni, and Garcia (1979), for example, used the term "clinical fears" to describe "those with a duration of over 2 years or an intensity that is debilitating to the client's routine life-style" (p. 805). Frequently, a distinction is made between fears and phobias, usually on the basis of their persistence, developmental and social appropriateness,

duration, intensity, and degree of interference in a child's life (Morris & Kratochwill, 1983, 1991). For example, Marks (1969) described phobia as a special form of fear which (a) is out of proportion to the demands of a situation; (b) cannot be explained or reasoned away; (c) is beyond voluntary control; and (d) leads to avoidance of the feared situation (p. 3). Subsequently, Miller, Barrett, and Hampe (1974) proposed additional criteria, noting that phobia persists over an extended period of time, is maladaptive, and is not age or stage specific.

The fourth edition of the *Diagnostic and Statistical Manual of Mental Disorders* (*DSM-IV;* American Psychiatric Association, 1994) identifies two phobic disorder subtypes that occur in childhood and adolescence: specific phobia (formerly simple phobia) and social phobia. For a diagnosis of specific phobia, criteria in Table 1 must be met. The criteria for specific and social phobia are similar, with the emphasis of the latter condition being on feared social situations. *DSM-IV* identifies five subtypes of specific phobia: animal, natural environment (e.g., heights, water), blood injection-injury (e.g., receiving an injection), situational (e.g., enclosed places), and "other" type (e.g., loud noises). Symptoms described as school phobia may or may not represent "true" phobias (see School Phobia, this volume, for a discussion of issues related to this phobia).

An example of a childhood fear that would meet the phobia criteria described in Table 1 concerns a 5-year-old boy referred to a school psychologist because of "social immaturity." The child had a phobia precipitated by his bad experiences while sitting on the toilet in the family bathroom. On the first occasion, a bookshelf mounted above the toilet fell on him, causing him to be lodged into the toilet. His parents were present and assisted him, and they were able to overcome his fear of going back into the bathroom and using the commode rela-

Table 1 DSM-IV *Diagnostic Criteria for Specific Phobia*

1. The fear is marked, persistent, and excessive or unreasonable and is triggered by the anticipation or presence of the feared object or situation.
2. Almost invariably, exposure to the phobic stimulus provokes an immediate anxiety response which can take the form of a situationally bound (or predisposed) Panic Attack. In children, the response may be in the form of freezing, clinging, crying, or tantrums.
3. The person recognizes that the fear is excessive or unreasonable. In children, this criterion may be absent.
4. The phobic stimulus is either avoided or endured with intense anxiety or distress.
5. The avoidance, anxious anticipation, or distress in the feared situation(s) significantly interferes with the individual's normal routine, occupational or academic functioning, or social relationships or activities, or there is marked distress about having the fear.
6. For children and adolescents (under age 18 years), the duration must be for at least 6 months.
7. The reaction to the feared stimulus is not better accounted for by other disorders, for example, Obsessive-Compulsive Disorder with the obsession content being fear of dirt.

Note. From *Diagnostic and Statistical Manual of Mental Disorders* (Fourth Edition, pp. 410–411), by the American Psychiatric Association, 1994, Washington, DC: Author. Copyright 1994 by the American Psychiatric Association. Adapted with permission.

tively quickly. Some time later, the exact same incident re-occurred. This time his parents were unavailable to assist him, and he was lodged in the toilet for an extended period of time and became extremely terrified. After this experience, his parents placed a small portable potty in the kitchen for him to use because he would not enter the bathroom. The child also developed a more severe phobic reaction to other toilets. He generally was able to avoid using public bathroooms but had toileting accidents due to his severe phobic reaction.

This case demonstrates that a particular kind of fear might develop as a consequence of certain specific negative emotional experiences. In fact, most children recover from these aversive experiences if they are not too intense and do not occur very often. However, in this case, the two aversive experiences were intense enough for the child to develop a rather severe clinical fear, or phobia.

Fear Versus Anxiety

Another term that is commonly used to describe children's fears, phobias, and related states is "anxiety" (see Anxiety, this volume). Anxiety traditionally has been distinguished from fears on the basis of the specificity of the eliciting stimuli and accompanying response (Jersild, 1954). Also, anxiety has been regarded as more diffuse reactions to nonspecific stimuli (Barrios & Hartmann,

1988). Nevertheless, fear, phobia, and anxiety often are interrelated as constructs.

Nietzel and Bernstein's (1981) social learning conceptualization of anxiety includes the following:

1. Anxiety is not a trait or personality characteristic internal to the individual.
2. Anxiety can be acquired through different learning mechanisms.
3. Anxiety consists of several response channels or components.
4. The response channels are not correlated highly. (pp. 216–220)

The last two dimensions need elaboration because they form the basis of how fears, phobias, anxiety, and related terms might be defined in terms of children's actual reactions. To begin with, as already mentioned, anxiety, fears, and phobias can be conceptualized in terms of three response systems or channels (Barrios & Hartmann, 1988; Lang, 1984)—motor, cognitive, and physiological. The cognitive channel is a subjective system in which the child self-reports cognitions, feelings, and emotions associated with the fear. For example, a child might report the feeling of "being afraid" of dogs while approaching or even thinking of dogs. The motor channel would be operating if the child also avoided any dog that he or she saw while walking outside or if the child refused to leave his or her house for fear of being confronted by a dog. The physiological channel involves reactions of the sympathetic portion of the autonomic nervous system. For example, a child might show basic physiological reactions such as elevated blood pressure, heart rate, or respiration rate as well as a galvanic skin response in anticipation of some feared event.

Evidence of a child's fear, phobia, or anxiety can be obtained from any one or any combination of the three channels. Interestingly, research has indicated that the three channels do not necessarily correlate highly when all three are assessed simultaneously and individuals are presented with a stimulus that is purportedly feared (Barrios & Hartmann, 1988).

The three channels can be measured by self-report or behavioral or physiological methods. For example, a self-report survey could include both items that assess the cognitive response channel and items that refer to motoric and physiological responses. Other examples of instruments include interviews, questionnaires, behavioral avoidance tests, fear "thermometers," direct observation, and the palmer sweat index (see Barrios and Hartmann [1988] for an extensive list and descriptions of instruments designed to assess one or more response channels of children's fears, phobias, and anxieties).

In summary, fear is a normal reaction to a perceived or real threat involving subjective feelings of discomfort, physiological changes, and avoidance behavior. Phobia involves a fear reaction that is disproportionate to the perceived threat, and anxiety is an enduring reaction without an obvious external precipitating threat (Morris & Kratochwill, 1983; Reed, Carter, & Miller, 1992).

Normative Research

Important foci of normative investigations on children's fears have been the unique fears that children experience at different age levels and by gender. Other important, but less researched, variables are socioeconomic status (SES), race, ethnicity, culture, and disability status. Before describing the literature in this area, it is important to understand some methodological issues that may account for differences across studies. The number and type of fears reported in epidemiological studies vary depending on a number of factors. For example, studies that require children to generate fears (such as list and rank) tend to report fewer fears than those using survey techniques (e.g., Lapouse & Monk, 1959; Ollendick, King, & Frary, 1989). Other variables that differ across studies include (a) varying definitions (e.g., "normal" fears vs. phobias); (b) type of informants (e.g., child, parent, or teacher); (c) length of fear surveys; (d) descriptors of intensity ratings (e.g., "unrealistic or excessive" fear and "a lot" of fear) used in surveys; and (e–j) the child's age, gender, SES, race, ethnicity, and disability status. Because of these differences across studies, few of the findings should be considered definitive.

Age Trends

Fears and phobias are found in children from infancy through adolescence and into the adult years. In early studies, four to five fears were reported for children ages 2 through 6 and 9 years (e.g., Jersild & Holmes, 1935a). In addition, a specific fear was reported at least once for 90% of 2- to 14-year-olds (MacFarlane, Allen, & Hozik, 1954), and greater than seven fears were reported for 43% of 6- through 12-year-olds (Lapouse & Monk, 1959).

In more recent studies, the average number of fears was 14 (with "a lot" intensity rating) for children ages 7 to 16 years (Ollendick et al., 1989), and 22 (with both "a little" and "very" intensity ratings) for children ages 6 to 13 years (Ramirez & Kratochwill, in press). Thus, the number of fears tend to fluctuate from 4 to about 20 in the various studies that have examined this question. Also, it has been found that severe fears tend to be experienced by a relatively large proportion of children and adolescents. However, the prevalence estimates for simple (specific) phobia have been much lower, 2% in children and 3% in adolescents (Anderson, Williams, McGee, & Silva, 1987; McGee, Feehan, Williams, & Anderson, 1992).

There is a tendency for the frequency of children's fears to decline with increasing age (Graziano et al., 1979; Morris & Kratochwill, 1983). However, this finding is in-

consistent across studies and even within studies. For example, Ollendick et al. (1989) reported that 7- to 10-year-olds reported significantly more fears than either 11- to 13-year-olds or 14- to 16-year-olds and that the two older groups did not differ significantly. Kendall et al. (1992), on the other hand, suggested that the number of fears do not differ greatly with age; rather, with increased age, the type of fears change.

Table 2 presents common fears at various age levels for infants and children through age 12 years. Children between 2 and 6 years of age appear to have less "reality-based" fears (e.g., monsters and ghosts) than those of other age groups (e.g., Bauer, 1976; Jersild & Holmes, 1935a). These authors as well as others (e.g., Lapouse & Monk, 1959) reported that young children say that the dark, animals, dogs, and bugs are common fears. Generally, it appears that children ages 2 to 6 years have more global and, from an adult perspective, irrational fears. However, Barrios and O'Dell (1989) warn that what may seem to be innocuous fears from an adult perspec-

Table 2 *Children's Common Fears*

Age	Object of fear
0–6 months	Loss of support, loud noises
7–12 months	Strangers; sudden, unexpected, and looming objects
1 year	Toilet, injury, strangers, separation from parent
2 years	A multitude of fears including loud noises (vacuum cleaners, sirens, alarms, trucks, and thunder), animals (e.g., large dog), dark room, separation from parent, large objects or machines, change in personal environment
3 years	Masks, dark, animals, separation from parent
4 years	Parent separation, animals, dark, noises (including at night)
5 years	Animals, "bad" people, dark, separation from parent, bodily harm
6 years	Supernatural beings (e.g., ghosts, witches, "Darth Vader"), bodily injuries, thunder and lightning, dark, sleeping or staying alone, separation from parent
7–8 years	Supernatural beings, dark, fears based on media events, staying alone, bodily injury
9–12 years	Tests and examinations in school, school performance, bodily injury, physical appearance, thunder and lightning, death, dark (low percentage)
13+	Crime, being hurt, being kidnapped, being alone, war, bad grades, tests, school failure, punishment, personal relations, sex issues (pregnancy, AIDS), being alone, family concerns

Note. From *Treating Children's Fears and Phobias: A Behavioral Approach* (p. 2), by R. J. Morris and T. R. Kratochwill, 1983, Elmsford, NY: Pergamon. Copyright 1983 by Pergamon. And from "Children's Fears: Toward a Preventive Model," by E. H. Robinson, J. C. Rotter, M. A. Fey, and S. L. Robinson, 1991, *The School Counselor, 38,* p. 189. Copyright 1991 by American School Counselor Association. Adapted with permission.

tive can be real threats to children because they are more physically vulnerable.

Children between the ages of 7 and 12 years appear to exhibit fears reflecting threatening situations, the consequences of which are more readily identifiable. These children appear to be concerned primarily with danger and death (e.g., Moracco & Camilleri, 1983; Morris & Kratochwill, 1983; Ollendick et al., 1989; Ramirez & Kratochwill, in press). It also appears that various school-related fears develop at this time, including such matters as the fear of getting poor grades (Ollendick et al., 1989). Other common fears regard concern for the well-being of loved ones. Moracco and Camilleri (1983) reported that the most common fear for their sample of third graders was that "something would happen to mother or father." Similarly, two of this chapter's authors (Ramirez & Kratochwil, in press) found that the fear of someone or something hurting people they love was a common fear for children (ages 6 to 13 years).

Few investigations have focused on the fears of adolescents compared with studies of younger children. It is evident from the studies reviewed that many of the fears expressed by younger children are present in adolescents. Ollendick et al. (1989) reported that 8 of the 10 most feared stimuli were the same regardless of age group (being hit by a car or truck, not being able to breathe, bombing attacks, getting burned, falling from a high place, a burglar breaking into the home, earthquakes, and death). The remaining two fears for 7- to 10-year-olds were getting lost in a strange place and being sent to the school principal. For older children and adolescents, the remaining two common fears were of having parents argue (for 11- to 13-year-olds) and failing a test (for 14- to 16-year-olds). In general, additional fears of adolescents tend to be of a social and evaluative nature (McGee et al., 1992; Robinson, Rotter, Fey, & Robinson, 1991).

Gender Differences

Different conclusions have been drawn from the results of research concerning gender differences in fears and related emotional states. The more consistent finding is that, generally, girls have scored higher than boys on fear measures (e.g., Ollendick et al., 1989; Ramirez & Kratochwill, in press). For example, Ollendick et al. (1989) reported that there was an average of 18 fears for girls and 10 fears for boys. One explanation for these differences has been sex-role stereotyping, with boys being socialized not to admit to fears. However, some studies have not found gender differences (e.g., Nalven, 1970). As with age-related differences, sex differences appear to vary depending on the type of fear being studied and its intensity (Graziano et al., 1979). In regard to qualitative differences in fears, Ollendick et al. (1989) reported that 9 of the 10 most prominent fears were the same for males and females (a burglar breaking into the home, being sent to

the principal, bombing attacks, being hit by a car or truck, falling from high places, earthquakes, not being able to breathe, getting burned, and death). The fears that differed were getting an illness for males and getting lost in a strange place for females.

Socioeconomic Status, Race, Ethnicity, and Culture

In regard to SES, studies typically define this variable in dissimilar ways, thus making comparisons across studies difficult. Nevertheless, some studies have reported differences in this dimension in either number or type of reported fears. Generally, lower SES children have more fears than higher SES children (e.g., Jersild & Holmes, 1935a). It also has been reported that lower SES children have more fear of some specific objects (e.g., rats), while higher SES children have more fear of other objects (e.g., car accidents; Fonseca, Yule, & Erol, 1994; Nalven, 1970). Differences between SES groups may be due to differing environmental experiences and perceptions of danger and differences in education and understanding (King, 1993).

Few studies have compared the fears of racial or cultural groups. Last and Perrin (1993) reported that, for their clinical sample of children with anxiety disorders, African-American children had higher total fear scores than White children; however, the results may have been confounded by SES because while only 17% of the White children were of low SES, 40% of the African-American children were. In early editions of the *DSM* classification system, there was little reference to the impact of culture on diagnosis. However, *DSM-IV* makes reference to considerations based on culture. For example, fears of spirits are present in many cultures, but according to *DSM-IV*, they should not be considered specific phobias if they are not excessive within the culture and do not cause significant impairment and distress. See Fonseca et al. (1994) for a discussion of (international) cross-cultural issues.

Disabilities and Fears

Although specific fears in children with disabilities rarely have been studied systematically, there have been consistent findings of differences between children with and without disabilities. For example, Deverensky (1979) found that children with disabilities reported a greater number of fears and had a wider range of fears than nondisabled children. Most fears were reported to be realistic, learned, and dependent upon the youth's intellectual and maturational level.

These findings have been supported by more recent studies comparing the fears of children with and without mental retardation. Vandenberg (1993) reported that the fears of children with mental retardation were more similar to those of younger children without mental retardation than to those of their similar-aged peers. Children with mental retardation and younger children without mental retardation reported more events of an imaginary nature and less of people-related events than older children without mental retardation. Two of this chapter's authors (Ramirez & Kratochwill, in press) found that children with mental retardation reported a greater number of fears than their same age-peers but did not differ in this regard from younger children without mental retardation. In this latter study, although children with mental retardation shared a majority of common fears with their younger and similar-age peers, there were some differences. For example, fire was among the most common fears for children with mental retardation and their younger age peers, while it was not among the most common fears for their similar-age peers without mental retardation.

Development of Fears and Phobias

How fears and phobias develop in children can be understood through looking at the various perspectives that have been advanced to explain these phenomena. These theoretical perspectives include psychoanalytic, biological, and behavioral, including cognitive-behavioral (see Morris & Kratochwill, 1983, for a review). In Freudian theory, phobias represent unconscious conflict (e.g., regarding sexual or aggressive impulses) with the conflict and anxiety being displaced on a symbolic object. In the biological perspective, individuals are viewed as having a biological predisposition for developing fears and phobias. Based on evolution, individuals are viewed as being predisposed to develop rapidly fear of certain "prepared" stimuli (e.g., snakes). Compared to other models, behavioral models of the development of fears and phobias in children and adolescents have considerably more empirical support and therefore will be discussed in greater detail here.

In behavioral psychology, five different theoretical perspectives have been advanced to conceptualize the development of fears and phobias, including classical (Pavlovian) conditioning, two-factor learning, operant conditioning, social learning, and cognitive-behavioral. *Classical conditioning* involves the pairing of an aversive unconditioned stimulus (UCS) with a previously neutral conditioned stimulus (CS). The trauma-induced bathroom phobia described earlier is an example of a phobia that may have developed with classical conditioning. Another theoretical framework, labeled *two-factor learning theory,* integrates both classical and instrumental conditioning (Mower, 1960). Mower combined classical conditioning with Hull's (1943) instrumental learning theory to account for the conditioning and maintenance of fears. For example, he noted that fear was a classically conditioned response (CR) that came about by pairing a UCS with a CS. The conditioned fear response (CR) was said to motivate avoidance behavior whenever the CS was present. This avoidance behavior reduced the CR, which

in turn reinforced the organism to engage in the avoidance behavior (Morris & Kratochwill, 1983).

Mower's initial work facilitated Wolpe's (1958) conceptualization of systematic desensitization in the treatment of fears, phobias, and anxiety. Wolpe noted that neurotic behavior (such as a severe fear) was a persistent and unadaptive habit individuals had learned and therefore could unlearn. He argued that these types of behavior patterns were learned through temporal contiguity of the stimulus and response (classical conditioning) and maintained by drive reduction (Hullian instrumental learning).

Another behavioral theory accounting for the development of fears is based on the *operant conditioning* model. In this theoretical model, the avoidance response, or motor behavior, is said to be reinforced through various conditions. For example, parents or teachers might reinforce a child's avoidance of certain situations or objects. This reinforcement, in turn, strengthens the actual fear and leads to future motor avoidance of the stimulus. Basically, the operant framework assumes that fear responses are learned and that aspects of the environment are responsible for this learning and for the maintenance of the behavior. Assessment can be focused on the functions of behavior or what is commonly called a functional analysis (Shill, Kratochwill, & Gardner, 1996). Some functional diagnostic scales have been developed for fear-related problems such as the *School Refusal Assessment Scale* (Kearney & Silverman, 1993).

Other behavioral models involve *social-learning theory* (Bandura, 1977) and *cognitive-behavioral theory* (Beck & Emery, 1985). In the social-learning model, vicarious learning may result in fears. In this case, the individual acquires a fear by directly observing exposure of a model to a traumatic or aversive event. Social-learning theory assumes that psychological functioning involves "a reciprocal interaction" between the individual and the environment. This theoretical model, as well as the cognitive-behavioral model, accommodate the belief that a great deal of self-directed behavior is involved in human performance. Additionally, the cognitive-behavioral model holds that children have negative thinking styles that lead to fear development and maintenance. They have internal fearful dialogues (e.g., "I will die if I have go to the school gym") when confronted with feared stimuli or situations (Kendall et al., 1992; Meichenbaum & Genest, 1980).

All the models just described have not done particularly well in accounting for a broad range of children's fears and phobias, and there have been few studies in this area. One exception is a study by Ollendick, King, and Hamilton (1991). They administered a questionnaire designed to assess the pathways of fear acquisition to 1,092 youth (ages 9 to 14 years) from Australia and the United States. The majority of the children indicated that instructional (89%) and vicarious factors (56%) were the most influential. However, it appeared that direct conditioning experiences also were sources of fear. This latter finding is consistent with Ollendick's (1979) notion that fears may be acquired and maintained by various interactive conditioning processes.

Problems and Implications

Fear is a normal part of children's development. The expression of fear is viewed as a positive feature in that normal fears help children avoid potentially harmful situations, adapt to their environment, and deal with various stressors in daily life (Morris & Kratochwill, 1983, 1991). Many mild fears and some phobias are transient in nature, but other fears and phobias continue through adulthood (King, 1993; Ollendick, 1979). While some children's fears and phobias may be "outgrown" with time, other childhood fears and phobias may have a poor prognosis if untreated. Studies have demonstrated positive relationships between anxious-inhibited behavior in infancy and adolescence and have documented the presentation of internalizing fearful-anxious behavior of children followed from preschool to junior high school (King, 1993).

Fears and phobias can affect a child's social and academic functioning and cause personal discomfort to the child and family (King, Hamilton, & Ollendick, 1988; King & Ollendick, 1989; Silverman & Nelles, 1990). The more severe the fear, the greater may be the avoidance and the interference with learning and adjustment. Treatment is usually sought when the disruption to functioning is fairly high. Problems include disruption not only in the child's daily functioning (e.g., relationships with peers) but also in the family's functioning.

Examples of the effects of fears and phobias on children's lives have been described in the literature (King et al., 1988; King & Ollendick, 1989; Morris, Kratochwill, & Aldridge, 1988; Silverman & Nelles, 1990; Strauss, 1990). Among the most maladaptive fears in the school setting are performance anxiety and social anxiety. A child may become housebound to avoid contact with a feared stimulus, which may result in severely impaired social and academic functioning, as well as somatic complaints. A fear of taking tests can interfere with optimal performance and ultimately can lead to school avoidance. A social phobia may result in the child interacting infrequently with his or her peers and a refusal to speak in class.

Other fears not traditionally perceived as academically related also can interfere in the school setting. For example, a fear of animals may interfere when pet animals are brought to class by classmates or when contact with animals is required in biology class. Also, a child's fear of dogs may interfere with the child walking to school, forcing the parents to drive the child to school, and in some cases has been known to lead to death when

the child panics and runs into a busy street to avoid dogs.

Finally, some fears are not related directly to school functioniong but can affect other facets of the child's life. A child may have a phobia of medical procedures that may affect the child's receiving proper treatment. Also, a child's phobia of the darkness may be manifested in panic and tantrums at bedtime. This child may avoid spending the night at the homes of friends and family members because of the embarrassment associated with the phobia.

The relationship of fears to anxiety and academic and other behavioral problems has been discussed in the literature. Avoidance of fear-evoking objects and situations is the most common behavioral response of phobic individuals. Reed et al. (1992) cited the results of studies (e.g., MacFarlane et al., 1954) in which relatively high correlations were reported between fears in children and timidity, overdependence, and mood swings. Miller et al. (1974) reported that phobic children differed significantly (i.e., had less desirable characteristics) from a matched sample of children in the general population on numerous variables including anxiety, fear, infantile aggression, hyperactivity, antisocial behavior, social withdrawal, sensitivity, academic disability, immaturity, normal irritability, rare deviance, prosocial behavior, need for achievement, and academic disability. Phobic children also were more likely to be extraverted, have fears of natural events, and have higher levels of social stress. Ollendick (1983) reported that fears are related to external locus of control, low self-concept, and overly anxious behavior. Also, Morris, Bergan, and Fulginiti (1991) found that school-related fears correlated with physical complaints (stomacheaches and headaches). Interestingly, Ollendick, Yule, and Ollier (1991) reported that, while anxiety was highly related with fears and depression, fears and depression did not correlate highly.

Relatively few guidelines have been established for making treatment decisions when working with children and adolescents experiencing fears, phobias, or anxiety. Barrios and Hartmann (1988) have raised some important issues related to making the decision whether treatment is indicated or not, as well as some guidelines for selecting specific procedures. First of all, taking a developmental perspective on children's fears, phobias, and anxiety reactions provides some helpful information for deciding whether intervention should be scheduled, given that much of the available evidence suggests that many common fears are part of normal development and are not a cause for alarm (Harris & Ferrari, 1983). Other issues raised by Barrios and Hartmann (1988) include

■ *Who is actually complaining?* This is the first issue that needs to be addressed. That is, what are the perceptions of the parents, teachers, child, and others toward the problem and treatment? Because most children are not self-referred to treatment but rather are brought to mental health professionals by parents, teachers, or others, it must be emphasized that the perceptions of adults are very important. Therapists also need to consider that a child may not necessarily be motivated to participate in treatment. Under these conditions, it is possible that adult demands or specific expectations of fearless behavior by the child are unreasonable. Thus, the focus of intervention may be on the parent or the adult caregiver rather than the child.

■ *Can the actual fear behavior be considered a problem?* As implied earlier, in defining a clinical fear or phobia, a problem is found to exist when the behavior disrupts the person's overall functioning; ability to adjust to the environment; and sense of comfort, satisfaction, and freedom as well as the pursuit of various personal goals (Karoly, 1980). It may, therefore, be important to consider not only the child but the entire family when making a decision to treat.

■ *Are the fear(s) related to other areas of the child's functioning and family dysfunctions?* One must be concerned with how fears are related to other areas of a child's functioning. It may be that another behavior problem should be the central focus for an intervention program. Thus, a child's fears or anxieties may be a reaction to other kinds of difficulties. Moreover, the child's fear may be linked to certain family dysfunctions or even child abuse.

■ *What are the costs of the treatment?* When developing an intervention program for a child experiencing a severe fear, it is necessary to consider the costs of the treatment (e.g., time, money, and effort), assuming demonstrated effectiveness of the procedure. A great deal of time, money, and effort often goes into treating a problem that is rather isolated and may become nonproblematic as the child gets older. Therapists need to be aware of the developmental course of fears and to use this information when deciding whether to intervene.

■ *What are the short- and long-term consequences for a child when a decision is made to treat or not to treat?* Another important question is: What would be different for the child in the absence of the fear or phobia? Basically, the mental health professional must consider short- and long-term consequences for a child when a decision is made to treat or not to treat. Answers to the aforementioned questions will determine whether more serious emotional problems for the child can be prevented or whether immediate intervention for more specific types of fears is necessary.

Alternative Actions

A variety of psychological intervention procedures have been used for children experiencing a broad range of fears and phobias. A number of major books have been published dealing with the treatment of childhood and adolescent fears, phobias, and anxiety (e.g., Craig & Dobson, 1995; Kendall et al., 1992; King et al., 1988; March, 1995; Ollendick, King, & Yule, 1994; Reynolds, 1992; see also the Recommended Resources). Much of the published empirical literature suggests that behavior therapy procedures can be used effectively to reduce various fears and phobias in children and adolescents.

Four major behavior therapy methods are used to treat children experiencing fears and phobias: desensitization (with variations), contingency-management procedures, modeling procedures, and cognitive-behavioral (self-control) methods. Flooding (and implosion), which confront the child with the feared stimulus at a high intensity level, are sometimes considered a part of the major behavior therapies. However, we do not recommend these procedures for treatment of most fears and phobias, and they will not be discussed here.

Systematic Desensitization

Systematic desensitization is the best known counterconditioning procedure (Morris & Kratochwill, 1983, 1991; Ollendick & Cerny, 1981). It was developed in the early 1950s by Wolpe (1958). In this form of intervention, it is assumed that a fear or anxiety response is learned and that it can be inhibited by substituting an activity antagonistic to this response. Usually, relaxation or some type of induced state of calmness is used during treatment to inhibit the anxiety response. Thus, the desensitization procedure involves exposing children in small graduated steps to some fear stimulus while they are performing the actual activity antagonistic to the feelings of tension or arousal. The graduated exposure to the fear or anxiety event can take place in real life or in an imaginary context.

Systematic desensitization has three major components: relaxation training, development of an anxiety hierarchy, and the actual systematic desensitization treatment procedure. In the relaxation phase, the child (typically, a child older than 9 years of age) is taught methods to relax, essentially through relaxing and tensing various muscle groups. In anxiety-hierarchy development, a therapist designs, with the child's assistance, a hierarchy of various situations or events from the least to the most anxiety provoking. The hierarchies usually differ in respect to the number of people present, particular settings in which fears occur, and the number of items in the hierarchy.

During systematic desensitization proper, the therapist actually pairs relaxation training with the components of the hierarchy. The child is asked to imagine each scene as vividly as possible while maintaining a relaxed condition. The hierarchy elements developed during the previous phase are then presented in ascending order while relaxation is paired with the condition. It is important that the counterconditioning response (i.e., relaxation) be sufficiently strong to inhibit the fear at each step of the hierarchy (Ollendick & Francis, 1988). Other variations have been used in place of relaxation as the anxiety-antagonistic state. These include story telling, game playing, eating, maternal and therapist contact, laughter, and anger (Barrios & O'Dell, 1989). Systematic desensitization can present difficulties with children who may find the relaxation training to be demanding and tedious, and the evocation and control of images can be difficult for younger children. There are a number of variations of systematic desensitization that may be especially applicable to children. For example, in vivo (or live) desensitization involves exposing children to actual situations in the hierarchy rather than relying on the imagination.

In vivo desensitization procedures would have obvious benefits for children who are unable to imagine or whose treatment might be better focused on real as opposed to symbolic representations of the problem area. Phelps, Cox, and Bajorek (1992) recommend using imagery with children over the age of 10 until they demonstrate a willingness to try the technique in vivo. With younger children, they recommend that the therapist use numerous in vivo sessions, beginning with innocuous settings and working up the fear hierarchy.

Another variation is called emotive imagery. It involves having children listen to the therapist describe particular anxiety-arousing scenes or scenarios that concern their favorite hero, usually from television, movies, fiction, or fantasy or from the child's imagination, such as Batman or Superman (Morris & Kratochwill, 1983). Then, they are requested to imagine a favorite hero successfully overcoming the anxiety or fear during a particular scene. After using muscular relaxation as the inhibiting agent unsuccessfully with a child with fear of the dark, noises, and shadows, Jackson and King (1981) used emotive imagery. They developed a fear hierarchy after determining that the child was fond of Batman. The child was asked to imagine that he was joining forces as a special agent with Batman. Then, he was asked to close his eyes and imagine the fear-producing stimuli in graduated steps, while accompanied by Batman. The following transcript illustrates the development of the imagery and introduction of the fear-producing stimuli. The child's words are in italics and demonstrate the active involvement:

Close your eyes. Now I want you to imagine that you are sitting in the lounge room watching TV with your family. You're dressed for bed and the last program before bedtime has finished. Your mother tells you it's time for bed but just then Batman, who you really wish you knew, appears out of nowhere and sits down next to you. Think about it as best you can. Can you see Batman in your head?
Yes.
Can you tell me what Batman is wearing? What color are his clothes?
He's got black and red clothes and big shoes and a gun.
Oh, you can see him with a gun?
Yeah, he needs it for the Joker.
That's terrific, M. Now I want you to imagine that Batman tells

you he needs you on his mission to catch robbers and other bad people and he's appointed you as his special agent. However, he needs you to get your sleep in your bedroom and he will call on you when he needs you. You're lucky to have been chosen to help him.
Yes.
Now your mother puts you in your bed and leaves both the lights on and the three blinds up. Batman is also there looking as strong as he always does. Think about it as clearly as you can. Can you see it?
Yes, I can see mummy (sic) and Batman in my room and all the lights are on.
Well if you're scared raise your finger. . . . (p. 327)

Other variations of systematic desensitization involve contact desensitization (also known as participant modeling and described next) and self-control desensitization (see Morris & Kratochwill, 1983, 1991). Also, children can often participate in systematic desensitization in a group format. In this case, children participate at the pace of the slowest member in the group.

Contingency Management

Contingency-management procedures are associated with the operant or applied behavior-analysis model of treatment. This particular model focuses on the environmental consequences for learning and unlearning of fear-related responses. A common therapeutic procedure used within contingency management is positive reinforcement. This procedure has been used alone and in combination with other behavioral procedures to facilitate children's adaptation to settings previously deemed fearful. To be most effective, the therapist must assess both the positive and negative consequences that maintain the fear response (Ollendick & Francis, 1988). For example, in one project Vaal (1973) used a contingency contracting system for a 13-year-old boy who had previously been afraid to attend school. The contingency-management program was set up to gradually get the child back to school. He was permitted various privileges (such as going bowling, attending a basketball game) that were contingent on meeting certain criteria for school attendance. The treatment program lasting approximately 6 weeks was generally successful.

A variety of other behavioral procedures have also been used within the contingency-management or operant approach to treatment. These procedures are outlined in great detail in many child therapy textbooks (see King et al., 1988; Kratochwill & Morris, 1991, 1993; Morris & Kratochwill, 1983; Ollendick & Cerny, 1981).

Modeling Interventions

Modeling approaches can be useful in the treatment of fears, phobias, and related anxieties where there appears to be a lack of skill on the part of the child; that is, the child does not know which specific behaviors are required to effectively deal with the feared situation (King, 1993).

Modeling treatment approaches are associated with the social learning theory of Bandura and his coworkers. The modeling procedures generally consist of having the therapist, teacher, peer, or parent model or demonstrate certain positive responses for the client observer. The model engages successfully in certain behaviors that are fear or anxiety provoking in the observer. The following requirements must be met for modeling to be successful: Clients must (a) attend to certain aspects of the modeling situation; (b) retain what has been learned in the modeling situation; (c) reproduce or match what has been observed; and (d) be motivated to carry out the observed behavior (Bandura, 1977). The therapist also must also be able to guarantee that the model does not experience any perceived or unsafe consequences in the fear or anxiety situation. Moreover, the model is typically instructed to approach the target situation gradually and with caution—in a coping fashion—so as to enhance the modeling effect (Morris & Kratochwill, 1983, 1991).

Three types of modeling have been described in the literature: in vivo modeling, filmed (or symbolic) modeling, and participant modeling (or contact desensitization). In live modeling, children view live models (usually with similar characteristics as the targeted children) participating successfully in various activities such as going to school without any fear. Symbolic modeling, a more common strategy, involves having children view a tape of individuals like themselves participating in a fear-laden experience. The third type, participant modeling, involves both in vivo modeling and physical contact with a therapist (or fearless peer) who physically guides the target child through the fearful situation. The child is provided with realistic information about the feared stimulus, encouragement to perform the modeled behavior, and positive verbal feedback regarding the imitated performance (Morris & Kratochwill, 1983).

Modeling treatments can be very helpful in working with children, and there has been empirical support for modeling with phobic children—with the greatest evidence for participant modeling and the least evidence for filmed modeling. Successful outcomes are influenced by other variables including the similarity of the model's age and gender, use of multiple models, and the child's level of initial anxiety (Ollendick & Francis, 1988). Unfortunately, while modeling procedures have been used extensively with children's non-school-related fears and anxieties, relatively little work has been published on school-related fears and anxieties other than the work on the treatment of social withdrawal/social isolation (Morris & Kratochwill, 1985; Morris et al., 1988).

Self-Control Methods

Self-control methods of treatment typically are associated with cognitive-behavior modification procedures (Meichenbaum & Genest, 1980). There are relatively few treatment studies focused on the school-related fears and anxieties of children and adolescents (King & Ollendick, 1989). The underlying approach in self-control therapies is the view that cognitive processes contribute substantially to any behavior-change program established and that children and adolescents can regulate their own behavior. Also, therapists serve the role of instigator or motivator, but the individual child is primarily responsible for carrying out the intervention program.

Self-control procedures involve the following major components of the therapeutic approach: (a) becoming aware of negative thinking styles that impede performance and lead to an emotional upset and inadequate performance; (b) generating in collaboration with the trainer a set of incompatible self-statements, rules, and strategies for use in fear-arousing situations; (c) learning specific, adaptive cognitive-behavioral skills (Meichenbaum & Genest, 1980, p. 403). Clients must be aware of their anxiety reactions, possibly across the three response channels, for the program to be effective.

An intervention reported by Craddock, Cotler, and Jason (1978) illustrates the use of a cognitive self-control program. These authors studied the relative effectiveness of cognitive-behavior rehearsal and a systematic desensitization program on reduction of speech anxiety in high school freshman girls. In the cognitive intervention treatment, the students were provided a treatment rationale and the steps they needed to take for speech preparation and delivery. The students also were guided through imaginary exercises. Subsequently, treatment sessions consisted of learning 18 hierarchical steps in preparing and giving a speech as well as studying potential coping strategies that could be used prior to and during the speech. For example, a girl might say to herself, "I can handle this step by taking a deep breath and remaining calm." Items in the hierarchy were presented for one minute, and then the students were requested to imagine themselves using a coping strategy at each step. When these results were compared to a more conventional systematic desensitization procedure, the cognitive rehearsal group demonstrated a significant reduction relative to a delayed treatment control group in scores on a speech anxiety measure. However, on motor measures such as stammering and hand tremors, no differences were found in this study.

Another self-control approach is that of problem solving which follows a sequential process of working through a problem until reaching a solution. Instead of avoiding the situation, the child is assisted in determining alternative ways of coping with the feared stimulus. Kendall et al. (1992) describe the case of a 13-year-old child who worried excessively about failing tests. With the therapist's assistance, the child used a problem-solving approach in making reasonable preparations for the test. The child generated numerous ideas, including checking with other students about how long they prepared for the test and reminding herself that any score above 80% would indicate mastery of the material.

The efficacy of cognitive procedures alone has been questioned, however, by some writers (e.g., King, 1993). Ollendick, Hagopian, and Huntzinger (1991) reported that, for the treatment of two nighttime fearful children, self-control training alone was ineffective. When reinforcement training was added to self-control training, there was improvement. Ollendick and Francis (1988) recommend an integrative treatment approach which includes exposure variants, modeling, and behavioral- and cognitive-based procedures. Heard, Dodds, and Conrad (1992) used such an approach in the treatment of three adolescents females with simple phobias. Their successful treatment consisted of strategies including the construction of hierarchies of anxiety-provoking stimuli for in vivo exposure, participant modeling, cognitive restructuring, the application of relaxation/regulated breathing techniques, and home contingency management.

Parents and teachers also need to be considered agents of therapuetic change (Heard et al., 1992; Robinson et al., 1991). Via consultation, parents can be involved in contingency management and learn information about the nature of their children's fears, more effective ways of supporting each other, and interacting with their children in more constructive ways. Also, parents and teachers can be taught ways of effectively preventing children's fears and phobias. Examples of primary and secondary prevention strategies (e.g., Jersild & Holmes, 1935b; Robinson et al., 1991) include

1. Provide an explanation of the nature of the feared stimulus (e.g., noise) combined with a partial introductory experience, demonstration, or example of fearfullness.
2. Promote skill attainment.
3. Anticipate the effects of maturation (e.g., accustoming the child to the dark in anticipation of the age when the child is likely to develop fear of the dark).
4. Display a casual attitude toward the feared stimulus with or without the use of explanation.
5. Prevent fear stimulation (e.g., by refraining from building on the child's fears for disciplinary purposes).
6. Conduct child guidance activities that address self-control and security issues.
7. Seek opportunities to explore and master feared objects (e.g., reading stories about the dark).

Selecting Interventions

When selecting an intervention program for a child experiencing fear, phobia, or anxiety, the therapist also must take into consideration the age appropriateness of the techniques and make whatever necessary modifications to ensure understanding and cooperation by children and their caretakers (King, Gullone, & Tonge, 1991). Some of the more common characteristics of the individual child that should be considered prior to the selection of treatment include the child's skills in language and imagery. Generally, the child's ability to participate in a self-management program should be assessed before this type of intervention is established.

Also, it is necessary to consider a series of questions that relate to conducting a carefully developed functional analysis of the problem (Shill et al., 1996). Specifically, it is important to identify the target response. As noted earlier, anxiety or fear can occur within physiological, cognitive, or motor response domains. Within the cognitive fear domains, various images, thoughts, and feelings may be an important focus of the intervention. In addition, the child may demonstrate problematic motor responses that involve escape or avoidance of various situations, such as school. In this regard, it is important to keep in mind that the various fear behaviors the child is demonstrating may be appropriate in a harmful, dangerous, or aversive environment. The child may also display social skills deficits or inability to perform various academic skills. Thus, the appropriate focus of intervention actually may be on teaching social skills or various areas of the academic curriculum.

Another question relates to the conditions in which the problem response occurs. A careful functional analysis of the environment can further help the clinician to determine whether there are basic skills deficits involved or whether there is a conditioned or learned emotional reaction to some anxiety-provoking stimulus. Other aspects of the child's environment must be assessed when the treatment program is selected. This assessment will often include a comprehensive review of the behavior, skills, and motivations of any adults involved, as they might contribute to the problem and treatment. In addition, characteristics of siblings, teachers, or others who are related to the child in the social environment would need to be assessed.

Summary

This chapter has presented an overview of definitions, incidence, diagnosis, theories, and treatment approaches related to children's fears and phobias. A common definitional conceptualization is a multidimensional one which takes into account motoric, cognitive, and psychophysiological systems. There is general consensus that most fears in children and adolescents are common, transient, and developmentally appropriate. Phobias are less common and can be severely disabling. With phobias, there is a severe anxiety reaction disproportionate to the actual threat.

Considerable research has been conducted on normative and developmental aspects of children's fears and phobias. While age-related differences in the content of fears is a consistent finding, the frequency of fears between younger and older children has been an inconsistent finding. Generally, girls have scored higher than boys on fear measures, and children with disabilities have scored higher than children without disabilities. Conclusions about the effects of other variables (e.g., SES and race) have been inconclusive.

Fears and phobias can disrupt the functioning of the child and others in a variety of settings, including social and academic. Childhood fears have been associated with a number of variables, including timidity, overdependence, mood swings, external locus of control, low self-concept, overly anxious behavior, and physical complaints.

A number of theories about the development of fears and phobias have been advanced, with behavioral models having the most empirical support. Desensitization (with variations), contingency management, modeling, and cognitive-behavioral treatment are among the most widely used and effective treatment procedures for children experiencing fears and phobias. Guidelines for making treatment decisions were suggested, and an integrative treatment approach is recommended.

Recommended Resources

Kendall P. C., Chansky, T. E., Kane, M. T., Kim, R. S., Kortlander, E., Ronan, K. R., Sessa, F. M., & Siqueland, L. (1992). *Anxiety disorders in youth: Cognitive-behavioral interventions.* New York: Allyn & Bacon.
This volume's focus is cognitive-behavioral interventions of anxiety disorders in youth. A cognitive-behavioral model is presented, and assessment methods are described. Other areas addressed include cognitive-behavioral treatment strategies, an integrated cognitive-behavioral treatment program, suggestions for working with families, dealing with potential difficulties, clinical case examples, and research results.

King, N. J., & Ollendick, T. H. (1989). Children's anxiety and phobic disorders in school settings: Classification, assessment, and intervention issues. *Review of Educational Research, 59,* 431–470.
The authors discuss normal fears, epidemiological issues, and classification schemes of childhood anxiety disorders. Also discussed are basic features and methodological issues from a cognitive-behavioral perspective. The authors review a range of assessment techiques and cognitive-behavioral treatments and stress the need for flexibility and use of integrative treatment methods in the school setting.

Morris, R. J., & Kratochwill, T. R. (1991). Fears and phobias. In T. R. Kratochwill & R. J. Morris (Eds.), *The practice of child therapy* (2nd ed. pp. 76–114). Boston: Allyn & Bacon.
Definitional and assessment issues related to children's fears and phobias are discussed and an overview of the various treatment approaches for reducing such fears and phobias is provided.

Ollendick, T. H., King, N. J. & Yule, W. (Eds.). (1994). *International handbook of phobic and anxiety disorders in children and adolescents.* New York: Plenum Press.
In this volume, the authors explore issues related to understanding phobic and anxiety disorders in children and adolescents. Various assessment strategies (ranging from structured diagnostic interviews to physiological assessment) are discussed along with theoretical underpinnings for their use, including case examples. Finally, treatment interventions and prevention strategies are presented.

References

American Psychiatric Association. (1994). *Diagnostic and statistical manual of mental disorders* (4th ed.). Washington, DC: Author.

Anderson, J. C., Williams, S., McGee, R., & Silva, P. A. (1987). The prevalence of DSM-III disorders in preadolescent children: Prevalence in a large sample from the general population. *Archives of General Psychiatry, 44,* 69–76.

Bandura, A. (1977). *Social learning theory.* Englewood Cliffs, NJ: Prentice-Hall.

Barrios, B. A., & Hartmann, D. P. (1988). Fears and anxieties. In E. J. Mash & L. G. Terdal (Eds.), *Behavioral assessment of childhood disorders* (2nd ed., pp. 196–262). New York: Guilford Press.

Barrios, B. A., & O'Dell, S. L. (1989). Fears and anxieties. In E. J. Mash & R. A. Barkley (Eds.), *Treatment of childhood disorders* (pp. 167–221). New York: Guilford Press.

Bauer, D. (1976). An exploratory study of developmental changes in children's fears. *Journal of Child Psychology and Psychiatry, 17,* 69–74.

Beck, A. T., & Emery, G. (1985). *Anxiety disorders and phobias: A cognitive perspective.* New York: Basic Books.

Craddock, C., Cotler, S., & Jason, L. A. (1978). Primary prevention: Immunization of children for speech anxiety. *Cognitive Therapy and Research, 2,* 389–396.

Craig, K. K. & Dobson, K. S. (Eds.). (1995). *Anxiety and depression in adults and children.* Thousand Oaks, CA: Sage.

Deverenski, J. L. (1979). Children's fears: A developmental comparison of normal and exceptional children. *The Journal of Genetic Psychology, 135,* 11–21.

Fonseca, A. C., Yule, W., & Erol, N. (1994). Cross-cultural issues. In T. H. Ollendick, N. J. King, & W. Yule (Eds.), *International handbook of phobic and anxiety disorders in children and adolescents* (pp. 67–84). New York: Plenum.

Graziano, A. M., DeGiovanni, I. S., & Garcia, K. A. (1979). Behavioral treatments of children's fears: A review. *Psychological Bulletin, 86,* 804–830.

Harris, S. L., & Ferrari, M. (1983). The developmental factors in child behavior therapy. *Behavior Therapy, 14,* 54–72.

Heard, P. M., Dodds, M. R., & Conrad, P. (1992). Assessment and treatment of simple phobias in children: Effects on family and marital relationships. *Behaviour Change, 9,* 73–82.

Hull, C. (1943). *Principles of behavior.* New York: Appleton-Century-Crofts.

Jackson, H. J., & King, N. J. (1981). The emotive imagery treatment of a child's trauma-induced phobia. *Journal of Behavior Therapy and Experimental Psychiatry, 12,* 325–328.

Jersild, A. T. (1954). Emotional development. In L. Car-michael (Ed.), *Manual of child psychology* (2nd ed., pp. 833–917). New York: John Wiley & Sons.

Jersild, A. T., & Holmes, F. B. (1935a). Children's fears. *Child Development Monograph, 20.*

Jersild, A. T., & Holmes, F. B. (1935b). Methods of overcoming children's fears. *Journal of Psychology, 1,* 75–104.

Karoly, P. (1980). Operant methods. In F. H. Kanfer & A. P. Goldstein (Eds.), *Helping people change* (2nd ed., pp. 210–247). New York: Pergamon.

Kearney, C. A., & Silverman, W. K. (1993). Measuring the function of school refusal behavior: The School Refusal Assessment Scale. *Journal of Clinical Child Psychology, 22,* 85–96.

Kendall P. C., Chansky, T. E., Kane, M. T., Kim, R. S., Kortlander, E., Ronan, K. R., Sessa, F. M., & Siqueland, L. (1992). *Anxiety disorders in youth: Cognitive-behavioral interventions.* New York: Allyn & Bacon.

King, N. J. (1993). Simple and social phobias. In T. H. Ollendick & R. J. Prinz (Eds.), *Advances in clinical child psychology* (pp. 305–341). New York: Plenum Press.

King, N. J., Gullone, E., & Tonge, B. J. (1991). Childhood fears and anxiety disorders. *Behaviour Change, 8,* 124–135.

King, N. J., Hamilton, D. I., & Ollendick, T. H. (1988). *Children's phobias: A behavioral perspective.* New York: John Wiley & Sons.

King, N. J., & Ollendick, T. H. (1989). Children's anxiety and phobic disorders in school settings: Classification, assessment, and intervention issues. *Review of Educational Research, 59,* 431–470.

Kratochwill, T. R., & Morris, R. J. (Eds.). (1991). *The practice of child therapy* (2nd ed.). New York: Pergamon Press.

Kratochwill, T. R., & Morris, R. J. (Eds.). (1993). *Handbook of psychotherapy with children and adolescents.* Boston: Allyn & Bacon.

Lang, P. J. (1984). Cognition in emotion: Concept and action. In C. E. Izard, J. Kagan, & R. B. Zajonc (Eds.), *Emotions, cognition, and behavior* (pp. 192–226). New York: Cambridge University Press.

Lapouse, R., & Monk, M. A. (1959). Fears and worries in a representative sample of children. *American Journal of Orthopsychiatry, 29,* 803–818.

Last, C. G., & Perrin, S. (1993). Anxiety disorders in African-American and White children. *Journal of Abnormal Child Psychology, 21,* 153–164.

MacFarlane, J. W., Allen, L., & Hozik, M. P. (1954). *A developmental study of the behavior problems of normal children between twenty-one months and fourteen years.* Berkeley, CA: University of California Press.

March, J. S. (Ed.). (1995). *Anxiety disorders in children and adolescents.* New York: Guilford Press.

Marks, I. M. (1969). *Fears and phobias.* New York: Academic Press.

McGee, R., Feehan, M., Williams, S., & Anderson, J. (1992). The DSM-III disorders from age 11 to age 15 years. *Journal of the American Academy of Child and Adolescent Psychiatry, 31,* 50–59.

Meichenbaum, D., & Genest, M. (1980). Cognitive behavior modification: An integration of cognitive and behav-

ioral methods. In F. H. Kanfer & A. P. Goldstein (Eds.), *Helping people change* (2nd ed., pp. 390–422). Elmsford, NY: Pergamon.

Miller, L. C., Barrett, C. L., & Hampe, E. (1974). Phobias of childhood in a prescientific era. In A. Davids (Ed.), *Child personality and psychopathology: Current topics* (pp. 89–134). New York: Wiley.

Moracco, J., & Camilleri, J. (1983). A study of fears in elementary school children. *Elementary School Guidance and Counseling, 18,* 82–87.

Morris, R. J., Bergan, J. R., & Fulginiti, J. V. (1991). Structural equation modeling in clinical assessment research with children. *Journal of Consulting and Clinical Psychology, 59,* 371–379.

Morris, R. J., & Kratochwill, T. R. (1983). *Treating children's fears and phobias: A behavioral approach.* Elmsford, NY: Pergamon.

Morris, R. J., & Kratochwill, T. R. (1985). Behavioral treatment of children's fears and phobias: A review. *School Psychology Review, 14,* 84–93.

Morris, R. J., & Kratochwill, T. R. (1991). Fears and phobias. In T. R. Kratochwill & R. J. Morris (Eds.), *The practice of child therapy* (2nd ed., pp. 76–114). Boston: Allyn & Bacon.

Morris, R. J., Kratochwill, T. R., & Aldridge, K. (1988). Fears and phobias. In J. C., Witt, S. N. Elliott, & F. M. Gresham (Eds.), *Handbook of behavior therapy in education* (pp. 679–717). New York: Plenum.

Mower, O. H. (1960). *Learning theory and behavior.* New York: Wiley.

Nalven, F. B. (1970). Manifest fears and worries of ghetto versus middle class suburban children. *Psychological Reports, 27,* 285–286.

Nietzel, M. T., & Bernstein, D. A. (1981). Assessment of anxiety and fear. In M. Hersen & A. S. Bellack (Eds.), *Behavioral assessment: A practical handbook* (2nd ed., pp. 215–245). New York: Pergamon.

Ollendick, T. H. (1979). Fear reduction techniques with children. In M. Hersen, R. M. Eisler, & P. M. Miller (Eds.), *Progress in behavior modification* (Vol. 8, pp. 127–168). New York: Academic Press.

Ollendick, T. H. (1983). Reliability and validity of the revised fear survey schedule for children. *Behaviour Research and Therapy, 21,* 685–692.

Ollendick, T. H., & Cerny, J. A. (1981). *Clinical behavior therapy with children.* New York: Plenum Press.

Ollendick, T. H., & Francis, G. (1988). Behavioral assessment and treatment of childhood phobias. *Behavior Modification, 12,* 165–204.

Ollendick, T. H., Hagopian, L. P., & Huntzinger, R. M. (1991a). Cognitive-behavior therapy with nighttime fearful children. *Journal of Behavior Therapy and Experimental Psychiatry, 22,* 113–121.

Ollendick, T. H., King, N. J., & Frary, R. B. (1989). Fears in children and adolescents: Reliability and generalizability across gender, age and nationality. *Behaviour Research and Therapy, 27,* 19–26.

Ollendick, T. H., King, N. J., & Hamilton, D. I. (1991b). Origins of childhood fears: An evaluation of Rachman's theory of fear acquisition. *Behaviour Research and Therapy, 29,* 117–123.

Ollendick, T. H., King, N. J., & Yule, W. (Eds.). (1994). *International handbook of phobic and anxiety disorders.* New York: Plenum Press.

Ollendick, T. H., Yule, W., & Ollier, K. (1991). Fears in British children and their relationship to manifest anxiety and depression. *Journal of Child Psychology and Psychiatry, 32,* 321–331.

Phelps, L., Cox, D., & Bajorek, E. (1992). School phobia and separation anxiety: Diagnostic and treatment comparisons. *Psychology in the Schools, 29,* 384–394.

Ramirez, S. Z., & Kratochwill, T. R. (in press). Self-reported fears in children with and without mental retardation. *Mental Retardation.*

Reed, L. J., Carter, B. D., & Miller, L. C. (1992). Fear and anxiety in children. In C. E. Walker & M. C. Roberts (Eds.), *Handbook of clinical child psychology* (pp. 237–260). New York: John Wiley & Sons.

Reynolds, W. W. (Ed.). (1992). *Internalizing disorders in children and adolescents.* New York: Wiley.

Robinson, E. H., Rotter, J. C., Fey, M. A., & Robinson, S. L. (1991). Children's fears: Toward a preventive model. *The School Counselor, 38,* 187–202.

Shill, M. A., Kratochwill, T. R., & Gardner, W. I. (1996). Conducting a functional analysis of behavior. In M. J. Breen & C. R. Fiedler (Eds.), *Behavioral approach to the assessment of youth with emotional and behavioral disorders.* (pp. 83–179). Austin, TX: Pro-ed.

Silverman, W. K., & Nelles, W. B. (1990). Simple phobia in childhood. In M. Hersen & C. G. Last (Eds.), *Handbook of child and adult psychopathology: A longitudinal perspective* (pp. 183–195). New York: Plenum.

Strauss, C. C. (1990). Anxiety disorders of childhood and adolescence. *School Psychology Review, 19,* 142–157.

Vaal, J. J. (1973). Applying contingency contracting to a school phobic: A case study. *Journal of Behavior Therapy and Experimental Psychiatry, 4,* 371–373.

Vandenburg, B. (1993). Fears of normal and retarded children. *Psychological Reports, 72,* 473–474.

Wolpe, J. (1958). *Reciprocal inhibition therapy.* Stanford, CA: Stanford University Press.

29

Selective Mutism

Thomas J. Kehle
John M. Hintze
University of Connecticut

George J. DuPaul
Lehigh University

Background and Development

Selective mutism was first reported in the psychological and medical literature over 100 years ago under the rubric "aphasia voluntaria" (Colligan, Colligan, & Dilliard, 1977). Since the 1930s, aphasia voluntaria has been replaced with the term *elective mutism*. Currently, *selective mutism* is the preferred term used to describe the disorder, due to the selective nature of the behavior. "Not only does the child elect when to speak, but the child selects the conditions under which to speak" (Porjes, 1992, p. 370). The essential feature of children exhibiting selective mutism is their failure to speak in specific settings, such as the school, although they freely converse in other settings. There appears to be considerable variation amongst children with selective mutism regarding the rate and production of speech as a function of the school or home settings.

In order to meet the criteria specified in the *Diagnostic and Statistical Manual of Mental Disorders-Fourth Edition* (*DSM-IV,* American Psychiatric Association, 1994), the condition has to be severe enough to impede the child's academic and social functioning and not be due solely to lack of knowledge of the spoken language or embarrassment as a result of some communication disorder. Associated features of selective mutism may include excessive shyness, social isolation and withdrawal, negativism, tantrumming, anxiety, and controlling oppositional behaviors, particularly in the home setting (*DSM-IV,* American Psychiatric Association, 1994). Wright and Cuccaro (1994) noted that some of the associated features are not mutually exclusive. As such, they recommend considering the possibility that the child's oppositional controlling behaviors develop as a consequence of both the parent-child interactions and the child's relative absence of other coping strategies.

The onset of selective mutism usually occurs around the time the child enters school (Kratochwill, 1981) and typically lasts for several months. However, it may persist throughout the child's educational career and even into adulthood. Black and Uhde (1992) have noted the coincidence of the onset of selective mutism with the child starting school and suggest that the disorder may be a manifestation of school refusal behavior.

Selective mutism is rare, occurring in perhaps no more than 1 per 1,000 children (Kolvin & Fundudis, 1981). Although it appears to be slightly more prevalent in females (Kaplan-Tancer, 1992), other demographic characteristics such as the child's intellectual competencies, ethnicity, and social economic background have not been shown to be related to the rate of incidence.

Several formulations regarding the etiology and treatment of selective mutism have been described. However, the overwhelming majority of the literature can be summarized under the two general approaches derived from either the psychoanalytic or learning-theories perspective (Porjes, 1992). From a psychoanalytic perspective, multiple causal factors are implicated including a predisposition for social reticence, trauma during a critical period of language development, an insecure environment, the use of mutism to reduce fear, and finally, a conflictual family environment (Colligan et al., 1977). Components of the conflictual family environment include social isolation, disharmony, an absent or emotionally distant father, and an overprotective depressed mother who establishes and maintains a highly enmeshed relationship with her child (Shvarztman, Hornshtein, Klein, Yechezkel, 1990).

In concert with the psychoanalytic assumption that selective mutism functions as a way to reduce fear, Shreeve (1991) suggested that the disorder originates as a freezing reaction from being exposed to a perceived dangerous event. In subsequent anxiety-provoking situations, such as the school, the child reduces fear through unresponsiveness.

Etiology based on learning theory suggests that selective mutism is a "learned response, perhaps with obscure origins, representing discriminative learning maintained by a differential pattern of idiosyncratic reinforcers" (Colligan et al., 1977, p. 10). Reed and Mees (1967) suggested that the child's selective mutism was maintained by significant individuals, such as parents and teachers, within the child's social environment.

Historically the condition has shown to be highly resistant to intervention (Dowrick & Hood, 1978; Yates, 1970). This resistance to intervention may be because children with selective mutism are often inadvertently reinforced for responding nonverbally. Teacher requests are often simply ignored or avoided by exhibiting distressed behavior. In either situation, requests for compliance are often suspended, and consequently the child is negatively reinforced. Furthermore, the child with selective mutism is reinforced for not speaking by classmates who may assume a protective attitude toward him or her and interpret the child's needs to the teacher (Scott, 1977; Sheridan, Kratochwill, & Ramirez, 1995).

Considering the outcomes of studies based on different theoretical orientations provides a way to evaluate the psychodynamic and learning-theories perspectives on the causes and effective treatment strategies for selective mutism. The majority of treatment procedures that have produced substantial and enduring changes in selective mutism have been based on learning theory and involved the behavior-therapy techniques of reinforcement, stimulus fading, modeling, token economies, and shaping (Kratochwill, 1981; Labbe & Williamson, 1984; Sheridan et al., 1995). Also there have been successful treatment outcomes that involve self-modeling combined with a variety of behavioral-therapy techniques (Kehle, Root, Spackman, Boyer, & Conte, 1995). Finally, Black and Uhde (1992), who believe that selective mutism is a manifestation of social phobia, have had treatment success with fluoxetine, a medication also effective with social phobia.

There is a dearth of experimental research supporting therapeutic approaches based on psychodynamic theory (Redford, 1977), family therapy (Pustrom & Speers, 1964), or joint mother-child therapy (Atoynatan, 1986). Scott (1977) states that traditional psychotherapy is of little value in treating children with selective mutism. In accord with the early work of Reed (1963), Sluckin, Foreman, and Herbert (1991) found that treatment gains are most often noted when behaviorally based strategies are employed.

Problems and Implications

In addition to the previously cited features associated with *DSM-IV,* selective mutism has also been related to a lack of eye contact (Louden, 1987), enuresis (Barlow, Strother, & Landreth, 1986), motor activity delays (Kolvin & Fundudis, 1981), apathy, and timidity (Rutter, 1977). According to Kanner (1957), selective mutism may also be a precursor to severe behavioral maladjustment.

It has been noted for some time (Salfield, 1950) that children with selective mutism may have other family members that also employ silence in reaction to difficult situations. Sluckin et al. (1991) noted, in an examination of factors associated with successful treatment outcome for children with selective mutism, a poor prognostic indicator was the presence of mental illness in an immediate family member.

The course of selective mutism may be relatively short, lasting for only a couple of months (American Psychiatric Association, 1994), or it can persist throughout the school years into adulthood. The longer selective mutism persists, the more delimiting it becomes. The senior author has attempted unsuccessfully to treat a 34-year-old female with selective mutism. This woman has been totally mute since kindergarten and currently will only converse with her mother and, to a lesser extent, her brother. In 29 years, she has not had any verbal communication with anyone else, including her father or other relatives. Her situation is desperate in that she cannot function independently outside of the home setting.

Perhaps one of the more serious problems associated with selective mutism in childhood is the restriction of social interactions with teachers and classmates. Friendship formation in the school setting is very limited when there is an absence of conversation. Additionally, although many children with selective mutism perform well academically, it is reasonable to assume that their educational experiences are also diminished by the lack of verbal engagement with their teachers and classmates. However, there is considerable variation among children with selective mutism with regard to their social interactions with their peers. Some children control their social environments to the extent that they use their classmates, and even teachers, to assist them in nonverbally fulfilling their needs; others are severely apathetic and socially withdrawn.

The theoretical orientation of either psychoanalytic or learning theory clearly influences one's consideration of the problems and implications associated with selective mutism. As stated by Porjes (1992), studies based on psychoanalytic theory assume that pathology exists and that it exists strictly within the child. Studies based on the learning-theory approach assume that the child's selective mutism is a learned pattern of behavior maintained by social reinforcement within the environment. Consequently, with the learning-theory perspective, it is assumed that many of the features associated with selective mutism will be diminished or eliminated when talking is reinstated through the aid of behavior therapy.

Alternative Actions

Because selective mutism is typically manifested around the time the child starts school, the school psychologist is likely to design an intervention and coordinate treatment efforts. In addition to the obvious delimiting effect that selective mutism has on the child's academic and social functioning within the school, there are often serious associated problems. Thus, interventions will ideally require collaboration between home and school. Establishing and maintaining an effective therapeutic relationship with the family, particularly the mother, to effect change in the maternal-child relationship can be a challenging task.

Within the home setting, perhaps a more troublesome problem is the child's controlling oppositional behavior. In one study, controlling oppositional behavior was noted in 90% of children with selective mutism (Krohn, Weckstein, & Wright, 1992). Further, a high rate (59%) of maternal-child overenmeshment was apparent (Krohn et al., 1992). It is reasonable to assume that the associated feature of controlling oppositional behavior is perhaps due in part to the overenmeshed style of maternal-child interaction, thus making this interaction an important focus of any family-based intervention.

The school setting also can be successfully employed to effect change (Bendar, 1974) and may even be better suited. According to Bendar, school personnel, particularly the school psychologist, ideally should attempt to involve the parents within the school-based treatment.

Interventions shown to be most effective with selective mutism have often employed behavior therapy approaches. These include contingency management, stimulus fading, shaping, escape or avoidance techniques, and self-modeling. Recently, pharmacological treatment and combined learning-theory and pharmacological approaches have been employed as effective treatment strategies. Most of these interventions have produced positive change with few treatment sessions.

The selection of treatment strategies will be substantially aided by carefully analyzing the function of the child's selective mutism (Mace & West, 1986). Treatment strategies designed on the basis of an accurate analysis of the conditions maintaining the selective mutism will obviously have a greater effect.

Contingency Management

Contingency management involves reinforcement for verbal behavior and extinction of the child's nonverbal responses. Williamson, Sewell, Sanders, Haney, and White (1977) employed a contingency-management procedure with an 8-year-old male who occasionally conversed with classmates, usually during recess. A 45-minute class party was made contingent upon the child making 45 verbalizations to his classmates during recess.

Public posting of the child's progress toward accumulating the necessary tokens promoted the participation of his entire class. The child earned the class party after 5 days. The treatment program continued with individual privileges, rather than the group reinforcer, contingent upon the child's verbal interactions. Speech production increased dramatically and was maintained at a one-year follow-up.

Piersel and Kratochwill (1981) suggested that greater gains will be realized when both verbal behaviors are reinforced and nonverbal communicative behavior is extinguished, in contrast to solely reinforcing the child's verbal behavior. Based on these recommendations, Morin, Ladouceur, and Cloutier (1982) employed a contingency-based variable-ratio reinforcement schedule, through which the teacher intermittently reinforced verbal behavior with "school money" that could be exchanged for a reward while ignoring all nonverbal communication. The intervention was shown to be effective with a 6-year-old boy with selective mutism. Follow-up observations after one year revealed the treatment effects were maintained to the extent that the child no longer refused to speak or answer questions.

Similarly, Sanok and Striefel (1979) used reinforcement contingent upon verbal responses and response cost as a consequence for not responding to increase the verbal production of an 11-year-old girl who had a 6-year history of selective mutism. In this study, the treatment effects also generalized to other settings. Colligan et al. (1977) employed contingency-management procedures to ameliorate selective mutism by making social reinforcement contingent upon the child's verbalizations. Social reinforcement, rather than secondary reinforcers such as tokens, may be more manageable in regular class settings. The subject was an 11-year-old male who was selectively mute for 6 years. Progress was rapid and the child's speaking generalized to other persons and settings within the school. Follow-up observations a year later showed that treatment gains were maintained to the extent that the child was indistinguishable from his classmates with respect to his verbal behavior.

Stimulus Fading

Stimulus fading involves the transfer of stimulus control by fading the discriminative stimulus. For example, a situation in which a normal rate of speech production was highly probable would be used to gradually fade the discriminative stimuli (i.e., classmates, teacher) by slowly introducing them into that situation.

Sheridan et al. (1995) used this approach with a 6-year-old girl ("Stacy"). A functional analogue assessment revealed that the child responded neither verbally nor nonverbally to any questions under any conditions typically encountered in the classroom setting. A stimulus-fading procedure was implemented that involved Stacy's mother, a person with whom Stacy would converse in the school setting. After speech was initiated with the mother in the school, a four-phase stimulus-fading procedure was implemented. Each phase involved the gradual fading of settings and other individuals, such as the teacher and classmates, into the child's increasingly normal verbal interactions. The first phase involved Stacy and her mother alone in the teacher's lounge. During this stage, the child audiotaped a "secret" message. The second phase involved stimulus fading of the setting. Stacy and her mother audiotaped messages to her teacher in the school's library. In the third phase, stimulus fading of individuals was initiated. Stacy's teacher was gradually introduced into the library setting where Stacy with her mother audiotaped her messages. The fourth phase involved the stimulus fading of both persons and settings. During this phase, Stacy evidenced talking sessions in the classroom setting with her peers. The stimulus-fading procedure continued for 31 days during which the child spoke to eight different persons, individually and in small groups, in three different school settings.

There is a good probability that employing stimulus fading as a treatment strategy for selective mutism, if done correctly, will be effective. Another advantage is that the child's parents are typically involved in treatment implementation because these are the persons with whom the child is usually conversant. Also having the parents closely associated with the school-based treatment allows them to observe the professional school staff's interactions with the child. This may lead to the parents developing more appropriate styles of interacting with the child which can carry over to facilitate more appropriate parent-child relations in the home setting. This is particularly advantageous in those cases where the child with selective mutism evidences controlling, oppositional home behaviors.

The disadvantage of using fading as a treatment variable is that it is relatively intrusive, requires considerable professional expertise and time, and necessitates a successful consultative relationship with the teachers. For example, in the Sheridan et al. (1995) study, the procedure required 31 days to implement. Although Sheridan did not stipulate the amount of time the child needed to devote to different aspects of the treatment, it would presumably be considerable and therefore intrusive. An effective consultative relationship with the teacher is fundamental to most stimulus-fading procedures. It is not uncommon for interventions that require a consultative service delivery model to be less than effective due to implementation difficulties (Kehle, Bray, & Nastasi, 1996).

Shaping

Shaping typically involves the reinforcement of successive graduated approximations toward normal speech.

Bendar (1974) employed a shaping technique in the treatment of a 10-year-old male student. The student was totally noncommunicative, refusing even to respond in writing to teacher questions. Consequently, he was initially reinforced for producing written responses. The next step involved administering reinforcement contingent upon a written response accompanied by a verbal noise. Subsequently, his verbal behavior was shaped by reinforcing verbal noise with his mouth open, humming, stating the letters of the alphabet, reading sentences, and eventually, performing patterns of vocalizations that approximated speech. The newly acquired verbal behavior was faded to the teacher, classroom, and classmates.

In those cases where it is also necessary to increase the loudness of the speech in a child with selective mutism, shaping with feedback has shown to be effective. For example, Norman and Broman (1970) used shaping and feedback to promote normal speech in a 12-year-old boy who had not uttered a sound outside his home in over 8 years. The experimenters used a view meter on a tape recorder to give the child feedback regarding the volume of his speech. The loudness of the child's speech was shaped by reinforcing increasingly greater levels of loudness of different sounds. In addition, the experimenters shaped the child's use of simple words (i.e., "yes" and "no"), naming objects, and reading aloud simple sentences. They also faded unfamiliar individuals into the treatment, and after several sessions, the child eventually began verbally interacting with other children.

Feedback procedures designed to increase the loudness of a child's speech were also successfully employed by Brown and Doll (1988). These experimenters used a talk light that lit only when the child's speech was sufficiently loud.

One of the major disadvantages associated with using shaping as an intervention in the schools, is that like stimulus fading, it also must rely on an effective consultative relationship with the relevant school personnel. For example, Watson and Kramer (1992), over a period of 29 weeks, employed a 21-step, school-based, shaping program with a 9-year-old boy with selective mutism. The moderate success of the shaping intervention was not maintained at follow-up. The most probable reason for the lack of maintenance was a flawed consultation process on which the shaping intervention was based. The teacher was not adequately trained in the implementation of the procedure, there was insufficient support staff to assist the teacher, and school personnel decided not to continue reinforcement for the child speaking and allowed the child to revert back to nonverbal means of communication.

Escape-Avoidance Techniques

Escape-avoidance techniques involve situations in which the child can avoid an unpleasant event contingent upon talking. Van der Koy and Webster (1975) reported rapid acquisition of normal speech in a 6-year-old boy by employing an escape-avoidance technique. The child had not spoken in nursery school or during kindergarten. The intervention was conducted in a swimming pool at a summer-camp experience designed for asocial children. Experimenters instructed the child that he could avoid being dunked under the water or splashed in the face by saying "no." The experimenters gradually withdrew from the intervention. Fading was facilitated by other children who would often comply with the requests of the child with selective mutism. Follow-up at 6 months indicated that the child maintained appropriate speech production across varied social settings, including school.

Escape-avoidance techniques have obvious disadvantages in that they are intrusive and probably unethical. It would be unlikely that they would be permitted within school settings.

Self-Modeling

Self-modeling is defined as the positive change in behavior that results from repeated and spaced viewings of oneself on edited videotapes depicting only appropriate or desired behaviors (Kehle, Owen, & Cressy, 1990). Self-modeling is an effective and unobtrusive intervention for different problematic disorders including behavior disorders (Kehle, Clark, Jenson, & Wampold, 1986; Kehle & Gonzalez, 1991), depression (Kahn, Kehle, Jenson, & Clark, 1990), and selective mutism (Kehle et al., 1990).

Kehle et al. (1990) used self-modeling with a 6-year-old selectively mute male who had not spoken since preschool, although the child conversed freely at home. The procedure involved having the mother come to the child's regular classroom, where she asked the child nine questions (e.g., "What is your favorite flavor of ice cream?" "Who is your best friend?"). No one else was in the classroom at the time. A video camera recorded the mothers' attempts to get her son to respond. With some prodding, he finally verbally responded to his mother's questions. Immediately thereafter, with all the children back in their classroom, the teacher was instructed to ask the same nine questions to several children including the child with selective mutism. As expected, the child with selective mutism did not respond. The videotape was edited to depict the selectively mute child supposedly responding to the teacher's questions during regular classroom activities.

The edited intervention tape, which was 5 minutes in duration, was shown back to the child on two different occasions over a period of a week. On the second day of intervention, the selectively mute child abruptly began to converse freely with the experimenters, his teachers, and other school children. A 9-month follow-up indicated that the treatment gains were maintained. Interestingly, the child could not remember why he chose not to talk for

over 3 years in preschool, kindergarten, and the first grade. His response to the question, "Why did you not talk?" was, "I don't remember not talking."

An obvious advantage of the self-modeling procedure is that it requires very little of the child's time and is therefore perhaps the least intrusive of all the procedures that have been successfully employed to treat selective mutism. In the study just described, the child probably did not have to devote more than 30 minutes of his time to the different treatment phases. However, the disadvantages of self-modeling involve the practicality of the procedure. Although the procedure is not intrusive with respect to the child's time, it does require inordinate amounts of professional expertise and time devoted to videotaping and editing. Furthermore, the editing equipment needed to construct high-quality intervention tapes is expensive. The time requirements for implementing the intervention and the initial expense of the editing equipment may seriously limit its use by practicing school psychologists.

Pharmacological Treatment

In a double-blind, placebo-controlled study, Black and Uhde (1994) evaluated the effects of fluoxetine (i.e., Prozac) with 16 children with selective mutism. Children in the experimental group were judged significantly more improved, in comparison to the placebo group, on measures of mutism, anxiety, and social functioning. However, even given substantial improvement on the basis of parental ratings, teacher ratings did not differentiate the groups.

Golwyn and Weinstock (1990) successfully used phenelzine with a 7-year-old female with a 2-year history of selective mutism. Some side effects were noted including mild constipation and weight gain.

The advantages of using medication are that it is relatively inexpensive and requires essentially no investment of the child's time. The disadvantages involve possible side effects, particularly with phenelzine. Also, there is concern over the long-term effects of using these types of pharmacological interventions with children.

Combined Treatment Strategies

Some difficulty with replication, generalizability, and maintenance (McCurdy & Shapiro, 1988; Shear & Shapiro, 1993; Watson & Kramer, 1992) has resulted in experimenting with combining several strategies. Watson and Kramer (1992) summarized the research on behavior treatment of selective mutism by stating the majority of effective treatment studies incorporated a combination of behavioral techniques. These combined approaches tended to result in the quickest acquisition of speech with the greatest generalizability.

In an example of a combined treatment strategy, Kehle, Sutilla, and Visnic (1994) employed self-modeling combined with behavior techniques to treat an intentional diurnal enuretic, who was also selectively mute. Intentional diurnal enuresis is rare; however, it has been reported as one of the accompanying behaviors of selective mutism (Barlow et al., 1986). Nevertheless, the combination of these two dysfunctional behaviors in a single child is extremely unusual.

The child ("Penny"), was a 9-year-old girl who had not talked or used any toilet facilities outside the home since the age of three. Apparently, Penny's elective mutism and intentional enuresis occurred shortly after a supposedly traumatic incident occurred in a public restroom at the beach. The parents do not know the details of what happened to Penny, and Penny will not say or does not remember. In any case, she stopped talking and using bathroom facilities outside the home.

According to teacher reports, from the very first day of preschool, Penny exhibited mutism and severely depressed behaviors. Outside the school setting, Penny's behavior was described as normal. She communicated easily, appeared happy, and engaged in many play activities with the neighborhood children.

A self-modeling intervention was designed that also incorporated the spacing effect, mystery motivators, controlled self-reinforcement, peer expectations, and stimulus fading.

Edited videotapes were constructed depicting Penny supposedly responding to the special education teachers' questions in ongoing class instruction. In reality, Penny was responding to her father's questions. To ensure a spacing effect, the 7-minute-long, edited self-modeling videotape was shown to Penny on five different occasions over a period of 4 weeks. Spacing effect refers to the fact that for a given amount of study time, spaced presentations of the material (i.e., appropriate verbal behavior depicted on the edited videotape) will yield better learning than would a single massed presentation. "The spacing effect is one of the most studied and remarkable phenomena to emerge in the 100-year history of research on learning" (Dempster, 1988, p. 627). The spacing effect, although not usually incorporated into intervention designs (Kehle, Jenson, & Clark, 1992), is reliable and very potent in that even as few as two spaced presentations are approximately twice as effective as two massed presentations. Further, the effect is ubiquitous in that it occurs in almost all learning paradigms (Dempster, 1988).

Before the beginning of the intervention, a manilla envelope was tacked to the bulletin board in the front of the class. On the envelope was a big question mark and the name "Penny." The class, including Penny, were told that the envelope contained a "mystery" motivator—a gift that Penny would really like and that she could have when she asked her teacher for it in a tone of voice clearly audible to the other children. Mystery motivators are de-

signed to increase the anticipation and value of a reinforcer (Rhode, Jenson, & Reavis, 1993). The decision of what to include as Penny's mystery motivator was determined after consultation with Penny's parents.

During the viewings of the 7-minute videotape, Penny was instructed to stop the tape (using a remote control) whenever she thought she responded appropriately to the teacher's questions. At each child-initiated cessation of the tape, she was allowed to choose from a variety of small reinforcers displayed on a table near the video monitor (i.e., controlled self-reinforcement). With Penny's permission, the edited videotapes were presented to her classmates to show them that she was clearly capable of normal conversation. This consequently increased peer expectations for Penny to speak.

Furthermore, it was learned that in the home setting, Penny was very verbal when playing a board game with her family. Her parents, grandmother, and brother were invited to play the game with Penny in the special education classroom after school when no other children or teachers were present. Penny conversed normally during the game. Employing a stimulus-fading technique, one of Penny's classmates, who volunteered to stay after school to help Penny, was gradually introduced to the room and finally invited to be involved in the board game. Subsequently, two other volunteer classmates were gradually introduced to the setting and eventually integrated into the game.

Following the fading technique, Penny's verbal behavior quickly assumed normal frequency to the point that she was indistinguishable from the other children. With the development of speaking behavior within school settings, the intentional enuresis was eliminated within a single day. On the first day after she regained use of normal verbal behavior, Penny was escorted to the bathroom with one of her friends without incident.

Nine months after this initial interview, Penny was asked to respond to a series of follow-up questions. Penny expressed liking of the mystery motivator, referring to it as "cool." She also expressed an appreciation of having viewed herself successfully responding to questions on the self-modeling tapes. However, in response to the question of why she did not talk and why she urinated in her clothes, Penny stated that she was just shy and that she did not know, respectively.

In another study, Kehle et al. (1995) employed a hierarchial model of combined intervention strategies that eventually led to the use of fluoxetine with a 9-year-old female. Besides selective mutism, the child ("Ellen") also exhibited intentional vomiting. She made no vocalizations within the school or school-related settings during her entire academic career. She was placed in a self-contained special education classroom upon entering school. In addition to the selective mutism, her academic placement was also due to below-average results on intelligence scales combined with other problematic behaviors.

Ellen's vomiting behavior typically occurred as a consequence of the teacher's request for compliance and was usually preceded by a slight cough. The incidences of vomiting episodes were approximately twice weekly and would occur both within the school and on field trips. The combination of these two dysfunctional behaviors, mutism and intentional vomiting, in a single child is extremely rare and very effective in negatively reinforcing the child. That is to say, when she was asked by the teacher to comply and Ellen's response was to vomit on her desk, the teacher's request for compliance stopped and in so doing served to reinforce the behavior of vomiting.

Intervention tapes were constructed in the same manner as described in Kehle (1991). Ellen viewed the initial 7-minute intervention videotapes on eight occasions extending over a period of 5 weeks. Concurrently, mystery motivators were employed for both Ellen and her classmates. Ellen received the first mystery motivator if she requested it from her teacher. A classmate received the second mystery motivator if he or she successfully encouraged Ellen to say the name of her cat. The class mystery motivator, together with the class viewing of the intervention videotapes, was intended to increase peer expectations for Ellen to speak.

Ellen began speaking in school during the stimulus-fading phase, which was implemented after five viewings of the videotapes. Ellen was initially engaged in conversation with a family member alone in a classroom that faded her discrimination between speaking outside and inside the school. To increase stimulus fading, several school personnel and peers were gradually faded into the treatment room.

However, despite continued spaced viewings of the intervention videotapes, Ellen's speech production within the school decreased from its initial postintervention level. Consequently, a pharmacological approach was incorporated into the intervention. This consisted of the administration of 10 milligrams of fluoxetine for 4 weeks. The dosage was increased to 20 milligrams, at which point Ellen's verbal behavior increased to an acceptable level. In addition her intentional vomiting was eliminated.

Ellen's dramatic increase in speech following the administration of fluoxetine enabled the production of much more sophisticated self-modeling intervention videotapes. The new intervention videotapes depicted her engaging in age-appropriate levels of conversation and could not have been made before the pharmacological treatment. The fluoxetine was gradually withdrawn while continuing the self-modeling intervention. A 6 month follow-up indicated that the treatment effects were maintained.

Summary

There is little evidence supporting therapeutic approaches for selective mutism based on psychoanalytic theory, family therapy, or joint mother-child therapy. For over 30 years, treatment gains have been most often associated when the application of behavior-therapy techniques, particularly in combined approaches. However, there is variability regarding the magnitude of effects.

In conclusion, selective mutism has historically been shown to be very resistant to intervention. Currently, behavior therapies appear to be the treatments of choice. Associated features are assumed to diminish or be eliminated after the selective mutism is successfully addressed.

Recommended Resources

Kaplan-Tancer, N. (1992). Elective mutism: A review of the literature. In B. B. Lahey & A. E. Kazdin (Eds.), *Advances in clinical child psychology* (Vol 14, pp. 265–288). New York: Plenum Press.
This review provides an excellent summary of the literature from 1970 to 1989. Included in the article are essential and associated features of elective mutism; clinical features including age of onset, gender differences, and prevalence; and the course of the disorder. A good source for those seeking epidemiological information, the article, however, does not include good coverage of treatment options.

Kehle, T. J., Owen, S. V., & Cressy, E. T. (1990). The use of self-modeling as an intervention in school psychology: A case study of an elective mute. *School Psychology Review, 19,* 115–121.
This clinical case study illustrates the application of self-modeling with a selectively mute child. The school-based intervention was effective, enduring, short-term, and inexpensive. In addition, it is argued that self-modeling as an intervention for selective mutism is perhaps the least restrictive and least intrusive of interventions currently employed for this disorder.

Sheridan, S. M., Kratochwill, T. R., & Ramirez, S. Z. (1995). Assessment and treatment of selective mutism: Recommendations and a case study. *Special Services in the School, 10,* 55–77.
The paper outlines an assessment protocol that can be employed for diagnosis of selective mutism and the formulation of treatment plans implemented through a consultation process. A case study in which a four-phase stimulus-fading treatment was successfully employed is presented to illustrate the assessment protocol and the consultative process.

References

American Psychiatric Association. (1994). *Diagnostic and statistical manual of mental disorders* (4th ed.). Washington, DC: Author.

Atoynatan, T. H. (1986). Elective mutism: Involvement of the mother in the treatment of the child. *Child Psychiatry and Human Development, 17,* 15–27.

Barlow, K., Strother, J., & Landreth, G. (1986). Sibling group play therapy: An alternative with the electively mute child. *The School Counselor, 34*, 44–50.

Bendar, R. A. (1974). A behavioral approach to treating an elective mute in school. *Journal of School Psychology, 12*, 326–337.

Black, B., & Uhde, T. W. (1992). Elective mutism as a variant of school phobia. *Journal of the American Academy of Child and Adolescent Psychiatry, 31*, 1090–1094.

Black, B., & Uhde, T. W. (1994). Treatment of elective mutism with fluoxetine: A double-blind, placebo-controlled study. *Journal of the American Academy of Child and Adolescent Psychiatry, 33*, 1000–1006.

Brown, B., & Doll, B. (1988). Case illustration of classroom intervention with an elective mute child. *Special Services in the Schools, 1988*, 107–125.

Colligan, R. W., Colligan, R. C., & Dilliard, M. K. (1977). Contingency management in the classroom treatment of long-term elective mutism: A case report. *Journal of School Psychology, 15*, 9–17.

Dempster, F. N. (1988). The spacing effect: A case study in the failure to apply the results of psychological research. *American Psychologist, 43*, 627–634.

Dorwick, P. W., & Hood, M. (1978). Transfer of talking behavior across settings using faked films. In E. L. Glynn & S. S. McNaughton (Eds.), *Proceedings of the New Zealand Conference for Research in Applied Behavior Analysis* (pp. 121–132). Auckland, New Zealand: University of Auckland Press.

Golwyn, D. H., & Weinstock, R. C. (1990). Phenelzine treatment of elective mutism: A case report. *Journal of Clinical Psychiatry, 51*, 384–385.

Kahn, J., Kehle, T. J., Jenson, W. R., & Clark, E. (1990). Comparison of cognitive-behavioral, relaxation, and self-modeling interventions for depression among middle-school students. *School Psychology Review, 19*, 196–211.

Kanner, L. (1957). *Child psychiatry* (3rd ed.). Springfield, IL: Charles C. Thomas.

Kaplan-Tancer, N. (1992). Elective mutism: A review of the literature. In B. B. Lahey & A. E. Kazdin (Eds.), *Advances in Clinical Child Psychology* (Vol 14, pp. 265–288). New York: Plenum Press.

Kehle, T. J. (1991). Use of self-modeling with elective mutes. *Communiqué, 20*, 18.

Kehle, T. J., Bray, M. A., & Nastasi, B. K. (1996). Problems with the school psychology service delivery model that affect the implementation of school-based intervention programs. *School Psychology International, 17*, 33–42.

Kehle, T. J., Clark, E., Jenson, W. R., & Wampold, B. E. (1986). Effectiveness of self-observation with behavior disordered elementary school children. *School Psychology Review, 15*, 289–295.

Kehle, T. J., & Gonzales, F. (1991). Self-modeling for emotional and social concerns of childhood. In P. W. Dowrick (Ed.), *A practical guide to video in the behavioral sciences* (pp 211–252). New York: John Wiley & Sons.

Kehle, T. J., Jenson, W. R., & Clark, E. (1992). Teacher acceptance of psychological interventions: An allegiance to intuition? *School Psychology International, 13*, 307–312.

Kehle, T. J., Owen, S. V., & Cressy, E. T. (1990). The use of self-modeling as an intervention in school psychology: A case study of an elective mute. *School Psychology Review, 19*, 115–121.

Kehle, T. J., Sutilla, H., & Visnic, M. (1994, March). *Augmentation of self-modeling with behavioral strategies: Case study of an intentional enuretic and electively mute child.* Paper presented at the annual meeting of the National Association of School Psychologists, Seattle, WA.

Kolvin, I., & Fundudis, T. (1981). Elective mute children: Psychological development and background factors. *Journal of Child Psychiatry and Psychiatry, 22*, 219–232.

Kratochwill, T. R. (1981). *Selective mutism: Implications for treatment and research.* Hillsdale, NJ: Erlbaum Associates.

Krohn, D. D., Weckstein, S. M., & Wright, H. L. (1992). A study of the effectiveness of a specific treatment for elective mutism. *Journal of the American Academy of Child and Adolescent Psychiatry, 31*, 711–718.

Labbe, E. E. & Williamson, D. A. (1984). Behavioral treatment of elective mutism: A review of the literature. *Clinical Psychology Review, 4*, 273–292.

Louden, D. M. (1987). Elective mutism. A case study of a disorder of childhood. *Journal of the Medical Association, 79*, 1043–1048.

Mace, F. C., & West, B. (1986). Analysis of demand conditions associated with reluctant speech. *Journal of Behavior Therapy and Experimental Psychiatry, 17*, 285–294.

McCurdy, B. L., & Shapiro, E. S. (1988). Self-observation and the reduction of inappropriate classroom behavior. *Journal of School Psychology, 26*, 371–378.

Morin, C., Ladouceur, R., & Cloutier, R. (1982). Reinforcement procedure in the treatment of reluctant speech. *Journal of Behavior Therapy and Experimental Psychiatry, 13*, 145–147.

Norman, A., & Broman, H. J. (1970). Volume feedback and generalization techniques in shaping speech of an electively mute boy: A case study. *Perceptual and Motor Skills, 31*, 463–470.

Piersel, W. C., & Kratochwill, T. R. (1981). A teacher-implemented contingency management package to assess and treat selective mutism. *Behavioral Assessment, 3*, 371–382.

Porjes, M. D. (1992). Intervention with the selectively mute child. *Psychology in the Schools, 29*, 367–376.

Pustrom, E., & Speers, R. W. (1964). Elective mutism in children. *Journal of the American Academy of Child Psychiatry, 3*, 287–289.

Redford, P. A. (1977). Psychoanalytically based therapy as the treatment of choice for a six-year-old elective mute. *Journal of Child Psychotherapy, 4*, 49–65.

Reed, J. B. (1963). Elective mutism in children: A reappraisal. *Journal of Child Psychology and Psychiatry, 4*, 99–107.

Reed, J. B., & Mees, J. L. (1967). A marathon behavior modification programme of an elective mute child. *Journal of Child Psychology and Psychiatry, 8*, 27–30.

Rhode, G., Jenson, W. R., & Reavis, H. K. (1993). *The tough kid book: Practical classroom management strategies.* Longmount, CO: Sopris West.

Rutter, M. (1977). Delayed speech. In M. Rutter & L. Hersov (Eds.), *Child psychiatry: Modern approaches* (pp. 698–716). Oxford, England: Blackwell Scientific.

Salfield, D. J. (1950). Observations on elective mutism in children. *Journal of Mental Science, 96,* 1024–1033.

Sanok, R. L., & Striefel, S. (1979). Elective mutism: Generalization of verbal responding across people and settings. *Behavior Therapy, 10,* 357–371.

Scott, E. (1977). A desensitization programme for the treatment of mutism in a seven year old girl: A case report. *Journal of Child Psychology and Psychiatry, 18,* 263–270.

Shear, S. M., & Shapiro, E. S. (1993). Effects of using self-recording and self-observation in reducing disruptive behavior. *Journal of School Psychology, 31,* 519–534.

Sheridan, S. M., Kratochwill, T. J., & Ramirez, S. Z. (1995). Assessment and treatment of selective mutism: Recommendations and a case study. *Special Services in the Schools, 10,* 55–77.

Shreeve, D. F. (1991). Elective mutism: Origins in stranger anxiety and selective mutism. *Bulletin of the Menninger Clinic, 55,* 491–504.

Shvarztman, P., Hornshtein, I., Klein, E., & Yechezkel, A., (1990). Elective mutism in family practice. *Journal of Family Practice, 31,* 319–320.

Sluckin, A., Foreman, N., & Herbert, M. (1991). Behavioural treatment programs and selectivity of speaking at follow-up in a sample of 25 selective mutes. *Psychologist, 26,* 132–137.

Van der Koy, D., & Webster, C. D. (1975). A rapidly effective behavior modification program for an electively mute child. *Journal of Behavior Therapy and Experimental Psychiatry, 6,* 149–152.

Watson, T. S., & Kramer, J. J. (1992). Multimethod behavioral treatment of long-term selective mutism. *Psychology in the Schools, 29,* 359–366.

Williamson, D. A., Sewell, W. R., Sanders, S. H., Haney, J. N., & White, D. (1977). The treatment of reluctant speech using contingency management procedures. *Journal of Behavior Therapy and Experimental Psychiatry, 8,* 151–156.

Wright, H. H. & Cuccaro, M. L. (1994). Selective mutism continued. *Journal of the American Academy of Child and Adolescent Psychiatry, 33,* 593–594.

Yates, A. J. (1970). *Behavior therapy.* New York: Wiley.

30

School Phobia, School Refusal, and School Avoidance

Leslie Z. Paige

Hays West Central Kansas Special Education Cooperative

Background and Development

The set of behaviors historically labeled "school phobia" has been discussed since the 1930s, yet there has been little agreement regarding the term *school phobia,* its etiology, characteristics, or the best treatment practices. This limited consensus is largely the result of shifts in the construct's definition over time, leading to a variety of behaviors of differing etiologies being merged under the general term (Kearney, Eisen, & Silverman, 1995). Other common terms to describe this set of behaviors include *school refusal* (Atkinson, Quarrington, & Cyr, 1985; Berg, 1982; Blagg & Yule, 1984; DiBacco, 1979; King, Ollendick, & Tonge, 1995) and *school avoidance* (Shaughnessy & Nystul, 1985; Taylor & Adelman, 1990). Despite being considered a low incidence behavior (Kearney et al., 1995; King et al., 1995), for many years school phobia has received extensive study and has been the focus of substantial debate (Kearney et al., 1995). This chapter will briefly review the controversial use of the term and describe the arguments in favor of the more recent use of terms such as school refusal and school avoidance. The heterogeneity of the behaviors associated with school refusal and avoidance will be explored. Assessment and treatment are complicated because (a) little agreement exists regarding etiology of school refusal and avoidance behaviors (Paige, 1993); (b) the causes of school refusal and avoidance behaviors vary; and (c) many factors may play a part in the development and maintenance of school refusal and avoidance behavior (King et al., 1995).

Historical Perspective

Broadwin (1932) was the first to describe school phobia, but Johnson, Falstein, Szurek and Svendsen (1941) generally receive credit for coining the term school phobia. Since that time, there have been many attempts to ex-

plain the acquisition of school phobic behaviors. There are three primary types of theoretical explanations: psychoanalytic, psychodynamic, and behavioral. The psychoanalytic models focus upon mother-child relationships characterized by repressed anxiety resulting from mutual dependency and hostility. According to Johnson et al. (1941) and other early researchers, children with school phobia were regarded to have acute anxiety and anxious mothers within an enmeshed relationship. The mother caused the child to be overdependent, resulting in a fear of separation and mutual repressed hostility. Case studies of overinvolved families were used for many years to support the separation-anxiety component within school phobia (Kearney et al., 1995).

Like the psychoanalytic model just described, psychodynamic explanations of school phobia tend to focus upon dysfunctional relationships between the child and parent. However, psychodynamic theories also emphasize the impact of the child's power struggles and resultant family behaviors. According to this view, anxiety results because of the child's social isolation when he or she returns to school (Eisenberg, 1958). The longer the child remains at home, the more these behaviors become reinforced, leading to increased academic and social deficits.

Learning theorists in the 1960s and 1970s considered school phobia to be a learned behavior resulting in school avoidance. The child learns to fear separation due to subtle parental cues, becomes conditioned, and links going to school with loss of the parent. From this perspective the primary fear is not of school but of separation from the family or loss of the mother (McDonald & Shepard, 1976). The child receives secondary reinforcement for staying at home through toys, snacks, TV, and parental attention and by a reduction in anxiety. Others conceptualize school phobia as an avoidance behavior motivated either by an intense fear of the school environment or of school social pressures (Lazarus, Davison, & Polefka, 1965). Age-related differences may be important. Heath (1985) reported that school refusal and avoidance behaviors are an expression of separation anxiety in younger children but are related to school-specific fears in older children.

School refusal has also been attributed to families who have maladaptive communication patterns, significant family dysfunction (Bernstein & Garfinkel, 1988), and marital conflict and psychopathology (Berg, Butler, & Pritchard, 1974). In these instances, the parents are frequently unable to facilitate needed interventions due to these factors and because they experience difficulty with parenting, problem solving and working together (King et al., 1995). Finally, a significant event can precipitate the onset of school refusal and avoidance behaviors, such as a new sibling, change of residence, or disease (King et al., 1995; Lazarus et al., 1965).

Prevalence and Demographics

Prevalence rates of school refusal and avoidance behaviors are difficult to determine due to differing opinions regarding diagnostic criteria (Phelps, Cox, & Bajorek, 1992), and reported rates depend upon the definition of the behaviors (King et al., 1995). However, most researchers agree that the prevalence rates are low (Kearney et al., 1995; King et al., 1995). Rates vary from 1.7% (Kennedy, 1965) to 5% (Granell de Aldaz, Vivas, Gelfand, & Feldman, 1984).

Similarly, demographic data vary across studies. Early studies reported an even distribution among males and females (Berg, Nichols, & Pritchard, 1969; Johnson, 1979; Kennedy, 1965). Recent studies have been inconsistent with some finding more males with these behaviors, whereas others find more females (King et al., 1995). Researchers also cannot agree upon the age of onset. Millman, Schaefer, and Cohen (1981) found school phobia to peak between the ages of 6 and 10 years, whereas Kearney et al. (1994) found most school refusers to be between 7 and 12 years old. King et al. (1995) reported that school refusal may occur at any age, but peak ages are associated with school entry and major school transitions.

The Term "School Phobia"

Much confusion has resulted because the same term, school phobia, has been used to describe both a general psychodynamic construct and a symptom of school avoidance or refusal (Kearney et al., 1995). Researchers and practitioners have historically used the term to describe a heterogeneous set of behaviors, sharing in common a significant difficulty with school attendance. Among others, Kearney et al. (1995) have criticized the use of the term because (a) there have been methodological problems in the research; (b) school phobia is not a true phobia; and (c) emphasis upon the separation anxiety com-

ponents may be the result of sampling bias toward younger children.

Methodological concerns
Researchers in the 1980s and 1990s criticized the early school-phobia research. Methodological flaws cited by Kearney et al. (1995) include

an overreliance on case reports, lack of control groups, poor sample size, referral bias and inadequate sampling procedures, incomparable diagnostic criteria, psychometrically unsound assessment methods, restricted sources of information (e.g., medical files, mothers, few children), and lack of normative data to evaluate the frequency and intensity of fears related to school. (p. 69)

Pilkington and Piersel (1991) made similar criticisms of the case-study approach, due to limited sampling, lack of control groups, poor reliability, and the emphasis on more severe cases (which tend to be referred). These problems make comparisons among studies difficult, if not impossible, and cast doubt on the conclusions drawn regarding etiology and diagnostic specificity.

School phobia as a true phobia
True phobias require excessive fear and avoidance of a specific object or situation (American Psychiatric Association [APA], 1994; see Tables 1 and 2). According to several researchers (Berg, et al., 1969; King et al., 1995),

Table 1 *Criteria for Specific Phobia*

A. Marked and persistent fear that is excessive or unreasonable, cued by the presence or anticipation of a specific object or situation (e.g., flying, heights, animals, receiving an injection, seeing blood).
B. Exposure to the phobic stimulus almost invariably provokes an immediate anxiety response, which may take the form of a situationally bound or situationally predisposed Panic Attack. Note: In children, the anxiety may be expressed by crying, tantrums, freezing, or clinging.
C. The person recognizes that the fear is excessive or unreasonable. Note: In children, this feature may be absent.
D. The phobic situation(s) is avoided or else endured with intense anxiety or distress.
E. The avoidance, anxious anticipation, or distress in the feared situation(s) interferes significantly with the person's normal routine, occupational (or academic) functioning, or social activities or relationships, or there is marked distress about having the phobia.
F. In individuals under age 18 years, the duration is at least 6 months.
G. The anxiety, Panic Attacks, or phobic avoidance associated with the specific object or situation are not better accounted for by another mental disorder.

Note. From *Diagnostic and Statistical Manual of Mental Disorders* (4th ed., p. 410–411), by the American Psychiatric Association, 1994, Washington, DC: Author. Copyright 1994 by the American Psychiatric Association. Reprinted with permission.

the intense emotional distress exhibited by some children with school-refusal behaviors may account for the popularity of labeling these behaviors a phobia. Further, some school-refusing children show specific fears of school or school-related situations (e.g., tests, bullies, teacher reprimands, undressing for gym; King et al., 1995), also suggesting the presence of truly phobic reactions. However, although many children labeled with school phobia exhibit anxiety regarding school attendance, their level of fear is not always excessive. For example, Kearney et al. (1995) reported that children's fears of non-school-related items on the *Fear Survey Schedule for Children's Fears-Revised (FSSC-R)* are at about the same level as school-related fears. Therefore, it appears that although some children commonly labeled with school phobia have genuinely phobic reactions to school, many others do not.

Separation anxiety

Separation anxiety is a normal and adaptive developmental stage from age 6 months to approximately age 2 or 3 years (Ainsworth, Blehar, Waters, & Wall, 1978). It is characterized by distressed behavior when infants and toddlers are separated from their primary caregivers. When these behaviors become severe or occur after the expected age, Separation Anxiety Disorder (SAD) is considered as a possible diagnosis (see Table 3). The child with SAD resists being separated from attachment figures, which frequently includes refusal to attend school. Therefore, some children exhibiting school refusal meet the diagnostic criteria for SAD. However, clearly not all children who refuse to go to school have SAD. For example, some children who exhibit severe anxiety reactions in school function adequately away from their parents in other, nonschool settings (Pilkington & Piersel, 1991). According to Pilkington and Piersel, separation anxiety does not explain the etiology of all school refusal and avoidance behaviors and it ignores the contribution of school-related fears. They suggested that it was likely linked to school phobias as a result of over-sampling of younger children.

Table 2 *Criteria for Social Phobia*

A. A marked and persistent fear of one or more social or performance situations in which the person is exposed to unfamiliar people or to possible scrutiny by others. The individual fears that he or she will act in a way (or show anxiety symptoms) that will be humiliating or embarrassing. Note: In children, there must be evidence of the capacity for age-appropriate social relationships with familiar people and the anxiety must occur in peer settings, not just interactions with adults.

B. Exposure to the feared social situation almost invariably provokes anxiety, which may take the form of a situationally bound or situationally predisposed Panic Attack. Note: In children, the anxiety may be expressed by crying, tantrums, freezing, or shrinking from social situations with unfamiliar people.

C. The person recognizes that the fear is excessive or unreasonable. Note: In children, this feature may be absent.

D. The feared social or performance situations are avoided or else are endured with intense anxiety or distress.

E. The avoidance, anxious anticipation, or distress in the feared social or performance situation(s) interferes significantly with the person's normal routine, occupational (or academic) functioning, or social activities or relationships, or there is marked distress about having the phobia.

F. In individuals under age 18 years, the duration is at least 6 months.

G. The fear or avoidance is not due to the direct physiological effects of a substance . . . or a general medical condition and is not better accounted for by another mental disorder. . . .

H. If a general medical condition or another mental disorder is present, the fear in Criterion A is unrelated to it.

Table 3 *Criteria for Separation Anxiety Disorder*

A. Developmentally inappropriate and excessive anxiety concerning separation from home or from those to whom the individual is attached, as evidenced by three (or more) of the following:
1. recurrent excessive distress when separation from home or major attachment figures occurs or is anticipated
2. persistent and excessive worry about losing, or about possible harm befalling, major attachment figures
3. persistent and excessive worry that an untoward event will lead to separation from a major attachment figure (e.g., getting lost or being kidnapped)
4. persistent reluctance or refusal to go to school or elsewhere because of fear of separation
5. persistently and excessively fearful or reluctant to be alone or without major attachment figures at home or without significant adults in other settings
6. persistent reluctance or refusal to go to sleep without being near a major attachment figure or to sleep away from home
7. repeated nightmares involving the theme of separation
8. repeated complaints of physical symptoms (such as headaches, stomachaches, nausea, or vomiting) when separation from major attachment figures occurs or is anticipated.

B. The duration of the disturbance is at least 4 weeks.

C. The onset is before age 18 years.

D. The disturbance causes clinically significant distress or impairment in social, academic (occupational), or other important areas of functioning.

E. The disturbance does not occur exclusively during the course of a Pervasive Developmental Disorder, Schizophrenia, or other Psychotic Disorder, and, in adolescents and adults, is not better accounted for by Panic Disorder with Agoraphobia.

Diagnostic Distinctions

In an effort to address the apparent heterogeneity in the etiology of school phobia, many researchers have attempted to develop classification systems (Atkinson et al., 1985; Coolidge, Hahn, & Peck, 1957; Kennedy, 1965; Sperling, 1967; Taylor & Adelman, 1990). Kennedy (1965) was one of the first to categorize types of school phobia. Age of onset was considered the critical factor, with Type I most common in younger children from well-functioning families and evoked by recent, school-related events. Type II, more prevalent in older children, was considered chronic and part of a pattern of generalized anxiety. However, this typology does not address some of the difficulties noted earlier in distinguishing phobias from anxiety disorders. According to several researchers, children with school phobia appear to be more diverse than was originally thought (Atkinson et al., 1985; Bernstein & Garfinkel, 1988; Burke & Silverman, 1987; Last & Strauss, 1990). Consequently, a number of authors have questioned whether the term school phobia should be avoided in developing typologies and replaced with more general, descriptive terms like school refusal and school avoidance.

School refusal has been used to describe those children who are frequently absent and/or attend school under duress or following tantrums or noncompliance (Kearney & Beasley, 1994). Unlike school phobia, the term school refusal has advantages in that it does not imply a specific etiology but is inclusive of children who do not attend or are reluctant to attend school for a variety of reasons (King et al., 1995; Pilkington & Piersel, 1991). Other researchers suggest that the term might be too inclusive, causing practitioners to ignore relevant differences between different disorders (Phelps et al., 1992). As Phelps et al. point out, the tendency to label all of these children as "school refusers" causes treatment providers to ignore treatment-relevant differences between distinctly different disorders, resulting in confusion regarding both treatment and diagnosis. At present, it may be best to consider school refusal and avoidance as specific behaviors that may be linked to several distinct disorders. The practitioner must consider a variety of etiologies and constellations of behaviors when making a diagnosis and planning appropriate treatment.

Several recent typologies are consistent with this approach (see Table 4). For example, Kearney et al. (1995) classify subgroups of children who refuse or avoid school based upon negative or positive reinforcement or both. Some children refuse to attend school in order to avoid situations causing negative affectivity (e.g., anxiety, depression, low self esteem) or to escape social or evaluative settings which are aversive (negative reinforcement). Other children are positively reinforced for refusing school through attention from parents or tangible rewards (e.g., watching television, playing with toys). Kear-

ney and Silverman (1993) found that these two factors are distinct, although they may combine to produce school refusal in some cases.

Other researchers, in distinguishing among school refusers, have relied more on criteria in the *Diagnostic and Statistical Manual of Mental Disorders,* (*DSM-IV;* APA, 1994). Although they retain the use of the term school phobia, Phelps et al. (1992) limit it to school refusal resulting from either a specific or social phobia. King et al. (1995) reported that children who exhibit school refusal and avoidance behaviors may meet the *DSM-IV* criteria for Specific Phobia, Social Phobia, SAD, or Major Depressive Disorder (MDD). Based on their observations, these authors described three primary types of school refusers: (a) phobic children who fear specific aspects of school such as tests or teasing; (b) separation-anxious children who fear harm to self or to major attachment figures; and (c) anxious/depressed children who fear harm to self and/or family *and* are anxious regarding school. The first two groups are regarded as acute, whereas the last group displays more chronic symptoms. King et al. (1995) acknowledge that school refusal may also arise from other, less frequently observed sources (e.g., post-traumatic stress, panic disorder, medical problems, parental psychopathology, or systemic school problems).

One other diagnostic distinction must be considered. Many researchers view truancy as separate from other school-refusal behaviors. Children exhibiting school-refusal behaviors are differentiated from truants in that the former have prolonged absences (Berg et al., 1969; Gordon & Young, 1976), lack antisocial behaviors (Berg et al., 1969; Gittleman, 1976; Want, 1983); and have parents who are aware of the absences (Berg et al., 1969; Gordon & Young, 1976). In contrast, truants stay away from home and school; engage in antisocial, rebellious, and delinquent behaviors; and have little interest in academics (Gittleman, 1976; Want, 1983). However, truant children tend to find school aversive in a similar way as other groups of school refusers (Pilkington & Piersel, 1991). In keeping with the King et al. (1995) typology, *DSM-IV* diagnoses such as Oppositional Defiant Disorder or Conduct Disorder might be appropriately applied to many students who are truant.

Clearly, the diagnosis and treatment of school refusal and avoidance behaviors pose a challenge for the practitioner because the same behaviors may be caused and maintained by the interaction of many factors (King et al., 1995). Whereas some children will have specific school-related fears, others may have convoluted histories involving chronic absenteeism, anxiety, depression, and complex family factors (King et al., 1995). Treatment goals must be built upon specific etiological variables, and therefore, diagnostic specificity is critical (Phelps et al., 1992).

Table 4   *Summary of Current Differential Diagnostic Criteria and School Refusal Subtypes*

Subtype by Author	Criteria or Characteristics
King, Ollendick, and Tonge (1995)	
Phobic*	Anxiety or fear regarding specific aspects of school (acute).
Separation-anxious**	Anxiety regarding harm to self or family (acute).
Anxious-depressed***	Anxious regarding harm to self or family and anxious regarding school (chronic).
Kearney, Eisen, and Silverman (1995)	
Avoids negative affectivity	Child refuses to attend school in order to avoid situations which cause negative feelings, such as anxiety, depression, low-self esteem (Negative reinforcement).
Escapes social/evaluative settings	Child refuses to attend school to escape aversive social or evaluative situations (Negative reinforcement).
Seeks positive reinforcement	Child stays at home to attain parent attention or tangible rewards (Positive reinforcement).
Phelps, Cox, and Bajorek (1992)	
School phobia	*DSM* criteria for Specific Phobia or Social Phobia.
Separation Anxiety	*DSM* criteria for Separation Anxiety Disorder.
School Refusal	Should be regarded only as a behavioral outcome, resulting from either school phobia or separation anxiety.

*May also meet *DSM-IV* criteria (comorbidity) for Specific or Social Phobia.
**May also meet *DSM-IV* criteria (comorbidity) for Separation Anxiety Disorder.
***May also meet *DSM-IV* criteria (comorbidity) for Major Depressive Disorder.

Problems and Implications

Untreated, children with school refusal and avoidance behaviors often have poor long-term outcomes. In a review of longitudinal studies, King et al. (1995) found that a significant number of children continue to experience psychopathology as adults. Among the problems related to school refusal behaviors are unusually high rates of psychiatric disorders (Berg, 1982), multiple refusal and avoidance behaviors (McDonald & Shepard, 1976), work and college avoidance (Moss, 1986), suicide (Shaughnessy & Nystul, 1985), academic deterioration, inability to establish meaningful peer relationships, school or legal conflicts (McDonald & Shepard, 1976; Want, 1983), panic attacks and agoraphobia (Perugi, Deltito, Soriani, & Musetti, 1988), and adult mood disorders (Adams, 1979).

Even if there has been a successful return to school, children who have evidenced school refusal and avoidance behaviors in the past tend to be at risk for further school attendance problems (Berg, Butler, & Hall, 1976). Transitions (e.g., following school vacations or moving from elementary to middle school or from middle school to high school) seem to be critical times for children who have previously experienced school refusal and avoidance behaviors (King et al., 1995; Paige, 1993).

Some researchers believe that school refusal and avoidance behaviors tend to occur in families that are dysfunctional and in conflict (Bernstein & Garfinkel, 1988). A recent divorce, family move, death, or illness of the child or a family member can "trigger" school refusal behavior. These children frequently believe that some-thing "terrible" will happen to someone at home while they are at school. However, some authors (King et al., 1995; Paige, 1994) urge caution in blaming the family for school refusal and avoidance behaviors. It is important to remember that the behavior may be due to other reasons, such as being afraid to read aloud in class, a panic attack at school, being teased or bullied, an unsafe school or neighborhood, or a distressing classroom environment. King et al. (1995) stated that school refusal and avoidance behaviors may be inevitable for children with certain personalities and temperament.

If forced to attend school, children with school refusal and avoidance behaviors can become extremely disruptive and may leave the school to return home. These children can be extremely distressed and very distressing when in school, as the following example illustrates:

Every morning Patty's screams preceded her entrance to school. Her mother would drag her up the sidewalk, detach her fingers one by one from the door jamb, and force her, step by step, to the third grade classroom. Her screams echoed down the hallway as the teacher blocked the doorway while Patty's mother left, sobbing. (Paige, 1993, p. 1)

Classmates and other children may become upset, especially if they observe the child being forced into the building or being restrained from leaving. Other parents and teachers may have questions, advice, or complaints regarding the disruption. At times the school staff may feel that the parents are contributing to the behavior. However, many families say that they feel unable to cope with this behavior and will look to the school staff or mental health professionals for help.

Alternative Actions

Given the considerable disagreement regarding etiology and identification of children with school refusal and avoidance behaviors, it is not surprising that there is also considerable disagreement regarding appropriate treatment. Treatment practices are highly variable and have traditionally been linked to theoretical orientations (Paige, 1993; Want, 1983). Behavioral treatments have received the most empirical support (King et al., 1995); these approaches also are generally economical and acceptable to school personnel and families. In particular, systematic desensitization has been the treatment of choice, particularly with fearful and anxious children (Kearney & Silverman, 1993). However, as noted earlier, most treatment studies have been methodologically flawed, casting doubt upon the effectiveness of the interventions (King et al., 1995).

Assessment and Treatment Planning

Because school refusal and avoidance behaviors may be maintained by a complex interaction of child, family, and school factors, treatment planning should begin with a functional analysis of the behavior (King et al., 1995). Assessment methods might include problem-focused behavioral interviews with the family and child, structured diagnostic interviews, self-report instruments, self-monitoring data, behavior checklists, behavioral observations, and family assessment instruments. The *School Refusal Assessment Scale* (SRAS, Kearney & Silverman, 1993) can assist in uncovering the reinforcement patterns that might be contributing to the problem. Other specific assessment measures are presented in King et al. (1995). The goal of assessment is to determine the specific factors involved in the school refusal and to develop prescriptive treatments addressing these factors. Clearly, a combination of treatments will be required in cases where multiple factors are involved (Kearney & Silverman, 1993; Kearney et al., 1995). King et al. (1995) caution that treatment should be developmentally appropriate and that "the use of behavioral procedures invariably requires considerable flexibility and creativity" (p. 68).

Consistent with the potential *DSM-IV* diagnoses discussed earlier, the child-focused portion of the diagnostic process should consider the possibility of learning disabilities, severe depression, and conduct disorders as maintaining the behavior in addition to phobic and anxiety disorders. Further, physical illness and health problems may precipitate school refusal and avoidance behaviors; medical investigation and collaboration with the family physician is recommended to determine the impact of any health problems (King et al., 1995).

If the assessment indicates that school refusal and avoidance are primarily related to the child avoiding stimuli that cause negative affectivity (anxiety, low self-esteem, depression), then systematic desensitization, relaxation, and gradual school re-entry would be indicated (Kearney et al., 1995). In these cases, flooding and forced school attendance are not recommended due to the stressful nature of the intervention (Phelps et al., 1992). Further, the desensitization hierarchies would be based on whether school refusal was related primarily to school-related stimuli or separation anxiety. In the former situation, the hierarchy would focus on the specific situations producing fearfulness. In the latter situation, separation from the attachment figure would be emphasized (Phelps et al., 1992)

Development of more appropriate coping skills might be needed in addition to desensitization. Some children may benefit from developing more effective social skills to manage aversive social or evaluative situations. Modeling, role-play, and other cognitive-behavioral techniques are helpful here (Kearney & Beasley, 1994; Phelps et al., 1992).

Parent training and contingency management are helpful for children who refuse to attend school in order to secure parental attention, whereas family therapy to reduce family conflict and foster appropriate contingency contracting is recommended for children who receive tangible rewards for remaining home (Kearney & Beasley, 1994). It is also important to consider the possibility that parental psychopathology may be contributing to school refusal, as it is not unusual for parents to be anxious, overprotective, or dependent (King et al., 1995). If parental problems are significant, it may be necessary to initially focus treatment on the parent(s).

In general, treatment based on psychotropic medications should be used cautiously due to the possibility of deleterious side effects. Medication may be helpful in treating separation anxiety disorder and depression; however, it should be used for school refusal primarily when symptoms are severe and cognitive-behavioral treatments have been ineffective (King et al., 1995).

Implementation of Treatment Strategies

The best predictor of a positive outcome for school refusal behaviors is early diagnosis and rapid initiation of a comprehensive treatment plan (e.g., Kearney & Beasley, 1994; McDonald & Shepard, 1976; Want, 1983). Some researchers even state that the type of treatment techniques used are not as important as the rapidity of treatment initiation (Adams, 1979; Coolidge et al., 1957). School refusal and avoidance behaviors must be identified early before becoming reinforced. Each day the child remains at home, it becomes more difficult to return to school. The complexity of the diagnostic and treatment process is challenging and requires the collaborative involvement of child, family, school, and community resources (Gittleman, 1976; Kearney & Beasley, 1994).

The treatment team should include some or all of the following: family members, such as parents, siblings, and extended family; principal or other administrator; teacher(s); school psychologist; school counselor; school nurse; family medical provider; community mental health provider; other community-based service providers (e.g., child protective services, church outreach services); and the child, when appropriate. Older children, in particular, will need to be involved in the treatment planning to increase the probability of treatment compliance.

Resources presented at the end of this chapter may be helpful to school-based teams in planning and implementing treatment plans. This chapter's author (Paige, 1993) developed a series of decision matrices to guide school-based teams through the process of identification, problem analysis, and the development of appropriate interventions based upon the behavioral consultation model. The matrices provide visual maps and decision trees to assist school personnel in determining if the child has school refusal and avoidance behaviors, evaluating the contexts in which they occur, and developing possible treatments. The decision matrices were designed to be flexible in recognition of the complex nature of school refusal and avoidance behaviors and to encourage rapid initiation of treatment and collaboration.

Although involving so many people in the intervention may seem cumbersome, the collaborative team can function as a support resource for its members, particularly when the current intervention seems ineffective. Parents may need support when specific strategies exclude them (e.g., having another adult bring the child to school) or when they are learning new behavior management and communication skills. Parents may particularly need support if the child is experiencing a high degree of distress. If there are significant family stressors, the family may need referral to appropriate services. Teachers, too, may need significant support. Teachers sometimes feel that they are responsible for the behavior or that they are being blamed. Their feelings of competence and confidence may be shaken. Encouragement and support may be needed as they learn new management and intervention strategies.

Inclusion of a variety of team members also will help ensure that certain contributing factors are not overlooked. For example, the school nurse or family physician will be alert to physical factors and somatic complaints and can guide the team regarding medical management, if appropriate. Teachers and administrators will contribute an in-depth understanding of classroom and school structures that may contribute to the problem and/or its resolution. School psychologists and counselors can assess the need for referral to community-based mental health services and coordinate school-based interventions. By including the expertise of multiple team members, strategies can be developed that are ethical, effective, and reasonable for the specific child, family, and school involved.

Prevention and Monitoring of At-Risk Students

Information about school refusal and avoidance behaviors is needed by early childhood providers and preschools in order to intervene early and prevent later difficulties. When does separation anxiety become problematic? Attention should be paid to the child who cannot stay in preschool or who remains excessively distressed when separated. Kindergarten and early elementary teachers need to monitor a child who is at risk and to know that asking for help with a child's behavior is not an admission of incompetence. Children who are chronically absent (without clear medical reasons), who frequently resist attending school, who have developmentally inappropriate separation difficulties, or who have high levels of anxiety or fear at school should be considered at risk. King et al. (1995) warn that unusually shy or fearful children who are behaviorally inhibited appear to be at risk for school refusal. Home or school stress such as moving, attending a new school, illness or surgery of the child or a family member, or an accident or a death in the family may precipitate school refusal.

Martin and Waltham-Greenwood (1995) urge parents to be concerned if their child

1) seems increasingly passive, withdrawn, shy, or fearful about participating in school activities;
2) is more frequently fighting, crying, or seeking attention at school;
3) seems to be torn [by] wanting to stay home, but at the same time being extremely anxious about missing school work;
4) frequently asks the teacher for permission to leave class, especially to go to the school nurse. (p. 210)

They also warn parents to be concerned about general anxiety, frequent unfounded somatic complaints, depression, perfectionism, self-criticism, and low self-esteem. These authors also point out that there may be cause for concern if parents (a) feel happier or less worried when the child is home; (b) have unusually strong attachments to their children; (c) are protective; or (d) are experiencing emotional, financial, or other problems.

A child who has experienced school refusal and avoidance behaviors in the past needs to be carefully monitored, particularly following vacations, the beginning of the school year, and school changes. Staff inservice, particularly in the early elementary grades and in the transition grades (i.e., first year in a middle or high school) can alert staff to the warning signs of school refusal and avoidance behaviors, and the need for early intervention. Attendance officers for the school need to watch for patterns of absences in at-risk children. Local pediatricians, family practitioners, county health departments, and community mental health providers may benefit from information regarding the diagnosis of school refusal and avoidance behaviors, and they need to be involved in collaborative treatment efforts. Communication and cooperation between the family, school staff, and involved community service providers is critical for comprehensive and consistent treatment.

Summary

Perhaps the only "truth" about the behaviors variously described as "school phobia," "school refusal," and "school avoidance" is that for many years the discussion in the literature has been and continues to be controversial. These terms have been used interchangeably to describe different behaviors. The term school phobia has recently fallen into disfavor, with a shift towards the terms school refusal or avoidance. However, school refusal and avoidance have also been used to describe a heterogeneous set of behaviors. Partially due to the confusion surrounding the use and misuse of all of these terms, the appropriate assessment and treatment of these behaviors has been difficult for the practitioner.

Although school refusal does not occur frequently, it can result in considerable negative consequences for the child, family, and school. Family factors, trauma, school environment, social and academic skills or experiences, and school safety may play a role in the development of school refusal and avoidance behaviors, but it is the multiplicity of these factors that causes the difficulty in identifying this disorder and developing appropriate treatment. "One size fits all" does not apply to children exhibiting school refusal and avoidance behaviors; each child needs to be approached on an individual basis.

Early diagnosis and a rapidly initiated, coordinated intervention plan are critical for successful outcomes. Several authors have proposed specific differential diagnostic procedures (Kearney et al., 1995; King et al., 1995; Paige, 1993). A team-based collaborative approach is recommended. Frequently used interventions include contingency contracting, systematic desensitization, relaxation training, modeling, shaping, emotive imagery, and contingency management. Appropriate interventions must be developed to address academic or social difficulties. The team needs to address concerns regarding possible family dysfunction, crisis, or psychopathology. Team members may be assigned to help families develop appropriate coping or parenting skills and provide emotional support during the treatment. Due to the need for rapid treatment, teachers, physicians, and community health and mental health providers should be provided with information regarding risk factors, warning signs, and the availability of treatment.

Recommended Resources

Kearney, C. A., Eisen, A. R., & Silverman, W. K. (1995). The legend and myth of school phobia. *School Psychology Quarterly, 10*(1), 65–85.
This article is an excellent discussion regarding the history and flaws of school phobia research. The authors also discuss classification, assessment, and treatment issues and make recommendations.

King, N. J., Ollendick, T. H., & Tonge, B. J. (1995). *School refusal: Assessment and treatment.* Boston: Allyn and Bacon.
This book is written from a clinical behavioral perspective. It provides the reader with an overview of school refusal and emphasizes procedures for behavioral assessment and treatment. Multisourced assessment is detailed, recommended instruments are included, and several case histories are presented to illustrate diagnosis and intervention strategies.

Paige, L. Z. (1993). *The identification and treatment of school phobia.* Silver Spring, MD: National Association of School Psychologists.
This book provides a practical, "user-friendly" framework to guide school-based teams through identification and treatment procedures. The etiology, characteristics, and evaluation of school phobia, as well as intervention and prevention issues, are presented. Decision matrices and numerous handouts are available for use by practitioners and school-based teams.

References

Adams, P. (1979). Psychoneurosis. In J. D. Nohpitz (Ed.), *Basic handbook of child psychiatry* (Vol. 2, pp. 194–235). New York: Basic Books.

Ainsworth, M. D. S., Blehar, M., Waters, E., & Wall, S. (1978). *Patterns of attachment.* Hillsdale, NJ: Lawrence Erlbaum Associates.

American Psychiatric Association. (1994). *Diagnostic and statistical manual of mental disorders* (4th ed.). Washington, DC: Author.

Atkinson, L., Quarrington, B., & Cyr, J. J. (1985). School refusal: The heterogeneity of a concept. *American Journal of Orthopsychiatry, 55,* 83–101.

Berg, I. (1982). When truants and school refusers grow up [CD-ROM]. *British Journal of Psychiatry, 141,* 208–210. Abstract from: SilverPlatter File: PsycLIT Item: 73-30928.

Berg, I., Butler, A. & Hall, G. (1976). The outcome of adolescent school phobia. *British Journal of Psychiatry, 121,* 509–514.

Berg, I., Butler, A., & Pritchard, J. (1974). Psychiatric illness in mothers of school-phobic adolescents. *British Journal of Psychiatry, 125,* 466–467.

Berg, I., Nichols, K., & Pritchard, C. (1969). School phobia: Its classification and relationship to dependency. *Journal of Child Psychology and Psychiatry, 10,* 123–141.

Bernstein, G. A., & Garfinkel, B. D. (1988). Pedigrees, functioning, and psychopathology in families of school phobic children. *American Journal of Psychiatry, 145,* 70–74.

Blagg, N. R., & Yule, W. M. (1984). The behavioural treatment of school refusal: A comparative study. *Behavioural Research and Therapy, 22*(2), 119–127.

Broadwin, I. T. (1932). A contribution to the study of truancy. *American Journal of Orthopsychiatry, 2,* 253–259.

Burke, A. E. & Silverman, W. (1987). The prescriptive treatment of school refusal. *Clinical Psychology Review, 7,* 353–362.

Coolidge, J. C., Hahn, P. B., & Peck, A. (1957). School phobia: Neurotic crisis or way of life? *American Journal of Orthopsychiatry, 27,* 296–306.

DiBacco, J. B. (1979, April). *School refusal: Diagnosis and treatment in the school setting.* Paper presented at the spring conference of the Arizona Association of School Psychologists, Phoenix.

Eisenberg, I. (1958). School phobia: A study in the communication of anxiety. *American Journal of Psychiatry, 14,* 712–718.

Gittleman, R. (1976). School phobic children. *Today's Education, 71,* 41–42.

Gordon, D. A., & Young, R. D. (1976). School phobia: A discussion of etiology, treatment, and evaluation. *Psychological Reports, 39,* 783–804.

Granell de Aldaz, E., Vivas, E., Gelfand, D. M., & Feldman, L. (1984). Estimating the prevalence of school refusal. A Venezuelan sample. *Journal of Nervous and Mental Disease, 172,* 722–729.

Heath, C. P. (1985, April). *School phobia: Etiology, evaluation, and treatment.* Paper presented at the national conference for the National Association of School Psychologists, Las Vegas, NV.

Johnson, A. M., Falstein, E. I., Szurek, S. A., & Svendsen, M. (1941). School phobia. *American Journal of Orthopsychiatry, 11,* 702–711.

Kearney, C. A., & Beasley, J. F. (1994). The clinical treatment of school refusal behavior: A survey of referral and practice characteristics. *Psychology in the Schools, 31,* 128–132.

Kearney, C. A., Eisen, A., & Silverman, W. (1995). The legend and myth of school phobia. *School Psychology Quarterly, 10*(1), 65–85.

Kearney, C. A., & Silverman, W. (1993). Measuring the function of school refusal behavior: The School Refusal Assessment Scale. *Journal of Clinical Child Psychology, 22,* 85–96.

Kennedy, W. A. (1965). School phobia: Successful treatment of 50 cases. *Journal of Abnormal Psychology, 70,* 285–289.

King, N. J., Ollendick, T. H., & Tonge, B. J. (1995). *School refusal: Assessment and treatment.* Boston: Allyn & Bacon.

Last, C. G., & Strauss, C. C. (1990). School refusal in anxiety-disordered children and adolescents, *Journal of the American Academy of Child and Adolescent Psychiatry, 29,* 31–35.

Lazarus, A. A., Davison, D. C., & Polefka, B. A. (1965). Classical and operant factors in the treatment of school phobia. *Journal of Abnormal Psychology, 70,* 225–229.

Martin, M., & Waltham-Greenwood, C. (1995). *Solve your child's school-related problems.* New York: Harper Collins.

McDonald, J. E., & Shepard, G. (1976). School phobia: An overview. *Journal of School Psychology, 14,* 291–306.

Millman, H. L., Schaefer, C. E., & Cohen, J. J. (1981). *Therapies for school behavior problems: A handbook of practical interventions.* San Francisco: Jossey Bass.

Moss, R. A. (1986). The role of learning history in current sickrole behavior and assertion. *Behavior Research and Therapy, 24,* 681–683.

Paige, L. Z. (1993). *The identification and treatment of school phobia.* Silver Spring, MD: National Association of School Psychologists.

Paige, L. Z. (1994). School phobia: Diagnosis and intervention strategies for school teams. *Communique, 23*(4), 13–14.

Perugi, G., Deltito, J., Soriani, A., & Musetti, L. (1988). Relationships between panic disorders and separation anxiety with school phobia. *Comprehensive Psychiatry, 29*(2), 98–107.

Phelps, L., Cox, D., & Bajorek, E. (1992). School phobia and separation anxiety: Diagnostic and treatment comparisons. *Psychology in the Schools, 29,* 382–393.

Pilkington, C. L., & Piersel, W. C. (1991). School phobia: A critical analysis of the separation anxiety theory and an alternative conceptualization. *Psychology in the Schools, 28,* 290–303.

Shaughnessy, M. F., & Nystul, M. B. (1985). Preventing the greatest loss—Suicide. *Creative Child and Adult Quarterly, 10,* 232–238.

Sperling, M. (1967). School phobias: Classification, dynamics, and treatment. *Psychodynamic Study of the Child, 22,* 375–401.

Taylor, L., & Adelman, H. S. (1990). School avoidance behavior: Motivational bases and implications for intervention. *Child Psychology and Human Development, 20,* 219–233.

Want, J. H. (1983). *Scale for the Identification of School Phobia: Manual.* Novato, CA: Academic Therapy Publications.

31

Depressive Disorders During Childhood

Kevin D. Stark
Dawn Sommer
Blair Bowen
Cameron Goetz
Meredith A. Doxey
Christy Vaughn

University of Texas

Background and Development

Depression in children and adolescents is a serious mood disorder which, if left unidentified and untreated, can lead to life-threatening behaviors including suicide (Cohen-Sandler & Berman, 1980). Depression negatively affects children's functioning at school, with peers, and at home (Stark, 1990). It is important for school psychologists to recognize the magnitude and clinical importance of this disorder and to become educated regarding the identification, assessment, and treatment of depression in youth (Reynolds, 1984). School psychologists can educate teachers and other school staff about the various symptoms and the ways they may be manifested in the classroom so that all staff members can assist in the identification process. School psychologists can utilize various assessment tools including self-report and clinical interviews to assess at-risk youngsters. They can refer those experiencing a severe mood disorder for in- or out-patient treatment and can coordinate school-based intervention efforts with other psychiatric or psychological treatments (Reynolds, 1984). Moreover, school psychologists can develop and implement classroom-based prevention programs.

Even though schools have many individuals concerned about children's social-emotional and educational development, the majority of depressed children are never identified (Stark, 1990). Perhaps the biggest reason for this oversight is that depressed children rarely act out. More commonly, they are quiet children who sit in the back of the classroom and attract little, if any, attention. As a result, it is easy for these children to be overlooked. Furthermore, school psychologists spend a majority of their time evaluating and treating children referred for special education services. However, when depression is discussed, it is usually in regard to regular education students while overlooking the possibility that depressive disorders can and do co-occur with intellectual deficits and learning disabilities (Reynolds, 1984).

To qualify for psychological and related services in the schools, a child must demonstrate an academic need. Commonly, an academic need is operationalized as poor classroom performance. The symptoms of depression including anhedonia, negative self-evaluations, difficulty concentrating, indecisiveness, fatigue, and psychomotor retardation or agitation may lead to decreased academic performance. These symptoms can affect the child's motivation as well as cognitive processing. A depressed child is likely to engage in negative self-evaluations, which can also be detrimental to the child's performance, motivation, and confidence regarding academic achievement (Stark, 1990). Research suggests that depressed children's academic achievement is significantly lower than that of nondisturbed controls but similar to that of other psychiatric groups (Puig-Antich et al., 1985).

Many school professionals have not had extensive training regarding the ways in which depression manifests itself during childhood. Thus, this population may be less likely to be identified and to receive treatment services. However, with education and training, school psychologists can effectively treat this emotional disorder within the educational setting. It is hoped that this chapter will alert school personnel to the growing problem of childhood depression and that it will promote greater involvement of school psychologists in the identification and treatment of depressed youth.

Definitions

Depression can be defined as a *symptom* (sad mood or unhappiness) which occurs across the entire age span and may last for a brief or extended period of time. The symptom of depression (dysphoric mood) is often related to specific environmental events and may or may not be indicative of a psychiatric disorder (Cantwell, 1990).

Depression can also be defined as a *syndrome,* or a constellation of behaviors and emotions that occur together and are not associated by chance. A depressive syndrome consists not only of sad mood but also of other emotional, cognitive, physiological and vegetative, and behavioral/motivational disturbances (Cantwell, 1990). A depressive syndrome is less common than a depressed mood (Cantwell). Furthermore, a depressive syndrome may be a primary problem, or it may occur (a) with other medical disorders, (b) as a result of life stressors such as loss, or (c) as a secondary disturbance in conjunction with other psychiatric disorders.

Depression can also be defined as a *disorder,* or a constellation of behaviors and emotions which occur together for a minimum duration of time. The *Diagnostic and Statistical Manual of Mental Disorders-Fourth Edition* (*DSM-IV,* American Psychiatric Association, 1994) recognizes three major diagnostic categories of unipolar depressive disorders: major depression, dysthymic disorder, and depressive disorder not otherwise specified. The primary difference between these disorders is the number, severity, and duration of depressive symptoms. All three categories of depressive disorders are associated with significant impairment in current functioning.

The diagnostic criteria for a major depressive episode stipulate that five or more symptoms must be present over a 2-week period including one symptom of either depressed mood, loss of interest or pleasure (anhedonia), or irritability. In addition to the mood disturbance, the syndrome also includes at least four of the following symptoms: (a) changes in weight or failure to make necessary weight gains, (b) sleep disturbance, (c) psychomotor agitation or retardation, (d) fatigue or loss of energy, (e) excessive feelings of worthlessness or guilt, (f) lack of concentration and decision-making ability, and (g) suicidal ideation, attempts, or plans (American Psychiatric Association, 1994).

Dysthymic disorder is characterized by a chronic mood disturbance of either dysphoria or anger and at least two other depressive symptoms. These symptoms must be present for a minimum of one year without more than two symptom-free months. Children who exhibit depressive symptoms but do not meet the diagnostic criteria for either major depression or dysthymic disorder may receive a diagnosis of depressive disorder not otherwise specified.

School-aged children and adolescents can experience both major and minor variants of depression (Kovacs, 1989). Early onset of a depressive disorder is related to more frequent and severe depressive episodes. Furthermore, the manner in which depressive symptoms cluster together may vary as a function of development (Kazdin, 1990). For example, Ryan and colleagues (1987) found that prepubertal children displayed depressed appearance, somatic complaints, psychomotor agitation and depressive hallucinations significantly more often and with greater severity than adolescents diagnosed with major depression. On the other hand, adolescents with major depression displayed hopelessness, hypersomnia, weight loss, and weight gain significantly more often and with greater severity than children with the same diagnosis (Ryan et al., 1987).

The sex ratio of depressive disorders during the elementary school years is about equal. However, beginning with the middle school years and extending through high school, the ratio of females to males experiencing a depressive disorder progressively increases until adulthood at which time a two-to-one ratio is evident (Stark, 1990). Existing evidence also suggests that there may be an increased risk for depression among various subgroups including children from lower-socioeconomic families, Native American children, and homosexual youth (Petersen et al., 1993).

Episodes of major depression and dysthymia during childhood naturally remit (Kovacs, 1989). However, children who have experienced an episode of depression are likely to develop a subsequent episode while still in their teens suggesting that, for many youths, depression represents a recurrent, and in some instances, a chronic disorder. Furthermore, childhood and adolescent depression is considered a serious risk factor for adult depression. Therefore, primary prevention and early intervention efforts in the educational setting become an important means by which school psychologists can impact the course of depression during the child's formative years (Reynolds, 1984).

Prevalence

A relatively large percentage of youths are experiencing a depressive disorder at any given point in time; the prevalence increases with age and dramatically increases at around the time of puberty. Much of the existing epidemiological research solely reports the prevalence of major depression and overlooks the prevalence of dysthymic disorder. Thus, these reported figures are an underestimate of the extent of the problem of depression in the general school population. It is equally important to report the prevalence of dysthymic disorder both because it is a serious, long-lasting disturbance that places the youngster at risk for later development of an episode of major depression and because it is resistant to treatment (Kovacs, Gatsonis, Paulauskas, & Richards, 1985). When cases of both major depression and dysthymic disorder are considered, between 5% and 7% of the general school population in the fourth, fifth, sixth, and seventh grades may be experiencing a depressive disorder at any given time (Stark, 1990). This figure progressively increases through the junior and senior high grades until it reaches the adult level of approximately 10%. The current prevalence rate for younger elementary aged children progressively decreases for each successive grade until kindergarten and preschool, where it is very uncommon and associated with extreme chaos or abuse in the home (Kashani, Ray, & Carlson, 1984).

Problems and Implications

There appear to be multiple etiological pathways that lead to the development of depressive disorders during childhood including cognitive, behavioral, environmental, familial, genetic, and biochemical disturbances (Akiskal & McKinney, 1975). There probably are disturbances in multiple areas of functioning that lead to the development and maintenance of a depressive disorder, and a different pattern of disturbances may be evident in different children. Thus, the dominant unidimensional models of depressive disorders probably present inadequate explanations of the etiology of depression. A more complete picture results from a multidimensional and integrated model recognizing the reciprocal influence of cognitive, behavioral, contextual/interpersonal, and biochemical factors (Bedrosian, 1989; Hammen, 1991).

Cognitive Variables

The major cognitive models (e.g., Abramson, Metalsky, & Alloy, 1988; Abramson, Seligman, & Teasdale, 1978; Beck, 1967) are stress-diathesis models in which cognitive variables are assumed to interact with stressful life events to produce depression. In Beck's model (e.g., Beck, 1967), the cognitive disturbance stems from maladaptive schemata activated by related negative events. Once activated, the schemata filter and guide the processing of information in a negatively distorted fashion, which leads to information-processing errors and a plethora of intrusive and believable (to the individual) negative cognitions. These cognitions produce the depressive symptoms. In the learned helplessness/hopelessness model, a depressogenic attributional style is assumed to mediate the impact of negative life events and depressive symptoms (Abramson et al., 1978, 1989). The individual prone to developing depression has a trait-like tendency to attribute negative events to internal, stable, and global causes and positive events to external, unstable, and specific causes. Attributional style is hypothesized to serve as a filter for certain types of information processing.

In both cognitive models, the cognitive disturbance is hypothesized to moderate the impact of stressful events on the individual and on the depressive symptoms. These models, which were developed for adults, need to be modified when they are applied to children. Stressful life events have a direct effect on depressive symptoms in children and an indirect effect on depressive symptoms through the cognitive disturbances. Thus, it appears as though stressful events impact, and may in fact lead to, the development of the disturbances in cognition (Cole & Turner, 1993). However, cognitive style appears to moderate the relation between stressful events and depressive symptoms in later childhood (Turner & Cole, 1994).

A number of the major tenets of Beck's model (e.g., Beck, 1967) have been evaluated for depressed children. Depressed individuals are hypothesized to experience a negative bias in their thoughts about the self, the world, and the future, which is referred to as the depressive cognitive triad (Beck, 1976). An association has been found between (a) each component of the depressive cognitive triad and (b) the severity of depressive symptoms in children. This association has differentiated youngsters with depressive disorders from those with anxiety disorders or no disturbance (Kaslow, Stark, Printz, Livingston, & Tsai, 1992). However, no research has evaluated the potential role that the cognitive triad may play in the development of depressive disorders.

Beck hypothesizes that each emotional disorder is characterized by a unique disturbance in cognition; this is referred to as the cognitive specificity hypothesis. Depressive disorders are characterized by cognitions of loss while anxiety disorders are characterized by cognitions about threat. Support for the cognitive specificity hypothesis has been reported for depressive and anxiety disorders, although the relationship between loss and threat cognitions and depression and anxiety may be more complex than initially hypothesized (Gerber, Weiss, & Shanley, 1993; Gotlib, Lewinsohn, Seeley, Rohde, & Redner, 1993; Laurent & Stark, 1993).

Another concept central to Beck's cognitive theory of depression is the self-schema: the individual's rules about the self. The depressed individual is hypothesized to feel inadequate, unlovable, and unacceptable. The self-schema is presumed to facilitate encoding, storage, and retrieval of negative self-relevant information and may account for such disturbances as selective attention to, and personalization of, salient negative events. Beck hypothesizes that a negative self-schema guides the information processing of depressed individuals. However, research with children has indicated that nondepressed youths possess a positive self-schema which depressed youngsters lack (Jaenicke et al., 1987) or that depressed youngsters possess more of a balance of negative and positive self-schema (Prieto, Cole, & Tageson, 1992). However, support for the existence of a stronger negative self-schema among depressed youths has been reported in one study (Zupan, Hammen, & Jaenicke, 1987). The self-schema seems to affect the acquisition of new positive and/or negative information much more than it affects retrieval. Thus, it appears to guide selective attention, encoding, and retrieval (Prieto et al., 1992).

According to cognitive theory, the negative self-schema and other maladaptive schemata are maintained through, and give rise to, errors in information processing which result in the depressed individual exhibiting a negatively biased distortion in active information processing. Support for this theoretical contention has been reported for youngsters who self-report depressive symptoms (Haley, Fine, Marriage, Moretti, & Freeman, 1985; Leitenberg, Yost, Carrol-Wilson, 1986). The negatively biased distortion found in depressed youngsters stands in contrast to early research with depressed youngsters in which the investigators found that children reporting elevated levels of depressive symptoms experienced a deficit in information processing (Schwartz, Friedman, Linsay, & Narrol, 1982). Results of a series of three investigations (Kendall, Stark, & Adam, 1990) were consistent and indicated that depressed youngsters suffered from a distortion in self-evaluative information processing and did not suffer from a deficit in active information processing.

As noted earlier, the central premise of the learned helplessness/hopelessness model of depression is that stress will interact with a stable negative attributional style (moderational effect) to produce depression in some individuals. Results of early studies provide support for the model as children self-reported internal, stable, and global attributions for negative events and external, unstable, and specific attributions for positive events. However, results for attributions regarding positive events were not as strong (Asarnow & Bates, 1988; Kaslow, Rehm, & Siegel, 1984; Seligman et al., 1984). Further, it appears that a negative attributional style is not specific to depressive disorders but occurs in a variety of psychiatric disorders (Cole & Turner, 1993). Finally, stress appears to interact with atributional style to produce depressive symptoms, but the mechanisms and magnitude of the effect are still unclear (Nolen-Hoeksema, Girgus, & Seligman, 1986).

Several researchers have studied how a depressive cognitive style develops. Depressive schemata are hypothesized to form through early learning experiences, especially those within the family (Beck, Rush, Shaw, & Emery, 1986). Repeated exposure to negative life events, stressors, or specific forms of pathogenic feedback to the child leads to the internalization of negative cognitions and the eventual development of dysfunctional schemata (Cole & Turner, 1993). These negative schemata may develop as a result of inadequate parenting or ongoing aversive experiences within the family milieu (Young, 1991) or through parental modeling (Bandura, 1977). A current hypothesis (Stark, Schmidt, & Joiner, in press) holds that children's sense of self, world, and future (i.e., the cognitive triad) could represent the internalization of messages, both verbal and nonverbal, that they receive from interactions with parents. Study results support this contention as children's cognitive triad ratings were highly predictive of the severity of their level of depressive symptoms. Partial support was found for a social

learning perspective as mothers' cognitive triad ratings were significantly related to their children's cognitive triad ratings.

Results also indicated that perceived parental messages about the self, world, and future not only predicted the children's level of depression but were also strongly predictive of the children's sense of self, world, and future. Analyses indicated that the effects of parental messages on the children's depression were completely, not partially, mediated by the child's view of self, world, and future. Thus, perceived parental messages about the self, world, and future are predictive of the children's depression but only as a function of their association with the children's sense of self, world, and future. Goodness-of-fit tests supported the model that perceived parental messages predicted the children's cognitive triad which would predict the children's level of depression. Overall, preliminary support was found for two mechanisms (modeling and communication of negative messages) that were hypothesized to be instrumental in the development of a depressogenic style of thinking (Stark, et al., in press).

Behavioral Variables

Social skills deficits have been hypothesized to be a primary causal variable in the development of depression through the resulting loss of social reinforcement and disruption of close interpersonal relationships (Lewinsohn, 1975). Deficits in social skills lead to a reduction in the amount of response-contingent, positive reinforcement that the individual receives. Furthermore, it has been posited that depressed individuals elicit a corresponding pattern of rejection in others that reinforces the depression (Coyne, 1976). In other words, a vicious cycle is established in which poor social skills lead to interpersonal rejection, which produces depression and social withdrawal. Depressive symptoms are aversive to others and lead to further interpersonal rejection which exacerbates the depression.

Research indicates that depressed youths experience disturbances in interpersonal relationships. They are less popular (e.g., Strauss, Forehand, Frame, & Smith, 1984), less liked (Blechman, McEnroe, Carella, & Audette, 1986), and more likely to be rejected by their peers (e.g., Kennedy, Spence, & Hensley, 1989) than undisturbed children, and they tend to elicit negative reactions from adults (Mullins, Peterson, Wonderlich, & Raven, 1986). Furthermore, the degree of impairment appears to be related to the duration of the depressive episode.

The interpersonal difficulties of depressed youth may result from a deficit in social skills (Kennedy et al., 1989; Matson, Rotatori, & Helsel, 1983) as well as disturbances in social cognition (Sacco & Graves, 1984). However, the social skills disturbance associated with depression may not be as straightforward as previously thought (Stark,

Linn, MacGuire, & Kaslow, in press). Based on teachers' and children's ratings, depressed children with and without a comorbid anxiety disorder were described as exhibiting significantly fewer appropriate social skills relative to their nondepressed classmates. The social behaviors of children with a depressive disorder were characterized by an angry, jealous, and withdrawn style of interacting with others. The social skills deficits did not appear to be due to a lack of social skills knowledge. The disturbed children knew what was appropriate and inappropriate social behavior, but they did not enact appropriate behaviors (performance deficit). They also reported experiencing more aversive physical arousal in social situations which may contribute to their inability to enact appropriate social behaviors. The performance deficit and the heightened physical arousal may result from a negative cognitive style. Specifically, these children tend to compare themselves unfavorably to others, are less satisfied with their social interactions, exhibit disturbances in social problem solving (Sacco & Graves, 1984), and negatively distort evaluations of their social competence (Bell-Dolan, Reaven, & Petersen, 1993).

Family Variables

Genetic basis

There is compelling evidence to support a link between a genetic vulnerability and depressive disorders during childhood (Clarkin, Hass, & Glick, 1988). Higher concordance rates for depressive disorders have been reported among monozygotic (MZ) twins relative to dizygotic (DZ) twins (Tsuang & Farone, 1990). In fact, MZ twins are approximately three times more likely to develop a depressive disorder than DZ twins (Clarkin et at., 1988). Furthermore, the concordance rate for MZ twins reared apart is very high (67%; Price, 1968).

A considerably higher rate of depressive disorders has been found among first-degree relatives of depressed probands (Gershon et al., 1982). Children with a depressed parent have a 15% risk of developing a depressive disorder, which is six times greater than that for children with nondepressed parents (Downey & Coyne, 1990). Furthermore, if both parents have a depressive disorder, the child's chances increase to 40% (Goodwin, 1982). In comparison, children who have second-degree relatives with a depressive disorder are not at any greater risk for developing a depressive disorder than the general population (Tsuang & Farone, 1990).

Psychosocial factors

While it is generally recognized that the family plays an influential role in the psychological and psychosocial adjustment of children, a minimum of relevant research has been conducted with depressed youths. Evidence from clinical observations and research indicates that many depressed youngsters come from disturbed families (for re-

views, see Burdach & Borduin, 1986, and Stark & Brookman, 1992). Early reports provided evidence for the existence of disturbances within the families of depressed youths, but they did not identify the specific nature of the disturbances (Kaslow et al., 1984). Other research indicates that the families of depressed youths are characterized by greater chaos, abuse, and neglect (Kashani et al., 1984); conflict (Forehand et al., 1988); a critical, punitive, and belittling or shaming parenting style (e.g., Arieti & Bemporad, 1980; Poznanski & Zrull, 1970); an autocratic parenting style; communication difficulties (Puig-Antich et al., 1985); less participation in social and religious activities (Stark, Humphrey, Crook, & Lewis, 1990); less cohesiveness; and structural disturbances (Grossman, Poznanski, & Banegas, 1983). When affection is expressed, it is contingent upon behavior consistent with parental expectations (Grossman et al., 1983). The tone of the mother-child, and to a somewhat lesser extent the father-child, relationship is characterized as cold, hostile, tense, and at times rejecting (Puig-Antich et al., 1985).

Psychophysiology and Depression

Psychophysiological variables have been widely researched in depressed adults and are now being explored in depressed children (Burke & Puig-Antich, 1990). This research generally recognizes the importance of a developmental perspective when conducting research into the biological characteristics of depressed youths. Differences are evident between pre- and postpubertal cases suggesting that particular physiological traits associated with depression have both a developmental and a neuromaturational basis (Riddle & Cho, 1988). Psychophysiological variables that may be implicated in childhood depressive disorders include neurotransmitter systems, neuroendocrine dysfunction, and biological rhythms (Kalat, 1992).

The monoamine neurotransmitter system model of depression implicates norepinephrine, serotonin, and dopamine in the expression of depressive symptoms. The central hypothesis of this model is that a decrease in norepinephrine and serotonin produce depression, and an increase in these neurotransmitters alleviates depressive symptoms. Depression may result from both a deficit in neurotransmitters and a deficit in the number of binding sites for the neurotransmitters.

The monoamine neurotransmitters and neuroendocrine systems are linked closely. Serotonin and norepinephrine both are found in the limbic system, highlighting the connection between behaviors controlled by the limbic system (e.g., eating, sleeping, and emotion) and depression. Two endocrine systems, the hypothalamic-pituitary-thyroid (HPT) axis and the hypothalamic-pituitary-adrenal (HPA) axis, are linked closely to depression. Neuroendocrine dysfunction and the role of both the HPA axis and the HPT axis in depression have been examined in adults and children (Shelton et al., 1991). Mild hypothyroidism is seen in some patients with clinical depression, and thyroid hormone replacement decreases depressive symptoms. This relationship between hypothyroidism and depression suggests that the HPT axis is implicated in depressive disorders. However, similar responses to thyroid hormone replacement have not been found in prepubertal depressed children (Burke & Puig-Antich, 1990) suggesting that this response may be mediated by age.

Hormonal changes, particularly the presence of estrogen in girls, have also been linked to depressive disorders. Estrogen accounts for some individual differences between boys and girls in growth hormone (GH) secretion with girls secreting significantly more GH than boys (Burke & Puig-Antich, 1990). GH release during sleep in depressed prepubertal children was found to be significantly greater than in controls; however, this finding was not found in depressed adolescents (Burke & Puig-Antich, 1990). Thus, age and puberty appear to interact in the control of GH release. The complex relationship between hormones and the HPA and HPT axes that are mutually regulated with the monoamine neurotransmitters contribute to the complexity of biological explanations for depression.

Biological rhythms determine human functioning and involve natural circadian and ultradian rhythms. These physical processes provide another competing explanation for the biological basis of depression and focus on the mutual influences of the sleep-wake cycle, neuroendocrine activity, and body temperature that follow the daily light-dark cycle. Disruptions in these processes are potential links to the expression of depressive symptoms.

Alternative Actions

Pharmacological Interventions

Surprisingly little research has been conducted on the effectiveness of antidepressant medication for depressed youths. Thus, while antidepressants are commonly prescribed to depressed youngsters, there is little empirical support for this practice. "While virtually all the antidepressant and mood stabilizing drugs found useful in the treatment of adults have been tested with children, systematic studies with results that can confidently be applied by child psychiatrists are rare" (Rancurello, 1985, p. 88). Historically, the most common drug group for treating depression in children has been the tricyclic antidepressants, with imipramine, amitriptyline, and nortriptyline being the most popular. The specific mechanisms of action are unclear, but it is thought that tricyclics

block the reuptake of norepinephrine and serotonin at the presynaptic terminal (Julien, 1988).

Conclusions regarding the effectiveness of tricyclics is mixed for children. Initial controlled studies indicated no difference between imipramine and placebos. In open-trial studies, some encouraging findings have been reported for the effectiveness of tricyclic antidepressants with depressed children and adolescents. In a study of 34 adolescents who received a diagnosis of major depression, 44% responded favorably to imipramine (Ryan et al., 1987). A higher response rate (75%) was reported for children in a study of the effectiveness of nortriptyline (Geller, Perel, Knitter, Lycaki, & Farvok, 1983). While these findings are encouraging, results of investigations controlling for the methodological limitations of open-trial research do not indicate that tricyclic antidepressants are any more effective than a placebo (Kashani, Shekim, & Reid, 1984; Kramer & Feiguine, 1981; Puig-Antich et al., 1987). In an evaluation of one of the new generation of antidepressants (fluoxetine whose trade name is Prozac) with adolescents, Simeon, Dinicola, Ferguson, and Coping (1990) did not find conclusive evidence to support the effectiveness of this pharmacological treatment for depressed adolescents.

There have not been any studies in which the relative effectiveness of antidepressants, psychotherapy, and a combination of the two forms of therapy have been compared for children and adolescents. Nonetheless, in a unique study, Robins, Alessi, and Colfer (1989) reported that 18 of 38 adolescents who received a diagnosis of major depression responded favorably to 6 weeks of psychotherapy. Of the 15 nonresponders who continued in the study, 12 responded to a combination of continued psychotherapy and a tricyclic medication (in one case, lithium was added). Given the widespread use of the new family of antidepressants (Prozac, Zoloft, Paxsil, Welbutrin) with children and adolescents, further research concerning their effectiveness relative to the tricyclics is warranted.

Psychosocial Interventions

Surprisingly little treatment-outcome research has been conducted with depressed youths. To date, two control-group outcome studies with depressed children have been published (Butler, Miezitis, Friedman, & Cole, 1980; Stark, Reynolds, & Kaslow, 1987), and a third investigation was reported (Stark, 1990). A few more investigations have been completed with depressed adolescents (Fine, Forth, Gilbert, & Haley, 1991; Kahn, Kehle, Jenson, & Clark, 1990; Lewinsohn, Clarke, Hops, & Andrew, 1990; Reynolds & Coats, 1986). In addition, clinical trial methodology has been used in two investigations that describe promising interventions (Brent, Poling, McKain, & Baugher, 1993; Mufson et al., 1994). A recent trend in the literature is the development and evaluation of prevention programs for youths who are at risk for developing depressive disorders (Clarke, Hawkins, Murphy, & Sheeber, 1993; Clarke et al., 1995; Jaycox, Reivich, Gillham, & Seligman, 1994). The paucity of research limits the breadth of the knowledge base and the conclusions that can be drawn.

Based on the existing treatment-outcome research with depressed children (Butler et al., 1980; Stark et al., 1987), it appears that various cognitive-behavioral interventions with and without a social skills component are effective at reducing the severity of depressive symptoms reported by depressed children. Cognitive-behavioral therapy is more effective than a traditional counseling program designed to enhance self-esteem (Stark, 1990), an attention placebo condition (Butler et al., 1980), and no-treatment waiting-list control conditions (Butler et al., 1980; Stark et al., 1987). These results suggest that the improvements associated with cognitive behavioral interventions are greater than those that would naturally occur over the course of 10 to 12 weeks and that the interventions may produce more change than any simply due to the nonspecifics of psychotherapy.

Cognitive behavioral therapy (Lewinsohn et al., 1990) and relaxation training (Kahn et al., 1990; Reynolds & Coats, 1986) relative to no-treatment waiting-list conditions have produced significantly greater improvements in decreasing depressive symptoms among adolescents. The addition of a parent-training component involving negotiation and conflict resolution skills has also resulted in parents reporting a reduction in behavior problems (Lewinsohn et al., 1990). Fine and colleagues (1991) reported that a therapeutic support group was more effective than social skills training at reducing the severity of depressive symptoms immediately following treatment. However, it is interesting to note that while the support group was more effective than social skills training immediately following treatment, youngsters in the social skills group continued to improve following treatment until there was no difference between groups at the 9-month follow-up assessment.

Due to the episodic nature of depressive disorders, it is crucial to evaluate the maintenance of treatment effects (Stark, Sommer, & Bowen, in press). In general, while the length of the follow-up periods varied across studies from 5 weeks to 22 months, it appears as though the treatment gains are maintained over short as well as long periods. In fact, improvements may continue to be made following completion of treatment (Fine et al., 1991; Stark, 1990; Stark et al., 1987).

Results of the investigations designed to evaluate prevention programs for depressed youths yield mixed, although generally encouraging results. Jaycox and colleagues (1994) reported that a 12-session prevention program emphasizing training in cognitive and social problem solving reduced the severity of depressive symptoms and behavior problems in the classroom immediately following completion of the prevention program and pre-

vented symptoms from recurring for 6 months. Clarke et al. (1993) did not find significant effects for a cognitive behavioral prevention program for a general high school population. In a second study with adolescents reporting subclinical levels of depressive symptoms which placed them at risk for the development of a depressive disorder, Clarke et al. (1995) demonstrated that the prevention program was effective at reducing the number of youths who developed diagnosable depressive disorders over a 12-month period. However, the researchers noted that a number of youths did develop depressive disorders. It would be interesting to identify the variables predicting those who did and did not develop depressive disorders.

It is evident from this brief summary of the existing treatment and prevention investigations that a great deal of future research, especially programmatic research, needs to be conducted in the area. While research results are encouraging and suggest that it is possible to identify and treat depressed youths in the school setting, it is apparent that modifications may be needed for youngsters who are experiencing a co-morbid condition or have a multiplicity of confounding difficulties such as histories of physical and sexual abuse, familial substance abuse, and severe parental and familial psychopathology. To meet these challenges, more comprehensive treatment programs will have to be developed which address the multitude of factors impacting the onset and maintenance of depressive disorders in youths.

Summary

Depressive disorders adversely impact children's functioning at school, with peers, and at home. School psychologists are in a unique position to assist in the identification, assessment, and treatment of childhood depression within the school setting. Knowledge regarding the cognitive, behavioral, environmental, familial, genetic, and biochemical disturbances contributing to the onset and maintenance of depressive disorders will aid professionals in the development of appropriate interventions aimed at reducing symptomatology.

According to the major cognitive theories of depression, youngsters experiencing a depressive disorder exhibit cognitive distortions characterized by a negative view of the self, world, and future; attribute negative life events to internal, stable, and global causes; and have developed a negative self-schema which guides information processing in a biased manner. Such depressive schemata likely are formed through early learning experiences within the family. Depressed children and adolescents also experience social skills deficits. Poor social skills lead to interpersonal rejection which in turn reinforces the depression. Moreover, research conducted regarding the contributions of genetic and biochemical factors in the development and maintenance of depressive disorders in youth has illustrated the importance of including such factors in an integrated and developmentally sensitive model of depression across the life span.

Pharmacological interventions are often implemented with youngsters, but the efficacy of their use with this population has not yet been proven. Research regarding the effectiveness of different psychosocial interventions, including cognitive behavioral interventions with children in the school setting, has been promising. Thus, intervention efforts in the educational setting are an important means by which school psychologists can play an active role in altering the course of depression in identified youth.

Recommended Resources

Stark, K. D. (1990). *The treatment of depression during childhood: A school-based program.* New York: Guilford Press.
This book provides the reader with background information about the nature of depressive disorders during childhood from the perspective of a psychologist working in the schools. A thorough description of the symptom picture is followed by a discussion about the diagnosis, special education classification, prevalence, natural course, and comorbid conditions associated with depression during the elementary school years. A school-based identification and assessment model are described. The strength of the book is its description of an empirically based treatment program for depressed youths. This group intervention program, which has been applied and evaluated in the public schools, teaches youngsters a number of cognitive, affective, and behavioral skills for coping with depression.

Stark, K. D., Swearer, S., Delaune, M., Knox, L., & Winter, J. (1995). Depressive disorders. In R. T. Ammerman & M. Hersen (Eds.), *Handbook of child behavior therapy in the psychiatric setting* (pp. 269–300). New York: John Wiley and Sons.
This chapter provides a comprehensive outline of protoypic assessment and treatment of childhood depression. Assessment should be multidimensional and include areas such as affective, academic, behavioral, and cognitive abilities. Symptoms of depression and their impact on the academic setting are presented. Treatments discussed include behavior management; individual, group, and family therapies; and parent training.

Stark, K., Linn, J., Maguire, M., & Kaslow, N. (in press). The interpersonal functioning of depressed and anxious children: Social skills, social knowledge, automatic thoughts, and physical arousal. *Journal of Abnormal Psychology*
In this article, social skills, knowledge of social skills, automatic thoughts, and physical arousal in social situations of depressed children are evaluated. Literature addressing the role of social skills in the development and course of depression is reviewed. Results of the study reported indicate that depressed children exhibit significant social skills deficits and experience negative automatic thoughts and aversive physical arousal in social situations.

References

Abramson, L. Y., Metalsky, G. I., & Alloy, L. B. (1989). Hopelessness depression: A theory-based subtype of depression. *Psychological Review, 96,* 358–372.

Abramson, L. Y., Seligman, M. E. P., & Teasdale, J. (1978). Learned helplessness in humans: Critique and reformulation. *Journal of Abnormal Psychology, 87,* 49–74.

Akiskal, H. S., & McKinney, W. T. (1975). Overview of recent research in depression: Integration of ten conceptual models into a comprehensive clinical frame. *Archives of General Psychiatry, 32,* 285–305.

American Psychiatric Association. (1994). *Diagnostic and statistical manual of mental disorders* (4th ed.). Washington, DC: Author.

Arieti, S., & Bemporad, J. R. (1980). The psychological organization of depression. *American Journal of Psychiatry, 137,* 1360–1365.

Asarnow, J. R., & Bates, S. (1988). Depression in child psychiatric inpatients: Cognitive and attributional patterns. *Journal of Abnormal Child Psychology, 16,* 601–615.

Asarnow, J. R., Carlson, G. A., & Guthrie, D. (1987). Coping strategies, self-perceptions, hopelessness, and perceived family environments in depressed and suicidal children. *Journal of Consulting and Clinical Psychology, 55,* 361–366.

Bandura, A. (1977). *A social learning theory.* Englewood Cliffs, NJ: Prentice-Hall.

Beck, A. T. (1967). *Depression: Clinical, experimental and theoretical aspects.* New York: Hoeber.

Beck, A. T. (1976). *Cognitive therapy and the emotional disorders.* New York: International Universities Press.

Beck, A. T., Rush, A. J., Shaw, B. F., & Emery, G. (1979). *Cognitive therapy of depression.* New York: Guilford Press.

Bedrosian, R. C. (1989). Treating depression and suicidal wishes within the family context. In N. Epstein, S. E. Schlesinger, & W. Dryden (Eds.), *Cognitive-behavioral therapy with families* (pp. 292–324). New York: Brunner/Mazel.

Blechman, E. A., McEnroe, M. J., Carella, E. T., & Audette, D. P. (1986). Childhood competence and depression. *Journal of Abnormal Psychology, 95,* 223–227.

Brent, D. A., Poling, K., McKain, B., & Baugher, M. (1993). A psychoeducational program for families of affectively ill children and adolescents. *Journal of the American Academy of Child and Adolescent Psychiatry, 32,* 770–774.

Brown, N. W. (1994). *Group counseling for elementary and middle school children.* Westport, CT: Praeger Publishers.

Burbach, D. J., & Borduin, C. M. (1986). Parent-child relations and the etiology of depression: A review of methods and findings. *Clinical Psychology Review, 6,* 133–153.

Burke, P., & Puig-Antich, J. (1990). Psychobiology of childhood depression. In M. Lewis & S. M. Miller (Eds.), *Handbook of developmental psychopathology* (pp. 327–339). New York: Plenum Press.

Cantwell, D. P. (1990). Depression across the early life span. In M. Lewis & S. M. Miller (Eds.), *Handbook of developmental psychopathology* (pp. 293–309). New York: Plenum Press.

Clarke, G. N., Hawkins, W., Murphy, M., & Sheeber, L. (1993). School-based primary prevention of depressive symptomatology in adolescents: Findings from two studies. *Journal of Adolescent Research, 8,* 183–204.

Clarke, G. N., Hawkins, W., Murphy, M., Sheeber, L. B., Lewinsohn, P. M., & Seeley, J. R. (1995). Targeted prevention of unipolar depressive disorder in an at-risk sample of high school adolescents: A randomized trial of a group cognitive intervention. *Journal of the American Academy of Child and Adolescent Psychiatry, 34,* 312–321.

Clarkin, J. F., Haas, G. L., & Glick, I. D. (1988). *Affective disorders and the family: Assessment and treatment.* New York: Guilford Press.

Cohen-Sandler, R., & Berman, A. L. (1980). Diagnosis and treatment of childhood depression and self-destructive behavior. *Journal of Family Practice, 11,* 51–58.

Cole, D., & Turner, J., Jr. (1993). Models of cognitive mediation and moderation in child depression. *Journal of Abnormal Psychology, 102,* 271–281.

Coyne, J. C. (1976). Toward an interactional description of depression. *Psychiatry, 39,* 28–40.

Fine, S., Forth, A., Gilbert, M., & Haley, G. (1991). Group therapy for adolescent depressive disorder: A comparison of social skills and therapeutic support. *Journal of the American Academy of Child and Adolescent Psychiatry, 30,* 79–85.

Forehand, R., Brody, G., Slotkin, J., Fauber, R., McCombs, A., & Long, N. (1988). Young adolescent and maternal depression: Assessment, interrelations, and predictors. *Journal of Consulting and Clinical Psychology, 56,* 422–426.

Frame, C., Matson, J. L., Sonis, W. A., Fialkov, M. J., & Kazdin, A. E. (1982). Behavioral treatment of depression in a prepubertal child. *Journal of Behavior Therapy and Experimental Psychiatry, 3,* 239–243.

Freeman, A. (1986). Understanding personal, cultural and family schema in psychotherapy. In A. Freeman, N. Epstein, & K. M. Simon (Eds.), *Depression in the family* (pp. 79–100). New York: Haworth Press.

Fristad, M. A., Weller, E. B., Weller, R. A., Teare, M., & Preskorn, S. H. (1988). Self-report versus biological markers in assessment of childhood depression. *Journal of Affective Disorders, 15,* 339–345.

Garber, J., Weiss, B., & Shanley, N. (1993). Cognitions, depressive symptoms, and development in adolescents. *Journal of Abnormal Psychology, 102,* 47–57.

Geller, B., Perel, J. M., Knitter, E. F., Lycaki, H., & Farooki, Z. Q. (1983). Nortriptyline in major depressive disorder in children: Response, steady-state plasma levels, predictive kinetics, and pharmacokinetics. *Psychopharmacology Bulletin, 19,* 62–65.

Gershon, E. S., Hamovit, J., Guroff, J. J., Dibble, E., Leckman, J. F., Sceery, W., Targum, S. D., Nurnberger, J. I., Goldin, L. R., & Bunney, W. E. (1982). A family study of schizoaffective, bipolar I, bipolar II, unipolar, and normal control probands. *Archives of General Psychiatry, 39,* 1157–1167.

Goodwin, F. (1982). *Depression and manic-depressive illness.* Bethesda, MD: National Institutes of Health.

Gotlib, I. H., Lewinsohn, P. M., Seeley, J. R., Rohde, P., & Redner, J. E. (1993). Negative cognitions and attributional style in depressed adolescents: An examination of stability and specificity. *Journal of Abnormal Psychology, 102,* 607–615.

Grossman, J. A., Poznanski, E. O., & Banegas, M. E. (1983). Lunch: Time to study family interactions. *Journal of Psychosocial Nursing and Mental Health Services, 21,* 19–22.

Haley, B. M. T., Fine, S. L., Marriage, K., Moretti, M. M., & Freeman, R. J. (1985). Cognitive bias and depression in psychiatrically disturbed children and adolescents. *Journal of Consulting and Clinical Psychology, 53,* 535–537.

Hammen, C. (1991). *Depression runs in families: The social context of risk and resilience in children of depressed mothers.* New York: Springer-Verlag.

Jaenicke, C., Hammen, C., Zupan, B., Hiroto, D., Gordon, D., Adrian, C., & Burge, D. (1987). Cognitive vulnerability in children at risk for depression. *Journal of Abnormal Child Psychology, 15,* 559–572.

Jaycox, L. H., Reivich, K. J., Gillham, J. & Seligman, M. E. P. (1994). Prevention of depressive symptoms in school children. *Behavior Research and Therapy, 32,* 801–816.

Julien, R. M. (1988). *A primer of drug reaction* (5th ed.). New York: Freeman.

Kahn, J. S., Kehl, T. J., Jenson, W. R., & Clark, E. (1990). Comparison of cognitive-behavioral, relaxation, and self-modeling interventions for depression among middle-school students. *School Psychology Review, 19,* 196–211.

Kalat, J. W. (1992). *Biological psychology.* Belmont, CA: Wadsworth Publishing.

Kashani, J. H., Ray, J. S., & Carlson, G. A. (1984). Depression and depressive-like states in preschool-age children in a child development unit. *American Journal of Psychiatry, 141,* 1397–1402.

Kashani, J. H., Shekim, W. O., & Reid, J. C. (1984). Amitriptyline in children with major depressive disorder: A double-blind crossover pilot study. *Journal of the American Academy of Child Psychiatry, 23,* 348–351.

Kaslow, N. J., Rehm, L. P., & Siegel, A. W. (1984). Social-cognitive and cognitive correlates of depression in children. *Journal of Abnormal Child Psychology, 12,* 605–620.

Kaslow, N. J., Stark, K. D., Printz, B., Livingston, R., & Tsai, Y. (1992). Cognitive triad inventory for children: Development and relationship to depression and anxiety. *Journal of Clinical Child Psychology, 21,* 339–347.

Kazdin, A. E. (1990). Childhood depression. *Journal of Child Psychology and Psychiatry, 31,* 121–160.

Kendall, P. C., Stark, K. D., & Adam, T. (1990). Cognitive deficit or cognitive distortion in childhood depression. *Journal of Abnormal Child Psychology, 18,* 255–270.

Kennedy, E., Spence, S. H., & Hensley, R. (1989). An examination of the relationship between childhood depression and social competence amongst primary school children. *Journal of Child Psychology and Psychiatry, 30,* 561–573.

Kovacs, M. (1981). Rating scales to assess depression in school aged children. *Acta Paedopsychiatrica, 46,* 305–315.

Kovacs, M. (1989). Affective disorders in children and adolescents. *American Psychologist, 44,* 209–215.

Kovacs, M., Gatsonis, C., Paulauskas, S. L., & Richards, C. (1989). Depressive disorders in childhood: Vol. IV. A longitudinal study of comorbidity with and risk for anxiety disorders. *Archives of General Psychiatry, 46,* 776–782.

Kramer, A. D., & Feiguine, R. J. (1981). Clinical effects of amitriptyline in adolescent depression: A pilot study. *Journal of the American Academy of Child Psychiatry, 20,* 636–644.

Laurent, J., & Stark, K. D. (1993) Testing the cognitive content-specificity hypothesis with anxious and depressed youngsters. *Journal of Abnormal Psychology, 102,* 226–237.

Leitenberg, H., Yost, L. W., & Carroll-Wilson, M. (1986). Negative cognitive errors in children: Questionnaire development, normative data, and comparisons between children with and without self-reported symptoms of depression, low self-esteem, and evaluation anxiety. *Journal of Consulting and Clinical Psychology, 54,* 528–536.

Lewinsohn, P. M. (1975). The behavioral study and treatment of depression. In M. Hersen, R. M. Eisler, & P. M. Miller (Eds.), *Progress in behavior modification* (Vol. 1, pp. 16–64). New York: Academic Press.

Matson, J. L., Rotatori, A. F., & Helsel, W. J. (1983). Development of a rating scale to measure social skills in children: The Matson Evaluation of Social Skills with Youngsters (MESSY). *Behavioral Research and Therapy, 41,* 335–340.

Mufson, L., Moreau, D., Weissman, M., Wickramaratne, P., Marin, J., & Samoilov, A. (1994). *Journal of the American Academy of Child and Adolescent Psychiatry, 33,* 695–705.

Mullins, L. L., Peterson, L., Wonderlich, S. A., & Reaven, N. M. (1986). The influence of depressive symptomatology in children on the social responses and perceptions of adults. *Journal of Clinical Child Psychology, 15,* 233–240.

Nolen-Hoeksema, S., Girgus, J. S., & Seligman, M. E. P. (1986). Learned helplessness in children: A longitudinal study of depression, achievement, and explanatory style. *Journal of Personality and Social Psychology, 51,* 435–442.

Petersen, A. C., Compas, B. E., Brooks-Gunn, J., Stemmler, M., Ey, S., & Grant, K. E. (1993). Depression in adolescence. *Psychological Bulletin, 48,* 155–168.

Petti, T. A., Bornstein, M., Delamater, A., & Conner, C. K. (1980). Evaluation and multimodality treatment of a depressed prepubertal girl. *Journal of the American Academy of Child Psychiatry, 19,* 690–702.

Poznanski, E. O., & Zrull, J. (1970). Childhood depression: Clinical characteristics of overtly depressed children. *Archives of General Psychiatry, 23,* 8–15.

Prieto, S. L., Cole, D. A., & Tageson, C. W. (1992). Depressive self-schemas in clinic and nonclinic children. *Cognitive Therapy and Research, 16,* 521–534.

Puig-Antich, J., Lukens, E., Davies, M., Goetz, D., Brennan-Quattrock, J., & Todak, G. (1985). Psychosocial functioning in prepubertal major depressive disorders: Vol. 1. Interpersonal relationships during the depressive episode. *Archives of General Psychiatry, 42,* 500–507.

Puig-Antich, J., Perel, J. M., Lupatikin, W, Chambers, W. J., Tabrizi, M. A., King, J., Goetz, R., Davies, M., & Stiller, R. L. (1987). Imipramine in prepubertal major depressive

disorder. *Archives of General Psychiatry, 44,* 81–89.

Rancurello, M. D. (1985). Clinical applications of antidepressant drugs in childhood behavioral and emotional disorders. *Psychiatric Annals, 15,* 88–100.

Reynolds, W. M (1984). Depression in children and adolescents: Phenomenology, evaluation, and treatment. *School Psychology Review, 13,* 171–182.

Riddle, M. A., & Cho, S. C., (1988). Biological aspects of adolescent depression. In G. R. Adams, R. Montemayor, & T. P. Gullotta (Eds.), *Biology of adolescent behavior and development* (pp. 223–249). London: Sage.

Robins, D. R., Alessi, N. E., & Colfer, M. V. (1989). Treatment of adolescents with major depression: Implications of the DST and the melancholic clinical subtype. *Journal of Affective Disorders, 17,* 99–104.

Ryan, N. D., Puig-Antich, J., Ambrosini, P., Rabinovich, H., Robinson, D., Nelson, B., Iyengar, S., & Twomet, J. (1987). The clinical picture of major depression in children and adolescents. *Archives of General Psychiatry, 44,* 854–861.

Sacco, W. P., & Graves, D. J. (1984). Childhood depression, interpersonal problem-solving, and self-ratings of performance. *Journal of Clinical Child Psychology, 13,* 10–15.

Schwartz, M., Friedman, R., Lindsay, P., & Narrol, H. (1982). The relationships between conceptual tempo and depression in children. *Journal of Consulting and Clinical Psychology, 50,* 488–490.

Seligman, M. E. P., Peterson, C., Kaslow, N. J., Tanenbaum, R. L., Alloy, L. B., & Abramson, L. Y. (1984). Attributional style and depressive symptoms among children. *Journal of Abnormal Psychology, 93,* 235–238.

Stark, K. D. (1990). *The treatment of depression during childhood: A school-based program.* New York: Guilford Press.

Stark, K. D., & Brookman, C. (1992). Childhood depression: Theory and family-school intervention. In M. J. Fine & C. Carlson (Eds.), *Family-school intervention: A systems perspective* (pp. 247–271). Boston: Allyn & Bacon.

Stark, K. D., Humphrey, L. L., Crook, K., & Lewis, K. (1990). Perceived family environments of depressed and anxious children: Child's and maternal figure's perspectives. *Journal of Abnormal Child Psychology, 18,* 527–547.

Stark, K., Humphrey, L., Laurent, J., Livingston, R., & Christopher, J. (1993). Cognitive, behavioral, and family factors in the differentiation of depressive and anxiety disorders during childhood. *Journal of Consulting and Clinical Psychology, 61,* 878–886.

Stark, K. D., Linn, J. D., MacGuire, M., & Kaslow, N. J. (in press). The social functioning of depressed and anxious children: Social skills, social knowledge, automatic thoughts, and physical arousal. *Journal of Clinical Child Psychology.*

Stark, K. D., Reynolds, W. M., & Kaslow, N. J. (1987). A comparison of the relative efficacy of self-control therapy and a behavioral problem-solving therapy for depression in children. *Journal of Abnormal Child Psychology, 15,* 91–113.

Stark, K. D., Schmidt, K., & Joiner, T. E. (in press). Depressive cognitive triad: Relationship to severity of depressive symptoms in children, parents' cognitive triad, and perceived parental messages about the child him or herself, the world, and the future. *Journal of Abnormal Child Psychology.*

Stark, K. D., Swearer, S., Delaune, M., Knox, L., & Winter, J. (1995). Depressive disorders. In R. T. Ammerman & M. Hersen (Eds.), *Handbook of child behavior therapy in the psychiatric setting* (pp. 269–300). New York: John Wiley and Sons.

Tems, C., Stewart, S., Skinner, J., Jr., Hughes, C., & Emslie, G. (1993). Cognitive distortions in depressed children and adolescents: Are they state dependent or trait like? *Journal of Clinical Child Psychology, 22,* 316–326.

Tsuang, M. T., & Farone, S. V. (1990). *The genetics of mood disorders.* Baltimore: Johns Hopkins University Press.

Turner, J. E., & Cole, D. A. (1994). Developmental differences in cognitive diatheses for child depression. *Journal of Abnormal Child Psychology, 22,* 15–33.

Young, J. (1991). *Cognitive therapy for personality disorders: A schema-focused approach.* Sarasota, FL: Professional Resource Exchange.

Zupan, B. A., Hammen, C., & Jaenicke, C. (1987). The effects of current mood and prior depressive history on self-schematic processing in children. *Journal of Experimental Child Psychology, 43,* 149–158.

32

Suicidal Ideation and Behaviors

Stephen E. Brock

Lodi (California) Unified School District

Jonathan Sandoval

University of California, Davis

The incidence of completed suicide among school-aged populations has increased dramatically over the past 40 years. Specifically, teen suicides have quadrupled since 1950. While only 2.7 per 100,000 15- to 19-year-olds committed suicide in 1950 (Centers for Disease Control, 1991), this rate climbed to 10.9 by 1992 (Centers for Disease Control, 1995). Suicide is the eighth leading cause of death in the United States across all age groups (National Center for Health Statistics, 1994); however, it is the third leading cause of death among 15- to 24-year-olds (Moscicki, 1995). More recently, there has also been a dramatic increase in the suicide rate of children. From 1980 to 1992 the rate among 10- to 14-year-olds increased 120%, rising from 0.8 to 1.7 (Centers for Disease Control, 1995).

Completed suicides are only part of the problem. Research estimates suggest that as many as 62.5% of high school students have suicidal thoughts (Smith & Crawford, 1986). Additionally, 8% to 13% of high school students have engaged in a suicidal behavior (Centers for Disease Control, 1991; Harkavy-Friedman, Asnis, Boe, & DiFiore, 1987; Smith & Crawford, 1986). For the school psychologist, these statistics highlight the importance of understanding and knowing how to respond to suicide.

Background and Development

Suicidal ideation and behaviors can be placed on a gradient of severity (Diekstra & Garnefski, 1995; Moscicki, 1995). Least severe are casual thoughts of suicide. Most severe are behaviors that result in death. All suicidal behaviors involve thoughts of suicide but differ in the degree to which the individual considers and acts upon these thoughts. As severity increases, behaviors become more lethal, less prevalent, and more strongly associated with psychopathology.

Range of Suicidal Behaviors

- *Suicidal ideation* refers to conscious thoughts of suicide. These cognitions may range from fleeting thoughts to a chronic preoccupation. Although some consideration may have been given to means of suicide, no self-destructive behaviors are displayed.
- *Suicidal gestures* are mild self-destructive behaviors displayed by individuals with thoughts of suicide. However, these behaviors do not cause physical harm (e.g., pointing an unloaded gun at one's head). Gestures range in purpose from a way to express distress to a rehearsal for a suicide attempt. They may or may not be a part of a suicide plan.
- *Parasuicide* is more severe, planned self-destructive behavior that has resulted in significant, nonfatal physical harm. Parasuicide is often referred to as attempted suicide, but some authors use the term parasuicide when the intent to die is low (Ramsay, Tanney, Tierney, & Lang, 1991). The individual who ingests barbiturates, knowing that the behavior will be discovered before it is lethal, might be considered to have displayed parasuicidal behavior. Obviously, there is a fine line between low-intent-to-die parasuicide and high-intent-to-die attempted suicide. Parasuicidal behavior can be lethal and may result in "accidental suicides."
- *Attempted suicide* refers to serious, planned, self-destructive acts that result in significant but nonfatal physical harm. Unlike parasuicidal behavior the individual's intent to die is high. These individuals might be thought of as "accidentally alive" (Ramsay et al., 1991). The means employed in attempted suicide are typically more lethal than those in parasuicide. The use of highly lethal means is correlated ($r = .67$) with high intent to die (Andrews & Lewinsohn, 1992).
- *Indirect suicide* refers to risk-taking behavior (e.g., reckless driving) resulting in death, when a causal sequence can be specified (e.g., suicidal thoughts lead to

reckless driving and subsequently a fatal traffic accident). In fact, many automotive fatalities among adolescent males are suspected to be suicides (Farberow, 1980). Indirect suicide is common among adolescents, and there is evidence to suggest that adolescent suicidal behaviors are particularly impulsive (Taylor & Stansfield, 1984).

■ *Completed suicide* refers to deaths that are the consequence of planned self-destructive behaviors. The suicidal individual believed that the planned behavior could result in death, and death was the result.

Prevalence of Suicidal Ideation and Behaviors

Frequency
By obtaining estimates of lethality (e.g., determining whether a behavior resulted in the need for medical attention), recent research has allowed for frequency estimates of the different types of suicidal behaviors. This research has revealed lethal and/or intentional attempts among adolescents to be relatively rare. These estimates suggest 1.6% to 2.6% of adolescents have made potentially lethal suicide attempts (Moscicki, 1995). Clearly, suicidal gestures and parasuicidal behavior are more frequent than is attempted suicide. The majority of individuals who engage in nonlethal suicidal behaviors do not intend to die (Meehan, Lamb, Saltzman, & O'Carroll, 1992).

Developmental trends
Suicidal ideation, attempted suicide, and completed suicide all appear to be relatively rare in childhood and to become more prevalent during adolescence (Diekstra & Garnefski, 1995; Moscicki, 1995). However, the ratio of attempted suicide to completed suicide in adolescents is considerably higher than it is among the aged population. The suicidal behavior of older individuals is much more lethal than that of adolescents. Finally, while the peak ages for attempted suicide fall within the first half of the life cycle (between 15 and 44 years of age), the risk of completed suicide increases as a function of age (the rate is highest among persons over the age of 75) (Diekstra & Garnefski, 1995; Moscicki, 1995).

Demographics
Attempted and completed suicides are reported more frequently among Whites than non-Whites (Diekstra & Garnefski, 1995; Moscicki, 1995). However, between 1980 and 1992 suicide rates increased most dramatically among young Black males (Centers for Disease Control, 1995). Other demographic data reveal differences between attempted and completed suicide. Although suicide ideation and attempts are especially prevalent among females, the majority of completed suicides are by males. Thus, younger females are more likely to *attempt* suicide, but older males are more likely to *commit* suicide.

Suicide methods
The methods of attempted suicide are typically less lethal than those of completed suicide. While drug overdoses appear to account for 70% of attempts (Moscicki, 1995), firearms account for 64.9% of completed suicides among individuals younger than 25 years. Within this age group, during 1980 to 1992, the proportions of suicides by poisoning, cutting, and other methods declined and the proportions by firearms and hanging increased. Hanging was the second most common means of suicide followed by poisoning. Among teenagers, 81% of recent suicide rate increases can be attributed to firearms (Centers for Disease Control, 1995).

Risk Factors

Psychopathological risk factors
Severe, and frequently comorbid, psychiatric disorders are the strongest risk factor for suicidal behavior in all age groups. Psychological autopsy research reveals 90% of suicides are associated with mental or addictive disorders (Garland & Zigler, 1993); among adolescents the most frequent disorders are affective and conduct disorders and substance abuse (Moscicki, 1995). Hopelessness is a strong indicator of suicide potential (Beck, 1986), and prior suicide attempts may be the best single predictor of suicidal behavior (Shaffer, Garland, Gould, Fisher & Trautman, 1988).

Substance abuse also plays an important role in suicide. It can increase overall vulnerability to suicide and can also act as a triggering event. For example, substance abuse can increase susceptibility to the effects of stresses that are eventually the proximal trigger of the suicide. Substances such as alcohol can contribute to depression, impaired judgment, and impulsivity that are in turn related to suicide. When compared to the general population, the suicidal substance abuser typically has more serious intent to die and higher levels of suicidal ideation. In adolescents, alcohol intoxication has been found in approximately half of all youth suicides (Moscicki, 1995).

Finally, it appears that psychiatric disorders are a characteristic of many, but not all, suicide attempters (Moscicki, 1995). For example, rates of depression among this group range from 20% to 55% (Diekstra & Garnefski, 1995).

Biological risk factors
Neurochemical research has found that persons who commit suicide and violent suicide attempters often have a deficit in the functioning of the neurotransmitter serotonin (Davis & Sandoval, 1991). Reduced central serotongenic activity is correlated more highly with suicidal behavior than with any particular psychiatric diagnosis

Brown & Goodwin, 1986). However, the relationship between reduced serotongenic activity and suicidal behavior is not clear. It is possible that the serotongenic changes may be associated with characteristics such as impulsivity or threshold for violence and not a direct cause of suicidal behavior (Moscicki, 1995).

Familial risk factors

Familial characteristics that increase adolescent suicide risk include a family history of suicide and of medical and psychiatric illness. Increased economic stress and higher levels of family strife, involving family loss, are also associated with increased suicide risk. Suicidal children experience more parental separations, divorces, and remarriages. The suicidal youth frequently views the family as high in conflict and low in support or cohesion. Suicide attempters often view their parents as indifferent, rejecting, and unsupportive. Family violence, parental arguments, and physical and sexual abuse are associated with suicidal behavior (Davis & Sandoval, 1991; Moscicki, 1995; Pfeffer, 1989).

Situational risk factors

While situational factors are most typically associated with suicidal behavior, they are, by themselves, insufficient to cause this behavior. However, when combined with other risk factors they create conditions that may lead to suicide (Moscicki, 1995).

One of the strongest situational risk factors in the United States is the presence of a firearm in the home. Even after other risk factors are taken into account, the presence of a gun increases the risk of suicide. This is true regardless of which type of weapon or of whether the weapon and ammunition are stored separately (Brent et al., 1991).

Recent severe life stress, especially from losses that result in a perceived devaluing of the individual's life, can also be situational factors associated with suicide (Ramsay et al., 1991). Among youth, the most frequent stresses include interpersonal loss or conflict (particularly in romance), economic problems, and legal problems. Incarceration is also a frequent factor in youth suicide (Moscicki, 1995).

Frequently, a precipitating event will push the teenager "over the edge." As many as 40% of youth suicidal behaviors appear to have identifiable precipitants (e.g., rejection, unwanted pregnancy, poor school performance, fights with friends, dispute and/or breakup with a romantic partner, or problems with parents). The most common event of this type is a disciplinary crisis (Pfeffer, 1989; Shaffer, 1974; Spirito, Overholser, & Stark, 1989).

Warning Signs of Suicidal Ideation and Behaviors

Although a single, traumatic event can trigger a sudden suicide without warning, individuals who are thinking about suicide usually give signals in advance that predict suicidal behavior (Ramsay, Tanney, Tierney, & Lang, 1990). Warning signs might be interpreted as cries for help or invitations to intervene. They are ways in which an individual communicates distress, but they are not necessarily predictive of impending suicidal behavior. They do signal the possibility that the individual has suicidal ideation and suggests it would be appropriate to ask: "Are you thinking of suicide?" Ramsay et al. (1990) group the common warning signs of suicidal behavior into three general classifications: suicidal threats; preoccupation with death; and changes in behavior, physical appearances, thoughts, or feelings. Specific warning signs are presented in Table 1, with the most dangerous warning signs listed first.

Implications of Suicidal Ideation and Behaviors

Educational implications

Suicidal ideation and behaviors have a tremendous impact on learning. Students who display these behaviors and/or have these thoughts will be mentally unavailable for instruction. Additionally, the impact of suicidal behavior on other nonsuicidal students cannot be ignored. Difficulty coping with another's suicidal behavior will also interfere with learning. Thus, even those who argue schools should only provide academic instruction must acknowledge there are educational reasons for school suicide prevention, intervention, and postvention.

Increasing danger

It frequently has been suggested that less severe forms of suicidal ideation and behaviors may evolve into more severe forms (Diekstra & Garnefski, 1995). Exactly how these transformations take place is unclear. However, it has been documented that a person with a history of suicidal behavior has a 35 times greater risk of suicide than does a member of the general population (Tanney & Motto, 1990). Therefore, both family members and school personnel must increase vigilance when suicidal behavior becomes evident, watch for warning signs, and ensure the provision of appropriate mental health services.

Risk assessment and referral

Assessing the severity of suicidal thinking and making appropriate referral decisions are important problems to be addressed by schools. These procedures are typically designed for school psychologists and counselors. These individuals are most likely to be designated as the staff members to whom all reports of suicidal students are brought. Specific risk assessment and referral procedures may include the following steps.

Table 1 *Common Warning Signs of Suicidal Behavior*

Warning Sign*	Discussion
Suicide notes	Suicide notes are a very real sign of danger and should always be taken seriously.
Direct and indirect suicide threats	Most individuals give clues they have suicidal thoughts. Clues include direct ("I have a plan to kill myself") and indirect threats ("I might as well be dead").
Making final arrangements	Making funeral arrangements, writing a will, paying debts, saying good-bye, and the like could be signs a youth is suicidal.
Giving away prized possessions	In effect, the youth is executing a will.
Talking about death	This could be a sign the youth is exploring death as a solution to problems.
Reading or writing, and/or creating art work about death	Sometimes warnings include writing death poems or filling sheets of paper with macabre drawings.
Hopelessness or helplessness	A youth who feels there is no hope problems will improve and who feels helpless to change things may consider suicide.
Social withdrawal and isolation	These behaviors may be a sign of depression and may be a precursor of suicide.
Loss of involvement in interests and activities	A youth who is considering suicide may see no purpose in continuing previously important interests and activities.
Increased risk taking	Youths who choose high-risk sports, daredevil hobbies, and other unnecessarily dangerous activities may be suicidal.
Heavy use of alcohol or drugs	Substance abusers have a six times greater risk for suicide than the general population.
Abrupt changes in appearance	Youths who no longer care about their appearance may be suicidal.
Sudden weight or appetite change	These changes may be a sign of depression that can increase the risk of suicide.
Sudden changes in personality or attitude	The shy youth who suddenly becomes a thrill seeker or the outgoing person who becomes withdrawn and unfriendly may be giving signals that something is seriously wrong.
Inability to concentrate or think rationally	This inability may be a sign of depression or other mental illness and may increase the risk of suicide.
Sudden unexpected happiness	Sudden happiness, especially following prolonged depression, may indicate the person is profoundly relieved after having made a decision to commit suicide.
Sleeplessness or sleepiness	This behavior may be a sign of depression and may increase the risk of suicide.
Increased irritability or crying easily	Depressed, stressed, and potentially suicidal youths demonstrate wide mood swings and unexpected displays of emotion.
Low self-esteem	Youths with low self-esteem may consider suicide.
Abrupt changes in attendance	Remain alert to excessive absenteeism in a student with a good attendance record, particularly when the change is sudden.
Dwindling academic performance	Question unexpected and sudden decrease in performance.
Failure to complete assignments	Sudden failure is often seen in depressed and suicidal students.
Lack of interest and withdrawal	One of the first signs of a potentially suicidal youth is withdrawal, disengagement, and apathy. A sudden lack of interest in extracurricular activities may be seen.
Changed relationships	Evidence of personal despair may be abrupt changes in social relationships.
Despairing attitude	Students may make comments about being unhappy, feeling like a failure, not caring about the future, or even not caring about living or dying.

Note. Adapted from *The California Helper's Handbook for Suicide Intervention* by R. F. Ramsay, B. L. Tanney, R. J. Tierney, & W. A. Lang (Primary Consultants), 1990, Sacramento, CA: State Department of Mental Health.

*Warning signs are presented in order beginning with the most dangerous ones.

1. Risk Assessment

Whenever a staff member refers a suicidal student, a risk assessment should be conducted by a school psychologist or counselor. A risk-assessment interview is a semi-structured interview protocol. Because school personnel do not routinely perform suicide evaluations, it should be prepared in advance. School mental health professionals quickly get out of practice and need a structure to help support and guide them (Davis & Sandoval, 1991).

From a model developed by Ramsay et al. (1991), Table 2 contains some questions for a risk-assessment interview. To supplement this interview, school psychologists might administer a general mental status examination at the conclusion of the Engagement phase (Davis & Sandoval, 1991). A mental status exam is a screening device to look for evidence of psychosis, depression, psychosomatic concerns, organicity, and disorientation due to drugs and alcohol. Additionally, school psychologists might use standardized measures to help in determining a course of action. One good device is the Suicidal Ideation Questionnaire (Reynolds, 1988). Developed for stu-

dents in Grades 7 through 12, this measure offers cut-off scores and items designated as critical indicators that can be used in determining the severity of suicidal ideation. With younger students, the Hopelessness Scale for Children (Kazdin, Rodgers, & Colbus, 1986) has been recommended (Fremouw, de Perczel, & Ellis, 1990). This measure is a self-report inventory designed for children 6 to 7 years of age and older.

2. Consultation

Following the risk assessment, the school psychologist should consult with another staff member or mental health professional who has training in suicide risk assessment. Peer review, when available, is desirable before taking action.

3. Determine a course of action

The risk assessment and consultation data should help to determine a course of action. If an outside referral is made, it would be appropriate to make copies of the in-

---

Table 2   *Student Interview Model: Suicide Risk Screening*

Engagement

- It seems things haven't been going so well for you lately. Your parents and/or teachers have said _____. Most teens/children would find that upsetting.
- Have you felt upset, maybe had some sad or angry feelings you have trouble talking about? Maybe I could help you talk about these feelings and thoughts?
- Do you feel like things can get better, or are you worried (afraid, concerned) things will just stay the same or get worse?
- Are you feeling unhappy most of the time?

Identification

- Other teenagers/children I've talked to have said that when they feel that sad and/or angry, they thought for a while that things would be better if they were dead. Have you ever thought that? What were your thoughts?
- Is the feeling of unhappiness so strong that sometimes you wish you were dead?
- Do you sometimes feel that you want to take your own life?
- How often have you had these thoughts? How long do they stay with you?
- Administer the Suicidal Ideation Questionnaire (Reynolds, 1988) or the Hopelessness Scale for Children (Kazdin, Rodgers, & Colbus, 1986) to further qualify and/or quantify the seriousness of the student's suicidal thinking.

Inquiry

- What has made you feel so awful?
- What problems or situations have lead you to think this way?
- Tell me more about what has led you to see killing yourself as a solution.
- What do you think it would feel like to be dead?

- How do you think your father and mother feel? What do you think would happen with them if you were dead?
- As appropriate administer items from the Mental Status Exam (Davis & Sandoval, 1991).

Assessment

Current Suicide Plan

- Have you thought about how you might make yourself die?
- Do you have a plan?
- On a scale of 1 to 10, how likely is it that you will kill yourself? When are you planning to or when do you think you will do this?
- Do you have the means with you now, at school, or at home?
- Where are you planning to kill yourself?
- Have you written a note?
- Have you put things in order?

Prior Behavior

- Has anyone that you know of killed or attempted to kill themselves? Do you know why?
- Have you ever threatened to kill yourself before? When? What stopped you?
- Have you ever tried to kill yourself before? How did you attempt to do so?

Resources

- Is there anyone or anything that would stop you?
- Is there someone whom you can talk to about these feelings?
- Have you or can you talk to your family or friends about suicide?

Summary

- Use a suicide risk assessment worksheet (e.g., Poland, 1989) to summarize the information gained during the interview(s).

Note. Adapted from procedures and suggestions made by the California State Department of Education (1987), Corder and Haizlip (1982), Davis and Sandoval (1991), and Ramsay, Tanney, Tierney, and Lang (1991).

formation obtained from the assessment and send them with the care provider who will be transporting the student to the community agencies and/or private practitioners providing assistance.

In making referral decisions, it is also important to assess whether the student's distress is the result of parent or caretaker abuse, neglect, or exploitation. If this is the case, it may not be appropriate to ask the student's parents to take responsibility for getting the student help. In these circumstances it would be appropriate to call child protective services, give them the facts, and ask them to intervene. Typically, however, an essential part of any action plan is to call the student's parents. It is preferable to meet with them in person.

Arvey and Petzold (1983) suggest that a "Notification of Emergency Conference" form should be completed as part of a school district's standard procedures for dealing with suicidal students. Such a record is especially important if it is feared that parents may not follow through with mental health referrals; a record protects staff members from potential liability for the actions of the suicidal student (Poland, 1989).

School staff should be prepared to respond appropriately if the parents are unavailable to assist staff in dealing with their suicidal child. In cases where the student's risk of suicide is extreme, it may be appropriate to call the police department immediately and have them transport the student to the appropriate crisis center. In cases where the risk is moderate, it may be appropriate to employ school and community resources to help the parents to assist in the crisis. In either case, it is important to tell the youth and the parents in advance about the steps of the process they will be going through. Also, if a student resists an emergency psychiatric referral and attempts to flee, it is best to avoid physical confrontation and let the police handle the situation (Davis & Sandoval, 1991).

Schools must also be prepared for parents who disagree with recommendations for a crisis center or other referral. If the school psychologist believes this referral is necessary to protect the student's life, it would be appropriate to inform the parents that child protective services will be called if they do not cooperate (Davis & Sandoval, 1991).

In cases where the student's risk is judged to be low, and after parents have been provided with noncrisis counseling referrals, it may be appropriate to write a no-suicide contract. This contract is a personal agreement not to harm oneself. With adolescents it is important for the contract to be clear, realistic, and short term in nature (Davis & Sandoval, 1991). Poland (1989) suggests that contracts be individualized, placed on school stationery, and signed by both the student and the counselor. Also, the student should be given a copy of the contract. The term of a contact can be as short as one day. Initially, a contract's term is between contacts with the counselor.

Contracts may include situations likely to provoke suicidal feelings and coping strategies. Typically, phone numbers to call if the individual becomes suicidal are included in the contract as a coping strategy. A sample contract is provided in Davis and Sandoval (1991, p. 59).

4. Follow-up

After the appropriate referrals have been made, the school psychologist should follow up with the suicidal student. It is important for school staff to stay informed about progress, plans for therapy, and the school's role in helping the youth return to school.

Alternative Actions

Alternative actions for responding to suicidal ideation and behaviors can be classified as suicide prevention (designed to reduce the incidence of suicidal thoughts and actions before they occur), suicide intervention (designed to prevent the individual with suicidal thoughts from engaging in suicidal behavior), and suicide postvention (which aims to repair damage caused by suicidal behavior).

Suicide Prevention

School-based suicide-prevention programs are the primary strategy through which school systems attempt to prevent suicidal ideation and behavior before they occur. Nationally, it is estimated that 25% of U.S. secondary schools have suicide prevention programs, with 15.9% offering a classroom curriculum-based program (Wass, Miller, & Thornton, 1990). Shaffer et al. (1988) report the goals of these programs typically include developing a heightened awareness of the problem, identifying suicidal teens, providing information about mental health resources, and improving coping skills. Table 3 provides recommendations for a comprehensive school-based suicide prevention program (Hicks, 1990).

Additional information regarding the characteristics of these prevention programs has been provided by a national survey (Garland, Shaffer, & Whittle, 1989). From an examination of 115 school-based programs, it was concluded that an almost universal component was the targeting of all adolescents regardless of their suicide risk. A large number also included training programs for school staff (90%) and parent programs (70%). Programs on the average lasted almost 4 hours.

Student body programs

Programs reviewed by Garland et al. (1989) provided information on suicide facts and warning signs and on accessing mental health resources. Other topics covered include breaking confidentiality, stress-reduction and

Table 3 *Components of a Comprehensive School-Based Suicide-Prevention Program*

1. Faculty Seminars
    Identification of At-Risk Youth
    Assessment Strategies
    Communication Strategies
    Referral of Suspected Youth

2. Parent Seminars
    Similar Content to Faculty Seminars
    Parental Denial That *Their* Child Could Be At Risk of
    Suicide
    Parenting the "Normal" Adolescent

3. Student-Peer Education
    Normal Adolescent Development
    Self-Evaluation of Emotional Well-Being
    Identification of a Peer At Risk
    Assisting the At-Risk Peer

Note. From Youth suicide: A Comprehensive Manual for Prevention and Intervention by B. B. Hicks, 1990, Bloomington, IN: National Educational Service.

coping strategies, psychological development in adolescence, signs of emotional disturbance, interviews with attempters, and death and dying education. About half of the programs were taught by a combination of school and mental health agency personnel. Most other programs were taught exclusively by agency staff. Only 2% of these prevention programs were presented by school psychologists or counselors.

Several concerns regarding school suicide-prevention programs have been raised. First is the observation that very few adolescents attending these programs commit suicide (Shaffer et al., 1988) and that most of these students already hold accurate views of suicide (Shaffer, Garland, & Whittle, 1987). From these observations it has been suggested that prevention resources should be allocated to programs for at-risk youngsters, instead of targeting the entire student body.

While this concern has validity, there are two points that weaken these arguments. First, although completed suicide is rare, suicidal ideation and behaviors are not unusual. Thus, these programs may be reaching more suicidal adolescents than Shaffer et al. (1988) acknowledge. Second, most programs have a dual purpose. Not only do they target the student at risk for suicide, but they also hope to reach the nonsuicidal student who may be the first to identify a peer's suicide thinking. Contrary to the assertions of Shaffer, Garland, and Whittle (1987), in a survey of students before participation in a suicide-prevention program, Ciffone (1993) found a large number of students to hold undesirable or inaccurate views of suicide.

A second concern regarding student programs is their tendency to normalize suicidal behavior. Ninety-five percent of the programs reviewed by Garland et al. (1989) employed a *stress model* of suicide (i.e., suicide as

a response to stress or pressures that could happen to anyone) rather than a *mental health model* (i.e., suicide as a consequence of mental illness). This view is contrary to research indicating suicide is typically associated with emotional disturbance. The stress model may increase the tendency to view suicidal behavior as a "mainstream" solution to problems (Garland et al., 1988; Garland & Zigler, 1993; Shaffer & Bacon, 1989).

In response to the concerns that suicide-prevention programs may normalize suicide, Ciffone (1993) investigated the effect of a program that made use of a mental health model (as opposed to the stress model). It emphasized suicide as an maladaptive act of poor judgment. This program had a positive effect on teens who, before program participation, had been identified as having undesirable attitudes toward suicide. It increased the number of teens who would refuse to keep a friend's suicidal thoughts secret and increased willingness to refer a friend to a counselor.

A final concern regarding student body programs is their effect on suicidal students. Garland et al. (1989) suggest students who had made suicide attempts and had attended a suicide-prevention program did not appear to respond as favorably to these programs as did nonattempters. When compared to suicide attempters who did not attend a suicide-prevention program, suicide attempters/program participants were less likely to reveal suicidal intentions, less likely to believe that a mental health professional could help them, and more likely to view suicide as a reasonable solution. Similarly, Shaffer et al. (1990) found that when compared to nonattempters, participants who indicated having previously attempted suicide continued to be more likely to feel that suicide is a possible solution for problems and that it is a good idea to keep depressed feelings to oneself. Program participation attempters were less likely than nonattempters to think that other students should participate and were more likely to believe that talking about suicide in the classroom makes some students more likely to try to kill themselves.

Thus, it appears classroom suicide-prevention programs have the potential to do harm. This evidence supports Shaffer's call (1988, cited in Poland, 1989) for a moratorium on school suicide-prevention curricula. At the very least it would appear appropriate to develop alternative programs for students who have made suicide attempts. It is unknown whether programs using a mental health model would have similar negative consequences on previous suicide attempters.

Peer programs

Increasingly school personnel are turning to peer programs to address the problems of suicide. These programs may be effective because adolescents are more likely to confide suicidal thoughts to a friend than to a parent or teacher (Shaffer, Garland, & Bacon, 1987).

Peers know about students in trouble and peer helpers or leaders become important bridges to assistance. Thus, an important prevention option is to provide peer counselors with suicide awareness training and to ensure that they know how to make referrals. As peer programs are not aimed at the at-risk student, this approach would appear to take into account the concerns of Garland et al. (1989) and Shaffer et al. (1990).

Peer programs cover the same topics as student body programs. However, there may be a greater emphasis on how to expedite a referral and why it is important not to hold dangerous information in confidence or attempt to "counsel" suicidal peers.

Staff programs

Another prevention option is to educate school employees about youth suicide. Community resources are often brought in to assist, and there are good audio-visual resources available to supplement lecture and discussion (see Davis & Sandoval, 1991, for a list). As with other prevention options, the emphasis should be on the warning signs of suicide (see Table 1) and steps to take if they are encountered. Topics emphasized with staff also include legal issues, school policy issues, crisis-management procedures, causes of suicide, and suicide intervention (Garland & Shaffer, 1988). The first author's experience and research suggest that the training program developed by Ramsay et al. (1991) is appropriate as both a staff- and peer-training program.

The importance of staff programs is emphasized by *Kelson v. the City of Springfield* (1985). Following the suicide of their son at school, the parents of 14-year-old Brian Kelson sued the school district. A federal court allowed them to bring this action against the school because the death resulted from inadequate staff training in suicide prevention. The parents charged that the school had a duty to provide staff suicide-prevention training and that it failed to do so. This case, which was eventually settled out of court, opens the door for lawsuits when a student's death can be linked to inadequate staff training (Slenkovitch, 1986).

Suicide Intervention

Despite prevention efforts, suicidal ideation and behaviors will continue to occur. Thus, there is a need for every school to develop procedures for responding to the suicidal student. Suicide intervention, like many other rare crisis events, has not often been researched using traditional experimental designs. Instead, the information presented is a distillation of well-documented clinical experience.

School psychologists often play a critical suicide-intervention role (see Table 4). In instances where the school psychologist or other school staff members do not have necessary training, alternative resources should be used. Community mental health agencies are a potential risk-assessment resource. Alternatively, participation in a suicide-intervention training program (e.g., Ramsay et al. 1991) may provide the needed risk-assessment training.

Suicide-intervention procedures should be used whenever a suicide threat is made. A threat includes any statement or communication indicating a desire to cause physical harm to oneself. Suicide may or may not be mentioned so staff should be alert to indirect threats as well as direct ones. Indirect threats of suicide often take the form of wishes or desires. However, they clearly indicate that the student feels he or she would be better off not alive. Even vague threats to "Do something bad" should be investigated. Direct threats are clear unequivocal statements that the student is considering suicide as a solution to problems. Even if a student makes a direct threat in a neutral and light tone, it must be followed up.

Suicide Postvention

Suicide postvention procedures are designed to help schools respond to the aftermath of suicide. Following a suicide it is not unusual for some students and staff members to enter into a crisis state. Postvention assists in the identification of these individuals and facilitates adaptive resolution of the crisis. An additional concern is the possibility of contagion. Although such copy-cat behavior accounts for only an estimated 1% to 3% of all adolescent suicides (Moscicki, 1995), the potential to imitate suicidal behavior appears to be a unique issue for teenagers (Davidson, 1989).

Because it is essential to respond quickly following crisis events (Ruof & Harris, 1988), preparedness is an essential component of an effective suicide postvention (Davidson, 1989; Lamb & Dunne-Maxim, 1987; Wenckstern & Leenaars, 1993). Delay fuels rumors and can make a bad situation worse (Garfinkel et al., 1988). However, an immediate response is difficult following crises as they tend to have immobilizing effects on survivors. Previously established postvention procedures can minimize these immobilizing effects (Brock, Sandoval, & Lewis, 1996).

The following procedures are important components of a suicide postvention. From the authors' experiences, they are presented in order of importance. Ideally, however, different staff members will be working on several of these tasks simultaneously.

1. Verify the death. Schools must not accept any report that a suicide has occurred without verifying the facts (Garfinkel et al., 1988). The legal classification of a death as suicide is complex and is usually made by medical examiners. Thus, it is advisable to avoid labeling even what appear to be obvious suicides as such until an official determination is made.

2. Assess impact on the school. As soon as the death is verified and the facts are known, the school should

Table 4 *Recommended School Suicide-Intervention Procedures*

1. A student who has threatened suicide must be constantly observed. A school staff member should stay with the student constantly and without exception until help is obtained. This is true regardless of whether the threat was direct or indirect. Every student who makes even a mild indirect threat should be viewed as suicidal until it is determined otherwise. Typically, school personnel will not have the training to make this determination. Thus, this procedure may frequently be used with students who are not truly suicidal. Clearly, however, it is better to err on the side of being too cautious.

2. Under no circumstances should a suicidal student be allowed to leave school. A student who has threatened suicide should not leave school before the appropriate professionals have assessed the degree of risk and have ensured that appropriate supervision has been provided. Again, this would be true regardless of whether the threat was direct or indirect.

3. Helpers to a suicidal student must not agree to keep suicidal intentions a secret. All staff members have a legal and professional responsibility not to honor confidentiality in any situation where maintaining the confidence might result in harm to a student. No matter how much a student implores a staff member, a suicide plan must not be kept secret. It is better to have a student angry for having a confidence betrayed than to have a student dead because a confidence was maintained. A teacher in California was sued by the parents of a 12-year-old student after the teacher was allegedly told by the student that he intended to commit suicide. The teacher did not inform the parents of the student's suicidal intent, and the suit was brought against the teacher after the student committed suicide (California State Department of Education, 1987).

4. If the means of the threatened suicide are present, determine if they can be voluntarily relinquished. This procedure is based upon a lawsuit generated in part because a student who shot himself at school was never asked to relinquish the gun used in the suicide. Staff members apparently knew that this student was suicidal and that he had a gun (McKee, Jones, & Richardson, 1991). However, school staff members should not use force to attempt to remove the means of a threatened suicide. This is especially true if the means have the potential to harm staff members (e.g., a gun). If a student refuses to voluntarily relinquish the means, the police should be called. Staff should never place themselves in danger.

5. Take the suicidal student to a prearranged room. As soon as possible take the suicidal student to a prearranged, nonthreatening room away from other students. There should be another adult and a telephone close by. Typically, this room would be a counselor's office (McKee et al., 1991).

6. Notify the "designated reporter" immediately. Schools should identify one or more individuals who receive and act upon all reports from teachers and others about students who may be suicidal (Davis & Sandoval, 1991). This individual is usually a school psychologist or counselor.

7. Inform the suicidal youth that outside help has been called and describe what the next steps will be. Before leaving a suicidal student with the "designated reporter," it is important to let the student know that help has been obtained and to describe what will happen next. It may be appropriate to tell the student that this individual will assist in finding help to deal with suicidal thoughts and impulses. Also, it is important to let the student know that his or her parents or guardians will need to be contacted. If the student is resistant to this idea, this information should be relayed to the designated reporter. If it is suspected that a student's resistance to parental contact is a consequence of abuse, a referral to child protective services must be made. While staff cannot promise that parents will not be informed of the suicidal threats, it would be appropriate to let a suicidal student know his or her concerns are understood.

---

assess the impact of the loss on the student body. Variables to consider when estimating the number of students affected by a suicide are offered in Table 5. This assessment will determine if site resources can manage the crisis or if outside assistance is needed. It is essential that these outside resources be identified before a suicide occurs (Garfinkel et al., 1988). Provisions should be made for how this assistance can be obtained during non-school hours, weekends, and holidays.

3. Notify the school district office and other sites that could be affected. When a suicide occurs, district administration should be notified as soon as possible. Once word of a suicide reaches the community it is not uncommon for district administrators to receive calls from concerned citizens and the media. Thus, they need to have knowledge of what happened and what is being done to assist students. Additionally, district administration may be able to provide support to the school.

Also, attention needs to be given to how other schools might be affected. Issues to examine include

whether the student(s) involved have siblings and/or friends that attend other schools. If a staff member commits suicide, it is important to determine if there are former students, now attending different schools, who may be affected.

4. Contact the parents of the deceased. Many times parental contact will be one of the first suicide postvention tasks as the school attempts to verify facts. It should focus on expressing sympathy and, if appropriate, providing information about community grief-support groups (Davis & Sandoval, 1991).

5. Determine what information is to be shared. The first issue considered is confidentiality. Student names should not be released without prior consent. Additionally, there may be circumstances that parents wish to remain confidential. It is recommended that school staff discuss with the student's parents which details about the death can be shared (Thompson, 1990).

Postvention should avoid glorifying or sensationalizing the death, while at the same time providing a timely

Table 5 *Variables to Consider When Assessing the Impact of a Suicide on a School*

Variable	Suicide Impact Issues
Popularity of person who committed suicide	If the individual was well known in the school and/or community, a more significant impact can be expected. For example, if the individual had just moved into the area the impact is likely to be less severe.
Exposure to or involvement in the suicide	The greater the exposure or involvement of students or staff the greater will be the impact.
History of similar crises	If other suicides happened to the school in the past, old crisis reactions may be rekindled.
Recency of other crises	If other crises occurred in the school recently, this may reduce resiliency and result in a more significant crisis reaction. On the other hand, a less dramatic impact can be expected if the suicide is an isolated incident.
Resources available	Fewer personal, family, school, and community resources are likely to result in more significant crisis reactions.
Suicide timing	If the suicide occurred during a vacation, its impact on the school may be less than if it occurred while school was in session. In this case it is possible that students will have dealt with the suicide away from school, on their own or with their family. Additionally, rumors are spread more quickly when students are congregating in groups at school. Finally, when a suicide occurs during a vacation, the school has more time to prepare and is thus able to respond more effectively.

Note. Adapted from *Preparing for Crises in the School: A Manual for Building School Crisis Response Teams,* by S. E. Brock, J. Sandoval, & S. Lewis, 1996, Brandon, VT: Clinical Psychology Publishing Company.

flow of accurate information (O'Carroll, Mercy, & Steward, 1988). Because it is important to avoid labeling the death as suicide before official notification by the coroner, the initial announcement will typically simply report that a death has occurred. As more information becomes available, the school will continue to determine what information will be shared.

Once the death is ruled a suicide, schools need to exercise discretion regarding what information it shares with students. It is critical to avoid presenting information that might be perceived as glorifying the suicide or providing details that can be copied. In general, it is not the responsibility of the school to provide the media with details of the suicide (Wenckstern & Leenaars, 1993). If school personnel speak to the media, details such as the time of death, circumstances under which the death occurred, or contents of a suicide note should be avoided (Garfinkel et al., 1988). Also, a spokesperson should work with the media to downplay the incident. Research indicates media coverage of suicide is associated with an increase in reported suicide (Davis & Sandoval, 1991). Thus, it is advisable not to include a photo of the person who committed suicide and not to place the word "suicide" in the caption (Ruof & Harris, 1988). Ideally, the media would include information about the community resources available for those with suicidal thoughts.

6. Determine how information is to be shared. The same message should be delivered to all students at the same time (Davis & Sandoval, 1991). It is important to avoid sharing information over a public address system

or in an assembly. The announcement should be made simultaneously in classes where a staff member can be present to directly handle students' concerns (Berman & Jobes, 1991; Ruof & Harris, 1988). It may be appropriate to share information individually or in small groups with students who are particularly vulnerable or were close to the student who committed suicide. It is important to avoid casting the deceased in the role of "villain" or "hero." Grieving and seeking to learn from the tragedy should be the focus.

7. Identify high-risk students and plan interventions. A list useful in identifying students at high risk following a suicide is offered in Table 6. The process of identifying students significantly affected by the suicide should begin as soon as possible (Wenckstern & Leenaars, 1993). Failure to identify and intervene with these students may result in a suicide cluster.

Although it is critical that high-risk students be provided with counseling assistance, such help should be available to other students as well (Davis & Sandoval, 1991). Intervention options include individual meetings, group counseling, classroom activities and presentations, parent meetings, staff meetings, and referrals to community agencies (Davis & Sandoval, 1991; Morrison, 1987).

The typical intervention tasks involve ensuring that students do not identify with the person who committed suicide, do not romanticize or glorify the person's behavior or circumstances, and do not dwell on real or imagined guilt (Davis & Sandoval, 1991). To avoid identifica-

Table 6 *Factors That Place Students "At Risk" Following the Suicide of a Peer*

Risk Factor	Examples
Facilitated the suicide	1. Were involved in a suicide pact. 2. Helped write the suicide note. 3. Provided the means of the suicide. 4. Knew about and did not try to stop the suicide.
Failed to recognize the suicidal intent	1. Observed events that were later learned to be signs of the impending suicide. 2. Did not take a suicide threat seriously. 3. Had been too busy to talk to a person who committed suicide and had asked for help.
Believe they may have caused the suicide	1. Feel guilty about things said or done to the victim before the suicide. 2. Recently punished or threatened to punish the person who committed suicide for some misdeed.
Had a relationship or identify with the person who committed suicide	1. Were mentioned in the suicide note. 2. Were relatives, best friends, or self-appointed therapists of the person who committed suicide. 3. Identify with the situation of the person who committed suicide. 4. Have life circumstances that parallel those of the suicide victim.
Have a history of prior suicidal behavior	1. Have previously attempted or threatened suicide. 2. Have family members, acquaintances, or role models who have died by suicide.
Have a history of psychopathology	1. Have poor baseline mental health. 2. Have substance abuse problems. 3. Have a history of impulsive or violent behavior directed either toward self or others.
Show symptoms of helplessness, hopelessness, or both	1. Are desperate and now consider suicide a viable alternative. 2. Feel powerless to change distressing life circumstances. 3. Are depressed.
Have suffered significant life stresses or losses	1. Had family members or acquaintances who have died by accident or homicide. 2. Had someone they were close to die violently. 3. Had recently broken up with a girlfriend or boyfriend. 4. Have been disrupted by changes in residence, schools, or parental figures.

Note. Adapted from "The School Psychologist's Role in Suicide Prevention," by J. Sandoval, & S. E. Brock, in press, *School Psychology Quarterly,* and based on Brent et al. (1989); Davidson (1989); Davidson, Rosenberg, Mercy, Franklin, & Simmons (1989); and Rouf and Harris (1988).

tion with the suicide, Ruof and Harris (1988) suggest that the crisis counselors point out how the survivors are different from the person who committed suicide. To avoid glorifying the act, Ruof and Harris recommend that counselors avoid making the suicide seem exciting or the person who committed suicide admirable. They state: "Point out that suicide is a poor choice" (p. 8).

When working with students following a suicide, help them to express feelings about the suicide and tell them that it is normal to feel not only grief but also fear, anger, and confusion. They should be helped to understand that death is irreversible, that the person who committed suicide will not witness or enjoy the postmortem events, and that suicide is a permanent solution to temporary problems. They should also be helped to understand that many people have suicidal thoughts when a suicide has occurred in the community (Davidson, 1989).

8. Inform the staff. A staff meeting should be held as soon as possible following a suicide (Berman & Jobes, 1991; Wenckstern & Leenaars, 1993). This meeting has

two purposes: to educate staff on how they can assist students cope with this loss and to help faculty members deal with their own feelings of grief, guilt, or anger generated by the suicide (Lamb & Dunne-Maxim, 1987). Dealing with these feelings is an important prerequisite before the faculty can assist students in coping with the suicide.

During this meeting staff should be given permission to feel uncomfortable about discussing the suicide with their students. These feelings may result in some staff members not being able to provide students with needed support and guidance. These individuals should be provided with alternative opportunities for helping students cope (Brock et al., 1996).

At this meeting school staff should be provided with the facts regarding the death, information regarding plans for the provision of crisis counseling services (Thompson, 1990), and a review of procedures and guidelines for discussions during a crisis (Brock et al., 1996). Staff members will also need to be made aware of the

Table 7   *Memorial Activities Following Suicide: A List of "Do's" and "Don'ts"*

Do	Don't
Do something to prevent other suicides from happening.	*Don't* make special arrangements to send all students from school to funerals.
Do develop living memorials (e.g., student assistance programs) that help other students cope with feelings and problems.	*Don't* have memorial or funeral services at school.
Do allow any student, with parental permission, to attend the funeral.	*Don't* stop classes for a funeral.
Do encourage affected students, with parental permission, to go to the funeral.	*Don't* put up plaques in memory of the suicide victim.
Do mention to families and ministers the need to distance the person who committed suicide from survivors and to avoid glorifying the suicidal act.	*Don't* dedicate yearbooks, songs, or sporting events to the person who committed suicide.
	Don't fly the flag at half staff.
	Don't have a moment of silence in all-school assemblies.
	Don't have mass assemblies focusing on the suicide victim.

Note. Adapted from "The School Psychologist's Role in Suicide Prevention," by J. Sandoval, & S. E. Brock, in press, *School Psychology Quarterly*, and based upon suggestions made by Berman and Jobes (1991); Davidson (1989); Garfinkel et al. (1988); McKee, Jones, and Richardson (1991); and Ruof and Harris (1988).

types of students who may be at risk for an imitative response to the suicide and will need to know how to make referrals (Berman & Jobes, 1991).

9. Hold a debriefing. Besides the initial staff meeting, debriefings should be held. Debriefings will allow for a review of the intervention process and the status of referrals (Berman & Jobes, 1991). Prioritization of needs and plans for follow-up actions should be discussed. Perhaps most importantly, the debriefing is an opportunity to assess how the faculty is coping. It is not uncommon for "caretakers" to deal with their grief by denying it and directing their energy to caring for others. This meeting will provide an opportunity for mutual support and allow staff to continue to deal with their own emotions and feelings (Brock et al., 1996).

10. Weigh benefits and liabilities of memorials. After a crisis event, many people feel the need to express their grief, say good-bye, and do something as a memorial. Working together on a memorial can help survivors focus their grief, fears, and anger constructively. However, when choosing memorials following a suicide, particular care should be taken not to romanticize the suicide. In fact, based upon the belief that memorials reinforce the message that death is a way to obtain attention, some authorities have recommended avoiding them completely (McKee, Jones, & Richardson, 1991). Table 7 provides a list of "do's and don'ts" regarding memorial activities following suicide.

One final point should be made. If there is no chance of students becoming aware of a suicide, it is not necessary to report the situation to them nor to provide crisis intervention services. Suicide is only contagious if other people know about it. If knowledge of suicidal behavior can be kept out of a school building, it is probably best

to do so (Ruof & Harris, 1988). However, the worst-case scenario is for students to know of a suicide and to have the school pretend that it did not occur (Ruof & Harris).

Summary

Suicide is a reality in America's schools. In a typical high school, based on prevalence data, one might expect one suicide in a 5-year period, and somewhere around 170 suicidal gestures, parasuicides, or suicide attempts each year (Davis & Sandoval, 1991), although many of these incidents will not come to the school's attention. Suicidal behavior is a problem that school psychologists in partnership with other school personnel and community-based professionals can do something about. In this chapter, we have reviewed issues in prevention and outlined intervention and postvention strategies. We hope readers will be stimulated to seek further education on this topic and to be better prepared for suicidal crises. To this end, the following resources are recommended.

Recommended Resources

Davis, J. M., & Sandoval, J. (1991). *Suicidal youth: School-based intervention and prevention.* San Francisco: Jossey-Bass.
This book written for school psychologists and other school professionals presents research, theory, and practical strategies for preventing youth suicide and intervening with suicidal youth.

Pfeffer, C. R. (1986). *The suicidal child.* New York: Guilford Press.
This book examines the psychology of suicide and the role of family systems. It does not deal with school issues but discusses in detail clinical intervention with suicidal children.

Poland, S. (1989). *Suicide intervention in the schools.* New York: Guilford Press.
This is another volume prepared for school-based personnel reviewing procedures for working with suicidal youth. The author's experiences provide a number of practical suggestions for work in school settings.

Silverman, M. M., & Maris, R. W. (Eds.). (1995). Suicide prevention toward the year 2000 [Special issue]. *Suicide and Life-Threatening Behavior, 25* (1).
This special issue of the prominent journal on suicide is a compendium of current research on the topic of adolescent suicide. Several authors cover topics such as the prevalence of the problem, prevention strategies, and clinical techniques.

References

Andrews, J. A., & Lewinsohn, P. M. (1992). Suicidal attempts among older adolescents: Prevalence and co-occurrence with psychiatric disorders. *Journal of the American Academy of Child and Adolescent Psychiatry, 31,* 655–662.

Arvey, H., & Petzold, C. (1983). *Suicide prevention and intervention program.* Houston, TX: Houston Independent School District.

Beck, A. T. (1986). Hopelessness as a predictor of eventual suicide. *Annals of the New York Academy of Science, 487,* 90–96.

Berman, A. L., & Jobes, D. A. (1991). *Adolescent suicide: Assessment and intervention.* Washington, DC: American Psychological Association.

Brent, D. A., Kerr, M. M., Goldstein, C., Bozigar, J., Wartella, M., & Allan, M. J. (1989). An outbreak of suicide and suicidal behavior in a high school. *Journal of the American Academy of Child and Adolescent Psychiatry, 28,* 918–924.

Brent, D. A., Perper, J. A., Allman, C. J., Moritz, G. M., Wartella, M. E., & Zelenak, J. P. (1991). The presence and accessibility of firearms in the home of adolescent suicides: A case-control study. *Journal of the American Medical Association, 266,* 2989–2995.

Brock, S. E., Sandoval, J., & Lewis, S. (1996). *Preparing for crises in the schools: A manual for building school crisis response teams.* Brandon, VT: Clinical Psychology Publishing.

Brown, G. L., & Goodwin, F. K. (1986). Cerebrospinal fluid correlates of suicide attempters and aggression. *Annals of the New York Academy of Science, 487,* 175–188.

California State Department of Education. (1987). *Suicide prevention program for the California Public Schools.* Sacramento, CA: Author.

Centers for Disease Control. (1991). Attempted suicide among high school students—United States, 1990. *Morbidity and Mortality Weekly Report, 40,* 633–635.

Centers for Disease Control. (1992). *Youth suicide prevention programs: A resource guide.* Atlanta, GA: U.S. Department of Health and Human Services.

Centers for Disease Control. (1995). Suicide among children, adolescents, and young adults—United States, 1980–1992. *Morbidity and Mortality Weekly Report, 44,* 289–291.

Ciffone, J. (1993). Suicide prevention: A classroom presentation to adolescents. *Social Work, 38,* 197–203.

Corder, B. F., & Haizlip, T. M., (1982, September). Recognizing suicidal behavior in children. *Medical Times,* 26–30.

Davidson, L. E. (1989). Suicide cluster and youth. In C. R. Pfeffer (Ed.), *Suicide among youth: Perspectives on risk and prevention* (pp. 83–99). Washington, DC: American Psychiatric Press.

Davidson, L. E., Rosenberg, M. L., Mercy, J. A., Franklin, J., & Simmons, J. T. (1989). An epidemiologic study of risk factors in two teenage suicide clusters. *Journal of the American Medical Association, 262,* 2687–2692.

Davis, J. M., & Sandoval, J. (1991). *Suicidal youth: School-based intervention and prevention.* San Francisco: Jossey-Bass.

Diekstra, R. F., & Garnefski, N. (1995). On the nature, magnitude, and causality of suicidal behavior. *Suicide and Life-Threatening Behavior, 25,* 36–57.

Farberow, N. L. (Ed.). (1980). *The many faces of suicide: Indirect self-destructive behaviour.* New York: McGraw-Hill.

Fremouw, W. J., de Perczel, M., & Ellis, T. E. (1990). *Suicide risk: Assessment and response guidelines.* New York: Pergamon Press.

Garfinkel, B. D., Crosby, E., Herbert, M. R., Matus, A. L., Pfeifer, J. K., & Sheras, P. L. (1988). *Responding to adolescent suicide.* Bloomington, IN: Phi Delta Kappa.

Garland, A. F., & Shaffer, D. (1988). *School-based adolescent suicide prevention programs.* Unpublished manuscript, College of Physicians and Surgeons of Columbia University, New York.

Garland, A. F., Shaffer, D., & Whittle, B. (1989). A national survey of school-based adolescent suicide prevention programs. *Journal of the American Academy of Child and Adolescent Psychiatry, 28,* 931–934.

Garland, A. F., & Zigler, E. (1993). Adolescent suicide prevention: Current research and social policy implications. *American Psychologist, 48,* 169–182.

Harkavy-Friedman, J., Asnis, G., Boe, M., & DiFiore, J. (1987). Prevalence of specific suicidal behaviors in a high school sample. *American Journal of Psychiatry, 144,* 1203–1206.

Hicks, B. B. (1990). *Youth suicide: A comprehensive manual for prevention and intervention.* Bloomington, IN: National Educational Service.

Kazdin, A. E., Rodgers, A., & Colbus, D. (1986). The hopelessness scale for children: Psychometric characteristics and concurrent validity. *Journal of Consulting and Clinical Psychology, 54,* 241–245.

Kelson v. the City of Springfield. (1985). 767 F.2d 651 (9th Cir. 1985).

Lamb, R., & Dunne-Maxim, K. (1987). Postvention in schools: Policy and process. In E. J. Dunne, J. L. McIntosh, & K. Dunne-Maxim (Eds.), *Suicide and its aftermath: Un-*

derstanding and counseling the survivors (pp. 245–260). New York: Norton.

McKee, P. W., Jones, R. W., & Richardson, J. A. (1991, November). *Student suicide: Educational psychological, and legal issues for schools.* LRP Publications Conference, San Francisco.

Meehan, P. J., Lamb, J. A., Saltzman, L. E., & O'Carroll, P. W. (1992). Attempted suicide among young adults: Progress toward a meaningful estimate of prevalence. *American Journal of Psychiatry, 149,* 41–44.

Morrison, J. L. (1987). Youth suicide: An intervention strategy. *Social Work, 32,* 536–537.

Moscicki, E. K. (1995). Epidemiology of suicidal behavior. *Suicide and Life-Threatening Behavior, 25,* 22–35.

National Center for Health Statistics. (1994). Advance report of final mortality statistics, 1991. *Monthly Vital Statistics Report* (Vol. 42, No. 2 Suppl.). Hyattsville, MD: Public Health Service.

O'Carroll, P. W., Mercy, J. A., & Steward, J. A. (1988). CDC recommendations for a community plan for the prevention and containment of suicide clusters. *Morbidity and Mortality Weekly Report, 37* (Suppl. 56), 1–12.

Pfeffer, C. R. (1986). *The suicidal child.* New York: Guilford Press.

Pfeffer, C. R. (1989). Life stress and family risk factors for youth fatal and nonfatal suicidal behavior. In C. R. Pfeffer (Ed.), *Suicide among youth: Perspectives on Risk and Prevention* (pp. 143–164). Washington, DC: American Psychiatric Press.

Poland, S. (1989). *Suicide intervention in the schools.* New York: Guilford Press.

Ramsay, R. F., Tanney, B. L., Tierney, R. J., & Lang, W. A. (Primary Consultants). (1990). *The California helper's handbook for suicide intervention.* Sacramento, CA: State Department of Mental Health.

Ramsay, R. F., Tanney, B. L., Tierney, R. J., & Lang, W. A. (1991). *A suicide intervention training program: Trainer's manual.* Calgary, AB: LivingWorks Education.

Reynolds, W. M. (1988). *Suicidal ideation questionnaire: Professional manual.* Odessa, FL: Psychological Assessment Resources.

Ruof, S. R., & Harris, J. M. (1988, May). Suicide contagion: Guilt and modeling. *Communiqué, 16,* 8.

Sandoval, J., & Brock, S. E. (in press). The school psychologist's role in suicide prevention. *School Psychology Quarterly.*

Shaffer, D. (1974). Suicide in childhood and early adolescence. *Journal of Child Psychology and Psychiatry, 15,* 275–291.

Shaffer, D. (1988, April). School research issues. In K. Smith (Chair), *How do we know what we've done? Controversy in evaluation.* Symposium conducted at the meeting of the American Association of Suicidology, Washington, DC.

Shaffer, D., & Bacon, K. (1989). A critical review of preventive intervention efforts in suicide, with particular reference to youth suicide. In Alcohol, Drug Abuse, and Mental Health Administration, *Report of the secretary's task force on youth suicide: Vol. 3. Prevention and interventions in youth suicide* (DHHS Publication No. ADM 89-1623, pp. 31–61). Washington, DC: U.S. Government Printing Office.

Shaffer, D., Garland, A., & Bacon, K. (1987). *Prevention issues in youth suicide* (Report prepared for Project Prevention, American Academy of Child and Adolescent Psychiatry). New York: Adolescent Study Unit, College of Physicians and Surgeons of Columbia University.

Shaffer, D., Garland, A. F., Gould, M., Fisher, P., & Trautman, P. (1988). Preventing teenage suicide: A critical review. *Journal of the American Academy of Child and Adolescent Psychiatry, 27,* 675–687.

Shaffer, D., Garland, A., & Whittle, B. (1987). *An evaluation of three youth suicide prevention programs in New Jersey.* Unpublished report, Division of Child Psychiatry, New York State Psychiatric Institute, Columbia University, New York.

Shaffer, D., Vieland, V., Garland, A., Rojas, M., Underwood, M., & Busner, C. (1990). Adolescent suicide attempters: Response to suicide prevention programs. *Journal of the American Medical Association, 264,* 3151–3155.

Silverman, M. M., & Maris, R. W. (Eds.). (1995). Suicide prevention toward the year 2000 [Special issue]. *Suicide and Life-Threatening Behavior, 25*(1).

Slenkovitch, J. (1986, June). School districts can be sued for inadequate suicide prevention programs. *The Schools' Advocate,* pp. 1–3.

Smith, K., & Crawford, S. (1986). Suicidal behavior among "normal" high school students. *Suicide and Life-Threatening Behavior, 16,* 313–325.

Spirito, A., Overholser, J., & Stark, L. J. (1989). Common problems and coping strategies: II. Findings with adolescent suicide attempters. *Journal of Abnormal Child Psychology, 17,* 213–221.

Tanney, B. L., & Motto, G. (1990). *Long-term follow-up of 1570 attempted suicides.* Paper presented at the meeting of the American Association of Suicidology, New Orleans, LA.

Taylor, E. A., & Stansfield, S. A. (1984). Children who poison themselves: I. Clinical comparison with psychiatric controls. *British Journal of Psychiatry, 145,* 127–135.

Thompson, R. (1990). Suicide and sudden loss: Crisis management in the schools. *Highlights: An ERIC/CAPS digest,* p. 1.

Wass, H., Miller, M. D., & Thornton, G. (1990). Death education and grief/suicide intervention in the public schools. *Death Studies, 14,* 253–268.

Wenckstern, S., & Leenaars, A. A. (1993). Trauma and suicide in our schools. *Death Studies, 17,* 151–171.

33
Grief

Gary W. Mauk
Jim D. Sharpnack
Utah State University

Background and Development

Most children will experience the death of a relative, friend, neighbor, or pet sometime during their school years (Sims, 1991). Nearly two decades ago, before the steep increases in deaths from a variety of unnatural causes (e.g., suicide, homicide incident to gang violence, AIDS), Ewalt and Perkins (1979) estimated that by the time they attain their senior year in high school, 90% of youths will have known a family member or friend who has died. Despite the recent increases in the numbers and types of deaths, children and adolescents continue to be exposed to both vicariously (e.g., through media and conversations) and directly. Wass, Miller, and Thornton (1990) found that only 11% of U.S. public schools offered a course or unit on death education and only 17% had grief support programs.

A study of middle school students in North Carolina revealed that more than 40% of the students had been personally involved with death within the past year (Glass, 1991). Oates (1993) asserts that, "If one adds to the deaths of parents and relatives the increasing number of violent deaths of school-age children, it seems unlikely that *any* school-age child will reach adulthood without experiencing a loss related to death" (p. 38). Unfortunately, as James and Cherry (1988) observe, "we are better prepared to deal with minor accidents than we are to deal with the grief caused by death. Simple first aid gets more attention in our world than death and emotional loss" (p. 12).

However, grief does not always entail death. *Grief* is not only a response caused by the death of someone loved but also a response characteristic of the loss of something or someone held to be significant in an individual's life (Sims, 1991). It can be as simple and as seemingly insignificant as the loss of a favorite old sweatshirt to the dispassionate ravages of time or as complex as the loss of a close friend or parent to the ravages of a pernicious disease. Grieving is the process of separating oneself from losses for survival, for effecting necessary changes in life, and for fostering new attachments and commitments (Floerchinger, 1991).

The entire response to death is called *bereavement,* which includes the grief process, and attempts to create meaning from the loss (Saunders, 1981). Attempts to discontinue some feelings surrounding the loss and reattaching those feelings to significant others is known as the *mourning process* (Stein, 1974).

Viewing grief as an emotional process that challenges a youth's ability to cope with loss poses unique opportunities for children's and adolescents' growth (Hipp, 1995). Healthy grief resolution means (a) placing the loss in perspective without permanently impairing one's competencies to function in various roles, (b) finding inner strengths as one struggles with bereavement, and (c) often uniting people who might otherwise have remained divided and isolated.

Although grief can be construed as a generic response to loss including the loss of inanimate objects, this chapter will focus on aspects of grieving in children and youth related to the death of significant others, specifically parents, siblings, and friends. Although death has always been a reality for children and adolescents, the nature of death in the lives of children and adolescents has become more violent in recent years and is more likely to involve peers (Brock, Sandoval, & Lewis, 1996). For example, homicide and suicide have historically alternated between second and third in a list of the leading causes of death among adolescents (ages 15 to 24), with accidents being the leading cause of death in this population (Gardner & Hudson, 1996). A recent U.S. Department of Justice survey found that 2% of students (approximately 400,000) had been the victims of a violent crime at school. In fact, during 1993 (the most recent reporting year for national data at the time this chapter was written) more than 86% of all deaths among youth ages 15 to 24 were unexpected (accidents) or had violent roots (suicide, homicide; Gardner & Hudson). Overall, the prevalence of death in the lives of children and adolescents is increasing (Deaton & Berkan, 1995).

The Purpose and Phases of Grief and Mourning

Loss is "a physical, mental, emotional, and spiritual wound" (Hipp, 1995, p. 25), and grief incident to the loss is composed of a wide variety of individual manifestations and reactions. Grief responses are natural reactions when children experience loss and separation from someone they were close to and/or loved. The grief responses of children and adolescents express three things: (a) feelings about the loss; (b) protest at the loss including the wish to undo it and have it not be true; and (c) the effects from the assault on the self caused by the loss (Rando, 1988). Young people's grief responses can include shock, fear, anger, guilt, isolation, loneliness, confusion, and helplessness (Bertoia & Allan, 1988).

Like adults, youth are often numbed or temporarily stunned by the news of a death. Shock is the body's physical denial and serves as a protective shield around the youth (Beckmann, 1990). The body systems of children and adolescents temporarily shut down, sometimes to the point that they are unable to cry. They might even laugh or appear quite calm. Some youth are fearful of letting down their emotional defenses and will deny that the person has died. Denial can be expressed by children and adolescents in several ways (e.g., they may refuse to talk about the deceased; they may act "extra good" to see if the deceased will return; they may deny that the deceased ever existed or may deny the importance of the deceased).

Fear and anger are other common grief responses (Beckmann, 1990). Children may describe panic or alarm as a sore throat, tightness in the chest, or difficulty in breathing. They may show signs of having an "anxiety attack" or may have nightmares. Bertoia and Allan (1988) observe that some children and adolescents may feel worried that classmates might inquire about the death, because then the possibility exists of crying at school and being embarrassed by the loss of control.

The anger of children and adolescents may be focused on God for taking their loved one, on the deceased for abandoning them, or on themselves if they feel they have in any way caused the death. Anger often may not be expressed toward the true target but may be displaced and focused on someone or something that is less threatening (e.g., parents, siblings, teachers, objects, or anyone who seemingly could have prevented the loss). Few adolescents can admit their anger, let alone cope with it (Beckmann, 1990).

The purpose of grief and mourning is to take the youth beyond these reactions to the loss (Rando, 1988). Attainment of this goal requires that the child or adolescent work actively to adapt to the loss. According to Rando, the ultimate task of grieving is learning to live with the changes associated with the loss. She asserts that all grief responses fall into three broad, general, and flexible categories, which actually constitute three major *phases* of response. The word *phase* is used in place of the more common word *stage,* because Rando believes that some professionals have misinterpreted previous work in this field. When grief is described in stages, it implies that grief is an orderly and unvarying process, that all people grieve in the same way. However, although people may share many aspects of grief, their responses are quite personal and idiosyncratic (Rando).

The first grief-response phase is *avoidance* characterized by shock, denial, and disbelief. The second phase is *confrontation,* a highly charged and emotional state in which the child or adolescent realizes that the significant other or loved one is dead and in which grief is most intense. The third grief response phase is *reestablishment* in which there is a gradual decline of acute grief and the beginning of an emotional and social reentry into the everyday world. Rando (1988) asserts that all of the descriptions of grief for any group include these three broad phases.

Grief and Guilt

Three kinds of guilt are often associated with grief (Beckmann, 1990). The first type of guilt is called *survivor syndrome* and involves the question, "Why did *they* die instead of me?" *Real guilt* is due to doing or not doing something while the deceased was alive (e.g., "I acted out of carelessness which caused the accident"). Also, some guilt is due to unexpressed anger that the surviving child or adolescent may possess. *Imaginary guilt* includes components such as "thoughts can kill" (e.g., "My brother died because I fought with him and I wished he were dead"). Imaginary (or unrealistic) guilt usually stems from a situation which was uncontrollable. This type of guilt is irrational and must be discussed with the aggrieved child or adolescent. Sometimes imaginary guilt is due to lack of knowledge or incomplete thinking. In any case, the effects of "unresolved guilt" can be mentally and physically harmful (Beckmann, 1990).

Developmental Aspects of Grief

The most common mistake that adults make when associating or working with young people who are grieving, particularly children, is to presume that children think like adults (Giblin & Ryan, 1991). Bertoia and Allan (1988) note that although each youth is unique, "understanding of death generally depends on developmental level, previous death experiences, and cognitive ability" (p. 31). To provide a context for the grief work of children and adolescents, professionals need to examine some of the perceptions which young people maintain about death and explore constructive measures for assisting aggrieved children and adolescents to confront and to accept such a loss, so that they can maintain a course of healthy physical and psychological development (Giblin & Ryan, 1991).

Knowledge of characteristics and behaviors often correlated with bereavement in children and adolescents can be useful for school psychologists in at least three ways. First, the characteristics and behaviors inform school psychologists of the kinds of reactions that can be expected in children and adolescents who have experienced a loss through the death of a significant person in their lives. Second, they serve as indicators of the depth and length of the youth's distress (i.e., the more pronounced and long-lasting the characteristics or behaviors, the more disturbing the event has been for the young person). Third, the disappearance of certain behaviors can suggest that the school psychologist is effectively assisting the child or adolescent in the grieving process (i.e., that the young person is adjusting constructively to the death; Thomas, 1990).

Preschool children

Prior to age 6, most children believe death is gradual, happens to very old people, and is reversible (Giblin & Ryan, 1991). For children in this age group, part of the difficulty in accepting the reality of death is normal egocentric thinking:

Death is perceived as something that happens to others, not to the self. Anxiety can be caused by the child's concern about who will look after basic needs, and by an egocentric belief that the child is, in some way, responsible for the death, through wishes or thoughts, bad behavior, anger, or neglect of responsibility. (Bertoia & Allan, 1988, p. 31).

Too often, adults presume erroneously that young children are unaffected by a death. However, preschoolers experience grief phases similar to those of adults (Duncan, 1992). Fear of abandonment, difficulty forming new attachments, and beliefs about causing the loss are problems that young children may encounter along their normal journey through the grief process (Ney & Barry, 1983). Adults who attempt to protect young children by providing inaccurate or ambiguous answers can further confuse children and delay their grieving process (Norris-Shortle, Young, & Williams, 1993). Regressive behaviors for this age group include thumb sucking, temper tantrums, excessive clinging, and bowel or bladder problems. Eating and sleeping problems may occur in children under age five. Children under age two may temporarily exhibit loss of speech.

School-age children

By middle childhood, most children understand the finality and universality of death and, therefore, exhibit typical reactions of fearing death and of seeking ways to avoid it (Betz & Poster, 1984). Characteristic grief-related behaviors among school-age children may include phobic responses, hypochondriacal symptoms, withdrawal, ag-

gressive acts, eating or sleeping problems, idealization of the deceased, and learning problems. Angry children may get involved in physical fights or display verbal tirades against the deceased individual, an attending physician, God, or surviving significant others. The display of aggression may also be an attempt by the child to gain attention from a grieving parent.

Adolescents

The peer group becomes increasingly important for adolescents, as they place less emphasis on family relationships. The fear of being rejected by their peers may keep adolescents from expressing their thoughts and feelings about the death (Osterweis, Solomon, & Green, 1984). Aggrieved adolescents may develop bowel or bladder problems, stomachaches, eating complications, headaches, rashes, or any combination of these symptoms. Sleep disturbances can result in adolescents getting more or less rest in comparison to their usual sleeping patterns. Some examples of regressive behavior include loss of interest in important peer activities, remaining at home to stay closer to family members, competing for parental attention with younger siblings, and engaging in defiant behaviors (Everstine & Everstine, 1993). The presence of antisocial behaviors such as stealing, vandalism, promiscuous sexual activity, and using drugs become a possibility for adolescents (Everstine & Everstine). Aggrieved adolescents' emotional pain incident to the death can lead to impulsive behaviors that serve as escape mechanisms from the feelings associated with loss.

Bereavement produces intense and enduring emotional distress that outsiders seldom appreciate (Osterweis et al., 1984). Effects of bereavement may affect many areas of an adolescent's life, for instance, self-concept and identity formation, interpersonal relations, schoolwork, family involvement, and overall psychological well-being. Heightened emotions among young people in this age group (i.e., anger, fear, depression) may well be normal characteristics of adolescent grievers striving for mastery and control over thoughts and feelings about separation and loss in relation to their own identities (Fleming & Adolph, 1986).

Problems and Implications

Contemporary society typically (a) avoids the discussion of death, (b) attempts to protect young people from death's influence, and (c) generally is not very supportive of grievers (Floerchinger, 1991). Many unhealthy grief reactions are exacerbated by the lack of societal support for, and understanding of, the aggrieved person (Paul, 1969). Denial of grief almost always leads to a delay and prolongation of bereavement, to more troublesome and inappropriate behavior toward others, and, in extreme cases, to psychological impairment. Naturally, there are many variables that will affect both the intensity of a child's or adolescent's reactions to the death of a significant other and the availability of support.

Grief reactions are influenced by emotional, intrapersonal, interpersonal, psychological, and social variables. However, in light of the unique combinations of factors that may facilitate or impair grief resolution in children and adolescents, the grief responses of each young person must be examined individually (see Table 1). For example, based on their review of clinical and research data, Osterweis and Townsend (1988) noted that the following factors increase the risk of long-term negative outcomes following the death of a parent or sibling:

- The loss occurred when the child was under 5 years of age or during early adolescence.
- The loss of a mother for girls under age 11 and loss of a father for adolescent boys.
- Preexisting emotional difficulties.
- Preexisting conflict between the child and the deceased.
- A surviving parent who becomes excessively dependent on the child.
- A lack of adequate family or community supports or a parent who cannot use support systems.
- Unstable, disruptive environments including numerous caretakers and broken routines.
- A parent who marries someone with whom the child has a bad relationship.
- A sudden or violent death (including homicide or suicide).

Similarly, Gerald Kliman (1968) in his book, *Psychological Emergencies of Childhood* (pp. 89–90), proposed a number of criteria that indicate the need for preventive intervention for children or adolescents following a death (see Table 2).

Table 2   *Criteria Indicating the Need for Preventive Intervention Following a Death*

Presence of one or more of the following:

Parental suicide.
Poor relationship between the youth and the deceased or the surviving parent.
While living with relatives, the deceased presented psychopathology a year before death.
The surviving parent manifests psychopathology.
A girl under 8 years of age whose mother died.

Presence of two or more of the following:

Youth is under 4 years of age.
Presence of psychopathological symptoms in youth.
Father died during the youth's adolescence.
The death causes a geographic move or severe economic hardship.
Unavailable surrogate object with same sex and age variables as the deceased.
The surviving parent has pathologic mourning.
Increasing physical intimacy between the surviving parent and the youth.
Crying does not occur in youth under age 8 in the first weeks after the death.
No discussion of the deceased or the death in a youth older than 4 years of age.
Refusal to participate in religious or funeral activities in youth under the age of 5 years.
An unusually cheerful mood beginning the first week after a parent's death.
Sudden and unexpected death.
The death was the result of a terminal illness that lasted more than six months; the terminal illness involved disfiguration, mental deterioration, or mutilation.
Childbirth or uterine, ovarian, or breast cancer caused death and the bereaved are girls or young women.
The illness was concealed, or the child was misinformed by family.
Family delayed information about the death for more than one day to the child.

Note. Some material in this table was adapted from *Psychological Emergencies of Childhood* by Gerald Kliman, 1968, New York: Grune and Stratton.

Table 1   *Selected Factors Associated with the Psychosocial Impact of a Death on Youth*

Relationship to the deceased (e.g., parent, friend, teacher)	Quality/nature of relationship with the deceased prior to the death
Stability of multiple environments (e.g., family, school)	Number/nature of previous losses and death experiences
Nature of the death (e.g., expected versus sudden)	Extant repertoire and effectiveness of coping skills
Chronological age	Extant life stressors
Pre-death and extant health status and emotional functioning	Number/quality of available and supportive human resources
Social/cultural mores and proscriptions surrounding death and grieving	Religious/spiritual beliefs of self, family, and community
Actual chronological time elapsed since the death (Time *Chronos*)	Personal perception of time elapsed since the death (Time *Kairos*)

Note. Some material in this table was adapted from *Helping Bereaved Children: A Booklet for School Personnel* by M. Osterweis and J. Townsend, 1988, Rockville, MD: U.S. Department of Health and Human Services, National Institute of Mental Health.

The Death of a Parent

One out of every twenty children will face the death of a parent or stepparent during their childhood, and one of every five children will experience the death of a parent by age 16 (Los Angeles Unified School District, 1994). The death of a mother or father is difficult for youth of all ages. Parents are the main recipients of their child's feelings. Parents fulfill a child's needs and represent a part of their child's personality. Parents are also considered instrumental in the further development of their child's personality. Costa and Holliday (1994) observe that:

To a child, the death of a parent is the worst thing imaginable. When it happens, the world turns upside down, security is shaken, and the pain is overwhelming. This traumatic event is one that will affect a child profoundly for the rest of his or her life (p. 206).

However, some youth may experience special difficulties when a parent dies. Parental rules and values serve as the foundation of principles among children between the ages of 4 to 7 (Furman, 1984). If a parent dies between these ages, conscience development tends to occur prematurely resulting in an unequal balance favoring punishment over reinforcement (Furman, 1984). Also, one of the most prevalent consequences of parental death, especially if the death occurs when the child is young, is lowered self-esteem (Costa & Holliday, 1994). When young children idealize the parent who died, they often have difficulty forming new relationships and integrating later adult roles and often do not complete the grief recovery process (Crenshaw, 1990). Adolescents, who engage in normal power struggles with and rebellion against their parents, often experience substantial guilt if the parent with whom they struggled and against whom they rebelled dies (Oates, 1993).

Bertoia and Allan (1988) note that the research literature "indicates that psychopathology in later years is much more common among individuals who experienced the denial or unresolved death of a parent in childhood" (p. 35). Although the death of a parent is traumatic and unforgettable, the child *can* recover. A key factor in this healing process involves a supportive relationship with the remaining significant adult (Costa & Holliday, 1994).

The Death of a Sibling

Although studies of youth grievers have focused most often on death of parents, some attention has been given to sibling death (McCown & Davies, 1995). Among almost half of the families who lose a child to death, siblings of the deceased young person manifest depressive symptoms and severe separation anxiety (Jewett, 1982). A young person's death represents a major change in a family (McCown & Davies, 1995). Not only has the surviving child's brother or sister gone away, but the parents' behavior is altered by their profound grief resulting

from the loss, grief which may rob them of their usual energy, interest, and vitality in their parent role with their surviving children (McCown & Davies). Memories of intense rivalries, teasing, fights, and other negative interactions with the sibling who died may leave a special burden of survivor guilt for remaining siblings (Wass, 1984). Although siblings often may be rivals, they usually have strong emotional bonds and frequently depend on each other for affection and companionship.

Thus, sibling grievers, in common with other children and adolescents who experience the loss of someone close, experience the normal gamut of reactions and emotions which include sadness, loss of trust, regret, and guilt (Davies, 1990). In a recent parent-report study of bereaved siblings, McCown and Davies (1995) found sex differences in grief responses. Although both boys and girls manifested predominantly aggressive behaviors characterized by instrumental attention-seeking actions, girls also frequently demonstrated depressive (internalizing) behavior. In contrast, boys possessed substantial inability to concentrate and hyperactive (externalizing) behavior. Research studies of youths' reactions to the death of a sibling (or a parent) have reported that such children and adolescents typically appear sad, angry, and fearful. They often are withdrawn, dependent, regressive, and restless. Frequently they have trouble concentrating, and, hence, they experience difficulties in school (Thomas, 1990).

The Death of a Friend

Although peers play an important role in the lives of youth, especially adolescents, the reactions of young people to peer death has not been a top priority in research literature. The paucity of research is doubling perplexing considering the incidence of violent deaths from accidents, suicide, and homicide that accompany adolescent risk taking.

Young people who are friends and classmates of a deceased peer are indirect victims, subject to survivor guilt manifested in physical and psychosomatic illness or acting-out behaviors, especially anger (Kliman, 1978). Many adolescents are affected by the death of a peer, but their grief may be ignored because the main priority of the bereavement process is on surviving family members (Raphael, 1983). Peer bereavement during childhood and adolescence is often a matter of "disenfranchised grief" (Doka, 1989, p. 4), and young people bereaved over a peer's or friend's death are often "forgotten grievers," who are seldom given appropriate attention as they struggle to cope with their loss (Doka, 1989).

A Special Case: The Death of a Friend or Peer by Suicide

Adolescent suicide is a particularly disturbing mode of death for friends and acquaintances who are left behind in its wake (Mauk & Rodgers, 1994). Suicide is a self-administered, separate, and distinct cause of death which cannot be compared to any other crisis. Further, the stigma and proscription that exist regarding suicide serve to intensify the survivors' feelings of blame, self-doubt, confusion, shame, resentment, and guilt. For the adolescent survivor, who views the self as indestructible, the death of a friend or acquaintance challenges his or her coping resiliency (Mauk & Weber, 1991). In most cases, survivors will have little time for anticipatory grief. Issues related to suicide and postvention are discussed in detail by Brock and Sandoval (see Suicidal Ideation and Behaviors, this volume).

Bereavement Versus a Major Depressive Episode

As a part of their reaction to a death, some individuals may exhibit characteristics of a *major depressive episode* (MDE) with symptoms such as feelings of sadness or worthlessness, sleeping problems, psychomotor retardation, daily functioning impairment, preoccupation with death, and eating disturbances. Ordinarily, a diagnosis of MDE is made only if symptoms are still present more than 2 months following the loss. However, diagnosis may be appropriate even within that time frame if the bereaved individual exhibits marked functional impairment and feelings of guilt, thoughts of death, and/or hallucinatory experiences associated with issues other than the loved one's death (American Psychiatric Association, 1994).

Time and the Bereavement Process

With respect to time, societal pressures to curtail grief expressions emanate from the assumption that "time heals." This is simply not true. In working with the bereaved, it is important to stress that it is not the time you have to use but how you use the time you have. Zinner (1990) notes that grief work has few shortcuts and takes longer than most people expect or contemporary culture allows. Raphael (1983) reported that the physiological and psychological effects of profound loss on survivors of all ages may continue in varying intensity for many years.

The concepts of time *Chronos* and time *Kairos* from the field of anthropology are useful in describing differences in the experience of time (Campbell & McMahon, 1985). Time *Chronos* is *chronological* time, and clocks and calendars measure this experience of time. In contrast, time *Kairos* refers to the duration it takes for the person to resume growth. Time *Kairos* is not measured by temporal means but rather indicates the changes youth experience as a result of moments of awakening or realization (Campbell & McMahon).

As children and adolescents experience the full grieving process, time *Chronos* is valuable only in that it gives them a span within which to experience time *Kairos*. The passing of days and weeks and months does not within itself bring resolution to their conflict. The time it takes children and adolescents to finish the work of their grieving depends completely on time *Kairos* which can only move forward through perceived and actual support provided by significant individuals in their world (Deaton & Berkan, 1995).

Typical Grief Symptoms Versus Grief Complications

There is much about the normal grief experience that is frightening, even terrifying, for adults let alone children and adolescents. Aspects of the normal grieving process (e.g., vulnerability, the fear of "going crazy," strange physical sensations, self-criticism) can leave the bereaved child or adolescent psychologically and physically shaken. The anxiety generated as one confronts this puzzling, unfamiliar, and frightening array of psychological and physical experiences can be reduced to manageable proportions through cognitive interventions designed to correct misconceptions regarding grief (Fleming & Adolph, 1986).

The extent and duration of grief reactions probably depend on the centrality of the relationship to the deceased person, as well as on the perceived preventability of the death (Bugen, 1979). If a young person's grief responses interfere with the resumption of his or her usual tasks and activities, grieving has become a problem (Beckmann, 1990). Other clues or indicators that a youth is *not* progressing adequately through the grieving process are provided by Beckman (see Table 3).

For many children and adolescents, professional help is needed before they evidence positive adaptation to the loss. Early loss experiences, such as the death of a significant other, are often carried by a youth throughout his or her life, only to be reawakened at other distressing and painful moments (Gaffney, 1988). However, these first significant loss experiences can provide valuable information and skills to ease the pain of future losses (Gaffney).

Alternative Actions

To be human and to live in the world is to experience loss. These losses can be small or great yet they are always personal and are mileposts along life's journey. If you accept that many children and adolescents experience personal loss through death, and that grief is a natural and normal reaction to such a loss, then grief-management techniques and tools should be an integral part of school support services (Deaton & Berkan, 1995).

Table 3 *Symptoms Indicating Grief Complications*

Problems in school (e.g., falling grades, underachievement, behaving
 aggressively toward others)
Delinquent behavior (acting out in school or at home)
Self-destructive behaviors (e.g., excessive use of alcohol or other
 drugs, increasing sexual activity without regard to sexually
 transmitted diseases, pregnancies)
Aggressive behaviors (e.g., slamming doors, smashing or destroying
 objects, loud cursing)
Lack of emotion/loss of feelings
Overactivity
Psychosomatic conditions (i.e., may acquire the symptoms of the
 deceased)
Personality changes (e.g., paranoid behavior ["everyone is against
 me"])
Withdrawing or retreating from social activities or becoming isolated
Suicidal ideation
Giving away possessions
Continual anger or depression
Unusual vulnerability to new separations

Note. Some material in this table was adapted from *Children Who Grieve: A Manual for Conducting Support Groups* by R. Beckmann, 1990, Holmes Beach, FL: Learning Publications.

Further, schools should be *proactive* in their endeavors to assist students who are grieving a death (Brock et al., 1996). That is, schools should *plan* for such contingencies as student death. As Sims (1991) observes: "One should not have to wait until a dramatic or traumatic life event occurs to begin preparation for life's crises" (p. 187). More recently, Oates (1993) asserted that when death affects a school community, there can be resultant chaos or an orderly resolution of the crisis and trauma: "The outcome largely depends on how effectively school staff respond, and effective responses require planning" (p. 93). The loss of a significant person in the life of a child or an adolescent is at once a *time of crisis* for the students caught up in the emotional and psychosocial aftermath of the death and a *time of opportunity* for the school psychologist and other helping professionals, who can provide timely assistance to the grieving student (McCoard, 1990).

Tasks for Bereaved Children and Adolescents

When a significant other dies, children or adolescents lose someone who has been a part of their lives and activities. Because the normal and predictable response to loss is grief, the concern is not whether the youth will grieve, but whether his or her grief will be healthy and functional or pathological and dysfunctional (Parkes, 1990). Adults can play an important role in ensuring that the grief is good grief (i.e., that it helps the aggrieved child or adolescent stay psychologically healthy and that it strengthens the individual's capacity to cope with future

losses; Fox, 1989). To grieve successfully, Fox notes that bereaved children and adolescents must accomplish four tasks:

1. *Understanding.* This task involves knowing that the person is no longer alive (his or her body has stopped working) and that the person will never again be around. Completion of this task requires the provision of honest and age-appropriate information that dispels rumors.
2. *Grieving.* The young person must experience and express the feelings that go with the loss, including sadness, anger, and guilt. The specific content of the grief will depend on the child's or adolescent's relationship with the person who died, on the cause of death, and on a variety of other factors (see Table 1).
3. *Commemorating.* This is the process of formally or informally remembering the life (rather than the death) of the person who died. Commemoration confirms both the reality of the death and the value of human life.
4. *Going on.* After completing the first three tasks, the young person needs to resume the usual activities of living, learning, and loving. However, it is not quite accurate to say that young people "forget." The reality is that the young person never completely "gets over" the death of a significant other; he or she simply learns to live with it. Certainly the acute phase of grief begins to subside, and the pain becomes less intense and more intermittent, with increasingly longer periods of peacefulness intervening. However, incidents such as the aggrieved child or adolescent hearing a favorite song or thinking he or she has seen the deceased in a crowd may trigger a grief response of astounding magnitude (Fleming & Adolph, 1986). After a child or an adolescent has dealt with the death and with its accompanying grief, he or she can go on with living (Fox, 1989).

The School as a Context for Grief Intervention

Death and grief education programs have become much more prevalent in schools in recent decades (Deaton & Berkan, 1995). A primary rationale for these programs is that education is known to be a beneficial intervention tool either prior to or after a loss (Oltjenbruns, 1991). Educational programs aimed at lessening the risk of post-bereavement morbidity need to be developed and implemented with young people (Fleming & Adolph, 1986).

Nelson and Slaikeu (1990) observe that schools are unique settings for crisis intervention, including grief work for two reasons. First, schools are the only public institutions to have daily contact with children for 6 or more hours, at least 9 months during the year, affording time and physical proximity for therapeutic work. Second, the goals of schools and therapeutic intervention services are extremely compatible, as both strive for individual growth and development based on learning. Deaton and Berkan (1995) assert that, "No other entity in the community has a better opportunity or the means to provide prevention, intervention, and postvention activities concerning death issues than the local school system" (p. 7).

Postvention is a form of tertiary prevention and, although the term is most often used to refer to efforts that address the effects of an individual's suicide on the victim's friends and family (Shneidman, 1981), it entails the provision of therapeutic assistance and support in the aftermath of any crisis. In the present context, postvention is (a) that process after the death of a significant person in the lives of children or adolescents during which they work toward psychological healing and readjustment to healthy living, and (b) the provision of both educational and therapeutic interventions to forestall bereavement complications in aggrieved youth.

When confronted with the death of a significant other, young people need a methodology whereby their often unspeakable fears and sorrows may find expression so that the cornerstones of the healing process may be laid (Cunningham & Hare, 1989). Assisting young people, especially the very young child, to understand the death of a significant other is never an easy task. "A child's perceptions of death may be couched in images which lie between fantasy and fact, while verbal command is not always available for the expression of feelings or fears. Nevertheless, most children have an awareness and sensitivity to which honest, yet simple explanations of death may be directed" (Salladay & Royal, 1981, p. 204).

In general, death is a very sensitive topic to discuss and address in a school setting (Considine & Steck, 1994). However, there are some strategies of which educators should be aware. Considine and Steck recommend various positive actions to take and numerous pitfalls to avoid (see Table 4).

Activities used to facilitate healthy grieving in children and adolescents may be *developmental* (i.e., used before a death occurs) or *responsive* (i.e., used after a death). Oates (1993) asserts that *how* various activities and strategies are implemented depends on the expertise and comfort level of the educator or helping professional, the age or grade level of the student(s), and the circumstances surrounding the death as well as the type of death (Cunningham & Hare, 1989). Excellent resources are available for adults who desire to engage in the challenging yet rewarding work of assisting young people in the grieving process. Many of these resources are listed in the annotated bibliography at the end of this chapter.

Also, it is important to educate parents, professionals, and paraprofessionals through various media regarding the nature of grief and adaptive processes to deal with it. Topics might include the necessity for the open expres-

sion of grief and frank discussion of the deceased (in effect, granting affected individuals permission to grieve), the need to recognize and accept support during this vulnerable period, the importance of good communication skills, the identification of behaviors helpful to the griever, and the recognition of the child or adolescent who may be at risk for bereavement complications.

Providing aggrieved children and adolescents with grief education and support can assist them to understand, process, and navigate through loss and, at the same time, help them to see themselves as competent, strong, resilient, and worthwhile individuals (Hipp, 1995). Toward this end, Sims (1991) makes the following observations:

Although painful things do happen in life, it is not "the end of the world" for long. . . . Loss hurts, and we cannot find the words to soothe that hurt—there aren't any. We cannot shield our children from the twists and turns of living. We cannot protect them from experiencing life. We can, however, build supports and safety nets, not only for our children, but for ourselves as well. That requires love and faith, strength and support. Hurt and pain have their lessons, and we cannot rob our children of the rich tapestry that hurt and love weave together. To eliminate one from the loom is to break the thread and steal away the fabric. . . . "Who am I now?" can become a real challenge rather than a despair if we allow our children and ourselves to claim every experience and support each other as we grow through the triumphs and the trials (p. 189).

Summary

Children and adolescents encounter loss quite frequently in their lives from a variety of expected and unexpected causes. Young people who experience the death of a significant other must ultimately come to emotional closure as individuals. Although grief resolution (if *complete* resolution exists) is very much a personal task, children and adolescents too often find themselves adrift alone in the stormy and frightening sea of loss by death and need the caring and efficacious assistance of adults to navigate and bring them safely to the port of resolution.

Because the majority of work in the area of grief and bereavement has focused on adults, there are still many unanswered questions surrounding the grieving patterns of children and adolescents. Yet, there are some general developmental and psychological guidelines for normal grieving and some risk indicators to be monitored for children and adolescents who do not appear to be approximating grief resolution adequately.

Van Ornum and Mordock (1990), in response to the question, "What can we do for youth struggling with grief?" assert that, as helpers, "We need to be available. We need to listen. We need to recognize, understand, and make allowances for the grieving process. We will not be

Table 4 *Positive Actions and Caveats for Addressing Death in the School Setting*

Permit students to express their feelings and opinions.
Use simple and direct language in explaining things about death.
Start with material that arouses the least emotion and progress to materials that arouses the most emotion.
Help students know that they are not responsible for the death.
Present material in a nonmoralistic fashion.
Be sensitive to students who may have emotional or negative reactions.
Tell students that sickness may be the cause of death but explain in detail.
Tell students the truth.
Tell students that you do not have all the answers about death.

Note. Some material in this table was adapted from *Working Together: When Death Comes to School* by A. S. Considine and L. P. Steck, 1994, A Paper presented at the 14th Annual National Conference of the American Council of Rural Special Education (ACRES), Austin, TX.

stronger than the grief, but we can help children do what they must do" (p. 79). School psychologists can experience substantial personal rewards when youth with whom they have worked learn to cope with and adapt to the deaths of significant persons in their lives. Ideally, in the shadow of such a death, professionals and aggrieved youth can manifest personal resilience and growth, a greater appreciation for life and people, and enhanced capacities for empathy, compassion, and caring.

Recommended Resources

Selected Resources for Educators

Balk, D. E. (Ed.). (1991). *Journal of Adolescent Research* (Special issue on death and adolescent bereavement), *6*(1), 1–156.
This special issue reviews current research and future directions in death and adolescent bereavement. Articles include such topics as dialectical themes in adolescent conceptions of death, positive outcomes of adolescents' experience with grief, aspects of sibling bereavement, and perspectives on grieving and postvention for peer survivors of adolescent suicide.

Deaton, R. L., & Berkan, W. A. (1995). *Planning and managing death issues in the schools: A handbook.* Westport, CT: Greenwood Press.
This excellent resource for educators describes prevention, intervention, and postvention activities regarding death issues and grief interventions for youth in school settings.

Essa, E. L., & Murray, C. I. (1994). Young children's understanding and experience with death. *Young Children, 49*(4), 74–81.
This article reviews the research literature and highlights young children's cognitive and emotional understanding of death. *The authors offer practical suggestions for helping young children cope with death.*

James, J. W., & Cherry, F. (1988). *The grief recovery handbook: A step-by-step program for moving beyond loss.* New York: Harper & Row.
Also appropriate for parents or caregivers, this inspirational book presents the authors' step-by-step grief recovery program. The specific down-to-earth advice in this book can help individuals work through their loss to create a richer, fuller life for themselves and those around them.

Oates, M. D. (1993). *Death in the school community: A handbook for counselors, teachers, and administrators.* Alexandria, VA: American Counseling Association.
A valuable resource for school administrators, faculty, and staff, this book can assist in planning for and managing various types of deaths in schools. The book provides an overview of death in schools, presents aspects of a plan for dealing with death contingencies, explicates the understanding of grief in school-age children, and supplies guidelines for leading loss and grief groups.

Selected Resources for Parents and Caregivers

Chaloner, L. (1962). How to answer the questions children ask about death. *Parent's Magazine, 37,* 100–102.
The author indicates how, before addressing the needs of one's own children, a parent must first be comfortable with their self-perception of death and its impact.

Grollman, E. A. (1970). *Taking about death: A dialogue between parent and child.* Boston: Beacon Press.
In an attempt to help parents talk to their children about death, this source addresses often-asked questions by children about death.

Monahon, C. (1993). *Children and trauma: A parent's guide to helping children heal.* New York: Lexington Books.
This book teaches parents about the effects of trauma, including the death of a significant other, and provides a blueprint for restoring a child's sense of safety and balance.

Stein, S. B. (1974). *About dying.* New York: Walker and Company.
To assist parents in the explanation of death to children, half of the book tells the story of the death of Snow, a bird, and the rest of the book focuses on information that is helpful to children about death and loss.

Selected Resources for Children

Cohen, J. (1987). *I had a friend named Peter.* New York: Morrow.
This story is about a young girl, Betsy, who is troubled and has many questions when her best friend dies. It is an excellent resource to help children age 6 through 12 who are grieving the death of a peer.

Gootman, M. E. (1994). *When a friend dies: A book for teens about grieving and healing.* Minneapolis: Free Spirit Publishing.

This well-written book helps adolescents handle one of life's most difficult and all-too-common events: the death of a friend. The author's advice and explanations are practical and perceptive, and she contributes many ideas to discuss with others to help grieve in healthy ways.

Hipp, E. (1995). *Help for the hard times: Getting through loss.* Center City, MN: Hazelden Publishing.
This book reviews, in very "youth-centered" language, the concepts of loss and grief, getting through and growing through the difficult times after a loss, healing after a loss, and supporting someone else who has experienced a loss.

Johnson, J., & Johnson, M. (1982). *Where's Jess?* Omaha, NE: Centering Corporation.
After the death of a son, parents attempt to answer death-related questions posed by their surviving child.

LeShan, E. (1988). *Learning to say goodbye: When a parent dies.* New York: Avon Books.
This book, for children ages 8 and older, describes common feelings after the death of a parent and discusses how to work through their grief. This book is also helpful for adults who seek more understanding about how loss affects children.

Richter, E. (1986). *Losing someone you love: When a brother or sister dies.* New York: Putnam.
Early adolescents through young adults (ages 10–24) frankly discuss their experiences following the death of a sibling.

White, E. B. (1952). *Charlotte's web.* New York: Harper and Row.
In this classic story, the relationship between Wilbur, a pig, and Charlotte, a spider, provides a setting for the triumphs and tragedies of the life cycle.

Relevant Organizations

Center for Trauma Information and Education (CTIE)
2522 Highland Avenue
Cincinnati, OH 45219.
The CTIE was established in 1992 for the purpose of promoting, developing, and implementing educational programs and publications in the field of psychological trauma. The overall mission of CTIE is the prevention and alleviation of psychological trauma in children, adolescents, and adults.

Good Grief Program, Judge Baker Children's Center
295 Longwood Avenue
Boston, MA 02115.
The Good Grief Program offers counseling to children in the Boston area and provides resource materials to helping professionals engaged in death education and bereavement counseling.

Institute for Trauma and Loss in Children (ITLC)
Corand Dex Plaza
2051 West Grand Boulevard
Detroit, MI 48208.
The ITLC is a nonprofit organization that provides knowledge, resources, and training to professionals so they can more effectively assist children and families who experience nonviolent and violent loss or trauma. The ITLC offers half-day, full-day, or multiple-day multimedia training to professionals in schools and other agencies.

References

American Psychiatric Association. (1994). *Diagnostic and statistical manual of mental disorders* (4th ed.). Washington, DC: Author.

Beckmann, R. (1990). *Children who grieve: A manual for conducting support groups.* Holmes Beach, FL: Learning Publications.

Bertoia, J., & Allan, J. (1988). School management of the bereaved child. *Elementary School Guidance and Counseling, 23,* 30–38.

Betz, C. L., & Poster, E. C. (1984). Children's concepts of death: Implications for pediatric practice. *Nursing Clinics of North America, 19,* 341–349.

Brock, S. E., Sandoval, J., & Lewis, S. (1996). *Preparing for crises in the schools: A manual for building school crisis response teams.* Brandon, VT: Clinical Psychology Publishing.

Campbell, P. A., & McMahon, E. M. (1985). *Bio-spirituality.* Chicago: Loyola University Press.

Considine, A. S., & Steck, L. P. (1994). *Working together: When death comes to school.* Paper presented at the 14th Annual National Conference of the American Council of Rural Special Education (ACRES), Austin, TX.

Costa, L., & Holliday, D. (1994). Helping children cope with the death of a parent. *Elementary School Guidance and Counseling, 28,* 206–213.

Cunningham, B., & Hare, J. (1989). Essential elements of a teacher in-service program on child bereavement. *Elementary School Guidance and Counseling, 23,* 175–182.

Davies, B. (1990). Long-term follow-up of bereaved siblings. In J. D. Morgan (Ed.), *The dying and bereaved teenager* (pp. 78–89). Philadelphia: The Charles Press.

Deaton, R. L., & Berkan, W. A. (1995). *Planning and managing death issues in the schools: A handbook.* Westport, CT: Greenwood Press.

Doka, K. J. (1989). Disenfranchised grief. In K. J. Doka (Ed.), *Disenfranchised grief: Recognizing hidden sorrow* (pp. 3–11). Lexington, MA: D. C. Heath.

Duncan, U. (1992). *Grief and grief processing for preschool children.* (ERIC Document and Reproduction Services No. ED 354 078)

Everstine, D. S., & Everstine, L. (1993). *The trauma response: Treatment for emotional injury.* New York: W. W. Norton.

Ewalt, P. L., & Perkins, L. (1979). The real experience of death among adolescents: An empirical study. *Social Casework, 60,* 547–551.

Fleming, S. J., & Adolph, R. (1986). Helping bereaved adolescents: Needs and responses. In C. A. Corr & J. N. McNeil (Eds.), *Adolescence and death* (pp. 97–118). New York: Springer.

Floerchinger, D. S. (1991). Bereavement in late adolescence: Interventions on college campuses. *Journal of Adolescent Research, 6,* 146–156.

Fox, S. S. (1989). Good grief: Preventive interventions for children and adolescents. In S. C. Klagsbrun, G. W. Kliman, E. J. Clark, A. H. Kutscher, R. DeBellis, & C. A. Lambert (Eds.), *Preventive psychiatry: Early intervention and situational crisis management* (pp. 83–93). Philadelphia: The Charles Press.

Furman, E. (1984). Children's patterns in mourning the death of a loved one. In H. Wass & C. A. Corr (Eds.), *Childhood and death* (pp. 185–203). Washington, DC: Hemisphere Publishing.

Gaffney, D. A. (1988). Death in the classroom: A lesson in life. *Holistic Nurse Practitioner, 2*(2), 20–27.

Gardner, P., & Hudson, B. L. (1996). Advance report of final mortality statistics, 1993. *Monthly Vital Statistics Report, 44*(7, Suppl.), 1–84. [This report was published in Hyattsville, MD, by the National Center for Health Statistics.]

Giblin, N., & Ryan, F. (1991). Reaching the child's perception of death. In J. D. Morgan (Ed.), *Young people and death* (pp. 3–10). Philadelphia: The Charles Press.

Glass, J. C. (1991). Death, loss, and grief among middle school children: Implications for the school counselor. *Elementary School Guidance and Counseling, 26,* 139–148.

Hipp, E. (1995). *Help for the hard times: Getting through loss.* Center City, MN: Hazelden Publishing.

James, J. W., & Cherry, F. (1988). *The grief recovery handbook: A step-by-step program for moving beyond loss.* New York: Harper & Row.

Jewett, C. L. (1982). *Helping children cope with separation and loss.* Cambridge, MA: The Harvard Common Press.

Kliman, A. S. (1978). *Crisis: Psychological aid for recovery and growth.* New York: Holt, Rinehart, & Winston.

Kliman, G. (1968). *Psychological emergencies of childhood.* New York: Grune and Stratton.

Los Angeles Unified School District. (1994). *A handbook for crisis intervention.* Los Angeles: Student Support Services.

Mauk, G. W., & Rodgers, P. R. (1994). Building bridges over troubled waters: School-based postvention with adolescent survivors of peer suicide. *Crisis Intervention and Time-Limited Treatment, 1*(2), 103–123.

Mauk, G. W., & Weber, C. (1991). Peer survivors of adolescent suicide: Perspectives on grieving and postvention. *Journal of Adolescent Research, 6,* 113–131.

McCoard, W. D. (1990). A crisis intervention model. In M. J. Rotheram-Borus, J. Bradley, & N. Obolensky (Eds.), *Planning to live: Evaluating and treating suicidal teens in community settings* (pp. 195–209). Norman: The University of Oklahoma, National Resource Center for Youth Services.

McCown, D. E., & Davies, B. (1995). Patterns of grief in young children following the death of a sibling. *Death Studies, 19,* 41–53.

Nelson, E. R., & Slaikeu, K. A. (1990). Crisis intervention in the schools. In K. A. Slaikeu (Ed.), *Crisis intervention: A handbook for practice and research* (2nd ed., pp. 329–347). Boston: Allyn and Bacon.

Ney, P. G., & Barry, J. E. (1983). The child and death: Children who survive. *New Zealand Medical Journal, 96,* 127–129.

Norris-Shortle, C., Young, P. A., & Williams, M. A. (1993). Understanding death and grief for children three and younger. *Social Work, 38,* 736–742.

Oates, M. D. (1993). *Death in the school community: A handbook for counselors, teachers, and administrators.* Alexandria, VA: American Association for Counseling and Development.

Oltjenbruns, K. A. (1991). Positive outcomes of adolescents' experience with grief. *Journal of Adolescent Research, 6,* 43–53.

Osterweis, M., Solomon, F., & Green, M. (Eds.). (1984). *Bereavement: Reactions, consequences, and care.* Washington, DC: National Academy Press.

Osterweis, M., & Townsend, J. (1988). *Helping bereaved children: A booklet for school personnel.* Rockville, MD: U.S. Department of Health and Human Services, National Institute of Mental Health.

Parkes, C. M. (1990). Risk factors in bereavement: Implications for the prevention and treatment of pathologic grief. *Psychiatric Annals, 20,* 308–313.

Paul, N. (1969). Psychiatry: Its role in the resolution of grief. In A. H. Kutscher (Ed.), *Death and bereavement* (pp. 174–195). Springfield, IL: Charles C Thomas.

Rando, T. A. (1988). What is grief? In T. A. Rando (Ed.), *Grieving: How to go on living when someone you love dies* (pp. 18–23). Lexington, MA: Lexington Books.

Raphael, B. (1983). *The anatomy of bereavement.* New York: Basic Books.

Salladay, S. A., & Royal, M. E. (1981). Children and death: Guidelines for grief work. *Child Psychiatry and Human Development, 11*(4), 203–212.

Sims, D. (1991). A model for grief intervention and death education in the public schools. In J. D. Morgan (Ed.), *Young people and death* (pp. 185–190). Philadelphia: The Charles Press.

Stein, S. B. (1974). *About dying.* New York: Walker and Company.

Thomas, R. M. (1990). *Counseling and life-span development.* Newbury Park, CA: Sage Publications.

Van Ornum, W., & Mordock, J. B. (1990). *Crisis counseling with children and adolescents: A guide for nonprofessional counselors.* New York: Continuum.

Wass, H. (1984). Parents, teachers, and health professionals as helpers. In H. Wass & C. A. Corr (Eds.), *Helping children cope with death: Guidelines and resources* (2nd ed., pp. 75–130). Washington, DC: Hemisphere Publishing.

Wass, H., Miller, M. D., & Thornton, G. (1990). Death education and grief/suicide interventions in the public schools. *Death Studies, 13,* 161–173.

Zinner, E. S. (1990). Survivors of suicide: Understanding and coping with the legacy of self-inflicted death. In P. Cimbolic & D. A. Jobes (Eds.), *Youth suicide: Issues, assessment, and intervention* (pp. 67–85). Springfield, IL: Charles C Thomas.

34

Achievement Motivation

Anastasia S. Morrone

University of Delaware

Paul R. Pintrich

University of Michigan

Background and Development

When faced with a challenging academic assignment, some students are likely to ask themselves, "What will I learn from the assignment?" and "What is the best way to approach the assignment?" Other students are likely to ask themselves, "Can I do this assignment?" and "Will I get a high grade on this assignment?" (Dweck & Leggett, 1988). These examples illustrate two different types of classroom goals, learning (mastery) and performance goals, which have been found to be related to achievement motivation (Ames, 1992; Ames & Archer, 1988). In this section, we present two of the most current theories of achievement motivation, attribution theory and achievement goal theory. We selected attribution theory because of its significant contributions to the study of achievement motivation and because it provides a theoretical foundation for achievement goal theory. Achievement goal theory provides the framework for the remainder of the chapter. We conclude with a review of the literature on how the classroom context influences the type of goals students select for themselves.

Attribution Theory

Attribution theory emphasizes causal attributions for success and failure outcomes. The theory begins at the point where a person experiences an outcome that is unexpected, negative, or important (Weiner, 1986). This causes the person to retrospectively search for possible reasons why the outcome might have occurred. For example, if a student expected to earn a B on an exam, but instead earns a D, the student is likely to search for an explanation that might explain why the grade is much lower than expected. The student would also go through a similar process if a higher than expected grade had been earned.

The perceived causes of success and failure in academic settings can be located along three causal dimensions, locus of causality (internal vs. external), stability (stable vs. unstable) and controllability (controllable vs. uncontrollable; see Table 1). Locus of causality refers to whether the cause of the outcome is attributed to something within the person (internal) or outside the person (external). Aptitude, temporary and long-term effort, skills and knowledge, and mood are internal attributions because they describe characteristics of the person, while perceived teacher bias, help from others, objective task difficulty, and chance are considered external because they are outside of the person. Stability refers to whether the cause of the outcome is attributed to something that will not change (stable) or something that is variable and can change (unstable). Therefore, long-term effort, aptitude, perceived teacher bias, and objective task difficulty are considered stable causes, while temporary effort, skills and knowledge, mood, help from others, and chance are considered to be unstable. The third causal dimension, controllability, reflects whether the cause is something over which students perceive themselves to have control. Long-term and temporary effort, perceived teacher bias, and help from others are considered controllable causes, while aptitude, mood, objective task difficulty, and chance are considered uncontrollable causes.

Generally, when students attribute an outcome to their aptitude, they consider information such as how successful they have been in the past with similar tasks as well as the objective difficulty of the task. In a failure situation, a student making an aptitude attribution might reason, "Even though this was a hard test, I never do well in math. I'm just not good at math." If the task is perceived to be based on skill, and if other variables such as objective task difficulty are held constant, then the cause is usually attributed to temporary effort. In the same failure situation, another student making an effort attribution might reason, "I have always been good at math, and this test was not that difficult. So I must not have studied hard enough."

Table 1 *Achievement Attributions Classified by Causal Dimensions* *

Student Attribution	Locus of Causality		Controllability		Stability	
	Internal	External	Controllable	Uncontrollable	Stable	Unstable
Long-term Effect	✓		✓		✓	
Temporary Effort	✓		✓			✓
Skills and knowledge	✓		✓			✓
Aptitude (Ability)	✓			✓	✓	
Mood	✓			✓		✓
Perceived Teacher Bias		✓	✓		✓	
Help from Others		✓	✓			✓
Objective Task Difficulty (Task Difficulty)		✓		✓	✓	
Chance (Luck)		✓		✓		✓

Note. Adapted from *An Attributional Theory of Achievement Motivation and Emotion* (pp. 46–49), by B. Weiner, 1986, New York: Springer-Verlag, and from *Motivation in Education: Theory, Research, and Applications* (p. 134), by P. R. Pintrich and D. H. Schunk, 1996, Englewood Cliffs, NJ: Merrill Prentice Hall. Words in parenthesis were the original terms used in the literature.
*Causes perceived by students to be internal, unstable, and controllable are most likely to evoke further student effort of toward mastery.

It is clear that these two explanations for failure will result in different future behavior. The reason for this is that the stability of a cause, rather than its locus, determines expectancy for future success (Weiner, 1986). For example, the student who attributed failure to low aptitude is likely to have low expectancy for future success. The reason for this is that aptitude is considered an internal, stable cause. This student is likely to conclude, "I will never do well in math, no matter how hard I study." But the student who attributed the cause of failure to insufficient effort is likely to have high expectancy for future success because temporary effort is an internal, unstable cause. This student is likely to conclude, "I just need to study harder next time. I know I can do better if I work harder."

The controllability dimension further highlights the importance of attributing past failures to insufficient effort. Not only is temporary effort an unstable cause, but it is also something over which students have full control. If students believe that working harder will produce success, they are likely to persist longer at the task and achieve at higher levels than if they attribute their failures to aptitude, which is an uncontrollable cause.

Note that the words in parentheses in Table 1 were the original names of the four primary perceived causes of academic success and failure (ability, effort, task difficulty, and luck). These names were included because they are still used extensively in the literature (Pintrich & Schunk, 1996). Weiner (1986) renamed these attributions because he acknowledged that the original names may have been misleading. For example, research by Dweck and Leggett (1988) has indicated that some children perceive their intellectual ability to be changeable such that the more they learn, the smarter they become, while other children perceive their intellectual ability to be fixed and unchangeable. To help clarify what was meant by ability, Weiner (1986) suggested that *aptitude* might better describe intellectual ability, which is considered relatively stable. Similarly, effort was renamed *temporary effort* to better differentiate it from sustained or long-term effort. Note that throughout this chapter the original names will be used when referring to studies that have examined effort and ability attributions. However, we acknowledge that we are actually referring to temporary effort and aptitude unless otherwise noted.

Whereas attribution theory has made important contributions to the study of achievement motivation, the theory primarily emphasizes reactions to events after they have occurred rather than how beliefs and cognitions might influence the way students approach new academic tasks. In other words, attribution theory provides an explanation for the way in which students retrospectively attribute the cause of achievement outcomes but is less clear about how students' *anticipatory* beliefs and cognitions influence the way in which they approach academic tasks. Achievement goal theory, to which we now turn, focuses on these anticipatory beliefs and cognitions.

Achievement Goal Theory

Ames (1992) defined an achievement goal orientation as an "integrated pattern of beliefs, attributions, and affect that produces the intentions of behavior (Weiner, 1986) and that is represented by different ways of approaching, engaging in, and responding to achievement-type activities" (p. 261). This quote by Ames underscores the way in which achievement goal theory has attempted to integrate and elaborate on the motivational processes proposed by previous theories of achievement motivation.

In keeping with this theme, Dweck and Leggett (1988) have proposed a model of achievement motivation derived from the attribution/learned helplessness approach. The model is presented from a social-cognitive developmental perspective and has as its primary focus two types of achievement goals: learning goals and performance goals. As illustrated in the introduction to this chapter, when students have learning goals, their primary focus is on learning or mastering something new. Because they value learning for its own sake, they tend to choose more challenging assignments and work harder in school. These students also tend to use more effective learning strategies while studying (Ames, 1992).

Conversely, when students have performance goals they tend to focus on the external reward associated with their learning. This reward is often to get a good grade and ideally to get a higher grade than other students in the class. Another aspect of performance goals is to avoid getting a bad grade in the class (Dweck, 1986). Students with performance goals often approach academic tasks by first determining how difficult the task will be and whether they believe they will be successful (Dweck, 1986). Because the focus is on the outcome, they spend less time deciding on the best learning strategies to use, which often results in the use of less effective strategies (Elliott & Dweck, 1988).

But what are the reasons behind the selection of one goal over another? Dweck and Leggett (1988) suggested that students may select achievement goals based on their own implicit theories of intelligence. The two implicit theories of intelligence that students differentially subscribe to, according to Dweck and Leggett, are the entity and incremental theories of intelligence.

Students with an entity theory of intelligence believe that intelligence is a fixed, global trait. In the context of attribution theory, the primary emphasis is on the internal, stable factor of ability (aptitude; Weiner, 1986). Thus, students with an entity view see effort as being *inversely* related to ability (Dweck & Leggett, 1988) such that if they have to work hard to succeed, they must not be very smart. Because this view of intelligence focuses on ability, students who subscribe to this view are likely to be mastery oriented in their approach to academic tasks only when they believe they are already good at something. The mastery-oriented pattern of behavior involves seeking challenging tasks, showing positive affect, and demonstrating high persistence. If a student believes that he or she is not very good at something, a very different behavioral pattern is likely to emerge. In this case, the student is likely to exhibit helplessness, which is characterized by challenge avoidance, negative affect, and low persistence, especially in the face of difficulty. The entity view of intelligence favors performance goals because these goals either reinforce students' ability (by getting good grades) or protecting students' ability from being evaluated negatively (by withdrawing from the task).

Conversely, students with an incremental theory of intelligence believe that intelligence increases as they acquire new skills and knowledge. The primary emphasis of this view of intelligence is on the unstable, internal factor of effort (temporary effort; Weiner, 1986). These students see a positive relationship between effort and ability, such that the harder they work, the smarter they will become. This view of intelligence favors learning goals in which students seek challenging tasks from which they will be able to learn. These students also understand that making mistakes is part of learning. It is important to note that these students are also aware of their present ability in a particular area, just as students with an entity view of intelligence are, but the former students place less importance on demonstrating that they are smart. Instead, they use what they know about their ability as a guide in determining the strategies that would best help them achieve their goals (Dweck, 1986).

An interesting question that emerges concerns the relationship between effort and ability and the ways in which the perceived relationship changes as children develop. Young children see effort and ability as positively related to one another (Nicholls, 1990), but gradually they become more concerned with how their ability compares with other children. For example, Harari and Covington (1981) found that high effort was increasingly less valued by students at higher grades until the college level at which time, the "progressive grade-linked reversal of effort valuation, from positive to negative, becomes complete" (p. 22). This developmental trend begins around age nine and continues until approximately eighth grade, at which time students have developed "adult-like" (entity theory of intelligence) views concerning the relationship between effort and ability (Nicholls, 1990).

With this developmental trend come changes in the way children approach achievement-related tasks. Dweck and Elliott (1983) proposed that there are two major factors contributing to these changes:

- Children encounter new tasks in school that are very different from the ones in which they are used to engaging (this often reflects a transition from physical to intellectual tasks).
- Children learn that ability is stable and uncontrollable which causes them to begin evaluating their ability compared to their peers.

But despite this developmental trend, Dweck and Elliott argued that some children, even as they grow older, continue to believe that their ability increases through effort (incremental theory of intelligence). One explanation for this may be the influence of the classroom context, which is discussed in the next section. Table 2 pro-

Table 2 *Achievement Goals and Behavioral Patterns*

Theory of Intelligence	Attributional Emphasis	Type of Goal	Perceived Ability	Behavioral Pattern
Entity	Ability	Performance	If High	Mastery
			If Low	Helplessness
Incremental	Effort	Learning	If High or Low	Mastery

Note. Adapted from "Motivational Processes Affecting Learning," by C. S. Dweck, 1986, *American Psychologist, 41,* p. 1,041.

vides a summary of the differences between students with learning and performance goals.

Note that the differences in behavior between students with performance goals and learning goals are similar to the behavioral differences between individuals who are ego involved and task involved (Nicholls, 1989). The term *ego involvement* refers to situations in which students seek to demonstrate their ability as compared to the ability of a normative reference group. *Task involvement,* on the other hand, refers to situations in which the focus is on improving mastery at a task rather than in demonstrating ability relative to others. The difficulty that arises with ego involvement is that individuals must determine whether they can master a task and to what extent this implies higher ability than others. If the amount of effort required to master the task is too high, this implies low ability. Ego involvement is seen more frequently in competitive situations while task involvement is more often present in noncompetitive situations (Nicholls, 1989).

Learning and performance goals are also conceptually similar to the distinctions between intrinsic and extrinsic motivation (Deci, Vallerand, Pelletier, & Ryan, 1991; Harter, 1992). Deci et al. defined intrinsic motivation as the desire to engage in activities for their own sake, without the necessity for an accompanying external reward. Conversely, extrinsically motivated behaviors were defined as being instrumental in acquiring some type of reward. Similarly, Harter (1992) defined an intrinsic motivational orientation as one in which children are curious and interested in learning. These children tend to seek challenges and opportunities for independent mastery. In contrast, an extrinsic motivational orientation was defined as one in which children tend to avoid challenges and opportunities for independent mastery. These children tend to focus on pleasing the teacher and earning good grades.

As the preceding discussion indicates, there are a variety of different ways of conceptualizing the differences between goal orientations. As Ames (1992) noted, these different goal-orientation distinctions are conceptually similar to one another. Therefore, she suggested the use of the terms mastery and performance goals. These terms will be used throughout the rest of this chapter.

The Role of the Classroom Context

To this point, we have discussed the differences between mastery and performance goals and some reasons why students might select each of these two goals. An important question that still remains concerns how the classroom might influence the type of goals students adopt. This question has been addressed recently in research examining the role of the classroom context in contributing to students' achievement goals. The results from both laboratory and classroom studies suggest that it is possible to manipulate achievement goals (Ames, 1984; Ames & Archer, 1988; Elliott & Dweck, 1988; Graham & Golan, 1991). A few of these studies will be reviewed next to highlight their contribution to understanding the role of the classroom context in students' goal orientation.

Ames (1984) examined whether competitive and individualistic goal structures would result in the patterns of achievement cognitions associated with helpless and mastery-oriented children, respectively. The goal structure was experimentally manipulated through the instructions given to the children. Children in the competitive structure were paired with a partner and told that the goal was to try to be the "winner" by solving more puzzles than their partner. In the individualistic structure, children worked alone and were encouraged to try to solve as many puzzles as possible and to improve their performance on the second set of puzzles. The results indicated that children in the individualistic structure selected more effort-attribution statements and self-instruction statements than children in the competitive structure. In contrast, children in the competitive structure selected more ability-attribution statements and fewer self-instruction statements. The findings are consistent with the attributional emphasis of children who have mastery and performance goals.

In a similar study, Elliott and Dweck (1988) found that children more frequently selected a learning task when the importance of acquiring new knowledge was emphasized, but selected a performance task more often when evaluation of their skill was emphasized. When mastery goals were highlighted, the children selected more challenging tasks and were more mastery oriented in their approach, regardless of their perceived ability. When performance goals were highlighted, children were more likely to show a helpless pattern of behavior, especially in the face of difficulty.

In a study done in an actual classroom rather than in the laboratory, Ames and Archer (1988) found that students who perceived mastery goals to be emphasized in their classrooms reported using more effective learning strategies, selected more challenging tasks, and had more positive attitudes toward the class. Conversely, students who perceived performance goals to be emphasized had more negative attitudes toward the class as well as lower perceived ability.

Graham and Golan (1991) examined the influence of task-involving versus ego-involving instructions on children's level of cognitive processing. (Recall that task involvement is conceptually similar to having mastery goals while ego involvement is similar to having performance goals.) The children who received the task-involving instructions were told that people often make mistakes when they first learn how to solve puzzles but that they usually get better at solving them over time. These children were also encouraged to see the activity as a challenge and to have fun trying to master it. Conversely, the children who received ego-involving instructions were told that based on their performance, the experimenter had a good idea about how good they were at solving puzzles compared with other children their age. The results indicated that when the task required deeper levels of processing, the ego-involved children showed poorer recall than the task-involved children. This study illustrates how the social context influenced information processing, which is an important aspect of any type of academic learning.

Problems and Implications

The previous section emphasized the importance of mastery goals and also illustrated that it is possible to influence the type of goals students adopt. Yet many teachers are frustrated in their attempts to motivate their students. They often express their frustration by saying, "My students seem so unmotivated. No matter what I do, it doesn't seem to make any difference in their motivation." This often causes teachers to rely on the use of extrinsic rewards such as stickers, candy, pizza coupons, and extra recess to motivate their students. The difficulty that arises from these types of rewards is that they tend to foster performance goals rather than mastery goals. Students often come to see engaging in academic tasks as a means to an end (the reward) rather than as an end in itself.

Ames (1992) suggested a framework for promoting mastery goals which includes the nature of academic tasks, authority in the classroom, and evaluation and recognition of student achievement (see also Maehr &

Midgley, 1991). We will use this framework to highlight some of the motivation problems that can arise in the classroom. Suggestions on ways to address some of these problems will be discussed in the Alternative Actions section that follows this section. In addition, Pintrich and Schunk (1996) and Stipek (1993) present many applications for teachers to use in the classroom.

With respect to the nature of academic tasks, it is not surprising that tasks students see as repetitive and boring tend to lower intrinsic motivation. A consistent finding in motivation research has been that students are the most motivated when they are given moderately challenging tasks (Lepper & Hodell, 1989). But many teachers say that it is difficult to provide challenging tasks to all students because their students have very different levels of ability. This often causes teachers to tailor their assignments so that all students can complete them. The difficulty that arises from this approach is that the assignments are often seen as unchallenging by many students. Even students who are generally motivated are less likely to feel motivated when the tasks are too easy. It is when students are not challenged that behavior problems also tend to surface, which often causes teachers to rely more on rewards and punishments to maintain control in the classroom. These rewards and punishments, while effective in maintaining control, often work to lower intrinsic motivation. The result is that students engage in academic tasks only to earn some external reward or to avoid some type of punishment.

Another aspect of academic tasks that often lowers intrinsic motivation is when the tasks seem to have little relevancy to the students. This has been described as the utility value of the task or the extent to which the task is seen as instrumental in helping students reach some long-term goal (Eccles, 1983). When students have low utility value for an academic task, they are likely to say, "I will never need to know this. Why should I learn it?" It is often possible to motivate these students by helping them understand how the information they are learning will be useful to them. This can be done by using problems that reflect real problems students might encounter rather than decontextualized problems. For example, calculating the area of a rectangle is likely to be viewed as less useful than calculating the area of a bedroom.

Although many academic tasks seem uninteresting to students, it is often difficult for teachers to know how to make the material interesting. To impress upon students that they will need this information in the future often increases the utility value associated with the task, but it does not guarantee that the task will be more interesting. Hidi (1990) described interesting information as "novel or unusual, has characters or life themes with which readers can identify, and/or involves high activity or intensity level" (p. 557). While we concede the difficulty of making every academic task extremely interesting to all students, we argue that it is possible for teachers to present the material in ways that might interest their students. Providing students with hands-on experiences or framing problems in interesting ways are two strategies likely to increase intrinsic motivation. For example, a particularly creative teacher in Delaware taught her students geometry during the World Cup Soccer tournament by illustrating how knowledge of angles helped soccer players be more effective.

With respect to the evaluation and recognition of student achievement, classroom practices that emphasize social comparison, especially as it relates to students' ability, frequently reduce the focus on mastery goals (Ames, 1992). For example, posting the top scorers or a grade distribution encourages social comparisons of ability. This shifts the focus from mastery to performance goals because how much students are learning becomes less important than how well they are doing compared to other students. While many teachers believe that a little "healthy competition" is helpful to students, there is evidence that these practices can be devastating to the child who consistently finds himself or herself at the bottom of the distribution (Covington, 1992). Children who constantly receive feedback that they have low ability come to believe that no matter how hard they try it will not make a difference. This can result in the helpless behavior pattern described earlier in this chapter.

Another aspect that relates to students' self-perceptions of ability is the way in which teachers attribute the causes of their students' successes and failures. Graham (1991) found that students make inferences about ability and effort based on the way the teacher responds to their failures. When teachers react with pity toward a student who fails, the student is likely to infer that the teacher believes that he or she has low ability. However, when a teacher reacts with frustration or anger, the student is likely to infer that the teacher is attributing the cause of failure to a lack of effort. These attributional inferences are important because ability (aptitude) is considered an internal, stable, uncontrollable cause while effort (temporary exertion) is considered to be an internal, unstable, controllable cause. Recall that these attributions are related to mastery and performance goals such that students with mastery goals are more likely to emphasize the importance of effort, while students with performance goals are more likely to emphasize the importance of ability. The role that teachers play is very important because if students come to believe that their success depends on how smart they are (ability attribution), they are more likely to adopt performance goals. But students who come to believe that the key to academic success is effort (effort attribution) are more likely to adopt mastery goals.

With respect to authority in the classroom, there is evidence that practices perceived as "controlling" by students tend to lower intrinsic motivation, while practices that promote student autonomy tend to increase intrinsic motivation (Ames, 1992). The reason for this is that students see themselves as "origins" when they have some control over what happens to them in the classroom but see themselves as "pawns" when a great deal of control is placed upon them (Deci et al., 1991). Whereas it is becoming clear that controlling strategies lower intrinsic motivation, recent research demonstrates that parents and teachers favor controlling classroom techniques to motivate children (Boggiano & Katz, 1991). One common use of a controlling strategy occurs when external rewards are used to control students' behavior. An example of this is when teachers say such things as, "If you complete your worksheets, you will be able to go to recess early." Many teachers (and parents) consider this technique to be effective because it does *seem* that the children are working hard to complete the task. The problem with these kinds of controlling strategies is that they tend to promote increased interest in the *reward* and decreased interest in the academic task (Boggiano & Katz, 1991). The reason for this, as noted earlier, is that engaging in the academic task becomes a means to an end. Thus, the children are doing their work not because they want to learn, but because it will lead to some external reward. Another problem is that rewards tend to increase motivation only as long as the possibility for additional rewards exists. When the rewards are not present, students often lack the motivation to engage in the task for its own sake. However, it is important to note that the detrimental effects of rewards are most pronounced when students are already intrinsically motivated. When students are not intrinsically motivated, rewards can have positive effects, especially when the rewards are used to convey information to the student (Cameron & Pierce, 1994). For example, verbal praise generally increases intrinsic motivation, especially when it provides specific information to students about their performance.

Alternative Actions

In this final section of the chapter, we offer suggestions that might promote mastery motivation in the classroom. We will again use the framework proposed by Ames (1992) to address some of the problems outlined in the previous section. We will conclude by summarizing the problems and alternative actions discussed in this and the previous section.

With respect to the nature of academic tasks, we believe that it is important for teachers to provide challenging tasks for students with different ability levels. This can be accomplished by designing activities with a *variety* of difficulty levels. For example, an assignment might have some problems that are relatively easy, some that are moderately difficult, and some that are quite difficult. Using this assignment, a teacher might say to students,

"Some of the problems at the end of this assignment are really hard, so don't worry if you can't solve them yet. You know how to do the problems at the beginning of the assignment, so practice on those first. Then just try some of the harder problems. You might just surprise yourself." The purpose of these kinds of assignments is to provide challenging problems to all students but also to make sure that students who are struggling do not feel bad if they are not immediately able to complete the more difficult problems.

To increase the utility value of academic tasks, we encourage teachers to think about the ways in which the information might be relevant to their students' lives. This can be done by first finding out about the students' interests and goals and then trying to incorporate them into the lesson. This approach is used in many whole language classrooms where children are encouraged to write about topics that are interesting and relevant (Oldfather, 1993). After writing and editing, children often spend the time to illustrate their story before it is "published," thus making their experiences in art class relevant to their interests as well. The whole language approach differs from more traditional approaches in which all of the children read and write about the same topics. The advantage to the whole language approach is that it increases students' utility value for reading and writing and also provides students with choices which increases intrinsic motivation (Lepper & Hodell, 1989).

To promote interest in the classroom, it is important that teachers make use of novel or unexpected tasks. This can be difficult because it requires not only a strong grasp of the content, but also creative thinking on the teacher's part about how to present the material in new and innovative ways. Despite the difficulty, we believe that thinking about how to make something interesting to students is fundamentally important in increasing intrinsic motivation. A classic example of the use of the unexpected is when a History teacher comes to class dressed as the person being discussed that day. The students do not expect this and therefore are intrigued by the novel approach. Of course, to simply dress and act as a famous historical figure does not guarantee students' learning. It is also important that the lesson be pedagogically sound such that the teacher conveys meaningful information about the historical figure.

We also recommend curtailing classroom practices that emphasize competition among students. As mentioned earlier, many teachers believe that competition will help motivate students. But the problem with competitive practices is that they highlight ability rather than effort (Covington, 1992). So students who have improved greatly, but who are still behind their classmates, will never receive the encouragement necessary to keep trying because they continue to see themselves at the bottom of the distribution. Rather than emphasizing how students compare with one another, we suggest the use of self-competition. With self-competition, students compete with themselves to see how much they have improved over their previous performance. This allows students to feel good about their academic gains, without the burden of being compared with other students. Self-competition is also much less likely to result in the pattern of learned helplessness discussed earlier in this chapter because the students understand that their effort, rather than their ability relative to other students, has resulted in their academic gains.

Another way to minimize the emphasis on competition among students is through the use of cooperative learning techniques. These techniques allow students of all ability levels to work together toward some common goal (Slavin, 1991). Cooperative learning also helps students focus on the effort needed to accomplish the goal and less on their ability relative to other students in the class.

In keeping with the importance of effort, it is also important that teachers emphasize that failures are due to lack of effort or ineffective strategy use. This reinforces an incremental rather than an entity view of intelligence. While we have discussed the importance of effort attributions, Weinstein, Hagen (Morrone), and Meyer (1991) argued that rather than suggesting to students that they should work harder, they should also be encouraged to "work smarter." This means that besides a lack of effort, another reason for academic failure is the use of ineffective learning strategies. The strategy attribution is especially important for students with learning disabilities (LD) because they are often working very hard and still having trouble in school (Borkowski, Carr, Rellinger, & Pressley, 1990). To continue to tell these students that they need to try even harder may cause them to give up and begin exhibiting the learned helplessness pattern of attributing failures to low ability. For these students, the importance of strategy use should be emphasized because attributing a failure to ineffective strategy use allows them to remain optimistic that with the right strategy they can be successful in the future.

As noted by Pintrich, Anderman, and Klobucar (1994), although many studies have shown that students with LD are more likely to exhibit learned helplessness, other studies have failed to show any differences between students with and without LD. For example, Pintrich et al. (1994) found no evidence of the learned helplessness pattern in students with LD. They also did not find any differences in the intrinsic motivation of students with and without LD. However, they did find that students with LD were more likely to attribute their successes and failures to external rather than internal causes. Because the students with LD who participated in this study spent a fair amount of time in a resource room, Pintrich et al. (1994) suggested that their external attributions may be due to the nature of the resource room in which they were given a great deal of help (an external attribution) from the special education teacher.

Finally, we believe that it is important to provide all students with opportunities to make choices in the classroom. This does not mean that students should be given the ability to do as they please, but rather that they be part of the decision-making process. For example, many classrooms have class rules that the students are expected to follow. Instead of the teacher giving these rules to the students, which is often perceived by students as controlling, it is better if teachers can allow the students to help come up with these rules (and also the consequences for not following these rules). Not only do the students feel more autonomous, they are also more likely to follow the rules if they helped establish them in the first place.

Summary

Table 3 provides a summary of some of the problems and alternative actions we have suggested together with some additional suggestions outlined by Brophy (1987).

Table 3 *Summary of Recommendations*

Problem	Alternative Action
Tasks not challenging to students	Provide assignments that have a range of difficulty levels. Allow students to respond actively. Provide timely feedback on students' responses. Include high-level questions in assignments.
Tasks not perceived as relevant	Design lessons that incorporate students' interests and goals. Design lessons that have a clear instructional purpose.
Tasks not perceived as interesting	Design lessons that are novel, unexpected, and reflect the interests of the students. Foster students' curiosity by posing interesting and/ or paradoxical questions.
Competition among students encouraged	Promote self-competition and make use of cooperative learning techniques. Incorporate game-like features into assignments.
Ability emphasized rather than effort	Attribute the cause of students' failures to a lack of effort or use of ineffective learning strategies. Provide appropriate strategy instruction as needed.
Controlling strategies used in classroom	Provide students with choices whenever possible to foster autonomy. Allow students to help establish class rules and procedures.

As reflected in Table 3 and throughout the chapter, we believe that it is important that teachers look for ways to increase the intrinsic motivation of children by shifting the emphasis away from practices such as the use of extrinsic rewards and competition among students. While such practices are prevalent in schools today, they are problematic in that they tend to shift the focus from mastery goals to performance goals. This often causes students to see engaging in academic tasks as a means to an end, rather than an end in itself. Therefore, we believe it is important that teachers and school psychologists look for ways to increase intrinsic motivation rather than continuing to rely on extrinsic rewards and competition to motivate children. While we acknowledge that this can sometimes be difficult to do, we believe it is critical to improving students' motivation for learning. It is our hope that we have highlighted some of the most important motivational problems facing schools right now and also provided you with helpful suggestions on how to begin solving some of these problems.

Recommended Resources

Ames, C. (1992). Classrooms: Goals, structures, and student motivation. *Journal of Educational Psychology, 84,* 261-271.
This article provides a synthesis of the research on achievement motivation and also discusses how the classroom environment might influence students' goals. The framework we discussed in this chapter is elaborated in more detail in this article, with an emphasis on instructional strategies that promote mastery goals in the classroom.

Brophy, J. (1987, October). Synthesis of research on strategies for motivating students to learn. *Educational Leadership, 45,* 40–48.
This article provides a highly readable synthesis of the research on strategies for motivating students to learn. The strategies include motivating students by promoting success expectations, motivating students through the use of extrinsic motivation, motivating students through the use of intrinsic motivation, and stimulating students' motivation for learning.

Hunter, M., & Barker, G. (1987, October). "If at first . . .": Attribution theory in the classroom. *Educational Leadership, 45,* 50–53.
This article provides a very readable overview of attribution theory applied to the classroom. Implications of attribution theory for both students and teachers are also discussed.

Pintrich, P. R., & Schunk, D. H. (1996). *Motivation in education: Theory, research, and applications.* Englewood Cliffs, NJ: Merrill/Prentice Hall.
This is a new textbook on motivation that reviews the major theories in motivation and also provides classroom applications of these theories. The book represents one of the most complete references on motivation in education.

Stipek, D. J. (1993). *Motivation to learn: From theory to practice.* (2nd ed.) Needham, MA: Allyn and Bacon.
This textbook does an excellent job of making motivation theories understandable. The classroom applications of these theories are particularly helpful, especially for elementary school teachers.

References

Ames, C. (1984). Achievement attributions and self-instructions under competitive and individualistic goal structures. *Journal of Educational Psychology, 76,* 478–487.

Ames, C. (1992). Classrooms: Goals, structures, and student motivation. *Journal of Educational Psychology, 84,* 261–271.

Ames, C., & Archer, J. (1988). Achievement goals in the classroom: Students' learning strategies and motivation processes. *Journal of Educational Psychology, 80,* 260–267.

Boggiano, A., & Katz, P. (1991). Maladaptive achievement patterns in students: The role of teachers' controlling strategies. *Journal of Social Issues, 47,* 35–51.

Borkowski, J. G., Carr, M., Rellinger, E., & Pressley, M. (1990). Self-regulated cognition: Interdependence of metacognition, attributions and self-esteem. In B. F. Jones & L. Idol (Eds.), *Dimensions of thinking and cognitive instruction* (pp. 54–92). Hillsdale, NJ: Lawrence Erlbaum Associates.

Brophy, J. (1987, October). Synthesis of research on strategies for motivating students to learn. *Educational Leadership, 45,* 40–48.

Cameron, J., & Pierce, W. D. (1994). Reinforcement, reward, and intrinsic motivation: A meta-analysis. *Review of Educational Research, 64,* 363–423.

Covington, M. V. (1992). *Making the grade: A self-worth perspective on motivation and school reform.* New York: Cambridge University Press.

Deci, E. L., Vallerand, R. J., Pelletier, L. G., & Ryan, R. M. (1991). Motivation and education: The self-determination perspective. *Educational Psychologist, 26,* 325–346.

Dweck, C. S. (1986). Motivational processes affecting learning. *American Psychologist, 41,* 1040–1048.

Dweck, C. S., & Elliott, E. S. (1983). Achievement motivation. In P. H. Mussen (Gen. Ed.) & E. M. Hetherington (Vol. Ed.), *Handbook of child psychology: Vol. IV. Socialization, personality, and social development* (pp. 643–691). New York: Wiley.

Dweck, C. S., & Leggett, E. L. (1988). A social-cognitive approach to motivation and personality. *Psychological Review, 95,* 256–273.

Eccles, J. (1983). Expectancies, values and academic behaviors. In J. T. Spence (Ed.), *Achievement and achievement motives: Psychological and sociological approaches* (pp. 75–146). San Francisco: W. H. Freeman.

Elliott, E. S., & Dweck, C. S. (1988). Goals: An approach to motivation and achievement. *Journal of Personality and Social Psychology, 54,* 5–12.

Graham, S. (1991). A review of attribution theory in achievement contexts. *Educational Psychology Review, 3,* 5–39.

Graham, S., & Golan, S. (1991). Motivational influences on cognition: Task involvement, ego involvement, and depth of information processing. *Journal of Educational Psychology, 83,* 187–194.

Harari, O., & Covington, M. V. (1981). Reactions to achievement behavior from a teacher and student perspective: A developmental analysis. *American Educational Research Journal, 18,* 15–28.

Harter, S. (1992). The relationship between perceived competence, affect, and motivational orientation within the classroom: Processes and patterns of change. In A. Boggiano & T. Pittman (Eds.), *Achievement and motivation: A social-developmental perspective* (pp. 77–114). New York: Cambridge University Press.

Hidi, S. (1990). Interest and its contribution as a mental resource for learning. *Review of Educational Research, 60,* 549–571.

Lepper, M. R., & Hodell, M. (1989). Intrinsic motivation in the classroom. In C. Ames & R. Ames (Eds.), *Research on motivation in education* (Vol. 3, pp. 73–105). San Diego, CA: Academic Press.

Maehr, M. L., & Midgley, C. (1991). Enhancing student motivation: A schoolwide approach. *Educational Psychologist, 26,* 399–427.

Nicholls, J. G. (1989). *The competitive ethos and democratic education.* Cambridge, MA: Harvard University Press.

Nicholls, J. G. (1990). What is ability and why are we mindful of it? A developmental perspective. In R. Sternberg & J. Kolligan (Eds.), *Competence considered* (pp. 11–40). New Haven, CT: Yale University Press.

Oldfather, P. (1993). What students say about motivating experiences in a whole language classroom. *Reading Teacher, 46,* 672–681.

Pintrich, P. R., Anderman, E. M., & Klobucar, C. (1994). Intraindividual differences in motivation and cognition in students with and without learning disabilities. *Journal of Learning Disabilities, 27,* 360–370.

Pintrich, P. R., & Schunk, D. H. (1996). *Motivation in education: Theory, research, and applications.* Englewood Cliffs, NJ: Merrill/Prentice Hall.

Slavin, R. E. (1991, February). Synthesis of research on cooperative learning. *Educational Leadership, 48,* 71–77.

Stipek, D. J. (1993). *Motivation to learn: From theory to practice* (2nd ed.) Needham, MA: Allyn and Bacon.

Weiner, B. (1986). *An attributional theory of achievement motivation and emotion.* New York: Springer-Verlag.

Weinstein, C. E., Hagen (Morrone), A. S., & Meyer, D. K. (April, 1991). Work smart . . . not hard: The effects of combining instruction in using strategies, goal using, and executive control on attributions and academic performance. In H. H. Marshall (Chair), *I can't because I don't know how: Links among and beyond attribution, strategy, and attribution to strategy.* Symposium conducted at the annual meeting of the American Educational Research Association, Chicago.

35

Reading

Kurtis S. Meredith
Jeannie L. Steele

University of Northern Iowa

Margaret M. Dawson

Center for Learning and Attention Disorders, Portsmouth, New Hampshire

Background

Discussion and research on reading, reading comprehension, reading to learn, literacy, and reading instruction have grown increasingly complex and at times confusing. It has become so in part because a full understanding of the cognitive and metacognitive processes involved in reading are elusive. But despite this complexity and confusion, it is essential that school psychologists have a grasp of the issues so that they can intervene when reading difficulties arise.

This is true for several reasons. First of all, as stated by Anderson, Hiebert, Scott and Wilkinson (1985, p. 1) in *Becoming a Nation of Readers,* "reading is a basic life skill. It is a cornerstone for a child's success in school and, indeed, throughout life. Without the ability to read well, opportunities for fulfillment and job success inevitably will be lost." With such an impact on one's life, many consider reading a basic human right. It is hard to imagine a skill that better exemplifies the purpose of schooling, particularly in the elementary years.

Secondly, school psychologists must be knowledgeable about reading processes and effective instruction because of the sheer numbers of students experiencing reading difficulties. Over 5 million students in the United States are served through special education and Title I. The latest government statistics showed a 4.2% increase in both populations in 1993–1994 compared to the previous year. Furthermore, the rate of growth in these programs exceeds the rate of growth of the number of children and youth enrolled in school. Over half of the students served in special education are learning disabled, and the vast majority of these experience reading problems (Meredith & Steele, 1985; Palinscar & Perry, 1995). It is estimated that almost 25% of 17-year-olds in school read below a level necessary to comprehend popular magazines (Slavin, 1989). These statistics speak

to the need to improve delivery of effective reading instruction and compensatory reading programs. They also demonstrate the need for all educators to be aware of fundamental issues of reading instruction and literacy development.

The good news from literacy research literature is that there is a developing consensus regarding effective instructional practices along with instructional models which show considerable promise for improving reading skills and overall literacy development. This does not mean that the disagreements regarding effective instruction have all been resolved. This debate has been joined not just by literacy theoreticians but by politicians, religious groups, and others outside the classroom. At the classroom level where instruction must occur every day, however, an instructional consensus appears to be evolving. Most classroom teachers blend the best elements drawn from a variety of instructional models. Their work is often guided by the basal readers acquired by their districts which in recent years have incorporated various theoretical stances into a single, coherent instructional text.

Further positive news is that several compensatory programs have been developed which show lasting remedial effects for students with reading delays who are identified early in elementary school. Two of the most widely used of these programs will be described in some detail later in this chapter.

Definition of Terms

A definition of terms may clarify some of the central issues of reading and literacy development. The definition of *reading* has received considerable attention yet remains a somewhat elusive term which varies with one's point of view toward reading. While some have described reading as the process of identifying words in print, most

397

now concede that a definition of reading must include the notion of comprehension, that is, the acquisition or construction by the reader of meaning from print. Reading comprehension is often viewed as the outcome of interactions among reader, text, and context. The act of comprehension is viewed as a constructive process, integrating meaning derived from text with the reader's own knowledge and experience.

Literacy has also proven difficult to define. While there is no single definition, the term generally refers to the interrelatedness of reading, writing, and oral communication and the mutual benefits of this interrelatedness to language learning. Most definitions make reading a central component of literacy development. In the broadest terms, "the concept of literacy involves a set of structures ranging from individual skills, abilities, and knowledge to social practices and functional competencies to ideological values and political goals" (Harris & Hodges, 1995, p. 140). More specifically, the aim of literacy development is to enable students to become lifelong active readers capable of independent engagement in literacy activities. By regarding literacy development as the primary outcome of instruction, reading is seen as a communication tool rather than an isolated subject. Reading then becomes one of four language tools—reading, writing, speaking, and listening—which enable students to access other literacies, such as computer and cultural literacy.

Specific instructional terms such as phonics-based instruction and whole language also require clarification. *Phonics,* or instruction which emphasizes the "systematic instruction of the relation of letter sounds to words" (Adams, 1990, p. 48), is code oriented and involves teaching sounds associated with individual letters and then blending the letters together to form words. Central to this approach is the teaching of the "alphabetic principle," or the concept that individual symbols (graphemes) are associated with individual sounds (phonemes) which can be combined in predictable ways to form syllables and words. Phonics then is "a way of teaching reading and spelling that stresses symbol-sound relationships, used especially in beginning instruction" (Harris & Hodges, 1995, p. 186). It is important to note that there are competing approaches to phonics instruction. For example, analytic or whole-word approaches first teach students sight words and phonic generalizations which are then applied to other words in a whole-to-part sequence. In contrast, synthetic-phonics approaches use a part-to-whole sequence, first teaching students the sounds represented by letters and letter combinations and then having them blend the sounds to create words.

Whole language is a broad concept incorporating a variety of approaches and philosophies. The implementation of whole-language programs depends on how schools or school districts define the concept. In its broadest sense, whole language encompasses beliefs

about all language learning and the context of that learning (Goodman, 1986). It is a philosophy about teaching and learning rather than a method, and it involves an abstract concept based mainly on beliefs and attitudes about learning and teaching (Cambourne, 1989).

The whole language philosophy translates into instruction in a variety of ways. Even the most respected researchers in the field of reading differ in their views of good whole-language teaching methodologies. Often misunderstandings arise as a result of an overemphasis on the application of whole language learning without a complete understanding of the theory. But while specific instructional practices may vary from class to class, whole-language teachers share a consensus of beliefs about language learning. Specifically, this involves students actively engaged in the process of learning. In such classrooms, teachers often integrate the child's prior knowledge and experiences with current instructional activities. They may also solicit input from students regarding instructional practices, materials, and topics to be covered. Texts include pieces by published authors as well as authentic texts written by students (Clay, 1972; Huck & Kuhn, 1968). Reading and writing are interwoven and integrated across the curriculum (Bergeron, 1990; Cambourne, 1988).

The Great Debate

Considerable tension has developed between avid proponents of whole-language instruction on the one hand and those who promote systematic phonics instruction as the single or central strategy taught. Beginning in the 1960s a debate has ensued in the United States over the efficacy of various reading instruction approaches. From the 1930s the predominant method of reading instruction was the "look-say" method (Liebling, 1994) in which sight words were emphasized over sound-symbol relationships. With the publication of *Why Johnny Can't Read* (Flesch, 1935) and *Learning to Read: The Great Debate* (Chall, 1967), a shift began as this approach was blamed for the failure of many children to become fluent readers. An emphasis on phonics was subsequently promoted. The debate continued and intensified with the emergence of whole-language instructional models in the 1980s. These models emerged as concern continued to grow, following National Assessment of Educational Progress (NAEP) reports regarding declining functional literacy rates and the steady decline of reading and writing performance of American school children.

While proponents of phonics-based instruction debate the best way to teach phonics, most maintain that learning to read requires, for most students, concentrated, "explicit" instruction in letter-sound correspondence to enable them to read unfamiliar words fluently. A central tenet is that reading instruction is hierarchical, systematic, and primarily teacher centered and teacher directed. Often phonics instruction relies on a drill-and-practice format where instruction in learning how to read receives primary emphasis until later elementary grades when emphasis shifts to reading to learn (Meredith & Steele, 1985).

Whole-language instruction occurs within the context of a literature-rich environment using predictable books, cooperative learning, paired reading, dictated stories, and the blending of writing with reading instruction. As discussed earlier, whole language classrooms vary depending upon philosophical orientation. While some proponents of whole language do not support explicit instruction in word analysis, others do. Explicit instruction in word-analysis skills, if included, is de-emphasized and integrated into a larger context which incorporates three language systems: graphophonemic (sound and symbol correspondence), syntactic (sentence patterns), and semantic (meanings; Goodman, 1986; Routman, 1988).

While there are many zealots at both extremes of this debate, many researchers and practitioners recognize that a reading program reaching the greatest number of students will incorporate the three primary language systems consistent with the specific needs of individual readers and within the context of a literature-rich environment. Stanovich (1993) notes that Chall has advocated that real literature and student writing be incorporated along with phonics into reading instruction. Many whole-language teachers recognize, as Stanovich suggests, that children who do not pick up the alphabetic principle through immersion in print and writing activities need explicit instruction in alphabetic coding. Furthermore, an extensive research base supports this stance (Adams, 1990).

The vast majority of teachers, however, are interested in application rather than theory, reflecting the urgency about what to do in the classroom tomorrow (Fountas & Hannigan, 1989). Consequently, there has been a resolution of the debate in the classroom where theory must yield to practice. What school psychologists will observe is that most classrooms make greater use of real literature either through the use of trade books or newer basal readers incorporating genuine literature rather than controlled vocabulary stories. These readers focus more on reading comprehension, higher level thinking, and metacognitive activities than previous basal readers. Newer basals typically incorporate explicit phonics instruction into the literature-based program and use the text as the source for this instruction rather than rely as heavily on workbooks or intensive drill or other decontextualized materials as in the past. In whole-language classrooms where teachers use whole books and stories rather than basal readers, teachers facilitate understanding of the language systems through structured interactions such as mini-lessons and individual conferences in the context of readers and writers workshops.

Developmental Aspects of Reading

Changes in the understanding of developing literacy have significantly altered what is done to facilitate children's movement toward fluent silent reading and conventional literacy. The foundation for learning to read is laid down in the home as soon as children are born. Substantial research reviewed in *Becoming a Nation of Readers* (Anderson et al., 1985) indicated that the type of interactions parents have with their children, their use of oral and written language, the knowledge base students develop through oral language, and the amount of reading in which parents and children engage, all determine how successfully children will learn to read. In fact, for young children "the single most important activity for building knowledge required for eventual success in reading is reading aloud to children." (Anderson et al., p. 25)

Viewing the development of literacy from the child's perspective has been a relatively recent focus of researchers. Teale and Sulzby (1989) used the term *emergent literacy* to describe a body of work relating to how reading and writing concepts and behaviors develop. The emergent literacy perspective looks at reading and writing development from the child's point of view, basing development on observations of what children actually do, examining changes over time in the strategies used and concepts developed by children in their journey toward maturity as readers and writers. The study of literacy development from the child's point of view provides important insights into learning to read and write. Strickland (1990, pp. 19–20) summarizes these understandings as follows:

- "Learning to read and write begins early in life and is ongoing.
- Learning to read and write are interrelated processes that develop in concert with oral language.
- Learning to read and write requires active participation in activities that have meaning in the child's daily life.
- Learning to read and write involves interaction with responsive others.
- Learning to read and write is particularly enhanced by shared book experiences."

School psychologists should be aware of instructional implications based on the emergent-literacy perspective. These implications include the basic principles of immersion in language; modeling practice in an encouraging, risk-free environment; and participation in communication activities that are functional and meaningful from the child's point of view. Classrooms and instruction based on emergent-literacy perspectives will provide print-rich environments where children engage in meaningful reading and writing experiences. Enjoyment and pleasure in reading and writing activities will be facilitated with the goal of developing positive attitudes for development of lifelong readers and writers.

Emerging literate children are discovering that meaning and experience can be derived from print. Reading and writing are linked, and children actively seek engagement in both activities. During the emergent-literacy stage, children gain knowledge of the layout of books, of the fact that both print and pictures are read, and of the general directional orientation of print from left to right and top to bottom (in English language text). Children begin to develop an understanding that writing has a beginning, middle, and end and that there are specific words and letters. They become aware that stories are meaningful, can be related to real experiences, and may be joyful or sad. Critical to mastering independent reading is the knowledge gained in this stage of the concept of word-in-print. This occurs when a child sees the white spaces between words and understands that the series of letters between the white spaces represents a discrete unit of meaning.

The next stage of reading development is characterized by children's abilities to transfer learned strategies to new books and reading experiences. Often this stage begins at the time of beginning reading instruction in school. These strategies include application of graphophonemic, syntactic, and semantic cues. Children learn the relationship between letters and sounds, recognize letter patterns, and blend letters to form words. Children cannot learn these skills until they have developed a concept of word-in-print, and premature efforts to teach graphophonics can be fruitless at the least or confusing at the worst. They also need to grasp the notion that words (both spoken and written) are made up of sounds, and until they are able to construct and deconstruct spoken words, phonics instruction is premature.

Children in this stage also begin to apply semantic, syntactic, and graphophonemic cues systematically to "crack the code." Children reflect on the meaning of what is being communicated in print, to understand words in print. Additionally, early readers use pictures to cue them to unknown words. Application of these strategies is typically variable in effectiveness, and generally students benefit from direct, explicit instruction in how and when to use them effectively.

The next stage of reading development is typified by rapid automaticity of the reading process. Readers are now more likely to engage in silent reading and apply various decoding strategies to decipher difficult text and unknown words. For many children, the transition from early reading to more automatic reading processes occurs during the early elementary grades. The time varies, however, with some students struggling to automate the reading process throughout elementary school.

The final stage in the development of fluent reading involves application of higher level metacognitive skills through which students carefully monitor comprehension, vary reading rate to accommodate text, and read more abstract material consistent with general cognitive development.

One area of confusion regarding the development of reading fluency has been the lack of a distinction between developmental processes and instructional sequencing. Several developmental models have been proposed which suggest that children first become familiar with books, then learn the code for reading. This knowledge is then applied through repeated practice until children have "learned to read." Once this has been accomplished children then can begin to "read to learn." Typically it is suggested this final stage begins around fourth grade. Substantial evidence contradicts this model and suggests that children engage in reading-to-learn activities from the very beginning of their exposure to print (Teale & Sulzby, 1989). Early readers have demonstrated the capacity to apply metacognitive strategies effectively to decode written text and to monitor comprehension. What has been proposed as a developmental model of sequencing learning-to-read followed by reading-to-learn is in reality not a developmental model based on human growth and development but simply an instructional sequence based upon mistaken beliefs about cognitive development.

Factors Contributing to Normal Growth and Development

The single most important factor contributing to successful acquisition of fluent silent reading is early and frequent exposure to oral and written language at a meaningful and purposeful level (Temple & Gillet, 1996). That is, young children exposed to a language-rich environment where books are read and discussed, where parents engage in meaningful dialog with their children, and where parents read and allow free and ready access to books will learn to read fluently and will read more frequently than children without these experiences. Adams (1990) estimates that in homes where parents have spent 30 to 45 minutes a day engaged in reading activities, children have accumulated 1,000 to 1,700 hours of reading experiences by the time they enter first grade. They may also have spent up to 1,000 hours watching "Sesame Street" and as many hours playing with magnetic letters, engaging in word games with parents and siblings, or using reading software on a home computer. Given that the average first grade teacher spends about 2 hours a day teaching reading, thereby exposing children over the course of the school year to 360 hours of reading instruction, it is apparent that the child who begins school with ample exposure to print and oral language will have a decided advantage compared to the child who has had little opportunity to read prior to the start of school (Adams, 1990).

Research also suggests that children exposed to a comprehensive reading program which provides a literature-rich environment and substantial opportunities for reading and writing as well as explicit and implicit instruction in decoding systems are more likely to become successful readers. Reading and writing develop best when children are reading meaningful literature and writing about meaningful events. As with emergent literacy, the single best way to improve reading ability is to read. Reading and writing are intimately connected. Readers who write become better readers and writers who read become better writers. It is through practice with both reading and writing and the belief that one is a reader and writer that children more easily approximate conventional reading and writing.

Finally, there is fairly conclusive evidence that phonemic awareness, or "the ability to identify, segment, and blend individual sounds within spoken words" (Liebling, 1994), is a strong predictor of first grade reading achievement. In fact Stanovich (1993) points out that measures of phonemic awareness are better predictors of early reading achievement than are measures of intelligence. While the connection between predictors of reading achievement and essential skills of reading achievement are not always direct, there is clear evidence that, for some children, implicit instruction in phonemic awareness is not sufficient and explicit instruction can enhance reading acquisition. However, early instruction in synthetic phonics before children have a concept of word-in-print can inhibit children's reading development and negatively impact on the goal of developing lifelong readers (Morris, 1981).

Problems and Implications

As the large numbers of children placed in compensatory programs indicate, not all children acquire fluent reading easily. The reasons for reading failure are many and varied. Some are extrinsic to the child (e.g., lack of sufficient exposure to literacy activities or poor instruction) while others relate to deficits in cognitive processes intrinsic to the child.

Stanovich (1986, 1991) has detailed those cognitive processes that appear to have the greatest impact on learning disabilities. Central to the reading difficulties of children he terms "dyslexic readers" are deficits in phonological processing. These readers "have difficulty making explicit reports about sound segments at the phoneme level, they display naming difficulties, their utilization of phonological codes in short-term memory is inefficient, and their categorical perception of certain phonemes may not be normal" (Stanovich, 1991, p. 156). This difficulty is a causal one; that is, children who have trouble with phonological processing subsequently have difficulty learning letter-to-sound correspondence. Furthermore, this affects the child's ability to gain reading speed and fluency.

Children who have difficulty learning to read tend to have smaller vocabularies than good readers and may have difficulty understanding complex syntax. Additionally, problems with verbal working memory impede comprehension because these students tend to forget what they have read earlier as the new information they are reading replaces previous reading (Jordan, 1994). Poor readers also frequently display a weak prior-knowledge base (Jordan). This hampers reading acquisition because children learn more easily and more fluently when what they are reading is related to information and knowledge they have already acquired.

Finally, poor readers are less likely to apply metacognitive strategies to the task of reading (Jordan, 1994). Metacognition refers to the ability to "think about thinking." Metacognitive strategies that good readers apply to reading include understanding the purpose of reading, modifying reading strategies and reading rates depending on task demands (e.g., skimming for main ideas versus reading slowly for details), and deciding how well material has been understood and applying strategies to cope with the failure to understand.

While these skills and cognitive processes are intrinsic to the child, there is an interaction between intrinsic and extrinsic variables which can have a particularly devastating effect on the acquisition of reading skills. Stanovich (1993) has referred to this as the "Matthew effect" (taken from the Gospel according to Matthew: "For unto every one that hath shall be given, and he shall have abundance; but from him that hath not shall be taken away even that which he hath" [XXV:29]). He notes that children who begin school with poor phonological awareness have difficulty learning the alphabetic principle. This in turn hinders their ability to recognize words. As word identification becomes a laborious process, this impedes reading comprehension. Reading without comprehension is unrewarding, thus children tend to avoid reading, which in turn means they fail to acquire the necessary practice in order for reading to become automatic, fluid, and enjoyable. This sets in motion a negative spiral which also has emotional ramifications as would be expected when a child encounters failure on a task considered central to the school experience.

Coincidentally, children who come to school with limited vocabularies due to limited exposure to oral and written language are less likely to understand and master phonics instruction. And if instruction focuses on phonemic awareness without also incorporating integrated literacy activities, these children will continue to lag behind their peers with respect to vocabulary development and reading interest.

Although it has been estimated (Slavin et al., 1989) that only 1% to 2% of the population has a learning disability or a mental disability so severe as to profoundly hinder the acquisition of reading, many more students are at risk for more minor reading problems. Using Stanovich's (1993) concept of the Matthew effect, this can lead not only to delayed acquisition of reading skills but to the need for compensatory services, special education, or ultimately to school failure and school leaving. It is imperative, therefore, that schools provide reading programs that are developmentally appropriate and effective for the vast majority of children and supplementary, more intensive programs for those children who need additional support.

Alternative Actions

Compensatory Reading Programs

Not all children learn to read fluently through developmental reading instruction alone but require additional support and targeted instruction. In recent years, a number of effective compensatory reading programs have been identified which can successfully remediate the vast majority of students who encounter difficulties learning to read. Pikulski (1994) recently reviewed a number of programs effective in combating reading failure and identified some common components:

1. Although pull-out models such as Reading Recovery (described later in this chapter) can be effective, whenever possible supplemental instruction should be coordinated with classroom instruction.
2. Children with reading problems should receive more reading instruction than students who learn to read easily. Although this appears self-evident, all too frequently remedial efforts simply replace classroom instruction without additional time for instruction and practice.
3. Instruction should be presented individually or in groups of four to five students at most.
4. Intervention programs should be targeted at the first grade level although some students will continue to need additional support in higher grades.
5. For young children, predictable texts are recommended. Some programs emphasize books with natural language patterns, while others use controlled vocabulary to reinforce specific word-identification skills. Research supports both approaches.
6. Repeated readings of the same text are beneficial to develop fluency.
7. Intervention programs should incorporate both phonemic-awareness training and phonics instruction.
8. There should be ongoing communication between home and school with daily reading activities taking place in the home.
9. The most effective intervention programs employ professionally trained teachers.

Effective compensatory programs place students in a literature-rich environment that is contextually relevant for the student. In this environment, teachers engage students in meaningful and extended dialog about relevant topics, and this dialog is related to students' reading and writing. Contextually relevant instruction integrates the student's remedial program with the general instructional program (Meredith & Steele, 1985).

What is perhaps most critical is that teachers, and eventually their students, come to understand what good readers do. Winograd (1984) identified a number of characteristics differentiating good from poor readers. He found that good readers better understand the goals of reading and apply the rules of reading more effectively. They are better at identifying the important elements of text and ways to use textural cues to identify important information. Good readers are better able to develop an internally meaningful representation of what is being read. They are also able to differentiate introductory and summary reading segments and to use them for comprehension and summarization. Poor readers are subject to serial position effect, summarizing more frequently information presented in the first part of the reading assignment, and utilizing subsequent information at a rapidly declining rate. Good readers also appear to be more organized and able to use more precise language to summarize materials read. They are more able to apply their own prior knowledge or "schema" to the information read, allowing greater personal understanding.

The work of Pearson and Fielding (1991), among others, describes good readers as purposeful, active, and thoughtful. They read to answer questions, to be entertained, and to learn. They are interested in what the writer has to say. While reading, the good reader actively applies relevant previous knowledge and develops an interest in what the writer has to say by engaging in prereading activity(s). When the reading assignment is completed, good readers think about what has been read and incorporate into experiences the new information, meanings, thoughts, and emotions elicited from the text.

Successful readers also take risks while reading (Steele, 1984). They will guess at words and make predictions regarding the writer's meanings and will read with an open mind, learning whether or not their predictions are accurate. They will vary reading rate of response to the level of difficulty of the text and their purpose for reading.

In summary, the good reader is absorbed in the reading process in an organized and intentional manner, and reads in order to learn from the written text.

Model Programs

In recent years, a fair number of remedial reading programs have been developed, many of which have good research support (see Pikulski, 1994; Wasik & Slavin,

1993, for descriptions of several). This section will focus on two which have a particularly strong track record and years of research support.

Reading Recovery

Brought to this country from New Zealand by Marie Clay, this program is widely used in schools throughout the country. It is built upon three major theoretical principles (Wasik & Slavin, 1993). First, reading is strategic, involving the coordination of a number of separate processes, including features of print (direction rules, space formats, and punctuation cues), letter-sound relationships, visual patterns, and the child's vocabulary and background knowledge. Secondly, reading and writing are integrally connected, and literacy development requires that the child grasp this concept. Third, children learn to read by having ample opportunities to practice reading in connected text.

Reading Recovery is a pull-out model. High-risk first graders are identified early in the school year and exposed to 12 to 15 weeks of daily 30-minute tutorial instruction individually tailored to the child's needs through daily, ongoing diagnostic assessment. The format of the daily tutorials are the same, although the content varies from child to child. It includes the following steps in a 30-minute lesson:

1. Reading easy stories read previously (stories the child can read with greater than 90% accuracy).
2. Reading a story independently from a book introduced the previous day.
3. Constructing a written message in the child's own writing book, during which time the teacher helps the child analyze sounds in words and construct words which cannot be spelled independently;
4. Reconstructing the written message after it has been transcribed on a strip and cut apart.
5. Introducing and talking about a new book carefully selected by the teacher to support the extension of the child's reading strategies.
6. Reading a new book with support from the teacher.

Reading Recovery has been shown to be effective with almost 75% of the students who participate in it (who are themselves in the bottom 20% of their class at the time they begin the program). Effects seem to be durable. Additionally, participation in Reading Recovery reduces the likelihood of retention and placement in special education. For a concise review of the research on Reading Recovery, see Wasik and Slavin (1993).

Success for All

Unlike Reading Recovery, which is a pull-out model, Success for All is a comprehensive school-wide literacy program designed for use in schools serving large numbers of disadvantaged children. Designed by Robert Slavin

and his colleagues at The Johns Hopkins University, components of the program include preschool and kindergarten programs, outreach to parents, and instruction in other basic skills in addition to offering individual tutoring by certified teachers for students in first through third grades who are delayed in learning to read (Wasik & Slavin, 1993). The instructional program combines reading in meaningful context with systematic phonics instruction. As with Reading Recovery, this program also views reading as a strategic process, with the strategies taught via a direct instruction model. Components of the program include having students read meaningful texts, direct phonics instruction with practice in texts with phonetically controlled vocabularies, an emphasis on the relationship between reading words and comprehension, and instruction in metacognitive strategies to assist in developing effective comprehension skills.

Unlike Reading Recovery, the tutoring component of Success for All is fully integrated with classroom instruction with the goal of ensuring that students are learning the skills and concepts being taught in the classroom. Tutoring takes place in daily 20-minute sessions, with assessment taking place every 8 weeks or so to determine whether more tutoring is necessary. Each tutor teaches a 90-minute reading class and spends the rest of the day tutoring three children each hour. Tutoring sessions are structured but flexible, with ongoing diagnostic assessment incorporated in the process. A tutoring session might begin with the students reading aloud a familiar story, followed by a drill on letter sounds. The major portion of the session is taken up with reading "shared stories" that complement stories they have read in the classroom. Listening, reading aloud, sounding out words, answering comprehension questions, and writing activities are all incorporated into the tutoring sessions.

Research conducted in disadvantaged schools where the program has been in place for 4 years provide strong support for Success for All, not only in improving reading scores but in reducing placement in special education and in virtually eliminating grade retentions.

Summary

Reading is a basic life skill forming the hub of school learning from kindergarten on. Despite national consensus that high literacy rates are essential to the economic success of this country and its citizens, such rates have yet to be achieved. Literacy programs are now being implemented which show considerable promise for improving overall literacy rates. Even as the political debate about reading rages, within many classrooms a consensus has been building regarding reading instruction which emphasizes a comprehensive instructional model. This model immerses students in meaningful literacy activities; provides explicit instruction, where needed, in the three basic coding processes of phonemic awareness and semantic and syntactic cues; regards reading as a tool for learning; and is based on a foundation of understanding of good reader characteristics and the goal of creating life long readers.

Compensatory reading programs require three components:

1. A prereading program which includes ample exposure to oral reading and prereading activities in the home as well as a kindergarten curriculum stressing a print-rich environment combined with instruction in phonemic awareness.
2. A developmental reading program which includes both systematic phonics instruction and extensive opportunities to engage in connected text reading with real literature.
3. Early and intensive intervention beginning in the first grade for those students at risk for reading failure.

In recent years, a number of compensatory reading programs have been developed for which there is strong research to support their efficacy. Two highlighted in this chapter are Reading Recovery, a short-term, intensive pull-out model of tutorial instruction designed for high-risk first graders, and Success for All, a comprehensive reading program in which well-designed classroom instruction is supplemented with daily tutorials for students who need it during the first 3 years of school.

Recommended Resources

Adams, M. J. (1990). *Beginning to read: Thinking and learning about print.* Cambridge, MA: MIT Press.
This is one of the most comprehensive reviews of reading research available. Written to resolve "the great debate," it not only consolidates the research to answer that question, it goes further to establish a relationship between thinking and learning as it applies to reading which gives the reader a clear understanding of the reading process. A summary version of this book is available from the Center for the Study of Reading at the University of Illinois at Urbana-Champaign. It should be noted that there exists some controversy surrounding this text within the literacy community but it can serve as a valuable resource.

Anderson, R. C., Hiebert, E. H., Scott, J. A., & Wilkinson, I. A. G. (Eds.). (1985). *Becoming a Nation of Readers: The Report of the Commission on Reading.* Washington, DC: National Institute of Education.
This brief text summarizes reading research across three broad areas—(a) studies of human cognition in the psychology of language, linguistics, child development, and behavioral science as they relate to reading processes; (b) environmental influences on reading acquisition; and (c) classroom practices, *especially studies of teaching as it impacts understanding of reading processes and instruction. This text also reviews reading processes, describing practices which have been shown to be effective while identifying those which are less effective but are consistently employed despite research support.*

Stanovich, K. E. (1986). Cognitive processes and the reading problems of learning-disabled children: Evaluating the assumption of specificity. In J. K. Torgeson & B. Y. L. Wong (Eds.), *Psychological and educational perspectives on learning disabilities* (pp. 87–131), Orlando, FL: Academic Press.
This book chapter provides a concise description of the body of reading research on the cognitive characteristics of students with reading disabilities. Stanovich is a leader in the field, and this article goes a long way toward debunking some of the myths regarding the nature of learning disabilities, while establishing the validity of other theories about the causes and effects of reading problems.

References

Adams, M. J. (1990). *Beginning to read: Thinking and learning about print,* Cambridge, MA: MIT Press.

Anderson, R. C., Hiebert, E. H., Scott, J. A., & Wilkinson, I. A. G. (1985). *Becoming a nation of readers: The report of the Commission on Reading,* Washington, DC: National Institute of Education.

Bergeron, B. S. (1990). What does the term whole language mean? Constructing a definition from the literature. *Journal of Reading Behavior, 22,* 301–329.

Cambourne, B. (1988). *The whole story: Natural learning and the acquisition of literacy in the classroom.* Auckland, New Zealand: Ashton Scholastic.

Chall, J. S. (1967). *Learning to read: The great debate.* New York: McGraw-Hill.

Clay, M. (1972). *Reading: The patterning of complex behavior.* Auckland, New Zealand: Heinemann.

Flesch, R. (1935). Developmental perspectives on reading disabilities. *Reading and Writing Quarterly: Overcoming Learning Difficulties, 10,* 297–311.

Fountas, I. C., & Hannigan, I. L. (1989). Making sense of whole language: The pursuit of informed teaching. *Childhood Education, 65,* 133–137.

Goodman, K. (1986). *What's whole in whole language?* Portsmouth, NH: Heinemann.

Harris, T., & Hodges, R. (1995). *The literacy dictionary: The vocabulary of reading and writing.* Newark, DE: International Reading Association.

Huck, C., & Kuhn, D. (1968). *Children's literature in the elementary classroom.* New York: Holt, Rinehart & Winston.

Jordan, N. C. (1994). Developmental perspectives on reading disabilities. *Reading and Writing Quarterly: Overcoming Learning Difficulties, 10,* 297–311.

Liebling, C. R. (1994). Beginning reading: Learning print-to-sound correspondences. In S. Brody (Ed.), *Teaching reading: Language, letters, and thought* (pp. 143–176). Milford, NH: LARC Publishing.

Meredith, K. S., & Steele, J. L. (1985). *The troubled reader: Access to intervention for the school psychologist.* Des

Moines: Iowa Department of Public Instruction.

Morris, D. (1981). Concept of word: A developmental phenomenon in the beginning reading and writing process. *Language Arts, 58,* 659–668.

Palinscar, A. S., & Perry, N. E. (1995). Developmental, cognitive, and sociocultural perspectives on assessing and instructing reading. *School Psychology Quarterly, 24,* 331–344.

Pearson, P. D., & Fielding, L. (1991). Comprehension instruction. In R. Barr, M. L. Kamil, P. Mosenthal, & P. D. Pearson (Eds.), *Handbook of Reading Research* (Vol. 2, pp. 815–860). White Plains, NY: Longman.

Pearson, P. D., & Johnson, P. D. (1979). *Teaching reading comprehension.* New York: Holt, Rinehart & Winston.

Pikulski, J. J. (1994). Preventing reading failure: A review of five effective programs. *The Reading Teacher, 48,* 30–39.

Routman, R. (1988). *Transition: From literature to literature.* Portsmouth, NH: Heinemann.

Slavin, R. E. (1989). Students at risk of school failure: The problem and its dimensions. In R. E. Slavin, N. L. Karweit, & N. A. Madden (Eds.) *Effective programs for students at risk* (pp. 3–19). Boston: Allyn and Bacon.

Slavin, R. E., Karweit, N. L., & Madden, N. A. (Eds.). (1989). *Effective programs for students at risk.* Boston: Allyn and Bacon.

Stanovich, K. E. (1986). Cognitive processes and the reading problems of learning-disabled children: Evaluating the assumption of specificity. In J. K. Torgeson & B. Y. L. Wong (Eds.), *Psychological and educational perspectives on learning disabilities* (pp. 87–131). Orlando, FL: Academic Press.

Stanovich, K. E. (1991). Reading disability: Assessment issues. In H. L. Swanson (Ed.), *Handbook on the assessment of learning disabilities: Theory, research and practice* (pp. 147–175). Austin, TX: Pro-Ed.

Stanovich, K. E. (1993). Romance and reality. *The Reading Teacher, 47,* 280–291.

Steele, J. L. (1985). Recall and comprehension: The interactive relationship of text and reader. Unpublished doctoral dissertation, University of Virginia, Charlottesville.

Strickland, D. S. (1990). Emergent literacy: How young children learn to read and write. *Educational Leadership, 47,* 18–23.

Teale, W., & Sulzby, E. (1989). Emergent literacy: New perspectives. In D. S. Strickland & L. M. Morrow (Eds.), *Emerging literacy: Young children learn to read and write* (pp. 1–15). Newark, DE: International Reading Association.

Temple, C., & Gillet, J. (1996). *Language and literacy: A lively approach.* New York: Harper Collins College Publishers.

Wasik, B. A., & Slavin, R. E. (1993). Preventing early reading failure with one-to-one tutoring: A review of five programs. *Reading Research Quarterly, 28,* 178–200.

Winograd, P. N. (1984). Strategic difficulties in summarizing texts. *Reading Research Quarterly, 19,* 404–425.

36

Study Skills

Maribeth Gettinger

University of Wisconsin-Madison

Molly Nicaise

University of Missouri-Columbia

Background and Development

Knowing how to study is a critical component in the learning process and essential for successful academic performance. For many learners, lack of success in school is associated with deficiencies in both their knowledge and application of effective study skills. Capable students at all grade levels may experience failure and frustration in school not because they lack ability but because they lack appropriate study strategies. Although the relationship between academic success and effective studying has been well documented, study skills are not taught directly in most classrooms (Scheid, 1993). Teachers often assume that students acquire basic study skills on their own. Some children, in fact, develop effective ways to study, often through trial and error, without having anyone teach them these skills directly. Many students, however, will never become proficient at studying without systematic instruction and repeated practice. Students referred to school psychologists for problems completing homework or poor test performance frequently lack the study skills necessary to succeed in regular classrooms. For example, research shows that low-achieving students use a restricted range of different strategies; can rarely explain why good study strategies are important for learning; and use the same, often ineffective, study approach for all learning tasks, regardless of the task content, structure, or expectations (Decker, Spector, & Shaw, 1992).

It is clear that deficits in knowing how to study and how to implement study skills pose substantial problems for many students. Research has shown that study skills are necessary for students to succeed in academic settings and that students can benefit greatly when a focus on study skills is incorporated into the teaching of academic content (Hoover, 1990). School psychologists may be called on to facilitate the development of classroom-based interventions for enhancing study skills, thus necessitating an understanding of the nature of study skills and ways to intervene when problems with studying occur.

There are several compelling reasons why educators should focus on study skills in classroom teaching. First, study skills are necessary for learning and retaining information. According to Devine (1987), study skills are the tools associated with critical components of learning, specifically "acquiring, recording, organizing, synthesizing, remembering, and using information and ideas found in school" (p. 5). Because these components apply to all learning, the ability to study effectively provides students the greatest chance for success with any learning task. Second, effective study skills offer students a means of enhancing their sense of personal control and self-efficacy. Students with good study skills experience feelings of competence and confidence as they learn. They are more likely to approach schoolwork with positive expectations and attitudes.

Finally, study skills are associated with basic "life skills" that are applicable to many activities outside of school, including work, athletics, and social situations. Through the use of effective study skills, individuals understand how to function in different situations and how best to acquire and retain important information. The goal of education is to maximize students' potential for learning, both during and after their formal schooling experience. Instruction not only helps students achieve their immediate learning goals but also prepares them to manage learning situations they will face after leaving school. Although the use of study skills usually occurs during school-related tasks, the development of study strategies contributes to individuals' continued growth as independent lifelong learners. In sum, study skills go well beyond helping students achieve success in a classroom; they help individuals function effectively in all environments, including academic, social, and vocational. Given the importance of study skills and the fact that learners may not acquire good study skills on their own (Hoover, 1990), the basic premise of this chapter is that greater attention should be given in classrooms at all grade levels toward helping students develop and maintain proficiency in study skills.

The issue of what should be considered in a definition of study skills is open to differences in interpretation. Current literature emphasizes the need for a definition that encompasses skill-based, organizational, and self-directed aspects of studying. Studying can be characterized in ways that distinguish it from other forms of learning (Hoover, 1990). First, studying is deliberate and effortful and usually must be self-instigated. For many learners, studying is performed in situations where alternative activities, such as watching TV or talking with peers, are distracting and more alluring. Studying is not incidental learning; it is purposeful and requires a deliberate and conscious effort on the part of the student. A second characteristic distinguishing studying from classroom learning is that studying is an isolated and individual activity. All learning is, to a certain extent, an individual activity; however, most classroom learning occurs within a social context with guidance or direction from others, such as peers or teachers. In contrast, studying is a highly personal, individualized, and autonomous process that occurs independent of others.

A third distinction is that studying has been described as a mixture of "skill and will." Studying requires not only the application of specific skills or competencies to learn information but also volition. Studying is as dependent on factors such as personal efficacy and motivation as it is on specific skills for processing and organizing information.

A final characteristic of studying is that it involves monitoring. When individuals study, they engage in a process of self-monitoring; they evaluate whether understanding is occurring and whether information is being remembered. In sum, studying can be distinguished from other forms of learning in several ways. Because of the unique characteristics of studying, individuals may be good learners but not good studiers.

Given these characteristics, what does it mean to have good study skills? *Study skills* is a broad term referring to a wide range of competencies that enhance the effectiveness and efficiency of students' learning. Researchers have come to view study skills as a complex phenomenon involving a number of coordinated cognitive skills and processes. A useful distinction has emerged in recent years to differentiate between a study tactic and a study strategy (Ellis, Deschler, Lenz, Schumaker, & Clark, 1991). A *study tactic* is a specific technique or skill such as underlining, note taking, outlining, summarizing, or self-questioning. A study tactic is often operationalized and taught through the specification of observable, isolated behaviors. For example, the steps for constructing an outline may be delineated by a teacher, taught systematically, and observed directly in students' work products. In teaching study skills, it is often as-

sumed that good studying means using specific tactics. However, researchers have produced no consistent empirical evidence that one tactic is any more effective than another (Ellis et al., 1991; Pressley, Goodchild, Fleet, Zajchowski, & Evans, 1990).

The application and effectiveness of a study tactic may be improved through the use of a study strategy. A *study strategy* is more than the use of a particular tactic. A strategy is a configuration of different tactics, deliberately selected by the learner for a specific purpose or a particular learning situation. A study strategy also has a metacognitive component; tactics become strategies when students demonstrate knowledge of where, when, and how to use them effectively. Study strategies are self-directed procedures used by students to complete learning tasks. Although a strategy requires knowledge of study skills, the focus is primarily on knowing how to study, on making decisions about the use of study tactics, and on taking responsibility for one's own learning. Good studiers are, in effect, good strategy users; they know how to use a variety of goal-specific tactics, to execute them in a planned sequence, and to monitor their use. In sum, study skills encompass a variety of tactics that are used both flexibly and purposefully by students in different learning situations. Good studying involves the ability to plan and control, to think and inquire, and to reflect and self-evaluate.

Research has shown that good studiers do not use one general study skill but rather choose from and use a collection of specific tactics in a purposeful way. Wade, Trathen, and Schraw (1990) identified six clusters of study strategies exhibited by students while engaged in studying an experimental text. The diversity of study tactics used and the purposefulness in using a particular tactic were the primary predictors of cluster membership. The six clusters or types of studiers included:

- "Good strategy user"—characterized by using the greatest diversity in tactics and being able to explain the purpose for using each different tactic.
- "Information organizer"—relying heavily on tactics aimed at highlighting and remembering main ideas, such as outlining.
- "Flexible reader"—using primarily reading study tactics such as rereading, adjusting reading rate, or skimming.
- "Text noter"—consistently using text-noting tactics including highlighting and focusing on chapter headings.
- "Mental integrator"—evidencing a high degree of self-questioning, self-checking, and other tactics involving active interaction with and integration of learning material.
- "Memorizer"—confining study tactics primarily to reviewing and rehearsing material or using mnemonic devices to learn the content. (Wade et al., 1990).

Diversity in the use of study tactics and being able to state a purpose for using a given tactic at a given time, rather than consistency in using a single tactic, were associated with effective studying (based on text recall). More important, Wade et al. (1990) found no relation between cluster membership and recall of the information presented in the experimental study text.

Thus, it appears that different collections of tactics exist among students, each reflecting different ways of studying the same materials under the same conditions. No study skill is appropriate for all students or for all academic tasks, and a number of strategies might be equally effective for learning and remembering information. Despite the flexibility and diversity of effective study skills, however, the development of effective study approaches may not occur among students without training. Instead, students may continue to use ineffective or inefficient techniques, such as passive rereading of material, as their primary study tool even when the method does not help them learn (Lenz, Ellis, & Scanlon, 1996).

Research has documented that success in most academic skill areas is often associated with effective study skills (Thomas & Rohwer, 1986). In the area of reading, for example, proficient readers have been shown to apply a variety of effective study skills that differentiate them from less successful readers. Specifically, successful readers are able to (a) assess the demands of different reading tasks and activities, (b) plan their reading approach, (c) allocate their attention appropriately to concentrate and focus on main ideas, and (c) monitor their comprehension through review and self-questioning (Scott, Wolking, Stoutimore, & Harris, 1990).

Study skills also have an effect on the quality of children's writing. Effective writers implement several study skills including (a) setting writing goals; (b) outlining or organizing related ideas into categories before they write; and (c) editing, reviewing, or asking themselves questions about what they wrote. Finally, study skills apply to mathematics performance as well. Students who are successful in math have a well-organized knowledge base and are able to assess the demands of math problems and to select appropriate problem-solving strategies and requisite computation facts (Harris & Pressley, 1991).

The importance of competence in study skills increases as students get older (Smith & Dowdy, 1989). As learners mature and advance in school, they face special challenges and expectations over and above academic content learning. In high school, students are expected to handle multiple courses (which are not as well integrated as elementary curriculum), to read dozens or hundreds of pages weekly, and to be skillful and motivated as studiers. In addition, organization and time-management skills are important components of effective studying for adolescent learners. For example, good studiers at the high school level typically have their own special routines for identifying and recording new terminology or information, and

they are less likely to study with distractions such as music or TV. When preparing to study, they organize necessary books, notes, and other related materials. They are also more proficient at organizing their time and are aware of their own strengths and weaknesses when approaching novel and challenging academic material (Jones, Slate, Blake, & Holifield, 1992).

In sum, students at all grade levels who have good study skills demonstrate an understanding of task demands and ability to implement flexible, effective strategies. In addition to knowing the steps associated with specific study tactics, good studiers understand why, how, and when to use them. Active learning is the essence of effective study skills. Good studiers are active learners, not passive recipients of facts and details as they study (Scheid, 1993). They have been characterized as "directors" of their own learning, able to determine what information is important and how to learn and retain information. As children develop cognitively, they tend to create their own strategies for learning and studying based on previous experiences (successes as well as failures) in school. Some students, however, do not develop their own strategies independently, and, consequently, their learning may be ineffective and disorganized. The implications of lacking good study skills for academic performance and general classroom learning can be significant.

Problems and Implications

Most study skills are needed when students are not under the direct guidance of a teacher, such as when completing independent homework assignments or preparing for tests. Consequently, study problems are generally ascribed to adolescents and older students. Problems with study skills, however, can be evidenced among elementary school children as well. Basic study deficits in elementary children often appear as weak study behaviors including poor attention, low persistence, or weak motivation (Henley, Ramsey, & Algozzine, 1996).

Beyond study habits and behaviors, study skills affect performance in academic skill areas as well. Inadequate study skills may be reflected in how learners approach reading, writing, and mathematics tasks. Poor readers, for example, display an array of problems with reading that, collectively, can be termed weak study skills. They typically do not monitor their own reading accuracy and understanding; they may not be aware of the purpose of reading; and they do not adjust their reading rate to match the demands of the reading task. Poor readers also show little evidence of study tactics such as skimming, looking back, or asking themselves about what they read (Scott et al., 1990). Poor writers, similarly, do little planning prior to writing. They tend to focus on organizing individual words rather than main ideas or the overall structure and seldom engage in reviewing, editing, or revising their written products. Finally, students with low success in math often do not organize information and fail to identify and select appropriate strategies to apply to a problem (Wong, 1992).

Many students with learning problems and many considered at risk for problems have not developed the study skills necessary for success in school, or they demonstrate weak and ineffective study skills (Gearheart, Weishahn, & Gearheart, 1992). Specifically, children with learning problems often assume a passive role in the learning process and may rely on external factors to regulate their own studying. Children with learning disabilities (LD), for example, do not exhibit an executive level of thinking in which they plan, evaluate, and develop approaches to studying and completing work (Wong, 1992). Their studying may be haphazard and not integrative in nature. Students with mild disabilities also experience problems with organization, which is important for success in the general education classroom (Gearheart et al., 1992). Particular areas of difficulty related to organization may include (a) keeping track of materials and assignments, (b) following directions, (c) completing class assignments, and (d) completing homework assignments.

When older students lack necessary study skills, they experience additional difficulty acquiring new information and understanding course material and often feel overwhelmed with the amount of material they are expected to learn. For example, high school students who have weak study skills rely heavily on passive study strategies such as rote memorization and rereading. They tend to memorize details to the exclusion of main ideas and do not establish goals or priorities when studying. When they do study, they study in long, infrequent sessions. Not surprisingly, they find studying to be unpleasant because they associate it with frustration and failure (Jones et al., 1992). The negative outcomes for older students who possess weak study skills are often significant. They may be forced to drop classes, receive failing grades, drop out of school, and ultimately not function successfully in a job.

In addition to deficits in study strategies, recent studies also report that high school students do not exhibit desirable study behaviors or habits (Shaw, Brinckerhoff, Kistler, & McGuire, 1991). Students with weak study skills do not evidence routine study habits or behaviors. They report that the purpose of studying is to remember material just long enough to take a test. A common strategy to prepare for an exam is to study alone the night before a test. In addition, students weak in study skills do not allocate sufficient time to study. When time is devoted to study, it is often interrupted by friends, daydreaming, music, or poor concentration. Finally, poor studiers lack self-regulation skills, do not monitor comprehension effectively, are not aware when a particular study skill is working or failing, and have few self-assessment or self-monitoring skills (Jones, Slate, Bell, & Saddler, 1991).

There are several explanations for why students may lack the strategies necessary for effective studying and independent learning. In some cases, students have not been taught good study strategies and do not have a repertoire of well-developed study skills. In other cases, there may be deficiencies in students' existing study strategies (Jones et al., 1992). Although students are expected to acquire study and test-taking skills during their school experience, these strategies are seldom taught systematically. Frequently, teachers may assume that students already have mastered them.

Another reason for poor studying is poor motivation. When confronted with competing goals or outside pressures, students may elect to engage in activities other than schoolwork. Also, environmental or instructional practices may inadvertently contribute to low motivation (Adams & Hamm, 1994). For example, because traditional instruction is primarily adult centered, with teachers, parents, and administrators defining learning objectives and methods, students may not gain experience in being self-directed and setting individual learning goals. As a result, students become overreliant on the structure imposed by teachers.

Finally, difficulty with studying may not be due to a lack of knowledge of effective strategies but rather to an inability to self-select and self-regulate their use. According to Resnick and Klopfer (1989), few high school students are able to regulate their own study strategies because they are "victims" of blind training or instruction. Blind training occurs when teachers fail to explain the when, where, how, or why in using a new strategy. Students, for example, may be able to recite the steps of a previewing procedure but do not know when to apply it, how to modify it for different tasks or content areas, or why it is even important to their own learning. In sum, the problem with many students who have poor study skills often lies with the lack of or type of training they have received, thus underscoring the need for preparing teachers to place greater emphasis on study skills (Lenz & Deshler, 1990).

Teachers may be either unaware that study skills must be taught to students or unfamiliar with how to teach these kind of skills. One way to determine if students need to improve their study skills is to ask them questions about their study habits and strategies or observe work samples and other evidence of study skills. Henley et al. (1996) recommended using a checklist for this purpose. Although informal inventories are available for assessing study skills (see Gettinger & Knopik, 1987), school psychologists are more likely to help teachers develop checklists that assess study skills important for successful performance in their specific classrooms. Because students must be aware of and responsible for their own study patterns, checklists or questionnaires may be completed at multiple times during the school year by students themselves (see example in Table 1). The objective of self-analysis is to provide information to students about their study skills and general classroom behavior so that students and teachers together can develop a plan of specific strategies to enhance skills. A necessary prerequisite for enhancing study skills is self-analysis; students must identify both effective and ineffective study behaviors and assume some responsibility for modifying their own study strategies (Jones et al., 1991).

Alternative Actions

There are many ways and resources available concerning how educators can train students to develop and regulate study strategies. Certainly, one way to increase student motivation and self-regulation is to reconstruct classrooms to be more student centered. Bringing about change in instructional environments through consultation and professional development activities may be the most critical role for school psychologists in enhancing the development of effective study skills among learners (Lenz & Deshler, 1990). Study skills training should be developed within an active, problem-solving framework (Adams & Hamm, 1994; Byrnes, 1996). Recent approaches have combined cognitive research on self-regulation and metacognition with strategic skill building (Harris & Pressley, 1991). In these combined approaches, students are made aware of cognitive learning strategies and practice using them during their regular classroom instruction and study periods. Effective study skills instruction incorporates three critical components:

- Simplification of the strategy so that the basic steps are explicit, justified, and amenable to individualization.
- Frequent modeling or demonstration of the learning strategy.
- Guided instruction, practice, and feedback to help students move from teacher-dependence to self-dependence in judging a strategy's utility and effectiveness.

The following paragraphs provide a summary of several alternative actions for promoting good study skills. These approaches are predicated on the assumption that study skills have a significant effect on students' school performance and can be taught at all ages and ability levels.

Table 1   *Self-Analysis of Study Skills*

	Almost Always	Some-times	Very Seldom
1. Do I understand directions provided in class?	_____	_____	_____
2. Do I take notes that are helpful?	_____	_____	_____
3. Do I ask questions when I don't understand?	_____	_____	_____
4. Do I understand lectures and discussions?	_____	_____	_____
5. Do I keep up with assigned work?	_____	_____	_____
6. Do I feel disorganized most of the time?	_____	_____	_____
7. Do I participate in class discussions?	_____	_____	_____
8. Do I find it difficult to complete assignments?	_____	_____	_____
9. Do I feel adequately prepared most of the time?	_____	_____	_____
10. Do I find vocabulary in reading too difficult?	_____	_____	_____
11. Do I have a regular place where I study?	_____	_____	_____
12. Do I have a regular time to study?	_____	_____	_____
13. Do I outline or summarize what I read?	_____	_____	_____
14. Do I keep a calendar of tests and assignments?	_____	_____	_____
15. Do I review class and reading notes regularly?	_____	_____	_____

When school psychologists are asked to consult with classroom teachers or parents about a student's study skill deficits, there are several different study approaches to consider for intervention. Although tactics may reflect different ways of studying material, the outcomes or benefits across methods are usually similar. In fact, research has failed to document consistent benefits of one study tactic over another (Pressley et al., 1990). The most critical issue related to effectiveness is how well students use any given approach to acquire and retain information, not the particular study method they use. Rather than requiring students to learn and use a specific study tactic, teachers should be advised to encourage students to consider the range of different learning strategies available, the reasons these strategies are useful, and ways to employ each strategy most effectively.

Any study tactic is beneficial if it enables students to process, organize, and retain relevant information in effective and efficient ways. Routine or rote application of a study technique does not ensure effective studying. Note taking is a good example. Students use a note taking tactic in several different ways. Some students routinely copy parts of a text verbatim and process information only superficially; others use their own words when they take notes or write notes that elaborate on the text and promote a deeper processing of information. Some students may take notes randomly; others may take notes strategically, selecting information that is important, relevant, or worthy of extra processing. How students take notes and what they do with a note-taking tactic affect how successful their studying will be, not the activity of note taking itself. Students need training or direction in how to use a technique effectively and to employ one that best fits the task they are studying. As with note taking, students can apply all study techniques with varying degrees of success and effectiveness. Rather than developing separate courses or using published instructional packages, the best context for enhancing study skills is the regular classroom content and curriculum. The following sections focus briefly on organization and individual study tactics before focusing in greater detail on cognitive strategy training and instruction that can be incorporated into classroom learning.

Organization

Lack of organization is a common deficit among students with poor study skills (Swanson & Keogh, 1990). Although students may demonstrate an understanding of good organizational skills, many do not have the motivation or self-discipline to use them. Several competencies underlie the development of good organization, including time management, material organization, and development of routines.

A typical problem for students with organizational deficits is the inability to structure their study time and to adapt their schedules to provide sufficient time for studying and work completion. Even students in elementary grades can be helped by teachers or parents to plan and organize their study time. A time-use chart, for example, enables students to "see" how their time is spent each week and to look for ways to build in sufficient study time (Archambeault, 1992). A personal organizational plan for studying should be constructed by students on several levels, including monthly (focusing on exams and long-term assignments), weekly (listing weekly goals and designated times for completion and review), and daily (identifying optimal and realistic study periods within a day and allocating time for breaks). After constructing a detailed daily schedule to organize study time and developing a list of all work to be accomplished in the day, students can convert their list into a plan of action following several guidelines:

1. Schedule challenging tasks during times when you are typically most alert and least distracted.
2. Save routine tasks for times when you may be more tired or most distracted.
3. Divide long assignments into shorter, more manageable units.
4. Spend minimal time on rote memorization of information (5 to 15 minutes).
5. Vary the type of study tasks (e.g., intersperse reading, writing, or artistic activities).
6. Be flexible to include periodic study breaks and to reschedule study time if conflicts arise.

Individual Study Tactics

Most students have difficulty generalizing a study tactic taught in isolation. Therefore, it is important to teach study techniques in conjunction with academic content and within the regular classroom. Skills such as note taking, outlining, summarizing, or self-questioning can be incorporated into daily instruction (Jones et al., 1991). Systematic efforts to teach study tactics should introduce simple variations of study skills in elementary grades and gradually increase to more complex variations as students progress through school. Training in any study tactic should highlight several key points for students, including (a) the importance of understanding the nature and expectations of the study task; (b) knowing why, when, and how to use a particular study strategy; (c) the need for continued practice, refinement, and personalization of an acquired study skill; and (d) knowing how to monitor or evaluate the usefulness and effectiveness of their study methods.

Cognitive Study Strategies

The most comprehensive approach to study skills training at all grade levels stems from an information-processing model. Within this model, the development of study skills is conceptualized as strengthening cognitive processes across many, human information-processing systems. Typically, four information-processing components are targeted for strategic study-skills training. These include (a) improving background knowledge, (b) developing schemata, (c) increasing metacognition, and (d) implementing expert learning control processes (learning skills). Although each component is thought to function somewhat independently, collectively, they provide the foundation for the development of effective and efficient learning and study techniques. Furthermore, each is thought to be environmentally influenced, such that students can be taught to convert their weak study skills into strategic ones (Harris & Pressley, 1991).

Building background knowledge

The greater knowledge students have about a specific topic or task, the more likely they are to understand it, learn from it, and use it. Thus, students need to develop sufficient background knowledge. They may do this individually or in groups by writing down all facts related to a topic they already know or any information they have acquired through listening or reading material on the topic. For example, students may review chapter summaries, classroom notes, and vocabulary lists to accrue background knowledge prior to studying. An effective technique is to write on individual index cards all key concepts, facts, terms, or principles associated with the topic. To monitor and evaluate background knowledge while studying, students should sort through their cards to check if they can identify facts and other important background information. In group study, students exchange index cards with friends or classmates to test their knowledge further, thus incorporating self-evaluation.

When terms, concepts, or important principles are unfamiliar or when students are unable to identify critical facts, their background knowledge base is likely to be insufficient for studying a topic. In this instance, additional background information must be obtained, for example, by locating and reading library resources such as magazines, newspapers, or technical articles that provide a detailed overview of related topics and concepts. Library usage skills, thus, are critical for enabling students to enrich their background knowledge for effective study. Teachers can help students acquire library skills by (a) emphasizing the use and importance of library materials for effective studying, (b) providing direct instruction and practice in the use of library resources and staff, and (c) creating instructional tasks that require students to use reference materials to develop appropriate background knowledge.

In addition to assembling background knowledge about topics, students need to compile facts associated with the task itself (paper, test, or project). This component of studying is often referred to as developing appro-

priate test-taking skills (Scruggs & Mastropieri, 1992). It includes understanding the essential details surrounding a task, such as knowing the number and type of questions that will be on an exam or understanding the criteria that will be used to evaluate a project or paper. Meeting with teachers and asking them about the style, format, and content of an exam or requesting specific evaluation criteria beforehand will assist students in collecting important background information.

In sum, it is important that students are taught how to collect sufficient background knowledge related to the content under study. This includes obtaining facts about the nature of the task and what is necessary to succeed. Students can use background knowledge to create a comprehensive understanding and context for seemingly discrete pieces of information. By assembling small pieces of information and relating them to a larger framework, students are developing powerful schemata for studying and acquiring new information.

Developing schemata

Similar to background knowledge, the extent to which learners' schemata are developed can make a significant difference in how effective their studying will be. Schema theory suggests that information is stored in long-term memory in networks of connected facts and concepts. Information that fits into an existing schema is more easily understood, learned, and retained than information that does not fit. It follows that good studying requires students to (a) relate and connect new ideas, information, or concepts to what they already know (background knowledge) or (b) develop a novel and effective schema to accommodate the content to be learned (Thomas & Rohwer, 1986).

To assist in the development of a new schema, students can implement a strategy called semantic or concept mapping (Novak & Gowin, 1984; Scanlon, Duran, Reyes, & Gallego, 1991). Mapping is a method to develop new schemata, to organize information, and to add or integrate new information into previous knowledge. Typically, a map contains a hierarchical diagram or arrangement of people, places, concepts, ideas, and facts concerning a subject. Concept maps often resemble a wheel surrounded by spokes of interrelated ideas. Maps can be enhanced by adding photographs and pictures as examples and elaborations. To make a concept map, students collect note cards they developed and used for building background knowledge and try to arrange the cards in a systematic fashion. In the process of arranging, students connect cards related to each other and describe in detail the relationship between or among cards. As their knowledge of content expands, students arrange and rearrange individual cards into meaningful and holistic diagrams. At this stage, not only can concept mapping assist in schema development, it can also serve as a form of self-assessment. When students have difficulty making a map, they are made aware that requisite background knowledge is not sufficiently developed. Students can also use their maps for self-assessment by comparing their maps to those developed by classmates, teachers, or other "experts." If discrepancies exist among different concept maps for the same topic, students can try to resolve differences through small-group discussions.

In addition to concept mapping, cooperative-learning and group-learning activities are important for schema development and, therefore, represent a critical study strategy. Studying in groups helps students to construct hypotheses and test them against reality. Moreover, cooperative grouping enables students to view knowledge and information from multiple perspectives. Conceptual growth occurs when students and teachers share different viewpoints and when understandings change in response to new perspectives and experiences. If students have difficulty working in cooperative groups, they can still use group-study techniques such as rehearsing study materials aloud or teaching content to other students. Both rehearsal and peer-tutoring strategies rely on verbalizations and help learners with limited strategic behavior to learn the material (Byrnes, 1996). Similar to concept mapping, peer tutoring and cooperative learning outcomes also serve as self-assessment. If students cannot teach another person, then their background knowledge and schemata are insufficiently developed. They will need to collect additional facts and reconstruct concept maps to improve their understanding.

It is also important to activate previously developed schemata and background knowledge when studying a new or related topic. Analogous to opening a file on a computer, students can promote studying by thinking about a topic prior to initiating a specific study strategy. For example, the following types of questions may assist in "warming up" a student's thinking: "What do I already know about this topic? How does this chapter relate to the previous chapter and to in-class discussion? How does this assignment relate to what we are supposed to do next in class?"

Another way to activate existing schemata and background knowledge is previewing. Previewing helps students develop an awareness about topics to be covered in a text, thus facilitating assimilation of new information. Students can use several types of questions to preview content: "What is this chapter about? Do I know anything about this topic? How does it relate to what was said during class? Based on this subheading, can I predict what is likely to come next in the chapter?"

Training in metacognition

Another way to facilitate studying is to help students develop their metacognitive skills or awareness concerning their own thinking processes and self-regulatory mechanisms. Metacognitive processes, such as knowing how and when to use a specific study strategy, being able to

detect problems in comprehending materials, or establishing realistic study goals, help individuals regulate their learning (Palincsar & Brown, 1989). Skilled studiers possess many metacognitive skills including being able to modify or generate an alternative strategy when the current strategy fails, engaging in self-monitoring of comprehension, knowing how to deal with frustration when failure occurs, knowing how to retrieve and add to existing information, and being able to evaluate performance (Scheid, 1993). Good studiers are especially aware of task demands and the requirements for completing or succeeding on school tasks; they also know when they have succeeded or failed. Furthermore, when task failure occurs, they have a repertoire of alternative actions to overcome the failure. Given these metacognitive strengths of good studiers, several techniques have been developed to assist less skilled studiers to learn and implement skills related to metacognition and self-regulation (Harris & Pressley, 1991).

Components of self-regulation are often incorporated into traditional study skills training approaches. These procedures include the techniques of scheduling, time management, self-rewarding, and increasing academic engaged time. Current approaches also incorporate procedures related to managing anxiety and monitoring comprehension. To illustrate, several metacognitive experts have identified important affective components of self-regulation. In study skills training, concentration may be hindered by debilitative or interfering emotional states such as performance anxiety. Maladaptive emotional states are often maintained through negative cognitive appraisals. Examples include "I'll never be able to remember this for the exam. I'll fail this course. I feel stupid. This comes easy to most people—why not me?" Therefore, interventions designed to control negative affect and self-talk fall within the area of metacognitive control and are often an imperative intervention focus for study skills training (Ellis et al., 1991).

To improve their affect related to studying, students first need to be informed that most individuals who experience consistent failure in school eventually begin to question their own abilities, self-confidence, and self-worth. Students who have academic difficulty are more likely to have low self-esteem, attribute their failures to a lack of ability as opposed to a lack of effort, and hold inaccurate perceptions of their true talents (Henley et al., 1996). After developing an awareness of their study and learning habits and the nature of their perceptions, students with debilitative self-talk often require cognitive training. They need to be told that negative thoughts make it impossible to study. Subsequently, students must question and challenge their negative thoughts and convert negative appraisals into positive and coping statements such as "I don't have an ability problem, I just lack effective study skills. If others have used these study strategies, then they may work for me too." Likewise, students should be trained to emit statements that help them focus on the study task, such as "Instead of talking badly to myself, I will survey the chapter headings to get a better picture of the topic and to develop expectations of what I'll be reading. One strategy I can use to better understand this is to summarize what I have just read. This seems to be an important concept; I'll write it down and add it to my concept map." After students develop a repertoire of positive or strategy-guiding self-statements, they should practice and rehearse them before, during, and after each study session and in the context of authentic study activities or classroom tasks.

Another metacognitive aspect of study skills is self-monitoring of goal completion and material comprehension. Comprehension-monitoring techniques, such as using concept maps, generating exam questions, engaging in self-questioning, or taking practice exams, enable students to check their own comprehension. If, for example, students are not able to generate an appropriate exam question, then comprehension has likely not occurred. Overall, metacognitive skills are necessary for enhancing effective study skills but are not sufficient in themselves as study strategies without the student's ability to implement effective study skills. Clearly, it is important to teach students how to monitor their own comprehension; students must be aware of problems in their studying and know when studying is not successful. If students do not know how to implement effective study techniques, however, they will have no strategy in their repertoire to rectify the problem. The next section, therefore, describes additional ways students can become stronger studiers.

Implementing effective learning strategies

Many of the strategies already described, such as concept mapping, surveying headings, and comprehension monitoring, are considered "learning strategies" (see Learning Strategies, this volume). This final section summarizes additional strategies that make learning more strategic and studying more effective. One obvious way to improve students' study skills, consistent with information-processing theory, is to train students how to use memory strategies (Mastropieri & Scruggs, 1991). The use of mnemonics has a long history in study skills training and includes teaching students how to use the key-word, loci, or initial-letter methods.

In addition to improving memory skills, cognitive psychologists advocate training in both goal setting and strategy planning. Educators have long recognized the role of goal setting in academic achievement. Not only does the process of setting goals help to maximize and organize study time, it also assists students in making the content personally relevant and meaningful. To help students develop these skills, they can be trained to ask themselves several questions prior to studying: "Why is it important to learn this? How can I relate this to my own life? What do I want to accomplish in this study session?

What specifically am I hoping to learn from reading this chapter? How long should I plan to spend studying? What benefits will I receive if I stick to my goal? Are there any possible or foreseeable distractions? How will I plan to manage these distractions?"

An important part of goal setting is that students record whether the goal was attained and think about what may have facilitated or posed a barrier to their goal completion. They may accomplish this by using a questionnaire similar to the one presented in Table 2. In addition to setting academic goals, students should identify and develop a plan of study strategies they will use to obtain their goals. Proactive strategic planning reminds students of the diversity of study skills they can use and encourages them to rely on alternative strategies when current approaches are not working.

Key Principles for School Psychologists

Research on teaching study strategies, particularly to students with mild disabilities, has been ongoing since the 1970s (Wong, 1992). Some school districts are so convinced of the need to teach study skills systematically that they have initiated system-wide programs as part of efforts to include students with special learning needs in regular education classrooms (Wong, 1994). Unfortunately, the translation of research into effective classroom-based practices has been limited. A critical role for school psychologists is to maximize the success of efforts to enhance study skills by encouraging several alternative actions. Two key principles derived from research on improving study skills are important to keep in mind.

First, students must recognize the need for varied approaches in studying. For example, students should understand that the most effective strategy for studying spelling words is different from the most effective one for studying for a history test and that any single study tactic will likely require some modification. In developing an awareness of different strategies, students should be asked to explain the appropriateness of a particular study strategy for different tasks.

Second, the key to effective study-strategy training is to help students guide their own thinking, organizing, and study behaviors. Effective study-strategy instruction helps children to develop strategies that work for them. Students should not be told or taught precise steps in developing a strategy (which is typically the focus of instructional packages for study skills training). Instead, they should be involved actively in developing their own personalized study strategies. This development facilitates internalization of strategies, involves students as self-governing learners, and enhances generalization to other study situations. Because students should understand the benefit of using diverse approaches to studying, information concerning alternative strategies and their effectiveness should also be stressed.

Table 2   *Self-Monitoring of Goal Attainment*

1. What was my study goal?

_____

2. Did I achieve my goal?   _____ yes   _____ no

3. How much time did I devote to this study goal? _____

4. How much of this devoted time did I spend actually engaged in study?

   10%   20%   30%   40%   50%   60%   70%   80%   90%   100%

5. Which types of distractions did I encounter?

_____

6. What was my plan for dealing with distractions?

_____

7. Did the plan work?   _____ yes   _____ no

8. What will I do differently next time?

_____

9. What is my new study goal?

_____

10. What is my new study plan?

_____

Summary

Study skills are as fundamental to school success as other academic skills taught in school. Furthermore, the principles and methods for effective study can be built into most school learning. The best content to use for training study skills includes the materials and texts that students encounter regularly in their schoolwork. Study skills are important for elementary as well as secondary students. Therefore, study strategies should be developed and reinforced during the elementary grades and applied continually as students progress through school. Study skills are of sufficient importance for academic success that they deserve attention from teachers and school psychologists alike. School psychologists can assist directly in the enhancement of study skills at all grade levels by helping teachers incorporate the guidelines and methods discussed in this chapter into the activities, assignments, and tasks already in classroom use.

In recent decades, much has been learned about the process of effective learning and study. It is generally accepted that studying is a complex process and requires active engagement. Recent developments related to intervention and training in study skills focus on equipping students with active strategies that direct learners to build their background knowledge and to acquire and practice specific expert strategies including previewing, goal setting, concept mapping, and self-monitoring. Furthermore, information-processing theory emphasizes training students how to study in groups and how to identify and understand the role of cognitive appraisal in studying.

Although much of this chapter has emphasized what students can do to improve their own study and learning strategies, there are several things teachers can be encouraged to do to foster successful studying among students. For example, educators can structure their learning environments to encourage student-regulated and student-guided learning. Likewise, they can provide students with inherently meaningful and authentic learning activities and with collaborative, hands-on learning opportunities. School psychologists have a responsibility to collaborate with schools, parents, and teachers in fostering effective study skills and creating effective study environments. Problems with studying can contribute to academic failure and inability to profit from even the most optimal instruction. Therefore, study skills represent a critical need for all school children and an important area for school psychological services.

Recommended Resources

Decker, K., Spector, S., & Shaw, S. (1992). Teaching study skills to students with mild handicaps: The role of the classroom teacher. *The Clearing House, 65,* 280–284.
This short, concise, and very readable summary of specific study tactics is designed to enhance study behavior among students with mild disabilities. The tactics described in this article are more organizational in nature than strategic and include suggestions for material organization and time management. Nonetheless, there is some attention given to the importance of self-regulation and self-awareness.

Hoover, J. J. (1990). *Using study skills and learning strategies in the classroom.* Lindale, TX: Hamilton Publications.
This book was written for teachers of general or special education students in elementary or secondary schools. It includes relevant information, guidelines, checklists, and sample materials to facilitate the incorporation of ongoing and effective study skills instruction into regular instruction.

Nowak, J. D., & Gowin, D. B. (1984). *Learning how to learn.* New York: Cambridge University Press.
Joseph Nowak was one of the originators of concept mapping. Details about creating, presenting, and evaluating concept maps are included in this book. The authors describe in detail how concept mapping lends itself to a variety of uses, for example, as a teacher assessment tool, for student self-assessment, and as an instructional aid.

Scheid, K. (1993). *Helping students become strategic learners: Guidelines for teaching.* Cambridge, MA: Brookline.
Scheid synthesizes findings from current research concerning strategic learning and presents this information in a practical and understandable fashion. The book focuses on many of the strategies and approaches addressed in this chapter, including collaborative learning methods, peer tutoring, and cooperative learning. Educators should find the chapter on media and classroom resources useful. Overall, this volume offers practical and research-based information for enhancing strategic learning among all students.

References

Adams, D., & Hamm, M. (1994). *New designs for teaching and learning: Promoting active learning in tomorrow's schools.* San Francisco: Jossey-Bass.

Archambeault, B. (1992). Personalizing study skills in secondary students. *Journal of Reading, 35,* 468–472.

Byrnes, J. P. (1996). *Cognitive development and learning in instructional contexts.* Boston: Allyn and Bacon.

Decker, K., Spector, S., & Shaw, S. (1992). Teaching study skills to students with mild handicaps: The role of the classroom teacher. *The Clearing House, 65,* 280–284.

Devine, T. G., (1987). *Teaching study skills: A guide for teachers* (2nd ed.). Boston: Allyn and Bacon.

Ellis, E. S., Deshler, D. D., Lenz, B. K., Schumaker, J. B., & Clark, F. L. (1991). An instructional model for teaching learning strategies. *Focus on Exceptional Children, 23,* 1–24.

Gearheart, B. R., Weishahn, M. W., & Gearheart, C. J. (1992). *The exceptional student in the regular classroom* (5th ed.). New York: Macmillan.

Gettinger, M., & Knopik, S. (1987). Children and study skills. In A. Thomas & J. Grimes (Eds.), *Children's needs: Psychological perspectives* (pp. 594–602). Washington, DC: National Association of School Psychologists.

Harris, K., & Pressley, M. (1991). The nature of cognitive strategy instruction: Interactive strategy construction. *Exceptional Children, 57,* 392–404.

Henley, M., Ramsey, R. S., & Algozzine, R. F. (1996). *Characteristics and strategies for teaching students with mild disabilities* (2nd ed.). Boston: Allyn and Bacon.

Hoover, J. J. (1990). *Using study skills and learning strategies in the classroom: A teacher's handbook.* Lindale, TX: Hamilton Publications.

Jones, C., Slate, J., Bell, S., & Saddler, C. (1991). Helping high school students improve their academic skills: A necessary role for teachers. *High School Journal, 74,* 198–202.

Jones, C. H., Slate, J. R., Blake, P. C., & Holifield, S. D. (1992). Two investigations of the academic skills of junior and senior high school students. *The High School Journal, 76*(1), 24–29.

Lenz, B. K., & Deschler, D. D. (1990). Principles of strategies instruction as the basis of effective preservice teacher education. *Teacher Education and Special Education, 13*(2), 82–95.

Lenz, B. K., Ellis, E. S., & Scanlon, D. (1996). *Teaching learning strategies to adolescents and adults with learning disabilities.* Austin, TX: Pro-Ed.

Mastropieri, M., & Scruggs, T. (1991). *Teaching students ways to remember: Strategies for learning mnemonically.* Cambridge, MA: Brookline.

Novak, J. D., & Gowin, D. B. (1984). *Learning how to learn.* New York: Cambridge University Press.

Palincsar, A., & Brown, A. (1989). Instruction for self-regulated reading. In L. Resnick & L. Klopfer (Eds.), *Toward the thinking curriculum: Current cognitive research* (pp. 19–39). Alexandria, VA: Association for Supervision and Curriculum Development.

Pressley, M., Goodchild, F., Fleet, J., Zajchowski, R., & Evans, E. (1990). The challenges of classroom strategy instruction. *The Elementary School Journal, 89,* 301–342.

Resnick, L., & Klopfer, L. (Eds.). (1989). *Toward the thinking curriculum: Current cognitive research.* Alexandria, VA: Association for Supervision and Curriculum Development.

Scanlon, D. J., Duran, G. Z., Reyes, E. I., & Gallego, M. A. (1991). Interactive Semantic Mapping: An interactive approach to enhancing LD students' content area comprehension. *Learning Disabilities Research & Practice, 7,* 142–146.

Scheid, K. (1993). *Helping students become strategic learners: Guidelines for teaching.* Cambridge, MA: Brookline.

Scott, J., Wolking, B., Stoutimore, J., & Harris, C. (1990). Challenging reading for students with mild handicaps. *Teaching Exceptional Children, 22*(3), 32–35.

Scruggs, T., & Mastropieri, M. (1992). *Teaching test-taking skills: Helping students show what they know.* Cambridge, MA: Brookline.

Shaw, S. F., Brinckerhoff, L. C., Kistler, J. K., & McGuire, J. M. (1991). Preparing students with learning disabilities for postsecondary education: Issues and future trends. *Learning Disabilities, 2,* 23–28.

Smith, T. E. C., & Dowdy, C. A. (1989). The role of study skills in the secondary curriculum. *Academic Therapy, 24,* 479–490.

Swanson, H. L., & Keogh, B. (Eds.). (1990). *Learning disabilities: Theoretical and research issues.* Hillsdale, NJ: Lawrence Erlbaum.

Thomas, J. W., & Rohwer, W. D. (1986). Academic studying: The role of learning strategies. *Educational Psychologist, 21,* 19–41.

Wade, S., Trathem, B., & Schraw, A. (1990). Spontaneous study strategies. *Reading Research Quarterly, 25,* 148–166.

Wong, B. Y. L. (1992). *Contemporary intervention research in learning disabilities.* New York: Springer-Verlag.

Wong, B. Y. L. (1994). Instructional parameters promoting transfer of learning strategies in students with LD. *Learning Disability Quarterly, 17,* 110–120.

37

Learning Strategies

Mary Ann Rafoth
Indiana University of Pennsylvania

Background and Development

Schools generally make little effort to teach students strategies for individual success, even though it is widely recognized that children learn differently with unique styles and abilities. Successful students differ from unsuccessful students in the degree to which they are able to attach meaning to new information, select appropriate strategies to aid in retention, and match the way in which information is encoded to the performance demands of the criterion task (Baker & Brown, 1984; Wittrock, 1988).

Researchers have investigated specific kinds of *learning strategies* children use to carry out a variety of tasks. A learning strategy is a voluntary activity that children can use toward the act of remembering or learning information (Moely et al., 1986). Strategies may be domain specific (applying a specific strategy to solve a particular kind of math problem) or higher order (using a strategy to sequence or coordinate other strategies; Bruning, Schraw, & Ronning, 1995). Thus, students with effective learning strategies (behaviors directed at improving the processing of new information to aid learning) become independent learners by acting as teachers to themselves. For example, they recognize when they are experiencing difficulty or successfully retaining information, and they adapt their strategies accordingly.

While the use of specific learning strategies has been shown to improve learning, the effectiveness of adapting instruction to match individual *learning styles* remains questionable. According to Dunn, Dunn, and Perrin (1994), learning styles are the unique ways in which each student begins to concentrate on, process, and retain new and difficult information. Theoretically, when schools conform more to the learning styles of students, student achievement will increase. Some authors argue that when variables such as lighting, temperature, activity level, preference for group-versus-individual work, and motivational factors are taken into account instructionally, increased achievement results (Dunn & Dunn, 1993).

However, research does not support the premise that matching an individual's learning style with particular instructional methods yields achievement gains (Arter & Jenkins, 1978; Kavale & Forness, 1987; Knight, Halpin, & Halpin, 1992; Snider, 1992; Snow, 1992; Stahl, 1988). For example, Stahl and Kuhn (1995) note the false dichotomy created by trying to teach reading (a task requiring a meaning match of auditory-visual symbols) in purely an auditory or visual format. Moreover, often those who seem to have an analytic "style" are matched with a phonics approach which they no longer require having already mastered part-to-whole decoding, while those who seem to have a holistic "style" are matched with a whole language approach, missing instruction in the very phonics skills they lack! Stahl and Kuhn conclude that any approach to teaching reading must include aspects of a variety of instructional strategies to match multiple aspects of reading. Thus, attending to learning styles does not appear to deter underachievement. For this reason, this chapter focuses on learning strategies, not learning styles.

In the classroom, teachers check students' comprehension and memory through questions, activities, and evaluations. Students do this for themselves when they learn which learning strategies to successfully employ. In the primary grades, teachers typically play a more directive role because younger children do not have the executive processing skills to set expectations; focus, direct, and maintain direction; choose appropriate strategies; and monitor their learning. As children mature and curriculum demands for independent learning escalate, teachers place an increasing amount of responsibility on the learner. This progression follows nicely the developmental sequence of learning strategies and metacognitive skills which emerge during the upper elementary grades and throughout middle and high school.

Teachers assume that young children lack learning strategies and metacognitive skills and that their learning needs to be directed to a large extent. Likewise, as students progress in school many teachers assume that students are aware of appropriate study strategies and are capable of greater monitoring their own learning. However, while some students may spontaneously develop strong metacognitive skills, many do not. Knowledge of appropriate learning strategies and the ability to choose them appropriately and judge their effectiveness may well differentiate successful from unsuccessful students more so than ability (Morris, 1990; Swanson, 1990). Likewise, students who believe that they control the learning process through the use of effective strategic techniques are more likely to be successful students than those who believe success is due to chance or luck (McCombs & Marzano, 1990; Palmer & Goetz, 1988).

Schmeck (1988) views strategy development as emerging from both personality and learning styles on a causal continuum leading to a specific learning outcome. Schmeck uses the term "learning style" to reflect the individual's preferred learning strategy, as well as elements of motivation, attitude, and cognitive styles. Cognitive style has been defined in various ways. Some learners are field dependent, preferring interactive learning and being sensitive to contextual factors. Others are field independent, being less sensitive to contextual factors and requiring less contextual support. Learners have also been described as analytic versus global depending on their preference for step-by-step, sequential presentation or for more holistic, meaningful introduction of new concepts. Similar dichotomies include inductive and deductive or sequential and simultaneous approaches.

Schmeck (1988) argues that the best way to aid students is to make the student's cognitive style more versatile by teaching strategies that allow for greater adaptation. Encouragement of the development of deeper, more elaborative cognitive styles (where students use strategies to enhance meaningfulness and accept personal responsibility for learning outcomes) should enhance learning. Thus, according to Schmeck, the best way to accommodate individual learning is to use diverse instructional strategies and to directly teach students the use of learning strategies.

Common Learning Strategies

Using categories recommended by Weinstein, Goetz, and Alexander (1988), learning strategies demonstrated to be effective in enhancing achievement, and their developmental progression, are described next. Within each category, strategies may be simple or complex (i.e., using a simple association to remember a date in history versus using a complex strategy for taking and elaborating notes to enhance remembering and comprehension). Students adopt increasingly more complex strategies as they mature.

Rehearsal
Rehearsal is a generic name for a variety of memory strategies that involve repetition as a method for remembering material. Writing each spelling word five times, silently or orally repeating the name of a toy seen on a television commercial until a parent is told that it is a desired birthday gift, or reciting multiplication facts aloud are all examples of rehearsal strategies. Use of rehearsal as a strategy for remembering and learning is not consistently reported before 6 years of age (Flavell, 1992). When children do begin to rehearse material, their method of rehearsal undergoes a qualitative change with age. For example, Ornstein, Naus, and Liberty (1975) examined the rehearsal strategies of third-, sixth- and eighth-grade students as they studied a list of words. When the third graders (9-year-olds) rehearsed the words, they tended to rehearse one item at a time (i.e., "desk, desk, desk, desk"). The older children combined the items into rehearsal sets ("desk-cat-shirt-sky, desk-cat-shirt-sky"). The older children also recalled more of the words, which Ornstein et al. attributed to their use of a more sophisticated rehearsal strategy.

Training studies have shown that, as early as first grade, children can be taught to use more sophisticated rehearsal strategies before they are observed using them spontaneously (Guttentag, 1984). Although material can eventually be learned using a rehearsal strategy, rehearsal is a rote strategy that does not promote the meaningful processing of information. In many learning situations, rehearsal is not the most effective strategy for remembering. As older children and adolescents acquire more sophisticated learning strategies, they are less likely to report that they use rehearsal as a study routine. Rehearsal is most effective when embedded within a meaningful context, such as when teachers allow children to practice multiplication facts in a classroom game like "Round the World" (Pressley et al., 1991).

Organizational and time-management strategies
Organizational strategies for remembering involve reorganizing information into meaningful groupings that are easier to remember. By organizing material, semantic processing of that material is promoted (McDaniel & Einstein, 1989). For example, one might organize spelling words for study based on identical prefixes or learn the crops produced in a state by grouping them according to their use. Although preschool children demonstrate knowledge about similarity relationships, they rarely use this information in deliberate attempts at remembering. By first grade children still fail to use category organization as a guide for study (Moely, Olson, Halwes, & Flavell, 1969). It is not until around 10 and 11 years of age (fifth grade) that children begin to successfully use organization as a purposeful study plan. Children as young as 5 years, however, can be trained to use organizational study strategies to their advantage (Paris & Jacobs, 1984). The development of organizational study strategies, therefore, parallels the development of rehearsal strategies, although rehearsal strategies develop earlier. Common strategies for organization include concept webbing (used with young children as well as high

school students; Hyerle, 1995), outlining, and note-taking methods. Time-management strategies include keeping assignment books, using calendars to plan study activity, and organizing study time around task difficulty and importance (Rafoth, Leal, & DeFabo, 1993).

Elaboration and note-taking strategies

Elaboration strategies involve creating connections that add meaning to the material to be remembered or understood. These connections can involve visual images or verbal phrases. For example, the phrase "*Every good boy does fine*" is a verbal elaboration for remembering e, g, b, d, and f, the lines of the treble clef in music. An example of visual elaboration is a teacher telling students to "visualize" what they think a fictional character looks like based on how that character is described in the text. As a strategy for remembering, elaboration works because it requires children to create connections that have special meaning to them. The first elaboration strategies that children use, however, are often ineffective because their elaborations are not memorable. In fact, research has found that younger children remember more when elaborations are suggested by the experimenter than when the children produce their own (Pressley, Borkowski, & Schneider, 1987). The performance of adolescents and adults is better when they produce their own elaborations. These results suggest that elementary-school students profit most when specific elaborations are provided either by the classroom teacher or in textbooks and other materials.

Providing students with "questions to consider" when reading or listening helps students form effective elaborative connections (King, 1992). Without such prompts, it is doubtful either that children will create their own elaborations or, if elaborations are created, that they will be memorable ones.

Elaboration is a late-developing strategy. Children do not use elaboration spontaneously until at least 11 years of age, with dramatic increases in their use occurring during adolescence (Pressley, 1982). Older adolescents are more likely than older elementary-school children to report that they use elaboration while studying. Elaboration is not a universally adopted study skill, however. Even university students rarely report using elaborative-type study techniques (Schneider & Pressley, 1989).

Ideally, note taking is a form of elaboration on what is learned as well as a written memory aid. Students should be encouraged to highlight, underline, and add to their notes to add meaning. Underlining and highlighting text, when possible, is also helpful when students know to underline important ideas and essential detail (McAndrew, 1983; Snowman, 1986). Note-taking styles should develop as students mature, with each individual developing a system which best matches his or her individual preference.

Problem-solving strategies

Strategy training in problem solving involves training in algorithmic and heuristic approaches. For example, students can be taught several methods of attack for word problems involving diverse strategies such as finding the correct algorithmic formula by locating key words and phrases or more heuristic approaches such as visualizing the problem or personalizing it (replacing names and situations with personally relevant information to concretize the problem). Some research indicates that problem-solving training is most effective when combined with self-monitoring instruction (Delclos & Harrington, 1991).

Self-testing and test-taking strategies

One of the last study strategies to develop during childhood involves activity aimed at determining if one can safely stop studying. Self-testing is one way to decide if study activity can be terminated, and this can be accomplished in several ways. Practice tests, looking away and reciting material, and flashcards are all methods for self-testing. Spontaneous self-testing behaviors are infrequent prior to the third grade (Brainerd & Pressley, 1985). Developmental differences in the quality of children's self-testing behaviors have also been noted. When children initially begin to self-test, they usually do not use the information they gain from self-testing. For instance, a third-grader may self-test by looking away from the spelling word she is studying and spell it to herself; she looks back and notes that she misspelled the word. She then stops studying. Fifth- or sixth-grade students are more likely to use the information that self-testing provides to their advantage. That is, they are more likely to continue studying the material they missed during a self-test until self-testing proves they have mastered the material. Self-testing is not a universal method, however. When seventh graders over a 3-year period were asked to describe their study behavior and charged with telling the teacher when "they were ready for a quiz," approximately one-third did not indicate they would self-test (Rafoth, 1994).

Students who do not self-test are unlikely to engage in strong test-taking strategies. Students often make errors because they fail to read all distractors or refer back to test questions (Scruggs, White, & Bennion, 1986). Instruction on time-use, error avoidance, guessing, deductive reasoning, and avoiding carelessness can significantly increase student test performance (Sarason, 1980). Length of training is related to success, as is developmental level. Programs are more effective when they last at least 5 weeks, and children in Grades 1 through 3 require much more training than children in middle or high school (Scruggs et al., 1986).

Retrieval strategies

Retrieval strategies are methods used to recall information from long-term memory. If a math homework assignment is lost, one method for retrieving it would be to begin looking in places where the homework is likely to be found (e.g., backpack, math text, notebook, kitchen counter). Retrieval strategies can vary from simple to complex. For instance, a basic strategy is not to give up trying to remember something that does not come to mind immediately (if you do not immediately locate your homework, you continue to search for it). More sophisticated strategies often involve the use of general knowledge, logic, and inference. Knowing that thinking about some related item or event may help you remember the specific, forgotten item or event is an example of a mature retrieval strategy (i.e., recalling when you last saw your homework, what you were wearing, who you were with). In general, older children are better than younger children at using retrieval strategies. From the ages of 4 to 12 years, children become more efficient and sophisticated in their use of retrieval strategies when they are having difficulty recalling information. The use of retrieval strategies prior to 4 years of age is infrequently reported in the literature (Rafoth et al., 1993).

Comprehension monitoring and reading strategies

Young children are very poor at monitoring their own comprehension; that is, they are often unaware that they do not understand something. Markman (1977) gave first through third-grade children incomplete instructions for performing a magic trick or playing a game. The older children almost immediately realized that the instructions were inadequate. The same was not true for the younger children; many were never aware that relevant information was missing. Markman concluded that the younger children were taking a more passive approach to processing instructions; they were merely listening to instruction without applying them.

Recent research indicates that, developmentally, children understand memory and memory strategies before they understand comprehension and comprehension strategies (Lovett & Flavell, 1990). These results imply that children, especially those in early elementary school, often will not realize when they do not understand material or instructions. In fact, evidence indicates that children may "learn" material through memorization that they do not comprehend but, at the same time, not realize that they do not understand, giving an "illusion of knowing" (Baker, 1989). Lovett and Flavell use the Pledge of Allegiance as an example. Many young children memorize the Pledge of Allegiance and yet not only do they not understand what it means, they also do not recognize their lack of comprehension. This is an important concern in the classroom because if children do not recognize when they do not understand what they are learning, they will not adjust learning strategies accordingly or otherwise indicate their lack of comprehension.

Research on reading comprehension has found similar results. Children often do not monitor comprehension problems while reading (Mayer, 1992). Ideally, good readers monitor their comprehension as they are reading and once miscomprehension is detected, they adjust their reading strategies accordingly. Adjusting reading strategies due to comprehension failures is a late-developing skill. It is rarely reported in children under 8 years of age. Moreover it is often reported that even college students and other skilled readers fail to monitor their comprehension while reading (Baker & Brown, 1984; Glenberg & Epstein, 1987).

Affective strategies

A final category of strategies are those used to lessen anxiety (e.g., relaxation training) or to self-motivate (goal setting, self-reinforcement, self-management). Students' beliefs about themselves and about specific school tasks affect school achievement (Ames, 1990; McCombs & Marzano, 1990). Strategy instruction concerning overcoming negative self-statements and belief systems can affect student belief systems (Duchardt, Deshler, & Schumaker, 1995) even in special populations.

Sex Differences

Research indicates that elementary-school girls may be more competent than boys of the same age in their use of study and learning strategies (Pressley, Levin, Ghatala, & Ahmad, 1987). Waters (1981) suggested that this developmental lag for males is maintained from elementary school to college at least in the use of organizational strategies. Cox and Waters (1986) demonstrated that consistent sex differences favoring girls occur across ages in the processing of verbal materials and in the use of organizational study strategies. Pressley et al. (1987) found that fourth- and fifth-grade girls were more aware than boys of the same grade level that they were unlikely to be correct on difficult multiple-choice test items. Boys are also more likely than girls to be oblivious to their past failures as they make predictions about future performance (Parsons & Ruble, 1977). After failure, girls make lower predictions about performance. If children are unaware of previous failures, it is unlikely that they will improve or adjust their study techniques accordingly.

The currently available evidence indicates that strategies for learning develop at a faster pace in girls than in boys. What causes this acceleration is unclear. It may be related to physical or cognitive maturation, to school achievement, or to other related factors. Because few studies of memory and learning have systematically looked for possible sex differences, those studies that do report sex differences should be interpreted cautiously. Of course, within a single elementary-school classroom there will be variability in the study-skill development of individual girls as well as individual boys.

Metacognition and Its Development

Metacognition refers to the knowledge an individual has about cognitive processes and their function. Metacognition has three components:

- *Metaknowledge* (e.g., knowledge of how memory works).
- *Metamonitoring* (the ability to know when something has or has not been retained).
- *Specific strategy use* (application of various strategies in specific situations).

Metamemory is a subset of metacognition and refers to knowledge about how memory works and about how to remember effectively. It is the onset of metacognitive maturity (coinciding with acquisition of concrete thinking and, later, formal thinking) which explains the increases in use of strategies and the improved memories of older children and adolescents. Actual short-term memory capacity reaches its potential (about seven meaningful units of information) by the time children are school age.

Flavell (1970) posited that metacognition consists of three major factors: person, task, and strategy. Everything one knows about oneself and others as processors and retainers of information make up *person factors*. For instance, knowing that older children are likely to remember more information on a memory task than younger children is person knowledge. Similarly, self-awareness about those tasks which are difficult for an individual is representative of person knowledge. As students become aware of their own learning, this information is incorporated into their knowledge of metacognition and makes it possible for them to increase the efficiency and accuracy of their learning. *Task factors* involve information about how a particular task can best be handled and how successful one is likely to be at it. Knowing that you should devote more study time to difficult material is an example of a task factor. Knowledge about potentially employable strategies and their effectiveness characterize *strategy factors*. Again, as students mature, strategy factors should become more individualized and matched to their personal preference. For example, students should be introduced to a variety of note-taking methods and taught to elaborate on their notes. By high school, students should have developed a note-taking strategy that best fits their needs. Knowing that writing down a homework assignment helps you to remember it is also an example of strategy knowledge. Children between 4 and 12 years of age become progressively more aware of person, task, and strategy variables as metacognitive awareness increases.

As with strategy use, distinct age-related changes in metacognitive knowledge have been reported in the literature, with older children demonstrating a better understanding of memory. For example, a number of studies have reported that preschool and young children make unrealistic (overly optimistic) predictions about their own memory capabilities, with the accuracy of predictions increasing with age (Baker, 1989; Flavell, Friedrichs, & Hoyt, 1970). Flavell et al. asked nursery-school, kindergarten, second-, and fourth-grade children to estimate how many items they would be able to remember before they carried out a memory task. The second and fourth graders predicted their memory performance more accurately than the preschoolers and kindergarteners. The younger children tended to overestimate their memory performance; in fact, many reported that their memories were always infallible!

First graders are more likely than younger children to know that studying improves learning and that noise hinders the ability to learn (Brainerd & Pressley, 1985). By fifth grade, children also know that recognition is easier than recall (Speer & Flavell, 1979), that relearning is easier than initial learning (Kreutzer, Leonard, & Flavell, 1975), and that it is easier to repeat the main points of a story than to recite the story verbatim (Kreutzer et al.). Older children are also more aware than younger ones that items they just failed to recall on a test are more in need of further study than ones they just succeeded in remembering (Masur, McIntyre, & Flavell, 1973).

By the end of elementary school children know that memory skills vary from person to person and from situation to situation and that they do not have equally good memories in all situations. Their knowledge of various memory strategies has increased dramatically from what it was in kindergarten (Bruning et al., 1995; Garner & Alexander, 1989; Kreutzer et al., 1975).

Metamemory, however, is not completely developed by the end of childhood. Many adolescents and college students have little knowledge about some important memory strategies (Schneider & Pressley, 1989). It is not unusual for college students to know little about elaborative or organizational study strategies, to have difficulty identifying what is important when studying from a text, or to fail to effectively monitor learning (Schraw, 1994; Weinstein, Goetz, & Alexander, 1988)

Problems and Implications

Research involving children with learning problems—in particular, mild to moderate retardation and learning disabilities—has shown these children's memories to be similar to that of younger, "normal" learners. For instance, children with reading disabilities have been found to lack study strategies appropriate for their age and intellectual level. Torgesen (1982) found that second-grade poor readers were less likely than average readers to use verbal rehearsal on memory tasks. Similarly, children with learning disabilities (LD) were less aware of how to effectively organize and study prose, spent less time studying, and were less likely than average readers to use an organization strategy on a memory task (Dallago & Moely, 1986; Wong & Wilson, 1984).

Moely, Leal, Taylor and Gaines (1981) found that third- and fifth-grade children with LD engaged in less self-testing than nondisabled children of the same grade level. In another study, second-grade children with LD tended to choose less effective 'strategies for remembering than their nondisabled peers (Conca, 1989). Wong, Wong, and Blenkinsop (1989) found that adolescents with LD performed at the level of younger children in quality and quantity of essay writing. Nondisabled peers wrote longer essays and were more aware of planning and audience in their writing. In general, learners with disabilities cannot make use of their knowledge base effectively because of metacognitive deficits (Baker & Brown, 1984; Torgeson, 1982). These students also have more difficulty generalizing strategies beyond the immediate task (Ryan, Ledger, Short, & Weed, 1982). Results similar to those reported for children with LD have been reported for children with mental retardation (Brown & Barclay, 1976).

Alternative Actions

Studies have shown that it is possible to instruct underachieving students in self-testing and other strategies (Leal, Crays, Moely, 1985; Weinstein, Ridley, Dahl, & Weber, 1989). Examples of successful strategy instruction with special populations, particularly students with learning disabilities are listed in Table 1.

Training Strategies

The many deliberate attempts reported in the literature to teach appropriate study strategies to those children who do not generate them spontaneously, as cited previously, show that both young children and children with learning problems can be trained to be more strategic on learning tasks and thereby improve their performance. Children as young as 9 years of age can be instructed in the use of elaborative techniques (Wood, Pressley, & Winne, 1988).

Research has also shown, however, that many children do not maintain the trained strategies once explicit instructions referring to the training are no longer present. Methods have been developed to encourage children to maintain trained strategies. These methods indicate, however, that strategy instruction is not easy and requires effort on the teacher's part. Providing multiple training sessions so that a study strategy is well-learned increases the likelihood that children will use the strategy in the future when not reminded to do so (Palinscar & Brown, 1984; Pressley, Harris, & Marks, 1992). For instance, a teacher instructs the class to give themselves (or to have their parents give them) a practice test while studying for their spelling test. Not only should the teacher remind the students of this strategy for several consecutive weeks and periodically thereafter, but the teacher should also demonstrate this strategy to the class and have students practice its use in class until the strategy is successfully executed. Table 2 suggests a mnemonic to help teachers provide strategy instruction.

Feedback

As mentioned earlier, young children are often unaware that memory strategies facilitate task performance. Successful memory training studies have also included telling children that the strategy will improve their performance and why (Pressley, Borkowski, & Schneider, 1987). For the spelling test example just given, the teacher should tell students that a practice test gives them important information about whether they can terminate their study activities. Students should also be informed that the results of the practice test will indicate which words they need to continue studying and whether they should continue studying until practice tests indicate they have mastered the material. The teacher should also tell students that by carrying out these procedures (by making sure they really know the material), they are likely to perform better on their spelling test. Additionally, teachers should specifically point out those instances when carrying out a study strategy has resulted in improved performance (Leal & Rafoth, 1991). For example, after the spelling test, the teacher should acknowledge those students with better grades resulting from use of the self-testing strategy.

Assessing Learning Strategies and Metacognition

The assessment of learning strategies has largely focused on older learners, particularly college-age students. Weinstein, Goetz, and Alexander (1988) provide an excellent discussion of issues and assessment of learning strategies in older students, noting limitations of self-report instruments. Perhaps the most well-developed self-report instrument is the Learning and Study Strategies Inventory (LASSI; Weinstein, Zimmerman, & Palmer, 1988). Instruments to assess study skills in school-age children exist but generally do not investigate learning strategies (see Chapter 3, Rafoth, Leal, & De-Fabo, 1993, for a discussion of these instruments). In general, learning strategies are perhaps best assessed by a combination of self-report instruments, direct observations, and interviews of a student.

Table 1 *Typical Problems and Suggested Alternative Intervention Strategies*

Learning Problem	Suggested Strategy	Research Reference
Difficulty with acquisition of "rote" information (e.g. times tables)	Embed into meaningful context; use rap, rhyme	Leal & Rafoth, 1991; Moely et al., 1986
Cannot organize ideas	Use visual maps, webs	Hyerle, 1995
Difficulty with comprehension and recall of new concepts	Teach elaboration strategies	Weinstein, Ridley, Dahl, & Weber, 1989; Colson & Mehring, 1990
Not motivated to self-regulate learning	Evaluate self in relation to study task, connect task to future goal	McCombs & Marzano, 1990; Duchardt, Deshler & Shumaker, 1995
Difficulty with problem-solving	Teach heuristics within specific domain context	Bransford, Sherwood, Vye, & Reisser, 1986
High test anxiety	Teach relaxation exercises, test-taking strategies	Sarason, 1980
Poor note-taking skills	Teach strategies for paraphrasing lecture information, using abbreviations and symbols, using review strategies	Suritsky & Hughes, 1991; McAndrew, 1983
Poor written expression	Provide structure through strategies for planning, production, and revision	MacArthur, Graham, Schwartz, & Schafer, 1995
	Use WRITER & COPS Model	Rafoth, Leal, & DeFabo, 1993
	Teach PLEASE strategy	Welch, 1992
Poor reading comprehension	Teach a strategy for comprehension and embed across disciplines	
	Use POSSE strategy	Englert & Mariage, 1991
	Teach awareness/analysis of text structure	Simmons, Kameenui, & Darch, 1988
Difficulty in recall of new vocabulary, essental detail	Use mnemonic instruction	Scruggs & Mastropieri, 1989; Mastropieri & Scruggs, 1989
Does not self-monitor or predict achievement accurately	Teach self-testing; monitor prediction of success	Reid & Harris, 1989

Assessment of skills should lead directly to interventions aimed at remediating deficits and enhancing strengths. For example, activities which help students learn how to monitor their work and evaluate their own learning should be incorporated into lessons. In preparation for a quiz, teachers might suggest that students check their work with a partner to ensure accuracy; review their worksheets with a model completed by the teacher and make corrections; and practice the questions on the worksheet with a parent, student partner, or older student tutor. Students need instruction in how to use the feedback that these activities provide (e.g. "Do my answers indicate that I understand the material or assignment? If not, what should I do? Have I mastered the material? If not, what should I do next?") These practices increase the likelihood that young students will recognize that one can evaluate learning and monitor understanding.

In the middle grades, teachers expect more mature learning strategies from their students. In fact, many children spontaneously demonstrate more mature understanding of how memory and learning work by fourth and fifth grades. Children by this time *know* more about memory and may begin to employ some learning strategies (especially rehearsal) in studying. By junior high school,

some students (usually the more successful ones) may have begun to self-test—a very important tool for monitoring learning. Most importantly, students at this age level have developed the potential to develop their own learning strategies and to benefit from mnemonic techniques as well as to self-test. To ensure and reinforce these developments, teachers should actively teach students these skills and provide opportunities for practice.

For example, picture a lesson on geography requiring students to learn and remember state capitals. The lesson would be facilitated by the teacher actively pointing out important characteristics to students, setting expectations for learning, structuring opportunities for practice, and providing students with feedback about their performance. Much can also be done to help students aid themselves in setting learning goals, encoding information in short-term memory, and transferring it into long-term memory. Even though students at this age have the ability to generate new learning strategies and to monitor their learning, they may not do so without instruction and reinforcement. A variety of techniques for encoding information including rehearsal, organizational, and elaboration strategies should be modeled. Because knowledge about memory and learning should increase,

Table 2 *M-I-R-R-O-R-S: TEACHING STRATEGY USE EFFECTIVELY*

Remember, children's failure to use a study strategy is often due to an instructional failure rather than a learning failure.

GOOD STRATEGY INSTRUCTION INCLUDES:

- Direct explanation and modeling of the strategy
- Information on when and how to use it
- Reminders to use the strategy
- Repeated use of the strategy
- Constant feedback about the strategy's usefulness
- Constant feedback about the student's improved performance when he or she uses the strategy
- Generalizing the strategy to other learning tasks

A HELPFUL MNEMONIC: M-I-R-R-O-R-S

M— Model the strategy; explain how to carry it out
I— Inform the students about when and how to use it
R— Remind them to use the strategy
R— Repeat the strategy: practice, practice, practice
O— Outline the strategy's usefulness via constant feedback
R— Reassess the student's performance as a result of using the strategy
S— Stress strategy generalization

Note. From *Strategies for Learning and Remembering: Study Skills Across the Curriculum* (p. 71), by M. A. Rafoth, L. Leal, and L. DeFabo, 1993, Washington DC: National Education Association Profession Library. Copyright 1993 by National Education Association. Reprinted with permission.

students in middle and junior high school can benefit especially from the modeling of elaborative and organizational techniques. In this example, teachers might discuss the nature of the task—a paired associate one—and the types of rehearsal which facilitate this kind of learning. (Rehearsal of the paired items in a rhythmic pattern may facilitate retrieval.)

This is also an excellent opportunity to demonstrate elaboration strategies that use visual imagery, rhymes, or other forms of meaningful connection to tie the two items to be remembered. For example, using a *key word method* students can remember the capital of Maine, Augusta, by picturing a horse's *mane* being blown by *a gust of* wind. Columbus, Ohio, might be remembered by imagining *Columbus* sighting land and shouting *Oh hi "O"*. Harrisburg, Pennsylvania, might be recalled by picturing an artist's *pencil* drawing a *"harrisburger."* As with any elaboration, the more personal and bizarre the image or rhyme the more easily remembered. Remembering state capitals is also an excellent opportunity to introduce organizational strategies. States can be organized according to geographical regions or historical significance. Students should be encouraged to make up their own mnemonic devices and strategies because individually generated strategies often work best at this age. Most importantly, this will allow for practice of the strategy and

enhance the likelihood of generalization of strategy to other study situations.

Teachers should also encourage students to consider which strategies work best for them, to predict their grades on tests, and to practice self-testing to increase their ability to know when they have mastered the task. At this juncture, students may begin to learn to tailor their learning strategies to match their individual learning needs. For example, students who are taught several problem-solving strategies as they learn to deal with the infamous "word problem" in the intermediate grades including algorithmic solutions, personalization strategies, and visualization strategies may choose the strategy which works best for them. Thus, students who tend to be analytical thinkers often feel comfortable identifying algorithmic patterns and solutions. Students who are person-oriented, field-dependent learners may prefer personalization strategies (where they substitute their name or friends' names and interests for details in problems to make them more concrete and solvable). Students who prefer spatial and visual learning like to visualize solutions by drawing pictures. Students, once exposed and reinforced with a variety of learning strategies, may choose those that complement their own learning so that a personal study approach emerges (Rafoth, 1993, 1994).

In high school, many of the skills described earlier for use in middle and junior high school will need to be reinforced. Most importantly, it is during these years that particular study skills need to be generalized and systems of skills such as note taking, test taking, and improving comprehension be developed and honed. Secondary teachers must consider how to reinforce the development of effective note taking. For example, not only should they present information in an organized fashion, cite frequent examples, and indicate key relationships to facilitate selective perception, semantic encoding, and retention, but they should also encourage students to do the same. This can be accomplished by making specific suggestions about how to record information in notes, providing a skeletal outline, and using a note-taking system as an advanced organizer. Teachers might also cue students to regularly generate their own examples to test their understanding of new concepts. Again, initially teachers will have to check examples and provide feedback to the learner about their accuracy. Likewise, requiring students to frequently paraphrase information they have read or heard in the form of oral and written responses aids in comprehension (Aaron & Joshi, 1992). It is critical that students are directly taught that this strategy will aid in comprehension and will help them monitor their learning (Paris, Cross, & Lipson, 1984; Paris & Jacobs, 1984). While systems for improving comprehension, such as the SQ3R technique and reciprocal teaching (Palinscar & Brown, 1984) are helpful in training students, frequent embedded practice is necessary for skill acquisition and generalization.

Summary

The results from many studies have shown that a major difference between mature and immature learners is the spontaneous use of efficient learning strategies. That is, in learning and study situations, mature learners employ a variety of acquisition and retrieval strategies that are not readily available to the less mature learner. These less mature learners are not only young children, but also those children who have been labeled as learning disabled, mentally retarded, or otherwise developmentally disabled in school. Study after study has shown that younger and less proficient students are less strategic in their learning efforts. They generally know fewer strategies and have little awareness of when and how to use the strategies that they do know.

Children become more active in initiating strategy use in a variety of situations as they become older. Older children also know more about the workings of memory. Improvements in performance can occur when children are taught to use more effective strategies. However, strategies should not be taught by discussion alone. Children require intensive training and practice in the use of any one study strategy as well as feedback about why and when they should employ the strategy. In addition, students should be encouraged to evaluate strategies. Which choices work best for them? Which strategies meet their individual needs? As students move through school, helping them develop a personally effective approach to learning and studying should be a priority.

Recommended References

Frender, G. (1990). *Learning to learn.* Nashville, TN: Incentive Publications.
This book includes informational handouts and exercises in the areas of learning styles, time management and organization, note-taking skills, memory, test-taking skills, problem solving, and independent study. It includes permission to copy for classroom use. Information is well presented and comprehensive.

McCarney, S. B., & Tucci, J. K. (1991). *Study skills for students in our schools.* Columbia, MO: Hawthorne Press.
This book provides study skills and instructional intervention strategies for elementary and secondary students according to "problem area." Numerous learning strategies are included to help students gain more from instruction and learn independently. While somewhat of a "cookbook" approach, it is helpful in locating a number of intervention strategies quickly.

Presseisen, B. Z., Sternberg, R., Fischer, K. W., Knight, C. C., & Feuerstein, R. (1990). *Learning and thinking styles: Classroom interaction.* Washington, DC: National Education Association Professional Library.
This publication provides insights and research on intellectual styles, cognitive development, and structural modifiability.

Book authors are recognized experts and couch their discussion within a research framework while describing practical classroom implications.

Rafoth, M. A., Leal, L., & DeFabo, L. (1993). *Strategies for learning and remembering: Study skills across the curriculum.* Washington, DC: National Education Association Profession Library.
This book reviews information-processing theory and makes connections between the ways children learn and the embedding of strategy instruction in teaching. Curriculum-specific strategies for teaching students of all levels effective ways to learn and remember are included. The implications of metacognitive development are also discussed.

References

Aaron, P. G., & Joshi, R. M. (1992). *Reading problems: Consultation and remediation.* New York: Guilford Press.

Ames, C. (1990). Motivation: What teachers need to know. *Teachers College Record, 91*(3), 409–421.

Arter, J. A., & Jenkins, J. A. (1979). Differential diagnosis-prescriptive teaching: A critical appraisal. *Review of Educational Research, 49,* 517–555.

Baker, L. (1989). Metacognition, comprehension monitoring, and the adult reader. *Educational Psychologist, 1,* 338.

Baker, L., & Brown, A. L. (1984) Metacognitive skills and reading. In P. D. Pearson, M. Kamil, R. Barr, & P. Mosenthal (Eds.), *Handbook of reading research* (pp. 353–394). New York: Longman.

Brainerd, C., & Pressley, M. (1985). *Basic processes in memory development.* New York: Springer-Verlag.

Bransford, J., Sherwood, R., Vye, N., & Riesser, J. (1986). Teaching thinking and problem solving. *American Psychologist, 41*(10), 1078–1089.

Brown, A. L., & Barclay, C. R. (1976). The effects of training specific mnemonics on the metamnemonic efficiency of retarded children. *Child Development, 47,* 71–80.

Bruning, R., Schraw, G., & Ronning, R. (1995). *Cognitive psychology and instruction.* Englewood Cliffs, NJ: Prentice Hall.

Colson, S., & Mehring, T. (1990). Facilitating memory in students with learning disabilities. *LD Forum, 16*(1), 75–79.

Conca, L. (1989). Strategy choice by LD children with good and bad naming ability in a naturalistic memory situation. *Learning Disability Quarterly, 12*(2), 87–107.

Cox, D., & Waters, H. S. (1986). Sex differences in the use of organization strategies: A developmental analysis. *Journal of Experimental Child Psychology, 41,* 18–37.

Dallago, M. L. L., & Moely, B. E. (1986). Free recall in boys of normal and poor reading levels as a function of task manipulations. *Journal of Experimental Child Psychology, 30,* 62–78.

Delclos, V., & Harrington, C. (1991). Effects of strategy monitoring and proactive instruction on children's problem-solving performance. *Journal of Educational Psychology, 83,* 35–42.

Duchardt, B. A., Deshler, D., & Shumaker, J. B. (1995). A strategic intervention for enabling students with learning disabilities to identify and change their ineffective beliefs. *Learning Disability Quarterly, 18*(3), 186–201.

Dunn, R., & Dunn, K. (1993). *Teaching secondary students through their individual learning styles.* Boston: Allyn & Bacon.

Dunn, R., Dunn, K., & Perrin, J. (1994). *Teaching young children through their individual learning styles.* Needham Heights, MA: Allyn & Bacon.

Englert, C. S., & Mariage, T. V. (1991). Making students partners in the comprehension process: Organizing the reading "POSSE." *Learning Disability Quarterly, 14*(2), 123–140.

Flavell, J. H. (1970). Developmental studies of mediated memory. In H. W. Reese & L. P. Lipsitt (Eds.), *Advances in child development* (pp. 181–211). New York: Academic Press.

Flavell, J. H., (1992). Perspectives on perspective taking. In H. Bailin & P. Pufall (Eds.), *Piaget's theory: Prospects and possibilities* (pp. 107–139). Hillsdale, NJ: Lawrence Erlbaum.

Flavell, J. H., Friedrichs, A. G., & Hoyt, J. D. (1970). Developmental changes in memorization processes. *Cognitive Psychology, 1,* 324–340.

Garner, R., & Alexander, P. (1989). Metacognition: Answered and unanswered questions. *Educational Psychologist, 24,* 143–158.

Glenberg, A., & Epstein, W. (1987). Inexpert calibration of comprehension. *Memory and Cognition, 15,* 84–93.

Guttentag, R. E. (1984). The mental effort requirement of cumulative rehearsal: A developmental study. *Journal of Experimental Child Psychology, 37,* 92–106.

Hyerle, D. (1995). Thinking maps: Seeing is understanding. *Educational Leadership, 53*(4), 85–89.

Kavale, K., & Forness, S. (1987). Substance over style: Assessing the efficacy of modality testing and teaching. *Exceptional Children, 54,* 228–239.

King, A. (1992). Facilitating elaborative learning through guided student generated questioning. *Educational Psychologist, 27,* 111–126.

Knight, C., Halpin, G., & Halpin, G. (1992, March). *The effects of learning environment accommodations on the achievement of second graders.* Paper presented at the annual conference of the American Educational Research Association, San Francisco, CA.

Kreutzer, M. A., Leonard, C., & Flavell, J. H. (1975). An interview study of children's knowledge about memory. *Monographs of the Society for Research in Child Development, 40*(1, Serial No. 159).

Leal, L., Crays, N., & Moely, B. E. (1985). Training children to use a self-monitoring study strategy in preparation for recall: Maintenance and generalization effects. *Child Development, 56,* 643–653.

Leal, L., & Rafoth, M., (1991). Memory strategy development: What teachers do makes a difference. *Intervention in School and Clinic, 26*(4), 234–237.

Lovett, S. B., & Flavell, J. H. (1990). Understanding and remembering: Children's knowledge about the differential effects of strategy and task variables on comprehension and memorization. *Child Development, 61,* 1842–1858.

MacArthur, C., Graham, S., Schwartz, S. & Schafer, W. (1995). Evaluation of a writing instruction model that integrated a process approach, strategy instruction, and word processing. *Learning Disability Quarterly, 18*(4), 278–292.

Markman, E. M. (1977). Realizing that you don't understand: A preliminary investigation. *Child Development, 48,* 986–992.

Mastropieri, M., & Scruggs, T. (1989). Constructing more meaningful relationships: Mnemonic instruction for special populations. *Educational Psychology Review, 1,* 83–111.

Masur, E. F., McIntyre, C. W., & Flavell, J. H. (1973). Developmental changes in apportionment of study time among items in a multitrial free recall task. *Journal of Experimental Child Psychology, 58,* 237–246.

Mayer, R. E. (1992). *Thinking, problem-solving, and cognition* (2nd ed.). New York: Freeman.

McAndrew, D. A. (1983). Underlining and note-taking: Some suggestions from research. *Journal of Reading, 27,* 103–108.

McCombs, B., & Marzano, R. (1990). Putting the self in self-regulated learning: The self as agent in integrated will and skill. *Educational Psychologist, 25*(1), 51–69.

McDaniel, M., & Einstein, G. (1989). Material appropriate processing. *Educational Psychology Review, 1,* 113–145.

Moely, B. E., Hart, S. S., Santulli, K., Leal, L., Johnson, T., Rao, N., & Burney, L. (1986). How do teachers teach memory skills? *Educational Psychologist, 21,* 55–72.

Moely, B. E., Leal, L., Taylor, E., & Gaines, J. G. (1981, August). *Memory in learning disabled children: Strategy use, self-monitoring, and metamemory.* Paper presented at the annual meeting of the American Psychological Association, Los Angeles, CA.

Moely, B. E., Olson, F. A., Halwes, T. G., & Flavell, J. H. (1969). Production deficiency in young children's clustered recall. *Developmental Psychology, 1,* 26–34.

Morris, C. C. (1990). Retrieval processes underlying confidence in comprehension judgements. *Journal of Experimental Psychology: Learning, Memory, and Cognition, 16,* 223–232.

Ornstein, P. A., Naus, M. J., & Liberty, C. (1975). Rehearsal and organizational processes in children's memory. *Child Development, 46,* 818–830.

Palinscar, A., & Brown, A. (1984). Reciprocal teaching of comprehension fostering strategies and comprehension monitoring strategies. *Cognition and Instruction, 1*(2), 117–175.

Palmer, D. J., & Goetz, E. (1988). Selection and use of study strategies: The role of the studier's beliefs about self and strategies. In C. E. Weinstein, E. Goetz, & P. Alexander (Eds.), *Learning and study strategies* (pp. 41–57). San Diego: Academic Press Inc.

Paris, S., Cross, D., & Lipson, M. (1984). Informal strategies for learning: A program to improve children's reading awareness and comprehension. *Journal of Educational Psychology, 76,* 1239–1252.

Paris, S. & Jacobs, J. (1984). The benefit of informed instruction for children's reading and comprehension. *Child Development, 55,* 2083–2093.

Parsons, J., & Ruble, D. (1977). The development of achievement-related expectancies. *Child Development, 48,* 1075–1079.

Pressley, M. (1982). Elaboration and memory development. *Child Development, 53,* 296–309.

Pressley, M., Borkowski, J., & Schneider, W. (1987). Cognitive strategies: Good strategy users coordinate metacognition and knowledge. In R. Vasta & G. Whitehurst (Eds.), *Annals of child development* (Vol. 5, pp. 89–129). Greenwich, CT: JAI.

Pressley, M., Gaskins, I., Cunicilli, E., Burdick, N., Schaub-Matt, M., Lee, D., & Powell, N. (1991). Strategy Instruction at Benchmark School: A Faculty Interview Study. *Learning Disabilities Quarterly, 14*(1), 19–48.

Pressley, M., Harris, K., & Marks, M. (1992). But good strategy instructors are constructivists! *Educational Psychology Review, 4,* 3–31.

Pressley, M., Levin, J. R., Ghatala, E. S., & Ahmad, M. (1987). Test monitoring in young grade school children. *Journal of Experimental Child Psychology, 43,* 96–111.

Rafoth, M. A. (1993, April). *Assessment of students' memory and study skills to facilitate remedial and intervention plans.* A paper presented at the annual conference of the National Association of School Psychologists, Washington DC.

Rafoth, M. A. (1994, March). *Assessment of metacognitive maturity and study skills: Successful intervention with underachieving students.* A paper presented at the annual conference of the National Association of School Psychologists, Seattle, WA.

Rafoth, M. A., Leal, L., & DeFabo, L. (1993). *Strategies for learning and remembering: Study skills across the curriculum.* Washington, DC: National Education Association Professional Library.

Reid, R., & Harris, K. (1989). Self-monitoring of performance. *LD Forum, 15*(1), 39–42.

Ryan, E., Ledger, G., Short, E., & Weed, K. (1982). Promoting the use of active comprehension strategies by poor readers. *Topics in Learning Disabilities, 2,* 53–60.

Sarason, I. (1980). *Test anxiety: Theory, research, and applications.* Hillsdale, NJ: Erlbaum.

Schmeck, R. (1988). Individual differences and learning strategies. In C. E. Weinstein, E. Goetz, & P. Alexander (Eds.), *Learning and study strategies* (pp. 171–188). San Diego, CA: Academic Press.

Schneider, W., & Pressley, M. (1989). *Memory development between 2 and 20.* New York: Springer-Verlag.

Schraw, G. (1994). The effect of metacognitive knowledge on local and global monitoring. *Contemporary Educational Psychology, 19,* 143–154.

Scruggs, T., & Mastropieri, M. (1989). Mnemonic instruction of LD students: A field-based evaluation. *Learning Disability Quarterly, 12*(2), 119–125.

Scruggs, T., White, K., & Bennion, K. (1986). Teaching test-taking skills to elementary-grade students: A meta-analysis. *Elementary School Journal, 87,* 69–82.

Simmons, D. C., Kameenui, E. J., & Darch, C. (1988). The effect of textual proximity on fourth- and fifth-grade L. D. students' metacognitive awareness and strategic comprehension behavior. *Learning Disability Quarterly, 11*(4), 380–395.

Snider, V. (1992). Learning styles and learning to read: A critique. *Remedial and Special Education, 13,* 6–18.

Snow, R. (1992). Aptitude theory: Yesterday, today, and tomorrow. *Educational Psychologist, 27*(1), 5–32.

Snowman, J. (1986). Learning tactics and strategies. In G. D. Phye & T. Andre (Eds.), *Cognitive classroom learning: Understanding, thinking, and problem-solving* (pp. 243–275). Orlando, FL: Academic Press.

Speer, J. R., & Flavell, J. H. (1979). Young children's knowledge of the relative difficulty of recognition and recall memory tasks. *Developmental Psychology, 15,* 214–217.

Stahl, S. (1988). Is there evidence to support matching reading styles and initial reading methods? *Phi Delta Kappan, 70,* 317–322.

Stahl, S., & Kuhn, M. (1995). Does whole language or instruction matched to learning style help children learn to read? *School Psychology Review, 24*(3), 393–404.

Suritsky, S., & Hughes, C. A. (1991). Benefits of note-taking: Implications for secondary and post-secondary students with learning disabilities. *Learning Disability Quarterly, 14*(1), 7–18.

Swanson, H. L. (1990). Influence of metacognitive knowledge and aptitude on problem-solving. *Journal of Educational Psychology, 82,* 306–314.

Torgeson, J. (1982). The learning disabled child as an inactive learner: Educational implications. *Topics in Learning and Learning Disabilities, 2,* 45–52.

Waters, H. S. (1981). Organizational strategies in memory for prose: A developmental analysis. *Journal of Experimental Child Psychology, 32,* 223–246.

Weinstein, C. E., Goetz, E., & Alexander, P. (1988). *Learning and study strategies: Issues in assessment, instruction, and evaluation.* San Diego, CA: Academic Press.

Weinstein, C. E., Ridley, D., Dahl, T., & Weber, E. (1989). Helping students develop strategies for effective learning. *Educational Leadership, 46*(4), 17–19.

Weinstein, C. E., Zimmerman, S. A., Palmer, D. R. (1988). Assessing learning strategies: The design and development of the LASSI. In C. E. Weinstein, E. Goetz, & P. Alexander (Eds.), *Learning and Study Strategies* (pp. 25–40). San Diego: Academic Press Inc.

Welch, M. (1992). The PLEASE strategy: A metacognitive learning strategy for improving the paragraph writing of students with mild learning disabilities. *Learning Disability Quarterly, 15*(2), 119–128.

Wittrock, M. C. (1988). A constructive review of research on learning strategies. In C. E. Weinstein, E. Goetz, & P. Alexander (Eds.), *Learning and study strategies.* San Diego, CA: Academic Press.

Wong, B. Y. L., & Wilson, M. (1984). Investigating awareness of and teaching passage organization in learning disabled children. *Journal of Learning Disabilities, 17,* 477–482.

Wong, B., Wong, P., & Blenkinsop, J. (1989). Cognitive and metacognitive aspects of LD adolescents' composing problems. *Learning Disability Quarterly, 12*(4), 300–323.

Wood, E., Pressley, M., & Winne, P. (1988, April). *Children's learning of arbitrary facts in prose as a function of type of elaborative activity.* Paper presented at the annual meeting of the American Educational Research Association, New Orleans, LA.

38

Giftedness

Carolyn M. Callahan

University of Virginia

Background

The Gifted Student—Why Worry?

The latent talent and potential for extraordinary accomplishments of children are the most valuable resource of any society. Eminent individuals contribute daily to public health through medical breakthroughs; society's spirits and souls through the arts; and to the overall well-being, safety, and comfort of society through science, mathematics, the social sciences, and technology. The argument for recognizing gifted students as a natural resource is often used as a basis for concern about their educational and developmental needs. However, a much stronger argument lies in the commitment to provide the best possible environment for all students, regardless of ability, to ensure the maximum development and realization of their academic, social, and personal potential. To address either of these objectives, school personnel need to understand ways to nurture the development of notable and valued talents of children and adolescents, ways to help children and adolescents with exceptional abilities lose the constraints placed on them by rigid curriculum and expectations, and ways to use resources available to these students to overcome the obstacles society may place in the way of achievement of full potential—both in terms of cognitive achievements and healthy adjustment.

Unfortunately, one segment of the school population often given minimal attention (and sometimes even negative attention) is the group of students variously labeled *gifted, talented,* or *able.* There are many reasons for general neglect of the needs and concerns of these children and young adults. First, gifted students generally achieve at or above the norm on standardized assessments and generally earn good grades; hence they are unlikely to be referred to school psychologists or counselors for academic reasons. Second, the myths that gifted children will "make it anyway," that they do not face the same difficulties academically as those faced by other children, and that they are helplessly mired in social isolation due to their uniqueness result in concern and efforts being directed

toward other populations deemed more "in need" of special services. Finally, the American public has harbored a "resentment and suspicion of the life of the mind . . . and a disposition to constantly minimize the value of that life" (Hofstadter, 1963, p. 29). The American public has long engaged in a "love-hate" relationship with gifted individuals—appreciating their accomplishments but at the same time feeling resentful of their success (see Gallagher, 1986, for a fuller discussion of this phenomenon).

The obvious negative ramifications for highly able students range from labels such as "dweeb," "nerd," or "geek" to the stereotyping of academically able individuals on television and in film. But there are many, less obvious and more serious dangers of ignoring the unique needs of this population. For example, seemingly high performance on tests and high grades hide some of the issues facing schools and the gifted child. The first is the failure of many gifted students to reach their potential (Callahan, 1993). This is evident in the decline of scores over time of highly able students on national standardized assessments and their relatively low standing in cross-cultural comparisons. "Compared with top students in other industrialized countries, American students perform poorly on international tests, are offered a less rigorous curriculum, read fewer demanding books, do less homework, and enter the workforce or postsecondary education less well prepared" (U.S. Department Education, 1993, p. 1).

A second obvious danger is that overgeneralizations about the academic accomplishments, as well as the social and emotional well-being, of gifted students tend to result in assumptions that they all are either unusually well-adjusted, resilient problem solvers who can work out their own solutions to problems or that they are really quite poorly adjusted, overachieving, and socially inept. Either of these overgeneralizations leads to inappropriate assumptions and responses to gifted students. Most gifted children are well-adjusted and cope quite adeptly in social situations. There is also ample evidence, to be presented in later sections, that many gifted children face problems associated with their unique talents and abilities. Further, there is considerable evidence that gifted

431

students usually do not make it on their own. Bloom (1985) amply documented in his study of talented young people that achievement of potential was closely related to appropriate instruction in the field:

No one reached the limits of learning in a talent field on his or her own. Families and teachers were crucial at every point along the way to excellence. The role of the home changed greatly over time, as did the qualities of the teaching and the qualifications of teachers. What the families and teachers do at different times and how they do it clearly sets the stage for exceptional learning in each talent field. (p. 507)

Davis and Rimm (1994) conclude that "inadequate curricula, social and emotional difficulties, inadequate parenting, and pressure can all extinguish the high potential accomplishment of gifted children and adolescents" (p. 4).

Those who do succeed in achieving their potential may draw from internal resources or from their families, their schools, and/or their communities in achieving healthy adjustment and academic success. Some succeed despite a failure of one of these resources because of strong support of another, while others fail to achieve or to adjust. But as Csikszentmihalyi, Rathunde, and Whalen (1993) noted in the conclusion of their study of the successes and failures of talented teenagers, "children must first be recognized as talented in order to develop a talent" (p. 243). Hence, I will begin with the basic questions that need to be asked to ensure the greatest fulfillment of the gifted population: Who are these children? What are their characteristics? What are the issues they face? What are the strategies for ensuring healthy development of talent potential?

Definitions of Giftedness

The issue of defining giftedness is complicated by the existence of both "official" and theoretical definitions. Most states and schools have adopted some variation of the definition known as the U.S.O.E. definition (U.S. Office of Education, 1972), also known as the Marland definition:

Gifted and talented children are those identified by professionally qualified persons who by virtue of outstanding abilities are capable of high performance. These are children who require differentiated educational programs and/or services beyond those normally provided by the regular school program in order to realize their contribution to self and society. (p. 2)

This definition goes on to delineate areas of giftedness that include general intellectual ability, specific academic ability, creative or productive thinking, leadership ability, visual and performing arts, and psychomotor ability. The most recent revision of this definition was written with the intention of broadening the concept of giftedness; dispelling the notion that giftedness is fixed and can be measured by one test; and focusing on the presence of talent in all cultural, economic, and racial groups.

Children and youth with outstanding talent perform or show the potential for performing at remarkably high levels of accomplishment when compared with others of their age, experience or environment.

These children and youth exhibit high performance capability in intellectual, creative, and/or artistic areas, possess an unusual leadership capacity, or excel in specific academic fields. They require services or activities not ordinarily provided by the schools.

Outstanding talents are present in children and youth from all cultural groups, across all economic strata, and in all areas of endeavor. (U.S. Department of Education, 1993, p. 3)

Both of these definitions reflect the current judgments by experts in the field that giftedness is broader than and determined by more than the score on an intelligence test.

Theoretical definitions also abound. The most popular of these is Renzulli's (1978) three-ring definition of giftedness which is based on a confluence of above-average ability, task commitment, and creativity in any recognized domain of productive behavior. Other definitions used in the field include Gardner's theory of multiple intelligences (1983), Sternberg's triarchic theory (1986), and locally derived conceptions of giftedness.

Identifying Giftedness

Whereas intelligence tests have historically been used to define giftedness and still are very often used as one indicator of giftedness, current literature on the appropriate definitions and identification of gifted students stress going beyond this narrow conception and assessment tool. My colleagues and I (Abeel, Callahan, & Hunsaker, 1994) identified general, recurring themes in current recommendations for defining and identifying gifted students. The first theme was the use of a broadened conception of giftedness, ranging from the inclusion of the categories defined by the U.S. Department of Education to the multiple intelligences as defined by Gardner (1983), the triarchic theory of giftedness espoused by Sternberg (1986), and Renzulli's (1978) three-ring definition of giftedness.

A second theme was the use of multiple criteria in identifying giftedness. In particular, practitioners are guided never to use a single score from a single test to determine whether a child is gifted. However, it is also critical that multiple assessments not become multiple hurdles for the child. Multiple sources of data should be used to form a profile of student accomplishments, potential, and needs. The literature also stresses using unique and appropriate instruments for identifying specific talents and areas of academic and intellectual giftedness. The misuse of tests of creativity, intelligence, and cognitive processing was widely noted in our study (Abeel et al., 1994). The use of reliable and valid instruments is, of course, recommended in all assessments, and we emphasized this recommendation in light of the findings of the National Research Center on the Gifted and Talented showing misuse of published tests and widespread use of locally constructed nomination forms, checklists, and rating scales that lack evidence of either reliability or validity (Callahan & Hunsaker, 1991; Hunsaker & Callahan, 1995).

A third theme in the general literature is the recommendation that giftedness be defined and identified on the basis of the need for unique programs or special interventions rather than by predetermined cut-off scores on matrices or according to "slots available" in a program. The final theme that emerged was the need to use instruments appropriate for screening and identifying underserved populations such as minorities, the very gifted child, the child with limited English proficiency, and the child with disabilities.

In a review of promising practices in identifying students from these underserved groups and in matching identification procedures and curricular offerings to gifted students, several commonalities in successful practice were identified (Callahan, Tomlinson, & Pizzat, n.d.). The first of these was acceptance of intelligence as multifaceted in accordance with the guidelines mentioned earlier. The second was the recognition of multiple manifestations of giftedness. Those systems most successful in identifying students from minority cultures accepted the premise that intelligence expresses itself differently in different contexts and cultures. Emphasis on authentic assessment tools and assessment over time evolved from a commitment to examine how students respond to instructional intervention that might be called "gifted teaching" rather than looking only at end products exhibited on tests. These assessments focused on carefully observing students in structured lessons over a period of time and collecting portfolio data as part of the identification process. The acceptance of the premises that intelligence may manifest itself in different ways and that authentic assessment is a valuable source of information led to the acceptance of many sources of evidence from outside the classroom as part of the identification process. Underlying all of these practices was a philosophy of inclusiveness rather than exclusiveness on the part of the school divisions examined. While they saw the value to the children of identifying and serving special needs, they were willing to err on the side of providing services that could be refused rather than denying services. Further discussion of the steps in identifying gifted students may be found in Boatman, Davis, and Benbow (1995).

Incidence

The original report which contained the Marland definition of giftedness stated, "It can be assumed that utilization of these criteria [actually the categories named] for

the identification of gifted and talented will encompass a minimum of 3 to 5 percent of the school population" (U.S. Office of Education, 1973, p. 2). This was most often taken not as a minimum figure but as a general guideline. At this time, only four states identify more than 10% of their students as gifted; fewer than 5% are identified in 21 states (U.S. Department of Education, 1993).

Renzulli (1978), in contrast, suggests that the talent pool of students who are offered special services from which gifted behaviors may emerge be set at approximately 20% of the school population. At any given point in time, demonstration of these gifted behaviors in a smaller subset of these talent-pool learners would suggest a need for even further specialized services.

Characteristics and Development

While many of the characteristics of gifted children are qualitatively different from those of other children, some indicators of giftedness in young children emerge relatively earlier, are more intense, or represent more profound accomplishments of developmental tasks, learning, or performances. Table 1 provides a list of 25 general characteristics of the intellectually gifted child, as documented in studies of intellectual giftedness. Although not appearing in the table, studies of eminent individuals and talented children have also identified specific traits by discipline (e.g., Bloom's 1985 study of six domains of giftedness). Mathematically precocious children, for example, may learn to count by two, five and ten or give surprisingly good reasoning for the solution to a mathematical problem at a relatively early age.

The development of talent has been characterized by a combination of innate abilities and the interactions of those abilities with family, school, and peer dynamics. Bloom's (1985) retrospective study and Csikszentmihalyi et al.'s (1993) longitudinal study of talented individuals have provided a framework for understanding the influences on the development of talent. Bloom and his co-investigators identified three phases of talent development. While the phases vary in onset from talent area to talent area (music and athletics beginning very young and science and mathematics beginning later), the stages are parallel. The early years of talent development are characterized as playful and filled with immediate rewards from parents and teachers. During the middle years, there is a much greater commitment of time, greater attention to detail, and the development of specific skill and process, with teachers becoming more focused on a productive critique of work and on more formal, disciplined, and systematic instruction. At this point the students set goals of becoming an "Olympic swimmer," a "concert pianist," or a "research mathematician." While external reinforcement is still important, greater

Table 1 *Characteristic Behaviors of the Intellectually and/or Academically Gifted Students*

- Displays advanced vocabulary for age group.
- Shows advanced logical reasoning.
- Uses language fluently and with unusual analogies, similes, and metaphors.
- Is very curious, inquisitive, and questioning.
- Has an excellent memory and a large store of information.
- Processes information efficiently.
- Learns new things quickly and easily.
- Becomes intensely involved in interests of own choosing.
- Generalizes from the specific instance to the principle easily.
- Likes to solve problems independently.
- Sees patterns and relationships easily.
- Has a keen sense of humor.
- Understands cause and effect, draws conclusions, and makes decisions from complex data.
- Is able to delay closure in problem solving.
- Thinks of many solutions to everyday problems.
- Understands complex, abstract concepts at an earlier age than other children.
- Thinks independently.
- Develops idealism and sense of justice at an earlier age.
- Is sensitive to incongruities and paradoxes.
- Has a high energy level.
- Shows originality in products.
- Exhibits an early ability to develop complex conceptual frameworks and strategies for learning.
- Thinks metacognitively (thinks about thinking).
- Is likely to be an early reader.
- Shows insight.

Note: This list is synthesized from Dunn, Dunn, and Treffinger, 1992; Clark, 1992; and Davis and Rimm, 1994. These characteristics may be present across one or more disciplines or talent areas.

intrinsic reinforcement is evident. Finally, the third phase of talent development is characterized by generalization and integration—a commitment to making the talent a significant part of one's life and future. Table 2 shows the major factors identified by Bloom (1985) as associated with the success of highly able individuals in mathematics, science, athletics, and music. The following additional factors and observations were noted by Csikszentmihalyi et al. (1993) in their study of successful talented teenagers:

1. Potential talents were recognized early, cultivated, and nurtured.
2. Talented students possessed personality traits conducive to concentration and were open to experience.
3. Talent development was easier for teens who had learned habits conducive to cultivating talent; who shared more active and challenging pursuits with friends such as hobbies or studying rather than just socializing or hanging out; who had learned to modulate their attention, exerting more concentration when in school and less when socializing, doing chores, and watching television; and who spent more time alone.
4. Talented teens did not have to invest unreasonable amounts of time or energy in chores or jobs.
5. Talented teens came from psychologically supportive families (more cohesive and flexible).
6. Talented teens were more conservative in sexual attitudes and aware of the conflict between productive work and peer relations.
7. Family support and challenge enhanced development of talent. Where family context was perceived as complex (both integrated and differentiated), teens spent more time doing homework and were more alert and goal directed.
8. Talented teens liked teachers best who were supportive and modeled enjoyable involvement in a field; who were intense people, often professionally involved in their fields outside the classroom; who held a presence and infectious enthusiasm; who did not just go through the motions; and who challenged students in a way commensurate with abilities.
9. Talent development required both expressive and instrumental rewards.

Much of the literature on the development of gifted children is based on the early work of Terman and his associates (Terman, 1925; Terman & Oden, 1947; Terman & Oden, 1959). In studying the academic, social, and emotional development of gifted children, Terman and his colleagues focused on comparisons of gifted students to nonidentified students rather than on the dynamic and developmental characteristics of the gifted. In addition, they limited their sample to individuals with high IQ scores on the Stanford-Binet. Many other researchers also have focused exclusively on high IQ students, thus warranting caution in generalizing findings to other gifted groups.

In general, these researchers concluded that most gifted students are well adjusted, both personally and socially. Terman's subjects were less neurotic and more emotionally stable than nonidentified students. More recent studies yielded similar findings: Gifted students tend to be as well adjusted as the general population, and in most cases their self-concept scores have been shown to be average or better (Davis & Rimm, 1994; Colangelo & Assouline, 1994). As Milgram and Milgram (1976) pointed out, gifted children are able to use their intellectual ability as an asset in coping with life's problems and in solving them.

Hollingworth (1942), however, concluded that social adjustment characterized the moderately but not the highly gifted (IQ above 145) students. Likewise, recent research by the National Research Center on the Gifted and Talented (Sowa & May, in press) suggests that intellectual resources of some gifted children fail to serve

Table 2 *Influences on the Development of Talent*

Parental/Home Influences

Parents:

- Were child-oriented.
- Stressed achievement, success, doing one's best at all times.
- Modeled the "work ethic."
- Believed work should come before play.
- Believed in working for distant goals.
- Taught values of achievement and work to their children.
- Were often the first teachers of the children in their talent area (or there was another family member who was).

In the home:

- Children were expected to share household chores (and to complete them before play).
- Family routines were structured to give children responsibilities and help them become self-disciplined.
- Emphasis was placed on excellence, doing one's best, working hard, and spending one's time constructively.
- An expectation existed that work values would be applied in talent area of interest.
- Of those who developed talent in music, art, and athletics, there was an emphasis in the home on the respective talent from an early age.
- Of mathematically and scientifically talented children, parents were interested in or involved in intellectual activity even if not formally educated; there was discussion of school learning and long-term educational planning; there was encouragement of curiosity and reading as a family activity; and children were read to until able to read themselves.
- In the middle years and later years of talent development, family routines were adjusted for practice or classes, as necessary.

Teacher Influences

In the early stages of talent development teachers:

- Made initial learning pleasant and rewarding with much playful activity and positive reinforcement for small gains.
- Were rarely critical but set standards, expected progress, and quickly rewarded steps toward reaching standards.
- Set tasks to be accomplished clearly and helped child correct flaws.
- Established good relationships with parents.
- Helped students grasp larger patterns and processes of subject.
- Encouraged discovery of underlying processes and ideas of the discipline.

In the middle stages of talent development teachers:

- Were more expert in the area of talent.
- Were either very selective in choosing students with whom they would work (tennis, swimming, piano) or were college or university instructors (mathematics, neurology).
- Expected high levels of attainment.
- Emphasized precision in the talent area.
- In music and athletics used tournaments and competitions.
- In mathematics (in addition to encouraging them to take more advanced—usually graduate-level—mathematics courses) encouraged students by discussing mathematics topics with them and pointed to the work of outstanding mathematicians.
- Helped students set short-term and long-term goals.

In the later years of talent development teachers:

- Were master teachers in their fields.
- Conveyed that selection to work/study with them (the master teacher) would mean the student would go far in the field.
- Conveyed that selection to work/study with them was conditional on "putting oneself in the hands of the teacher without reservation."
- Raised demands and expectations constantly to the point where it was clearly communicated that the student was expected to do what had never been done before (set Olympic records, solve unknown mathematics problems, etc.).
- Taught students to evaluate their own performance.
- Conveyed that learning was based on doing what the experts in the field do.

Peer Influences

In the middle years close friends:

- Were usually from the same talent field.
- Helped the student see self in relation to the field.
- Were aspiring to the same goals and became friends as well as competitors.

In the later years:

- Exchanges with peers were often a way of sharing ideas and observing how others attacked problems.

Note. Synthesized from *Developing Talent in Young People*, edited by B. S. Bloom, 1985, New York: Ballatine.

them well. That is, despite the generally positive conclusions about the psychological and social well-being of gifted students, aspects of being gifted may contribute to problems such as social isolation, perfectionism, and underachievement. However, these problems are often related to developmental differences, as well as to gender, educational practice, and other factors.

Differential rates of development across domains within the gifted child, as well as between the gifted child and other children, are believed to be one source of social and emotional problems. The uneven development of gifted children has been labeled *dyssynchrony* by Terrasier (1985). More recently the term *internal dyssynchrony* proposed as a replacement for dyssynchrony because of the negative associations with the prefix "dis" (Silverman, 1993) has been used to refer to imbalances within the individual child in the rates of physical, psychomotor, language, and affective development. While the gifted child's intellectual or academic achievements may be more like those of older children or adults, their physical, psychomotor, and emotional development may be age appropriate. This may lead to frustrations or anxieties on the part of gifted children who are able to understand the seriousness and complexity of social issues or advanced concepts such as war, the holocaust, or death but feel helpless to effect the world or unable to process the accompanying emotions.

Social dyssynchrony refers to the differential between the development of the gifted child and the development of age peers along any of the dimensions mentioned earlier. Children may seek to be with older children who are processing information at an equivalent level of sophistication rather than with their age peers (Silverman, 1993). The early work of Leta Hollingworth (1931) and the more recent work of Roedell (1984), Dembrowski (1964, 1972), and Tolan (1989) suggest that higher levels of intellectual and academic functioning are associated with more intense emotions. Furthermore, the more different the child is from peers, the more the child is aware of and sensitive to differences and responses of others. This leads to greater social and emotional vulnerability if the child is rejected by either age peers or older, more intellectually able peers (Silverman, 1993). However, recent research by Oram, Cornell, and Rutemiller (1995) failed to support the assumption that children will be maladjusted because of high academic ability or that a curvilinear relationship exists between adjustment and aptitude or achievement (with moderately high academic aptitude an asset, but higher levels acting as a liability).

Research on students who are not easily recognizable as gifted through traditional intelligence testing is just now emerging. Only recently have psychologists and educators begun to look at the developmental patterns—cognitive, social, and emotional—of gifted students and to study the populations of traditionally underserved gifted students such as those with physical disabilities

(Willard-Holt, 1994), those with learning disabilities (Reis, Neu, & McGuire, 1995), the very young gifted child (Robinson, 1993), or those from differing cultural backgrounds (Ford, 1994a; Plucker, 1994). (For a fuller discussion of the cognitive development of gifted students see Monks & Mason, 1993; Shore & Kanevsky, 1993; and Sternberg & Davidson, 1985.)

Problems and Implications

A common misperception about gifted children is that they will be "okay" and do well in school regardless of the curriculum or program provided or the environment in which they live. Considerable evidence exists that this myth should be debunked. First, while there is evidence that gifted students are less prone to feelings of loneliness, anger, and anxiety than the general population and are less likely to exhibit somatic problems such as depression, withdrawal, psychosis, or hyperactivity, the incidence of severe adjustment difficulties are similar to those of the general population (Bland, Sowa, & Callahan, 1994).

Whereas the characteristics generally used as indicators of giftedness are usually regarded as positive and desirable, these same characteristics cause difficulties for some gifted students. This is especially true among children who have not been identified as gifted but who exhibit gifted characteristics regarded by others as inappropriate behaviors. Table 3 summarizes characteristics of gifted children and their possible association with social and emotional problems.

Intense Sensitivity and Empathy

Perhaps foremost among emotional characteristics of gifted children is intense sensitivity and empathy (Clark, 1992, Genshaft & Broyles, 1991), which is closely related to their advanced cognitive development. It may manifest itself as an unusually grave concern for the well-being of others in the world (e.g., concern for the homeless, the poor or hungry, or the environment). When the expression of this intensity is translated into extreme anxiety, it may be considered emotional immaturity by those unaware of the ways in which the gifted child perceives the world (Silverman, 1993).

Frustration, Boredom and Noncomformity

Several difficulties may manifest themselves as the young gifted child enters school. The first of these relates to the asynchrony described earlier. The very young gifted child may be frustrated by an inability to communicate ideas because of the lack of motor skills to write quickly enough. Children with advanced vocabularies and ad-

Table 3 *Characteristics of Gifted Children As They Relate to Issues and Difficulties These Children May Face*

Differentiating Characteristics	Possible Concomitant Problems
Extraordinary quantity of information, unusual retentiveness	Boredom with regular curriculum; impatience with "waiting for the group."
Advanced comprehension	Poor interpersonal relationships with less able children of the same age; adults considering children "sassy" or "smart aleck"; a dislike of repetition of already understood concepts.
Unusually varied interests and curiosity	Difficulty in conforming to group tasks; overextending energy levels, taking on too many projects at one time.
High level of language development	Perceived as a "show off" by children of the same age.
High level of verbal ability	Dominates discussions with information and questions deemed negative by teachers and fellow students; use of verbalism to avoid difficult thinking tasks or expression of emotions.
Unusual capacity of processing information	Resents being interrupted; perceived as too serious; dislikes routine and drill.
Accelerated pace of thought processes	Frustration with inactivity and absence of progress.
Flexible thought processes	Seen as disruptive and disrespectful to authority and tradition.
Comprehensive synthesis	Frustration with demands for deadlines and for completion of each level prior to starting new inquiry.
Early ability to delay closure	If products are demanded as proof of learning, may refuse to pursue an otherwise interesting subject or line of inquiry.
Heightened capacity for seeing unusual and diverse relationships, integration of ideas and disciplines	Frustration at being considered "off the subject" or irrelevant in pursuing inquiry in areas other than subject being considered; considered odd or weird by others.
Ability to generate original ideas and solutions	Difficulty with rigid conformity; may be penalized for not following directions; may deal with rejection by becoming rebellious.
Early differential patterns for thought processing (e.g., thinking in alternatives, abstract terms, sensing consequences, making generalizations; visual thinking; use of metaphors and analogies)	Rejection or omission of detail; questions generalizations of others, which may be perceived as disrespectful behavior; considers linear tasks incomplete and boring.
Early ability to use and form conceptual frameworks	Frustration with inability of others to understand or appreciate original organization or insights; personally devised systems or structure may conflict with procedures of systems later taught.
An evaluative approach toward self and others	Perceived by others as elitist, conceited, superior, too critical; may become discouraged from self-criticism; can inhibit attempting new areas if fear of failure is too great; seen by others as too demanding, compulsive; can affect interpersonal relationships as others fail to live up to standards set by gifted individual; intolerant of stupidity.
Unusual intensity; persistent, goal-directed behavior	Perceived as stubborn, willful, uncooperative.

(continued)

vanced knowledge may become unpopular, and perhaps social isolates, because they lack the social skill of "hiding" their ability. Their enthusiasm dominates group discussions, and they take over group tasks out of an eagerness to get the task done.

In school, gifted children may become quickly bored because they have already mastered the curriculum. Some children who are bored and/or frustrated by the lack of challenge engage in inappropriate behaviors (according to their teachers) as they seek ways to engage themselves in interesting activities. Teachers may find

them disruptive if they ask questions which appear contradictory, if they challenge tasks and assignments, or if they refuse to conform because of their own sense of moral justice in a particular situation.

Stress and Anxiety

Perhaps the most serious issues faced by young, as well as older, gifted students are the development of stress and anxiety. It is unclear exactly how prevalent stress and anxiety are among gifted students or exactly how the en-

Table 3 *Continued*

Differentiating Characteristics	Possible Concomitant Problems
Unusual sensitivity to the expectations and feelings of others	Unusually vulnerable to criticism of others; high level of need for success and recognition.
Keen sense of humor—may be gentle or hostile.	Use of humor for critical attack upon others resulting in damage to interpersonal relationships.
Heightened self-awareness, accompanied by feelings of being different	Isolates self, resulting in being considered aloof, feeling rejected; perceives difference as negative attribute resulting in low self-esteem and inhibited growth emotionally and socially.
Idealism and sense of justice, which appear at an early age	Attempts unrealistic reforms and goals with resulting intense frustration.
Earlier development of an inner locus of control and satisfaction	Has difficulty conforming; rejects external validation and chooses to live by personal values that may be seen as a challenge to authority or tradition.
Unusual emotional depth and intensity	Unusual vulnerability; has problems focusing on realistic goals for life's work.
High expectations of self and others, often leading to high levels of frustration with self, others, and situations; perfectionism	Discouragement and frustration from high levels of self-criticism; has problems maintaining good interpersonal relations as others fail to maintain high standards imposed by gifted individual; immobilization due to high levels of frustration resulting from situations that do not meet expectations of excellence.
Strong need for consistency between abstract values and personal actions	Frustration with self and others leading to inhibited actualization of self and interpersonal relationships.
Advanced levels of moral judgment	Intolerance of and lack of understanding from peer group, leading to rejection and possible isolation.
Involvement with the meta-needs of society (e.g., justice, beauty, truth)	Involvement in obscure groups with narrow, perfectionistic beliefs.
Unusual quantity of input from the environment through a heightened sensory awareness	Attention moving diffusely toward many areas of interest; overexpenditure of energy due to lack of integration; seeming disconnectedness.
Unusual discrepancy between physical and intellectual development	Results in gifted adults who function with a mind/body dichotomy; gifted children who are only comfortable expressing themselves in mental activity, resulting in limited development both physically and mentally.
Low tolerance for the lag between athletic skills and standards	Refuse to take part in any activities where they do not excel; limiting their experience with otherwise pleasurable, constructive physical activities.
Early involvement and concern for intuitive knowing and metaphysical ideas and phenomena	Ridiculed by peers; not taken seriously by elders; considered weird or strange.

Note. Adapted from *Growing Up Gifted: Developing the Potential of Children at Home and School* (Fourth Edition) by B. Clark, 1992, New York: Macmillan. Copyright 1994 by Macmillan. Adapted with permission.

vironment and individual characteristics interact to produce stress. However, there is ample evidence that some gifted students experience extreme stress resulting from sensitivity to the adult world and the expectations of parents and teachers. As mentioned earlier, for some students this may stem from their capacity for greater perceptions and insights and their ability to take in and retain greater amounts of information from their environment and a consequent frustration with the inability to change an unfair world (Delisle, 1986). Stress for other gifted students appears to result from factors in the external environment including pressure from parents and teachers to achieve, which may result in setting extremely high self-standards (Genshaft & Broyles, 1991).

Perfectionism

A second serious manifestation of adjustment issues with young gifted children is the development of perfectionistic tendencies. The experience of always having the right answer and always being the one of whom much is expected may result in an internalization of unrealistic self-expectations, intense self-scrutiny, self-doubt, and self-criticism (Blatt, 1995; Sowa, McIntire, May, & Bland, 1994). As a result, students may internalize a need to present perfect products regardless of the task, the time or resource parameters, or the expectations of others. Consequently, they may be unable to complete and/or share products because of fear of having them judged to be inadequate. At early ages this may manifest itself in the re-copying and re-editing of seemingly exemplary products, disappointment in final products even after maximum effort has been expended, refusal to submit products because of the belief that the product fails to meet standards, and the like. At its extreme the child may frequently express frustration through tears or anger directed at self. At later ages, this tendency may underlie the underachievement syndrome (see the following section). If the student makes a decision (consciously or unconsciously) that it is better to fail by virtue of not trying than to be judged as less than perfect, then he or she may begin unconsciously to simply not finish or submit work for judgment, preferring to fail on the basis of no product rather than an inferior product.

In addition to the parental issues noted earlier, Blatt's 1995 analysis of the literature on perfectionism suggests that parental rejection and excessive authoritarian control predict the level of self-criticism in early adolescence and level of depression in later adolescence and young adulthood. Further, excessive concerns about making mistakes and worry about the judgments of others appear to be associated with "childhood experiences with non-approving or inconsistently approving parents whose love is always conditional upon performance" (p. 1010). Blatt notes that Barrow and Moore (1983) described four parenting modes or conditions conducive to the development of perfectionistic thinking: (a) overly critical or demanding, (b) parental standards which imply criticism, (c) absence of parental standards, and (d) parental behaviors which themselves serve as models for perfectionism.

Perceptions of Being Different

Advocates for gifted children have considered the label necessary for bringing about identification of education needs and services and for securing funding at local, state, and national levels. Some contend that the label may be a liability for the child because of stereotypic images and unrealistic expectations that adults may impose (Davis & Rimm, 1994). However, there is little evidence that elementary school children object to the label, find it detrimental, or reject participation in programs labeled for gifted students.

Nevertheless, preadolescence and adolescence are developmental periods during which the effects of being "different" (regardless of a label) have the most serious ramifications for the gifted individual. During these periods, the developmental task is one of individuation and separation from family and identification with peers. Dif-

ferences associated with giftedness at this time loom large for some gifted students and may negatively impact social, emotional, or even academic development. Davis and Rimm (1994) suggest that when gifted students become "conformity-conscious adolescents, many do not want such a label and they drop out of secondary gifted programs" (p. 401). Gifted adolescents believe people treat them differently when aware of their giftedness (Cross, Coleman, & Stewart, 1993), and they engage in pairing neutral or disclaiming statements to counterbalance any positive statements about themselves (Coleman & Cross, 1988). Studies of families of gifted students suggest that the presence of a gifted child in the family may cause sibling rivalry and competition but that the effects seem to decrease over time (Colangelo & Brower, 1987a, 1987b; Cornell, 1983). Further, earlier manifestation of problems may become more serious issues as the child no longer feels a need to please the adults in his or her life. One of the most serious school-related problems that begins to emerge at this time is underachievement.

Underachievement

One group of students likely to come to the attention of school psychologists are gifted underachievers. Parents and educators alike experience acute frustration when students of great potential begin to fall short of expectations in school. Perfectionism is sometimes noted in elementary children; underachievement is more common in the preadolescent or adolescent. While the underachievement of any child is a perplexing problem for parents and educators, the underachievement of the gifted child or adolescent seems particularly distressing—perhaps because of the expectation levels set by prior performance or evidence of ability.

Lists of characteristics of gifted underachievers include traits ranging from simple laziness to a "heightened sense of omnipotence" (Newman, Dember, & Krug, 1973, p. 109) accompanied by a belief that their verbal abilities will be a sufficient resource for solving any problem or achieving any goal. Drawing from her clinical observations, Rimm (1986) distinguished between categories of underachievement (manipulative, assertive, conforming, or nonconforming). Based on their review of the empirical literature and experience with underachievers, Mandel and Marcus (1988) created the underachiever categories of overanxious, impulsive and manipulative, situation specific (school), identity disorder (lacking strong self-image and insecure), and oppositional (negative, antisocial, and defiant).

Unfortunately, whereas a great deal of research effort has been expended on identifying family-functioning factors, personality characteristics, and educational issues associated with underachievement among gifted students, empirical data about causes/etiologies or successful interventions are scarce. Many theorists and practitioners (e.g., Rimm, 1986) have written about the "causes" of underachievement in talented children and youth and the factors associated with discrepancies between performance and expectations. Analyses of the problem have been based on premises ranging from psychoanalytic (Newman et al., 1973) to family systems theory (Zuccone & Amerikaner, 1986). As a result, underachievement has been attributed to factors ranging from Oedipal striving, castration anxiety, narcissism, eroticism, and ego imbalance to family practices such as overindulgence or unclear messages (Rimm, 1986). More recently, Baum, Renzulli, and Hébert (1995) categorized the causes of underachievement into emotional issues (dysfunctional families, student need for extraordinary attention, perfectionism, and depression), social/behavioral issues (influence of inappropriate peer group, questioning of social values, and lack of behavioral controls and social skills), lack of appropriate curriculum (lack of motivation stemming from lack of challenge, and emphasis on memorization of content), and learning disabilities and poor self-regulation.

Underachievement has often been attributed to family-achievement orientation, with a curvilinear relationship being posited between achievement and family expectations. Csikszentmihalyi et al. (1993) described the family structure of highly successful students as stable and their environment as stimulating. Parents devoted time and energy to meeting the needs of their highly able children, held high expectations in the children's talent areas, and emphasized productive work and goal directedness. However, the extreme of these parent behaviors has been associated with underachievement among gifted children. Inordinately high expectations, overinvolvement, placing too great a responsibility on children for achievement, and tying affection to achievement have been identified as characteristics of families of underachieving gifted children (Fine, 1967; McCall, Evahn & Kratzer, 1992).

The basis of underachievement also has been attributed to the schools. Delisle (1994) claimed that gifted underachievers are nonconformists who refuse to accept the mediocrity in education. Likewise, Whitmore (1988) argued that school work is too easy for these students, resulting in their failure to acquire appropriate learning behaviors necessary for later success. Similarly, Redding (1989) criticized the educational programs of gifted underachievers as routine, easy, and boring. Ziv (1977) concluded that achieving high grades with little effort results in gifted students developing poor study habits.

The lack of challenge also may lead to passive resistance regarding school assignments and required activities. Bruns (1992) identified a combination of traits suggestive of passive resistance—not overtly refusing, but only doing assignments of interest and never bothering to turn in other assignments. In this way the student exerts control over the home or school environment without outward conflict but with the consequence of low grades.

Overreliance on Process Adjustment or Achievement Adjustment

In a recent study of gifted middle school students, Sowa and May (in press) examined the themes emerging from extended qualitative interviews and observations of the children and their teachers, peers, and family. The information was used as the basis for developing a model of adjustment and adjustment difficulties in gifted children. The researchers found that some children rely almost exclusively on achievement adjustment, "engaging in socially acceptable behaviors which include purposeful attempts to comply or adjust to the detriment of self" (p. 14). These children were seen as model students by teachers; however, they often suppressed their beliefs in order to conform to peer, parent, or teacher expectations. They experienced considerable conflict when peer and parent expectations conflicted or when their belief systems were consistently in conflict with expected behaviors. The children who exhibited these behaviors were from families where a sense of belonging was emphasized to the detriment of a sense of self and where the families relied on rigid rules, rewards were based on conformity to family expectations, and the family took precedence over the individual.

Gifted children who were characterized as overly reliant on process adjustment experienced congruence between their beliefs and their behaviors but experienced conflict when the actions resulting from their beliefs were seen as inappropriate by others. Thus it appears that, in this case, the gifted adolescent's internal appraisal mitigates against behaviors which facilitate achievement adjustment. As noted by Sowa and May (in press, p. 18), for these children "emotional adjustment exists at the expense of social adjustment." These children are usually from families characterized as having an "exaggerated sense of individual importance, . . . erratic rules, individual domination (often by the gifted child), and expectations of system modification to individual needs" (p. 17).

Gender Differences

The challenges faced by the gifted adolescent seem to vary by gender, as well as by race and age. For example, Colangelo and Assouline (1994) found that while gifted students' self-concepts are generally much above average, gifted high school boys had significantly lower behavioral self-concept than any other group (elementary through high school male or female); physical appearance self-concept of gifted students was considerably lower than behavioral, intellectual, and social status scales for all gifted groups. By junior high, gifted girls had begun to show greater anxiety and feelings of isolation. By high school, gifted girls rated themselves lowest of all groups. Similarly, high school gifted girls saw themselves much below average in popularity even though the overall sample was average on this domain. Finally, the high school gifted students had lower scores on happiness and satisfaction scales than the elementary students.

Gifted females are one group that has received considerable attention in the study of changes that occur in the development process, particularly as these young women enter middle school and high school. Any generalizations about the achievement of gifted students, as well as their social and emotional adjustment, need to be tempered by consideration of the adolescent female. While the achievement levels of gifted females and males are equally high when measured by school grades and honors, significant gender differences emerge in academic achievement as measured by standardized tests. Differences favoring males are particularly apparent in test scores used in awarding scholarships and determining college entrance, as well as in scores in the areas of math, science, and technology. Likewise, gifted females and males differ in career aspirations, with males favoring careers in science and technology and females selecting careers in the social sciences and humanities (Callahan, 1993; Callahan & Reis, 1996).

Underachievement among gifted girls begins to reveal itself as early as fifth grade, becomes prevalent in middle school, and extends into adulthood (Arnold, 1993; Bell, 1989). In late elementary school, gifted girls begin to lose self-confidence, increasingly doubt their intellectual competence, perceive themselves as less capable than they actually are, believe that boys can rely on innate ability while they must work hard, and value their personal achievements less than males (Callahan & Reis, 1996). In Arnold's study of valedictorians (1993), the percentage of females perceiving themselves as being "far above average" declined from 21% at the time of high school graduation to 4% at the end of their sophomore year in college, while the self-perceptions of males remained nearly the same. None of the five females in a qualitative study of gifted adolescents attributed her success in school to extraordinary ability (Callahan, Cunningham, & Plucker, 1994). Noble (1989) found that even when girls acknowledged their achievements, they reported hiding their abilities and achievements to gain social acceptance at some point in their lives. Some studies have even documented decreased participation of females in programs for the gifted, with females making up a slight majority of students in gifted programs in elementary school but being in the minority by the end of high school (Read, 1991; Silverman, 1986).

As discussed earlier, gifted females also face peer pressure to conform to stereotypic expectations of behavior, career goals, and achievement. Noble (1989) noted a tendency of peers to reject girls who reveal their intelligence. Parental attitudes have been identified as sources of lowered self-esteem. For example, parents note giftedness in females at older ages than they note it in males, and they tend to underestimate their daughters' abilities (Eccles & Jacobs, 1985).

Barriers to gifted females' achievement exist in schools in many forms. Gifted girls receive less attention in classrooms than any other group (Eccles & Blumfield, 1985); they are more likely to be rejected by others and are more negatively affected by that rejection than gifted boys (American Association of University Women, 1992). They also experience differential treatment from teachers and are exposed regularly to stereotyping (Cramer, 1989).

Cultural, Racial, and Social Factors

Other issues and problems for gifted students may derive from culturally and/or socially based factors. For example, high achieving African-American students are often haunted by accusations of "acting White" and by peer pressure to avoid academic excellence leading to internal conflicts and a perceived need to make difficult choices between cultures (Duru, 1991; Ford, 1994b). Children commonly identified as at risk in the school population, minority or poor children, face a unique set of pressures as gifted students. Ford (1994a), for example, found that many highly able African-American students hid their academic abilities behind the facade of class clown, invested in athletics rather than academics, dropped out, or refused to exert the effort required for excellent performance. To achieve was often perceived as "acting White." Students from other cultures, from impoverished backgrounds, or with disabling conditions may face additional stressors or constraints. These range from the pressure to achieve often placed on Asian-Americans by parents with high academic expectations, and by teachers with stereotypic assumptions about interests in mathematics and science, to a lack of recognition of abilities. A consequence is the lack of challenge and opportunity to achieve full potential because of language, experiential backgrounds, or a disabling condition (e.g., Hispanic children, poor children, children with physical disabilities or learning disabilities).

Alternative Actions

The roles of school psychologists and others in the helping professions include assisting in the identification of talent, providing guidance in educational placement decisions, and providing services aimed at developing the maximum potential in conjunction with healthy social and emotional adjustment. To fully encompass these functions, the school psychologist and counselor must be concerned with those students who have been identified as

Table 4 *Summary of Recommended Interventions*

Adjustment Issue	Recommendation

Stress	■ Work with students on strategies to
	  a. Identify stresses and physiological reactions including faulty beliefs that exacerbate the stress (Genshaft & Broyles, 1991).
	  b. Develop a checklist of warning signs to use in avoiding the escalation of stress (Genshaft & Broyles, 1991).
	  c. Use adaptive coping strategies and decision making (Genshaft & Broyles, 1991; Genshaft, Greenbaum, & Borovsky, 1995).
	  d. Activate stress management (Genshaft & Broyles, 1991).
	  e. Increase relaxation and calming (Broyles, Greenbaum, & Borovsky, 1995; Richter, 1984).
	■ Provide instruction in
	  a. Controlling and using energy (Genshaft & Broyles, 1991).
	  b. The use of physical exercise to reduce stress (Genshaft & Broyles, 1991).
	  c. The use of diaries or journals.
	■ Help parents set realistic expectations and clarify expectations to the child.
	■ Reward the child for both success and attempts at success; to learn that winning is not everything (Genshaft, Greenbaum, & Borovsky, 1995).
	■ Help the child learn to compartmentalize thinking and stress (Genshaft, Greenbaum, & Borovsky, 1995).
	■ Help the child use humor to diffuse tense situations (Genshaft, Greenbaum, & Borovsky, 1995).

Perfectionism	■ Teach the child to set realistic standards (Burns, 1980) and to distinguish between pursuit of excellence and perfectionism (Adderholt-Elliot, 1991). ■ Teach self-talk, relaxation, imagery, and role-playing (Barrow & Moore, 1983). ■ Use reality therapy (Glasser, 1975). ■ Encourage the child to laugh at his or her mistakes (Adderholt-Elliot, 1991). ■ Encourage an internal locus of control (Adderholt-Elliot, 1991).
Underachievement	■ Focus on interactive dynamics of individual, family, and school (Moore, 1996). ■ Implement curricular changes that give the student an opportunity to focus on self-selected topics, using strengths, acting as professionals, and addressing real-world problems (Baum, Renzulli, & Hébert, 1995).

(continued)

gifted and with discerning behaviors which may be indicative of talent overlooked or mislabeled. The first realm of involvement for the school psychologist may be that of identification and educational placement.

Identification and Placement

The identification of gifted students relies on the appropriate interpretation of test scores and performance information. A fair and unbiased identification process is also dependent on the alertness of professionals within and outside the classroom to behaviors that are indicative of giftedness even in the absence of high grades or scores on traditional measures of intellectual ability or achievement. An important first step is to look for characteristics presented in this chapter, especially in Tables 1 and 4, and to make sure students with a constellation of these characteristics are considered for special program options.

The educational placement of a gifted student should be predicated on the match of the student's needs with curricular and instructional options. There are many options available to the gifted and talented student; how-

ever, schools often limit the options to "the program" for gifted students. A more appropriate strategy is to ask the question, "What do we need to do to meet the needs of this child?" The question should be answered both in terms of administrative arrangement (how the child is placed or grouped) and curricular options (what the child learns). It is not always clear where the administrative decision ends and the curricular option begins; however, the most important decision lies in the level of challenge offered to the child.

Alternatives for Promoting Academic Achievement

Acceleration

In some cases, early entrance to kindergarten, grade skipping, or other forms of acceleration are appropriate. Radical acceleration is most warranted when a child is considered highly intellectually gifted and academically advanced across the disciplines. Another acceleration option is for students to be accelerated in a single subject area either within the classroom or by the child going to another classroom or school for instruction. This is the

Table 4 *Continued*

Adjustment Issue	Recommendation
Inappropriate Process	■ Work with teachers and parents to create belief in the student (Baum, Renzulli, & Hébert, 1995). ■ Help the student find a strong model for role identification (Rimm, 1995). ■ Diagnose and provide alternatives for manipulative processes of parent and child (Rimm, 1995). ■ Help parents foster *simultaneous* adjustment mechanisms (Sowa & May, in press). ■ Develop personal identity which includes trust in cognitive self-appraisal, especially among those students over-reliant on achievement adjustment (Sowa & May, in press). ■ Help the student incorporate others into his or her appraisal process (Sowa & May, in press).
Female Underachievers	■ Provide role modeling and mentorships (Hollinger, 1991). ■ Provide nonstereotypic career counseling (Hollinger, 1991). ■ Encourage exploration of strengths and learning to self-evaluate and acknowledge talents (Hollinger, 1991). ■ Encourage career development, particularly development of skills in lifework planning, decision making, negotiation, and compromise (Hollinger, 1991). ■ Arrange support groups (Hollinger, 1991, 1995). ■ Alter conflicting messages from significant others (Hollinger, 1995). ■ Provide parents with guidelines for nonstereotypic child-rearing practices (Davis & Rimm, 1994; Hollinger, 1995). ■ Enhance perceptions of self-efficacy (Hollinger, 1995). ■ Encourage exploration of issues of sex-role stereotyping and socialization, assertiveness, achievement motivation, and comfort with success (Hollinger, 1995). ■ Work with librarians and teachers to ensure gender-role stereotyped books, classroom materials, films, and the like are not used (Davis & Rimm, 1994). ■ Examine all assessment tools for stereotypic examples or gender bias (Davis & Rimm, 1994). ■ Encourage females to participate in leadership roles (Davis & Rimm, 1994). ■ Encourage females to take advanced courses across all disciplines (Davis & Rimm, 1994). ■ Provide assertiveness training (Davis & Rimm, 1994). ■ Provide parents with guidelines or suggestions for creating nonsexist environments (Davis & Rimm, 1994). ■ Help females learn task values of mathematics and science (Hollinger, 1991). ■ Provide biographies of gifted females (Reis, 1987).

most likely action for reading, language arts, or mathematics. For further discussion of acceleration, see Boatman et al. (1995). In any accelerative option, the assumption is being made that the curriculum will either be covered at a faster pace or learned material will be skipped. The intention is to move the child through the regular curriculum at a faster pace to reduce boredom and consequent frustration.

In considering candidates for early entrance, the following questions should be addressed (adapted from Davis & Rimm, 1994):

1. Is the child considered intellectually precocious (with an IQ over 130 or two standard deviations above the mean for the system)?
2. Does the child have the eye-hand coordination skills necessary for the activities expected (e.g., cutting, pasting, drawing, writing)?
3. Is the child ready to read?
4. Does the child have the appropriate social maturity? Has the child adapted to preschool experiences with other children? Does the child have friends of the same age as the grade he or she is about to enter?
5. Is the child mature enough to follow directions and handle the routine of school?
6. Does the child have a history of good health? (Frequent absences may create too much stress for the child.)
7. Is the receiving teacher willing to help the child and able to adjust to the developmental differences?
8. Does the family value education and academic achievement?
9. Is the family flexible and willing to consider adjustments if early entrance does not seem to be appropriate?

Likewise, the following guidelines, adapted from Davis and Rimm (1994) should be considered whenever grade skipping is at issue:

1. A child should have an IQ score over 130.
2. Although older students (after about age 14) have successfully moved directly from middle school to col-

lege, a young child should only skip one grade at a time.

3. Gaps in skills and knowledge should be assessed, and steps should be taken to provide the necessary basic skills.

4. The teacher and parents must be supportive.

5. The child should be assessed for social and emotional maturity as well as the intellectual ability to handle grade skipping.

6. Teachers, counselors, and peers should be available to help deal with social problems if they occur.

7. Every grade-skipping decision needs to made separately and should include consideration of physical maturity, emotional stability, motivations, ability to handle challenge, *and the child's willingness to skip a grade.*

8. Every grade-skipping placement should be considered a trial placement, and the option for returning to age-appropriate placement should be clear to the student and the parent without the stigma of failure.

Enrichment

Enrichment options may be offered either within the regular classroom or for specially arranged groups of children. In either case, the child remains with age peers or is provided instruction within cross-age groupings. The curriculum offered within these settings is considered to be more in-depth, advanced, and/or extensions of the regular content of the curriculum. One of the most popular enrichment options is that described by Renzulli and Reis (1985) called the Schoolwide Enrichment Model focusing on maximizing the above-average ability, creativity, and task commitment of gifted students in the production of products reflecting the methodology, problems, and products of the disciplines. Enrichment programs are constructed around a variety of goals but generally include maximizing the development of skills related to creative productivity; higher level thinking skills; broadened, abstract, transformed knowledge; independent and self-directed learning; and the like.

Compacting

One strategy which cuts across enrichment and acceleration programs is compacting. This procedure, in short, is a system for identifying the skills and knowledge already mastered by the child in order to eliminate repetitive instruction. While this may seem a logical instructional practice, Westberg, Archambault, Dobyns, and Slavin (1993) report "little differentiation in the instructional and curricular practices, grouping arrangements, and verbal interactions for gifted and talented students in the regular classroom" (p. 120). Reis et al. (1993) reported that even when more than 50% of the regular curriculum in reading and mathematics is eliminated from their programs, gifted students still achieve at a higher level on standardized achievement tests than gifted students whose programs are not compacted.

Alternatives for Promoting Social and Emotional Development

The development of healthy social relationships and emotional maturity of gifted students entails a complex interaction of the family, school, and individual (Moore, 1996; Sowa et al., 1996). In most cases, gifted individuals negotiate developmental stages successfully. However, in those cases where the gifted child does have adjustment difficulties, it is imperative that professionals and parents not assume that the child will be able to solve the problem or know which resources to bring to bear in seeking a solution.

If intervention is called for, the first stage is obviously an assessment of the seriousness and importance of the difficulty faced by the child. For example, parents of a gifted child may worry about friendships when the child has only one or two friends. However, parents may be confusing popularity with social adjustment. The critical variable is the degree to which the child has significant peers to whom she can relate and how comfortable she feels with herself in the home and school environment. Because evidence on the development of behaviors such as those associated with underachievement suggest a very complex dynamic (Moore, 1996), professionals need to examine and intervene at multiple levels when gifted children face problems they themselves cannot resolve.

The second stage is to identify the individual, family, and school resources that can be brought to bear on the problem. Gifted students obviously have greater intellectual and problem-solving resources to use, but these skills can also be used to rationalize behavior. Great facility with verbal expression can help the child bring the problem to the attention of professionals, but it can also be used to hide the real issues or problems from the teacher, counselor, or psychologist.

There are many circumstances in which adjustment issues present special challenges to gifted students and may require the intervention of the school psychologist and counselor. Among these are stress management, perfectionism, underachievement, issues facing gifted females, issues of achievement and process adjustment and peer pressure brought on minorities. Table 4 presents a brief summary of recommendations for interventions emanating from research on gifted children with difficulties and clinicians' experiences with intervention practices.

Summary

Many myths and folktales surround the gifted child. One common misconception is that gifted children are so superior that they "will make it" academically no matter what is offered by the school program. Another mistaken view is that genius and insanity are closely tied and that very gifted individuals are likely to be maladjusted emotionally or socially. In reality, the majority of gifted students are well adjusted and experience considerable success in school. However, as with all populations of human beings, some will experience academic difficulties and some will have problems in the areas of social or emotional adjustment. Some problems arise, as they might for any child or adolescent, as a result of the interactions of that child's personality with his or her family, school, and/or environment. In addition, some of the very characteristics which result in the identification of these children as gifted will make them more vulnerable to academic problems of perfectionism or underachievement or to social and emotional adjustment problems. For example, characteristics such as more highly developed perceptual abilities and sensitivities may create undue anxieties; increased adult or self-imposed pressures to achieve unrealistic standards may create perfectionistic behaviors; and boredom with the school curriculum may create underachieving behaviors. Further, the peer pressures brought to bear on African-American students may create conflict between the expectations of the adult world of parents and schools and the child or adolescent's need for relationships with peers. Stereotypes of male and female behaviors may impede the development of the full potential of female gifted students and may act as a deterrent for appropriate choices by male gifted students.

The school—including teachers, counselors, and psychologists—and the family of the child both play roles in ensuring appropriate development of these children. Providing both a challenging and appropriate curriculum and supportive, encouraging learning environments that set high goals but do not create unnecessary stress should be the first priority of the school. However, the issues which children and adolescents face outside the classroom may impact both academic and social/emotional development and present issues to the school psychologist and counselor that require expedient diagnosis and intervention.

Recommended Resources

Bireley, M., & Genshaft, J. (1991). *Understanding the gifted adolescent: Educational, developmental, and multicultural issues.* New York: Teachers College.
This volume ranges from personal and social issues in general to the specifics of perfectionism, eating disorders, stress management, underachievement, and multicultural issues.

Butler-Por, N. (1993). Underachieving gifted students. In K. A. Heller, F. J. Monks, & A. H. Passow (Eds.), *International handbook of research and development of giftedness and talent* (pp. 649–668). Oxford, England: Pergamon.
This comprehensive, cross-cultural review of the literature on underachievement provides the reader with information on etiologies and the various treatments that have been used in treating underachievement.

Genshaft, J. L., Bireley, M., & Hollinger, C. L. (1995). *Serving gifted and talented students: A resource for school personnel.* Austin, TX: Pro-Ed.
Designed for support personnel in schools including school psychologists and counselors, this volume covers developmental perspectives, assessment and evaluation issues, curricular issues, personal and interpersonal issues, and intervention strategies.

Monks, F. J., & Mason, E. J. (1993). Developmental theories and giftedness. In K. A. Heller, F. J. Monks, & A. H. Passow (Eds.), *International handbook of research and development of giftedness and talent* (pp. 89–101). Oxford, England: Pergamon.
In this chapter, the authors provide a comprehensive discussion of the various theoretical approaches to conceiving and defining giftedness.

Shore, B. M., & Kanevsky, L. S. (1993). Thinking processes: Being and becoming gifted. In K. A. Heller, F. J. Monks, & A. H. Passow (Eds.), *International handbook of research and development of giftedness and talent* (pp. 133–147). Oxford, England: Pergamon.
In this chapter, the authors provide a comprehensive description of the ways in which the thinking of the gifted child differs from that of the average student with an emphasis on both speed of processing and quality of processing abilities.

Swassing, R. (Ed.). (1994). Affective dimensions of being gifted [Special issue]. *Roeper Review, 17.*
A compendium of recent research on social and emotional development of gifted students, this special issue includes articles dealing with general issues of adjustment as well as special issues of African-American, Asian, and female gifted students.

References

Abeel, L. B., Callahan, C. M., & Hunsaker, S. L. (1994). *The use of published instruments in the identification of gifted students.* Washington, DC: National Association for Gifted Children.

Adderholdt-Elliot, M. (1991). Perfectionism and the gifted adolescent. In M. Bireley & J. Genshaft (Eds.), *Understanding the gifted adolescent: Educational, developmental, and multicultural issues* (pp. 65–75). New York: Teachers College.

American Association of University Women. (1992). *How schools shortchange girls.* Washington, DC: Author/National Education Association.

Arnold, K. D. (1993). Academically talented women in the 1980s: The Illinois Valedictorian Project. In K. Hulbert & D. Schuster (Eds.), *Women's lives through time: Educated American women of the twentieth century* (pp. 314–393). San Francisco: Jossey-Bass.

Barrow, J., & Moore, C. (1983). Group interventions with perfectionistic thinking. *Personnel and Guidance Journal, 61,* 612–615.

Baum, S. M., Renzulli, J. S., & Hébert, T. P. (1995). Reversing underachievement: Creative productivity as a systematic reform. *Gifted Child Quarterly, 39,* 224–235.

Bell, L. A. (1989). Something's wrong here and it's not me: Challenging the dilemmas that block girls' success. *Journal for the Education of the Gifted, 12,* 118–130.

Bland, L. C., Sowa, C. J., & Callahan, C. M. (1994). An overview of resilience in gifted children. *Roeper Review, 17,* 77–80.

Blatt, S. J. (1995). The destructiveness of perfectionism: Implications for the treatment of depression. *American Psychologist, 50,* 1003–1020.

Bloom, B. S. (Ed.). (1985). *Developing talent in young people.* New York: Ballantine.

Boatman, T. A., Davis K. G., & Benbow, C. P. (1995). Gifted education. In A. Thomas & J. Grimes (Eds.), *Best practices in school psychology-III* (pp. 1083–1095). Bethesda, MD: National Association of School Psychologists.

Burns, D. (1980, November). The perfectionist's script for self-defeat. *Psychology Today,* pp. 34–54.

Burns, J. H. (1992, Winter). They can but they don't: Helping students overcome work inhibition. *American Educator, 16,* 38–47.

Callahan, C. M. (1993). *The performance of high ability students in the United States on national and international tests.* Washington, DC: National Association for Gifted Children.

Callahan, C. M., Cunningham, C. M., & Plucker, J. A. (1994). Foundations for the future: The socio-emotional development of gifted, adolescent women. *Roeper Review, 17,* 99–105.

Callahan, C. M., & Hunsaker, S. L. (1991, April). *The National Research Center: Identification and Evaluation Project.* Paper presented at the Annual Meeting of the Council for Exceptional Children, Atlanta, GA.

Callahan, C. M., & Reis, S. M. (1996). Gifted girls: Remarkable women. In K. D. Arnold, R. B. Subotnik, & K. D. Noble (Eds.), *Remarkable women.* Creskill, NJ: Hampton Press.

Callahan, C. M., Tomlinson, C. A., & Pizzat, P. M. (n.d.). *Contexts for promise: Noteworthy practices and innovations in the identification of gifted students.* Charlottesville, VA: National Research Center on the Gifted and Talented.

Clark, B. (1992). *Growing up gifted: Developing the potential of children at home and at school* (4th ed.). New York: Macmillan.

Colangelo, N., & Assouline, S. A. (1994). Self-concept of gifted students: Patterns by self-concept domain, grade level, and gender. In M. W. Kazko & F. J. Monks (Eds.), *Nurturing talent: Individual needs and social ability.* Assen, Netherlands: Van Corcum.

Colangelo, N., & Brower, P. (1987a). Gifted youngsters and their siblings: Long-term impact of labeling on their academic and social self-concepts. *Roeper Review, 10,* 101–103.

Colangelo, N., & Brower, P. (1987b). Labeling gifted youngsters: Long-term impact on families. *Gifted Child Quarterly, 31,* 75–78.

Coleman, L. J., & Cross, T. L. (1988). Is being gifted a social handicap? *Journal for the Education of the Gifted, 11,* 41–56.

Cornell, D. G., (1983). Gifted children: The impact of positive labeling on the family system. *Journal of Orthopsychiatry, 53,* 322–355.

Cramer, R. H. (1989). Attitudes of gifted boys and girls toward math. *Roeper Review, 11,* 128–130.

Cross, T. L., Coleman, L. J., & Stewart, R. A. (1993). The social cognition of gifted adolescents: An exploration of the stigma of giftedness paradigm. *Roeper Review, 16,* 37–40.

Csikszentmihalyi, M., Rathunde, K., & Whalen, S. (1993). *Talented teenagers: The roots of success and failure.* Cambridge, England: Cambridge University Press.

Davis, G. A., & Rimm, S. B. (1994). *Education of the gifted and talented* (3rd ed.). Boston: Allyn and Bacon.

Delisle, J. R. (1986). Death with honors: Suicide among gifted adolescents. *Journal of Counseling and Development, 64,* 558–560.

Delisle, J. R. (1994). Dealing with the stereotype of underachievement. *Gifted Child Today, 17,* 20–21.

Dembrowski, K. (1964). *Positive disintegration.* London: Little Brown.

Dembrowski, K. (1972). *Psychoneurosis is not an illness.* London: Gryf.

Dunn, R., Dunn, & K., Treffinger, D. (1992). *Bringing out the giftedness in your child.* New York: Wiley.

Duru, N. J. (1991, May 19). You're just trying to act white. *Washington Post,* p. D7.

Eccles, J. S., & Blumfield, P. (1985). Classroom experiences and student gender: Are there differences and do they matter? In L. C. Wilkinson & C. B. Marret (Eds.), *Gender influences in classroom interaction* (pp. 79–114). Greenwich, CT: JAI Press.

Eccles, J. S., & Jacobs, J. E. (1985). Gender differences in math ability: The impact of the media on parents. *Educational Researcher, 14,* 20–25.

Fine, B. (1967). *Underachievers: How they can be helped.* New York: Dutton.

Ford, D. Y. (1994a). Nurturing resilience in gifted black youth. *Roeper Review, 17,* 80–84.

Ford, D. Y. (1994b). *The recruitment and retention of African-American students in gifted education programs: Implications and recommendations* (Research Based Decision Making Monograph No. 9406). Storrs, CT: University of Connecticut, National Research Center on the Gifted and Talented.

Gallagher, J. J. (1986). Our love-hate affair with gifted children. *Gifted Child Quarterly, 33,* 12–19.

Gardner, H. (1983). *Frames of mind.* New York: Basic Books.

Genshaft, J., & Broyles, J. (1991). Stress management and gifted adolescents. In M. Bireley & J. Genshaft (Eds.), *Understanding the gifted adolescent: Educational, developmental, and multicultural issues* (pp. 76–88). New York: Teachers College.

Genshaft, J., Greenbaum, S., & Borovsky, S. (1995). Stress and the gifted. In J. L. Genshaft, M. Bireley, & C. L. Hollinger (Eds.), *Serving gifted and talented students: A resource for school personnel* (pp. 257–268). Austin, TX: Pro-Ed.

Glasser, W. (1975). *Reality therapy.* New York: Harper and Row.

Hofstadter, R. (1963). *Anti-intellectualism in America.* New York: Vintage Books.

Hollinger, C. (1991). Career choices for gifted adolescents: Overcoming stereotypes. In M. Bireley & J. Genshaft (Eds.), *Understanding the gifted adolescent* (pp. 201–213). New York: Teachers College.

Hollinger, C. (1995). Stress as a function of gender: Special needs of gifted girls and women. In J. L. Genshaft, M. Bireley, & C. L. Hollinger (Eds.), *Serving gifted and talented students: A resource for school personnel* (pp. 269–284). Austin, TX: Pro-Ed.

Hollingworth, L. S. (1931). The child of very superior intelligence as a special problem in social adjustment. *Mental Hygiene, 15*(1), 3–16.

Hollingworth, L. S. (1942). *Children above 180 IQ Stanford-Binet: Origin and development.* Yonkers-on-Hudson, NY: World Book.

Hunsaker, S. L., & Callahan, C. M. (1995). Creativity and giftedness: Published instrument uses and abuses. *Gifted Child Quarterly, 39,* 110–114.

Kaufman, F. (1991). The courage to succeed: A new look at underachievement. Keynote address at AEGUS (Association for the Education of Gifted Underachieving Students) conference, University of Tuscaloosa, Tuscaloosa, AL.

Mandel, H. P., & Marcus, S. I. (1988). *The psychology of underachievement: Differential diagnosis and differential treatment.* New York: Wiley.

McCall, R. B., Evahn, C., Kratzer, L. (1992). *High school underachievers.* Newbury Park, CA: Sage.

Milgram, R. M., & Milgram, N. A. (1976). Personal characteristics of gifted Israeli children. *Journal of Genetic Psychology, 125,* 185–192.

Monks, F. J., & Mason, E. J. (1993). Developmental theories and giftedness. In K. A. Heller, F. J. Monks, & A. H. Passow (Eds.), *International handbook of research and development of giftedness and talent* (pp. 89–101). Oxford, England: Pergamon.

Moore, B. J. (1996). *Three case studies of underachieving gifted high school students.* Unpublished doctoral dissertation, University of Virginia, Charlottesville, VA.

Newman, C. J., Dember, C. F., & Krug, O. (1973). "He can but he won't." *The Psychoanalytic Study of the Child, 28,* 83–129.

Noble, K. D. (1989). Counseling gifted women: Becoming the heroes of our own stories. *Journal for the Education of the Gifted, 12,* 131–141.

Oram, G. D., Cornell, D. G., & Rutemiller, L. A. (1995). Relations between academic aptitude and psychosocial adjustment in gifted program students. *Gifted Child Quarterly, 39,* 236–244.

Plucker, J. A. (1994). Issues in the social and emotional adjustment and development of a gifted Chinese-American student. *Roeper Review, 17,* 89–94.

Read, C. R. (1991). Gender distribution in programs for the gifted. *Roeper Review, 13,* 188–193.

Redding, R. E. (1989). Underachievement in the verbally gifted: Implications for pedagogy. *Psychology in the Schools, 26,* 275–291.

Reis, S. M. (1987). We can't change what we don't recognize: Understanding the special needs of gifted females. *Gifted Child Quarterly, 31,* 83–88.

Reis, S. M., Neu, T. W., & McGuire, J. M. (1995). *Talents in two places: Case studies of high ability students with learning disabilities who have achieved* (Research Monograph No. 95114). Storrs, CT: University of Connecticut, National Research Center on the Gifted and Talented.

Reis, S. M., Westberg, K. L., Kulikowick, J., Caillard, F., Hébert, T., Plucker, J., Purcell, J. H., Rogers, J. B., & Smist, J. M. (1993). *Why not let high ability students start school in January? The curriculum compacting study.* (Monograph No. 93106). Storrs, CT: University of Connecticut, National Research Center on the Gifted and Talented.

Renzulli, J. S. (1977). *The enrichment triad model: A guide for developing defensible programs for the gifted.* Mansfield Center, CT: Creative Learning Press.

Renzulli, J. S. (1978). What makes giftedness: Reexamining a definition. *Phi Delta Kappan, 60,* 180–184.

Renzulli, J. S., & Reis, S. M. (1985). *The schoolwide enrichment model: A comprehensive plan for educational excellence.* Mansfield Center, CT: Creative Learning Press.

Richter, N. C. (1984). The efficacy of relaxation training with children. *Abnormal Child Psychology, 12,* 319–344.

Rimm, S. B. (1986). *Underachievement syndrome: Causes and cures.* Watertown, WI: Apple Publishing.

Rimm, S. B. (1995). Underachievement syndrome in gifted students. In J. L. Genshaft, M. Bireley, & C. L. Hollinger (Eds.), *Serving gifted and talented students: A resource for school personnel* (pp. 173–200). Austin, TX: Pro-Ed.

Robinson, N. M. (1993). *Parenting the very young, gifted child* (Research Based Decision-Making Series Report No. 9308). Storrs, CT: University of Connecticut, National Research Center on the Gifted and Talented.

Roedell, W. (1984). Vulnerabilities of highly gifted children. *Roeper Review, 6,* 127–130.

Shore, B. M., & Kanevsky, L. S. (1993). Thinking processes: Being and becoming gifted. In K. A. Heller, F. J. Monks, & A. H. Passow (Eds.), *International handbook of research and development of giftedness and talent* (pp. 133–147). Oxford, England: Pergamon.

Silverman, L. K. (1986). What happens to gifted girls? In C. J. Maker (Ed.), *Defensible programs for the gifted* (pp. 43–89). Rockville, MD: Aspen.

Silverman, L. K. (1993). Counseling needs and programs for the gifted. In K. A. Heller, F. J. Monk, & A. H. Passow (Eds.), *International handbook of research and development of giftedness and talent* (pp. 631–647). Oxford, England: Pergamon Press.

Sowa, C. J., & May, K. M. (in press). Conceptual model of social and emotional adjustment of gifted children and adolescents. *Gifted Child Quarterly.*

Sowa, C. J., McIntire, J., May, K. M., & Bland, L. (1994). Social and emotional adjustment themes across gifted children. *Roeper Review, 17,* 95–98.

Sternberg, R. J. (1986). The triarchic theory of intellectual giftedness. In R. J. Sternberg & J. E. Davidson (Eds.), *Conceptions of giftedness* (pp. 223–246). Cambridge, England: Cambridge University Press.

Sternberg, R. J., & Davidson, J. E. (1985). Cognitive development in the gifted and talented. In F. D. Horowitz & M. O'Brien (Eds.), *The gifted and talented: Developmental perspectives* (pp. 75–98). Washington, DC: American Psychological Association.

Terman, L. M. (1925). *Genetic studies of genius: Vol. 1. Mental and physical traits of a thousand gifted children.* Stanford, CA: Stanford University Press.

Terman, L. M., & Oden, M. H. (1947). *Genetic studies of genius: Vol. 4. The gifted child grows up.* Stanford, CA: Stanford University Press.

Terman, L. M., & Oden, M. H. (1959). *Genetic studies of genius: Vol. 5. The gifted group at midlife.* Stanford, CA: Stanford University Press.

Terrasier, J. C. (1985). Dyssynchrony-uneven development. In J. Freeman (Ed.). *The psychology of gifted children* (pp. 265–274). New York: John Wiley.

Tolan, S. (1989). Special problems of highly gifted children. *Understanding Our Gifted, 1* (5), 7–10.

U.S. Department of Education. (1993). *National excellence: A case for developing America's talent.* Washington, DC: U.S. Government Printing Office.

Westberg, K. L., Archambault, F. X., Dobyns, S. M., & Slavin, T. J. (1993). The classroom practices observation study. *Journal for the Education of the Gifted, 16,* 120–146.

U.S. Office of Education. (1972). *Education of the gifted and talented: Report to the Congress of the United States by the U.S. Commissioner of Education.* Washington, DC: U.S. Government Printing Office.

Whitmore, J. R. (1988). Gifted children at risk for learning difficulties. *Teaching Exceptional Children, 20,* 10–14.

Willard-Holt, C. (1994). *Recognizing talent: Cross-case study of two high potential students with cerebral palsy* (Collaborative Research Study Report No. CRS94308). Storrs, CT: University of Connecticut, National Research Center on the Gifted and Talented.

Ziv, A. (1977). *Counselling the intellectually gifted child.* Toronto: Guidance Center, University of Toronto.

Zuccone, C. F., & Amerikaner, M. (1986). Counseling underachievers: A family systems approach. *Journal of Counseling and Development, 64,* 590–592.

39

Creativity

Jack H. Presbury
A. Jerry Benson

James Madison University

E. Paul Torrance

Georgia Studies of Creative Behavior
University of Georgia

Background and Development

It should be obvious to the most casual observer that, without creativity, humankind would have made no progress at all. Necessity may be the "mother of invention," but without creativity invention is stillborn. The literature is replete with attempts to define creativity. Vernon (1989) has offered a comprehensive definition of creativity that seems to condense most of the others: "Creativity means a person's capacity to produce new and original ideas, insights, restructuring, inventions, or artistic objects, which are accepted by experts as being of scientific, aesthetic, social, or technological value" (p. 94).

Creativity is not a possession of a few genius thinkers. Lefrancois (1982) noted that "just as very low intelligence is stupidity, so very low creativity is ordinariness" (p. 264). Creativity is viewed by most theorists and educators (Ford & Harris, 1992; Sternberg & Lubart, 1995; Torrance, 1967, 1995) as an identifiable process, verified through the acceptance of the uniqueness and value of the product, which is modifiable. Research (e.g., Michael & Bachelor, 1992) has substantiated the multidimensional nature of creative thinking.

Creativity is generally viewed as an important characteristic of giftedness. In attempting to differentiate giftedness, talent, and creativity, Gagné (1995) noted that giftedness includes creativity as well as intellectual, socioaffective, and sensorimotor abilities. Likewise, *gifted*, in the Javits Gifted and Talented Education Act of 1988, is defined as high performance capability in intellectual, *creative*, and/or artistic areas; possessing unusual leadership capacity; or excelling in specific academic fields (U.S. Department of Education, 1993). One does not, however, have to be intellectually gifted to be creative. Piizto (1995) suggested that a minimum of intellectual ability was all that was necessary to display creative talent

in any domain, though some domains are more demanding of this ability than others. Creativity then is an aspect of giftedness that can be observed in many areas of endeavor. Talent, on the other hand, is the realization of such abilities within certain domains, for example, academics, games of strategy, technology, the arts, social action, business, and athletics (Gagné, 1995).

Creativity is a combination of intelligence, knowledge, thinking style, personality, motivation, and environment (Sternberg & Lubart, 1995). Using a stock market analogy, Sternberg and Lubart suggest that people who successfully manifest their creativity "buy low and sell high." By this, they mean that when everyone else is unwilling to risk, creative people, being divergent thinkers and nonconformists, tend to take the plunge. They accomplish this by combining a number of abilities. Sternberg and Lubart suggest that creative people tend to

1. Generate the options that other people do not think of and recognize which are the good ones (intelligence).
2. Know what other people have done in their field of endeavor so that they will know what others are not doing or have not yet thought to do (knowledge).
3. Think and act in creative and contrarian ways and see the forest from the trees (thinking styles).
4. Take risks and overcome the obstacles that confront those who buy low and sell high (personality).
5. Not only think in contrarian ways but have the drive to do so (motivation).
6. Work at a job, live in a country, or be in a relationship to others that lets them do all these things (environment).

The results of a longitudinal study spanning 22 years (Torrance, 1995) indicate the likelihood of a general ability that can be called creativity but also the reality that this ability takes many forms and displays itself in many domains, thereby dispelling the notion that there can be such a thing as a creativity quotient. Baer (1993) suggests that, if domain-general factors do exist, likely candidates would be divergent thinking (Guilford, 1959) and associative thinking (Mednick, 1962). Sternberg and Lubart (1995) view creativity as an amalgamation of factors, though they maintain that creativity tends to occur in specific areas of endeavor. For example, one may be highly creative in music but not in science. While Sternberg and Lubart consider creativity to be a type of giftedness, they state that it is a somewhat more domain-specific type of giftedness than an across-the-board ability.

Tardif and Sternberg (1988) attempted to sum up the research findings of 20 experts in the field of creativity. In doing so, they used a category system that has become known as "the four Ps": One can focus on the creative *person;* the cognitive/affective *process;* the created *product;* or the domain, the *place* in which the work is done. The last P, the place, not only includes the area or discipline in which the person works, but also the study of the kind of environment in which creativity thrives. The following discussion is primarily based on the synthesis of creativity studies by Tardif and Sternberg.

The Person

Descriptions of the creative person typically fall into three categories: cognitive characteristics; personality and motivational qualities; and special events or experiences during one's development. It is generally acknowledged that creative people tend to be drawn to particular domains. In other words, they fall in love with something and pursue it (Torrance, 1988). This may be due to inborn sensitivities to particular types of information or modes of operation or a unique combination of "intelligences."

Regardless of the domain, however, creative people seem to possess certain traits, abilities, and processing styles in common. The traits that have been identified are relatively high intelligence, originality, articulateness and verbal fluency, and a good imagination. Abilities include the knack for thinking metaphorically, flexibility and skill in decision making, independence of judgment, seeking and coping well with novelty, logical thinking skills, internal visualization (the ability to see past surface appearances), the ability to break out of conventional categories or sets, and the desire to find order in apparent chaos. Commonly mentioned processing styles are using wide categories and images of broad scope, a preference for nonverbal communication, building new structures (rather than accepting old ones), questioning norms and assumptions by asking "why?", being alert to novelty and gaps in knowledge, and going beyond an existing knowledge base to develop new ideas.

Creative persons can recognize "good" problems and apply themselves to these while ignoring others. They seem to possess a certain "aesthetic sense" that allows them to imagine new patterns and ways of doing things. Motivationally, they seem drawn to problems. They are willing to confront hostility, express an unusual degree of curiosity and inquisitiveness, and display a driving absorption and commitment to whatever may be the focus of their interest. They set their own rules rather than follow the rules set by others. They may often be withdrawn and internally preoccupied. It should be apparent to the reader that many of the characteristics listed for creative persons could lead to difficulty in school settings.

A partial list of developmentally unique experiences in the lives of creative persons includes being a firstborn, having survived the loss of a parent, experiencing an unusual life situation, being reared in a stimulating environment, being exposed to a wide range of ideas, being happier with books than with people, having a mentor or good role model, and learning outside of class as the large part of their education.

The Process

Tardif and Sternberg (1988) suggest that perhaps the most important elements in the creative process are the cognitive and emotional tensions the person experiences when dealing with a problem. The first tension is one of conflict between staying with the traditional view versus breaking new ground. The second may be in the ideas themselves, as different paths to solutions become apparent in the process. There is the tension between the apparent chaos of the situation and the drive for a new organization. And finally, because the ideas are novel, there is the tension between the individual's view and society's way of seeing the situation.

One of the more enduring descriptions of the creative process is one developed by Helmholtz and Poincaré and proposed as four stages by Graham Wallas (1926). The first stage, *preparation,* involves a long period of conscious work, without success. During this period, the person is captivated by the problem and dogged by the lack of its solution. Then, the problem is set aside and not considered consciously. This stage is called *incubation.* During incubation, the assumption is that the problem is still being worked on but unconsciously being blended together as a "supra-rational stew." The incubation process has been called "creative worrying," because one is never really far from the problem and remains distracted by it until the next stage is reached. That is when the person experiences *illumination,* in which the solution, or the path to the solution, becomes clear enough to proceed. Some people have reported feeling a sense of elation that they have solved the problem even before the solution is clear. The *verification* stage of the process is the actual working out of the solution. This stage requires the crafting or testing of the product and the public exhibition of it.

The Product

The main product of the creative process is the problem solution. Of course, this varies widely with the domain in which the person is working. Technical innovations, artistic artifacts, novel ideas, new styles and designs, and altered paradigms, all fall under the heading of the creative product. Sometimes, creative products are obvious and enduring, such as a painting or a building. Sometimes, they are less obvious, such as in images and abstract ideas, or less enduring, such as in a single dance or musical performance (unless such performances are recorded).

Some products can be immediately produced, while others take a lifetime to verify. Products are occasionally scorned by those who evaluate them because of their radical break with convention. Luigi Pirandello's play, *Six Characters in Search of an Author,* culminated in a fistfight between the cast and the audience when first performed (Matthaei, 1973), and Igor Stravinsky's work, *Le sacre du printemps,* opened to hisses and catcalls (Gardner, 1993). While somewhat extreme, these stories illustrate the need for another major trait which must be possessed by a creative person: He or she must have courage (Torrance, 1995).

The Place

As noted, the audience for the creative product can make a great deal of difference as to whether the person persists in the creative effort. One must be encouraged by significant others in order to be able to meet criticism and to maintain self-esteem. Being a creator is a lonely business. By definition, someone with a novel idea is an "N of 1": a person unlike all others in some way. Focusing on issues of maintaining and enhancing creativity in children and making suggestions as to how school personnel and families might help to provide encouragement entails making the fourth P; the *place,* a supportive environment in which the creative gifts of all children can survive and thrive.

Csikszentmihalyi (1993) has spent decades researching the subjective experiences people report when they are involved in creative and joyful states of mind. He calls this experience *flow.* Flow is when someone is totally absorbed in whatever they may be doing. Furthermore, when a person is away from the absorbing activity that they love, they sometimes experience a vicarious kind of flow just by thinking about it and imagining their involvement in the activity. This often happens when the task they are actually doing is a repetitive and boring one. Of course, they are "daydreaming" when this happens, and if they are a child in a classroom and not paying attention to the task at hand, this can be a problem.

Research has revealed the elements of flow (Csikszentmihalyi, 1993). Briefly, they are (a) goal-directed thought and the felt-sense that one knows how the goal is to be accomplished; (b) the belief that one's skills are equal to the challenge; (c) the merging of action and awareness; (d) total concentration on the task; (e) the sense of being in control of the situation; (f) the lack of any self-consciousness; (g) an altered sense of time; and (h) the feeling that the task is worth doing for its own sake. Flow usually happens when one experiences an urge toward a goal, and, as each step is taken toward it, there is the sense that one is on the right track. Something about it just feels right. Flow involves intrinsic motives, which may be at odds with what other people want us to be doing at the moment and extrinsic reward systems such as grades.

In the flow experience, the person becomes so absorbed as to lose all sense of time and space orientation. Csikszentmihalyi (1993) calls this the merging of action and awareness. This unified consciousness is the most telling aspect of the experience. It is an ecstatic state, and when one is immersed in it, intrusions are very frustrating. The person emerging from the flow state may appear to be ill-tempered to those around. For example, children sometimes report that, just as they were beginning "to get into" something in a class at school, the bell would ring. So they arrived at the next class somewhat disoriented and in a bad mood. Getting into flow takes time, and one cannot simply pick up where he or she left off. Interruptions "break the spell." Those around them—who have been living in the real world—find it difficult to understand why they should be so grumpy.

Experiencing flow is such an ecstatic feeling that it tends to be addictive. Csikszentmihalyi (1993) believes that flow is part of our biological inheritance, that our desire for this experience is programmed into us. "Every human being has this creative urge as his or her birthright. It can be squelched and corrupted, but it cannot be completely extinguished. This enjoyment that comes from surpassing ourselves, from mastering new obstacles" (pp. 175–176). It is the journey, not the goal, that brings happiness. This means that joy must come from what we are doing, from flow. "Children—provided they are healthy and not too severely abused—seem to be in flow constantly; they enjoy 'unfolding their being' as they learn to touch, throw, walk, talk, read, and grow up" (pp. 191–192).

Problems and Implications

Can children truly be regarded as creative given the notion that creative products must be original and viewed as good? If one considers whether a product is new and good for that age group, then children can be considered as generators of creative products (Russ, 1993; U.S. Department of Education, 1993). Indeed, children appear to be constantly creating—inventing and testing new ideas. But something happens to many of them as they develop and become formally educated. "Many people with the potential for creativity probably never realize it: They believe that creativity is a quality they could never have" (Sternberg & Lubart, 1995, p. vii). What happens to these potentially creative children? Why do they arrive at adulthood having lost their creative potential?

It appears that some of the attitudes of our culture and practices in our schools are implicated in this loss of creativity. In their book *Defying the Crowd,* Sternberg and Lubart (1995) state that creativity can be developed but suggest one reason why we are not more creative is that creativity is generally undervalued and overlooked in our culture. The *National Excellence: A Case for Developing America's Talent* report (U.S. Department of Education, 1993) notes that the American tendency to hold low expectations in education and intellect and to favor conformity over deviation from the norm is not new, but it is more visible today. Creative students thus receive mixed messages: Creativity is both a valuable human resource and a troublesome expression of eccentricity.

Descriptions of the creative thinker as a "contrarian" suggest that the creative person might be seen by others as oppositional or rebellious (Sternberg & Lubart, 1995; Torrance, 1995). Critics of schools, such as Gardner (1991) and Goleman (1995), view school as a place that values only the traditional cognitive, convergent, and conforming ways of learning which are antithetical to students developing creative thinking.

Researchers (e.g., Torrance, 1963; Carroll & Howieson, 1992) have studied teachers' attitudes toward creative behaviors in their students and their ability to recognize creative talent in the classroom. The research indicates that conforming behavior (being courteous and obedient, handing work in on time, accepting the judgment of authorities, etc.) were most prized, while creative behaviors were consistently listed as least desirable.

One of this chapter's authors (Torrance, 1967) identified what is called the "fourth-grade slump." At about this stage of education, an alarming number of children display a marked decline in their creative production. It is then that male and female roles become important, peers become significant evaluators, children are expected to behave in more adult-like ways, and the school curriculum changes:

Curriculum content begins to emphasize the realistic and the factual. Lessons become more formal and organized. Students are invited to be critical of other people's ideas; guessing and hazarding uncommon responses are discouraged. Credit is given only for what is written down, and marks become an indicator of acceptability.... Children, it is thought, need to learn that the world isn't all roses, that animals don't talk, that competition is keen, and that the rewards of life go to persons who are alert, practical and realistic (Strom & Bernard, 1982, p. 309).

Imagination, a precondition for original thought, is often given up as a liability at this stage (Collangelo & Zaffran, 1979). Whether the child enters adolescence equipped to preserve creative thinking or experiences the virtual extinction of creativity depends on whether the home and school environments value the thought processes that support creativity.

The developing student also faces increasing expectations that his or her thinking be free of emotional bias. Dispassionate, logical, and critical thinking are the hallmarks of science. Perkins (1981) stated, however, that feeling is a major criterion for judgment in the creative process. The inexplicable feeling of the rightness of an idea seems to guide the creative person toward a useful solution; "creating is too much work to be worth the bother, were it not a passionate enterprise" (p. 115).

Russ (1993) asserts that affect is crucial to creative thinking and suggests that one can be cognitively (academically) talented but not be creative because of the inability to use affective cues. She has compiled a list of the cognitive, affective, and personality variables that are associated with each stage of the creative process and which should aid in our understanding of the abilities important for creativity.

At the *preparation* stage, cognitive abilities include sensitivity to problems and a wide breadth of knowledge or a mastery of a certain knowledge base. Affectively, children need to take pleasure in a challenge. Their personality features would include curiosity, tolerance of ambiguity, risk taking, intrinsic motivation, and a preference for challenge and complexity.

The *incubation* stage requires the cognitive abilities of divergent thinking, transformation skills, and the tendency to consider alternative solutions. The affective abilities are the flexibility to access emotionally laden, primary-process thoughts and an openness to affective states. Primary-process thought was first discussed by Freud in 1915 and is defined by Dudeck (1980) as "the mechanism by which unconscious instinctual energy surfaces in the form of images or ideas" (p. 520). The personality variables associated with this stage are openness to experience, tolerance of ambiguity, self-confidence, and a preference for challenge.

At the *illumination* stage, the cognitive ability of insight is most important, together with an ability to evaluate. Affective access and openness remain important at this stage and are accompanied by the pleasure of problem solving. We would add to Russ's list an element of emotional evaluation—the "feels right" component of judgment. The personality factor paramount at this stage is self-confidence.

Finally, the *verification* stage requires the cognitive ability of evaluation, the affective pleasure in problem solving, and the integration of cognitive and affective information. It should be noted that primary-process thought is not the type of thinking valued in school. It is by nature "undirected and freely wandering . . . not oriented toward reality . . . takes no account of time or logical contradiction . . . [and is] driven by motives, emotions and wishes" (Martindale, 1981, p. 297). Russ (1993) states that as the child develops more secondary process thinking (logical and critical thought), it becomes dominant and supplants primary process thinking. A repressive barrier develops that controls the flow of this content into cognition. If this barrier becomes too repressive, then the child can no longer employ the "illogical thinking, condensation (fusion of two ideas or images), and loose associative links" which are the well-spring of creativity (Russ, 1993, p. 18).

Another problem is that as children begin to work for grades, then motivation becomes extrinsic and immediate gratification is more controlled. Hennessey and Amabile (1988) have found that when a child is rewarded for creative production, his or her creativity actually decreases! It is important that the child be allowed to pursue interests that are intrinsically motivating and immediately satisfying. At all levels of development, the locus of control and evaluation should rest with the developing child. To impose conventional standards upon a child runs the risk of inviting the child to work for the approval of others before the child has learned to approve of himself or herself.

According to Maxwell (1991), some personality traits that would aid children in being creative are also possible liabilities. She proposes that we understand these traits and reframe them in the best possible light, so that children do not develop a belief that they are weird or bad. An emotional intensity underlies much of the creative process "showing up in strong concentration, deep emotional sensitivity, persistent curiosity, elation or anguish, enthusiasm or inhibition" (p. 20). Because of this, these children experience strong fears, joys, caring, a vivid fantasy life, "and a mind that simply will not quit because there are too many fascinating things that compel investigation" (p. 20). Sometimes, the richness of their fantasies makes it difficult for them to differentiate between imagination and reality. This clouds the distinction of fact and fiction, so adults may view them as liars. Lenba (1985) suggests that lying is the first clear indicator of intellectual creativity. Children's imaginations are rich with fiction and the reporting of their fantasies is, by harsh definition, a lie. The intensity of their emotional life may leave them inconsolable with grief at the death of a pet or enraptured by the shape of a snowflake, leaving adults with the impression that they are too emotionally labile.

Alternative Actions

If some portion of creative ability is domain-general, then those aspects that tend to endure across domains (e.g.,

divergent thinking, originality, fluency, elaboration, etc.) should be measurable. Of those instruments designed to do this, the Torrance Tests of Creative Thinking (T.T.C.T.) have been the most widely used (Baer, 1993). Three-quarters of the studies of school-aged children conducted in the 1970s and early 1980s used the T.T.C.T. (Baer, 1993; Torrance & Presbury, 1984). However, as Treffinger (1986) noted, "creativity is one of the most complex of human functions; it is unrealistic to expect that there will ever be a single, easily administered, simply scored test booklet that educators can use" (p. 16). Ford and Harris (1992), in a review of the literature on identifying creativity, noted that "with meager research on bias in creativity tests, particularly as they relate to the culturally diverse, one can justly wonder whether such tests tap the creative potential or abilities of culturally diverse students" (p. 191). As an alternative to current practice, Sternberg and Lubart (1995) suggest "a better model for assessing creative giftedness . . . would be to find an area (or those areas) in which a person excels and help him or her realize as fully as possible his or her giftedness in those areas" (p. 290).

Because emotion is central to motivation and judgment in creativity, more attention should be paid to it in school. Gardner (1991) has called for a complete restructuring of the school experience and an expansion of the curriculum to include, among other things, the "personal intelligences" which have a strong affective component. Goleman (1995) echoed this sentiment and proposed that because emotional intelligence is so crucial to success in many areas, schools should adopt the "Self-Science Curriculum" on the model of Stone and Dillehunt (1978). The main components of this curriculum include the following:

- self-awareness.
- Personal decision making.
- Managing feelings.
- Handling stress.
- Empathy (understanding others' feelings and concerns and taking their perspective).
- Self-disclosure (valuing openness and building trust in a relationship).
- Insight (identifying patterns in your emotional life).
- Self-acceptance.
- Personal responsibility (including following through on commitments).
- Assertiveness.
- Group dynamics (knowing when and how to lead, when to follow).
- Conflict resolution (the win/win model for negotiating compromise).

The school psychologist, through consultation with parents, teachers, and administrators, can work toward creating a better environment for children in which they can entertain, and retain, their creative energies. Reviewing advice to adults wishing to encourage the growth of creativity in children from a number of authors (Harrington, Block, & Block, 1987; Russ, 1993; Sternberg & Lubart, 1995; Torrance, 1979, 1984), an analysis suggests that it can be arranged into three categories: Anyone wishing to encourage creative thinking in children must *support, challenge,* and *lead* them.

Support means honoring the way children think and helping them understand and use their creative ability. Do not be so quick to dismiss answers as wrong, inappropriate, unrealistic, or useless. Be interested in what the child is currently doing—rather than focusing too much on the future. Provide a refuge somewhere in the system; producing an original idea or product automatically places one in the minority, at least for a time, and is thus stressful. Almost inescapably, the creative child will come into conflict with the "authorities" in the system and must have a spokesperson to advocate for his or her creative style, and against compulsive conformity. Accept the child's tendency to look at things differently and do not dismiss unusual perspectives as weird. Be accepting of the child's expression of feelings and give verbal permission for expression of feelings. Listen to the child and empathize. Enjoy the child's play and fantasy. Honor your own "crazy" ideas and curiosity and divergent thoughts. Be a role model.

Challenge by gently pushing for increasing production while giving the gift of the right to fail. Encourage risk-taking behaviors and ground-breaking thoughts. Encourage the child to speculate and hypothesize, rather than rely on the mere rightness or factualness of a response. For example, if teachers ask who discovered America, they will get a memorization response. If they ask in what way Columbus and Neil Armstrong were alike, they generate more thought but little creativity. But if they ask what might have been different today if Columbus had, instead, landed in California or Alaska, then they are likely to have stimulated some creative thought.

Provide toys, games, and activities which develop imagination. Permit time for thinking or daydreaming, but articulate the need for the completion of a project. Encourage the child to look at or read something twice and to find ideas that were previously overlooked, especially if the child expresses further interest. Be careful about asking for too much conformity, but emphasize the importance of communicating a product or idea so that others will understand. Edit, criticize, and question children's ideas with great caution. Encourage children to "mess around" with words, drawings, rules to games, and the like. Encourage children not to accept facts and ideas solely on the basis of authority. Ask children to guess and follow up on their hunches, and then take a stand for their position.

Lead by providing mentors to children. The term *mentor* originates from Homer's epic, "The Odyssey" (Goff & Torrance, 1991). Before Ulysses embarked on his 10 year journey, he asked his wise and trusted friend, Mentor, to guide and teach his son and to look out for his son's well-being. The mentor's task is to use his or her superior knowledge, wisdom, and skill to help the protégé navigate through the snares and around the pitfalls that the world leaves in the protégé's path. Freiberg (1995) cited a study of 2,026 scientists, 771 artists, 2,012 philosophers, and 696 composers in which it was found that mentors played a crucial part in the development of productive creativity. Children who have the benefit of mentors are more likely to grow into creative adults (Torrance, 1984). Some things that mentors can do for children include

- Arrange for the protégé to see the mentor at work.
- Expose the protégé to unusual or innovative ideas and objects.
- Call attention to the creative production of the protégé and discuss career plans in terms of specific talents.
- Publicly praise original, unusual work.
- Encourage participation in suitable clubs or organizations.
- Give the protégé information about appropriate summer camps or other summer activities.
- Participate with the protégé in some kind of investigation of another project.
- Help the protégé prepare for local science fairs, auditions, performances, presentations, publications, or other forums for expression of their creativity.
- Help the protégé obtain information about colleges and college scholarships, field experiences in an area of interest, and work opportunities.
- Assist the protégé in gaining admission to settings that will further creative production, such as college, apprenticeships, specific training, and the job market.

Schools need to tap into human resources such as parent volunteers, financial resources, and potential supporters such as local businesses and industry.

Summary

Creativity is a misunderstood and overlooked construct. Everyone is creative to some extent, and this ability can be enhanced given the proper environment.

Schools, and the culture at large, appear to be ambivalent toward creative behaviors in children. While everyone would likely agree that creativity is important, there seems to be a paradoxical suspicion of nonconforming attitudes and unusual ideas. Emotion appears to be basic to the inspiration and judgment aspects of the creative process; one must emotionally sense the correctness of ideas and be carried away by an idea or project, losing the realization of the peripheral aspects of the current environment. This can produce off-task behaviors and over-excitability and irritability in children. Emotion is traditionally viewed as an impediment to good thinking (i.e., dispassionate, objective thinking). Schools tend to reward correct answers and critical thought. Children, because of their need to fit in, will often give up their creative ways of thinking in favor of those of their peers and may become satisfied with facts and concepts given by authorities. When this happens, they either come to regard themselves as uncreative or to see creativity as irrelevant—an obstacle to success.

Some reformers have called for a complete restructuring of the school curriculum to include training in previously overlooked aspects of intelligence and the emotions. Other authors, seeking to make modifications within the existing system, offer advice which sorts into three categories: adults who wish to free children to be creative must support, challenge, and lead them. The recommendations of authors who specialize in creativity should be applied to all children and all areas of education. While this may be criticized as a "shotgun" approach to this issue, it must be remembered that all children are potentially creative and, therefore, our creative production as a society could be increased by such interventions.

Recommended Resources

Books for Professionals

Hofstadter, D., & the Fluid Analogies Research Group. (1995). *Fluid concepts and creative analogies: Computer models of the fundamental mechanisms of thought.* New York: Basic Books.
For years, Douglas Hofstadter, a cognitive scientist and computer wizard at the University of Indiana, has attempted to develop a computer program that will think creatively. In this book, the reader is led through several attempts that have fallen short but have advanced our understanding. Hofstadter makes the mechanisms of creative thinking clearer than those who have attempted to keep creative thought a mystery. But of course, so far, machines cannot create like humans.

Sternberg, R. J. (Ed.). (1988). *The nature of creativity: Contemporary psychological perspectives.* Cambridge, England: Cambridge University Press.
This edited volume contains the research of 20 acknowledged experts in the field of creativity. It includes many illuminating chapters on topics such as psychometric approaches; cognitive approaches; the study of creative lives; and the study of creative systems and environments. Anyone interested in recent concepts of creativity and the enhancement of creative thinking within the school setting will find these chapters interesting.

Books for Parents and Professionals

Csikszentmihalyi, M. (1990). *Flow: The psychology of optimal experience.* New York: Harper & Row.
You may never learn to pronounce his name, but the experiences this author describes will be familiar to you. Through years of qualitative research, Csikszentmihalyi has assembled testimonials and descriptions of people involved in peak experiences, such as creative absorption and illumination. This book makes creativity seem more within the reach of all of us. It is clearly written and easily understood. Also worth reading is his 1993 book The Evolving Self.

Gardner, H. (1993). *Creating minds: The anatomy of creativity seen through the lives of Freud, Einstein, Picasso, Stravinsky, Eliot, Graham, and Ghandi.* New York: Basic Books.
As with all Howard Gardner books, this one is well researched and scholarly but written so that anyone would find it very readable. Based on his Theory of Multiple Intelligences, Gardner picked one creative person who worked roughly within the domain of each of the "seven intelligences." The biographies are interesting, and Gardner's analysis provides new insights into the lives of creative people.

Weisberg, R. W. (1993). *Creativity: Beyond the myth of genius.* New York: W. H. Freeman.
With all the mystery and superstition that surrounds creativity, Weisberg sets out to bring naturalistic explanations to our understanding of the process. He debunks some of the cherished notions about what it takes to be creative and explains that truly inventive ideas do not come out of nowhere. Weisberg's attempt is to apply the methods of science to the study of creativity.

Programs for Creative Development

The Future Problem Solving Program: This program was developed by E. Paul and Pansy Torrance. Students use the six steps of the creative problem-solving model (Osborn, 1963; Parnes, 1967). These problems include predicting future events by creatively extrapolating from what is known today. The Program has been in existence nearly 20 years and has grown into an international competition. Contact Bonnie Jensen, International Office, Future Problem Solving Program, 318 West Ann Street, Ann Arbor, MI, 48104-1337.

Odyssey of the Mind: This program was initiated in 1978 by Sam Micklus and Theodore Gourley. First known as Olympics of the Mind, it was meant to be the cognitive olympics for children. It provides structured, creative problem-solving activities which promote exciting competition and learning. Contact Odyssey of the Mind Association, Inc., P.O. Box 27, Glassboro, NJ 08028.

Invent America: Developed by the U.S. Patent Model Foundation, this relatively new program was designed to help children develop their creativity. Students create inventive solutions to problems in school, the community, and the home. Competition begins at the local school level and culminates when winners are presented patents for their inventions in Washington, D.C. Contact U.S. Patent Model Foundation, 1331 Pennsylvania Ave., Suite 903, Washington, DC 20004.

References

Baer, J. (1993). *Creativity and divergent thinking: A task-specific approach.* Hillsdale, NJ: Lawrence Erlbaum Associates.

Carroll, J., & Howieson, N. (1992). Recognizing creative thinking talent in the classroom. *Roeper Review, 14(4),* 209–212.

Collangelo, N., & Ziffran, R. (1979). *New voices in counseling the gifted.* Dubuque, IA: Kendall/Hunt.

Csikszentmihalyi, M. (1993). *The evolving self: A psychology for the third millennium.* New York: Harper Collins.

Dudeck, S. (1980). Primary process ideation. In R. H. Woody (Ed.), *Encyclopedia of clinical assessment* (Vol. 1, pp. 520–530). San Francisco: Josey-Bass.

Ford, D. Y., & Harris, J. J. (1992). The elusive definition of creativity. *Journal of Creative Behavior, 26(3),* 186–198.

Freiberg, P. (1995). Creativity is influenced by our social networks. *Monitor, 26(8),* 21.

Gagné, F. (1995). Hidden meanings of the "talent development" concept. *The Educational Forum, 59,* 350–362.

Gardner, H. (1991). *The unschooled mind.* New York: Basic Books.

Gardner, H. (1993). *Creating minds: An anatomy of creativity seen through the lives of Freud, Einstein, Picasso, Stravinsky, Eliot, Graham, and Gandhi.* New York: Basic Books.

Goff, K., & Torrance, E. P. (1991). *Mentor's guide and protégé's handbook.* Bensenville, IL: Scholastic Testing Service.

Goleman, D. (1995). *Emotional intelligence.* New York: Bantam Books.

Guilford, J. P. (1959). Three faces of intellect. *American Psychologist, 14,* 469–479.

Harrington, D. M., Block, J. W., & Block, J. (1987). Testing aspects of Carl Rogers' theory of creative environments: Childrearing antecedences of creative environments in young adolescents. *Journal of Personality and Social Psychology, 52,* 851–856.

Hennessey, B. A., & Amabile, T. M. (1988). The conditions of creativity. In R. J. Sternberg (Ed.), *The nature of creativity: Contemporary psychological perspectives* (pp. 11–38). Cambridge, England: Cambridge University Press.

Lefrancois, G. R. (1982). *Psychology for teaching: A bear rarely faces the front.* Belmont, CA: Wadsworth Publishing.

Lenba, C. A. (1985). New look at curiosity and creativity. *Journal of Higher Education, 29,* 132–140.

Martindale, C. (1981). *Cognition and consciousness.* Homewood, IL: Dorsey.

Matthaei, R. (1973). *Luigi Pirandello.* New York: Federich Ungar Publishing.

Maxwell, E. (1991). The changing developmental needs of the gifted: Birth to maturity. In M. Bireley & J. Genshaft (Eds.), *Understanding a gifted adolescent: Vol. 5. Education and psychology of gifted services* (pp. 17–30). Columbia University, NY: Teachers College Press.

Meador, K. S. (1992). Emerging rainbows: A review of the literature on creativity in preschoolers. *Journal for the Education of the Gifted, 15(2),* 163–181.

Mednick, S. A. (1962). The associative basis of the creative process. *Psychological Review, 69,* 220–232.

Michael, W. B., & Bachelor, P. (1992). First-order and higher-order creative ability factors in structure-of-intellect measures administered to sixth-grade children. *Educational and Psychological Measurement, 52,* 261–273.

Perkins, D. N. (1981). *The mind's best work.* Cambridge, MA: Harvard University Press.

Piizto, J. (1995). Deeper and broader: The Pyramid of Talent Development in the context of a giftedness construct. *The Educational Forum, 59,* 363–370.

Russ, S. W. (1993). *Affect and creativity: The role of affect and play in the creative process.* Hillsdale, NJ: Lawrence Erlbaum Associates.

Sternberg, R. J., & Lubart, T. I. (1995). *Defying the crowd: Cultivating creativity in a culture of conformity.* New York: The Free Press.

Stone, K. F., & Dillehunt, H. Q. (1978). *Self-science: The subject is me.* Santa Monica: Goodyear Publishing.

Strom, R. D., & Bernard, H. W. (1982). *Educational psychology.* Monterey, CA: Brooks/Cole Publishing.

Tardif, T. Z., & Sternberg, R. J. (1988). What do we know about creativity? In R. J. Sternberg (Ed.), *The nature of creativity: Contemporary psychological perspectives* (pp. 429–440). Cambridge, England: Cambridge University Press.

Torrance, E. P. (1963). The creative personality and the ideal pupil. *Teachers College Record, 65,* 220–226.

Torrance, E. P. (1967). *Understanding the fourth-grade slump in creative thinking* (Final Report). Washington, DC: U.S. Office of Education.

Torrance, E. P. (1979). Unique needs of the creative child and adult. In National Society for the Study of Education (Ed.), *The gifted and the talented: Their education and development* (pp. 352–371). Chicago: University of Chicago Press.

Torrance, E. P. (1984). *Mentor relationships.* Buffalo, NY: Bearly Limited.

Torrance, E. P. (1988). The nature of creativity as manifest in its testing. In R. J. Sternberg (Ed.), *The nature of creativity: Contemporary psychological perspectives* (pp. 43–75). Cambridge, England: Cambridge University Press.

Torrance, E. P. (1995). *Why fly?: A philosophy of creativity.* Norwood, NJ: Ablex.

Torrance, E. P., & Presbury, J. H. (1984). The criteria of success used in 242 recent experimental studies of creativity. *Creative Child and Adult Quarterly, 9,* 238–243.

Treffinger, D. J. (1986). Research on creativity. *Gifted Child Quarterly, 30(1),* 15–118.

U.S. Department of Education. (1993). *National excellence: A case for developing America's talent.* Washington, DC: Author.

Vernon, P. E. (1989). The nature-nurture problem in creativity. In J. Glover, R. Ronning, & C. R. Reynolds (Eds.), *Handbook of creativity* (pp. 93–110). New York: Plenum.

Wallas, G. (1926). *The art of thought.* London: Watts.

40

Ability Grouping

Carl M. Ross
Patti L. Harrison
The University of Alabama

Ability grouping is the educational practice of placing students of similar ability into groups for instructional purposes. Ability-grouping structures range from relatively restricted within-class ability grouping (e.g., reading groups) to extensive whole-class ability grouping (e.g., tracking). Historically, several key assumptions have supported the practice of ability grouping (Oakes, 1987). Proponents of the practice argue that students can be fairly and accurately placed into appropriate ability groups and that the task of teaching such homogeneous groups is more efficient and effective. It is assumed that students will learn best when they learn with others who have similar characteristics. It is also argued that ability grouping alleviates the potential negative emotional impact slower students might experience by making negative self-comparisons with brighter students in heterogeneous classes.

For many years, however, a debate has raged over the effectiveness and appropriateness of ability grouping, particularly extensive grouping practices such as tracking. Comprehensive reviews of ability grouping first appeared in the 1920s and continue to the present (Oakes & Guiton, 1995; Raze, 1984). Researchers have examined a wide range of issues, including the effects of ability grouping on students' academic achievement and self-esteem and the possible discriminatory effects of ability grouping. Currently, debates over ability-grouping practices continue, and both sides fervently argue their position. Some researchers appear to find no benefit in ability-grouping practices (e.g., Oakes, 1985), others support certain types of ability grouping but question others (e.g., Slavin, 1987b), while still other researchers view ability grouping as "a tool for educational excellence" (Gallagher, 1993, p. 21).

In this chapter we examine research and issues concerning this debate. In addition to a review of the literature, special topics, such as ability grouping for gifted children and the importance of specific classroom practices when considering ability grouping, will be reviewed. Finally, while the special education practice of grouping students according to disability will not be directly addressed in this chapter, many of the ability-grouping issues discussed would seem to be relevant to special education practices and the current move toward greater inclusion of students with disabilities into the general education program.

Background and Development

Ability grouping has been a common practice in education for many years, and a number of important characteristics define the practice. A major aspect in understanding ability grouping is the many different forms of ability groups that exist in schools; there is no one standard form of ability grouping. A description of the various forms of ability grouping and a review of some key terms illustrate the wide variety of practices (Gamoran, 1992; Mills & Durden, 1992; Slavin, 1987a).

- *Homogeneous grouping:* A general term that refers to arrangements in which students are grouped according to some preset criteria, usually academic ability, with each resulting group containing only one ability level.
- *Heterogeneous grouping:* Another general term that refers to arrangements in which students are grouped systematically or randomly, with each resulting group containing students of all ability levels.
- *Within-class ability grouping:* A grouping arrangement in which students from an otherwise heterogeneous class are grouped together within the class for instruction in one or more subjects. This practice is common at the elementary-school level for reading and mathematics instruction.
- *Regrouping entire classes for instruction in specific subjects:* An arrangement in which students spend most of the day in heterogeneous classes but are regrouped into separate classes for instruction in specific sub-

jects. This practice is also most common for reading and mathematics instruction at the elementary-school level.

- *Joplin and other cross-grade plans:* Arrangements in which students are primarily assigned to heterogeneous classes but are regrouped—according to ability and across grade levels—for instruction in specific subjects. The Joplin plan is a cross-grade plan specific to grouping across grade lines for reading instruction.
- *Comprehensive nongraded plans:* Arrangements such as nongraded schools in which students are not assigned to grades. Instead, students are heterogeneously mixed by age and ability and are served by teams of teachers who regroup the students frequently within the larger heterogeneous group dependent upon the task.
- *Whole-class ability grouping* (also referred to as *tracking* and *XYZ grouping*): The most extensive ability grouping arrangement in which students are separated into distinct classes by ability (generally low, average, and high) and remain in those classes throughout most or all of the school day.
- *Enrichment classes:* Homogeneous classes, typically for gifted students, in which students are grouped together for all or part of a day.
- *Accelerated classes:* Arrangements in which students, typically gifted students, are allowed to advance to higher grades or educational levels than their same-age peers.
- *Cooperative learning groups:* Small heterogeneous grouping structures in which students work cooperatively on a task. This practice is often offered as an alternative to homogeneous grouping.

Problems and Implications

As the advantages and disadvantages of homogeneous ability grouping have been debated over the years, many issues and concerns have been raised (National Association of School Psychologists, 1993; Oakes & Guiton, 1995; Slavin & Braddock, 1993):

- *Ability grouping may not result in improvements in students' achievement and may be harmful to some students.* One of the major assumptions about ability grouping has been that students learn better in homogeneous ability groups. However, this assumption has been questioned, particularly for students with lower ability. Many educators express the belief that students with lower ability are labeled and stigmatized and may even be harmed by participating in homogeneous classes.
- *Ability grouping may be inconsistent with the democratic ideal that all students should have an equal opportunity to learn.* Concerns have been raised that homogeneous grouping results in students in lower ability groups receiving inferior instruction. Concerns also have been raised that heterogenous grouping is unfair to students with higher ability because the instruction is "watered down" to focus on the needs of the students with lower ability.
- *Ability grouping may promote a view that students' abilities are fixed and stable and that schooling cannot alter the abilities.* Many educators express the belief that homogenous-ability groups accommodate students' inherent abilities and skills and that students should not be expected to accomplish any more than the limits of their fixed abilities. On the other hand, other educators believe that homogenous ability grouping results in a "self-fulfilling prophecy," with students with lower ability always performing poorly and students with higher ability always performing well. These educators believe that the abilities and skills of all students, even those with lower ability, *can* be altered through quality instruction and high expectations.
- *Ability grouping may result in discrimination based on race, ethnicity, and socioeconomic status.* Specific race, ethnic, and socioeconomic status groups may be overrepresented or underrepresented in homogeneous-ability groups. Some educators express the belief that the ability groups are not discriminatory but that they simply reflect the typical ability and motivational levels associated with race, ethnicity, and socioeconomic status groups. Other educators feel that homogeneous-ability groups promote a continuation of discriminatory practices, including poorer quality schooling and lower expectations for poor or minority students in lower ability groups.

Researchers are not entirely consistent in their conclusions about the appropriateness and effectiveness of ability grouping. It is easier to understand the conclusions drawn by these various researchers when the different variables they considered are examined. Some of the different variables examined by researchers include (a) the type of grouping utilized (e.g., between-versus within-class grouping), (b) the curriculum used with the various groups (e.g., differentiated or undifferentiated), (c) the different instructional practices used in the various groups, (d) the outcomes being assessed (e.g., academic achievement or social-emotional factors), and (e) the ability level of the students in the groups (e.g., high ability or low ability).

Research has largely focused on differences between homogeneously and heterogeneously grouped students on standardized achievement tests (e.g., Kulik & Kulik, 1982, 1984; Slavin, 1987a, 1990, 1993). To a lesser extent, student social-emotional outcomes and teacher and classroom factors have also been investigated (Gamoran, 1992; George, 1993; Oakes, 1985; Rosenbaum, 1976). While past research on the effects of ability grouping has generally been quasi-experimental in design, more recent research has used advanced statistical research designs such as meta-analyses to effectively and objectively combine past research on the topic (Kulik & Kulik, 1982, 1984; Slavin, 1987a, 1990, 1993).

Effects on Student Achievement

Research results

Research consistently shows that the homogenous-ability-grouping practice of *tracking,* or whole-class ability grouping, is ineffective and does not improve student achievement. Meta-analyses conducted by Kulik and Kulik (1992) and Slavin (1987a) compiled effects of numerous research studies comparing elementary students' achievement in whole-class homogenous-ability groups and heterogenous-ability groups. All meta-analyses at the elementary-school level yielded effect sizes of nearly zero, indicating that tracking did not result in increases nor decreases in student achievement. The effect sizes for all groups, including low-, middle-, and high-ability groups, were similar. These results are contrary to the popular belief that whole-class ability groups may be more effective for students with high ability than for students with low ability.

Meta-analyses for middle and high school students conducted by Slavin (1990, 1993) have resulted in similar findings. Tracking can take several forms at the secondary level, including placement in high, middle, or low tracks; in advanced or basic tracks; and in college preparatory or vocational/technical tracks. In comparing the achievement between students in tracked, whole-class ability groups with those in heterogenous-ability groups, Slavin (1990, 1993) found no group differences, regardless of the level of ability of the students. In a review of research on tracking in secondary schools, Oakes (1987) concluded that tracking was generally ineffective for all students and indicated that it may be detrimental to the achievement of students with low ability. Oakes noted that some forms of tracking, such as a college preparatory track, may *appear* to show positive effects on achievement of students with high ability but noted that these findings may be related to factors such as the academic subjects taken, rather than to homogeneous grouping per se.

Although research consistently has shown that student achievement is not generally enhanced by tracking, research results on other forms of ability grouping have been less consistent. At the elementary level, Slavin (1987a) conducted meta-analyses of several other forms of ability grouping: regrouping into distinct classes for reading, mathematics, or both; the Joplin Plan and other cross-grade plans; and within-class ability grouping. All forms of ability grouping were compared to heterogenous-grouping arrangements. The effects of regrouping into distinct classes for reading and mathematics were inconclusive, with no consistent support across studies. However, Slavin found consistent support for the effectiveness of the Joplin Plan and similar nongraded, homogenous grouping plans. The studies analyzed by Slavin that compared effects across ability levels indicated that the Joplin/cross-grade plans showed inconsistent results: Some studies found greater benefits for students with lower ability, some for students with higher ability, and some studies for all ability groups. However, none of the ability groups gained at the expense of another ability group. Slavin's results for within-class ability grouping also provided consistent support for this grouping practice and evidence that the greatest gains in within-class groups were for students with lower ability.

Very little research has investigated other forms of ability grouping with students older than elementary level. Slavin (1993) identified only four studies that investigated within-class grouping and nongraded plans for middle school students. Unlike research with elementary students, Slavin reported no differences in the effectiveness of within-class or cross-graded plans for middle school students when compared to other grouping methods.

Results, while fairly consistent, have been controversial with respect to the ability grouping of gifted students. Slavin (1987a) did not include gifted programs in his meta-analyses, noting that these programs had certain features (e.g., changes in curriculum, class size, goals) that made them fundamentally different from comprehensive ability-grouping structures. However, enriched and accelerated classes for gifted students in elementary and secondary schools were included by Kulik and Kulik (1992) in their meta-analyses and were found to be effective.

Implications

It appears that tracking is not effective for the majority of students and generally has no significant impact on student achievement, regardless of grade or student-ability level. Given these research findings, there is little support for the continuation of traditional whole-class tracking programs in elementary, middle, or high schools. Other forms of ability grouping, however, have been shown to be effective.

Evidence for elementary students indicates that two forms of homogeneous-ability grouping—cross-graded/Joplin plans and within-class grouping—*can* increase student achievement. Slavin (1987a) suggested that these two grouping plans are of maximum benefit when groups homogeneous in the specific skills being taught are created, when the plans are flexible enough to allow for changes in groups after initial placement, when teachers modify their pace and instructional level to be consistent with the students' levels, and when teachers conduct frequent and careful assessments of student performance.

Although research on tracking at the middle and high school levels is extensive, there is very little research on the use of other grouping practices with older students. Perhaps tracking is so entrenched at the secondary level that no other grouping practices are attempted on a large-scale basis, despite the consistent research on the ineffectiveness of tracking. It is recommended that secondary schools systematically develop and implement other grouping strategies, such as the cross-grade and within-class plans used with elementary students, and evaluate the effectiveness of these alternative strategies.

While the students who occupy the upper end of the high-ability spectrum appear to benefit substantially from enriched or accelerated classes (Kulik & Kulik, 1992), ability grouping for gifted children appears to be particularly controversial. Even though Slavin and Braddock (1993) agreed that accelerated programs were effective for gifted students, they expressed concern that enrichment programs were only available to the upper 3% to 5%: "Even if there were evidence in favor of enrichment programs for the gifted, there would still be no evidence whatsoever to deny that such enrichment programs might be effective for all students, not just gifted ones" (p. 14).

Others make the argument that gifted students, like students in special education at the other end of the spectrum, have special needs and require special attention. Is it just as appropriate, for example, to have special services for students with IQs over 130 as it is for students with IQs under 70? In response to critics who suggest that the achievement effects of enrichment and accelerated programs are due to differentiated instructional practices, Allan (1991) responded that this is precisely the point for effective grouping; changes should be made to meet the unique needs of the different groups. When these curriculum changes are made, Kulik and Kulik (1992) argue that all students, not just the gifted, benefit.

Gallagher (1993) considered the philosophical concepts of equity and excellence surrounding ability grouping and the gifted and suggested that sometimes the two concepts clash. While some philosophically question offering enrichment programs only to the gifted, others would argue that abolishing ability-grouping programs for gifted students on the premise that equity should be maintained clashes with the studies that show educational excellence is promoted and that substantial achievement gains are made by gifted students in accelerated and enrichment programs (Gallagher, 1993). A continuing question appears to be whether both equity and excellence can be accomplished.

Other Considerations in Ability Grouping

Research results

Other factors such as teachers' behaviors and practices, teachers' expectations, teacher tracking, student social-emotional factors, students' access to knowledge, measurement and placement, and discrimination have been examined. However, research on these factors has focused primarily on their impact on students in lower ability groups, particularly when the practice of tracking is used. These factors are reviewed next.

Social-emotional factors, such as self-esteem, self-concept, aspirations, and attitudes toward school have been shown to be affected by tracking or whole-class ability grouping. A primary assumption in support of ability grouping is that students with lower ability will experience a negative social impact in heterogeneous classes through self-comparisons with more able peers. Oakes (1987) reported that research does not support this assumption. In fact, Oakes noted that high school students with lower ability in tracked classes experienced lower self-esteem and aspirations and had more negative attitudes toward school than their counterparts in less rigidly tracked classes. Similarly, Slavin and Braddock (1993) concluded that low-achieving elementary students in lower tracks, when compared to low achievers in heterogenous groups, exhibited lower self-esteem, greater feelings of inferiority, and higher external locus of control.

Marsh and Parker (1984), however, describe a "frame of reference" model in which students' academic self-concepts are largely influenced by self-comparisons. They asserted that students compare their perceived academic ability with that of their peers and use this relativistic impression as a primary basis for their academic self-concept. They found that after controlling for actual ability, students in low-socioeconomic (SES)/low-ability schools had higher academic self-concepts than students in high-SES/high-ability schools. Marsh (1984) suggested that this frame-of-reference model could be applicable to ability-grouped situations and that academic self-concept, thus, could be affected positively by placement in a low-ability group and negatively by placement in a high-ability group.

There is evidence to support that *student motivation and behavior* differs in the higher and lower tracks (Dawson, 1995; Gamoran, 1992). Students in higher tracks, when compared to those in lower tracks, may have more on-task behavior, spend more time on homework, turn in more assignments, and have better work habits and motivation. These behaviors may interact with the differing teacher practices in tracked classes, discussed next, which are likely to impact student achievement.

Teachers' behaviors and practices may vary significantly between higher and lower ability classes when whole-class ability grouping is used (Dawson, 1995; Oakes, 1985). Teachers with lower ability classes often communicate less effectively with their students, focus more on behavior management and less on academic skills, and use generally poorer instructional strategies. The result appears to be a poorer overall classroom environment for students in lower tracked classes.

Good (1981) concluded that teachers treat low and high achievers differently in such ways as paying less attention and calling on low achievers less often, providing them with less helpful feedback, waiting less time for them to respond, requiring less effort from them, and positively reinforcing them less often for correct responses. Research investigating teachers' behaviors in elementary reading classes also showed systematic differences in reading classes grouped by ability. For example, Allington (1980) found that teachers were far more likely to interrupt poor readers than good readers when they made an oral mistake. Hiebert (1983) reviewed ability grouping in reading and noted that students with high ability engaged in more silent reading than students with low ability. Gambrell, Wilson, and Gantt (1981) found that students with high ability spent more time in meaningful, contextual reading than students with low ability. A study at the secondary level (Evertson, 1982) also found different teacher behaviors and practices in high- and low-ability classes. While teachers in low-ability classes spent more time on classroom management activities, teachers in high-ability classes were better able to maintain task orientation, deal more consistently with behavior, and present instructional objectives more clearly.

Oakes (1985) related that instructional quality has been found to be generally poorer in lower tracked classes where a variety of instructional inequalities have been enumerated. It appears that teachers in higher tracked classrooms provide their students with more time to learn, give more productive feedback, avoid criticism more often, are better organized, provide greater variety, and are more enthusiastic than teachers in lower tracked classes. At the other extreme, classroom climates in lower tracked classes are marked by more student-teacher hostility, disruption, and alienation.

Teachers' expectations of their students may vary across homogeneously grouped classes as well, with teachers in lower ability classes having lower expectations of their students. In summarizing 10 years of teacher expectation research, Good (1981) asserted that differences in teacher expectancies for students with high and low achievement may be accentuated in ability grouped classrooms. Likewise, Oakes (1985) found that whereas teachers in lower ability classes emphasized mainly behavioral requirements and expected such things as conformity, following rules, and working quietly, teachers in higher ability classes were more likely to expect such things as active participation, critical thinking skills, creativity, and self-direction.

In addition to students in lower tracked classes receiving poorer quality instruction and being held to lower expectations, *teacher tracking* may occur. That is, as noted by Rosenbaum (1976), lower ability groups are often taught by less experienced and less qualified teachers. Rosenbaum also noted that when teachers teach more than one level, their higher track classes tend to consume most of their energy and attention. Moreover, as stated by George (1992), few teachers desire to teach the lower tracked classes, and higher tracked classes are often bestowed as a reward to the best teachers.

Students in lower ability groups may have *limited access to knowledge* compared to higher tracked students. Gamoran (1986) reported that students in lower tracks are offered fewer math and science classes and are required to take fewer academic courses. Oakes (1985) related that lower tracked classes focused on low-level topics and skills, while higher tracked classes focused on higher order skills, concepts, and processes. Students in lower tracked classrooms were generally not exposed to these higher level forms of knowledge.

Many of the *procedures used to place students* in homogeneously grouped classes are questionable. Once placed, students may become locked into their track placement. George (1992) related that track placements are sometimes made based on test-score differences as small as one point; thus, placement decisions that can have an enormous impact on a student's academic future can be based on a statistically insignificant test-score difference. After being placed in lower tracked classes, George (1992) indicated it becomes "virtually impossible" for students to move to a higher track.

Student segregation by race, ethnicity, and socioeconomic status has been found to be a factor in homogenous ability grouping. George (1992) indicated that poor and minority students are placed in lower tracked classes in disproportionate numbers compared to their representation in the overall school population. He suggested this overrepresentation might be due to such factors as a lack of advocacy for students of lower socioeconomic status and biased testing and identification procedures (George, 1992). Slavin and Braddock (1993) also noted that tracking has been shown to segregate students based on racial or social groups and related that students in the lower tracks are less likely to complete their education and are more likely to be delinquent. Oakes (1987) reported that disproportionate numbers of poor, African-American, and Hispanic students are placed in noncollege preparatory and vocational classes in high schools. Likewise, Oakes and Guiton (1995) found that teachers' perceptions of students' suitability for various high school tracks and ability groups were linked to the students' race, ethnicity, and social class.

Implications

When considering ability grouping research, the influence of within-child variables must be recognized. Certain factors, such as a lack of motivation or disruptive behavior, may exist independent of the environmental influence of a particular student-grouping structure and confound research results. However, in combination with these within-child variables, the influence of traditional tracking on students in lower tracked classes appears to be consistently negative.

Based primarily on studies focusing on lower tracked classes, research suggests that whole-class ability grouping may have a negative impact on students' self-esteem, attitude, and class behavior and that teacher and instructional factors significantly differ across ability grouped classes. Moreover, evidence clearly shows that lower socioeconomic status students, African-Americans, and Hispanic students are overrepresented in lower tracked classes. These findings led Gamoran (1992) to conclude, "Grouping and tracking do not increase overall achievement in schools but they do promote inequity, research suggests. To reduce inequality, we should decrease the use of both practices" (p. 11). The inequality appears to go far beyond the actual placement of students into groups. Many students in lower ability groups receive poorer quality instruction and fewer academic advantages than students in higher ability groups. As such, the actual practices used by teachers in classrooms, such as behavioral management, instructional strategies, expectations for student achievement, provision of feedback, teacher tracking, and the like should be carefully monitored across all classrooms.

Alternative Actions

Research suggests that rigid tracking is detrimental to students in lower tracked classes and has no benefit for most other students. However, other alternative forms of ability grouping are likely to yield more favorable outcomes and may be beneficial in reducing inequity. In the following paragraphs, we describe alternative grouping practices and general classroom strategies likely to result in such positive academic and social-emotional outcomes.

Partial Untracking and More Flexible Tracking

If tracking cannot be eliminated altogether, the lowest tracks should be. If tracking is necessary, ways in which it could be implemented more effectively in the earlier grades include (a) regularly reassessing students' capabilities, (b) regularly rotating high quality teachers among the tracks, (c) using tutorials to allow students in lower tracked courses to make up work and advance to higher tracks, and (d) experimenting with new methods of placement and creating better tracking placement criteria (Braddock & McPartland, 1990; Gamoran, 1992).

Other Forms of Ability Groups

Along with improving the use of ability grouping, investigators have suggested alternatives to traditional homogeneous-ability grouping and tracking. Slavin (1987a) suggests that the most effective grouping practices gen-

erally combine heterogeneous and homogeneous grouping strategies. He recommended that students should have a primary association with a heterogeneous group but that, for specific activities, small homogeneous groups may be appropriate. Dawson (1995), George (1992), and Slavin (1987a) provide a number of specific alternatives:

- Flexible grouping/team teaching: A very flexible grouping scheme in which grouping arrangements are changed based upon the current instructional purpose; team teaching is sometimes combined with this arrangement.
- Mixed-ability grouping with additional support: All students are placed in heterogeneous classes and extra support is provided to individual students as needed.
- Cross-graded grouping, also known as the Joplin plan when used with reading: Students are primarily assigned to heterogeneous classes but are regrouped according to ability across grade levels for instruction in specific subjects.
- Nongraded schools: Students are not assigned to grades but rather are heterogeneously mixed by age and ability and are served by teams of teachers who regroup the students frequently within the larger heterogeneous group dependent upon the task.
- Teacher autonomy grouping: Teachers are given the authority to group students in the way they feel is most effective for instruction.
- Before- and after-school programs: Lower or remedial tracks are eliminated during the regular school day and shifted to before school, after school, or on weekends.
- Split-level grouping (Winchester Plan): Ability grouping is both maintained and minimized; students are divided into ability groups and remain with those groups, but the groups are rotated during the day and no one ability group remains with any other one single ability group throughout the day.
- Administrative or student choice grouping: Both students and administrators have more choice in where the students are placed; test scores, for example, may have less weight than student preferences or administrative decisions.

Implementing changes to entrenched, rigid tracking arrangements will be very difficult. Perhaps due to mistaken assumptions, many parents and teachers resist changes to traditional tracked classrooms. Parents of bright students may feel that any move to de-track may be harmful to their children, while teachers used to teaching tracked classes may be hesitant to teach heterogeneous classes. George (1992) asserts that these fears and concerns must be addressed for successful de-tracking to occur, and a long-term plan must be implemented that begins by promoting viable ability-grouping alternatives to both school personnel and the public. Along with providing many viable alternatives to tracking, Dawson (1995) also gives suggestions on how implementation of these alternatives should take place.

Improving All Classroom Practices

One consistent theme emerges between the various researchers with divergent conclusions concerning ability grouping. Most assert that what actually goes on in the grouped classrooms is not adequately considered in the research (Dawson, 1987; Gallagher, 1993; George, 1993; Slavin, 1987a, 1990). Effective classroom practices are required for both heterogeneously and homogeneously grouped arrangements to be successful. Gallagher (1993) may have made this point most clearly: "Merely clustering students who have similarities does not guarantee that anything useful will occur. It is what *happens* to these students *after* they have been grouped that makes the difference" [italics in original] (p. 23). Grouping may, in fact, be of only secondary importance when these other areas are considered.

To ensure that all students are given the best opportunity to learn, effective classroom practices are essential. A number of investigators have enumerated practices that have proven to be effective in promoting achievement in the classroom (Brophy, 1986; Dawson, 1987; Dweck & Leggett, 1988; Good, 1981; Pressley & McCormick, 1995). Suggestions are that

- Teachers spend most of their school days in direct, brisk academic instruction of students, and students should spend most of their day engaged in learning.
- Teachers develop clear academic objectives and relate these objectives to students.
- Teachers incorporate instructional strategies that promote active learning and peer interaction, including cooperative learning, peer tutoring/cross-age teaching, seminar discussions, hands-on experiential learning, project-oriented learning, and individualized instruction.
- Teachers actively question students at an appropriate level and promote student questioning and discourse.
- Teachers engage students in activities with difficulty levels that ensure moderate to high success rates and ensure continuous progress with minimal frustration.
- Teachers use effective classroom management and organization that results in less time being spent in disciplinary activities and more time being used in direct instruction.
- Teachers promote reward systems that foster intrinsic motivation and students' belief that learning and mastery can occur.
- Teachers maintain high expectations for all students, regardless of student ability, and emphasize all students' mastery of important academic objectives.
- Teachers encourage parental involvement in schooling and classroom activities.

Summary

Ability grouping is a broad term that encompasses a wide variety of grouping practices. These practices range from tracking to various forms of within-class ability groups. The basic premise underlying all homogeneous-grouping practices is that students will benefit both academically and emotionally from being grouped with peers of like ability and achievement level.

This premise, however, has not always been supported by research. One of the more prevalent and extensive forms of ability grouping, tracking, has not been shown to increase student achievement. Research also suggests that it may produce social-emotional and sociological detriments, particularly for students in low-ability classes. Given this, there are few, if any, good reasons to continue tracking as currently employed.

Other forms of ability grouping have been shown to effectively increase academic achievement. Research supports the effectiveness of placing students primarily into heterogeneous groups but organizing students into small homogeneous groups for specific activities, such as the organizations used in within-class or cross-graded grouping plans. Very little research, however, has been conducted on the effectiveness of these alternative forms of ability grouping at the middle and secondary school level.

There is disagreement about the appropriateness of targeting gifted students for homogeneous-grouping arrangements. There is agreement that accelerated programs for gifted students will substantially increase achievement for those students and that enrichment programs may also be beneficial. There is great debate, however, about the appropriateness of offering enrichment programs only to gifted students. The question of gifted students and ability grouping evokes an even broader, philosophic question: Is the purpose of education to provide equity or excellence, or can both be accomplished? This question lies at the heart of the ability-grouping issue for gifted students, and there is no easy answer.

An even more pressing and more practical question requires attention. Are grouping practices, themselves, of primary importance in education? Most researchers appear to agree that the actual instructional practices occurring within the grouping structures must receive more attention in future ability-grouping studies. Slavin (1987a) stated that a complete conceptual understanding of the effects of ability grouping on achievement will not be possible "until the relationship between alternative grouping plans, teacher and student behaviors and perceptions, and student achievement are better understood" (p. 297). A systematic way to incorporate these other variables must be found. Regardless of grouping arrangement, the use of effective classroom practices are required for students to be successful, and classroom practices must be considered in any ability-grouping discussion.

Recommended Resources

Dawson, M. M. (1995). Best practices in promoting alternatives to ability grouping. In A. Thomas & J. Grimes (Eds.), *Best Practices In School Psychology-III* (pp. 347–357). Washington DC: National Association of School Psychologists.
This is a well written, easily read, concise yet comprehensive overview of the topic that focuses on alternatives to rigid tracking structures and suggestions on how to de-track. It is a good source for educators and parents who are interested in the subject and wish to explore alternatives to traditional tracking.

Gamoran, A. (1993). Alternative uses of ability grouping in secondary schools: Can we bring high-quality instruction to low ability classes? *American Journal of Education, 102,* 1–22.
This article offers a practical middle ground in the ability-grouping debate. A description of high quality instruction in low ability classrooms is provided.

Kulik, J. A., & Kulik, C. C. (1992). Meta-analytic findings on grouping programs. *Gifted Child Quarterly, 36,* 73–77.
Offered to contrast Slavin's 1987 study, this is also a comprehensive meta-analytic study. Gifted programs are included in this research, and the conclusions are somewhat different than those reached by Slavin (see later entry).

Oakes, J. (1987). Tracking in secondary schools: A contextual perspective. *Educational Psychologist, 22,* 129–153.
An extension of the 1985 book **Keeping Track: How Schools Structure Inequality** *(Yale University Press, 1985), this article covers a wide variety of factors that, taken together, effectively condemn the practice of tracking. For more complete coverage of these factors, see the aforementioned book.*

Slavin, R. E. (1987). Ability grouping and student achievement in elementary schools: A best-evidence synthesis. *Review of Educational Research, 57,* 293–336.
This comprehensive meta-analytic research study examines various grouping structures in elementary schools. It appears to be one of the preeminent research studies of ability grouping and is cited often in the literature. Conclusions and recommendations appear to be well-balanced and objective.

References

Allan, S. D. (1991). Ability grouping research reviews: What do they say about grouping and the gifted? *Educational Leadership, 48,* 60–65.

Allington, R. L. (1980). Teacher interruption behaviors during primary-grade oral reading. *Journal of Educational Psychology, 72,* 371–377.

Braddock, J. H., & McPartland, J. M. (1990). Alternatives to tracking. *Educational Leadership, 47,* 76–79.

Brophy, J. (1986). Teacher influences on student achievement. *American Psychologist, 41,* 1069–1077.

Dawson, M. M. (1987). Beyond ability grouping: A review of the effectiveness of ability grouping and its alternatives. *School Psychology Review, 16,* 348–369.

Dawson, M. M. (1995). Best practices in promoting alternatives to ability grouping. In A. Thomas & J. Grimes (Eds.), *Best Practices In School Psychology-III* (pp. 347–357). Washington DC: National Association of School Psychologists.

Dweck, C. S., & Leggett, E. L. (1988). A social-cognitive approach to motivation and personality. *Psychological Review, 95,* 256–273.

Evertson, C. E. (1982). Differences in instructional activities in average- and low-achieving junior high English and mathematics classes. *Elementary School Journal, 82,* 329–350.

Gallagher, J. J. (1993). Ability grouping: A tool for educational excellence. *College Board Review, 168,* 21–27.

Gambrell, L. B., Wilson, R. M., & Gantt, W. N. (1981). Classroom observations of task-attending behavior of good and poor readers. *Journal of Educational Research, 74,* 400–404.

Gamoran, A. (1986). The stratification of high school learning opportunities. Madison: Wisconsin University. (ERIC Document Reproduction Service No. ED 269 901)

Gamoran, A. (1992). Is ability grouping equitable? *Educational Leadership, 50,* 11–17.

Gamoran, A. (1993). Alternative uses of ability grouping in secondary school: Can we bring high-quality instruction to low-ability classrooms? *American Journal of Education, 102,* 1–22.

George, P. S. (1992). *How to untrack your school.* Alexandria, VA: Association for Supervision and Curriculum Development. (ERIC Document Reproduction Service No. ED 348 752)

George, P. S. (1993). Tracking and ability grouping in the middle school: Ten tentative truths. *Middle School Journal, 24,* 17–24.

Good, T. L. (1981). Teacher expectations and student perceptions: A decade of research. *Educational Leadership, 38,* 415–427.

Hiebert, E. H. (1983). An examination of ability grouping for reading instruction. *Reading Research Quarterly, 18,* 231–255.

Kulik, C. C., & Kulik, J. A. (1982). Effects of ability grouping on secondary school students: A meta analysis of evaluation findings. *American Educational Research Journal, 19,* 415–428.

Kulik, C. C., & Kulik, J. A. (1984). Effects of ability grouping on elementary school pupils: A meta analysis. Ann Arbor: University of Michigan. (ERIC Document Reproduction Service No. ED 255 329)

Kulik J. A., & Kulik, C. C. (1992). Meta-analytic findings on grouping programs. *Gifted Child Quarterly, 36,* 73–77.

Marsh, H. W. (1984). Self-concept, social comparison, and ability grouping: A reply to Kulik and Kulik. *American Educational Research Journal, 21,* 799–806.

Marsh, H. W., & Parker, J. W. (1984). Determinants of student self-concept: Is it better to be a relatively large fish in a small pond even if you don't learn to swim as well? *Journal of Personality and Social Psychology, 47,* 213–231.

Mills, C. J., & Durden, W. G. (1992). Cooperative learning and ability grouping: An issue of choice. *Gifted Child Quarterly, 36,* 11–16.

National Association of School Psychologists. (1993). *Position statement on ability grouping.* Silver Spring, MD: Author.

Oakes, J. (1985). *Keeping track: How schools structure inequality.* New Haven, CT: Yale University Press.

Oakes, J. (1987). Tracking in secondary schools: A contextual perspective. *Educational Psychologist, 22,* 129–153.

Oakes, J., & Guiton, G. (1995). Matchmaking: The dynamics of high school tracking decisions. *American Educational Research Journal, 32,* 3–33.

Pressley, M., & McCormick, C. B. (1995). *Advanced educational psychology for educators, researchers, and policymakers.* New York: HarperCollins.

Raze, N. (1984). Overview of research on ability grouping. Redwood City, CA: SMERC Information Center. (ERIC Document Reproduction Service No. ED 252 927)

Rosenbaum, J. E. (1976). *Making inequality: The hidden curriculum of high school tracking.* New York: Wiley.

Slavin, R. E. (1987a). Ability grouping and student achievement in elementary schools: A best-evidence synthesis. *Review of Educational Research, 57,* 293–336.

Slavin, R. E. (1987b). Grouping for instruction in the elementary school. *Educational Psychologist, 22,* 109–127.

Slavin, R. E. (1990). Ability grouping and student achievement in secondary schools: A best-evidence synthesis. *Review of Educational Research, 60,* 471–499.

Slavin, R. E. (1993). Ability grouping in the middle grades: Achievement effects and alternatives. *The Elementary School Journal, 94,* 535–552.

Slavin, R. E., & Braddock, J. H. (1993). Ability grouping: On the wrong track. *College Board Review, 168,* 11–18.

41

Grades and Grading Practices

William Strein

University of Maryland, College Park

Grades are a pervasive feature of education from elementary to graduate school. Despite well-meaning calls for ending or deemphasizing grades, especially the traditional A-to-F system, grades continue to be widely used in today's schools (Polloway et al., 1994) and are viewed as important by educators, parents, prospective employers, and students themselves (Evans & Engelberg, 1988). Grading practices have complex effects on students' achievement, attitudes, and self-perceptions of competence (Natriello, 1987). Without question, grades have a significant impact on the lives of children and adolescents.

Much about grades and grading practices is controversial, with debates documented in the literature for at least a century (Laska & Juarez, 1992). Although articles and position papers about grades are numerous, research is scant (Polloway et al., 1994). In fact, grading policies and practices are most often guided primarily by philosophical considerations and are likely to remain so (Terwilliger, 1977). Nonetheless, thoughtful analysis, including understanding of the relevant literature, will inform all of those for whom grades are an issue.

Although *grades* is an everyday term, it is helpful to have a working definition before continuing this analysis. The following definition, adopted with revision from Natriello (1992, p. 772) will be used:

Grades are those summary symbols assigned by teachers to some significant portion of student performance for purposes of both reporting on the performance and recording the information in the student's permanent file.

Note that while "symbols" are most often letter grades, they can also be numeric or categorical descriptors, such as "excellent," or "average."

Nature of Grades

All grades are inherently a subjective, evaluative judgment of the student's performance regardless of the method used (Ornstein, 1994). Whereas a teacher may assess a student's skills in an objective manner, the resulting grade is an evaluative judgment as to what level of quality this work represents. For example, a teacher in a school where few students excel academically might view a score of 85/100 on a challenging nationally standardized math exam as outstanding, meriting an A. The same performance might be seen as only adequate, receiving a B or C, at a highly selective school. Such possibilities are not merely speculative. Based on an analysis of a nationwide, longitudinal database, researchers recently documented that students in high poverty schools who reported getting "mostly A's" in either English or math scored similarly, as a group, on tests of reading and math, respectively, as did students who reported receiving "mostly C's" or "mostly D's" in affluent schools (Office of Educational Research and Improvement [OERI], 1994).

Another aspect critical to the understanding of grades is that they serve multiple purposes that are often in conflict with one another (Natriello, 1992). Grading may serve one of four basic purposes: (a) *certifying* that the student has achieved a specific level of accomplishment or mastery, for example, high school graduation; (b) *selecting* students for some educational or occupational path, e.g., college admission or employment; (c) *informing* the students and parents about the student's progress; and (d) *motivating* the student.

Grading policies and practices that serve one function particularly well may actually hinder another function. For example, although the certification function may best be served by a simple two-part distinction between those who have and have not reached some set of criteria (graduate vs. nongraduate), such a system would not serve well employers or colleges who want to select the best graduates. As another example, the certification and selection functions are often well served by "high" standards and "competitive" grading practices, but these approaches to grading tend to be the most motivating to already high-achieving students and may actually decrease the motivation of lower achieving students (Natriello, 1987). Given these tensions it is not surprising that teachers, especially at the elementary school level, find grading to be one of their most difficult, least liked, and least comfortable tasks (Brookhart, 1993).

467

Although various methods of grading exist, there are only two basic types of grading systems, comparative and mastery. *Mastery grading* will be discussed later in this chapter (in the Alternative Actions section). A *comparative grading* system uses two or more hierarchical categories; uses a fixed time period for the assignment of a grade; implicitly grades students relative to one another; and embodies an expectation that not all students will, or should, attain the highest grade (Laska & Juarez, 1992; Strein, 1988). Grading in the United States is almost entirely of the comparative type (Juarez, 1994). Using categorical descriptors or percentages instead of the familiar letter-grades does not alter the comparative nature of the system.

Grading Policies and Practices

Given the difficulties surrounding grading, how do teachers grade students? Recent survey research provides some interesting answers. A national survey of school system policies (Polloway et al., 1994) indicated that a majority of school systems have a formalized, written policy on grading. Consistent with recommendations made by measurement experts (Terwilliger, 1989), system policies strongly emphasize grading based on demonstrated achievement (e.g., tests, homework, projects). However, such nonachievement factors as attendance, behavior, and extra credit were endorsed by 33%, 24%, and 40% of the systems, respectively.

Not surprisingly, teachers responding to a large, nationally representative survey (Nava & Loyd, 1992) also accented achievement- or performance-related criteria. However, teachers reported using other factors in their grading, such as effort and ability level, even more strongly than school system policies would advocate. This study also showed that elementary and secondary teachers use substantially different criteria for grading. Elementary teachers were much more likely to include improvement in their grading, whereas secondary teachers placed more emphasis on demonstrated achievement in the form of tests and homework. The best conclusion based on this and other studies (e.g., Brookhart, 1993; Rojewski, Pollard, & Meers, 1990) is that teachers use multiple criteria and weigh these criteria variably, such that "grades become classroom-specific and must be interpreted as such" (Nava & Loyd, 1992, p. 19).

Teachers' reluctance to follow the measurement experts' recommendation to assign grades based solely on achievement is likely related to teachers' understanding that grades serve functions in addition to indicating some level of skills. In a creative study using various scenarios about grading dilemmas, Brookhart (1993) researched the meanings and values that teachers use when assigning grades. Brookhart concluded that teachers' grading practices reflect an attempt to balance their often-conflicting roles of advocate and judge. Teachers weigh the effects of grading on the student (e.g., motivation, self-esteem) against the certification and information-providing functions. Primarily, teachers in the Brookhart study saw grades as the "pay for work done." Grades were used as a part of teachers' classroom management strategies in a token-economy-like fashion. Thus, teachers' meaning and values attached to grades conflicted with the achievement-only approach to grading that deemphasizes the function of grades as a pedagogical tool. Consistent with this interpretation, Brookhart found that having a course in measurement had little effect on teachers' grading practices.

Grading of students with disabilities is of special consideration to school psychologists and others whose work focuses on this population. The diverse functions of grades are especially likely to conflict for these students. Assigning grades to students with disabilities strictly on "merit" (i.e., emphasizing the certification, information, and selection functions) is likely to result in a perpetual string of low grades, which almost certainly has a negative effect on these students' motivation. The most commonly advocated solution to this problem is to grade students with identified disabilities on a modified basis, especially with an emphasis on mastery grading (Polloway et al., 1994; Rojewski et al., 1990). This practice seems to be widespread. In the Polloway et al. study of school systems' grading policies, over half of those systems with written policies formally allowed for modifications for students with disabilities.

One must be careful, however, when using some sort of modified grading system with children with disabilities, especially when these students can clearly see that they are being graded differently than their nondisabled peers. Selby and Murphy (1992), in a qualitative interview study of six mainstreamed, middle-school students with learning disabilities, found that the students uniformly devalued "good" grades that they perceived as being based on some lesser standard than was being used with the general education students. These students desperately wanted to *earn* good grades, even though their achievement levels precluded them receiving such grades using the usual criteria. This paradox led Selby and Murphy to conclude that students with learning disabilities are "in a no-win situation—they may not be able to achieve high letter-grades within the regular program and they derive little satisfaction from high letter-grades achieved in the modified program" (1992, p. 98). Suggestions for grading students with disabilities are included in the Alternative Actions section later in this chapter.

Effects of Grades on Students

Teachers are often more concerned about the effects grades have on students than they are about the other functions grades serve (Brookhart, 1993). It is likely that practicing psychologists share this priority. Unfortunately, the answer to the question of how grades affect students is complex. What research exists suggests that the effects of grades may be very different on different types of students (Natriello, 1987).

One of the most striking research findings is that students often do not understand, and may be incapable of understanding, the basis on which they receive grades. In a questionnaire study of over 300 students from Grades 4 to 11, Evans and Engelberg (1988) found that understanding of even simple systems was incomplete for the younger students. Moreover, less than one-third of the 9th and 11th graders understood such important, but more complex, ideas as grade point averaging. The youngest students in this study were fourth graders, suggesting even less comprehension by early elementary students. It is unlikely that students will be motivated by a system that they fail to understand.

Actual research on the effects of grades has been sparse, and much of it is confounded by the fact that "grades" versus "no grades" conditions correspond to different instructional approaches. Existing research is generally not very supportive of traditional grading. Yarborough and Johnson (1980) identified 23 research studies between the 1950s and 1980s that studied the effects of graded versus nongraded settings on reading achievement. Of these, 11 studies found advantages for nongraded settings, 9 found no differences, and 3 were inconclusive. None of the 23 studies found clear advantages for the graded settings. However, these findings do not contradict the possibility of differential effects for differing types of students.

The effect of grades on motivation and self-perceptions is widely debated. Defenders of traditional, comparative grading (Ebel, 1992) emphasize the motivational value of maintaining high standards, while critics (Juarez, 1994) emphasize the destructive effects of repeated negative feedback for lower achieving students. Although it may sound trivially circular, one of the most supportable conclusions is that traditional, comparative grading has positive effects on students who typically receive good grades and negative effects on those who do not. For example, in a 1987 review of the literature, Natriello concluded that higher evaluation standards lead to higher student performance, but only when students perceive the standards to be attainable. When a student perceives the standards to be unattainable, higher standards *decrease* performance.

Lower achieving students tend to attribute grades to external factors such as task difficulty and luck, whereas higher achieving students tend to make internal attributions, such as ability, for grades received (Evans & Engelberg, 1988). Given that grades and skills are consistently correlated *within* a given school (OERI, 1994), it is reasonable to predict that those receiving higher grades

will attribute their success to effort and will see the grading standards as being attainable, thus leading to continued or increased motivation. The converse is likely true for lower achieving students.

The logic that traditional, comparative grading differentially affects students with differing abilities is supported by direct evidence from empirical research (Evans & Engelberg, 1988; Yarborough & Johnson, 1980). Such research shows that compared to their lower achieving peers, higher achieving students are more likely to favor traditional grading and view it as being fair. Reinforcing the idea of differential effects, Natriello's (1987) review uncovered research suggesting, for example, that the competition engendered by comparative grading only has positive effects on the academic performance of the top one-third of the class and that different systems of grading differentially affected the academic performance of students depending on their level of self-esteem and causal attributions.

Interestingly, the teacher's emphasis on grading may be much less important than is the distribution of grades in the class. Using data from a 2-year, 3000-student longitudinal study of the transition from elementary to secondary school, MacIver (1988) found that it was the dispersion of grades within a class that affected student self-concepts, not the frequency or importance placed on grading, even when controlling for ability. For example, in classes where there was high dispersion of math grades, a greater proportion of pupils believed themselves to be poor in math.

Defenders of traditional grading usually emphasize the motivational value of grades and their efficiency in providing a succinct evaluation of the student's progress. Ebel (1992) observes that failure is often as instructive as success and that guaranteeing "success" by awarding satisfactory grades does not avoid failure to master academic material. To illustrate, he points to the rising need for "remedial" courses in college for students with acceptable high school grades. Terwilliger (1977) defended comparative grading on the grounds that identification of relative strengths and weaknesses is beneficial both to society and the students. Such information is particularly helpful to students in making career choices.

Issues Related to Traditional Grading

The most frequently addressed issue related to traditional letter grading has been its subjectivity. For example, research showing a range of grades from 92 to 42 for the same high school history exam appeared over 80 years ago (Laska & Juarez, 1992). Since that time numerous studies have documented that different teachers give widely varying evaluations to the same student performance. This is true especially for activities such as essays in which the teacher must make a double judgment—first, a judgment as to how the student performed and secondly, a judgment as to what level of quality that performance represents. However, given that all grading inherently involves a subjective judgment (Ornstein, 1994), the relevant question is not whether grading is subjective but whether the subjective standards used by the school are appropriate.

Research in the 1970s and 1980s found grading to be influenced by such irrelevant factors as penmanship (in classes other than writing); discipline problems; and the student's reputation, race, or sex (Strein, 1988). Consistent with this earlier research, the more recent Nava and Loyd (1992) national survey found that at least half of the teachers reported "definitely" or "probably" including factors such as cooperativeness and attention in class. Over one-third would "definitely" or "probably" include handwriting neatness (other than in writing), aggressive behavior, and consideration for other students. Accordingly, before attempting to interpret a grade one must ascertain what comprised the grade in question. Without such additional information, the accurate interpretation of low grades is unlikely.

Grades are more related to specific classroom or school achievement than they are to broader measures of achievement such as scores on standardized tests (Leiter & Brown, 1985; OERI, 1994). To the extent that a teacher's grades represent valid measurements of something, they are largely a measure of *classroom performance* rather than of skills or knowledge. A highly skilled student who is not motivated to perform in class or who has poor work habits may get low grades, whereas a student who has somewhat lesser skills but who performs well in class may receive higher grades.

Another frequently asked question is whether grades matter at all. Do scholastic grades predict anything important? The answer to this question largely depends on which criteria one chooses. Elementary school grades do correlate with high school grades, and grades from year to year in high school are moderately related (r equals about .6) to one another. High school grades are about equally related to college grades (Evans, 1976) and are the best single predictor of college performance for most students. By contrast, research has generally found little or no relationship between college grades and "real-life" outcomes. However, numerous technical problems pervade this area of research, making the true relationship between grades and adult accomplishments difficult to discern. These problems include the large variability in grading criteria from school to school, highly skewed grade distributions within schools or classrooms, and varying definitions of real-life outcomes, all of which confound the issue of how grades relate to out-of-school variables.

Developmental Aspects of Grades

Because grades are almost universally given relative to some grade-based expectations (e.g., 1st vs. 3rd vs. 11th grade), grades do not typically change in a predictable developmental sequence. Nonetheless, parents of elementary students often wonder if their children's grades will likely get much better or worse in the future. In general the answer is a simple "no," but with reference to a specific child the issue can be quite complex. Grades in general are moderately stable over time (Evans, 1976) and from one subject to another (Leiter & Brown, 1985). In other words and using broad categories, students' grades do not change much. Elementary school students who obtain average, or above or below average, grades tend to continue to do so. Similarly, most students who receive A's in math do not receive D's in language arts.

Notwithstanding the general stability of grades over time and subject matter, there are some predictable deviations. Mastery of curriculum objectives plays an important role in grading, and the demands of the curriculum change in predictable ways thorough the elementary school years. In early elementary school, the curriculum largely requires rote memory skills, such as learning phonics rules or number facts. In the latter elementary grades, the curriculum begins to require some modest conceptual skills, such as the ability to comprehend reading material or to apply math facts to solve problems. Students who have an uneven development of abilities may experience rather abrupt changes in grades as a result of the shifting curriculum demands. Children who have relatively good memory compared to their conceptual skills often receive satisfactory grades in the early years, but their grades rapidly decline when they enter the later elementary school years. This pattern is common for children with learning disabilities or even for children with mild developmental delays, if these children are motivated and have good memory skills.

At several points demands of the curriculum also change in regard to students' self-sufficiency. In later elementary school students are increasingly expected to work independently during seatwork periods or on homework assignments. As the students move into the departmentalized structures more typical of middle and high school in which each student has several teachers, demands for self-sufficiency and organizational skills take another leap. Most students are able to adjust to these shifting demands, but for those students who have difficulty working independently, who have strong needs for frequent approval from adults, or who are disorganized, these shifts can be disastrous, resulting in dramatically lower grades. Students with certain learning disabilities, especially Attention Deficit/Hyperactivity Disorder, and students with emotional problems frequently follow this pattern.

Developmental changes caused by an increasingly poor match between the student's skills and curricular demands typically occur gradually. A review of previous report cards or interviews with previous teachers can often confirm the developmental pattern. More abrupt changes in grades, assuming that the student has not changed schools, are more likely to be the result of other factors. Stress resulting from such outside factors as family strife, death of a sibling, and so on is the most frequent cause of such abrupt changes.

Changes in grades in early adolescence are not confined to low-achieving students. In fact, Eccles et al. (1993) report that in many schools the *majority* of students experience a decrease in grades in the transition between elementary and junior high school. Greater use of normative grading criteria and more public forms of grading by junior high school teachers appear to explain this decline more than do changes in the students themselves. The Eccles et al. research also indicates that there is a greater mismatch for *most* students between features of the junior high school classroom environment and students' developing maturational needs than is true in elementary school. This mismatch is thought to have substantial negative effects on both grades and self-perceptions of competence. Although Eccles and her colleagues did not specifically look at grade changes for low-achieving students, they found that transition from elementary to junior high school typically had the strongest negative effects on the self-perceptions of low-achieving students.

Problems of Grades and Grading

Some form of grades, most likely traditional letter grades, will probably continue to pervade the lives of children, parents, and teachers for the foreseeable future. Accordingly, it is instructive to look at some of the major problems associated with grades and ways to lessen these problems' impact.

Perhaps the first challenge facing teachers and policy makers (and to a lesser extent parents, who apply pressure to these people) is the question of which of the varying functions of grades to emphasize. To the extent that the multiple functions of grades are in tension with one another (Natriello, 1992), teachers and schools must decide where to place the most emphasis. Teachers tend to accent the motivational functions of grades more than measurement experts would recommend (Brookhart, 1993). Advocates for students with disabilities carry this emphasis even further (Polloway et al., 1994). However, there are substantive arguments against this practice (Ebel, 1992; Terwilliger, 1989). Expedient criteria for awarding grades are not an acceptable substitute for clearly reasoned policy.

Closely related to this problem is the issue of the interpretability of grades and the understanding of the students receiving them. Grades are relatively poor vehicles for communication, even though this is one of their primary purposes. In addition to serving multiple functions, grades are assigned based on varying achievement- and nonachievement-related criteria (Nava & Loyd, 1992). Grades reflect classroom performance more than achievement per se (Leiter & Brown, 1985) and vary dramatically from school to school (OERI, 1994). Clearly, there is much room for misinterpretation. Accordingly, grades should be interpreted cautiously. If one needs specific information about a student's mastery or progress, information in addition to grades is needed. On top of all this, many students likely do not understand the system by which they are graded (Evans & Engelberg, 1988).

Contemporary society is mobile. Students move from school to school, often several times during their school career. The vast differences in grading criteria (OERI, 1994) pose a special problem for students who change schools. Students who transfer to a school with higher expectations will predictably experience a lowering of grades. The converse is true for students who transfer to a less competitive school. Such changes in grades do not reflect changes in mastery of material but in relative standing. Receiving substantially lower grades for the same effort and skills could create significant mental health problems and disaffection from school. Even for students who do not change schools, the school-referenced nature of grades can be problematic with regard to realistic self-appraisal of skills. For example, students in high-ability schools tend to underrate their own abilities (Strein, 1993).

A third problem is putting grades in the proper perspective. Whereas students are less positive about grades as they progress through the school system, they consistently believe that others view grades as being important. Parents attach even more importance to grades (Evans & Engelberg, 1988). Grades *are* important because we, as a society, believe they are. Despite numerous technical problems with grades, colleges and employers place a high value on them (Evans, 1976). The common-sense belief that students who receive better grades in school generally have more opportunities available to them and are more likely to advance professionally should not be quickly dismissed. However, although grades are important factors in securing highly selective opportunities, they are only moderate predictors of college performance and are questionable predictors of adult accomplishments (Evans, 1976). Similarly, although grades are often thought of as motivators for student achievement, this appears to be true only for relatively high achievers (Natriello, 1987). Accordingly, teachers and parents need not overly fear that alternative grading systems for low-achieving students will be detrimental.

Alternative Actions

Consulting with School Staff About Grades

Psychologists do not carry the burden of assigning grades. However, grading is an excellent example of an issue on which psychologists can serve as collaborative consultants (Conoley & Conoley, 1992) and as experts on assessment (Fairchild, 1982). Psychologists can help school policy makers with the development or clarification of system-wide grading policies. Although teachers are often not free to choose the types of grades that will be given, they do decide on which basis to assign grades and must make the delicate judgments of students' performance that grading entails. With teachers, psychologists may provide either case- or consultee-focused consultation around grading issues.

Consistent with a collaborative consultation approach, the place to start when consulting about grading is a discussion about the teacher's (or school's) educational philosophy. The major challenges surrounding grading have less to do with narrow technical measurement issues than with the overall issue of how grades are used (Brookhart, 1993). Although it is necessary to sort through nuances of teachers' philosophies, Terwilliger (1977) offers a handy gross guide to matching philosophies and grading systems. Given the large number of position statements on how grading should be done and the paucity of research on this topic, psychologists can also help teachers to sort through conflicting recommendations and come to a reasoned approach to grading.

Addressing the General Problems with Grades

School staffs need to address several general problems with grades. First, because of the problems stemming from the multiple functions of grades and the difficulty in interpreting them, school personnel and parents need to give more detailed thought to which grading systems they want to use and then make such policies clear in writing. Psychologists could help individual teachers or parent-teacher organizations to clarify their thinking about how best to evaluate students. Once classroom and school policies are clearly defined, schools need to find ways to inform their students as to how grades will be assigned.

Second, students and their parents need to understand the contextualized nature of grades. This will prepare them for transitions to other schools, where applicable, or for transition to postsecondary societal institutions, such as college or the workplace, which tend to reference evaluations to a wider standard. Schools should develop procedures, similar to college orientation programs, to ease student transitions, especially for students

transferring from other systems. Exploring possible differences in grading would be an important part of such programs. Additionally, schools need to provide students and their parents with information that ties students' performance to a frame of reference broader than their particular school building. This is especially relevant at the secondary level. Including the results of standardized achievement testing in the assignment of grades would be one way to serve this goal.

Use of Alternative Grading Methods for All Students

Schools are likely to continue to use traditional letter grading because it is (a) familiar to educators, parents, and postsecondary consumers of this information; (b) administratively cost-efficient in terms of reporting on student progress; and (c) arguably beneficial for high-achieving students. However, in most cases this does not prohibit teachers, especially at the elementary level, from using alternative methods for assigning grades.

Educators and measurement experts have proposed a variety of alternatives to the typical, inherently comparative grading system. Two alternatives are reviewed briefly here.

Mastery grading (Juarez, 1994) is the most commonly recommended alternative, especially for lower achieving students. In mastery grading the teacher sets specific, minimal learning objectives to be mastered by all students or in accordance with a given student's individualized program. "Grading" consists of dichotomously indicating mastery or nonmastery of the objectives. Mastery grading is most consistent with a "pass/fail" or "credit/no credit" grading system. Mastery grading also typically puts little emphasis on learning within a set period of time (Laska & Juarez, 1992). Although mastery grading is widely used, some experts believe that it is appropriate only for assessing minimal competencies and should be supplemented by a more comparative system to indicate better-than-minimal performance (Terwilliger, 1989).

Given the limitations of younger children's understanding of grades (Evans & Engelberg, 1988) and the focus of much of the elementary school curriculum on mastery of basic literacy and numeracy competencies required by all members of our society, a strong case can be made for using mastery grading throughout the elementary school years. Extending this logic further, Juarez (1994) asserts that mastery grading is most consistent with the goals of middle schools that emphasize success opportunities for all adolescents and reengagement of their families in the educational process.

In *self-referenced grading,* often referred to as grading based on improvement, students are graded on progress relative to their own earlier level of performance rather than by comparison to an externally defined absolute or comparative standard. Self-referenced grading is popular with teachers (Nava & Loyd, 1992) and systems-level policy makers (Polloway et al., 1994), who emphasize the motivational value of this system. However, it is generally discouraged by measurement experts because the resulting grade is not a measurement of mastery (Brookhart, 1993).

Reinforcing educators' beliefs that self-referenced feedback serves the motivational aspects of grading well, Slavin (1980) found that a carefully designed system of awarding points based on improvement produced significantly higher achievement gains in English grammar for a set of middle school students than did traditional grading of quizzes. McColsky and Leary (1985) found that students experiencing failure in a self-referenced feedback condition had higher expectancies for future performance and attributed their performance more to their own effort than did students in a norm-referenced condition.

Grading Students with Disabilities

Most experts highly recommend using alternative grading methods with low-achieving students or students with disabilities (Polloway et al., 1994; Rojewski et al., 1990). An important recommendation is that general and special education teachers share grading responsibilities for students in inclusive programs, rather than having grading be the sole responsibility of the general education teacher in whose class the student is officially enrolled. The Polloway et al. study found that general and special education teachers shared grading responsibilities in only about 12% of the relevant cases. Faced with the challenges posed by the inclusion movement, shared responsibilities for grading such students would provide needed support and perspective for both groups of teachers.

Shared grading of students with disabilities needs to be taken one step further to include not only teachers but parents and the students themselves (Selby & Murphy, 1992). Many students with learning disabilities appear to most highly value traditional letter grades based on the same criteria as those being used with their general education peers. By contrast, special educators prefer grading with reference to the special education class or with reference to effort or improvement. Parents put great stock in letter grades and interpret them as an indication of their child's status relative to other children. School systems need to seek input from all of these stakeholders and then develop and articulate a grading policy that communicates clearly to all concerned.

Mastery and self-referenced grading, already described, are the two most commonly recommended alternatives for grading students with disabilities because their noncomparative nature reduces the failing grades that accrue to students with disabilities when compared normatively to general education students. However, the Selby and Murphy (1992) research suggests that such grading may not be motivational, at least for students with mild disabilities, if the rest of the school system is following a traditional letter-grade approach. Accordingly, teachers should be cautious in using these grading systems as modifications specifically for students with disabilities. The clear, although challenging, implication here is that significant improvement in the grading of students with disabilities may not be possible without reforming the grading practices for *all* students within a given school system.

A final note involves the use of portfolio assessment. Currently popular as a part of educational reform that stresses "authentic" and classroom-based assessments, portfolio assessment has the potential to be useful for students with disabilities (Nolet, 1992; Swicegood, 1994). Although more a form of "assessment" than of "grading," portfolio assessment rests on the premise that comparative methods, such as standardized tests and letter grades, are less valuable than are classroom- and individual-referenced evaluation. In portfolio assessment student work samples and teacher's attached annotated comments are gathered into a cumulative collection that can then be used for either diagnostic or summary assessment of the student's work in that class. Notwithstanding the current popularity of this approach, there are several unresolved issues regarding portfolio assessment. Empirical evaluation of technical adequacy is virtually nonexistent (Nolet, 1992). The questions of which types of materials constitute a portfolio and the purposes for which portfolios will be used are open to debate. Advocates typically stress the value of portfolios in instructional planning (Swicegood, 1994) rather than for grading. Using portfolios as an assessment and learning tool, as generally advocated in educational literature, is probably most closely related to self-referenced grading that focuses on demonstrated improvement.

Summary

Psychologists need to understand the grading process because grades pervasively impact the lives of children, their parents, and their teachers. The many difficulties associated with grades are not likely to be soon resolved. In their roles as collaborative consultants and applied measurement experts, psychologists can make meaningful contributions to improving the grading process and the understanding of it.

Although likely to persist, the traditional grading system works well for only a relatively small proportion of students and works poorly as a vehicle for communicating information about a student's knowledge or skills. For the kinds of students most typically referred to psychologists, grades produce a murky picture of students' performance and often function as a disincentive for improvement. Psychologists need to help children and parents understand and cope with the grading system and help teachers and policy makers develop creative systems that validly represent student accomplishment without destroying the conditions promoting further academic progress and realistically positive attitudes toward work, self, and school. Mastery, or even substantial progress, on these twin tasks certainly merits an A.

Recommended Resources

Ornstein, A. C. (1994). Grading practices and policies: An overview and some suggestions. *NASSP Bulletin, 78,* 55–64.
This brief article provides a succinct overview of the key issues underlying grading and 10 recommendations for teachers to follow. The article is well-referenced yet written in a straight-forward, readable style.

Ory, J. C., & Ryan, K. E. (1993). *Tips for improving testing and grading.* Newbury Park, CA: Sage Publications.
Although written for college faculty, this book includes numerous practical recommendations for secondary school teachers about both classroom grading and testing. The 20-page chapter on assigning grades includes sections on purposes of grading, grading issues, conceptual basis for grade assignment, grading methods, and evaluating one's grading strategy.

Schurr, S. (1992). *The ABC's of evaluation: 26 alternative ways to assess student progress.* Columbus, OH: National Middle School Association.
Designed for middle school teachers, this book creatively includes exercises for assessing one's beliefs about the evaluation process and provides numerous specific classroom-based techniques for evaluating student work. Although the book does not address the grading issue per se, it does a nice job of leading the reader through the process of rethinking assessment practices that are alternatives to the traditional testing approach.

Terwilliger, J. S. (1977). Assigning grades: Philosophical issues and practical recommendations. *Journal of Research and Development in Education, 10,* 21–39.
In an exceptionally clear analysis of the issues surrounding grading, Terwilliger identifies the philosophical assumptions underlying various approaches to grading and analyzes on technical grounds several common grading procedures. The author makes recommendations within an admittedly pragmatic belief system.

References

Brookhart, S. M. (1993). Teachers' grading practices: Meaning and values. *Journal of Educational Measurement, 30,* 123–142.

Conoley, J. C., & Conoley, C. W. (1992). *School consultation: Practice and training* (2nd ed.). Boston: Allyn & Bacon.

Ebel, R. L. (1992). The failure of schools without failure. In J. A. Laska & T. Juarez (Eds.), *Grading and marking in American schools: Two centuries of debate* (pp. 105–112). Springfield, IL: Charles C. Thomas.

Eccles, J. S., Midgley, C., Wigfield, A., Buchanan, C. M., Reuman, D., Flanagan, C., & MacIver, D. (1993). Development during adolescence: The impact of stage-environmental fit on young adolescents' experiences in schools and in families. *American Psychologist, 48,* 90–101.

Evans, F. B. (1976). What research says about grading. In S. B. Simon & J. A. Belanca (Eds.), *Degrading the grading myths: A primer of alternatives to grades and marks* (pp. 30–50). Washington, DC: Association for Supervision and Curriculum Development.

Evans, E. D., & Engelberg, R. A. (1988). Student perceptions of school grading. *Journal of Research and Development in Education, 21,* 45–54.

Fairchild, T. N. (1982). The school psychologist's role as assessment consultant. *Psychology in the Schools, 19,* 200–208.

Juarez, T. (1994). Mastery grading to serve student learning in the middle grades. *Middle School Journal, 26,* 37–41.

Laska, J. A., & Juarez, T. (Eds.). (1992). *Grading and marking in American schools: Two centuries of debate.* Springfield, IL: Charles C. Thomas.

Leiter, J., & Brown, J. S. (1985). Determinants of elementary school grading. *Sociology of Education, 58,* 166–180.

MacIver, D. (1988). Classroom environments and the stratification of pupils' ability perceptions. *Journal of Educational Psychology, 80,* 495–505.

McColsky, W., & Leary, M. R. (1985). Differential effects of norm-referenced and self-referenced feedback on performance expectancies, attributions, and motivation. *Contemporary Educational Psychology, 10,* 275–284.

Natriello, G. (1987). The impact of evaluation processes on students. *Educational Psychologist, 22,* 155–175.

Natriello, G. (1992). Marking systems. In M. C. Alkin (Ed.), *Encyclopedia of Educational Research* (6th ed., pp. 772–775). New York: Macmillan.

Nava, F. J., & Loyd, B. H. (1992). *An investigation of achievement and nonachievement criteria in elementary and secondary school grading.* Paper presented at the annual meeting of the American Educational Research Association, San Francisco, CA. (ERIC Document Reproduction Services No. ED 346 145)

Nolet, V. (1992). Classroom-based measurement and portfolio assessment. *Diagnostique, 18,* 5–26.

Office of Educational Research and Improvement. (1994). *What do student grades mean? Differences across schools.* Washington, DC: U.S. Department of Education. (ERIC Document Reproduction Services No. ED 367 666)

Ornstein, A. C. (1994). Grading practices and policies: An overview and some suggestions. *NASSP Bulletin, 78,* 55–64.

Polloway, E. A., Epstein, M. H., Bursuck, W. D., Roderique, T. W., McConeghy, J. L., & Jayanthi, M. (1994). Classroom grading: A national survey of policies. *Remedial and Special Education, 15,* 162–170.

Rojewski, J. W., Pollard, R. R., & Meers, G. D. (1990). Grading mainstreamed special needs students: Determining practices and attitudes of secondary vocational educators using a qualitative approach. *Remedial and Special Education, 12,* 7–15.

Selby, D., & Murphy, S. (1992). Graded or degraded: Perceptions of letter-grading for mainstreamed learning-disabled students. B.C. *Journal of Special Education, 16,* 92–104.

Slavin, R. E. (1980). Effects of individual learning expectations on student achievement. *Journal of Educational Psychology, 72,* 520–524.

Strein, W. (1988). Children and grades. In J. Grimes & A. Thomas (Eds.), *Children's Needs: Psychological Perspectives* (pp. 241–246). Bethesda, MD: National Association of School Psychologists.

Strein, W. (1993). Advances in research on academic self-concept: Implications for school psychology. *School Psychology Review, 22,* 273–284.

Swicegood, P. (1994). Portfolio-based assessment practices: The uses of portfolio assessment for students with behavioral disorders or learning disabilities. *Intervention in School and Clinic, 30,* 6–15.

Terwilliger, J. S. (1977). Assigning grades: Philosophical issues and practical recommendations. *Journal of Research and Development in Education, 10,* 21–39.

Terwilliger, J. S. (1989). Classroom standard setting and grading practices. *Educational Measurement: Issues and Practices, 8*(2), 15–19.

Yarborough, B. H., & Johnson, R. A. (1980). How meaningful are marks in promoting growth in reading? *Reading Teacher, 33,* 644–651.

42

Homework

Timothy Z. Keith
Michelle DeGraff

Alfred University

Background

The purposes, efficacy, and effects of homework have been debated since the early 1900s (Foyle, 1984) and continue to be debated in both the professional (Barber, 1986) and popular (Gallo, Van Zuidam, Warner, & Block, 1995; Homework, Sweet Homework, 1995) press. For example, a Phi Delta Kappa booklet designed to review homework research and draw practical implications for teachers concluded that *little* was known about the effects of homework (England & Flatley, 1985). On the other hand, research compiled by the U.S. Department of Education (1987) concerning teaching and learning argued that both the quality and the quantity of homework affect student learning. Given such inconsistency, this chapter will begin with a review of homework research with the assumption that psychologists need to understand the effects of homework before they can develop coherent recommendations concerning homework. *Homework* is here defined as work assigned for completion outside the normal class period; it may be completed at home or at school, but it is assumed that most is completed at home. Furthermore, it is assumed that the primary purpose of homework is to supplement and improve academic learning.

Effects of Homework on Learning

Does homework substantially improve learning and achievement? If not, the reasons for assigning homework seem weak at best. Research provides some evidence about the effects of homework on learning, although, interestingly, most homework research has focused on issues of quantity rather than quality. Perhaps this is because of the difficulty of categorizing the *quality* of assignments, whereas all homework takes time to complete so time is a natural measure of the *quantity* of homework. Thus, much of the homework research has focused on time spent on homework or homework versus no homework and the effects of such conditions on learning.

Quantity

Much of the available homework research has been conducted at the high school level, with researchers often using large, representative data sets and nonexperimental research techniques for such analyses. For example, in a series of studies on the effects of homework and other variables on school learning, Keith and colleagues have consistently shown that the amount of time high school students spend working on homework has an important—although sometimes small—effect on their achievement (Fehrmann, Keith, & Reimers, 1987; Keith, 1982; Keith, in press; Keith & Benson, 1992; Keith & Cool, 1992; Keith & Page, 1985; Keith, Reimers, Fehrmann, Pottebaum, & Aubey, 1986). In this research, homework had meaningful effects across different ages of students (sophomores and seniors), for cross-sectional as well as longitudinal analyses, and when a variety of other important influences (e.g., motivation, parental involvement, quality and quantity of instruction) were controlled. Time spent on homework was an important influence on learning whether it was measured by grades or by test scores and even after important background characteristics were controlled (cf. Natriello & McDill, 1986). Perhaps of most interest is the observation that many of the background variables used in such analyses (e.g., socioeconomic status and intellectual ability) are not easily manipulable by schools, whereas homework is manipulable by parents, by schools, and by students themselves.

The importance of homework for high school students has been demonstrated in experimental research as well. For example, in a well-designed quasi-experiment using 10th grade students and social studies assignments, students assigned homework achieved at a higher level than those receiving no homework assignments (Foyle, 1984). Of course not all research is consistent in its support for the influence of homework on high school learning (e.g., Cool & Keith, 1991; Walberg, Pascarella, Haertel, Junker, & Boulanger, 1982), but the majority of research indeed suggests positive effects for homework on high-school-student learning and achievement (Cooper, 1989).

Similarly, homework seems an important influence on the learning of middle school youth (Keith et al., 1993; Peng & Wright, 1994), although some reviewers suggest that the effects of homework may be smaller for middle than for high school youth (Cooper, 1989). One recent study suggested that homework may help explain the positive effects of parental involvement. In that study, eighth graders with more involved parents completed more homework, and that homework, in turn, resulted in higher achievement test scores (Keith et al., 1993).

There seems to be less research on the effects of homework for younger children. Mathematics homework has been a common focus of study, and a number of researchers have found significant positive effects for homework for elementary-level students. Results suggest that homework may improve arithmetic computation (Maertens & Johnston, 1972), problem-solving skills (Hudson, 1966; Maertens & Johnston), and concept understanding (Koch, 1965). Yet, consistency is not a hallmark of social science research: Others have shown no differences for elementary students assigned homework over those assigned none (Gray & Allison, 1971; Maertens, 1969). Still, several such "no effect" studies have used very narrow definitions of "homework" (e.g., Gray & Allison). In a 1979 review of homework research in mathematics, Austin concluded that the results of homework studies in mathematics suggested the superiority of homework over no homework, at least down to the fourth-grade level.

Homework may have inconsistent positive effects for elementary students in other subject-matter areas as well. Time variables, especially homework, were important influences on the achievement of elementary (10-year-olds) through high-school-level students for a variety of subject-matter areas (science, reading, literature) in international data (Wolf, 1979). Similar results have been demonstrated in analyses of the effects of homework on reading, mathematics concepts, writing, and other subject-matter areas with students as young as the fourth-grade level (Harnischfeger, 1980). But again, homework findings are less consistent for elementary than for older students. Meloy (1987), for example, showed positive effects for homework on language arts achievement for fourth graders but *negative* effects for third graders. Other variables were confounded with homework at the third-grade level in this quasi-experiment (e.g., instructional time was greater for the no-homework group), but the conclusion remains that the evidence for homework's positive effects is stronger for older youth. Thus, a recent, comprehensive meta-analysis of homework research showed a significant but smaller effect for homework over no homework for elementary students (Cooper, 1989, Chapter 5).

Quality

It seems logical that the quality of homework assignments should also be important. And while quality is more difficult to define than quantity, there is evidence to support this assumption as well. For example, homework that is graded or commented on has a stronger impact on achievement than does homework that is not (Austin, 1976; Paschal, Weinstein, & Walberg, 1984). Evidence from in-class assignments suggests that positive comments are particularly beneficial (Page, 1958, 1992). Furthermore, well planned, systematic homework, closely tied to the instruction in the classroom, appears more effective than vague, less well-planned assignments (Leonard, 1965). Consequences for homework completion or noncompletion (Harris, 1973) and parental checking of homework (Maertens & Johnston, 1972) may add to its effectiveness. On the other hand, in one of the few studies designed to compare the effectiveness of various types of homework, Foyle (1984) found no difference in the effects of practice homework, designed to review and reinforce skills and materials covered in class, and preparation homework, designed to prepare students for an upcoming class topic. Such results do not necessarily mean that the two types of homework result in no meaningful differences; the lack of differences in the two experimental conditions may simply point to the need for the type of homework to be tied closely to the *purpose* of the assignment (Keith, 1986).

Other Time Variables, Effects, and Purposes

Research with other time variables (e.g., in-school learning time, time needed for learning, time spent learning) generally supports homework research in suggesting the importance of such time variables for learning (Fredrick & Walberg, 1980; Gettinger, 1984), and it appears that homework is an important influence on college achievement as well (Polachek, Kniesner, & Harwood, 1978). In addition, homework may have compensatory effects; less able students may be able to compensate for their lower ability through increased study (Polachek et al.).

The effects of homework may be greater for minority students than for majority youth. In particular, homework may have stronger effects on the achievement test scores of Black and Hispanic than White youth (Keith, 1993), and stronger effects on the grades of students of Asian descent (Keith & Benson, 1992). Some researchers speculate that homework may further improve achievement by reducing leisure TV viewing (Paschal et al., 1984), although several analyses of the effects of both variables found little support for this hypothesis (Keith et al., 1986; Keith et al., 1993).

Few researchers have examined the effects of homework specifically for special education youth. There is evidence, however, that homework is as effective for low-ability as for high-ability youth (Keith, 1982; Keith & Page, 1985) and that it can help compensate for low ability (Polachek et al., 1978). The few studies conducted with students with learning disabilities suggest similar effects as for regular education students but also suggest that "(a) simple, short assignments; (b) careful monitoring by and prominent rewards from teachers; and (c) parental involvement, especially to provide structure, conducive environments, and immediate rewards" are needed for students with learning disabilities (Cooper & Nye, 1994, p. 470). One study suggested that percentage completion and percentage correct should exceed 70% for homework to be effective (Rosenberg, 1989). Teachers perceive that accommodations such as additional assistance, more frequent checking concerning assignments and expectations, the use of learning aids such as computers, and alternative-response formats are particularly useful for students with learning disabilities (Polloway, Epstein, Bursuck, Jayanthi, & Cumblad, 1994).

Although the primary purpose of homework may be the improvement of learning, homework may have other purposes and effects as well, although research support for such effects is generally limited. Parents see homework as developing responsibility, providing independent study and preparation for future study, and strengthening the home-school bond (Friesen, 1978). Olympia, Sheridan, and Jenson (1994) argued that homework is "a natural means of home-school collaboration." Other possible purposes of homework include the development of good work habits, the extension of the school day, the opportunity for practice and review, and the assessment of students' understanding of the lesson (for a more detailed discussion of these purposes, see Keith, 1986). Homework may also aid in attempts to individualize instruction if individual students or small groups of students are given different assignments based on their instructional levels. There is, in fact, preliminary evidence that individualized homework assignments may produce higher achievement than "blanket" assignments (Bradley, 1967). Nevertheless, such secondary purposes of homework need additional research support (Cooper, 1989).

Developmental Issues

Education and school curricula are developmental in nature, and thus it follows that homework should change at different ages and grade levels. At the simplest level, the time students spend working on homework should vary depending on the child's age and grade level. Guidelines for the "right" amount of homework are difficult because this depends a great deal on the individual community, school, and teacher. Even more important, there will be wide variability within a classroom for the same assignment; the assignment that takes one student 10 minutes to complete may take another an hour. Despite such caveats, several authors have made suggestions for general homework guidelines; these suggestions are summarized in Table 1 (cf. Cooper, 1989; Keith, 1986). It has already been noted that homework seems to have stronger and more consistent effects for older students.

Types of homework assignments should also vary by grade level and subject-matter area. Lee and Pruitt (1979) classified homework as falling into one of four categories:

- *Practice homework*, the most frequent type, is designed to review materials and reinforce skills developed in the classroom.
- *Preparation assignments* are designed to prepare students for an upcoming class topic and often involve activities such as reading in a text or library research.
- *Extension homework* is designed to extend or generalize concepts or skills learned from familiar to new situations (e.g., writing an essay on the similarities and differences in the causes of the American and the French Revolutions [Lee & Pruitt, 1979, p. 34]).
- *Creative homework* assignments require the integration, extension, and creative application of a variety of skills (e.g., a TV production on some topic).

It is not the case that one type of assignment is always better than another; each serves its own purpose and has its own strengths and weaknesses. Practice, for example, while a necessary component of learning, tends to be the most frequently used type of homework assignment and can degenerate into busy work if overused. Preparation assignments, on the other hand, require considerable initiative and thought but may not be helpful if vague (e.g., "read the next chapter in your Social Studies text").

While one type of assignment is not always better than another, it seems likely that both the purposes and types of assignments should vary by grade level. If one of the purposes of homework is to increase students' initiative and responsibility as they grow older, then the mix of types of assignments should change accordingly as students enter higher grades. Thus, if the types of homework are placed on a continuum from practice to creative assignments, the proportion of higher order (extension and creative) assignments should increase as children enter higher grades. Similarly, some of the other purposes of homework would seem to become more or less important as children grow. For example, the purpose of strengthening the home-school relation may be more important at younger than older grade levels, while the purpose of extending the school day may be more important at higher grade levels. Individualization as a purpose of homework is important for any student having learning difficulties.

Table 1 *Recommendations for Normal Homework Duration and Quantity*

Grade Level	Guidelines #1	Guidelines #2
Grades 1–3	10 to 45 minutes per day, geared toward the "average" student	1 to 3 assignments per week, 15 minutes or less each
Grades 4–6	45 to 90 minutes per day	2 to 4 assignments, 15 to 45 minutes each
Grades 7–9	1 to 2 hours per day	3 to 5 assignments, 45 to 75 minutes each
Grades 10–12	1 1/2 to 2 1/2 hours per day	4 to 5 assignments, 75 to 120 minutes each

Note. The data in column 2 are from *Homework* by T. Z. Keith, 1986, West Lafayette, IN: Kappa Delta Pi. The data in column 3 are from *Homework* by H. Cooper, 1989, New York: Longman

Problems and Implications

It seems obvious that homework should be closely tied to the curriculum and to a child's instructional level. Thus, the hallmarks of well-developed classroom instruction would seem to hold for homework as well. Homework assignments should have a clear purpose, with explicit, even foolproof directions. Similarly, the product of the assignment should be clear. Is the student expected to answer the questions at the end of the chapter or to complete an essay? Finally, homework generally should be evaluated in some way either by grading assignments, quizzing the students on the assignment topic, or commenting on their assignments (cf. Paschal et al., 1984). Whatever system is chosen, work completed outside of school should be followed up in school, both to correct problems that arise and to reinforce the learning that has occurred. Many homework problems likely are the result of homework being poorly tied to the in-school curriculum.

Homework can be viewed from a variety of perspectives. On the one hand, homework can be seen as a means to an end or as a method of raising achievement or improving learning. Such a perspective leads to the notion of homework as an educational intervention (Keith & Page, 1985), a technique school psychologists could prescribe to improve the achievement of individuals or groups having learning problems (Olympia, Sheridan, Jenson, & Andrews, 1994). Homework may also be important in itself, in which case the problem might be compliance with homework assignments or the extent to which assigned homework is being correctly completed (Fish & Mendola, 1986; Miller & Kelley, 1991, 1994). Parents' and teachers' questions commonly come from this perspective: homework is being assigned, why isn't the student completing it?

Homework concerns and questions can also come from a group or an individual perspective. A child may be referred to a school psychologist for problems in homework or with a problem (such as low achievement) for which homework might be a suitable intervention. Many school districts and schools are in the process of developing homework policies; school psychologists may and should be involved in designing such policies. Similarly, school psychologists' input would seem valuable when developing less formal policies at a school or classroom level.

Thus, the *perspective* underlying the question may be among the first considerations of school psychologists when faced with questions concerning homework. Other information which may affect the school psychologist's possible action toward the presenting question include both school- and home-related concerns. At the school level, the school psychologist will want to know if homework is being assigned and, if so, how much is being assigned. How long does it take the student to do the homework? What types of homework are being assigned? Are the types of assignments and the amount of homework appropriate for the child's grade and ability level? Is the purpose of the assigned homework clear? Do the children understand what they are to do and the expected product of the assignments? Is the homework being reviewed in some meaningful fashion in the classroom? Does the homework supplement classroom instruction?

Assigned homework will not fulfill any purpose if it is not completed. When homework problems arise, it may be valuable to assess patterns of homework completion and noncompletion. Is assigned homework generally being completed? Are there clear contingencies for the completion or noncompletion of homework? How much homework is being completed? Are there differences in the types of homework students are completing as compared to homework not completed? Is completed homework done accurately? If the concern is with an individual student, are other students in the class completing homework correctly? If homework is being completed, but inaccurately, adjustments may be needed in directions for, types of, or difficulty level of homework assignments. Homework that is clearly defined, regularly assigned, of appropriate difficulty level, positively evaluated, and properly integrated into the curriculum will probably produce more learning and be completed more correctly than homework that is not. Furthermore, students will likely complain less about homework that is expected, relevant, and appropriate.

Student attitudes toward homework are obviously important. What are student reactions to the homework they are assigned? Do they have valid reasons for not completing assignments? What changes would they suggest?

Homework is a shared school-home responsibility, and thus assessment of what happens in the home is needed when homework problems arise (Olympia, Sheridan, & Jenson, 1994). What are parents' and other family members' attitudes towards homework? Do the parents convey a belief that homework completion and learning in general are important? There is evidence that such an orientation toward learning, called "the curriculum of the home," may be an important influence on learning (Walberg, 1984). Is there a quiet place—even if only the kitchen table—for the child to study? Is homework time planned, or is homework done hurriedly and only when there is extra time available? Is additional structure, such as a consistent place and time for study, needed? For some students, specifying regular times for homework may be necessary while for other students it may be better simply to specify a time by which homework must be completed. Is a parent too involved with the child's homework, such that homework is viewed as a shared responsibility rather than the child's responsibility? It is easy for parents to become over involved in children's homework, especially for children who are having academic difficulties.

Table 2 lists many of the questions that are asked in this section and that may shed light on the locus or possible solution of homework problems. Beside each question is a continuum from positive to negative. To use the listing, the psychologist should simply mark his or her impressions of the answer to each question after interviewing the teacher, student, or parent and after reviewing relevant records. The listing is intended as an *organizer* for collecting information, *not* as an interview or checklist. An alternative, more formalized assessment is provided by the Homework Problem Checklist, a valuable tool for assessing the extent of homework problems (Anesko, Schoiock, Ramirez, & Levin, 1987). This short checklist provides parents' perspective on homework problems. Both lists may be useful in determining homework strengths and weaknesses and in designing interventions.

Alternative Actions

The action taken in response to a homework question will depend on the nature of the problem. It has been noted that homework questions may focus on homework as an intervention (homework as a means to an end) or on issues of homework completion (homework itself as the focus). In addition, homework questions may be at the group or the individual level. Thus, discussion of possible actions will be grouped in four categories, although

readers should keep in mind the overlap among the possible actions.

Homework as a Group Intervention

School districts are increasingly expressing an interest in the development of formal homework policies, and school psychologists can provide constructive input for the development of such policies. Informal policies at the district, school, or class level are also possible, and there are advantages and disadvantages to either the formal or informal approach. For example, a district-wide policy creates consistent standards which let parents, children, teachers, and administrators know what is expected. On the other hand, informal policies or class-level policies may provide greater flexibility for individual classes and individual students. The general homework policy presented in Cooper (1989) may provide a good starting point for the development of individual district policies.

Whatever the approach taken, the policy developed should be flexible. It should communicate different expectations for different grade levels and allow flexibility within grade levels, subject-matter areas, and individual classes. An inflexible, unworkable homework policy is probably worse than none at all. The policy should be shared with students and parents to ensure that they are aware of expectations as well; the policy may also provide guidelines for parental involvement in homework. The policy should emphasize the need for variety in homework assignments and should encourage homework on a consistent basis. Such regularly assigned homework will likely produce more learning than less consistently assigned homework (Paschal et al., 1984), and students who expect homework on a regular basis will also likely complain less about assignments than those who do not expect homework. Homework policies should be developed with input from administrators, teachers, parents, and even students (Bond & Smith, 1965). Finally, when district-wide homework policies are developed, setting up a "homework hotline" to help answer student questions concerning homework should be considered (Blackwell, 1979), although students can also be encouraged to call classmates with homework questions.

A number of homework "programs" also may be appropriate for use in groups, such as classes, or with individual students. Such programs can focus on helping parents, teachers, or the students themselves intervene with homework problems. Olympia, Sheridan, and Jenson (1994) provide a valuable review of such programs.

Any district, school, or class that institutes a homework policy or a homework program should be prepared to hear objections to them. Homework takes time for students to complete and time for teachers to check over and grade. Some contend that students have too many other important out-of-school activities to spend time on homework, although the finding that many high school

Table 2 *Information about homework; this information may be useful in planning homework interventions.*

Student Name: _____

Information of Interest Concerning Homework	Positive .... Negative	
How many classes report homework problems?	0 .... All	

Information from Teacher (from Interview and Observation). Class: _____

Is homework assigned regularly?	Always .... Rarely
Is the homework tied to the curriculum?	Closely .... Loosely
Is it appropriate for grade level?	Very appropriate .... Not appropriate
Is it appropriate for ability level?	Very appropriate .... Not appropriate
Is the purpose of the homework clear?	Very clear .... Vague
Are the directions explicit?	Very explicit .... Vague
Is the expected product of the homework clear?	Very clear .... Vague
Is the homework evaluated in some way?	Always .... Rarely
Is the student provided feedback about homework?	Always .... Rarely
Are there clear contingencies for failure to complete homework?	Always .... Rarely
Is reinforcement provided for completed homework?	Always .... Rarely
How much time is expected for homework?	Consistent with guidelines .... None or excessive
Are other students completing homework accurately?	All .... Few
Is individualization of homework possible?	Easily .... Difficult
Are different types of assignments used?	Variety .... No variety

Information from Student and Review of Homework Products:

How much time is spent on homework?	Consistent with guidelines .... None or excessive
Are student reports of time consistent with teacher expectations?	Consistent .... Inconsistent
Does the student write down the assignment?	Always .... Rarely
Does the student understand the assignment?	Always .... Rarely
Does the student bring home needed materials?	Always .... Rarely
Normal rate of completion of homework	100% .... <60%
Normal rate of homework accuracy	100% .... <60%
Does the student have a quiet place to study?	Always .... Rarely
Does the student study at a consistent time?	Always .... Rarely
Student attitude toward homework?	Positive .... Negative

Information from Parents:

Do parents believe education is important?	Very important .... Not important
Do parents believe homework is important?	Very important .... Not important
Does the student have a quiet place to study?	Always .... Rarely
Does the student study at a consistent time?	Always .... Rarely
Do parents check or supervise homework?	Always .... Rarely
Do parents make sure all assignments are completed?	Always .... Rarely
Are parents willing to check, supervise, reinforce, or help with homework?	Very willing .... Not willing

Note. This listing of questions is intended as a means of organizing information collected concerning homework problems. After discussing the problem with the teacher, student, and parent, the school psychologist may use this form to check off areas that are problematic and that represent no problems by placing an X in the appropriate place along each continuum. The list is *not* intended as an interview or checklist to be completed by teachers, parents, and students.

students spend more time watching TV *per day* than they spend *per week* on homework would seem to suggest the fallacy of this concern (Keith, 1986). Student objections to homework can be minimized if homework is expected, its purpose is clear, time requirements are not excessive, and the scope and product of the assignment are explicit. High school teachers may be advised to let students know in advance what their assignments will be for the week to avoid having several classes "bunch up" their assignments.

Homework also requires a time commitment from teachers. Good homework assignments are well planned and an integral part of the curriculum. Most assignments should be graded, and practice homework may be followed profitably by a quiz. Students may also occasionally correct each other's assignments.

Most objections to homework revolve around the issue of time commitment, commitment on the part of students, teachers, and parents. Yet homework does seem to pay off in higher achievement. If it is decided that homework is important and that it produces desirable outcomes, then time will need to be budgeted for its assignment, completion, and correction.

Homework as an Individual Intervention

Homework can also be conceived as an intervention for an individual child; a hypothetical case may best illustrates this possibility (see Olympia, Sheridan, Jenson, & Andrews, 1994, for a research example). The school psychologist receives a referral from a teacher concerning a sixth-grade boy achieving below the level of his peers; the teacher questions whether special class placement is needed. Screening and record review suggests low-average abilities and achievement and a consistent history of marginal classroom performance. Special class placement seems inappropriate yet some sort of classroom intervention is obviously needed. Further checking reveals the presence of low homework demands (or alternatively, the regular assignment of homework that is too difficult and not completed).

A homework intervention may be appropriate for such a case, and the efficacy of such an intervention could be demonstrated using single-case design techniques. For example, the teacher may give weekly quizzes in math, and reading could be assessed weekly using curriculum-based assessment (CBA). The quiz and CBA scores for the first several weeks would serve as a baseline for the intervention. The school psychologist would then work with the teacher to develop appropriate-level, nightly mathematics homework and would work with the student and the parents to explain the mathematics intervention, to enlist their support, and to set up some guidelines for homework completion at home. Weekly assessment would be continued in both mathematics and reading, with the expectation being that the mathematics

weekly quizzes would improve while the reading assessments would remain relatively stable. After such a pattern emerged, reading homework assignments could similarly be started, with the expectation of subsequent improvement in the weekly reading CBA scores.

Such an intervention would keep the child in the regular classroom; would enlist the aid of the teacher, parents, and the child in improving his achievement; would clearly demonstrate whether the intervention was effective; and would require relatively little in-class individualization. Of course, several assumptions are made in this hypothetical case. The first is that the assigned homework is appropriate for the child's age and achievement level and is closely tied to the in-class curriculum. Homework that does not meet these criteria will likely be ineffective. The second major assumption is that the child complies with the homework intervention; if not, adjustments would be needed in the intervention. The appropriateness of the level and time commitment of the assignments would need to be checked, as would the commitment of the parents and the student. It would also be relatively easy to build in some type of reinforcement for successful homework completion.

Ensuring Homework Completion—Groups

Many questions about homework center around methods of ensuring its completion: Homework that is not completed will not fulfill any of its purposes. In working with teachers of classes in which homework is not being completed, the school psychologist should encourage them to assign homework on a regular basis and to make every effort to ensure that the assignments are consistent with in-class goals and activities. Teachers should strive to convey the purpose of each assignment and to make sure that the directions and expected products of assignments are so clear that they are virtually foolproof. It may be worthwhile to *start* assignments in class to clear up any questions or problems that arise, although the majority of the assignment should be completed at home.

Teachers should provide a mix of assignments; practice homework is necessary but should not be overused. Other types of assignments will often fulfill the purpose better than practice assignments. Teachers should be encouraged to individualize assignments for students who are unlikely to benefit from the normal assignment, as such individualization may benefit students' learning (Bradley, 1967). For example, the majority of the class may be given extension homework in science, whereas several low-achieving children may be served better by an assignment using some of the new, important science vocabulary in writing sentences. Excessively long assignments will also reduce compliance; teachers should be encouraged to think about how long a similar assignment would take in the classroom. It may be worthwhile occasionally to ask a reliable student how long an assignment took to complete. Such efforts to ensure the relevance and quality of homework assignments should also go far towards increasing homework completion.

Finally, assignments completed should be assessed in some way; grades and positive comments on homework assignments will likely produce more learning and will also convey that the teacher thinks the assignments are important. Assignments may also be followed up by a short quiz on the assigned material. Contingencies also can be added to increase motivation for homework completion (e.g., Moore, Waguespack, Wickstrom, Witt, & Gaydos, 1994).

Ensuring Homework Completion— Individuals

Teachers and parents are often concerned about a child who does not complete or poorly completes assigned homework. The first step in such a referral should be an assessment of the assigned homework using some of the guidelines for group-level completion. The homework should be appropriate for the child's ability, achievement, and in-class performance. Individualization of homework assignments may be needed for a child performing below the average classroom level. The purpose of the assignment and the directions should be clear and the products well defined; homework assignments should be graded or somehow evaluated. Given the adequacy of the assigned homework, individual cases of noncompletion of homework will often require working with the child and the child's parents to improve homework completion. The child may be questioned concerning reasons for noncompletion of homework, and realistic objections and concerns should be addressed (see also Table 2).

Behavior management techniques can be very useful for increasing homework compliance (Kahle & Kelley, 1994). Student-managed interventions have been shown to improve homework completion and accuracy (Fish & Mendola, 1986; Olympia, Sheridan, Jenson, & Andrews, 1994). Goal setting and contingency contracting have also shown promise as methods for improving homework performance (Kahle & Kelley; Miller & Kelley, 1994).

Parental cooperation and support can be an important and effective aspect of homework interventions (Kahle & Kelley, 1994; Miller & Kelley, 1991; Olympia, Sheridan, & Jenson, 1994). If nothing else, parents should be informed of their child's noncompletion of homework and the extent to which they should expect the child to bring assignments home. If parents do not know how often homework is assigned, it is easy for their children to pretend they have no homework. Thus, reg-

ularly assigned homework will help ensure clear parental expectations as well.

Parents should be encouraged to provide a quiet, nondistracting place for their child to study as well as a regularly scheduled time for study. They should also be encouraged to convey a belief in the importance of homework and the expectation that homework will be completed well. The extent of parental involvement in a child's homework, while negotiable, should also be discussed. Extensive involvement should probably be rare. Even when parents have the academic and teaching skills to help their children with homework, it is difficult to serve as teacher and parent at the same time. Parents should generally provide the structure and encouragement for homework completion and should be available to answer an occasional question and to review completed assignments, if they feel comfortable in this role.

Completion of homework is a first step; successful completion is obviously a more important goal. A child experiencing difficulty with homework may need adjustments in the nature and type of assignment and may also need help in developing good study skills. The school psychologist may need to work with the child to teach him or her basic organizational and study strategies. For example, the SQ3R (Survey, Question, Read, Recite, Review; Robinson, 1961) approach is a valuable tool for ensuring understanding of texts and can easily be applied to a variety of situations. The chapters on study skills and learning strategies in this volume may be valuable resources for the development of learning interventions.

Summary

Research evidence suggests that homework is an important influence on academic learning, and homework may fulfill other worthwhile purposes as well. Yet to fulfill these purposes, homework needs to be a well-planned part of the curriculum and be appropriate for the students who are to complete it.

Questions from teachers and parents concerning homework are likely to focus on groups or individuals and on homework as a means to an end (improving achievement) or on homework itself (is homework being completed?). As with other types of referrals, school psychologists faced with homework questions will need to understand the perspective and needs of the person asking the question and then to gather additional information about the child, the child's classroom, and the nature of the homework. Unlike many other types of school concerns, homework provides an excellent opportunity for working collaboratively with the school, the child, and the home in an effort to improve a child's functioning.

Homework can be viewed as a cost-effective intervention for improving achievement or as a method of accomplishing other purposes. Yet homework requires a considerable time commitment, both from teachers and from students. For this reason, care is needed to ensure that homework assignments fulfill their purposes and that they are clear, well-aligned with the curriculum, and appropriate for the students who are to complete them. Such a focus on the quality of homework assignments should help ensure that assignments are treated as important components of the curriculum rather than as busy work. Furthermore, with such a focus on quality, and with appropriate feedback, it is likely that homework's effect on learning will be even greater than that shown in research, where the quality of assignments is rarely controlled.

Recommended Resources

For Professionals

Cooper, H. (1989). *Homework.* New York: Longman.
This book presents a fairly comprehensive meta-analysis of homework research, along with a "generic" homework policy. Of interest to researchers, Cooper outlines homework research that needs to be done.

Hodapp, A. F., & Hodapp, J. B. (1992). Homework: Making it work. *Intervention in School and Clinic, 27,* 233–235.
The Hodapps provide an A to Z list of homework suggestions.

Keith, T. Z. (1986). *Homework.* West Lafayette, IN: Kappa Delta Pi.
This short booklet summarizes current homework research and provides practical advice, primarily aimed toward teachers, on how to devise a homework policy and meaningful homework assignments. A section on parental involvement and homework is also included.

Miller, D. L., & Kelley, M. L. (1991). Interventions for improving homework performance: A critical review. *School Psychology Quarterly, 6,* 174–185.
This review summarizes research findings on interventions designed to increase homework completion and accuracy. Miller and Kelley particularly focus on parental involvement and parent-child conflict and their relation to homework.

Olympia, D. E., Sheridan, S. M., & Jenson, W. (1994). Homework: A natural means of home-school collaboration. *School Psychology Quarterly, 9,* 60–80.
Olympia and colleagues provide a fine review of homework programs that can be used in the service of group or individual interventions. Programs may focus on parents, teachers, or students as the primary locus of the interventions.

Walberg, H. J. (1984). Improving the productivity of America's schools. *Educational Leadership, 41*(8), 19–30.
This is an excellent synthesis of thousands of research studies on a number of variables, including homework, that affect academic learning. Must reading for psychologists concerned with improving school learning.

Walberg, H. J., Paschal, R. A., & Weinstein, T. (1985). Homework's powerful effects on learning. *Educational Leadership, 42*(7), 76–79.
This article provides a discussion of a homework meta-analysis (see Paschal et al., 1984, in the reference list), discusses issues related to homework (students' time budgets, policy constraints), and practical suggestions for schools and parents concerning homework.

For Parents and Students

Dawson, P. (1994). Homework survival guide: Parent handout. *NASP Communiqué, 22*(7), insert, 1–8.
This insert provides a structured approach for parents interested in improving their children's homework completion and accuracy. The handout is also available from Multi-Health Systems, Inc., 908 Niagara Falls Blvd., North Tonawanda, NY 14120-2060.

Nathan, A. (1994). The homework report. *Zillions, 4*(4), 15–17.
Nathan provides advice for students by students on how to complete homework.

Olympia, D. E., Sheridan, S. M., & Jenson, W. (1994). Homework: A natural means of home-school collaboration. *School Psychology Quarterly, 9,* 60–80.
As noted in Recommended Resources for Professionals, this article reviews homework programs. Although the article itself is not appropriate for parents, five commercially available parent-based programs are reviewed.

Radencich, M. C., & Schumm, J. S. (1988). *How to help your child with homework.* Minneapolis: Free Spirit.
This book provides detailed, concrete suggestions for parents for helping their children with homework. The authors specify how to help with homework in each subject matter area (reading, spelling and writing, math, science and social studies, and foreign languages) and how to approach common assignments within each subject. A chapter of "resources and tools," such as lists of sight words, multiplication tables, book report outlines, and games, will be especially appreciated. This is an excellent resource for committed, capable parents.

References

Anesko, K. M., Schoiock, G., Ramirez, R., & Levin, F. M. (1987). The homework problems checklist: Assessing children's homework difficulties. *Behavioral Assessment, 9,* 179–185.

Austin, J. D. (1976). Do comments on mathematics homework affect student achievement? *School Science and Mathematics, 76,* 159–164.

Austin, J. D. (1979). Homework research in mathematics. *School Science and Mathematics, 79,* 115–121.

Barber, B. (1986). Homework does not belong on the agenda for educational reform. *Educational Leadership, 43*(8), 55–57.

Blackwell, W. R. (1979, November). *An analysis of Dial-A-Teacher assistance program (Dataline)*. Paper presented at the National Urban League Conference, Detroit. (ERIC Document Reproduction Service No. ED 183 647)

Bond, G. W., & Smith, G. J. (1965). Establishing a homework program. *Elementary School Journal, 66,* 139–142.

Bradley, R. M. (1967). An experimental study of individualized versus blanket-type homework assignments in elementary school mathematics. *Dissertation Abstracts International, 28,* 3874a.

Cool, V. A., & Keith, T. Z. (1991). Testing a model of school learning: Direct and indirect effects on academic achievement. *Contemporary Educational Psychology, 16,* 28–44.

Cooper, H. (1989). *Homework.* New York: Longman.

Cooper, H., & Nye, B. (1994). Homework for students with learning disabilities: The implications of research for policy and practice. *Journal of Learning Disabilities, 27,* 470–479.

Dawson, P. (1994). Homework survival guide: Parent handout. *NASP Communiqué, 22*(7), insert, 1–8.

England, D. A., & Flatley, J. K. (1985). *Homework—And why.* Bloomington, IN: Phi Delta Kappa Educational Foundation.

Fehrmann, P. G., Keith, T. Z., & Reimers, T. M. (1987). Home influence on school learning: Direct and indirect effects of parental involvement on high school grades. *Journal of Educational Research, 80,* 330–337.

Fish, M. C., & Mendola, L. R. (1986). The effect of self-instruction training on homework completion in an elementary special education classroom. *School Psychology Review, 15,* 268–276.

Foyle, H. C. (1984). The effects of preparation and practice homework on student achievement in tenth-grade American history. (Doctoral dissertation, Kansas State University, 1984). *Dissertation Abstracts International, 45,* 2474-A.

Fredrick, W. C., & Walberg, H. J. (1980). Learning as a function of time. *Journal of Educational Research, 73,* 183–204.

Friesen, C. D. (1978). *The results of surveys, questionnaires, and polls regarding homework.* Iowa City: University of Iowa. (ERIC Document Reproduction Service No. ED 159 174).

Gallo, J., Van Zuidam, J., Warner, C., & Block, L. (1995, September 1). Homework: To have or not to have. *Family Circle, 108,* 68.

Gettinger, M. (1984). Achievement as a function of time spent in learning and time needed for learning. *American Educational Research Journal, 21,* 617–628.

Gray, R. F., & Allison, D. E. (1971). An experimental study of the relationship of homework to pupil success in computation with fractions. *School Science and Mathematics, 71,* 339–346.

Harnischfeger, A. (1980). Curricular control and learning time: District policy, teacher strategy, and pupil choice. *Educational Evaluation and Policy Analysis, 2*(6), 19–30.

Harris, V. W. (1973). Effects of peer tutoring, homework, and consequences upon the academic performance of elementary school children. *Dissertation Abstracts International, 33,* 6175A.

Hodapp, A. F., & Hodapp, J. B. (1992). Homework: Making it work. *Intervention in School and Clinic, 27,* 233–235.

Homework, sweet homework. (1995, May 6). *The Economist, 335,* 15–16.

Hudson, J. A. (1966). A pilot study of the influence of homework in seventh grade mathematics and attitudes toward homework in the Fayetteville public schools. *Dissertation Abstracts International, 26,* 906.

Kahle, A. L., & Kelley, M. L. (1994). Children's homework problems: A comparison of goal setting and parent training. *Behavior Therapy, 25,* 275–290.

Keith, T. Z. (1982). Time spent on homework and high school grades: A large-sample path analysis. *Journal of Educational Psychology, 74,* 248–253.

Keith, T. Z. (1986). *Homework.* West Lafayette, IN: Kappa Delta Pi.

Keith, T. Z. (1993). Causal influences on school learning. In H. J. Walberg (Ed.), *Analytic methods for educational productivity* (pp. 21–47). Greenwich, CT: JAI Press.

Keith, T. Z. (in press). Structural equation modeling in school psychology. In C. R. Reynolds & T. B. Gutkin (Eds.), *The handbook of school psychology* (3rd ed.). New York: Wiley.

Keith, T. Z., & Benson, M. J. (1992). Effects of manipulable influences on high school grades across five ethnic groups. *Journal of Educational Research, 86,* 85–93.

Keith, T. Z., & Cool, V. A. (1992). Testing models of school learning: Effects of quality of instruction, motivation, academic coursework, and homework on academic achievement. *School Psychology Quarterly, 7,* 207–226.

Keith, T. Z., Keith, P. B., Troutman, G. C., Bickley, P. G., Trivette, P. S., & Singh, K. (1993). Does parental involvement affect eighth grade student achievement? Structural analysis of national data. *School Psychology Review, 22,* 474–496.

Keith, T. Z., & Page, E. B. (1985). Homework works at school: National evidence for policy changes. *School Psychology Review, 14,* 351–359.

Keith, T. Z., Reimers, T. M., Fehrmann, P. G., Pottebaum, S. M., & Aubey, L. W. (1986). Parental involvement, homework, and TV time: Direct and indirect effects on high school achievement. *Journal of Educational Psychology, 77,*.

Koch, E. A. (1965). Homework in arithmetic. *The Arithmetic Teacher, 12,* 9–13.

Lee, J. F., & Pruitt, K. W. (1979). Homework assignments: Classroom games or teaching tools? *The Clearing House, 53*(1), 31–35.

Leonard, M. H. (1965). An experimental study of homework at the intermediate-grade level. *Dissertation Abstracts International, 26,* 3782.

Maertens, N. (1969). An analysis of the effects of arithmetic homework upon the arithmetic achievement of third-grade pupils. *The Arithmetic Teacher, 16,* 383–384.

Maertens, N., & Johnston, J. (1972). Effects of arithmetic homework upon the attitude and achievement of fourth, fifth, and sixth grade pupils. *School Science and Mathematics, 72,* 117–126.

Meloy, L. L. (1987). Effects of homework on language arts achievement in third and fourth grades. (Doctoral dissertation, The University of Iowa, 1987). *Dissertation Abstracts International, 49,* 725-A.

Miller, D. L., & Kelley, M. L. (1991). Interventions for improving homework performance: A critical review. *School Psychology Quarterly, 6,* 174–185.

Miller, D. L., & Kelley, M. L. (1994). The use of goal setting and contingency contracting for improving children's homework performance. *Journal of Applied Behavior Analysis, 27,* 73–84.

Moore, L. A., Waguespack, A. M., Wickstrom, K. F., Witt, J. C., & Gaydos, G. R. (1994). Mystery motivator: An effective and time efficient intervention. *School Psychology Review, 23,* 106–118.

Nathan, A. (1994). The homework report. *Zillions, 4*(4), 15–17.

Natriello, G., & McDill, E. L. (1986). Performance standards, student effort on homework, and academic achievement. *Sociology of Education, 59,* 18–31.

Olympia, D. E., Sheridan, S. M., & Jenson, W. (1994). Homework: A natural means of home-school collaboration. *School Psychology Quarterly, 9,* 60–80.

Olympia, D. E., Sheridan, S. M., Jenson, W., & Andrews, D. (1994). Using student-managed interventions to increase homework completion and accuracy. *Journal of Applied Behavior Analysis, 27,* 85–99.

Page, E. B. (1958). Teacher comments and student performance: A seventy-four classroom experiment in school motivation. *Journal of Educational Psychology, 49,* 173–181.

Page, E. B. (1992). Is the world an orderly place? A review of teacher comments and student achievement. *Journal of Experimental Education, 60,* 161–181.

Page, E. B., & Keith, T. Z. (1981). Effects of U.S. private schools: A technical analysis of two recent claims. *Educational Researcher, 10*(7), 7–17.

Paschal, R. A., Weinstein, T., & Walberg, H. J. (1984). The effects of homework on learning: A quantitative synthesis. *Journal of Educational Research, 78,* 97–104.

Peng, S. S., & Wright, D. (1994). Explanation of academic achievement of Asian American students.

Polachek, S. W., Kniesner, T. J., & Harwood, H. J. (1978). Educational production functions. *Journal of Educational Statistics, 3,* 209–231.

Polloway, E. A., Epstein, M. H., Bursuck, W. D., Jayanthi, M., & Cumblad, C. (1994). Homework practice of general education teachers. *Journal of Learning Disabilities, 27,* 500–509.

Radencich, M. C., & Schumm, J. S. (1988). *How to help your child with homework.* Minneapolis: Free Spirit.

Robinson, F. P. (1961). *Effective study* (4th ed.). New York: Harper & Row.

Rosenberg, M. S. (1989). The effects of daily homework assignments on the acquisition of basic skills by students with learning disabilities. *Journal of Learning Disabilities, 22,* 314–323.

U.S. Department of Education. (1987). *What works: Research about teaching and learning* (2nd ed.). Washington, D.C.: Author.

Walberg, H. J. (1984). Improving the productivity of America's schools. *Educational Leadership, 41*(8), 19–30.

Walberg, H. J., Pascarella, E., Haertel, G. D., Junker, L. K., & Boulanger, F. D. (1982). Probing a model of educational productivity in high school science with National Assessment samples. *Journal of Educational Psychology, 74,* 295–307.

Walberg, H. J., Paschal, R. A., & Weinstein, T. (1985). Homework's powerful effects on learning. *Educational Leadership, 42*(7), 76–79.

Wolf, R. M. (1979). Achievement in the United States. In H. J. Walberg (Ed.), *Educational environments and effects: Evaluation, policy, and productivity* (pp. 313–330). Berkeley, CA: McCutchan.

43

Issues in School Readiness

Gilbert R. Gredler
University of South Carolina

Background

School readiness is a concept long used in discussions about education. In general, readiness implies that the child is able to benefit from structured educational experiences. The topic is of particular interest today because of the differing theoretical perspectives on the nature of readiness and the associated implications for educational practice.

Until the 1980s, the major perspectives proposed divergent conceptions of readiness. For example, the developmental-growth or maturational perspective views the child as an organism whose readiness is inextricably linked with biological unfolding. According to this perspective, the environment exerts limited influence on the unfolding process. Therefore, school entry and the introduction of some school subjects should be postponed until the child shows "signs" of readiness.

In contrast, the other major perspective emphasizes the skills developed by the child that are essential prerequisites to successful learning. Developed by Robert Gagné (1985), the cumulative-skills perspective views determining readiness as documenting the child's acquisition of identified prerequisite skills.

In the 1980s, a third perspective advanced by Lev S. Vygotsky, a Russian psychologist, began to influence educational practices related to readiness. Vygotsky (1930–35/1978) questioned the assumption defining developmental level as the tasks that the child can carry out independently. He maintained that a more adequate measure of the child's potential for further development consists of the tasks that the child can complete in collaboration with an adult. Guided problem solving, in other words, indicates the tasks that the child is ready to learn because the child can imitate only those processes within the limits set by the state of his or her development (Vygotsky, 1934/1962, p. 103). Referred to as the zone of proximal development, this concept of readiness places major emphasis on the child's interactive social experiences with more knowledgeable members of the culture (Gredler, 1997).

The different theories of the relationships between development and learning have each influenced educational practices and the choices of school experiences for children. Educational policies such as increasing the kindergarten entrance age, retaining children in the early grades, and using transition rooms are based largely on the maturational model. In contrast, the Reading Recovery program, a nationwide reading program for first graders at risk for reading difficulties, is grounded in the Vygotskian perspective (Clay & Cazden, 1990). The teacher and child first participate in shared reading which allows the teacher to explore the child's knowledge of reading and use of strategies. After 2 weeks, instruction begins with shared reading of a new selection which the child should be able to read aloud independently the next day. If not, the selection is inappropriate.

How old a child must be to enter school is guided less by theoretical models per se than by state law. That is, states (somewhat arbitrarily) set cut-off dates for kindergarten entrance. These dates vary greatly, with 43 states applying 12 different dates (Education Commission of the States, 1995). Over the last 32 years (1963 to 1995), the required entrance age for kindergarten and first grade has risen steadily, in part a result of the influence of the maturational model. In 1963, only 14% of the schools required a kindergarten entrance age of 5.0 by September 1. By 1995, this age was required by 56% of the schools (Education Commission of the States, 1995; Gredler, 1992; Smith & Shepard, 1988). Obviously, increases in the kindergarten entry age also raise the age at which children enter all succeeding grades.

In an important review of research and policy options, Gray (1985) made the following important observations about entrance age:

1. Chronological age is a useful criterion for school entry because it clearly states the obligations of the government for the provision of educational services for its citizens and is administratively convenient.
2. Research literature indicates that the majority of the youngest children who enter kindergarten achieve as well as the older children.

3. Many children with disabilities who are in need of specialized educational services are not served until they enter school. Raising the entry age would delay the provision of such services.
4. Disadvantaged children, who are in special need of early educational services, would be hampered in skill development by delay in entrance age.
5. Parents in many states currently do *not* have to enter their children if they believe they are not ready. However, arbitrarily raising the entry age would discriminate against the children who are ready for school. (p. 15)

Other issues that have entered into discussions of school readiness are the developmental and experiential factors that may be related to school success and the social and emotional adjustment of younger children. A brief overview of these factors follows.

Developmental and Experiential Factors

Chronological age

The entrance-age issue is more complicated than it first appears. The concept of a young, and therefore possibly at-risk child, is a relative one. Because September is now the accepted cut-off date by which children must reach 5 years of age to enter kindergarten in many states, the at-risk and youngest child is now born in the summer months (June through September). However, according to the December cut-off used in the 1960s, the summer child would not be at risk.

Also of importance is that school admission occurs only once each year. Therefore, children's ages in any one classroom vary by at least 12 months. The key question becomes that of the relationship of these age differences to school performance. Differential rates of referral to psychological services and retention rates for children young for grade when they enter kindergarten or first grade cannot be considered as valid indicators of at-risk status because these decisions are strongly influenced by teachers' beliefs about age (Smith & Shepard, 1988).

Frequently, the performance of older children on achievement tests will be somewhat higher at the end of first grade than that of the younger children. This difference is not unexpected because the older children come to school knowing more (Gredler, 1992; Green & Simmons, 1962). Thus, one cannot expect that the younger group should be *equal* to the older group on achievement measures at the end of the school year.

Shepard and Smith (1986), in the discussion of their research on kindergarten children in Boulder, Colorado, noted that only small differences in reading and math were found between the oldest and youngest children in first grade. They also found that the differences between the two groups that did exist were the result of a combination of youngness *and* low ability. Further, they noted that the disadvantage of youngness reported in some studies usually disappeared by the third grade.

Gender differences

A common view is that gender differences in readiness occur because boys mature later than girls. As indicated by McGuinness (1985), girls have a distinct advantage in comprehension skills, in producing language, and in fine motor skills, while boys are superior in gross motor skills. The girls' advantages facilitate learning to write. However, McGuinness adds that the major differences between girls and boys are found mainly in the lower range of the verbal skills distribution which includes more boys than girls. As noted by Berk (1994), gender differences, especially in verbal abilities, are not necessarily biologically based. She states that girls' superior reading performance is probably due to their more extensive experiential backgrounds. Children consider reading as feminine, and parents rate their daughters as more competent readers. Also the school setting is considered to be "feminine-biased" because boys are more active than girls and, therefore, receive more reprimands than girls (Berk, 1994, p. 545). While girls begin to talk earlier and show more rapid vocabulary growth during the first grade, boys later catch up. Berk further states that a simple biological explanation for differences in verbal abilities must be discounted because the superiority of girls in reading is found to be nonexistent in countries where reading and school learning are more highly regarded activities for males. Although girls obtain better grades in all subjects through the third grade, these differences disappear in subsequent years.

Two recent studies of the effects of age and gender on school achievement shed additional light on the relationship between these three variables. Flynn and Rahbar (1993) investigated reading development over 3 years of schooling (kindergarten through third grade) in a sample of 3,400 students in Wisconsin and Minnesota schools. Results of their analyses failed to support the current practice of enrolling and promoting children based on the child's age at time of entrance or considering gender differences in such practices. Children entering kindergarten in these states were 5 years old before September 1. For purposes of the study, younger children were defined as 5 years 6 months (5–6) or younger and the older children as those from 5–6 to 5–11 in age. The gender effects that were found were too small to be of practical significance. Moreover, younger boys did not perform at lower academic levels than did their older peers in first, second, or third grade.

In another study, Flynn, Rahbar, and Bernstein (1996) studied the association between season of birth and reading problems in a population of 3,200 second-grade children also in Minnesota and Wisconsin schools. Flynn et al. found similar rates of reading failure for boys and girls and no relationship between season of birth and reading failure. Because the entrance age to first grade in Minnesota and Wisconsin schools is 6–0 by September 1, summer birth children would be considered to be most at risk, but no such relationship was found.

Social and Emotional Adjustment of Younger Children

Much of the published research on the differences in the social and emotional adjustment of younger and older children in kindergarten and first grade was undertaken in the 1950s and 1960s. These studies, however, lack sophistication in research design and instrumentation.

Much of the current research consists of unpublished doctoral dissertations. However, four published studies address some aspects of social or emotional adjustment. Bickel, Zigmond, and Strayhorn (1991) studied the relationship of first-grade entrance age to elementary-school success in the Pittsburgh school system. No relationship was found between entry age and social and work habits as measured by the children's report card ratings. In addition, no relationship was found between entry age and first-grade retentions, remedial assistance in reading or mathematics after first grade, or placement in special education classes. This latter group included placement in classes for the socially and emotionally disturbed.

Social adjustment, defined as social acceptance, was studied by Spitzer, Cupp, and Parke (1995). They measured acceptance by peer sociometric ratings, teacher reports of social acceptance and adjustment, and kindergarten report card grades. The study included 512 children from 41 classrooms in 9 schools from 2 southern California school districts. Results indicated that kindergarten entrance age was not related to peer sociometric ratings either in kindergarten or first grade. That is, the youngest children were not more likely to be rejected by their peers. Although rating scales completed by both kindergarten and first grade teachers indicated some differences between younger and older children, no significant differences were found for report card grades for language, mathematics, physical skills, or social skills. The authors concluded that the evidence does not support an educational policy that would exclude younger children from school.

Another perspective on social adjustment is reflected in statements in both the press and professional journals on the possible relationship between school entry age and youth suicide. Uphoff and Gilmore (1984) studied youth suicides in an Ohio county and determined that a large percentage of the victims had entered school at a younger age. They concluded that the academic problems of the younger children "who were unready at school entrance often last throughout their school careers and sometimes even into adulthood" (Uphoff & Gilmore, 1984, p. 34). Limitations of the research include the small sample size ($N = 28$) and the brief time span

(1½ years) included in the study. A more recent study included 173 youth suicides for the five largest population centers in South Carolina for a 5-year period (Gredler, 1992). The suicide rate for those who were youngest or oldest when they entered school did not differ from expected (random) frequency. Conceptually, the premise that school entry age is closely linked to student suicide is difficult to accept because various other important events have occurred in the students' lives since they entered school.

Socioeconomic Status and Early Intervention Programs

A substantial relationship between socioeconomic status (SES) and success in school has been reported consistently over the years. The effect of SES is greater than that of age. For example, in a recent study of the reading achievement of 1,900 children, the risk of failure in the first grade was found to be twice as great for lunch-assisted children (i.e., those with low SES) than for the youngest children in the sample (Jones & Mandeville, 1990).

For more than 30 years, a number of programs have provided intensive educational intervention for children from low-income families. Once the province of middle-class parents (and provided privately), the complex of preschool programs currently available has many more provisions for the children of low-SES families. In addition to Operation Headstart, which is found in most school districts, many schools are offering early childhood programs for 3- and 4-year-olds. A survey of such programs in 1991 found that one-half of all 3- to 5-year-olds were enrolled in an early childhood program. The programs ranged from Operation Headstart to all-day child-care centers (West, Hausken, & Collins, 1993).

Several intervention programs, such as Operation Headstart, have been shown to increase readiness test scores, achievement test scores, and IQ scores and to reduce the number of children retained or placed in special education (Clarke & Clarke, 1989; Neisser et al., 1996; Powell, 1995). During the first 2 to 3 years of school, children in these programs scored higher than controls on measures of IQ and achievement. Unfortunately, some decline in scores followed. However, a one- or two-year educational program cannot be expected to cancel all the negative aspects of low SES. Thus, educators should emphasize the importance of providing educational support programs through the elementary years (Berk, 1994).

The Carolina Abecedarian Project is another example of a successful early-intervention program for children in low-SES homes. This project consisted of (a) high-quality child-care programs for infants and preschoolers and (b) additional school-age intervention for several years beginning in kindergarten (Campbell & Ramey, 1994; Powell, 1995). Intervention was all-inclusive with a home/school teacher assigned to each child. The teachers' responsibilities included providing additional curriculum materials in reading and math to be utilized in the home and providing help to the families in obtaining community services. Intellectual and academic gains lasted through 7 years. IQ scores of the treatment groups were higher at age 2 than for the control group; at age 12 there was a 5-point difference, 7 years after intervention treatment had ended (Niesser et al., 1996; Powell, 1995).

Differences in Curriculum and Instructional Practices

The primary goals of kindergarten have undergone several cyclic changes over the past 25 years (Katz, Raths, & Torres, 1987). As noted by Walsh (1989), kindergarten has become the center of increased scrutiny due to (a) increased concern about public education in general and (b) conflict over which educational group is going to "control" the kindergarten curriculum. One group, for example, emphasizes the teaching of academic skills; others, however, focus on developmental motivation. Such policy differences mask the real problem, which is that a number of students are not doing well in school. That is, schools define the problem in inadequate ways such as "the 'problem' of the late birthday child; the problem of the immature child" (Walsh, 1989, p. 388). As indicated by Walsh, the failure of children in kindergarten cannot be solved by redefining it away.

In an interesting study of instructional practices of teachers, a close relationship was found between teacher beliefs and kindergarten retention rates (Smith & Shepard, 1988). Open-ended interviews of teachers revealed four different belief systems:

- *Nativist*—belief in the physiological unfolding of abilities.
- *Remediationist*—the belief that children of legal age are ready for school and should be taught.
- *Diagnostic-prescriptive*—the belief that specialized training for the child's deficits will correct them.
- *Interventionist*—the view that learning is a complex interaction between the psychological characteristic of the child and the environment arranged by the teacher.

The teachers who were nativists had the highest retention rates, judging retained children as being not developmentally ready for the next grade.

Problems and Implications

Measuring Readiness

Screening programs in education are based on the assumption that learning and behavioral problems can be predicted accurately from early childhood assessment and that children's potential problems can be measured accurately and reliably. However, the accurate prediction of success in the early grades is often problematic, as indicated next.

Two types of instruments are commonly used to screen children for kindergarten and first grade: *developmental screening* measures and *readiness* measures. Developmental screening measures are designed to assess the developmental level of the child's potential to acquire skills, rather than the degree to which a specific skill has been acquired (Meisels, 1994). Such screening tests typically examine motor coordination, memory of visual sequences, verbal expression, language comprehension, and social-emotional status (Lichenstein & Ireton, 1991; Meisels, 1994). See Table 1.

Readiness tests tend to tap skills believed to be related to school learning tasks and to be predictive of school success. Areas included on readiness tests are cognitive skills, language, motor skills, copying shapes, concept development, and perceptual processes (Lichenstein & Ireton, 1991).

Although these descriptions indicate differences between developmental screening tests and school readiness tests, as seen in Table 1, Lichenstein and Ireton (1991) note that "it is difficult to make clear content distinctions between developmental and school readiness measures" (p. 493). (See the next section on analysis of procedures).

Unfortunately, many school districts make placement decisions based almost completely on the results of the administration of some type of instrument. It is important to reiterate that, regardless of whether the instrument is a developmental screening measure or a readiness test, there appears to be little difference as to the kinds of decisions made by educational personnel. A survey of kindergarten screening in school districts in the state of New York indicated that 30% of the districts used developmental screening measures, 28% used readiness measures, 20% made use of informal observations, and 33% used school-constructed tests (May & Kundert, 1993). (The total is more than 100% because many school districts used more than one measure). Results also showed that 45% of the school districts recommended that parents delay school entry for "unready" children, and 21% recommended placement in a readiness kindergarten. These recommendations were based primarily on the results of screening tests.

Effective Screening Measures: Analysis of Procedures

The selection of developmental screening and readiness tests should be based on an adequate standardization sample, low cost, ease of administration, appropriate content, and adequate validity and reliability. Essential types

Table 1   *Screening Instruments*

Skills Assessed by Tests	Brigance[1]	Dial-R[1]	Early Screening Inventory[2]	Denver II[2]	Gesell[1]
Gross Motor Skills	X	X	X	X	X
Fine Motor Skills	X	X	X	X	X
Social Skills	X	–	–	X	X
Self-Help Skills	X	X	X	X	X
Cognitive Skills	X	X	X	X	X
Academic/Procedures	X	X	X	X	X
Expressive Language	X	X	X	–	X
Receptive Language	X	X	X	X	X
Articulation Skills	X	X	–	X	–
Behavioral/Self Control	X	–	–	X	X

Note. From *A Validation Study and the Psychometric Properties of the Brigance Screens* (p. 30) by F. P. Glascoe, 1995, North Billerice, MA: Curriculum Associates. Copyright 1995 by Curriculum Associates. Adapted with permission. A more indepth analysis of a large number of developmental screening measures and readiness tests may be found in Glascoe, 1995.
[1]Readiness Measure
[2]Developmental Screening Measure

of information for assessing the value of a screening instrument are illustrated in Table 2. The index of sensitivity

$$\left(\frac{a}{a + b}\right)$$

indicates the number of children who actually performed poorly that also were originally selected by the screening measures. The index of specificity

$$\left(\frac{d}{c + d}\right)$$

compares the number of children who actually performed satisfactorily with the number who were originally considered not at risk by the screening test (a retrospective view). The positive predictive value

$$\left(\frac{a}{a + c}\right)$$

indicates the number of children who were predicted to be at risk and actually demonstrated learning problems, school failure, or the like. The last of the four indices

$$\left(\frac{d}{b + d}\right)$$

indicates the number of those predicted *not* to be at risk but who actually performed satisfactorily.

Although all four indices are important in determining the effectiveness of a screening measure, the positive predictive value

$$\left(\frac{a}{a + c}\right)$$

is the index that most school personnel consider to be the most important. That is, school districts act mainly on the number of children who are classified as at risk. Thus, if the positive predictive value is low (i.e., .20 to .50) and the school district subsequently places children in a special program such as a prekindergarten or a transition room, a large number of such children would be misplaced because in reality they do *not* have learning or behavioral deficits. Note that data from Table 3 indicate that only 23% of children who scored low on the Denver II actually experienced later academic difficulties. Such a high level of inaccuracy results in waste of diagnostic resources, undue parental anxiety, and waste of programming resources.

Finally, reference should be made to the utility of the Gesell School Readiness Test (Ilg, & Ames, 1972), one of the most widely used of readiness measures. Graue and Shepard (1989) investigated the progress of kindergarten children who had been administered the Gesell School Readiness Test as they progressed to first grade. Analysis of the relationship between Gesell scores and the outcome criteria (i.e., standardized tests and teachers' ratings of maturity and achievement) indicated low predictive validity. Graue and Shepard concluded that the use of the Gesell for placement decisions was unwise.

The measures shown in Table 3 are illustrative of the kinds of developmental screening and readiness measures currently in use in a number of school districts. In this table, it is particularly important to note the performance criteria used with a particular measure. Two examples of the use of the Brigance are given. The performance criterion for the Wenner (1995) study indicates the relationship of the readiness measure to promotion decisions and referrals to special services. In contrast, the Glascoe (1995) study uses achievement test scores as a criterion. While both criteria are important, it is doubtful that school psychologists should recommend use of a readiness/developmental screening measure based

Table 2 *Assessing the Validity of a Screening Test*

Criterion	Screening Measure		Indices
	At Risk	Not At Risk	
Poor Performance on Criterion Measure	Valid Positive **a**	False Negative **b**	Index of sensitivity $\left(\dfrac{a}{a+b}\right)$ The percentage of poor performers correctly identified originally by the screening test.
Adequate Performance on Criterion Measure	**c** False Negative	**d** Valid Positive	Index of specificity $\left(\dfrac{d}{c+d}\right)$ The percentage of adequate performers correctly identified originally by the screening test.
	Positive predictive value $\left(\dfrac{a}{a+c}\right)$ Percentage of 'at risk' subjects who later performed poorly on criterion measure.	Negative predictive value $\left(\dfrac{d}{b+d}\right)$ Percentage of children identified as <u>not</u> at risk who later performed adequately.	

Table 3 *Analysis of Effectiveness of Selected Readiness/Developmental Screening Measures*

Measures	Subjects	Performance Criteria	Positive Predictive Value	Not At Risk Children Who Later Performed Adequately	Sensitivity	Specificity
Brigance K-1 Screen[a]	Prekindergarten (4- and 5-year-olds)	Promotion decisions and referrals by teachers to special services	.56	.93	.45	.94
Merrill Language Screening Test[a]	Same as above	Same as above	.86	.93	.50	.99
Denver II[b]	X̄ age 39 months	Concurrent psychological assessment	.23	.83	.43	.93
Brigance K-1 Screen[c]	Kindergarten (5-3 to 5-8)	Achievement test scores	.63	.77	.75	.86
Dial-R[d]	Prekindergarten (4- to 5-year-olds)	Special education placement	.53	.97	.43	.98

[a]Results were taken from Wenner, 1995.
[b]Results were taken from Glascoe et al., 1992.
[c]Results were taken from Glascoe, 1995.
[d]Results were taken from Jacob, Snider, and Wilson, 1988.

solely on its relationship to promotion/retention decisions. Also, while the Merrill Language Screening test generally shows low error rates, further information is needed as to the relationship between the Merrill and actual achievement in Grades 1 and 2.

Alternative Actions

Important topics in the consideration of alternatives are school policy decisions, parental and legal issues, and the role of the school psychologist.

Policy Decisions

Raising the minimum age for entrance to school remains a popular yet questionable course of action for increasing the number of children deemed "ready" for schooling. Many school districts are convinced that children are still entering school at too early an age; thus, the entry age has risen considerably in the past three decades. However, as indicated earlier, school personnel are still confronted with a wide range of individual differences because there is always at least 12 months between the youngest and oldest children who enter school. This range of 12 months has expanded in recent years as a result of parents holding their children out an extra year in expectation that they will be more "ready" for kindergarten if they are a year older. For example, in their study of three California school districts, Cosden, Zimmer, and Tuss (1993) found that 10% to 11% of children were "held out" by their parents. Additionally 6% to 8% of the students were retained in kindergarten. Consequently, 16% to 19% of children enrolled in kindergarten the next year were a year older than the average age set for kindergarten by the state. Such an increase in the range of abilities and skills among kindergartners makes the teacher's instructional task much more difficult and challenges the wisdom of raising the minimum age for school entrance.

A common alternative to delaying entrance is to admit all children at the specific chronological age required by state law but then either place at risk children in a prekindergarten or junior kindergarten followed by a year of regular kindergarten. In the absence of a prekindergarten program, children would be retained in kindergarten. While some educators believe that early retention does little damage to the child's self-esteem, interviews of retained children and their parents indicated many negative feelings about the experience (Brynes, 1989).

Another popular course of action for children judged not ready for first grade is to place them in a transition/readiness, or prefirst, program after their first year in kin-

dergarten. Ostensibly, the transition-room program provides an opportunity for young children to "mature" within an appropriately structured environment. However, research studies clearly indicate that the achievement of transition-room children is less than, or at best equal to, the achievement of children eligible for placement in a transition room but placed instead in regular classrooms (Gredler, 1992; Mantzicopoulos & Morrison, 1990; May & Kundert, 1993; May & Welch, 1984; Shepard, 1989; Shepard & Smith, 1987; Southward & May, 1996). A recent study of the relationship between extra year programs (i.e., kindergarten retention or transition classroom placement) indicated that the retained kindergarten children, despite their extra year of school, performed significantly lower on achievement measures than children who were recommended for retention but went on to first grade (Dennebaum & Kulberg, 1994).

Perhaps it is important to note that whether referred to as a developmental kindergarten, pre-first-grade, readiness-room program, or transition class, the result is the same. That is, a minimum of an extra year is added to the child's educational program.

Within the past 10 years, a number of schools have emphasized new instructional approaches for children who appear to be at risk either in kindergarten or first grade. One such approach is described in a study of the progress of kindergarten children placed in two different kindergarten programs in Tulsa, Oklahoma. Whereas one program emphasized nonacademic activities, the other emphasized academics to a small degree and included the Writing to Read Program (Martin & Freidberg, 1986; Zenka & Keatley, 1985). One purpose of this study was to investigate the relationship between readiness for first grade, readiness test scores (Gesell developmental age status), and instructional techniques used in kindergarten. A child had to obtain a score equal to the 40th percentile on the Metropolitan Readiness Test in order to be placed in first grade. Results showed that 73% of "immature" children in the nonacademic kindergarten failed to reach the 40th-percentile cut-off score. However, only 44% of the immature children in the Writing to Read Program scored below the 40th percentile. It should also be noted that the percentage of mature children subsequently considered eligible for first grade placement increased by 13%. Thus, instructional modification in the kindergarten program resulted in improved performance of a larger percentage of the kindergarten children.

Another instructional intervention program found to be of value is Reading Recovery. Targeting at-risk first-grade students, this program, developed by Marie Clay in New Zealand in the late 1970s, was adopted in the Columbus, Ohio, schools in 1984 (Clay, 1987). The program provides individual tutoring of children 30 minutes per day for 12 to 20 weeks. The children are removed from the classroom for the tutoring and work with a specially trained teacher. A critical feature of the program is that the first 2 weeks are spent in establishing a close relationship with the child and in assessing the child's learning strategies and knowledge in a thorough manner. Research studies over the past several years attest to the value of this type of intervention when working with children labeled at risk or considered not ready for first grade (Pinnell, 1989; Wasik & Slavin, 1993).

When a school offers no alternatives other than retention in kindergarten or a prefirst program to help at-risk children, then high retention rates can be expected. Research shows that schools with high kindergarten retention rates typically set inflexible grade expectations and do not set adapting instruction to children's special needs as a priority. First-grade teachers in such schools are often unwilling to accept children who cannot begin a reading program the first week of school (Shepard, 1991; Shepard & Smith, 1985).

Parental and Legal Issues of Concern

Few references in the literature include discussion of parental concerns about assessment and placement policies relating to kindergarten and first-grade children. In-depth parent interviews by this chapter's author (Gredler, 1992) revealed a number of such concerns. Parents questioned the adequacy of tests utilized to measure readiness and the examiner's qualifications to administer the tests. They were also concerned about the lack of opportunity to discuss screening results and stated that there was too much emphasis on the child's "late" birthday to the exclusion of other characteristics of the child.

Parental concerns have led to various legal actions. For example, the Commonwealth of Pennsylvania has specifically encoded into law educational regulations to ensure certain educational rights of parents of kindergarten and first-grade children. These regulations state that children who have reached the requisite age for entry to kindergarten must be enrolled in kindergarten and cannot be placed instead in a prekindergarten or kept out of regular first grade without the express approval of parents. In addition, a child cannot be required to repeat kindergarten (Wall, 1988).

An important legal decision concerning developmental kindergarten placement occurred in New York State (State of New York Department of Education, 1987). Children in a northern New York State school district were required to take the Gesell Readiness Test in June prior to entrance to kindergarten in September. A mother objected to the fact that her daughter was assigned to the developmental kindergarten and felt her concerns were not adequately addressed by school personnel. Legal action resulted in the following decisions:

The child in question was transferred to regular kindergarten and no kindergarten aged child was to be assigned to the developmental kindergarten without written consent from the parent. It was further stated that the readiness test (e.g., Gesell) did not meet professional standards of reliability and validity; and that the school failed to place students in a regular educational environment first, to determine whether the child could satisfactorily function within the regular school setting. Also the court stated that the school failed to evaluate students individually in order to assess specific areas of educational need; and that the school failed to make use of information from a variety of sources. Also students who were suspected of possible problems should have been referred for further diagnostic assessment. The court concluded that the school did not attempt to implement an intervention program before placing these children in a segregated setting (State of New York Department of Education, 1987).

Obviously, the issues raised by this lawsuit will need to be addressed by other school districts because of their possible impact on screening and placement decisions.

Role of the School Psychologist

School psychologists can aid school personnel by providing consultation in the following areas:

1. Select screening instruments that will accurately predict possible learning problems with appropriate indices ratios for sensitivity, specificity, and positive predictive values. A proper approach to the use and interpretation of screening tests is provided by Mardell-Czudnowski and Goldenberg (1990), who state that a readiness test is not an end in itself but rather should be a first step in an evaluation process which will be many tiered. Therefore, part of the process will always entail a more thorough assessment of the child's capabilities.
2. Help educational personnel to implement suitable screening programs in first grade and evaluate their effectiveness.
3. Provide information on effective intervention programs for at-risk children such as Reading Recovery and Writing to Read.
4. Undertake indepth assessment of children who fail to progress after appropriate interventions have been implemented. The school psychologist is still the only school-system professional who is trained to undertake such a task.
5. Expand consultation sessions with teachers by encouraging them to discuss with you the behavior of children about whom there are questions of emotional and social adjustment.
6. Provide leadership in evaluating the effects of an intervention program. School psychologists can definitely expand their role and responsibility by encouraging

school personnel to implement some of the interventions previously described in this chapter. Such a move will help reduce the perception by some school personnel that the school psychologists only administer standardized or curriculum-based measures.

Summary

School readiness issues have become quite prominent in education in recent years. Questionable school practices include the continual manipulation of the school entrance age and use of retention and transition rooms as the only intervention programs for children deemed to be at risk. School personnel must choose screening measures carefully and provide an ongoing evaluation as to their validity and reliability.

Examples of effective interventions for young children with possible learning problems have been described. When implemented, such programs will reduce learning problems in children and also reduce the need for assessments of young children by school psychologists.

Recommended Resources

Glascoe, F. P. (1995). *A validation study and the psychometric properties of the Brigance Screens.* North Billerica, MA. Curriculum Associates.
This book provides the results of a careful investigation of the psychometric properties of one screening instrument and offers a helpful guide to school psychologists who plan to evaluate screening measures.

Gray, R. (1985). *Criteria to determine entry into school: A review of the research.* Springfield, IL: Illinois State Board of Education, (ERIC Document Reproduction Service No. ED 260 826).
This remains one of the best discussions of school entry variables available. An outstanding research study sponsored by a state board of education is detailed.

Graue, M. E., & Shepard, L. A. (1989). Predictive validity of the Gesell School Readiness Tests. *Early Childhood Research Quarterly, 4,* 303–315.
This article presents an indepth analysis of the validity of the Gesell. This is an important study given that the Gesell is still one of the most frequently used readiness measures.

Gredler, G. R. (1992). *School readiness: Assessment and educational issues.* New York: John Wiley & Sons.
This publication provides the reader with an overall view of the many issues in early childhood education. It is one of the few that discusses parental concerns about assessment and placement decisions as well as legal issues. The book also provides extensive coverage on choosing a screening or readiness test that is both valid and reliable.

Powell, D. R. (1995). *Enabling young children to succeed in school.* Washington, DC: American Educational Research Association.
This excellent monograph covers a number of topics concerning readiness and provides a good discussion of early childhood programs.

Shepard, L. A., & Smith, M. L. (Eds.), (1989). *Flunking grades: Research and policies on retention.* Philadelphia: The Falmer Press.
This book contains 11 chapters written by prominent educators and psychologists on the hazards of retention practices. It presents solid research describing teachers' beliefs about retention, the results of kindergarten retention, attitudes of students and parents about retention, and policy implications of retention practices.

Wasik, B. A., & Slavin, R. E. (1993). *Preventing early reading failure with one-to-one tutoring: A review of five programs. Reading Research Quarterly, 28,* 179–206.
This article discusses prevention programs with which school psychologists should be familiar. It provides an excellent summary of Reading Recovery along with discussion of a number of research studies of Reading Recovery.

References

Berk, L. E. (1994). *Child development* (3rd ed.). Boston: Allyn & Bacon.

Bickel, D., Zigmond, N., & Strayhorn, J. (1991). Chronological age at entrance to first grade: Effects on elementary school success. *Early Childhood Research Quarterly, 6,* 105–117.

Byrnes, D. A. (1989). Attitudes of students, parents, and educators toward repeating a grade. In L. A. Shepard & M. E. Smith (Eds.), *Flunking grades: Research and policies on retention* (pp. 108–131). Philadelphia: The Falmer Press.

Campbell, F. A. & Ramey, E. T. (1994). Effects of early intervention on intellectual and academic achievement: A follow-up study of children from low-income families. *Child Development, 65,* 684–698.

Challenge to Gesellian Kindergarten Placement Exam. (1988). *Fair Test Examiner, 2,* 5–6.

Clarke, A. M. & Clarke, A. D. (1989). The later cognitive effects of early intervention. *Intelligence, 13,* 289–297.

Clay, M. C., & Cazden, C. B. (1990). A Vygotskian interpretation of Reading Recovery. In L. C. Moll (Ed.), *Vygotsky and education* (pp. 206–222). New York: Cambridge University Press.

Clay, M. M. (1987). Implementing reading recovery: Systematic adaptations to an educational innovation. *New Zealand Journal of Educational Studies, 22,* 35–38.

Cosden, M., Zimmer, J., & Tuss, P. (1993). The impact of age, sex, and ethnicity on kindergarten entry and retention decisions. *Educational Evaluations and Policy Analysis, 15,* 209–222.

Dennebaum, J. M., & Kulberg, J. M. (1994). Kindergarten retention and transition classrooms: Their relationship to achievement. *Psychology in the Schools, 31,* 5–12.

ECS Clearinghouse Notes (1995). *State characteristics: Kindergarten.* Denver, CO: Education Commission of the States.

Flynn, J. M., & Rahbar, M. (1993). The effects of age and gender on reaching achievement: Implications for pediatric counseling. *Journal of Developmental and Behavioral Pediatrics, 14,* 301–307.

Flynn, J. M., Rahbar, M. H., & Bernstein, A. J. (1996). Is there an association between season of birth and reading disability? *Journal of Developmental and Behavioral Pediatrics, 17,* 22–26.

Gagné, R. M. (1985). *The conditions of learning* (4th ed.). New York: Holt, Rinehart, & Winston.

Glascoe, F. P. (1995). *A validation study and the psychometric properties of the Brigance Screens.* North Billerica, MA: Curriculum Associates.

Glascoe, F. P., Byrne, K. E., Chang, B., Strickland, B., Ashford, L., & Johnson, K. (1992). The accuracy of the Denver II in developmental screening. *Pediatrics, 89,* 1221–1225.

Graue, M. E., & Shepard, L. A. (1989). Predictive validity of the Gesell School Readiness Tests. *Early Childhood Research Quarterly, 4,* 303–315.

Gray, R. (1985). *Criteria to determine entry into school: A review of research.* Springfield, IL: Illinois State Department of Education.

Gredler, G. R. (1984). Transition classes: A viable alternative for the at-risk child? *Psychology in the Schools, 21,* 463–470.

Gredler, G. R. (1992). School readiness: Assessment and educational issues. Brandon, VT: Clinical Psychology Publishing.

Gredler, M. E. (1997). *Learning and instruction: Theory into practice* (3rd ed.). Upper Saddle River, NJ: Prentice-Hall.

Green, D. R. & Simmons, S. V. (1962). Chronological age and school entrance. *Elementary School Journal, 63,* 41–47.

Ily, F. L. & Ames, L. B. (1972) *School readiness behavior tests used at the Gesell Institute.* New York: Harper & Row.

Jacob, S., Snider, K., & Wilson, J. (1988). Validity of the DIAL-R for identifying children with special education needs and predicting early reading achievement. *Journal of Psychoeducational Assessment, 6,* 289–297.

Jones, M. M., & Mandeville, G. K. (1990). The effect of age at school entry on reading achievement scores among South Carolina students. *Remedial and Special Education, 11,* 56–62.

Katz, G. L., Raths, J. D., & Torres, R. D. (1987). *A place called kindergarten.* Urbana, IL: Clearinghouse on Elementary and Elementary Childhood Education.

Kelly, F. J. (1987). Rights of child to attend kindergarten (Opinion # 6467). Lansing, MI: Office of Attorney General.

Lichenstein, R., & Ireton, H. (1991). Preschool screening for developmental and educational problems. In B. A. Bracken (Ed.), *Psychoeducational assessment of preschool children* (pp. 486–513). Boston: Allyn & Bacon.

Mantzicopoulos, P., & Morrison, D. (1990). Character-

istics of at-risk children in transitional and regular kindergarten programs. *Psychology in the Schools, 27,* 325–332.

Mardell-Czudnowski, C., & Goldenberg, D. S. (1990). *DIAL-R: Developmental indicators for the assessment of learning—Manual* (Rev.). Circle Press, MN: American Guidance Service.

Martin, J. & Fredberg, A. (1986) *Writing to read.* New York: Warner.

May, D. C., & Kundert, D. K. (1993). Pre-first placement: How common and how informed? *Psychology in the Schools, 30,* 161–167.

Meisels, S. J. (1994). *Developmental screening in early childhood: A guide* (4th ed.). Washington, DC: National Association for the Education of Young Children.

Neisser, U., Boodoo, G., Bouchard, T. J., Boykin, A. W., Brody, N., Ceci, S. J., Halpern, D. F., Loehlin, J. C., Perloff, R., Sternberg, R. J., & Urbina, S. (1996). Intelligence: Knowns and unknowns. *American Psychologist, 51,* 77–101.

Pinnell, G. S., DeFord, E. E., & Lyons, C. A. (1988). *Reading recovery: Early intervention for at risk first graders.* Arlington, VA: Educational Research Service.

Powell, D. R. (1995). *Enabling young children to succeed in school.* Washington, DC: American Educational Research Association.

Shepard, L. A. (1989). A review of research on kindergarten retention. In L. A. Shepard & M. E. Smith (Eds.), *Flunking grades: Research and policies on retention* (pp. 64–78). Philadelphia: The Falmer Press.

Shepard, L. A. (1991). Readiness testing in local school districts: An analysis of back door policies. *Journal of Education Policy, 5,* 159–179.

Shepard, L. A., & Smith M. L. (1985). *Boulder Valley kindergarten study: Retention practices and retention effects.* Boulder: University of Colorado, Laboratory of Educational Research.

Shepard, L. A., & Smith, M. E. (1986). Synthesis of research on school readiness and kindergarten retention. *Educational Leadership, November,* 78–86.

Shepard, L. A., & Smith, M. E. (1987). Effects of kindergarten retention at the end of first grade. *Psychology in the Schools, 24,* 346–357.

Shepard, L. A., Smith, M. E., & Marion, S. F. (1996). Failed evidence on grade retention. *Psychology in the Schools, July,*

Smith, M. E., & Shepard, L. A. (1988). Kindergarten readiness and retention: A qualitative study of teachers' beliefs and practices. *American Educational Research Journal, 25,* 307–3337.

Southward, N. A., & May, D. C. (1996). The effects of prefirst grade programs on reading and mathematics achievement. *Psychology in the Schools, 33,* 132–142.

Spitzer, S., Cupp, R., & Parke, R. D. (1995). School entrance age, social acceptance and self-perceptions in kindergarten and 1st grade. *Early Childhood Research Quarterly, 10,* 433–450.

State of New York Department of Education. (1987). Appeal Case of Diane and David Liebfred, Nov. 30.

Uphoff, J. K., & Gilmore, J. E. (1984). Local research ties suicide to early school entrance stress. *Dayton Daily News,* p. 34.

Vygotsky, L. S. (1934; 1962). *Thought and language.* Cambridge, MA: Massachusetts Institute of Technology.

Vygotsky, L. S. (1930–35; 1978). *Mind in society: The development of higher psychological processes.* Cambridge, MA: Harvard University Press.

Wall, D. D. (1988). Rules and regulations covering the establishment and operation of kindergarten, early admission policy and admission of beginners in Pennsylvania. Harrisburg, PA: State Department of Education.

Walsh, D. J. (1989). Changes in kindergarten: Why here? Why now? *Early Childhood Research Quarterly, 4,* 377–391.

Wasik, B. A., & Slavin, R. E. (1993). Preventing early reading failure with one-to-one tutoring: A review of five programs. *Reading Research Quarterly, 28,* 179–206.

Wenner, G. (1995). Kindergarten screen as tools for the early identification of children at risk for remediation or grade retention. *Psychology in the Schools, 32,* 249–254.

West, J., Haushen, E. G. & Collins, M. (1993) Profile of preschool children's child care and early education program participation. Washington, D.C. National Center for Education Statistics, Office of Educational Research & Improvement, U.S. Department of Education, (NCES 93–133).

Zenka, L. L., & Keatley, M. J. (1985). Progress toward excellence: Tulsa's kindergarten program, *ERS Spectrum, 3,* 3–8.

44

Inclusion

Nancy L. Waldron
Indiana University

Few recent topics in education have generated the fervor and produced such a firestorm of debate as the inclusion of students with disabilities in general education classrooms. The professional literature has been replete with commentaries, reflections, and pronouncements which have often served to highlight the extremes in this debate (Fuchs & Fuchs, 1994; Kauffman & Hallahan, 1995; Stainback & Stainback, 1990), rather than the commonalities upon which professionals and parents can reasonably agree. The rhetoric and emotional tone of the debate reflects the complexity of the issues involved in inclusive school programs and the deep beliefs of individuals on each side of the debate regarding the purpose, goals, and quality of special education services for students with disabilities.

While there are multiple definitions of *inclusion,* present use of the term refers to educating students with disabilities in general education classrooms for much or all of the school day. Inclusion is conceptualized differently than past practices such as mainstreaming, in that inclusive school programs are developed based on a belief that students with disabilities belong and have a right to participate fully within a general education classroom with age-appropriate peers. This is reflected in the effort to bring special services and supports to the child in the general education classroom instead of removing the child from the classroom to provide such services. In addition, participation in a general education classroom is not based on a student's ability to meet specific age and grade standards but instead is based on the acceptance and accommodation of the general education environment to meet the student's individual needs. Inclusion is often conceptualized as the full realization of the least restrictive environment mandate contained in Public Law (P.L.) 94-142, along with the provision in the Individuals with Disabilities Education Act (IDEA) which states that students with disabilities should be removed from the general education environment "only when the nature and severity of the disability is such that education in regular classes with the use of supplemental aids and services cannot be achieved satisfactorily."

While some who review the current professional literature on the topic may feel that inclusion is an either/ or choice based upon the extremes often taken in the present debate, recent research has begun to document that, in practice, most inclusion reflects a reasoned middle ground. In this chapter, this middle ground will be explored and a responsible view of inclusion (Vaughn & Schumm, 1995) presented—one which considers the limitations of the current system of special education services, while recognizing the difficulties inherent in implementing a program of inclusion that works for most, but not all, students with disabilities (McLeskey & Waldron, 1996).

Background and Development

The current inclusion movement began in the early 1980s under the rubric of the Regular Education Initiative (REI) and has undergone changes in definition and terminology in the succeeding years. Fuchs and Fuchs (1994) chronicle the development of two reform efforts in special education, the REI and the inclusive schools movement. These two distinct reform movements represent differences in the population of students with disabilities addressed and the type of proposed reform efforts considered appropriate for special education. The REI largely addressed the interests of students with mild disabilities (e.g., learning disabilities) and called for a merger of general and special education (Will, 1986). This merger was often conceptualized as bringing "the best special education has to offer" into general education for the benefit of students with mild disabilities and other students deemed at risk for school failure. In contrast, the beginning of the inclusive schools movement was based upon the needs and goals of students with more substantial disabilities and focused on the need to reduce the isolation and segregation often experienced by these students in self-contained classrooms and separate school facilities (Stainback & Stainback, 1990).

In more recent years, the term *full inclusion* has been used to characterize an extreme position within the inclusive schools movement, with advocates taking the position that special education as we have come to know it should be dismantled and all students with disabilities should be placed in general education settings. From the perspective of these advocates, *all* students should be included for *all* of the school day in *every* school setting, preschool through high school, with appropriate supports and services (Lipsky & Gartner, 1989; Stainback & Stainback, 1990).

While some have termed the burgeoning development of inclusive programs part of an educational fad or bandwagon mentality (Fuchs & Fuchs, 1994; Kauffman, 1993), others have noted multiple forces that are contributing to the rapid development of such programs, including forces within special education, general education, and society at large. The primary reason cited by proponents of inclusion for the development of these programs is that special education has failed to live up to its promise as mandated in P.L. 94-142, especially in that special education programs have not been shown to be effective for a large number of students with disabilities. Inclusion advocates largely reject separate classes, which are so predominant in special education, with the expressed concern that special education in these settings is often not individualized for student needs.

Proponents of inclusion contend that one reason separate class programs have often failed is that these programs have not met the high standards set by those describing the ideal program (Haynes & Jenkins, 1986; Pugach & Warger, 1993; Smith, 1990). As Kauffman (1993) points out, "A central problem is that too many students are poorly served by special education because their programs are not really special—no more appropriate than the programs they would receive in general education" (p. 7). For example it has proven difficult to individualize or differentiate instruction for students in these separate class programs (Haynes & Jenkins, 1986). Furthermore, the curriculum offered by special education often consists of disjointed activities that are used to develop basic literacy and numeracy skills, do not constitute a coherent curriculum, do not focus on higher level cognitive skills, and lack the richness of the general education curriculum (Pugach & Warger, 1993; Smith, 1990). Finally, the curriculum offered in separate special education classes is most often not coordinated with or supportive of the curriculum in the general education classroom (McGill-Franzen & Allington, 1991).

In addition to the belief that special education separate-class programs have not been successful for many students with disabilities, inclusion proponents also focus on the growing number of students with disabilities (especially students with learning disabilities) and the continuing reliance on separate special education programs (Gartner & Lipsky, 1987; McLeskey & Pacchiano, 1994). For example, despite the mandate to educate students with disabilities in the least restrictive environment, surprisingly little progress has been made with educating students with mild disabilities in general education classrooms. A recent investigation of placement settings for students with learning disabilities revealed that in the 1990–1991 school year, 24% of students with learning disabilities and 70% of students with mental retardation were substantially segregated from their peers without disabilities, receiving their education in special classes or other separate settings for the majority of the school day. Moreover, only 23% of students with learning disabilities and 7% of students with mental retardation were educated in a typical classroom setting for 80% or more of the school day (McLeskey & Pacchiano, 1994). While the number of students with disabilities in general education classes has increased, this appears to be largely due to students moving from resource to more inclusive settings and not to any changes in the number of children served in more restrictive special education settings (Kauffman & Hallahan, 1995).

Other reasons cited by advocates for the expansion of inclusive school programs include

- Concerns about the validity of the referral and evaluation system currently used to identify students with disabilities.
- Lack of evidence that students grouped by disability learn differently or are in fact taught differently than other students.
- Disproportionate numbers of students who are from low-income and racial/linguistic minority backgrounds in special education.
- Restrictiveness of special education placements determined more by available service delivery options than severity of students' disabilities.
- Limited success of students with disabilities in completing educational programs and participating actively in employment upon the termination of secondary education. (Epps & Tindal, 1987; Reschly, 1988)

Critics of the inclusive schools movement (e.g., Fuchs & Fuchs, 1995; Kauffman & Hallahan, 1995) are not necessarily opposed to the expansion of less restrictive placement options for students with disabilities. In fact, inclusion critics have acknowledged the validity of many of the issues raised by inclusion proponents, such as the overidentification of students with learning disabilities, the lack of success achieved by special education for many students, the need for greater collaboration between general and special education, and the realization that general education classrooms can be changed to better accommodate student diversity. However, critics challenge the conclusions of inclusion advocates regarding the lack of effectiveness and need for separate class placements for some (or perhaps many) students with disabilities. Critics of inclusion generally believe that there are limits on just how resourceful and responsive general education classrooms can become, especially in the face of increasing student diversity in general education. Thus, they emphasize the need to maintain the full service delivery continuum, while developing inclusive school programs for those who can benefit from them.

Other issues frequently addressed by critics of the inclusive schools movement include

- General education cannot be trusted to respect the needs of some students with disabilities.
- General education is uninterested in changing the special education service delivery system.
- Special education presently provides individualized instruction, smaller classes, and more highly trained teachers for students with disabilities.
- Supporters of inclusion do not attempt to disaggregate the population of students with disabilities, and therefore differentiate the goals, needs, and feasibility of inclusion for varying groups of students with disabilities, (Fuchs & Fuchs, 1995; Kauffman, 1993; Semmel, Abernathy, Butera, & Lesar, 1991)

Clearly, there is no resolution to the debate about inclusion, primarily because the proponents and critics have chosen to focus on different aspects of special education. Critics largely have focused on the technology and instructional methods that research has demonstrated to be effective in teaching students with disabilities literacy and numeracy skills. In contrast, proponents of inclusion often focus on issues of equity in education and the need for students with disabilities to function effectively in general education settings. What seems unequivocal from the research is that there are good special education separate-class programs and there are good inclusive programs. One critical question that must be addressed is, "How quickly should schools move toward ever more inclusive educational opportunities for students with disabilities?" As Pugach (1995) has stated, "while debates over the appropriateness of inclusion as special education policy continue to be rancorous, these are not really debates about the merits of inclusion as a basic philosophy or ethical stance. Rather, they are debates over the degree of optimism various stakeholders have regarding the capacity for the educational system which includes special and general education alike—to recreate itself with inclusion as a basic premise and achievement as a tangible goal" (p. 213). A second critical question is, "To what extent should separate-class options be preserved?" As Fuchs and Fuchs (1995) have stated, "We are not suggesting that all students with disabilities require such (separate class) settings—in fact relatively few do. Nor do we suggest that all special education placements are successful: alas, they are not. But none of this diminishes the fact that separate is better for some children, and that to abolish special education

placements in the name of full inclusion is to deprive many of an appropriate education" (p. 525).

Problems and Implications

Recent evidence reveals that effective inclusive school programs can be developed, as classrooms and schools are restructured to better meet student needs (Affleck, Madge, Adams, & Lowenbraun, 1988; Banerji & Dailey, 1995; Bear & Proctor, 1990; Zigmond et al., 1995). However, evidence also exists to indicate that some poor inclusive school programs have been implemented, where students with disabilities are returned to general education classrooms with little planning, minimal changes in the classroom, and insufficient support for general education teachers (Baines, Baines, & Masterson, 1994; Baker & Zigmond, 1995; Houck & Rogers, 1994).

To further elucidate factors which may contribute to the success or failure of these programs, consideration must be given to why these disparate experiences and perceptions of inclusive school programs exist. As Kauffman, Lloyd, Baker, and Reidel (1995) have noted in their call for a more restrictive definition of inclusion for students with emotional and behavioral disorders, "while we attempt to make regular schools and classrooms inclusive in the best sense for as many students as possible, we should not be guided by overgeneralizations or become detached from the realities of classroom teaching" (p. 542). The following sections will address the realities of an inclusive classroom for teachers and students by reviewing research in the areas of teacher attitudes regarding inclusion, general education curriculum and instruction, and the achievement and behavior of students in inclusive classrooms.

Teacher Attitudes Regarding Inclusion

Initial investigations of attitudes toward inclusion seemed to indicate strong teacher opposition to these programs (e.g., Semmel et al., 1991). Teacher survey responses suggested that teachers do not believe the instructional needs of students with disabilities can be met in the general education classroom. Based on this belief, these teachers expressed the perspective that separate-class special education programs are needed to meet the needs of students with disabilities and, thus, should be maintained.

In more recent years, studies of teacher attitudes have been conducted with teachers directly involved in inclusive programs. The results of these investigations contrast the results of the earlier studies. For example, Minke, Bear, Deemer, and Griffin (1996) conducted a survey in a school district that has had inclusive programs for children with mild disabilities for almost 20 years. Both general and special education teachers in these inclusive settings reported more positive views of inclusion, higher levels of personal efficacy, and higher ratings of their own competence than teachers in traditional classes. Other studies involving observations and interviews have found teachers to be accepting of individual students and enthusiastic in their desire to teach students with disabilities in inclusive settings (Baker & Zigmond, 1995; McIntosh, Vaughn, Schumm, Haager, & Lee, 1993).

Several recent studies have also addressed teacher attitudes toward working with students with substantial needs in inclusive settings (Giangreco, Dennis, Cloninger, Edelman, & Schattman, 1993; Janney, Snell, Beers, & Raynes, 1995). For example, Giangreco et al. (1993) found that while most classroom teachers responded negatively to the initial placement of a student with a substantial disability in their class, 17 of the 19 teachers who participated in this study described a gradual transformation of their attitudes as they worked with these students over the course of a school year. This transformation was described as involving their willingness to become directly involved with the student and the perceived benefits of these interactions for their teaching and for the nondisabled students in their classrooms.

To explain the differing results of investigations regarding teacher attitudes toward inclusion of students with disabilities in general education classes, two key variables must be considered: actual experience with students with disabilities and sufficient resource support to meet teacher-identified needs in inclusive classes. Prior to the implementation of inclusive school programs, teachers often expressed very real concerns about their ability to meet student needs and to deal with the changes which would occur in their classes due to the presence of students with disabilities (Giangreco et al., 1993). However, after such programs are successfully implemented, teacher attitudes have been found to change significantly (Baker & Zigmond, 1995; Giangreco et al., 1993).

A second variable influencing teacher attitudes toward inclusive programs is appropriate resources to support these programs. Minke et al. (1996) found that teachers who were part of inclusive programs viewed allocation of resources as a critical factor for effective inclusion. Furthermore, studies which have found less favorable attitudes toward inclusion (e.g., Houck & Rogers, 1994) have also found the presence of limited resource supports available to teachers in these settings.

General Education Curriculum and Instruction

Students with disabilities are labeled and removed from the general education classroom because, after the best efforts of the classroom teacher, the needs of the student are not being met. To return the student to the same classroom, under the same circumstances (e.g., same level of teacher support) is irresponsible and will not lead to an appropriate instructional program for the student (e.g., Baines et al., 1994). Indeed, unless major changes occur in general education classrooms and schools, the likelihood is high that students with disabilities who are placed back in these settings will not receive significant benefits.

Concerns about the ability of general education teachers to provide specialized instruction and curricular adaptations that meet the needs of students with disabilities is one of the most significant concerns of those individuals critical of inclusive school programs. A number of studies have addressed this concern. While teachers may endorse the desirability of making adaptations to meet students needs, they often do not find these adaptations to be feasible within their classrooms (Schumm & Vaughn, 1991). In fact, observations of general education classrooms have led to the conclusion that while teachers make "routine" adaptations to facilitate the learning of the whole class, they make few adaptations to meet the individual learning needs of students with disabilities nor other students with learning difficulties (McIntosh et al., 1993).

It is noteworthy that the vast majority of studies addressing classroom adaptations have been conducted with general education teachers who were not supported nor provided resources to assist in finding ways to adapt for individual student needs (Schumm et al., 1995). Vaughn and Schumm (1995) note that such support and resources are qualities of any "responsible" inclusive program. In an investigation where teachers were provided with this support and prompted in developing adaptations, more specialized adaptations for individual students were implemented (Fuchs, Fuchs, Hamlett, Phillips, & Karns, 1995). Although further research is needed to confirm and provide a better understanding of the results of the Fuchs et al. (1995) investigation, this finding suggests that well-developed inclusive school programs may result in more use of teacher adaptations to address individual student needs.

At the crux of the issue regarding the ability of general education teachers to adapt for the needs of students with disabilities is the question of how specialized and individualized these adaptations must be. Some contend that for inclusion to be successful, special education must be *replicated* in the general education classroom. In contrast, others feel that successful inclusion is reflected in a very good general education program (McLeskey & Waldron, 1996).

These different perspectives are illustrated by a critique of inclusive school programs provided by Baker and Zigmond (1995). These investigators, who provided anecdotal descriptions of five inclusive school programs, noted that the students with disabilities in these programs were taught willingly; special education teachers provided support to general education teachers; accommodations were generally implemented (though usually for the whole class); and special instruction was often provided as needed by peers, teachers, and/or paraprofessionals. In short, these programs had successfully fostered the participation of students with learning disabilities in age-appropriate curriculum and all activities of the general education classroom. Some would consider such a program to be a significant success. However, the authors critiqued these programs by noting, "students with learning disabilities in these models of inclusive education were getting a very good *general* education" (p. 175). They also criticized these programs for their lack of "specially designed instruction delivered uniquely to the student with a disability" (p. 178). Thus, while all agree that major changes are needed in general education classrooms if students with disabilities are to succeed in these settings, the nature and scope of such changes depend on the perspective taken regarding which types of adaptations are needed in the general education classroom.

Impact of Inclusion on Student Achievement and Behavior

Those who advocate for responsible inclusion programs emphasize program outcomes for students with disabilities (Vaughn & Schumm, 1995). In this regard, inclusion becomes student centered—focused on specific student outcomes—and therefore not solely focused on the organization and delivery of special education support services. The primary question must be "Are students with disabilities making academic and social progress in inclusive general education classrooms?"

Most studies addressing the achievement of students with disabilities in inclusive programs have concluded that achievement gains in these programs are comparable to or greater than gains made by students in traditional, special education pull-out programs (Banerji & Dailey, 1995; Bear & Proctor, 1990; Jenkins et al., 1994). The predominant focus of most of these studies has been students with learning disabilities who were provided services in restructured general education classrooms. Across the studies, a range of individual and group standardized achievement measures and curriculum-based measures have been employed, and program effects have been studied for varying time periods from one to three years.

Academic gains demonstrated by students with disabilities in inclusive settings have been found in different academic areas. For example, Bear and Proctor (1990) compared students with disabilities in inclusive classes

and others in resource classes and found that equivalent gains existed in reading and language, but greater gains for students with disabilities in inclusive classrooms occurred in math. Another study (Jenkins et al., 1994) resulted in greater gains for students in inclusive settings in written expression, reading, and language. These different outcomes are likely influenced by the differences which exist across programs described as inclusive. These programs vary with respect to organization (some use team teaching, others use consultative support and instructional assistants), instruction (some spend time on language arts and mathematics only, while others emphasize all school subjects), and curriculum (some emphasize exposing students to the general education curriculum, while others emphasize more ability grouping in reading and mathematics). These differences likely account for the varying achievement outcomes reported in the professional literature.

When evaluating the effectiveness of inclusive school programs, proponents have typically used a criterion indicating these programs are "at least as effective" or equivalent to traditional pull-out special education programs to indicate the success of a program (McLeskey & Waldron, 1995). In contrast, critics of inclusion have argued with this conclusion, stating that to significantly change special education services for students with disabilities, there should be evidence that new approaches are more effective than current or past ones (Zigmond et al., 1995).

The debate concerning how to evaluate the effectiveness of inclusive programs continues to be contentious. Recently, Zigmond et al. (1995) argued that, if inclusive programs are to be deemed effective, achievement gains for students with learning disabilities in these programs should be greater than gains made by "average" students. These authors found that 61% of the students with learning disabilities in their sample made meaningful gains in reading achievement, improving their standing when compared to the achievement of typical students in reading. Based on this finding, the authors concluded that "for a significant proportion of students with learning disabilities, enhanced educational opportunities provided in the general education setting ... do not produce desired achievement outcomes" (p. 540). They go on to note that there is "no basis for the conclusion that satisfactory outcomes can be achieved in the general education setting" (p. 540). In contrast to the conclusions of Zigmond et al. (1995), others find these results to be highly supportive of inclusive school programs (McLeskey & Waldron, 1995). The question thus remains, "What is an acceptable level of academic gain for students with disabilities in inclusive settings?"

Another important question regarding achievement in inclusive settings relates to outcomes for students without disabilities in these settings. Specifically, "What effect do inclusive school programs have on the learning opportunities and outcomes for students without disabilities in these classrooms?" One pressing concern of teachers and parents is that average and above-average students in inclusive classes will get less instructional time and make less-than-average gains as teacher attention and resources are shifted to the lowest achieving students in the classroom.

A number of investigations have addressed achievement outcomes for students without disabilities who receive their education in inclusive classrooms. These studies have consistently found that these students achieve gains equivalent to or greater than gains made by comparable students educated in noninclusive settings. For example, Jenkins et al. (1994) studied the effects of a program which included students with mild disabilities in general education classrooms. These investigators found that students without disabilities demonstrated gains in vocabulary, reading, and language which were greater than gains made by a control group of students in noninclusive settings. In a similar study, Bear and Proctor (1990) found that students without disabilities in inclusive classes outperformed students in noninclusive classes in reading, math, and language. Staub and Peck (1995) also report that academic progress of students without disabilities is not negatively influenced by the inclusion of a student with a substantial disability in the general education classroom. In addition to the academic benefits which often accrue for students without disabilities in inclusive settings, investigators also report social and interpersonal gains such as reduced fears of individual differences; increased tolerance of others; increased self-esteem; and reinforcement of values such as caring, belonging, community, and acceptance.

A final consideration regarding student outcomes is attention to social progress and competence of students with disabilities. To a large extent, inclusion has been justified by many proponents as providing potentially greater social benefits for students with disabilities. The potential benefits cited by inclusion advocates include the modeling of appropriate social behavior by age-appropriate peers, removing the stigma associated with pull-out special education services, and improving the social status of students with disabilities. Although some research has been conducted to address these issues, there remains a considerable need for research to address whether these benefits can be actualized for students with disabilities in inclusive classrooms.

Research has addressed social status and competence of students with disabilities in inclusive settings by considering the perspectives of peers, teachers, and students with disabilities themselves. When studies have reviewed peer ratings, students with disabilities in inclusive classrooms have been shown to make modest gains in social status when compared to students with disabilities in resource programs (Madge, Affleck, & Lowenbraun,

1990). However, studies have repeatedly shown that students with disabilities are less frequently accepted and are given lower social preference ratings than their peers without disabilities, even when they are in inclusive classrooms (Madge, et al., 1990; Roberts & Zubrick, 1992).

Teacher ratings of classroom behaviors for students with disabilities in inclusive classrooms indicate perceived improvements in self-esteem and acceptance, while concurrently reporting less positive overall perceptions of these students when compared with nondisabled peers. These results indicate that teachers perceive no significant improvement in general social competence and classroom behavior when students with disabilities are educated in inclusive school programs (Banerji & Dailey, 1995; Jenkins et al., 1994).

Research addressing the perceptions of students with disabilities regarding their own social progress in inclusive settings tends to support the results of the foregoing investigations. For example, Bear, Clever, and Proctor (1991) found that students with disabilities had poorer self-perceptions of scholastic competence and behavioral conduct when compared to nondisabled students in inclusive classrooms.

Finally, the complexity of this issue is reflected in a study conducted by Jenkins and Heinen (1989), which considered student preferences for different special education service-delivery options. This investigation found that most students were influenced by their current type of program (i.e., in-class services or pull-out services) as well as a desire to avoid embarrassment. The majority of students preferred to receive additional assistance from their classroom teacher as opposed to a specialist. In explaining this preference, students stated that the classroom teacher better understood their individual needs. These results demonstrate that the important issue may not be where students receive special education services, but rather that services are provided in a manner which avoids stigmatization and embarrassment. This may occur in a pull-out program but could occur in an inclusive program as well.

While investigations addressing the social status and competence of students with disabilities in inclusive settings reveal that benefits may accrue for students with disabilities in these settings, concerns continue regarding whether these benefits will enable students with disabilities to fit into these settings and not be stigmatized or socially isolated. It is clear from these studies that improved social status and competence does not occur simply by closer proximity to typical peers. It must be recognized that many students with disabilities have deficits in social interaction skills, and these students will continue to experience lower social acceptance and possible rejection by peers unless inclusive school programs promote the development of needed social skills and provide support to ensure that positive social interactions occur between students with disabilities and typical peers.

Table 1 *Instructional and Curricular Accommodations for Inclusive Classrooms*

Classroom Instruction Accommodations	Establish consistent classroom routines.
	Present information using a multisensory approach (visual, auditory, hands-on).
	Preteach critical vocabulary.
	Activate necessary background knowledge and prior learning.
	Provide advanced organizers in written or diagram form.
	Write key points on the board or an overhead.
	Use frequent demonstrations and models to convey new concepts.
	Provide study guides that identify key concepts and vocabulary.
	Use samples of finished products as models.
	Provide several options (oral, written, diagrams) for students to demonstrate knowledge.
	Give directions orally, specifying small, distinct steps.
	Use written backup for oral directions.
	Check often for student understanding.
	Allot time for teaching learning strategies (test-taking, note-taking) as well as content.
	Use computers to enhance learning of basic skills.
	Provide students with ongoing feedback about performance.
Testing and Grading Adaptations	Provide the opportunity to have the test read orally.
	Read directions orally, give oral explanation of directions.
	Reduce the number of test items.
	Simplify terminology or concepts.
	Highlight key words in questions.
	Teach students test-taking skills.
	Preview language of test questions.
	Allow additional time for test taking.
	Modify the test format (e.g., short answer, multiple choice).
	Allow use of learning aids during tests (e.g., calculators, notes, books).
	Provide a menu of options for student to demonstrate knowledge other than or in addition to tests (e.g., projects, extra credit).
	Allow student to take tests with classmates in pairs or small groups.
	Provide study guides with key concepts, vocabulary in advance of test.
	Allow test retakes and give credit for improvement.
	Create a modified grading scale or grade on a pass/fail basis.
	Provide information on the standard report card indicating adaptations have been made.

(continued)

Alternative Actions

As the movement toward ever more inclusive program options for students with disabilities progresses, the debate concerning the benefits and limitations of these programs continues. However, emerging evidence regarding these programs indicates that successful, effective inclusive school programs can and are being developed in practice. Unfortunately, evidence also reveals that poorly designed inclusive school programs are being implemented in some settings. As the development and implementation of inclusive school programs continues, it is critical that educators use the research and reflections on practice presently available to promote the development of inclusive school programs that are responsive to student needs and ensure maximal benefits for students with disabilities. There are three areas that deserve the close attention of educators as they develop and implement responsible and effective inclusive school programs (McLeskey & Waldron, 1996; Vaughn & Schumm, 1995).

First, it is important that educators discern and address teacher attitudes and beliefs concerning inclusive schooling. It has been demonstrated that, when teachers are initially approached about the development of inclusive programs, their attitudes are often negative. However, current evidence reveals that these attitudes change over time, as (a) more information is provided about the specific students with disabilities who are to be included, (b) teachers are involved in the development of the inclusive program, (c) the supports and resources to be provided in the general education classroom are clarified, and (d) teachers become involved in implementing these programs.

In addressing teacher attitudes and beliefs, critical areas to explore are the beliefs teachers hold about students (both typical students and those with disabilities) and about how schools should be organized to more effectively meet the needs of students and the value teachers place on the education of students with disabilities. These areas must be examined, reflected upon, and often

Table 1 *Continued*

Adapting Reading and Written Assignments	Provide stories and chapters on tape.
	Preview reading assignment in small group or with peer buddy.
	Allow student to work with a peer on reading assignments.
	Recognize the value of listening comprehensions.
	Ask parents to provide extra practice with reading assignments at home.
	Simplify written directions by limiting words and numbering steps.
	Highlight reading materials and study guides.
	Reduce length and/or complexity of written assignments.
	Allow extra time for written work.
	Do not penalize for errors in spelling, punctuation, penmanship.
	Provide a copy of a peer's class notes.
	Mark items correct on paper, not items wrong.
	Provide credit for partially completed assignments.
	Allow student to dictate answers to peers, tape recorders, parents.
	Pair student for completion of written assignments.
	Use cooperative group arrangements with designated responsibilities for reading and/or writing across members.
Homework Adaptations	Communicate homework expectations to parents.
	Specify modifications to be used for homework assignments.
	Use homework log to communicate directions and timelines.
	Specify time student should spend on homework.
	Provide home set of texts/materials for preview/review.
	Reduce homework assignments.
	Allow homework papers to be typed by student or dictated or recorded by someone else.
	Have student start homework assignments in class.
	Give homework on skills student can already perform.

Note. Adapted from *Adapting Curriculum and Instruction in Inclusive Classrooms: A Teacher's Desk Reference,* (p. 53) by C. Deschenes, D. G. Ebeling and J. Sprague, 1994, Bloomington, IN: The Institute for the Study of Developmental Disabilities. Adapted with permission.

changed if inclusion programs are to be effective. A dialogue concerning these beliefs should include all teachers in a setting as well as administrators.

While research indicates that teacher attitudes toward inclusion will continue to vary as programs are developed and implemented, one way to ensure more supportive teacher attitudes is to have teachers volunteer or choose to participate in inclusive classrooms (McLeskey & Waldron, 1996; Vaughn & Schumm, 1995). This self-selection by teachers to be involved in inclusion should ensure that participants have attitudes and beliefs more consonant with inclusive school programs as well as ensuring the active support of participants in program implementation.

Secondly, it is important to consider how the planning of an inclusive school program will occur. Decisions regarding inclusive school programs must be school based. Inclusion programs will then differ from school to school depending on the strengths and weaknesses of the faculty involved, the characteristics of the student population, resources available in the school setting, administrative support for inclusion, and a plethora of other factors (McLeskey & Waldron, 1996). Furthermore, there is no model of inclusion that will be successful in all schools, but instead different programs which capitalize on teacher and school strengths must be developed

and tailored to specific school needs. This planning process necessarily involves teachers and must address the provision of adequate resources, support to teachers to make necessary classroom adaptations to meet student needs, the specific design of the program, the nature and scope of teacher collaborative efforts, the specific students who will participate in inclusive school program options, teacher roles and functions in addressing student needs, and many other factors.

A primary concern for teachers involved in planning inclusion programs is the nature and scope of adaptations which will be needed to accommodate students with disabilities in general education classrooms. For many teachers, inclusion has served as a catalyst for altering instruction and curriculum to better accommodate the diverse needs of all students in general education classrooms, not just those of students with disabilities (McLeskey & Waldron, 1996; Zigmond et al., 1995). Given that research studies have consistently found that students without disabilities in inclusive classrooms show achievement gains equivalent to or greater than gains made by comparable students in noninclusive classrooms, it appears that these instructional changes can be effective for a broad range of students. While the nature of instructional and curricular changes instituted in any one classroom or school will necessarily differ based on

tudent needs, teacher preferences, and desired outcomes, Table 1 provides a range of accommodations that
ould be used in inclusive classrooms.

Finally, it is important to consider the need to evaluate and continually adapt inclusive school programs. If
an inclusive school program is to be successful in the
long term, it is necessary to view the program as a "work
in progress" rather than as a fixed model which will not
change. The involvement of new teachers in the program,
as well as changes in the student population of a school,
will lead to changes in programs from one school year to
the next. In addition, adjustments may be made in the
program during the school year in response to evaluation
information concerning factors such as outcomes of present services (e.g., academic outcomes for students with
disabilities, effectiveness of collaborative efforts between
general and special education teachers), refinement of
curriculum and instructional approaches in response to
student needs, and participation in ongoing professional
development activities.

Summary

From the foregoing review, it is apparent that research
is not currently available to end the debate regarding inclusive school programs. Indeed, in every area of research, there seems to be investigations which may be
used to support the position of both proponents and op-
ponents of inclusion. While some have shown that teachers oppose inclusion, others have shown teacher support
for these programs. In addition, there is some evidence
of improved academic achievement outcomes for students with disabilities in inclusive settings, while others
have found no difference in achievement outcomes.

Perhaps the only area of research related to inclusive
programs that is very nearly unequivocal relates to positive academic outcomes for students without disabilities
who are educated in these settings. However, even these
results may be used to both support and oppose inclusion. For example, supporters of inclusion may use these
results to conclude that inclusive programs result in improved classroom instruction, which benefits all students
including those without disabilities. In contrast, oppo-
nents of inclusion may interpret this same evidence to
mean that resources intended to benefit students with
disabilities are being inappropriately used to support students without disabilities.

In spite of the ongoing controversy regarding inclusive school programs, educators continue to develop and
implement these programs in every state and scores of
school districts across the country. The current proliferation of inclusive school programs is unlikely to abate as
teachers, parents, and advocates for students with disabilities press for increased opportunities and access to
the mainstream of general education. As some programs
have been able to show, successful inclusion is possible
in some schools, with some teachers, for some students
with disabilities. These mixed results leave obvious questions unanswered: Can successful inclusion programs be
developed in all schools and with all teachers? For which
students can inclusion work? There must be a continuing,
concerted effort to investigate these questions as well as
issues concerning the development, implementation, and
evaluation of inclusive school programs. It is only
through these efforts that a better understanding will
come of the possibilities and limitations that inclusion offers to students with disabilities.

Recommended Resources

Goodlad, J., & Lovitt, T. (Eds.). (1993). *Integrating general
and special education.* New York: Macmillan.
*This edited book is organized around different issues that must
be addressed to facilitate the integration of special and general
education. Chapters address curriculum, financial issues, service delivery options, program evaluation, administrative perspectives, and teacher roles.*

Kauffman, J. M., & Hallahan, D. P. (1995). *The illusion of
full inclusion.* Austin, TX: Pro-Ed.
*This book is a compilation of articles that have been printed
elsewhere, each addressing concerns about the "rhetoric of full
inclusion." Articles are organized around the topics of historical perspectives, conceptual and policy issues, and issues of concern for groups with specific disabilities.*

Vaughn, S., & Schumm, J. S. (1995). Responsible inclusion
for students with learning disabilities, *Journal of Learning
Disabilities, 28,* 264–270.
*The authors of this article present guidelines for the develop-
ment of responsible inclusion programs including adequate resources for inclusion classrooms, teacher choice in participating, maintaining a continuum of special education services,
and the provision of ongoing professional development.*

References

Affleck, J. Q., Madge, S., Adams, A., & Lowenbraun, S.
(1988). Integrated classroom versus resource model: Academic viability and effectiveness. *Exceptional Children, 54,*
339–348.

Baines, L., Baines, C., & Masterson, C. (1994). Mainstreaming: One school's reality. *Phi Delta Kappan, 76*(1),
39–40, 57–64.

Baker, J. M., & Zigmond, N. (1995). The meaning and
practice of inclusion for students with learning disabilities:
Themes and implications from the five cases. *The Journal of
Special Education, 29*(2), 163–180.

Banerji, M., & Dailey, R. (1995). A study of the effects
of an inclusion model on students with specific learning disabilities. *Journal of Learning Disabilities, 28,* 511–522.

Bear, G. G., Clever, A., & Proctor, W. A. (1991). Self-
perceptions of nonhandicapped children and children

with learning disabilities in integrated classes. *The Journal of Special Education, 24,* 409–426.

Bear, G. G., & Proctor, W. A. (1990). Impact of a full-time integrated program on the achievement of nonhandicapped and mildly handicapped children. *Journal of Exceptionality, 1,* 227–238.

Deschenes, C., Ebeling, D. G., & Sprague, J. (1994). *Adapting curriculum and instruction in inclusive classrooms: A teacher's desk reference.* Bloomington, IN: The Institute for the Study of Developmental Disabilities.

Epps, S., & Tindal, G. (1987). The effectiveness of differential programming in serving students with mild handicaps: Placement options and instructional programming. In M. C. Wang, M. C. Reynolds, & H. J. Walberg (Eds.), *Handbook of special education: Research and practice* (pp. 213–248). New York: Pergamon Press.

Fuchs, D., & Fuchs, L. S. (1994). Inclusive schools movement and the radicalization of special education reform. *Exceptional Children, 60,* 294–309.

Fuchs, D., & Fuchs, L. S. (1995). What's "special" about special education? *Phi Delta Kappan, 77,* 522–530.

Fuchs, L. S., Fuchs, D., Hamlett, C. L., Phillips, N. B., & Karns, K. (1995). General educators' specialized adaptation for students with learning disabilities. *Exceptional Children, 61,* 440–459.

Gartner, A., & Lipsky, D. K. (1987). Beyond special education: Toward a quality system for all students. *Harvard Educational Review, 57,* 367–395.

Giangreco, M. F., Dennis, R., Cloninger, C., Edelman, S., & Schattman, R. (1993). "I've counted Jon": Transformational experiences of teachers educating students with disabilities. *Exceptional Children, 59,* 359–372.

Haynes, M. C., & Jenkins, J. (1986). Reading instruction in special education resource rooms, *American Educational Research Journal, 23,* 161–190.

Houck, C. K., & Rogers, C. J. (1994) The special/general education integration initiative for students with specific learning disabilities: A "snapshot" of program change. *Journal of Learning Disabilities, 27,* 435–453.

Janney, R. E., Snell, M. E., Beers, M. K., & Raynes, M. (1995). Integrating students with moderate and severe disabilities into general education classes. *Exceptional Children, 61,* 425–439.

Jenkins, J. R., & Heinen, A. (1989). Students' preferences for service delivery: Pull-out, in-class, or integrated models. *Exceptional Children, 55,* 516–523.

Jenkins, J. R., Jewell, M., Leicester, N., O'Connor, R. E., Jenkins, L. M., & Troutner, N. M. (1994). Accommodations for individual differences without classroom ability groups: An experiment in school restructuring. *Exceptional Children, 60,* 344–358.

Kauffman, J. M. (1993). How we might achieve the radical reform of special education. *Exceptional Children, 60,* 6–16.

Kauffman, J. M., & Hallahan, D. P. (1995). *The illusion of full inclusion.* Austin, TX: Pro-Ed.

Kauffman, J. M., Lloyd, J. W., Baker, J., & Reidel, T. M. (1995). Inclusion of all students with emotional or behavioral disorders? Let's think again. *Phi Delta Kappan, 77,* 542–546.

Lipsky, D. K., & Gartner, A. (1989). *Beyond special education: Quality education for all.* Baltimore: Paul Brookes.

Madge, S., Affleck, J., & Lowenbraun, S. (1990). Social effects of integrated classrooms and resource room/regular class placements on elementary students with learning disabilities. *Journal of Learning Disabilities, 23,* 439–445.

McGill-Franzen, A., & Allington, R. (1991). The gridlock of low reading achievement: Perspectives on practice and policy. *Remedial and Special Education, 12,*(3), 20–30.

McIntosh, R., Vaughn, S., Schumm, J. S., Haager, D., & Lee, O. (1993). Observations of students with learning disabilities in general education classrooms. *Exceptional Children, 60,* 249–261.

McLeskey, J., & Pacchiano, D. (1994). Mainstreaming students with learning disabilities: Are we making progress? *Exceptional Children, 60,* 508–517.

McLeskey, J., & Waldron, N. L. (1995). Inclusive elementary programs: Must they cure students with learning disabilities to be effective? *Phi Delta Kappan, 77,* 300–303.

McLeskey, J., & Waldron, N. L. (1996). Responses to questions teachers and administrators frequently ask about inclusive school programs. *Phi Delta Kappan, 78,* 150–156.

Minke, K. M., Bear, G. G., Deemer, S. A., & Griffin, S. M. (1996). Teachers' experiences with inclusive classrooms: Implications for the special education reform. *Journal of Special Education, 30,* 152–186.

Pugach, M. C. (1995). On the failure of imagination in inclusive schooling. *Journal of Special Education, 29,* 212–223.

Pugach, M., & Warger, C. (1993). Curriculum considerations. In J. Goodlad & T. Lovitt (Eds.), *Integrating general and special education* (pp. 125–148). New York: Macmillan.

Roberts, C., & Zubrick, S. (1992). Factors influencing the social status of children with mild academic disabilities in regular classrooms. *Exceptional Children, 59,* 192–202.

Schumm, J. S., & Vaughn, S. (1991). Making adaptations for mainstreamed students: General classroom teachers' perspectives. *Remedial and Special Education, 12*(4) 18–27.

Schumm, J. S., Vaughn, S., Haager, D., McDowell, J. Rothlein, L., & Saumell, L. (1995). General education teacher planning: What can students with learning disabilities expect? *Exceptional Children, 61,* 335–352.

Semmel, M. I., Abernathy, T. V., Butera, G., & Lesar, S. (1991). Teacher perceptions of the Regular Education Initiative. *Exceptional Children, 56,* 9–24.

Smith, S. (1990). Individualized education programs (IEPs) in special education: From intent to acquiescence. *Exceptional Children, 57,* 6–14.

Stainback, W., & Stainback, S. (1990). *Support networks for inclusive schooling.* Baltimore: Paul H. Brookes.

Staub, D., & Peck, C. A. (1995). What are the outcomes for nondisabled students? *Educational Leadership, 6,* 36–40.

Vaughn, S., & Schumm, J. S. (1995). Responsible inclusion for students with learning disabilities. *Journal of Learning Disabilities, 28,* 264–270.

Will, M. (1986). Educating children with learning problems: A shared responsibility. *Exceptional Children, 52,* 411–415.

Zigmond, N., Jenkins, J., Fuchs, L. S., Deno, S., Fuchs, D., Baker, J. N., Jenkins, L., & Couthino, M. (1995). Special education in restructured schools. *Phi Delta Kappan, 5,* 531–540.

45

School Dropout

Larry J. Kortering

Appalachian State University

Robyn S. Hess

University of Nebraska at Kearney

Patricia M. Braziel

Appalachian State University

The noncompletion of school is a serious concern for today's educational and economic systems. By leaving school before graduation, many dropouts have considerable educational deficiencies that limit their financial and social well-being throughout their lives (Rumberger, 1987). Society associates the school-dropout phenomenon with crime, low wages, unemployment, and immersion in a cycle of poverty. Moreover, those who drop out of school represent lost tax revenue and reduce the nation's economic productivity necessary for competitiveness in today's technologically advanced global market (Wehlage, Rutter, Smith, Lesko, & Fernandez, 1989). The problems associated with noncompletion of school are considered so serious that reducing the dropout rate has become a national priority, as reflected in the Education Goals 2000 program objective that 90% of students graduate from high school.

acteristics; surveying self-reported reasons for dropping out; and, finally, examining the schools themselves and their characteristics and educational environments that contribute to placing students at risk of dropping out (Miller, 1989). Despite these concerted efforts, much of the research to date ignores the long-term process that takes place before the actual decision to leave school is reached. Indeed, explanations of the dropout process are often limited to single descriptors assigned to the students who drop out such as at risk, low income, or ethnically diverse without an appreciation of the intricacy of the relationship between individual characteristics and the contexts of home, school, and community.

Background and Development

Over the long term, the rate of high school dropout has decreased. For example, in 1940 more than 60% of all persons age 25 to 29 years old had not completed high school; by 1980, that proportion had fallen to less than 16% (U.S. Census Bureau, 1985). However, the short-term trend has remained steady and even increased, especially for some minority groups (Rumberger, 1987). Furthermore, high school graduation is now viewed as a prerequisite to most entry-level occupations. Educational personnel have struggled for years to identify the variables that determine why one student drops out and another persists. The research has moved through a number of focus areas including accurately assessing the numbers and defining dropouts; examining student char-

Problems and Implications

Key Concepts

The school dropout

Most educational professionals believe they have a good understanding of the meaning of *dropping out of school*. However, the variations in the process and the difficulty in determining whether a student is actually a dropout can be confusing. In general, the term refers to students who leave high school before completion without re-enrolling in another school or enrolling in a related educational program. Mandatory attendance laws limit the dropout label to those students age 16 and over. By using this definition, however, students who drop out before reaching high school are overlooked or mislabeled. For example, the often cited *High School and Beyond* database (e.g., Eckstrom, Goertz, Pollock, & Rock, 1986; Wehlage & Rutter, 1986) employed a sample of high school sophomores. As a result, this database missed all students who were school age but had already left school prior to reaching the 10th grade. This oversight is particularly misrepresentative for Hispanics for whom it is estimated that 40% leave school before the 10th grade (Hirano-Nakanishi, 1986). In addition, in North Carolina alone, up to 15% of dropouts leave before age 16 (North Carolina Department of Public Instruction, 1994). Those who leave school at such an early age often are referred to as *truants* rather than dropouts. Moreover, some students leave school without any forwarding address or information and in essence are "lost" without ever receiving the label "dropout."

The "at-risk" student

This term is used to denote students who are considered to be in danger of ending their formal education because of exposure to one or more external risk-producing conditions or circumstances. The term has become increasingly popular in the literature and has been misused to describe entire populations of children. For example, it is frequently noted in the literature that a culturally diverse background places a child "at risk" for dropping out of school (e.g., Miller, 1989; Rumberger, 1987). This information is of little use in school districts where the majority of students meet this criterion and implies that minority children are inherently at risk. Furthermore, this term becomes counterproductive when used to place sole responsibility for failure on students and their families.

The school dropout process

School dropout is conceptualized best as a process and not a single event. The process generally evolves over time with initial warning signs in elementary school. By as early as the third grade, attendance, grades, and discipline data can be used to identify many of the students who will drop out (e.g., Barrington & Hendricks, 1989; Ensminger & Slusarcick, 1992). Moreover, many dropouts do not abandon their education when they drop out but rather return to high school, enter adult education programs, or pursue a General Education Development (GED) diploma. This feature suggests that initial school learnings are interruptions in one's education, a pattern which has led to the term *stopouts* rather than dropouts. After returning to high schools, however, most stopouts eventually drop out again (Kortering, Haring, & Klockars, 1992).

Researchers interested in the school-dropout phenomenon increasingly conceptualize poor educational performance and dropping out as the process of disengagement that may begin with the child's entry into school (e.g., Finn, 1989, Wehlage et al., 1989). During the elementary years, a student may have his or her first experience with school failure. As previously noted, increasing pattern of absences and lower expectations for graduating can be found as early as third grade (Hess &

D'Amato, in press). Once established, a negative trend becomes difficult to reverse. If the child consistently performs below grade level academically, retention is often practiced in the belief that this extra year will help the child to "catch up." However, students who are over age at the time of high school entrance are more likely to drop out (Hess, 1986). At the secondary level, this process of disengagement often continues and is accelerated by an increase in disciplinary problems, truancy, and friendships with peers who also are uninvolved in school. It is at this level that the actual act of dropping out occurs. Although those who drop out frequently report financial reasons, pregnancy, or simply "not liking school," it is unlikely that any one reason can easily summarize this long history of withdrawal and failure.

Those students who are considered at risk and yet avoid the dropout process are, conversely, more likely to be involved, to have stronger levels of academic performance, to feel connected to peers and staff, and to have a mentor or role model. In the developmental cycle outlined by Finn (1989), successful students experience positive events at school which enhance their identification with school and result in increased participation, thus creating a positive pattern of school engagement.

Correlates and Contributing Factors

Research indicates that dropping out of school has no single cause. Individual, family, and school variables work, in combination, to create a dropout. Put another way, no single factor can predict who will drop out of school; rather a variety of concurrent characteristics interact with various inherent or developed limitations and life events to create a dropout. Any effort that fails to consider various features would be less than optimal in meeting the educational and related needs of these students. Thus, an ecological approach for examining the different contexts of a student's environment (i.e., individual, family, peers, school, and community) may provide the most complete framework from which to understand the theories and research related to those students who drop out of school.

Individual characteristics

In pursuit of an explanation for dropping out, researchers have historically attempted to find the cause for failure within the student (Wehlage et al., 1989). The implicit assumption of this approach is that if students demonstrate deficiencies or differences in language, behavioral, or emotional competencies, they are at risk of experiencing subsequent school failure. An alternative view promotes the idea that students possess individual characteristics that are neither positive nor negative but rather that are viewed in terms of their appropriateness within specific settings or environments (Bronfenbrenner, 1979).

Individual variables such as ethnicity, gender, academic achievement, and attitudes toward school have been identified as variables related to dropout behavior. Research has consistently demonstrated that ethnicity is one of the background characteristics most strongly related to noncompletion of school (Ekstrom et al., 1986; Rumberger, 1987) with Hispanic and Black youth having the highest rates of dropping out. The relationship between gender and dropping out behavior is not as clear. Although both Rumberger (1987) and Ekstrom et al. (1986) concluded that males were slightly more likely than females to drop out of school, this finding was not supported by Barrington and Hendricks (1989). A consistent finding, however, is differences in the reasons females and males provide for dropping out. Females are more likely to leave school because of pregnancy and marriage whereas males are more likely to leave to seek employment or work full time because of financial difficulties (Rumberger, 1983). Males also are twice as likely as females to report leaving high school because of behavior problems (Ekstrom et al., 1986).

Low academic achievement in school is the most consistently reported predictor related to dropping out or staying in school (e.g., Barrington & Hendricks, 1989; Ekstrom et al., 1986). Research findings have repeatedly indicated that unsuccessful academic experiences, such as poor classroom performance and failing grades, are correlated with dropping out (Hess, 1986; Rumberger, 1987). Ensminger and Slusarcick (1992) found that students earning C and D grades in first grade are twice as likely to drop out as peers with higher grades. Similarly, Fernandez and Shu (1988) found a connection between standardized math scores and the dropout rate. Specifically, the odds of dropping out doubled for students with scores below the 50th percentile. Despite low achievement levels when compared to non-college-bound peers who graduate, most dropouts have comparable skill levels (Ekstrom et al., 1986; Kortering et al., 1992). In fact, Toby and Armor (1992) speculate that only 10% to 15% of dropouts leave high school because they are not capable of success. This finding suggests that deficiencies do not prevent a student from graduating but may hinder success at learning and grade promotion, while contributing to his or her frustration and subsequent disengagement from school.

Grade retention is one sign of failing to attain success in school and is more likely to have occurred to students who drop out than those who complete high school. Specifically, in one study students who repeated a grade were three times more likely to drop out than those students who were not retained (Roderick, 1993). Likewise, North Carolina reported that 62% of dropouts in 1992–93 had grade retentions (North Carolina Department of Public Instruction, 1994).

Patterns of school failure are frequently accompanied by behavioral problems. Students who drop out display more behavioral problems, often of a more serious nature (e.g., assault, theft, or incidents with the police) than similar students who do not drop out of school (Ekstrom et al., 1986; Roderick, 1993). Alpert and Dunham (1986), in their comparison of at-risk students who stayed in school and those who dropped out, found that the number of times a student was sent out of the classroom for disciplinary reasons was the single most important variable to distinguish those who dropped out. Ensminger and Slusarcick (1992) found evidence that the disciplinary problems related to dropping out emerged as early as first grade.

Behavior problems present a significant challenge to any prevention effort. Some suggest that schools be more accommodating with their norms (Fine, 1991; Goodlad, 1984). Others, like some local school principals, note that schools run more efficiently without these students. A more constructive view recognizes discipline problems as a sign of pending disengagement from school, rather than a challenge to authority. It also has been suggested that behavioral problems constitute a "confrontational practice" which the students engage in when they feel alienated from educational goals (Velez, 1989). Accordingly, schools should view these problems as warning signs that students have problems likely to lead to their dropping out. From this perspective, underachievement and behavior problems may be considered symptoms of the dropout process rather than an indication of a student's lack of ability, motivation, or self-control.

Chronic absenteeism might also be viewed as a symptom of the dropout process. Researchers have consistently reported that dropouts have higher rates of absenteeism and tardiness than graduates (Barrington & Hendricks, 1989; Ekstrom et al., 1986; Rumberger, 1987; Velez, 1989). Daily attendance is crucial to success in school and requires parental support and individual motivation. Roderick (1993) found that dropouts over age 17 missed twice as much school in the 9th and 10th grade, while younger dropouts showed higher levels of absenteeism in 4th to 6th grade. Likewise, a sample of 100 rural dropouts, on average, had already missed one of every four days before being identified as a dropout (Kortering, 1995). Nonattendance is often an early warning that students do not view regular school attendance as important or relevant to their own lives. For many students, attendance patterns are influenced by a concern for social mobility, college plans, or parental support. For others, the school setting offers a rewarding sense of belonging. Students who see no relevance in school, feel alienated, or lack parental support often display an early pattern of nonattendance.

Working in conjunction with a student's skills, abilities, and behaviors are the attitudes and perceptions that the student holds in relation to the educational environment. For most students, staying in school is a motivated behavior. They stay in school when they accept the order of schools and perceive a benefit for coming. Many at-risk students lack such motivation and feel degraded or ignored by the school system. These students often come to see the school as an alienating setting. This perception, regardless of its accuracy, affects a student's social reality and thwarts school success. Eventually, the student becomes disengaged, leaving the educator with a reluctant and, perhaps, disruptive learner. Several authors offer ways to understand this process through the use of theories of attachment, bonding, and alienation (Finn, 1989; Tinto, 1987) and educational engagement (Wehlage et al., 1989). These theories suggest that staying in school hinges on a psychological attachment or investment with the institution, the key to which entails successful learning experiences and satisfying relationships with peers and teachers.

Family characteristics

Family background is one of the most widely studied factors relative to educational attainment and is thought to exert a powerful influence on a child's decision to stay in or drop out of high school (Rumberger, 1983, 1987; Rumberger, Ghatak, Poulos, Ritter, & Dornbusch, 1990). Family socioeconomic status (SES) is the most common characteristic predictive of dropping out (Barrington & Hendricks, 1989; Ekstrom et al, 1986; Rumberger, 1987). Many of the other family-related variables considered to be predictive of dropping out are no doubt associated with family income. For example, parental education level (Ekstrom et al., 1986), single-parent home (Kortering et al., 1992; Rumberger, 1983), and amount of available reading material (Ekstrom et al., 1986; Rumberger, 1983) would seem to be related to the income earnings of the family. Another finding related to SES is that students from economically disadvantaged backgrounds tend to score lower on tests of ability, have lower levels of academic achievement, and display more behavioral problems in the classroom (Montgomery & Rossi, 1994). Economic disadvantage correlates highly with these measures of student performance, which in turn are related to dropping out. Thus, the relationship between SES and dropping out, though powerful, is indirect (Rumberger, 1991).

Although the relation between dropping out and family descriptors such as SES is informative, it reveals little about the complex interactional process within the family that leads to dropping out (Rumberger et al., 1990). It has been argued that family influence variables can tell more about the process that leads to dropping out than descriptive variables such as SES (Rumberger et al.). For example, parenting style is thought to influence academic achievement by fostering the development of autonomy and maturity (Rumberger, 1991). An authoritative parenting style is considered the most conducive to academic success; parents of dropouts tend to be more permissive, to use negative sanctions and emotions in

reaction to their children's academic performance, and to be less engaged with their children's schooling (Rumberger et al.). As shown in a study of Chicano students (Delgado-Gaitan, 1988), dropouts tend to come from families in which education holds little value and the parents fail to help their children adjust to the expectations of school or get involved in their child's education. Indeed, access to adults who provide social and emotional support (Coleman, 1988; Delgado-Gaitan) and the parent's view of the importance of a high school education (Okey & Cusick, 1995) are important to a student's success in school.

Not only are parents influential in academic decisions, but so too are siblings who often serve as role models. There is a significant correlation between dropping out and having a sibling who dropped out (e.g., Valverde, 1987). As early as elementary age, younger siblings of high school dropouts rate themselves as less likely to complete high school and have a higher number of absences than the younger siblings of high school persisters (Hess & D'Amato, in press).

The theory of "social capital" also helps to illustrate how the family contributes to a student's ability and motivation to finish school (Coleman, 1988). Coleman notes that students need positive interactions with educated and supportive parents and siblings. These interactions are more important than monetary resources, mere access to parents, or the number of adults in the home. The importance of supportive interactions manifests itself in the completion of homework, encouragement to stay in school, access to positive role models, and resources to do school work.

An alternative view for understanding the family's role suggests that American schools have failed to adequately educate culturally diverse and economically disadvantaged families about the U.S. school system and its expectations. Consequently, these parents may feel uncomfortable talking with teachers and participating in school-sponsored events. This behavior is often misinterpreted as a lack of concern for their child's educational success and in turn, some educators may give up trying to involve parents in educational efforts (Manning, 1995).

Peer relationships

Although peer relationships have not often been studied in association with high school completion, evidence suggests children with poor peer acceptance are especially at risk for dropping out (Parker & Asher, 1987). Dropouts, in general, appear to feel alienated from school life as indicated by their lack of involvement in extracurricular activities (Valverde, 1987). They are also less likely to report feeling popular with other students and tend to choose friends who are also alienated from school (Ekstrom et al., 1986). Whereas graduates tend to participate in school-related activities, dropouts engage in nonschool activities like community-sponsored dances, "hanging around" with friends, and neighborhood sports (Delgado-Gaitan, 1988; Valverde, 1987). Such participation is most influential for males as it improves their social status and popularity in school (Edar & Kinney, 1995).

Finn (1989) describes a Participation-Identification Model that explains the relationship between extracurricular activities and school engagement. He believes that participation in school activities allows a student not only to become socially connected but also to identify with the school. This identification leads to a sense of belonging and a perception that school is relevant, qualities that appear to be missing from the school experiences of those who drop out.

School-related characteristics

Since the mid-1980s, there has been a growing recognition that the school itself plays an important role in increasing or decreasing the number of dropouts, especially among minorities (e.g., Wehlage & Rutter, 1986). In support of this idea, Fine (1991) and Goodlad (1984) stress that an understanding of dropping out demands a consideration of school characteristics. Organizational practices and the actions of staff often prove detrimental to students. For example, schools in which students reported unfair discipline practices and widespread truancy have relatively high dropout rates (Wehlage & Rutter). Related research has indicated that rigid retention policies, tracking procedures, competency examinations, and the practice of reassigning a student to a new school for reasons other than relocation or promotion also negatively affect the dropout rate (Bryk & Thum, 1989; Goodlad). So too, large school or class size (Wehlage et al., 1989), overall school climate (Montgomery & Rossi, 1994), and high teacher turnover rates (Carrennza, 1988) can contribute to a student's decision to leave school.

In terms of individual teacher behaviors, low teacher expectations and frustration with at-risk students are likely to encourage dropping out. Indeed, some students are *pushed out* of school because they pose discipline problems or are simply expendable in an overcrowded school system (Fine, 1991; Goodlad, 1984). "Pushouts" often do not "fit" in with the existing school structure. "Pushouts" include special education students who present behavioral problems warranting expulsion if the student were not disabled. By encouraging these students to drop out, the school avoids the extensive due process procedures invoked by the usual expulsion process.

Research also suggests that school settings often fail to meet the perceived needs of dropouts. Students who drop out exhibit a number of signs which imply a sense of dissatisfaction with the school environment including a dislike of teachers or school, reported mistreatment, general disaffection, and boredom. A review of the *High School and Beyond* data revealed that 33% of the dropouts reported dropping out because they disliked school, while 15% left because they could not get along with

teachers (Ekstrom et al., 1986). More recently, Kortering (1995) interviewed 100 general and special education dropouts for their suggestions about how to reduce local dropout rates. He found that the dominant suggestion among dropouts was for teachers and administrators to provide more and better interpersonal support.

The academic needs of at-risk students are often overlooked. As a result, these students seldom experience success in school and eventually become alienated. Successful experiences can help to offset alienation and eventual withdrawal. In fact, Bloom (1980) postulates that positive experiences provide an inoculation to bad experiences, a sort of armor if you will. Accordingly, students with sufficient armor tolerate a low grade or bad experience. Students who drop out, however, tend to have a history dominated by negative experiences. For illustration, Lichenstein (1993) chronicles the experiences of four special education dropouts, three of whom left to simply "reclaim their lives and self-esteem." He described their schooling as one of consistent failures and reminders that they were not valued, events that would drive almost any student from school.

Community characteristics

Community characteristics also can serve as predictors of changes in school dropout rates. School systems are a reflection of society's values. Yet some educational policies and practices contribute to high dropout rates. For example, despite the educational reforms sweeping the country, many researchers remain concerned about the fate of disadvantaged and minority youth (e.g., Fine, 1991; McDill, Natriello, & Pallas, 1985). While new policies seek to challenge students and ensure minimal levels of competency for standard diplomas, little is said about the kinds of programs that will be developed to help students achieve these goals. The idea of establishing a minimum level of competency for all students is compelling, but the impact on at-risk youth may be devastating unless it includes adequate attention and funding for academic assistance and support programs. Some believe changes mandating academic competency will only increase the rate of dropping out among marginal students (McDill et al., 1985).

Employment opportunities in the community also play a role in the educational decisions of students who are at risk for dropping out. Rising dropout rates correspond to increases in entry-level employment openings and conversely, high unemployment rates correspond to a rise in the number of dropouts returning to school (Borus & Carpenter, 1983). Local entry-level employment options offer students opportunities for immediate mobility, income, and freedom. These options appear more attractive than waiting for an education or diploma that they perceive as not enhancing their job prospects for adulthood. For example, Alpert and Dunham (1986) found that at-risk students who stayed in school believed that finishing high school would help them get a desired job. This characteristic distinguished them from their at-risk peers who eventually dropped out.

It has been suggested that many ethnic minority youths believe their community does not offer them employment, job advancement, good salaries, and other benefits of education equal to those of Whites. These concerns were supported by Rumberger (1991) who concluded that there are fewer economic incentives for Hispanic males to finish high school than other male students. This is true because the relative rewards for finishing school are lower for Hispanics than for Blacks or Whites. Exchange theory, as supported by Fine (1991), helps explain the role of this perception by suggesting that students continue to come to school when they perceive a benefit in exchange for their effort.

In review, given these numerous variables related to school failure and the variety of reasons that a student gives for dropping out, it seems clear that two main forces help to keep students in school: engagement in the school community (Finn, 1989; Goodlad, 1984) and connecting school learning to an improvement in one's life (Fine, 1986). The key question becomes how to alter the operation of schools so as to facilitate these forces in the lives of at-risk students?

Alternative Actions

To properly respond to the problem of school dropout, educators must consider not only the factors contributing to a student's decision to drop out but also steps schools can take to avert the situation. Because students drop out of school for multiple reasons at various times, prevention and intervention strategies need to be multifaceted and tailored to local conditions. Standardized solutions, like those derived from national or state-level sources, are not the answer, nor can educators expect a simple, immediate solution. Educational personnel must combine their understanding of the factors that impact school completion with their knowledge of local schools, students, communities, and resources to create potential points of intervention.

The persistence of a high dropout rate suggests a failure to successfully educate many students. Catterall (1987a), like many others, argues that appreciable progress on the dropout rate requires the school, not the marginal student, to change. Alternative actions offer a way to refocus existing programs. These actions may help schools to be more responsive to students by closing the gap between what is offered and what is needed. The fact that the needs of many of these students become visible long before they become a dropout statistic only magnifies the school's failure at early intervention efforts. The focus must shift to an awareness of what to do rather than on knowing what goes wrong or why. Therefore, the challenge involves understanding how to structure local responses so as to create intervention strategies that address several levels of the dropout process. The suggested framework includes early identification models, prevention program components, retrieval and reentry programs, and program evaluation.

Early Identification Models

Early identification models allow the local school to identify students before they drop out and to uncover key facets of the local problem. The models range in complexity from simple univariate comparisons to complex multivariate analyses. For the former, schools compare two sets of students (e.g., dropouts and graduates) across a series of variables. The respective group comparisons are completed one variable at a time. This model is easy to understand but does not account for more sophisticated features like the interaction between variables. For the latter model, schools can simultaneously compare students across a set of variables. This type of model allows for an examination of how the variables interact. In either case, the school can readily develop and validate local identification models (see, e.g., Barrington & Hendricks, 1989; Kortering et al., 1992). Regardless of the statistical model, a validated early identification system provides a justifiable method for identifying youths who will most likely become dropouts, while reducing the likelihood of false positive identifications. A validated model also allows schools to direct available resources toward keeping at-risk youths in school.

A second aspect of early identification lies with which variables to use. Table 1 provides examples of variables readily available in most schools. It bears repeating that dropping out of school is often a function of a number of variables whose respective influence varies according to school and community features. For example, student absenteeism would be a more powerful predictor in a school requiring students attendance at afterschool or weekend programs to make up for missed school days. Districts also should avoid identifying likely dropouts on the basis of a single variable. For example, identifying all low achievers as likely dropouts would miss the point that many will in fact graduate and might well be penalized by being labeled a likely dropout.

Prevention and Intervention Program Components

A number of factors affect engagement in school and the perception that school is relevant. These factors evolve over time, and initial warnings of pending problems often appear in elementary school (Roderick, 1993). The factors, if ignored, eventually amplify family or student character-

Table 1 *School-Based Indicators of Likely School Dropouts and Ways to Measure These Indicators*

Indicator	Suggested Measures
Individual Characteristics	
Low Achievement Levels	Standardized test scores
Course Failures	Student transcripts
Retentions	School history records
Limited Success in School	Student rankings; grade point average
Discipline Problems	School records; student or teacher interviews
Absenteeism	Daily attendance records
Limited School Involvement	Participation in school activities
Perception of School	Student satisfaction surveys; student interviews
Failure to Pass Required Competency Tests	Competency test scores
Family Characteristics	
Low Socioeconomic Status	Free/Reduced lunch status; indices of household income
Parent Educational Level	Student interview or survey
Siblings Who Dropped Out	Student interview or survey
Level of Family Support	Student interview or survey
Peer Characteristics	
School Involvement	Student survey
Achievement Status	Transcripts of peers

istics associated with dropping out. The specific factors important to any prevention and intervention program include school engagement, relevant school experiences, attendance incentives, supportive school climate, mentoring programs, and family-school-community ties.

The connection between learning and school engagement is not a new idea. Indeed, Dewey (1916) recognized that the social context of learning was the basis for mastering new material. More recent research confirms the importance of a student's sense of belonging to a learning community (Wehlage et al., 1989). Four precursors to such engagement were outlined by Hirschi (1969, cited in Wehlage et al., 1989): attachment by way of social and emotional ties; commitment as reflected by an acceptance of key goals; involvement in activities of the institution; and a belief or faith in the institution. Although difficult to evaluate, Wehlage et al. (1989) found support for each of these variables in an examination of successful dropout prevention programs.

Students need to view coming to school as relevant to their lives. For many, the promises of future social mobility or the skills necessary for success in college prove sufficient. Many dropouts, however, fail to identify with such promises. Educational practices can make schooling meaningful and help students feel more engaged. Curriculum changes that recognize the importance of a child's culture and teaching strategies that embrace a more holistic philosophy can accommodate greater variation in student abilities. Experiencing academic success and positive school experiences is central to a student's investment in school. Thus, it is important that school personnel provide opportunities for success. Compensatory education programs, such as Chapter I, also play an important role in narrowing the achievement gap between disadvantaged and nondisadvantaged students. However, schools must not rely solely on add-on programs but instead focus on school-wide and classroom practices that acknowledge learner differences and individual progress. Furthermore, school districts need to acknowledge the large body of literature that demonstrates the negative effects and financial cost of potentially harmful practices such as retention and tracking.

Motivating school attendance can occur through promoting daily attendance as well as encouraging long-term participation in school. Educators have employed a number of approaches which commonly include punitive measures, social reinforcement, and tangible reinforcers. One successful approach to improving the daily attendance patterns of students included using tangible (e.g., fast-food coupons) and social reinforcers (e.g., movie passes for groups of students) to improve daily attendance among special education students (Licht, Gard, & Guardino, 1991). West Virginia was the first state to try withholding driving licenses from dropouts. Although this effort proved a failure (Toby & Armor, 1992), it remains a popular idea among many educators. In a much different way, the successful C.D. Lang Project promised financial assistance for a college education to a group of inner city students. Such promises are beyond the resources of most schools, but the general idea may be a good one (i.e., give students a reason to stay in school, one they can "bank" on). School psychogists can work with attendance liasons, community businesses, and school administrators to develop incentive programs for students beginning to show high absentee rates.

Student success is a function of caring, learning environments. For illustration, in an ethnographic study of a low-track English class, Dillion (1989) uncovered the importance of a risk-free environment, home visits, carefully planned lessons based on existing student knowledge, meaningful learning, and active student participation. Similarly, Tinto (1987) demonstrated that universities could retain minority students by developing supportive learning environments. He specifically suggested early orientation activities, upper-class mentors, introductory activities, advisory periods, and post-transition support—all of which could be a part of any high school dropout-prevention program.

Mentoring programs have become a popular intervention strategy to help create a more supportive school environment. Upon leaving for the Trojan War, Odysseus recognized that his son, Telemachus, needed a role model, counselor, and teacher. He asked his servant and advisor, Mentor, to take on these responsibilities. The actions of Odysseus still hold true for today as students need access to skilled and caring mentors. The promise in mentoring programs lies in their ability to be a source of support for students during troubled times and encouragement at other times. Hamilton and Hamilton's (1992) evaluation of a joint university/school mentoring program led them to offer recommendations including looking within one's ranks for mentors (e.g., central office staff, teachers), concentrating on students in need, providing support to mentors, offering a contextual setting for mentoring efforts, and highlighting the benefits for the mentor. These recommendations offer a good starting point for developing an effective mentoring program.

By strengthening school-family-community ties, the educational system can better meet the needs of children and their families (Rossi & Montgomery, 1994). Programs which serve to educate parents, increase shared decision making, and encourage parental involvement have proven successful in establishing home-school partnerships. As parents perceive the school as meeting their own needs, they are more likely to embrace the values set forth by school. In fact, a survey by Epstein and Dauber (1991) confirmed that parents were more involved with their children's schools when the schools had strong programs to encourage parental involvement. On a community level, the creation of school-business partnerships can help students to see the importance of their education and provide them an opportunity to meet local business leaders.

Fine's (1991) ethnographic study of a New York City high school led her to conclude that many dropouts simply saw no connection between school and their lives. Work-centered education can make a direct connection between future work roles and the student's life. Effective work-related venues should serve to teach academics to avoid becoming a dead-end learning track. In fact, Catterall (1987b) notes that work-based interventions have little impact on school completion unless they also focus on needed educational skills. To be successful, programs must prepare students for real occupational tracks, involve responsible roles, and offer a portal of entry into adulthood and suitable employment.

Dropout Retrieval and Reentry Efforts

Once a student has stopped attending school, retrieval efforts can be as simple as a phone call or entail more involved efforts including formal interviews. These efforts provide a means to accomplish three important outcomes. First, they offer a way to reconnect with the former student. This contact provides a chance to get a student back into school or into a GED alternative. Second, such efforts allow school personnel the opportunity to collect crucial information about the local dropout problem. An interviewer can easily obtain information on strategies or services that might prove helpful to other dropouts while evaluating a student's willingness to return. Third, it sends the message that the school values the student who has dropped out. This message carries with it an understanding that the student is welcome to try again. In fact, local educators report that many dropouts return with a renewed motivation to become educated and stay in school.

Successful retrieval and reentry programs need to help the student's transition back into school. It is unrealistic to expect students to simply return to the same conditions that helped lead them to dropping out. Support strategies, such as counseling, support groups, a caring teacher, and mentors, can help the student readjust to school. Flexible scheduling and childcare programs also can help accommodate the needs of students who are employed or responsible for childcare. So too, alternative programs, when characterized by lower student-to-teacher ratios, individualized curriculum, and flexible programming, can meet the educational needs of many dropouts (Wehlage et al., 1989).

Project Evaluation

Project evaluation should be central to any effort to reduce the local dropout rate. In practice, evaluation seeks to identify what works. Generally, schools identify success by way of easy, and often vague, indices. For example, schools often use student test scores or projected college attendance rates as the main indication of their school's educational quality. In turn, these indices drive school decisions. Such indices, however, fail to provide insight into whether the school setting is responsive to the needs of eventual dropouts. Schools seldom evaluate postschool outcomes of non-college-bound students, student or parent satisfaction, teacher satisfaction, and other indices of student learning.

Dropout prevention programs face two evaluation dilemmas. First, they must confront the reality that many efforts are ineffective or the results are not immediately apparent. This reality is contrary to what most administrators or taxpayers want to see. Nonetheless, a genuine concern for dropout students demands an honest and prolonged effort to understand what works and what does not. Second, some aspects of dropout prevention are difficult to measure. At a minimum, programs should evaluate dropout rates, course failures, and daily attendance. Schools also should develop ways to evaluate complex factors including learning outcomes other than test scores; postschool adjustment; and teacher, community, and student satisfaction (see, e.g., Gottfredson, 1984).

Summary

The primary challenge lies less with changing students or their families than mastering how to redistribute existing resources so that educators can do extraordinary things in the lives of more at-risk students. Unfortunately, existing school settings seldom empower teachers to fully exercise their influence (Fine, 1991). The school structure seems more conducive to getting rid of challenging and troubled students than helping them to experience success (Goodlad, 1984).

Educators often feel powerless to change the social forces of poverty, unequal employment opportunities, and the influences of these factors on individual lives. Accordingly, many feel that schools can do little to alter the life space course of students experiencing numerous stressors associated with problems outside of school. It is also naive to wait for legislation or policy that changes what actually happens to students once they are inside the classroom or expect prepackaged programs or additional pull-out options to be the answer. Instead, schools need to value and pursue responsive schooling for at-risk students, especially strategies that correspond to the nature of the local dropout problem. These efforts should include components that help students to experience academic success; to feel part of a caring, learning environment; and to understand the relevance of education in their lives. So too, school psychologists, teachers, administrators, social workers, and counselors must work together to develop effective supports. Local schools, working with parents and community members, must plan for these components through fundamental change. Com-

prehensive and collaborative efforts can (and must) help schools to respond to the unique needs of at-risk students.

Recommended Resources

Finn, J. D. (1989). Withdrawing from school. *Review of Educational Research, 59*(2), 117–142.
This article offers two models for understanding school dropout. Both models examine characteristics that he feels schools can change. First, he proposes a Frustration/Self-Esteem model. Second, he describes a Participation/Identification Model.

Lovitt, T. (1989). *Preventing school dropouts: Tactics for at-risk, remedial, and mildly handicapped adolescents.* Austin, TX: Pro Ed.
This book offers a practical guide on what to do with at-risk students. The text includes 11 sections ranging from study skills and attendance to goals and attitude. In between lie some 100 practical ideas. A unique feature of the text is its quick and ready-to-implement strategies.

Rossi, R. J. (1995). *Schools and students at risk: Context and framework for positive change.* New York: Teachers College Press.
By focusing on an ecological perspective, Rossi provides a thorough discussion of the variables that place a child at risk. His work also focuses on the importance of cultural background within school. The final section of this book highlights effective dropout prevention and intervention programs in a variety of settings.

Wehlage, G. G., Rutter, R. A., Smith, G. A., Lesko, N., & Fernandez, R. R. (1989). *Reducing the risk: School dropouts as communities of support.* New York: Falmer Press.
An insightful commentary on the need to have schools that respond to at-risk students, this book combines a solid research base with practical expertise. The text focuses on the importance of having a sense of community within the school.

References

Alpert, G., & Dunham, R. (1986). Keeping academically marginal students in school. *Student and Society, 17,* 346–361.

Barrington, B. L., & Hendricks, B. (1989). Differentiating characteristics of high school graduates, dropouts, and nongraduates. *Journal of Educational Research, 82*(6), 309–319.

Bloom, B. (1980). The new direction in educational research: Alterable variables. *Phi Delta Kappan, 61,* 382–385.

Borus, M., & Carpenter, S. (1983). A note on the return of dropouts to high school. *Students and Society, 14,* 501–506.

Bronfenbrenner, U. (1979). *The ecology of human development: Experiments by nature and design.* Cambridge, MA: Harvard University Press.

Bryk, A., & Thum, Y. (1989). The effects of high school organization on dropping out: An exploratory investigation. *American Educational Research Journal, 26,* 353–383.

Carrennza, E. (1988). The impact of teacher life changes and performance on school dropouts. *Educational Research, 17*(2), 122–127.

Catterall, J. (1987a). An intensive group counseling dropout prevention intervention: Some comments on isolating at-risk adolescents within high schools. *American Educational Research Journal, 24,* 521–540.

Catterall, J. (1987b). On the social costs of dropping out of school. *The High School Journal, 71*(1), 19–30.

Coleman, J. (1988). Social capital in the creation of human capital. *American Journal of Sociology, 94,* S95–S120.

Delgado-Gaitan, C. (1988). The value of conformity: Learning to stay in school. *Anthropology & Education Quarterly, 19,* 354–380.

Dewey, J. (1916). *Democracy and education: An introduction to the philosophy of education.* New York: McMillan.

Dillon, D. (1989). Showing them that I want them to learn and that I care about who they are: A microethnography of the social organization of a secondary low-track English-reading classroom. *American Educational Research Journal, 26,* 227–259.

Ekstrom, R., Goertz, M., Pollock, J., & Rock, D. (1986). Who drops out and why: Findings from a national study. *Teachers College Record, 87,* 356–373.

Edar, D., & Kinney, D. (1995). The effect of middle school extracurricular activities on adolescents' popularity and peer status. *Student and Society, 26,* 298–324.

Ensminger, M., & Slusarcick, A. (1992). Paths to high school graduation or dropout: A longitudinal study of a first-grade cohort. *Sociology of Education, 65,* 95–113.

Epstein, J. L. & Dauber, S. L. (1991). School programs and teacher practices of parent involvement in inner-city elementary and middle schools. *Elementary School Journal, 91,* 289–305.

Fernandez, R., & Shu, G. (1988). School dropouts: New approaches to an enduring problem. *Education and Urban Society, 20,* 363–386.

Fine, M. (1991). *Framing dropouts: Notes on the politics of an urban public high school.* Albany, NY: State University of New York.

Finn, J. D. (1989). Withdrawing from school. *Review of Educational Research, 59*(2), 117–142.

Goodlad, J. (1984). *A place called school: Prospects for the future.* New York: McGraw-Hill Book Company.

Gottfredson, G. (1984). *The effective school battery.* Odessa, FL: Psychological Assessment Resources.

Hamilton, S., & Hamilton, A. (1992). Mentoring programs: Promise and paradox. *Phi Delta Kappan, 71,* 546–551.

Hess, G. A. (1986). Educational triage in an urban school. *Metropolitan Education, 1*(2), 39–52.

Hess, R. S., & D'Amato, R. C. (in press). High school completion among Mexican American children: Individual and familial risk factors. *School Psychology Quarterly.*

Hirano-Nakanishi, M. (1986). The extent and prevalence of pre-high-school attrition and delayed education for Hispanics. *Hispanic Journal of Behavioral Sciences, 8,* 61–76.

Kortering, L. (1995). *Dropout report summary: A look at Wilkes County's dropouts.* Unpublished Report, Appalachian State University, Boone, NC.

Kortering, L. J., Haring, N. G., & Klockars, A. (1992). The identification of LD high school dropouts: Evaluating the utility of a discriminant analysis function. *Exceptional Children, 58,* 422–435.

Lichenstein, S. (1993). Transition from school to adulthood: Case studies of adults with learning disabilities who dropped out of school. *Exceptional Children, 59,* 336–347.

Licht, B., Gard, T., & Guardino, C. (1991). Modifying high school attendance of special education high school students. *Journal of Educational Research, 84,* 368–373.

Manning, M. L. (1995). Understanding culturally diverse parents and families. *Equity & Excellence in Education, 28,* 52–57.

McDill, E. L., Natriello, G., & Pallas, A. M. (1985). Raising standards and retaining students: The impact of the reform recommendations on potential dropouts. *Review of Educational Research, 55,* 415–433.

Miller, A. P. (1989). Student characteristics and the persistence/dropout behavior of Hispanic students. In J. M. Lakebrink (Ed.), *Children at risk* (pp. 119–139). Springfield, IL: Charles C. Thomas.

Montgomery, A. F., & Rossi, R. J. (1994). Becoming at risk for failure in America's schools. In R. J. Rossi (Ed.), *Schools and students at risk: Context and framework for positive change* (pp. 3–22). New York: Teachers College Press.

North Carolina Department of Public Instruction. (1994). *1992–93 dropout data report and program summary.* Raleigh, NC: Author.

Okey, T., & Cusick, P. (1995). Dropping out: Another side of the story. *Educational Administration Quarterly, 31,* 244–267.

Parker, J. G., & Asher, S. R. (1987). Peer relations and later personal adjustment: Are low-accepted children at risk? *Psychological Bulletin, 102,* 357–389.

Roderick, M. (1993). *The path to dropping out: Evidence for intervention.* Westport: NC: Auburn House.

Rumberger, R. W. (1983). Dropping out of high school: The influence of race, sex, and family background. *American Educational Research Journal, 20*(2), 199–220.

Rumberger, R. W. (1987). High school dropouts. A review of issues and evidence. *Review of Educational Research, 57,* 101–121.

Rumberger, R. W. (1991). Chicano dropouts: A review of research and policy issues. In R. R. Valencia (Ed.), *Chicano school failure and success: Research and policy agendas for the 1990s* (pp. 64–89). New York: Falmer Press.

Rumberger, R., Ghatak, R., Poulos, G., Ritter, P., & Dornbusch, S. (1990). Family influences on dropout behavior in one California high School. *Sociology of Education, 63,* 283–299.

Tinto, V. (1987). *Leaving college: Rethinking the causes and cures of student attrition.* Chicago: University of Chicago Press.

Toby, J., & Armor, D. (1992). Carrots or sticks for high school dropouts? *The Public Interest, 92,* 76–93.

Valverde, S. A. (1987). A comparative study of Hispanic high school dropouts and graduates. Why do some leave school early and some finish? *Education and Urban Society, 19*(3), 320–329.

Velez, W. (1989). High school attrition among Hispanic and non-Hispanic White youths. *Sociology of Education, 62,* 119–133.

U.S. Bureau of Census. (1985). *Statistical abstract of the United States, 1986* (196th ed.). Washington, DC: U.S. Government Printing Office.

Wehlage, G. G., & Rutter, R. A. (1986). Dropping out: How much do schools contribute to the problem? *Teachers College Record, 87*(3), 376–392.

Wehlage, G. G., Rutter, R. A., Smith, G. A., Lesko, N., & Fernandez, R. R. (1989). *Reducing the risk: School dropouts as communities of support.* New York: Falmer Press.

46

English as a Second Language

Emilia C. Lopez
Queens College of the City University of New York

Sharon-ann Gopaul-McNicol
St. John's University

Background

The number of children who speak *English as a second language* (ESL) has increased significantly as a result of the influx of many immigrant groups into the U.S. Students who speak ESL enter schools demonstrating a wide range of language, academic, and behavioral abilities. Many are well adjusted and demonstrate appropriate social and academic abilities. Others enter classroom situations demonstrating a variety of difficulties. These difficulties are sometimes related to the second language acquisition process and to the demands of adjusting to a new culture. However, children who speak ESL often demonstrate problems not necessarily related to their linguistically and culturally different backgrounds (e.g., disabilities).

It is beyond the purposes of this chapter to address the many different types of problems that children who speak ESL encounter. This chapter will instead focus on the developmental issues encountered by these students within the context of language acquisition and the process of acculturation. Factors influencing their classroom performance are emphasized, particularly educational background, first and second language skills, motivation issues, adjustment to the bicultural experience, disabilities, and placement and instructional issues. We also recommend a variety of strategies that seek to enhance their classroom functioning.

In this chapter children who speak ESL are defined as those who (a) live in homes where a language other than English is used as the primary communication mode; (b) demonstrate heterogenous proficiency profiles in their ability to use language ranging from limited English proficiency (LEP) to bilingualism; and (c) come from culturally different backgrounds. According to the U.S. Bureau of the Census (1990), 31.8 million Americans speak a language other than English at home, with Spanish, French, and German as the three most common languages spoken by individuals over the age of five. The fastest growing immigrants in the U.S. are Asians and Pacific Islanders who speak a variety of languages including Chinese, Korean, Tagalog, Vietnamese, and Mon-Khmer (Cheng, Ima, & Labovitz, 1994).

Children who speak ESL demonstrate diverse *language proficiency* profiles. Language proficiency is defined as the degree to which individuals exhibit "control over the use of language, including the measurement of expressive and receptive language skills in the areas of phonology, syntax, vocabulary, and semantics and including the area of pragmatics" (Payan, 1989, p. 127). LEP children are most proficient in their native language because their English language skills are significantly less well developed. Although the term *bilingual* refers to individuals who have developed skills in two languages, bilingual children demonstrate considerable variation in their proficiency across both languages. For example, some bilingual children exhibit a higher level of proficiency in their native language, while others are more proficient in their second language. Balanced bilinguals demonstrate similar levels of proficiency in both languages.

Children who speak ESL come from diverse cultural backgrounds and, therefore, may exhibit behaviors and values that vary from those of the mainstream American culture. The degree to which these children demonstrate different behaviors and values is often related to their level of acculturation. Acculturation is defined as a "culture change which results from continuous first hand contact between two distinct cultural groups" (Berry, Kim, Minde, & Mok, 1987, p. 494). Several variables have a strong influence on the process of acculturation including the characteristics of the acculturating group (e.g., values, beliefs, attitudes, and behaviors), social variables (e.g., socioeconomic status, family and social network structure), and individual characteristics (e.g., coping skills and educational status). For a more detailed discussion of these variables, see Aponte & Barnes, 1995, and Berry, 1986.

Developmental Issues

First and Second Language Acquisition

Children learn their first language within environments that provide meaningful communicative interactions with significant others (e.g., parents, siblings, other family members, peers). As language skills evolve, children typically advance through various stages in the process of acquiring expressive and receptive language skills in their native language. The stages include playing with sounds (e.g., cooing, babbling), imitating sounds, using isolated words, using telegraphic speech or short phrases, and finally using more complex sentences (Gleason, 1985).

The development of a second language is similar to the development of a first language in that children acquire most of their second language skills through social interactions (Krashen, 1982). Children exposed to a second language at home and during their early years learn vocabulary and meaning as they interact with their parents and siblings. Many school-age children first gain access to a second language through communicative experiences with school personnel, peers, and community members (e.g., neighbors). The development of a second language mirrors the first language in that children generally advance through similar developmental stages. Children learning a second language progress through several stages as follows (Krashen, 1982):

1. Preproduction. During this stage, expressive language skills in the second language are minimal or missing, but comprehension skills are beginning to develop. Similar to children learning a first language, children learning their second language initially focus on comprehension skills by listening to the new language and its corresponding sounds. Dulay, Burt, and Krashen (1982) report that many second language learners go through an initial, silent period as they acquire meaning for many new words but do not communicate orally in the new language. They can, however, often follow directions related to physical activities and movement (e.g., a game during which children point to objects as they are labeled).

2. Early Production. Comprehension skills, though still limited during this stage, are progressively improving. The use of single words or short phrases in the second language emerges. During this stage, children learning ESL typically use telegraphic speech or produce short sentences that are missing articles or other language structures.

3. Speech Emergence. As second language learners are introduced to new vocabulary, they begin to produce longer phrases and more complete and complex sentences. Comprehension continues to increase during this stage, as many children who speak ESL are able to follow directions and to retell stories in English. Errors in the use of plurals, verb tenses, and semantics are frequent (Dulay et al., 1982). Such errors often are related to the transference of rules from the first language to the second language. For example, instead of saying "Do you like pizza?" Spanish speaking children often omit the "Do" because the corresponding construction in Spanish does not need such a verb.

4. Intermediate Fluency. During this stage, receptive language skills are adequate. Children are now able to produce more complex and longer sentences with fewer errors in the second language. However, information processing is generally slower in the second language than in the first largely because the children frequently still translate to understand the content of the communication (Dornic, 1979).

5. Advanced Fluency. This stage includes individuals who demonstrate advanced receptive and expressive skills in their second language. Although fluent, many bilingual children continue to process information at a slower rate in the second language than in their native language, especially in such areas as memorization, retrieval, and encoding. According to Dornic (1979), slower processing occurs even after many years of using the second language simply because the process of decoding in a new language requires time and practice.

Throughout the second-language acquisition stages, parents, teachers and other individuals can help children gain meaning in their second language by exposing them to language embedded within paralinguistic cues that include facial expressions, objects, and hands-on experiences (Supancheck, 1989). Meaning is also facilitated by helping children relate newly acquired concepts in the second language to concepts previously mastered in their native language (Cummins, 1984).

Variations in the Rate of Second Language Acquisition

Early studies examining the aptitude and achievement functioning of bilingual children concluded that bilingualism and the acquisition of a second language led to cognitive, academic, and language deficits (see Diaz, 1983, for a review of the literature). However, such studies were criticized for their failure to control for language proficiency. Peal and Lambert (1962) were the first investigators to adequately define bilingualism and to control for language proficiency. Their study and other subsequent investigations have found that bilingual individuals outperform monolingual ones on tasks measuring originality elaboration, flexibility, and metalinguistic awareness (Diaz, 1983; Lemmon & Goggin, 1989). Despite these findings, educators often attribute "slow progress" in the acquisition of a second language to the bilingual experience with little understanding of the factors contributing to the second-language acquisition process.

Variations in the rate of second language acquisition are due to a number of interactive factors, including individual learner characteristics, the quality of language programs, and the social conditions in which the second language is learned (see Wong Fillmore & Valdez, 1986). Two individual learner characteristics often perceived to be important are intellectual ability and level of motivation. However, Wong Fillmore and Valdez (1986) argue these are not decisive factors because bright and very motivated children with LEP can experience difficulties acquiring a second language. Other individual factors which can significantly influence the rate of second language acquisition are differences in social skills (e.g., children who are social, outgoing, and talkative may learn a second language at a faster rate) and learning styles (e.g., learners who apply a variety of cognitive strategies in the task of learning a second language are often more successful). Age also has a significant impact on the rate of second language acquisition with older children making more progress due to their greater cognitive maturity. In general, the studies suggest that older children "appear to be more accurate in figuring out how the language works than do young learners" (Wong Fillmore & Valdez, 1986, p. 677). In contrast, younger learners have an advantage in "gaining control over the sound system of the language" (p. 677).

The quality of language programs also influences the rate of second language acquisition. For example, bilingual programs that allocate time to use the two languages at separate times (e.g., the alternate-days approach in which each language is used every other day) are generally more effective in developing first and second language skills than programs that use the two languages interchangeably. Finally, social conditions also have a significant impact. Among the social variables that promote second language acquisition are opportunities for speakers and learners of the second language to interact within cooperative situations.

The Process of Acculturation

In addition to learning a new language, children who speak ESL often face the challenges of adjusting to a new culture. Acculturation is a fluid, ongoing process which encompasses learning facts about the new culture (e.g., history, traditions); incorporating behaviors representative of individuals within the host culture (e.g., the language, making friends); and adopting values, norms, and worldviews representative of the host culture (Aponte & Barnes, 1995).

It is not uncommon for children who speak ESL to have to cope with a myriad of changes in their immediate environment as they are exposed to a new culture. To illustrate, children must adjust to physical changes (e.g.,

living in a new country and a new community), biological changes (e.g., changes in diet), cultural changes (e.g., language), social changes (e.g., new social networks), and psychological changes (e.g., stress experienced as a result of adjusting to a new culture; Thomas, 1995).

According to Berry (1986), the acculturation process involves three phases. During the contact phase, minority group members establish contact and interact with members of the majority group. In the conflict phase, members of the minority group experience dissonance between yielding their values and embracing the values of the host culture. Culture shock is often experienced as children attempt to employ familiar problem-solving strategies and interactive patterns that are not effective within a new cultural context (Lynch, 1992). During the adaptation phase, the minority group members adopt one of several modes of acculturation that can vary from full assimilation to participation in both the mainstream culture and the native cultures to exclusive commitment to the native culture (Berry, 1986; Thomas, 1995).

Backler and Eakin (1991) found that children who retain their native culture but fail to learn adaptive behaviors within the new culture demonstrate low levels of adjustment. Although more research is needed in this area, the literature suggests that good mental health stems from the blend of retaining traditional cultural variables while also incorporating elements from the host culture.

Problems and Implications

Students who speak ESL are a heterogeneous group, the majority of whom do not experience academic problems. However, a significant percentage of these children are at risk for academic failure. According to the National Center for Education Statistics (1993), children whose first language is not English are twice as likely to drop out of school, and 38% are enrolled below their age-appropriate grade level.

Among factors influencing the academic performance of children who speak ESL are educational background, first and second language skills, motivation, adjustment to the bicultural experience, disabilities, and placement and instruction.

Educational Background

The limited educational background of many children who speak ESL is often cited as a reason for underachievement (Gage, 1990). This most commonly applies to those children who arrive in school with little or no formal educational experience. Many lack the basic, native, language and literacy skills necessary to succeed in the classroom and consequently are often referred for special education due to their poor achievement. See Lopez, 1995, for a discussion of issues related to the assessment of bilingual children.

First and Second Language Skills

Competencies in expressive and receptive language are necessary for successful performance of almost all academic tasks, including reading, writing, and participation in classroom discussions (Woolfolk, 1995). Children who lack such language skills typically experience academic difficulties (Cummins, 1979; Wong Fillmore, 1982).

Language proficiency, both in English and the native language, strongly influences academic performance. Research suggests that children with well-developed social and academic language abilities in the native language develop high levels of language skills in the second language (Cummins, 1984). This is generally accepted to be valid because the common underlying proficiency between the two languages allows children to transfer their skills from the first language to the second language. Thus, when children acquire a first language, they also develop a conceptual and linguistic proficiency strongly related to the development of literacy and general academic skills in the second language. For example, children who learn the concepts of relativity in a science class in Chinese are also developing a conceptual framework of the concept of relativity which can be easily transferred to English when the children are sufficiently exposed to that language.

Empirical evidence also suggests that when children who speak ESL do not develop adequate skills in either language, their academic performance levels decline. According to Cummins (1984), "if bilingual children attain only a very low level of proficiency in one or both of their languages, their long-term interaction with their academic environment through these languages, both in terms of input and output, is likely to be impoverished" (p. 107).

To succeed in the classroom, children need to acquire English language proficiency at the interpersonal and the academic levels. Wong Fillmore (1982) examined the language skills students need in classroom situations and concluded that

"There are indeed differences between the language skills that enable individuals to function competently in everyday social situations and those that enable them to think and to read. It seems clear, however, that both kinds of skills are necessary for a child's competent functioning in the classroom, for understanding the instruction received, for participating in recitations and question-and-answer exchanges, for reading text material with comprehension, and, in general, for formulating ideas orally or in writing. (p. 154)."

Cummins (1984) posits that proficiency in English is first acquired through basic interpersonal communicative

skills (BICS). It generally takes 2 to 3 years to develop BICS which entail acquiring language skills needed to communicate in everyday social situations. In school, BICS are needed to communicate with peers as well as teachers and other school personnel. As children are exposed to academic activities in English, they acquire cognitive, academic language-proficiency skills (CALPS), which are necessary to succeed in such academic tasks as reading, writing, and discussions of the curriculum content. Children need 5 to 7 years to acquire CALPS in English.

As Cummins (1984) warned, children exposed to English as a second language for 2 to 3 years are often inaccurately described as possessing adequate language skills. However, in spite of having acquired BICS in English, these children may not have developed the sufficient CALPS to function in English-only academic tasks (e.g., writing an essay in English). Thus, sufficient time must be provided for these children to acquire the CALPS needed to function in academic situations where the language used is often more abstract and the demands are for automatized academic skills.

The process of acquiring a second language is facilitated when learners are provided with experiences that are context-embedded or supported by a wide range of meaningful paralinguistic and contextual cues (Cummins, 1984). Context-reduced communicative interactions are more difficult because the receiver of the message must depend on a well-established knowledge base of the language. Communicative tasks that are cognitively demanding (i.e., tasks not previously mastered or automatized) are particularly difficult for children with limited-English-language proficiency. Cummins' research suggests that children not provided with context-embedded learning experiences in the newly acquired language will have greater difficulty in classroom situations.

Motivation

An important motivational factor is one's reason(s) for learning a second language. Integrative motivation, or "the desire to achieve proficiency in a new language in order to participate in the life of the community that speaks the language," can contribute to the process of learning a second language (Dulay et al., 1982, p. 47). The desire to learn a language in order to identify with a particular social group may also be instrumental in the process of second language acquisition. However, motivation factors can also hinder this process. For example, children who do not want to participate in or be associated with the host community are likely to demonstrate slow progress in second language acquisition.

Adjustment to the Bicultural Experience

As children who speak ESL proceed through the process of acculturation, they often encounter a number of difficulties that can influence their academic performance. Many of these children enter school demonstrating cultural differences in communicative styles, behaviors, values, and beliefs (Hanson, 1992). These differences often are associated with academic difficulties, particularly in schools that expect strict adherence to traditional cultural norms. Cultural differences between school professionals and ESL children can lead to miscommunications and misinterpretations, as well as mislabeling these children as uncooperative, uncommunicative, or unmotivated.

Culture shock and identity problems, which are likely to interfere with school functioning, can also emerge as the children are introduced to a second culture (Lynch, 1992). When "basic values, beliefs, and patterns of behavior are challenged by a different set of values, beliefs, and behaviors" (Lynch, pp. 23–24), the result may be frustration, depression, withdrawal, lethargy, aggression, or illness.

Cross-cultural conflicts between children and family members also cause stress and adjustment difficulties. As the children integrate themselves into the new culture, conflicts can arise with those parents and other family members who continue to follow traditional cultural patterns. Similarly, children also experience emotional difficulties when the cultural expectations of the home and school vary significantly.

Disabilities

Baca and Cervantes (1989) estimate that the number of students who speak ESL and who have disabilities is close to one million. Other statistics indicate that over 40% of special education students are from culturally different backgrounds (Hardman, Drew, Winston Egan, & Wolf, 1993). The question of how many of these students are truly disabled remains in dispute as claims persist of overrepresentation and misplacements of minority-culture children in special education programs (Ortiz & Yates, 1983).

Placement and Instructional Issues

The overrepresentation of children who speak ESL in classes for students with disabilities causes concern because many of them may have been placed inappropriately and special education programs may not meet their educational needs. As Gersten and Woodward (1994) indicate, many bilingual educators are concerned that "the task-analytic, skill-building approach used in many special education programs is both functionally and philosophically incompatible with the natural language ... approach increasingly used in mainstream classrooms serving students from language minority groups" (p. 317).

The quality of instruction provided to children who speak ESL is also a source of concern. Yates and Ortiz (1991) found that a shortage of classroom personnel with training in second-language instructional techniques and bilingual education has contributed to poorly designed programs for these children. Ovando and Collier (1985) reported that language minority children are sometimes underrepresented in special education programs in some areas of the country because many bilingual and LEP students with disabilities are placed in bilingual education programs as an alternative to special education. Consequently, some language minority children with learning and behavioral difficulties are not receiving the services they need.

Alternative Actions

Programs for Children Who Speak ESL

Both bilingual education and immersion programs are available for children who speak ESL. Bilingual education is defined as "the use of two languages as media of instruction" (p. 31). Several designs (e.g., transitional and maintenance) as well as models (e.g., alternate-day plan, half-day plan) are available for bilingual programs. Because it is beyond the scope of this chapter to review the research regarding the bilingual education designs and models, readers are referred to Wong Fillmore and Valadez (1986) for a review of the literature. Immersion programs use English as the medium of instruction and emphasize the presentation of content instruction at levels comprehensible to the students.

Many ESL students with disabilities have access to bilingual education programs (Baca & Cervantes, 1989). If bilingual special education programs are not available, students are usually placed in all-English special education classes or in bilingual education classes for nondisabled children.

According to Gernsten and Woodward (1994), longitudinal studies comparing the bilingual and immersion programs "have shown little or no difference in achievement between students taught with a native-language-emphasis approach and those taught with a more sheltered-English or structured immersion model" (p. 315). The authors conclude that the type of program selected may be "less important than the quality of instruction provided" (p. 316).

Overall, the effectiveness of special education programs for children with disabilities who speak ESL has not been investigated. In addition to this limited knowledge base, the lack of educational materials suggests that much is yet to be accomplished in the quest to provide adequate services for this population of students.

Strategies That Contribute to Greater Academic Achievement

Although there is little consensus on the effectiveness of academic programs for students who speak ESL, a few studies (see Tharp, 1989, for a review of psychocultural variables and achievement) have found certain specific strategies to be effective in promoting the achievement of ESL students.

Develop first and second skills through diverse curriculum and language strategies

A number of curriculum and language strategies are appropriate for increasing the academic functioning of children who speak ESL. Among the recommended strategies are:

1. Provide language input, whether in the first or second language, that is interesting, relevant, challenging, of sufficient quantity, and comprehensible (Krashen, 1982). While Krashen does not specify what is sufficient quantity, he argues that it is critical that students be provided ample opportunities to utilize the second language. In addition to ample opportunities, the material presented must be comprehensible. To be comprehensible, language should be at a level that is easy or only slightly difficult to understand. Thus, placing children with LEP in sheltered English classrooms where the language level is not comprehensible to these students will not lead to a faster rate of language acquisition nor to higher levels of academic performance (McLaughlin, 1990).

2. For a bilingual program, provide language activities in both English and the native language with different time periods devoted to instruction in different languages to promote adequate development in both languages (Lindholm, 1990; Wong Fillmore & Valdez, 1986).

3. Develop cognitive skills through a curriculum that emphasizes higher thinking skills rather than factual knowledge (Lindholm, 1990).

4. Utilize instructional interventions that place concepts within real-life contexts and that integrate the students' background knowledge (Fletcher & Cardona-Morales, 1990; Tharp, 1989). Greater sensitivity to context should improve comprehension and integration of information in the native language and English (Aaronson & Ferres, 1987). Likewise, activities that place reading in the context of a real task or application should help provide the students with a more compelling reason to read.

5. Encourage language use within natural communication exchanges (Krashen, 1982; Tharp, 1989). Within this approach, effective instruction avoids continuous correction of dialect-type "errors." Instead, students are encouraged to produce language within natural interactions and settings.

6. Teach students to use metacognitive strategies when learning their first and second languages (Bartolome, 1992). Among the metacognitive strategies of benefit to children who speak ESL are self-management, functional planning, advance organization, directed attention, selective attention, delayed production, self-monitoring, and self-evaluation.

7. Encourage students to integrate their background knowledge into their writing activities (Fletcher & Cardona-Morales, 1990). Within this sociocognitive framework (Bakler & Eakin, 1991; Langer, 1986), the focus is on recognizing the context within which a person learns to write (Hayes & Flower, 1980) and on acknowledging the impact of the students' background. This background provides students not only with a context, but also with varying forms of expression that shape their view of written communication. Thus, the focus is on the home, the community, and the classroom.

8. Emphasize a whole language approach that integrates writing, reading, and oral expression (Altwerger, Edelsky, & Flores, 1987). This approach conveys to learners via a broad set of communication cues clear, authentic, and important purposes for engaging in literacy activities. Students are given more responsibility for mastering and creating innovative and authentic texts based on natural activities that involve written and other forms of expression (e.g., oral).

9. Apply meaning-oriented reading approaches (Collins, Brown & Newman, 1987; Duffy, 1987). Such approaches emphasize the search for meaning in written text very early in the process of learning to read in both the first and second languages.

Employ culturally sensitive pedagogical approaches

Research examining culturally sensitive pedagogical approaches suggests that children's achievement levels increase when interventions are matched to the students' cultural backgrounds (Cummins, 1989; Haynes & Gebreyesus, 1992; Tharp, 1989). Cooperative learning strategies, for example, are described as culturally sensitive interventions (Haynes & Gebreyesus). Many students are reared in communities in which communal sharing is a normative pattern of social interaction. Thus, cooperative learning is a culturally sensitive, pedagogical and social-learning approach that is consistent with the values and reward structures of many children, their homes, and their communities. In addition to increasing the academic performance of children from ESL backgrounds, cooperative learning has also been found to be effective in improving relations among groups of students and in fostering positive feelings about learning and school. In a summary of the literature, Kagan (1986) concludes that cooperative learning activities also improve students' ethnic relations.

Tharp's (1989) research in the area of psychocultural variables suggests that employing the social structure with which culturally different children are most familiar can result in higher student productivity and achievement. For example, in the Hawaiian culture, collaboration, cooperation, and peer assistance are encouraged. Educational programs that emphasized those patterns of behavior resulted in higher academic performances of Hawaiian children. Tharp also refers to the importance of applying sociolinguistic classroom practices that are compatible with students' backgrounds. He specifically refers to classroom-discourse research indicating that there are cross-cultural differences in waiting-time, rhythm (e.g., tempo used by teacher to present materials), and participation practices. Tharp concludes that classrooms utilizing sociolinguistic compatibilities encourage children to participate and to demonstrate their skills.

Address the emotional needs of language-minority children

Social support networks are important in helping children negotiate the stages of acculturation. According to Lucas, Henze, and Donato (1989), counseling programs supporting children as they adjust to environmental changes (e.g., school, acculturation issues) promote the academic success of language minority students. For children going through the acculturation process, Gopaul-McNicol (1993) recommends a more comprehensive, multisystem approach focusing on children's strengths and their interactions with various systems (e.g., educational, social, religious, and home). The goal is to empower children and families by helping them utilize all of the available sources within these systems. Rivers and Morrow (1995) recommend individual counseling, group counseling, and family therapy as other alternatives.

Apply collaborative consultation approaches

The School Development Program at Yale University Child Study Center has achieved great success in addressing the academic underachievement of students who speak ESL. Strategies include constant collaboration among governing members of the school, mental health teams, and parents. The goals are to increase the children's coping skills and to build their self-esteem through a series of lessons infused into the curriculum under the aegis of a school/home model (Comer, 1980). Parents are taught how to improve their children's study habits by creating a quiet home atmosphere conducive to studying. With this preventive psychological model, improvement in all academic and social skills areas have been noted among minority children.

Provide a supportive school environment

Research emerging from the effective schools literature has identified organizational factors present in school settings where minority children succeed academically. The findings indicate that

1. Administration personnel and other school personnel are supportive of programs for children from ESL backgrounds (Carter & Chatfield, 1986; Lucas et al., 1990).
2. School personnel are well trained to work with these children and to utilize effective methods of instruction (e.g., bilingual and ESL instruction; Lindholm, 1990).
3. A variety of courses and programs are offered that target the first and second languages (Lucas et al., 1990).
4. Positive interactions exist between school staff and language minority children and between language majority and language minority students (Lindholm, 1990).
5. Value is placed on the students' languages and cultures (Lucas et al., 1990).
6. School personnel hold high expectations for all students and provide a challenging curriculum (Carter & Chatfield, 1986; Lucas et al., 1990).
7. Schools have effective leaders who make the education of students from ESL backgrounds a priority (Lucas et al., 1990).
8. School staff members share a strong commitment to empower students through education (Lucas et al., 1990).

Summary

This chapter addresses issues related to the achievement of children who speak ESL. A profile of these children reflects their heterogenous linguistic and cultural backgrounds. Attention is also given to the processes of language development and acculturation for these children. Factors impeding their academic progress and approaches that enhance their academic achievement are presented.

Empirical research indicates that effective strategies for improving academic achievement include developing language skills through diverse curricula, addressing the students' emotional needs, employing culturally sensitive pedagogical techniques, applying collaborative consultation efforts, and providing a supportive school environment. Further research is needed in the fields of psychology and education to explore the numerous variables impacting the academic achievement of children who speak English as a second language. Among the variables that need to be examined are methods of generalizing the strengths that these children demonstrate in their homes and communities to school settings and environmental factors (e.g., curriculum, program effectiveness) that contribute to their academic achievement.

Recommended Resources

Baca, L. M., & Cervantes, H. T. (Eds.). (1989). *The bilingual special education interface* (2nd ed.). New York: Merrill.

This book addresses the needs of children in bilingual education programs. Assessment as well as intervention issues are explored by a number of different authors.

Cummins, J. (1989). *Empowering minority students.* Sacramento, CA: California Association of Bilingual Education.
The comprehensive nature of this book makes it a excellent resource for educators and psychologists. The author addresses issues that enhance the functioning of linguistically and culturally different children within the school context.

Homel, P., Palif, M., & Aaronson, D. (Eds.). (1987). *Childhood bilingualism: Aspects of linguistic, cognitive and social development.* Hillsdale, NJ: Lawrence Erlbaum.
Language development and second language acquisition issues are discussed by various authors. The authors further examine the interaction between language variables and cognitive/social factors.

Tharp, R. G. (1989). Psychocultural variables and constants. *American Psychologist, 44,* 349–359.
This article addresses the psychological and cultural variables that contribute to the successful academic functioning of all children. In particular, the author explores innovative culturally sensitive curriculum strategies that enhance the learning experiences of language minority children.

References

Aaronson, D., & Ferres, S. (1987). The impact of language differences on language processing: An example from Chinese-English bilingualism. In P. Homel, M. Palif, & D. Aaronson (Eds.), *Childhood bilingualism: Aspects of linguistic, cognitive and social development* (pp. 75–119). Hillsdale, NJ: Lawrence Erlbaum.

Altwerger, B., Edelsky, C., & Flores, B. (1987). Whole language: What's new? *Reading Teacher, 41,* 144–154.

Aponte, J. F., & Barnes, J. N. (1995). Impact of acculturation and moderator variables on the intervention and treatment of ethnic groups. In J. F. Aponte, R. Y. Rivers, & J. Wohl (Eds.), *Psychological intervention and cultural diversity* (pp. 19–39). Boston: Allyn & Bacon.

Baca, L. M., & Cervantes, H. T. (Eds.). (1989). *The bilingual special education interface* (2nd ed.). New York: Merrill.

Backler, A., & Eakin, S. (1991). *Every child can succeed: Readings for school improvement.* Indiana: Agency for Instructional Technology.

Bartolome, L. I. (1992). Effective transitioning strategies: Are we asking the right questions? In J. V. Tinajero & A. F. Ada (Eds.), *The power of two languages* (pp. 209–219). New York: MacMillan/McGraw.

Berry, J. W. (1986). The acculturation process and refugee behavior. In C. L. Williams & J. Westermeyer (Eds.), *Refugee mental health in resettlement countries* (pp. 25–37). Washington, DC: Hemisphere.

Berry, J. W., Kim, U., Minde, T., & Mok, D. (1987). Comparative studies of acculturative stress. *International Migration Review, 21*(3), 491–511.

Carter, T. P., & Chatfield, M. L. (1986). Effective bilingual schools: Implications for policy and practice. *American Journal of Education, 95,* 200–232.

Cheng, L., Ima, K., & Labovitz, G. (1994). Assessment of Asian and Pacific Islander students for gifted programs. In S. R. Garcia (Ed.), *Addressing cultural and linguistic diversity in special education* (pp. 30–45). Reston, VA: Council for Exceptional Children.

Collins, A., Brown, J. S., & Newman, S. E. (1987). *Cognitive apprenticeship: Teaching the craft of reading, writing and mathematics.* Technical Report. Urbana, IL: University of Illinois Center for the Study of Reading.

Comer, J. (1980). *The school program: School power.* New York: Free Press.

Cummins, J. (1979). Linguistic interdependence and the educational development of bilingual children. *Review of Educational Research, 49,* 222–251.

Cummins, J. (1984). *Bilingualism and special education: Issues in assessment pedagogy.* San Diego: College-Hill Press.

Cummins, J. (1989). *Empowering minority students.* Sacramento, CA: California Association of Bilingual Education.

Diaz, R. M. (1983). Thought and two languages: The impact of bilingualism on cognitive development. *Review of Research in Education, 10,* 23–54.

Dornic, S. (1979). Information processing in bilinguals: Some selected issues. *Psychological Research, 40,* 329–348.

Duffy, G. (1987). Effects of explaining the reasoning associated with using reading strategies. *Reading Research Quarterly, 22*(3), 347–366.

Dulay, H., Burt, M., & Krashen, S. (1982). *Language two.* New York: Oxford University Press.

Fletcher T. V., & Cardona-Morales, C. (1990). Implementing effective instructional interventions for minority students. In A. Barona & E. E. Garcia (Eds.), *Children at risk: Poverty, minority status, and other issues in educational equity* (pp. 151–170). Washington, DC: National Association of School Psychologists.

Gage, N. L. (1990). Dealing with the dropout problem. *Phi Delta Kappan, 72*(4), 280–285.

Gersten, R., & Woodward, J. (1994). The language-minority student and special education: Issues, trends, and paradoxes. *Exceptional Children, 60,* 310–322.

Gleason, J. B. (1985). *The development of language.* Columbus, OH: Merrill.

Gopaul-McNicol, S. (1993). *Working with West Indian families.* New York: Guilford Press.

Hanson, M. J. (1992). Ethnic, cultural and language diversity in intervention settings. In E. W. Lynch & J. Hanson (Eds.), *Developing cross-cultural competence* (pp. 3–18). Baltimore: Paul H. Brookes.

Hardman, M. L., Drew, C. J., Winston Egan, M., & Wolf, B. (1993). *Human exceptionality: Society, school, and family.* Needham Heights, MA: Simon & Schuster.

Hayes, J. R., & Flower, L. S. (1980). Writing as problem solving. *Visible Language, 14,* 383–399.

Haynes, N. M., & Gebreyesus, S. (1992). Cooperative learning: A case for African American students. *School Psychology Review, 21,* 577–585.

Henderson, A., Donly, B., & Strang, W. (1994). *Summary of the Bilingual Education State Educational Agency*

Program survey of States' limited English proficient persons and available educational services, 1992–1993. Washington, DC: Office of Bilingual Education and Minority Language Affairs.

Kagan, S. (1986). Cooperative learning and sociocultural factors in schools. In Bilingual Education Office (Ed.), *Beyond language: Social and cultural factors in schooling language minority students* (pp. 231–298). CA: Evaluation, Dissemination, and Assessment Center, California State University.

Krashen, S. D. (1982). *Principles and practice in second language acquisition.* New York: Pergamon.

Langer, J. (1986). *Children reading and writing.* Norwood, NJ: Albex.

Lemmon, C. R., & Goggin, J. P. (1989). The measurement of bilingualism and its relationship to cognitive ability. *Applied Psycholinguistics, 10,* 133–155.

Lindholm, K. J. (1990). Bilingual immersion education: Educational equity for language-minority students. In A. Barona & E. E. Garcia (Eds.), *Children at risk: Poverty, minority status, and other issues in educational equity* (pp. 77–89). Washington, DC: National Association of School Psychologists.

Lopez, E. C. (1995). Best practices in working with bilingual children. In A. Thomas & J. Grimes (Eds.), *Best practices in school psychology-III* (pp. 1111–1121). Washington, DC: National Association of School Psychologists.

Lucas, T., Henze, R., & Donato, R. (1990). Promoting the success of Latino language-minority students: An exploratory study of six high schools. *Harvard Educational Review, 60,* 315–340.

Lynch, E. W. (1992). From culture shock to cultural learning. In E. W. Lynch & J. Hanson (Eds.), *Developing cross-cultural competence* (pp. 19–34). Baltimore: Paul H. Brookes.

McLaughlin, B. (1990). Development of bilingualism: Myth and reality. In A. Barona & E. E. Garcia (Eds.), *Children at risk: Poverty, minority status, and other issues in educational equity* (pp. 65–89). Washington, DC: National Association of School Psychologists.

National Center for Education Statistics. (1993). *Language characteristics and schooling in the United States, a changing picture: 1979 and 1989.* Washington, DC: Author.

Ortiz, A. A., & Yates, J. R. (1983). Incidence of exceptionality among Hispanics: Implications for manpower planning. *NABE Journal, 7,* 41–54.

Ovando, C. J., & Collier, V. P. (1985). *Bilingual and ESL classrooms: Teaching on multicultural contexts.* New York: McGraw-Hill.

Payan. (1989). Language assessment for the bilingual exceptional child.

Peal, E., & Lambert, W. E. (1962). The relation of bilingualism to intelligence. *Psychological Monographs, 76,* 1–23.

Rivers, R. Y., & Morrow, C. A. (1995). Understanding and treating ethnic minority youth. In J. F. Aponte, R. Y. Rivers, & J. Wohl (Eds.), *Psychological intervention and cultural diversity* (pp. 164–180). Boston: Allyn & Bacon.

Supancheck, S. P. (1989). Language acquisition and the bilingual exceptional child. In L. M. Baca & H. T. Cervantes (Eds.), *The bilingual special education interface* (2nd ed., pp. 101–123). New York: Merrill.

Tharp, R. G. (1989). Psychocultural variables and constants. *American Psychologist, 44,* 349–359.

Thomas, T. N. (1995). Acculturative stress in the adjustment of immigrant families. *Journal of Social Distress and Homeless, 4,* 131–142.

U.S. Bureau of the Census. (1990). *Languages spoken at home and ability to speak English for United States, Regions, and States: 1990* (Report No. CPH-L-133). Washington, DC: Author, Population Division, Statistical Information Office.

Wong Fillmore, L. (1982). Language minority students and school participation: What kind of English is needed. *Journal of Education, 164,* 143–156.

Wong Fillmore, L., & Valdez, C. (1986). Teaching bilingual learners. In M. C. Wittrock (Ed.), *Handbook of research on teaching* (pp. 648–685). New York: Macmillan.

Woolfolk, A. E. (1995). *Educational psychology* (6th ed.). Needham Heights, MA: Allyn and Bacon.

Yates, J. R., & Ortiz, A. A. (1991). Professional development needs of teachers who serve exceptional language minorities in today's schools. *Teacher Education and Special Education, 14(1),* 89–98.

47

Career Development

Edward M. Levinson

Indiana University of Pennsylvania

John Brandt

University of New England

Background

Unfortunately, schools have all too often done an inadequate job of preparing young people for work. A 1993 Gallup Poll (Hoyt & Lester, 1995) indicated that 60% of American adults said high schools devote enough attention to preparing students for college but *not* enough attention to helping non-college-bound students get jobs. Most schools direct the majority of their resources toward preparing students for college. Yet only about 15% of incoming ninth graders go on to graduate from high school and then obtain a 4-year college degree within 6 years of their high school graduation (Morra, 1993). Stern, Finkelstein, Stone, Latting and Dornsife (1995) note that after leaving school, most young people "spend a number of years 'floundering' from one job to another, often with occasional spells of unemployment" (p. 5). Relatedly, a recent report from the U.S. Government Accounting Office (1993) notes that "many youth are ill prepared for work when they leave high school, often with long term negative consequences. For example, about 30% of youth aged 16 to 24 lack the skills for entry level employment, and 50% of adults in their late twenties have not found a steady job" (p. 1). As noted by Halloran (1989):

Students reach the end of their public school experience poorly prepared for competitive employment or independent living. As students approach the end of their formal schooling, we frequently ask what they will be doing after school ends. Unfortunately, when we look back to determine what preparations have been made for students to live and work in our communities, we see a series of disjointed efforts lacking a focus on skills necessary to confront the expectations of adult life. (p. xiii)

Most adults now agree that there is a clear need for career development programs for all students at all ages (Hoyt & Lester, 1995). Recent legislation (e.g., the School-to-Work Opportunities Act, the Individuals with Disabilities Education Act) has set in motion a program to assist schools in developing new curricula designed to better prepare students for future careers. Such efforts have also been fueled by the June 1991 report from SCANS (Secretary's Commission on Achieving Necessary Skills). Commissioned by the Secretary of Education, SCANS was made up of representatives of the nation's schools, businesses, unions, and government and was designed to examine the demands of the workplace and to determine which skills students would need to function adequately in the next century. The resulting list of skills and competencies is designed to prepare students to find meaningful, rewarding jobs and to lead fulfilling lives (Krieg, Brown & Ballard, 1995).

Development

Career development has been defined as "the total constellation of psychological, sociological, educational, physical, economic, and chance factors that combine to shape the career of any individual over the life span" (Hoyt, 1991, p. 23). As Seligman (1994) rightly notes, career development encompasses not only paid employment but also leisure activities, volunteer work, time spent on education, and time spent at home caring for a family. As such, this chapter focuses on developmental factors that affect an individual's ability to make a successful transition from school to work and community living and to effectively adapt to the various roles one will assume in life. Career development is a lifelong process. It is beyond the scope of this chapter to deal with all of the career development stages and issues which will confront individuals throughout their life spans. Hence, this chapter focuses on stages and issues spanning the school years and on concerns associated with childhood, adolescence, and young adulthood.

At least 10 different theories of career development have been developed and subjected to research. At present, even the best of these theories are incomplete, not well substantiated by research, or still in the process of being developed and refined (Seligman, 1994). Though many of these theories have common themes and there has been at least one recent attempt at theory convergence (Savickas & Lent, 1994), Dawis (1994) likened such attempts at unified theory to the quest for the Holy Grail—elusive, ephemeral, perhaps unattainable. Two prominent career development theorists have argued that (a) such theory convergence was ill-advised (Holland, 1994; Krumboltz, 1994), (b) work should continue on renovating existing theories (Holland, 1994), and (c) practitioners should adopt different theories for different purposes (Krumboltz, 1994).

Therefore, we do not attempt any theory convergence in this chapter but rather briefly review two of the "Big Four" theories of career development (Osipow, 1990): those of Holland (1968; 1985; 1992) and of Super (1957; 1990). Many of the concepts embedded within these theories have utility across genders, racial groups, and socioeconomic status (Kidd, 1982; Salomone & Slaney, 1978). Unfortunately, consideration of all four theories is prevented by space limitations. Readers interested in the theory of work adjustment (Dawis, England & Lofquist, 1964; Dawis, Lofquist & Weiss, 1968) or the social learning theory of career development (Krumboltz, 1979) may wish to consult the references listed at the end of this chapter. Additionally, readers interested in social cognitive theory may wish to consult Lent and Hackett (1994).

Holland's Theory of Vocational Personalities and Work Environments

Holland's (1968; 1985; 1992) work has had a tremendous influence on the vocational psychology and counseling fields. Research suggests that his constructs are generally valid (Latona, 1989; Spokane, 1987). Holland's trait-factor theory emphasizes factors that influence career choice at any given point in time but de-emphasizes cumulative factors. Based on extensive factor analytic studies, Holland identified six major personality orientations: realistic, investigative, artistic, social, enterprising, and conventional. According to Holland, each personality orientation is a theoretical or ideal "type" that consists of relatively well defined and distinct characteristics and that can be used as a model for measuring individuals. An individual's personality can be adequately described by some combination of these six orientations. Most people resemble one type (dominant type) more than others (secondary types). How personality orientations develop is not clear in his theory, although he does suggest that they are a product of heredity and environment. Once developed, these interests and skills create a particular disposition that lead individuals to think, perceive, and

act in certain ways. Characteristics of these six types (realistic, investigative, artistic, social, enterprising, conventional) are presented in Figure 1.

Holland argues that each of the six personality types has a corresponding model work environment, with unique requirements and demands, which is typically populated by individuals of similar personality orientations. That is, realistic work environments are populated by realistic types, investigative work environments are dominated by investigative types, and so forth. Similarly, each of these work environments reinforces certain basic traits in people, while withholding reinforcement (and sometimes punishing) other traits. For example, *realistic* work environments, like a machine shop or a coal mine, require and reinforce physical skills or strength and manual, practical, mechanical, and manipulative problem-solving skills. These work environments also discourage idealism; overt displays of compassion and warmth; and symbolic, abstract, higher level language.

Investigative work environments, such as a university research laboratory, require creative, higher level, abstract thought to solve problems related to symbolic, scientific, and mathematical phenomena. Learning, intelligence, and scientific accomplishments are valued and reinforced. *Artistic* work environments, such as dance or recording studios, present demands and requirements of an unstructured nature, usually involving the creative and imaginative use or production of art forms. Creativity, originality, independence, autonomy, and freedom are valued. *Social* work environments (e.g., churches, schools) present demands that require extensive social and interpersonal contact, usually for the purpose of helping and teaching. In these environments compassion, concern, understanding, empathy, and cooperation are valued. *Enterprising* work environments (e.g., car dealerships, real estate offices, political offices) require the manipulation of others to attain self-interest or organizational-related goals. Thus, aggressiveness, ambition, influence, and persuasiveness are valued. Power, wealth, status, or all three are important. *Conventional* work environments (e.g., accounting and business offices) present tasks that require the explicit, systematic organization and ordering of verbal and mathematical data. Tasks usually are repetitive and routine and require little interpersonal contact. Persistence, conscientiousness, efficiency, orderliness, and compliance are valued.

Holland believes that people search for work environments that will let them exercise their skills and abilities, express their attitudes and values, and take on agreeable problems and roles. He uses the term "congruence" to explain the relationship between personality and work environment. The greater the match is between one's personality characteristics or traits and the requirements existing in a work environment, the greater the congruence. Congruence can be used to make predictions about job satisfaction, job performance, and job stability. Generally,

	Realistic	Investigative	Artistic	Social	Enterprising	Conventional
Personality Characteristics	Stable Materialistic Practical Frank Self-reliant	Analytical Independent Curious Intellectual Precise	Imaginative Idealistic Original Expressive Impulsive	Cooperative Understanding Helpful Tactful Sociable	Persuasive Dominating Energetic Ambitious Flirtatious	Conscientious Orderly Persistent Conforming Efficient
Activities	Working with Tools Building Things Repairing mechanical & electrical machinery Planting Trees	Solving Math Puzzles Doing Scientific Experiments Reading Scientific Articles	Reading Fiction Sketching Attending Concerts Writing Poetry or Stories Dramatizing	Socializing Helping Others Belonging to Clubs Organizing People Activities	Influencing Others Giving Talks Discussing Politics Selling Conducting Meetings Debating	Typing Keeping Records and Files neat Bookkeeping Proofreading Operating Office Machines
Occupational Characteristics	Includes Skilled Trades & Some Technical Jobs Tasks Include Working With tools machines plants animals - frequently outdoors	Includes Scientific and Some Technical Jobs Tasks Include Observing Learning Analyzing Evaluating	Includes Artistic Musical Acting and Literary Jobs Tasks Include Creating Innovating Imagining Expressing Designing	Includes Educational and and Working-With-People Jobs Tasks Include Helping Training Informing Enlightening Curing Explaining	Includes Managerial/Sales Jobs Tasks Include Influencing Persuading Leading Managing Others for Economic Gain or Organizational Goals	Includes Clerical and Office occupations Tasks Include Following Through on Details Clerical Tasks Working with Data
Sample Occupations	Forester Radio Operator Mechanical Engineer Civil Engineer Aircraft Mechanic Surveyor Dental Technician	Economist Anthropologist Astronomer Biologist Math Teacher Oceanographer Veterinarian Detective Pharmacist	Drama Coach English Teacher Philosopher Critic Decorator Public Relations Associate Artist Writer	Employment Rep. Speech Therapist Counselor Teacher Occupational Therapist Training Director Nurse Personnel Dir. Director of Social Service	Banker Executive Contractor Lawyer Personnel Recruiter Labor Arbitrator Warehouse Manager	Accountant Time-Study Analyst Credit Manager Cashier Secretary Proofreader Statistician Financial Analyst

Figure 1. *Holland's Personality Orientations and Characteristics*

the construct of congruence is well substantiated in the research literature. High congruence has been shown to be associated with overall personal well-being, including decreased anxiety (Healy & Mourton, 1985), and to positive vocational outcomes, particularly job satisfaction, among both individuals without disabilities (Assouline & Meir, 1987; Gottfredson & Holland, 1990) and those with disabilities (Jagger, Neukrug, & McAuliffe, 1992). Low levels of congruence have been associated with chronic career indecision (Conneran & Hartman, 1993). In a comprehensive review of the major studies on person-environment congruence in Holland's theory, Spokane (1985) concluded that such research "reveals a consistent relationship between congruence and a number of measures of vocational satisfaction and adjustment" (p. 336). However, because much of the research on congruence has methodological flaws, continued research on this construct is needed (Spokane, 1994).

Using a hexagonal model with each point on the hexagon representing a personality type, Holland uses the term "calculus" to describe the degree of relatedness among the personality types and work environments. In this model, the distances between personality types is inversely proportional to the supposed relationship among the types (Erwin, 1988). For example, social and enterprising types are more similar to one another than are social and realistic types. The construct of calculus has also been well supported in the research literature (Seligman, 1994).

Individuals whose dominant and secondary types are adjacent on the hexagon are said to have a more consistent personality. Finally, some persons may closely resemble a single type and show little resemblance to other types. Similarly, certain occupations and jobs may closely resemble one type of work environment and show little resemblance to other types of work environments. Holland uses the term "differentiation" to describe the degree to which an individual's personality, or a particular work environment, more closely resembles a single type rather than multiple types. Personalities comprised of a relatively equal number of characteristics from several types are considered to be less differentiated than are personalities dominated by characteristics from one type.

Although the degree of congruence between one's personality and one's work environment is the primary basis for predicting potential work adjustment (job satisfaction, job performance, and job stability), consistency and differentiation allow one to assess the degree of confidence that can be placed in the prediction. According to Holland, consistent and highly differentiated personality profiles allow for more confident prediction about behavior than do less differentiated and inconsistent personality profiles. Research on differentiation and consistency, however, has not provided the same degree of support for these constructs as that received by other constructs in Holland's theory (Leung, Conoley, Scheel,

& Sonnenberg, 1992). Despite its shortcomings, Holland's theory has been extensively studied over the past 25 years and has considerable value for counseling (Seligman, 1994).

Super's Theory of Vocational Development

Among the developmental approaches to career development, Super's has received the most continuous attention, stimulated the most research, is the most comprehensive, and has had the most influence on the field of vocational psychology (Herr & Cramer, 1988). Developmental theories like Super's assume that the choice of a career is an orderly and rather predictable process consisting of a series of well-defined and hierarchical stages that extend from birth to death. As is true with other aspects of development, the age and rate at which individuals progress through each vocational stage vary. Although career development theorists provide age ranges associated with each stage, one must interpret these cautiously.

Super based his theory on his Career Pattern Study, a longitudinal study of 100 ninth-grade boys who were subsequently studied at ages 21, 25, and 36 (Super, 1985). He proposed five major stages: Growth, Exploration, Establishment, Maintenance, and Decline. Each is comprised of several substages, and each is associated with several developmental tasks. Figure 2 summarizes these stages, substages, and developmental tasks. Although only two major stages generally occur during the traditional school years (Growth and Exploration), all stages are listed and summarized in keeping with the birth-to-death perspective inherent in developmental theory.

The growth stage, which extends from birth to age 14 years, includes the fantasy, interest, and capacity substages. During the fantasy substage (birth to 10 years), expressed choices are often unrealistic, closely related to play life, and usually have little long-term significance. Careers such as professional athlete, rock star, television performer, teacher, or police officer are typical examples. Boys tend to select active, physically oriented occupations, while girls tend to select people-oriented occupations in the helping professions (Miller, 1989). Earliest choices within this substage are often derived from parental roles, whereas later choices tend to be based on occupations of "heroes." Children at the fantasy substage have little understanding of the requirements and demands of various jobs and are unaware of potential obstacles to attaining such jobs (Seligman, 1994).

As Isaacson (1986) notes, however, many adolescents and even adults do not advance beyond this substage. Their self-awareness or occupational awareness never sufficiently develops to allow more realistic career choices to be generated. Only as children become more aware of their interests (interest substage, ages 11-12) and abilities (capacity substage, ages 13-14) and begin to relate these to the world of work through exploration are

STAGE	GROWTH			EXPLORATION			ESTABLISHMENT		MAINTENANCE	DECLINE	
Substage	Fantasy	Interest	Capacity	Tentative	Transition	Trial	Commitment & Stabilization	Advancement		Deceleration	
Age Range	0-10	11-12	13-14	15-17	18-21	22-24	25-30	31-44	45-64	65-70	71 & on
Primary Task(s)	Increase Self Awareness and Awareness of the World of Work			Explore various vocational Options and Implement A Vocational Choice			Settle and Advance Within Chosen Occupation		Preserve Vocational Status and Gains	Cope With Declining Vocational Abilities and Begin to Adjust to Retirement	

Figure 2. *Super's Stages of Career Development*

more realistic career options identified. During the interest substage, children begin to reject many of their earlier idealistic choices and focus upon activities and future goals that relate to present interests (Seligman, 1994). During the capacity substage, young adolescents become more knowledgeable of their strengths and weaknesses and begin to realize that ability and aptitude must be considered along with interest in making career plans (Farmer, 1985).

The exploration stage (ages 15–24) consists of three substages: tentative (ages 15–17), transition (ages 18–21), and trial (ages 22–24). During the tentative substage individuals, having explored a variety of occupational areas and having compared the requirements and demands of jobs in these areas to their abilities and interests, begin to narrow their occupational choices. Most adolescents are able to express a tentative occupational preference and can explain the reasons for these preferences (Seligman, 1994). Once tentative choices are made, they are then explored further (often by means of part-time work experience, enrollment in certain courses, or training programs). During the transition substage (ages 18–21), these tentative choices are converted into a specific choice. It is during this stage that the individual makes the transition from school to work or from school to further education and training. During the trial substage (ages 22–24), a seemingly appropriate occupation is identified and a beginning job in the area is found and tried out as life's work. Commitment to the occupation is still limited, and many people make changes as a result of the experience encountered on the job or in training.

Embedded within these stages are the multiple roles that individuals assume during their lifetimes (e.g., child, student, leisurite, citizen, worker, spouse, homemaker, parent). Termed the life-career rainbow (Super, 1990), the sequencing, importance, and combination of these roles for a particular individual shape career development. As individuals begin to assume new roles in life, they may recycle through earlier stages of development.

Like Holland, Super argues that individuals have a unique set of personality characteristics (interests, abilities, values, attitudes, etc.) qualifying them for an array of occupations. Although all occupations require a given set of abilities, interests, and personality traits, there is enough variability (tolerance) inherent in each occupation to accommodate different kinds of people (providing the variability inherent in the traits possessed by these individuals are within the occupation's tolerance range). Super believes, as do most vocational theorists, that there is no one right occupation for people. There are many right occupations for everyone.

The traits that characterize an individual's personality, and thereby qualify him or her for jobs, develop as a result of one's progression through the five stages detailed in Figure 2 and are influenced by environmental factors like socioeconomic status, parents, family, friends, and schooling. The initial choice of a career is influenced by one's self perceptions, which then are influenced by and change as a function of the experiences one has in his or her career. Thus, career development becomes a continuous process of adjustment, change, and readjustment in both self-concept and in choice of work throughout the life span.

Common Perspectives on Career Development

There is considerable overlap among the different theories of career development discussed in the literature. Career development is commonly viewed as a lifelong process influenced by both environmental and genetic factors and characterized by progression through a series of hierarchical stages, each with certain developmental tasks. The process entails a series of ongoing, interrelated career-development decisions that are influenced by vocational or career experiences and personality development and traits. Self-concept, one's feelings about oneself (whether accurate or not), also influences career development and choice. How well an individual adjusts to work is at least partially determined by the extent to which that individual is satisfied with the work and performs it well. Both job satisfaction and job performance may be influenced by the "match" between one's personality traits and self-concept and the demands and requirements inherent in one's work environment. Lastly, because personality traits, self-concept, and demands inherent in the work environment all change somewhat over time, adjustment to a particular job or occupation is also likely to change over time. Thus, career development or choice is a process characterized by continuous adjustment and readjustment.

Problems and Implications

The problem of choosing a career has garnered much attention in the career counseling literature. Gottfredson (1986) identified 12 factors that impact career choice and place certain populations at risk for experiencing career choice difficulties. These risk factors, which are attributes of the person or of the person's environment, are based upon (a) comparing the individual with the general population, (b) identifying differences within one's own social circle, and (c) identifying family responsibilities (Gottfredson, 1986). Risk factors include low intelligence, poor education, cultural isolation, low self-esteem, functional limitations, nontraditional interests, social isolation, low or high intelligence compared to family and peers, primary caretaker, and primary economic provider. These factors place women, racial and ethnic minorities, and individuals with disabilities at particularly high risk for career-choice problems.

Career Choices Among Women

Leong (1995) notes that in 1980 women constituted 42.5% of the American workforce and are expected to constitute 47.2% of that workforce by the year 2000. During this same period the percentage of women who work outside the home will increase from 51.5% to 61.1%. Despite these increases, women continue to experience discrimination in hiring and in career opportunities (Flanders, 1994). Full-time female employees earn 34% less than do their male counterparts and are underrepresented in many high-level management positions (Seligman, 1994). The politics of the workplace contribute to this being the norm (Pfeffer, 1989).

Though the source of much debate (Hackett & Lent, 1992), most agree that a combination of environmental factors, race, age, socioeconomic status, parental work histories, educational levels and behaviors, teachers' attitudes and behaviors, and role-models contribute to the career-related difficulties experienced by women (Betz &

Fitzgerald, 1987). Gottfredson (1986) argues that cultural isolation, educational attainment, nontraditional interests, and family responsibilities place women at risk for career-choice problems. Because most societies continue to expect women to serve in the roles of "homemaker" and caretaker for children, women are presented with a role conflict that most men do not experience. As families have changed from the traditional two-parent structure over the last two decades, the expectations for women to serve in these roles have not. Even among "dual-career" couples, the role of homemaker often falls to women (Fitzgerald & Betz, 1983).

Career Choices Among Ethnic and Racial Minorities

Members of minority groups will make up 15.5% of the American workforce by the year 2000, up from 13.6% in 1980 (Leong, 1995). In the period from 1986 to 2000, the number of White workers in the country will increase 14.6% while the number of African-Americans will increase by 28.8% (Leong, 1995). Similarly, the percentage of Hispanic and Asian workers are also projected to increase. Unfortunately, there is a paucity of dynamic research in the area of career development as it relates to ethnicity, racial, and cultural differences, and research in this area is flawed by a lack of consistency in the definitions used to describe these groups (Hackett & Lent, 1992). Whereas social movements and legislation over the past 30 years have generally improved educational and career opportunities for members of minority groups, individuals in these groups still experience discrimination and income limitations (Leong, 1995). For example, Brown (1995) notes that the average income for African American families is 58% of White families and that unemployment rates for African Americans is about 2.5 times higher than for Whites. Minority group members are overrepresented among the poor, among high school dropouts, and in occupations declining in employment and are underrepresented in higher education and in high growth occupations (Seligman, 1994).

For many members of minority groups, the physical environment is impoverished, lacking in quality educational resources, and replete with hardships and stressors not commonly found in middle- and upper-class American homes—factors believed to inhibit the career development of racial and ethnic minorities (Gottfredson, 1986). Career choices may also be limited by expectations and aspirations that differ significantly from Whites (Brown, 1995). Research with other ethnic and racial minorities demonstrate a similar pattern.

Career Choices Among Individuals with Disabilities

Outcome studies have suggested that youth with disabilities have failed to attain desirable levels of self-dependency, largely as a result of unemployment and underemployment (Kohler, Johnson, Chadsey-Rusch, & Rusch, 1993). In a national study on school-to-work transition, Wagner and her colleagues (1991) found that after leaving high school, students with disabilities were significantly less likely to be employed than their nondisabled counterparts. Between 44% and 47% of students with disabilities do not graduate from high school with either a diploma or a certificate of completion (U.S. Department of Education, Office of Special Education and Rehabilitative Services, 1990; Wagner & Shaver, 1989). While 67% of students with learning disabilities were employed in 1989, only 48% of students with emotional disturbance, 56% of students with mental retardation, and 10% of students with multiple disabilities were employed (Marder & D'Amico, 1992).

Although the factors that place individuals with disabilities at risk vary by disability category, low intelligence, poor academic background, social isolation, and disability-specific limitations have all been implicated (Gottfredson, 1986). Heal and Rusch (1995) note that personal and family characteristics were the best predictor of postschool employment for students with disabilities.

Unfortunately, educational planning for students with disabilities is often directed toward academic rather than vocational and independent living goals (Cummings & Maddux, 1987). As a result, many students with disabilities are ill prepared for the world of work. The Individuals with Disabilities Education Act now requires schools to develop a plan designed to assist students with disabilities make a successful transition from school to work and community living. The law requires the identification of those services needed by a student to make a successful transition and their inclusion in the student's Individual Education Plan by (IEP) age 16. As a result, schools are increasingly developing school-to-work transition programs to meet this federal requirement.

Types of Career-Choice Problems

No agreed-upon system for classifying career-choice problems exists, though many systems have been developed (Rounds & Tinsley, 1984). Few classification systems have attracted much interest from researchers or practitioners, a situation which may suggest that none have been found to be particularly useful (Gottfredson, 1986). At the high school level, practitioners are likely to confront students who have made no career choice, have made a tentative career choice but are uncertain about it and seek confirmation, or have made an unwise career choice. Though there are many reasons why such problems may develop, Gottfredson (1986) has suggested four underlying causes:

- Lack of knowledge (e.g., an individual possesses insufficient or inaccurate knowledge of self or occupational options).

- Internal conflicts (e.g., an individual's interests are inconsistent with his or her abilities).
- External conflicts (e.g., an individual's goals are inconsistent with parental aspirations).
- Perceived barriers and opportunities (e.g., an individual believes a preferred occupation is inaccessible or unattainable).

Using these four underlying causes and the risk factors discussed earlier, Gottfredson (1986) has developed a problem-analysis framework for career-choice problems that practitioners may find useful.

Alternative Actions

Generally, research has suggested that career interventions have positive effects and that no one intervention is more effective than another (Fretz, 1981; Savickas, 1989). More research is needed to determine which interventions seem to be most effective for whom and under what circumstances (Savickas, 1989). Interventions designed to facilitate the career development of school-aged youth can be categorized as systemic or individualized. Systemic interventions involve the development of school-wide programs designed to assist all students or targeted (at-risk) groups. Examples include the development of career education programs or school-to-work transition programs. Individualized interventions are specific strategies that can be used by a professional with one or several students. All interventions should have the purpose of facilitating one or more of the following, each of which is critical to mature decision making about careers (National Occupational Information Coordinating Committee, 1992): increasing self-awareness, increasing educational and occupational awareness, improving decision-making skills, and facilitating job readiness and placement.

Systemic Actions

Developing career education programs
Career education programs usually follow a model similar to that depicted in Figure 3 and are based on normal career development theory. Activities and experiences usually include career assessment, career counseling, and the provision of educational and occupational information (Seligman, 1994). These programs are usually

- Integrated into the regular education curriculum.
- Implemented by a variety of school personnel.
- Developed by a team of professionals, including administrators, parents, counselors, psychologists, teachers, and employers.
- Cooperative efforts between grades, schools, community resources, and businesses.

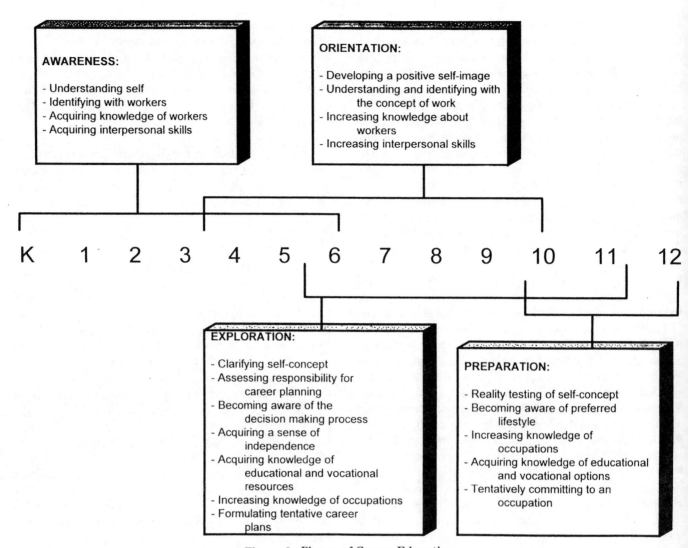

Figure 3. *Phases of Career Education*

■ Based upon the developmental needs of the involved students (Splete & Stewart, 1990; Walz & Benjamin, 1984).

A meta-analysis of 18 studies of K-12 career development programs concluded that moderate, positive outcomes were present across studies (Baker & Popowicz, 1983). In general, career education programs appear to have positive effects (Herr & Cramer, 1988).

Developing school-to-work transition programs

As stated earlier, recent federal legislation has provided the impetus for the development of school-to-work transition programs. Unfortunately, many of these programs are designed to serve only students with disabilities, focus solely on employment as a goal, and are not made available to students until age 16. As Szymanski (1994) rightly notes, current knowledge of career development clearly suggests that transition services should incorporate a longitudinal, career-oriented focus rather than a single-time, occupational-choice perspective. Though transition is conceptualized by many as a process that begins several years prior to high school graduation, it is better thought of as part of the broader phenomenon of career development. The knowledge and skills individuals need to make a successful transition from school to work and community living actually begin to develop at birth and continue throughout the life span. Hence, issues like understanding oneself and getting along with others ultimately affect transition from school to work and thus should be included in transition plans as early as elementary school. Transition planning, therefore, should be understood to be an ongoing process which is inextricably linked to career development and begins the moment a student sets foot in school (Levinson, 1995).

Moreover, a major goal of transition planning should be to empower individuals (Szymanski, 1994). That is, individuals need to be provided with the knowledge and skills necessary to negotiate the various developmental tasks throughout the life span, not just tasks specific to the transition from school to work and community. While the latter is important, focusing solely on it as a career-related objective may foster dependency and render individuals unprepared to deal with other, similar development issues later in their lives.

Halloran (1989) suggests that effective transition programs for students with disabilities have three essential components: (a) the involvement of families as equal partners in the planning and implementation of activities designed to facilitate independent functioning; (b) community involvement that provides opportunities to succeed in employment and other aspects of community life; and (c) the use of working interagency partnerships among schools, businesses, and community agencies. Additionally, effective programs ensure that

- Planning for postschool adjustment begins early in a student's educational career.
- Written, individualized plans specifying transition services are a part of each student's IEP.
- Attempts are made to integrate individuals with disabilities with individuals without disabilities.
- The educational curriculum focuses upon instruction of relevant and functional life skills.
- A large part of instruction takes place in the community.
- The curriculum include academic, vocational, and social skills instruction.
- Program planning is based upon a comprehensive, transdisciplinary vocational assessment (Levinson, 1993; 1995).

Individualized Actions

Increasing self-knowledge

Vocational assessment is one technique that can be used to increase a student's self-understanding. Vocational assessment programs often are dual-level programs involving a variety of school personnel. Level I assessments typically include measures of mental ability, academic achievement, motor coordination, personality, vocational interests, vocational aptitudes, vocational adaptive behavior, and career maturity. They utilize paper-and-pencil tests, performance tests, interviews, and observations. Level II evaluations may assess these same areas but typically emphasize vocational adaptive behavior, vocational interests, and vocational aptitudes and utilize more expensive and time-consuming techniques such as work samples and real and simulated work experiences.

A variety of commercial materials are also available which can be used to promote self-awareness. Self-understanding can be promoted by assigning students classroom jobs, evaluating their performance, and providing feedback. Discussions following job performance can focus on how well the student enjoyed the job, how well the student performed the job, and so on. Students can be asked to keep a diary or book to compile information learned about themselves as a result of these experiences. Classroom discussions focusing on topics like "What I Like About My Classmates" can also be helpful in developing self-awareness.

Increasing occupational awareness

A number of commercial materials, including filmstrips, books, and activity kits, are available and can be used to promote occupational awareness. *The Dictionary of Occupational Titles* (U.S. Employment Service, 1991) and the *Occupational Outlook Handbook* (U.S. Department of Labor, 1994) are particularly valuable publications for use with junior or senior high school students. Local business and labor organizations are a particularly good source of printed occupational information. At the elementary level, units on "community helpers," field trips to local work establishments or vocational training facilities, or Career Days featuring guest lecturers in various occupational areas will also aid in increasing occupational awareness. Weisgerber, Dahl, and Appleby (1981) have suggested initiating class discussion of a Job of the Week and playing a game of "What's My Job" in quiz show format. Students can also involve themselves in the role-playing of various workers and can join work-related organizations (e.g., Future Farmers of America, Distributive Education Clubs of America), which exist in many schools.

Additionally, the following activities can be useful to increase occupational awareness (adopted from Levinson, 1993):

- *Structured site visits.* Students participate in field trips to specific work settings, gather information about jobs during these visits, and share information with one another in post-trip discussions.
- *Shadowing.* Students follow an individual worker around for a period of time and acquire information about jobs via observation and limited hands-on experience.
- *Simulated site visits.* Students are exposed to slide or tape presentations which simulate actual work settings.
- *Simulated work samples.* Students are exposed to work tasks which are representative of the various vocational course options available to them and the local jobs which emanate from training in these courses.
- *Vocationally related classroom experiences.* Students are involved in industrial arts, home economics, and other vocationally related classes.
- *Academic classroom experiences.* Guest speakers, media resources, and role-playing activities are incorporated into regular academic instruction that expose students to various vocational options. Students receive career information on occupational areas of high interest and are introduced to such job-seeking skills as finding jobs, writing résumés, filling out applications, and interviewing.

■ *Visits to vocational settings.* Students visit work settings where jobs consistent with their interests are performed.

Facilitating adequate decision making

Because high school students frequently make decisions based upon limited information and knowledge, it is important to ensure that they have adequate understanding of themselves and of the world of work before entering into the decision-making process. Even with adequate information, however, inadequate decision making may still occur. Because decision making is such an anxiety-provoking task, young people frequently postpone it for so long that their options become limited or decisions occur by default. As Krumboltz (1993) noted "Young people are sheltered from having to make important decisions about structuring their life until they graduate. The educational system is a co-dependent in enabling them to avoid difficult career decisions. Then suddenly they are turned loose with little skill and a strong case of zeteophobia" [fear of zeteophobia] (p. 146).

It can be helpful to hold group discussions designed to encourage the acceptance of such anxiety yet stimulate an understanding of the necessity and importance of making timely decisions. If significant personal or emotional conflicts appear to be precluding decision making, individual counseling (either in a school or mental health facility) is recommended. Such problems should be addressed prior to encouraging decision making. Adolescents are often overly influenced by parents and peers when making decisions. Individual and group counseling are appropriate actions to consider in situations in which a student's decision is being overly influenced by peers. Family counseling sessions may be indicated when parents are dictating decisions.

Professionals can encourage adequate decision making in students by setting up classes to specifically teach and model these skills. Activities can be initiated that require students to role-play actual decision-making situations, allowing the students to improve these skills by practice and feedback. Students can be asked to discuss important decisions they have made in their lives and be encouraged to discuss and evaluate the process they have used to make these decisions. A variety of commercial materials designed to promote decision making are also available.

Facilitating job readiness and placement

Facilitating job readiness involves the development of positive job attitudes and work-related behaviors. Such attitudes and behaviors include punctuality, concern for quality workmanship, responding to criticism, relationships with coworkers, and so forth and are best encouraged by modeling and work-related experiences. In public schools, transforming a classroom into a simulated work situation (in which the teacher is a supervisor or employer and the

students are employees) can help teach students positive job attitudes and behaviors. Such a program, developed for students with emotional disabilities, has been described by Levinson (1984). Part-time jobs, internships, and other types of work experiences can be valuable to students in learning appropriate work-related behavior, if accompanied by evaluation and feedback. Research with students with disabilities (Ohler, Levinson, & Barker, 1996) and without disabilities (Magee & Pumfrey, 1986; Nelsen, 1990) suggests that students with work-related experiences demonstrate higher levels of career maturity than those without such experiences. Vocational rehabilitation facilities frequently offer work-adjustment training programs that facilitate job readiness of students not quite prepared for job placement. Weisgerber et al. (1981) suggest including such things as sign-in sheets, "tool licenses," competency checks, job evaluations, and Worker of the Week awards in elementary school classes to facilitate positive job attitudes and behaviors.

Kimeldorf and Tornow (1984) describe job clubs that can be established to facilitate both job readiness and job placement. Job clubs utilize a curriculum based upon "job search education" (Kimeldorf, 1984), peer support, and behavioral principles and encourage the development of job-seeking skills and job acquisition. Students are taught to write application letters, complete applications, construct résumés, read employment ads, prepare for interviews, and make employer contacts. Phillips (1992) noted that these programs have been found effective in facilitating job-search skills and improving self-presentation skills. When attempting to encourage job placement, professionals should consult with local employment agencies and various business, industry, and labor organizations for assistance.

Summary

A necessary first step in assisting children and adolescents in the career-development process is recognizing the influence that work has on the lives of people and the responsibility that schools have to assist students in the process. Though the majority of students who progress through our schools do not enter college and many experience difficulties in obtaining and maintaining employment, schools continue to emphasize an academic curriculum geared toward preparation for college. As a result of recent legislation, however, schools are beginning to place more emphasis on preparation for work and adult living. Programs designed to facilitate the career development of students should be based upon career development theory and should begin in the elementary grades. Although career-development services should be afforded to all students, females, minorities, and individuals with disabilities are at particularly high risk for experiencing career-related difficulties. Consequently, practitioners may wish to target these groups for special services.

To effectively assist a student in the career-planning process, a professional must understand the normal developmental tasks that confront students at different ages and must understand the process by which realistic and informed career decisions are made. Professionals must know how to assess the degree to which students need assistance and what kind of assistance is needed. In particular, they must be able to recommend activities designed to aid students in understanding themselves and the world of work and in making sound, informed decisions. Because the career-planning process is a multidisciplinary effort, perhaps most importantly, professionals must involve parents and recognize and utilize the expertise of other school and community-based professionals.

Recommended References

Herr, E. L., & Cramer, S. H. (1988). *Career guidance and counseling through the lifespan: Systematic approaches* (3rd. ed.). Boston, MA: Scott Foresman.
This text summarizes research and practice in career development and planning in a variety of settings through the lifespan.

Kapes, J. T., Mastie, M. M., & Whitfield, E. A. (1994). *A counselor's guide to career assessment instruments* (3rd ed.). Alexandria, VA: National Career Development Association.
This book describes uses and technical characteristics of instruments designed to assess career development needs. Sections on selecting instruments for special populations are included.

Levinson, E. M. (1993). *Transdisciplinary vocational assessment: Issues in school-based programs.* Brandon, VT: Clinical Psychology.
This book summarizes theories of career development; discusses assessment techniques which can be used to assess aspects of career development; and discusses the development and implementation of vocational assessment, career education, and school-to-work transition programs in the schools. Six school-based vocational assessment program models are discussed, and sample forms are included.

Levinson, E. M. (1995). Best practices in transition services. In A. Thomas & J. Grimes (Eds.), *Best practices in school psychology- III* (pp. 909–915). Washington, DC: National Association of School Psychologists.
This chapter provides an overview of legislation related to transition from school to work, discusses the development of effective transition programs, addresses issues associated with individual transition programming, and discusses roles of school psychologists in the transition process.

Savickas, M. L., & Lent, R. W. (1994). *Convergence in career development theories: Implications for science and practice.* Palo Alto, CA: CPP Books.

This contemporary text includes chapters by each of the major career development theorists and attempts to promote a unified theoretical base for the practice of career psychology.

Seligman, L. (1994). *Developmental career counseling and assessment.* Thousand Oaks, CA: SAGE Publications.
This book summarizes research on the career development of individuals at various life stages and discusses appropriate assessment and counseling approaches that can be used with clients at various developmental stages. Case studies and descriptions of assessment tools are included.

References

Assouline, M., & Meir, E. I. (1987). Meta-analysis of the relationship between congruence and well-being measures. *Journal of Vocational Behavior, 31,* 319–332.

Baker, S. B., & Popowicz, C. L. (1983). Meta-analysis as a strategy for evaluating effects of career education interventions. *Vocational Guidance Quarterly, 31,* 178–186.

Betz, N. E., & Fitzgerald, L. F. (1987). *The career psychology of women.* San Diego, CA: Academic Press.

Brown, M. T. (1995). The career development of African Americans: Theoretical and empirical issues. In F. T. Leong (Ed.), *Career development and vocational behavior of racial and ethnic minorities* (pp. 7–35). Mahwah, NJ: Lawrence Erlbaum.

Conneran, J. M., & Hartman, B. W. (1993). The concurrent validity of the Self Directed Search in identifying chronic career indecision among vocational education students. *Journal of Career Development, 19,* 197–208.

Cummings, R. W., & Maddux, C. D. (1987). *Career and vocational education for the mildly handicapped.* Springfield, IL: Charles C. Thomas.

Dawis, R. V. (1994). The theory of work adjustment as convergent theory. In M. L. Savickas & R. W. Lent (Eds.), *Convergence in career development theories: Implications for science and practice* (pp. 33–44). Palo Alto, CA: CPP Books.

Dawis, R. V., England, G. W., & Lofquist, L. H. (1964). *A theory of work adjustment* (Minnesota Studies in Vocational Rehabilitation, No. 25). Minneapolis, MN: Industrial Relations Center, University of Minnesota.

Dawis, R. V., Lofquist, L. H., & Weiss, D. J. (1968). *A theory of work adjustment: A revision* (Minnesota Studies in Vocation Rehabilitation, No. 23).

Erwin, T. D. (1988). Some evidence for the construct validity of the Map of College Majors. *Measurement and Evaluation in Counseling and Development, 20*(4), 158–161.

Farmer, H. S. (1985). Model of career and achievement motivation for women and men. *Journal of Counseling Psychology, 32*(3), 363–390.

Fitzgerald, L. F., & Betz, N. E. (1983). Issues in the vocational psychology of women. In W. B. Walsh & S. H. Osipow (Eds.), *Handbook of vocational psychology* (Vol. 1, pp. 83–151). Hillsdale, NJ: Lawrence Erlbaum.

Flanders, M. L. (1994). *Breakthroughs: The career woman's guide to shattering the glass ceiling.* (ERIC Document Reproduction Service No. ED 377 369).

Fretz, B. R. (1981). Evaluating the effectiveness of career interventions. *Journal of Counseling Psychology, 28*(1), 77–90.

Gottfredson, G. D. & Holland, J. L. (1990). A longitudinal test of the influence of congruence: Job satisfaction, competency utilization, and counterproductive behavior. *Journal of Counseling Psychology, 37*(4), 389–398.

Gottfredson, L. S. (1986). Special groups and the beneficial use of vocational interest inventories. In W. B. Walsh & S. H. Osipow (Eds.), *Advances in vocational psychology* (pp. 127–188). Hillsdale, NJ: Lawrence Erlbaum.

Hackett, G., & Lent, R. W. (1992). Theoretical advances and current inquiry in career psychology. In S. D. Brown & R. W. Lent (Eds.), *Handbook of counseling psychology* (2nd ed., pp. 420–451). New York: J. Wiley.

Halloran, W. (1989). Foreword. In D. E. Berkell & J. M. Brown (Eds.), *Transition from school to work for persons with disabilities* (pp. xiii–xvi). New York: Longman.

Heal, L. W., & Rusch, F. R. (1995). Predicting employment for students who leave special education high school programs. *Exceptional Children, 61,* 472–487.

Healy, C. C. & Mourton, D. L. (1985). Congruence and vocational identity: Outcomes of career counseling with persuasive power. *Journal of Counseling Psychology, 32* (3), 441–444.

Herr, E. L. & Cramer, S. H. (1988). *Career guidance and counseling through the lifespan* (3rd ed.). Boston, MA: Scott, Foresman.

Holland, J. L. (1968). Explorations of a theory of vocational choice: Vol. 6. A longitudinal study using a sample of typical college students. *Journal of Applied Psychology Monographs, 52* (1, Pt. 2).

Holland, J. L. (1985). *Making vocational choices: A theory of vocational personalities and work environments* (2nd ed.). Englewood Cliffs, NJ: Prentice-Hall.

Holland, J. L. (1992). *Making vocational choices: A theory of vocational personalities and work environments* (2nd ed.). Odessa, FL: Psychological Assessment Resources.

Holland, J. L. (1994). Separate but equal is better. In M. L. Savickas & R. W. Lent (Eds.), *Convergence in career development theories: Implications for science and practice* (pp. 45–52). Palo Alto, CA: CPP Books.

Hoyt, K. B. (1991). The concept of work: Bedrock for career development. *Future Choices, 2*(3), 23–30.

Hoyt, K. B., & Lester, J. N. (1995). *Learning to work: The NCDA Gallup Survey.* Alexandria, VA: National Career Development Association.

Isaacson, L. E. (1986). *Career information in counseling and career development* (4th ed.). Boston, MA: Allyn and Bacon.

Jagger, L., Neukrug, E., & McAuliffe, G. (1992). Congruence between personality traits and chosen occupation as a predictor of job satisfaction for people with disabilities. *Rehabilitation Counseling Bulletin, 36,* 53–60.

Kidd, J. M. (1982). *Self and occupational concepts in occupational preferences and entry into work.* Unpublished doctoral dissertation, National Institute of Careers Education and Counseling, Cambridge, MA.

Kimeldorf, M. (1984). *Job search education.* New York: Education Design.

Kimeldorf, M., & Tornow, J. A. (1984). Job clubs: Getting into the hidden labor market. *Pointer, 28,* 29–32.

Kohler, P. D., Johnson, J. R., Chadsey-Rusch, J., & Rusch, F. R. (1993). *Transition from school to adult life: Foundations, best practices, and research directions* (Research report). City: Transition Research Institute at Illinois. (ERIC Document Reproduction Service No. 358 607)

Kreig, F. J., Brown, P., Ballard, J. (1995). *Transition: School to work.* Bethesda, MD: National Association of School Psychologists.

Krumboltz, J. D. (1979). A social learning theory of career decision making. In A. M. Mitchell, G. B. Jones, & J. D. Krumboltz (Eds.), *Social learning and career decision making.* Cranston, RI: Caroll Press.

Krumboltz, J. D. (1993). Integrating career and personal counseling. *Career Development Quarterly, 42,* 143–148.

Krumboltz, J. D. (1994). Improving career development theory from a social learning perspective. In M. L. Savickas & R. W. Lent (Eds.), *Convergence in career development theories: Implications for science and practice* (pp. 9–32). Palo Alto, CA: CPP Books.

Latona, J. R. (1989). Consistency of Holland code and its relation to persistence in a college major. *Journal of Vocational Behavior, 34,* 253–265.

Lent, R. W. & Hackett, G. (1994). Sociocognitive mechanisms of personal agency in career development: Pantheoretical prospects. In M. L. Savickas & R. W. Lent (Eds.), *Convergence in career development theories: Implications for science and practice* (pp. 77–102). Palo Alto, CA: CPP Books.

Leong, F. T. L. (Ed.). (1995). *Career development and vocational behavior of racial and ethnic minorities.* Mahwah, NJ: Lawrence Erlbaum.

Leung, S. A., Conoley, C. W., Scheel, M. J., & Sonnenberg, R. T. (1992). An examination of the relation between vocational identity, consistency, and differentiation. *Journal of Vocational Behavior, 40,* 95–107.

Levinson, E. M. (1984). A vocationally oriented secondary school program for the emotionally disturbed. *Vocational Guidance Quarterly, 33* (1), 76–81.

Levinson, E. M. (1993). *Transdisciplinary vocational assessment: Issues in school based programs.* Brandon, VT: Clinical Psychology.

Levinson, E. M. (1995). Best practices in transition services. In A. Thomas & J. Grimes (Eds.), *Best practices in school psychology-III* (pp. 909–916). Washington, DC: National Association of School Psychologists.

Magee, M., & Pumfrey, P. D. (1986). Vocational maturity: Does occupational interest testing and feedback of results help students? *British Journal of Guidance and Counseling, 14,* 280–291.

Marder, C., & D'Amico, R. (1992). *How well are youth with disabilities really doing? A comparison of youth with disabilities and youth in general.* Menlo Park, CA: SRI International.

Miller, M. J. (1989). Career counseling for the elementary school child: Grades K–5. *Journal of Employment Counseling, 26,*(4), 169–177.

Morra, L. G. (1993). *Transition from school to work: H. R. 2884 addresses components of comprehensive strategy*

(GAO/HRD-93-32; Testimony before the Committee on Education and Labor, U.S. House of Representatives). Washington, DC: General Accounting Office.

National Occupational Information Coordinating Committee, U.S. Department of Labor. (1992). *The National Career Development Guidelines Project.* Washington, DC: U.S. Department of Labor.

Nelsen, K. K. (1990). *How relevant career experiences influence career decision making.* Unpublished master's thesis, University of Texas at Austin.

Ohler, D. L., Levinson, E. M., & Barker, W. F. (1996). Career maturity in college students with and without learning disabilities. *Career Development Quarterly, 44*(3), 278–288.

Osipow, S. H. (1983). *Theories of career development* (3rd ed.). New York: Appleton Century-Crofts.

Osipow, S. H. (1990). Convergence in theories of career choice and development: Review and prospect. *Journal of Vocational Behavior, 36,* 122–131.

Pfeffer, J. (1989). A political perspective on careers: Interests, networks, and environments. In M. B. Arthur, D. T. Hall, & B. S. Lawrence (Eds.), *Handbook of career theory* (pp. 381–396). New York: Cambridge University Press.

Phillips, S. D. (1992). Career counseling: Choice and implementation. In S. E. Brown & R. W. Lent (Eds.), *Handbook of counseling psychology* (2nd ed., pp. 513–547). New York: J. Wiley.

Rounds, J. B. & Tinsley, H. E. A. (1984). Diagnosis and treatment of vocational problems. In S. D. Brown & R. W. Lent (Eds.), *Handbook of counseling psychology* (pp. 137–177). New York: John Wiley & Sons.

Salomone, P. R. & Slaney, R. B. (1978). The applicability of Holland's theory to nonprofessional workers. *Journal of Vocational Behavior, 19,* 25–35.

Savickas, M. L. (1989). Annual review: Practice and research in career counseling and development, 1988. *Career Development Quarterly, 38*(2), 100–134.

Savickas, M. L. & Lent, R. W. (1994). *Convergence in career development theories: Implications for science and practice.* Palo Alto, CA: CPP Books.

Seligman, L. (1994). *Development career counseling and assessment* (2nd ed.). Thousand Oaks, CA: Sage Publications.

Splete, H. H., & Stewart, A. (1990). *Competency based career development strategies and the National Career Development Guidelines* (Information series No. 345). Columbus, OH: ERIC Clearinghouse on Adult, Career, and Vocational Education. (ERIC Document Reproduction Service No. ED 327 739).

Spokane, A. (1985). A review of research on person-environment congruence in Holland's theory of careers. *Journal of Vocational Behavior, 26,* 217–221.

Spokane, A. (1987). Conceptual and methodological issues on person-environment congruence in Holland's theory of careers. *Journal of Vocational Behavior, 31,* 217–221.

Spokane, A. (1994). The resolution of incongruence and the dynamics of person-environment fit. In M. L. Savickas & R. W. Lent (Eds.), *Convergence in career development theories* (pp. 119–138). Palo Alto, CA: CPP Books.

Stern, D., Finkelstein, N., Stone, J. R., Latting, J., & Dornsife, C. (1995). *School-to-Work: Research on programs in the United States.* Bristol, PA: Falmer Press.

Super, D. (1957). *The psychology of careers.* New York: Harper & Row.

Super, D. (1985). Coming of age in Middletown. *American Psychologist, 40*(4), 405–415.

Super, D. (1990). A life-span, life-space approach to career development. In D. Brown & L. Brooks (Eds.), *Career choice and development: Applying contemporary theories to practice* (2nd ed., pp. 197–261). San Francisco: Jossey-Bass.

Szymanski, E. M. (1994). Transition: Life-span and Life-space considerations for empowerment. *Exceptional Children, 60,* 402–410.

U.S. Department of Education, Office of Special Education and Rehabilitative Services. (1990). *Twelfth annual report to Congress on the implementation of the Education of the Handicapped Act.* Washington, DC: U.S. Government Printing Office.

U.S. Department of Labor. (1994). *The occupational outlook handbook.* Washington, DC: U.S. Government Printing Office.

U.S. Employment Service. (1991). *Dictionary of occupational titles.* Washington, DC: U.S. Government Printing Office.

U.S. Government Accounting Office. (1993, September). *Transition from school to work: States are developing new strategies to prepare students for jobs* (Report to Congressional Requesters by the General Accounting Office; GAO/HRD-93-139). Washington, DC: Author.

Wagner, M., Newman, L., D'Amico, R., Jay, E. D., Butler-Nalin, P., Marder, C., & Cox, R. (1991). *Youth with disabilities: How are they doing? The first comprehensive report from the National Longitudinal Transition Study of special education students* (Research/Technical Report 143). Menlo Park, CA: SRI International.

Wagner, M. & Shaver, D. M. (1989). *The transition experiences of youth with disabilities: A report from the National Longitudinal Transitional Study.* Menlo Park, CA: SRI International.

Walz, G. R. & Benjamin, L. (1984). A systems approach to career guidance. *The Vocational Guidance Quarterly, 33*(1), 26–34.

Weisgerber, R. A., Dahl, P. R., & Appleby, J. A. (1981). *Training the handicapped for productive employment.* Rockville, MD: Aspen Systems.

48

Family Systems and the Family-School Connection

Harleen S. Vickers
Kathleen M. Minke
University of Delaware

Families exist in many forms. They vary in ethnic, religious, and cultural backgrounds; socioeconomic status; family shape (e.g., one or two parents, blended family, extended relatives as caretakers); employment status; and educational level of parents. Although researchers have studied these demographic or status variables extensively for potential links with children's academic outcomes, studies have increasingly focused on investigating another way that families differ—family-system functioning. Families' ways of interacting, both within the family unit and with other social systems, provide a context for understanding particular individual behaviors. This *ecological-systemic* (or *eco-systemic*) perspective proposes a framework of multiple, overlapping systems that affect the developmental course of individuals (for discussion see among others Bronfenbrenner, 1986; Fine, 1992). The family, one of these systems, is a dynamic, interdependent unit interacting with other units in a larger context. Eco-systemic thinking differs from other explanations of human behavior because the emphasis is on circular, mutually reciprocal, interactional processes (Watzlawick, Beavin, & Jackson, 1967).

A significant advantage of the eco-systemic approach is the assumption that systems' interaction is amenable to change, if needed, whereas the demographic/status variables enumerated in the previous paragraph typically are not. Additionally, with its attention to family process rather than specific family configurations, the eco-systemic view is useful in studying the diverse range of family situations that have emerged in recent decades (e.g., greater cultural variation, increased family poverty). A family, as a unit of study, can be any collection of individuals who assert long-term emotional commitment to each other and live in a family-like setting.

Although systems theory is the major model currently in use to study families, this theory has not been adequately utilized to aid in the understanding of families in the school setting (Doherty & Peskay, 1992). Understanding family systems and the ways families differ in their behavioral interactions should be an essential component of school psychologists' and school counselors' knowledge base. The alternative methods of observation and analysis promoted by a systems approach not only encourage a nonblaming framework for understanding families and family-school relationships but also offer additional, context-sensitive avenues of intervention.

Background and Development

The Family as a System

Family functioning refers to the ways that a family works to meet the needs of the family system, its individual members, and other connected systems (e.g., community, workplace, school). Family-systems theorists (e.g., Minuchin, 1974; Watzlawick et al., 1967) use a variety of constructs to explain family organization and the processes governing family functioning. We describe wholeness, patterns, family organization, and family process below.

Wholeness

Families are composed of subsystems that unite and organize in an interdependent whole. Changes in any member influence the other members and the group as a whole. Each member contributes to the family's identity as a unit. A central assumption is that summing the descriptions of individual members cannot describe a family; thus, the family as a whole is greater than the sum of its parts (Bertalanffy, 1969).

Patterns

Circular, reciprocal behavioral sequences, called *patterns,* develop as family members interact. Descriptions of any interaction vary according to how one "punctuates" that interaction (i.e., what is chosen as the *first* action). Typically, experiences are punctuated according to the perceptions of the participants, each of whom focuses on a sequence that supports his or her ascription of power, responsibility, and blame in the interaction. For example, a son may describe an interaction with his parent by saying, "My mom is on my back all the time, so I just refuse to do anything to help around the house." His mother might share that "Sammy will not help with anything and consequently all I do is holler at him." Punctuation is, therefore, arbitrary and one cannot go far enough back in time to "know" who did what first and further, it does not matter. It is the patterned "dance" between mother and son that maintains the behavior of each (Minuchin, 1974). Such patterns serve to stabilize the relationship as each member performs complementary roles. Each expects the other to continue his or her behavior.

Family Organization

The boundaries, hierarchy, alliances, and rules that are idiosyncratic to each family further define patterns. These evolve over time, are fluid and ever changing, and comprise the organization (sometimes called structure) of family functioning. (The term *structure* can have two different meanings in the family literature: One is the family organization [hierarchy, boundaries, alliances, etc.], and the other refers to the configuration of the family [one-parent, two-parent, etc.] herein referred to as *family shape.*)

Boundaries

Boundaries between subsystems function as filters that regulate access to information about feelings, perceptions, understandings, and expectations. They protect the differentiation of subsystems and, in turn, the whole system. Filters that allow appropriate (functional) access to thoughts, feelings, and behaviors (clear boundaries) are considered optimal; those that permit too much access or inhibit most access can be less effective (Minuchin, 1974). A too-permeable boundary is present if parents share intimate details about their marital lives with their child; likewise a nonpermeable boundary is evident if a family member is left out of all decision making. Clear boundaries are associated with unambiguous communication, in which family members share relationship-appropriate information with each another. Boundaries limit who knows what and offer predictability in relationships (Rosenblatt, 1994).

Hierarchy

Establishment of a hierarchy among subsystems involves the allotment of power and control and determines who is in charge. A may give B an order, but whether B follows the order concerns *both* B and A. Each influences the other. If a mother tells her daughter to pick up her toys and she refuses, she is challenging the hierarchy in the family. Whether the daughter is successful in this challenge will influence future hierarchal processes. Methods of exerting power and control vary. A higher ranking person utilizes direct, overt methods to influence a lower ranking person, whereas a lower ranking person may use a more covert method. For example, a father may instruct his son to go to bed, but the son may send messages of refusal by acting out a repertoire of behaviors (e.g., crying, stalling) that keep the father engaged (Rosenblatt, 1994).

Alliances

Members form alliances (sometimes referred to as "coalitions") to achieve a goal or to oppose someone inside or outside the family unit. The alliance may be:

- Temporary—mother and son align together to convince dad to agree to a large purchase.
- Shifting—different siblings join at different times to meet particular needs.
- Long-standing—father and daughter unite against the mother on all major issues.

Alliances function either to advance or inhibit the needs of the family. If parents align to carry out their parenting duties, it is generally considered a functional alliance (Minuchin, 1974). On the other hand, if a cross-generational alliance forms between a child and parent or a child and a grandparent, it may produce confusion about the hierarchy.

Family rules

Implicit interaction rules that guide and regulate family behavior are the infrastructure of family functioning. Although frequently challenged and modified, rules keep behavior within certain limits through the use of sanctions such as disapproval, anger, criticism, withdrawal of affection, or even termination of the relationship. Hierarchy, alliances, and boundaries are reflections of the family rules. Rules determine who may do what, where, when, how, and with whom (Rosenblatt, 1994). The rules both prescribe and proscribe behaviors related to expressing feelings, dealing with conflict, sexuality, independence, and achievement (Barbarin, 1992). They embrace the beliefs, myths, rituals, attitudes, attributions, and expectations in family life. In essence, rules are the members' shared assumptions about their family and the family's relationship to the environment. Families often transmit rules through the generations.

Family Process

The organizational constructs just outlined assist in the description of family functioning; however, researchers have also identified a number of process constructs that provide additional information about family interaction (see, for example, Beavers, 1981, and Olson et al., 1983). Although theorists use different construct labels, most of the process constructs fall under two rubrics—connection and change. The following discussion draws primarily from the work of Olson and colleagues (1983).

Connection

Connection or cohesion refers to the closeness or bonding experienced by family members and the quality of their affective relationships. Members seek a balance between supportiveness and autonomy. Supportiveness is embodied in the feelings of emotional closeness, loyalty, and concern about each other's well being. Autonomy, on the other hand, describes the individual freedom, individuation (extent of differentiation from other members), and emotional distance experienced by members. A family's experience of connection is determined by how they balance the competing processes of support and autonomy.

Families can vary in their degree of connection from too much (enmeshed) to too little (disengaged; see discussion in Minuchin, 1974). Enmeshed family members experience such a high degree of supportiveness that they have very little individual freedom. Because the hierarchy in this type of family is likely to be confused, children may have excessive power. The boundaries between the subsystems permit extreme and inappropriate sharing of information (too-permeable boundaries). Members may feel emotionally smothered; rely on other members as their reference points for cues about what to think, feel, or do (Rosenblatt, 1994); equate disagreement with disloyalty; and reveal little tolerance for individual differences. They do not permit each other to perform their family roles without interference (Minuchin, 1974). This type of family often aligns together to shut out the community or school.

A family with very low connection (i.e., disengaged) values individual autonomy over support for its members. Members behave independently of one another (Rosenblatt, 1994). Boundaries are nonpermeable as members share little information with each other. Inadequate bonding may prevent effective functioning. Members may feel neglected, undervalued, and indifferent to the needs of others.

Families who achieve a symmetry between support and autonomy are characterized by clear boundaries. They balance physical and emotional togetherness with reasonable degrees of individual freedom. Although invested in one another's needs, such closeness does not preclude individuation. Adults align together in charge of the children.

Change

Change involves a family's ability to adapt its patterns of interaction when needed. Two opposing pressures influence family change. The first, *homeostasis,* promotes stability and provides the continuity of family interaction. This force fosters resistance to change. However, systems must often change and restructure to survive. The force toward change is called *adaptation.* A natural tension occurs between these conflicting forces. A family's ability to change when needed can vary from too little (rigid) to too much (chaotic). Rigidly functioning families maintain fixed patterns, do not permit negotiation, and display an inability to adjust their previous functioning style to meet new needs of members. By contrast, chaotically functioning families are characterized by constantly shifting, confusing, arbitrary rules and endless negotiation (Gaughan, 1982). As a result, members cannot count on consistency or predictability. The middle level of this dimension is characterized by a productive balance between the resistance to change and the need to change (Barbarin, 1992).

Change may occur on two levels as families attempt to meet the needs of individual members. First-order change refers to the ability of families to adapt to internal (within the family) and external (societal) demands during day-to-day interaction. Although this type of change requires family flexibility, significant change in family organization and process is not necessary. For example, in a family accomplished at first-order change, parents would encourage developmentally appropriate personal responsibility in their children by allowing more active participation in decision making and problem solving as the children get older.

However, other types of stressors impinge on families over time, requiring significant interactional change if they are to function effectively. Second-order change involves a profound reorganization that may include rules, boundaries, hierarchy, and/or alliances. Families generally need this level of change whenever they experience either expected developmental concerns such as the birth of a baby or unexpected crises such as the death of a child.

In summarizing the eco-systemic theoretical framework, hallmarks of effective family functioning include both a constructive balance of support and autonomy and the willingness and capability to adapt to changing needs. These families organize with the caretakers aligning to take charge of the children and all family members contributing to the maintenance of clear boundaries. Clear boundaries optimize opportunities for parties to express thoughts and feelings and to negotiate points of disagreement. However, families can tolerate a great deal of diversity in functioning. Although a family's ways of behaving may differ from generally accepted notions of what is effective, they may be as successful in meeting each other's needs as a family that uses more conventional modes of interaction. It is when conflicts or stresses are associated with a particular interactional style that symptoms emerge and are maintained by the system.

Problems and Implications

Traditionally, attention in the study of families has been given to the relatively unchangeable "social addresses" or statuses of families (Dornbusch & Wood, 1989), such as socioeconomic status (SES) or ethnicity. Differences in child outcomes based on these variables have been well documented. However, a number of problems are associated with this approach. First, although many studies are correlational in nature, causation is frequently inferred. Second, the effects of these status variables are not independent. For example, studying the effects of living in a step-family on child outcomes may be confounded with a variety of other effects (e.g., divorce, a period of living in a single-parent family, change in family income, or moves to different schools; see Hetherington & Arasteh, 1988). Third, status variables may be defined differently across studies. Perhaps the best example of these problems is the use of SES as a status variable.

White (1982) conducted a meta-analysis of 101 studies of the relationship between SES and academic achievement. He noted that a strong, positive relationship between these variables is typically considered a given. However, his study showed that, when the individual is the unit of analysis, the correlation between these variables is quite low and accounts for less than 5% of the variance in academic achievement. Where SES appears to have a higher correlation with achievement, studies frequently used definitions of SES that included "home atmosphere" variables (e.g., availability of reading materials, educational aspirations for children, taking children to library and cultural events), variables that are more amenable to change than parental income or education levels. White noted, however, that "complete interpretation of the contribution of home atmosphere to students' academic achievement is fraught with problems of third variables and directionality" (p. 470). Similarly, in a discussion of the wide range of status variables often studied, Menaghan (1996) stated

The unobserved variables that lead to exit from high school without a diploma or exit from college without a bachelor's degree, to an early marriage or pregnancy, or to an unfortunate partner choice may explain later outcomes as much or more than the subsequent occupational conditions or marital status that we observe (p. 186)

Family functioning may be an important "unobserved variable" that both influences, and is influenced by, these status variables. Further, it is likely to have a direct influence on child outcomes. If certain aspects of family functioning that can be learned and changed are associated with better child outcomes, then greater hope for intervention can be inferred. Research can shift "from subdividing social groups ever more finely in a search for differences in academic performance to identifying the mechanisms that account for the observed group differences" (Dornbusch & Wood, 1989, p. 68). Of particular interest for the present chapter are child outcomes related to academic achievement.

Connection, Change, and Child Outcomes

Research into the influence of family functioning on child outcomes has frequently examined families' connectedness and capacity for change. Olson et al. (1983) use the terms *cohesion* and *adaptability* to refer to these constructs. They typically are measured using the Family Adaptability and Cohesion Evaluation Scale (FACES III; Olson, Portner, & Lavee, 1985). The instrument yields scores for each factor (cohesion and adaptability) and allows classification of families using a curvilinear model (Circumplex Model). Because the variables are considered curvilinear, extreme scores (very high or very low) on either scale indicate less effective functioning; optimal functioning is associated with more moderate scores on both scales.

Although the curvilinearity of the variables has been questioned (e.g., Daley, Sowers-Hoag, & Thyer, 1991), children in families with some patterns of extreme FACES scores have been shown to have a variety of difficulties. Adolescents attending an alternative school due to severe behavior problems (e.g., suspension, probation, substance abuse) lived in families rated as significantly less cohesive than a matched group of public school adolescents (Masselam, Marcus, & Stunkard, 1990). Similarly, in a study of 5- to fourteen-year-old children, Amerikaner and Omizo (1984) found that families of children with learning disabilities and emotional disturbance rated their families as significantly more chaotic (extremely high adaptability scores) and less cohesive than families of children without disabilities. Young children (Grades 1 to 3) considered at risk for dropping out of school based on a combination of factors (i.e., attendance, achievement, grade retention, and nominations by school personnel) also were identified as living in families with less than optimal functioning: Almost two-thirds of the families fell in the extreme disengaged category and fully half were in the rigid category (Vickers, 1994). It is important to note that family functioning appears to be independent of family composition; that is, more effective family functioning is not associated with specific family shapes (e.g., two parent, divorced; McFarlane, Bellissimo, & Norman, 1985).

Some studies, rather than assessing the entire family system, have focused on specific, dyadic relationships within the system. These studies suggest a significant association between academic achievement and the nature of the affective relationship between parents and children. For example, one longitudinal study showed that a positive mother-child affective relationship at age four had a significant effect on academic achievement at age twelve, independent of maternal IQ and SES (Estrada, Arsenio, Hess, & Holloway, 1987). Although this study included only the mother-child dyad, which is itself affected by a variety of other family processes, the findings indicate that having at least one positive affective relationship early in life provides a continuing influence on achievement even into adolescence. Christenson, Rounds, and Gorney (1992) concluded their review of affective environment studies by stating "Parents who accept, nurture, encourage, and are emotionally responsive to their child's developmental needs tend to have children who are successful in school. This affective relationship is not associated with IQ, SES, or gender of the child" (p. 188).

Erickson and Pianta (1989) suggest a path by which children's early affective experiences may lead to a difficult transition to school. Children who experience ineffective early attempts to influence their environments are likely to become anxiously attached. These children develop a "working model" of relationships in which they expect that their efforts to interact with adults will not lead to consistent or supportive responses. Thus, their avoidant and/or resistant behavior with their caregivers may be a self-protective, adaptive response. However, if they generalize these response patterns to the school environment, a cycle may be created in which teachers respond with lowered expectations and punishing behavior that inadvertently reinforces the child's negative working models of relationships. Unless an improved parent-child relationship or a supportive teacher-child relationship breaks the cycle, poor academic performance can be expected.

Other Aspects of Family Functioning and Child Outcomes

Although useful in demonstrating relationships between overall family functioning and children's school success, the studies just cited generally do not illuminate the underlying, specific family processes that influence children's performance. Dornbusch and Wood (1989) in their review of the literature outlined a number of these processes; their findings are summarized in Table 1.

The relationships identified are not simple or clearly directional (i.e., causal); multiple influences interact to affect academic success and other child outcomes. Because of these multiple influences, one cannot identify certain family functioning patterns as "good" and others as "bad." For example, Humphries and Bauman (1980) found authoritarian and controlling attitudes positively correlated with hostility and rejection for mothers of nor-

mally achieving children but virtually uncorrelated for mothers of children with learning disabilities. The authors speculated that mothers of children with learning disabilities were responding appropriately to their children's need for greater behavioral control, but they exercised this control in a nonhostile manner. Similarly, although a rigid style of family functioning is generally considered less than optimal, Veerman (1995) found that several years after discharge from a day and residential treatment program, those adolescents who exhibited fewer problems at follow-up also reported more rigid family functioning. Again, greater structure in these families may have contributed to better outcomes in adolescents with severe behavior problems.

A number of studies have shown an indirect effect of family functioning on child outcomes. For example, family functioning variables (e.g., parental acceptance, family conflict) may be more salient predictors of adolescents' suicidal ideation than nonfamily variables (e.g., peer involvement and school performance). However, the effect of one of the family variables, family conflict, appears to be mediated by self-derogation; that is, high levels of conflict are associated with self-derogation, which in turn influences suicidal ideation (Shagle & Barber, 1995). Similarly, family functioning and parenting appear to influence the development of self-regulatory skills in children; these skills then become important in limiting delinquent behavior in adolescence (Feldman & Weinberger, 1994). These studies highlight the complex paths by which family functioning influences children's development.

It is clear that family functioning is an important influence on child and adolescent functioning in a variety of developmental areas. A growing body of research supports that it accounts for more variance in child outcomes than the traditional, unchangeable statuses of families. However, the family is only one of the microsystems in which a child develops; the school as a system is also critical. Although a comprehensive review of the literature investigating the influences of teacher, classroom-climate, and school-system variables on children's development is beyond the scope of this chapter (see, e.g., Fraser & Walberg, 1991), a brief summary of what is known about the connections between the systems is important.

The Family-School Interface and Child Outcomes

There are studies indicating that varying amounts and types of parent involvement influence child academic outcomes. There is also evidence that relates numerous variables specific to teachers and parents to the quality of parent-teacher interaction (e.g., see Christenson, Rounds & Franklin, 1992). These variables include attitudes toward and perceptions of one another; styles of communication; particular needs, roles, and expectations of each party; and factors that limit family involvement such as

Table 1 *Family Processes Associated with Academic Success*

Process	Sample Findings
Communication style	Emphasis on conformity with others' opinions is associated with lower grades; emphasis on diversity of ideas is associated with higher grades.
Decision making	Too early autonomy in decision making is associated with delinquent behavior; joint decision making in adolescence is associated with higher grades.
Parental reaction to grades	For average high school students, extrinsic rewards and punishments are associated with declining grades; parental encouragement is associated with higher grades. For low-achieving high school students, no parental response was found that increased grades.
Parenting styles	Authoritarian and permissive parenting tends to be negatively associated with grades; authoritative parenting tends to be associated with higher grades; cross-ethnicity and gender differences are apparent.
Educational expectations	Higher expectations are associated with higher achievement, especially among lower socioeconomic families.
Parental interest and involvement in education	Across family background variables, parental involvement is associated with better academic performance.
Parental monitoring	Parental knowledge of adolescent behavior and adolescents' beliefs that parents will find out about their behavior are associated with better grades.

Note. Findings summarized from Dornbusch and Wood, 1989. See also the chapter on Parenting Styles, this volume.

time and family demands. However, relatively few studies have applied systems constructs to the study of the family-school interface. Most available studies have examined differences between home and school cultures. That is, schools often mirror White, middle class values and expectations, thereby placing students from minority and poor families at a disadvantage (e.g., Colbert, 1991; Lareau, 1987). However, because schools are also systems with their own hierarchy, rules, alliances, etc., the potential is great for a mismatch between families' preferred ways of functioning and schools' expectations for family behavior, even within cultural groups.

Hansen (1986) conducted one of the few studies that examined both families and schools as individual systems. More specifically, he identified patterns of *how* things are done in each setting (rather than *what* things are said) and investigated how a mismatch between the systems' organizations might impede student progress. He categorized families and classrooms as cohesive, coercive, or laissez-faire in their rule structures. As expected, children performed best in classrooms in which the rules governing adult-child interactions were similar to those of their homes. That is, no particular type of classroom organization or family organization was associated with good grades for all children. Any child could be relatively disadvantaged in a classroom highly dissimilar in rule structure to that child's home and relatively advantaged in a classroom with a rule structure similar to that in the family. This study further supports conceptualizing child achievement problems from a broad, systems perspective rather than as strictly intrachild phenomena.

Interestingly, there has been little investigation of the association between family-school conflict and child outcomes. However, because the family and the school are the major interactive contexts of the child's life, it is reasonable to assume that conflict between the two makes it difficult for children to perform optimally. The current interest in family-school partnerships may lead to needed further study in this area.

Alternative Actions

A knowledge of family systems can be useful to school psychologists and counselors in understanding child problems from a broader perspective. Perhaps its greatest potential, however, is in improving the connections between family and school systems through encouraging collaborative interactions. To use family systems knowledge in this way, counselors and psychologists must first consider the systemic perspective as a viable, alternative frame of reference for viewing family-school issues. Second, through modeling and teaching, they can encourage other school personnel to develop a systemic perspective.

Essential Attitudes for Systemic Problem Solving

True collaboration requires a significant shift in a number of attitudes commonly held by school staff. In their search for causal explanations for child behavior problems, school professionals may blame the problems on family factors, leading to a sense of hopelessness about control over solutions. A systemic, collaborative framework involves different attributions about the nature of problems and different attitudes about the source of solutions. Some prerequisite attitudes for enacting a systemic approach are outlined next.

Problems are system problems

Probably the most critical attitude shift involves changing common problem attributions. Typically, school professionals consider intrachild factors as primary in the description of a problem. The systemic perspective differs from more traditional frameworks (e.g., intrapsychic and medical models) by characterizing children's problems as maintained by a lack of balance in the system. This imbalance may concern "a disparity between an individual's particular characteristics and abilities, and the demands or expectations of the system, or a 'failure to match' between child and system" (Christenson & Cleary, 1990, p. 231).

Thus, instead of analyzing a problem by focusing solely on the child's attributes (e.g., IQ, achievement scores, ratings of behavior), the search for contributors to the problem is expanded. These contributors might include aspects of the classroom environment (e.g., interaction rules, style of discipline), aspects of the family environment (e.g., parenting style, level of cohesion and adaptability), and, most significantly, the ways in which these factors are interwoven with child characteristics to contribute to the presenting problem. Conoley (1987) offers numerous strategies for school psychologists and counselors to use in assessing families and schools, including interview, self-report, and observational methods. This information is combined to develop data-based hypotheses about the child's characteristics and preferences and the ways in which these attributes enhance or impede the child's progress in multiple settings.

Although there are obvious within-child problems, such as learning difficulties secondary to head injury, it is the systems' organization and capacity for coping with the problem that may be amenable to intervention. Thus, even problems with clear intrachild origins are considered system problems rather than individual problems.

No one person is blamed

Related to the first attitude change is the notion of a blame-free approach. In the absence of collaboration, families tend to blame schools for problems and schools tend to blame families. Ascribing blame to others allows each party to avoid responsibility for change. The standard practice of beginning meetings by describing the child's shortcomings and then listing prior interventions with the child functions as an effort by school personnel to avoid being blamed by the family (Carlson, Hickman, & Horton, 1992). It may also serve to reinforce parents'

perceptions that their summons to the school is little more than an invitation to listen to multiple strangers list their child's failures and, by implication, their failures as parents. Not surprisingly, blaming solves few problems because those who blame feel the problem is outside their control and those who feel blamed become resentful and are unlikely to be motivated to change.

Systemic explanations of behavior assume interactions are circular. Problems may be related to discrepancies between the needs of the individual and the needs of the educational system or to conflicts between family culture and school culture (Barbarin, 1992). Because multiple factors combine to contribute to the problem, assigning blame to any particular person or system is futile. Instead of searching for the cause of the problem, family members and school personnel can search for the part of the system most amenable to change. Whenever energies are solution focused instead of blame focused, there is greater opportunity for productive encounters with families.

Parents and teachers do the best they can

Rarely are parents deliberately indifferent to their children's education and rarely are teachers simply mean or cruel to particular children. Clearly, these situations may occur, but they are exceptions rather than the rule. Because interactions are circular, people are often unaware of how they are contributing to the maintenance of a problem. It is, therefore, more productive to assume that people's behavior makes sense from their frame of reference and to work toward understanding in what ways a particular behavior supports the system's stability. Similarly, the technique of reframing or searching for a positive explanation of a given behavior can help all parties view the interaction differently. Successful reframing involves listening carefully to what a person says and attempting to find an alternative way to describe the experience. For example, in response to a teenager complaining about her "overprotective" father "spying" on her to see where she goes and with whom, a reframe of the father's behavior might be: "He must love you very much to go to such lengths to protect you." Reframing emphasizes the positive quality of caring over the negative quality of overprotectiveness. This consideration should be shown to all involved members, including school personnel.

Power and responsibility are shared

A commonly held institutional belief among school professionals is that they are required to be the experts on all problems, large and small. This attitude has two unfortunate ramifications. First, it encourages advice giving as a primary intervention. Advice, by its nature, implies that the other is responsible for the problem. However, it also allows the other to blame the advice-giver for poor outcomes. This pattern is reflected in the frequently heard response of parents and teachers: "Well, they told me to try behavior modification and it did not work!" Secondly, an expert approach precludes using the most valuable problem-solving resource available—parents. Parents know more about their children than anyone else. As such, they can make valuable contributions to any problem-solving process. Actively listening to how a family interprets events validates their expertise, implicitly conveying the belief that they are doing the best they can. When school staff resort to teaching and telling rather than listening and gathering information, they derail the collaborative problem-solving process that can empower all participants.

In collaboration, a problem is examined from the perspective of how all involved contribute to its maintenance. It is assumed that each concerned individual has a say in how to approach the problem and which solutions to attempt. Although it is probably necessary for practical reasons to focus on specific behavior sequences or a particular part of the system in introducing an intervention, the selection is based on consensus. Both the power to select an intervention and the responsibility for success or failure are shared.

Children are included

The child is part of all the relevant systems: family, school, and family-school. Thus, the basic problem-solving interactional unit is, at a minimum, composed of teacher, parent, and child (O'Callaghan, 1993). Ideally, however, problem solving should include all relevant adults working together with the child, rather than multiple dyads such as parent/teacher, parent/counselor, or psychologist/child. Reasons abound for inclusion of the child. The child's perspective of the problem is as valid as that of parents, teachers, and other involved participants. In addition, being present when problems are discussed offers the child an opportunity to observe parents and others working together to help him or her, hear expectations shared by parents and others, and contribute solutions that invest the child in success. There are two possible reasons to exclude the child as a protective measure: (a) if there is sexual or physical abuse in the family or (b) if parents' disagreements of how to manage the child are so severe that they inhibit the problem-solving process.

Problem-Solving Meetings

Problem-solving meetings in which the child and all significant adults come together to explore the problem and generate potential solutions provide opportunities for school psychologists and counselors to model collaborative attitudes and behaviors. These meetings provide a chance to expand the observational lens to include connections between systems. With each of the two major systems represented by involved participants (i.e., school

and family), school counselors and psychologists can observe interactions and relationships and facilitate movement of the meeting toward a common goal.

A number of researchers and practitioners have described protocols for such meetings (e.g., see O'Callaghan, 1993; Weiss & Edwards, 1992). Carlson and her colleagues drew from both an enablement/empowerment model (Dunst & Trivette, 1987) and a family-systems therapy model, Solutions-Oriented Brief Therapy (de Shazer, 1985; O'Hanlon & Weiner-Davis, 1989) to develop the Solution-Oriented Family-School Consultation Model (see Carlson et al., 1992, for a thorough discussion).

The enablement model guides assumptions about how help should be provided. That is, clients are viewed as capable of demonstrating competence if provided the opportunity; helpers are to be alert to client strengths and to create opportunities for clients to demonstrate or develop their competencies. The helping relationship is a collaborative partnership with joint responsibility for eliciting solutions. Solution-Oriented Brief Therapy is based on the notion that when a particular problem is resolved, systems reorganize themselves as needed. Thus, the focus of intervention is solely on resolving the immediate problem. Clients are expected to be active participants in generating solutions; the therapist works collaboratively with clients to examine situations in which the problem does *not* occur. In this way, they may generate new solutions.

Problem-solving meetings in the family-school venue may cast counselor or psychologist in the helper and facilitator role. Included in the role of the "client" are all of the stakeholders in the problem (e.g., teacher, parents, child, principal). All parties are brought together and, after introductions, the facilitator briefly describes the solution-oriented approach, making clear that discovering solutions (rather than blame-based causes) is the focus of the meeting. The initial task of the facilitator is to join with all participants by acknowledging each individual's point of view and the expertise each brings to the meeting (including parents as experts on the child). Participants are invited to describe their complaints as clearly as possible so that they can negotiate a solvable complaint. Various aspects of the problem are explored as the group searches for strengths, past solutions, and exceptions (i.e., times when the problem does not occur). Once the participants agree upon a solvable complaint, attention turns toward gaining consensus on an attainable goal and identifying multiple solutions for accomplishing it. They develop a mutual plan of action; clarify individual responsibilities; and determine how the plan will be monitored, followed up, and evaluated. Follow-up is critical to the success of any solutions, and it is the responsibility of the facilitator to take an active role in this area.

Initial evaluations of this approach suggest that parents found the meetings more successful than teachers. Carlson et al. (1992) speculated that more inservice training might have been needed to help teachers focus on child strengths and possible solutions rather than problems. Thus, the essential attitudes described earlier in the chapter may need to be imparted through direct means rather than simply modeled through the collaboration process.

School-Wide Interventions

Collaborative problem solving with parents is an important use of school professionals' knowledge of family functioning. However, this approach is clearly challenging to both school staff and family members. Strong family-school relationships, developed before problems arise, enhance the chance that families will participate in effective, collaborative problem solving (Epstein, 1996). Therefore, it is important that schools develop systematic efforts to make families feel that they are welcome in their children's schools and an important part of their children's education.

The evidence is strong that parental interest and involvement in their children's schooling results in better academic outcomes across SES and ethnic groups (e.g., Henderson, 1987). Further, schools can have a dramatic impact on the level of parent involvement depending on the activities they select (e.g., Dauber & Epstein, 1993). Schools have a basic obligation to inform parents about specific ways that their involvement can help their children succeed academically. School psychologists and counselors, through delivery of parent programs, can be at the forefront of delivering this information. Still, to reach the maximum number of families, expectations must be individualized according to each family's strengths and needs, and a variety of valued options for family participation in education must be available. Numerous programs have been developed, many of which utilize a systemic perspective.

A sample program

Weiss and Edwards (1992) provide a detailed description of the Family-School Collaboration Project at the Ackerman Institute. This project demonstrates the use of both family-school problem-solving meetings and more broadbased school-climate activities that are attentive to individual family preferences and styles of interaction. The project is based on the premise that a commitment to family-school partnerships will be enhanced when all parties come to view family-school collaboration as a key ingredient in their shared goal of children's academic success, rather than an additional burden unrelated to this goal. In this program, a small team of school stakeholders, including teachers, parents, administrators, and support staff (e.g., school psychologists, counselors), are trained in the required collaboration skills. The team then involves the rest of the school. One team member is designated as the family-school coordinator and takes primary responsibility for organizing relationship-building

activities. Counselors and psychologists are good candidates for this role.

Although each school should develop its own unique program based on the strengths and needs of staff and families, Weiss and Edwards (1992) outline a number of activities that demonstrate collaborative attitudes and processes. For example, some schools in the project replaced traditional parent-teacher conferences addressing student progress with family-teacher conferences. These conferences involve parent(s), teacher(s), and the student whose progress is the topic of the meeting. Each party makes preparations prior to the meeting as appropriate to the student's developmental level. Students may be asked to prepare by completing a sample report card or listing areas in which they are doing well and areas in which they need to improve. Parents and teachers might share in advance any questions or concerns that they wish to discuss. The products of these preparatory activities form the basis for the meeting. The desired outcome of the meeting is a plan for continued progress or improvement, as needed. As in the problem-solving meetings described earlier, the value of this approach is that it sets up an expectation that all concerned parties (teachers, parents, and students) are involved in the student's educational progress. Because the student is present, he or she does not have to rely on others' perceptions of the meeting. This direct communication decreases the likelihood of misunderstandings. Working together to develop a consensus on the nature of the problems and mutual participation in planning solutions increases the likelihood of each person's investment in following through with the plans.

A note about parent involvement

Parent involvement, as defined in the literature, appears to be a multidimensional construct; that is, it involves factors such as parent behavior toward the school, parent provision of cognitive activities for the child, and child perceptions of the parents' availability to the child (Grolnick & Slowiaczek, 1994). Traditionally practiced, it has often meant attempting to engage parents in activities that help the school achieve its goals, without concern for parents' understandings, wishes, or functioning styles. Parents' perceptions of their level of involvement and their view of appropriate interactions with school personnel may be quite disparate from the school staff's perceptions (Lareau, 1996). That is, parents may see themselves as more concerned and involved than school staff perceive them to be.

True collaboration occurs when families and school personnel work together to develop shared goals and find common ground on which to work toward those goals. In collaboration there is a sense of shared responsibility for children's development, tempered with a respect for individual family functioning. Parent involvement from a collaborative perspective involves empowering families and school staff to be active participants in the educational enterprise (see the chapter on the Meaning and Implications of Empowerment, this volume). Delgado-Gaitan (1991) provides an excellent example of how one school district's efforts to involve Spanish-speaking parents in nontraditional ways led to the parents independently developing their own organization and implementing their own agenda for school improvement.

What every school psychologist or counselor can do to encourage collaboration

Clearly, implementation of family-school collaboration programs requires a significant commitment by schools and families. It may take several years of concerted effort to institutionalize more collaborative approaches with families. School psychologists and counselors who already have skills in consultation may be better prepared than most school staff to implement a collaboration program. However, they might need additional training in family-systems assessment and collaborative problem solving. School counselors and psychologists also frequently find themselves overwhelmed with other responsibilities and may not have time for activities they are already prepared to implement.

There are steps that *all* school counselors and psychologists can take to improve their preparation for collaboration and increase the chances that they will be given the opportunity to implement a collaboration program. First, upgrade your own skills. Use continuing education requirements as a means to take courses, attend workshops, or invite speakers to provide training in collaborative problem solving. Second, model systemic thinking in your daily work. Avoid seeking simple causal explanations for problems and assigning blame for them. Encourage a focus on solutions. Third, educate your administrators, school board members, and parent-teacher-organization members about the value of parent involvement in children's education and the success of collaborative approaches. Fourth, start small. Create one project or activity that does not add significantly to your workload but helps others in your schools begin to think differently about families. For example, work with one teacher who is willing to develop new ways of communicating with families. Make one or more small changes in "business as usual" (e.g., send home more positive comments, find a volunteer to translate weekly messages into families' primary languages, or develop helpful hints for homework completion). Evaluate the outcome of the intervention and broadcast your successes to all who will listen. Such incremental progress may eventually lead to a demand by families and/or a commitment by administrators for a more comprehensive program. The systemic concept of wholeness predicts that even small changes in any member influence the rest of the system, sometimes in dramatic ways. School psychologists and counselors can be leaders in introducing such changes.

Summary

In this chapter we outlined several, basic family-systems constructs that can assist school psychologists and counselors in understanding families. These constructs may have greater intervention potential than the traditionally studied status variables (e.g., SES, ethnicity) because they inform school professionals more fully about particular families. Families characterized by a balance of connection and autonomy, stability with the capacity for change as needed, and clear organization are more likely to have children who function well within and outside the family. However, there is no single optimal organizational style, as individual characteristics of family members and the particular challenges faced by each family also influence child outcomes. Studies were reviewed that reveal the correlation between more balanced family functioning and child achievement; some specific family processes that appear to underlie effective family functioning were presented as well.

The organization of schools as systems also influences children's academic success. Whenever there is a better match between the ways in which a child's family functions and the ways in which the classroom functions, better academic achievement may result. School psychologists and counselors can apply their knowledge of family functioning by using it to build more collaborative relationships between families and schools. We reviewed a number of essential attitudes for a collaborative approach and presented several activities that can be used to assist families and schools in working more productively together. All school counselors and psychologists were challenged to find at least one small step that can be taken to develop stronger working relationships between families and schools.

Recommended Resources

Booth, A., & Dunn, J. F. (Eds.). (1996). *Family-school links. How do they affect educational outcomes?* Mahwah, NJ: Lawrence Erlbaum.
This book is based on papers and commentaries presented at a national symposium on family-school links held at the Pennsylvania State University in 1994. It will be of interest primarily to school psychologists concerned with the research related to parent involvement in education. However, many of the commentaries provide recommendations for interventions as well. A strength of this volume is the number of contrasting perspectives included.

Christenson, S. L., & Conoley, J. C. (Eds.). (1992). *Home-school collaboration: Academic and social competence.* Washington, DC: National Association of School Psychologists.
This volume is an essential resource for school psychologists who wish to promote collaborative processes in their schools. A

number of chapters present model collaboration programs; others provide examples of collaboration applied to specific groups or problems (e.g., preschool programs, homework completion, families experiencing divorce). The empirical basis supporting attempts at collaboration is also covered.

Fine, M. J., & Carlson, C. (Eds.). (1992). *The handbook of family-school intervention: A systems perspective.* Boston: Allyn-Bacon.

This book has 28 chapters devoted to understanding families and the ways their characteristics affect child outcomes. Sections are provided related to theory, ethnicity, exceptionality, specific family problems, and intervention models. School psychologists facing specific issues (e.g., giftedness, depression, multi ethnic settings) will find substantial guidance in ways to involve families for school-based solutions.

References

Amerikaner, M., & Omizo, M. (1984). Family interaction and learning disabilities. *Journal of Learning Disabilities, 17,* 540–543.

Barbarin, O. A. (1992). Family functioning and school adjustment: Family systems perspectives. In F. Medway & P. Cafferty (Eds.), *School psychology: A social psychological perspective* (pp. 131–163). Hillsdale, NJ: Lawrence Erlbaum.

Beavers, W. (1981). A systems model of family for family therapists. *Journal of Marriage and Family Therapy, 7,* 299–307.

Bertalanffy, L. C. (1969). *General system theory: Essays in its foundations and development.* New York: Braziller.

Bronfenbrenner, U. (1986). Ecology of the family as a context for human development: Research perspectives. *Developmental Psychology, 22,* 723–742.

Carlson, C., Hickman, J., & Horton, C. (1992). From blame to solutions: Solution-oriented family school consultation. In S. L. Christenson & J. C. Conoley (Eds.), *Home-school collaboration: Enhancing children's academic and social competence* (pp. 193–214). Washington, DC: National Association of School Psychologists.

Christenson, S. L., & Cleary, M. (1990). Consultation and the parent-educator partnership: A perspective. *Journal of Educational and Psychological Consultation, 1,* 219–241.

Christenson, S. L., Rounds, T., & Franklin, M. J. (1992). Home-school collaboration: Effects, issues, and opportunities. In S. L. Christenson & J. C. Conoley (Eds.), *Home-school collaboration: Enhancing children's academic and social competence* (pp. 193–214). Washington, DC: National Association of School Psychologists.

Christenson, S. L., Rounds, T. & Gorney, D. (1992). Family factors and student achievement: An avenue to increase students success. *School Psychology Quarterly, 7,* 178–206.

Colbert, R. D. (1991). Untapped resource: African American parental perceptions. *Elementary School Guidance and Counseling, 26,* 96–105.

Conoley, J. C. (1987). Schools and families: Theoretical and practical bridges. *Professional School Psychology, 2,* 191–203.

Daley, J. G., Sowers-Hoag, K. M., & Thyer, B. A. (1991). Construct validity of the Circumplex Model of family functioning. *Journal of Social Service Research, 15,* 131–147.

Dauber, S. L., & Epstein, J. L. (1993). Parents' attitudes and practices of involvement in inner-city elementary and middle schools. In N. F. Chavkin (Ed.), *Families and schools in a pluralistic society* (pp. 53–71). New York: State University of New York Press.

Delgado-Gaitan, C. (1991). Improving parents in the schools: A process of empowerment. *American Journal of Education, 100*(1), 20–46.

de Shazer, S. (1985). *Keys to solution in brief therapy.* New York: W. W. Norton.

Doherty, W. J., & Peskay, V. E. (1992). Family systems and the school. In S. L. Christenson & J. C. Conoley (Eds.), *Home-school collaboration: Enhancing children's academic and social competence* (pp. 1–18). Washington, DC: National Association of School Psychologists.

Dornbusch, S. M., & Wood, K. D. (1989). Family processes and educational achievement. In W. J. Weston (Ed.), *Education and the American family: A research synthesis* (pp. 66–95). New York: New York University Press.

Dunst, C. J., & Trivette, C. M. (1987). Enabling and empowering families: Conceptual and intervention issues. *School Psychology Review, 16,* 443–456.

Epstein, J. L. (1996). Perspectives and previews on research and policy for school, family, and community partnerships. In A. Booth & J. F. Dunn (Eds.), *Family-school links: How do they affect educational outcomes?* (pp. 209–246). Mahwah, NJ: Lawrence Erlbaum.

Erickson, M. F., & Pianta, R. C. (1989). New lunch box, old feelings: What kids bring to school. *Early Education and Development, 1*(1), 35–48.

Estrada, P., Arsenio, W. F., Hess, R. D., & Holloway, S. D. (1987). Affective quality of the mother-child relationship: Longitudinal consequences for children's school relevant functioning. *Developmental Psychology, 23,* 210–215.

Feldman, S. S., & Weinberger, D. A. (1994). Self-restraint as a mediator of family influences on boys' delinquent behavior: A longitudinal study. *Child Development, 65,* 195–211.

Fine, M. J. (1992). A systems-ecological perspective on home-school intervention. In M. J. Fine & C. Carlson (Eds.), *The handbook of family-school intervention: A systems perspective* (pp. 1–17). Boston: Allyn and Bacon.

Fraser, B. J., & Walberg, H. J. (Eds.). (1991). *Educational environments: Evaluation, antecedents, and consequences.* Oxford, England: Pergamon.

Gaughan, L. D. (1982). Structural theory of family mediation. In L. D. Messinger (Ed.), *Therapy with remarriage families* (pp. 93–103). Rockville, MD: Aspens Systems Corporation.

Grolnick, W. S., & Slowiaczek, M. L. (1994). Parents' involvement in children's schooling: A multidimensional conceptualization and motivational model. *Child Development 63,* 237–252.

Hansen, D. A. (1986). Family-school articulations: The effects of interaction rule mismatch. *American Educational Research Journal, 88,* 313–334.

Henderson, A. (1987). *The evidence continues to grow: Parent involvement improves student achievement.* Columbia,

MD: National Committee for Citizens in Education.

Hetherington, E. M., & Arasteh, J. D. (Eds.). (1988). *Impact of divorce, single parenting, and stepparenting on children.* Hillsdale, NJ: Lawrence Erlbaum.

Humphries, T. W., & Bauman, E. (1980). Maternal child rearing attitudes associated with learning disabilities. *Journal of Learning Disabilities, 13*(8), 54–57.

Lareau, A. (1987). Social class differences in family-school relationships: The importance of cultural capital. *Sociology of Education, 60,* 73–85.

Lareau, A. (1996). Assessing parent involvement in schooling: A critical analysis. In A. Booth & J. F. Dunn (Eds.), *Family-school links: How do they affect educational outcomes?* (pp. 57–64). Mahwah, NJ: Lawrence Erlbaum.

Masselam, V. S., Marcus, R. F., & Stunkard, C. L. (1990). Parent-adolescent communication, family functioning, and school performance. *Family Therapy, 62,* 177–179.

McFarlane, A. H., Bellissimo, A., & Norman, G. R. (1985). Family structure, family functioning, and adolescent well-being: The transcedent influence of parental style. *Journal of Child Psychology and Psychiatry, 36,* 847–864.

Menaghan, E. G. (1996). Family composition, family interaction, and children's academic and behavior problems: Interpreting the data. In A. Booth & J. F. Dunn (Eds.), *Family-school links: How do they affect educational outcomes?* (pp. 185–196). Mahwah, NJ: Lawrence Erlbaum.

Minuchin, S. (1974). *Families and family therapy.* Cambridge, MA: Harvard University Press.

O'Callaghan, J. B. (1993). *School-based collaboration with families: Constructing family-school-agency partnerships that work.* San Francisco: Jossey-Bass.

O'Hanlon, W. H., & Weiner-Davis, M. (1989). *In search of solutions: A new direction psychotherapy.* New York: W. W Norton & Company.

Olson, D. H., McCubbin, H. I., Barnes, H. L., Larsen A. S., Muxen, M. J., & Wilson, M. A. (1983). *Families: what makes them work.* Beverly Hills, CA: Sage.

Olson, D. H., Portner, J., & Lavee, Y. (1985). *FACES III.* St. Paul, MN: Department of Family Social Science.

Rosenblatt, P. C. (1994). *Metaphors of family systems theory.* New York: Guilford.

Shagle, S. C., & Barber, B. K. (1995). A social-ecological analysis of adolescent suicidal ideation. *American Journal of Orthopsychiatry, 65*(1), 114–124.

Veerman, J. W. (1995). Family stress, family functioning, and emotional/behavioural problems following child psychiatric treatment. *European Child and Adolescent Psychiatry, 4*(1), 21–31.

Vickers, H. S. (1994). Differences in family system functioning of young children at risk for academic failure. *Journal of Educational Research, 87,* 262–270.

Watzlawick, P., Beavin, J., & Jackson, D. (1967). *Pragmatics of human communication.* New York: Gardner Press.

Weiss, H. M., & Edwards, M. E. (1992). The family school collaboration project: Systemic interventions for school improvement. In S. L. Christenson & J. C. Conoley (Eds.), *Home-school collaboration: Enhancing children's academic and social competence* (pp. 215–244). Washington, DC: National Association of School Psychologists.

White, K. R. (1982). The relation between socioeconomic status and academic achievement. *Psychological Bulletin, 91,* 461–481.

49

Parenting Styles

Patricia B. Keith

Alfred University

Sandra L. Christensen

University of Minnesota, Minneapolis

Background

Once people become parents their lives are never the same. Parenting can provide fulfilling and rewarding moments, while at other times it can be challenging and humbling. So much in the ecology and social network that surrounds the family affects the relationship between parent and child. The parents' life experiences, values, and expectations for the child, as well as the temperaments and cognitive abilities of both parent and child, influence this critical relationship. Religious doctrine, cultural traditions, family values, social movements, divorce rates, and research all have a real impact on the way parents view their roles. In an era when the media continues to be the message, it will come as no surprise to school psychologists that television programming may sway parents' ways of dealing with their children. From the early family situation programs, such as *Ozzie and Harriet* and *Father Knows Best,* to the *Brady Bunch* and *Bill Cosby,* to *Roseanne* and *Me and the Boys,* art has imitated life and vice versa.

The importance of parenting styles lies in the fact that the parent-child relationship has a critical impact on the growth and development of the child and the adolescent. Although school psychologists cannot control the decisions parents make about their parenting styles, research can be synthesized and presented to parents. In addition, teachers, schools, and the community benefit from information about parenting practices, because it helps them understand the socialization of the child and adolescent in the context of the family. By providing this information and assistance, school psychologists can work to promote positive child outcomes through collaborative efforts between home and the school (Christensen, 1995) and can function as a distributor of research results (Keith, 1995).

What Is "Parenting Style"?

Parenting style is "a constellation of attitudes toward the child that are communicated to the child and that, taken together, create an emotional climate in which the parents' behaviors are expressed" (Darling & Steinberg, 1993, p. 493). Parenting styles are believed to be independent of a specific socialization context and evident across a wide range of parent-child interactions. They convey the parents' attitude toward the child rather than the parents' attitude toward the specific behavior of the child. These attitudes include parenting practices such as helping an adolescent choose high school courses and aspects of parent-child interaction that communicate an emotional attitude, such as tone of voice, body language, bursts of temper, or inattention.

An important differentiation between parenting styles and *parenting practices* is offered by Darling and Steinberg (1993). Although both parenting styles and practices are believed to result from goals and values held by parents, each influences outcomes for the child through different processes. Parenting practices are conceptualized as having a direct effect on the development of specific child behaviors (from toilet training to academic performance) and child characteristics (e.g., self-confidence). Parenting practices are the "mechanisms through which parents directly help their children attain their socialization goals" (Darling & Steinberg, p. 493). Parenting styles, in contrast, are conceptualized as having an indirect influence on child development; they moderate the relation between parenting practices and child outcomes. "Parenting style alters the parents' capacity to socialize their children by changing the effectiveness of their parenting practices" (Darling & Steinberg, p. 493). In essence, parenting styles may enhance or inhibit the effectiveness of a specific parenting practice.

Development of the Construct

The theories of human growth and development proposed by Erik Erikson, Sigmund Freud, Abraham Maslow, and other psychologists influenced the development of this construct. At the turn of the century, the psychoanalytic theory of psychosexual development suggested that parents should meet infants' sucking, excretory, and genital needs. If the child's needs were met at each psychosexual stage, then the child would grow up into a secure and healthy adult. These ideas were often used as the basis for "guidelines" about breast feeding, toileting, discipline, and other parenting practices. This theoretical framework influenced the work of Benjamin Spock (1946), who originally advocated unlimited acceptance of a child's need for gratification and recommended lenient or permissive disciplinary practices. Later, Spock and Rothenberg (1985) wrote about the need for parents to establish controls, ideals, and standards for their children.

By the early 1970s, the popularity of the construct of parenting styles was increasing and psychologists were taking a closer look at Diane Baumrind's research (1968). She defined three kinds of parenting styles: authoritative, permissive, and authoritarian. Each parenting style was based on different parent-child interaction patterns, values, and expectations for the child. Authoritative parents are guided by a desire to balance pleasure with duty and freedom with responsibility, who encourage children to reason and communicate in an issue-oriented manner, and who establish standards for children's behavior. Permissive parents are guided by a desire to let children regulate their own activities; these parents encourage children to define their own standards and rules and generally do not enforce adult rules or standards. And, finally, authoritarian parents are guided by a set of standards developed by a higher authority, encourage children to preserve the social order and traditional structure, and generally are not open to discussions regarding standards of behavior.

More recently, the construct of parenting styles has been expanded with the work of Maccoby and Martin (1983). Although their parenting-style model builds on Baumrind's work, it describes four kinds of parenting styles and measures them along two scales (demandingness and responsiveness of the parent and the child). Parents are believed to have one of the following parenting styles:

- Authoritative-reciprocal—high demandingness and high responsiveness.
- Authoritarian-autocratic—high demandingness and low responsiveness.
- Indulgent-permissive: low demandingness and high responsiveness.
- Indifferent-uninvolved—low demandingness and low responsiveness. Indifferent-uninvolved parents may

not be committed to parenting and the day-to-day activities children need (support, encouragement, discipline, etc.).

In summary, these theoretical frameworks suggest that parenting practices can be categorized, that parenting practices are directional or bidirectional in nature (i.e., parents' actions influence child development), and that parenting styles influence the children's personality and academic achievement.

Development

Because research literature uses various labels to define developmental stages of children and the role that parents have in this process, our review will be guided by the developmental stages found in the *Handbook of Parenting* (Bornstein, 1995a) and a three-phase developmental process of parental regulation (Maccoby, 1984).

Child development can be organized into four stages: infancy, toddler, middle childhood, and adolescence. As the child develops and goes through various stages, parents may need to change their regulation practices with the child. The regulation roles that parents have are parental-regulation, co-regulation, and finally self-regulation. Each role can be found at any stage of development, but parent-regulation generally is found in the infancy and toddler stages, co-regulation starts in the middle childhood stage and continues into the adolescent stage, and self-regulation begins in adolescence. If the child meets the parent's expectations for a developmental stage, then the parent may become more inclined to decrease future regulation of the child's behavior.

During infancy, parents must provide their child with basic needs (food, clothing, shelter, security, etc.). Because the child is dependent on the parent, parent-regulation is found at this stage of development. Parenting styles during infancy are influenced by maternal mood and verbal interactions with the child during feeding (Vibbert & Bornstein, 1989). Additionally, parents' beliefs about parenting (Goodnow & Collins, 1990), along with their feelings about their own lives and relationships, influence their parenting style. Other factors such as the amount of engagement time, temperament, and genetic makeup of the child affect parenting styles and practices (Plomin & DeFries, 1985). Parenting practices during this stage provide a model for the child's language and emotional attachment and often serve as a basis for the child's understanding of the environment. When parents are happy to be parents, secure in their relationships, and have the needed resources to parent (time, support systems, finances, sleep, etc.), positive outcomes for the child can be expected.

As the child becomes a toddler, parenting practices are influenced by the child's increased mobility, language, reasoning and cognitive development, gender identity, toileting habits, and emotional and social attachments. Children's self-recognition, desire to do what they want (Lewis, Sullivan, Stranger, & Weiss, 1989), and testing of limits (Caplan & Caplan, 1977) may require the parent to use different parenting practices. The demandingness and responsiveness of the child to the parent influences the parent-child relationship significantly at this time (Dubin & Dubin, 1963). During this stage of development, parents need to understand children's demandingness and help them develop impulse- and self-control. At the same time parents must assist children in learning how to become members of the family and peer group.

During middle childhood, children become more self-regulatory, autonomous, and independent; parent-school partnerships begin; and the peer group becomes more important. These developmental changes require parents to become more child-directed and base their parenting practices on the child's personality, temperament, and cognitive skills. Generally, parenting practices during middle childhood become more co-regulatory in orientation, because the child spends more time away from the home and has more responsibilities. Yet, children continue to need emotional support, parental monitoring, and, when necessary, parental discipline (Dekovic & Janssens, 1992). During this stage of development, parents tend to establish expectations for the child in the family, school, and community (Vuchinich, Bank, & Patterson, 1992). Parenting styles and practices that are child-specific, follow core family values, and are consistent over time should produce positive child outcomes (Collins, 1990).

The adolescent developmental stage is characterized as a period of rapid changes (Paikoff, Brooks-Gunn, & Carlton-Ford, 1991). Some of these rapid changes can be influenced by adolescents' physical and emotional development, stability of family and peer relationships, growing awareness of life outside the family and school, and their ability to meet the ecological and social demands around them. Additionally, during this stage most adolescents expect to become more, if not totally, self-regulatory (Holmbeck & Hill, 1991). If parents want to maintain the status quo of their parenting practices, conflicts will most likely occur (Hauser, Powers, & Noam, 1991). Much has been written about conflict during this developmental stage. Arguments happen between adolescents and parents about once every three days (Montemayor, 1983) and are part of every close relationship (Kelley et al., 1983). Yet, typically, arguments do not undermine the parent-adolescent relations (Collins, 1990) and can help the adolescent learn conflict-resolution skills (Holmbeck & Hill, 1991). When parenting practices and adolescent self-regulation needs are similar, better outcomes for children and parents will result (Collins, 1990).

Parenting-Styles Research

Parenting-styles research typically uses nonexperimental research designs; data are collected from parents, teachers, or children using behavioral observations forms, self-reports, school records, and questionnaires. Generally, investigators measure parenting styles—authoritarian, permissive, or authoritative and demandingness and responsiveness—or parenting practices—support, interactions, discipline. The styles are then used to find correlates or predictors of academic achievement, peer relationships, or personality characteristics. The majority of available research is said to be embedded in European-American cultural traditions that tend to stress independence, individualism, individual choice, self-expression, and uniqueness (Chao, 1994).

Seminal articles on parenting-styles research report the more "optimal" parenting style to be authoritative. This style is distinguished from the authoritarian style by a democratic type of firm control, autonomous self-will, and warmth (Baumrind, 1968, 1971). Authoritative parenting styles were found to be related to positive peer relations, academic achievement, and independence among children. The authoritarian and permissive parenting styles were found to be less positively related to the same variables. Later research with high school students found similar results for some students, but differences were found between Asian-American and White students (Dornbusch, Ritter, Leiderman, Roberts, & Fraleigh, 1987). Asian students rated their parents higher on the authoritarian parenting scale and lower on the authoritative parenting scale and yet they had the highest grade-point averages. Steinberg, Dornbusch, and Brown (1992) found similar results and suggested that parental influences were good predictors of school success among White and Hispanic students, whereas peer influences were more effective as predictors for Asian students. Still, one should not conclude that parental influences are not important for school success for all students. Perhaps parental concern, involvement, and parenting practices can be more organized and direct in nature, in some families, to foster family harmony (Lau & Cheung, 1987) or help other families survive difficult living situations (Baumrind, 1991) without negative effects on academic achievement or peer relationships.

Other research suggests verbal aggressiveness and argumentativeness may be related to authoritarian or non-child-centered parenting practices (Bayer & Cegala, 1992; Grusec & Goodnow, 1994). Harsh or inconsistent parental discipline practices can be associated with conduct problems (Frick, 1993) or conduct disorders (Short & Shapiro, 1993) and negatively influence children's home and school outcomes (Pettit, Bates, & Dodge, 1993).

Directions for Future Research

Parenting styles is a construct that needs to be further researched. Much is still not understood about the process of parenting and the role parenting styles and parenting practices have on children's outcomes. Future research should be developmental in perspective, longitudinal in nature, multivariate in orientation, interactional in direction, and should focus on ecological and social networks. Because parenting is a lifelong experience, it is critical that school psychologists understand how parenting practices evolve from a parent-regulation to a self-regulation state as the child and the parent go through various developmental stages. Longitudinal research will help to examine how the process of parenting does or does not change over time and how the quantity and quality of the relationship at various stages influence outcomes. Without using a multivariate approach that controls for critical variables, the generalizability and validity of the research results may be limited. Because parenting practices can be measured on a demandingness and responsiveness scale, research should be interactional to detect different parenting styles and their influence on outcomes for children and adolescents. Without considering the ecology and social networks that surround this relationship, research results may be difficult to translate into practice.

Problems and Implications

Children, adolescents, and parents experience challenges daily. Although the media constantly presents tragic parenting events (e.g., neglect, abuse), most parents, regardless of their ideology about parenting styles and practices, desire positive outcomes for their children. Parents want their children to be happy, healthy, safe, and successful in school and community. Additionally, parents want their children to be socially and academically competent or what Baumrind (1973) refers to as instrumentally competent.

No longer are parenting styles or practices thought to be the sole reason children and adolescent have problems. Rarely do single experiences or events determine personality characteristics; however, inconsistencies in parenting practices over time can influence development (Bornstein, 1995b). Parenting problems can have many origins and are rarely simple in nature. For example, problems can arise when parents are not sensitive to their children's maturational level or developmental needs. These problems can be compounded when parents themselves may not be sensitive to their own evolving physical and emotional needs, and situational demands (job, relationship, financial status, etc.). Differences between parents and children's temperaments (e.g., explosive vs implosive, communicative vs. noncommunicative, impulsive vs. slow to respond) may also complicate parenting practices.

School psychologists are in a unique position to share information with parents and educators, while pro-

moting positive child outcomes through collaborative relationships between home and schools. Using a comprehensive review of parenting-styles literature, some cautions, considerations, and guidelines for practice are summarized next.

Caution should be applied to rigidly describing (or diagnosing) parents as authoritarian, authoritative, or permissive because a single category may not accurately represent the styles of both parents in a family (Fischer & Crawford, 1992; Noller & Callan, 1988) or one parent may not represent a "pure" style under all situations (Grusec & Goodnow, 1994). Furthermore, little is known about the stability of parenting styles over time and about the antecedents of parenting styles (Darling & Steinberg, 1993). It is necessary to discern the general emotional climate or style established by parents in relation to their roles, expectations, and interactions with their children, while recognizing that a particular instance could be an "exception to the rule."

Parenting style is a helpful construct if viewed as a context within which to socialize children and youth. Although parents may not be one "pure" type, it may be helpful to examine the similarity between authoritarian and permissive styles. According to Lamb, Ketterlinus, and Fracasse (1992), authoritarian and permissive parents are similar because neither provide children and youth with opportunities to be effective participants in their own socialization. For example, authoritarian parents require children to adhere and conform to their expectations, rules, and restrictions, whereas permissive parents place few, if any, constraints on children's behavior. In both cases, children receive little opportunity to experience rational, issue-oriented, cooperative interactions and little opportunity to develop responsibility. Conversely, authoritative parents teach their children that "social competence emerges within a context of interpersonal give and take" (p. 488). Thus, the authoritative parenting style provides opportunities for children to develop responsibility and to learn important skills like problem solving, negotiation, and decision making.

Parenting styles offer implications for the effectiveness of discipline. Baumrind (1971, 1991) has shown that authoritative parents discipline children and youth and that socially competent children are disciplined. Thus, punishment is an effective means of controlling children's behavior when specific conditions are applied. Punishment is effective when it occurs shortly after the transgression, is consistently applied, and is paired with examples of behaviors deemed more appropriate (e.g., Aronfreed, 1968). Furthermore, parent use of reasoning or induction, sometimes accompanied with power assertion, has been shown to be a more successful disciplinary approach than exclusive use of power assertion (Hoffman, 1994). Grusec and Goodnow (1994) suggest that Baumrind's emphasis and terminology for parenting styles are congruent with Hoffman's position. Both present a consistent picture of child-rearing effects, "namely, that parents who tend to be harshly and arbitrarily authoritarian or power assertive in their parenting practices are less likely to be successful than those who place substantial emphasis on induction or reasoning, presumably in an attempt to be responsive to and understanding of their child's point of view" (Grusec & Goodnow, 1994, p. 6). By the same token, Lamb et al. (1992) cite Baumrind's work (1973) and state "parental warmth is not beneficial in the absence of firm control" (p. 490).

It is important to note the remarkable similarity of the underlying dimensions of parenting styles proposed by different researchers over two decades. Specifically, two dimensions of parental practices integral to healthy, positive child outcomes have emerged from this literature: demandingness (expectations, monitoring, supervisory control) and support (responsiveness, warmth). Examples of demandingness include establishing clear, rational guidelines for behavior; communicating expectations and the rationale for them; and supervising, monitoring, and confronting child behavior. Examples of support include encouragement, support for child-initiated efforts, open communication between parents and children, and recognition of rights of both parents and children. It appears that both dimensions are essential for optimal child outcomes. Collins, Harris, and Susman (1995) state, "Current models of socialization imply that the most effective parental response to changes in children's behavior is a combination of child-centered flexibility and adherence to core values and expectations for approved behavior" (p. 82). They speculate that the parents' capacity for age-appropriate adaptation is inherent in the characteristics of effective parenting practices at every age.

Adaptation must also occur in relation to specific goals and situations (Dix, 1991). Grusec and Goodnow (1994) speculate that variations in methods of discipline or parenting practices yield an advantage for child outcomes. The importance of these variations lies "in the possibility that the methods per se may be less important than the flexibility of their use" (p. 7). For school psychologists working with parents, it is necessary to understand parents' goals for the child and to recognize that responses to a disciplinary situation will be influenced by the nature of the misdeed and the nature of the parental reaction as well as child characteristics (e.g., temperament, age) and parent characteristics (e.g., responsiveness to child's wishes). Thus, differences in parenting practices are not inherently bad. However, flexibility in use of methods must be differentiated from inconsistent application of punishment, which has been shown to lead to negative outcomes for students (Hetherington, Stouwie, & Ridberg, 1971).

School psychologists are encouraged to consider the two dimensions of parenting styles for at least two reasons. Extensively replicated findings indicate that a parenting style marked by authoritativeness toward children, coupled with child-centered attitudes and concerns, is related to positive outcomes for students in middle childhood (e.g., peer acceptance, school success) and is predictive of successful adaptation in later life (Collins et al., 1995). As a corollary, parenting behaviors, attitudes, and practices dominated by parental concerns rather than child needs, which characterizes both the authoritarian and permissive styles, are correlated with less positive child outcomes on these same variables. Additionally, the dimensions have relevance to families of differing structures and cultural backgrounds. Research has shown that an authoritative parenting style facilitates the socialization of children in middle-class, American, two-parent families (Lamb et al., 1992) and that parenting styles vary markedly among ethnic groups in contemporary America (Steinberg et al., 1992). It is also known that some form of demandingness and parental responsibility influence child outcomes regardless of ethnicity (Grusec & Goodnow, 1994).

Parenting styles and practices must be understood in reference to the realities faced by families. For example, socialization methods that appear authoritarian or punitive by middle-class, White standards may have utility in preparing African-American adolescents to cope with the hazards of contemporary urban life (Baumrind, 1991). Other situations have been found to moderate parenting practices, such as parental work demands (McLoyd, Jayaratne, Ceballo, & Borquez, 1994) and single parenting (Health & MacKinnon, 1988). With respect to parenting practices in single-parent homes, Health and MacKinnon found that single mothers used lax control more often with their sons than with their daughters. Similarly, Dornbusch et al. (1985) found that adolescents in single-parent families were more likely to make decisions without direct parental input.

Finally, the bidirectional nature of the parent-child relationship is a factor. Some children and adolescents are more difficult to parent. With some children it is more difficult to negotiate specific behaviors (i.e., demandingness) or to support their interests and individuality (i.e., responsiveness). For example, the relationship of authoritative parenting style and school outcomes has been shown to be mediated by adolescent psychosocial maturity (Steinberg, Elmen, & Mounts, 1989). These examples support the contention of Darling and Steinberg (1993) that parenting style is best understood as a context that facilitates or undermines parents' efforts to socialize their children by using specific parenting practices. They contend that the effectiveness of any practice will vary as a function of this context. The role for school psychologists in supporting families through parent consultation and educationally oriented parent-support groups is evident.

Miller, Cowan, Cowan, Hetherington, and Clingempeel (1993) have shown that parents' individual and marital adjustment has a strong connection with the quality of their parenting styles. Thus, these authors conclude that interventions for families with aggressive, antisocial children must also help parents improve their personal adjustment or quality of their marriage.

Findings from parenting-styles literature require that school psychologist think comprehensively about interventions involving families. For example, family environments characterized by conflict, lack of cohesion, or over- or under-control may best be viewed by school psychologists as signs of disturbing contexts for socialization of children. By changing the context for socialization of the child, family interventions may "ultimately benefit both parent-child relationships and the child's development" (Miller et al., 1993, p. 13). Finally, it is essential to differentiate highly verbal family dialogue and argumentativeness from aggression and inadequate family problem solving. Parents characterized by authoritativeness engage in much verbal dialogue and debate with their children (Bayer & Cegala, 1992).

Alternative Actions

One of the school psychologist's goals should be to enhance the contexts for socialization for children and youth. Translating theory and research findings from the parenting-styles literature into practice suggests that school psychologists should concentrate on the broad dimensions of demandingness and support. Optimal child outcomes result when children and youth receive both assertive control and support. Although the balance of these factors may change with developmental stage, both assertive control and support are important regardless of the child's age. It should also be remembered that parents may articulate or demonstrate their commitment to control and support in multiple ways. The parenting styles literature suggests (a) working with parents to determine their goals for socializing their children and the practices they desire to use to achieve their goals and (b) working to bring consistency of influence for children's outcomes by promoting collaborative efforts between home and school (Christensen, 1995). To this end, we suggest that school psychologists consider the following activities:

1. Provide information about child and adolescent development in multiple formats (print and nonprint) to parents on a regular basis. School psychologists need to share with parents knowledge about the predictors of positive and negative outcomes for children. The routine sharing of this information is an example of primary prevention that may assist schools in creating a collaborative approach for working with parents to achieve positive outcomes for students. Another benefit of disseminating this information is that in a nonthreatening way it enhances the probability of increas-

ing parents' sensitivity to children's maturational and developmental levels.

2. Provide information about the needs of children and youth: the need for monitoring and supervision, the need for rules, the need for learning from consequences of personal decisions, the need for time together, and the need for ongoing relationships with parents.

3. Provide parents with specific examples of ways to improve assertive control and support for children and youth. An example would be information on positive parenting discipline strategies or alternatives to physical punishment.

4. Provide consultation to parents to assist them in establishing personal goals for their children and specific practices to achieve the goals, and support parents as they implement new strategies and develop new behaviors. School psychologists could be actively involved in establishing parent groups based on parent-identified needs for promoting positive outcomes for students.

5. Provide referrals and serve as a liaison for families living in difficult circumstances, which can negatively influence the parent-child relationships and child or adolescent development. (Baumrind, 1968, 1971)

Summary

Parenting styles is a helpful construct because it assists school psychologists in understanding children's needs, parent-child relationships, and parenting practices. School psychologists cannot control the decisions made by parents with respect to the specific parenting practices they use or the overall emotional climate (support and warmth) in the home. Yet, school psychologists can learn about parents' fulfilling, rewarding, challenging, and humbling moments with their children and help them identify areas that they would like to work on in their parent-child relationships. Additionally, this construct provides information to assist school psychologists in developing home- and school-based interventions, guiding consultation practices, forming parent-education and parent-support groups, and assisting parents and teachers to work toward positive outcomes for children. When school psychologists "give psychology away," they contribute to the building of better contexts for socialization of children in homes and schools while positively influencing outcomes for children and youth.

Recommended Resources

Baumrind, D. (1991). Effective parenting during the early adolescent transition. In P. A. Cowan & M. Hetherington

(Eds.), *Family transitions* (pp. 111–161). Hillsdale, NJ: Lawrence Erlbaum Associates.

In this chapter, Baumrind provides a historical perspective for the construct of parenting styles and describes a conceptual framework for predicting the impact of various facets of parental demandingness and responsiveness on adolescents. The chapter reports the results of research and contrasts the classic and contemporary view of effective parenting.

Baumrind, D. (1991). The influence of parenting style on adolescent competence and substance use. *Journal of Early Adolescence, 11*(1), 56–95.

In this article, Baumrind describes findings from the longitudinal program of research on the Family Socialization and Developmental Competence Project that has yielded varied categorizations of parenting styles. The benefits and limitations of the parenting-styles construct and adolescent competence are comprehensively described. For example, Baumrind explains that an authoritative upbringing, although sufficient, is not a necessary condition to produce competent children.

Bornstein, M. H. (Ed.). (1995). *Handbook of parenting*. Hillsdale, NJ: Lawrence Erlbaum Associates.

More than 60 chapters divided into four volumes describe different types of parents, basic considerations of parenting, forces that shape parenting, and practical aspects of parenting. Recent research and conceptualizing of issues in the parenting field are covered for each type.

Darling, N. & Steinberg, L. (1993). Parenting style as context: An integrative model. *Psychological Bulletin, 113*(3), 487–496.

In this article, parenting style is conceptualized as a context for child socialization that moderates the effect of specific parenting practices on child and adolescent outcomes. Directions for future socialization are clearly articulated.

Dinkmeyer, D. Sr. and McKay, G. D. STEP: Systematic Training for Effective Parenting. American Guidance Association, Circle Pines, MN. (1-800-328-2560).

Using audiocassettes or videocassettes, leader's manual, participants handbook and parent survey, this kit assists parents with understanding behavior and misbehavior, disciplining with natural and logical consequences, developing communication skills, leading family meetings, and communicating more effectively with children. Cassettes are appropriate for non-reading parents or busy parents who spend time commuting to work. If this training program does not cover areas of interest there are a number of other kits worth checking out (STEP/teen: Systematic Training for Effective Parenting of Teens; Early Childhood STEP; the Next STEP; STEP and STEP/teen Biblically; PECES: Padres Eficaces Con Entrenamiento Sistematico; Strengthening Stepfamilies; and TIME: Training in Marriage Enrichment).

Parent to Parent Parenting for Safe and Drug Free Youth. Prepared by PRIDE Parent Training Center, Marietta, Georgia, 30068 (1-800-487-7743).

Although the primary purpose of Parent to Parent is to help parents become informed and confident in dealing with rising drug use in their communities, this organization's videos and other materials can be very useful to school psychologists. This

program works to empower parents with an understanding of their legal, moral, and ethical responsibilities for their children's well-being. Parents learn how to communicate, make rules, and set standards for their children; parenting skills are presented in basic and realistic terms that parents can use.

References

Aronfreed, J. (1968). *Conduct and conscience.* New York: Academic Press.

Baumrind, D. (1968). Authoritarian vs. authoritative parental control. *Adolescence, 3,* 255–272.

Baumrind, D. (1971). Current patterns of parental authority. *Developmental Psychology Monograph, 4,* (1, pt. 2).

Baumrind, D. (1973). The development of instrumental competence through socialization. In A. D. Pick (Ed.), *Minnesota Symposia on Child Psychology* (Vol. 7, pp. 3–46). Minneapolis: University of Minnesota Press.

Baumrind, D. (1991). The influence of parenting style on adolescent competence and substance use. *Journal of Early Adolescence, 11,* 56–95.

Bayer, C. L., & Cegala, D. J. (1992). Trait verbal aggressiveness and argumentativeness: Relations with parenting style. *Western Journal of Communication, 56,* 301–310.

Bornstein, M. H. (Ed.). (1995a). *Handbook of parenting.* Hillsdale, NJ: Lawrence Erlbaum Associates.

Bornstein, M. H. (1995b). Parenting infants. In M. H. Bornstein (Ed.), *Handbook of parenting: Vol. 1. Children and parenting* (pp. 3–30). Hillsdale, NJ: Lawrence Erlbaum Associates.

Caplan, F., & Caplan, T. (1977). *The second twelve months of life: A kaleidoscope of growth.* New York: Grossett & Dunlap.

Chao, R. K. (1994). Beyond parental control and authoritarian parenting style: Understanding Chinese parenting through the cultural notion of training. *Child Development, 65,* 1111–1119.

Christensen, S. L. (1995). Supporting home-school collaboration. In A. Thomas & J. Grimes (Eds.), *Best practices in school psychology-III* (pp. 253–268). Washington, DC: National Association of School Psychologists.

Collins, W. A. (1990). Parent-child relationships in the transition to adolescence: Continuity and change in interaction, affect, and cognition. In R. Montemayor, G. Adams, & T. Gullotta (Eds.), *Advances in adolescent development: From childhood to adolescence: A transitional period?* (Vol. 2, pp. 85–106). Beverly Hills, CA: Sage.

Collins, W. A., Harris, M. L., & Susman, A. (1995). Parenting during middle childhood. In M. H. Bornstein (Ed.), *Handbook of parenting: Vol. 1, Children and parenting* (pp. 65–86). Hillsdale, NJ: Lawrence Erlbaum Associates.

Darling, N., & Steinberg, L. (1993). Parenting style as context: An integrative model. *Psychological Bulletin, 113,* 487–496.

Dekovic, M., & Janssens, J. M. A. M. (1992). Parents' child-rearing style and child's sociometric status. *Developmental Psychology, 28*(5), 925–932.

Dix, T. (1991). The affective organization of parenting:

Adaptive and maladaptive processes. *Psychological Bulletin, 110,* 3–25.

Dornbusch, S. M., Carlsmith, J. M., Bushwall, S. J., Ritter, P. L., Leiderman, R. H., Hastorf, A. H., & Gross, T. T. (1985). Single parents, extended households, and the control of adolescents. *Child Development, 56,* 326–341.

Dornbusch, S. M., Ritter, P. L., Leiderman, P. H., Roberts, D. F. and Fraleigh, M. J. (1987). The relation of parenting style to adolescent school performance. *Child Development, 58,* 1244–1257.

Dubin, E. R., & Dubin, R. (1963). The authority inception period in socialization. *Child Development, 34,* 885–898.

Fischer, J. L., & Crawford, D. W. (1992). Codependency and parenting styles. *Journal of Adolescent Research, 7*(3), 352–363.

Frick, P. J. (1993). Childhood conduct problems in a family context. *School Psychology Review, 5*(3), 376–385.

Goodnow, J. J., & Collins, W. A. (1990). *Development according to parents: The nature, sources, and consequences of parents' ideas.* London, England: Lawrence Erlbaum Associates.

Grusec, J., & Goodnow, J. J. (1994). The impact of parental discipline methods on the child's internalization of values: A reconceptualization of current points of view. *Developmental Psychology, 30,* 4–19.

Hauser, S. T., Powers, S. I., & Noam, G. G. (1991). *Adolescents and their families: Paths of ego development.* New York: Free Press.

Health, P. A., & MacKinnon, C. (1988). Factors related to the social competence of children in single-parent families. *Journal of Divorce, 11*(3/4), 49–66.

Hetherington, E. W., Stouwie, R. J., & Ridberg E. H. (1971). Patterns of family interaction and child-rearing attitudes related to three dimensions of juvenile delinquency. *Journal of Abnormal Psychology, 78,* 160–176.

Hoffman, M. L. (1994). Discipline and internalization. *Developmental Psychology, 30,* 26–28.

Holmbeck, G. N., & Hill, J. P. (1991). Conflictive engagement, positive affect, and menarche in families with seventh-grade girls. *Child Development, 62,* 1030–1048.

Keith, T. Z. (1995). Best practices in applied research. In A. Thomas & J. Grimes (Eds.), *Best practices in school psychology-III* (pp. 135–143). Washington, DC: National Association of School Psychologists.

Kelley, H. H., Berscheid, E., Christensen, A., Harvey, J. H., Huston, T. L., Levinger, G., McClintock, E., Peplau, L. A., & Peterson, D. R. (1983). *Close relationships.* New York: Freeman.

Lamb, M. E., Ketterlinus, R. D., & Fracasse, M. P. (1992). Parent-child relationships. In M. H. Bornstein & M. E. Lamb (Eds.) *Developmental psychology: An advanced textbook* (pp. 465–502). Hillsdale, NJ: Erlbaum Associates.

Lau, S., & Cheung, P. C. (1987). Relations between Chinese adolescents' perceptions of parental control and organization and their perception of warmth. *Developmental Psychology, 23*(5), 726–729.

Lewis, M., Sullivan, M., Stranger, C., & Weiss, M. (1989). Self development and self-conscious emotions. *Child Development, 60,* 146–156.

Maccoby, E. E. (1984). Middle childhood in the context of the family. In W. A. Collins (Ed.), *Development during middle childhood: The years from six to twelve* (pp. 184–239). Washington, DC: National Academy of Sciences Press.

Maccoby, E. E., & Martin, J. (1983). Socialization in the context of the family: Parent-child interaction. In E. M. Hetherington (Vol. Ed.) & P. H. Mussen (Series Ed.), *Handbook of child psychology: Vol. 4, Socialization, personality, and social development* (pp. 1–101). New York: Wiley.

McLoyd, V. C., Jayaratne, T. E., Ceballo, R., & Borquez, J. (1994). Unemployment and work interruption among African-American single mothers: Effects on parenting and adolescent socioemotional functioning. *Child Development, 65,* 562–589.

Miller, N. B., Cowan, P. A., Cowan, C. P., Hetherington, E. M., & Clingempeel, R. (1993). Externalizing in preschools and early adolescence: A cross-study replication of a family model. *Developmental Psychology, 29*(1), 3–18.

Montemayor, R. (1983). Parents and adolescents in conflict: All families some of the time and some families most of the time. *Journal of Early Adolescence, 3,* 83–103.

Noller, P., & Callan, V. J. (1988). Understanding parent-adolescent interactions: Perceptions of family members and outsiders. *Developmental Psychology, 24*(5), 707–714.

Paikoff, R. L., Brooks-Gunn, J., & Carlton-Ford, S. (1991). Do parent-child relationships change during puberty? *Psychological Bulletin, 110,* 47–66.

Pettit, G. S., Bates, J. E., & Dodge, K. A. (1993). Family interactional patterns and children's conduct problems at home and school: A longitudinal perspective. *School Psychology Review, 5*(3), 403–420.

Plomin, R., & DeFries, J. C. (1985). *The origins of individual differences in infancy: The Colorado Adoption Project.* New York: Academic Press.

Short, R. J., & Shapiro, S. K. (1993). Conduct disorders: A framework for understanding and intervention in schools and communities. *School Psychology Review, 22*(3), 362–375.

Spock, B. (1946). *Baby and child care.* New York: Simon & Schuster.

Spock, B., & Rothenberg, M. B. (1985). *Baby and child care.* New York: Simon & Schuster.

Steinberg, L., Dornbusch, S. M., & Brown, B. B. (1992). Ethnic differences in adolescent achievement: An ecological perspective. *American Psychologist, 47,* 723–729.

Steinberg, L., Elmen, J. D., & Mounts, N. S. (1989). Authoritative parenting, psychosocial maturity, and academic success among adolescents. *Child Development, 60,* 1424–1436.

Vibbert, M., & Bornstein, J. H. (1989). Specific associations between domains of mother-child interaction and toddler referential language and pretense play. *Infant Behavior and Development, 12,* 163–184.

Vuchinich, S., Bank, L., & Patterson, G. R. (1992). Parenting, peers, and the stability of antisocial behavior in preadolescent boys. *Developmental Psychology, 28*(3), 510–521.

50

Working Parents

Lisa G. Bischoff
Susan M. Wilczynski
Indiana State University

Background and Development

For children growing up in the 1990s, dual-income families or families headed by a single working parent are the rule rather than the exception. Research conducted on the effects of parental employment on parents, children, and family relationships has suggested a complex relationship among issues. To provide appropriate services to today's children, youth, and families, school psychologists need to be cognizant of the issues facing dual-income and single-parent families.

Employment of mothers outside the home has increased steadily over the course of the 20th century. In 1950, 18% of mothers with children under the age of 18 were employed; by 1990, this figure had risen to 63% (Moen, 1992). The increase is particularly striking in employment rates of mothers of infants and preschool children. In 1950, only 12% of married mothers of children under the age of 6 were employed; by 1990, this rate had risen to 59.4% (Moen, 1992). (Information is not available for single or divorced mothers prior to 1970.) The rates for women raising children alone have also risen: In 1970, 36.9% of single mothers with children age three to five were employed; by 1986, this figure had increased to 64.5%. Rates of employment for married mothers of children from birth to age three rose from 24% in 1970 to 51% in 1986 and for women raising children alone to 50.9% (Matthews & Rodin, 1989).

As mothers have begun to enter the workforce in increasing numbers, the role of the mother in the home and the family has changed. The changing role of the mother in dual-income families has led to a changing role, or at least changing expectation, for the father. Furthermore, changes in parental roles and responsibilities may impact children and family relationships.

Although parental roles and responsibilities have changed over time, research concerning parental employment has been predominantly designed to identify negative effects of maternal employment. Possible benefits of maternal employment and parenting activities of fathers have often been ignored. A new research agenda promoting social change is needed that (a) addresses the role of fathers, child-care providers, and extended family members in child development; (b) documents the negative effects of inadequate, unaffordable child care; and (c) identifies child-care factors related to positive outcomes for children and families (Matthews & Rodin, 1989; Silverstein, 1991).

It is difficult to isolate the impact of parental employment on children and families. Factors related to parental employment such as income level, marital relationships, family structure, and child-care arrangements also influence children and families. Furthermore, the effect of factors such as family income and parental education on children and families may be compounded by the influence of such factors as the quality of child care. Poor-quality child care has been associated with low socioeconomic status and family stress in some studies (Belsky, 1990). Child-care issues are discussed elsewhere in this volume and will not be covered in detail in this chapter. In the present chapter, the impact of parental employment on parent, child, and family functioning are addressed.

Problems and Implications

Parents

Fathers and mothers may be affected by stress related to multiple roles as they fulfill both workplace and household responsibilities. In the following section, the effects of structural and psychosocial variables and the impact of dual-role stress on family roles, parental (maternal) health, and parent-child relationships are discussed.

The concept of dual-role stress encompasses role overload and role conflict. Role overload occurs when role demands require more time and energy than available, and role conflict occurs when incompatible demands of roles are experienced (Moen, 1992). The effects of dual-role stress as discussed in the literature are primarily addressed in relation to their influence on women, although recent research has addressed effects on men as well.

Family structure variables

Research suggests that the time parents spend in work activities affects their availability for participation in family activities including being at home, interacting with other family members, and completing household tasks. In one study of family activities, mothers employed full-time spent less time than mothers employed part-time, and mothers employed part-time spent less time than nonemployed mothers. Differences in time spent in family activities by fathers did not differ significantly based on employment status. Interestingly, time spent in *child-related* activities did not differ for mothers or fathers by employment status, although mothers were found to spend more time in household and child-related activities than fathers overall (Larsen, Richards, & Perry-Jenkins, 1994).

Mothers and fathers in dual-income families may be affected by the time factor in different ways. Research indicates that modern fathers have slightly increased the time spent in child-care activities (Pittman & Kerpelman, 1993), yet mothers continue to be primarily responsible for children regardless of employment status. Further, women who are employed, especially women with children, have less leisure time than men (Ferber, O'Farrell, & Allen, 1991). Fathers in dual-income households have been found to spend more time engaged in care-taking tasks than fathers whose wives are not employed outside the home (Lamb, 1987, cited in Deater-Deckard & Scarr, 1996), although mothers continue to be primarily responsible for direct physical care of children (Parcel & Menaghan, 1994). However, husbands whose wives work outside the home do not spend more time engaged in household tasks than husbands whose wives do not work outside the home (Pittman & Kerpelman, 1993).

The degree to which fathers care for children may be related differentially to maternal employment as a function of gender and age of the child. In dual-income families, fathers have been found to spend less weekday and weekend time alone with children than mothers (Greenberger, O'Neil, & Nagel, 1994). Fathers are more likely to play with preschoolers when mothers are employed full-time (Bailey, 1994) and are less likely to touch, hold, or play with infants when mothers are not employed (Zaslow, Pederson, Suwalsky, Cain, & Fivel, 1985).

In families with young children, fathers in dual-income families appear to be more involved in caregiving activities when children are very young, yet to be similar to fathers in single-income families in time spent in leisure or in activities involving both wife and children. Child-care activities of mothers in dual-income families appear to be related to number of hours worked—the higher the number of hours, the fewer the activities. However, employed mothers displayed higher rates of some parenting behaviors, such as verbalization, then did nonemployed mothers (Crouter & McHale, 1993).

The preponderance of evidence suggests mothers tend to be responsive to their children's caregiving needs regardless of maternal employment status (Moorehouse, 1991; Zaslow et al., 1985). However, the gender of the child may differentially impact the amount of attention a child receives in maternal employed and nonemployed families. Families with employed mothers are more likely to give daughters more attention whereas families with nonemployed mothers give sons more attention (Stuckey, McGee, & Bell, 1982).

Discrepancies between time spent with children by employed and nonemployed mothers appear to decrease as a child's age increases. Research on paternal involvement demonstrates a more complex relationship. Fathers in both dual-income and single-income families spend a similar amount of time with their children. However, fathers in dual-income families spend an equal amount of time with sons and daughters, while fathers in single-income families spend more time with sons and less time with daughters (Crouter & McHale, 1993).

Psychosocial variables

Research regarding the impact of parent gender on work and family roles of men and women provides limited information. Research conducted on mothers has generally focused on the effect of employment on family adjustment while research on fathers has generally focused on the effect of specific job characteristics on work-related issues such as job satisfaction and motivation (Lambert, 1990). Scarr, Phillips, and McCartney (1989) reviewed research on family relationships of employed mothers and reported spousal support to be an important factor in the relationship between maternal employment and family functioning. Components of spousal support discussed in the literature include positive attitude toward employment as well as engagement in household and child-related tasks. Research on spousal support has focused almost exclusively on the effect of husband support for wives.

Scarr et al. (1989) suggest that fathers with more egalitarian beliefs who participate more in family activities and take more responsibility for household tasks tend to be more supportive of their wife's employment. They are more likely than fathers with less egalitarian views to view maternal employment as an opportunity for their wife to experience an independent identity, greater social interaction, and more intellectual companionship. When actual roles of parents conflict with sex-role attitudes, parents were less satisfied with their marital relationship and less satisfied with their spouses (Crouter & McHale, 1993).

Greenhaus and Beutell (1985) suggest that spousal support reduces work-family conflict by (a) reducing role pressures, thus producing fewer demands on time and greater flexibility of expectations and (b) buffering the effect of work-family conflict on psychological well-being. Specifically, fathers' participation in child-care and household tasks and demonstration of positive attitude about spousal employment is associated with greater maternal satisfaction (Crouter & McHale, 1993). Emotional support, particularly spousal support, as well as involvement of fathers in child care may be related to decreased parental stress for both mothers and fathers (Deater-Deckard & Scarr, 1996).

Stress and health

Stress arising from conflict and guilt related to dual roles of worker and caregiver has been the focus of recent research, primarily as related to the health of women. Results indicate that the effects of dual-role stress on parents vary based on income, marital status, social supports, and adequacy of child-care arrangements (Shipley & Coats, 1992). The impact of dual-role stress on the physical and mental health of parents is discussed in the following paragraphs.

The relationship of multiple-role stress and behavior to health is complex and research has provided conflicting results. In one study, employed mothers of toddlers reported greater stress and a less healthy lifestyle than nonemployed mothers of toddlers. Conversely, research also suggests that employed women may have better physical health than nonemployed women. The relationship between employment and health is difficult to interpret because of a selection effect: Mothers who are employed may be more likely to be those who are healthy than women who are not employed (Facione, 1994).

Research regarding the impact of employment on the health of women suggests few negative but possibly some positive effects of employment on the health of mothers. Effects are mediated by marital status, spousal participation with household tasks, parental status, attitude toward employment, and job characteristics. Although employed mothers have been found to experience greater role overload and role conflict than nonemployed mothers and other employed women, most longitudinal studies have not found employed mothers to experience fewer beneficial effects on health, suggesting that multiple-role strain does not necessarily adversely affect health. Effects of employment on health did not differ based on parental status for White middle class women, and employment appeared to provide health advantages for Black women with children living at home.

Finally, cross-sectional studies found a stronger association between good health and employment for women with positive attitudes toward employment and for women who preferred employment outside the home to nonemployment. Specific job characteristics such as heavy job demands, lack of control, and lack of support at work were found to be associated with health risks, whereas social support at work was related to improved physical and psychological health (Repetti, Matthews, & Waldron, 1989).

Research on the emotional state of parents in work and home settings suggests differences between mothers and fathers. Employed women report more positive affect than their husbands at their jobs and less positive affect than their husbands at home. This difference may be related to the differences in at-home activities in which mothers and fathers engage. Mothers spend more time at home engaged in housework than fathers, and fathers spend more time at home engaged in leisure activities than mothers (Facione, 1994).

Results of a study on the impact of dual roles on women's moods indicated increased negative mood in mothers when simultaneously responding to demands of multiple roles. However, concurrent multiple-role demands accounted for only a small percentage of the variance in mood, suggesting role juggling may not be a major stressor for employed mothers (Williams, Suls, Alliger, Learner, & Wan, 1991). Results of a study on the impact of role stress on depression in women suggest that women who are married and employed have lower levels of depression than women who are married and not employed or single. Furthermore, mothers reported lower levels of depression than women who were not parents, regardless of work or marital status. The lower level of depressive symptomatology in women with the most complex configuration of roles (married employed mothers) suggests that either multiple roles have a positive effect on health or that women with fewer depressive symptoms seek out more complex role configurations (Kandel, Davies, & Raveis, 1985).

Children

Literature regarding the effect of parental employment on child outcomes has primarily addressed the impact of parental employment on children's physical development and health, academic achievement, and behavior. A consistent relationship between parental employment and child outcomes has not emerged from the literature to date.

Physical development and health

In the area of physical development, research has focused on the impact of maternal employment on children during infancy. Physical development, as measured by the Physical Development Index (PDI) of the Bayley Scales of Infant Development, does not differ significantly among premature infants whose mothers are employed, not employed, or taking a leave of absence when the infants are 3, 9, or 12 months of age (Youngblut, Loveland-Cherry, & Horan, 1993). While maternal employment does not appear to directly impact physical development during infancy, consistency between maternal employment status (employed versus not employed) and employment attitude (want to be employed versus do not want to be employed) when infants are 3 months of age predicts PDI scores when children are 1 year old. Outcomes are best for infants whose mothers experience consistency between their employment status and employment attitude. The impact of inconsistency between employment status and attitude is equally strong for infants of mothers who want to work but are not employed as for infants of mothers who are employed but do not wish to be employed outside the home.

In the area of physical health, maternal employment has been associated with greater levels of chronic and non-chronic physical health problems in school-aged children (Hong & White-Means, 1933). Hong and White-Means suggest that nonemployed mothers are able to take their children to the physician with greater frequency, thus increasing their children's physical health status. If this hypothesis is correct, it may mean fathers or extended family members are not offsetting this decrease in visits to the physician when the mother is employed.

Academic achievement

Early maternal employment has not been consistently associated with beneficial or deleterious achievement outcomes for children (Baydar & Brooks-Gunn, 1991; Desai, Chase-Lansdale, & Michael, 1989). The reason no clear pattern has emerged in the literature may be because intervening variables such as timing of entry into the workforce, family income, and gender of the child can mediate the relationship between early maternal employment and academic achievement. For example, academic achievement of boys from high income families may be negatively influenced by maternal employment during the first year of life or when employment is continued through the second year. In contrast, girls from high income families whose mothers enter the workforce when the girls are 2 years of age perform better on tests of academic achievement than girls whose mothers were not employed during this time period (Desai et al., 1989).

Parental work conditions may have a strong impact on children's academic skills (Parcel & Menaghan, 1994). For example, children of mothers working overtime score lower on standardized measures of academic achievement than children of mothers working full-time, and children of mothers working full-time score lower than children of mothers working part-time. Further, children whose mothers were employed part-time when the children were 3 to 5 years old had higher overall grades in school than children whose mothers worked full-time or overtime (Williams & Radin, 1993). These results should be interpreted with caution because outcomes may be influenced by intervening economic variables. The benefits to academic achievement that could be

gained by having a parent remain a full-time caregiver may be limited only to those families in which occupational prospects for the mother were poor (Parcel & Menaghan, 1994).

The negative impact of longer hours spent at work by employed mothers may be mediated by the number of activities shared between mother and child (Moorehouse, 1991). Shared activities may include a wide range of child-focused interactions including reading aloud; looking at picture books; talking about the child's friends, plans, and school; making up stories; and singing. Maternal employment may be negatively related to academic performance only when shared activities are infrequent. Parents who are aware of this relationship and who actively take measures to engage in shared activities with their children may ameliorate any problems full-time or overtime employment could create.

A review of the shared activities just enumerated suggests an overlap may exist between shared activities of parents with children and parental involvement in school activities. The concept of parental involvement in schooling is not restricted to parent volunteer work in the classroom but rather includes engagement in learning activities at home (Epstein & Dauber, 1991). Indeed, parental communication with children about short- and long-term plans (i.e., having high educational aspirations for children and discussing school and school activities) may be a more relevant factor in predicting children's achievement than either the degree to which the home is structured toward learning or direct parental participation in school activities (Keith et al. 1993; Kurdek & Sinclair, 1988). Further, high school students to whom parents convey high educational aspirations and whose mother or father monitor school progress are more likely than students without such support to maintain their grades and attend school and less likely to drop out of school. Parental aspirations are also associated with students' desire to attend college, attitude toward school, and likelihood of achieving a high school diploma or graduate equivalency diploma (GED, Astone & McLanahan, 1991).

Behavioral characteristics

Research investigating the relationship between maternal employment and children's behavior has produced mixed results. Maternal employment does not appear to have a direct effect on children's behavior; however, timing of employment may be an important factor (Baydar & Brooks-Gunn, 1991). Maternal employment during the first year of life was found to have a significantly negative impact on children's internalizing and externalizing behaviors (e.g., antisocial, anxious-depressed, hyperactive, immature, peer-conflict, and social withdrawal behaviors) when children were 3 or 4 years of age. While the impact of maternal employment on later behavior during their children's first year of life was statistically significant, it should be noted that timing of maternal employment accounted for only 6% of the variance in behavior. Maternal employment during the child's second or third year did not have a significant effect on behavior (Baydar & Brooks-Gunn, 1991).

The relationship between maternal employment and children's behavior is complex and should be examined within a larger set of variables (McCartney, 1991). Working conditions may influence maternal values, which may further affect the behavioral characteristics of children (Luster, Rhodes, & Haas, 1989). For example, higher levels of maternal occupational prestige are positively related to self-direction values (Luster et al., 1989). If maternal values are related to child outcomes, children of mothers with higher levels of occupational prestige may be provided more opportunities to engage in self-directed behavior than children of mothers with lower levels of occupational prestige. The emphasis placed on self-directed behavior may teach children of employed mothers to control their behavior more than children of nonemployed mothers. Indeed, mothers who earn more money report lower levels of behavioral problems in their children (Rogers, Parcel, & Menaghan, 1991).

Children's behavior and maternal workplace activities may be associated through parental role satisfaction. Parents who are satisfied with their roles (employed parent, nonemployed parent, participant in activities in and out of the home) may behave differently toward their children and teach their children different skills than parents who are not satisfied with their roles. Parental satisfaction at home and at work may be related to the type of workplace activities in which parents engage. Parents whose employment is challenging and requires complex work with people are more likely to use firm but flexible discipline with their children and are less likely to treat their children harshly (Greenberger et al., 1994). The workplace activities in which parents with complex jobs engage may be more satisfying than jobs requiring routine activities. In addition, these parents may be more likely to emphasize the importance of using interpersonal skills in problem resolution because of the need to effectively utilize these skills in the workplace. Children whose mothers interact with "things" (i.e., manipulation of tools or machinery) in the workplace rather than with people demonstrate greater behavioral problems (Rogers et al., 1991).

Consistency between parents' views about women's roles and employment status may also contribute to parental role satisfaction. Role satisfaction may be higher for parents who experience a greater level of consistency between beliefs and employment status (e.g., nonemployed mothers with traditional beliefs or employed mothers with nontraditional beliefs). In contrast, parents who hold beliefs which are inconsistent with their employment status may experience lower role satisfaction. The level of consistency between beliefs and employment status can affect parental behavior toward children. Parents who experience consistency between beliefs and employment status are less likely to exhibit negative affect, whereas parents who experience inconsistency between beliefs and employment status are more likely to demonstrate negative affect toward their children (Stuckey et al., 1982).

Experiences in the workplace may be associated with parental commitment to work and home, which may in turn be related to parental behavior toward children. Parents with high commitment to work are less likely to report being harsh disciplinarians, and mothers committed to both work and parenting are most likely to have an authoritative parenting style. Fathers with high work commitment are more likely to report making demands of their children to demonstrate maturity in self-control and prosocial behavior (Greenberger & Goldberg, 1989). Each of these trends may be related: Parents with a challenging and interpersonally stimulating workplace may have greater levels of role satisfaction and commitment to work and home. In turn, they may be in a better position to provide a rich, structured, and caring environment for their children (Menaghan & Toby, 1991) and may have higher expectations for interpersonal behavior. Therefore, the children of parents who experience high levels of role satisfaction and commitment may demonstrate fewer behavioral problems because of the environment their parents can provide.

At this time, no direct relationship between maternal employment and children's behavior has been clearly established. However, research to date has focused on behaviors as expressed in early childhood. Little research has examined the long-term effects of maternal employment on behavioral and emotional factors. Gottfried, Bathurst, and Gottfried (1994) found few significant differences between preadolescent children with employed and nonemployed mothers. Indeed, no significant differences were identified for preadolescent children whose mothers were employed and whose mothers were nonemployed when assessing academic motivation, academic anxiety, and socio-emotional or behavioral factors, as measured by the Child Behavior Checklist (parent and teacher versions), Vineland Total Adaptive Score, Baltimore Self-Esteem, and Self-Description Questionnaire. Further, college students whose mothers were either employed or nonemployed when they were children report similar levels of self-esteem (Wise & Joy, 1992).

Alternative Actions

The literature regarding the impact of parental employment on parent-child relationships and child outcomes provides a mixed view. No clear pattern of relationships, positive or negative, has emerged. It is evident that maternal employment status in and of itself does not predict parent, family, or child outcomes. Perhaps McCartney

(1991) provides the clearest perspective when she suggests that understanding the influence of parental employment on children can only be understood within a larger social ecology.

"It takes a village to raise a child" is an African saying. School psychologists need to recognize their role in the larger social ecology and become leaders in the "village." School psychologists can play a critical role within the community by consulting with parents and families about issues relevant to working parents. An important factor emerging in the literature is that shared activities may compensate for time spent away from children due to work demands. School psychologists can provide preventive services to families within the community by informing them about the importance of shared activities and by providing direct instruction in the types of shared activities that can be helpful. Furthermore, school psychologists can provide support and consultation for parents to increase the efficacy of the home learning environment (Christenson, 1990).

School psychologists can consult with employed parents by helping them learn to coordinate various aspects of their lives. Stress-reduction and time-management techniques can be provided to parents and children so that they can learn to reduce frustration and anxiety associated with juggling multiple roles. Further, school psychologists should be aware of services within the community available to parents and children. For example, providing parents with pertinent child-care information may assist them in adequately meeting the needs of their children (see the chapter on Child-Care Arrangements, this volume).

Silverstein (1991) suggests that researchers need to consider the role of the father and the family, not merely the role of the mother. While the number of fathers staying home with their children is increasing, there has been a dearth of research conducted in this area. Silverstein's edict is well-suited for practitioners as well. School psychologists must ask themselves: "What can I do differently to demonstrate to fathers that school personnel recognize the critical role they play in their children's lives?" and "How can I increase paternal involvement in school activities?" It is important for school psychologists to be aware of their own attitudes, values, and beliefs concerning family roles and responsibilities in order to reduce the likelihood of ignoring the contributions of *all* families members. Fathers, grandparents, and other family members are typically concerned about providing children with a safe and secure environment and may be willing to work with the schools if made to feel welcome.

School psychologists can also be leaders in the village by becoming change agents within the school. Working collaboratively with teachers and administrators, school psychologists may provide impetus for institutional change in order to accommodate the unique needs of dual-income families. For example, the parent-child shared activities described earlier include child-focused interactions associated with parental involvement in school. Teachers' attitudes are more positive when they perceive a high degree of support for parental involvement from their colleagues and from students' parents (Epstein & Dauber, 1991). School psychologists could provide inservice presentations to describe the many ways parents can be involved in their children's schooling (see Epstein, 1990, and Epstein & Dauber, 1991, for details), thus fostering a climate that encourages parental involvement through a wide range of avenues. By recognizing the varied contributions parents make to children's schooling (e.g., reading with them or talking with them about school and their plans), teachers' attitudes may become more positive, and teachers may become more willing to make accommodations to meet parents' needs (e.g., meeting in the evening instead of during school hours).

School psychologists can also offer consultation services to schools that provide, or are willing to provide, after-school care. Many schools already recognize the need to provide services to children in dual-income families once the school day is over. Programs allowing children to remain on the school campus with supervision until their parents can pick them up is one attempt to meet this demand. School psychologists can help locate adequate providers of after-school services within the community and can assist in establishing an environment that provides positive outcomes for children, parents, and child-care providers.

Schools can actively help working families by providing an opportunity for networking among parents. Parents need to network with employed and nonemployed parents to see that they are not alone in the stresses associated with parenting and the concerns they have regarding their children's current and future needs. As agents of change, school psychologists can encourage administrators to make parent groups feel welcome within the school and can also help to establish parent groups.

Finally, school psychologists should ensure that support materials are available to working families. For example, *Both My Parents Work* by Katerine Leiner (1986) can be read by children to help them recognize that other children's parents work and that children have different feelings about parental employment. Another resource is *The Kids' Self-Care Book* by Lyneete Long (1984). This book provides activities that help prepare children to take care of themselves when their parents are not home.

Clearly, school psychologists can engage in a wide range of activities that will assist working families. Merely recognizing the needs of dual-income families, school personnel, and the community may assist school psychologists in exploring the range of services they provide. The list of services suggested here are not exhaustive and should serve only as a starting point for school psychologists concerned with the needs of working families.

Summary

As mothers have entered the workforce in increasing numbers over the course of the 20th century, the role of the mother in the home and the family has changed. The evolving role of the mother in dual-income families has led to an alteration in role and expectations for the father. Research conducted on the effects of parental employment on parents, children, and family relationships has suggested a complex relationship among issues.

Parental employment status in and of itself does not predict parent, family, or child outcomes. The influence of parental employment on children can only be understood within a larger social ecology. In order for knowledge of parental employment to contribute to the school psychologist's understanding of children and families, the psychologist must consider the child's gender, parents' educational and income level, family structure and roles, and the occupational complexity and prestige associated with parental employment. School psychologists need to be cognizant of the issues facing today's dual-income families in order to provide appropriate services to children, youth, and families.

Recommended Resources

Crouter, A. C., & McHale, S. M. (1993). The long arm of the job: Influences of parental work on childrearing. In T. Luster & L. Okagaki (Eds.), *Parenting: An ecological perspective* (pp. 179–202). Hillsdale, NJ: Lawrence Erlbaum.
This chapter discusses the influences of parental work on childrearing from the perspectives of workplace and family.

Gottfried, A. E., & Gottfried, A. W. (1994). *Redefining families: Implications for children's development.* New York: Plenum Press.
This book provides an overview of the diverse factors influencing today's families.

Moorehouse, M. J. (1991). Linking maternal employment patterns to mother-child activities and children's school competence. *Developmental Psychology, 27*(2), 295–303.
This article reports the results of a research study relating maternal employment to mother-child activities and to children's school competence. It also presents a model for evaluating the impact of these activities on child outcomes.

Scarr, S., Phillips, D., & McCartney, K. (1989). Working mothers and their families. *American Psychologist, 44,* 1402–1409.
This article provides a comprehensive review of the impact of maternal employment on mothers, children, and marital relationships.

Silverstein, L. B. (1991). Transforming the debate about child care and maternal employment. *American Psychologist, 46*(10), 1025–1032.
Research agendas related to maternal employment and child care over the past two decades are reviewed, and a new agenda for research and policy is proposed.

References

Astone, N. M., & McLanahan, S. S. (1991). Family structure, parental practices, and high school completion. *American Sociological Review, 56,* 309–320.

Bailey, W. T. (1994). A longitudinal study of fathers' involvement with young children: Infancy to age 5 years. *The Journal of Genetic Psychology, 155,* 331–339.

Baydar, N., & Brooks-Gunn, J. (1991). Effects of maternal employment and child-care arrangements on preschoolers' cognitive and behavioral outcomes: Evidence from the children of the National Longitudinal Survey of Youth. *Developmental Psychology, 27,* 932–945.

Belsky, J. (1990). Parental and nonparental child care and children's socioemotional development: A decade in review. *Journal of Marriage and the Family, 52,* 885–903.

Christenson, S. L. (1990). Differences in students' home environments: The need to work with families. *School Psychology Review, 19,* 505–517.

Crouter, A. C., & McHale, S. M. (1993). The long arm of the job: Influences of parental work on childrearing. In T. Luster & L. Okagaki (Eds.), *Parenting: An ecological perspective* (pp. 179–202). Hillsdale, NJ: Lawrence Erlbaum.

Deater-Deckard, K., & Scarr, S. (1996). Parenting stress among dual-earner mothers and fathers: Are there gender differences? *Journal of Family Psychology, 10,* 45–59.

Desai, S., Chase-Lansdale, P. L., & Michael, R. T. (1989). Mother or market? Effects of maternal employment on the intellectual ability of four-year-old children. *Demography, 26,* 545–561.

Epstein, J. L. (1990). School and family connections: Theory, research, and implications for integrating sociologies of education and family. *Marriage and Family Review, 15,* 99–126.

Epstein, J. L., & Dauber, S. L. (1991). School programs and teacher practices of parent involvement in inner-city elementary and middle schools. *Elementary School Journal, 91,* 289–305.

Facione, N. C. (1994). Role overload and health: The married mother in the waged labor force. *Health Care for Women International. 15,* 157–164.

Ferber, M. A., O'Farrell, B., & Allen, L. R. (Eds.). (1991). *Work and family: Policies for a changing work force.* Washington, DC: National Academy Press.

Gottfried, A. E., Bathurst, K., & Gottfried, A. W. (1994). Role of maternal and dual-earner employment status in children's development: A longitudinal study from infancy through early adolescence. In A. E. Gottfried, & A. W. Gottfried (Eds.), *Redefining families: Implications for children's development* (pp. 221–229.) New York: Plenum Press.

Greenberger, E., & Goldberg, W. A. (1989). Work, parenting, and the socialization of children. *Developmental Psychology, 25,* 22–35.

Greenberger, E., O'Neil, R., & Nagel, S. K. (1994). Linking workplace and homeplace: Relations between the nature of adults' work and their parenting behavior. *Developmental Psychology, 30,* 990–1002.

Greenhaus, J. H., & Beutell, N. J. (1985). Sources of conflict between work and family roles. *Academy of Management Review, 10,* 76–88.

Hong, G., & White-Means, S. (1993). Do working mothers have healthy children? *Journal of Family and Economic Issues, 14,* 163–186.

Kandel, D. B., Davies, M., & Raveis, V. H. (1985). The stressfulness of daily social roles for women: Marital, occupational and household roles. *Journal of Health and Social Behavior, 26,* 64–78.

Keith, T. Z., Keith, P. B., Troutman, G. C., Bickley, P. G., Trivette, P. S., & Singh, K. (1993). Does parental involvement affect eighth-grade student achievement? Structural analysis of national data. *School Psychology Review, 22,* 474–496.

Kurdek, L. A., & Sinclair, R. J. (1988). Relation of eighth graders' family structure, gender, and family environment with academic performance and school behavior. *Journal of Educational Psychology, 80,* 90–94.

Lambert, S. J. (1990). Processes linking work and family: A critical review and research agenda. *Human Relations, 43,* 239–257.

Larsen, R. W., Richards, M. H., & Perry-Jenkins, M. (1994). Divergent worlds: The daily emotional experience of mothers and fathers in the domestic and public spheres. *Journal of Personality and Social Psychology, 67,* 1034–1046.

Leiner, K. (1986). *Both my parents work.* New York: Franklin Watts.

Long, L. (1984). *The kids self-care book: On my own.* Washington, DC: Acropolis Books.

Luster, T., Rhodes, K., & Haas, B. (1989). The relation between parental values and parenting behavior: A test of the Kohn hypothesis. *Journal of Marriage and the Family, 51,* 139–147.

Matthews, K. A., & Rodin, J. (1989). Women's changing work roles: Impact on health, family, and public policy. *American Psychologist, 44,* 1389–1393.

McCartney, K. (1991). Maternal employment should be studied within social ecologies. *Journal of Marriage and the Family, 53,* 1103–1107.

Menaghan, E. G., & Toby, L. P. (1991). Determining children's home environments: The impact of maternal characteristics and current occupational and family conditions. *Journal of Marriage and the Family, 53,* 417–431.

Moen, P. (1992). *Women's two roles: A contemporary dilemma.* New York: Auburn House.

Moorehouse, M. J. (1991). Linking: Maternal employment patterns to mother-child activities and children's school competence. *Developmental Psychology, 27,* 295–303.

Parcel, T. L., & Menaghan, E. G. (1994). Early parental work, family social capital, and early childhood outcomes. *American Journal of Sociology, 99,* 972–1009.

Pittman, J. F., & Kerpelman, J. L. (1993). Family work of husbands and fathers in dual-earner marriages. In J. Frankel (Ed.), *The employed mother and the family context.* New York: Springer Publishing.

Repetti, R. L., Matthews, K. A., & Waldron, I. (1989). Employment and women's health: Effects of paid employment on women's mental and physical health. *American Psychologist, 44,* 1394–1401.

Rogers, S. J., Parcel, T. L., & Menaghan, E. G. (1991). The effects of maternal working conditions and mastery on child behavior problems: Studying the intergenerational transmission of social control. *Journal of Health and Social Behavior, 32,* 145–164.

Scarr, S., Phillips, D., & McCartney, K. (1989). Working mothers and their families. *American Psychologist, 44,* 1402–1409.

Shipley, P., & Coats, M. (1992). A community study of dual-role stress and coping in working mothers. *Work and Stress, 6,* 49–63.

Silverstein, L. B. (1991). Transforming the debate about child care and maternal employment. *American Psychologist, 46,* 1025–1032.

Stuckey, M. F., McGee, P. E., & Bell, N. J. (1982). Parent-child interaction: The influence of maternal employment. *Developmental Psychology, 18,* 635–644.

Williams, E., & Radin, N. (1993). Paternal involvement, maternal employment, and adolescents' academic achievement: An 11-year follow up. *American Journal of Orthopsychiatry, 63,* 306–312.

Williams, K. J., Suls, J., Alliger, G. M., Learner, S. M., & Wan, C. K. (1991). Multiple role juggling and daily mood states in working mothers: An experience sampling study. *Journal of Applied Psychology, 76,* 664–674.

Wise, P. S., & Joy, S. S. (1992). Working mothers, sex differences, and self-esteem in college students' self-descriptions. *Sex Roles, 8,* 785–790.

Youngblut, J. M., Loveland-Cherry, C. J., & Horan, M. (1993). Maternal employment, family functioning, and preterm infant development at 9 and 12 months. *Research in Nursing and Health, 16,* 33–43.

Zaslow, M. J., Pederson, F. A., Suwalsky, J. T. D., Cain, R. L., & Fivel, M. (1985). The early resumption of employment by mothers: Implications for parent-infant interactions. *Journal of Applied Developmental Psychology, 6,* 1–16.

51
Child Care

Deborah Lowe Vandell
Kim Pierce
University of Wisconsin-Madison
Anne Stright
Indiana University

Background and Development

During the 1950s, an idealized view that young children are best reared by their mothers was well-established in the professional and popular literature (Scarr, Phillips, & McCartney, 1990). This view was reflected in the extensive use of mothers as the primary care provider for young children. The last 40 years have witnessed major changes in beliefs and practices pertaining to who cares for young children in the United States. These changes are, in part, a response to significant increases in maternal employment, particularly for mothers of infants and young children, and to increases in the numbers of female-headed households (Scarr et al., 1990). By 1995, fully 60% of children under the age of 6 years were cared for on a regular basis by individuals who were not their parents (U.S. Department of Education, 1995). Percentages of children in nonparental care systematically increase with age across the first 5 years: 45% of infants less than one year of age, 78% of 4-year-olds, and 84% of 5-year-olds are in a nonparental child-care arrangement on a regular basis.

A critical question raised by parents, education and health professionals, and policymakers is how this fundamental change in child rearing has affected children's development. A substantial research literature (Hayes, Palmer, & Zaslow, 1990) has demonstrated that a simple answer to the question is not possible. A much more accurate and useful response has been to identify the conditions under which child care supports children's development as well as the conditions under which development is undermined. One important set of conditions to consider is the broader ecological context of children's families in which child care is embedded. A second set of critical conditions pertains to the wide variations that characterize child care in the United States. Both of these sets of qualifying conditions are examined in this chapter.

Child Care and Family Connections

Multiple connections between child care and the family must be considered. It is clear that child-care placement is influenced by family characteristics, including financial resources and demographic features such as family size as well as by parents' work schedules and jobs (U.S. Department of Education, 1995). Families who lack the financial resources to pay for child care are more likely to use fathers, grandparents, and other relatives as care providers. When mothers provide higher proportions of family income, children are placed into child care earlier and for more hours (NICHD Early Child Care Research Network, 1996b). Child-care centers are more likely to be used when mothers are employed full time during standard work weeks; father care is more common when mothers work nonstandard (weekends or evenings) or irregular hours. In-home care is more common when there are more children in the household.

Parents' values and beliefs about child rearing contribute to child-care usage. Parents who utilize nonparental child care are more likely to believe that maternal employment and child care are beneficial for their children (NICHD Early Child Care Research Network, 1996b), whereas families who rely solely on parental care express reservations about their children being cared for by others. Also, families who use nonparental care are more likely to endorse egalitarian sex roles.

Family characteristics and resources are reflected in the quality of child care that families select or use. Affluent and/or highly educated families are more likely to utilize high-quality child-care settings in comparison to families with fewer resources. Emotionally stressed families are more likely than less stressed families to utilize poor-quality and unstable arrangements. Some of the most problematic care occurs for the "near poor" children whose families do not qualify for subsidized child-care programs (Hayes et al., 1990).

The extensive associations between family characteristics and child-care arrangements underscore the difficulty of determining how child care affects children. An ostensible child-care "effect" may actually be the result of preexisting family characteristics or experiences. Consequently, a standard approach adopted in much of the current research is to control statistically for preexisting family characteristics when testing for child-care effects. A second strategy is to consider the joint contributions of family and child care to children's development within different ecological niches, such as determining the impact of child care for children growing up in poverty. A third approach is to examine the cumulative impact on children of both environmental contexts (i.e., family and child-care situation).

Recent studies suggest that early child-care experiences have the potential of offsetting some of the influence of family experiences on children's development. Whereas children reared in families in which mothers are the primary or sole caregiver are heavily influenced by the quality of that experience (Bretherton, 1992), children who have regular child-care experiences appear to be less affected by the quality of the mother-child relationship (Egeland & Hiester, 1995; Howes, Matheson, & Hamilton, 1994). Thus, attending day care as infants appears to have beneficial effects for children who are insecurely attached. These children are rated as more socially competent than home-reared children who are insecurely attached to their mothers (Egeland & Hiester, 1995), suggesting that child care may act as a protective factor for children when home circumstances are less advantageous.

For children who are in child care, the quality of their early relationships with child-care providers appears to be critical (Howes et al., 1994). The socialization practices of child-care providers (not mothers' socialization practices) are powerful predictors of behavior problems and kindergarten difficulties for children who attend child-care programs during the infant and preschool years. For children who are not enrolled in child care, family socialization practices are the major predictors of behavior problems and adjustment in kindergarten. These findings indicate strongly that the quality of early child-care experiences can have powerful effects on children's adjustment.

Child Care Variations

Even a cursory look at child care in the United States reveals that this care varies along many dimensions, including (a) the settings (e.g., centers, child-care homes, children's homes) and (b) the quality of care within those settings. Variations also occur in the timing of different child-care experiences. The relevance of these variations for children's development is examined next.

Center-based care

Child-care centers provide care for groups of children in school-like settings. Child-care centers vary widely in the United States. These variations are reflected in child-staff ratios, staff training, and physical facilities (Helburn, 1995; Howes, Phillips, & Whitebook, 1992). For example, observed child-staff ratios for infants have been found to range from 1:1 to 1:14. Staff training varies from less than a high school degree to advanced academic degrees. Infants are cared for in groups as large as 30 (NICHD Early Child Care Research Network, 1996a).

These regulatable features are systematically related to children's experiences in the centers. Children are more likely to experience positive, sensitive caregiving from more highly educated caregivers in centers with smaller group sizes and ratios. Caregivers with fewer children to care for provide more sensitive caregiving and developmentally appropriate activities. They are more responsive, socially stimulating, and less restrictive than caregivers who are responsible for more children. Children in centers with higher staff turnover are more likely to wander aimlessly and to play less with peers (Whitebook, Howes, & Phillips, 1989).

These differences in programs are not trivial because they are associated with children's concurrent development. When ratios and group sizes are smaller, children are more likely to be emotionally attached to their caregivers, socially competent with peers, and cooperative with staff and peers. They are less likely to appear hostile and aimless (Howes et al., 1992). Preschoolers in such programs appear to benefit cognitively from the experience. They demonstrate better vocabularies, receptive language, and math skills (Helburn, 1995). Children who experience fewer changes in teachers are rated as more gregarious and less withdrawn or aggressive (Howes et al., 1994).

There is evidence that these child-care effects can be persistent or long lasting. Children who attended poor-quality centers as infants and toddlers have been rated as less compliant and self-regulated as preschoolers. In contrast, high-quality child care is associated with children subsequently displaying more complex play, more positive affect, less hostility, and better peer relationships. Some of these effects associated with child-care quality are maintained into the early elementary years. Poor-quality child care during the preschool years is associated with problems in behavioral adjustment in kindergarten and with poorer social competence and less positive emotion in third grade. Frequent staff turnover during the preschool years is associated with poorer academic achievement in first grade, even after family factors are controlled (Clarke-Stewart, 1992).

Center-based care appears to be particularly important for children from low-income families. Participation in high-quality child care mitigates against declines in cognitive and language development that are found when low-income children do not attend programs. Participation in high-quality programs is associated with improved cognitive development, language development, attention, adaptive behavior (McCartney, Scarr, Phillips, & Grajek, 1985), and mathematics and reading achievement (Caughy, DiPietro, & Strobino, 1994). There is evidence that the positive effects of high-quality center-based programs for low-income children's intellectual development and academic achievement are maintained through 12 years of age (Campbell & Ramey, 1994). By the same token, poor-quality child care for children from low-income families may be particularly detrimental.

Center-based or formal programs have been developed to meet the needs of school-age children for those time periods when their schools are not in session. The National Child Care Survey (Hofferth, Brayfield, Deich, & Holcomb, 1991) reported that 21% of 5-year-olds attend such before- or after-school programs, whereas only 9.1% of children ages 6 to 9 and 2.6% of children ages 10 to 12 do. There is evidence that young school-age children can benefit from attending high-quality after-school programs. In one study, middle-class kindergarteners who attended an extended day program at their school had better relationships with peers than did classmates who did not attend the program, perhaps because of additional opportunities to develop peer relationships (Howes, Olenick, & Der-Kiureghian, 1987). High-quality, formal, after-school programs also appear to be beneficial for low-income children. Improved math achievement, reading achievement, work habits, and peer relationships have been linked to attending after-school tutorials and recreational activities (Vandell & Posner, in press).

The quality of children's experiences in after-school programs is related to some of the same regulatable features important for younger children. For example, negative staff-child interactions are more frequent when child-staff ratios are larger and when staff have less education and training (Rosenthal & Vandell, in press). School-age programs also must be sensitive to school-age children's press for autonomy and independence. A program attractive to the older child provides opportunities for children to select activities and to interact with peers. The environment is fun and relaxing, rather than rigidly structured, and children are included in the planning of activities and development of rules. Also, activities are developmentally appropriate, and children are given opportunities to pursue their individual interests. Children assess their after-school experiences more positively when programs are smaller, when they offer a greater diversity of activities, and when there are fewer negative staff-child interactions (Rosenthal & Vandell, in press).

Child-care homes

Another common child-care arrangement in the United States is the child-care home (sometimes called family day care). Of families with employed mothers, 20% use this kind of child care for their infants and toddlers. Figures are somewhat lower for preschoolers. Substantially fewer school-age children (4.5%) are enrolled in child-care homes after school (Hofferth et al., 1991). In this arrangement, the provider cares for a small group of children in the provider's home. Families often prefer child-care homes for young children because they see it as providing a home-like setting with one stable caregiver and relatively few other children. Generally, the other children are of different ages, giving the child the opportunity to play with children in a mixed-age group setting.

The training and education of child-care home providers vary, with some providers having considerable training and education and others having very little. Licensing requirements differ substantially by state and community (Phillips, Lande, & Goldberg, 1990). Some states do not regulate child-care homes, whereas other states have rules regarding group size, age configurations, and caregiver training.

Researchers have recorded differences between licensed and nonlicensed care. Licensed homes typically receive higher ratings in terms of the quality and quantity of materials, activities, and furnishings. Children in nonlicensed homes have been reported to watch more television and to have fewer informative interactions with caregivers. Observations in child-care homes reveal additional differences associated with regulatable features. As numbers of children increase, caregivers appear less sensitive, positive, and stimulating. More time is spent controlling and restricting children (Clarke-Stewart, Gruber, & Fitzgerald, 1994). Quality of caregivers' behaviors is influenced by their child-rearing beliefs and training in child development. Caregivers with nonauthoritarian child-rearing attitudes and specialized training appear warmer and more "in tune" with children's needs.

Differences in children's developmental outcomes are associated with these variations in the quality of child-care homes. Children who attend licensed child-care homes evidence higher language scores than those who attend nonlicensed facilities, even after controlling for family differences (Goelman & Pence, 1987). Controlling for family factors, children who attend higher quality child-care homes demonstrate more competent play with peers, toys, and caregivers than do children who are placed in poorer quality child-care homes (Howes & Stewart, 1987).

In-home care

Another child-care arrangement is for families to employ a person to care for the child in the child's own home. This arrangement is sometimes preferred by parents because the child is believed to receive one-to-one attention in a familiar, safe environment (the child's own home). This arrangement is sought by families who need the flexibility it provides them. Because of the high financial costs, this type of care tends to be used by affluent families in which mothers are highly educated and have high-status professions (NICHD Early Child Care Research Network, 1996b). Families also are more likely to use in-home care if they have several small children requiring child care.

As is the case for other forms of child care, the training and education of in-home providers vary. Some are college-educated professional nannies with specialized child-care training, whereas others have minimal education or training and view child care as a temporary job. Caring for fewer children, having more training in child development, and having less authoritarian child-rearing beliefs are associated with more sensitive and stimulating in-home child care (NICHD Early Child Care Research Network, 1996a).

Relative care

Relatives, often grandmothers or aunts, are another source of child care. This arrangement is used by 16% of all families with children younger than 6 years and by 21% of school-age children (Hofferth et al., 1991). Relative care is more common when mothers are employed part time and when families have fewer financial resources. Because the care is often free of charge or offered at a reduced cost, it is used by low-income families who lack the financial resources to pay for other care. For example, Hofferth et al. (1991) report that 43% of low-income families use relative care. Parental beliefs also contribute to the use of this type of care. Families who have concerns about their children being cared for by nonfamily members are more likely to use relative care.

Wide variations have been observed in the quality of child care provided by grandmothers and other relatives. In one study that focused on relative care in low-income families (Galinsky, Howes, Kontos, & Shinn, 1994), 69% of the care was rated as insensitive to the needs of young children and half of the children were judged to be insecurely attached to their relative caregiver. A second study (NICHD Early Child Care Research Network, 1996a), however, observed that grandmothers did provide sensitive and stimulating care when they were caring for fewer children and when they had nonauthoritarian child-rearing beliefs.

It is important to consider grandparent care in juxtaposition to other care options available to a family. Using a national data set, Baydar and Brooks-Gunn (1991) found that grandmother care during the first year was associated with fewer behavior problems and better cognitive performance at age 3 years than were either father care or community-based day-care centers.

Father care

In some families, fathers serve as child-care providers while mothers are employed or attending school. According to Hofferth et al. (1991), 19% of fathers of children under 5 years and 18% of fathers of school-age chil-

dren provide such care. In most cases, this care occurs in dual-earner households in which mother and father are employed on different shifts. Father care tends to occur in combination with other arrangements that families piece together. It is more likely when families need both parents' incomes to sustain an adequate standard of living but feel that they cannot afford to pay for the costs of child care (Presser, 1989). Larger families turn to father care because they cannot afford to pay child-care costs for several children. Sometimes father care is motivated by parents' beliefs that young children should be cared for within the family and/or by an ideological belief in the benefits of paternal involvement in child rearing (Vandell, Hyde, Plant, & Essex, 1996).

Father care has been associated with both beneficial and negative effects on children and the family. On the positive side, within middle-income families who adopt father care because it is a preferred form of care, father care is associated with improvements in marital relationships and mothers' mental health (Vandell et al., 1996). Infants are also more likely to display secure attachment relationships with their mothers when their fathers serve as child-care providers (Belsky & Rovine, 1988). On the negative side, shift work combined with mother and father trading off child care can result in increased marital problems. For families living in poverty (and the father is available for child care because he is unemployed), father care is associated with increased child behavior problems and poorer receptive vocabulary scores (Baydar & Brooks-Gunn, 1991).

Self-care

Yet another child care alternative is self-care. Self-care refers to a range of situations in which children are without adult supervision. Children may be at home or elsewhere; they may be alone or with siblings or peers. In the National Child Care Survey (Hofferth et al., 1991), parents rarely reported using self-care as their primary child-care arrangement for children younger than 13 years (some 2% of children between 5 and 12 years of age). Families were more likely to report self-care as a supplemental or secondary arrangement; 12% of children aged 5 to 12 years were reported to be in self-care at least some of the time. When broken down by age group, it is clear that use of self-care increases as children get older (2.2% for children 5 to 7 years old, 10.7% for children 8 to 10 years, and 31.5% for 11- and 12-year-olds).

Conflicting results are available regarding the effects of self-care experiences on children's adjustment. Some have found that self-care children are more fearful and are more likely to act out and to perform poorly in school than children supervised by adults during the after-school hours. Others, however, have found no differences between self-care and adult-supervised children in behavioral adjustment, self-esteem, anxiety, and social adjustment (cf. Galambos & Maggs, 1991).

Several factors must be considered in determining the consequences of self-care. These include the child's age, the amount of time spent in self-care, the specific type of self-care arrangement, the neighborhood in which the child resides, and the quality of the parent-child relationship.

Generally, children who are younger than fourth grade do not have the skills necessary to deal effectively with caring for themselves during their out-of-school time. There is clear evidence that negative consequences of self-care are more common with younger school-age children than with older children. Parents of children in kindergarten through third grade often report that their children are fearful and apprehensive about being alone. As children get older and desire greater autonomy, self-care may represent an opportunity to exhibit their ability to regulate their own behavior within the context of rules set by parents (Vandell & Posner, in press). Use of a self-care arrangement in this case acknowledges the child's responsibility and independence and his or her developmental press for autonomy. With older children who are ready for some self-care, additional factors must be considered.

One critical factor is the duration of the self-care experience. Children who spend 30 minutes caring for themselves after school experience the arrangement differently than children who spend 2 hours without adult supervision (Vandell & Posner, in press). The number of days each week that self-care is used is another relevant factor. One day per week in self-care is a different experience for children than 5 days a week in self-care. Children's behavior problems increase as the amount of time in self-care increases.

The effects of self-care are influenced by the presence of other children and by the degree of adult supervision. Some children are home alone, others are home with a sibling, others are at the home of a friend without adult supervision, and still others spend their self-care time "hanging out" at places such as shopping malls and video arcades. Children monitored by telephone and those with parental rules to follow while caring for themselves are less likely to experience harmful effects from the arrangement (Galambos & Maggs, 1991). Unsupervised time with peers appears to be particularly problematic (Vandell & Posner, in press) and is associated with behavior problems for grade school, middle school, and high school students.

Neighborhood characteristics such as actual and perceived safety must be considered (Vandell & Posner, in press). Self-care children who live in urban areas with attendant problems of crime appear more fearful and isolated than their classmates who are supervised after school. These children also evidence more antisocial behaviors and greater drug, tobacco, and alcohol use than children who are supervised by adults after school. Research with children in suburban and rural areas has not found negative effects of self-care, perhaps because these children experience fewer restrictions on outdoor play and fewer threats of physical harm.

Another factor that plays a role in moderating the effects of self-care is the quality of the parent-child relationship. Emotionally supportive parents who establish firm rules for their children's self-care time may protect children from negative consequences. Children who report a strong attachment to their parents have been shown to experience fewer fears about being home alone in an urban environment, and parents who provide a great deal of emotional support protect their self-care children from exhibiting behavior problems (Vandell & Posner, in press). The quality of children's experiences within their families is an important determinant of the outcomes of self-care arrangements.

Timing of child-care experiences

Child-care experiences must be evaluated in terms of children's developmental status or readiness. One area which has sparked considerable debate pertains to the use of extensive nonmaternal care during infancy. Some (e.g., Belsky, 1988) have argued that the repeated mother-child separations associated with early child-care experiences can interfere with infants establishing secure attachment relationships with their mothers. Using a laboratory procedure called the Strange Situation, which assesses infant reaction to a series of brief separations and reunions, they report somewhat elevated incidents of "avoidant" behaviors. Others, however, have questioned the validity or meaning of the Strange Situation for children who regularly experience mothers' comings and goings (Clarke-Stewart, 1989).

More recent findings (NICHD Early Child Care Research Network, 1996c) indicate that there is no overall effect of child-care quality, type, or hours on the quality of infant-mother attachment. Under certain home/child-care combinations, however, the incidence of insecure attachments is elevated. When children receive insensitive, poor-quality caregiving from their mothers and in their child-care setting, the highest rates of attachment insecurity occur (about 55% of the children in that group). When children are in less risky conditions such as better child care or better maternal care, the rates of insecurity are lower (about 38%). Maternal insensitivity coupled with extensive hours or with frequent child-care changes also increase the rates of insecurity (from about 37% to 48%). These results underscore the importance of considering child-care timing within the context of family functioning.

A second timing issue pertains to children's movement from informal home-based child-care settings to more formal center-based programs. Families are more likely to use centers for preschoolers (37%) and kindergarten children (28%) than for infants (7%) and toddlers (15%), whereas in-home providers and child-care homes are favored for infants and toddlers (Hofferth et al., 1991).

These enrollment figures mirror parental beliefs. Parents often state preferences for center-based programs for preschoolers because of their perceived social and intellectual opportunities. Informal home-based settings, in contrast, often are preferred for infants and toddlers because they are thought to offer more one-to-one attention and "family-like" interactions. Observations of children's experiences in these different settings provide evidence in support of these parental beliefs (Clarke-Stewart et al., 1994). Centers tend to have more didactic materials and small-group learning activities, whereas child-care homes and sitters offer more informal learning activities and more one-to-one interaction and interactions with mixed-aged peers. Preschoolers' language and preacademic skills appear to benefit from the more formal learning activities that occur in centers (Clarke-Stewart et al., 1994). Researchers have not determined an "optimal" age period for children to begin some center-based experiences, although the usage patterns suggest that parents see this transition as occurring between the third and fourth year.

A third timing issue pertains to after-school care. Options for school-age child care can be viewed as lying along a continuum from full adult supervision to no supervision (Todd, Albrecht, & Coleman, 1990). Adult supervision with a high degree of accountability is provided when children are cared for by parents or other relatives and in child-care homes and formal programs. In these situations, adults directly supervise children and have full responsibility for their welfare. Further along the continuum is adult supervision with some accountability as provided by library programs, sports teams, and youth groups. Adults provide monitoring, but children have greater choice in attending the activities. Neighborhood check-in programs and self-care with parental monitoring by telephone typify a third point on the continuum in that they offer some distal supervision. In these cases, children have major responsibilities for their own care, but adults are aware of where the children are, what they are doing, and whom they are with. The final point on the continuum reflects a complete lack of supervision, typified by children in self-care who have little or no contact with adults.

A family's choice of arrangements for the school-age child should be dictated by considerations of the child's age and readiness for new responsibilities. Younger school-age children need close adult supervision; self-care would be inappropriate. Children who receive adult supervision during their out-of-school time can be given opportunities to make choices and explore their own interests with the help of a supportive adult. As children get older, they experience a desire for increasing autonomy and become ready to take on greater responsibility. They may become ready for less-structured supervision. Adult monitoring can become more distal as children internalize rules for appropriate behavior and acquire the skills and knowledge needed to follow those rules (Todd et al., 1990). Throughout the process of selecting care arrangements, parents need to consider their child's individual needs and ability to regulate his or her own behavior, particularly when considering use of a self-care arrangement.

Problems and Implications

Families often have to "make do" with the child care that they can find and that they can afford. Many families piece together child-care arrangements. Families often rely on several arrangements, and changes in settings and caregivers are the norm. The NICHD Study of Early Child Care, for example, found the average infant experienced three different nonparental arrangements during the first year. High-quality child care is particularly difficult for families to find. According to several national multisite studies, much of the available child care is of poor or barely adequate quality. In one study of 50 nonprofit and 50 for-profit child-care centers in California, Colorado, Connecticut, and North Carolina, only 14% of the classrooms were rated as providing developmentally appropriate, good-quality care, 74% of the classrooms were rated as providing only mediocre care, and 12% provided poor-quality care (Helburn et al., 1995). Center-based programs for infants appeared to be particularly problematic; 8% of the infant and toddler rooms were rated as being of good quality, and 40% were rated as poor quality. Another multisite study of 414 children in two states (Howes et al., 1992) also found that centers offered poorer quality care for infants and toddlers. In that study, 70% of the infants and 52% of the toddlers were in classrooms rated as barely adequate or inadequate in terms of providing appropriate caregiving.

Several factors are believed to contribute to these worrisome figures. Child-care standards vary widely in the United States; there are no common standards enforced across the states. For example, required center adult-child ratios for infants range from 1:3 to 1:12 (Phillips et al., 1990). In addition, many state regulations do not meet recommended guidelines for quality care. Over 20 states do not meet recommended *minimum* guidelines of adult-infant ratios of 1:4, adult-toddler ratios of 1:6, and adult-preschooler ratios of 1:10 (Phillips et al., 1990). A second factor contributing to poor-quality center-based care is substantial staff turnover (41% in 1988), which has been linked to poor staff salaries and benefits (Whitebook et al., 1989).

Quality of care also is a concern in child-care homes (family day care) and relative care. In a study of 226 toddlers and preschoolers (predominantly low-income African-American and Hispanic children) who were being cared for in child-care homes and by relatives, only 9% were rated as receiving good-quality care, 56% received adequate or custodial care, and 35% received inadequate care (Galinsky et al., 1994). Children were less likely to receive sensitive and stimulating care when the caregiver provided child care "to help the mother out" or when the providers felt coerced into providing care. Many states have been reluctant to regulate child-care homes. In fact, only 39 states have such regulations, and these vary widely in terms of numbers of children that are permitted and staff training (Phillips et al., 1990). Relative care is viewed as a family matter and is not regulated.

One reason so many working poor and unemployed families use parental care or relative care is that other forms of child care place considerable financial strain on these families. Only one fourth of families of the working poor and one third of working-class families use paid child care. When these families must pay for care, it requires a substantial portion of the family's income. Hofferth et al. (1991) report that of the families who do pay for child care, the working poor devote 33% of their income to child care, and working-class families spend 13%. In contrast, middle-class families spend only 6% of their income on child care. There are other distinctions among household types as well. Whereas two-parent families devote 9% of their income to child care, single-parent families use 21% of their income for child care. It is clear that child-care costs can be an onerous burden for single parents and for low-income families.

Infant care is the most expensive form of child care for all families. Because of the need to approach one-to-one ratios, staff or personnel costs are substantial. Many centers and child-care homes do not offer infant care because of its heavy staffing demands relative to care for older children. Mothers appear to be emotionally stressed by the demands of finding and maintaining infant child-care arrangements (Vandell et al., 1996).

The provision of developmentally appropriate after-school arrangements is another challenge for families, schools, and communities. Older school-age children sometimes complain that the formal programs are "for babies" and that the activities are "boring" (Vandell & Corasaniti, 1988). The children press for an opportunity to have some unstructured time after school when they can relax, play with friends, and set their own agenda. This push is often balanced against parents' and other adults' legitimate concerns about the dangers and risks associated with children being unsupervised by adults during the after-school hours. The challenge, then, is to develop after-school care arrangements in which children's needs to exercise greater autonomy and independence are met along with the children's continuing needs for contact and support from caring adults. An additional challenge for families is the financial one of paying for this care because most after-school programs are funded by parent fees.

Alternative Actions

Historically, the United States has been very reluctant to develop a national child-care policy because child care is viewed as a family matter. The assumption is that parents should select and monitor the quality of their children's child care. However, parents may have difficulty recognizing high-quality child care. In a recent study of 100 centers in four states, 90% of parents rated their children's centers as good, while trained observers rated these same programs as poor or mediocre (Helburn, 1995). An important step in improving the quality of care available to children is to educate parents on the dangers of poor-quality care for their children's development and to help parents identify high-quality care. School psychologists can play a key role in this educational effort.

There is evidence that the quality of children's experiences in child care can be improved by instituting federal standards for regulatable features such as group size and ratio as well as caregiver qualifications. States that require more favorable group sizes, adult-child ratios, and caregiver education have centers with better quality care than states with less demanding licensing standards (Helburn, 1995). One set of proposed standards, which focus on child-staff ratios, group size, and staff training, is the Federal Interagency Day Care Requirements (FIDCR). Proposed group sizes are 6, 12, and 16 for infants, toddlers, and preschoolers, respectively. Proposed ratios for infants, toddlers, and preschoolers are 3:1, 4:1, and 8:1. Adopting such national standards will require concerted efforts by citizens as well as professional organizations. While the United States has been willing to introduce federal standards for food and drug production because of health and safety concerns, concerns about the effects of poor-quality child care have not yet yielded federal standards. In the absence of federal standards, individual states can adopt appropriate safeguards.

Because compliance with higher child-care standards will increase the costs of care, it will be necessary to develop ways to offset such costs, especially for families who cannot afford them. Federal and state financial support of low-income families' use of high-quality care programs is particularly needed because this support helps low-income families in three ways. First, government support reduces the financial strain child care places on these families. Second, these programs serve as enrichment experiences that can contribute to the children's ability to succeed at school. Third, these programs act as a respite for parents, reducing the stress in their lives and improving the quality of their parenting. Following a major review of existing research on child care, the National Research Council recommended that federal and state governments expand support for low-income families' use of high-quality child-care programs. The "near poor" is another group in need of additional support.

A national child-care policy also should include a modification of existing parental leave policies as a way of meeting the need for high-quality infant care. Most industrialized countries offer a parent an opportunity to stay home and care for the infant for at least part of the first year. Countries such as Spain, Israel, Canada, Finland, Italy, Belgium, and Ireland provide mothers or fathers with paid leave lasting from 3 to 11 months at 75% to 80% of the parent's original salary. Other countries (Norway, Austria, Portugal, Netherlands, Sweden, Denmark, France, and the United Kingdom) provide periods of paid leave at 90% to 100% of the parent's salary and additional periods of unpaid leave (Kamerman, 1989). As a result of these parental leave policies, child care for infants is uncommon in Europe.

The United States has a much more restricted parental leave policy. Currently, parents employed by firms with more than 50 employees are allowed by federal law to take up to 3 months of unpaid leave. There is no federal policy of paid leave, although some companies allow employees to use sick leave or other benefits for a period following the birth of a baby. The development of a more comprehensive parental leave policy is one way of meeting the need for infant care. The National Research Council recommends that job-protected leave be mandated by the federal government for parents of infants less than one year of age.

One way of meeting the need for high-quality after-school care is to make more effective use of public schools. School psychologists can serve as strong advocates within their districts for the development of age-appropriate programs and activities. Schools are an ideal location for before- and after-school child-care programs because they have classrooms, gyms, equipment, and outdoor play areas. School-based programs make transportation to another setting unnecessary. For these programs to appeal to older school-age children and to middle schoolers, changes in programming and activities and inclusion of youth in program planning will be necessary.

School psychologists also can work, within their schools and communities, on the development of self-care training programs. These programs can help children and families to evaluate children's readiness for self-care and to institute appropriate safety and monitoring features. These programs must be implemented with considerable care because they may be viewed as an endorsement of self-care for children who are not yet ready for such care and they may provide children and families with a false sense of security. Several organizations such as the American Red Cross and the National Campfire, Incorporated, have begun to develop programs that can serve as models.

Unfortunately, school psychologists also may have to address both short-term and long-term failures in the child-care system as they are manifested in individual children's school adjustment. Children who have experienced poor-quality and unstable child care are more likely than their classmates to appear uncooperative, aggressive, distractible, and withdrawn. Individual and small-group activities to address these behavior problems may be needed in conjunction with consideration of changes in the children's current child care.

Summary

The majority of children in the United States participate in nonparental child-care arrangements on a regular basis. These child-care environments in conjunction with family environments represent two major contexts in which children develop. Child care can vary in structural and regulatable features such as child-staff ratio, group sizes, and caregiver education and training. Arrangements also vary in terms of caregivers' warmth and sensitivity to children and the provision of age-appropriate activities. Positive caregiving experiences and age-appropriate activities are more likely when group sizes and ratios are smaller and caregivers have more child-related training and education.

High-quality child care can serve a compensatory function for children when families are stressed or are unable to meet children's needs. High-quality child care can contribute to children developing better language and cognitive skills as well as more competent interactions with peers. Poor-quality child care, in contrast, is associated with children having behavioral difficulties including noncompliance to adult requests, less complex play, and problems interacting with peers. There is evidence that effects of early child-care experiences are maintained into elementary school.

Families' child-care needs continue through middle childhood. The quality of school-age child-care programs is influenced by some of the same regulatable features (group size, ratio, staff training) as child care for younger children. School-age child care also requires close attention to children's press for autonomy and independence. Toward the end of grade school, many children are moving into self-care. Formal programs and self-care may be seen as representing points along a continuum of adult supervision during the after-school hours. The effects of these self-care experiences are dependent on multiple factors including the child's maturity and competence, the amount of time spent in self-care, the presence of peers, parental monitoring and support, and neighborhood characteristics.

The importance of child-care experiences, as both positive and negative contributors to children's development, underscores the need for a national child-care policy to ensure that children have access to care that does not compromise development.

Authors Note

This research was supported, in part, by grants from the National Institute of Child Health and Human Development (RO1 HD#30587-03 and U10 HD#27040-07) to Deborah Lowe Vandell.

Recommended Resources

For Professionals

Barton, M., & Williams, M. (1993). Infant day care. In C. H. Zeanah, Jr. (Ed.), *Handbook of infant mental health* (pp. 445–461). New York: Guilford Press.
This chapter presents a careful review of research examining the effects of infant day care, with special attention devoted to attachment issues.

Booth, A. (ed.). (1992). *Child care in the 1990s: Trends and consequences.* Hillsdale, NJ: Lawrence Erlbaum.
An edited volume that examines major child care issues including quality, availability, costs, and effects on children and parents. Each review is followed by commentaries by leading figures in the field.

Campbell, F. A., & Ramey, C. T. (1994). Effects of early intervention on intellectual and academic achievement: A follow-up study of children from low-income families. *Child Development, 65,* 684–698.
A careful longitudinal study of the effects of high-quality child care on low-income children's development is detailed in this article.

Hayes, C. D., Palmer, J. L., & Zaslow, M. J. (1990). *Who cares for America's children?: Child care policy for the 1990s.* Washington, DC: National Academy Press.
This book presents a summary of the findings and recommendations of the Panel on Child Care Policy which was convened by the National Research Council of the National Academy of Science.

Posner, J., & Vandell, D. L. (1994). Low-income children's after-school care: Are there beneficial effects of after-school programs? *Child Development, 65,* 440–456.
This article compares the school adjustment of low-income urban children in four types of after-school arrangements: self-care, formal programs, mother care, and informal adult-supervision.

For Parents and Children

Swan, H. L., & Houston, V. (1985). *Alone after school: A self-care guide for latchkey children and their parents.* Englewood Cliffs, NJ: Prentice-Hall.
This training manual for children in self-care includes separate sections for parents, school-age children, and early adolescents. Information is provided for parents so that they can judge their child's readiness for self-care and help their children prepare for being on their own. Exercises are offered to help build children's self-care skills, including preparation for emergency situations. Other sections deal with sibling relations, telephone use, health and safety, and summer vacation.

Zigler, E. F., & Lang, M. E. (1991). *Child care choices: Balancing the needs of children, families, and society.* New York: Free Press.
This is an easy-to-read summary of the latest research on child care by experts in child development.

References

Baydar, N., & Brooks-Gunn, J. (1991). Effects of maternal employment and child-care arrangements on preschoolers' cognitive and behavioral outcomes. Evidence from the children of the National Longitudinal Survey of Youth. *Developmental Psychology, 27,* 932–945.

Belsky, J. (1988). The "effects" of infant day care reconsidered. *Early Childhood Research Quarterly, 3,* 235–272.

Belsky, J., & Rovine, M. (1988). Nonmaternal care in the first year of life and the security of infant-parent attachment. *Child Development, 59,* 157–167.

Bretherton, I. (1992). Attachment and bonding. In V. B. Van Hasselt, & M. Hersen (Eds.), *Handbook of social development: A lifespan perspective* (pp. 133–155). New York: Plenum Press.

Campbell, F. A., & Ramey, C. T. (1994). Effects of early intervention on intellectual and academic achievement: A follow-up study of children from low-income families. *Child Development, 65,* 684–698.

Caughy, M. O., DiPietro, J. A., & Strobino, D. M. (1994). Day-care participation as a protective factor in the cognitive development of low-income children. *Child Development, 65,* 457–471.

Clarke-Stewart, K. A. (1989). Infant day care. Maligned or malignant? *American Psychologist, 44,* 266–273.

Clarke-Stewart, K. A. (1992). Consequences of child care for children's development. In A. Booth (Ed.), *Child care in the 1990s: Trends and consequences* (pp. 63–82). Hillsdale, NJ: Lawrence Erlbaum.

Clarke-Stewart, K. A., Gruber, C., & Fitzgerald, L. (1994). *Children at home and at day care.* Hillsdale, NJ: Lawrence Erlbaum.

Egeland, B., & Hiester, M. (1995). The long-term consequences of infant day-care and mother-infant attachment. *Child Development, 66,* 474–485.

Galambos, N. L., & Maggs, J. L. (1991). Out-of-school care of young adolescents and self-reported behaviors. *Developmental Psychology, 27*(14), 644–655.

Galinsky, E., Howes, C., Kontos, S., & Shinn, M. (1994). *The study of children in family child care and relative care: Highlights of findings.* New York: Families and Work Institute.

Goelman, H., & Pence, A. (1987). Children in three

types of day care: Daily experiences, quality of care, and developmental outcomes. In A. Honig (Ed.), *Optimizing early child care and education* (pp. 67–76). New York: Gordon & Breach Science Publishers.

Hayes, C. D., Palmer, J. L., & Zaslow, M. J. (Eds.). (1990). *Who cares for American's children?* Washington, DC: National Academy Press.

Helburn, S. (1995). *Cost, quality, and child outcomes in child care centers: Technical report.* Denver, CO: University of Colorado.

Hofferth, S. L., Brayfield, A., Deich, S., & Holcomb, P. (1991). *National Child Care Survey, 1990: A National Association for the Education of Young Children (NAEYC) study.* Washington, DC: Urban Institute Press.

Howes, C., Matheson, C. C., & Hamilton, C. E. (1994). Maternal, teacher, and child care history correlates of children's relationships with peers. *Child Development, 65,* 264–273.

Howes, C., Olenick, M., & Der-Kiureghian, T. (1987). After-school child care in an elementary school: Social development and continuity and complementarity of programs. *Elementary School Journal, 88,* 93–103.

Howes, C., Phillips, D. A., & Whitebook, M. (1992). Thresholds of quality: Implications for the social development of children in center-based child care. *Child Development, 63,* 449–460.

Howes, C., & Stewart, P. (1987). Child's play with adults, toys, and peers: An examination of family and child care influences. *Child Care Quarterly, 14,* 140–151.

Kamerman, S. B. (1989). Child care, women, work, and the family: An international overview of child care services and related policies. In J. S. Lande, S. Scarr, & N. Gunzenhause (Eds.), *Caring for children: Challenge to America* (pp. 93–110). Hillsdale, NJ: Lawrence Erlbaum.

McCartney, K., Scarr, S., Phillips, D., & Grajek, S. (1985). Day care as intervention: Comparisons of varying quality programs. *Journal of Applied Developmental Psychology, 6,* 247–260.

NICHD Early Child Care Research Network. (1996a). Characteristics of infant child care: Factors contributing to positive caregiving. *Early Childhood Research Quarterly.*

NICHD Early Child Care Research Network. (1996b). *Factors affecting parental selection of infant child care.* Manuscript submitted for publication.

NICHD Early Child Care Research Network. (1996c). *Infant child care and attachment security.* Paper presented at invited symposium conducted at the International Conference for Infant Studies, Providence, RI.

Phillips, D., Lande, J., & Goldberg, M. (1990). The state of child care regulations: A comparative analysis. *Early Childhood Research Quarterly, 5,* 151–179.

Presser, H. B. (1989, November). Can we make time for children? The economy, work schedules, and child care. *Demography, 26*(4), 523–543.

Rosenthal, R., & Vandell, D. L. (in press). Quality of care at school-aged child care programs: Regulatable features, observed experiences, child perspectives, and parent perspectives. *Child Development.*

Scarr, S., Phillips, D., & McCartney, K. (1990). Facts, fantasies, and the future of child care in the United States. *Psychological Science, 1,* 26–35.

Todd, C. M., Albrecht, K. M., & Coleman, M. (1990, Spring). School-age child care: A continuum of options. *Journal of Home Economics, 82,* 46–52.

U.S. Department of Education. (1995, October). *Statistics in brief: Child care and early education program participation of infants, toddlers, and preschoolers,* NCES 95–824. Washington, DC: Author.

Vandell, D. L., & Corasaniti, M. A. (1988). The relationship between third graders' after-school care and social, academic, and emotional functioning. *Child Development, 59,* 868–875.

Vandell, D. L., Hyde, J. S., Plant, E. A., & Essex, M. J. (1996). *Fathers and "others" as child care providers during the first year: Predictors of parents' emotional well-being and marital relationships.* Manuscript submitted for publication.

Vandell, D. L., & Posner, J. (in press). Conceptualization and measurement of children's after-school environments. In S. L. Friedman & T. D. Wachs (Eds.), *Assessment of the environment across the lifespan.*

Whitebook, M., Howes, C., & Phillips, D. (1989). *Who cares? Child care teachers and the quality of care in America* [Final Report, National Child Care Staffing Study]. Oakland, CA: Child Care Employee Project.

52

Short-Term Family Separation

Frederic J. Medway
University of South Carolina

Background

The psychological study of the modern family typically has focused on one of two situations, those in which family members have frequent and stable interactions with each other and those in which the interaction is ended by some type of permanent separation of children from parent or parents such as happens in death and divorce. In many cases, however, separations of family members are imposed upon the family as the result of external factors. These separations, often short-term and frequently repeated, include the demands of various occupations and military service. Included in the former category are executives and sales personnel who must travel as part of their jobs, those in the travel industry such as pilots and bus drivers, construction workers, missionaries, seasonal workers, and those whose job schedules (e.g., shift work) separate parents and children (Riggs, 1990). Included in the latter category are both full-time, active military and those in the Reserves and National Guard. A different and often more damaging forced separation results from the incarceration of a parent in a family with children (Gabel, 1992; Hale, 1987). Such separations can also result when a parent must be away from home for personal reasons (e.g., to be with an ill relative or to go on vacation).

For the most part, there has been relatively little attention paid to children's reactions to brief periods of family separation during which normal family relations must be maintained. The few early papers addressing reactions to these separations, growing out of the separation of children from fathers during World War II, tended to equate these phenomena with grief and mourning (Hill, 1949). Recent research, however, has addressed family separation in terms of family systems theory, personality differences in coping with separation, individuals' cognitions and beliefs about separation, and various situational variables associated with the separation (Hale, 1987; Vormbrock, 1993).

Intermittent separations of children from their families are presumed to create a temporary disruption in the family unit (Riggs, 1990) which can have direct effects on children or, in the case of one parent away from home, can be mediated by the coping style of the parent who remains at home with the child. Children's reactions can take a variety of forms which tend to be nonspecific and relate to the developmental stage of the child (Gabel, 1992). These reactions include behavioral and emotional problems, many of which are manifested in school. Consequently, it is important for school psychologists to understand the dynamics of these situations in order to develop prevention and intervention strategies. This chapter focuses primarily on parent absence due to work and military requirements. Some attention also is given to the psychological reactions of children whose parents are incarcerated. However, because of space considerations and the breadth of this topic, readers desiring additional information on incarceration should see Gabel (1992) and Gouke and Rollins (1990). Issues of child hospitalization are covered elsewhere in this volume. For related information on commuter marriages readers should see Gerstal and Gross (1984).

Problems of family separation touch the lives of millions of adults and children daily. Riggs (1990) estimated that over 37 million adults or 34% of the labor force are in occupations involving business travel away from home. Nearly 210 million business trips are taken yearly, and business travelers are away from home about 3 to 4 days at a time. Although business travel primarily affects males, almost a third of the trips are taken by women (U.S. Travel Data Center, 1994). About 3.5% of the U.S. population are in the active military, National Guard, or Reserves or depend on someone who is (Black, 1993). About half of all enlisted personnel have children of preschool age (Black, 1993). During the Persian Gulf War, approximately 645,000 troops were deployed, most of whom were married and with children (Department of Defense, 1992). At their return, 19% reported moderate or severe family adjustment problems, and many reported problems in dealing with their children (Figley, 1993). Finally, estimates indicate that over one million men and women are incarcerated in the United States, more than half of whom are married, separated, or supporting other persons (King, 1993). "Millions of children . . . either currently have a parent who is incarcerated or have had an incarcerated parent at some point in their lives" (Gabel, 1992, p. 303).

Short-term family separations are defined as temporary, but often repetitive, physical separations of family members who anticipate and hope to be reunited and expect to resume normal family life, at least until the next separation. Most of the research in this area is based on studies of children who undergo brief parent absence primarily due to parent military obligations (e.g., Hunter, 1982; Jensen, Lewis, & Xenakis, 1986; Kaslow, 1993; McCubbin, Dahl, & Hunter, 1976), and, to a lesser extent, to work demands (Piotrkowski & Gornick, 1987; Riggs, 1990; Vormbrock, 1993). There is general consensus that these separations should be viewed as stressors for the family and that some type of coping or family readjustment is required for successful resolution. There also is evidence to support the notion that these separations are not necessarily negative. For example, husband absence often is associated with reports of increased independence and adoption of sought-after responsibility on the part of wives remaining at home. Additionally, both positive and negative reactions might be observed in children. These reactions may be short-term and transient or be long-term and modify previously acquired behavior patterns. Short-term family separations involve a series of interrelated stages. At each stage the stay-at-home spouse and any children may develop coping difficulties. And at each stage there may be opportunities for school psychologists to intervene with the parents, the child, and the entire family unit.

Beginning with the notion that not all temporary separations are alike and that different types of separations will produce different reactions in parents and children, Medway and Cafferty (1991) developed a simplified conceptual framework to organize the study of intermittent temporary separation. Drawing on military and organizational studies, Medway and Cafferty view separation as consisting of three phases: (a) anticipation and preparation, (b) physical separation, and (c) reunion (see Figure 1).

Anticipation involves the processes which families go through once separation is imminent. During this stage, both the adults and children may have anticipatory anxiety and be preoccupied with the upcoming separation. The parent leaving home may become preoccupied with work that must be finished before departing and, therefore, become "psychologically absent." Separation involves the actual physical separation of one or more family members from the rest of the unit. It commonly involves changes in family routines necessitated by parent absence although, as just indicated, it may have both positive and negative outcomes for individuals. Finally, reunion refers to a series of interpersonal processes and renegotiations of relationships which begin once separated individuals are reunited and may continue well beyond the actual day(s) of home-

Conceptual Framework for Intermittent Separation

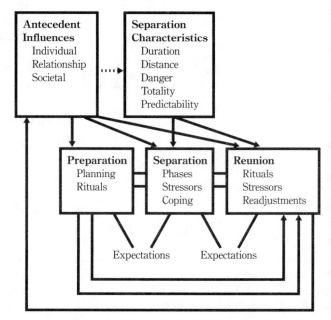

Note. From *A Model of Intermittent Family Separations: Practice Implications,* a paper presented at the August 1991 meeting of the American Psychological Association in San Francisco by F.J. Medway and T. P. Cafferty. Copyright 1991 by F.J. Medway and T.P. Cafferty. Reprinted with permission.

Figure 1. *Conceptual Framework for Intermittent Separation*

coming. Further, according to the model, anticipation, separation, and reunion are influenced by certain antecedent conditions and by the nature of the separation. Finally, the stress of separation appears to depend on one's marital beliefs and expectations such that holding realistic expectations about anticipation, separation, and reunion tends to minimize marital dissatisfaction during these stages (cf. Jones & Stanton, 1988).

Figure 1 shows that antecedent conditions impacting on separation may include individual, relationship, and social influences. Individual factors include family members' gender, personality characteristics, attachment styles, life experiences with separation, self-sufficiency, coping styles, and attitudes about the separation. To illustrate, boys appear to be more vulnerable than girls to father absence (Gabel, 1992). Relationship factors include the level of marital satisfaction, number of children in the home, existing social supports provided by siblings and the caretaking parent, and prior family experience in dealing with separation. Societal influences include how the society views the separation and the social supports available through the extended family and community. For example, military service does not carry a stigma as incarceration does, particularly when it involves a middle-class family who may try and keep the reason for the parent's absence hidden from young children and neighbors.

The conceptual framework of Figure 1 shows that separations themselves vary in many ways including

- The length of time a parent is away.
- The frequency of these separations (one-time occurrence or regular aspect of family life).
- The geographic distance between parent(s) and child (e.g., a stateside versus overseas business trip, confinement to a local jail or federal prison).
- The opportunity for contact or written and oral communication.
- The danger faced by the separated parent (e.g., war combat, incarceration) and the possible danger to those who remain at home (e.g., increased vulnerability to crime).
- The correspondence with key life events (i.e., separation of family members during holidays and birthdays).
- The predictability or suddenness of separation (Piotrkowski & Gornick, 1987).
- The opportunity for family members to exercise control over when separation occurs.
- The extent to which the separation is required to meet larger goals such as economic realities and national defense.
- The presence of other exogenous stressors during the phases such as family crises, illness, or the like.

Medway, Davis, Cafferty, Chappell, and O'Hearn (1995) found that separations can reliably be rated on these different dimensions and these ratings in turn relate to ultimate separation costs. In a study of 158 spouses of soldiers deployed during the Persian Gulf War, it was found that spouse personal distress was primarily due to perceptions that the soldiers' deployment was lengthy, dangerous, and unexpected; involved little choice; entailed little opportunity for contact; and involved high uncertainty regarding the time when the soldier would return home. This distress, in turn, was related to a variety of behavior problems on the part of children in the family.

Finally, cognitive processes are important in all phases of the model. These include memories (of past separations, of characteristics of the loved one) and unmet expectations (Epstein & Eidelson, 1981). For example, in a modern business climate characterized by family relocation, low job security, world markets, shift work, and dual earner families, it is unrealistic to assume that, in a two-parent family, both parents should always be available to care for the children. Holding such unrealistic expectations ultimately will negatively impact relationship satisfaction. Rather, it is better to focus thoughts on how one can use time during separation productively. Finally, within the phases of separation and reunion, one can examine how families cope and readjust. These coping and adjustment factors, in turn, serve to highlight useful intervention strategies to reduce family separation stress.

Developmental Issues

An excellent starting point for considering the effects of short-term separations on children is Miller's (1978) biopsychological model. This model holds that families should be viewed as systems whose members are interconnected in terms of their personal relationships. When one or more caregivers are separated from the child, the family system must reorganize and the remaining adults and children must adopt new roles and responsibilities to reduce system strain. Hill (1949) was the first to observe that war-time separations cause families to establish new roles and that the family left behind is not necessarily the same one to which the separated family member returns. According to Figley (1993), "families affected by major life events can respond in complex ways. These can best be understood by identifying the sources of stress (stressors), stress reactions (both individual and interpersonal), and the methods by which families cope with these stressors and reactions to control or eliminate them" (p. 54).

Short-term separations are highly disruptive for the adults in families (Vormbrock, 1993). The parent at home suffers depressive behavior, anxiety, irritability, resentment, sexual problems, and psychosomatic complaints (e.g., Amen, Jellen, Merves, & Lee, 1988; Kelley, 1994b). Often there are conflicting emotions with anger and resentment over spouse separation mixed with feelings of depression and anxiety over spouse loss (Vormbrock, 1993). The adults may become apprehensive about changes in themselves and anticipated changes in their partners. At-home spouses are at increased risk for ineffective coping and substance abuse (Figley, 1993). They may withdraw from their caregiving duties or become overly punitive with children (Kelley, 1994a). Departing spouses typically report guilt about having to be away from the family and fears that the quality of the marriage and family relationships will suffer (Hunter, 1982; McCubbin & Dahl, 1976; McCubbin, Dahl, & Hunter, 1976; Piotrkowski & Gornick, 1987). These reactions are reported in research on occupational and military separation as well as incarceration.

Parent absence has significant effects on children's behavior (Black, 1993; Gabel, 1992; Riggs, 1990). An unanswered question is whether these separations have a direct effect on the children or whether children's reactions are mediated by the remaining caretaker's separation reaction. There is a strong association between maternal dysfunction and abnormal behavior in children (Downey & Coyne, 1990; Gabel, 1992; Kelley, 1994b; Medway et al., 1995). In all likelihood children must deal with both separation losses and changes in the parenting environment. A study of military families during the Persian Gulf War found that children's behavior was related more to the reported distress of the stay-at-home parent than to the stress caused by parent absence (Medway et al., 1995).

Estimates suggest that between 20% and 70% of children faced with short-term parent separation exhibit some behavioral changes. The numbers of children affected cannot be precisely estimated because children's reactions are influenced by the type of family separation experience, children's developmental levels and coping mechanisms, and existing family supports. Among the behaviors cited in the literature are oppositional behavior, truancy, delinquency, anxiety, fearfulness, withdrawal, dependency, depression, and academic problems. Children express feelings of anger, insecurity, loneliness, abandonment, and insecurity (Figley, 1993; Riggs, 1990). For example, 22% of the children of soldiers deployed during the Persian Gulf War showed increased discipline problems, although serious problems were reported in only 7% (Department of Defense, 1992). Behavioral changes may begin before actual parent separation when children become anxious over the upcoming separation and sense changes in their parents' availability (Kelley, 1994a).

While there appear to be certain developmental stages during which short-term separations increase children's problems, there is little conclusive evidence on this issue at this time. One critical age period is between ages two and five years. Infants, toddlers, and preschoolers are vulnerable to feelings of abandonment and fears that the parent will not return (Yeatman, 1981). These children are less likely to understand the need for parental absence, and caring for their developmental needs is difficult for the parent at home (Kelley, 1994b). The early marital years, and the years when children are young, also are times when business travel may make the greatest demand on parents (Riggs, 1990). Problems can occur during the elementary school years when children rely on their parents to fulfill a wide variety of needs including socialization, development of self-image, and academic competence. Separation from fathers for young males is associated with greater dependency and academic problems (Gullotta & Donohue, 1981). Early adolescence also appears to be a difficult time for children to deal with separation (Shinn, 1978), particularly separation due to incarceration. Young males around the age of puberty are particularly susceptible to separation stresses associated with fathers' incarcerations and often resort to acting-out behavior (Gabel & Shindledecker, 1993).

The role of the parent or substitute caregiver in helping children adjust to these separations has received little attention. However, related literature on parenting following a family divorce suggests that the custodial parent may be less affectionate and consistent and suffer some loss of parental control (Wallerstein & Blakeslee, 1989). Articles by Amen et al. (1988) and Jensen et al. (1986) describe military spouses separated from soldiers as overwhelmed, as relaxing household rules and routines,

as overprotective and impatient with children, and as withdrawing emotionally from them. Mothers reported yelling more at their sons during separation as compared to changes in other disciplinary methods (Kelley, 1994a).

Reintegration of the absent member into the family unit poses additional challenges for the system. Reunion is not only a time of significant family stress, it may actually be more stressful than separation (Vormbrock, 1993). Some of the positive benefits of separation for the at-home spouse such as increased feelings of personal freedom may end at reunion (McCubbin, Dahl, & Hunter, 1976). Among the factors that seem most closely related to successful coping with separation and to readjustment on reunion are the degree of preparation for separation, the subjective level of hardship involved, and preexisting marital satisfaction. Upon reunion, the returning parent feels out of touch with the family and the home spouse may perceive the returnee as a "stranger" (Bey & Lange, 1974). As a result, there are conflicts around child discipline and family management.

Problems and Implications

In determining the emotional and behavioral impact of short-term separations on children, school psychologists must take a systemic view and realize that these family disruptions will result in greater conflict when there are preexisting family problems, poor marital relationships, and low family cohesiveness. Repeated, externally imposed separations of the adults may impair communication; decrease marital spontaneity; and increase feelings of anger, jealousy, distrust, and unfaithfulness (Lang, 1988).

The effects of short-term separations on families can be understood through the conservation of resources model (Hobfoll et al., 1991). According to this theory, two factors moderate a family's reaction to separation and other stresses. The first element is the actual or perceived stress on the family. These stressors include family-life disruptions; assumptions of new family tasks; possible changes in standards of living; deprivation of spouse support; dealing with the procedures and policies of the work, military, or correctional setting; and fears and uncertainties about the welfare of the separated parent (Figley, 1993). Situations that put the separated parent in potential danger, limit family communication, or require extended separation (e.g., incarceration or war) should, therefore, put more stress on family members than those that are routine. Although the research literature supports this notion (e.g., Kelley, 1994a; Medway et al., 1995), even routine separations can be difficult for children, especially in families where preexisting stressors, such as financial hardships and parent mental health problems, are already in place (Lang, 1988).

The second factor in the conservation of resources model (Hobfoll et al., 1991) is the availability and use of existing resources for coping with separation stress. These coping responses can be separated into two types: (a) the supportive resources in the social environment and (b) the parents' and child's characteristic way of coping with separation and stress. Thus, the nature and severity of separation stress interacts with personal resources to heighten or mitigate the stress reaction.

There are several effective ways families can use the social environment to moderate stress (Figley, 1993). One method is by increasing social contact with others, especially those in similar situations. Another is to increase the quality and quantity of family communication. A third is to increase the flexibility within the family to meet multiple demands. Specific examples of these and other effective coping mechanisms will be provided later in this chapter.

In terms of personal characteristics available for dealing with separation, much recent research has focused on the role of childhood and adult attachment styles (Cafferty, Davis, Medway, O'Hearn, & Chappell, 1994; Vormbrock, 1993). The attachment theory of Bowlby (1969, 1973, 1980) appears to have major implications for separation and reunion reactions. According to Bowlby, attachment is a behavioral system enacted with the goal of bringing the infant into the proximity of an adult caregiver so as to minimize danger, threat, and novelty. The system becomes organized by the infant through the development of working (or representational) models of the self and the relevant caregiver—usually the mother or "mother figure." These models are stored in memory on either the conscious or unconscious level or both and are strongly influenced by interactions between child and caregiver early in the child's life. Bowlby developed an extensive analysis of grief and mourning in children faced with the perceived loss of a parent or attachment figure. He described the common separation reactions of protest, despair, and detachment.

Ainsworth, Blehar, Waters, and Wall (1978) described three childhood attachment styles: secure, insecure avoidant, and insecure anxious/ambivalent. Securely attached children adjusted easily to both separation from caregivers and reunion with them. Insecure avoidant children showed little separation protest and tended to avoid or ignore their caregivers at reunion. Insecure anxious children reacted to both separation and reunion poorly. They strongly protested separation and tended to resist contact upon reunion, often vacillating between anger and dependency. These attachment styles, in turn, appear related to parents' caregiving styles such that parents of securely attached children tend to be consistent and available and engage in high levels of physical contact. Further, these styles tend to be stable until age six (Main, Kaplan, & Cassidy, 1985) and potentially into adulthood (Hazan & Shaver, 1987). Recent research and theory suggest that adults with secure attachment styles, although distressed by separation, maintain the affectionate relationship and tend to have children with fewer behavior problems during separation than parents with less secure styles (Medway et al., 1995; Vormbrock, 1993).

Alternative Actions

Because separation-related problems can give rise to a host of nonspecific internalizing and externalizing problems which are not unique to the separation experience as compared to other family stressors, a family history is necessary to (a) establish the influence of separation and other stressors on the family and (b) reveal available supports to the child in his or her environment. In some cases school psychologists will almost immediately recognize the causative role of parent separation as in the case of military deployments, parent incarcerations, and other relatively public events. In the wake of the Persian Gulf War in January 1991, both the National Association of School Psychologists and the School Psychology Division of the American Psychological Association mobilized and coordinated referrals and other services. Diagnosing the role of more routine separations, such as business travel or temporary marital separation, will be more difficult. To do this almost certainly will require an extensive interview with the parent and a sensitivity to the issues raised in this chapter.

The bulk of the literature on assisting children and families deal with short-term separations comes from studies involving military families. The military, through its Family Assistance Programs, often working with the base schools for military dependents, has taken the lead in developing and implementing effective support services to deal with family separation (Department of Defense, 1992; Figley, 1993), although efforts were modest prior to the Vietnam War (Jensen et al., 1976). By contrast, providing assistance to families dealing with separations has not been widely addressed by social service agencies, educators, the business sector, and correctional facilities. Separation-related services for prisoners' families has largely resulted from advocacy efforts of inmate groups themselves (Hairston & Lockett, 1987).

With appropriate training in assessment, including family assessment, child development, intervention, and prevention, school psychologists should have the necessary skills to aid both families dealing with separation-related crises and teachers whose students may have difficulty learning because of concern over parent absence. Psychologists can serve an important educative function on the nature of stress, coping, developmental reactions, and parenting. In most cases school psychologists will be called in to assist when children's behavioral changes are relatively serious. They are less likely to learn about the separation distresses of the caretaking parent in the absence of a serious change in the school performance or behavior of the child. Accordingly, by the time that school psychologists are involved with the child there may well be others involved with the primary caretaker at home such as family therapists, clergy, military support personnel, and social workers. This should not, however, preclude school psychologists from becoming key providers of mental health services to children and families faced with separation stresses. Recommended services involve (a) developing support programs to aid families with separation issues and (b) working directly with children experiencing separation difficulties.

Prevention

No studies designed to prevent short-term separation stress have been conducted, although the literature suggests several factors that school psychologists should consider in designing such programs (Figley, 1993). First, educational efforts are important. These efforts can take the form of school-based workshops for families and teachers concerned with separation issues. Topics might include separation phases, the importance of family flexibility and maintaining open communication with the departed parent, the role of individual attachment styles and developmental variables, and effective rather than ineffective coping styles. A program sharing some similarities with this recommended school-based effort is one called Parents in Prison, instituted by inmates of the Tennessee State Penitentiary (Hairston & Lockett, 1987). The program seeks to strengthen separated families, improve communication, and develop effective parenting styles.

Second, school psychologists can serve an important function by linking families faced with intermittent separation circumstances so that they may provide mutual, informal support. And third, the school psychologist should indicate to supervisors that he or she has expertise in this area and can be the first contact point to provide services should routine or more dramatic family separation events occur. This role will require the school psychologist to be knowledgeable regarding outside mental health services in a community. In an extreme situation, such as military conflict or hostage taking involving a community family, services will be needed not only by those immediately affected but by all children with fears, anxieties, and questions. To illustrate, during the Persian Gulf War, a school in Norfolk, Virginia, sponsored a Deployed Dad program. Each day the students tracked the deployment journey of a different father on a map and learned about the various places. The child brought stamps, postcards, and other items sent from the father, and all children in the class wrote the absent father letters. In this way, deployment became an educational experience for all children, and all became a part

of the support system (Department of Defense, 1992). Similar programs could be modeled on this one for children whose parents do frequent business travel or are away from home on other emergencies.

Assessment and Counseling

The most effective assessment and counseling programs (a) adopt a family systems orientation, (b) attempt to empower families (and children) and build on their strengths, (c) are brief and focused, (d) are sensitive to the long-term outcomes of separation, (e) encourage the family to take a positive view of the separation, and (f) teach the family to be more prepared to deal with future separations (Figley, 1993). It is important to look at what else is going on in the family and in the child's life and at how the system is coping. School-age children could be advised to write letters and send audiotapes and photos to the separated parent(s), to keep a log or diary of family events occurring during separation, to have a specific list of chores and duties, and to take opportunities to talk to others about their feelings. Children can be helped to understand that birthdays and other events may have to be celebrated after the parent returns and that the returning parent may be tired and may act a bit differently depending upon the length of the separation.

Support Groups

During the Persian Gulf War there was an impressive effort by the military to set up support groups to help children of affected personnel cope (Department of Defense, 1992). Numerous support groups were organized by local communities, religious organizations, social service organizations such as the Red Cross, and professional associations. These support groups appeared beneficial for children and adults with separation problems, although some evidence indicated that the groups were particularly valuable when initial stress levels were high (Medway et al., 1995). It is important, however, for school psychologists to realize that such groups should not be limited to the separation period but should extend into the reunion period.

Summary

School psychologists typically have been involved with children whose families face permanent separations from parents such as occur in divorce and death. However, many children find themselves in short-term, intermittent separations from parents due to external circumstances such as work, military demands, and incarceration. These situations stress the ability of the family to adjust, often result in distress and conflicting emotions for the at-home parent, and can result in child behavior problems, many of which occur in school.

Families can deal successfully with these crises by learning coping skills which increase their control over the separation-related stressors, improve communication among all family members, and provide opportunities for children to express potential anxieties and fears. In addition, schools can facilitate important educational and support functions for these families. As indicated, millions of children potentially are impacted by these family separations. Unfortunately, these problems have been largely ignored by community organizations (Hairston & Lockett, 1987) with the exception of situations involving massive family separation such as occur during military deployment. School psychologists, however, can provide needed services both by making the issues of family separations salient in their schools and communities and by serving as key resources, along with other mental health professionals, to help school children and their parents effectively adjust to family separations and reunions.

Recommended Resources

Barrett, J. M. (1978). *No time for me.* New York: Human Sciences Press.
This book tells the story of Jimmy who feels hurt and abandoned because his parents' work leaves little time for him. It is intended for children between ages four and eight and is useful for dealing with separation feelings.

Bauer, C. F., (1981). *My mom travels a lot.* New York: F. Warne.
This is a picture book designed for young children whose parents work requires frequent travel.

Bloom-Feshbach, J., & Bloom-Feshbach, S. (Eds.). (1987). *The psychology of separation and loss.* San Francisco: Jossey-Bass.
In this edited book, various scholars address how separation experiences affect development throughout the life span. Included are discussions of divorce, daily parental absence, parental death, school adjustments, and other topics. This is an excellent theoretical reference.

Lang, D. V. (1988). *The phantom spouse: Helping you and your family survive business travel or relocation.* White Hall, VA: Betterway.
Lang, a journalist and teacher, writes of the emotions and challenges faced by executive spouses based on personal experience, interviews, and expert advice. This book, aimed at the at-home spouse, contains many suggestions, tips, and strategies for dealing with separation.

Vormbrock, J. K. (1993). Attachment theory as applied to wartime and job-related marital separation. *Psychological Bulletin, 114,* 122–144.
*This comprehensive review article is a rich resource of integrative theory on numerous articles dealing with short-term sep-*aration. *The focus is primarily on relationship issues rather than child reactions.*

References

Ainsworth, M. D. S., Blehar, M. C., Waters, E., & Wall, S. (1978). *Patterns of attachment: A psychological study of the strange situation.* New York: Wiley.

Amen, D. J., Jellen, L., Merves, E., & Lee, R. E. (1988). Minimizing the impact of deployment on military children: Stages, current preventive efforts, and system recommendations. *Military Medicine, 153,* 441–446.

Bey, D. R., & Lange, J. (1974). Waiting wives: Women under stress. *American Journal of Psychiatry, 131,* 283–286.

Black, W. G., Jr. (1993). Military-induced family separation: A stress reduction intervention. *Social Work, 38,* 273–280.

Bowlby, J. (1969). *Attachment.* New York: Basic Books.

Bowlby, J. (1973). *Attachment and loss: Vol. 2. Separation.* New York: Basic Books.

Bowlby, J, (1980). *Attachment and loss: Vol. 3. Loss.* New York: Basic Books.

Cafferty, T. P., Davis, K. E., Medway, F. J., O'Hearn, R. E., & Chappell, K. D. (1994). Reunion dynamics among couples separated during Operation Desert Storm: An attachment theory analysis. In K. Bartholomew & D. Perlman (Eds.), *Advances in personal relationships* (Vol. 5, pp. 309–330). London: Jessica Kingsley.

Department of Defense. (1992). *DoD Report on Title III of the Persian Gulf conflict and supplemental authorization and Personnel Benefits Act of 1991, Public Law 102–25.* Arlington, VA: Department of Defense.

Downey, G., & Coyne, J. C. (1990). Children of depressed parents: An integrative review. *Psychological Bulletin, 108,* 50–76.

Epstein, N., & Eidelson, R. J. (1981). Unrealistic beliefs of clinical couples: Their relationships to expectations, goals, and satisfaction. *American Journal of Family Therapy, 9,* 13–22.

Figley, C. R. (1993). Coping with stressors on the home front. *Journal of Social Issues, 49,* 51–71.

Gabel, S. (1992). Behavioral problems in sons of incarcerated or otherwise absent fathers: The issue of separation. *Family Process, 31,* 303–314.

Gabel, S., & Shindledecker, R. (1993). Characteristics of children whose parents have been incarcerated. *Hospital and Community Psychiatry, 44,* 656–660.

Gerstal, N., & Gross, H. (1984). *Commuter marriage.* New York: Guilford Press.

Gouke, M. N., & Rollins, A. M. (1990). *One-parent children, The growing minority: A research guide.* New York: Garland.

Gullotta, T. P., & Donohue, K. C. (1981). The corporate family: Theory and treatment. *Journal of Marital and Family Therapy, 7,* 151–158.

Hairston, C. F., & Lockett, P. W. (1987). Parents in prison: New directions for social services. *Social Work, 32,* 162–164.

Hale, D. C. (1987). The impact of mothers' incarceration on the family system: Research and recommendations. *Marriage and Family Review, 12,* 143–154.

Hazan, C, & Shaver, P. (1987). Conceptualizing romantic love as an attachment process. *Journal of Personality and Social Psychology, 52,* 511–524.

Hill, R. (1949). *Families under stress: Adjustment to the crises of war separation and reunion.* New York: Harper Brothers.

Hobfoll, S. E., Spielberger, C. D., Breznitz, S., Figley, C., Folkman, S., Lepper-Green, B., Meichenbaum, D., Milgram, N., Sandler, I., Sarason, I., & van der Kolk, B. (1991). War-related stress: Addressing the stress of war and other traumatic events. *American Psychologist, 46,* 848–855.

Hunter, E. J. (1982). *Families under the flag.* New York: Praeger.

Jensen, P., Lewis, R., & Xenakis, S. (1986). The military family in review: Context, risk, and prevention. *Journal of the American Academy of Child Psychiatry, 6,* 51–63.

Jones, M. E., & Stanton, A. L. (1988). Dysfunctional beliefs, belief similarity, and marital distress: A comparison of models. *Journal of Social and Clinical Psychology, 7,* 1–14.

Kaslow, F. (1993). *The military family in war and peace.* New York: Springer.

Kelley, M. L. (1994a). The effects of military-induced separation on family factors and children's behavior. *American Journal of Orthopsychiatry, 64,* 103–111.

Kelley, M. L. (1994b). Military-induced separation in relation to maternal adjustment and children's behavior. *Military Psychology, 6,* 163–176.

King, A. E. O. (1993). The impact of incarceration on African American families: Implications for practice. *Families in Society, 74,* 145–153.

Lang, D. V. (1988). *The phantom spouse: Helping your family survive business travel or relocation.* White Hall, VA: Betterway.

Main, M., Kaplan, N., & Cassidy, J. (1985). Security in infancy, childhood, and adulthood: A move to the level of representation. In I. Bretherton & E. Waters (Eds.), *Growing points of attachment theory and research* (pp. 66–104). Chicago: University of Chicago Press for the Society for Research in Child Development. Monographs of the Society for Research in Child Development 50: 1–2, Serial No. 209, 66–104.

McCubbin, H. I., & Dahl, B. B. (1976). Prolonged family separation in the military: A longitudinal study. In H. I. McCubbin, B. B. Dahl, & E J. Hunter (Eds.), *Families in the military system* (pp. 112–144). Beverly Hills, CA: Sage.

McCubbin, H. I., Dahl, B. B., & Hunter, E. J. (1976). *Families in the military system.* Beverly Hills, CA: Sage.

Medway, F. J., & Cafferty, T. P. (1991, August). *A model of intermittent family separations: Practice implications.* Paper presented at the meeting of the American Psychological Association, San Francisco.

Medway, F. J., Davis, K. E., Cafferty, T. P., Chappell, K. D., & O'Hearn, R. E. (1995). Family disruption and adult attachment correlates of spouse and child reactions to separation and reunion due to Operation Desert Storm. *Journal of Social and Clinical Psychology, 14,* 97–118.

Miller, J. G. (1978). *Living systems.* New York: McGraw-Hill.

Piotrkowski, C. S., & Gornick, L. K. (1987). Effects of work-related separations on children and families. In J. Bloom-Feshbach, & S. Bloom-Feshbach (Eds.), *The psychology of separation and loss* (pp. 267–299). San Francisco: Jossey-Bass.

Riggs, B. A. (1990). Routine-work-related absence: The effects on families. *Marriage and Family Review, 15,* 147–160.

Shinn, M. (1978). Father absence and children's cognitive development. *Psychological Bulletin, 85,* 295–324.

Vormbrock, J. (1993). Attachment theory as applied to war-time and job-related marital separations. *Psychological Bulletin, 114,* 122–144.

Wallerstein, J. S., & Blakeslee, S. (1989). *Second chances: men, women, and children a decade after divorce.* NY: Ticknor & Fields.

U.S. Travel Data Center (1994). *Travel printout: Review of travel in America.* Washington, DC.

Yeatman, G. (1981). Parental separation and the military dependent child. *Military Medicine, 146,* 320–322.

53

Divorce

Howard M. Knoff

University of South Florida

M. Denise Bishop

University of Southern Maine

Background and Development

Parents' divorce is one of the most significant life crises experienced by a child or adolescent. Indeed, from a psychological perspective, divorce often has a long-term impact on children's—especially boys'—development and adjustment. Critically, this impact may be evident in all settings and environments, especially at school and in the home (Mitchell, 1987). In schools, for example, divorce has been related to children's increased anxiety, aggressiveness, and other emotional reactions; to poorer social and academic competence ratings and scores; and to the increased likelihood of grade retentions and referrals to school psychologists. In the home, divorce has been related to poorer general family health, lower ratings of children's social competence, significant changes in parents' personal functioning and interactions with their children, and decreased financial stability for the custodial parent (who often is the mother). While some have suggested that many of the social-emotional reactions to divorce are first evident in school, because the child does not feel comfortable expressing his or her feelings at home, the psychological effects of divorce do occur in both home and school settings (Guidubaldi, Cleminshaw, Perry, & McLoughlin, 1983; Guidubaldi & Perry, 1985; Hetherington, 1979; Hetherington, Cox, & Cox, 1978; Kurdek, 1983; Kurdek, Blisk, & Siesky, 1981; Wallerstein, 1984, 1987, 1991; Wallerstein & Kelly, 1976).

For both parents and children, divorce should be conceptualized as a long-term, multistage process dependent on (a) the age of the child at the time of the divorce; (b) the length of time since the divorce; (c) the child's gender; (d) financial, custodial, and other changes after the divorce, including the availability of support systems to cushion the effects of the divorce; (e) home and school conditions and their preparations and responses to the divorce situation; and (f) home, school, and community intervention as needed (Ellwood & Stolberg, 1991; Guidubaldi, Perry, & Nastasi, 1987; Holloway & Machida, 1991; Kurdek, 1981). These different variables will be discussed here along with the impact and implications of divorce and the intervention directions that can best assist children and adolescents to adjust to divorce in the most favorable way possible.

Incidence of Divorce

The number of children affected by divorce is staggering. For example, census and other data suggest that approximately 50% of all current marriages will end in divorce (1,215,000 divorces, for example, were granted in the United States in 1994) and that 40% to 50% of all children born during the past decade will spend some time living in a single-parent family (Hodges, 1991; National Center for Health Statistics, 1995). Further, although the divorce rate has recently stabilized primarily among younger couples, it doubled between 1970 and 1981, and it has more than tripled since 1960. Today, the divorce rate among middle-aged and older individuals is still on the rise (Cooney, 1993). More specifically, in 1970, 11.9% of all children in the United States were living in single-parent homes, partly due to divorce; this percentage increased to 22.5% in 1983 and 25.1% in 1994. Some of these numbers, however, actually are underestimates because children living in remarried households are not typically included.

Children's Ages and Reactions to Divorce

Although developmental status and gender appear to be mediating variables, children from divorced homes seem to be at greater social-emotional and academic-intellectual risk than those from intact families. In fact, children or adolescents at different ages appear to demonstrate a range of different reactions to the divorce situation (Kurdek, 1981; Wallerstein, 1987; Wallerstein & Kelly, 1976, 1980). These age-related effects are summarized next.

593

Infants

Infants' reactions to divorce are closely related to their primary caretakers' emotional status and adjustment. Thus, because of the parent-child bonding, nurturing, and identification processes that begin early in life, infants are potentially at physical and emotional risk during a divorce when the primary caretaker is unable to parent appropriately. In fact, given research suggesting that adults' adjustments to divorce may take 2 years or longer (Hetherington et al., 1978), primary caretakers need to take special care to protect their infants from divorce-related stress responses that impede normal physical, social-emotional, and other developmental milestones.

In investigating another area of early childhood development, Hodges, Landis, Day, and Oderberg (1991) conducted an initial exploration of the relationship between post divorce parental access to infants and toddlers and language development. Significantly, a relationship between visitation and the children's language development was noted with poor visitation patterns being associated with greater language development delays. In addition, they found that fathers who were more involved with their children before the divorce visited more frequently after the separation and that the predivorce conflict between the parents was associated with irregular visitation patterns following separation. Finally, in discussing visitation patterns for children under 3 years old in general, the authors concluded that the child's need for stability, predictability, and security should be taken into account. Overnight visits with the noncustodial parent were not recommended.

Given the important developmental milestones that occur during infancy and the potential impact of divorce on them, far more research and focus on this age level is needed. Despite their predominant focus on school-aged students, practitioners need to understand how divorce functionally impacts infants. For example, when they know of a divorce situation in the schools, school psychologists might investigate whether the parents of school-aged children also have infants at home so that appropriate information and support can be offered. This preventive step might decrease an infant's later need for social and emotional support due to ongoing poor divorce adjustment.

Toddlers

Preschoolers have sometimes reacted to their parent's divorce with diverse emotional manifestations: anxiety, nightmares, depressed play, eating disturbances, bed wetting, sexual identity difficulties, irritability, aggressiveness, bewilderment, self-blame, and guilt. Much concern has been expressed for preschoolers experiencing divorce because their level of cognitive development may cause them to misunderstand or misinterpret why their parents have separated. While more definitive research

on this concern is needed, the behavioral and emotional reactions of the child are indeed real. Interventions for preschool children in single-parent settings, therefore, must be made available if needed. School psychologists, with their knowledge of child development, should take the lead in helping others to discriminate between typical developmental patterns and those specific to divorce at this, and other, age levels.

School-aged children

Young children commonly react to their parents' divorce with depression, withdrawal, grieving, fear, fantasies of responsibility and reconciliation, anger, decreased academic and other school performance, a sense of loss or rejection, requests for explanations, shame, and conflicts over which parent to express loyalty to. Guidubaldi et al. (1983), controlling for IQ differences across their divorced and intact family samples, found that first-, third-, and fifth-grade children from divorced parents scored more poorly on the following scales of the Hahnemann Elementary School Behavior Rating Scale (HESBRS): Originality, Independent Learning, Involvement, Productive with Peers, Intellectual Dependency, Failure Anxiety, Unreflectiveness, Irrelevant Talk, Social (Over)Involvement, Negative Feelings, Holding Back/Withdrawn, Critical/Competitive, Blaming, and Inattention. In addition, teachers' ratings of competence in communication and social interactions, teacher and parents' ratings of the child's popularity, and Wide Range Achievement Test (WRAT) reading and spelling scores were negatively affected. The children from divorced homes also had more school absences and poorer school grades in reading and math, and they were more likely to have been retained. Controlling for socioeconomic status (SES), children from divorced homes scored poorer on all of the HESBRS scales noted except the Originality and Productive with Peers scales. These results indicate that, with the differences across the two samples due to IQ and SES partialed out, children from this national sample of divorced families were at greater social and academic risk than their peers in families unaffected by divorce.

While others (e.g., Kurdek et al., 1981) have found that older children generally exhibit relatively more positive levels of adjustment to divorce, the Guidubaldi et al. study (1983) reported that first graders also showed significantly fewer negative effects from the divorce experience than fifth graders. For example, first graders showed better adjustment than the older children on five of the HESBRS scales (Productive with Peers, Failure Anxiety, Negative Feelings, Critical/Competitive, and Blaming), on three of the Vineland Scale domains (Communication, Socialization, Motor), on the WRAT math scores, and on the regular class versus special class placement measure. The fifth graders showed better adjustment on the Vineland's Daily Living domain, the optimism and locus of control measures, and on parents' ratings of the number of current adjustment problems.

The age measure in the Guidubaldi study, however, was often significantly confounded with the gender variable. Briefly, divorce more seriously affected boys than girls, and *older* boys manifested more significant adjustment problems than younger boys. Conversely, first-grade girls in the Guidubaldi study manifested significant divorce-related problems, while these problems were not more seriously represented in the fifth-grade female sample. More recent data suggest that the ongoing impact of divorce may be related to the gender of the parent who has custody of the male child rather than the fact that boys are more vulnerable during divorce simply because of their gender (Wallerstein, 1991). Comparable results for girls have not been found.

Adolescents

Finally, *adolescents* reportedly react to their parents' divorce, even after 10 years, with interpersonal-relationship, self-identity, and independence problems. Signs of sadness, shame, embarrassment, anxiety about the future and their own potential marriages, and withdrawal also are noted (see Buchanan, Maccoby, & Dornbusch, 1991; Wallerstein, 1991). While some researchers believe that adolescents should more easily adjust to their parents' divorce because they can cognitively understand the separation and divorce process, others feel that the adjustment is more likely to be difficult because the adolescents have experienced more exposure to the parental conflicts. Longitudinally, Wallerstein's (1987) 10-year follow-up of 16- to 18-year-old adolescents ($n = 38$) who experienced their parents' divorce as 8- to 10-year-olds revealed wide variability in individual levels of adjustment. Indeed, only 6 of the 16 girls and 8 of the 22 boys were considered to be psychologically and socially adjusted at the time of the follow-up. Clearly, while the age of the child at the time of a divorce is a predictor of subsequent adjustment, adjustment difficulties do manifest themselves differently as a function of other intervening variables such as the length of time since the divorce (discussed next).

Length of Time Since the Divorce

While some children are able to adjust to their parents' divorce and decrease their resulting emotional reactions, a significant proportion continue to exhibit troublesome behavioral and academic patterns for a period of years. For example, in the one-year follow-up study of Wallerstein and Kelly (1976, 1980), it was estimated that 44% of preschool children, 23% of younger latency-aged children, and 50% of older latency-aged children continued to have similar or worse levels of adjustment problems.

These problems persisted at a 5-year follow-up, in which more than one-third of the original sample was deemed to be at moderate to severe levels of depression, and at a 10-year follow-up, in which preliminary data indicated some emotional traces of sorrow and anger (Wallerstein, 1984).

Kurdek et al. (1981), reporting on a 2-year follow-up of a previous Dayton, Ohio sample, found that children whose parents had been separated for about 4 years were not experiencing severe adjustment problems related to the divorce. However, these children still expressed primarily negative feelings toward the divorce experience, and their parents felt that their children's adjustment was more related to resolving their feelings toward the divorce and not their understanding of why the divorce occurred. Assessments of the children in the sample 2 years later generally revealed no severe problems related to the divorce experience. Overall, the more well-adjusted children were older, had parents who had been divorced a longer period of time, and were characterized by an internal locus of control and high levels of interpersonal functioning and reasoning.

Guidubaldi et al. (1987) reported the comprehensive results of their 2-year follow-up of the 1983 national sample of elementary-school children. Their results indicated that children of divorce (average length of time since divorce = 6.41 years) continued to demonstrate poorer mental health, social competence, and overall adjustment and a broad range of deviant behavior. Specifically, the children from divorced homes were rated more poorly (a) by parents on indices of hostility to adults, peer popularity, nightmares, and anxiety and (b) by teachers on indices of school-related behavior, dependency, anxiety, aggression, withdrawal, inattention, peer popularity, locus of control, and maladaptiveness. Furthermore, they scored more poorly on (a) WISC-R IQ scores; (b) WRAT reading, spelling, and math scores; (c) Vineland Teacher Rating scores in the daily living, social skills, and communications domains; (d) classroom reading and math grades; and (e) physical health ratings. The children of divorce also were more likely to repeat a grade and be referred to the school psychologist. Guidubaldi's findings were consistent with those of Hetherington, et al. (1979) and Wallerstein (1984). Therefore, the discrepancies noted earlier in Kurdek et al. (1981) might have been the result of their methodology and sampling procedures, the assessment tools used, or some idiosyncrasy of the specific sample.

While the preceding section has focused on adjustments that children and youth need to make due to divorce and while some children do exhibit long-term difficulties, most children can adjust to divorce over a period of years. This is especially true when adults recognize the developmental nature of divorce adjustment and respond accordingly.

Problems and Implications

Gender of the Child and Reactions to Divorce

There is consistent, significant evidence that boys experience far more problems due to divorce than girls across the areas of general social-emotional and academic-intellectual development, that these problems get more serious from Grades 1 to 5, that they have a stronger relationship to the time since the parental separation than for girls, and that they persist through Grade 7 (Buehler & Legg, 1992; Guidubaldi & Perry, 1985; Heath & Lynch, 1988; Kurdek, 1981; Wallerstein & Kelly, 1980). For example, Guidubaldi et al. (1983) found that boys from homes affected by divorce manifested significantly poorer adjustment than girls from divorced homes on

■ 10 HESBRS scales: Independent Learning, Productive with Peers, Unreflectiveness, Irrelevant Talk, Social (Over)Involvement, Negative Feelings, Holding Back/Withdrawn, Critical/Competitive, Approach to Teacher, and Inattention.
■ The Vineland Daily Living domain.
■ Measures of peer popularity and optimism.
■ Reading, math, and classroom-conduct grades.
■ WRAT reading, spelling, and math scores.

In addition, girls from the divorced sample were statistically indistinguishable from the intact-family sample of girls as they got older; boys from homes of divorce maintained their poorer adjustment than intact-family boys over time.

From a longitudinal perspective (Guidubaldi et al., 1983), fifth-grade divorced-family boys scored more poorly than fifth-grade intact-family boys on 11 of the 16 HESBRS scales (all except the Originality, Involvement, Productive with Peers, Intellectual Dependency, and Approach to Teacher scales), the Vineland Social domain, a peer-rejection measure, and grades in mathematics. Two years later (Guidubaldi & Perry, 1985), these divorced-family boys still manifested more problems than their intact-family peers, specifically higher frequencies of maladaptive symptoms on the Child Behavior Checklist and the Teacher Report Form (Achenbach, 1991); lower ratings for appropriateness of behavior, work effort, and happiness; and lower scores on an internal locus of control measure.

Relative to relationships in the divorced family, gender differences favoring girls persisted. Boys exhibited poorer adjustments both to parents' authoritarian child-rearing styles (results for girls were mixed) and to their permissive parenting styles (girls responded positively to this style). However, boys seemed better adjusted than girls when the custodial parent was satisfied with the ex-spouse's parenting support.

In a different study based on a 1981 national sample of 1,400 children aged 12 to 16 years, Peterson and Zill (1986) investigated the effects of marital disruption on children's behavior while accounting for differences in living arrangements (e.g., custody), the effects of parent-child relationships, and the degree of marital conflict. The children were separated into three groups: living with both biological parents, living with the biological mother with father absent, or living with biological father with mother absent. The families then were subdivided by the level of conflict between the parents. Low Conflict was defined as couples who were "very happy" and who had arguments in no more than two of nine specified interrelationship areas. High Conflict was defined as couples who were "not too happy" or who indicated that they argued about five or more of the nine interrelationship areas. Five child outcome variables were investigated. Three were based on the Child Behavior Checklist (Achenbach, 1991) and included depressed/withdrawn behavior, impulsive/hyperactive behavior, and antisocial behavior. The other two variables involved discipline referrals for the child at school and school suspensions or expulsions.

Within low-conflict/intact homes, 62% of the children reported a positive relationship with both parents. In contrast, only 29% of the children from high-conflict homes reported a positive relationship with both parents. Girls reported poorer relationships with parents than boys, but children from divorced homes reported more positive relationships when in the custodial care of their same-gender parent. Within divorce situations, the best outcomes for both boys and girls occurred when the children had a positive relationship with both parents. The least favorable outcomes occurred when girls had a poor relationship with both parents. Finally, girls who lived with their fathers had more problems at home than at school. Overall, boys were found to be better adjusted when they lived in a stable environment with fathers who were psychologically well-adjusted. Girls were better adjusted when living with a psychologically well-adjusted mother under similar stable conditions.

Changes after the Divorce and the Availability of Support Systems

Many longitudinal studies have investigated different variables or factors that facilitate children's long-term adjustment to the divorce experience. Summarized by Guidubaldi et al. (1987), Kurdek (1981), and Walsh and Stolberg (1989), these factors include

■ A relatively limited financial loss or impact to the custodial parent, the family, and its predivorce routine and standard of living.
■ The ability of the child to find and use support systems and personal coping skills.

- Low interparent conflict and hostility preceding and following the divorce.
- Postdivorce consistency between the parents with respect to child rearing and disciplinary practices and good single-parenting skills.
- Approval, love, and positive relationships with both parents.
- Authoritative (as opposed to authoritarian) discipline approaches from the custodial parent.
- An emotional climate that permits child and family discussions of divorce-related issues and concerns.
- More frequent and reliable visitations with the non-custodial parent.
- Specific school characteristics such as smaller school populations, environments emphasizing structure and orderliness, traditional rather than open-classroom structures, and proximity of school to home (i.e., shorter distances requiring less busing).
- Family-support factors such as the availability of and interaction with helpful relatives (especially relatives of the noncustodial parent), friends, child-care assistance (e.g., nursery schools), and involvement by the custodial parent in social/recreational groups and experiences.

The parents' own emotional stability has been clearly related to their children's divorce adjustment. In general, the research (reviewed in Kurdek, 1981, and Walsh and Stolberg, 1989) suggests that many divorced parents may need up to 2 years to overcome the emotional effects of the divorce. During the first year, these parents are characterized as (a) less able to accomplish their parenting tasks, (b) less likely to have age-appropriate expectations for their children, (c) more inconsistent in disciplinary approaches and parent-child communication processes, and (d) less interactive and affectionate with the children. Mother-son interactions also were observed to be particularly tense during this time period with increased acts of aggression by boys, increased attempts to be authoritarian by mothers, and increased feelings of incompetence and helplessness in parenting by mothers. By the end of the second, postdivorce year, significant decreases in poor parenting practices, conflictual parent-child relationships, and poor parental social-emotional adjustment were noted.

Expanding on parental disciplinary styles relative to children's divorce adjustment, Guidubaldi evaluated Baumrind's (1968) three patterns of child rearing in his longitudinal study: the *authoritarian* parent who often uses punishment, force, and rejection to control; the *permissive* parent who allows the child to set his or her own controls; and the *authoritative* parent who directs the child using reason and problem solving yet firm structure (see chapter on Parenting Styles, this volume). Overall, boys from divorced homes exhibited poorer adjustment to both the authoritarian and permissive styles. Girls, however, demonstrated mixed adjustment patterns with authoritarian parents and positive adjustment with permissive parents. While clear results have been observed for authoritative parents with children of either sex, custodial mothers often are more controlling and restrictive (authoritarian) with their children after a divorce, whereas noncustodial fathers are more permissive and indulgent. Thus, these parents appeared to be using parenting styles that are least helpful to their children's long-term adjustment.

More recently, Holloway and Machida (1991) investigated the child-rearing effectiveness of divorced mothers as related to their levels of coping and social support systems. In all, 58 divorced mothers and their preschool children (mean age = 4.5 years) were included in the study which used a questionnaire, a maternal-coping scale, and a personal interview to collect the coping and social support data. Results suggested that the use of active cognitive-behavioral problem-solving coping strategies and self-reinforcement were associated with a sense of control in child-rearing situations and with an authoritative parenting style. Coping strategies that involved distancing and escape/avoidance behavior and that were associated with *high* levels of social support were related to greater symptoms of distress. In fact, support from friends accounted for more of the distress and parenting variance than the mother's educational level, current financial stability, time since separation, or geographic place of residence. The availability of family members was associated with *less* authoritative parenting styles *and* less distress, while the availability of friends was related to *more* authoritative parenting but *more* distress. Some of these results seem counter-intuitive and may have been a function of the scales used to collect data. Nonetheless, the social-support literature does suggest that some types of social support are helpful while other types are detrimental. Clearly, more research in this area as it relates to divorce is needed.

Overall, this research indicates that some, but not all, types of social-support systems are helpful to the custodial mother during the adjustment period following divorce. However, it confirms that an authoritative parenting style is most likely to evoke a sense of control over and effectiveness with child management for the single parent.

To summarize, the research suggests that divorced parents (a) should use the same disciplinary approaches and styles with their children, (b) need to communicate about and support one another's disciplinary decisions, and (c) should maintain overt expectations for their children's appropriate behavior and continued social maturation. The research also suggests (a) the need to avoid using authoritarian and permissive disciplinary styles for boys and (b) the relationship between permissive disciplinary styles and girls' positive adjustment.

Alternative Actions

Home Conditions and Preparations Prior to Divorce

A number of predivorce family conditions may be found that will help children's postdivorce adjustment and development. These "preparations" prior to the divorce may be considered preventive; however, it is likely that children living in environments fraught with interparental conflict, threats of divorce, or parental separation are already experiencing social-emotional reactions to significant stresses (Emery, 1982).

The child's perspective

Children need to receive information, appropriate to their chronological, developmental, and social-emotional age levels, about an upcoming separation or divorce and the broad implications of those actions. This communication hopefully emanates from both parents in a joint discussion, but it also can occur during sessions coordinated by a psychologist or marriage and family therapist. With the parents' permission, discussions with a school psychologist, individually or in divorce or separation counseling groups, could further support these children—even before the divorce is final. Among the important themes that can be expressed continually to children of a future divorce are that

1. Their parents still love them.
2. They are not responsible for the divorce; rather it is a problem between their parents independent of themselves.
3. Their physical, social-emotional, and other needs will be taken care of as much as possible.
4. Their parents will be available as much as possible to talk with them about their concerns or fears.
5. Everyone will try to work together to make the situation as comfortable as possible, but they themselves are still expected to perform their responsibilities with respect to home and school.
6. It is alright to feel badly about the situation, but there are people who do care and can help them through these bad feelings.

The parent's perspective

For parents, the predivorce period also should include preparations for the broad implications of the divorce. As noted by Guidubaldi, et al. (1987), family- and community-support factors (e.g., the availability of relatives, friends, community education, and recreation resources) are important to divorced children's adjustment. Clearly, they also are important to the parents' adjust-

ment. During the predivorce or marital separation period, it is important for people facing divorce to receive some guidance or personally to explore their supportive resources. While close relatives or friends often provide the most support, the availability of legal, mental health, community-oriented, educational/vocational, and religious support systems also should be investigated. More specifically, predivorce preparations should address the financial stability of the custodial parent (usually the mother), the custody and visitation arrangements themselves, and the development of predivorce joint-parenting agreements.

The relationship between the custodial parent's (and family's) financial stability and children's postdivorce adjustment has been well-documented (as discussed previously). If the importance of this issue is known by the divorcing parents, attending lawyers, divorce judges, and state and federal legislators, perhaps more binding and equitable predivorce agreements protecting children's financial interests can be reached. Federally, the Child Support Enforcement Amendments of 1984 (P. L. 98-378) were developed to ensure that a divorce's financial stipulations are met. However, this act has been inconsistently implemented state by state, resulting nationally in significant amounts of unpaid child support (Guidubaldi et al., 1987). On a more personal level, perhaps the message that custody payments may facilitate children's overall divorce adjustment will diffuse some of the resistance that often occurs when noncustodial parents are forced to support, but not participate in, a household responsible for rearing their biological children. This message would emphasize the noncustodial parents' continuing role as a parent while de-emphasizing the notion that child support (as opposed to alimony) is provided for the ex-spouse's personal use.

Custody arrangements, visitation decisions, and joint-parenting agreements prior to a divorce also can significantly affect children's postdivorce adjustment. These decisions may occur through (a) discussions between divorcing parties that are formalized in a divorce agreement; (b) lawyer-mediated discussions that are later formalized; (c) independently mediated discussions using a certified or licensed mediation specialist; and/or (d) stipulations rendered by a divorce, family, or other relevant court. Once again, through a school psychologist or others, parents and significant others need to understand the research correlating these variables with children's adjustment over time. Briefly, it appears that joint-custody arrangements may have the greatest potential to positively affect children's long-term adjustment so long as the respective parents can agree to and use consistent parenting styles. An increase in joint-custody decisions, however, will necessitate radical changes in divorce courts' conceptualizations of divorce settlements and divorcing parents' pleas for child custody. Indeed, mothers alone continue to receive custody of their children in the vast majority (90%) of custody cases (Guidubaldi et al., 1987).

Predivorce agreements encouraging consistent, on-going, and important amounts of visitation by the non-custodial parent are extremely important to the adjust-ment of the children. Such agreements hopefully can minimize the effects of postdivorce difficulties in this area, thus decreasing future parental conflict, another variable related to children's postdivorce adjustment. Visitation agreements should particularly target male children who appear to have the more severe and long-lasting postdivorce adjustment difficulties. The longitu-dinal research emphasizes that divorced boys' relation-ships with their fathers and post-divorce father-son interactions (often during visitation, given the custody statistics just noted) significantly predict their general ad-justment. The overall implications, then, are clear. First, divorcing parents need to understand the reasons for and develop a *parenting package* describing the practices they agree to use consistently with their children after the di-vorce. Second, significant amounts of tension-free, non-custodial visitation after the divorce should be part of this parenting package.

Discipline is another important issue that parents should agree upon as part of the parenting package. Dif-ferential discipline styles, both before and after a divorce, are often a source of considerable tension. Predivorce agreements, again whether developed informally, through mediation, or by a court, may decrease this tension and result in more positive parent-child interactions. From a preventive perspective, predivorce agreements in this and other parenting areas can open a needed communication process that must continue after the divorce. This process should focus away from parents' personal divorce traumas and onto the reality that their children still need support, guidance, and joint parenting efforts. Emery (1982) has suggested that many children's adjustment problems are related not to the divorce but to continuing interparental conflict after the divorce. If true, then the agreements within the parenting package may decrease subsequent parental conflicts, thereby increasing the probability of children's more positive adjustment.

Obviously, the sensitivity of the issues just dis-cussed—and the possibility that they helped precipitate the divorce—sometimes make them difficult to resolve. However, as their psychological importance to the ad-justment of the children of divorce is clear, school psy-chologists need to emphasize these issues while advo-cating respect for the children and their psychological rights. From a practitioner perspective, the social-emotional and academic-intellectual effects of divorce on children also need to be publicized so that parents and community systems (e.g., legislative, judicial, mental health) can consider the entire family system when mak-ing decisions that at first appear only to involve a divorc-ing husband and wife.

School Conditions and Preparations Responding to Students' Divorce Situations

Because divorce is a phenomenon of the family or home, its effects in the school system or classroom are indirect. Thus, for school psychologists and other school support staff, interventions addressing the effects of divorce must occur with the full knowledge and support of the divorced parents (or of the custodial parent if the noncustodial parent abdicates responsibility) and often should be co-ordinated with other nonschool interventions such as pri-vate counseling or community-based support. Once pa-rental consent has been received, however, these interventions should focus particularly on ways to mini-mize the *school-related* social-emotional and academic-in-tellectual effects of the divorce. That is, the more perva-sive issues and family-related effects of divorce should remain the responsibility of community or private mental health services if they are called on by the parents. With-out parental consent, the school system is limited to in-terventions that are available to all children and that do not unduly target the children of divorce.

In developing supportive interventions at school for children of divorce, both general and divorce-specific information is needed. The general information should include baselines of the child's predivorce and presepar-ation social-emotional and academic-intellectual devel-opment for comparative purposes. This information should include results from previous standardized and individual tests; academic grades and teacher ratings or comments on classroom conduct and effort; referrals or records for behavioral or learning problems or services; and documentation of psychological or other supportive intervention. The divorce-specific information should pro-vide school staff with an understanding of the divorce situation and the current home/divorce environment, and it should be related to those variables that the re-search literature has identified as important to children's divorce adjustment. This information, ideally collected from both parents' perspectives, should include an un-derstanding of

- The parents' desired involvement with the school and the specific interactions they want from the school. For example, does the noncustodial parent wish to receive report cards and other communications from the teacher or principal?
- The custodial arrangements chosen. For example, have any siblings been separated between the parents? Is a joint custody arrangement in force?
- The parents' approaches to discipline and ways they might affect school behavior or adjustment.
- Other mental health and community support services being used by the parents or child, for example, coun-seling, Big Brother/Big Sister support.

In collecting all of this information, school psychologists must limit themselves to questions and information relevant to the school and any school-based interventions; care should be taken to avoid irrelevant and unnecessarily personal (voyeuristic) questions and to maintain the child's, parents', and family's right to confidentiality.

Two other factors are important to any potential intervention process: the actual need for intervention and the coordination and cooperation of school support staff and teachers. In considering the first factor, school psychologists cannot automatically assume that all children of divorce will have adjustment difficulties and require intervention services. Some children, in cases of acrimonious predivorce home environments, may actually demonstrate better psychological development and overall adjustment after the divorce, whereas others may possess individual coping skills or already-existing emotional support systems that minimize any negative reactions. School psychologists must ensure that behavior motivating the referral of any of these children is significant in frequency, duration, and/or intensity and must determine whether these difficulties are related, to some degree, to the divorce experience and not to some other coincidental issue or condition.

As with almost any comprehensive, school-intervention initiative, the coordination and cooperation of school support staff and teachers is critical. This is especially true given the sensitive nature of divorce for both the parents and children experiencing it. Coordination between relevant individuals on a school staff should result in everyone clearly understanding which procedures are being used with children experiencing divorce difficulties and which intervention programs and techniques are available for use within the district. Part of these procedures may involve a "case manager" approach, in which one individual is chosen as the primary contact between the home and school so that confusing, multiple intervention messages are avoided. Other procedures should ensure the periodic review and evaluation of any district policy or process that might be related to divorce situations and the implementation of divorce-specific interventions. Clearly, this coordination is most easily accomplished when the school district uses a mental health/child study team approach at either the district or individual-building level and the team meets regularly to plan and consider all identified child problems. However, if the need existed, a district could form a special district-wide mental health team to specifically address the needs of children of divorce.

School-based interventions

From a school psychologist's perspective, intervention programs addressing the impact of divorce can focus on primary, secondary, or tertiary prevention. While most school psychological interventions occur in schools with specific children, divorce-related preventive interventions may also involve family or community programs. For example, parent or family support groups around divorce issues have been especially highlighted in the intervention literature, and comprehensive community education or in-service programs are also important considerations.

There are three ways, minimally, that schools can prepare children for the effects of a divorce. They can (a) serve children who have actually experienced a divorce by maintaining school conditions and programs that correlate with their postdivorce social and academic adjustment (tertiary prevention); (b) develop preventive programs for children experiencing a parental separation or significant parent or family conflict *before* a divorce occurs (secondary prevention); and (c) develop programs for *all* school children in a particular school district to help them understand and deal with divorce as a common life crisis (primary prevention). Across all three levels of prevention, school psychologists first must convince school personnel that divorce is a significant problem in the community and that its effects do cross into and affect the school environment and everyday classroom experience. This process involves in-service programs to educate and inform all administrators, teachers, and support and other staff regarding (a) the possible effects of divorce on children at various age levels, (b) ways to identify divorce-related maladjustment, and (c) which support staff to contact for a coordination of services and interventions. Once a staff understands the potential impact of divorce and is committed to supporting children in this area, specific child-focused programs can be developed and implemented.

From a tertiary perspective, five school-climate dimensions were identified by Guidubaldi et al. (1983) as affecting students' adjustment to divorce: a safe and orderly environment, continued high expectations for these students, maintenance of the level of time a student remains on task and exposed to opportunities to learn, frequent monitoring of student progress, and appropriate reinforcement practices. In developing or maintaining these positive conditions, teachers and other school officials should attempt to involve *both* parents in the education of their children (unless, of course, the approaches are rejected by one of the parents or prohibited by a court decision or ruling). This effort may involve duplicate report cards or progress reports for both parents, separate conference invitations, or two phone calls to communicate positive or negative classroom information. When both parents are involved, children of divorce will realize that they are still accountable to both parents and, significantly, that both parents care for them and feel that their academic development is important.

As an example of a specific tertiary intervention, Stolberg and Mahler (1994) evaluated a school-based Children's Support Group process that helped 103 third through fifth graders to cope with their parents' separation or divorce through (a) supportive discussion; (b) supportive discussion plus self-control and problem-solving skill building; or (c) support, skill-building, skill-transfer, and parent-training procedures. After analyzing multiple measures of student affect, cognition, home behavior, and school behavior across a one-year period of time, Stolberg and Mahler found that (a) the skill-building components provided the most significant gains in student adjustment; (b) the skills and support condition provided the most immediate gains in reducing inappropriate behavior in the home; (c) the addition of the transfer and parent-training procedures resulted in immediate reductions in the students' self-ratings of anxiety, but delayed reports of improvements in home behavior until the one-year follow-up; and (d) those students participating in the two skill-based conditions had higher ratings of adjustment at the one-year follow-up than those in the divorce control group.

From both a secondary and tertiary program perspective, many programs for children of separation or divorce are described in the school counseling, social work, and psychology literatures. These include (a) counseling groups for children from homes headed by single, previously divorced, or separated parents; (b) programs that integrate stories or other books about other children's divorce experiences and feelings that then stimulate program participants to discuss and express personal experiences and feelings; (c) programs that coordinate crisis intervention, coping, and social skills training for children; and (d) programs emphasizing brief psychotherapeutic interventions. Very few of these programs have collected data or completed program evaluations to demonstrate their efficacy relative to children's social or academic changes. School psychologists, therefore, need to formatively and summatively evaluate such programs if they utilize them in the schools.

From a primary prevention perspective, divorce education programs should be developed to systematically include all children in a school district. Such programs could help children, at their various individual age and developmental levels, to (a) understand the broad implications of divorce, (b) relate more effectively with peers who have gone or are going through that experience, (c) cope with their own natural fears that *their* parents also might get divorced, and (d) be better prepared if they themselves face divorce at some time in the future. Similar to the drug education and other preventive programs of the past two decades, these divorce programs address divorced and nondivorced children's social and academic problems by preparing children's families, schools, and communities with positive approaches and responses to the divorce experience and its multifaceted effects.

As one example of a primary prevention intervention, Dubow, Schmidt, McBride, Edwards, and Merk (1993) taught fourth-grade students specific coping skills over a 13-session school-based program. Focusing on five common stressful experiences (i.e., parental separation/di-

vorce, loss of a loved one, a move to a new home or school, spending significant amounts of time in "self-care," and being "different"), the intervention involved teaching cognitively based problem-solving and coping skills. Students were able to generate a wide variety of effective solutions to stressful situations after the program, and these results were maintained or strengthened at a 5-month follow-up. This study demonstrates the feasibility of conducting school-based primary prevention programs. It also reinforces the importance of teaching problem-solving and cognitively based coping skills to help students deal with significant life events.

In the community
Within the community setting, school psychologists can (a) help to develop support services for children of divorce, for example, Big Brother/Big Sister programs; (b) participate in parent- or family-support groups addressing divorce or separation issues; (c) sponsor comprehensive community-education programs or open houses to acquaint the public with the effects of divorce and with the programs available in the schools or community; and (d) develop a school-community coordinating board or system organizing all mental health and supportive service agencies toward a more unified approach to divorce services and interventions. As one example of a community-based preventive program, Stolberg and Cullen (1983) developed a Divorce Adjustment Project (DAP) which targeted families of divorce and their adjustment and other difficulties during the first 2 years after a divorce. The DAP has three primary components: a children's support group, a discussion sequence focused on the planning process beyond the divorce, and a parents' group providing "parenting alone" suggestions and supports. Collectively, the program attempted to (a) provide a supportive environment among people all experiencing the same life crisis; (b) identify problem behavior and maladjustment patterns related to the divorce experience and the processes that influence those patterns; (c) teach both parents and children specific coping skills and procedures which can enhance their adaptive responses to the divorce; and (d) replace social support systems lost when the divorce occurred. Initial results of this program indicated that the DAP showed promise as an integrated, preventive response to divorce for parents and their children.

Primary, secondary, and tertiary programs in the community provide a wraparound layer of services that complement those provided by the schools to children of divorce. School psychologists need to take every opportunity to coordinate with community programs and agencies such that comprehensive services are available to students and their families as needed.

Encouraging research in the field
A final "alternative action" for school psychologists involves the need to do field-based research in the area of

divorce so that information remains current and has impact. Longitudinal research in this area is particularly important, because it allows professionals to follow a cohort of individuals and track the developmental progression of divorce. To date, there have been four major longitudinal studies on the effects of divorce on school-aged children (Guidubaldi et al., 1983; Guidubaldi & Perry, 1985; Hetherington, 1979; Hetherington et al., 1978; Kurdek, 1983; Kurdek et al., 1981; Wallerstein, 1984, 1987, 1991; Wallerstein & Kelly, 1976). The samples in the studies involved the following:

1. Wallerstein and Kelly (1971) investigated a sample of 131 children between the ages of 2 1/2 and 18 years from 60 divorced families of Marin County, California, just after parental separation and then 1, 5, and 10 years following the divorce. In 1987, Wallerstein reported findings from the 10-year follow-up data relative to 38 adolescents, who were 6 to 8 years old when their parents divorced.
2. Over a 2-year period, Hetherington, Cox, and Cox (1978) collected personality, cognitive, and social development data on a sample of 48 divorced and 48 intact middle-class families and their preschool children from Virginia matched on age, gender, birth order, and nursery school attendance of the child, and by the parents' age, education, and length of marriage.
3. Kurdek, Blisk, and Siesky (1981) investigated 74 White, divorced, middle-class families from Dayton, Ohio (60 mothers and 14 fathers); 33 of these single parents were members of the local chapter of Parents Without Partners and 41 were friends of these members. In total, these families accounted for 132 children ranging in age from 5 to 19 (mean = 12.56) years. This longitudinal study initially involved 58 children from ages 8 to 17 (mean = 13.09) years whose parents had been separated from 1 to 14 years (mean separation = 14.54 years). The follow-up assessment occurred 2 years later involving 24 of the original group (mean age = 13.32 years) and 14 siblings (mean age = 13.53 years) as a supplemental group.
4. Guidubaldi, Cleminshaw, Perry, and McLoughlin (1983) completed a nationwide study (representing 38 states and 144 school psychologists) of 699 children in Grades 1, 3, or 5 from divorced and intact families during the 1981–1982 school year. These researchers attempted to overcome the methodological limitations of past research, namely, (a) small, biased samples; (b) inadequate or nonexistent control groups; (c) poor or absent control of socioeconomic status and other potentially confounding variables; and (d) lack of multisetting, multimethod, and multifactored assessments. At least one follow-up of the original sample has been completed.

School psychologists should consider how to contribute additional information to this important area, whether through longitudinal, assessment, intervention, or program-efficacy research. In the end, it is through this research that students and their families will be most effectively understood and served. School psychologists cannot assume to understand the impact of divorce simply through experience. Data and research are critical components to clinical effectiveness.

Summary

The rate of divorce continues at a staggering pace, and its social and academic effects on children constitute a major mental health and educational problem for schools and communities. School psychologists need to understand that children appear to react differently to the divorce experience depending on their age, developmental maturity, gender, the length of time since the divorce, and the support systems available. Children's reactions, however, must be analyzed and considered within the context of their school and family environments. Clearly, some children of divorce are able to weather the experience with minimal discomfort, but others appear to require specific emotional and other supports in order to adapt. Thus, analyzing each child as an individual and each child's individual school and home ecologies is of paramount importance.

From an intervention standpoint, school psychologists should target school staffs and the community at large by working to increase understanding and sensitivity to the problems and issues of divorce. They also should work to coordinate programs for children of divorce (and their parents), children at risk for divorce, and all other children—as it is inevitable that they will interact with divorced children and, perhaps, feel the emotions related to this life event. Furthermore, school psychologists should become involved in practical research that identifies the variables and intervention programs or strategies that most effectively affect children's social and academic adjustments.

In a sense, *every* child in today's society is at risk for experiencing the separation and divorce of his or her parents. Divorce appears relatively indiscriminate in its presence across the different demographic characteristics comprising today's communities. Divorce must be viewed as a significant public and mental health problem. School psychologists must utilize their special training and skills in human behavior and mental health development and begin to address the special problems of children of divorce. School psychologists also must assume leadership positions in the schools and community to encourage comprehensive, coordinated, and community-wide responses. Given that 40% to 50% of all children born during the past decade will spend some time living in a single-parent family, the problems associated with divorce clearly will not go quietly away. School psychologists must acknowledge these problems and begin to develop sound solutions.

Recommended Resources

For the Professional

Hodges, W. F. (1991). *Interventions for children of divorce: Custody, access, and psychotherapy* (2nd ed.). New York: Wiley.
An integrated, single-authored text that provides over 600 research references related to children and divorce. Among the chapters and topics addressed are child development and the response of children to separation and divorce; mediation; custody evaluations; visitation and parent access patterns and problems; unique problems of single parenting and remarriage; interventions for children and with families; and group intervention strategies in school and community settings.

Guidubaldi, J., Perry, J. D., & Nastasi, B. K. (1987). Growing up in a divorced family: Initial and long-term perspectives on children's adjustment. In S. Oskamp (Ed.), *Annual review of applied social psychology* (pp. 202–237). New York: Sage Publications.
This chapter provides a critical and in-depth description of one of the major longitudinal studies investigating the effects of divorce on children and adolescents. It describes a nationwide study undertaken by the National Association of School Psychologists and Kent State University, the various results, and their implications.

Wallerstein, J. S. (1987). Children of divorce: Report of a ten-year follow-up of early latency-age children. *American Journal of Orthopsychiatry, 57,* 199-211.
This article reports the findings from a 10-year follow-up of 38 adolescents (aged 16 to 18 years old) and the impact to them relative to their parents' divorce. Issues related to age, gender, and the circumstances around the separation and divorce were investigated and are reported. This study is one of the very few longitudinal investigations available in the research.

A Sampling of Books For Children and Adolescents

Brown, L. K. (1986). *Dinosaurs divorce.* Boston: Altantic Monthly Press.

Krementz, J. (1984). *How it feels when parents divorce.* New York: Knopf.

Ives, S. B. (1985). *The divorce workbook; A guide for kids and families.* Burlington, VT: Waterfront Books.

Nickman, S. L. (1986). *When mom and dad divorce.* New York: Messner.

For the Parent

Gardner, R. (1991). *The parents' book about divorce* (Rev.). New York: Bantam Books.
One of a number of books available at the local bookstore and providing advice to parents about the divorce process and ways its affects children. Contents of this book include: how to tell the children; postseparation adjustment and specific child problems; telling neighbors, teachers, and friends; helping children to adjust to two households; dealing with issues or feelings of anger, insecurity, blame, guilt, abandonment, sadness, and preoccupations about reconciliation; money, visitation, and custody concerns; and ways to interact with grandparents and step-parents down the road.

The following books provide unique, personal perspectives on divorce in an attempt to help parents understand their reactions to the experience and those of their children:

Glass, S. M. (1980). *A divorce dictionary: A book for you and your children.* Boston: Little, Brown.

Stein, S. B. (1979). *On divorce: An open family book for parents and children together.* New York: Walker.

Salk, L. (1978). *What every child would like parents to know about divorce.* New York: Harper and Row.

References

Achenbach, T. M. (1991). *Manual of the Child Behavior Checklist/4-18 and 1991 Profile.* Burlington, VT: University of Vermont Department of Psychiatry.

Baumrind, D. (1968). Authoritarian versus authoritative parental control. *Adolescence, 3,* 255-272.

Buchanan, C. M., Maccoby, E., & Dornbusch, S. M. (1991). Caught between parents: Adolescents' experience in divorced homes. *Child Development, 62,* 1008-1029.

Buehler, C., & Legg, B. H. (1992). Selected aspects of parenting and children's social competence post-separation: The moderating effects of child's sex, age, and family economic hardship. *Journal of Divorce and Remarriage, 15,* 177-195.

Child Support Enforcement Amendments of 1984, Pub. L. No. 98-378, 98th Congress, August 16, 1984.

Cooney, T. M. (1993). Recent demographic changes: Implications for families planning for the future. *Marriage and Family Review, 18,* 37-55.

Drake, E. A., & Shellenberger, S. (1981). Children of separation and divorce: A review of school programs and implications for the psychologist. *School Psychology Review, 10,* 54-61.

Dubow, E. F., Schmidt, D., McBride, J., Edwards, S., & Merk, F. L. (1993). Teaching children to cope with stressful experiences: Initial implementation and evaluation of a primary prevention program. *Journal of Clinical Child Psychology, 22,* 428-440.

Ellwood, M. S., & Stolberg, A. L. (1991). A preliminary investigation of family systems' influences on individual divorce adjustment. *Journal of Divorce and Remarriage, 14,* 157-174.

Emery, R. E. (1982). Interparental conflict and the children of discord and divorce. *Psychological Bulletin, 92,* 310-330.

Guidubaldi, J., Cleminshaw, H. K., Perry, J. D., McLoughlin, C. S. (1983). The impact of parental divorce on children: Report of the nationwide NASP study. *School Psychology Review, 12,* 300-323.

Guidubaldi, J., & Perry, J. D. (1985). Divorce and mental health sequelae for children: A two-year follow-up of a nationwide sample. *Journal of the American Academy of Child Psychiatry, 24,* 531-537.

Guidubaldi, J., Perry, J. D., & Nastasi, B. K. (1987). Growing up in a divorced family: Initial and long-term perspectives on children's adjustment. In S. Oskamp (Ed.), *Annual review of applied social psychology* (pp. 202-237). New York: Sage Publications.

Heath, P. A., & Lynch, S. (1988). A reconceptualization of the time since parental separation variable as a predictor of children's outcomes following divorce. *Journal of Divorce, 11,* 67-76.

Hetherington, E. M. (1979). Divorce: A child's perspective. *American Psychologist, 34,* 851-858.

Hetherington, E. M., Cox, M., & Cox, R. (1978). Effects of divorce on parents and children. In M. E. Lamb (Ed.), *Nontraditional families: Parenting and child development* (pp. 233-288). New Jersey: Lawrence Erlbaum.

Hodges, W. F. (1991). *Interventions for children of divorce: Custody, access, and psychotherapy* (2nd ed.). New York: Wiley.

Hodges, W. F., Landis, T., Day, E., & Oderberg, N. (1991). Infant and toddlers and post divorce parental access: An initial exploration. *Journal of Divorce and Remarriage, 14,* 239-252.

Holloway, S. D., & Machida, S. (1991). Child-rearing effectiveness of divorced mothers: Relationship of coping strategies and social support. *Journal of Divorce and Remarriage, 14,* 179-201.

Kelly, J, B., & Wallerstein, J. S. (1977). Brief interventions with children in divorcing families. *American Journal of Orthopsychiatry, 47,* 23-36.

Kurdek, L. A. (1981). An integrative perspective on children's divorce adjustment. *American Psychologist, 36,* 856-866.

Kurdek, L A. (Ed.). (1983). *Children and divorce.* San Francisco: Jossey-Bass.

Kurdek, L. A., Blisk, D., & Siesky, A. E. (1981). Correlates of children's long-term adjustment to their parents' divorce. *Developmental Psychology, 17,* 565-579.

Mitchell, A. (1987). Children's experience of divorce. *Children & Society, 2,* 136-147.

National Center for Health Statistics. (1995). Births, marriages, divorces, and deaths for 1994. *Vital Statistics of the United States: Annual, 44.* Hyattsville, MD: Public Health Service.

Peterson, J. L., & Zill, N. (1986). Marital disruption, parent-child relationships, and behavior problems in children. *Journal of Marriage and the Family, 48,* 295-307.

Stolberg, A. L., & Cullen, P. M. (1983). Preventive interventions for families of divorce: The Divorce Adjustment Project. *New Directions for Child Development, 19,* 71-81.

Stolberg, A. L., & Mahler, J. (1994). Enhancing treatment gains in a school-based intervention for children of divorce through skill training, parental involvement, and transfer procedures. *Journal of Consulting and Clinical Psychology, 62,* 147-156.

Wallerstein, J. S. (1984). Children of divorce: Preliminary report of a ten-year follow-up of young children. *American Journal of Orthopsychiatry, 54,* 444-458.

Wallerstein, J. S. (1987). Children of divorce: Report of a ten-year follow-up of early latency-age children. *American Journal of Orthopsychiatry, 57,* 199-211.

Wallerstein, J. S. (1991). Tailoring the intervention to the child in the separating and divorced family. *Family and Conciliation Courts Review, 29,* 448-459.

Wallerstein, J. S., & Kelly, J. B. (1976). The effects of parental divorce experiences of the child in later latency. *American Journal of Orthopsychiatry, 46,* 256-267.

Wallerstein, J. S., & Kelly, J. B. (1980). *Surviving the breakup: How children and parents cope with divorce.* New York: Basic Books.

Walsh, P. E., & Stolberg, A. L. (1989). Parental and environmental determinants of children's behavioral, affective, and cognitive adjustment to divorce. *Journal of Divorce, 12,* 265-282.

54

Issues of Visitation and Custody

Christy M. Buchanan

Wake Forest University

This chapter focuses on problems and benefits of different custody and visitation arrangements for children following their parents' divorce. Visitation and custody as defined in this chapter refer to a child's *actual* living arrangements. When parents divorce, they get a legal custody decree specifying how the children are supposed to split their time between parents. The custody or visitation plan specified in the legal decree, however, does not always match what parents do in practice (Maccoby & Mnookin, 1992). Thus, one should not assume that the specifications of a legal divorce document reflect what actually takes place in a child's life.

Very little information is available on issues of visitation and custody for children of never-married parents. Thus, although some of the information contained herein may be relevant to those children, it is important to acknowledge that children of never-married parents may face somewhat different issues than children of divorce. Current studies of custody and visitation also have not identified how the issues surrounding visitation and custody vary for individuals from different ethnic and socioeconomic backgrounds. Although some study samples are drawn from representative populations, researchers have not typically conducted analyses separately by ethnic or economic groups. Thus, much of the following information applies to White, middle- and upper-middle-class families, and its relevance to other groups is not known.

Background and Development

An inevitable outcome of divorce is that children are faced with having to split their time between homes and between parents. This reality may affect the school-aged child in ways that range from relatively minor, such as leaving homework at one parent's home when making a transition to the other parent's home, to more substantial, such as experiencing ongoing problems in mood or behavior that stem from relational or parenting problems in the family. This chapter focuses on the latter kinds of problems.

Prevalence of Alternative Arrangements

After divorce in the United States, most children (approximately 70%) live primarily with their mothers. However, there are now substantial numbers of children who, after their parents separate, either live primarily with their fathers or split their time fairly equally between their mothers' and fathers' homes (the latter arrangement is called joint custody or, less commonly, dual residence). Father custody is more likely among adolescents than among younger children, and rates of joint custody tend to be highest for children in the late preschool and early elementary school years (Maccoby & Mnookin, 1992).

Initial studies of the amount of contact children have with their noncustodial parent, conducted with families whose divorces occurred in the 1970s, painted a dismal picture. Up to half of fathers completely dropped out of their children's lives, and loss of contact occurred very quickly following divorce (Furstenberg & Harris, 1992; Furstenberg, Nord, Peterson, & Zill, 1983). More recent national and regional studies find that current rates of contact with noncustodial parents are significantly higher. For example, one recent national survey found that only 11% of children under age 18 whose parents had been separated for 5 years or less had not seen their noncustodial father within the previous year (Seltzer, 1991). This study and others suggest that, currently, complete absence of contact with noncustodial fathers is rare, although irregular and infrequent contact is not uncommon, especially as the time since parental separation increases (Buchanan, Maccoby, & Dornbusch, 1996; Furstenberg & Harris, 1992). For instance, only one-third of the children in Seltzer's (1991) study saw their noncustodial fathers weekly; 58% saw him once a month. Rates of contact with noncustodial mothers appear to be somewhat higher than those with noncustodial fathers (Buchanan et al., 1996).

What is "Optimal" for Children of Divorce?

Based on research that examines the factors promoting good adjustment among children of divorce, professionals can paint a picture of the "ideal" world for such children. In this ideal scenario, divorced parents would get along well with one another and encourage positive relationships between the child and each parent. Children would spend enough time with each parent to sustain close relationships with each and to allow both to be well-informed about the child's activities, interests, struggles, hopes, and concerns. Parents would have similar rules and expectations in both households, and those rules and expectations would be appropriate to the child's age and personality and tempered with warmth and responsiveness between parent and child. There also would be adequate financial and material resources in the child's primary residence.

As different custody and visitation arrangements are presented in this chapter, this ideal scenario should be kept in mind. Of course, no family (divorced or otherwise!) will meet all aspects at all times, but it is helpful to examine those aspects of ideal functioning enhanced or jeopardized by different custody or visitation arrangements. For example, some arrangements may be more likely than others to provoke conflict between parents, and some may be more conducive to consistency in rules and routines. Armed with such knowledge, school personnel can be alert to possible "risk factors" for a particular student in a particular kind of situation. Of course, any one student or family might not fit the "average" description for their particular custody or visitation arrangement, so this information should be used only to guide inquiry into a particular situation, rather than to make absolute judgments about what must be happening for any particular family.

Problems and Implications

The issues of custody and visitation overlap with one another: They both involve the amount of contact a child has with each parent after divorce. In many cases, findings about high levels of visitation (e.g., overnights every other weekend plus a midweek visit with the noncustodial parent) are similar to those concerning joint custody (e.g., often defined as spending at least one-third of the time with each parent). Yet, there are also some distinct issues arising in joint custody situations that do not apply to cases of clear sole custody with high visitation. So, in the following section, visitation is discussed first, followed by information on custody arrangements, which refers back to information about visitation where appropriate.

Visitation with the Noncustodial Parent

Most information about the effects of different levels of visitation on family functioning and children's adjustment comes from mother-custody families and refers to visitation with the noncustodial father. Father custody has only recently become common enough for investigators to study it seriously, and there are still very few studies that have directly investigated issues of visitation among father-custody children. Thus, the bulk of the discussion in this section refers to visitation with noncustodial fathers, although information on noncustodial mothers is included where available.

In general, visitation itself does not appear to increase the amount of conflict between parents. Initial levels of conflict between parents seem to influence the initial choices they make about custody: Parents with higher levels of conflict are less likely to implement high visitation (and joint custody) arrangements to begin with, even when the legal decree calls for such arrangements, and they are less likely to sustain such arrangements over time. But for families that sustain arrangements permitting high levels of access to both parents, conflict does not appear to be either exacerbated or reduced simply by virtue of the arrangement (Maccoby, Depner, & Mnookin, 1990; Maccoby & Mnookin, 1992).

Several studies have further examined the direct relation between the amount of contact a child has with a noncustodial father and that child's adjustment. The results of these studies are mixed, with most studies indicating a positive link between visitation and adjustment but with smaller numbers indicating either no link or a negative link (Amato, 1993; Amato & Rezac, 1994; King, 1994). When a link between visitation and adjustment is found, the link is typically small. On the basis of the modest and mixed findings, experts tend to agree on two things: First, the quality of the relationship between the noncustodial parent and child is very likely more important to the child's adjustment than is visitation per se. Second, the impact of visitation depends on other factors, including the amount of conflict that exists between the parents. Some experts have also suggested that visitation promotes child-support compliance, which is beneficial for the child.

Quality of the noncustodial parent-child relationship
It is impossible to maintain a close relationship with a parent if you never see that parent. Conversely, having a lot of contact with a parent ought to increase the odds of maintaining a close relationship with that parent. Furthermore, children are most likely to maintain contact with noncustodial parents to whom they already feel close. It is not surprising, then, that researchers have found high visitation to be associated with greater levels of reported closeness to a noncustodial parent (e.g., Buchanan et al., 1996; Furstenberg & Harris, 1992).

In a large study of adolescents, this chapter's author and colleagues (Buchanan et al., 1996) found that having visitation with the noncustodial parent—mother or father—was associated with greater adolescent-reported closeness to that parent and with very little else (i.e., visitation was not directly associated with adolescent adjustment or with any feature of parenting in the custodial or noncustodial home.) Interestingly, for adolescents in this study, it did not take very high levels of visitation to promote feelings of closeness. Adolescents who visited their noncustodial parent for only 2 weeks in the summer felt about as close to that parent as did adolescents who visited on a weekly or biweekly basis during the school year. The suggestion in these data is that even small amounts of visitation may serve to maintain or promote emotional ties between children and noncustodial parents.

The level of closeness maintained between children and noncustodial fathers is generally not as high as that between children and custodial mothers or between children and nondivorced fathers (Buchanan et al., 1996; Furstenberg & Harris, 1992). Closeness to noncustodial mothers appears to be maintained at a somewhat higher level than closeness to noncustodial fathers, especially for boys (Buchanan et al., 1996). But clearly, having at least some contact with the noncustodial parent—mother or father—enhances the chances for having a good relationship with that parent.

Maintaining a close relationship with both parents after divorce appears to be advantageous for children (Buchanan et al., 1996; Thomas & Forehand, 1993; Wallerstein & Kelly, 1980), and this may be particularly true for children in father custody (Buchanan et al., 1996). Of course, it is possible that any benefits of a close relationship with the noncustodial parent are an artifact of other factors present in families in which noncustodial parents and children manage to remain close. However, there is no evidence that a positive relationship between children and their noncustodial parents is detrimental for the child.

In sum, although visitation is no guarantee of a good relationship between children and noncustodial parents, it enhances the chances for one. And a good relationship with the noncustodial parent appears to be a generally positive factor in children's adjustment to divorce.

Moderating factors

Although visitation generally appears to be positive for children, it would be naive to assume that visitation and the maintenance of a relationship with the noncustodial parent is equally good for all children and in all circumstances. One factor that may be of special importance in whether visitation with a noncustodial parent has positive outcomes is the level of conflict remaining between the parents. The bulk of the evidence suggests that visitation is, at minimum, less likely to be beneficial, and that it may hold a greater potential for harm, if interparental conflict is high (Amato & Rezac, 1994; Johnston & Campbell, 1988; also see Felner & Terre, 1987, for a review). These findings are bolstered by similar findings concerning joint custody.

The failure of visitation to be helpful to children in the face of interparental conflict may occur simply because the negative effects of conflict cancel any positive effects of visitation. Or it may be that conflict between parents interferes with a close relationship between children and their noncustodial parents, and such closeness is one of the proposed mechanisms by which visitation has a positive effect. For example, in our study (Buchanan et al., 1996) hostility toward the noncustodial parent on the part of the custodial parent was associated with less closeness between adolescent children and the noncustodial parent, but closeness to the custodial parent was not influenced by the level of interparental conflict. Any actual harm from visitation in high-conflict situations may result from increased exposure to conflict or an increased likelihood that children will become caught up in the conflict (Buchanan, Maccoby, & Dornbusch, 1991; Johnston, Kline, & Tschann, 1989).

In contrast to the research cited thus far, a few studies suggest that visitation may actually be helpful in situations of high interparental conflict, presumably because maintenance of the relationship with the noncustodial parent buffers the negative effects of the conflict. In one study of early adolescents whose parents were divorced, levels of social and academic competence were low only for children whose parents were in high conflict *and* who did not visit their noncustodial fathers (Forehand et al., 1990). Adolescents whose parents were in high conflict but who also visited their noncustodial fathers scored as well as adolescents whose parents experienced low levels of conflict. These results suggest that early adolescents might be better off in some respects by visiting a noncustodial parent when there is high conflict between their parents.

The mixed findings with regard to whether visitation is good, bad, or of no consequence when parents are in high conflict suggest that the impact of visitation in high-conflict situations depends on yet other factors. Although high conflict might make visitation more risky, it does not guarantee negative outcomes. For example, although some parents might take advantage of a child's contacts with the other parent to use the child in the conflict, not all parents will do so. If parents can avoid the temptation to involve children in the conflict, visitation (or the continued positive relationship that visitation enables) may in fact benefit the child in spite of the high levels of conflict.

Early studies of divorce also pointed to the adjustment and maturity of the noncustodial parent and the children's predivorce relationship with that parent as important factors in determining the effects of visitation. Visitation was shown to be beneficial if the previous relationship was good and if the father was not "poorly adjusted or extremely immature" (Kelly, 1993, p. 38). The quality of the parent-child relationship and what actually takes place during visitation are also important. For example, the amount of time spent alone with fathers, rather than the frequency of visitation, was linked to the adjustment of late-elementary-school-aged children (Kurdek & Berg, 1983).

Studies also suggest that regular and predictable visitation is more beneficial, especially for younger children (Healy, Malley, & Stewart, 1990; Kelly, 1988), perhaps in part because a regular schedule reduces parental conflict over visitation (Isaacs, 1988). Adolescents, in contrast to younger children, desire and appear to benefit more from flexibility in visitation (Bray, 1991; Buchanan et al., 1996; Hodges, 1991). Data from our large study of adolescents suggested that adolescents value time spent with the noncustodial parent and want to have visitation but experience frustration and resentment when visitation plans do not accommodate their peer and extracurricular activities and when they have little say in when or how much visitation occurs (Buchanan et al., 1996). In all likelihood, some kind of predictable schedule is still warranted, so that visitation does not fall by the wayside, but parents of adolescents need to be prepared to alter that schedule to meet the adolescent's needs for increasing involvement outside of the family.

The number of transitions the child has to make from one home to another in a given period of time has also been identified as an important variable with respect to the impact of visitation. The time of transition, especially for younger children and if parents are still in high conflict, can be stressful (Johnston, Campbell, & Mayes, 1985; Wallerstein & Blakeslee, 1989). Thus, to the extent that the visitation plan minimizes the number of transitions, and to the extent that parents try to make those times as low-stress as possible, the child will be better off.

Child-support compliance

Visitation appears to be related to more reliable payment of child support (Seltzer, Schaeffer, & Charng, 1989), although it is not clear whether visitation privileges lead to better compliance or whether it is simply the case that more committed fathers both visit their children and pay child support. In any case, children who visit their noncustodial fathers appear more likely to benefit from adequate financial and material resources. Child-support compliance has been found in several studies to be an important factor predicting better child adjustment after divorce, particularly in the area of cognitive and academic development (King, 1994).

Custody Arrangement

Although mother custody of children after divorce is still the most common arrangement, father custody and joint custody have become more prevalent since 1970. Thus, a substantial number of today's children of divorce, especially school-aged and adolescent children, experience these "alternative" forms of custody. Unfortunately, given the relative infrequency of father and joint custody, it is currently impossible to fully untangle the effects of being in one of these alternative arrangements from the effects of other factors that initially influence the choice of custody arrangements. It is possible, however, to point to some of the potential risks or benefits of one form of custody over another, without drawing conclusions about causes.

Comparison of mother custody and father custody

Despite the emphasis on gender equality in the United States today and despite the fact that many mothers, as well as fathers, are employed outside the home, women still perform the majority of child-care and household-management duties in most homes. The implication of this fact is that, when parents divorce, fathers do not typically have as much experience in primary child care and household management. Coupled with the entrenched notion that mothers are the more "natural" and competent parent, especially for young children, most families, as well as courts, continue to assume that mother custody is a better option for children than father custody.

Research comparing mother custody and father custody suggests that the two arrangements are similar in many ways (Buchanan et al., 1996; Warshak, 1986). My colleagues and I, in an extensive comparison of the two custody arrangements among families with adolescents, found no differences on many aspects of family and household functioning (Buchanan et al., 1996). There were no differences in children's trust of parents, conflict between the child and parent, family decision-making practices, curfews, household organization and routines, the presence of a parent in the home after school, or assignment of chores. There were a few differences of note, however. Adolescents reported feeling somewhat closer to custodial mothers than to custodial fathers, and custodial fathers were reported to be less effective monitors of their children's activities. In line with the greater emotional closeness between children and mothers, custodial mothers confided more in their children, and these children worried more about her and felt a greater need to take care of her.

Father-custody adolescents were somewhat less well-adjusted (using an index that measured the adolescent's worst score on depression, deviant behavior, or school effort) than mother-custody adolescents. The difference was partly accounted for by the differences in emotional closeness to and monitoring by custodial parents (Buchanan et al., 1996). Thus, father-custody children—at least adolescent children—may be at a somewhat elevated risk compared to mother-custody children. In part, this is because fathers get custody of more difficult children and under more difficult family circumstances. In our study, (Buchanan et al., 1996), father-custody adolescents were more likely to have moved into father custody after initially living with the mother or in dual residence (in comparison with adolescents in mother custody, more of whom had lived in mother residence all along). The reasons for a change into father custody, although sometimes positive, were more likely to be negative (e.g., due to conflict with the mother or to behavior problems that the mother could not handle) than were changes to other arrangements over time. Furthermore, father-custody arrangements were characterized by somewhat higher levels of hostility between the parents and higher levels of overall life stress as reported by the adolescent. Thus, the average single father may face a more difficult parenting situation than the average single mother.

However, the poorer adjustment of the father-resident adolescents and the relations among lower closeness, lower monitoring, and adjustment were not eliminated when background factors such as the stability of the residential arrangement and the hostility between parents were accounted for. This indicates that the more difficult circumstances of some father-custody cases did not completely explain the original findings (Buchanan et al., 1996) and that fathers' lower levels of experience in parenting may also contribute to the differences in parenting and in adolescent adjustment. In line with the hypothesis that fathers have had less experience in parenting prior to the divorce, and may need extra support as they face the challenge of primary caretaking, Warshak (1987) found that single fathers felt a need for help with parenting skills. Regardless of the cause of the higher levels of problems in father-resident adolescents, however, these data illuminate some of the risk factors that children living in the sole custody of their fathers might face.

There are mixed findings concerning the question of whether children are better off with their same-sex parent. A few early and often-cited studies suggest that boys are better off in the custody of their fathers and girls in the custody of their mothers (Camara & Resnick, 1988; Santrock & Warshak, 1979; Warshak & Santrock, 1983). The samples for these studies, however, were small in size, and factors influencing the selection of boys versus girls into father residence were not considered. Some more recent studies have supported the original findings (e.g., Peterson & Zill, 1986), but others have not (e.g., Buchanan et al., 1996). Data supporting the conjecture that girls are better off with mothers is stronger than that indicating boys are better off with fathers. To the extent that there are greater risks for girls than for boys in father custody, it is not clear how much those risks stem from the difficulty fathers have in parenting girls, a girl's "need" for "mothering," or the often unusual circumstances under which many girls end up in the custody of their fathers (e.g., because mothers have abandoned them or because these girls have troubled relationships with their mothers). Father custody of girls is rare, and it may be misleading to extrapolate any findings from research concerning this group to the population as a whole. However, it may be useful for practitioners to know that girls in father custody are more likely than other children of divorce to have been exposed to a variety of unusual, and potentially troubling, family background factors.

All of the documented differences between custody arrangements are relatively small in magnitude. Furthermore, there is a great deal of variability of family functioning within both mother custody and father custody. Thus, several recent reviewers of the literature on custody rightly conclude that a child's custody arrangement per se is a less important factor in his or her adjustment than is the parenting and the nature of the relationships to which he or she is exposed (Bray, 1991; Grych & Fincham, 1992).

Joint versus sole custody

Like high levels of visitation in sole-custody arrangements, the major potential benefit of joint custody is that children are able to maintain relationships with both parents (Buchanan et al., 1996; Luepnitz, 1982, 1986). For example, adolescents in joint custody had a higher combined level of closeness to both parents than children in either mother or father custody in our study (Buchanan et al., 1996). The higher closeness to both parents resulted in somewhat higher levels of overall adjustment (using a measure that incorporated depression, deviance, and school effort) in joint-custody adolescents compared to those in sole custody (particularly those in father custody). Joint-custody adolescents were also the most satisfied with the division of time between their parents, compared to mother-custody or father-custody adolescents.

As with visitation, however, there is evidence that joint custody has less favorable outcomes for children when parents are in high conflict and when joint custody is imposed on families rather than chosen voluntarily. Studies of joint custody based on samples of families where conflict between parents is relatively low (and who typically choose joint custody voluntarily) show good adjustment in children, often better than the adjustment of sole-custody children (Luepnitz, 1986; Shiller, 1986). In contrast, studies based on samples of families with relatively high conflict (where joint custody was often court imposed) show problems in adjustment of the children (Johnston et al., 1989; Steinman, Zemmelman, & Knoblauch, 1985). A constellation of factors is typically present in well-functioning joint-custody arrangements (Felner & Terre, 1987): The child has good relationships with both parents, the parents are in little to no conflict, and parents are supportive of and cooperative with each other. In addition, voluntary joint custody is more often implemented by highly educated, high-income families. All of these factors are probably responsible for any advantages children in joint custody experience, although our study, which looked at several of these factors jointly, found that closer relationships with both parents were an important and direct predictor of better outcomes even after accounting for other factors (Buchanan et al., 1996).

Some have argued against joint custody on the grounds that it will increase loyalty conflicts in children. At least among adolescents, this argument appears to hold only for high-conflict cases. Adolescents in joint custody and whose parents were not in high conflict experienced a *lower* level of loyalty conflicts than sole-custody adolescents. When parents were in high conflict, joint-custody adolescents experienced the highest levels of loyalty conflicts (Buchanan et al., 1991). So, once again, the impact of joint custody depends on the level of conflict that exists between parents.

Joint custody itself does not appear to affect the level of conflict between the parents. High-conflict families tend not to choose joint custody in the first place, and when they do (or when it is court imposed), they tend not to maintain the joint custody arrangement over time. Joint custody does not appear to increase conflict for low-conflict families that choose it (Maccoby et al., 1990; Maccoby & Mnookin, 1992), although most joint-custody parents do not actively cooperate in parenting (Furstenberg & Nord, 1985; Maccoby & Mnookin, 1992; Steinman, 1981).

Another potential misgiving about joint custody is that when a child spends a substantial part of each week or month in each home, it might become more difficult for each individual parent to monitor and supervise the child effectively. The evidence available provides little support for this concern (Buchanan et al., 1996). Joint-custody adolescents, by and large, experience the same rules and expectations and the same degree of monitoring and supervision as do mother-resident adolescents. Consistency in rules and expectations across homes appears to be *higher* for adolescents in joint-custody arrangements (Buchanan et al., 1996), probably because of the kinds of parents who choose this arrangement more so than because the arrangement itself promotes consistency.

In sum, when families voluntarily elect joint custody and are motivated to make it work for the sake of preserving the child's relationship with both parents, there is substantial evidence that it can be beneficial to the children. In contrast, imposed joint custody in families where parents are still doing battle with one another can lead to a great deal of stress and potential maladjustment for children. As was the case with visitation of a noncustodial parent, other factors may influence the success of the arrangement, including the number and kind of transitions between homes, the distance between homes, and the temperament of the child. Not surprisingly, joint custody seems to work better for children who have more flexible, easygoing temperaments (Wallerstein & Blakeslee, 1989). Joint custody also appears to work better for

preadolescent school-aged children than for adolescents, perhaps for the same reasons that high and regular visitation becomes more problematic for adolescents. Yet some adolescents do maintain a joint-custody arrangement and seem to do so without significant stress or problems in managing and organizing their life in two homes. As noted earlier, joint-custody adolescents were not only satisfied with their arrangement, they were more satisfied than mother-custody or father-custody adolescents (Buchanan et al., 1996).

Alternative Actions

School personnel may be asked for advice about custody and visitation arrangements, or they may have to evaluate the extent to which children's functioning is affected by such arrangements. The research reviewed in this chapter points to the following conclusions about what is in the best interests of children.

Visitation should generally be encouraged, in the spirit of promoting a good relationship between a child and each parent. In instances where conflict between parents is low or nonexistent, there is little reason to think that children will be harmed by visitation; in fact, there is some evidence that children can benefit from the ongoing relationship such visitation provides. In situations of high conflict, there is probably more reason to be concerned about the negative effects of visitation and to be alert for signs of poor adjustment. However, some families are able to manage their conflict in such a way that the child can continue to benefit from the relationship with the noncustodial parent. In fact, in some cases that relationship buffers the otherwise negative effects of the conflict. Although ideally visitation and a good relationship between the nonresidential parent and child should be promoted, personnel clearly need to consider each situation individually.

Other factors to consider include (a) whether a particular set of parents are likely to use visitation as an excuse to involve the child in the conflict (e.g., ask the child to carry messages, ask the child questions about the other parent or home), (b) how well adjusted the parents are, and (c) the strength of the existing relationship between the noncustodial parent and child. In addition, one should consider the temperament of the child. Some children tolerate changes in routine and transitions from one home to another better than others. For those with easygoing temperaments, frequent visitation or transitions between homes may pose little problem. For less adaptable children, more time in one, consistent home environment may be preferable, although as long as the routine of visitation is consistent, they may adapt quite well to spending time in both homes on a regular basis.

As with visitation, joint custody can be encouraged if both parents are supportive of the arrangement and if parents are either amiable or able to handle their conflicts between themselves, with minimal exposure of the child to the conflict. Under these circumstances, joint custody seems best able to promote over time (or allow maintenance of) good relationships between a child and both parents. It also does not appear to interfere with effective supervision of children or consistency of rules and management within or across homes. In and of itself, joint custody does not promote conflict between parents. Thus, if parents are not in high conflict to begin with, this custody option may be most beneficial for children.

With regard to handling the logistics of high visitation or joint custody, there are no data on specific schedules that are best for children. However, schedules that minimize the number of transitions between homes, especially for younger children, and that are relatively predictable seem to work best. Adolescents, as compared to younger children, need more flexibility within their routine to accommodate friends, jobs, and other extracurricular interests. Even so, a predictable schedule viewed as flexible is more likely to promote continued visitation and the positive outcomes that may ensue than is allowing visitation to occur in a haphazard, spontaneous fashion.

Concerning father custody, each situation needs to be considered individually. Any parent—whether mother or father—experiences challenges and difficulties in parenting alone (Hetherington, Cox, & Cox 1982; also see chapters on Divorce and Single Parenting and Stepparenting, this volume), and in many ways the parenting of single fathers is similar to that of single mothers. Fathers, however, because they often have less experience in primary caretaking than mothers and because of the unusual circumstances under which they often get custody, may need extra support in creating a healthy, effective, family environment. In particular, attention should be given to their efforts to develop close relationships with their children and to their monitoring of children's activities.

To what extent should children have a voice in their custody and visitation arrangements? Most experts believe that if children have opinions, those opinions should be considered in the decision about visitation or custody. However, children—even adolescent children—should not be forced to give an opinion or to make a decision about what custody will be or how much visitation will occur. Even seemingly minor decisions about where to spend a weekend or a holiday can be stressful because children feel as if they are choosing between their parents and they worry about hurting their parents' feelings (Buchanan et al., 1996). Thus, parents and counselors must walk a fine line between, on the one hand, gently eliciting and considering children's wishes when they are offered and, on the other hand, not making children feel responsible for decisions concerning the amount of contact with each parent. Ultimately, parents need to assume

such responsibility, even if their decision is influenced by the child's wishes.

On a related note, it is quite normal for adolescents to express interest in changing custody or visitation arrangements, either to accommodate new activities and interests or simply as a reflection of the identity exploration process. Changes expressing an interest in "trying out something new" as opposed to those reflecting attempts to escape from or manipulate parents are generally seen as reasonable and worth considering (Bray, 1991).

More important to children's adjustment than specific custody or visitation arrangements are the quality of children's relationships with each parent, the quality of parenting that children receive from each parent, and the level of conflict between parents after divorce. To enhance children's relationships with their noncustodial parents, school personnel might consider sending information about children's school activities and achievements to the noncustodial parent as well as to the primary custodian. Parent-teacher conferences could be conducted with both parents, either individually or together, depending on what particular parents can handle. Noncustodial parents could also be invited to attend school events, as there is evidence that "attendance by the noncustodial parent at special events can facilitate the parent-child relationship" (Bray, 1991, p. 426). Individual counseling or group parenting education focused on issues faced by single parents can help parents recognize the importance of the child's relationship with each parent as well as other aspects of parenting and can provide resources and support for those parents who want and need to make adjustments in their parenting (see Barber, 1995, and Stolberg & Cullen, 1983, for examples of specific intervention programs; see also chapter on Parenting Styles, this volume).

Reducing conflict between parents is a more complex issue. Aside from generally educating parents about the negative effects of conflict on children, perhaps one of the most helpful things that school personnel can do is to intervene to limit or stop parents from involving their children in the conflict. In some cases, simply alerting parents that behaviors such as asking children to carry messages between homes, quizzing them about the other home, or denigrating the other parent in front of the child are stressful for the child may help to stem some of those behaviors. Counseling children about how to handle such situations would also be helpful. In more extreme cases, facilitating more extensive family or individual counseling is also an option.

Summary

By and large, children seem to want and benefit from sustained contact with both parents. The benefits, however, depend on a variety of factors including the level of conflict between parents, characteristics of the child (age, sex, temperament), and the logistics of the arrangement (distance between homes, regularity of contact, frequency of transitions, flexibility of the arrangement, etc.). Joint custody (or sole custody with high visitation of a custodial parent) may come closest to approximating the ideal postdivorce scenario if it is chosen voluntarily by the parents and if they do not have high levels of initial conflict between them. However, joint custody may be risky in some situations (for example, where there is a lot of conflict between parents or the child's temperament is such that he or she has trouble adapting to changes in routine). Father custody may be associated with some risks for the average child in the average situation, although it can work well for many children.

School personnel can use the information provided here to understand some of the processes and outcomes that might be more or less likely given a child's visitation or custody arrangement but ought not to be surprised to find situations that do not fit the average profile for that arrangement. Ultimately, encouraging and supporting parents in efforts to minimize conflict, develop and maintain positive relationships with their child, and provide consistent, authoritative parenting in each home in which the child resides will do the most to improve children's functioning after divorce.

Recommended Resources

Bray, J. H. (1991). Psychosocial factors affecting custodial and visitation arrangements. *Behavioral Sciences and the Law, 9,* 419–437.
This article notes that the custody arrangement that is best for any individual child depends on many different factors. The factors discussed include (a) child characteristics (e.g., age, sex, intelligence, and temperament); (b) parental adjustment and parenting skills; (c) family relationships; and (d) other contextual factors.

Felner, R. D., & Terre, L. (1987). Child custody dispositions and children's adaptation following divorce. In Weithorn, L. A. (Ed.), *Psychology and custody determinations: Knowledge, roles, and expertise* (pp. 106–153). Lincoln, NE: University of Nebraska Press.
This is an extensive literature review on mother custody (including data on visitation), father custody, and joint custody. The chapter addresses major questions of interest (e.g., "does joint custody reduce interparental conflict?") and concludes there is no one "best" custody arrangement.

Hodges, W. F. (1991). *Interventions for children of divorce: Custody, access, and psychotherapy* (2nd ed.). New York: John Wiley & Sons.
This book is written for practitioners but has a solid grounding in the clinical as well as developmental research. Some of the

more practical, as well as emotional and psychological, issues surrounding divorce, visitation, and custody are discussed.

Kelly, J. B. (1993). Current research on children's postdivorce adjustment: No simple answers. *Family and Conciliation Courts Review, 31,* 29–49.
This article reviews some of the major factors associated with children's adjustment after divorce, including data on custody and visitation arrangements. It includes references to classic studies of divorce as well as more recent studies.

References

Amato, P. R. (1993). Children's adjustment to divorce: Theories, hypotheses, and empirical support. *Journal of Marriage and the Family, 55,* 23–38.

Amato, P. R., & Rezac, S. J. (1994). Contact with nonresident parents, interparental conflict, and children's behavior. *Journal of Family Issues, 15,* 191–207.

Barber, B. L. (1995). Preventive intervention with adolescents and divorced mothers: A conceptual framework for program design and evaluation. *Journal of Applied Developmental Psychology, 16,* 481–503.

Bray, J. H. (1991). Psychosocial factors affecting custodial and visitation arrangements. *Behavioral Sciences and the Law, 9,* 419–437.

Buchanan, C. M., Maccoby, E. E., & Dornbusch, S. M. (1991). Caught between parents: Adolescents' experience in divorced homes. *Child Development, 62,* 1008–1029.

Buchanan, C. M., Maccoby, E. E., & Dornbusch, S. M. (1996). *Adolescents after divorce.* Cambridge, MA: Harvard University Press.

Camara, K. A., & Resnick, G. (1988). Interparental conflict and cooperation: Factors moderating children's postdivorce adjustment. In E. M. Hetherington & J. D. Arasteh (Eds.), *Impact of divorce, single parenting, and stepparenting on children* (pp. 169–195). Hillsdale, NJ: Lawrence Erlbaum Associates.

Felner, R. D., & Terre, L. (1987). Child custody dispositions and children's adaptation following divorce. In L. A. Weithorn (Ed.), *Psychology and custody determinations: Knowledge, roles, and expertise* (pp. 106–153). Lincoln, NE: University of Nebraska Press.

Forehand, R., Wierson, M., Thomas, A. M., Armistead, L., Kempton, T., & Fauber, R. (1990). Interparental conflict and paternal visitation following divorce: The interactive effect on adolescent competence. *Child Study Journal, 20,* 193–202.

Furstenberg, F. F., Jr., & Harris, K. M. (1992). The disappearing American father?: Divorce and the waning significance of biological parenthood. In S. J. South & S. E. Tolnay (Eds.), *The changing American family* (pp. 197–223). Boulder, CO: Westview Press.

Furstenberg, F. F., Jr., & Nord, C. W. (1985). Parenting apart: Patterns of childrearing after marital disruption. *Journal of Marriage and the Family, 47,* 893–904.

Furstenberg, F. F., Jr., Nord, C. W., Peterson, J. L., & Zill, N. (1983). The life course of children of divorce. *American Sociological Review, 48,* 656–668.

Grych, J. H., & Fincham, F. D. (1992). Interventions for children of divorce: Toward greater integration of research and action. *Psychological Bulletin, 111,* 434–454.

Healy, J. M., Jr., Malley, J. E., & Stewart, A. J. (1990). Children and their fathers after parental separation. *American Journal of Orthopsychiatry, 60,* 531–543.

Hetherington, E. M., Cox, M., & Cox, R. (1982). Effects of divorce on parents and children. In M. E. Lamb (Ed.), *Nontraditional families* (pp. 233–288). Hillsdale, NJ: Erlbaum.

Hodges, W. F. (1991). *Interventions for children of divorce: Custody, access, and psychotherapy* (2nd ed.), New York: John Wiley & Sons.

Isaacs, M. B. (1988). The visitation schedule and child adjustment: A three year study. *Family Process, 27,* 251–256.

Johnston, J. R., & Campbell, L. E. G. (1988). *Impasses of divorce: The dynamics and resolution of family conflict.* New York: Free Press.

Johnston, J. R., Campbell, L. E. G., & Mayes, S. S. (1985). Latency children in post-separation and divorce disputes. *Journal of the American Academy of Child Psychiatry, 24,* 563–574.

Johnston, J. R., Kline, M., & Tschann, J. M. (1989). Ongoing post-divorce conflict in families contesting custody: Effects on children of joint custody and frequent access. *American Journal of Orthopsychiatry, 59,* 576–592.

Kelly, J. B. (1988). Longer-term adjustment in children of divorce: Converging findings and implications for practice. *Journal of Family Psychology, 2,* 119–140.

Kelly, J. B. (1993). Current research on children's post-divorce adjustment: No simple answers. *Family and Conciliation Courts Review, 31,* 29–49.

King, V. (1994). Nonresident father involvement and child well-being. *Journal of Family Issues, 15,* 78–96.

Kurdek, L. A., & Berg, B. (1983). Correlates of children's adjustment to their parents' divorces. In L. A. Kurdek (Ed.), *New directions for child development: No. 19. Children and divorce* (pp. 47–60). San Francisco: Jossey-Bass.

Luepnitz, D. A. (1982). *Child custody: A study of families after divorce.* Lexington, MA: Lexington Books/D.C. Heath & Company.

Luepnitz, D. A. (1986). A comparison of maternal, paternal, and joint custody: Understanding the varieties of post-divorce family life. *Journal of Divorce, 9,* 1–12.

Maccoby, E. E., Depner, C. E., & Mnookin, R. H. (1990). Coparenting in the second year after divorce. *Journal of Marriage and the Family, 52,* 141–155.

Maccoby, E. E., & Mnookin, R. H. (1992). *Dividing the child: Social and legal dilemmas of custody.* Cambridge, MA: Harvard University Press.

Peterson, J. L., & Zill, N. (1986). Marital disruption, parent-child relationships, and behavior problems in children. *Journal of Marriage and the Family, 48,* 295–307.

Santrock, J. W., & Warshak, R. A. (1979). Father custody and social development in boys and girls. *Journal of Social Issues, 35,* 112–125.

Seltzer, J. A. (1991). Relationships between fathers and children who live apart: The father's role after separation. *Journal of Marriage and the Family, 53,* 79–101.

Seltzer, J. A., Schaeffer, C., & Charng, H. W. (1989). Family ties after divorce: The relationship between visiting and paying child support. *Journal of Marriage and the Family, 51,* 1013–1032.

Shiller, V. M. (1986). Joint versus maternal physical custody for families with latency age boys: Parent characteristics and child adjustment. *American Journal of Orthopsychiatry, 56,* 486–489.

Steinman, S. B. (1981). The experience of children in a joint-custody arrangement: A report of a study. *American Journal of Orthopsychiatry, 51,* 403–414.

Steinman, S. B., Zemmelman, S. E., & Knoblauch, T. M. (1985). A study of parents who sought joint custody following divorce: Who reaches agreement and sustains joint custody and who returns to court. *Journal of the American Academy of Child Psychiatry, 24,* 554–562.

Stolberg, A. L., & Cullen, P. M. (1983). Preventive interventions for families of divorce: The Divorce Adjustment Project. In L. A. Kurdek (Ed.), *New directions for child development: No. 19. Children and divorce* (pp. 71–81). San Francisco: Jossey-Bass.

Thomas, A. M., & Forehand, R. (1993). The role of paternal variables in divorced and married families: Predictability of adolescent adjustment. *American Journal of Orthopsychiatry, 63,* 126–134.

Wallerstein, J. S., & Blakeslee, S. (1989). *Second chances: Men, women and children a decade after divorce.* New York: Ticknor & Fields.

Wallerstein, J. S., & Kelly, J. B. (1980). *Surviving the breakup: How children and parents cope with divorce.* New York: Basic Books.

Warshak, R. A. (1986). Father-custody and child development: A review and analysis of psychological research. *Behavioral Sciences and the Law, 4,* 185–202.

Warshak, R. A. (1987). Father-custody families: Therapeutic goals and strategies. *The Family Therapy Collections, 23,* 101–124.

Warshak, R. A., & Santrock, J. W. (1983). The impact of divorce in father-custody and mother-custody homes: The child's perspective. In L. A. Kurdek (Ed.), *New directions for child development: No. 19. Children and divorce* (pp. 29–46). San Francisco: Jossey-Bass.

55

Single Parenting and Stepparenting

Cindy Carlson

The University of Texas at Austin

Background

In 1990, 21.6% of children under age 18 lived with their mother only, 3.1% lived with their father only, 11.3% lived in a stepfamily, and 6.3% lived with neither parent or were "unknown or unaccounted for"; 57.7% lived with both their biological parents (U.S. Bureau of the Census, 1992, cited in Popenoe, 1994). Thus, 4 of every 10 children in any given classroom, measured at a single point in time, could be residing in a home that does not include two biological parents. While these national demographics are ample to underscore the importance of understanding the effects of single-parent and stepfamily life on the achievement and school-related behavior of children, a static view of the statistics underestimates the magnitude and impact of these family forms on the development of children. All children in a stepparent home, for example, previously resided in a single parent or extended family home. Sixty-two percent of remarriages end in divorce with rates higher for remarriages involving children, resulting in a return to a single-parent family situation (Furstenberg & Cherlin, 1991). Looking at the picture more broadly, it is estimated that one-half of children born in the 1980s will spend some time living in a one-parent situation (Bianchi, 1995). One out of every three Americans is now a stepparent, a stepchild, a stepsibling, or some other member of a stepfamily, and more than half of Americans today have been, are now, or will eventually be in one or more step situations during their lives. (Popenoe, 1994).

Contrary to the recent view of some social scientists who believed that the effects of family fragmentation were both modest and short-lived, there is now substantial evidence to indicate that the child outcomes on average of single-parent families and stepfamilies are significantly inferior to those of families consisting of two biological parents as settings for child development (Popenoe, 1994). Also contrary to the common view that stepfamilies, with the addition to the one-parent home of economic resources and a second parent figure, were preferable childrearing situations, recent studies find that children of stepfamilies have as many, and possibly more, behavioral and emotional problems as children in single-parent families (Popenoe, 1994). Importantly, child problems associated with single-parent and stepfamily homes remain significant when parental variables of race and socioeconomic status are controlled.

Compared to children in homes with two biological or adoptive parents, children in divorced, single-parent, and stepfamily homes are significantly more likely to have emotional and behavior problems, to receive the professional help of psychologists, to have health problems, to perform poorly in school and drop out, and to leave home early (Popenoe, 1994). Adolescents (grades 6–12) in mother-only and mother-stepfather families, compared with mother-father families, are significantly more likely to repeat a grade, be suspended or expelled from school, and achieve in the bottom half of their class; they are also 50% more likely to have their parents contacted by the school or teacher regarding a behavior problem (Zill, 1994). Overall rates of behavior problems are similar in stepparent and single-parent families. Although many of these statistics relate to children's adjustment problems as a function of marital transitions, additional concern is raised by the increasing rates of never-married single-parent homes, which characteristically have the most adverse effects on children. Recent statistics indicate that currently 37% of children under 18 live with a divorced single parent but almost as many (35.8%) live with a never-married single parent (U.S. Bureau of the Census, 1994).

Although coming from a single-parent or stepfamily significantly increases the relative risk that a child will experience problems in school, it is important to note that residing in these family forms does not automatically result in school problems. As noted by Zill (1994), "one can correctly say, for example, that three quarters of children from stepfamilies have not had to repeat a grade, more than 80% have never been suspended or expelled from school, and a majority are in the upper half of their classes. This is true despite the fact that these children have experienced marital conflict and parental divorce, or birth outside marriage and the entrance of a new, and perhaps, unwelcome adult into the family constellation" (p. 100). Further, differences in child outcomes between homes with two biological parents and those with one or fewer biological parents, while reflecting statistically significant differences in the distributions of large national samples, may represent only small differences, practically speaking, in the behavior or achievement of children (Amato, 1994). Others have argued, however, that statistically different coefficients mean sizable differences in the risk that children in single-parent and stepfamilies face when compared with two biological parent families. "In epidemiological terms, the doubling of a risk is hardly trivial. Many well-known medical risk factors are far weaker in their impact" (Zill, 1994, p. 100).

In summary, while the majority of children in single-parent and stepfamily homes will demonstrate insignificant differences in behavior problems or school achievement, risk for problems is clearly increased for children in both of these family forms. Viewed broadly, one-third to one-half of the students in any school setting may experience increased vulnerability associated with the stress of single-parent or stepfamily home life or with the transition between these family forms. It is the purpose of this chapter to present the most recent research regarding risk and vulnerability of children in single-parent and stepparent homes and to make recommendations for assessment and intervention when appropriate. The focus of this chapter is on a review of literature published since 1990. The interested reader is referred to previous chapters by the author for discussion of earlier research (Carlson, 1985, 1987), theoretical perspectives on the topic (Carlson, 1991b), and broader suggestions for intervention regarding single-parent and stepparent family life as it affects children's school-related development (Carlson, 1995).

Definitions and Related Issues

Both single-parent and stepparent families are complex and diverse systems. The following discussion serves to underscore the diversity of these families before committing the unavoidable error of oversimplification from categorization that will result when the research literature on the effects of these family types on children is reviewed.

Single-Parent Families

The most simple definition of a single-parent home is a household in which an adult raises children alone without the presence of a second adult (Weiss, 1979). This definition, however, does not address the diversity of this family form. Moreover, the diversity of single-parent homes is largely related to ethnic diversity. First, there

is considerable racial variation in the incidence of single-parent homes. Black children are most likely to live in a mother-child family (54% in 1992), followed by Native American (30%), Hispanic (23%), European-American (14%), and Asian (11%) children (Bianchi, 1995). The high rates of single-parent homes among the African-American population are related to higher birth rates to never married women, higher rates of divorce in first marriages, lower remarriage rates, and more years between marriages compared with European-American women (Bianchi, 1995).

Single-parent homes also differ in the antecedents of single parenthood, head of household, and economic well-being. Data regarding this diversity appear in Table 1. Recent statistics indicate that while divorce rates are dropping, never-married rates are increasing. Thus, as Table 1 indicates, there are currently almost equivalent population percentages of never-married and divorced single mothers (*USA Today,* 1994). Race is a clearly distinguishing feature of never-married versus divorced single parent homes. Most European-American children will reside in a postdivorce single-parent home whereas most African-American children will reside with a never-married mother (Bianchi, 1995).

Single-parent homes also differ in who is head of the household. The single parent may be a mother or a father, a grandparent, or other related or unrelated adult. The most prevalent family form is the one headed by a single mother (over 90%; Angel & Angel, 1993). Although the rates of father-headed homes increased from 13% to 18% in the 1980s, the number of children residing in single-father homes remains low (3%; Bianchi, 1995). Racial differences are extremely large regarding head of household in single-parent families. A significant percentage of African-American children are being reared by a grandparent alone, with neither parent present (George & Dickerson, 1995), whereas the dramatic increase in father-headed single-parent homes in the past decade (from 13% to 18%) is primarily among European-American fathers (Bianchi, 1995).

The social and psychological issues related to each of these single-parent family forms are distinctive (see Carlson, 1985, for further discussion), as are the economic disadvantages. Half of children living in a mother-only family resided in poverty in 1991 (Bianchi, 1995). As evident from Table 1, although the economic ramifications of divorce are dramatic, the economic disadvantage of the never-married mother by comparison is alarming. The high incidence of poverty among never-married single mothers is related to their younger age, lower education (40% are not high school graduates), lower rates of employment (38% vs. 79% of divorced mothers), and inability to garner income from the father of their children (Bianchi, 1995). In contrast with both single post-divorce mothers and never-married mother headed homes, economic resources are generally higher in

Table 1 *Demographic Profile of Variations in Single-Parent Families*

Parenting Group	Demographic Indicators		
	Percentage of Single-Parent Population	Percentage of Children in These Homes by Ethnicity	Median Income Compared to That of Two-Parent Homes
Postdivorce/Separated Mothers	37%	50% of European-American Children	69% Lower
Postdivorce/Separated Fathers	18%	Primarily European-American Children	43% Lower
Never-Married Mothers	36%	50% of African-American Children	85% Lower
Widowed Parents	6%	No Ethnic Differences	Most closely approximates two-parent homes
Other Caretaking Adults (e.g., Grandparent)	Unknown	38% of African-American Children	Unknown

Note. Figures may not sum to 100% because statistics are drawn from multiple sources including Bianchi, 1995; George and Dickerson, 1995; Lino, 1995; and *USA Today,* 1994.

single-father and single-parent widow homes (Bianchi, 1995).

Although discussion has focused on single-parent homes with one adult provider/caretaker, it is important to note that many families identified as single parent in research, school records, or earlier census statistics may, in fact, have additional adults in residence who, to a greater or lesser degree, provide support to the household. In 1992, 15% of children in mother-child and 37% of children in father-child situations had at least one non-relative living in the household (Bianchi, 1995). Within the African-American community, many single mothers reside in extended households with the maternal grandmother and sometimes the great grandmother (Bianchi, 1995). While these homes would not technically fall within our definition of a single-parent family, they provide a more realistic picture of the resources potentially available to children in single-parent households.

Stepfamilies

The simplest definition of a stepfamily is a family in which at least one member of the adult couple is a stepparent (Popenoe, 1994). Stepfamilies are commonly distinguished in research as stepfather families (only the mother has residential children from a previous marriage), stepmother families (only the father has residential children from a previous marriage), and complex families (both parents have residential children from a previous marriage; Hetherington & Jodl, 1994). Perhaps most useful from a treatment perspective is the view of stepfamilies as a linked family system (LFS; Jacobson, 1995). In LFS, the child is seen as related to two households, each of which is viewed as a subsystem of a dual-

household conceptualization. People in both households are seen as part of the child's family environment. The child is viewed as the "link" who is both influenced by and influencing members in two (or more) households. Six possible LFS types derive from this conceptualization:

- Family Type 1—child lives with a single mother and visits a remarried father.
- Family Type 2—child lives with a remarried mother and visits a remarried father.
- Family Type 3—child lives with a remarried mother and visits a single father.
- Family Types 4, 5, and 6—parallel Types 1–3, except the child lives with the father.

Each of these stepfamily variations may have distinctive family stressors (Carlson, 1991b).

As with the ethnic variation in single-parent homes, stepparenting is more common among some ethnic groups than others. White single parents are most likely to remarry and form a stepfamily; Hispanic single parents are least likely to remarry; African-American single mothers represent an intermediate group. European-American single mothers are most likely to remarry quickly, many within the first year following divorce, with a median of 3 years between marriages (Bumpass & Sweet, 1989, cited in Furstenberg and Cherlin, 1991). Among both African-Americans and European-Americans, mothers who are less educated are most likely to remarry (Coleman & Ganong, 1991). This would appear to be a wise strategy as the primary route out of poverty for single mothers is marriage or remarriage (Angel & Angel, 1993), and virtually all demographic studies point to the relative economic well-being of two-parent, dual-earner versus one-parent, single-earner incomes.

Common Family Forms: Implications for Child Development

Despite the heterogeneity of single-parent and stepparent families, research to guide understanding of these family forms as they influence children's school-related development is limited to certain common variations. Thus, in this section, normal family functioning and expected child outcomes will be reviewed for the more commonly studied single-parent and stepparent types. The term, *normal,* carries multiple meanings (Walsh, 1993). Normal may mean the family is asymptomatic, is optimal in functioning, is average in functioning, or has transactional processes that are characteristic. In the following discussion, normal will refer to average functioning as defined in research by statistical means; normal will also be used to refer to characteristic transactional processes as observed by clinicians and social science researchers. Average functioning and characteristic transactional processes in single-parent and stepfamilies, although normal, may result in problems for children.

Postdivorce Single-Parent Families

Marital dissolution is the largest single contributor to the increasing number of children living with a single parent, particularly European-American children. It is, therefore, impossible to disentangle the effects of living in a single-parent home from the effects of divorce for these children, and it should be assumed that this family type represents confounded effects. Moreover, divorce should not be considered a single static life event but rather be seen as part of a complex chain of marital transitions and family reorganizations associated with alterations in family roles and relationships and adjustment of family members (Hetherington & Jodl, 1994; see also chapter on Divorce, this volume). Thus, it is important to differentiate the short- from long-term effects on children of postdivorce single-parent homes.

Marital transitions, such as separation, divorce, and remarriage, are consistently found to have adverse short-term effects on both parents and children. Parenting skills weaken in the disequilibrium associated with marital transitions, and children display higher rates of learning and behavior problems (Hetherington, 1991). Moreover, marital transitions are usually associated with multiple losses for children including loss of a parent; loss of income; changes in maternal employment; geographical relocation; and related changes in school, friends, and neighborhood. Because extensive literature exists on the effects of divorce on children, this discussion of development in the postdivorce single-parent home will focus on long-term child outcomes.

Mother-Headed Families

The majority of postdivorce single-parent homes are headed by mothers (90%; Angel & Angel, 1993). The postdivorce mother-headed home as a setting for development of children has been clearly articulated by Hetherington in a series of studies on marital transitions (1991), and the following discussion, unless otherwise indicated, is based on the results of her data.

Age and sex differences are relevant in the childrearing effects of single-parent homes. For younger children the adverse effects of divorce and life in a single mother-headed household are more marked and enduring for sons than daughters. Whereas both boys and girls show increases in externalizing and internalizing behavior disorders in the first 2 years following divorce (with marked improvement after the first year), by 2 years girls' rates of disorder do not differ from girls in homes with two biological parents. In contrast, boys continue to show higher rates of behavior problems, as well as problems with academic achievement, compared with boys in nondivorced homes. The more negative outcomes for boys associated with the single-mother homes appear, in part, to be related to parenting style. Parent-child interactions between single mothers and sons tend to be coercive (as defined by Patterson, 1982) and marked by nagging, nattering, complaining, ambivalence, inconsistency of rules and punishments, and escalating conflict. In short, it appears to be more difficult, but necessary, for single mothers to be authoritative with younger sons in the absence of fathers in the home.

With the onset of adolescence, sons and daughters in single-mother homes tend to look more similar behaviorally, although girls continue to do better than boys in school performance. Although both divorced mothers and their adolescent children report more involvement and time together compared with peers in two-biological-parent families, there are also higher levels of acrimonious, coercive, and conflictual exchanges between mothers and both adolescent sons and daughters. The changed parent-child relationship is particularly marked for early maturing girls. As described by Hetherington (1991):

The relationship between divorced mothers and adolescent children is an intensely emotional and ambivalent one. . . . The sense of intimacy, affection, camaraderie, concern, involvement, even enmeshment, accompanied by anger and conflict was notable in these families with adolescent children. Over the course of these early adolescent years, divorced mothers were becoming more active in attempting to control and monitor their children's behavior, especially their daughter's behavior. However, the attempt seemed to be initiated too late. . . . It is reactive rather than proactive and preventive (pp. 334–335).

Single-mother-headed homes are notable for allowing both sons and daughters more responsibility, independence, and power in decision making compared with children in nondivorced families (Weiss, 1979). Although younger children in single-parent homes do not perceive their mothers to be less authoritative, adolescents report that their mothers exert significantly less control and that they have considerably more independence and decision-making autonomy compared with youth in nondivorced two-parent homes (Dornbusch, Ritter, Leiderman, Roberts, & Fraleigh, 1987). Related to the greater independence given to children in single-parent families, single mothers engage in significantly less monitoring of their children's whereabouts, and children in single-mother homes are less likely to be supervised by an adult when home alone compared with children in two-biological-parent families (Hetherington, 1991).

In sum, the single mother establishes a relationship with her child that is characteristically more egalitarian and affectively intense and with greater time spent together compared with children reared in nondivorced families. In some cases this results in a mutually supportive relationship between mother and child. Mothers and daughters, in particular, express considerable satisfaction with their congenial relationship in stabilized single-mother homes. In other cases, however, where the emotional demands or responsibilities placed by the single mother are age inappropriate, extend beyond the capabilities of the child, or interfere with the child's normal activities, children respond with resentment, rebellion, or behavior problems (Hetherington, 1991). The burden of a close parent-child relationship may be particularly onerous in adolescence.

These descriptions of normal family processes in the single-mother home help to explain differences between single-parent and two-biological-parent homes in long-term outcomes related to being reared by a single mother. Reviews of the literature (Barber & Eccles, 1992), meta-analyses of the literature (Amato & Keith, 1992), and large scale national survey studies (Downey & Powell, 1993; Zimilies & Lee, 1991) all find adolescents reared in single-parent homes to be more susceptible to peer influence and more likely to engage in deviant behavior, even when sex, age, socioeconomic status, maternal employment, and family decision making are controlled. Relatedly, adolescents, particularly male adolescents, in single-mother-headed homes were found to be three times as likely to drop out of high school before graduation, compared with adolescents in two-biological-parent families, despite school achievement comparable to peers (Zimilies & Lee, 1991). Given the comparable school achievement, the higher rate of school dropout for adolescents in single-mother homes appears to be more a function of social deviancy than cognitive deficiency. Because parental monitoring is a key predictor of adolescent deviancy across family structure, single mothers' lack of active monitoring would appear to place their children at risk.

Father-Headed Families

The numbers of single custodial fathers increased in the past decade at a rate exceeding the increase in mother-headed families. Nevertheless, because only 3% of children reside in single-father families, there is limited research on this family form, and with few exceptions, existing research tends to focus on middle-class European-American fathers who are also most likely to have custody of children (Grief & DeMaris, 1995).

Fathers gain custody of children for a variety of reasons including maternal incompetence or rejection of the children, children choosing the father, the father having more financial resources, and custody being won via prearrangement or in a brief or extended battle (Grief & DeMaris, 1995). Just as with single mothers, the antecedents to single fatherhood influence parenting quality. Fathers who choose to have custody or who fight for and win custody tend to have more positive attitudes toward their children than fathers who have custody thrust upon them or who gain custody without a court battle (Grief & DeMaris). In addition, these researchers found that comfort with single fathering was greatest for men who (a) had been in that role for a number of years, (b) had a satisfactory social life, (c) had a good relationship with the children, (d) had a higher income, (e) rated themselves highly as a parent, (f) reported that visitation with the mother was amicable or there was no visitation, and (g) did not have strong religious affiliations (Grief & DeMaris, 1990, cited in Grief & DeMaris, 1995).

There is limited data on the outcomes for children of being reared in single-father homes. Zimilies and Lee (1991) found adolescent girls in father custody homes to be at higher risk for high school dropout, compared with girls in single-mother or two-biological-parent homes. The reasons for this finding are unclear. One explanation is that a permissive parenting style characterizes single fathers as well as single mothers (Dornbusch et al., 1987). A second explanation that has been proposed (given the difficulties single mothers have with sons in both their younger years and adolescence) is that opposite-sex single-parent childrearing has associated risks. An early classic study (Santrock & Warshak, 1979) found preadolescent children's socio-emotional well-being to be strongly correlated to residence with a same-sex parent, with boys showing more maturity and sociability when reared in father-custody homes and girls more social competence in mother-custody homes; however, the sample size ($N = 65$) of this study was too small to be conclusive. In a more recent national representative survey of eighth graders ($N = 24,599$), only 2 of the 35 outcome criteria showed differences between mother-custody and father-custody homes, and neither supported the same-sex custody argument (Downey & Powell, 1993). Rather, for both boys and girls, living with fathers meant children were more likely to have money saved for their college education and to have a computer in the home. As concluded by Downey and Powell, "the benefits of living in a father-only household owe to background factors, most notably greater income" (p. 67). These findings would suggest, consistent with many studies, that an authoritative parenting style, regardless of the sex of the child or sex of the parent, produces the best child development outcomes for youth, particularly those of European-American ethnicity.

African-American Single-Mother Families

Incidence and family forms

As of 1990, more than half of all African-American children under 18 years of age lived with their mother, making the mother-headed single-parent family the most prevalent or normative among African-Americans. Extended family systems are common among African-Americans, and many never-married single mothers may reside in an extended versus single-parent family household. Three extended family forms have been identified among African-Americans: Three-generation systems, four-generation systems, and two single sisters with children. The most prevalent extended family form is the four-generation family comprised of child and three generations of single mothers (adolescent mother, grandmother, and great-grandmother). Burton (1991) found that in these homes the great-grandmother assumes most of the parenting responsibility for the adolescent mother while the grandmother assumes most of the responsibility for the child. This organization may serve a functional protective role for all family members. A more mature caregiver is responsible for the child and conflict between the two closest generations (mother/grandmother, grandmother/great-grandmother) is minimized with these role distinctions. It should also be noted that the members of these multigenerational family systems, with transgenerational adolescent pregnancies, are primarily responsible for childrearing at an age equivalent to the birth timing in the European-American population. A grandmother in her late 20s to mid 30s, for example, is likely to be parenting her grandchild and a great-grandmother in her mid-40s is parenting an adolescent.

In contrast to the potential functionality of the four-generation extended family for rearing children, the functionality of the three-generation extended family appears to vary with the age of the adolescent mother (Chase-Lansdale, Brooks-Gunn, & Zamsky, 1994). For young adolescent mothers, coresiding with a grandmother results in higher quality parenting. For older adolescent mothers, however, this family form was characterized by mother-grandmother conflict over parenting, confusion among children regarding who was the parent, and conflict related to sharing economic resources. Although national statistics indicate a rise in the third type of ex-

tended family, that is, two-single-mother sisters sharing a household, there are no empirical data regarding the impact of this family form on children.

Economic issues and maternal education

Over half of African-American single-parent never-married families live in poverty, and family economic hardship is a critical variable in the functioning of these families (Randolph, 1995). There appears to be a complex interrelationship among family structure, maternal functioning, family economic experience, and children's adjustment. McLoyd, Jayaratne, Cebello, & Borquez, 1994) found that adolescents who perceived their families to be experiencing more severe economic hardship reported higher anxiety, more cognitive distress, and lower self-esteem. Adolescent functioning was also influenced by economic hardship indirectly via the mother's psychological functioning and parenting behavior. Economic stressors of work interruption and unemployment negatively predicted mother's psychological functioning, which, in turn, negatively affected parenting behavior and the mother-child relationship. Specifically, unemployment predicted maternal depressive symptomatology, which predicted more frequent maternal punishment and was mediated by mother's negative perceptions of maternal role. More frequent maternal punishment was associated with adolescent cognitive distress and depressive symptoms. Thus, economic hardship, maternal mental health, and parenting skill are interrelated in creating a stressed childrearing environment.

Another important and related factor in the African-American single-mother household is the education level of the parent. Employed African-American single mothers with education beyond high school perceived their children (both boys and girls) significantly more positively than mothers with no education beyond high school (Jackson, 1993). In contrast, having no education beyond high school and a male child predicted significantly higher role strain and maternal depression, lower ratings of overall life satisfaction, and a less favorable view of one's children. Highest levels of strain were related to reluctant employment, whereas mothers who preferred to be employed were more energetic in their response to the demanding role of raising sons. Higher educational attainment, regardless of poverty, would appear to better prepare these mothers both to cope with raising sons and to access social support networks that moderate role strain.

Extrafamilial support

African-American never-married mothers, whether single heads of household or members of an extended family, are embedded in a culture characterized by augmented families and community support. The augmented family refers to adult nonrelatives who reside in the same households as single mothers. No recent research has been conducted on the augmented family form, although earlier research (1970s) found these adult nonrelatives to assume significant family roles, including the parenting of children (Randolph, 1995). Although not necessarily in residence or serving in economic provider roles, adolescent fathers and older fathers of children born to adolescent mothers do appear to function as companions to their children (Staples & Boulin Johnson, 1993). Moreover, once paternity is acknowledged, the father's family becomes an important resource for the mother (Boyd-Franklin, 1995). The African-American community also provides supports to the children of never-married mothers. Formal institutions, such as churches and mosques, provide extensive social support services including educational and recreational activities, male role models and mentors, surrogate fathers, parental support, job training, child care, scholarships, transportation, and health support (Billingsley, 1993).

Summary

It should be apparent from the discussion of the African-American single-mother home that this is a distinctive family form associated with enormous risk or enormous strength depending upon the mother's level of education, economic well-being, and ability to use family and community resources. Significant risks to children in this family form are associated with poverty; low maternal education; multiple siblings; family conflict; lack of social support; and unsafe, underresourced urban neighborhoods. In contrast, strengths of African-American single-mother families include role flexibility, spirituality, sense of community, and positivity (Randolph, 1995).

Stepparent Families

As previously noted, remarriage has commonly been viewed as a panacea to the deficit model of the single-mother, father-absent family. Recent studies, however, find significant differences between two biological parent families and two-parent stepfamilies, with child outcomes in the latter no better than for children reared in a single-parent home. In short, stepfamilies, like single-parent families, differ from biological or adoptive, nondivorced two-parent families in their patterns of functioning, organization, and relationships. Moreover, as noted earlier, stepfamilies represent diverse structures, and the family processes associated with each structure will vary to some extent (see Carlson, 1985, 1991b, 1995). Unfortunately, available research typically focuses on the most common stepfamily form, the stepfather family, in which a custodial mother with residential children marries. Studies seldom differentiate this family type further; thus, little consideration has been given to whether the stepfather has children or the degree to which these children are residents of the household.

The distinctiveness of the stepfamily from non-divorced two-parent families should be obvious when one considers the starting point. The typical stepfamily is comprised of a weak couple system, with a tightly bonded parent-child alliance, and potential interference in family functioning from an "outsider" (*Papernow*, 1984, cited in Hetherington & Jodl, 1994). This is not a starting point that would be viewed as auspicious from a family systems perspective and is in stark contrast with the nondivorced family which optimally begins with a strong couple system, no children until the system is stabilized, and clear boundaries limiting interference from outsiders. Not surprisingly, constructive marital and parent-child relationships in stepfamilies may differ significantly from those in first marriages. Changes in family membership are often a source of stress and rivalry. These may be especially marked if the remarriage involves not only the entrance of a stepparent but the blending of children from both previous marriages. Problems of cross-generational alliances, establishment of appropriate boundaries, scapegoating, and loyalty conflicts are common, as are more conflicts about childrearing and financial support, less family cohesion, more ambiguous roles, more stress, and more problems in child rearing and child adjustment (Hetherington & Jodl, 1994).

Developmental issues

Adjustment of children to the complex relationship matrix created by remarriage varies with the age and sex of the child (Hetherington & Jodl, 1994). As with marital transitions in general, younger boys and girls are initially resistant to remarriage of their mother and show disruptive, primarily externalizing behavior problems and declines in social and academic competence. Although both boys and girls adapt over time, girls' adjustment problems are both more marked and more sustained. Two years after remarriage, boys reared in a home with an authoritative stepfather show behavior comparable to boys in nondivorce homes and behavior that is much improved compared with boys in single-mother homes. Girls, although adapting, continue to show more externalizing problems compared with girls in either nondivorced or nonremarried single-parent homes. Beneficial outcomes derived from remarriage are most likely to be found in preadolescent boys and when the remarriage occurs at an early age (Hetherington & Jodl). In a consistent finding, perceived levels of support and control from stepfathers do not differ significantly from perceptions of biological fathers in nondivorced families when remarriages are of 6 years or longer in duration; stepfathers, however, are never viewed by children as being equivalently involved in punishment (Amato, 1987).

As children enter adolescence, adjustment to remarriage is severely compromised. Both early adolescent boys and girls show significant increases in externalizing behavior problems with remarriage, and there is no significant improvement in adjustment for children across a 26-month post-remarriage period. As noted by Hetherington & Jodl (1994):

It may be that early adolescents take longer to adjust than do younger children, and that 26 months following remarriage is not a sufficient time for adaptation to occur. Or it may be, as proposed, that early adolescence is an especially inauspicious time to have a remarriage occur and that the adolescents may never accept or benefit from their new family situation and a relationship with a stepfather (p. 330)

Early adolescent developmental tasks are proposed to exacerbate remarriage adaptation problems. These tasks include (a) developing independence while maintaining appropriate levels of attachment to family members; (b) experiencing, but containing, sexual feelings and fantasies associated with puberty; and (c) practicing good judgment in the face of acute self-consciousness and egocentrism associated with the cognitive developmental shift from concrete to formal operational thought. Remarriage is in direct conflict with these adolescent tasks. Remarriage pulls for family cohesion and the imposition of a new parental authority in the face of adolescent striving for autonomy; remarriage inserts a sexual couple relationship (i.e., the remarried parent) and the potential for a sexual stepparent-stepchild relationship in the face of adolescent puberty; remarriage demands major adjustments of roles within the family and definition of self to others outside the family at the point in cognitive development when youth are most vulnerable to feelings of shame regarding parents' behavior.

The antecedent single-parent home

The stress of remarriage on early adolescents also must be viewed against the background of the divorced mother's relationship with her preadolescent children (Hetherington & Jodl, 1994). As mentioned earlier, the single-mother home generally includes high involvement and much time spent between single mothers and their children, unusual reported closeness between divorced mothers and daughters, conflict and coercion between mothers and sons, and independence and decision-making power for both boys and girls. The entrance of a stepfather into this affectively charged and somewhat closed system is understandably difficult and affects all family relationships.

Remarriage in general is accompanied by higher levels of conflict between mothers and early adolescents and lower levels of maternal monitoring and control (Amato, 1987, 1994; Hetherington & Jodl, 1994). Although high levels of conflict may ease over the 2-year stabilization period, it is observed to be at the cost of intimacy with both adolescent sons and daughters communicating less and being less warm, more sullen and avoidant, and more coercive in their interactions with mothers (Hetherington & Jodl, 1994). Early adolescents' relationships with their stepfathers are highly aversive. Early in a remarriage, adolescent children behave significantly more negatively to stepfathers than do adolescents to biological fathers. Stepfathers tend to remain initially pleasant in the face of aversive interactions with stepchildren but soon lose patience and get involved in extremely angry and prolonged interchanges, especially with stepdaughters. Stepdaughters tend to view their new stepfathers as hostile, punitive, and unreasonable on matters of discipline. Conflicts between stepfathers and stepdaughters tend to focus on issues of parental authority and respect for the mother. This relationship differs markedly from that of daughters and fathers in nondivorced families.

It is not clear who is more influential in the reciprocal coercive cycles of interaction common in stepfamilies with early adolescents. Hetherington & Jodl (1994) found adolescents in stepfamilies to be more effective in shaping the behavior of their parents in the early stages of remarriage than parents were in shaping the behavior of their adolescents. In contrast, Papernow (1995) found that, although effects between parent and child were reciprocal, the effect of parental rejection, negativity, and punitiveness in stepfamilies was more powerful in shaping children's negative behavior than vice versa. What is known is that children's social competence is associated with positivity directed toward them by both custodial mothers and stepfathers (Hetherington & Jodl, 1994).

Characteristic roles

Given the initial reaction of stepchildren to remarriage, it may not be surprising that stepfathers, when compared with nondivorced biological fathers, remain significantly less affectively involved; less supportive; less willing to criticize; and less engaged in the control, monitoring, or discipline of stepchildren (Hetherington & Jodl, 1994). Stepfathers are also less authoritative with their stepchildren than with their biological children or compared with fathers in nondivorced homes (Hetherington & Jodl). Stepfathers of younger children, over the course of a long-term remarriage, may become equivalently authoritative in their parenting style (Amato, 1987, 1994). Remarried mothers, in contrast, are as warm and controlling with their children as are single mothers and nondivorced mothers except when the remarriage occurs during early adolescence. In this situation, maternal monitoring and control has been found to stabilize over the 2-year adjustment period at levels lower than for either stabilized single mothers or nondivorced mothers (Hetherington & Jodl). In summary, except with remarriages that occur during children's adolescence, biological custodial mothering tends to restabilize in remarriage to premarital levels of warmth and control. In contrast, except with remarriages that are long-term and that occur when children are very young, stepfathers remain more disengaged and less authoritative in parenting their stepchildren in stabilized families. Not surprisingly, both young children and adolescents in stepfamilies report feeling less close to stepfathers than to custodial mothers and less close than children report feeling to fathers in nondivorced families (Amato, 1987). Commonly, even after 2 years of remarriage, many stepfathers and stepchildren do not mention each other when asked to identify members of their family (Hetherington & Jodl).

Many adolescent children in stepfamilies cope with perceived family stress by disengaging from family life. Approximately one-third of boys and one-fourth of girls in both divorced single-parent and remarried families were found to spend little time at home compared with adolescents in nondivorced homes (Hetherington & Jodl, 1994). Many became involved with a surrogate family, with school extracurricular activities, or with a job. If the disengagement involved a close relationship with a caring, involved adult, it was sometimes a constructive solution. If disengagement involved association with antisocial peers or little or no adult supervision, it was associated with substance abuse, low school achievement, school dropout, sexual activity, and delinquency. Older siblings were found to have a significant impact on the externalizing and delinquent behaviors of younger siblings in remarried families (Hetherington, 1991).

Stepmothers

Far less data are available illuminating stepmother-stepchild processes. Stepmothers report greater difficulty than do stepfathers in rearing stepchildren; they also report greater difficulty rearing their stepchildren compared with rearing their biological children (MacDonald & DeMaris, 1996). While one might assume from stepmothers' reported distress that their relationships with stepchildren are highly conflictual, Hetherington & Jodl (1994) found that stepmother-stepchild interaction was actually less negative and coercive than typical exchanges between children and their biological mothers, whether in nondivorced or remarried families. It has been argued based on role theory that stepmothers experience greater stress in their role due to the social expectations to be more involved in a close and nurturing parent role with children. The typically closer relationships between single mothers and children may intensify the role competition between biological and stepmothers, as well as intensify the loyalty conflicts faced by children, making it difficult for children to establish a close relationship with a stepmother.

Summary

Although remarriage may increase the economic resources available to single mothers (especially if the stepfather has no biological children), stepfathers do not replace biological fathers except in long-term stable remarriages that occur early in the life of the child. Even in long-term stable remarriages, close stepfather-stepson relationships appear more easily accomplished than close stepfather-stepdaughter relationships. Finally, remarriage during early adolescence appears to be particularly stressful for all family members and may exacerbate the risks already inherent for children in this developmental stage.

Factors Contributing to Child Development

Although single-parent and stepparent families are more characterized by heterogeneity than homogeneity, there are six major factors that, broadly speaking, contribute to the normal growth and development of children in these homes or, alternatively, the absence of which increases vulnerability to problems. These factors include family resources, parenting skill, interparental cooperation, quality of sibling relations, child characteristics, and an authoritative school environment.

Family Resources

Family resources refer to the economic, interpersonal, and cultural resources that parents bring to children's lives (Downey, 1995). Economic resources include such things as personal income and materials conditioned by income, such as the number of books and other educational resources in the home. Interpersonal resources refer, for example, to the number of adults available to interact with and supervise the child, time devoted to childrearing activities, the number of siblings with whom the child has to compete for parental time and attention, parenting ability and education level of adults, parental discussions about school, and daily activities that serve the child (Zill, 1994). Cultural resources reflect activities, such as visits to museums or the library, that support school learning and child development. On a general level, as noted by Zill, there is extensive evidence to support that the more resources a family can apply to the task of raising a child, the better will be the outcomes for the child, all other things being equal.

Studies find that children in both single-parent and stepfamilies, compared with children in nondivorced two-parent homes, have fewer family resources. The deficit in family resources would appear to be obvious in the comparison of the single-parent and two-parent home. Single-parent homes with one adult serving the multiple roles of provider, caretaker of children, manager of the household, social/recreational director, and emotional supporter will be resource strained. Family resource factors that reduce strain and enhance the normal development of children in single-parent homes include adequate income, higher levels of parent education, parental involvement in school, and family internal and external social support. For example, "thrivers" from single-parent homes were twice as likely as youth at high risk to report living in a home characterized by internal family support (i.e., being able to turn to a parent for help and having a parent involved in their schooling) as well as external support (i.e., positive peer influence, positive school climate, and involvement in structured activities outside the home, such as church, extracurricular activities, and lessons; Benson & Roehlkeparten, 1993). "Many of the differences in assets between single-parent youth who thrive and those who do not point toward the support systems around families. It may be this external network of support is key to success in single parenting" (Benson & Roehlkeparten, 1993, p. 9).

Children in stepfamilies, both stepmother and stepfather, are also deprived from a family-resource perspective even when socioeconomic status and other background variables are considered. Using a large-scale national sample, Downey (1995) found significant differences in level of parental resources between stepparent and nondivorced two-parent families. Furthermore, most of the difference in children's school performance between these households could be explained as a result of differences in parental resources. Although differences in family resources emerged across economic, interpersonal, and cultural domains, differences in interpersonal resources were sufficient in explaining the entire difference in educational performance between stepchildren and children reared in a nondivorced home. In general, parental attention to children is less in stepfamily homes compared with nondivorced intact homes. Although still significantly lower than intact homes, stepfather homes were found to have greater parental resources than stepmother homes, and relatedly children scored higher on math tests in stepfather homes.

A recent large scale survey by Zill (1994) addressed more pointedly the issue of family resources and, specifically, the role of parental involvement in school as it affects children's school behavior and achievement in single-parent and stepparent families. These data show that rates of parental involvement in school are lower for single-parent families, stepfamilies, and families in which neither parent lives with the child compared with families where both biological or adoptive parents live with the child. Again these results hold even when education level of parents, family income, and other related factors are controlled. Children with parents who were relatively uninvolved in school activities were more likely to have experienced problems in school, whereas students whose parents reported high levels of school involvement tended to have a low incidence of learning and behavior problems. Zill found that the increased risk for children in stepfamilies of having school behavior problems was reduced to rates comparable to children in nondivorced homes when *all* parents in stepfamilies were highly involved in their children's schooling.

In summary, family resources are significant factors in the normal development of children in single-parent and stepfamily homes. Of particular importance to children's school learning and behavior are parent interpersonal resources that focus time, attention, and positivity on children and involve parents in the education of their children. Given that family resources may be lacking in many single-parent and stepfamily homes, the role of extrafamilial social support may be viewed as more critical to normal child development in these family forms.

Parenting Style

The second factor related to normal development of children in single-parent and stepparent homes is parenting skill. Parents who are authoritative, that is, who engage in a warm and child-centered style coupled with active control and monitoring, enhance the normal development of their children (see chapter on Parenting Styles, this volume). In single-parent homes, authoritative parenting has been associated with children's social competence (Hetherington & Clingempeel, 1992), school achievement (Dornbusch et al., 1987; Hetherington & Clingempeel, 1992), lower levels of deviance (Dornbusch et al., 1987), and fewer externalizing behaviors (Hetherington & Clingempeel, 1992). Unfortunately, research finds that, as a group, single parents (both mothers and fathers) are more likely to engage in permissive, nonauthoritative parenting (Dornbusch et al., 1987). Permissive parenting appears to contribute to behavior problems in younger sons and to social deviancy in adolescent sons and daughters in single-parent homes.

The benefits of authoritative parenting in stepfamilies is less straightforward. Authoritative parenting by the custodial parent (Hetherington, 1991; Hetherington & Jodl, 1994) and the stepmother (Fine, Voydanoff, & Donnelly, 1993) is related to better outcomes for children. The benefits to children of authoritative parenting by stepfathers, however, varies with the age of the child and the stage of the remarriage (Hetherington & Jodl, 1994). With younger children, adjustment and development are enhanced when stepfathers first establish a warm relationship with the child, support the biological mother's authoritative parenting, and only later become more authoritative themselves. This approach is associated with greater acceptance of the stepfather by stepchildren and with more positive adjustment over time, particularly for boys. In contrast, for early adolescents, immediate authoritative parenting by the stepfather is associated with better outcomes. It is important to note, however, that adolescent adjustment was more strongly predicted by the affective quality of the stepparent-stepchild relationship than by the capacity of the stepfather to establish rules, regulations, and discipline. A disengaged stance by stepfathers predicts the worst adjustment in stepchildren (Hetherington & Jodl).

Although an authoritative parenting style is optimal for children's development, "good-enough" parenting is essential. Children in both single-parent and stepfamilies are at high risk for physical abuse. Numerous studies have indicated that children are far more likely to be abused by a stepfather than by the biological father, leading one researcher to claim stepchildren are not merely "disadvantaged" but "imperiled" (for review, see Popenoe, 1994). Explanations for this pattern include the lack of biological ties between stepparent and stepchild, failure of stepfathers psychologically to assume the role of father, the ambiguity of roles and boundaries inherent in stepfamilies, and the supposedly normal higher level of conflict in stepfamilies.

Parenting ability, particularly among single parents, is directly influenced by the economic resources available to the family. Several studies have documented that single mothers in poverty have higher rates of stress related to economic, family, intimate relationships, and personal health, all of which are related to high rates of depressive symptoms; in turn, maternal depression predicts negative maternal attitudes and ineffective parenting (Hall, Gurley, Sachs, & Kryscio, 1991). Children who live in single parent homes in poverty are not only at risk related to ineffective parenting, they are also at particularly high risk for physical abuse. Gelles (1989), based on a national survey of 6,000 households, found rates of severe and very severe violence toward children highest in single-mother and single-father homes with annual incomes below $10,000. Impoverished single fathers reported the highest rates of very severe violence toward children (406 per 1000), rates higher than any other subpopulation of parents. These data converge with self-reports of adolescents regarding environmental deficits in single-parent homes. The average youth in a single-parent home was more likely to have experienced physical abuse, sexual abuse, parental addiction, time alone, stress, and television overexposure when compared with youth in nondivorced two-parent homes (Benson & Roehlkeparten, 1993).

Involvement with the noncustodial parent might be expected to offset the negative effects of ineffective custodial parenting, whether in single or stepparent families, or the effects of disengaged stepparents. Unfortunately, Hetherington & Jodl (1994) found that noncustodial parents, both mothers and fathers, when they remain involved in the lives of their children, are less authoritative than custodial, biological parents. Following divorce, noncustodial fathers either become more permissive and indulgent or more disengaged from their children. Those who remain involved are more likely to assume a recreational, companionate role rather than an instrumental role of disciplinarian or teacher. It will be recalled that this is also the role most likely to be played by fathers of children in never-married single-parent families. Noncustodial mothers are more likely to remain involved with their children than noncustodial fathers, but like single mothers, they are more vulnerable to permissive parenting styles. Children's reports confirm the lack of support, control, and punishment from noncustodial parents (Amato, 1994). Because the worst outcomes for children are related to no involvement with noncustodial parents, it is important to note that maintenance of contact with children was associated with geographical proximity, remarriage of parents in either family system, feelings of control over decisions in the child's life, and fewer obstacles placed on visitation by the custodial parent (Hetherington & Jodl, 1994).

Interparental Conflict

The third key factor related to normal and symptomatic child development in single-parent and stepfamilies is a cooperative relationship between the adults who are responsible for the rearing of the children. For the never-married mother, conflict between grandmothers and mothers or mothers and other kin have adverse consequences for children (Randolph, 1995). Compelling evidence regarding the adverse effects of interparental hostility on children is provided by Amato and Keith (1992) who concluded after a meta-analysis of 92 studies that family conflict was the most significant predictor of children's adjustment in postdivorce single-parent homes. Hostile and noncooperative relationships between divorces spouses directly relate to diminished parenting capacity of the biological parent and thus indirectly predict worse child outcomes (e.g., Fauber, Forehand, Thomas, & Wierson, 1990; Johnston, 1990). As children become adolescents, the effect of interparental hostility and conflict may not be mediated by ineffective parenting. A recent study of adolescents, interviewed 4.5 years following divorce of their parents, found higher rates of symptomatic levels of anxiety and depression when adolescents felt emotionally "caught between parents" (Buchanan, Maccoby, & Dornbusch, 1991). Parental conflict only related to adolescent adjustment indirectly through feelings of being caught between parents. These researchers conclude:

Our results suggest that parental conflict has negative effects by altering family interaction in such a way that either the child is explicitly drawn into the conflict and/or becomes fearful of what effect a positive relationship with one parent will have on the other parent. . . . These results also indicate, however, that parental conflict need not affect children negatively. (Buchanan, Maccoby, & Dornbusch, 1991, p. 1026)

In this study, feeling close to both parents predicted better adjustment. In sum, another key factor in the normal development of children is cooperation and support between biological parents, regardless of family form.

Sibling Relationships

Although little empirical attention has been directed to the role of sibling relationships in children's well-being in single- and stepparent homes, this emerging area of inquiry has yielded some important findings. Hetherington & Jodl (1994) finds conflictual and rivalrous sibling relationships commonly accompany marital transitions and may add to family strain. In more established stepfamilies, however, no differences are found in sibling relationship between single-parent, stepfamily, or nondivorced homes (see also Amato, 1994). Sibling relationships do appear to play a role in adolescent social deviance, however, with older siblings significantly influencing the externalizing behavior of younger female siblings (Hetherington, 1991). Older siblings may serve to introduce early maturing female siblings (in both divorced and remarried families) to older peers who are more likely to be involved in norm-breaking, externalizing behaviors. The negative influence of older siblings appears to be stronger in single-parent and stepfamilies than in nondivorced two-parent families and would appear to interact with factors, such as family resources and parenting style, that have previously been discussed.

Individual Characteristics

Child characteristics will ease or exacerbate the tensions inherent in single-parent and stepparent family relationships. In younger children, difficult temperament predicts more negative outcomes, especially for boys, in both single-parent and stepparent homes. In contrast, high self-esteem, motivation to achieve, and valuing of sexual restraint serve to protect single-parent youth from social deviancy risk (Benson & Roehlkeparten, 1993). Acting-out behaviors and social incompetence in adolescence play strong roles in preventing the establishment of any relationship between stepfathers and stepchildren (Hetherington & Jodl, 1994). For further discussion of child characteristics as mediators, see my earlier chapters on this topic (Carlson, 1985, 1987, 1990).

School Environment

A final factor in the normal development of children is the school environment. An authoritative school that provides a structured, predictable environment is related to greater social and academic competence and a lower incidence of behavior problems among children and early adolescents (Hetherington & Jodl, 1994). Hetherington (1993, cited in Hetherington, 1994) found that structure, control, responsiveness, warmth, and demands for maturity on the part of teachers all contributed to the adjustment of children in postdivorce single-parent and remarried homes. Effects were more marked for early adolescents in the middle school environment compared with younger children in the elementary school setting. Interestingly, teacher warmth, responsiveness, and demands for maturity were more critical for girls, whereas structure and control within the school setting were more salient for boys. It should be noted that the effects of an authoritative school environment vary in significance with the degree to which parents are authoritative. If the single parent or both stepfamily parents were authoritative in their parenting style, no enhancing effect of the school environment was demonstrated. However, if only one residential parent or neither residential parent (in the case of stepfamilies) was authoritative, an authoritative school contributed to increased academic achievement, social responsibility, and a lower incidence of behavior problems in children (Hetherington, 1993, cited in Hetherington & Jodl, 1994). These data underscore the importance of school environment in supplementing parental roles for youth in single-parent and stepparent homes.

Conclusions

Although the majority of youth in single-parent and stepparent homes will not experience serious problems related to their family situation, the risk of problems is clearly higher for this population. The primary implication for children being reared in a single-parent or stepparent home is that a significant percentage may not reach their potential, in part as a function of being reared in homes with inadequate family resources, including inadequate parenting skill and lack of parental involvement with the child or the school. A second concern is the health and safety risks faced by these youth who are more likely to engage in social deviancy during adolescence. A third concern is the socioemotional well-being (i.e., levels of anxiety and depression) of children who experience frequent family transitions, multiple emotional losses, high rates of family stress and conflict, or child abuse or neglect. A final concern is related to the fact that children in single-parent and stepparent homes are more likely than children in nondivorced homes to drop out of school and leave home. Without education, their ability to attain adequate family resources is clearly limited and will affect their parenting of future generations.

The implications for the family of children's problems in single-parent and stepfamilies is primarily related to the reciprocal strain placed on family relationships. Although single-parent and stepfamily processes directly influence the development of child problems, acting-out behavior on the part of adolescents in these homes reciprocally strains family relations and paradoxically leads to a further deterioration of the very affective bonds most needed or desired by the adolescent. Parent-child conflict plays a significant role in the breakup of remarriages, resulting in further family instability.

The school is directly affected by both the problems children develop as a result of residing in single-parent and stepparent homes and the family processes associated with these family forms. To the degree parents provide an insufficiently authoritative childrearing setting, schools bear the responsibility of providing an authoritative structure and coping with the social deviant outcomes related to permissive and disengaged parenting. Schools also suffer to the degree that single parents and stepfamily parents are less involved in school. This not only negatively affects children's educational achievement but reduces parental resources available to the school and limits communication between home and school.

Alternative Actions

Recommendations for assessment and intervention with single parent and stepfamilies have been discussed at length previously (Carlson, 1985, 1987, 1990, 1991a, 1991b, 1992a, 1992b, 1995). In this section, broad guidelines for assessment and intervention, based on the previously reviewed literature, will be provided.

Assessment

Six factors were discussed that influence the development of children in single-parent and stepparent homes: family resources, parenting style and skill, interparental cooperation versus conflict, quality of sibling relationships, individual child characteristics, and quality of the school environment. Each of these factors represents an important focus of assessment and intervention. When combined, these factors represent a profile of risk or resiliency for children in single-parent and stepparent homes. Key factors and related questions are listed in Table 2.

Stress and Coping Framework

It is recommended that when children exhibit school-based behavior or learning problems requiring attention, assessment and intervention with single-parent and stepfamilies adopt a nondeficit (Rich, 1987) and normative stress and coping framework (Crosbie-Burnett, 1989). The nondeficit approach to school-family relations (adapted here for single-parent and stepfamilies) is based on the following assumptions:

1. All children have meaningful experiences in their families. Children in single-parent and stepparent homes have different experiences.

2. Home environments, no matter how disadvantaged or troubled, are contexts of care and concern for children.
3. All parents intrinsically possess the abilities to help their children succeed in school.
4. Family concern can readily be translated into practical support for children and for schools.
5. Schools should start with what the family has, instead of worrying about or blaming the family for what it lacks.
6. Schools, no matter how understaffed or ill equipped, have the capabilities of reaching out and affecting parent involvement.

Approaching single-parent and stepparent families from a nondeficit framework is essential to enhancing the self-esteem and sense of self-efficacy of single parents and stepparents who, on average, may be more permissive and less involved in the schooling of their children.

The normative stress and coping approach (Crosbie-Burnett, 1989) assumes that stress associated with transitions is normative, whether the transition is marital, developmental, or a move between schools. The stress and coping model encourages clinicians to focus their assessment on three aspects of family functioning: the perceived stressor(s) and associated losses and hardships, the adaptive resources available for coping, and the family's definition or meaning of the total situation including their respective roles and responsibilities. Numerous stressors and adaptive resources for coping have been discussed in this chapter. A particularly important aspect of assessment from this framework, however, is family members' perceptions of role and responsibility. Whereas the two-parent nondivorced family typically has well-defined family roles, appropriate roles for adults in single-parent and stepparent families are more ambiguous.

Role ambiguity and conflict may be particularly common in never-married three-generation extended families, for noncustodial parents in single- and stepparent families, and for stepparents in stepfamilies. Failure of all parental figures in these systems to assume clear, active, and authoritative parental roles appears to be the single most common deficit of these family systems related to child adjustment. For this and other reasons, it is important to involve in assessment and intervention as many family members as possible from the linked households in which the child resides and visits. Because a notable shortcoming of these family forms is a resource deficit, expansion of the responsible system while clarifying roles should produce a more effective intervention than one targeted to a single member or subsystem of the family. Intervention from a normative life-transitions perspective focuses on normalizing the perceived stressor, enhancing coping ability and resources, and clarifying family roles and responsibilities regarding the child.

Table 2 *Assessment Domains and Questions for Single-Parent and Stepparent Families*

I. **Family Resources**
- How may adults are available to care for the child?
- What is the education level of adult caretakers?
- What is the physical and mental health of adult caretakers?
- How much time is spent with the child and in what activities?
- How many siblings reside in the home?
- Are parents/adult caretakers employed?
- Are economic resources adequate?
- What educational resources are in the home, if any?
- If few, what community resources are available and are they utilized?
- Are parental figures involved in school? If not, what barriers exist to parental involvement?

II. **Parenting Style and Skills**
- Who are the adult caretakers in the life of the child (check for all possible across households)?
- Who establishes rules for the child? Does the child view rules as having to be followed?
- Who disciplines the child? How is the child disciplined?
- Who monitors the whereabouts of the child?
- Who does the child view as being in charge?
- Do parental figures agree on rules and punishments? If not, how is disagreement handled?
- How do parental figures view their role and responsibilities vis-a-vis the child?
- To whom does the child feel close?
- To whom does the child feel he or she can go for help?
- Check for possible abuse by any adult caretaker.

III. **Interparental Conflict***
- Does the child report conflict in the family? If so, between whom? How often? What form does it take?
- Does the child express loyalty conflicts or stress related to "being in the middle"?
- Does the child have access to the noncustodial parent? How does he or she describe the relationship?

IV. **Sibling Relationships**
- How many siblings and stepsiblings are in the family? What are their ages, sex, and characteristics?
- What is the quality of the sibling/stepsibling relationships (e.g., rivalrous, supportive)?
- Are older siblings/stepsiblings involved in deviant activities?

V. **Child Characteristics**
- What is the age and sex of the child?
- Does the child have inborn qualities that making mothering more difficult (e.g., difficult temperament, Attention Deficit/Hyperactivity Disorder, mental retardation)?
- Assess the child's level of social skill, maturity, self-control, achievement motivation, and self-esteem.

VI. **School Characteristics**
- Is the child's school structured? responsive? warm? with high expectations for children?
- How involved are all parents in the school?
- How adequate are school practices and policies related to parent involvement?

*Note that interparental here refers to cooperation between any adult figures who play a caretaking role with the child. Cooperation, for example, between a biological adolescent parent and caretaker grandparent is as critical as cooperation between a custodial mother and a noncustodial father.

School Policies

In addition to the adoption of a nondeficit and normative stress and coping framework for assessment of individual families, school personnel are encouraged to examine carefully their school policies, procedures, and available resources for single-parent and stepfamilies. Are policies, procedures, and programs in place that accommodate the special needs of these families and their children? In particular, given the importance of parental involvement to the prevention of academic and social deviance in single-parent and stepfamily adolescents, implementing programs specifically targeted to increasing the involvement of these parents would appear critical. How many schools, for example, have programs specifically designed to involve noncustodial fathers or stepfathers in the schooling of their children and stepchildren?

School policies are also critical regarding prevention of child problems in the never-married, impoverished single-mother home. In particular, does the school have an effective program to retain pregnant adolescents? Between 32% and 80% of pregnant adolescents drop out of school (Linares, Leadbeater, Kato, & Jaffe, 1991) perpet-

uating a cycle of poverty, inadequate family resources, and less effective parenting (Angel & Angel, 1993). Comprehensive school-based programs that support high school completion by pregnant adolescents are significantly related to the ability of these mothers to access social support, maintain economic viability, limit future pregnancies, and more effectively parent their children. Because school dropout during pregnancy, school dropout following pregnancy, and multiple pregnancies during adolescence (which guarantees school dropout) are predicted by adolescent depression and school failure, effective programs will need to be broader than policies permitting pregnant teens to attend classes and the provision of child care in schools; comprehensive mental health services are essential to these would-be mothers (Linares et al., 1991).

Summary

Children reared in single-parent and stepparent homes *on average* are at greater risk than children in nondivorced two-parent homes for lowered educational achievement, especially school dropout; for increased susceptibility to peer deviant influence during adolescence; and for higher rates of anxious and depressive symptomatology. Research has not advanced to a stage where it can be predicted clearly which risk factors in single-parent and stepfamilies contribute to specific child outcomes and under which conditions. Rather children's risk and vulnerability in these family forms appear to be linked with multiple, interrelated environmental factors.

Children's problems associated with rearing in single-parent and stepfamily homes adversely affect the child, exacerbate conflictual family relations, and place resource demands on the school. It is important for schools to assume responsibility for creating authoritative environments for children's learning and to develop policies and programs that increase the involvement of single, noncustodial, and stepparents in school; and that prevent the high school dropout of pregnant adolescents. It is further recommended that assessment and treatment of single-parent and stepfamilies in crisis is best conceptualized within nondeficit and normative-transition stress and coping frameworks that enhance parental self-efficacy in relationships with their biological and stepchildren.

Recommended Resources

Dickerson, B. J. (Ed.). (1995). *African American single mothers.* Thousand Oaks, CA: Sage Publications.
This book written both for professionals and scholars provides up-to-date information on a single-parent population that receives far less attention than postdivorce European American single mothers. It is an invaluable resource for psychologists working with children from this family form.

Furstenberg, F. F. Jr., & Cherlin, A. J. (1991). *Divided families: What happens to children when parents part.* Cambridge, MA: Harvard University Press.
This is a user friendly summary of the intervention implications of research on the effects on children of divorce, single parenting, and remarriage. It is well-researched and authoritative but also clearly written without jargon. It is very useful background reading for both professionals and parents.

Ganong, L. H., & Coleman, M. (1994). *Remarried family relationships.* Thousand Oaks, CA: Sage Publications
This book, authored by two eminent scholars on stepfamilies, provides up-to-date information about remarried families, including partners, stepparents and stepchildren, biological parents and children, and grandparents. The book is both scholarly and readable.

Grief, G. L. (1990). *The daddy track and the single father.* Lexington, MA: Lexington Books.
This self-help book for single fathers provides both a view of characteristics of this growing population and information useful to single fathers. Chapters address dealing with common myths; running a household; parenting children; balancing work and family; conducting one's social life; getting along with the noncustodial mother; dealing with the courts and child support and joint custody; and facing fatherhood after the death of a spouse.

Kissman, K., & Allen, J. A. (1993). *Single-parent families.* Newbury Park, CA: Sage Publications.
This book written primarily for professionals provides a comprehensive discussion of the heterogeneity of the single-parent family. Chapters are devoted to mother-headed families, ethnic families, adolescent parents, single father-headed families, and noncustodial parents. Specific suggestions for intervention are provided. This book is unusually sensitive in discussion of issues of gender, ethnicity, race, and social class.

Visher, E. B., & Visher, J. S. (1988). *Old loyalties, new ties: Therapeutic strategies with stepfamilies* New York: Brunner/Mazel Publishers.
No book compares with this one—a classic—in providing mental health professionals with sensitive, authoritative, and useful advice on both the challenges of stepfamilies and effective strategies for resolving problems. The authors have remained the most authoritative clinicians in the field for over a decade.

References

Amato, P. R. (1987). Family processes in one-parent, stepparent, and intact families: The child's point of view. *Journal of Marriage and the Family, 49:* 327–337.

Amato, P. R. (1994). The implications of research findings on children in stepfamilies. In A. Booth & J. Dunn (Eds.), *Stepfamilies: Who benefits? Who does not?* (pp. 81–87). Hillsdale, NJ: Lawrence Erlbaum Associates.

Amato, P. R., & Keith, B. (1992). Paqrental divorce and the well-being of children: A meta-analysis. *Psychological Bulletin, 110* (4), 26–43.

Angel, R., & Angel, J. L. (1993). *Painful inheritance: Health and the new generation of fatherless families.* Madison, WI: The University of Wisconsin Press.

Barber, B. L., & Eccles, J. S. (1992). Long-term influence of divorce and single parenting on adolescent family- and work-related values, behavior, and aspirations. *Psychological Bulletin, 111*(1), 108–126.

Benson, P. L., & Roehlkeparten, E. C. (1993). *Youth in single-parent families: Risk and resiliency.* Minneapolis, MN: Search Institute.

Bianchi, S. M. (1995). The changing demographic and socioeconomic characteristics of single parent families. *Marriage and Family Review, 20* (1 & 2), 71–97.

Billingsley, A. (1993). *Climbing Jacob's ladder: The enduring legacy of African American families.* New York: Simon & Schuster.

Boyd-Franklin, N. (1989). *Black families in therapy: A multisystems approach.* New York: Guilford.

Buchanan, C. M., Maccoby, E. E., & Dornbusch, S. M. (1991). Caught between parents: Adolescents' experience in divorced homes. *Child Development, 62,* 1008–1029.

Burton, L. (1990). Teenage childbearing as an alternative life-course strategy in multigeneration Black families. *Human Nature, 12,* 123–143.

Carlson, C. I. (1985). Best practices for working with single-parent and stepparent families. In A. Thomas & J. Grimes (Eds.), *Best practices in school psychology—I* (pp. 43–60). Kent, OH: National Association of School Psychologists.

Carlson, C. I. (1987). Children and single parent homes. In A. Thomas & J. Grimes (Eds.), *Children's needs: Psychological perspectives* (pp. 560–570). Washington, DC: National Association of School Psychologists.

Carlson, C. I. (1990). Best practices for working with single-parent and stepparent families. In A. Thomas & J. Grimes (Eds.) *Best practices in school psychology—II* (pp. 837–858). Kent, OH: National Association of School Psychologists.

Carlson, C. I. (1991a). Assessing the family context. In R. Kamphaus & C. R. Reynolds (Eds.), *Handbook of psychological and educational assessment of children: Vol. II. Personality, behavior, and context* (pp. 546–575). New York: Guilford Press.

Carlson, C. I. (1991b). Single parent and stepparent family systems: Problems, issues, and interventions. In M. J. Fine & C. I. Carlson (Eds.), *Handbook of family-school intervention: A systems approach* (pp. 188–214). Boston: Allyn & Bacon.

Carlson, C. I. (1992a). Single-parent families. In M. E. Procidano & C. B. Fisher (Eds.), *Families: A handbook for school professionals* (pp. 36–56). New York: Teachers College Press.

Carlson, C. I. (1992b). Single-parent homes. In H. Knoff (Ed.), *Helping children grow up in the 90's: A resource book of handouts for parents and teachers* (pp. 315–319). Kent, OH: National Association of School Psychologists.

Carlson, C. I. (1995). Best practices for working with single-parent and stepparent families. In A. Thomas & J. Grimes (Eds.), *Best practices in school psychology—III* (pp. 1097–1110). Washington, DC: National Association of School Psychologists.

Chase-Lansdale, P. L., Brooks-Gunn, J., & Zamsky, E. S. (1994). Young African-American multigenerational families in poverty: Quality of mothering and grandmothering. *Child Development, 65,* 373–393.

Coleman, M., & Ganong, L. H. (1991). Remarriage and stepfamily research in the 1980s. In A. Booth (Ed.), *Contemporary families* (pp. 192–207). Minneapolis, MN: National Council on Family Relations.

Crosbie-Burnett, M. (1989). Application of family stress theory to remarriage: A model for assessing and helping stepfamilies. *Family Relations, 38,* 323–331.

Dornbusch, S. M., Ritter, P. L., Leiderman, P. H., Roberts, D. F., & Fraleigh, M. J. (1987). The relation of parenting style to adolescent school performance. *Child Development, 58,* 1244–1257.

Downey, D. B. (1995). Understanding academic achievement among children in stephouseholds: The role of parental resources, sex of stepparent, and sex of child. *Social Forces, 73*(3), 875–894.

Downey, D.B., & Powell, B. (1993). Do children in single-parent households fare better living with same-sex parents? *Journal of Marriage and the Family, 55,* 55–71.

Fauber, R., Forehand, R., Thomas, A. M., & Wierson, M. (1990). A mediational model of the impact of marital conflict on adolescent adjustment in intact and divorced families: The role of disrupted parenting. *Child Development, 61,* 1112–1123.

Fine, M.. A., Voydanoff, P., & Donnelly, B. W. (1993). Relations between parental control and warmth and child well-being in stepfamilies. *Journal of Family Psychology, 7*(2), 222–232.

Furstenberg, F.F. Jr., & Cherlin, A. J. (1991). *Divided families: What happens to children when parents part.* Cambridge, MA: Harvard University Press.

Gelles, R. J. (1989). Child abuse and violence in single-parent families: Parent absence and economic deprivation. *American Journal of Orthopsychiatry, 59*(4), 492–501.

George, S. M., & Dickerson, B. J. (1995). The role of the grandmother in poor single-mother families and households. In B. J. Dickerson (Ed.), *African American single mothers* (pp. 146–163). Thousand Oaks, CA: Sage Publications.

Grief, G. L., & DeMaris, A. (1995). Single fathers with custody: Do they change over time? In W. Marsaglio (Ed.), *Fatherhood* (pp. 193–210). Thousand Oaks, CA: Sage Publications.

Hall, L. A., Gurley, D. N., Sachs, B., & Kryscio, R. J. (1991). Psychosocial predictors of maternal depressive symptoms, parenting attitudes, and child behavior in single-parent families. *Nursing Research, 40*(4), 214–220.

Hetherington, E. M. (1991). Presidential address: Families, lies, and videotapes. *Journal of Research on Adolescence, 1*(4), 323–348.

Hetherington, E. M., & Clingempeel, W. G. (1992). Coping with marital transitions. *Monographs of the Society for Research in Child Development, 57*(2–3),

Hetherington, E. M., & Jodl, K. M. (1994). Stepfamilies as settings for child development. In A. Booth & J. Dunn (Eds.), *Stepfamilies: Who benefits? Who does not?* (pp. 55–79). Hillsdale, NJ: Lawrence Erlbaum Associates.

Jackson, A. (1993). Black, single, working mothers in poverty: Preferences for employment, well-being, and perceptions of preschool-age children. *Social Work, 38,* 26–34.

Jacobson, D. S. (1995). Critical interactive events and child adjustment in the stepfamily: A linked family system. In D. K. Huntley (Ed.), *Understanding stepfamilies: Implications for assessment and treatment* (pp. 73–86). Alexandria, VA: American Counseling Association.

Johnston, J. R. (1990). Role diffusion and role reversal: Structural variation in divorced families and children's functioning. *Family Relations, 39,* 405–413.

Linares, L. O., Leadbeater, B. J., Kato, P. M., & Jaffe, L. (1991). Predicting school outcomes for minority group adolescent mothers: Can subgroups be identified? *Journal of Research on Adolescence, 1*(1), 379–400.

Lino, M., (1995). The economics of single parenthood: Past research and future directions. *Marriage and Family Review, 20*(1 & 2), 99–114.

MacDonald, W. L., & DeMaris, A. (1996). Parenting stepchildren and biological children. *Journal of Family Issues, 17*(1), 5–25.

McLoyd, V. C., Jayaratne, T. E., Ceballo, R., & Borquez, J. (1994). Unemployment and work interruption among African American single mothers: Effects on parenting and adolescent socioemotional functioning. *Child Development, 65,* 562–589.

Papernow, P. L. (1995). What's going on here? Separating (and weaving together) step and clinical issues in remarried families. In D. K. Huntley (Ed.), *Understanding stepfamilies: Implications for assessment and treatment* (pp. 3–24). Alexandria, VA: American Counseling Association.

Patterson, G. R. (1982). *A social learning approach: Vol. 3. Coercive family process.* Eugene, OR: Castalia.

Popenoe, D. (1994). The evolution of marriage and the problem of stepfamilies: A biosocial perspective. In A. Booth & J. Dunn (Eds.), *Stepfamilies: Who benefits? Who does not?* (pp. 3–27). Hillsdale, NJ: Lawrence Erlbaum Associates.

Randolph, S. M. (1995). African American children in single mother families. In B. J. Dickerson (Ed.), *African American single mothers* (pp. 117–145). Thousand Oaks, CA: Sage Publications.

Rich, D. (1987). *Schools and families: Issues and actions.* Washington, DC: National Education Association.

Santrock, J. W., & Warshak, R. A. (1979). Father custody and social development of boys and girls. *Journal of Social Issues, 35*(4), 112–125.

Staples, R., & Boulin Johnson, L. (1993). *Black families at the crossroads: Challenges and prospects.* San Francisco: Jossey-Bass.

USA Today, USA Snapshots. January 17, 1994.

Walsh, F. (1993). Conceptualization of normal family processes. In F. Walsh (Ed.), *Normal family processes* (2nd ed, pp. 3–69). New York: Guilford.

Weiss, R. (1979). *Going it alone.* New York: Basic Books.

Zill, N. (1994). Understanding why children in stepfamilies have more learning and behavior problems than children in nuclear families. In A. Booth & J. Dunn (Eds.), *Stepfamilies: Who benefits? Who does not?* (pp. 97–106). Hillsdale, NJ: Lawrence Erlbaum Associates.

Zimiles, H., & Lee, V. E. (1991). Adolescent family structure and educational progress. *Developmental Psychology, 27*(2), 314–320.

56
Siblings

Karen T. Carey

California State University, Fresno

Background and Development

Although we are not given a choice as to whom our siblings will be (nor, for that matter, who our parents are), we are required as children to interact daily and intimately with our siblings. Due to differences in heredity, family environment as the number of siblings increase, and chance life experiences for individual children, our siblings are often quite different from ourselves (Dunn & Plomin, 1991). However, following the parent-child relationship, the sibling relationship is the first significant social relationship experienced by individuals whereby they learn to rehearse social interaction skills (Newman, 1994). These interactions can be a significant, intense, long-lasting, socializing force for many children, and the socialization skills learned from siblings often generalize to relationships with persons outside of the family (e.g., Newman, 1994). Thus, the sibling relationship is one of the most important contexts for the development of interpersonal skills.

Approximately 80% of all children grow up with one or more siblings (Dunn, 1995). As children's initial peer group, siblings provide the first opportunity to engage in social-comparison or competition processes. The learning of these processes can result in the development of skills for support and friendship or, conversely, maladjustment and social difficulties.

Youniss (1980) defined interpersonal relationships as either reciprocal or complementary. Reciprocal relationships are those that exist between peers, while complementary relationships are generally hierarchical, such as those between adults and children. Sibling relationships, however, can be characterized as both reciprocal and complementary, which may result in awkward and difficult interactions. For example, older children may at times engage in reciprocal relationships with their siblings, as during play. At other times, the relationship can be viewed as complementary, as when an older sibling has responsibility for the younger child. Thus, the interactions can be strained and confusing for all children involved.

Research on siblings' interactions has been limited. While there are a number of "self-help" books for parents related to dealing with sibling interactions, empirical studies are lacking. Investigators examining sibling interactions have primarily focused on siblings with disabilities. Information on this topic is included in the chapter on Families of Children with Disabilities (this volume).

Studies conducted with siblings without disabilities have generally focused on the rivalry between brothers and sisters and on the birth order in relationship to intellectual and personality characteristics (e.g., Newman, 1994). White (1975) and others maintain that conflict between siblings is the most prevalent family problem. However, more recent research indicates that there is much more harmony between siblings than there is rivalry (Dunn, 1985). Thus, the family may experience stress or peace depending on the relationships of siblings (Newman, 1994).

One of the difficulties in reviewing this body of literature is that diverse methodologies have been employed in the investigations (Dunn, Stocker, & Plomin, 1990). Some studies include observational, naturalistic data, while others utilize self-report of parents' and childrens' feelings regarding the sibling interaction. Self-reports, however, are not necessarily congruent with behavior observed in the natural setting (Newman, 1994). Observational studies conducted in the natural environment reveal that, while sibling conflict is not uncommon, prosocial behavior appears to occur much more often (Abramovitch, Corter, Pepler, & Stanhope, 1986; Dunn & Munn, 1987). However, when parents and siblings are asked to respond to questionnaires or interviews related to sibling relationships, they tend to report those instances where family harmony is disrupted, making it appear as if such negative interactions were the norm. Thus, in many families, positive sibling interactions are overlooked or ignored.

Sibling Interactions

Most of the research related to sibling interactions has been conducted with young children between birth and 6 years of age. Many investigators are primarily concerned with the interactions that occur immediately following the birth of a second child and the effects of the birth on the older child. Firstborn children often react with ambivalence to the birth of a second child and can either demonstrate interest or hostility toward the newborn (Dunn, 1985). Generally, the hostility is not directed at the newborn per se but toward the mother, particularly when she is providing care for the younger child. Some older siblings exhibit regressive behavior by clinging to the mother, having sleep disturbances, experiencing breakdowns in toilet training, or some combination of these (Nadelam & Begun, 1982). Other children demonstrate mature and independent behaviors following the birth of the second child by imitating their parents or pretending to engage in caregiving (Dunn, 1985).

The results of these studies indicate that the sibling relationship is most affected by the mother's initial introduction of the new sibling to the family and her interactions with both children over time (e.g., Hetherington, 1994; Leung & Robson, 1991). The firstborn child who is allowed by the mother to touch, talk to, and play with a newborn infant develops more positive feelings toward the infant (Hetherington). As the siblings grow, family harmony can be established by the mother who does not take sides in sibling disputes, intervenes in disputes only when necessary, and structures activities for the children (Hetherington, 1994). Thus, mothers' interactions with individual children and with the children together can have lifelong effects on the interactions between the siblings (Hetherington, 1994). Empirical studies investigating the father's contribution to positive sibling interactions are extremely limited.

Children appear to learn early in life that they must compete with their siblings for parental attention, approval, and affection, as well as for recognition of achievement and competence (Newman, 1994). In addition they must assert themselves to gain access to favorite activities such as toys or television programs. While this type of rivalry does occur between siblings, the research findings related to the interaction of preschool-age siblings tends to be contradictory.

Kramer and Schaefer-Hernan (1994) found that 3- to 5-year-old children who had positive interactions with younger siblings engaged in solitary fantasy play longer, engaged in solitary play that was relevant to being a sibling, and had more positive interactions with peers than did children who had less positive interactions with younger siblings. Four- and five-year-olds, when playing with younger siblings, primarily engaged in parallel, solitary play (Berndt & Bulleit, 1985) and, when engaged in cooperative play, required parental input to structure social interactions (e.g., Dunn, 1985).

The nature and amount of sibling conflict changes during the transition from the preschool years to the school-age years with more negative interactions occurring between preschoolers than between school-age chil-

dren. Individual differences in children's relationships with their siblings in middle childhood are marked (e.g., Dunn, 1995). Links have been found between the quality of children's relationships with their siblings and antisocial behavior (e.g., Patterson, 1986), sociocognitive development (e.g., Dunn, 1993), and resilience to marital disharmony (Jenkins, 1992). While some researchers have found that ambivalence tends to be a primary characteristic of sibling relationships in middle childhood (Furman & Buhrmester, 1985), others have found that sibling interactions increase during middle childhood (Berndt & Bulleit, 1985). Some children are affectionate and supportive to their siblings while others are hostile and aggressive. When sibling aggression does occur, such conflicts provide children with experiences in how to upset another and the consequences of doing so (Dunn & Munn, 1987). Depending on the siblings' and mother's reactions to the conflict, children can learn important skills for later interpersonal interactions. Interestingly, children from high socioeconomic families express more warmth and intimacy with their siblings than do children from low socioeconomic families (Dunn, Slomkoski, & Beardsall, 1994). This is possibly due to the stress families of low socioeconomic status are under and the fact that day-to-day living, such as working two jobs, can impede quality family interaction time.

The most prevalent interactions between siblings seem to be prosocial play and verbal behaviors (e.g., Dunn, 1993). Physical aggression, when it does occur, is generally directed by the older sibling at the younger sibling. Older siblings, particularly girls, tend to initiate prosocial interactions, whereas the younger siblings primarily tend to display imitative behaviors (Pepler, Corter, & Abramovitch, 1982). Older brothers in same-sex dyads tend to initiate more aggressive behaviors toward younger siblings (Pepler et al., 1982). However, as the younger siblings approach the ages of 4 and 5, they tend to initiate both prosocial and aggressive physical behaviors more frequently, while older siblings, both male and female, initiate both prosocial and verbally aggressive behaviors. Mixed-sex dyads tend to engage in more aggressive behaviors than do same-sex dyads (Berndt & Bulleit, 1985). Overall, interactions between preschool-age siblings tend to be much more antagonistic than do their interactions when they reach school age.

For example, as children become older, relationships with siblings become more egalitarian and less intense and include experiences influenced by the child's birth order (Buhrmester & Furman, 1990). Firstborn children prefer to interact with parents whereas last-born children, when they reach the same age, pay equal attention to parents and older siblings. By late middle-childhood, older sisters are more likely than older brothers to be in confiding relationships with their younger siblings. In play, older girls tend to tolerate interaction with younger siblings in some activities, such as school role-play, while older boys tend to physically dominate their younger siblings (Buhrmester & Furman, 1990).

Late middle-childhood students (i.e., fifth- and sixth-grade students) were interviewed about their current relationships with one of their siblings (Furman & Buhrmester, 1985). Of those interviewed, 91% mentioned antagonism with their sibling while 79% reported quarrelling; however, children also reported that positive relationships were equally characteristic of their sibling relationships.

Few studies of the sibling interaction have been undertaken with middle-school-age children and older adolescents. Steinmetz (1977) found that when parents were questioned about sibling conflicts they reported many more problems as children entered adolescence. Felson (1983) questioned adults about their early sibling relationships and found that verbal aggression was more common than physical aggression and that many continued to interact with siblings in the same manner as they did as adolescents.

Verbal Interactions

The sibling relationship is also important in teaching children verbal interaction skills. One of the most important activities for increasing language and developing emotional understanding in young children is "family talk" (Dunn, Brown, & Beardsall, 1991). Young children raised in families where feelings are discussed are better able to recognize the emotions in siblings and others as they become older and provide both physical and verbal comfort to younger siblings when younger siblings are distressed (e.g., Howe & Ross, 1990; Stewart & Martin, 1984).

Young, preschool-aged, oldest siblings, however, are often not competent in making pragmatic adjustments that propel young siblings into the world of conversation, although they are able to structurally accommodate their own language in order to allow their younger siblings to understand them (Mannle, Barton, & Tomasello, 1992). When compared to 7- to 8-year-old siblings, preschool-aged siblings were not able to provide the necessary conversational support to their 1- to 2-year-olds siblings or alter their speech to the younger siblings' understanding (Hoff-Ginsberg & Krueger, 1991). However, as younger siblings develop language and an understanding of the feelings of others, the verbal interactions between the siblings change, and they are able to offer support in both reciprocal and complementary ways (Dunn, 1993).

In studies investigating the ability of middle-school-age siblings to influence the conversational interactions of younger siblings, older siblings asked fewer questions of their younger siblings and tended to give them more direct commands than did mothers (Mannle et al., 1992). While many older siblings have direct responsibility for younger siblings, such direct command giving may limit the learning experiences of the preschool-aged child. Thus, mothers and individual siblings differ in the way they converse with other children in the family (Brown & Dunn, 1992). Children, when conversing with siblings, tend to draw attention to their own feelings most often rather than the feelings of their siblings, as mothers might do (Brown & Dunn, 1992). When siblings are engaged in conversation, they are found to talk more about feelings in humorous ways, share child jokes, and tease one another about gender-based toy preferences. Stoneman, Brody, and MacKennon (1984) studied how children played with friends, their verbal interactions, and the influence of these factors upon siblings. Some younger siblings interacted and then withdrew from the interaction while others engaged with the older children and formed an interactive group. When the siblings were engaged, the older siblings tended to give advice or orders to the younger children and often the younger child actively sought the information (Stoneman et al., 1984). Furthermore, siblings of different gender or very different ages were less likely to have activities in common, and most children, when given a choice, would select a peer for play rather than a sibling. For children closer in age, sharing a bedroom, doing chores, or going to school together provided many opportunities for verbal interaction.

Caregiving and Teaching

In many families, older siblings have the responsibility of caring for younger siblings. For some children this is a daily activity, while others are left to watch their siblings once a week or less. Children who possess affective knowledge and skills are better caregivers to their younger siblings than children who have a cognitive perspective on caregiving (Garner, Jones, & Miner, 1994). For some older siblings it is more important to demonstrate to parents that they can handle the caregiving situation rather than actually care for the needs of the young child. Thus, while the older sibling may avert any major catastrophe (e.g., fire-setting) while the younger siblings are in his or her care, younger siblings miss out on opportunities for learning, support, and encouragement, resulting in delayed development and lack of challenge for younger siblings.

In relation to the effectiveness of sibling teaching, older children are quite effective in teaching younger siblings cognitive or construction tasks (Azmitia & Hesser, 1993). Further, younger siblings apparently do not learn as well from their peers as they do from older siblings because they are reluctant to ask peers for help but feel comfortable requesting help from older siblings (Azmitia & Hesser). Older sisters and more widely spaced older siblings were the most effective teachers for younger siblings (Cicirelli, 1976). As girls tend to be more engaged in the process of caregiving to younger siblings and older siblings in general tend to have more caregiving responsibilities, older siblings of both genders tend to assist younger siblings more often than those siblings who are closer in age. The benefits of teaching a young sibling can be intellectually beneficial to the older child as well, as the older child practices previously learned skills (Zajonc & Markus, 1975).

Problems and Implications

School

The schooling process may result in problems between siblings, particularly when an older sibling experiences academic success or begins to broaden his or her social networks. Younger siblings often feel jealous or resentful of the older sibling's behavior or successes (Dunn, 1993). Such jealousy or hurt feelings occur most often when the two children have been close and the older sibling enters adolescence.

Negative school experiences can also add fuel to sibling difficulties. Conflicts can occur due to embarrassment by one sibling of the other's negative behavior or lack of school success (Dunn, 1993). In cases where the family moves and the children enter new schools or one sibling changes schools, as from elementary to middle school, unhappiness that can result from such moves can be played out in the sibling relationship. Problems in the sibling relationship can be intensified when one child likes the new setting and the other child does not (Dunn, 1995).

Effects of Divorce

The effects of divorce on the sibling relationship have also been investigated. Findings vary with some indicating that the quality of the relationship increases in hostility following a divorce (Hetherington, 1994) and others indicating that some siblings prove to be significant sources of support for one another (Jenkins, 1992). In general, hostile or supportive sibling relationships tend to be a result of the parents' interactions and of the decision of which parent with whom children eventually reside. In cases where mothers raise girls following a divorce and fathers raise boys, hostility between the girls and boys tends to increase (Hetherington, 1994). In other cases where siblings reside with one parent and visit the other parent at selected times or in cases where the mother is required to return to work, siblings tend to rely on one another for support (Jenkins, 1992).

Increased sibling conflict occasionally occurs when children feel that their siblings are responsible for the divorce or believe that one sibling is given preferential treatment (Dunn, 1993). Hetherington (1994) found that following a divorce the presence of a stepfather was re-lated to poor sibling relationships. When two families combine, relationships can also become strained between siblings in the same family (Hetherington, 1994).

Sibling Abuse

In contrast to the attention that has been given to parental abuse of children, little has been done to combat sibling abuse, and such abuse does occur. Although the most prevalent behavior in siblings is prosocial behavior, some children can be very abusive to one another (e.g., Felson, 1983), resulting in carryover to later violence with peers (Steinmetz, 1977). Patterson (1986), who worked with boys, demonstrated how aggression by one child and the resulting submission by the other can become consistent features of sibling and peer relationships, resulting in mutual reinforcement. For girls, however, almost all of their violent acts are directed at siblings rather than peers. In most cases violence between siblings is tolerated and viewed by many parents as normal behavior. The most extreme violence between siblings generally occurs when parents are not present and, thus, are unable to intervene (e.g., Pepler et al., 1982).

Alternative Actions

There are few specific, research-based interventions for improving sibling interactions in the literature. In most cases it would appear that one would need to make logical generalizations from the peer-intervention literature in order to design interventions for siblings. Those interventions that have been developed for sibling interactions will be briefly discussed next.

Of particular concern to most parents is the reaction of the firstborn child to the arrival of the second. As mentioned previously, many firstborn children experience difficulties stemming from the mother's lack of attention as she attends to the newborn. Dunn (1995) provides some useful information for parents preparing for the birth of a second child and the means by which parents can assist the older child in accepting the newborn. First, during the pregnancy, parents should talk with the older child about the coming birth of the new baby. Such preparation can occur by discussing the wants, needs, and emotions of the new child and can often ease the transition for the older child. Mothers need to ensure that they are giving the firstborn individual attention at times when the newborn's needs are met. Talking, playing, and engaging in activities can provide the older child with the necessary adult attention. Providing the older child with activities while caregiving of the newborn is taking place can also help the older child deal with the lack of attention during that time (Dunn, 1995). Most importantly, the firstborn should be made to feel a part of the experience and allowed to assist the parent with caregiving activities (Dunn, 1995). Children given such opportunities are much more accepting of their new siblings and develop more positive interactions with their siblings in the long term (Dunn, 1995).

Arguments over possessions or chores or simply due to boredom or differences in child temperaments do occur even for those children who have good relationships with one another. Dunn (1995) outlines the means by which parents can alleviate these arguments. For example, parents often label children as the "smart one," the "helpful one," or the "lazy one." Dunn points out that such labeling should be avoided as much as possible as children may feel unnecessary conflict with their brothers and sisters. Comparisons about looks, academic achievements, athletic achievements, or other talents should also be avoided. Such comparisons can spur jealously between the children and result in lifelong rivalry (Leung & Robson, 1991).

Younger siblings should be shielded from no-win situations. Many younger children feel inferior to their older brothers and sisters who are stronger, smarter, and simply older. Encouraging the older child to assist the younger child can be beneficial to both children as younger children often look up to their older siblings (Dunn, 1995). Older siblings may benefit from such interactions by learning to teach and understand the experiences of others.

When engaged in his or her own activities, the older child also needs to be protected from the interference of the younger child. Younger children do not always need to be included in the activities of older siblings. Keeping both children busy and engaged in age-appropriate activities can reduce boredom and the often ensuing conflicts (Dunn, 1995).

Rules and limits can also reduce many sibling conflicts. Rules related to the use of others' possessions within the home, daily assignments of chores, and rules for home behavior can assist children in respecting others and limiting conflict (Dunn, 1995). Providing consistent consequences and mediating in conflicts can help children learn tolerance and acceptance of others.

When physical aggression occurs, Dunn (1995) recommends that children be separated and isolated. Time-out and role-play techniques can be effective in preventing aggression and helping children learn alternative methods for dealing with their problems. Parents should also attend to the victim in a physical conflict and isolate the aggressor. While both children need to be reassured that they are loved, attending to the victim defies what the aggressor actually wants to occur—that he or she receives parental attention (Dunn, 1995).

Parents should encourage cooperative play, and children should be rewarded or praised when they engage in harmonious activities (e.g., Dunn, 1995). If either child initiates inappropriate or undesirable behavior, neither child obtains the reward. Time-out for both children regardless of who started the conflict can also be effective for keeping problems at a minimum. Such actions should be explained to the children in advance. Specific, consistent parenting skills that can reduce sibling conflict include the use of patience, love, understanding, common sense, and humor (Leung & Robson, 1991). Remaining calm and matter of fact and letting children know that they have behaved in inappropriate ways but are still loved can assist children in resolving their own conflicts.

Using the strategies discussed in this section, school psychologists can work with parents in brief consultation sessions to reduce many sibling conflicts. However, in cases where the sibling rivalry is intense, long-term intervention may be required. Acts of extreme violence or any sexual assault certainly call for intensive interventions and require referrals to mental health professionals outside of the school setting.

Summary

The literature related to sibling interactions is limited and contradictory. Most researchers would agree, however, that the sibling relationship is the most important one, following that of the parent-child relationship, for children to learn prosocial behaviors. Whereas most of the literature focuses on sibling rivalries, prosocial behaviors including altruism, affection, and cooperation tend to be much more prevalent among brothers and sisters than previously assumed. As stated earlier, when family members are asked to respond to questionnaires related to sibling relationships, they tend to identify situations when disruptions occur.

Older siblings often take responsibility for younger siblings by caregiving, teaching, or defending, while younger siblings tend to imitate the behavior of their older siblings. Parents can have a significant impact on the interactions that occur between siblings by enforcing rules, communicating, and providing each child with individual attention. School psychologists can assist parents in these tasks by consulting with them and helping them monitor their behaviors. Such consultations can result in a more peaceful daily existence for all family members.

Recommended Resources

Professionals

Dunn, J. (1993). *Young children's close relationships: Beyond attachment.* Newbury Park, CA: Sage.

This volume reviews the literature on individual child differences, research on parenting, and sibling relationships. Factors that affect the overall family atmosphere and relationships with persons outside of the family are discussed.

Dunn, J., & Plomin, R. (1991). Why are siblings so different? The significance of differences in sibling experiences in the family. *Family Process, 30,* 271–283.
This article reviews the behavioral genetics research and the environmental effects on individual child development. Factors regarding both the genetic and environmental differences between siblings are discussed.

Leung, A. K., & Robson, W. L. (1991). Sibling rivalry. *Clinical Pediatrics, 30,* 314–317.
This brief article quickly reviews the problem of sibling rivalry and suggests preventative and treatment strategies.

Newman, J. (1994). Conflict and friendship in sibling relationships: A review. *Child Study Journal, 24,* 119–152.
This article reviews the research on sibling relationships across the lifespan.

Parents

Butchee, B. (1992). *For parents' sakes: A survival kit for parents and kids.* Oklahoma City: Oklahoma State Department of Health, Office of Child Abuse Prevention.
This free volume is divided into three parts. The development of children's self-esteem is discussed in the first section. The second section provides information for parents on family communication, sibling issues, family routines, discipline in public places, and ways to solve family problems. The final section provides information on how to discipline children who physically harm others.

Dunn, J. (1995). *From one child to two: What to expect, how to cope, and enjoy your growing child.* New York: Fawcett.
This book is a valuable resource for parents with two children or for those expecting their second child. The topics include the first 2 years after the birth of a second child, conflict and rivalry between siblings, and the individual differences evidenced by siblings. Tips on how to handle sibling problems are given throughout.

References

Abramovitch, R., Corter, C., Pepler, C. J., & Stanhope, L. (1986). Sibling and peer interaction: A follow-up and a comparison. *Child Development, 57,* 217–229.

Azmitia, M., & Hesser, J. (1993). Why siblings are important agents of cognitive development: A comparison of siblings and peers. *Child Development, 64,* 430–444.

Berndt, T. J., & Bulleit, T. N. (1985). Effects of sibling relationships on preschoolers' behavior at home and at school. *Developmental Psychology, 21,* 761–767.

Brown, J., & Dunn, J. (1992). Talk with your mother or your sibling? Developmental changes in early family conversations about feelings. *Child Development, 63,* 336–349.

Buhrmester, D., & Furman, W. (1990). Perceptions of sibling relationships during middle childhood and adolescence. *Child Development, 61,* 1387–1398.

Cicirelli, V. G. (1976). Siblings helping siblings. In V. L. Allen (Ed.), *Children as teachers: Theory and research on tutoring* (pp. 63–85). New York: Academic Press.

Dunn, J. (1985). *Sisters and brothers: The developing child.* Cambridge, MA: Harvard University Press.

Dunn, J. (1993). *Young children's close relationships: Beyond attachment.* Newbury Park, CA: Sage.

Dunn, J. (1995). *From one child to two: What to expect, how to cope, and enjoy your growing child.* New York: Fawcett.

Dunn, J., Brown, J., & Beardsall, L. (1991). Family talk about feeling states and children's later understanding of others' emotions. *Developmental Psychology, 27,* 448–455.

Dunn, J., & Munn, P. (1987). Development of justification in disputes with mother and sibling. *Developmental Psychology, 23,* 791–798.

Dunn, J., & Plomin, R. (1991). Why are siblings so different? The significance of differences in sibling experiences within the family. *Family Process, 30,* 271–283.

Dunn, J., Slomkowski, C., & Beardsall, L. (1994). Siblings relationships from the preschool period through middle childhood and early adolescence. *Developmental Psychology, 30,* 315–324.

Dunn, J., Stocker, C., & Plomin, R. (1990). Assessing the relationship between young siblings: A research note. *Journal of Child Psychology and Psychiatry, 31,* 983–991.

Felson, R. B. (1983). Aggression and violence between siblings. *Social Psychology Quarterly,* December.

Furman, W., & Buhrmester, D. (1985). Children's perceptions of the qualities of sibling relationships. *Child Development, 56,* 448–461.

Garner, P. W., Jones, D. C., & Miner, J. L. (1994). Social competence among low-income preschoolers: Emotion socialization practices and social cognitive correlates. *Child Development, 65,* 622–637.

Hetherington, E. M. (1994). Siblings, family relationships, and child development: Introduction. *Journal of Family Psychology, 8,* 251–253.

Hoff-Ginsberg, E., & Krueger, W. M. (1991). Older siblings as conversational partners. *Merrill-Palmer Quarterly, 37,* 465–481.

Howe, N., & Ross, H. (1990). Socialization, perspective-taking, and the sibling relationship. *Developmental Psychology, 26,* 160–165.

Jenkins, J. (1992). Sibling relationships in disharmonious homes: Potential difficulties and protective effects. In F. Boer & J. Dunn (Eds.), *Children's sibling relationships* (pp. 125–138). Hillsdale, NJ: Erlbaum.

Kramer, L., & Schaefer-Hernan, P. (1994). Patterns of fantasy play engagement across the transition to becoming a sibling. *Journal of Child Psychology and Psychiatry and Allied Disciplines, 35,* 749–767.

Leung, A. K., & Robson, W. L. (1991). Sibling rivalry. *Clinical Pediatrics, 30,* 314–317.

Mannle, S., Barton, M., & Tomasello, M. (1992). Two-year-olds' conversation with their mothers and preschool-aged siblings. *First Language, 12,* 57–71.

Nadelman, L., & Begun, A. (1982). The effect of the newborn on the older sibling: Mother's questionnaires. In

M. E. Lamb & B. Sutton-Smith (Eds.), *Sibling relationships: Their nature and significance across the lifespan* (pp. 13–37). Hillsdale, NJ: Erlbaum.

Newman, J. (1994). Conflict and friendship in sibling relationships: A review. *Child Study Journal, 24*(3), 119–152.

Patterson, G. R. (1986). The contribution of siblings to training for fighting: A microsocial analysis. In D. Olweus, J. Block, & M. Radke-Yarrow (Eds.), *Development of antisocial and prosocial behavior* (pp. 235–261). San Diego, CA: Academic Press.

Pepler, D., Corter, C., & Abramovitch, R. (1982). Social relations among children: Comparison of sibling and peer interaction. In K. H. Rubin & H. S. Ross (Eds.), *Peer relationships and social skills in childhood* (pp. 209–227). New York: Springer-Verlag.

Steinmetz, S. K. (1977). *The cycle of violence: Assertive, aggressive, and abusive family interaction.* New York: Praeger Publishers.

Stewart, R. B., & Martin, R. S. (1984). Sibling relations: The role of conceptual perspective-taking in the ontogeny of sibling caregiving. *Child Development, 55,* 1322–1335.

Stoneman, Z., Brody, G. H., & MacKinnon, C. (1984). Naturalistic observation of children's activities while playing with their siblings and friends. *Child Development, 55,* 617–627.

Watanabe-Hammond, S. (1988). Blueprints from the past: A character work perspective on siblings and personality formation. In M. D. Kahn and K. G. Lewis (Eds.), *Siblings in therapy: Life span and clinical issues* (pp. 356–378). New York: Norton.

White, B. L. (1975). *The first three years of life.* New York: Prentice Hall.

Youniss, J. (1988). *Parents and peers in social development.* Chicago: University of Chicago Press.

Zajonc, R. B., & Marcus, G. B. (1975). Birth order and intellectual development. *Psychological Review, 82,* 74–88.

57

Adoption

Gretchen Miller Wrobel

Bethel College

Harold D. Grotevant

University of Minnesota

Adoption in the 1990s cannot be characterized by any one description. Adoptive parents are married, unmarried but living in committed relationships, and single. They adopt infants and older children, children of differing races and from different countries, one child at a time or sibling groups together, and children with known disabilities. Adoptive parents, birth parents, and adopted children have varying amounts of contact with each other. Some families only have access to nonidentifying medical information about the adopted child, whereas others have continued exchange of information mediated by an adoption agency or face-to-face meetings. Adoptive families encounter unique adoption-related tasks in addition to the normative developmental milestones faced by all families and children.

School psychologists will encounter within their schools adoptive families, adopted children, and teenage birth mothers. In 1990, approximately 118,800 adoptions were completed in the U.S. Of these, 51% were adoptions by relatives (e.g., stepparents) and 9% were of children from outside the U.S. (AdoptINFO, 1996). Although data about U.S. adoptions are not maintained in a uniform manner, it is estimated that 2% to 4% of children in the U.S. are adopted. There are approximately 1.5 million adoptive families in the U.S. (Adoptive Families of America, 1996).

Background

Adoption is a value-laden social arrangement that changes in response to sociocultural contexts (Hartman & Laird, 1990). In the U.S., adoption has traditionally been a vehicle to form families that mimic the nuclear biological family. This approach supported the tacit but strong bias that families formed by adoption were second best. Efforts were made to match the biological characteristics of adoptive parents and babies. Older children and children with disabilities were considered not adoptable. Confidentiality was a primary consideration; agencies placed children in adoptive families with the legal agreement that no identifying information would be exchanged between the birth mother, adoptive parents, and adopted child. This approach assumed that once the adoption was legally finalized, families could deny the differences created by adoption and birth mothers would get on with their lives (Hartman & Laird, 1990).

Several societal trends have reshaped the practice of adoption. Today there are fewer infants available to place with adoptive families than in the past. The lessened stigma attached to an unmarried mother raising her children and the greater availability of abortion have increased the number of alternatives to adoption for birth mothers. The belief that all children are adoptable and have the right to a permanent home, founded in the child rights movement, has focused attention on the needs of children other than healthy, Caucasian infants. Desire on the part of adopted individuals to know their birth history and families, as well as the desire for birth mothers to know the welfare of the child they placed for adoption, has placed a greater emphasis on communication between birth families and adoptive families. The shrinking supply of healthy infants for adoption has given the birth mother more power to determine who will adopt her baby and under what conditions the adoption will proceed. These trends have forced adoptive parents to consider forming their families through special needs, transracial, and international adoptions or arrangements that include some form of communication with birth families. The traditional confidential adoption is no longer the norm.

Openness in Adoption

Openness can be described as a continuum with confidential adoption at one end and fully disclosed (open) adoption at the other. In open adoption the birth mother and adoptive family maintain direct ongoing communication after placement of the child. Midway on the continuum is mediated (semi-open) adoption, where non-identifying information is communicated between the birth mother and adoptive family through a third party (McRoy, Grotevant, & White, 1988). The move toward openness in adoption has generated much debate. Critics of openness have cautioned that the development of a secure attachment with adoptive parents could be inhibited (Kraft et al., 1985) and that children could misinterpret information given to them about their birth parents (Bevan & Pierce, 1994). Providing information to early-school-aged children about birth parents could increase fantasies and fears because the children are not yet able to cognitively understand the concept of adoptive permanence (Rosenberg, 1992).

Berry (1991) supports the idea of open adoptions for older children who have had an extended history with birth parents rather than younger children for whom there is less evidence regarding impact of such a relationship on their development. She believes it is more natural and less detrimental for an older child to retain ties with birth relatives. Others suggest that openness in adoption provides an essential link with birth parents through the exchange of information. This link is seen as important because it provides children a sense of continuity with their personal history which enhances their self-esteem (Kirk, 1964, 1981). Further, it will result in adopted children gaining a better understanding of their birth parents' situations, resulting in a lessened sense of rejection (Pannor & Baran, 1984). Finally, it is viewed as the right of children to have all known information available to them (Melina & Roszia, 1993). Birth parent and adopted-individual activist groups (e.g., Concerned United Birthparents, Adoptees Liberty Movement Association) also view access to available information a human rights issue. They strongly advocate for openness in adoptive relationships as a means of gaining this information.

Empirical research regarding the impact of openness on the development of the adopted child, including the perspective of the child, is only now forthcoming. One recent study (Wrobel, Grotevant, Ayers-Lopez, McRoy, & Friedrick, in press) compared adopted children in varying levels of openness on self-esteem, satisfaction with the amount of openness in the adoptive relationship, curiosity about birth parents, and understanding of adoption. All children reported positive levels of self-esteem. Older children were most curious and least satisfied with the exception of older children in fully disclosed relationships. These children were also curious about their birth parents but reported being satisfied with the current amount of openness in the relationship with their birth mothers. Also, children with more information about their own adoption had a more sophisticated understanding of adoption than children with less information. These results are not compatible with assertions of poor self-esteem and confusion associated with adoptive open-

ness, nor do they support the position that openness will enhance these outcomes.

Special Needs Adoption

Children with special needs constitute a significant number of those adopted each year. Approximately 30,000 American adoptions annually are of older children or children with special needs (Adoptive Families of America, 1996). Children in this group include (a) those over age 3 without permanent homes; (b) children of ethnicity differing from the adoptive parents; (c) children with developmental, behavioral, or health-related problems; (d) children adopted internationally; and (e) children adopted in sibling groups. Adoptions involving special needs children are considered to be at higher risk for disruption, which includes "all placements that end with the return of the child to the adoption agency whether before or after the formal legalization of the adoption and the official end of the agency's involvement with the family" (Barth, Berry, Yoshikami, Goodfield, & Carson, 1988, p. 227). Acting out, aggression, self-abuse and punishment-seeking behavior, in addition to older age at placement, are strongly associated with risk for disruption (Rosenthal & Groze, 1991).

Westhues and Cohen (1990) concluded, based on their review of the literature, that special needs adoption-disruption rates are rising, with the majority of reported disruption rates falling between 10% and 15%. Despite the number of disrupted adoptions, the majority of parents are generally satisfied with their decision to adopt even though their children exhibit non-normative behavior (Rosenthal & Groze, 1991). While it is clear that many special needs children exhibit more behavioral difficulties, especially in the category of externalizing behaviors, interpretation of results must be made with caution when several types of adoptions are categorized together. A clearer picture of adjustment can be seen by looking independently at some differing categories of special needs adoptions.

Older children and children with behavioral difficulties

Children who are older at the time of placement experience more behavioral difficulties and more problematic parent-child relationships. These problems can lead to adoption disruption. Children who are older at placement have a more complex preplacement history, often involving multiple placements and serious behavioral difficulties (Festinger, 1990). Externalizing behaviors create more problems than internalizing behaviors for these adoptive families. The difficult behaviors are associated with perceptions of the adoption having a negative impact on the family, higher rates of referral for professional intervention, and a greater percentage of adoption disruption (Rosenthal & Groze, 1991; Rosenthal, Groze, & Aguilar, 1991). Increasingly, cases of "wrongful adoption" are being filed in the courts. Adoptive parents in these cases contend that relevant information about the adopted child's preplacement history relating to his or her current emotional and behavioral difficulties was not fully disclosed. Therefore, the adoptive parents claim, they were not able to anticipate the extent of the adopted child's difficulties and make a fully informed decision about their choice to adopt the child.

Children with disabilities

Better child and family outcomes are associated with families who adopt children with physical disabilities, mental retardation, or serious medical conditions than with behavioral difficulties, developmental delays, or learning disabilities (Rosenthal, Groze, & Aguilar, 1991). It has been suggested that better outcomes are realized because the families are better prepared to deal with disabilities known at the time of placement. Behavioral difficulties, developmental delays, and learning disabilities, all of which typically present problems years after the adoption, may, therefore, be unexpected by the parents. Thus, adoptive parents should be carefully prepared for potential disability-related problems (Rosenthal, Groze, & Aguilar, 1991).

Transracial adoption

It is estimated that 1,000 to 2,000 domestic transracial adoptions occur yearly (Silverman & Feigelman, 1990), most often involving the adoption of African-American children by Caucasian parents. Typically, adjustment for these children has been defined through the use of measures most closely associated with middle-class Caucasian culture. Given this context, children adopted transracially report good self-esteem and feeling as if they are a part of and belong to their families (McRoy & Zurcher, 1983; Silverman & Feigelman, 1990; Tizard, 1991). Emotional and developmental problems that do exist in childhood appear to be influenced more by pre-adoptive experiences than by post-adoptive prejudice and ethnic hostility met by the adopted individuals (Silverman & Feigelman, 1990). However, little is currently known about adult outcomes for transracially adopted persons, especially when they live in contexts very different from those in which they were raised.

An area of importance for transracially adopted children is racial identification. Little research has been done on the task of integrating the dual inheritance of the transracially adopted individual's own racial background and that of their adoptive family, especially for those of Asian and Latin American descent (Tizard, 1991). For African-American children, this task can be eased by parents who accept their child's racial identification with the African-American community, acknowledge the importance of connections to that community, and take actions to facilitate such connections (Silverman & Feigelman, 1990).

It should be noted, however, that the practice of transracial adoption is controversial. Those against it argue that African-American children need to be raised in their own cultural group in order to adapt successfully to their environments and to the racism they will encounter (National Association of Black Social Workers, 1972). Proponents of inracial adoption contend that the large number of African-American children available for adoption is due to institutional barriers preventing their adoption rather than unwillingness on the part of African-American parents to adopt. Many point out the need for adoption agencies to undergo organizational change so that African-American families willing to adopt African-American children can be better served (McRoy, 1989).

International adoptions

Between 8,000 and 10,000 international adoptions occur annually in the U.S. (Ramos, 1990). The majority of these adoptions involve Korean, Indian, and Hispanic children adopted by Caucasian parents. While the issues surrounding transracial adoption are salient for many children adopted internationally, there are specific issues related to international adoptions. Parents and physicians of internationally adopted children must often make decisions about a child's health status based on incomplete records which do not include a health history prior to the child's arrival in this country. Upon arrival, the child must be examined by a physician to determine health status, and many physicians do not have extensive experience making this kind of evaluation which requires knowledge of the variety of health problems that may afflict these children (Hostetter & Johnson, 1989). The lack of reliable and specific information about a child's medical history and experiences prior to placement can have important implications because early adverse experiences place a child at greater risk for later maladjustment.

A large sample of internationally adopted children (aged 10 to 15 years) from the Netherlands was studied to evaluate the connection between early adverse experiences and behavioral difficulties (Verhulst, Althaus, & Versluis-den Bieman, 1992). It was concluded that adopted children from developing countries ran a greater risk of maladjustment because of early neglect, abuse, numerous caretaker changes, and health risks but also appeared to be functioning quite well based upon parent report using the Achenbach Child Behavior Checklist.

For children who are adopted at older ages, evaluating their proficiency with English is important. In addition, environmental factors will influence newly arrived children's ability to make their ideas known (Ramos, 1990). Are the adoptive parents fluent in their child's native language? In school, is the child in an English as a second language, bilingual transitional, or English-only program? It is also important to evaluate the amount and type of the child's formal education to adequately serve the child academically (Ramos, 1990).

Factors associated with successful special needs adoptions

It is important that families who participate in special needs adoption have the support and information they need to meet both the adoption and the disability-related needs of their children. Positive functioning for families with special needs adoptions is enhanced by (a) active participation of the father in addition to the mother, (b) strong problem-solving skills on the part of the parents, and (c) a motivation to adopt characterized by acceptance that the adopted child with special needs will not be similar to a birth child the adoptive parents may have had (Westhues & Cohen, 1990).

A consistent finding in the literature is that adoptive parents want all possible information about their child's preplacement history and/or disability. Obtaining this information is associated with greater satisfaction with the adoption and an increased ability to understand the child's behavior and to meet his or her needs (Berry, 1990; Groze, 1994; Rosenthal, Groze, & Aguilar, 1991). Groze (1994) found that families with high expectations for their special needs children were more likely to seek clinical intervention than families with lesser expectations for their children. Having more information about their child's background may help adoptive parents create an appropriate level of expectation for their child with special needs, so that the level of expectation itself does not become a stressor.

Developmental Issues

Adopted children and their families encounter unique developmental tasks in addition to the normative tasks all families face. Acknowledgment of the differences associated with adoptive families is essential for facilitating parental communication with children about adoption-related issues and concerns (Kirk, 1964, 1981). It is important to understand that although adoption adds to the stressors children and families face, the majority of children and families function in a healthy manner. This section will focus on the unique developmental tasks encountered by adopted children and their families.

Adoptive Families and Society

Society places a stigma on adoptive families easily identified by adoptive parents. Negative societal attitudes and beliefs identified by one group of adoptive parents included (a) the biological tie is important for bonding and love (suggesting that bonding and love in adoptive families is inferior), (b) adopted children are second rate because of an unknown genetic past, and (c) adoptive parents are not their child's real parents (Miall, 1987). While adoptive parents do not personally hold these attitudes

and are satisfied with their decision to adopt, they and their children must cope with the negative attitudes residing in the larger society. For parents adopting children across racial or national lines, additional prejudices may be encountered.

Adoption and Loss

Adoptive families must deal with the losses inherent in adoption. Roszia (as cited in Melina, 1990) outlined seven core issues of adoption and their implications for development (see Table 1). The issues of loss, rejection, guilt and shame, grief, identity, intimacy, and control are important for understanding the experience of adoption. Knowing that these seven core issues will present themselves throughout a person's lifetime can help the school psychologist better meet the needs of adopted children and their families. It is important to note that not all adopted children and their families will need assistance dealing with these issues. Many families and individuals possess the problem-solving skills and insights to deal with these issues effectively in their own experiences.

Growing Up Adopted

Brodzinsky and colleagues (Brodzinsky, 1987; Brodzinsky, Lang, & Smith, 1995) have placed adoption-related developmental tasks into the context of an adoptive-family life cycle. At each stage families encounter tasks similar to nonadoptive families but also experience tasks unique to adoptive families. These adoption-related issues interact with and complicate the way in which adoptive families meet the universal tasks of family life (Brodzinsky et al., 1995). Some of the adoption-related tasks families face include transition to adoptive parenthood, explaining adoption to the children, coping with adoption-related loss, supporting curiosity regarding birth parents, forming positive identities regarding adoption status, and coping with negative societal attitudes regarding adoption. Four developmental tasks adopted children face will be discussed in this chapter: attachment, understanding of adoption, curiosity, and identity development. These tasks are considered central to the development of a healthy self-concept that incorporates adoption as a important theme.

Attachment

Formation of an affectional bond between children and those who care for them has long been recognized as an important developmental factor. The first influential attachments to primary caregivers develop over the first 6 to 8 months of a child's life and provide a context of security within which the child grows (Bowlby, 1969). Disruption of this process is thought to have deleterious effects upon the developing child. Attachment theory has important implications for adopted children, especially

Table 1 *Adoption and Loss*

Key Issue	Influence on Adopted Children	Influence on Adoptive Parents
Loss-Adoption is beneficial for forming families but it is a formation based on loss	1. Loss of birth parents 2. Lack of personal history 3. Insecurity about permanence of relationship	1. Loss of fertility associated with loss of immortality 2. Loss of biological child that would have been born to parents
Rejection-Loss is personalized by feeling rejected. Individuals feel they did something wrong to cause the loss	1. Adoptive placement is seen as a rejection by birth parents 2. Rejection ideas based on poor self-image; can only be chosen if first rejected 3. Anticipate rejection	1. Feel their bodies have rejected them 2. Keenly feel societal attitude that adoption is second best 3. Concerned others will reject their parenting style
Guilt/Shame-Guilt can develop over perceived wrongdoing that facilitated the loss and shame that others may know	1. Feel shame at being different or not being good enough for birth parents to keep from rejecting them 2. Feel deserving of misfortune 3. Take defensive or angry stance	1. Feel shame about infertility and that they are not their child's biological parents
Grief-A normal reaction to loss that is often overlooked in adoptive families; members are supposed to be happy because needs for family relationships have been met	1. Denied grief can lead to depression and acting-out behavior 2. Grieve lack of fit in adoptive family	1. Difficulty attaching emotionally to their child 2. Inhibit grief in their children because it feels like rejection to the adoptive parent
Identity-Identity is based on information gained about yourself though several sources	1. In traditional adoptions, the lack of information can make identity formation process difficult 2. Feeling of borrowing adoptive family's identity 3. May become people pleasers to create sense of belonging	1. May not fully identify with the parenting role because they do not have a genetic link to the child
Intimacy-Loss and confusion about identity can make it difficult to develop emotional intimacy.	1. Avoids emotional intimacy for fear of experiencing loss again 2. Fear being involved with a birth relative	1. Unresolved grief over losses may present itself through difficulties in the marital relationship
Control-Adoption may be seen as a loss of control because it is not a first choice by those involved	1. Adoption alters life course without child's involvement in the decision 2. May have difficulty understanding cause and effect, leading to an inability to take responsibility for own actions	1. May develop a sense of learned helplessness because mastery linked decision to procreation 2. Lack generativity

Note. Adapted from material in "NACAC Speakers Describe Seven Core Issues of Adoption" by L. Melina, Winter 1990, *AdopTalk,* pp. 2–5, and in *Seven Core Issues in Adoption,* a brochure by D. Silverstein and S. Kaplan, 1986, Tustin, CA.

those adopted after the age of 6 months, where a first attachment may be broken or, because of neglect, not developed at all.

The literature is equivocal about the assumption that mother-infant attachments are less secure in adoptive families than nonadoptive families. Singer, Brodzinsky, Ramsay, Stein, and Waters (1985) found no difference in attachment status using the strange situation for non-adopted and adopted infants with an average placement age of one month. Portello (1993) suggested that when early neglect has hindered the formation of secure attachments the initial adoptive-mother/infant attachment process may be prolonged. Groze (1992) found a relationship between attachment (as measured by parent report of behavioral indicators) and self-esteem in a group of adopted children with special needs. The children who described better parent-child relationships and who did not exhibit anxious-ambivalent attachment behaviors had higher self-esteem as measured by the Piers-Harris Self-Concept Scale.

Recent emphasis in attachment theory has focused on the development of affectional bonds across childhood, no longer considering infancy the only important developmental phase for attachment. Johnson and Fein (1991) offer a definition of attachment as a developmental process that allows relationships to stabilize and change over time. The ability of the child to maintain multiple attachments and behavioral expectations of others is thus viewed as adaptable. Providing a warm and stable environment to explore positive and negative feelings of loss, curiosity, and identity will facilitate attachments with those who care for the adopted child. Understanding attachment as a developmental process provides room for the negative effects of poor attachments to be influenced and remediated. Instead of seeing attachment as occurring only in critical periods of development with a dichotomous good or bad outcome, professionals can look for developmentally appropriate ways of intervening throughout the attachment process (Portello, 1993). The use of family rituals, such as marking the anniversary of the adopted child joining the family, will facilitate feelings of entitlement associated with attachment (Groze, 1992). School psychologists can help parents and school personnel understand the dynamic, developmental nature of attachment in order to refute the popular belief that the lack of a mother/infant "bond" will dictate poor childhood adjustment.

Understanding of adoption

Children's understanding of adoption follows a systematic developmental course that parallels their general cognitive development. Brodzinsky, Singer, and Braff (1984) describe a continuum that represents degrees of cognitive sophistication in understanding the concept of adoption. At first, understanding of adoption is characterized by the child verbalizing, but not differentiating, the ideas of adoption and birth. The concepts are fused together. Joining the adoptive family is viewed by the preschool child as a singular process involving both birth and adoption. By age six, children are able to clearly differentiate between adoption and birth as alternative paths to parenthood and to accept that the adoptive family relationship is permanent but not understand why. They are most likely repeating without understanding what their parents have told them about permanence. At the next level, ages 8 to 11 years, children view adoptive family relationships as a quasi-legal sense of permanence which invokes an authority figure, such as a judge or social worker, who in a vaguely described way makes the relationship permanent. Finally, adopted children in early to middle adolescence view adoptive family relationships as permanent based on the legal transfer of rights from birth to adoptive parents.

Curiosity

Middle childhood and adolescence is a time of heightened questioning by children about their adoptive status. As children mature cognitively, they come to realize that to be adopted means also that birth parents must relinquish a child for adoption (Brodzinsky, 1987). Adopted children begin to process what it means to lose one family while gaining another, leading to an increased desire for information about birth family members. The adoption story told to children as preschoolers may no longer satisfy their need to know. Their new need to know can lead to stress, confusion, and uncertainty. These feelings are normative for adopted children and should not be viewed as psychopathology or as reflecting a deficit in parenting skills (Brodzinsky et al., 1995).

The degree of openness has implication for the impact of the adoption story told adopted children. While children in all types of openness arrangements are curious about their birth parents, having different amounts of information about birth parents influences the child's perspective about the reasons why the birth mother placed her child and the child's affective reaction to the adoption story. Children ages 8 to 12 years, in more open relationships, more often reported hearing adoption stories that contained a personal characteristic of their birth mother (e.g., she was too young) as the reason for adoption (Wrobel, Grotevant, & McRoy, 1995). These children also most frequently identified both positive and negative feelings regarding the story they were told. Children in confidential arrangements more often reported not knowing the content of the adoption story they were told or why their birth mothers placed them for adoption. These children reported not knowing how they felt about their adoption story. Having more information to process may lead to mixed feelings about the adoption story as children sort out what all the information means for their family relationships. The impact these mixed feelings may have on developmental outcomes has not been determined.

Although most children experience adoption as more positive than negative, there is occasional stress related to their adoptive status. In a nonclinical sample, Smith and Brodzinsky (1994) found children ages 6 to 9 years reported being the least ambivalent about their adoptive status, but they reported more intrusive thoughts and feelings about their adoption than children in early to later adolescence. This higher degree of intrusiveness of thought and feeling coincides with the greater curiosity experienced by adopted children in this age group but should not lead one to assume that older children do not think about the implications of their adoptive status. Parents and school professionals need to provide a caring environment in which adopted children can work through their issues of loss and curiosity. Professionals should not overreact to the children's feelings of confusion and ambivalence. Rather, they should view the feelings as normative calls to support children through the sometimes difficult process of understanding their adoptive status.

Identity

Adoptive status has important consequences for the social and personality development of adopted individuals, particularly for their developing sense of identity. Personal identity refers to the distinctive combination of personality characteristics and social style by which one defines oneself and by which one is recognized by others. It represents the meshing of personality with historical and situational context. Secondly, it refers to one's subjective sense of coherence of personality and continuity over time. Identity is not just an abstract construct; it is related to behavior in the daily lives of adolescents. Understanding the linkages between identity and behavior requires a developmental perspective (Grotevant, in press).

In examining the process through which identity develops, the assigned components of identity over which the adolescent has no control (e.g., gender, ethnicity, adoptive status) provide a context for those aspects of identity over which adolescents have greater personal choice (e.g., occupations, values, relationships; Grotevant, 1987, 1992, 1993). For example, adopted children might feel that they are missing a crucial piece of their personal history because of lack of knowledge about their birth parents and consequently find the process of identity development more complex. Adolescents are often preoccupied with the lack of physical resemblance between themselves and their family members. Linkages between assigned and chosen aspects of identity should be most intertwined developmentally when there is a direct connection between specific aspects of the two. For example, adoptive status might have little to do with political values but might have much to do with views about personal and family relationships. When the child's adoptive status is undervalued by those around him or her or when parents do not effectively match their communication about adoption with what the child is seeking to understand, there is greater potential for difficulty (Grotevant, 1992).

Benson, Sharma, and Roehlkepartain (1994), using closed-ended survey questions, found that 27% of adopted teenagers said "adoption is a big part of how I think about myself," and 41% said they think about adoption from at least 2 to 3 times per month to on a daily basis. Girls were more likely than boys to report that adoption played an important role in their identity formation, and they reported thinking about adoption more frequently than boys. On average, the adopted adolescents in this study demonstrated levels of self-esteem comparable to that of nonadopted peers but also reported that adoption is on their minds frequently, influencing how they think about themselves.

Problems and Implications

Adoption-related issues arise in the context of general development and are not necessarily problematic. Adoption is an important aspect of a child's identity to consider but should not be made the primary focus of responses to adjustment problems, which are often related to multiple and interacting factors.

Mental Health of Adopted Children

Wierzbicki (1993) conducted a meta-analysis of 66 published studies which demonstrated that adopted children had higher levels of maladjustment, externalizing disorders, and academic problems than nonadopted children. However, Brodzinsky, (1993) found developmental level

had a moderating influence: Relatively few differences were typically found between adopted and nonadopted children during infancy or preschool years, but by middle childhood and adolescence when issues of grief and loss become salient, differences began to emerge).

Adopted children are referred for psychological treatment two to five times more frequently than their nonadopted peers (McRoy, Grotevant, & Zurcher, 1988). One controversial explanation for this higher referral rate is a specific pattern of adoption-related psychopathology, involving acting-out behaviors, specific personality and interpersonal difficulties, and ideational content. Kirschner (1995) calls this pattern the "adopted-child syndrome." This syndrome is defined as having psychosocial roots that distinguish it from related diagnoses such as conduct disorder. By assessing only the behavioral patterns of a child it is believed that the "adopted-child syndrome" may be missed and a label of conduct disorder applied. "The adopted child syndrome can be differentiated from [conduct disorders] by underlying adoption-specific psychodynamics, greater emotional vulnerability, accessibility to and motivation for therapy, and better prognosis" (Kirschner, 1995, p. 3).

The adopted-child-syndrome label is problematic. It is stigmatizing and misleading because the label attributes characteristics of some individuals in a group to the entire group. Further, there are other alternative explanations for the higher mental health referral rates of adoptive children. First, adoptive parents may feel greater comfort with human services providers. Their experiences in completing the adoption process may make them more likely than nonadoptive parents to refer their children when problems are relatively minor and fewer (Warren, 1992). Second, studies related to the mental health of adopted children primarily involve children in confidential adoptions. It is speculated that greater openness in adoption could buffer adopted children from such problems, because secrecy and uncertainty regarding their origins would be greatly reduced. The effect of open adoptive relationships on mental health referral rates of adopted children is unknown.

Educational Implications of Adoption

There is little research regarding the prevalence rates of adopted children in special education. Brodzinksy and Steiger (1991) surveyed 84 public and private schools in the state of New Jersey to determine prevalence rate of adopted children in three special education categories: (a) students with neurological impairment (NI), (b) students with perceptual impairment (PI), or students with emotional disturbance (ED). These special education groups were chosen because they tend to manifest symptoms (academic difficulty and externalizing behaviors) commonly reported in adopted children. Similar to patterns observed in mental health studies, adopted children were overrepresented in special education. Adopted children accounted for 6.7% of students with NI, 5.4% of students with PI, and 7.2% of students with ED; however, adopted children comprised only 1% to 2% of the population under the age of 18.

The perception of poor school adjustment was supported by a group of adoptive mothers and teachers who rated adopted children lower on school achievement and social competence and higher on school-related problems that nonadopted peers (Brodzinsky, Schechter, Braff, & Singer, 1984). Brodzinsky and Steiger (1991) argue that the feelings of grief and loss experienced by adopted children during the school years may be a contributor to academic difficulty. These stressors may leave less mental energy for successfully completing the academic and social tasks of school. They further state that adopted children with learning disabilities may find it more difficult to interpret the circumstances of their adoption because of their problems processing and comprehending information in interpersonal areas, prolonging the resolution of adoption-related grief. To consider that academic problems may in part be related to the grief process can normalize the difficulties identified by parents and teachers. Involvement in a support group for adopted children before a special education referral is made may help (Brodzinsky & Steiger).

It is important to note that a recent analysis of data from the 1987 follow-up of the 1983 Ontario Child Health Study found that for a group of 104 adopted school-age children there were no significant differences in school performance or substance abuse between adopted and nonadopted children. Adoption itself did not have an independent effect on these outcomes but was an influence when grouped with other predictors. It was postulated that adoptive status was a relatively small contributor to prediction of poor school performance and substance abuse when compared with other known predictors such as gender (Lipman, Offord, Boyle, & Racine, 1993).

Benson et al. (1994) surveyed a national U.S. sample of adopted adolescents and their nonadopted public school counterparts. Rates of school absenteeism and the desire to drop out of high school before graduation for adolescents aged 12 to 18 were similar for adopted adolescents and the general public-school population. Of the adopted adolescents, 4% of those aged 12 to 15 and 14% of those aged 16 to 18 reported "skipping" school 2 or more days in the previous month. The percentage of public school students reporting the same absenteeism were 8% and 15% respectively. One percent of adopted adolescents (ages 12 to 18) reported the desire to drop out of school. The same prevalence rate was reported for public school students. This same group of adopted adolescents reported having a B or better school average (62%), high achievement motivation (72%), and the desire to pursue postsecondary education (94%).

The picture of academic difficulty and school adjustment for adopted children is equivocal. It is clear that more research is needed to delineate special education prevalence rates, types of academic problems experienced in the school setting, and the contributors to the development of these difficulties.

Alternative Actions

School psychologists are in a position to educate other school professionals and families about adoption while serving the unique needs of adopted students. Through consultation with staff and students, adoption-related issues can be thoughtfully considered in a developmental context. The following list contains actions school psychologists can take when dealing with the issues faced by adopted children, their families, and their teachers.

1. Remember that there is no typical adopted child. Given the numerous forms of adoption practiced today, it is important to ask adopted children and their families what type of adoption arrangement they have. This knowledge will guide the school psychologist to information that may be useful in helping the student. Preadoption history, special needs, and cultural differences can vary tremendously and are critically important background issues to understand.

2. Helping adoptive families identify and utilize their strengths and resources is important in helping them meet the demands of their growing adopted child. The school psychologist is uniquely qualified to facilitate family strength by educating parents about how adoption influences normative and atypical development. If applicable, educating parents about their child's disability, including appropriate behavioral and educational expectations and interventions for their child, is well within the expertise of the school psychologist.

3. Adoption must be considered an influence on development across the life span. The availability of postplacement services beyond the first 2 to 3 years is important for healthy functioning (Berry, 1990). The school psychologist should be familiar with postplacement services available in the community so appropriate referrals can be made.

4. Do not automatically construe children's adoptive status as the cause of their behavioral or academic problems. The simplistic belief that any one variable can have such power as to overshadow other contributors to behavioral difficulties is detrimental to the student's well-being. Adoptive status and issues should be considered when determining a course of assess-

Table 2 *Adoption Terminology*

Person or Situation	Appropriate Terminology	Inappropriate Terminology
Parents of adopted child	Mother	Adoptive mother[1]
	Father	Adoptive father[1]
Biological parent	Birth mother	Natural mother
	Birth father	Natural father
		Real mother
		Real father
Adopted person	Adopted individual	Adoptee
Placing a child for adoption	Making an adoption plan for the child	Putting up for adoption
	Signing an agreement for adoption	Giving the child up for adoption

[1]Adoptive parents should only be referred to as adoptive mother or adoptive father in adoption-related discussions. An adopted child's mother would not be introduced as "Pat's adoptive mother" but rather "Pat's mother."

ment and intervention, but only in the context of other developmental and environmental factors.

5. It is possible that the school psychologist will be unaware of a child's adoptive status and thus not have an important context to evaluate a child's behavior. When gathering demographic information about a child, it is appropriate to ask if the child is adopted. Some parents may be reluctant to share this information for fear that their child's adoptive status will become the only explanation for their difficulties. The school psychologist should covey to parents their understanding that the salient issue of adoption must be considered in the wider developmental and environmental context.

6. School psychologists can help adoptive parents have realistic but challenging expectations for their children by helping them to understand the unique tasks adopted children face within the context of normative development.

7. The use of constructive adoption terminology is the mark of a well informed professional. Birth mother and birth father refer to the child's biological parents, while mother and father refer to the child's adoptive parents. Children's and parents' adoptive status should only be referred to in the context of adoption-related discussions. It is inappropriate to ask parents who have had children enter their family through adoption and birth which children are "their own." Table 2 provides a limited overview of appropriate and inappropriate terminology. Spencer (1994) provides a complete discussion of constructive adoption terminology.

8. School psychologists should familiarize themselves with adoption issues by reading adoption-related literature. The ideas presented by adoption professionals, first-person accounts, and those contained in the empirical literature should be consulted for a well-balanced view of adoption. This information will allow the school psychologist to combat any uninformed negative attitudes, stereotypes, expectations, and attributions school personnel may have about adoption

and will enhance the healthy development of adopted children. Many of these resources are also suitable for sharing directly with adopted children and their families.

9. Curricula should be reviewed to evaluate if they are sensitive to the feelings of adopted children. In discussions of differing family types, adoption should be presented as a viable way to form a family. Assignments should also be reviewed for their sensitivity. Children adopted internationally do not automatically want to study the country of their birth and should not automatically be considered "experts." Genealogies, autobiographies, and comparisons of inherited traits should be developed in such a way that all students can complete the assignment as presented. Modifications made only for adopted students single them out unnecessarily.

Summary

The changing and multifaceted nature of adoption does not allow for professionals to view adopted children through a single lens. Adoptive families take many forms. Special needs adoptions are increasing in number. The traditional confidential adoption is no longer the norm; varying degrees of communication between birth parents, adoptive parents, and adopted children are found. It is important for school psychologists to understand the developmental implications that the varying forms of adoption can have for a child. Adopted children face unique developmental tasks in addition to the normative tasks all children encounter. These additional tasks can be stressors that manifest themselves in behavioral and academic difficulties. Although adoptive children and their families often require support from mental health and educational professionals, most families and children function in a healthy manner. It is essential that school psychologists view adoption as only one important factor among other developmental and environmental influences when considering a course of intervention for school difficulties. School psychologists, as informed and effective child advocates, can make an important difference in the lives of adopted students.

Recommended Resources for Professionals

Brodzinsky, D. M., & Schechter, M. D. (Eds.). (1990). *The psychology of adoption.* New York: Oxford University Press.
This volume is a compilation of writings covering a broad spectrum of adoption-related topics. The work is especially useful because it contains not only reviews of empirical research but also chapters covering theoretical perspectives on adoption, clinical issues in adoption, and social policy in adoption.

Brodzinsky, D. M., Schechter, M. D., & Henig, R. M. (1992). *Being adopted: The lifelong search for self.* New York: Doubleday.
This book describes the lifelong developmental process for adopted individuals, drawing from the empirical and clinical work of the authors. It is a good source for gaining information about the developmental course of adopted adults. An acknowledged limitation is that the work is based primarily on the experiences of individuals in traditional confidential adoptions.

McRoy, R. G., Grotevant, H. D., & White, K. L. (1988). *Openness in adoption: New practices, new issues.* New York: Praeger.
This book provides a comprehensive discussion of the issues involved in openness in adoption. Included are a review of the literature related to confidentiality and openness in adoption, a discussion of theoretical perspectives and agency practices, and a description of a pilot study of families involved in open adoptions.

Recommended Resources for Parents and Children

Krementz, J. (1982). *How it feels to be adopted.* New York: Alfred A. Knopf.
In this powerful book, 19 children ranging in age from 9 to 16 tell their adoption stories using their own words. Each story is accompanied by a picture of the child author. The children are involved in a variety of adoptive relationships and express their feelings in a way that will impact readers' ideas about adoption.

Register, C. (1991). *"Are those kids yours?": American families with children adopted from other countries.* New York: Free Press.
*This book offers practical parenting advice related to raising children adopted internationally. In addition, the controversies and ethical issues surrounding adoption across culture, race, and social class inherent in international adoption are ex-*plored. *A good resource for those considering international adoption, as well as current adoptive parents.*

van Gulden, H., & Bartels-Rabb. L.M. (1993). *Real parents, real children: Parenting the adopted child.* New York: Crossroad.
This book balances theory and practical suggestions for dealing with the everyday issues adoptive parents encounter. A developmental approach is used to discuss issues faced by adoptive families without ignoring the concerns of those who have arranged for transracial, international, and older-child adoptions. Preparing to become an adoptive parents is also discussed.

Adoptive Families Magazine. Published by Adoptive Families of America, 3333 Highway 100 North, Minneapolis, MN 55422.
This bimonthly magazine features relevant and informative articles on all aspects of adoptive family life. A regular feature "Growing up adopted" addresses particular issues faced by adopted children in five developmental time periods ranging from infancy to later adolescence. A free review issue may be obtained by calling Adoptive Families of America (800-372-3300).

References

AdoptINFO: Research-based information on adoption. (1996). *Quick stats about adoption* [on-line]. Available: http://www.fsci:.umn.edu/cyfc/AdoptINFO.htp

Adoptive Families of America. (1996). *Adoption fact sheet* [on-line]. Available: http://www.AdoptiveFam.org

Barth, R. P., Berry, M., Yoshikami, R., Goodfield, R. K., & Carson, M. L. (1988). Predicting adoption disruption. *Social Work,* May–June, 227–233.

Benson, P. L., Sharma, A. R., & Roehlkepartain, E. C. (1994). *Growing up adopted: A portrait of adolescents and their families.* Minneapolis, MN: Search Institute.

Berry, M. (1990). Preparing and supporting special needs adoptive families: A review of the literature. *Child and Adolescent Social Work, 7*(5), 403–418.

Berry M. (1991). The effects of open adoption on biological and adoptive parents and the children: The arguments and the evidence. *Child Welfare, 70*(6), 637–651.

Bevan, C. S. & Pierce, W. (1994, November). *Secrecy, privacy, and confidentiality in adoption.* Paper presented at Building Families: Ethical and Policy Issues in Adoption Conference, Minneapolis, MN.

Bowlby, J. (1969). *Attachment.* New York: Basic Books.

Brodzinsky, D. (1987). Adjustment to adoption: A psychosocial perspective. *Clinical Psychology Review, 7,* 25–47.

Brodzinsky, D. (1993). Long-term outcomes in adoption. *The Future of Children, 3,* 153–166.

Brodzinsky, D., Lang, R., & Smith, D. (1995). Parenting adopted children. In M. Bornstein (Ed.), *Handbook of parenting: Vol. III. Status and social conditions of parenting* (pp.209–232). Hillsdale, NJ: Erlbaum.

Brodzinsky, D., Schechter, D., Braff, A. & Singer L. (1984). Psychological and academic adjustment in adopted children. *Journal of Consulting and Clinical Psychology, 52*(4), 582–590.

Brodzinsky, D., Singer, L., & Braff, A. (1984). Children's understanding of adoption. *Child Development, 55,* 869–878.

Brodzinsky, D., & Steiger, C. (1991). Prevalence of adoptees among special education populations. *Journal of Learning Disabilities, 24*(8), 484–489.

Festinger, T. (1990) Adoption disruption: Rates and correlates. In D. M. Brodzinsky & M. D. Schechter (Eds.), *The Psychology of adoption* (pp. 201–218). New York: Oxford University Press.

Grotevant, H. D. (1987). Toward a process model of identity formation. *Journal of Adolescent Research, 2,* 203–222.

Grotevant, H. D. (1992). Assigned and chosen identity components: A process perspective on their integration. In G. R. Adams, R. Montemayor, & T. Gulotta (Eds.), *Advances in adolescent development* (Vol. 4, pp. 73–90). Newbury Park, CA: Sage.

Grotevant, H. D. (1993). The integrative nature of identity: Bringing the soloists to sing in the choir. In T. Kroger (Ed.), *Discussions on ego identity* (pp. 121–146). Newbury Park, CA: Sage.

Grotevant, H. D. (in press). Family processes, identity development, and behavioral outcomes at adolescence: What can we learn from adoptive families? *Journal of Adolescent Research.*

Groze, V. (1992). Adoption, attachment and self-concept. *Child and Adolescent Social Work Journal, 9*(2), 169–191.

Groze, V. (1994, February). Clinical and non-clinical adoptive families by special needs children, *Families in Society: The Journal of Contemporary Human Services,* 90–104.

Hartman, A., & Laird, J. (1990). Family treatment after adoption: Common themes. In D. M. Brodzinsky & M. D. Schechter (Eds.), *The psychology of adoption* (pp. 221–239). New York: Oxford University Press.

Hostetter, M., & Johnson, D. (1989). International adoption: An introduction for physicians. *American Journal of Diseases of Children, 143,* 325–332.

Johnson, D., & Fein, E. (1991). The concept of attachment: Applications to adoption. *Children and Youth Services Review, 13,* 397–412.

Kirk, H. D. (1964). *Shared fate.* New York: Free Press.

Kirk, H. D. (1981). *Adoptive kinship: A modern institution in need of reform.* Toronto: Butterworths.

Kirschner, D. (1995) Adoption psychopathology and the "Adopted Child Syndrome." *Directions in Child and Adolescent Therapy, 2*(6), 2–14.

Kraft, A., Palombo, R., Woods, P., Mitchell, D., Schmidt, A., & Tucker, N. (1985). Some theoretical considerations on confidential adoption: Part III. The adopted child. *The Child and Adolescent Social Work Journal, 2*(3), 139–153.

Lipman, E., Offord, D., Boyle, M., & Racine, Y. (1993). Follow-up of psychiatric and educational morbidity among adopted children. *Journal of the Academy of Adolescent Psychiatry, 32*(5), 1007–1012.

McRoy, R. G. (1989). An organizational dilemma: The case of transracial adoptions. *The Journal of Applied Behavioral Science, 25,* 145–160.

McRoy, R. G., Grotevant, H. D., & White, K. L. (1988). *Openness in adoption: New practices new issues.* New York: Praeger.

McRoy, R. G., Grotevant, H. D., & Zurcher, L. (1988). *Emotional disturbance in adopted adolescents: Origins & development.* New York: Praeger.

McRoy, R. G., & Zurcher, L. (1983). *Transracial and inracial adoptees.* Springfield, IL: Charles C. Thomas.

Melina, L. (1990, Winter). NACAC speakers describe seven core issues of adoption. *Adoptalk,* 2–5.

Melina, L., & Roszia, S. (1993). *The open adoption experience.* New York: Harper Collins Publishers.

Miall, C. (1987). The stigma of adoptive parent status: Perceptions of community attitudes toward adoption and the experience of informal social sanctioning. *Family Relations, 36,* 34–39.

National Association of Black Social Workers. (1972, April). *Position statement on transracial adoptions.* Presented at the National Association of Black Social Workers Conference, Nashville, TN.

Pannor, R., & Baran, A. (1984). Open adoption as standard practice. *Child Welfare, 63,* 245–250.

Portello, J. Y. (1993). The mother-infant attachment process in adoptive families. *Canadian Journal of Counseling, 27*(3), 177-190.

Ramos, J. (1990). Counseling internationally adopted children. *Elementary School Guidance and Counseling, 25,* 147–152.

Rosenberg, E. B. (1992). *The adoption life cycle.* New York: Free Press.

Rosenthal, J., & Groze, V. (1991). Behavioral problems of special needs adopted children. *Children and Youth Services Review, 13,* 343–361.

Rosenthal, J., Groze, V., & Aguilar, G. (1991). Adoption outcomes for children with handicaps. *Child Welfare, 60*(6), 625–635.

Silverman, A. R., & Feigelman, W. (1990). Adjustment in interracial adoptees: An overview. In D. M. Brodzinsky & M. D. Schechter (Eds.), *The psychology of adoption* (pp. 187–200). New York: Oxford University Press.

Silverstein, D., & Kaplan, S. (1986). *Seven core issues in adoption* [brochure]. Tustin, CA: Author.

Singer, L. M., Brodzinsky, D. M., Ramsay, D., Stein, M., & Waters, E. (1985). Mother-infant attachment in adoptive families. *Child Development, 56,* 1543–1551.

Smith, D., & Brodzinsky, D. (1994). Stress and coping in adoption: A developmental study. *Journal of Clinical Child Psychology, 23,* 91–99.

Spencer, M. (1994). Constructive adoption terminology: A statement of basic philosophy underlying specific adoption terms. (Available from the Children's Home Society of Minnesota, 2230 Como Avenue, St. Paul, MN, 55108)

Tizard, B. (1991). Intercountry adoption: A review of the literature. *Journal of Child Psychology and Psychiatry, 32*(5), 743–756.

Verhulst, F., Althaus, M., & Versluis-den Bieman, H. (1992). Damaging backgrounds: Later adjustment of international adoptees. *Journal of the American Academy of Child and Adolescent Psychiatry, 31,* 518–524.

Warren, S. (1992). Lower threshold for referral for psychiatric treatment for adopted adolescents. *Journal of the*

American Academy of Child and Adolescent Psychiatry, 31(3), 512–517.

Westhues, A., & Cohen, J. S. (1990). Preventing disruption of special-needs adoptions. *Child Welfare, 69*(2), 141–155.

Wierzbicki, M. (1993). Psychological adjustment of adoptees: A meta-analysis. *Journal of Clinical Child Psychology, 22,* 447–454.

Wrobel, G., Grotevant, H., Ayers-Lopez, S., McRoy, R., & Friedrick, M. (in press). Open adoption and the level of child participation. *Child Development.*

Wrobel, G., Grotevant, H., & McRoy, R. (1995, November). *The impact of the adoption story from the perspective of the adopted child.* Poster session presented at the annual conference of the National Council on Family Relations, Portland, OR.

58

Adolescent Pregnancy and Parenting

Karen Callan Stoiber

University of Wisconsin-Milwaukee

Background

Adolescent pregnancy is increasingly receiving attention as a major challenge to American society. For example, Dryfoos (1994) targeted adolescent pregnancy as one of the so-called "social morbidities" affecting youth in America. A recent report by the Alan Guttmacher Institute (AGI, 1994) entitled *Sex and America's Teenagers* provides a compendium of statistics documenting adolescent pregnancy and parenting as leading contemporary threats to America's youth. The AGI report indicated more than one million adolescents become pregnant each year, with nearly half of them (478, 000) becoming adolescent mothers. Sexual activity or heterosexual intercourse among adolescents is also occurring at alarming levels. Recent estimates suggest more than one in five 15-year-olds are sexually active (AGI, 1994). Davis (1989) reported 45% of females aged 15 to 19 years were sexually active before marriage.

Students at risk for adolescent pregnancy, pregnant adolescents, and parenting adolescents emerge as groups of youth who demonstrate particular mental health, health care, and education needs. Several national policy initiatives have promoted schools as critical sites for responding to the diverse needs of America's youth (e.g., the Health Promotion and Disease Prevention objectives highlighted in *Healthy People 2000*, and the National Education Goals specified in *America 2000: An Educational Strategy*). Schools are considered to be in an especially strategic position for responding to the adolescent pregnancy crisis because of their accessibility and potential for coordination of mental health, health care, and educational services (Carlson, Paavola, & Talley, 1995). Although schools are common sites for information-based sex education programs, recent evidence suggests a need for schools to go beyond didactic information modalities to address adolescent pregnancy and parenthood (Stoiber, 1995).

School psychologists represent a unique group of mental health professionals who are well-trained to perform diverse roles related to innovative pregnancy prevention and intervention. For example, school psychologists can present to entire classes of students classroom-based prevention programs aimed at altering adolescents' sexual behaviors. They are also able to augment classroom-based services through consultation. Direct prevention and intervention services through either individual counseling or groups can also be provided by school psychologists. However, the capacity of school psychologists to design and implement effective, adolescent pregnancy-prevention and intervention programs depends upon their understanding of adolescent pregnancy as well as their knowledge of the at-risk conditions surrounding it.

Adolescence is generally conceptualized as the developmental period ranging from 13 to 19 years. Examining adolescent sexual patterns and pregnancy rates makes it clear that younger and older adolescents differ in experience and behavior. The likelihood of having intercourse increases steadily over the teen years, with 80% of males and 76% of females being sexually active by their 20th birthday (AGI, 1994). Perhaps most disturbing are data indicating an increase in sexual activity and births among *young* adolescents. For example, Stoiber, Anderson, and Schowalter (in press) found that one-third of seventh- and eighth-grade culturally diverse students attending an urban middle school reported being sexually active. AGI (1994) reported that the greatest increase in adolescent births has occurred for teens aged 15 to 17 years, who show an increase of 23% since 1986. Coercion is often involved for younger females who are sexually active. Approximately 75% of girls who had sex before 14 and 60% of girls having intercourse before age 15 reported being forced to have sex against their will. The fact of young adolescent American women being at risk for teen pregnancy is most striking when compared to patterns of sexual activity in other industrialized countries. The U.S. rate of birth for girls 14 years or under is approximately 5 births per 1,000. The number of births to very young adolescents in the U.S. is four times that of Canada, the only other comparable developed country with a rate of 1 per 1,000 for this age group (Jones et al., 1985).

At the same time that greater proportions of adolescents are experiencing sexual activity than in previous decades, marriage is being entered 3 to 4 years later than in the 1950s (AGI, 1994). Hence, although a smaller proportion of teenagers are marrying, a larger proportion are beginning sex both earlier and prior to marriage. AGI (1994) estimated that young people typically begin sexual activity approximately 8 years before marriage, with the gap being considerably longer for African American youth. On the average, African American men initiate sex 19 years prior to marriage, and African American women experience a 12-year gap.

Among the statistics related to adolescent parenting are data showing adoption rates as steadily dropping among single mothers. Prior to the late 1950s about 90% of single mothers opted for adoption. Today more than 90% of single mothers assume the responsibility of caregiver. Recent data on European American unmarried mothers indicated that from 1982 to 1988 only 3% chose adoption (AGI, 1994). Hence, in contemporary society, teen pregnancy is likely to be accompanied by single parenthood.

Development

The reasons underlying adolescent pregnancy are complex with no one factor considered adequate to explain this developmentally disruptive phenomenon (Stoiber, 1995). It is generally accepted that adolescence is a period of rapid and dramatic physical and psychological transition (Kazdin, 1993). Because of the emotional upheaval and ongoing changes that usually accompany adolescence, it is also generally believed that pregnancy during this period can exacerbate even typical developmental challenges. An analysis of adolescent pregnancy and parenting suggests that there are two broad categories of contributing factors: (a) dispositional characteristics and (b) situational factors (Byrne, Kelley, & Fisher, 1993; Trad, 1994).

Dispositional Characteristics

Dispositional factors refer to one's orientation or approach to thinking and behaving (Trad, 1994). For example, adolescents are more prone to risk-taking behavior because, when compared to adults, they demonstrate less developed decision-making competence and reflective-thinking dispositions. In adjusting to the changes faced during adolescence, teenagers often engage in risk-taking behaviors that can result in negative outcomes. *Risk-taking behaviors* are defined as those behaviors or activities that promote the probability of adverse psychological, social, and health consequences (Kazdin, 1993). Examples of risk behavior include substance use and abuse, school failure and dropout, gang membership, violence, and early and unprotected sexual activity. Though a certain level of risk taking is considered a con-

comitant aspect of adolescence, greater risk taking in areas such as drug and alcohol abuse and delinquency behavior has been found for sexually active young adolescents (Small & Luster, 1994). Small and Luster (1994) reported that alcohol use emerged as the strongest predictor of sexual experience in youth. If an adolescent is prone to taking risks, there may be a greater likelihood not to seek medical care early in the pregnancy. Also, behaviors such as alcohol and drug use may continue in risk-taking pregnant adolescents because they tend not to associate them with detrimental effects for the unborn offspring (Trad, 1994).

Sexual activity among adolescents in America is often characterized as "contraceptively careless" (Byrne et al., 1993). Contraceptives (e.g., condoms) reduce the risk of unintended pregnancy. Despite the well-publicized risks of sexually transmitted diseases (STDs), ineffective contraceptive use is more often the rule among adolescents (DiClemente et al., 1992). Many adolescents engage in unprotected sexual activity despite having knowledge of the risk of contracting STDs or of becoming pregnant (DiClemente et al., 1992). A dispositional impediment associated with adolescence is the belief that one will uniquely escape misfortunes, such as illness, accident, or unintended pregnancy. Negative peer influence (e.g., peer perspective that condoms reduce sexual pleasure or that condoms are not necessary as protection against pregnancy or AIDS if you shower after sex), embarrassment about purchasing or using condoms, and beliefs that condoms are too expensive also influence condom use (DiClemente et al., 1992).

Among dispositional characteristics linked to adolescent pregnancy, the cognitive profiles and attitudes of pregnant adolescents have been shown to differ significantly from those of teens who do not become pregnant (Sommer et al., 1993). Adolescent girls who believe they will not become pregnant or contract AIDS and STDs are the group least likely to use contraception (AGI, 1994). This naive disposition implies an unrealistic cognitive capacity to grasp the probable consequences of one's actions. A related at-risk disposition, then, is not being future oriented. Adolescents who become pregnant tend to lack specific academic motivation and realistic career orientations (Stoiber et al., in press). They harbor unrealistic expectations about what they need to do to achieve academically and to attain educational goals. The combination of being unable to plan for the future and to predict realistically the consequences of one's behavior often leads to the unfortunate outcome of too-early pregnancy.

Another important dispositional characteristic is one's effective and attitudinal reaction to sexual information, sexual cues, and contraception. Sex guilt and erotophobia (fear or phobia regarding erotic stimuli) have been linked to failure to take an elective sex education course, in particular when the adolescent has high self-esteem (Byrne et al., 1993). Underestimating the likelihood of one's own sexual activity or parents' under-estimation of their child's sexual activity decreases the probability of contraceptive preparedness and knowledge of contraceptive use. Similarly, adolescents who consider themselves to be invulnerable to negative events such as pregnancy and AIDS are at particular risk of unprotected sexual activity. Erotophobic sexual attitudes tend to promote unpleasant emotional and cognitive reactions to the experience of purchasing contraceptives (e.g., embarrassment) and, hence, the avoidance of this event (Bryne et al., 1993). An obvious outcome is that negative sexual attitudes interfere with an adolescent's capacity to obtain and use contraceptives. However, DiClemente et al. (1992) reported that adolescents who believe condoms prevent HIV transmission and who had fewer sexual partners were significantly more likely to use condoms.

A final dispositional quality that characterizes many pregnant and parenting adolescents is the belief of pregnancy as a means of establishing independence (Trad, 1994). For many troubled or rebellious adolescents, pregnancy may be viewed as a way to separate from their parent(s) and to establish their own unique identity. An adolescent may view pregnancy as a "rite of passage" in pursuing financial independence. Paradoxically, a pregnant adolescent may find that she needs to rely on her parent(s) as a coping strategy in facing the challenge of too-early pregnancy and parenting. In addition, child care responsibilities will force her to relinquish the freedom she might have experienced with peers.

Situational Factors

Situational factors refer to educational, family, and economic conditions that may promote or mediate whether one is sexually active or becomes pregnant. Poverty is considered the major underlying situational factor related to adolescent childbearing (AGI, 1994). In a recent analysis of teen pregnancy by Males (1994), a correlation of .812 was reported between youth poverty and adolescent childbearing, providing strong evidence for poverty as a common condition surrounding teenage parenthood. Geronimus and Korenman (1991) pointed out that little positive motivation exists among economically poor young women to avoid pregnancy. Teenagers from troubled or impoverished homes may believe pregnancy provides a path to escape a dysfunctional family that has little prospect of improving. Economically poor teens may also view adolescent parenting as a means toward economic support provided through welfare assistance programs. Abortion rates, too, vary significantly across socioeconomic groups. Whereas nearly three-quarters of higher income pregnant adolescents have abortions, fewer than half as many poor or low-income pregnant adolescents choose this alternative.

Race and ethnicity also emerge as important situational variables related to adolescent pregnancy rates

(AGI, 1994). Nearly 20% of all African American women aged 15 to 19 years become pregnant each year, compared with 13% of Hispanic Americans and 8% of European Americans. The relation between ethnic-minority status and adolescent pregnancy needs to be better understood. Perhaps African American, Hispanic American, and other ethnic minority youth do not have identities that match those of the majority culture. In addition, African Americans are at greater risk for pregnancy because they (a) attain menarche and hormonal fertility at an earlier age, (b) are more likely to be sexually experienced at younger age, and (c) are less likely to use a contraceptive or to use it effectively (AGI, 1994).

Though Hispanic Americans comprise the second largest ethnic minority in America, less is known about their early sexual patterns. The contraceptive practices of Hispanic American youth appear to more closely resemble African Americans than European Americans. European American youth are significantly more likely to use contraception, usually the male condom, than African American, Hispanic American, and lower income teenagers (AGI, 1994). Hispanic Americans and African Americans are also similar in being more likely to continue their pregnancy while a teenager. Approximately 60% of European American adolescents choose abortion, but less than 50% of Hispanic American and African American youth choose this option (AGI, 1994).

On the other hand, some differences between Hispanic American and African American adolescents have been noted. The intention to become pregnant, or at least being less concerned about whether one becomes pregnant while a teenager, has been observed more for Hispanic Americans when compared to other adolescents. For Hispanic Americans, culture-specific positive attitudes toward early pregnancy combined with a de-emphasis on educational attainment likely contribute to higher levels of adolescent pregnancy (Byrne et al., 1993). Another important distinguishing feature of Hispanic American teens is that many were born outside the U.S. making the adjustment during adolescence more challenging than for native-born youth. Socioeconomic levels among Hispanic Americans appear to be related to adolescent pregnancy. Approximately 3% of Cuban descent young women aged 15 to 19 years give birth; these teens tend to be the most financially advantaged group of Hispanic Americans. A rate of 10% to 11% occurs for similar aged teens of Mexican and Puerto Rican descent, who tend to be less advantaged. Unfortunately, variations in sexual attitudes and behaviors among Hispanic American populations (Cubans, Puerto Ricans, and Mexicans to name a few groups), and among newly immigrant and later generation Hispanic Americans, remain generally unexplored. Most surveys of adolescent sexuality and childbearing are not sufficiently large to examine smaller ethnic groups, such as Southeastern Asians (Hmong), Native Americans, or Asians.

Several researchers (Small & Luster, 1994; Stoiber & Anderson, 1996; Wasserman, Rauh, Brunelli, Garcia-Castro, & Necos, 1990) have begun to use a sociocultural paradigm that emphasizes the importance not only of race and class, but also of family structure for understanding early motherhood among ethnic minorities. That is, consideration is given to an adolescent's family structure, such as single parenthood, in attempting to understand the path toward adolescent pregnancy. AGI (1994) reported that 14-year-old poor girls are twice as likely to live in a family headed by a single female than their higher income counterparts. Perhaps more striking, if 14 years of age and African American, you are three times more likely than your European American age peers to be raised in a family headed by a single female. In a recent study, more than two-thirds of African American pregnant adolescents reported that their mothers were unmarried teens during their first pregnancy (Stoiber et al., in press). Intergenerational adolescent parenting is a reality that contextualizes the motherhood expectations of African American young women. Perhaps the earlier initiation of sexual intimacy and single parenthood fits more into the social norm of African American culture than European American culture (AGI, 1994; Sonenstein, Pleck, & Ku, 1991).

Educational disadvantage, school failure, and school dropout are additional situational variables that place an adolescent at risk for pregnancy. The life experiences of those in economic poverty has a synergistic impact on educational goals and aspirations. Sexually inactive youth tend to have higher educational goals and grades. Although pregnant and sexually inactive adolescent youth may hold similar educational values (believe education is important) and life expectations (expect to marry, have a good marriage, desire purpose and meaning in their lives), pregnant teens are less likely to hold accurate perceptions and economic means to attain productive goals. Adolescent pregnancy rates are disproportionately higher in schools having high dropout rates and in families having parents with lower education levels (AGI, 1994). Students who become pregnant are at much greater risk for reduced educational achievement and attainment and low-status employment, thus perpetuating a financially disadvantaged life.

Pervasive messages about sex in contemporary adolescent life also emerge as impacting on teen sexuality, pregnancy, and parenting. In *Sex and America's Teenagers,* AGI (1994) pointed out the many complex and conflicting sexual messages that teens face in today's society and provided the following illustrative situations. For students in grades 8 to 11, more than 80% reported being the recipient of unwelcome sexual messages or advances, which were usually initiated by another student. Interestingly, nearly 60% of same-aged students admitted to subjecting another student to unwanted sexual comments or actions. In addition, adolescents are bombarded

with media encouraging them toward sexual intimacy (Byrne et al., 1993). In contrast, little is stated about the importance of responsible sexual activity. The three major television networks have historically resisted advertising condoms. Although most teenagers report concern about STDs, in particular AIDS, almost half of 15- to 19-year-olds believe that the average young person lacks adequate information about sexuality and reproduction (AGI, 1994). Communication breakdowns within families regarding the topic of sex are not unusual. Approximately one-third of 15-year-old girls reported that neither parent had discussed with them how pregnancy occurs. One-half of 15-year-old females stated that their parents had not discussed contraceptive methods or STDs with them (AGI, 1994).

When reviewing research on adolescent parents, one observes a noticeable lack of information on teenage fathers. There are at least two reasons for this apparent gap in the literature. First, consensus has not occurred among researchers about which ages constitute "teenage" with reference to fathers. More specifically, whether adult males who impregnate adolescent females should be considered "adolescent fathers" remains an unresolved issue. Second, male adolescents are often missed as a target, both of pregnancy prevention and of parent intervention. One study showed that males and females were equally uninformed in the area of fertility and contraception, with the majority of both genders identifying the most fertile time as "safe." However, males were less likely to endorse using contraceptives for occasional sex (44% of males felt it was important compared to 64% of females) and more likely to endorse the idea of unprotected sex as an expression of greater love (21% of males compared to 10% of females; Freeman & Rickels, 1993). Readers interested in greater detail about adolescent fathers are referred to Freeman and Rickels and Stoiber et al. (in press).

Problems and Implications

A decade ago the National Academy of Sciences Panel on Early Childbearing (Hayes, 1987) urged public institutions and policy makers to place priority on designing and implementing pregnancy prevention programs. Nonetheless, adolescent pregnancy rose 20% from 1986 to 1990 (AGI, 1994). The failure of American society to reduce levels of adolescent pregnancy becomes more sobering when consideration is given to the consequences of adolescent pregnancy. Whether the newfound sexual freedom evidenced among contemporary adolescents is viewed positively or negatively, teens involved in early sexual activity have a greater likelihood of experiencing (a) the threat of incurable and fatal STDs, (b) unintended pregnancy, (c) abortion or adoption, (d) poor economic outcomes, and (e) cognitive and behavioral problems for the offspring (AGI, 1994; Stoiber, 1995).

Sexually Transmitted Diseases

Every year, three million adolescents contract a STD. Hence, adolescents now account for a quarter of all new cases of STDs. A sexually active adolescent's chance of contracting sexually transmitted infection, then, is considered significantly greater than that of becoming pregnant. Approximately 25% of sexually active adolescents become infected with an STD each year, with roughly 13% of all teens acquiring these infections annually. Factors that influence whether a STD is contracted include one's gender, the number of sexual partners one has and whether they have STDs, and the type of STD (see also the chapter on communicable diseases in this volume).

Women are at much greater risk of acquiring a sexual transmitted infection because their physical anatomy make them more prone to STD transmission (AGI, 1994). For example, in a single act of unprotected sexual behavior with an infected partner, a woman is twice as likely as a man to become infected with gonorrhea, chlamydia, and hepatitis B. Although the number of reported AIDS cases among adolescents is relatively small, some 20% of AIDS cases are diagnosed in individuals while in their twenties, most of whom likely contracted HIV during adolescence (AGI, 1994). Obviously, the more partners that one has increases the risk of contracting STDs. Women who have more sexual partners tend to use an oral contraceptive rather than a condom, which also increases the chance of STDs.

Young adolescents are at particular risk for STDs for at least four important reasons. First, the younger the age at which sexual activity is initiated, the greater the likelihood of contraceptive nonuse (Byrne et al., 1993). Second, adolescent women appear biologically to be more susceptible to STDs than older women. Adolescents have a higher risk of infection both because their cervix has not completely developed and because they have fewer protective STD antibodies. For example, sexually active adolescents aged 15 to 19 years have the highest incidence of gonorrhea than for any other 5-year age group between 20 and 44. Another trend affecting STDs in adolescent women is that most of their sexual partners tend to be several years older. Third, due to young adolescents' sexual activity being more erratic, they are less likely to plan for contraceptive use. Fourth, contraceptives may be difficult or too expensive for young adolescents to obtain.

The consequences of sexually transmitted infection are often very serious—including infertility, cancer, HIV infection, and AIDS. STDs have an especially devastating impact on women because these diseases are both transmitted more easily and more difficult to detect in women. As another unfortunate consequence, women can transmit STDs to their infants during pregnancy or childbirth, which can have far-reaching and life-threatening repercussions.

Unintended Pregnancy

Of the more than one million teenage pregnancies, approximately 85% are unintended. Differences in the adolescents' social economic level and ethnicity distinguish whether the pregnancy was intended. For example, pregnancies among lower income and Hispanic American teens are more likely to have been intentional when compared to other adolescents. Pregnancies among married teens are more intentional than for unmarried teens. Some one-third of married women aged 19 or younger reported that their pregnancy was planned, compared to 7% of unmarried pregnant teens.

Unintended pregnancies in adolescents can cause serious emotional turmoil. Stoiber et al. (in press) found that a full three-quarters of pregnant teens characterized their pregnancy as being mostly negative emotionally. An estimated 13% of pregnant teens attempt suicide, suggesting that the prospects of being a mother and caring for an infant may be overwhelming for many teens (Trad, 1994). Adolescents who experience unintended pregnancy may be more prone to depression and to develop gross misperceptions of the infant (e.g., view the infant as having devil-like qualities, consider the infant to be "greedy" because he or she needs to eat frequently). These distorted images seem to interfere with the adolescents' capacity to develop an emotionally satisfying bond with the infant. In turn, a failure to bond between the adolescent mother and child increases neglect and abuse of the infant. Not surprisingly, grim child consequences are associated with unintended pregnancy, including a higher than average incidence of low birth weight, cognitive and emotional problems, and maladaptive behaviors (AGI, 1994).

Abortion and Adoption

Pregnant adolescents often consider abortion as an option. One-third of the more than one million adolescent pregnancies end in abortion (AGI, 1994). Most adolescents who choose abortion indicate that their young age and low income influenced their decision. In just three states—Connecticut, Maine, and Wisconsin—and the District of Columbia are there laws permitting a minor to consent on her own to have an abortion. Conversely, 21 states require a minor to either obtain consent or notify a parent (in some states, both parents) prior to having an abortion. In most of these states, however, an adolescent can avoid parent involvement by obtaining the legal option of a judge's authorization for an abortion. However, knowledge of this legal option as well as an understanding of legal procedures often are not apparent to a pregnant adolescent. In the remaining states, the law is silent with regard to the parent's role in minors' accessibility to an abortion.

Whether an adolescent is married while pregnant influences the outcome of the pregnancy. Married adolescents are more prone to continue their pregnancy than unmarried adolescents. Married teens are believed less likely to terminate an unintended pregnancy because of spousal and family support, a better employment and income level, and more willingness to have children. Nonetheless, approximately 25% of unintended pregnancies among married teens result in an abortion (AGI, 1994). The termination of an unintended pregnancy is more common among higher income and European American youth and among those who have higher educated parents and a strong future orientation. Those adolescents covered by Medicaid are less likely to have abortions, which may be due to the fact that most states do not include the cost of abortion as a Medicaid benefit.

Few studies have evaluated pregnant adolescents' decision making related to abortion, adoption, or pregnancy continuation. Indications are that adolescents who choose to discontinue their pregnancy tend to be more similar to nonpregnant teens. For example, both groups of teens have higher family incomes and academic aspirations than pregnant adolescents who give birth (AGI, 1994). Several factors seem to influence whether a teen relinquishes her child after birth, including the adolescents' (a) relationship with family members, (b) bonding with the baby in utero, (c) level of family support, (d) cognitive development, (e) participation in guided decision-making activities, and (f) opportunity to weigh options (Cervera, 1993). Adolescents who receive positive feedback and support from family and friends about the pregnancy and who are less realistic about the future for themselves and their child tend to raise the child (Cervera, 1993). Unmarried adolescent mothers exposed to structured counseling wherein the burdens and benefits of relinquishing or keeping their babies are explored (e.g., imagine your life with and without the baby) have a greater tendency to release their babies (Mech, 1986).

Studies suggest that adolescents who choose to abort or to relinquish their babies may exercise prolonged feelings of loss and grief. Recent evidence indicates that open adoption may lessen the emotional pain of relinquishing a baby (Cervera, 1993). Cervera recommends counseling and emotional support during the grieving process that may follow adoption or abortion.

Economic Ramifications

As increasing numbers of young women begin early parenting, the problem of inadequate economic and social support for these youth has also heightened. The cost of adolescent parenting to public taxpayers has risen at exponential levels. Each year more than 50% of the federal budget for welfare aid goes to families begun by women who were teens when they first gave birth (Center for Population Options, 1992). In 1990, families started by teens were estimated to cost over $25 billion for Aid to Families With Dependent Children, Medicaid, and food stamps (Center for Population Options). The issue of whether the opportunity for welfare payments has contributed to childbearing among low income adolescents continues to be hotly debated. Nonetheless, it remains disconcerting that adolescent parenting perpetuates the poverty cycle. Recent estimates by AGI (1994) suggest that nearly 70% of adolescent mothers and their children live in poverty, and only 2% eventually complete college. In contrast only 7% of women who delay their first childbearing beyond adolescence are poor during adulthood, demonstrating the long-term economic advantage of postponing early pregnancy.

Children of Adolescent Parents

Recent studies have documented the likelihood of a high-risk environment as characteristic of adolescent-parent families (AGI, 1994; Small & Luster, 1994; Stoiber & Houghton, 1994). Children of adolescent parents may represent a group of youngsters most seriously predisposed to developmental and social problems. Risk factors such as limited social and economic support are considered to be fused with the quality of adolescent parenting, which, in turn, impacts negatively on the development of their children. Because teenage parents are more likely to come from low income families and to resist accepting their pregnancy, adolescents tend to receive inadequate prenatal health care. Babies born to younger mothers when compared to older mothers are at greater risk for health problems during childhood and more likely to need hospitalization.

Unrealistic expectations about children and about their role as parents are more prevalent in adolescent parents, which mediate important parent-child bonding, attachment, and communication patterns. In general, adolescent mothers have been found to hold more authoritarian idealogies about parenting, tending to view typical developmental behaviors of their children as negative unless taught to think differently (Furstenberg, Brooks-Gunn, & Chase-Lansdale, 1989). The immature developmental status of adolescent parents provides one explanation for their tendency toward unrealistic expectations; another reason is their failure to adopt child-oriented or empathic concerns. At the heart of both hypotheses is the belief that the self-oriented needs of adolescents limit their capacity to adapt and be sensitive to their children's concerns and developmental needs (Stoiber & Houghton, 1994).

One important consequence for children of adolescent parents is that they demonstrate lower cognitive abilities and more educational problems. Their poorer cognitive and academic performance is not believed to be a direct result of birth to a young parent. Rather, the increased multiple risks associated with poor economic conditions, lower parent educational level, and single parenthood appear to produce adverse consequences for these children (Stoiber & Anderson, 1996). The risk environments of adolescent mothers have an accumulative effect on their children, increasing the level of academic and behavioral difficulties that they experience while growing older.

Children of adolescent mothers are more likely to develop social-emotional and coping problems (Furstenberg et al., 1989; Stoiber & Anderson, 1996). More specifically, lower competence in adapting to situations or in initiating social interactions with peers and adults has been observed for these children compared to other groups of children (Furstenberg et al., 1989; Stoiber & Anderson, 1996). Furthermore, the stresses surrounding adolescent parent families can be detected early in the development of their children (Stoiber & Anderson, 1996; Stoiber & Houghton, 1994). For example, the study by Stoiber and Anderson showed that behavioral indicators of less competent coping behaviors (e.g., poorer self-regulation, greater irritability, negative or sad affect, poorer social engagement) were observed for children of adolescent mothers, especially for those who seemed to experience greater distress in their lives. Stoiber and colleagues have demonstrated that risk factors associated with adolescent parenting are linked to their children's poorer coping competence. Pervasive environmental factors associated with poverty, including parental depression, community violence, and less adult supervision, seem to influence the child's social and affective development negatively. Also a greater tendency toward harsh parenting techniques, child neglect, and not meeting their children's psychological needs have been reported for adolescent parents (Furstenberg et al., 1989). Because family qualities are thought to provide the context of risk, the coping competencies of the children of adolescent mothers are often seriously compromised.

Not all children of adolescent mothers display problems in development (Stoiber & Anderson, 1996; Stoiber & Houghton, 1994). Various protective factors have been found to promote coping competence in children of adolescent mothers. Adolescent mothers who have positive and realistic expectations about their children and who demonstrate responsive parental behaviors (e.g., verbal interactions, behavioral involvement and monitoring) seem to have children who fare better than other children of adolescent mothers (Stoiber & Anderson, 1996; Stoiber & Houghton, 1994). Children of adolescent mothers who experience other cognitive, developmental, or neurological challenges (e.g., exposure to cocaine, fetal alcohol syndrome, low birth weight) represent a group of children believed to be among the most at-risk children due to the exponential effect of adverse environmental,

family, and individual factors. Further research aimed at disentangling the impact of specific and interrelated risk conditions as well as their long-term effects must occur. Nonetheless, most agree that the initial disadvantages experienced by the too-early parent are projected on their offspring, often having detrimental effects on the child's cognitive, social, and emotional well-being.

Alternative Actions

A clear need for school- and community-based pregnancy prevention and intervention programs emerges from the preceding overview. The search for effective programs is catalyzed by the social, economic, educational, and health consequences of adolescent pregnancy and parenting for the child, for the adolescent parents, and for society. A review of literature on pregnancy prevention and intervention reveals diverse perspectives on what constitutes the best strategies for altering early sexual behavior. There are two major types of pregnancy-prevention programs: primary and secondary. The goal of primary prevention programs is to foster responsible sexual behavior by delaying early sexual activity. The goal of secondary prevention is to encourage the use of contraceptives as a means of reducing unintended pregnancy. Unfortunately, little evaluation data on the impact of programs aimed at reducing either adolescent sexual behavior or adolescent pregnancy are available. There are several reasons underlying the inadequate evaluative status of these programs (AGI, 1994; Stoiber et al., in press):

1. Funding for many programs is linked to direct services, not permitting monies for evaluation.
2. Sensitivity about questions on sexuality makes schools and community agencies reluctant to survey participants.
3. Program organizers are overly confident of their program's impact, de-emphasizing their need to determine its effects.
4. Attrition rates of programs do not permit a large enough sample size to measure effects.
5. Program evaluation often focuses only on short-term effects, and the program may not have had an adequate duration to demonstrate sustained effects.
6. Control participants are usually exposed to some level of sexuality education, which presents a confound in comparing program participants and nonparticipants.

Particular attention will be given in this section to approaches that incorporate an evaluation component. In general, research has consistently demonstrated that the most effective primary prevention programs reach adolescents prior to their initiating sexual activity; once initiated, sexual activity is difficult to stop (Miller, Card, Paikoff, & Peterson, 1992). Readers interested in a more comprehensive review should consult Dryfoos (1994), Robinson, Watkins-Ferrell, Davis-Scott, and Ruch-Ross (1993), and Stoiber et al. (in press). Programs designed to alter adolescent sexual practices and adolescent parenting can generally be categorized into five types (Robinson et al., 1993; Stoiber et al., in press): (a) traditional sex education programs emphasizing sexual knowledge, (b) skill-based programs aimed at promoting decision-making, communication, and assertiveness abilities, (c) contraceptive-access-oriented programs, (d) life-options programs that stress career awareness and training, and (e) collaborative school-community support and mentoring programs. In general, the most effective pregnancy prevention programs focus on social, cognitive, and behavioral competencies to address the diverse and complex needs of adolescents (St. Lawrence et al., 1995).

Sexuality Education Programs

Perhaps the most common strategy used to prevent adolescent pregnancy is school-based sexuality education classes (AGI, 1994). Today, most young people have been exposed to sexuality education in their schools. To date, 46 states and the District of Columbia either mandate or recommend that schools provide some instruction about sexuality, and all 50 states and the District of Columbia mandate or recommend AIDS education. Kenney et al. (1989) reported that 94% of sexuality education programs promote increased decision-making skills about sexuality, 77% provide knowledge about reproduction, and 40% emphasize abstinence. Few school-based programs provide information on birth control techniques or on where to obtain contraceptives (AGI, 1994).

Outcome data on traditional sexuality education indicated that this form of prevention has been successful in increasing students' knowledge about male and female anatomy, birth control methods (when included in curricula), the probability of pregnancy, and STDs. However, evaluations of the effects regarding changes in sexual behavior or in increasing responsible contraceptive use have been less promising. Increased knowledge may not be enough to promote responsible behavior. Programs that take a very narrow approach, such as promoting abstinence until marriage ("just say no"), have not been shown to delay intercourse or reduce sexual activity (AGI, 1994). Rather, when participants of narrow-focused abstinence programs become sexually active they may be at greater risk for pregnancy and STDs because they have less accurate information and strategies regarding protection (Byrne et al., 1993). In general, increased use of contraceptives have only generally been documented when specific information is included on how to resist sexual pressures and how to use contraceptives. There is no conclusive information that sexuality education programs reduce adolescent pregnancy

among participants. Research does show that high school students who receive formal instruction on AIDS are more knowledgeable about STD and HIV transmission than those not receiving such instruction. In addition, evidence suggests that students receiving AIDS education may be less likely to engage in risky sexual behaviors (AGI, 1994).

In sum, the majority of teens receive some sex education through programs offered in their school, church, or other community organization. Often school and other public programs are limited in scope, emphasizing mostly facts and knowledge related to sex. In addition, explicit information about sex often occurs too late (i.e., during high school rather than junior high), after the adolescent has already become sexually experienced.

Skill-Based Instruction

Knowledge alone does not seem sufficient to change adolescents' early sexual behaviors. Hence, curricula have been designed that combine sexuality education with instruction in decision-making and effective-communication skills. The rationale for this dual-oriented prevention program stems from research and theory indicating that adolescents who have specific skill deficits (such as in assertive communication or future-oriented problem solving) are at greater risk for unintended early pregnancy. Hence, students are taught specific skills through interactive strategies, including role plays, group discussion, and peer modeling. The intent is to provide adolescent participants with practice in communication strategies to "say no" or "not yet" in refusing unwanted sexual initiations, to resist coercions, to negotiate safely, and to implement self-protective behavior by recognizing their vulnerability to sexual activity. Although research on effects of skill-based programs show inconsistent results, some school-based programs have demonstrated a positive impact on students' reported sexual behavior (AGI, 1994). Studies have reported at least three benefits of skill-based programs (AGI, 1994): (a) participants postpone the initiation of sexual activity; (b) contraceptives, including condoms, are used more by participants than control students; and (c) a greater proportion of participants reported being in monogamous relationships, and a smaller proportion reported having sexual relations with high-risk partners than control students.

Byrne et al. (1993) suggested that effective prevention of unwanted pregnancies requires five discrete steps: (a) acquiring and retaining information about conception and contraception, (b) acknowledging the possibility of sexual intercourse, (c) obtaining contraceptives, (d) communicating about contraception with one's sexual partner, and (e) utilizing contraception correctly. Successful contraceptive use, based on Byrne's model, requires a variety of decision-making and communication skills. Consistent with Byrne's approach is the belief that American society should both accept and deal with the sexual behavior of adolescent youth. Those adolescents who are not prepared to expect their own engagement in sexual intercourse tend to be nonusers of contraceptives. Byrne and others argue that an important aim of prevention programs should be to help adolescents accept their own sexuality and acknowledge their possible participation in sexual intercourse.

Effective skill-based programs share at least five qualities. First, they are based upon theoretical approaches, such as social learning or social influence theory that recognizes the impact of peers and other social forces on sexual behavior. Second, these programs provide participants with instruction on which types of social pressure to expect and how to respond assertively. Third, they include experiential-based activities highlighting the risks of unprotected sexual activity and draw on real-life scenarios related to sexual risks. Fourth, skill-based programs use group support and norms that reinforce attitudes against unprotected sexual behaviors. Finally, programs incorporate activities designed to increase relevant communication and decision-making skills and build participants' confidence in using them.

Access to Contraceptives

School-based health clinics have emerged as a primary mechanism for providing adolescent students with contraception counseling and with access to contraceptives. A proliferation of school-based clinics occurred during the last decade, with recent estimates indicating 400 to 500 exist (AGI, 1994; Dryfoos, 1994). Despite their recent growth, school-based clinics remain somewhat controversial. Many clinics offer related health care (e.g., physical exams), education and reproductive health care, and counseling. There are no data on service provision by school psychologists in school-based clinics. However, school psychologists seem well suited to provide services such as counseling and support groups. Although condom distribution is favored by 60% of adults, only 8% of middle and high school students live in school districts where condoms are distributed. To date, no data are available on the impact of condom-distribution programs on students' use or STD incidence levels.

Statistics indicating that nearly half of America's adolescent females are sexually active 9 or more months prior to making their first visit to a family planning clinic provide a strong rationale for school-based clinics. A few evaluations of school-based clinics have demonstrated significant benefits, including higher levels of sexual and contraceptive knowledge, delay in the initiation of first intercourse, and declines in pregnancy rates and birthrates among students. For example, Zabin and associates (Zabin, Hirsch, Smith, Streett, & Hardy, 1986) reported that students involved in a school-based clinic program for 3 years showed a 30% decrease in pregnancy rates

when compared to previous pregnancy rates for the school. This rate contrasted sharply with a comparison school, which had a 58% increase in pregnancy during that same period. Unfortunately, the evaluation did not examine which aspects of the program (i.e., counseling, access to contraceptives, education) most impacted on pregnancy rates. A comprehensive nationwide evaluation of six school-based clinics suggested encouraging results in increasing students' contraceptive use and reducing their consumption of alcohol and tobacco (Kirby, Waszak, & Ziegler, 1991). However, the evaluation by Kirby et al. (1991) found no difference in pregnancy rates between clinic and comparison schools.

Approaches Emphasizing Life Options

Comprehensive programs that focus on increasing positive self-esteem and educational and career aspirations characterize life-option programs. The primary basis of such programs is research indicating adolescents with high grades and educational or career aspirations tend to postpone sexual involvement and not become pregnant. One of the primary theoretical underpinnings of life-option programs is that adolescents must be motivated to delay child bearing, especially when surrounded by poor educational, social, and economic conditions. Life option programs attempt to foster links between education, postponing pregnancy, and career opportunities for at-risk adolescents. These programs, which are usually sponsored by a community agency, often occur as an after-school format involving small-group discussion and support. Program goals include (a) reducing school suspension, dropout rates, and unintended pregnancy and (b) increasing educational aspirations, life planning, and career goal setting.

Evaluations of life-option programs have suggested initial short-term effects in reducing school dropout and adolescent pregnancy rates. However, long-term data suggested that over time these positive benefits were no longer evident and pregnancy rates returned to preintervention rates (AGI, 1994). Though conceptually it is reasonable to believe that attention to the motivational elements of teen pregnancy makes sense, more research on life-option programs needs to occur.

Multicomponent Collaborative School-Community Programs

Because available research points to numerous contributive factors in adolescent pregnancy, multicomponent prevention programs are supported as a viable intervention alternative (St. Lawrence et al., 1995). Multicomponent programs may incorporate (a) imparting knowledge, (b) enhancing cognitive and behavioral competencies (e.g., decision making, assertiveness), (c) exploring motivational elements and future options (e.g., values clarification), (d) providing sexually active teens access to contraceptives, and (e) promoting a positive social and community network (Robinson et al., 1993; Stoiber et al., in press). The intent of multicomponent programs is to use a competency-building model grounded in developmental, social, and cognitive-behavioral theory (Robinson et al., 1993). Generally, sessions span from 10 weeks to 2 years. Ideally, this school-based approach constitutes a psychosocial intervention that is coordinated and/or implemented by a school psychologist, social worker, or other mental health professional. Program facilitators should be comfortable both with adolescents and with sexuality issues and have specific training in small-group intervention. Groups consist of 8 to 10 homogeneous-gender students, who meet each week on a regular basis. Because multicomponent programs often incorporate a therapeutic or counseling component, an open relationship among group members and the facilitator is considered critical.

One multicomponent program, Teens Learning to Cope (TLC), spans 13 weeks and targets skill areas such as self-esteem enhancement, human relationships and social values clarification, sexual-social decision making, sexual assertiveness, and birth control methods (Robinson et al., 1993). In TLC a collaborative working relationship is established allowing a diverse group of planners (e.g., school officials, students, community leaders) through a variety of feedback loops (e.g., staff meetings at school, community group meetings, one-to-one student interviews) to develop the program's goals and construct the program's content. To encourage commitment and program bonding, all involved parties are encouraged to share their values and preferences. Evaluation data supported intervening with males, who showed the most promising changes. Male TLC participants were significantly more likely to report use of effective birth control, to demonstrate knowledge of contraception, and to develop problem-solving skills in sexual social situations. TLC findings for female participants were less impressive. Although when compared to wait-list control participants, the TLC female participants demonstrated greater knowledge of contraception, significant differences were not noted on other important sexual behavior variables (condom usage, problem-solving skills). The greater incidence of sexual activity among male participants may explain the more powerful findings related to their condom usage. Nonetheless, TLC represents one of the first programs to target adolescent males and yields important data to support future efforts aimed at them.

In a recent study by St. Lawrence et al. (1995), support was found for a multicomponent cognitive-behavioral intervention that targeted African American adolescents. The intervention combined education with behavioral skills training (e.g., correct condom use, sexual assertion, problem solving, risk recognition). When compared to participants who received information alone, adolescents involved in the combined education and skill-training program had reduced unprotected intercourse and increased condom-protected behavior. Furthermore, sexual risk reduction continued at one-year follow-up for the skill-trained group. St. Lawrence found that 31% of youth in the education group who were abstinent at baseline had initiated sexual activity one year later. In contrast, only 11% of comparable adolescents from the skills-training program were sexually active.

Interventions for Pregnant and Parenting Adolescents

Schools represent a critical site for service delivery and service coordination for pregnant and parenting teens. Intervention programs for pregnant and parenting students should be varied to meet the diverse social, educational, and cultural needs of these at-risk youth. A variety of opportunities for intervention are appropriate for school settings, including (a) individual counseling, (b) parent education groups, (c) social support groups, and (d) groups focusing on the parent-child relationship. School psychologists can play an essential role in designing, coordinating, and implementing intervention services. See Stoiber et al. (in press) for a more expansive description of intervention groups for pregnant and parenting teens.

Interventions for pregnant teens may address the following issues: (a) basic knowledge related to human reproduction and body changes during pregnancy; (b) pregnancy continuation and adoption options; (c) nutrition education; (d) effects of risk-taking behaviors such as smoking, drinking, and doing drugs; (e) expectations and fears about labor and delivery; and (f) family coping and relationship problems. Many of these issues lend themselves to a group approach, which permit more efficient use of the school psychologist's time and resources.

Interventions for parenting teens may focus on several issues especially relevant for this group of students. One primary intervention aim is to help adolescent parents continue their education. Because adolescents who have a second child show a much greater likelihood of school dropout (AGI, 1994), avoidance of subsequent pregnancy emerges as an important topic. In early intervention sessions, topics such as coping with a newborn, bonding, and family change might be covered. Beliefs, expectations, and knowledge about child development are also useful areas to discuss with parenting teens. Peer and family support are also critical foci of intervention efforts for parenting adolescents. In addition, economic needs, educational and career development, and job training are usually included in effective parent intervention programs (Stoiber et al., in press). A final focus of adolescent parent interventions targets the young parents' behavioral functioning and attitudes. Relationship-focused intervention components attempt to improve quality of attachment, behavioral involvement, and parenting practices; these are often facilitated through guided parent-child activities (e.g., shared snack time, game and song activities, caregiving role plays). Increased attention by school psychologists to the development and evaluation of adolescent parent intervention is needed to determine program outcomes.

Future Directions

More research is needed to better understand the transition to sexual activity and adolescent pregnancy. In particular, more empirical attention should be aimed at clarifying the relationship between ethnic-minority status and adolescent pregnancy. Little is known about why some at-risk adolescents become parents whereas others with similar risk characteristics do not. Empirical knowledge on what places an adolescent at particular risk for becoming pregnant is essential to developing useful prevention programs. Clearly, increased sensitivity to the needs and realities of at-risk youth is required to construct socially valid and meaningful pathways to preventing adolescent pregnancy. Similarly, active participation in intervention work with pregnant and parenting teens by school psychologists appears as an important goal for the profession. Schools and school psychologists must be an integral partner in pregnancy prevention and intervention to develop system-level intervention and change.

Summary

Sexual activity is increasing among all American youth. A compelling list of negative social, economic, and health consequences continues to be associated with early sexual intercourse, pregnancy, and parenting. Concern about unprotected sexual activity has especially become heightened due to its link to STDs and AIDS. Obviously, both the societal context and consequences of adolescent sexual activity and pregnancy must be further explored. If American society is serious about preventing adolescent pregnancy, then policy and political support for broad-based intervention programs should occur. Such programs need to be based on current understanding about contributive factors and situations associated with adolescent sexual activity, pregnancy, and parenting. The apparent shift in recent years of conceptualizing adolescent pregnancy as one facet in a constellation of adolescent risk behavior holds promise (Small & Luster, 1994). Though schools cannot be solely responsible for program implementation, they serve as a critical resource due to their unique capacity to reach a broad spectrum of youth.

The manner in which pathways to pregnancy prevention are constructed can be diverse. Choices about program content and design carry poignant ramifications, both for the program's implementation and its effects. In considering the possible approaches to prevention of adolescent pregnancy, no single approach emerges as appropriate for all teens in all schools. To date, the most effective programs appear to be those that have multiple goals and focus on increasing reproductive knowledge, improving social assertion and decision-making skills, promoting an adolescent's motivation to avoid risky sexual behavior and pregnancy, and developing their career goals and life options (AGI, 1994; Stoiber, 1995). Recent studies suggest that competency-based sexuality education does not increase levels of adolescents' sexual activity (St. Lawrence et al., 1995).

Because the contributive factors leading to early pregnancy and parenting tend to be complex, multimodal intervention strategies are needed to target individual risk characteristics, including poor communication patterns with parents and persuasive peers, co-existing risk behaviors, lack of a school identity, low academic or career aspirations, coping issues, and unrealistic attitudes about early pregnancy and parenting. Intervention work with pregnant and parenting students is a challenging task. The developmental needs of these adolescents should be addressed through coordinated assessment and monitoring of their psychosocial and schooling needs.

A collaborative web across schools, parents, community agencies, and community leaders is essential for ensuring powerful and effective pregnancy prevention and intervention. A need for programs having a valid theoretical base, as well as more applied research on adolescent pregnancy, prevention, and intervention looms widely. The overwhelming societal consequences of adolescent pregnancy make it imperative that resources, both at the level of individual school psychologists and at the level of institutional systems, be directed to further prevention and intervention efforts. Perhaps only through the concerted commitment of educators, school psychologists, and other mental health workers can at-risk adolescents be prevented from taking the hazardous path toward unprotected sexual activity and too early pregnancy.

Recommended Resources

Alan Guttmacher Institute. (1994). *Sex and America's teenagers.* New York: Author.
This latest report by The Alan Guttmacher Institute (AGI) is based on more than a decade of research, analysis, and thought by AGI staff members and researchers. Within this nearly 100-page report is an extensive compendium of research and statistics related to the "problem" of adolescent pregnancy and parenting, the risks of unprotected sexual behavior and unin-

tended pregnancy, outcomes of adolescent pregnancies, and organized responses to adolescent sexual and reproductive behavior. It is considered an invaluable resource for any individual who has contact with preadolescents and adolescents, especially those who desire greater understanding of adolescent pregnancy and parenting.

Robinson, W. L., Watkins-Ferrell, P., Davis-Scott, P., & Ruch-Ross, H. S. (1993). Preventing teenage pregnancy. In D. S. Glenwick & L. A. Jason (Eds.), *Promoting health and mental health in children, youth, and families* (pp. 99–124). New York: Springer.

This chapter was written for scholars, students, and practitioners wishing for an overview of specific contextual issues related to adolescent pregnancy. It focuses on significant factors that impact on the problem of teenage pregnancy and parenting. In addition, there is a brief overview of strategies for preventing early pregnancy, including sexuality-education programs, skill-based programs, and life-option programs. Realistic information is contained in an in-depth description and analysis of the process of establishing a school-based, multicomponent, pregnancy-prevention program known as Teens Learning to Cope (TLC).

Stoiber, K. C., Anderson, A. J., & Schowalter, D. S. (in press). Group prevention and intervention with pregnant and parenting adolescents. In K. C. Stoiber & T. R. Kratochwill (Eds.), *Group prevention and intervention in school and community.* Needham Heights, MA: Allyn & Bacon.

The purpose of this chapter is to provide students and practitioners with practical suggestions for group-oriented prevention and intervention of adolescent pregnancy. Following a discussion of current thinking and research on issues associated with adolescent pregnancy, the authors offer an empirically based rationale for group interventions. In addition, practical guidelines for designing and implementing multicomponent, group prevention and intervention strategies are outlined. A unique feature of this chapter is the inclusion of actual goals, techniques, and scripts for conducting groups aimed at preventing teen pregnancy.

Stoiber, K. C., & Houghton, T. G. (1994). Adolescent mothers' cognitions and behaviors as at-risk indicators. *School Psychology Quarterly, 9,* 295–316.

This article presents research on the relation between what adolescent mothers' think and do and their child's social-emotional competence. Findings highlight the importance of adolescent mothers' attitudes and beliefs in affecting the development of their child. The discussion section presents useful information for designing interventions for adolescent parents and their children.

Trad, P. V. (1993). Adolescent pregnancy: An intervention challenge. *Child Psychiatry and Human Development, 24,* 99–113.

After reviewing the contributive influences on adolescent pregnancy, Trad presents a theoretical perspective of adolescent pregnancy as a form of risk-taking behavior. In addition, he offers a developmental analysis helpful in understanding the experience of pregnancy and parenting for an adolescent. A specific intervention strategy, known as previewing, is dis-cussed as a method for assisting pregnant adolescents in envisioning future outcomes and for developing coping techniques.

References

Alan Guttmacher Institute. (1994). *Sex and America's teenagers.* New York: Author.

Byrne, D., Kelley, K., & Fisher, W. A. (1993). Unwanted teenage pregnancies: Incidence, interpretation, and intervention. *Applied & Preventive Psychology, 2,* 101–113.

Carlson, C. I., Paavola, J., & Talley, R. (1995). Historical, current, and future models of schools as health care delivery settings. *School Psychology Quarterly, 10,* 184–202.

Center for Population Options. (1992). *Teenage pregnancy and too early childbearing: Public costs, personal consequences* (5th ed.). Washington, DC: Author.

Cervera, N. J. (1993). Decision making for pregnant adolescents: Applying reasoned action theory to research and treatment. *Families in Society, 73,* 355–365.

Davis, S. (1989). Pregnancy in adolescents. *Pediatric Clinics of North America, 36,* 665–668.

DiClemente, R. J., Durbin, M., Siegel, D., Krasnovsky, F., Lazarus, N., & Comacho, T. (1992). Determinants of condom use among junior high school students in a minority, inner-city school district. *Pediatrics, 89,* 197–202.

Dryfoos, J. G. (1994). *Full-service schools.* San Francisco: Jossey-Bass.

Freeman, E. W., & Rickels, K. (1993). *Early childbearing.* Newbury Park, CA: Sage.

Furstenberg, F., Brooks-Gunn, J., & Chase-Lansdale, L. (1989). Teenaged pregnancy and childbearing. *American Psychologist, 44,* 313–320.

Geronimus, A. T., & Korenman, S. (1991). *The socioeconomic consequences of teen childbearing reconsidered.* Cambridge, MA: National Bureau of Economic Research.

Hayes, C. (Ed.). (1987). *Risking the future: Adolescent sexuality, pregnancy, and child-bearing* (Vol. 1). Washington, DC: National Academy.

Jones, E. F., Forrest, J. D., Godmen, N., Henshaw, S. K., Lincoln, R., Rosoff, J. I., Westoff, C. F., & Wulf, D. (1985). Teenage pregnancy in developed countries: Determinants and policy implications. *Family Planning Perspectives, 17,* 53–62.

Kazdin, A. E. (1993). Adolescent mental health. *American Psychologist, 48,* 127–141.

Kirby, D., Waszak, C., & Ziegler, J. (1991). Six school-based clinics: Their reproductive health services and impact on sexual behavior. *Family Planning Perspectives, 23,* 6–16.

Males, M. (1994). Poverty, rape, adult/teen sex: Why pregnancy prevention programs don't work. *Phi Delta Kappan, 54,* 407–410.

Mech, F. (1986). Pregnant adolescents: Communicating the adoption option. *Child Welfare, 65,* 555–567.

Miller, B. C., Card, J. J., Paikoff, R. L., & Peterson, J. L. (1992). *Preventing adolescent pregnancy.* Newbury Park, CA: Sage.

Robinson, W. L., Watkins-Ferrell, P., Davis-Scott, P., & Ruch-Ross, H. S. (1993). Preventing teenage pregnancy. In

D. S. Glenwick & L. A. Jason (Eds.), *Promoting health and mental health in children, youth, and families* (pp. 99–124) New York: Springer.

Small, S. A., & Luster, T. (1994). Adolescent sexual activity: An ecological, risk-factor approach. *Journal of Marriage and the Family, 56,* 181–192.

Sommer, K., Whitman, T. L., Borkowski, J. G., Schellenbach, C., Maxwell, S., & Keogh, D. (1993). Cognitive readiness and adolescent parenting. *Developmental Psychology, 29,* 389–398.

Sonenstein, F. L., Pleck, J. H., & Ku, L. C. (1991). Levels of sexual activity among adolescent males in the United States. *Family Planning Perspectives, 23,* 162–167.

St. Lawrence, J. S., Brasfield, T. L., Jefferson, K. W., Alleyne, E., O'Bannon, R. E., & Shirley, A. (1995). Cognitive-behavioral intervention to reduce African American adolescents risk for HIV infection. *Journal of Consulting and Clinical Psychology, 63,* 221–237.

Stoiber, K. C. (1995). Using research on adolescent pregnancy to construct prevention pathways. *The School Psychologist, 49,* 56–57.

Stoiber, K. C., & Anderson, A. J. (1996). Behavioral assessment of coping strategies in young children at-risk, developmentally delayed, and typically developing. *Early Education and Development, 7,* 25–42.

Stoiber, K. C., Anderson, A. J., & Schowalter, D. S. (in press). Group prevention and intervention with pregnant and parenting adolescents. In K. C. Stoiber & T. R. Kratochwill (Eds.), *Group prevention and intervention in school and community.* Needham Heights, MA: Allyn & Bacon.

Stoiber, K. C., & Houghton, T. G. (1994). Adolescent mothers' cognitions and behaviors as at-risk indicators. *School Psychology Quarterly, 9,* 295–316.

Trad, P. V. (1994). Teenage pregnancy: Seeking patterns that promote family harmony. *The American Journal of Family Therapy, 22,* 42–56.

Wasserman, G. A., Rauh, V. A., Brunelli, S. A., Garcia-Castro, M., & Necos, B. (1990). Psychosocial attributes and life experiences of disadvantaged minority mothers: Age and ethnic variations. *Child Development, 61,* 566–580.

Zabin, L. S., Hirsch, M. B., Smith, E. A., Streett, R, & Hardy, J. B. (1986). Evaluation of pregnancy prevention program for urban teenagers. *Family Planning Perspectives. 18,* 119–126.

59

Families of Children with Disabilities

Kelly A. Powell-Smith
Stephanie A. Stollar
University of South Florida

Background and Development

During the 1991–1992 school year, approximately 4.9 million children and youth with disabilities (ages 3 through 21) were served in schools in the United States (U.S. Bureau of the Census, 1994). Historically, the primary responsibility for care of children with disabilities has alternated between families and institutions (Newman, 1991). The current trend in the United States is away from institutional treatment of people with disabilities and toward more community-based care. Community-based services (e.g., Easter Seals, Association for Retarded Citizens, community mental health centers) assist parents in shouldering the responsibility for care of their children with disabilities. Although families may no longer have the full responsibility for care of children with disabilities, family participation and the rights of parents and children are protected in laws such as Public Law 94-142, the Education for All Handicapped Children Act (EHA, 1977), Public Law 99-457 (the 1986 amendments to EHA, 1986), Public Law 101-476 the Individuals with Disabilities Education Act (IDEA, 1991), and the Americans with Disabilities Act (ADA, 1991).

Federal laws including IDEA acknowledge the important role that families play in their children's education by requiring schools to actively seek parent participation in processes like developing Individual Education Plans (IEPs). Federal legislation also has expanded the role of school psychologists and other school professionals to include service to younger children as they progress from home to school and to older students as they transition from school to work through the passage of Public Law 99-457. This legislation increased the emphasis on family involvement in children's education by requiring collaborative relationships between school professionals and families of children with disabilities.

In 1992, more than 32% of school-aged children with disabilities were served in general education classrooms (U.S. Bureau of the Census, 1994). As special education continues to move toward inclusion of children with disabilities and expanded general education alternatives, the need for school-based professionals skilled at working with families of children with disabilities becomes more critical. No longer are children with disabilities the sole responsibility of special educators or staff of residential facilities. To a large extent, the success of a child with a disability is related to the environment's ability to adapt to the child's special developmental needs both at school and at home. Families of children with disabilities face many unique challenges, in addition to the typical rewards and difficulties of parenting. It is the responsibility of school-based professionals to develop an awareness of the complex issues confronting families of children with disabilities, so that they can assist families and schools in creating environments where children can be successful.

To work closely with families, professionals need to move beyond the traditional focus on mothers and their children with disabilities. Family can be defined more broadly as "two or more people who regard themselves as a family and who perform some of the functions that families typically perform. These people may or may not be related by blood or marriage and may or may not usually live together" (Turnbull, Turnbull, Shank, & Leal, 1995, p. 24–25). Professionals also require a framework for understanding families' complexity. Family-systems theory (Minuchin, 1974; Turnbull & Turnbull, 1990) provides such a framework. The theory maintains that family structure is composed of four family subsystems: marital, sibling, parental, and extrafamilial. Effective family functioning depends on the clarity of family boundaries and rules as well as family cohesiveness and flexibility during life-cycle changes. The interrelatedness of the subsystems is central to family-systems theory. Life events, such as the birth of a child with a disability, will affect not only the parents, but also the siblings, grandparents, and family friends. An important implication of the family-systems framework is that professionals are part of the extrafamilial subsystem and therefore affect each family member, even though they may be involved directly with only one family member.

Family Reactions Across the Life Span

Just as all families do not respond to the birth of a child in the same way, all families do not respond to having a child with a disability in the same way. Although researchers have attempted to document the ways families respond to having a child with a disability (e.g., Friedrich & Friedrich, 1981; Kazak & Marvin, 1984), it is not possible to be aware of all potential family reactions, and it is not recommended to predict a family's reaction based on child or family characteristics (Bailey, Blasco, & Simeonsson, 1992). Anticipation of a continual cycle of adjustment and adaptation may be more appropriate. Individual families may experience and/or re-experience stress at various stages as the result of their own individual characteristics, needs, and circumstances. Professionals should recognize that each family has unique needs and concerns and support the family in accessing resources and developing coping strategies. Facilitation of and support for the family's strengths and capacity to engage resources may be the most significant role for school professionals (Dunst, Trivette, & Deal, 1988; Laborde & Seligman, 1991).

Awareness of the components of family needs and concerns begins with a general understanding of events and experiences across the child's life span. The challenges facing families of children with disabilities may be ongoing throughout the child's life. Thus, a primary goal of professionals is to empower the family to work for continual environmental adaptations that will address their needs.

Anticipation of Birth

Differences in parents' initial reactions to the diagnosis of a disability may be related to factors and events that occur prior to the child's birth. Parents may view their child as an extension of themselves, a chance to fulfill their own unachieved dreams (Garguilo, 1985). During pregnancy, parents develop an image of the unborn child. This image often involves the desire for a perfect baby and the fear of having a child with a disability (Ross, 1964). These dreams and anxieties are shared with family, friends, and doctors who attempt to reassure the parents by discounting worries about the baby's health. Even with a prenatal diagnosis of a disability, parents may still hope that there has been a mistake.

Diagnosis

The birth of a child with a disability, or the diagnosis of a disability later in the child's life, may challenge the family's hopes, dreams, and expectations for the child. The contradiction between the family's expectations and reality can present a serious challenge to the family's coping abilities (Garguilo, 1985). The realization that their child has a disability may produce a wide range of emotions from families. This response should be considered natural and typical. Negative reactions to diagnosis are understandable given our culture's negative stereotypes about people with disabilities, parental fantasies and expectations that may need adjustment, and the often secretive or negative reactions of delivery room doctors and nurses (Darling, 1991). Not only do parents have negative reactions to the diagnosis but the impact may be felt throughout the family system. However, not all families react with the same degree of emotional response. It is important to acknowledge that a period of emotional adjustment should be expected, regardless of the nature of the disability or the time of diagnosis (Garguilo). This acknowledgment is especially important for school professionals who may work with families in circumstances surrounding an accident or identifying the need for special education.

After Diagnosis

One of the most widely reported parental needs at the time of diagnosis is the request for information about their child's disability (Kornblatt & Heinrich, 1985). Because uncertainty leads to worry, families want and need information from professionals (Laborde & Seligman, 1991). Additionally, parents may request information about the possible course of the child's development and practical strategies for home management (Upshur, 1991). Parents need to have accurate information so they can begin to adjust expectations if necessary and, if they choose, take an active role in their child's education. Many families feel powerless until they start to do something to assist the child's development.

Following a diagnosis, some families seek further evaluation. Although this may be interpreted by professionals as denial, Laborde and Seligman (1991) suggest that it may reflect the continued search for more information. Families also may seek additional evaluation to gain a particular diagnosis that will give them access to services. Professionals should attempt to determine the function of the family's "shopping" behavior before assuming they are denying the child's diagnosis.

Infancy

When the child's disability is apparent at birth or soon after, the process of attachment may be impeded by the child's appearance, unpleasant crying, atypical activity level, feeding difficulties, or life-threatening medical conditions (Barnard & Kelly, 1990; Blacher, 1984; Collins-Moore, 1984). If the infant does not respond to the parents, the parent will not be rewarded and may not continue to seek interaction with the infant (Stone & Chesney, 1978). Most parents, however, do form strong attachments with their children regardless of the nature of the child's disability (Stone & Chesney).

Early childhood

Many children with severe disabilities begin receiving formal medical and educational services at birth or a very young age. In such cases, their families will be introduced to a system of care before school entry. When a child's disability is diagnosed at a later age, the preschool years may be the family's first encounter with the special education system. Locating an appropriate early intervention program can be a difficult task for some families.

There are several reasons why the preschool years may be when a child's disability is first identified. The family may become concerned about their child when they notice that typical developmental milestones are not being achieved, especially in families where older siblings are used as a reference point. The differences between children also may become noticeable during this age period because children should be increasing their social interactions. Parents may observe other same-age children and notice that their child is not performing at the same level.

School-age

Alternately, entry into public school may be the family's first encounter with the special education system. Special education legislation entitles children with disabilities to a free and appropriate public education in the least restrictive environment. However, some families have difficulty securing appropriate educational services for their children. A frequent concern for families with children in the primary grades is success in learning. Families want to be sure their children are learning and achieving at a pace consistent with their abilities. It may be particularly difficult for families of children with disabilities to negotiate what they view as an appropriate educational program when the special education system appears to be adversarial and inflexible.

Adolescence

All adolescents struggle with issues related to their physical development and independence. However, a disability may limit the level of independence a child achieves. Continuing dependence may be highlighted for the family during these years as they struggle with issues related to the child's independent functioning beyond the immediate-family support system. Depending upon the nature of the disability, families may need to deal with the following issues during the child's adolescence: (a) planning for the transition from school to work, (b) securing appropriate housing, (c) navigating social issues related to peers and dating, and (d) arranging for the child's support after parents' death.

Summary

Individual families of children with disabilities may or may not experience the challenges identified in the developmental stages just outlined. Family needs can be complex and varied. The most reasonable goal for professionals may be to develop (a) a basic understanding of common needs of families with children with disabilities and (b) the strategies for identifying needs unique to individual families. Fostering a working environment of mutual respect will promote the family's confidence and skills for taking the lead in addressing their own needs.

Problems and Implications

Families of children with disabilities encounter a variety of needs across the life span of the child. Some of these needs may be unique to certain members of the family, such as parents or siblings. Other issues impact the family as a unit, such as financial and respite-care needs.

Needs of Specific Family Members

The child with the disability

The needs of children with disabilities vary greatly with the unique skills and attributes of each child, the severity of the disability, the environmental conditions, and the demands placed upon the child. Therefore, any discussion of needs must be tempered by respect for the individual variability that exists.

Children with disabilities may have daily-care, educational, vocational, informational, and social-emotional needs beyond those of children without disabilities. Many children with disabilities have daily-care needs which include medical and health-care concerns (e.g., dialysis, physical therapy, medication). Thus, children with disabilities also may require more frequent hospitalization than other children (Darling, 1991). As the child with the disability ages, needs related to transportation (e.g., knowing how to use public transportation because the person is unable to drive a car) and finding appropriately supportive housing (e.g., group home or assisted living center) become important.

With more early intervention services now available, educational needs within the service delivery system become a priority shortly after the child is diagnosed (Darling, 1991). Children with disabilities may have needs in traditional academic skill areas (e.g., reading, math, writing), independent living skills, and specific vocational or career-related skills (e.g., computer skills). As the child approaches adolescence and early adulthood, needs may shift more toward finding appropriate housing, finding suitable job opportunities, and planning for future financial needs (Darling, 1991). Children with disabilities also may require extra assistance in learning how to interact appropriately with peers. As children get older, their public behavior may become more of a concern for parents while concerns regarding physical needs tend to decrease (Baxter, as cited in Darling, 1991). Coupled with this concern is the likelihood that these children may experience some stigma related to their disability which may limit their social opportunities in the community.

Children with disabilities often have communication needs related to their academic and social-emotional needs. They may require adaptations, such as the use of a hearing aid, or need speech and language services. Finally, the child with the disability may have informational needs. Gaining information and understanding the nature of their disabilities as well as their own strengths and limitations are part of developing self-advocacy skills (Turnbull & Turnbull, 1990). School psychologists are a logical choice to help meet these informational needs. They can explain the nature and future implications of the disability in understandable terms, and they can answer any questions the child might have.

Siblings

Meeting the needs of siblings is an important part of serving families of children with disabilities. The first step in this process is recognizing the feelings and needs of siblings (Turnbull & Turnbull, 1990). Needs of siblings of children with disabilities fall into two broad categories: informational and social-emotional. Siblings have a need for information beginning at the time of diagnosis and continuing through the life span. This information can help siblings understand the nature of their brother or sister's disability and alleviate worries and anxieties they may experience. For example, siblings may wonder if they carry a defective gene and worry that they may become parents of a child with a disability (Featherstone, 1980; Garland, 1993).

In the social-emotional area, siblings may need to learn coping skills for dealing with less attention from their parents, while having to cope with the emotional impact of having a brother or sister with a disability (Harris, 1987; Mullins, 1987). These coping skills are important as parents may become less sensitive to their other children because their attention is focused on the needs of the child with the disability (Turnbull & Turnbull, 1990). As a result, siblings may not have as much interaction with parents as they might need or want, and they may be asked to defer their needs (Siegel & Silverstein, 1994). Additional problems can include (a) siblings thinking that their assistance is taken for granted, (b) siblings resenting the differing behavioral expectations for the child with the disability, and (c) siblings feeling embarrassed by their brother or sister with the disability (Siegal & Silverstein, 1994).

Siblings may spend less time in social activities with their peers and/or less time in activities outside the family, such as participating in scouting or organized clubs and sports. One reason for this decreased time may be because of increased caregiving demands for their brother or sister with a disability. As the sibling ages, he

or she will need to cope with increased demands in child care and income needs (Harris, 1987; Siegal & Silverstein, 1994). As adults, siblings may be expected to have some degree of lifetime responsibility for a brother or sister with a disability. Feelings of distress about leaving other family members with the burden of care for the child with the disability may complicate the process of siblings separating from their families (Harris, 1987).

Despite the various issues siblings of children with disabilities encounter, a number of positive outcomes also may result from this experience. Siblings sometimes report that they benefited from growing up with a brother or sister with a disability because they have become more altruistic, empathetic, and understanding of others with problems (Siegal & Silverstein, 1994). Also, siblings may learn to be less judgmental of others (Turnbull & Turnbull, 1990), and relationships with siblings may serve as the model for future peer relationships (Siegal & Silverstein).

Parents

Parents also have needs in the informational and social-emotional areas. For example, parents need accurate information to understand their child's disability because diagnostic ambiguity and the lack of congruence between a child's appearance and parental behavioral expectations for the child can lead to stress (Minnes, 1988). Handbooks specifically for parenting children with disabilities are less available than more general parenting handbooks. Also, reliance on information from family and friends can be problematic because their frame of reference may be so different as to make their advice much less useful (Suelzle & Keenan, 1981). Even other parents of children with disabilities may not be adequate informational resources because children with disabilities vary so greatly (Wikler, 1981). Thus, parents may come to rely more upon the professional community for information (Suelzle & Keenan, 1981). For example, in one survey of 330 parents of children with developmental disabilities, parents of young children relied more heavily on recommendations of doctors than parents of older children to find appropriate schools and programs for their children (Suelzle & Keenan, 1981). Parents also require information about provisions for their child under federal and state laws (e.g., IDEA) as well as their legal rights. This knowledge can help promote a more active role in their child's education and help parents serve as advocates for their children.

Parents' need for information is considered to be ongoing because the information for one situation does not necessarily generalize to the next (Wikler, 1981). School professionals may be the most consistent informational resource available to parents across the life span of the child. In fact, parents may increasingly seek the recommendations of school personnel over the course of the child's life (Suelzle & Keenan, 1981).

The social-emotional needs of parents parallel those of siblings and the child with the disability. For example, they may encounter stigma and social isolation. These problems may become compounded as the child ages. Suelzle and Keenan (1981) found that parents of older children believed their neighbors were less likely to accept their children in roles such as friends, coworkers, or fellow citizens. Parental hopes for their child may be defeated by this lack of acceptance of their child by those in their community (Fewell, 1991).

Parents may experience re-emergent grief during times such as holidays and family reunions, when they hear parents of children without disabilities discuss their children (Wikler, 1981). Additionally, emotional stress may occur as parents realize that certain parental roles cannot be undertaken with this child (e.g., coaching in a particular sport). Grief will tend to emerge when the discrepancy between reality and expectation is large (Wikler, 1981).

Conflicting research exists regarding the impact that the stress of raising children with disabilities has on the marital relationship. A study of families of eighth-grade students with and without disabilities (Hodapp & Krasner, 1994–1995) found a higher incidence of divorce and separation among the families of children with disabilities. Others claim that having a child with a disability strengthens marriages (Turnbull & Turnbull, 1990). Another study, in which parents of nearly 2,000 children with disabilities were interviewed, found that the effect on marriage may be much less than the effect on the family in other areas (e.g., job situation; Palfrey, Walker, Butler, & Singer, 1989). Only a small percentage (4.1% to 15%) of the parents interviewed said that having a child with a disability in the family had *any* effect on their marriage. One concern with much of the research on marital stress is that the degree of marital stress prior to the birth of a child with a disability has not been taken into account (Minnes, 1988).

Parental coping may impact family functioning. Parents who are struggling to cope may not be good role models for their children, and the degree to which expressions of emotion are permitted may affect the reactions of other family members such as siblings (Siegal & Silverstein, 1994). Conversely, parents who learn to cope effectively may be excellent role models for their children and others. Mullins (1987), in an analysis of books written by parents of children with disabilities, found that despite incredible demands on these families' physical and financial resources, very few of the parent authors summarized the course of their lives as being a negative experience. In fact, many viewed their lives as being more meaningful because of the experience.

Extended family members

"Since the early 1980's, there has been a growing recognition that a child's disability or illness will affect more than the child and his or her mother" (Meyer, 1993, p. 88). Increasingly, the term "family" is replacing the term "parents" in literature about children with disabilities. Despite the broader family focus, extended family members such as grandparents, aunts, and uncles still are excluded frequently in the literature (Meyer, 1993). Extended families may consist of relatives (aunts, uncles, grandparents), friends, neighbors, and professionals. Extended family members provide a valuable support network to parents and positively affect the quality of life for the child with the disability (Turnbull & Turnbull, 1990). Therefore, extended family members' needs are important for school professionals to consider.

Extended family members experience needs similar to those of parents. For example, extended family members have a need for (a) information and education (e.g., the nature of the disability, available programs and services); (b) empowerment (e.g., training in strategies for being supportive of the child and family); and (c) support and encouragement (e.g., from other grandparents who share similar experiences; Meyer, 1993). Parents express concern over grandparents who have difficulties in seeing the "good things" involved in having a child with a disability (Garland, 1993). Grandparents may not know when, or even how, to help or they may want to help when the parents believe such help is not necessary. Professionals should encourage grandparents and other extended family members to participate in the child's education (e.g., participation in IEP conferences, visiting the child's classroom; Turnbull & Turnbull, 1990). This kind of participation may help extended family members gain a more complete picture of the child, access information that otherwise may not be provided to them, and become a better support resource to the immediate family.

Unfortunately, extended family members rarely have a peer group with whom to share common experiences regarding a family member's disability. Despite the growth of parent-to-parent support groups, a much smaller percentage of other family member support programs exist. Yet, extended family members (e.g., grandparents) need such support services for many of the same reasons parents do (e.g., emotional support to deal with grief). Because of this lack of access to peers, extended family members often learn to cope in isolation (Meyer, 1993).

The Needs of the Family as a Unit

As discussed previously, any family member may experience social-emotional and informational needs as well as prolonged caregiving demands. "Children with disabilities inevitably challenge families by making inordinate demands on their time, psychological well-being, relationships, economic resources, and freedom of movement" (Brantlinger, 1991, p. 250). It is important to know at which time periods families are at risk so that preventative efforts can be pursued (Wikler, 1981).

Respite care

One of the greatest needs for families is the need for respite care (Palfrey et al., 1989). Families have an on-going need for help with everyday issues, whereas help during crises apparently is easier to receive (Palfrey et al., 1989). The daily-care needs of the child with a disability may cause family members to overlook their own daily-care or socialization needs. Resources are needed especially at transition times, when families may experience several stressors at once, referred to as the pile-up factor (Minnes, 1988). In such cases, respite-care services may be helpful. Respite-care services provide temporary care for a person with a disability for a period of time (e.g., an hour, all day, or for extended periods of time; Turnbull & Turnbull, 1990). Such services can provide families with opportunities to relax and take time for themselves. Also, respite services free up time for family members to engage in socialization opportunities (e.g., going out with friends, playing sports, participating in parenting groups). These opportunities can relieve stress and serve a preventative function. Unfortunately, however, respite services sometimes are provided only in emergencies rather than on a routine basis (Upshur, 1991). In a survey of parents of children with disabilities, the need for respite care was one of the highest perceived unmet needs of parents of preschoolers and young adults (Suelzle & Keenan, 1981).

Finally, the need for respite-care services is not consistent across all families. It is *not* always the case that a child with a disability causes great stress in family functioning in daily-care or socialization areas. Family independence and flexibility may help mediate stress (Minnes, 1988) and perhaps lessen the need for respite.

Financial needs

Families of children with disabilities may experience extraordinary demands on their financial resources (Mullins, 1987). Costs, in part, depend on the type of disability, with multiple disabilities being associated with the greatest costs. Financial impact may occur both directly and indirectly. Examples of direct costs are those associated with medical bills, adaptive equipment, communication devices, changes to home architecture for accessibility purposes (Morris, 1987), tutoring or other educational supports beyond what is provided by public schools, and residential placement. Indirect costs are those associated with loss of income due to one parent needing to stay at home or take time off from work to care for the child with the disability.

According to a survey conducted by the United Cerebral Palsy Association, reported by Morris (1987), the costs of raising a child with a disability were $5,282 to $7,035 per year. These costs were *in addition to* costs associated with raising a child without a disability. However, another recent survey found no differences in extra money spent on schooling between families of eighth-grade students with and without disabilities (Hodapp & Krasner, 1994–1995).

Adding to cost-related stress on families is the often limited access parents have to appropriate health care and related services for their children with disabilities (Morris, 1987). "All too frequently they have been forced to bankrupt themselves in an effort to meet on-going health care costs" (Morris, 1987, p. 38). Some families may not have access to insurance. Even with health insurance coverage, some devices and equipment are not covered adequately and lifetime caps are often met early, leaving families without adequate coverage (Morris, 1987). Thus, financial stress often increases as the child ages.

The financial burden of caring for a child with a disability may impact family functioning in terms of stress management and coping skills as well as willingness to implement interventions for the child with the disability. When family resources are not adequate, the needs of the child with the disability may seem less immediate than the needs of the family as a whole (Dunst, Leet, & Trivette, 1988).

Cultural Diversity and the Needs of Families of Children with Disabilities

Culturally diverse families of children with disabilities have many needs in common with any family of a child with a disability. Especially pertinent to families from minority cultures are the need for adequate representation in parent organizations and the need for information to be provided in their native language (Marion, 1980). School-based professionals should allocate enough time to communicate thoroughly and without holding back information from families (Marion, 1980). Families from nonmajority cultures also may have needs and/or reactions to having a child with a disability that differ from members of the majority culture. For example, the meaning of the disability to the family varies among cultural and/or ethnic groups which, in turn, impacts their need for services (Turnbull & Turnbull, 1990). Families from minority groups "experience dual stigma—the stigma of being racially or ethnically different from the dominant culture and the stigma of having a child who is seen as 'different' because of a disability" (Rounds, Weil, & Bishop, 1994, p. 3). The overrepresentation of ethnic minority children in classes for persons with mental retardation and emotional disturbance often produces anger in family members (Marion, 1980). Because of this history of discrimination, families may be cautious in seeking information or assistance from service agencies or schools (Turnbull & Turnbull, 1990).

Alternative Actions

Communicating with Families of Children with Disabilities

The link between families and school-based professionals becomes critical when there is a child with a disability in the family. Often, however, even with the best intentions, the efforts of professionals to communicate with families are unsuccessful. Families report that professionals seem to have little empathy for the daily difficulties of parenting a child with a disability and do not value the parent's role as an acute observer of their child's developmental skills, problems, and needs (Darling, 1979; Featherstone, 1980; Turnbull & Turnbull, 1985). Communication breaks down from the professionals' viewpoint when families do not implement recommendations and are then viewed as resistant, unwilling to participate, and part of the child's problem rather than part of the professional team.

Professionals need to consider the multiple needs of families and the complex reasons for difficulties in forming effective partnerships. It may be tempting to see the child with a disability as the "problem" in a family. An alternative framework for collaborative work with families includes the ecological perspective supported by family-systems theory (e.g., Dunst, Trivette, & Deal, 1988; Powers, 1991) and school-based consultation (e.g., Gutkin & Curtis, 1990). In addition to a theoretical framework for understanding families, professionals must have effective collaboration skills. School-based consultation provides a useful model for working with families. The foundation of the consultation service-delivery model is a nonhierarchical, collaborative relationship for the purpose of mutual problem solving (Gutkin & Curtis). Professionals are cautioned to avoid an expert role by recognizing families as the true experts on their children. This recognition is operationalized by including the family in meaningful ways in all decision making throughout the referral, assessment, and strategy development stages.

Delivering Sensitive Information to Families

Parents often report that professionals seem to experience difficulty informing them of their child's disability. This difficulty may occur because the professional's first interaction with the family may be at the time of initial diagnosis (Upshur, 1991). It is especially stressful for a family to hear sensitive information from a stranger. When children are diagnosed, there is likely to be anger directed at the professional for being evasive, using jargon, not providing enough information, and being either too optimistic or too pessimistic (Darling, 1979; Featherstone, 1980). Guidelines for delivering sensitive information to families are included in Table 1.

Preparing Parents to Work with Agencies

Given the socio-demographic patterns and trends over the last 20 years (increased number of single-parent homes, decreased family size, high geographic mobility, etc.), families can no longer be expected to rely solely on the resources and support of extended family members (Kagan, Klugman & Zigler, 1983). A broader view of family needs has become necessary for social policy as well as educational practice. Connecting families to the network of agencies that offer services to families with children with disabilities is essential. Yet, the large number of agencies and the lack of coordination among them may present an additional challenge to the family. Boggs (1984) reported that there are as many as eight federal agencies involved with children with disabilities, each with different eligibility criteria, application procedures, services, and state administration. Although there is some overlap in services provided by various agencies, little consistency exists across states or counties, and very little coordination of services within states exists. The services traditionally provided by schools and federal agencies have focused on the needs of the child alone and have not accounted for the complexity of issues in the child's environment.

Some families are not aware of the services available in their community. School professionals often have abundant information about state and local agencies and the services they offer and about area chapters of advocacy and support groups as well as on community information and referral services. The information in Table 2 may be helpful to provide to parents when making referrals to outside agencies.

Although respite-care services may not be needed by all families, school professionals should be prepared to assist families in obtaining information about the variety of respite-care services available in their community or to assist the school's parent group in organizing such a service. School psychologists also may be able to link families of children with disabilities with other families in the area who have had similar experiences as sources of informal support.

For families to work with professionals as partners, they need to have information that will allow them to become full participants. Useful information includes (a) familiarity with the language and jargon used by educational, medical, and mental health professionals; (b) full knowledge of the rights given to parents and their children by federal and state legislation; and (c) awareness of the available service options. An important component of preparing families to work with agencies involves teaching parents how to interact with other professionals (e.g., feeling empowered to ask questions and to challenge school placement). Unfortunately, many professionals are reluctant to give parents complete information (Bailey, Buysse, Edmondson, & Smith, 1992; Minke &

Table 1 *Delivering Sensitive Information to Families*

Include the Family System	■ Allow the family to identify significant people in the child's life and to invite whom they choose to all informational and decision-making meetings.
Demonstrate Empathy	■ Put yourself in their shoes.
	■ Recognize that the family may feel overwhelmed by the amount or type of information being presented. They may be hearing the information for the first time.
	■ Schedule a private meeting space.
	■ Provide ample time for the meeting.
	■ Eliminate distractions and interruptions.
	■ Allow the expression of emotions.
Provide Accurate Information	■ Be prepared with accurate information about the child's disability.
	■ Provide printed material that the family can take home and digest in their own time.
Communicate Clearly and Honestly	■ Deliver information clearly and slowly without jargon or technical terms.
	■ Pause periodically to allow the family to ask questions.
	■ Be honest if you do not know the answer.
	■ Promise to locate the information and follow through by providing it promptly.
Follow-up	■ Schedule a follow-up meeting.
	■ Encourage the family to write out questions and concerns to bring to the next meeting.
Referral	■ Provide information about resources that allow family members to become involved with the child's disability at a level consistent with their needs and goals.

Table 2 *Information to Provide Parents When Making a Referral*

1. Purpose of the agency, name, phone number, address, and contact person.
2. Appointment procedures (including acceptance of walk-in clients, waiting lists, scheduling of appointments by nonfamily members).
3. Cost of services (including insurances accepted and sliding scales for payment).
4. Location of services (including in-home vs. agency-based, availability of transportation).
5. Required paperwork (including forms to be completed prior to first appointment, documentation that should be brought to the appointment).

Note. Adapted from Lubker (1983, p. 124) as cited in Apter (1992, p. 496).

Scott, 1995). Differences of opinion have been additional obstacles to collaboration. Regardless of agreement with the family's point of view, it is the professional's responsibility to provide information about the available alternatives and community resources.

Including Families in Assessment

Federal laws mandate the inclusion of families in the assessment process through their requirements for informed consent and participation in IEP development. Family members are a valuable resource to those conducting assessments and should be included as part of a "best practice" approach to assessment beyond these legal requirements. Such an approach is consistent with a consultative service-delivery model, NASP's Standards for the Provision of School Psychological Services (National Association of School Psychologists, 1995b) and both NASP and APA ethical standards (National Association of School Psychologists, 1995a; American Psychological Association, 1992). Including the family in the assessment process also is consistent with viewing the child within the context of the family system. Active encouragement of parents (and other family members) in the assessment and problem-solving process parallels efforts to increase home-school collaboration (Christenson, 1995).

Little argument can be raised regarding the fact that the child's family knows the child better than anyone else. Families bring valuable information about developmental milestones, what the child is like at home, which activities the child is involved in, and any interests the child has. Inclusion of parents should occur at the beginning of the assessment process rather than at the end when the assessment is complete. Including the family from the beginning allows for valuable information to be gathered that might not otherwise come to light. For example, school professionals can gain information about the family's expectations for the child, the parent's attitude toward the school system and education in general (Wise, 1995), and the child's developmental skills in home and community environments (Turnbull & Turnbull, 1990).

Including families in the assessment process accrues more than just informational benefits. By including families, they become an integral part of the problem-solving process rather than just spectators who may feel left out and frustrated by a lack of attention to their needs and input. Including families in the assessment process increases rapport and empowers families by providing them with the opportunity to ask questions about proce dural issues related to the child's assessment and to voice their concerns (Wise, 1995). When school professionals include families in the assessment process, they increase the social validity of their assessment information and open communication lines that facilitate family participation in intervention implementation.

Family Goals in Developing Plans

Including families in developing the Individual Family Service Plan (IFSP) and Individual Education Plan (IEP) is critical for developing trust and collaborative relationships between parents and professionals. Families should have the option to participate in all stages of IEP or IFSP development. After assessment information has been integrated and shared with the family, they should be given the opportunity to identify their intervention goals and priorities (Bailey, 1989). Like an IEP for preschool and school-age children, the IFSP for infants and toddlers requires a statement of the child's present functioning. The infant/toddler legislation also requires that the IFSP must include, among other things, a statement of present family strengths and needs (Bondurant-Utz & Luciano, 1994).

Family goals may be included in the IFSP if the family desires. A family goal is "any goal that involves a change in behavior or skill for a family member other than the child with a disability" (Bailey & Wolery, 1992, p. 123). It is becoming accepted practice to collaborate with families in writing family goals related directly to caring for children as well as goals related to other aspects of family functioning. Whether goals have been met should be validated by families (Dunst, Trivette, & Deal, 1988) and professionals. Family goals and services are strictly voluntary and should not be imposed by professionals.

In considering goals to be included in IEPs and IFSPs, it is suggested that service providers assess the needs of families of children with disabilities to determine the likelihood that parents will have the time and energy necessary to carry out interventions (Dunst, Leet, & Trivette, 1988). School professionals should be sensitive to financial and other needs of families in their efforts to develop IFSP and IEP goals. To help meet the financial needs of families, Turnbull and Turnbull (1990) suggest (a) connecting parents to community resources that can help with estate planning, disability benefits, or family subsidies; (b) providing information about scholarships and financial aid; and (c) making financial planning information available. Freeing families from some of the financial burden may lead to increased involvement in interventions.

Several concerns related to effective use of IEPs and IFSPs exist, including (a) the inability of professionals to write collaborative plans with each other, (b) the difficulty in writing long-range plans that will stay applicable when the family's needs change so rapidly, (c) the faulty

assumption that child-related concerns always take precedence over family needs in other areas, (d) the failure to recognize the power of informal interventions, and (e) the reliance on a case manager rather than the family to secure resources (Dunst, Trivette, & Deal, 1988).

Additional concerns have been raised by parents themselves. For example Harry, Allen, and McLaughlin (1995) reported that parents voiced concern that their children's IEPs were repetitive from one year to the next, meetings were routine, and they had little influence in the process. The five professional actions primarily found to discourage parent participation included (a) inflexibility in scheduling or notices sent out late, (b) not allowing enough time for the meetings, (c) too much emphasis on signing the documents without supporting meaningful parent participation, (d) use of language or jargon unfamiliar to the parents, and (e) team dynamics that set up a power structure or "we-them" posture that made parent advocacy efforts difficult (Harry et al., 1995). When problems like those identified by the parents in this study occur, communication between parents and school professionals breaks down, collaborative problem solving is inhibited, and it is unlikely that family goals in IEPs or IFSPs will be encouraged.

To avoid the types of concerns raised here, school professionals must change the way they work with each other and with families (Duwa, Wells, & Lalinde, 1993). Turbiville, Turnbull, Garland, and Lee (1993) suggest some best-practice indicators for IFSPs and IEPs:

1. The family is the decision maker in the process of generating the IEP or IFSP.
2. The plan has importance for family outcomes. The IEP or IFSP should reflect all the services and supports the family has identified as priorities and emphasize the need for collaboration among professionals and agencies.
3. The role of the professional should focus on helping the family meet their own needs and support them in decision making.

Facilitating Transitions

Transitional crises may occur throughout the child's life span (e.g., upon learning the diagnosis, at the time the child enters school). "Across various age phases, transition points are often stressful periods that bring new demands with which families need to cope" (Heller, 1993, p. 202). Although transition times are difficult for any family, they may be especially stressful for the family of a child with a disability. In part, additional stress is caused by transitions occurring at unexpected times or without the typical rituals or ceremonies that mark transitions for "typical" families (e.g., graduation) leading to uncertainty about the future (Turnbull & Turnbull, 1990). When transitions are delayed, occur earlier than expected (e.g., when a young child leaves home to live elsewhere), or do not occur at all (e.g., child remains living at home through adulthood), the family may experience a variety of feelings including guilt, inadequacy, and grief (Turnbull & Turnbull, 1990). Knowledge about predictable times of crisis may help reduce their impact because families may be less critical of their own reactions if they know these reactions are not unusual (Wikler, 1981).

Stress at times of transition also can be caused by a lack of planning for the child's future. Although transition planning is now a mandated requirement in a student's IEP, parents and the students themselves may choose not to participate in this process (Morningstar, Turnbull, & Turnbull, 1995). Additional concerns are (a) the planning process may not begin early enough, (b) students may not believe they are prepared for the future because of the lack of responsibility and decision-making power given to them by their families, and (c) families may not see how quickly the future actually is approaching (Morningstar et al., 1995). For these reasons, school professionals should be proactive in gaining the family's involvement early in the child's school career.

School-based professionals can help families by assisting them in planning ahead for transitions. For example, Turnbull and Turnbull (1990) suggest (a) discussing goals and objectives in terms of the child's future needs (e.g., 1 to 5 years from now); (b) arranging for parents to visit various schools and future classrooms and meet the teachers in those classrooms; and (c) familiarizing parents with possible career options and future opportunities for their child and arranging visits to potential community job sites. Family members, including extended family members, should be encouraged to help create a vision for the student's future (Morningstar et al., 1995). Despite the necessity to plan for the future, a balance needs to be achieved by ensuring that the planning is both appealing and relevant to the family and child in their current circumstances (Morningstar et al., 1995). All families should be allowed to enjoy the childhood years.

As the child reaches adolescence and young adulthood, the need for coordinated transition services becomes paramount as families begin to consider future employment and housing options. Schools might want to consider placing more emphasis than they currently are on careers found within the student's family to increase the student's motivation and interest in planning for the future (Morningstar et al., 1995). School professionals also might facilitate the ease of transitions by arranging for parents beginning the transition process to meet and talk with "veteran" parents (Turnbull & Turnbull, 1990). During childhood, helping families prepare for IEP meetings and arranging for family support groups can help family members cope with the variety of emotions they may experience during transitions.

Finally, a student's exit from the educational system and transition to adulthood can be especially difficult due to the abrupt end to mandated services. The idea of placing their adult son or daughter in a setting outside the home may be more stressful to the parents than the child (Heller, 1993). Families often play an important and ongoing role in the lives of persons with disabilities throughout their adulthood (Morningstar et al., 1995). Thus, identifying immediate and extended family members who will support the family member with the disability after his or her school exit is a vital element in transition planning (Morningstar et al., 1995). Several excellent resources have been identified by Turnbull and Turnbull (1990) to assist families with this transition. For example, *Disability and the Family: A Guide to Decisions for Adulthood* (Turnbull, Turnbull, Bronicki, Summers, & Roeder-Gordon, 1989) is a resource written specifically for families. School professionals should be mindful that some families may be so accustomed to taking one day at a time that such planning for the future actually may be stress producing (Turnbull & Turnbull, 1990).

Developing Support Groups

Support groups can play an important role in providing assistance to families of children with disabilities. During the child's early childhood years, support groups may help a variety of family members cope with the social-emotional and informational needs brought on by the diagnosis of a disability. Support groups can provide a forum for gaining skills and learning to cope with the demands of caring for a child with a disability. Support groups also provide a way for family members to benefit from other families' experiences with and knowledge about the education system and various community agencies. These groups also can provide parents and other family members with friendships that counter the social isolation they sometimes experience. When the child with a disability reaches adolescence, family support groups can help parents cope with the emotional and physical changes that occur during puberty, help families identify leisure activities available in their community, and assist families in identifying skills needed for future career or vocational settings (Turnbull & Turnbull, 1990).

Support groups for siblings can be especially helpful for (a) developing their skills in coping with less attention from their parents than they may want or desire and (b) dealing with the emotional concerns created by having a brother or sister with a disability. Such groups may allow siblings to vent their feelings in a safe environment where they know others understand and empathize. The formation of sibling-support groups may provide an avenue for increased social activities and peer interactions which tend to occur less for siblings of children with disabilities. Finally, it should be noted that support groups should not be considered a panacea as not all needs will be served by them (Meyer, 1993).

Support groups attempt to accomplish a variety of goals. Among these goals are to (a) allow family members the opportunity to meet with other family members of children with disabilities in a relaxed setting, (b) provide opportunities to discuss commonly experienced joys or concerns, (c) provide opportunities to learn how others have handled situations experienced by many family members of children with disabilities, (d) provide opportunities to learn about the implications of being a family member of a child with a disability, and (e) provide school professionals and other concerned parties with opportunities to learn more about the opportunities and concerns shared by family members of children with disabilities (adapted from Meyer & Vadasy, 1994). The actual activities designed to achieve these goals will vary depending on the population for which the support group is intended (e.g., parents, siblings, grandparents).

Published curricula are available for those interested in beginning a support program for grandparents (see Meyer & Vadasy, 1986) and siblings (see Meyer & Vadasy, 1994). Less information is available on support groups for other family members (e.g., extended family members such as aunts and uncles), although peer support programs also may be useful for these extended family members. General suggestions for developing a support group, adapted from Meyer and Vadasy (1994), are listed in Table 3.

Summary

Families of children with disabilities may encounter a wide range of experiences and challenges throughout the family's life cycle and the life span of their child. Individual differences are expected in terms of reaction to diagnosis and subsequent family needs. This individual family variation necessitates that a more individualized approach be taken in meeting the needs of families of children with disabilities. School-based professionals are encouraged to take a proactive role in assisting families in identifying their needs and accessing services to meet them. Ongoing problem solving is facilitated by developing an environment of mutual respect in which family members and school professionals become equal partners in decision making.

Authors' Notes

Both authors contributed equally to the development and completion of this book chapter.

Table 3   *Suggestions for Developing Support Groups*

Sponsors	■ Consider inviting other agencies to cosponsor your support group.
	■ Inform the cosponsoring agency about why support groups are important.
	■ Request that the cosponsoring agency send representatives to planning meetings.
	■ Encourage and seek family participation in developing the support group.
Population	■ Examine the needs of the population your support group will serve.
	■ Determine which geographic area your support group will serve.
	■ Determine if enrollment will be limited to those served by sponsoring agencies.
	■ For sibling-support groups, decide which ages will be served.
Finances	■ Determine how many people will be served by the support group.
	■ Determine if facilitators need to be hired.
	■ Examine how much materials and food will cost.
	■ Determine costs of accessing a meeting space (e.g., renting building space).
	■ Examine incidental costs (e.g., advertisements, postage, telephone).
	■ Determine if a fee will be charged to support group participants.
	■ Develop a budget.
Logistics	■ Determine the number of facilitators needed and their background.
	■ Decide on a location of the meeting place (e.g., centrally located).
	■ Determine when and how often the group will meet.
	■ Decide how the group will be advertised.
	■ Determine how to handle registrations and money.

Note. Adapted from *Sibshops: Workshops for Siblings of Children with Special Needs* by D. J. Meyer and P. F. Vadasy, 1994, Baltimore: Brookes. Copyright 1994 by Brookes. P.O. Box 10624, Baltimore, MD 21285–0624. Adapted with permission.

The authors would like to express their sincere appreciation to Cametra L. Reed for her assistance with the references and recommended resources for this chapter.

Recommended Resources

Resources for Professionals

Meyer, D. J., & Vadasy, P. F. (1994). *Sibshops: Workshops for siblings of children with special needs.* Baltimore: Brookes. *This guide serves as a helpful tool in organizing and conducting support groups, called Sibshops, for siblings of children with special needs. The first half of the book focuses on concerns in approaching such a workshop and ways to address specific needs of the children. The second half of the book introduces program games and activities which could be utilized during a support-group session. The authors include extensive appendices covering a Sibshop model, information concerning specific disabilities, and an introduction to national organizations.*

Seligman, M. (Ed.). (1991). *The family with a handicapped child* (2nd ed.). Needham Heights, MA: Allyn and Bacon.
Contributors to this edited book discuss the dimensions of the family and ways families cope with a child who has a disability. The authors examine the historical, legislative, and philosophical perspectives of persons with disabilities in the United States, including an investigation of the role of the family. The family's relationship with the child with a disability is analyzed from various viewpoints including an ecological model; the "world view" of parents, professionals, and siblings; and the collaborative effort of all involved. This volume provides useful insights into exceptional families for professionals working in mental health, educational, and medical settings. Chapters include in-depth descriptions of children with autism and other pediatric chronic illnesses as well as best practices in counseling and family therapy.

Turnbull, A., & Turnbull, H. R., III (1990). *Families, professionals, and exceptionality: A special partnership* (2nd ed.). New York: Macmillan.
Turnbull and Turnbull offer a value-based text which serves as a professional's guide through a systematic and scholarly analysis of families with children who have exceptionalities. The information is presented through six identifiable and operational values (positive contributions, great expectations, choices, relationships, full citizenship, and inherent strength) which should govern family-professional partnerships. The authors focus on applied family-systems theory and specific ways of incorporating it into professional practice. This book is not restricted to disabilities but is inclusive of the full range of exceptionalities including the gifted and explores issues across the life span.

Resources for Families

Beckman, P., & Boyes, G. B. (1993). *Deciphering the system: A guide for families of young children with disabilities.* Cambridge, MA: Brookline.
This comprehensive guide provides extensive information about the service delivery system for young children with disabilities. Parents are encouraged to become advocates for their child through an integration of and negotiation with the various service systems. The authors present an informative review of current legislation and parental rights. The chapters address step-by-step suggestions to ensure that the educational system is geared to provide the services necessary for the individual child's development.

The Exceptional Parent (Begun June/July 1971), Boston: Psy-Ed Corporation.
An excellent resource magazine for parents of children and young adults with disabilities and special health care needs. The mission of the magazine is to (a) provide a worldwide network of caring parents, (b) encourage parents to become advocates for their children by joining local and national organizations, and (c) enable parents as caregivers by providing information and support from other parents and professionals.

Turnbull, H. R., Turnbull, A. P., Bronicki, G. J., Summers, J. A., & Roeder-Gordon, C. (1989). *Disability and the family: A guide to decisions for adulthood.* Baltimore: Brookes.
This book serves as a guide in answering the basic questions about the daily interactions, living arrangements, jobs and leisure activities that must be addressed by families with children who have disabilities. The authors focus on planning as the cornerstone to an increased quality of life for children with disabilities and their families. Issues discussed include (a) the child's competency to make decisions; (b) governmental benefits and resources available; (c) ways to determine the child's preferences and selection of jobs, leisure activities and residences; and (d) advocacy. The text also includes tips on creating new programs and increasing self-advocacy in daily living. Although this book was created for families, it would also serve as a helpful tool for professionals working with families in planning.

References

American Psychological Association. (1992). Ethical principles of psychologists and code of conduct. *American Psychologist, 47,* 1597–1611.

Americans with Disabilities Act of 1990, Pub. L. No. 101-336, Sec. 12101 *et. seq.,* 104 Stat. 328 (1991).

Apter, D. (1992). Utilization of community resources: An important variable for the home-school interface. In S. L. Christenson & J. C. Conoley (Eds.), *Home-school collaboration* (pp. 487–498). Silver Spring, MD: National Association of School Psychologists.

Bailey, D. B. (1989). Assessment and its importance in early intervention. In D. B. Bailey and M. Wolery (Eds.), *Assessing infants and preschoolers with handicaps* (pp. 1–21). New York: Merrill.

Bailey, D. B., Blasco, P. M., & Simeonsson, R. J. (1992). Needs expressed by mothers and fathers of young children with disabilities. *American Journal on Mental Retardation, 97,* 1–10.

Bailey, D. B., Buysse, V., Edmondson, R., & Smith, T. M. (1992). Creating family-centered services in early intervention: Perceptions of professionals in four states. *Exceptional Children, 58,* 298–309.

Bailey, D. B., & Wolery, M. (1992). *Teaching infants and preschoolers with disabilities.* New York: Merrill.

Barnard, K. E., & Kelly, J. F. (1990). Assessment of parent-child interaction. In S. J. Meisels & J. P. Shonkoff (Eds.), *Handbook of early childhood intervention* (pp. 278–302). Cambridge, England: Cambridge University Press.

Blacher, J. (1984). Sequential stages of parental adjustment to the birth of a child with handicaps: Fact or artifact? *Mental Retardation, 22,* 55–68.

Boggs, E. M. (1984). Feds and families: Some observations on the impact of federal economic policies on families with children who have disabilities. In M. A. Slater & P. Mitchell (Eds.), *Family support services: A parent professional partnership* (pp. 65–78). Stillwater, OK: National Clearinghouse of Rehabilitation Training Materials.

Bondurant-Utz, J. A., & Luciano, L. B. (1994). Family involvement. In J. A. Bondurant-Utz & L. B. Luciano (Eds.),

A practical guide to infant and preschool assessment in special education (pp. 41–57). Boston: Allyn and Bacon.

Brantlinger, E. (1991). Home-school partnerships that benefit children with special needs. *The Elementary School Journal, 91,* 249–259.

Christenson, S. L. (1995). Best practices in supporting home-school collaboration. In A. Thomas & J. Grimes (Eds.), *Best practices in school psychology-III* (pp. 253–267). Washington, DC: National Association of School Psychologists.

Collins-Moore, M. S. (1984). Birth and diagnosis: A family crisis. In M. C. Eisenber, L. C. Sutkin, & M. A. Jansen (Eds.), *Chronic illness and disability through the life span: Effects on self and family* (pp. 39–46). New York: Springer.

Darling, R. B. (1979). *Families against society: A study of reactions to children with birth defects.* Beverly Hills, CA: Sage.

Darling, R. B. (1991). Initial and continuing adaptation to the birth of a disabled child. In M. Seligman (Ed.), *The family with a handicapped child* (pp. 55–89). Needham Heights, MA: Allyn and Bacon.

Dunst, C. J., Leet, H. E., & Trivette, C. M. (1988). Family resources, personal well-being, and early intervention. *Journal of Special Education, 22*(1), 108–116.

Dunst, C. J., Trivette, C. M., & Deal, A. G. (1988). *Enabling and empowering families: Principles and guidelines for practice.* Cambridge, MA: Brookline Books.

Duwa, S. M., Wells, C., & Lalinde, P. (1993). Creating family-centered programs and policies. In D. M. Bryant & M. A. Graham (Eds.), *Implementing early intervention: From research to effective practice* (pp. 92–123). New York: Guilford Press.

Education for All Handicapped Children Act of 1975, Pub. L. No. 94-142, Sec. 1401 *et. seq.,* 88 Stat. 773 (1977).

Education of the Handicapped Act, Pub. L. No. 99-457, Sec. 1400 *et. seq.,* 100 Stat. 1145 (1986).

Featherstone, H. (1980). *A difference in the family.* New York: Basic Books.

Fewell, R. R. (1991). Parenting moderately handicapped persons. In M. Seligman (Ed.), *The family with a handicapped child* (pp. 203–236). Needham Heights, MA: Allyn and Bacon.

Friedrich, W., & Friedrich, N. (1981). Psychosocial assets of parents of handicapped and nonhandicapped children. *American Journal of Mental Deficiency, 86,* 551–553.

Garguilo, R. (1985). *Working with parents of exceptional children.* Boston: Houghton Mifflin.

Garland, C. W. (1993). Beyond chronic sorrow: A new understanding of family adaptation. In A. P. Turnbull, J. M. Patterson, S. K. Behr, D. L. Murphy, J. G. Marquis, & M. J. Blue-Banning (Eds.), *Cognitive coping, families, and disability* (pp. 67–80). Baltimore: Brookes.

Gutkin, T. B., & Curtis, M. J. (1990). School-based consultation: Theory, techniques, and research. In C. R. Reynolds & T. B. Gutkin (Eds.), *The handbook of school psychology* (Vol. 2, pp. 577–611). New York: Wiley.

Harris, S. L. (1987). The family crisis: Diagnosis of a severely disabled child. *Marriage and Family Review, 11,* 107–118.

Harry, B., Allen, N., & McLaughlin, M. (1995). Communication versus compliance: African-American parents'

involvement in special education. *Exceptional Children, 61,* 364–377.

Heller, T. (1993). Self-efficacy coping, active involvement, and caregiver well-being throughout the life course among families of persons with mental retardation. In A. P. Turnbull, J. M. Patterson, S. K. Behr, D. L. Murphy, J. G. Marquis, & M. J. Blue-Banning (Eds.), *Cognitive coping, families, and disability* (pp. 195–206). Baltimore: Brookes.

Hodapp, R. M., & Krasner, D. V. (1994–1995). Families of children with disabilities: Findings from a national sample of eighth-grade students. *Exceptionality, 5*(2), 71–81.

Individuals with Disabilities Education Act, Pub. L. No. 101-476, Sec. 1400 *et. seq.,* 104 Stat. 1142 (1991).

Kagan, S. I., Klugman, E., & Zigler, E. (1983). Shaping child and family policies: Criteria and strategies for a new decade. In S. L. Kagan & E. Klugman (Eds.), *Children, families and government: Perspectives on American social policy* (pp. 415–438). Cambridge, England: Cambridge University Press.

Kazak, A. E., & Marvin, R. S. (1984). Differences, difficulties and adaptations: Stress and social networks in families with a handicapped child. *Family Relations, 33,* 67–77.

Kornblatt, E. S., & Heinrich, J. (1985). Needs and coping abilities of children with developmental disabilities. *Mental Retardation, 20,* 2–6.

Laborde, P. R., & Seligman, M. (1991). Counseling parents with children with disabilities: Rationale and strategies. In M. Seligman (Ed.), *The family with a handicapped child* (pp. 337–368). Needham Heights, MA: Allyn and Bacon.

Marion, R. L. (1980). Communicating with parents of culturally diverse exceptional children. *Exceptional Children, 46,* 616–623.

Meyer, D. J. (1993). Lessons learned: Cognitive coping of overlooked family members. In A. P. Turnbull, J. M. Patterson, S. K. Behr, D. L. Murphy, J. G. Marquis, & M. J. Blue-Banning (Eds.), *Cognitive coping, families, and disability* (pp. 81–92). Baltimore: Brookes.

Meyer, D., & Vadasy, P. (1986). *Grandparents workshops: How to organize workshops for grandparents of children with handicaps.* Seattle: University of Washington Press.

Meyer, D. J., & Vadasy, P. F. (1994). *Sibshops: Workshops for siblings of children with special needs.* Baltimore: Brookes.

Minke, K. M., & Scott, M. M. (1995). Parent-professional relationships in early intervention: A qualitative investigation. *Topics in Early Childhood Special Education, 15,* 335–352.

Minnes, P. M. (1988). Family stress associated with a developmentally handicapped child. *International Review of Research in Mental Retardation, 15,* 195–226.

Minuchin, S. (1974). *Families and family therapy.* Cambridge, MA: Harvard University Press.

Morningstar, M. E., Turnbull, A. P., & Turnbull, H. R., III. (1995). What do students with disabilities tell us about the importance of family involvement in the transition from school to adult life? *Exceptional Children, 62,* 249–260.

Morris, M. W. (1987). Health care: Who pays the bills? *Exceptional Parent, 17*(5), 38–42.

Mullins, J. B. (1987). Authentic voices from parents of exceptional children. *Family Relations, 36,* 30–33.

National Association of School Psychologists. (1995a). Principles for professional ethics. In A. Thomas & J. Grimes (Eds.), *Best practices in school psychology-III* (pp. 1143–1159). Washington, DC: Author.

National Association of School Psychologists. (1995b). Standards for the provision of school psychological services. In A. Thomas & J. Grimes (Eds.), *Best practices in school psychology-III* (pp. 1161–1172). Washington, DC: Author.

Newman, J. (1991). Handicapped persons and their families: Historical, legislative, and philosophical perspectives. In M. Seligman (Ed.), *The family with a handicapped child* (pp. 1–26). Needham Heights, MA: Allyn and Bacon.

Palfrey, J. S., Walker, D. K., Butler, J. A., & Singer, J. D. (1989). Patterns of response in families of chronically disabled children: An assessment in five metropolitan school districts. *American Journal of Orthopsychiatry, 59* (1), 94–104.

Powers, M. D. (1991). Intervening with families of young children with severe handicaps: Contributions of a family systems approach. *School Psychology Quarterly, 6,* 131–146.

Ross, O. (1964). *The exceptional child in the family.* New York: Grune & Stratton.

Rounds, K. A., Weil, M., & Bishop, K. K. (1994). Practice with culturally diverse families of young children with disabilities. *Families in Society: The Journal of Contemporary Human Service, 75* (4), 3–15.

Siegal, B., & Silverstein, S. (1994). *What about me? Growing up with a developmentally disabled sibling.* New York: Plenum

Stone, N. W., & Chesney, B. H. (1978). Attachment behaviors in handicapped infants. *Mental Retardation, 16,* 8–12.

Suelzle, M., & Keenan, V. (1981). Changes in family support networks over the life cycle of mentally retarded persons. *American Journal of Mental Deficiency, 86* (3), 267–274.

Turbiville, V., Turnbull, A., Garland, C., & Lee, I. (1993). IFSPs and IEPs. In *DEC task force on recommended practices: Indicators of quality in programs for infants and young children with special needs and their families* (pp. 30–36). Reston, VA: Council for Exceptional Children.

Turnbull, A. P., & Turnbull, H. R. (1985). *Parents speak out: Then and now.* New York: Merrill.

Turnbull, A. P., & Turnbull, H. R., III. (1990). *Families, professionals, and exceptionality: A special partnership* (2nd ed.). New York: Macmillan.

Turnbull, A. P., Turnbull, H. R., Shank, M., & Leal, D. (1995). *Exceptional lives: Special education in today's schools.* Englewood Cliffs, NJ: Merrill.

Turnbull, H. R., Turnbull, A. P., Bronicki, G. J., Summers, J. A., & Roeder-Gordon, C. (1989). *Disability and the family: A guide to decisions for adulthood.* Baltimore: Brookes.

Upshur, C. C. (1991). Families and the community service maze. In M. Seligman (Ed.), *The family with a handicapped child* (pp. 91–118). Needham Heights, MA: Allyn and Bacon.

U. S. Bureau of the Census. (1994). *Statistical abstract of the United States: 1994* (114th Ed.). Washington, DC: Author.

Wikler, L. (1981). Chronic stresses of families of mentally retarded children. *Family Relations, 30,* 281–288.

Wise, P. S. (1995). Best practices in communicating with parents. In A. Thomas & J. Grimes (Eds.), *Best practices in school psychology-III* (pp. 279–287). Washington, DC: National Association of School Psychologists.

60

The Meaning and Implications of Empowerment

Kim R. Galant
Carol M. Trivette

Western Carolina Center, North Carolina

Carl J. Dunst

Allegheny-Singer Research Institute and
Medical College of Pennsylvania and Hahneman University

The nature of relationships in the field of education is changing. Educational reform efforts, changing roles for professionals, and the centrality of the family in federal legislation for young children are among the multiple factors that challenge the context in which help is offered in contemporary society. Traditionally, parents have had a passive role as help-seekers; they were told by professionals what was wrong with their child, what to do to correct the problems, how often and for how long. New approaches emphasize inviting parents to join with professionals as partners in the planning, implementing, and evaluating of educational services. Similar changes are occurring in professional-to-professional interactions. At the school level, administrators are being asked to share power and responsibility with parents and school staff. These constituents work together to develop a school vision, redesign school structure and policy, and implement organizational change. School districts, through site-based management plans, are attempting to share power and decision making with individual schools.

These changes have at their core a belief that parents, teachers, and administrators have the knowledge, skills, and support to manage their resources and make informed choices that will enhance the quality of their outcomes and the process by which they achieve these outcomes. These broad-based changes in relationships call for a thorough understanding of the effects of this transformation and the implications of sharing power as partners with families, school personnel, and administrators. The concept of empowerment is a foundation for understanding and implementing this shared responsibility.

The call for the adoption of empowerment as an ideology to guide both theory and practice has been cham-

pioned by a diverse array of behavioral and social scientists and practitioners, including community psychology (Rappaport, 1981), organizational psychology (Belasco, 1990), education (Bowman, 1994), early childhood intervention (Dunst, Trivette, & Deal, 1988), public policy (Berger & Neuhaus, 1977), social work (Pinderhughes, 1995), and speech pathology (Damico & Armstrong, 1990/91). The concept of empowerment has served as a major challenge to entrenched thinking about the capabilities of people and the roles they can play in shaping their own destinies.

In its broadest sense, empowerment has been used as a framework for addressing a range of social, economic, and political concerns (Swift, 1984), including how human needs are viewed, how concerns and desires should be addressed, and how intervention outcomes should be operationalized and evaluated (Rappaport, 1984). The term embodies a wide array of participatory endeavors directed at influencing a sense of control over important life events. When applied to education, the empowerment of parents has been linked to notions of parents as recipients of knowledge (Cochran, 1992), parents as advocates for their children (Bowman, 1994), parents as an extra pair of hands (Bowman, 1994), and parents as partners in general education reform efforts (Riley, 1994). Thus, empowerment is a broad term that can apply to individuals, groups, organizations, and communities (Whitmore & Kerans, 1988); it can refer to process as well as outcome.

The major purposes of this chapter are to (a) define and illustrate three components of empowerment, (b) explore the problems and implications of empowerment, and (c) describe what empowerment might look like in an education setting. The chapter is relevant for school personnel who will be called on to serve increasing numbers of young children for whom partnerships with families are considered best practice under federal law. Recent literature in school psychology indicates a need for the profession to respond to the expanding roles and responsibilities of the field including an empowering service-delivery model (Epps & Jackson, 1991).

Background and Development

Empowerment approaches are an alternative to the deficit approach that is well entrenched in the field of disability. Professionals working from a deficit model assess children to determine the presence of deficits or weaknesses and then devise professionally implemented interventions to ameliorate the identified problems. Because families are passive recipients of expert advice, this process may foster a sense of helplessness and powerlessness in the families of children with disabilities as they lose control over the decisions that affect their children. The empowerment model described here enables individuals to make informed decisions and take control of their lives by imparting information, skills, and resources to strengthen families.

Definitions of Empowerment

It is difficult to find a generally agreed upon operational definition of the term *empowerment*. Rappaport (1984) asserts, "Empowerment is a little bit like obscenity; you have trouble defining it but you know it when you see it" (p. 17). Two of this chapter's authors and a colleague (Dunst, Trivette, & LaPointe, 1994) conducted a content analysis across various literatures in an attempt to develop a definition. We found a number of commonalities among definitions now in use. This led to the development of a complex model of empowerment that has been reduced to three components for the present discussion: empowerment ideology, participatory experiences, and empowerment outcomes.

Empowerment Ideology

Empowerment ideology, the foundation of the model, consists of two parts: (a) adopting beliefs and attitudes that involve positive attributions about people's capabilities and roles in affecting decisions and (b) embracing behaviors that promote the families' competencies and capabilities (Bond, 1982). A number of authors have attempted to delineate the principles or beliefs that uniquely define the empowerment ideology (Cornell Empowerment Group, 1989; Rappaport, 1981). For example, in his pioneer work,

Rappaport (1981) delineated three guiding principles of an empowering philosophy. These are

1. All people have existing strengths and capabilities as well as the capacity to become more competent.
2. The failure of a person to display competence is *not* due to deficits within a person but rather the failure of social systems to provide or create opportunities for competencies to be displayed or acquired.
3. In situations where existing capabilities need to be strengthened or new competencies need to be learned, they are best learned through experiences that lead people to make self-attributions about their capabilities to influence important life events.

Implicit in this philosophy is the belief that parents must have choices regarding interventions for their children and the power to exercise those choices. Because families vary significantly in their beliefs and values, it is expected that parents' choices will be as diverse as the families themselves.

The empowerment ideology suggests a proactive rather than reactive approach to problems. Therefore, anticipatory actions by helpers that support and strengthen individual or group functioning are valued (Cowen, 1985). Building on an individual's strengths rather than rectifying weaknesses helps people become more adept not only in dealing with difficult life events, but in achieving growth-oriented goals and personal aspirations. Because skills are learned or demonstrated in important real-life situations, individuals are more likely to internalize skills and apply them to other areas of their lives. Adopting an empowerment ideology is important because it provides the foundation and perspective through which professionals view situations and actions encountered in everyday experiences with families.

Participatory Experiences

The second component of this conceptual model, participatory experiences, describes the process of working with families and the nature of the relationships between parents and professionals. Many theorists and practitioners argue that process is the most important dimension when defining empowerment (Cornell Empowerment Group, 1989; Lord & Farlow, 1990), particularly with respect to the application of the construct. Process in empowerment involves providing parents various opportunities, or participatory experiences, that promote the acquisition of new competencies by building on the families' existing strengths and capabilities. These experiences are designed to make parents feel competent and in control. Useful strategies include actively eliciting participation of families in the helping process, assisting families in the process of identifying needs and concerns, providing information necessary for families to make informed decisions, encouraging families' decisions about courses of action to meet needs and achieve goals, and enhancing and promoting families' knowledge and skills needed to take action (Maple, 1977).

Professional relationships with families take the form of partnerships. These partnerships are an important part of the participatory experiences that influence a parent's sense of control. When partnerships are developed, families play an active, valued role in the relationship. Professionals must not only acknowledge families' decisions but must accept and support these decisions. This process affirms the family's central role in the help-giving process and leads to empowerment outcomes.

Empowerment Outcomes

Empowerment outcomes, the third model component, include parent behaviors that are strengthened or learned as a result of participatory experiences and parents' subsequent appraisal of their own capabilities and control over important events in their children's lives. Empowerment outcomes include attributions and beliefs that reflect a sense of control over one's own behavior. These outcomes encompass constructs such as personal control, internal locus of control, self-efficacy, self-esteem, personal power, intrinsic motivation, and political efficacy. Collectively, these terms describe the types of changes that result from an individual's efforts to produce desired effects and outcomes (Lord & Farlow, 1990; Zimmerman & Rappaport, 1988). "The confluence of these (various) areas of perceived control is hypothesized to represent psychological empowerment" (Zimmerman & Rappaport, 1988, p. 727). Research has shown that these attributions of control both influence, and are influenced by, empowering ideology and participatory experiences (Trivette, Dunst, & Hamby, in press). Service providers who consistently work with families in ways that maximize families' control over services, facilitate the skill development of individual family members, and support the families' decisions increase parental perceptions of self-efficacy and control.

It could be argued that having parents feel in control is a "nice idea" but one that has limited educational relevance. However, research shows that empowerment outcomes such as parental self-efficacy are linked positively with child development measures. Specifically, parental perceptions of self-efficacy are related to parental well-being (Dunst & Trivette, in press). When parents feel that they have control over important events in their lives, they express a greater sense of personal well-being. This increased sense of personal well-being influences family functioning, which, in turn, is related to styles of interactions that promote child development (Dunst & Trivette, 1988). In these families, parents respond contingently to child behavior and encourage children to explore their world and their abilities. These interactions positively support children's cognitive development. Thus, encouraging parental empowerment can have an important influence on children's educational outcomes.

Problems and Implications

The application of these empowerment concepts to education requires an examination of the structure, roles, and relationships of the individuals involved in the school ecology. In the education literature, the analysis of empowerment has focused in three areas: parents (Seifert, 1992), professionals (Barrett, Crimando, & Riggar, 1993), and school organizations (Johnson, 1991).

Much of the work related to the empowerment of parents in the schools has been developed around the construct of a home-school collaboration or partnership. This focus on partnership has come from a number of sources in both regular and special education. From regular education there is an awareness that (a) schools can no longer meet all children's needs without help, (b) children are part of a larger ecological system that must be involved in the learning process (see Family Systems and the Family-School Connection, this volume), and (c) the best learning environment is one connected to the families' perspectives (Christenson, Rounds, & Franklin, 1992). This awareness suggests the importance of involvement of parents in the school. It does not, however, define the type of parent involvement that would be most beneficial to children's development.

There are a number of perspectives on parent involvement in the schools (Seifert, 1992), including parent education, parents as advocates, and parents as informants and decision makers. In the parent education model, parents are offered information about their children's learning through lectures, individual meetings, and the like where the emphasis is on experts (school personnel) relaying information to less knowledgeable recipients (parents). It is assumed that if the information is understood and followed, the child's problems will be eliminated. Educating parents may be empowering only if the family has indicated a need or desire for information and/or skills. There is an unspoken but fundamental expectation of incompetence inherent in the assumption that all families need education and skills. This attitude characterizes the deficit approach discussed earlier that has been prevalent in the field of special education. There is a tendency to focus on deficit areas of children with disabilities and their parents: what they cannot do, what they do not do well, or what needs to be "fixed." In contrast, an empowering approach is based on identifying and building on children's and parents' strengths and capabilities and responding to issues that *they* identify as areas of need.

Much of the work in the special education field has focused on parents as advocates for their children's rights (Nelson, Howard, & McLaughlin, 1993). Nelson and her colleagues describe strategies for parents to advocate for their children with disabilities and for professionals to support this advocacy and have positive outcomes for children. In many cases, families of children with disabilities exercise a level of involvement with their children's education that is not part of the education process of families with typically developing children. However, all families should be invited to participate and then choose the degree to which they wish to be involved.

From special education also comes the idea that parents are holders of important information professionals need to consider—that parents know their children best (Seifert, 1992). This information is considered critical if teachers are to be effective. Related to this belief is the notion that parents should be given some voice in deciding the direction of their children's educational paths with the awareness that these decisions are best made when the school and family work collaboratively. It involves families understanding all the information necessary to make informed decisions and professionals trusting families and assuming they are competent to make decisions meaningful for them and their children.

However, Seifert (1992) suggests that one of the barriers raised by this concept is the desire of teachers for greater professionalism. The voice of parents within the educational setting may be interpreted by teachers as a threat to their professional status. Partnership requires sharing power traditionally reserved for school personnel. Riley (1994) states that, if there is to be a real partnership, the "traditional educational hierarchy must begin to question itself and the ways it does business." One common obstacle to the implementation of an empowerment model is the philosophical and paradigmatic shift that needs to be made by staff and the system. Based on our own experience in moving a human service program toward an empowerment model and our research findings, this chapter's authors agree that the threat to professional status will be an issue. The issue of teacher empowerment is directly related to the empowerment of the organization. School personnel cannot be expected to empower families unless their organizations empower them as professionals.

In schools and organizations, a trend known as the democratization of professionalism is changing the manner in which administrators interact with their employees. One of the keys to developing human resource potential in an organization is empowered employees. Employee empowerment can be defined as strengthening an employee's self-efficacy—one's belief in his or her capability to perform a task and/or affect the outcomes of the organization. The role of an administrator is to ensure that employees have opportunities to acquire the knowledge, resources, and support necessary to perform optimally. To empower employees requires that they have input into the vision and goals of the organization, set personal goals related to their work, and are involved in the implementation and evaluation of organizational change (Barrett et al., 1993). Today's movement toward school-based management (Riley, 1994) represents organization-level attempts at empowerment.

As part of this movement, a primary question that must be addressed is the notion of who has power. In school-based management, the power for decision making is given to local schools and parents are closely involved in the school reform efforts (Etheridge & Hall, 1992). Dixon (1992) describes a model in which most school professionals want parents to be limited partners in the school, allowing school personnel to be primarily responsible for the education of students. In this situation, school personnel are the experts and parents are viewed as helpers to the school personnel, not full partners. She argues that when there is full partnership, the assumption becomes that both family and school are responsible for the learning of children and that families share in the decision-making process. Clearly, full partnership requires that school personnel rethink the meaning of control and power.

Alternative Actions

The remainder of the chapter will present ideas about the new relationships that are necessary between parents, school personnel, and administrators to build schools that support and strengthen all. An empowerment model is not easy to implement system wide, but there are many steps an individual school and school personnel can take toward including parents in the educational system.

The empowerment philosophy, as defined by Rappaport (1981), suggests the need to develop a set of principles to guide interactions with parents. Many educational systems and schools have a mission statement and/or guiding principles. Examining existing principles with a focus on the extent to which they reflect empowering beliefs about parents may be a way to begin to operationalize an empowerment philosophy. If a system or school does not have guiding principles, then the task is writing and adopting them. Parents may be invited to participate in the development of the philosophy and principles. A diverse group of parents should be included to represent all families, not just the well educated. Developing principles that include beliefs about parents' roles within the system is important for staff and parents, for it provides guidance and sets up a standard against which practices can be measured.

Working with families through collaborative partnerships requires open communication, full disclosure of information, mutual respect and trust, and shared responsibility (Riley, 1994). This connection with families is not limited to families who are easy to reach. Those most difficult to reach may have the greatest need to feel welcomed and accepted in the school community, to have open and responsive communication with school personnel, and to receive clear information on how to help their children succeed in school (Epstein, 1992). The process of developing partnerships with families occurs over time. As with all relationships, partners must work to develop trust, appreciate each others' contributions, and understand one another. The work will begin at different points with different families and proceed at varying rates over time. All families deserve educators' best efforts at creating partnerships; any progress made with families benefits their children.

Partnerships between parents and school personnel require effort and a willingness to share power and decision making. These partnerships begin with the establishment of routine positive communication that is the foundation for shared understanding, particularly when problems arise (U.S. Department of Education, 1994). For information to be helpful to families, it should be provided in their primary language and be jargon free. Written information must be provided at a level appropriate for all families. Effective oral communication will, at times, require the use of an interpreter. School psychologists can play a leadership role in supporting improved communication between parents and school personnel.

Schools interested in developing collaborative partnerships with parents must examine the existing parental roles and responsibilities within the educational setting. School personnel should then ask parents in what ways they would like to be involved. School staff may invite parents to act as tutors to other children; raise money for fund drives; or become leaders on committees, activists for change, or advocates for the school at a school board level. Jennings (1992) suggests a number of ways to increase parental involvement. Activities such as the development of a family center, esteem-building activities to promote school/family relations, and staff development for teachers to increase their understanding of diverse family situations are a few ways to support families' involvement in schools.

Schools may want to develop relationships with families before children enter schools through summer enrichment programs, parenting classes, and Family Fun Days. Restructuring school-entry practices may include a spring orientation and summer visitation program to support children's success and families' sense of belonging. Classrooms should be inviting for both children and their families. Schools may house and organize activities that have appeal to families, begin to make them feel comfortable and safe within the school, and help them view the school as a community building. Many of these activities match the strengths of school psychologists, although they are not typically viewed as part of their role.

In special education, very specific strategies have been and can continue to be used to promote families' involvement in their children's education. The development of the Individual Education Plan (IEP) offers the opportunity for family empowerment. Families should play a major role in the identification of the child's and family's needs. This implies initial interviews that are open ended and responsive to parents' issues and concerns. The role of the school psychologist becomes more than an evaluator; it includes working with families to assist them in identifying family strengths and resources and in prioritizing their concerns. The family is treated as a major source of information abut the child's past history as well as the child's current abilities. Parental information about what has worked with the child in the past can be a critical building block for the development of a current plan for the child. Parents should be viewed as having such crucial information about their child that their presence at meetings is essential. Meetings must be scheduled at times convenient to the parents, even if they occur in the evenings. The role taken by parents in the IEP meeting is the parents' choice, including the role of facilitator, if they desire. Control over details such as where meetings are held and who attends meetings should lie with the family to the extent possible under special education regulations.

The schools have traditionally looked to school professionals to meet students' needs. An empowering approach might involve a conversation with families about others in the family network who could act as support for their children's educational goals. A family may identify a neighbor who enjoys reading with the child, a grandparent who might attend Saturday morning story hour at the library, or the use of a home computer with a CD-ROM encyclopedia program as their contributions to meeting their child's educational goals.

School psychologists can assist school staff in developing empowering relationships with families. However, to do so, the role of the school psychologist will need to be expanded from traditional diagnosis and placement to consultation with families and school personnel (Shriver, Kramer, & Garnett, 1993). The school psychologist may need to work with parents and teachers to facilitate communication and overcome any barriers to collaboration. He or she can help both school staff and families to understand a child's learning style or to deal with challenging behaviors. To the extent that educators believe that this type of special attention should be paid to every student, then the notion of empowerment applies to work with all families.

Family-level goals should also be included in the IEP process to enable families to get the information, skills, or support they need. An example from our work with families involved the mother of a young boy with a severe hearing loss. The mother was in the process of transitioning her child into prekindergarten services and wanted to determine the educational approach that would be most beneficial for her child. The local school for the deaf advocated using American Sign Language (ASL) with the child and emphasized the importance of his inclusion in the deaf community. The mother decided that she needed more information about educational options for her child. She worked with the school psychologist to research the various educational approaches, find professionals who would discuss these approaches with her, and find parents who had made different choices for their children. After acquiring some basic information, the mother took courses in deaf education at a local college and developed skills in ASL, cued speech, and auditory verbal techniques. She also researched assistive technology such as Frequency Modulation (FM) systems and new advances in hearing aides to support her son's interactions within the hearing community. The mother gained knowledge and skills that enabled her to support her son's development and provide parent-to-parent support to other families of young children who are deaf.

The empowerment of this mother to take control over the educational decisions for her son began with very small steps that were built upon to develop new competencies and learn new skills. For example, when this mother first began talking to the school psychologist about her concerns, she had little information about available options and few ideas about how to get the information she needed. She was, however, motivated to gather the information and very capable of following through with ideas once she knew how to get started. The psychologist and mother brainstormed ideas about how to get information: Read, talk to professionals, talk to parents, take classes, and so forth. Then they got more specific: what kinds of professionals would be helpful (audiologists, deaf educators, school psychologists, speech/language pathologists, etc.) and how she could locate those people within the community (referrals from people she already knew; the National Association for Parents of the Deaf; the American Speech, Language, and Hearing Association; the family resource program on the campus of the School for the Deaf, etc.). The mother and psychologist worked together to analyze the tasks and to identify strategies and resources to get the information and assistance she needed. Using skills developed through this process, this mother now assists other parents working through a similar process. Ultimately, families come to rely less on professionals and more on their own resources when they have opportunities to build their skills and competencies.

These same principles of working with families can be applied to school personnel and organizations. Teachers and staff are much less resistant to sharing their power when they have an opportunity to be a part of a larger system in which they have input, when their skills and ideas are valued and respected, and when they have some control over how they do their jobs. In our pro-gram, meetings are open and working groups have a rotating representative assigned as part of the management team. As issues and concerns are identified, teams of interested people are formed to clarify the issues, develop a plan for making changes, and then implement the changes. Successes are shared and celebrated by the group and ongoing unresolved issues are put back out to the group for another attempt to develop solutions. This personal experience with being empowered as an employee helps staff understand the importance of empowering families with whom they work. The collaboration process brings together the ideas, concerns, strengths, and visions of parents, school personnel, and administrators and removes the blame from any one group. An empowered organization is a key element to responding to challenging issues in today's schools (Barrett et al., 1993; U.S. Department of Education, 1994).

Summary

This chapter has attempted to define the empowerment construct in a way that includes the most common current uses of the term. The definitions of empowerment and the insights from relevant research support the application of the construct in an educational setting. Small steps toward empowering parents made by individual school personnel can make a significant difference in the nature of home-school relationships and the outcomes for children and families. The challenge is not just to meet children's educational goals, but to do so in a way that respects families' values and choices for their children, ensures full disclosure of unbiased information, and creates partnerships between families and school personnel that honor each member's strengths and contributions.

If empowerment goals are to be realized, a system must be created in which all members are valued and have real input into decisions that affect their lives. By empowering families, school personnel can do much to strengthen families in their roles as caregivers. Empowered personnel send supportive messages to families through their attitudes, relationships, and responsiveness. Empowered systems create policies and programs that address the total ecology of the child, family, and community.

Authors Note

Appreciation is extended to Nancy Gordon and Wendy Jodry for editing this paper and verifying references and to Heidi Simonetti and Pat Condrey for preparation of the manuscript.

Recommended Resources

Christenson, S. L., & Conoley, J. C. (Eds.). (1992). *Home-school collaboration: Enhancing children's academic and social competence.* Silver Springs, MD: The National Association of School Psychologists.
This book addresses many of the concepts included in empowerment as a partnership. There are four major sections: Conceptual/Empirical Bases for Home-School Collaboration, Programs and Models for the 90s, Approaches for Enhancing Home-School Collaboration, and Implications for Facilitating Change Toward Home-School Collaboration. This book is intended for participants within the schools who are or want to be working with parents on a regular basis to develop the educational opportunities possible for all children.

Martin, S., & Everts, J. (Eds.). (1992). Parent empowerment [Special Issue]. *Family Science Review, 5* (1&2).
The focus of this special issue on parental empowerment examines both the empowerment programs and issues. There are a number of conceptual articles in this issue including one by Moncrieff Cochran of the Cornell Empowerment Group. Crosbie-Burnett then takes the Cornell Empowerment model and provides strategies for working with nontraditional families within an educational setting. Several articles describe how their authors have used the empowerment construct in work with various populations, including families dealing with divorce and Hispanic families. The last article by Weiss and Greene focuses on the importance of evaluation efforts in empowerment projects and examines a variety of approaches to address this issue.

Rappaport, J. (1981). In praise of paradox: A social policy of empowerment over prevention. *American Journal of Community Psychology, 9*(1), 1–23.
Julian Rappaport is one of the leading empowerment theorists within the community psychology literature and has published on numerous occasions about the construct. This article identifies the important underlying assumptions from which an empowerment philosophy is developed.

U.S. Department of Education. (1994). *Strong families, strong schools: Building community partnerships for learning.* Washington, DC: U.S. Government Printing Office.
This research-based document provides a strong rationale for why parent involvement in the schools is important to the educational system and to children. It also provides many examples of how to involve families in schools, develop family partnerships, and connect communities to families and schools. The document also points out some of the challenges that schools and families face when trying to form partnerships as well as solutions to these challenges.

Zimmerman, M. A. (1990). Toward a theory of learned hopefulness: A structural model analysis of participation and empowerment. *Journal of Research in Personality, 24,* 71–86.
This article provides research data to support Zimmerman's model but also strongly suggests roles that are important for practitioners to play. Zimmerman describes the concept of learned hopefulness as one where the process of learning and using problem-solving skill leads to the perceptions of control by the family. His discussion of the various processes by which one can learn hopefulness offers many ideas for the development of best practice in many human services fields including education.

References

Barrett, K., Crimando, W., & Riggar, T. F. (1993). Becoming an empowering organization: Strategies for implementation. *Journal of Rehabilitation Administration, 17,* 159–167.

Belasco, J. A. (1990). *Teaching the elephant to dance: Empowering change in your organization.* New York: Crown Publishers.

Berger, P. L., & Neuhaus, R. J. (1977). *To empower people: The role of mediating structures in public policy.* Washington, DC: American Enterprise Institute for Public Policy Research.

Bond, L. (1982). From prevention to promotion: Optimizing infant development. In L. Bond & J. Joffe (Eds.), *Facilitating infant and early childhood development* (pp. 5–39). Hanover, NH: University Press of New England.

Bowman, B. T. (1994). Home and school, the unresolved relationship. In S. L. Kagan & B. Weissbourd (Eds.), *Putting families first: America's family support movement and the challenge of change.* San Francisco: Jossey-Bass.

Christenson, S. L., Rounds, T., & Franklin, M. J. (1992). Home-school collaboration: Effects, issues, and opportunities. In S. L. Christenson & J. C. Conoley (Eds.), *Home-school collaboration: Enhancing children's academic and social competence* (pp. 19–52). Silver Springs, MD: The National Association of School Psychologists.

Cochran, M. (1992). Parent empowerment: Developing a conceptual framework. *Family Science Review, 5*(1&2), 3–21.

Cornell Empowerment Group. (1989). Empowerment through family support. *Networking Bulletin: Empowerment and Family Support, 1*(1), 1–3.

Cowen, E. L. (1985). Person-centered approaches to primary prevention in mental health: Situation-focused and competence-enhancement. *American Journal of Community Psychology, 13,* 31–48.

Damico, J. E., & Armstrong, M. B. (1990/91). Empowerment in the clinical context: The speech-language pathologist as advocate. *National Student Speech Language Hearing Association Journal, 18,* 34–43.

Dixon, A. P. (1992, April). Parents: Full partners in the decision-making process. *NASSP Bulletin, 76*(543), 15–18.

Dunst, C. J., & Trivette, C. M. (1988). Determinants of parent and child interactive behavior. In K. Marfo (Ed.), *Parent-child interaction and developmental disabilities* (pp. 3–31). New York: Praeger Publishers.

Dunst, C. J., & Trivette, C. M. (in press). Empowerment, effective helpgiving practices, and family-centered care. *Pediatric Nursing.*

Dunst, C. J., Trivette, C. M., & Deal, A. G. (1988). *Enabling and empowering families: Principles and guidelines for practice.* Cambridge, MA: Brookline Books.

Dunst, C. J., Trivette, C. M., & LaPointe, N. (1994). Meaning and key characteristics of empowerment. In C. J. Dunst, C. M. Trivette, & A. G. Deal (Eds.), *Supporting and strengthening families: Volume 1. Methods, strategies and practices.* Cambridge, MA: Brookline Books.

Epps, S. & Jackson, B. J. (1991). Professional preparation of psychologists for family-centered service delivery to at-risk infants and toddlers. *School Psychology Review, 20,* 498–509.

Epstein, J. L. (1992). School and family partnerships: Leadership roles for school psychologists In S. L. Christenson & J. C. Conoley (Eds.), *Home-school collaboration: Enhancing children's academic and social competence.* Silver Spring, MD: National Association of School Psychologists.

Etheridge, C. P., & Hall, M. L. (1992, March). *The impact of school-based decision making: A case study.* (ERIC Document Reproduction Service No. ED 345 361.)

Jennings, J. M. (1992, December). Parent involvement strategies for inner-city schools. *NAASP Bulletin,* 63–68.

Lord, J., & Farlow, D. M. (1990). A study of personal empowerment: Implications for health promotion. *American Journal of Health Promotion, 5,* 2–8.

Maple, F. F. (1977). *Shared decision making.* Beverly Hills, CA: Sage.

Nelson, D., Howard, V. F., & McLaughlin, T. F. (1993). Empowering parents to become advocates for their own children with disabilities. *British Columbia Journal of Special Education, 17*(1), 62–72.

Pinderhughes, E. (1995). Empowering diverse populations: Family practice in the 21st century. *Families in Society: The Journal of Contemporary Human Services, 76*(3), 131–140.

Rappaport, J. (1981). In praise of paradox: A social policy of empowerment over prevention. *American Journal of Community Psychology, 9*(1), 1–23.

Rappaport, J. (1984). Studies in empowerment: Introduction to the issues. In J. Rappaport, C. Swift, & R. Hess (Eds.),

Studies in empowerment: Steps toward understanding and action (pp. 1–7). New York: Haworth Press.

Riley, A. (1994). Parent empowerment: An idea for the Nineties? *Education Canada,* 15–20.

Seifert, K. L. (1992). *Parents and teachers: Can they learn from each other?* (ERIC Document Reproduction Service No. ED 352 202.)

Shriver, M. D., Kramer, J. J., & Garnett, M. (1993, July). Parent involvement in early childhood special education: Opportunities for school psychologists. *Psychology in the Schools, 30,* 264–273.

Swift, C. (1984). Empowerment: An antidote for folly. In J. Rappaport, C. Swift, & R. Hess (Eds.), *Studies in empowerment: Steps toward understanding and action* (pp. xi–xv). New York: Haworth Press.

Trivette, C. M., Dunst, C. J., & Hamby, D. W. (in press). Factors associated with perceived control appraisals in a family-centered early intervention program. *Journal of Early Intervention.*

Trivette, C. M., Dunst, C. J., Hamby, D. W., & LaPointe, N. J. (1996). Key elements of empowerment and their implications for early intervention. *Infant-Toddler Intervention, 6,* 59–74.

U. S. Department of Education, (1994). *Strong families, strong schools: Building community partnerships for learning.* Washington, DC: U.S. Government Printing Office.

Whitmore, E., & Kerans, P. (1988). Participation, empowerment and welfare. *Canadian Review of Social Policy, 22,* 51–60.

Zimmerman, M. A. (1990). Toward a theory of learned hopefulness: A structural model analysis of participation and empowerment. *Journal of Research in Personality, 24,* 71–86.

Zimmerman, M. A., & Rappaport, J. (1988). Citizen participation, perceived control, and psychological empowerment. *American Journal of Community Psychology, 16,* 725–750.

61

Homelessness

Laurie Ford
Catherine C. Cantrell
University of South Carolina

Background and Development

The problem of homelessness, although not new, has increased in magnitude since the early 1980s. Currently, approximately two million Americans do not have a place to call home (National Alliance to End Homelessness, 1994). Homeless people are found in virtually every American community. Along with the increase in the number of homeless individuals, the "face" of the homeless has also changed dramatically within the last decade. The stereotype of a middle-aged male with alcoholism as the typical homeless person no longer holds true.

Statistics regarding the demographic characteristics of the homeless population vary greatly, and national counts are constantly changing due to difficulty in record keeping, inconsistent definitions, and methodological variables. What is known, however, is that women and families with children are joining the ranks of the homeless at a higher percentage than any other group. Families currently make up 43% of all homeless people in the United States (U.S. Conference of Mayors, 1993). Eighteen percent of homeless people are in families with children present. For the first time since statistics have been available in the United States, the percentage of families without homes has begun to surpass the number of single homeless men (Jenks, 1994).

Homeless families differ in their characteristics from the population of single homeless women or men. According to Burt and Cohen (1989), 80% of homeless women with children have no history of hospitalizations for mental illness, inpatient substance abuse treatment, or imprisonment. In contrast, 50% to 55% of the homeless population in general have a drug or alcohol problem, about a third have a mental illness, and a high percentage are HIV positive. Most homeless families are headed by single mothers between the ages of 25 and 30 years, are often from ethnic minority groups, and are likely to be pregnant or to have recently had a child. The typical homeless family has, on average, two or three children (Shinn, 1992). Children are the fastest growing segment

of the homeless population in the United States. On any given night, as many as 100,000 children are homeless (Children's Defense Fund [CDF], 1994) and children younger than 5 years now compose over half the population of children without homes. Another subgroup of the homeless population are older children and adolescents, the number of these homeless youth continues to increase. These youth include those who (a) have left home without parental permission (runaways), (b) have been thrown out of their homes (throwaways), (c) have left problematic social service placements (system youth), and (d) lack basic shelter (street youth). While many school psychologists and other education professionals will be faced with addressing the needs of this homeless subgroup, a discussion of their needs goes beyond the scope of this chapter. The reader is referred to Rotherman-Borus, Koopman, and Ehrhardt (1991) to begin the exploration of issues related to homeless youth living outside their family.

Homelessness cannot be considered independent of poverty. Homelessness is an extreme manifestation of poverty with more persons who are homeless at the bottom of the poverty ladder. Almost 40% of all children in the United States are born into poverty, and children under age six are more likely to be poor than any other age group (Shinn & Weitzman, in press). Of even greater concern is that the group of children who live in extreme poverty (i.e., less than $55.93 per week for a family of three which is halfway down the poverty level) are the more common. Further, a racial gap exists in that individuals from African-American, Hispanic, and Native American populations experience poverty at a higher percentage rate than their representation in the population at large (CDF, 1994). While the focus of this chapter is on homelessness and its impact on children, readers interested in the topic of homelessness are encouraged to gain a better understanding of the impact of poverty on children as well (see Huston, McLloyd, & Garcia-Coll, 1994).

The condition of homelessness has an impact on children's development in a variety of ways. Hundreds of thousands of homeless children spend their earliest, most formative years in unstable, chaotic, and developmentally unresponsive environments (Klein, Bittel, & Molnar, 1993). The trauma of homelessness is immense and often disrupts social networks, family routines, and emotional grounding in one's home. Young children, who represent over half of the population of children without homes, are at a stage in their lives when a secure environment is critical to the development of a stable sense of self. Stability is central to children's growth and development, and children, particularly young children, are completely dependent on their families, especially their mothers. Typically, homeless families do not have a stable living environment and move frequently from shelter to shelter. The effects of disorganization and chaos that accompany homelessness make it increasingly difficult to develop autonomy and trust in the physical and social world (Klein et al., 1993).

Children who have moved three or more times in their lives are more likely than other children to have emotional and behavioral problems, to have repeated a grade, or to be expelled or suspended from school. Homeless children confront many threats to their well-being including a tendency to have increased levels of health problems, developmental delays, psychological problems such as anxiety and depression, and educational underachievement (Rafferty & Shinn, 1991). Such consequences of homelessness rarely operate in isolation. The problems are typically interrelated. For example, when young children's nutritional needs are not met, growth is affected, physical health deteriorates, mental health is adversely affected, behavioral problems increase, the ability to concentrate is compromised, and academic performance suffers (Rafferty & Shinn, 1991).

Historically, many homeless children have been unable to attend school due to their living and financial situations. Schools require a parental address to determine attendance zones, immunization records to enter school, supplies to participate in activities, and previous records to continue special education services. With no place to call home, children who are homeless often have no address. Their immunizations are frequently not up to date, or if immunizations have been completed, records are difficult to locate. Frequent school changes increase the likelihood that special education records are not current as well.

Although school psychologists and other professionals working with children with disabilities are familiar with the Individuals with Disabilities Education Act (P. L. 102-119, 1990), few are familiar with the Stewart B. McKinney Homeless Assistance Act (P. L. 100-77, 1987). However, this act contains language likely to sound familiar. The McKinney Act is a federal law that provides funding for education, training, community service, and family support for individuals who are homeless. It requires that "each state educational agency shall assure that each child of a homeless individual and each home-

less youth have access to a free, appropriate public education" (42 U.S.C. Sec. 11431). Amendments to the original McKinney Act in 1990 called for better efforts to facilitate school success and access (Helm, 1993; Stronge, 1993). The law and associated funding have served to improve awareness of the problem and access to education (Helm, 1993).

Like IDEA, which provides specific definitions of disabilities categories, the McKinney Act provides a definition of homeless under which states are to operate if they are to receive federal assistance. While the Act addresses funding for services to people of all ages who are homeless, subsections of the Act address literacy and education. Coordinating services between state agencies such as education, social service, and health is discussed. In addition, states are encouraged to "develop relationships and coordinate relevant education, child development, and preschool programs and providers of services to children who are homeless" in order to improve the provision of such services to children and their families (p. 68). The state is also encouraged to adopt policies and practices to "ensure that homeless children and homeless youths are not isolated or stigmatized" (p. 69). Further, the act provides that children who become homeless during an academic year or between academic years may continue in their school of origin, that is, the school that they attended at the time they became homeless. Funding is also provided for individuals in local education agencies to serve as liasons between the school districts and service providers and the advocates working with children who are homeless. Finally, the act provides for local educational agency grants for the education of homeless children and youth. While the act is strong in provision, much like IDEA, the funding for many of the provisions has unfortunately not followed.

Homelessness is relatively new to social science research (Jones, Levine, & Rosenberg, 1991). The available literature largely consists of descriptive studies and theories of homelessness untested with children and families. This information, with its focus on adult populations, may be useful in providing an initial understanding of the problem and related issues. However, the literature, especially as it relates to children and families, should be read with a critical eye as much of what is known about homelessness is still untested.

The problems faced by children living in homeless situations and the implications for school psychologists and other education professionals working with these children and their families will be addressed in the remainder of this chapter. In addition, strategies for addressing the unique needs of these children in the school environment will be highlighted. The problem of homelessness is multidimensional and the issues for children are complex. The reader is encouraged to review other related topics in this book (e.g., foster care, stress, abuse, and neglect) when trying to gain a better understanding of ways to address the needs of children who are homeless.

Problems and Implications

The problem of homelessness is a daunting challenge. Theorists and researchers in the area approach the issue in multiple ways with no single approach to solving the problem having unanimous support in the literature. Research on homelessness is plagued by methodological concerns. The nature of the very problems researchers try to address are the source of many methodological challenges. Jones et al. (1991) argue that as a result of the limited "codified research, practice or intervention knowledge, each analysis reflects a slice in time from the vantage of the author" (p. 1110). Of the research and writing in the area, little has found its way to the school psychology and education literatures. Research from the fields of sociology, social work, anthropology, community psychology, and epidemiology among others has helped professionals working with children in education settings better understand the range of problems associated with homelessness. Addressing the unique challenges faced by homeless children and families is complex. What is clear, however, is that problem solving in the school setting for children who are homeless must be interdisciplinary. The importance and necessity of collaborative work by professionals across multiple domains and agencies cannot be understated.

Homeless children share many characteristics of children living in poverty who have homes. They are at risk for a variety of health, academic, developmental, and social-emotional and behavior difficulties (Shinn & Weitzman, 1990). The more common risk factors include poverty, single parent families, welfare dependent families, poorly educated parents, inadequate prenatal care, inadequate health care, elevated lead levels, frequent school transfers, and high exposure to life stressors (McChesney, 1993; Rafferty & Shinn, 1991; Shinn & Weitzman, in press). However, homeless children represent a more extreme group than children in low-income housing situations based on their cumulative risk (Masten, Miliotis, Graham-Bermann, Ramirez, & Neeman, 1993). For example, risk factors such as low educational status of mothers, single parents, poor health care, and foster care are common in both groups. However, homeless children also experience challenges unique to their situation including limited or inadequate access to education and the social stigma of living in a shelter or on the streets (Rafferty & Shinn, 1991). Still, when identifying a "peer group" for children who are homeless, school psychologists should make comparisons with other children living in extreme poverty.

Rafferty and Shinn (1991) and Shinn and Weitzman (in press) provide comprehensive reviews of the impact of homelessness on children, and McChesney (1993) offers a critical exploration of the literature examining homeless families and the implications for education. These researchers provide a framework to conceptualize the problems faced by children who are homeless. These problems and the implications for professionals working with children who are homeless are discussed next.

Health and Nutrition

The health risks faced by children who are homeless begin before birth. Women who are homeless and/or living in shelters receive less prenatal care than other pregnant mothers and those who do receive prenatal care do so much later in pregnancy (Chavkin, Kristal, Seaborn, & Guigli, 1987). Further, children born to mothers in homeless shelters are more likely to be born at a lower birth weight, as well as more likely to need hospitalizations and have delayed immunization schedules. They often have elevated lead levels in their blood and face an infant mortality rate one and one half times that of infants born to women in other public housing (Alperstein, Rappaport, & Flanigan, 1988; Rafferty & Shinn, 1991).

It is often a struggle to maintain an adequate and nutritionally balanced diet while living in a homeless shelter. Although children in shelters typically have more opportunities to eat than adults, they still report long periods of hunger, and the nutrition content of the food often is inadequate (Milburn & D'Ercole, 1991). One study reported families stretching infant formula with water (Rafferty & Shinn, 1991). Children who are homeless are more likely to be hungry and to have nutritional problems and subsequent health problems. Interestingly, some homeless children experience obesity due to poor diets (Wood, Valdez, Hayashi, & Shen, 1990).

Families who live in shelters rely heavily on entitlement programs such as Aid to Families with Dependent Children (AFDC) and the Special Supplemental Food Program for Women, Infants, and Children (WIC). However, the procedures to obtain benefits from entitlement programs are often complex, and families have to repeat the process many times due to relocation. Thus, homeless families are more likely than housed families to have had their AFDC cases closed and WIC benefits reduced (Rafferty & Shinn, 1991). Families not receiving AFDC and WIC often are left dependent on emergency food assistance facilities that frequently must turn people away because of lack of resources (Rafferty & Shinn).

Children living in homeless shelters have a greater incidence of upper respiratory tract infections, asthma, gastrointestinal disorders, chronic physical disorders, diarrhea, and intestinal ailments (Alperstein et al., 1988). Living conditions, poor sanitation, and noise that prevents adequate sleep contribute to the spread of communicable diseases and inhibit the child's ability to recuperate when he or she is sick. Families may be required to leave the shelter during the day further exacerbating potential health problems (U.S. Conference on Mayors, 1993).

Social-Emotional
and Behavioral Problems

Children who are homeless are more likely than their housed peers of all socioeconomic statuses to experience social-emotional and behavioral difficulties (Fox, Barrnett, Davies, & Bird, 1990). Children suffer substantial physical, psychological, and emotional damage from homelessness (Molnar, Rath, & Klein, 1990), including internalizing problems of depression and anxiety and externalizing problems such as aggression (Rafferty & Shinn, 1991). Interestingly, among homeless children, younger girls appear to have more overall behavioral and emotional problems (Masten et al., 1993).

Children who are homeless often have difficulty developing lasting friendships because they move so often (Eddowes, 1993). They may be less likely to seek friendship from children at school because of their own moving history and concern over the difficulty adjusting to the loss of friends when they move. They cannot invite friends over to play at their houses, have slumber parties, or engage in many social rituals typical of childhood. In many instances their physical appearance is different due to poverty, leading to a lack of acceptance by other children. Thus, homeless children's social development is hindered due to the unavailability of a stable social group.

Bassuk and her colleagues (see Bassuk and Gallagher, 1990; Bassuk and Rosenberg, 1990) were among the first to publish studies of mental health problems of children and mothers in homeless families. In their studies, mothers reported that after moving into a homeless shelter, many of their children's behaviors changed noticeably. Some children regressed and began to behave in ways more typical of younger children. Many developed eating and sleeping difficulties and started bedwetting again. Mothers also reported that their children became more aggressive and noncompliant or shy and withdrawn. The children were reportedly angry, cried for no reason, were provocative, and generally were hard to control. Children also tended to develop mothering behaviors. Siblings who seemed to be searching for adults to nurture and protect them from a dangerous, uncertain world turned to each other for nurturance and protection. Behavior problems scores were elevated, as were self-report symptoms of anxiety.

The research on the long-term consequences of homelessness is unclear. The effect of homelessness on children's social-emotional functioning may be transitory and limited to the time in which the stress of homelessness occurs (Shinn & Weitzman, in press). However, there is some evidence that emotional and behavioral problems persist after the family moves to a more permanent housing situation (Stanford Center, 1991). For example, many children continue to demonstrate significant behavioral difficulties and are likely to have difficulty with peer inter-

actions. Many also continue to experience low self-concept and high levels of anxiety and fear.

Developmental Delay

Children who are homeless are more likely to show developmental delays in all areas (e.g., cognitive functioning, language development, reading, motor development) than children in the general population (McChesney, 1993; Rescorla, Parker, & Stolley, 1991). However, few significant differences are found on measures of development when comparing children who are homeless to housed poor children. Rafferty and Shinn (1991) conclude that "poverty may be a key mediator of developmental problems" (p. 1173). Shelter conditions, unstable child care, and parental factors also appear to mediate developmental problems (Rafferty & Shinn, 1991). For example, many parents under the stress of homelessness are unable to interact with their children in ways that best promote development. In addition, crowded conditions in shelters, limited access to space and materials for play, and the unavailability of same-age peers may impact development in a variety of domains including language, motor, social, and cognitive.

Educational Problems

Homelessness appears to impede a child's access to early childhood education programs (Shinn & Weitzman, in press). Of children who are homeless, those not living in shelters are the least likely to have access to adequate child care and early education experiences. Further, those children not living in shelters are more likely to "lack developmentally appropriate toys and may not have appropriate places to play" (Shinn & Weitzman, in press). Little research has been conducted on the educational achievement of children who are homeless (Rafferty & Shinn, 1991). The few studies that have been conducted indicate that homeless children often face barriers to education, attendance problems, transportation problems, and academic delays and often repeat grades (Rafferty, 1991; Rafferty & Shinn, 1991; Stanford Center, 1991). In addition, children who are homeless, on average, score significantly lower on measures of academic achievement and behavior than nonhomeless and higher socioeconomic status peers (Rescorla et al., 1991). Further, the conditions in the shelter are not typically conducive to education and facilities often do not provide adequate student work space (Rafferty & Shinn, 1991).

Despite the passage of the McKinley Act, obtaining and maintaining access to school appears to be a major factor in the educational underachievement of children who are homeless. While residency requirements may have lessened in some parts of the U.S., they continue to pose a challenge to school attendance for most families who are homeless. Other problems such as the inability to obtain previous school records, inadequate immunization records, transportation problems, lack of clothing and supplies, and hostility from students and teachers also remain (Eddowes, 1993; Shinn & Weitzman, in press). In addition, due to the difficulty in re-establishing eligibility for services, many children who are homeless often lose special educational services (e.g., special education, gifted and talented enrichment programs, and bilingual education) as they move from school to school (Rafferty, 1991).

Social Policy Implications

School professionals working with children who are homeless face many challenges. Solutions to these children's problems are complex and cannot be considered in isolation of social policy. At the time of this writing, many of the programs of greatest benefit to homeless children are experiencing drastic budget cuts (e.g., Headstart, school breakfast and lunch programs, AFDC, and WIC), and some are at risk for total elimination. Professionals familiar with the needs of homeless argue more, not less, is needed.

Schools must address residency requirements that prevent children from maintaining a stable school environment and often prevent them from even entering school. Community-based programs for at-risk children and families and the movement toward school-based health and mental health services show great promise in addressing the multifaceted needs of children who are homeless.

Alternative Actions

Professionals must realize that first consideration should be given to the life stressors the child is experiencing and then consideration to the family's living situation (Masten et al., 1993). Admittedly, homelessness places multiple, complex stressors on the family which are not easily unraveled. However, if even a portion of the stressors that plague families who are homeless could be alleviated, the psychological risks for children could be greatly reduced (Rafferty & Shinn, 1991; Shinn & Weitzman, 1990).

School psychologists in settings providing services to children who are homeless must work to increase their level of awareness of the issues and concerns. The process is similar to the manner in which professionals increase their awareness of many issues of diversity. The easiest and best way to learn more about a population is to spend time with these individuals in their own area. For example, professionals who work with homeless children may find it helpful to volunteer time at a local food bank, community shelter, or community health clinic.

Such volunteer work allows professionals to learn about the community and populations with whom they will be working. In addition, contact with local community agencies providing services to children who are homeless and their families such as the state department of mental health, social service, housing, and the like may assist school professionals in making contacts with other relevant professionals. This can in turn help to provide a more comprehensive model of interdisciplinary service to children in the school setting.

The research on effective and promising intervention alternatives in education settings for children who are homeless is brief and plagued with many methodological concerns. However, a number of themes emerge that appear likely to assist school psychologists and other educational professionals as they attempt to address these children's needs.

Individuality

Just as "the homeless" are not one undifferentiated mass, children and families who are homeless are not homogeneous (McChesney, 1993). Children and families are homeless for many reasons, and each story is unique. The individual situation of each child must be carefully explored to arrive at understanding appropriate techniques and areas for intervention.

McCormick and Holden (1992) and Klein et al. (1993) provide excellent reviews of ways education professionals can address the needs of children who are homeless. Their suggestions are easy to implement and provide not only a manner of effective service delivery to children who are homeless but also good intervention for all children.

According to McCormick and Holden (1992), education staff need to understand the following:

1. Children are embarrassed about being homeless.
2. Their parents are dealing with many problems in addition to homelessness.
3. Parents care about their children.
4. Intrusive questions about their living conditions and home environments may make parents uncomfortable because answers are often not easy.
5. Parents should not be blamed for children's problems.
6. Requests to bring things to school can pose a hardship for the family.
7. Just because they are homeless does not mean that the family is necessarily dysfunctional.

Teachers in the study believed the following to be important areas of consideration when working with children who are homeless:

1. Children who are homeless are more similar to their peers than they are different.

2. Peer friendships may need to be actively encouraged because such friendships do not always occur naturally.
3. Play and social activities are particularly important for children who are homeless because they often have no time or place to play when they are not at school.
4. Stress is unavoidable for children who are homeless. Although some children may appear to be coping well, they cannot escape the stressors that being homeless places on the family.
5. Even the most basic health and safety concerns may seem overwhelming to families who are already overstressed. Patience and sensitivity are essential.

Interdisciplinary Activities

Given the complexity of stressors and problems experienced by children who are homeless, work across disciplines is crucial. While this may sound simple to do, the reality is that work across disciplines is often difficult. The school psychologist should develop contacts with professionals working in community agencies that provide services to children and families who are homeless. It may be helpful to develop a list of available services with addresses and phone numbers. Such a list might include WIC; the local housing authority; community food banks; local shelters; free and reduced cost medical clinics; physicians and mental heath workers who see patients without insurance; and community organizations that provide items such as clothing and school supplies to children who are homeless. It may also be helpful to highlight these places on a map with locations related to the school the child attends and with local bus routes marked if available.

In addition to contacts with professionals in other disciplines, school psychologists should remember that professionals each have different areas of expertise within their own discipline. Homelessness issues could be developed as an area of expertise. Finally interdisciplinary and collaborative work is essential in providing the best and most effective service to children who are homeless.

District-Level Change

Many of the barriers faced by children who are homeless cannot be addressed by individual teachers, school psychologists, or educational staff. School psychologists with their skills in consultation and systems-level change are in a unique position to effect changes likely to assist children who are homeless. For example, streamlined school-entry processes could be developed and school residency requirements examined in light of their impact on children who are homeless. Extended school-day programs can provide children with (a) opportunities to develop friendships outside of the classroom; (b) a place to complete outside-of-class assignments in an environment conducive to studying; and (c) supervision when their parents are away. Finally, school-based health and mental health services could provide opportunities for intervention in areas that mediate school performance.

Summary

While the problem of homelessness is not new, the face of homelessness is. Children are the fastest growing segment of the homeless population. Of the children who are homeless, young children appear to be at greatest risk. Children who are homeless face problems in health and nutrition, social-emotional and behavioral problems, developmental delays, and educational underachievement.

Homelessness is a manifestation of extreme poverty. As a result, the problems of homelessness in children cannot be addressed without considering ways to address the problems of poverty. Such issues must be addressed at the national, state, and community levels. While this chapter has stressed the complexity of the challenges posed in providing effective services to children who are homeless, perhaps the most important point to remember in addressing their needs is the least complicated. Good teaching is good teaching for all students. Focus on the strength of the students and their families. Remember that they are children first and homeless second.

Recommended Resources

Eddowes, E. A. (1993). Education of younger homeless children in urban settings. *Education in Urban Society, 25,* 381–393.
The article provides an excellent review of the literature on educational problems of elementary and preschool age children. Of particular interest is the review of programs successful in serving the educational needs of homeless preschool, elementary, and middle-school children.

Jones, J. M., Levine, I. S., & Rosenberg, A. A. (Eds). (1991). Homelessness [Special issue]. *American Psychologist, 46*(11).
The entire issue of the November 1991 **American Psychologist** *is devoted to the topic of homelessness. It contains empirical studies, theoretical discussion pieces, and position articles on the topic. Especially relevant to professionals working with children and families are the five articles on homeless women, children, and families.*

Kozol, J. (1988). *Rachel and her children: Homeless families in America.* New York: Fawcett Columbine.
Kozol presents a graphic picture of life for the homeless in New York City. The strength of this book for practitioners working in school settings is the manner in which Kozol paints pictures of these families. The book is a powerful tool in gaining an appreciation of the issues faced by homeless children and their families.

Massachusetts State Department of Education. (1991). *Faces of homelessness: A teacher's guide.* Quincy, MA: Author.
This guide accompanies two 15-minute video segments on homelessness. Multiple cases of homelessness are highlighted. The tapes and guide are useful in discussions with students and are available from the author.

Timmer, D. A., Eitzen, S., & Talley, K. D. (1994). *Paths to homelessness: Extreme poverty and urban housing crisis.* Boulder, CO: Westview Press.
While not directly focused on issues related to children, this book provides an excellent overview of the condition of homelessness through the use of case studies. Specific subtypes of homelessness are highlighted including old people who are homeless, runaway teens, and young families. Implications for politics and policy are also discussed.

References

Alperstein, G., Rappaport, C., & Flanigan, J. M. (1988). Health problems of homeless children in New York City. *American Journal of Public Health, 78,* 1232–1233.

Bassuk, E. L., & Rosenberg, L. (1990). Psychosocial characteristics of homeless children and children with homes. *Pediatrics, 85,* 257–261.

Burt, M. R., & Cohen, B. E. (1989). Differences among homeless single women, women with children, and single men. *Social Problems, 36,* 508–524.

Chavkin, W., Kristal, A., Seaborn, C., & Guigli, P. E. (1987). Reproductive experience of women living in hotels for the homeless in New York City. *New York State Journal of Medicine, 87,* 10–13.

Children's Defense Fund. (1994). *The state of America's children 1994.* Washington, DC: Author.

Eddowes, E. A. (1993). Education of younger homeless children in urban settings. *Education in Urban Society, 25,* 381–393.

Fox, S. J., Barrnett, J. R., Davies, M., & Bird, H. R. (1990). Psychopathology and developmental delay in homeless children: A pilot study. *Journal of the American Academy of Child and Adolescent Psychiatry, 29,* 732–735.

Helm, V. M. (1993). Legal rights to education of homeless children and youth. *Education and Urban Society, 25,* 323–339.

Huston, A. C., McLloyd, V. C., & Garcia-Coll, C. (1994). Children and poverty: Issues in contemporary research. *Child Development, 65,* 275–282.

Individuals with Disabilities Education Act of 1991, Pub. L. No. 102-119.

Jenks, C. (1994). *The homeless.* Cambridge, MA: Harvard University Press.

Jones, J. M., Levine, I. S., & Rosenberg, A. A. (Eds.). (1991). Homelessness [Special issue]. *American Psychologist, 46*(11).

Klein, T., Bittel, C., & Molnar, J. (1993). No place to call home: Supporting the needs of homeless children in the early childhood classroom. *Young Children, 48,* 22–31.

Masten, A. S., Miliotis, D., Graham-Bermann, S. A., Ramirez, M., & Neemann, J. (1993). Children in homeless families: Risks to mental health and development. *Journal of Consulting and Clinical Psychology, 61,* 335–343.

McChesney, K. Y. (1993). Homeless families since 1980: Implications for education. *Education and Urban Society, 25*(4), 361–380.

McCormick, L., & Holden, R. (1992). Homeless children: A special challenge. *Young Children,* 61–67.

Milburn, N., & D'Ercole, A. (1991). Homeless women, children, and families. *American Psychologist, 46,* 1159–1160.

Molnar, J., Rath, W., & Klein, T. (1990). Constantly comprised: The impact of homelessness on children. *Journal of Social Issues, 46,* 109–124.

National Alliance to End Homelessness. (1994). *Annual report.*

Rafferty, Y. (1991). *And miles to go: Barriers to academic achievement and innovative strategies for the delivery of educational services to homeless children.* New York: Advocates for Children.

Rafferty, Y., & Shinn, M. (1991). The impact of homelessness on children. *American Psychologist, 46*(11), 1170–1179.

Rescorla, L., Parker, R., & Stolley, P. (1991). Ability, achievement, and adjustment in homeless children. *American Journal of Orthopsychiatry, 61,* 210–220.

Rotheram-Borus, M. J., Koopman, C., & Ehrhardt, A. A. (1991). Homeless youths and HIV infection. *American Psychologist, 46*(11), 1188–1197.

Shinn, M. (1992). Homelessness: What is a psychologist to do? *American Journal of Community Psychology, 20*(1), 1–24.

Shinn, M., & Weitzman, B. C. (1990). Research on homelessness: An introduction. *Journal of Social Issues, 46*(4), 1–11.

Shinn, M, & Weitzman, B. C. (in press). Homeless families are different. In J. Baumohl (Ed.), *Homeless in America: A reference book.* New York: National Coalition for the Homeless and Oryx Press.

Stanford Center for the Study of Families, Children, and Youth. (1991). *The Stanford studies of homeless families, children and youth.* Palo Alto, CA: Author.

Stewart B. McKinney Homeless Assistance Act, 42 U.S.C.A. § 11443 *et seq.* (West, 1987).

Stronge, J. H. (1993). From access to success: Public policy for educating urban homeless students. *Education and Urban Society, 25,* 340–360.

U.S. Conference of Mayors. (1993). *A status report on hunger and homelessness in America's cities: 1993.* Washington, DC: U.S. Conference of Mayors.

Wood, D., Valdez, R., Hayashi, T., & Shen, A. (1990). Health of homeless children and housed poor children. *Pediatrics, 86,* 858–866.

62

Foster Homes

Nancy McKellar

Wichita State University

Background and Development

Children are entitled to reach adulthood having experienced a safe, healthy, and nurturing environment and to experience the benefits of a family that advocates for them and offers them the opportunity to develop into responsible and self-sufficient adults (Barth, Courtney, Berrick, & Albert, 1994, p. 274).

Children in foster care are at risk for not having the benefits of such an upbringing. They have been removed from their biological home to protect them and to improve their well-being (Dubowitz et al., 1994).

Foster care is similar to group homes and institutional care because children live apart from their biological families. It is distinguished from these other arrangements in that children live with a substitute family who is given some financial compensation by the state for the child's care. About three fourths of children in out-of-home placement are in family foster homes (Lewit, 1993). Unlike adoption which results in a permanent home placement, foster care is intended as temporary care.

Foster homes are recruited and supervised by public and private social service agencies that are authorized and monitored by the state. The agencies are staffed by social workers, one of whom is assigned as the foster child's case manager. The Federal Adoption Assistance and Child Welfare Act of 1980 (P.L. 96-272) requires permanency planning within specified time limits to prevent children from languishing in foster care without a goal being set for either reunification with the biological family, adoption, guardianship, or long-term foster care until emancipation.

The experiences of children in foster homes are affected by the length of time they have been in foster care and the age at which they were first removed from the biological home. The stability of their placement history is described in terms of the number of their different foster parents, living arrangements (foster homes, group homes, institutions), and returns to the biological family. The placement of siblings is also important to understanding foster children.

The overall number of children currently or formerly in foster care makes it likely that school psychologists

work with these students. Bauer (1993) estimated that there are about 400,000 children in foster care on any given day. The school-related needs of foster children also raise the likelihood that school psychologists serve students who are in the foster care system. Foster children experience higher rates of poor school achievement (Dubowitz et al., 1994) and emotional and physical disabilities (Barth et al., 1994). Also, there is a disproportionate number of foster children in special education (Bauer, 1993; Goerge, Voorhis, Grant, Casey, & Robinson, 1992).

Since the mid-1980s, the number of children in foster care has risen dramatically, with disproportionate increases among young children, particularly infants (Barth et al., 1994), and in large, urban areas (Wulczyn & Goerge, 1992). In 1992, approximately six of every thousand U.S. children were in foster care (Lewit, 1993). By 1995 almost 900,000 children were expected to live away from their biological parent(s) in foster homes, group homes, or institutions (Children's Defense Fund, 1992).

Reasons Children Enter Foster Care

Most children enter foster care because their parents provide inadequate care (Lewit, 1993). Biological parents may voluntarily request that their children enter foster care, but typically children are removed from the home after the state's child protective services agency or a law enforcement agency has received a report of abuse or neglect (Davis & Ellis-MacLeod, 1994). Barth and his associates (1994) analyzed the reasons for placement of a sample of California children. Most of these children were removed from a single-parent home (mother 79%; father 4.5%), primarily due to neglect (40%), abuse (28%), or caretaker absence or incapacity (26%). Figures for two large states in 1991 indicate that 68% of children were removed due to neglect, caretaker absence or incapacity, relinquishment, or voluntary placements (U.S. General Accounting Office, 1994).

Social and economic conditions, such as divorce, substance abuse, disease, and family violence, lead to a greater probability of family poverty or diminished ability to parent and increase the chances of a child entering the foster care system. In recent years, more and more of the families from which children are removed have complex, multiple problems (Tatara, 1994). The drug epidemic that began in the mid-1980s differs from those in earlier decades in the increase of women of childbearing age using cocaine, often in combination with alcohol and other drugs (U.S. General Accounting Office, 1990, 1994). The impact has been an increase in the foster care population due to many drug-dependent infants entering the system at birth and additional young children entering as victims of abuse and neglect by their biological parent(s) who are abusing drugs (Lewit, 1993; Stahl, 1990).

For many children, foster care results in long-term instability. About 40% of the children in one study (Barth et al., 1994) spent at least 3 years in foster care. Most children who leave foster care do so by being reunited with their biological families (Barth et al., 1994; Kansas Legislative Division of Post Audit, 1991). The more frequent the visitation between the child and biological family members, the greater likelihood that the child will be reunited rather than continue in foster care (Lawder, Poulin, & Andrews, 1986).

Elementary-school children (between ages 4 and 12) have the fastest rate of return to their biological parents (Barth et al., 1994). Poor children, however, return home at a slower rate. The rate of reunification with the biological parent(s) is particularly slow for infants. Unfortunately, a quick return to the biological home is associated with a greater risk that the child will be returned to foster care (Barth et al., 1994).

As has been true for many years, children who are poor and from minority homes, particularly African-American, enter the foster care system at a higher rate than other children (Barth et al., 1994). There is a difference of 2.5 years between the age when White children first experience total separation from both their mothers and fathers (average age of 7.4 years) and when minority children experience this disruption (average age of 4.9 years; Fanshel, Finch, & Grundy, 1989). Once in foster care, Black children are significantly less likely to receive health care or ancillary services (Benedict, White, Stallings, & Cornely, 1989). Also, they exit foster care by returning to their biological homes at only half the rate of White children (McMurtry & Lie, 1992).

The lives of foster children are characterized by many situation changes. While they are with their biological families between birth and placement, their families are characterized by divorce, separation, and widowhood (Hulsey & White, 1989). Two different placements while in foster care are not unusual (Pardeck, 1983). Children whose parents have fewer resources to care for them, particularly those with divorced or widowed biological parents with economic problems, have a higher probability of multiple placements, as do older children and

those who experience high caseworker turnover (Pardeck, Murphy, & Fitzwater, 1985). Although children are typically not placed in foster care due to any of their behaviors or characteristics, the most common reason for moving them from home to home once in the state's custody is that they run away, have behavior problems, or both (Kansas Legislative Division of Post Audit, 1991). Foster families that are emotionally involved with the child, able to share feelings and handle anger well, and communicate effectively under stress are better able to provide longer, more stable care (Walsh & Walsh, 1990).

Alternate Types of Foster Care

Two variations of foster care expected to expand in the future are *kinship care* and *specialized care* (Barth et al., 1994). Foster care by members of the child's extended biological family is called kinship care. This form of foster care has grown rapidly in the last decade (Berrick & Barth, 1994). Children in kinship care are more likely to be poor children of color and to return to their biological parent(s) at a slower rate than children in nonkinship care (Barth et al., 1994). They tend to have more contact with their biological parents (Dubowitz et al., 1994) and a much lower probability of multiple placements (Berrick, Barth, & Needell, 1994) than children in conventional foster care. They are also more likely to remain in the same school and neighborhood after entering care (Barth et al., 1994).

The kinship foster parent is often a single grandmother or aunt employed outside the home but with a low income, who may not have the energy or good health needed to raise a young child (Berrick et al., 1994; Kelley, 1992). In a study of the quality of care for children whose mothers were incarcerated, Gaudin and Sutphen (1993) found that the needs of infants and toddlers were met equally well in kinship and conventional foster care but that preschoolers (ages 3–6) received more attention and cognitive stimulation in conventional care. Research is needed on the long-term effects of kinship care on the general well-being of children (Barth et al., 1994).

Specialized foster care, also called *treatment or therapeutic foster care,* is designed for children with extreme behavior problems or with complex medical needs, such as HIV infection (Anderson, 1990; Barth et al., 1994). Often there was a combination of chaos, abuse, neglect, substance abuse, and sexual abuse in their biological homes. Children from such chaotic backgrounds have the most pressing needs and pose the most difficult problems for foster parents (Stahl, 1990). Treatment foster care is critical to providing these children with the specialized, coordinated care they need (Barth et al.). These placements are powerful alternatives to residential or group home placements, especially for young children (Barth et al.). Usually foster parents providing this type of care receive more training and significantly more compensation (U.S.

General Accounting Office, 1994), report more satisfaction from being a foster parent, and are more involved in the case planning for the child than are foster parents providing conventional care. Because a majority of parents providing therapeutic foster care are White, minority children have less chance of being placed with a foster family of similar ethnicity (Barth et al.).

Impact of Foster Care on Children

A professor of special education who is also the adoptive parent of several special needs children explained:

In our constant learning about our children and how to parent them, one factor has emerged as the most significant. Living in foster care has an incredible impact on your life, not only at that time, but throughout your development. As you enter each developmental stage, you will again deal with issues that emerged from your neglect, abandonment, or abuse. (Bauer, 1993, p. 140)

Attachment and separation are the dominant psychological issues in describing how children at different developmental levels react to removal from the biological parent(s) and how they adapt to foster care (Stahl, 1990; see Table 1). When interviewed as adults, former foster children relate that the core issues in their lives as children were "their feelings about loss of their parents, their difficulty in getting over a disrupted adoption, and their dealing with expectations of their foster parents" (Fanshel et al., 1989, p. 474).

The psychological attachment process of foster children is threatened in several ways when there is substance abuse by their biological parents. First, drug-exposed infants may not adequately attach to their foster parents because they can be difficult children to parent. They may be stiff, reluctant to cuddle, irritable, and easily overstimulated. Some have varying combinations of tremors, feeding problems, impaired organizational abilities, depressed interactive abilities, and abnormal sleep patterns (Kelley, 1992). These babies have an increased likelihood of health problems related to prematurity, retarded intrauterine growth, and low birth weight. Second, children who are with their drug-dependent mothers for the first months and years of life also are at risk of not having accomplished the psychological task of attachment with the primary caregiver because their mothers' drug dependence may have impeded the mother's ability to parent effectively. This weak attachment to the parental figure leaves the toddler poorly prepared for the developmental task of separation and individuation (Stahl, 1990).

The impact of poor attachment to the biological parents can be ameliorated to some extent by better quality attachment to foster parents (Marcus, 1991). "Children who feel more secure with their foster parents, who experience more positive emotional ties with them, and who receive physical affection from them are psychologically better adjusted and experience fewer achievement problems in school" (p. 385).

Separation from one's biological parent(s) represents a significant loss for the foster child (Stahl, 1990). But the loss is more pervasive than just losing one's parent(s) because the child usually loses siblings, grandparents, pets, and belongings when placed in foster care (Bauer, 1993). The experience of removal from the biological home has been described as "being told by a stranger to get your things, get into a car, and simply go to live with someone we don't know, with no information about when we would see our parents or home again" (Bauer, 1993, p. 141).

The shock, anger, despair, and acceptance that comprise the grieving process are experienced by foster children as they mourn the loss of their biological home (Stahl, 1990). Feeling psychologically vulnerable is the primary effect of being removed from one's biological parent(s). In response to this vulnerability and in addition to the feelings associated with the grieving process, foster children may experience confusion, anger, alienation, and ambivalence. They may withdraw and isolate themselves, test rules excessively, engage in wishful and magical thinking, be dependent and passive, and/or have limited self-confidence.

Children who have experienced several out-of-home placements may feel like they have no control over their lives, leading to learned helplessness behaviors (Bauer, 1993). Each time the child moves to a new home, time must be spent learning the new rules and routines and ways to fit in. The more life situation changes experienced, the more likely the child will be hostile and oppositional. In their longitudinal study of children in foster care, Fanshel et al. (1989) found that children who are hostile when they enter foster care do not adapt well. They tend to have less financial security and more antisocial behavioral tendencies as adults. However, this pattern can be broken if an intervention is implemented to overcome their oppositional behavior.

Problems and Implications

Problems Common to Most Foster Children

Foster children may go for long periods of time without information about or contact with their biological families (Bauer, 1993). They may worry about their siblings who remain in the biological home or have gone into other foster homes. Children who have few contacts with their biological families and little chance of being reunited with them have the most complex problems involving low self-esteem and identity confusion.

Because they have often been abused, neglected, or both in their biological families, foster children are at risk for discontinuous and inadequate medical care, poor health and nutrition, undetected health problems, and very low weight and height (Benedict et al., 1989; Dubowitz et al., 1994). Anemia, asthma, and dental problems are common (Dubowitz et al., 1994). Their health records may be very limited (Hochstadt, Jaudes, Zimo, & Schachter, 1987). Children frequently enter foster care with multiple, complex health problems that adults in the foster care system are unprepared or unable to deal with (Simms & Halfon, 1994). Social workers are not used to focusing on medical issues, and foster parents often underestimate the extent of foster children's health problems (Cain & Barth, 1990). The parents may need to take the child to numerous appointments at which they sometimes receive conflicting recommendations (Simms & Halfon, 1994). Follow-up care is jeopardized because foster parents usually are not legally able to make major decisions regarding the child's medical treatment and because changes in foster home placements and case managers are common.

Children who start school prior to foster care placement may have a history of inadequate instruction. The biological parents may have moved often, not consistently gotten the child to school, and failed to support the child in getting homework done.

Behavior problems are found more frequently in foster children than their age-mates (Hochstadt et al., 1987). These problems more often involve multiple symptoms (McIntyre & Keesler, 1986) and tend to be most severe in foster children with a history of having been abused (Stein, Rae-Grant, Ackland, & Avison, 1994). Delinquency, aggression, social problems, and attention-seeking behaviors are common (Dubowitz et al., 1994). Conduct disorder is the most prevalent single disorder (Stein et al., 1994).

In his work with foster families, Stahl (1990) found that foster parents are able to handle the typical problematic behaviors that children at different developmental stages exhibit. However, foster parents have more difficulty handling other problem behaviors that occur often in foster children, including aggression, lying, stealing, regressive behaviors, passive-aggression, and destructive behavior. Foster homes with higher quality child-rearing and a greater variety of stimulation are correlated with foster children's better emotional functioning, less aggression, and greater social competence (Smith, 1994).

When Drugs Are Involved

Infants are placed in foster care typically because their parents are drug dependent and the infants were drug exposed. These babies have a low probability of returning to their biological parent(s) and, thus, may enter school having spent their entire lives in a form of care meant to be temporary. In 1991, 79% of the families from which young children were removed had other children in foster care and 78% involved at least one parent who was abusing drugs or alcohol (U.S. General Accounting Office, 1994). Because most treatment programs are not designed for pregnant women and mothers, there are few alternatives to foster care for drug-abusing single mothers who continue using drugs (U.S. General Accounting Office, 1994).

Children who have been prenatally exposed to drugs are at an increased risk of developmental delays; neurological abnormalities; and problems with language, adaptive behavior, fine motor coordination, and cognitive skills (U.S. General Accounting Office, 1990). These children are likely to have come from impoverished environments with the concomitant problems of poor nutrition and health care, homelessness, and violence (Lester & Tronick, 1994). The complex interaction of biological and environmental factors that determine the developmental outcomes for drug-exposed children is not fully understood (Garrity-Rokous, 1994). Surprisingly, some preschool children show few of the negative behavioral characteristics that have been predicted for them based on their prenatal drug exposure (Cohen & Erwin, 1994). Because a child-centered early environment is positively related to developmental outcomes (Black, Schuler, & Nair, 1993), the biological mother's participation in a treatment program and her ability to provide such an environment are important considerations in whether the goal for the foster child should be family reunification or adoption.

When the Child Was Neglected or Abused

Children placed in foster care often have histories of being neglected, abandoned, or abused. They may have been without adequate care or control or may not have attended school regularly (Kansas Legislative Division of Post Audit, 1994). Many children have suffered "a massive interaction of both abuse and neglect" (Stahl, 1990, p. 7). Explosiveness and a basic distrust of parental figures are common in children who have suffered abuse or extreme neglect. Anger and fantasies about parental-child relationships characterize children who have been abandoned or who have been entangled in a mutually hostile relationship with their biological parents (Fanshel et al., 1989). If the child's emotional development has been hampered by neglect, abuse, or other circumstances that prompted the removal, the child may have an especially difficult time with the grieving process (Stahl). Fanshel et al. found that among boys in foster care, those who had been physically abused did less well in foster care, had a higher probability of experiencing a disturbing sexual event, and were more likely to engage in criminal activity as adults.

School-Related Issues

The foster child's rights to confidentiality and privacy may result in less background information than the school team typically has for assessment and intervention services. Social workers do not always give foster parents complete information about the child's past. Likewise, foster parents are obligated to keep information about their foster children confidential (Stahl, 1990).

Truancy and school refusal are common among foster children. Stahl (1990) explained these behaviors as being due to prior hurt, anger at their biological parents, and fear of being hurt by new authority figures.

Foster children often do poorly in unstructured activities, such as recess (Stahl, 1990). Their tendency to be easily victimized or start fights can result in peers treating them as their biological parents did and reinforcing their belief that they are bad and deserving of abuse. They are at a higher risk than their age-mates to be disliked or rejected by their peers (McIntyre, Lounsbury, Berntson, & Steel, 1988). Foster children also may have difficulty with authority figures both at school and in the foster home (Stahl). They may test the limits of authority, have angry outbursts when asked to do something, or avoid contact with authority figures.

Over half the school-aged children entering foster care in Cook County, Illinois, in a single month were identified as needing a review of their academic records or an evaluation due to potential school-related problems (Hochstadt et al., 1987). In the Fanshel et al. (1989) longitudinal study, a third of the children were achieving below their grade level both when entering and when leaving foster care. Dubowitz and his associates (1994) found in their study of Baltimore foster children that 45% of them had repeated a grade and almost 30% were in special education. Teachers noted particularly the children's poor attention and work study habits. The most common handicapping conditions among foster children are learning disabilities (Berrick et al., 1994), mental retardation, and emotional disturbance (Hill, Hayden, Lakin, Menke, & Amado, 1990). When children are assessed shortly after their initial foster care placement, older children are more likely to be identified as having developmental problems that are cognitive, behavioral, and/or motor in nature (Horwitz, Simms, & Farrington, 1994).

School achievement tends to be lower among children placed in foster care because of suspected neglect or abuse than among children placed for other reasons (Aldgate, Heath, Colton, & Simm, 1993). In a British longitudinal study comparing children in foster care with those from similar home circumstances who remained with their biological parents while the family received social work support, no difference was found in educational progress (Heath, Colton, & Aldgate, 1994). However, foster children who were removed from their parents because of deprivation or maltreatment made slower educational progress than those removed due to parental illness or economic hardship.

Concerns of Foster Parents

At the same time that the demand for foster care has been increasing, the availability of foster homes has been diminishing. This pattern has been attributed to demographic factors, such as more women working outside the home, and to the frustrations experienced by foster parents (Barth et al., 1994).

Foster parents may feel that they are not appropriately informed, respected, valued, supported, or compensated (Barth et al., 1994). Social service workers may not provide essential information about the child being placed. Although foster parents are the individuals who have spent extensive time and effort with the child, they are not typically included by the social service agency as an active team member serving the child, let alone consulted by the social worker or the juvenile courts about the child's progress. They may not receive adequate training for their responsibilities and may receive stipends that fail to cover the child's expenses.

Alternative Actions

When one former foster child was asked to describe the most gratifying experience while in foster care, the adult replied,

That I finally belonged somewhere. . . . This simple fact, that I belonged, was the most healing. It may not sound like much, but when one grows up in a world of continual crisis and disorganization, it means everything. That I had a chance. They gave me an opportunity to change my life. . . . They gave me hope. (Fanshel et al., 1989, p. 477)

The adult described how receiving birthday and Christmas cards and knowing that one's photo was in the agency office signalled this sense of belonging by the foster care agency. Foster children, like all children, need to have the repeated message that they are valued unconditionally (Bauer, 1993).

Questions to Ask During Problem Analysis

Given the length of time that many children spend in foster care, educational planning should not be postponed until the child is in a more permanent home. The following questions should be answered in planning educational interventions:

1. What are the history and circumstances of the child's out-of-home placements?

Caution is needed in interpreting data from evaluations of children whose adjustment to foster care has not stabilized (Kates, Johnson, Rader, & Strieder, 1991). When children must be evaluated soon after placement in foster care, re-evaluation in a few months should be planned. As stated earlier, children at various developmental levels respond differently to placement in foster care (see Table 1).

2. Who is the child's legal guardian and who is providing daily care of the child?

A determination needs to be made of who must sign whenever parental permission is required. The answer may be dependent upon the reason for permission, for example, a field trip versus special education services. Because state laws vary as to parental rights and legal guardianship, the state education agency (SEA) should be consulted for the relevant requirements. To begin to gather information needed to apply these requirements, school officials can ask the foster parents for the name and telephone number of the child's case manager. In situations in which kinship care is occurring without the involvement of the social service agency, the foster parents should be asked the conditions of any power of attorney related to the child that they have.

It is unlikely that the foster parents will be the individuals who must give parental permission in decisions related to special education services. However, the foster parents are very important in the implementation of educational interventions because they provide the child's daily care. The school staff needs to establish and maintain a good relationship with foster parents, just as with all parents, to facilitate their involvement in the child's education. Also, as interventions are planned, decisions need to be made about the ways and extent that the foster parents can be involved.

3. Does the child have unmet or undetected health needs?

If so, these will need to be addressed so that the child can benefit fully from the educational program. Therefore, the involvement of the school nurse is very important when evaluating a child in foster care.

4. What is the child's school attendance record and level of academic achievement?

No assumptions should be made that a child has not benefitted from prior education unless information can be obtained to substantiate that the child has received adequate instruction. Prior to foster care placement, the child may not have attended school regularly, limiting the opportunity to learn academic skills and appropriate school behaviors (Stahl, 1990). Foster children may not have been reinforced by their biological parents for their efforts and encouraged to do homework. Placement in foster care may have required that the child change schools (Berrick et al., 1994). Because poverty is highly associated with placement in foster care, these children may lack experiences, such as playing with age-appropriate toys and being read to, that are common to other children (Bauer, 1993). Error and task analyses will help to identify curriculum content that the foster child has missed.

5. Does the child have a history of abuse, neglect, or both?

Abused children typically become either defiant or overly compliant (Bauer, 1993). Interventions helpful for these children include behavior management, self-management, and natural consequences (Bauer). Neglected children are quite emotionally needy. They benefit from a structured, predictable environment coupled with much individual attention. For both groups of children and for those who have been both abused and neglected, the environment needs to have clear limits and consequences that are consistently enforced (Smith, 1994). Ignoring inappropriate behavior should be avoided because these children often increase the behavior being ignored to dangerous levels (Bauer). However, punishment of any type, particularly corporal punishment, should not be used with foster children, whether or not prior abuse is suspected (Piers, 1984).

6. What is the goal of the permanency plan for this child?

The social service agency should develop a permanency plan for each foster child, indicating whether the goal is to reintegrate the child with the biological parent(s); to have the child adopted; or to keep the child, usually an adolescent, in foster care until emancipation. The child's case manager should be asked the goal of the permanency plan and the extent to which it has been shared with the child. When children are not informed about decisions and plans regarding their future, they fill the void with fantasies of their own.

7. Is the foster child currently receiving counseling?

Foster children need help to accept and understand their feelings, such as anger and sadness, and to learn appropriate behaviors in response to those feelings (Stahl, 1990). They need to be told that it is all right for them to be concerned about their biological families (Bauer, 1993).

The school psychologist should inquire as to whether the foster child is receiving private therapy. If so, it may be helpful for the school psychologist to communicate with the private therapist about the child's behavior at school. If the child is not receiving private therapy, a consideration needs to be made as to whether the child should receive counseling at school.

Table 1 *Problematic Responses to Foster Care Placement by Children at Different Developmental Levels*

Age of Entry to Foster Care	Prominent Psychological Concerns
I. Newborns	Attachment not accomplished
	(Possible drug dependency)
II. Young Children	Delays in development, particularly talking, socialization, and toileting
	Regression
	Immaturity
A. Toddler	Regression in emotional functioning
	Clingy and dependent
	Strong feelings of vulnerability, exhibited as temper tantrums, depression, withdrawal, and destructiveness
B. Preschoolers	May see self as bad and deserving of prior abuse—can manipulate circumstances to "prove" badness
	Fears continual hurt
	Poor impulse control
	Frequent temper tantrums
	Poor self-esteem and socialization with peers
	Depression
	Destructiveness
	Difficulty separating from foster parents
III. Elementary-Aged Children	Difficulty following rules
	Poor listening
	Isolates self from others
	Extreme lack of self-confidence
	Not emotionally free to risk failure
	Fearful
	Anxious
	Misses biological families
	Thinks often of home and family problems
	Depression
	Hyperactivity (as a defense against depression)
	Withdrawal exhibited as lethargy, daydreaming, and failure to complete work
	Poor frustration tolerance
	Difficulty in unstructured activities
	Difficulty dealing with authority figures
	Denial
	Anger, often expressed through teasing
IV. Adolescents	Behavior problems
	Struggles with authority figures
	Conflicting loyalties between biological and foster families
	Anxiety over approaching emancipation
	Angry
	Misses biological families
	Denial
	Rage (repressed)
	Bravado expressing self-sufficiency (boys)
	Feelings of inferiority and worthlessness
	Unresolved sexuality issues
	Negative feelings about school
	Dislikes feeling "different"
	Resentful

Note. Developed from information found in "A Forum for Foster Children," by D. L. Rice and E. J. McFadden, 1988, *Child Welfare, 67*(3), 231–243, and *Children on Consignment: A Handbook for Parenting Foster Children and Their Special Needs* by P. M. Stahl, 1990, Lexington, MA: D.C. Heath.

8. Which adults have supportive relationships with the child?

Adults who experienced foster care placement themselves often cite the support and encouragement of a teacher, a foster parent, or other adult, as a major reason for their attaining satisfying, productive adult lives (Rhodes & Hoey, 1994). "Every effort should be made to help the child develop a relationship with at least one other person who really cares about him/her and can affirm the child's worth" (Horejsi, 1979, p. 131).

Home-School Cooperation

It is very important that the school invite and encourage the involvement of the foster parents in the child's education. The reality that the child may move soon and the constraint of foster parents in making certain legal decisions concerning the child may lead school staff to make less effort to involve foster parents. However, the foster parents need to support the child in completing homework assignments. Any intervention involving home-school contingencies requires full cooperation of the foster parents.

The extent, timing, and type of involvement of the biological parents in the child's education should be discussed by the school team and the child's case manager. This involvement will vary depending on the permanency plan for the child.

Additional Intervention Considerations

"Life books," like those used with adopted children, can be an important therapeutic tool to use with foster children (Backhaus, 1984). These books are tailored to the individual child and describe the child's life from birth until the present in the child's own words. Life books help children to integrate their past, present, and future and to understand that they were not to blame for the unfortunate things that have happened to them. To improve the chances that an adequate health record will accompany the child into future placements, a section of the life book can be devoted to a health diary, including the child's physical development; dental history; immunization records; and reports of accidents, illnesses, and allergies (White, Benedict, & Jaffe, 1987).

Many foster children have good interpersonal skills and are eager for approval and affection (Dubowitz et al., 1994). For these children, interventions that capitalize on such characteristics, like cooperative learning and positive reinforcement, should be sought.

Children with a history of multiple placements may be overly concerned with how the classroom works, instead of what is being taught. Teachers can make the classroom more predictable for these children by giving them such aids as schedules and advance organizers.

Foster children whose biological homes were chaotic need more structure than their classmates (Stahl, 1990). Teachers need to monitor the completion of assignments and work with the foster parents to make sure that homework is completed. The child's anxiety level may be reduced if the foster parents structure after-school time for homework, snacks, play, and television.

Interventions should be planned to address the child's hostility. Giving children a quiet place in the classroom to use when they cannot cope provides an alternative to aggression (Bauer, 1993).

Summary

Children are removed from their biological parents and placed with foster families, who may be strangers or relatives, to protect them and/or to give them the adequate care that their parents failed to provide. There has been a dramatic increase in the number of children placed in foster care in the last decade. More and more infants, as well as children who have suffered extreme neglect and abuse, are being placed.

Foster care is meant to be temporary, but for many children it becomes long-term instability. Some children remain in foster care for years and may be moved from foster home to foster home. The enormous vulnerability felt by foster children impedes their accomplishment of developmental tasks related to attachment and separation. They are at risk for poor health and medical care, as well as poor school adjustment.

School psychologists, teachers, and others in the school can positively impact the lives of foster children. Good information gathering will enable the school team to pinpoint interventions to the needs of the foster child. Teachers, as well as foster parents, need to establish clear limits and consequences. Adults in the school who are sensitive to the issues faced by foster children can provide the sense of belonging that these children need.

Recommended Resources

Bauer, A. M. (1993). Children and youth in foster care. Intervention in School and Clinic, 28(3), 134–142.
The author is a professor of special education who has adopted four special needs children, all of whom had been in foster care previously. Bauer explains the feelings and behaviors of foster children related to the circumstances that they have had to face. She gives specific recommendations to teachers who have students in foster care.

Davis, I. P., & Ellis-MacLeod, E. (1994). Temporary foster care: Separating and reunifying families. In J. Blacher (Ed.), *When there's no place like home: Options for children living*

apart *from their natural families* (pp. 123–161). Baltimore: Paul H. Brooks.
This chapter is an excellent reference on the history of foster care and on important issues, including children's physical and mental health, special-risk populations, and family contact during foster care placement. Lists of research implications and of practice and policy implications conclude the chapter.

Kates, W. G., Johnson, R. L., Rader, M. W., & Strieder, F. H. (1991). Whose child is this? Assessment and treatment of children in foster care. *American Journal of Orthopsychiatry, 61*(4), 584–591.
This article provides helpful background on issues specific to foster children for those counseling them. The psychological issues and possible responses for the foster child, the biological family, and the foster family are discussed.

Lewit, E. M. (1993). Children in foster care. *The Future of Children, 3*(3), 192–200.
Lewit provides a concise overview of recent national data concerning the foster care system. Several helpful figures are included.

Stahl, P. M. (1990). *Children on consignment: A handbook for parenting foster children and their special needs.* Lexington, MA: D.C. Heath.
This book is intended for foster parents but contains much practical information on parenting foster children that can be adapted for school-based interventions. The emotional impact of foster care placement on children, the needs of foster children at different developmental stages, and specific problem behaviors, such as regressive behavior and aggression, are discussed.

References

Aldgate, J., Heath, A., Colton, M., & Simm, M. (1993). Social work and the education of children in foster care. *Adoption and Fostering, 17*(3), 25–34.

Anderson, G. R. (Ed.). (1990). *Courage to care: Responding to the crisis of children with AIDS.* Washington, DC: Child Welfare League of America.

Backhaus, K. A. (1984). Life books: Tool for working with children in placement. *Social Work, 29*(6), 551–554.

Barth, R. P., Courtney, M., Berrick, J. D., & Albert, V. (1994). *From child abuse to permanency planning.* Hawthorne, NY: Aldine De Gruyter.

Bauer, A. M. (1993). Children and youth in foster care. *Intervention in School and Clinic, 28*(3), 134–142.

Benedict, M. I., White, R. B., Stallings, R., & Cornely, D. A. (1989). Racial differences in health care utilization among children in foster care. *Children and Youth Services Review, 11,* 285–297.

Berrick, J. D., & Barth, R. P. (1994). Research on kinship foster care: What do we know? Where do we go from here? *Children and Youth Services Review, 16*(1–2), 1–5.

Berrick, J. D., Barth, R. P., & Needell, B. (1994). A comparison of kinship foster homes and foster family homes: Implications for kinship foster care as family preservation. *Children and Youth Services Review, 16*(1–2), 33–66.

Black, M., Schuler, M., & Nair, P. (1993). Prenatal drug exposure: Neurodevelopmental outcome and parenting environment. *Journal of Pediatric Psychology, 18,* 605–620.

Cain, C. E., & Barth, R. P. (1990). Health beliefs and practices of foster parents. *Social Work in Health Care, 15,* 49–61.

Children's Defense Fund. (1992). *The state of America's children: 1992.* Washington, DC: Author.

Cohen, S., & Erwin, E. J. (1994). Characteristics of children with prenatal drug exposure being served in preschool special education programs in New York City. *Topics in Early Childhood Special Education, 14,* 232–253.

Davis, I. P., & Ellis-MacLeod, E. (1994). Temporary foster care: Separating and reunifying families. In J. Blacher (Ed.), *When there's no place like home: Options for children living apart from their natural families* (pp. 123–161). Baltimore: Paul H. Brooks.

Dubowitz, H., Feigelman, S., Harrington, D., Starr, R., Zuravin, S., & Sawyer, R. (1994). Children in kinship care: How do they fare? *Children and Youth Services Review, 16*(1–2), 85–106.

Fanshel, D., Finch, S. J., & Grundy, J. F. (1989). Foster children in life-course perspective: The Casey Family Program experience. *Child Welfare, 68*(5), 467–478.

Garrity-Rokous, F. E. (1994). Punitive legal approaches to the problem of prenatal drug exposure. *Infant Mental Health Journal, 15,* 218–237.

Gaudin, J. M., & Sutphen, R. (1993). Foster care vs. extended family care for children of incarcerated mothers. *Journal of Offender Rehabilitation, 19,* 129–147.

Goerge, R. M., Voorhis, J. V., Grant, S., Casey, K., & Robinson, M. (1992). Special-education experiences of foster children: An empirical study. *Child Welfare, 71*(5), 419–437.

Heath, A. F., Colton, M. J., & Aldgate, J. (1994). Failure to escape: A longitudinal study of foster children's educational attainment. *British Journal of Social Work, 24,* 241–260.

Hill, B. K., Hayden, M. F., Lakin, K. C., Menke, J., & Amado, A. R. N. (1990). Special report: State-by-state data on children with handicaps in foster care. *Child Welfare, 69*(5), 447–462.

Hochstadt, N. J., Jaudes, P. K., Zimo, D. A., & Schachter, J. (1987). The medical and psychological needs of children entering foster care. *Child Abuse & Neglect, 11,* 53–62.

Horejsi, C. R. (1979). *Foster family care: A handbook for social workers, allied professionals, and concerned citizens.* Springfield, IL: Charles C. Thomas.

Horwitz, S. M., Simms, M. D., & Farrington, R. (1994). Impact of developmental problems on young children's exits from foster care. *Developmental and Behavioral Pediatrics, 15,* 105–110.

Hulsey, T. C., & White, R. (1989). Family characteristics and measures of behavior in foster and nonfoster children. *American Journal of Orthopsychiatry, 59*(4), 502–509.

Kansas Legislative Division of Post Audit. (1991). *Performance audit report: Kansas' foster care program: Part II. Placement of children and delivery of service* (State of Kansas Publication No. 91-34). Topeka, KS: Author.

Kansas Legislative Division of Post Audit. (1994). *Per-*

formance audit report: Reviewing the department of social and rehabilitation services' procedures for handling complaints against foster homes (State of Kansas Publication No. 94-40). Topeka, KS: Author.

Kates, W. G., Johnson, R. L., Rader, M. W., & Strieder, F. H. (1991). Whose child is this? Assessment and treatment of children in foster care. *American Journal of Orthopsychiatry, 61*(4), 584–591.

Kelley, S. J. (1992). Parenting stress and child maltreatment in drug-exposed children. *Child Abuse and Neglect, 16,* 317–328.

Lawder, E. A., Poulin, J. E., & Andrews, R. G. (1986). A study of 185 foster children 5 years after placement. *Child Welfare, 65*(3), 241–251.

Lester, B. M., & Tronick, E. Z. (1994). The effects of prenatal cocaine exposure and child outcome. *Infant Mental Health Journal, 15,* 107–120.

Lewit, E. M. (1993). Children in foster care. *The Future of Children, 3*(3), 192–200.

Marcus, R. F. (1991). The attachments of children in foster care. *Genetic, Social, and General Psychology Monographs, 117*(4), 365–394.

McIntyre, A., & Keesler, T. Y. (1986). Psychological disorders among foster children. *Journal of Clinical Child Psychology, 15*(4), 297–303.

McIntyre, A., Lounsbury, K. R., Berntson, D., & Steel, H. (1988). Psychosocial characteristics of foster children. *Journal of Applied Developmental Psychology, 9,* 125–137.

McMurtry, S. L., & Lie, G. (1992). Differential exit rates of minority children in foster care. *Social Work Research & Abstracts, 28,* 42–48.

Pardeck, J. T. (1983). Marital status and family source of income: Potential predictors for determining the stability of foster family care? *Adolescence, 18*(71), 631–635.

Pardeck, J. T., Murphy, J. W., & Fitzwater, L. (1985). Profile of the foster child likely to experience unstable care: A re-examination. *Early Child Development and Care, 22,* 137–146.

Piers, J. C. (1984). *Fostering the school age child: Instructor's manual.* Ypsilanti, MI: Eastern Michigan University, Institute for the Study of Children and Families, Foster Parent Education Program.

Rhodes, W. A., & Hoey, K. (1994). *Overcoming childhood misfortune: Children who beat the odds.* Westport, CT: Praeger.

Rice, D. L., & McFadden, E. J. (1988). A forum for foster children. *Child Welfare, 67*(3), 231–243.

Simms, M. D., & Halfon, N. (1994). The health care needs of children in foster care: A research agenda. *Child Welfare, 73,* 505–524.

Smith, M. C. (1994). Child-rearing practices associated with better developmental outcomes in preschool-age foster children. *Child Study Journal, 24,* 299–326.

Stahl, P. M. (1990). *Children on consignment: A handbook for parenting foster children and their special needs.* Lexington, MA: D.C. Heath.

Stein, E., Rae-Grant, N., Ackland, S., & Avison, W. (1994). Psychiatric disorders of children "in care": Methodology and demographic correlates. *Canadian Journal of Psychiatry, 39,* 341–347.

Tatara, T. (1994). The recent rise in the U.S. child substitute care population: An analysis of national child substitute care flow data. In R. Barth, J. D. Berrick, & N. Gilbert (Eds.), *Child welfare research review* (Vol. 1, pp. 126–145). New York: Columbia University Press.

U.S. General Accounting Office. (1990). *Drug-exposed infants: A generation at risk* (GAO/HRD-90-138). Gaithersburg, MD: Author.

U.S. General Accounting Office. (1994). *Foster care: Parental drug abuse has alarming impact on young children* (GAO/HEHS-94-89). Washington, DC: Author.

Walsh, J. A., & Walsh, R. A. (1990). Studies of the maintenance of subsidized foster placements in The Casey Family Program. *Child Welfare, 69,* 99–114.

White, R. B., Benedict, M. I., & Jaffe, S. M. (1987). Foster child health care supervision policy. *Child Welfare, 66*(5), 387–398.

Wulczyn, F. H., & Goerge, R. M. (1992). Foster care in New York and Illinois: The challenge of rapid change. *Social Service Review, 66,* 278–294.

63

Psychological and Physical Abuse

Marla R. Brassard

Teachers College, Columbia University

S chools have an essential role to play in both the prevention and treatment of psychological and physical abuse of children. Schools are already providing special education and mental health services to many abused children through special education classes, services for pregnant teens, dropout programs, substance-abuse programs, and violence-prevention programs. Under our current educational system, fragmented programs have been developed within and outside of the school to address student needs without focusing on the underlying problems shared by abused children and adolescents. Schools can provide an enormous service by developing a coordinated classroom and mental health program to meet the needs of these children.

Schools have many advantages for the delivery of services to this population:

1. They already have trained staff members who are skilled in home, family, and community collaboration including school psychologists, social workers, guidance counselors, and nurses.
2. The schools have intimate, daily knowledge of how a given child or adolescent is functioning.
3. School-based services may be more acceptable to families, increasing the likelihood of parent involvement, and are often more accessible to children.
4. Schools can be therapeutic environments in that they have a clear mandate to promote development and educational attainment in children.
5. Schools can be powerful advocates for children by sending a clear message to the community that they will not tolerate abuse and can demonstrate this through reporting and advocating for abused children.
6. School personnel are the most reliable source of compensatory relationships and role models for children who do not have good relationships or positive role models in their life.

The purpose of this chapter is to provide guidance for school psychologists when confronted with cases of physical and psychological abuse. The chapter focuses on two major findings of the literature: First, psycholog-ical abuse/neglect is the most frequent type of maltreatment, and second, it is responsible for most of the mental injuries and adverse developmental outcomes associated with all forms of child abuse and neglect. The types of problems faced by psychologically and physically abused children and adolescents and their families, and the problems they present for schools, are reviewed. Then three research models are discussed which outline a variety of actions that schools might take in dealing with psychological and physically abused children.

Background

Psychological Abuse: Definition and Incidence

Psychological maltreatment is defined as "a repeated pattern of caregiver behavior or extreme incident(s) that convey to children that they are worthless, flawed, unloved, unwanted, endangered, or only of value in meeting another's needs" (Brassard, Hart, & Hardy, 1991, p. 255). Psychological abuse consist of acts of commission in which caregivers spurn (criticize, belittle, or ridicule), threaten, or exploit/corrupt children through encouraging antisocial behavior (see Table 1). These definitions come from the work of Hart and this chapter's author (see Brassard, Hart, & Hardy, 1993) and are consistent with the national incidence study definition (National Center on Child Abuse and Neglect [NCCAN], 1988) and with the psychological abuse categories of other researchers (see Hardy & Brassard, in press).

Published studies on the incidence of psychological abuse and neglect are highly discrepant, ranging from a reported incidence of 0.54 cases per 1,000 (American Humane Association, 1987) to 900 cases per 1,000 (Bouchard, Tessier, Fraser, & Laganieve, in press) depending on the definition used, the population studied, and the method used to gather information. Incidence figures based on the extent to which psychological abuse comes to the attention of human service professionals or official

Table 1 *Elements of Psychological Abuse*

Element	Definition	Examples
Spurning	Verbal and nonverbal caregiver acts that reject and degrade a child.	■ Belittling, degrading, and other nonphysical forms of overtly hostile or rejecting treatment. ■ Shaming and/or ridiculing the child for showing normal emotions such as affection, grief, or sorrow. ■ Consistently singling out one child to criticize and punish, to perform most of the household chores, or to receive fewer rewards. ■ Public humiliation.
Exploiting/ Corrupting	Caregiver acts that encourage the child to develop inappropriate behaviors (self-destructive, antisocial, criminal, deviant, or maladaptive behaviors).	■ Modeling, permitting or encouraging antisocial social behavior (e.g., prostitution, performance in pornographic media, initiation of criminal activities, substance abuse, violence to or corruption of others). ■ Modeling, permitting, or encouraging developmentally inappropriate behavior (e.g., parentification, infantilization, living the parent's unfulfilled dreams). ■ Encouraging nor coercing abandonment of developmentally appropriate autonomy through extreme overinvolvement, intrusiveness, and/or dominance (e.g., allowing little or no opportunity or support for child's views, feelings, and wishes; micromanaging child's life). ■ Restricting or interfering with cognitive development.
Threatening	Caregiver behavior that threatens or is likely to physically hurt, kill, abandon, or place the child or child's loved ones/objects in recognizably dangerous situations	■ Placing a child in unpredictable or chaotic circumstances. ■ Placing a child in recognizably dangerous situations. ■ Setting rigid or unrealistic expectations with threat of loss, harm, or danger if they are not met. ■ Threatening of perpetrating violence against the child. ■ Threatening or perpetrating violence against a child's loved ones or objects.

Note. From Office for the Study of the Psychological Rights of the Child, Indiana University—Purdue University at Indianapolis and University of Massachusetts at Amherst. Used with permission.

child protection agencies are the lowest, and population-based self-reports of all abuse occurring in the family are the highest.

The 1986 national incidence study of the NCCAN (1988) identified 211,100 cases of emotional abuse and 223,100 cases of emotional neglect which combined represented an annual incidence of 6.0 per 1,000. There were no sex differences in reported emotional abuse or neglect. Girls are just as likely to be identified by professionals as emotionally abused as sexually abused; boys are likely to be identified as emotionally abused at a rate of two times that of child sexual abuse. Family income was found to have an effect on the incidence of emotional abuse and neglect, although not to the same extent as with physical neglect. Emotional abuse was nearly five times more frequent for the lower income group than for the higher income group. This income-related difference may reflect poorer parenting on the part of families under economic stress (and related stressors linked to poverty), personality and interpersonal characteristics of some families living in poverty, or both. No racial or ethnic differences were noted. In interpreting the results of the

NCCAN study, it is important to bear in mind that only 5% to 7% of the cases of child maltreatment come to the attention of authorities and that psychological abuse and neglect go unidentified even more often than other forms of maltreatment (Claussen & Crittenden, 1991) and, if identified, are less likely to receive serious attention or court involvement. For these reasons, studies with samples drawn from the general population are believed to provide more accurate estimates of the incidence of psychological abuse.

Two studies using samples drawn from the general population have investigated the incidence of verbal/symbolic aggression (includes spurning, threatening, and denying emotional responsiveness) using a set of items from the Conflict Tactics Scale (CTS, Straus, 1995), an instrument developed to measure interpersonal conflict in families. A nationally representative telephone survey of 3,346 parents revealed that 63.4% of children experienced at least one incident of verbal/symbolic aggression during the preceding year with the average being 12.9 incidents (Vissing, Straus, Gelles, & Harrop, 1991). As there are no accepted criteria for how frequent verbal/symbolic aggression needs to be in order to qualify as psychological abuse, incidence estimates vary depending on the criteria used: 267 per 1,000 if 10 or more incidents are used, and 113 per 1,000 if more than 20 incidents are used (14% of all children). Because the CTS is based on self-report data, even these figures are likely to be lower bound estimates.

In order to further correct for social desirability bias and to get better information on all the psychological and physical abuse children were exposed to, Bouchard and his colleagues (Bouchard et al., in press) asked parents to report on the conflict tactics (using the CTS) they had witnessed in the family in the last year. In this population survey in Quebec, 84% of the fathers and 90% of the mothers acknowledged witnessing verbal/symbolic violence directed toward their children in the last year. This finding suggests that the incidence of psychological abuse is very high.

Physical Abuse: Definition and Incidence

Physical abuse is defined as an act of commission on the part of caregivers or parents that is characterized by infliction of overt physical violence (Wolfe, 1988). It may include beating; squeezing; burning; lacerating; suffocating; binding; exposing to excessive heat or cold; poisoning; and subjecting to sensory overload such as excessive light, sound, stench or aversive taste and preventing sleep (Williams, 1983). In addition to death, physical injuries may include skeletal injuries, neurological and ocular damage, loss of consciousness, interrupted breathing, broken bones, and third degree burns, with the most common types of abuse being bruises, lacerations, and contusions. Identification of physical abuse is usually done through physical inspection by trained social workers or medical professionals. They most often use a combination of x-ray and diagnostic experience in determining that injuries could not have occurred accidentally.

Estimates of the incidence of physical abuse in the United States, from state reports and research projections, in their most conservative formulations, have suggested that approximately 358,300 children are physically abused each year (American Humane Association, 1987; NCCAN, 1988). The NCCAN study (1988) found that approximately 5.7 children per 1,000 were physically abused, and it was estimated that 0.02 per thousand (or 1,100 children) died from maltreatment in 1986. Estimates of incidence from the National Family Violence Resurvey in 1985, based on parents' self-reports, reveals a much greater incidence; physical abuse rates of 23 per 100 were reported (Straus & Gelles, 1990).

The NCCAN (1988) study found that physical abuse was equally common for male and female children in the sample. Children in larger families, those with four or more children, were significantly more likely to be abused than children from smaller families. Physical abuse was related to income. Children from families with incomes of less than $15,000 per year were physically abused at a rate four times higher than that of children from higher-income families. It is unclear whether the relationship between physical abuse and socioeconomic status is due to socioeconomic bias in reporting, because of the greater likelihood that low-income families will come under public scrutiny.

The co-occurrence of physical and psychological maltreatment was examined by Claussen and Crittenden (1991). Their study included 175 families that had been referred to child protective services (CPS; 96% of which involved physical abuse), 39 families in which a child was receiving mental health services, and 175 control families who were recruited through community preschools. For the CPS-involved sample, 91% of the cases with physical abuse also involved psychological abuse and neglect. In the community sample, 93% of the cases of physical abuse and 91% of the cases of neglect involved psychological maltreatment but in the community sample, only 19% of the psychological maltreatment cases involved any physical abuse.

What these studies suggest is that psychological abuse almost always co-occurs with physical abuse and physical neglect. As a result, it seems clear that cases of physical abuse and neglect should always include assessments of psychological maltreatment. As the rate of psychological maltreatment in the Claussen and Crittenden (1991) community sample and the population survey of Vissing et al. (1991) were five times that of physical abuse, it underscores that psychological abuse may be far more common than other forms of maltreatment in the population at large. This is of tremendous concern as research suggests that milder forms of abuse may be as related to negative child outcomes as severe forms (Barnett, Manly, & Cicchetti, 1993).

Development

There is consensus that assessment for suspected psychological and physical abuse should include a consideration of the child's developmental level, although relatively little is actually known about the developmental implications of abuse at particular ages. What is known is that there are age differences in psychological (emotional) abuse cases recognized and reported by community professionals (NCCAN, 1988). Children ages birth to 2 were significantly less likely to be identified as emotionally abused than children ages 6 and older, and 3- to 5-year-old children were less likely to be identified than children ages 12 years and older.

The pattern for physical abuse was a little different. Preschool children were particularly at risk for physical abuse. Their small size increases their vulnerability both to parental assault and in their lack of ability to defend themselves and, because of their early-stage development, makes them more vulnerable to damage as a result of whatever maltreatment is inflicted. Over 60% of all abuse fatalities and over 50% of all cases of permanent disability occur among children under 2 years of age. Most of these damages are the result of head injuries. Obviously these injuries can have lasting implications for children's educational success and social adjustment.

Children have developmental tasks that are particularly salient at each age level (American Professional Society for the Abuse of Children [APSAC], 1995). Caregiver behavior may thwart or undermine a child's competence in these tasks. For example, in the preschool years an important developmental task is the development of self-control through the use of language to regulate impulses, store information, and develop structures to make sense of the world. A caregiver who does not use language to regulate impulses, who models out-of-control angry behavior, and whose actions disregulate (emotionally and physically upset) the child is undermining the child's competence in this area. Important tasks for infancy are attachment and assistance in the regulation of bodily states and emotion. Tasks for toddlerhood include development of symbolic relations (language and other mental models), a continuation of self-other differentiation (developing an increasingly refined sense of self and of other), problem solving, pride, and mastery motivation. Preschool tasks include self-control (already mentioned), the development of verbally mediated or semantic memory, gender identity, moral reasoning, and the development of relationships beyond the family. In the elementary years, tasks include the development of peer relationships, adaptation to the school environment, and continued development of moral reasoning. In adolescence, identity issues are particularly important, specifically sexuality, future orientation, peer acceptance, and ethnicity. Assessments to determine the impact of abuse on development and to design relevant interventions can benefit from an examination of the developmental tasks and the success a child has had in accomplishing these tasks (see APSAC, 1995, for an application of this model).

It is particularly important to attend to factors promoting normal growth and development in the case of psychologically and physically abused children. The literature on resiliency, with its examination of risk and protective factors in development, is encouraging, and it suggests that protective factors or buffers are more powerful than risk factors (Werner & Smith, 1992). Family factors identified as providing protection include time with an adult who expresses care and interest, having a parent who is a high school graduate or above, expressions of caring and affection within the family, support from family members and strong bonds with them, financial security, four or fewer offspring, two years or more

between siblings, informed parent/child conversations, regular consistent routines, monitored TV watching, frequent storybook reading and discussion, expectation that the child will remain in school 10 to 12 years and become literate, involvement with the child's schooling, sense of control over circumstances, strong religious orientation, and strong work orientation. School factors related to resilience include stable schooling, quality programs tied to children's strengths and needs, an atmosphere of support for children's efforts, policies that discourage retention, active linguistic models, encouragement of parental involvement, and a focus on child-environmental interactions. Community factors related to better outcomes for children at risk include support from friends or religious groups; child-care and educational opportunities; and community programs such as literacy, job training, and the like (Boehm & Brassard, in press).

Resiliency research suggests that caring relationships with one or more adults; consistent routines at home and at school; and home, school, and community efforts to promote competence are related to good outcomes for children at risk. Schools that foster positive staff-student relationships; offer a consistent, predictable routine; and work hard to promote competence in educational as well as extracurricular areas (e.g., band, drama, athletics) for all children are providing support that is particularly needed for abused children.

Problems and Implications

Most of the findings of negative effects for both psychological abuse and physical abuse appear to be the result of a hostile and rejecting form of caregiving. Physical abuse almost always co-occurs with psychological abuse, and psychological abuse accounts for most of the negative developmental outcomes observed in children psychologically abused or physically and psychologically abused. Very few studies of physical abuse have assessed for psychological abuse, but those that have found it accounting for most of the variance in child and adult functioning (Hardy & Brassard, in press). It is difficult to determine the effects of physical abuse apart from psychological abuse except when head injury or other forms of permanent damage occur (see Brassard et al., 1993, and Hardy & Brassard, in press, for reviews). The material in the following sections should be interpreted in light of this evidence.

Overview of Research

Crittenden (1988) found that families who abuse but do not neglect their children differed from other maltreating families in a number of distinctive ways. In these families, the couple relationship was often violent, and the families tended to have only a few young children. Both parents had parents who tended to be harsh or neglecting, and the parents perceived this harshness as a necessary parental characteristic. There was a tremendous emphasis in these families on being perfect parents, which involved reading books and attending parenting classes. They were very concerned that their children reflect well on them, and they had high standards both for themselves and for their children. They typically had conflictual relationships with relatives and other families in the community. Most of their relationships were acrimonious and short-term. Their parental coping strategies involved power-assertive techniques, where they sought to dominate if possible but were willing to take the alternative role and submit to more powerful authorities such as husbands or courts. Their children responded by being either difficult and acting out or compliant and inhibited. Compliance tended to reduce the risk of physical abuse. Many of the children were overachievers, but others were delayed. There was some role-reversal (child in parental role) among compulsively compliant children. On the whole, these families tended to have a better prognosis than the other maltreating patterns studied. The parents were motivated, had appropriate goals in wanting to be good parents, tended to be more intellectually competent, and understood and responded to the authority presented by CPS. Little is known about families that psychologically abuse their children in the absence of physical or sexual abuse or neglect because they are rarely identified.

Erickson, Egeland, and Pianta (1989) in a longitudinal prospective study of high-risk families found that when maltreated children entered school, a variety of patterns emerged, depending on the caregiving patterns that they had received. Teacher reports indicated that physically abused children (who were also verbally abused) functioned more poorly on cognitive tasks than nonmaltreated peers. Half of these children were referred for special intervention and attention by the end of their first year at school because of the high rates of regressive, noncompliant, and acting-out behavior that they exhibited.

Not only does the rejecting and aggressive behavior of psychologically and physically abused children predispose teachers, other adults, and peers who interact with them to respond to them in ways that parallel the ways in which they are treated at home, but other unfortunate patterns related to learning develop as well. Cicchetti, Toth, and Hennessey (1989) found that physically abusive parents demonstrated a combination of high-achievement expectations for their children along with a controlling, non-reasoning-based style of interaction with their children. These behaviors had a highly negative effect on their children's classroom performance. These authors noted that behavior problems exhibited by maltreated children in a classroom are likely to elicit over-

controlling teaching styles that tend to undermine an intrinsic motivation to learn and emphasize a learning style based on extrinsic rewards or punishment.

Physically abused children often have cognitive delays relative to nonmaltreated peers. This may be the result of either mild head injuries occurring in the course of physical abuse or just an additional result of environments that do not provide the nutritional, emotional, and intellectual support needed for appropriate cognitive development. These cognitive delays appear early in life, and as children begin attending school, they often have difficulty maintaining attention. In addition, they both receive less and are less able to elicit adult support for learning. There is evidence that mothers who maltreat their young children communicate with them in a less sensitive, contingent, and stimulating manner than do adequate mothers. Most preschool maltreated children master basic language but appear to have some specific deficits in the use of internal-state language (language about emotions and feelings). Additionally, they have a tendency to talk less about themselves than about their ongoing activities (Cicchetti et al., 1989).

Verbal abuse (spurning and threatening) has been implicated in contributing to poor outcomes in a number of studies on diverse populations. When compared to other forms of maltreatment, children who are verbally abused are more likely to experience low enjoyment in living and to perceive poor chances of living to old age. A combination of psychological and physical abuse is correlated with problems in self-esteem and sexual behavior and with anger and aggression. Psychological abuse appears more likely to be transmitted intergenerationally than physical violence and leaves deeper scars. Children who experience frequent psychological abuse (referred to in some studies as verbal/symbolic aggression) from parents have elevated rates of physical aggression, delinquency, and interpersonal problems. These effects are consistent across all age groups and segments of the population (Vissing et al., 1991).

Research findings demonstrate that psychological abuse is more closely related to psychosocial problems than is physical abuse (unless severe), but that together they create an even greater risk factor. Hostile rejection (spurning) by parents has been related to a history of psychiatric problems in parents; to deficits of self-esteem, social instability, and excessive aggression in children; and to difficulty controlling aggression, inappropriate responses to distress in others (e.g., anger, hitting, giggling), and self-isolating tendencies in preschoolers. Repeated threats of abandonment, beating, and killing from caregivers (threatening) discriminated between the childhood histories of physically abusive and demographic control mothers (see Hardy & Brassard, in press, for a review).

Research in other types of maltreatment not explicitly focused on psychological abuse indicates that the psychological climate of the family or quality of relationships with the caregiver determines the developmental course of the victim. To give an example, a number of studies suggest that the negative psychological outcomes associated with sexual abuse are not related to the sexual abuse per se but to aspects of the family environment such as lack of parental affection, parental impulsivity, alcoholism, negative or hostile patterns of interaction, and response to the abuse disclosure (see Hardy & Brassard, in press, for review).

In summary, victims of psychological and physical aggression demonstrate attachment problems with parents and relationship difficulties with peers and teachers. Both groups suffer from problems with the regulation of emotions, particularly anger and aggression. Some physical abuse victims demonstrate cognitive deficits which may be related to mild head injuries as well as to the lack of appropriate stimulation in their environment. Both groups may have difficulty using language to identify and understand their own and others' emotions.

Useful Theoretical Models

There are two theoretical models, attachment theory and Wolfe's transactional model, that seem particularly useful for understanding and treating cases of psychological and physical abuse. Resiliency research, just reviewed, also provides a useful framework for thinking about maltreatment cases as it focuses on social and environmental circumstances which seem to promote coping in children who are at risk. For other theoretical models of maltreatment, the reader is referred to Krugman, Kempe, and Helfer (in press).

Attachment theory

Attachment theory, based on the work of John Bowlby (Bowlby, 1980) and Mary Ainsworth (Ainsworth, Blehar, Waters, & Wall, 1979) and their associates, has significant empirical support. Attachment theory suggests that children develop a model of the world and, in particular, of themselves and others in the context of reciprocal interactions with their early caregivers. A secure attachment develops if the care that a child receives is reliably available, adequate, and in response to the child's signaled cues. A securely attached child constructs a model of self as effective and of the environment as responsive to the child's signaled needs. There are two styles of anxious attachment. If the care received is inconsistent in quality and availability, the child constructs a model of the world as unreliably responsive and a model of self as inept in being able to impact the environment to have his or her needs met. This is anxious-ambivalent attachment. Other children, based on noncontingent care, construct a model of the environment as adverse and intrusive. Children in these anxious-avoidant relationships learn that they are most likely to be rebuffed when they signal

neediness. They cope but by avoiding the caregiver when needy and minimizing awareness of attachment-related feelings. All three primary attachment styles have major implications for the child's developing sense of self and sense of other.

There is considerable research support for the attachment perspective as it relates to child maltreatment. Almost all maltreated children that have been studied appear to have anxious attachments to their parents (Crittenden, 1985; Erickson et al., 1989). Because of their early experiences with caregivers, maltreated children appear to see others as either hostile or rejecting. Physically abused toddlers have been found to be less likely to approach their teachers and to resist the advances of both their teachers and their peers, compared to non-abused toddlers. The abused toddlers were also much more likely to direct aggression at their teachers, and they had a pattern of responding to distress in their peers with aggression. This avoidance or aggression occurred in response to friendly overtures as well as to neutral or negative behavior from peers and teachers. This type of response makes it much more likely that abused youngsters will be rejected by adults and peers, thereby confirming their wariness, distrust, and anger toward others. A similar pattern of behavior was observed in children who were rejected by their mothers but who were not physically abused (Main & Goldwyn, 1984).

Based on this theory-driven research, one would expect that maltreated children would have difficulties in early adaptation to school. Their concerns over safety and search for acceptance would be likely to impede their successful school adaptation (Cicchetti et al., 1989). Maltreated children have been found to have a less-secure readiness to learn when they enter preschool. There is a correlation between this readiness to learn and maternal reports of social withdrawal, regression, and depression in the maltreated preschoolers. Cicchetti et al. (1989) suggest that the maltreatment disrupts the balance between the child's desire for safety in relationships and age-appropriate motivation to explore an environment in order to master it. School-based intervention approaches designed to address attachment-related safety issues are described in Sroufe (1983) and Pavenstedt (1967).

Wolfe transactional model

Wolfe (1987) presents what he calls the transactional model of child physical abuse. In his model, child abuse develops as a result of a gradual transformation of the parent-child relationship, from a relatively benign pattern of interaction to, over time, a fairly toxic pattern. This pattern interferes with the parent-child relationship and increases the probability of aggressive behavior on the part of the parent and, later on, on the part of both parent and child. The model assumes that psychological processes are important in that they are linked to the expression of anger, arousal, and coping reactions in adults.

These processes include (a) basic principles of acquiring and maintaining behavior; (b) cognitive-attributional processes that influence individuals' interpretations and reactions to events; and (c) the emotional conditioning processes that influence the degree of physiological arousal, discomfort, and self-control when under stress. Wolfe sees these processes as responsible for determining the positive or negative resolution of each stage in the development of the parent-child relationship. The psychological processes accentuate the impact of many of the major factors associated with child abuse.

The model illustrates how unfortunate preconditions can start with (a) the parents' own weak preparation for parenting, often as a result of poor modeling in the parent's family of origin, and (b) current ineffective style of dealing with crises as they occur in the immediate environment. Parents lacking competent ways of dealing with interpersonal relationships and managing stress are more likely to find themselves overwhelmed by routine difficulties of living. Poor management of daily living and crises that arise may reduce parents' tolerance for child behavior and increase the likelihood that he or she will feel angry, overly aroused, and distressed. At this point, even typical child behavior may serve as a triggering event that results in a parent losing control. The child is a target of anger and frustration related more to current events and past relationships than the child's behavior. In the final stage, a habitual pattern of irritability and aversive interaction, or avoidance, may become established, leading to either consistent or alternating patterns of using force or reducing involvement with the child.

Alternative Actions

Develop Clearly Articulated Reporting Policies

The school has both a legal and a moral responsibility to report child abuse. A clearly articulated reporting policy that is known to staff and parents can serve a preventative function by signaling that a school will not tolerate maltreatment and will take whatever steps it can to ensure the safety of children in its care. A written policy should be developed with the input of teachers, administrators, parents, and support personnel and reviewed by legal counsel prior to implementation to ensure that it complies with state statutes. A policy is of little use unless it is actively backed by school administrators and supported by in-service training dealing with the identification of child abuse and neglect and the special needs of this population. It is advisable to have one person in the school, usually the principal, school psychologist, or school social worker, serve as the designated reporter.

Having one designated person, if legally permitted by the state, works well because this individual can build a collaborative relationship with CPS, take responsibility for the school's communications with a concerned parent, and develop a workable strategy for dealing with families. A feedback loop should be established to inform the reporting teacher on the status of the report and increase confidence in the reporting process. The policy should designate someone to support the child through the process of being interviewed by CPS. Finally, parents should be provided the reasons for filing a report. Even though parents are likely to be upset and angry with the school for reporting, informing them of the report in a nonjudgmental fashion (it is not the school's responsibility to determine whether abuse has occurred and who is at fault) demonstrates concern for all parties and a desire to maintain a relationship with the family whatever the outcome of the investigation.

Assess Referred Children for Maltreatment

The Conflict Tactics Scale (CTS; Straus, 1995) is the only nationally normed measured of psychological and physical abuse. This simple, 19-item, 7-point measure takes 3 minutes to administer; provides data on the incidence, prevalence, and chronicity of physical and psychological abuse; and does not seem to be confounded with social desirability. It has three scales: reasoning, verbal/symbolic aggression (psychological abuse defined as "a communication intended to cause psychological pain to another person or communication perceived as having that intent" [Straus, 1995]), and physical abuse. The CTS may be given to parents, for which it is normed, and to children as an informal measure of how conflicts are resolved between family members. While the CTS does not necessarily produce the quality of information that would lead to a report to CPS, it provides a picture of the methods by which family members resolve conflicts, some of which may, with follow-up questions, lead to a report to CPS. School psychologists who would like to screen for sexual abuse and neglect as well may want to consider the CTS-2 and its supplemental scales although the psychometric data have yet to be published.

Address the Special Needs of Foster Children

Abused and neglected children make up the majority of foster children. The National Adoption and Assistance and Child Welfare Act requires that social services make reasonable efforts to find a foster placement in the same community as the family home, when a child is placed in care. It is sometimes possible and preferable, if a local foster placement is available, for the child to remain in the same school. Schools can offer stability in the lives of these children who have experienced so much chaos and now find themselves in the insecure world of foster care.

Foster children need to be screened for academic and emotional problems because of the very high base rate of these problems in this population (APSAC, 1995). A very high percentage of these children need services and, unless referred for special education programs, often do not receive treatment. Some states require or permit all children entering a district to be screened. In other states, permission would need to be obtained from the parent or guardian, often the local CPS agency. Because schools are not always informed of foster placements, school personnel may need to be alert in attempting to identify such children and any special needs they may have. A close relationship with CPS may facilitate this process. CPS may also take advantage of a teacher's intimate knowledge of children's functioning as it evaluates changes in children's placements, such as a return home from foster care. On file, with a checklist to make sure it is complete, should be important information such as the name, address, and telephone number of the foster parent, biological parents, and case worker; the last school attended and Individual Education Plan (IEP), if relevant; health records and copies of court orders (see chapter on Foster Homes, this volume).

Provide Individual or Group Treatment for Psychologically and Physically Abused Children

Careful reviews of the literature illustrate that currently there is no effective treatment for abusive and neglecting families. In general, families continue to maltreat despite intervention. In addition, primary prevention of the different forms of maltreatment is no more effective than its remediation (Cohn & Daro, 1987; MacMillan, MacMillan, Offord, & Griffith, 1994). However, there is strong evidence that if maltreatment is identified and appropriate treatment is provided to victims, much of the associated emotional distress and social/emotional delays victims experience can be mitigated (Cohn & Daro, 1987) and may prevent maltreatment of future offspring (see Egeland, Jacobvitz, & Sroufe, 1988; Main & Goldwyn, 1984). For this reason, treatment of all identified victims of psychological and physical abuse (including those who have witnessed spousal violence), as well as for neglect and child sexual abuse, is strongly indicated. Although the specific components of a successful treatment program have not been empirically identified, treatment programs have been developed (see Gil, 1991) which deal with the mental injuries that may arise from all forms of maltreatment. In general, interventions attempt to (a) challenge abused children's assumptions about their own worthiness and what they can expect from selected others in a relationship, (b) provide symptom relief, (c) allow the expression of negative feelings in a safe environment as needed, and (d) promote competence and mastery of age-appropriate tasks.

The school is one of the most appropriate settings for the provision of mental health services to abused children. Although most schools and some parents would prefer that mental health services be provided elsewhere, they often are not. Abusive parents are more likely to come from lower income families with less money and possibly less time to secure mental health care; they are often quite defensive about external judgments of their parenting but may feel less stigmatized by having a child participate in a school-based treatment program. Service provision within the schools may give abused children a chance to secure treatment on their own initiative. Some states, such as New York, allow an abused or neglected child to receive mental health services without the permission of a parent if a licensed psychologist or physician determines that such treatment is necessary. This is, obviously, an option of last resort. In New York, to qualify, a minor must be voluntarily seeking such service, the service must be clinically indicated and necessary for the child's well being, and requiring parental consent would either have a detrimental effect on the treatment or the parent or guardian has refused to give consent for treatment determined to be necessary and in the best interests of the minor (New York State Mental Hygiene Law 33.21).

Providing treatment to psychologically and physically abused children and adolescents is not something one should do without appropriate training and/or supervision (see Brassard & Appellaniz, 1990). Some school psychologists may have appropriate training for individual and group treatment of this population; others may seek outside supervision, colead groups with a trained colleague or consultant, or invite a community mental health team into the school. The great need of these children for services and the convenience and appropriateness of a school setting for the provision of these services suggest this as a way that the school can directly intervene and attempt to improve the behavior, mental health, and academics of abused children.

Modify School Structure and Procedures

A number of ways in which classrooms can be restructured to potentially help maltreated children are detailed next.

1. Find an adult who will take a special interest in the abused child

If children do not receive acceptance of worth at home, it is very important that they get adequate attention from adults in other sectors of their lives. Research has shown that what separates invulnerable from vulnerable children (those that cope compared with those in the same adverse life circumstances who do not) is adults who take an interest, who make a commitment to the child, and who are available to the child for support and encouragement (Egeland et al., 1988; Werner & Smith, 1992). Frequently, these individuals are teachers, coaches, lunchroom helpers, church youth group leaders, therapists, and other relatives. Mental health professionals in the schools do not have the time to build this relationship with every needy child they encounter, but often they can help the child find another adult who is available and willing to fill this role (Brassard & Appellaniz, 1990).

Sroufe (1983) found that, when several warm, skillful teachers of both sexes were available to a preschool class, maltreated children were able to form secure attachments to at least one teacher (often of the same sex). Sroufe suggested employing several teachers per classroom, particularly in the early grades. If this is not possible, a child should be moved to another classroom if a good relationship does not develop between a vulnerable child and his or her teacher. Sroufe states that "all children deserve to be in a program where someone cares for them unconditionally," although "no teacher should be expected to unconditionally love every child" (p. 75).

2. Provide a Predictable, Routine Environment

Clinical experience and some research suggest that abused children are positively affected by structured discipline, responsible and dependable adult role models, and a routine schedule at school (Brassard & Appellaniz, 1990; Crittenden, 1989; Pavenstedt, 1967). Curriculum approaches that provide high degrees of structure better meet the needs of maltreated children than those that depend on a child's initiative and acceptance of responsibility for their own use of time. Predictable environments may also provide a context in which abused children gain experience in competently signaling needs and reading appropriately the cues of others (Crittenden, 1989).

3. Teach and Practice Good Communication and Problem-Solving Skills

Abusive parents and their children tend to be quite poor at accurately identifying their own emotional states (Crittenden, 1989; Main & Goldwyn, 1984), and they are inclined to attribute negative intent to others' neutral behavior. As a result, abused children may benefit from school situations that give them experience in using and interpreting emotional communications that are clear and consistent (see Crittenden, 1989; Pavenstedt, 1967). Classroom or group training in problem-solving skills have been shown repeatedly to improve outcomes for children at risk for violence, a group that includes many abused children (see Tolman, 1994, for a review).

For this approach to be effective, staff need assistance in responding appropriately to provocative emotional communications from abused children. These chil-

dren often expect adults to interact with them coercively and may provoke many of the angry, coercive responses they receive from principals, teachers, and peers. School personnel can benefit from in-service training and ongoing consultation on how to step back from provocative communications and respond to the unspoken message being conveyed. For example, a student who says, "This assignment stinks!" might be given this response from the teacher, "It sounds like you are upset about the assignment I gave. Could you tell me what problems you have with it?" This is not always easy to do, particularly at first, but it is effective. It not only reduces explosive incidents between school personnel and acting-out students, but it models good communication skills. If staff can see these students as emotionally needy and deprived rather than threatening, they are better able to respond in healing, or at least nonharmful, ways.

4. Promote Self-Control and Competence

Schools that give at-risk students a sense of competence through (a) successful experiences in academics, art, music, athletics, or social interaction and (b) teaching them to plan and make conscious choices about important events in their lives have significantly better student outcomes than those that do not (Rutter & Rutter, 1992). The cognitive deficits of some physically abused children may exacerbate their behavior problems if they are unable to keep pace with peers academically. Psychologically abused children may have low self-esteem and poor mastery motivation. Both types of children may feel great pressure at home to do well at school and lack an interest in learning for its own sake. Encouraging learning as a source of self-esteem and autonomy, independent of parental wishes, promotes competence, reducing classroom behavior problems.

Thus, efforts on the part of school psychologists to emphasize and support the competencies, self-control, and planning skills of abused children (and of all children) may well be rewarded in better outcomes than efforts that focus strictly on attempts to remediate or treat a difficult family situation. Competencies and planning ability offer abused children opportunities to modify their own life course even if it does not stop the abuse in the short-term.

5. Do Not Tolerate Abuse of Children by School Personnel

Staff awareness can also be increased as to the powerful negative impact that teachers can have on children, an impact that is particularly devastating for children who are maltreated at home. Krugman and Krugman (1984) and Hyman (see chapter on Corporal Punishment, this volume) reported a few case studies of teachers who were emotionally maltreating children. These teachers exhibited a variety of maltreating patterns that included the ridiculing of children who did not do perfect work and making the class join in the belittling of one particular child, maintaining total classroom silence, restricting access to the bathroom, and taping children's mouths shut. The teachers' behaviors were only discovered after the children's reactions became serious enough to alarm parents. Children were becoming fearful and adamant about not going to school; avoided unfamiliar men (in one case with a male teacher); developed nightmares, sleep difficulties, and headaches; and demanded that their parents review homework to make sure it was perfect. Teacher abuse or neglect in the classroom can be as damaging and long-lasting as other forms of abuse.

Abusive teachers can be identified by (a) asking referred children about their class(es) and teacher(s) (e.g., how they feel about coming to school and why, asking them about their best experience in school and why, their worst experience and why); (b) asking parents about their child's feelings about school and his or her relationship with the teacher(s) (fear, anger, or marked withdrawal of interest can indicate a problem); (c) listening to teachers talk about children in their class (disrespectful, degrading remarks to colleagues are likely to be conveyed just as clearly to students), and (d) overhearing or observing classroom interaction (some abusive teachers yell and scream at children, some create such a tense atmosphere that children are afraid to make a sound).

Intervening with a teacher (or other member of the school staff) suspected of abuse should follow ethical guidelines coupled with a keen sense of how one would like to be approached if one were the person suspected of abuse. A private meeting should be arranged as soon after the event(s) as possible. The professional can, using "I" statements, describe the behavior he or she observed and the interpretations that were made, raising the possibility that the behavior was misinterpreted. The professional can then attempt to clarify and understand the teacher's response. If the behavior was misinterpreted, both individuals may feel relieved that the issue was clarified. If there was no misinterpretation, the teacher may attempt to repair the situation and modify his or her future behavior with input from the professional. If there was no misinterpretation and the teacher is not interested in changing or does not change, or if the behavior is severe, then a report should be made to the administration and, in some states, to CPS.

Through training, staff can be sensitized to the powerful impact they have on students. Staff training (including role-plays) on conflict resolution, prevention and defusing of potentially violent situations, and stress and anger management can help all teachers cope better with provocative children (many of whom have been abused). Some teachers lack skills in creating a positive and cooperative learning environment and, as a result, are forced to rely on coercive strategies which exacerbate the situation. Many of these teachers are relieved to find that there are alternative approaches for maintaining or-

der in the classroom and, if offered a nonjudgmental and supportive training environment, are eager, or at least willing, to try new approaches.

Summary

Psychologically and physically abused children demonstrate attachment problems with parents and relationship difficulties with peers, teachers, and themselves. Both groups of abused children suffer from problems with the regulation of emotions, particularly anger and aggression. Some physical abuse victims demonstrate cognitive deficits which may be related to mild head injuries as well as to the lack of appropriate stimulation in their environment. Both groups may have difficulty using language to identify and understand their own and others' emotions. They are at great risk for special education classification, interpersonal problems, and delinquency. Neither primary prevention of abuse nor treatment of abusive families have been found to be effective. Mental health treatment of abuse victims and schools that promote competence in and plan for at-risk students are effective in ameliorating symptoms and changing life courses in a positive direction. This chapter argues that schools are one of the most appropriate, and certainly the most convenient, setting for the provision of services to abused children, and recommended actions and services are described.

Recommended Resources

American Professional Society on the Abuse of Children. (1995). *Practice guidelines: Psychosocial evaluation of suspected psychological maltreatment in children and adolescents.* Chicago: Author.
These guidelines, although designed for forensic practice, provide guidance in the identification and assessment of psychological abuse and neglect.

Brassard, M. R., & Hart, S. N. (1987). *Words can hurt.* Chicago: National Committee for Prevention of Child Abuse.
This public-service pamphlet for parents and children is written at a fourth-grade reading level. Cartoons are used to illustrate the points, and suggestions are offered for parents who find themselves saying or doing some of the emotionally abusive acts described. It is ideal for waiting rooms or side tables and can be ordered individually or in bulk from the NCPCA (they also have many good pamphlets on related topics such as alcoholism).

Fraiberg, S., Adelson, E., & Shapiro, V. (1980). Ghosts in the nursery: A psychoanalytic approach to the problems of impaired infant-mother relationships. In S. Fraiberg (Ed.),

Clinical studies in infant mental health (pp. 164–196). New York: Basic Books.
This is one of the most influential papers ever written on the topic of child abuse and neglect and the reader will immediately see why. Fraiberg and her colleagues present a powerful theory of maltreatment illustrated with compelling clinical examples. I have used it in different classes for over 10 years and it is always one of the favorite readings assigned.

Garbarino, J., & Merrow, J. (1985). *Psychological maltreatment of children: Assault on the psyche* [videotape]. University Park, PA: Pennsylvania State University.
This powerful videotape can be used in health classes, parenting groups, and child/adolescent treatment groups to generate discussions about psychological abuse.

Pavenstedt, E. (Ed.). (1967). *The drifters: Children of disorganized lower-class families.* Boston: Little and Brown.
This is an excellent research study conducted in the early 1960s. Particularly relevant to school psychologists and other school personnel are the descriptions of the structure of the nursery school classroom, teacher-child interactions, and outreach to families. The book provides an understanding of the mental health and educational challenges these children face and what might prove helpful to them in a school context.

Topics in Early Childhood Special Education, 1989, 9.
This is a special issue devoted to research on child maltreatment and its application to early educational settings. It offers many ideas for teachers in how to deal with young abused children in the classroom.

References

Ainsworth, M., Blehar, M., Waters, E., & Wall, S. (1978). *Patterns of attachment.* Hillsdale, NJ: Lawrence Erlbaum.

American Professional Society for the Abuse of Children (APSAC). (1995). *Guidelines for the psychological evaluation of suspected psychological maltreatment in children and adolescents.* Chicago: Author.

Barnett, D., Manly, J., & Cicchetti, D. (1993). Defining child maltreatment: The interface between policy and research. In D. Cicchetti & S. Toth (Eds.), *Child abuse, child development, and social policy* (pp. 7–74). Norwood, NJ: Ablex.

Boehm, A., & Brassard, M. (in press). *Preschool assessment: Strategies and tools.* New York: Guilford.

Bouchard, C., Tessier, R., Fraser, A., & Laganière, J. (in press). La violence familiale envers les enfants: Prevalence dans la Basse-ville et etude de validite de la mesure (Family violence toward children: Prevalence in the "Basse-ville" a study of the validity of measures). In R. Tessier, C. Bouchard, & G. M. Tarabulsy (Eds.), *Enfance et famille: Contextes de developement* (Childhood and family: Developmental contexts). Quebec: Presses de l'Universite Laval.

Bowlby, J. (1973). *Attachment and loss. Volume II: Separation.* New York: Basic Books.

Brassard, M. R., & Appellaniz, I. (1990). The abusive family: Theory and intervention. In M. Fine & C. Carlson (Eds.), *The handbook of family-school intervention* (pp. 215–230). Boston: Allyn & Bacon.

Brassard, M. R., Hart, S. N., & Hardy, D. (1993). The psychological maltreatment rating scales. *Child Abuse and Neglect, 17,* 715–729.

Cicchetti, D., Toth, S., & Hennessy, K. (1989). Research on the consequences of child maltreatment and its application to educational settings. *Topics in Early Childhood Special Education, 9,* 33–55.

Claussen, A. H., & Crittenden, P. M. (1991). Physical and psychological maltreatment: Relations among types of maltreatment. *Child Abuse and Neglect, 15,* 5–18.

Cohn, A. H., & Daro, D. (1987). Is treatment too late: What ten years of evaluative research tell us. *Child Abuse and Neglect, 11,* 433–442.

Crittenden, P. (1985). Maltreated infants: Vulnerability and resilience. *Journal of Child Psychology and Psychiatry, 26* (1), 85–96.

Crittenden, P. (1988). Family and dyadic patterns of functioning in maltreating families. In K. Brown, C. Davies, & P. Stratton (Eds.), *Early prediction and prevention of child abuse* (pp. 161–189). New York: John Wiley and Sons.

Crittenden, P. M. (1989). Teaching maltreated children in the preschool. *Topics in Early Childhood Special Education, 9,* 16–32.

Egeland, B., Jacobovitz, D., & Sroufe, L. A. (1988). Breaking the cycle of abuse. *Child Development, 59,* 1080–1088.

Erickson, M. F., Egeland, B., & Pianta, R. (1989). The effects of maltreatment in the development of young children. In D. Cicchetti & V. Carlson (Eds.), *Child maltreatment: Theory and research on the causes and consequences of child abuse and neglect* (pp. 647–684). New York: Cambridge University Press.

Gil, E. (1991). *The healing power of play: Working with abused children.* New York: Guilford.

Hardy, D., & Brassard, M. R. (in press). In R. Krugman, R. Kempe, & M. E. Helper (Eds.), *The battered child* (5th ed.). Chicago: University of Chicago Press.

Krugman, R., Kempe, R., & Helper, M. E. (Eds.). (in press). *The battered child* (5th ed.). Chicago: University of Chicago Press.

Krugman, R., & Krugman, M. (1984). Emotional abuse in classrooms. *American Journal of Diseases of Children, 138,* 284–286.

MacMillan, H., MacMillan, J., Offord, D., & Griffith, L. (1994). Primary prevention of child physical abuse and neglect: A critical review. *Journal of Child Psychology and Psychiatry and Allied Disabilities, 35* (5), 835–856.

Main, M., & Goldwyn, R. (1984). Predicting rejection of her infant from mother's representation of her own experience: Implications for the abused-abusing intergenerational cycle. *Child Abuse and Neglect, 8,* 203–217.

Mueller, E., & Silverman, N. (1989). Peer relations in maltreated children. In D. Cicchetti & V. Carlson (Eds.), *Child maltreatment: Theory and research on the causes and consequences of child abuse and neglect* (pp. 529–578). New York: Cambridge University Press.

National Center on Child Abuse and Neglect (NCCAN). (1988). *Study findings: Study of national incidence and prev-*

alence of child abuse and neglect: 1988. Washington, DC: U.S. Department of Health and Human Services.

Pavenstedt, E. (Ed.). (1967). *The drifters: Children of disorganized lower-class families.* Boston: Little & Brown.

Rutter, M., & Rutter, M. (1992). *Developing minds: Challenge and continuity across the life span.* New York: Basic Books.

Sroufe, L. A. (1983). Infant-caregiver attachment and patterns of adaptation in preschool: The roots of maladaptation and competence. *The Minnesota symposium on child psychology* (Vol. 16, pp. 41–83). Hillsdale, NJ: Erlbaum.

Straus, M., & Gelles, R. (1990). *Physical violence in American families: Risk factors and adaptations to violence in 8,145 families.* New Brunswick, NJ: Transaction.

Tolan, P., & Guerra, N. (1994). *What works in reducing adolescent violence: An empirical review of the field.* Boulder, CO: Center for the Study of Prevention of Violence, Institute of Behavioral Sciences. (Available from the University of Colorado, Box 442, Boulder, CO 80309-0442)

Vissing, Y. M., Straus, M. A., Gelles, R. J., & Harrop, J. W. (1991). Verbal aggression by parents and psychosocial problems of children. *Child Abuse and Neglect, 15,* 223–238.

Werner, E., & Smith, R. (1992). *Overcoming the odds: High risk children from birth to adulthood.* Ithaca, NY: Cornell University.

Wolfe, D. A. (1987). *Child abuse: Implications for child development and psychopathology.* Beverly Hills, CA: Sage.

64

Child Sexual Abuse

Connie B. Horton
Tracy K. Cruise
Illinois State University

Since the passage of the Child Abuse Prevention and Treatment Act (Public Law 93-247) in 1974, child sexual abuse, among other forms of maltreatment, has received significantly increased attention. Since that time, many expert clinicians have described the effects of this form of abuse on their client victims, and numerous researchers have investigated multiple aspects of this phenomenon. Thus, child sexual abuse, while a virtually unrecognized and unstudied phenomenon 20 years ago, has, over the last few years, been the subject of numerous books, over 500 research articles, and even journals dedicated specifically to the topic. Given this explosion of information, concerned practitioners may find it difficult to keep current. The focus of this chapter, therefore, will be to update professionals on what is presently known about child sexual abuse, including definitions, incidence and prevalence, effects, and mediators.

Background

Definitions and Demographics

There is no universal definition of *child sexual abuse*. Conceptually, sexual abuse has been defined as "the involvement of dependent, developmentally immature children in sexual activities that they do not fully comprehend and therefore to which they are unable to give informed consent and/or which violate the taboos of society" (Krugman & Jones, 1987, p. 286). Thus, the dominant position of an adult perpetrator is recognized as allowing the offender to coerce the child, who lacks the power to refuse the act, into sexual compliance (Finkelhor, 1979).

Legally, there is much ambiguity in sexual abuse terms as definitions vary significantly from state to state. Most definitions, however, note that abuse occurs when there is sexual activity between a child and an adult or significantly older child or adolescent (usually more than 5 years; Larson, Terman, Gomby, Quinn, & Behrman,

1994). These sexually abusive behaviors are not restricted solely to attempted, simulated, or actual intercourse. Contact and noncontact sexual abuse may consist of any one, or more commonly a combination of, any of the following behaviors: voyeurism, child pornography, kissing, masturbation, oral-genital contact, digital (finger) penetration of the anus or vagina, and vaginal or anal intercourse (Sgori, Blick, & Porter, 1982).

While early definitions referred to adult-child sexual contact, increasingly, sexual abuse circumstances involving peer perpetrators are also being recognized (Horton, 1995b). In these situations, there may not be a significant age difference, but coercion or force is used, thus creating an experience far different than normal sexual play or experimentation. Normal child sexual experimentation has been described as an "information gathering process of limited duration wherein children of similar ages explore each other's bodies, visually and tactually" (Johnson, 1990, p. 64). Empirical research confirms that children exhibit a variety of sexual behaviors at a relatively high frequency. Studies of young children, for example, document that kissing nonfamily children and adults is a fairly typical behavior (Friedrich et al., 1992). Many parents also report that their children undress in front of others and touch sex parts at home (Friedrich, Gramsch, Broughton, Kuiper, & Beilke, 1991). Children coercing or forcing others into compliance with sexual activity, however, is far beyond normal and should be considered abusive behavior, which requires immediate assessment and intervention (Berliner & Rawlings, 1991).

Incidence and Prevalence

Although most mental health professionals and researchers treating and studying sexual abuse would agree that this form of maltreatment occurs with great frequency, no accurate national statistics on the incidence and prevalence of child sexual abuse exist (Finkelhor, 1994). Incidence data are derived from two primary sources: the National Incidence Study of Child Abuse and Neglect (NIS) and state child-protection agencies. Prevalence data are gathered mostly from adult retrospective studies.

Perhaps the most reliable figures for annual incidence come from the NIS in which cases known to professionals, but not necessarily reported to child protection agencies, are calculated (Sedlak, 1991). This study revealed 133,600 cases of sexual abuse known to professionals or a rate of about 2.1 cases per 1,000 American children in 1986. Another national incidence study conducted in 1986 concluded that 3.5 females per 1,000 and 0.9 males per 1,000 were reported as being sexually abused each year (National Center on Child Abuse and Neglect, 1988). A compilation of the reports made to child protection agencies in 50 states indicates that sexual abuse makes up 11% of reported cases (Wiese & Daro, 1995). It is important to note, however, that such rates are probably based solely upon reports of children abused by adults and do not include those cases involving child or juvenile offenders, cases that may be reported to law enforcement but not forwarded to child protection agencies, cases disclosed but unreported, or those incidents that are simply never disclosed. Thus, incidence data based on reports must clearly be interpreted as serious underestimates of the overall number of children experiencing sexual abuse.

Because so much sexual abuse remains undisclosed, prevalence data gathered through adult retrospective studies may provide a more accurate picture of the scope of the problem. Some individuals, in light of the recent "false memory syndrome" controversy, have questioned the accuracy of such data sources, suggesting that numbers may be inflated as some respondents may fabricate abuse scenarios. In his review of this literature, Finkelhor (1994) concludes that "while this may occur occasionally, no evidence suggests that fabrication is a major threat to the validity of victimization surveys" (p. 42). In fact, he concludes, there is a much greater likelihood that retrospective studies are underestimates, as many subjects may not remember or may choose not to disclose such personal information.

The percentage of adults disclosing child sexual abuse in a review of retrospective studies ranged from 2% to 62% for females and 3% to 16% for males (Finkelhor, 1994). A good, conservative estimate is that approximately 20% of females and approximately 5% to 10% of males experience sexual abuse by adults (Finkelhor, 1994).

Offenders

While studies vary in their findings regarding whether the most common sexual offenders are fathers, stepfathers, or other male family members, it is clear that the majority (70% to 90%) of sexual offenders are family members or those known to the child (Finkelhor, 1994). Thus, sexual abuse by strangers is a relatively rare event. Males

are apparently more likely to be sexually abused by someone outside of the family, while females are more likely to be sexually abused by someone within the family (Courtois, 1993). The vast majority (85% to 95%) of sexual abuse is perpetrated by males, though there certainly are some cases in which females victimize male or female children (Larson et al., 1994).

As mentioned earlier, a newly recognized type of sexual perpetrator is a child who uses force or coercion in sexual contact with other children and may have begun planning, calculating, rationalizing their behavior, grooming their victims, and carrying out sexual assaults as early as ages 6 to 11 (National Adolescent Perpetrator Network, 1988). Although prevalence figures are unavailable, it is clear that both male and female child perpetrators exist (Johnson, 1988, 1989).

Females make up the overwhelming majority of sexual abuse victims; the ratio of female to male victims is four to one (Larson et al., 1994). Although cases involving male victims constitute only about 20% of cases reported to child protection agencies, the actual number of male victims is estimated to be much higher (Finkelhor, 1994). Males are underrepresented in research samples. Therefore, more information is needed on this population of victims. Another group of victims which may be underreported is children with disabilities. The very nature of certain disabilities make some children more dependent and, thus, more vulnerable to abuse. Moreover, disabilities may interfere with the child's ability to make a clear, credible report (Horton & Kochurka, 1995; Tharinger, Horton, & Millea, 1990).

Contrary to commonly held beliefs, children who are from minority cultures do not appear to be at greater risk for sexual abuse than their majority peers (Finkelhor, 1994). Low socioeconomic status has been found to be an inconsistent risk factor. Parenting factors such as unavailability and inadequacy are somewhat more predictive. These factors may increase risk because children of inadequate or unavailable parents are less closely supervised and more emotionally deprived and, therefore, vulnerable (Finkelhor, 1994). Children of virtually every age, socioeconomic level, and racial group have been identified as victims of sexual abuse.

Problems and Implications

Clinical literature and empirical investigations in the past decade have documented that a range of psychological (e.g., depression, anxiety, guilt, fear) and behavioral problems (e.g., sexual dysfunctions, withdrawal, acting-out) are more prevalent among those who have been sexually abused than among those with no such experiences (Beitchman, Zucker, Hood, DaCosta, & Akman, 1991). The few longitudinal studies conducted have also provided supportive evidence that sexual abuse does lead to subsequent psychological difficulties in the short and longer term (Erickson, Egeland, & Pianta, 1989; Gomez-Schwartz, Horowitz, & Cardarelli, 1990).

Initial Effects

Initial effects, sometimes referred to as short-term effects, are those reactions that a victim has during and/or immediately following the sexual abuse. These usually occur within 2 years of the termination of the abuse (Browne & Finkelhor, 1986) and may include a number of emotional and behavioral responses. In their review of empirical studies, Browne and Finkelhor found that one-fifth to two-fifths of abused children manifest pathology in the immediate aftermath of abuse.

The immediate effects of child sexual abuse may vary according to the developmental age of the child. The following are general effects noted across different developmental periods, with specific characteristics of sexual abuse provided for each developmental phase.

Sexual abuse may occur at any time in a child's life and may result in physical damage to the child's body (e.g., rectal and vaginal tears, sexually transmitted diseases, pregnancy) as well as leave emotional scars. Child victims of sexual abuse may initially experience fear, anxiety, depression, anger, or hostility (Browne & Finkelhor, 1986). Somatic complaints are also commonly noted symptoms (Kendall-Tackett, Williams, & Finkelhor, 1993).

Behavioral manifestations that may be exhibited by an abused child during or immediately following the sexual abuse include the following:

- Regressed behaviors such as thumb-sucking or bed-wetting.
- Sleeping problems, including insomnia and nightmares.
- Eating disturbances.
- School problems, including an inability to concentrate, a sudden drop in performance, and nonparticipation in school activities (e.g., not changing clothes for gym class).
- Relationship difficulties such as not being able to make friends (Beitchman et al., 1991; Browne & Finkelhor, 1986).

Victims of sexual abuse may also develop fear and anxiety regarding the opposite sex or sexual issues (Brassard, Tyler, & Kehle, 1983) and may display inappropriate sexual behavior (Browne & Finkelhor, 1986). In children, this tendency is observed as heightened interest in or preoccupation with sexuality which is manifested in a number of ways including sexual play, excessive masturbation, seductive or sexually aggressive behavior, and age-inappropriate sexual knowledge. Ado-

lescent sexual difficulties include sexual dissatisfaction, promiscuity, and an increased risk for revictimization (Beitchman et al., 1991).

In addition to these general effects that may be seen across individuals and across developmental periods, the following are the most notable effects of sexual abuse observed for each developmental period.

Preschool years

Children ages 2–5, prior to entering elementary school, are at a period where significant cognitive and social growth is occurring. The sexually abused preschooler may have feelings of shame or guilt, be confused about what has happened, and be leery of turning to another adult for help because it has most commonly been a trusted adult who has violated them.

The most distinguishing behavioral effect of child sexual abuse among preschoolers is persistent and inappropriate sexual interest or play with self, peers, and toys (Beitchman et al., 1991; Cole & Putnam, 1992). This type of behavior has been a relatively constant marker of sexual abuse during early years (Kendall-Tackett et al., 1993). Thus, young children who have sexual information beyond their years (e.g., a 4-year-old who describes ejaculation, a 3-year-old who demonstrates sexual intercourse with Barbie dolls or initiates such activities with peers) should be observed carefully as they are quite likely victims of sexual abuse.

School-age years

The initial effects of sexual abuse occurring during school-age years have been documented as more widespread than those observed among preschoolers. These children may also feel intense shame and guilt about the abuse and yet have no one with whom they can share those feelings. Another common response by children is that of fear—fear of whether to disclose, fear of punishment, or fear of not being believed (Browne & Finkelhor, 1986). Although girls may show more internalizing behaviors such as withdrawal, which may lead to depressive symptoms, boys may display more externalizing or acting-out behaviors (Beitchman et al., 1991). Again, while most of these symptoms may be indicative of child distress caused by any number of stressors, sexualized behaviors are much more suggestive of child sexual abuse (Beitchman et al., 1991; Cole & Putnam, 1992).

Adolescence

Although adolescence is a time of exploration of the self and a challenge to the rules and values of others, the typical acting-out behaviors of sexually abused adolescents are attempts to escape or to understand what has happened to them (Cole & Putnam, 1992). These behaviors include running away, promiscuity, and substance abuse (Beitchman et al., 1991). The preoccupation with suicide and self-destructive behaviors (e.g., bingeing and purging, cutting or burning oneself) have also been shown to be elevated among sexually abused females (Beitchman et al., 1991). Higher levels of depression have been found to distinguish between those adolescents with a history of sexual abuse than those without. Continued self-blame and feelings of guilt may also result in lowered self-esteem for these individuals.

Long-Term Effects

The negative effects of child sexual abuse may extend years beyond the initial impact for many victims. The long-term effects of child sexual abuse also cover a wide range of emotional and behavioral responses. It is important for mental health professionals to be aware of the long-term effects because adolescents who were abused as children may display many of the following responses.

Emotionally, depression is the symptom most commonly reported by adults who were sexually abused as children (Browne & Finkelhor, 1986). These individuals may also display self-destructive behaviors such as suicide, problematic eating behavior, and cutting or burning oneself (Beitchman et al., 1992). High levels of tension or anxiety among survivors of sexual abuse may manifest as insomnia, nightmares, anxiety attacks, or person- or situation-specific increases in anxiety.

Victims of child sexual abuse also report feeling isolated and stigmatized during adolescence and adulthood. They may perceive that others cannot understand or relate to their experience and feel a need to keep the abuse a secret out of fear or feelings of shame (Cole & Putnam, 1992). Many sexual abuse victims encounter additional problems in relationships, especially in the realm of sexual functioning (Beitchman et al., 1992; Browne & Finkelhor, 1986). Impaired trust may be a direct result of the abuse, while dysfunctional sexual behaviors and decreased sexual satisfaction may also indirectly or directly result from the sexual trauma.

Revictimization is another long-term effect associated with child sexual abuse that has received little research attention. Higher rates of rape or attempted rape have been found in several studies for those having also experienced child sexual abuse (Beitchman et al., 1992). In addition, victims of a battering relationship have also been shown to have higher levels of sexual abuse than their nonabused counterparts (Beitchman et al., 1992; Browne & Finkelhor, 1986). It is important for professionals to keep in mind that those who may have been abused at an early age may be more likely to experience date rape or some other sexual assault before graduating from high school or college (Aizenman & Kelley, 1988).

Although the effects of child sexual abuse are wide ranging, there is no uniform impact of child sexual abuse. Great heterogeneity is found in the extent and type of symptoms of sexual abuse victims. There is no "child sexual abuse syndrome" or specific diagnostic label to be given to children who may have experienced abuse. Furthermore, not all victims of child sexual abuse show negative effects. A substantial minority of sexually abused children (21% to 49%) report no psychological distress (Kendall-Tackett et al., 1993).

A number of reasons for this lack of reported distress have been discussed. Some children may actually be more resilient in handling the abuse. Others with "no reported psychological distress" may be denying distress via an avoidant coping style. Still others may have "sleeper effects," symptoms which, though not present immediately after the abuse, develop later (Finkelhor & Berliner, 1995). Other explanations for the variety in postabuse sequelae involve mediators of the effects.

Mediators of the Effects

Researchers have examined factors that may mediate the impact of sexual abuse (Barnett et al., 1995; Browne & Finkelhor, 1986; Hindman, 1989). Initially, the factors considered among victims of adult-perpetrated abuse consisted of those that were a direct part of the sexual abuse experience. These factors include the age of the victim, duration, frequency, intrusiveness of the sexual behavior, degree of force, and the relationship of the abuser to the child.

It has been generally believed that greater trauma occurs the younger a child was at the time of the abuse, the longer and more often the abuse took place, and the more intrusive the abuse (i.e., penetration). It was also thought that if the perpetrator was a father-figure, force was used to engage the child, or both, then the child would be more affected (Hindman, 1989). However, empirical investigations have produced inconsistent results regarding the degree to which these factors predict later psychological trauma (Browne & Finkelhor, 1986). None of these single factors *consistently* predict later negative effects. For example, evidence suggests that a one-time sexual assault by a trusted family friend involving fondling may also have a severe negative impact on the child. Conversely, a victim subjected to violent, invasive abuse over many years may not be as traumatized as one might think, depending on multiple other factors.

Based on inconsistent research results and the assumption that more factors may be mediating the effects of sexual abuse than aspects of the abuse itself, current research has begun to examine factors related to victims' interpretations of the abuse and their disclosure experience (Barnett et al., 1995; Hindman, 1989). Although data are limited, it appears that these newly proposed factors are equally, if not more, predictive of later trauma compared to the direct factors of the abuse (Barnett et al.; Hindman).

Clinicians and researchers have suggested several cognitive interpretations that may be critical in predicting a victim's outcome. One aspect that has been examined is the victim's attribution of responsibility for the abuse. Victims who have been severely traumatized are often unable to place blame for the act onto the offender because they feel they had some role to play in the abuse and often blame themselves (Cole & Putnam, 1992; Hindman, 1989). This sense of self-blame may lead to depressive symptoms and lowered self-esteem. Additionally, as a result of being unable to control or prevent the abuse, many survivors feel powerless at the time of the abuse and may continue to feel helpless in other aspects of their lives (Spaccarelli, 1994). Survivors may feel they have no control over where their lives are headed or what happens to them on a daily basis. Some survivors may also have a sense that they are "damaged goods"—that they are not worthy of having a trusting relationship with another person, that they are somehow tarnished by the abuse, or that they are less important than those around them (Spaccarelli).

In addition to these cognitive factors, issues related to disclosure are also believed to affect the resulting trauma (Barnett et al., 1995; Hindman, 1989). How others respond to disclosures of abuse, the length of time the child keeps the abuse a secret, and the amount of support and continued information the victim receives regarding sexual abuse and normal sexuality have all been examined as promising mediators of the effects of sexual abuse.

Child victims who find that significant people in their lives believe and support them and clearly place the responsibility for the abuse with the offender are likely to experience less trauma. In fact, it has been shown that the belief and support by just one significant person in the child's life can offset the severe negative impact of the abuse (Briere & Elliott, 1994).

It has been demonstrated that victims who disclose more quickly may be less traumatized than those who "keep the secret" for years (Hindman, 1989). Also, those child victims who are provided ongoing support and information regarding sexual abuse and healthy sexuality are believed to fare better than those from whom information is withheld (Hindman). Thus, abuse-related variables alone do not consistently predict how traumatized a victim may be. Instead, multiple factors, including cognitive- and disclosure-related variables, may be critical in predicting child abuse sequelae.

Alternative Actions

Based on the literature just discussed, mental health professionals who want to respond sensitively and effectively to child sexual abuse situations have a number of important areas in which to keep current. Roles for school psychologists and other professionals in responding to child abuse and sexual abuse, in particular, have been described in some detail elsewhere (see Horton, 1995;

Vevier and Tharinger, 1986). Thus, the following section will highlight aspects of the roles for school psychologists and other professionals, paying particular attention to applying the most current available information to practice situations.

Detecting Abuse

Awareness of the prevalence and effects of sexual abuse allows professionals to consider abuse as a possible cause of some behaviors, affect, or changes in school performance. Commonly observed symptoms of child sexual abuse such as those discussed earlier, while not conclusive in isolation, are indicators of possible abuse (Gil, 1991). It is important to remember that, while many effects of child sexual abuse (e.g., fear, depression, anxiety) are common in a variety of situations in which a child is distressed, sexual behavior problems do appear to be a unique effect, which should lead to a stronger suspicion that a child has been sexually abused.

Children who do act out sexually may victimize other children. Because neither under- nor overreactions to children's sexual behavior are helpful, professionals must make determinations regarding what is typical, exploratory, normal sexual behavior and what sexual behavior is abnormal and victimizes a child. In determining when sexual behavior is a concern, there are number of issues to consider and questions to ask (Berliner & Rawlings, 1991; Gil & Johnson, 1993). Specifically,

1. Are there power differences that exist between the children involved? Differences in age, size, strength, social status, or intellectual ability should raise more concern.
2. How did the child gain compliance? When a child uses coercion or force, the situation should be treated seriously.
3. What was the affect of the children involved when "caught" by an adult? While giggly embarrassment is not unusual when children are involved in normal experimentation, reactions such as shame, anger, or anxiety suggest the incident may be beyond normal sexual play.
4. How does the child respond to correction? If the child compulsively and/or defiantly repeats the behavior despite adult correction, the situation warrants assessment and intervention.
5. Which specific sexual behaviors were involved? Attempted or actual intercourse, for example, should be treated much more seriously than "peeking" games.

Whether a child is being abused by an adult, an adolescent, or another child, it should be noted that accurate, early detection of the abuse may be an important positive mediator in predicting a child's recovery. Because "keeping the secret" for longer periods of time may further traumatize a child, early detection and disclosure may help prevent more extensive suffering.

Child Interviews

Often, school professionals may have concerns regarding possible child sexual abuse due to physical, emotional, or behavioral indicators but may need additional information. In other cases, a child may make a direct disclosure regarding abuse to the school psychologist or other school personnel. In either of these situations, the school psychologist or school counselor may need to interview the child further to gain enough information to make a report.

In addition to following standard "good interview procedures" (see Horton, 1995, for specifics), it is critical that the interviewer keep in mind the cognitive and disclosure variables that may mediate recovery. For example, in interviewing children, school personnel may unintentionally suggest thoughts of blame ("Why didn't you tell someone sooner? Or run away?"), helplessness ("It's OK, you couldn't have helped it, you were too little." "There is nothing you could have done."), or "damaged goods" ("Oh, you poor thing! You must feel terrible."). Instead, the interview can be the beginning of a supportive response from significant others. Rather than expressing shock or outrage, the interviewer should use basic listening skills to facilitate an understanding of what the child is trying to express. If the child feels supported through the process and is not blamed or treated as helpless or damaged, the child victim may experience less trauma.

Reporting Abuse

Once there is enough information from physical, behavioral, or emotional indicators and/or child interviews to suspect abuse, a report must be made to the appropriate child protection agency. School personnel should be familiar with the laws in their state on reporting child abuse. Although school personnel are mandated reporters in all states, the specifics such as which agency should be contacted and the time frame within which the sometimes-required written report (which follows the immediate oral report) must be made varies from state to state.

Reporting, though sometimes a traumatic step for victims, may be an additionally important phase in breaking the silence. The key to avoiding the promotion of a sense of helplessness throughout this phase may be to give the child as much power and as many choices in the process as possible. For example, the child may be given options regarding what room at school will be used for the interview with the child protection agency social worker or who will drive him or her to the child protection office or police station. In some cases, for certain parts of the interviews, children may be allowed to re-

quest that a supportive person such as a teacher or school psychologist remain in the room. Such choices, while they may seem trivial, may give the child some sense of control in an otherwise overwhelming situation.

Consultation with Teachers and Parents

Because the response of others to the child victim is so critical in preventing additional trauma and promoting recovery, perhaps the most important message that the school psychologist can convey to teachers (who are aware of the situation) and parents is that their response is also critical and will make a significant difference in the child's life.

Just as school psychologists themselves must strive to treat victims in ways that dispel myths of self-blame, helplessness, and damaged goods, school psychologists can encourage others to do so as well. Modeling a supportive response and educating others on how not to react to a disclosure may significantly lessen the extent of the trauma for the child.

Teachers may be reminded that sexually abused children often need and can benefit greatly from a special attachment with a concerned teacher (Gelardo & Sanford, 1987). The role of the nonoffending caretaker (often mothers in sexual abuse cases) is typically even more critical. Studies repeatedly demonstrate that the mental health of nonoffending caretaking parents and the relationships they maintain with their children are closely related to the recovery of their children who have been victimized (Tharinger & Horton, 1992). Thus, mental health professionals' support of teachers and parents in their efforts to provide a healthy recovery environment for child victims may make an invaluable contribution to the victim's recovery.

Making Referrals

School counselors and psychologists, because of limited opportunities, expertise, or both, will not typically be the primary therapists for child victims of sexual abuse. Further, because the child may find it difficult to return to class after discussing such an emotional topic, school may not be the best location for the primary individual therapy to take place. Helping parents locate available resources may be among the most valuable services the school psychologist provides (Brassard et al., 1983).

School psychologists who appreciate the importance of mediators which promote recovery will recommend therapists who will likely (a) provide a significant supportive relationship, (b) assist in correcting possible cognitive distortions, and (c) provide ongoing information regarding healthy sexuality as well as sexual abuse.

Direct Interventions

School-based counseling is typically not as intensive as outside therapy; however, school-based groups conducted by school psychologists, other school mental health professionals, or both may still be an important adjunct to victim treatment and recovery. Specifically, school-based educational or cognition-focused groups for victims may be helpful in addressing a number of the needs of victims. For example, as noted earlier, children who have been abused often lack basic information about sex and sexuality and may have more questions or concerns than their nonabused peers. School-based groups can provide such accurate information. School-based groups may also address and help correct the cognitive distortions many victims experience (e.g., "I must be to blame" or "This makes me a bad person"). Finally, school-based groups assist victims in realizing they are not the "only one" who has experienced abuse, hopefully lessening the sense of isolation or of being "damaged goods."

Prevention

An additional role for school psychologists, with the interest and resources for involvement, is in the area of child sexual abuse prevention. School psychologists may have the opportunity to develop and/or implement prevention programs for school districts.

If they do have this opportunity, school psychologists must be aware of possible unintended consequences, limitations, and strengths of implementing prevention programs (Consentino, 1989). Unintended consequences to consider include the possibilities that (a) some children may become fearful, (b) school personnel such as teachers may feel overwhelmed at the tasks of identifying and reporting suspected victims, and (c) society as a whole may feel less concerned about the epidemic of child sexual abuse because the problem is now "handled" through school-based prevention programs (Consentino; Reppucci & Haugaard, 1989).

There are many issues to consider when selecting a prevention program, including the developmental sensitivity of the program, empirical support for the specific program, and the complex mixed messages that some programs may unintentionally send (see Tharinger et al., 1988, for further discussion). One important observation regarding "prevention" programs directed at children is that there are no data demonstrating that they prevent anything. In fact, it is probably unrealistic and developmentally inappropriate to expect children to prevent their own abuse (Tharinger et al.). Better programs are multifaceted and include parent and public education components, support groups for vulnerable children and adults, and interventions for those already victimized (Daro, 1994).

School-based prevention programs directed at child audiences do, however, offer a potentially critical role, in that they tend to promote disclosures of both current and past abuse (Daro, 1994). Thus, given the importance of breaking the silence described earlier, these programs, when carefully implemented, may significantly reduce the amount of time a victim suffers in silence and experiences long-term trauma.

Summary

The information available regarding child sexual abuse is growing rapidly. Thus, practitioners can be more effective in recognizing, reporting, and responding to child sexual abuse if they are informed about recent developments in the field. Professionals should be aware of the high incidence of this form of maltreatment, have knowledge of the short- and long-term effects of such abuse, be fully aware of the factors which may mediate the impact of sexual abuse, and use best practices when working on such cases. This is a sensitive and complex area, but being fully informed may ease some of the concerns for those who wish to work effectively with issues of child sexual abuse.

Recommended Resources: Professionals

Behrman, R. E. (Ed.). (1994). *The future of children: Sexual abuse of children, (vol. 4)*. Los Altos, CA: The Center for the Future of Children, The David and Lucile Packard Foundation.
This book is a biannual publication on specific topics related to children. This specific issue reviews the latest research in the area of child sexual abuse. Chapters address the incidence and prevalence, effects, mediators, treatment, prevention, and offenders of child sexual abuse. This is a good desk resource for the school psychologist.

Friedrich, W. N. (1990). *Psychotherapy of sexually abused children and their families*. New York: Norton.
This book reviews the literature regarding the impact of child sexual abuse and suggests a model of coping. Treatment goals and specific suggestions for therapeutic work with sexually abused children are also given. Family issues are carefully considered throughout this work.

Gil, E. (1991). *The healing power of play: Working with abused children*. New York: Guilford, Press.
Following a discussion of the impact of child maltreatment and resulting therapeutic issues, the author provides practical suggestions for play-based, child-oriented therapy with abused children. In addition, clinical vignettes of treatment with victims of various forms of child maltreatment are included.

Gil, E., & Johnson, T. C. (1993). *Sexualized children: Assessment and treatment of sexualized children and children who molest*. Rockville, MD: Launch Press.
This book covers the continuum of sexual behavior problems and provides descriptions for distinguishing between sexually

reactive behavior and more severe child molesting behaviors. The authors provide information to aid in the diagnosis of children exhibiting behavior problems and discuss intervention techniques and strategies for this population.

Hindman, J. (1991). *When mourning breaks.* Ontario, OR: AlexAndria Associates.
Hindman provides a discussion of the factors that mediate the impact of child sexual abuse, dispelling myths about the impact of aspects of the abuse experience. A model of trauma assessment is proposed. Also included is a compilation of over 100 specific treatment activities, indexed by age, many that could be appropriate for school-based individual or group sessions.

Recommended Resources: Parents

Allen, S., & Dlugokinski, E. (1992). *Ben's secret.* Raleigh, NC: Feelings Factory.
This book may be read with a child who is suspected to have been sexually abused or may be read by a child alone. This book uses the story of a turtle to encourage the disclosure to a trusted adult of touching that makes a child feel uncomfortable. The book reinforces that the abuse was not the child's fault and that the best thing to do is tell an adult who will believe them.

Hindman, J. (1985). *A very touching book.* Ontario, OR: AlexAndria Associates.
This book is to be read by a parent or other adult with a child. It outlines sexual body parts and describes why this is an issue that makes many people uncomfortable. The book, along with wonderful illustrations, teaches children about secret touching and allows the child to interact with the reader to determine if secret touching is involved in specific scenarios. Designed for the professional or parent wanting to introduce the issue of touching to children.

Wachter, O. (1983). *No more secrets for me.* Boston: Little, Brown and Company.
This book is designed to introduce various types of touching that may make a young child feel uncomfortable. The book provides four separate ministories that detail a specific type of touching, including hugs that feel uncomfortable, having your privacy invaded in the bathroom, being observed in the nude by another person, and having private parts touched by an adult. This book includes two scenarios involving male victims (one with a male adult and one with a female adult) and two scenarios involving female victims (one with a stepfather and one with an older man). This book may elicit questions and comments from children about their own experiences.

References

Aizenman, M., & Kelley, G. (1988). The incidence of violence and acquaintance rape in dating relationships among college men and women. *Journal of College Student Development, 29,* 305–311.

Barnett, D., Glancy, L., Meade, J., Behen, M., Standish, J., Jones, D., & Richardson, K. (1995, March). *Factors that mediate the effects of sexual abuse.* A poster presented at the Biennial Meeting of the Society for Research in Child Development, Indianapolis, IN.

Beitchman, J. H., Zucker, K. J., Hood, J. E., DaCosta, G., & Akman, D. (1991). A review of the short-term effects of child sexual abuse. *Child Abuse & Neglect, 15,* 537–556.

Beitchman, J. H., Zucker, K. J., Hood, J. E., DaCosta, G., Akman, D., & Cassavia, E. (1992). A review of the long-term effects of child sexual abuse. *Child Abuse & Neglect, 16,* 101–118.

Berliner, L., & Rawlings, L. (1991). *A treatment manual: Children with sexual behavior problems.* Unpublished manuscript.

Brassard, M. R., Tyler, A., & Kehle, T. J. (1983). Sexually abused children: Identification and suggestions for intervention. *School Psychology Review, 12,* 93–96.

Briere, J., & Elliott, D. M. (1994). Immediate and long-term impacts of child sexual abuse. In R. E. Behrman (Ed.), *The future of children: Sexual abuse of children,* (Vol. 4, pp. 54–69). Los Altos: The Center for the Future of Children, The David and Lucile Packard Foundation.

Browne, A., & Finkelhor, D. (1986). Impact of child sexual abuse: A review of the research. *Psychological Bulletin, 99,* 66–77.

Cole, P. M., & Putnam, F. W. (1992). Effects of incest on self and social functioning: A developmental psychopathology perspective. *Journal of Consulting and Clinical Psychology, 60,* 174–184.

Consentino, C. E. (1989). Child sexual abuse prevention: Guidelines for the school psychologist. *School Psychology Review, 18,* 371–383.

Courtois, C. A. (1993). *Adult survivors of child sexual abuse.* Milwaukee, WI: Families International.

Daro, D. A. (1994). Prevention of child sexual abuse. In R. E. Behrman (Ed.), *The future of children: Sexual abuse of children* (Vol. 4, pp. 198–223). Los Altos: The Center for the Future of Children, The David and Lucile Packard Foundation.

Erickson, M. F., Egeland, B., & Pianta, R. (1989). The effects of maltreatment on the development of young children. In D. Cicchetti & V. Carlson (Eds.), *Child maltreatment* (pp. 647–685). Cambridge, England: Cambridge University Press.

Finkelhor, D. (1979). *Sexually victimized children.* New York: The Free Press.

Finkelhor, D. (1994). Current information on the scope and nature of child sexual abuse. *The future of children: Sexual abuse of children* (Vol. 4, pp. 31–53). Los Altos: The Center for the Future of Children, The David and Lucile Packard Foundation.

Finkelhor, D., & Berliner, L. (1995). Research on the treatment of sexually abused children: A review and recommendations. *Journal of the Academy of Child and Adolescent Psychiatry, 34,* 1408–1423.

Friedrich, W. N., Grambsch, P., Broughton, D., Kuiper, J., & Beilke, R. L. (1991). Normative sexual behavior in children. *Pediatrics, 88,* 456–464.

Friedrich, W. N., Grambsch, P., Damon, L., Hewitt, S.,

Koverola, C., Lang, R. A., Wolfe, V., & Broughton, D. (1992). Child sexual behavior inventory: Normative and clinical comparisons. *Psychological Assessments, 4,* 303–311.

Gelardo, M. S., & Sanford, E. E. (1987). Child abuse and neglect: A review of the literature. *School Psychology Review, 16,* 137–155.

Gil, E. (1991). *The healing power of play.* New York: Guilford, Press.

Gil, E., & Johnson, T. C. (1993). *Sexualized children: Assessment and treatment of sexualized children and children who molest.* Rockville, MD: Launch Press.

Gomez-Schwartz, B., Horowitz, J. M., & Cardarelli, A. P. (1990). *Child sexual abuse: The initial effects.* Newbury Park, CA: Sage.

Hindman, J. (1989). *Just before dawn.* Ontario, OR: AlexAndria Associates.

Horton, C. B. (1995). Best practices in the response to child maltreatment. In A. Thomas & T. Grimes (Eds.), *Best Practices in School Psychology*-III (pp. 963–976). Washington, DC: National Association of School Psychologists.

Horton, C. B. (in press). Children who molest other children: The school psychologist's response to the sexually aggressive child. *School Psychology Review.*

Horton, C. B., & Kochurka, K. (1995). The assessment of children with disabilities who report sexual abuse: A special look at those most vulnerable. In T. Ney (Ed.), *True and false allegations of child sexual abuse: Assessment and case management* (pp. 275–289). New York: Brunner Mazel.

Johnson, T. C. (1988). Child perpetrators—Children who molest other children: Preliminary findings. *Child Abuse & Neglect, 12,* 219–229.

Johnson, T. C. (1989). Female child perpetrators: Children who molest other children. *Child Abuse & Neglect, 13,* 571–585.

Johnson, T. C. (1990). Children who act out sexually. In J. McNamara & B. H. McNamara (Eds.), *Adoption and the sexually abused child.* Human Services Development Institute, University of Southern Maine.

Kendall-Tackett, K., Williams, L. M., & Finkelhor, D. (1993). Impact of sexual abuse on children: A review and synthesis of recent empirical studies. *Psychological Bulletin, 113,* 164–180.

Krugman, R., & Jones, D. P. H. (1987). Incest and other forms of sexual abuse. In R. E. Helfer & R. E. Kempe (Eds.), *The battered child.* Chicago: University of Chicago Press.

Larson, C., Terman, D., Gomby, D., Quinn, L., & Behrman, R. (1994). Sexual abuse of children: Recommendations and analysis. In R. E. Behrman (Ed.), *The future of children: Sexual abuse of children* (Vol. 4, pp. 4–30). Los Altos: Center for the Future of Children, The David and Lucile Packard Foundation.

National Adolescent Perpetrator Network, (1988). Preliminary report from the national task force of juvenile sex offending. *Juvenile and Family Court Journal, 39,* 5–52.

National Center on Child Abuse and Neglect. (1988). *Study findings: Study of national incidence and prevalence of child abuse and neglect* (DHHS Publication No. 105-85-1702). Washington, DC: Government Printing Office.

Reppucci, N. D., & Haugaard, J. J. (1989). Prevention of child sexual abuse: Myth or reality. *American Psychologist, 44,* 1276–1286.

Sedlak, A. (1991). *National incidence and prevalence of child abuse and neglect: 1988* (Revised report). Rockville, MD: Westat.

Sgori, S. M., Blick, L. C., & Porter, F. S. (1982). A conceptual framework for child sexual abuse. In S. M. Sgori (Ed.), *Handbook of clinical intervention in child sexual abuse* (pp. 9–37). Lexington, MA: D. C. Heath & Company.

Spaccarelli, S. (1994). Stress, appraisal, and coping in child sexual abuse: A theoretical and empirical review. *Psychological Bulletin, 116,* 340–362.

Tharinger, D., & Horton, C. B. (1992). Family-school partnerships: The response to child sexual abuse as a challenging example. In S. L. Christenson & J. C. Conoley (Eds.), *Home school collaboration: Enhancing children's academic and social competence* (pp. 467–486). Silver Spring, MD: National Association of School Psychologists.

Tharinger, D., Horton, C. B., & Millea, S. (1990). Sexual abuse and exploitation of children and adults with mental retardation and other handicaps. *Child Abuse and Neglect, 14,* 301–312.

Tharinger, D. J., Krivacska, J. J., Laye-Donough, M., Jamison, L., Vincent, G. G., & Hedlund, A. D. (1988). Prevention of child sexual abuse: An analysis of issues, educational programs, and research findings. *School Psychology Review, 17,* 614–634.

Vevier, E., & Tharinger, D. J. (1986). Child sexual abuse: A review and intervention framework for the school psychologist. *The Journal of School Psychology, 24,* 293–311.

Weise, D., & Daro, D. (1995). *Current trends in child abuse reporting and fatalities: The results of the 1994 annual fifty state survey* (Working Paper No. 808. Prepared by the National Center on Child Abuse Prevention Research). Chicago: National Committee for Prevention of Child Abuse.

65

Child Neglect

Kathleen D. Paget
University of South Carolina

Background and Development

In the educational preparation of school psychologists and other school-based service providers, child neglect is not a topic that receives much attention. And yet, as a risk factor, it exists in the family background of many children in educational settings. Children eligible for special education services may have learning and behavioral difficulties resulting from neglect, and some children, although not eligible for special services, are predisposed by the experience of neglect to need consultation and other intervention services. In addition, there is some evidence that children with special needs are particularly at risk of neglect (Jaudes & Diamond, 1986). The fact that educational personnel comprise the most frequent source of maltreatment reports to child protective services (U.S. Department of Health and Human Services, 1995) indicates keen awareness within school settings of the seriousness of child maltreatment, but methods for serving these children and their parents through the school system are less clear. Nevertheless, increased awareness of the unique needs of children who have experienced neglect should challenge school systems to supplement the reporting role with prevention and intervention activities for these children and their parents.

A principal reason for the lack of preparation to serve these children is that only recently has neglect been recognized in the literature as a phenomenon or set of phenomena conceptually separate from other forms of child maltreatment. Early efforts to study neglect (e.g., Giovannoni & Billingsley, 1970; Polansky, Hally, & Polansky, 1975) were overshadowed quickly by political, social, and educational forces associated with physical and sexual abuse and resulted in what Wolock and Horowitz (1984) termed "the neglect of neglect." More recent attention to child neglect has stimulated discussion of basic issues related to child rearing, the overall societal value placed on children, the availability of support services to families, and the culpability of parents who do not meet the needs of their children. Recent terminology describes neglected children as "children in the shadows" who are

being killed softly (Wattenberg, 1995). As school-based, support-service professionals provide increased services to these children and their parents, it is important that child neglect emerges from the shadows and becomes a topic of vigorous discussion among school psychologists and within the educational support services community.

Conceptual Issues Related to Child Neglect

The narrowness with which state statutes treat the broad range of issues related to neglect has spawned much discussion in the literature among researchers, practitioners, and policy makers. The simple, traditional textbook assertion that neglect is a willful act of omission on the part of a parent to provide food, clothing, shelter, and protection from danger (Gelles, 1975) has raised many questions. In an attempt to address the questions, the focus of discussion has comprised a range of etiological theories, definitions, and subtypes of parenting behaviors and children's needs.

Etiological theories and models

Because current understanding of the diverse causes of neglect is in the initial stages, a broad spectrum of theoretical foundations has been advocated. As emphasized by McGee and Wolfe (1991) in reference to psychological maltreatment, creation of paradigmatic boundaries would only deter efforts to broaden the breadth and scope of understanding. Numerous theories and models have been posited, which Ammerman (1990) synthesized into two broad categories. "Traditional" models focus on parental psychiatric disorders (psychopathological); the role of stress engendered by poverty, unemployment, and educational disadvantage (socio-cultural); and combinations of parental, child, and situational characteristics (social-situational). "Integrative" models delineate multiple levels of influence in the etiology of abuse and neglect (ecological), propose interactive effects from variables that increase or decrease the likelihood of maltreatment (transactional), and hypothesize stages of parent-child interactions that progressively heighten the probability of maltreatment (transitional).

The literature reflects a growing emphasis on transitional models, including those related to attachment theory (Crittenden, 1992). A provocative addition to the theoretical discussion is Crittenden's (1993) information-processing theory, which is based upon the premise that neglecting mothers lack or are limited in the cognitive and social skills of perceiving, interpreting, and responding to signals their children send them. Broader than any of these theories, however, is a model initially proposed by Lally (1984) and later widely adopted. The model structures an understanding of neglect on three levels: the microanalytic (individual), the mesoanalytic (social systems), and the macroanalytic (societal). Only by using a multi-tiered framework, according to Lally, is it possible to capture the complexities of the problem of neglect and understand the scope of necessary interventions. In the absence of sufficient support and resources at each of these levels, Lally emphasizes the difficulty of determining the extent to which individual parents are responsible for the neglect of their children.

Definitions of child neglect

The question of what constitutes adequate care of children lies at the very heart of the challenges in defining child neglect. This question is complicated by the issues of adequate care for children at varying stages and in all domains of development. In addition to the failure to provide for children's basic physical needs, an increasing number of states are including in their definition a failure to provide for the psychological needs of the children. This includes a lack of nurturance and affection; social and emotional support; verbal, intellectual and cultural stimulation; psychological involvement and social interaction; and socialization. When these psychological variables are included in the state's definition, the line between neglect and emotional abuse becomes very blurred. This line becomes even more blurred when neglect and abuse co-occur in the same family and/or when failure on the part of a caregiver to protect children from the physical and psychological harm of abuse defines the neglect charge. (For more discussion of the distinction between neglect and abuse, the reader is urged to read the chapters on physical abuse and sexual abuse, this volume.)

The major distinction between neglect and abuse lies in the difference between the omission of behavior or the failure to act (the former) and the commission of behavior (the latter). The issue of behavioral omissions raises several key questions, which must be answered on a case-by-case basis: What is the best way to document a behavioral omission? Must the omission be intentional or willful? Is the omission a result of poverty or of neglect? Must actual harm to the child be evident, or does the threat of harm also constitute neglect? Should the overall focus be on the parent and his or her parenting behaviors or on the child and his or her unmet needs?

Attempts to answer these questions have resulted in differing definitions from legal, research, and practice vantage points. Legal professionals advocate that the parents' behavior must result in some specific physical or emotional damage or impairment to a child, with clear evidence of serious harm to a child before court intervention takes place. For professionals intervening with a family to prevent foster care placement and to protect a child from further harm, the definition of neglect must focus on parental omissions in care that are likely to increase the risk of harm to the child. For researchers studying the long- and short-term consequences of neglect for a child, definitions tend to focus on parental behaviors that result in harm to the child.

Zuravin (1991) asserts that when the definitional focus is on parents, sharpest attention should be on parental *behaviors* (or lack of behaviors) rather than on culpability or intentionality. Nevertheless, a strong stance has been taken by key theorists and researchers (Dubowitz, Black, Starr, & Zuravin, 1993) that the definitional focus should be on children's needs rather than parental behaviors. These authors propose "a single, broad definition of neglect based on the concept that neglect occurs when basic needs of children are not met, *regardless of cause....* Basic needs include adequate shelter, food, health care, clothing, education, protection, and nurturance" (p. 12). Thus, practitioners must read the results of research studies with an understanding of which definition of neglect was used and the extent to which the definition is similar to and different from their state's legal definition of neglect.

Typologies of child neglect

The search for an understanding of the causes and consequences of neglect has resulted in a number of typologies, each using different language to classify neglect subtypes. Hegar and Yungman (1989) subdivided neglect into physical, developmental, and emotional neglect (including general emotional neglect and nonorganic failure to thrive). They discuss how differing combinations of stress, personality, lack of skill, culture and belief, and role and relationship problems are associated with each type of neglect. Zuravin (1991) significantly advanced existing classification systems by emphasizing the importance of previously overlooked variables in the literature. These variables include the child's age, the frequency and chronicity of neglecting behavior, the time period involved, and the differentiation between delays in providing adequate child care and refusals to provide such care. Applying these variables to an elaborated typology of neglect, the author proposed 14 subtypes of neglect, which advance definitional efforts in four substantial ways:

1. By specifying that both refusal to provide care and delays in providing care should be considered neglectful behavior.

2. By describing how custody refusal in divorce proceedings constitutes neglectful behavior as do other omissions related to custody disputes.

3. By explicating mental health care as a particular type of care that a neglectful caregiver may refuse to provide or delay providing.

4. By emphasizing the importance of a child's developmental age rather than chronological age as the marker for determining adequacy of care.

The specificity and range of these subtypes clearly reflect the complexity of the issues. Although there are numerous unanswered questions related to the neglect of young children, an equally large number can be raised for preadolescent and adolescent youth. At what age and maturity level, for example, should youth be allowed to stay home by themselves for extended periods of time or with caretaking responsibilities for others? More detailed delineation of subtypes and cogent discussions of their operational definitions and implications are provided by Zuravin (1991).

In addition to the conceptual issues already discussed, there are others related to chronic-versus-acute neglect, severe-versus-moderate or mild neglect, as well as community and cultural variations in definition and concomitant variation in the reporting of neglect to authorities. Clearly, the topic of child neglect is as complex as the topic of caregiving itself; the lack of consensus about some basic issues concerning neglect is related to the same lack of consensus regarding national standards of adequate child care. This complexity is reflected in more depth in the recommended resources at the end of this chapter.

The Prevalence of Child Neglect

Issues related to prevalence figures are intimately connected to which definition is used, whether threat of harm versus actual harm is counted, whether duplicated counts exist, whether cases referred to agencies other than child protective services are counted, and substantiation-versus-reporting rates. Further complicating the picture is the reality that levels of evidence to substantiate reports of neglect vary from state to state. Some states require "some credible evidence," others require "credible evidence," and still others require "a preponderance of evidence" (U.S. Department of Health and Human Services, 1995). The most recent study on the nationwide prevalence of child maltreatment (U.S. Department of Health and Human Services, 1995), based on various state definitions of neglect, indicates that nearly half (49%) of all substantiated, unduplicated child maltreatment cases are for neglect. Comparisons with the frequency of abuse in-

dicate the percentage of victims of physical neglect is more than double the percentage of victims of physical abuse (24%) and more than triple the percentage of victims of sexual abuse (14%). Medical neglect and emotional maltreatment are reported for about 7% of the victims, and about 15% are reported with other types of maltreatment, such as abandonment, congenital drug addiction, and threats to harm the child. Interestingly, the overall prevalence figures on neglect doubled during the period of time between this incidence report and the first national incidence study (U.S. Department of Health and Human Services, 1980) because children who were endangered, but not actually harmed from neglect, were counted in the second study but not in the first.

Other key findings from the second national incidence study indicate that effects of family income and family size are important variables in understanding neglect. Neglect represents a greater percentage of maltreatment cases for lower income groups (less than $15,000 annual income), where 68% of the children experience neglect compared with 37% who experience abuse. In contrast, the proportions for the upper income group (more than $15,000 annual income) are approximately equivalent, with 51% of the reported upper income children experiencing neglect and 56% experiencing abuse. With respect to family size, the rate of neglect for larger families is nearly double what it is for families with three or fewer children. Larger families exhibit nearly double the rate of physical neglect than smaller families, and children in larger families are three to four times more likely to be endangered.

Problems and Implications

Despite the lack of consensus on the etiology, definition, and typology of child neglect, research investigations have begun to illuminate the correlates and consequences of neglect. Based upon comparisons between abusing and neglecting families, Zuravin (1986, 1989) concluded that (a) the influence of poverty emerges more consistently for child neglect than abuse; (b) neglect is associated more strongly with household crowding than is abuse; (c) low-income single-family dwellings, numerous vacant houses, and the number of families who recently have moved into a neighborhood are more related to neglect than abuse; and (d) the number of live births and unplanned conceptions increase the probability of neglect more than abuse. Other empirical data support the contention that chronic neglect is associated with maternal depression as well as alcohol and other substance abuse (Nelson, Saunders, & Landsman, 1993).

When trying to address the question of whether child neglect has unique developmental correlates and consequences, it is essential to distinguish the effects of poverty on children's development from the sole effects of parental omissions. The judgment concerning parental adequacy must be made with the assumption that the parent has adequate physical resources available to provide appropriately but is not doing so. In many cases, the factors that distinguish neglect from poverty pertain to the "psychological adequacy" and decision-making skills of the primary caregiver and the degree of adequate support he or she receives for caregiving (Gaudin, 1993). Ironically, although child neglect receives more attention in families with limited resources (because these families come to the attention of authorities more frequently), the parental omissions comprising neglect are more obvious when they occur in middle- to upper-income families who have adequate to more-than-adequate resources. Readers are urged to stay current with knowledge about poverty and the limited access to physical resources experienced by a growing number of children in poverty (Hernandez, 1994) and the limited access to nonphysical resources experienced by a growing number of children in affluence.

Neglect-Related Child Fatalities

Studies of fatalities related to child maltreatment indicate that children die from neglect almost as often as from physical abuse. A review of 556 child fatality cases reported to child protective services agencies indicated that 44.3% were related to physical neglect (American Humane Association, 1986, cited in Gaudin, 1993). In addition, Margolin (1990) discovered that, over an 8-year period, as many as 40% of the child fatality cases reviewed were from neglect. The typical neglect fatality was a male child under the age of 3 years, living with a single mother and two or three siblings. The child typically died because a caregiver was not there at a critical moment, and the fatality was most often an accident associated with a single, life-threatening incident. Often, it would have been difficult to prevent the accident because, in two-thirds of the cases, the families were not known previously to child protective services agencies.

Effects of Neglect on Physical Development

Neglect has its most profound effect on children's physical development during the earliest stages of life (Crouch & Milner, 1993). Because a child's need for a safe and nurturing environment begins prior to conception and continues throughout pregnancy, the potential for neglect to occur actually begins before birth. The neglect of very young children may result from a variety of parental behaviors (e.g., failing to feed properly, leaving the child alone for inappropriate periods of time). The most specialized and researched form of neglect is non-

organic failure to thrive (NOFTT), a syndrome that is receiving increased attention in the school psychology literature (Black, 1995; Phelps, 1991). The syndrome manifests as an early deceleration of weight gain or failure to gain weight according to age expectations, and it has long-term consequences for children's health and development. The consequences of the syndrome may include growth deficits, decreased immunologic resistance, diminished physical activity, depressed performance in assessments of cognitive development, and poor academic performance (Blackman, 1990). These effects are likely to persist into school-age years if intervention does not occur (Vondra, Barnett, & Cicchetti, 1990).

An increased research emphasis on interaction patterns within the mother-child dyad has led some researchers to conceptualize NOFTT as a form of neglect in which the key feature is a breakdown in caretaker-child interaction. Substantial evidence suggests that mothers of NOFTT infants have less adaptive social interactional behavior, less positive affective behavior, and more arbitrary termination of feedings (Drotar, Eckerle, Satola, Pallotta, & Wyatt, 1990). Nevertheless, other researchers emphasize the importance of recognizing the potential diversity of factors (both organic and nonorganic) that may interact in the etiology of any given child's failure to thrive (Ayoub & Milner, 1985).

Effects of Neglect on Intellectual and Language Development

The effects of neglect on children's language, cognitive, and academic functioning comprise a much-needed and growing research focus. A brief review of findings thus far suggests that:

- Neglect is associated with both expressive and receptive language deficits, with deficits for children in neglect-only groups being greater than those in combined abuse and neglect groups (Hoffman-Plotkin & Twentyman, 1984).
- Neglected children are rated by parents and teachers as having difficulty in cognitive activities (Vondra et al., 1990).
- When compared to other forms of maltreatment, neglect is the only significant predictor for measures of auditory comprehension and verbal ability in preschool-age children (Allen & Oliver, 1982).
- Neglected school-age and adolescent children obtained lower scores on composite measures of overall school performance as well as on tests of language, reading, and math skills (Wodarsky, Kurtz, Gaudin, & Howing, 1990).
- Gender differences exist, with neglected boys scoring significantly lower than physically abused and non-maltreated boys in full-scale IQ scores, and neglected

girls scoring similarly to physically abused girls but lower than nonmaltreated girls (Rogeness, Amrung, Macedo, Harris, & Fisher, 1986).

Collectively, the emerging evidence suggests that neglect contributes to early changes in a child's intellectual and language abilities that, in turn, may affect the interaction between the child and environment in such a manner that later academic, social, and behavioral difficulties become more likely. The existing research not only suggests relationships between neglect and certain cognitive abilities but also illustrates the importance of considering issues of gender and severity of neglect when exploring these relationships.

Effects of Neglect on Social, Behavioral, and Affective Development

In an effort to examine the effects of neglect on children's social, behavioral, and affective development, an intensive focus of research activity has been the relationship between neglect and patterns of caregiver-child attachment. When compared to nonmaltreated children, neglected children have been reported to (a) display higher frequencies of avoidant, resistant, and anxious-dependent attachments to their primary caretaker (Erickson & Egeland, 1995; Lamb, Gaensbauer, Malkin, & Schultz, 1985); (b) be more passive (Crittenden, 1992); and (c) display fewer overtures of affection and produce less frequent initiations of play behavior in interactions with their mothers (Bousha & Twentyman, 1984).

Neglected children also have been reported to adopt different styles of social interaction with peers. Neglected preschool and school-age children tend to remain isolated during opportunities for free play with other children (Crittenden, 1992). Neglected preschool children also display fewer interactions during classroom observations than nonmaltreated or physically abused children and exhibit fewer prosocial behaviors than nonmaltreated children (Hoffman-Plotkin & Twentyman, 1984). Egeland, Sroufe, and Erickson (1983) reported that neglected preschool children were more apathetic, withdrawn, and dependent in their social interactions than were nonmaltreated children. Although these studies reveal that neglected children initially may be passive in social interactions, other studies indicate that under the care of neglectful (but not physically abusive) parents, children's behavior becomes increasingly difficult (Crittenden & DiLalla, 1988). Neglectful mothers rate their children as having more behavior problems than do nonmaltreating mothers (Williamson, Borduin, & Howe, 1991). Both neglected and physically abused preschool- and school-age children display greater amounts of physical and verbal aggression in interactions with their mothers than do nonmaltreated children (Bousha & Twentyman, 1984), although neglected children have

also scored significantly lower than physically abused and control children on some measures of aggression (Kaufman & Cicchetti, 1989). Males who experience neglect are at higher risk of later violent criminal activity than females (Rivera & Widom, 1992), and neglected girls are less likely than physically abused girls to be diagnosed with a conduct disorder (Rogeness et al., 1986). The extent to which neglected children are diagnosed with depression is unclear; Kaufman (1991) reported significant relationships between experiences of physical and emotional abuse and levels of depression in school-age children but failed to find an association between neglect and depression scores.

Collectively, the studies examining the effects of neglect on children's functioning suggest both the need for and potential effectiveness of school-based assessment and intervention activities. Children whose risk of negative developmental effects is high from multiple out-of-home placements, multiple life stresses, and parental depression greatly need intervention and preventive consultation activities (Nelson et al., 1993), especially in light of the fact that negative developmental consequences are not inevitable. Augoustinos (1987) found that when a child's living environment can be stabilized and higher cognitive functioning reached, negative outcomes can be moderated. Therefore, understanding the effects of neglect requires attention to the interaction between the nature of the neglectful omission, the child's developmental needs, and other contextual issues in the child's life. This level of understanding is possible only from carefully conducted assessments focused on the type, severity, and chronicity of neglect. To this end, items from some measures of child and family functioning (e.g., The Childhood Level of Living Scale; Polansky, Ammons, & Weathersby, 1983) have been shown to predict severe inadequacy in parental judgment. Although the assessment process is vital to intervention, discussion of assessment measures and strategies is beyond the scope of this chapter. Interested readers are referred to Gaudin (1993) and Nelson and Landsman (1995) for more complete coverage of specific assessment measures and strategies.

Children's Perceptions of Competence

Examination of children's perceptions of their competence and life situations comprises a line of research leading to counter-intuitive findings and serving as a reminder that children's perceptions vary according to age. The results of studies suggest that (a) children who experience neglect and emotional abuse have lower self-esteem and behavior ratings than controls but have higher ratings than those experiencing only neglect or physical or emotional abuse (Kaufman & Cicchetti, 1989); (b) younger neglected children perceive themselves as more competent and accepted than control children, especially in physical competence, whereas older neglect children describe themselves as less competent and accepted than controls (Vondra, Barnett, & Cicchetti, 1989); and (c) neglected children tend to give themselves higher ratings of physical competence and peer acceptance than nonmaltreated children (Vondra et al., 1990). Examining the moral functioning of maltreated children, Smetana, Kelly, and Twentyman (1984) found that neglected children considered the unfair distribution of resources more universally wrong than did abuse- and control-group children. These findings reflect the sensitivity of neglected children to unfair circumstances and are an important, initial step toward understanding their moral functioning. In general, then, existing knowledge identifies children's perceptions as important mediating variables that must be considered when designing interventions children find acceptable.

Alternative Actions

Existing research into the effectiveness of intervention strategies with neglecting parents and neglected children has promising implications for practice; the greatest challenge lies in establishing a range of services for individuals, groups, and systems within the context of educational settings. In this respect, three overarching principles challenge existing educational practice:

1. Traditional, in-office, one-to-one counseling by professionals is ineffective with neglect.
2. Intervention design must address the difficulty of neglecting parents in the very initial steps of seeking and receiving help.
3. Supplementing the services provided by professionals with those of paraprofessionals is a cost-effective way to enhance the effectiveness of interventions.

Clearly, the normalizing environment of school settings is an appropriate context for the necessary informal interventions that are not punitive or intrusive (Gracia, 1995). To implement this kind of intervention, however, school-based service providers must be creative and flexible in applying the results of research to school settings, and school systems must support and encourage nontraditional interventions with families where neglect is evident or suspected.

A Context for the Design of Interventions

Because intervention with neglecting families is new territory for school psychologists, a practical context for the design of interventions is important. With this in mind, the following guidelines are offered to assist in the trans-

lation of effectiveness evidence to the practical design of interventions (Paget & Abramczyk, 1994).

- Ecological validity is important to intervention accessibility, acceptability, and effectiveness. Stated differently, interventions should take place in the environment where the participants spend time, and they should be part of the participants' regular experiences. The number of office-visit "no-shows" among at-risk populations underscores the reality that the context in which interventions are offered is as important as the interventions themselves.
- Contingent helping, in contrast to noncontingent helping, is key to the participants' feelings of self-worth during the intervention process. Participants feel better and more in control when they are required to do something in return for the assistance they receive.
- Interventions should be designed to address the initial difficulty experienced by some people in seeking and receiving help.
- Interventions should be designed to take place over time to encompass the major developmental phases experienced by parents and children. This developmental continuity is surprisingly missing from most intervention programs serving families and children.
- The acceptability of interventions to address a particular problem is dependent upon the target person's perception of the problem and his or her own perceived competence in the problem area, whether the perception is a parent's belief about how well she nurtures her child or a child's belief about how well he interacts with peers in school.
- Normalizing the parenting experience also is important to intervention acceptability and effectiveness for parents who are experiencing difficulty.
- At the end of a professionally delivered intervention, participants should be capable of sustaining the benefits of the intervention with less direct assistance from the professional. Thus, parents should be helping other parents with the challenges of childrearing by serving as resources for each other and establishing a sense of community. This is particularly true for neglecting mothers in light of empirical evidence of difficulty with social isolation and social distancing.
- Interventions that involve choices meet with less resistance than those that are coercive and limit the freedom of participants to design and choose the intervention they need.

An understanding of these guidelines optimizes the likelihood that the following interventions, supported by research and targeted for parents, children, and families will be both acceptable to and effective with the participants they are designed to serve.

Interventions with Parents: Evidence from Research

Interventions with neglecting parents, which have been examined empirically, encompass behavioral approaches with individual parents (especially mothers), social network approaches, and group approaches.

Behavioral interventions

Studies with neglecting parents have been conducted in several different areas, including the training of problem-solving abilities, skills in maintaining a hazard-free and clean home environment, nutrition and personal cleanliness skills, and the provision of adequate stimulation for children. Many of these interventions have been conducted by Lutzker and colleagues (cf. Lutzker, 1990; Watson-Perczel, Lutzker, Greene, & McGimpsey, 1988). Results of interventions suggest (a) parents are able to incorporate problem-solving training into child-care dilemmas and generate additional, effective solutions (Dawson, de Armas, McGrath, & Kelly, 1986); (b) personal cleanliness of children can be improved through involvement of the mother or another family member; (c) neglectful conditions in the homes of mothers with mental retardation can be alleviated through behavioral intervention; (d) skills related to the proper nutrition of children can be learned by mothers with mental retardation; (e) infant stimulation skills can be trained successfully, including the use of appropriate affect; and (f) the number of hazards in a home can be reduced. Overall, these results suggest that skill and motivational difficulties resulting in child neglect are reasonable targets of behavioral interventions and that neglecting mothers, including those with limited intellectual capacity, can be receptive and responsive to a variety of interventions.

Numerous avenues exist for service providers and researchers interested in exploring new behavioral intervention approaches. Creative strategies are needed for circumventing the low literacy skills of some parents in areas such as knowledge of child development, and a focus on appropriate parental affect should be expanded to the initiating and responding behaviors of smiling, laughing, using affectionate words and physical touch, eye-to-face behavior, leveling (i.e., parent is on the same physical plane as the child), eliciting speech, and using guided play. Behavioral systems strategies (cf. Mash, 1989) offer promising avenues for the examination of behaviors manifested by neglecting mothers, not only within the mother-child dyad, but also outside the context of the dyad. In this respect, it is important to identify which reinforcers outside the dyad are more potent for the parent than the reinforcement he or she receives from dyadic interactions with the child. Crittenden's (1993) information-processing model holds much potential for the design of interventions that assist mothers to perceive their children's needs accurately and to implement appropriate behaviors in response to those needs.

Social network interventions

Research conducted by Polansky and associates has contributed significantly to the development of key concepts associated with child neglect. The terms "psychological ecology" (Polansky, Gaudin, Ammons, & Davis, 1985) and "social distancing" (Gaudin & Polansky, 1986) are key to understanding the isolation experienced by neglecting parents. Intervention approaches emerging from this line of research enhance the social network supports for neglecting parents. These approaches are discussed by Gaudin (1993) and include (a) direct intervention by a professional into the family's support network to facilitate communication, problem solve, and modify dysfunctional perceptions of potentially supportive relationships; (b) use of volunteers and parent aides to expand the resources within the network; (c) social skills training to teach basic communication, social, and friendship-making skills individually and in parent-support groups through modeling, practice, rehearsal, and reinforcement; and (d) linking with indigenous neighborhood helpers and other supportive resources in the neighborhood and community.

Coohey (1995) examined specific problems in the reciprocal exchange of resources between neglecting mothers and their partners and between them and their own mothers. Beeman (1995) examined differences between neglecting and non-neglecting mothers in their use of social networks. Results underscore the importance of perceptions of social support as important additions to objective indices of such support. Parents' perceptions of support (e.g., stability of support, the opportunity to reciprocate support, overall satisfaction with support), combined with views on when to ask for help and what it means to need help, were found to be distinguishing characteristics between neglecting and non-neglecting mothers. Consequently, an understanding of how these perceptions may be more negative for neglecting mothers is important to the success of social network interventions for them.

Group-based interventions

Interventions that take place in a group format hold much promise for neglecting parents. Their sense of isolation is alleviated because group participants are able to experience "connectedness" with other parents and develop and practice social and friendship-making skills. As a result of research with neglecting families, Abramczyk and this chapter's author (Abramczyk & Paget, 1993, 1994) enthusiastically endorse the use of groups with neglecting mothers and with neglected children. We found that the "constructing" of content through group discussion substantially elaborated the information given in individual interviews, and participants provided a rich repertoire of responses to each other. Thus, the group format is likely to be a valuable departure point for parents and children to learn information while building a more satisfying social network. The interested reader is encouraged to read Gaudin (1993) for more specific guidelines for conducting group-based interventions.

Interventions with Children: Evidence from Research

Intervention studies focusing on neglected children have been conducted to validate strategies in the areas of social initiation and language stimulation. With respect to social initiation, results suggest that (a) a peer social-initiation intervention can be effective in increasing the positive social responses of withdrawn, neglected preschoolers, with moderate maintenance and generalization effects (Fantuzzo, Stovall, Schachtel, Goins, & Hall, 1987) and (b) neglected children are more responsive in peer-mediated than adult-mediated social interactions (Davis & Fantuzzo, 1989). These results, which are replicated across several studies, support the effectiveness of intervention strategies for enhancing social relationships between neglected children and their peers. These results should challenge school personnel interested in research to develop and validate interventions to enhance interactions between neglected children and adults.

Examining language interventions, McLaren (1988) modified the Mother-Child Home Program of Levenstein (1979) to emphasize affective goals. Combining child's play with mother-child dialogue promoted the child's learning and improved relationships between mothers and children. However, this study's findings are weakened because of a simple pre-post design and a lack of control for maturation effects. Nevertheless, because of the importance of affective communication between parent and child and the potential for improvement in both the child and the parent(s), these findings should stimulate future replication studies and continued examination of intervention strategies for enhancing communication between neglecting parents and their children.

System-Level Interventions: Evidence from Demonstration Projects

In addition to empirical research studies, evaluations of demonstration projects serving neglecting families are an important source of information on intervention effectiveness. Demonstration projects have provided a wide range of multiservice and family-focused interventions to neglecting families.

Multiservice interventions
The challenge of intervention with neglecting families, especially when the neglect is chronic and severe, is described well by Gaudin (1993) when he states, "Success-ful intervention requires the delivery of a broad range of concrete, supportive community services from multiple sources and a combination of individual, family, and group methods that include individual counseling, behavioral methods, individual and group parenting education, and family therapy" (p. 36). Multidisciplinary teams are necessary to coordinate the therapeutic and supportive services provided by a variety of agencies. They also can coordinate legal interventions, when necessary, to ensure the child's safety. For handling child abuse and neglect, some states now mandate the establishment of such teams that include representatives from child welfare, law enforcement, the courts, schools, hospitals, health departments, and mental health agencies. Thus, an important first step toward effective intervention with the most severe cases of child neglect is an understanding of the state statutes surrounding child maltreatment and multidisciplinary teams.

Family-focused interventions
In a review of demonstration projects, Daro (1988) concluded that interventions including family members, rather than focusing only on the principal care provider, were more successful. According to Polansky et al. (1985), assertive, intrusive interventions sometimes are necessary with neglectful families to achieve a more "functional" family system balance that does not sacrifice the needs of the children. Family preservation services are specialized services designed to treat the entire family when two conditions are met: (a) the family is experiencing a "crisis" for the first time and (b) at least one child is at imminent risk of placement in out-of-home care. Although different family preservation models exist, characteristics that unite the models are small caseloads, around-the-clock availability of staff to families, and a range of instrumental, supportive, and therapeutic services (Gaudin, 1993). Other innovative approaches to community-based services for neglecting families, which serve as alternatives to formal, investigative tracks, are being examined. Two promising approaches are the Hennepin County Family Demonstration Project (AuClaire, 1995) and Project Empowerment (Schaefer & Jackson, 1995), a collaboration between Family and Children's Services in Minneapolis and Hennepin County Child Protection Services. The reader is referred to these sources and to the chapter on family empowerment (this volume) for additional information about family-focused services.

Despite the promising results from research studies and demonstration projects, the knowledge base must be expanded to maximize the scope of intervention effectiveness. Future projects need to (a) include fathers as participants; (b) train parents to combine verbal and nonverbal behaviors; (c) train children to reciprocate positive behaviors; (d) train self-sufficiency and friendship skills of parents; (e) determine the cost-effectiveness of various intervention strategies; (f) develop longitudinal designs;

and (g) document the type, severity, and chronicity of neglect in situations targeted for change.

Specific Activities for School Psychologists

Information on intervention effectiveness supports the need for action on multiple levels. Very evident is the need to supplement individual- and group-based services to parents, children, and families with activity on the social-systems level. The following activities are suggested as departure points from which school psychologists and other school-based service providers may initiate and expand services to neglecting families:

- Refer to your state's codes and statutes for the state definition of neglect and the requirements regarding team interventions. This information may be obtained from the legal department in the central office of your state's social services or human services agency.
- Consult with your school system's administration to bring attention to the problem of child neglect.
- Continue to refer families to state social services department when child neglect is suspected. Supplement the investigative nature of this intervention with support services for these families.
- Identify existing services provided by the school system to at-risk children and families. Determine how these services could be modified or supplemented to serve in a more intentional way the needs of children who have been neglected and their parents or caregivers.
- Identify key personnel within the school system who are trained to work with families (e.g., school social workers). Design and coordinate the implementation of activities with them.
- Implement assessment procedures for children at risk of neglect and their families.
- Develop individual and group-based interventions for parents and children at the preschool, elementary, middle, and high school levels. Design these interventions to be sensitive to the motivational needs of families and their difficulties in seeking and receiving help.
- Learn the resources and support services in the community and the surrounding region. Connect families with these resources.
- Coordinate with agencies outside of education and make referrals when the complexities of a case exceed training limitations. Refer to other agencies for needs such as counseling for chemical dependency and mental illness.
- Seek information concerning the processes of foster care placement. Understand the needs of children in the foster care system and the effects of the current placement on their functioning and adjustment. Understand the effects of previous, multiple placements on children's adjustment and relationship difficulties.
- Replicate research studies from the literature. Expand sample selection to encompass a range of socioeconomic backgrounds.
- Design and conduct evaluations of interventions.
- Provide inservice training and consult with teachers about the needs of children in their classrooms who have experienced neglect.

Summary

Despite the prevalence of child neglect, attention to it as a problem separate from other forms of maltreatment, such as physical and sexual abuse, has occurred only recently. The effects of neglect on children's language, social, intellectual, behavioral, and affective development challenge service providers in educational settings to address the needs of these children in an intentional way. Although these children and their families receive some kind of intervention through reports made to child protective services, the nature of these services often is investigative and coercive. School systems are in an opportune position to serve neglected children and their parents in a way that is supportive and more acceptable to the families. The knowledge base from which to design services, while in the formative stages and developed largely outside the field of education, offers initial guidance to service providers in educational settings. School psychologists are in a unique position to develop the knowledge base further and to mobilize public school systems to apply new knowledge to the challenges of child neglect.

Recommended Resources

Gaudin, J. M. (1993). *Child neglect: A guide for intervention*. Washington, DC: U.S. Department of Health and Human Services.
This monograph provides a detailed, practical, and comprehensive discussion of all relevant issues pertaining to child neglect. Written from an accurate and readable research perspective, the discussions are replete with information pertaining to defining neglect, understanding the causes of neglect, the short- and long-term consequences of neglect, assessment, intervention, prevention, and social policy implications. Additional sources of information, including national organizations, are provided.

Milner, J. S. (Ed.). (1993). Child neglect: Theory, research, and intervention. *Criminal Justice and Behavior, 20 (1)*.
This special journal issue is devoted entirely to child neglect and provides one of the most thorough discussions available.

Six articles written by key researchers and theorists provide much detail related to theory, research, intervention, and prevention. Discussed are issues related to definitions, an information-processing model of the behavior of neglectful parents, and the effects of neglect on children.

Nelson, K., & Landsman, M. J. (1995). Child neglect. In B. K. Williams (Ed.), *Family-centered services: A handbook for practitioners.* (pp. 184–200). Iowa City: The National Resource Center for Family-Centered Practice.
Written specifically for practitioners, this chapter provides very readable and pragmatic information related to child neglect. The authors review relevant issues but emphasize what practitioners can do in their work settings to assess and intervene in cases of child neglect. Copies can be obtained by writing The National Resource Center for Family-Centered Practice, School of Social Work, The University of Iowa, 112 North Hall, Iowa City, Iowa 52242-1223.

Paget, K. D., Philp, J. D., & Abramczyk, L. W. (1993). Recent developments in child neglect. In T. H. Ollendick and R. J. Prinz (Eds.), *Advances in clinical child psychology* (Vol. 15, pp. 121–174). New York: Plenum Press.
This chapter is a critical review of research on child neglect, and it provides much detail of key issues. Conceptual issues, including definitions and typologies, are discussed. An extensive review of research is given on a range of topics, including perceptions of neglect and resulting reporting behaviors, sociodemographic correlates of neglect, characteristics of neglecting parents, effects of neglect on children, and intervention effectiveness.

Pecora, P. J., Whittaker, J. K., & Maluccio, A. N. (1992). *The child welfare challenge: Policy, practice, and research.* New York: Walter de Gruyter.
This book contains an excellent chapter on child neglect and the associated research, practice, and policy issues. The chapter presents the complexities of child neglect as one of the challenges facing contemporary human service providers. The authors present a comprehensive overview of issues from research, practice, and policy perspectives. There is much practical information in the chapter on strategies for prevention and promising treatment approaches.

U.S. Department of Health and Human Services. (1995). *Chronic neglect symposium proceedings.* Washington, DC: Author.
This monograph is a compilation of presentations from a 2-day conference focused on chronic child neglect. Although most of the presentations resulted from empirical research studies, numerous practice and policy implications also were discussed. Chapters include information on arriving at a consensus on definitions, strategies for change through empowerment of neglectful families, culturally competent services to chronic neglect families, substance abuse and child neglect, effects of neglect on children, clinical treatment issues for children and neglectful families, family functioning in neglectful families, and policy implications. Copies can be obtained by writing to the National Clearinghouse on Child Abuse and Neglect Information, P.O. Box 1182, Washington, DC 20013-1182, or calling 1-800-394-3366.

References

Abramczyk, L. W., & Paget, K. D. (1993). Family functioning in neglecting families. Final report to the National Center on Child Abuse and Neglect. Washington, DC: U.S. Department of Health and Human Services.

Abramczyk, L. W., & Paget, K. D. (1994). Children in neglecting families. Final report to the National Center on Child Abuse and Neglect. Washington, DC: U.S. Department of Health and Human Services.

Allen, R. E., & Oliver, J. M., (1982). The effects of child maltreatment on language development. *Child Abuse and Neglect, 6,* 299–305.

American Humane Association. (1986). *Highlights of official child neglect and child abuse reporting.* Washington, DC: Author.

Ammerman, R. T. (1990). Etiological models of child maltreatment: A behavioral perspective. *Behavior Modification, 14,* 230–254.

AuClaire, P. (1995). Amplifying choice for neglecting families: Early findings from a research study. In E. Wattenberg (Ed.), *Children in the shadows: The fate of children in neglecting families* (pp. 127–128). Minneapolis: The Center for Advanced Studies in Child Welfare and the Center for Urban and Regional Affairs, University of Minnesota.

Augoustinos, M. (1987). Developmental effects of child abuse: Recent findings. *Child Abuse and Neglect, 11,* 15–27.

Ayoub, C. C., & Milner, J. S. (1985). Failure to thrive: Parental indicators, types, and outcomes. *Child Abuse and Neglect, 9,* 491–499.

Beeman, S. (1995). Reconceptualizing social support: The results of a study on the social networks of neglecting mothers. In E. Wattenberg (Ed.), *Children in the shadows: The fate of children in neglecting families* (pp. 61–84). Minneapolis: The Center for Advanced Studies in Child Welfare and the Center for Urban and Regional Affairs, University of Minnesota.

Black, M. (1995). Failure to thrive: Strategies for evaluation and intervention. *School Psychology Review, 24,* 171–185.

Blackman, J. A. (1990). *Medical aspects of developmental disabilities in children birth to three* (2nd ed.). Rockville, MD: Aspen Publishers.

Bousha, D. M., & Twentyman, C. (1984). Mother-child interaction style in abuse, neglect, and control groups: Naturalistic observations in the home. *Journal of Abnormal Psychology, 93,* 106–114.

Coohey, C. (1995). Neglectful mothers, their mothers, and partners: The significance of mutual aid. *Child Abuse and Neglect, 19,* 885–895.

Crittenden, P. M. (1992). Children's strategies for coping with adverse home environments: An interpretation using attachment theory. *Child Abuse and Neglect, 16,* 329–343.

Crittenden, P. M. (1993). An information-processing perspective on the behavior of neglectful parents. *Criminal Justice and Behavior, 20,* 27–48.

Crittenden, P. M., & DiLalla, D. L. (1988). Compulsive compliance: The development of an inhibitory coping strategy in infancy. *Journal of Abnormal Child Psychology, 16,* 585–599.

Crouch, J. L., & Milner, J. S. (1993). Effects of child neglect on children. *Criminal Justice and Behavior, 20,* 49–65.

Daro, D. (1988). *Confronting child abuse: Research for effective program design.* New York: Free Press.

Davis, S., & Fantuzzo, J. W. (1989). The effects of adult and peer social initiations on social behavior of withdrawn and aggressive maltreated preschool children. *Journal of Family Violence, 4,* 227–248.

Dawson, B., de Armas, A., McGrath, M. L., & Kelly, J. A. (1986). Cognitive problem-solving training to improve the child-care judgment of child neglectful parents. *Journal of Family Violence, 1,* 209–221.

Drotar, D., Eckerle, D., Satola, J., Pallotta, J., & Wyatt, B. (1990). Maternal interactional behavior with nonorganic failure-to-thrive infants: A case comparison study. *Child Abuse and Neglect, 14,* 41–51.

Dubowitz, H., Black, M., Starr, R. H., Jr., & Zuravin, S. (1993). A conceptual definition of child neglect. *Criminal Justice and Behavior, 20,* 8–26.

Egeland, B., Sroufe, L. A., & Erickson, M. (1983). The developmental consequences of different patterns of maltreatment. *Child Abuse and Neglect, 7,* 459–469.

Erickson, M., & Egeland, B. (1995). Throwing a spotlight on the developmental outcomes for children: Findings of a seventeen-year follow-up study. In E. Wattenberg (Ed.), *Children in the shadows: The fate of children in neglecting families* (pp. 113–126). Minneapolis: The Center for Advanced Studies in Child Welfare and the Center for Urban and Regional Affairs, University of Minnesota.

Fantuzzo, J. W., Stovall, A., Schachtel, D., Goins, C., & Hall, R. (1987). The effects of peer social initiations on the social behavior of withdrawn maltreated preschool children. *Journal of Behavior Therapy and Experimental Psychiatry, 18,* 357–363.

Gaudin, J. M. (1993). *Child neglect: A guide for intervention.* Washington, DC: U.S. Department of Health and Human Services.

Gaudin, J. M., & Polansky, N. A. (1986). Social distancing of the neglectful family: Sex, race, and social class influences. *Children and Youth Services Review, 8,* 1–12.

Gelles, R. J. (1975). The social construction of child abuse. *American Journal of Orthopsychiatry, 45,* 363–371.

Giovannoni, J. M., & Billingsley, A. (1970). Child neglect among the poor: A study of parental adequacy in families of three ethnic groups. *Child Welfare, 49,* 196–204.

Gracia, E. (1995). Visible but unreported: A case for the "not serious enough" cases of child maltreatment. *Child Abuse and Neglect, 19,* 1083–1093.

Hegar, R. L., & Yungman, J. J. (1989). Toward a causal typology of child neglect. *Children and Youth Services Review, 11,* 203–220.

Hernandez, D. J. (1994). *Children's changing access to resources: A historical perspective* (Social Policy Report). Chicago: Society for Research in Child Development.

Hoffman-Plotkin, D., & Twentyman, C. T. (1984). A multimodal assessment of behavioral and cognitive deficits in abused and neglected preschoolers. *Child Development, 55,* 794–802.

Jaudes, P. K., & Diamond, L. J. (1986). Neglect of chronically ill children. *American Journal of Diseases of Children, 140,* 655–658.

Kaufman, J. (1991). Depressive disorders in maltreated children. *Journal of the American Academy of Child and Adolescent Psychiatry, 30,* 257–265.

Kaufman, J., & Cicchetti, D. (1989). Effects of maltreatment on school-age children's socioemotional development: Assessments in a day-camp setting. *Developmental Psychology, 25,* 516–524.

Lally, J. R. (1984). Three views of child neglect: Expanding visions of preventive intervention. *Child Abuse and Neglect, 8,* 243–254.

Lamb, M. E., Gaensbauer, T. J., Malkin, C. M., & Schultz, L. A. (1985). The effects of child maltreatment on security of infant-adult attachment. *Infant Behavior and Development, 8,* 35–45.

Levenstein, P. (1979). Building concepts through verbal interactions: The key to future success in schools? *Carnegie Quarterly, 1,* 1–4.

Lutzker, J. R. (1990). Behavioral treatment of child neglect. *Behavior Modification, 14,* 301–315.

Margolin, L. (1990). Fatal child neglect. *Child Welfare, 69,* 309–319.

Mash, E. J. (1989). Treatment of child and family disturbance: A behavioral-systems perspective. In E. J. Mash & R. A. Barkley (Eds.), *Treatment of childhood disorders* (pp. 3–36). New York: Guilford Press.

McGee, D. A., and Wolfe, D. A. (1991). Between a rock and a hard place: Where do we go from here in defining psychological maltreatment? *Development and Psychopathology, 3,* 119–124.

McLaren, L. (1988). Fostering mother-child relationships. *Child Welfare, 67,* 353–365.

Nelson, K., & Landsman, M. (1995). Child neglect. In B. K. Williams (Ed.), *Family-centered services: A handbook for practitioners* (pp. 184–200). Iowa City, IA: The National Resource Center for Family-Centered Practice.

Nelson, K., Saunders, E. J., & Landsman, M. (1993). Chronic neglect in perspective. *Social Work, 38,* 661–671.

Paget, K. D., & Abramczyk, L. W. (1994). *Parents' exchange.* Unpublished manuscript. The Center for Child and Family Studies, University of South Carolina.

Paget, K. D., Philp, J. D., & Abramczyk, L. W. (1993). Recent developments in child neglect. In T. H. Ollendick & R. J. Prinz (Eds.), *Advances in clinical child psychology* (pp. 121–159). New York: Plenum Press.

Pecora, P. J., Whittaker, J. K., & Maluccio, A. N. (1992). Child neglect and psychological maltreatment: Prevention and treatment. In P. J. Pecora, J. K. Whittaker, & A. N. Maluccio (Eds.), *The child welfare challenge: Policy, practice, and research* (pp. 191–226). New York: Aldine de Gruyter.

Phelps, L. (1991). Non-organic failure-to-thrive: Origins and psychoeducational implications. *School Psychology Review, 20,* 417–427.

Polansky, N. A., Ammons, P. W., & Weathersby, B. L. (1983). Is there an American standard of child care? *Social Work,* September–October, 341–346.

Polansky, N. A., Gaudin, J. M., Jr., Ammons, P. W., & Davis, K. B. (1985). The psychological ecology of the neglectful mother. *Child Abuse and Neglect, 9,* 265–275.

Polansky, N. A., Hally, C., & Polansky, N. (1975). *Profile of neglect: A survey of the state of knowledge of child neglect.* Washington, DC: U.S. Department of Health, Education, and Welfare.

Rivera, B., & Widom, C. S. (1992). Childhood victimization and violent offending. *Violence and Victims, 5,* 19–35.

Rogeness, G. A., Amrung, S. A., Macedo, C. A., Harris, W. R., & Fisher, C. (1986). Psychopathology in abused and neglected children. *Journal of the American Academy of Child Psychiatry, 25,* 659–665.

Schaefer, N., & Jackson, C. (1995). Empowering families to disconnect from public agencies as they find resources within their own communities. In E. Wattenberg (Ed.), *Children in the shadows: The fate of children in neglecting families* (pp. 128–130). Minneapolis: The Center for Advanced Studies in Child Welfare and the Center for Urban and Regional Affairs, University of Minnesota.

Smetana, S. G., Kelly, M., & Twentyman, C. T. (1984). Abused, neglected, and nonmaltreated children's conceptions of moral and social-conventional transgressions. *Child Development, 55,* 277–287.

U.S. Department of Health and Human Services. (1980). *Study findings: Study of national incidence and prevalence of child abuse and neglect.* Washington, DC: U.S. Government Printing Office.

U.S. Department of Health and Human Services. (1990). *Study findings: Study of national incidence and prevalence of child abuse and neglect: 1988.* Washington, DC: U.S. Government Printing Office.

U.S. Department of Health and Human Services. (1995). *Child maltreatment 1993: Reports from the states to the National Center on Child Abuse and Neglect.* Washington, DC: U.S. Government Printing Office.

Vondra, J., Barnett, D., & Cicchetti, D. (1989). Perceived and actual competence among maltreated and comparison school children. *Development and Psychopathology, 1,* 237–255.

Vondra, J., Barnett, D., & Cicchetti, D. (1990). Self-concept, motivation, and competence among preschoolers from maltreating and comparison families. *Child and Abuse and Neglect, 14,* 525–540.

Watson-Perczel, M., Lutzker, J. R., Greene, B. F., & McGimpsey, B. J. (1988). Assessment and modification of home cleanliness among families adjudicated for child neglect. *Behavioral Modification, 132,* 57–81.

Wattenberg, E. (1995). Introduction. Neglected children: Killing them softly. In E. Wattenberg (Ed.), *Children in the shadows: The fate of children in neglecting families* (pp. 1–10). Minneapolis: The Center for Advanced Studies in Child Welfare and the Center for Urban and Regional Affairs, University of Minnesota.

Williamson, J. M., Borduin, C. M., & Howe, B. A. (1991). The ecology of adolescent maltreatment: A multilevel examination of adolescent physical abuse, sexual abuse, and neglect. *Journal of Consulting and Clinical Psychology, 59,* 449–457.

Wodarsky, J. S., Kurtz, P. D., Gaudin, J. M., Jr., & Howing, P. T. (1990). Maltreatment and the school-age child: Major academic, socioemotional, and adaptive outcomes. *Social Work, 35,* 506–513.

Wolock, I., & Horowitz, B. (1984). Child maltreatment as a social problem: The neglect of neglect. *American Journal of Orthopsychiatry, 54,* 530–543.

Zuravin, S. J. (1986). Residential density and urban child maltreatment: An aggregate analysis. *Journal of Family Violence, 1,* 307–322.

Zuravin, S. J. (1989). The ecology of child abuse and neglect: Review of the literature and presentation of data. *Violence and Victims, 4,* 101–120.

Zuravin, S. J. (1991). Research definitions of child physical abuse and neglect: Current problems. In R. H. Starr, Jr., & D. A. Wolfe (Eds.), *The effects of child abuse and neglect: Research issues.* New York: Guilford Press.

66

Ethnic and Racial Diversity

Craig L. Frisby
University of Florida

The study of America is the study of the racial and ethnic diversity of its people. This presents a formidable challenge, as there are a variety of approaches to the study of race and ethnicity among social scientists. For example, a social scientist may study the political, cultural, or economic contributions of various racial and ethnic groups to a host society (history); the social variables that influence intergroup harmony or conflict (sociology); the ways an individual's thinking, attitudes, and behavior is manifested toward members of different groups (psychology); genetic and environmental differences within and between racial and ethnic groups (biological anthropology); as well as a synthesis of these perspectives (sociobiology).

School psychology practitioners can draw from knowledge bases within a variety of these disciplines in order to understand how ethnic and racial diversity plays a role in the psychology of schooling. The ethnic and racial diversity of communities is intricately linked with the influence of social class on schooling; the values, attitudes, and beliefs shared by families (and how these characteristics may influence children's classroom behavior); school decision making on curriculum and instructional issues; and an understanding of historical contexts behind contentious local school board politics. These issues also influence the selection of topics deemed most important for study by school psychology researchers.

Background

Race

Race is a biological concept that refers to a genetically distinct inbreeding division within a species (Rushton, 1995). As such, races are recognized by a combination of geographic, ecological, and morphological factors and gene frequencies of biochemical components (e.g., blood groups). Traditional racial classification systems have rec-

ognized three major evolutionary subdivisions: Caucasoid groups (who originally inhabited Europe, North Africa, western Asia, and India), Mongoloid groups (who originally inhabited the Americas, the northern and eastern Pacific, and all of Asia except India), and Negroid groups (who originally inhabited all of sub-Saharan Africa).

Due to extensive interbreeding among and between these major racial groups, there are no "pure" races. This is particularly true in America. Unfortunately, popular discourse on race in America associates groups with generic color labels. African, Hispanic, Native, Asian, and Caucasian Americans are often referred to as Black, Brown, Red, Yellow, and White people respectively. However, a moment's reflection illustrates the obvious problems with this informal taxonomy. For example, certain Americans from India have a darker skin pigmentation than African Americans yet are still considered Caucasian. Most African Americans are Negroid-Caucasoid hybrids to some degree and average about 25% of Caucasian admixture (Chakraborty, Kamboh, Nwankwo, & Ferrell, 1992). Lighter skinned African Americans can "pass" for White but are still classified (and identify themselves psychologically) as "Black." Native Americans are called "Red people" but are descended from early Asians ("Yellow people") who migrated to the New World 20 to 40 thousand years ago across the land bridge from Asia to Alaska (Mattson & Mattson, 1990). American Hispanics come in all colors, including the whitest of white (e.g., Americans from Spain) to dark brown (e.g., Afro-Cubans). This reflects the rich mixture of Spanish, Native American, and African sexual unions through the centuries.

It has become clear that race is a vague word that can be used very loosely and has sparked much debate in psychology (see issues of *American Psychologist,* Vol. 48, Nos. 6 & 11; Vol. 50, No. 1). At one time, race was a more or less inflammatory term used by unenlightened persons to describe an ethnic group (e.g., "Jewish race," "Irish race," "Mexican race"). For these and other politically sensitive reasons, many investigators avoid usage of the term "race" as much as possible and prefer the term "population" (Rushton, 1995).

Ethnicity

Whereas the concept of race emphasizes biological differences between groups, the concept of ethnicity emphasizes the influence of psychosocial variables on intra- and intergroup relationships. Ethnicity is characterized by the following nine interrelated principles (Hraba, 1979):

1. Although racial group differences can play an important role in ethnic group differences, ethnicity is not synonymous with race. Widely differing ethnic groups can be found among people who are racially similar.
2. Ethnic group relations cannot be comprehensively understood as being synonymous with a majority group/ minority group model. Although the majority/minority model may have some explanatory power, it oversimplifies ethnic relations and is ahistorical and static. That is, it ignores the fact that many "majority" groups have at one time been minority group members (and vice versa).
3. Ethnic groups are self-conscious collectives of people.
4. Members of ethnic groups usually (but not always) share a common origin or hold a common set of traditions not shared by others with whom they are in contact.
5. Ethnic groups may or may not exist in cultural/physical isolation from outgroups. Because physical isolation of a group is not observed, it does not mean that there is no ethnicity.
6. Members of ethnic groups maintain distinctions between themselves and outsiders, which may be manifested in territorial segregation of a group, circumscribed social participation of its members, distinct patterns of thinking and/or sentiment, or a consciousness of historical continuity.
7. Characteristics that distinguish ethnic groups can be symbolic or psychological. The symbols may be arbitrary but are purposeful in order to consciously differentiate themselves from other groups or achieve certain objectives in society.
8. Progress toward the assimilation of ethnic groups with other groups and increased competition/conflict over coveted resources with other groups can exist simultaneously.
9. As American society changes and relations among ethnic groups evolve, the expression of ethnicity and the nature of intergroup relations change and evolve as well.

America's Racial and Ethnic Diversity

The regions of the country (states) in which five racial/ethnic groups are in the highest proportions are listed in Table 1. It bears emphasizing that these five labels are overly broad and woefully imprecise. Considerable ethnic

diversity exists within each of these five groupings. For example, Native-Americans are organized according to language groups called "nations" (Mattson & Mattson, 1990), which are subdivided into over 500 tribes. Within the broad term "White," a distinction is often made between "WASPs" (persons descending from a core culture of British and North European groups from which later immigrant groups have had to adapt), and "White ethnics" (non-Protestant caucasians of non-British ancestry such as the Irish, Italians, Germans, and Jews). The broad designation "Black" refers to those persons originally descended from Africans brought to America against their will by early slave traders, as well as small populations of West Indian Blacks and Africans who later freely immigrated to America. The term "Hispanic" is an umbrella term widely used in describing Spanish-speaking Americans of Mexican, Puerto Rican, Dominican, Cuban, Portugese, and Central/South American descent. The term "Asian" encompasses the Chinese, Japanese, Filipinos, south Asians from India and Pakistan, Koreans, and various Indo-Chinese ethnic groups such as the Vietnamese, Cambodians, and Laotians.

For a detailed discussion of the history, immigration and settling patterns, language, and religious diversity within the five broad grouping in Table 1, readers are encouraged to consult Edmonston and Passel (1994), Feagin and Feagin (1993), Mattson and Mattson (1990), Min (1995), Paisano (1991), Sowell (1981), and Weaver (1993).

Problems and Implications

Racial and ethnic diversity among children and youth is not a problem in and of itself. However, problems are identified within the context of an American society that places a high social value on equality of educational outcomes, intergroup harmony, and individual mental health. Such problems often lead to both political and social conflicts among psychologists and educators who hold differing interpretations as to reasons why these ideals have not been realized in American schooling (e.g., see *School Psychology Review,* Vol. 21, No. 4; Vol. 24, No. 1). Such problems can be categorized as universal problems that disproportionately affect ethnically and racially diverse children, youth, and families versus problems that are unique to the psychology of race or ethnicity.

Universal Problems That Disproportionately Affect Groups

Racial and ethnic group inequalities have been observed in childbirth, poverty level, family constellation, health variables, average intelligence and academic achievement scores, and dropout rates. These variables have

Table 1 *Broad Racial or Ethnic Groupings in the United States*

Group	Percentage of U.S. Population*	States with the Highest Proportions of This Group (Percentage Range)
Native Americans	0.8%	AK, NM, OK, AZ (5–15%)
Whites (non-Hispanic)	75.2%	ID, IA, ME, MN, NH, ND, VT, WV, WY (95–99%)
Blacks	12.1%	AL, DC, GA, LA, MS, SC (25–35%)
Hispanics	9.0%	AZ, CA, CO, NM, TX (20–35%)
Asians	2.9%	CA, HI, NY (2–5%)

*Based on 1990 Census figures obtained from Edmonston and Passel (1994).

been repeatedly shown in the social science literature to covary with children's school success or failure.

Childbirth

According to 1992 figures, the percentage (within ethnic/racial group) of expectant mothers receiving prenatal care beginning in the first trimester of their pregnancies was 62% to 64% for Native American, Mexican American, and African American women; 67%–68% for Central American, South American, and Puerto Rican mothers; 70% for Hawaiian mothers; and 84% to 88% for non-Hispanic White, Chinese, Cuban, and Japanese mothers (National Center for Health Statistics, 1995).

Similarly, Black and Chinese groups have consistently fallen at opposite ends of the spectrum on a number of other childbirth variables. In 1992, the percentage of live births to unmarried mothers within the total population was 30.1%. Within various racial or ethnic groups, these figures (in order from highest to lowest) were 68.1% (Blacks), 57.5% (Puerto Ricans), 55.3% (Native Americans), 45.7% (Hawaiians), 43.9% (South/Central Americans), 36.3% (Mexican Americans), 22.6% (whites), 20.2% (Cubans), 16.8% (Filipinos), 9.8% (Japanese), and 6.1% (Chinese). Again, using 1992 figures, the percentage of live births for mothers under 18 was at 4.9% in the general population, with the highest percentages observed within Black subgroups (10.3%) and the lowest percentages observed within the Chinese (0.3%). In the same year, figures for the percentage of low birthweight (under 2,500 grams) babies fall at 7% for the general population, with the highest percentages observed within Black subgroups (13.3%) and the lowest percentages observed within the Chinese (4.9%; National Center for Health Statistics, 1995).

Family

According to 1993 figures, the percentages of one-parent family households with children under 18 were 30% for the total population, 25% for Whites, 35% for Hispanics, and 63% for Blacks (U.S. Department of Commerce, 1994). According to 1992 figures, the percentages of families living below poverty level were 11.7% for the total population, 8.9% for Whites, 26.2% for Hispanics, and 30.9% for Blacks (U.S. Department of Commerce, 1994).

Of the total number of Black children living in poverty, 81.8% live in a female-headed household with no husband present (National Center for Education Statistics, 1994).

Health/Mortality

The Native American mortality rates for tuberculosis, alcoholism, accidents, diabetes mellitus, homicide, pneumonia, influenza, and suicide are considerably higher than general population averages (Indian Health Services, 1994). According to 1990 figures, for example, Native Americans between the ages of 1 and 14 years die from accidents at nearly twice the rate as the general population. Native Americans between the ages of 15 and 24 years die from accidents, suicide, viral hepatitis, and liver disease at a rate of 2.5, 2.8, 6 and 9 times the rate (respectively) of the general population (Indian Health Services, 1994).

Intelligence/Academic Achievement

Chinese and Japanese groups (both in America and abroad) obtain higher average nonverbal IQ and achievement test scores than American Caucasian groups, although the precise size of this difference is unclear (Herrnstein & Murray, 1994). In contrast, African American groups obtain average IQ scores that converge at 1 standard deviation below the mean of Whites. Not enough reliable data are aggregated for other American subgroup comparisons, so no firm conclusions can be drawn. In general, students' average standardized achievement test scores go up with concomitant rises in the social class standing of the family (Miller, 1995). However, data on school achievement scores both within and across social classes tend to reflect a consistent pattern of racial or ethnic group differences, although these differences may be more pronounced in different subject areas. For example, the mean Scholastic Aptitude Test scores of college-bound seniors between 1987 and 1993 show Whites consistently ranking highest in the verbal subtest, while Asians consistently ranked highest in the math subtest. Blacks consistently ranked lowest in both verbal and math subtests (National Center for Education Statistics, 1994).

According to 1993 estimates, the percentage of high school dropouts among persons between the ages of 14 and 34 was 10.6%. The corresponding figures are 7.3% for Whites, 12.5% for Blacks, and 30.7% for Hispanics (National Center for Education Statistics, 1994).

Summary

According to these data, Asians tend to fare well on variables that support school success. Native Americans tend to fare worst on variables that shorten life expectancy. Unfortunately, the quadruple problems of out-of-wedlock births, single-parent families, lower IQ scores, and poverty are so interrelated among Black and Latino families (Roth, 1994; Weaver, 1993) that school failure is disproportionately represented within these groups. Illegitimacy tends to be more common among younger women who themselves have experienced difficulties in school and live in poor, disorderly, and crime-ridden neighborhoods (Roth, 1994). These neighborhoods, in turn, are breeding grounds for youth gangs. While youth gang research conducted during the 1920s involved primarily the study of European immigrants, contemporary youth gangs are predominantly African American, Hispanic, and Asian (Joe, 1993).

Problems Unique to the Psychology of Race or Ethnicity

The previous section addressed demographic variables shown to be related to disproportionate school failure among ethnic groups. A complementary research agenda addresses how race and ethnicity may interact with psychological constructs (e.g., self-esteem, acculturation, ethnic identity) to undermine school success and mental health. Most of this research focuses on African, Hispanic, and Native American children and youth, because school failure is most salient for these groups. Implicit in such research is the "minority/majority" paradigm, in which it is assumed that problems have their origin in an awareness of minority group status in the midst of a majority European-American cultural ethos. For a general discussion on theories of psychological development as it relates to race or ethnicity, readers are encouraged to consult Ponterotto, Casas, Suzuki and Alexander (1995). The following brief discussion focuses on how psychological constructs may negatively influence the social and educational adjustment of racial or ethnic minority children and youth. This discussion can be summarized under three hypotheses:

- Does racial or ethnic minority status lead to lower levels of self-esteem?
- Are lower levels of acculturation related to impaired school success and mental health?
- Is impaired ethnic-identity development related to school problems, mental health problems, or both?

Self-esteem hypothesis

There is little or no consistent evidence that African American children manifest lower levels of self-esteem compared to White children (see review by Whaley, 1993). Research with a variety of ethnic groups across school and college ages is inconclusive regarding the relationship between self-esteem and an ethnic minority individual's attitudes toward, knowledge about, and commitment to their group. Various assessment paradigms corroborate the finding of no relationship between racial attitudes or preferences and self-esteem in African American children (Whaley, 1993). However, there is some evidence that higher levels of self-esteem are associated with individuals who display both high levels of ethnic identity and positive attitudes toward mainstream culture (Phinney, 1991).

The role of ethnicity as a moderator variable in the relationship between levels of self-esteem and antisocial acts is difficult to interpret. For example, Leung and Drasgow (1986) examined the relationship between self-esteem and delinquency in large national subsamples of White, Hispanic, and African American adolescents. A significant negative relationship between self-esteem and delinquency was found for Whites, but not for Hispanics and African Americans (Leung & Drasgow, 1986).

Acculturation hypothesis

Acculturation refers to the degree to which an individual from an ethnic minority group accepts and adheres to both majority and minority values, norms, and traditions. According to some theorists, school success and mental health levels of racial or ethnic group children are directly related to their level of acculturation. One popular theory explains the higher instances of social problems among Native American adolescents to "acculturative stress," which is defined as physiological discomfort experienced from attempts to negotiate both tribal and "Western" cultures (Ponterotto et al., 1995). Similarly, immigrant or first-generation Asian families in which the children are newly exposed to (or born into) American culture may experience significant parent-child conflicts that have their origins in acculturation differences. In such cases, the quality of the family environment can either facilitate or hinder children's development of ethnic pride and belongingness (Ponterotto et al., 1995).

According to some theorists, when students who are not acculturated interact with American schools, "cultural discontinuities" occur which lead to academic failure and poor mental health (see review by Bernal, Saenz, & Knight, 1991). Primary support for this theory comes from the observation that language-minority groups (e.g., Hispanics) and older immigrant children experience greater academic problems than non-language-minority and younger immigrant children. This hypothesis is undermined by the observation that some immigrant language minorities (e.g., some Asian groups) have been found, on average, to display greater school success than nonimmigrant English-speaking minorities (e.g., African Americans).

Ethnic-identity hypothesis

While acculturation involves changes in the cultural or behavioral patterns shown by groups when they come into contact with one another, ethnic identity deals with attitudes towards in- versus out-groups and self-identification preferences. Whaley's (1993) literature review suggests that children's cultural identity, like other cognitive psychological contructs, is heavily influenced by cognitive development. Here, the course of young children's ethnic identity development begins with an undifferentiated view of the self, followed by concrete self-descriptions, and ending in abstract self-descriptions as they mature. Cognitive limitations have been cited as a plausible explanation for the finding that young racial and ethnic minority children often display a pro-White identity "bias" or self-misidentification (Spencer & Markstrom-Adams, 1990).

The period of adolescence creates problems in identity development that are universal to all Americans irrespective of race or ethnicity. However, race and ethnicity factors create other problems not addressed by generic, adolescent identity-development theories. Within adolescence through adulthood, ethnic-identity theories posit a "developmental" pattern starting from a point of unexamined ethnic identity, which is followed by an "encounter" experience that initiates psychological disequilibrium and self-evaluation, ending with a period of personal integration, equilibrium, and commitment to an ethnic identity (see reviews in Ponterotto et al., 1995; Spencer & Markstrom-Adams, 1990). However, the nature and outcome of this process is moderated by family socialization practices, gender, the racial or ethnic makeup of the community in which the child grows up, the extent to which the ethnic or racial minority person accepts or rejects the dominant group (and vice versa), and the extent to which the person feels a sense of belonging to their own ethnic or racial minority group (Ponterotto et al., 1995; Spencer & Markstrom-Adams, 1990). When the adolescent is biracial, another layer of complex issues is added (Ponterotto et al., 1995; also, see Biracial Identity, this volume).

Research suggests that ethnic identity and self-esteem are independent constructs; this undermines the proposition that negative ethnic-identity development must necessarily lead to low self-esteem (see reviews by Phinney, 1991; Whaley, 1993). However, Bernal et al. (1991) argue that when academic success is a value embedded within a minority student's ethnic identity, behavior that promotes success is more likely, even in instances where cultural disparities exist between home and school environments. This is borne out in research by Matute-Bianchi (1986) and Fordham and Ogbu (1986). Fordham and Ogbu identified some Mexican and

African American secondary school students who believed that maintenance of their ethnic identity must necessarily involve engaging in behaviors that reduce the chances for academic success. In contrast, academically successful Japanese American students who were interviewed by Matute-Bianchi did not see components of their ethnicity to be in conflict with their identities as students. For further examples of clinically referred ethnic or racial minority children and youth with disturbed identity development, see Canino and Spurlock (1994).

Alternative Actions

School professionals who want to familiarize themselves with counseling issues relevant to racial or ethnic minority children and youth are encouraged to consult Ponterotto et al. (1995) and Thomas (1992). This concluding discussion focuses on two salient issues relevant to multiracial or ethnic education: school curriculum and instruction and testing/assessment.

School Curriculum

There has always been a rich tradition of debate among educators as to the proper curriculum for children of differing racial or ethnic groups. Some educators complain that education in general, and social studies education in particular, trivializes or distorts the contributions of racial or ethnic minorities. They argue that racial or ethnic minority children, in order to develop healthy attitudes and self-identities, require immersion in a curriculum centered around academic role models and cultural contributions from a variety of groups (i.e., multiculturalism) or specifically from the learner's own racial or ethnic group (i.e., particularism).

A more detailed treatment of the complex issues inherent in "multiethnic" education is given by Banks (1994). Unfortunately, some recommendations found in the multiethnic education literature are shaped by an explicit sociopolitical ideology, are lacking in a consistent body of rigorous and controlled evaluation studies, and have been carried to questionable extremes that can lead to highly contentious battles in integrated settings (see case studies described in Bernstein, 1994).

Some researchers have investigated the extent to which the "culture" of low-achieving racial or ethnic minority children may be incompatible with the "culture" of schools. If disparities are found, the conventional wisdom is that teachers and schools must modify their practices to reduce the disparity (which should improve academic achievement). Miller (1995) reviews research summarizing four dimensions in which disparities may be found: classroom social organization preferences, teacher/student sociolinguistic differences, children's cognitive characteristics or styles, and children's motivational needs. The strength of this research lies in its attention to classroom processes often overlooked by global achievement test scores. Such information can orient school psychological consultants as to variables that may be most amenable to teacher modification. The weakness of this research lies in its inability to explain consistent racial or ethnic group disparities in school achievement that persist despite a wide range of individual teaching styles, coupled with its implicit (but debatable) assumption that requiring students to modify "natural" cultural traits in deference to classroom expectations is undesirable.

There is little doubt that children whose primary language is not English pose unique educational problems. The 1975 Supreme Court decision in *Lau v. Nichols* provided constitutionally protected school remedies to meet the academic needs of language-minority children. There exists considerable debate, however, over the extent to which schools should promote or discourage the maintenance of a students' primary language as they learn English. Positions on this issue are based on theories of language learning, political-ideological considerations, and/or hard data from large-scale evaluation studies. Many bilingual educators argue that the preferred approach is for limited English proficient students to be taught academic subjects in their primary language for the first few years, with English taught as a second language (called transitional bilingual education, or TBE). As the students develop their academic English skills over time, instruction in academic subjects is gradually shifted to English (Miller, 1995). Some data suggest that late-exit TBE programs have been found to result in greater academic gains compared to early-exit TBE or English immersion for Spanish speaking elementary school students (see reviews of evaluation studies in Miller, 1995). However, many educators argue that bilingual education programs have been abused and are obstacles to both English learning and academic progress (see Chavez, 1991; Porter, 1990). Decisions as to the "best" curriculum for any particular child appear to be based on the complex interplay of the child's cognitive ability, functional competence and adaptive behavior, quality of school resources, and parental goals.

Testing and Assessment

Cervantes and Arroyo (1995) and Dana (1993) level criticisms at the clinical use of various instruments and taxonomies (e.g., *Diagnostic and Statistical Manual of Mental Disorders,* or *DSM-IV*) in the diagnosis of pathology in ethnic or racial minority clients. In addition, there is an extensive literature base critiquing the appropriateness of school practices in the referral, assessment, and labelling of ethnic and racial minority students as behavior disordered and emotionally disturbed (Peterson &

Ishii-Jordan, 1994). The gist of these criticisms is that ethnic or racial minority persons run the high risk of being misdiagnosed (and hence mistreated) as a result of a school professional's or service provider's ignorance about cultural factors that may assist in explaining disturbing behaviors. These criticisms, and the supporting research on which they are based, are relevant for school psychology practitioners who find themselves serving populations that are so culturally distinct from the mainstream that "traditional" literature on psychological pathologies appears to have limited usefulness. As such, this literature fills a long-standing void in school psychology.

Nevertheless, much work needs to be done in evaluating the validity of these criticisms. For example, some are minor offshoots of more fundamental criticisms of (a) the subjectivity of teacher referrals (Algozzine, 1976, 1977; Algozzine, Christenson, & Ysseldyke, 1982), (b) the unreliability and questionable validity of projective techniques (see *School Psychology Review,* Vol. 12, No. 4; *School Psychology Quarterly,* Vol. 8, No. 3), and (c) the questionable treatment utility in the diagnosis of mental disorders (see *School Psychology Quarterly,* Vol. 7, No. 2; Kratochwill & Plunge, 1992).

In addition, many writers base their accusations of the cultural inappropriateness of diagnostic and labelling practices solely on statistical disparity evidence (Peterson & Ishii-Jordan, 1994). Here, it is reasoned that if the proportion of a group receiving special education services or labels does not match their proportion in the general population, then this represents prima facie evidence of "cultural bias." Hence, schools can be criticized for "mislabelling" a group overrepresented in a socially undesirable category and for denying services to groups underrepresented in socially desirable categories. Some writers may or may not buttress this conclusion with anecdotal descriptions of blatant malpractice. Despite the simplicity and appeal of this logic, there are two serious problems with this reasoning.

First, in their emphasis on comparisons of proportional representation, writers are prone to overlook appropriate analyses of proportional representations *within* groups. Specifically, the proportions of ethnic or racial minority children who are *not* in special education classes for students with emotional or behavioral disorders or learning disabilities is far greater than those who are. Thus, how can overrepresentation be attributed solely to "cultural factors" (associated with race/ethnicity) when the majority of children in these groups are not labelled in this fashion? Second, various ethnic or racial groups do not show identical distributions across key factors (e.g., poverty, single-parent families) that play a role in the development of undesirable school behaviors. Because writers are extremely sensitive to social perceptions of ethnic or racial minority group persons as "inferior," "pathological," or "deviant," there is a reluctance to

openly discuss the possibility that some disturbing behaviors have a universal validity and are simply over- or
underrepresented in a particular group. To seriously address these two shortcomings, writers would have to acknowledge that the sum total of an individual's school
behavior cannot be adequately explained solely through
knowledge of cultural traits associated with racial or ethnic group membership.

With respect to cognitive testing, massive reviews of
the test bias literature have come to the conclusion that
well-developed standardized cognitive tests maintain the
same psychometric properties when used with American-
born English-speaking groups (Jensen, 1980; Wigdor &
Garner, 1982). For immigrant children not born in America and non-English speakers, the choice of appropriate
tests is more complex. To assist in this regard, Hamayan
and Damico (1991) detail proper guidelines for conducting assessments of bilingual students. Because the cultural distance between various ethnic and racial groups
is multidimensional, efforts to reduce the cultural loading
of mental test items may be appropriate for one dimension of cultural differences but may not make a difference
for another dimension of cultural differences. The variety
of ways in which the culture loading of a test can be reduced is listed in Table 2. It cannot be assumed, however,
that a "culturally reduced" test on any of these dimensions necessarily makes a test less biased or more fair
for a particular racial or ethnic group. Questions of culture bias and test fairness must be answered empirically
(e.g., through an analysis of test reliability, test validity,
item characteristic curves, selection outcomes) for each
test used for each group (e.g., see Camilli & Shepard,
1994).

Summary

American racial and ethnic diversity is not problematic
per se. However, racial or ethnic disparities become problematic in the context of a society which values egalitarian principles, intergroup harmony, and individual mental
health. As a group, Native Americans experience the
highest rates for health factors detrimental to a long life
span. National statistics on a variety of birth, family, and
economic factors that covary with school success indicate
that Caucasian and Chinese subgroups fare best, while
African Americans fare worst (on average). The same relationship holds for IQ and academic achievement test
scores. Hispanic groups experience the highest school
dropout rates of all American racial or ethnic groups.
There are interesting research questions that explore the
relationship between self-esteem, acculturation, ethnic
identity, and academic achievement in racial or ethnic
minority children and youth. Although firm relationships
(or lack thereof) have been established in some cases,
the influence of complex mediating variables have resulted in inconclusive findings.

A brief overview of issues and problems related to
school curriculum/instruction was given in this chapter,
with particular emphasis placed on debates over multiculturalism and the efficacy of bilingual education. The
chapter concluded with a brief discussion of testing and
assessment issues with ethnically and racially diverse
populations. Much more work needs to be done in examining the validity of criticisms of the cultural appropriateness of diagnoses of behavioral and emotional pathologies. Variables that reduce the culture loading of
cognitive tests were highlighted, circumscribed by the

Table 2 *Methods of Reducing the Culture Loading of Tests (Reprinted from Jensen, 1980, p. 637)*

Culture Loaded	Culture Reduced
Paper-and-pencil tests	Performance tests
Printed instructions	Oral instructions
Oral instructions	Pantomine instructions
No preliminary practice	Preliminary practice items
Reading required	Purely pictorial
Pictorial (objects)	Abstract figural
Written response	Oral response
Separate answer sheet	Answers written on test itself
Language	Nonlanguage
Speed tests	Power tests
Verbal content	Nonverbal content
Specific factual knowledge	Abstract reasoning
Scholastic skills	Nonscholastic skills
Recall of past-learned information	Solving novel problems
Content graded from familiar to rare	All item content highly familiar
Difficulty based on rarity of content	Difficulty based on content complexity of relation education

Note. From *Bias in Mental Testing* by Arthur R. Jensen. Copyright 1980 by Arthur Jensen. Reprinted with permission of The Free Press, a Division of Simon & Schuster.

need to apply empirical analyses in the investigation of test bias and fairness.

Recommended Resources

Arias, B., & Casanova, U. (Eds.). (1993). *Bilingual education: Politics, practice, and research.* Chicago, IL: University of Chicago Press.
This edited volume of nine chapters by 14 authors addresses the complex political, curricular, and instructional issues inherent in bilingual education for Hispanic language minority students. The book includes informative anecdotes from the field, as well as a glossary of acronyms and specialized terms for the uninitiated.

Banks, J. A. (1994). *Multiethnic education: Theory and practice (3rd ed.).* Needham Heights, MA: Allyn and Bacon.
This text, written by one of America's leading scholars in multicultural education, outlines historical, conceptual, political, and philosophical issues inherent in the multiethnic education movement in American schools. Included are curriculum guidelines for multiethnic education.

Peterson, R. L., & Ishii-Jordan, S. (Eds.). (1994). *Multicultural issues in the education of students with behavioral disorders.* Cambridge, MA: Brookline.
This edited volume of 20 chapters addresses relevant community, family, and cultural issues related to the assessment and diagnosis of behavior disorders in populations that are substantially atypical from the mainstream. An appendix contains a "Best Assessment Practices" document endorsed by the Council for Children with Behavioral Disorders.

Roth, B. M. (1994). *Prescription for failure: Race relations in the age of social science.* New Brunswick, NJ: Transaction.
This book represents a significant departure from traditional social science explanations for the poor achievement of underclass Black children, youth, and families. Professor Roth demonstrates how crime, out-of-wedlock births, and school failure act in combination to erect barriers to African American social advancement.

References

Algozzine, B. (1976). The disturbing child: What you see is what you get? *The Alberta Journal of Educational Research, 22,* 330–333.

Algozzine, B. (1977). The emotionally disturbed child: Disturbed or disturbing? *Journal of Abnormal Psychology, 5,* 205–211.

Algozzine, B., Christenson, S., & Ysseldyke, J. (1982). Probabilities associated with referral to placement process. *Teacher Education and Special Education, 5,* 19–23.

Banks, J. A. (1994). *Multiethnic education: Theory and practice (3rd ed.).* Needham Heights, MA: Allyn and Bacon.

Bernal, M. E., Saenz, D. S., & Knight, G. P. (1991). Ethnic identity and adaptation of Mexican American youths in school settings. *Hispanic Journal of Behavioral Sciences, 13*(2), 135–154.

Bernstein, R. (1994). *Dictatorship of virtue: Multiculturalism and the battle for America's future.* New York: Alfred A. Knopf.

Camilli, G., & Shepard, L. A. (1994). *Methods for identifying biased test items.* Thousand Oaks, CA: Sage.

Canino, I. A., & Spurlock, J. (1994). *Culturally diverse children and adolescents.* New York: Guilford Press.

Cervantes, R. C., & Arroyo, W. (1995). Cultural considerations in the use of DSM-IV with Hispanic children and adolescents. In A. M. Padilla (Ed.), *Hispanic psychology: Critical issues in theory and research* (pp. 131–147). Thousand Oaks, CA: Sage.

Chakraborty, R., Kamboh, M. I., Nwankwo, M., & Ferrell, R. E. (1992). Caucasian genes in American blacks: New data. *American Journal of Human Genetics, 50,* 145–55.

Chavez, L. (1991). *Out of the barrio: Toward a new politics of Hispanic assimilation.* New York: Basic Books.

Dana, R. H. (1993). *Multicultural assessment perspectives for professional psychology.* Boston, MA: Allyn and Bacon.

Edmonston, B., & Passel, J. S. (Eds.). (1994). *Immigration and ethnicity.* Washington, DC: Urban Institute Press.

Feagin, J. R., & Feagin, C. B. (1993). *Racial and ethnic relations.* Englewood Cliffs, NJ: Prentice-Hall.

Fordham, S., & Ogbu, J. (1986). Black students' school success: Coping with the burden of "acting white." *The Urban Review, 18,* 176–206.

Hamayan, E. V., & Damico, J. S. (1991). *Limiting bias in the assessment of bilingual students.* Austin, TX: Pro-ed.

Herrnstein, R. J., & Murray, C. (1994). *The bell curve: Intelligence and class structure in American life.* New York: The Free Press.

Hraba, J. (1979). *American ethnicity.* Itasca, IL: Peacock Publishers.

Indian Health Services. (1994). *Trends in Indian health - 1994.* Washington, DC: U.S. Department of Health and Human Services.

Jensen, A. R. (1980). *Bias in mental testing.* New York: Free Press.

Joe, K. A. (1993). Getting into the gang: Methodological issues in studying ethnic gangs. In M. R. De La Rosa & J. R. Adrados (Eds.), *Drug abuse among minority youth: Advances in research and methodology* (pp. 234–257). Rockville, MD: National Institute on Drug Abuse.

Kratochwill, T. R., & Plunge, M. (1992). DSM-III-R, treatment validity, and functional analysis: Further considerations for school psychologists. *School Psychology Quarterly, 7*(3), 227–232.

Leung, K., & Drasgow, F. (1986). Relation between self-esteem and delinquent behavior in three ethnic groups: An application of item response theory. *Journal of Cross-Cultural Psychology, 17,* 151–167.

Mattson, C. M., & Mattson, M. T. (1990). *Contemporary atlas of the United States.* New York: Macmillan.

Matute-Bianchi, M. E. (1986). Ethnic identities and patterns of school success and failure among Mexican-descent and Japanese-American students in a California high school: An ethnographic analysis. *American Journal of Education, 95,* 233–255.

Miller, L. S. (1995). *An American imperative: Acceler-*

ating minority educational advancement. New Haven, CT: Yale University Press.

Min, P. G. (Ed.). (1995). *Asian Americans: Contemporary trends and issues.* Thousand Oaks, CA: Sage.

National Center for Education Statistics. (1994). *The condition of education.* Washington, DC: U.S. Department of Education, Office of Educational Research and Improvement.

National Center for Health Statistics. (1995). *Health United States 1994.* Hyattsville, MD: Public Health Service.

Paisano, E. L. (1991). *Major findings on American Indian and Alaska Native populations from the 1990 census.* Washington, DC: U.S. Bureau of the Census, Racial Statistics Branch.

Peterson, R. L. & Ishii-Jordan, S. (Eds.). (1994). *Multicultural issues in the education of students with behavioral disorders.* Cambridge, MA: Brookline Books.

Phinney, J. S. (1991). Ethnic identity and self-esteem: A review and integration. *Hispanic Journal of Behavioral Sciences, 13*(2), 193–208.

Ponterotto, J. G., Casas, J. M., Suzuki, L. A., & Alexander, C. M. (Eds.). (1995). *Handbook of multicultural counseling.* Thousand Oaks, CA: Sage.

Porter, R. P. (1990). *Forked tongue: The politics of bilingual education.* New York, NY: Basic Books.

Roth, B. M. (1994). *Prescription for failure: Race relations in the age of social science.* New Brunswick, NJ: Transaction.

Rushton, J. P. (1995). *Race, evolution, and behavior.* New Brunswick, NJ: Transaction.

Sowell, T. (1981). *Ethnic America: A history.* New York: Basic Books.

Spencer, M. B., & Markstrom-Adams, C. (1990). Identity processes among racial and ethnic minority children in America. *Child Development, 61,* 290–310.

Thomas, T. N. (1992). Psychoeducational adjustment of English-speaking Caribbean and central American immigrant children in the United States. *School Psychology Review, 21*(4), 566–576.

U.S. Department of Commerce. (1994). *Statistical abstract of the United States: 1994.* Lanham, MD: Bernan Press.

Weaver, T. (Ed.). (1993). *Handbook of Hispanic cultures in the United States: Anthropology.* Houston, TX: Arte Publico Press.

Whaley, A. L. (1993). Self-esteem, cultural identity, and psychosocial adjustment in African American children. *Journal of Black Psychology, 19*(4), 406–422.

Wigdor, A. K., & Garner, W. R. (Eds.) (1982). *Ability testing: Uses, consequences, and controversies.* Washington, DC: National Academy Press.

67

Biracial Identity

Maria P. P. Root
University of Washington

Background and Development

Ms. Okamura looks pridefully at her third-grade classroom. She makes one more sweep around the room, quickly checking the bulletin boards, the tables, and the desks. Ms. Okamura slows her perusal as she fondly looks at each of the five houses the children have team-built from cardboard and other found objects. She remembers conversations about their families—extended, blended, adoptive, small, large, single-parent, two-parent, interracial. Her children are living the diversity of family life in the 1990s. Race emerged in the conversations as they made figures to represent the families living in their houses. They were curious and engaged in figuring out the answers to "Why is race so important?" "Can a person be more than one 'race'?" "How can a brother and sister be different 'races'?"

Much of the journey to comprehending race is travelled during the school age years. Unfortunately, along the way, children learn to repeat the same errors that have fueled racial tensions throughout the history of the United States. Omi and Winant (1994) suggest that these errors are indelibly etched into the fabric of American society, shaping the journeys and the paths taken in race relations. Subsequently, in a society that is heterogeneous in physical appearance and continues to live with faulty beliefs, appearance becomes racialized and turned into a social address.

Fortunately, many strides toward righting the inequities of race relations have been achieved in the last half of the 20th century. Children and teenagers in the 1990s are the beneficiaries of legislation that hypothetically protects the civil rights to education, housing, and employment of all people in the U.S. The Supreme Court's repeal of the last anti-miscegenation laws in 1967 critically impacts the racial environment children grow up in today because a biracial baby boom has followed the erosion of the interracial marriage taboo.

Since 1967, the rates of interracial marriage have approximately doubled each decade. The numbers of biracial babies born since 1970 has grown approximately 260% while the numbers of monoracial babies has grown only 15%. Black-White baby numbers have grown 500%, and more biracial babies of Japanese American heritage are now born in this country than babies with two Asian American parents (U.S. Bureau of the Census, 1992). The historical result is the first significant cohort of biracial children visible in educational systems across the country, most noticeably in large cities. For this reason, governmental bodies are attending to the meaning of this demographic change. Education professionals need to consider how multicultural education may inadvertently apply the following three rules of race which negatively impact the racial environment in the classroom or school for these children.

Race Rules

Children acquire three general rules about race in this country. These rules provide the foundation for repeating America's history of race relations. Whereas children (as well as their parents) may not be able to articulate the rules that govern racial assignment in this country, they can apply them from the early primary grades forward. First, children learn that there are "distinct" races. Second, they learn that there is a racial hierarchy. All of this learning takes place within a monoracial framework. To be able to believe in distinct races and clear boundaries, children must learn to apply the third rule of *hypodescent* which originated during slavery. This rule simply means that if a person's heritage is drawn from two racial groups, they are assigned the status of the group that has lower social value in the racial hierarchy. Thus, Biracial children born of African female slaves were essentially stripped of privileges associated with their white paternity and, in most cases, increased white slavemaster's holdings (Tenzer, 1990).

Continuing to modern times, children soon learn to think of multiracial Black and White children as Black. Asian and White children are racially classified as something other than White, often being misidentified as Latino. The rule serves to keep the border between White and not White distinct. Biracial children from two non-

White groups do not threaten the border between White and non-White, explaining why children of Chicano and African, Asian and Latino, Native American and African, or African and Asian heritage receive little notice in the media or the literature.

Racial Classification

Today's visible cohort of biracial children and their families has become large enough to cause the U. S. Bureau of the Census to seriously consider the need to rethink the racial classification categories for the year-2000 decennial census (Evinger, 1995; Root, 1996). Inconsistent rules for classifying multiracial people have been used by the U. S. Bureau of the Census in previous decennial population counts. The country's embarrassing history of race is also observed in recent changes in guidelines for classifying biracial children. Prior to 1989, children were identified by the race of the father unless they were biracial. If biracial, children were identified by the race of their non-White parent. Since 1989, the laws have eliminated this inconsistent classification scheme but still apply a monoracial framework in the classification of children. All children are now identified by their mother's race regardless of how the children identify themselves (Waters, 1994).

Within a monoracial framework, biracial children's parents are initially forced to "choose just one" racial identifier or "other" (Hall, 1992). When filling out their own applications in junior or senior high school or for job employment, biracial children and teenagers are confronted repeatedly with the same monoracial paradigm. Many parents assert that their biracial children are "both" (Brown & Douglass, 1996; Graham, 1996). This accounts for some of the growth in the "other" category of the 1990 U.S. Census and the tremendous growth in the number of people writing in multiracial designators (Waters, 1994). As a result of such problems, many interracial family and student grassroot groups throughout the nation and national groups such as the Association for Multiethnic Americans (AMEA) and Project Reclassify All Children Equally (RACE) are assertively pointing out the fallacies and inadequacies of the rules of racial classification to local, state, and federal governments (Brown & Douglass, 1996; Graham, 1996). Currently, six states have passed legislation to include a multiracial designator in school forms: Ohio, Illinois, Georgia, Indiana, and Michigan. Maryland's legislature recommended this change, but the governor vetoed it. Several other states are working on similar legislation (Graham, 1996).

Racial Identity

The impact of U.S. political and social construction of race is evident in the most widely accepted models of racial identity development—even in their updated forms (e.g.,

Atkinson, Morten, & Sue, 1979; Cross, 1991; Helms, 1990; Parham, 1989). All models describe a similar process. A person of color progresses through stages of awareness of how their racial designation and physical appearance affects their social interactions and life chances. Individual factors, family, community, and larger social spheres intersect. At times they collide. Existential or critical incidences promote a conflict which in the course of resolution moves the individual through stages of awareness.

These stages begin with a denial that one's race makes a difference in daily social interactions. An individual may even uphold discriminatory attitudes toward other persons of color. Subsequently, in response to some critical racial incident, one may insulate oneself from the European American influence while immersing in one's own racial experience. Eventually, one is able to venture into transacting within both racial environments. In some models, there is a value in being able to transcend race while recognizing its influence in daily life (e.g., Cross, 1991).

Ramirez (1983) has been one of the few researchers of identity development who addressed the bicultural mind and negotiation of living in two worlds. Highly regarded, his research on Mexican Americans and Chicanos has not been adapted in the field of racial identity development. This is probably because his research moved beyond a monoracial and monocultural framework before much of social and political science was able to accommodate the integration of multiple heritages.

Since the 1980s, a growing body of research and theory suggests that prevailing models of racial identity development do not universally apply to biracial people. For example, the process of immersing oneself in the singular race of one's origin may be to deny one parent. In contemporary times, such an emotional cutoff may more accurately reflect an essential disturbance in the parent-child relationship than the normal process of racial identity development. A more normative process for many biracial children and adults is to shift emphasis of what heritage one may be from foreground to background in different social contexts.

What may be the normative process for racial identity development of biracial children and teenagers may be interpreted pathologically out of context. For example, several researchers, using nonclinical samples of high school and college-age students, have found that a common element of the biracial experience is the ability to be "both" (Hall, 1992; Stephan, 1992; Williams, 1992), to change identities contextually (Stephan, 1992), and to change identities over a lifetime, but not necessarily in a stepwise progression (Root, 1990). Furthermore, the experimentation or conscious manipulation of identity in which an individual gives different identities in different contexts may be confusing to someone with a monoracial framework. For example, Black Japanese American teenagers may join both an African American and an Asian American club at school, with their behavior conforming to the cultural mores for that specific group. They may assert they are African American in some situations; Asian American in others; Japanese American in still others; biracial in other situations; and refuse to give an ethnic or racial label in still another situation.

Several researchers have offered models for understanding the identity choices of biracial children and young adults. Three will be mentioned here for their diversity of perspective and their focus on school-age children. Based on his study of biracial Japanese White children and youth, Kich (1992) provided a progressive model by which a teenager comes to understand and take on a biracial identity. Three stages were observed from childhood to adolescence to young adulthood. In the first stage, conflict exists between self-perception and others' perceptions of the child. This dissonance rests in the significant meaning given to race and the three rules of race mentioned previously. The second stage reflects a normal developmental progression to focus on peer acceptance and the struggle for acceptance from others. This struggle is confounded by the increased inculcation of racial rules by peers and an increasingly poor fit of the monoracial paradigm for many youth. By late adolescence or young adulthood the individual may be more at ease with asserting a biracial and bicultural identity. Kich (1992) noted that "the major developmental task for biracial people is to differentiate critically among others' interpretations of them, various pejorative and grandiose labels and mislabels, and their own experiences and conceptions of themselves" (pp. 305–306).

Jacobs (1992) carefully explored biracial children's understanding of color and race, focusing on biracial Black-White children. Like Kich (1992), he found that several factors emerged frequently throughout the interviews with children. These factors, which formed the experiences behind their identity development, were (a) the degree to which these children understood the concept of racial colors and applied these notions consistently to themselves and family members; (b) their access and internalization of a biracial label; (c) the grappling and resolution of racial ambivalence that stems from their increased understanding of the social implications of color and race in the wider social context; and (d) the process of cognitive distortions of color that a child uses to make accurate social racial identifications.

Jacobs (1992) proposed three stages of development in children up to 12 years of age. In stage one, usually prior to 4.5 years of age, color has nominal rather than evaluative value. Thus, the color applied to people may change based on the child's sense of whimsy or attention to other environmental cues. By the second stage, starting around 4.5 years of age, the child has more understanding of social categories of color. This increased understanding introduces an ambivalence about the child's

racial status. The child has color constancy and no longer freely experiments with color. A biracial label becomes familiar to children during this stage. In the third stage, ages 8 to 12 years, the grasp of the social meaning of race unfortunately shows signs of America's history of race relations. The child realizes that objective color does not necessarily correlate with racial status; racial group is determined by parentage and hypodescent. The child can apply all the social rules of race.

Gibbs (1989) adopted an Eriksonian model of development to describe developmental tasks faced by biracial children. In contrast to the majority of researchers on biracial identity development, she drew her observations from clinical samples of adolescents who were distressed, though the origin of their distress was not clear. She posed five conflictual tasks to be resolved by biracial adolescents: (a) racial/ethnic identity, (b) social marginality, (c) sexuality, (d) autonomy, and (e) educational and occupational aspirations (pp. 332–337). Gibbs asserted that these tasks are more difficult for the biracial child; thus, they may contribute to pathological development.

The Phenomenological Experience of a Multiracial Social Address

There is a distinct phenomenological experience to being multiracial or biracial. In a monoracial framework, these children lack a consistent or unambiguous social address based upon race. When they are with both parents, most biracial children have experienced "triangle" stares; the onlooker looks at the child and each parent and back and forth to comprehend the relationship of the child to the parents and the adults to each other. Many biracial children have been in conversations or witnessed conversation that implies that they were a mistake of a sexual liason or that their parents are deviant for marrying interracially. These types of comments also imply rules around race and the social taboos around intimate race mixing. Many biracial children acquire the rules of race and other assumptions about the boundaries between ethnic and racial groups by their differential experiences with their separate parents or relatives. Many more White parents than parents of color have been asked where they "got" their child. Implicit in this question is that a White parent would not have chosen to bring a "child of color" into this world.

Unlike among monoracial children, the phenomenological experience of many biracial children is replete with repeated questions about who they are and where they fit based upon their racial ambiguity. Biracial children eventually all face the question "What are you?" The question is an implicit demand to state where one fits in the racial framework. The question is not simply motivated by the biracial person's physical ambiguity but may be motivated because of their multiple allegiances or varied friendship networks. Thus, this experience is further layered upon the experience of usually being perceived as a person of color and the implicit demands of solidarity—only identifying with one group as proof of authentic membership. As they grasp the political nature of this question, some children will give subversive answers "What do you mean?" "What are you?" "melange" "hapa" "Amerasian" "mulatto." And in fact this is what many young adults did with the 1990 decennial census. Such answers make the inquisitor pause when the child refuses to apply the monoracial framework for giving their "social address" based upon race or, alternately, decides to strain the artificial monoracial framework.

In summary, this country's embarassing and tragic history of race relations is colliding with a cohort of young people, more visible than ever, who are challenging the rules of racial classification and, as their parents before them, the boundaries between racial and ethnic groups. For the first time ever in the history of this country, a biracial cohort of school age children is visible, particularly in large cities. Unlike previous periods in history, these children and their parents are making the choices to identify as biracial and "both" or "all," defying some of the implicit rules around race relations that assure the onlooker security in knowing the "other's" social address. In general, research has been conducted on nonclinical samples and suggests that while some of the tasks of identity and acceptance may be more difficult and leave indelible memories (Root, 1996), these children are much like their monoracially identified peers and particularly peers of color in terms of social adjustment and self-esteem (Cauce et al., 1992; Field, 1996; Johnson & Nagoshi, 1986). How racial identity is measured may predict the result as situational cues become that much more important to negotiating one's way in a racially insensitive and sensitized country (Duffy, 1978; Nakashima, 1988; Stephan, 1992; Williams, 1996). The importance of context appears to be associated with increased cognitive flexibility around perceiving race. Cognitive flexibility also appears to allow these children to move in and out of varied friendship networks more fluidly (Cauce et al., 1992; Hall, 1992; Root, 1996).

Problems and Implications

There is general consensus by researchers on biracial identity development that being biracial in and of itself carries no inherent harm (Root, 1990). Whereas parents of biracial children may provide a positive family atmosphere for understanding race and cultural difference, once the child goes to school they are subject to their peers' and teachers' socialization around race. Usually without exception, rules of hypodescent and application of a monoracial framework will be applied assertively. A child's assertion of biraciality or assertion to have friends from all different groups may be misunderstood. Unfortunately, teachers' ideologies about race may contribute to the conflicts the children will have. Thus, this section will include a discussion on some of the missing pieces of multicultural education.

Recent research on nonclinical populations has provided information on the normal development of biracial children. In general, research does suggest that the children are well-adjusted (Cauce et al., 1992; Field, 1996; Johnson & Nagoshi, 1986; Johnson, 1992). For example, Cauce et al. (1992) investigated the self-esteem and well-being of junior high school African American and Asian American students in the Seattle public schools. These investigators found that although mixed heritage children were as well-adjusted as their monoracial heritage peers, the experience of being a child of color influenced their orientation to life.

When they are not well-adjusted (e.g., Gibbs, 1989), it is not clear that the maladjustment is due to being biracial. It is possible that the difficulties arise in family relations, problem parenting, lack of resources to parents, or a combination of factors—some of which may be confounded with the stress of being a person of color or family of color in this country. Field's (1996) research suggests that race-related adjustment difficulties may be present when the child is not able to understand other people's inability to allow him or her the choice to proceed in the world while insisting on a White identity and requiring affirmation from others for this identity. Concomitant with a preference for a White identity and distress over not receiving corroboration for it may be the internalization of negative values associated with being a person of color (Root, 1995).

Until very recently, the problems discussed in the literature about biracial children have echoed social and moral objections to race mixing in the guise of concern for the children. Thus, if this chapter had been written 20 or 30 years previously, undoubtedly, there would be overt concern that biological mixing would produce physical anomalies (Provine, 1973). Within that same time frame, moral doctrine might also be spewed as to how race mixing was not intended by God and how harm might come to the children. Even in contemporary time, pleas are made to interracial couples to "think of the children" that may result from their union. These concerns acknowledge the reality that social racial tensions are very real in this country. And as the literature shows, different types of adjustments and additional processes to integrating racial identity into one's whole identity may be more complicated for the biracial child.

The contemporary literature, largely produced during the last decade, provides an optimistic outlook on the resolution of racial identity and concomitant social adjustment. However, while concerns about biological inferiority or moral inferiority do not have a place in this literature, evidence of new misconceptions exist. In popular literature or media, biracial children are talked about as special, especially beautiful, or smarter than their monoracial counterparts. None of these conclusions are supported by research. These notions of the biracial person set a foundation for only continuing to objectify them as exotic rather than humanize them. However, many of the studies already cited do find increased cognitive complexity in the ability to comprehend and discuss race.

Preadolescent adjustment may be easier than during adolescence because adolescence is replete with increasingly complex social relationships particularly related to sexuality and dating (Root, 1990). Racial segregation may prevail in dating relationships although not necessarily in friendships. Biracial teenagers may have some poignant experiences that remind them of society's difficulties and irrationalities around race. Whereas many biracial teenagers are able to see the illogical way in which race is constructed and performed in daily life, they are not immune to the hurtful way in which it affects them. Gibbs (1989) suggests that these teenagers are subject to repeated external assaults on their self-esteem while trying to ascertain where they fit in. Likewise, Root (1990) suggests that these teenagers are often caught in a "squeeze of oppression." Rather than rendering one marginal, racial politics in this country constricts social behavior by demanding more racially stereotypical behavior of racially ambiguous people.

As is true with problems faced by others, individual resilience—or hardiness—and social support may be critical to minimizing the degree to which the personal and social adjustment of biracial children is effected by negative reactions of others. Teachers, parents, and friends can take a significant role in reshaping race relations on a daily level which will make the identity process and social process of belonging easier for the biracial child.

Education and Diversity

Despite a movement toward multiculturalism, most American classrooms are still limited by a monoracial paradigm (Wardle, 1996). Educators seeking to broaden multicultural education, particularly around issues of race and ethnicity, suggest direct intervention in elementary education. Wardle (1996) notes that the history of mixed race people in this country and their contributions are systematically ignored. The mere teaching of the five-race framework, which originated in the 1970s (Sanjek, 1994), reinforced the squeeze of oppression that biracial children often experience during their school-age years. They are either moved to the margins or must choose one heritage over the other to be part of the discussion. Their racial "complexity" adds to the reality of the history of this country rather than complicating it. Efforts to preserve and regenerate the monoracial paradigm have com-

plicated this country's racial and ethnic history. Taunting on the playground, such as stating that another child is not ethnically legitimate or is mixed up, may stem from the teachings about the meaning of race. Too often, it is taught that race is about racial purity, reinforced by discussion only of distinct borders between groups.

Glass and Wallace (1996) suggest that educational approaches might be classified as cultural understanding, cultural competence, and cultural emancipation. The former two approaches are limited because they lack a systemic focus on the the societal institutions maintaining a value structure that still precludes a significant appreciation of what differs from European-originated values and symbols. Perhaps a more radical approach is their revisioning of multicultural education, which requires teachers to be more personally involved in the challenging of institutions and contradictions within them so that they are examples to students.

If the goal of multicultural education is to facilitate pride and mutual respect among all children, teaching about America's history of race mixing is an essential part of deconstructing the harmful way in which most of us were originally taught about race. The usual objections are *lack of literature to support this goal, complexity that may confuse the children, and insistence that the "real world" does not recognize race mixture.* All of these objections reflect a resistance to the effort and responsibility to move towards correcting the human errors in race relations committed by people who lived before us. None of which should be difficult to address in contemporary times.

Is there is a lack of literature on multiracial children and multiracial families? Brown and Douglass (1996) and Wardle (1996) suggest avenues by which to find this literature. Additionally, there is now a magazine, *Biracial Child,* that is a source of information. There are numerous support groups throughout the country that help educators and parents to gain resources toward a goal of critically reevaluating the way we think, talk, and live race (see Brown & Douglass, 1996).

Will talking about racial mixture confuse children? Discussions with children, particularly before they are brainwashed into the rules of race, will be neither confusing nor complicated. It is complicated for many adults because such discussions require that we undo much of what we were taught. I suggest that the cognitive capacity for thinking about race is stunted because the reality of race mixture has not been addressed (Root, 1996a). Increasingly, with the biracial baby boom, teachers will be confronted with questions and the need for discussion. With background education and consultation, teachers can facilitate discussions that acknowledge the growing reality of the demographics of the U.S. population as the twenty-first century approaches.

Does the real world outside of family, friends, and school recognize race mixture? Much of our society has not and does not, but it is changing and will necessarily change as the biracial baby boom and parents' orientation of their children toward identifying as multiracial and multiethnic increases. Even before the current support existed for such a multiracial movement (Nakashima, 1996), many individuals, well into their middle adult years, verified that they identified as multiracial in many contexts (Hall, 1992; Williams, 1992). Note that the numbers are now critical enough that legislation is being passed to support a multiracial category in several states and within more school districts (Graham, 1996). The U.S. Bureau of the Census is seriously considering the implications of changing the census forms for the year 2000 to accommodate the growing proportion of the U.S. population who identifies as multiracial (Evinger, 1995).

Alternative Actions

One of the benefits that might be derived from today's increasingly self-centered, individualistic society is the insistence on creations and recognitions of individual realities and rights. This affords the opportunity to form interest groups to advocate for marginalized individuals. As a result, being biracial has a chance of being a socially acknowledged existence that ultimately strains the standard five-race framework. Many actions can be taken by educators to facilitate antiracism and a more realistic understanding and appreciation of the social complexity of race in the U.S. Educators have a chance to provide different information than parents might have access to. Such exposure may make only a small amount of difference, but small differences can cumulatively result in a hope for significant change (Freire, 1994).

Whereas information about identity development was provided earlier in this chapter, elsewhere I have suggested that one must keep in mind how much history interacts with the psychosocial elements that inform the identity process (Root, 1990). Even within the U.S., the process of identity formation for multiracial people is differentially felt in different geographical locations. But all educators need to understand not only the process some individuals progress through but also that this is not a uniform process for all people *and* that monoracial identity theories were researched and established before a significant cohort of multiracial families and individuals existed. Intervening variables (e.g., U.S. Census consideration of racial categories, magazines and books for interracial individuals and families, support groups for multiracial families and individuals, dominant themes of interracial relationships on television and in the movies) all create a contemporary context that has not previously existed for multiracial people. Educators should consider that flexibility and malleability of identity is important and that no single endpoint is "right." For example, it would

be an error for a teacher to insist that a multiracial African American and Filipino American child identify as both if the child does not. However, it would be important for that teacher to acknowledge the possibility that the child may identify with both and at other times as one or the other.

Several theorists, therapists, lecturers, educators, and students on the topic of racially mixed people advocate several key "ingredients" to the education of children that facilitate antiracist education and acceptance of current racial realities. Most of these persons have already been cited in this chapter. *The cumulative suggestions at an individual level are:*

1. Provide multiracial children with an understanding of the racism directed at them and with the defenses to constructively deal with these personal assaults.
2. Develop secure, positive relationships with these children.
3. Foster social and physical competencies.
4. Encourage them to talk about the hurts, rejections, confusion, or pride they feel in their racial existence.

Suggestions to support educators in effecting a change in how they advocate for multiculturalism are:

1. Read publications by and for multiracial families and individuals.
2. If available in your area, attend community conferences on multiracial identity or families.
3. Discuss your feelings, hesitations, and insecurities about broadening multicultural education such that it includes the acknowledgement of multiracial individuals and race mixing.
4. Seek consultation from individuals who have been integrating multicultural education into their curriculum.
5. Read some of the reference material in chapters, such as this one, for background on parts of history that were likely left out of your education.
6. Explore your use of language connoting race and the limitations and exclusions of this language.

At the educational level in the classroom, the following suggestions can be supported by many of the materials cited within this chapter:

1. Provide a classroom map of the peoples of the world. This global picture serves as a concrete reminder of the lack of clear lines between races.
2. Note that race mixing is the natural consequence of people living adjacent to one another.
3. Facilitate discussions on use of language regarding race, culture, and ethnicity.
4. Provide visual images of multiracial people, families, and children.

5. Expose children to multiracial role models.
6. Provide a complex and comprehensive understanding of race relations and racial classification. For example, explore the development of racial categories and provide a critique of it (Wright, 1994).
7. Suggest autobiographies of multiracial persons.
8. Include in discussions of racism the racism against multiracial people and the reasons why this is harmful.
9. Discuss interracial dating and marriage. This is a useful vehicle for linking many of these pieces together.
10. Observe the cognitive distortions around "color" that a person must make to place many people into racial groups.
11. Consciously separate race from the definition of culture or ethnicity. Point out that race is not a necessary nor sufficient variable for knowing about a person's culture, ethnicity, or both.
12. Discuss the fact that there is more physical and personality variability of people within racial groups than between racial groups.
13. Definitely help students understand that race is largely a social and political construction rather than a biological fact.

Summary

A helpful piece that facilitates race discussion is being used in classrooms and multicultural educational workshops and by multiracial support groups. I titled it a *Bill of Rights for Racially Mixed People* and organized it around three themes: resistance, revolution, and change (see Figure 1; Root, 1996a). Resistance refers to refusal to adhere to a racial system that has been destructive. Revolution depicts the assertion of identity despite others' conflicts with one's identity. Change is a continuation of revolution in which language, process, and social interaction are integrated into one's life in a way that emancipates one from an intimately segregated life. Children of all ages are willing and able to consider our relationships with ourselves and each other in this framework.

Recommended Resources

Biracial Child. This is a bimonthly publication to provide information for parents of biracial children. Information helpful to teachers is provided also.

Funderburg, L. (1994). *Black, white, other: Biracial Americans talk about race and identity.* New York: William Morrow and Company.
Journalist Lise Funderburg shares the experiences of 46 adult biracial black white adults exploring their resolution of racial

identity in this country. This foray exposes the legacy of centuries of racial politics in this country.

Gay, K. (1995). *I am who I am: Speaking out about multiracial identity.* New York: Franklin Watts.
This is a short book which covers race relations past and present related to this country's perspective on multiracial people and in the context of other nations' perspectives on multiracial people. She explains some of the multiracial movement in terms of grassroots organizations and suggests multiracial families and their children as change agents in this society.

Omi, M., & Winant, H. (1994). *Racial formation in the United States from the 1960s to the 1990s.*
This volume serves as a thoughtful primer on race relations in the United States and its evolution and transformation over the last 30 years. It is clear yet sophisticated and complex in its presentation of the discussion of race separating as well as placing it in the context of ethnicity, class, and nation.

Root, M. P. P. (1992). *Racially mixed people in America.* Thousand Oaks, CA: Sage Publications.
This edited volume is a compilation of dissertations, theses, and original contemporary theory on biracial identity development and race relations relative to biracial persons across various mixes, black white, black Japanese American, Vietnamese Amerasians, and Mexican American and Native American perspectives on mixed people. The U.S. Bureau of the Census has used this as one of the documents guiding their reformulation of racial categories for the year 2000.

Root, M. P. P. (1996). *The multiracial experience: Racial borders as the new frontier.* Thousand Oaks, CA: Sage Publications.
This edited volume tackles current conceptualizations of race, human rights in a monoracial versus multiracial framework, multicultural education, and the co-influence of race and gender on identity.

I HAVE THE RIGHT . . .

Not to justify my existence in this world.
Not to keep the races separate within me.
Not to be responsible for people's discomfort with my physical ambiguity.
Not to justify my ethnic legitimacy.

I HAVE THE RIGHT . . .

To identify myself differently than strangers expect me to identify myself.
To identify myself differently from how my parents identify me.
To identify myself differently from my brothers and sisters.
To identify myself differently in different situations.

I HAVE THE RIGHT . . .

To create a vocabulary to communicate about being multiracial.
To change my identify over my lifetime—and more than once.
To have loyalties and identification with more than one group of people.
To freely choose whom I befriend and love.

Figure 11–1. *Bill of Rights for Racially Mixed People*

References

Atkinson, D. R., Morten, G., & Sue, D. W. (Eds.). (1979). *Counseling American minorities.* Dubuque, IA: William C. Brown.

Brown, N., & Douglass, R. (1996). Making the invisible visible: The role of community network organizations. In M. P. P. Root (Ed.), *The multiracial experience: Racial borders as the new frontier* (pp. 323–340). Thousand Oaks, CA: Sage Publications.

Cauce, A. M., Hiraga, Y., Mason, C., Aguilar, T., Ordonez, N., & Gonzales, N. (1992). Between a rock and a hard place: Social adjustment of biracial youth. In M. P. P. Root (Ed.), *Racially mixed people in America* (pp. 91–107). Thousand Oaks, CA: Sage Publications.

Cross, W. E., Jr. (1991). *Shades of black: Diversity in African-American identity.* Philadelphia, PA: Temple University Press.

Duffy, L. K. (1978). *The interracial individuals: Self-concept, parental interaction, and ethnic identity.* Unpublished master's thesis, University of Hawaii, Honolulu.

Evinger, S. (1995). How shall we measure our nation's diversity? *Change, 8* (1), 7–14.

Field, L. D. (1996). Piecing together the puzzle: Self-concept and group identity in biracial black/white youth. In M. P. P. Root (Ed.), *The multiracial experience: Racial borders as the new frontier* (pp. 211–226). Thousand Oaks, CA: Sage publications.

Freire, P. (1994). *Pedagogy of hope: Reliving pedagogy of the oppressed.* New York: Continuum Publishing Company.

Gibbs, J. T. (1989). Biracial adolescents. In J. T. Gibbs, L. N. Huang and Associates (Eds.), *Children of color: Psychological intervention with minority youth* (pp. 322–350). San Francisco: Jossey-Bass Publishers.

Glass, R. D., & Wallace, K. R. (1996). Challenging race and racism: A framework for educators. In M. P. P. Root (Ed.), *The multiracial experience: Racial borders as the new frontier* (pp. 341–358). Thousand Oaks, CA: Sage Publications.

Graham, S. (1996). The real world. In M. P. P. Root (Ed.), *The multiracial experience: Racial borders as the new frontier* (pp. 37–48). Thousand Oaks, CA: Sage Publications.

Hall, C. I. I. (1992). Please choose one: Ethnic identity choices for biracial individuals. In M. P. P. Root (Ed.), *Racially mixed people in America* (pp. 250–264). Thousand Oaks, Ca: Sage Publications.

Helms, J. E. (1990). *Black and white racial identity: Theory, research, and practice.* New York: Greenwood Press.

Jacobs, J. (1992). Identity development in biracial children. In M. P. P. Root (Ed.), *Racially mixed people in America* (pp. 190–206). Thousand Oaks, CA: Sage Publications.

Johnson, R. C. (1992). Offspring of cross-race and cross-ethnic marriages in Hawaii. In M. P. P. Root (Ed.), *Racially mixed people in America* (pp. 239–249). Thousand Oaks, CA: Sage Publications.

Johnson, R. C., & Nagoshi, C. T. (1986). The adjustment of offspring of within-group and interracial intercultural marriages: A comparison of personality factor scores. *Journal of Marriage and the Family, 48,* 279–284.

Kich, G. K. (1992). The developmental process of asserting a biracial, bicultural identity. In M. P. P. Root (Ed.), *Racially mixed people in America* (pp. 304–317). Thousand Oaks, CA: Sage Publications.

Nakashima, C. (1988). Research notes on Nikkei Happpa identity. In G. Y. Okihiro, S. Hune, A. A. Hansen, & J. M. Liu (Eds.), *Reflection on shattered windows: Promises and prospects for Asian American studies* (pp. 206–213). Pullman: Washington State University Press.

Nakashima, C. (1996). Voices from the movement: Approaches to multiraciality. In M. P. P. Root (Ed.), *The multiracial experience: Racial borders as a new frontier in race relations* (pp. 79–97). Thousand Oaks, CA: Sage Publications.

Omi, M., & Winant, H. (1994). *Racial formation in the United States from the 1960s to the 1990s.* New York: Routledge.

Parham, T. A. (1989). Cycles of psychological nigrescence. *Counseling Psychologist, 17* (2), 187–226.

Provine, W. B. (1973). Geneticists and the biology of race crossing. *Science, 182,* 790–796.

Ramirez, M., III. (1983). *Psychology of the Americas: Mestizo perspectives on personality and mental health.* New York: Pergamon Press.

Root, M. P. P. (1990). Resolving other status: Identity development of biracial individuals. In L. Brown & M. P. P. Root (Eds), *Complexity and diversity in feminist theory and therapy* (pp. 185–205). New York: Haworth Press.

Root, M. P. P. (1992). Within, between, and beyond race. In M. P. P. Root (Ed.), *Racially mixed people in America* (pp. 3–11). Thousand Oaks, CA: Sage Publications.

Root, M. P. P. (1995). The psychological browning of America. In N. Zack (Ed.), *American mixed race: The culture of microdiversity* (pp. 231–236). Lanham, MD: Rowman & Littlefield.

Root, M. P. P. (1996a). A Bill of Rights for racially mixed people. In M. P. P. Root (Ed.), *The multiracial experience: Racial borders as a new frontier in race relations* (pp. 3–14). Thousand Oaks, CA: Sage Publications.

Root, M. P. P. (1996b). The multiracial experience: Racial borders as a significant frontier in race relations. In M. P. P. Root (Ed.), *The multiracial experience: Racial borders as a new frontier in race relations* (pp. xii–xxviii). Thousand Oaks, CA: Sage Publications.

Sanjek, R. (1994). Intermarriage and the future of races in the United States. In S. Gregory & R. Sanjek (Eds.), *Race.* New Brunswick, NJ: Rutgers University Press.

Spickard, P. R. (1992). The illogic of American racial categories. In M. P. P. Root (Ed.), *Racially mixed people in America* (pp. 12–23). Thousand Oaks, CA: Sage Publications.

Stephan, C. W. (1992). Mixed-heritage individuals: Ethnic identity and trait characteristics. In M. P. P. Root (Ed.), *Racially mixed people in America* (pp. 50–63). Thousand Oaks, CA: Sage Publications.

Tenzer, L. R. (1990). *A completely new look at interracial sexuality: Public opinion and select commentaries.* Manahawkin, NJ: Scholars' Publishing House.

U.S. Bureau of the Census. (1992). Marital status and living arrangements: March 1992. (*Current Population Re-*

ports, Population characteristics, Series P20-468, December). Washington, DC: Government Printing Office.

Wardle, F. (1996). Multiracial Education. In M. P. P. Root (Ed.), *The multiracial experience: Racial borders as the new frontier* (pp. 380–391). Thousand Oaks, CA: Sage Publications.

Waters, M. C. (1994, April). The social construction of race and ethnicity: Some examples from demography. Paper presented at the Center for Social and Demographic Analysis Conference, State University of New York, Albany.

Williams, T. K. (1992). Prism lives: Identity of binational Amerasians. In M. P. P. Root (Ed.), *Racially mixed people in America* (pp. 280–303). Thousand Oaks, CA: Sage Publications.

Williams, T. K. (1996). Race as process: Reassessing the "what are you?" encounters of biracial individuals. In M. P. P. Root (Ed.), *The multiracial experience: Racial borders as the new frontier* (pp. 191–210). Thousand Oaks, CA: Sage Publications.

Wright, L. (1994, July 25). One drop of blood. *The New Yorker,* pp. 46–48.

Zack, N. (1995). Life after race. In N. Zack (Ed.), *American mixed race: The culture of microdiversity* (pp. 297–307). Lanham, MD: Rowman & Littlefield.

68
Religion

Harriet Cobb

James Madison University

Background

An increasing diversity of religious beliefs are practiced in the United States, as reflected in religious services ranging from the informal and spare meetings of Quakers and Amish to the ceremonious gatherings of Roman Catholics and Jews. As when our country was first founded, religion continues to be present in the lives of a majority of Americans. However, just as the freedom of religion and the separation of church and state greatly altered religious practices over 200 years ago, so too have recent social changes influenced this important aspect of life experience. Whereas the mainstream American culture previously had been influenced predominantly by Judeo-Christian traditions, exposure to belief systems different from those of one's parents is now a nearly universal experience of the "baby boomer" generation. Intermarriage among religious groups is common, and from these marriages children are often exposed to at least two belief systems or a blended version of the two.

Families also are more geographically mobile, which means that parents often decide on a particular place of worship in the new community that fits their spiritual and social needs, rather than one that is identical to the church or synagogue of their childhoods. Furthermore, the infusion of religious beliefs from other cultures has provided more of a marketplace of religions from which to choose. Some religions have included an integration of a scientific perspective into the explanation of life's beginnings and a greater role for women as spiritual leaders, while others have admonished their constituents for straying from longstanding beliefs and traditions. The growing secularization of U.S. society has contributed to increased emphasis on spirituality as a personal, individual journey that may or may not be connected with an organized religion (Roof & McKinney, 1987).

Nevertheless, most Americans identify with an organized religion. Religions can be categorized by examining belief, lifestyle, customs and rituals, and degree of institutionalization. As recently reported by Kosmin and Lachman (1993), the vast majority of Americans (86.2%)

consider themselves to be Christians, with Roman Catholics being the largest subgroup (26.2%). Those who report having no religion or describing themselves as agnostic or humanist comprise 8.2%. Jews represent about 2% of the population, while Muslims comprise 0.5%, a slightly higher percentage than Buddhists and Hindus. The majority of African-Americans (81.8%) report membership in Protestant denominations; a growing percentage (9.2%) are Catholic, with the remaining respondents in "other" categories. Eighty-two percent of African-Americans describe religion as "very important" in their lives, compared to 55% of Whites. The majority of Hispanics are Catholic (65.8%), with most of the remaining Protestant. Martin Luther King, Jr., once said that "11 A.M. on Sunday morning is the most segregated hour in America." For the most part, Blacks attend church with other Blacks; Whites belong to predominantly White congregations (Roof & McKinney, 1987).

In spite of increased tolerance and support for spirituality as a matter of personal choice, the public schools often are battlegrounds for conflicting values. In the past two decades, there have been numerous court cases involving religious liberty (Roof & McKinney, 1987). Controversies continue to emerge in many communities regarding school prayer, the teaching of "creation," family-life education, and counseling services in the schools. These issues have yet to be resolved, although some states (e.g., Virginia) have adopted new religious-activity policies in response to this political pressure.

It is not unusual then that school psychologists encounter issues related to religion when working with children. (In this chapter, religion, faith, and spirituality are treated as socio-psychological constructs, rather than theological/philosophical concepts.) Regardless of the personal attitudes and beliefs of the school psychologist, an understanding of the individual, developmental perspective is important, as is an appreciation for cultural and group differences. An awareness of and sensitivity to these issues has clear implications for developing rapport, understanding psychological dynamics, and generating interventions for children. In completing a psychological assessment or in providing counseling/consultation interventions, knowledge of sociocultural factors is critical for a comprehensive understanding of a child's individual psychological development. This includes the values, beliefs, and religious practices of the family. It is essential for school psychologists to become acquainted with beliefs and practices that are foreign to their own experience. This knowledge can assist in establishing rapport with a child or parent and help to avoid discomfort when certain issues are raised. For example, one would not want to compliment an Amish girl about her hair because of this religion's attitude toward vanity or personal pride, nor expect a Jehovah's Witness child to be excited about a birthday party because birthdays are not celebrated in that religion. Awareness of the state and local political issues with regard to religion is also important for effective relationships with school personnel and the community. Removing a child from the "Bible Bus" (a part of a weekly religious education program) for testing may be a serious political error in some communities.

Development

Numerous studies have examined children's concept of God and other religious issues by a variety of approaches, including clinical interviews, projective techniques, structured inventories, and standardized tests (see Ratcliff, 1985, for a review). Studies have been conducted across a variety of cultures, both Eastern and Western. The vast majority of these studies included children whose parents were members of formal religions. Recent interview-based studies have also included children of agnostic parents (Coles, 1990; Fay; 1994). Whether or not children are brought up in a religious home, they raise the "big" questions with their parents, such as "Why are we here?", "If there is a God, why is there so much suffering?", and "What happens after we die?" Children pose philosophical reflections about the meaning of their lives and the creation of the universe by calling on what they have been told by parents and religious leaders. They then construct their own ideas as well, which may be very idiosyncratic. Robert Coles, in *The Spiritual Life of Children* (1990), interviewed children in several different countries who belonged to Christian, Islamic, Jewish, and secular belief systems. He came to perceive children as "pilgrims" who are aware that life is a finite journey and who are as eager as adults to make sense of the universe. Coles concluded that the psychological themes of desires, hopes, and fears are often connected with religious and/or spiritual thinking. Regardless of specific religious background or training, there are clear similarities among children's concepts, particularly prior to the third or fourth grade. In a study of 4,800 children from different religious backgrounds Ratcliff (1985) found that religious development progressed through three major stages:

(a) fairy tale stage (3–6 years); (b) realistic stage (7–12 years); and (c) individualistic stage (13–18 years; Ratcliff, 1985). This research demonstrates that religious concepts are highly correlated with cognitive development, following a pattern comparable with other classes of abstract concepts. Table 1 depicts religious stages in relation to Piaget's cognitive developmental stages and Kohlberg's (1981) stages of moral development.

Nye and Carlson (1984) specifically examined the development of the concept of God in children and found it to be compatible with Piaget's stages of cognitive development. Protestant, Jewish, and Catholic children between the ages of 5 and 16 years were asked questions such as "Where does God come from?", "What does God look like?", "Can God see and hear you?" The children's responses were classified either as "concrete" or "abstract." The criterion for a concrete-level response was its tangibility or measurability; the criterion for an abstract response was its generality, that is, the absence of relation to specific descriptors. As was expected, younger children were significantly more concrete in their responses than the older children. The more abstract concept of a deity was found to be relatively more dependent on developmental level than on religious training. Although the Jewish children in the 5- to 8-year-old group gave significantly more abstract responses than those in the other two groups, no other differences were found among the three groups.

Some gender differences in children's concept of God were noted by Nye and Carlson (1984). Although both girls and boys perceived a masculine deity, girls tended to include more aesthetic qualities, for example, drawing God surrounded by flowers. Boys tended to emphasize the physical prowess and strength of God. When asked, "What if God were the opposite sex?", boys tended to completely reject the idea, whereas some girls took a decidedly feminist perspective: One girl stated that there would be less violence if God were a woman. The results of this study are consistent with an earlier study by Goldman (1964), which assessed the readiness of children to learn certain religious concepts. Both studies support the notion that religious instruction has little impact on the child's concrete concept of God before the age of 10.

Heller (1986) studied children's conceptions of God and how these constructs change with normal intellectual growth. He interviewed children brought up in homes affiliated with Judaism, Catholicism, Protestantism (Baptists), and Hinduism. The 4- to 6-year-old children tended to associate God with a happy state and, in an attempt to reconcile "bad" things, constructed a separate "bad" God. These results indicate that children at the preoperational level gradually come to perceive God as occupying about the same level of significance as their parents, whom they perceive as responsible for providing for their needs. Young children often imagine God as looking like their grandfather or state that He lives in the clouds. Children

Table 1   *A Comparison of Concepts by Developmental Stages*

Piaget (cognitive development)	Kohlberg (moral development)	Harms (concept of religion)	Heller (concept of God)	Fowler (stages of faith)
I. Preoperational	Punishment-reward	Fairy tale (3–6 years)	Good versus bad God—unquestioning acceptance	Intuitive, projective faith (imitation of adults; 3–7 years)
II. Concrete Operational	Instrumental hedonism (reciprocal fairness)	Realistic (7–12 years)	Personalization of God (preadolescence) (7–12 years)	Mythic, literal faith (literal interpretation)
III. Early formal operations	Interpersonal expectations and concordance	Individualistic (13–18 years)		Synthetic, conventional (reliance on authority; 7–15 years)
IV. Formal Operations	Societal perspective; reflective relativism or class-biased universalism			Individuating reflexive (personal reference point; adolescence)
V. Formal Operations	Prior to society, principled higher law (universal and critical)			Paradoxical, consolidative faith (acceptance of religions and objective paradox; adolescence)
VI. Formal Operations	Loyalty to being			Universalizing faith (acceptance of the oneness of being)

at this stage tend to unquestioningly accept statements about God.

As children approach adolescence, they tend to project their own emotions and issues onto God. According to Heller (1986), this occurs when they observe that God does not always operate as they had originally concluded. At this point, they will change their concept of the deity to meet their individual psychological needs. These findings are similar to the observations of Deconchy (cited in Elkind, 1971, p. 673), whose 8- to 10-year-olds associated God with strength, beauty, and goodness. Older adolescents expressed worries related to doubt, fear, obedience, and love.

Concepts of Prayer

Differences among religious groups with regard to prayer emerged in Heller's (1986) study. Roman Catholic children interpreted God as an active participant in family events and were more likely to stress the importance of informal dialogues with God. Jewish children were more likely to bring in rituals. Hindu children preferred chanting. Most of the preadolescent children expressed a dislike of rituals, especially a scheduled period for silent prayer, which they perceived as "routine."

Other studies have found that the belief among children that prayer actually produces results decreases with age (Elkind, 1971). Children's concept of prayer transforms from a magical to a sacramental orientation. As Elkind's research indicated, children aged 5 to 7 years did not understand prayer, although they recited certain phrases as expected of them and used the word "God" frequently. After the age of 7, children usually focused on making specific requests. At approximately age 10 to 12 years, children conceptualized prayer as a conversation with God and became generally more satisfied with it.

Goldman (1964) also researched prayer in children and identified several stages. Younger children tended to believe that immediate answers from God were to be expected. Unanswered prayer was explained by their own misbehavior or an incorrect manner of responding. Events occurring soon after prayer were attributed to the prayer and not to other causes. In the second stage, extending until the age of 12, Goldman's subjects believed that failure of prayer to be answered was a consequence of selfish or materialistic requests. In the third stage answers to prayer were attributed to the faith or effort of the individual praying. Later in adolescence, a lack of results was explained as "God knows best."

Ratcliff (1985) examined the concept of God as judge. He found that children perceive God as using rewards and punishments, such as good weather, or conversely, flood or fire, in a concrete manner. In contrast, about half of the adult respondents focused on the uniqueness of

God's judgments and resorted to more abstract descriptions of love and justice.

Research on children's perceptions of the specific activities of God were also reviewed by Ratcliff (1985). As described by Ratcliff, Piaget reported such perceptions as the following: During the preoperational stage, all origins are thought to be caused by a deity (e.g., clouds are made by God smoking a pipe). During the concrete stage, natural explanations are included with supernatural solutions. Beginning at about age 10, children perceive God as a controller of nature. Understandably, the rational and scientific approach comes into direct conflict with the authoritative and miraculous aspects of religion, which remain contradictory. At about the age of 12, children attempt to understand God as working within the known laws of nature, with divine communication being an internal event.

Fowler (1981), who might be described as a theistic developmentalist, studied how faith changes with age, positing a six-stage progression of faith similar to Kohlberg's stages of moral development (see Table 1). Fowler defines faith broadly as the individual's construction of "ultimate conditions of existence" and proposes that faith is necessary for the justification of a moral position. Stage 1 (3–7 years of age) is characterized primarily by the imitation of adults through story and example, with fantasy playing a major role. Stage 2 (7–12 years) is characterized by an increasing distinction between fantasy and reality, with literal interpretation of symbols. The concrete thinking of this stage personalizes the beliefs and rituals. Adolescence brings more self-awareness, and according to Fowler, faith progresses through stages similar to Kohlberg's moral development sequence. Stage 3 continues to be authority-bound, whereas Stage 4 requires responsibility for one's actions. In Stage 5, individuals act affirmatively upon their espoused values and beliefs. The final stage, which Fowler states is rare, is characterized by a sense of oneness of all persons.

According to Goldman (1964), children also progress through stages in perceiving the concept of "church." At first, children focus on the physical building as the place God lives. Later, until they are approximately 14, church is seen as a place to pray, learn about God, or receive help. In the third stage, church attendance is associated with fellowship, altruism, and spirituality.

With regard to identification with a particular church denomination, as would be expected, Elkind (1971) found that the onset of formal operations is associated with the abstract concept of holding specific beliefs. Prior to this stage, children first perceive their denomination as a name, confusing it with nationality or race, and later associating it with the characteristic traditions and rituals.

The conclusion to be drawn from the studies just summarized is that the child's perspective on religion/spirituality is a reflection of developmental stage and should be recognized as such.

Problems and Implications

In a review of the literature, Thomas and Cornwall (1990) tentatively concluded that religious involvement and commitment are related to increasing social competence. They attributed this positive relationship to the role that religion plays in integrating young people into social orders. Coles (1990) presented considerable evidence that children look primarily to their parents for moral guidance. Belonging to a church or synagogue often provides moral guidelines that reinforce parental values of social responsibility, compassion and charity, and self-actualization. It may also provide individuals with additional feelings of belonging and emotional support during life crises. However, it also is clear that religion per se does not necessarily promote moral development. Moreover, certain religious beliefs can create problems, or challenges, for school psychologists, especially those engaged in counseling.

To what extent is the actual moral development of children related to religion? According to Kohlberg (1981), few studies have shown moral reasoning to be directly related to religious instruction. Children progress through similar stages of moral reasoning (see Moral Reasoning and Behavior, this volume). When differences related to religion have been found, studies have shown that college students who are conservative in their Christian faith are less likely to reason at principled, level stages than students who are liberal in their religious beliefs (Clouse, 1985). Instead, the conservative Christians' moral reasoning tends to be based more on respect for law, order, and authority.

There is mixed evidence that religion per se contributes to moral behavior. Moral reasoning reflects the child's quality of thinking. It may or may not reflect what the child actually does behaviorally. Cross-cultural comparisons of honesty, for example, have found that religious education is neither necessary nor sufficient for the expression of honest behavior. Dishonesty and theft, for example, are low in some atheistic societies such as the Israeli atheistic kibbutzim, as well as some Christian and Buddhist groups, but high in some strongly religious countries such as Italy and Mexico. These findings indicate that the family remains the strongest influence on the moral behavior of children.

Differences in parenting styles have been shown to be associated with religious affiliation and beliefs. For example, parents who frequently use the threat that "God will punish" to ensure compliance in their children tend to punish their children more frequently than parents who do not form an alliance with a punitive God. Catholic parents and those with Protestant fundamentalist beliefs tend to use this threat more than other Protestant denominations (Nelson & Kroliczak, 1984).

In their study of religion and parenting orientation, Ellison and Sherkat (1993) found that conservative Protestants and Catholics value obedience more than other Americans. While intellectual autonomy is valued by most Americans, Bible literalists value conformity to dogma. Catholics have a modest but persistent tendency to value autonomy less than parents in liberal Protestant or other groups. Parents who perceive people as essentially moral tend to be gentler in their child rearing (Clayton, 1988, cited in McIntosh & Spilka, in press).

For the vast majority of children, religious organizations and spiritual belief systems provide a source of strength, emotional support, and reinforcement of compassion and self-regulated behavior. However, a minority of children may have a negative experience involving religious issues that contributes to emotional distress or conflict. A dilemma that may be encountered by school psychologists whenever they counsel children is the difficulty of reconciling certain beliefs with accepted notions of what promotes psychological well-being. Much research has been conducted documenting the importance of developing a positive self-concept in children (see Self-Concept, this volume). While most religions support this fairly universally accepted criterion for mental health, a child may belong to a congregation that emphasizes the "evil" nature of humankind and the need to punish sinners.

Most counseling theories place a value on the development of good problem-solving skills. Decision-making models emphasize the importance of considering several alternatives to solving a problem; there is often not just one "right" way. This is in direct conflict with some religious groups' teaching that there *is* only one right way to live, which may be based on their literal interpretation of the Bible. In some of these groups there is an explicit assumption of the moral superiority of one religious sect over all others, discouraging acceptance of those with different belief systems. The emphasis on dogma and acceptance of authority in certain denominations can make the challenging individuation tasks of adolescence even more difficult.

School psychologists (particularly those who provide counseling services) may encounter a number of situations related to religion that require sensitivity and skill in handling. For example, some parents may be mistrustful of a professional who is not a member of their religion and may question the school psychologist's ability to understand their point of view. A compassionate approach will be essential to establish trust and a therapeutic alliance with the family. It is unusual (except in extreme cases) for a parent to resist counseling services after a session in which the psychologist communicates understanding and acceptance of their particular religious beliefs. The school psychologist may need to reassure the parents that he or she will work within the faith perspective of the family.

Some adolescents may express concerns in counseling that are specifically related to religious issues. Adolescents experiencing sexual identity or homosexuality issues from families with religious beliefs that view homosexuality as a sin encounter additional obstacles to self-acceptance and resolution of conflict. The following example highlights the importance of establishing rapport with the family. A 15-year-old African-American male, whose family were Seventh Day Adventists, was referred to a school psychologist for expressing suicidal ideation. It became immediately clear that this young man, "Richard," was in a crisis due to his awakening attraction to other males. A loyal member of his church, he feared disapproval and ostracism by his family and other church members.

Establishing rapport and developing trust helped the family be open to the psychologist working with Richard. The parents were genuinely concerned about their son but horrified about the possibility of him being gay. A warm, nonjudgmental stance contributed to the family's willingness to read books about homosexuality that took a more tolerant perspective than their church leader. Richard eventually "came out," and with supportive therapy, the family did not reject their son during this crisis.

Alternative Actions

When encountering any of the situations just described, it is important for school psychologists to learn as much as possible about the child's family and community. This means acquiring an understanding of the various cultural beliefs, including those related to religion. It is particularly relevant if a school psychologist is employed in an area with unfamiliar or less common religious practices. Flanagan and Miranda (1995) provide guidelines for working with children and families from diverse cultures. Their suggestions clearly apply to religious differences as well. An important first step is to develop an awareness of the beliefs, customs, and practices of mainstream and minority religions. This involves examining one's own belief system as well as obtaining information about other specific religions and belief systems. Acquiring knowledge may occur through reading literature and interacting with members of the religion in the same way one would become familiar with diverse cultures.

An overview of U.S. religions by Roof (1993) may be helpful in gathering information about specific religions. In addition, although members of some religious sects are reluctant to talk with "outsiders," speaking with various community members or former believers is another way to learn about local customs and beliefs.

Without offering their own judgment of a belief or practice at issue, school psychologists can assist older children or adolescents in clear thinking about a particular problem. Awareness of the overlap between a child's mental life with his or her spiritual life is essential. Psychologists who engage in counseling must develop a comfort level with sensitive topics such as spirituality and sexuality. This requires training and supervised practice beyond a basic counseling techniques course. It particularly requires the psychologist to be aware of his or her own beliefs and to learn to appreciate religious/spiritual practices different from one's own experience. Furthermore, the school psychologist must understand that encouraging individuals to come to their own conclusions about a particular matter has certain implications. The adolescent, for example, may begin to experience considerable distress during the process of considering alternative choices that are in conflict with religious teachings. The school psychologist must be sensitive to the client's dilemma; the warmth and caring of a good psychologist-client relationship is especially important. On the other hand, assisting the child and family in marshalling the supportive and motivating forces that many religious/spiritual communities offer can be a powerful tool in counseling. Consulting with parents about child rearing may certainly intersect with religious issues. A nonjudgmental, approachable stance can be the most effective way of establishing a therapeutic alliance with the parents in order to facilitate positive outcomes for the child.

The following case illustrates the need for the school psychologist to be comfortable with spiritual issues that arise in counseling with children. A 9-year-old girl, "Sarah," was referred to the school psychologist for assessment and counseling following Sarah's involvement in a serious car accident. Sarah suffered broken bones and internal injuries. Her father experienced severe head trauma, and his recovery was a slow and frightening process for the family. Sarah was understandably quite phobic about automobile rides (and had developed a number of other fears related to the accident as well). An aspect of the counseling involved cognitive behavioral techniques, including systematic desensitization and relaxation. Sarah, whose family was Catholic, progressed using prayer as a part of her coping strategy. Sarah's prayers were incorporated easily into the intervention, and she was eventually able to ride in cars knowing she had a special way to comfort herself. This exemplifies the natural integration of many children's spirituality with their emotional issues in a positive way.

Summary

The topic of children and religion is a controversial one. Most people, school psychologists included, have strong beliefs in this realm. A wide range of positions exist on the various issues that have been raised in this chapter. Reflection and debate about the religious and spiritual status of American children and families will continue into the next century. Most probably, discussion of religious-

political issues such as separation of church and state will go on. Schools will continue to struggle with differing viewpoints about such issues as school prayer and the teaching of evolution. There is increasing religious pluralism in the United States. African-Americans, Hispanics, and Asian immigrants are influencing the mainstream culture with regard to religion. The "new" spirituality of the "baby boomer" generation, with its emphasis on exploration and personal choice, will be an interesting trend to follow (Albanese, 1993). Intellectual, social/emotional, and spiritual issues are indeed connected. The school psychologist interested in a "best practice" approach to working with children must assess his or her own sensitivity and skill level with regard to this integrated conceptualization of mental health.

A knowledge of the world view that children and their parents possess is essential for truly understanding the psychological dynamics involved in many emotional problems. Practicing psychologists should acquire extensive information on the children with whom they work, including their religious practices, beliefs, and customs. Additionally, it is suggested that school psychologists thoroughly explore their own values regarding religion as part of the general self-awareness that is expected of a mental health professional. Genuineness, a belief in the essential worth of the client, and an effective psychologist/client relationship are also crucial for providing psychological services that are in the best interests of children, regardless of their religious orientation.

Recommended Resources

For Mental Health Practitioners

Coles, R. (1990). *The spiritual life of children.* Boston: Houghton Mifflin.
Coles presents a fascinating compilation of interviews with children around the world about their spiritual life. His observations and interpretations are touching and insightful.

Munsey, B. (Ed.). (1980). *Moral development, moral education, and Kohlberg: Basic issues in philosophy, psychology, religion and education.* Birmingham, AL: Religious Education Press.
This book provides a good collection of essays regarding moral development, several of them specifically focusing on the issue of religion.

Williams, J. P. (1969). *What Americans believe and how they worship.* New York: Harper & Row.
Williams offers a comprehensive overview of most of the various religions practiced in the United States. The book is quite readable, providing history, structure, and custom related to each religion.

For Parents and Children

Blume, J. (1970). *Are you there God? It's me, Margaret.* New York: Bradbury. (Ages 10–16).
This is the story of an 11-year-old girl who decides to investigate different religions for a school project when her grandparents come for a visit and start an argument with her about her religious views. Margaret is upset by this and gives up talking to God for a time.

Boritzer, E. (1990). *What is God?* Willowdale, Ontario: Firefly Books.
This book for children ages 5 to 10 years presents the concept of God as a spiritual feeling that each child experiences personally.

Fay, M. (1994). *Children and religion: Making choices in a secular age.* New York: Fireside.
The author interviewed a number of parents who are in the process of dealing with the spiritually related questions their children have. The parents, who are from a variety of belief systems, discuss their ways of sensitively responding to these questions.

Lickona, T. (1983). *Raising good children.* New York: Bantam Books.
This book integrates moral development theory into a consistent approach to parenting. It focuses on assisting parents in helping children learn responsible behavior, without relating to specific religious ideology.

Thomas, M. A., & Ramey M. L. (1987). *Many children: Religions around the world.* 2055 Royal Fern Court, Reston, VA 22091 Reston, VA: M. Angele Thomas.
This comparative religion book for children ages 8 to 12 provides brief highlights of the major religions across world cultures.

References

Albanese, C. L. (1993). Fisher kings and public places: The old new age in the 1990s. In W. C. Roof (Ed.), Vol. 527, May 1993, 10–25. *The annals of the American Academy of Political and Social Science.* Newbury Park, CA: Sage Periodical Press.

Clouse, B. (1985). Moral reasoning and Christian faith. *Journal of Psychology and Theology, 1*(33), 190–198.

Coles, R. (1990). *The spiritual life of children.* Boston: Houghton Mifflin.

Elkind, D. (1971). The development of religious understanding in children and adolescents. In M. Stommen (Ed.), *Research on religious development: A comprehensive handbook.* New York: Hawthorn Books.

Ellison, C. G., & Sherkat, D. E. (1993). Obedience and autonomy: Religion and parental values reconsidered. *Journal for Scientific Study of Religion, 32*(4), 313–329.

Fay, M. (1994). *Children and religion: Making choices in a secular age.* New York: Fireside.

Flanagan, D., & Miranda, M. (1995). Working with culturally different families. In A. Thomas, & J. Grimes (Ed.), *Best practices in school psychology*-III (pp. 1049–1060). Washington DC: National Association of School Psychologists.

Fowler, J. (1981). *Stages of faith.* San Francisco: Harper & Row.

Goldman, R. (1964). *Religious thinking from childhood to adolescence.* New York: Seabury.

Heller, D. (1986). *The children's God.* Chicago: University of Chicago Press.

Kohlberg, L. (1981). Moral and religious education and the public schools: A developmental view. In L. Kohlberg (Ed.), *Essays on moral development: Vol 1. The philosophy of moral development* (pp. 294–306). San Francisco: Harper & Row.

Kosmin, B. A., & Lachman, S. P. (1993). *One nation under God: Religion in contemporary American society.* New York: Harmony Books.

McIntosh, D. N., & Spilka, B. (in press). Religion and the family. In B. R. Neff, & D. Ratcliff (Eds.), *Handbook of family religious education.* Birmingham, AL: Religious Education Press.

Nelson, H. M., & Kroliczak, A. (1984). Parental uses of the threat "God will punish": Replication and extension. *Journal for the Scientific Study of Religion, 23*(3), 267–277.

Nye, W. C., & Carlson, J. S. (1984). The development of the concept of God in children. *Journal of Genetic Psychology, 145,* 137–142.

Piaget, J. (1973). *The Child and Reality.* New York, NY: Grossman Publications.

Ratcliff, D. (1985). The development of children's religious concepts: Research review. *Journal of Psychology and Christianity, 4*(1), 35–43.

Roof, W. C. (Ed.). (1993). *The annals of the American Academy of Political and Social Science.* Newbury Park, CA: Sage Periodical Press.

Roof, W. C., & McKinney, W. (1987). *American mainline religion: Its changing shape and future.* New Brunswick, NJ: Rutgers University Press.

Thomas, D. L., & Cornwall, M. (1990). Religion and family in the eighties: Discovery and development. *Journal of Marriage and the Family, 52*(4).

Williams, J. P. (1969). *What Americans believe and how they worship.* New York: Harper & Row.

69

Sexual Minority Youth

Jon Lasser
Deborah Tharinger
University of Texas at Austin

Background

Although adult homosexuality has received considerable attention in the literature little has been written until recently about homosexual and bisexual youth (D'Augelli & Dark, 1995; Uribe & Harbeck, 1991). Several factors may explain the absence of gay, lesbian, and bisexual youth in the literature. Many adults fail to acknowledge children's sexuality (see Sexual Development, this volume) and are even less likely to acknowledge children's homosexual desires. In addition, as a socially stigmatized group, sexual minority youth[1] are disenfranchised and left without a voice in social spheres, let alone scholarly publications. Nevertheless, the past 5 to 10 years have witnessed a significant increase in awareness of and research on sexual minority youth and the developmental challenges that they may face (Uribe & Harbeck, 1992). In addressing the needs of sexual minority youth and adolescents who are questioning their orientation, schools and school psychologists have the opportunity to play an important role in ways that both decrease the current, widespread discrimination and oppression these young people experience and enhance their development, health, and mental health.

In 1993, the American Psychological Association (APA) and the National Association of School Psychologists (NASP) passed a joint Resolution on Lesbian, Gay, and Bisexual Youths in the Schools (APA, 1995), an important first step that sets a standard for psychologists and their professional organizations. In this document, APA and NASP jointly resolved that they:

- Shall take a leadership role in promoting societal and familial attitudes and behaviors that affirm the dignity and rights, within educational environments, of all lesbian, gay, and bisexual youths, including those with physical or mental disabilities and from all ethnic/racial backgrounds and classes.
- Support providing a safe and secure educational atmosphere in which all youths, including lesbian, gay, and bisexual youths, may obtain an education free from discrimination, harassment, violence, and abuse, and which promotes an understanding and acceptance of self.
- Encourage psychologists to develop and evaluate interventions that foster nondiscriminatory environments and lower risk for HIV infection and decrease self-injurious behavior in lesbian, gay, and bisexual youths.
- Advocate efforts to ensure the funding of basic and applied research on and scientific evaluations of interventions and programs designed to address the issues of lesbian, gay, and bisexual youths in the schools and enhance HIV prevention targeted at gay and bisexual youths (p. 14).

This chapter focuses on the development of sexual minority youth but does not preclude the potential for other factors to affect and interact with sexual minority development. In addition to struggling with developmental issues specific to sexual orientation, gay, lesbian, and bisexual adolescents face many of the same developmental challenges as heterosexual adolescents, such as the need for peer approval, body image issues, and the desire for greater autonomy (Anderson, D., 1987). Parents, educators, and psychologists need to maintain an awareness that sexual minority youth are first and foremost teens. Their sexual orientation is but one of their many characteristics. Furthermore, sexual minority youth come from both genders and all races, religions, and ethnic groups (Hetrick & Martin, 1987). For example, al-

---

[1]Throughout this chapter we refer to persons with same-sex attractions as sexual minorities, homosexuals, or gays/lesbians/bisexuals (Sullivan, 1994). The term "lesbian" refers to girls and women with same-sex attractions, whereas "gay" refers to boys and men with same-sex attractions. Those who are attracted to members of both sexes are referred to as "bisexual."

though it may be convenient to conceive of an individual as lesbian *or* African-American, in reality, lesbian African-American adolescents may be subject to homophobia, sexism, *and* racism.

Discussions of lesbian, gay, and bisexual development also need to include the impact of homophobia and heterosexism on heterosexual adolescents, as many theoretical models of homosexual development implicate homophobia and heterosexism as the factors that make the development of sexual minority youth unique (Anderson, D., 1994; Patterson, 1995). *Homophobia* is used to describe a set of negative attitudes about homosexuality and is therefore better understood as a prejudice rather than a phobia or irrational fear as the name implies (Haaga, 1991). *Heterosexism* refers to the assumption that everyone is heterosexual or that heterosexuality is inherently superior to homosexuality (Francoeur, 1991). Teens who may be questioning their sexual orientation or are perceived mistakenly to be gay, lesbian, or bisexual may be targeted and stigmatized like homosexual youth (D'Augelli & Dark, 1995; Schneider & Tremble, 1985). Also, sanctioned prejudice and discrimination regarding any group of individuals perpetuates the vulnerability in all persons. Thus, while lesbian, gay, and bisexual youth are clearly the focus of this chapter, it is acknowledged that the impact of sexual minority development extends beyond sexual minorities.

Estimates of the prevalence of homosexuality vary greatly (Price & Telljohann, 1991). Although social changes such as the gains made by the lesbian/bisexual/gay rights movement have created a climate in which more sexual minority youth have opportunities to "come out" and disclose their sexual orientation (Herdt, 1989), the number of sexual minority youth is frequently underestimated. This may be due to the unwillingness of many gays, lesbians, and bisexuals to disclose their sexual orientation in a climate of hostility and discrimination. Therefore, self-reports may only reflect the number of open homosexual youth. Furthermore, the various ways in which social scientists determine a person's sexual orientation may yield significantly different outcomes. For example, some sexual minority youth may be more willing to report same sex attraction than the label "homosexual" given the negative images often associated with the term. However, it is generally held that 5% to 10% of the population is exclusively homosexual, meaning that these individuals are attracted only to members of the same sex (Gonsiorek, 1988; Treadway & Yoakam, 1992). Most prevalence studies report slightly more male homosexuals than female homosexuals (Paroski, 1986). This estimate translates to approximately 3 million homosexual adolescents in the United States (Herdt, 1989). Their unique developmental experiences need to be understood.

Gay, Lesbian, and Bisexual Identity Development

The etiology of sexual orientation is unknown, and a wide range of often conflicting theories exist regarding the cause of sexual orientation (Patterson, 1995). Biological explanations have attempted to attribute sexual orientation to hormones (Meyer-Bahlburg et al., 1995), genetic factors (Bailey & Pillard, 1991), and brain structure (LeVay, 1993), whereas some theorists have focused on environmental and social constructivist perspectives (Kitzinger & Wilkinson, 1995). Critics of biological explanations argue that sexual orientation, like many other traits, results as a combination of both biological and psychosocial influences and that efforts to identify a single cause of sexual orientation are overly simplistic given the complexity of human sexual behavior (Parker & De Cecco, 1995). Given the high level of uncertainty regarding the determinants of sexual orientation, this chapter places emphasis on the development of homosexual identities rather than the etiology of sexual orientation.

Troiden's (1989) model of sexual minority identity development, like most others, is based on the formation of a homosexual identity in the shadow of discrimination and oppression. Although this model fails to describe developmental differences between male and female sexual minority youth, it provides a useful framework for understanding the major challenges faced by same-sex-oriented youth. Troiden (1989) cautions that identity formation as operationalized in his model is not linear, but rather "emergent: never fully determined in a fixed or absolute sense, but always subject to modification and further change" (p. 68). Furthermore, Troiden shares Herdt's (1989) assumption that "sexual identities and meanings are, like other areas of human life, profoundly shaped by culture and social structure" (p. 18).

According to Troiden (1989), a fully realized homosexual identity is actually a composite of three identities: self, perceived, and presented. *Self-identity* refers to the incorporation of a homosexual identity in one's self-concept. In other words, seeing oneself as a homosexual. *Perceived identity* refers to the perception from others that an individual is a sexual minority. *Presented identity* is achieved when an individual comes out or publicly announces that she or he is lesbian, gay, or bisexual. This conceptualization of three distinct (yet related) identities has empirical support from research examining milestones in sexual minority development. For example, D'Augelli and Hershberger (1993) found that in their sample of 194 gay and lesbian youth, expression of identities similar to those described by Troiden appeared at distinct times: The mean age of self-labeling preceded the mean age of first disclosure, which preceded the mean age of first disclosure to a family member. Developmental models proposed by Cass (1979) and Troiden describe lesbian, gay, and bisexual development as a process by which self-identity, perceived identity, and presented identity emerge and shape one another as the individual becomes aware of his or her orientation and interacts with others.

The six-stage model of identity development proposed by Cass (1979) provides a more detailed account of identity formation and evolution. According to this model, the initial awareness of same-sex attraction results in *identity confusion* (Stage 1). At this stage, the individual has a difficult time trying to reconcile this awareness with his or her previous self-concept. *Identity comparison* (Stage 2) is marked by a tentative acceptance of a new self-concept as lesbian, gay, or bisexual but often with negative feelings about this identity. Over time one moves to *identity tolerance* (Stage 3), still short of full acceptance yet tolerating this new identity. Stage 4 in the Cass model is *identity acceptance,* in which one's sexual orientation becomes normative. In support of this newly accepted orientation *identity pride* (Stage 5) may be adopted. Cass's model ends with an *identity synthesis* (Stage 6) that facilitates alliances between heterosexuals and homosexuals. This model is useful for detailing some of the transitions neglected by other models of development, and four of the six stages have received some empirical support (Cass, 1984). However, when compared to other models of development, the Cass model seems to complicate sexual minority development with superfluous detail. For example, Cass's last three stages are subsumed under Troiden's (1989) fourth and final stage. For the purposes of this chapter, Troiden's model will serve as a framework for understanding sexual minority youth development. The Troiden model divides sexual minority development into four stages which are described next.

First Stage: Sensitization

The first stage, *sensitization,* is characterized by a general sense of isolation and feeling different from same-sex peers and by most accounts occurs between the ages of 5 and 7 years (Treadway & Yoakam, 1992). Although other stage models mark the beginning of homosexual development with an awareness of identity (Cass, 1979), Troiden (1989) suggests that sensitization is the antecedent to identity awareness. This stage precedes an awareness of the self as homosexual, but the feeling that one is different may be associated with gender neutral/inappropriate behaviors. However, gender atypical behavior does not indicate homosexuality; heterosexuals may be gender atypical and homosexuals may be gender typical.

Sexual minority youth in the sensitization stage, or "prehomosexuals," are unlikely to consider the possibility that they are homosexual because their thoughts and feelings are not understood in terms of attraction or sex-

uality. Rather, the notion that one is different often comes from interest in activities usually restricted to members of the other sex as a means of enforcing gender-role expectations. This is not to say that girls who like sports are prehomosexual, but that many adult homosexuals recall gender atypical interests as children. Interestingly enough, approximately 80% of Paroski's (1987) sample of gay and lesbian adolescents believed that all gay men are effeminate and all lesbians are masculine, thereby supporting the notion that sexual minority youth incorporate societal stereotypes into their own world views.

Unfortunately, much more is known about adult homosexuals' retrospective thoughts than the thoughts of youth during the sensitization stage, and retrospective data may not be valid for understanding sexual minority youth today (Boxer & Cohler, 1989). Feelings and experiences during the sensitization stage become more salient as they are reinterpreted retrospectively. "The reinterpretation of past events as indicating a homosexual potential appears to be a necessary (but not sufficient) condition for the eventual adoption of homosexual identities" (Troiden, 1989, p. 52).

Second Stage: Identity Confusion

Due to heterosexism, most prehomosexual children assume that they are heterosexual before they are aware of their homosexuality (Troiden, 1989). Heterosexism is a bias that leads to the assumption that all people are heterosexual. Heterosexist beliefs and practices (e.g., telling a young boy that someday he'll marry a beautiful woman) may cause dissonance for adolescents discovering that they are something other than what they once believed. This often results in *identity confusion* (Hetrick & Martin, 1987; Troiden, 1989). The age at which homosexual youth reach the identity confusion stage varies. Although previous data have suggested that sexual minority youth first become aware of their sexual orientation between the ages of 12 and 14 (Anderson, D., 1987), more recent studies have found mean ages of first awareness as low as 10 years (D'Augelli & Hershberger, 1993). The identity confusion stage may be characterized by inner turmoil, for the gay or lesbian adolescent is almost certain that he or she is homosexual and must contend with a major change in self-concept. During identity confusion, sexual minority youth gain a greater awareness of their attraction to members of the same sex and begin to associate cultural homophobia with their own developing identity.

Several other factors contribute to identity confusion. Many homosexual teens will also experience attraction to members of the other sex and may feel forced to adopt either a homosexual or heterosexual identity in the midst of their confusion. The social stigma attached to homosexuality acts as a barrier to discussions of conflicted feelings, placing many sexual minority youth in social, emotional, and cognitive isolation (Hetrick & Martin, 1987). Social isolation is characterized by a lack of access to friends and social networks for communication and friendly interactions. Again, stigma plays an important role because sexual minority youth may feel a need to hide their identity through isolation (Anderson, D., 1987). *Emotional isolation* is a feeling of affectional detachment from others, especially family members.

Cognitive isolation refers to a lack of awareness concerning accurate information about homosexuality. The adoption of myths and stereotypes (e.g., homosexuality is a mental illness or unnatural) rather than the facts results in cognitive isolation and presents a barrier to identity formation. Acclimating to a stigmatized identity without appropriate information can be challenging (Uribe & Harbeck, 1991). "Before they can see themselves as homosexuals, people must realize that homosexuality and homosexuals exist, learn what homosexuals are actually like as people, and be able to perceive similarities between their own desires and behaviors and those of people labeled socially as homosexual" (Troiden, 1989, p. 55).

Homosexual youth actively create their own coping strategies to deal with identity confusion (Zera, 1992). Many will deny or avoid their homosexual feelings with the hope that same sex desire will abate. Others actively try to alter their sexual orientation by engaging in heterosexual behavior. Hetrick and Martin (1987) speculate that some young lesbians may even get pregnant as a result of "heterosexual sexual acting out" in an effort to conceal and/or deny their true desires. Others may redefine their feelings and experiences to explain themselves as something other than homosexual. Same sex attraction may be redefined as bisexuality, a passing phase, or the result of extraneous circumstances (e.g., "I was really drunk and had no idea what I was doing"). However, Troiden's (1989) model predicts that most sexual minority youth will emerge from identity confusion with acceptance of the label "homosexual" (or "gay," "lesbian," "bisexual," "queer," etc.) for themselves. With this acceptance comes the understanding that to be gay, lesbian, or bisexual is to be a member of a socially stigmatized group.

Third Stage: Identity Assumption

When sexual minority youth move beyond confusion, they proceed to the next stage of *identity assumption*. It is at this stage that sexual minority youth first know with certainty that they are homosexual and accept the identity of gay, lesbian, or bisexual. The move from confusion to identity assumption should not be oversimplified; Troiden's (1989) model is not linear and allows for movement back and forth between stages. There are empirical data that demonstrate a gap between knowledge of one's sex-

ual orientation and assumption of the identity. In D'Augelli and Hershberger's (1993) sample of gay and lesbian youth, the mean age difference between age of first awareness and age of self-labeling was 5 years for males and 4 years for females. The mean age of first awareness of males and females was 10 years and 11 years, respectively. The mean age of self-labeling for males and females was 15 years. In light of Troiden's model, self-awareness seems to fall into the identity confusion stage and self-labeling represents identity assumption. During this stage, sexual minority youth begin to "come out" and disclose their sexual orientation to others. This is a risky endeavor given the unpredictability of responses. Therefore, many sexual minority youth may begin coming out to other homosexuals to test the waters. In D'Augelli and Hershberger's (1993) sample, the average age of first disclosure was 17 years for males and 16 years for females, and first disclosure tended to be to a friend rather than to a family member.

Because many sexual minority youth do disclose their orientation during the identity assumption stage, a brief discussion of coming out is appropriate. Coming out of the closet is a not an event but rather a process (Savin-Williams, 1990) and has been characterized as a rite of passage for sexual minority adolescents (Herdt, 1989). Stage models of the coming out process overlap with models of gay and lesbian development, so a thorough discussion of coming out will not be included here. However, for the purposes of this chapter, a brief consideration of parents' reactions to disclosure of a child's homosexuality is appropriate.

Strommen (1989) reviewed the literature on family members' reactions to disclosure of homosexuality and concluded that (a) many families will apply their negative beliefs and attitudes toward homosexuality to their child, and (b) feelings of guilt and/or failure are likely to follow the disclosure if the parents mistakenly believe that homosexuality is a consequence of poor parenting. Compounded with a traditional view of gender roles and strong religious doctrines against homosexuality, these reactions to disclosure can amount to a psychological crisis for families. Support from groups such as Parents and Friends of Lesbians and Gays (PFLAG; see Additional Resources at the end of this chapter) can be a valuable resource for families.

Coming out often leads to contact with other homosexuals. This contact can be extremely important, for it has the potential to reduce isolation, provide sexual minority youth with information about homosexuality, and allow them to form a better developed understanding of homosexuality. Sexual experimentation and a greater awareness of a homosexual community/culture are hallmarks of the identity assumption stage.

Troiden (1989) notes that self-identification as a homosexual requires the adoption of a strategy for the management of stigmatization. Some sexual minority youth will capitulate by avoiding homosexual behavior. In other words, the social punishment of homophobia and/or internalized homophobic attitudes may be powerful enough for some sexual minority youth to believe that their feelings are wrong and that acting on those feelings exacerbates the "problem." Others may engage in "minstrelization," which involves playing the role of the stereotype by adopting extreme cross-gendered behavior and dress (Hetrick & Martin, 1987; Troiden, 1989). Passing, or living separate public and private lives, may be the choice of stigma management for others. Whereas most racial minority youth cannot "pass" as White to gain acceptance because their minority status is visible (with some exceptions), sexual minority youth can pass as heterosexual by avoiding discussion of their private lives or by fabricating a heterosexual private life for public consumption. Finally, many gay and lesbian youth will manage stigma by aligning themselves with the gay community via organizations, clubs, and support groups.

Fourth Stage: Commitment

The final stage of Troiden's (1989) identity formation model is *commitment* to a way of life that is accepting of homosexuality internally and externally. Internally, commitment manifests itself as an appreciation for homosexuality as a valid orientation and as satisfaction with one's identity. Externally, commitment is realized with coming out to heterosexuals, engaging in homosexual relationships, and making a change in stigma management. Passing is less common among homosexuals at the commitment stage, whereas assimilating and alignment with a homosexual community become more common. Troiden's commitment stage, analogous to Cass's (1979) synthesis stage, is characterized by greater happiness and diminished conflict. Although the path to commitment may be one of conflict, pain, and turmoil, most lesbians, gays, and bisexuals are happy and well adjusted (Hooker, 1957; Reiss, 1980; Zera, 1992). At this stage, pressure to change one's sexual orientation is not desirable (Treadway & Yoakam, 1992). The fact that these models do not imply linear development suggests that sexual minority youth may be found at any of these stages, and professionals working with these youth should be aware of the various ways in which these stages are experienced.

Problems and Implications

Due to the negative attitudes and behaviors directed toward homosexuals in today's society, sexual minority youth face unique developmental challenges not experienced by heterosexual adolescents (Hetrick & Martin,

1987). These challenges and obstacles include the social risks of discrimination, violence, and social rejection; the personal risk of the possibility of a compromised self-acceptance; health and mental health risks, including suicide and HIV infection; and educational risks, specifically the challenge to succeed in a hostile climate.

Social Risks

Discrimination against sexual minorities is pervasive in the United States on interpersonal and institutional levels (Sullivan, 1994). A study of homophobia on a college campus concluded that "homophobic attitudes among freshmen may be so common as to be normative" (D'Augelli & Rose, 1990, p. 490). According to Herek (1986), homophobia is an integral component of socially constructed, idealized masculinity, and that "to be a man in contemporary American society is to be homophobic—that is, to be hostile toward homosexual persons in general and gay men in particular" (p. 563).

The effects of homophobia and heterosexism can have serious negative consequences for sexual minorities. Violence against gays and lesbians is the most frequently occurring type of bias-related violence (Herek, 1989). Pilkington and D'Augelli (1995) assessed the various forms of victimization to which gay and lesbian youth are subjected and found that 44% of their sample had received threats of physical violence, 33% had objects thrown at them, 31% had been chased or followed, approximately 20% had been physically assaulted, and 22% had been sexually assaulted. Violence against gays and lesbians may come from strangers, acquaintances, or family members. In Harry's (1989) study which compared gay and heterosexual male college students, gay males were found to be more likely to experience abuse by parents during adolescence than heterosexual males.

Sexual minority youth may also find that social rejection as a result of disclosing their sexual orientation is common (Uribe & Harbeck, 1991). While racial/ethnic minority youth may have the opportunity to commiserate with parents over discrimination, gay and lesbian youth are frequently rejected by their families of origin and must look elsewhere for support (Strommen, 1989; Uribe & Harbeck, 1991). This problem is compounded by the fact that homophobia and heterosexism operate not only on an interpersonal but also on institutional level. Thus, sexual minority youth face discrimination at school, with counselors, and at treatment facilities (Gonsiorek, 1988). Institutional discrimination is particularly harmful because it denies sexual minority youth access to much needed resources. While heterosexual teens can discuss family and social problems with school counselors, homosexual teens may find that school counselors hold negative attitudes toward sexual minorities and are therefore inaccessible.

Personal Risks

The most important factor contributing to the mental health of sexual minority youth may be self-acceptance (Hershberger & D'Augelli, 1995). Self-acceptance, or a positive feeling about one's sexual orientation, corresponds with the commitment stage of Troiden's (1989) developmental model and may mediate negative consequences from victimization and social stigma. The self-acceptance of gay and lesbian youth may be compromised by internalized homophobia (Zera, 1992). Most children, including those who will later identify as gay, lesbian, or bisexual, are socialized in a homophobic and heterosexist culture that teaches, both directly and indirectly through schools, churches/synagogues, and mass media, that homosexuality is unnatural, sinful, abnormal, and inferior to heterosexuality. When lesbian, gay, and bisexual youth hear "faggot" and "dyke" used as derogatory terms, hatred of gays and lesbians is reinforced in their minds.

If discrimination against gays and lesbians erodes self-acceptance, professionals working with sexual minority youth need to develop creative strategies to help homosexual adolescents achieve a more positive self-image. Greater self-acceptance can be facilitated by support groups (Proctor, 1994), exposure to good role models (Gonsiorek, 1988), socialization with other sexual minorities (Cass, 1979), and access to accurate information about homosexuality (Hetrick & Martin, 1987). Given the importance of a positive self-concept for all students, the role of schools in protecting and fostering the self-concept of sexual minority youth is extremely important.

Health and Mental Health Risks

Homophobia and heterosexism may have negative health consequences for sexual minority youth. It appears that homosexual adolescents may present a number of mental health problems related to their sexual orientation. In a recent sample of sexual minority youth, D'Augelli and Hershberger (1993) found

- 77% of males and 62% of females reported that they were troubled by depression.
- 73% of males and 53% of females were troubled by anxiety.
- 24% of males and 22% of females expressed concern about excessive drug use.
- 90% of males reported that they worry about HIV/AIDS (very few females expressed this concern).
- 69% of males and 61% of females were troubled by the thought of coming out to family members.
- 42% of the sample had attempted suicide.

The incidence of these problems more than doubles that of heterosexual adolescents. Therefore, sexual minority youth are more likely to suffer severe mental health problems due to their victimization, placing them at risk for suicide. The literature on suicide and HIV/AIDS with respect to sexual minority youth is discussed due to the seriousness of these life-threatening problems.

Suicide

It has been reported that 20% to 66% of lesbian, gay, and bisexual youth have attempted suicide (Hershberger & D'Augelli, 1995; Proctor, 1994; Schneider, Farberow, & Kruks, 1989). These figures are shocking in comparison to the 6% to 10% of suicide attempts by adolescents in the general population (Garland & Zigler, 1993). The fact that sexual minority youth are significantly more likely to commit suicide has launched an effort to determine some of the risk factors associated with gay, lesbian, and bisexual adolescents' suicides, and several studies have produced some consistent findings. For example, the following factors have been associated with sexual minority youth suicide: dealing with the stress and pain of identity confusion, alcoholism and physical abuse in the family, lack of family support, earlier awareness of one's sexual orientation, and alienation (Hershberger & D'Augelli, 1995; Schneider et al., 1989).

Although these risk factors have been identified, they must be understood in terms of their interaction with the adolescent and his or her environment. For example, Hershberger and D'Augelli (1995) found that although the mental health/suicidality of gay and lesbian youth (in response to victimization) was mediated by family support and self-acceptance, further analysis demonstrated that neither of these factors acted as a buffer independently, but that their combined impact lowered the risk. It is also noteworthy that in a high school sample of sexual minority youth, very few of the students who attempted suicide sought help from school (Uribe & Harbeck, 1991). Efforts to prevent adolescent suicide need to (a) include the fact that a disproportionate number of sexual minority youth are suicidal and (b) focus on meeting the needs of this population.

HIV/AIDS infection

Most young gay males report that they are worried about HIV infection (D'Augelli & Hershberger, 1993). This concern may be justified, given many sexual minority youths' high risk for HIV infection (Feldman, 1989; Gonsiorek, 1988). Sexual exploration, both heterosexual and homosexual, as a means to clarifying identity issues, may put homosexual and questioning youth at a high risk for infection if they are not practicing safe sex (e.g., condom/dental dam use; Paroski, 1987). Young lesbians who heterosexually act out to conceal their homosexual orientation may also place themselves at risk for HIV infection. Sexual minority youth are at an even greater risk for HIV infection than their heterosexual peers because education and prevention strategies often fail to reach them due to heterosexist curricula and social/cognitive isolation (Coleman & Remafedi, 1989; D'Augelli & Hershberger, 1993).

Sexual minority youth may also be at risk for HIV infection if they are involved in drug use and/or prostitution. Sexual minority youth may attempt to cope with stress through substance abuse (Coleman & Remafedi, 1989), which could put them at risk for HIV infection if they share needles or are less likely to practice safe sex when high. Although prostitution among sexual minority youth is not well studied, Coleman (1989) suggests that sexual minority youth who have run away from home or have been thrown out due to conflicts with family members over sexual orientation may end up in prostitution for survival. Clearly this would have a dramatic impact on these youths' risk of HIV infection. Further research is needed in this area. (For more information, see Chapter 70, this volume.)

Educational Risks

While the personal, social, health, and mental health risks faced by sexual minority youth certainly impact their educational experiences, factors specific to educational institutions are also significant. The existence of sexual minority youth typically is denied or ignored by curricula, administrators, and teachers. School personnel may assume that all students are heterosexual or hold hostile attitudes toward lesbian, gay, and bisexual youth (Sears, 1991). In extreme cases, some school districts have prohibited any discussion of homosexuality as a normal variation. Sexuality education classes often fail to address sexual orientation (especially when the focus of the curriculum is on reproduction) and may even reinforce myths and misinformation about homosexuality (Morrow, 1993; Sears, 1992). Discussions of homosexuality that are limited to an association with AIDS perpetuate a disease model of homosexuality and fail to acknowledge positive aspects of sexual variation (Treadway & Yoakam, 1992). Unfortunately, "cultural taboos, fear of controversy, and a deeply rooted, pervasive homophobia have kept the educational system in the United States blindfolded and mute on the subject of childhood and adolescent homosexuality" (Uribe & Harbeck, 1991).

Thus, the educational experiences of sexual minority youth may be affected by a number of factors including level of homophobia in the school environment; attitudes of teachers, counselors, and other school staff toward homosexual youth; the degree to which homosexuality is incorporated in (or ignored by) the curriculum; opportunities for lesbian, gay, and bisexual students to meet and share their experiences; and the level of support for sexual minority students as expressed by heterosexual students. There is a paucity of research on homosexual students' educational experiences. Research on teachers' and counselors' attitudes is reviewed here, as well as

some data on both heterosexual and homosexual students' assessment of school environment.

Schools have traditionally been an unfriendly place to lesbian, gay, and bisexual students, often reinforcing societal hate of sexual minorities. Most schools fail to protect lesbian, gay, and bisexual students from physical violence. In their review of victimization of sexual minority youth, D'Augelli and Dark (1995) note that approximately one-third to one-half of gay and lesbian students are victimized verbally or physically in schools (perhaps a greater proportion of homosexual youth would report victimization if their sexual orientation were readily identifiable by outsiders). Harassment often comes from teachers as well as peers and may include destruction of personal property (Treadway & Yoakam, 1992; Uribe & Harbeck, 1991). Lesbian, gay, and bisexual students often find that harassment (e.g., "queer jokes") is ignored or otherwise condoned and endorsed by teachers and that a failure to provide accurate information about homosexuality in sexuality education classes sends a clear message that schools are unwilling to recognize sexual minority youth (Morrow, 1993).

In an effort to gain a better understanding of the factors contributing to this hostile school environment, Sears (1991) assessed the attitudes and feelings toward homosexual youth of prospective teachers and school counselors. Separate measures were used to assess attitudes (cognitive) and feelings (affective). Negative attitudes toward gay men and lesbians were held by 80% of Sears's sample of prospective teachers. When asked how much their own high school teachers knew about homosexuality, 21% reported that they "don't know," which suggests that many teachers never discuss homosexuality with students. Prospective teachers' scores on a test of knowledge about homosexuality demonstrated inadequate knowledge as a group.

Approximately two-thirds of Sears's sample of school counselors expressed negative attitudes toward sexual minorities. The negative feelings were significantly stronger than the negative beliefs, which is regrettable given that "situations that place school counselors in direct contact with homosexual men and women create among many intensely negative feelings" (Sears, 1991, p. 59). Price and Telljohann's (1991) sample of school counselors grossly underestimated the number of gay and lesbian students in their schools, with 16% claiming that there were no homosexual students in their schools and almost two-thirds claiming that 1% to 5% of the students were gay or lesbian (as mentioned earlier, the best estimates are around 5% to 10%). Self-evaluation revealed that only one in four school counselors feel that they are "very competent" in working with sexual minority youth, and 41% believed that schools are not doing enough to help this population.

Little data exist on the attitudes and feelings of sexual minority youth and their educational experiences. Uribe and Harbeck (1991) interviewed 50 lesbian, gay, and bisexual youth to assess their needs before implementation of a school-based intervention program at Fairfax High School in Los Angeles called PROJECT 10 (for the 10% of students who are homosexual). Sexual minority students indicated that verbal harassment from other students and teachers was pervasive, and every lesbian, gay, and bisexual student interviewed knew at least one student who dropped out of school in response to the abuse. Students reported that "overt discrimination, in the form of verbal and physical harassment, occurs with such regularity that it is an accepted part of the life of an openly gay male" (p. 24). Although males were more likely to be victimized than females, the lesbian and female bisexual students in the study felt a need to keep their sexual orientation private given the hostile climate toward homosexuals.

Alternative Actions

Schools that attempt to address the needs of sexual minority youth may face a number of challenges including religious opposition, insufficient funding, and the absence of professionals trained to work with lesbian, gay, and bisexual youth (Anderson, D., 1994; Taylor, 1994). By working with agencies that have experience with this population, school psychologists can develop programs that are both cost-effective and tailored for homosexual adolescents. Opposition to such programs should be dealt with professionally by affirming the right of every sexual minority student to equal educational opportunities.

Some school psychologists may find participating in activities to promote the health and educational attainment of sexual minority youth to be overly challenging and uncomfortable due to a number of potential barriers. Some school psychologists may

- Fear that they will be perceived as gay or lesbian if they are involved in programming for sexual minority youth.
- Object to developing interventions for this population on religious or moral grounds.
- Face opposition from external sources such as churches, parents, or both.
- Fear that their jobs are in jeopardy.

Given these obstacles, how can school psychologists effectively meet the needs of lesbian, gay, and bisexual students?

School psychologists who are worried that others will perceive them as gay or lesbian may find that examining their own attitudes and feelings about homosexuality eases this discomfort. Similarly, those who object

on religious or moral grounds may find working with this population easier after a thorough examination of their own beliefs. Working with agencies that have experience with sexual minority youth can provide school psychologists with helpful information and resources that would otherwise be unavailable, thereby easing the difficulty of developing entirely new programs. When faced with opposition to interventions for sexual minority youth, school psychologists may find support in school district antidiscrimination policies; the APA/NASP resolution on lesbian, gay, and bisexual youth; and the APA and NASP ethical codes. School psychologists who fail to intervene on behalf of a gay or lesbian student in need may be in violation of their professional codes of ethics.

Professional activities designed to address the needs of sexual minority youth can be discussed by using the framework of the APA/NASP resolution, presented earlier. Although four separate goals are presented in the resolution and reflected in the following discussion, in practice the first three overlap and are intervention focused, and the last one advocates for funding for research and evaluation activities. School psychologists can be key school personnel in providing leadership for change in attitudes and behaviors regarding sexual minority youth, in helping to create safe educational atmospheres, and in implementing and evaluating interventions for homosexual youth.

Promote Supportive Societal and Familial Attitudes and Behaviors

The resolution on lesbian, gay, and bisexual youth states that psychologists need to promote positive attitudes and behavior regarding homosexual youth. Perhaps the most important recommendation is that accurate and nonbiased information about sexual orientation be provided in schools. When asked how they learned about homosexuality, gay and lesbian youth reported that sexual encounters, television, and word of mouth were sources of information, yet none reported school as a place where information could be obtained (Paroski, 1987). There is clearly a need for accurate information, not just for homosexual students, but also for heterosexual students. In fact, 79% of heterosexual and homosexual students at Fairfax High School reported that PROJECT 10's greatest contribution was the accessibility to information about sexual orientation (Uribe & Harbeck, 1991). School psychologists can serve as a source of accurate information about sexual orientation for students, parents, teachers, and administrators, as well as ensure that this information is present in sexuality education curricula and in books on the shelves of school libraries. Furthermore, they can provide support for school faculty and administrators who are working toward the promotion of positive attitudes and behaviors concerning sexual orientation.

School psychologists can also help promote positive attitudes by working with faculty and administrators on developing community support for sexual minority youth services.

Attitudinal change can also be facilitated through modification of existing curricula and teacher training. Discussions of homosexuality need not be relegated to health education or sexuality education classes. History, art, and literature classes can include relevant information about homosexuals and homosexuality, providing role models for sexual minority youth in schools. Teachers unfamiliar with lesbian, gay, and bisexual history may need additional training to familiarize themselves with famous homosexuals (see Recommended Resources). Furthermore, teachers should not suggest that all students are heterosexual.

School psychologists can also play a role in developing and implementing educational workshops for the parents of sexual minority and sexual majority youth. Parents educated accurately about homosexuality can help their homosexual children through developmental challenges and teach their heterosexual children that homophobia is wrong and harmful. Additionally, school psychologists can help parents of homosexual children to gain access to information by providing referrals to support groups, books, and other community resources (see Recommended Resources).

Promote Safe and Secure Educational Atmospheres

Making schools safe for sexual minority youth is a controversial topic in most communities. As a first step, promoting the health and development of sexual minority youth can be advanced under the context of less controversial initiatives, such as prevention of violence, health education, and drug and alcohol programs. Furthermore, work that improves the educational experiences of sexual minority youth should be promoted as a set of programs that help all students regardless of their sexual orientation.

However, although all the activities just outlined are important, additional steps are needed (direct interventions are further discussed in the following section), such as the codified, institutional support of gays and lesbians in schools. While the presence of a support group for sexual minority youth may demonstrate implicit recognition of homosexual students, explicit protection from verbal and physical abuse needs to be written into school policy to demonstrate that discrimination against lesbians and gays will not be tolerated. Teachers and students alike should be held accountable for their homophobia just as they would be for their racism, and the inclusion of an anti-homophobia statement in school conduct codes and discrimination policies would facilitate this. Also, just as racist remarks would be deemed unacceptable in the classroom, teachers need to challenge homophobic comments (Treadway & Yoakam, 1992).

Thus, although school personnel cannot prevent homophobia or its effects on sexual minority students, they can work toward making schools safer for lesbian, gay, and bisexual youth by writing anti-discrimination policies that specifically prohibit harassment based on sexual orientation, thus providing these students with institutional support and protection (Harbeck, 1994). Furthermore, support groups or "gay-straight alliances" can be formed to give students an opportunity to share their feelings of being a sexual minority in school and to recognize that the school acknowledges their presence (Blumenfeld, 1994; Williams, Doyle, Taylor, & Ferguson, 1992). Finally, school psychologists can communicate to students that the psychologist's office is a safe haven by placing books about homosexuality in plain view, putting up posters about homosexuality on the office wall, or verbally communicating a willingness to talk with students about sexual orientation. Some sexual minority students may believe that their school is an inherently unsafe place for disclosure and may seek services at another school. Meeting the needs of these students may require networking between schools so that support groups can be promoted throughout a district.

Other efforts to make the educational experiences of sexual minority youth safer include a district-wide counseling and education program (Uribe & Harbeck, 1991) and a separate school established for lesbian, gay, and bisexual youth experiencing abuse in their regular school (D'Augelli & Dark, 1995). Although separate schools may be necessary when regular schools fail to meet the needs of sexual minority youth, emphasis should be placed on improving the educational environment of regular schools, given the fact that separate is inherently unequal.

Promote the Development and Evaluation of Interventions

As just stated, the overriding principle for school psychologists when designing and implementing interventions to address discrimination and hostility against homosexual youth in schools is to be a source of accurate, nonbiased information for students, parents, and teachers. School psychologists may involve themselves in the development of sexuality education curricula, staff- and parent-training programs to raise awareness of sexual minority youth, and HIV/AIDS education programs that are relevant to students of all sexual orientations. Programs developed for staff and teachers could address important issues such as ways to handle homophobia in the classroom, students who "came out" or disclose their orientation, and the concerns of students who have been labeled "queer" or gay by their peers. Interventions targeted at students need to stress that homosexuality is not pathological and that discrimination against homosexuals is not tolerated at school.

Evaluation of school-based interventions designed to help lesbian, gay, and bisexual youth are much needed. Which programs are most effective? How is success measured? Are services reaching all sexual minority youth or only subpopulations? What obstacles do these programs face and which factors facilitate implementation of new services? All of these questions will need to be answered to build support for interventions and to monitor the quality of services.

School psychologists need to be prepared to counsel teenagers with varied concerns regarding sexual orientation. Some students may come for support and empathy, whereas others may be confused and scared about their orientation. Similarly, school psychologists may also work with parents with a range of beliefs and concerns. Some may come for support, whereas others may object to the sexual orientation of their child. School psychologists can listen to parents and adolescents, provide empathy and support, and serve as a source of accurate information with respect to the development of sexual minority youth. School psychologists can also place adolescents and their parents in contact with community services designed to help sexual minority youth and their families.

Recommendations for Research

Many unanswered questions remain about the social, personal, health, mental health, and educational experiences of sexual minority youth. What are the survival strategies employed by lesbian, gay, and bisexual youth in schools? Is there a relationship between one's identity formation and the school experience? What proportion of sexual minority youth are dropping out of school? In short, what is needed is a better picture of how sexual minority students perceive their educational environment and interact with it in the face of developmental and institutional challenges. Efforts to meet the needs of gay, lesbian, and bisexual students must take into consideration the heterogeneity of this population so that interventions serve as many students as possible.

Research on sexual minority development must continue to provide empirical support for theoretical models. Furthermore, there is still a need for more longitudinal studies and a recognition that growing up as a sexual minority in the 1990s and beyond may be very different than growing up as a sexual minority individual in earlier times (Boxer & Cohler, 1989). If lesbian, gay, and bisexual development does indeed follow a circuitous path, then the study of sexual minority identity development must capture the changes that occur in the lives of homosexual youth over time within specific cultural contexts.

Summary

Sexual minority youth face unique developmental challenges. Raised in a homophobic and heterosexist culture, gay, lesbian, and bisexual youth form identities that may be initially confusing and conflicted. Through a process mediated by rejection and acceptance, committed homosexual and bisexual identities emerge. Nevertheless, abuse and discrimination in the family and at school may compromise the mental health and educational experiences of sexual minority youth. School psychologists can play an important role in meeting the needs of sexual minority youth in schools by providing leadership that promotes supportive attitudes and behaviors, by promoting safe and secure educational environments, and by developing and evaluating interventions.

Recommended Resources

Cass, V. C. (1984). Homosexual identity formation: Testing a theoretical model. *Journal of Sex Research, 20,* 143–167.
Published 5 years after Cass' initial article on homosexual identity formation, this article offers some empirical support not only for specific stages of development but also for the ordering of stages. The article includes an introduction to Cass's six-stage model of development along with the methods used to test the model. Given the need to test theoretical models of sexual minority development, this article provides a framework for developing similar studies.

D'Augelli, A. R., & Hershberger S. L. (1993). Lesbian, gay, and bisexual youth in community settings. *American Journal of Community Psychology, 21,* 421–448.
Data collected from a sample of 194 lesbian, gay, and bisexual youth are presented, yielding information regarding developmental challenges, significant developmental milestones, and suicidality. Attention is given to the need for interventions in community settings (e.g., schools, lesbian/gay/bisexual youth centers). Valuable information regarding self-labeling and coming out is provided.

Hersberger, S. L., & D'Augelli, A. R. (1995). The impact of victimization on the mental health and suicidality of lesbian, gay, and bisexual youths. *Developmental Psychology, 31,* 65–74.
This study examined the relationships between family support, self-acceptance, and mental health of sexual minority youth. The authors provide an excellent account of the extent to which lesbian, gay, and bisexual youth are victimized. Especially helpful in this article are models that explain the mediating effects of family support and self-acceptance on the impact of victimization. Also discussed are the relationships between victimization and suicide.

Patterson, C. J. (1995). Sexual orientation and human development: An overview. *Developmental Psychology, 31,* 3–11.
The impact of sexual orientation on development as well as the impact of development on sexual orientation are both discussed

in this theoretical overview paper. The author reviews contemporary research and theory in the area of sexual orientation and development, followed by a discussion of future research and theory trends. This article provides an excellent introduction to the developmental issues of sexual orientation and is part of a special issue on sexual orientation in Developmental Psychology.

Sears, J. T. (1991). Educators, homosexuality, and homosexual students: Are personal feelings related to professional beliefs? *Journal of Homosexuality, 22,* 29–79.
Sears provides data regarding school counselors' and prospective teachers' attitudes toward sexual minority youth. This article also features data on lesbian, gay, and bisexual youths' perceptions of their school environment. Qualitative interview data provide a rich complement to the attitudinal measures. Sears concludes that although many counselors and teachers believe that there is a need for interventions for sexual minority youth, ignorance and prejudice interfere with the implementation of services.

Troiden, R. R. (1989). The formation of homosexual identities. *Journal of Homosexuality, 17,* 43–73.
This article proposes a four-stage model of homosexual identity development. In his description of the four stages, Troiden integrates a review of theoretical and empirical studies. In addition to detailing the stages of identity formation, Troiden offers broad theoretical considerations regarding the development and application of stage models. Troiden's model is particularly helpful for understanding homosexual identity formation in the context of discrimination and oppression.

Additional Resources for Sexual Minority Youth, Parents, and Educators

Out Youth Toll-Free Helpline: 1-800-96-YOUTH
Daily 5:30–9:30 p.m. (central time)

Cowan, T. D. (1988). *Gay Men and Women Who Enriched the World.* New Canaan, CT: Mulvey Books.

Fairchild, B., & Hayward, N. (1979). *Now That You Know: What Every Parent Should Know About Homosexuality.* Harcourt Brace Jovanovich.

Parents and Friends of Lesbians and Gays (PFLAG), P.O. Box 27605, Washington, DC 20038, (202) 638-4200

Public Education Regarding Sexual Orientation Nationally (P.E.R.S.O.N.), 586 62nd St., Oakland, CA 94609-1245

Sexuality Education and Information Council
of the United States (SIECUS), 130 W. 42nd St., Suite 2500, New York, NY 10036, (212) 819-9770

Hetrick-Martin Institute for the Protection of Lesbian and Gay Youth, 401 West St., New York, NY 10014, (212) 633-8920

Internet Newsgroup: soc.support.youth.gay-lesbian-bi

References

American Psychological Association. (1995). *Policy statements on children, youth, and families.* Washington, DC: Author.

Anderson, D., (1987). Family and peer relations of gay adolescents. *Adolescent Psychiatry, 14,* 162–178.

Anderson, D., (1994). Lesbian and gay adolescents: Social and developmental considerations. *The High School Journal, 77,* 13–19.

Anderson, J. D., (1994). School climate for gay and lesbian students and staff members. *Phi Delta Kappan, 76,* 151–154.

Bailey, J. M., & Pillard, R. C. (1991). A genetic study of male sexual orientation. *Archives of General Psychiatry, 48,* 1089–1096.

Blumenfeld, W. J. (1994). Gay/straight alliances: Transforming pain to pride. *The High School Journal, 77,* 113–121.

Boxer, A. M., & Cohler, B. J. (1989). The life course of gay and lesbian youth: An immodest proposal for the study of lives. *Journal of Homosexuality, 17,* 315–355.

Cass, V. C. (1979). Homosexual identity formation: A theoretical model. *Journal of Homosexuality, 4,* 219–235.

Cass, V. C. (1984). Homosexual identity formation: Testing a theoretical model. *Journal of Sex Research, 20,* 143–167.

Coleman, E. (1989). The development of male prostitution activity among gay and bisexual adolescents. In G. Herdt (Ed.), *Gay and lesbian youth.* New York: Haworth Press.

Coleman, E., & Remafedi, G. (1989). Gay, lesbian, and bisexual adolescents: A critical challenge to counselors. *Journal of Counseling and Development, 68,* 36–40.

D'Augelli, A. R., & Dark, L. J. (1995). Vulnerable populations: Lesbian, gay and bisexual youth. In L. D. Eron, J. Gentry, & P. Schlegel (Eds.), *Reason to hope: A psychosocial perspective on violence and youth* (pp. 177–196). Washington, DC: American Psychological Association.

D'Augelli, A. R., & Hershberger, S. L. (1993). Lesbian, gay, and bisexual youth in community settings. *American Journal of Community Psychology, 21,* 421–448.

D'Augelli, A. R., & Rose, M. L. (1990). Homophobia in a university community: Attitudes and experiences of heterosexual freshmen. *Journal of College Student Development, 31,* 484–491.

Feldman, D. A. (1989). Gay youth and AIDS. *Journal of Homosexuality, 17,* 185–193.

Francoeur, R. T. (1991). *Becoming a sexual person.* New York: Macmillan.

Garland, A. F., & Zigler, E. (1993). Adolescent suicide prevention. *American Psychologist, 48,* 169–182.

Gonsiorek, J. C. (1988). Mental health issues of gay and lesbian adolescents. *Journal of Adolescent Health Care, 9,* 114–122.

Haaga, D. A. (1991). "Homophobia?" *Journal of Social Behavior and Personality, 6,* 171–174.

Haffner, D. W., & de Mauro, D. (1991). Winning the battle: Developing support for sexuality and HIV/AIDS education. New York: Sexuality Education and Information Council of the United States.

Harbeck, K. M. (1994). Invisible no more: Addressing

the needs of gay,lesbian, and bisexual youth and their advocates. *The High School Journal, 77,* 169–176.

Harry, J. (1989). Parental physical abuse and sexual orientation in males. *Archives of Sexual Behavior, 18,* 251–261.

Herdt, G. (1989). Introduction: Gay and lesbian youth, emergent identities, and cultural scenes at home and abroad. *Journal of Homosexuality, 17,* 1–42.

Herek, G. M. (1986). On heterosexual masculinity. *American Behavioral Scientist, 29,* 563–577.

Herek, G. M. (1989). Hate crimes against lesbians and gay men. *American Psychologist, 44,* 948–955.

Hershberger, S. L., & D'Augelli, A. R. (1995). The impact of victimization on the mental health and suicidality of lesbian, gay, and bisexual youths. *Developmental Psychology, 31,* 65–74.

Hetrick, E. S., & Martin, A. D. (1987). Developmental issues and their resolution for gay and lesbian adolescents. *Journal of Homosexuality, 17,* 25–43.

Hooker, E. (1957). The adjustment of the male overt homosexual. *Journal of Projective Techniques, 21,* 18–31.

Kitzinger, C., & Wilkinson, S. (1995). Transitions from heterosexuality to lesbianism: The discursive production of lesbian identities. *Developmental Psychology, 31,* 95–104.

LeVay, S. (1993). *The sexual brain.* Cambridge, MA: MIT Press.

Meyer-Bahlburg, H. F. L., Ehrhardt, A. A., Rosen, L. R., Gruen, R. S., Veridiano, N. P., Vann, F. H., & Neuwalder, H. F. (1995). Prenatal estrogens and the development of homosexual orientation. *Developmental Psychology, 31,* 12–21.

Morrow, D. F. (1993). Social work with gay and lesbian adolescents. *Social Work, 38,* 655–660.

Parker, D. A., & De Cecco, J. P. (1995). Sexual expression: A global perspective. *Journal of Homosexuality, 28,* 427–430.

Paroski, P. A. (1987). Health care delivery and the concerns of gay and lesbian adolescents. *Journal of Adolescent Health Care, 8,* 188–192.

Patterson, C. J. (1995). Sexual orientation and human development: An overview. *Developmental Psychology, 31,* 3–11.

Pilkington, N. W., & D'Augelli, A. R. (1995). Victimization of lesbian, gay, and bisexual youth in community settings. *Journal of Community Psychology, 23,* 33–55.

Price, J. H., & Telljohann, S. K. (1991). School counselors' perceptions of adolescent homosexuals. *Journal of School Health, 61,* 433–438.

Proctor, C. D.. (1994). Risk factors for suicide among gay, lesbian, and bisexual youths. *Social Work, 39,* 504–513.

Reiss, B. F. (1980). Psychological tests in homosexuality. In J. Marmor (Ed.), *Homosexual behavior* (pp. 00–00). New York: Basic Books.

Savin-Williams, R. C. (1990). *Gay and lesbian youth: Expressions of identity.* New York: Hemisphere.

Schneider, M., & Tremble, B. (1985). Gay or straight? Working with the confused adolescent. *Journal of Social Work and Human Sexuality, 4,* 71–83.

Schneider, S. G., Farberow, N. L., & Kruks, G. N. (1989). Suicidal behavior in adolescent and young adult gay men. *Suicide and Life-Threatening Behavior, 19,* 381–394.

Sears, J. T. (1991). Educators, homosexuality, and homosexual students: Are personal feelings related to professional beliefs? *Journal of Homosexuality, 22,* 29–79.

Sears, J. T. (1992). Dilemmas and possibilities of sexuality education: Reproducing the body politic. In J.T. Sears (Ed.), *Sexuality and the curriculum: The politics and practices of sexuality education.* New York: Teachers College Press.

Strommen, E. F. (1989). "You're a What?": Family members reactions to the disclosure of homosexuality. *Journal of Homosexuality, 18,* 37–58.

Sullivan, T. R. (1994). Obstacles to effective child welfare service with gay and lesbian youths. *Child Welfare, 73,* 291–304.

Taylor, N. (1994). Gay and lesbian youth: Challenging the policy of denial. in T. DeCrescenzo (Ed.), *Helping gay and lesbian youth.* Binghamton, NY: Harrington Park Press.

Treadway, L., & Yoakam, J. (1992). Creating a safer school environment for lesbian and gay students. *Journal of School Health, 62,* 352–357.

Troiden, R. R. (1989). The formation of homosexual identities. *Journal of Homosexuality, 17,* 43–73.

Uribe, V., & Harbeck, K. M. (1991). Addressing the needs of lesbian, gay, and bisexual youth: The origins of PROJECT 10 and school-based intervention. *Journal of Homosexuality, 22,* 9–28.

Williams, K. L., Doyle, M. S., Taylor, B. A., & Ferguson, G. (1992). Addressing sexual orientation in a public high school. *Journal of School Health, 62,* 154–156.

Zera, D. (1992). Coming of age in a heterosexist world: The development of gay and lesbian adolescents. *Adolescence, 27,* 849–854.

70

HIV and AIDS

Steven Landau
Christy Mangione
John B. Pryor
Illinois State University

Background and Development

As of June 1995, nearly one-half million Americans have been reported with AIDS (Centers for Disease Control and Prevention [CDC], 1995). Since the onset of this epidemic, more Americans have died from AIDS than three times the death toll in the Vietnam War. There is no cure, only prevention and treatments to help alleviate the symptoms.

Because victims of HIV/AIDS include children and adolescents, the presence of infected children in the classroom is an issue of growing concern. Although pediatric HIV (i.e., HIV in patients under the age of 13 years) represents only 1.3% of all known cases in the United States (CDC, 1995), school psychologists should become knowledgeable in HIV-related matters for a variety of reasons. First, although there is no cure, treatment drugs continue to improve, thereby resulting in an increasing number of children living to reach school age (Palfrey et al., 1994). Second, rates of HIV infection among children are growing at an alarming rate. For example, the 12-month period of July 1994 to June 1995 witnessed almost 1,000 new cases (CDC, 1995). In fact, infants born to infected mothers represent one of the fastest growing groups testing positive for HIV (CDC, 1995).

In addition, many epidemiologists argue that the current prevalence estimate of HIV is grossly understated, and it is likely that many cases of adolescent infection are undetected. In fact, due to the modal incubation period of 9 1/2 years between HIV infection and symptomatic AIDS, one should conclude that cases of clinical AIDS in young adults resulted from exposure during adolescence, a time when most of these individuals were still in school. Third, recent (and alarming) research demonstrates that stressors experienced by the child will have adverse affects on the medical course of pediatric HIV (Bose, Moss, Brouwers, Pizzo, & Lorion, 1994). Thus, mental health professionals—and school psychologists in particular—must play a role regarding the child's psychological adjustment. Supportive efforts to protect the child with HIV from additional stress and trauma may enhance longevity.

Finally, AIDS affects entire families. Even if a school-age child does not present with the disease, children who have a family member with AIDS may be subjected to social stigma and personal strain (Pryor & Reeder, 1993). By the year 2000, maternal deaths caused by HIV and AIDS will have orphaned over 80,000 children and adolescents in the United States (Michaels & Levine, 1992). Thus, HIV/AIDS is a growing concern in the school setting. As such, school psychologists need to become familiar with issues surrounding HIV infection and the psychoeducational and psychosocial sequelae of the disease in order to meet the growing needs of involved children and their families.

Overview of HIV/AIDS

Many laypersons are confused about the different, progressive medical milestones associated with this disease. A patient's medical status, and the attending classification, changes as degree of impairment changes. *HIV infection* refers to infection with human immunodeficiency virus, regardless of the presence of overt illness or clinical manifestations. *HIV-related disease* refers to the presence of HIV infection and the presence of clinical manifestations which may or may not be life threatening. *Acquired immunodeficiency syndrome* (AIDS) represents essentially the later stages of HIV disease. The HIV virus attacks and ultimately compromises a person's immune system. Persons with AIDS are vulnerable to a variety of opportunistic diseases which rarely infect people with healthy immune systems. The onslaught of such opportunistic illnesses in a weakened immune system eventually results in death for the person with AIDS (Weiss, 1993). Clinical diagnosis of AIDS hinges in part upon the presence of these opportunistic infections. Progression through these stages is consistent across patients, but timing may differ.

Transmission of HIV

There are three major ways by which the HIV virus is transmitted: (a) perinatally from an infected mother, (b) from exposure to infected blood or blood products, and (c) from unprotected sex with an infected person. Approximately 90% of infected children have acquired HIV through perinatal transmission (CDC, 1995). Modes of perinatal transmission include intrauterine or transplacental (e.g., during early or late pregnancy), intrapartum (e.g., at delivery), and postpartum (e.g., through breast feeding; Levenson & Mellins, 1992). The HIV virus also has been isolated in amniotic fluid.

All babies born of HIV-infected mothers carry maternal antibodies to HIV; however, only about one-third are actually infected with the virus. Distinct groups exist representing the spectrum of HIV disease in infants (CDC, 1994). Infants born to known-infected mothers are classified in a transitional category and not clinically confirmed as to their HIV status. These infants will test positive to HIV antibody tests because they carry maternal antibodies until 15 months of age. At this time, they will lose the passively acquired maternal antibodies. Approximately 70% of these infants will test negative when their own antibodies are tested. The classification for these infants is called *seroreverters*. If the infant's antibodies continue to test positive for the HIV infection, four classifications are possible: Category N (Not Symptomatic) is used to classify those infants testing positive who will remain relatively healthy and asymptomatic for a number of years. However, when an infant or child becomes symptomatic (e.g., progressive neurological disease, pneumonia) a classification of Category A (Mildly Symptomatic), B (Moderately Symptomatic), or C (Severely Symptomatic) is used.

Exposure to contaminated blood is possible through transfusions, the use of tainted clotting agents in treating hemophilia, and accidental needle pricks encountered by medical personnel. Approximately 10% of infected children acquired HIV through blood transfusions or hemophilia/coagulation disorder (CDC, 1995). Fortunately, systematic screening of the blood supply in the United States has greatly reduced the number of infections related to transfusions and the use of clotting agents. In addition, the institution of CDC (1985) universal precautions has significantly reduced the infection risk to medical personnel.

In adolescents and adults, the primary means of transmission is still unprotected sex with an infected person. The HIV virus may be present in either the semen or vaginal secretions of an infected person. Sexual activity in which a partner comes in contact with either of these fluids runs a risk for HIV transmission. Most cases (i.e., 33%) of adolescent sexual transmission in boys 13 to 19 years of age has been attributed to a homosexual contact risk factor, with 3% due to heterosexual contact. In con-

trast, heterosexual risk factors accounted for 53% of HIV cases in adolescent females (CDC, 1995).

An alternate mode of transmission in children is through sexual abuse. The prevalence rates are unclear and more research is needed to establish these rates. One study examined the histories of 96 HIV-infected children and found that sexual abuse was the source of transmission for 4, and possibly an additional 6, children (Gutman et al., 1991).

HIV is not spread through casual contact (Task Force on Pediatric AIDS, 1988). In studies of hundreds of households where family members have lived with and cared for AIDS patients (even when it was not known that the person was infected with HIV), there is no known case of transmission through casual contact, including circumstances where kitchen and bathroom facilities, meals, eating and drinking utensils, and even toothbrushes were shared repeatedly for prolonged periods of time (CDC, 1993). There are no reports that HIV has been casually transmitted in other social situations such as schools and day-care settings (Task Force on Pediatric AIDS, 1988).

Epidemiology of HIV/AIDS

One explanation for the increasing prevalence of AIDS has to do with a changing definition. The National Centers for Disease Control and Prevention (CDC, 1993) have revised the defining characteristics of AIDS three times: in 1985, 1987, and 1992. These revisions have broadened the range of AIDS-indicator diseases and conditions and have used HIV diagnostic tests to improve the sensitivity and specificity of the definition. In June 1995, the CDC reported a cumulative total of 9,238 cases of AIDS in persons under the age of 20 in the United States. Most of these were children under the age of five. The vast majority of preschool children were infected perinatally by their mothers. Moving from childhood to adolescence, one finds a different characteristic pattern of infection. For example, for adolescents aged 13 to 19, 47% of the males and 69% of the females were infected via intravenous drug use, sexual contact, or both. Minority children and adolescents have been hardest hit by this epidemic. More than 80% of pediatric AIDS cases have been among African-American or Hispanic youth, with African-Americans accounting for 57% of all cases (CDC, 1995).

Regional patterns with respect to the annual rate of AIDS per 100,000 population show that the Northeast and Southeast regions of the U.S. are the epicenters of the epidemic, with California reporting a very high rate as well (CDC, 1995). In terms of pediatric cases reported through June 1995, New York, New Jersey, and Florida had the highest prevalence rates (CDC, 1995). Metropolitan areas with a population of 500,000 or more present a much higher AIDS rate than less densely populated areas. This is consistent with findings that the cluster of socioeconomic problems related to inner-city living is causally related to eventual HIV infection through drug taking and unprotected sexual intercourse (National Commission on AIDS, 1994).

Problems and Implications

Neurological Sequelæ

In addition to its effects upon the immune system, the HIV virus has been found to affect the nervous system directly (Fletcher et al., 1991; Navia, Cho, Petito, & Price, 1986). The dementia aspect of AIDS (e.g., brain atrophy, encephalopathy) is believed to be separate from the immunodeficiency aspects and may be caused by direct infection of the brain with HIV. Indicators of neurological involvement in adults include general mental slowness, impaired concentration, mild memory loss, and motor skills impairment (e.g., progressive loss of balance, leg weakness). Younger children, particularly those infected perinatally, are especially susceptible to neurological damage from HIV infection because their nervous systems are still developing (Epstein, Sharer, & Goudsmit, 1988). Thus, in adult cases, the infection is compromising a fully developed, intact nervous system, while in pediatric cases, brain development is interrupted by HIV infection. While the exact cause of neurodevelopmental dysfunction is unknown, some hypotheses have been suggested including the release of neurotoxins and/or demyelinization of glial cells (Cohen, Papola, & Alvarez, 1994). Neurological damage is one of the most common causes of death in children with AIDS (CDC, 1995). The HIV virus appears to have a profound effect upon brain development in pediatric cases and, subsequently, upon the attainment of motor, intellectual, and developmental milestones (Cohen et al., 1994).

In children with HIV, CT scans show cerebral atrophy, enlarged ventricles, and microcephaly, which are related to low intelligence or retardation. Some children may show cerebral-palsy-like conditions due to pyramidal tract dysfunction (Levenson & Mellins, 1992). In addition, the infection may cause visual and auditory short-term memory difficulties as well as attentional deficits (Butler, Hittelman, & Hauger, 1991).

Most children with pediatric HIV show delays in motor milestones plus brain impairment leading to language disorders and problems in spatial and mathematical abilities. In its progressed state, the disease causes cognitive delays and specific lesions at various sites in the brain (Levenson & Mellins, 1992). As a consequence, the HIV-infected child who lives to reach school age is likely to have a variety of academic problems.

Research indicates that treatment with AZT (Aziodothymidine) may alleviate some of the AIDS dementia consequences found in children (Seachrist, 1995; Wood, 1995). Also, drug trials have found that other antiretroviral drugs, such as didanosine (ddI), in combination with AZT are more effective than AZT alone, although success depended on the stage and progression of the disease (Stephenson, 1995; Wood, 1995). The most common adverse effects of AZT therapy include anemia, leukopenia, severe headaches, nausea and vomiting, skin rashes, insomnia, and hyperpigmentation of nails (Wood, 1995).

Psychosocial Sequelæ

In addition to cognitive difficulties, children with HIV present with higher rates of depression and anxiety (Spiegel & Mayers, 1991). They are more likely to have problems with separation-individuation and must deal with the effects of living with a chronic illness. These effects include fear of death, loss of abilities, and social stigma. These children must confront frequent hospital visits that result in disruptions in routine and poor school attendance. In addition, they are faced with painful medical treatments and side effects of medications (Crandles & Jean, 1990).

Common behavior problems experienced by HIV-infected children include attention deficits, sometimes associated with hyperactivity (Armstrong, Seidel, & Swales, 1993). Some HIV-infected children have been labeled "autistic-like" because they present severe withdrawal behaviors (Seidel, 1991). It is not clear whether these behavioral outcomes are due to the disease itself or to efforts at coping with the disease plus other environmental stressors commonly experienced by HIV-infected children.

Confounding this discussion of the consequences of HIV is the fact that HIV-infected children are typically from ethnic minorities, inner cities, and poverty. These factors alone put a child at risk for social and economic hardship. In addition, HIV-infected infants are more likely to have been exposed to deficient prenatal and postnatal care and are at greater risk for in-utero exposure to heroin, cocaine, alcohol, and nicotine (Landau, Pryor, Haefli, 1995). Each of these factors could impair the development of the child. Thus, the deleterious consequences uniquely attributable to HIV infection are yet to be established; more research is clearly needed to clarify this issue.

HIV/AIDS Stigma and Disclosure

A diagnosis of HIV/AIDS, unlike most other terminal diseases, carries with it intense negative reactions and fear. As such, a unique problem in dealing with HIV/AIDS in the school is the additional concern of the stigma associated with HIV-infection. For example, negative attitudes espoused by others is known to have a deleterious effect on the child with HIV (Bose et al., 1994), and there are unsettling data to suggest that these attitudes mitigate any therapeutic effects derived from an AIDS patient's support network (Collins, in press). As such, there are costly consequences that accrue from the blame and social stigma associated with HIV/AIDS (Pryor, Reeder, & Landau, 1996).

The majority of research done in the area of AIDS stigma involves adult attitudes toward adult infection. More research is needed to assess the reaction among children to an HIV-infected child. Generally, people fear coming in close proximity with a diagnosed person, and this fear will affect the number and quality of interpersonal exchanges (Mooney, Cohn, & Swift, 1992). In addition, research has shown that victim-blaming is associated with an HIV diagnosis; thus, people may hold the belief that infected persons get what they deserve (Anderson, 1992). With increased AIDS education programs in school, young adolescents are becoming more knowledgeable about AIDS-related matters (Brown & Fritz, 1988). However, many misconceptions still persist related to developmental differences in understanding this information. For example, children may be able to explain that people get AIDS through sex, but further probing may reveal many different age-related explanations of how and why (Walsh & Bibace, 1991).

Stigmatization of children with HIV/AIDS can lead to social isolation when peers perceive them as different or tainted (Korniewicz, O'Brien, & Larson, 1990). This social isolation will in turn affect the child's self-concept and self-esteem. A 1991 study by Kann et al., which involved a national survey of 9th- through 12th-grade students, is emblematic of a hostile social perspective: Although 91% of the students believed they could not be infected by being in the same class with an HIV-infected student, only one-half felt that students with HIV should be allowed to attend their school, and only 56% were willing to be in class with an HIV-infected student. Another study that assessed AIDS concerns in fourth- through eighth-grade students reported that students knew they should not blame the peer for having AIDS but privately thought the HIV-infected student could have prevented the infection (Whalen, Henker, Burgess, & O'Neil, 1995). This is especially unsettling as it is clear that pediatric HIV infection does not occur through risk-taking behavior on the child's part. Finally, there are recent adolescent data that further indicate the cost of HIV/AIDS stigma. Westerman and Davidson (1994) found that anti-gay prejudice predicted teenagers' sense of invulnerability to HIV infection. In a study of 80 high school students, more intense homophobic attitudes were related to reduced likelihood of condom use during sex and reduced behavioral intentions to be discriminating when selecting a sexual partner. Thus, a negative attitude toward gay men can be quite costly (i.e., it increases one's risk of HIV infection).

Traditional means of conceptualizing the psychosocial impact of HIV/AIDS focus upon the infected individual. However, it is important to realize that the stigma of HIV/AIDS also may affect uninfected children living in the context of AIDS (Fair, Spencer, Weiner, & Riekert, 1995). Having a parent or other family member with HIV/AIDS may result in shame, guilt, or even suicide ideation (Aronson, 1995). One reason for these feelings may be the negative social reactions these children experience from peers. Research in our laboratories at Illinois State University has found that children react negatively to the prospect of interacting with an uninfected child whose sibling has HIV/AIDS. Younger children (Grades 1 and 2 in our sample) were generally more negative in their reactions than children in Grades 4 through 11 (Pryor & Landau, 1994). While HIV is generally spread though sexual contact, contact with contaminated blood, or perinatally, the stigma of HIV may spread through kinship lines and other means of social affiliation (Pryor & Reeder, 1993). The social reactions of both children and adults to possible contact with HIV/AIDS-infected persons seem to reflect magical contagion beliefs: The taint or stigma of the disease is presumed to be transmitted to *affiliated* persons and may, as a consequence, be potentially transmitted to others (Rozin, Markwith, & Nemeroff, 1992).

Because half of all HIV-infected children live to reach school age (Palfrey et al., 1994), many practitioners will be confronted by pediatric HIV. A major issue in the schools is the confidentiality of a child's HIV status. The most commonly recommended policy is that only those who have a legitimate need to know of a child's HIV-status should be informed (Fraser, 1989). Federal and state laws regulate the disclosure of HIV status (see Legal Issues later in this chapter). Often, disclosure of HIV status may reveal information about parental drug use, sexual orientation, and fidelity that can affect the entire family system (Levenson & Mellins, 1992). Recent clinical findings suggest that it may be beneficial for children of normal cognitive development to know about their diagnoses and be able to discuss them with trusted adults (Lipson, 1994). However, a child's knowledge of his or her own HIV status makes self-disclosure a likely consequence. Thus, regardless of the school's policy on disclosure, school personnel must be prepared to handle the rapid transmission of HIV rumors across the school community. However a school chooses to handle confidentiality issues, education of school personnel about physical, psychosocial, and developmental aspects of HIV is strongly advocated (e.g., Haiken, Hernandez, Mintz, & Boland, 1991; Landau et al., 1995).

Alternative Actions

Because of the multitude of issues and concerns that emanate from HIV-related cases, the school psychologist will be only one among many professionals who must address the complex needs of an HIV-infected child. These needs transcend many domains of functioning and will challenge the professional acumen of multiple disciplines. As such, it has become increasingly evident that schools can no longer respond to the urgencies of society simply by focusing on academics; instead, they must adjust the educational mission to meet the changing needs of the community. This perspective, as well as increased political and social pressure for health care reform, suggests that the institution of public education must also address the general health of its students *and* their family members (DeMers, 1995). Although several models exist that portray different interpretations of this mission (see Carlson, Paavola, & Talley, 1995, for a review), each is predicated on the notion that the community has failed some of its constituents regarding medical or mental health services or both. This problem is particularly acute in disadvantaged urban centers where the risk-taking behaviors leading to HIV infection are concentrated. Thus, it is argued that school services must compensate for insufficient community resources, thereby becoming "full-service schools" (Dryfoos, 1994).

One feature of the full-service school involves delivery of school-based or school-linked medical and mental health services. According to Tharinger (1995), these services should encompass the assessment, identification, and treatment of health-related conditions (also including a concentration on psychological aspects of health disorders and a focus on high-risk behaviors). Second, schools should develop conscious health education and promotion programs designed to reduce students' risk status for preventable medical and mental health disorders. Finally, schools should concentrate efforts to enhance educational outcomes and decrease the incidence of school failure. To accomplish these objectives, collaboration between schools and communities, especially regarding the delivery of health care, must be promoted (Tharinger, 1995). In those instances of deficient community resources, it is feasible that the community health clinic be situated on a school campus. Students tend to be the primary beneficiary, but these school-based health services are also extended to family members, preschool-age siblings of enrolled students, and even school personnel (Tharinger, 1995). By so doing, these full service schools represent a return to the school's historic role as community center.

In this context, some school psychologists will be encouraged to pursue a new and exciting specialty that is evolving to meet the needs of students whose school-based adaptation is compromised by medical phenomena. As suggested by Power, DuPaul, Shapiro, and Parrish (1995), *pediatric school psychologists* will

1. Advocate for the educational needs of children with medical conditions.

2. Conduct evaluations of the school's ability to implement adaptations to meet the needs of pediatrically involved students.
3. Serve as liaison and promote effective communication between school and pediatric professional communities.
4. Influence educators to design curricular programs that promote health among all students.

See Power et al., 1995, for a detailed discussion of these roles.

These various activities indicate the multiple ways that a school psychologist can contribute to school-based efforts to meet the needs of children with medical problems. However, there are some particularly salient issues when confronting pediatric HIV in the classroom. These include knowledge of legal issues, safety precautions, psychoeducational consequences of AIDS, and strategies to address the bereavement experience in school. In addition, school psychologists must be able to contribute to the development of a curricular response to the AIDS epidemic. These issues will be briefly discussed next; greater detail is presented in Landau et al. (1995).

Legal Issues

Most states have developed policies concerning the HIV-infected child's legal right of access to unimpeded education in the public school setting (Katsiyannis, 1992). Because of the negative reactions and stigma associated with HIV/AIDS, confidentiality and right of privacy become central issues. The Education for All Handicapped Children Act (EHA) of 1975, as well as the 1991 Individuals with Disabilities Act (IDEA) and the Family Education Rights and Privacy Act require that consent be given before disclosure of a student's HIV condition. These laws consider disclosure necessary only when justified by public health or other legitimate reasons. Thus, it may be appropriate for the principal and/or superintendent exclusively to know the status of an infected student.

Disclosure to other individuals and agencies can have both positive and negative consequences. It is possible that disclosure could benefit the infected child by increasing resources available to the family and providing greater social support. However, it could also lead to discrimination (Agency for Health Care Policy and Research [AHCPR], 1994). Discriminatory practices affecting the family include loss of housing, employment, and child custody as well as reduced health benefits and social ostracism (AHCPR, 1994). The disclosure of a person's HIV status carries with it the potential for negative reactions from other children and parents (Pryor & Reeder, 1993). Efforts to educate parents, students, and school staff about HIV/AIDS can help to reduce discrimination and lead to more humane practices (Schmitt & Schmitt, 1990). In addition, because the majority of pediatric HIV cases are the result of parental drug use and/or high-risk sexual activity, public knowledge of a child's serostatus could have implications for the parents' reputation in the community (Landau et al., 1995). Thus, disclosure is a difficult issue for families of HIV-infected children to face. Health care providers, school psychologists, and administrators should help families with issues of confidentiality and ensure that appropriate support is available for the family during this process.

Safety Precautions

Regardless of the disclosed presence of an HIV-infected student, adherence to the Centers for Disease Control's universal precautions (CDC, 1987, 1988) and appropriate training in these guidelines should be an important component of teacher education. Students and teachers should be made aware of modes of HIV transmission, and the myths surrounding this issue should be dispelled. Because commonly spread viruses such as colds and influenza can have serious impact on the weakened immune system of an HIV-infected child, increased attention to good hygienic practices is appropriate (CDC, 1985). All schools should adopt policies regarding the handling of blood regardless of known attendance of an HIV-infected student.

Psychoeducational Issues

Pediatric HIV cases will be a challenge for school personnel because of the individual differences in children with HIV-related CNS disease and because the pattern of functioning can change within individual children across time (Meyers, 1994). A longitudinal perspective is necessary to identify changes due to deteriorating CNS functioning, and intervention programs should be flexible to account for changes in cognitive functioning across time (Wolters, Brouwers, & Moss, 1995). It should be noted, however, that impairment resulting from HIV infection is not unique to this disease. Therefore, regardless of the cause of impairment, children can benefit from existing early intervention and special education services for children with developmental disabilities (Armstrong et al., 1993). Most HIV-infected children will be eligible for special education and related services under Section 504 due to physical and cognitive impairment as well as discrimination and ostracism related to the perceived contagiousness of the disease (Katsiyannis, 1992).

Because neuropsychological disabilities may be global or specific in nature, a thorough neurodevelopmental assessment is important to determine the exact areas of impaired functioning. These children will likely have multifaceted needs that require interdisciplinary services. Interdisciplinary teams should assess multiple areas known to be affected by HIV, such as cognitive functioning, language, perceptual-motor abilities, memory, and adaptive behavior (Wolters et al., 1995). If an HIV-infected child is developmentally delayed, it may be necessary to use tests standardized on younger children to obtain age-equivalent scores and to identify areas of strength and weakness (Wolters et al., 1995). A number of disciplines should be involved in assessments including psychology, physical therapy, occupational therapy, speech pathology, special education, social work, and nursing. In addition, some psychological and neurodevelopmental evaluations may be done through a medical setting.

With parental consent, results of evaluations should be shared across the medical and school settings (Wolters et al., 1995). Assessments should be family centered, including a family and developmental history, especially given the prevalence of poverty and drug use among mothers of pediatric HIV children (Brouwers, Belman, & Epstein, 1991). Interdisciplinary teams should assess for special family needs related to stress, financial hardships, respite care, and infection of other family members (Wolters et al., 1995). The reader is encouraged to consult Wolters et al. (1995) for further details regarding an excellent, pediatric-HIV, and psychoeducational-assessment protocol.

It is important to realize that HIV-infected children will differ significantly from HIV-infected adolescents in many ways, including the respective mode of virus exposure, the locus of impairment, the severity of the illness, and school-based interventions that are required. Given the limitations of current medical treatment, it is likely that HIV-infected children who live to reach school age will enter school with an advanced state of HIV disease. In these cases, cognitive and physical complications may already compromise the child's ability to function in school. Thus, school psychologists must be able to deal with psychoeducational as well as psychosocial sequelæ of AIDS and be prepared to ultimately address the bereavement experience faced by family members, classmates, and school personnel.

In contrast, the HIV-positive adolescent was most likely exposed through unprotected sexual activity or intravenous (IV) drug use. Due to the virus's typical 10-year post-exposure latency period, these infected adolescents will remain asymptomatic *and undetected* throughout their tenure in the school setting. Indeed, most of these students will not become aware of their seropositive status until sometime later in adulthood. As a consequence, the school's preeminent response to the AIDS epidemic in junior and senior high school should involve HIV prevention programs dispensed at all grade levels, even before students reach the age of potential sexual activity. In addition, the systematic implementation of universal precautions in all school settings is critical.

Bereavement Issues

As previously stated, approximately 50% of pediatric HIV cases will succumb to the illness before reaching school age. Those who do endure long enough to attend school will present to others the portentous indicators of a terminal illness. Because the course of HIV is progressive, the illness will involve a gradual deterioration over time; the child will grow weaker and weaker and eventually depart school for hospital-based care. Not only will schools need to address school-based bereavement resulting from the death of a student, they may also have to confront AIDS-related deaths of teachers and other school staff, as well as family members of school children. Thus, school-based bereavement needs cut across multiple populations.

There are two approaches to bereavement counseling. One offers support to the individual exposed to a specific death, while the other is aimed at educating every student in a preventative mental health capacity (Schonfeld, 1989). The 1980s saw a proliferation of literature concerning death education. This literature included information on children's developmental differences in understanding death and provided general and specific helping behaviors to use in the schools (e.g., Reeves & Knowles, 1981). For example, it was suggested that adults in school explore their own attitudes toward death before addressing the concerns of children. Even though many of the prescriptions inherent in this literature have high intuitive appeal, and many are borrowed from best-practice schemes in the counseling setting, few methodologically sound outcome-evaluation studies have examined these procedures. Instead, efficacy information is essentially limited to case study testimonials (see the chapter on grief, this volume, for additional discussion of grief and bereavement issues). In addition, the scientific literature has yet to describe school-based bereavement programs that specifically address pediatric HIV.

As a consequence, information regarding AIDS-related bereavement in school is scarce. The majority of published AIDS bereavement studies focus on the adult, gay male population and the caregivers of persons with AIDS. Existing bereavement studies pertaining to children focus on the family system, including such issues as survivor isolation, multiple infection within the family, and dissolution of the home (Bergeron & Handley, 1992).

One could consult the suicide postvention literature for information on bereavement in the school setting (see the chapter on suicide, this volume). This literature generally advocates consultation by a mental health professional after a suicide event in the school (Mauk, Gibson, & Rodgers, 1994; Range, 1993; Wenckstern & Leenaars, 1993). Goals of the postvention include improving the emotional environment of the school, reducing the likelihood of imitation, extending services, providing in-service for teachers to address crisis situations, and al-leviating guilt from those who feel they might have prevented the suicide (Mauk et al., 1994; Range, 1993).

An obvious limitation of applying this body of literature to AIDS-related cases results from its focus on the catastrophic nature of the suicidal event and the likelihood of students imitating suicidal behavior. In addition, the stigma associated with AIDS-related deaths is certainly not addressed. Finally, this research predominantly involves a high-school population. Younger school-age children have a much different understanding of death, different death concerns, and, as a consequence, a different bereavement experience. Epidemiological data strongly indicate that it is the young child who would most likely be exposed to the AIDS-related death of a classmate.

The idea of consultation and coordination by staff and administration after a death in the school can be applied to AIDS-related cases. The death of a student affects the entire school to some extent. If school staff talk to each other before talking to the students, they may feel more support in their own grieving. As a team, principal, teachers, and psychologists can work out a plan of action for presenting the news to students (Wenckstern & Leenaars, 1993). AIDS-related bereavement issues in the school will be an increasingly important concern to address as medical treatments improve for HIV-infected students. However, because of the growing incidence of pediatric problems, sound outcome-evaluation investigations need to undertaken before a best-practice paradigm can be prescribed.

It is important for school psychologists to remember that, according to the current demographic and epidemiological data, the most likely AIDS-related bereavement scenario will involve a healthy child who loses a family member. There are many ways in which this child's bereavement experience is no different than if a parent or older sibling was lost to any other terminal disease. Thus, the extant child-focused bereavement literature may provide guidance to the professional trying to meet the needs of students affected by this loss.

However, there are some important, if not unique, attributes of AIDS-related bereavement that diminish the utility of this literature. According to Fair et al. (1995), these issues include the likelihood of losing multiple family members to AIDS due to a family concentration of risk-taking behaviors. Second, these children may not be able to grieve openly in school because of the stigma attached to AIDS; surviving family members may exert pressure to behave in a secretive manner. Also, many of these bereaved children assume, albeit erroneously, they are now more vulnerable to HIV infection. Finally, disintegration of the family is not uncommon: AIDS not only creates many orphans, it is the cause of other major stressors, including a move to the residence of extended family members and legal battles regarding custody. School psychologists must keep in mind that, prior to the AIDS-related loss of a parent, these children not only witnessed the conspicuous deterioration of a loved one but, in many cases, also had to assume the role of caregiver to a dying parent.

HIV/AIDS Prevention

Schools are an obvious place to reach the majority of young people to provide information and prevention strategies regarding HIV infection. While some may question whether this type of program falls in the realm of school responsibility, others believe that, as a major social institution, schools cannot afford to ignore the increasing impact of the AIDS epidemic on children and adolescents (Robenstine, 1995). The National Association of State Boards of Education (NASBE) provides a position statement that schools cannot be successful in their primary mission of educating children if they fail to address social and health problems that interfere with current and future student learning (National Commission on AIDS, 1994).

Crocker et al. (1994) provide best-practice guidelines for supporting children with HIV infection in school. They advocate having an advisory committee on HIV-related issues and HIV infection, staff education and in-service training, universal precautions relating to blood-borne infections, and education relating to the prevention of HIV infection for all students in grades K-12 (Crocker et al., 1994). Currently, the majority of AIDS education programs focus on adolescents in higher grade levels (Landau et al., 1995). It is possible to provide appropriate AIDS education to all grade levels while being sensitive to developmental differences across the ages. Clearly, implementing prevention programs in earlier grades can help to prevent high-risk behavior patterns before they become firmly established and more difficult to change (American Academy of Pediatrics Committee on Adolescents, 1990).

Walsh and Bibace (1990) provide guidelines for a developmentally based AIDS education program. Education in the younger grades should focus on reassurance that young children do not usually get AIDS. Young children generally do not have the ability to comprehend cause and effect relationships; thus, it makes little sense to explain specific causes of AIDS or specific prevention strategies. Intermediate grade children are beginning to distinguish between cause and effect; therefore, children in this age group might respond that "sex causes AIDS," but this understanding will likely be concrete and non-specific. Because these children are just beginning to understand the cause-effect relationship between certain at-risk behaviors and HIV infection, it is best to focus on general healthy lifestyle habits and general prevention of illness. Older children will benefit from more detailed explanations of HIV transmission and prevention. These children understand that HIV infection can be prevented and that certain high-risk behaviors increase the proba-

bility of HIV infection. All age groups should have access to a resource professional in the school who can address specific AIDS-related questions and concerns (Walsh & Bibace, 1990).

Research has found that effective HIV prevention programs are designed around the peer group and its influence (DiClemente, 1993; National Commission on AIDS, 1994; Robenstine, 1995). Peer educators have been an effective tool for providing information, modeling preventive behaviors, and socially validating behavior change (Robenstine, 1995). Other effective activities have included theatrical presentations written and performed by students who discuss risk for HIV infection, health fairs with presentation about HIV/AIDS, presentations by young people who are infected with HIV, discussion sessions on sexual and social issues, and health columns in the school paper (Kirby, 1992). In addition, Robenstine (1995) advocates adapting traditional programs to be more culturally sensitive, especially to African-American youth who are disproportionately affected by the AIDS epidemic. Such programs should reflect African-American cultural style by including African-American literature, storytelling, music, role-playing, group learning, and games.

Providing information to children and adolescents is easy, but invoking behavior change is more difficult. Students must practice critical-thinking and decision-making skills and must also be encouraged to explore their values (National Commission on AIDS, 1994). School personnel can support behavioral change by recognizing and supporting all efforts toward change. By providing ongoing support and making resources accessible, school personnel can focus on the positive benefits of behavior change.

Perhaps the most important confound in understanding the effectiveness of adolescent-focused HIV prevention programs is the multitude of problems that compromise the likelihood of behavior change. When consideration is given to the social and economic contexts of those young people at greatest risk for infection with HIV, it is not surprising that messages to "just say no" or "use contraceptives" are doomed to fail (Elders, 1994). Many of these teenagers are raised in poverty, lack adequate medical care and social support, and may feel helpless in their efforts to create change for the future. In this context, HIV infection is only one symptom of a failing social and economic system. Therefore, if HIV infection is to be prevented, the larger social and economic issues must be addressed as well. The National Commission on AIDS (1994) supports HIV education in the context of a comprehensive health curriculum.

Summary

It is critical that schools and school psychologists be poised to respond to the educational and psychosocial problems evoked by HIV/AIDS. Epidemiological data indicate a growing enrollment of HIV-infected students and a greater number of bereaving children. School psychologists must address numerous contentious HIV-related issues, including disclosure of HIV status, stigma associated with HIV/AIDS and its psychosocial effects on the infected child, psychoeducational challenges that confront HIV-infected students, the death of family members with AIDS, and the implementation of prevention programs to educate students about behaviors that place them at risk for HIV infection.

Authors Note

The preparation of this work was supported, in part, by a grant from the Ronald McDonald's Children's Charities awarded to the first and third authors.

Address all correspondence to Steven Landau, Ph.D., Department of Psychology, Campus Box 4620, Illinois State University, Normal, IL 61790-4620. (E-mail: selandau@rs6000.cmp.ilstu.edu)

Recommended Resources

For Professionals

The reader is strongly encouraged to consult the HIV web site maintained by *The Journal of the American Medical Association* (JAMA) at the following address: <http://www.ama-assn.org/special/hiv/hivhome.htm> As of this writing, this site may be the most up-to-date source of information available to professionals and laypersons alike and is organized to cover the following areas: Journal Scan, *JAMA* Archives and Libraries, Newsline, Practice Guidelines, Ethics Update, Expert Advice, Training and Treatment Centers, Information for Patients (including Support Groups), and a Glossary.

The National Centers for Disease Control and Prevention (CDC) AIDS Clearinghouse maintains a regularly updated information web site. This can be found at ⟨http://cdcnac.aspensys.com:86/aidsinfo.htm1#Youth⟩ The site offers current epidemiological information, as well as extensive attention devoted to cases of pediatric and adolescent HIV/AIDS.

Fair, C. D., Spencer, E. D., Weiner, L., & Riekert, K. (1995). Healthy children in families affected by AIDS: Epidemiological and psychosocial considerations. *Child and Adolescent Social Work Journal, 12,* 165-181.
This article focuses on the impact of AIDS within families. Special attention is given to healthy children living in families with HIV-infected members.

Katsiyannis, A. (1992). Policy issues in school attendance: A national survey. *Journal of Special Education, 26,* 219–226.
This is an important paper discussing school policies and legal issues for children with AIDS. The article reviews state policies and discusses trends regarding the education of children with AIDS.

Wolters, P. L., Brouwers, P., & Moss, H. A. (1995). Pediatric HIV disease: Effects on cognition, learning, and behavior. *School Psychology Quarterly, 10,* 305-328.
This article is an excellent review of HIV-related consequences in pediatric cases. The authors provide details in specific areas of impairment, such as expressive language, attention, motor skills, and behavioral functioning. The role of the school psychologist is discussed regarding legal, assessment, consultation, intervention, and education issues.

(1994). Supports for children with HIV infection in school: A project to identify best practices guidelines for including children with HIV infection in the nation's schools (Special issue). *Journal of School Health, 64*(1).
This special issue provides background papers regarding transmission and consequences of HIV as well as confidentiality and public policy issues. It reports project findings investigating schoolchildren with HIV, school health services, and best-practice guidelines for the school. The issue includes a report from the National Commission on AIDS regarding HIV prevention programs.

For Children

The following books were recommended by *Library Journal* as valuable resources regarding AIDS education for adolescents:

Hyde, M. O. (1994). *Know about AIDS* (rev. ed.). Walker & Co.

Hyde, M. O. (1995). *AIDS: What does it mean to you?* (5th ed.). Walker & Co.

Lerner, E. A. (1987). *Understanding AIDS.* Lerner Publishing.

Silverstein & Silverstein (1989). *Learning about AIDS.* Enslow Publishing.

References

Agency for Health Care Policy and Research. (1994). *Quick reference guide for clinicians* (AHCPR Publication No. 94-0573). Washington, DC: CDC National Clearinghouse.

American Academy of Pediatrics Committee on Adolescence. (1990). Contraception and adolescents. *Pediatrics, 86,* 134-138.

Anderson, V. N. (1992). For whom is this world just?: Sexual orientation and AIDS. *Journal of Applied Social Psychology, 22,* 248-259.

Armstrong, F. D., Seidel, J. F., & Swales, T. P. (1993). Pediatric HIV infection: A neuropsychological and educational challenge. *Journal of Learning Disabilities, 26,* 92-103.

Aronson, S. (1995). Five girls in search of a group: A group experience of adolescents of parents with AIDS. *International Journal of Group Psychotherapy, 45,* 223-235.

Bergeron, J. P., & Handley, P. R. (1992). Bibliography on AIDS-related bereavement and grief. *Death Studies, 16,* 247-267.

Bose, S., Moss, H. A., Brouwers, P., Pizzo, P., & Lorion, R. (1994). Psychologic adjustment of human immunodeficiency virus-infected school-age children. *Developmental and Behavioral Pediatrics, 15,* S26-S33.

Brouwers, P., Belman, A. L., & Epstein, L. G. (1991). Central nervous system involvement: Manifestation and evaluation. In P. A. Pizzo & C. M. Wilfert (Eds.), *Pediatric AIDS: The challenge of HIV infection in infants, children, and adolescents* (pp. 318-335). Baltimore: Williams & Wilkins.

Brown, L. K., & Fritz, G. K. (1988). Children's knowledge and attitudes about AIDS. *Journal of the American Academy of Child and Adolescent Psychiatry, 27,* 504–508.

Butler, C., Hittelman, J., & Hauger, S. B. (1991). Approach to neurodevelopmental and neurological complications in pediatric HIV infection. *Journal of Pediatrics, 119,* S41–S46.

Carlson, C. I., Paavola, J., & Talley, R. (1995). Historical, current, and future models of schools as health care delivery settings. *School Psychology Quarterly, 10,* 184–202.

Centers for Disease Control and Prevention. (1985, August 30). Education and foster care of children infected with HTLV-III/LAV. *Morbidity and Mortality Weekly Report, 34,* 517–521.

Centers for Disease Control and Prevention. (1987, August 21). Recommendations for prevention of HIV transmission in health-care settings. *Morbidity and Mortality Weekly Report, 36*(2S), 3S–12S.

Centers for Disease Control and Prevention. (1988). Guidelines for effective school health education to prevent the spread of AIDS. *Journal of School Health, 58,* 142–146.

Centers for Disease Control and Prevention. (1993, May). *HIV/AIDS Surveillance Report* (Vol. 5, No. 1). Atlanta, GA: National Centers for Disease and Prevention.

Centers for Disease Control and Prevention. (1994, September 30). 1994 revised classification system for human immunodeficiency virus infection in children less than 13 years of age. *Morbidity and Mortality Weekly Report, 43*(RR-12), 2–8.

Centers for Disease Control and Prevention. (1995, June). *HIV/AIDS Surveillance Report.* (Vol. 7, No. 1). Atlanta, GA: National Center for Disease and Prevention.

Cohen, H. J., Papola, P., & Alvarez, M. (1994). Neurodevelopmental abnormalities in school-age children with HIV infection. *Journal of School Health, 64,* 11–13.

Collins, R. L. (in press). Social support provision to HIV-infected gay men. *Journal of Applied Social Psychology.*

Crandles, S., & Jean, A. (1990). Caregivers' perceptions of their school-age children with perinatally acquired HIV infection. *Sixth International Conference on AIDS: Abstracts, 6,* 328.

Crocker, A. C., Lavin, A. T., Palfrey, J. S., Porter, S. M., Shaw, D. M., & Weill, K. S. (1994). Supports for children with HIV infection in school: Best practices guidelines. *Journal of School Health, 64,* 32–34.

DeMers, S. T. (1995). Emerging perspectives on the role of psychologists in the delivery of health and mental health services. *School Psychology Quarterly, 10,* 179–183.

DiClemente, R. J. (1993). Preventing HIV/AIDS among adolescents: Schools as agents of behavior change. *Journal of the American Medical Association (JAMA), 270,* 760–762.

Dryfoos, J. G. (1994). *Full-service schools.* San Francisco, CA: Jossey-Bass.

Elders, M. J. (1994, August/September). Sexuality education for communities of color. *SIECUS Report.* Washington, DC.

Epstein, L. G., Sharer, L. R., & Goudsmit, J. (1988). Neurological and neuropathological features of human immunodeficiency virus in children. *Annals of Neurology, 23,* 19–23.

Fair, C. D., Spencer, E. D., Weiner, L., & Riekert, K. (1995). Healthy children in families affected by AIDS: Epidemiological and psychosocial considerations. *Child and Adolescent Social Work Journal, 12,* 165–181.

Fletcher, J. M., Francis, D. J., Pequegnat, W., Raudenbush, S. W., Bornstein, M. H., Schmitt, F., Brouwers, P., & Stover, E. (1991). Neurobehavioral outcomes in diseases of childhood: Individual change models for pediatric human immunodeficiency viruses. *American Psychologist, 46,* 1267–1277.

Forrest, J. D., & Silverman, J. (1989). What public school teachers teach about preventing pregnancy, AIDS, and sexually transmitted diseases. *Family Planning Perspective, 21,* 65–72.

Fraser, K. (1989). *Someone at school has AIDS.* Alexandria, VA: National Association of State Boards of Education.

Gutman, L. T., St. Claire, K. K., Weedy, C., Herman-Giddens, M. E., Lane, B. A., Niemeyer, J. G., & McKinney, R. E. (1991). Human immunodeficiency virus transmission by child sexual abuse. *American Journal of Diseases of Children, 145,* 137–141.

Haiken, H., Hernandez, M., Mintz, M., & Boland, M. (1991). School-aged HIV-infected children and access to education. *Pediatric AIDS and HIV Infection: Fetus to Adolescent, 2,* 74–79.

Kann, L., Anderson, J. E., Holtzman, D., Ross, J., Truman, B. I., Collins, J., & Kolbe, L. J. (1991). HIV-related knowledge, beliefs, and behaviors among high school students in the United States: Results from a national survey. *Journal of School Health, 61,* 397–401.

Katsiyannis, A. (1992). Policy issues in school attendance: A national survey. *Journal of Special Education, 26,* 219–226.

Kirby, D. (1992). School-based prevention programs: Design, evaluation, and effectiveness. In R. DiClemente (Ed.), *Adolescents and AIDS: Generation in jeopardy* (pp. 00–00). Newbury Park, CA: Sage Publishers.

Korniewicz, D. M., O'Brien, M. E., & Larson, E. (1990). Coping with AIDS and HIV. *Journal of Psychosocial Nursing and Mental Health Services, 28*(3), 14–21.

Landau, S., Pryor, J. B., & Haefli, K. (1995). Pediatric HIV: School-based sequelæ and curricular interventions for infection prevention and social acceptance. *School Psychology Review, 24,* 213–229.

Levenson, R. L., & Mellins, C. A. (1992). Pediatric HIV disease: What psychologists need to know. *Professional Psychology: Research and Practice, 23,* 410–415.

Lipson, M. (1994, June). Disclosure of diagnosis to children with human immunodeficiency virus or acquired immunodeficiency syndrome. *Developmental and Behavioral Pediatrics, 15,* s61–s65.

Mauk, G. W., Gibson, D. G., & Rodgers, P. L. (1994). Suicide postvention with adolescents: School consultation practices and issues. *Education and Treatment of Children, 17,* 468–483.

Meyers, A. (1994). Natural history of congenital HIV infection. *Journal of School Health, 64,* 9–10.

Michaels, D., & Levine, C. (1992). Estimates of the number of motherless youth orphaned by AIDS in the United States. *Journal of the American Medical Association, 268,* 3456–3461.

Mooney, K. M., Cohn, E. S., & Swift, M. B. (1992). Physical distance and AIDS: Too close for comfort? *Journal of Applied Social Psychology, 22,* 1442–1452.

National Commission on AIDS. (1994). Preventing HIV/AIDS in adolescents. *Journal of School Health, 64,* 39–51.

Navia, B. A., Cho, E. S., Petito, C. K., & Price, R. W. (1986). The AIDS dementia complex: II. Neuropathology. *Annals of Neurology, 19,* 525–535.

Palfrey, J. S., Fenton, T., Lavin, A. T., Porter, S. M., Shaw, D. M., Weill, K. S., & Crocker, A. C. (1994). Schoolchildren with HIV infection: A survey of the nation's largest school districts. *Journal of School Health, 64,* 22–26.

Power, T. J., DuPaul, G. J., Shapiro, E. S., & Parrish, J. M. (1995). Pediatric school psychology: The emergence of a subspecialization. *School Psychology Review, 24,* 244–257.

Pryor, J. B., & Landau, S. (1994). *Psychological reactions to persons with HIV/AIDS: An associative model of stigma.* Paper presented at the Fifth International Language and Social Psychology Conference, Brisbane, Australia.

Pryor, J. B., & Reeder, G. D. (1993). Collective and individual representations of HIV/AIDS stigma. In J. B. Pryor & G. D. Reeder (Eds.), *The social psychology of HIV infection* (pp. 263–286). Hillsdale, NJ: Erlbaum.

Pryor, J. B., Reeder, G. D., & Landau, S. (1996, April). *A social psychological analysis of stigmatization: Lessons from the HIV epidemic.* Paper presented at the National Institutes of Mental Health Symposium on AIDS Stigma, Bethesda, MD.

Range, L. M. (1993). Suicide prevention: Guidelines for schools. *Educational Psychology Review, 5,* 135–154.

Reeves, N., & Knowles, D. (1981). Helping children deal with death concerns. *Journal of Special Education, 5,* 41–48.

Robenstine, C. (1995). Providing HIV/AIDS education for African American high school students. *The High School Journal, 78,* 133–141.

Rozin, P., Markwith, M., & Nemeroff, C. (1992). Magical beliefs and fear of AIDS. *Journal of Applied Social Psychology, 22,* 1081–1092.

Schmitt, T. M., & Schmitt, R. L. (1990). Constructing AIDS policy in the public schools: A multimethod case study. *Journal of Contemporary Ethnography, 19,* 295–321.

Schonfeld, D. J. (1989). Crisis intervention for bereavement support: A model of intervention in the children's school. *Clinical Pediatrics, 28,* 27–33.

Seachrist, L. (1995). AZT: Attacking AIDS early and hard. *Science News, 148,* 116.

Seidel, J. F. (1991). The development of a comprehensive pediatric HIV developmental service program. In A. Rudigier (Ed.), *Technical report on developmental disabilities and HIV infection* (No. 7, pp. 1–4). Silver Spring, MD: American Association of University Affiliated Programs.

Spiegel, L., & Mayers, A. (1991). Psychosocial aspects of AIDS in children and adolescents. *Pediatric Clinics of North America, 38,* 153–167.

Stephenson, J. (1995). Other AIDS drug regimens beat AZT alone, reduce clinical progression and mortality. *JAMA, 274*(15), 1183–1184.

Task Force on Pediatric AIDS. (1988). Pediatric guidelines for infection control of human immunodeficiency virus (acquired immunodeficiency virus) in hospitals, medical offices, schools, and other settings. *Pediatrics, 82,* 801–806.

Tharinger, D. (1995). Roles for psychologists in emerging models of school-related health and mental health services. *School Psychology Quarterly, 10,* 203–216.

Walsh, M. E., & Bibace, R. (1990). Developmentally-based AIDS/HIV education. *Journal of School Health, 60,* 256–261.

Walsh, M. E., & Bibace, R. (1991). Children's conceptions of AIDS: A developmental analysis. *Journal of Pediatric Psychology, 16,* 273–285.

Weiss, R. (1993). How does HIV cause AIDS? *Science, 260,* 1273–1279.

Wenckstern, S., & Leenaars, A. A. (1993). Trauma and suicide in our schools. *Death Studies, 17,* 151–171.

Westerman, P. L., & Davidson, P. M. (1994). Homophobic attitudes and AIDS risk behavior of adolescents. *Journal of Adolescent Health, 14,* 208–213.

Whalen, C. K., Henker, B., Burgess, S., & O'Neil, R. (1995). Young people talk about AIDS: "When you get sick, you stay sick." *Journal of Clinical Child Psychology, 24,* 338–345.

Wolters, P. L., Brouwers, P., & Moss, H. A. (1995). Pediatric HIV disease: Effects on cognition, learning, and behavior. *School Psychology Quarterly, 10,* 305–328.

Wood, G. E. (1995). Antiretoviral therapy in infants and children with HIV. *Pediatric Nursing, 21,* 291–296.

71

Communicable Diseases

Stephen C. Eppes

Division of Infectious Diseases, duPont Hospital for Children, Wilmington, Delaware

Background and Development

Despite advances in microbiology, improvements in sanitation, the availability of immunizations and antibiotics, and various other public health measures, diseases due to microorganisms remain common in modern society. While some (e.g., polio and smallpox) have been effectively controlled or eliminated by vaccination, other diseases have only recently emerged (e.g., AIDS and Lyme disease). Many infectious diseases are most frequently observed in the childhood population. This fact results from many factors, including relative immaturity of the immune system and unique patterns of exposure to infections, such as would be encountered in a day-care or school situation.

The school setting unavoidably invites the spread of certain communicable diseases. Children who acquire viruses or bacteria from their siblings or playmates bring those microorganisms to the classroom, school cafeteria, restrooms, and other frequented areas, resulting in risk of transmission of infection to other students. Staff may similarly infect students and vice versa. Objects shared by students may become contaminated and act as fomites to assist in the spread of certain diseases. Sexually active adolescents may acquire and transmit venereal diseases, some of which have become common among high school students. Measures to prevent the entry of microorganisms into the school setting (e.g., quarantine, requiring physician permission for absentee returns, and disinfection) have met with variable success.

Compared with adolescents and adults, young children are immunologically immature. Their immune systems are less fully developed (particularly in the case of infants and preschool children), and because they have not come in contact with as many infections, they are more susceptible. Children who spend their early years in day care may have a dozen or more respiratory and gastrointestinal infections each year, as some parents are acutely aware. The silver lining to that cloud is that these children become ill less often in elementary school because their immune defenses have already been challenged by many infectious agents and are more protective. Most teenagers have a reasonably well developed repertoire of defenses against common respiratory and gastrointestinal infections.

This chapter will discuss several of the most common and most serious of the infectious diseases encountered in schools. Where appropriate, disease manifestations, treatment, and prevention measures will be outlined. When the disease is likely to cause social or psychological consequences, those problems will be addressed (see Table 1).

Problems and Implications: Common Communicable Diseases

Respiratory Tract Infections

Infection of the upper and lower respiratory tract is common, with many young children experiencing 8 to 10 infections, mostly viral, each year (Turner & Hayden, 1995). In some cases, the symptomatology is related directly to the respiratory tract and includes cough, congestion, and hoarseness. However, for some infections spread by the respiratory route (either by direct contact or airborne transmission), the most troublesome symptoms do not involve the respiratory tract; Examples here include infectious mononucleosis, parvovirus B-19, and chicken pox.

The common cold

Colds are caused by many different viruses but generally result in easily recognizable symptoms of nasal pain and discharge, cough, and low-grade fever. Symptoms may last 7 to 10 days, and school absenteeism is common despite the fact that the disease is comparatively mild. Individuals vary with respect to how well this common illness is tolerated, possibly related to genetic and immunologic factors as well as psychological makeup. Sinus and ear infections are bacterial complications that may require antibiotics. Contact with respiratory secretions is usually required for transmission of cold viruses; hand washing and the use of disposable tissues can decrease the chances of spread within the classroom.

793

Table 1 *School Problems Posed by Infectious Diseases*

School-Related Issue	Disease Examples	Helpful Measures
Prolonged absence	Mononucleosis Hepatitis Meningitis	Send assignments home Homebound schooling Assess readiness to return to school
Classroom transmission of infection	Colds and flu Gastroenteritis Head lice Chicken pox	Hand washing Environmental disinfectant Selective temporary school exclusion
Stigmatization and social isolation	Hepatitis Tuberculosis Scabies Sexually transmitted diseases	Appropriate education of students and families Maintain confidentiality
Occupational hazard for school employees	Influenza Chicken pox Cytomegalovirus (CMV) Parvovirus B-19 Rubella	Immunization (children and staff) Hand washing Education of staff
Public health implications	Tuberculosis Shigellosis Sexually transmitted diseases	Encourage reporting to public health authorities Selective temporary school exclusion Treatment of infection
Health maintenance	Vaccine-preventable diseases Sexually transmitted diseases Other lifestyle-associated conditions	Immunization Health/sex education School-based health centers

Tonsillitis and pharyngitis

Viruses are also the most frequent causes of sore throat; these infections are generally mild and self-limited. Streptococcal pharyngitis (strep throat) is also notoriously common in school-aged populations. With strep, sore throat may be mild or severe, and other symptoms, such as fever, headache, and abdominal pain, may be pronounced. Because of widespread concern about streptococcal infection and its complications (e.g., rheumatic fever and scarlet fever), significantly sore throats are frequently treated by physicians. Children with positive throat cultures are given an antibiotic, usually for 10 days. A student with streptococcal pharyngitis is less contagious after 1 to 2 days of antibiotic therapy and may return to school.

Conjunctivitis

Inflammation of the lining of the eye results in redness and frequently in pain, itching, or discharge. Allergic conjunctivitis is common in certain geographic areas and is often accompanied by sneezing and nasal congestion. Viral conjunctivitis is common in young children and may be seen with concomitant cold symptoms or sore throat. Both the eye discharge and nasal secretions are likely to be contagious. Bacterial conjunctivitis sometimes occurs following viral conjunctivitis; here, the discharge is thicker and the symptoms often more severe. Antibiotic

eyedrops are useful for bacterial conjunctivitis only. Students are sometimes excluded from school because of conjunctivitis, but the risk of transmission in the school setting is no greater than that associated with colds and pharyngitis.

Bronchitis and pneumonia

Acute bronchitis is usually viral in origin and is associated with a good prognosis. Chronic bronchitis is a disease seen mainly in adults and is often associated with cigarette smoking. Pneumonia in the preschool and young school-aged child is usually viral, and no specific therapy is required although hospitalization is occasionally necessary. Bacterial pneumonia, especially due to pneumococcus, is usually more symptomatic and more likely to require antibiotics, either in hospital or at home. The classic "walking" pneumonia of school-aged children is due to a bacterium named Mycoplasma; students may miss little or no school and are usually treated with oral antibiotics.

Specific infections

Pertussis, or whooping cough, is most severe in infants but is common in school-aged children whose immunity from prior immunization has waned. The early 1990s saw a significant increase in reported cases of pertussis in the United States. The disease is associated with a characteristic cough lasting several weeks, but older children may lack the classic whoop. Because it is quite contagious, it can rapidly spread through susceptible students and staff in a school. While the school-aged and adult populations can act as a reservoir to pass infection along to susceptible infants (in whom severe disease can develop), the infection is relatively mild in older children and adults. Antibiotics are used to reduce infectivity.

Influenza (the flu) refers to a specific illness caused by influenza A and B viruses. Symptoms usually begin abruptly with achiness, fever, headache, and upper respiratory symptoms. Lower respiratory tract involvement follows, often with a deep cough producing chest pain. Influenza is extremely contagious by airborne droplets and has a short incubation period; hence, in a susceptible school-aged population, spread may be explosive. The illness lasts 5 to 10 days and usually results in significant school absence. In fact, when influenza strikes a community, public health officials may recognize an outbreak because of febrile respiratory illness causing extensive school absenteeism. Usually, people are less contagious by the time fever subsides, which is when they may return to school.

Treatment of flu involves rest and supportive measures; amantadine and rimantidine are antiviral drugs which may be helpful if given early in the illness. The most common complication of influenza is pneumonia, which can be severe. Prevention is possible for people at high risk for influenza and its complications, particularly those who are aged or have underlying medical problems (including asthma). Yearly influenza vaccination is effective but significantly underutilized (Centers for Disease Control, 1993). Of those recommended to receive flu shots, about half of individuals over age 65 years and only 10% of children with moderate to severe asthma actually get immunized (Szilagyi, Rodewald, Savageau, Yoos, & Doane, 1992). People whose occupations place them at greater risk for influenza or who are essential for the community (e.g. teachers, health care workers, police) may also be advised to get flu shots.

Often considered a rite of passage, chicken pox (varicella) is a common, usually mild infection of childhood. However, various complications can result and there are about 100 deaths per year in the U.S., mostly in otherwise normal children (Jenson & Leach, 1995). Adults have a greater rate of severe disease than do children. Because it is highly communicable, students are kept out of school until the skin lesions are crusted, usually about one week. This results not only in days missed from school but frequently causes time away from work for parents. In 1995, a vaccine for varicella was approved for routine immunization of both children and adults who are susceptible to infection. The vaccine is safe, effective in disease prevention, and expected to be economically cost-effective (Lieu et al., 1994). School staff who are not immune to varicella (usually defined by blood test in addition to negative his-

tory of chicken pox) may be advised to receive immunizations.

Until the late 1980s when many areas of the U.S. suffered minor epidemics, measles had been a forgotten disease, especially among younger parents who had never seen a case. Complacency with immunizations, particularly in urban areas, was largely responsible for the increased susceptibility and spread of the disease. The classic symptoms of rash, congestion, cough, conjunctivitis, and fever result in a miserable illness lasting a week. However, complications, such as pneumonia and encephalitis, may have a fatal outcome. Measles is highly preventable by appropriate immunization in the second year of life, with a second dose of vaccine either before kindergarten or during middle school.

Mumps is a viral infection with generally mild symptoms that include fever and swelling of the salivary glands. Complications may be significant, however, especially meningitis and encephalitis that sometimes occur. It is for this reason that immunization is routinely given in the second year of life, usually in the form of the MMR (measles, mumps, and rubella) vaccine. Rubella (german measles) is a mild illness in children characterized by rash, lymph node enlargement, and low-grade fever. This infection is more problematic when young women acquire infection because of the risk of congenital rubella syndrome (described later). MMR vaccine usually induces adequate immunity.

Acute infection with Epstein-Barr virus (EBV) frequently results in a clinical disease known as infectious mononucleosis. Young children often have mild or subclinical infections with EBV. The typical adolescent will initially develop sore throat, enlarged lymph nodes in the neck, fever, and fatigue. Mononucleosis is usually distinguishable from other causes of tonsillitis by the severity of the fatigue and the duration of the symptoms. While the fever and sore throat may last a week or two, the fatigue, often debilitating, may resolve much more slowly over several weeks or months. In general, students are able to return to school during convalescence from infectious mononucleosis; however, they may not have normal stamina and may need to refrain from physical education and other strenuous activities. Teenagers who try to resume activities too quickly may experience worse fatigue which interferes with school performance. School absence may become a problem for students whose symptoms are more severe; homebound teaching is often recommended in such cases. If that option is chosen, efforts should be periodically made to determine if the student is able to return to school as the potential exists for students or families to find secondary gain from the situation. For athletes, mononucleosis poses an additional hazard. If the spleen is enlarged and prone to rupture, contact sports are to be avoided until full recovery.

Transmission of EBV occurs from person to person and usually involves saliva or other respiratory secretions; ill or convalescing students should avoid sharing their secretions with others. Treatment for mononucleosis mainly involves supportive measures as no current antiviral therapies are effective. Some physicians may prescribe prednisone or other similar steroid medications in an effort to shorten the duration of acute symptoms. For students with final examinations or other key responsibilities, this is a reasonable option. Mononucleosis may be a miserable experience and complications are possible, but immunity is solid and recurrences do not occur. In the 1980s, "chronic EBV infection" or "chronic mono" were popularly thought to cause chronic fatigue syndrome, but current evidence does not support the role of EBV in that disorder (Ablashi, 1994).

Meningococcus (*Neisseria meningitidis*) is a bacterium that can normally inhabit the upper respiratory tract of some individuals. Infrequently, it can get into the bloodstream (sometimes following influenza) and cause life-threatening infection. Meningitis, as the name implies, can also result and can be severe. The infection is spread by the respiratory route and frequently occurs in crowded situations, such as military barracks and schools. When a case of meningococcal disease occurs in a school, it inevitably produces widespread concern, even panic, because of the often severe nature of the disease. However, single cases, rather than outbreaks, are usually what is observed. Preventive antibiotics are advised for household and other close contacts of a child with meningococcal disease because some of them may harbor the bacterium. This is also done for nursery school contacts, but prophylaxis of older school-aged contacts is not routine. Sometimes, depending on the nature of the situation and on whether other cases have occurred in a community, public health officials may recommend that other individuals receive immunization or antibiotic prophylaxis. There are other forms of meningitis in childhood, some dangerous and some less so, which are not to be confused with meningococcal disease.

Through the late 1980s and the 1990s, a significant resurgence of tuberculosis was observed throughout many areas of the United States, in part due to AIDS and to urban problems such as homelessness. Certain populations, including some ethnic minorities, the homeless, persons with AIDS, and the elderly, are at particular risk for tuberculosis. Young children, when infected with the tuberculosis bacterium, are apt to become symptomatic. However, for a variety of biological reasons, school-aged children are more likely to acquire pulmonary infection and remain asymptomatic. These children and adolescents are frequently identified as infected by tuberculin skin testing, often done as part of routine physical examinations. A chest x-ray should be done on every person with a positive skin test. Those who have evidence of active tuberculosis (the minority of school-aged children) are considered potentially infectious until treatment is underway and microbiologic studies are negative. The more

likely situation is for the child to have no symptoms and a negative chest x-ray; these children pose no risk of infection to others. All skin-test-positive children should be treated with antituberculous antibiotics because latent infection can progress to pulmonary tuberculosis as the children grow older. The evaluation of any school-aged child with a positive skin test should include investigation of contacts. Usually an adult with active tuberculosis is responsible for transmitting infection to the child. School staff who have untreated tuberculous infection, usually defined by a positive tuberculin skin test, need to be evaluated for possible infectivity before returning to the school setting.

Infections harmful for the fetus

Pregnant teachers and other school personnel are frequently worried about exposure to infectious diseases. In particular, three viruses encountered in the school setting cause concern. Cytomegalovirus (CMV) is a ubiquitous agent frequently acquired and shed by young children. It generally causes mild symptoms, if any at all, but can produce a mononucleosis-like syndrome. When a pregnancy is complicated by maternal CMV, especially in the first months, severe fetal abnormalities and death sometimes results. It is important to recognize that over half of the adult females in the U.S. are immune to CMV because of prior infection. A woman who is not immune, which can be determined by blood tests, would be susceptible. However, CMV is not highly communicable, and studies have shown that infection-control procedures, especially hand washing, effectively prevent transmission.

The second agent is parvovirus B-19 which causes a common childhood illness called "fifth" disease (erythema infectiosum). This generally mild illness is manifested by low-grade fever and a characteristic rash; older girls and women can develop a transient arthritis. As with CMV, maternal infection can result in fetal death, but the risk is less than 10% for infection occuring in the first half of pregnancy and negligible thereafter. The child with fifth disease is not contagious by the time symptoms occur so isolation of the child from the pregnant woman at that point does no good. Because of the high level of immunity in the population, the relatively low risk for the fetus, and the low risk of transmission from student to teacher, it is not recommended that pregnant women be excluded from school when cases of fifth disease have been identified (American Academy of Pediatrics, 1994).

Rubella is now less common because of widespread use of immunization, but cases of congenital rubella syndrome still occur when nonimmune women become infected. Brain, eye, and heart malformations in the fetus are the most frequent manifestations. All women considering pregnancy should know their rubella immune status.

Gastrointestinal Infections

Gastrointestinal infections, as a group, occupy second place in frequency in school-aged children. Diarrheal disease, although frequent, is less likely to be severe or to require hospitalization, compared with the situation in infants. Also, in distinction to infants and toddlers, school-aged children are more likely to practice reasonable hygiene and are less likely to place objects in their mouths, both of which contribute to a higher rate of such infections in younger children.

Gastroenteritis

This common condition is usually attributable to viruses and is manifested by diarrhea and variable amounts of fever and vomiting. The most common complication is dehydration, but this is less likely as the child gets older. The degree of symptomatology determines whether and how long school absence is required. Good hand washing is the most important method of controlling spread of disease in the classroom setting. The use of disinfectants is recommended for contaminated areas or articles.

Bacterial diarrheal disease

Though less frequent than viral infection, bacterial agents often cause more severe disease and may have public health implications. Salmonella infections are the most prevalent in this country and are sometimes linked to occupational exposure (e.g., poultry farms) or to ingestion of improperly cooked eggs or poultry. However, person-to-person spread may also occur, especially in the home or day-care situation. Diarrhea, often bloody and sometimes accompanied by fever, is the usual presentation. Most cases of Salmonellosis do not require specific therapy, but persons who are ill or those who have typhoid fever are usually treated with antibiotics. Shigella infections are associated with fever and bloody diarrhea and are treated with antibiotics; outbreaks may occur (e.g., in day care centers) and are more likely to be a public health problem.

Hepatitis

Hepatitis can be caused by a number of viruses as well as by non-infectious conditions. However, infectious hepatitis, when it occurs in a school setting, is usually due to hepatitis A virus (HAV). Many young children acquire HAV and develop only mild symptoms resembling viral gastroenteritis. When older children and adults become infected, liver-related symptoms, including jaundice, are likely to occur. The vast majority of HAV infections resolve completely with no lasting liver damage. The spread of HAV is via feces; infection can occur as a result of person-to-person contact or, less commonly, from contaminated foods. By the time symptomatic HAV infection is identified, however, very little virus is present in the stool. Given these facts and the likelihood that most school-aged children are toilet trained and use reasonable hygiene, significant outbreaks of infectious hepatitis are unlikely to occur in the school setting. It is not uncommon for schools to inform parents when a case is identified. This practice may create anxiety for parents but does very little good. Education of staff and students about proper hygiene, especially hand washing, is more appropriate. Stigmatization of the student should be avoided. For close contacts of the child with hepatitis, an injection of gamma globulin can prevent infection. As a safety measure, the student should remain out of school for one week after the onset of symptoms.

Skin Infections and Infestations

In contrast to respiratory and gastrointestinal infections, skin conditions are frequently visible and often recognizable. Hence, even though these conditions are often of less medical importance, school personnel are more likely to notice them and advise medical evaluation or school exclusion.

Impetigo

Superficial infections with staph or strep bacteria can result in weeping sores which can spread over the skin rapidly. This condition can be transmitted person to person but simple hand washing usually interrupts the spread. Antibiotics by mouth or topically are effective.

Scabies

Mites are microscopic skin parasites that can tunnel into the skin and cause scabies, an intensely itchy condition that may be localized to certain areas of skin or be more widespread. It can be spread person to person, usually by direct (including intimate) contact. More troublesome by far than ordinary insect bites, scabies can last weeks to months and frequently requires scabicidal lotion or cream to resolve. Parents often are alarmed or resentful of the diagnosis of scabies, presumably because of the implication of filth or poor living conditions (which can be a risk factor). However, scabies knows no socioeconomic boundaries. Children may return to school after treatment is completed, but the resolution of skin lesions may take weeks. Household and sexual contacts should be treated prophylactically.

Pediculosis

This term refers to the itching and inflammation caused by head lice, body lice, and pubic lice. Pubic lice are transmitted sexually or, less commonly, by shared items such as towels. Head lice are most common in school-aged children and, while not serious, are a source of frustration for school personnel and parents alike. The condition is recognizable by the nits (eggs) which are attached to hairs and easily seen with a magnifying glass. A synthetic pyrethroid shampoo is effective in eliminating lice and communicability such that children may return to school after treatment. Removal of nits by using a fine tooth comb is for cosmetic purposes, not for eradication of infestation. "No nits" policies, preventing students from returning to school as long as nits are visible, have not been shown to reduce classroom transmission (American Academy of Pediatrics, l994). Recurrent infestation is more common than treatment failure. Contacts of the child with head lice should be examined and treated if infestation is demonstrated. Clothing and bedding may be disinfected by laundering in hot water. Environmental insecticides are not recommended.

Cold sores

Herpes labialis is caused by herpes simplex virus (generally a different strain than that associated with genital infection). The infection may reactivate time after time to cause the distinctive sore on the edge of the lip. Adolescents are particularly bothered by the unsightly appearance. Herpes labialis clears up spontaneously in about a week, sometimes more quickly with antiviral medication. The virus can be transmitted by kissing and during sexual contact but also by less intimate direct contact. Students do not require exclusion from school but should use common-sense hygiene and refrain from sharing drink containers, eating utensils, and the like.

Sexually Transmitted Diseases

The epidemic of human immunodeficiency virus (HIV) infection and AIDS has heightened the awareness of the general public about sexually transmitted diseases (STDs). Nevertheless, HIV infection and other venereal diseases are occurring with alarming frequency in adolescents and young adults. The "classic" STDs, syphilis and gonorrhea, are only two of the many microorganisms transmitted in this fashion. STDs can result in a variety of symptoms including those relating primarily to the genital tract (e.g., chlamydia), diseases not affecting the genital tract at all (e.g., hepatitis B), and diseases with widespread manifestations (e.g., syphilis). Most STDs can be transmitted not only between sexual partners but also from mother to baby as a result of transplacental spread or contact with infected secretions.

In a national survey of high school students, 54% responded they had had sexual intercourse (Centers for Disease Control, 1992b). African-American students are significantly more likely to be sexually active than white or other ethnic populations. Roughly one fourth of the 12 million sexually active teenagers in the U.S. will acquire a STD each year (Hammerschlag & Rawstron, 1995). Many individuals will be asymptomatic, will not seek treatment, and may unknowingly transmit the infection to other partners. The use of condoms can help prevent, in addition to unwanted pregnancy, transmission of HIV and other sexually transmitted diseases. Nevertheless,

studies have suggested that at least half of sexually active adolescents use condoms inconsistently or not at all (Centers for Disease Control, 1992b).

The use of drugs and alcohol affect sexual behavior and is associated with a lower rate of condom use. Adolescents who are not in school are more likely to engage in risky sexual behaviors than those in school (Centers for Disease Control, l994). In addition to teenagers who willingly engage in sex, younger children and adolescents can acquire STDs as a result of sexual abuse. An estimated 100,000 to 500,000 children are victims of such abuse in the U.S. each year. In one report, 7% of adolescent males and females under 15 years of age reported nonvoluntary sexual encounters (Chacko & Taber, l993). When prepubertal children are discovered to have gonorrhea or syphilis, sexual abuse should be assumed.

The subject of AIDS/HIV is addressed in another chapter in this volume; a discussion of some of the most prevalent STDs follows.

Specific infections

Gonorrhea was the most frequently reported STD through the 1980s, though rates have declined somewhat in the 1990s (Hammerschlag & Rawstron, l995). About one fourth of cases occur in adolescents, and it is the most common STD in sexually abused children. Gonorrhea most frequently involves the urethra in males and the cervix in females, but other sites may become infected, for example, from orogenital sex. Pain and discharge are frequent symptoms, but asymptomatic infection may occur, mainly in females. Spread of infection up the fallopian tubes can lead to pelvic inflammatory disease and ultimately to infertility. Treatment with either injectable or oral antibiotics is effective in eradication of infection but may not reverse damage to the fallopian tubes and ovaries. Recurrences are common, particularly if contact tracing and treatment have not been performed.

The most common STD in the U.S. today is probably *Chlamydia trachomatis* (Hammerschlag & Rawstron, 1995). Among males, it is the most frequent cause of nongonococcal urethritis. Adolescent females have the highest rate of chlamydial infection, often exceeding 15%. Pelvic inflammatory disease and infertility can result as can ectopic pregnancy. Infection of the newborn baby, resulting in conjunctivitis and/or pneumonia, is common when the mother has had untreated genital infection. Therapy should always be given for chlamydial infection when gonorrhea is being treated, as the two infections often occur together.

The rates of syphilis have increased over the past decade concomitant with the era of AIDS, crack cocaine use, and "sex for drugs" (Hammerschlag & Rawstron, 1995). After exposure, the individual develops the characteristic genital lesion (chancre). If treatment is not received, signs of secondary syphilis, including rash and generalized illness, develop within several weeks. Without treatment, recurrences of secondary syphilis may occur, and years later, tertiary syphilis can cause chronic neurologic and cardiovascular damage. Congenital syphilis can result when pregnancy is complicated by secondary or latent syphilis. Affected babies may have severe disease involving the central nervous system, bones, liver, and other internal organs; 40% are stillborn or die in the neonatal period. Penicillin treatment usually cures the infection.

Genital herpes simplex infection is caused by a virus similar to the one which causes cold sores. It is characterized by lesions of the genitalia which are frequently painful and may recur with great frequency. Antiviral therapy can ameliorate the symptoms but does not get rid of the latent infection which persists for life. When herpes simplex is transmitted to a newborn, the infection can be devastating. Because of central nervous system involvement, survivors are frequently severely retarded. The genital lesions which occur with both syphilis and herpes can increase the likelihood of transmission of HIV during sexual intercourse.

Alternative Actions

As noted in the previous section, many communicable diseases affecting school-aged children are benign and self-limited and require little in the way of intervention. More serious infections will be seen by health professionals, especially pediatricians, family physicians, and public health clinics. School personnel are in a unique position to recognize and refer students with infectious diseases. The school health nurse, on the front line, is likely to deal with communicable diseases on a regular basis. Teachers frequently notice diminished stamina and poor concentration in children who have been ill with diseases such as infectious mononucleosis. They may also be the first to notice other respiratory infections and skin infections and infestations. Sexually active students who have or fear they may get sexually transmitted diseases are often hesitant to tell their parents or independently seek medical attention from the family physician. Such students may seek attention from the school counselor or psychologist.

Hand washing is the single most important way to prevent disease transmission in the classroom setting. Particularly in the preschool and early elementary grades, disinfectants are useful for cleaning contaminated areas. Schools (and their respective districts and states) should have policies enumerating infectious conditions which require temporary school exclusion and other measures which may be required to deal with outbreaks. These policies are best developed in consultation with local physicians and public health authorities or based on recommendations from organizations such as the American Academy of Pediatrics. While protecting the health of other students is of prime importance, the privacy of individual students should be treated with sensitivity, particularly in the context of diseases with potential for social stigmatization such as tuberculosis and STDs. School authorities should provide sufficient, accurate, and consistent information to allow parents to make individual decisions regarding their children without causing unnecessary fear. Explaining the mechanisms of disease transmission and immunity is useful in this regard.

In addition to state and local STD clinics, which specialize in the evaluation, treatment, prevention, partner notification, and public health aspects of STDs, schools have an important role to play with regard to sex education and prevention of STDs. School health curricula, mandatory AIDS education, and school-based health centers are examples of such efforts. National surveys conducted from 1989 through 1991 (Centers for Disease Control, 1992a) indicated that high school students received increasing amounts of AIDS-related health education, discussed it more frequently with parents, and exhibited a reduction of high-risk sexual activities during that time frame, suggesting effectiveness of school health education. School-based health and wellness centers can play an important role in identifying and referring students with STDs and other communicable diseases and in providing preventive services and counseling. Advice to abstain from sexual intercourse is the safest message, but for sexually active adolescents recommendations for appropriate condom usage is reasonable. The issue of condom distribution in schools for the prevention of teen pregnancy as well as of infectious diseases has been hotly debated; some school districts have adopted this practice. For maximum effectiveness, any condom-distribution program should be accompanied by age and culturally appropriate counseling, in addition to required sex and AIDS education in the classroom. Clearly, an effective health curriculum in schools has the potential for improving both individual students' health and the public health.

Summary

Public health measures have had a major impact on preventing the spread of infectious diseases. Immunization has been, and will remain, a mainstay of protecting children and adults from infectious diseases. In the school setting, children learn hygiene and basic principles of health and disease as part of an ongoing curriculum from preschool through high school. This instruction should promote healthy behaviors in an effort to prevent lifestyle-associated diseases which result in morbidity and premature mortality. It should also help reduce the frequency of diseases transmitted from one person to another. Infection-control measures in the school setting include hand washing, use of disinfectants, temporary school exclusion, and appropriate education of staff and students.

As noted in Table 1, several aspects of communicable diseases are relevant to school psychologists as well as to teachers, school nurses, and other personnel. School absence can be a significant issue for some illnesses. To maintain continuity with studies as well as to prevent repetition of a grade, students may need to perform schoolwork at home. Psychologists may be involved with the psychosocial aspects of the child's illness and with making a determination about readiness to return to school. Helping a school deal with a serious illness in one of its students and to protect the privacy and dignity of affected students should be the responsibility of, among others, school psychologists. Efforts to promote the general health of students should be coupled with education of not only the children but also their families and school professionals.

Recommended Resources

American Academy of Pediatrics. (1993). *School health: Policy and practice.* Elk Grove, IL: Author.
This handbook outlines the functions and responsibilities of personnel in school health programs, normal and abnormal health and development, and health assessment of students through the range of ages. Health education, physical education, and competitive sports are discussed. A variety of medical issues, including communicable disease control, are treated in succinct, authoritative fashion.

American Academy of Pediatrics. (1994). *1994 red book: Report of the Committee on Infectious Diseases.* Elk Grove, IL: Author.
This has become the "bible" for pediatricians and other health care providers who deal with children. Arranged alphabetically, the major infectious diseases affecting children in the U.S. are dealt with in concise form, with special emphasis on epidemiology, diagnosis, treatment, prevention, disease control, and care of exposed persons. Recommendations are based on the latest available information and expert consensus.

Jenson, H. B., & Baltimore, R. S. (1995). *Pediatric infectious diseases: Principles and practice.* Norwalk, CT: Appleton and Lange.
This authoritative textbook in the field will be found mainly in medical libraries. While more exhaustive in its treatment of infectious diseases than the previous resource, much of it can still be read and understood by paramedical and nonmedical readers.

McMillan, J. A. (1995). Control of infections in schools. *Pediatrics in Review, 16,* 283–289.
This current reference is likely to be owned by most pediatricians as well as medical libraries. Dr. McMillan reviews current data and recommendations concerning management of students exposed to communicable diseases in schools.

References

Ablashi, D. V. (1994). Summary: Viral studies of chronic fatigue syndrome. *Clinical Infectious Diseases, 18,* S130–133.

American Academy of Pediatrics. (1994). *1994 red book: Report of the Committee on Infectious Diseases,* (23rd ed.). Elk Grove Village, IL: Anonymous.

Centers for Disease Control. (1992a). HIV instruction and selected HIV risk behaviors among high school students—United States, 1989–1991. *MMWR, 41,* 866–868.

Centers for Disease Control. (1992b). Sexual behavior among high school students—United States, 1990. *MMWR, 40,* 885–888.

Centers for Disease Control. (1993). Comprehensive delivery of adult vaccination—Minnesota, 1986–1992. *Journal of the American Medical Association, 270,* 2790.

Centers for Disease Control. (1994). Health risk behaviors among adolescents who do and do not attend school. *MMWR, 43,* 129–132.

Chacko, M. R., & Taber, L. H. (1993). Epidemiology of sexually transmitted diseases in adolescents in the United States. *Seminars in Pediatric Infectious Diseases, 4,* 71–72.

Hammerschlag, M. R., & Rawstron, S. A. (1995). Sexually transmitted infections. In H. B. Jenson & R. S. Baltimore (Eds.), *Pediatric infectious diseases: Principles and practice* (pp. 1249–76). Norwalk, CT: Appleton and Lange.

Jenson, H. B., & Leach, C. T. (1995). Chicken pox and zoster. In H. B. Jenson & R. S. Baltimore (Eds.), *Pediatric infectious diseases: Principles and practice* (pp. 415–428). Norwalk, CT: Appleton and Lange.

Lieu, T. A., Cochi, S. L., Black, S. B., Halloran, E., Shinefield, H. R., Holmes, S. J., Wharton, M., & Washington, E. (1994). Cost effectiveness of a routine varicella vaccination program for U.S. children. *Journal of the American Medical Association, 271,* 375–381.

Szilagyi, P. G., Rodewald, L. E., Savageau, J., Yoos, L., & Doane, C. (1992). Improving influenza vaccination rates in children with asthma: A test of a computerized reminder system and an analysis of factors predicting vaccination compliance. *Pediatrics, 90,* 871–875.

Turner, R. B., & Hayden, G. F. (1995). The common cold. In H. B. Jenson & R. S. Baltimore (Eds.), *Pediatric infectious diseases: Principles and practice* (pp. 873–878). Norwalk, CT: Appleton and Lange.

72

Epilepsy

Laura L. Bailet
William R. Turk

The Nemours Children's Clinic, Jacksonville, Florida

Background

Epilepsy is a common medical problem in school-age children. It is estimated that the cumulative incidence of epilepsy by age 20 is 1% (Hauser, Annegers, & Kurland, 1991). The potentially adverse impact of childhood seizures on academic achievement, psychosocial adjustment, social development, and eventual adult functional status is of major concern for psychologists, educators, physicians, and parents. The school psychologist who is knowledgeable about seizures and epilepsy can provide numerous assessment, counseling, and consultative services for students with this disorder.

Definitions

Significant confusion exists regarding the use and meaning of the terms *seizure, epilepsy,* and the newer concept of *epilepsy syndrome.* A seizure is an isolated event that can be individually described and classified. Over 100 years ago Hughlings Jackson described a seizure as an "occasional, sudden, excessive, rapid discharge of gray matter" (Jackson, 1873, p. 317). This concept is still accepted although the precise mechanisms of neuronal excitability remain the subject of intense speculation and research. The manifestations of a seizure can vary dramatically. As far back as the first century A.D., Galen proposed a classification system for seizures. However, it was not until 1964 that the International League Against Epilepsy (ILAE) successfully introduced and then in 1981 revised, a classification scheme that is now widely accepted (Commission, 1981; see Table 1). Seizures are classified as being either partial or generalized based on their behavioral or electrographic features. *Partial seizures* demonstrate features that begin in one brain hemisphere, whereas *generalized seizures* begin simultaneously in both hemispheres.

The behavioral manifestations of partial seizures depend on the region of the brain from which they arise. A seizure arising from the left frontal lobe may manifest as jerking of the right arm, whereas a seizure arising from either occipital lobe may manifest as altered visual perceptions. Partial seizures are subclassified as simple partial or complex partial. In simple partial seizures consciousness is preserved; in complex partial seizures consciousness is impaired. Either type of partial seizure may spread to involve other brain regions or generalize.

Generalized seizures present a diverse array of clinical features and are subclassified into nonconvulsive and convulsive seizures. Types of nonconvulsive seizures include *absence* seizures, commonly referred to as petit mal seizures. During absence seizures the predominant manifestation is a brief lapse in consciousness usually lasting less than 10 seconds. This lapse may be associated with subtle motor phenomena such as eye fluttering or automatisms, which are involuntary, often semipurposeful stereotyped behaviors during seizures. Automatisms may be a continuation of activity that was occurring when the seizure began or a new behavior that began with the onset of the seizure. Examples of motor automatisms include chewing, swallowing, gesturing, picking, and buttoning motions. Automatisms are also commonly seen in partial complex seizures. Absence seizures end abruptly. The person frequently is unaware that a seizure has occurred and continues as though nothing had happened.

In *myoclonic* seizures, the predominant manifestation is a rapid muscle jerk. Depending on the muscles involved, the person may lose postural control or fall to the ground. *Atonic* seizures or drop attacks are characterized by a brief sudden loss of tone in postural muscles. When mild, the patient may have a simple head drop with brief loss of awareness. When more severe, the person suddenly collapses to the floor. Continuous use of a helmet to prevent a head injury may be necessary for a child with this seizure type.

Generalized convulsive seizures, commonly referred to as grand mal seizures, are classified as *tonic* when the principal manifestation is stiffening, *clonic* when the principal manifestation is jerking, and, most commonly, *tonic-clonic* when there is a mixture of stiffening and jerking.

Table 1 *International Classification of Epileptic Seizures*

Seizure Type	Subtypes
Partial Seizures	Simple partial
	Complex partial
	Partial seizures evolving to secondarily generalized seizures
Nonconvulsive Generalized Seizures	Absence
	Myoclonic
Convulsive Generalized Seizures	Clonic
	Tonic
	Tonic-clonic
Unclassified	

Note. Data from "Proposal for Revised Clinical and Electroencephalographic Classification of Epileptic Seizures," by the Commission on Classification and Terminology of the International League Against Epilepsy, 1981, *Epilepsia, 22,* pp. 489–501. Copyright 1981 by International League Against Epilepsy.

In contrast to a seizure, which is an isolated event, *epilepsy* is a term describing individuals who have recurrent seizures. Despite many common misperceptions, it is a simple descriptive term similar to the use of diabetes to describe individuals with persistently elevated blood sugars. Unfortunately, epilepsy still has negative connotations for many people because of misperceptions about its meaning. The term "epilepsy" does not denote seizure type; severity; frequency; prognosis; or associated neurological, cognitive, behavioral, or developmental disabilities. Individuals with seizures caused exclusively by identifiable and specifically treatable systemic processes such as fever, low blood sugar, or drug withdrawal are not generally considered to have epilepsy.

Individuals caring for patients with seizure disorders have long recognized the limitations of a diagnosis based only on seizure type for guiding therapeutic decisions, identifying comorbid conditions, anticipating complications, or allowing accurate prognostication. Thus, the concept of epilepsy syndrome has been developed to describe epileptic disorders characterized by a cluster of signs and symptoms that commonly occur together. In addition to seizure type, a syndrome may include etiology, anatomy, precipitating factors, age of onset, severity, response to treatment, and prognosis. Over the past 20 years, the utility of the concept of epilepsy syndromes has become increasingly evident, particularly for children as new syndromes are identified and classified (Commission, 1989). Currently approximately 15% of children with epilepsy can be identified as having an epilepsy syndrome. Table 2 lists some of the commonly identified epilepsy syndromes of childhood. The utility of the concept is demonstrated by the syndrome of Benign Rolandic Epilepsy (see Table 3), the most commonly identified epilepsy syndrome in childhood, which is estimated to account for between 10% and 20% of all epilepsy that

Table 2 *Common Epileptic Syndromes of Childhood*

Benign Neonatal Convulsions
Benign Rolandic Epilepsy
Childhood Absence Epilepsy
Lennox-Gastaut Syndrome
Juvenile Absence Epilepsy
Juvenile Myoclonic Epilepsy
West Syndrome (Infantile Spasms)

starts in children ages 3 years and up. Information regarding specific epilepsy syndromes can be found in excellent reviews by Roger et al. (1992) and Dulac (1995).

Etiology and Developmental Patterns

The most common cause of seizures in children is fever leading to usually brief, generalized seizures called *febrile convulsions.* These seizures occur in 5% of all children between ages 6 months and 5 years, with a peak incidence between ages 1 and 2 years. Febrile seizures are felt to result from an immaturity of the developing nervous system and rarely require antiepileptic drug (AED) therapy. A number of large, longitudinal studies have demonstrated that febrile seizures do not adversely affect development or subsequent neuropsychological status (Nelson & Ellenberg, 1978). As febrile seizures are considered to be triggered by fever and reflect immaturity rather than a defect in the nervous system, these children are not considered to have epilepsy.

Children with epilepsy can be placed in two etiological groups, *idiopathic* and *symptomatic.* For the majority of children with epilepsy, particularly those whose seizures begin after infancy, no specific cause for the child's epilepsy can be determined. These children are considered to have idiopathic epilepsy. This diagnosis is often frustrating for parents and teachers who assume that, with current metabolic and neuroradiological techniques, a cause should be found for each child's seizures. There are many theories as to why children and adults have idiopathic seizures (Schwartzkroin, 1993), but more questions than answers exist.

Symptomatic epilepsy patients, who constitute a minority of children with epilepsy, have either an acute or prior (remote) nervous system insult or injury that predisposes them to seizures. Symptomatic causes include trauma, hemorrhage, stroke, inherited metabolic disorders, congenital brain malformations, prenatal or perinatal brain injury, meningitis, encephalitis, intoxications, hypoxia, and tumors. A genetic role in the etiology of epilepsy has long been suspected but remains poorly defined. Infrequently epilepsy is a manifestation of a neurological disorder with a dominant or recessive pattern of inheritance, such as tuberous sclerosis, which is autosomal dominant. More commonly, there is either no

Table 3 *Benign Rolandic Epilepsy*

Epidemiology	Onset at age 3 to 13, peak age 7 to 8. Accounts for 10% to 20% of all seizure disorders in school-age children.
Seizure Type	Brief partial simple involving face and oropharyngeal muscles with drooling and speech arrest. May spread to involve arm on affected side or secondarily generalize. Seizures most commonly are nocturnal (80%).
Electroencephalogram (EEG) Findings	Characteristic pattern of frequent centro-temporal spikes (in region of the rolandic fissure), particularly during sleep.
Seizure Frequency	Infrequent but perhaps underreported as many occur during sleep. 10% to 15% have only one seizure.
Treatment	Many require no treatment as seizures are infrequent, nocturnal, and brief. If frequent or during waking state they are typically easily controlled with drugs effective against partial seizures. Carbamazepine often agent of first choice.
Prognosis	Excellent with consistent remission by age 16, most commonly between ages 9 and 12. Children tend to be neurologically, developmentally, and intellectually normal before onset and after remission. Nocturnal occurrence minimizes peer stigmatization, and good control with either no treatment or low therapeutic treatment minimizes drug toxicity.

family history of epilepsy or a mildly elevated prevalence of epilepsy in near relatives that does not approach the prevalence that would be observed in first-degree relatives with a completely penetrant, dominantly inherited disorder (Andermann, 1982). Rare epilepsies have been mapped to specific chromosome locations, such as juvenile myoclonic epilepsy, which has been mapped to the short arm of chromosome 6 (Treiman & Treiman, 1993). It is anticipated that continued application of modern molecular genetic techniques, in combination with population and family studies of epilepsy, will further define the role of inheritance in childhood epilepsy.

Fortunately for the majority of children with epilepsy, there is a high probability of a permanent remission of their seizure disorder after withdrawal of medication. Most children are treated until a 2-year, seizure-free interval is reached, at which time their ongoing need for medication is assessed. When medication is tapered after an appropriate seizure-free interval, approximately 30% will have a recurrence of their seizures. Factors that may adversely influence recurrence risk are an abnormal neurological examination, mental retardation, continuing electroencephalogram abnormalities, the need for multiple medications to control seizures, the occurrence of many seizures prior to control, and a progressive neurological disorder (Arts et al., 1988; Brorson & Wranne, 1987; Shinnar et al., 1990). However, even for many children with these risk factors, an attempt is made to wean medication after a several-year seizure-free interval.

Evaluation

The most crucial element in establishing a diagnosis of epilepsy is accurate observation and reporting of seizures that occur. Because they are usually brief and stop before medical attention is sought, seizures are only rarely ob-

served by medical personnel. Thus, in cases of suspected epilepsy, parents, siblings, care providers, and teachers should be educated as to proper observation and documentation of any events.

Often history alone, particularly for convulsive seizures, is sufficient to establish a diagnosis of epilepsy. However, for more subtle seizures, such as absence seizures that can easily be confused with daydreaming, history alone may be insufficient. Thus, most patients will have an electroencephalogram (EEG) that records brain electrical activity. Unfortunately more than 25% of children with epilepsy may have a normal EEG when recorded between seizures, and 3% to 5% of children without a history of seizures may have abnormalities on their EEG suggesting a predisposition to seizures. Thus, the adage "treat the patient and not the EEG" remains a cornerstone of epilepsy diagnosis and management. In recent years increased utilization of new EEG techniques, including ambulatory monitoring and prolonged video-EEG monitoring, have been helpful in establishing a diagnosis in difficult cases. With ambulatory monitoring, wires are attached to the child's head and connected to a waist recording pack the size of a cassette player, which records EEG activity while the child pursues normal activity, including attending school. For prolonged video-EEG monitoring, children are kept in a laboratory for hours or days at a time while being continuously recorded in an attempt to capture seizures. The proliferation of home and school video cameras also has enabled parents and teachers to record events for medical review.

When a diagnosis of epilepsy is suspected, tests are typically performed in an attempt to determine the cause of the seizures. These tests usually include blood tests looking for metabolic or toxic disorders and either a Computerized Axial Tomography (CAT) or Magnetic Resonance Imaging (MRI) scan to look for structural brain abnormalities. As noted previously, most children experiencing seizures have idiopathic seizures, and these tests therefore often are unrevealing.

Treatment

Until recent years, virtually any child with a seizure was automatically started on long-term AED therapy. This procedure was based on assumptions that (a) the child would have more seizures if not treated, (b) AEDs have minimal side effects, and (c) seizures, even brief ones, could lead to permanent brain damage. These assumptions have been challenged in recent years, leading to significant changes in the therapeutic management of epilepsy.

Results of studies measuring the risk of recurrence after a single unprovoked seizure vary from 27% to 71%, depending on the definitions and study design. Factors that have been demonstrated to increase recurrence risk include an abnormal EEG, preexisting neurological disease such as cerebral palsy, past history of meningitis or major head trauma, and partial as opposed to generalized seizures (Shinnar et al., 1990). Thus, in many patients who present with a first seizure, the physician elects to observe them for recurrent seizures prior to committing to AED therapy.

The cornerstone of epilepsy therapy remains AEDs. Beginning with bromides in the 19th century and phenobarbital in the early 20th century, a small number of drugs have been available to treat seizures. However, after a 15-year drought with no new AEDs since valproate was approved for use in the United States in 1978, a number of new drugs are being developed and will be brought into use during this decade (see Table 4).

The goal of AED therapy is to control all seizure activity without any significant drug side effects. Unfortunately, this goal cannot be achieved in all patients, as 30% to 40% continue to have seizures despite AED therapy and many patients report side effects. Although recurrent seizures may occur because of poor treatment compliance,

AEDs may not completely control seizures, even when taken as prescribed. In many patients a balance must be sought between the degree of seizure control and the dosage of AEDs. Many physicians prefer to tolerate a few seizures and have no drug side effects, rather than have complete seizure control in a child who is having significant, daily drug side effects.

Physicians usually select an AED based on consideration of the child's type of seizures, age, and any individual factors that may predispose the child to drug side effects. For infants and toddlers, phenobarbital remains the drug of preference for most types of seizures. However, phenobarbital is rarely used in children beyond the toddler stage due to concern about potential behavioral and attentional effects, which will be discussed in subsequent sections of this chapter. Currently, carbamazepine and at times, phenytoin and valproate, are the AEDs of choice for partial seizures, while valproate is the preferred drug for generalized convulsive, myoclonic, and atonic seizures. Ethosuximide or valproate are the drugs of choice for absence seizures. With the proliferation of new AEDs, it is anticipated these preferences may change over the next several years.

The treatment strategy for use of AEDs after selection of the most optimal drug is to initiate therapy based on the patient's weight. Dosages are adjusted based on the degree of seizure control, reported side effects, and measured blood levels. Most physicians take a deliberate and long-term approach to medication adjustments. Thus, for many patients it may take several weeks or months before the dose and effect of medication are optimized. If satisfactory seizure control is not attained or significant side effects occur, a second AED is usually started, and ultimately the first AED is weaned. Whenever possible it is advised to treat seizures with one medication to minimize the potential side effects.

AEDs can be associated with many types of side effects. They may potentially affect functions of the liver, blood, skin, central and peripheral nervous system, and endocrine system. Fortunately, severe or life-threatening medical side effects are rare. Physicians monitor patients closely for indicators of medical side effects with laboratory studies, including blood levels of medication, periodic physical examinations, and careful review of complaints. Patients and their parents also are educated extensively about the need to monitor for and report symptoms suggestive of side effects.

One potential side effect of valproate that educators and psychologists may observe is a hand tremor, which occurs in about 10% of patients. This can affect fine-motor and visual-motor functions. A reduction in dose often alleviates the tremor. Cosmetic effects can be worrisome for patients and their parents. Valproate may result in weight gain, which can be controlled by a reduction in calorie intake. Phenytoin may cause gum hyperplasia in a few patients, although this can be minimized by good

Table 4 *Commonly Used Antiepileptic Drugs*

Chemical Name	Brand Name	Year Introduced
Phenobarbital	N/A	1912
Phenytoin	Dilantin	1938
Ethosuximide	Zarontin	1960
Carbamazepine	Tegretol	1974
Valproate	Depakote	1978
Felbamate	Felbatol	1993
Gabapentin	Neurontin	1993
Lamotrigine	Lamictal	1994
Vigabatrin	N/A	Currently in clinical trials
Topiramate	N/A	Currently in clinical trials
Tiagabine	N/A	Currently in clinical trials

dental hygiene. Hirsutism (excess body hair) occurs in some patients taking phenytoin but is rarely significant enough to be of concern.

Subtle side effects such as fatigue, drowsiness, nausea, tremor, and dizziness are commonly reported, particularly just after starting a new medication or a significant increase in dosage. For many patients these side effects are transient and resolve after a period of adjustment to the medication. Evaluation of persistent subtle side effects is a major challenge for physicians. Many double-blind studies of patients and normal controls report a significant incidence of subtle effects but often with only a small difference in incidence between the treatment and the placebo groups. The observations of parents, teachers, and other caregivers are often important in confirming their presence and excluding other medical, psychological, or social factors that may enhance or masquerade as apparent AED toxicity.

AEDs may cause impaired behavior, attention, memory, reaction time, and psychomotor speed in some patients, especially at higher doses. Phenobarbital in particular may have an adverse effect on cognition and behavior (e.g., Calandre, Dominguez-Granados, Gomez-Rubio, & Molina-Font, 1990). Except in infants and toddlers, physicians are using phenobarbital less frequently for this reason. An increased incidence of depression for patients taking phenobarbital also has been reported (Brent, Crumrine, Varma, Brown, & Allan, 1990). Older studies also suggested adverse cognitive effects of phenytoin. However, studies of AED cognitive side effects often have had serious methodological flaws, such that some of the results may have been spurious. Effects often have been dose related; subjects with higher AED blood levels demonstrated the most significant effects (Dodrill & Troupin, 1991). In a large-scale study with improved methodological controls, results indicated minor AED effects from carbamazepine, valproate, and phenytoin on psychomotor speed, attention, and memory functions in children (Aldenkamp et al., 1993). Ethosuximide, used to treat absence seizure disorders, often results in markedly improved cognitive functioning, due to the diminution of seizures that typically occur very frequently prior to treatment. There have been no consistent research findings to indicate significant adverse cognitive effects of ethosuximide.

Cull, Trimble, and Wilson (1992) found that behavioral problems in children ages 7 to 18 years decreased as AED dosages were lowered. In particular, there were decreases in anxiety levels, socially inappropriate behaviors, impulsivity, and hyperactivity. Other studies have found improved behavioral and emotional functioning when the total number of prescribed drugs was reduced.

Cull et al. (1992) found some behavioral improvements in a sample of children with epilepsy whose AED dosages were increased. Their behavioral profile was quite different than that of the subjects with decreasing AED dosages. In the sample with increasing AED dosages, improvement was seen on a psychosomatic factor, suggesting an improved sense of physical well-being. Improved mood has been reported with initiation of carbamazepine (Herranz, Armijo, & Arteaga, 1988). Results of these and other studies indicate that AEDs can have both positive and negative effects on behavior. The behavioral construct of concern needs to be specifically defined when considering the impact of AED therapy.

When assessing possible cognitive and behavioral side effects of AEDS, the ongoing confounding effect of seizure condition must be considered. Even for patients who appear clinically seizure free, there may be abnormal epileptic electrical activity within the brain that subtly disrupts cognition and behavior (Aldenkamp et al., 1993). This is known as subclinical seizure activity, which has been the focus of neuropsychological studies in children with epilepsy (Binnie & Marston, 1992; Rugland, 1990). If subclinical seizure activity is occurring, it could cause the cognitive impairment often attributed to AEDs. For children with persistent cognitive or behavioral impairment despite initiation of medical treatment, repeat EEGs, particularly video or ambulatory EEGs, may be helpful in identifying subclinical seizure activity.

Avoidance of *precipitants* of seizures is important for persons with epilepsy. Some patients may have a specific precipitant for their seizures, such as exposure to flashing lights or computer screens in individuals with photosensitive epilepsy. Although frequently reported in the lay press, photosensitive video-game epilepsy is uncommon and usually is readily diagnosed on an EEG with photic stimulation.

For all individuals with epilepsy, there are several nonspecific precipitants of seizures that should be avoided. These include sleep deprivation and alcohol or drug use. Unfortunately for many college students during exams, sleep deprivation followed by binge drinking is a common behavior pattern that precipitates seizure activity. Common sense, moderation, and prior individual experience should guide specific recommendations regarding avoidance of precipitants.

In recent years there has been renewed interest in the ketogenic diet as a treatment for epilepsy (Freeman, Kelly, & Freeman, 1994). This treatment is based on the consumption of a diet high in fat to produce a state of ketosis, where the brain is relatively deprived of glucose as an energy source and must shift to utilization of ketone bodies as a primary energy source. However, the mechanism by which this diet produces seizure control has not been determined. The diet is used most frequently in children with intractable seizures, particularly myoclonic and atonic seizures. Efficacy has also been reported for generalized tonic-clonic and partial seizures. It is not currently recommended as primary therapy for new onset or uncomplicated epilepsy. The diet is most effective in young children and rarely is used over age 10. Most reports of dietary efficacy are anecdotal, as are reports that the diet improves alertness and behavior. These issues are currently being studied prospectively in an attempt to determine ketogenic dietary efficacy and discriminate between dietary effects, placebo effects, drug withdrawal, and drug side effects.

The diet is initiated in the hospital with a fast, followed by introduction of a carefully calculated and controlled high fat diet that most children consider unpalatable. Rigorous attention to all aspects of the diet and oral intake is essential, as even small amounts of unplanned carbohydrate found in medication syrups or chewing gum may cause loss of ketosis and abrupt loss of seizure control. Thus, children cannot partake in traditional school holiday and birthday celebrations. For children attending school, a special snack and lunch dietary program must be established in collaboration with the medical dietitian. These students often require emotional and psychological support to deal with issues of peer stigmatization.

Epilepsy surgery has been increasingly utilized in the treatment of children with epilepsy over the past decade, but it is still considered a treatment option for less than 1% of this population. Surgery is considered most commonly for children with intractable seizures who fail to respond to medication or children whose seizures arise from a brain lesion that can be surgically removed. In recent years there has been a trend toward earlier surgical evaluation of children to avoid the cumulative developmental and psychological sequelae of prolonged uncontrolled epilepsy. Epilepsy surgery in children requires intensive presurgical evaluation and should be performed only in centers with resources for the comprehensive medical, psychological, social, and behavioral evaluation of surgical candidates.

Problems and Implications

Many factors have been considered as possible causes of learning, attentional, and behavioral problems in children with epilepsy, including the seizures themselves, AED side effects, underlying brain abnormalities, preexisting learning disabilities, specific attentional and memory deficits, and psychological adjustment factors. The frequency and type of seizure, as well as degree of seizure control, may influence the child's daily performance pattern and scores on formal psychological and educational tests. For example, if a child is continuing to have absence seizures despite AED therapy, academic and perhaps behavioral or emotional functioning may be adversely affected intermittently. Patient responses to various AEDs and specific doses are to some extent individual. Some may experience either transient or

chronic subtle cognitive side effects that undermine learning and performance.

The importance of understanding the potential impact of specific medical variables on the performance of a child with epilepsy cannot be overemphasized. However, these factors typically account for only a small portion of the variance in educational test scores and social outcomes of children and adolescents with epilepsy (Camfield, Camfield, Smith, Gordon, & Dooley, 1993; Seidenberg et al., 1986). Factors such as preexisting learning disabilities, parental income and educational levels, and psychosocial problems within the family remain strong outcome predictors for children with epilepsy, as they are for children in general (Camfield et al., 1993; Freeman, Jacobs, Vining, & Rabin, 1984; Hermann, Whitman, Hughes, Melyn, & Dell, 1988; Mitchell, Chavez, Lee, & Gregman, 1991).

Intelligence

Several studies have investigated intelligence in children with epilepsy, with varied findings (Bailet & Turk, 1993; Bourgeois, Prensky, Palkes, Talent, & Busch, 1983; Dreifuss, 1992). Differences across studies often reflect differences in patient samples and research methods. Most investigators agree that, as a group, children with epilepsy display average intelligence but with a shift toward the lower end of the normal range. Children with developmental disabilities (e.g., mental retardation, cerebral palsy, and autism) or language, learning, or emotional handicaps are more likely to have epilepsy than children without developmental disabilities (Frank, 1985). Children with symptomatic epilepsy are less likely to have average cognitive capabilities than children with idiopathic epilepsy (Sachs & Barrett, 1995). Although there are many exceptions, seizure onset prior to five years of age also is associated with poorer cognitive and psychosocial outcomes.

Historically, it was postulated that seizures themselves might cause brain damage and subsequent intellectual decline. This hypothesis has been largely refuted for the epilepsy population overall. However, Bourgeois et al. (1983) identified a subset of children with epilepsy who displayed a persistent IQ decline (8 of the 72 children in the study). They had seizures that started at a younger age and were more difficult to control than subjects with stable IQs. They also tended to have mixed seizure types and more instances of AED levels in the toxic range. The presence of these seizure-related factors indicated severe epilepsy.

Specific Cognitive Process Deficits

In addition to concerns about general intellectual ability, specific deficits in memory, attention, and psychomotor speed have been associated with epilepsy. Again, delineating the precise cause of these deficits is difficult at best, due to the confounding effects of the seizures, AED side effects, and perhaps preexisting but previously undiagnosed cognitive processing deficits. Although the majority of studies investigating these cognitive processes have included adults with epilepsy, a few studies have been conducted with children. Chronic verbal memory deficits have been reported primarily in patients with seizures originating in the left temporal lobe of the brain. Persistent visual memory deficits have been reported for patients with right temporal lobe foci. Patients with bilateral temporal lobe involvement often have more severe, pervasive memory deficits, as the temporal lobes are essential for memory. A recent study found that children with epilepsy displayed verbal memory deficits, but there were no differences according to seizure type (McCarthy, Richman, & Yarbrough, 1995). Decreased psychomotor speed and reaction time also have been extensively documented in individuals with epilepsy.

Attentional deficits have been reported in both children and adults with epilepsy. For some children, these deficits may be due to frequent subtle seizure activity, as may occur with absence seizures (Stores, 1978; Trimble, 1987). For others, Attention-Deficit/Hyperactivity Disorder may be present in addition to seizures. A recent study of children with epilepsy who had at least average intelligence found that they demonstrated increased impulsivity as compared with youngsters without epilepsy but no impairment in sustained attention (Mitchell, Chavez, Zhou, & Guzman, 1993). AEDs may contribute to attentional deficits, as previously described.

Academic Achievement

Despite normal intelligence in most children with epilepsy, academic underachievement is widespread in this population. Seidenberg et al. (1986) found that 33% of their subjects with epilepsy displayed significant arithmetic deficits relative to their IQ. An earlier age of seizure onset, higher lifetime seizure total, and the presence of generalized seizures were significantly associated with underachievement in arithmetic. However, these medical factors in combination with age and sex accounted for only a modest proportion (17%) of the variance in arithmetic scores for their epilepsy subjects. The authors speculated that other cognitive factors were contributing significantly to school achievement problems in children with epilepsy.

Camfield et al. (1993) found that a history of more than 20 seizures before treatment correlated with poor social and educational outcome, including the need for special education services or grade retention. Of their sample, 35% required special education services over the course of the study, as compared to 11.7% for the general school population in their geographic area. Children with simple partial seizures experienced the most favorable long-term outcomes. However, the strongest predictor of poor outcome was the presence of learning deficits at the time epilepsy was initially diagnosed. These results occurred even when children with known mental retardation were excluded from data analyses (Camfield et al., 1993).

Our own longitudinal study of children with epilepsy has demonstrated similar findings (Turk, 1993). The subjects with epilepsy scored significantly lower than their nonepileptic siblings and children with migraine headaches on reading and spelling tests, and these differences persisted across serial reevaluations. Of our subjects with epilepsy, 17% had received special education services, and 32% had repeated a grade. Among the 23 siblings, only one had received special education, and three had repeated a grade (13%). The study included only subjects with IQ scores of at least 80.

Behavioral Functioning

Behavioral problems are frequently reported among children with epilepsy, including emotional lability, anxiety, irritability, and hyperactivity. A recent population-based study found significantly greater likelihood of hyperactivity, short attention span, and argumentative temperament in children with epilepsy as compared to children with cardiac problems and control subjects (McDermott, Mani, & Krishnaswami, 1995). Children with epilepsy have more psychiatric problems than children with diabetes (Hoare, 1984) and children with asthma (Austin, 1989). Our longitudinal study identified significant behavioral and emotional problems among the subjects with epilepsy, as compared with their siblings, although the subjects with migraine displayed behavioral problems as significant as those observed in the epilepsy sample (Turk, 1993). As is the case for the learning deficits seen in children with epilepsy, these behavioral problems often have an underlying neurological basis but may also result from adverse AED effects.

Emotional Functioning

For anyone with a chronic illness such as epilepsy, quality of life is determined as much by the person's perception of symptoms and psychological response to them as by the illness itself (Santilli, 1993). A number of affective and adjustment issues may impair school and social functioning for children and adolescents with epilepsy. Fundamentally, there is anxiety associated with the loss during a seizure of physical control, mental control, or both. The physical manifestations of a generalized convulsive seizure can be especially embarrassing. There may be confusion and stress regarding who and what to tell about one's seizures. These concerns often provoke significant fears of seizure recurrence in public settings. Physical safety during a seizure also is a legitimate concern, including injuries from falls, bicycle or motor vehicle accidents, and drowning. Children and adolescents often perceive a loss of independence for these reasons. AED side effects can cause physical changes, which further undermine self-esteem. Treatment compliance may diminish in the presence of any side effects, with a potential for exacerbation of seizures.

These issues often are most problematic during adolescence, when the desires for independence and peer acceptance become more pronounced, along with the urge to deny differences or handicaps. Chronic feelings of helplessness, dependency, and reduced self-esteem may result in social withdrawal (Taylor, 1989). Prejudice and stigmatization of individuals with epilepsy persist and contribute to social ostracism (Baumann, Wilson, & Wiese, 1995). Restrictions on driving for persons with epilepsy exist in most states. This and other possible restrictions on recreational activities further contribute to anxiety and anger associated with chronic illness as well as loss of social status.

Family Issues

The presence of epilepsy introduces some degree of stress to family structure and resources (Austin, Risinger, & Beckett, 1992). Initially, there may be fear that the child will die. Most seizures are not associated with life-threatening neurological problems, such as brain tumors or severe trauma. In addition, significant injury or death as a result of a seizure is very uncommon in children. Nonetheless, some types of seizures can be terrifying to observe, and the person may look as though death is possible (Taylor, 1989). The fear of injury, understandably, may evoke overprotective efforts by caregivers, which lead to reduced expectations (Hartlage & Green, 1972). The child may respond by becoming increasingly dependent and manipulative, identifying primarily with the sickness rather than with more positive personal attributes. McDermott et al. (1995) found a significantly higher occurrence of dependency among children with epilepsy as compared with control subjects and children with cardiac problems. Emotional adjustment to chronic illness is required by the patient, parents, siblings, and extended family members.

In addition to fear and overprotection, unidentified and unresolved feelings of guilt, anger, and depression are not uncommon and may contribute to maladaptive family interaction patterns (Sachs & Barrett, 1995; Taylor, 1989). For example, one parent may blame the other for a head injury to a child, if the injury is perceived to be a possible cause of the seizures. Siblings may resent the extra attention a child with epilepsy receives, feel guilty that they are healthy, or worry that they may have

to care for the sibling with epilepsy in the parent's absence. Additional doctor appointments and medical tests result in school absences for the child and missed work for the parent. Financial resources may be strained, particularly for children with more complicated epilepsy. Level of family stress and degree of extended family support have been shown to correlate significantly with behavioral problems in children with epilepsy (Austin et al., 1992). A restored sense of control is essential to stress reduction in the patient and family members. It will contribute to more successful long-term epilepsy management and improved educational, vocational, and psychosocial outcomes.

Alternative Actions

The school psychologist has many opportunities to provide direct and indirect services for students with epilepsy and to serve as a source of information about epilepsy for other school personnel and parents. Factual information about seizure recognition and management at school, recommendations about discussions on epilepsy with students, principles of psychoeducational assessment and educational management, and counseling issues are described in this section.

Seizure Recognition

As discussed previously, the manifestations of a seizure may vary widely. Careful observation and documentation of the behavior or event in question, duration, time of day, and events both before and immediately following a suspected seizure can be helpful to the physician in making a diagnosis of seizures and deciding upon appropriate treatment. Specific information to record is summarized in Table 5. If a diagnosis of seizures is made, it is crucial to continue observing the child for persistent seizure symptoms and for changes in alertness, behavior, affect, and academic performance. Improvement may reflect the beneficial effects of the child's AED. Ongoing seizure symptoms or decline in academic, behavioral, or emotional functioning may indicate a lack of optimal seizure control, a progressive neurological disorder causing the seizures, or significant AED side effects. Such information, both favorable and unfavorable, may assist the physician in patient management.

Response to Seizures Occurring at School

The appropriate response to a seizure occurring at school obviously varies according to the type of seizure. Most seizures are not medical emergencies and do not require acute medical intervention. Generalized convulsive sei-

Table 5 *Seizure Observation*

For any of the following symptoms observed, describe in as much detail as possible:

1. What was the child doing before the seizure?

_____ Was ill
_____ Had a fever
_____ Suffered an injury
_____ Experienced a behavior change

2. What happened first? _____

3. What did the child's body do?

_____ On one side
_____ On both sides

4. What did the child's face do?

_____ Eye rolling, twitching, or deviation
_____ Jerking
_____ Chewing movements

5. Were there unusual movements or behaviors?

_____ Speech, vocalizations
_____ Automatisms
_____ Responsiveness to verbal, auditory, visual, or tactile stimuli
_____ Urine or fecal incontinence

6. How long did the seizure last? _____

7. How was the child after the seizure?

_____ Tired, sleepy
_____ Confused, disoriented
_____ Was weak on one side
_____ Was weak on both sides
_____ Had a headache
_____ Vomited

Table 6 *Acute Management of Seizures*

1. Clear the area around the individual.
2. Place the individual on a flat, soft surface.
3. Turn on side with head down slightly.
4. Loosen clothing, but do not restrain movements or place objects in mouth.
5. Carefully observe seizure, including duration (time with a watch) and manifestations: onset, facial movements, automatisms, stiffening or jerking, one sided or bilateral, incontinence, and behavior after seizure stops.
6. Emergency medical services should be called if
   ■ The convulsive seizure activity continues for more than 5 minutes.
   ■ The person has repetitive seizures without awakening in between.
   ■ The person has no known prior history of seizures.
   ■ The person sustained a significant injury before or during the seizure.
   ■ Normal breathing does not resume quickly.
7. When the seizure activity stops, the person should be observed and allowed to rest in a quiet environment. It is not uncommon to vomit during a seizure or have a headache and sleepiness after a seizure. Post-seizure management of a child with known epilepsy should be customized for each student based on the condition after the seizure, experience with prior seizures, parental desires, and recommendations from medical personnel.

zures are the most frightening to observe and historically have provoked unhelpful and potentially dangerous responses. Contrary to the widely held myth, the tongue cannot be swallowed during a convulsive seizure; consequently, no effort should be made to place a pencil or any other object into the person's mouth, to force the mouth open, or to hold the tongue. Table 6 summarizes acute seizure management procedures. A relatively quick return to normal classroom activities following a seizure is recommended if possible. Keeping a change of clothes at school is essential for children who lose bladder or bowel control during seizures.

Helping Students Understand Epilepsy

Remaining calm and reassuring the child who had the seizure and others who were present will make epilepsy management and resumption of the normal routine easier. Discussion of factual information about epilepsy, as well as emotions that arise in students as a result of ob-

serving a seizure, should be undertaken. The school psychologist can be instrumental either in leading the discussion or consulting with teachers who will be discussing epilepsy in the classroom. Students with seizures should be asked their opinions about such a discussion with classmates and be given the option of not attending class at that time. Details of the discussion should always be reviewed with the child who elects not to attend.

Students frequently fear that seizures are contagious and should be reassured that they are not. They may worry that the child having a seizure will die or never return to normal. Honest explanations of seizures and direct reassurances about the students' fear should alleviate these concerns. Reviewing the appropriate response to seizures also is important in classrooms with a student likely to experience recurrent seizures. Discussion of the fears and embarrassment felt by the student who has seizures may create greater empathy toward that student among classmates and facilitate normal social interaction (Frank, 1985).

Participation in School, Recreational, and Vocational Activities

It is generally advised that children with seizures pursue normal childhood activities with few restrictions. When in doubt, parents and teachers should use common sense to guide specific decisions. School activities are not generally restricted for children with epilepsy. For the child with frequent seizures, a buddy system often works well to assist the student during class changes. Full participation in physical education is encouraged.

Because seizures are often abrupt in onset and may cause both loss of consciousness and motor control, situations should be avoided where there is a high probability of injury. For persons of all ages with epilepsy, avoidance of heights is strongly advised, and all water activities should be supervised. The most dangerous body of water is the bathtub. Children and teenagers should never be left alone in the bathtub and should be encouraged to take showers. All states have regulations regarding driving restrictions for individuals with epilepsy. Students should be encouraged to contact their local Department of Motor Vehicles for specific information. Bicycling generally is not restricted unless children have frequent seizures, but it is recommended that they ride only on nonbusy streets or sidewalks, always wear a helmet, and ride with a buddy. These precautions are taken in all children following their first seizure. If the child is placed on medication, these precautions generally continue throughout their period of treatment and for one year after their AED is stopped. For children who have a single seizure and are not placed on treatment, precautions should apply for a minimum of one year.

Children with epilepsy are not usually restricted from athletic participation unless their seizures are poorly controlled. Boxing is forbidden for all children with epilepsy due to the high probability of a head injury. Contact football is not specifically restricted, although consideration of alternative sports with a lower probability of head injury is recommended.

Vocationally, children with epilepsy generally should be encouraged to pursue their interests commensurate with their abilities, particularly as many children have a permanent remission of their seizure disorder. For a few professions, such as commercial airline pilot, a history of seizures may be an absolute contraindication to entry. For some occupations that require use of heavy equipment or exposure to potentially dangerous equipment, some changes in job activities may be indicated. Thus, exposure to high speed saws in wood shop or the deep fryer or grill at a fast food restaurant should be restricted. Students should be advised to disclose their history of seizures when applying for work. Should they sense that an employer is concerned about their seizure disorder, they should request advice, information, and if necessary, assistance from their physician, counselor, and local epilepsy foundation.

Psychoeducational Consultation and Assessment

Ideally, increased monitoring of educational performance, behavior, and psychosocial functioning should take place for all students diagnosed with epilepsy. How-

ever, the presence of seizures may not always be documented in student records. For any child undergoing assessment of school performance problems, a medical history should be obtained that includes questions about seizures. Information should be collected regarding seizure type, age at seizure onset, medications, date when medication treatment began, and date of last seizure.

School psychologists are among the best trained school personnel to observe and record a student's behavior, for the purpose of identifying a significant medical problem, documenting response to medical treatment, or identifying learning and behavior problems. The information gathered through a structured observation should be conveyed to the student's parent, who in turn should be encouraged to contact the child's physician. An interview with the child can elicit previously unexpressed feelings and provide insights into the child's coping capabilities. All of this information will influence the precise educational, behavioral, or counseling strategies employed to alleviate school-based problems.

Many children with epilepsy display chronic mild learning, memory, and performance speed deficits, as previously described in this chapter. The school psychologist can provide instructional consultation for classroom teachers to devise educational strategies that lessen the impact of these deficits on daily performance. See Rosenfield, 1987, Aaron, 1995, and Mather and Roberts, 1995, for comprehensive discussions of general instructional consultation issues, assessment and remediation of reading problems, and assessment and remediation of writing problems, respectively.

In the event that these alternative educational strategies are not sufficient to improve classroom performance, formal assessment and consideration for special education will need to be undertaken. Students with epilepsy may qualify for special education services using criteria specified under the Individuals With Disabilities Education Act (IDEA), either by meeting criteria for services to students with learning disabilities, emotional disorders, or mental handicaps or through the Other Health Impaired category. They may also be eligible for regular classroom accommodations under Section 504 of the Rehabilitation Act of 1973.

In general, a comprehensive assessment approach used for any student experiencing learning, behavioral, or emotional difficulties is appropriate for students with epilepsy. Psychological and educational testing should usually be postponed if medication has been initiated within the preceding 8 weeks or changed within the preceding 2 weeks, or if a convulsive seizure has occurred within the past week. The student should be closely observed throughout the evaluation for any subtle mental or physical indications of seizure activity. An interview with the child and parents regarding their knowledge and concerns about epilepsy also should be incorporated into the assessment process.

Occasionally, a student with epilepsy will fail to improve following psychoeducational assessment and intervention at school. In such cases, referral for more in-depth neurological, psychiatric, or neuropsychological evaluation is recommended, preferably to a clinic that provides comprehensive services to patients with epilepsy.

Counseling

Counseling may be appropriate for a student who displays acute or chronic problems adjusting to the diagnosis of epilepsy and developing effective coping strategies. At some point, nearly all children with epilepsy and their families need counseling. The focus may be to educate the child and family about epilepsy, to provide support during difficult periods of adjustment, or to teach social problem-solving skills. Depending on the age of the child, different medical, psychological, and psychosocial issues will arise (see Santilli, 1993, for a comprehensive discussion).

Educational counseling focuses on what the child and the family need to know about seizures, medications, and other aspects of management and on how and when to initiate contact with medical personnel. This information may need to be presented on multiple occasions to ensure adequate understanding. Knowledge alone, however, rarely ensures compliance. The child and family must have confidence in the diagnosis and management plan, as well as opportunities to practice application of their knowledge with constructive feedback from medical personnel.

Supportive counseling may occur briefly to encourage acknowledgment of feelings resulting from the presence of seizures, to alleviate stress, and to foster more positive adaptation. Prejudice and stigmatization in regards to epilepsy contribute to rejection, which in turn causes a loss of social group membership and a loss of opportunities to compete educationally, socially, and vocationally (Taylor, 1989). Problem-solving and social skills training, including role-playing, may facilitate increased self-confidence, as well as greater social and educational initiative. Early counseling intervention may also prevent overprotectiveness by caregivers and adoption of a sick role as the primary feature of the child's social interactions, both of which compound the adverse effects of the medical condition itself (Sachs & Barrett, 1995; Taylor, 1989). For children with both seizures and developmental disabilities, play or art therapy may be beneficial (Santilli, 1993).

Although it is widely accepted that children with chronic medical conditions are at increased risk for behavioral and emotional problems, the majority receive no mental health or social service support (Gortmaker, Walker, Weitzman & Sobol, 1990). The reasons for this pattern remain unclear but may include limited accessibility due to financial and managed health care constraints, lack of appropriate referrals by physicians, and failure of parents to acknowledge the child's behavioral difficulties and stresses within the family.

School psychologists may be in a unique position to provide essential counseling support, at least in cases where the child's school performance is in jeopardy. An assessment, counseling, and work experience program implemented through a large public school system demonstrated improved academic performance, decreased dropout rate, and increased post-high-school employment for adolescents with epilepsy (Freeman et al., 1984).

Summary

Epilepsy is a central nervous system disorder characterized by recurrent seizures; it affects approximately one percent of children and adolescents. It is often associated with significant problems in academic achievement, psychological adjustment, social development, and eventual adult functional status. Antiepileptic drugs remain the primary method of treatment at present. For rare patients, brain surgery or the ketogenic diet may decrease seizure activity. Avoidance of known seizure precipitants and psychosocial interventions to decrease stress and increase treatment compliance also may lessen the severity and adverse impact of this disorder.

In the school setting, school psychologists can be instrumental in documenting behaviors that may indicate seizure activity or response to treatment and the need for educational or psychological intervention. Information regarding the child's seizure type, characteristics, and treatment should be obtained, as it may impact conceptualization of the child's school problems, timing of a formal psychoeducational assessment, and formulation of an educational plan. Many children with epilepsy display academic underachievement and may qualify for special education services or other classroom accommodations.

The school psychologist can provide information to classroom teachers, students, and parents about seizures, seizure management, and adjustment issues deriving from the presence of a chronic medical disorder. Counseling often is warranted for students with epilepsy and their families to provide factual information about epilepsy and its treatment and to address fear, anger, depression, and reduced self-esteem that may result from the perceived loss of physical or mental control and possible activity restrictions. Excellent support groups exist locally and nationally that can provide factual information about epilepsy, including community resources, advocacy programs, and job placement (see Recommended Resources).

Recommended Resources

For Professionals

Hermann, B., & Seidenberg, M. (1989). *Childhood epilepsies: Neuropsychological, psychosocial and intervention aspects.* New York: John Wiley.
This is the most comprehensive textbook written for psychologists on childhood epilepsy. Chapters are included on effects of AEDs on cognitive functioning, adjustment issues, and therapeutic interventions.

For Parents

Freeman, J. M., Vining, E. P. G., & Pillas, D. J. (1990). *Seizures and epilepsy in childhood: A guide for parents.* Baltimore: The Johns Hopkins University Press.
This book provides comprehensive medical information about childhood epilepsy, along with extensive information on coping with the diagnosis and long-term management. Brief cases are presented throughout the book to illustrate issues described. A glossary of medical terms is included.

Reisner, H. (Ed.). (1988). *Children with epilepsy: A parents' guide.* Kensington, MD: Woodbine House.
This is an edited volume written for parents, which includes chapters by physicians, therapists, educators, lawyers, and parents of children with epilepsy. Many practical issues are addressed, and quotes from parents appear frequently throughout the book. It has an extensive annotated bibliography, as well as addresses for national and state agencies that provide assistance to persons with epilepsy and developmental disabilities.

Support Organizations

The Epilepsy Foundation of America (EFA) provides numerous services nationwide for individuals with epilepsy and their families. Many excellent pamphlets are available through their toll-free information service at 1-800-EFA-1000. State- and local-affiliated EFA programs offer training to school personnel, advocacy, recreational opportunities, brief counseling, and employment assistance.

References

Aaron, P. G. (Ed.). (1995). Recent advances in reading instruction and remediation (mini-series). *School Psychology Review, 24,* 327–442.

Aldenkamp, A. P., Alpherts, W. C. J., Blennow, G., Elmqvist, D., Heijbel, J., Nilsson, H. L., Sandstedt, P., Tonnby, B., Wahlander, L., & Wosse, E. (1993). Withdrawal of antiepileptic medication in children—effects on cognitive function: The multicenter Holmfrid study. *Neurology, 43,* 41–50.

Andermann, E. (1982). Multifactorial inheritance of generalized and focal epilepsy. In V. E. Anderson, W. A. Hauser, J. K. Penry, & C. F. Sing (Eds.), *Genetic basis of the epilepsies* (pp. 355–374). New York: Raven Press.

Arts, W. F. M., Visser, L. H., Loonen, M. C. B., Tjiam, A. T., Stroink, H., Stuurman, P. M., & Poortvliet, D. C. J. (1988). Follow-up of 146 children with epilepsy after withdrawal of antiepileptic therapy. *Epilepsia, 29,* 244–250.

Austin, J. K. (1989). Comparison of child adaptation to epilepsy and asthma. *Journal of Child and Adolescent Psychiatric and Mental Health Nursing, 2,* 139–144.

Austin, J. K., Risinger, M. W., & Beckett, L. A. (1992). Correlates of behavior problems in children with epilepsy. *Epilepsia, 33,* 1115–1122.

Bailet, L. L., & Turk, W. R. (1993). Selective anticonvulsant effect on academic achievement in childhood-onset epilepsy. *Annals of Neurology, 34,* 500.

Baumann, R., Wilson, J., & Wiese, H. (1995). Kentuckians' attitudes toward children with epilepsy. *Epilepsia, 36,* 1009–1016.

Binnie, C. D., & Marston, D. (1992). Cognitive correlates of interictal discharges. *Epilepsia, 33* (Suppl. 6), S11–S17.

Bourgeois, B. F. D., Prensky, A. L., Palkes, H. S., Talent, B. K., & Busch, S. G. (1983). Intelligence in epilepsy: A prospective study in children. *Annals of Neurology, 14,* 438–444.

Brent, D., Crumrine, P., Varma, R., Brown, R., & Allan, M. (1990). Phenobarbital treatment and major depressive disorder in children with epilepsy: A naturalistic follow-up. *Pediatrics, 85,* 1086–1091.

Brorson, L. O., & Wranne, L. (1987). Long-term prognosis in childhood epilepsy: Survival and seizure prognosis. *Epilepsia, 28,* 324–330.

Calandre, E., Dominguez-Granados, R., Gomez-Rubio, M., & Molina-Font, J. (1990). Cognitive effects of long term treatment with phenobarbital and valproic acid in school children. *Acta Neurologica Scandinavia, 81,* 504–506.

Camfield, C., Camfield, P., Smith, B., Gordon, K., & Dooley, J. (1993). Biologic factors as predictors of social outcome of epilepsy in intellectually normal children: A population-based study. *Journal of Pediatrics, 122,* 869–873.

Commission on Classification and Terminology of the International League Against Epilepsy. (1981). Proposal for revised clinical and electroencephalographic classification of epileptic seizures. *Epilepsia, 22,* 489–501.

Commission on Classification and Terminology of the International League Against Epilepsy. (1989). Proposal for revised classification of epilepsies and epileptic syndromes. *Epilepsia, 30,* 389–399.

Cull, C. A., Trimble, M. R., & Wilson, J. (1992). Changes in antiepileptic drug regimen and behaviour in children with epilepsy. *Journal of Epilepsy, 5,* 1–9.

Dodrill, C. B., & Troupin, A. S. (1991). Neuropsychological effects of carbamazepine and phenytoin: A reanalysis. *Neurology, 41,* 141–143.

Dreifuss, F. E. (1992). Cognitive function: Victim of disease or hostage to treatment? *Epilepsia, 33* (Suppl. 2), S7–S12.

Dulac, O. (1995). Epileptic syndromes in infancy and childhood: Recent advances. *Epilepsia, 36* (Suppl. 1), 51–57.

Frank, B. B. (1985). Psycho-social aspects of educating epileptic children: Roles for school psychologists. *School Psychology Review, 14,* 196–203.

Freeman, J. M., Jacobs, H., Vining, E., & Rabin, C. E. (1984). Epilepsy and the inner city schools: A school-based program that makes a difference. *Epilepsia, 25,* 438–442.

Freeman, J. M., Kelly, M. T., & Freeman, J. B. (1994). *The epilepsy diet treatment.* New York: Demos.

Gortmaker, S. L., Walker, D. K., Weitzman, M., & Sobol, A. M. (1990). Chronic conditions, socioeconomic risks, and behavioral problems in children and adolescents. *Pediatrics, 85,* 267–276.

Hartlage, L. L., & Green, J. B. (1972). The relation of parental attitudes to academic and social achievement in epileptic children. *Epilepsia, 13,* 21–26.

Hauser, W. A., Annegers, J. F., & Kurland, L. T. (1991). The prevalence of epilepsy in Rochester, Minnesota, 1940–1980. *Epilepsia, 32,* 429–445.

Hermann, B. P., Whitman, S., Hughes, J. R., Melyn, M. M., & Dell, J. (1988). Multietiological determinants of psychopathology and social competence in children with epilepsy. *Epilepsy Research, 2,* 51–60.

Herranz, J. L., Armijo, J. A., & Arteaga, R. (1988). Clinical side effects of phenobarbital, primidone, phenytoin, carbamazepine, and valproate during monotherapy in children. *Epilepsia, 29,* 794–804.

Hoare, P. (1984). The development of psychiatric disorders among school children with epilepsy. *Developmental Medicine and Child Neurology, 26,* 3–24.

Jackson, J. H. (1873). On the anatomical, physiological, and pathological investigation of epilepsies. *West Riding Lunatic Asylum Medical Reports, 3,* 315–332.

Mather, N., & Roberts, R. (1995). *Informal assessment and instruction in written language.* Brandon, VT: Clinical Psychology Publishing.

McCarthy, A. M., Richman, L. C., & Yarbrough, D. (1995). Memory, attention and school problems in children with seizure disorders. *Developmental Neuropsychology, 11*(1), 71–86.

McDermott, S. Mani, S., & Krishnaswami, S. (1995). A population based analysis of specific behavior problems associated with childhood seizures. *Journal of Epilepsy, 8,* 110–118.

Mitchell, W. G., Chavez, J. M., Lee, H., & Gregman, B. C. (1991). Academic underachievement in children with epilepsy. *Journal of Child Neurology, 6,* 65–72.

Mitchell, W. G., Chavez, J. M., Zhou, Y., & Guzman, B. L. (1993). Effects of antiepileptic drugs on reaction time, attention, and impulsivity in children. *Pediatrics, 91,* 101–105.

Nelson, K. B., & Ellenberg, J. H. (1978). Prognosis in children with febrile seizures. *Pediatrics, 61,* 720–727.

Roger, J., Bureau, M., Dravet, C., Dreifuss, F. E., Perret, A., & Wolf, P. (1992). *Epileptic syndromes in infancy, childhood and adolescence* (2nd ed.). London: John Libby.

Rosenfield, S. A. (1987). *Instructional consultation.* Hillsdale, NJ: Lawrence Erlbaum Associates.

Rugland, A. L. (1990). Neuropsychological assessment of cognitive functioning in children with epilepsy. *Epilepsia, 31*(Suppl. 4), S41–S44.

Sachs, H. T., & Barrett, R. P. (1995). Seizure disorders: A review for school psychologists. *School Psychology Review, 24,* 131–145.

Santilli, N. (1993). Psychosocial aspects of epilepsy: Education and counseling for patients and families. In E. Wyllie (Ed.), *The treatment of epilepsy: Principles and practice* (pp. 1163–1167). Philadelphia: Lea & Febiger.

Schwartzkroin, P. A. (1993). Basic mechanisms of epileptogenesis. In E. Wyllie (Ed.), *The treatment of epilepsy: Principles and practice* (pp. 83–98). Philadelphia: Lea & Febiger.

Seidenberg, M., Beck, N., Geisser, M., Giordani, B., Sackellares, J. C., Berent, S., Dreifuss, F. E., & Boll, T. J. (1986). Academic achievement of children with epilepsy. *Epilepsia, 27,* 753–759.

Shinnar, S., Berg, A. T., Moshe, S. L., Petix, M., Maytal, J., Kang, H., Goldensohn, E. S., & Hauser, W. A. (1990). Risk of seizure recurrence following a first unprovoked seizure in childhood: A prospective study. *Pediatrics, 85,* 1076–1084.

Stores, G. (1978). School-children with epilepsy at risk for learning and behavior problems. *Developmental Medicine and Child Neurology, 20,* 502–508.

Taylor, D. C. (1989). Psychosocial components of childhood epilepsy. In B. P. Hermann & M. Seidenberg (Eds.), *Childhood epilepsies: Neuropsychological, psychosocial and intervention aspects* (pp. 119–142). Chichester, England: John Wiley & Sons.

Treiman, L. J., & Treiman, D. M. (1993). Genetic aspects of epilepsy. In E. Wyllie (Ed.), *The treatment of epilepsy: Principles and practice (pp. 145–156).* Philadelphia: Lea & Febiger.

Trimble, M. R. (1987). Anticonvulsant drugs and cognitive function: A review of the literature. *Epilepsia, 28*(Suppl. 3), 537–545.

Turk, W. R. (1993). Academic achievement in childhood onset epilepsy. *Epilepsia, 34*(6), 25.

73

Brain Injury

Elaine Clark
University of Utah

Background and Development

More than one million children and adolescents sustain brain injuries each year. Brain injuries are not new to educators; however, the more severe ones may be. Given recent advancements in life-saving techniques (e.g., jaws of life) and medical technology (e.g., acute trauma management), many children are surviving serious brain injuries. It is estimated that 65% of children with severe injuries now survive (Michaud, Rivara, & Grady, 1992). Although this rate is lower than the total number of survivors of all ages, estimated to be around 95% (Rosen & Gerring, 1986), it still represents a substantial number of students who will need some accommodation in the regular classroom or additional rehabilitation or special education services.

Public schools are probably in the best position to provide services to students with brain injuries given the diversity of the specialists employed and their access to both families and students. A number of obstacles, however, can interfere with the provision of service. Because traumatic brain injuries are unexpected, the number of students requiring service cannot be anticipated from one year to the next. Further, the nature of brain injuries vary, as do the sequelae, making it difficult to anticipate the extent of services that may be needed. Costs cannot be predicted as easily as they can for other special education populations (e.g., intellectual disabilities) who remain in the system year after year (Lash, 1994). While some schools may have 20 students enrolled with brain injuries, others may have only one or two. This poses particular problems for sharing resources. Perhaps the most serious obstacle to service, however, is the lack of knowledge on educators' part as to how brain injuries impact a student's learning and behavior (Blosser & DePompei, 1991). Research has shown that relatively few educators have had any formal coursework, or even inservice training, in this area (Anderson, 1995; Mira, Meck, & Tyler, 1988).

Educational Definition of Brain Injury

In 1990 the U.S. government enacted legislation that mandates special education services for students who have sustained a traumatic brain injury (TBI) that interferes with their learning. Public Law 101-476, the Individuals with Disabilities Education Act (IDEA), specifies that:

Traumatic brain injury means an acquired injury to the brain caused by an external physical force, resulting in total or partial functional disability or psychosocial impairment, or both, that adversely affects a child's educational performance. The term applies to open or closed head injuries resulting in impairments in one or more areas, such as cognition; language; memory; attention; reasoning; abstract thinking; judgement; problem-solving; sensory; perceptual and motor abilities; psychosocial behavior; physical functions; information processing; and speech. The term does not apply to brain injuries that are congenital or degenerative, or brain injuries induced by birth trauma (Definition from 1992 Federal Register/Vol. 57, No. 189, p. 44802).

Whereas the majority of states have adopted guidelines that parallel the federal definition, some state guidelines include students who otherwise would be ineligible for service by federal standards (Katsiyannis & Conderman, 1994). For example, in New York, Utah, and Wisconsin, students who sustain brain injuries from strokes, brain tumors, central nervous system infections, toxic exposure, and hypoxia secondary to events other than near drowning (i.e., cardiac arrest and electrocution) are eligible for TBI services if their brain injury interferes with academic and social success. Some states, such as Utah, based their decision to include these students on the fact that their impairments and educational needs were virtually indistinguishable from those of students with "external" injuries. However, because head injuries are the most common cause of disabling brain injuries in children and adolescents (Moloney, 1989), head injuries that cause brain injury will be specifically addressed in this chapter.

Epidemiology of Head Injury

Research shows that males are one and a half times more likely than females to sustain a traumatic brain injury and that both sexes are likely to have the highest incidence of injury during the first year of life (Henry, Hasuber, & Rice, 1992). Typically, these injuries are the result of falls and are less severe than those that occur later on in development (Di Scala, Osberg, Gans, Chin, & Grant, 1991). Traffic-related accidents, however, account for nearly half of all brain injuries and for the majority of serious ones (Di Scala et al., 1991). While the automobile is considered to be the most lethal weapon in a child's environment (Tepas, Di Scala, Ramenofsky, & Barlow, 1990), especially for adolescents who drive, recent research on recreational equipment suggests that sport-related accidents may be a close second. Studies show that head injury is the primary diagnosis made for children injured on playground equipment and other recreational equipment such as skate boards and roller skates (Baker, Fowler, Li, Warner, & Dannenberg, 1994). Other sports-related activities such as horseback riding have been associated with head injury, especially when children ride without helmets (Christey, Nelson, Rivara, Smith, & Condie, 1994).

Brain injury is also found among children who are physically abused, especially among abused children under one year of age. Both mortality and morbidity are high for this group. Researchers have found that more than half of the survivors have persistent and serious neurologic sequelae as a result of the injury (Sinal & Ball, 1987).

Neuropathology of Head Injury

Head injuries are typically referred to as open or closed. Open injuries are typically caused by a penetrating object such as a knife or bullet. The injury to the brain tends to be along the path of penetration. The damage is generally circumscribed unless high velocity missiles are used that interrupt blood flow and cause substantial tissue swelling (Lezak, 1995) or complications occur such as infection and seizure (Feler & Watridge, 1992).

Closed head injuries result from a number of sources and are the most frequent causes of brain injury (Di Scala et al., 1991). Closed head injuries can be caused by a direct, though blunt, blow to the head, the head hitting something, or the acceleration-deceleration events of a motor vehicle accident. In a closed head injury, damage to the brain is caused by the brain having impact with the skull when it is depressed or the brain striking the inside of the skull during sudden acceleration and deceleration. The extent to which the brain is actually injured in an open or closed head injury situation depends on the primary effects of the injury and the secondary complications.

Primary effects.

The primary effects of brain injury include diffuse axonal injury, contusions, and skull fractures. Diffuse axonal injury refers to widespread damage to axons, or nerve pathways, that is often associated with high velocity injuries where rotational acceleration and deceleration occurs. As different brain layers move at different rates, stretching and shearing of axons occurs, which in turn, interferes with transmission of messages (Bigler, 1987).

Contusions (bruising) can also be caused by rapid acceleration/deceleration. Other causes, however, include skull fracture and focal injury to the brain. Contusions are most often found in the orbitofrontal and anterior temporal regions of the brain where the skull is rough and irregular (Mapou, 1992). Bruising that occurs at the point where the brain makes contact with the skull is referred to as a coup injury, whereas bruising opposite this site is a contre-coup injury.

Skull fractures tend to occur in the area of direct impact (Bigler, 1990). Some fractures do not result in brain injury, although brain injury almost always occurs with more serious fractures (Graham, Adams, & Gennarelli, 1993).

Secondary complications.

Secondary complications include increased intracranial pressure, edema (swelling), and hemorrhaging. Survival often depends on the immediate and effective treatment of these complications. Increased pressure is the most common cause of death in head injury cases and predicts poor outcomes for those who survive (Lezak, 1995). Pressure can be caused by an increase in fluid around damaged brain tissue (swelling) or an increase in blood flow within the skull or brain (hemorrhaging). These complications can disrupt normal blood flow necessary for adequate oxygenation and nourishment of the brain and can lead to death of brain tissue (Bigler, 1990). When brain tissue dies, ventricles begin to enlarge. This enlargement may not be visible on (CT) or (MRI) for 6 weeks or more following injury (Bigler, Kurth, Blatter, & Abildskov, 1992; Bowen et al., in press). While ventricle enlargement has been found to be a reliable index of severity in adults (Wilson & Wyper, 1992), very few studies have examined this relationship in children. Those that have show variable results (e.g., Bowen et al., in press), making it impossible to draw conclusions at this time.

Predicting Outcomes

Researchers estimate that 90% of more severely injured patients are subsequently disabled to some degree (Knights et al., 1991). However, when all survivors of brain injury are included (e.g., survivors with mild, moderate, and severe brain injuries), only 20% have long-term disabilities (Kraus, Rock, & Hemyarai, 1990). Research has shown fairly consistently that outcome is related to injury severity, that is, the more serious the brain injury the worse the outcome (Fay et al., 1994). There are, however, exceptions where injuries that appear minor result in extremely poor outcomes (Savage & Wolcott, 1994). To what extent this has to do with how severity is defined, age at the time of injury, or some other factor is unclear.

Severity.

Severity of brain injury is typically defined by the extent of intracranial damage (e.g., skull fracture and hemorrhage) and length of unconsciousness and post-traumatic amnesia (PTA). Although severity indicators, such as coma and PTA, have been shown to be relatively good predictors of outcome (Ewing-Cobbs & Fletcher, 1990; Michaud, Duhaime, & Batshaw, 1993), these indicators may be less reliable or valid for children. For example, the Glasgow Coma Scale (GCS), which measures impaired consciousness, requires verbal response in addition to motor response (e.g., movement or eye opening in response to verbal command or pain). For children with more limited language skills, the score may not mean the same as it does for adults. The scoring criteria and range (3, no response, to 15, oriented and conversing) are, nonetheless, the same for children and adults. Measures of amnesia are even more problematic because the assessment of PTA means determining the extent to which memories of ongoing events are stored (e.g., recalling in the evening what transpired that morning). PTA scores for children whose developmental stage precludes the accurate and reliable reporting of facts will, therefore, be difficult to interpret. Scales are available to measure coma and PTA in children, specifically, the Children's Coma Scale (CCS; Raimondi & Hirschauer, 1984) and the Children's Orientation and Amnesia Test (COAT; Levin, Fletcher, Miner, & Eisenberg, 1989). However, these measures are not as frequently used and have their own shortcomings (e.g., the CCS relies on physiological indicators such as reactive pupils instead of cognitive functioning; the COAT is primarily used for research).

No coma or amnesia scale takes into account extracranial variables that can compound physical trauma as well as psychological stress. Arm and leg fractures and damage to organs such as the spleen and liver can cause shock, hypotension, hypoxia, and metabolic disruption that lead to an underestimation of brain injury severity (Di Scala et al., 1991; Tepas et al., 1990). Measures that assess the process of recovery over time may be more beneficial in determining what impact these and other psychological factors play. The Rancho Los Amigos' Level of Cognitive Functioning Scale provides a means to assess early, middle, and late stages of recovery. Eight levels, ranging from no response to fully alert, oriented,

and purposeful, are measured by the Rancho Scale (the scale can be adapted for children under five).

The majority of pediatric brain injury cases in the literature are considered mild (Kraus, 1993). Mild is typically defined as brief or no loss of consciousness (CCS greater than 12), brief PTA (e.g., less than 30 minutes), and no signs of neurologic injury to the brain (e.g., hemorrhage). Although some researchers have indicated that children with mild head injuries have persistent functional impairments (e.g., Greenspan & MacKenzie, 1994), prospective studies tend to show that mild injuries have rather negligible effects (Jaffe et al., 1993; Knights et al., 1991). In one study that compared children with mild head injuries to children with burns and lacerations, children with head injuries actually performed better on cognitive measures (Bijur, Haslum, & Golding, 1990). Longitudinal research at the University of Washington has also shown that mild injuries are not associated with deterioration in learning, behavior, or family functioning (Jaffe et al., 1993; Rivara et al., 1992).

Although the majority of mildly injured children require no medical treatment and seem to have no significant sequelae, according to some researchers (e.g., Lehr, 1990), there are children with apparent mild brain injuries who have problems with headache, dizziness, fatigue, irritability, and deficits in attention and memory (Lehr, 1990). Teachers may describe these children as being inattentive in class, slow to respond to instructions and to complete assignments, and easily frustrated. Children with mild injuries may not be readily distinguished from peers with more moderate injuries.

Moderate brain injury is typically defined by a loss of consciousness (GCS between 9 and 12), PTA greater than 30 minutes but less than 24 hours, and in some cases an abnormal CT or MRI findings indicative of neurologic signs of injury (i.e., skull fracture and hemorrhage). Teachers may find that these children have difficulty learning, cannot concentrate or control their behaviors as well as same-age peers, and may even have coordination problems and personality changes. Although research has shown that moderate brain injuries can have a negative effect on outcome (Fay et al., 1994; Jaffe et al., 1993), the findings are not as consistent as they are for severe injuries. Fletcher and his colleagues (Fletcher, Ewing-Cobbs, Miner, Levin, & Eisenberg, 1990) failed to find any difference between their subjects in the "moderate" group and subjects in the control and "mild" groups. Clearly, the most consistent and significant findings of impairment are among children who sustain severe brain injuries.

A severe brain injury is typically defined as loss of consciousness, PTA for more than 24 hours, and definite (and serious) signs of neurologic damage to the brain. Cerebral contusions and intracranial hematomas are found among this group, as are skull fractures and evidence of brain swelling (edema) and increased intracranial pressure. Children with severe brain injuries have been shown to have serious learning delays as well as multiple physical, psychological, and social problems (Fletcher et al., 1990). Subjects in the Washington study (Fay et al., 1994) who sustained severe brain injuries were found to perform worse than matched controls on 40 out of 53 variables, even 3 years after the initial injury took place. The finding of significant and persistent impairments among children with severe brain injuries can be seen throughout the literature with rates of impairment as high as 90% (Knights et al., 1991). These children may return to the classroom in wheelchairs, no longer be able to write with their dominant hand, have problems keeping track of what is going on in the classroom, fail to understand and/or complete homework assignments, and exhibit immature and inappropriate behaviors (e.g., telling jokes when inappropriate). Social rejection and social withdrawal are serious concerns for these children.

Age

Although severity of injury is related to outcome, the age at which a child sustains a brain injury also plays a critical role. While children are more likely to survive brain injuries than adults (Tepas et al., 1990), long-term outcomes have been found to be worse for children, especially children younger than 2 years (Lehr, 1990; Levin, 1993). Although research suggests that the immature skull and brain give infants and young children some advantage in terms of fewer contusions, lacerations, and axonal injuries (Spreen, Risser, & Edgwell, 1995), the fact that this time period involves rapidly emerging skills means that these children are likely to be more vulnerable to the impact from their injuries (Thompson et al., 1994). Studies have shown that brain injured infants are three times more likely to have poor outcomes than children between the ages of two and three (Raimondi & Hirschauer, 1984).

For infants, brain injuries can impact developing sensory and motor functions (e.g., hearing, vision, and fine/gross motor skill). While this does not mean that other areas of functioning are not impacted, it does mean that the effects may not be apparent until years after the initial injury. Damage at very young ages may affect functions not expected to develop for years after injury; therefore, the impact cannot be assessed. The same can be said of toddlers. Injury during this period of life when children are so actively engaged in learning (e.g., climbing on and getting into things and playing with toys) puts them at risk for not developing adequate learning strategies and achieving cognitive and social competence. According to Lehr (1990), even if there is no loss of previously acquired skills, losing the capacity to learn puts young children at risk for later learning problems. Although it is not entirely clear what the long-term impact is from injuries sustained during the early years of life, educators and parents need to be aware that some problems may resolve but others may arise later on.

Preschool-age children, who like toddlers, are at high risk for brain injuries from falls are also vulnerable to the impact of injury on learning ability, especially social learning (Lehr, 1990). School-age children are at risk for serious, and persistent, cognitive deficits from their injuries (Levin, Benton, & Grossman, 1982), despite the fact they have a much better chance than very young children to survive their injuries. According to Lehr (1990), for latency-age children injury "threatens the very core of childhood; that is, learning to be in control of one's self, being able to function as part of a group, and being able to master the skills and information that are important" (p. 70).

Adolescents, whose injuries tend to be more serious given the fact most occur in motor-vehicle-related accidents, are also at risk for impact on cognitive skill development (i.e., higher level cognitive functions such as the ability to plan and evaluate goals). This age group, however, is at particular risk for psychosocial and emotional problems as a result of their injuries. Peer relationships so critical during this stage are threatened, and in turn, the adolescent's sense of identity and direction is altered (Lehr, 1990).

Problems and Implications

The range of impairments that are seen is broad and includes physical complaints and deficits in sensory and motor functioning, language, cognition, achievement, and behavior (Ewing-Cobbs, Levin, Eisenberg, & Fletcher, 1987; Jaffe et al., 1993; Thompson et al., 1994).

Physical Complaints

One of the most common physical complaints following injury is headache. Headaches are estimated to affect around 20% of children within the first 6 months (Lanser, Jennekens-Schinkel, & Peters, 1988). Headaches are a symptom of concussion, along with nausea, dizziness, lack of environmental awareness, poor concentration and memory, sleep problems, and irritability (Bigler, 1990). Headaches, unlike some of the other postconcussive symptoms, have been shown to persist for months, even years, following injury (Klonoff, Clark, & Klonoff, 1993). The relationship of these headaches to the injury, however, is unclear years later.

Seizures are not as common as headaches and are actually infrequent in closed head injury cases (Levin, Benton, & Grossman, 1982). Whereas the rate of seizures is 50% in children with penetrating injuries, it is only 5% with closed injuries (Begali, 1992). Like headaches, when seizures do occur they can have a significant impact on learning and level of activity. Wesson et al. (1989) found that these children's level of participation in social and physical activities drops dramatically.

Sensory and Motor Deficits

Problems with vision and hearing can also affect learning and are often seen following brain injury (Michaud, Duhaime et al., 1993). Typical visual impairments include double vision, tracking problems, visual field defects, and cortical blindness. Hearing problems can include reduced acuity, sensorineural deafness, and ringing in the ears. Other sensory problems that can result from brain injury include a distorted sense of smell and taste and difficulty swallowing.

Brain injuries can result in a range of motor impairments, including disturbance in gait and coordination, weakness, rigidity, tremor, and spasticity (Levin et al., 1982). Motor skills are usually the first to recover, although some deficits can persist (e.g., tremor and spasticity). The more rapid recovery of motor functions than cognitive and psychosocial functions (Livingston & McCabe, 1990; Ylvisaker, 1986) may result in more subtle deficits going unnoticed. Educators and family members may see the child as being "back to normal" following motor recovery and may develop unrealistic expectations for a similarly fast rate of recovery of other functions.

Language Deficits

Expressive language skills, such as naming and written language, have been shown to be more frequently affected by brain injury than receptive language skills (Ewing-Cobbs et al., 1987), but they tend to recover at about the same rate as motor skills. However, problems with pragmatics, verbal fluency, word finding, concept formation and verbal comprehension recover at a much slower pace and tend to be more persistent (Michaud, Duhaime et al., 1993). Because problems with receptive language are at times more difficult to detect, researchers have shown that they are more likely to interfere with learning than are expressive skills (Blosser & DePompei, 1989; Ylvisaker, 1986).

Cognitive Deficits

Cognitive impairments are considered to be the most disabling sequelae of brain injury, particularly for the younger child (Capruso & Levin, 1992). The cognitive problems typically found include inattention, slowed information-processing speed, poor memory, difficulty planning and initiating, and impaired visual-spatial skills and visual-motor integration (Ewing-Cobbs, Fletcher, & Levin, 1986).

Although most children continue to function in the average to low-average range following injury, IQ declines between 10 to 30 points have been found shortly after severe brain injuries (Klonoff, Low, & Clark, 1974). Studies, however, tend to show substantial recovery of intellectual skills within the first 6 to 12 months; after that time, recovery slows (Levin, 1987). Initial improvement is likely to be related to the faster recovery of motor skills (Kolb & Whishaw, 1990). In some cases, a decline on IQ tests can be seen over time (Ewing-Cobbs et al., 1986). It is unclear to what extent declines in performance on IQ tests are related to interference with later development of higher level cognitive functioning or some other factor, such as persistent problems with psychomotor slowing having more weight in terms of performance test scores as children get older.

Attention deficits, similar to those found in children with Attention Deficit/Hyperactivity Disorder (i.e., difficulty focusing and sustaining attention, and distractibility), are also commonly found in this population (Begali, 1992; Ewing-Cobbs et al., 1986). This finding is not surprising given the number of neural structures associated with attention that are impacted by brain injury. Nor is it surprising that the persistence of these problems has been shown to significantly interfere with post-injury learning (Auerbach, 1986).

Memory problems are also a characteristic feature of brain injury. According to Levin (1989), memory problems are among the most frequent cognitive sequelae, with nearly 50% of children exhibiting some memory deficit. Diffuse axonal injury from shearing has been considered to be a contributory factor in the occurrence of memory deficits (Levin, 1989). Damage to other areas of the brain, including the hippocampus, frontal region, and anterior temporal region have also been associated with memory deficits (Adams, Graham, Scott, Parker, & Doyle, 1980; Kolb & Whishaw, 1990).

Achievement Problems

Although deficits in achievement may not become apparent for months or years following injury, research has consistently shown an impact on achievement. For example, Levin and Benton (1986) found arithmetic scores to be significantly below the expected level 6 months post-injury, and Jaffe et al. (1993) found that one year post-injury these children had significant math problems. The subjects also had problems with spelling and reading. Although modest gains were observed in spelling at one year, this recovery was attributed more to improvements in motor skill than written language. Even smaller gains were observed in reading and math. When these children were retested 2 years later, there were negligible change in mean test scores (Fay et al., 1994). In fact, children with moderate or severe injuries continued to perform significantly below controls on all academic measures.

The Washington studies (e.g., Fay et al., 1994) are important for a number of reasons. Not only do they demonstrate persistent academic problems among children with brain injuries, but they stress the importance of using appropriate comparison groups for these children and appropriate achievement measures (i.e., curriculum-based measures). Although many children with a history of moderate to severe injuries earned academic scores within the average range, the mean scores of the subjects who had brain injuries were significantly lower than those of the matched controls.

Behavior Problems

Behavior problems are reported to be the most troublesome sequelae for families (Levin, 1987). Common behavioral sequelae from injury include increased aggression, anger, hyperactivity, anxiety, depression, emotional liability, social withdrawal, and somatization (e.g., Filley, Cranberg, Alexander, & Hart, 1987). Some of the emotions and behaviors likely are responses to the sudden and dramatic changes in these children's lives (e.g., irritability and feelings of hopelessness). However, damage to brain areas that regulate emotional controls also will result in maladaptive behaviors (McAllister, 1992). These behaviors have the potential to disrupt not only learning but also social relationships.

Researchers have provided considerable data to support a causal link between behavior problems and brain injury. In addition to demonstrating the emergence of behavior problems in children who did not have difficulties before (Asarnow, Satz, Light, & Lewis, 1991), researchers have found evidence that the more severe the injury, the more severe the behavior problems (e.g., Michaud, Rivara, Jaffe, Fay, & Dailey, 1993). Michaud and her colleagues found that children with brain injuries are three times more likely than the general population to develop serious behavior disorders and the rate of brain injury among students in special education classes for behavior/emotional disorders is three times higher than for the regular education population. However, educators may not always attribute behavior problems seen in the classroom to brain injury (Michaud, Rivara et al., 1993).

The problem with attribution may be due to the fact that some children who display behavior problems after injuries had pre-existing problems. Research has shown that worse outcomes are associated with pre-existing problems (Telzrow, 1990) such as constitutional factors, a predisposition to psychological disturbance, and previous cognitive and psychosocial problems (Rutter, 1981).

Family Problems

Family functioning and readjustment have been shown to be significant problems following a child's brain injury (Bragg, Klockars, & Berninger, 1992). The impact is especially acute in families that had pre-injury dysfunction (Rivara et al., 1992). Persistent problems from both the physical burden of caring for the child and the distress caused by the presence of the child's cognitive and behavioral disabilities contribute to family stress (Brooks, 1991). Although the physical burden improves with time, the psychological stress worsens and affects many facets of family life (Rivara et al., 1992). For example, family members report increased employment and substance use problems. Sadly, as parents and siblings struggle to reorganize their lives, they often become increasingly more isolated and lose important social networks over time (Kozloff, 1987).

Alternative Actions

Interventions are likely to be as diverse as the sequelae of injury. They likely will require the combined efforts and talents of a number of staff members. A well planned and informed team is critical for transitioning the child from the hospital to the school and setting up an appropriate educational plan (Blosser & DePompei, 1989; Clark, in press; Mira, Tucker, & Tyler, 1992). School psychologists will often be called on to head this team and to plan the school-based interventions for these students.

A successful transition from the hospital or rehabilitation facility to the school requires that planning begin early, preferrably right after the child is injured. Communication lines need to be set up with the medical rehabilitation team to keep school personnel informed about the child's condition and the needs of the family. Information from medical personnel will help in timing the child's return to school, scheduling the school day, and modifying the classroom and curriculum to meet individual needs. To further ensure that the most effective interventions are implemented, frequent follow-up evaluations of academic performance and social-emotional adjustment are needed.

Although considerable information is available in the literature addressing the issue of intervening with these children in an educational setting (e.g., Savage & Wolcott, 1994), the empirical support for these interventions is almost nonexistent. Instead, the majority of research with this population has focused on the use of medications to control behaviors (e.g., Clark, Baker, Gardner, Pompa, & Tait, 1990). However, armed with what is known about effective interventions for problems similar to the ones faced by these children and what is known about the sequelae of injury, educators can adapt interventions to meet these children's needs just as they would with other children. Savage and Wolcott (1994) and many others have provided excellent suggestions for adapting interventions.

Behavioral Management

Franzen and Lovell (1987) have outlined two general principles of behavioral management for children with brain injuries. The first principle involves reduction of the antecedents that elicit inappropriate behavior, and the second involves reducing the probability that an inappropriate behavior will be reinforced in the first place.

According to Deaton (1994), the procedures most likely to succeed with children who have brain injuries are those that require the fewest possible resources and are the least intrusive. Antecedent-based strategies seem to meet both criteria. Antecedent strategies are also more positive than some of the consequential strategies because they communicate more clearly to the student which behaviors are expected and will be rewarded. Posted rules help to define expected behaviors and serve as reminders for students who have difficulty remembering what they are expected to do. Structuring the classroom and providing a consistent schedule can increase predictability and reduce the impact of impaired memory (e.g., remind them of expectations). Careful scheduling of the school day can also minimize opportunities for off-task behaviors and maximize rest periods. Seating these students who have problems with distractibility and impulsivity nearer the teacher and away from peers with similar problems can also increase immediate monitoring and opportunity for reinforcement (Cohen, 1986; Rhode, Jenson, & Reavis, 1993).

Because antecedent strategies are not always possible, teachers often rely on consequence based strategies. Reprimands are the most common and most preferred method that teachers employ as a consequence for an undesired behavior (Reavis, Jenson, Kukic, & Morgan, 1993). Often embedded within these reprimands, however, are threats of punishment if compliance is not forthcoming. According to Malec (1984), when individuals already perceive themselves negatively, as is the case with many children with brain injuries, punishment lowers self-esteem further, reduces motivation, and causes a depressed mood. Given the fact that rates of reprimands have been shown to be particularly high with students who have cognitive and social difficulties (Heller & White, 1975), students with brain injuries may receive more reprimands than other students.

Reprimands, if used appropriately, however, have been shown to be effective in increasing compliance and improving academic competence (Reavis et al., 1993). To ensure that reprimands have a positive and enduring effect with these children, however, it is recommended that their use be limited; that consequences be preplanned and reasonable; and that they be used in combination with other interventions, such as praise (Reavis et al., 1993).

While the effectiveness of praise has been well documented (e.g., Rhode et al., 1993), teachers do not use it very often; in fact, it is used with decreasing frequency over successive grade levels (White, 1975). Positive attention, however, has been shown to effectively reduce unwanted behaviors, including tantruming behaviors of children with brain injuries (Reavis et al., 1993). According to Reavis and his colleagues, to increase the effectiveness of praise, teachers should first establish eye contact, describe in detail the expected behavior (this serves as a reminder for those with memory problems), then deliver the praise immediately, frequently, and with enthusiasm.

Other interventions that may be effective with these students include precision requests and self-modeling. Although these interventions have been found to reduce maladaptive behaviors and increase adaptive functioning in non-injured children (e.g., Kehle, Sutilla, & Visnic, 1994; Reavis et al., 1993), they may require some augmentation. For example, self-modeling may be more effective if used in combination with other cognitively and behaviorally based strategies (e.g., spacing effects, positive rewards, and self-reinforcements).

Even reductive techniques such as time-out and overcorrection may be appropriate for these children. According to Franzen and Lovell (1987), the effectiveness of time-out depends on how negatively reinforcing the time-out setting is to the child. While time-out has been shown to be potent in reducing unwanted behaviors (Rhode et al., 1993), the degree of restrictiveness needs to be carefully considered when implementing this strategy with injured children. For children with brain injuries, like many others, it may be preferred to leave the student at his or her desk or in the instructional setting for the time-out. This practice will ensure safety and provide the child with greater exposure to the learning and social environment. As overcorrection is even more intrusive than time-out, the costs need to be weighed against the potential benefits. The benefit of overcorrection, however, is that it is designed to eliminate a maladaptive behavior while at the same time teach an appropriate one (Franzen & Lovell, 1987).

Pharmacologic Treatments

Pharmacologic treatments have been used to a great extent for behavior management of children with brain injuries. Medications typically used to manage behavior include stimulants (e.g., Ritalin and Dexedrine), antidepressants (e.g., Tofranil, Prozac, and Zoloft), anticonvulsants (e.g., Tegretol and Depakote), benzodiazepines (e.g., Clonidine and Valium), neuroleptics (e.g., Haldol), and lithium salts. Yudofsky, Silver, and Schneider (1987) found medications to be useful in reducing emotional outbursts and aggressive behaviors, while Clark et al. (1990) found stimulant medications to improve attending behaviors. Stimulant medications have also been found to have a calming effect on children with brain injury; they may actually be more effective than sedatives in managing aggressive behaviors, at least initially (Glenn, 1987).

Researchers warn, however, that too little is known about traumatic brain injury to accurately predict individual children's responses to medication (Cope, 1987). Because various neurochemical mechanisms can be involved in the development of inappropriate behaviors following brain injury, determining an effective medication protocol may be difficult and should be approached cautiously. Cope (1987) suggests that unless a true behavioral emergency exists, environmental or behavioral interventions should be used first. These interventions can establish a baseline for evaluating the effectiveness of pharmacologic interventions if these become necessary. Further, because the medications used control maladaptive behavior by depressing arousal, control may be gained at the expense of reducing the child's capacity to function (Cope, 1987).

Family Interventions

School personnel can also help by working directly with the parents and siblings of the injured child. Families are unprepared for the sudden and dramatic change in their lives following injury (Hartman, 1987). They also lack basic information as to how a brain injury affects behavior and what can be expected in terms of recovery (Resnick, 1993). Families report feeling angry and disillusioned by professionals, especially medical professionals (Resnick, 1993). According to families, understandable information from supportive individuals is of primary importance during this time of crisis (Miller, 1993). Educators may be in a particularly good position to provide this information or at least put families in touch with those who can (e.g., state brain injury associations and rehabilitation facilities and specialists).

Some families will need more than what schools can provide in terms of consultation. They may need individual counseling to deal with their own issues of grief, and some may need financial planning to assist with the high costs of caring for the injured child (Conoley & Sheridan, in press). Family therapy can give parents and siblings the opportunity to express their feelings of loss, their resentments about one child receiving all the attention (and resources), and their guilt about their own feelings. Conflicts among family members can also be aired and worked on. Family therapy may also give the injured child the chance to express his or her feelings about the injury and get constructive feedback from family members about problematic behaviors. School psychologists and counselors can identify those families at greatest risk for problems, that is, families who showed dysfunction before or have had difficulties coping with stress (Rivara et al., 1992).

In addition to these intervention activities, school personnel can play a vital role in providing other information, including ways to help children establish friendships and ways to avoid further injury. Because bicycle helmets have been shown to reduce the risk of serious brain injury by as much as 85% (Thompson, Rivara, & Thompson, 1989), this may be the easiest part. Helping parents to help their children make and keep friends, however, is not so easy. While research at the Teaching Research Institute in Eugene, Oregon, has shown that teachers can play an important role in developing friendship groups, even these friendships are tenuous (Glang, personal communication, December 4, 1995). For family members who bear the sole burden of being their child's friend, however, educator involvement may still be quite valuable.

Academic Interventions

Given that children with brain injury may experience disruption of underlying information processes, academic interventions may need to be focused on the learning process, not achievement in subject areas (Cohen, 1986). Although even children with moderate to severe injuries have been shown to perform in the average range on standardized tests, they have also been shown to be quite deficient when compared to case controls (Jaffe et al., 1993). Assessments, as well as interventions, need to be sensitive to subtle changes in cognitive functioning so that potential areas of difficulty can be identified. Failure to detect these changes can lead to the decline in academic performance seen across studies with this population (e.g., Fay et al., 1994; Levin & Benton, 1986).

Deficits in areas such as attention, memory, and problem solving can greatly interfere with efforts to learn math, as well as learning any new concept in school. Problems with speed of processing can further impede the student by making him or her unable to keep up with the pace of the classroom and the learning that is required. Traditional educational practice requires rapid assimilation of new information, thus making it very difficult for these children to learn and maintain their motivation to keep trying (Jaffe et al., 1993). Additional problems, such as poor fine motor control or having to use a nondominant hand to do class work, can compound the risk of these children falling hopelessly behind. As Cohen (1986) suggests, educators should delay trying to teach new content until some of the underlying deficits are remediated.

The focus should be placed on the process of learning, not the product (Cohen, 1986). Children with attentional and memory problems may need to be taught memory aids before being expected to learn multiplication tables. Similarly, children with organizational problems are likely to need help with organizers before tackling the task of writing a term paper.

Summary

The chronic nature of the problems children with brain injuries face argue for the serious attention of educators. Educators need to know more about the way brain injuries can potentially affect a child's functioning; this includes knowing how differently children are affected. The severity of injury and the age at which children sustain injuries are only two of many variables that predict which children will have what problems and for how long. Research is just beginning to expose which variables are critical to consider when setting up interventions, especially interventions intended to prevent future problems. Researchers are still trying to understand how these children's reactions to their own injuries affect the recovery process and outcome.

Given the breadth, and potential chronicity, of these children's problems, educators are faced with a formidable task. Designing effective teaching strategies and behavior-management systems will depend on increasing their knowledge base about brain injuries and being exposed more to these children in the classroom. Knowing how these children differ from peers with learning and behavior problems is just a start. Research would suggest that it is critical to take into consideration the latent as well as the manifest problems these children have. Recognizing that these children have problems learning new concepts may not be enough for intervening, but understanding how to improve the speed and efficiency of information processing may be.

Recommended Resources

Begali, V. (1992). *Head injury in children and adolescents: A resource and review for school and allied professionals.* Brandon, VT: Clinical Psychology Publishing Company.
This book provides an excellent overview of the topic of head injuries and addresses educationally relevant issues. Although the author provides comprehensive background information about the mechanisms of head injury and factors that affect outcome, the book is written in an easy-to-understand manner. Readers will appreciate the organization of the book and will probably find themselves referring to it for suggestions about how to work with these students (e.g., conducting assessments).

Bigler, E. D. (Ed.) (1990). *Traumatic brain injury: Mechanisms of damage, assessment, intervention, and outcome.* Austin, TX: Pro-Ed.
This book compiles the writing of some of the foremost experts in the field of neuropsychology. While the text addresses traumatic brain injury issues for all ages, several chapters are devoted to child and adolescent issues. These chapters include topics such as management of behavioral disturbances, attention problems, and academic difficulties following injury. Family interventions are also covered in the text.

Hynd, G. W., & Willis, W. G. (1988). *Pediatric neuropsychology.* Orlando, FL: Grune & Stratton.
This text is one of the best available in addressing a variety of neurologic diseases and disorders that affect children and adolescents. Although it is somewhat dated, the information is presented in a way that readers with little or no background in neuropsychology can understand. The authors provide readers with background information in normal development of the central nervous system.

Mira, M. P., Tucker, B. F., & Tyler, J. S. (1992). *Traumatic brain injury in children and adolescents: A sourcebook for teachers and other school personnel.* Austin, TX: Pro-Ed.
This book addresses the problems that children and adolescents with moderate to severe brain injuries face, and it is specifically designed for use by school personnel. The authors provide practical suggestions on how to work with these students, including reintegrating them into the classroom and setting up interventions to deal with problems with attention, problem solving, and motivation.

Savage, R. C., & Wolcott, G. F. (Eds.) (1994). *Educational dimensions of acquired brain injury.* Austin, TX: Pro-Ed.
The authors have provided an excellent up-to-date text for educators working with students who have traumatic brain injuries. The information is practical and provides professionals in the schools a resource to consult regarding a variety of problem behaviors (e.g., cognitive, psychosocial, and behavioral) that affect these students and ways they might intervene. Although the majority of interventions presented have not been empirically validated with this population, they are based on the clinical experience of experts in the field. Secondary educators may be particularly interested in the chapters on work transition issues.

In addition, educators may want to contact state-level brain injury organizations. To obtain information about these organizations, the national organization can be called. The toll-free number for the Brain Injury Association, Inc., formerly the National Head Injury Foundation, is 1-800-444-6443.

References

Adams, J. H., Graham, D., Scott, G., Parker, L. S., & Doyle, D. (1980). Brain damage in fatal non-missile head injury. *Journal of Clinical Pathology, 33,* 1132–1145.

Anderson, N. (1995). *Perceptions of school-based professionals regarding traumatic brain injury.* Unpublished masters thesis, University of Utah, Salt Lake City.

Asarnow, R. F., Satz, P., Light, R., & Lewis, R. (1991). Behavior problems and adaptive functioning in children with mild and severe closed head injury. *Journal of Pediatric Psychology, 16*(5), 543–555.

Auerbach, S. H. (1986). Neuroanatomical correlates of attention and memory disorders in traumatic brain injury: An application of neurobehavioral subtypes. *Journal of Head Trauma Rehabilitation, 1,* 1–12.

Baker, S. P., Fowler, C., Li, G., Warner, M., & Dannenberg, A. L. (1994). Head injuries incurred by children and young adults during informal recreation. *American Journal of Public Health, 84*(4), 649–652.

Begali, V. (1992). *Head injury in children and adolescents.* Brandon, VT: Clinical Psychology Publishing Company.

Bigler, E. D. (1987). The clinical significance of cerebral atrophy in traumatic brain injury. *Archives of Clinical Neuropsychology, 2,* 293–304.

Bigler, E. D. (1990). Neuropathology of traumatic brain injury. In E. D. Bigler (Ed.), *Traumatic brain injury: Mechanisms of damage, assessment, intervention, and outcome* (pp. 13–49). Austin, TX: Pro-Ed.

Bigler, E. D., Kurth, S. M., Blatter, D., & Abildskov, T. J. (1992). Degenerative changes in traumatic brain injury: Post-injury magnetic resonance identified ventricular expansion compared to pre-injury levels. *Brain Research Bulletin, 28,* 651–653.

Bijur, P. E., Haslum, M., & Golding, J. (1990). Cognitive and behavioral sequelae of mild head injury in children. *Pediatrics, 86* (3), 337–344.

Blosser, J. L., & DePompei, R. (1989). The head-injured student returns to school: Recognizing and treating deficits. *Topics in Language Disorders, 9*(2), 67–77.

Bowen, J. M., Clark, E., Bigler, E. D., Gardner, M. K., Nilsson, D., Gooch, J., & Pompa, J. L. (in press). Childhood traumatic brain injury: Neuropsychological status at time of hospital rehabilitation discharge. *Developmental Medicine and Child Neurology.*

Brooks, D. N. (1991). The head-injured family. *Journal of Clinical and Experimental Neuropsychology, 13,* 155–188.

Capruso, D., & Levin, H. S. (1992). Cognitive impairment following closed head injury. *Neurology Clinics, 10*(4), 879–893.

Christey, G. L., Nelson, D. E., Rivara, F. P., Smith, S. M., & Condie, C. (1994). Horseback riding injuries among children and young adults. *Journal of Family Practice, 39*(2), 148–152.

Clark, E. (in press). Children and adolescents with traumatic brain injury: Reintegration challenges in educational settings. *Journal of Learning Disabilities.*

Clark, E., Baker, B. K., Gardner, M. K., Pompa, J. L., & Tait, F. V. (1990). Effectiveness of stimulant drug treatment for attention problems. *School Psychology International, 11,* 227–234.

Cohen, S. B. (1986). Educational reintegration and programming for children with head injuries. *Journal of Head Trauma Rehabilitation, 1*(4), 22–29.

Conoley, J. C., & Sheridan, S. M. (in press). Pediatric traumatic brain injury: Challenges and interventions for families. *Journal of Learning Disabilities.*

Cope, D. N. (1987). Psychopharmacologic considerations in the treatment of traumatic brain injury. *Journal of Head Trauma Rehabilitation, 2,* 2–5.

Deaton, A. (1994). Changing the behaviors of students with acquired brain injuries. In R. C. Savage & G. F. Wolcott (Eds.), *Educational dimensions of acquired brain injury* (pp. 257–275). Austin, TX: Pro-Ed.

Di Scala, C., Osberg, J. S., Gans, B. M., Chin, L. J., & Grant, C. C. (1991). Children with traumatic head injury: Morbidity and postacute treatment. *Archives of Physical Medicine & Rehabilitation, 72,* 662–666.

Ewing-Cobbs, L., & Fletcher, J. M. (1990). Neuropsychological assessment of traumatic brain injury in children. In E.D. Bigler (Ed.), *Traumatic brain injury* (pp. 107–128). Austin, TX: Pro-Ed.

Ewing-Cobbs, L., Fletcher, J. M., & Levin, H. (1986). Neurobehavioral sequelae following head injury in children: Educational implications. *Journal of Head Trauma Rehabilitation, 1,* 57–65.

Ewing-Cobbs, L., Levin, H. S., Eisenberg, H. M., & Fletcher, J. M. (1987). Language functions following closed-head injury in children and adolescents. *Journal of Clinical and Experimental Neuropsychology, 9,* 575–592.

Ewing-Cobbs, L., Levin, H. S., Fletcher, J. M., Miner, M. E., & Eisenberg, H. M. (1989). Post-traumatic amnesia in head-injured children: Assessment and outcome. *Journal of Clinical and Experimental Neuropsychology, 11,* 58.

Fay, G. C., Jaffe, K. M., Polissar, N. L., Liao, S., Rivara, J. B., & Martin, K. M. (1994). Outcome of pediatric traumatic brain injury at three years: A cohort study. *Archives of Physical Medicine Rehabilitation, 75,* 733–741.

Feler, C. A., & Watridge, C. B. (1992). Initial management of head trauma. In C. L. Long & L. K. Ross (Eds.), *Handbook of head trauma* (pp. 19–31). New York: Plenum.

Filley, C. M., Cranberg, L. D., Alexander, M. P., & Hart, E. J. (1987). Neurobehavioral outcome after closed head injury in childhood and adolescence. *Archives of Neurology, 44,* 194–198.

Franzen, M. D., & Lovell, M. R. (1987). Behavioral treatments of aggressive sequelae of brain injury. *Psychiatric Annals, 17,* 389–396.

Glenn, M. B. (1987). A pharmacological approach to aggressive and disruptive behaviors after traumatic brain injury: Part 1. *Journal of Head Trauma Rehabilitation, 2,* 71–73.

Graham, D. I., Adams, J. H., & Gennarelli, T. A. (1993). Pathology of brain damage in head injury. In P. R. Cooper (Ed.), *Head injury* (pp. 91–114). Baltimore: Williams & Wilkins.

Greenspan, A. L., & MacKenzie, E. J. (1994). Functional outcome after pediatric head injury. *Pediatrics, 94*(2), 425–432.

Haas, J. F., & Cope, N. (1985). Neuropharmacologic management of behavior sequelae in head injury: A case report. *Archives in Physical Medicine Rehabilitation, 66,* 472–474.

Hartman, S. (1987). Patterns of change in families following severe head injuries in children. *Australian and New Zealand Journal of Family Therapy, 8*(3), 125–130.

Heller, M. S., & White, M. A. (1975). Rates of approval and disapproval to higher and lower ability classes. *Journal of Educational Psychology, 67,* 769–800.

Henry, P. C., Hasuber, R. P., & Rice, M. (1992). Factors associated with closed head injury in a pediatric population. *Journal of Neuroscience and Nursing, 24*(6), 311–316.

Jaffe, K. M., Fay, G. C., Polissar, N. L., Martin, K. M., Shurtleff, H. A., Rivara, J. B., & Winn, H. R. (1993). Severity of pediatric traumatic brain injury and neurobehavioral recovery at one year: A cohort study. *Archives of Physical Medicine & Rehabilitation, 74,* 587–595.

Katsiyannis, A., & Conderman, G. (1994). Serving individuals with traumatic brain injury. *Remedial and Special Education, 15*(5), 319–325.

Kehle, T. J., Clark, E., & Jenson, W. R. (in press). Interventions for students with traumatic brain injury: Managing behavioral disturbances. *Journal of Learning Disabilities.*

Kehle, T. J., & Gonzales, F. (1991). Self-modeling for emotional and social concerns of childhood. In P. W. Dowrick (Ed.), *A practical guide to video in the behavioral sciences* (pp. 221–252). New York: Wiley.

Kehle, T. J., Sutilla, H., & Visnic, M. (1994, March). *Augmentation of self-modeling with behavioral strategies: Case study of an intentional enuretic and electively mute child.* Paper presented at the annual meeting of the National Association of School Psychologists, Seattle, WA.

Klonoff, H., Clark, C., & Klonoff, P. (1993). Long-term outcome of head injuries: A 23 year follow-up of children with head injuries. *Journal of Neurology, Neurosurgery and Psychiatry, 56,* 410–415.

Klonoff, H., Low, M. D., & Clark, C. (1977). Head injuries in children: A prospective five year follow-up. *Journal of Neurology, Neurosurgery, and Psychiatry, 40,* 1211–1219.

Knights, R. M., Ivan, L. P., Ventureyra, E. C., Bentivoglio, C., Stoddart, C., Winogron, W., & Bawden, H. N. (1991). The effects of head injury in children on neuropsychological and behavioral functioning. *Brain Injury, 5*(4), 339–351.

Kolb, B., & Whishaw, I. Q. (1990). *Fundamentals of human neuropsychology.* New York: W.H. Freeman.

Kozloff, R. (1987). Networks of social support and the outcome from severe head injury. *Journal of Head Trauma Rehabilitation, 2*(3), 14–23.

Kraus, J. F. (1993). Epidemiological aspects of brain and spinal cord injuries. In A. Sances, D. J. Thomas, C. L. Ewing, S. J. Larson, & F. Unterharnscheidt (Eds.), *Mechanisms of head and spine trauma* (pp. 49–68). New York: Aloray.

Kraus, J. F., Rock, A., & Hemyarai, P. (1990). Brain injuries among infants, children, adolescents and young adults. *American Journal of Diseases of Children, 144,* 684–691.

Lanser, J. B., Jennekens-Schinkel, A., & Peters, A. C. (1988). Headache after closed head injury in children. *Headache,* 176–179.

Lash, M. (1994). Families and students get caught between medical and educational systems. *REHAB Update.* Boston: Research and Training Center in Rehabilitation and Childhood Trauma.

Lehr, E. (1990). *Psychological management of traumatic brain injuries in children and adolescents.* Rockville, MD: Aspen.

Levin, H. S. (1987). Neurobehavioral sequelae of head injury. In P. R. Cooper (ed.), *Head injury* (2nd ed.). Baltimore: Williams and Wilkins.

Levin, H. S. (1989). Memory deficit after closed head injury. In J. Boller & J. Grafman (Eds.), *Handbook of neuropsychology* (pp. 183–207). TX: Elsevier Science.

Levin, H. S. (1993). Head trauma. *Current Opinions in Neurology, 6*(6), 841–846.

Levin, H. S., & Benton, A. L. (1986). Developmental and acquired dyscalculia in children. In I. Flemhig & L. Sterns (Eds.), *Child development and learning behavior* (pp. 317–322). Stuttgart, West Germany: Gustav Fischer.

Levin, H. S., Benton, A., & Grossman, R. G. (1982). *Neurobehavioral consequences of closed head injury.* New York: Oxford University Press.

Lezak, M. D. (1995). *Neuropsychological assessment.* New York: Oxford.

Livingston, M. G., & McCabe, R. J. (1990). Psychosocial consequence of head injury in children and adolescents: Implications for rehabilitation. *Pediatrician, 17*(4), 255–261.

Malec, J. (1984). Training the brain-injured client in behavioral self-management skills. In B. A. Edelstein & E. T. Couture (Eds.), *Behavioral assessment and rehabilitation of the traumatically brain damaged* (pp. 121–150). New York: Plenum.

Mapou, R. L. (1992). Neuropathology and neuropsychology of behavioral disturbances following traumatic brain injury. In C. L. Long & L. K. Ross (Eds.), *Handbook of head trauma* (pp. 75–89). New York: Plenum.

McAllister, T. W. (1992). Neuropsychiatric sequelae of head injuries. *Psychiatric Clinics of North America, 15*(2), 522–534.

Michaud, L. J., Duhaime, A., & Batshaw, M. L. (1993). Traumatic brain injury in children. *Pediatric Clinics of North America, 40*(3), 553–565.

Michaud, L. J., Rivara, F. P., & Grady, M. S. (1992). Predictors of survival and severity of disability after severe brain injury in children. *Neurosurgery, 31,* 254–264.

Michaud, L. J., Rivara, F. P., Jaffe, K. M., Fay, G., & Dailey, J. L. (1993). Traumatic brain injury as a risk factor for behavioral disorders in children. *Archives of Physical Medicine and Rehabilitation, 74,* 368–375.

Miller, L. (1993). Family therapy of brain injury: Syndromes, strategies, and solutions. *The American Journal of Family Therapy, 21,* 111–121.

Mira, M. P., Meck, N. E., & Tyler, J. S. (1988). School psychologists' knowledge of traumatic head injury: Implications for training. *Diagnostique, 13,* 174–180.

Mira, M. P., Tucker, B. F., & Tyler, J. S. (1992). *Traumatic brain injury in children and adolescents: A sourcebook for teachers and other school personnel.* Austin, TX: Pro-Ed.

Moloney, H. (1989). Pediatric issues in multisystem trauma. *Critical Care Nursing: Clinics of North America, 1*(1), 85–95.

Raimondi, A. J., & Hirschauer, J. (1984). Head injury in the infant and toddler. *Child's Brain, 11,* 12–35.

Reavis, H. K., Jenson, W. R., Kukic, S. J., & Morgan, D. P. (Eds.). (1993). Reprimands and precision requests. In *Utah's BEST project: Behavioral and educational strategies for teachers.* Salt Lake City: Utah State Office of Education.

Resnick, C. (1993). The effect of head injury on family and marital stability. *Social Work in Health Care, 18*(2), 49–62.

Rhode, G., Jenson, W. R., & Reavis, H. K. (1993). *The tough kid book: Practical classroom management strategies.* Longmont, CO: Sopris West.

Rivara, J. B., Fay, G. C., Jaffe, K. M., Polissar, N. L., Shurtleff, H. A., & Martin, K. M. (1992). Predictors of family functioning one year following traumatic brain injury in children. *Archives of Physical Medicine and Rehabilitation, 73,* 899–910.

Rosen, C. D., & Gerring, J. P. (1986). *Head trauma: Educational reintegration.* San Diego, CA: College-Hill.

Rutter, M. (1981). Psychological sequelae of brain damage in children. *American Journal of Psychiatry, 138,* 1533–1544.

Rutter, R. M., Cullum, C. M., & Luerssen, T. G. (1989). Brain imaging and neuropsychological outcome in traumatic brain injury. In E. D. Bigler, R. A. Yeo, & E. Turkheimer (Eds.), *Neuropsychological function and brain imaging* (pp. 161–183). New York: Plenum.

Savage, R. C., & Wolcott, G. F. (1994). *Educational dimensions of acquired brain injury.* Austin, TX: Pro-Ed.

Shutte, R. C., & Hopkins, B. L. (1970). The effects of teacher attention on following instructions in a kindergarten class. *Journal of Applied Behavior Analysis, 3,* 117–122.

Sinal, S. H., & Ball, M. R. (1987). Head trauma due to child abuse: Serial computerized tomography in diagnosis and management. *Southern Medical Journal, 80*(12), 1505–1512.

Spreen, O., Risser, A. H., & Edgwell, D. (1995). *Developmental neuropsychology.* New York: Oxford.

Telzrow, C. F. (1990). Management of academic and educational problems in traumatic brain injury. In E. D. Bigler (Ed.), *Traumatic brain injury* (pp. 251–272). Austin, TX: Pro-Ed.

Tepas, J. J., Di Scala, C., Ramenofsky, M. L., & Barlow, S. (1990). Mortality and head injury: The pediatric perspective. *Journal of Pediatrics and Surgery, 25*(1), 92–95.

Thompson, N. M., Francis, D. J., Stuebing, K. K., Fletcher, J. M., Ewing-Cobbs, L., Miner, M. E., Levin, H. S., & Eisenberg, H. M. (1994). Motor, visual-spatial and somatosensory skills after closed head injury in children and adolescents: A study of change. *Neuropsychology, 8*(3), 333–342.

Thompson, R. S., Rivara, F. P., & Thompson, D. C. (1989). A case-controlled study of the effectiveness of bicycle safety helmets. *New England Journal of Medicine, 320*(21), 1361–1367.

Wesson, D. E., Williams, J. I., Spence, L. J., Filler, R. M., Armstrong, P. F., & Pearl, R. H. (1989). Functional outcome in pediatric trauma. *Journal of Trauma, 29*(5), 589–592.

White, M. A. (1975). Natural rates of teacher approval and disapproval in the classroom. *Journal of Applied Behavior Analysis, 8,* 367–372.

Wilson, J. T. L., & Wyper, D. (1992). Neuroimaging and neuropsychological functioning following closed head injury: CT, MRI, and SPECT. *Journal of Head Trauma Rehabilitation, 7,* 29–39.

Wood, R. L. (1987). *Brain injury rehabilitation: A neurobehavioral approach.* Rockville, MD: Aspen.

Ylvisaker, M. (1986). Language and communication disorders following pediatric head injury. *Journal of Head Trauma Rehabilitation, 1*(4), 48–56.

Yudofsky, S. C., Silver, J. M., & Schneider, S. E. (1987). Pharmacological treatment of aggression. *Psychiatric Annals, 17*(6), 397–404.

74

Allergies and Asthma

Gretchen A. Meyer MD
Nathan J. Blum MD

Children's Seashore House, Philadelphia, Pennsylvania

Background and Development

Allergic diseases are among the most common medical problems during childhood. They account for one third of all chronic conditions in childhood and affect as many as one in five children (Evans, 1993). These disorders include anaphylaxis (an immediate, severe reaction), allergic rhinitis (hay fever), asthma, skin allergies, and food allergies. As with other chronic illnesses, persistent symptomatology, medical treatments, and psychological reactions to the presence of allergic diseases may create unique problems for the school-aged child. In this chapter, basic information about the function of the body's immune system will be reviewed followed by an overview of treatment alternatives. Then, specific aspects of common allergic diseases of children will be presented including their etiology, clinical manifestations, and treatment methods. Finally, there will be a discussion of the ways in which allergic diseases may impact school functioning. The information presented here is for educational purposes only. It is not intended to be used as a replacement for consultation with trained medical personnel in making treatment recommendations for allergic diseases.

Allergic diseases affect between 5% and 20% of school-aged children (Evans, 1993). The incidence of most allergic diseases is similar in boys and girls. Asthma, however, is twice as common in boys prior to adolescence (Evans, 1993). It is thought that one is born with a genetic predisposition toward allergic disease (Zeiger, 1993). However, an environmental exposure to a foreign substance is needed to induce the illness. The overall tendency for a person's immune system to react excessively to allergens is called *atopy*. The word *atopic* is often used synonymously with *allergic*.

Allergic diseases are caused by an overreaction of the immune system to a foreign substance, or *allergen*. An allergen is any substance that stimulates the body's immune system causing an allergic reaction. Allergens may enter the body in many ways, as inhalants (pollens, fungi, animal dander), ingestants (food, medications), injectants (insect venom, medications), or contactants (medications, food, clothing).

To understand allergic diseases it is helpful to have a basic understanding of how some components of the immune system function. *Immunoglobulins* (antibodies) are proteins in the body which recognize and bind to foreign substances (allergens, bacteria, viruses, etc.). There are many different types of immunoglobulins, but the one responsible for most allergic diseases is known as Immunoglobulin E (IgE). When IgE binds to a foreign substance, it activates specific cells of the immune system known as *mast cells*. These cells are found in the lining of the respiratory tracts, nose, eyes, and in the skin. Upon activation, a mast cell releases allergic *mediators* which then act on the body's organ systems to cause the symptoms of allergic disease. *Histamine* is the most well known of the many mediators and is responsible for some, though not all, allergic symptoms. *Inflammation* (swelling and congestion of bodily tissues) is one result of the effects of allergic mediators.

Allergies develop after the body's immune system trains itself to recognize allergens. Individuals do not experience allergic reactions the first time they encounter an allergen. Rather, with repeated exposures the immune system makes enough antibodies to cause allergic symptoms. Symptoms may occur with the second exposure or may develop in a child after multiple exposures. Over time, the characteristics of a child's allergic symptoms may change. For example, in infancy, foods are among the most common allergy-inducing substances, and the symptom is most often atopic eczema. Later, this pattern may disappear to be replaced by respiratory allergies (allergic rhinitis or asthma). As an individual matures, particularly by the fourth or fifth decade of life, the body's tendency to mount allergic reactions decreases.

Treatment for most allergic diseases involves two basic principles—prevention (prophylaxis) and symptomatic treatment. *Prophylaxis* is achieved mainly through aggressive avoidance of allergens, whenever possible. If a child is allergic to inhalants (pollens, molds, or house dust), there are a variety of ways to reduce allergen levels in the home. If a child is allergic to a pet, then removal of the animal from the home should help alleviate symptoms. If a food is an allergen, then it should be eliminated from the diet. Similarly, in skin allergies, topical contactants (soaps, certain types of clothing, etc.) may need to be avoided.

If symptoms are severe enough and specific allergens have not been identified, then *skin testing* may be performed so that the exact allergen or allergens in a particular child can be determined. In this procedure, a few drops of an extract of each allergen to be evaluated are placed on the child's skin and the skin pricked to allow penetration. If an allergy to a particular extract exists, redness and swelling appear at the site. Identification of specific allergens may facilitate environmental manipulations and avoidance techniques.

Because complete avoidance is not possible for some types of allergies, medications can also be used to prevent symptoms of allergies and asthma. Prophylactic drugs are those which can help prevent the release of allergic mediators from mast cells. One such drug is *cromolyn sodium.* Cromolyn works best when delivered directly to the site of symptoms and is available in nasal sprays, inhalers, and eye drops. Because it prevents the release of mediators, it does not work acutely to reduce symptoms. Rather, it must be taken regularly for it to be effective.

Another, more aggressive method of preventing allergy symptoms is with *immunotherapy* (allergy shots). This procedure is usually reserved for older children with severe symptoms and is given under the supervision of a physician with expertise in the area of allergy and immunology. Small amounts of allergenic extract are injected, usually into the upper arm. Shots are given weekly for a period of at least 3 years. They "desensitize" the immune system by building up blocking antibodies that resemble IgE antibodies enough to fool the immune system but are different enough that symptoms do not result.

Once allergic symptoms have appeared, treatment is based upon medications to help alleviate these symptoms. A frequently used class of drugs, the *antihistamines,* are used to block the effects of histamine once it has been released into the system. There are many brands of antihistamines available (see Table 1). These drugs may relieve symptoms of sneezing, itching, and rhinorrhea (runny nose). Classically, antihistamines have side effects of dry mouth and sedation; however, newer, less sedating types have recently become available.

Nasal congestion often does not improve with antihistamines. For this symptom, a *decongestant* may be prescribed. In fact, many allergy medications contain both an antihistamine and decongestant. Oral decongestants have many side effects such as nervousness, insomnia, irritability, headache, or rapid heart rate (see Table 1). Nasal decongestant sprays and drops are quite effective but should never be used for more than 2 or 3 days due to possible development of "rebound congestion" (more severe congestion when medication is stopped).

Lastly, corticosteroids are used to help alleviate the inflammation that is universally present when allergic symptoms appear. They are useful both in the prevention and treatment of swelling during an allergy exacerbation. They may be topically applied (creams), inhaled, or taken orally. Topical and inhaled corticosteroids, when used properly, are generally safe and have few side effects. If oral corticosteroids are used, they are usually prescribed for short periods (5–14 days), and this practice has also not been associated with severe side effects. Daily use of oral corticosteroids for prolonged periods is associated with adverse side effects in many organ systems and should only used in the most severe cases. *Corticosteroids* are not to be confused with *anabolic steroids,* commonly abused compounds which are derivatives of testosterone and are used to enhance athletic performance.

Problems and Implications

Anaphylaxis

The most severe manifestation of allergic disease is called *anaphylaxis.* This is a severe reaction characterized by coughing, vomiting, itching, hives, swelling, redness, and difficulty breathing. It is most commonly seen after exposures to antigens such as insect venom, medications, or specific food items (peanuts, walnuts, legumes, seafood). An anaphylactic reaction can begin within seconds of exposure to the offending allergen or may be delayed for several hours. It represents a medical emergency requiring immediate treatment and can be fatal. During anaphylaxis, the immediate injection of a medication called *epinephrine* can be life-saving. Children with a known severe allergy resulting in anaphylaxis should carry epinephrine with them at all times. Kits containing an antihistamine and a prefilled syringe of epinephrine are available. The child's teacher, the school nurse, and the child should all be instructed in the use of these kits.

Allergic Rhinitis

Etiology/Epidemiology

Allergic rhinitis (hay fever) is the most common of all the allergic diseases. It affects up to 10% of children and 20% to 30% of adolescents in the United States (Evans, 1993). The term *hay fever* is actually a misnomer because affected patients do not have fever and are not typically allergic to hay. The incidence of allergic rhinitis increases

Table 1   *Medications for Allergic Disease*

Antihistamines and Decongestants	
Antihistamines (brand name)	Side Effects[a]: Drowsiness, irritability, blurred vision
	Least sedating
Brompheniramine (Bromfed*, Dimetane*)	Astemizole (Hismanal)
Chlorpheniramine (Rynatnan*, Extendryl*, Atrohist*)	Loratadine (Claritin)
Carbinoxamine (Rondec*)	Terfenadine (Seldane)
Clemastine (Tavist)	
Diphenhydramine (Benadryl)	
Hydroxyzine (Atarax)	
Triprolidine (Actifed)	
*Also contains a decongestant	

Decongestants-Intranasal	Side Effects[a]: Rebound congestion (see text)
Oxymetazoline	
Pseudoephedrine	
Xylometazoline	
Decongestants-Oral	Side Effects[a]: Agitation, insomnia, hallucinations, tremor
Ephedrine	
Phenylepherine	
Phenylepherine	
Phenylpropanolamine	

Anti-inflammatory medications	
Steroids-Intranasal (brand name)	Side Effects[a]: Irritation, nose bleeds
Beclomethasone (Beconase AQ, VAncenase AQ)	
Budesonide (Rhinocort)	
Trimcinalone (Nasacort)	
Steroids-Inhaled (brand name)	Side Effects[a]: Cough, dry mouth, rinse mouth after administration to prevent infection of the mouth.
Beclomethasone (Beclovent, Vanceril)	
Flunisolide (Aerobid)	
Trimcinalone (Aristocort, Azmacort)	
Steroids-Oral	Side Effects[a]: Mild side effects with short-term use.
Dexamethasone (Decadron, Dexacort)	Many side effects including mood and behavior changes with long-term use.
Methylprednisolone (Medrol)	
Prednisolone (Prelone)	
Prednisone	
Steroids-creams/ointments	Side Effects: Few side effects with low potency medications. Intermediate to high potency medications may cause many side effects if used for prolonged periods.

Low Potency	*Intermediate Potency*	*High Potency*
0.05% Alclometasone dipropionate (Aclovate)	0.10% Betamethasone valerate (Valisone)	0.05% Clobetasol propionae (Temovate)
0.05% Desonide (Tridesilon)	0.025% Fluocinolone (Synalar)	0.05% Betamethasone dipropionate (Diprolene)
1% Hydocortisone (Hytone, Synacort)	0.10% Triamcinolone acetonide (Aristocort, Kenalog)	0.25% Desoximetasone (Topicort)
		0.05% Diflorasone diacetate (Psorcon, Florone)
		0.05% Fluocinonide (Lidex)
		0.20% Fluocinolone (Synalar)

Other Anti-inflammatory medications	
Cromolyn Sodium	Side Effects[a]: Throat irritation, cough

Bronchodilators	
Beta-adrenergic agonists	Side Effects[a]: Few side effects when inhaled. They are less effective and have more side effects when given orally. Side effects include increased heart rate, tremor, hyperactivity, insomnia.
Albuterol (Ventolin, Proventil)	
Metaproterenol (Alupent, Metaprel)	
Salmeterol (Serevent)	
Terbutaline (Brethine)	
Bronchodilators-other	
Theophylline	Side Effects[a]: Many, including hyperactivity and decreased attention span.
Ipatropium Bromide (Atrovent)	Side Effects[a]: Increased heart rate, blurred vision, headache, dry mouth.

[a]Does not include all possible side effects.

with age and it is rarely observed before 4 to 5 years of age. Individuals with hay fever become sensitized to the airborne pollens of trees, grasses, weeds, and molds. Symptoms tend to be seasonal based on the varied pollination patterns of these airborne allergens. Because pollination patterns and plant types differ in different regions of the country, a child who had no symptoms while living in one area of the country might develop severe symptoms after relocating to another.

In contrast to classic hay fever, perennial (chronic) allergic rhinitis is diagnosed when symptoms are present year-round. Causative allergens are most often indoor inhalants such as house dust, feathers, and animal dander. Mold spores may also induce chronic allergic rhinitis, particularly in humid climates.

Manifestations

Allergic rhinitis is characterized by sneezing; profuse and watery rhinorrhea (runny nose); nasal congestion; and itching of the nose, mouth, or ears. The eyes may also be involved and may itch, water, and become reddened (allergic *conjunctivitis*). The child with allergic rhinitis may frequently wrinkle or rub the nose. A horizontal crease may appear near the tip of the nose from repeated rubbing in an upward direction. Dark circles under the eyes (allergic shiners) are often seen. Many children with allergic rhinitis may breathe predominantly through the mouth causing dry mouth or sore throat. Nasal secretions dripping down the back of the throat (postnasal drip) may cause a child with allergic rhinitis to have a chronic cough.

Other irritating airborne substances, such as tobacco smoke, components of air pollution, chalk dust, aerosolized cosmetics, or other strong smells, may cause symptoms in children who suffer from allergic rhinitis. Reaction to one of these irritants may not indicate a typical IgE-mediated *allergy,* but rather a hypersensitivity to the substance. Changes in temperature may also induce symptoms in some children. Lastly, periods of psychological and emotional stress can trigger the onset of symptoms or exacerbate them when present. Although allergic rhinitis is generally not a serious medical condition, there are occasional complications. The presence of allergic rhinitis may predispose a child to colds and recurrent ear or sinus infections. The nasal secretions of allergic rhinitis are generally clear and watery. The presence of thick, discolored, or malodorous drainage should raise suspicion of the presence of a viral or bacterial infection.

Chronic mouth breathing may eventually lead to structural problems of the teeth, gums, or even the jaw. Halitosis (bad breath) may result from mouth breathing, sinusitis, or postnasal drip. The senses of smell and taste may be temporarily lost during allergic flare-ups.

Lastly, children with allergic rhinitis have an increased risk of developing other types of allergic diseases as well. For example, nearly half of the children who suffer from allergic rhinitis also have asthma (Evans, 1993).

Treatment

Allergic rhinitis is best treated using a combined approach. The most effective treatment is prevention through avoidance of allergens, but medications are also useful. With currently available treatments, relief of a child's discomfort is generally possible. Usually, the first drugs prescribed are the *antihistamines* (see Table 1). Cromolyn sodium or intranasal corticosteroids are also used to reduce the frequency of exacerbations. For severe allergic conjunctivitis, antihistamine or decongestant eye drops may help decrease the itching and watering. When symptoms of allergic rhinitis or conjunctivitis are extremely severe, a limited course of oral corticosteroids may be prescribed—usually for a period of 5 days to 2 weeks. If drugs and avoidance are not sufficient to alleviate a child's symptoms, and they are deemed to be severe, then *immunotherapy* (allergy shots) may be instituted.

Asthma

Etiology/Epidemiology

Asthma (reactive airway disease) is one of the most common chronic diseases affecting children in the United States. It is the most serious and complicated of the allergic disorders, mainly because it is chronic and can be life-threatening if not treated appropriately. It is a disorder characterized by wheezing which occurs when the airways through which air is passed into and out of the lung become narrowed or occluded. Two factors contribute to this airway obstruction. First, the air tubes are surrounded by muscles which, when stimulated by allergic mediators, may go into spasm narrowing the airway. This is called *bronchospasm.* Second, the mucous membrane lining becomes inflamed and swollen.

The frequency of asthma attacks varies widely among children. Some with mild asthma may have an episode as infrequently as once or twice a year. A child with moderate asthma may experience wheezing or coughing more than once or twice a week. Children with severe asthma may be wheezing daily or almost constantly.

Certain types of asthma are said to be nonallergic because IgE is not felt to be involved. Wheezing induced by exercise or cold or hot ambient air are examples. Many children with asthma will experience an increase in symptoms during a viral illness, cold, or other upper respiratory tract infection. In addition, as with allergic rhinitis, asthma can be triggered by exposure to irritating substances such as tobacco smoke, perfumes, paint fumes, dusts, air pollutions, or soap powders. Some children have asthma attacks which occur without pattern or clear evidence of specific triggers.

Manifestations

During an asthma attack a child may experience difficulty breathing or "tightness" in the chest. In mild cases, wheezing may only be detectable with a stethoscope. When it is loud enough to hear with the naked ear, significant narrowing of the airways has occurred. Untreated, the child may develop obvious difficulty breathing and may be so short of breath that speaking is difficult. This is a life-threatening situation, and urgent medical care is necessary.

Treatment

The treatment of asthma is multifaceted. As with other types of allergic diseases, prevention of symptoms is a key element of disease management. Avoidance of identified triggers combined with the use of cromolyn sodium or inhaled corticosteroids may be recommended so that severe restrictions need not be placed on a child's daily life or extracurricular activities.

During an asthma attack treatment focuses on opening the narrowed airways. This is usually done with medications known as *bronchodilators*. Bronchodilators relax the muscle lining of the bronchial tubes thereby dilating the airways. The most commonly used type of bronchodilators are called *beta-adrenergic agonists* (see Table 1). They are most effective when delivered directly into the lungs using a metered-dose inhaler (MDI). Proper use of the inhaler is crucial to its effectiveness, and timing of the inhalation and spray can be difficult. Younger children may benefit from the use of a "spacer" (a baglike device which helps the child to coordinate the timing of the spray). Alternatively, beta-adrenergic agonists may be delivered using a *nebulizer* (an electrical machine that aerosolizes the medication; the mist can then be inhaled through a mask or tube). Nebulizers are most often used for children unable to operate an MDI. They are much less convenient, usually require some adult assistance, and take longer to administer.

Beta-adrenergic agents are most useful when a child is in the midst of an asthma attack. Although some children with severe asthma take these medications daily, in most cases they are used only for acute wheezing. Common side effects of these drugs include increased heart rate, "jitteriness," and muscle tremors. They are generally quite safe when used properly. *Theophylline,* another type of bronchodilator, was used regularly in the past as first-line therapy for asthma. Because of the advent of the newer anti-inflammatory and bronchodilator drugs, it is now used only rarely in the severe asthmatic (usually in the hospital setting). Lastly, *ipatropium bromide* is a bronchodilator used rarely in acute asthma attacks which are unresponsive to the just listed therapies.

Cromolyn sodium is also commonly used in the treatment of asthma. It is delivered via MDI or nebulizer directly into the lungs. It is important to note that it does not act to relieve bronchospasm directly and, therefore, does not work acutely in an attack as do the beta-adrenergic agonists. Because of its preventive properties, children with chronic asthma often use cromolyn daily even in the absence of symptoms.

Lastly, corticosteroids have become a mainstay of asthma treatment because of their potent anti-inflammatory properties. Similar to cromolyn sodium, these drugs work to prevent the onset of airway inflammation or to reduce ongoing swelling. Therefore, they are useful even in the absence of symptoms. Most commonly, corticosteroids are administered via MDI, with or without a spacer. Children with severe disease may need to take oral corticosteroids for short periods. Very rarely, a child's asthma is severe enough to require continuous oral corticosteroids.

Antihistamines, used commonly in other types of allergic diseases, are not felt to be useful in the treatment of asthma. A child with asthma may take antihistamines, however, to combat symptoms of allergic rhinitis or eczema which often accompany asthma.

In the past several years, the use of the home peak-flow meter has revolutionized the care of children with asthma. During an asthma attack, air will move out of the lung more slowly. A peak-flow meter measures the peak expiratory flow rate (PEFR) which is the greatest flow velocity that can be obtained during a forced expiration of the lung. It provides a simple, reproducible measure of the degree of airway obstruction present. Before any amount of wheezing will be noticed by a patient or observer, the child may have some degree of airway obstruction. Once wheezing is noticeable, the PEFR will have already decreased by 25% (National Asthma Education Program, 1991). Regular measurement of the PEFR with a peak-flow meter permits the child to record his or her baseline PEFR. A PEFR decreased from the normal baseline value alerts the child that an attack is beginning. This allows bronchodilator and anti-inflammatory medications to be instituted earlier in the disease process, often interrupting the progression of the attack. All children with asthma should use a peak-flow meter daily. A specific therapeutic plan designed by the child's physician will instruct the child on an appropriate therapeutic action depending on the measured PEFR.

Education of children with asthma and their parents is paramount to the successful treatment and prevention of asthma attacks. Therefore, children with asthma should have a basic understanding of the disease process, its triggers, and the rationale behind the proper use of medication. Children should be active in the monitoring of their own PEFR and should recognize the need for additional medication. Given this degree of understanding by the child, and agreement of the parents and physician, the child may be allowed to carry an inhaler at all times. In addition, teachers and school nurses should be familiar with the child's condition, known triggers, and prescribed course of treatment.

Skin Allergies

There are three distinct categories of skin allergies. They are *eczema* (often called atopic dermatitis), *urticaria* (hives), and *contact dermatitis.*

Etiology/Epidemiology

Of the three types of skin allergies, eczema is the most chronic, causing continuous symptoms in some children. Eczema often appears in infants and young children with a family history of allergy or eczema. Of children with eczema, one half or more may go on to develop allergic rhinitis or asthma as they enter the school-age years (Evans, 1993). Symptoms of eczema may wax and wane for years and usually decrease as the child ages. Sometimes flare-ups are seasonal. While eczema is linked to specific allergies in some children, in most cases the exact cause of eczema is unknown. Occasionally allergies to foods may cause the eczema to flare. Rarely, flare-ups are linked with airborne allergens. Some children may react to certain soaps, detergents, or even clothing materials (e.g., wool).

Urticaria (hives) in contrast to eczema is an episodic condition. It may be induced by a variety of allergens. Food allergies (especially nuts, berries, cheese, sesame oils, shellfish, eggs, and milk) or medications are often responsible. Rarely, a child will develop hives in response to an inhaled allergen. It is not clear why some children develop eczema to an allergen while others manifest hives. Nonallergic causes of urticaria include cold water, pressure or vibration on the skin, infections, or exposure to sunlight.

The third type of allergic skin disorder is contact dermatitis. It is caused by a different immune mechanism than eczema and the respiratory allergies. Allergies to fabrics and dyes, the leather or rubber in shoes, cosmetics, jewelry, or topically applied creams are often causes of contact dermatitis. The most familiar type of contact dermatitis is what is known as poison ivy.

Manifestations

Eczema usually appears as slightly raised, itchy, scaly eruptions on the skin. It is most often present on the bends of the elbows, backs of the wrists and ankles, or behind the knees but can also occur on the face, trunk, and scalp. Acutely, it may be moist and ooze. If it persists for an extended period of time, the skin may thicken and become dry. Most problematic for the child, however, is the intense itching. In some children, the itching can become so severe that, through repeated scratching, the skin becomes raw and easily infected.

Urticaria is typified by a skin rash with the characteristic appearance of raised, red bumps, often with a pale central area. In response to an inciting agent, a child may develop a single hive or multiple lesions, and they may appear on any portion of the face and body. Often, they are migratory and locations of specific lesions may change within minutes or hours. They are always associated with *intense* itching.

Hives are not, themselves, life-threatening. The most serious problem is usually the intense itching. However, urticaria is occasionally accompanied by swelling of the lips, ears, eyes, or genitals. When this occurs, anaphylaxis should be suspected and effective treatment instituted immediately. Treatment for anaphylaxis was described earlier in this chapter.

The rash accompanying contact dermatitis consists of reddened bumps or blisters and dry, scaly, itchy skin. It, like eczema, may initially be moist and oozing. Contact dermatitis differs from eczema in that it is generally located on a discretely defined portion of the child's skin where contact with an allergen has occurred. In fact, the location of the rash is often what helps determine the offending agent. Symptoms of contact dermatitis may take 1 to 2 days to erupt.

Treatment

Treatment of skin allergies is aimed at prevention as well as amelioration of symptoms. Food is often a trigger of eczema in infants and young children but is much less likely to cause symptoms in school-aged children. Known allergenic contactants such as laundry detergents or wool clothing should be avoided.

Topical corticosteroid creams are prescribed to help decrease inflammation in the skin during flare-ups. They come in varying strengths (see Table 1) and should be used only as prescribed to avoid systemic side effects. Antihistamines are often prescribed to help prevent itching which further damages the skin and predisposes it to secondary infection. As in other allergic diseases, if symptoms of skin allergy are extremely severe, systemic corticosteroids are used for short periods of time. Immunotherapy is generally not helpful in the control of skin allergies.

Food Allergies

Etiology/Epidemiology

Food as an allergen is discussed separately because of the large variety of symptoms attributed to food allergies. In considering symptoms thought to be caused by foods, one should distinguish true allergies (caused by an immunologic reaction to the food item) from negative food reactions *not* related to the immune system. The latter reactions are best termed "food intolerances" or "food sensitivities."

True food allergies occur in 2% to 8% of infants and young children (Sampson, 1993). Although allergies to some foods may be particularly persistent (mainly nuts, peanuts, buckwheat, shellfish, and cottonseed), many of these food sensitivities tend to abate after the ages of 2 or 3 years. Thus, food allergies in the school-aged child are rare.

Manifestations

Food allergies may manifest themselves in different ways. Most dramatic is anaphylaxis (described earlier). Usually, however, children will react less dramatically with symptoms resembling hives or, less frequently, allergic rhinitis.

Food intolerances may cause gastrointestinal symptoms or headaches. For example, some children may have adverse reactions (bloating, stomach cramps, diarrhea) after ingesting milk or lactose-containing items. This is not a true allergy to milk but is due to a deficiency in one's ability to digest lactose, a condition called "lactose-intolerance." In addition, children who suffer from migraine headaches often report that foods will trigger an attack. This, too, is not felt to be a true food allergy but a sensitivity not fully understood. The concept that sensitivity to food or food additives can produce symptoms of nervousness, problems in concentration and learning, behavior disorders, or hyperactivity is controversial and will be discussed later in this chapter.

The diagnosis of food allergies can be difficult and time consuming. Because foods are generally consumed in combinations and food items are often disguised in recipes, identifying the allergen may require detective work. Skin tests may be helpful in certain cases. Food challenges (systematic removal and then reintroduction of certain foods) may be conducted under the supervision of a qualified physician.

Treatment

Treatment of food allergies and food intolerance depends mainly on avoidance. This can be exceedingly difficult if the item is a component of food products. Nutritional information about purchased foods is now generally available on packaging which has helped food-allergic individuals to monitor their intake. If anaphylaxis is encountered, it is treated as described earlier. For skin reactions to food, treatment is similar to that outlined for skin allergies.

Allergies and School Problems

The presence of allergic diseases can create special problems for the school-aged child. Difficulties may arise from the allergic symptomatology, the treatment, or the psychological impact of chronic illness. This situation is not unique to children with allergies; rather, some of the problems encountered are similar to those experienced by children with any type of chronic illness or disabling condition.

A number of factors related to allergic diseases in childhood may potentially interfere with academic performance and behavior in the classroom. These include excessive absenteeism, impaired concentration and inattention, possible intellectual impairment, and the effects of medication used to control symptoms.

Several studies have demonstrated an increased incidence of school absenteeism among children with allergies and asthma (Gutstadt et al., 1989; Richards, 1992). Estimates are that as many as 25% of all school absences may be due to these conditions (Steiner, Hilliard, Fritz, & Lewiston, 1982). School absences because of allergies and asthma may be brief but frequent. The impact of these absences on school performance may vary among children. McLoughlin and colleagues (1983) showed correlation between excessive absences and lower scores on teachers' perceptions of students' educational achievement and psychological well-being. Some researchers found that children who miss school frequently are less likely to finish school and tend to perform less well (Richards, 1992). In contrast, Gustadt et al. (1989) found no correlation between the rate of school absence and academic performance.

Even when present in the classroom, the child with allergies may experience difficulty with attention to specific tasks and with concentration. Symptoms of allergic diseases such as sneezing, sniffing, difficulty breathing, and coughing are often worse at night leading to poor quality or an insufficient quantity of sleep. Excessive fatigue can make it hard for a child to concentrate. In addition, when these symptoms occur in the classroom, they may be distracting and contribute to problems with attention and concentration. A child with allergies who develops difficulties with attention should be evaluated for intermittent hearing impairment. Respiratory allergies cause swelling which can obstruct proper drainage of the middle ear. The result is often a build-up of fluid which can interfere with normal hearing.

Concentration and attention may also be negatively affected by medications used to treat allergies. Antihistamines, the most commonly used class of drugs for allergies, can have effects on the central nervous system such as sedation, diminished alertness, and slowed reaction time (Milgrom & Bender, 1995). Inhaled beta-adrenergic agonists (bronchodilators), used extensively in the treatment of asthma, have been implicated as a cause for hyperactivity with some children reporting "tremors" and "shakiness" after appropriate doses (McLoughlin, 1983; Milgrom & Bender, 1995). Theophylline, an oral bronchodilator, has been shown to impair concentration, visuomotor retention, memory, and reading skills (Furukawa, 1984). It has also been reported to alter attention and cause restlessness and irritability (Rachelefsky et al., 1986). In contrast, Lindgren (1992) demonstrated that theophylline, when used in appropriate doses, did not impair academic performance. Finally, the use of oral corticosteroids has also been implicated in the impairment of school performance and behavior (Suess, Stump, Chai, & Kalisker, 1986). There may be mood and/or memory changes even in low doses, and these alterations may be seen more frequently in children with a preexisting history of emotional difficulty (Milgrom & Bender, 1995). In spite of all these findings, it is important to note that most children do not experience negative side effects as a result of the medical treatment of their allergic disease. As with any treatment that may have cognitive or behavioral side effects, monitoring is vital. Collaboration between physicians and school psychologists may facilitate the early detection of these side effects.

Symptomatology and medical treatment effects aside, do allergies themselves *cause* learning, attentional, or behavioral problems? There is a large body of conflicting literature discussing whether a relationship exists between allergies and learning disabilities and allergies and Attention Deficit/Hyperactivity Disorder (ADHD). Many researchers have postulated that a common etiologic aberration of chemicals within the brain ultimately leads to immune problems (allergies) and abnormalities of brain function (learning problems or attentional difficulties.) As early as the 1940s, Randolph (1947) described what he called "allergic toxemia," characterized by fatigue and impaired cognitive functioning. Subsequently, Speer (1954) introduced the concept of the "allergic-tension-fatigue syndrome." This syndrome was described as periods of extreme fatigue alternating with hyperkinesis or tension. It was contended that it represented some sort of "cerebral allergy," and food was implicated in most cases (Speer, 1954). While these "syndromes" have not been accepted, the idea that food allergies can cause behavioral and cognitive symptoms has persisted.

In 1989, Marshall proposed that allergic reactions engender chemical imbalances in the central nervous system leading to poorly regulated arousal levels and ADHD-type behaviors in some children. Roth and colleagues (1991) reported that, in tests sensitive to attentional capacity and behavioral inhibitory functions, children with allergies performed less well. He felt that this finding supported the theory of a common predisposing factor in both allergic diseases and attentional or behavioral disorders. Rawls, Rawls, and Harrison (1971) also found that allergic children were "significantly less aggressive, more nervous, and required more frequent discipline" than their nonallergic peers. In contrast, McLoughlin et al. (1983) found no significant difference in parent perceptions of behavior problems between allergic and nonallergic children. Moreover, in a recent report of a cohort of 1,037 children followed prospectively from birth, McGee, Stanton, and Sears (1993) found no association between allergies and symptoms consistent with ADHD.

In addition to attentional and behavioral problems, allergies have been suggested to be a cause for learning disabilities. Some researchers have reported specific cognitive deficits in cohorts of children with asthma. Deficits were detected in visuospatial configurations, incidental memory, and the planning and execution of visual and tactile motor tasks (Dunleavy, 1980). Gustadt et al. (1989), however, found that academic achievement and intelligence, measured by standardized tests, did not differ between children with and without asthma. Rawls et al. (1971) also reported finding no differences in achievement and intelligence tests between allergic and nonallergic children. In addition, McLoughlin et al. (1983) found no significant difference in parent perceptions of academic performance, retention, or classification as "handicapped" between the children with and without allergies.

In summary, when asking whether there is a relationship between allergies and difficulties with attention, behavior, and learning, one must attempt to discern whether allergies themselves *cause* school problems through some physiologically mediated mechanism, whether the *treatment* of allergies causes them, whether one is not causative of the other but they merely coincide in a particular child because of a common predisposing factor, or lastly, whether the "association" between these two different types of problems in a single child may be mere coincidence. A good deal more scientific investigation must take place before these questions can be answered.

In addition to difficulties in academic performance and behavior in the classroom, allergies have been reported to have effects on the emotional state of the school-aged child and on peer interactions. Chronic allergies potentially have a deleterious effect on self-esteem through embarrassment over symptoms, treatment, or bodily appearance (eczema). Often children with allergic rhinitis may have a "nasal" quality to their voice or halitosis (bad breath) which may be aversive to peers. Also, missed or restricted activities may have a significant impact on the child's self-esteem.

At times, the prescribed treatment regimen may create conflicts for the child in the home or school. If these difficulties lead to failure to adhere to medical regimens, this may further exacerbate the allergic symptoms and escalate the conflict. Alternatively, parents or teachers may provide excessive amounts of attention to the allergic child related to the symptoms or to compliance with treatments. If attention related to allergic symptoms replaces more typical interactions between the child and the parent or teacher, overreporting of symptoms may occur. Reinforcement for displaying allergic symptoms or wheezing may also include avoidance of task demands or school absence (Lowenthal & Lowenthal, 1995). If excessive attention is related to difficulties in getting the child to cooperate with treatment, then the child's noncompliance may be inadvertently reinforced (Christiaanse, Lavigne, & Lerner, 1989). In these cases, assessment and treatment planning can be very difficult. Collaboration between a physician and psychologist may be necessary to develop a safe and effective treatment plan.

Children with significant allergic disorders, especially asthma, may also develop excessive anxiety surrounding their condition. The child with asthma who has been hospitalized, has suffered numerous repeated attacks, or has experienced anaphylaxis may live in constant fear that an attack is imminent. Up to two thirds of children with asthma report feeling "panic" at the start of an asthma attack (Butz & Alexander, 1993). This fear and anxiety may interfere with academic performance and social competence. Moreover, there may be anxiety on the part of the child's parents or peers. Parental anxiety may cause significant problems, occasionally exacerbating the child's symptoms (Butz & Alexander, 1993). Worried parents may be overprotective and place restrictions on a child's activities. Lastly, because allergic symptoms may mimic infections, the child may be rejected by peers over fear of contagion. To help alleviate anxiety, education about the disease process and its treatment can be extremely helpful.

Although it is generally accepted that periods of psychological or social stress may cause a child with allergies to experience an exacerbation of symptoms, it is not felt that psychosocial factors can actually *cause* allergies in a child not otherwise affected. The primary abnormality of the immune system cannot be explained by psychosocial stress alone.

Controversial Treatments

Scientifically based investigative procedures have led to advances in the understanding of the pathophysiology, etiology, and treatment for most of the allergic diseases which affect children. Traditional therapies for allergies and asthma in children have been touched on in this chapter and include allergen avoidance, treatment with medications, and immunotherapy. There are "nontraditional" therapies proposed by a small number of practitioners that bear mentioning. These therapies are controversial and unproven, set apart as such by a paucity of both scientifically based studies of their effectiveness and publication of results in peer-reviewed scientific journals.

In the past 30 years, a group of individuals who call themselves "clinical ecologists" has emerged. They propose that the root cause of many disorders of behavior and learning actually represent sensitivities to various environmental toxins including food and food additives. The notion that dietary factors can have a deleterious impact on the function of the central nervous system is not new. Rather, it has been a recurring theme throughout medicine's history. In the early 1900s, Rowe described what he termed "cerebral allergy" characterized by drowsiness, confusion, and memory loss. He attributed these symptoms to food sensitivities (Rowe, 1928). Investigation over the years resulted in a myriad of unproven treat-

ments that continue to be promoted in the orthomolecular and homeopathic literature.

In 1975, Feingold proposed a relationship between "hyperactivity" and the ingestion of food additives such as food colorings, flavorings, preservatives, and naturally occurring salicylates. This theory received widespread publicity. Subsequent attempts to substantiate this hypothesis have yielded inconclusive and conflicting results (Conner, Goyette, & Southwick, 1976; Levine & Liden, 1976). Many of the studies have been plagued by methodological difficulties. In 1982 the National Institutes of Health published a consensus statement formulated by researchers investigating the role of food and food additives in determining behavior. Their conclusion was that data existing at that time did not support Feingold's hypothesis (Consensus Conference, 1982).

The current "gold standard" for determining whether a particular food or food additive is responsible for a specific symptom is called a double-blind, placebo-controlled food challenge (DBPCFC). Recently, two research groups using the DBPCFC scientific method reported significant differences in parent ratings of home behavior between challenge food days and placebo days in small samples of children (Boris & Mandel, 1994; Carter et al., 1993). Although these results are interesting, neither of these studies evaluated the effects of food challenges on school performance or behavior. In general, the opinion of those who work routinely with children with attentional problems and behavior disorders is that there may be a *very* small subset of children whose symptoms are exacerbated by ingested food or chemicals. It is not believed, however, that food sensitivities *cause* ADHD.

Extreme caution must be used in attributing behavioral symptomatology to food allergies. The proposed method of treatment involves "elimination" diets or "few food" diets. These often require rigid dietary restrictions that are difficult to impose and may significantly alter the family life and social life of the patient. Nevertheless, many parents remain adamant that their children react negatively to the ingestion of a certain food coloring or food item. If elimination of this food item is simple and does not negatively affect the child's nutritional status, then a trial of dietary treatment may be warranted. If a strict elimination diet is used, it should be guided by a physician or nutritionist.

Another controversial theory is that of the "yeast overgrowth syndrome" popularized by Crook (1989) with the publication of his book *The Yeast Connection: A Medical Breakthrough.* Proponents of this theory believe that some individuals, whether by "allergy" or mere "sensitivity," demonstrate an overpopulation of *candida,* a yeast that normally inhabits the gastrointestinal tract. Excess candida leads to the production of a "toxin" which is said to cause any of a myriad of somatic difficulties including autism, learning disabilities, and behavior disorders.

There are no well-designed scientific studies to support these claims.

Neutralization therapy is another unproven method of treating allergies. In this procedure allergen extracts are administered to the patient, usually sublingually (under the tongue). It is not to be confused with allergen immunotherapy (allergy shots), a well-established therapy already described in this chapter.

The use of vitamins, minerals, amino acids, antioxidant supplements, or enzymes in the treatment of allergic disorders and asthma has also been suggested. This treatment is called *orthomolecular* therapy. Treatment with these dietary supplements is standard in the extremely rare case of a proven deficiency. However, improper use of large doses can be harmful in a nondeficient individual. There is no evidence to substantiate the theory that vitamin or nutritional deficiency is a mitigating factor in allergic diseases, nor any to suggest that "mega" doses of these substances have therapeutic benefit (Terr, 1993).

The role of emotional factors in allergies, particularly asthma, may vary among children. At one time, allergic symptoms were attributed to difficulties in mother-child interactions (French & Alexander, 1941). Most experts now agree that, although allergies and their symptoms are multifactorial in origin, psychological factors are not a primary cause of allergies. It is accepted, however, that allergic symptoms may be precipitated or exacerbated by psychological factors in an individual with known allergic disease. Furthermore, psychological factors may interfere with adaptation to the illness and adherence to medical treatments. The role of psychological interventions in the treatment of asthma is discussed in the following section.

Alternative Actions

A variety of psychological approaches have been used as adjuncts to pharmacologic therapy in the treatment of asthma and other allergic diseases. In general, these approaches involve improving the child's and parents' understanding and monitoring of the disease, improving adherence to medical regimens, decreasing anxiety or tension related to the disease, and providing counseling to help manage psychosocial or family stressors that impact on the disease or its management (Lask, 1991). While these approaches to treatment will not be needed for many children with mild disease, they can be an essential component of a comprehensive treatment plan for children who are having difficulty adjusting to their disease or whose disease is negatively impacting on their home, school, or peer functioning.

A comprehensive treatment plan requires collaboration between physicians, school personnel, family members, and the child. This plan may include education about the disease, guidelines for monitoring symptom severity and administration of medications in school, and guidelines for participation in activities and school attendance. If the child's illness severely impacts school performance, then the child may be classified as "other health impaired" under the Individuals with Disabilities Education Act (IDEA) and therefore eligible for assistance in school.

Self-management or family management programs for asthma have been the most commonly studied adjunctive psychological interventions for allergic disease. Typically these programs involve education of the child and parents about the disease in combination with behavioral interventions designed to increase the likelihood of the child engaging in appropriate asthma self-care strategies. Many programs incorporate relaxation training into the intervention package (Wigal, Creer, Kotses, & Lewis, 1990).

Outcome studies of asthma self-management programs usually demonstrate an increase in the child and parents' knowledge about asthma and a more positive attitude toward the disease. Some programs have demonstrated decreased numbers of asthma attacks and decreased absenteeism (Wigal et al., 1990), but a recent meta-analysis concluded that self-management programs did not reduce asthma morbidity (Bernard-Bonnin et al., 1995). However, this analysis only included the results of a limited number of programs. The program factors which make for effective self-management programs have not been clearly delineated. Self-management programs seem to be most effective for children who are experiencing the lowest levels of appropriate self-care prior to the intervention (Vasquez & Buceta, 1993).

Clark and colleagues (1984) conducted a study of the effects of an asthma family education and management program on school performance. The intervention involved monthly one-hour training sessions with separate sessions for parents and children. The intervention took place over 6 months. Children in the intervention group maintained slightly better academic performance than did children in the control group, and there was a trend toward increased participation in physical education. In this study no difference was found between the two groups in school absenteeism.

Other psychological treatments that have been used in allergic diseases include hypnosis and biofeedback. A number of studies of hypnosis for children with asthma have demonstrated that it improves subjective ratings of symptoms, while variable findings have been reported when objective measures of airway obstruction are used (Aronoff, Aronoff, & Peck, 1975; Isenberg, Lehrer, & Hochron, 1992). A randomized study of the effects of hypnosis on response to an allergen challenge in adults with asthma showed small improvements in objective measures of airway obstruction in the hypnosis group. When the treatment and control groups with a high susceptibility to hypnosis were evaluated alone, there was a 75% improvement in airway hyperresponsiveness to the allergen in the hypnosis group (Ewer & Stewart, 1986). These findings suggest that hypnosis may be an effective adjunct to treatment in some, but not all, individuals with asthma.

Lastly, some children with asthma have difficulty recognizing the degree of airway obstruction present when they develop symptoms. These individuals may overreact to changes or not recognize large changes in airway resistance. While monitoring of PEFR (discussed earlier) is essential for these children, biofeedback has also been used to increase awareness or ventilatory problems (Falliers, 1988). Biofeedback has also been used to manage itching associated with chronic skin allergies.

Summary

Allergic diseases, including asthma, are a common cause of chronic illness in children. They are caused by a malfunction of the immune system and include allergic rhinitis and conjunctivitis (hay fever), asthma, eczema, hives, other contact skin allergies, and food allergies. The symptoms produced are varied but can range from annoying (itching, runny nose) to life-threatening in the cases of asthma and anaphylaxis.

The treatment for allergic diseases consists mainly of preventative measures and symptomatic relief. Prevention is achieved through avoidance and environmental control measures. Medications may be used to prevent or treat symptoms. In children with severe disease, immunotherapy (allergy shots) may be considered.

Children with allergic diseases may experience difficulties in the classroom both academically and behaviorally. Problems may include poor concentration, attentional difficulties, and underachievement. The precise reason for such problems may differ from child to child. Many of the medications used cause drowsiness or slowed reaction times. Others may make a child shaky or "jittery." A few have been shown to impair cognitive performance directly. Aside from medication use, a child may suffer the psychological and emotional effects of having a chronic illness. Despite these considerations, and although much has been written in this area, there is little evidence to suggest that allergies cause learning disabilities, behavioral disorders, or ADHD.

Through avoidance techniques, proper use of medications, and a comprehensive education plan, the effects of allergies or asthma on a child's development, behavior, and academic achievement can be greatly minimized. The child, the parents, involved teachers, and school nurses should all recognize the child's triggering events/ exposures and understand the proposed treatment plan.

Goals should include keeping school absences to a minimum, optimizing medical treatment, and normalizing the child's participation in activities to the maximum extent possible.

Recommended Resources

American Academy of Allergy and Immunology. (n.d.). *Tips to remember*. (Available from Author, 611 E. Wells St. Milwaukee, WI 53202)
This series of 24 concise, understandable brochures covers many aspects of allergies including prevention and treatment.

The Asthma and Allergy Foundation of America. (n.d.). *ACT (Asthma Care Training) for KIDS*. (Available from Author, 1302 18th St. NW, Washington, DC 20036)
This training kit is designed for children to learn about the causes and treatment of asthma. Also, methods for achieving better control of symptoms are reviewed. It is written for children ages 6 to 12 years and their parents.

The Asthma and Allergy Foundation of America. (n.d.). *Managing asthma in the school: An action plan (video)*. (Available from Author, 1320 18th St. NW, Washington, DC)
This video illustrates the basics of asthma and discusses how school personnel can work in tandem with physicians in managing children with asthma.

Mendoza, G., Garcia, M. K., & Collins, M. A. (1989) *Asthma in the school: Improving control with peak flow monitoring*. Healthscan
This is a brief, very useful summary of the principles of asthma prevention and treatment. Included are several flow charts and handouts to help the teacher, school nurse, and child better manage the symptoms of asthma.

Steinmann, M. (1992). *A parent's guide to allergies and asthma*. The Children's Hospital of Philadelphia Series. New York: Dell
This informative book contains basic information for parents on the physical and psychological aspects of allergies and asthma. It includes a discussion of etiology, diagnosis, and treatment. A full chapter is dedicated to environmental avoidance techniques.

Tinkelman, D. G., Falliers, J., & Naspitz, C. K. (Eds.). (1987). *Childhood asthma: Pathophysiology and treatment*. New York: Marcel Decker.
This comprehensive monograph explains methods of differential and etiologic diagnosis. It reviews all aspects of treatment and discusses theories on the pathogenesis of asthma. Additionally, there is a section on the environmental, family, and psychosocial aspects of the disease.

Wood, R. A. (1995). *Taming Asthma and Allergies by Controlling Your Environment*. Washington, DC: Asthma and Allergy Foundation of America.
This brief monograph discusses how children and their parents can successfully minimize allergen exposure in the home and at school.

References

Aronoff, G.M., Aronoff, S., & Peck, L. W. (1975). Hypnotherapy in the treatment of bronchial asthma. *Annals of Allergy 34*, 356–362.

Bernard-Bonnin, A. C., Stachen K.D.S., Bonin, D., Charette, C., Rousseau, E. (1995). Self-management teaching programs and morbidity of pediatric asthma: A meta-analysis. *Journal of Allergy and Clinical Immunology, 95*, 34–41.

Boris, M., & Mandel, F.S. (1994). Foods and additives are common causes of the attention deficit hyperactive disorder in children. *Annals of Allergy, 72*, 462–468.

Butz, A. M., & Alexander, C. (1993). Anxiety in children with asthma. *Journal of Asthma, 30*(3), 199–209.

Carter, C.M., Urbanowicz, M., Hemsley, R., Mantilla, L., Strobel, S., Graham, P.J., & Taylor, E. (1993). Effects of a few food diet in attention deficit disorder. *Archives of Diseases of Childhood, 69*, 564–568.

Christiaanse, M. E., Lavigne, J. V., & Lerner, C. V. (1989). Psychosocial aspects of compliance in children and adolescents with asthma. *Developmental and Behavioral Pediatrics, 10*(2), 75–80.

Clark, N. M., Feldman, C. H., Evans, D., Wasilewski, Y., & Levison, M. J. (1984). Changes in children's school performance as a result of education for family management of asthma. *Journal of School Health, 54*(4), 143–145.

Conners, C. K., Goyette, C. H., & Southwick, D. A. (1976). Food additives and hyperkinesis: A controlled double-blind experiment. *Pediatrics, 58*, 154–66.

Consensus Conference, National Institutes of Health. (1982). Defined diets and childhood hyperactivity. *Journal of the American Medical Association, 248*(3), 290–292.

Crook, W. G. (1989). *The Yeast Connection: A medical breakthrough* (3rd ed.) Jackson, TN: Professional Books.

Dunleavy, R. A. (1980). Neuropsychological correlates of severe asthma in children 9–14 years old. *Journal of Consulting and Clinical Psychology, 48*, 214–219.

Evans, R., III. (1993). Epidemiology and natural history of asthma, allergic rhinitis, and atopic dermatitis. In E. Middleton, C. E. Reed, E. F. Ellis, N. F. Adkinson, J. W. Yunginger, & W. W. Busse (Eds.), *Allergy: Principles and practice* (4th ed, pp. 1109–1136). St. Louis, MO: Mosby.

Ewer, T. C., & Stewart, D. E. (1986). Improvement in bronchial hyperresponsiveness in patients with moderate asthma after treatment with a hypnotic technique: A randomised controlled trial. *British Medical Journal, 293*, 1129–1132.

Falliers, C. J. (1988). Global perspectives in the management of asthma. *Journal of Asthma, 25*, 285–91.

Feingold, B. (1975). Hyperkinesis and learning disabilities linked to artificial food flavors and colors. *American Journal of Nursing, 75*(5), 797–803.

French, T. M., & Alexander, F. (1941). Psychogenic factors in bronchial asthma. *Psychosomatic Medicine Monograph, 4*.

Furukawa, C.T., DuHamel, T.R., Weimer, L., Shapiro, G.G., Pierson, W.E., & Bierman, C.W. (1988). Cognitive and behavioral findings in children requiring inpatient rehabilitation. *Journal of Allergy and Clinical Immunology, 81*, 83–88.

Gutstadt, L.B., Gillette, J.W., Mrazek, D.A., Fukuhara, J.T., LaBrecque, J.F., & Strunk, R.C. (1989). Determinants of school performance in children with chronic asthma.

American Journal of Diseases of Childhood, 143, 471–475.

Isenberg, S. A., Lehrer, P. M., & Hochron, S. (1992). The effects of suggestion on airways of asthmatic subjects breathing room air as a suggested bronchoconstrictor and bronchodilator. *Journal of Psychosomatic Research, 36*(8), 769–776.

Lask, B. (1991). Psychological treatments of asthma. *Clinical and Experimental Allergy, 21,* 625–626.

Levine, M. D., & Liden, C. B. (1976). Food for inefficient thought. *Pediatrics, 58*(2), 145–148.

Lindgren, S., Lokshin, B., Stromquist, A., Weinberger, M., Nassif, E., McCubbin, M., Frasher, R. (1992). Does asthma or treatment with theophylline limit children's academic performance? *New England Journal of Medicine, 327,* 926–930.

Lowenthal, B., & Lowenthal, J. (1995). The effects of asthma on school performance. *Learning Disabilities, 6*(2), 41–46.

Marshall, P. (1989). Attention deficit disorder and allergy: A neurochemical model of the relation between the illnesses. *Psychological Bulletin, 106*(3), 434–446.

McGee, R., Stanton, W. R., & Sears, M. R. (1993). Allergic disorders and attention deficit disorder in children. *Journal of Abnormal Child Psychology, 21*(1), 79–88.

McLoughlin, J., Nall, M., Isaacs, B., Petrosko, J., Karibo, J., Lindsey, B. (1983). The relationship of allergies and allergy treatment to school performance and student behavior. *Annals of Allergy, 51,* 506–510.

Milgrom, H., & Bender, B. (1995). Behavioral side effects of medications for asthma and allergic rhinitis. *Pediatrics in Review, 16,* 333–336.

National Asthma Education Program. (1991). *Guidelines for the diagnosis and Management of Asthma* (No. 91-3042). Bethesda, MD: U.S. Department of Health and Human Services.

Rachelefsky, G.S., Wo, J., Adelson, J., Mickey, M.R., Spector, S.L., Katz, R.M., Siegel, S.C. & Rohr, A.S. (1986). Behavior abnormalities and poor school performance due to oral theophylline usage. *Pediatrics, 78,* 1133–1138.

Randolph, T. G. (1947). Allergy as a causative factor of fatigue, irritability, and behavior problems of children. *Journal of Pediatrics, 31,* 560–572.

Rawls, D. J., Rawls, J. R., & Harrison, C. W. (1971). An investigation of six- to eleven-year-old children with allergic disorders. *Journal of Consulting and Clinical Psychology, 36*(2), 260–264.

Richards, W. (1992). Asthma, allergies, and school. *Pediatric Annals, 21*(9), 575–579.

Roth, N., Beyreiss, J., Schlenzka, K., & Beyer, H. (1991). Coincidence of attention deficit disorder and atopic disorders in children: Empirical findings and hypothetical background. *Journal of Abnormal Child Psychology, 19*(1), 1–13.

Rowe, A. H. (1928). Food allergy and its manifestations, diagnosis, and treatment. *Journal of the American Medical Association, 91,* 1623–1631.

Rowe, K. S. (1988). Synthetic food colourings and "hyperactivity": A double-blind crossover study. *Australian Pediatrics Journal, 24,* 143–147.

Sampson, H. A. (1993). Adverse reactions to foods. In E. Middleton, C. E. Reed, E. F. Ellis, N. F. Adkinson, J. W.

Yunginger, & W. W. Busse (Eds.), *Allergy: Principles and practice* (4th ed., pp. 1661–1686). St. Louis, MO: Mosby.

Speer, F. (1954). Allergic-tension-fatigue in children. *Annals of Allergy, 12,* 168–171.

Steiner, H., Hilliard, J., Fritz, G. K., & Lewiston, N. J. (1982). A psychosomatic approach to childhood asthma. *Journal of Asthma, 19*(2), 111–121.

Suess, W. M., Stump, N., Chai, H., & Kalisker, A. (1986). Mnemonic effects of asthma medication in children. *Journal of Asthma, 23,* 291–296.

Terr, A. I. (1993). Unconventional theories and unproven methods in allergy. In E. Middleton, C. E. Reed, E. F. Ellis, N. F. Adkinson, J. W. Yunginger, & W. W. Busse (Eds.), *Allergy: Principles and practice* (4th ed., pp. 1767–1793). St. Louis, MO: Mosby.

Vazquez, M. I. & Buceta, J. M. (1993). Psychological treatment of asthma: Effectiveness of a self-management program with and without relaxation training. *Journal of Asthma, 30*(3), 171–183.

Wigal, J. K., Creer, T. L., Kotses, H., & Lewis, P. (1990). A critique of 19 self-management programs for childhood asthma: Part I. Development and evaluation of the programs. *Pediatric Asthma, Allergy, and Immunology, 4*(1), 17–39.

Zeiger, R. S. (1993). Development and prevention of allergic disease in Childhood. In E. Middleton, C. E. Reed, E. F. Ellis, N. F. Adkinson, J. W. Yunginger, & W. W. Busse (Eds.), *Allergy: Principles and practice* (4th ed., pp. 1137–1172). St. Louis, MO: Mosby.

75

Visual Impairments

Sharon Bradley-Johnson
Rena J. Sorensen
Central Michigan University

Background and Development

It is not uncommon for school psychologists to have little or no experience with individuals who are visually impaired. Therefore, they may feel uncomfortable planning an assessment or consulting on instruction for these students. Obtaining sufficient background information on the student and the student's visual loss, as well as conducting classroom observations before working directly with a student, will be helpful in beginning to understand the needs of these students. Information in this chapter should also be useful in understanding the nature of visual impairment, its relevance to assessment and instructional planning, and the role of the school psychologist as a member of an interdisciplinary team serving students with visual impairments.

Definitions

Confusion surrounds definitions for the terms *visually impaired* and *blind*. The term "visually impaired" refers, in a general sense, to students with visual losses who require more than corrective lenses to enable them to function.

The term "legally blind" is used to document eligibility for governmental benefits. Because an individual is classified as legally blind does not mean that he or she is totally blind. In fact, the American Foundation for the Blind (undated) reported that more than 75% of individuals classified as blind in the United States retain some usable vision. The certification of legal blindness is applied when visual acuity is 20/200 or less in the better eye with corrective lenses or when the visual field is limited to an angle no greater than 20° at its widest diameter. This definition is not very useful for educational planning because many of these individuals can, for example, use large-type print and other visual materials.

Functionally, a "blind" student is one who must rely primarily on tactile and auditory means for learning. Many of these students are Braille readers.

"Visually impaired" applies not only to students who are blind but also to students who can learn through vision yet require more than corrective lenses to do so. Thus, all students who are blind are visually impaired, but not all students who are visually impaired are blind.

The terms used to describe students who are visually impaired but not blind vary from state to state. Terms used include *partially sighted, low vision,* and *limited vision*. These students may be able to see regular or large-type materials held close to their eyes, or they may use magnifiers to aid their vision. Additional tactile and auditory material may be needed for instruction.

For clarity, in this chapter the term "visually impaired" will refer to the general population of students with a visual loss who require more than corrective lenses to function, whereas "blind" will refer to students who must rely primarily on senses other than vision for learning. The term "low vision" will be used to describe students who are visually impaired but not blind.

Prevalence

Though visual loss is common among older adults, it occurs infrequently among school-age students. During the 1990–91 school year, 17,783 students classified as visually impaired were served under the Individuals with Disabilities Education Act of 1990 (IDEA; U.S. Department of Education, 1992). These students made up only 0.4% of special education students between the ages of 6 and 21.

Etiology

Etiology of visual loss can vary widely from student to student. Scholl (1985) reported that most visual losses in school-age children are congenital. Congenital losses may be due to genetic factors where vision problems are inherited or to prenatal damage resulting from factors such as mothers contracting rubella while pregnant, or they may occur because of trauma during birth. Often the specific etiology of congenital losses is unknown (Finkelstein, 1989). Examples of congenital losses include an-ophthalmos (absence of the eyeball), aniridia (absence or near absence of the iris), and retinopathy of prematurity (abnormal development of blood vessels in the eye with possible scar tissue, bleeding, and detachment of the retina, sometimes resulting in total blindness).

The other type of visual loss is termed *adventitious,* occurring as a result of disease or an accident. Adventitious losses may result, for example, from bacterial or viral infections, diabetes, or tumors, or they may be the result of an accident such as a blow to the head or eye. Examples of adventitious disorders include

- Optic nerve atrophy: damage to fibers of the optic nerve because of infections, tumors, or injury. (This condition could alternately be due to lack of oxygen at birth or malformation.)
- Corneal disease (scarring of the cornea from injury, infection, or allergic reactions).
- Retinoblastoma: malignant tumor on the retina.

For a discussion of specific types of visual losses, see Happe and Koenig (1987).

Onset and Progression

Knowing the child's age at onset and the progression of a visual loss has important implications for assessment and instruction. Visual memories, such as memories of color and images, are typically retained by children who lose vision after the age of 5 years. It is easier for a child with visual memories to learn certain language concepts and motor skills. For example, it is easier to teach the concept "horse" if a student remembers what horses or other large animals look like than it is to teach the concept to a student who is congenitally blind. If a student who is congenitally blind were given a model of a horse to explore tactually, he or she would have a very limited understanding of the concept. If the student were encouraged to touch a real horse, information would be received in parts and it would be necessary to integrate the information to develop a complete concept of horse. Integration of this information may be difficult for some students resulting in inadequate concept development.

Students who lose their vision prior to age five and have an inadequate understanding of some concepts may still use the concepts correctly on occasion because they have acquired the terms through rote learning. Consequently, to determine during assessment and instruction whether a student has an adequate understanding of certain concepts, it is wise to probe questionable responses and observe use of the concepts in several situations.

The type of onset of the visual loss has implications for educational planning. Though a student with a visual loss present from birth would require special instruction, he or she would not have to adjust to a loss of vision.

Students with adventitious visual losses, however, are likely to require considerable support and counseling to assist them in adapting to this dramatic change in their lives. Their families also are likely to need assistance. The emotional adjustment of these students, and their need to learn new adaptive behaviors to enable them to cope with the requirements of daily living, will be priorities for instruction. Once they are emotionally ready, new modes of learning may need to be taught, such as use of low-vision equipment and listening skills.

Whether the onset is progressive or sudden also has implications for educational planning. Progressive visual losses allow students to acquire new methods of learning, such as the use of Braille, while they still have vision. Counseling and support also will be important as the student's visual condition changes.

Some time will be required for students who experience a sudden loss of vision to make the adjustment to this loss. Once they do, however, it is important to begin instruction as soon as possible in new modes for learning and use of adaptive devises, if needed, to minimize loss of instructional time.

The prognosis for the visual loss is important, especially for older students. If the condition will progressively worsen, this information will be an important consideration in making future educational or vocational plans.

Whatever the cause or progression of the visual loss, a multidisciplinary approach is necessary to work effectively with these students. Consultation with a student's medical specialist will be important in understanding the visual loss. Communication with the classroom teacher and consultant certified for working with students who are visually impaired will aid in understanding the factors affecting the student's ability to function.

Interpreting Medical Reports

Information in medical reports can be helpful in planning assessment and instruction for students who have a vision loss. The terminology and abbreviations encountered in these reports, however, can be confusing. Reports from ophthalmologists and optometrists may contain required medical interventions, prescriptions, and restrictions on eye use.

Descriptions of visual acuity are reported separately for each eye as well as with and without correction (glasses). Changing visual conditions may result in changing visual needs. Hence, vision evaluations should be current; that is, they should be completed at least annually. Also, hearing should be evaluated annually because students who are visually impaired rely heavily on auditory input for learning and mobility. Further, students who are visually impaired often have multiple impairments that can include hearing losses. Definitions for common abbreviations encountered in medical reports are provided in Table 1.

Titles of medical specialists also can be confusing. An ophthalmologist is a physician able to diagnose and treat defects as well as diseases of the eye. He or she can prescribe lenses and medication, perform surgery, and use other types of medical treatment. An optometrist is a licensed nonmedical specialist who can measure muscle disturbances and refractive errors and prescribe lenses. An optician is a technician who grinds lenses to fill prescriptions, fits contact lenses, and adjusts frames of eyeglasses.

Functional Vision Assessment

Because testing conditions in a clinic are very different from classroom conditions, recommendations contained in medical reports may or may not apply to classroom settings. Hence, a functional vision assessment carried out within the school setting is needed for instructional planning and for ensuring that appropriate accommodations are made in the classroom. This type of assessment is conducted by a teacher certified in working with students who are visually impaired. These assessments are relatively new and currently not required in all states.

Results from these assessments provide invaluable information concerning a student's use of vision for classroom instruction. These results indicate how a particular student uses vision for routine tasks, including academic tasks and daily living. Reports from these assessments may include information regarding size of print needed, appropriate lighting, viewing distance for materials, and recommendations for low-vision equipment. Some functional vision assessments will also include an environ-mental assessment, which evaluates the compatibility of the environment with a student's capabilities (Kelley, Davidson, & Sanspree, 1993).

Recommendations from functional vision assessments are equally important both for creating an optimal learning environment for students who are visually impaired and for understanding a particular student's visual needs when planning a psychoeducational assessment. Hence, this information should be sought prior to direct testing or planning educational programs.

Problems and Implications

As with all students who have a physical disability, students who are visually impaired present unique needs and challenges to professionals working within the educational system. Many of these needs, and their implications, are discussed in this section.

Early Intervention

A number of delays in development are common for children who are visually impaired, especially in the areas of language, adaptive behavior, and motor skills (Bradley-Johnson, 1994). Many of these delays can be lessened or eliminated if early intervention is provided.

An important component of early intervention is helping parents learn how to provide appropriate educational experiences for young children with visual impairments. Fortunately, there are a number of materials in this area designed for parents and professionals. Providing appropriate educational experiences for these children also can

Table 1 *Common Abbreviations Used in Medical Reports*

Abbreviation	Terminology	Meaning
O.D.	ocular dexter	right eye
O.S.	ocular sinister	left eye
O.U.	oculi unitas	both eyes
W.N.L.	within normal limits	
S., S.S., S.C.	without correction	without lenses
C., C.C.	with correction	with lenses
L.P.	light perception	is aware of light
N.L.P.	no light perception	not able to distinguish light from dark
C.F.	counts fingers	visual acuity less than that measured by Snellen chart (20/400), shown as ability to count fingers held up at varying distances
H.M.	hand movements	describes vision that is less than Snellen chart and counting fingers. Ability to see hand movement at varying distances from the eyes
V.A.	visual acuity	sharpness of vision in terms of ability to perceive detail
N.V.	near vision	what can be seen at 16 inches

foster healthy emotional development and adult/child interactions and aid the development of social skills. For example, *On the Way to Literacy: Early Experiences for Visually Impaired Children* (Stratton & Wright, 1993) is a program consisting of storybooks specifically designed to be read to children about 2 to 5 years of age who are visually impaired. The books have both tactile and visual illustrations as well as Braille and print text. A handbook includes suggestions on how to use the program.

Discovering the Magic of Reading (Wright, 1995) is a video and brochure package for parents and teachers of children from birth to age 5. The material covers, for example, ways to involve a child in a story and choosing books most likely to interest children who are visually impaired.

Other materials for working with these children and their parents are available through both the American Printing House for the Blind (APH) and the American Foundation for the Blind (see Recommended Resources).

Special Equipment and Materials

Without specialized equipment and materials, many students who are visually impaired will not be able to function adequately during an assessment or in the classroom. Many materials in large print and Braille as well as recorded materials are available for testing and instruction from APH. In some cases it will be necessary to enlarge classroom materials by photocopying. In this case it is important to ensure that adequate contrast is maintained between the print and paper. Yellow plastic laminate may be used over printed material to increase the contrast; however, it may cause a glare and reduction in color for some students.

Low-vision equipment may be required. This equipment should be used for both assessment and instruction, if recommended. Examples of low-vision equipment include magnifiers held or mounted on a stand, on the student's glasses, or on a headband; monocular or binocular telescopes to aid distance viewing; closed-circuit television which magnifies text displayed on a television monitor; and book stands to lessen fatigue from holding materials close to the eyes. Students with little or no useful vision may benefit from computer systems that scan written material and provide output in speech or Braille. Computers, Braille writers, or a manual slate and stylus may be used for writing. A Braille writer is a machine similar to a typewriter, used to produce embossed Braille symbols. A slate and stylus are used to write Braille by hand. The slate is a metal plate that holds the paper; the stylus is held in the hand and used to press the Braille dots in the paper. Signature guides, an abacus (for math calculation), as well as Braille rulers, clocks, and watches are available also.

Braille reading should be taught using a systematic approach. *Patterns* (Caton, Pester, & Bradley, 1980) is a basal Braille reading program. For students who use Braille as their main writing medium, a companion program, *Patterns: The Primary Braille Spelling and English Program* (Caton, Pester, Bradley, Modaressi, & Hamp, 1996; Caton, Pester, Bradley, Modaressi, Hamp, & Otto, 1993; Caton, Pester, Bradley, & Hamp, 1992) also is available in three levels for elementary-age students. Included are lessons in Brailling, spelling, syntax, mechanics, and composition.

Orientation and Mobility Training

A visual impairment makes it difficult to move about safely and orient to the demands of the environment. To enable many students with a visual impairment to achieve adequate independence, assessment and instruction by a specialist in orientation and mobility should be an integral part of their educational program. Specialists in orientation and mobility are able to recognize factors that will increase orientation and mobility skills that may go undetected by others not trained in this area. Examples of skills taught in orientation and mobility instruction include using an appropriate gait and stride when walking, seeking help with orientation and mobility from the public, finding and using telephones and public transportation systems, and traveling safely within school and home environments. Instruction in these skills, which increase independence and enhance learning, can begin as early as the preschool years.

Social Interaction

Many students who are visually impaired do not have the opportunity to learn some of the social skills that sighted students acquire by observing others. Hence, students with visual impairments may need to be taught some social skills directly, especially those pertaining to nonverbal communication such as orienting to a speaker and use of gestures. When this is the case, these behaviors should be written into the Individual Educational Plan (IEP). Consideration should also be given to the emotions of students with visual impairments. Their emotions may be misinterpreted or difficult to understand if these students are not taught to express their feelings through forms of nonverbal communication used by sighted persons.

Any individual with a disability is more likely than nondisabled peers to require assistance from others. For example, they may require assistance in locating new materials or equipment in the classroom or in finding a seat during an assembly. Consequently, in order to establish and maintain friendships within the classroom, students with visual impairments should be able to request help as well as accept and refuse help appropriately. Some students may require direct instruction regarding how to respond courteously in these situations.

Information from classroom observation, teacher interviews, and rating scales should be sufficient to determine whether social skills need to be targeted for instruction.

Daily Living Skills

Many daily living skills are difficult to carry out when a student has a severe visual loss, such as the tasks involved in food preparation and use of an alarm clock. Some students with a visual loss will require specialized equipment designed specifically for their needs in order to complete tasks of daily living independently.

Examples of specialized equipment for this area include Braille watches, Braille alarm clocks, knife-slicing guides, and large-print cookbooks. Such equipment can be obtained from APH or the American Foundation for the Blind. Catalogs of publications and equipment are available from both agencies.

When assessing adaptive behavior, professionals should credit a student with performing a skill if he or she can demonstrate the skill when using adaptive equipment. In the report it is helpful to note the types of adaptive equipment used.

Accommodations for Braille or Large-Type Readers

Braille takes about 2½ times longer to read than regular type; large type also takes more time to read than regular type. In addition, the use of residual vision (vision remaining after damage to the eye) is very tiring. Unless special accommodations are made, fatigue from reading Braille or large type will negatively affect performance during assessment and classroom instruction.

Data collected for the purpose of administering the Federal Act to Promote the Education of the Blind (American Printing House for the Blind, 1995) indicate that a variety of reading media are used by students who are visually impaired. That is, 26% read large print or regular type, 10% are primarily Braille readers, 8% use a reader or recorded material (auditory readers), 24% are at a readiness level or the primary reading medium has not yet been determined (prereaders), and 32% are non-readers.

Because reading is so tiring for these students, it is important to watch for signs of fatigue. Breaking an assignment into several short parts rather than one long one enables students with a visual impairment to take needed breaks. Frequent breaks will be necessary to maximize performance during testing also.

Language Development

Especially during the preschool years, concept development may be delayed for children with visual impairments (Bradley-Johnson, 1994). Also, children without visual memories may have only a limited understanding of some concepts. Higgins (1973), for example, found that some of these students demonstrated meaningful use of a word in one context but not in another, indicating an incomplete understanding of the word.

Particularly during preschool and the early elementary grades, providing additional instruction in concept development, and checking to see that students who are visually impaired have an adequate understanding of difficult constructs, is beneficial. Results from verbal tests must be interpreted with caution, and questionable responses probed, to ensure valid conclusions for educational planning.

For orientation and mobility as well as language development, knowledge of position or relational concepts such as *up, left,* and *inside* are very helpful to teach. Understanding these concepts will aid independence as well as language development. Thus, position concepts should be given special attention during assessment and instruction.

If a student with a visual impairment is having difficulty following directions, a thorough assessment of skills related to receptive language should be carried out. Though students who are visually impaired must depend to a large extent on auditory input, good listening skills often are not learned automatically. Thus, assessment of a student's receptive vocabulary and syntax development, hearing, memory, attending in class, and motivation to perform should be completed. This information should help to determine the specific nature of the problem.

Because of the importance of listening skills to these students, if listening skills are problematic, they should be targeted for instruction. Listening skills may have to be taught directly, and sufficient practice with feedback provided, in order to make the skills functional.

Classroom Skills

Because of the loss of vision, it is difficult for students with low vision or who are blind to be well organized. Yet, to function independently and efficiently in the classroom, these students need to be particularly well organized. In fact, being well organized is more important for these students than for their sighted peers. For preschoolers, teaching organization can begin with having a specific place for storing their toys and providing guidance to them to return the toys to the storage place when they have finished playing.

If older students do not routinely return materials and equipment to appropriate places, they need to be taught to do so in order to be able to retrieve the materials and equipment easily and efficiently. Feedback from the teacher may be necessary to encourage them to keep their desks neat, well organized, and free of unnecessary material. Observation in the classroom or preschool will indicate whether there is a need to focus on organization as part of a student's educational plan.

Some methods used for studying by these students are quite different from those used by their sighted peers. Special techniques are necessary, for example, to keep one's place when reading, for reading maps and graphs, and for use of low-vision aides. Students with low vision reported having severe difficulty reading atlases and maps in the classroom (Kalloniatis & Johnston, 1994). Specialized study skills are needed to address such problems for both students with low vision and those who are blind. These skills should be taught by a consultant for students who are visually impaired.

Self-Stimulation

Everyone, sighted or not, engages in some level of self-stimulation, especially when bored, tired, or under stress. For example, observe the behavior of individuals in their cars in a traffic jam on a hot day. No doubt you will see some body rocking, finger tapping, hair twisting, and head rolling. However, self-stimulatory behaviors may seem bizarre when exhibited by students with visual impairments because the behaviors may occur more frequently or intensely than for sighted students. Types of self-stimulation shown by some of these students include head rolling, body rocking, finger waving or flicking, and light gazing. These behaviors are often transitory.

Young children who are visually impaired commonly engage in a form of self-stimulation referred to as eye pressing or poking which can make the child look strange to others. Eye poking can begin as early as 12 months of age as frequent eye rubbing and by the age of 18 months progress to the habit of frequently pressing the thumbs against the eyes. Children who engage in this behavior often have deeply depressed eyes with discoloration around them (Scott, Jan, & Freeman, 1985). Eye poking and body rocking were found to be the most frequent and stable forms of self-stimulation observed in blind preschool children (Brambring & Troster, 1992). Because self-stimulatory behaviors occur in many sighted students who are emotionally impaired or mentally impaired, self-stimulatory behaviors of students who are visually impaired sometimes cause others to assume the behaviors are a sign of emotional or mental impairment. These behaviors also can interfere with learning and, in extreme cases, may result in physical harm.

Self-stimulatory behaviors that make a student look unusual to others, interfere with instruction, or result in physical harm should be targeted for remediation as soon as possible. The longer these behaviors are allowed to occur, the more difficult they will be to eliminate. For a discussion of treatment procedures, see Sisson (1992).

Emotional Adjustment

Some students who are visually impaired do not understand their visual impairment and are uncomfortable talking about it. Yet, as noted by Hazekamp and Huebner (1989), to deal effectively with the stereotypes and prejudice they are likely to encounter, they need to understand and accept the impairment. Hazekamp and Huebner also suggest that if students are comfortable discussing their visual impairment, others will be more comfortable and accepting of them.

It is important to assist students who are visually impaired in understanding their visual impairment and to provide supportive counseling when appropriate. Several social skills programs have beneficial lessons on coping with teasing (Elliott & Gresham, 1991; Walker et al., 1983; Walker, Todis, Holmes, & Horton, 1988).

Alternative Actions

Family Involvement

As for any child with a disability, family members of a child with a visual impairment may need support and counseling to discuss the shock, grief, anger, and resentment they feel when first informed that their child has a disability. They may be frightened at the prospect of raising a child who has a visual impairment. This fear may be more pronounced if the family has not had prior contact with individuals with visual impairments.

It is important to emphasize to family members that most children who have low vision or are blind become well-adjusted, productive adults. Arranging for the family to talk to adults who have visual impairments or with other parents raising children with visual impairments can be very beneficial.

Parents should be provided with information on agencies and groups involved with children and adolescents who are visually impaired. For example, the National Association for Parents of the Visually Impaired provides information, peer support, and services to families of students who are visually impaired. Addresses of local chapters are available from the national headquarters. The American Foundation for the Blind provides information and technical assistance to individuals who are visually impaired and to their families. They also have a toll-free hotline. The Council for Exceptional Children provides information to parents and has a Division for the Visually Handicapped. Addresses for these agencies are listed under Recommended Resources later in this chapter. Information about diagnostic centers and summer programs usually can be obtained from state residential schools for students who are visually impaired.

Some family members may be overly protective of a child with a visual loss. Such overprotection can interfere with learning and the development of an appropriate degree of independence. Counseling may be required for the family members in order to modify expectations and to promote normal adaptive behavior for the student.

Parents need to be involved in the educational planning for their child. This will help them keep abreast of their child's needs and set appropriate expectations for development. It may help to conduct a family assessment to determine the families' needs in raising a child with a visual loss.

Parents will need assistance with understanding reports and test results. Jargon should be avoided when discussing test results and remediation techniques in order to ensure parents' understanding as well as increase parent satisfaction in working with the school. Also, activities can be provided for parents to work with their children, especially when the child is young.

Inclusion

The current emphasis on inclusion raises many questions regarding how, in general education settings, to best meet the unique needs of students who are visually impaired. There is very little information, and almost no research, on this topic. The limited information is, no doubt, due in part to the low prevalence of visual impairments.

There is definitely a need for evaluation of various models for serving these students in general education settings. Integration has several advantages including allowing equal access to educational opportunities, allowing students to remain with their families and in their communities rather than attending residential schools, preparing students with life competencies to participate fully in society, and providing both the positive and negative information necessary to form a realistic representation about the world (Erwin, 1991). Erwin also noted, however, that some individuals have concerns about integration in terms of being able to adequately adapt instruction and curricula and to provide appropriate social and recreational activities, career education, and independent living skills. Though research is minimal in this area, Erwin presents guidelines for integrating young children who are visually impaired into general education settings. A brief overview of these guidelines follows.

1. Because children who are visually impaired tend to interact less frequently in integrated settings than typical peers (Hoben & Lindstrom, 1980), there is a need for systematic promotion of social interaction by the classroom teacher.
2. Active involvement of a certified teacher of visually impaired students is critical.
3. Weekly conferencing of the classroom teacher and the certified teacher of visually impaired students is needed.
4. In the curriculum, much of what is needed by sighted students is important for students who are visually impaired, though modifications in materials and the environment may be required to make the curriculum functional.
5. Systematic data-based instructional planning to individualize instruction is needed to ensure success.

6. Programs that emphasize the teacher's role in structuring learning activities based on students' needs is important.
7. Bishop (1986) found that an accepting and flexible classroom teacher is one of the most critical components to successful integration of these students.
8. It is important for someone to be responsible for coordinating services and resolving conflicts for the family and school as well as seeking new resources when necessary.
9. Involvement of the family in selecting and designing programs is critical.
10. Liaisons with community agencies such as Head Start and agencies serving individuals who are visually impaired can be helpful.
11. Professionals trained in the field of vision should teach sighted students about visual impairment through informal and ongoing activities.

Readers are encouraged to see Erwin (1991) for a further discussion of these issues.

Suggestions for School Psychologists

Following are guidelines describing the role school psychologists can play in ensuring successful educational experiences for students with visual impairments.

1. Before working with a student who is visually impaired, obtain adequate background information on the student's visual loss and educational and medical history. This information can be obtained from a review of records, interviews, and classroom observation.
2. Put this information in perspective in terms of issues presented under this chapter's headings of Onset and Progression and Interpreting Medical Reports.
3. If possible, ensure that a functional vision assessment, and if needed, an orientation and mobility assessment, are completed prior to psychoeducational assessment and program planning.
4. Work as part of a multidisciplinary team. This is essential to successful educational planning for these students.
5. Involve parents in program planning as early as possible. For parents of young children, ensure that materials designed for parents of young children are available to them.
6. When planning assessment and instruction,
   - Ensure that the needed adaptive materials and equipment are used.
   - Emphasize social skills, especially those that are particularly difficult for these students.
   - Emphasize thorough development of language concepts, especially position concepts.
   - Consider the effects of reading fatigue.

- ■ Emphasize organizational skills to ensure independent and efficient functioning.
- ■ Target self-stimulation for remediation, if needed.
7. Provide supportive counseling when appropriate.
8. Ensure that adequate support and information is provided to family members as described under this chapter's Family Involvement heading.
9. Work with the multidisciplinary team in designing and monitoring inclusion efforts. School psychologists can be particularly helpful in ensuring systematic and frequent evaluation of student progress toward desired outcomes.
10. Assist the multidisciplinary team by interpreting relevant research in this area that could assist in program planning and evaluation.

Summary

Many unique issues are involved in working with students who are visually impaired. A multidisciplinary team made up of the student's parents, a teacher certified in working with students with visual impairments, an orientation and mobility instructor, medical specialists, and a school psychologist are necessary in order to coordinate efforts to meet the educational and emotional needs of these students. There are a number of factors pertinent to educational progress, including degree and type of visual loss, progressive or sudden onset, and age at the time of the visual loss.

Skills of particular importance for consideration in educational planning include orientation and mobility, language development, study skills, adaptive behavior, organizational skills, and social skills. Self-stimulation, a common occurrence in students who are visually impaired, may need immediate remediation. Also, families may require information and emotional support to deal with issues surrounding their child's visual loss. Fortunately, there are many materials and programs available to assist school psychologists in working with these students and their families.

RECOMMENDED RESOURCES

Agencies

AMERICAN FOUNDATION FOR THE BLIND (AFB), 15 West 16th Street, New York, NY 10011, 212-620-2000 or 800-232-5463.
AFB provides technical assistance services to individuals who are visually impaired, their families, professionals, and organizations. AFB is a national clearinghouse for information regarding visual impairment and provides catalogs of publications, equipment, and media.

AMERICAN PRINTING HOUSE FOR THE BLIND (APH), P.O. Box 6085, Louisville, KY 40206, 1-800-223-1839.
APH has the latest in educational materials and assessment instruments. APH publishes adapted and transcribed materials in Braille or large type as well as recorded books and magazines. Videotapes also are available for professionals on functional vision assessment and psychoeducational assessment. The Printing House is a national nonprofit organization that publishes materials solely for persons who are visually impaired.

BLIND CHILDREN'S CENTER, 4120 Marathon Street, Los Angeles, CA 90020, 1-800-222-3566.
This center publishes a number of helpful booklets for parents of infants and preschoolers who are visually impaired. Some topics include play, language, and movement. Copies are free to parents and inexpensive for professionals. Most booklets are available in English and Spanish.

COUNCIL FOR EXCEPTIONAL CHILDREN (CEC), 1920 Association Drive, Reston, VA 20191, 1-703-620-3660.
This organization publishes a newsletter, a magazine, and position papers for parents and professionals. It has a Division for the Visually Handicapped.

NATIONAL ASSOCIATION FOR PARENTS OF THE VISUALLY IMPAIRED (NAPVI), P.O. Box 562, Camden, NY 13316, 1-800-562-6265.
This organization provides peer support, information, and services to families of students who are visually impaired or multiply impaired. Addresses for local chapters can be obtained from NAPVI's national headquarters.

NATIONAL FEDERATION OF THE BLIND (NFB), 1800 Johnson Street, Baltimore, MD 21230, 301-659-9314.
This is an organization of blind persons that provides assistance to school staff and parents and has a public education program. Addresses of state affiliates are available from NFB's national headquarters.

Materials

Blind Children's Center. (1993). *First Steps: A handbook for teaching young children who are visually impaired.* Los Angeles, CA: Author.
This comprehensive and easily understood book is written for students, professionals, and parents working with children who are visually impaired. Topics cover infancy through preschool and include the family, behavior management, orientation and mobility, and self-help skills.

Bradley-Johnson, S. (1994). *Psychoeducational assessment of students who are visually impaired or blind: Infancy through high school* (2nd ed.). Austin, TX: PRO-ED.
This edition emphasizes information useful for planning instruction. Extensive checklists are included for organizing assessment information. Also, checklists of procedures for each phase of the assessment are presented along with detailed reviews of tests for social skills, play, language, cognition, achievement, and adaptive behavior.

Duckworth, B., & Bradley-Johnson, S. (1995). *An Introduction to Psychoeducational Assessment,* Louisville, KY: American Printing House for the Blind.

This videotape, prepared primarily for school psychologists, presents an overview of issues relevant to carrying out an educationally useful assessment of students who are visually impaired.

National Federation of the Blind. (undated). *The blind child in the regular preschool program.* Baltimore: Author.
This fact sheet presents useful recommendations for helping regular classroom teachers understand the needs of young children. The fact sheet is free from the National Federation for the Blind.

Olson, M. R. (1981). *Guidelines and games for teaching efficient Braille reading.* New York: American Foundation for the Blind.
These games and guidelines to help teach efficient Braille reading are based on research in rapid reading and precision teaching. Also presented are methods for adapting a general reading program for Braille readers.

Scott, E. P., Jan, J. E., & Freeman, R. D. (1985). *Can't your child see?* Austin, TX: PRO-ED.
This easily understood book is written for parents of children who are visually impaired, but it is also a good resource for professionals unfamiliar with visual impairment. Topics include eyes and what can go wrong, parent problems and some solutions, and play and playthings.

Wright, S. (1995). *Discovering the magic of reading: "Elizabeth's Story."* Louisville, KY: American Printing House for the Blind.
This videotape and brochure package makes a compelling presentation of the value of reading to young children who are visually impaired. Recommended for parents and teachers of children from birth to 5 years of age. The video is narrated by a parent and covers infancy through preschool. Illustrations as well as Braille and print text are included.

References

American Foundation for the Blind. (Undated). *Facts about blindness.* New York: Author.

American Printing House for the Blind. (1995). *Distribution of federal quota.* Louisville, KY: Author.

Bishop, V. E. (1986). Identifying the components of success in mainstreaming. *Journal of Visual Impairment and Blindness, 80,* 939–946.

Bradley-Johnson, S. (1994). *Psychoeducational assessment of students who are visually impaired or blind.* Austin, TX: PRO-ED.

Brambring, M., & Troster, H. (1992). On the stability of stereotyped behaviors in blind infants and preschoolers. *Journal of Visual Impairment and Blindness, 86,* 105–110.

Caton, H., Pester, E., & Bradley, E. J. (1980). *Patterns: The Primary Braille Reading Program.* Louisville, KY: American Printing House for the Blind.

Caton, H., Pester, E., Bradley, E. J., & Hamp, E. (1992). *Patterns: The Primary Braille Spelling and English Program* (Readiness-primer reader level). Louisville, KY: American Printing House for the Blind.

Caton, H., Pester, E., Bradley, E. J., Modaressi, B., & Hamp, E. (1996). *Patterns: The Primary Braille Spelling and English Program* (Second reader level). Louisville, KY: American Printing House for the Blind.

Caton, H., Pester, E., Bradley, E. J., Modaressi, B., Hamp, E., & Otto, F. (1993). *Patterns: The Primary Braille Spelling and English Program* (First reader level). Louisville, KY: American Printing House for the Blind.

Elliott, S. N., & Gresham, F. M. (1991). *Social skills intervention guide.* Circle Pines, MN: American Guidance Service.

Erwin, E. J. (1991). Guidelines for integrating young children with visual impairments in general educational settings. *Journal of Visual Impairment and Blindness, 85,* 253–260.

Finkelstein, S. (1989). *Blindness and disorders of the eye.* Baltimore: National Federation of the Blind.

Happe, D., & Koenig, A. (1987). Children and vision. In A. Thomas & J. Grimes (Eds.), *Children's Needs* (pp. 658–667). Washington, DC: National Association of School Psychologists.

Hazekamp, J., & Huebner, K. M. (1989). *Program planning and evaluation for blind and visually impaired students: National guidelines for educational excellence.* New York: American Foundation for the Blind.

Higgins, L. C. (1973). *Classification in the congenitally blind.* New York: American Foundation for the Blind.

Hoben, M., & Lindstrom, V. (1980). Evidence of isolation in the mainstream. *Journal of Visual Impairment and Blindness, 74,* 289–292.

Kalloniatis, M., & Johnston, A. W. (1994). Visual environmental adaptation problems of partially sighted children. *Journal of Visual Impairment and Blindness, 88,* 234–243.

Kelley, P., Davidson, R., & Sanspree, M. J. (1993). Vision and orientation and mobility consultation for children with severe multiple disabilities. *Journal of Visual Impairment and Blindness,* 397–401.

Scholl, G. T. (1985). Visual impairments. In G. T. Scholl (Ed.), *The school psychologist and the exceptional child* (pp. 203–218). Reston, VA: Council for Exceptional Children.

Scott, E. P., Jan, J. E., & Freeman, R. D. (1985). *Can't your child see?* Austin, TX: PRO-ED.

Sisson, L. A. (1992). Positive behavioral support: New foci in the management of challenging behaviors. *Journal of Visual Impairment and Blindness, 86,* 364–369.

U. S. Department of Education. (1992). Fourteenth Annual Report to Congress on the Implementation of the Individuals with Disabilities Education Act. Washington DC: Author.

Walker, H. M., McConnell, S., Holmes, D., Todis, B., Walker, J., & Golden, J. (1983). *The ACCEPTS program: A curriculum for children's effective peer and teacher skills.* Austin, TX: PRO-ED.

Walker, H. M., Todis, B., Holmes, D., & Horton, G. (1988). *The ACCESS program: Adolescent curriculum for communication and effective social skills.* Austin, TX: PRO-ED.

Wright, S. (1995). *Discovering the magic of reading: "Elizabeth's story."* Louisville, KY: American Printing House for the Blind.

76

Prematurity

Gloria C. Maccow
Cynthia L. Elias
Mark E. Swerdlik
Illinois State University

Background and Development

Premature birth accounts for more than 60% of perinatal mortality and morbidity (American College of Obstetricians and Gynecologists, 1989). In spite of major advances in obstetric care, the past 25 years have not seen any significant reduction in the incidence of premature births, and premature birth is now the single most common cause of poor pregnancy outcome for infants (Creasy, 1993; Morrison, 1990). The international definition of *prematurity* is an infant born preterm, prior to 37 weeks (less than 259 days) from the first day of the mother's last menstrual period (World Health Organization, 1977). Because of the difficulty of establishing gestational age, many studies of prematurity have used a birth-weight definition of prematurity. Low birth weight (LBW) refers to those infants weighing less than 2,500 grams or 5 pounds 8 ounces; very low birth weight (VLBW) infants weigh less than 1,500 grams or 3 pounds 5 ounces; extremely low birth weight (ELBW) refers to those infants weighing less than 1,000 grams or 2 pounds 3 ounces. Approximately one-third of LBW infants are born full-term (Michielutte, Moore, Meis, Ernest, & Wells, 1994).

Whether premature or full-term, LBW infants are 40 times more likely to die in the neonatal period than heavier infants, and infants born both preterm and LBW are at a higher risk of dying than all other infants (Michielutte et al., 1994). In the United States, which has a rate of prematurity higher than in 18 other industrialized nations (Morrison, 1990), the incidence of premature births increased from 9.4% in 1981 to 10.7% in 1989 (Creasy, 1993).

Approximately 20% of premature births are deliveries necessitated by medical disorders in the mother or fetus, but for the remaining 80%, prevention of premature birth is desirable (Morrison, 1990). The survival rate of premature infants, particularly those with ELBW, has increased significantly over the last decade (Fuchs, Fuchs, & Stubblefield, 1993). The economic costs of caring for these infants have also risen. Neonatal intensive care is the most expensive health care service in the medical system (Morrison, 1990). The average cost of the initial hospital stay for a sick infant in neonatal intensive care is between $20,000 and $100,000, and infants weighing less than 1,000 grams cost an average of $140,000 (Morrison, 1990). In addition, the longer term costs for medical care are also high.

Although 70% of all infants who require neonatal care have no disabling conditions identified during the preschool years, the risk of school failure for this population is high (Fuchs et al., 1993). Separating out the contribution of prematurity to school failure can be difficult, however. Rates of premature births are higher in disadvantaged populations, but these populations are at higher risk for problems in school irrespective of premature births. Although it is difficult to quantify the effects of prematurity and socioeconomic status, it is clear that developmental outcome can be compromised by organismic or environmental variables or both (Horowitz, 1987). As such, in assessing the risks to a child's development, professionals must consider the degree to which the organism is impaired, and the extent to which the environment is facilitative.

School psychologists are uniquely trained to promote the healthy development of children and families. In the educational environment, school psychologists assess the current functioning of children to identify the special services each child needs to achieve cognitive, behavioral, and affective competence. Because of their specialized needs, many children born prematurely will require services provided by school psychologists. In identifying the developmental needs of children born prematurely, school psychologists must consider the effects of biomedical conditions, as well as family, school, and community variables. The predictions for the individual child will be more accurate when they are based on assessment of multiple dimensions including perinatal and environmental-demographic variables (Siegel et al., 1982).

Factors That Increase the Risk of Prematurity

Although remediation of their deleterious effects is important, premature births must be prevented if social, economic, and personal costs are to be minimized and benefits maximized. Prevention of preterm labor and LBW has become one of the nation's health care priorities (Fuchs et al., 1993). Current understanding of the basic etiology of premature labor is limited (Morrison, 1990), but researchers have identified numerous risk factors that indicate an increased statistical likelihood of premature birth. It should be noted, however, that approximately 40% of mothers who deliver prematurely have no risk factors (Morrison, 1990). A recent study (Heffner, Sherman, Speizer, & Weiss, 1993) described the relationship between several reproductive factors and the magnitude of risk for premature labor. Factors associated with very high risk included third-trimester bleeding, multiple gestation, and chorioamnionitis (inflammation of fetal membrane as a result of infection). Moderate risk was associated with smoking and drug use, prior preterm delivery, bleeding in early pregnancy, uterine anomalies, maternal exposure to diethylstilbestrol (DES), and urinary tract infection.

Low socioeconomic status, a history of induced second-trimester abortion, and assisted reproduction techniques also raise the risk of premature delivery. A study of all live single births in the United States in 1974 found the following factors to be associated with LBW: race other than White, previous reproductive loss, short interpregnancy interval, out-of-wedlock birth, lack of prenatal care, and maternal age under 18 or over 35 years (Eisner, Brazie, Pratt, & Hexter, 1979). The greater the number of risk factors present, the higher the incidence of LBW. Certain maternal illnesses are also associated with LBW, including severe juvenile diabetes mellitus, chronic hypertension, chronic renal disease, the collagen vascular diseases, cyanotic heart disease, and pregnancy toxemia (Fuchs et al., 1993). Excessive physical activity and hard work have been linked with prematurity in European studies, but this connection has been difficult to prove in the United States.

Differential Effects by Ethnicity

There are significant differences among ethnic groups in their risk for prematurity. For example, of the infants born in the United States in 1991, the LBW rate was between 5% and 6% for infants of Chinese, Mexican, White, and Native American descent, but greater than 13% for African American infants. In addition, the rate of preterm delivery for African American infants was twice that of Whites (National Center for Health Statistics, 1993). However, because factors associated with ethnicity are also correlated with socioeconomic disadvantage, it is difficult to separate out the contributions of each to pre-

maturity. A number of studies using multivariate analysis techniques, adjusting for relevant variables such as maternal age, education, marital status, employment, parity, and smoking and drug use, have nevertheless found that ethnicity itself strongly predicts the rate of premature birth. In one such study of 28,330 women in California, the adjusted-odds ratios for preterm delivery rates were as follows: African American women (1.79), Mexican American and Asian women (1.4), and White women (1.0; Shiono & Klebanoff, 1986). A study of differences in premature delivery among enlisted women in the United States Army found that very low rates of illicit drug use, uniform access to prenatal care, and good maternal health reduced, but did not eliminate, the Black-White differences (Adams et al., 1993). Higher prevalence of adverse social conditions during the mothers' gestations, infancies, or childhoods that compromised reproductive capability may explain at least some of the differences in rates of prematurity.

Differential Effects by Age

As previously indicated, teenage mothers have a greater risk of premature deliveries and LBW infants. They are also at greater risk for neonatal deaths and complications from delivery (Smith, Weinman, Reeves, Wait, & Hinkley, 1993). There is grave concern about mothers in this age group for several reasons. First, the birth rate for teenagers rose almost 20% between 1986 and 1989 (Creasy, 1993). Second, mothers in this age group often are unmarried, drop out of school, experience financial hardship, and become dependent on welfare (Rosenheim, 1992). As single parents, they may be unable to provide the medical services and environmental stimulation required by their vulnerable infants.

Biomedical Risk Factors

The survival of prematurely born infants has increased markedly over the last decade. Among the factors responsible for better outcomes are fetal monitoring to identify infants at high risk and delivery of high-risk infants in perinatal centers with sophisticated equipment and expertise in the management of high-risk newborns. Nevertheless, a number of the infants who survive have complex medical needs. Resulting biomedical complications, such as brain damage, increase the risk of subsequent developmental disability (Allen, 1991). These medical needs and complications are the result of diseases experienced by premature infants due to the immaturity of their organ systems (see Table 1).

Breathing problems may be caused by Respiratory Distress Syndrome (RDS; Manginello & DiGeronimo, 1991). Treatment requires increased oxygen concentration and, for infants with severe RDS, respirators. The effect of using respirators for more than a month may be complications such as chronic lung disease, upper airway

Table 1 *Common Diseases of Premature Infants and Possible Complications*

Disease	Possible Complications
Hyperbilirubinemia (jaundice)	▪ Kernicterus (mental retardation, cerebral palsy) ▪ Inner ear damage
Intraventricular Hemorrhage (IVH)	▪ Neurological impairment ▪ Hydrocephalus ▪ Cerebral palsy ▪ Mental retardation ▪ Hearing impairment ▪ Visual impairment
Necrotizing Enterocolitis (NEC)	▪ Damage to intestines
Patent Ductus Arteriosus (PDA)	▪ Congestive heart failure ▪ Necrotizing enterocolitis ▪ Pulmonary edema ▪ Oxygen or respirator dependency
Respiratory Distress Syndrome (RDS)	▪ Bronchopulmonary dysplasia ▪ Upper airway damage ▪ Recurrent lower respiratory tract infections
Retinopathy of Prematurity (ROP)	▪ Impaired vision (myopia, partial loss of field of vision) ▪ Blindness

damage, and recurrent lower respiratory tract infections (Brown, 1993). Oxygen or respirator dependency itself may result when the blood vessel connecting the aorta and the pulmonary artery does not close as it should shortly after birth (Patent Ductus Arteriosus [PDA]; Manginello & DiGeronimo, 1991).

Brain damage may result from an overabundance of bilirubin (a yellowish-red pigment) in the blood (Hyperbilirubinemia or Jaundice). Abnormal bleeding on the surface of the brain, in the substance of the brain, or in the ventricles (Intraventricular hemorrhage [IVH]) may also damage the brain (Manginello & DiGeronimo, 1991). IVH occurs in 24 to 40% of infants weighing less than 1,500 grams at birth, and its likelihood of occurrence is inversely related to birth weight. About 28% of premature infants with IVH will die. Those who survive have a high risk of neurologic or developmental disability (Brown, 1993). The degree of risk is related to the severity of the bleeding. The least severe would be a localized hemorrhage without ventricular blood, while the most severe indicates a major hemorrhage with bleeding extending into the brain (Papile, Burstein, Burstein, & Koffler, 1978).

Psychosocial Risk Factors

While some effects of biomedical complications can be ameliorated by a facilitative environment (Horowitz, 1987), parents are sometimes unable to provide the care and stimulation required by an already vulnerable infant. In the first place, mothers may be preoccupied with their own feelings about the birth of the premature infant and may feel anxious and less than confident about their ability to parent an infant with multiple needs. This may be true especially during the first year of the child's life. Even though most parents develop competence in caring for the premature infant, feelings of anxiety and inadequacy are likely to persist as changing needs of the child demand different parenting skills. Secondly, many premature infants are born into families with lower socioeconomic status, where parenting skills may be limited (Minde, 1992). Some parents may not receive the education they need to develop effective parenting skills because their time is consumed by decisions regarding medical and daily care for the infant, as well as by the economic needs of the family.

Parents of a premature infant face many challenges after the birth of their child. They may experience feelings of grief, anxiety, shock, panic, denial, anger, sadness, guilt, emptiness, and depression (Manginello & DiGeronimo, 1991). Generally, parents go through four stages when adapting to parenting a premature infant. At Stage 1, parents experience anticipatory grief as they prepare for the possible loss of their child. At Stage 2, parents acknowledge and accept failure to deliver a normal full-term infant. At Stage 3, they bond and resume a relationship with the infant. Finally, in Stage 4, parents come to understand the ways in which premature infants differ from full-term infants (Caplan, Mason, & Kaplan, 1965).

Normal living patterns of parents are likely to be disrupted by longer hospital stays of the premature infant, and concern about the infant may cause parents to neglect siblings and other family members. Once they come home, premature infants as a group tend to be more irritable and less easily consoled than full-term infants. Sometimes they require special home-care equipment which may be quite involved. Socializing with premature infants may require patience and understanding because they are fragile and not as "organized" in behavior as a full-term infant. The premature infant is easily overstimulated and has more difficulty than a full-term infant in focusing and disconnecting attention.

Problems and Implications

Although premature infants face many medical challenges, approximately 95% of those born in the United States survive (Manginello & DiGeronimo, 1991). Most manifest developmentally appropriate skills by the time they are 2 to 3 years of age, but about 10 to 20% carry lifelong consequences of their preterm delivery and/or low birth weight. The effects may range from mild conditions, such as muscular weakness, learning disabilities, and poor socialization, to more severe disabilities, such as cerebral palsy, blindness, deafness, or mental retardation. These children require varying degrees of adaptation in the school setting.

Developmental Outcomes

Advances in obstetric and neonatal care have increased the survival rate of infants born as much as 17 weeks early and with birth weights below 500 grams (Allen, 1991). With these technological improvements, concern about premature infants has shifted from survival to the effects of complex medical problems on subsequent health and development (Gross, Brooks-Gunn, & Spiker, 1992; Manginello & DiGeronimo, 1991). The majority of premature infants are free of major disability, but infants with birth weights below 800 grams are at greater risk for developmental disability than infants of higher birth weights (Allen, 1991). Because of biological vulnerability, these ELBW children are more likely than full birth weight (FBW) children to experience neurosensory and health problems (Gross et al., 1992), which, in turn, compound clinical and educational outcomes (Hack, Klein, & Taylor, 1995).

In general, birth weight is inversely related to positive developmental outcomes. LBW children have more health-related problems than normal-birth-weight children, and children with VLBWs have the greatest number of such problems. Premature infants may require numerous surgeries and rehospitalizations. Medical problems contribute to school absences and may adversely affect school performance. In addition, children from disadvantaged backgrounds fare worse than socially advantaged children. These biological and environ-

mental risk factors have both short- and long-term effects on the child's physical, mental, and emotional development (Hack et al., 1995).

Because birthweight and gestational age at the extremes are strong predictors of developmental outcome (Allen, 1991), studies of developmental outcome tend to focus on VLBW infants, although they constitute less than 15% of LBW births (Hack et al., 1995). Compared to infants of moderately low birth weight (1,500 to 2,499 grams), VLBW infants are at greater risk for disability and for having school difficulty (Hack et al., 1995). In following the long-term development of infants who weighed 1,360 grams or less at birth, Drillien (1958) found that the majority (75%) had difficulty functioning in the regular school environment because of physical and/or mental disabilities. Deficits in intellectual ability are more common in children born with LBW compared to FBW, and IQ scores show a decline with decreasing birth weight during the first 4 years of life (Drillien, 1964). In school, LBW children score lower than FBW children on measures of language development, and experience less overall school success (Gross et al., 1992).

Whereas the sequence in which developmental milestones are achieved does not differ for most premature infants and full-term infants, premature infants initially acquire skills at a slower pace. If their development is compared to infants their own chronological age during their first 2 years of life, premature infants may appear to be significantly delayed in their attainment of developmental milestones. For this reason, professionals often adjust for prematurity in evaluating the development of preterm or LBW infants younger than 2 or 3 years. The child's development is compared to the development of children of the same corrected, or adjusted age. This corrected age is computed by subtracting from the chronological age the number of weeks the infant was premature. For example, a child evaluated 6 months after birth who was born 8 weeks prematurely (at 32 weeks gestation) would have a corrected age of 4 months. This child's functioning would be considered developmentally appropriate if the child demonstrates skills typical of 4-month-old infants (see Table 2 for a comparison of developmental milestones). In fact, to avoid lengthy explanations, parents are sometimes advised to respond with the child's corrected age when strangers ask the age of the infant (Manginello & DiGeronimo, 1991).

In general, there are low correlations between the performance of normal children on developmental tests in infancy and intelligence test scores obtained in later childhood (Sattler, 1992). For ELBW infants, this holds true even when adjusted ages are used. One study found the Bayley Mental Development Index at age 2 years to be an inaccurate predictor of scores on the WPPSI at age 5½ years for a number of ELBW children (Kitchen, Ford, Rickards, Lissenden, & Ryan, 1987). For this reason, there is controversy about whether to use chronological

Table 2 *Major Developmental Milestone for Infants*

Six Months	Four Months
Gross-motor	
Turns from stomach to back to stomach.	Holds back firm while hips are supported in sitting position.
Plays with toes.	When prone, lifts head and chest up off table.
First crawling reaction—Pushes on hands, draws up knees, and the like.	Holds head erect while sitting supported.
Fine-motor	
Uses hand to reach, grasp, crumble, hang, or splash.	Hands come together.
Thumb opposes in grasping 1″ cube.	Thumb does not participate when grasping 2″ cube.
Communication	
Combines vowel and consonant sounds, such as "ma," "da."	Laughs aloud in response to others.
Talks and gestures to objects.	Localizes sounds.
Conceptual	
Regards object.	Follows movements with eyes.
Reaches for object.	Manipulates object provided.
Social	
Smiles and vocalizes at mirror image.	Cries if adult stops playing with him.
Discriminates strangers, may cry.	Smiles at approach of mother.

Note. To evaluate the development of low birth weight infants, their "age" can be "corrected" by subtracting from their chronological age the number of weeks each was premature. Thus, a 6-month-old who was born 8 weeks prematurely would be evaluated using the developmental milestones for a 4-month-old of normal birth weight.

age or corrected age in assessing cognitive development. However, there is agreement that corrected age should be used in assessing motor development. For language, preliminary data suggest using chronological age for children older than 9 months. It is generally accepted that motor development proceeds according to corrected age, but the findings for cognitive ability and language are equivocal at this time (Allen, 1991).

Because of the interrelated nature of early development, specifically because motor skills affect performance on measures of mental ability (e.g., Bayley Scales of Infant Development; Bayley, 1993), it is difficult to justify the use of corrected age for motor ability and not for mental ability. Until further research is completed, school psychologists should use caution in deciding whether to adjust for degree of prematurity (Cohen & Spenciner, 1994). In making these decisions, school psychologists should consider the purpose of the assessment. When the goal is to provide early intervention services, an uncorrected age will most accurately identify the child's developmental strengths and needs.

Motor Development

Premature infants generally master motor skills in the same sequence as the normally developing infant. However, they tend to accomplish the motor milestones at later ages. For example, at the age of 4 months, typical children born at term gestation are able to hold their heads erect while being supported in a sitting position. By six months of age, they would demonstrate readiness to crawl. However, at the age of 6 months, typical children who were 8 weeks premature would be holding their heads erect while supported.

In engaging in motor activities, children use senses, such as vision, hearing, and touch. They begin to develop tactile discrimination skills by first accepting touch from their parents or caregivers. They respond reflexively to cuddling, patting, and stroking and are soon able to visually track the movements of the caregiver, establish eye contact, and reach and grasp for objects in the environment. They also are able to attend to sounds in the environment and locate the source of the sounds. Soon they are able to distinguish their mother's voice from the phone ringing and associate environmental sounds with certain events or conditions. Because of damage to the central nervous system, infants who were born prematurely may be delayed in their development of the muscular strength required to navigate the environment.

For example, infants with cerebral palsy may have difficulty controlling their muscles or may display stiffness in their movements. This muscular weakness interferes with the development of coordinated motor movements. Cerebral palsy is the most common neurological abnormality seen in LBW children, and a higher incidence rate is associated with decreasing birth weight (Hack et al., 1995).

Touch, Vision, and Hearing

Children with neurological impairments may be intolerant to tactile stimulation and may have visual or auditory impairments. Infants with a tactile impairment may be unresponsive to touch, stiffening or withdrawing when cuddled, fed, or clothed. This protective response interferes with the child's ability to tolerate weight-bearing in all positions (Benner, 1992). At the other extreme, some infants may crave tactile stimulation so much that they engage in self-stimulatory and self-injurious behaviors, such as patting their cheeks or banging their head.

Retinopathy of prematurity (ROP) affects the visual ability of approximately 33% of premature infants (Manginello & DiGeronimo, 1991). Blindness occurs at a rate of 5% to 6% among children with birth weights below 1,000 grams, but 22% to 44% with birth weights below

1,000 grams have scarring from ROP (Hack et al., 1995). Myopia or nearsightedness (5% to 21%) and strabismus, sometimes referred to as crossed eyes (4% to 21%), also occur among premature infants. Infants with a visual impairment do not see the caregiver's smile and therefore do not, themselves, develop a distinct smile. There is no visual stimulation for them to reach out toward objects and people in the environment, limiting the amount of tactile stimulation they experience.

Complications of prematurity, such as perinatal asphyxia, use of ototoxic drugs, and hyperbilirubinemia can cause hearing loss. The rate of deafness among LBW infants is approximately 3% (Hack et al., 1995). Infants with an auditory deficit do not hear the voices of their caregivers and are therefore limited in their ability to perceive differences in sound, which is important for the development of language. These impairments make it more difficult for infants to explore their environment and integrate information from different sensory modalities.

Language and Cognitive Development

Children with delayed sensorimotor development will have difficulty touching and visualizing objects in their environment. They may not hear the sound of their mother's voice nor develop the ability to differentiate auditory stimuli. Because the understanding and production of first words is based on objects in the environment, the lack of visual input delays development of a one-word vocabulary. The lack of visual incentive to explore the environment inhibits the spontaneous use of touch and audition, which are important in developing understanding of concepts. This may result in impairments in expressive language. Such impairments have been identified for children with VLBW of average intelligence (Hack et al., 1995).

Infants with neurological impairments have difficulty paying attention. They tend to be irritable and have difficulty sleeping. As preschoolers, they have difficulty with fine motor tasks, such as cutting with scissors, coloring, buttoning, and tying shoes, and with gross motor activities, such as running (Benner, 1992). They have difficulty maintaining their balance and completing tasks requiring eye-hand coordination, such as throwing and catching a ball and copying. Because these skills are assessed by scales of infant development, children with neurological impairments are likely to score below the expected levels for their chronological ages on these instruments. Whereas research has documented mean IQs for LBW children in the average range, the rates of quotients below 70 and between 70 and 84 are significantly higher than among control groups of children with normal birth weight. Furthermore, the rates increase as birth weight decreases. For example, 8% to 13% of children born weighing less than 1,000 grams have IQs between 70 and 84, compared with 20% of those born weighing less than 750 grams (Hack, Taylor, Klein & Eiben, 1994).

In general, the verbal abilities of LBW children are less impaired than their perceptual-performance skills (Hack et al., 1995). Compared to full-term children in control groups, VLBW children display selective impairments in mental arithmetic, visual-motor and fine-motor skills, spatial abilities, expressive language, and memory.

Social and Emotional Development

Attachment, the lasting affective bond between infants and their caregivers, has long been identified as a precursor to healthy emotional development. Because the development of healthy attachment depends on the relationship between the child and the caregiver, the attachment of children with disabilities may be compromised by child characteristics such as temperament and behavior. Children with disabilities may be at higher risk for demonstrating a behavioral style characterized by withdrawal, intense reactions, and overactivity. In addition, infants with disabilities may have difficulty getting their needs met because the caregiver is unable to understand their signals and cues. Add to this the unusual caregiving demands of some premature infants, and it is clear that child characteristics may produce parental stress, which in turn, may affect the parent-child relationship.

Greater rates of behavioral problems are identified with decreasing birth weight. These problems are attributed, in part, to brain injury because they tend to occur in children with cognitive deficits and neuromotor dysfunction. For example, Attention Deficit Hyperactivity Disorder has been diagnosed in 16% of children with birth weights less than 1,000 grams, compared with 6.9% of a matched control group. While no differences were noted in the temperament of LBW children and normal controls, the behavior of LBW children was characterized by more shyness, unassertiveness, and withdrawal (Hack et al., 1995). At greatest risk for emotional and behavioral disorders are males who are small for gestational age, show signs of early neurological problems, and have a nonfacilitative social environment (Buka, Lipsitt, & Tsuang, 1992).

Effects on Education and Instruction

Most children born prematurely will require few modifications to succeed in school. Nevertheless, the incidence of those requiring modifications is expected to increase as technological advances make it possible for even smaller infants to survive. According to parental reports, learning difficulties tend to increase as birth weight decreases. Parents also report that VLBW children achieve at lower levels compared to full-term children. For example, in a recent study (Hack et al., 1995), 34% of parents of VLBW children reported school problems, as defined by repeating a grade or receiving special education services. Of the parents of normal birth weight children, only

14% reported such problems. Thus, it is clear that low birth weight places children at risk for later school problems. This risk could be compounded by inadequate environments. It is therefore important for professionals to identify biological and environmental factors that could compromise developmental outcome so that modifications can be made to improve the prognosis for the individual child.

Predicting Developmental Outcome

As previously indicated, reproductive variables such as the amount of maternal smoking during pregnancy and the number of previous abortions increase the risk of prematurity. Once the infant has been delivered prematurely, developmental outcome can be predicted by a number of perinatal variables. Birth weight and gestational age are both related to later development. The risk of disability is higher in premature infants with perinatal asphyxia, as defined by low APGAR scores (Allen, 1991). The infant's *A*ppearance, *P*ulse rate, *G*rimace, *A*ctivity, and *R*espiration are evaluated immediately following birth and a score below 7 out of a possible 10, indicates the infant is experiencing some distress (Manginello & DiGeronimo, 1991). Developmental outcome is also adversely affected by severe or persistent apnea and/or need for mechanical ventilation and by the degree of intraventricular hemorrhage (Allen, 1991).

The following data about reproductive and perinatal variables (described by Barsky & Siegel, 1992) would allow professionals to make some predictions about development outcome.

Jim was born at 30 weeks gestation weighing 3 pounds 3 ounces. His initial APGAR score was 6. He was administered oxygen for intraventricular hemorrhage with mild respiratory distress syndrome. Jim was the result of his mother's first and only pregnancy. His parents had been married for 2 years before he was conceived, and neither parent had ever smoked. Jim's parents, who are both attorneys, were very concerned about his development. His mother decided to take a year off work to provide care for Jim.

Reproductive and perinatal variables are good predictors of performance on tasks requiring visual-spatial skills and attention (Siegel et al., 1982). On the basis of these data, professionals would predict that Jim will experience some motor difficulties related to central nervous system damage from the IVH-RDS (Barsky & Siegel, 1992).

In addition to biological risk, information on environmental-demographic variables allows professionals to identify whether an already vulnerable infant is at risk of further harm because of inadequate or nonfacilitative environments (Benner, 1992; Horowitz, 1987). Socioeconomic status, sex, and parental education are good predictors of a child's performance on language measures (Siegel et al., 1982). In general, environmental factors,

including caregiving interactions, play, and stimulation, are good predictors of intellectual outcomes (Aylward, 1988). Thus, once perinatal risk factors have been identified, social workers should obtain information to describe the characteristics of the family and the family needs that should be met to facilitate the development of the child. On the basis of family data, they would predict that Jim's language is likely to develop normally and that his intellectual ability is likely to be in the above-average range. As illustrated, perinatal variables, environmental-demographic variables, and reproductive variables allow professionals to predict developmental outcome. However, the data on VLBW infants do not allow us to predict functioning beyond the age of 8 years (Barsky & Siegel, 1992).

Identifying Developmental Needs

In order to identify services likely to enhance the development of the child and family, professionals should describe the child's strengths and needs in five developmental areas: cognition; communication; social and emotional development; adaptive or self-help; and physical, including motor, vision, and hearing. Although the five domains are specified by law, professionals and parents recognize that such an analytic approach can provide an inaccurate picture of a child's development. For example, delays in motor performance may be misinterpreted if the effects of blindness are not taken into account. Furthermore, it is difficult to separate cognitive development from motor and language abilities, because cognition is often measured by physical and verbal tasks (e.g., Bayley Scales of Infant Development; Bayley, 1993). Because of the interrelated nature of early development, assessment of the child's strengths and needs is typically conducted by a team of professionals from different disciplines. In collaboration with families, the physical and occupational therapist, speech/language pathologist, psychologist, and social worker should identify the current functioning of the child in several developmental areas. This family-centered approach to assessment of infants and toddlers is described by Toni Linder (1990) as Transdisciplinary Play-Based Assessment and by Child Development Resources (n.d.) in Lightfoot Virginia, as Transdisciplinary Arena Assessment. Linder (1990) provides observation checklists for the different developmental domains. Other instruments that assess multiple domains can be used with the arena assessment approach (see Table 3).

To effectively assess the child's development and adaptive functioning within the home environment, the assessment team needs to consider a number of family variables. Professionals collaborate with families to identify strengths, developmental needs, and outcomes for the child and family.

Table 3 *Multidomain Instruments Suitable for the Developmental Assessment of High-Risk Premature Infants and Children*

Instrument	Age Range	Description
Assessment, Evaluation, and Programming System (AEPS) for Infants and Children (Bricker, 1992)	Birth to 3 years	Evaluates the child's functioning in six domains: fine-motor, gross-motor, adaptive, cognitive, social-communication, and social. Also assesses family functioning. The AEPS links assessment, intervention, and evaluation.
Battelle Developmental Inventory Screening Test (Newborg, Stock, Wnek, Guidubaldi, & Sviniski, 1988)	Birth through 8 years	Uses structured testing, parent interviews, and observations of the child to assess personal and social development, adaptive behavior, motor development, communication, and cognitive development.
Bayley Scales of Infant Development-II (Bayley, 1993)	1 month to 42 months	Assesses current level of cognitive, language, personal-social, fine and gross motor development, and behavior during the testing situation.
Brigance Diagnostic Inventory of Early Development-Revised (Brigance, 1991)	Birth to 7 years	Uses comprehensive skill sequences to assess functioning in 12 developmental domains including motor skills, prespeech behaviors, social and emotional functioning, and general knowledge.
Transdisciplinary Play-Based Assessment (Linder, 1990)	Functional level: Infancy to 6 years	Professionals from different disciplines and parents use play-based techniques to assess the child's cognitive, social-emotional, communication and language, and motor development.

As previously indicated, the rate of prematurity in the United States is much higher among African Americans. In addition, poverty has been identified as a factor that places preterm or LBW children at environmental risk. Because a disproportionate number of children of color live in poverty (Edmunds, Martinson, & Goldberg, 1990), their biological risks due to prematurity are likely to be compounded by environmental effects. Professionals must be sensitive to such adverse effects in identifying developmental needs of premature infants. At the same time, it is important to recognize that the effects of neonatal illness and treatment on developmental outcome can be mediated by familial factors.

Alternative Actions

Prematurity puts a child at biological risk for developing physical, mental, or emotional disabilities. To reduce the risks and improve the developmental outcome for premature infants, intervention must focus on reducing both the incidence and effects of prematurity.

Reducing the Incidence of Prematurity

Because it is less costly to prevent prematurity than to remediate the effects, much attention has been focused on prevention efforts. Premature birth is a syndrome with many etiologies, therefore reduction of its incidence requires effort at many levels (Fuchs et al., 1993). At the first or primary prevention level (also referred to as the universal level: Gordon, 1983) are approaches that can be used prior to pregnancy or in early pregnancy to reduce the incidence of new cases of prematurity. These approaches include increased participation of females in family planning activities that focus on delaying childbirth beyond age 17 and/or extending intervals between births. In addition, primary prevention programs seek to increase concern about nutrition and weight gain of pregnant women, reflected in widespread use of supplemental nutritional programs. Emphasis also is placed on cessation of risk behaviors, such as smoking and the use of licit and illicit drugs, including alcohol. The need for universal prenatal care is stressed, as is the importance of resting from jobs with prolonged standing, treating specific illnesses early, and preventing genital infections. Many of these approaches have been emphasized through nationwide public information campaigns. In addition, primary prevention efforts have included the role of obstetrical medical technology such as home monitoring of uterine activity, tocolytic drugs to suppress uterine contractions, corticosteroids to accelerate fetal lung maturity, and the use of bed rest to prevent preterm deliveries.

Although a number of "expert panels" have defined and recommended these primary or universal prevention programs (U.S. Public Health Services . . . , 1989), there exists a paucity of research supporting their effectiveness. There are some data indicating pregnancy rates can be reduced by providing school-based health clinics (Dryfoos, 1994).

Efforts to reduce the incidence of low birth weight infants have been directed primarily at the individual health consequences of economic and social disadvantage. These efforts have included educational programs related to the negative consequences of cigarette smoking, alcohol and drug abuse, and lack of adequate nutrition during pregnancy. Outcome studies investigating these educational programs have produced mixed results. Equivocal findings were also obtained for the efforts directed at the underlying causes of social and economic disadvantage, such as improving access to prenatal health care through Medicaid and providing income support such as Aid to Families of Dependent Children (Alexander & Korenbrot, 1995; Hughes & Simpson, 1995). The use of obstetrical medical technology, such as home monitoring of uterine activity, has had little impact on the reduction of low birth weight and preterm births (Ricciotti, Chen & Sachs, 1995).

Despite the lack of clear empirical support for primary or universal prevention efforts, there is a need for more and better designed empirical studies investigating these programs. Research agendas for the future are proposed by a number of experts (Center for Children, 1995; Zeanah, 1993).

Secondary prevention efforts focus on early identification of symptoms, such as increased uterine contractility or premature dilatation of the cervix, that may cause premature delivery. To assess the risk, and eliminate specific risks for individual pregnant women, education is provided for pregnant women and health professionals. This training improves the ability of women to recognize symptoms of early preterm labor and to use home uterine monitoring. At the same time, health professionals are educated to respond early, to provide special prenatal care for patients who are at high risk for prematurity, and to administer effective drugs to stop premature labor.

Preventive prenatal care is particularly important for teenage mothers. Intervention programs for economically disadvantaged pregnant adolescents, including programs in hospitals or clinics, maternity shelters, and home visitation by nurses, have improved birth outcome by reducing infant mortality, morbidity, and pregnancy (Seitz & Apfel, 1994). To maximize the positive outcomes of these prevention programs, it is necessary for the teenager to enroll before midgestation. Specific services provided as part of these intervention programs include onsite prenatal care to students and psychosocial support. Counseling services have focused on a family-management approach that assists the pregnant teenagers in planning for their immediate and long-term future. First and foremost, teenagers are encouraged to remain in school to complete their education. During their pregnancy, the teenagers attend classes on prenatal devel-

opment, labor and delivery, family planning, and infant care. The importance of regular prenatal care is stressed, and the instructions of the obstetricians are reinforced. Once the infant arrives, provisions are made for day care, and assistance in finding suitable living arrangements is provided for teenagers who cannot reside with their parents or relatives.

A recent study found that education, psychological support, and monitoring (but no prenatal examinations) from health care professionals (i.e., nurses) in a public school setting substantially reduced the incidence of premature deliveries (Seitz & Apfel, 1994). For this reason, and because the law prevents girls from being excluded from schools because of pregnancy, increased numbers of educational programs are being established in segregated special schools or in regular school buildings. Teenage mothers who continue to make progress toward their high school diploma during the pregnancy maximize their ability to obtain gainful employment after their infants are born. Their rate of graduation is increased by programs that allow pregnant teenagers to receive services in their home school. This practice reduces their risk of dropping-out because their relationships with supportive school friends and significant adults (teachers, counselors, school psychologists) are not disrupted. A comprehensive review of outcome studies of secondary prevention programs is provided by Barnard, Morisset, and Spieker (1993).

Reducing the Effects of Prematurity

Most of the direct intervention research with premature infants has been consistent with the assumption that biomedical risk interacts with environmental inadequacy to depress the development of many premature infants. The infant's attributes, which are affected by biomedical complications, operate continuously and reciprocally with environmental forces such as schools and families in determining the outcome for the infant. Thus, the developmental outcome of premature infants could be enhanced by (a) reducing the biomedical risks, (b) creating a facilitative environment, and (c) providing early intervention programs.

Reducing Biomedical Risks

Tertiary preventive approaches seek to improve the outcome for the neonate when premature delivery is inevitable (Fuchs et al., 1993). These approaches include transportation of mothers to a perinatal center, treatment of the mother with specialized drugs and therapies after premature rupture of the membranes, and expert neonatal care. Research on early intervention suggests that high technological care of premature infants may significantly improve their immediate and long-term outcomes (Als, 1992; Brooks-Gunn, McCarton, Casey, & McCormick, 1994). Supplemental stimulation has been used in

Neonatal Intensive Care Units (NICUs) to counteract neonatal sensory deprivation. This stimulation includes:

- Visual, for example, pictures and mobiles.
- Auditory, for example, tape recordings of the mother's voice and of heartbeat sounds and music therapy.
- Tactile-kinesthetic.
- Vestibular, for example, the use of oscillating water-beds, rocking cribs, cuddling, stroking, and flexing of limbs and the provision of physical and occupational therapy.

Nonnutrituve sucking during tube feedings (Field, et al., 1982) and massaging of preterm neonates (Field, et al., 1986) have been demonstrated to be effective in increasing weight gain of premature infants.

Although most of the sensory-based interventions have been provided by medical staff, attempts have been made to teach parents to provide these types of stimulation and engage in appropriate interaction with their infants during hospitalization. For example, intervention has focused on incorporating at least the mother into a more active feeding and holding role (Als, 1992). Positive outcomes of these sensory-based interventions have included short-term reductions in crying and apnea, improved weight gain, increased activity, visual exploration and attention, better habituation, and facilitation of neonatal motor development (Als, 1992). Barnard et al. (1993) also provide a useful review of outcome studies of a variety of tertiary prevention programs.

Creating a Facilitative Environment

Interventions have been developed to address parental feelings of loss and increased stress that typically occur after the birth of premature infants. The stress results from real and perceived loss of freedom and added responsibilities, uncertainty, and lack of confidence in their own parenting skills when the infant is released from the hospital. Interventions with parents have also focused on modifying parental attitudes related to the prematurity stereotype (Stern & Karraker, 1992). A specific target of intervention has been the low level of self-confidence of the primary caretaker, typically the mother. Successful intervention programs have included education aimed at increasing parental knowledge of infancy and the premature infants' mental and psychomotor competence during the first year of life and parental understanding of child development processes, caregiving, childrearing issues, and developmental norms (Dichtelmiller et al., 1992).

There has been an increased recognition of the importance of the attachment process to positive psychological and physical developmental outcomes for premature infants. Interventions have focused on mother-child interactions and stressed the importance of frequent and consistent maternal and family visits to the neonatal intensive care unit (Brooks-Gunn, Klebanov, Liaw-Fong, & Spiker, 1993). Short-term self-help groups (Lowenthal, 1987) have specifically targeted facilitating the attachment process during identified critical periods and alleviating family stress. Programs (e.g., Nurcombe et al., 1984) that focus on supporting the family and facilitating the attachment process have reported many positive effects. These effects include enhanced satisfaction with and confidence in mothering, more favorable attitudes towards child-rearing, reduced degree of infant temperamental difficulty perceived by the mother, greater appreciation of the infant's motor capacity, and improved ability to recognize the infant's social and physiological cues and to engage the infant's attention and sustain social interaction. Although short-term increases in cognitive abilities have been reported for children as a result of these interventions, these increases tend to attenuate when many of the children enter inner city schools with fewer educational resources.

Increases in parental feelings of competence and enhancement of their self-esteem are linked to early "hands-on experiences" with their infant. These positive feelings are maintained by a problem-solving approach to education, which allows parents to develop their own skills for assessing the needs of their child and family and to design a program to address these identified individualized needs (Dichtelmiller et al., 1992). In addition, successful programs capitalize on the strengths of families and recognize that assessment of family and infant needs must be ongoing and respond to changes in factors that impact the family over time (Beckman & Pokorni, 1988). The types of support likely to mediate the stress of families vary with the individual characteristics of the child and the family. Services must be tailored to meet these individualized needs at a given point in time and assist families in developing and mobilizing support networks.

Early Intervention

Research has documented that early education can improve the developmental outcome for at-risk children and their families (e.g., Berrueta-Clement, Schweinhart, Barnett, Epstein, & Weikart, 1984; Ramey & Campbell, 1987). Such early education is available for at least some children born prematurely through the Individuals with Disabilities Education Act (IDEA; 1990). Participating states are legally required to serve all infants, toddlers, and preschool-age children with developmental delays or disabilities (Bowe, 1995). States may also elect to serve at-risk infants and toddlers who have neither delays nor disabilities but may develop them if intervention does not occur. These services are designed not only to enhance the development of infants and toddlers with disabilities, but also to minimize the potential of all infants and toddlers for developmental delay (Education for All Handicapped Children Act, Amendments of 1986, p. 1145). Professionals from different disciplines typically are involved in early intervention programs due to the complex biological, medical, and environmental factors that contribute to the developmental delays of these children.

Comprehensive early intervention programs integrate psychological, instructional, and therapeutic services. These services may be center based, home based, or a combination of the two (McDonnell, Hardman, McDonnell, & Kiefer-O'Donnell, 1995). The majority (52%) of infants and toddlers with special needs are served in center-based programs (Karnes & Stayton, 1988), located in hospitals, churches, schools, or other community facilities. Because they are heavily furnished with therapeutic equipment, the centers may appear to be more like hospital rooms than educational settings (Noonan & McCormick, 1993). Nevertheless, many of the programs represent a downward extension of preschool programs for the disadvantaged. The most successful programs include a strong parent, educator, and physician partnership (Saylor, Levkoff, & Elksnin, 1989; Sparling et al., 1991). Consistent with P.L. 99-457 (Education for All Handicapped Children Act, Amendments of 1986), and after a comprehensive assessment of the infant, an Individualized Family Service Plan (IFSP) is developed which stresses an integrated approach to service delivery.

Successful educational interventions have focused on spontaneous interactions with premature infants and enhancing their ability to learn through play, rather than the direct teaching of specific skills that are likely to emerge following their own individualized developmental course (Sparling et al., 1991). For example, parents are taught exercises and games to facilitate the infant's cognitive development, coordination, language, and socialization skills and are provided with information about infant development and caretaking skills, such as feeding. A central part of these early intervention educational programs is parent education. Provided by the school psychologist or school social worker, this component focuses on the normal development of the premature infant, atypical development, health-related problems that require immediate intervention, and effective parenting skills.

ties such as specific learning disabilities and attentional difficulties, to severe cerebral palsy, profound mental retardation, or sensory impairments. While the developmental outcome differs for each child, some early data allow relatively accurate predictions of the effects of prematurity. Birth weight, gestational age, amount of birth asphyxia, and severity of respiratory distress can all affect subsequent development. These factors can cause neurological damage that can adversely affect the child's cognitive, motor, and language development. Because the biological risks to the child can be mediated by the environment, assessment of environmental variables will increase the accuracy of predictions about later development.

Having identified the risks to development, professionals can provide interventions to improve developmental outcomes. A review of intervention research indicates that an unified developmental approach to intervention extending to the infant, the family, and the community is necessary to maximize the positive outcomes for children born prematurely. The approach must include medical, psychological, and developmental/educational experiences and target the "whole child," including the infant's physiological and psychological needs and the needs of the family. Once the premature infant leaves the hospital, the family must be linked to a community-based support system, including the school and the services of the school psychologist. Intervention services must support the family in their capacity to care for and facilitate the continued growth and development of their infant.

In addition to the provision of direct services to the premature infants and their families, the school and the school psychologist play an important role in the prevention of premature births. The school represents the primary site for prevention efforts, including education, with the goal of reducing the increasing number of infants born preterm.

Summary

Advances in neonatal care have made it possible for many premature infants to survive. However, these increased survival rates are not without cost. The medical costs of caring for extremely premature infants are enormous, but the long-term costs due to complications from prematurity are less easily quantified. Most children born preterm show no signs of their premature birth by the time they are school age. For other children, however, the effects of prematurity may range from mild disabili-

Recommended Resources

Castle Connolly. (1995). *How to find the best doctors, hospitals, and HMOs for you and your family.* New York: Castle Connolly Medical Ltd.
This resource guide provides excellent information for professionals and families concerned about selecting good medical care. Certain sections address the specific needs of women and children.

Center for the Future of Children. (1995, Spring). *The future of children: Low birth weight.* Volume 5, number 1.
This special issue discusses the impact of low birth weight on medical and social systems. While physicians strive to reduce the mortality rate of infants with low birth weight, social systems must find ways to absorb the costs due to medical compli-

cations and special educational needs of children born prematurely.

Cohen, L. G., & Spenciner, L. J. (1994). *Assessment of young children.* White Plains, NY: Longman Publishing Group.
This comprehensive textbook describes assessment of infants, toddlers, and preschool-age children. It provides a thorough discussion of legislation and of assessment issues relative to these age groups.

Friedman, S. L., & Sigman, M. D. (Eds.). (1992). *The psychological development of low birthweight children: Advances in applied developmental psychology.* Norwood, NJ: Ablex Publishing Corporation.
A number of authors contributed to this edited text. The chapters cover directions for research on low birth weight children and epidemiological, medical, and theoretical considerations, as well as social and emotional development and academic competence of children born prematurely. Several chapters on interventions and their effects are especially useful for school psychologists interested in prevention programs.

Manginello, F. P., & DiGeronimo, T. F. (1991). *Your premature infant.* New York: Wiley.
The information in this book is useful for parents and professionals. It describes the characteristics of infants born at different gestational ages and details the emotions parents of premature infants are likely to experience. The authors describe the medical complications, and these are made more comprehensible by case studies written by parents.

References

Adams, M. M., Read, J. A., Rawlings, J. S., Harlass, F. B., Sarno, A. P., & Rhodes, P. H. (1993). Preterm delivery among black and white enlisted women in the United States Army. *Obstetrics & Gynecology, 81,* 65–71.

Alexander, G. R. & Kernbrot, C. C. (1995). The role of prenatal care in preventing low birth weight. *Future Child J* (1), 103–120.

Allen, M. C. (1991). Prematurity. In A. J. Capute, & P. J. Accardo (Eds.), *Developmental disabilities in infancy and childhood* (pp. 87–99). Baltimore: Paul H. Brookes.

Als, H. (1992). Individualized, family-focused developmental care for the very low-birthweight preterm infant in the NICU. In S. L. Friedman, & M. D. Sigman (Eds.), *The psychological development of low birthweight children: Advances in applied developmental psychology* (pp. 341–388). Norwood, NJ: Ablex.

American College of Obstetricians and Gynecologists. (1989). *Preterm labor.* ACOG Technical Bulletin no. 133. Washington, DC: Author.

Aylward, G. P. (1988). Issues in prediction and developmental follow-up. *Developmental and Behavioral Pediatrics, 9,* 307–309.

Barnard, K. E., Morisset, C. E., Spieker, S. (1993). Preventive interventions: Enhancing parent-infant relationships. In Zeanah, C. H. (Ed.), *Handbook of infant mental health* (pp. 386–401). New York: Guilford Press.

Barsky, V. E., & Siegel, L. S. (1992). Predicting future cognitive, academic, and behavioral outcomes for very-low-birthweight (<1,500 grams) infants. In S. L. Friedman, & M. D. Sigman (Eds.), *The psychological development of low birthweight children: Advances in applied developmental psychology* (pp. 275–298). Norwood, NJ: Ablex.

Bayley, N. (1993). *Bayley Scales of Infant Development-II.* San Antonio, TX: The Psychological Corporation.

Beckman, P. J., & Pokorni, J. L. (1988). *Developmental and Behavioral Pediatrics, 9,* 307–309.

Benner, S. M. (1992). *Assessing young children with special needs: An ecological perspective.* White Plains, NY: Longman.

Berrueta-Clement, J. R., Schweinhart, L. J., Barnett, W. S., Epstein, A. S., & Weikart, D. P. (1984). *Changed lives: The effects of the Perry Preschool Program on youths through age 19.* (Monograph of the High/Scope Educational Research Foundation No. 8). Ypsilanti, MI: High/Scope Press.

Bowe, F. G. (1995). Population estimates: Birth-to-5 children with disabilities. *Journal of Special Education, 28,* 461–471.

Bricker, D. (Ed.). (1992). *Assessment, evaluation, and programming system (AEPS) for infants and children: Vol. 1. AEPS measurement for birth to three years.* Baltimore: Paul H. Brookes.

Brigance, A. H. (1991). *Brigance diagnostic inventory of early development-revised.* North Billerica, MA: Curriculum Associates.

Brooks-Gunn, J., Klebanov, P. K., Liaw-Fong, R., & Spiker, D. (1993). Enhancing the development of low-birthweight, premature infants: Changes in cognition and behavior over the first three years. *Child Development, 64,* 736–753.

Brooks-Gunn, J., McCarton, C. M., Casey, P. H., & McCormick, M. C. (1994). Early intervention in low-birthweight premature infants: Results through age 5 years from the Infant Health and Development Program. *Journal of the American Medical Association, 272,* 1257–1262.

Brown, E. R. (1993). Long-term sequelae of preterm birth. In A. R. Fuchs, F. Fuchs, & P. G. Stubblefield (Eds.), *Preterm birth: Causes, prevention, and management* (2nd ed.; pp. 465–475). New York: McGraw-Hill.

Buka, S. L., Lipsitt, L. P., & Tsuang, M. T. (1992). Emotional and behavioral development of low-birthweight infants. In S. L. Friedman, & M. D. Sigman (Eds.), *The psychological development of low birthweight children: Advances in applied developmental psychology* (pp. 187–214). Norwood, NJ: Ablex.

Caplan, G., Mason, E. A., & Kaplan, D. M. (1965). Four studies of crisis in parents of prematures. *Community Mental Health Journal, 1,* 149–161.

Center for Children. (1995). *The future of children: Low birth weight, 5* (1). Los Altos, CA: The David and Lucile Packard Foundation, Center for the Future of Children.

Child Development Resources. (n.d.). *Transdisciplinary Arena Assessment Process: A resource for teams.* Lightfoot, VA: Author.

Cohen, L. G., & Spenciner, L. J. (1994). *Assessment of young children.* New York: Longman.

Creasy, R. K. (1993). Preterm birth prevention: Where are we? *American Journal of Obstetrics and Gynecology, 168,* 1223–1230.

Dichtelmiller, M., Meisels, S. J., Plunkett, J. W., Bozynski, M. E., Clafin, C., & Mangelsdorf, S. C. (1992). The relationship of parental knowledge to the development of extremely low birth weight infants. *Journal of Early Intervention, 16,* 210–220.

Drillien, C. M. (1964). *Growth and development of the prematurely born infant.* Edinburgh: Livingstone.

Drillien, C. M. (1958). Growth and development in a group of children of very low birth weight. *Archives of Diseases in Childhood, 33,* 10–18.

Dryfoos, J. F. (1994). *Full-service schools: A revolution in health and social services for children, youth and families.* San Francisco, CA: Josey-Bass.

Edmunds, P., Martinson, S., & Goldberg, P. (1990). *Demographics and cultural diversity in the 1990s: Implications for services to young children with special needs.* Chapel Hill, NC: NEC*TAS.

Education for all Handicapped Children Act, Amendments of 1986, Pub. L. No. 99–457, 100, Stat. 1145.

Eisner, V., Brazie, J. V., Pratt, M. W., & Hexter, A. C. (1979). The risk of low birth weight. *American Journal of Public Health, 69,* 887–893.

Field, T., Ignatoff, E., Stringer, S., Brennan, J., Greenberg, R., Widmayer, S., & Anderson, G. (1982). Nonnutritive sucking during tube feeding: Effects on preterm neonates in an ICU. *Pediatrics, 70,* 381–384.

Field, T., Schanberg, S. M., Scafidi, F., Bauer, C. R., Vega-Lahr, N., Garcia, R., Nystrom, J., & Kuhn, C. M. (1986). Tactile/kinesthetic stimulation effects on preterm neonates. *Pediatrics, 77,* 654–658.

Fuchs, A. R., Fuchs, F., & Stubblefield, P. G. (Eds.). (1993). *Preterm birth: Causes, prevention, and management* (2nd ed.). New York: McGraw-Hill.

Gordon, R. (1983). An operational definition of prevention. *Public Health Reports, 98,* 107–109.

Gross, R. T., Brooks-Gunn, J., & Spiker, D. (1992). Efficacy of comprehensive early intervention for low-birthweight premature infants and their families: The Infant Health and Development Program. In S. L. Friedman & M. D. Sigman (Eds.), *The psychological development of low birthweight children: Advances in applied developmental psychology* (pp. 411–433). Norwood, NJ: Ablex.

Hack, M., Klein, N. K., & Taylor, H. G. (1995, Spring). Long-term developmental outcomes of low birth weight infants. *The Future of Children, 5(1),* 176–196.

Hack, M., Taylor, G., Klein, N., & Eiben, R. (1994). Outcome of 750 gm birthweight children at school age. *New England Journal of Medicine, 331,* 753–759.

Heffner, L. J., Sherman, C. B., Speizer, F. E., & Weiss, S. T. (1993). Clinical and environmental predictors of preterm labor. *Obstetrics and Gynecology, 81,* 750–757.

Horowitz, F. D. (1987). *Exploring developmental theories: Toward a structural/behavioral model of development.* Hillsdale, NJ: Erlbaum.

Hughes, D. & Simpson, L. (1995). The role of social changes in preventing low birthweight. *Future of Children, 5(1),* 87–102.

Individuals with Disabilities Education Act of 1990, 20 U.S.C. 1400, as amended by the IDEA Amendments of 1991, Pub. L. No. 102–119.

Karnes, M. B., & Stayton, V. D. (1988). Model programs for infants and toddlers with handicaps. In J. B. Jordan, J. J. Gallagher, P. L. Hutinger, & M. B. Karnes (Eds.), *Early childhood special education: Birth to three* (pp. 67–106). Reston, VA: Council for Exceptional Children and the Division for Early Childhood.

Kitchen, W. H., Ford, G. W., Rickards, A. L., Lissenden, J. V., & Ryan, M. M. (1987). Children of birth weight <1000 g: Changing outcome between ages 2 and 5 years. *Journal of Pediatrics, 110,* 283–288.

Linder, T. W. (1990). *Transdisciplinary play-based assessment: A functional approach to working with young children.* Baltimore: Brookes.

Lowenthal, B. (1987). Stress factors and their alleviation in parents of high risk pre-term infants. *Exceptional Child, 34,* 21–30.

Manginello, F. P., & DiGeronimo, T. F. (1991). *Your premature infant.* New York: Wiley.

McDonnell, J. M., Hardman, M. L., McDonnell, A. P., & Kiefer-O'Donnell, R. (1995). *Introduction to persons with severe disabilities.* Boston: Allyn and Bacon.

Michielutte, R., Moore, M. L., Meis, P. J., Ernest, J. M., & Wells, H. B. (1994). Race differences in infant mortality from endogenous causes: A population-based study in North Carolina. *Journal of Clinical Epidemiology, 47,* 119–130.

Minde, K. (1992). The social and emotional development of low-birthweight infants and their families up to age 4. In S. L. Friedman, & M. D. Sigman (Eds.), *The psychological development of low birthweight children: Advances in applied developmental psychology* (pp. 157–185). Norwood, NJ: Ablex.

Morrison, J. C. (1990). Preterm birth: A puzzle worth solving. *Obstetrics and Gynecology, 76,* 5S–12S.

National Center for Health Statistics. (1993). Advance report of final natality statistics, 1991. *Monthly Vital Statistics Report, 42(3),* Suppl. Hyattsville, MD: Public Health Service.

Newborg, J., Stock, J. R., Wnek, L., Guidubaldi, J., & Sviniski, J. (1988). *Battelle developmental inventory screening test.* Allen, TX: DLM.

Noonan, M. J., & McCormick, L. (1993). *Early intervention in natural environments: Methods and procedures.* Pacific Grove, CA: Brooks/Cole.

Nurcombe, B., Howell, D. C., Rauh, V. A., Teti, D. M., Ruoff, P., & Brennan, J. (1984). An intervention program for mothers of low-birthweight infants: Preliminary results. *Journal of the American Academy of Child Psychiatry, 23,* 319–325.

Papile, L., Burstein, J., Burstein, R., & Koffler, H. (1978). Incidence and evolution of subependymal and intraventricular hemorrhage: A study of infants with birthweights less than 1500 g. *The Journal of Pediatrics, 92,* 529–534.

Ramey, C. T., & Campbell, F. A. (1987). The Carolina Abecederian Project: An educational experiment concerning human malleability. In J. J. Gallagher & C. T. Ramey (Eds.), *The malleability of children* (pp. 127–139). Baltimore: Paul H. Brookes.

Ricciotti, H. A., Chen, K. T. & Sachs, B. P. (1995). The role of obstetrical medical technology in preventing low birth weight. *The future of children: Low birth weight.* 5(1), 71–86.

Rosenheim, M. K. (1992). Teenage parenthood: Policies and perspectives. In M. K. Rosenheim & M. F. Testa

(Eds.), *Early parenthood and coming of age in the 1900s* (pp. 200–206). New Brunswick, NJ: Rutgers University Press.

Sattler, J. M. (1992). *Assessment of children* (Revised & Updated 3rd ed.). San Diego, CA: Jerome M. Sattler.

Saylor, C. F., Levkoff, A. H., & Elksnin, N. (1989). Premature infants with intraventricular hemorrhage: A need for early intervention. *Topics in Special Education, 9,* 86–98.

Seitz, V., & Apfel, N. H. (1994). Effects of a school for pregnant students on the incidence of low-birthweight deliveries [Special issue]. *Child Development, 65,* 666–676.

Shiono, P. H., & Klebanoff, M. A. (1986). Ethnic differences in preterm and very preterm delivery. *American Journal of Public Health, 76,* 1317–1321.

Siegel, L. S., Saigal, S., Rosenbaum, P., Morton, R. A., Young, A., Berenbaum, & Stoskopf, B. (1982). Predictors of development in preterm and full-term infants: A model for detecting the at risk child. *Journal of Pediatric Psychology, 7,* 135–148.

Smith, P. B., Weinman, M., Reeves, G. C., Wait, R. B., & Hinkley, C. M. (1993). Educational efforts in preventing preterm delivery among inner city adolescents. *Patient Education and Counseling, 21,* 71–75.

Sparling, J., Lewis, I., Ramey, C. T., Wasik, B. H., Bryant, D. M., & LaVange, L. M. (1991). Partners: A curriculum to help premature, low birthweight infants get off to a good start. *Topics in Early Childhood Special Education, 11,* 36–55.

Stern, M., & Karraker, K. H. (1992). Modifying the prematurity stereotype in mothers of premature and ill full-term infants. *Journal of Clinical Child Psychology, 21,* 76–82.

U.S. Public Health Service (USPHS) Expert Panel on the Content of Prenatal Health Care. (1989). *Caring for our future: The content of prenatal care.* Washington, DC: U.S. Government Printing Office.

World Health Organization. (1977). Recommended definitions, terminology, and formulae for statistical tables related to the perinatal period and use of a new certificate for cause of perinatal death. *Acta Obstet Gynaecol Scand. 56,* 247–253.

Zeanah, C. H. (1993). *Handbook of infant mental health.* New York: Guilford.

77

Sleep and Sleep Problems

Deidre L. Donaldson

Rhode Island Hospital/Brown University School of Medicine

Judith Owens-Stively

Rhode Island Hospital/Brown University School of Medicine

Natalie C. Frank

University of North Carolina at Chapel Hill

Anthony Spirito

Rhode Island Hospital/Brown University School of Medicine

Background and Development

In the last two decades, the role of sleep in child development has received increased attention from clinicians and researchers. The exact function of sleep across the life span is uncertain despite several theoretical explanations, including the restoration of physiological deficits incurred during wakefulness, energy conservation, the enhancement of learning and memory, and unlearning spurious information obtained during wakefulness (Sheldon, Spire, & Levy, 1992). The importance of children's sleep became of great interest to child development professionals when the prevalence and impact of pediatric sleep problems were realized.

Sleep problems are reportedly among the most common behavior problems confronted by pediatricians (Kataria, Swanson, & Trevathan, 1987). Recent estimates suggest that as many as 30% of children between birth and 4 years of age experience difficulty sleeping through the night (e.g., Lozoff, Wolf, & Davis, 1985). Bedtime struggles and night awakenings are common among preschool and latency-aged children (Adair & Bauchner, 1993; Lozoff et al., 1985). Estimates of sleep problems during adolescence, particularly insomnia and daytime fatigue, range from 33% to 75% (Morrison, McGee, & Stanton, 1992; Strauch & Meier, 1988). Prevalence estimates for sleep problems vary due to normative developmental patterns in all aspects of sleep. To properly assess and treat childhood sleep problems, professionals need to understand the typical development of sleep phenomena.

Sleep Patterns Across Development

The temporal organization of sleep involves both circadian sleep/wake and REM/non-REM cycles. The circadian sleep/wake cycle involves transitions from wakefulness to sleep and eventually back to wakefulness. Changes in circadian rhythm with increased age include (a) shorter sleep and longer wake periods, (b) increased duration between sleep and wakefulness, and (c) greater reliance on external cues for the onset and cessation of sleep (Anders, Sadeh, & Appareddy, 1995).

REM (rapid eye movement) sleep refers to active sleep, or sleep characterized by a desynchronized EEG pattern, rapid respirations, dream activity, and muscle atonia (Sheldon et al., 1992). Non-REM sleep, or quiet sleep, is differentiated into four sleep stages. Each stage represents a progressively deeper state of sleep. REM and non-REM sleep states in the fetus become organized during the last trimester of pregnancy (Anders et al., 1995). General changes in this cycle across development include (a) increased duration between REM and non-REM cycles, (b) a shift from sleep onset REM to non-REM sleep onset, (c) a modest decrease in the proportion of the sleep period spent in REM sleep, and (d) increasingly longer REM periods concentrated later in the sleep period (Anders, et al., 1995; Sheldon et al., 1992). To better understand the developmental patterns of sleep, it is helpful to consider the characteristics of sleep during four separate developmental periods, including infancy, early childhood, middle childhood, and adolescence.

Infancy (0–1 Year)

During the first year of life, there are significant developmental changes in sleep. Neonates spend approximately 70% of every 24 hours asleep (Sheldon et al., 1992). Frequent awakenings are common at 1 to 2 months. Sleep-wake patterns occur in 3- to 4-hour cycles (Anders et al., 1995). Between 3 and 4 months of age, however, the sleep-wake cycle becomes more stable, diurnal, and established with the light-dark cycle. Between 6 and 8 months of age, sleep periods may last 6 hours, and total sleep time decreases to 13 hours from the 16 to 24 hours per day exhibited by newborns (Sheldon et al.). Sleep onset decreases from approximately 30 minutes for 2-month-olds to approximately 15 minutes by age 9 months. Repetitive, self-soothing behaviors such as body rocking or head banging are common (Anders et al.). By 1 to 2 years of age, infants exhibit regular, nighttime sleep patterns electrophysiologically similar to those exhibited during adulthood (Ferber, 1995b). Because sleep irregularity is typical, formal sleep disorders are infrequently diagnosed unless there is a sudden or drastic change in sleep patterns or behaviors (Adair & Bauchner, 1993). Nevertheless, parents are often concerned by such irregularity and may seek pediatric consultation as a result.

Early Childhood (2–5 Years)

By the end of the first year of life, most children sleep through the night. Transient awakenings are common but resolve quickly when the child's physiological needs are met and parents remain neutral in response to such occurrences (Anders & Weinstein, 1972). Sleep changes during preschool or early childhood occur more gradually than those during infancy. Between the ages of 2 and 3 years, sleep becomes consolidated into one long nocturnal period of approximately 10 hours with naps common during the day (Sheldon et al., 1992). By the time children reach the age of 4 or 5, daytime naps are no longer needed (Edwards & Christophersen, 1994). Bedtime routines become established around 2 years of age and often involve toileting, drinking, reading a story, and separating from parents (Beltramini & Hertzig, 1983). Typical bedtime routines last 30 minutes with longer periods required for older preschool children (Beltramini & Hertzig). Preschool children also exhibit increasingly longer sleep onset latency with age, ranging from approximately 15 minutes for younger children to 30 minutes for ages 5 and 6 (Sheldon et al.).

During the preschool period the sleep-wake schedule becomes more reliant on external cues (light and adult schedules). Children become more socially interactive and, as a result, often exhibit resistance to bedtime. To cope with separation from significant others, children may request objects such as stuffed toys and blankets or engage in self-soothing behaviors to ease the transition (e.g., thumbsucking). Preschool-aged children typically desire a certain bedtime, call out for parents after being put in bed, awaken frequently during the night, and experience nightmares or nighttime fears (Beltramini & Hertzig, 1983). For the most part, these disturbances are transient and require minimal intervention. Bedtime routines and self-soothing behaviors enhance the initiation and maintenance of sleep.

Middle Childhood (6–12 Years)

Few studies have examined sleep patterns during this age range. Existing information suggests that gradual changes in the sleep/wake and REM/non-REM cycles continue to approach adult sleep patterns. Total sleep duration for school-aged children averages between 9 and 11 hours per night with older children exhibiting shorter sleep periods than younger children (Anders et al., 1995). Naps are rare for this age group, and school-aged children usually remain quite alert throughout the day (Sheldon et al., 1992).

Adolescence (13–18 Years)

Adolescents experience dramatic physiological, sociological, and psychological changes that impact sleep. Average sleep duration during adolescence decreases from a prepubescent average of 10 hours to 8 1/2 hours by age 16 (Sheldon et al., 1992). There is a significant discrepancy in total sleep time on school nights compared to nonschool nights, a trend that is not exhibited during middle childhood (Carskadon, 1992). Decreased sleep duration on school nights occurs largely as a function of environmental demands such as earlier school starting times, homework, and limits set by parents. Research with this age group shows that adolescents do *not* experience a concurrent decrease in daily sleep requirements coinciding with the decreased sleep obtained on school nights (Carskadon). Thus, daytime sleepiness is a common adolescent complaint. Research also suggests that sleep on weekends is more natural and represents a sleep rebound effect to compensate for the deprivation experienced during the week (Carskadon).

The evaluation of sleep behaviors during adolescence requires clinical sophistication due to the developmental complexities that characterize this period (Carskadon, 1992). Potential sleep problems include those evident in childhood, those that first emerge during adolescence, and precursors to adult disorders.

Problems and Implications

Broadly defined, a *sleep problem* "is a condition . . . that interferes with the refreshing nature of a child's sleep or that significantly disrupts other people" (Adair & Bauchner, 1993, p. 156). Childhood sleep problems differ from adult sleep problems in that complaints are most often reported by adult caregivers and not children themselves (Ferber, 1995a). It is important to recognize that adult reports reflect caregiver expectations of sleep development and desired sleep behaviors in addition to the child's actual sleep behaviors. For example, a child who takes short naps may not allow a busy parent sufficient respite from childcare, resulting in parental complaints about the child's sleep patterns. Thus, the assessment of sleep problems should include factors central to the reported problem as well as the ways these factors relate to adult expectations and desired child behaviors.

The International Classification of Sleep Disorders (ICSD; Thorpy, 1990) provides criteria for the classification of adult sleep disorders and is presently utilized to diagnose sleep problems in school-aged children and adolescents. Primary sleep disorders in this classification system are grouped into two major categories: dyssomnias and parasomnias. Sleep disorders secondary to other medical and psychiatric disorders are categorized separately and, for space reasons are not included in this chapter. Some sleep difficulties such as prolonged bedtime routines, delayed sleep onset, and frequent awakenings commonly occur between infancy and 5 years of age and promote serious concern and frustration for parents (Beltramini & Hertzig, 1983). In the absence of problems in other areas of child functioning, however, such sleep disturbances are probably age-appropriate phenomena and do not constitute a formal sleep disorder.

Dyssomnias

The dyssomnias are a diagnostic grouping of sleep disorders characterized by problems initiating or maintaining sleep (DIMS) or excessive somnolence (DOES). This grouping includes intrinsic sleep disorders, extrinsic sleep disorders, and circadian-rhythm sleep disorders (Thorpy, 1990).

Intrinsic Dyssomnias

Intrinsic sleep disorders originate from causes within the body (Thorpy, 1990). Disorders that may arise during childhood or adolescence include, among others, obstructive sleep apnea and narcolepsy.

Obstructive sleep apnea. Obstructive sleep apnea (OSA) is a medical condition in which brief, repeated episodes of obstructed airflow through the nose and mouth occur during sleep. These periods of airflow cessation, or apneic episodes, result in two problematic conditions. First, chronic reduction in oxygen levels (hypoxia) and increases in carbon dioxide levels (hypercapnia) during the apneic periods are believed to result in cognitive impairment (Carroll & Laughlin, 1995). Empirical data are only now being col-

lected in children, but clinical reports suggest subtle learning problems may result rather than generalized developmental delays. Second, frequent, partial awakenings often accompany the apneic episodes. Over the course of many nights, these awakenings result in poor sleep quality, chronic sleep deprivation, and daytime sleepiness.

Increasing numbers of children and adolescents are being diagnosed with sleep apnea (Sheldon et al., 1992). The age range for this disorder is 2 to 15 years, with a peak incidence between 3 and 4 years (Thorpy, 1990). Males and females are equally affected. Certain populations show an increased incidence of OSA, including children with facial and oral anomalies, genetic syndromes such as Down's syndrome, neuromuscular conditions, and morbid obesity. The most common underlying cause of OSA in children is enlarged tonsils and adenoids.

Symptoms of OSA may be divided into sleep-related symptoms and daytime symptoms. The most common sleep-related symptom of OSA is loud snoring. This is usually accompanied by noticeable pauses in breath sounds during the night, gasping, or choking. Children with OSA may also experience restless sleep, exhibit nocturnal sweating, and sleep in abnormal positions to breathe more easily. Children with OSA commonly have an increased incidence of parasomnias, including bedwetting, nightmares, and night terrors. Daytime symptoms of OSA include chronic mouth breathing, a nasal vocal quality, and growth failure. Growth failure may result from the child's relative difficulty in eating and breathing simultaneously, decreased taste sensation secondary to nasal obstruction, and interruption of the regular nocturnal secretion of growth hormone due to frequent partial awakenings. Other symptoms include morning headaches and difficult awakenings with subsequent morning irritability.

Behavioral symptoms of OSA may include decreased attention span, increased distractibility, low frustration tolerance, behavioral impulsivity, aggressive behavior, daytime sleepiness, social withdrawal, learning problems, and compromised academic performance (Sheldon et al., 1992). Many of these symptoms result from chronic sleep deprivation and overlap considerably with symptoms of other problems, including Attention-Deficit/Hyperactivity Disorder (ADHD). Differential diagnosis is made difficult by the fact that OSA and ADHD may coexist. If the daytime behavioral symptoms are accompanied by nocturnal symptoms of OSA, referral for a physical examination should be made. When a child fits the criteria for ADHD, school personnel should question parents about the child's sleep to help rule out the possibility of OSA. The diagnosis of OSA is typically made on the basis of the child's medical history, physical examination, or an overnight sleep study.

Narcolepsy. The diagnosis of narcolepsy is rarely made in childhood. However, many narcoleptic adults report the onset of symptoms in later childhood and adolescence. Peak onset is approximately 14 years (Thorpy, 1990). The hallmarks of narcolepsy include (a) sudden, dramatic, and irresistible sleep attacks of less than one hour in duration; (b) cataplexy, a sudden decrease in muscle tone triggered by emotions that may result in falling to the ground; (c) sleep paralysis, the perceived inability to move as the individual is falling asleep; and (d) hypnagogic hallucinations, visual and auditory hallucinations that occur at the beginning or end of the sleep period (Challamel et al., 1994). Secondary symptoms may include poor school performance and behavioral problems as a result of excessive daytime sleepiness. Narcolepsy, a rare condition with quite dramatic symptoms, is, therefore, usually distinguishable from nonpathological daytime sleepiness.

Extrinsic Dyssomnias

Extrinsic sleep disorders are problems in initiating and maintaining sleep that originate from factors *outside* the body. The extrinsic sleep disorders most pertinent to childhood and adolescence include adjustment sleep disorder, limit-setting sleep disorder, sleep-onset association disorder, and allergy-related sleep disturbances.

Adjustment sleep disorder. Children may experience difficulty initiating sleep secondary to life stress that results in emotional arousal (Mindell, 1993). Examples of life stress that may affect sleep include family conflict, traumatic events, and major life changes such as moving, parental separation, or the death of a family member. The essential features of this problem include sleep disturbance that differs from the child's typical pattern and an identifiable stressor associated with the disturbance. The symptoms and features of this disturbance remit in the absence of the stressor or with improved psychological adaptation to the precipitant (Thorpy, 1990).

Children affected by this problem often present with insomnia, although daytime sleepiness may also be a symptom. Additional symptoms, including irritability, lethargy, tearfulness, or anxiety, usually begin within 3 months of the onset of the stressor (Thorpy, 1990). Impairment in social and educational functioning may result. The disorder tends to persist longer in response to chronic versus acute stressors. However, if the condition lasts longer than 6 months, the potential for other contributing factors should be reassessed, including medical and psychiatric conditions that may compromise sleep, exposure to environmental toxins, and parent-child interactions (Thorpy).

Limit-setting sleep disorder. Research suggests that children of all ages experience difficulty falling asleep (e.g., Beltramini & Hertzig, 1983; Morrison et al., 1992). Young children, particularly between the ages of 2 and 6, may refuse to go to bed despite being physiologically ready

(Adair & Bauchner, 1993; Ferber, 1995c). As a result, bedtime struggles commonly arise, and caregivers may experience increasing difficulty separating from their child at night. This presents serious difficulty for 5% to 10% of the childhood population (Thorpy, 1990). Parents of children with this problem typically report conflicts around bedtime (Adair & Bauchner), and children may also present with other complications as a result of inadequate sleep, including irritability, diminished attentional abilities, decreased academic performance, and family conflict.

Parents who wish to avoid conflict with their child, who lack knowledge regarding appropriate limit-setting, or who are too tired to set firm limits may repeatedly allow a child to sleep in a place other than the child's bed. Psychosocial stressors (e.g., substance abuse, depression, marital conflict) also may minimize a caregiver's ability to effectively maintain bedtime limits (Ferber, 1995c). Busy family schedules may also result in inconsistent bedtimes that compromise sleep onset. As a child experiences repeated difficulty falling asleep to which parents respond with ineffective limits or inconsistency, he or she may increasingly cry out for caregivers, use delay tactics, refuse to stay in bed, or tantrum during attempts by caregivers to separate.

Caregivers often try a variety of strategies to quiet the child and minimize escalation, including sleeping in the child's bed, allowing the child to sleep in the caregivers' bed, using physical punishment, or allowing the child to fall asleep anywhere, at anytime. Unfortunately, these methods may only serve to exacerbate the problem.

Sleep-onset association disorder. Stage 1 non-REM sleep consists of light sleep during which an individual can be easily aroused. It is typical for children to awaken during light sleep stages, independently settle, and fall back to sleep. In sleep-onset association disorder, which occurs primarily between ages 6 months and 3 years (Thorpy, 1990), children are unable to transition back to sleep once aroused because the factors associated with sleep onset (e.g., bottle feeding, music) are not sustained or maintained during the night. These children are unable to self-soothe and depend on external assistance for sleep onset at bedtime or following night awakenings. Parents of children with sleeponset association disorder report that their children have difficulty sleeping through the night in contrast to the bedtime struggles reported by parents of children with limit-setting sleep disorder. Sleep-onset association disorder also may manifest itself in an association between eating and sleep such that a child requires food or drink in order to fall asleep (i.e., Nocturnal Eating Disorder; Thorpy).

Allergy-related sleep disturbances. Allergies may have adverse effects on children's sleeping habits. There are several possible etiologies for the sleep difficulties associated with allergies. Cow's milk allergies, which typically begin in infancy and resolve by 2 to 4 years of age, may cause gastrointestinal distress that results in restless sleep and frequent night awakenings (Sheldon et al., 1992). Children with allergies often have symptoms of asthma, which may result in respiratory problems during the night and restless, disordered sleep (Dahl, Bernhisel-Broadbent, Scanlon-Holdford, Sampson, & Lupo, 1985). In addition, medications used to treat allergies, although sedating in nature, may paradoxically result in difficulties initiating and maintaining sleep.

Circadian Rhythm Disorders

This group of dyssomnias causes problems because of misalignment between the child's actual sleep pattern and that desired, required, or expected by society (Thorpy, 1990). In most cases, individuals with these disorders experience difficulty sleeping when sleep is desired or necessary, forcing the corresponding wake periods also to occur at undesirable times.

Delayed sleep phase syndrome. This problem most commonly occurs as adolescents acquire responsibility for their own sleep schedule or experience changes in biologic timing mechanisms causing delayed sleep onset (Carskadon, 1992). The disorder affects approximately 7% of all adolescents (Thorpy, 1990) and usually results from staying up later than usual, sleeping in, or taking late afternoon naps (Dahl & Carskadon, 1995). Bedtimes occur later and are inconsistent with the biologic sleep cycle. Individuals with this problem report sleep onset insomnia as a result of the body's inability to shift sleep rhythms to earlier hours. Excessive morning sleepiness is also a problem.

If allowed to sleep whenever desired, most adolescents with this problem experience no difficulties with sleep onset, sleep for over 9 hours, and feel refreshed upon awakening. Children or adolescents whose primary problem is insomnia may exhibit similar symptoms but often intentionally choose a late-night schedule and are not distressed by the pattern (Dahl & Carskadon, 1995). Alternatively, other children and adolescents may experience prolonged sleep onset periods regardless of bedtime but awaken refreshed in the morning.

Advanced sleep phase syndrome. In contrast to delayed sleep onset problems, children may also present with sleep onset that is advanced in relation to the desired or required bedtime. The symptoms of advanced sleep phase disorder include the inability to stay awake at night, early morning awakenings prior to 5:00 a.m., or both (Thorpy, 1990). Although daytime activities are rarely hindered, this problem may interfere with the ability to accomplish homework or chores in the evening due to excessive somnolence between the hours of 6:00 and 8:00 p.m. (Thorpy). This syndrome is much less common

than delayed sleep phase syndrome and is particularly rare in children and adolescents (Thorpy).

Parasomnias

Parasomnias are a group of disorders associated with sleep staging or partial arousals during sleep (Thorpy, 1990). These disorders often begin in early childhood and can be disruptive to children and their families. Although the exact cause of parasomnias is unknown, one hypothesis is that they result from immaturity of the central nervous system (Sheldon et al., 1992). Parasomnias can be precipitated by several factors, including sleep deprivation, a chaotic sleep-wake cycle, life stress, illness or fever, full bladder, obstructive sleep apnea, loud noises, and certain medications (Sheldon et al.).

Partial-Arousal Disorders

Partial-arousal disorders are non-REM parasomnias associated with slow-wave sleep (Sheldon et al., 1992). Typically, children enter the deepest sleep of the night during the first 90-minute sleep cycle. Under normal conditions they will briefly arouse before descending into another deep, slow-wave sleep cycle. It is at this point when partial-arousal disorders are most likely to occur. Children with partial arousals do not fully arouse and do not transition normally between deep, slow-wave sleep and lighter sleep stages. Thus, they demonstrate characteristics indicative of both wakefulness (getting out of bed or talking) and sleep (eyes closed, incoherent speech; Rosen, Mahowald, & Ferber, 1995). These disorders share a number of characteristics, including occurrence during the first third of the night, amnesia for the event, and family history of partial-arousal disorders. Consultation with a sleep center or neurologist assists with the differential diagnosis of partial arousals and seizure disorders.

Confusional arousals

Confusional arousals, exhibited most often by infants and toddlers, can be extremely frightening for parents. These incidents typically begin with moaning or crying during the first third of the night. The symptoms may gradually escalate to the point of moderate agitation or disorientation and persist for up to 45 minutes. The child may get out of bed and walk around the room or become combative if an attempt is made to wake him or her. While the child often appears to be awake, he or she neither responds appropriately to tactile or verbal stimuli nor has recall of the event (Guilleminault, 1987). Although very disturbing for other family members, the symptoms of this disorder tend to dissipate with age (Thorpy, 1990).

Sleep terrors

Sleep terrors present similar to confusional arousals. However, there are important differences that distinguish the two disorders. Sleep terrors affect approximately 3% of older children, with peak incidence during school age or preadolescence (Thorpy, 1990). Whereas confusional arousals begin gradually, the onset of sleep terrors is sudden and intense. The child may sit up in bed, emit a piercing scream, and exhibit autonomic nervous system manifestations such as increased heart and respiratory rates, dilated pupils, and sweating. Some children also may get out of bed and run hysterically around the room yelling and crying. They often report the fear that something is going to get them. As with confusional arousals, attempts to console or wake the child will often exacerbate the incident (J. D. Kales, Kales, & Soldatos, 1980). The episodes usually end as quickly as they began, lasting approximately 1 to 5 minutes.

Sleepwalking

Some studies estimate that 40% of children exhibit sleepwalking sometime during childhood (Klackenberg, 1982). Sleepwalking may occur any time after a child learns to walk, with a peak incidence between 4 and 8 years of age (Thorpy, 1990). Sleepwalking behavior may range from calm to agitated. Children may perform complex tasks while sleepwalking, such as preparing and eating food or unlocking a door. The child may also display inappropriate behavior such as urinating in a corner. Although their activities appear purposeful, their actions are often uncoordinated and clumsy. Vocalizations may occur but are typically senseless or unintelligible (A. Kales, Soldatos, & Caldwell, 1980). The risk of self-injury is a central concern.

Sleep-Stage Transition Disorders

Sleep-stage transition parasomnias occur during sleep onset or between sleep stages. Any of these problems may occur in otherwise healthy individuals; thus, they are considered to be disorders of altered physiology as opposed to pathophysiology (Thorpy, 1990). Two of the most common problems in children include sleep talking and rhythmic-movement disorders.

Sleep talking

Sleep talking is common in children and rarely indicative of underlying psychological problems. Children of any age may exhibit sleep talking, which occurs during REM or non-REM sleep and can be triggered by talking to the child. During sleep talking episodes, the content of vocalizations may or may not be easily understood. Generally, sleep talking is of little concern unless it is extremely loud and disturbs others in the household.

Rhythmic-movement disorders

Rhythmic-movement disorders are repeated, stereotyped movements involving large-muscle groups. Examples include body rocking, head rolling, and head banging. These behaviors are common in infants: Bodyrocking has a mean-age onset of approximately 6 months, headbanging begins at 9 months, and headrolling begins at approximately 10 months (Thorpy, 1990). These behaviors typically remit between 2 and 4 years of age (Sheldon et al., 1992). Persistence of these behaviors into childhood and adolescence constitutes disorders with an associated psychogenic component (Sheldon et al.). Although there appear to be both a genetic component and gender predisposition (more males than females), rhythmic-movement parasomnias are also associated with central nervous system trauma and severe developmental delay. Rhythmic-movement disorders can be alarming to parents, but physical injury rarely results.

REM Sleep Disorders and Other Parasomnias

Pathophysiological REM mechanisms are assumed to underlie parasomnias that occur during REM sleep (Thorpy, 1990). Nightmares are a common example in children and are difficult to distinguish from partial arousals. Other parasomnias exist that also affect children and adolescents but are not associated with slow-wave sleep, sleep-stage transitions, or REM sleep. These include bruxism and sleep enuresis (Sheldon et al., 1992).

Nightmares

Between the ages of 3 and 6 years, 10% to 50% of children experience nightmares that bother their caregivers (Thorpy, 1990). Nightmares are long, frightening dreams that usually awaken the child from REM sleep. They may begin as early as 2 to 3 years, although children do not typically report having nightmares until they are 3 or 4 years old (Thorpy). The content of nightmares often involves some threat to the child or family members. If the child awakens screaming, nightmares can be difficult to distinguish from arousal disorders. However, there are several important defining characteristics which can be utilized to differentiate between the two.

Nightmares usually occur during the longest REM period in the last third of the night, whereas arousal disorders occur during the first third of the night. Generally, when the child awakens from a nightmare, there is clear recall, and the child is alert and oriented. Further, the child usually responds well to comforting. In arousal disorders, the child will usually appear confused and disoriented in response to awakenings, and adult intervention often exacerbates the symptoms (Sheldon et al., 1992). Unlike arousal disorders, nightmares rarely result in displacement from bed or self-injury.

Bruxism

Bruxism involves clenching or grinding the teeth while asleep and is common in infancy as teeth begin to develop. Typical onset of the clinical disorder occurs between the ages of 10 and 20 months, and approximately 5% of children present with clinical symptoms of the disorder (Thorpy, 1990). The child is unaware of episodes as they occur. Others in the household often report hearing loud grinding sounds emanating from the child's room. Bruxism may occur during any stage of sleep and usually consists of a 5- to 15-second interval repeated several times throughout the night. It may result in damage to the gums and crowns of the teeth, jaw and facial pain, and headaches (Gallagher, 1980). This problem may be associated with mental retardation and cerebral palsy.

Sleep enuresis

Bedwetting during the night is considered a diagnosable problem after age six (Thorpy, 1990). Considerable controversy exists about whether nocturnal enuresis constitutes a sleep problem. A thorough discussion of this issue is presented elsewhere (see Encopresis and Enuresis, this volume).

Factors Contributing to Sleep Problems

Limited information exists regarding the etiology of childhood sleep problems. Several studies have identified factors related to the presence of such problems that may play a role in problem maintenance. These include factors related to individual child functioning (biological or psychological factors) as well as factors that influence caregiver perceptions and behavior in response to the sleep pattern exhibited (social/environmental influences; Adair & Bauchner, 1993). In general, sleep problems may arise from and be maintained by the complex interaction of these factors. Thus, to understand sleep problems and effectively intervene, professionals need information regarding each of these areas (Marks & Monroe, 1976).

Child functioning: Biological factors

Neurophysiological development is central to the development of sleep patterns. Brain maturation and internal regulatory processes play an integral role in sleep and are particularly salient as the consolidation of sleep patterns evolves in infancy. In addition to the neurological substrate responsible for regulating sleep, evidence suggests that perinatal factors, such as asphyxia or premature birth, may contribute to night awakenings and problems with sleep organization (Adair & Bauchner, 1993). Variations in child temperament have also been found to affect sleep patterns. For example, low sensory threshold and high activity level have been found to distinguish children with sleep disturbances from those with no sleep problems (Richman, 1987). These factors influence the development of sleep early in childhood.

Other biological factors that may emerge during a child's development include acute and chronic medical conditions. In particular, those causing discomfort due to pain, fever, or respiratory difficulties (e.g., asthma) place children at risk for sleep disturbances (Mrazek, Anderson, & Strunk, 1985). Additionally, medications commonly prescribed to children and adolescents may negatively affect sleep quality. For example, antibiotics used to treat infections may be associated with delayed sleep onset or disturbed sleep. Psychostimulants, anticonvulsants, and preparations for asthma symptoms may also affect arousal and cause sleep disturbance. Thus, children with health problems may also have difficulty in daily functioning as a result of sleep disruptions secondary to their physical condition.

Child functioning: Psychological factors

Emotional problems and psychiatric conditions are often associated with sleep disturbance (Marks & Monroe, 1976). One of the most common psychiatric diagnoses in childhood that may be accompanied by sleep problems is Attention-Deficit/Hyperactivity Disorder (ADHD). Parents of children diagnosed with this disorder frequently report difficulty with bedtime struggles. Fragmented, restless sleep and frequent night awakenings have also been described (Kaplan, McNicol, Conte, & Moghadam, 1987). Children with ADHD tend to have shorter sleep durations and more frequent early morning awakenings than nondiagnosed children. Children with ADHD and chronic sleep problems may be sleep deprived, which contributes to the daytime symptoms of ADHD. Alternatively, some children are erroneously diagnosed with ADHD due to daytime behavior problems that mimic ADHD symptoms but are actually due to primary sleep problems and chronic sleep deprivation. School professionals working with children exhibiting symptoms of ADHD should consider assessing the child's sleep patterns. If sleep disturbances are also present, further assessment of symptom duration and quality may be helpful in differentiating the problem. For example, diagnosis of ADHD requires at least a 6-month duration and onset prior to age seven. Referral for further evaluation may assist in proper diagnosis and treatment. However, behavioral interventions for sleep problems can be helpful even if the cause of the sleep disturbance is not well understood.

Other psychiatric disorders, such as anxiety and depression, often present with secondary sleep problems. Of all children referred for the treatment of phobias, 15% suffer from severe nighttime fears (Graziano & De-Giovanni, 1979). Clinical anxiety also has been found to be associated with nightmares (Mindell, 1993). Separation anxiety often becomes an issue at bedtime and may result in bedtime struggles. Similarly, children with depressive disorders may experience insomnia or restlessness. Even psychosocial stress that does not cause marked clinical symptoms may interfere with sleep. For example, marital problems, parental affective illness, or the start of school may interfere with the child's ability to sleep or the caregivers' ability to be supportive of the child and set consistent bedtime limits. Adolescents report that the most frequent causes of chronic poor sleep are worries, tensions, and personal problems (Carskadon, 1992). Thus, in instances where sleep problems occur secondary to chronic psychiatric disturbance, it is important to consider referral for treatment of the primary problem.

Children with developmental delays have been known to experience serious sleep problems. Neuropathology accompanying or causing mental impairment may interfere with sleep architecture and circadian rhythms. Despite the fact that many studies fail to properly control for different subtypes of cognitive disabilities, research suggests that individuals with Down's syndrome, cerebral palsy, and other nonspecific mental disabilities have a higher prevalence of sleep problems compared to children with no mental impairment (Stores, 1992). The most common sleep problems for children with mental disabilities include insomnia, night awakenings, and short sleep duration (Stores). Children with certain types of developmental syndromes may exhibit a predisposition for specific sleep problems. For example, obstructive sleep apnea is common in children with Down's syndrome (Stores). Children with mental disabilities also may experience sleep problems as a result of psychiatric disturbances associated with their conditions (Stores).

Social/Environmental influences: Sleep hygiene

Sleep hygiene includes those "conditions and practices that promote continuous and effective sleep" (Sheldon et al., 1992, p. 246). When sleep hygiene is inadequate, increased arousal or disruptions in sleep organization may result in insomnia. Poor sleep hygiene practices are often used to combat the insomnia, inadvertently contributing to the sleep problem. For example, parents of children exhibiting separation difficulties or bedtime struggles may allow the child to sleep in the parents' room, further exacerbating the child's separation anxiety and inability to fall asleep in his or her own bed.

Sleep research has identified several general guidelines applicable to all levels of development. Common suggestions for younger children include:

- Consistency between parents regarding bedtime.
- Calming activities at bedtime such as a bath or a story.
- A regular bedtime that occurs when the child is sleepy as opposed to when it is convenient for parents.
- Transition objects for the child to take to bed as a source of comfort (e.g., stuffed animal).
- A comfortable and inviting room environment (e.g., a night-light).
- Maintaining positive parent-child interactions at bedtime.

- A consistent bedtime routine that includes going to the bathroom prior to getting into bed. (Cuthbertson & Schevill, 1985).

Suggestions for older children and adolescents include a quiet sleep environment, comfortable room temperature (<75 degrees), a consistent bedtime schedule and routine, minimizing fluids and vigorous activity prior to bedtime, and avoiding caffeine and theophylline (Hauri, 1982).

Social/Environmental influences: Social stressors

Stressful social situations such as poor housing, financial burdens, and illness are more common in families whose children have problematic sleep patterns than in those whose children are good sleepers (Lozoff et al., 1985). Social stresses that affect a child's sleep may also directly minimize the caregiver's ability to effectively manage bedtime behavior and sleep difficulties (Richman, 1987). Rates of marital conflict and maternal depression have been found to be higher in children with sleep problems compared to children with no sleep problems (Richman, 1981).

Social/Environmental influences: Parent-child interactions

Interpersonal relationships may also impact sleep behaviors, especially early in life when children depend on the caregiver to structure the bedtime routine. Some of the sleep problems discussed previously are directly influenced by caregiver behaviors, and many sleep problems may be perpetuated by caregiver responses. Some practitioners have emphasized the role of parent-child attachment issues in sleep problems (Daws, 1993). Significantly greater numbers of children with sleep problems have insecure attachments to their mothers compared to children with no sleep problems (Adair & Bauchner, 1993).

A practice relevant to the issue of attachment is cosleeping, or sleeping with caregivers. Cosleeping is not socially sanctioned in the United States but is a common practice in some American families with young children as well as in other cultures and most nonindustrialized countries (Lozoff, 1995). Sleeping with caregivers has been linked to disrupted sleep in American children, particularly bedtime struggles and night awakenings (Lozoff). Although it is unclear whether cosleeping *causes* disrupted sleep or results from it, cosleeping usually only resolves sleep problems in the short term (Lozoff).

Contribution of Sleep to Daily Functioning

Children with sleep problems may experience decrements in daily functioning, which are particularly problematic for school-aged children and adolescents. For example, sleep deprivation may result in oversleeping in the morning; excessive sleepiness during the school day; behavioral problems in the classroom; and decrements in academic functioning, including perceptual, cognitive, and psychomotor capabilities (Dahl & Carskadon, 1995; Mindell, 1993). Children who are tardy to school, exhibit changes in academic performance for the worse, persistently look physically fatigued, or nap during classes should be suspect for potential sleep disturbances. Although these behaviors may occur as a matter of course for adolescents, they may also be indicative of sleep deprivation and insomnia in this age group (Carskadon, 1992). One study reported that 21% of a sample of preadolescent poor sleepers had failed at least one year of school (Kahn et al., 1989).

Sleep problems not only affect the child's well-being but have an impact on others as well (Bootzin & Chambers, 1990). Caregivers stand to benefit from changes in the child's sleep patterns, particularly for bedtime struggles, frequent awakenings, problems napping, and several of the parasomnias (Ferber, 1995b). Parents of children with sleep problems often report marital difficulties, disruptions in social activities, and adverse effects on siblings (particularly those who share the same room with the child). Successful treatment for children with sleep problems has been shown to be associated with improvements in parental sleep and family satisfaction (Mindell & Durand, 1993). Given the prevalence and impact of childhood sleep problems, the importance of treatments which improve child functioning, improve the sleep and well-being of all family members residing in the home, and reduce caregiver frustration should not be underestimated.

Alternative Actions

Unfortunately, medical professionals often recommend ineffective strategies to address childhood sleep problems, including changing the child's diet, consoling the parents, and prescribing sedatives for the child (Mindell & Holst, 1991). Moreover, many sleep problems in children go undiagnosed and untreated until daytime symptoms such as excessive somnolence, learning problems, and behavioral difficulties are observed in the school setting (Bootzin & Chambers, 1990). Thus, school professionals may play an important role in assisting the child and family with appropriate referrals or suggestions to effectively manage sleep problems. Although research regarding the etiology and nature of childhood sleep problems is limited, several treatment strategies have been borrowed from adult practice (Bootzin & Chambers). As illustrated in Table 1, different strategies are effective for each type of sleep problem or disorder, and both medical and behavioral interventions should be considered (Edwards & Christophersen, 1994).

Medical Interventions

Based on their success with adults, medications have been used to help children who have problems falling asleep or sleeping through the night. Chavin and Tinson (1980) reported that 71% of the children referred to them with sleep problems had been previously prescribed medications. However, limited research has been conducted regarding the effectiveness of medications for child sleep problems (Edwards & Christophersen, 1994). The potential side effects associated with medications (convulsions, decreased mental alertness, etc.) continue to be of concern to parents and medical professionals.

Of the medications utilized with children and adolescents, antihistamines such as Benadryl, tricyclic antidepressants, and benzodiazepines or antianxiety agents such as Clonidine provide the most effective pharmacological treatment for sleeplessness and night awakenings (Adair & Bauchner, 1993). Hypnotics (e.g., chloral hydrate) may also be prescribed. Antidepressants and anticonvulsants are often used to suppress Stage IV and REM sleep in patients with narcolepsy or parasomnias. The major disadvantage of these agents is their marginal impact and short-term effectiveness in managing sleep problems. In addition, many agents have paradoxical effects that can exacerbate sleep problems. Thus, it is recommended that pharmacological interventions only be used to provide short-term amelioration of sleep problems and in combination with behavioral interventions for long-term problem management.

Some sleep problems require medical interventions that are not pharmacological in nature. For example, children with OSA may have their tonsils and adenoids removed, use a breathing device at night called "nasal-continuous positive-airway pressure" to deliver air under pressure through a face mask, or be required to lose weight if obesity is a contributing factor. These interventions do not usually interfere with the child's daily routines.

Behavioral Interventions

Behavioral strategies may be helpful irrespective of the presenting sleep problem. These strategies include improving sleep hygiene, charting the sleep problem in a diary format, and improving the match between child and caregiver sleep patterns or between child sleep patterns and caregiver expectations. Written instructions and self-help manuals to assist parents with interventions may also be useful.

Other behavioral interventions have been found to be effective in managing specific sleep problems. Several effective behavioral strategies are available for extrinsic dyssomnias. For example, treatment of adjustment sleep disorder typically involves stimulus-control procedures to

Table 1 *Common Treatments for Childhood Sleep Problems*

Sleep Problem	Type of Treatment	
	Medical	**Behavioral**
Obstructive sleep apnea	Tonsil/adenoidectomy, nasal steroids, C-PAP	Weight loss, positional therapy
Narcolepsy	Tricyclic antidepressants, stimulants	Supportive therapy to address coping with symptoms
Adjustment sleep disorder	Not usually indicated	Therapy targeting precipitating life stressor, stimulus control
Limit-setting sleep disorder	Not usually indicated	Systematic ignoring, graduated extinction, bedtime routine
Sleep-onset association disorder	Not usually indicated	Systematic ignoring, graduated extinction, bedtime routine
Delayed sleep phase syndrome	Melatonin (experimental)	Gradually advance morning awakenings, advance bedtime
Advanced sleep phase syndrome	Not usually indicated	Delay bedtime
Insomnia	Short-term use of sedatives, hypnotics	Stimulus control procedures, sleep hygiene
Confusional arousals	Not usually indicated	Safety precautions, do not arouse child, sleep hygiene
Sleep terrors	Benzodiazepenes or antidepressants (rarely used)	Scheduled awakenings, safety precautions, do not arouse child, sleep hygiene
Sleep walking	Not usually indicated	Scheduled awakenings, safety precautions, do not arouse child, sleep hygiene
Nightmares	Not usually indicated	Comforting by parent, removal of frightening stimuli, relaxation training, hypnosis
Sleep talking	Not usually indicated	Reassure parents
Sleep paralysis	Not usually indicated	Comforting by parent
Bruxism	Not usually indicated	Dental management, biofeedback

manage the symptoms of insomnia. The goals of stimulus-control procedures are to minimize behaviors incompatible with sleep and to regulate the circadian rhythm. For example, children are not allowed to play games or do homework in bed. In the event that sleep onset does not occur within 20 minutes of being in bed, the child is instructed to get up and engage in a monotonous, quiet activity until he or she feels sleepy (Bootzin & Nicassio, 1978). This typically involves sitting in a straight-back chair and reading a nonstimulating book. These steps are repeated as often as necessary until sleep onset occurs.

Systematic ignoring and graduated extinction are two similar interventions that have been found to be helpful with bedtime struggles and night awakenings—behaviors commonly present in preschool or school-age children with limit-setting sleep disorder or sleep-onset association disorder. Systematic ignoring refers to intentionally refraining from contact with the child during the child's attempts to gain interaction (e.g., crying, screaming, calling out for a caregiver). Because this is so difficult for many parents, particularly those setting minimal lim-

its, a modified approach, called graduated extinction, was developed. Graduated extinction allows the caregiver to respond to distress from the child on a progressively less frequent basis. Adults initially enter the child's room; limit their visit to a few minutes regardless of the child's responses; provide brief, minimally stimulating contact and reassurance; and gradually increase the duration between return visits to the child's room until the child falls asleep without their presence (Ferber, 1985c). It is helpful to advise caregivers that initial attempts to set limits around the child's bedtime behavior may result in increased behavioral resistance from their child as the child attempts to get what he or she wants, for example, to stay up or stay with the adults. It is common for caregivers to respond to a child's crying or screaming by physically or verbally consoling the child and removing the bedtime limit. Setting limits will only be effective when caregivers continue to ignore the child's resistance and maintain the limit being set. Once a child learns that they are not going to give in and revoke the limit, the undesirable behavior will dissipate quickly. It is important to give the parents or caregivers permission to maintain bedtime limits despite the child's distressful displays and support them when they are effective in doing this.

For delayed sleep-phase disorder, the child's bedtime needs to be advanced to an earlier hour. Because this proves difficult for many caregivers and children, interventions have been designed to gradually advance the morning awakening to maximize the child's sleepiness in the evening. In severe cases, chronotherapy is recommended. This treatment requires the child's bedtime to be progressively delayed later around the clock each evening until the desired bedtime is attained. The stimulus-control procedures described earlier may minimize concomitant insomnia. Problems due to advanced sleep-phase disorder are very rare but, when present, require shifting the schedule to a later bedtime while morning awakenings occur progressively later.

Caregivers may become quite distressed in response to the dramatic symptoms that often accompany the parasomnias. However, parasomnias are rarely indicative of psychopathology (Rosen et al., 1995). Reassurance to parents may decrease their distress. For those disorders that may potentially result in harm to children, instructions regarding how parents can ensure their child's safety without being overly invasive and thus exacerbating the symptoms should be provided. Other symptoms of partial arousals (irregular sleep patterns and sleep deprivation) may threaten the child's safety. Thus, sleep hygiene is also important (Dahl & Williamson, 1990). Relaxation and mental imagery may also be used to decrease stress in children with partial arousal disorders (Kohen, Rosen, & Mahowald, 1992). Another effective intervention for partial arousals is the use of scheduled awakenings. Awakening the child until alert approximately 30 minutes prior to the time he or she typically has a partial-arousal incident is hypothesized to disrupt slow-wave deep sleep and eliminates night terrors and sleepwalking (e.g., Lask, 1988).

Sleep-stage transition disorders, REM-associated disorders, and the other parasomnias typically require minimal intervention. For example, unless disturbing to family members, sleep talking is not usually problematic, and no interventions are recommended. Children with nightmares usually respond well to comforting by caregivers and will often quickly return to sleep. Frightening stories and television programs should be eliminated for children with frequent nightmares. Rhythmic movement disorders rarely cause serious injury. Placing rhythmic objects in the child's room, such as a clock or a metronome, and moving the child's bed away from the walls are two strategies commonly recommended for younger children. In older children, these behaviors are often associated with emotional factors that may warrant evaluation for psychotherapy. The symptoms of bruxism can be controlled with a mouth guard worn at night to prevent teeth from grinding together. Because stress can precipitate nonarousal parasomnias, stress management procedures

such as relaxation, biofeedback, and mental imagery may be beneficial in minimizing these problems (Mahowald & Thorpy, 1995).

In general, behavioral management procedures can be useful in addressing most childhood sleep problems. Implementing effective behavioral interventions requires that professionals have regular contact with the child's caregivers and be active in helping monitor and address the child's behaviors at home.

Summary

The development of sleep involves complex changes in the sleep/wake and REM/non-REM cycles. Many of these changes begin during the first year of life and continue into adulthood. As changes occur, deviations from normal sleep may result in sleep problems. Bedtime struggles and frequent night awakenings are common during preschool or latency age. Complaints of insomnia and daytime fatigue are common during adolescence. Some problems may evolve into formal sleep disorders. Sleep disorders include dyssomnias (i.e., difficulties initiating and maintaining sleep, excessive sleepiness) and parasomnias (i.e., problems associated with sleep or sleep-stage transitions). Several factors may exacerbate or play a role in maintaining sleep problems, including individual child functioning and socioenvironmental factors.

Sleep problems that persist over time may result in decreased academic performance and behavioral changes such as inattentiveness, problems concentrating, and increased irritability. Medical and behavioral strategies may improve children's sleep and consequently benefit others living in the home. Medications are only rarely indicated and may be limited by their potential side effects, short-acting effects, or minimal data supporting their use with children. Several behavioral interventions have been found to provide effective, long-term amelioration of several types of childhood sleep problems. Given the number of children who experience sleep problems and the potential impact of poor sleep on children's behavioral, socioemotional, and academic functioning, school professionals play an important role in assisting children and their families to identify and address sleep problems.

Recommended Resources

Books for Parents and Practitioners

Cuthbertson, J., & Schevill, S. (1985). *Helping your child sleep through the night.* New York: Double Day.
The authors present age-appropriate information about sleep

patterns and practical strategies to use with children between the ages of infancy and 5 years.

Ferber, R. (1985). *Solve your child's sleep problems.* New York: Simon & Schuster.
Ferber summarizes years of clinical experience into a helpful guide for parents. The book provides information for parents about how to recognize children's sleep problems, how to intervene with many types of problems, and when to pursue professional help.

Schaefer, C. E., & Millman, H. L. (1981). *How to help children with common problems.* New York: Van Nostrand Reinhold.
A subsection of this book (pp. 177–200) is devoted specifically to sleep problems. Several common sleep disturbances in children are reviewed with examples and strategies for managing each type provided.

Huntley, R. (1991). *The sleep book for tired parents: Help for solving children's sleep problems.* Seattle, WA: Parenting Press.
This is a user-friendly guide to common sleep problems in young children. Parents are presented with several suggestions to assist them in problem definition and developing an individualized family plan. Supportive information and resources for parents are provided.

Lansky, V. (1991). *Getting your child to sleep and back to sleep.* Deephaven, MN: Book Peddlers.
This easy-to-read book addressing bedtime routines, colic, night fears, cosleeping, parasomnias, and parental loss of sleep is written from the perspective of a parent with a sleepless child. It directs parents to several relevant services and written resources.

Weissbluth, M. (1987). *Healthy sleep habits, happy child.* New York: Fawcett Columbine.
Information regarding typical sleep patterns, potential problems, and practical interventions are specifically detailed for five different age categories. Sleep disorders and special concerns (e.g., working moms) also are discussed.

Books for Children

Berry, J. W. (1987). *Every kid's guide to understanding nightmares.* Sebostopol, CA: Living Skills Press.
Using vivid cartoons, the author describes nightmares, typical emotional responses children feel in response to nightmares, and steps children can take in preventing and coping with nightmares.

Berry, J. W. (1987). *Teach me about bedtime.* Sebostopol, CA: Living Skills Press.
This is a colorfully illustrated book about a toddler's need for sleep and her nap and bedtime routines.

Coatsworth, E. (1972). *Good night.* New York: MacMillan.
As darkness falls, a star rises and watches over the animals and a boy down below.

Mayer, Mercer (1983). *Just go to bed.* New York: Western Publishing.
A young "critter" and his parents demonstrate the steps of a bedtime routine, despite the "critter's" desire to just play.

Ormerod, J. (1993). *Midnight pillow fight.* Cambridge, MA: Candlewick Press.
After awakening in the middle of the night, a young girl engages in a fight with several pillows and independently falls back to sleep.

References

Adair, R. H., & Bauchner, H. (1993). Sleep problems in childhood. *Current Problems in Pediatrics,* 147–170.

Anders, T. F., Sadeh, A., & Appareddy, V. (1995). Normal sleep in neonates and children. In R. Ferber & M. H. Kryger (Eds.), *Principles and practice of sleep medicine in the child* (pp. 7–18). Philadelphia: W. B. Saunders.

Anders, T. F., & Weinstein, P. (1972). Sleep and its disorders in infants and children: A review. *Pediatrics, 50*(2), 312–324.

Beltramini, A. U., & Hertzig, M. E. (1983). Sleep and bedtime behavior in preschool-aged children. *Pediatrics, 71*(2), 153–158.

Bootzin, R. R., & Chambers, M. J. (1990). Childhood sleep disorders. In A. M. Gross & R. S. Drabman (Eds.), *Handbook of clinical behavioral pediatrics* (pp. 205–229). New York: Plenum Press.

Bootzin, R. R., & Nicassio, P. M. (1978). Behavioral treatment for insomnia. In M. Hersen, R. Eisler, & P. Miller (Eds.), *Progress in behavior modification* (pp. 1–45). New York: Academic Press.

Carroll, J. L., & Laughlin, G. M. (1995). Obstructive sleep syndromes in infants and children: Clinical features and pathophysiology. In R. Ferber & M. Kryger (Eds.), *Principles and practice of sleep medicine in the child* (pp. 163–191). Philadelphia: W. G. Saunders.

Carskadon, M. A. (1992). Sleep disturbances. In S. B. Friedman, M. Fisher, & S. K. Schonberg (Eds.), *Comprehensive adolescent health care* (pp. 747–754). St. Louis, MO: Quality Medical Publishing.

Challamel, M., Mazzola, M., Nevsimalva, S., Cannard, C., Louis, J., & Revol, M. (1994). Narcolepsy in children. *Sleep, 17,* 517–520.

Chavin, W., & Tinson, S. (1980). Child with sleep difficulties. *Health Visitor, 53,* 477–480.

Cuthbertson, J., & Schevill, S. (1985). *Helping your child sleep through the night.* New York: Double Day.

Dahl, R., Bernhisel-Broadbent, J., Scanlon-Holdford, S., Sampson, H., & Lupo, M. (1995). Sleep disturbances in children with atopic dermatitis. *Archives of Pediatric and Adolescent Medicine, 149,* 856–860.

Dahl, R. E., & Carskadon, M. A. (1995). Sleep and its disorders in adolescence. In R. Ferber & M. Kryger (Eds.), *Principles and practice of sleep medicine in the child* (pp. 19–27). Philadelphia: W. G. Saunders.

Dahl, R., & Williamson, D. E. (1990). Aggressive partial arousal preceding competitive football games. *Sleep Research, 19,* 160–167.

Daws, D. (1993). *Through the night: Helping parents and sleepless infants.* London: Free Association Books.

Edwards, K. J., & Christophersen, E. R. (1994). Treating common sleep problems of young children. *Developmental and Behavioral Pediatrics, 15*(3), 207–213.

Ferber, R. (1995a). Assessment of sleep disorders in the child. In R. Ferber & M. Kryger (Eds.), *Principles and practice of sleep medicine in the child* (pp. 45–53). Philadelphia: W. B. Saunders.

Ferber, R. (1995b). Introduction: Pediatric sleep disorders medicine. In R. Ferber & M. Kryger (Eds.), *Principles and practice of sleep medicine in the child* (pp. 1–5). Philadelphia: W. B. Saunders.

Ferber, R. (1995c). Sleeplessness in children. In R. Ferber & M. Kryger (Eds.), *Principles and practice of sleep medicine in the child* (pp. 79–89). Philadelphia: W. B. Saunders.

Gallagher, S. J. (1980). Diagnosis and treatment of bruxism: A review of the literature. *General Dentistry, 28,* 62–80.

Graziano, A. M., & DeGiovanni, I. S. (1979). The clinical significance of childhood phobias: A note on the proportion of child-clinic referrals for treatment of children's fears. *Behavior Research Therapy, 17,* 161–162.

Guilleminault, C. (1987). Narcolepsy and its differential diagnosis. In C. Guilleminault (Ed.), *Sleep and its disorders in children* (pp. 181–194). New York: Raven Press.

Hauri, P. (1982). *Current concepts: The sleep disorders.* Kalamazoo, MI: Upjohn Company.

Kahn, A., Van de Merckt, C., Rebuffat, E., Mozin, M. J., Sottiaux, M., Blum, D., & Hennart, P. (1989). Sleep problems in healthy preadolescents. *Pediatrics, 84,* 542–546.

Kales, A., Soldatos, C. R., & Caldwell, A. B. (1980). Somnambulism: Clinical characteristics and personality patterns. *Archives of General Psychiatry, 37,* 1406–1412.

Kales, J. D., Kales, A., & Soldatos, C. R. (1980). Night terrors: Clinical characteristics and personality patterns. *Archives of General Psychiatry, 37,* 1413–1421.

Kaplan, B., McNicol, J., Conte, R., & Moghadam, H. (1987). Sleep disturbance in preschool-aged hyperactive and nonhyperactive children. *Pediatrics, 80*(6), 839–844.

Kataria, S., Swanson, M., & Trevathan, G. E. (1987). Persistence of sleep disturbances in preschool children. *The Journal of Pediatrics, 110*(4), 642–646.

Klackenberg, G. (1982). Somnambulism in childhood: Prevalence, course, and behavioral correlations. *Acta Paediatrics Scandinavia, 71,* 495–501.

Kohen, D., Rosen, G. M., & Mahowald, M. W. (1992). Sleep terror disorder in children: The role of self-hypnosis in management. *The American Journal of Self Hypnosis, 34,* 233–239.

Lask, B. (1988). Novel and non-toxic treatment for night terrors. *British Medical Journal, 297,* 592.

Lozoff, B. (1995). Culture and family: Influences on childhood sleep practices and problems. In R. Ferber & M. Kryger (Eds.), *Principles and practice of sleep medicine in the child* (pp. 69–73). Philadelphia: W. G. Saunders.

Lozoff, B., Wolf, A. W., & Davis, N. S. (1985). Sleep problems seen in pediatric practice. *Pediatrics, 75*(3), 477–483.

Mahowald, M. W., & Thorpy, M. J. (1995). Nonarousal parasomnias in the child. In R. Ferber & M. Kryger (Eds.), *Principles and practice of sleep medicine in the child* (pp. 115–123). Philadelphia: W. G. Saunders.

Marks, P. A., & Monroe, L. J. (1976). Correlates of adolescent poor sleepers. *Journal of Abnormal Psychology, 85*(2), 243–246.

Mindell, J. A. (1993). Sleep disorders in children. *Health Psychology, 12*(2), 151–162.

Mindell, J. A., & Durand, V. M. (1993). Treatment of childhood sleep disorders: Generalization across disorders and effects on family members. *Journal of Pediatric Psychology, 18*(6), 731–750.

Mindell, J. A., & Holst, S. K. (1991). Pediatricians and sleep problems in young children: Views and treatment recommendations. *Sleep Research, 20,* 105.

Morrison, D. N., McGee, R., & Stanton, W. R. (1992). Sleep problems in adolescence. *Journal of the American Academy of Child and Adolescent Psychiatry, 31*(1), 94–99.

Mrazek, D., Anderson, I., & Strunk, R. (1985). Disturbed emotional development in severely asthmatic preschool children. In J. Stevenson (Ed.), *Recent research in developmental psychopathology* (pp. 81–94). Oxford: Pergamon Press.

Richman, N. (1981). Sleep problems in young children. *Archives of Disease in Childhood, 56,* 491–493.

Richman, N. (1987). Surveys of sleep disorders in children in a general population. In C. Guillemnault (Ed.), *Sleep and Its Disorders in Children* (pp. 115–127). New York: Raven Press.

Rosen, G., Mahowald, M. W., & Ferber, R. (1995). Sleepwalking, confusional arousals, and sleep terrors in the child. In R. Ferber & M. Kryger (Eds.), *Principles and practice of sleep medicine in the child* (pp. 99–106). Philadelphia: W. B. Saunders.

Sheldon, S. H., Spire, J. P., & Levy, H. B. (1992). Parasomnias. In J. Fletchers (Ed.), *Pediatric sleep medicine.* Philadelphia: W. B. Saunders.

Stores, G. (1992). Sleep studies in children with a mental handicap. *Journal of Child Psychiatry, 33*(8), 1303–1317.

Strauch, I., & Meier, B. (1988). Sleep need in adolescents: A longitudinal approach. *Sleep, 11*(4), 378–386.

Thorpy, M. J. (Ed.). (1990). *International classification of sleep disorders: Diagnostic and coding manual.* Rochester, MN: American Sleep Disorders Association.

78

Encopresis and Enuresis

Mark W. Steege
University of Southern Maine

Encopresis and *enuresis* are biobehavioral problems that present a complex set of diagnostic and intervention issues. These disorders typically have multiple causes, topographies, and social-emotional consequences. From a biobehavioral perspective, behaviors such as encopresis and enuresis are often directly related to biological constraints. However, through the application of learning-based treatments, and resulting behavior change, these biological constraints themselves are altered (Mellon & Houts, 1995). Effective interventions for encopresis and enuresis should be based on multidisciplinary evaluations, thorough behavioral assessment, and individually tailored treatment approaches that address biological and behavioral components of the disorder.

Encopresis

Background and Development

Functional encopresis refers to the repeated passage of feces into inappropriate places (e.g., clothing or floor). For a formal diagnosis, the behavior occurs at least once per month for 3 months, although children with this disorder may experience several soiling episodes per day (Mellon & Houts, 1995). The child must be at least 4 years of age for formal diagnosis, and physical disorders that cause incontinence such as aganglionic megacolon must be ruled out (American Psychiatric Association, 1994).

Estimates of the prevalence of encopresis among children vary, ranging from 0.5% to 10% with most figures ranging between 2% and 3% (Mellon & Houts, 1995). The incidence of encopresis tends to diminish with age. Approximately 1% of 5-year-olds experience encopresis (American Psychiatric Association, 1994) and the incidence lowers to 0.75% for 10- to 12-year-olds. The incidence rate is considerably higher in males than females, with male/female estimates ranging from 6:1 to 2:1 (Levine, 1982; Mellon & Houts, 1995).

Subtypes

Several classification systems have been proposed as means of identifying various subtypes of encopresis. The American Psychiatric Association proposed one classification system in 1987 and a modified method of classifying encopresis in 1994. The former classification system distinguishes between primary and secondary encopresis. Children with primary encopresis have not, at any time, attained bowel continence for a period of at least one year. Children with secondary encopresis have attained fecal continence of at least one year at some point in their development (American Psychiatric Association, 1987). In 1994, the American Psychiatric Association specified two subtypes: Encopresis with constipation and overflow incontinence involves (a) evidence of constipation, (b) poorly formed feces and continuous fecal leakage, occurring both during the day and during sleep, (c) passage of only small amounts of feces during bowel movements, and (d) resolution of the encopresis upon treatment of constipation (American Psychiatric Association, 1994). With the second subtype, encopresis without constipation and overflow incontinence, there is no evidence of constipation. Feces tend to be of normal form and consistency and soiling is intermittent (American Psychiatric Association, 1994).

Boon and Singh (1991) and Mellon and Houts (1995) draw a distinction between retentive encopresis and nonretentive encopresis. Children with retentive encopresis experience chronic constipation, reports of abdominal pain, painful passage of large diameter stools, and frequent daily accidents. Nonretentive encopresis is characterized by one to two soiling accidents per day with normal stool size and consistency. The role of the school psychologist is to clearly identify and describe the referred child's bowel history and habits. The classification of a child's particular type of encopresis is helpful to the degree that it leads to the identification and implementation of effective treatment methodologies.

Etiology

Approximately 80% of children who experience encopresis present a history of chronic constipation (Christophersen, 1994). Christophersen (1994) identified three factors that play a role in constipation: (a) insufficient bulk or roughage in the diet; (b) bland diet, such as one too high in dairy products, without enough counteracting bulk; and (c) insufficient intake of fluids by mouth. Other factors reported to contribute to the development of encopresis are family problems, changing schools, doorless toilet stalls, travel, birth of a sibling, early toilet training, fecal retention, and medications (Christophersen & Edwards, 1992). Any of these factors or combinations of them may contribute to constipation and encopresis.

The development of normal bowel control involves specific prerequisite skills. The skills necessary for the muscular coordination involved in normal bowel control are (a) using bodily cues to discriminate the need to defecate, (b) finding the appropriate place to have a bowel movement, (c) undressing and sitting on the toilet, (d) executing the valsalva maneuver (i.e., the muscular mechanisms that force the passage of feces), and (e) receiving reinforcement for this complex sequence of events (Mellon & Houts, 1995). Encopresis results when this chain of behaviors is broken. Children with chronic constipation may over time experience difficulty in detecting bodily signals that cue the need to defecate.

Christophersen (1991) and Christophersen and Edwards (1992) described a pattern of constipation and encopresis. Often times children with chronic constipation will experience seepage around the hard stool that results in a smearing, staining, or streaking of fecal matter in the underwear. Although these children are constipated, it appears that they are experiencing numerous watery, foul-smelling soiling accidents. Occasionally, a child will pass excessively large stools and will then have a period of several days of no soiling followed by the recurrence of constipation (Christophersen & Edwards, 1992). This constipation-encopresis cycle continues until the constipation is resolved and the child is taught appropriate bowel habits.

Problems and Implications

Encopresis can play a significant role in the development of related inappropriate behaviors and feelings of frustration, guilt, and helplessness. Many children who experience encopresis report fears of discovery and ridicule by parents, siblings, and peers (Simonson, 1987). For example, children with encopresis frequently hide soiled clothing to avoid discovery (Steege & Harper, 1989).

Some children who evidence encopresis also present social-emotional problems (Friman, Mathews, Finney, Christophersen, & Leibowitz, 1988; Gabel, Chandra, & Schindledecker, 1988). Some children display acting out behaviors such as verbal opposition and/or aggression while other children are socially withdrawn. Discovery of occurrences of encopresis often lead to parent-child con-

flicts. In most cases, social-emotional problems are considered to be the result of soiling or the ramifications of encopresis (Christophersen, 1994). Psychological problems associated with encopresis are most likely consequential rather than antecedent (Christophersen & Edwards, 1992).

Alternative Actions

Assessment of encopresis typically begins with a thorough medical evaluation involving a clinical history, full physical, and a rectal examination. This evaluation should determine the presence or absence of organic involvement and any medical causes of encopresis (Mellon & Houts, 1995). A behavioral assessment should be conducted to determine the behavioral components associated with encopresis and as the foundation for designing an intervention strategy.

Behavioral assessment of encopresis should address the following variables: (a) developmental milestones, (b) previous attempts at toilet training, (c) readiness skills for development of appropriate toileting, and (d) antecedents and consequences associated with soiling accidents that may be maintaining encopresis. Behavioral interviews with the parents/caregivers and the child are recommended. While behavioral observations of the child's toileting skills are also recommended (e.g., Mellon & Houts, 1995), this practice may not be appropriate for the school psychologist. Interviews with those familiar with the child's toileting habits, parents, caregivers, and/or teachers, are recommended. To establish baseline rates of responding and to evaluate the frequency and topography of soiling, behavioral ratings should be completed for 2 weeks by parents and/or other caregivers measuring the following variables: (a) soiling accidents, (b) appropriate bowel movements in the toilet, (c) the size and consistency of soiling accidents and appropriate bowel movements, (d) time and place of soiling accidents and appropriate bowel movements (Mellon & Houts, 1995).

A wide variety of intervention strategies have been used to successfully treat encopresis. Most treatments for encopresis have included a combination of medical and behavioral approaches (Christophersen & Edwards, 1992). Specific medical procedures have included the use of suppositories and enemas, high fiber diets, and stool softeners such as mineral oil (Mellon & Houts, 1995). Specific behavioral approaches have included toileting skills training, discrimination training, mild punishment for soiling accidents, positive reinforcement for appropriate toileting, biofeedback, and positive reinforcement for clean underwear (Christophersen & Edwards, 1992; Mellon & Houts, 1995). In general treatment packages that incorporate several approaches are more successful than intervention plans based on singular methodologies.

Moreover, it is important to tailor the intervention to the specific needs of the student. Intervention packages based on the results of thorough behavioral and medical assessments and designed in collaboration with parents and team members generally have the highest probability of success.

Because most cases of encopresis are related to biological factors that the child is unable to control, the role of punishment in the treatment of encopresis deserves special attention. The use of procedures such as overcorrection, time-out from reinforcement, and social disapproval have not been shown to be effective as singular treatments and may lead to the development of negative reactions and behaviors within the child. Incorporation of naturally occurring consequences (e.g., cleaning underwear, changing clothes) contingent on occurrences of encopresis is recommended and has been included as a component of several successful treatment protocols.

O'Brien, Ross, and Christophersen (1986) used a multicomponent intervention package involving scheduled toileting, suppositories, overcorrection, positive reinforcement for appropriate bowel movements, skill training, and dietary modification to successfully treat two encopretic children. With two other children, the addition of time-out from reinforcement, positive practice, and increased scheduled toiletings were used successfully.

Steege and Harper (1989) successfully treated an 11-year-old boy who had a 6-year history of chronic constipation and encopresis. They developed an intervention package that included (a) enemas, (b) suppositories, (c) milk of magnesia, (d) positive reinforcement for the nonoccurrence of soiling accidents, (e) positive reinforcement for the occurrence of appropriate bowel movements, (f) diet modifications (high fiber), (g) positive practice, (h) individual counseling/self-monitoring, and (i) labelled underwear. Labelling of underwear was used because the child frequently hid soiled clothing, up to five pairs of underwear per day. The child was provided with one pair of underwear specifically marked for each day, and two additional pairs for use in the event of soiling accidents. This procedure eliminated the hiding of soiled underwear and resulted in accurate estimates of the frequency of daily soiling accidents. The self-monitoring component involved the child self-recording occurrences of appropriate bowel movements and clean underwear at scheduled monitoring times. These procedures focused only on positive outcomes of the intervention thereby deemphasizing the negative consequences of encopresis. To increase parental and child long-term compliance with the treatment protocol, the parents and child were provided with verbal and written explanations of all treatment procedures, copies of all data-collection forms, toileting schedule charts, items from the reinforcement menu, self-monitoring recording forms, a high fiber diet, schedule for administering milk of magnesia, and the labelled underwear. Followup was conducted over a 2-year period. No further occurrences of encopresis were reported.

Individual and group counseling has also been shown to be an effective treatment for encopresis. For example, Gumaer (1990) demonstrated the efficacy of multimodal therapy in the treatment of encopresis in a 13-year-old boy. The treatment approach involved individual counseling focusing on behavior affect, imagery, cognition, and interpersonal relationships between variables such as sensation, medications, and diet. Wells and Hinkle (1990) used a family systems approach incorporating strategic homework assignments, thoughtful predictions about family behavior, and restructuring of family roles and boundaries to successfully treat encopresis in two boys aged 7 and 8 years respectively.

Enuresis

Background and Development

Enuresis is defined as the repeated voiding of urine during the day or at night into bed or clothing beyond the approximate age at which most children attain bladder control. *Nocturnal enuresis,* the passage of urine only during nighttime sleep, is the most common form of the disorder. The passage of urine during waking hours is referred to as *diurnal enuresis* (American Psychiatric Association, 1994). Most children achieve daytime bladder control by age three, although occasional accidents occur through 5 years of age (Christophersen, 1994). Approximately 49% of all children experience nocturnal enuresis at three years of age, 36% at 5 years, 16% at 10 years, and 8% at 12 years (Christophersen & Edwards, 1992). Diurnal enuresis can occur with or without bedwetting (Houts, 1987).

Subtypes

An important distinction in classification is based on the child's history of bladder control. *Primary enuresis* refers to the condition in which the child has never achieved urinary continence. *Secondary enuresis* refers to the condition in which urinary incontinence develops after a period of urinary continence. The vast majority of children with enuresis fall into the category of primary nocturnal enuresis (i.e., bedwetting in a child who has not achieved at least a 2-month period of consecutive dry nights). Approximately 10% of children who experience nocturnal enuresis exhibit secondary enuresis, with the average age of onset for secondary enuresis between 5 and 8 years (Houts, 1987).

Etiology

A history of enuresis among family members of enuretic children is often present. For example, according to one study, when both parents had been enuretic, 77% of the children experienced enuresis; when one parent was enuretic, 43% of the children were enuretic; and when neither parent had a history of enuresis, only 15% of the children were enuretic (Christophersen & Edwards, 1992).

A number of etiological factors have been associated with enuresis. However, no definitive cause has been identified. Enuresis may be conceptualized as a biobehavioral problem in which the application of medical, learning, and conditioning methodologies lead to behavioral and physiological changes that cause or maintain the problem (Mellon & Houts, 1995). Organic causes of enuresis include seizure disorders, diabetes, renal disorders, and urinary tract infection. For example, with nocturnal enuresis, the two leading etiological hypotheses are (a) deficiency in nocturnal secretion of antidiuretic hormone and (b) deficiency in muscular responses needed to inhibit urination during sleep (Mellon & Houts, 1995).

Maturational delays are also associated with enuresis. A widely accepted nonorganic etiology of enuresis is based on learning theory models. Doleys (1977) reported that inadequate toileting learning experiences, the development of bad habits, and inappropriate reinforcement contingencies lead to the formation and continuation of enuresis. In many cases of enuresis, the child is conditioned to urinate in bed or clothing and has not been properly conditioned to urinate in a toilet.

Problems and Implications

Generally, enuretic children are normally adjusted children who do not display excessive behavior problems or overt psychological problems (Wagner & Geffken, 1986). However, they may show evidence of withdrawal and tend to report feelings of anxiety, guilt, and embarrassment. Moreover, children with nocturnal enuresis are often reluctant to go on overnight visits or camping trips (Butler, Redfern, & Forsythe, 1990).

Children who evidence diurnal enuresis, regardless of whether they also experience nocturnal enuresis, tend to have significantly more medical problems than children who exhibit only nocturnal enuresis. Moreover, children who present diurnal enuresis will often require extensive medical evaluations and benefit from drug treatments for urinary tract infection or from antispasmodic medications that reduce spontaneous bladder contraction (Mellon & Houts, 1995).

Secondary enuresis is frequently linked with stressors in a child's life. Specifically, it is most frequently associated with traumatic experiences such as parental death or divorce, birth of a sibling, and child abuse (Javyelin, Moilaen, Vikevainen-Terronen, & Huttenen, 1990).

Alternative Actions

Prior to developing or recommending an intervention strategy, professionals should refer the child for a thorough medical evaluation and a behavioral assessment of enuresis patterns. By thoroughly assessing the behaviors of concern, the school psychologist will be able to identify the critical variables associated with enuresis and use the assessment information to tailor an intervention strategy for the unique behaviors of the referred child. As with encopresis, behavioral assessment of enuresis should include interviews and systematic measurement of the frequency, topography, and variables associated with its occurrence. The purpose of the interview is to determine the type of enuresis behavior exhibited by the child and to develop tentative hypotheses regarding causes and possible maintaining variables. Specific information is needed regarding the type, onset, and frequency of urination accidents. It is important to distinguish between nocturnal and diurnal and primary and secondary enuresis.

Direct measures of enuresis should begin with a 2-week baseline phase. The baseline phase serves not only to determine the frequency of enuresis, but to identify the times of the day in which urination accidents occur and to evaluate if there are trends or patterns of incontinence. Moreover, the baseline can be used as a measure to evaluate the effectiveness of subsequent intervention. With nocturnal enuresis, parents should be provided with and asked to complete forms that include columns for wet and dry nights, the size of the wet spot, and whether the child spontaneously awakened to go to the bathroom (Mellon & Houts, 1995). With diurnal enuresis, behavioral assessment of urination accidents could include hourly monitoring of the child's clothing to determine continence and incontinence and records of the frequency of urination in the toilet or potty chair.

A wide variety of intervention strategies have been developed to address the various types and etiologies of enuresis. If the possible cause of enuresis is due to maturational delay, waiting for the child to develop bladder control may be a viable option. Of the 15% to 20% of five-year-olds who experience maturational delays the vast majority will experience spontaneous resolution of their symptoms by the time they reach adolescence (Fitzwater & Macklin, 1992). However, such a "wait and see" attitude allows enuresis to continue and the child continues to experience related social-emotional difficulties.

Treatment of enuresis has frequently involved the use of medications. Historically, the drug most commonly used to treat enuresis is imipramine (Tofranil ™), a tricyclic antidepressant that has been shown to stop enuresis completely in 60% of enuretic children. However, the relapse rate is high, with approximately two-thirds of enuretics resuming enuresis after the medication is discontinued (Christophersen & Edwards, 1992).

Thompson and Rey (1995) reported the effectiveness of desmopressin in the treatment of functional enuresis. They suggest that this medication may be particularly useful with older children who fail to respond to behavioral interventions. They cautioned that additional research is needed on the long-term effectiveness and unwanted side affects of desmopressin.

Individual counseling has been found to be effective in cases of nonorganic secondary enuresis. However, counseling is usually considered an indirect treatment of enuresis. For example, if counseling addresses traumatic events experienced by the child, the treatment is directed at the psychopathology and not the enuresis (Christophersen & Edwards, 1992). It is expected that by addressing traumatic events through counseling that enuresis will resolve. More direct methods of intervention are typically needed, however.

With children who experience diurnal enuresis, a proactive method of treatment involves the use of traditional toilet training procedures. Central to the task of toilet training is the concept of readiness (Christophersen, 1994). Behavioral treatment approaches for enuresis should be initiated only in those cases wherein the child has developed a physiological readiness to learn appropriate toileting skills. Physiological readiness can be determined by evaluating a combination of physical and psychological factors. Information about a child's readiness should be determined during the medical and behavioral assessments. Physical readiness criteria include (a) reflex sphincter control and (b) myelinization of pyramidal tracts. Psychological readiness criteria are (a) established motor milestones of sitting and walking, (b) verbal comprehension skills, (c) positive relationships with adults, (d) identification and imitation of adults and significant others, and (e) the desire for independence (Christophersen, 1994). Azrin and Foxx (1974) identified the following readiness criteria: (a) bladder control, (b) physical readiness, and (c) instructional readiness.

The most successful methods of treating enuresis have involved behavioral conditioning techniques, including retention control training (Doleys, 1983), urine alarm training (Mellon & Houts, 1995) and dry bed training (Azrin, Sneed & Foxx, 1972). As with encopresis, punishment procedures have not been shown to be effective as singular strategies in the treatment of enuresis. The use of naturally occurring consequences (e.g., changing wet clothes) has been included as a component within comprehensive treatment packages.

Azrin and Foxx (1974) developed a training program that has been successfully used to teach toilet training skills. The components of this program include (a) practice and reinforcement in dressing skills, (b) immediate reinforcement for appropriate toileting (i.e. urination in the toilet), (c) positive practice contingent upon toileting accidents, and (d) learning by imitation/social learning methods.

With children who evidence maturational delays or poor learning histories, treatment of enuresis, particularly diurnal enuresis, often involves the use of operant conditioning procedures. The focus of treatment is on teaching appropriate toileting behavior. This method involves a multicomponent training package incorporating:

- Frequent liquids to increase opportunities for appropriate urination.
- Scheduled toileting.
- Prompting the child to urinate in a potty chair or toilet.
- Positive reinforcement of appropriate toileting (i.e., voiding in the toilet).
- Natural consequences of changing wet clothes, cleaning self, and putting on dry clothes.
- Self-monitoring, by instructing the child to record on a chart at each scheduled toileting time his or her dry-wet status and occurrences of appropriate toileting.

The most comprehensive approach used in the treatment of nocturnal enuresis is Full Spectrum Treatment (Houts & Liebert, 1984; Mellon & Houts, 1995). Full Spectrum Treatment has been used to effectively treat medically uncomplicated nocturnal enuresis. This is a multicomponent treatment package that includes (a) urine alarm treatment, (b) cleanliness training, (c) retention control training, and (d) overlearning (Houts & Liebert, 1984; Mellon & Houts, 1995).

Urine alarm training involves the use of a urine alarm device that is activated immediately upon the passage of urine. When the alarm goes off, children are instructed to stand and turn off the alarm and finish urinating in a toilet. Cleanliness training involves having the child remake the bed and to self-record on a chart either "wet" or "dry" for each night of the training. Retention control training is practiced once daily. The child is reinforced (e.g., money, tangible rewards) for postponing urination for an increasing amount of time up to a 45-minute holding time. In some cases the child is also prompted to gradually increase liquid intake while simultaneously withholding the urge to urinate. With overlearning, once the child has achieved 14 consecutive dry nights in the treatment program, he or she drinks 16 ounces of water during the hour before bedtime. Mellon and Houts (1995) reported a 70% success rate with Full Spectrum Treatment.

Treatment Adherence

The success of interventions for either enuresis or encopresis is directly related with the degree of adherence to the treatment protocol. It is important for the school psychologist to determine the degree to which parents, teachers, and the child will adhere to a specific treatment program before recommending its implementation. Indeed, unimplemented treatments are not treatments at all (Reimer, Wacker, & Koeppl, 1987). Parental and child noncompliance with intervention packages has been cited as an important factor in long-term encopresis (Wright & Walker, 1992). Walker (1978) devised an intervention package incorporating behavioral and medical treatments for 200 children and reported that up to 15% of the families failed to complete the training program.

Similar findings occur within the area of enuresis. Telzrow (1995) reported that successful interventions are determined by the degree of intervention adherence (i.e., the parent and/or child actively implements the treatment components) and treatment integrity (i.e., the parent and/or child accurately and assiduously implements the treatment components). Moreover, treatment adherence may be influenced by (a) personal variables associated with the school psychologist, parent, child, and/or teacher and (b) systemic variables, such as the type of intervention and the associated support structures available (Telzrow, 1995).

Reimers et al. (1987) in evaluating treatment adherence identified two variables that are critical to the acceptability of an intervention and that increase the probability of treatment adherence: (a) the consumer's understanding of the intervention and (b) the proven effectiveness of the intervention. Telzrow (1995) reported that intervention adherence and treatment integrity can be enhanced by the following practices:

- Use of participatory planning procedures.
- Use of a collaborative problem-solving approach among the school psychologist, parent, child, teacher, and others involved to increase understanding of and commitment to the intervention.
- Selection of interventions that are feasible, applicable, and effective.
- Provision of cognitive and affective training/support.
- Use of data-based monitoring systems that measure both implementation and effectiveness of intervention.

The team also needs to constantly monitor interventions and consider revision of interventions to meet the changing needs of the child, the course of treatment, and changes in the support structure. Involving parents, the referred child, and teachers in the collaborative design of the intervention often leads to increased understanding of the intervention and an increased expectation of intervention effectiveness.

Finally, it is highly recommended that prior to beginning any intervention addressing elimination disorders that the school psychologist educate the parent(s) and child. It is important to emphasize that many other children have similar problems, that the problem and course of treatment can be long term, and that there is no one to blame for the problem (Christophersen & Edwards, 1992).

Summary

Encopresis and enuresis are biobehavioral problems that frequently occur within children. With appropriate assessment and intervention, these behaviors can be effectively treated. School psychologists, because they are often in the position to provide ongoing behavioral consultation, play an important role in the treatment of those disorders. School psychologists could orchestrate an intervention package that involves the following phases: (a) behavioral assessment, (b) design of individually tailored intervention, (c) implementation of intervention, (d) systematic measurement of target behaviors, and (e) evaluation of the effectiveness of the intervention. Effective interventions should incorporate thorough medical and behavioral assessments, multicomponent treatments including when necessary medical and behavioral interventions, and a collaborative problem-solving approach that fully considers issues related to treatment adherence and treatment integrity.

Recommended Resources

Christophersen, E. (1994). *Pediatric compliance: A guide for the primary care physician.* New York: Plenum Publishing. *This book includes a chapter focusing on methods of addressing enuresis and encopresis. Topics include toilet training, toileting refusal, constipation and encopresis, and nocturnal enuresis. While targeted towards physicians, this chapter and book are very applicable to the practice of school psychology. The chapter includes several sample handouts useful in the evaluation and treatment of enuresis and encopresis. They include a toilet-training readiness checklist, methods for dealing with toilet-training resistance and toileting refusal, enuresis and encopresis structured interview forms, high fiber diet instructions, and specific step-by-step intervention methods.*

Mellon, M., & Houts, A. (1995). Elimination disorder. In R. Ammerman & M. Hersen (Eds.), *Handbook of child behavior therapy in the psychiatric setting* (pp. 341–365). New York: Wiley. *This chapter presents a biobehavioral perspective on the acquisition, evaluation, and treatment of nocturnal enuresis and functional encopresis. The authors' position that enuresis and encopresis are biobehavioral problems best treated through a combination of medical and behavioral treatment approaches is supported by a thorough review of the literature.*

Christophersen, E., & Edwards, R. (1992). Treatment of elimination disorders: State of the art 1991. *Applied and Prevention Psychology, 1,* 15–22.

This article reviews data-based research on encopresis and enuresis, reviewing the efficacy of chemotherapy and behavioral conditioning procedures in the treatment of nocturnal enuresis and multifaceted approaches for treating encopresis.

Steege, M. & Harper, D. (1989). Enhancing the management of secondary encopresis by assessing acceptability of treatment. *Journal of Behavior Therapy and Experimental Psychiatry, 20* (4), 333–341.
This article emphasizes the importance and methods for determining the acceptability of an intervention package and in increasing intervention adherence during the treatment of encopresis. The use of self-monitoring procedures is also described.

Azrin, N. & Foxx, R. (1974). *Toilet training in less than a day.* New York: Simon and Schuster.
This book describes a set of procedures for the acquisition of toilet-training skills with children.

Telzrow (1995). Best practices in facilitating intervention adherence. In A. Thomas & J. Grimes (Eds.), *Best practices in school psychology-III* (pp. 501–510). Washington, DC: National Association of School Psychologists.
This chapter provides a conceptual and practical framework of treatment adherence and treatment integrity. Included is a comprehensive problem-solving assessment and intervention form that could be a useful tool for the school psychologist providing evaluation and intervention services to children with encopresis and enuresis.

References

American Psychiatric Association. (1987). *Diagnostic and statistical manual of mental disorders* (3rd ed. rev.). Washington, DC: Author.

American Psychiatric Association. (1994). *Diagnostic and statistical manual of mental disorders* (4th ed.). Washington, DC: Author.

Azrin, N., & Foxx, R. (1974). *Toilet training in less than a day.* New York: Simon & Schuster.

Boon, F., & Singh, N. (1991). A model for the treatment of encopresis. *Behavior Modification, 15*(3) 355–371.

Butler, R., Redfern, E., & Forsythe, W. (1990). The child's construing of nocturnal enuresis: A method of inquiry and prediction of outcome. *Journal of Child Psychology and Psychiatry, 31*(3), 447–454.

Christophersen, E. (1994). *Pediatric compliance: A guide for the primary care physician.* New York: Plenum Publishing.

Christophersen, E., & Edwards, K. (1992). Treatment of elimination disorder: State of the Art 1991. *Applied and Prevention Psychology, 1*(1), 15–22.

Doleys, D. (1977). Behavioral treatment for nocturnal treatment of enuresis in children: A review of the recent literature. *Psychological Bulletin, 84*(1), 30–54.

Fitzwater, D., & Macklin, M. (1992). Risk/benefit ratio in enuresis therapy. *Clinical Pediatrics,* 308–310.

Gumaer, J. (1990). Multimodal counseling of childhood encopresis: A case example. *School Counselor, 38*(1), 58–64.

Houts, A. (1987). Children and enuresis. In A. Thomas & J. Grimes (Eds.), *Children's needs: Psychological perspectives* (pp. 194-202). Washington DC: National Association of School Psychologists.

Houts, A., & Liebert, R. (1984). *Bedwetting: A guide for parents and children.* Springfield, IL: Charles C Thomas.

Javyelin, M., Moilaen, Vikevainen-Terronen & Huttenen (1990). Life changes and protective capacities in enuretic and nonenuretic children. *Journal of Child Psychology and Psychiatry, 31*(5), 763-774.

Mellon, M., & Houts, A. (1995). Elimination disorders. In R. Ammerman & M. Hersen (Eds.), *Handbook of child behavior therapy in the psychiatric setting* (pp. 341–365). New York: Wiley.

O'Brien, S., Ross, L., & Christophersen, R. (1986). Primary encopresis: Evaluation and treatment. *Journal of Applied Behavior Analysis, 19*(2), 137–145.

Reimers, T., Wacker, D., & Koeppl, G., (1987). Acceptability of behavioral interventions: A review of the literature. *School Psychology Review, 16,* 212–227.

Simonson, D. (1987). Children and encopresis. In A. Thomas & J. Grimes (Eds.), *Children's needs: Psychological perspectives* (pp. 189-194). Washington, DC: National Association of School Psychologists.

Steege, M., & Harper, D. (1989). Enhancing the management of secondary encopresis by assessing acceptability of treatment. *Journal of Behavior Therapy and Experimental Psychiatry, 20* (4), 333–341.

Telzrow, C. (1995). Best practices in facilitating intervention adherence. In A. Thomas & J. Grimes (Eds.), *Best practices in school psychology-III* (pp. 501–510). Washington, DC: National Association of School Psychologists.

Wagner, W., & Geffken, G. (1986). Enuretic children: How they view their wetting behavior. *Child Study Journal, 16*(1), 13–18.

Walker, C. (1978). Toilet training, enuresis, encopresis. In P. Magrab (Ed.), *Psychological management of pediatric problems* (Vol. 1, pp. 129–182). Baltimore: University Park Press.

Wells, M., & Hinkle, J. (1990). Elimination of childhood encopresis: A family systems approach. *Journal of Mental Health Counseling, 12* (4) 520–526.

Wright, G., & Walker, E. (1977). Treatment of the child with psychogenic encopresis. *Clinical Pediatrics, 16,* 1042–1045.

Wright, G. (1975). Outcome of a standardized program for treating psychogenic encopresis. *Professional Psychology, 6,* 453–456.

79

Tic Disorders

Thomas J. Power
Marianne Mercugliano

University of Pennsylvania School of Medicine

Tic disorders are patterns of behavior characterized by the presence of involuntary, brief, repetitive movements and/or vocalizations, which can fluctuate in frequency and severity over time (Singer, 1993). Tics may be difficult to distinguish from behaviors commonly viewed as "nervous habits." An important difference is that habits, such as nail biting or hair twirling, usually have a continuous, effortful, "writhing" quality, while tics, such as eye blinking or throat clearing, usually have a very brief, automatic, "staccato" quality. Tics are often misunderstood by laypersons and professionals; they may be ascribed to visual disturbances, allergies, "nerves," purposeful attention-seeking behavior, and disruptive or antisocial behavior.

Tic disorders can have a significant impact on school functioning. In fact, it has been estimated that 35% of children with Tourette's syndrome (TS), the most severe tic disorder, receive special education services (Comings, 1990). Tics can interfere with attention to instruction, productivity on written tasks, and willingness to participate in class discussions. Tics also can be a source of distraction to other students and disruption to classroom routines. Furthermore, children who exhibit tics, particularly the more severe types, may become victims of peer rejection (Stokes, Bawden, Camfield, Backman, & Dooley, 1991).

In addition to problems arising directly as a result of tics, tic disorders are frequently associated with other conditions which interfere with school functioning. For instance, a high percentage of children with tic disorders have Attention Deficit/Hyperactivity Disorder (ADHD); obsessive-compulsive disorder (OCD); or symptoms of anxiety, aggressive behavior, and learning problems (Singer & Walkup, 1991).

Background and Development

Characteristics of Different Tic Disorders

Individual tics can be differentiated by their topology (motor or vocal) and complexity (simple versus com-

plex). Table 1 shows common examples of each type of tic. Simple motor tics involve only one or a few muscle groups while complex motor tics involve several muscle groups acting in a series. Simple vocal tics are noises while complex vocal tics consist of whole words or phrases.

The essential features of tic disorders, as defined by the *Diagnostic and Statistical Manual of Mental Disorders, Fourth Edition* (*DSM-IV;* American Psychiatric Association, 1994) are presented in Table 2. The *DSM-IV* criteria are very similar to those developed by the Tourette Syndrome Classification Study Group (1993). Tic disorders are relatively common in the general population. Transient tic disorder is the most common form and is estimated to occur in 5% to 24% of children (Singer, 1993). Chronic tic disorder, consisting of single or multiple tics which are either motor or vocal in nature, occurs in an estimated 1% to 2% of the school-age population (Comings, 1990). Tourette's syndrome, the least common form of tic disorder, is estimated to occur in 4 to 5 individuals per 10,000 (American Psychiatric Association, 1994), although there is evidence that this may be a conservative estimate (Comings, 1990). Tourette's syndrome, like all tic disorders, is much more common in males than females. The diagnosis of a specific type of tic disorder requires observation over time; there is no way to predict at initial presentation whether the disorder will be transient or chronic.

Development Course

Most of the research on tic disorders has focused on TS, so this discussion will summarize the literature regarding its developmental course. Given the substantial amount of evidence to suggest that different forms of tic disorders are genetically and functionally related and that tic disorders lie along a continuum from least severe (transient tic disorder) to most severe (Tourette's syndrome; Kurlan, 1994), it is safe to assume that conclusions drawn from children with TS have implications for children with other tic disorders.

Table 1 *Examples of Common Tics*

Simple Motor Tics	Simple Vocal Tics
Blinking	Throat clearing
Grimacing	Grunting
Rolling or darting eyes	Sniffing
Squinting	Snorting
Lip licking	Inspiratory or expiratory
Shoulder shrugging	noises
	Humming

Complex Motor Tics	Complex Vocal Tics
Manipulating clothing	Repeating parts of words, words,
Dystonic posturing	or phrases
Hopping/Jumping	Stuttering
Touching rituals	Animal Noises
Thrusting of body parts	Altered speech quality
Sequences of simple motor	Talking to oneself
tics	

Table 2 *Diagnostic Criteria for Tic Disorders*

Diagnostic Type	Criteria
Transient Tic Disorder	Single or multiple motor or vocal tics
	Almost daily occurrences
	Duration less than 12 months
	Onset before age 18
	Not due to other medical conditions
Chronic Motor or Vocal Tic Disorder	One or more motor or vocal tics (not both)
	Almost daily occurrences
	Duration more than 12 months
	Onset before age 18
	Not due to other medical conditions
Tourette's syndrome	Multiple motor and at least one vocal tic
	Almost daily occurrences
	Duration more than 12 months
	Onset before age 18
	Location, frequency, and severity may fluctuate over time
	Not due to other medical conditions

Note. Adapted from the *Diagnostic and Statistical Manual of Mental Disorders, Fourth Edition* by American Psychiatric Association, 1994, Washington, DC: Author Copyright 1994 by the American Psychiatric Association.

There is often a long latency between onset of symptoms and definitive diagnosis. Children who eventually show symptoms of TS often present to pediatricians or psychologists in early childhood for a variety of behavioral concerns well before the onset of tics. They are often, though certainly not always, "temperamentally difficult." They may have difficulty with new situations or transitions, seem overly anxious or fearful, have rapid changes in mood and behavior, and display compulsive or ritualistic behaviors. Some are diagnosed within the pervasive developmental disorder spectrum (Comings & Comings, 1991). Children with TS frequently demonstrate signs of ADHD, and these behaviors usually present prior to the onset of tics as well (Singer, 1993).

The first tic usually appears between 6 and 8 years of age (almost always by 13) and is usually a simple motor tic. Gradually other tics begin, some replacing ones which disappear, and others being added to the preexisting repertoire. One or more vocal tics typically emerge later (approximately 8–10 years of age) and complex tics occur later still (Bruun & Budman, 1993). After having tics for a period of time, some children will describe the presence of an unusual sensation in the area of a motor tic. This sensation usually feels something like an itch or an urge, and performing the motor tic relieves the buildup of this sensation. These sensations are sometimes referred to as sensory tics. Many children, when asked if the behavior in question is involuntary, will state that it is not, because they have the sense that they are choosing to perform the tic in order to relieve the uncomfortable sensation (Lang, 1993). Tics are most common in the face, neck, and shoulders. Coprolalia, a complex vocal tic consisting of the involuntary repetition of taboo words, is a famous, though relatively uncommon, characteristic of TS. Children with TS may display other vocal or motor tics with sexual content, such as obscene ges-

tures, pelvic thrusting, or sexually explicit words or phrases (Shapiro, Shapiro, Young, & Feinberg, 1988).

Tourette's syndrome and chronic tic disorders are usually lifelong, worsening from onset into adolescence, and decreasing in severity during late adolescence and adulthood (Bruun & Budman, 1993). In addition to fluctuating over the life span, tics vary in severity over much shorter time frames. Anxiety, stress, and fatigue can exacerbate tics, while relaxation and sleep decrease them (Singer & Walkup, 1991). Tics may be suppressed for short periods of time, such as during public speaking or a doctor's visit, but such periods will usually be followed by a "flurry" of tics.

Etiology

The etiology of tic disorders is primarily genetic, though sometimes an individual with a tic disorder has no family history and appears to be the first affected in a pedigree. Tic disorders vary greatly in severity but probably have a common genetic etiology. It is not uncommon to have one individual in a family with a chronic, single-motor tic disorder and another with the full TS presentation. In addition, OCD and possibly also ADHD are not just common comorbid features, but also part of the same genetic etiology (Comings, 1990). It is possible for different individuals in a pedigree to manifest OCD, OCD and tics, and tics alone. The analogous situation exists with ADHD. Females inheriting the genetic disposition for TS are far more likely to have OCD than males, but males are more likely to have tics than females (Singer & Walkup, 1991).

The genetics of TS are not entirely understood, but it behaves as an autosomal dominant disorder with variable penetrance. That is, an individual can inherit TS if just one parent has it or is a carrier, and multiple factors can modify the severity of expression. The final genetic explanation of TS awaits identification of the gene(s) involved. Many researchers have been seeking the TS gene; however, thus far, over two-thirds of the entire human genome has been searched without success.

Nongenetic factors also play a role in the expression of TS. Monozygotic (identical) twins share the same genetic makeup but do not always share TS nor have it to the same degree of severity. Clearly, being male affects the expression of tics, and it is theorized that testosterone or other testosterone-like hormones may play a role in early brain development which influences the expression of the TS gene. Twin studies also indicate that the smaller twin is frequently affected to a greater degree. Because the smaller twin may have had less placental blood flow or nutrition, it has been hypothesized that the quality of the intrauterine environment may also affect the expression of the TS gene. Finally, in animal studies, maternal stress during pregnancy results in abnormalities in the offspring which may be analogous to those found in individuals with TS. Thus, maternal stress during pregnancy, and the release of hormones and catecholamines it causes, may influence the expression of the TS gene (Leckman & Peterson, 1993).

Neurological Basis of Tic Disorders

A substantial body of evidence suggests that alterations in brain functioning underlie the motor and nonmotor symptoms of TS. The induction of repetitive movements in rodents and primates by destruction or stimulation of certain brain regions, manipulation of certain neurotransmitter systems, or the administration of stimulant drugs such as methylphenidate or dextroamphetamine, has been well described in the scientific literature for over 20 years (see Comings, 1990). These studies, as well as neuropsychological studies of humans with brain injuries and neurologic diseases, have helped to focus researchers on the brain regions and neurotransmitter systems that are likely to be involved in the etiology of tics.

The frontal cortex, basal ganglia, and/or limbic system are probable sites of altered functioning in TS (Singer & Walkup, 1991). The frontal cortex is important in the planning of voluntary motor activity; the integration of emotional information with the selection of a response; and the functioning of the executive cognitive processes, including filtering and selecting from among multiple streams of incoming stimuli, self-regulation, and response inhibition. The basal ganglia are a group of several small brain regions which work together in a highly organized fashion to integrate motor, cognitive, and affective information from higher and lower brain centers. Although performing many complex functions, the basal ganglia are best known for their role in the regulation of movement. The limbic system is a group of brain nuclei which work in concert to regulate emotional functioning.

The frontal cortex, basal ganglia, and limbic system are linked to other parts of the cortex and to each other in a loop which also includes the thalamus. Alterations in neural transmission in this loop are proposed to underlie many neuropsychiatric disorders, but the specifics are known for only a few. Tourette's syndrome, unfortunately, is not among them. It is important to note that the basal ganglia and frontal cortex have also been implicated in ADHD and OCD, and the frontal and temporal cortices and limbic system have been implicated in affective disorders and serious impulse control disorders (Comings, 1990). Thus, the same regions implicated in TS have also been implicated in the disorders frequently associated with TS. A very simplified and general current theory hypothesizes that TS results when the basal ganglia and limbic system are somehow structurally or neurochemically "disconnected" from the voluntary, inhibitory influence of the frontal cortex. In particular, it is thought that an abnormality in the dopamine neurotransmitter system may be involved in the pathology leading to tics, because drugs which increase dopamine transmission, such as the stimulants, increase stereotypic movements, but drugs which block dopamine transmission, such as neuroleptics, decrease stereotypic movements (Singer & Walkup, 1991).

Problems and Implications

Tic disorders are commonly associated with other behavioral, emotional, and learning problems. Most of the research regarding the comorbidity of tic disorders has focused on children with TS. Not as much information is available about rates of comorbidity with less severe tic disorders. Given that the pattern of neuropsychological functioning, level of ADHD, and level of obsessive-compulsive behaviors tends to worsen as a function of the severity of tic behavior (Hyde & Weinberger, 1995), it is reasonable to hypothesize that the prevalence of comorbid conditions is higher among children with TS than children with less severe tic disorders (Kurlan, 1994).

Attention Deficit/Hyperactivity Disorder

Children with tic disorders frequently display characteristics of ADHD, including short attention span, poor concentration, lack of productivity, hyperactive behavior, and problems with social discourse. Components of ADHD have been found in an estimated 50% to 60% of children with TS. Behaviors related to ADHD typically precede the onset of tics by 2 to 3 years (Singer & Walkup, 1991). The ADHD-related problems of children with tic disorders often result in a greater degree of impairment than the tics themselves (Shapiro et al., 1988). ADHD is known to be associated with enormous academic, social, and emotional risks. Children with ADHD underachieve academically, are frequently the victims of peer rejection, are subjected to relatively high rates of criticism by parents and teachers, and often become demoralized (Barkley, 1990). ADHD is known to be chronic in nature; the effects of this disorder typically persist through adolescence and into adulthood (see the chapter on ADHD in this volume).

Obsessive-Compulsive Behavior

Obsessive-compulsive behavior is genetically related to tic disorders (Comings, 1990). It is estimated that the prevalence of obsessive-compulsive behavior in children with TS is about 50% (Singer & Walkup, 1991). Obsessions are recurrent thoughts or images that are experienced by a person as intrusive and senseless and which can result in escalating levels of distress and anxiety. Compulsions are stereotyped, repetitive behaviors that have the purpose of relieving distress and anxiety (American Psychiatric Association, 1994). For instance, a student may worry obsessively about germs on the hands. The child becomes increasingly distressed the longer time passes since the last hand washing. The discomfort can be relieved by performing a compulsive ritual involving leaving the classroom, going to the bathroom, and washing his or her hands.

Obsessions and tics are functionally related. An urge to exhibit a tic, like an obsession, can lead to distress. The individual typically will try to repress the tic or obsession, which results in escalating levels of discomfort. The performance of a tic or compulsion may lead to a temporary relief from distress. The similarity between tics and obsessive-compulsive behaviors has led some experts to speculate that obsessive-compulsive behaviors are actually examples of highly complex motor and/or vocal tics (Shapiro et al., 1988).

Cognitive and Learning Problems

Studies investigating the cognitive and neuropsychological functioning of children with TS have shown that most of these individuals perform at least within the normal range. Abnormalities on neuropsychological measures generally are mild in nature; problems on motor tasks, in particular writing and drawing activities, as well as written and mental arithmetic appear most common (Bornstein, 1990). There is evidence that the severity of tic symptoms is related to the significance of deficits in cognitive functioning and academic performance.

Aggression

Children with tic disorders frequently display aggressive behavior toward adults and peers (Singer & Walkup, 1991). Their aggressiveness may take the form of oppositional, defiant behavior toward persons in authority; anger outbursts associated with screaming, hitting, and kicking when frustrated, as well as verbal and physical aggression toward peers. Aggression is strongly related to peer rejection (Price & Dodge, 1989) and has been shown to be a primary risk factor for negative outcome in adolescence and adulthood (Weiss & Hechtman, 1993).

Anxiety

Children with tic disorders are more likely to exhibit symptoms of anxiety and phobia than children in the general population (Comings, 1990). Symptoms of anxiety at times may contribute to school avoidance, resulting in high rates of school absence and frequent trips to the nurse's office in school. Phobias may also be highly disruptive of daily routines. For instance, one child with a chronic tic disorder treated through our program had a phobia of bees which prevented him from going outdoors and attending camp in the summertime.

Factors Contributing to Problems

Child Factors

Children with tic disorders demonstrate a high degree of variability in the topology of their tic symptoms; patterns of comorbid psychological problems; and severity of learning, behavioral, and emotional problems. Developmental factors can have a marked impact on problems faced by children with tic disorders. During the preschool years, these children generally do not display tics, although they may present with symptoms of ADHD, aggression, and stereotyped patterns of behavior (Comings, 1990; Comings & Comings, 1991). In the early elementary years, tic symptoms typically emerge, symptoms of ADHD and aggression crystallize, and other comorbid psychological problems, such as obsessive-compulsive behaviors and anxiety symptoms, may arise. Behavioral and emotional problems may become even more complex and severe during the adolescent years. Research regarding children with related behavioral and emotional problems has shown that child factors, such as academic competence, self-control in social situations, and peer acceptability are associated with more favorable outcomes during adolescence and adulthood (Weiss & Hechtman, 1993).

Parenting Factors

Children with tic disorders, particularly those with complex patterns of psychiatric comorbidity, can be extremely difficult to parent. Parents differ markedly with regard to their skills in addressing the problems presented by these children. Research has demonstrated that lower socioeconomic status, marital discord, parental psychopathology, and parental isolation have a significant impact on parents' ability to use effective behavior management techniques with their children (Wahler & Dumas, 1989). Given that tic disorders are inherited, it is common for parents of children with tic disorders to experience many of the problems associated with these disorders, which may impair their ability to parent effectively. For instance, the impulsivity and disorganization associated with ADHD may contribute to a parent's problems in managing his or her child's ADHD-related behaviors.

School Variables

Children with tic disorders often need special accommodations in the school environment to function adaptively. For instance, these children may need intensive behavior modification interventions in the classroom to enhance their work productivity and compliance with classroom rules. The teacher and school nurse may need to collaborate on a protocol to address a child's somatic complaints, reduce anxiety, and decrease trips to the nurse's office during the school day. In addition, the teacher may need to communicate frequently with parents to address issues of school avoidance and to increase school attendance. Teachers can vary markedly with regard to their willingness to employ behavioral interventions and collaborate with parents to resolve children's problems. Moreover, schools can differ greatly with regard to the resources available (e.g., expertise of consultants, time available for school psychologist to provide behavioral consultation, responsiveness of school administrators to teachers' professional needs) to address the complex needs of children with tic disorders.

Alternative Actions

Assessment of Tic Disorders

The diagnosis of a tic disorder is based primarily on the presence of the diagnostic criteria, as determined by parent report, teacher report, and direct observation of behavior (see Table 2). The diagnosis is generally made by a team of professionals, consisting of the child's pediatrician and one or more specialists familiar with TS, such as a neurologist, psychiatrist, developmental pediatrician, or clinical psychologist. Additional information important to diagnostic decision making includes the family history and the absence of symptoms of other neurologic disease, acquired brain injury, or medications which can induce tics (e.g., stimulant medications for ADHD). If a child is on medication at the onset of the tic disorder, the diagnostic team usually finds it necessary to stop the medication for a trial period to clarify its role in the occurrence of tics. Few other neurologic conditions mimic tic disorders, but in unusual cases the clinician may need to rule out other neurologic disorders (e.g., Huntington's chorea) with additional studies. There are no specific physical exam findings, laboratory studies, or findings on neuroimaging scans which denote or confirm the diagnosis of a tic disorder.

The observation of tic behavior in a clinic setting is useful but often of questionable significance, because tics fluctuate greatly in severity across situations and time, and a child may be able to suppress tics in the doctor's office (Gadow, Nolan, & Sverd, 1992). It is often extremely helpful in clarifying the frequency and severity of tic behaviors to have direct observations or videotaped recordings of the child's behavior in familiar settings (see Gadow et al., 1992) and to ask parents and teachers to complete rating scales, such as the Yale Global Tic Severity Scale (Leckman et al., 1989) or the Hopkins Motor/Vocal Tic Scale (Walkup, Rosenberg, Brown, & Singer, 1992). Because school psychologists are in an excellent position to obtain observation data and rating scale information from teachers (Power, Atkins, Osborne, & Blum, 1994), they can be extremely helpful to external consultants in assessing the disorder and developing an effective treatment plan.

Whenever a child is being evaluated for a tic disorder, the assessment of associated problems is as important as the assessment of tics in terms of the child's overall management. Describing the assessment of academic skill deficits, ADHD, OCD, and other disruptive, affective, and anxiety disorders is beyond the scope of this chapter; however, a few brief points are important. The evaluation of associated problems, with the possible exception of learning disorders, is based primarily on data obtained through a behavioral assessment. There are no physical examination or laboratory findings that confirm these diagnoses. Most clinicians use the criteria in the *DSM-IV* as a starting point, with the assistance of one or more structured diagnostic interview tools, standardized rating scales, and direct observation procedures to determine the presence and severity of symptoms needed to make a diagnosis.

The decision to refer a child for assessment of tics should be based on the level of functional problems encountered by a child, and not merely on the presence or chronicity of tic-like symptoms. Functional difficulties may arise from the tics themselves, or more likely, from coexisting problems with attention, learning, behavior, or mood.

Pharmacologic Treatment

Treatment of tic disorders with medication involves two separate considerations: treatment of tics and treatment of associated symptoms. The vast majority of children with tics have mild enough symptoms that the tics themselves are not usually treated with medication. The medications effective in decreasing tic severity have significant side effects that limit their use to relatively severe cases of TS. However, many children with mild TS, or one of the less severe tic disorders, can be helped by pharmacologic treatment for ADHD, anxiety, obsessive compulsive behaviors, or mood problems. Two factors complicate the medication management of children with tic disorders:

1. Medication for one type of problem often has behavioral side effects that exacerbate another problem (e.g., stimulants can exacerbate tics, and neuroleptics can impair concentration).
2. The chronically fluctuating course of the disorder makes it difficult to monitor medication effects (Singer & Walkup, 1991).

Some children with TS require multiple medications. Table 3 describes medications used to treat tics, along with common dose ranges and potential side effects. Neuroleptics are the most effective medications for the treatment of tics (Shapiro & Shapiro, 1993). In severe cases, a benzodiazepine (valium-related medication) may be used to augment the effects of a neuroleptic.

Table 4 shows analogous information for the treatment of associated disorders. These medications fall into several categories. The stimulants are generally most effective for ADHD-related behaviors but may exacerbate tics (Bruun, Cohen, & Leckman, 1995). In this case, particularly if ADHD is the more disabling condition, a small dose of a neuroleptic may be added to suppress the tics. The tricyclic antidepressant medications, the newer antidepressant medication, bupropion, and the antihypertensive, clonidine, are second-line choices for ADHD behaviors and tics (Singer et al., 1995). The antidepressants may also be effective for depression and mood lability. The new serotonin re-uptake inhibitors are particularly effective for obsessive-compulsive features but can also be helpful for anxiety and depression. They appear to have fewer cardiovascular side effects than the tricyclic antidepressants.

Most medications are increased and decreased gradually. Some require laboratory monitoring of EKGs and blood tests. Feedback from teachers about the effects and side effects of medication addition, discontinuation, and substitution, as well as dose and timing changes is critical to effective intervention.

Behavioral Treatment

Behavioral treatments can be effective in treating tics as well as many of the behavioral and emotional problems associated with tic disorders. Azrin and colleagues have demonstrated the efficacy of a combination of behavioral techniques in the treatment of tic symptoms (Azrin & Peterson, 1990). One approach, known as a habit reversal procedure, consists of (a) awareness training to detect the occurrence and antecedents of tics; (b) relaxation training to reduce contributory stress; (c) competing response training, involving performance of a response antithetical to the tic; and (d) contingency management, consisting of the administration of positive reinforcers for practicing the procedures and reducing the frequency of tics. This treatment procedure, which can take about 20 sessions to complete, was demonstrated to be effective in reducing the frequency and severity of tics in a group of 10 individuals diagnosed with TS (Azrin & Peterson, 1990).

Behavioral interventions also have been successful in treating many behaviors associated with comorbid conditions. For the treatment of obsessive-compulsive rituals, effective behavioral interventions typically consist of (a) gradual exposure to the situation evoking the obses-

Table 3 *Medications Used to Treat Tics*

Medication Type	Dose Range	Potential Side Effects
Neuroleptics		
Haloperidol (Haldol)	.5–10 mg/day	Fatigue, weight gain, decreased ability to think/remember, movement disorders, akathisia, depression
Pimozide (Orap)	1–20 mg/day	Same as above; also EKG changes
Fluphenazine (Prolixin)	.5–4 mg/day	Similar to haloperidol
Benzodiazapine		
Clonazepam (Klonopin)	0.5–5 mg/day	Sedation, irritability, dizziness
Antihypertensive		
Clonidine (Catapres)	.05–.5 mg/day	Sedation, sleep disturbance, dry mouth, blurred vision, hypotension, depression, anxiety

Note. Dose ranges start with common starting doses and end with usual maximal doses.

Table 4 *Medications to Treat Disorders Associated with Tic Disorders*

Medication Type	Dose Range		Potential Side Effects
Stimulants			
Methylphenidate (Ritalin)	5–60	mg/day	Appetite loss, headache, stomachache, rebound irritability, increased tics
Dextroamphetamine (Dexedrine)	2.5–40	mg/day	Same as methylphenidate
Magnesium pemoline (Cylert)	18.75–150	mg/day	Same as methylphenidate, also liver inflammation
Tricyclic Antidepressants			
Imipramine (Tofranil)	10–300	mg/day	Dry mouth, blurred vision, constipation, fatigue, appetite and sleep changes, EKG changes
Desipramine (Norpramin)	100–300	mg/day	Same as imipramine
Nortriptyline (Pamelor)	10–150	mg/day	Same as imipramine
Serotonin Re-uptake Inhibitors			
Fluoxetine (Prozac)	10–80	mg/day	Agitation, insomnia, upset stomach
Sertraline (Zoloft)	10–300	mg/day	Same as fluoxetine
Clomipramine (Anafranil)	25–250	mg/day	Same as imipramine
Other Antidepressants			
Bupropion (Wellbutrin)	75–300	mg/day	Agitation, dry mouth, insomnia, headache, nausea, constipation, tremor
Antihypertensives			
Clonidine (Catapres)	.05–.5	mg/day	Sedation, sleep disturbance, dry mouth, blurred vision, hypotension, depression, anxiety

sive-compulsive behavior; (b) response prevention, which involves stopping the child from emitting the compulsive behavior associated with an obsession; (c) relaxation training to reduce the distress arising when the child does not perform the compulsive act; and (d) contingency management, involving the provision of positive reinforcers for using the procedures and not performing the compulsive behaviors (March, 1995). Behaviors associated with ADHD have been treated effectively using differential reinforcement, token economy techniques, school-home notes with home-based consequences, and response cost procedures (Pfiffner & O'Leary, 1993). The treatment of fears and anxieties may consist of a combination of gradual exposure, systematic desensitization, adult and/or peer modeling, and contingency management (Barrios & O'Dell, 1989). Finally, anger-coping interventions may include training children in self-instruction and problem-solving strategies and training parents and teachers to cue and reinforce strategy use and adaptive social behavior (Lochman, Dunn, & Klimes-Dougan, 1993).

Child Advocacy

Effective treatment may include providing teachers with information about tic disorders and their academic, be-

havioral, and emotional correlates. Collaboration with teachers also may be useful in developing instructional and behavioral interventions for these children. For instance, the teacher and school psychologist might collaborate on a behavioral strategy to reduce a distracting vocal tic. The strategy might involve having the teacher (a) cue the child periodically and unobtrusively to use a specialized deep breathing procedure to prevent the occurrence of the tic and (b) reinforce the child frequently for using the strategy and reducing the occurrence of the tic.

Interventions targeted at the peer groups of children with tic disorders may also be helpful. Peers may misinterpret the meaning of tics and other behaviors related to tic disorders, resulting in rejection of the child with tics. Providing peers with information about tic disorders and coaching a child with a tic disorder to communicate with one or more peers about how specific peer-oriented behaviors are helpful and harmful to the child may be beneficial. Certainly, it is important that interventions with peers be designed and monitored carefully to reduce the risk of peer rejection as a side effect of the intervention.

Choosing the Right Intervention

The choice of an intervention strategy depends on several factors, including (a) the problems targeted for intervention and the availability of effective behavioral and/or pharmacological interventions to treat the problem(s); (b) the severity of the target behavior(s); (c) the effects of prior attempts to treat the targeted behavior(s); (d) the resources available within the family and school to treat the problem; and (e) the acceptability of possible treatment options to the child, parents, and teachers. For instance, if the primary behavior targeted for intervention is a vocal tic (e.g., barking), which results in frequent disruption of classroom routines and significant peer rejection, the school psychologist could consider using a habit-reversal procedure or consulting with the parents about obtaining a neurological evaluation to determine the usefulness of medication. If a behavioral intervention has not yet been attempted, if the parents would prefer a nonpharmacological approach initially, and if the school can coordinate the resources needed to provide an intensive behavioral intervention, then the use of a behavioral approach could be considered initially. If an intensive behavioral intervention is employed but does not reduce classroom disruption and peer rejection markedly, then adding a pharmacological component to the intervention program would probably be advisable. As another example, if the primary targets are obsessive-compulsive behaviors or symptoms of anxiety, an intensive behavioral intervention generally would be the first choice because, thus far, research validating behavioral interventions for these symptoms in children is more impressive than research regarding the efficacy of pharmacological treatments.

Evaluating Treatment Outcome

The school psychologist can serve a critical role in evaluating the effects of behavioral and pharmacological treatments for children with tic disorders and related problems (Kubiszyn, 1994). School psychologists work in a context where it is relatively easy to acquire naturalistic data regarding a child's academic and social functioning on repeated occasions in diverse settings from multiple informants. The role of the school psychologist in evaluating treatment outcome has been described repeatedly in the literature (see Kubiszyn, 1994; Power et al., 1994 for a review). When evaluating treatment effects for children with tic disorders, the following practices are recommended:

- Colloborate with the prescribing physician, classroom teachers, and parents in designing and refining the outcome measurement procedures.
- Use multiple methods of assessment, including direct observation of tic behaviors and other relevant target behaviors (e.g., off-task behavior, inappropriate vocalizations, aggression toward peers) and teacher ratings

of tic severity as well as academic productivity and behavior problems.
- Gather samples of academic work in two or more subject areas.
- Employ single-case research methods, preferably using double-blind procedures with placebo control.
- Extend the length of treatment phases to achieve a stable rate of responding within phase due to the fluctuating nature of tic behavior.

Summary

Tic disorders represent a spectrum of problems that range in severity from transient tic disorders, the most common and least severe form, to Tourette's syndrome (TS), the least common and most severe type. Tic disorders can be differentiated according to their topology, complexity, chronicity, and severity. The etiology of tic disorders is primarily genetic, but environmental factors can contribute to the manifestation and severity of symptoms. A genetic disposition toward tic disorders may manifest itself in a variety of ways, including tic symptoms, obsessive compulsive behaviors, and symptoms of ADHD. The assessment of tic disorders should be conducted by a team of professionals including the child's pediatrician and one or more specialists in the fields of medicine and psychology. Treatment of tic disorders and related problems may include behavioral and pharmacologic methods of treatment. The choice of treatment strategy depends on the availability of effective treatments for the primary target behavior(s); the severity of the target behavior(s); the child's response to previous interventions; the resources of the family and school; and the acceptability of various methods of treatment to the child, parents, teachers, and treating physician. A systematic, multimethod assessment of treatment outcome is strongly recommended.

Recommended Resources

Professional Organization

Tourette Syndrome Association
42-40 Bell Blvd.
Bayside, New York 11361
(718) 224-2999
Available information: Articles, pamphlets, and videos for parents, children, and professionals about all aspects of TS; inservice materials for educators and peers; local professional referrals for assessment and treatment; and a membership newsletter detailing clinical and research updates.

Resources for Parents

Haerle, T. (Ed.) (1992). *Children with Tourette syndrome: A parent's guide*. Rockville, MD: Woodbine House. (To order, call 1-800-643-7323.)

Hughes, S. (1990). *Ryan: A mother's story of her hyperactive/Tourette syndrome child.*

Duarte, CA: Hope Press. (To order, call 1-800-321-4039).

Resources for Professionals

Azrin, N. H., & Peterson, A. L. (1990). Treatment of Tourette syndrome by habit reversal: A waiting-list control group comparison. *Behavior Therapy, 21,* 305–318.

The authors present the results of a control-group study investigating the effectiveness of a behavioral intervention for the treatment of tics in 10 children diagnosed with Tourette's syndrome. The behavioral protocol consisted of self-monitoring, relaxation, and competing response procedures. The 20-session protocol was successful in markedly reducing the frequency and severity of vocal and motor tics.

Comings, D. E. (1990). *Tourette syndrome and human behavior.* Duarte, CA: Hope Press.

This text provides extensive information regarding the diagnosis of tic disorders and comorbid conditions associated with this spectrum of disorders. The author, a geneticist, offers an excellent description of the genetics and neurobiology of tic disorders. In addition, this text describes many of the medications used to treat tic disorders and outlines the potential advantages and side-effect profiles of the pharmacologic approaches.

Gadow, K. D., Nolan, E. E., & Sverd, J. (1992). Methylphenidate in hyperactive boys with comorbid tic disorder: II. Short-term behavioral effects in school settings. *Journal of American Academy of Child and Adolescent Psychiatry, 31,* 462–471.

In this study the authors describe a school-based protocol for evaluating the effects and side effects of medications for treating children with ADHD and tic disorders. Eleven children were administered a double-blind, placebo-controlled trial of methylphenidate. Effects and side effects were monitored in classroom, playground, and lunchroom settings using direct observation and rating scale procedures. This study provides an excellent model of how school psychologists can evaluate the efficacy of interventions for treating children with tic disorders.

Kurlan, R. (Ed.). (1993). *Handbook of Tourette's syndrome and related tic and behavioral disorders.* New York: Marcel Dekker.

This book is a collection of papers reviewing several important aspects of TS, including its developmental course, neurobiology, and comorbidity with other psychiatric disorders. The author includes several articles addressing the pharmacologic, behavioral, and educational treatment of children with TS.

Singer, H. S., & Walkup, J. T. (1991). Tourette syndrome and other tic disorders: Diagnosis, pathophysiology, and treatment. *Medicine, 70,* 15–32.

This review article describes the history and development of TS as a diagnosis as well as the characteristics of tics and tic disorders. The paper also includes sections on epidemiology, ge-netics, comorbid features, pathophysiology, and treatment options. Case examples are provided.

References

American Psychiatric Association. (1994). *Diagnostic and statistical manual of mental disorders* (4th ed.). Washington, DC: Author.

Azrin, N. H., & Peterson, A. L. (1990). Treatment of Tourette syndrome by habit reversal: A waiting-list control group comparison. *Behavior Therapy, 21,* 305–318.

Barkley, R. A. (1990). *Attention Deficit Hyperactivity Disorder: A manual for diagnosis and treatment.* New York: Guilford.

Barrios, B. A., & O'Dell, S. L. (1989). Fears and anxieties. In E. J. Mash & R. A. Barkley (Eds.), *Treatment of childhood disorders* (pp. 167–221). New York: Guilford.

Bornstein, R. A. (1990). Neuropsychological performance in children with Tourette's syndrome. *Psychiatry Research, 33,* 73–81.

Bruun, R. D., & Budman, C. L. (1993). The natural history of Gilles de la Tourette syndrome. In R. Kurlan (Ed.), *Handbook of Tourette's syndrome and related tic and behavioral disorders,* New York: Marcel Dekker. (pp. 27–42).

Bruun, R. D., Cohen, D. J., & Leckman, J. F. (1995). *Guide to the diagnosis and treatment of Tourette syndrome.* Bayside, NY: Tourette Syndrome Association.

Comings, D. E. (1990). *Tourette syndrome and human behavior.* Duarte, CA: Hope Press.

Comings, D. E., & Comings, B. G. (1991). Clinical and genetic relationships between autism-pervasive developmental disorder and Tourette syndrome: A study of 19 cases. *American Journal of Medical Genetics, 39,* 180–191.

Gadow, K. D., Nolan, E. E., & Sverd, J. (1992). Methylphenidate in hyperactive boys with comorbid tic disorder: II. Short-term behavioral effects in school settings. *Journal of American Academy of Child and Adolescent Psychiatry, 31,* 462–471.

Hyde, T. M., & Weinberger, D. R. (1995). Tourette's syndrome: A model neuropsychiatric disorder. *Journal of American Medical Association, 273,* 498–501.

Kubiszyn, T. (1994). Pediatric psychopharmacology and prescription privileges: Implications and opportunities for school psychologists. *School Psychology Quarterly, 9,* 26–40.

Kurlan, R. (1994). Hypothesis II: Tourette's syndrome is part of a clinical spectrum that includes normal brain development. *Archives of Neurology, 51,* 1145–1150.

Lang, A. E. (1993). The premonitory ("sensory") experiences. In R. Kurlan (Ed.), *Handbook of Tourette's syndrome and related tic and behavioral disorders* (pp. 17–26). New York: Marcel Dekker.

Leckman, J. F., & Peterson, B. S. (1993). The pathogenesis of Tourette's syndrome: Epigenetic factors active early in CNS development. *Biological Psychiatry, 34,* 425–427.

Leckman, J. F., Riddle, M. A., Hardin, M. T., Ort, S. I., Swartz, K. L., Stevenson, J., & Cohen, D. J. (1989). The Yale

Global Tic Severity Scale: Initial testing of a clinician-rated scale of tic severity. *Journal of Academy of Child and Adolescent Psychiatry, 28,* 566–573.

Lochman, J. E., Dunn, S. E., & Klimes-Dougan, B. (1993). An intervention and consultation model from a social cognitive perspective: A description of the anger coping program. *School Psychology Review, 22,* 458–471.

March, J. S., (1995). Cognitive-behavioral psychotherapy for children and adolescents with OCD: A review and recommendations for treatment. *Journal of American Academy of Child and Adolescent Psychiatry, 34,* 7–18.

Pfiffner, L. J., & O'Leary, S. G. (1993). School-based psychological treatments. In J. L. Matson (Ed.), *Handbook of hyperactivity in children* (pp. 234–255). Boston: Allyn & Bacon.

Power, T. J., Atkins, M. S., Osborne, M. L., & Blum, N. J. (1994). The school psychologist as manager of programming for ADHD. *School Psychology Review, 23,* 279–291.

Price, J. M., & Dodge, K. A. (1989). Reactive and proactive aggression in childhood: Relations to peer status and social context dimensions. *Journal of Abnormal Child Psychology, 17,* 455–471.

Shapiro, A. K., & Shapiro, E. (1993). Neuroleptic drugs. In R. Kurlan (Ed.), *Handbook of Tourette's Syndrome and related tic and behavioral disorders (pp. 347–375).* New York: Marcel Dekker.

Shapiro, A. K., Shapiro, E. S., Young, J. G., & Feinberg, T. E. (1988). *Gilles de la Tourette syndrome* (2nd ed.). New York: Raven Press.

Singer, H. S. (1993). Tic disorders. *Pediatric Annals, 22,* 22–29.

Singer, H. S., Brown, J., Quaskey, S., Rosenberg, L. A., Mellits, E. D., & Denckla, M. B. (1995). The treatment of Attention-Deficit Hyperactivity Disorder in Tourette's syndrome: A double-blind placebo-controlled study with clonidine and desimpramine. *Pediatrics, 95,* 74–81.

Singer, H. S., & Walkup, J. T. (1991). Tourette syndrome and other tic disorders: Diagnosis, pathophysiology, and treatment. *Medicine, 70,* 15–32.

Stokes, A., Bawden, H. N., Camfield, P. R., Backman, J. E., & Dooley, J. (1991). Peer problems in Tourette's disorder. *Pediatrics, 87,* 936–942.

Tourette Syndrome Classification Study Group. (1993). Definitions and classification of tic disorders. *Archives of Neurology, 50,* 1013–1016.

Wahler, R. G., & Dumas, J. E. (1989). Attentional problems in dysfunctional mother-child interactions: An interbehavioral model. *Psychological Bulletin, 105,* 116–130.

Walkup, J. T., Rosenberg, L. A., Brown, J., & Singer, H. S. (1992). The validity of instruments for measuring tic severity in Tourette's syndrome. *Journal of American Academy of Child and Adolescent Psychiatry, 30,* 472–477.

Weiss, G., & Hechtman, L. (1993). *Hyperactive children grown up* (2nd ed.). New York: Guilford.

80
Obesity

David V. Sheslow
Sandra G. Hassink

Alfred I. duPont Institute

Background and Development

Importance of Topic

Obesity affects as many as one of every four children in the United States. From the 1970s to the 1990s, prevalence rates have increased by more than 50% for children in the 6- to 11-year age range and by 40% during adolescence (Gortmaker, Dietz, Sobol, & Wheeler, 1987). Not only has there been a precipitous rise in the rate of childhood obesity, but the prevalence rate of superobesity (above the 95th percentile) has increased most rapidly, leading to Dietz's (1991) conclusion "America's children are not only getting fatter, but the fattest of the group are getting fatter at a more rapid rate" (p. 290).

Reasons for the increasing rates of obesity in childhood are mulifactorial and include declining activity in children, increased access to calorically dense fast food, and the hurried pace of many American families. It is now reasonably clear that most children do not outgrow their weight problems. An adolescent with obesity is at a 50% to 70% risk of becoming an adult with obesity (Dietz, 1991; Garn, 1986).

Definition

Obesity may be defined simply as excess body fat. There are several measures that attempt to quantify the percentage of body weight accounted for by fat, including the weight-height-age tables commonly used by pediatricians, measurement of tricep fat-fold thickness, and even total water immersion (Foreyt & Goodrick, 1988). While weight is a commonly employed indirect assessment, measures that take height into consideration are more highly correlated with percentage of body fat. Many research studies employ the "Body Mass Index" (BMI) as a cost-effective, close estimate of body fat. BMI is calculated by dividing weight (in kilograms) by height squared (in meters). For example, an average, 85-pound (38.6 kg), 11-year-old female who is 4 feet 9 inches (1.45 m) tall would have a BMI of 13.3. An obese, 11-year-old, 155-pound (70.5 kg) female who is 5 feet 2 inches tall (1.57 m) would have a BMI of 28.2. Criteria for childhood obesity have included BMI above the 95th percentile, weight above the 95th percentile, and tricep skin-fold above the 85th percentile available from standardized tables that account for age and gender.

Etiology

Since the 1950s, the conceptualization of the causes of obesity has undergone a marked change. From viewing obesity as a manifestation of unconscious psychic conflict, current conceptualization suggests that obesity is a heterogeneous disorder with an interplay of both environmental and genetic factors (Brownell & Wadden, 1992).

Environmental Factors

Among the most salient environmental factors influencing the development of childhood obesity are diet, activity patterns, and parental influences. Findings are often inconsistent and vary with (a) age, (b) general versus treatment-seeking populations, (c) gender, and (d) socioeconomic level. Still, some general conclusions may be warranted.

Although families are spending increasing portions of their food expenditures eating outside the home, results of most national nutritional surveys suggest that today's children and adolescents have equivalent energy and fat intake with children of two decades ago (Albertson, Tobelmann, Engstrom, & Asp, 1992). However, children who are obese consume a greater proportion of their calories in fat than do children of normal weight, independent of total energy intake (Gazzaniga & Burns, 1993). It is important to note that children do not have to eat excessively to become obese. An excess of the equivalent of one glass of soda beyond what is needed to maintain appropriate weight for age can result in over 10 pounds (4.5 kg) of weight gain per year (Klish, 1995).

Recently, the Committee on Sports Medicine and Fitness of the American Academy of Pediatrics reported that low physical activity was the primary factor contributing to excessive fat accumulation in young children. Only half of all high schoolers, according to the Youth Risk Behavior Survey, reported being enrolled in physical education programs (Heath, Pratt, Warren, & Kahn, 1994). As with food intake, minor changes in activity can have marked long-term effects. Waxman and Stunkard (1980) found obese males were far less active at home, slightly less active outside the home, and equally active in school compared to controls. In an interesting early study examining the development of obesity, Griffiths and Payne (1976) found children of obese parents expended 300 kilocalories less per day than did children of nonobese parents. Also provocative was a case-controlled study by Muecke, Simons-Morton, Huang, and Parcel (1992) that found neither high-fat food intake nor reported level of physical activity distinguished obese from normal weight children, but together these variables synergistically combined to confer a 38% increase in risk for obesity. The braiding of diet and activity may well vary in subtle ways for obese children.

Studies on television viewing have reported inconsistent results. Whereas data from the National Health Examination Surveys have suggested a 2% increase in the prevalence of obesity for each additional hour of television viewed (Dietz & Gortmaker, 1985), other studies have failed to find a clear relationship (Shannon, Peacock, & Brown, 1991). Yet, it is likely that passive television viewing has an influence on youth at risk for obesity. Children spend four times as much time watching television—more than 25 hours per week—as they do preparing their homework. By the time children graduate from high school, they have spent more time watching television than engaging in any other activity except sleep (Rice, 1992).

Family factors also are intertwined in the multicausal etiology of childhood obesity. Larger families have a lower prevalence of obesity. Obesity is more common in "only children," in the last born in the family, and in children of older parents (Dietz, 1991). Perhaps the most influential factor, however, is obesity in the parents. If both parents are obese, more than two-thirds of their offspring will be obese. The risk drops to 10% if neither parent is obese (Stunkard et al., 1986). Again, the interactive nature of etiological factors should be stressed as suggested by Klesges, Eck, Hanson, Haddock, and Klesges (1990) who found parental obesity to be associated with lower activity levels in their preschoolers.

Genetic Factors

There is little if any dispute over the major role genetics play in the development of obesity. However, the mode of transmission and the exact mechanism underlying the inheritance (i.e., metabolic factors, activity levels) are still unresolved. Three major avenues of investigation have contributed to the understanding of the heritability patterns of obesity: adoption studies, twin studies, and family aggregate studies.

The majority of adoption studies find high correlations between obesity in children and their biological parents. Little relationship between adoptees and their adoptive parents is found (Stunkard et al., 1986). As well, there is little weight relationship between commonly reared adoptive children with different biological parents.

Twin studies are the most powerful ways to evaluate familial components of a trait. Identical twins, unlike fraternal twins, share all of their genes and, depending on adoption, vary in the degree to which they share rearing environments. Significant correlations are found consistently between BMIs of identical twins, with relatively little variability between those reared together or apart (.75 vs. .61 respectively). A .33 correlation between the BMIs of fraternal twins reared together has been reported (Grilo & Pogue-Geile, 1991), only slightly higher than siblings reared together (generally about .28).

Broadly, population surveys generally report that heritability does not exceed 30% to 40% with about a .25 correlation between parent and offspring weights (Grilo & Pogue-Geile, 1991). Yet, as indicated earlier, having an obese parent significantly raises the risk of being an obese child. Thus, while a genetic vulnerability is clearly inherited, nature finds itself intermingled with nurture in a complex and likely heterogeneous way to result in an obese child.

Prevalence: Socioeconomic, Racial, and Gender Factors

Research on the relationship between socioeconomic status (SES) and obesity has yielded a complex picture, interacting at times with ethnicity and gender. Generally, overall prevalence rates of obesity are increasing among all ages, races, and ethnic groups. Results from the recent National Health and Nutrition Examination Survey (NHANES III) found an overall prevalence of 22% for children 6 to 17 years with adolescents presenting higher rates than school-age children (Troiano, Flegal, Kuczmarski, Campbell, & Johnson, 1995). Some studies have found an inverse relationship between weight and SES while others have found a direct relationship. Generally, trends suggest that overweight is lowest in the very poor and in the wealthy and highest in the somewhat poor. There are few studies comparing obesity in urban versus rural areas of the country. Poverty in urban areas may confer a particular risk for obesity due to high levels of stress in families, few safe places to play, the high cost of fresh fruit and vegetables, and the easy access to fast food (Stunkard, d'Aquili & Fox, 1972).

Ethnicity and cultural factors associated with different racial groups affect prevalence rates. Generally, Hispanic children of both sexes are shorter and heavier than Caucasian or African-American peers. Most surveys typically associate less overweight with African-American children across gender. This relationship breaks down in adolescence for females. During adolescence, the prevalence of obesity for African-American girls increases markedly leading to a 50% rate of obesity in African-American women, twice the rate of Caucasian women (Melnyk & Weinstein, 1994).

Generally, the prevalence of obesity tends to increase with age with a corresponding decrease in physical activity (24% higher in elementary school than high school; Griffiths & Payne, 1976). Activity also appears to vary with ethnic background. Asian and Hispanic children are reported to be less active than Caucasian and African-American children. In contrast to research in the 1960s suggesting malnutrition as a health concern, Brousard et al. (1991) reported Native American adolescents and preschool children now have higher rates of overweight and of obesity than for all United States races combined. Along with changes in activity levels, changes in nutrition and availability of health care are reported to be significant etiological factors in the rising rates of obesity in Native American children (Davis, Gomez, Lambert, & Skipper, 1993).

Changes with Development

This section will highlight some of the developmental changes associated with children who present with obesity in the general population and to describe some of the clinical phenomena often present in a significant minority of children who seek treatment. Despite the high and growing prevalence rates, little is known about obesity across developmental stages. In part, this is due to viewing obesity as one entity, despite wide agreement as to the heterogeneous nature of its etiology. Few studies have attempted to subdivide children by race, age, degree of obesity, family factors, and variables in the clinical versus general populations (Kimm, Sweeney, Janosky, & MacMillan, 1991). Whereas studies examining childhood obesity in the general population often fail to find marked differences between children with obesity and controls on such factors as self-esteem, children presenting for treatment of their weight appear to be at greater psychological risk. For example, Epstein, Valoski, Wing, and McCurely (1994) reported that 29% of children entering one of their treatment studies met cutoff criteria for anxiety/depression and social problems on a behavior problem checklist. Similar findings were reported by Sheslow, Hassink, Wallace, and deLancey (1993) with obese patients seeking treatment. Interestingly, their psychological status was not correlated with weight.

Obesity and Developmental Delay

There are several syndromes in which obesity is associated with developmental delay. The most common genetic syndrome is the Prader-Willi Syndrome with an incidence of 1 in 10,000 newborns. During preschool years, this syndrome is associated with compulsive eating, an absence of satiation, and obsession with and stealing food. In later childhood, excessive stubbornness, poor impulse control, and aggression are reported (Hom et al., 1993). Other syndromes in which obesity figures prominently are Bardet-Biedl Syndrome, associated with progressive visual acuity loss; polydactly and kidney disease; and Alstrom Syndrome, associated with blindness, hearing loss, and kidney failure. These disorders are considerably more rare than the Prader-Willi Syndrome.

Obesity often coexists with other syndromes such as Down Syndrome and with mental retardation in general as a result of problems with coordination, limitations in play skill, and, at times, sheltering children at home where food and snacking may take on increased importance. Parents report that exclusion from peer opportunities in the neighborhood often means that passive, solitary activities replace activities that burn energy. The move to greater inclusion for all identified special populations may present school personnel with a special challenge to provide appropriate physical education activities that are active, inclusive, and oriented to lifestyle as opposed to calisthenic-type activities (Epstein, Valoski, et al., 1994).

Obesity and Preschool-Age Children

Clearly, the younger the child the more influence parents have over their children's food and activity levels. In one survey, almost 90% of parents reported that they decided when their preschoolers ate and believed that their own levels of between-meal snacking influenced their children's snacking behavior (Contento, Manning, & Shannon, 1992). Data from the Framingham Children's Study (Oliveria et al., 1992) indicated that preschoolers whose parents consumed diets high in saturated fat were over five times more likely to have a diet high in saturated fat than were preschoolers whose parents ate low-fat diets. Similarly, Klesges and colleagues (Klesges et al., 1983; Klesges, Mallot, Boshee, & Weber, 1986) in a series of studies reported significant positive correlations between parental prompts to eat and the amount of time that preschoolers actually spent eating. Parents of overweight children gave more encouragement to eat and more food prompts than did parents of normal weight children.

In a study of 132 nonreferred preschool children, Klesges et al. (1992) concluded that family functioning assessed across normal and overweight children did not correlate with measures of body fat nor with parental ratings of their preschooler's self-esteem. Given the heterogenous phenomena associated with the etiology of obesity, it is not surprising that global assessment measures do not consistently distinguish between overweight and control children. Even within the same family, parent-child interactions for the obese and nonobese child can be quite different. As noted by Waxman and Stunkard (1980), mothers served larger portions to their obese children more frequently than they did their normal weight children.

Many obese preschoolers presenting for treatment are reported by their parents to be demanding and to have challenging temperaments. Carey, Hegrik; and McDevitt (1988) reported that rapid weight gain in 4- and 5-year-old children was correlated with a difficult temperamental style. They hypothesized that children with difficult temperaments experience more stress in their social interactions and use eating as a technique for comforting or they may be less flexible about changing their eating patterns or both. In our weight-management program, this chapter's authors have observed two common family systems associated with preschoolers presenting for treatment. In one family system, consistent with a hypothesis proposed by Carey et al. (1988), the child's behavior was marked by temperamental intensity, disinhibition, and persistence. The child's demands for food or snacks and demands for video games or television viewing appear to be negatively reinforced by parents who value the momentary calm engendered by "giving in."

The second, common, clinically observed preschool family system, also observed by Neumann and Jenks (1992) in their weight management program, presents with a child who has suffered a difficult birth or a life-threatening illness or is a product of divorce whose parents are "making up" for past injuries to the child. These children often have an easy temperamental style, wear the latest clothing, snack and eat out frequently, and often choose their own diets.

Obesity in School-Age Children

The rate of obesity during the school-age years may be as high as one in four children (Dietz, 1991). This rate clearly exceeds the base rates for depressive disorders, anxiety disorders, and other common emotional problems in childhood. Thus, it is illogical to think that mental health or self-esteem problems would globally coexist with childhood obesity. Studies examining the relationship between self-esteem and obesity in school-aged children offer mixed results: Some find lowered self-esteem while others find no differences between control children and children with obesity (Friedman & Brownell, 1995). It is more reasonable to treat obesity as an independent risk factor for psychological morbidity the way it is treated as a risk factor for medical morbidity. In this way, it is possible to conclude that, at least for some populations of school-aged children, obesity increases the likelihood of emotional distress (Wallace, Hassink, & Sheslow, 1993).

In one study examining the risk for depression in obese children referred for treatment, almost 30% were found to be at some increased risk on a commonly used depression self-report instrument (Wallace et al., 1993). Kimm et al. (1991) found average ratings in self-esteem for a large group of referred obese children, but a further look at their data suggested some within-group differences. Analysis of their African-American subgroup revealed lower self-esteem ratings for younger females and older males. Obese children with a period of normal weight gain followed by a rapid rise in weight appeared to have higher self-esteem than did children with chronic obesity (Hassink, Sheslow & deLancey, 1993). Epstein, Klein, and Wisnewski (1994) examined the effects of parental psychopathology on the self-esteem of obese children. Parental psychopathology, but not weight, was found to be, associated with lowered self-esteem in obese children.

It is during the mid-elementary-school years that vulnerable children with weight problems withdraw or perhaps, more accurately, are pushed away by their peers. Whether obese children internalize it or not, almost all are teased and many suffer from a societally more tolerated prejudice. In an often quoted study, Goodman, Richardson, Dornbucsh, and Hastorff (1963) asked 10- and 11- year-olds to rank order six drawings of children from the most to least liked. Pictures depicted children physically disabled, disfigured, obese, and "normal." Consistently, the normal child was rated most desirable and the child with obesity least desirable. In another study, silhouettes of children differing in body type were presented to girls 7 to 11 years old with a list of adjectives (Staffieri, 1972). Words like "ugly" or "stupid" were used to describe the obese silhouettes, even by overweight raters.

Clinically, referred school-aged children with obesity report feeling lonely and often have only one child willing to play with them. Family becomes more important as a source of reinforcement and, because it is typical for at least one parent also to be obese, socialization is often around such adult (nonaerobic) activities as going out to eat.

During this period, parents often believe that their children should be responsible for their own diets. Conflict can arise when the overweight child is singled out to exercise self-control when others in the family have access to high-calorie snack foods or second servings.

Obesity in Adolescence

During the high conformity years of adolescence, when being with the "right" crowd and showing up at the "right" places influence one's sense of self, the impact of obesity may be felt most keenly, at least for Caucasian middle-class adolescents. Body ideals appear to depart between Caucasion and African-American and Hispanic teens during this period. Caucasian teenagers from middle and upper socioeconomic levels strive for an ultra-thin ideal (Striegel-Moore, Silberstein & Rodin, 1986) increasing their risk of anorexia nervosa and bulimia. Cultural attitudes about body ideal appear to provide some protection from these disorders for African-American and Hispanic females (Melnyk & Weinstein, 1994; Silber, 1986). Cultural tolerance toward overweight, however, may prevent necessary attention to weight management. Gortmaker et al. (1987) analyzed trends in obesity from 1963 to 1980 and reported a 35% increase in adolescent obesity for Caucasians with a 53% percent increase for African-Americans.

Between 50% and 70% of obese adolescents become obese adults (Dietz, 1991; Garn, 1986) resulting in increased risk for high blood pressure, diabetes, cardiovascular disease, and some forms of cancer. A dramatic demonstration of the socioeconomic costs of not normalizing weight in adolescence was provided by Gortmaker and colleagues (Gortmaker, Must, Perrin, Sobol & Dietz, 1993) in their 7-year follow-up study of adolescents presenting with obesity, matched with controls for initial education and socioeconomic levels. Results revealed that women who were obese completed fewer years in school, were significantly less likely to be married, and had lower household incomes and higher rates of poverty.

Clinically, obese adolescents present with concerns common to this developmental period. As teenagers begin to explore relationships in earnest, feelings about one's body and physical attractiveness become intertwined with identity formation. The self-concept of obese teens seems to suffer at this developmental period when "watching and being watched" by peers seems so important. Unlike research reporting inconsistent findings as to self-esteem in school-age children, studies examining self-concept in the adolescent age group consistently suggest lower scores on self-report measures (Friedman & Brownell, 1995). It is also during this developmental period that adolescents seeking treatment present with clinical levels of depression and isolation, a willingness to confront previously undisclosed sexual abuse, or with insights into family dysfunctions that directly relate to their weight management concerns.

Problems and Implications

Medical Problems

Medical concerns related to obesity in childhood can range from early physical maturation to orthopedic disease when children with morbid obesity are unable to support their weight. Generally, children who are obese are more accurately seen as at risk for medical problems which become apparent in adulthood. There are, however, several medical complications and comorbidities of childhood obesity that have implications for school personnel.

Children with significant obesity who demonstrate excessive sleepiness to the point of falling asleep in class may have Obstructive Sleep Apnea Syndrome (Guilleminalult, 1985). Other symptoms may range from externalizing behavior such as hyperactivity and aggression to internalizing behavior such as withdrawal. Medical evaluation is warranted. Temporizing interventions are aimed at increasing airflow while definitive treatment requires weight loss.

Asthma, the most common reason for school absence, may be both a contributor and result of weight problems. Exercise-induced asthma may prevent a child from participating in active physical education, and increased weight may also affect pulmonary function (Kaplan & Montana, 1993). Orthopedic problems of the hip or knees also can dramatically affect activity levels. Treating the asthma and the orthopedic problems is instrumental for weight-management efforts by opening opportunities for outdoor activities and exercise tolerance.

Children with chronic obesity may be at greater risk for Type II diabetes, hypertension, stroke, and cardiovascular disease (Hassink et al., 1993). As adults, the constellation of obesity, glucose intolerance, hyperinsulinemia, and low HDL ("good") cholesterol has been termed "Syndrome X" (Reaven, 1991). Adults and some children with obesity have higher then expected levels of insulin leading to some degree of insulin resistance (Hassink, Sheslow, & Wallace, 1993). Blood sugar levels then remain high, and the body converts the excess blood sugar into fat, often stored at the mid-body. As the pancreas reaches its capacity, Type II diabetes ensues, blood vessels constrict causing high blood pressure, and plaque builds in the arteries increasing the risk of stroke and heart disease. Given the rise in obesity rates in childhood and the poor health prospects of adult obesity, the development of child and adolescent weight-management programs should be considered a health priority.

Psychological Problems

Just as obesity increases risk associated with medical morbidities, obesity also increases psychological risk on a dimension ranging from no demonstrable effect to mental disorder (e.g., Depressive Disorders). As is also the case with potential medical problems, increasing the number of risk factors increases the probability of negative outcome. The risk of injury to self-esteem appears to increase with development (Friedman & Brownell, 1995). Children presenting for treatment of their obesity appear to be at increased risk for social anxiety and mood disorders (Epstein, Valoski, et al., 1994). Difficulties with peers may further exacerbate a withdrawal from energetic activities and increase dependency on family as a main source of support. We have worked with a child who was frightened to leave the house, participated in home-bound instruction, lived mostly in her bedroom, and socialized only with family. Another child in our program presented with depression, reporting that he was teased by the "jerks" in the neighborhood and at school. He turned to his obese grandmother for companionship who inadvertently foiled his attempt at weight management. A teenager with significant body disparagement, disclosed her history of sexual abuse, as factors related to the onset of her rapid weight gain were discussed.

Thus, obesity may be seen most appropriately as resulting from heterogeneous factors that increase the risk of stress in childhood. Whether obesity is an independent risk factor for psychopathology or interacts with other factors such as parental psychopathology (Epstein, Klein, et al., 1994) is unclear.

Alternative Actions

Treatment Approaches

Dieting

As early as 1967, Dwyer, Feldman, and Mayer reported that 45% of third to sixth graders wanted to be thinner, and 37% had already tried to lose weight. Dieting is generally associated with adolescence and most particularly with Caucasian adolescent females. Broad health surveys typically report approximately 40% of females (47% Caucasian vs. 30% African American) and 20% of males attempt to lose weight while another 20% of females and 10% of males attempt not to gain weight. About 25% of females who reported themselves to be the "right weight" still were trying to lose weight (Serdula et al., 1993). Emmons (1994) found that dieters and nondieters could not be distinguished by weight but rather by their perception of being overweight, and this perception of being overweight was associated with actually being overweight sometime in childhood. The effects of dieting can include impaired growth, discontinuation of menses, feelings of failure, lowered self-esteem, and symptoms of depression (Nylander, 1971; Wilson, 1993). Several lines of research have shown that anorexia nervosa and bulemia nervosa are associated with dieting. Yet, given the high rates of dieting and the lifetime prevalence rates of 1.5% to 2% for these eating disorders, clearly additional risk factors need to be considered in predicting who is most prone to these serious eating disorders (Wilson, 1993).

As will be discussed in the next section, supervised dieting (or perhaps more appropriately termed "alterations in lifestyle eating behavior") as part of a comprehensive program of weight management can add to a positive outcome. Self-initiated dieting often ends in frustration which may lead to stress and the abandonment of weight management efforts. Medically supervised, very low calorie diets (i.e., less than 800 calories) for morbidly obese adolescents have reported some positive short-term results, but long-term weight loss has been discouraging (Stallings, Archibald, Pencharz, Harrison, & Bell, 1988). Other extreme forms of weight reduction such as liposuction or jaw wiring are clearly not appropriate forms of treatment for juvenile populations as the short-term benefits are outweighed by their medical risks.

Clinically Based Treatment

The long-term ineffectiveness of behavioral and dietary approaches to the treatment of adult obesity is a matter of record (National Institutes of Health, Technology Assessment Conference Panel, 1992). It is therefore noteworthy to report a more positive outcome for the treatment of obese children. In their meta-analysis of 41 controlled-outcome studies, Haddock and colleagues, (Haddock, Shadish, Klesges, & Stein, 1994) conclude that "comprehensive behavioral treatments employing behavior modification techniques, a special diet and a special exercise program are moderately successful in reducing weight or obesity status measures" (p. 241), and these results are maintained at follow-up.

Although a number of studies report on programs that employ behavioral principles, nutritional education, and exercise with good outcomes, only the work of Epstein and his colleagues (Epstein, Valoski, et al., 1994) can boast impressive results on 10-year follow-up. Long-term results of their family-based treatment program indicate a 34% decrease in overweight by 20% of children and 30% of treated children who were no longer obese.

Components of the program were varied to investigate their effectiveness, but the basic approach remained constant. The basic treatment package consisted of weekly meetings stressing behavior management for 8 to 12 weeks, followed by monthly meetings for 6 to 12 months. The Traffic Light Diet (Epstein, Wing, & Valoski, 1985) was employed where foods were characterized as "red," "yellow," or "green" on the basis of nutrient content. Green foods like vegetables were "a go" while red foods like potato chips or candy were limited to seven per week. Exercise, also a cornerstone of the program, was found to result in superior outcome when compared to diet alone, with lifestyle exercise (e. g., increasing walking, biking) superior to calisthenics. Lastly, improved effects were reported by including the parent in treatment (Epstein, Valoski, et al., 1994). Israel, Guile, and Baker (1994) employed a standard multicomponent treatment and contrasted giving the major responsibility for interventions to the parents or to the child. For the latter condition, children were given enhanced training in self-management (i.e., self-goal setting, formulating plans for change, self-evaluation, self-reward). Results supported both approaches in terms of percentage of overweight changed, but the child's enhanced self-regulation training appeared superior on 3-year follow-up.

Recently, Epstein et al. (1995) provided support for the notion that decreasing sedentary behavior in children treated for obesity might be a useful treatment component. The family-based treatment targeted increasing exercise, decreasing sedentary behavior, or a combined approach in 8- to 12-year-olds. At the one-year follow-up, the "sedentary" group demonstrated a greater loss in percentage of body weight and body fat than the other two groups.

Because behavioral interventions are a large part of effective interventions packages, it is important to underscore some of the skills taught. According to Foreyt and Cousins (1989), there are five behavioral methodologies commonly employed in the treatment of obese children. Self-monitoring involves the recording of the where, what, when, and with whom of eating and exercise behavior; these records are used to determine baselines and patterns of behavior. Stimulus control involves the systematic altering of cues that lead to excessive eating and sedentary behavior. Eating-management techniques focus on such behaviors as slowing the pace of eating, eating on smaller plates, or having portions served rather than eating family style. Operant conditioning principles of rewards and sanctions are applied to goals set in order to increase awareness and affect the strength of habitual behaviors. In one of the few studies investigating individual aspects of the "behavioral package," Epstein, McKenzie, Valoski, Klein, and Wing (1994) reported that reinforcing participants for mastery of diet, exercise, weight loss, and parenting versus noncontingently reinforcing participation resulted in significantly greater weight loss at one-year follow-up. This effect, however, was not maintained at the 2-year follow-up.

As noted by Kumanyika, Morssink, and Agurs (1992), a weight-management program may be technically well constructed but not effective for individuals with different ethnic backgrounds as a result of lifestyle issues, food preferences, or family structure. One of the few studies to demonstrate success with African-American teens, a particularly at-risk group, was described by Wadden et al. (1990). A multidisciplinary program (Weight Reduction and Pride) proved successful that emphasized behavioral weight counseling, nutritional counseling, physical activity, and eating management, and also included the teen's mother in treatment. The more sessions attended by the girl's mothers the more weight was lost. Melnyk and Weinstein (1994) stressed that using the language, social settings, peer supports, and professional networks within a culture will enhance the likelihood of success of the weight-control program.

It is well known that support from both family and peers is a key factor contributing to the adjustment of children with chronic illnesses (Wallander & Varni, 1989). Combining nutritional education, activity management, and behavioral interventions in ways that support the social needs of children and families holds the most promise for future treatment efforts.

School-Based Programs

Schools can provide unique opportunities for weight management unavailable in other settings. The school environment allows easy access to children and to educational programming that can be concentrated (a course) and longitudinal (increasing sophistication across grades). Interventions can include significant members of the child's natural environment and provide both active (e.g., physical education) and passive (e.g., groups) aspects of effective weight-control methods. Despite these advantages, there have been few recent studies focusing on weight control in the schools. Competition with other health needs such as substance abuse or AIDS appears to have moved weight concern to the "back burner" (Resnicow, 1993). While 77% of principals interviewed in one study endorsed the importance of a curriculum focusing on childhood obesity, only 39% viewed weight-management programs as appropriate for the school environment and only 28% believed the school to be the best place to prevent weight problems (Price, Desmond, & Seltzer, 1987).

School-based obesity programs can be classified as schoolwide or high risk: delivering services to the whole student body or exclusively to children who are overweight (Resnicow, 1993). Generally, programs specifically aimed at children with weight concerns appear more successful. These programs also provide a wider service delivery model. High-risk programs have included behavior modification, nutrition education, exercise, and peer and parent support. School-wide programs primarily are classroom based and provide nutrition information, some skills training, and some parent involvement. While few programs provide follow-up data to support long-term outcome, most programs report positive short-term results. Of the six "high-risk" programs reviewed by Resnicow (1993), all reported reductions in the percentage overweight compared to expected weight for height, with many participating students reporting weight loss. All were multicomponent treatment programs that varied aspects of the interventions such as peer leaders or parental involvement. "Holding the line" on weight gain while growing into growing bodies may be a reasonable weight-management goal particularly in light of the report that many control children increase their weight during the treatment interval. Only one-third of school-wide programs reported significant positive weight-related outcomes. It should be noted that the majority of short-term school-based treatment programs typically yield small changes in actual weight lost.

A now classic study by Brownell and Kaye (1982) highlighted the unique potential of the school environment for weight control. A behavioral component (self-monitoring, eating management, contracting, and rewards for changes) was combined with dietary education and exercise. This study was the first to enlist social supports from the child's network. Teachers, parents, peers, the physical education teacher, and food service personnel had a role in the intervention. Of the children treated, 95% lost weight and 97% showed a reduction in percentage overweight for expected height. Of the control children, 71% gained weight. Other multicomponent treatment programs altered program components or student populations. For example, Foster, Wadden, and Brownell (1985) trained peer counselors to recommend changes in eating and exercise habits. Nelson, Catchings, and Pendleton (1983) reported successful outcomes employing behavior modification approaches with obese children who were mentally retarded. An early study by Epstein, Masek, and Marshall (1978) demonstrated that young children attending a Head Start program could successfully participate in a weight-management program.

Although more is now known about the factors that improve weight loss and maintenance, these ideas have not percolated into school-based treatment programs. Brownell and Wadden (1992) noted several factors that might enhance outcome in the school environment including employing the concept of reasonable weight-change expectancy (i.e., reducing weight gain in children might be appropriate), extending the length of treatment (as longer treatment intervals are associated with greater success), teaching relapse-prevention skills, building coping skills for children's specific needs, integrating treatment of body image, and emphasizing a low-fat diet. Including these concepts within the multicomponent treatment model in a school environment that can provide concentrated and longitudinal contact with children may hold the most promise for stemming the rising rates of obesity in children.

Summary

Since the 1970s, there has been more than a 50% rise in the prevalence of childhood obesity. It is no longer in dispute that there are both biological and behavioral factors associated with the etiology of obesity.

It is clear that most obese children do not suffer emotional damage as a result of their obesity. It may be more reasonable to view obesity as a risk factor that influences and is influenced by intrapsychic issues, peer relationships, family relationships, and developmental issues. In early childhood, parents exert greater control over their youngster's diet and activity pattern. Obesity does not

appear to play a formative role in the young obese child's self-esteem. By adolescence, obesity appears to be associated with a more pervasive effect on self-concept. Prejudice in the form of social devaluation and economic devaluation of obese children and adolescents has been documented.

In contrast to poor treatment outcomes with obese adults, there is reason for measured optimism in the treatment of obese children. Multicomponent treatment programs that include behavior modification, nutritional training, and exercise or activity management can boast moderately successful long-term outcomes. Family-oriented approaches that also stress lifestyle exercise appear to be most successful.

School programs also appear to be successful with obese children if they are comprehensive in scope. School programs oriented to obese children specifically rather than to the whole student population generally have been found to be more effective. However, the lack of follow-up data from school-based programs prevents a clear statement of their long-term effectiveness. Schools may be the most logical site for obesity intervention given the need for long-term management, the school's potential for physical education and nutritional education, and the potential for rallying important people in the child and adolescent's networks.

Recommended Resources

Brownell, K. D., & Kaye, F. S., (1982). A school-based behavior modification, nutrition education and physical activity program for obese children. *The American Journal of Clinical Nutrition, 35,* 277–283.
Brownell and Kaye present one of the most well-designed, controlled studies of a comprehensive treatment approach effective in the school environment. Most impressively, the program marshalled support from the child's network including participation by parents, the nurse's aide, teachers, food service personnel, the physical education teacher, and peers. Compared to controls, 71% of whom gained weight, 97% of program children lost weight. This study may be unique in including child's social network in weight management.

Brownell, K. D., & Wadden, T. A. (1992). Etiology and treatment of obesity: Understanding a serious, prevalent, and refractory disorder. *Journal of Consulting and Clinical Psychology, 60,* 505–517.
Brownell and Wadden present a clear overview of the heterogeneous factors related to the treatment of obesity. The authors suggest integrating information on etiology, social beliefs, and exercise and then setting reasonable goals for weight loss to form a comprehensive and compassionate model for intervention.

Epstein, L. H., Valoski, A., Wing, R. R., & McCurley, J. (1994). Ten-year outcomes of behavioral family-based treatment for childhood obesity. *Health Psychology, 13,* 373–383. *Outcomes from four studies employing a family-based, behaviorally oriented treatment program are discussed. Studies by this group have consistently reported lasting, positive results. Significant effects were reported when parents and children were both treated and when lifestyle exercise was stressed. The basic treatment program is described and reasons for the long-term success discussed.*

References

Albertson, A. M., Tobelmann, R. C., Engstrom, A., & Asp, E. H. (1992). Nutrient intake in 2–10-year-old American children: Ten-year trends. *Journal of the American Dietetic Association, 92,* 14–20.

Brousard, B. A., Johnson, A., Himes, J. H., Story, M., Fichtner, R., Hauck, F., Bachman-Carter, J., Hayes, J., Frolich, K., Valay, S., & Gohdes, D. (1991). Prevalence of obesity in American Indians and Alaska Natives. *American Journal of Clinical Nutrition, 53,* 1535S-1542S.

Brownell, K. D., & Kaye, F. S. (1982). A school-based behavior modification, nutrition education and physical activity program for obese children. *American Journal of Clinical Nutrition, 35,* 277–283.

Brownell, K. D., & Wadden, T. A. (1992). Etiology and treatment of obesity: Understanding a serious prevalent and refractory disorder. *Journal of Consulting and Clinical Psychology, 60,* 505–517.

Carey, W. B., Hegrik, R. L., & McDevitt, S. C. (1988). Temperamental factors associated with rapid weight gain and obesity in middle childhood. *Developmental and Behavioral Pediatrics, 9,* 194–194.

Contento, I. R., Manning, A. D., & Shannon, B. M. (1992). Research perspectives on school-based nutrition education. *Journal of Nutrition Education, 24,* 247–260.

Davis, S., Gomez, Y., Lambert, L., & Skipper, B. (1993). Primary prevention of obesity in American Indian children. In C. L. Williams & S. Y. S. Kimm (Eds.), *Prevention and treatment of childhood obesity* (pp. 167–180). New York: The New York Academy of Sciences.

Dietz, W. (1991). Factors associated with childhood obesity. *Nutrition, 7,* 290–291.

Dietz, W. H., & Gortmaker, S. L. (1985). Do we fatten our children at the television set: Obesity and television viewing in children and adolescents. *Pediatrics, 75,* 807–812.

Dreizen, D., Sprikakis, C. N., & Stone, R. E. (1967). A comparison of skeletal growth and maturation in undernourished and well nourished girls before and after menarche. *Journal of Pediatrics, 70,* 256–263.

Dwyer, J. F., Feldman, J. J., & Mayer, J. (1967) Adolescent dieters: who are they? Physical characteristics, attitudes and dieting practices of adolescent girls. *American Journal of Clinical Nutrition, 20,* 1045–1046.

Emmons, L. (1994). Predisposing factors differentiating adolescent dieters and nondieters. *Journal of the American Dietetic Association, 94,* 725–729.

Epstein, L. H., Klein, K. R., & Wisnewski, L. (1994). Child and parent factors that influence psychological problems in obese children. *International Journal of Eating Disorders, 15,* 151–157.

Epstein, L. H., Masek, B. J., & Marshall, W. R. (1978). A nutritionally based school program for control of eating in obese children. *Behavior Therapy, 9,* 766–788.

Epstein, L. H., McKenzie, S. J., Valoski, A. M., Klein, K. R., & Wing, A. (1994). Effects of mastery criteria and contingent reinforcement for family-based child weight control. *Addictive Behaviors, 19,* 135–145.

Epstein, L. H., Valoski, A. M., Vara, L. S., McCurely, J., Wisnewski, L., Kalarchian, K. M., Klein, K. R., & Shrager, L. R. (1995). Effects of decreasing sedentary behavior and increasing activity on weight change in obese children. *Health Psychology, 14,* 109–115.

Epstein, L. H., Valoski, A., Wing, R., & McCurley, J. (1994). Ten-year outcomes of behavioral family-based treatment for childhood obesity. *Health Psychology, 13,* 373–383.

Epstein, L. H., Wing, R. R., & Valoski, A. (1985). Childhood obesity. *Pediatric Clinics of North America, 32,* 363–379.

Foreyt, J. P., & Cousins, J. H. (1989). Obesity. In E. J. Marsh & R. A. Barkley (Eds.), *Treatment of childhood disorders* (pp. 405–422). New York: Guilford Press.

Foreyt, J. P., & Goodrick, G. K. (1988). Childhood obesity. In E. J. Marsh & L. G. Terdal (Eds.), *Behavioral assessment of childhood* (2nd ed., pp. 528–551). New York: Guilford Press.

Foster, G. D., Wadden, T. A., & Brownell, K. D. (1985). Peer-led program for the treatment and prevention of obesity in the schools. *Journal of Consulting and Clinical Psychology, 53,* 538–540.

Friedman, M. A., & Brownell, K. D. (1995). Psychological correlates of obesity: Moving to the next research generation. *Psychological Bulletin, 117,* 3–20.

Garn, S. M. (1986). Family-line and socioeconomic factors in fatness and obesity. *Nutrition Reviews, 44,* 381–386.

Gazzaniga, J., & Burns, R. L. (1993). Relationship between diet composition and body composition and body fatness with adjustment for resting energy expenditure and physical activity in preadolescent children. *American Journal of Clinical Nutrition, 58,* 21–28.

Goodman, N., Richardson, S. A., Dornbusch, S. M., & Hastorff, A. H. (1963). Variant reactions to physical disabilities. *American Sociological Review, 28,* 429–435.

Gortmaker, S. L., Dietz, W. H., Sobol, A. M., & Wheeler, C. A. (1987). Increasing pediatric obesity in the United States. *American Journal of Diseases of Children, 141,* 535–540.

Gortmaker, S. L., Must, A., Perrin, J. M., Sobol, A. M., & Dietz, W. (1993). Social and economic consequences of overweight in adolescence and young adulthood. *New England Journal of Medicine, 329,* 1008–1012.

Griffiths, M., & Payne, P. R. (1976). Energy expenditure in small children of obese and nonobese patients. *Nature, 260,* 698–700.

Grilo, C. M., & Pogue-Geile, M. F. (1991). The nature of environmental influences on weight and obesity: A behavior genetic analysis. *Psychological Bulletin, 110,* 520–537.

Guilleminalult, C. (1985). Obstructive sleep apnea: The

clinical syndrome and its historical perspective. *Medical Clinics of North America, 69,* 1187–1203.

Haddock, C. K., Shadish, W. R., Klesges, R. C., & Stein, R. J. (1994). Treatments for childhood and adolescent obesity. *Annals of Behavioral Medicine, 16,* 235–244.

Hassink, S., H., Sheslow, D. V., & deLancey, E. (1993, May). *Chronic and reactive weight gain history in obese children: Differential risk assessment for future morbidity.* Paper presented at the American Academy of Pediatrics, Seattle, WA.

Hassink, S. H., Sheslow, D. V., & Wallace, W. (1993). Hyperinsulinemia: Incidence and risk in an obese pediatric population. In C. L. Williams & S. Y. S. Kimn (eds.) *Prevention and treatment of childhood obesity* (pp. 271–272). New York: New York Academy of Sciences.

Heath, G. H., Pratt, M., Warren, C. W. & Kahn, L. (1994). Physical activity patterns in American high school students. *Archives of Pediatric Adolescent Medicine, 148,* 1131–1136.

Hom, V. A., Cassidy, S. B., Butler, M. G., Hanchett, J. M., Greenway, L. R., Whitman, B. Y., & Greenberg, F. (1993). Prader-Willi Syndrome consensus diagnostic criteria. *Pediatrics, 91,* 398–402.

Israel, A. C., Guile, C. A., & Baker, J. E. (1994). An evaluation of enhanced self-regulation training in the treatment of childhood obesity. *Journal of Pediatric Psychology, 19,* 737–749.

Kaplan, T. A., & Montana, E. (1993) Exercise induced bronchospasm in nonasthmatic obese children. *Clinical Pediatrics, 32,* 220–225.

Klesges, R. C., Coates, T. J., Holzer, B., Moldenhauer, L. M., Woolfey, J., & Vollmer, J. (1983). Parental influences on children's eating behavior. *Journal of Applied Behavior Analysis, 16,* 371–378.

Klesges, R. C., Eck, L. H., Hanson, C. L., Haddock, C. K., & Klesges, L. M. (1990). Effects of obesity, social interactions, and physical environment on physical activity in preschoolers. *Health Psychology, 9,* 435–449.

Klesges, R. C., Haddock, C. K., Klesges, L. M., Stein, R. J., Eck, L. H., & Hanson, C. L. (1992). Relationship between psychosocial functioning and body fat in preschool children: A longitudinal investigation. *Journal of Consulting and Clinical Psychology, 60,* 793–796.

Klesges, R. C., Mallot, J. M., Boshee, P. F., & Weber, J. M. (1986). The effects of parental influences on children's food intake, physical activity, and relative weight. *International Journal of Eating Disorders, 5,* 335–346.

Klish, W. J. (1995). Childhood obesity: Pathophisiology and treatment. *Acta Paediatrica Japonica, 37,* 1–6.

Kimm, S. Y., Sweeney, C. G., Janosky, J. E., & MacMillan, J. P. (1991). Self-concept measures and childhood obesity: A descriptive analysis. *Developmental and Behavioral Pediatrics, 12,* 19–24.

Kumanyika, S. K., Morssink, C., & Agurs, T. (1992). Models for dietary and weight change in African-American women: Identifying cultural components. *Ethnicity Discourse, 2,* 166–175.

Melnyk, M. G., & Weinstein, E. (1994). Preventing obesity in Black women by targeting adolescents: A literature review. *Journal of the American Dietetic Association, 94,* 536–540.

Meucke, L., Simons-Morton, B., Huang, I. W., & Parcel, G. (1992). Is childhood obesity associated with high-fat foods and low physical activity? *Journal of School Health, 62,* 19–23.

National Institutes of Health, Technology Assessment Conference Panel. (1992). Methods for voluntary weight loss and control. *Annals of Internal Medicine, 116,* 942–949.

Nelson, E. C., Catchings, M. W., & Pendleton, T. B. (1983). Weight reduction and maintenance for overweight mentally retarded students, ages 9–17. *Journal of School Health, 53,* 380–381.

Neumann, C. G., & Jenks, B. H. (1992). Obesity. In M. L. Levine, W. B. Carey, & A. C. Crocker (Eds.), *Developmental-Behavioral pediatrics* (pp. 354–363). Philadelphia: W. B. Saunders.

Nylander, I. (1971). The feeling of being fat and dieting in a school population. *Acta Sociology Scandinavia, 1,* 17–26.

Oliveria, S. A., Ellison, R. C., Moore, L., Gillman, M. W., Garraahhie, E. J., & Singer, M. R. (1992). Parent-child relationships in nutrient intake: The Framingham Children's Study. *American Journal of Clinical Nutrition, 56,* 593–598.

Price, J. H., Desmond, S. M., & Seltzer, C. M. (1987). Elementary school principals' perception of childhood obesity. *Journal of School Health, 57,* 367–370.

Reaven, G. (1991) Beyond cholesterol concentration: Other abnormality of lipid metabolism associated with coronary heart disease. *Diabetes-Metabolism Reviews, 7,* 137–138.

Resnicow, K. (1993). School-based obesity prevention. In C. L. Williams & S. Y. Kimm (Eds.), *Childhood obesity* (pp. 154–167). New York: New York Academy of Sciences.

Rice, B. (1992). Mixed signals: TV's effect on children continues to stir debate. *American Health, 62,* 24–30.

Serdula, M. K., Collins, E., Williamson, D. F., Anda, R. F., Pamuk, E., & Byers, T. E. (1993). Weight control practices of U.S. adolescents and adults. *Annals of Internal Medicine, 119,* 667–671.

Shannon, B. M., Peacock, J., & Brown, M. J. (1991). Body fatness, television viewing and calorie intake in a sample of Pennsylvania sixth graders. *Journal of Nutrition Education, 23,* 262–268.

Sheslow, D. V., Hassink, S. G., Wallace, W., & deLancey, E. (1993). The relationship between self-esteem and depression in childhood obesity. In C. L. Williams & S. Y. S. Kimm (Eds.), *Prevention and treatment of childhood obesity* (pp. 289–291). New York: New York Academy of Sciences.

Silber, T. J. (1986). Anorexia nervosa in Blacks and Hispanics. *International Journal of Eating Disorders, 5,* 121–128.

Staffieri, J. R. (1972). Body build and behavior expectancies in young females. *Developmental Psychology, 6,* 125–127.

Stallings, V. A., Archibald, E. H., Pencharz, M. B., Harrison, J. E., & Bell, L. E. (1988). One-year follow-up of weight, total body potassium and total body nitrogen in obese adolescents treated with protein-sparing modified fast. *American Journal of Clinical Nutrition, 48,* 91–94.

Striegel-Moore, R., & Rodin, J. (1986). The influence of psychological variables in obesity. In K. D. Brownell & J. P. Foreyt (Eds.), *Handbook of eating disorders: Physiology, psychology and treatment of obesity, anorexia and bulimia* (pp. 99–121). New York: Basic Books.

Stunkard, A. J., d'Aquili, E., & Fox, S. (1972). Influence of social class on obesity and thinness in children. *Journal of the American Medical Association, 221,* 579–585.

Stunkard, A. J., Sorenson, T., Hanes, C., Teasdale, R., Chakraborty, W., Schull, J., & Shulsinger, F. (1986). An adoption study of human obesity. *New England Journal of Medicine, 314,* 193–198.

Troiano, R. P., Flegal, K. M., Kuczmarski, R. J., Campbell, S. M., & Johnson, C. L. (1995). Overweight and obesity prevalence trends for children and adolescents. *Archives of Pediatric and Adolescent Medicine, 149,* 1085–1091.

Wadden, T. A., Stunkard, A. J., Rich, L., Rubin, C. J., Sweidel, G., & McKinney, S. (1990). Obesity in Black adolescent girls: A controlled clinical trial of treatment by diet, behavior modification, and parental support. *Pediatrics, 85,* 345–352.

Wallace, W., Hassink S., & Sheslow, D. (1993). Obesity in children: A risk factor for depression. In C. L. Williams & S. Y. S. Kimm (Eds.), *Prevention and treatment of childhood obesity* (pp. 301–303). New York: New York Academy of Sciences.

Wallander, J. L., & Varni, J. W. (1989). Social support and adjustment in chronically ill and handicapped children. *American Journal of Community Psychology, 17,* 185–201.

Waxman, M., & Stunkard, A. J. (1980). Caloric intake and expenditure of obese boys. *Journal of Pediatrics, 96,* 187–193.

Wilson, G. T. (1993). Relation of dieting and voluntary weight loss to psychological functioning and binge eating. *Annals of Internal Medicine, 119,* 727–730.

81

Adolescent Eating Disorders, Chronic Dieting, and Body Dissatisfaction

LeAdelle Phelps

State University of New York at Buffalo

Kristine Augustyniak

Children's Hospital of Buffalo

Linda D. Nelson

Niagara Falls Memorial Medical Center

David S. Nathanson

West Seneca Central Schools

Background and Development

The adolescent with an eating disorder is characterized by an intense preoccupation to be thin. The pathological fear of weight gain is manifested through the acts of self-starvation or cyclic bingeing and purging of food. *The Diagnostic and Statistical Manual of Mental Disorders, Fourth Edition* (*DSM-IV,* American Psychiatric Association, 1994 [APA]) identifies two separate types of eating disorders: *anorexia nervosa* and *bulimia nervosa.* Diagnostic criteria for anorexia require *loss of menses* and body weight *less than 85%* of that expected, whereas a diagnosis of bulimia dictates bingeing and purging episodes at least *twice a week.* Although less than 5% of adolescents manifest symptoms to the severity necessary for a *DSM-IV* diagnosis, some aggressive methods of weight control and reduction have become common including chronic and severe dieting; excessive exercise; self-induced vomiting; and abuse of laxatives, diet medications, and water pills. For example, fasting for one or more days has been reported by up to 37% of high school females, self-induced vomiting by 16%, and abuse of diet drugs or medications by 28% (Phelps, Andrea, & Rizzo, 1994).

Scientific data generally support the notion of a robust biogenetic predisposition to maintain weight within a certain range (i.e., set-point theory) and the ineffectiveness of most diets (Lissner, Steen, & Brownell, 1992; Stunkard, Harris, Pedersen, & McClearn, 1990). Yet current sociocultural mores place adolescent and young adult females under significant pressure to epitomize the thin yet unrealistic ideal.

Concomitant with the 30-year movement toward exaltation of slimness is the significant increase in disordered eating. For example, bulimia was not even described in the *DSM* until the 1980 edition, and virtually no research articles were devoted to the topic. Yet not all racial groups or countries embrace the thin model. For example, eating disorders in non-industrialized cultures are rare and in the United States, there are significant differences in disordered eating symptomatology among socioeconomic and race or ethnic groupings. American Asian, Caucasian, and Hispanic females as well as Black women of higher socioeconomic status (SES) are more likely to embrace the thin ideal whereas Black women of lower SES perceive a heavier body size as more attractive (Alan, Mayo, & Michael, 1993). From this perspective, eating disorders have been typically analyzed as socially induced neuroses.

Gender is a key component in eating disorders as 90% to 96% of patients so diagnosed are female (APA, 1994; Stice, 1994). The cultural ideal for female thinness and male muscularity appears to be well incorporated into adolescent mores. As early as the sixth grade, early maturing females who are typically heavier and less lean than their later developing cohorts are significantly dissatisfied with their bodies. Even before the onset of puberty, females as young as nine express concern about being or becoming overweight (Thelan, Powell, Lawrence, & Kuhnert, 1992). Thus, although an increase in

Table 1 *Possible Warning Signs of Disordered Eating*

1. Frequent complaints regarding current weight.
2. Obsessive concern with shape or size of hips, buttocks, thighs, and stomach.
3. Intense preoccupation to be thin.
4. Pathological fear of weight gain.
5. Chronic and severe dieting.
6. Excessive exercise.
7. Purchase or possession of diet medications, laxatives, or diuretics.
8. Evidence of self-induced vomiting.
9. Evidence of frequent bingeing of food.
10. Picky eating.
11. Either lack of interest *or* obsessive interest in food.

body fat is a normal characterization of female puberty, many adolescent girls assimilate the current cultural standards of attractiveness and desire the prepubescent look.

Eating disorders typically appear in adolescence with the mean age of onset being 17 years. This pattern is not unusual considering how preoccupied adolescents are with conformity, acceptance, and appearance issues. Some data suggest bimodal peaks at ages 14 and 18 years for anorexia (APA, 1994). However, youngsters as early as age 7 have been diagnosed. Given this developmental pattern, school psychologists are in an ideal position to assist in identification, consultation, prevention, and early intervention service provision with this population. In their interactions with students, school personnel can identify weight variations, eating habits, and behavioral indices that are sometimes concealed from family members, physicians, or community mental health personnel. As prevention, early identification, and timely treatment are key variables for affirmative long-term outcomes, this chapter will be devoted to predictors and early indices of disordered eating. Because the *DSM-IV* diagnostic criteria for anorexia and bulimia are very stringent, professionals should also be concerned with adolescents who do not meet the "letter" of the criteria but certainly meet the "spirit" (i.e., at risk) due to chronic dieting; excessive exercise; less than twice weekly self-induced vomiting; and abuse of laxatives, diet medications, and water pills (see Table 1). By educating school personnel and parents, developing prevention curricular materials, and providing direct intervention with at-risk or borderline cases, the school psychologist can impact this frequently ignored problem.

Problems and Implications

The role of the media in promoting society's ideal cannot be overstated. Garner, Garfinkel, Schwartz, and Thomp-son (1980) were among the first to examine the media's contribution. They concluded, after reviewing height and weight data from *Playboy* magazine centerfolds and Miss America contestants between 1959 and 1978, that there was a *10% decrease* in reported weight-to-height measurements over the 20-year period. Concomitantly, they discovered a six-fold increase in the number of diet articles in popular women's magazines. In a 1992 update of that study, Wiseman, Gray, Mosimann, and Ahrens (1992) found that this trend magnified during the 1980s. The "ideal" body weight portrayed in magazines then stabilized at between 13% and 19% below-average weight expectancy. The authors described the leveling off of idealized body weight in terms of a "floor effect" because any further reduction would be nearly impossible and dangerously unhealthy. Interestingly, if one frames the current body ideal in terms of *DSM-IV* criteria for anorexia (body weight 15% below expectancy), there is a strong suggestion that the media, and the societal values that the media mirrors, is idealizing one of the major symptoms of an eating disorder.

Stice, Schupak-Neuberg, Shaw, and Stein (1994) utilized path analyses to examine the direct effects of media exposure on eating disorder symptomatology. Using a sample of 238 college undergraduates, they found that women who had higher levels of exposure to media (i.e., number of fashion and beauty magazines studied, number of hours spent watching television game and comedy shows) were at greatest risk for developing eating disorder symptoms if they endorsed traditional gender roles for women and men. Such an endorsement led to the internalization of the ideal body stereotype. Subsequently, these women become dissatisfied with their own body shape and weight.

Similar findings have been reported with younger adolescents. For example, Levine, Smolak, and Hayden (1994) surveyed 363 female middle school students (Grades 6–8) regarding the impact of media, peers, and family on weight dissatisfaction. Using multiple regression analyses, the authors reported that the strongest predictors of disturbed eating and use of weight-control techniques were information from magazines followed by family teasing or criticism. The research team conducted a further analysis regarding whether some girls live in a "subculture of dieting" by determining those who perceive high levels of weight messages from all three cultural sources: media, peers, and family. By comparing this subgroup with the remaining sample, the researchers found that these specific females had significantly higher levels of body dissatisfaction, engaged in far more frequent weight-control activities, and evidenced elevated disturbed-eating behaviors.

For females, social and media pressure are not the only antecedents for weight dissatisfaction and dieting regime. Although the cultural mores and media models of thinness are ubiquitous, the majority of teenagers do not develop long-term dysfunctional eating and weight-related behavioral patterns. Identification of factors which place youngsters at risk for developing disordered eating habits as well as components which are protective or attenuate the societal influence would be most beneficial. Not only would such information assist in understanding the etiology of bulimia and anorexia, it would significantly aid in the development of prevention and early intervention programming by tailoring multidimensional strategies to the specific needs of a population at notable risk.

Self-Concept

After completing an extensive review of the literature, Stice (1994) outlined an etiological model for eating disorders wherein sociocultural pressures (e.g., the thin ideal, the centrality of appearance to females, the importance of appearance for success) were filtered through the mediational influences of family, peers, and the media and then internalized. He proposed that moderators of low self-esteem and identity confusion increased that internalization. A factor-analytic study of adolescent girls clearly supports that model by suggesting that endorsement of the thin model generally first requires psychological distress, such as feelings of insecurity and social self-doubt (Phelps & Wilczenski, 1993). Perhaps the broadest appropriate terminology for these feelings or beliefs is a profound sense of personal ineffectiveness. Patients with eating disorders have a sense of both attitudinal and behavioral impotency over personal control, social interactions, and life outcomes (Butow, Beumont, & Touyz, 1993).

Three recent studies with adolescent females have documented that several distinct aspects of self-concept are strongly related to eating disorder symptomatology. First, Bennett, Spoth, and Borgen (1991) surveyed 2,042 female high school students (Grades 9–12). They found that subjects with the highest scores on measures of bulimic symptoms had the lowest levels of self-efficacy. Likewise, Adams, Katz, Beauchamp, and Zavis (1993) analyzed the relationship of physical self-esteem to eating disorder symptomatology with a co-ed sample of 599 students in Grades 5, 8, and 12. A body-image subscale used to assess positive feelings about one's body was negatively associated with both eating disordered behaviors and depression.

In the third study, Phelps, Augustyniak, and Johnston (1995) measured four areas of self-concept: Physical (i.e., how one feels about her or his physical appearance and ability), Social (i.e., peer relationships and social success), Competence (i.e., personal efficacy, goal attainment, problem solving) and Academic (i.e., success in scholarly pursuits; Bracken, 1992). Surveying 830 middle school and high school females (Grades 6–12), the researchers found that all four areas had significant negative correlations with

bulimic behaviors. Using multiple regressions and path analyses, the researchers reported that low scores on Competence and Physical self-concept coupled with high scores on the Eating Disorders Inventory-2 (EDI-2; Garner, 1991) variables of Body Dissatisfaction (i.e., unhappiness with and disapproval of one's body shape and size) and Drive for Thinness (i.e., endorsement and pursuit of an extremely slim body standard) resulted in excessive use of weight-control methods. Stated in the positive direction, the results suggested that increasing an adolescent female's sense of personal efficacy or power, coupled with assisting her in recognizing the positive attributes of her own physical appearance, may result in less internalization or acceptance of current sociocultural mores. Less internalization would then result in less body dissatisfaction and lowered compliance or endorsement of the thin model (i.e., drive for thinness) which would then reduce disordered eating.

Body Dissatisfaction

According to the sociocultural model, body dissatisfaction occurs when an individual internalizes a culturally determined body ideal and then upon self-comparison, determines her or his body to be discrepant from that ideal. A large amount of research identifies body dissatisfaction as *one of the* primary precursors and predictors of later eating-disorder symptomatology. Button (1990) developed an eating disorder risk-status score by prospectively surveying 937 11- and 12-year-old females on measures of personality, self-concept, and eating attitudes and patterns as well as current weight, and then followed the sample to determine long-term eating-disorder status. Longitudinal data analyses indicated that body dissatisfaction was the *single strongest predictor* of risk for developing an eating disorder. In a similar study, Leon, Fulkerson, Perry, and Cudeck (1993) examined 937 females in Grades 7 to 10 on measures of personality, self-concept, eating patterns, and attitudes. Results of hierarchical multiple regression analyses found the strongest predictor variables for risk were body dissatisfaction, negative emotionality, and lack of interoceptive awareness, defined as difficulty in labeling emotions and feelings.

Body dissatisfaction can vary from generalized displeasure, such as dislike of the entire body shape or size, to vexation with a specific part. Typically, females report displeasure with hips, thighs, buttocks, and stomach. Breasts are seldom, if ever, mentioned. This seems to reflect the attitude that formation of breasts is not development of fat and is thus welcomed, because breasts might be considered an attractive asset and socially desirable commodity. However, the pubertal acquisition of fat in the areas of stomach, hips, buttocks, and thighs is not socially desirable nor acceptable and is thus not welcomed by these females.

Research examining body dissatisfaction indicates profound gender disparity. In a study examining gender and age differences in body dissatisfaction, figure preference, and body distortion with 454 female and male students in Grades 7 to 12, Phelps et al. (1993) reported significant gender differences with females preferring a thinner ideal and expressing higher rates of body dissatisfaction. The adolescent males expressed only a desire for a slightly heavier build. Both males and females perceived their own body sizes to be larger than viewed by objective adult raters, suggesting an "enhancing" body distortion for males (i.e., boys desire a heavier more muscular build) yet a "disparaging" body distortion for females (i.e., girls yearn for a thinner one). Likewise, body dissatisfaction for the females increased in a significant linear fashion. As the female sample moved from childhood to early and then middle to late adolescence, body dissatisfaction increased, reaching elevated levels far exceeding those reported by adult women. In sum, the acquisition of a mature body with flesh and curves for females is experienced as a problem, perhaps even a crisis, whereas an increase in muscles and bulk is seen as an improvement for males.

Any model of etiology and maintenance of eating-disorder symptomatology that relies on body dissatisfaction should necessarily consider the possibility of a positive association between body dissatisfaction and actual weight. Can it be concluded that the typical eating-disordered female experiences body dissatisfaction as a function of simply being overweight and therefore realistically assesses her shape against an appropriate criterion matched for her age and weight? Research data suggest not. Large epidemiological studies have shown the majority of adolescent females to be dissatisfied with their bodies yet few are overweight (Bunnell, Cooper, Hertz, & Shenker, 1992). Likewise, body dissatisfaction is intimately tied to *subjective opinions* of weight, and this subjective view is more predictive of dieting behaviors than actual weight (Button, 1990; Bunnell et al., 1992).

Chronic Dieting

Because weight has become the lay person's measure of health and beauty, many children, teenagers, and their parents view dieting as an innocuous practice. Unfortunately, "normal" chronic dieting in preteen and teenage girls poses sober health threats. Malnutrition during maturation can lead to delayed puberty, physical retardation, and an increase in the risk of future osteoporosis (Kreipe & Forbes, 1990). Of particular importance is the association between dieting and eating disorders. Pressured with societal mores for thinness and at war with the natural weight and fat gain concurrent with pubertal onset, many adolescents begin to diet, often following rigorous caloric regimes. Soon hunger triumphs, resulting in the temptation to eat. Binge eating frequently begins during

or after such an episode of dieting in adolescent females (Huon, 1994). Self-induced vomiting, laxative or diuretic abuse, and excessive exercise then begin to unfold as a compensatory compromise between the need to pursue thinness and self-control yet the need to eat. Herein lies the significant difference among nonsymptomatic dieters and persons with disordered eating behaviors. Following harsh restrictive dietary intake, "normal" dieters eat moderately, persons with bulimic tendencies eat excessively, and those with anorexia attempt to deny their hunger and refuse to eat.

Generally, prospective studies substantiate that a sizable minority of adolescent females on chronic and severe diets develop eating disorders. For example, Patton, Johnson-Sabine, Wood, Mann, and Wakeling (1990) surveyed 1,010 London adolescents between the ages of 14 and 16 years. Dieting was reported by 31% of the sample. At a 12-month follow-up, 21% ($n = 66$) of the dieters in the initial survey had developed bulimia or anorexia. The authors estimated the relative risk of dieters becoming clinical cases at seven to nine times that of nondieters. Similarly, Marchi and Cohen (1990) interviewed a sample of over 800 children and their mothers on the subject of specific eating disorders including food avoidance, pica, anorexia, and bulimia. The families were interviewed three times: when the children were one to 10 years of age, when they were 9 to 18 years old, and 2.5 years later when they were an average of 12 to 20 years of age. The authors found that "picky eating" (defined as the presence of three of the following four behaviors: does not eat enough, often choosy about food, usually eats slowly, and is usually not interested in food) at 8 to 18 years of age was strongly associated with anorexic symptoms at 12 to 20 years of age. Attempts at weight reduction at 8 to 18 years of age were significantly associated with bulimic symptoms at 12 to 20 years of age. These two studies clearly suggest a link between food-restriction and weight-reduction behaviors and future development of eating disorders.

A return to physiological normalcy after chronic caloric restriction may be difficult as the most insidious effect of dieting is the distortion of hunger and satiety signals. These mixed signals can lead to exaggerated cycles of food restriction, bingeing, or both. Furthermore, chronic and severe dieting can trigger physiological mechanisms which suppress metabolic rates (Prentice et al., 1991), making it more difficult to achieve weight goals and prompting the dieter to consider more drastic means to weight loss.

Alternative Actions

The American College of Physicians (ACP) and several research groups have called for public education to prevent eating disorders while promoting healthy weight regulation among adolescents (ACP, 1986). Given that the mean age of onset for eating disorders is 17, an effective prevention model should target middle school and early high school adolescents. Likewise, an ideal prevention program could be integrated into existing classes with numerous sessions spread throughout the school year and devoted to such topics as the impact of sociocultural mores for thinness, the role of media, natural weight and fat gain during puberty, normative reference points for body mass, appropriate methods of weight modification and maintenance, the enhancement of physical self-esteem, and the building of personal competence. These variables are selected due to their demonstrated relationship with disordered eating behaviors via past research (e.g., Adams et al., 1993; Button, 1990; Leon et al., 1993; Levine et al., 1994; Phelps, et al., 1995; Stice et al., 1994).

Only two efficacy studies with young adolescents have been published. The first was the Killen et al. (1993) study wherein 967 females in Grades 6 and 7 were randomly assigned to either experimental or no-treatment control groups. The authors developed an extensive 18-lesson program using slide presentations and workbooks with written assignments. Three main components comprised the intervention: (a) information on harmful effects of unhealthy weight control; (b) education regarding nutrition, dietary principles, and regular exercise; and (c) emphasis on resisting sociocultural influences promoting thinness and dieting. Posttesting sessions were conducted immediately and at 7, 14, and 24 months after program completion. Results indicated the intervention was not successful in effecting notable change in attitudes or behaviors, although a significant difference in knowledge was found between the treatment and control groups. Secondary analyses comparing only high-risk students (i.e., high scores on a weight concern scale) found such girls in the experimental group to possess significantly more knowledge than the high-risk control females, yet no significant differences were found on eating attitudes or weight-control practices. However, both the experimental and control groups showed fairly large differences between pre- and posttesting, suggesting that treatment generalization may have occurred. That is, given the tendency for adolescent girls to discuss and share relevant information, it is possible they discussed details of the program and thus effectively negated statistical impact.

To avoid such possible contamination, Moreno and Thelan (1993) conducted a second efficacy study utilizing three different junior high schools: one school served as the experimental group ($n = 80$) and two other schools operated as the control group ($n = 139$). This intervention consisted of only one session that showed a 6 1/2-minute videotape of two sisters discussing bulimia, its prevalence and harmful effects, sociocultural attitudes re-

garding thinness and dieting, and suggestions for weight management and resistance to peer pressure. Following the video, either a graduate student or the classroom teacher led a discussion for 30 minutes. Both experimental and control groups were assessed three times (i.e., 2 days prior to intervention, 2 days after intervention, and one month later). Using a 23-item questionnaire, the researchers reported no significant differences between the experimental and control groups prior to the intervention session (an important consideration given the lack of random assignment of subjects). Posttesting resulted in significant group differences with the experimental group indicating greater knowledge, more positive attitudes, and healthier intentions about weight management than the control group. However, it is essential that this intervention be cross-validated as the positive findings are based on a 23-item author-developed questionnaire which has not undergone the rigors of validation and reliability assessment.

A significant limitation of both these intervention efforts is their reliance upon didactic presentations of factual information. Past research on prevention models for AIDS, unprotected sex, drug use, and drinking and driving programs have proven that increasing an adolescent's knowledge about the dangers associated with certain behaviors is simply not enough to significantly change future actions (Dielman, 1994). It is hypothesized that an effective prevention program would necessarily be designed toward building skills and ego strength that attenuate the sociocultural pressures promoting disordered-eating behaviors (e.g., physical self-esteem and personal competence). By addressing only negative risk factors (e.g., chronic dieting, peer pressure, body dissatisfaction), the participants may not develop the necessary adaptive coping skills that past research has shown to mitigate future eating-disorder symptomatology. Likewise, it is hypothesized that interactive lessons which include group discussions and problem solving, cooperative exercises, and active student participation would prove efficacious (see Table 2). However, no research to date has substantiated these hypotheses.

Finally, although the vast majority of individuals suffering from eating disorders are female, the role of males in the development and maintenance of symptoms should not be overlooked. It appears appropriate for adolescent males to be included in prevention programming so that they can be challenged to examine their own beliefs regarding beauty and become aware of the pressures they may be placing on their female peers to engage in unhealthy eating practices.

Summary

Eating disorders have become more prevalent in recent decades, resulting in 5% of the population, primarily ad-

Table 2 *Proposed Characteristics of Prevention and Early Intervention Program*

A. Reduce internalization of sociocultural pressures by
   1. Discussing the impact of sociocultural mores for thinness.
   2. Illustrating the role of media, peers, and family modeling.

B. Decrease body dissatisfaction by
   1. Illustrating the natural weight and fat gain during puberty.
   2. Depicting visual normative reference points for body shape and size.

C. Educate regarding appropriate methods of weight control by
   1. Elucidating the negative consequences of restrictive dieting and other weight reduction or maintenance techniques.
   2. Providing information regarding appropriate methods of weight modification and maintenance.

D. Increase physical self-esteem by
   1. Focusing on positive physical attributes.
   2. Improving physical fitness and strength.

E. Build personal competence by
   1. Developing an internal locus of control.
   2. Cultivating adaptive coping skills.

olescent females, meeting restrictive *DSM-IV* criteria for anorexia or bulimia. Likewise, over one-third of the adolescent female population report participation in such aggressive methods of weight control and reduction as chronic dieting; excessive exercise; self-induced vomiting; and abuse of laxatives, diet medications, and water pills. Research supports an etiological model which links sociocultural pressures to the acceptance of a thin, yet unrealistic, ideal. The internalization of this ideal leads to body dissatisfaction, which in turn, provides motivation for one to adopt the use of stringent weight-control methods. The use of various weight-management techniques, particularly restrictive dieting, provides significant risk toward the establishment of an eating disorder. However, protective factors have been identified (i.e., physical self-esteem and personal competence) which serve as buffers to the development of disordered symptomatology. Utilizing this etiological model, it is recommended that prevention programming be directed toward female and male young adolescents with an orientation toward increasing factors which attenuate risk status while reducing elements placing teenagers in jeopardy.

Recommended Resources

For the Practitioner

Kinoy, B. P. (Ed.). (1994). *Eating disorders: New directions in treatment and recovery.* New York: Columbia University Press.

A valuable resource for the mental health provider working with more severe cases of anorexia and/or bulimia.

Smukler, G., Dare, C., & Treasure, J. (Eds.). (1995). *Handbook of eating disorders: Theory, treatment, and research.* New York: Wiley.
This is an excellent resource for school psychologists. The book contains a fairly current review of the literature. Most beneficial are recommended, empirically validated treatment interventions written with the busy practitioner in mind.

For the Client

Dolan, B., & Gitzinger, I. (1994). *Why women? Gender issues and eating disorders* (rev. ed.). London: Athlone Publishing.
This is recommended reading for older adolescent/young adult women who desire further information regarding the feminist perspective on eating disorders.

Pipher, M. B. (1995). *Hunger pains: From fad diets to eating disorders—What every woman needs to know about food, dieting, and self-esteem* (rev. ed.). Holbrook, MA: Adams Publishing.
This is a helpful book for young women who are engaged in disordered eating. It is recommended reading for adolescent females in treatment.

For Parents and Teachers

Lemberg, R. (Ed.). (1992). *Controlling eating disorders with facts, advice, and resources.* Phoenix, AZ: Oryx Press.
This is a helpful resource which outlines key issues without all the medical jargon.

References

Adams, P. J., Katz, R. C., Beauchamp, K., & Zavis, D. (1993). Body dissatisfaction, eating disorders, and depression: A developmental perspective. *Journal of Child and Family Studies, 2,* 37–46.

Alan, J. D., Mayo, L., & Michael, Y. (1993). Body size values of white and black women. *Research in Nursing and Health, 16,* 323–333.

American College of Physicians. (1986). Eating disorders: Anorexia nervosa and bulimia. *Annals of Internal Medicine, 105,* 790–794.

American Psychiatric Association. (1994). *Diagnostic and statistical manual of mental disorders* (4th ed.). Washington, DC: Author.

Bennett, N. M., Spoth, R. L., & Borgen, F. H. (1991). Bulimic symptoms in high school females: Prevalence and relationship with multiple measures of psychological health. *Journal of Community Psychology, 19,* 13–28.

Bracken, B. A. (1992). *Multidimensional Self Concept Scale.* Austin, TX: Pro-Ed.

Bunnell, D. W., Cooper, P. J., Hertz, S., & Shenker, I. R. (1992). Body shape concerns among adolescents. *International Journal of Eating Disorders, 11,* 79–83.

Butow, P., Beumont, P., & Touyz, S. (1993). Cognitive processes in dieting disorders. *International Journal of Eating Disorders, 14,* 319–329.

Button, E. (1990). Self-esteem in girls aged 11–12: Baseline findings from a planned prospective study of vulnerability to eating disorders. *Journal of Adolescence, 13,* 407–413.

Dielman, T. E. (1994). School-based research on the prevention of adolescent alcohol use and misuse: Methodological issues and advances. *Journal of Research on Adolescence, 4,* 271–293.

Garner, D. M. (1991). *Eating Disorder Inventory-2.* Odessa, FL: Psychological Assessment Resources.

Garner, D. M., Garfinkel, P. E., Schwartz, D., & Thompson, M. (1980). Cultural expectations of thinness in women. *Psychological Reports, 47,* 483–491.

Huon, G. F. (1994). Dieting, binge eating, and some of their correlates among secondary school girls. *International Journal of Eating Disorders, 15,* 159–164.

Killen, J. D., Hammer, L. D., Litt, L., Wilson, D. M., Rich, T., Hayward, C., Simmonds, B., Kraemer, H., & Varady, A. (1993). An attempt to modify unhealthful eating attitudes and weight regulation practices of young adolescent girls. *International Journal of Eating Disorders, 13,* 369–384.

Kreipe, R. E., & Forbes, G. B. (1990). Osteoporosis: A "new morbidity" for dieting female adolescents. *Pediatrics, 86,* 478–480.

Leon, G. R., Fulkerson, J. A., Perry, C. L., & Cudeck, R. (1993). Personality and behavioral vulnerabilities associated with risk status for eating disorders in adolescent girls. *Journal of Abnormal Psychology, 102,* 438–444.

Levine, M. P., Smolak, L., & Hayden, H. (1994). The relation of sociocultural factors to eating attitudes and behaviors among middle school girls. *Journal of Early Adolescence, 14,* 471–490.

Lissner, L. L., Steen, S. N., & Brownell, K. D. (1992). Weight reduction diets and health promotion. *American Journal of Preventive Medicine, 8,* 154–158.

Marchi, M., & Cohen, P. (1990). Early childhood eating behaviors and adolescent eating disorders. *Journal of the American Academy of Child and Adolescent Psychiatry, 29,* 112–117.

Moreno, A. B., & Thelan, M. H. (1993). A preliminary prevention program for eating disorders in a junior high school population. *Journal of Youth and Adolescence, 22,* 109–124.

Patton, C. G., Johnson-Sabine, E., Wood, K., Mann, A. H., & Wakeling, A. (1990). Abnormal eating attitudes in London schoolgirls: A prospective epidemiological study: Outcome at 12-month follow-up. *Psychological Medicine, 20,* 383–394.

Phelps, L., Andrea, R. K., & Rizzo, R. G. (1994). Weight control techniques among female adolescents: A comparative study. *Journal of School Psychology, 32,* 283–292.

Phelps, L., Augustyniak, K., & Johnston, L. S. (1995). Correlates of self-esteem, gender role adherence, and body dissatisfaction to eating disorder symptomatology. Manuscript in preparation.

Phelps, L. Johnston, L. S., Jimenez, D., Wilczenski, F. L., Andrea, R. K., & Healy, R. W. (1993). Figure preference, body dissatisfaction and body distortion in adolescence. *Journal of Adolescent Research, 8,* 297–310.

Phelps, L., & Wilczenski, F. (1993). Eating Disorders Inventory-2: Cognitive-behavioral dimensions with nonclinical adolescents. *Journal of Clinical Psychology, 49,* 508–515.

Prentice, A. W., Goldberg, G. R., Jebb, S. A., Black, A. E., Murgatroyd, P. R., & Diaz, E. O. (1991). Physiological responses to slimming. *Processing of the Nutrition Society, 50,* 441–458.

Stice, E. (1994). Review of the evidence for a sociocultural model of bulimia nervosa and an exploration of the mechanisms of action. *Clinical Psychology Review, 14,* 633–661.

Stice, E., Schupak-Neuberg, E., Shaw, H. E., & Stein, R. I. (1994). Relation of media exposure to eating disorder symptomatology: An examination of mediating mechanisms. *Journal of Abnormal Psychology, 103,* 836–840.

Stunkard, A. J., Harris, J. R., Pedersen, N. L., & McClearn, G. E. (1990). The body-mass index of twins who have been reared apart. *New England Journal of Medicine, 322,* 1483–1487.

Thelan, M. H., Powell, A. L., Lawrence, C., & Kuhnert, M. E. (1992). Eating and body image concern among children. *Journal of Clinical Child Psychology, 21,* 41–46.

Wiseman, C. V., Gray, J. J., Mosimann, J. E., & Ahrens, A. H. (1992). Cultural expectations of thinness in women: An update. *International Journal of Eating Disorders, 11,* 85–89.

82

Substance Use and Abuse

Susan G. Forman
Allison Pfeiffer

Rutgers, The State University of New Jersey

Substance use and abuse have long been issues of special concern to those who work with children and adolescents. Although prevalence rates declined in the 1980s, the most recent surveys of high school students indicate alarming rises in alcohol and other drug use. Such behavior has a wide range of potential negative consequences on physical, psychological, behavioral, and social functioning and thus should be of major concern to school psychologists.

Background and Development

Prevalence

The prevalence of substance use and abuse among adolescents has been the subject of a comprehensive annual survey conducted since 1975 (Johnston, O'Malley, & Bachman, 1994). Results from the 1993 survey are summarized in Table 1. Although current prevalence rates are below the peak rates of the late 1970s and early 1980s, the rates have been rising sharply in recent years. The level of use of illicit drugs in the United States is greater than that for any other industrialized nation. Over 60% of 12th-grade students have tried cigarettes, 87% have tried alcohol, 35% have tried marijuana, and 46% have tried other illicit drugs. In addition to marijuana, the illicit drugs most often used are cocaine, stimulants, LSD, and inhalants. Perhaps more important in illustrating the seriousness of the problem are data showing that

- 28% of high school seniors had had five or more drinks in a row at least once in the two weeks prior to the survey.
- 30% of seniors are current cigarette smokers and 19% are current daily cigarette smokers.
- 9.6% of seniors had been daily marijuana smokers at some time for at least a month prior to the survey. (Johnston et al., 1994)

Concurrent with the recent rise in prevalence rates, the survey also found that teens' attitudes and beliefs about the harmfulness of drug use have begun to soften. The downturn in prevalence rates in the 1980s was believed to be related to increases in perceived risk and disapproval of substance use. These beliefs and attitudes were probably influenced by the amount and nature of public attention being paid to the substance use issue. This attention has declined substantially in recent years, possibly explaining the change in attitudes and concomitant increase in prevalence rates (Johnston et al., 1994).

The Johnston et al. (1994) survey also obtained information about substance use in younger children by asking questions about age of initiation. After examining retrospective responses from students in Grades 8, 10, and 12, the authors estimate that by the end of sixth grade between 18% and 29% of students have had their first cigarette; between 11% and 37% have had their first drink and 2% to 4% have tried marijuana.

In his response to questions from the press about recent survey findings indicating a rise in substance use among teenagers, Lloyd Johnston, the survey's principal investigator, stated that many parents today have themselves tried drugs and may feel awkward about giving their children lectures on drugs' dangers because they feel conflicted about it. He further stated that it is critical for parents to warn their children of the hazards of drug use. Parents can explain that when they were young less was known about the dangers of drugs and that the drugs available today are stronger and more addictive ("Drug and Alcohol Use," 1995).

Risk Factors

A variety of risk factors have been identified for adolescent substance abuse. A risk factor is a characteristic or condition that increases the probability of substance abuse. Genetic-biological, temperament, psychological, behavioral, and social-environmental factors have been identified. No single factor has been found to determine adolescent substance abuse, and it is generally thought

917

Table 1 *Prevalence of Adolescent Substance Use*

	Lifetime	30-Day	Daily
Cigarettes			
Grade 8	45.3	16.7	8.3
Grade 10	56.3	24.7	14.2
Grade 12	61.9	29.9	19.0
Alcohol			
Grade 8	67.1	26.2	0.8
Grade 10	80.8	41.5	1.6
Grade 12	87.0	51.0	2.5
Marijuana			
Grade 8	12.6	5.1	0.4
Grade 10	24.4	10.9	1.0
Grade 12	35.3	15.5	2.4
Any Illicit Drug			
Including Inhalants			
Grade 8	32.3	12.0	
Grade 10	38.7	15.5	
Grade 12	46.5	19.3	

Note. Numbers represent percentages of the sample reporting use. Adapted from *National Survey Results on Drug Use from Monitoring the Future Study, 1975–1993: Vol. 1. Secondary School Students,* (pp. 6–9), by L. D. Johnston, P. M. O'Malley, and J. G. Bachman, 1994, Rockville, MD: National Institute on Drug Abuse.

that the greater number of risk factors an individual has, the greater the likelihood of substance abuse (Newcomb, Maddahian, & Bentler, 1986). Recent research indicates that personal, social, and family maladjustment precursors to substance abuse can be identified as early as age 7 (Shedler & Block, 1990). Direct intervention is possible with some risk factors and can lead to a reduction in the likelihood of substance abuse (Clayton, 1992).

Studies involving monozygotic and dizygotic twins, adopted-away children of alcoholics, and genetic markers associated with substance abuse indicate that substance abuse may have genetic-biological determinants. However, the precise contribution of an individual's genetic background remains in question (Kaminer, 1994).

Various temperament characteristics have also been implicated as precursors to substance abuse. One characteristic related to increased risk for adolescent substance abuse is difficult temperament in early childhood, defined as slow adaptability, social withdrawal, negative mood, high intensity of emotional reactions, and dysrhythmia (Lerner & Vicary, 1984). In addition, high behavior-activity level, low attention span and persistence, low sociability, and low soothability have been associated with vulnerability to alcoholism (Tarter & Mezzich, 1992).

Psychological factors related to adolescent substance abuse include external locus of control, low self-esteem, high degree of dissatisfaction and pessimism, high need for social approval, low social confidence, high anxiety, low assertiveness, and a tendency to impulsivity and rebelliousness (Flay, d'Avernas, Best, Kersell, & Ryan, 1983). Sensation seeking—the need for novel experiences and the willingness to take risks to engage in these experiences—is also related to adolescent substance abuse (Cloninger, 1987). Stress and coping skills are additional psychological factors associated with adolescent substance abuse. Adolescent substance abusers report experiencing a greater number of negative life events and use substances as a way of dealing with problems, negative feelings, and stressful situations (Forman & Linney, 1991).

Behavioral factors related to adolescent substance abuse include disruptive, antisocial, and delinquent behaviors. Poor academic performance and dropping out of school also are precursors of substance abuse (Hawkins, Lishner, Catalano, & Howard, 1986). In addition, early initiation of substance use is predictive of later substance-abuse problems.

Social and environmental factors strongly influence the probability of adolescent substance abuse. Adolescents whose parents or siblings engage in substance abuse and whose parents have permissive or approving attitudes toward substance use tend to abuse substances themselves (Merikangas, Rousaville & Prusoff, 1992). The quality of family interactions also affect the potential for adolescent substance abuse. Adolescents who have been neglected or abused are more likely to become substance abusers (Clayton, 1992; Shedler & Block, 1990). Low levels of parental support and control, poor family communication, and high family conflict also are correlated with high levels of substance use in adolescents (Barnes, 1984).

The peer group plays an especially influential role in the initiation and maintenance of substance use and the transition to substance abuse. Adolescents with friends who use substances are likely to be substance users themselves (Kandel, 1982). This pattern has been attributed to the importance of the peer group at this age and adolescent responsiveness to pressures to conform.

Community environmental factors, such as availability of psychoactive substances, also must be considered when examining risk for substance abuse. Adolescents who live in neighborhoods where drug use is widespread are more likely to engage in it. In addition, adolescents who come from economically deprived communities are more likely to have substance use problems.

Protective Factors

A protective factor is a characteristic or condition that inhibits, reduces, or buffers the probability of substance abuse. Recently, researchers have begun to identify these factors and are using this information as the basis for developing prevention programs.

Social protective factors and the role of the family have the potential to moderate the effects of exposure to the risk of substance abuse. These factors include close family relationships, strong positive bonds, sufficient monitoring, clear standards and messages, and attractive alternatives to substance use and abuse (Bry, 1993; Hawkins & Catalano, 1992). Family relationships that protect against substance use and abuse are defined by closeness and warmth, effective and positive discipline, and successful problem solving and communication. The risk of adolescent substance abuse is also lowered when parents are aware of how their children are spending time. In addition, if adolescents know that substance use will result in negative physical and psychological effects, as well as parentally imposed sanctions, they are less likely to engage in use. Provision of opportunities to participate in high-interest, challenging activities and religious activities also protect against substance use and abuse. Finally, the likelihood of substance abuse is reduced when parents have been able to instill hope for a successful future in their children.

A number of genetic-biological and personality factors also appear to reduce the probability of substance abuse (Norman, 1995). These include easy temperament, good intellectual capabilities (particularly verbal skills), self-efficacy (positive perception of one's competence), realistic appraisal of the environment, social problem-solving skills, sense of direction or mission, empathy, humor, and adaptive distancing (children's ability to separate themselves from troubled parents).

Use Versus Abuse

There has been substantial discussion in the literature on the issue of defining adolescent substance abuse and distinguishing use from abuse at this age level. A large number of adolescents experiment with drugs and do not repeat the experience (Newcomb & Bentler, 1989). Some adolescents engage in substance use occasionally without suffering any negative consequences. In fact, in their longitudinal study of adolescent drug use and psychological health, Shedler and Block (1990) found experimenters to be more psychologically healthy than frequent users or abstainers.

There seems to be general agreement that any regular use of a psychoactive drug by a child is abuse (Newcomb & Bentler, 1989). For adolescents, the distinction between use and abuse is less clear-cut. Frequency, quantity, and negative consequences such as health problems, injuries, arrests, and school discipline or academic problems are usually considered.

Occasional use of beer, wine, or marijuana at a party among adolescents is not always considered abuse (Newcomb & Bentler, 1989). However, abuse occurs with overindulgence in the substance, frequent regular use, negative outcomes, or all three conditions. Glantz and

Pickens (1992) state that while any illicit drug use may be viewed as abuse, use typically refers to "experimentation with or low-frequency irregular use of illicit drugs," and abuse refers to "regular or compulsive use of illicit drugs" (p. 3). Thus, the distinguishing factor in this definition is whether illicit drug use has become a regular part of the individual's lifestyle. Most researchers currently view use and abuse as a continuum from first use to regular and excessive use to the point of impairment (Clayton, 1992).

Transition to Abuse

A number of authors have written about "the stages of substance abuse." Typically, use starts with beer, wine, or cigarettes, moves to hard liquor and marijuana, and then to other illicit drugs such as amphetamines and cocaine. Whereas use at one stage does not necessarily lead to use at the next stage, use at a given stage is unlikely without prior involvement in the previous stage (Newcomb & Bentler, 1989).

The cycle of use and abuse has been conceptualized as consisting of five stages (Clayton, 1992). Initiation, that is, movement from being a nonuser to a user, is the first stage. In the second stage the individual makes a decision to continue use. In Stage 3, the individual escalates quantity, frequency, or both within a class of drugs. During the fourth stage use progresses across drug classes. This stage involves experimenting with simultaneous use of multiple drugs. In stage 5 regression, cessation, and relapse cycles may occur a number of times before an individual succeeds in stopping substance use or remains dependent. Progression from one stage to another is related to the variety of risk and protective factors discussed earlier and can be influenced by participation in prevention and treatment programs.

Currently, the majority of adolescents engage in experimental substance use (Johnston et al., 1994). Peak ages for the initiation of cigarette smoking are 6th and 7th grades. Initiation of alcohol use occurs somewhat later, typically in the 7th through 9th grade. For marijuana, the highest initiation rates are seen from 9th to 11th grade. This experimentation, as indicated earlier, does not necessarily lead to abuse.

Personality and parenting antecedents of individuals who are likely to abstain, experiment, and become frequent users can be differentiated as early as age 7 (Shedler & Block, 1990). At this early age those who became frequent users were found to be unable to form good relationships, were insecure, and showed signs of emotional distress. Their mothers were perceived as cold, unresponsive, and underprotective. They gave their children little encouragement, while pressuring them for good performance. These and similar findings indicate that rather than assuming that any experimental substance use will lead to substance abuse, signs of emotional, social, and family maladjustment should be considered in predicting the transition from use to abuse.

Problems and Implications

A variety of short- and long-term negative effects are associated with substance abuse. In general, the more substances used and the more often they are used, the greater the negative effects. However, some researchers have pointed out that because most of the studies in this area are correlational, it is difficult to determine if some identified psychological and behavioral problems are actually consequences or antecedents (Dryfoos, 1990).

Serious negative consequences on physical, psychological, behavioral, and social functioning have been found for short- and long-term substance use (Dryfoos, 1990). Even the most frequently used substances—tobacco, alcohol, and marijuana—have been related to significant problems.

Short-term cigarette use can lead to respiratory problems, and long-term use can cause serious illness and decrease an individual's life span. Cigarette smoking is linked with cancer of the lungs, larynx, oral cavity, esophagus, pancreas, and bladder, as well as cardiovascular disease, atherosclerosis, respiratory infections, chronic bronchitis, emphysema, and peptic ulcers (U.S. Department of Health and Human Services, 1982). Adolescent smokers have small-airway dysfunctions and a high incidence of coughing, phlegm production, wheezing, and other respiratory symptoms (Botvin & McAlister, 1981).

Serious short-term consequences of alcohol use include impaired school performance, automobile accidents, and accidental death (Dryfoos, 1990). A significant percentage of fatal automobile accidents of teenagers involve alcohol (Mayer, 1983). Alcohol use has also been related to problems involving the law resulting from decreased behavioral control (Cohen, 1981). In addition, many adolescent suicides involve alcohol (Forrest, 1983). Long-term consequences include serious health problems such as cirrhosis of the liver and stomach cancer, as well as psychiatric illness and significant problems in social functioning (Dryfoos).

Short-term consequences of marijuana and other illicit drug use include impaired psychomotor performance, impaired psychological functioning, and short-term memory loss. Long-term consequences include psychological disorders, serious health problems, marital instability, job instability, and financial problems (Dryfoos, 1990).

These significant negative effects on adolescent functioning and potential make it imperative that school psychologists view substance abuse as a major concern. School psychologists working with adolescents should be cognizant that some behavioral and academic referral problems may be the result of substance abuse and should consider assessment of this area. Substance abuse assessment methods include prereferral questionnaires, information gathered during the initial interview, behavioral observation, and standardized assessment instruments (Fisher & Harrison, 1992). In addition to assessing students, school psychologists can play a variety of roles in substance abuse prevention such as providing training for school personnel regarding the nature and scope of the problem, planning and implementing prevention programs, and referring students for treatment.

Alternative Actions

Prevention

Over the past 25 years, many substance abuse prevention programs have been developed, implemented, and evaluated. In a meta-analysis of the outcome results of 143 adolescent drug-prevention programs, Tobler (1986) identified five program types:

- Knowledge-only programs focus on provision of substance information and use of scare tactics.
- Affective-only programs focus on personal and social growth through strategies such as self-esteem building and values clarification.
- Peer programs are based on approaches assuming that peer pressure is of major importance in the initiation and maintenance of substance use. These programs teach interpersonal resistance skills, and social and personal coping skills.
- Knowledge-plus-affective programs are based on the notion that attitudes and values must change in order to change behavior and focus on information and decision-making skills.
- Alternative programs provide positive alternative activities for youth such as various types of recreation.

Peer programs appear to be superior for the magnitude of their effects on all outcome measures for the average school-based population (Tobler, 1986). Tobler found that programs focusing on social influence and coping skills were effective in changing overall substance use, as well as in changing individual substance outcomes (i.e., cigarette, alcohol, marijuana, and other drug use). Alternatives programs were effective for specific high-risk subpopulations, such as delinquents, and for drug abusers.

More recent reviews of the literature support these findings (Hansen, 1992; Meyer, 1995) but raise questions about the long-term effectiveness of any of the currently used school-based programs. Based on their review of existing prevention programs, Hawkins and Catalano (1992) concluded

1. Information alone has little or no effect on substance use.
2. Short-term approaches, especially one-shot presentations, are ineffective. Consistent, extended programs are needed.
3. Programs that teach resistance skills do affect substance use; however, these effects often dissipate after 2 to 3 years.
4. Programs with more lasting effects have used either booster sessions or a multilevel approach that includes involvement of parents, the media, and the community.
5. School-based programs have been less effective in reducing substance use in those at greatest risk for abuse than in preventing substance use in the general population.

Life Skills Training, developed by Gilbert Botvin (1983), is a school-based, substance-abuse prevention program that has repeatedly shown positive effects in the research literature and has the most empirical evidence of effectiveness. Life Skills Training teaches general personal and social coping skills as well as skills and knowledge specifically related to substance use.

The training is typically conducted in 18 sessions during the seventh grade, with 10 booster sessions in the eighth grade, and 5 booster sessions in the ninth grade. It consists of five major components (Botvin & Tortu, 1988). The knowledge and information component provides information about prevalence and effects of tobacco, alcohol, and marijuana use. The decision-making segment addresses decision-making skills and ways advertisers and others attempt to influence substance use. The self-directed behavior-change portion focuses on how self-image can be improved through a self-improvement plan. Students complete a self-directed, behavior-change project as part of this component. Sessions on coping with anxiety teach students how to use imagery, breathing, and muscle relaxation as coping strategies. The social skills component addresses verbal and nonverbal communication skills including guidelines for avoiding misunderstandings; skills to initiate, maintain, and end conversations; and skills needed to maintain romantic relationships. In addition, this component teaches assertiveness skills that can be used to resist peer pressure to smoke, drink, or use drugs.

Life Skills Training was initially evaluated with respect to prevention of cigarette smoking (Botvin & Eng, 1982; Botvin, Eng, & Williams, 1980; Botvin, Renick, & Baker, 1983). These studies indicated that after Life Skills Training conducted either by project staff, peer leaders, or teachers, middle and high school students had lower rates of smoking onset and made more positive changes on cognitive, attitudinal, affective, and social measures than did no-treatment, control-group students. These changes were found to maintain at 1-year follow-up. The impact of Life Skills Training on alcohol and marijuana use has also been documented in a study of over 1,300 seventh-grade, White, middle-class students from suburban New York City schools. Significant treatment effects were found for substance use, substance knowledge, substance attitudes, locus of control, and influenceability (Botvin, Baker, Renick, Filazolla, & Botvin, 1984).

The final report of a 5-year investigation of Life Skills Training funded by the National Institute on Drug Abuse (Botvin, 1987) indicated that, at initial posttest, students participating in a peer-led group were significantly different from control-group students with regard to tobacco, alcohol, and marijuana use as well as mediating variables. Students participating in a teacher-led intervention, however, did not differ significantly from those in the control group. The ineffectiveness of the teacher-led groups was attributed to possible problems with teacher training. Results were maintained at 1- and 2-year follow-up while booster sessions were implemented. After the 2-year follow-up, booster sessions were terminated. One year after termination no effects were present.

These findings suggest the need for more comprehensive, multilevel interventions to address the numerous substance-abuse risk factors and to build on the protective factors that may be present. The Midwestern Prevention Project, also called Project STAR (Students Taught Awareness and Resistance), developed by Mary Ann Pentz and her colleagues (Pentz, Cormack, Flay, Hansen, & Johnson, 1986), is the comprehensive, community-based intervention that has the most evidence of effectiveness at this time. The project has involved over 100 middle schools in Kansas City and Indianapolis in a program that focuses on resistance and other coping skills as well as environmental support strategies.

The project has five major components. The school-based curriculum consists of 10 sessions for sixth or seventh graders that focus on resistance skills, with homework assignments consisting of interviews and role-plays with family members. Parent programs consist of parent-student-principal groups formed to promote a drug-free school environment and parent training in family communication skills. Through community organization, community leaders are trained in drug-prevention strategies and develop task forces, mass media appeals, community events, award ceremonies, networking, and referrals. Through health policy change, government officials promote antismoking policies, enforce drunk driving laws, and create neighborhood watches for drugs. Mass media efforts include press kits, commercials, news features, and other television programs to promote drug prevention.

An evaluation of 42 of the Kansas City schools showed that after 18 months the prevalence of cigarette, alcohol, and marijuana use was significantly lower than in control schools, for students as well as for their parents (Pentz et al., 1989). At the 3-year follow-up, the rate of increase for tobacco and marijuana use was less in experimental schools than in control schools, and the program was found to be as successful for high-risk youth as for youth with lower risk levels (Johnson et al., 1990).

Treatment

When overindulgence, frequent episodes, negative outcomes, or all three conditions are present, treatment for substance abuse should be considered. The concept of the least restrictive environment is an important consideration in examining treatment options for the adolescent (Kaminer, 1994). Effective treatments address the substance-use problem, help the individual achieve other aftercare objectives such as academic success and positive family functioning, and require the least lifestyle change. There is general agreement that substance-abuse treatment programs must address underlying causes such as family dysfunction and psychological disorders, as well as the substance abuse itself.

Some schools have student assistance programs. Through these programs a team of trained school personnel can intervene with students who have substance-abuse problems. Referral to this type of program is appropriate for a student who is engaging in alcohol or other drug use that is causing problems or who has been in treatment for substance abuse and is in an aftercare program (Anderson, 1987).

Unfortunately, very few substance-abuse treatment programs are designed specifically for adolescents. Although 20% of all patients in these programs are under the age of 19, only 5% of programs have adolescents as their main clientele (Kaminer, 1994). The most prevalent types of substance-abuse treatment for adolescents are outpatient treatment, partial hospitalization, inpatient or residential treatment, individual therapy, self-help groups, and family therapy. Ideally treatment facilities should offer more than one level of treatment to make transitions easy for clients and to allow therapists to follow their clients through different levels of treatment (Kaminer).

Most adolescents are treated on an outpatient basis (81.5%); adolescents who are appropriate for this type of treatment have behavior that is manageable at home and do not have suicidal ideation or other mental disorders (Lawson & Lawson, 1992). These programs vary widely but generally include hotlines; individual therapy; group therapy; self-help groups; family therapy; and educational, vocational, and social services. Most outpatient programs emphasize counseling.

Partial hospitalization is a transitional setting for those individuals who have successfully completed inpatient care hospitalization but are not yet ready for outpatient treatment. Typically, clients receive care and therapy 5 days a week, including family therapy and educational therapy.

Inpatient treatment is indicated when outpatient therapy has failed, when the client is a clear danger to himself or herself or others, when behavior is unmanageable outside of a controlled setting, or when medication management is required (Lawson & Lawson, 1992). Such adolescents may be frequent runaways, be frequently truant, expelled or suspended from school, demonstrate conduct disorders, or refuse to participate in outpatient programs. Inpatient programs are usually highly structured with an emphasis on group therapy and substance-abuse education. These programs tend to base treatment on the 12-step Alcoholics or Narcotics Anonymous approach in which belief in a power greater than oneself is emphasized. The environment is tightly controlled, and the length of stay typically ranges from 20 to 60 days.

Residential communities typically treat adolescents who have serious psychological or social problems in addition to a substance use problem, and the length of treatment is usually 6 to 9 months. The goal is to change substance-use behavior and to build social, educational, and vocational skills; self-esteem; and confidence. These communities also use the 12-step approach. The programs include confrontational encounter groups, individual counseling, and tutoring (Schinke, Botvin & Orlandi, 1991).

There are indications that as many as 75% of all inpatient, outpatient, and residential programs for adolescent substance-abuse treatment use the Alcoholics or Narcotics Anonymous 12-step philosophy or model (Lawson & Lawson, 1992). Unfortunately, very few studies have examined the effectiveness of these treatment programs, and the ones that have do not provide evidence that the programs significantly affect substance abuse or that one treatment is more effective than another (Schinke et al., 1991).

Summary

Although adolescent substance use and abuse has declined over the last two decades, the most recent prevalence data indicate that this trend has reversed. Substance abuse continues to be a problem for many adolescents, and the problem has increased substantially in the past few years. At the same time, knowledge about causes, effects, problem development, and the effectiveness of prevention and intervention programs has grown, although much remains to be explained and determined.

Researchers in this area agree that experimental substance use and abuse are not the same. A majority of adolescents engage in experimental use, and most of these will not become substance abusers. Thus, prevention and intervention efforts should be focused primarily on abuse rather than experimental use.

There are also increasing indications that early personal, social, and family maladjustment are precursors of substance abuse. Therefore, prevention and intervention programs must be comprehensive and multilevel and address the personal, social, and family issues that appear to influence risk for substance abuse. Given the current knowledge in this area, such programs are likely to be more successful than those that only focus directly on substance-use issues without addressing the underlying risk and protective factors.

Recommended Resources

Glantz, M., & Pickens, R. (Eds.) (1992). *Vulnerability to drug abuse.* Washington, DC: American Psychological Association.
This edited volume provides extensive reviews of the literature on a variety of risk factors and protective factors for substance abuse. Chapters address genetic factors, family factors, environmental factors, psychological and psychosocial factors, and the transition from use to abuse.

Gullotta, T. P., Adams, G. R., & Montemayor, R. (Eds.) (1995). *Substance misuse in adolescence.* Newbury Park, CA: Sage.
This edited volume provides comprehensive overviews of the literature on personal, family, and social/community factors associated with adolescent substance use and abuse. In addition, chapters address urban youth, rural youth, prevention programs, and treatment programs.

Kaminer, Y. (1994). *Adolescent substance abuse.* New York: Plenum.
This volume provides a comprehensive overview of issues related to adolescent substance use. Areas addressed include epidemiology, etiology, diagnosis, prevention, assessment, and treatment. There are also chapters on the relationship between substance abuse and suicide and between HIV/AIDS and substance abuse.

Cohen, P. (1991). *Helping your chemically dependent teenager recover: A guide for parents and other concerned adults.* Minneapolis, MN: Johnson Institute.
This guide for parents recognizes that both substance abusing adolescents and their parents need guidance in recovery. Chapters describe in detail the stages of recovery and the specific tasks of each stage, as well as the problems one is likely to encounter during the process.

DuPont, R. L. (1984). *Getting tough on gateway drugs: A guide for the family.* Washington, DC: American Psychiatric Press.
*This book, written for parents, addresses the dangers of using the "gateway" drugs—alcohol, marijuana, and cocaine. It ex-*plains the pharmacological effects of drugs, provides psychological explanations behind substance abuse, and stresses the importance of the family in helping a loved one recover. This is a very readable resource with practical advice and guidance in prevention and available treatment options.*

References

Anderson, G. L. (1987). *The student assistance program model.* Greenfield, WI: Community Recovery Press.

Barnes, G. M. (1984). Adolescent alcohol abuse and other problem behaviors: Their relationship and common parental influences. *Journal of Youth and Adolescence, 13,* 329–348.

Botvin, G. J. (1983). *Life skills training: A self-improvement approach to substance abuse prevention.* New York: Smithfield Press.

Botvin, G. J., Baker, E., Renick, N., Filazolla, A. D., & Botvin, E. M. (1984). A cognitive-behavioral approach to substance abuse prevention. *Addictive Behaviors, 9,* 137–147.

Botvin, G. J., & Eng, A. (1982). The efficacy of a multicomponent approach to the prevention of cigarette smoking. *Preventative Medicine, 11,* 199–211.

Botvin, G. J., Eng, A., & Williams, C. (1980). Preventing the onset of cigarette smoking through life skills training. *Preventative Medicine, 9,* 135–143.

Botvin, G. J., & McAlister, A. (1981). Cigarette smoking among children and adolescents: Causes and prevention. In C. B. Arnold (Ed.), *Annual review of disease prevention* (pp. 222–249). New York: Springer.

Botvin, G. J., Renick, N., & Baker, E. (1983). The effects of scheduling format and booster sessions on a broad spectrum psychosocial approach to smoking prevention. *Journal of Behavioral Medicine, 6,* 359–379.

Botvin, G. J. (1987). Factors inhibiting drug use: Teacher and peer effects. Report presented to the National Institute on Drug Abuse, Rockville, MD.

Botvin, G. J., & Tortu, S. (1988). Peer relationships, social competence, and substance abuse prevention: Implications for the family. *Journal of Chemical Dependency Treatment, 1,* 245–273.

Bry, B. H. (1993). *Research on family setting's role in substance abuse.* Springfield, VA: National Technical Information Service. (NTIS No. PB 94-175 692)

Clayton, R. R. (1992). Transitions in drug use: Risk and protective factors. In M. Glantz & R. Pickens (Eds.), *Vulnerability to drug abuse* (pp. 15–51). Washington, DC: American Psychological Association.

Cloninger, C. R. (1987). Neurogenetic adaptive mechanisms in alcoholism. *Science, 236,* 410–416.

Cohen, S. (1981). *The substance abuse problem.* New York: Haworth Press.

Drug and alcohol use rising among teenagers, study finds. (1995, December 17). *The New York Times,* p. 45.

Dryfoos, J. G. (1990). *Adolescents at risk: Prevalence and prevention.* New York: Oxford University Press.

Fisher, G. L., & Harrison, T. C. (1992). Assessment of alcohol and other drug abuse with referred adolescents. *Psychology in the Schools, 29,* 172–178.

Flay, B. R., d'Avernas, J. R., Best, J. A., Kersell, M. W., & Ryan, K. B. (1983). Cigarette smoking: Why young people do it and ways of preventing it. In P. J. McGrath & P. Firestone (Eds.), *Pediatric and behavioral medicine* (pp. 132–183). New York: Springer.

Forman, S. G., & Linney, J. A. (1991). School-based social and personal coping skills training. In L. Donohew, H. E. Sypher, & W. J. Bukoski (Eds.), *Persuasive communication and drug abuse prevention* (pp. 263–282). Hillsdale, NJ: Erlbaum.

Forrest, G. G. (1983). *How to cope with a teenage drinker.* New York: Atheneum.

Glantz, M., & Pickens, R. (1992). Vulnerabilities to drug abuse: Introduction and overview. In M. Glantz & R. Pickens (Eds.), *Vulnerability to drug abuse* (pp. 1–14). Washington, DC: American Psychological Association.

Hansen, W. (1992). School based substance abuse prevention: A review of the state of the art in curriculum, 1980–1990. *Health Education Research, 7,* 403–430.

Hawkins, J. D., & Catalano, R. F. (1992). *Communities that care: Action for drug abuse prevention.* San Francisco: Jossey Bass.

Hawkins, J. D., Lishner, D. M., Catalano, R. F., & Howard, M. D. (1986). Childhood predictors of adolescent substance abuse: Toward an empirically grounded theory. *Journal of Children in Contemporary Society, 18,* 11–49.

Johnson, C. A., Pentz, M., Weber, M., Dwyer, J., Baer, N., MacKinnon, D., & Hansen, W. (1990). Relative effectiveness of comprehensive community programming for drug abuse prevention with high-risk and low-risk adolescents. *Journal of Consulting and Clinical Psychology, 58,* 447–456.

Johnston, L. D., O'Malley, P. M., & Bachman, J. G. (1994). *National survey results on drug use from monitoring the future study, 1975–1993: Vol. 1. Secondary school students.* Rockville, MD: National Institute on Drug Abuse.

Kaminer, Y. K. (1994). *Adolescent substance abuse: A comprehensive guide to theory and practice.* New York: Plenum.

Kandel, D. B. (1982). Epidemiological and psychosocial perspective on adolescent drug use. *Journal of the American Academy of Child Psychiatry, 20,* 328–347.

Lawson, G. W., & Lawson, A. W. (1992). *Adolescent substance abuse: Etiology, treatment, and prevention.* Gaithersburg, MD: Aspen.

Lerner, J., & Vicary, J. (1984). Difficult temperament and drug use: Analysis from the New York longitudinal study. *Journal of Drug Education, 14,* 1–8.

Mayer, W. (1983). Alcohol abuse and alcoholism: The psychologist's role in prevention, research, and treatment. *American Psychologist, 38,* 1116–1121.

Merikangas, K. R., Rousaville, B. J., & Prusoff, B. A. (1992). Familial factors in vulnerability to substance abuse. In M. Glantz & R. Pickens (Eds.), *Vulnerability to drug abuse* (pp. 75–97). Washington, DC: American Psychological Association.

Meyer, A. L. (1995). Minimization of substance use: What can be said at this point? In T. P. Gullotta, G. R. Adams, & R. Montemayor (Eds.), *Substance misuse in adolescence* (pp. 201–232). Newbury Park, CA: Sage.

Newcomb, M. D., & Bentler, P. M. (1989). Substance use and abuse among children and teenagers. *American Psychologist, 44,* 242–248.

Newcomb, M. D., Maddahian, E., & Bentler, P. M. (1986). Risk factors for drug use among adolescents: Concurrent and longitudinal analyses. *American Journal of Public Health, 76,* 525–531.

Norman, E. (1995). Personal factors related to substance misuse: Risk abatement and/or resiliency enhancement? In T. P. Gullotta, G. R. Adams, and R. Montemayor (Eds.), *Substance misuse in adolescence* (pp. 15–35). Newbury Park, CA: Sage.

Pentz, M. A., Cormack, C., Flay, B., Hansen, W., & Johnson, C. A. (1986). Balancing program and research integrity in community drug abuse prevention: Project STAR approach. *Journal of School Health, 56,* 389–393.

Pentz, M. A., Dwyer, J. H., MacKinnon, D. P., Flay, B. R., Hansen, W. B., Wang, E. Y. I., & Johnson, C. A. (1989). A multicommunity trial for primary prevention of adolescent drug abuse. *Journal of the American Medical Association, 261,* 3259–3266.

Schinke, S. P., Botvin, G. J., & Orlandi, M. A. (1991). *Substance abuse in children and adolescents: Evaluation and Intervention.* Newbury Park, CA: Sage.

Shedler, J., & Block, J. (1990). Adolescent drug use and psychological health: A longitudinal inquiry. *American Psychologist, 45,* 612–630.

Tarter, R. E., & Mezzich, A. C. (1992). Ontogeny of substance abuse: Perspectives and findings. In M. Glantz & R. Pickens (Eds.), *Vulnerability to drug abuse* (pp. 149–178). Washington, DC: American Psychological Association.

Tobler, N. S. (1986). Meta-analysis of 143 adolescent drug prevention programs: Quantitative outcome results of program participants compared to a control or comparison group. *Journal of Drug Issues, 16,* 537–568.

U.S. Department of Health and Human Services. (1982). *The health consequences of smoking: Cancer, A report of the Surgeon General* (DHHS Publication No. PHS 82-50179). Washington, DC: U.S. Government Printing Office.

83

Pediatric Psychopharmacology

Tom Kubiszyn

American Psychological Association

Ronald T. Brown

Emory University

Stephen T. DeMers

University of Kentucky

Background and Development

Many medications, both prescription and nonprescription or over the counter (OTC), are frequently administered to school-age children to treat a variety of medical problems. In addition to the intended or beneficial therapeutic effects, all medications have attendant side effects, some of which may even be detrimental to learning (e.g., somnolence, impaired attentional ability, emotional/behavioral lability). Thus, both prescription and OTC drugs can affect a child's emotional functioning, learning needs, and ultimate school success.

Psychotropic drugs, which are administered by prescription only (e.g., antidepressants, antipsychotics, antianxiety agents, stimulants), target attention, cognition, emotion, and behavior. In addition, many nonpsychotropic drugs also may affect attention, cognition, emotion, and behavior. These effects may be due to their intended therapeutic effects or to side effects associated with these agents. Examples of these pharmaceutical agents include anticonvulsants, antiasthmatics, antihistamines, decongestants, expectorants, antibiotics, and antihypertensives. Thus, if a child is receiving any type of medication, educational, social, emotional, or behavioral functioning in the school setting may be affected.

School Psychologists' Concern With Medication

School psychologists need to be concerned with the effects of medication on children for several reasons. First, the use of prescription medication to control children's behavior in the schools has increased significantly and is expected to continue to increase in future years (Biederman & Steingard, 1990; Gadow & Pomeroy, 1993). Swanson, Lerner, and Williams (1995) reported that the number of outpatient visits for attention-deficit/hyperactivity disorder and the amount of methylphenidate (the generic name for Ritalin) manufactured more than doubled between 1990 and 1993.

Second, clinical and anecdotal evidence suggests that school psychologists frequently work with children receiving psychotropic medication and see medication evaluation as an important part of their future role. Findings from a recent survey (Kubiszyn & Carlson, 1995) support these conclusions. A sample of school psychologists ($N = 571$) were asked to assess their attitudes and experiences with pediatric psychopharmacology. The sample reported that over the course of their careers,

- 97.6% dealt with children receiving stimulant medication.
- 83.6% dealt with children receiving anticonvulsants.
- 82.6% dealt with children receiving antidepressants.
- 68.4% dealt with children receiving antipsychotics.
- 42.2% dealt with children receiving antianxiety agents.

More importantly, a strong consensus emerged in the survey regarding increased involvement of school psychologists in the field of pediatric psychopharmacology (Kubiszyn & Carlson, 1995). Expansion of the already busy school psychologist's role to include psychotropic medication evaluation was supported by 77.1% of the respondents. At the same time, dissatisfaction with existing medication evaluation methods was evident. Only 15.4% of the sample endorsed agreement regarding the adequacy of current methodology to evaluate the efficacy of psychotropic drugs for children.

A third reason for involvement of school psychologists in psychopharmacology relates to the inclusion movement. In recent years, full inclusion in the regular classroom of special learners, including those with multiple and severe disabilities, has gained momentum (Conte, 1994). These children may receive one or more medications that affect learning. Classroom teachers and other educators with limited training and experience with challenged learners and psychopharmacology will work with these children. Thus, there are likely to be even more medication-related questions posed by educational personnel than has been the case in the past. Because few prescribers are school based, questions regarding the effects of medication on behavior and learning are likely to fall increasingly upon the school psychologist. With appropriate psychopharmacological training, school psychologists may help bridge the gap between the physician's office and the school environment.

Finally, teachers and significant others react to children's behavior in ways which vary from supportive to critical depending on the attributions they make about the cause of the child's behavior, particularly if it is disruptive. An adult who concludes "it's the medicine" is likely to respond to a behavioral aberration in an understanding and supportive way, whereas a conclusion that "it's the child" is more likely to result in a punitive judgement in response to the same behavior (for a review, see Brown, Dingle, and Landau, 1994). Without valid and reliable means to identify the cause of a child's behavior, subjective impressions rather than objective data will be employed to make sense of a child's behavior (Brown, Lee, & Donegan, in press). By utilizing appropriate evaluation techniques, school psychologists can help acquire the objective data needed to help evaluate attributional accuracy.

General Issues in Pharmacology

Generic and trade names
In the applied practice of pharmacology, medications typically are referred to by either their generic name (e.g., methylphenidate) or their brand or trade name (e.g., Ritalin). Generic formulations are usually less expensive than brand-name drugs, because brand names are patent protected by pharmaceutical corporations driven by profit motives. In theory, there should be no difference in safety or efficacy between trade and generic formulations. However, in clinical practice physicians tend to prefer one over the other. In the authors' experience, this choice often is based on clinical experience, on clinical lore regarding potency, and primarily on the marketing efficacy of the drug's manufacturer.

Safety of OTC drugs
While many psychologists and other health care professionals have voiced concern over the use of prescription drugs with children, less concern has been expressed about nonprescription, or OTC, drugs. Greater acceptance of OTC medication may be a function of the passage of time and increased familiarity because prescription drugs can only be sold as OTC medications after patent protection lasting decades has expired. Yet, these agents are no more safe or effective as OTCs than when prescription limited their availability. For example, aspirin is considered to be safe and effective, but potential side effects can be life threatening, with Reyes' Syndrome in children being a prime example. Thus, a change from prescription to OTC status should not be considered to ensure a formulation's safety and efficacy.

Dosage
A common misconception has been that because children are smaller than adults, proportionately lower doses of a drug should be prescribed for them. However, this is not necessarily true. A drug may be metabolized and/or excreted quicker and/or more completely by a child than by an adult (American Medical Association, 1991). Thus, proportionately more of a drug actually may be necessary to obtain a therapeutic level in a child (Werry & Aman, 1993).

Mechanism of action
Nerve cells form the basis for one of the body's primary communication and control systems (others are genetic, hormonal, and immunological). Alteration in nerve cell function can elicit a cascade of profound effects on the function of other nerve cells, tissues, organs, and glands (i.e., affecting the entire organism). Psychotropic drugs and those medications with behavioral actions alter nerve cell functioning directly and indirectly and can thereby trigger deleterious and even fatal effects (Riddle et al., 1991; Riddle, Geller, & Ryan, 1993).

All pharmaceutical agents, regardless of their classification, circulate throughout the blood stream until they reach electrochemically attractive receptor sites on nerves or other cells. Then, like iron filings attracted to a magnet, they are drawn to the receptor sites. The drug binds with, or remains attached to, the receptor until an electrochemical change releases it. These activities affect a nerve cell's capacity to transmit or receive information by affecting intracellular and extracellular changes that lead to alterations in cellular membranes, receptors, neurotransmitters, and other molecules. The reader is referred to Werry and Aman (1993) for a detailed review of these changes.

Receptors may be localized in a small area or dispersed throughout the body. The terms *affinity* and *specificity* are used to describe the binding strength of a drug's and receptor's chemical structure and the magnitude of the electrochemical status and attraction. Affinity and specificity affect how much of a drug is needed to achieve sufficient receptor binding (i.e., saturation) to elicit a therapeutic effect. In short, as specificity and affinity increase, the amount of a drug needed to achieve a particular level of saturation is reduced. If less of a drug is needed, all other factors being equal, the lower the probability of unwanted side effects.

This dynamic pertaining to pharmacology may be understood in relation to the difference between a rifle and a shotgun. A well-aimed rifle hits its target with a single projectile (i.e., a bullet). When the single bullet hits the specific intended target there is no "side affect" or collateral damage. A shotgun, on the other hand, always incurs substantial collateral damage because it fires multiple, even hundreds of projectiles at a specific target. This results in facility at hitting the target but at the cost of unwanted and perhaps multiple side effects. Stated generally, the task of modern psychopharmacological research is to identify the most accurate "bullet." That is, the goal of such researchers is to develop agents that are increasingly specific in their capacity to bind with selected and/or localized receptor sites without affecting undesired receptor sites. A drug able to target a specific type of receptor(s) would affect those receptors and not others. Thus, there hopefully would be nonexistent or minimal collateral or side effects.

Major Pediatric Psychopharmacologic Medications

Table 1 (Brown, Dingle, & Landau, 1994) presents the major psychopharmacologic agents administered to children; their indications; and common as well as infrequent, but serious, side effects. For more in depth information the reader is referred to Brown, Dingle, and Dreelin (1997), to Campbell and Cueva (1995), and to two recent mini-series on pediatric psychopharmacology published in *School Psychology Quarterly* (see Brown et al., 1994) and *School Psychology Review* (see Pelham, Jr., 1993).

Problems and Implications

Differences Between Adult and Pediatric Psychopharmacology

Modern pharmaceuticals are an improvement from the drugs of a decade or more ago, but particularly with children, their specificity is not what most clinicians would like. Thus, side effects are an ever present reality. With the pediatric population, the frequency of these side effects is especially relevant. Systematic study has not yet been done on the effects of psychotropic drugs on children whose complex, immature, and evolving neurophysiological control systems are bidirectionally linked to hormonal and immunological control systems. Drugs may affect these developing systems and their interplay, and

as a result the developing organism, in different ways than they affect mature organisms.

Possible Dose-Response Relationships

In addition, little research is available that has systematically assessed the effects of varied doses of psychotropics on children to determine differential dose effects on behavior, cognition, learning, and affect. For example, with regard to stimulants, initial research indicated that learning and behavior respond differently to various doses of stimulants (Brown & Sleator, 1979). However, subsequent research has failed to confirm this finding (Rapport & Kelly, 1991). Nonetheless, it is important to examine the effects of various doses of other medications on learning and behavior.

Prescribing Practices for Psychotropic Drugs

Psychotropic agents comprise about 20% of all drugs prescribed, and about 70% or more of all psychotropic drugs are prescribed by non-psychiatrically-trained physicians, including pediatricians and family practice physicians (Baldessarini, 1990). Most prescribers have little familiarity with pediatric psychopharmacology (Barkley et al., 1991) and even less with schools and curricula. In addition, other than for stimulants, there is a dearth of research in this area and there are few data to guide physicians in prescribing psychotropics for the pediatric population. Thus, even if prescribers are available for consultation with school personnel, their knowledge of the effects of medications on learning and behavior is limited.

In fact physicians sometimes turn to psychologists to obtain information regarding psychotropic drug use with children (Barkley et al., 1991; Kubiszyn & Carlson, 1995). It has been reported that 79% of clinical child psychologists (Barkley et al., 1991) and 38% of doctoral school psychologists (Kubiszyn & Carlson, 1995) were consulted at least once in their careers by physicians regarding psychotropics for child patients of the physician (i.e., the psychologists did not know the child in question). Psychologists were consulted even more frequently by physicians about psychotropic medication for child clients collaboratively treated by both the physician and the psychologist.

The State of the Art in Evaluating Pediatric Psychotropic Drugs

Gadow (1986, 1991) has reviewed contemporary practices in pediatric psychopharmacotherapy. Historically, prescribers have relied on parent or child self-report to make decisions about the initiation of psychopharmacological treatment, titration of drug dosages, or termination

Table 1. *Major Psychopharmacologic Agents Administered to Children*

Agent (Brand Name)	Indications	Common Side Effects	Infrequent, Serious Side Effects
ANTIDEPRESSANTS *Tricyclics*			
Imipramine (Tofranil)	Enuresis Depression	Sedation Dry mouth Constipation Urinary retention	Cardiac conduction slowing with heart block Decrease in seizure threshold Exacerbation of glaucoma
Amitriptyline (Elavil/Endep)	Enuresis	Blurred vision Cardiac conduction slowing	
Desipramine (Norpramin)	ADHD Depression	Mild tacycardia Elevated blood pressure	
Noritriptyline (Palemor)	ADHD Depression	Weight gain Orthostatic hypotension	
ANTIPSYCHOTICS *Phenothiazines*			
Chloropromazine (Thorazine)	Acute psychotic states	Sedation Orthostatic hypotension	Tardive dyskinesia Neuroleptic malignant syndrome Elevated liver enzymes
Thioridazine (Mellaril)	Autistic disorder Pervasive developmental disorder	Akathisia motor restlessness Parkinsonian symptoms Cognitive blunting Photosensitivity	Agranulocytosis Acute dystonic reactions Seizures Eye changes (retinopathy) Rebound hypertension
Trifluperazine (Stelazine)	Tourette's disorder Dyskinetic movements	Sedation Hypotension Headache Gastrointestinal upset Anticholinergic effects Insomnia	Depression Cardiac arrythmias
STIMULANTS			
Dextroamphetamine (Dexadrine)	ADHD	Insomnia Dysphoria Behavioral rebound	Depression Tachycardia or hypertension Psychotic symptoms
Methylphenidate (Ritalin)	ADHD	Impaired cognitive performance Anorexia Weight loss or failure to gain	Growth retardation Motor tics
Pemoline (Cylert)	ADHD	Weight loss or failure to gain	
ANTIHISTAMINES			
Diphenhydramine (Benadryl)	Anxiety Insomnia	Dizziness Oversedation Agitation	
Hydroxyzine (Atarax)	Sleep induction Agitation	Incoordination Abdominal pain Blurred vision	
Propanolol (Inderal)	Aggression	Dry mouth	

(Continued)

Table 1 *Continued*

Agent (Brand Name)	Indications	Common Side Effects	Infrequent, Serious Side Effects
ANXIOLYTIC (Antianxiety agent) *Benzodiazepine*			
Diazepam (Valium)	Seizures Anxiety disorders Behavior disorders	Substance abuse	Sedation Diminished cognitive performance Confusion Emotional lability
ANTICONVULSANTS			
Phenobarbital	Seizures	Memory and attention disturbance Hyperactivity	
Diphenylhydamtoin (Dilantin)	Seizures	Irritability Aggression Depressed mood	
Carbamazepine (Tegretol)	Aggression Emotional lability Irritability Seizures	Drowsiness Nausea Rash Eye problems	Reversible bone marrow effects Irritability Agitation Mania
Valproic acid (Depakene)	Mania Seizures	Nausea Gastrointestinal distress Weight gain	Tremor
OTHER DRUGS			
Lithium carbonate	Bipolar disorders Aggression	Gastrointestinal upset Tremor Headache Polyuria/polydipsia	Possible renal injury Thyroid dysfunction Toxicity Ataxia Slurred speech Dizziness Sedation Weakness Leukocytosis
Clonidine (Catapres)	Tourette's disorders ADHD Aggression	Sedation	Dry mouth Photosensitivity Hypotension Dizziness

of medication treatment. When school data were obtained, they typically were either anecdotal or incomplete, even though data collected to evaluate psychosocial and educational interventions could have been employed to evaluate drug safety and efficacy. Given that most prescribers are not school based, this situation is not surprising, yet it is unacceptable. It should be noted, however, that failure to collect valid data is characteristic of many psychosocial and educational interventions as well. Further, because most prescribers lack sufficient training and experience in psychosocial and educational intervention, medication treatment is seldom integrated with other types of nonsomatic interventions.

Clearly, further research efforts are needed to study the effects of psychotropics on learning and behavior in pediatric populations. In concluding their recent review

of child and adolescent psychopharmacology, Campbell and Cueva (1995) note that "carefully designed and closely monitored multisite studies are essential to assess adequately the efficacy and safety of psychopharmacological agents in this young age group" (p. 1269). Continuing to follow typical or common models to initiate, adjust, and terminate psychotropic treatment with the pediatric population will add little to the knowledge base (Barkley et al., 1991; Kubiszyn, 1994).

With the exception of stimulants, little is known about psychopharmacology for the pediatric population. Beyond the general issues of safety and efficacy, more specific issues in pediatric psychopharmacology remain unanswered. These include identification of the variables that may affect interaction effects, dose-response relationships, long-term effects, medication holidays, and differential effects within and between developing children. Stated differently, each time a psychotropic drug is prescribed for a child, the probability of therapeutic and untoward side effects is largely unknown, and possible confounding effects are unable to be controlled. Thus, careful, systematic analysis of ecologically valid data across settings is indicated, both for clinical drug evaluations and for research drug trials.

The Need for Ecologically Valid Evaluation

The term *ecological validity* has been used to describe data-collection methods that have maximum generalizability to the classroom environment (Whalen & Henker, 1991). This methodology employs techniques such as structured observations by trained observers in the classroom, lunchroom, and play areas; structured interviews with pupils, parents, and teachers; completion of behavior rating scales with established reliability and validity; and use of psychometric instruments to assess medication efficacy and safety under "double-blind" conditions that may include medication as the independent variable. Fischer and Newby (1991) and Gadow, Nolan, Paolicelli, and Sprafkin (1991) have described the classroom-based, double-blind trial in detail.

Rigorous systematic observations of drug effects are employed primarily within laboratory settings, and only recently has the assessment of drug effects been employed in natural settings. In reality physicians seldom observe children in the school setting, and communication with teachers or other school personnel is infrequent. Even when such input is sought by prescribers, because educators and school psychologists do not have a great deal of training in psychopharmacology monitoring and evaluation, conclusions that the prescriber draws about titrating or terminating a medication often are influenced primarily by anecdotal data from school personnel, parents, and the child. Adjustment of medication is infrequently dictated by objective, valid evidence (Gadow, 1986, 1991). For this reason, one of the extant needs is for ecologically valid and reliable methods to evaluate and render judgments about such medication effects within the school setting.

The systematic use of medication-sensitive rating scales and questionnaires and direct observation is recommended as a formal means of assessing pediatric medication effects. Future research should be designed to assess in ecologically appropriate fashion both the beneficial and untoward effects of medications in the classroom setting.

Factors Complicating Medication Evaluation

Beyond issues of instrumentation, methodology, and training, various psychological and physiological factors also complicate the evaluation of pediatric psychotropic safety and efficacy.

Psychological factors

Psychotropic drugs especially may be influenced by emanative effects (Brown et al., 1994). Emanative effects refer to the cognitive, affective, attributional, or social effects of the act of taking medication. In some cases such emanative effects may be desirable. Increased self-confidence and self-efficacy may be evident if a child attributes behavioral improvement to the self and views taking medication in a favorable way. However, such emanative effects also may be undesirable. Decreased self-confidence and self-efficacy may be evident if a child attributes improvements in school work to the medication rather than the child's own efforts or if the child's view of the self is deficient because of the need to take medication. For a review of the emanative effects of medication in the pediatric population see Brown et al. (in press).

Another complicating psychological factor is the expectancy effect. It has been well documented that expectancies influence perceptions of behavior, and for this reason the perceived efficacy of a drug may be influenced by expectancies. Expectancies make it somewhat difficult to assess objectively the adequacy of a medication through an interview alone (Whalen & Henker, 1991). Thus, if a child (or parent or teacher or other observer) endorses the efficacy of a medication it may be due to any of the following factors: (a) accuracy of perception, (b) emanative factors associated with medications, (c) need for approval or desire to respond in a socially desirable fashion, (d) expectancy effects, or, finally, (e) a combination of the aforementioned or other possible factors.

Physiological factors

As noted previously, a lack of receptor site specificity increases the likelihood of side effects. However, receptor specificity is not static. It can vary depending on a variety of internal and external events. Alterations in specificity, as well as a myriad of other variables, in turn can affect the probability of therapeutic and untoward side effects. As a result there can be individual differences in therapeutic response. For example, variation may be expected in side-effect proclivity and resistance for identical doses of medications in the same individual at different points in time, as well as across individuals. This is true for adults, yet it is particularly an issue for pediatric populations characterized by immature nervous system development. Finally, younger children in particular have difficulty in the identification and/or accurate reporting of interoceptive stimuli associated with both therapeutic and side effects (American Medical Association, 1991).

Children also differ more widely and less predictably than adults in their rates of medication absorption, distribution, metabolism, and excretion (American Medical Association, 1991). This also makes prediction of therapeutic and side effects more difficult than with adults. In summary, accurate evaluation of pediatric medication safety and efficacy is complex, dynamic, and time consuming.

Legal and Ethical Implications

Complex legal and ethical dilemmas surround the school psychologist's involvement in pediatric psychopharmacology (DeMers, 1994). A case described by Jacob and Hartshorne (1991) involved a malpractice suit brought against a school district in California in 1980. In response to perceived pressure from the schools to medicate their children, the parents of a group of 18 children successfully litigated against the district and its staff (including the school psychologist) for "intrusion into the decision of whether or not a child should take Ritalin to control what the schools alleged was hyperactive behavior" (Jacob & Hartshorne, 1991, p. 46). Obtaining proper informed consent, avoiding coercive tactics to ensure medication acceptance and compliance, and providing recognized collateral behavioral interventions would likely have protected the district from the litigation (DeMers, 1994).

Ensuring confidentiality of records also may be problematic if school psychologists become more involved with physicians in the collaborative evaluation of the safety and efficacy of psychotropic medication (DeMers, 1994). Collaboration will increase the need to share medical, special education, and mental health information or files among physicians, school psychologists, and possibly other school or health care personnel. Minimally, procedural safeguards to protect confidential information and to ensure that written, informed consent is obtained by all concerned parties will need to be developed and implemented.

However, there may be cases in which consent is not granted or obtained. In such cases, the legal and ethical ramifications of revealing or not revealing medication information are unclear. For example, if the school psychologist does not inform the school staff that a child is receiving medication and the child suffers from significant, deleterious side effects that go unrecognized, issues of liability and ethics could be raised. If the school psychologist informs the staff against the wishes of the individual holding privilege, confidentiality becomes an issue. These are difficult issues that must be given serious consideration; interested readers are referred to DeMers (1994) for more detailed discussion.

Several other ethical concerns attendant to increased psychopharmacological involvement by school psychologists have been noted (DeMers, 1994). For example, school psychologists are ethically bound to practice only within their areas of competence. Thus, only those school psychologists who have had appropriate training and experience should participate in medication evaluation (DeMers & Bricklin, 1995). Logically, because all school psychologists deal with children taking medication, it follows that all school psychologists should have training and experience in pediatric psychopharmacology.

Finally, parents, school staff, and third-party payors frequently exert pressure to resolve quickly a child's complex problem. This pressure may compromise a school psychologist's intention to structure an intervention in an ethically appropriate, comprehensive manner, by implementing both psychosocial and educational interventions as well as pharmacotherapy. A related danger involves medications being perceived as panaceas, with needed psychosocial and educational interventions overlooked or provided with less than optimal levels of attention (DeMers, 1995).

Alternative Actions

Multimodal Treatment

As noted previously, all medications have side effects. Thus, it may be argued that biological therapies should be avoided in favor of psychosocial treatments. However, it also may be argued that all treatments are subject to side effects. Further, as the biological markers of cognitive, emotional, and behavioral difficulties are better delineated, employing psychotropics in the treatment of selected disorders may become the standard of practice. With increased emphasis on economy in treatment, and as managed care increasingly comes to control public as well as private health care, there will be added pressure to consider treatments that are less labor intensive and as a result less costly than traditional psychosocial treatments. Psychopharmacologic treatment may increasingly be viewed by business-oriented health-care decision makers as the most, or only, viable, cost-effective, reasonable, and attractive treatment option.

Given the strength of the powerful societal, fiscal, and political forces affecting health-care decision making today, it may make little sense for school psychologists to expend limited resources rigidly resisting such forces. Instead advocating for the incorporation of pharmacotherapy into an integrated, multimodal treatment plan may be more effective. Such a treatment plan would include collaboration with physicians, educators, and other professionals to develop integrated pharmacological, psychosocial, and educational interventions and could be evaluated in an ecologically valid fashion. Thus, the standard of care in working with children in the schools would include coordination and integration of psychosocial and educational interventions, with consideration then given to the addition of pharmacotherapy. The palatability of this position among school psychologists is suggested by the finding that 90% of the earlier cited sample of school psychologists "endorsed the use of psychosocial and educational interventions in conjunction with prescription of psychoactiove medications" (Kubiszyn & Carlson, 1995, p. 254).

Recent Developments

In recent years there has been increased collaboration between physicians and school personnel regarding medication decisions (Brown et al., 1994). Increasingly prescribers are asking teachers and parents to complete standardized questionnaires and checklists that have demonstrated sensitivity to medication effects at school and/or at home (Brown et al., 1996). In addition, school psychologists are becoming increasingly aware of the need to provide prescribers with ecologically valid data on which to base their medication decisions.

Professional organizations have begun to recognize the needs of school psychologists for information about pediatric psychopharmacology. This is illustrated by the mini-series on school and pediatric psychopharmacology published in the *School Psychology Quarterly,* a journal of the Division of School Psychology of the American Psychological Association (APA), and the *School Psychology Review,* a journal of the National Association of School Psychologists (NASP).

The mini-series followed the release of the Report of the (APA) Board of Directors Ad Hoc Task Force on Psychopharmacology in 1992, which recommended the development of curricula for three levels of graduate training in psychopharmacology (Smyer et al., 1993) and recommended that all doctoral trainees be required to obtain at least the first level of psychopharmacology training. Further, in 1995 the APA Council of Representatives formally endorsed the development of a three-level psychopharmacology graduate curriculum for applied psychologists. With this endorsement, graduate psychopharmacology training became official APA policy.

Finally, it must be noted that while medication can alleviate symptoms, it does not train a child in social skills, problem solving, self-regulation, or any of the academic skills. Similarly, medication does not directly alter (a) inappropriate family interactions, (b) teacher and peer reactions to the child, (c) the maladaptive family, or (d) social and school systems that may exacerbate a child's symptoms. Furthermore, symptoms often reappear soon after medication is terminated (Brown, Borden, Wynne, Schleser, & Clingerman, 1986; Whalen & Henker, 1991). Drugs do not permanently eliminate the child's symptomatology, in large part because the underlying problem frequently is a complex function of genetics, anatomy, physiology, learning, and environment. Thus, multimodal treatment appears to be an appropriate match to the underlying biological, psychosocial, and educational issues of pupils. However, powerful financially driven forces will be in direct conflict with such efforts.

Summary

There is a clear trend toward increased psychopharmacological intervention with school children. Despite this trend, adequate empirical support for the safety and efficacy of various psychotropics is lacking, other than for the stimulants. In addition, myriad legal, ethical, methodological, and procedural concerns remain unresolved. Methods to evaluate safety and efficacy range from limited parent and child interviews in the physician's office to elaborate, double-blind, and ecologically valid but expensive school-based methodologies. While there have been increased efforts to collect classroom data pertaining to safety and efficacy, the literature regarding most medications remains scant.

School psychologists, with appropriate training, can contribute substantively to overcome the dearth of information that too often is characteristic of decisions about the initiation, adjustment, and termination of psychotropic medications. Further, as experts in psychosocial and educational intervention, school psychologists, with appropriate training, can help ensure that children receive the integrated and comprehensive health-care services they deserve. Professional associations have recently begun to respond to the training needs of school psychologists in this area.

Finally, however well-intended such efforts may be, school psychologists, like other health care providers, likely will find themselves operating in an increasingly financially driven environment that may attach little value to the concerns raised in this chapter.

Recommended Resources

Barkley, R. A. (1990). *Attention-Deficit Hyperactivity Disorder: A handbook for Diagnosis and treatment.* New York: Guilford.
This is an excellent reference regarding issues and techniques in the assessment and treatment of ADHD. It provides a comprehensive literature review, addresses diagnosis from several perspectives, and emphasizes the incorporation of medication into a multimodal treatment program.

Barnhardt, E. R. (Eds.). (1996). *Physicians' desk reference.* Oradell, NJ: Medical Economics.
More commonly known as the PDR, this encyclopedic reference provides comprehensive information about drugs approved by the Food and Drug Administration through its publication date. Supplements also are published during the year as new drugs are released. The PDR includes a wealth of information including trade and generic names, drug category, mechanism of action, approved uses and dosages, indications, contraindications, drug interactions, side effects, titration schedules, and special considerations.

Brown, R. T., Dingle, E., & Dreelin, A.D. (1997). Neuropsychological effects of stimulant medication on children's

learning and behavior. In C. R. Reynolds & E. Fletcher-Janzen (Eds.), *Handbook of clinical child neuropsychology*. New York: Plenum.
This chapter provides a thorough and scholarly review of current research findings related to all aspects of stimulant use with this population.

Mini-series published by Division 16 of the American Psychological Association (*School Psychology Quarterly*, [1994], 9[1], 1-53), by the National Association of School Psychologists (*School Psychology Review*, [1993], 22[2], 158-251), and by the Child Clinical Section of Division 12 of American Psychological Association (*Journal of Clinical Child Psychology*, [1991], 20[3].)
Taken together these three recent mini-series provide a wide-ranging overview of the state of the art in pediatric psychopharmacology. All issues raised in this chapter are discussed in detail in one or more of these mini-series' chapters.

References

American Medical Association (AMA). (1991). *Drug evaluations annual 1991.* Milwaukee, WI: Author.

Baldessarini, R. J. (1990). Drugs and the treatment of psychiatric disorders. In A. Goodman Gilman, T. W. Rall, A. S. Niles, & P. Taylor (Eds.), *The pharmacological basis of therapeutics* (8th ed., pp 383–534). New York: Pergamon Press.

Barkley, R., Connors, C., Barclay, A., Gadow, K., Gittleman, R. Sprague, R., & Swanson, J. (1991). Task force report: The appropriate role of clinical child psychologists in the prescribing of psychoactive medication for children. *Journal of Clinical Child Psychology, 19* (Suppl.), 1–38.

Biederman, J., & Steingard, M. R. (1990). *Psychopharmacology of children and adolescents: A primer for the technician.* (Technical Paper No. 27), Washington, DC: World Health Organization.

Brown, R. T., Borden, K. A., Wynne, M. E., Schleser, R., & Clingerman, S. R. (1986). Methylphenidate and cognitive therapy with ADD children: A methodological reconsideration. *Journal of Abnormal Child Psychology, 14,* 481–497.

Brown, R., Dingle, A., & Dreelin, E. (1997). Neuropsychological effects of stimulant medication on children's learning and behavior. In C. R. Reynolds & E. Fletcher-Janzen (Eds.), *Handbook of clinical child neurospychology.* New York: Plenum.

Brown, R., Dingle, A., & Landau, S. (1994). Overview of psychopharmacology in children and adolescents. *School Psychology Quarterly, 9*(1), 4–23.

Brown, R.T., Lee, D., & Donegan, J. (in press). Psychopharmacotherapy in school-aged children. In C. R. Reynolds and T. Gutkin (Eds.), *Handbook of school psychology* (2nd Ed.). New York: Wiley.

Brown, R. T., & Sleator, E. K. (1979). Methylphenidate in hyperkinetic children: Differences in dose effects on impulsive behavior. *Pediatrics, 64,* 408–411.

Campbell, M., & Cueva, J. E. (1995). Psychopharmacology in child and adolescent psychiatry: A review of the past seven years, Part II. *Journal of the American Academy of Child and Adolescent Psychiatry, 34*(10), 1262–1272.

Conte, A. E. (1994). Blurring the line between regular and special education. *Journal of Instructional Psychology, 21*(2), 103–113.

DeMers, S. (1994). Legal and ethical issues in school psychologists participation in psychopharmacological interventions with children. *School Psychology Quarterly, 9*(1), 41–52.

DeMers, S. (1995). Emerging perspectives on the role of psychologists in the delivery of health and mental health services. *School Psychology Quarterly, 10*(3), 179–183.

DeMers, S., & Bricklin, P. (1995). Legal, professional, and financial constraints on psychologists' delivery of health care services in school settings. *School Psychology Quarterly, 10*(3), 217–235.

Fischer, M., & Newby, R. (1991). Assessment of stimulant response in ADHD children using a refined multimethod clinical protocol. *Journal of Clinical Child Psychology. 20*(3), 232–244.

Gadow, K. D. (1986). *Children on medications: Hyperactivity, learning disabilities, and mental retardation.* San Diego: College Hill Press.

Gadow, K. D. (1991). Clinical issues in child and adolescent psychopharmacology. *Journal of Clinical and Consulting Psychology, 59,* 842–852.

Gadow, K. D., Nolan, E., Paolicelli, L., & Sprafkin, J. (1991). A procedure for assessing the effects of methylphenidate on hyperactive children in public school settings. *Journal of Clinical Child Psychology, 20*(3), 268–276.

Gadow, K. D., & Pomeroy, J. C. (1993). Pediatric psychopharmacology: A clinical perspective. In T. R. Kratochwill & R. J. Morris (Eds.), *Handbook of psychotherapy with children and adolescents* (pp. 356–402). Boston: Allyn & Bacon.

Jacob, S. & Hartshorne, T. (1991). *Ethics and Law for School Psychologists.* Brandon, VT: Clinical Psychology Publishing Co., p. 46.

Kubiszyn, T. (1994). Pediatric psychopharmacology and prescription privileges: Implications and opportunities for school psychology. *School Psychology Quarterly 9*(1), 26–40.

Kubiszyn, T., & Carlson, C. (1995). School psychologists' attitudes toward an expanded health care role: Psychopharmacology and prescription privileges. *School Psychology Quarterly, 10*(3), 247–270.

Pelham, W. E., Jr. (1993). Guest editor's comments: Recent developments in pharmacological treatment for child and adolescent mental health problems. *School Psychology Review, 22*(2), 158–161.

Rapport, M. D., & Kelly, K. L. (1991). Psychostimulant effects on learning and cognitive function: Findings and implications for children with attention-deficit/hyperactivity disorder. *Clinical Psychology Review, 11,* 61–92.

Riddle, M., Geller, B., & Ryan, N. (1993). Case study: Another sudden death in a child treated with desipramine. *Journal of the American Academy of Child and Adolescent Psychiatry, 32,* 792–797.

Riddle, M., Nelson, C., Kleinman, C., Rasmusson, A., Leckman, J., King, R., & Cohen, D. (1991). Sudden death in children receiving norpramin: A riddle of three reported cases and commentary. *Journal of the American Academy of Child and Adolescent Psychiatry, 30*(1) 104–108.

Smeyer, M. A., Balster, R. L., Egli, D., Johnson, D. L., Kilbey, M. M., Leith, N. J., & Puente, A. E. (1993). Summary of the report of the Ad Hoc Task Force on Psychopharmacology of the American Psychological Association. *Professional Psychology: Research and Practice, 24*(4), 394–403.

Swanson, J. M., Lerner, M., & Williams, L. (1995, October 5). More frequent diagnosis of attention-deficit hyperactivity disorder. *The New England Journal of Medicine,* 944.

Werry, J. S., & Aman, M. G. (1993). *Practitioner's guide to psychoactive drugs for children and adolescents.* New York: Plenum.

Whalen, C. K., & Henker, B. (1991). Therapies for hyperactive children: Comparisons, combinations, and compromises, *Journal of Clinical and Consulting Psychology, 59,* 126–137.

84

Hospitalization

Ronald T. Brown

Emory University School of Medicine and Rollins School of Public Health

Natalie Frank

University of North Carolina at Chapel Hill

Ronald L. Blount
Adina Smith

University of Georgia

Background and Development

For many children, being in the hospital can be a frightening occasion. Children experience a new environment in which they are exposed to strange odors, meet individuals frequently wearing unusual uniforms or even masks, and possibly endure procedures both horrifying and excruciatingly painful (Blount, Smith, & Frank, in press). Even benign and nonpainful procedures such as magnetic resonance imaging (MRI) and computerized tomography (CT), can be both intimidating and frightening.

Children, their families, and health care providers are all challenged by the multitude of stressors associated with hospitalization. The reactions of children, families, and staff to hospitalization are diverse and are a complex function of numerous interacting variables. Such variables include children's developmental level and coping style, socioeconomic status, family financial and personal resources, and environmental contingencies that reinforce specific behaviors in the child, the family, and the hospital staff.

A number of psychological sequelae may emerge from either the hospitalization, the physiological process associated with the disease, the iatrogenic effects of treating the disease, or finally, the general experiences associated with any chronic illness or injury (see Table 1). As a symptom of their disease or injury, many children endure significant cognitive changes requiring an initial evaluation while the child is hospitalized. In addition, some children may experience medication-induced side effects that may affect their cognitive functioning. Other diseases for which hospitalization is necessary frequently involve developmental delay, coping with intense pain following an injury or procedure, and adjustment to disfig-

urement or a disability. Many school psychologists provide psychological services to chronically ill children (Brown, 1996). For example, they may be involved in coordinating the needs for children who require home schooling due to medical problems or in providing therapeutic services for these children in an outpatient clinic setting. Because of the school psychologist's expertise in child development, behavioral analysis, consultation, intervention design, family systems, and educational needs, this individual is in a prime position to work with hospital staff and families during the course of the child's hospitalization and in the subsequent process of reintegration into the school.

Hospital-Related Issues

Children's adjustment to the stressors associated with the hospitalization experience frequently is determined by the physical environment and the contingencies established within the hospital that shape children's behavior.

Hospital environment

The optimal hospital environment for children is a facility designed for them. These hospitals, designed for children by trained pediatrics staff, are very flexible and accommodating to the child's needs (Cahners, 1979). However, in some smaller cities, older hospitals, or rural areas, this ideal situation may not be available, and children with illnesses or injuries may be in the same facilities as adults. In this type of hospital setting, a unit devoted to pediatrics is most desirable. Regardless of the type of unit, a good understanding of the organization and structure of the unit is vital to identifying stressors and possible resources that may be beneficial during the child's stay (Gillman & Mullins, 1991).

Table 1 *Common Psychological Issues Associated with Pediatric Subspecialties*

Subspecialty	Condition	Representative Psychological Aspects
Trauma (surgery)	Orthopedic trauma, burns	Coping with intense postinjury pain, adjustment to disfigurement, disability
	Head injury	Cognitive deficits
Cardiology	Congenital heart defects	Impaired cognitive function secondary to hypoxia, parental guilt about responsibility for anomaly
	Acquired heart defects	Restriction of activity secondary to blood thinner used in valve replacement
	Hypertension	Cognitive or mood effects of antihypertensive medication
Endocrinology	Diabetes mellitus	Nonadherence to complex self-care regimen
	Short stature	Self-concept, peer relations
Gastroenterology	Encopresis	Coercive parent-child interactions around toileting, impaired child self-esteem
	Nonorganic recurrent abdominal pain	Reinforcement of child's "sick" behavior, family dysfunction
	Ileitis (Crohn's disease)	Impaired self-esteem
Hematology	Sickle cell	Recurrent pain, cognitive changes
	Hemophilia	Chronic arthritic pain
Infectious Diseases	AIDS	Cognitive deterioration, depression
	Meningitis	Cognitive changes
Neonatology	Bronchopulmonary	Feeding disorders, developmental delays, dysplasia
	Apnea	Sleep regulation
Nephrology	Renal failure	Treatment nonadherence, cognitive symptoms
	Cushing's Syndrome	Muscle weakness, body composition changes
Neurology	Headaches	Stress
	Seizures	Medication-induced changes in cognitive functioning
Oncology	Leukemia	Coping with aversive medical diagnostic and treatment procedures
	Solid tumors	Pain, treatment-related changes, death and dying issues
Pulmonology	Asthma	Activity restrictions
	Cystic fibrosis	Repeated rehospitalization, decreased life expectancy

Note. From "Psychological Aspects of Pediatric Disorders" by K. J. Tarnowski and R. T. Brown, 1995b, in *Advanced Abnormal* Child Psychology (M. Hersen & R. T. Ammerman, Editors), Hillsdale, NJ: Erlbaum. Copyright 1995 by Erlbaum. Adapted with permission.

In a hospital designed specifically for children, a number of services are provided to improve child and family adjustment throughout the course of hospitalization. These services include:

- Social services to provide instrumental resources (e.g., financial support, transportation, meal vouchers for family members during hospital stays, temporary local housing for families who live farther away from the hospital).
- Psychological and psychiatric services to decrease the emotional stress of the child and family, to develop behavioral contingency plans during the hospitalization, and to prevent treatment nonadherence which may necessitate further hospitalizations.
- Child life specialists to prepare the child for surgery and encourage developmental progress while the child is hospitalized.
- Tutoring and school services as a means of maintaining academic skills in the hospital.

Thus, various team members often play differential roles for the purpose of assisting the child and family to adjust to the hospitalization experience.

For some children, such as patients undergoing bone marrow transplantation or situations where the threat of infection is paramount, a major stressor of hospitalization is the requirement for stringent isolation. Separation from caregivers and support systems actually may be more aversive than the illness itself (Tarnowski & Brown, 1995b). The process of isolation, which may include masks and gowns prior to entering a child's room, frequent hand washings, and avoidance of physical contact, may be very threatening and confusing, particularly to younger children (Brown, Dingle, & Koon-Scott, 1994).

Environmental contingencies

The environmental context of any hospitalization is critical for the child's adjustment to the hospital setting. The availability of basic resources (e.g., finances to secure appropriate treatment, medication, transportation) as well as psychological resources (e.g., parental support and caring) are important determinants of how well children will function when hospitalized (Tarnowski & Brown, 1995b). It also is important to carefully evaluate the behavioral contingencies in effect for an ill or injured child in the hospital (Routh, 1988; Tarnowski & Brown, 1995). Behavioral reactions of pediatric patients while hospitalized include crying, flailing, attempts to escape, seeking parental comfort, and withdrawal. These reactions may come in response to certain aversive treatments (Varni, Blount, Waldron, & Smith, 1995) or to a particular symptom of an illness such as pain related to a sickle cell crisis. They are a function of biological differences across children, such as pain threshold and temperament, as well as developmental factors including understanding of the need for a painful procedure. However, it should be remembered that the responses of significant others (families, staff, and peers) to the child's behavior highly influence and shape the topography, intensity, and duration of child responding while in the hospital (Tarnowski & Brown, 1995a; Varni et al., 1995). In short, although it is critical that parents and staff create a consistently supportive and nurturant environment for the child while hospitalized, it also is imperative that behavioral contingencies are in force in the hospital environment that promote developmentally appropriate self-regulation and self-care skills.

Child Issues Pertaining to Hospitalization

Developmental issues

Children's levels of cognitive development influence their conceptualization of illness and injury, their understanding of hospitalization, and their cooperation with specific medical procedures. For example, a preschooler will have very different reactions and issues of adjustment related to being in the hospital than will an adolescent. The child's level of development also determines the level of understanding of the injury and treatment, as well as the type and extent of explanations provided by the hospital staff regarding the illness and necessary procedures. Bibace and Walsh (1980) have expanded on Piaget's theory of cognitive development to conceptualize children's understanding of hospitalization and illness at various stages:

- The sensorimotor stage is characteristic of infants; they understand their environment through manipulation and activity. An infant who is hospitalized is likely to have limited opportunity to explore the environment and for this reason frequent contact with caregivers is critical.
- The prelogical thinking of children from ages 2 to 7 years is characterized by phenomenism (attribution of illness to a remote cause) and contagion (attribution of illness to a proximate object). For example, a two-year-old in the hospital for a burn injury may attribute the pain experienced not to the actual injury but rather directly to hospital events such as wearing a dressing, seeing staff in gowns and masks, and being separated from his or her parents.
- Children between the ages of 7 and 11 rely on concrete logical explanations of illness based on contamination

(i.e., person, object, or bad behavior) and internalization (looking for the source of the illness inside the body). Children with leukemia in this phase of development may attribute the experience of frequent venipunctures in the hospital as being caused by the staff or may believe it to be a function of their character.
- Formal logical thinking, which develops after the age of 12 years, involves cause-and-effect relationships that are physiological. Adolescents in this phase of development have a more realistic and accurate understanding of the etiology and process of disease and the need for hospitalization. An adolescent typically comprehends the needs and goals for hospitalization. (Bibace & Walsh, 1980)

Given that children experience hospitalization and illness in accordance with their development (Bibace & Walsh, 1980), it is important to tailor interventions to their developmental level. The stressors associated with hospitalization frequently result in emotional and cognitive regression, which should be considered in the assessment and intervention phases of treatment. It also should be noted that chronological age is only a very general indicator of children's developmental levels.

Socioemotional issues

Children who are hospitalized and are seriously ill or injured often have to cope with extended hospitalizations; separation from parents or caregivers, siblings, and peers; and frequent painful medical procedures. Such challenges may become a source of stress to children resulting in anxiety, overt distress, regressive behaviors, difficulty in coping with pain, and depression (Tarnowski & Brown, 1995). Further, although adaptive family functioning can serve to provide support to the child who is hospitalized, a child's illness can diminish significantly family financial and psychological resources. More importantly, a premorbidly dysfunctional family environment serves as an additional risk factor that may potentiate socioemotional maladjustment (Tarnowski & Brown, 1995a). Again, it is important to note that adaptive functioning for children is developmentally mediated. For younger children in the hospital, parental separation will be emotionally stressful, while for older children, disrupted peer relationships will constitute a major stressor of the hospitalization experience. Finally, for adolescents, coping with personal identity issues represents a critical stressor during hospitalization.

Summary

When considering the psychological aspects of hospitalization, it is important to begin with an assessment of the basic developmental level of the child who is hospitalized (Brown et al., 1994; Tarnowski & Brown, 1995b). The nature of the illness or injury should be evaluated, coupled with the treatments and their associated side effects, and a determination subsequently made as to whether the hospitalization may have disrupted child developmental and familial functioning which are integral to adjustment (Brown, Doepke, & Kaslow, 1993). It will be important to assess carefully the child's environment including the hospital, the staff, and the family support systems that are available to the child (Brown et al., 1993). Finally, both financial and psychological resources should be identified to maximize adjustment.

Problems and Implications

Children undergoing hospitalization must cope with unfamiliar aspects of a strange and threatening environment, their medical condition, and often painful treatments. Early studies suggested enduring behavioral problems, learning difficulties, and delinquency—sometimes lasting up to 20 years following hospitalization (Douglas, 1975). In contrast, the current and more widely accepted results indicate that the majority of adjustment problems subsequent to hospitalization remit after two weeks (Thompson & Vernon, 1993). However, while some children cope well before, during, and after hospitalization, other children do not. Recognizing factors associated with the variability in children's responses to hospitalization and identifying specific medical procedures that place children at risk may help determine high-risk individuals and specify targets for intervention.

Child Factors Influencing Adaptation

Myriad factors influence the child's adaptation to the anxieties associated with the hospital environment and the stressors associated with the various procedures performed while the child is hospitalized. While a discussion of each of these factors is not possible within the limited scope of this chapter, the most salient determinants of the child's adjustment include the capacity for stress and coping, overall coping styles, and specific strategies employed for coping during stressful procedures. The child's temperament also has been found to be a central ingredient in predicting adjustment to the hospital experience.

Temperament
Temperament, while not easily modifiable, may help identify those children at risk and most in need of intervention. In one investigation (McClowry, 1990), the temperament dimensions of predictability, approach or withdrawal, mood, threshold of responsiveness, and intensity

of reaction accounted for 50% of the variance in the behavior of 8- to 12-year-olds prior to, one week following, and one month after hospitalization. Consistent with this research, Carson, Council, and Gravley (1991) found that children who adjusted better to hospitalization for tonsillectomies were adaptable, positive in mood, generally predictable in behavior, approaching and approachable, distractible, and less reactive to stimuli and had less intense emotional reactions. Finally, Lumley, Abeles, Melamed, Pistone, and Johnson (1990) investigated the combined effects of children's temperamental characteristics and maternal behavior on children's reactions to stressful situations. They found that children rated by their mothers as "difficult" were more distressed if their mothers were not involved with them following the medical procedure. Thus, difficult children with involved mothers demonstrated less distress.

Stress and coping, coping style, and coping strategies
Coping is most often defined as "constantly changing cognitive and behavioral efforts to manage specific external and/or internal demands that are appraised as taxing or exceeding the resources of the person" (Lazarus & Folkman, 1984, p. 141). A stressor is perceived, coping is employed, and better or worse adjustment is the outcome. For children, the study of coping usually involves investigating the influence of their general coping styles or specific coping strategies. Coping style, in contrast to the dynamic definition of coping given at the start of this paragraph, is seen as the person's usual way of responding to a stressor. The typical nosology is to divide coping styles into information-seeking and information-avoiding styles (Blount, Davis, Powers, & Roberts, 1991). Those with the former seek information about the procedure and direct their attention toward the threatening stimulus, while those with the latter style ignore or refuse to attend and use repression, denial, or distraction when confronting the stressful procedure (Fanurik, Zeltzer, Roberts, & Blount, 1993). In general, children who use an information-seeking style of coping demonstrate superior adjustment to hospitalization.

Suls and Fletcher (1985) performed a meta-analysis, primarily with studies that had investigated adults' coping style, to determine whether there was evidence for the efficacy of one coping style over the other. They found that avoiding styles of coping were associated with better adjustment when confronting short-term stressors. In contrast, information seeking was associated with better outcomes when confronting long-term stressors. We have extended these and other findings to suggest that a prescriptive model based on a "coping strategy by stressful situation" is needed to help determine whether to provide children with more information or to encourage them to engage in distraction or avoidance coping strategies (Blount et al., in press). For short-term stressors, such as injections, lumbar punctures, and other acute painful procedures, we encourage the use of parental or staff-directed distraction of the child's attention away from the threatening aspects of the medical stressor, perhaps in the form of using a blower, talking about nonprocedural topics, deep breathing, or counting. Some procedural information can be provided during a brief role-play in the service of training the children and adults to use the coping and coping prompting behaviors. For longer term stressors, such as impending hospitalization, information should be provided in age-appropriate terms at critical junctures, or stress points, such as prior to admission, before surgery, and prior to discharge (e.g., Visintainer & Wolfer, 1975). By considering aspects of the stressful situation, this model provides practical suggestions about the types of coping strategies to teach children, while avoiding the less clinically useful construct of coping style.

Familial and Parental Factors

The parents' relationship with their child is related to the child's coping with hospital stays and surgery. High levels of maternal anxiety, rejection, overindulgence, and overprotectiveness have been related to poorer child adjustment during hospitalization (Carson et al., 1991). In addition, Zabin and Melamed (1980) found that parents who reported using positive reinforcement, modeling, and persuasion had children with lower anxiety and fear levels during hospitalization, in contrast to those parents who reported relying more on punishment, force, and reinforcement of dependency.

As noted previously, separation from caregivers represents a major stressor of the hospitalization experience. Thus, children's separation from their parents is another factor associated with hospitalized children's distress. Children who have been allowed to have constant parental contact during their hospital stay have been rated as better adjusted during hospitalization and demonstrating fewer maladaptive behaviors at discharge and at follow-up than children whose mothers were not allowed to room-in (Douglas, 1975). In contrast to the results of studies of parental presence during hospitalization, Shaw and Routh (1982) found that children whose mothers were present during injections were more distressed than those children whose mothers were absent. Similarly, in a study of children ranging in age from 1 to 7 years, Gonzalez et al. (1989) found that older children displayed more behavioral distress when the parent was present. However, despite these findings, the same children strongly preferred their parent to be present for future injections. Blount, Davis, et al. (1991) speculated that it was not the parents' presence or absence but what the parents did while present during the procedure that influenced the children's distress. Also, because a child's hospitalization can be anxiety provoking for parents, and

few parents have been trained to manage their own distress or effectively assist their child with coping, Blount, Davis, et al. (1991) recommend that parents receive training to promote their own and their children's coping prior to admission and during the course of hospitalization.

School Issues

Teachers may wish to consult with school psychologists regarding visitation by the teacher and other children to the hospitalized child, information to the hospitalized child's peers, and means of communication to the hospitalized child from classmates. In addition, a major role in the social rehabilitation of any child who has been hospitalized for any length of time is the return to school. For some children, particularly for those having sustained a long-term hospitalization or those who may suffer from a disfigurement such as a burn injury or limb amputation, returning to school may be a formidable task. It has become apparent that school adjustment is highly significant in children's overall adaptation to their illness, and thus a smooth transition from the hospital back to the classroom is of utmost importance. Unfortunately, there are few data available on school reintegration for children who have been hospitalized.

Cahners (1979) has supported the need for a strong hospital-school liaison in the process of school reentry to assist children who have been disfigured from injuries, as well as to assist school personnel in reintegrating these children into the classroom. Some investigators have suggested that children who have endured multiple hospitalizations are at risk for learning and academic problems (Woodward, 1959), while others have suggested that only specific groups of children who have had multiple hospitalizations are at risk for such difficulties (Fowler, Johnson, & Atkinson, 1985). With some diseases, the neuropsychological processes involved in the specific chronic illness may place children at risk for learning problems, such as children who have early onset of insulin-dependent diabetes mellitus (Holmes, O'Brien, & Greer, 1996; Rovet, Ehrlich, Czuchta, & Ackler, 1993), children diagnosed with leukemia who have undergone radiation or chemotherapy (Brown et al., 1992), and pediatric patients who have sustained cerebral vascular accidents (strokes; Brown, Armstrong, & Eckman, 1993). Some investigators have attributed academic delays to extended school absences for children who have been hospitalized for prolonged periods (Brown, Armstrong et al., 1993), while other investigators have found little association between school attendance and achievement (Weitzman, 1986). Finally, for children hospitalized due to traumatic injuries, poor achievement and learning problems are posited to be premorbid factors which may precede the injury, rather than an injury itself being causal in children's learning problems (Tarnowski & Brown, 1995a).

Alternative Actions

Preparation for Hospitalization

It is estimated that 75% of pediatric hospitals utilize some sort of program to prepare children for hospitalization (Peterson & Ridley-Johnson, 1980). Commonly, hospitals provide prehospitalization tours, presentation of and play activities with medical equipment, and group discussions (Azarnoff & Woody, 1981). However, the effectiveness of such individual programs at decreasing child and parent distress is rarely evaluated which raises questions about their utility (Blount, 1987). Several types of interventions, however, have received empirical support of their effectiveness in preparing the child and parent for upcoming hospitalization. These methods include providing information to the child and parent, modeling, and coping skills training.

Providing information

One of the earliest interventions for decreasing distress in hospitalized children and their parents is information provision. Often, one of the most frightening aspects of hospitalization for families is not knowing what to expect. Providing information to the child and parent about upcoming procedures has been demonstrated to be effective in reducing distress for these individuals (Haller, Talbert, & Dombro, 1967).

In addition to providing information to the child and parents, health care professionals have included stress-point nursing care to improve the effectiveness of the intervention. Stress-point care consists of providing information regarding medical procedures at several critical times during the course of hospitalization. Nurses also provide support and reassurance to the family and may help children rehearse responses expected of them during the stressful procedures.

Wolfer and Visintainer (1975) demonstrated that children admitted to a hospital for elective surgery who received information regarding stressful medical procedures were less distressed and more cooperative at different points during the hospitalization than were control children who received standard nursing care. Parents who received information reported less anxiety, perceived the information provided as more adequate, and reported more satisfaction with the care of their child than did parents in the control group. It should be noted that all major demographic data for both groups were controlled including race, socioeconomic status, age, and parental education. Thus, there was no bias in either the treatment or control group. This research also demonstrated that children who received preparation in managing stress were less distressed in response to preoperative medication than children who received information at a single point in time (Visintainer & Wolfer, 1975).

A later study by these investigators demonstrated that this intervention could be enhanced by adding preparatory booklets sent to the home 3 to 4 days prior to hospital admission (Wolfer & Visintainer, 1979). These booklets explained what to expect during the hospitalization and included pictures of children undergoing various medical procedures. Children also were provided with appropriate toy medical equipment along with the book illustrations.

The model of information provision and supportive interactions throughout the times of stressful procedures appears to be a better intervention than information provided at a single point in time. Although more time consuming, this repeated intervention may help the family with the necessary information through repetition and prompting of appropriate responses at the appropriate times. Further, the supportive environment in which the information is offered may aid in decreasing family anxiety and distress and in assisting parents and other family members in emotionally supporting the hospitalized child.

Modeling

Much of the research in the area of preparing children for hospitalization has focused on modeling of upcoming procedures. Modeling allows the child to gain exposure to the situation, often through observation of another child in a similar situation. Live models demonstrating what will occur during the hospitalization have been used, along with videotapes, slide shows, and illustrated materials. Inanimate objects such as dolls and puppets also have been used in modeling interventions. The best recognized example of modeling through the use of video materials is Melamed and Siegel's (1975) film *Ethan Has an Operation*. The film presented a child going through all the steps involved in hospitalization for hernia repair. The film was demonstrated to be more effective than a non-medically-related control film in reducing distress in 4- to 12-year-old children. In addition, locally produced films created and utilized in specific hospitals have been shown to be effective in decreasing child and parent hospital distress (Peterson, Schultheis, Ridley-Johnson, Miller, & Tracy, 1984). Inexpensive puppet models demonstrating the use of medical equipment and showing the steps that occur during a procedure also have been used to aid pediatric patients in adjusting to hospitalization (Schultz, Raschke, Dedrick, & Thompson, 1981).

On the other hand, some research has indicated that modeling may not be an effective intervention for children with previous medical experience. Melamed, Dearborn, and Hermecz (1983) suggested that young children with previous medical experience may be sensitized by filmed modeling. This sensitization may actually result in increased distress. Thus, previous medical experience and the developmental stage of the child should be taken into consideration when deciding whether to use a modeling intervention.

Coping-skills training

Coping-skills training is frequently employed with children to help them adjust to anxiety-producing situations. Three types of coping strategies taught include distraction, relaxation, and self-talk. Distraction consists of focusing on external stimuli, such as a book or movie. Relaxation consists of deep breathing or imagery-based exercises. Self-talk consists of teaching the child to use statements such as "It will be over soon," "I can handle this," or "Everything is alright." These strategies, alone or in combination with information provision and modeling, have proven effective in decreasing distress in children who are hospitalized.

Peterson and Shigetomi (1981) demonstrated that children who were trained during a 15-minute presentation/practice session of relaxation, self-talk, and distraction were less distressed than were untrained children as indicated by greater food intake, nurses' ratings of anxiety and cooperativeness, and child reports of fear and anxiety. In addition, parents of the trained children reported less anxiety than parents of the untrained children. Faust, Olson, and Rodriguez (1991) reported similar results for children trained in coping skills, such as deep breathing and imagery, that were taught through the use of a modeling, slide and audio show. Instructional videotapes and booklets sent to parents one week prior to their child's surgery also have been used in training parents to teach their children to utilize these coping strategies. Children coached during their hospital stay by their parents were shown to be less distressed and to display less problematic behavior in the week prior to and after the hospitalization (Meng & Zastowny, 1982).

While standard hospital preparation programs may provide components of the previously mentioned strategies, the failure to monitor their actual effectiveness is problematic. When imposing any intervention, it is important to demonstrate that it actually makes a difference. Examining which components of a program are most effective at producing the desired outcome provides the ability and opportunity to create the most useful and practical intervention possible for a particular setting. While the research presented here is useful in providing implications for intervention programs, the components most beneficial for a particular hospital and particular family can be ascertained only through careful monitoring and assessment. Thus, future research must identify the component parts of intervention programs most effective with particular children and families.

School Reentry

In their review of school reentry for hospitalized children, Sexson and Madan-Swain (1993, 1996) focused on the common types of school problems encountered, the process of school reentry, and recommendations for school personnel and the child's family. This review is particularly relevant for the practicing school psychologist who may be the only mental health provider available to coordinate the reentry plan. Specifically, Sexson and Madan-Swain provide recommendations for a reentry plan for the teacher, delineate questions typically raised by peers, and provide school psychologists with recommendations for preparing the hospitalized child's class regarding the illness and associated treatments. They recommend that school psychologists employed within the schools could serve as excellent liaisons and consultants to parents and pediatric health care providers in planning for the child's transition back to school. It should be noted that a number of legal protections are available for children under special education legislation. Thus, children with chronic illnesses may become eligible for special education services under the classification of "Other Health Impaired." The school psychologist will be an important person in determining whether the student's needs can be met without an Individualized Education Plan (IEP).

Blakeney (1994) recommends that plans for each child be individualized according to chronological age, developmental level, visibility of disfigurement, degree of physical impairment, and the child's level of premorbid functioning. Sexson and Madan-Swain (1993, 1996) recommend that a member of the health care team from the hospital work directly with school personnel during the latter part of hospitalization and at follow-up periods until the child has attained good adjustment. Again, ongoing assessment in the cognitive and social arena is critical.

Adjustment to school is an important quality-of-life factor that may predict later adjustment for children and adolescents who have endured frequent and lengthy hospitalizations. Assistance with appropriate transition is imperative. Written and videotape materials specific to the burn injured child have been developed to assist with school reintegration and are described in detail in Blakeney (1994). Limited empirical data are available on the efficacy of school reintegration programs for children who have sustained long periods of hospitalization. As Blakeney (1994) has suggested, further empirical elucidation of school reentry represents an important objective in understanding children who have survived long periods of hospitalization.

Assisting children and their families in coping with the stressors of hospitalization and the associated side effects of treatment for various diseases, as well as the successful reintegration of these children back to the classroom, will necessitate the joint working efforts of school psychologists and pediatric health-care providers. The collaboration emerging over the past two decades between child clinical psychologists and pediatricians has been decidedly successful and productive and serves as a model in both the provision of clinical services and research productivity (Roberts, 1995). The programs developed to date have been designed to assist children and their families in coping with the ongoing stressors of disease and associated treatments during hospitalization. As a great number of children and adolescents survive diseases and injuries previously considered fatal, there will be more children with learning problems and greater numbers of children who must face the challenge of reintegrating to school. The school psychologist is a collaborator in providing consultation and liaison services in attempting to secure mental health services for these children.

Finally, as many health care systems and hospitals endeavor to prevent injuries and some childhood illnesses, there is an excellent match between the training of school psychologists in psychological assessment, consultation, and intervention design and the services needed by health care providers. Further, with the recent emphasis on involving schools in health promotion and the prevention of disease and injury, it is anticipated that individuals trained in school psychology will benefit from future employment opportunities concomitant with the growth in health education and disease and injury prevention.

tant to conduct ongoing assessment and monitoring regarding the efficacy of the approach as well as the intervention components most promising in enhancing coping.

A major role for the school psychologist in assisting children with the transition from the hospital environment to the school is consultation and liaison between hospital staff and the school regarding the nature of the illness, explanations regarding any disabilities, and sensitizing other children and school personnel about disfigurement. There also is a viable role for the school psychologist in the assessment of children's educational performance in determining whether specific learning difficulties are either a function of the disease process, an iatrogenic effect of treatment, or the result of excessive absenteeism from school due to lengthy hospitalizations. It is recommended that a reentry plan should be individualized in accordance with the child's specific illness or injury and developmental level. Finally, the promotion of health-related behaviors and training in the prevention of injuries and specific diseases is a future role to be assumed by school psychologists.

Summary

Hospitalization involves a unique set of challenges for children and their families. These challenges frequently vary depending upon disease type, treatments prescribed during the course of hospitalization, and the iatrogenic effects associated with such treatments. Children's understanding of the need for hospitalization and their conceptualization of illness are largely influenced by their level of cognitive development. For this reason, the assessment of the child's functioning during the hospital stay, as well as interventions designed to assist in mitigating the stressors associated with the hospitalization, must be considered within the context of the child's developmental level. Factors influencing adaptation to hospitalization include the child's style of coping and the use of active coping strategies. Issues of temperament also are related to children's adjustment to hospitalization and associated medical procedures. Finally, premorbid familial and parental factors and parents' capacity to manage their own stressors have been demonstrated to be highly associated with the children's adjustment to hospitalization.

Numerous programs are available to prepare children to cope with the stressors of hospitalization and associated procedures during the course of the hospitalization. These interventions are included within the areas of patient education and provision of specific information regarding procedures, modeling, and coping-skills training. Regardless of the intervention employed, it is impor-

Authors' Note

This chapter was supported in part by a grant award to the first author from the National Institute of Health, Heart, Lung, and Blood Branch, HL-48-482-02.

Recommended Resources

Ammerman, R. T., & Campo, J. V. (1997). *Handbook of pediatric psychology and psychiatry.* Needham Heights, MA: Allyn and Bacon.
This is an outstanding collection of works by leading practitioners in the field to assist children and their families in adapting to the hospitalization experience.

Children's Health Care. Hillsdale, NJ: Erlbaum.
This journal designed for child health care workers, other allied health professionals, and parents publishes a potpourri of topics relating to hospitalization and chronic illness. Topics have ranged from pain management to child abuse and neglect.

Journal of Pediatric Psychology. New York: Plenum Press.
This scholarly journal disseminates excellent empirical articles on characteristics and intervention programs with hospitalized and chronically ill children. It is the journal of the Society of Pediatric Psychology *and the premiere in pediatric chronic illness.*

Mini-series published by Division 16 of the American Psychological Association [*School Psychology Quarterly,* 1996,

10(4)] and by Pro-Ed, *Journal of Learning Disabilities,* 1993, 26(1–3).

Taken together, these two recent mini-series provide a wide-ranging overview regarding hospitalization and chronic illness. All issues raised in this chapter are discussed in detail in one or more of these series.

Roberts, M. (1995). *Handbook of pediatric psychology* (2nd ed.). New York: Guilford.

This is an excellent compendium of issues relating to hospitalization and chronic illness. The text contains topics ranging from legal issues to theory development with chronically ill children.

References

Azarnoff, P., & Woody, P. D. (1981) Preparation of children for hospitalization in acute care hospitals in the United States. *Pediatrics, 68,* 361–138.

Bibace, R., & Walsh, M. E. (1980). Development of children's concepts of illness. *Pediatrics, 66,* 912–917.

Blakeney, B. (1994). School reintegration. In K. J. Tarnowski (Ed.), *Behavioral aspects of pediatric burns* (pp. 217–241). New York: Plenum.

Blount, R. L. (1987). The dissemination of cost-effective psychosocial programs for children in health care settings. *Children's Health Care, 15,* 206–213.

Blount, R. L., Davis, N., Powers, S., & Roberts, M. C. (1991). The influence of environmental factors and coping style on children's coping and distress. *Clinical Psychology Review, 11,* 93–116.

Blount, R. L., Smith, A. J., & Frank, N. C. (in press). Preparation to undergo medical procedures. In A. J. Gorecnzy & M. Hersen (Eds.), *Handbook of pediatric and adolescent health psychology.* Needham Heights, MA: Allyn and Bacon.

Brown, R. T. (1996). Introduction to the special series: Cognitive and academic issues related to chronic illness. *School Psychology Quarterly, 10,* 271–273.

Brown, R. T., Armstrong, F. D., & Eckman, J. (1993). Neurocognitive aspects of sickle cell disease. *Journal of Learning Disabilities, 26,* 33–45.

Brown, R. T., Dingle, A. D., & Koon-Scott, K. (1994). Inpatient consultation and liaison. In K. J. Tarnowski (Ed.), *Behavioral aspects of pediatric burns* (pp. 217–241). New York: Plenum.

Brown, R. T., Doepke, K., & Kaslow, N. J. (1993). Risk-resistance-adaptation model for pediatric chronic illness: Sickle cell syndrome as an example. *Clinical Psychology Review, 13,* 119–132.

Brown, R. T., Madan-Swain, A., Pais, R., Lambert, R., Sexson, S. B., & Ragab, A. (1992). Chemotherapy for acute lymphocytic leukemia: Cognitive and academic sequelae. *Journal of Pediatrics, 121,* 885–889.

Cahners, S. S. (1979). A strong hospital-school liaison: A necessity for good rehabilitation planning for disfigured children. *Scandinavian Journal of Plastic and Reconstructive Surgery, 13,* 167–168.

Carson, D. K., Council, J. R., & Gravley, J. E. (1991). Temperament and family characteristics as predictors of children's reactions to hospitalization. *Developmental and Behavioral Pediatrics, 12,* 141–147.

Douglas, J. W. B. (1975). Early hospital admission and later disturbances of behavior and learning. *Developmental Medicine and Child Neurology, 17,* 456–480.

Fanurik, D., Zeltzer, L. K., Roberts, M. C., & Blount, R. L. (1993). The relationship between children's coping styles and psychological interventions for cold pressor pain. *Pain, 53,* 213–222.

Faust, J., Olson, R., & Rodriguez, H. (1991). Same-day surgery preparation: Reduction of pediatric patient arousal and distress through participant modeling. *Journal of Consulting and Clinical Psychology, 59,* 475–478.

Fowler, M. G., Johnson, M. P., & Atkinson, M. S. (1985). School achievement and absence in children with chronic health conditions. *Journal of Pediatrics, 106,* 683–687.

Gillman, J. B., & Mullins, L. L. (1991). Pediatric pain management: Professional and pragmatic issues. In J. P. Bush & S. W. Harkins (Eds.), *Children in pain: Clinical and research issues from a developmental perspective* (pp. 117–148). Berlin: Springer Verlag.

Gonzalez, J., Routh, D., Saab, P., Armstrong, F. D., Shifman, L., Guerra, E., & Fawcett, N. (1989). Effects of parent presence on children's reactions to injections: Behavioral, physiological, and subjective aspects. *Journal of Pediatric Psychology, 14,* 449–462.

Haller, J. A., Talbert, J. L., & Dombro, R. H. (1967). *The hospitalized child and his family.* Baltimore: Johns Hopkins University Press.

Holmes, C. S., O'Brien, B., & Greer, T. (1996). Cognitive functioning and academic achievement in children with insulin-dependent diabetes mellitus (IDDM). *School Psychology Quarterly, 10,* 280–290.

Lazarus, R. S., & Folkman, S. (1984). *Stress, appraisal and coping.* New York: Springer.

Lumley, M. A., Abeles, L. A., Melamed, B. G., Pistone, L. M., & Johnson, J. H. (1990). Coping outcomes in children undergoing stressful medical procedures: The role of child environment variables. *Behavioral Assessment, 12,* 223–238.

McClowry, S. G. (1990). The relationship of temperament to the pre- and post-behavioral responses of hospitalized school-age children. *Nursing Research, 39,* 30–35.

Melamed, B. G., Dearborn, M., & Hermecz, D. A., (1983). Necessary conditions for surgery preparation: Age and previous experience. *Psychosomatic Medicine, 45,* 517–525.

Melamed, B. G., & Siegel, L. J. (1975). Reduction of anxiety in children facing hospitalization and surgery by use of filmed modeling. *Journal of Consulting and Clinical Psychology, 43,* 511–521.

Meng, A., & Zastowny, T. (1982). Preparation for hospitalization: A stress inoculation training program for parents and children. *Maternal-Child Nursing Journal, 11,* 87–94.

Peterson, L., & Ridley-Johnson, R. (1980). Pediatric hospital response to survey on prehospital preparation for children. *Journal of Pediatric Psychology, 5,* 1–7.

Peterson, L., Schultheis, K., Ridley-Johnson, R., Miller, D. J., & Tracy, K. (1984). Comparison of three modeling procedures on the presurgical and postsurgical reactions of children. *Behavior Therapy, 15,* 197–203.

Peterson, L., & Shigetomi, C. (1981). The use of coping techniques to minimize anxiety in hospitalized children. *Behavior Therapy, 12,* 1–14.

Roberts, M. (1995). *Handbook of Pediatric Psychology.* (2nd ed.). New York: Guilford.

Routh, D. K. (1988). *Handbook of pediatric psychology.* New York: Guilford.

Rovet, J. F., Ehrlich, R. M., Czuchta, D., & Ackler, M. (1993). Psychoeducational characteristics of children and adolescents with insulin-dependent diabetes mellitus. *Journal of Learning Disabilities, 26,* 7–22.

Schultz, J. B., Raschke, D., Dedrick, C., & Thompson, M. (1981). The effects of a preoperational puppet show on anxiety levels of hospitalized children. *Journal of the Association for the Care of Children's Health, 9,* 118–120.

Sexson, S. B., & Madan-Swain, A. (1993). School reentry for the child with chronic illness. *Journal of Learning Disabilities, 26,* 115–125.

Sexson, S. B., & Madan-Swain, A. (1996). The chronically ill child in the school. *School Psychology Quarterly, 10,* 292–300.

Shaw, E. G., & Routh, D. K. (1982). Effect of mother presence on children's reaction to aversive procedures. *Journal of Pediatric Psychology, 7,* 32–42.

Suls, J., & Fletcher, B. (1985). The relative efficacy of avoidant and nonavoidant coping strategies: A meta-analysis. *Health Psychology, 4,* 249–288.

Tarnowski, K. J., & Brown, R. T. (1995a). Pediatric burns. In M. Roberts (Ed.), *Handbook of pediatric psychology* (2nd ed., pp. 446–462). New York: Guilford.

Tarnowski, K. J., & Brown, R. T. (1995b). Psychological aspects of pediatric disorders. In M. Hersen & R. T. Ammerman (Eds.), *Advanced abnormal child psychology* (pp. 393–410). Hillsdale, NJ: Erlbaum.

Thompson, R. H., & Vernon, D. T. A. (1993). Research on children's behavior after hospitalization: A review and synthesis. *Developmental and Behavioral Pediatrics, 14,* 28–35.

Varni, J. W., Blount, R. L., Waldron, S. A., & Smith, A. (1995). Management of pain and distress. In M. Roberts (Ed.), *Handbook of pediatric psychology* (2nd ed., pp. 105–123). New York: Guilford.

Visintainer, M. A., & Wolfer, J. A. (1975). Psychological preparation for surgical pediatric patients: The effect on children's and parent's stress responses and adjustment. *Pediatrics, 56,* 187–202.

Weitzman, M. (1986). School absence rates as outcome measures in studies of children with chronic illness. *Journal of Chronic Disease, 39,* 799–808.

Wolfer, J. A., & Visintainer, M. A. (1975). Pediatric surgical patients and parents stress responses and adjustment. *Nursing Research, 24,* 244–255.

Wolfer, J. A., & Visintainer, M. A. (1979). Prehospital psychological preparation for tonsillectomy patients: Effects on children and parents' adjustment. *Pediatrics, 64,* 646–655.

Woodward, X. (1959). Emotional disturbances of burned children. *British Medical Journal, 1,* 1009–1113.

Zabin, M. A., & Melamed, B. G. (1980). Relationship between parental discipline and children's ability to cope with stress. *Journal of Behavioral Assessment, 2,* 17–38.

85

Health Promotion

Joseph E. Zins
Donald I. Wagner

University of Cincinnati

Increasing numbers of students arrive at school suffering from the ill effects of substance abuse, interpersonal violence, sexually transmitted diseases, a sedentary life style, physical and emotional abuse, poor nutrition, excessive stress, and unwanted pregnancies. Although often viewed as public health or societal problems outside the domain of the schools, these issues cannot be ignored by educators because students experiencing them are not fully prepared to benefit from schooling and are less likely to learn despite the best educational efforts (Kolbe, Collins, & Cortese, in press). Moreover, some of these behaviors (e.g., drinking and driving) can have irrevocable outcomes, and other conditions (e.g., stress management and blood pressure) can sometimes be the difference between life and death (Goleman, 1995). In addition, the onset of many negative behavioral patterns and lifestyles often begins early in life and establishes an increased susceptibility to a variety of conditions responsible for the decline in the health of many Americans (Millstein, Petersen, & Nightingale, 1993; Wagner & Zins, 1985). In fact, there is evidence that lifestyle is a 50% contributor to the causation of the leading mortalities (U.S. Department of Health, Education, and Welfare, 1979).

Problem-solving approaches that merely emphasize individual intervention and treatment are likely to overwhelm available educational and community resources. Instead, the promotion of health-enhancing behaviors and the prevention of high-risk ones must be emphasized because of the potential cost benefits and the opportunities to avoid the human suffering associated with the onset of these problems. To encourage greater emphasis on prevention efforts, however, the connection between behavioral health-risk factors and negative physical and emotional outcomes must be recognized. School psychologists, by virtue of their expertise in understanding and changing behavior, can apply their skills toward addressing such issues, thereby becoming major contributors to school wellness efforts.

This chapter begins by defining health promotion and then examines the need for health promotion programs in some detail. Risk and protective factors associated with health are identified next, followed by discussion of alternative actions that school psychologists can take to address health-related issues.

Background and Development

Health promotion is broadly defined as a combination of behavioral, educational, social, spiritual, economic, and environmental efforts that support the establishment, maintenance, and enhancement of behaviors and lifestyles conducive to overall emotional and physical well-being (Wagner & Zins, 1985; Zins & Wagner, 1987). Socially competent students are more likely to engage in health-enhancing behaviors and to avoid ones that may lead to negative outcomes (Consortium, 1994), thereby increasing their potential to be effective learners. Health promotion efforts can focus on (a) increasing skills and competencies to facilitate the development of positive, health-enhancing behaviors (e.g., regular physical exercise, effective stress management, use of car safety belts) and (b) eliminating or reducing health-compromising actions (e.g., quitting smoking, teaching behavioral self-control skills, avoiding unprotected sexual intercourse). Because many of the behaviors associated with adult morbidity and mortality begin early in life, emphasis is placed on developing healthy behavioral patterns during a young person's formative years to bring about both immediate and long-term positive effects.

Today, health promotion and the prevention of maladaptive behaviors are no longer considered outside the domain of the school or the function of a single discipline or institution. Rather, they are viewed as cooperative endeavors in which professionals from many fields work alongside general education teachers, students, and parents to provide comprehensive school health programs.

945

Comprehensive school health involves the collaborative, coordinated, and integrative efforts of disciplines such as health education, nursing, physical education, nutrition (food) services, counseling, and school psychology directed toward health education, prevention, and promotion activities. Professionals in these areas work together to develop comprehensive health education curricula, provide appropriate health services, maintain a healthful school environment, and mobilize community resources to enhance health promotion efforts in schools (Kolbe et al., in press). Viewing health promotion as the responsibility of several disciplines or institutions rather than just one provides multiple opportunities for health promotion. Furthermore, schools are ideal settings for health-promotion activities as they provide access to virtually all children and youth and have a professional staff that is prepared or can become prepared to deliver such services (Zins, Wagner, & Maher, 1985).

Health Issues and Implications

To serve the health needs of youth, professionals need both a short- and long-term perspective on the specific health issues that may jeopardize a young person's longevity and/or quality of life. A great deal of attention has been devoted to the health concerns of young people by several groups (e.g., American Medical Association, 1990; U.S. Department of Health and Human Services, 1995; U.S. Preventive Services Task Force, 1989). The outcomes of these reports are very similar and demonstrate the variance in morbidity and mortality concerns for today's youth.

Leading Causes of Mortality

According to the most recent (1993) Youth Risk Behavior Study (YRBS) data, the leading causes of death for youth ages 10 to 24 in rank order (percentage of total mortality in parentheses) are: (a) motor vehicle crash (37%), (b) other causes (e.g., congenital heart disease) (24%), (c) homicide (14%), (d) other injury (12%), (e) suicide (12%), and (f) HIV infection (1%). In contrast, the leading causes for all ages are (a) heart disease (35%), (b) cancer (22%), (c) stroke (7%), and (d) other causes (36%) (Kolbe, 1995). Thus, the diseases and conditions that kill young people are very different from the leading causes of mortality in later life. However, the common denominator for all ages is the role that lifestyle plays as a contributor to the causation of these mortalities. Lifestyle risk factors such as driving behaviors, exercise practices, nutritional decisions, and tobacco use play significant roles in a person's eventual cause of death.

The mortality rankings indicate that youth are most vulnerable to intentional and unintentional injury and acts of violence. However, mortality is not the exclusive focus of health concerns that impact young people.

Leading Morbidities of Children and Youth

The primary morbidities affecting students are readily recognized by school psychologists. Among the most common are obesity, vision problems, diminished hearing, signs of abuse or neglect, abnormal bereavement, injuries, alcohol and drug use, pregnancy, sexually transmitted diseases, anorexia, bulimia, and depression. Primary care providers should conduct age-specific screening for the early detection and intervention of these problems and their associated risk factors (U.S. Department of Health and Human Services, 1990). Likewise, school psychologists and other members of the school health team are positioned to recognize many of these problems in their earliest stages. Unfortunately, the health interests and concerns of young people are not closely correlated with the leading morbidities and mortalities. Trucano (1984) surveyed children in Grades 7 through 12 to ascertain their health interests. Table 1 indicates the diversity of viewpoints between young people's health interests and the realities of health problems that affect this age group. As outlined later, school-based programs that address the underlying health risk and

Table 1   *Primary Health Interests of Youth*

Grade 7	Mental Health
	Family Relationships
	Drugs
	Nutrition
Grade 8	Drugs
	Nutrition
	Mental Health
	Family Relationships
Grade 9	Family Relationships
	Mental Health
Grade 10	Family Relationships
	Mental Health
	Drugs
	Safe Living/First Aid
	Nutrition
Grade 11/12	Family Relationships
	Mental Health
	Drugs
Other Issues of Low/Moderate Interest	
	Disease Control/Prevention
	Physical Well-Being
	Human Growth and Development
	Health Care System

Note. Adapted from *Students Speak: A Survey of Health Interests and Concerns: Kindergarten through Twelfth Grade,* by L. Trucano, 1984, Seattle, WA: Comprehensive Health Education Foundation.

protective factors associated with specific health conditions are one method for closing the gap between young people's health interests and the actual health events that affect them.

Risk and Protective Factors

Although a number of conceptual frameworks can guide prevention efforts (Zins, Garcia, Tuchfarber, Clark, & Laurence, 1994), examining health promotion from the perspective of risk factors and protective mechanisms is particularly useful (see Hawkins, Catalano, & Associates, 1992; Jessor, 1991). Risk factors are associated with an increased likelihood of susceptibility to a problem. For example, tobacco use is a risk factor for cancer. On the other hand, regular exercise can serve to protect or buffer an individual from the risk of coronary heart disease and can help to mediate the effects of stress.

A study by Benson (1993) examined risk and protective factors with 47,000 youth in Grades 7 through 12. This research identified 20 at-risk indicators, as shown in Table 2, associated with negative health outcomes. These results are generally consistent with those from the YRBS (Kolbe, 1995) mentioned earlier.

Benson (1993) likewise identified 30 assets, more commonly referred to as protective factors, associated with positive health outcomes (see Table 2). His work indicated that there is an additive effect of these assets and that the optimal number for youth to acquire is 25 or 30. However, he found that the average young person has only 17 of these assets.

Although risk behavior can become a problem when the magnitude of the behavior creates health- and life-compromising outcomes, it is important to recognize that risk behavior may also reflect a young person's normal developmental processes. Thus, it may be difficult to effect change when a young person views the risk behavior from a developmental and not a health perspective. Adolescents, for example, may not perceive the importance of not smoking because the adverse health effects are delayed until middle age or later. At the same time, however, this group may be a particularly receptive audience because of their sense of curiosity about themselves (Millstein et al., 1993). Clearly, risk behavior is complex, and single variable interventions are not easily applied in this framework. Further, Benson's (1993) additive view of assets also implies the need for multimodal interventions. Thus, widespread consensus is emerging on the necessity of multicomponent, coordinated prevention and promotion programs (Consortium, 1994).

Key Objectives for Reducing Health Risks in Children

The U.S. Department of Health and Human Services (1990) has conducted a baseline study of the prevalence

Table 2   *Factors Associated with Health Outcomes for Youth, Grades Six through Twelve*

Factors	Percentage
Risk Factors and Percent Involved	
Used alcohol six or more times in the last 30 days	11
Had five or more drinks in a row during the last 2 weeks	23
Smoked 1 or more cigarettes per day	12
Used an illicit drug six or more times in last 12 months	8
Had sexual intercourse two or more times	30
Sexually active and not using contraceptives	47
Sad or depressed "most" or "all" of the time	15
Attempted suicide one or more times	13
Destroyed property "just for fun" two or more times in last 12 months	10
Took part in a fight between two groups or gangs two or more times in last 12 months	13
Got into trouble with the police two or more times in last 12 months	7
Stole something from a store two or more times in last 12 months	10
Skipped school before completing high school	10
Drove after drinking two or more times in last 12 months	11
Rode with a driver who had been drinking two or more times in last 12 months	33
Does not use seat belts "all" or "most" of the time	50
Protective Factors and Percent Possessing	
Cares about people's feelings	88
Has educational aspirations	86
Displays assertiveness skills	82
Parental monitoring is present	77
Parental standards exist	75
Has friendship-making skills	74
Is motivated to achieve	72
Spends time at home	70
Has positive view of personal future	68
Possesses decision-making skills	68
Is involved in extra curricular activities	62
Is aware of parental discipline	60
Is involved in church or synagogue	57
Has planning skills	57
Acknowledges family support	56

Note. Table includes only risk factors endorsed by over 5% and assets endorsed by over 50% of the respondents. Adapted from *The Troubled Journey: A Portrait of Sixth-Twelfth Grade Youth* by P. Benson, 1993, Minneapolis, MN: Search Institute.

of critical risks that impact the health outcomes of children. In this report, key objectives are outlined for improving the health status of children in the United States (see Tables 3 and 4). These objectives provide a framework for school psychologists and others on a comprehensive school health team to assess the needs of their students and to develop and monitor specific health-promotion interventions.

Table 3 *Key Risk-Reduction Objectives Targeting Children*

1.3	Increase to at least 30% the proportion of people aged 6 years and older who engage regularly, preferably daily, in light to moderate physical activity for at least 30 minutes per day.
1.4	Increase to at least 20% the proportion of people aged 18 and older and to at least 75% the proportion of children and adolescents aged 6 to 17 who engage in vigorous physical activity that promotes the development and maintenance of cardiorespiratory fitness three or more days per week for 20 minutes or more per occasion.
1.5	Reduce to no more than 15% the proportion of people aged 6 and older who engage in no monthly leisure time physical activity.
1.6	Increase to at least 40% the proportion of people aged 6 and older who regularly perform physical activities that enhance and maintain muscular strength, muscular endurance, and flexibility.
3.5	Reduce the initiation of cigarette smoking by children and youth so that no more than 15% have become regular smokers by age 20.
3.8	Reduce to no more than 20% the proportion of children aged 6 and younger who are regularly exposed to tobacco at home.
8.3	Achieve for all disadvantaged children and children with disabilities access to high quality and developmentally appropriate preschool programs that help prepare children for school, thereby improving their prospects with regard to school performance, problem behaviors, and mental and physical health.
9.12a	Increase the use of occupant protection systems, such as safety belts, inflatable safety restraints, and child safety seats to at least 95% of children aged 4 and younger who are motor vehicle occupants.
17.1	Increase to at least 80% the proportion of providers of primary care for children who routinely refer or screen infants and children for impairments of vision, hearing, speech and language, and assess other developmental milestones as part of well-child care.

Note. Based on *Healthy People 2000: National Health Promotion and Disease Prevention Objectives,* Conference Edition, 1990, by the U.S. Department of Health and Human Services, Washington, DC: U.S. Government Printing Office.

Table 4 *Key Risk-Reduction Objectives Targeting Adolescents and Young Adults*

3.9	Reduce smokeless tobacco use by males aged 12 through 24 to a prevalence of no more than 4%.
4.5	Increase by at least 1 year the average age of first use of cigarettes, alcohol, and marijuana by adolescents aged 12 through 17.
4.6a	Reduce alcohol use during the past month by young people aged 12 to 17 to a prevalence of no more than 12.6%.
4.6b	Reduce marijuana use during the past month by young people aged 12 to 17 to a prevalence of no more than 3.2%.
4.6c	Reduce cocaine use during the past month by young people aged 12 to 17 to a prevalence of no more than 0.6%.
4.10	Increase the percentage of high school seniors who associate risk of physical or psychological harm with the heavy use of alcohol to 70%.
4.11	Reduce to no more than 3% the proportion of male high school seniors who use anabolic steroids.
5.4	Reduce the proportion of adolescents who have engaged in sexual intercourse to no more than 15% by age 15 and no more than 40% by age 17.
5.5	Increase to at least 40% the proportion of ever sexually active adolescents aged 17 and younger who have abstained from sexual activity for the previous three months.
5.6	Increase to at least 90% the proportion of sexually active, unmarried people aged 19 and younger who use contraception.
7.9	Reduce by 20% the incidence of physical fighting among adolescents aged 14 to 17.
7.10	Reduce by 20% the incidence of weapon carrying by adolescents aged 14 through 17.
8.2	Increase the high school graduation rate to at least 90%, thereby reducing risks for multiple problem behaviors and poor mental and physical health.
18.4a	Increase to at least 60% the proportion of sexually active, unmarried young women aged 15 through 19 who used a condom at last intercourse.
18.4b	Increase to at least 75% the proportion of sexually active, unmarried young men aged 15 through 19 who used a condom at last sexual intercourse.

Note. Based on *Healthy People 2000: National Health Promotion and Disease Prevention Objectives,* Conference Edition, 1990, by the U.S. Department of Health and Human Services, Washington, DC: U.S. Government Printing Office.

Two important elements must be focused on when planning health-promotion interventions. First, known or suspected behavioral risk factors that contribute to negative health outcomes need to be reduced by delaying the onset of the risk or, ideally, avoiding the onset of the risk. With existing behavioral risk factors, interventions must be developed to reduce, mediate, or eliminate the impact of the behavioral risk. Second, emphasis should be placed on developing protective factors (assets) that build resilience and assist in the promotion of positive health outcomes.

Alternative Actions: Promoting Wellness

A transformation in the delivery of school psychological services is needed to address students' health-related needs. Rather than continuing to emphasize the remediation of individual student problems in practice and in university training as has been done traditionally, an expanded emphasis that also includes the prevention of problem behaviors and the promotion of healthy ones must assume greater importance (Zins, Conyne, & Ponti, 1988). Moreover, it is time to more explicitly recognize by action the connection of social, emotional, and physical well-being with one another and with students' academic performance.

Key Ingredients of Prevention Programs

Although widespread societal change may be necessary to enable most children to grow up to become responsible and productive citizens, activities at the local school and community level are the foundation on which these large-scale changes can be based. To this end, a number of characteristics or active ingredients associated with effective prevention programs have been identified by a variety of researchers (e.g., Consortium, 1994; Dryfoos, 1991; W. T. Grant Consortium, 1992). Among the key elements are that programs should be comprehensive and multiyear and involve the support, involvement, and coordinated efforts of the many individuals, organizations, and institutions who affect young people's lives.

Further, health promotion involves far more than a lecture on the evils of tobacco use, a visit to a detention center to demonstrate the consequences of ineffective interpersonal conflict resolution, or viewing a film on injuries sustained in car crashes when not wearing seatbelts. These strategies may be important, but they will be most effective when implemented in the context of a comprehensive health-promotion program. The active participation of students, parents and the community is required, and activities such as role-playing, behavioral rehearsal, performance feedback, and positive reinforcement should be provided. The program should take place within a supportive, safe, and caring environment that values diversity and respects cultural differences. In addition, developmentally appropriate instruction on specific topics such as substance abuse and conflict resolution is needed, along with assistance on developing more generic skills such as problem solving and social decision making (Consortium, 1994; W. T. Grant Consortium, 1992).

Coordinated and Comprehensive Services

It is becoming increasingly clear that the current system of providing health-related services is not working effectively. Many services are provided in a piecemeal fashion, sometimes there is much overlap, and other times services are not even provided despite being available (e.g., Dryfoos, 1994; Illback, Joseph, & Cobb, in press; Illback & Nelson, 1995). Hence, interest has been growing within the fields involved in school health to make these services more integrated and coordinated and to ensure that they address the spectrum of needs (Talley & Short, 1995). As noted earlier, health-promotion efforts should:

- Be established as part of the counseling and social services program.
- Be developed in conjunction with health education, health services, physical education, nutrition services, and health promotion programs for staff.
- Occur within a supportive, safe, and caring school environment.
- Include the active participation of parents and the community (Kolbe, 1995).

Consequently, an array of integrated pupil support services will be created, and school and community resources and energies coordinated (Dryfoos, 1994). Recent federal statutes also emphasize the importance of coordination between the educational and health care systems (e.g., P.L. 102-531: Preventive Health Amendments of 1992; P.L. 102-321: Alcohol, Drug Abuse, and Mental Health Administration Reorganization Act of 1992; and P.L. 99-457: Education of the Handicapped Act Amendments of 1986).

Examples of Activities

As noted earlier, schools are important environments for the development of young people, and students' experiences in this setting help to determine their vulnerability to a number of health-related problems. Some school characteristics such as a psychosocial culture that is uncaring, harsh, punitive, or inconsistent, or an environment that implicitly condones alcohol use have been shown to be predictive of negative outcomes for students. Academic success and school attachment can reduce the risk of involvement in behaviors such as violence and substance abuse, and a predictable, consistent, safe, and well-organized environment can decrease behavioral problems (Hawkins & Catalano, 1990; Hawkins, Jenson, Catalano, & Lishner, 1988; Nelson & Colvin, 1996; Talley, Short, & Kolbe, 1995).

Accordingly, psychologists can help schools play a central role in reducing the many health risks that young people face by assisting in the development of relevant policies, practices, and organizational arrangements conducive to health enhancement. Examples of health-promotion activities in which school psychologists might participate are listed in Table 5, and brief summaries of several programs follow. Included are programs that address several organizational levels and that illustrate a variety of types of preventive interventions.

Transitions such as moving from elementary to junior high school are periods of particular vulnerability that increase the risk for engaging in health-compromising behaviors (Hirsch & Rapkin, 1987; Jason & Associates, 1992). To address this predictable life event, Felner and Adan (1988) developed a prevention program that increased bonding to school by expanding the amount of

Table 5 *Examples of Health Promotion Activities for School Psychologists*

- *Consult with School Staff.* Assist in the development of specific interventions with individual and groups of students in areas such as conflict-resolution and social skills, and help create a supportive, safe environment in which these interventions occur.
- *Consult with Parents/Guardians.* Help to develop appropriate supervisory and disciplinary practices; encourage ongoing parent-child communication; work to increase their involvement in and support for school programs.
- *Conduct School and Community Risk Assessments for Program Planning.* Determine the availability of alcohol within the community through an analysis of establishments that serve or sell it; examine convictions for sales to minors, especially around schools.
- *Collaborate with Health Service Providers to Develop and Implement Programs.* Programs to prevent smoking and alcohol use or premature sexual activity can be developed and directed toward students beginning in the elementary grades, in cooperation with the nursing, counseling, physical education, and health education staffs.
- *Conduct Direct Behavioral Health Interventions with Individuals and Groups of Students.* Teach behavioral self-management skills to help reduce loss of control which may result in conflict or interpersonal violence; provide instruction in relaxation techniques.
- *Promote Organizational Change.* Help develop health-enhancing district policies such as prohibiting corporal punishment, promoting use of cooperative learning, and requiring bicycle safety helmets to be worn if riding to school.
- *Ensure That Health Promotion Information Is Blended Throughout Curriculum.* Problem-solving skills can be taught beginning in kindergarten and continuing through Grade 12; applied to a variety of problems; and emphasized in all classes, on the playground, and in extracurricular activities.
- *Provide Program Evaluation Services.* Assess the outcomes of health-promotion efforts or of integrated-services-delivery programs for use in making decisions about program continuance, modification, or elimination.
- *Conduct Staff Training and Development Programs.* Provide instruction in stress or time-management techniques; offer training in identifying risk factors for engaging in interpersonal violence or suicide.
- *Act as Liaison in Coordination and Integration of School and Community Services.* Work with community professionals such as the local YMCA or Boys/Girls Club who are delivering prevention and health-promotion services to ensure continuity and mutual support and to avoid overlap.

interaction occurring among participating students and between students and teachers. As a result, they were able to reduce absenteeism and decrease school drop-out.

As another example, school psychologists can use their knowledge of research to help in *policy and curriculum development.* It has been shown that schools which provide smoking areas for their students have significantly more smokers than those that do not (Crow, 1984) and that students' attachment to school and community can serve as a protective factor against involvement in a variety of negative behaviors (Hawkins, Catalano, & Miller, 1992). By sharing such information with educational decision makers, school psychologists can help create a health-enhancing environment.

The social-decision-making curriculum developed by Elias and Clabby (1989) is also useful for classroom-based intervention in which school psychologists and teachers collaborate. In this program, elementary students learn self-control, group participation, and social-awareness skills while also developing critical-thinking and decision-making skills. The program has a strong prevention orientation and can be used to prepare students for entry into middle school and with the refusal skills necessary to decrease drug abuse. A related book provides a good description of the development of the curriculum and of the supporting research (Elias & Clabby, 1992).

Finally, health-promotion efforts can also be *directed toward school staff.* Blair, Collingwood, Smith, Upton, and Sterling (1985) demonstrated that a wellness program for teachers in a large district can result in important changes in employee health practices, including increased exercise, weight loss, and a reduction in blood pressure. In addition, it had a beneficial effect on their absenteeism, which may enhance children's opportunity to learn by reducing instructional disruptions. Of course, in addition to developing and/or implementing any of these programs, school psychologists might also be involved in developing and conducting appropriate program evaluations.

Training

Many school psychologists currently do not have the specific training to contribute substantially to health-promotion programs as few university training programs place much emphasis on a health promotion or prevention role (Fagan, 1990). However, the majority of these programs teach relevant skills such as consultation and behavioral-change strategies that could readily be adapted and applied to these issues. To accomplish this goal, a significant change in philosophical orientation in most training programs would be required. Students would have to acquire a far deeper understanding of the potential benefits of prevention and promotion programs and of the relationship between physical and mental health. In addition, development of specific skills related to collaborating effectively with health, medical, and social service professionals is essential. One concrete example of how school psychologists can become better prepared for this expanded role is the pediatric school psychology program proposed by Power, DuPaul, Shapiro, and Parrish (1995) although it would be improved with greater emphasis on the health-promotion and prevention aspects.

Several constraints can be identified that may keep school psychology programs from providing training in the health promotion area. For example, because most schools are not demanding these skills in the psychologists they hire, it is easy for training programs not to attend to these issues. Further, nondoctoral programs already are hard pressed to provide training in what they perceive to be the essential "survival" skills their students will need and may see health promotion as an added-on "frill." Although these issues are real, it should be noted that the foundation skills needed to become a contributing member of the school health team already are provided by most training programs. In most instances, a modification in orientation and skill applications are required rather than extensive new coursework.

Further, programs need to carefully consider educational and related trends and the possible relationship between these trends and the role of the school psychologist. In addition, faculty members' own roles as educational change agents need to be examined. As they work with schools, they have a wonderful opportunity to assist these institutions in better meeting young people's needs by advocating for more emphasis on health promotion through their own efforts and through the preparation that their trainees receive. Ultimately, difficult judgments need to be made about how children and youth in schools today and in the future might best be served by school psychologists.

Summary

In this chapter the case was made for schools and school psychologists to address proactively a wide variety of problem areas that can affect young people's learning and lifelong health. Despite the rhetoric prevalent in the literature, our observation and various surveys of school psychologists strongly suggest that the individually focused approach continues to be prevalent in most school psychology service delivery and training programs. However, we anticipate that such a model will not be as relevant in the 21st century as less emphasis is placed on traditional activities such as intellectual assessment and special education categorization, and perhaps even on individual intervention. Comprehensive school health programs are being developed in many states (Kolbe, 1995), and school psychologists must act quickly if they are to be included in this promising approach to assisting large numbers of students in this crucial area. Preparation of students for the next century must begin now.

It is clear that students who are physically and emotionally healthy and competent in general are better prepared to be effective learners. Teachers who can address the multiple needs that students bring to school and who work with them to develop lifelong health behaviors may produce the best long-term outcomes, that is, assisting them in becoming responsible, productive citizens. How-

ever, teachers' efforts will be greatly enhanced with the support of and through the joint efforts of special services and health staff including school psychologists. There are a vast number of relevant applications of psychological principles in health promotion endeavors.

There is no doubt that more prevention and health promotion services will be provided routinely in the future and that comprehensive school health programs will be an important component of schools. The only unanswered question is, who will be the providers of these services? We hope that school psychologists will take up this challenge and be contributing members of the school health team!

Recommended Resources

For Professionals

American Medical Association. (1990). *Healthy youth 2000: Health promotion and disease prevention objectives for adolescents.* Chicago: Author.
This brief book contains a comprehensive review of the national objectives associated with adolescent health and related issues.

Benson, P. Galbraith, J., & Espeland, P. (1994). *What kids need to succeed.* Minneapolis, MN: Free Spirit Publishing.
More than 500 ideas for building assets in youth can be found in this resource, which includes strategies for families, schools, communities, and congregations.

Dejong, W. (1994). *Preventing interpersonal violence among youth.* Washington, DC: U.S. Department of Justice.
This informative report examines school-based, community-based, and mass media strategies for reducing conflict and preventing violence.

Dryfoos, J. G. (1991). *Adolescents at risk: Prevalence and prevention.* New York: Oxford University Press.
This book provides an overview of the prevention issues for delinquency, substance abuse, teen pregnancy, and school failure and dropout. The components of successful programs and findings from youth surveys and evaluations are reported.

Haggerty, R. J., Sherrod, L. R., Garmezy, N., & Rutter, M. (Eds.). (1994). *Stress, risk, and resilience in children and adolescents: Processes, mechanisms, and interaction.* New York: Cambridge University Press.
In this book the interrelated concepts of risk, resilience, and development are investigated, as are the multiple causes of many problem behaviors.

Millstein, S. G., Petersen, A. C., & Nightingale, E. O. (Eds.). (1993). *Promoting the health of adolescents: New directions for the twenty-first century.* New York: Oxford University Press.
The contributors to this book discuss social, environmental, and behavioral factors that can be targeted to enable adolescents to form good health-related behaviors.

Simeonsson, R. J. (Ed.). (1994). *Risk, resilience, and prevention: Promoting the well-being of all children.* Baltimore: Paul H. Brookes.

This innovative book is a helpful resource that uses a wellness model and demonstrates how children at risk can be influenced before a variety of problems manifest themselves.

Resource Organizations

American Cancer Society
3340 Peachtree Road, N.E.
Atlanta, GA 30326
404/320-3333

This national organization provides a variety of services and resources related to the prevention and treatment of cancer. Included are programs on comprehensive school health, smoking, cancer risks (e.g., sun), and self-exams.

American Heart Association
7272 Greenville Avenue
Dallas, TX 75231
800/527-6941

This organization is dedicated to preventing heart disease. It provides relevant information on nutrition, health disease risk, and fitness. The AHA has a new, school-site, educational program entitled *Heart Power.*

American Lung Association
1740 Broadway
New York, NY 10019
212/315-8700

This organization addresses diseases of the lung (asthma, emphysema, etc.) through its research and educational programs. Among their school curricula available are *Huff and Puff* for preschool students and *Growing Healthy,* Grades K-6, which is approved by the National Diffusion Network.

Collaborative for the Advancement of Social and Emotional Learning (CASEL)
Yale Child Study Center, P.O. Box 207900
230 South Frontage Road
New Haven, CT 06520
203/785-6107

CASEL is a new organization that serves as a clearinghouse to help educators all over the country interested in learning about school-based social and emotional learning programs. CASEL periodically publishes an informative newsletter.

National Mental Health Association
1021 Prince Street
Alexandria, VA 22314
703/684-7722

A national advocacy organization dedicated to addressing all aspects of this country's mental health and mental illness. In addition to materials for the general public, they have available a variety of professional publications on mental and emotional disorders, general mental health, prevention, and program development.

Youth Update (published by Search Institute)
Thresher Square West
700 South Third Street, Suite 210
Minneapolis, MN 55415
800/888-3820

A free quarterly newsletter published by the Lutheran Brotherhood, that highlights issues in positive youth devel-opment and shares strategies on how communities can build their asset base.

References

American Medical Association. (1990). *Healthy youth 2000.* Chicago: American Medical Association.

Benson, P. (1993). *The troubled journey: A portrait of sixth-twelfth grade youth.* Minneapolis, MN: Search Institute

Blair, S. N., Collingwood, T. R., Smith, M., Upton, J., & Sterling, C. L. (1985). Review of a health promotion program for school employees. *Special Services in the Schools, 1*(3) 89–98.

Consortium on the School-Based Promotion of Social Competence [Elias, M. J., Weissberg, R. P., Hawkins, J. D. Perry, C. L., Zins, J. E., Dodge, K. A., Kendall, P. C., Gott fredson, D., Rotheram-Borus, M. J., Jason, L. A., & Wilson Brewer, R. J.]. (1994). The school-based promotion of social competence: Theory, research, practice, and policy. In R. J Haggerty, L. R. Sherrod, N. Garmezy, & M. Rutter (Eds.) *Stress, risk, and resilience in children and adolescents: Pro cesses, mechanisms, and interaction* (pp. 268–316). New York: Cambridge University Press.

Crow, C. S. (1984). Smoking areas on school grounds Are we encouraging teenagers to smoke? *Journal of Adoles cent Health Care, 5,* 117–119.

Dryfoos, J. G. (1991). *Adolescents at risk: Prevalence and prevention.* New York: Oxford University Press.

Dryfoos, J. G. (1994). *Full-service schools: A revolution in health and social services for children, youth, and adoles cents.* San Francisco: Jossey-Bass.

Elias, M. J., & Clabby, J. F. (1989). *Social decision-mak ing skills: A curriculum guide for elementary grades* Gaithersberg, MD: Aspen.

Elias, M. J., & Clabby, J. F. (1992). *Building social prob lem-solving skills.* San Francisco: Jossey-Bass.

Fagan, T. K. (1990). Best practices in the training of school psychologists: Considerations for trainers, prospec tive entry-level and advanced students. In A. Thomas & J Grimes (Eds.), *Best practices in school psychology-II* (pp. 723-741). Washington, DC: National Association of School Psy chologists.

Felner, R. D., & Adan, A.M. (1988). The school transi tional environment project: An ecological intervention and evaluation. In R. H. Price, E. L. Cowen, R. P. Lorion, & J Ramos-McKay (Eds.), *14 ounces of prevention* (pp. 111–122) Washington, DC: American Psychological Association.

Goleman, D. (1995). *Emotional intelligence.* New York Bantam.

Hawkins, J. D., & Catalano, R. F. (1990). Broadening the vision of education: Schools as health promoting envi ronments. *Journal of School Health, 60,* 178–181.

Hawkins, J. D., Catalano, R. F., & Associates. (1992) *Communities that care: Action for drug abuse prevention.* Sai Francisco: Jossey-Bass.

Hawkins, J. D., Catalano, R. F., & Miller, J. (1992). Risk and protective factors for alcohol and drug problems in ado lescence and early adulthood: Implications for substance abuse prevention. *Psychological Reports, 112,* 64–105.

Hawkins, J. D., Jenson, J. M., Catalano, R. F., & Lishner, D. M. (1988). Delinquency and drug use: Implications for social services. *Social Services Review, 62,* 258–284.

Hirsch, B. J., & Rapkin, B. D. (1987). The transition to junior high school: A longitudinal study of self-esteem, psychological symptomatology, school life, and social support. *Child Development, 58,* 1235–1243.

Illback, R. J., Joseph, H., Jr., & Cobb, C. (Eds.). (in press). *Integrated services for children and families: Opportunities for psychological practice.* Washington, DC: American Psychological Association.

Illback, R. J., & Nelson, C. M. (1995). School-based integrated service programs: Toward more effective service delivery for children and youth with emotional and behavioral disorders. *Special Services in the Schools, 10,* 1–6.

Jason, L. A., & Associates. (1992). *Helping transfer students.* San Francisco: Jossey-Bass.

Jessor, R. (1991). Risk behavior in adolescence: A psychosocial framework for understanding and action. *Journal of Adolescent Health, 12,* 597–605.

Kolbe, L. J. (1995, April). *Building the capacity of schools to improve the health of the nation: A call for assistance from school psychologists.* Paper presented at the annual meeting of the National Association of School Psychologists, Chicago.

Kolbe, L. J., Collins, J., & Cortese, P. (in press). Building the capacity of schools to improve the health of the nation: A call for assistance from psychologists. *American Psychologist.*

Millstein, S. G., Petersen, A. C., & Nightingale, E. O. (Eds.). (1993). *Promoting the health of adolescents: New directions for the twenty-first century.* New York: Oxford University Press.

Nelson, J. R., & Colvin, G. (1996). Designing supportive school environments. *Special Services in the Schools, 11,* 169–186.

Power, T. J., DuPaul, G. J., Shapiro, E. S., & Parrish, J. M. (1995). Pediatric school psychology: The emergence of a subspecialization. *School Psychology Review, 24*(2), 244–257.

Talley, R. C., & Short, R. J. (1996). Schools as health service delivery sites: Current status and future directions. *Special Services in the Schools, 11,* 37–56.

Talley, R. C., Short , R. J., & Kolbe, L. J. (1995). *School health: Psychology's role.* Washington, DC: American Psychological Association.

Trucano, L. (1984). *Students speak: A survey of health interests and concerns: Kindergarten through twelfth grade.* Seattle, WA: Comprehensive Health Education Foundation.

U.S. Department of Health and Human Services. (1990). *Healthy people 2000: National health promotion and disease prevention objectives.* Washington, DC: U.S. Government Printing Office.

U.S. Department of Health and Human Services. (1995). *Healthy people 2000: Midcourse review and 1995 revisions.* Washington, DC: U.S. Government Printing Office.

U.S. Department of Health, Education, and Welfare. (1979). *Healthy people: The Surgeon General's report on health promotion and disease prevention* (DHEW [PHS] Publication No. 79-55071). Washington, DC: U.S. Government Printing Office.

U.S. Preventive Services Task Force. (1989). *Guide to clinical preventive services; an assessment of the effectiveness of 169 interventions.* Baltimore: Williams and Wilkins.

Wagner, D. I., & Zins, J. E. (1985). Health promotion in the schools: Opportunities and challenges for special services providers. *Special Services in the Schools, 1*(3), 5–7.

W. T. Grant Foundation Consortium on the School-Based Promotion of Social Competence [Elias, M. J., Weissberg, R. P., Dodge, K. A., Hawkins, J. D., Jason, L. A., Kendall, P. C., Perry, C. L., Rotheram-Borus, M. J., & Zins, J. E.]. (1992). Drug and alcohol prevention curricula. In J. D. Hawkins & R. F. Catalano, *Communities that care: Action for drug abuse prevention* (pp. 129–148). San Francisco: Jossey-Bass.

Zins, J. E., Conyne, R. K., & Ponti, C. R. (1988). Primary prevention: Expanding the impact of psychological services in schools. *School Psychology Review, 17* (4), 540–547.

Zins, J. E., Garcia, V. F., Tuchfarber, B. S., Clark, K. M., & Laurence, S. C. (1994). Preventing injuries in children and youth. In R. J. Simeonsson (Ed.), *Risk, resilience, and prevention: Promoting the well-being of all children* (pp. 183–202). Baltimore: Paul H. Brookes.

Zins, J. E., & Wagner, D. I. (1987). Children and health promotion. In A. Thomas & J. Grimes (Eds.), *Children's needs: Psychological perspectives* (pp. 258–267). Washington, DC: National Association of School Psychologists.

Zins, J. E., Wagner, D. I., & Maher, C. A. (Eds.). (1985). *Health promotion in the schools: Innovative approaches to facilitating physical and emotional well-being.* New York: Haworth.

Index